2006/07	2007/08	2008/09	2009/10	2010/11		Para No.
10%	10%	—	—	—	Starting rate	3, 5
—	—	10%	10%	10%	Starting rate for savings	7
£2,150	£2,230	£2,320	£2,440	£2,440	Starting rate limit	3, 5, 7
20%	20%	—	—	—	Savings rate	3, 7
22%	22%	20%	20%	20%	Basic rate	3, 5
£31,150	£32,370	£34,800	£37,400	£37,400	Basic rate band	3, 5
£33,300	£34,600	£34,800	£37,400	£37,400	Basic rate limit	3, 5
40%	40%	40%	40%	40%	Higher rate	3, 5
—	—	—	—	£150,000	Higher rate limit	3
—	—	—	—	50%	Additional rate	3
10%	10%	10%	10%	10%	Dividend ordinary rate	6
32.5%	32.5%	32.5%	32.5%	32.5%	Dividend upper rate	6
—	—	—	—	42.5%	Dividend additional rate	6
—	—	—	—	—	Children's tax credit (10%)	17
—	—	—	—	—	—year of birth	
					PERSONAL RELIEFS	
£5,035	£5,225	£6,035	£6,475	£6,475	Personal allowance	15
—	—	—	—	£100,000	Income limit	15
					Age-related allowances:	15, 16
£7,280	£7,550	£9,030	£9,490	£9,490	Personal (65 or over)	
£7,420	£7,690	£9,180	£9,640	£9,640	Personal (75 or over)	
£6,065	£6,285	£6,535	—	—	Married couple's (born before 6.4.1935)	
£6,135	£6,365	£6,625	£6,965	£6,965	Married couple's (75 or over)	
£20,100	£20,900	£21,800	£22,900	£22,900	Income limit	
£2,350	£2,440	£2,540	£2,670	£2,670	Basic married couple's allowance	
£1,660	£1,730	£1,800	£1,890	£1,890	Blind person's allowance	18
					CLASS 4 NIC	
8%	8%	8%	8%	8%	Rate	
£5,035–£33,540 plus 1% on excess	£5,225–£34,840 plus 1% on excess	£5,435–£40,040 plus 1% on excess	£5,715–£43,875 plus 1% on excess	£5,715–£43,875 plus 1% on excess	Band	
					Accumulated or discretionary income	
40%	40%	40%	40%	50%	Trust rate	
32.5%	32.5%	32.5%	32.5%	42.5%	Dividend trust rate	
£1,000	£1,000	£1,000	£1,000	£1,000	'Basic rate' band	

Tolley's Income Tax

Tolley's Income Tax 2010-11

95th Edition

by

David Smailes FCA

Consultant Editor Rebecca Benneyworth BSc FCA

LexisNexis®

Members of the LexisNexis Group worldwide

United Kingdom	LexisNexis, a Division of Reed Elsevier (UK) Ltd, Halsbury House, 35 Chancery Lane, London, WC2A 1EL, and London House, 20–22 East London Street, Edinburgh EH7 4BQ
Australia	LexisNexis Butterworths, Chatswood, New South Wales
Austria	LexisNexis Verlag ARD Orac GmbH & Co KG, Vienna
Benelux	LexisNexis Benelux, Amsterdam
Canada	LexisNexis Canada, Markham, Ontario
China	LexisNexis China, Beijing and Shanghai
France	LexisNexis SA, Paris
Germany	LexisNexis Deutschland GmbH, Munster
Hong Kong	LexisNexis Hong Kong, Hong Kong
India	LexisNexis India, New Delhi
Italy	Giuffrè Editore, Milan
Japan	LexisNexis Japan, Tokyo
Malaysia	Malayan Law Journal Sdn Bhd, Kuala Lumpur
Mexico	LexisNexis Mexico, Mexico
New Zealand	LexisNexis NZ Ltd, Wellington
Poland	Wydawnictwo Prawnicze LexisNexis Sp, Warsaw
Singapore	LexisNexis Singapore, Singapore
South Africa	LexisNexis Butterworths, Durban
USA	LexisNexis, Dayton, Ohio

© Reed Elsevier (UK) Ltd 2010

Published by LexisNexis
This is a Tolley title

A CIP Catalogue record for this book is available from the British Library.

ISBN 9 780754 539032

Printed in the United Kingdom by CPI Books Ltd

Visit LexisNexis at www.lexisnexis.co.uk

About This Book

Welcome to your new look Tolley Tax Annual. We have re-launched the books this year, aiming to make them easier to use and more practical. They still contain the same trusted, valuable content but now you can find the answer you need even quicker than before.

The first difference you'll notice is the new front cover. However, that's not the only change – the text has been revised too.

What are the other key changes?

- New key points – to direct you to matters that are of use in planning, or to areas of difficulty you may come across in practice.
- There are further practical examples – highly valued interpretation to help you understand the effects of the legislation on your day to day work. Examples are set in shaded boxes so they stand out if you need to go straight to practical interpretation.
- More contributions from practitioners using their own valuable experience.
- New, clearer text design – larger font and more white space for a more comfortable reading experience.
- Clearer contents – easier to read.
- The law and practice for the last four years is included and we have dispensed with any unnecessary historical text and statutory references.
- There are introductions for chapters – so that you can see quickly what is covered.
- We have split chapters where relevant – to break down the information into more manageable chunks and the structure of chapters has been improved.
- More headings have been introduced, with more distinct levels so that you can find the section that you want to read easily.
- Where appropriate, text has been converted to tables and lists to save you time and sentences shortened.

We hope that the new style meets your requirement for greater accessibility to the changing tax legislation and the ever increasing demands on you as a practitioner. We would be pleased to receive your feedback on the new style and any suggestions for further improvements. You can do this by e-mailing the Editor, Gemma Furniss at gemma.furniss@lexisnexis.co.uk. Technical queries will be dealt with by the author.

Contributors

Rebecca Benneyworth BSc FCA

Rebecca Benneyworth is an independent lecturer, author and consultant on a wide range of tax subjects. She lectures for Tolley CPD seminars and Tolley's Online, a wide range of professional bodies and commercial providers, and has presented sessions for HMRC and HM Treasury. She is Tax Editor of Accountingweb.co.uk and is the General Editor of Tolley's Taxwise. She also has a small practice in Gloucestershire comprising small owner managed businesses.

Contents

Contents

Abbreviations and References

Abbreviations

Art	article.
CAA	Capital Allowances Act.
CA	Court of Appeal.
CCA	Court of Criminal Appeal.
CCAB	Consultative Committee of Accountancy Bodies.
CES	Court of Exchequer (Scotland).
Cf.	compare.
CGT	Capital Gains Tax.
CIR	Commissioners of Inland Revenue.
Ch D	Chancery Division.
CJEC	Court of Justice of the European Communities.
CS	Scottish Court of Session.
CTA	Corporation Tax Act.
EC	European Communities.
ECHR	European Court of Human Rights.
EEC	European Economic Community.
ESC	Extra-Statutory Concession.
EU	European Union.
Ex D	Exchequer Division (now absorbed into Chancery Division).
FA	Finance Act.
F(No 2)A	Finance (No 2) Act.
FRS	Financial Reporting Standard.
FTT	First-tier Tribunal.
GAAP	Generally Accepted Accounting Practice.
HC	High Court.

HC(I)	High Court of Ireland.
HL	House of Lords.
HMRC	Her Majesty's Revenue & Customs.
ICAEW	Institute of Chartered Accountants in England and Wales.
ICTA	Income and Corporation Taxes Act.
IHT	Inheritance Tax.
IHTA 1984	Inheritance Tax Act 1984.
IR	Inland Revenue.
ITA 2007	Income Tax Act 2007.
ITEPA 2003	Income Tax (Earnings and Pensions) Act 2003.
ITTOIA 2005	Income Tax (Trading and Other Income) Act 2005.
KB	King's Bench Division.
LIFFE	London International Financial Futures Exchange.
NI	Northern Ireland.
NIC	National Insurance Contributions.
oao	on application of.
Pt	Part.
PC	Privy Council.
PDA	Probate, Divorce and Admiralty Division. (Now Family Division).
QB	Queen's Bench Division.
Reg	regulation.
s	section.
SC(I)	Irish Supreme Court.
Sch	Schedule.
SI	Statutory Instrument.
SP	Statement of Practice.
Sp C	Special Commissioners.
SR&O	Statutory Rules and Orders.
SSAP	Statement of Standard Accounting Practice.
TCGA 1992	Taxation of Chargeable Gains Act 1992.
TIOPA 2010	Taxation (International and Other Provisions) Act 2010.
TMA 1970	Taxes Management Act 1970.

| VAT | Value Added Tax. |
| VATA 1994 | Value Added Tax Act 1994. |

References

AER	All England Law Reports (Lexis Nexis , Halsbury House, 35 Chancery Lane, London WC2A 1EL).
All ER (D)	All England Reporter Direct (Lexis Nexis as above).
ATC	Annotated Tax Cases (Gee & Co. (Publishers) Ltd., South Quay Plaza, 183 Marsh Wall, London E14 9FS).
ITC	Irish Tax Cases (Government Publications, 1 and 3 G.P.O. Arcade, Dublin 1).
LTR	Law Times Reports.
SC	Special Commissioners.
SFTD	Simon's First-tier Tax Decisions (Lexis Nexis, as above).
SLR	Scottish Law Reporter.
SLT	Scots Law Times.
SSCD	Simon's Tax Cases Special Commissioners' Decisions (Lexis Nexis, as above).
STC	Simon's Tax Cases (Lexis Nexis, as above).
STI	Simon's Weekly Tax Intelligence (Lexis Nexis, as above).
TC	Official Tax Cases (The Stationery Office, PO Box 276, London, SW8 5DT).
TLR	Times Law Reports.
TR	Taxation Reports (Gee & Co., as above).

The first number in the citation refers to the volume, and the second to the page, so that [1995] 1 AER 15 means that the report is to be found on page fifteen of the first volume of the All England Law Reports for 1995. Where no volume number is given, only one volume was produced in that year.

Some series have continuous volume numbers.

Where legal decisions are very recent and in the lower courts, it must be remembered that they may be reversed on appeal. But references to the official Tax Cases ('TC') may generally be taken as final.

In English cases, Scottish and N. Irish decisions (unless there is a difference of law between the countries) are generally followed but are not binding, and Republic of Ireland decisions are considered (and vice-versa).

Acts of Parliament, Cmnd. Papers, 'Hansard' Parliamentary Reports and Statutory Instruments (SI) formerly Statutory Rules and Orders (SR & O)) are obtainable from The Stationery Office, PO Box 29, Norwich NR3 1GN, tel. 0870 600 5522, fax 0870 600 5533, online bookshop www.tsoshop.co.uk. Many items are available free of charge at www.opsi.gov.uk. **Hansard** references are to daily issues and do not always correspond to the columns in the bound editions. **N.B.** Statements in the House, while useful as indicating the intention of enactments, have no legal authority if the Courts subsequently interpret the wording of the Act differently, but see **5.32 APPEALS** for circumstances in which evidence of parliamentary intent may be considered by the Courts.

1

Allowances and Tax Rates

Introduction

[**1.1**] This chapter deals primarily with the computation of income tax liability (**1.7–1.10** below), the personal reliefs available to individuals (**1.14–1.16** below) and the rates of income tax to be applied (**1.3–1.6** below). A number of worked examples illustrating the operation of rates and allowances for the current tax year are included at the end of the chapter (**1.18** below). All income tax rates and personal reliefs for the last four years are listed in this chapter. A separate **ten-year summary** of allowances and tax rates appears inside the front cover.

The tax year

[**1.2**] The 'tax year' (or 'year of assessment' or 'fiscal year') runs from 6 April in one calendar year to 5 April in the next (e.g. the tax year 2010/11 starts on 6 April 2010 and ends on 5 April 2011). [*ITA 2007, s 4; ICTA 1988, s 832(1)*].

Rates of tax — 2010/11

[1.3] The main rates of income tax **for 2010/11** are as follows.

	Rate	On Taxable Income	Cumulative tax
Basic Rate	20%	£0–37,400	£7,480.00
Higher Rate	40%	£37,401–150,000	£52,520.00
Additional Rate	50%	Over £150,000	

[*ITA 2007, ss 6, 10; FA 2010, s 1*].

For 2009/10 and earlier years, see **1.4** below.

The figure of £37,400 is known as the basic rate limit. The 0–£37,400 band is known as the basic rate band. The figure of £150,000 is known as the higher rate limit. The higher and additional rates apply only to individuals. [*ITA 2007, ss 6, 10, 11, 20; ICTA 1988, s 1(2)(2A)(3); FA 2006, s 23; FA 2008, ss 4, 5, Sch 1 paras 3, 4, 10, 65; FA 2009, s 6(1)–(3), (6), Sch 2 paras 2, 4, 25; SI 2007 No 943*].

A special rate of **10%** (the **starting rate for savings**) applies to **savings income** (other than dividend income) to the extent that such income does not exceed a 'starting rate limit' (£2,440 for 2010/11), treating savings income as the highest part of an individual's income other than dividend income. The starting rate for savings applies only to individuals. See **1.6** below.

Note that the starting rate for savings must be distinguished from the more general starting rate in force for 2007/08 and earlier years (for which see **1.4** below). There was a separate starting rate band below the basic rate band, and the starting rate applied to all types of income to the extent that they fell within the starting rate band. That general starting rate and starting rate band were abolished for 2008/09 onwards.

Where income tax at the basic rate has been deducted from income, and that income is chargeable at the starting rate for savings, repayment of the excess tax deducted can be claimed. [*ITA 2007, s 17; ICTA 1988, ss 1(6A), 1A(6A); FA 1992, s 9(8); FA 1999, s 22(6)(7); FA 2008, Sch 1 paras 8, 65*].

A special rate of **10%** (known as the **dividend ordinary rate**) applies to **dividend income** to the extent that such income does not exceed the basic rate limit (treating that income as the highest part of an individual's income). A special rate of **32.5%** (known as the **dividend upper rate**) applies to dividend income to the extent that such income exceeds the basic rate limit but does not exceed the higher rate limit. A special rate of **42.5%** (known as the **dividend additional rate**) applies to dividend income to the extent that such income exceeds the higher rate limit. See **1.5** below.

See **1.13** below as to indexation of rate bands.

See **68.1, 68.11** SETTLEMENTS as regards income tax rates applicable to trusts.

See **56.5** PENSION INCOME for special rules on the taxation of State pension lump sums.

Scottish variable rate

The Scottish Parliament has the power (not yet utilised) to increase or reduce the basic rate of income tax in any tax year by up to three percentage points (in half-point steps). The rate so varied will apply to the income of Scottish taxpayers other than income from savings or distributions to which the dividend rate (or savings rate) applies (see **1.5, 1.6** below). An individual is treated as a Scottish taxpayer in relation to any tax year if he is treated as UK resident for income tax purposes (see **62 RESIDENCE, ORDINARY RESIDENCE AND DOMICILE**) and either:

• he spends at least as much time during the year in Scotland as elsewhere in the UK;
• he is a member of Parliament for a Scottish constituency, a member of the European Parliament for Scotland or a member of the Scottish Parliament; or
• his principal UK residence is located in Scotland for at least as much of the tax year as it is not located in Scotland and he spends at least part of the tax year in that Scottish residence.

[*Scotland Act 1998, Pt IV*].

See also Revenue Press Release 23 February 1998 for a Government technical paper commenting on the tax varying power of the Scottish Parliament, and setting out the Government's policy intentions where that power interacts with other parts of the tax system.

Rates of tax — 2009/10 to 2006/07

[1.4]
Basic and higher rate for 2009/10 [*ITA 2007, ss 6, 10; FA 2009, ss 1, 2*]

	Rate	On taxable income	Cumulative tax
Basic Rate	20%	£0–£37,400	£7,480.00
Higher Rate	40%	Over £37,400	

There was no additional rate of income tax (see **1.3** above) before 2010/11.

Basic and higher rate for 2008/09 [*ITA 2007, ss 6, 10; FA 2008, ss 1, 4, 5, Sch 1 para 3*]

	Rate	On taxable income	Cumulative tax
Basic Rate	20%	£0–£34,800	£6,960.00
Higher Rate	40%	Over £34,800	

Starting, basic and higher rate for 2007/08 [*ITA 2007, s 6; FA 2007, s 1; SI 2007 No 943*]

	Rate	On taxable income	Cumulative tax
Starting Rate	10%	0–£2,230	£223
Basic Rate	22%	£2,231–£34,600	£7,344.40
Higher Rate	40%	Over £34,600	

The figure of £2,230 is known as the starting rate limit and the figure of £34,600 as the basic rate limit. The 0–£2,230 band of income is known as the starting rate band and the £2,231–£34,600 band as the basic rate band. The starting rate and higher rate apply only to individuals. [*ITA 2007, ss 6, 10, 11, 20; ICTA 1988, s 1(2)(2A)(3); FA 1999, s 22(2)(3); FA 2006, s 23; SI 2007 No 943*].

A special rate of **20%** applies to **savings income** (other than dividend income) to the extent that such income does not exceed the basic rate limit (treating that income as the highest part of an individual's income other than dividend income). For 2007/08, this is known as the **savings rate**; previously it was known as the lower rate. The starting rate applies to such income instead of the 20% rate to the extent that the income does not exceed the starting rate limit. See **1.6** below.

Where income tax at the basic rate has been deducted from income, and that income is chargeable at the starting rate or savings rate, repayment of the excess tax deducted can be claimed. [*ITA 2007, s 17; ICTA 1988, ss 1(6A), 1A(6A); FA 1992, s 9(8); FA 1999, s 22(6)(7)*].

Similar principles apply for the other tax years set out below.

Starting, basic and higher rate for 2006/07 [*ICTA 1988, s 1(2); FA 2006, s 23; SI 2006 No 872*]

	Rate	On taxable income	Cumulative tax
Starting Rate	10%	0–£2,150	£215
Basic Rate	22%	£2,151–£33,300	£7,068
Higher Rate	40%	Over £33,300	

Rates of tax on dividend income

[1.5] In addition to receiving the cash amount of a UK dividend or other qualifying distribution, a UK resident receives a 'tax credit' of a proportion of the dividend etc. received. See *CTA 2010, s 1136* for meaning of 'qualifying distribution'. The tax credit is a fixed proportion (the 'tax credit fraction') of the dividend etc. This is set at **one-ninth** (see **64.8 SAVINGS AND INVESTMENT INCOME**). The income chargeable on the UK resident is the sum of the dividend etc. and the attached tax credit, with the tax credit being available against the liability (see **64.7 SAVINGS AND INVESTMENT INCOME**). A dividend paid (or other distribution made) in a tax year is chargeable as income of that tax year.

Non-qualifying distributions from UK resident companies do not carry a tax credit (see **64.10** SAVINGS AND INVESTMENT INCOME). This also used to be the case as regards qualifying distributions from non-UK resident companies, but in this case tax credits *are* available, in specified circumstances for 2008/09 onwards (see **64.13** SAVINGS AND INVESTMENT INCOME).

Tax credits cannot be repaid and can only be set against liability in respect of dividend income brought into charge (see **64.8** SAVINGS AND INVESTMENT INCOME and the example at **1.18** (v)(c) below). See, however, **30.21** EXEMPT INCOME for a five-year extension of tax credit payments in certain cases.

Special rates of tax apply to 'dividend income' (as defined below). Where the income falls within an individual's basic rate (and also, for 2007/08 and earlier years, where it falls within his starting rate band), the rate applied is the **dividend ordinary rate**, set at **10%** (so that the liability is met by the tax credit where applicable). To the extent that the income exceeds an individual's basic rate limit but does not exceed his higher rate limit, the rate applied is the **dividend upper rate**, set at **32.5%** (equivalent to a further liability of 25% of the actual amount of a dividend carrying a tax credit). To the extent that the income exceeds an individual's higher rate limit, the rate applied is the **dividend additional rate**, set at **42.5%** (equivalent to a further liability of 36.1% of the actual dividend). See **1.3** above for the basic rate band, basic rate limit and higher rate limit (and see **1.4** above for the starting rate band). The higher rate limit applies only for 2010/11 onwards.

For the purpose of determining whether dividend income falls within an individual's basic rate band or starting rate band) or exceeds his basic rate limit or (for 2010/11 onwards) his higher rate limit, it is treated as the highest part of his total income. This is apart from chargeable event gains on life policies etc. (see **44.3** LIFE ASSURANCE POLICIES) and income chargeable under *ITEPA 2003, ss 401–416* (payments and benefits on termination of office or employment — see **20.5** COMPENSATION FOR LOSS OF EMPLOYMENT). The above reference to chargeable event gains on life policies does not include any that do not carry a notional tax credit; examples are certain friendly society policies (see **44.22** LIFE ASSURANCE POLICIES) and offshore policies (see **44.20** LIFE ASSURANCE POLICIES).

The dividend *ordinary* rate does not apply (instead of the basic rate or, before 2008/09, the starting rate) to income chargeable on the REMITTANCE BASIS (**61**). For years up to and including 2004/05, the dividend *upper* rate did not apply (instead of the 40% higher rate) to income chargeable on the remittance basis either. For 2005/06, 2006/07 and 2007/08, due to a legislative error, the dividend upper rate *did* apply in these circumstances (HMRC Tax Bulletin August 2006 pp 1303, 1304). For 2008/09 onwards, the error is corrected, so that dividend income chargeable on the remittance basis is once again chargeable at the 40% higher rate to the extent that it exceeds the basic rate limit.

Dividend income received by income taxpayers other than individuals is generally chargeable at the dividend ordinary rate if it would otherwise be chargeable at the basic rate (unless the remittance basis applies). (The dividend upper rate does not apply to such persons.) But see **68.11** SETTLEMENTS as regards income chargeable at the trust rate or the dividend trust rate (generally applicable to, but not restricted to, the income of discretionary trusts and accumulation trusts). See also **75.9 UNIT TRUSTS ETC.** for an exception applicable to the income of an unauthorised unit trust.

'Dividend income' comprises:

(a)   dividends and other distributions from UK resident companies (see **64.7 SAVINGS AND INVESTMENT INCOME**);

(b)   dividends from non-UK resident companies (see **64.12 SAVINGS AND INVESTMENT INCOME**);

(c)   stock dividends from UK resident companies (see **64.14 SAVINGS AND INVESTMENT INCOME**);

(d)   income within **64.16 SAVINGS AND INVESTMENT INCOME** (release of loan to participator in a close company); and

(e)   income within **49.7 MISCELLANEOUS INCOME** (income not otherwise charged) which constitutes a distribution from a non-UK resident company which falls outside the charge under (b) above but which would be chargeable under (a) above if the company were UK resident.

Strictly speaking, the dividend upper rate did not apply (instead of the higher rate) before 2007/08 to income within (c) or (d) above. Apparently it was applied in practice and this is given statutory effect for 2007/08 onwards (see Change 1 in Annex 1 to the Explanatory Notes to *ITA 2007*).

[*ITA 2007, ss 8, 13, 14, 16, 19, 31(3)(4), 946; ICTA 1988, ss 1A, 1B, 833(3), 835(6);FA 2008, s 68, Sch 1 paras 6, 7, 65; FA 2009, Sch 2 paras 3, 5, 25*].

See **73.111 TRADING INCOME** as regards dealers in securities.

See **64.9 SAVINGS AND INVESTMENT INCOME** as regards qualifying distributions received by persons *not* entitled to tax credits.

Certain payments (and other items normally treated as distributions) made by a company for the redemption, repayment or purchase of its own shares are not treated as distributions and consequently have no tax credit and are not treated as income. See Tolley's Corporation Tax under Purchase by a Company of its own Shares.

A non-resident individual who claims personal reliefs (see **50.2 NON-RESIDENTS**) is entitled to a tax credit in respect of any qualifying distribution as if he were resident in the UK. [*ITTOIA 2005, s 397; ITA 2007, Sch 1 para 515; FA 2008, s 34, Sch 12 para 3*].

Tax credits set off or repaid which ought not to have been set off or repaid may be assessed, the tax due on such an assessment being payable (subject to the normal appeal procedures) within 14 days after the issue of the notice of assessment. [*ITTOIA 2005, s 401A; ICTA 1988, s 252; CTA 2010, Sch 1 para 456*].

Simon's Taxes. See D5.141, D5.414, E1.101A, E1.415, E1.603, E6.201.

Rates of tax on savings income

[1.6] For 2008/09 onwards, 'savings income' is chargeable to income tax at the basic rate to the extent that it falls within an individual's basic rate band. To the extent that savings income exceeds the basic rate limit, it is chargeable at the higher rate. To the extent that savings income exceeds the higher rate limit for 2010/11 onwards, it is chargeable at the additional rate. See **1.3** above for the basic rate band, the basic rate limit, the higher rate and the higher rate limit.

However, to the extent that an individual's savings income does not exceed the starting rate limit, it is taxed at the **starting rate for savings**, which is **10%**. The starting rate limit is as follows.

For	2008/09	£2,320
For	2009/10	£2,440
For	**2010/11**	£2,440

For the purpose of determining whether savings income exceeds an individual's starting rate limit, it is treated as the highest part of his total income apart from dividend income (as in **1.5** above) and income chargeable under *ITEPA 2003, ss 401–416* (payments and benefits on termination of office or employment — see **20.5 COMPENSATION FOR LOSS OF EMPLOYMENT**). Chargeable event gains on life policies etc. (see **44.3 LIFE ASSURANCE POLICIES**) have priority over both dividend income and other savings income. This does not apply to life assurance gains that do not carry a notional tax credit, though such gains do still have equal priority to other types of savings income; examples are certain friendly society policies (see **44.22 LIFE ASSURANCE POLICIES**) and offshore policies (see **44.20 LIFE ASSURANCE POLICIES**). Note also that the personal allowance is treated as reducing income of different descriptions in the order which will result in the greatest reduction in tax liability (see Step 3 at **1.7** below).

It follows that wherever the amount of an individual's taxable income, apart from savings income and dividend income, equals or exceeds the starting rate limit, the starting rate for savings cannot apply to any of his income.

See the example at **1.18**(iii) below.

Savings income received by income taxpayers other than individuals is generally chargeable at the basic rate. But see **68.11 SETTLEMENTS** as regards income chargeable at the trust rate or the dividend trust rate (generally applicable to, but not restricted to, the income of discretionary trusts and accumulation trusts).

For 2007/08 and earlier years, 'savings income' was chargeable to income tax at the savings rate, which was 20%, to the extent that it fell within an individual's basic rate band. Before 2007/08, the savings rate was known as the 'lower rate'. (The savings rate/lower rate did not apply to the extent that savings income fell within an individual's starting rate band.) To the extent that savings income exceeded the basic rate limit, it was chargeable at the higher rate. See **1.4** above for the basic and starting rate bands and limits and the higher rate.

For the purpose of determining whether savings income falls within an individual's basic rate or starting rate bands or exceeds his basic rate limit, it is treated as the highest part of his total income apart from dividend income (as in **1.5** above) and income chargeable under *ITEPA 2003, ss 401–416* (payments and benefits on termination of office or employment — see **20.5 COMPENSATION FOR LOSS OF EMPLOYMENT**). Chargeable event gains on life policies etc. (see **44.3 LIFE ASSURANCE POLICIES**) have priority over both dividend income and other savings income. For 2004/05 onwards, this does not apply to life assurance gains that do not carry a notional tax credit, though such gains do still have equal priority to other types of savings income; examples are certain friendly society policies (see **44.22 LIFE ASSURANCE POLICIES**) and offshore policies (see **44.20 LIFE ASSURANCE POLICIES**).

Savings income received by income taxpayers other than individuals was generally chargeable at the savings rate if it would otherwise be chargeable at the basic rate. But see **68.11 SETTLEMENTS** as regards income chargeable at the trust rate or the dividend trust rate (generally applicable to, but not restricted to, the income of discretionary trusts and accumulation trusts). A further exception was the savings income of an unauthorised unit trust (see **75.9 UNIT TRUSTS ETC.**), which is charged at basic rate.

For all years, *'savings income'* comprises:

(a) any income chargeable under *ITTOIA 2005, ss 369–381* (interest — see **64.2 SAVINGS AND INVESTMENT INCOME**), *ITTOIA 2005, ss 422–426* (purchased life annuities — see **64.17 SAVINGS AND INVESTMENT INCOME** and **24.11**(c) **DEDUCTION OF TAX AT SOURCE**) or *ITTOIA 2005, ss 427–460* (deeply discounted securities — see **64.18–64.25 SAVINGS AND INVESTMENT INCOME**), except for any income chargeable on the **REMITTANCE BASIS (61)**, but otherwise including foreign income, and except for annuities within *ITTOIA 2005, s 718(2)*;

(b) income chargeable under the **ACCRUED INCOME SCHEME (2)**; and

(c) chargeable event gains on life policies etc. on which an individual or the personal representatives of a deceased individual are liable to income tax (see **44.3 LIFE ASSURANCE POLICIES**).

Tax at the basic rate (previously the savings rate) is deductible at source from most UK savings income; see, for example, **8.2 BANKS** and **9.1 BUILDING SOCIETIES** (which also cover some exceptions to the rule). See generally **24 DEDUCTION OF TAX AT SOURCE**. In some other cases, notional tax is treated as having been paid at source (but is not refundable), e.g. chargeable event gains on life policies. This leaves a higher rate taxpayer to pay the excess of tax at the higher rate over tax at the basic/savings rate. Income from which a deduction of tax at source falls to be made (or is treated as made) at the basic/savings rate in force for a tax year is chargeable as income of that tax year.

[*ITA 2007, ss 7, 12, 16, 18, 31(2)(4), 946; ICTA 1988, ss 1A, 833(3), 835(6); FA 2008, Sch 1 paras 2, 5, 7, 12, 65; FA 2010, s 1; SI 2008 No 3023*].

Calculation of income tax liability

[1.7] The calculation of an individual's income tax liability for a tax year proceeds as follows.

Step 1.

Identify and add together the amounts of income on which the individual is chargeable to income tax. This may include, for example, TRADING INCOME (**73**), EMPLOYMENT INCOME (**27**), PROPERTY INCOME (**60**), SAVINGS AND INVEST-MENT INCOME (**64**), PENSION INCOME (**56**), SHARE-RELATED EMPLOYMENT INCOME (**69**), FOREIGN INCOME (**32**), income from PARTNERSHIPS (**52**), income from SETTLEMENTS (**68**), estate income (see **23** DECEASED ESTATES), income from INTELLECTUAL PROPERTY (**40**), income of UNDERWRITERS AT LLOYD'S (**74**), MISCELLANEOUS INCOME (**49**) and income deemed to arise under certain ANTI-AVOIDANCE (**4**) provisions. Expenses deductible in computing the amount of a particular type of income, e.g. trading expenses and most CAPITAL ALLOWANCES (**10** and **11**), should be duly deducted before arriving at the income to be included at this Step. An alphabetical list of some of the income exempt from income tax (and thus not to be included) forms the basis of **30** EXEMPT INCOME. Separate exemptions are covered in other chapters where appropriate, e.g. in SHARE-RELATED EMPLOYMENT INCOME AND EXEMPTIONS (**69**).

The aggregate of all income included at Step 1 is the individual's **total income**. (Before 2007/08, the term 'total income' was used inconsistently in the legislation and often referred to income *after* the deductions at Step 2 below.)

Certain stand-alone income tax liabilities are not included in this calculation and the related income should therefore not be included. These are mainly liabilities arising from the recovery of excessive tax relief, liabilities arising from specified anti-avoidance provisions, certain charges that can arise in connection with registered pension schemes and certain liabilities that are not directly connected to the individual's own tax position, e.g. tax deducted at source from payments made by him (for which see **24** DEDUCTION OF TAX AT SOURCE). A full list of the liabilities in this category is given at *ITA 2007, s 32* (as amended).

Step 2.

Identify and deduct from the income in Step 1 those deductions than can be made from total income (other than personal reliefs, which are deductible in Step 3 or given effect at Step 6 depending on their nature). A full list of the potential deductions at this Step for 2007/08 onwards is given at *ITA 2007, s 24*. It includes, for example, various allowable LOSSES (**45**), allowable INTEREST PAYABLE (**43**), annual payments and patent royalties (see **1.9** below), specified capital allowances (other than those deductible in arriving at amounts included at Step 1 above), relievable gifts of assets to CHARITIES (see **16.21**), contributions to registered pension schemes in the limited circumstances where these are deductible from income on the making of a claim (see **57.7** PENSION PROVISION), post-cessation expenditure (see **59.5** POST-CESSATION RECEIPTS AND EXPENDITURE) and post-employment deductions (see **27.52** EMPLOYMENT INCOME). The temporary extended carry-back relief at **45.5** LOSSES is deemed to be included in *ITA 2007, s 24* for these purposes.

In order, for example, to apply the correct rates of tax at Step 4 below, the deductions at Step 2 must be set against the various components of total income, in other words against income of different descriptions. The general rule is that these deductions are treated as reducing income of different descriptions in the order which will result in the greatest reduction in tax liability. However, there are various provisions dictating that a particular deduction must be set against a particular type of income, and these take priority over the general rule; for example, certain reliefs for trading losses can only be set against profits from the same trade. These provisions are covered throughout this work where relevant; a list of them is given at *ITA 2007, s 25(3)* as extended by *FA 2009, Sch 6 para 1(6)*.

A deduction from a component of income cannot produce a negative figure; the deduction is restricted to the amount required to reduce the component to nil. In some cases the excess deduction can then be set against other components. If it is one of those deductions that can only be made against a specified type of income, there may be rules enabling the excess to be carried forward or back to other tax years; such rules are covered throughout this work where relevant. Where more than one deduction can be made against a single component, the general rule is again that deductions are made in the order most beneficial to the taxpayer (even if in such case the benefit arises in a different tax year).

The figure remaining after carrying out Step 2 is the individual's **net income**. (Before 2007/08, this figure was often referred to as total income.)

Step 3.

Deduct from the individual's net income his personal allowance (see **1.14** below) and, where applicable, his entitlement to blind person's allowance (see **1.16** below). These deductions must be set against the various components of net income; they are treated as reducing income of different descriptions in the order which will result in the greatest reduction in tax liability.

This gives the individual's **taxable income**.

Step 4.

Apply the appropriate tax rates (see **1.3**, **1.5** and **1.6** above) to the various components of taxable income.

Step 5.

Add together the amounts of tax calculated at Step 4.

Step 6.

Deduct from the total in Step 5 any tax reductions to which the individual is entitled for the year — see **1.8** below. Subject to Step 7, the resultant figure is the individual's income tax liability for the year.

Step 7.

Where relevant, certain amounts of tax must be added to the figure resulting from Step 6 in order to arrive at the individual's income tax liability for the year. These comprise:

- any tax to which the individual is liable as a donor under the Gift Aid rules, i.e. where there are insufficient tax liabilities to cover the tax treated as deducted at source from the donation — see **16.16 CHARITIES**;
- any tax liability due on a State pension lump sum — see **56.5 PENSION INCOME**;
- any tax to which the individual is liable under the lifetime allowance provisions or the annual allowance provisions (see respectively **57.15** and **57.17 PENSION PROVISION**);
- any tax to which the individual is liable under **57.19**(a), (b), (d) or (e) **PENSION PROVISION**;
- the special annual allowance charge at **57.10 PENSION PROVISION**; and
- (for 2011/12 onwards) the high income excess relief charge at **57.9 PENSION PROVISION**.

The above calculation also applies to other persons within the charge to income tax, e.g. trusts and estates, but with the necessary modification allowing for the fact that such persons are not entitled to all the same tax reliefs as individuals.

[*ITA 2007, ss 22–25, 30, 31(5), 32, Sch 1 para 27; FA 2008, Sch 27 paras 27(2)(3), 30; FA 2009, Sch 1 paras 6, 7, Sch 6 para 1(5)*].

The amount of income tax (if any) payable directly by the individual to HMRC (or repayable) is subject to, for example, any tax he has paid under PAYE, tax deducted at source from his savings income and tax credits on dividends (except that the latter cannot create a repayment). These and similar items are not deductions from the tax liability as such but a means by which the liability is settled (or partially settled). They do not enter into the above calculation.

Tax reductions

[1.8] The tax reductions referred to at Step 6 of **1.7** above are set out below. To the extent that they are relevant in his case, the reductions in (1) to (7) below must be deducted from an individual's tax liability in the order in which they are listed.

(1) Venture capital trust investment relief (see **76.3 VENTURE CAPITAL TRUSTS**).

(2) Enterprise investment scheme relief (see **28.4 ENTERPRISE INVESTMENT SCHEME**).

(3) Community investment tax relief (see **19.3 COMMUNITY INVESTMENT TAX RELIEF**).

(4) Interest relief on pre-9 March 1999 loan to purchase a life annuity (see **43.12 INTEREST PAYABLE**).

(5) Relief for qualifying maintenance payments (see **47.9 MARRIED PERSONS AND CIVIL PARTNERS**).

(6) Relief under *ITA 2007, s 459* (or its predecessor) (certain payments for benefit of family members — see **44.2 LIFE ASSURANCE POLICIES**).

(7) Married couple's allowance (see **1.15** below).

Before 2007/08, items (6) and (7) above were expressed as a single item and there was no stated priority between them.

The total reductions within (1)–(3) above cannot exceed the individual's tax liability after Step 5 at **1.7** above less any tax deemed to have been deducted by him from Gift Aid donations (see **16.16 CHARITIES**).

The reductions in the following list are made in the order which will result in the greatest reduction in the individual's income tax liability for the tax year. To that end, any of the following may be made before, in between or after those in (1) to (7) above:

- life assurance top slicing relief (see **44.8 LIFE ASSURANCE POLICIES**);
- life assurance deficiency relief for 2007/08 onwards (see **44.13 LIFE ASSURANCE POLICIES**); before 2007/08, this relief did not fall to be given by way of a tax reduction;
- spreading relief in respect of patent royalties received (see **40.4 INTELLECTUAL PROPERTY**);
- relief under *ITTOIA 2005, s 401* (non-qualifying distributions — see **64.10 SAVINGS AND INVESTMENT INCOME**); and
- relief under *ITTOIA 2005, ss 677, 678* where income is received from a foreign estate that has borne UK income tax (see **23.10 DECEASED ESTATES**).

Finally, if the individual is entitled to relief for foreign tax (by way of reduction in UK income tax liability), whether under a double tax treaty or unilaterally (see respectively **26.2** and **26.6 DOUBLE TAX RELIEF**), that reduction is made after all other reductions have been made.

In all cases, a tax reduction must be restricted to the extent (if any) that it would otherwise exceed the individual's income tax liability before Step 7 at **1.7** above (or his remaining income tax liability after other reductions have been made).

For persons other than individuals, any reductions are made in the order which will result in the greatest reduction in the person's income tax liability for the tax year, except that a reduction in respect of double tax relief is made after all other reductions (apart from any reduction available at **68.19 SETTLEMENTS** (trusts with vulnerable beneficiaries), which is made last of all).

[*ITA 2007, ss 26–29, Sch 1 para 27; TIOPA 2010, Sch 8 paras 73–76; SI 2009 No 2859, Art 4(2)*].

Annual payments and patent royalties

[1.9] For 2007/08 onwards, subject to the detailed provisions below, relief for annual payments and payments of patent royalties is given by means of a deduction in computing net income for the tax year in which the payment is made (see Step 2 at **1.7** above). The amount deductible in computing net income is the *gross* amount of the payment, i.e. the amount before deduction of income tax. For 2006/07 and earlier years, such payments were relieved as charges on income (see **1.10** below and Change 81 in Annex 1 to the Explanatory Notes to *ITA 2007*).

The relief is available for payments from which income tax is required to be deducted at source under *ITA 2007, s 900(2)* (qualifying annual payment by an individual for commercial reasons in connection with his trade etc.) or *ITA*

2007, s 901(3) (qualifying annual payment by person other than an individual) or *ITA 2007, s 903(5)* or *(6)* (certain payments of patent royalties by an individual or another person). For the first two of those provisions and for the meaning of 'qualifying annual payment', see **24.7–24.10** DEDUCTION OF TAX AT SOURCE. For the provisions on patent royalties, see **24.13**. For the manner in which the payer accounts for the tax he deducts at source, see **24.17**. If a payment is deductible in calculating the payer's income from any source (e.g. his trading income), it cannot be deducted in computing net income. See below for restriction by reference to 'modified net income'. Certain payments made by persons other than individuals are ineligible for relief (see below).

Restriction by reference to 'modified net income'

The total amount for which relief can be obtained as above for a tax year cannot exceed the amount of the payer's 'modified net income' for that year.

A person's *'modified net income'* is defined (by *ITA 2007, s 1025*) as what would have been his net income if Steps 1 and 2 at **1.7** above applied with the following modifications.

(1) Ignore any relief that may be due for annual payments and patent royalties.

(2) Omit any 'non-qualifying income' (see below) from the person's total income.

(3) Ignore any relief for trading losses incurred (or treated as incurred) in a tax year subsequent to the one under review.

(4) Ignore any carry back of a post-cessation receipt from a tax year subsequent to the one under review (see **59.4** POST-CESSATION RECEIPTS AND EXPENDITURE).

(5) Ignore any relief for post-cessation expenditure (see **59.5** POST-CESSATION RECEIPTS AND EXPENDITURE) incurred (or treated as incurred) in a tax year subsequent to the one under review.

(6) Ignore any adjustment of profits resulting from an averaging claim by a creative artist or by a farmer or market gardener (see respectively **73.52, 73.74** TRADING INCOME) in respect of which the year under review is the first of the two years being averaged.

(7) Ignore the making, amending or revoking of any claim for tax relief if such action would have been out of time had it not been for an averaging claim by a creative artist or by a farmer or market gardener (see respectively **73.52, 73.74** TRADING INCOME).

'*Non-qualifying income*' (in (2) above) is any of the following:

(a) distributions from UK resident companies on which there is no entitlement to tax credit but on which income tax is treated as paid (see **64.9, 64.10** SAVINGS AND INVESTMENT INCOME);

(b) stock dividends issued to individuals or trustees (see **64.14** SAVINGS AND INVESTMENT INCOME);

(c) income treated as arising from the release of a loan to a participator in a close company (see **64.16** SAVINGS AND INVESTMENT INCOME);

(d) chargeable event gains arising to individuals or trustees and carrying a notional tax credit (see **44.7** LIFE ASSURANCE POLICIES);

(e)   income corresponding to that in (b), (c) or (d) above but arising to personal representatives and included in the aggregate income of an estate (see **23.5**(c)–(e) DECEASED ESTATES);

(f)   discretionary income from a settlor-interested trust and carrying a notional tax credit under *ITTOIA 2005, s 685A* (see **68.26** SETTLEMENTS); and

(g)   (before 2010/11) income treated as arising under **26.9**(e) DOUBLE TAX RELIEF (recovery of excess credit for foreign tax where overlap profits relieved).

The 'modified net income' rule mirrors the pre-2007/08 position under which certain types of income were treated as 'not brought into charge to income tax' and so were not available to cover charges on income. However, it was not explicit in the pre-2007/08 legislation that items originating in a year subsequent to the year under review — see (3) to (7) above — should be disregarded (see Change 154 in Annex 1 to the Explanatory Notes to *ITA 2007*).

Where **4.9**(b) ANTI-AVOIDANCE (purchase and sale of securities — now repealed) applied to a person, such that interest on securities that would otherwise have been exempt from income tax in his hands is not exempt, that interest could not be used to cover qualifying annual payments. See *ITA 2007, s 451* for the mechanism by which this was achieved after 2006/07; for 2006/07 and earlier years, a similar result was achieved by *ICTA 1988, s 733(2)*.

Ineligible payments by persons other than individuals

A payment otherwise within the above relief provisions and made by a person other than an individual is ineligible for relief if, or in so far as:

- the payment can lawfully be made only out of capital or out of income that is exempt from income tax; or
- it is charged to capital; or
- it is treated by the payer as made out of income that is exempt from income tax, but only if such treatment makes a difference to the current or future rights or obligations of any person; or
- it is not ultimately borne by the payer, unless the reason it is not ultimately borne is that the payer receives (or benefits from) an amount on which he is liable to income tax.

The above bullets are largely derived from case law concerned with the earlier requirement that payments be made 'out of profits or gains brought into charge to income tax', but have statutory authority for 2007/08 onwards (see Change 82 in Annex 1 to the Explanatory Notes to *ITA 2007*).

[ITA 2007, ss 447–452, 1025, 1026; FA 2008, s 66(4)(l), (8); TIOPA 2010, Sch 8 para 86].

Charges on income before 2007/08

[1.10] The term 'charges on income' covered annual payments (other than interest) and patent royalties paid under deduction of tax at source (see **24.20, 24.21** DEDUCTION OF TAX AT SOURCE), but subject to the exclusion of many annual payments made by individuals. In earlier years (but at no time in the six years immediately preceding 2007/08), the term had covered many other types of payment, for example interest, certain mining rents and royalties and payments under both charitable and non-charitable deeds of covenant. Charges on income in the six years preceding 2007/08 were limited to the types of payment now deductible under **1.9** above.

The concept of 'charges on income' was abolished for 2007/08 onwards and replaced by the deduction at **1.9** above, and also by the repeal of *ITTOIA 2005, s 51* which previously denied a deduction for patent royalties in computing trading profits (see **73.99 TRADING INCOME**); see Change 81 in Annex 1 to the Explanatory Notes to *ITA 2007*.

Charges on income were effectively allowable for income tax purposes to the extent that they were payable out of profits or gains brought into charge to income tax. But the tax saving was restricted to the excess of the taxpayer's marginal rate over the basic rate. In law, this was achieved by treating the (gross) amount of income out of which the charges were paid as liable at basic rate tax only. In practice, a similar result could be achieved by extending the basic rate band by the gross amount of the charges.

[*ICTA 1988, s 3, s 348(1)(2)(a), s 349(1); FA 1997, Sch 18 Pt VI(2)*].

The payer, having deducted tax at source, fell to be assessed to that tax to the extent, if any, that it exceeded the tax he had borne on his income. [*ICTA 1988, s 350(1)(1A)*]. If he failed to deduct tax, he obtained no relief for the payment. [*ICTA 1988, s 276*].

An annual payment made by *an individual* (or an individual's personal representatives), or by a Scottish partnership in which at least one partner is an individual, was excluded from relief as a charge on the income of the person making it. A payment which fell due before 6 April 2000 (even if made on or after that date) did not fall within this exclusion if it was made under an 'existing obligation'; broadly, this referred to a pre-15 March 1988 obligation, but see the 2005/06 and earlier editions for details. A payment made for *bona fide* commercial reasons in connection with the individual's trade, profession or vocation was not within this exclusion.

[*ICTA 1988, s 347A(1)(2) as amended, (2A)*].

With certain exceptions, annual payments made for non-taxable consideration are payable gross and are not deductible, as charges on income or otherwise — see **4.39 ANTI-AVOIDANCE**.

In *Bingham v CIR* Ch D 1955, 36 TC 254 a deduction was refused for alimony payable under a foreign Court Order as the payer was not empowered to deduct tax at source (cf. *Keiner v Keiner* QB 1952, 34 TC 346). Tax is deductible only if the payment is 'pure income profit' in the hands of the recipient and not, for example, an element entering into the computation of his business receipts. Hence a deduction was refused for insurance premiums payable under covenant on policies lodged as part of a mortgage security (*Earl Howe v CIR* CA 1919, 7 TC 289).

Where an interest in a business is transferred in consideration for periodical payments based on subsequent profits, whether the payments are 'annual payments' rests on the facts. See *Ramsay* CA 1935, 20 TC 79 and *Ledgard KB 1937*, 21 TC 129 in which a deduction was refused and contrast *Hogarth* CS 1940, 23 TC 491.

Claims

[1.11] Allowances unclaimed or not deducted from assessments (and relief for tax suffered by deduction at source) may be claimed within four years after the end of the tax year for which the claim is made. Where made before 1 April 2010, such claims had to be made within five years after 31 January following the tax year for which the claim was made. [*TMA 1970, s 43; FA 2008, Sch 39 para 12; SI 2009 No 403*]. See **18 CLAIMS** (and, in particular, **18.4**).

Relief is given only in respect of tax actually borne by the claimant, i.e., no relief on income the tax on which he is entitled to charge at the basic rate against, or deduct from any payment to, any other person. But this ceases to be relevant for 2007/08 onwards as a result of the abolition of the concept of 'charges on income' — see **1.10** above. [*ICTA 1988, ss 256(3)(c)(ii), 276; ITA 2007, Sch 1 paras 27, 38*].

Allowances depend upon 'the facts as they exist at the time' and cannot afterwards be withdrawn (or fresh assessments made) by reason of facts 'which arose after the year of assessment' (*Dodworth v Dale* KB 1936, 20 TC 285). Tax credits on dividends are not repayable (see **1.5** above).

See **7 BANKRUPTCY** for claims by bankrupts.

Non-residents

[1.12] Non-UK residents generally pay income tax at the normal rates on UK chargeable income, and are not entitled to personal reliefs *except* as stated in **1.14**, **1.15** and **1.16** below and at **50.2 NON-RESIDENTS**. See, however, **50.3 NON-RESIDENTS** for a limit on the income tax chargeable on the income of a non-resident. Non-residents may also be entitled to reliefs and exemptions under **DOUBLE TAX RELIEF** (**26**) agreements. See **62.5 RESIDENCE, ORDINARY RESIDENCE AND DOMICILE** as regards the year that UK residence begins or ends.

Indexation of personal reliefs and tax thresholds

[1.13] The basic rate limit, the starting rate limit for savings, the personal allowance, the married couple's allowance, the blind person's allowance and the income limit for age-related allowances are increased by the same percentage as the percentage increase (if any) in the retail prices index for the September preceding the tax year over that for the previous September. The resultant figures in the case of the basic rate limit and the income limit for age-related allowances are rounded up to the nearest £100 and in the case of the starting rate limit and the personal reliefs to the nearest £10.

An '*interest period*' is normally the period beginning with the day after one interest payment day (or the day after issue) and ending with the next (or first) such day. If, however, an interest period would otherwise exceed twelve months, it is divided into successive twelve month interest periods with any remaining months forming a separate interest period. The last interest period normally ends with the last interest payment day. For the purpose of determining when an interest period ends, conversions and exchanges of gilt-edged securities for strips are ignored. [*ITA 2007, s 673; ICTA 1988, s 711(3)(4)*].

The '*settlement day*', where securities are transferred through a recognised market such as the Stock Exchange, is the agreed settlement day or, if the transferee may settle on more than one day, the day he settles. If the transfer is not through such a market and the consideration is money alone and there is no interest payment day between the agreement for transfer and the agreed payment day or days, that day (or the latest such day) is the settlement day. If the transfer is not through such a market and either there is no consideration, or it is treated as a transfer by virtue of special provisions in *ITA 2007, s 620(1)(b)(c), s 648(1)(3), s 650, s 651, s 652* (see **2.13, 2.15, 2.20, 2.12, 2.7, 2.17** respectively below), the settlement day is the day of transfer. If the settlement day is not established by one of the above, it is decided by an officer of HMRC, subject to review by the Appeal Tribunal on appeal. [*ITA 2007, s 674; ICTA 1988, s 712; SI 2009 No 56, Sch 1 para 454*].

Deemed payments

[2.3] When securities are transferred, interest is effectively apportioned between the old and new owners so that the former is charged to income tax on the interest accrued up to the date of transfer while the latter is similarly charged on the interest accruing from that date. This is achieved by a system of deemed payments between transferor and transferee, described below.

The interest actually received is chargeable to tax in the normal way. It may, however, be reduced, or a further charge may arise — see **2.4** below.

Subject to exceptions in **2.5** below, if the transfer is *with accrued interest* (i.e. with the right to receive the next interest due, or 'cum div'), the transferor is treated as receiving a payment from the transferee. The amount of the payment is either the gross interest accruing to the settlement day (see **2.2** above) where this is accounted for separately by the transferee (as happens with short-dated gilts), or the proportion of the interest that has accrued between the last interest payment day (or the beginning of the first interest period of the securities) and the settlement day. This is given by the formula I x A/B, where I is the interest due on the first payment day following the settlement day, A is the number of days in the interest period up to and including the settlement day and B is the number of days in the whole period.

If, on the other hand, the transfer is *without accrued interest* (i.e. 'ex div') the transferor is treated as making a payment to the transferee. The amount of the payment is either the gross interest accruing from the settlement day to the next interest payment day (see **2.2** above) where this is accounted for separately by the transferor, or the proportion of the interest that has accrued during that period. This is given by the formula I x A/B, where I is the interest due on the first payment day following the settlement day, A is the number of days from the day after the settlement day up to and including the payment day and B is the number of days in the whole period.

Where the transfer of securities is a *Pt 5* transfer under *Proceeds of Crime Act 2002* (as in **10.2**(x) CAPITAL ALLOWANCES) and no compensating payment is made to the transferor, these provisions do not apply. [*ITA 2007, ss 623, 624, 632, 633, Sch 1 para 424; ICTA 1988, ss 711(5), 713; Proceeds of Crime Act 2002, Sch 10 paras 4, 10*].

Euroconversions

Where, in any interest period, there is both a transfer of securities and a *'euroconversion'* of those securities, i.e. a change from the currency of a State which has adopted the euro into euros, the adjustment to be made under the accrued income provisions is such amount as is just and reasonable. A euroconversion does not generally of itself give rise to a transfer within these provisions (see **2.2** above), but certain capital sums received in connection with euroconversions of securities which, on a just and reasonable view, may be attributable to a reduction or deferral of interest on those securities may give rise to adjustments under these provisions. [*SI 1998 No 3177, regs 3, 34, 35*].

Determination of accrued income profit/loss

[2.4] The various payments which a person is deemed to have made or received as in **2.3** above and which relate to securities of a particular kind in an interest period (see **2.2** above) are aggregated to give either an accrued income profit or loss. If the overall result is a profit, the full amount is taxed as income received at the end of the interest period. [*ITA 2007, s 616, s 617(1)(2)*]. If, on the other hand, the overall result shows a loss, relief is given by way of an exemption in relation to the actual interest received at the end of the interest period so that only the amount exceeding the loss is charged to tax. If this exemption is not possible because no interest is received at the end of the interest period, the loss is carried forward to be taken into account as a payment in calculating the accrued income profits or losses in the next interest period. [*ITA 2007, ss 637, 679; ICTA 1988, s 714; FA 1996, Sch 41 Pt V(3)*].

Income on which tax is chargeable under these provisions is charged at the rate of tax applicable to savings income — see **1.6** ALLOWANCES AND TAX RATES.

See **49.11** MISCELLANEOUS INCOME for the set-off of miscellaneous losses against accrued income scheme income.

See **2.9** below for the application of the remittance basis for 2008/09 onwards to accrued income profits arising as a result of a transfer of foreign securities.

Excluded transferors/transferees

[2.5] The following are excluded from being transferors or transferees under the accrued income scheme. Payments made by or to such persons are ignored. [*ITA 2007, s 638*].

(a)   Persons who account for such transfers in the computation of their trading profits or losses (e.g. financial traders).

(b)   Individuals, personal representatives and trustees of a disabled person's trusts (as defined in *TCGA 1992, Sch 1 para 1(1)*), provided that the nominal value of securities held in the capacity in question does not exceed £5,000 on any day in the year of assessment in which the interest period ends or in the preceding year of assessment. Special rules apply to transfers with unrealised interest and transfers of variable rate securities (see *ITA 2007, ss 639(2)–(4), 640(2)–(4), 641(2)–(4)*).

(c)   Persons neither resident nor ordinarily resident in the UK in the tax year in which the transfer is made, unless trading in the UK through a branch or agency. However, where such a person does so trade in the UK, the accrued income scheme only applies to securities situated in the UK (within the meaning of *TCGA 1992, s 275*) and acquired for use by, or for, the purposes of the branch or agency.

(d)   (Where the settlement day fell before 6 April 2008) individuals who would be liable to tax on actual interest on the securities on the **REMITTANCE BASIS (61)** (see now **2.9** below) see.

(e)   Charitable trusts (see **2.17** below).

(f)   Pension scheme trustees (see **2.18** below).

(g)   Makers of manufactured payments (see **2.25** below).

Note that no liability to income tax arises in respect of profits from FOTRA securities (see **64.3 SAVINGS AND INVESTMENT INCOME**) where the appropriate conditions are met.

[*ITA 2007, ss 638–647; ICTA 1988, ss 710(9), 715; FA 2008, Sch 7 paras 158, 160*].

Example

[2.6]

The following transactions take place between individuals during the year ended 5 April 2011.

Settlement day	Sale by	Purchase by	Securities
14.8.10	X (cum div)	Y	£4,000 6¼% Treasury Loan 2015
17.9.10	X (ex div)	P	£4,000 8% Treasury Loan 2013
4.4.11	S (cum div)	Y	£2,500 4% Treasury Loan 2012

Interest payment days are as follows.

6¼% Treasury Loan 2015	25 May, 25 November
8% Treasury Loan 2013	27 March, 27 September
4% Treasury Loan 2012	7 March, 7 September

Both X and Y owned chargeable securities with a nominal value in excess of £5,000 at some time in either 2009/10 or 2010/11, and both are resident and ordinarily resident in the UK. P is not resident and not ordinarily resident in the UK throughout 2010/11. The maximum value of securities held by S at any time in 2010/11 and 2011/12 is £4,000.

14.8.10 transaction

The transaction occurs in the interest period from 26.5.10 to 25.11.10 (inclusive).

Number of days in interest period	184
Number of days in interest period to 14.8.10	81
Interest payable on 25.11.10	£125

The deemed payment is

$$£125 \times \frac{81}{184} = £55$$

X is treated as receiving a payment of £55 on 25.11.10. Assuming no other transfers in this kind of security in the interest period (see **2.2** above), this will also be the figure of accrued income profit chargeable.

Y is treated as making a payment of £55. Assuming no other transfers in this kind of security in the interest period (see **2.2** above), this will also be the figure of accrued income loss to set against the interest of £125 he receives on 25.11.10. £70 remains taxable.

17.9.10 transaction

The transaction occurs in the interest period from 28.3.10 to 27.9.10 (inclusive).

Number of days in interest period	184
Number of days in interest period from 17.9.10	10
Interest payable on 27.9.10	£160

The deemed payment is:

$$£160 \times \frac{10}{184} = £9$$

X is treated as making a payment of £9. Assuming no other transfers in this kind of security in the interest period (see **2.2** above), this will also be the figure of accrued income loss to set against the interest of £160 he receives on 27.9.10. £151 remains taxable.

P is an excluded transferee as he is neither resident nor ordinarily resident in the UK.

4.4.11 transaction

The transaction occurs in the interest period from 8.3.11 to 7.9.11 (inclusive).

Number of days in interest period	184
Number of days in interest period to 4.4.11	28
Interest payable on 7.9.11	£50

The deemed payment is:

$$£50 \times \frac{28}{184} = £7$$

S is an excluded transferor as his holdings do not exceed £5,000 at any time in 2010/11 or 2011/12 (the year in which the interest period ends).

Y is treated as making a payment of £7. Assuming no other transfers in this kind of security in the interest period (see **2.2** above), this will also be the figure of accrued income loss to set against the interest of £50 he receives on 7.9.11 so £43 remains taxable.

Special cases

Nominees and trustees

[2.7] Transfers made by or to a nominee, or by or to a trustee of a person or persons absolutely entitled as against the trustee (including persons who would be so entitled if not an infant or under a disability), are treated for accrued income scheme purposes as being made by or to the person on whose behalf the nominee or trustee acts. [*ITA 2007, s 666; ICTA 1988, s 720(1)(2)*].

A person who becomes entitled to securities as trustee immediately after holding them in another capacity is treated as making a transfer within the new legislation. Such a transfer is 'with accrued interest' (see **2.3** above) if the person was entitled to receive any interest payable on the day of transfer where that is also an interest payment day, or in any other case on the next interest payment day. Where the person is not so entitled, the transfer is 'without accrued interest'. [*ITA 2007, ss 651, 623(1)(4), 624(4), 674(4)(5); ICTA 1988, ss 711(6), 720(4)*].

Trustees' accrued income (i.e. excluding that deemed to be that of a beneficiary, see above) is chargeable at the trust rate (see **68.12** SETTLEMENTS).

Where the trustees of a settlement are treated as making accrued income profits (see **2.4** above), or where they would have been treated as making, or making a greater amount of, accrued income profits if they had been UK resident or domiciled, the SETTLEMENTS (**68**) provisions apply with the effect that the accrued amount is, broadly, treated as income of the settlor where any actual income would be so treated. (Before 6 April 2006, 'settlement' had for this purpose its wider meaning given by *ITTOIA 2005, s 620* (see **68.28**(a) SETTLEMENTS).) [*ITA 2007, s 667; ICTA 1988, s 720(6)–(8); FA 1995, Sch 17 para 17; FA 2006, Sch 13 paras 21, 27*].

Interest payable in foreign currency

[2.8] Provision is made for establishing the rate of exchange to be used in converting into sterling certain figures used in calculating accrued income profits.

Deemed payments (see **2.3** above). Where accrued interest is accounted for separately and the parties specify a sterling equivalent themselves, this figure is used. Otherwise a deemed payment is converted at the rate of exchange (the London closing rate) on the settlement day.

Nominal values are converted at the London closing rate for the day in question.

[*ITA 2007, ss 664, 677; ICTA 1988, s 710(12), s 713(7)–(9)*].

Foreign securities — application of the remittance basis

[2.9] If, as a result of a transfer of 'foreign securities' where the settlement day is on or after 6 April 2008, accrued income profits are made by an individual to whom the remittance basis applies (i.e. he is within any of **61.2**(1)–(3) REMITTANCE BASIS for the tax year in which the profits are made), those profits are treated as 'relevant foreign income' (as in **32.2 FOREIGN INCOME**), with the consequences in **61.4 REMITTANCE BASIS**. For this purpose, securities are '*foreign securities*' if income from them would be relevant foreign income.

See **61 REMITTANCE BASIS** for the meaning of 'remitted to the UK' etc. For the purpose of applying the provisions in that chapter to a remittance of accrued income profits:

(a)   if the individual is the transferor (but subject to (b) below), treat any consideration for the transfer as deriving from the accrued income profits;

(b)   if the individual is the transferor and he does not receive consideration equal to (or exceeding) the market value of the securities, treat the securities as deriving from the accrued income profits; and

(c)   if the individual is the transferee, treat the securities as deriving from the accrued income profits.

[*ITA 2007, s 670A; FA 2008, Sch 7 paras 159, 160, 171*].

Previously, individuals to whom the remittance basis would have applied in relation to actual interest on the securities were excluded transferors/transferees (see **2.5**(d) above).

Foreign securities — delayed remittances

[2.10] A person (or his personal representatives) may claim to reduce accrued income profits by the amount of any payments deemed to be made to him in respect of transfers of a foreign security where the transfer proceeds are unremittable. If the amount of such payments exceeds accrued income profits, those profits are reduced to nil.

Transfer proceeds are unremittable if the person was unable to bring them to the UK, either because of the laws or government action of the territory in question or because of the impossibility of obtaining transferable foreign currency there. Prior to 2007/08 there was a further requirement that there was no want of reasonable endeavour to remit the proceeds, but this was dropped in the rewrite process (see Change 104 listed in Annex 1 to the Explanatory Notes to *ITA 2007*).

The claim must be made on or before the fifth anniversary of the normal filing date for the tax year in which the profits would have been chargeable. Where the claim is made on or after 1 April 2010 (and see **18.4** CLAIMS), it must be made no later than four years after that tax year. (Prior to 2007/08, the claim had to be made within six years of the end of the interest period in which the transfer occurred.)

Such reductions in accrued income profits are brought back into account in the chargeable period in which the transfer proceeds cease to be unremittable.

[*ITA 2007, ss 668–670; ICTA 1988, s 723; FA 2008, Sch 39 paras 61, 62; SI 2009 No 403*].

Death

[**2.11**] Death is *not* treated as giving rise to a transfer to the personal representatives (see **2.2** above). Where a transfer by the personal representatives to a legatee takes place in the interest period in which the death occurs, the transfer is disregarded for the purposes of the current provisions. [*ITA 2007, s 636; ICTA 1988, ss 711(6), 721; FA 1996, s 158*].

Trading stock — appropriations etc

[**2.12**] A transfer is deemed to be made under these provisions where a person appropriates to trading stock securities previously held as investments, and vice versa. Such a transfer is 'with accrued interest' (see **2.3** above) if the person was entitled to receive any interest payable on the day of transfer where that is also an interest payment day, or in any other case on the next interest payment day. Where the person is not so entitled, the transfer is 'without accrued interest'. [*ITA 2007, ss 650, 623(1)(4), 624(4), 674(4)(5); ICTA 1988, ss 711(6), 722*].

Conversions

[**2.13**] On a conversion of securities within *TCGA 1992, s 132*, the person entitled to them immediately before the conversion is treated as transferring them on the day of the conversion (if there is no actual transfer). The transfer is 'with accrued interest' (see **2.3** above) if the person was entitled to receive any interest payable on the day of conversion or on the next interest payment day thereafter. Where the person is not so entitled, the transfer is 'without accrued interest'. The 'interest period' (see **2.2** above) in which the conversion is made is treated as ending on the day on which it would have ended but for the conversion. [*ITA 2007, ss 620(1)(b),(7), 623(3)(4), 624(3)(4), 673(4), 674(4)(5); ICTA 1988, ss 710(13), 711(6)*].

Transfer of unrealised interest (bearer securities)

[**2.14**] Provision is made to ensure that accrued interest which has already become payable before the settlement day (e.g. on bearer securities) does not escape the accrued income scheme. The transferor is treated as receiving a payment equal to the unrealised interest. However, the transferee is not deemed to have made any payment and is not taxed when he actually receives the interest. Where, exceptionally, the settlement day falls after the last or only interest period of the securities, the transferor is treated as making accrued income profits equal to the unrealised interest and arising in the tax year which contains the settlement day.

The exceptions at **2.5** above apply to a charge so arising on the transferor and to the relief arising to the transferee. The capital gains tax calculation of the gain on the disposal by the transferor is adjusted to exclude the accrued interest from the consideration received and the transferee's base cost is similarly reduced by the amount of the relief obtained as above. Where necessary, the unrealised interest is converted into sterling at the London closing rate of exchange on the settlement day. Where the transfer of securities is a *Pt 5* transfer under *Proceeds of Crime Act 2002* (as in **10.2**(x) CAPITAL ALLOWANCES) and no compensating payment is made to the transferor, these provisions do not apply. [*ITA 2007, ss 617(3), 625, 630, 631, 634, 664(5), 681, Sch 1 paras 308, 424; ICTA 1988, s 716; TCGA 1992, s 119(4)(5); Proceeds of Crime Act 2002, Sch 10 paras 4, 10*]. See also **2.16** below where there is a default in interest payments.

Variable rate bonds

[2.15] Special rules apply to the transfer of securities unless either:

(a) they carry interest from issue to redemption at one, and only one, of the following rates:
    (i) a constant fixed rate (see *Cadbury Schweppes plc and another v Williams* CA 2006, [2007] STC 106); or
    (ii) a rate fixed in relation to a standard published base rate or the retail prices index (or foreign equivalent), or

(b) they were deep discount securities (prior to their abolition from 6 April 1996) for which the rate of interest for each interest period did not exceed the yield to maturity.

Where an interest rate change may arise solely from provision for actions required to effect a 'euroconversion' of a security, i.e. a change from the currency of a State which has adopted the euro into euros, this does not of itself bring the security concerned within these provisions (see *SI 1998 No 3177, regs 3, 33*).

Where securities not within (a) or (b) above are transferred at any time between issue and redemption, then:

(1) there is a deemed payment to the transferor;
(2) the deemed payment is equal to such amount (if any) as is just and reasonable; and
(3) no one is treated as making the payment, so there is no deemed payment in calculating the transferee's accrued income profit/loss (see **2.4** above).

The redemption of variable rate securities is itself a transfer for the purposes of the accrued income scheme if there has been a previous transfer.

Where the settlement day in relation to a transfer falls after the end of the only or last interest period in relation to the securities the transferor is treated as making accrued income profits of a just and reasonable amount. Such profits are treated as made in the tax year in which the settlement day falls.

[*ITA 2007, ss 617(3), 620(1)(c), 627, 630, 631; ICTA 1988, s 717; SI 2007 No 1820, reg 2*].

Interest in default

[2.16] Where there has been a failure to pay interest on the securities, deemed payments under the accrued income scheme on transfer are calculated by reference to the value of the right to receive the interest on the interest payment day in question rather than the full amount of the interest payable. The provisions regarding transfers of unrealised interest (see **2.14** above) similarly apply by reference to the value of the right to receive the interest (if less than the amount of the unrealised interest). Any unrealised interest subsequently received by the transferee is exempt in so far as it does not exceed the value of the right to receive the interest at the time of purchase. If he transfers the securities with the unrealised interest, the accrued income profit is restricted to any increase in the value of the right to receive the interest between purchase and re-sale. Special rules apply where unrealised interest is partially repaid and where part of a holding of securities is transferred. [*ITA 2007, ss 659, 660, 661, 681, Sch 1 para 308; ICTA 1988, ss 718, 719; TCGA 1992, s 119(5)*]. For the application of these provisions in practice, see HMRC Savings and Investment Manual SAIM4290, 4300.

Charities

[2.17] Charities are excluded from the accrued income scheme if any interest actually received would be exempt under **16.6 CHARITIES,** but where securities cease to be subject to charitable trusts the trustees are treated for the purposes of the legislation as making a transfer at that time. Such a transfer is 'with accrued interest' (see **2.3** above) if the trustees were entitled to receive any interest payable on the day of transfer or on the next interest payment day thereafter. Where the trustees were not so entitled, the transfer is 'without accrued interest'. [*ITA 2007, ss 623(3)(4), 624(3)(4), 645, 652; ICTA 1988, s 711(6), s 715(1)(d)(2)(3)*].

Retirement schemes

[2.18] Transfers to or by pension funds are excluded from the accrued income scheme as regards the pension fund if any interest received would be exempt under *FA 2004, s 186* or, before 2006/07, under *ICTA 1988, s 592(2)*. [*ITA 2007, s 646; ICTA 1988, s 715(1)(k)*].

Sale and repurchase of securities

[2.19] On a sale and repurchase of securities the accrued income scheme provisions are disapplied to both transfers. A sale and repurchase of securities involves an agreement (or agreements entered into under the same arrangement) for securities to be sold and the transferor, or a person connected with him (within **21 CONNECTED PERSONS**) to buy them, or similar securities, back. The repurchase may be triggered by an obligation to purchase, or the exercise of an option (put or call) under the agreement or a related agreement. However, if the sale and repurchase rules are themselves disapplied because the agreements are not arm's length or the interim holder assumes the risks and benefits of ownership, then the accrued income scheme provisions will apply.

Securities are 'similar' for this purpose if they entitle the holder to the same rights against the same persons as to capital and interest, and to the same enforcement remedies, and where securities are converted from the currency of a State which has adopted the euro into euros (a *'euroconversion'*), the new securities are treated as 'similar' (see *SI 1998 No 3177, regs 3, 14 as amended*).

[*ITA 2007, ss 654, 655; ICTA 1988, s 727A*].

The Treasury has broad powers to make regulations providing for the above provisions to apply with modifications (including exceptions and omissions) in relation to cases involving non-standard arrangements. These include any arrangement for the sale and repurchase of securities where the obligation to repurchase is not performed, or the repurchase option not exercised, or where provision is made by or under any agreement:

(a)   for different or additional securities to be treated as, or included with, securities which, for the purposes of the repurchase, are to represent securities transferred in pursuance of the original sale; or

(b)   for any securities to be treated as not included with securities which, for repurchase purposes, are to represent securities transferred in pursuance of the original sale; or

(c)   for the sale or repurchase price to be determined or varied wholly or partly by reference to fluctuations, in the period from the making of the agreement for the original sale, in the value of securities transferred in pursuance of that sale, or in the value of securities treated as representing those securities; or

(d)   for any person to be required, where there are such fluctuations, to make any payment in the course of that period and before the repurchase price becomes due.

Regulations may also make such modifications in relation to cases where corresponding arrangements are made by an agreement, or by related agreements, in relation to securities which are to be redeemed in the period after their sale, those arrangements being such that the vendor (or a person connected with him), instead of being required to repurchase the securities or acquiring an option to do so, is granted rights in respect of the benefits that will accrue from their redemption.

[*ITA 2007, ss 656–658; ICTA 1988, s 737E*].

Gilt strips

[2.20] Where a person exchanges a gilt-edged security for strips of that security, that person is deemed to have transferred the security with accrued interest (unless the exchange is after the balance has been struck for a dividend on the security but before the day the dividend becomes payable), without any person being treated as the transferee for the purposes of the deemed payment provisions (see **2.3** above), and without affecting the end of the interest period in which the exchange takes place. Similarly where strips are reconstituted by any person into the security from which they derived, the security is deemed to have been transferred to that person with accrued interest (unless the reconstitution is after the balance has been struck for a dividend on the security but before the day the dividend becomes payable) without any person being treated as the transferor. [*ITA 2007, ss 648, 673(4)(5); ICTA 1988, s 710(13A)(13B), s 722A*].

Stock lending

[2.21] The accrued income scheme provisions are specifically disapplied in relation to stock lending transactions disregarded for chargeable gains purposes under *TCGA 1992, s 263B(2)*. [*ITA 2007, s 653; ICTA 1988, s 727*].

New issues

[2.22] Where:

(a) securities of a particular kind are issued (being the original issue of securities of that kind),

(b) new securities of the same kind are issued subsequently,

(c) a sum (the 'extra return') is payable by the issuer in respect of the new securities, to reflect the fact that interest is accruing on the old securities and calculated accordingly, and

(d) the issue price of the new securities includes an element (separately identified or not) representing payment for the extra return,

then, for the purposes of the accrued income scheme,

(i) the new securities are treated as transferred *to* the person to whom they are issued, but are not treated as transferred *by* any person; and

(ii) the transfer is treated as being 'with accrued interest' (see **2.3** above) and as made on the actual day of issue of the new securities (the 'new issue day'), that day being treated as the settlement day (notwithstanding *ITA 2007, s 674* — see **2.2** above).

These rules do not apply if the new securities are variable rate securities (see **2.15** above).

If the new securities are issued under an arrangement whereby the 'extra return' (see (c) above) is accounted for separately to the issuer by the person to whom the securities are issued, the deemed payment (see **2.3** above) is equal to the extra return so accounted for. If there is no such separate accounting, the deemed payment by the transferee is a proportion of the interest payable on the new securities on the first 'interest payment day' (see **2.2** above) after the new issue day (subject, however, to the rules on interest in default: see **2.16** above). This is the proportion that the number of days in the period from the last interest payment day prior to the new issue (or, if there is no such day, the day on which the original securities were issued) to the new issue day (the 'relevant period') bears to the number of days from the beginning of the relevant period to the first interest payment day after the new issue day.

For foreign currency securities, the deemed payment is the sterling equivalent calculated by reference to the London closing rate of exchange on the settlement day.

[*ITA 2007, ss 649, 662, 664; ICTA 1988, s 726A*].

Interaction with capital gains tax

[2.23] Adjustments are necessary to capital gains tax computations where the accrued income scheme applies. The consideration for the disposal is adjusted to exclude or add the deemed payments as appropriate (see **2.3** above) and the sums allowed as a deduction to the transferee on a future disposal are correspondingly adjusted. [*TCGA 1992, s 119(1)–(3); ITA 2007, Sch 1 para 308*]. Where there is a CGT disposal which is not a transfer (see **2.2** above) for accrued income scheme purposes but which would give rise to deemed payments if it were such a transfer, a transfer is deemed to be made on the day of the disposal and the capital gains tax consideration and sums deductible are adjusted accordingly as above. [*TCGA 1992, s 119(6)–(9); ITA 2007, Sch 1 para 308*]. Where there is a conversion of securities within *TCGA 1992, s 132* or an exchange not involving a disposal within *TCGA 1992, Pt IV, Ch II* (reorganisations etc.) a capital gains tax adjustment is made to allow for the effect of the accrued income scheme. Any payment which the transferor is treated as receiving (see **2.3** above) is first treated as reducing any consideration receivable on the conversion etc., and then to the extent it exceeds any consideration receivable it is treated as consideration given for the conversion etc., while any deemed payment by the transferor is treated as consideration received for the conversion etc. [*TCGA 1992, s 119(10)(11); ITA 2007, Sch 1 para 308*].

Double tax relief

[2.24] Where a person is treated as making accrued income profits (see **2.4** above) and any interest actually received would be liable both to UK tax and to foreign tax, he is allowed unilateral credit (see **26.6** DOUBLE TAX RELIEF) against the UK tax on accrued income profits. The credit is for foreign tax at the rate at which such tax would be payable on interest on the securities.

Where a person is entitled to a credit for foreign tax against UK tax on interest treated as reduced under the accrued income scheme (see **2.4** above), the credit is also reduced. It is reduced to the same proportion that the interest actually taxable bears to the interest which would have been taxable without the reduction. There is a similar reduction where double tax relief is allowed by way of deduction of the foreign tax from the interest received (see **26.9**(a)(iii) DOUBLE TAX RELIEF).

[*TIOPA 2010, ss 10, 39, 112(1)(2); ICTA 1988, s 807; ITA 2007, Sch 1 para 198*].

Anti-avoidance

[2.25] Certain anti-avoidance measures are affected by the accrued income scheme legislation.

Transfer of assets abroad

Where a non-UK resident or non-UK domiciled person would have been treated as making accrued income profits (see **2.4** above) if he had been so resident or domiciled, the accrued income profits which he would have been treated as making are treated as income becoming payable to him for the purposes of *ITA 2007, Pt 13 Ch 2* (transfer of assets abroad). A corresponding reduction in interest payable for these purposes is made where an exemption arises under the accrued income scheme (see **2.4** above). See **4.14–4.17** ANTI-AVOIDANCE. [*ITA 2007, s 747; ICTA 1988, s 742(4)–(7)*].

Other matters

The provisions relating to manufactured dividends and interest (see **4.10** ANTI-AVOIDANCE) take precedence over the accrued income scheme, which does not apply to the extent that the transfer is covered by those provisions. [*ITA 2007, ss 647, 663; ICTA 1988, s 715(6)(7)*].

3

Alternative Finance Arrangements

Introduction

[3.1] The legislation described below provides for the taxation of certain finance arrangements (known as '*alternative finance arrangements*') that do not involve the receipt or payment of interest. It is intended to provide a tax regime for financial products that are economically equivalent to conventional banking products but which, instead of interest, involve arrangements of the kind described in **3.2–3.8** below. The legislation seeks to ensure that such products are taxed no more or less favourably than equivalent products involving interest. Such products are usually aimed at individuals who wish to adhere to Shari'a law, which prohibits the receipt or payment of interest. Prior to *FA 2005*, the tax treatment of such products was in some areas uncertain and in others could produce anomalous results. For example, finance arrangements based on asset sale and purchase might have fallen within the CGT rules, but this in turn could have depended on the nature of the asset; and returns from profit-share arrangements could have been treated as distributions.

The legislation is not restricted to Shari'a-compliant products but applies to any finance arrangement that falls within its terms. It does not change the nature of the financial arrangements, nor does it deem interest to arise where there is none. Instead, it brings certain types of finance arrangements, and the returns from those arrangements, within the pre-existing tax regime for receipts and payments of interest.

The Treasury have power by statutory instrument to designate arrangements further to those in **3.2**, **3.4**, **3.7** and **3.8** below as alternative finance arrangements and to amend pre-existing legislation in response to commercial and other developments. Any newly designated arrangements must equate in substance to a loan, deposit or other transaction that does not involve the payment of interest but achieves a similar effect. [*TIOPA 2010, s 366; FA 2006, s 98; FA 2008, s 156*]. See, for example, **19.28** COMMUNITY INVESTMENT TAX RELIEF.

For an article on alternative finance arrangements, with particular reference to Shari'a law, see *Taxation Magazine*, 6 October 2005, p 10.

The provisions at **3.2–3.8** below are subject to **3.10** below.

Simon's Taxes. See A1.3.

Alternative finance return — purchase and re-sale

[3.2] These provisions apply to arrangements entered into between two persons, X and Y (at least one of whom is a 'financial institution' — see **3.3** below), whereby X buys an asset and sells it, either immediately or in circumstances where both the conditions below are met, to Y for a consideration which is greater than the purchase price and at least part of which is deferred, such that the excess of sale price over purchase price (the '*effective return*') equates, in substance, to the return on an investment of money at interest. The conditions are that X is a 'financial institution' and that the asset was purchased by X for the purpose of entering into any such arrangements.

Where the whole of the sale price is paid on one day, the whole of the effective return is treated as '*alternative finance return*' (i.e. the equivalent of interest) included in the sale price. Where the sale price is to be paid by instalments, each instalment is taken to include alternative finance return equal to an amount of interest that would have been included in the instalment if:

(i)   the effective return were interest payable on a loan by X to Y of an amount equal to the purchase price of the asset;

(ii)   the instalment were a part repayment of the principal with interest; and

(iii) the loan were made on arm's length terms and accounted for under generally accepted accounting practice (see **73.18** TRADING INCOME).

The alternative finance return is treated for income tax purposes in the hands of X as if it were interest and thus within the charge at **64.2** SAVINGS AND INVESTMENT INCOME. The rules relating to relief for interest payable under *ITA 2007, s 383* (see **43.5** INTEREST PAYABLE) apply as regards Y as if the arrangements involved the making of a loan by X to Y and as if the alternative finance return were the interest on that loan. Insofar as a person is a party to alternative finance arrangements for the purposes of a trade, profession or vocation or of a property business (see **60.2** PROPERTY INCOME), alternative finance return paid by that person is to be treated as an expense of the trade etc. Relief under *ITTOIA 2005, s 58* for incidental costs of obtaining finance (see **73.93** TRADING INCOME) applies as if references to a loan included references to alternative finance arrangements and references to interest included references to alternative finance return. The alternative finance return is excluded in determining the consideration given for the purchase or sale of the asset for any other income tax purpose.

Foreign currency

If the alternative finance return is paid in a currency other than sterling by or to a person other than a company and otherwise than for the purposes of a trade, profession, vocation or property business, then, as regards that person, the alternative finance return is to be calculated in that other currency, and each payment of alternative finance return is to be translated into sterling at a spot rate of exchange for the day on which the payment is made.

[*ITA 2007, ss 564C, 564I, 564J, 564M–564O, 564V(1), Sch 1 para 598; ICTA 1988, s 367A; FA 2005, ss 47, 48(1), 51, 53, 56(1); FA 2006, s 96(1)(2); TIOPA 2010, Sch 2 paras 4, 10, 11, 14–16, 23, 47*].

Simon's Taxes. See **A1.301, A1.302.**

Meaning of 'financial institution'

[3.3] '*Financial institution*' for the purposes of the alternative finance return provisions means:

- a bank (within *ITA 2007, s 991*) or a wholly-owned subsidiary of a bank;
- a building society (within the meaning of *Building Societies Act 1986*) or a wholly-owned subsidiary of a building society;
- a person authorised by a licence under *Consumer Credit Act 1974, Pt 3* to carry on a consumer credit business or a consumer hire business within the meaning of that *Act*;
- a person authorised in a non-UK jurisdiction to receive deposits or other repayable funds from the public and to grant credits for its own account;
- (after 14 October 2009) an insurance company (as defined); or
- (after 14 October 2009) a person who is authorised in a jurisdiction outside the UK to carry on a business which consists of effecting or carrying out contracts of insurance or substantially similar business but not an insurance special purpose vehicle (as defined); or
- a bond-issuer within **3.5** below, but only in relation to any bond assets which are rights under purchase and re-sale arrangements (**3.2** above), diminishing shared ownership arrangements (**3.4** below) or profit share agency arrangements (**3.8** below).

[*ITA 2007, s 564B; FA 2005, s 46(2)(3); FA 2007, s 53(3); TIOPA 2010, Sch 2 para 3; SI 2009 No 2568*].

Alternative finance return — diminishing shared ownership

[3.4] These provisions apply to arrangements under which a financial institution (X) (see **3.3** above) acquires a beneficial interest in an asset and another person (Y):

(a)   also acquires a beneficial interest in the asset;

(b)   is to make a series of payments to X amounting in total to the amount paid by X for its beneficial interest;

(c)   is to acquire (in stages or otherwise) X's beneficial interest as a result of those payments;

(d)   is to make additional payments to X (whether under a lease or otherwise);

(e)   has the exclusive right to occupy or otherwise use the asset; and

(f)   is exclusively entitled to any income, profit or gain arising from or attributable to the asset, including, in particular, any increase in its value.

It is immaterial whether or not X acquires its beneficial interest from Y (for example, in a case where there is an initial conveyance of real property to Y followed by a sub-sale from Y to X), whether Y (or some person other than X and Y) has an interest in the asset as well as X and whether or not X has a legal interest in the asset.

The condition in (e) above does not preclude Y's granting an interest or right in the asset to someone else, e.g. he may sub-let the asset; but the person to whom the interest or right is granted cannot be X, a person controlled by X, or a person controlled by a person who also controls X, and the grant must not be required by X or by arrangements to which X is a party. The condition in (f) above does not preclude X's having to bear any loss (or a share of any loss) resulting from a decrease in the asset's value (and the total payments in (b) above may be reduced to reflect any such loss).

Payments made by Y under these arrangements are treated as alternative finance return, except insofar as they are the payments within (b) above or they constitute arrangement fees or legal or other expenses.

In the event that X is within the charge to income tax, the alternative finance return is treated for income tax purposes in his hands as if it were interest and thus within the charge at **64.2 SAVINGS AND INVESTMENT INCOME**. Generally, other income tax consequences ensue as they do for alternative finance arrangements involving purchase and resale (see **3.2** above), for example the treatment of alternative finance return as an expense of the payer's trade etc. Although arrangement fees and legal costs etc. are not treated as alternative finance return, relief may be available for these items as incidental costs of obtaining finance (see **73.93 TRADING INCOME**). The alternative finance return is excluded in determining the consideration given for the purchase or sale of the asset for any other income tax purpose.

Arrangements within these provisions are not to be treated as a partnership for tax purposes.

[*ITA 2007, ss 564D, 564K, 564M–564O, 564V(2), 564W, Sch 1 para 597; FA 2005, ss 46, 47A, 51, 53; FA 2006, s 96(1)(3)(6)(8); CTA 2009, Sch 1 para 649; TIOPA 2010, Sch 2 paras 5, 12, 14–16, 23, 24*].

An example of an arrangement that the above is intended to cover is the Shari'a compliant finance product known as diminishing musharaka. 'Musharaka' denotes a partnership or joint venture, and covers a wide spectrum, including arrangements identical to a normal partnership under which the partners share income or profits from a business or other asset. The above conditions are intended to exclude such arrangements (which are taxed in the same way as a conventional partnership — see **52 PARTNERSHIPS**) from the scope of these provisions. (Treasury Explanatory Notes to the 2006 Finance Bill).

Capital allowances

HMRC consider that Y is the person entitled to any plant and machinery capital allowances available in respect of the asset in question — in accordance with the rules at **11.61 CAPITAL ALLOWANCES ON PLANT AND MACHINERY** (HMRC Brief 26/07, 21 March 2007).

Simon's Taxes. See A1.302.

Alternative finance return — investment bond arrangements

[3.5] These provisions apply to arrangements which:

- are entered into after 5 April 2007 (but see also below under 'Transitional');
- provide for one person ('the bond-holder') to pay a sum of money ('the capital') to another ('the bond-issuer');
- identify assets (or a class of assets) which the bond-issuer will acquire for the purpose of generating a return ('the bond assets');
- specify the period for which the arrangements are to have effect ('the bond term'),

and under which the bond-issuer undertakes to dispose of the bond assets at the end of the bond term, to make a repayment of capital to the bond-holder during or at the end of the bond term (whether or not in instalments) and to make one or more additional payments to the bond-holder either during or at the end of the bond term, with the total additional payments not exceeding what would be a reasonable commercial return on a loan of the capital.

The provisions apply only if the following further conditions are met:

- under the arrangements the bond-issuer undertakes to arrange for the management of the bond assets with a view to generating income sufficient to make the above payments to the bond-holder;
- the bond is transferable, is a listed security on a recognised stock exchange (within *ITA 2007, s 1005* but see also below) and, under international accounting standards, falls to be accounted for as a financial liability of the bond-issuer (or would so fall if the bond-issuer applied those standards).

Certain additional stock exchanges are designated as recognised stock exchanges for the purposes of these provisions only (Order of the Commissioners of HMRC, 20 July 2007).

See also *ITA 2007, s 564G(2)* which allows for a range of possibilities within the above conditions; for example, the bond may (but need not) be convertible into, or exchangeable for, shares or securities at the end of its term.

Where these provisions apply (and subject to what is said below under 'Discount'), the additional payments are treated as alternative finance return. Generally, the income tax consequences are the same as for alternative finance arrangements involving purchase and resale (see **3.2** above), e.g. the treatment of the alternative finance return as interest.

The following additional consequences ensue for tax purposes:

- the arrangements are treated as securities (and, if appropriate conditions are met, may be corporate bonds for CGT purposes);
- the arrangements are not treated as a unit trust scheme or as an offshore fund;
- the bond-holder is not treated as having a legal or beneficial interest in the bond assets and is not entitled to relief for capital expenditure in connection with the assets;
- the bond-issuer is not treated as a trustee of the bond assets;
- profits accruing to the bond-issuer in connection with the bond assets are profits of the bond-issuer and not of the bond-holder (and do not arise to the bond-issuer in a fiduciary or representative capacity);
- the payments made by the bond-issuer to the bond-holder are not made in a fiduciary or representative capacity;
- the alternative finance return is excluded in determining, for any other income tax purpose, the consideration given for any sale of an asset by one party to the arrangements to the other party.

Discount

If part of the additional payments equates in substance to discount, that part is not treated as alternative finance return for income tax purposes but is taxed under the rules applicable to discounts (see **64.2** and **64.18** *et seq.* SAVINGS AND INVESTMENT INCOME). One consequence of this is that there can be no requirement to deduct tax (as in **24.12** DEDUCTION OF TAX AT SOURCE) from the discount element of the payments.

[ITA 2007, ss 564G, 564L(3)–(6), 564M–564O, 564R–564U, 564V(3), 1005(2A); FA 2005, ss 46, 48A, 48B, 51, 51A, 53, 56(1); FA 2007, s 53(1)–(3)(5)(7)(13); CTA 2009, Sch 1 paras 650, 651; FA 2009, Sch 61 para 27; TIOPA 2010, Sch 2 paras 8, 13–16, 19–23, 55].

The main effect of the above provisions are to apply the rules on alternative finance arrangements to a form of Shari'a compliant investment bond known (in the plural) as sukuk that is similar in economic substance to a debt security (Treasury Explanatory Notes to the 2007 Finance Bill).

Transitional

The above provisions apply additionally for income tax purposes in relation to payments of alternative finance return made after 5 April 2007, but under arrangements entered into on or before that date. In relation to a disposal after 6 April 2007 of arrangements within these provisions (whenever entered into), the provisions are deemed always to have had effect; this may be of significance for CGT purposes. [FA 2005, s 56(2)(3); FA 2007, s 53(13)(14)].

Stamp duty land tax, CGT and capital allowances

FA 2009, Sch 61 facilitates the issue of alternative finance investment bonds based on real property. With effect on and after 21 July 2009, it seeks to ensure that disposals and acquisitions of interests in land in connection with such bonds do not incur liabilities to stamp duty land tax or CGT and that entitlements to capital allowances on plant or machinery or industrial buildings are preserved.

Alternative finance return — profit share return

[3.6] Profit share return (for which see **3.7** and **3.8** below) is a type of alternative finance return and is treated for income tax purposes as if it were interest and thus within the charge at **64.2 SAVINGS AND INVESTMENT INCOME.** Where a person is a party to alternative finance arrangements for the purposes of a trade, profession or vocation, or of a property business (see **60.2 PROPERTY INCOME**), profit share return paid by that person is to be treated as an expense of the trade etc. Relief under *ITTOIA 2005, s 58* for incidental costs of obtaining finance (see **73.93 TRADING INCOME**) applies as if references to a loan included references to alternative finance arrangements and references to interest included references to profit share return. [*ITA 2007, ss 564M–564O; FA 2005, s 51; CTA 2009, Sch 1 para 655; TIOPA 2010, Sch 2 paras 14–16*].

Simon's Taxes. See **A1.304.**

Profit share return — deposit arrangements

[3.7] These provisions apply to arrangements under which a person deposits money with a financial institution (see **3.3** above), which is used by that institution, together with other money deposited, with a view to profit. Payments out of that profit are then made or credited to the depositor in proportion to the amount deposited, such that the return equates, in substance, to the return on an investment of money at interest.

Amounts paid or credited as above are profit share return, with tax consequences as in **3.6** above.

[*ITA 2007, ss 564E, 564L(1); FA 2005, ss 46, 49; FA 2006, s 95(1)(2); CTA 2009, Sch 1 para 652; TIOPA 2010, Sch 2 paras 6, 13*].

Simon's Taxes. See **A1.303, A1.306.**

Profit share return — agency arrangements

[3.8] These provisions apply to arrangements under which:

- a person ('the principal') appoints an agent;
- one or both of the principal and agent is a financial institution (see **3.3** above) or, before 15 October 2009, the agent is a financial institution;
- the agent uses money provided by the principal with a view to producing profits;

- the principal is entitled to those profits to a specified extent;
- the agent is entitled to any profits in excess of those to which the principal is entitled (and may also be entitled to be paid a fee by the principal); and
- the payment to the principal of his entitlement to profits equates, in substance, to the return on an investment of money at interest.

Amounts paid or credited in satisfaction of the principal's profit entitlement as above are profit share return, with tax consequences as in **3.6** above. For tax purposes, the agent, and not the principal, is treated as entitled to the profits themselves.

[ITA 2007, ss 564F, 564L(2), 564X; FA 2005, ss 46, 49A; FA 2006, s 95(1)(3); FA 2007, s 54; CTA 2009, Sch 1 para 653; TIOPA 2010, Sch 2 paras 7, 13, 25].

An example of an arrangement that the above is intended to cover is the Shari'a compliant finance product known as wakala (Treasury Explanatory Notes to the 2006 Finance Bill).

Simon's Taxes. See **A1.303, A1.306**.

Non-residents

[3.9] Where income arising to a non-UK resident consists of alternative finance return within **3.4, 3.5** or **3.8** above, neither the other party to the alternative finance arrangements nor any person acting for the non-resident in relation to the arrangements is regarded as the UK representative (within **50.6 NON-RESIDENTS**) of the non-resident in relation to the income. [ITA 2007, s 835J; FA 1995, s 127(1)(ca); FA 2006, s 95(10); FA 2007, s 53(11); CTA 2009, Sch 1 para 401; TIOPA 2010, Sch 6 para 8].

Arrangements not at arm's length

[3.10] The arrangements at **3.2, 3.4, 3.5, 3.7** and **3.8** above are not treated as alternative finance arrangements if:

- they are not entered into at arm's length,
- the transfer pricing rules at **4.18** et seq. **ANTI-AVOIDANCE** require the alternative finance return or profit share return (or amount representing it) to be recomputed on an arm's length basis, and
- the party receiving the return is not subject to income tax or corporation tax, or a corresponding tax under a foreign jurisdiction, on the return.

In any such case, the person paying the return is not entitled to any deduction in respect of it in computing profits for income tax purposes or in calculating net income.

[*ITA 2007, ss 564H, 564Y, Sch 1 para 599; FA 2005, s 52; FA 2006, ss 95(5), 96(5); FA 2007, s 53(6); CTA 2009, Sch 1 para 656; TIOPA 2010, Sch 2 paras 9, 26*].

Simon's Taxes. See **A1.304.**

4

Anti-Avoidance

Cross-references. See **2** ACCRUED INCOME SCHEME; CAPITAL ALLOWANCES at **10.8** and **10.22** for sales between connected persons; CAPITAL ALLOWANCES ON PLANT AND MACHINERY at **11.63** for sales between connected persons and **11.51** *et seq.* re certain leasing arrangements; **26** DOUBLE TAX RELIEF for amounts taxed abroad; **26.5** DOUBLE TAX RELIEF for wide-ranging anti-avoidance provisions concerning relief under double tax agreements; **43.2** INTEREST PAYABLE for certain interest; **45.11–45.19** LOSSES for restrictions relating to the use of losses in a trade, profession or vocation; **51** OFFSHORE FUNDS; **52.13–52.17** PARTNERSHIPS for restrictions on loss reliefs and interest reliefs due to non-active partners; **52.19** PARTNERSHIPS in relation to certain company partnership arrangements; **52.22, 52.24** PARTNERSHIPS for restrictions on loss reliefs due to, respectively, limited partners and members of limited liability partnerships; **60.17** PROPERTY INCOME for certain transactions in leases; **68.26–68.33** SETTLEMENTS for provisions treating income of settlements as income of the settlor.

Simon's Taxes. See A7.2, D9.1, D9.2, D9.7, E1.11, E1.12, I3.7.

Introduction

[4.1] For the general approach of the Courts to transactions entered into solely to avoid or reduce tax liability, leading cases are *Duke of Westminster v CIR* HL 1935, 19 TC 490; *W T Ramsay Ltd v CIR, Eilbeck v Rawling* HL 1981, 54 TC 101; *CIR v Burmah Oil Co Ltd* HL 1981, 54 TC 200 and *Furniss v Dawson (and related appeals)* HL 1984, 55 TC 324. See also *Cairns v MacDiarmid* CA 1982, 56 TC 556; *Ingram v CIR* Ch D, [1985] STC 835; *Craven v White and related appeals* HL 1988, 62 TC 1; *Shepherd v Lyntress Ltd* Ch D 1989, 62 TC 495; *Moodie v CIR and Sinnett* HL 1993, 65 TC 610; *Hatton v CIR* Ch D, [1992] STC 140; *Ensign Tankers (Leasing) Ltd v Stokes* HL 1992, 64 TC 617; *Countess Fitzwilliam and Others v CIR and related appeals* HL, [1993] STC 502; *Pigott v Staines Investment Co Ltd* Ch D 1995, 68 TC 342; *CIR v McGuckian* HL 1997, 69 TC 1; *MacNiven v Westmoreland Investments Ltd* HL 2001, 73 TC 1; *CIR v Scottish Provident Institution* HL 2004, 76 TC 538 and *Barclays Mercantile Business Finance Ltd v Mawson* HL 2004, 76 TC 446.

The classical interpretation of the constraints upon the Courts in deciding cases involving tax avoidance schemes is summed up in Lord Tomlin's statement in the *Duke of Westminster* case that ' . . . every man is entitled if he can to order his affairs so that the tax attaching . . . is less than it otherwise would be.' The case concerned annual payments made under covenant by a taxpayer to his domestic employees, which were in substance, but not in form, remuneration. The judgment was thus concerned with the tax consequences of a single transaction, but in *Ramsay*, and subsequently in *Furniss v Dawson*, the Courts have set bounds to the ambit within which this principle can be applied in relation to modern sophisticated and increasingly artificial arrangements to avoid tax. *Ramsay* concerned a complex 'circular' avoidance scheme at the end of which the financial position of the parties was little changed, but it was claimed that a large CGT loss had been created. It was held that where a preconceived series of transactions is entered into to avoid tax, and with the clear intention to proceed through all stages to completion once set in motion, the *Duke of Westminster* principle does not compel a consideration of the individual transactions and of the fiscal consequences of such transactions taken in isolation.

The HL opinions in *Furniss v Dawson* are of outstanding importance, and establish, inter alia, that the *Ramsay* principle is not confined to 'circular' devices, and that if a series of transactions is 'preordained', a particular transaction within the series, accepted as genuine, may nevertheless be ignored if it was entered into solely for fiscal reasons and without any commercial purpose other than tax avoidance, even if the series of transactions as a whole has a legitimate commercial purpose.

However, in *Craven v White* the House of Lords indicated that for the *Ramsay* principle to apply all the transactions in a series have to be pre-ordained with such a degree of certainty that, at the time of the earlier transactions, there is no practical likelihood that the transactions would not take place. It is not sufficient that the ultimate transaction is simply of a kind that was envisaged at the time of the earlier transactions.

The inheritance tax case *Fitzwilliam v CIR* appears to further restrict the application of the *Ramsay* principle, in that the HL found for the taxpayer in a case in which all their Lordships agreed that, once the scheme was embarked upon, there was no real possibility that the later transactions would not be proceeded with. There is, however, some suggestion that a decisive factor was that the first step in the transactions took place before the rest of the scheme had been formulated. Again, in the case of *MacNiven v Westmoreland Investments Ltd* it was held that the *Ramsay* principle did not apply where a company loaned money to a subsidiary to enable it to pay up outstanding interest and thus crystallise tax losses. The interest had been paid within the meaning of the legislation and the manner in which the payment was funded was irrelevant.

The HL judgments in *MacNiven v Westmoreland Investments Ltd* and, in particular, *Barclays Mercantile Business Finance Ltd v Mawson*, suggest that the essence of the current approach of the Courts to the *Ramsay* principle is 'to give the statutory provision a purposive construction in order to determine the nature of the transaction to which it was intended to apply and then to decide whether the actual transaction (which might involve considering the overall effect of a number of elements intended to operate together) answered to the statutory description'.

Simon's Taxes. See A2.117–A2.122.

Anti-avoidance legislation is intended to counteract transactions designed to avoid taxation, but bona fide transactions may sometimes be caught also. The provisions relating to income tax are detailed below and as further indicated in the cross-references above.

4.2– 4.5	Transactions in securities. [*ITA 2007, ss 682–713*].
4.6	Transfers of rights to receive income from securities. [*ICTA 1988, s 730 now repealed*].
4.7	Transfers of rights to receive annual payments. [*ICTA 1988, s 775A now repealed*].
4.8	Treatment of price differential on sale and repurchase of securities. [*ITA 2007, ss 607–611*].
4.9	Income on securities held for short periods. [*ICTA 1988, ss 731–735 now repealed*].
4.10– 4.13	'Manufactured' payments. [*ITA 2007, ss 565–614, 918–927*].
4.14– 4.17	Transfer of assets abroad. [*ITA 2007, ss 714–751*].
4.18– 4.27	Transfer pricing. [*ICTA 1988, s 770A, Sch 28AA*].
4.28	Sales of occupation income. [*ITA 2007, ss 773–789*].
4.29	Transactions in land. [*ITA 2007, ss 752–772*].
4.30	Land sold and leased back — payments connected with transferred land. [*ITA 2007, ss 681A–681AN*].
4.31	Land sold and leased back — new lease of land after assignment or surrender. [*ITA 2007, ss 681B–681BM*].
4.32	Leased trading assets. [*ITA 2007, ss 681C–681CG*].
4.33	Leased assets — capital sums. [*ITA 2007, ss 681D–681DP*].
4.34	Transfers of income streams. [*ITA 2007, ss 809AZA–809AZF*].
4.35	Factoring of income receipts etc. [*ITA 2007, ss 809BZA–809BZS*].
4.36	Loan or credit transactions. [*ITA 2007, ss 809CZA–809CZC*].
4.37	Leases of plant and machinery. [*ITA 2007, ss 809ZA–809ZD*].
4.38	Rent factoring of plant or machinery leases. [*ICTA 1988, s 785A now repealed*].
4.39	Annual payments for non-taxable consideration etc. [*ITA 2007, ss 843, 904*].
4.40	Dealings in commodity futures. [*ITA 2007, s 81*].

4.41 Futures and options — transactions with guaranteed returns. [*IT-TOIA 2005, Pt 4 Ch 12*].

4.42 Arrangements to pass on value of dividend tax credit. [*F(No 2)A 1997, s 28*].

4.43 Benefits from pre-owned assets. [*FA 2004, s 84, Sch 15*].

Disclosure of tax avoidance schemes

FA 2004 imposes a disclosure obligation on promoters of certain tax avoidance schemes and in some cases on persons entering into transactions under such schemes. See **4.44–4.51** below.

Transactions in securities

[4.2] There are provisions for counteracting income advantages obtained or obtainable in specified circumstances in respect of a transaction or transactions in securities. [*ITA 2007, Pt 13 Ch 1, Sch 2 para 129; ICTA 1988, ss 703–709; FA 2010, Sch 12 paras 2–7, 15(1)(2)*].

Subject to the exception below, the provisions apply where, in consequence of one or more 'transaction(s) in securities' combined with any of the circumstances listed below, a person is able to obtain an 'income tax advantage' (see **4.3** below). The circumstances were amended in relation to income tax advantages obtained after 23 March 2010. 'Securities' includes shares and stock, and, in the case of a company not limited by shares, includes an interest of a member of the company in whatever form. HMRC may make adjustments to counteract the tax advantage (see **4.4** below).

In relation to income tax advantages obtained after 23 March 2010, the provisions apply only if a main purpose of the person in being a party to the transaction or, as the case may be, any of the transactions is to obtain an income tax advantage. In relation to income tax advantages obtained before 24 March 2010, the provisions do not apply if the person shows (i) that the transaction or transactions are made (ii) for genuine commercial reasons or in the ordinary course of making or managing investments, and (iii) that enabling income tax advantages to be obtained is not a main object of the transaction or any of the transactions.

[*ITA 2007, ss 684, 685, 713; ICTA 1988, ss 703(1)(2), 709(2); FA 2010, Sch 12 paras 2, 15*].

On the question of whether a tax advantage was a 'main object' of a transaction, see *Marwood Homes Ltd v CIR, Tribunal 1998*, [1999] SSCD 44 and *Snell and another v HMRC (Sp C 699)*, [2008] SSCD 1094. See also *CIR v Laird Group plc Ch D 2001*, 75 TC 399.

For advance clearance, see **4.5** below.

A '*transaction in securities*' means a transaction, of whatever description, relating to securities, and includes in particular:

- the purchase, sale or exchange of securities;
- issuing or securing the issue of new securities;
- applying or subscribing for new securities; and
- altering or securing the alteration of the rights attached to securities.

[*ITA 2007, ss 684(2), 713; ICTA 1988, s 709(2); FA 2010, Sch 12 paras 2, 15*].

See also *CIR v Joiner* HL 1975, 50 TC 449 (in which a variation of rights prior to a liquidation was held to be a transaction in securities) and *CIR v Laird Group plc* HL 2003, 75 TC 399 (in which the payment of a dividend representing previously undistributed profits was held not to be).

For 'genuine commercial reasons' see *CIR v Laird Group, CIR v Brebner* HL 1967, 43 TC 705, *Clark v CIR* Ch D 1978, 52 TC 482 and *Marwood Homes Ltd v CIR, Tribunal* 1998, [1999] SSCD 44. In *Lewis (as a trustee of the Redrow Staff Pension Scheme) v CIR* (Sp C 218), [1999] SSCD 349, a distribution by way of purchase of its own shares by a company from the trustees of its pension scheme, pursuant to legislation requiring the trustees to reduce their holding, was held to be a transaction carried out by the trustees both for genuine commercial reasons and in the ordinary course of investment management.

Circumstances after 23 March 2010

In relation to income tax advantages obtained after 23 March 2010, the circumstances mentioned above, only one of which needs to be met, are those in (a) or (b) below, but see also below under Excluded circumstances.

(a)   As a result of the transaction in securities (or any one or more of the transactions in securities) the person receives 'relevant consideration' in connection with:

(i)   the distribution, transfer or realisation of assets of a 'close company'; or

(ii)   the application of assets of a close company in discharge of liabilities; or

(iii)   the direct or indirect transfer of assets of one close company to another close company;

and does not pay or bear income tax on the consideration.

(i)   In connection with the transaction in securities (or any one or more of the transactions in securities) the person receives 'relevant consideration';

(ii)   two or more close companies are concerned in the transaction(s); and

(iii)   the person does not pay or bear income tax on the consideration.

For the purposes of (a)(i) and (ii) above, '*relevant consideration*' means consideration which:

- is or represents the value of assets available for distribution by way of dividend by the company (or which would have been so available apart from anything done by the company); or
- is received in respect of future receipts of the company; or
- is or represents the value of trading stock of the company.

For the purposes of (a)(iii) and (b) above, 'relevant consideration' means consideration which consists of any share capital or any security issued by a close company and which is or represents the value of assets which:

• are available for distribution by way of dividend by the company (or would have been so available apart from anything done by the company); or
• are trading stock of the company.

'Close company' has the meaning given in CTA 2010, Pt 10 Ch 2 (broadly a company under the control of five or fewer participators) but also includes a company that would be a close company if it were resident in the UK.

The references in (a)(i) and (ii) above to 'assets' do not include assets which are shown to represent a return of sums paid by subscribers on the issue of securities, despite the fact that under the law of the country in which the company is incorporated assets of that description are available for distribution by way of dividend.

As regards (a)(iii) and (b) above, in so far as the consideration consists of non-redeemable share capital these provisions are triggered only so far as the share capital is repaid (in a winding-up or otherwise, including any distribution made in respect of any shares in a winding-up or dissolution).

Excluded circumstances

If the circumstances are as in (a) or (b) above, there is nevertheless a let-out if:

• immediately before the transaction in securities (or the first of two or more such transactions) the person concerned (P) holds shares (or an interest in shares) in the close company in question, and
• there is a 'fundamental change of ownership' of the close company.

There is a 'fundamental change of ownership' of the close company if, as a result of the transaction(s) in securities, at least 75% of the close company's ordinary share capital is held beneficially by one or more persons who are not connected with P and have not been connected with P at any time in the two years preceding the transaction (or the first transaction). The shares held by that person (or those persons) must carry an entitlement to at least 75% of the company's distributions and must carry at least 75% of the total voting rights in the company.

ITA 2007, s 993 applies to determine if persons are connected. See **21 CONNECTED PERSONS.**

[ITA 2007, ss 685, 686, 989; CTA 2010, Sch 1 para 562(4); FA 2010, Sch 12 paras 2, 7, 15].

Circumstances before 24 March 2010

In relation to income tax advantages obtained before 24 March 2010, the circumstances mentioned above, only one of which needs to be met, are as follows.

(A)   In connection with:

- a purchase of securities followed by the sale of the same or other securities; or
- a sale of securities followed by the purchase of the same or other securities; or
- a sale of securities followed by the purchase of the same or other securities; or
- the distribution, transfer or realisation of assets of a company; or
- the application of such assets in discharge of liabilities;

the person receives an 'abnormal amount by way of dividend' which is taken into account for purposes of;

- any exemption from income tax; or
- the setting off of losses against profits or income; or
- the giving of relief under *ITA 2007, s 383* (relief for interest payments — see **43.5 INTEREST PAYABLE**).

(B) In connection with any of the matters listed in (A) above, a person becomes entitled to a deduction from profits because of a decrease in value of securities held, formerly held, or sold which arises from payment of a dividend thereon or from any other dealing with a company's assets. This condition is repealed with effect for transactions in securities on or after 1 April 2008.

(C) In consequence of a transaction whereby (see *CIR v Garvin* HL 1981, 55 TC 24 and *Bird v CIR* HL 1988, 61 TC 238, and contrast *Emery v CIR* Ch D 1980, 54 TC 607) another person has received or subsequently receives an 'abnormal amount by way of dividend', the person to whom these provisions potentially apply receives consideration which:

- is not otherwise chargeable to income tax; and
- represents the value of:
  (i)   a company's trading stock or future receipts; or
  (ii) assets which are, or would otherwise have been, available for distribution (see *CIR v Brown* CA 1971, 47 TC 217) by a company as dividend, and which, in the case of a company incorporated abroad, do not represent a return of capital to subscribers.

For transactions entered into before 1 April 2008, the above applied equally if, instead of receiving an abnormal amount by way of dividend, the other person had become, or subsequently became, entitled to a deduction as in (B) above.

(D) In connection with the distribution, transfer or realisation of assets of a 'relevant company', or the application of such assets in discharge of liabilities, the person potentially within these provisions receives consideration which represents the value of:

(i)   the relevant company's trading stock or future receipts; or
(ii) assets which are, or would otherwise have been, available for distribution (see *CIR v Brown* CA 1971, 47 TC 217) by the relevant company as dividend, and which, in the case of a company incorporated abroad, do not represent a return of capital to subscribers,

and receives the consideration in such a way that it is not otherwise chargeable to income tax.

(E)   In connection with (i) the transfer of assets of a 'relevant company' to another such company, or (ii) a transaction in securities in which two or more relevant companies are concerned, the person potentially within these provisions receives consideration which:
- consists of any share capital or any security issued by a relevant company;
- is not otherwise chargeable to income tax; and
- represents the value of:
  (i)   a relevant company's trading stock; or
  (ii)   assets which are, or would otherwise have been, available for distribution (see *CIR v Brown* CA 1971, 47 TC 217) by a relevant company as dividend.

In so far as the consideration consists of non-redeemable share capital, it triggers these provisions only so far as the share capital is repaid (in a winding-up or otherwise, including any distribution made in respect of any shares in a winding-up or dissolution).

The provisions apply equally where the income tax advantage is obtainable due to the combined effect of the transaction(s) and the liquidation of a company.

[*ITA 2007, ss 686–690, 713, 989, 1005, Sch 2 paras 129, 130; ICTA 1988, ss 704, 709(2)(3); FA 2007, Sch 26 paras 1, 12(11)(12); FA 2008, s 66(2)(5)*].

(C), (D) and (E) above are in practice unlikely to apply unless the company in question has (or has recently had) distributable reserves (HMRC Company Taxation Manual CTM36835–36845).

For cases within (C) and (D) above, see *CIR v Cleary* HL 1967, 44 TC 399; *Anysz v CIR* Ch D 1977, 53 TC 601; *Williams v CIR* HL 1980, 54 TC 257; *CIR v Wiggins* Ch D 1978, 53 TC 639; *Lloyd v HMRC* (Sp C 672), [2008] SSCD 681. In determining 'under the control' in (D), the relevant date is the date of the dividend (*CIR v Garvin* above).

For the purposes of (A) and (C) above, an 'abnormal amount by way of dividend' is received if an officer of HMRC, the Commissioners of HMRC or the Appeal Tribunal (whichever is determining the question) is satisfied that the condition in (a) below is met and also, in relation to fixed rate dividends only, that the condition in (b) below is met.

(a)   This condition is that the dividend substantially exceeds a normal return on the consideration provided by the recipient for the securities (or, if those securities are derived from securities previously acquired by the recipient, those securities). In determining 'normal return', regard must be had to the length of time the securities were held and to dividends paid and other distributions made in respect of them during that time. If the recipient acquired the securities for nil consideration or for greater than market value, the recipient is treated for the purposes of this test as having acquired them at market value.

(b)   This condition is that the fixed rate dividend substantially exceeds the amount which the recipient would have received if the dividend had accrued from day to day and the recipient had been entitled to only so much of it as accrued while the recipient held the securities. But this condition is not met if during the six months beginning with the purchase of the securities the recipient does not dispose of them (or dispose of similar securities) or acquire an option to sell them (or to sell similar securities).

[*ITA 2007, ss 692–694; ICTA 1988, s 709(4)–(6); SI 2009 No 56, Sch 1 para 455*].

In any of (A)–(E) above, references to a dividend include any other qualifying distribution and also include interest. [*ITA 2007, s 713; ICTA 1988, s 709(2)*]. The amount of a qualifying distribution includes the related tax credit for these purposes (*CIR v Universities Superannuation Scheme Ltd* Ch D 1996, 70 TC 193). In the case of a purchase by a company of its own shares treated as a distribution (see Tolley's Corporation Tax under Distributions), it was held that the return was not abnormal (*CIR v Sema Group Pension Scheme Trustees* CA 2002, 74 TC 593).

In any of (C)–(E) above, references to consideration include money's worth. [*ITA 2007, s 688(8), 689(6), 690(8); ICTA 1988, s 709(3)*].

For the purposes of (D) and (E) above, a 'relevant company' is:

• a company under the control of five or fewer persons; or
• any other company none of whose shares or stocks (disregarding any debenture stock, preferred shares or preferred stock) is included in the Official UK list and dealt in on a recognised stock exchange in the UK (or before 19 July 2007 was listed in the Official List of the Stock Exchange, and dealt in on the Stock Exchange).

But a company is not a relevant company if it is under the control of one or more companies which are not themselves relevant companies. 'Control' is defined as in *CTA 2010, s 450*. In determining 'under the control', the relevant date is the date of the dividend (*CIR v Garvin* HL 1981, 55 TC 24).

[*ITA 2007, s 691, Sch 2 para 130; ICTA 1988, s 704; FA 2007, s 109, Sch 26 para 12(11)*].

Simon's Taxes. See D9.1.

Meaning of 'income tax advantage'

[4.3] For the purposes of **4.2** above, the meaning of 'income tax advantage' differs according to whether the circumstances are those in **4.2**(a) or (b) above (circumstances after 23 March 2010) or those in any of **4.2**(A)–(E) above (circumstances before 24 March 2010).

Circumstances after 23 March 2010

A person obtains an '*income tax advantage*' if the amount of income tax (if any) which would be payable by him in respect of the 'relevant consideration' (see **4.2** above) if it constituted a qualifying distribution exceeds the amount of capital gains tax payable in respect of it (which may be a nil amount). The amount of the income tax advantage is equal to the amount of that excess. For this purpose only, the relevant consideration is limited (if it would otherwise be greater) to the maximum amount that could in any circumstances have been paid to the person by way of a qualifying distribution at the time when the relevant consideration is received.

[ITA 2007, s 687; FA 2010, Sch 12 paras 2, 15].

Circumstances before 24 March 2010

An *'income tax advantage'* means any of the following:

- a relief (or increased relief) from income tax;
- a repayment (or increased repayment) of income tax;
- the avoidance or reduction of a charge to income tax or an assessment to income tax; or
- the avoidance of a possible assessment to income tax.

'Relief from income tax' includes a dividend tax credit. As regards the last two items, it does not matter whether the avoidance or reduction is effected by receipts accruing in such a way that the recipient does not pay income tax on them or by a deduction in calculating profits or gains.

[ITA 2007, s 683; ICTA 1988, s 709(1)(2A)].

For 'tax advantage' see *CIR v Cleary* HL 1967, 44 TC 399 (tax advantage obtained where taxpayers' company purchased shares from them) and contrast *CIR v Kleinwort, Benson Ltd* Ch D 1968, 45 TC 369 (no tax advantage where merchant bank purchased debentures with interest in arrear shortly before redemption). The decision in *Sheppard and another (Trustees of the Woodland Trust) v CIR (No 2)* Ch D 1993, 65 TC 724 that no tax advantage could arise where relief was obtained by virtue of charitable exemption was doubted in *CIR v Universities Superannuation Scheme Ltd* Ch D 1996, 70 TC 193, in which the opposite conclusion was reached. Prior to the hearing of the latter case, the Inland Revenue had, in any event, indicated that they would continue to proceed under the legislation on the footing that tax-exempt bodies obtain a tax advantage whenever they receive abnormal dividends, since they considered that there would have been good grounds for challenging the earlier decision had it not been for a defect in the assessment under appeal. This continues to be the HMRC approach. (Revenue Tax Bulletin August 1993 p 90, April 1998 p 537, October 1998 pp 590–592). For the quantum of the tax advantage, see *Bird v CIR* HL 1988, 61 TC 238.

Procedure

[4.4] The following procedure applies if an officer of HMRC believes that the provisions at **4.2** above may apply in a particular case.

(i)   The officer must notify the person (or his personal representatives if deceased) that he has reason to believe that the provisions may apply to him in respect of transaction(s) specified in the notification. *[ITA 2007, ss 695, 712; ICTA 1988, s 703(9)(11)].* See *Balen v CIR* CA 1978, 52 TC 406.

(ii)   The person notified may make a statutory declaration that in his opinion the provisions do not apply, stating supporting facts and circumstances, and send it to the HMRC officer within 30 days. [*ITA 2007, s 696; ICTA 1988, s 703(9)*]. For acceptance of late statutory declarations, see Revenue Tax Bulletin April 1999 p 656.

(iii)   The HMRC officer must then either take no further action or send the declaration together with a certificate that he sees reason to take further action (and any counter-statement he wishes to submit) to the Appeal Tribunal. The Tribunal will consider the declaration and certificate and counter-statement (if any) and decide whether there is a *prima facie* case for proceeding further. Such a determination does not affect the application of these provisions in respect of transactions including not only the ones to which the determination relates but also others. [*ITA 2007, s 697; ICTA 1988, s 703(10); SI 2009 No 56, Sch 1 paras 456, 458*]. HMRC have no right of appeal if the determination goes against them ad must take no further action. The taxpayer is not entitled to see HMRC's counter-statement nor to be heard by the Tribunal (*Wiseman v Borneman* HL 1969, 45 TC 540). See also *Howard v Borneman* HL 1975, 50 TC 322 and *Balen v CIR* CA 1978, 52 TC 406.

(iv)   If the Tribunal decides there is a case, or if no statutory declaration is made under (ii) above by the person, HMRC will make adjustments to counteract the corporation tax advantage. The adjustments required to be made, and the basis on which they are to be made, must be specified in a notice (a '*counteraction notice*') served on the person by an HMRC officer. The adjustments may take the form of an assessment, the cancellation of a tax repayment and/or a recalculation of profits or gains or liability to income tax. No assessment may be made later than six years after the tax year to which the tax advantage relates. [*ITA 2007, s 698; ICTA 1988, s 703(3); FA 2010, Sch 12 paras 3, 15; SI 2009 No 56, Sch 1 para 457*].

If **4.2**(a)(iii) or (b) above or **4.2**(E) above is in point, and is triggered by the repayment of share capital, the assessment must be for the tax year in which that repayment occurs. [*ITA 2007, s 700; ICTA 1988, s 704; FA 2010, Sch 12 paras 5, 15*].

The income tax payable by a person under **4.2**(D) or (E) above is limited to that which would arise in respect of a qualifying distribution of an amount equal to the consideration referred to in **4.2**(D) or (E) above (as appropriate) received on the same day as that consideration. [*ITA 2007, s 699; ICTA 1988, s 703(3A)*].

(v)   A person on whom a counteraction notice has been served may appeal, by giving notice to the Commissioners for HMRC within 30 days of the service of the notice, on the grounds that the provisions do not apply to him in respect of the transaction(s) in question or that the stated adjustments are inappropriate. The Tribunal may then affirm, vary or cancel the counteraction notice or affirm, vary or quash an assessment made in accordance with the notice. [*ITA 2007, ss 705–707, Sch 2 para 131; ICTA 1988, ss 705–705B; SI 1994 No 1813; SI 2009 No 56, Sch 1 paras 459, 460*].

(vi)   The application of these provisions is outside self-assessment, so that returns should be made without having regard to a possible charge (although taxpayers may wish to draw HMRC's attention to any correspondence with the Clearance and Counteraction Team (see **4.5** below) in connection with any particular transaction). Enquiries into the possible application of these provisions will accordingly be carried out independently of any enquiry into the self-assessment return (see **63.6 RETURNS**). (Revenue Tax Bulletin April 2000 pp 742, 743).

Following legal advice, HMRC changed the date from which they charge interest on tax due on an assessment within (iv) above (HMRC Tax Bulletin August 2006 pp 1304, 1305). The 'relevant date' (within **42.2 INTEREST AND SURCHARGES ON OVERDUE TAX**) is 31 January following the tax year in question.

Clearance

[4.5] Where **4.2** above may be in point, the taxpayer may take the initiative by submitting to HMRC particulars of any transaction effected or contemplated; HMRC may, within 30 days of receipt, call for further information (to be supplied within 30 days). Subject to this, they must notify their decision within 30 days of receipt of the particulars or further information, and if they are satisfied that no liability arises the matter is concluded as regards that transaction by itself, provided that all facts and material particulars have been fully and accurately disclosed. [*ITA 2007, ss 701, 702; ICTA 1988, s 707*]. HMRC are not obliged to give reasons for refusal of clearance but where the applicant has given full reasons for his transactions the main grounds for refusing clearance will be indicated. A refusal to give clearance indicates that counteraction would be taken if the transaction were completed. (HMRC SP 3/80).

Applications for clearance should be directed to Clearance and Counteraction Team, Anti-Avoidance Group, First Floor, 22 Kingsway, London WC2B 6NR (or, if market-sensitive information is included, to 'Team Leader' at the same address). Applications may be faxed to 020 7438 4409 or emailed to reconstructions@hmrc.gsi.gov.uk. Applications containing sensitive information should not be emailed at all and should be faxed only after telephoning Eric Gardner on 020 7438 6585. Only a single application need be made as above for clearances under any one or more of: *ITA 2007, s 701* or *ICTA 1988, s 707* (transactions in securities — see **4.2** above), *CTA 2010, ss 1091, 1092* or *ICTA 1988, s 215* (demergers), *CTA 2010, s 1044* or *ICTA 1988, s 225* (purchase of own shares), *ITA 2007, s 247(1)(f)* or *ICTA 1988, s 304A(1)(f)* (EIS company becoming wholly-owned subsidiary of new holding company — see **28.22 ENTERPRISE INVESTMENT SCHEME**), *TCGA 1992, s 138(1)* (share exchanges), *TCGA 1992, s 139(5)* (reconstructions involving the transfer of a business), *TCGA 1992, s 140B* (transfer of a UK trade between EU member states), *TCGA 1992, s 140D* (transfer of a non-UK trade between EU member states) and *CTA 2009, ss 832, 833* (previously *FA 2002, Sch 29 para 88*) (various clearances under the corporation tax intangible assets regime). For these and further details, see www.hmrc.gov.uk/cap/index.htm.

Revenue 'Working Together' Bulletin August 2001 pp 8, 9 contained a checklist of the items of information whose omission from clearance applications most commonly causes delay in the processing of applications.

Transfers of rights to receive income from securities

[4.6] The provisions described below are repealed with effect for transfers on or after 22 April 2009 and are superseded by the more general provisions on transfers of income streams at **4.34** below.

Where the owner of company shares sells or transfers the right to distributions (e.g. dividends) therefrom *but not to the shares themselves*, such distributions are treated for tax purposes as income of that owner (or, where the owner is not the beneficial owner, of the beneficiary entitled to the income) for the tax year in which the right to receive the distributions was sold. If tax would have been chargeable on the REMITTANCE BASIS (**61**) on the interest etc., the charge is correspondingly limited to the amounts remitted. If the proceeds of sale or transfer are otherwise chargeable to tax there is no charge under these provisions. HMRC have power to obtain information for the purposes of these provisions.

The charge is on the full amount of such income arising in the tax year but with credit for any tax already borne.

[*ICTA 1988, s 730; FA 2006, Sch 6 para 2; FA 2009, Sch 25 paras 9(1), 10*].

Simon's Taxes. See **D9.302–D9.309.**

Transfers of rights to receive annual payments

[4.7] The provisions described below are repealed with effect for transfers on or after 22 April 2009 and are superseded by the more general provisions on transfers of income streams at **4.34** below.

If a person sells or transfers the right to receive an annual payment and the consideration for the sale etc. would not otherwise be chargeable to tax, the seller or transferor is liable to income tax, for the tax year in which the sale etc. occurs, on an amount equal to the market value of the right to receive the annual payment. However, this does not apply in the case of a life annuity or pension annuity (both as defined), or an annual payment in respect of which, by virtue of *ITTOIA 2005, s 727* (annual payments made by individuals and arising in the UK), no liability to income tax arises under *ITTOIA 2005, Pt 5* (miscellaneous income).

These provisions also apply in relation to parts of annual payments. The transfer of *all* the rights under an agreement to receive annual payments is also within the scope of the provisions.

[*ICTA 1988, s 775A; CTA 2009, Sch 1 para 230; FA 2009, Sch 25 paras 9(1), 10*].

Simon's Taxes. See D9.320.

Price differential on repo agreements

[4.8] [*ITA 2007, ss 569, 607–611, Sch 2 paras 119–124; ICTA 1988, ss 730A, 730B, 730BB*].

Subject to the exception mentioned below, where a person (the 'original owner') has transferred securities to another person (the 'interim holder') under an agreement to sell them, and the original owner or a CONNECTED PERSON (21) is required to buy them back under, or in consequence of the exercise of an option (whether a put or a call option) acquired under, the same or a 'related' agreement, any difference between the sale and repurchase price is treated for income tax purposes as a payment of interest which:

(a)   where the repurchase price is greater than the sale price, is made by the repurchaser on a deemed loan from the interim holder of an amount equal to the sale price; and

(b)   otherwise is made by the interim holder on a deemed loan from the repurchaser of an amount equal to the repurchase price.

In either case, the deemed interest is treated for income tax purposes as becoming due when the repurchase price becomes due and, accordingly, as paid when that price is paid. For income tax purposes (other than those of the current provisions and the provisions governing deemed manufactured payments in relation to repos — see **4.13** below), and for the purposes of *TCGA 1992* (unless *TCGA 1992, s 263A*, see below, applies), the repurchase price is treated as reduced by the amount of the deemed interest where (a) above applies or as increased by that amount where (b) above applies. With effect for arrangements coming into force on or after 1 October 2007, a company within the charge to corporation tax is not treated as a result of these provisions as making a payment of interest for income tax purposes. [*ITA 2007, ss 607, 609, Sch 1 para 331; TCGA 1992, s 261G*].

The repurchase price, in a case where the rules relating to deemed manufactured payments in relation to repos operate to deem an increase in the repurchase price (see **4.13** below), is that price as increased by the deeming provisions. [*ITA 2007, s 610*]. In cases involving the exercise of an option (whether a put or a call option), the sale price must be adjusted for any consideration given for the option. [*ITA 2007, s 607(7)*].

HMRC generally accept that the deemed interest is short interest, except where it is clear that the transaction was entered into as a substitute for long term finance, and in particular where it is clear finance was arranged in this way specifically to avoid deduction of tax at source (Revenue Tax Bulletin December 1995 p 266).

The exception referred to above disapplies these provisions (unless regulations under *ITA 2007, ss 612–614*, see below, otherwise provide) if the agreement(s) in question are non-arm's length agreements, or if all the benefits and risks arising from fluctuations in the market value of the securities accrue to, or fall on, the interim holder. The Treasury has extensive powers to make modifications by regulation to the provisions governing price differences under repos in cases where the non-arm's length exception applies. [*ITA 2007, ss 608, 611*].

The Treasury also has power to make regulations providing for an amount of deemed interest under these provisions to fall within the exemptions for pension business of insurance companies, for registered pension schemes, exempt approved pension schemes or superannuation funds or certain other such schemes, or for funds held for pre-2006/07 personal pension schemes or retirement annuity contracts. See *SI 1995 No 3036* (as amended). [*ITA 2007, s 609(5) (6)*].

See also *SI 1998 No 3177, regs 16, 17* as regards securities which, prior to their repurchase, are converted from currencies of States which have adopted the euro into euros.

[*ITA 2007, ss 607–611; ICTA 1988, ss 730A, 730BB; FA 2007, s 47, Sch 14 para 23; SI 2007 No 2483, reg 3*].

Where the above provisions apply, the acquisition and disposal by the interim holder, and (except where the repurchaser is or may be different from the original owner) the disposal and acquisition (as repurchaser) by the original owner, are disregarded for CGT purposes. This does not, however, apply:

(A)   if the agreement(s) in question are non-arm's length agreements, or if all the benefits or risks arising from fluctuations in the market value of the securities accrue to, or fall on, the interim holder; or

(B)   in relation to any disposal or acquisition of qualifying corporate bonds (see Tolley's Capital Gains Tax under Qualifying Corporate Bonds) where the securities disposed of by the original owner, or those acquired by him or another person as repurchaser, are not such bonds.

With effect for arrangements coming into force on or after 1 October 2007, the following additional rules have effect where the above disregard applies.

•   If at any time after the acquisition by the interim holder it becomes apparent that he will not dispose of the securities to the repurchaser, he is treated for CGT purposes as acquiring them at that time at their then market value.

•   If at any time after the disposal by the original owner it becomes apparent that he will not acquire the securities (as repurchaser), he is treated for CGT purposes as disposing of them at that time at their then market value.

See also *SI 1998 No 3177, regs 14–18* (as amended) as regards conversions of securities from currencies of States which have adopted the euro into euros.

[*TCGA 1992, s 263A; ITA 2007, Sch 1 para 334; FA 2007, s 47, Sch 14 para 12; SI 2007 No 2483, reg 3*].

Interpretation. For the above purposes, the following apply.

(i)   Agreements are 'related' if entered into in pursuance of the same arrangement, regardless of the date on which either agreement is entered into.

(ii)   References to buying back securities include buying back similar securities, and 'repurchase' is construed accordingly. Securities are 'similar' if they give entitlement to the same rights against the same persons as to capital, interest and dividends, and to the same enforcement remedies. Where securities are converted from the currency of a State which has adopted the euro into euros (a *'euroconversion'*), the new securities are treated as 'similar' (see *SI 1998 No 3177, regs 3, 14 as amended*).

(iii)   'Securities' has the same meaning as it does for the purposes of manufactured payments (see **4.10** below).

[*ITA 2007, ss 571, 566, 567, 570; ICTA 1988, s 730B*].

The Treasury has power to make regulations providing for *ITA 2007, ss 607–610* and *TCGA 1992, s 263A* above to apply with modifications in relation to non-standard repo cases (as defined by *ITA 2007, s 612*) and cases involving redemption arrangements (where the securities are redeemed during the currency of the repo). See *SI 2007 No 2486* where the original transfer of the securities takes place on or after 1 October 2007, and see previously *SI 1995 No 3220*. These SI's provide for such modifications in cases where other securities are substituted for those originally transferred and in cases involving redemption arrangements.

[*ITA 2007, ss 612–614, Sch 1 paras 332, 336–338; TCGA 1992, s 261H, ss 263F–263H*].

See also **4.10** below, **73.111** TRADING INCOME and Tolley's Corporation Tax under Income Tax in Relation to a Company. For a brief overview of the changes made by *FA 2003* to the tax provisions on sale and repurchase agreements, see Revenue Tax Bulletin August 2003 pp 1052, 1053.

Simon's Taxes. See D9.1001, D9.1002, D9.1015–D9.1018.

Income on securities held for short periods

[4.9] The following provisions relate to income received on securities held for one month or less or held for more than one month but not more than six months. They apply where *either* purchase or sale was not at current market price *or* agreement regarding sale was made at, or before, purchase (see *ICTA 1988, s 731(3)*).

[*ICTA 1988, ss 731–735 repealed by FA 2008, s 66(1)(c), (6)*].

These provisions are repealed in relation to cases where the initial purchase is made on or after 1 April 2008. Otherwise, effects as regards various classes of recipient are as in (a) to (c) below.

In calculating the period of one or six months, sale under prior option is regarded as a sale at option date [*ICTA 1988, s 731(4)*], and a sale of 'similar securities' is taken into account. [*ICTA 1988, s 731(5)(10)*]. A purchase or sale effected as a direct result of the exercise of a 'qualifying option' (broadly, a traded or financial option within *TCGA 1992, s 144(8)*) is treated as being at current market price (and so excluded from these provisions) if the first buyer acquired, or became subject to, the option on arm's length terms. [*ICTA 1988, s 731(4A)–(4C)*]. The '*appropriate amount*' is the pre-acquisition portion of the dividend, interest etc. calculated from last 'ex-div' day. [*ICTA 1988, s 735(3)*]. See *ICTA 1988, s 735(4)* (as amended) if no last 'ex-div' day. In the case of (a) below, the portion taken is of net interest after deduction of tax and the amounts of actual dividends. In the case of (b), (c) and (d) below, it is the gross amount of interest and the amounts of dividends plus related tax credits. [*ICTA 1988, s 731(9)–(9B), s 735(1)(2)*].

These provisions do not apply where the purchaser is required by the purchase agreement to make to the vendor, before his re-sale of the securities, a payment representative of the interest, or where the purchaser is treated by *ITA 2007, s 602(1)* (or previously by *ICTA 1988, s 737A(5)*) as being required to make such a payment (see the provisions on manufactured payments at **4.10** below). [*ICTA 1988, s 731(2A); ITA 2007, Sch 1 para 167(2); FA 2007, s 47, Sch 14 para 6(2); SI 2007 No 2483, reg 3*].

Where there is a 'repo agreement' in relation to any securities, neither their purchase or repurchase, nor their sale or sale back, is taken into account under these provisions. The securities purchased by the original owner from the person to whom securities were sold under the agreement (the '*interim holder*') are instead treated under these provisions as the same securities, and as purchased at the same time, as his original holding. This does not, however, apply if the agreement(s) under which the arrangements are made are on non-arm's length terms, or if the interim holder bears any of the benefits or risks of market value fluctuations before the securities are repurchased. There is a '*repo agreement*' if the original owner sells the securities in pursuance of an agreement, and under the same or a 'related' agreement either:

- is required to buy back the securities, either as a result of a straight-forward obligation or the interim holder's exercise of an option; or
- acquires an option to buy them back which he subsequently exercises; or
- is entitled to receive from the interim holder an amount equal to any redemption proceeds.

Agreements are '*related*' for these purposes if entered into in pursuance of the same arrangement. The above references to buying back securities include buying 'similar' securities (as defined).

[*ICTA 1988, s 731(2B)–(2G); FA 2007, s 47, Sch 14 para 6(3); SI 2007 No 2483, reg 3*].

(a) **Share dealers.** The net 'appropriate amount' of the interest etc. is treated for all tax purposes as a reduction of the purchase price. This treatment does not apply if the interest falls to be taken into account in computing the first buyer's trading profits (see **73.111 TRADING INCOME**). It also does not apply to overseas securities if *ICTA 1988, s 732(4)* complied with.
[*ICTA 1988, s 732*].
See *ICTA 1988, s 731(7)(8)* (as amended) regarding change in ownership, or commencement, of trade.

The Commissioners of HMRC may make regulations by statutory instrument, effective from a day to be appointed therein, imposing conditions for the exclusion of market makers to apply, and making appropriate provision in regard to recognised investment exchanges other than the Stock Exchange. [*ICTA 1988, s 738(1)*].

(b)   **Person otherwise entitled to exemption from tax.** Exemption does not extend to the gross 'appropriate amount' of the interest etc. [*ICTA 1988, s 733; ITA 2007, Sch 1 para 168*]. That interest cannot be used to cover qualifying annual payments (see **1.9 ALLOWANCES AND TAX RATES**).

(c)   **Traders other than share dealers.** The gross 'appropriate amount' of the interest etc. and tax thereon is ignored in calculating loss repayment claim under *ITA 2007, s 64* or *72* (previously *ICTA 1988, s 380* or *381*) (see **45.2**, **45.9 LOSSES**). [*ICTA 1988, s 734(1); ITA 2007, Sch 1 para 169*].

'Securities' are defined to exclude those within the **ACCRUED INCOME SCHEME** (**2**). [*ICTA 1988, s 731(9); ITA 2007, Sch 1 para 167(3)*].

Simon's Taxes. See D9.2.

'Manufactured' payments

[4.10] The legislation governing manufactured payments is contained in *ITA 2007, Pt 11*.

The provisions of *ITA 2007, Pt 11 Ch 2 (ss 572–591)* have effect in relation to certain cases (see (a)–(c) below) where, under a contract or other arrangement for the transfer of shares or securities, a person is required to pay to the other party an amount representing a dividend or payment of interest thereon.

ITA 2007, Pt 11 Ch 3 (ss 592–595) operates to deny tax credits in certain cases involving stock lending or repurchase agreements (repos) (see **4.12** below).

ITA 2007, Pt 11 Ch 4 (ss 596–606) contains rules relating to deemed manufactured payments in relation to certain stock lending or repo arrangements (see **4.13** below).

The circumstances in which the provisions in *ITA 2007, Pt 11 Ch 2* apply are as follows.

(a)   **Manufactured dividends on UK shares.** This applies where one of the parties to a transfer of UK equities is required to pay the other an amount (a '*manufactured dividend*') representative of a dividend thereon.

(b)   **Manufactured interest on UK securities.** This applies where one of the parties to a transfer of UK securities is required to pay the other an amount ('*manufactured interest*') representative of a periodical payment of interest thereon. (See Tolley's Corporation Tax under Loan Relationships special cases for the corporation tax treatment of manufactured interest.)

(c)   **Manufactured overseas dividends.** This applies where one of the parties to a transfer of overseas securities is required to pay the other an amount (a '*manufactured overseas dividend*') representative of an overseas dividend thereon.

Where these provisions apply, the intention is that both payer and recipient of the amount in question should be in the same position, for tax purposes, as if the payment had in fact been a dividend or payment of interest. See *ITA 2007, ss 573, 578, 581* for the detailed mechanism by which this is achieved in each case.

In cases within (a) above, the payer is given an income tax deduction in arriving at net income for the tax year in question (see Step 2 at **1.7 ALLOWANCES AND TAX RATES**). The deduction is limited to the lower of the manufactured payment and the underlying dividend that the manufactured payment represents. Where the manufactured payment exceeds the original dividend, the excess is treated as a separate fee for entering into the transfer arrangement. In addition, a manufactured payment made before 31 January 2008 is deductible only to the extent that it can be matched with a taxable amount: either the original dividend, which must have been received in the same tax year as that in which the person makes the manufactured payment or in the preceding or following tax year; or with deemed interest arising from a repo price differential (see **4.8** above). Where the taxable amount is the original dividend, the deduction is made from the taxable amount instead of from total income. There are separate rules governing manufactured property income dividends in relation to Real Estate Investment Trusts.

There is legislation to the effect that a manufactured payment is not allowable as a deduction for income tax purposes if it is incurred in connection with avoidance arrangements (see **4.11** below).

A payer of a manufactured dividend who is not within the charge to corporation tax must give the recipient a statement setting out the amount of the manufactured dividend, the date of payment and the amount of the associated tax credit.

In cases within (b) above, manufactured interest paid before 31 January 2008 must be matched with a taxable amount of interest: either the underlying interest that the manufactured payment represents, or deemed interest under the accrued income scheme or a repo price differential.

In cases within (b) and (c) above, where a manufactured payment is less than the underlying payment it represents, any deduction in respect of the manufactured payment is limited to the gross amount of the manufactured payment itself. Conversely, if the underlying payment is less than the manufactured payment, the excess is treated as a separate fee for entering into the transfer arrangement.

Manufactured payments within (b) and (c) above are subject to deduction of tax at source:

- in the case of (b) above, at the basic rate (for 2008/09 onwards, previously the savings rate) in force for the year of payment (unless the underlying interest is payable gross, e.g. gilts, or the payment falls into the exception for payments between companies, see **24.18** DEDUCTION OF TAX AT SOURCE);
- in the case of (c) above, income tax equal to the relevant withholding tax (as defined).

Where the manufactured payment is made by a non-UK resident (and otherwise than in the course of a trade carried on through a branch or agency in the UK) there is a 'reverse charge' procedure where the recipient must account for and pay an equivalent amount of tax.

[*ITA 2007, ss 572, 573–581, 582–591, 918–927; ICTA 1988, s 736A, Sch 23A; FA 2006, s 139(1)(2)(7); ITA 2007, Sch 1 para 621; FA 2008, s 63, Sch 1 paras 31, 65, Sch 23 paras 1–9; CTA 2010, Sch 1 paras 537–539, 555; TIOPA 2010, Sch 7 paras 112, 113; SI 1992 No 173; SI 1992 No 1346; SI 1993 No 933; SI 1997 No 991*].

The Treasury has wide power to make regulations concerning all types of manufactured payments and the administrative procedures surrounding them. Such regulations may, *inter alia*, extend the circumstances in which (a)–(c) above may apply. See *SI 1993 No 2004* and *SI 1996 No 1826*.

The Treasury also has power to make regulations providing for any manufactured payment within (a)–(c) above to be treated as falling within the exemptions for pension business of insurance companies, for registered pension schemes, exempt approved pension schemes or superannuation funds or certain other such schemes. See *SI 1995 No 3036*.

Simon's Taxes. See D9.7.

Denial of income tax deduction

[4.11] Legislation was introduced by *FA 2008* to ensure that a manufactured payment is not allowable as a deduction for income tax purposes if it is incurred in connection with income tax avoidance arrangements (as widely defined). The legislation applies in relation to manufactured payments within each of **4.10**(a)–(c) above (including deemed manufactured payments — see **4.13** below) made (or treated as made) on or after 31 January 2008. Where part of a manufactured payment falls to be treated as a separate fee (see **4.10** above), the restriction applies to that part also. [*ITA 2007, ss 572A, 574(3), 579(3), 581A, 583(5); FA 2008, s 63, Sch 23 paras 2, 4, 7, 9, 10*].

Where a manufactured dividend is paid by an individual in connection with a transaction that produces a chargeable gain, *TCGA 1992, s 263D* applies instead of the above. This treats the manufactured dividend as a capital loss that can be relieved only against the capital gain produced by the wider arrangement.

Denial of tax credit

[4.12] Where a manufactured dividend is paid under certain stock lending arrangements or repos involving UK shares, the borrower (in the case of stock lending arrangements) or the interim holder (in the case of a repo) is not entitled to a tax credit in respect of the underlying dividend and, if UK resident, is not treated as having paid income tax at the dividend ordinary rate. Where, unusually, the original holder does not pass entitlement to dividends to the interim holder under a repo arrangement, but a manufactured dividend is nonetheless paid, the original holder is denied a tax credit. For 2008/09 onwards, the denial of tax credits is extended to certain stock lending arrangements or repos involving shares in a non-UK resident company where the tax credit would otherwise be available under **64.13 SAVINGS AND INVESTMENT INCOME**. [*ITA 2007, ss 567(1A), 592–595, Sch 2 paras 108–110; ICTA 1988, ss 231AA, 231AB; FA 2008, s 34, Sch 12 paras 26–30*].

Deemed manufactured payments

[4.13] Special rules apply as below as regards stock lending arrangements and repos.

Stock lending arrangements

Where, under such a stock lending arrangement, interest (including dividends) on stock transferred is paid to a person other than the lender, with no provision for the lender to receive a payment representative of that interest, the rules on manufactured payments apply as if the borrower were required to make, and did make, such a payment on the date the interest it represents is paid. For deemed payments, the borrower is not entitled to any deduction in computing profits or gains for income tax purposes or against total income. [*ITA 2007, s 596, Sch 2 paras 111, 113; ICTA 1988, s 736B; FA 2006, s 139(1)(3)(7), Sch 6 para 4(1); SI 1997 Nos 987, 991, 993; SI 1999 No 621*].

Legislation applies, to prevent a tax avoidance device using stock lending arrangements whereby a person effectively swaps taxable interest on cash for income on securities transferred to him under the arrangement which is either not taxable or taxable at a lower rate. The legislation treats that person (i.e. the borrower) as receiving an amount of taxable interest on any cash transferred as collateral for the securities borrowed. The interest is treated as received on the date on which the borrower transfers the securities back to the lender, and is computed, at a commercial rate, in respect of the period between the securities being transferred to the borrower and their being transferred back. The chargeable amount is reduced by the amount of any interest that the borrower actually receives in respect of the collateral for that period. No tax relief is available to anyone for the interest which the borrower is treated as receiving. If it becomes apparent that the borrower will not return the securities, he is treated for these purposes as having returned them on the date on which it becomes so apparent.

In relation to any stock lending arrangement in respect of which the amount of the cash collateral varies at any time before the securities are returned to the lender, the interest is computed on the highest amount of the collateral; otherwise it is computed on the amount as at the date of return of securities.

[*ITA 2007, ss 597, 598, Sch 2 para 112; ICTA 1988, s 736C; FA 2006, Sch 6 paras 3, 4(2); CTA 2010, Sch 1 para 540*].

There are additional provisions designed to prevent people circumventing *ITA 2007, ss 597, 598* above by entering into quasi-stock lending arrangements or providing quasi-cash collateral (both as defined). [*ITA 2007, ss 599, 600; ICTA 1988, s 736D; FA 2006, Sch 6 para 4(3)(4)*].

See generally HMRC Corporate Finance Manual CFM17300 *et seq*. Guidance notes to help people in the financial markets to comply with the tax rules on manufactured payments are available on the HMRC website.

Sale and repurchase of securities (repos)

The rules on manufactured payments apply where a person (the 'transferor') agrees to sell any 'securities', and under the same agreement (or under another agreement under the same arrangement) he (or a person connected with him (within **21 CONNECTED PERSONS**)) is required to buy back the same or 'similar' securities (whether as a result of a straightforward obligation or the exercise of a put option), or acquires an option (which he subsequently exercises) to buy them back, and either of the following two sets of conditions is fulfilled. The first set of conditions is that:

- as a result of the transaction, a 'distribution' is receivable by a person other than the transferor;
- the agreement(s) do not contain a requirement for an amount representative of the 'distribution' to be paid to the transferor on or before the date the repurchase price becomes due; and
- it is reasonable to assume that the repurchase price took into account the fact that the 'distribution' was receivable by a person other than the transferor.

The second set of conditions is that:

- a 'distribution' which becomes payable in respect of the securities is receivable otherwise than by the transferor;
- the transferor (or a person connected with him) is required to make a payment representative of the 'distribution';
- there is no requirement for a person to pay to the transferor an amount representative of the 'distribution' on or before the date the repurchase price becomes due; and
- it is reasonable to assume that, in arriving at the repurchase price, account was taken of these circumstances.

For these purposes, a '*distribution*' means, in the case of UK shares, a dividend; in the case of UK securities, a periodical payment of interest; and in the case of overseas securities, an overseas dividend.

The provisions apply as if the person from whom the securities are repurchased (or from whom the transferor has the right to repurchase them) were required under the arrangements for transfer of the securities to pay the transferor an amount representative of the said distribution, and a payment were accordingly made by that person to the transferor on:

- (with effect in relation to arrangements coming into force on or after 1 October 2007) the date the distribution is payable; or

- (with effect in relation to earlier arrangements) the date the repurchase price of the securities becomes due.

Where the person from whom the securities are repurchased (X) is not the same as the person to whom they were initially transferred, X is not entitled to any tax deduction for the deemed payment to the transferor; this applies where the agreement to sell the securities is made after 26 June 2006, or the agreement under which X acquired the securities is made after that date, and reverses the effect of the decision in *Bank of Ireland Britain Holdings Ltd v HMRC* (Sp C 544), [2006] SSCD 477 (which itself was confirmed on appeal — CA, [2008] STC 398).

'*Securities*' means UK equities and securities and overseas securities (as defined), and securities are '*similar*' if they carry the same entitlement as to capital and interest (or dividends) and the same enforcement remedies. [*ITA 2007, ss 566, 567, 570*]. Where securities are converted from the currency of a State which has adopted the euro into euros (a '*euroconversion*'), the new securities are treated as 'similar' (see *SI 1998 No 3177, regs 3, 14*).

There are special provisions (in *ITA 2007, ss 602–605*) for determining the amount of the deemed manufactured dividend or interest for these purposes, and for a corresponding adjustment to be made for tax purposes to the repurchase price of the securities.

See also *SI 1998 No 3177, reg 17* as regards securities which, prior to their repurchase, are converted from currencies of States which have adopted the euro into euros.

[*ITA 2007, ss 601–606, Sch 1 para 330, Sch 2 paras 114–118; ICTA 1988, ss 737A, 737B, 737C; TCGA 1992, s 261F; FA 2006, s 139(1)(4)(5)(7), Sch 6 para 5; FA 2007, s 47, Sch 14 para 22; CTA 2010, Sch 1 paras 541–544; SI 1995 No 1007; SI 1996 No 2645; SI 2007 No 2483, reg 3*].

The Treasury has power to make regulations providing for *ITA 2007, ss 601–606* above to apply with modifications in relation to non-standard repo cases (as defined by *ITA 2007, s 612*) and cases involving redemption arrangements (where the securities are redeemed during the currency of the repo). See *SI 2007 No 2486* where the original transfer of the securities takes place on or after 1 October 2007, and see previously *SI 1995 No 3220* (revoked by *SI 2007 No 2484*). These SI's provide for such modifications in cases where other securities are substituted for those originally transferred and cases involving redemption arrangements.

[*ITA 2007, ss 612–614, Sch 1 paras 332, 336–338; ICTA 1988, s 737E; TCGA 1992, ss 261H, 263F–263H*].

See also **4.9** above and, as regards application of accrued income scheme to such securities, **2.19 ACCRUED INCOME SCHEME.**

Transfer of assets abroad

Liability of transferor

[**4.14**] Where, as a result of a transfer of assets, either alone or in conjunction with any associated operations (see below), income becomes payable to non-UK residents, or to persons not domiciled in the UK, then, subject to the exemption at **4.16** below, the following provisions apply.

(a) If, by virtue of the transfer, one or more associated operations, or the transfer in conjunction with associated operations (see *Vestey v CIR* HL 1979, 54 TC 503 overruling *Congreve v CIR* HL 1948, 30 TC 163; and also *CIR v Pratt and Others* Ch D 1982, 57 TC 1), the transferor, being an individual ordinarily resident in the UK, has power to enjoy, forthwith or in the future, any income of a 'person abroad' (see below) which would be taxable if it were the income of the resident individual received in the UK, that income is treated as arising to that individual.

(b) If such a resident individual receives, or has received in any earlier year, or is entitled to, any capital sum by way of loan etc. (see *Lee* KB 1941, 24 TC 207), or other non-income payment not for full consideration, which is in any way connected with the transfer etc., the income which, by virtue of the transfer etc., has become payable to the 'person abroad' is treated as arising to the resident. A sum which a third person receives, or is entitled to receive, at the individual's direction or by assignment of the right to receive it, is treated as such a capital sum. There is no deemed income for a year of assessment in respect of a loan to the individual which has been wholly repaid before the beginning of that year.

These provisions apply:

(I) regardless of whether the income is otherwise chargeable to income tax;
(II) regardless of whether or not the individual with power to enjoy the income was ordinarily resident in the UK when the transfer of assets took place;
(III) regardless of whether a purpose of the transfer is the avoidance of income tax (thus the legislation can apply where any form of direct taxation is avoided, and not just income tax).

[*ITA 2007, ss 721(5), 728(3); ICTA 1988, s 739; FA 1997, s 81*].

The charge to tax under (a) and (b) above is made under *ITA 2007, s 720* and *ITA 2007, s 727* respectively for 2007/08 onwards.

Where a non-UK resident or non-domiciled person realises a profit from the discount on a deeply discounted security, it is treated for these purposes as income of that person (see **64.24 SAVINGS AND INVESTMENT INCOME**).

For the above purposes an individual is deemed to have power to enjoy income of a non-resident or non-domiciled person if:

(i) the income is so dealt with by *any* person so as to benefit the individual at some point of time, whether as income or not; or
(ii) the income increases the value to the individual of assets held by him or for his benefit; or

(iii)   the individual receives, or is entitled to receive, at any time any benefit provided out of the income, or out of money available by the effect of associated operations on that income or assets representing it, directly or indirectly; or

(iv)   the individual may obtain beneficial enjoyment of the income in the event of the exercise of one or more powers, by whomsoever exercisable and whether with or without the consent of any other person; or

(v)   the individual is able to control application of the income,

regard being had to the substantial effect of the transfer and associated operations and bringing into account all resultant benefits to the individual whether or not he has rights in law or equity to those benefits. [*ITA 2007, ss 722, 723; ICTA 1988, s 742(2)(3)*].

A '*person abroad*' means a person who is resident or domiciled outside the UK. Companies incorporated abroad are, for this purpose, always to be treated as resident abroad, even if technically resident in UK. Persons treated as neither UK resident nor ordinarily resident under the rules relating to settlements (see **68.5 SETTLEMENTS**) and personal representatives (see **62.5 RESIDENCE**) are treated as resident outside the UK for these purposes. [*ITA 2007, s 718, Sch 2 paras 134–137; ICTA 1988, s 742(8); FA 1990, s 66*].

Reference to an individual includes the individual's spouse or civil partner. [*ITA 2007, s 714(4); ICTA 1988, s 742(9)(a)*].

An '*associated operation*' is an operation of any kind effected by any person in relation to any of the assets transferred (or any assets representing those transferred) or to the income from those assets or to any assets representing accumulations of the income from those assets. (See also *Corbett's Exors* CA 1943, 25 TC 305; *Bambridge* HL 1955, 36 TC 313 and *Fynn* CD 1957, 37 TC 629.) With effect after 4 December 2005 it is made clear that:

•   associated operations are to be taken into account for the purposes of these provisions whether they are effected before, at the same time as or after the transfer;

•   income which arises by virtue of associated operations alone is to be taken into account for the purposes of the charging provisions; and

•   income which an individual has power to enjoy includes income which he has power to enjoy by virtue of associated operations alone.

These points are reflected in the rewritten provisions of *ITA 2007* (see Change 110 listed in Annex 1 to the Explanatory Notes to *ITA 2007*).

[*ITA 2007, ss 719(2), 721(2), 728(1), Sch 2 para 141; ICTA 1988, s 742(1)(1A)(1B); FA 2006, Sch 7 para 6*].

Income falling under the above headings is not chargeable at the basic rate, starting rate for savings, savings rate (before 2008/09) or dividend ordinary rate to the extent that it has borne such tax by deduction or otherwise. Income that would be dividend income if it were not for these provisions is charged to tax as if it were dividend income (see **1.5 ALLOWANCES AND TAX RATES**).

All deductions and reliefs to be given to the individual assessed as if he had actually received the income. If the income deemed to arise to the individual is subsequently received, it is not again assessed.

Prior to 2008/09, a non-UK domiciled individual was only chargeable on any income *deemed* to be his if he would have been chargeable if it had in fact been his income. Unless transactions were part of a wider arrangement, HMRC practice was not to charge a UK-domiciled individual on income of a non-domiciled spouse or civil partner arising from a transfer of assets by the spouse etc., which, by virtue of this rule, would not have been chargeable on the spouse etc. (Revenue Tax Bulletin April 1999 p 652; HMRC Tax Bulletin December 2005 p 1254).

For 2008/09 onwards, the rules for non-UK domiciled individuals are clarified and tightened; they are also brought into line with the rules at **61 REMITTANCE BASIS**. They apply where income is deemed to arise to an individual under (a) or (b) above in a tax year, the individual is not domiciled in the UK in that year and the remittance basis applies to him for that year (by virtue of his being within any of **61.2(1)–(3) REMITTANCE BASIS**). 'Foreign deemed income' is treated as 'relevant foreign income' (see **32.2 FOREIGN INCOME**) of the individual, with the consequences in **61.4 REMITTANCE BASIS**. The income deemed to arise is *'foreign deemed income'* if it would be relevant foreign income if it were the individual's own income. See **61 REMITTANCE BASIS** for the meaning of 'remitted to the UK' etc. For the purposes of applying the provisions described in that chapter, treat so much of the deemed income as would be relevant foreign income if it were the individual's as deriving from the foreign deemed income.

[*ITA 2007, ss 726, 730, 743, 745, 746; ICTA 1988, s 743; FA 2008, Sch 1 paras 24, 65, Sch 7 paras 165, 167, 170*].

HMRC have power to require from any person, under penalty, particulars of transactions where he acted for others (even if he considers no liability arises), and of what part he took in them. The request must be reasonable with regard to the purposes of the legislation. [*ITA 2007, s 748; ICTA 1988, s 745*]. These powers limited in the case of *solicitors* (but not accountants or others), and *bankers* are not obliged to furnish particulars of any *ordinary* banking transactions carried out in the *ordinary* course of a banking business. [*ITA 2007, ss 749, 750*]. 'Bank' for this purpose is defined by *ITA 2007, s 991* (see **8.1 BANKS**). See *Royal Bank of Canada* Ch D 1971, 47 TC 565, where held particulars required were not ordinary banking transactions and *Clinch v CIR* QB 1973, 49 TC 52 for powers of Revenue.

See *Philippi v CIR* CA 1971, 47 TC 75 for burden on taxpayer to prove that avoidance was not a purpose.

For general principles see the above cases and *Cottingham's Exors* CA 1938, 22 TC 344; *Beatty cases* KB 1940, 23 TC 574; *Lord Howard de Walden* CA 1941, 25 TC 121; *Aykroyd* KB 1942, 24 TC 515; *Latilla* HL 1943, 25 TC 107; *Sassoon* CA 1943, 25 TC 154; *Vestey's Exors* HL 1949, 31 TC 1; *Ramsden* Ch D 1957, 37 TC 619; *Chetwode v CIR* HL 1977, 51 TC 647; *Vestey (Nos 1 & 2)* HL 1979, 54 TC 503; *CIR v Schroder* Ch D 1983, 57 TC 94; *CIR v Brackett* Ch D 1986, 60 TC 134, 639; *CIR v Botnar* CA, [1999] STC 711.

In the case of *CIR v Willoughby* HL 1997, 70 TC 57, the Inland Revenue's refusal of exemption under *ICTA 1988, s 741* (now *ITA 2007, s 739*) in relation to 'personal portfolio bonds' (the holder of which has a degree of control of the management of the underlying investments but no proprietary interest therein) was overturned on appeal.

Simon's Taxes. See E1.1113.

Liability as non-transferor

[4.15] Where, as a result of a transfer of assets, one or more associated operations, or a transfer of assets in conjunction with associated operations (see **4.14** above), income becomes payable to a non-resident, or to a person not domiciled in the UK, *and* an individual ordinarily resident in the UK who is not liable as the transferor under *ITA 2007, ss 720, 727* receives a benefit provided out of those assets, then, subject to the exemption at **4.16** below, the following provisions apply to benefits received and relevant income arising after 9 March 1981 irrespective of when the transfer or associated operations took place. [*ITA 2007, ss 731, 732; ICTA 1988, s 740(1); FA 2008, Sch 7 paras 168, 170*].

Where a non-UK resident or domiciled person realises a profit from the discount on a deeply discounted security, it is treated for these purposes as income of that person (see **64.24 SAVINGS AND INVESTMENT INCOME**).

The value of the benefit, up to the amount of relevant income of years of assessment up to and including the year in which received, is treated as arising to the resident individual for that year and charged to income tax accordingly. Any excess of benefit is carried forward against relevant income of subsequent years and taxed accordingly. For 2007/08 onwards, the 'carrying forward' process is clarified in line with HMRC practice whereby for each year the figure for total untaxed benefits (as defined) is compared with the figure for available relevant income (as defined), the lower figure being the amount of income treated as arising (see Change 113 listed in Annex 1 to the Explanatory Notes to *ITA 2007*). [*ITA 2007, s 733; ICTA 1988, s 740(2)(4); ITTOIA 2005, Sch 1 para 304(2)(3)*].

'*Relevant income*' of a year of assessment is any income arising in that year to a non-resident or non-domiciled person and which by virtue of the transfer or associated operations mentioned above can directly or indirectly be used for providing a benefit for the resident individual. [*ITA 2007, s 733; ICTA 1988, s 740(3)*].

Prior to 2008/09, a non-UK domiciled individual was not taxable on a benefit not received in the UK in respect of any 'relevant income' on which, if he had received it, he would not, because of his domicile, have been taxable. *ITTOIA 2005, ss 833, 834* (formerly *ICTA 1988, s 65(6)–(9)* — income applied outside UK treated in certain cases as received in UK — see **61.27 REMITTANCE BASIS**) applied as if the benefit were 'relevant foreign income' (as in **32.2 FOREIGN INCOME**) or, before *ITTOIA 2005* came into effect, as if it were income arising from possessions outside the UK.

For 2008/09 onwards, the rules for non-UK domiciled individuals are clarified and tightened; they are also brought into line with the rules at **61 REMITTANCE BASIS**. They apply where income is deemed to arise to an individual as above in a tax year, the individual is not domiciled in the UK in that year and the remittance basis applies to him for that year (by virtue of his being within any of **61.2**(1)–(3) REMITTANCE BASIS). 'Foreign deemed income' is treated as 'relevant foreign income' (see **32.2** FOREIGN INCOME) of the individual, with the consequences in **61.4** REMITTANCE BASIS. The income deemed to arise is *'foreign deemed income'* if it would be relevant foreign income if it were the individual's own income. See **61** REMITTANCE BASIS for the meaning of 'remitted to the UK' etc. For the purposes of applying the provisions described in that chapter, treat relevant income, or a benefit, that 'relates to' any part of the foreign deemed income as deriving from that part of the foreign deemed income. Special 'matching' rules in *ITA 2007, s 735A* are used to determine how income *'relates to'* relevant income and to benefits.

[*ITA 2007, ss 735, 735A; ICTA 1988, s 740(5); ITTOIA 2005, Sch 1 para 304(4); FA 2008, Sch 7 paras 169, 170*].

Where a benefit otherwise giving rise to a charge under these provisions is in whole or part a capital payment giving rise to a chargeable gain or an offshore income gain (see **51** OFFSHORE FUNDS), it is regarded to that extent as having already been treated as income under these provisions. [*ITA 2007, s 734; ICTA 1988, s 740(6); FA 2000, Sch 26 para 6; FA 2008, Sch 7 paras 97, 98; SI 2009 No 3001, reg 129(5)*].

The provisions at **4.14** above relating to 'person abroad' and information powers apply equally here.

Exemption from above liabilities

[4.16] In relation to transactions on or after 5 December 2005, an individual is not liable under the transfer of assets abroad rules at **4.14, 4.15** above by reference to the 'relevant transactions' if he satisfies HMRC that:

- it would not be reasonable to draw the conclusion, from all the circumstances of the case, that the purpose of avoiding liability to taxation was the purpose, or one of the purposes, for which the 'relevant transactions' or any of them were effected; or that
- all the 'relevant transactions' were genuine 'commercial transactions' *and* it would not be reasonable to draw the conclusion, from all the circumstances of the case, that any one or more of them was more than incidentally designed for the purpose of avoiding liability to taxation.

In determining the purposes of 'relevant transactions', the intentions and purposes of any person who designs or effects them or provides advice on them must be taken into account.

'Relevant transactions' means the transfer and any 'associated operations' (see **4.14** above). Transactions are *'commercial transactions'* only if they are effected in the course of, or with a view to setting up, a trade or business and, in either case, for the purposes of that trade or business. The making and/or managing of investments is not regarded as a trade or business for this purpose unless the person by whom and the person for whom it is done are independent persons (i.e. persons not connected with each other as in **21** CONNECTED PERSONS) dealing at arm's length. Non-arm's length transactions are not

commercial transactions. Any associated operation that would not otherwise fall to be taken into account can nevertheless be taken into account if it would cause either of the above tests to be failed.

Any decision taken by HMRC on these tests is subject to review by the Appeal Tribunal on appeal.

[*ITA 2007, ss 737, 738, 751; ICTA 1988, s 741A; FA 2006, Sch 7 para 3; SI 2009 No 56, Sch 1 para 461*].

In relation to transactions before 5 December 2005, an individual is not liable under the transfer of assets abroad rules if he can show to the satisfaction of HMRC that either:

- the avoidance of taxation was not the purpose, or one of the purposes, for which the transfer or associated operations (or any of them) were effected; or
- the transfer and any associated operations were bona fide commercial transactions not designed for the purpose of avoiding liability to taxation.

HMRC's decision on such matters is subject to review by the Appeal Tribunal on appeal.

[*ITA 2007, ss 739, 751; ICTA 1988, s 741; FA 2006, Sch 7 para 2; SI 2009 No 56, Sch 1 para 461*].

If one or more of the relevant transactions was entered into before 5 December 2005 and one or more of them is entered into on or after that date and the exemption tests are failed by reference only to any of the transactions entered into on or after that date:

- income arising before that date is not brought into account in determining the liability of the transferor (under *ITA 2007, ss 720, 727* — see **4.14** above); and
- for the purposes of the rules relating to the liability of non-transferors (under *ITA 2007, s 731* — see **4.15** above), the value of any benefit received in 2005/06 is time-apportioned to the extent that it fell to be enjoyed before 5 December 2005; but in relation to any benefit received in that year or any later year, relevant income is *not* restricted to income arising on or after 5 December 2005.

[*ITA 2007, s 740; ICTA 1988, ss 741B, 741C; FA 2006, Sch 7 para 4*].

There is provision for apportionment in a case where a transfer and any associated operations met the second of the two exemption tests (whether those applicable before 5 December 2005 or those applicable on or after that date), but one or more subsequent associated operations result in liability under *ITA 2007, ss 720, 727* as a result of their failing to meet the second of the two tests applicable on or after 5 December 2005. The amount otherwise chargeable under *ss 720, 727* is to be reduced to the proportion of it (if any) that is considered by HMRC to be justly and reasonably attributable to the subsequent associated operations. Again, the Appeal Tribunal has jurisdiction, on appeal, to review any decision of HMRC on this matter.

[ITA 2007, ss 741, 742, 751; ICTA 1988, s 741D; FA 2006, Sch 7 para 5; SI 2009 No 56, Sch 1 para 461].

The stated intention of the changes made to the exemption tests with effect from 5 December 2005 is to ensure that all the relevant facts of the case, including the actual outcome of the transactions, are taken into account in deciding whether exemption is due, and to make clear that exemption will not be due solely on the basis of an assertion by the taxpayer that tax avoidance was not his subjective intention (Treasury Explanatory Notes to Finance Bill 2006).

For successful appeals against HMRC refusals of relief, see *Beneficiary v CIR* (Sp C 190), [1999] SSCD 134 (in which the grounds were that a transfer involved tax mitigation rather than tax avoidance) and *Carvill v CIR* (Sp C 233), [2000] SSCD 143 (in which the Special Commissioner accepted that the transfer had been for bona fide commercial purposes).

Miscellaneous

[4.17] The following miscellaneous matters apply.

Exclusion of double charge

No income can be charged more than once under the provisions at **4.14–4.16** above, and, where there is a choice as to persons to be assessed, HMRC may allocate income as appears just and reasonable. Appeal can be made to the Appeal Tribunal against HMRC's decision. Income is treated as having been charged to tax:

- in full, where charged under *ITA 2007, ss 720, 727* as income;
- to the extent of the value of any benefit charged under **4.14**(iii) above, and
- to the amount of relevant income taken into account in charging any benefit under *ITA 2007, s 731*.

[ITA 2007, ss 743, 744, 751; ICTA 1988, s 744; SI 2009 No 56, Sch 1 para 461].

Trustees and personal representatives

In relation to benefits received on or after 15 June 1989, relevant income for the purposes of *ITA 2007, s 731* (see **4.15** above) includes income arising to trustees or personal representatives before 6 April 1989, notwithstanding that one or more of the trustees or personal representatives was not resident outside the UK, unless they have been charged to tax in respect of that income. *[ITA 2007, Sch 2 para 135; ICTA 1988, s 685F(2); FA 1989, ss 110(9), 111(8); FA 2006, Sch 13 para 1(1)(5), para 28(2)(c)(6)].*

Accrued income on certain securities

See **2.25 ACCRUED INCOME SCHEME** as regards deemed income arising on transfer of certain securities.

Offshore funds

The transfer of assets abroad rules apply in relation to an offshore income gain arising to a person resident or domiciled outside the UK as if it were foreign income becoming payable to that person (see **51.10 OFFSHORE FUNDS**).

Controlled foreign companies

See Tolley's Corporation Tax under Controlled Foreign Companies as regards *ITA 2007, s 720* relief in certain cases where a charge is made in respect of profits of such companies. [*ITA 2007, s 725*].

HMRC interpretation

For an article giving HMRC's interpretation of a number of aspects of the transfer of assets abroad provisions, see Revenue Tax Bulletin April 1999 pp 651, 652.

Transfer pricing

[4.18] The transfer pricing legislation at *TIOPA 2010, Pt 4 (ss 146–217)* (previously at *ICTA 1988, Sch 28AA*) is to be construed so as best to secure consistency between the effect given to the basic statutory rule (see **4.19** below) and the principles of *Article 9* of the OECD Model Tax Convention and transfer pricing guidelines. [*TIOPA 2010, s 164; ICTA 1988, Sch 28AA para 2; CTA 2009, Sch 1 para 291(3)*]. The guidelines are published by the OECD (Organisation for Economic Co-operation and Development — www. oecd.org) as 'Transfer Pricing Guidelines for Multinational Enterprises and Tax Administrations', and can be purchased from the OECD or The Stationery Office. See also HMRC International Manual at INTM463000 *et seq*.

The transfer pricing legislation applies not only to international transactions but to transactions both parties to which are in the UK.

There are exemptions (see **4.21** below) for small and medium-sized businesses.

See HMRC International Manual at INTM431000 *et seq*. for further guidance.

The HMRC International Division, Room 311, Melbourne House, Aldwych, London WC2B 4LL may be approached for pre-transaction guidance on the likely tax treatment in particular cases when financial arrangements are in the process of being put in place. See Revenue Tax Bulletin October 1998 pp 579–582 for guidance on the nature of the risk assessment carried out by HMRC before undertaking a transfer pricing enquiry and a suggested timetabling framework for such enquiries.

See Tolley's Corporation Tax under Transfer Pricing for matters relevant only to companies.

See **Simon's Taxes D2.668**.

The basic rule

[4.19] The transfer pricing legislation applies where:

(a) provision (the '*actual provision*') has been made or imposed as between two persons (the '*affected persons*') by means of a transaction or series of transactions;

(b) the 'participation condition' is met (see **4.20** below); and

(c) the actual provision differs from the provision (the '*arm's length provision*') which would have been made as between independent enterprises.

If the actual provision confers a 'potential advantage' in relation to UK taxation on one (or both) of the affected persons, the profits and losses of the potentially advantaged person (or both of them) are computed for tax purposes as if the arm's length provision had been made or imposed instead of the actual provision. The resulting increase in profits (or decrease in losses) is often referred to as the '*transfer pricing adjustment*'.

The above applies equally if provision is made or imposed as between two persons but no provision would have been made as between independent enterprises. In such a case, the reference to the 'arm's length provision' is a reference to no provision being made.

See **4.21** below for exemptions to the basic rule above. There is also an exemption for certain oil transactions (see *TIOPA 2010, s 147(7)*) and special rules for oil-related ring-fence trades.

The actual provision confers a '*potential advantage*' on a person in relation to UK taxation where its effect, compared to that of the corresponding arm's length provision, would be a reduction in that person's profits or income or an increase in his losses for any chargeable period. Any income of a non-UK resident that is 'disregarded income' (within **50.3 NON-RESIDENTS**) is left out of account in determining whether there is any such reduction or increase. 'Losses' for these purposes include relief under *ITTOIA 2005, s 57* for pre-trading expenditure (see **73.102 TRADING INCOME**) and relief for interest paid under the trade losses rules (see **63 RETURNS** and **45 LOSSES**).

A 'transaction' for these purposes includes arrangements, understandings and mutual practices (whether or not legally enforceable). An 'arrangement' means any scheme or arrangement of any kind. A 'series' of transactions includes a number of transactions entered into (whether or not consecutively) in pursuance of, or in relation to, the same arrangement. A series of transactions is not prevented from being regarded as the means by which provision has been made or imposed between two persons by reason only that:

• there is no transaction in the series to which both those persons are parties; or

• the parties to any arrangement in pursuance of which the transactions are entered into do not include one or both of those persons; or

• there is one or more transactions in the series to which neither of those persons is a party.

[*TIOPA 2010, ss 147, 149–151, 155, 156; ICTA 1988, Sch 28AA paras 1, 3, 5, 14; ITA 2007, Sch 1 para 239*].

The participation condition

[4.20] The '*participation condition*' in **4.19**(b) above is met if:

(a)   one of the affected persons was directly or indirectly participating in the management, control or capital of the other; or

(b)   the same person (or persons) was (or were) directly or indirectly participating in the management, control or capital of each of the affected persons.

See below as to what is meant by 'directly or indirectly participating' in (a) and (b) above.

Generally, the participation condition is met only if (a) or (b) above is fulfilled at the time the actual provision is made or imposed. However, if and insofar as the actual provision is provision relating to 'financing arrangements', the participation condition is met if (a) or (b) above is fulfilled at that time or at any time in the next six months; so transfer pricing adjustments may be triggered by events occurring up to six months before the necessary relationship exists between the parties.

'Financing arrangements' means arrangements made for providing or guaranteeing, or otherwise in connection with, any debt, capital or other form of finance. For more details on the 'financing arrangements' rules, see www.hmrc. gov.uk/international/transferpricing.pdf and the links at www.hmrc.gov.uk/int ernational/transfer-pricing.htm under the heading 'Finance (No 2) Act 2005'.

Direct participation

For the purposes of (a) and (b) above, a person (B) is directly participating in the management, control or capital of another person (C) at a particular time if and only if, at that time, C is a body corporate or partnership which B controls (within *CTA 2010, s 1124*).

Indirect participation

For the purposes of (a) and (b) above (but subject to the special rules for financing arrangements), a person (P) is indirectly participating in the management, control or capital of another person (A) at a particular time:

(i)   if P would be *directly* participating in the management, control or capital of A at that time if certain rights and powers (see *TIOPA 2010, ss 159(3)–(7), 163*) were attributed to him; these include *future* rights and powers; or

(ii)   if P is, at that time, one of a number of 'major participants' in A's enterprise.

A person (Q) is a '*major participant*' in the enterprise of another person (B) if B is a body corporate or partnership, and Q is one of two persons who control B (within *CTA 2010, s 1124*), each of whom has at least 40% of the holdings, rights and powers which give them that control. In deciding whether this test is met, certain rights and powers are attributed as in (i) above.

In cases involving 'financing arrangements' (see above), the meaning of indirect participation is extended to include circumstances where a number of parties act together in relation to the financing arrangements of a business and could collectively control the business. So, for the purposes of (a) above, a person (X) is treated as indirectly participating in the management etc. of another person (Y) if:

- the actual provision relates, to any extent, to financing arrangements for Y (where Y is a body corporate or partnership);
- X and other persons acted together in relation to the arrangements; and
- X would be taken to have control of Y if, at a 'relevant time', there were attributed to X the rights and powers of each of those other persons (taking into account any additional rights or powers that would be attributed to any person under (i) above if it were being decided whether that person is indirectly participating).

'*Relevant time*' means any time when X and the other persons were acting together in relation to the financing arrangements or any time in the six months after they ceased to do so.

For the purposes of (b) above, the rule applies where the actual provision relates to financing arrangements for one of the affected persons and X would be taken to have control of each of the affected persons. It is immaterial whether the persons acting together did so at the time the actual provision is made or imposed or did so at some earlier time.

[*TIOPA 2010, ss 148, 157–163, 217(1); ICTA 1988, Sch 28AA paras 4, 4A, 4B, 14(2)*].

Exemptions from the basic rule

[4.21] No transfer pricing adjustment (as in **4.19** above) is made in computing profits or losses of a potentially advantaged person (see **4.19** above) for a tax year for which that person is a 'small enterprise' or a 'medium-sized enterprise'. See below for exceptions to this rule.

For this purpose, a '*small enterprise*' is one defined as such in the Annex to *Commission Recommendation 2003/361/EC* published by the EC on 6 May 2003 (as modified by *TIOPA 2010, s 172(4)–(7)*) and a '*medium-sized enterprise*' is one which falls within the category of micro, small and medium-sized enterprises as defined in that Annex (as modified) but which is not a 'small enterprise'. Broadly, the entity must meet the following criteria (see HMRC guidance at www.hmrc.gov.uk/international/small-medium-ent.pdf).

	Maximum number of staff	And less than one of these limits	
		Annual turnover	*Balance sheet total*
Small enterprise	50	10 million euros	10 million euros
Medium-sized enterprise	250	50 million euros	43 million euros

'Balance sheet total' means, broadly, total assets (without netting off liabilities). Associated entities etc. must be taken into account in determining whether the criteria are met. The modifications made to the Annex ensure, in particular, that qualification as small or medium-sized depends on the entity's data for the tax year under review and without reference to past history.

A small or medium-sized enterprise may make an irrevocable election to disapply the exemption for a particular tax year.

HMRC may override the exemption for any tax year (in relation to one or more particular provisions made or imposed) where the potentially advantaged person is a *medium-sized* enterprise. They do so by issuing a '*transfer pricing notice*' to the potentially advantaged person. A transfer pricing notice can be given only after an enquiry has been opened into the person's tax return (and an enquiry can be opened specifically for this purpose) potentially advantaged person can appeal against the notice (within 30 days) but only on the grounds that he is not a medium-sized enterprise. A person in receipt of a transfer pricing notice has 90 days in which to make the necessary amendments to his tax return, beginning on the date of issue of the notice or, where relevant, on the date the appeal against the notice is finally determined or abandoned. Failure to do so results in the return becoming an incorrect return (so that penalties potentially apply — see, for example, **55.10 PENALTIES**). The enquiry into the tax return cannot be closed until either the amendment is made or the 90-day period expires. (See **63.6** *et seq.* **RETURNS** for enquiries into returns generally.)

The exemption does not apply to either a small or a medium-sized enterprise in relation to an actual provision made or imposed if, at the time the provision is made or imposed, the other affected person or a 'party to a relevant transaction' is a 'resident' of a 'non-qualifying territory' (regardless of whether he is also a resident of a 'qualifying territory'). A person is a '*party to a relevant transaction*' if the actual provision was imposed by means of a series of transactions and he was a party to one or more of them. For these purposes, a person is a '*resident*' of a territory if he is liable to tax there by reason of his domicile, residence or place of management, unless he is so liable only in respect of income from sources in that territory or capital situated there.

'*Qualifying territory*' means the UK or any territory with which the UK has a double tax agreement (see **26.2 DOUBLE TAX RELIEF**) containing a standard non-discrimination provision (see HMRC International Manual INTM432112 for a list of countries with which the UK had an appropriate agreement at 1 April 2008). '*Non-qualifying territory*' is construed accordingly. However, territories may also be designated as 'qualifying' or 'non-qualifying' by Treasury regulations made for the purposes of these provisions.

[*TIOPA 2010, ss 166–173, Sch 8 para 107; ICTA 1988, Sch 28AA paras 5B–5E; TMA 1970, s 9A(4)*].

Elimination of double counting

[4.22] Where:

- a potential advantage is conferred (as in **4.19** above) on only one of the affected persons (the '*advantaged person*'); and

- the other person (the '*disadvantaged person*') is within the charge to income tax or corporation tax in respect of profits arising from the activities in relation to which the actual provision was made or imposed,

then the disadvantaged person may claim application of the arm's length provision rather than the actual provision (overriding any applicable time limits for the necessary adjustments).

The above claim can be made only if the arm's length provision has similarly been applied in the case of the advantaged person (in his return or as a result of a determination). The claim must be consistent with the calculation made in the case of the advantaged person. The claim must be made within two years after the making of the return by the advantaged person or the giving of the notice taking account of the determination, as the case may be. A claim based on a return which is subsequently the subject of such a notice may be amended within two years after the giving of the notice.

If notice taking account of a transfer pricing determination is given to the advantaged person, HMRC have a duty to inform a disadvantaged person of the potential for a claim. If there is a breach of this duty, the Commissioners of HMRC have discretion to extend the time allowed for the making or amendment of a claim.

Where the conditions at **4.20**(a) and (b) above are satisfied only by virtue of the special rules for financing arrangements, no claim by the disadvantaged person can be made where the actual provision is provision in relation to a security issued by one of the affected persons and the security is guaranteed by a person with whom the issuer of the security has a 'participatory relationship'. Appropriately modified versions of **4.20**(a) and (b) above apply to determine the existence or otherwise of a '*participatory relationship*' (see *TIOPA 2010, s 175(2)*).

A claim by the disadvantaged person to apply the arm's length provision does not affect the amount he is required to bring into account as closing trading stock or work in progress for any accounting period of his which ends on or after the last day of the accounting period of the advantaged person in which the actual provision was made or imposed. In the absence of such a rule, the benefit to him of applying the arm's length provision would effectively be delayed until the stock were sold or the work in progress realised.

Where the above claim is made, it is assumed, as respects any foreign tax credit which has been (or may be) given to the disadvantaged person:

- that the foreign tax does not include any tax which would not be (or would not have become) payable if the arm's length provision had also been made or imposed for the purposes of that tax; and
- that the profits from the activities in relation to which the actual provision was made or imposed and in respect of which the tax credit relief arises are reduced to the same extent as they are treated as reduced by virtue of the claim.

Where the application of the arm's length provision in a computation following such a claim involves a reduction in the amount of any income, and that income also falls to be treated as reduced under *TIOPA 2010, s 112(1)* by an amount of foreign tax (where credit relief is not available), the first-mentioned reduction is treated as made before the latter. The deductible foreign tax excludes that paid on so much of the income as is represented by the amount of the first-mentioned reduction.

Any adjustment to double tax reliefs as above may be given effect by set-off against any relief or repayment arising from the claim, and may be made without regard to any time limit on assessments or amendments.

Where one or more payments ('*balancing payments*') are made to the advantaged person by the disadvantaged person to compensate for the transfer pricing adjustment, they are not taken into account in computing either person's taxable profits or allowable losses to the extent that they do not in aggregate exceed the 'available compensating adjustment'. The '*available compensating adjustment*' is the difference between the profits/losses of the disadvantaged person computed on the basis of the actual provision and those profits/losses computed on the basis that the disadvantaged person makes a claim as above to apply the arm's length provision instead.

[*TIOPA 2010, ss 174–178, 180, 185, 186, 188–190, 195, 196, 216; ICTA 1988, Sch 28AA paras 6, 6A, 7, 7A; FA 1998, s 111; CTA 2009, Sch 1 para 291(4)*].

Determinations requiring HMRC sanction

[4.23] A determination of an amount falling to be brought into account under **4.19** above, other than in certain cases where an agreement has been reached between HMRC and the person concerned (see *TIOPA 2010, s 209*), requires the sanction of the Commissioners for HMRC. Where such a determination is made for the purpose of giving a closure notice, making a discovery assessment or giving a discovery notice amending a partnership return, and the notice or assessment is given to a person:

- without the determination, so far as taken into account in the notice or assessment, having been approved by HMRC; or
- without a copy of the Commissioners' approval having been served on that person at or before the time the notice was given,

the closure or amendment notice or discovery assessment is deemed to have been given or made (and in the case of an assessment notified) as if the determination had not been taken into account. The Commissioners' approval must be given specifically to the case in question and must apply to the amount determined, but may otherwise be given (either before or after the making of the determination) in any such form or manner as the Commissioners may determine. An appeal relating to a determination approved by the Commissioners may not question the the Commissioners' approval except to the extent that the grounds for questioning the approval are the same as the grounds for questioning the determination itself.

[*TIOPA 2010, ss 208-211; FA 1998, s 110*].

Appeals

[4.24] The following rules apply in so far as the question in dispute on an appeal:

- is or involves a determination of whether the transfer pricing legislation has effect; and
- relates to any provision made or imposed as between two persons each of whom is within the charge to income tax or corporation tax in respect of profits arising from the activities in relation to which the actual provision was made or imposed.

The rules are that:

- each of the persons as between whom the actual provision was made or imposed is entitled to be a party in any proceedings;
- the Appeal Tribunal is to determine the question separately from any other question in the proceedings; and
- the Tribunal's determination on the question has effect as if made in an appeal to which each of those persons was a party

[*TIOPA 2010, ss 212, 216; ICTA 1988, Sch 28AA para 12; SI 2009 No 56, Sch 1 para 162*].

Miscellaneous

Capital allowances

[4.25] The transfer pricing provisions do not generally affect the computation of capital allowances or balancing charges under *CAA 2001*. However, this does *not* apply for the purposes of **4.22** above (elimination of double counting). [*TIOPA 2010, s 213; ICTA 1988, Sch 28AA para 13*].

Interest paid

Where a person pays interest under the actual provision and a transfer pricing adjustment falls to be made, such that some or all of the interest paid is disallowed, then, if the recipient makes a claim under **4.22** above (elimination of double counting), the disallowed interest is not chargeable to income tax or corporation tax in his hands and the payer is not required to deduct tax at source. [*TIOPA 2010, s 187; ICTA 1988, s 28AA, para 6E; CTA 2009, Sch 1 para 291(5); SI 2007 No 3506, reg 2(4)*].

Employee share schemes

For an article on the application of the transfer pricing rules to employee share scheme costs, in particular in relation to the decision in *Waterloo plc v CIR* (Sp C 301), [2002] SSCD 95, see Revenue Tax Bulletin February 2003 pp 1002–1007.

Advance pricing agreements (APAs)

[4.26] A person ('the taxpayer') may apply to the Commissioners for HMRC for a written agreement (an advance pricing agreement) determining a method for resolving pricing issues in advance of a return being made. Provided the terms of the agreement are complied with, they provide assurance that the treatment of those pricing issues will be accepted by both HMRC and the enterprise for the period covered by the agreement.

An advance pricing agreement (APA) must contain a declaration that it is an agreement made for the purposes of *TIOPA 2010, s 218* (or predecessor legislation). It may contain provision relating to chargeable periods ending before the agreement is made. If the taxpayer is not a company (and subject to special provision for oil-related ring-fence trades), the APA must relate to one or more of the following.

(a)   The attribution of income to a branch or agency through which the taxpayer has been carrying on, or is proposing to carry on, a trade in the UK.

(b)   The attribution of income to any permanent establishment of the taxpayer's (wherever situated) through which the taxpayer has been carrying on, or is proposing to carry on, any business.

(c)   The extent to which income which has arisen or which may arise to the taxpayer is to be taken for any purpose to be income arising outside the UK.

(d)   The treatment for tax purposes of any provision made or imposed (whether before or after the date of the APA) as between the taxpayer and any 'associate' of his.

For the purposes of (d) above, persons are 'associates' for this purpose if (at the time of the making or imposition of the provision).

•   one of them is directly or indirectly participating in the management, control or capital of the other; or

•   the same person or persons is or are directly or indirectly participating in the management, control or capital of each of the two persons,

with further special provision in relation to sales of oil. For the meaning of direct and indirect participation, see **4.20** above.

Where an APA is in force in relation to a chargeable period, questions relating to the matters in (a)–(d) above are, to the extent provided for in the APA, to be determined in accordance with the APA rather than by reference to the legislative provisions which would otherwise have applied. However, where the relevant matter falls within (e) above and not within (a), (b) or (c) above, the only legislative provisions which can be displaced are those contained in the transfer pricing legislation. Where an APA relating to a chargeable period beginning or ending before the date of the APA provides for the manner in which consequent adjustments are to be made, those adjustments are to be made in the manner provided for in the APA.

An APA does not, however, have effect in relation to the determination of any question which relates to:

•   a time after that from which an officer of HMRC has revoked the APA in accordance with its terms; or

•   a time after or in relation to which any provision of the APA has not been complied with, where the APA was conditional upon compliance with that provision; or

- any matter as respects which any other essential conditions have not been, or are no longer, met.

The application for the APA must be an application for the clarification by agreement of the effect in the taxpayer's case of provisions by reference to which questions relating to any one or more of the matters in (a)–(d) above are to be, or might be, determined. The application must set out the taxpayer's understanding of what would in his case be the effect, in the absence of any agreement, of the provisions in relation to which clarification is sought, and in what respects clarification is required. It must also propose how the clarification might be effected in a manner consistent with that understanding.

It is for HMRC to ensure that the APA is modified so as to be consistent with any mutual agreement made under, and for the purposes of, a double taxation treaty.

Where the APA makes provision for its modification or revocation by HMRC, this may take effect from such time (including a time before the modification or revocation) as HMRC may determine.

A party to an APA must provide HMRC with all such reports and other information as he may be required to provide under the APA or by virtue of any request made by an officer of HMRC in accordance with the APA.

If, before an APA was made, the taxpayer fraudulently or negligently provided HMRC with false or misleading information in relation to the application for the APA or in connection with its preparation, the APA is deemed never to have been made. HMRC must notify the taxpayer that the APA is nullified by reason of the misrepresentation. A penalty of up to £10,000 may apply for so giving such false or misleading information.

Effect of APA on third parties

Where an APA has effect in relation to any provision between the taxpayer and another person, then in applying the double counting rules in **4.22** above to the other person, the arrangements set out in the APA similarly apply in determining any question as to:

- whether the taxpayer is a person on whom a potential advantage in relation to UK taxation is conferred by the actual provision; or
- what constitutes the arm's length provision in relation to the actual provision.

This is subject to any APA made between HMRC and the other person.

[*TIOPA 2010, ss 218-230; FA 1999, ss 85–87*].

For a detailed explanation of how APAs are administered, see HMRC SP 3/99. The contact address for APA applications and other information is Ian Wood, CT & VAT (International CT), 100 Parliament Street, London, SW1A 2BQ. See also Revenue Tax Bulletin October 1999 pp 697, 698 for a note on the scope of agreements, and for procedural guidance relating to bilateral agreements in the light of HMRC's experiences and observations in concluding agreements with treaty partners under double tax treaty mutual agreement procedures.

EU Arbitration Convention

[4.27] The Convention (*90/436/EEC*) on the elimination of double taxation in connection with the adjustment of profits of associated enterprises requires EU member States to adopt certain procedures and to follow the opinion of an advisory commission in certain cases of dispute relating to transfer pricing adjustments. The Convention contains a provision which enables the bilateral application of the Convention between those member States that have ratified it, which include the 15 older member States. For further information, see http://ec.europa.eu/taxation_customs/taxation/company_tax/transfer_pricing/arbitration_convention/index_en.htm.

There is legislation providing for UK domestic enactments to be overridden where necessary to give effect to a Convention determination. The legislation also provides powers and imposes confidentiality requirements in relation to disclosures of information to an advisory commission. [*TIOPA 2010, ss 126–128; ICTA 1988, ss 815B, 816(2A); FA 1989, s 182A*].

Sales of occupation income

[4.28] Where:

(i)   transactions or arrangements are made (having as their *main* object, or one of their main objects, the avoidance or reduction of income tax) which enable some other person to enjoy income or receipts, including copyrights, licences or rights etc., deriving, directly or indirectly, from occupational activities, past or present, which an individual carries on wholly or partly in the UK; and

(ii)   in connection therewith, or in consequences thereof, that individual obtains, for himself or for some other person, *a capital amount* (i.e. any amount not otherwise includible in any computation of income for tax purposes),

any such amount is (subject to certain exceptions, as below) to be treated as income arising to that individual when the capital sum is receivable (or, if it consists of property or a right, when it is sold or realised). That income is chargeable to income tax on the full amount so treated as arising in the tax year. [*ITA 2007, s 776(2)*]. Note that apportionment is necessary where a non-resident carries on an occupation partly in the UK (see *ITA 2007, ss 1015, 1016*; see also Change 115 listed in Annex 1 to the Explanatory Notes to *ITA 2007*).

Capital amounts from the disposal of:

(a)   shares in a company, so far as their value is attributable to the value of the company's business as a going concern: or

(b)   assets (including goodwill) of a profession or vocation, or a share in a professional or vocational partnership, so far as their value is attributable to the value of the profession etc., as a going concern,

are exempted from the above treatment. But these exemptions do not apply to any part of the capital amount which represents any part of the going-concern value of the business, profession etc., as above, materially deriving from prospective income etc., from the individual's activities in the occupation, whether as partner or employee, for which he will not receive full consideration (disregarding all capital amounts).

Where the person charged to tax is not the one for whom the capital amount was obtained (see (ii) above) he may recover from the latter person any part of that tax which he pays (for which purpose HMRC will supply, on request, a certificate of income in respect of which tax has been paid).

[*ITA 2007, ss 773–789; ICTA 1988, ss 775, 777, 778; SI 2009 No 2859, art 4(5)*].

Provisions similar to *ITA 2007, ss 761, 762 and 944* (for which see **4.29** below under 'General') apply for the purposes of these provisions. [*ITA 2007, ss 780, 781, 787(3)*].

See **27.20** EMPLOYMENT INCOME for possible treatment as employment income of any excess of the value of goodwill transferred to a company on incorporation of a business over its true value.

Simon's Taxes. See E1.12.

Transactions in land

[4.29] Certain gains on disposals of land are treated as income chargeable to income tax where:

(a)   the land (or any property deriving its value from the land) is acquired with the sole or main object of realising a gain from disposing of it; or
(b)   the land is held as trading stock; or
(c)   the land is developed with the sole or main object of realising a gain from disposing of it when developed.

The provisions apply if all or any part of the land in question is in the UK and a gain of a capital nature is obtained (for himself or for 'another person') from the disposal of all or part of the land by the person acquiring, holding or developing it or by any connected person (within **21** CONNECTED PERSONS), or a person party to, or concerned in, any arrangement or scheme to realise the gain indirectly or by a series of transactions.

For this purpose, a gain is of a capital nature if it does not (apart from these provisions and the equivalent corporation tax provisions) fall to be included in any computation of income for tax purposes. Any number of transactions may be treated as a single arrangement or scheme if they have, or there is evidence of, a common purpose. '*Another person*' may include a partnership or partners in a partnership, the trustees of settled property and personal representatives and for this purpose these are regarded as persons distinct from the individuals or persons who are for the time being partners, trustees or personal representatives.

'*Land*' is as defined in *Interpretation Act 1978, Sch 1.*

'*Property deriving its value from land*' includes any shareholding in a company, partnership interest, or interest in settled property, deriving its value, directly or indirectly, from land, and any option, consent or embargo affecting the disposition of land. See, however, 'Exemptions' below.

Land is *'disposed of'* for the above purpose if, by any one or more transactions or by any arrangement or scheme (whether concerning the land or any property deriving its value therefrom), the property in, or control over, the land is effectively disposed of. See also under 'General' below.

The gain from the disposal is treated as income arising when the gain is realised and the charge for any tax year is on the full amount of any such income treated as arising in that year. The person liable for the tax is the person whose income it is. Usually this will be the person realising the gain, but, if all or part of any gain is derived from value provided directly or indirectly by another person (as above) or from an opportunity of realising a gain provided directly or indirectly by another person, the income is that other person's.

An amount treated as arising under these provisions to a non-UK resident is treated as being from a source in the UK only to the extent that the land to which the disposal relates is in the UK.

The above provisions apply subject to *ITTOIA 2005, Pt 5 Ch 5* (amounts treated as income of settler — see **68.26 SETTLEMENTS**) and to any other provision treating income as belonging to a particular person.

[ITA 2007, ss 752–759, 763, 772; ICTA 1988, s 776(1)–(3)(3A)(3B)(4)(5) (8)(13)(14); CTA 2010, Sch 1 para 547; SI 2009 No 2859, art 4(4)].

See *Yuill v Wilson* HL 1980, 52 TC 674 and its sequel *Yuill v Fletcher* CA 1984, 58 TC 145; *Winterton v Edwards* Ch D 1979, 52 TC 655; and *Sugarwhite v Budd* CA 1988, 60 TC 679. *Bona fide* transactions, not entered into with tax avoidance in view, may be caught by the legislation — see *Page v Lowther and Another* CA 1983, 57 TC 199.

For the date of the capital gain where instalments are involved, see *Yuill v Fletcher* CA 1984, 58 TC 145.

Computation of gain

Gains are to be computed 'as is just and reasonable in the circumstances', taking into account the value of what is obtained for disposing of the land and allowing only for expenses attributable to the land disposed of. The following may be taken into account:

(A)   if a leasehold interest is disposed of out of a freehold, the treatment under *ITTOIA 2005, Pt 2* (trading income) in computing the profits in such a case of a person dealing in land (see **73.103 TRADING INCOME**); and

(B)   any adjustments under *ITTOIA 2005, s 158* for tax on lease premiums.

Any necessary apportionments of consideration, expenses etc., are to be made on a just and reasonable basis.

[ITA 2007, ss 760, 764; ICTA 1988, s 776(6)].

Where the computation of a gain in respect of the development of land (as under (c) above) is made on the footing that the land or property was appropriated as trading stock, that land etc., is also to be treated for purposes of capital gains tax (under *TCGA 1992, s 161*) as having been transferred to stock. *[TCGA 1992, s 161(5); ICTA 1988, s 777(11); ITA 2007, Sch 1 para 321].*

Trustees

Income treated as above as arising to trustees of a settlement is treated as being income chargeable at the trust rate. See **68.12 SETTLEMENTS.**

Exemptions

(i)   An individual's gain made from the *sale etc., of his residence* exempted from capital gains tax under *TCGA 1992, ss 222–226* or which would be so exempt but for *TCGA 1992, s 224(3)* (acquired for purpose of making a gain).

(ii)   A gain on the sale of *shares in a company holding land as trading stock* (or a company owning, directly or indirectly, 90% of the ordinary share capital of such a company) *provided that* the company disposes of the land by normal trade and makes all possible profit from it, and the share sale is not part of an arrangement or scheme to realise a land gain indirectly. This does not apply if the person obtaining the gain is only a party to, or concerned in, an arrangement or scheme to realise the gain indirectly or by a series of transactions. See *Chilcott v CIR* Ch D 1981, 55 TC 446.

(iii)   (If the liability arises solely under (c) above.) Any part of the gain fairly attributable to a period *before the intention was made* to develop the land.

[*ITA 2007, ss 765–767; ICTA 1988, s 776(7)(9)(10)); ITTOIA 2005, Sch 1 para 312(5)*].

Recovery of tax

Where tax under the above provisions is assessed on, and paid by, a person other than the one who actually realised the gain, the person paying the tax may recover it from the other party (for which purpose HMRC will, on request, supply a certificate of income in respect of which tax has been paid). [*ITA 2007, ss 768, 769; ICTA 1988, s 777(8)*].

Clearance

The person who made or would make the gain may (if he considers that (a) or (c) above may apply), submit to HMRC particulars of any completed or proposed transactions. If he does so HMRC must, within 30 days of receiving those particulars, notify the taxpayer whether or not they are satisfied that liability under these provisions does not arise. If HMRC are so satisfied the gain is not chargeable to income tax, provided that all material facts and considerations have been fully and accurately disclosed. [*ITA 2007, s 770; ICTA 1988, s 776(11)*].

General

See *ITA 2007, s 761* (previously *ICTA 1988, s 777(2)(3)*) for provisions to prevent avoidance by the use of indirect means to transfer any property or right, or enhance or diminish its value, e.g., by sales at less, or more, than full consideration, assigning share capital or rights in a company or partnership or an interest in settled property, disposal on the winding-up of any company, partnership or trust etc. For ascertaining whether, and to what extent, the value of any property or right is derived from any other property or right, value may be traced through any number of companies, partnerships and trusts, at each stage attributing property held by the company, partnership or trust to its shareholders etc., 'in such manner as is appropriate to the circumstances'. [*ITA 2007, s 762; ICTA 1988, s 777(5)*].

Where the person liable is non-UK resident, HMRC may direct that any part of an amount taxable under these provisions on that person be paid under deduction of income tax at the basic rate (for the tax year of payment). [*ITA 2007, s 944; ICTA 1988, s 777(9)*].

For the above purposes HMRC may require, under penalty, any person to supply them with any particulars thought necessary, including particulars of:

(I)   transactions or arrangements in which he acts, or acted, on behalf of others; and

(II)   transactions or arrangements which in the opinion of HMRC should be investigated; and

(III)   what part, if any, he has taken, or is taking, in specified transactions or arrangements. (A *solicitor* who has merely acted as professional adviser is not treated as having taken part in a transaction or arrangement.)

A solicitor who has merely acted as professional adviser is not compelled to do more than state that he acted and give his client's name and address.

[*ITA 2007, s 771; ICTA 1988, s 778*].

The transactions of which particulars are required need not be identified transactions (*Essex v CIR* CA 1980, 53 TC 720).

Simon's Taxes. See B5.235–B5.246.

Land sold and leased back — payments connected with transferred land

[4.30] The consequences described below ensue where land (or any interest or estate in land) is transferred (by sale, lease, surrender or forfeiture of lease etc.) and, as a result of:

*   a lease of the land, or any part of it, granted at the time of transfer or subsequently by the transferee to the transferor; or
*   another transaction or transactions affecting the land or interest or estate,

the transferor, or a person associated (see below) with the transferor, becomes liable to make a payment of rent under a lease of the land or part of it (including any premium treated as rent — see **60.19 PROPERTY INCOME**), or any other payment connected with the land or part of it (whether it is a payment of rentcharge or under some other transaction), which would be allowable as a deduction:

- in computing the profits of a trade, profession or vocation; or
- in computing the profits of a UK property business; or
- in computing profits or income under any of the provisions listed at *ITA 2007, s 1016* (previously *ICTA 1988, s 836B*) (see **49.8** MISCELLANEOUS INCOME) or in computing losses for which relief is available as in **49.11** MISCELLANEOUS INCOME; or
- from earnings, under *ITEPA 2003, s 336*; or
- in calculating losses in an employment.

A transfer of an estate or interest in land includes:

(a)   the granting of a lease or another transaction involving the creation of a new estate or interest in the land;

(b)   the transfer of the lessee's interest under a lease by surrender or forfeiture of the lease; and

(c)   a transaction or series of transactions affecting land or an estate or interest in land, such that some person is the owner (or one of the owners) before and after the transaction(s) but another person becomes or ceases to be one of the owners.

With regard to (c), a person is to be regarded as a transferor for the purposes of these provisions if the person is an owner before the transaction(s) and is not the sole owner afterwards.

The consequences are that the deduction for tax purposes in respect of the rent or other payment is limited to the 'commercial rent' of the land to which it relates for the period for which the payment is made. In fact, except where the deduction is made against earnings or in computing an employment loss, the position is judged on a cumulative basis. For any 'relevant period', amount E (which may be nil) is the expense or total expenses to be brought, in accordance with generally accepted accounting practice (GAAP), into account in the period in respect of the payments made (excluding any just and reasonable portion which relates to services, tenant's rates, or the use of assets other than land). A *'relevant period'* is generally a period of account, but if no accounts are drawn up it is the basis period for a trade, profession or vocation or otherwise a tax year. Take the amount of E for the current relevant period and for every previous relevant period ending on or after the date of the transfer. Subtract from the aggregate amount the total deductions given for every such previous relevant period. What remains is the cumulative unrelieved expenses for the current period, and it is this figure which is then compared to the commercial rent for the period and restricted if necessary. The cumulative unrelieved expenses cannot, however, be carried forward to a relevant period beginning after the payments have ceased; no deduction is available under these provisions for any such expenses.

Where the deduction is made against earnings or in computing an employment loss, it must not exceed the commercial rent for the period for which the payment is made. There is provision for carrying forward non-deductible amounts but not to a period beyond that for which the final payment is made (see *ITA 2007, s 681AF*). To the extent that a payment is actually made for a period more than twelve months ahead, it is treated as made for the period comprising the next twelve months.

In the case of a lease, '*commercial rent*' means the open-market rent, at the time the actual lease was created, under a lease whose duration and maintenance/repair terms are the same as under the actual lease but stipulating a rent payable at uniform intervals at a uniform rate, or progressively increasing proportionately to any increases provided by the actual lease. For other transactions, it is the open market rent which would be payable under a tenant's repairing lease (as defined by *ITA 2007, s 681AK(3)*) for the period over which payments are to be made (subject to a maximum of 200 years.

In these provisions, 'lease', as well as having its normal meaning, includes (i) an underlease, sublease, tenancy or licence, (ii) an agreement for a lease, underlease, sublease, tenancy or licence, and (iii) in the case of land outside the UK, an interest corresponding to a lease. 'Rent' includes any payment under a lease.

For the purposes of these provisions, the following persons are associated with one another:

(i)   the transferor in an 'affected transaction' and the transferor in another affected transaction, if the two persons are acting in concert or if the two transactions are in any way reciprocal;

(ii)   any person who is an associate of either of the associated transferors in (i);

(iii)   two or more bodies corporate if they participate in, or are incorporated for the purposes of, a scheme for the reconstruction, or amalgamation, of a body corporate or bodies corporate.

In addition, persons are associated with one another if they are associates as defined in *ITA 2007, s 681DL* (see **4.33** below). In (i) above, an 'affected transaction' is a transfer within these provisions or within the corresponding corporation tax provisions.

[*ITA 2007, ss 681A–681AN; ICTA 1988, s 779; TIOPA 2010, Sch 4 para 2*].

Simon's Taxes. See B5.247.

Land sold and leased back — new lease of land after assignment or surrender

[4.31] In certain circumstances where a lease of land is assigned or surrendered and another lease is granted or assigned, consideration received for the assignment or surrender of the first lease is chargeable to income tax and tax relief is allowed for rent under the other lease. These provisions apply where all of the following conditions are met:

(a)   a person (L) is a lessee of land under a lease which has 50 years or less to run ('the original lease') and is entitled to income tax relief on the rent;

(b)   L assigns the original lease to another person or surrenders it to the landlord, and the consideration for the assignment or surrender would not be taxable except as capital in L's hands;

(c)   another lease ('the new lease') for a term of 15 years or less is granted, or assigned, to L (or to a person linked to L);

(d)   the new lease comprises or includes all or part of the land which was the subject of the original lease; and

(e)   neither L (nor a person linked to L) had, before 22 June 1971, a right enforceable at law or in equity to the grant of the new lease.

The reference in (a) to income tax relief is to any of the allowable deductions listed in **4.30** above. For the purposes of (c) and (e), a person is linked to L if he is a partner of L, an associate of L or an associate of a partner of L. Persons are associated with one another if they are associates as defined in *ITA 2007, s 681DL* (see **4.33** below).

A proportion of the consideration mentioned in (b) above (the 'appropriate proportion') is taxed as income (and not treated as a capital receipt). If it is received by L in the course of a trade, profession or vocation and the rent payable under the new lease is allowable as a deduction in calculating the profits or losses of a trade, profession or vocation for tax purposes, the appropriate proportion is treated as a receipt of L's trade etc. If not, it is treated as an amount chargeable to income tax. The *'appropriate proportion'* is the proportion of the consideration found by applying to it the formula

$$\frac{16 - N}{15}$$

where N = the term of the new lease expressed in years (taking part of a year as an appropriate proportion of a year).

If the consideration is paid in instalments, the formula is applied to each instalment. If the term of the new lease is one year or less, the appropriate proportion of the consideration or instalment is the whole of it. If the property which is the subject of the new lease does not include all the property which was the subject of the original lease, the consideration must be reduced as is reasonable before applying the formula.

Provided the rent under the new lease is payable by a person within the charge to income tax, all provisions of *ITTOIA 2005* providing for deductions or allowances by way of income tax relief in respect of payments of rent apply in relation to the rent payable under the new lease.

There are provisions (see *ITA 2007, ss 681BE–681BI*) whereby for the above purposes the term of the new lease is deemed to end (i) on an earlier date if the rent is reduced or (ii) if the lessor or lessee has power to determine the lease or the lessee has power to vary its terms, on the earliest date on which it can be so determined or varied.

If conditions (a)–(d) above are met but condition (e) is not (such that the above provisions do not apply), and the rent under the new lease is payable by a person within the charge to income tax:

*   no part of the rent paid under the new lease is to be treated as a payment of capital; and

- all provisions of *ITTOIA 2005* providing for deductions or allowances by way of income tax relief in respect of payments of rent apply accordingly in relation to that rent.

In these provisions, 'lease', as well as having its normal meaning, includes (i) an agreement for a lease, and (ii) any tenancy, but does not include a mortgage. 'Rent' includes a payment by a tenant for work to maintain or repair leased land or premises which the lease does not require the tenant to carry out.

Consequences ensue if all of the following conditions are met:

(A)   a person (M) is a lessee of land under a lease which has 50 years or less to run ('the original lease') and is entitled to income tax relief on the rent;

(B)   M varies the original lease by agreement with the landlord;

(C)   under the variation, M agrees to pay a rent greater than that payable under the original lease and, does so in return for a consideration which would not be taxable except as capital in M's hands; and

(D)   under the variation, the period during which the greater rent is to be paid not more than 15 years after the date on which the consideration is paid to M (or, where applicable, the final instalment of the consideration is paid to M).

The consequences are that M is treated as having surrendered the original lease for the consideration mentioned in (C) and as having been granted a new lease for a term of 15 years or less but otherwise on the terms of the original lease varied as mentioned in (B). The provisions described above are then applied accordingly.

[ITA 2007, ss 681B–681BM; ICTA 1988, s 780; ITA 2007, Sch 1 para 188; TIOPA 2010, Sch 4 para 3, Sch 9 para 41].

Simon's Taxes. See B5.248.

Leased trading assets

[4.32] In certain circumstances where a payment is made under a lease of a trading asset, income tax relief for the payment is restricted. The provisions apply where:

- a payment is made by a person under a lease of an asset (other than land or an interest in land) created after 14 April 1964;
- a deduction is allowed for the payment in calculating the profits of a trade, profession or vocation for income tax purposes; and
- at a time before the lease was created the asset was used for the purposes of the trade etc. or for the purposes of another trade etc. carried on by the lessee, and was then owned by the person carrying on the trade etc. in which it was used.

The deduction for the payment is limited to the 'commercial rent' of the asset to which it relates for the period for which the payment is made. In fact, the position is judged on a cumulative basis in similar manner to that described in

4.30 above, taking into account the payments for every previous 'relevant period' ended on or after the date the lease was created. It is the cumulative unrelieved expenses for the current period which is then compared to the commercial rent for the period and restricted if necessary. The cumulative unrelieved expenses cannot, however, be carried forward to a relevant period beginning after the payments have ceased; no deduction is available under these provisions for any such expenses. A '*relevant period*' is generally a period of account, but if no accounts are drawn up it is the basis period for the trade etc. for the tax year.

The '*commercial rent*' is the rent which might at the time the lease is created be expected to be paid under a lease of the asset if the lease were for the rest of the asset's 'expected normal working life' (as defined), the rent were payable at uniform intervals and at a uniform rate, and the rent gave a reasonable return for the asset's market value at that time, taking account of the terms and conditions of the actual lease. If the asset is used at the same time partly for the purposes of the trade etc. and partly for other purposes, the commercial rent is to be determined by reference to what would be paid for such partial use.

For the above purposes, a lease is an agreement or arrangement under which payments are made for the use of, or otherwise in respect of, the asset. It includes an agreement or arrangement under which the payments (or any of them) represent instalments of, or payments towards, a purchase price.

The above provisions do not apply to payments due on or after 1 April 2006 under a lease which is a long funding finance lease as regards the lessee (see **11.45** CAPITAL ALLOWANCES ON PLANT AND MACHINERY).

[*ITA 2007, ss 681C–681CG; ICTA 1988, ss 782, 785; FA 2006, Sch 9 para 3; TIOPA 2010, Sch 4 para 4*].

Simon's Taxes. See B5.413.

Leased assets — capital sums

[4.33] In certain circumstances where a payment is made under a lease of an asset (other than one created on or before 14 April 1964), and a 'capital sum' is obtained in respect of an interest in the asset, income tax is chargeable. This does not apply if **4.32** above (or corporation tax equivalent) applies to the payment or would do so were it not for the exclusion in **4.32** of payments under long funding finance leases. A lease is defined as in **4.32** above. A '*capital sum*' is any sum of money, or any money's worth, except in so far as it falls to be taken into account as a trading receipt or is chargeable to income tax as miscellaneous income).

The provisions apply where a payment is made under a lease of an asset (other than land or an interest in land), the payment is one for which a tax deduction is available (see below) and any one of the following conditions is met:

- the person making the payment (P) obtains a capital sum in respect of the lessee's interest in the lease; or
- 'an associate' (see below) of P obtains a capital sum by way of consideration in respect of the lessee's interest in the lease; or

- the lessor's interest in the lease, or any other interest in the asset, belongs to an associate of P, and the associate obtains a capital sum in respect of the interest; or
- the lessor's interest in the lease, or any other interest in the asset, belongs to an associate of P, and an associate of that associate obtains a capital sum by way of consideration in respect of the interest.

Conditions (a)–(d) may be met before, at or after the time when the payment is made, but can be met only if the person obtaining the capital sum is within the charge to income tax. The conditions are not met if the lease is a hire-purchase agreement for plant or machinery and the capital sum has to be brought into account as the whole or part of the capital allowances disposal value of the plant or machinery (and provided, in the case of (c) or (d), that the capital sum is obtained in respect of the lessee's interest in the lease).

The reference above to a tax deduction is to a deduction allowable:

- in computing the profits of a trade, profession or vocation for income tax purposes; or
- in computing profits or income under any of the provisions listed at *ITA 2007, s 1016* (previously *ICTA 1988, s 836B*) (see **49.8 MISCELLANEOUS INCOME**) or in computing losses for which relief is available as in **49.11 MISCELLANEOUS INCOME**; or
- against earnings, under *ITEPA 2003, s 336*; or
- in calculating losses in an employment; or
- in computing trading profits for corporation tax purposes; or
- (for accounting periods ending on or after 1 April 2009) in computing profits or income under any of the provisions listed at *CTA 2010, s 1173* (miscellaneous income) or in computing losses for which relief is available under *CTA 2010, s 91* (miscellaneous losses); or
- (for accounting periods ended before 1 April 2009) in computing profits or losses for corporation tax under Schedule D, Case VI; or
- under *CTA 2009, s 1219* (management expenses of a company's investment business) (previously as a management expense under *ICTA 1988, s 75*); or
- under *ICTA 1988, s 76* (expenses of insurance companies).

The person obtaining the capital sum is treated as receiving, at the time the sum is obtained, an amount chargeable to income tax. The amount is equal to the amount(s) of the payment for which the above-mentioned tax deduction is made, but is not to exceed the capital sum. Where the lease is a hire-purchase agreement and the capital sum is obtained in respect of the lessee's interest in the lease, the recipient's capital expenditure on the asset is taken as reducing the capital sum for the purpose of applying this rule (see *ITA 2007, s 681DE*).

If a payment or part of a payment is taken into account in deciding the chargeable amount in respect of a capital sum, the payment or part must be left out of account in deciding whether a charge arises under these provisions in respect of another capital sum and, if so, the chargeable amount. This rule is applied in the order in which capital sums are obtained. If the capital sum is received before the payment is made, any necessary adjustment to the recipient's tax position can be made within the period ending with the fifth anniversary of 31 January following the tax year in which the payment is made.

If a person disposes of an interest in an asset to a person who is his 'associate' (as below), he is regarded as obtaining the greatest of the actual sum obtained, the open market value and the value of the interest to the person to whom it is transferred.

Reference above to any sum obtained in respect of an interest in an asset includes any insurance money obtained in respect of the interest and any sum representing money or money's worth obtained in respect of the interest by a transaction or series of transactions disposing of it. Reference to any sum obtained in respect of the lessee's interest in a lease of an asset includes any sums representing consideration for a surrender of the interest to the lessor, an assignment of the lease, the creation of a sublease or another interest out of the lease or a transaction or series of transactions under which the lessee's rights are merged in any way with the lessor's rights or with any other rights as respects the asset.

There is provision for payments to be apportioned where made by persons in partnership and for sums to be apportioned where obtained by persons in partnership or by persons jointly entitled to the interest in an asset (see *ITA 2007, ss 681DJ, 681DK*).

Meaning of 'associates'

For the above purposes, the following are associated with each other:

- an individual and the individual's spouse, civil partner or relative (meaning a brother, sister, ancestor or lineal descendant);
- an individual and a spouse or civil partner of a relative of the individual;
- an individual and a relative of the individual's spouse or civil partner;
- an individual and a spouse or civil partner of a relative of the individual's spouse or civil partner;
- a trustee of a settlement and an individual who is the settlor or any person associated with that individual;
- a person and a body of persons (which may be a partnership) of which he has control (within the meaning of *ITA 2007, s 995*);
- a person and a body of persons of which persons associated with the person have control;
- a person and a body of persons of which the person and persons associated with the person have control;
- two or more bodies of persons associated with the same person;
- in relation to a disposal by joint owners, the joint owners and any person associated with any of them.

[*ITA 2007, ss 681D–681DP; ICTA 1988, ss 781, 783–785; ITA 2007, Sch 1 paras 189, 190; CTA 2009, Sch 1 paras 234, 236; TIOPA 2010, Sch 4 para 5; SI 2009 No 56, Sch 1 para 156*].

Simon's Taxes. See B5.411, B5.412, B5.414.

Transfers of income streams

[4.34] The legislation described below is designed to prevent the avoidance of tax where a person transfers to another person **on or after 22 April 2009** a right to taxable receipts without transferring any asset from which the right to the receipts arises. It supersedes the legislation summarised at **4.6** and **4.7** above and at **4.38** below as well as parts of other provisions which deal with such transfers.

The legislation applies where a person within the charge to income tax transfers to another person a right to 'relevant receipts' without transferring to him an asset from which a right to relevant receipts arises. '*Relevant receipts*' means any income which, but for the transfer, would fall either to be charged to income tax as the transferor's income or to be included in computing his taxable profits. The legislation additionally applies if a person within the charge to income tax transfers to another person a right to relevant receipts in consequence of a transfer to him of all the rights under an agreement for annual payments.

The consideration for the transfer of the right is treated as income of the transferor and is brought into the charge to income tax in the same way and to the same extent as the relevant receipts would have been brought into charge had the transfer not taken place. If the consideration is substantially less than the market value of the right at the time of the transfer, of if the consideration is nil, the market value is brought into charge instead of the consideration.

The income is treated as arising in the tax year in which the transfer takes place. A special rule applies, however, if any of the relevant receipts would have been taken into account in computing the profits of a trade, profession, vocation or property business and, in accordance with generally accepted accounting practice (GAAP), would have been recognised otherwise than wholly in the tax year in which the transfer takes place. If the income is based on the amount of consideration, it is treated as arising in the tax year(s) in which the consideration is recognised under GAAP. If the income is based on market value, it is treated as arising in the tax year(s) in which the consideration would have been recognised under GAAP if it had been equal to market value.

Income is not to be brought into account as above to the extent (if any) that it is otherwise brought into the charge to income tax. Also, these provisions do not apply if the consideration for the transfer is the advance under a structured finance arrangement (see **4.35** below) in relation to either the transferor or a partnership of which he is a member. Also excepted from these provisions are transfers of (i) a right to annual payments under a life annuity, or (ii) a right to annual payments under an annuity which is pension income.

For the purposes of applying this legislation, the grant or surrender of a lease of land is to be regarded as a transfer of the land, and the disposal of an interest in an oil licence is to be regarded as a transfer of the oil licence. However, the transfer of an asset under a sale and repurchase agreement is not regarded for these purposes as a transfer of the asset. A 'transfer' includes a sale, an exchange, a gift, an assignment and any other arrangement which equates in substance to a transfer. A transfer to or by any partnership of which the transferor or transferee is a member counts as a transfer for the purposes of this legislation, as does a transfer to the trustees of any trust of which the transferor is a beneficiary.

If the transferor is a member of a partnership and the transfer of a right to relevant receipts consists of a reduction in his profit share, he is to be regarded as transferring an asset (i.e. the partnership property) from which the right arose, but only if at least one of the following two conditions are met.

- The first condition is that there is a reduction in the transferor's share in the partnership property, and the reduction in his profit share is proportionate to that reduction.
- The second condition is that the avoidance tax by any partner on the relevant receipts is not a main purpose of the transfer.

Thus, if at least one of the conditions is met, the transfer will not fall within the above provisions.

[ITA 2007, ss 809AZA–809AZG; FA 2009, Sch 25 paras 7, 10; TIOPA 2010, Sch 8 para 273].

Factoring of income receipts etc.

[4.35] The provisions described below are intended to counter, from 6 June 2006 (but see below for extension of the provisions from 6 March 2007), the situation in which a person enters into financing arrangements that equate in substance to his taking out a loan but which are structured in such a way as to effectively give him tax relief for repayment of principal as well as for finance charges.

Say, for example, B has the opportunity to take out a loan of £50,000 with L, under which B would repay the loan over five years together with total interest of £5,000. Tax relief might be available for the £5,000 interest but not for the repayment of the £50,000 principal. As an alternative, B transfers to L for £50,000 an asset that is fully expected to produce income of £55,000 over the next five years, at the end of which the asset will be transferred back to B for nothing. L receives £55,000 for an outlay of £50,000. B then claims that the transfer of the asset to L either gives rise only to a chargeable gain (which may be relatively small due to high base cost and available reliefs) or is not taxable at all, and that he is not chargeable on the income of £55,000 which is received not by him but by L. B effectively obtains tax relief on £55,000 (less any CGT payable).

Sometimes, instead of the borrower forgoing income, the arrangements generate a tax deduction for the borrower. Say B grants a long lease of freehold property to L for a premium of £50,000. L then grants a five-year sub-lease back to B at a rent of £11,000 per year. The arrangements will provide for the benefits of ownership to revert to B at the end of the five years. Again, L receives £55,000 for an outlay of £50,000. B obtains tax relief for rent payments of £55,000. Before 6 June 2006, this type of scheme may have been countered by the rent factoring legislation at *ICTA 1988, ss 43A–43G* (repealed by *FA 2006, Sch 6 para 1* for transactions entered into on or after 6 June 2006 as a consequence of the introduction of the wider provisions described below).

Commencement and transitional

Except where otherwise indicated, the following provisions apply in relation to any arrangements whenever made. However, in relation to any arrangements made before 6 June 2006, any amount otherwise falling to be brought into account as a result of these provisions in determining taxable income is to be brought into account only if the amount arises on or after that date. In relation to the second type of arrangement described above, the following provisions do not apply in relation to a pre-6 June 2006 arrangement insofar as the (now repealed) rent factoring legislation applies to that arrangement.

Arrangements involving disposals of assets

The anti-avoidance provisions apply where there is a '*structured finance arrangement*'. Such an arrangement exists where:

- under the arrangement a person (the borrower) receives from another person (the lender) any money or other asset (the advance) in any period;
- in accordance with generally accepted accounting practice (GAAP) the accounts of the borrower for that period record a financial liability in respect of the advance;
- the borrower (or a person connected with him) disposes of an asset (the security) under the arrangement to or for the benefit of the lender (or a person connected with him);
- the lender (or a person connected with him) is entitled under the arrangement to payments in respect of the security; and
- in accordance with GAAP those payments reduce the amount of the financial liability recorded in the borrower's accounts.

For these purposes, the rules in **21 CONNECTED PERSONS** apply to determine whether persons are connected, except that the borrower and lender cannot be regarded as a connected with one another. If the borrower is a partnership, references above to accounts are to the accounts of any member of the partnership as well as the partnership itself. 'Arrangement' is widely defined for the purposes of these provisions to include any agreement or understanding (whether or not legally enforceable). 'Payments' is also widely defined to include any obtaining of value or benefit, and encompasses the situation where an asset replaces the original asset within the arrangement. Where it is not the case, these provisions apply as if the accounts in question had been prepared in accordance with GAAP. On and after 19 July 2007, in determining whether accounts record an amount as a financial liability in respect of an advance, it has to be assumed that the period of account in which the advance is received ended immediately after the receipt of the advance.

If an arrangement is a structured finance arrangement, then:

(a)   if, as a result of the arrangement, an amount of otherwise chargeable income would escape tax in the hands of the borrower (or a person connected with him), it does not escape tax;

(b)   if, as a result of the arrangement, any amount would otherwise not fall to be taken into account in computing income of the borrower (or a person connected with him) for tax purposes, that amount shall be so brought into account; and

(c)   if, as a result of the arrangement, the borrower (or a person connected with him) would otherwise be entitled to a deduction in computing any taxable income, or a deduction against total income, he shall not be so entitled.

If the borrower is a partnership, the above have effect by reference to any member of the partnership.

With effect for disposals on or after 6 March 2007, if a structured finance arrangement would *not* have had the result mentioned in (a), (b) or (c) above, the payments to which the lender (or a person connected with him) is entitled under the arrangement are treated as income of the borrower in respect of the security. This applies whether or not the payments are also the income of another person for tax purposes. If, however, the arrangement was entered into before 6 March 2007, only amounts arising on or after that date are so treated.

In all the above cases, if the borrower is within the charge to income tax and, in accordance with GAAP, his accounts record a finance charge in respect of the advance, he can treat the finance charge as if it were interest on a loan. The intended effect is to place the borrower in the same position for tax purposes as if he had taken out a loan instead of entering into the structured finance arrangement. (If the borrower is a partnership, it is the partnership itself that is deemed to be paying interest, even if the finance charge appears in the accounts of a member.) The time at which this notional interest is to be treated as having been paid depends on the timing of the payments made to the lender in respect of the security; each such payment is treated as if it were part repayment of principal and part interest.

See also below under Exceptions.

Arrangements involving partnership changes

More complex types of arrangement might be involved where the 'borrower' is a partnership. For example, B might transfer an income-producing asset to a partnership of which he is a member. L then joins the partnership for a capital contribution of £50,000 in return for the right to receive partnership profits of £55,000 over the next 5 years but no profits beyond that period. B claims not to be taxable on the £55,000 of partnership profits diverted to L. In another scenario, an established partnership may already hold an income-producing asset and the above steps then follow without the need for the initial transfer of an asset by B. In this case, the members of the partnership whose profits are thereby reduced claim not to be taxable on the partnership profits diverted to L.

There are similar anti-avoidance provisions to catch these types of arrangement. See *ITA 2007, ss BZF–BZL* (previously *ICTA 1988, ss 774C, 774D*). These provisions rely on alternative definitions of 'structured finance arrangement', tailored to the type of arrangement at which they are aimed. If, as a result, an arrangement is a structured finance arrangement in relation to the borrower partnership, the partnership change is treated for tax purposes as if it had not occurred. For this purpose, the 'partnership change' might be the admission of the lender as a partner or a change in profit sharing ratios affecting the lender's share. The provisions are widely drawn so as also to catch changes made indirectly and/or involving a person connected with the lender. Again, as above, there is provision for a finance charge to be treated as if it were interest paid on a loan.

See also below under Exceptions.

Exceptions

The above provisions are disapplied if the whole of the advance under the structured finance arrangement falls to be brought into account in determining the taxable income of a 'relevant person'. (The effect of the rent factoring legislation at **4.38** below, where relevant, is to be ignored for this purpose.) This includes a case where the advance falls to be brought into account as a disposal receipt, or in otherwise computing a balancing charge, for capital allowances purposes, but not if any such balancing charge would fall to be restricted under the capital allowances legislation. A '*relevant person*' means the borrower under the arrangements or a person connected with the borrower or, if the borrower is a partnership, a member of the partnership.

There are also exclusions in cases where other statutory provisions specified in *ITA 2007, s 809BZN* do in any case result in the arrangement being properly taxed. These include, for example, certain repo and stock lending arrangements, ALTERNATIVE FINANCE ARRANGEMENTS (3) and certain sale and finance leaseback transactions. The Treasury have power to specify further exclusions by statutory instrument, and any such exclusions may be given retrospective effect.

Miscellaneous

The lease premium rules at *ITTOIA 2005, ss 277–281* (see **60.16 PROPERTY INCOME**) are disapplied where the grant of the lease constitutes the disposal of an asset for the purposes of these provisions.

See *TCGA 2002, s 263E* as regards the CGT consequences of structured finance arrangements.

[*ITA 2007, ss 809BZA–809BZS; ICTA 1988, ss 774A–774G; FA 2006, Sch 6 para 6; FA 2007, s 47, Sch 5 paras 3–7, 17(4)–(9), Sch 14 para 9; FA 2008, Sch 20 paras 6(18)(19), 12(11)(12); CTA 2009, Sch 1 paras 226–229; FA 2009, Sch 25 paras 9(3), 10; TIOPA 2010, Sch 5 paras 2–6; SI 2007 No 2483, reg 3*].

Loan or credit transactions

[4.36] Where, with reference to lending money or giving credit (or varying the terms of a loan or credit):

(i)   a transaction provides for the payment of an annuity or other annual payment (other than interest) — that payment is treated as if it were a payment of yearly interest.

(ii)   any person surrenders, waives or forgoes income on property — that person is chargeable to income tax on a sum equal to the income surrendered, waived etc. This does not apply if the person concerned is chargeable, as a result of **4.35** above, on the income surrendered etc.

(iii)   (before 22 April 2009 — see now the more general provisions at **4.34** above) any person *assigns* income on property (without a sale or transfer of the property) — that person is chargeable to income tax on a sum equal to the income assigned. This does not apply if the person concerned is chargeable, as a result of **4.35** above, on the income assigned;

(iv)   if credit is given for the purchase price of property and during the subsistence of the debt, the buyer's rights to income from the property are suspended or restricted — he is treated for the purpose of (ii) above as if he had made a surrender of that income.

Transactions with CONNECTED PERSONS (21) are included.

[ITA 2007, ss 809CZA–809CZC; ICTA 1988, s 786; FA 2006, Sch 6 para 8; FA 2009, Sch 25 paras 9(1), 10; TIOPA 2010, Sch 5 para 7].

Simon's Taxes. See E1.824.

Leasing of plant and machinery

[4.37] If, under a lease of plant or machinery, there is an unconditional obligation, first arising after 12 December 2007, to make a 'relevant capital payment' or if such a payment is made after that date without obligation, the lessor is treated for income tax purposes as receiving income attributable to the lease of an amount equal to the 'capital payment'. The income is treated as income for the period of account in which the obligation first arose or, as the case may be, income for the period of account in which the payment is made. These provisions apply to long funding leases (see **73.94** TRADING INCOME) as well as to other plant or machinery leases. The provisions apply equally if the obligation arises, or the payment is made, under an agreement or arrangement relating to a lease of plant or machinery, whether made before, during or after the currency of the lease itself.

For these purposes, a payment includes the provision of value by whatever means. A *'capital payment'* is any payment other than one which, if made to the lessor, would fall to be included in the lessor's income for tax purposes or which would fall to be included were it not for *ITTOIA 2005, s 148A* (which determines the amount to be brought into account as taxable income from such a lease — see **73.95** TRADING INCOME).

A capital payment is a *'relevant capital payment'* if either:

•   it is payable by lessee to lessor in connection with the grant, assignment, novation or termination of the lease or with any provision of the lease or, as the case may be, the agreement or arrangement (including the variation or waiver of any such provision); or

- the lease rentals are less than (or payable later than) they might reasonably be expected to be if there were no obligation to make the capital payment and the capital payment were not made.

However, a capital payment is *not* a '*relevant capital payment*' if, or to the extent that:

- it reduces the lessor's expenditure for the purposes of plant and machinery capital allowances — see the rules on expenditure met by another's contributions at **11.2**(vi) CAPITAL ALLOWANCES ON PLANT AND MACHINERY — or would do so if the circumstances were not such that the contributions rules are disapplied; or
- it represents compensation for damage to, or damage caused by, the plant or machinery in question.

Where a capital payment is an initial payment under a long funding lease (see **11.43** *et seq.* CAPITAL ALLOWANCES ON PLANT AND MACHINERY) whose inception is on or after 13 November 2008 and before 22 April 2009, the commencement of the term of the lease is an event that requires the lessor to bring a disposal value into account, the payment is not a relevant capital payment. If the inception of the lease is on or after 22 April 2009, the payment *is* a relevant capital payment but only to the extent (if any) that it exceeds the disposal value. Before 13 November 2008, a capital payment was not a relevant capital payment if, or to the extent that, it was a disposal value (see **11.24** CAPITAL ALLOWANCES ON PLANT AND MACHINERY) for the purposes of the lessor's plant and machinery capital allowances computations.

'*Lease*' is defined to include a licence and also the letting of a ship or aircraft on charter or any other asset on hire. For these purposes, if the obligation to make the relevant capital payment arises, or the payment is made, after 11 March 2008, a lease of plant or machinery includes a lease of plant or machinery together with other property, in which case the payment is apportioned on a just and reasonable basis and only the amount apportioned to the plant or machinery is chargeable under these provisions. It does not, however, include a lease all the lessor's income from which (if any) would be chargeable as **PROPERTY INCOME** (**60**) or a long funding lease of plant or machinery on which the lessor would have been treated as having incurred qualifying expenditure for the purposes of plant and machinery capital allowances if it were not for *CAA 2001, s 34A* at **11.46** CAPITAL ALLOWANCES ON PLANT AND MACHINERY. If the obligation to make the relevant capital payment arises, or the payment is made, on or before 11 March 2008, a lease of plant or machinery does not include a lease of plant or machinery together with other property, though it does include an equipment lease within **11.35** CAPITAL ALLOWANCES ON PLANT AND MACHINERY.

There is bad debt relief if the above provisions have applied by virtue of an unconditional obligation and at any time the lessor reasonably expects that the relevant capital payment will not be paid (or will not be fully paid). The lessor is allowed a deduction for the expected shortfall in computing his profits for the period of account in which that time falls.

[*ITA 2007, ss 809ZA–809ZF; FA 2008, Sch 20 para 2; FA 2009, Sch 32 paras 10, 11; CTA 2010, Sch 1 paras 548–551, 581(2)*].

Rent factoring of plant or machinery leases

[4.38] The provisions described below are repealed with effect for transfers on or after 22 April 2009 and are superseded by the more general provisions on transfers of income streams at **4.34** above.

Where a person arranges to transfer his right to receive taxable rentals under a lease of plant or machinery for consideration, all or some of which is neither chargeable (to income tax or corporation tax) as income nor liable to be treated as a disposal receipt for plant and machinery capital allowances purposes, the otherwise non-taxable consideration is taxable as rental income by reference to the period(s) of account in which it is receivable. A transfer of a right to receive rentals includes any arrangement that results in the rental receipts otherwise ceasing to be taxed as income, and 'lease' is widely defined to include, for example, an underlease, sublease, tenancy or licence.

Where the arrangement for the transfer of rights takes place after 11 March 2008, the charge to tax is on the market value of the rights transferred, and the chargeable income arises at the time of transfer. It is also specified that the provisions apply where the transfer is to a person in which the transferor has an interest, e.g. a partnership of which he is a member or a trust of which he is a beneficiary, just as they do where the transfer is not to such a person.

The provisions at **4.35** and **4.37** above each take priority over these provisions where more than one set of provisions would otherwise apply.

[*ICTA 1988, s 785A; FA 2004, s 135; FA 2006, Sch 6 para 7; FA 2008, Sch 20 para 3, Sch 22 para 1; FA 2009, Sch 25 paras 9(1), 10*].

Simon's Taxes. See B5.415.

Annual payments for non-taxable consideration etc.

[4.39] Any payment (whenever the liability to make it was incurred, but subject to exceptions as below) of an annual payment (which includes an annuity but does not include interest) satisfying the conditions below can be neither a qualifying annual payment (see **24.8** DEDUCTION OF TAX AT SOURCE) nor a patent royalty subject to deduction of tax (see **24.13** DEDUCTION OF TAX AT SOURCE). Consequently it is paid without deduction of tax. It is not allowed as a deduction in computing a person's income from any source. The conditions are that the payment:

- is charged to income tax under *ITTOIA 2005, Pt V* (miscellaneous income) (otherwise than as relevant foreign income — see **32.2** FOREIGN INCOME), or is chargeable to corporation tax under specified provisions of *CTA 2009* (previously under Schedule D, Case III); and
- is made under a liability incurred for consideration in money or money's worth, all or any of which either (a) consists of, or of the right to receive, a dividend, or (b) is not required to be brought into account in calculating for tax purposes the income of the person making it.

Exceptions to the above provisions are any payments:

(i)   which fall within **68.29**(i) or (ii) SETTLEMENTS; or
(ii)   to an individual for surrendering, assigning or releasing an interest in settled property to a person having a subsequent interest; or
(iii)   of any annuity granted in the ordinary course of a business of granting annuities; or
(iv)   any annuity charged on an interest in settled property and granted before 30 March 1977 by an individual to a company whose business was wholly or mainly in acquiring such interests or which was carrying on life assurance business in the UK. (This exception is not reproduced in the rewritten legislation in *ITA 2007, s 904*: presumably considered obsolete.)

For Scotland, reference to settled property refers to property held in trust and references to an individual include a Scottish partnership if at least one partner is an individual. For position prior to these provisions see *CIR v Plummer* HL 1979, 54 TC 1, and *Moodie v CIR and Sinnett* HL 1993, 65 TC 610, in which the decision in *Plummer* on similar facts was reversed on *Ramsay* principles (see **4.1** above).

As regards the recipient, a payment to which these provisions apply is excluded from the exemption of annual payments from tax at **30.4 EXEMPT INCOME**.

[*ITA 2007, ss 843, 904; ICTA 1988, s 125; CTA 2009, Sch 1 para 708; SI 2009 No 23, regs 1, 5(4)*].

Simon's Taxes. See E1.802.

Dealing in commodity futures — denial of loss relief

[4.40] Where there is a trade of dealing in commodity futures carried on in partnership in which one or more partners is a company and arrangements are made or a scheme effected (whether by the partnership agreement or otherwise) after 5 April 1976 so that the sole or main benefit expected from the partnership is tax relief under *ITA 2007, s 64* (trading losses set-off against general income of an individual — see **45.2 LOSSES**) or *ITA 2007, s 72* (losses in early years of a trade set-off against general income of an individual — see **45.9 LOSSES**) or their predecessors, such relief is not available. Where relief has been given, it will be withdrawn by an assessment. In relation to 2008/09 and 2009/10 losses, the restriction applies also to the extended carry-back relief under *FA 2009, Sch 6* (see **45.5 LOSSES**).

The above restriction is superseded by the broader legislation outlined in **45.18 LOSSES** and does not apply to a loss to which **45.18** potentially applies.

[*ITA 2007, s 81, Sch 2 para 24; ICTA 1988, s 399; FA 2009, Sch 6 para 1(11)(e); FA 2010, Sch 3 paras 9, 11*].

Simon's Taxes. See E1.1006.

Futures and options — transactions with guaranteed returns

[4.41] The special provisions described below apply to a 'disposal of a future or option' if it is one of two or more 'related' transactions, and it is reasonable to assume that a main purpose of the transactions, taken together, is or was to produce a 'guaranteed return', either from the disposal itself or together with another such disposal or disposals. The likely effect of the transactions, and/or the circumstances in which they, or any of them, is or are entered into, are taken into account for this purpose.

A *'future'* is any outstanding rights and obligations under a commodity or financial futures contract, and an *'option'* is one listed on a recognised stock or futures exchange or otherwise relating to currency, shares, stock, securities, an interest rate or rights under a commodity or financial futures contract. The existence or timing of a disposal is determined in accordance with *TCGA 1992, ss 143(5)(6), 144, 144A* (see Tolley's Capital Gains Tax under Disposal) and other relevant provisions of that *Act*, modified as necessary for this purpose, on the assumption that all futures are assets. However, a disposal consisting in the grant of an option, which precedes at least one 'related' transaction which is a disposal other than the grant of an option, is deemed for these purposes to be made at the time of (or of the first) such subsequent disposal (except insofar as the provisions of *TCGA 1992* referred to above require the grant of an option and the transaction entered into to fulfil obligations under the option to be treated as a single transaction, and determine the time at which that single transaction is treated as entered into).

Transactions are *'related'* for these purposes if they are entered into in pursuance of the same scheme or arrangements (including understandings of any kind, whether or not legally enforceable). This may include transactions with different parties, or with parties different from the parties to the scheme or arrangements. It also includes any case in which it would be reasonable to assume, from the likely effect of the transactions and/or the circumstances in which they, or any of them, is or are entered into, that neither or none of them would have been entered into independently of the other(s).

A *'guaranteed return'* is produced wherever risks from fluctuations in the subject matter to which the futures or options (or their value) are referable are so eliminated or reduced as to produce a return equating, in substance, to interest and not significantly attributable (otherwise than incidentally) to any such fluctuations. This includes any case where a main reason for the choice of subject matter is that it appears that there is no (or only an insignificant) risk that it will fluctuate. The return from one or more disposals is for these purposes that represented by the total net profits or gains (or all but an insignificant part of those profits or gains), aggregating where appropriate profits or gains of persons who are 'associated' (as specially defined) in relation to the disposals.

Profits or gains realised from a transaction to which these provisions apply (whether capital or not) are chargeable to income tax for the tax year in which the disposal takes place. The person liable for any tax charged is the person realising the profits or gains. Any charge to tax on trading profits takes priority. [*ITTOIA 2005, s 366(1)*].

Losses are relieved under the rules relating to losses from miscellaneous transactions in *ITA 2007, s 152*.

The charge is extended to cases where there are related transactions one of which is or would be the creation or acquisition of a future or option, and another of which is or would be the running of the future to delivery or the exercise of the option, and the latter transaction is not treated under the current provisions as a disposal of a future or option. The provisions of *TCGA 1992, s 144(2)* and *(3)*, which in certain cases treat the grant or exercise of an option and the transaction in fulfilment of the obligations under the option as a single transaction (see Tolley's Capital Gains Tax under Disposal), are ignored for these purposes. The current provisions then apply to the parties to the future or option as if there was a disposal of the future or option under the arrangements for the related or associated transactions immediately before the future runs to delivery or, as the case may be, the option is exercised. The disposal is treated, in the case of a person whose rights and entitlements under the future or option have a market value at that time, as at that value, or in the case of any other person as made for nil consideration with costs equivalent to those required at arm's length to obtain release of his obligations and liabilities under the future or option. There are provisions preventing double charge or relief under these provisions and capital gains tax.

Trusts

Where profits or gains are treated as income arising to trustees under these provisions, the trust rate applies to so much of that income as is not treated as income of the settlor. Also excluded from this treatment are income arising under charitable trusts and income from property held for certain retirement benefit or personal pension schemes. For 2006/07 onwards, the charge at the trust rate applies by virtue of **68.12**(5) SETTLEMENTS, having previously applied under *ITTOIA 2005, s 568(5)*, but the position effectively remains unaltered.

Transfer of assets abroad

Any profit or gain realised by a person resident or domiciled outside the UK from a transaction within these provisions is treated as income becoming payable to that person under *ITA 2007, Pt 13 Ch 2* (see **4.14–4.17** above) in determining whether a UK ordinarily resident individual has an income tax liability in respect of the profit or gain.

[*ITTOIA 2005, ss 555–569; TCGA 1992, ss 148A–148C; FA 2006, Sch 13 para 32(1)(4); ITA 2007, Sch 1 paras 543, 544*].

Recovery of assets under Proceeds of Crime Act 2002, Pt 5

Where the transfer of futures or options is a *Pt 5* transfer under *Proceeds of Crime Act 2002* (as in **10.2**(x) CAPITAL ALLOWANCES) and no compensating payment is made to the transferor, it is not treated as a disposal for the purposes of these provisions. [*Proceeds of Crime Act 2002, Sch 10 paras 8, 10*].

Simon's Taxes. See B8.608, E1.462–E1.465.

Arrangements to pass on value of dividend tax credit

[4.42] Special provisions apply where:

(a)   a person ('A') is entitled to a tax credit in respect of a qualifying distribution;

(b)   arrangements (as widely defined) subsist such that another person ('B') obtains, whether directly or indirectly, a payment representing any of the value of the tax credit;

(c)   the arrangements (whether or not made directly between A and B) were entered into for an 'unallowable purpose'; and

(d)   had B been entitled to and received the distribution when it was made, he would not have been entitled to payment of the tax credit and, if a company, could not have used the income consisting of the distribution to frank a distribution made in the same accounting period (after using any actual franked investment income).

They apply equally where an amount representing any of the value of the tax credit is applied at the direction of, or otherwise in favour of, some other person, as if that other person had obtained a payment representing that value.

Where these provisions apply:

(i)   no claim may be made for payment of the tax credit or for set-off against tax on other income;

(ii)   the income consisting of the distribution is not regarded as franked investment income; and

(iii)   no transitional charity relief payment may be claimed.

This does not, however, apply to the extent that the tax advantage otherwise obtained under the arrangements is cancelled or reduced by any other provision. 'Tax advantage' for this purpose has the meaning given by *CTA 2010, s 1139*. It also includes the obtaining of a payment representing any of the value of a tax credit where, had the person obtaining the payment been entitled to and received the distribution when it was made, he would not have been entitled to payment of the tax credit and, if a company, could not have used the income consisting of the distribution to frank a distribution made in the same accounting period (after using any actual franked investment income).

Arrangements are entered into for an *'unallowable purpose'* if any person is a party to the arrangements for purposes which include a purpose other than a business or commercial purpose (which includes the efficient management of investments). The purpose of obtaining a tax advantage for any person is not a business or commercial purpose unless it is not a main purpose of entering into the arrangements.

[*ICTA 1988, s 231B; F(No 2)A 1997, s 28; ITA 2007, Sch 1 para 26; CTA 2010, Sch 1 para 19*].

Benefits from pre-owned assets

[4.43] Subject to certain exemptions, a *de minimis* limit and a transitional right to elect to disapply these provisions (with inheritance tax (IHT) consequences), an income tax charge applies for 2005/06 onwards as described below on the annual benefit of using property previously owned by the user and not disposed of by him at arm's length. The legislation is intended to counter avoidance schemes which bypass the IHT 'gifts with reservation' rules, for which see Tolley's Inheritance Tax, but is not restricted to cases where such schemes have been used. HMRC have published detailed guidance notes on these pre-owned assets rules (see www.hmrc.gov.uk/poa/index.htm).

The main charge applies where an individual (whether alone or together with others) occupies any land or is in possession of, or has the use of, any chattel and *either* of the following two conditions is met.

The *first condition* is that, at some time after 17 March 1986, the individual owned the land or chattel, or owned other property the proceeds of disposal of which were applied, directly or indirectly, by another person towards the acquisition of the land or chattel, and the individual has disposed of all or part of his interest in the land, chattel or other property other than by way of an 'excluded transaction' (see below).

The *second condition* is that, at some time after 17 March 1986, the individual has provided, directly or indirectly but other than by way of an 'excluded transaction', any of the consideration given by another person for the acquisition of the land or chattel or of any other property the proceeds of disposal of which were applied by another person towards the acquisition of the land or chattel.

The above references to land include an interest in land, ownership of a chattel means sole or joint ownership, and references to the acquisition or disposal of any property generally include acquisitions and disposals of an interest in that property.

A disposition which creates a new interest in land or a chattel out of an existing interest is treated as a part disposal of the existing interest.

Where the above applies to an individual at any time in 2005/06 or any subsequent tax year, then subject to the exemptions from charge detailed below, the chargeable amount computed as below is treated as income of his, chargeable to income tax, for the tax year in question.

Excluded transactions

Any of the following disposals of the land, chattel or other property in question is an '*excluded transaction*' for the purposes of the first condition above:

- a disposal of the individual's entire interest in the property (except for any right expressly reserved by him over the property) by a transaction made at arm's length with a person not connected with him or by a transaction such as might be expected to be made at arm's length between persons not connected with each other;
- a transfer of the property to the individual's spouse or civil partner (or, by court order, to his former spouse or civil partner);
- a gift (or a transfer for the benefit of a former spouse or civil partner made in accordance with a court order) by virtue of which the property became settled property in which the individual's spouse or civil partner

or former spouse or civil partner has an interest in possession which either still subsists or has come to an end on the death of the spouse or civil partner or former spouse or civil partner;

- a disposition which is exempt from IHT under *IHTA 1984, s 11* (dispositions for maintenance of family);
- an outright gift to an individual which is covered by the IHT annual exemption or small gifts exemption;
- a disposal, made at arm's length and otherwise than to a connected person, of part of the vendor's interest in the property; and
- a disposal before 7 March 2005, by way of a transaction such as might be expected to be made at arm's length between persons not connected with each other, of part of the vendor's interest in the property;
- a disposal on or after 7 March 2005, by way of a transaction such as might be expected to be made at arm's length between persons not connected with each other, of part of the vendor's interest in the property for a consideration not in the form of money or 'readily convertible assets' (as defined by *ITEPA 2003, s 702* — see **53.4**(a) PAY AS YOU EARN).

For the purposes of these provisions, the rules in **21 CONNECTED PERSONS** apply to determine whether or not persons are connected with each other *but* as if a relative also included an uncle, aunt, nephew or niece and as if 'settlement', 'settlor' and 'trustee' had the meaning they have for IHT purposes.

For the purposes of the second condition above, the provision by the individual of consideration for another person's acquisition of property is an *'excluded transaction'* if:

- the other person is the individual's spouse or civil partner (or, where the transfer has been ordered by the court, his former spouse or civil partner); or
- on its acquisition the property became settled property in which the individual's spouse or civil partner or former spouse or civil partner has an interest in possession which either still subsists or has come to an end on the death of the spouse or civil partner or former spouse or civil partner; or
- the provision of the consideration was an outright gift of money made at least seven years before the individual first occupied the land in question or had possession of, or the use of, the chattel in question; or
- the provision of the consideration is a disposition which is exempt from IHT under *IHTA 1984, s 11* (dispositions for maintenance of family); or
- the provision of the consideration is an outright gift to an individual which is covered by the IHT annual exemption or small gifts exemption.

Exemptions from charge

The charge under these provisions does not apply by reference to any property at a time when that property would fall to be treated for IHT purposes as property which, in relation to the individual concerned, is property subject to a reservation (or would fall to be so treated were it not for specified IHT exemptions). See generally Tolley's Inheritance Tax under Gifts with Reservation. This exemption also applies at any time where property deriving its value from the property in question would fall to be so treated; however, if such other property reflects some of, but substantially less than the whole of, the value of the property in question, the exemption does not apply but the chargeable amount is scaled down accordingly.

The charge does not apply by reference to any property at a time when the individual's estate for IHT purposes includes that property or includes other property whose value is derived from it. If such other property reflects some of, but substantially less than the whole of, the value of the original property, the exemption does not apply but the chargeable amount is scaled down accordingly. This exemption (or partial exemption) is subject to anti-avoidance provision where the value of the estate is reduced by certain associated liabilities.

The above exemption is removed in a case where the property (or any derived property) falls into the individual's estate by virtue of it being an interest in possession in settled property created after the property originally left his estate or after he provided consideration for its acquisition. Such property is also not to be treated as property subject to a reservation, so that the first of the above exemptions is also disapplied. The removal of the exemptions in these circumstances has effect for the part of the tax year 2005/06 that begins with 5 December 2005 and for 2006/07 and subsequent years. This removal of the exemptions is apparently aimed at the situation where the settled property may in due course revert to the settlor (or to the spouse or civil partner or the widow, widower or surviving civil partner of the settlor) in circumstances such that, by virtue of *IHTA 1984, s 53(3)* or *s 53(4)* or *s 54*, no IHT charge arises when the individual's interest in possession comes to an end (see Treasury Explanatory Notes to Finance Bill 2006). The CIOT has discovered that the legislation as drafted may have wider and unintended implications in that it fails to distinguish between reverter to settlor trusts and trusts in which the settlor has an interest in possession; for details see www.tax.org.uk/showarticle.pl?id=5139;n=232.

The provisions do not apply to a person for any tax year during which he is not UK-resident. If in any tax year a person is UK-resident but not UK-domiciled (as defined for IHT, not income tax, purposes — see Tolley's Inheritance Tax under Domicile), the provisions apply to him only if the land or chattel is situated in the UK. In applying the provisions to a person previously domiciled outside the UK, no regard is to be had to any property which is 'excluded property' as defined for IHT purposes (see Tolley's Inheritance Tax under Excluded Property).

The Treasury may confer additional exemptions by regulations. See below for *de minimis* limit.

The chargeable amount

In the case of an individual chargeable under these provisions as a result of his occupation of **land**, the amount chargeable to tax in respect of any tax year is the 'appropriate rental value' less any payments made, under a legal obligation, by the individual to the owner for his occupation of the land. The *'appropriate rental value'* is:

$$R \times \frac{DV}{V}$$

where R = the 'rental value' of the land, V = the value of the land, and DV = (depending on the circumstances) (i) the value of the interest in the land that the individual disposed of or (ii) such part of the land's value as can reasonably be attributed to the other property that the individual disposed of, or (iii) (where it is the second condition above that is met) such part of the land's value as can reasonably be attributed to the consideration provided by the individual. So, in the most straightforward case where the individual disposed of the whole of the land he now occupies, the value of DV/V will be one and the tax charge will be on the rental value (subject to any deduction for payments made). Where it is the first condition above that is met and the disposal (whilst not being an excluded transaction as above) was a money sale of the individual's entire interest in the land or other property at less than market value, DV is scaled down proportionately so as to only take account of the gift element.

The *'rental value'* of land is the rent that would have been payable by the individual for the tax year if the land had been let to him at an annual rent equal to that which might reasonably be expected under a standard lease under which the landlord bears the cost of repairs, maintenance and insurance and the tenant pays all taxes, rates and other charges usually paid by a tenant. Regulations prescribe the continuing use of such rental value for five tax years.

In the case of an individual chargeable under these provisions as a result of his use or possession of a **chattel**, the amount chargeable to tax in respect of any tax year is the 'appropriate amount' less any payments made, under a legal obligation, by the individual to the owner for his use or possession of the chattel. The *'appropriate amount'* is:

$$N \times \frac{DV}{V}$$

where N = a notional amount of interest (at a rate prescribed by regulations) on the value of the chattel, and V and DV have similar meanings as in the above formula for land.

Where the individual is within these provisions during part only of a tax year, references above to the tax year, as regards both land and chattels, are to that shorter period within the tax year. The date at which *valuations* are to be made for these purposes is to be prescribed by statutory instrument, which may also prescribe the continuing use of such valuations for subsequent tax years (subject to any prescribed adjustments).

Regulations prescribe 6 April in each tax year as being the date at which valuations are to be made (or, if later and where applicable, the date in the tax year on which the asset first becomes chargeable). Land and chattels are to be valued every five years, with the valuation arrived at for the first year being used for that year and each of the next four years. The prescribed rate of interest for chattels is the same as the official rate (i.e. the rate applied to cheap employee loans — see **27.40 EMPLOYMENT INCOME**) as at the valuation date. The official rate is 5% throughout 2005/06 and 2006/07, 6.25% from 6 April 2007 to 28 February 2009 inclusive, 4.75% from 1 March 2009 to 5 April 2010 inclusive and 4% from 6 April 2010 onwards.

De minimis limit

A person is not chargeable under these provisions for a particular tax year if, for that year, the aggregate of any amounts given by the above formulae and (where applicable) the chargeable amount for intangible property in a settlement (see below) is £5,000 or less. Note that in determining whether or not the *de minimis* applies, no deduction is made at this stage for any payments made under legal obligation by the individual for occupation of land or for use or possession of chattels; it is thus possible for a tax charge to arise on an amount equal to or less than the *de minimis*.

Miscellaneous

The **value** of any property for the purposes of these provisions is its open market value, disregarding any potential reduction on the ground that the whole of the property is placed on the market at the same time.

A disposition made in relation to an interest in a deceased person's estate is disregarded for the purposes of these provisions if, by virtue of *IHTA 1984, s 17*, it is not a transfer of value for IHT purposes. This takes into account **instruments of variation, disclaimers etc.** — see Tolley's Inheritance Tax under Deeds Varying Dispositions on Death. So, for example, an individual is not treated as having formerly owned and disposed of any property simply by virtue of a will or intestacy that was subsequently varied.

A person who merely acts as **guarantor** in respect of a loan taken out by another person to acquire a property is not regarded for the purposes of these provisions as having thereby funded the acquisition.

Where for any tax year amounts are chargeable, in respect of a person's occupation of any land or his use or possession of any chattel, both under these provisions and, under *ITEPA 2003*, as **earnings** (including benefits in kind), the charge under *ITEPA 2003* takes priority and the charge under these provisions is limited to the excess (if any) of the amount otherwise chargeable under these provisions over the amount chargeable as earnings.

Election to disapply these provisions

An election may be made, in prescribed form (Form IHT 500), to disapply the above provisions by reference to any particular property, with the consequence described below. (With effect on and after 14 November 2007, HMRC will not accept an election made other than on Form IHT 500.) Such election has effect for the first tax year for which a charge under these provisions would otherwise arise by reference to enjoyment of the property in question (or any substituted property) and for all subsequent tax years. It must be made on or before **31 January** following that first tax year or such later date as an officer of HMRC may, in a particular case, allow. For circumstances in which HMRC may accept a late election, see www.hmrc.gov.uk/poa/poa_guidance3.htm. The election can be revoked or varied (but only by the chargeable person and not by his personal representatives) at any time on or before the said 31 January. The consequence of the election is that, for as long as that person continues to enjoy the property (or any substitute property), the property is treated for IHT purposes as property subject to a reservation; it will thus potentially attract an IHT charge if the person dies whilst continuing to enjoy the property or within seven years after ceasing to do so (see Tolley's Inheritance Tax under Gifts with Reservation). There are rules to eliminate a potential double IHT charge that could otherwise arise in certain limited circumstances where the election is made (see *SI 2005 No 724, reg 6*). If the property falls into the chargeable person's estate by virtue of it being an interest in possession in settled property, the consequence of the election is instead to disapply the exemptions otherwise available under *IHTA 1984, s 53(3)(4)* and *s 54* on the coming to an end of the interest in possession. Where, in the absence of an election, the charge to income tax would arise by reference to only a proportion of the value of the property, only a proportion of the property is brought into the scope of IHT as above. The foregoing references to enjoyment of property are to occupation of the property where it is land and to use or possession of the property where it is a chattel.

If these provisions would otherwise apply to an individual as a result of his having an interest in possession in settled property and he died before 19 July 2006 (the date of Royal Assent to *FA 2006*, which first applied these provisions in such circumstances), the election could be made by his personal representatives. If the individual died before that date but after making the election, the due date for payment of any IHT otherwise falling due before that date was deferred until 1 August 2006.

If, instead of making the election, a taxpayer chooses to avoid the charge by dismantling pre-owned assets arrangements previously made, there are regulations to eliminate a double IHT charge that could otherwise potentially arise in certain circumstances (*SI 2005 No 3441*). These apply where an individual enters into arrangements under which there are transfers both of property and of a debt owed to him, the debt is then written off and, on the individual's death on or after 6 April 2005, both the property and the debt are chargeable to inheritance tax.

Intangible property comprised in a settlement

Also included in these provisions is a charge on certain intangible property comprised in a settlement in which the settlor has an interest. The charge applies where:

(a)   the terms of a settlement, as they affect any property comprised in it, are such that any income arising from the property would be treated by virtue of *ITTOIA 2005, s 624* (previously *ICTA 1988, s 660A* — see **68.29** SETTLEMENTS) as the settlor's income (but *not* where it would be so treated only because the settlor's spouse or civil partner could benefit from the settlement); and

(b) that property includes any intangible property (meaning any property other than chattels or interests in land) which is, or which represents, property which the settlor settled, or added to the settlement, after 17 March 1986.

Where the above applies at any time in a tax year, an amount is treated as income of the settlor for that tax year. That amount is N minus T, where N is a notional amount of interest (at a rate prescribed by regulations) on the value of the intangible property in (b) above and T is the amount of income tax and/or capital gains tax payable (if any) by the settlor under specified enactments including *ITTOIA 2005, s 624*, so far as that tax is attributable to that property. The prescribed rate of interest is the same as the official rate (i.e. the rate applied to cheap employee loans — see **27.40 EMPLOYMENT INCOME**) as at the valuation date. The official rate is 5% throughout 2005/06 and 2006/07, 6.25% from 6 April 2007 to 28 February 2009 inclusive, 4.75% from 1 March 2009 to 5 April 2010 inclusive and 4% from 6 April 2010 onwards.

The exemptions etc. described above apply equally in relation to this charge. Where for any tax year a person would be chargeable under the above provisions by reason of his enjoyment of any land or chattel and also by reference to intangible property which derives its value (wholly or partly) from that land or chattel, he is chargeable only under whichever provision produces the greater chargeable amount; and only that amount is taken into account for the purposes of applying the *de minimis* limit above.

With appropriate modifications, the above election to disapply is also available, with similar consequences, in relation to the charge on intangible property.

[*FA 2004, s 84, Sch 15; FA 2006, s 80; ITA 2007, Sch 1 para 482; FA 2007, s 66; SI 2005 No 724; SI 2005 No 3229, reg 179; SI 2007 No 3000*].

Simon's Taxes. See I3.7.

Disclosure of tax avoidance schemes

[4.44] *FA 2004, ss 306–319* impose obligations on promoters of certain tax avoidance schemes, and in some cases on persons entering into transactions under such schemes, to disclose those schemes to HMRC. See **4.45–4.51** below. The primary legislation provides the framework for these disclosure rules, with the detail provided by regulations made by statutory instrument.

HMRC have published detailed guidance notes on the disclosure rules (see www.hmrc.gov.uk/aiu/disclosure-nov08.pdf supplemented by www.hmrc.gov.uk/avoidance/guidance-march.htm). The legislation is policed by the HMRC's Anti-Avoidance Group (Intelligence) unit; see www.hmrc.gov.uk/avoidance/index.htm, which includes links to the legislation and the official guidance plus various forms to be used for making disclosures. The address of the unit is HM Revenue & Customs, Anti-Avoidance Group (Intelligence), 1st Floor South, 22 Kingsway, London, WC2B 6NR.

Simon's Taxes. See A7.2.

Arrangements covered by the rules

[4.45] Prior to 1 August 2006, the *Tax Avoidance Schemes (Prescribed Descriptions of Arrangements) Regulations 2004 (SI 2004 No 1863 as amended by SI 2004 No 2429 and revoked by SI 2006 No 1543 below)* applied the disclosure rules only to certain arrangements related to *financial products* and certain arrangements connected with *employment* (in both cases with the features described in those regulations) and limits the scope of the rules to income tax, corporation tax and capital gains tax advantages. These regulations provided for, inter alia, a *premium fee* and *confidentiality* test whereby arrangements are excluded from the rules if:

• it might reasonably be expected that no promoter, and no person connected with a promoter, of arrangements that are the same as, or substantially similar to, the arrangements in question would be able to obtain a 'premium fee' for them, *and*

• the tax advantage expected to be obtained under the arrangements does not arise from any element of the arrangements (including the way in which they are structured) which, disregarding any duty of confidentiality owed to any person, a promoter might reasonably be expected to wish to keep confidential from other promoters.

For this purpose, a *'premium fee'* is a fee which is chargeable by virtue of any element of the arrangements from which the anticipated tax advantage arises and is a fee the amount of which is to a significant extent attributable to, or which is to any extent contingent upon the obtaining of, that tax advantage.

In *HMRC v Mercury Tax Group Ltd* (Sp C 737), [2009] SSCD 307, it was held that disclosure had not been required as the tax advantage expected to be obtained under the arrangements did not, as required, arise, to a significant degree, from the inclusion in those arrangements of the financial product, in this case a company share.

On and after **1 August 2006**, the *Tax Avoidance Schemes (Prescribed Descriptions of Arrangements) Regulations 2006 (SI 2006 No 1543 as amended)* extend the disclosure rules to potentially any kind of income tax, corporation tax or capital gains tax avoidance scheme, but a scheme need only be disclosed if it falls within any one or more of the following descriptions (described by HMRC as 'hallmarks').

• **Confidentiality in cases involving a promoter.** A scheme falls within this description if the promoter would wish to keep confidential from other promoters the way in which any element of the scheme (including the way the scheme is structured) secures the expected tax advantage or if (in order to facilitate its continued or repeated use in the future) he would wish such a matter to be kept confidential from HMRC. In a case involving a non-UK promoter or a case in which duty to disclose is transferred from promoter to client due to legal professional privilege (see **4.49** below), the second part of the test instead considers whether the scheme user wishes to keep the matter confidential from HMRC.

- **Confidentiality where no promoter involved.** A scheme falls within this description if there is no promoter (e.g. it is an in-house scheme), the intended user is a business which is *not* a 'small or medium-sized enterprise', and the user wishes to keep confidential from HMRC (in order to facilitate its continued or repeated use in the future) the way in which any element of the scheme (including the way the scheme is structured), secures the expected tax advantage.
- **Premium fee.** A scheme falls within this description if it might reasonably be expected that a promoter (or a person connected with a promoter) of arrangements that are the same as, or substantially similar to, the arrangements in question would be able to obtain for them a 'premium fee' (as above) from a person experienced in receiving services of the type being provided, e.g. tax advice. However, a scheme does not fall within this description if there is no promoter *and* the tax advantage is intended to be obtained by an individual or a business which is a 'small or medium-sized enterprise'.
- **Financial products: off market terms.** A scheme falls within this description if the tax advantage expected to be obtained arises, to more than an incidental degree, from the inclusion in the scheme of one or more financial products (as defined) to which the promoter is party and which is priced significantly higher than similar products in the open market. This hallmark is intended to catch schemes that would otherwise fall outside the premium fee hallmark above, due to the fee being incorporated into the price of the product.
- **Standardised tax products.** A scheme falls within this description if it is a standardised tax product, i.e. it has standardised documentation that is not significantly tailored to meet the circumstances of the client, requires the client to enter into a specific transaction or series of transactions that are standardised in form and it is made available by a promoter to more than one person. Excluded are schemes first made available (by anyone, not necessarily the promoter in question) before 1 August 2006. There are other specific exclusions. This hallmark is aimed at what are generally known as 'mass-marketed schemes'.
- **Loss schemes.** A scheme falls within this description if the promoter expects more than one individual to implement substantially the same arrangements and it is such that an informed observer could reasonably conclude that its main benefit is to generate losses for the purpose of reducing liability to income tax or capital gains tax. This appears to be aimed at schemes that generate tax losses greater than the amount the individual has, in economic substance, contributed.
- **Leasing arrangements.** This hallmark applies only to certain high value plant and machinery leases. See *SI 2006 No 1543, regs 13–17*. A scheme does not fall within this description if there is no promoter *and* the tax advantage is intended to be obtained by an individual or a business which is a 'small or medium-sized enterprise'.
- (On and after 1 September 2009, subject to transitional rules) certain **pension arrangements** (see below).

For detail as to how HMRC interpret these hallmarks, see the HMRC guidance notes referred to in **4.44** above. For the purposes of the hallmarks, the definition of *'small or medium-sized enterprise'* is based on *Commission Recommendation 2003/361/EC* published by the EC on 6 May 2003 (as modified for these purposes by *SI 2006 No 1543, reg 4*); it operates by reference to specified maxima for turnover, assets and staff, similar to those quoted for transfer pricing purposes at **4.21** above.

With effect on and after 1 September 2009, a new hallmark is introduced covering pension arrangements. A scheme falls within this description if it involves the accrual or expected accrual of benefits in a pension scheme and the main benefit is to avoid or reduce the special annual allowance charge described at **57.10 PENSION PROVISION**. Transitional rules require disclosure of schemes where the trigger event occurred between 23 April 2009 and 31 August 2009 inclusive; in such cases the deadline for making the disclosure is deferred until 31 October 2009. Guidance on this hallmark is available at www.hmrc.gov.uk/avoidance/income-corp.htm.

[*SI 2004 No 1863, 2429; SI 2006 No 1543; SI 2007 No 2484, reg 4; SI 2009 No 2033*].

Obligations to disclose

[4.46] The *Tax Avoidance Schemes (Information) Regulations 2004 (SI 2004 No 1864* as amended) set out the procedural rules for disclosure, dealing with the manner and timing of disclosure and the information to be provided.

On and after 1 November 2008, information to be provided under any of the provisions in *FA 2004, s 316* must be provided in the prescribed form and manner or the provision will not be regarded as complied with.

Obligations of promoters

A person who is a 'promoter in relation to a notifiable proposal' (see below) must provide HMRC (on form AAG1) with specified information on the proposal within five business days after the 'relevant date'. The *'relevant date'* is the earliest of the following:

- (with effect from a date to be appointed) the date he first makes a 'firm approach' (see below) to another person,
- the date on which he makes the proposal available for implementation by any person, and
- the date he first becomes aware of any transaction forming part of arrangements implementing the proposal.

The five-day period is extended if the promoter intends to apply to HMRC for clearance under certain specified statutory provisions — see *SI 2004 No 1864, reg 5*.

A *'notifiable proposal'* is a proposal for arrangements which, if entered into, would be *'notifiable arrangements'*, i.e. arrangements falling within any description prescribed by regulations (see **4.45** above) which enable (or might be expected to enable) any person to obtain a tax advantage (as widely defined) and are such that the main benefit, or one of the main benefits, that might be expected from them is the obtaining of that advantage.

There is a separate requirement for a person who is a 'promoter in relation to notifiable arrangements' (see below) to provide HMRC (on form AAG1) with specified information relating to the arrangements and to do so within five business days after the date on which he first becomes aware of any transaction forming part of those arrangements; but this does not apply if the arrangements implement a proposal which has been notified as above.

If a promoter has discharged his obligations in relation to a proposal or arrangements, he is not required to notify proposals or arrangements which are substantially the same as those already notified (whether or not they relate to the same parties).

Broadly, where any two persons are promoters in relation to the same (or, on and after 1 November 2008, substantially the same) proposal or arrangements, notification by one promoter discharges the obligations of the other. On and after 1 November 2008, the promoter who makes the notification must give HMRC the other promoter's identity and address unless the other promoter has the reference number allocated to the arrangements (see **4.47** below), and the other promoter must have details of the information provided to HMRC by the first promoter in discharge of his obligation.

Meaning of promoter

A person is a *'promoter in relation to a notifiable proposal'* if, in the course of a 'relevant business',

(i)   he is to any extent responsible for the design of the proposed arrangements, or

(ii)   (with effect from a date to be appointed) he makes a 'firm approach' to another person with a view to making the proposal available for implementation by that person or any other person; or

(iii) he makes the notifiable proposal available for implementation by another person.

The *Tax Avoidance Schemes (Promoter and Prescribed Circumstances) Regulations 2004 (SI 2004 No 1865)* exclude from the definition of 'promoter' (i) a company providing taxation services to another company in the same 51% group and (ii) an employee of the promoter or of a person entering into the proposed arrangements, and they also prescribe various circumstances in which a person to some extent responsible for the design of proposed arrangements is not to be regarded as a promoter by virtue of that fact alone.

A person is a *'promoter in relation to notifiable arrangements'* if

- he is a promoter by virtue of (ii) or (iii) above in relation to a notifiable proposal which is implemented by the arrangements, or
- in the course of a 'relevant business', he is to any extent responsible for the design or the organisation or management of the arrangements.
- he is to any extent responsible for the organisation or management of the arrangements.

A '*relevant business*' is any trade, profession or business which involves the provision to other persons of taxation services or is carried on by a bank or a securities house. Where companies form a 51% group, anything done by one group company for the purposes of another company's relevant business is brought within the above disclosure requirements.

For these purposes, a person makes a '*firm approach*' to another person if he makes a 'marketing contact' with that person when the proposed arrangements have been 'substantially designed'. A promoter makes a '*marketing contact*' with another person if he communicates information about the proposal, including an explanation of the tax advantage to be obtained, with a view to that person or any other person entering into transactions forming part of the proposed arrangements. Arrangements have been '*substantially designed*' at such time when the nature of the transactions to form part of them has been sufficiently developed for it to be reasonable to believe that a person wishing to obtain the tax advantage might enter into such transactions (or transactions which are not substantially different).

Obligation of person dealing with non-UK promoter

A person who enters into any transaction forming part of notifiable arrangements in relation to which there is a non-UK resident promoter (and no UK resident promoter) must himself provide HMRC (on forms AAG2) with specified information relating to those arrangements. He must do so within five business days after entering into the transaction. This obligation is discharged if a promoter makes disclosure of the notifiable proposal for the arrangements in question.

Obligation of parties to notifiable arrangements not involving a promoter

A person who enters into any transaction forming part of notifiable arrangements in respect of which neither he nor any other person in the UK has an obligation as above must himself provide HMRC (on form AAG3) with specified information relating to those arrangements. For arrangements implemented before 1 August 2006, he could make such disclosure at any time after the date of the transaction and before he was first required to quote a reference number for the arrangements (see **4.47** below). For arrangements implemented on or after 1 August 2006, he must make the disclosure within 30 days after the first transaction forming part of the notifiable arrangements.

[*FA 2004, ss 306, 307, 308, 309, 310, 316, 318(1), s 319; FA 2007, s 108(3)(10); FA 2008, s 116, Sch 38 para 6; CTA 2010, Sch 1 para 429; FA 2010, Sch 17 paras 2(2)(3)(5)(7), 3, 7, 11; SI 2004 Nos 1864, 1865, 2613; SI 2006 No 1544; SI 2007 Nos 2153, 3104; SI 2008 No 1935*].

Reference numbers allocated to arrangements

[4.47] Where a person has made a disclosure as in **4.46** above, HMRC may within 30 days allocate a reference number to the arrangements in question and must notify the number to that person (and, on and after 1 November 2008 where relevant, to any other person whose obligation is discharged by the first person's disclosure).

On and after 1 November 2008, a person who is a promoter in relation to notifiable arrangements and who is providing (or has provided) services to a client in connection with those arrangements must pass on to the client (on form AAG6) the reference number for those arrangements or for arrangements which are substantially the same as those arrangements. He must do so within 30 days after the later of the date he first becomes aware of any transaction which forms part of the arrangements and the date on which the reference number is notified to him (by HMRC or any other person). However, if the promoter is also a promoter in relation to a notifiable proposal which is substantially the same as the notifiable arrangements and he provides services to the client in connection with both the arrangements and the proposal, his above duty is discharged if he has provided the client with the reference number for the proposed arrangements. On and after 1 November 2008 HMRC may give notice that, in relation to notifiable arrangements specified in that notice, promoters do not have to notice.

Before 1 November 2008, a promoter who is providing services to a client in connection with notifiable arrangements must pass on to the client the reference number for those arrangements or for arrangements which are substantially the same as those arrangements. He must do so within 30 days after the date he first becomes aware of any transaction forming part of the arrangements or, if later, the date on which the reference number is notified to him by HMRC.

On and after 1 November 2008, where the client receives a reference number he must pass it on (on form AAG6) to any other person:

- who he might reasonably be expected to know is, or is likely to be, a party to the notifiable arrangements or proposed arrangements; and
- who might reasonably be expected to gain an income tax, corporation tax or capital gains tax advantage by reason of the arrangements or proposed arrangements.

The period during which the client must comply with the above is the 30 days beginning with the later of the date the client becomes aware of any transaction forming part of the arrangements and the date the reference number is notified to the client. The regulations may exempt a client from complying with this duty in prescribed circumstances; initially, an employer is given such exemption where the other party is his employee and the tax advantage arises by reason of the employment. HMRC may give notice that, in relation to notifiable arrangements or a notifiable proposal specified in that notice, clients do not have to pass on reference numbers after the date specified in the notice.

Where the duty to notify a reference number arises on or after 1 April 2009, further information must also be provided. Form AAG6 is revised accordingly.

A party to any notifiable arrangements giving rise to an income tax or capital gains tax advantage must quote the allocated reference number in his personal tax return for the year in which the person first enters into a transaction forming part of the arrangements and in all subsequent returns until the advantage ceases to apply to him. He must also quote the tax year in which, or the date on which, the advantage is expected to arise. Comparable provisions apply for corporation tax. For arrangements connected with employment, the obligation falls on the employer to quote the reference number etc. in a return in such form as HMRC may specify (form AAG 4). Persons not required to file a tax return must instead provide HMRC (on form AAG4) with specified information no later than what would have been the filing date for such a return. If the notifiable arrangements give rise to a claim (made on or after 1 April 2009 and outside a tax return) to relieve a trading loss, the claimant must provide HMRC (on form AAG4) with specified information at the time the claim is made.

If the reference number was notified to the above party before 1 April 2009, he had to first quote it in his tax return for the year in which the number was notified to him (or, if earlier, the year in which the tax advantage was expected to arise).

On and after 1 November 2008, HMRC may give notice that, in relation to notifiable arrangements specified in that notice, the above obligation does not apply after the date specified in the notice. To this end, a list of withdrawn scheme reference numbers is now published at www.hmrc.gov.uk/aiu/srn.htm. Clients and other parties who have received any of these reference numbers no longer have a duty to notify them to HMRC on their tax returns or on form AAG4 from the date shown on the list.

[FA 2004, ss 311, 312, 312A, 313, 319; FA 2008, s 116, Sch 38 paras 3–5; SI 2004 No 1864, regs 7, 7A, 7B, 8; SI 2006 No 1544, reg 6; SI 2008 Nos 1935, 1947; SI 2009 No 571, art 36; SI 2009 No 611].

Duty of promoter to provide client details

[4.48] The following applies from a date to be appointed by the Treasury by statutory instrument. It applies if a promoter of notifiable arrangements provides services to any client in connection with the arrangements and either

- the promoter is subject to the requirement to provide the client with specified information relating to the reference number of the arrangements (see **4.47** above) or
- he would be subject to that requirement if he had not failed to make the necessary disclosure of the proposal or arrangements.

The promoter must provide HMRC with specified information about the client within a period to be prescribed by regulations. (This does not apply if HMRC have cancelled the obligation to notify the reference number to the client — see **4.47** above.)

[FA 2004, s 313ZA; FA 2010, Sch 17 paras 6, 11].

The information to be provided as above must be provided in the prescribed form and manner or the duty will not be regarded as complied with. [FA 2004, s 316; FA 2010, Sch 17 paras 7, 11].

Legal professional privilege

[4.49] These provisions do not require the disclosure of privileged information, i.e. information with respect to which a claim to legal professional privilege (or Scottish equivalent) could be maintained in legal proceedings.

However, after 13 October 2004, the obligation to disclose is simply transferred from the promoter to the client; this is achieved by treating a case in which the promoter claims the protection of legal professional privilege as a case involving notifiable arrangements not involving a promoter (for which see **4.46** above). In these circumstances, the client must make disclosure (on form AAG3) within the period of five business days after entering into the transaction. Alternatively the client has the option of informing the promoter that he does not wish to maintain a claim to legal privilege, in which case the obligation is passed back to the promoter (www.hmrc.gov.uk/aiu/suppguide.htm).

[*FA 2004, ss 314, 319*].

HMRC powers where non-compliance suspected

[4.50] With effect from 19 July 2007, HMRC have powers as listed below in relation to cases in which they suspect non-compliance with the obligations at **4.46** above. These powers may be exercised on or after that date in relation to, or by virtue of, matters arising at any time, even if they arose wholly or partly before that date.

(a)   Where HMRC suspect that a person is the promoter of a proposal or arrangements that may be notifiable, they may by written notice require him to state his opinion as to whether or not the specified proposal or arrangements are notifiable by him as in **4.46** above and, if not, to state the reasons why. Any reasons given must be based on the legislation and cannot merely point to the fact that professional advice has been received; if the assertion is that the scheme does not fall within any of the hallmarks at **4.45** above, sufficient information must be provided to enable HMRC to confirm that this is so. The person must comply with the notice within ten days or such longer period as HMRC may direct. With effect from a date to be appointed by the Treasury by statutory instrument, the above applies equally where HMRC suspect that a person is an 'introducer' (as in (f) below) of a proposal.

(b)   Where HMRC have received a statement of reasons (whether or not under (a) above) as to why a proposal or arrangements are not notifiable by a particular person, they may apply to the Appeal Tribunal for an order requiring that person to supply specified information or documents in support of those reasons. The person must comply within 14 days after the date of the order or such longer period as HMRC may direct.

(c)   HMRC may apply to the Appeal Tribunal for an order that a specified proposal or arrangements be treated as notifiable. The application must specify the promoter. The Tribunal can grant the application only if satisfied that HMRC have taken all reasonable steps to establish whether the proposal or arrangements are notifiable and have reasonable grounds (see, for example, *FA 2004, s 306A(5)*) for suspecting that they may be. Where such an order is made, the promoter must comply within ten days after the date of the order.

(d)   HMRC may apply to the Appeal Tribunal for an order that a specified proposal or arrangements is notifiable. This is a separate power to that in (c) above. The application must specify the promoter. The Tribunal can grant the application only if satisfied that the arrangements in question fall within the statutory definition of 'notifiable arrangements' (see **4.46** above under 'Obligations of promoters').

(e)   If a promoter has supplied information in purported compliance with his normal obligations under these provisions (see **4.46** above) but HMRC believe that he has not provided all the necessary information, they may apply to the Appeal Tribunal for an order requiring the promoter to provide specified information or documents. The Tribunal can grant the application only if satisfied that HMRC have reasonable grounds for suspecting that the information or documents form part of the information required under the promoter's normal obligations or will support or explain it. Where such an order is made, the promoter must comply within ten days after the date of the order or such longer period as HMRC may direct. The requirement imposed by the order is treated as part of the promoter's normal disclosure obligations.

(f)   With effect from a date to be appointed by the Treasury by statutory instrument, where HMRC suspect that a person (P) is an 'introducer' in relation to a proposal and that the proposal is notifiable, they may by written notice require P to provide them with prescribed information in relation to each person who has provided P with information relating to the proposal. P must comply within period to be prescribed in regulations or such longer period as HMRC direct. A person is an *'introducer'* in relation to a proposal if he makes a 'marketing contact' (see **4.46** above) with another person in relation to the proposal. A person is not, however, an introducer by reason of anything done in circumstances to be prescribed in regulations.

[*FA 2004, ss 306A, 307(1A)(5)(6), 308A, 313A, 313B, 313C, 314A, 317A; FA 2007, s 108(2), (4)–(7), (10); FA 2010, Sch 17 paras 2(4)(6)(7), 4, 9, 11; SI 2004 No 1864, reg 8A; SI 2007 No 2153; SI 2009 No 56, Sch 1 paras 429–433*].

Penalties

[4.51] Penalties are chargeable for failures to comply with the following duties under the disclosure rules:

(a)   duty of promoter to notify HMRC of notifiable proposals or arrangements (*FA 2004, s 308(1)(3)*) (**4.46** above);

(b)   duty of taxpayer to notify where the promoter is not UK-resident (*FA 2004, s 309(1)*) (**4.46** above);

(c)   duty of parties to arrangements to notify where there is no promoter (*FA 2004, s 310*) (**4.46** above);

(d)   duty of promoter to notify parties of the scheme reference number (*FA 2004, s 312(2)*) (**4.47** above);

(e)   (from 1 November 2008) duty of client to notify parties of the reference number (*FA 2004, s 312A(2)*) (**4.47** above);

(f)   (from a date to be appointed) duty of promoter to provide details of clients (*FA 2004, s 313ZA*) (**4.48** above);

(g)   (from 19 July 2007) duty of promoter to respond to inquiry (*FA 2004, ss 313A, 313B*) (**4.50**(a)(b) above); and

(h)   (from a date to be appointed) duty of introducer to give details of persons who have provided information (*FA 2004, s 313C*) (**4.50**(f) above).

There is an initial penalty of up to £5,000 for any failure to comply with any one of the above duties. However, with effect from a date to be appointed by the Treasury by statutory instrument, where the failure relates to (a), (b) or (c) above, the initial penalty is up to £600 for each day during the 'initial period'. The *'initial period'* begins with the day after that on which the time limit for complying with the requirement expires and ends with the earlier of the day on which the penalty is determined and the last day before the failure ceases. The actual amount of the daily penalty should be arrived at after taking account of all relevant considerations, including the desirability of providing a deterrent and the amount of fees likely to be received by a promoter or the tax saving sought by the taxpayer. If, after taking account of those considerations, the maximum daily penalty seems inappropriately low, it can be increased to any amount up to £1 million.

Penalties are determined by the First-tier Tribunal — see **55.27 PENALTIES**. Where HMRC consider that a daily penalty has been determined to run from a date later than it should, they can commence proceedings for a redetermination of the penalty.

A further penalty or penalties of up to £600 applies for each day on which the failure continues after the initial penalty is imposed.

Wherever daily penalties apply, the maximum is increased to £5,000 per day where, in relation to the proposal or arrangements in question, an order has been made by the Tribunal under **4.50**(c) or (d) above. Where the order is made under **4.50**(d), the increased maximum only applies to days falling after the period of ten days beginning with the date of the order. From a date to be appointed, this will also apply where the order is made under **4.50**(c).

Where an order is made by the Tribunal under **4.50**(d) above or, from a date to be appointed, **4.50**(c), doubt as to notifiability is not a reasonable excuse for the purposes of *TMA 1970, s 118(2)* (see **63.23 RETURNS**) after the expiry of ten days beginning with the date of the order.

Parties to notifiable arrangements who fail to notify HMRC of the scheme reference number etc. are liable to a penalty of £100 in respect of each scheme to which the failure relates. The penalty is increased for a second failure, occurring within three years from the date on which the first failure began, to £500 in respect of each scheme to which the failure relates (whether or not the same as the scheme to which the first failure relates). Any further such failures occurring within three years from the date on which the previous failure began, result in a penalty of £1,000 in respect of each scheme to which the failure relates (whether or not the same as the schemes to which any of the previous failures relates).

The Treasury has the power to amend the above maxima of £5,000, £600 and £1 million by statutory instrument.

A party to notifiable arrangements who fails to give the reference number (for example, by including it in his tax return) as required by **4.47** above is liable to a penalty of £100 for each scheme (i.e. each set of notifiable arrangements) to which the failure relates. A second such failure within a period of 36 months gives rise to a penalty of £500 per scheme. A third or subsequent failure within 36 months gives rise to a penalty of £1,000 per scheme. The normal penalty regime for incorrect tax returns does not, however, apply in relation to any such failure.

[*TMA 1970, s 98C; FA 2004, ss 315, 319; FA 2007, s 108(9); FA 2008, s 116, Sch 38 para 7; FA 2010, Sch 17 paras 10, 11; SI 2004 No 1864, reg 8B; SI 2007 Nos 3103, 3104; SI 2008 No 1935*].

5

Appeals

Cross-references. See **18.3** CLAIMS for appeals in connection with claims and elections made outside returns; **38** HMRC INVESTIGATORY POWERS; **51.28** OFFSHORE FUNDS; **54.5, 54.6** PAYMENT OF TAX for payment of tax in relation to appeals; **55.24, , 55.26, 55.27,** PENALTIES for appeals relating to penalties; **62.8** RESIDENCE, ORDINARY RESIDENCE AND DOMICILE.

Simon's Taxes. See A5.1, A5.2, A5.3, A5.5, A5.6, E1.268.

Introduction

[5.1] A taxpayer who disagrees with an assessment or other decision made by HMRC can appeal against it. This is done by giving notice in writing to HMRC, stating the grounds of appeal. The notice must normally be given within 30 days after the date of issue of the assessment or decision, although late appeals can be made in some circumstances (see **5.3** below).

The appeal process has changed dramatically with effect from 1 April 2009. Appeals made, but not concluded, before that date are generally dealt with under the new process, but there are some transitional rules, for which see **5.33** below.

After a taxpayer appeals there are three main options:

* a different HMRC officer can carry out a review of the decision;
* the taxpayer can ask the Tribunal to decide the matter in dispute;
* the appeal can be settled by agreement at any time.

Reviews are not compulsory, and where HMRC carry out a review but the taxpayer still disagrees with the decision, he can ask the Tribunal to decide the issue (or continue negotiations with HMRC in order to settle the appeal by agreement).

For HMRC reviews, see **5.5** below and for settlement by agreement, see **5.8** below.

Where the taxpayer asks the Tribunal to decide the appeal, the case is usually dealt with by the First-tier Tribunal. The appeal is allocated to one of four categories, default paper, basic, standard or complex, and the process differs according to the category. Basic, standard and complex cases are normally decided at a hearing at which the taxpayer (or his representative) and HMRC are able to present their cases.

Default paper cases can also be decided at a hearing where one of the parties requests a hearing. Complex cases may be transferred for hearing by the Upper Tribunal.

For the First-tier Tribunal process, see **5.10–5.22** below.

If either the taxpayer or HMRC disagree with a decision of the First-tier Tribunal, there is a further right of appeal to the Upper Tribunal, but only on a point of law. Permission to appeal must be obtained from the First-tier Tribunal, or where it refuses permission, from the Upper Tribunal.

For the Upper Tribunal process, see **5.23–5.31** below. Where either party disagrees with an Upper Tribunal decision, there is a similar right of appeal to the Court of Appeal. See **5.32** below.

Where there is no right of appeal or a taxpayer is dissatisfied with the exercise by HMRC or the Tribunal of administrative powers, he may in certain circumstances seek a remedy by way of application for judicial review. See **5.34** below.

Costs can be awarded to or against a taxpayer in cases dealt with by either Tribunal or by the courts. See **5.22**, **5.32** and **5.35** below.

See generally HMRC Appeals, Reviews and Tribunals Guide.

Right of appeal

[5.2] A taxpayer can appeal against:

(a)   any assessment other than a self-assessment (see **6.2** ASSESSMENTS);

(b)   any conclusion stated, or amendment made, by a closure notice on completion of an enquiry into a personal, trustees' or partnership tax return (see **63.9** RETURNS);

(c)   any HMRC amendment (of a self-assessment) made, during an enquiry, to prevent potential loss of tax to the Crown (see **63.10** RETURNS);

(d)   any amendment of a partnership return where loss of tax is 'discovered' (see **6.6** ASSESSMENTS).

The right of appeal in (b) above includes a right of appeal by a partnership member against amendments made to his own tax return in consequence of an enquiry into the partnership return (*Philips v HMRC* FTT (TC 276), [2010] SFTD 332).

The hearing of an appeal within (b) above should not be limited to the conclusions stated, or amendments made, by the closure notice. Any such limitation 'might prevent a taxpayer from advancing a legitimate factual or legal argument which had hitherto escaped him or deprive, on the other hand, the public of the tax to which it is entitled'. The only limitation on issues which might be entertained by the First-tier Tribunal is that those issues must arise out of the subject-matter of the enquiry and consequently its conclusion, and they must be subject to the case management powers of the Tribunal. (*Tower MCashback LLP 1 v HMRC* CA, [2010] STC 809).

An appeal within (c) above cannot be taken forward until the enquiry has been completed.

[*TMA 1970, s 31(1)(2); SI 2009 No 56, Sch 1 para 19*].

A number of enactments give the right of appeal against a decision of the Commissioners of HMRC or an officer of HMRC in specified circumstances or an HMRC notice or determination (see, for example, *SI 2003 No 2682, Reg 18* as regards PAYE codings). Such rights are referred to in the appropriate section of this work. Further, certain matters are dealt with as appeals (see, for example, **73.112** TRADING INCOME as regards disputes as to the transfer price of trading stock on a discontinuance). There is, however, no right of appeal against a determination of liability made by HMRC in the event of non-submission of a self-assessment tax return (see **63.12** RETURNS). For appeals in connection with claims and elections made outside the tax return, see **18.3** CLAIMS.

Unless otherwise stated or required by context, the remainder of this chapter applies to all appeals and all matters treated as appeals, and not only to appeals within (a)–(d) above. [*TMA 1970, s 48; TIOPA 2010, Sch 7 para 31; SI 2009 No 56, Sch 1 para 28*].

Making an appeal

[5.3] An appeal is made by giving notice in writing, to the officer of Revenue and Customs concerned and specifying the grounds of appeal. Notice must normally be given within 30 days after the date of issue of the assessment or determination, the closure notice or the notice of amendment. [*TMA 1970, s 31A(1)–(5)*].

Late appeals

If a taxpayer fails to make an appeal within the normal time limit, an appeal can still be made if HMRC agree or, where HMRC do not agree, the Tribunal gives permission.

HMRC must agree to a written request for a late appeal if they are satisfied that there was a reasonable excuse for not making the appeal within the time limit and that the request was made without unreasonable delay after the reasonable excuse ceased.

Before 1 April 2009, HMRC could accept a late appeal only if satisfied that there was such a reasonable excuse and no unreasonable delay. Otherwise, HMRC had to refer the application to the Commissioners (normally the General Commissioners) for their decision.

[*TMA 1970, s 49; SI 2009 No 56, Sch 1 para 29*].

In the event of refusal to accept a late appeal, the decision is not subject to further appeal (*R v Special Commrs (ex p. Magill)* QB (NI) 1979, 53 TC 135), but is subject to judicial review (see *R v Hastings and Bexhill General Commrs and CIR (ex p. Goodacre)* QB 1994, 67 TC 126, in which a refusal was quashed and the matter remitted to a different body of Commissioners and *Advocate General for Scotland v General Commrs for Aberdeen City* CS 2005, 77 TC 391 in which HMRC successfully sought to overturn a decision to allow a late appeal). In *R (oao Browallia Cal Ltd) v General Commissioners of Income Tax* QB 2003, [2004] STC 296, it was held that the Appeal Commissioners had a wider discretion than HMRC in considering a late appeal. The court held that the Commissioners in that case had misunderstood their powers and that the lack of any reasonable excuse was 'potentially relevant' but was 'not conclusive'. The decision was followed in *R (oao Cook) v General Commissioners of Income Tax* QB, [2007] STC 499 in which the General Commissioners' refusal of a late appeal application was quashed because they had only considered the lack of a reasonable excuse and did not consider the possible merits of the appeal itself. (When the case was remitted to the General Commissioners, however, they again refused the late appeal, and the court upheld their decision — see *R (oao Cook) v General Commissioners of Income Tax (No. 2)* QB, [2009] STC1212.

Withdrawing an appeal

An appeal once made cannot, strictly, be withdrawn unilaterally (see *R v Special Commissioners (ex p. Elmhirst)* CA 1935, 20 TC 381 and *Beach v Willesden General Commissioners* Ch D 1981, 55 TC 663). If, however, a taxpayer or his agent gives HMRC oral or written notice of his desire not to proceed with an appeal, the appeal is treated as if settled by agreement, so that the provisions at **5.8** below apply (and the appeal is settled without any variation). Agreement is effective from the date of the taxpayer's notification. This does not apply if HMRC give written notice of objection within 30 days of the taxpayer's notice. [*TMA 1970, s 54(4)(5)*].

Payment of tax

For postponement of tax pending appeal and for payment of tax on determination of the appeal, see respectively **54.5** and **54.6** PAYMENT OF TAX.

The appeal process from 1 April 2009

[5.4] When an appeal to HMRC is made, there are four options for the appeal to proceed:

(a)   the appellant can require HMRC to review the matter in question;

(b)   HMRC can offer to review the matter in question;

(c)   the appellant can notify the appeal to the Tribunal for it to decide the matter in question; or

(d)   the appeal can be settled by agreement between HMRC and the appellant.

Where the appellant requires an HMRC review, he can still notify the appeal to the Tribunal if he disagrees with the review's conclusions or HMRC fail to complete a review within the required time. If HMRC offer a review and the appellant does not accept the offer, he can likewise notify the appeal to the Tribunal. Taking any of options (a) to (c) above does not prevent the appeal from being settled by agreement at any time.

[*TMA 1970, s 49A; SI 2009 No 56, Sch 1 para 30*].

For details of the review process, see **5.5** below; for notifying an appeal to the Tribunal, see **5.7** below; and for settlement of appeals by agreement, see **5.8** below.

Notices

All notices given under the appeal provisions must be made in writing. Notifications by the appellant can be made by a person acting on his behalf, but all HMRC notifications must be made directly to the appellant (although copies can be sent to his agent). [*TMA 1970, s 49I; SI 2009 No 56, Sch 1 para 30*].

HMRC review

[5.5] Where an appellant notifies HMRC that he requires them to review the matter in question, HMRC must first notify him of their view of the matter. They must do this within the 30 days beginning with the day on which they receive the notification from the appellant, or within such longer period as is reasonable. They must then carry out a review of the matter in question, as described at **5.6** below.

The appellant cannot request a second review of the matter in question and neither can he request a review if he has already notified the appeal to the Tribunal.

If it is HMRC who offer to review the matter in question, they must, when they notify the appellant of the offer, also notify the appellant of their view of the matter. The appellant then has 30 days beginning with the date of the document notifying him of the offer to notify HMRC of acceptance of it. If the appellant does so, HMRC must then carry out a review of the matter in question, as described at **5.6** below. Alternatively, the appellant can, within the same 30-day period, notify the appeal to the Tribunal for it to decide the matter in question.

If the appellant does not either accept the offer of review or notify the appeal to the Tribunal within the 30-day period, then HMRC's view of the matter in question is treated as if it were an contained in a written agreement for the settlement of the appeal, so that the provisions at **5.8** below apply (and the appeal is settled on the basis of HMRC's view). The appellant's normal right to withdraw from such agreements does not apply to the deemed agreement. The Tribunal may, however, give permission for the appellant to notify the appeal to it after the 30-day period has ended.

HMRC cannot make a second offer of a review or make an offer if the appellant has already required a review or has notified the appeal to the Tribunal.

[TMA 1970, ss 49B, 49C, 49H; SI 2009 No 56, Sch 1 para 30].

Conduct of the review

[5.6] The nature and extent of HMRC's review will be determined by them as seems appropriate in the circumstances, but they must take into account the steps taken before the start of the review both by them in deciding the matter in question and by anyone else seeking to resolve the disagreement. They must also take into account representations made by the appellant, provided that these are made at a stage which gives HMRC a reasonable opportunity to consider them.

The review must be completed and HMRC's conclusions notified to the appellant in writing within 45 days beginning with:

- (where the appellant required the review) the day HMRC notified him of their view of the matter in question; or
- (where HMRC offered the review) the day HMRC received notification of the appellant's acceptance of the offer.

HMRC and the appellant can, however, agree any other period for completion of the review.

If HMRC fail to notify the appellant of their conclusions within the required period, the review is treated as if the conclusion was that HMRC's original view of the matter in question were upheld. HMRC must notify the appellant in writing accordingly.

[*TMA 1970, s 49E; SI 2009 No 56, Sch 1 para 30*].

Effect of conclusions

HMRC's notice stating the conclusions to the review is treated as a written agreement for the settlement of the appeal, so that the provisions at **5.8** below apply (and the appeal is settled on the basis of those conclusions). The appellant's normal right to withdraw from such agreements does not apply to the deemed agreement.

The appellant does, however, have a further opportunity to notify the appeal to the Tribunal for them to determine the matter in question. This must normally be done within the period of 30 days beginning with the date of the document notifying the conclusions of the review. Where, however, HMRC have failed to notify the conclusions within the required period, the time limit is extended to 30 days after the date of the document notifying the appellant that the review is to be treated as if concluded on the basis of HMRC's original opinion. The Tribunal may give permission for an appeal to be notified to them after the time limits have expired.

[*TMA 1970, ss 49F, 49G; SI 2009 No 56, Sch 1 para 30*].

HMRC practice

Reviews are carried out by HMRC officers who have experience of the subject matter of the appeal but are independent of the decision maker and the decision maker's line management (HMRC Appeals, Reviews and Tribunals Guide, ARTG4310).

The review officer will consider whether the case is one which HMRC would want to defend before the Tribunal, and in particular will consider:

- whether the facts have been established, and whether there is disagreement about the facts;
- the technical and legal merits of the case;
- whether it would be an efficient or desirable use of resources to proceed with an appeal that will cost more than the sum in dispute;
- the likelihood of success; and
- whether the appeal raises unusual questions of law or general policy or may in some other way potentially have an effect on future decisions.

(HMRC Appeals, Reviews and Tribunals Guide, ARTG4080).

Review officers are instructed generally to avoid discussing the case with the caseworker during the review in order to ensure that the review remains independent. If exceptionally it is necessary discuss a case with the caseworker in any depth during the review the review officer will tell the appellant and offer equivalent telephone or face to face contact with him or his agent, so the appellant has an equal opportunity to make representations. (HMRC Appeals, Reviews and Tribunals Guide, ARTG4620).

See further HMRC Appeals, Reviews and Tribunals Guide, ARTG4000–4860.

Appeal to the Tribunal

[5.7] A taxpayer who has appealed to HMRC can notify the appeal to the Tribunal without requesting an HMRC review first. If he does so, HMRC cannot then make an offer of a review. [*TMA 1970, s 49D; SI 2009 No 56, Sch 1 para 30*].

An appellant can also notify an appeal to the Tribunal if he does not wish to accept an HMRC offer of a review or if he disagrees with the conclusions of a review. In both cases there are short time limits within which notification must be made, although the Tribunal can give permission for notification to be made outside those limits: see **5.5** and **5.6** above.

There is no provision for HMRC to notify an appeal to the Tribunal (unlike under the appeals system before 1 April 2009 where HMRC was responsible in most cases for listing appeals for hearing by the Commissioners — see **5.37** below).

Notice of appeal must include the appellant's details, details of the decision etc. appealed against, the result the appellant is seeking and the grounds of appeal. The notice must be accompanied by a copy of any written record of the decision and the reasons for it that the appellant has or can reasonably obtain. If the notice is made late it must also include a request for extension of time and the reason for lateness. [*SI 2009 No 273, Rule 20*].

Appeals should be notified to the Tribunal by e-mail to taxappeals@tribunals.gsi.gov.uk or by post to the Tribunals Service, Tax, 2nd Floor, 54 Hagley Road, Birmingham B16 8PE. A Notice of Appeal form can be obtained from the Tribunals Service web site (www.tribunals.gov.uk) or by phoning 0845 223 8080.

See **5.9** onwards below for the process by which an appeal notified to the Tribunal is decided.

Settlement by agreement

[5.8] At any time before an appeal is determined by the Tribunal, it may be settled by agreement between HMRC and the appellant or his agent. Where such an agreement is reached, in writing or otherwise, the assessment or decision as upheld, varied, discharged, or cancelled by that agreement, is treated as if it had been determined on appeal. Oral agreements are, however, effective only if confirmed in writing by either side (the date of such confirmation then being the effective date of agreement).

The taxpayer may withdraw from the agreement by giving written notice within 30 days of making it.

[*TMA 1970, s 54(1)–(3)(5); SI 2009 No 56, Sch 1 para 33*].

The agreement must specify the figure for assessment or a precise formula for ascertaining it (*Delbourgo v Field* CA 1978, 52 TC 225).

The agreement only covers the assessments (or decisions) which are the subject of the appeal, and does not bind HMRC for subsequent years, for example where relievable amounts are purported to be carried forward from the year in question (*MacNiven v Westmoreland Investments Ltd* HL 2001, 73 TC 1 and see also *Tod v South Essex Motors (Basildon) Ltd* Ch D 1987, 60 TC 598).

The issue of an amended notice of assessment cannot in itself constitute an offer for the purposes of a *section 54* agreement; nor can a lack of response by the taxpayer constitute acceptance of an offer (*Schuldenfrei v Hilton* CA 1999, 72 TC 167). For the general requirements for an agreement, see *Cash & Carry v Inspector* (Sp C 148), [1998] SSCD 46.

An agreement based on a mutual mistake of fact was as a result invalid, so that the taxpayer could proceed with his appeal (*Fox v Rothwell* (Sp C 50), [1995] SSCD 336).

See *Gibson v General Commissioners for Stroud* Ch D 1989, 61 TC 645 for a case where there was held not to have been a determination and *R v Inspector of Taxes, ex p. Bass Holdings Ltd; Richart v Bass Holdings Ltd* QB 1992, 65 TC 495 for one where rectification of an agreement was ordered where a relief had been deducted twice contrary to the intention of Revenue and taxpayer.

See *CIR v West* CA 1991, 64 TC 196 for a case where the taxpayer was unsuccessful in seeking leave to defend a Crown action for payment of tax on the ground that the accountant who had entered into an agreement had no authority to do so given him by the taxpayer.

An appeal that has been settled by the taxpayer's trustee in bankruptcy cannot subsequently be reopened by the taxpayer (*Ahajot (Count Artsrunik) v Waller* (Sp C 395), [1994] SSCD 151).

For the extent to which further assessments or error or mistake relief claims are permissible if an appeal has been determined by agreement, see **6.6 ASSESS-MENTS.**

The Tribunal

[5.9] Under the unified tribunal system established by the *Tribunals, Courts and Enforcement Act 2007*, there are two Tribunals; the First-tier Tribunal and the Upper Tribunal. The Tribunals are presided over by a Senior President of Tribunals. [*TCEA 2007, s 3*].

The First-tier Tribunal. Tax appeals notified to the Tribunal are in most cases initially heard and decided by the First-tier Tribunal. [*TMA 1970, s 47C; SI 2009 No 56, Sch 1 para 27*].

The First-tier Tribunal is organised into separate chambers each with responsibility for different areas of the law and with its own Chamber President. With certain exceptions, the Tax Chamber is responsible for all appeals, applications, references or other proceedings in respect of the functions of HMRC. It is also responsible for appeals etc. in respect of the exercise of Revenue functions by the Serious Organised Crime Agency (see **34.11** HMRC — ADMINISTRATION). The exceptions relate to certain tax credit and national insurance matters and to matters for which the Upper Tribunal is responsible. [*TCEA 2007, s 7; SI 2008 No 2684, Arts 2, 5A; SI 2009 No 196, Arts 3, 5*].

The Upper Tribunal

The Upper Tribunal is a superior court of record, so that its decisions create legally binding precedents. [*TCEA 2007, s 3(5)*].

It is similarly divided into chambers, including the Tax and Chancery Chamber. In relation to tax matters, the Chamber is responsible for:

(a)   further appeals against decisions by the First-tier Tribunal Tax Chamber (see **5.25** below);

(b)   applications by HMRC for a tax-related penalty under *FA 2008, Sch 36 para 50* in respect of failure to comply with an information notice or obstruction of an inspection (see **55.17 PENALTIES**);

(c)   complex appeals, applications or references transferred from the First-tier Tribunal (see **5.27** below);

(d)   matters referred to the Upper Tribunal following a decision by the First-tier Tribunal Tax Chamber to set aside its own original decision (see **5.28** below); and

(e)   applications for judicial review (see **5.34**below).

[*SI 2008 No 2684, Arts 6, 8; SI 2009 No 196, Arts 6, 8; SI 2009 No 1590, Art 8*].

Overriding objective

The Tribunal Procedure Rules which govern the operation of the Tribunals include an explicit statement of their overriding objective, which is to deal with cases fairly and justly. The Tribunals are required to deal with each case in ways proportionate to its importance, its complexity and the anticipated costs and resources of the parties to the appeal etc. They must avoid unnecessary formality and delay and seek flexibility in the proceedings. They must ensure that the parties are able to participate fully in the proceedings.

The parties to the appeal etc. are in turn required to help the Tribunal to further the overriding objective and to co-operate with the Tribunal generally. [*SI 2008 No 2698, Rule 2; SI 2009 No 273, Rule 2*].

Alternative dispute resolution

The Tribunals also have an explicit duty to point out to the parties the availability of any alternative procedure for resolving the dispute and to facilitate the use of the procedure if the parties wish. [*SI 2008 No 2698, Rule 3; SI 2009 No 273, Rule 3*].

Composition of Tribunals

Both the First-tier and Upper Tribunal consist of judges who have particular legal qualifications or experience, and other members who are not legally qualified but meet specified selection criteria. Judges of the Upper Tribunal are appointed by the Crown on the recommendation of the Lord Chancellor. Judges and members of the First-tier Tribunal, and members of the Upper Tribunal, are appointed by the Lord Chancellor. See *TCEA 2007, ss 4, 5, Schs 2, 3.*

First-tier Tribunal procedure

Case management

[5.10] The Tribunal has wide powers to regulate its own procedures and to give directions about the conduct or disposal of cases. In particular it can, by direction:

- consolidate or hear two or more cases together or treat a case as a lead case (see *SI 2009 No 273, Rule 18*);
- permit or require a party to the case or another person to provide documents, information or submissions to the Tribunal or another party;
- hold a hearing to consider any matter, including a case management hearing;
- decide the form of any hearing;
- require a party to produce a bundle of documents for a hearing.

The Tribunal can also substitute a party to a case where necessary or add a person to the case as a respondent. A person who is not a party to the case can apply to the Tribunal to be added as a party.

Either party to a case can apply for the Tribunal to make a direction, either in writing or orally at a hearing, or the Tribunal can make a direction on its own initiative. Applications for a direction must include the reason for making it. Directions can be challenged by applying for a further direction.

Any action required to be done in relation to a case on or by a particular day must be done before 5pm on that day (or, if that day is not a working day, by 5pm on the next working day).

[*SI 2009 No 273, Rules 5, 6, 9, 12*].

Administration of cases referred to the Tribunal, including the categorisation of cases (see **5.12** below), is carried out by the Tribunals Service.

Starting proceedings

See **5.8** above for how to notify an appeal to the Tribunal. There are also rules for proceedings to be determined without notice to a respondent (*Rule 19*), and for proceedings started by originating application or reference (*Rule 21*).

Representation

A party to a case can appoint a representative to represent him in the proceedings. The representative does not need to be a lawyer. The party has to notify the Tribunal and the other parties of the appointment of a representative and they will then treat the representative as authorised until notified otherwise.

Where no such person has been appointed, a party can, with the Tribunal's permission, nevertheless be accompanied at a hearing by another person who can act as a representative or assist in presenting the case.

[*SI 2009 No 273, Rule 11*].

Withdrawal from a case

Subject to any legislation relating to withdrawal from or settlement of particular proceedings, a party can notify the Tribunal of the withdrawal of its case, or part of it. This can be done in writing before a hearing or orally at a hearing. If the case is to be settled without a hearing, written notice must be given before the Tribunal disposes of the case.

A party who has withdrawn its case can, however, apply (in writing) to the Tribunal to reinstate it. The application must be received by the Tribunal within 28 days after it received the withdrawal notice or the date of the hearing.

[*SI 2009 No 273, Rule 17*].

Failure to comply with rules

[5.11] An irregularity resulting from any failure to comply with the Tribunal Procedure Rules, a practice direction or a direction by the Tribunal does not in itself make the proceedings void.

Where a party fails to comply with the Rules etc. the Tribunal can take such action as it considers just. This could be to require compliance or waive the requirement, to strike the case out (see below) or, in certain cases, to refer the failure to the Upper Tribunal.

The Tribunal can refer to the Upper Tribunal any failure to:

- attend a hearing, or otherwise be available, to give evidence;
- to swear an oath in connection with giving evidence;
- to give evidence as a witness;
- to produce a document; or
- to facilitate the inspection of a document or other thing (including premises).

The Upper Tribunal then has the same powers as the High Court to deal with the failure (which may include financial penalties).

[*TCEA 2007, s 25; SI 2009 No 273, Rule 7*].

Striking out a case

A case will automatically be struck out if the appellant fails to comply with a direction which states that failure to comply will lead to striking out.

The Tribunal can also strike out a case if the appellant fails to comply with a direction which states that failure to comply may lead to striking out, if the appellant has failed to co-operate with the Tribunal to such an extent that the case cannot be dealt with fairly and justly, or if the Tribunal considers that there is no reasonable prospect of the appellant's case succeeding. In the last two cases, however, the Tribunal must first give the appellant an opportunity to make representations.

If the case is struck out because of the appellant's failure to comply with a direction, the appellant can apply for the case to be reinstated. This must be done in writing within 28 days after the date the Tribunal sent the notification of the striking out.

The above rules also apply to respondents except that, instead of the case being struck out, the respondent is barred from taking any further part in the case.

[*SI 2009 No 273, Rule 8*].

Categorisation of cases

[5.12] When an appeal, application or reference is notified to the Tribunal, the Tribunals Service allocate it to one of four categories of case:

(a)   default paper;
(b)   basic;
(c)   standard; or
(d)   complex.

Cases may be re-categorised by the Tribunal at any time either on the application of one of the parties or on the Tribunal's own initiative.

[*SI 2009 No 273, Rule 23(1)–(3)*].

The process by which the appeal etc. will be decided varies according to the category to which the case is allocated as described below.

Default paper cases

[5.13] The following types of cases must normally be categorised as default paper cases:

(a)   appeals against penalties for late self-assessment tax returns (see **55.5 PENALTIES**) and certain other late returns or notifications;
(b)   appeals against surcharges for late payment of tax under *TMA 1970, s 59C* (see **42.3 INTEREST AND SURCHARGES ON OVERDUE TAX**); and
(c)   applications for a daily penalty for a late personal self-assessment tax return (see **55.5 PENALTIES**).

Cases can be allocated to a different category if the Tribunal considers it appropriate to do so.

(Tribunals Practice Direction, 10 March 2009).

In a default paper case, the respondent (i.e., in an appeal, HMRC) must provide a statement of case to the Tribunal, the appellant and any other respondents to be received within 42 days after the Tribunal sends it notice of the proceedings (or by such time as the Tribunal directs). The statement must state the legislation under which the decision in question was made and set out the respondent's position. If the statement is late it must also include a request for a time extension and give the reason for lateness.

The statement can also contain a request for the case to be dealt with either at or without a hearing.

Once such a statement has been given to the appellant, he may send a written reply to the Tribunal. The reply must be received within 30 days after the date on which the respondent sent its statement to the appellant and must be sent also to each respondent. The reply may include the appellant's response to the respondent's statement of case, provide any further relevant information and contain a request for the case to be dealt with at a hearing. If the reply is late it must also include a request for a time extension and give the reason for lateness.

The Tribunal must hold a hearing before determining a case if any party has requested one in writing. Otherwise, on receipt of the appellant's reply or the expiry of the time limit for such a reply, the Tribunal will determine the case without a hearing, unless it directs otherwise.

[*SI 2009 No 273, Rules 25, 26*].

Default paper cases are decided by one judge or other member of the First-tier Tribunal. (Tribunals Practice Statement, 10 March 2009).

Basic cases

[5.14] The following types of cases must normally be allocated as basic cases (unless they must be allocated as default paper cases:

(a) appeals against penalties for late filing and late payment, including daily penalties;

(b) appeals against penalties under *FA 2007, Sch 24* (errors in documents and failure to notify HMRC of errors in assessments — see **55.25, 55.26 PENALTIES**);

(c) appeals against indirect tax penalties on the basis of reasonable excuse and certain construction industry scheme decisions;

(d) appeals against information notices (including those at **38.4** and **38.11**(d) HMRC INVESTIGATORY POWERS and **63.8** RETURNS);

(e) applications for permission to make a late appeal (see **5.3** above);

(f) applications for the postponement of tax pending an appeal (see **54.5 PAYMENT OF TAX**); and

(g) applications for a direction that HMRC close an enquiry (see **63.9 RETURNS**).

Appeals against penalties for deliberate action or where an appeal is also brought against the assessment to which the penalty relates are excluded from (b) above (as are indirect tax cases).

Cases can be allocated to a different category if the Tribunal considers it appropriate to do so.

(Tribunals Practice Direction, 10 March 2009).

Basic cases normally proceed directly to a hearing, without the need for the respondent to produce a statement of case. Where, however, the respondent intends to raise grounds at the hearing of which the appellant has not been informed, the appellant must be notified of those grounds as soon as is reasonably practicable. The respondent must include sufficient detail to enable the appellant to respond to the grounds at the hearing. [*SI 2009 No 273, Rule 24*].

A decision in a basic case that disposes of proceedings or determines a preliminary issue made at, or following, a hearing must be made by either one, two or, where the Chamber President so decides, three members. The members can be judges or other members as the Chamber President decides, and he will choose one of them to be the presiding member. Any other decision will be made by one judge or other member. (Tribunals Practice Statement, 10 March 2009).

Standard cases

[5.15] In a standard case, the respondent (i.e., in an appeal, HMRC) must provide a statement of case to the Tribunal, the appellant and any other respondents to be received within 42 days after the Tribunal sends it notice of the proceedings (or by such time as the Tribunal directs). The statement must state the legislation under which the decision in question was made and set out the respondent's position. If the statement is late it must also include a request for a time extension and give the reason for lateness.

The statement can also contain a request for the case to be dealt with either at or without a hearing.

Within 42 days after the date on which the respondent sent the statement of case, each party to the case must send to the Tribunal and each other party a list of documents of which that party has possession (or the right to take possession or make copies) and on which the party intends to rely or to produce in the proceedings. The other parties must then be allowed to inspect or copy those documents, except for any which are privileged.

The case will then normally proceed to a hearing (see **5.17** below).

[*SI 2009 No 273, Rules 25, 27*].

A decision in a standard case that disposes of proceedings or determines a preliminary issue made at, or following, a hearing must be made by one judge or by one judge and one or two members as determined by the Chamber President. The judge will be the presiding member, unless one or more of the other members is also a judge, in which case the Chamber President will choose the presiding member. Any other decision will be made by one judge. (Tribunals Practice Statement, 10 March 2009).

Complex cases

[5.16] A case can be classified as a complex case only if the Tribunal considers that it will require lengthy or complex evidence or a lengthy hearing, involves a complex or important principle or issue, or involves a large financial sum. [*SI 2009 No 273, Rule 23(4)*].

The procedures in a complex case are the same as those described at **5.15** above for standard cases. The same rules regarding the membership of the Tribunal also apply.

Transfer to Upper Tribunal

The Tribunal can, with the consent of the parties, refer a complex case to the Chamber President with a request for transfer to the Upper Tribunal. The Chamber President can then, with the agreement of the President of the Tax and Chancery Chamber of the Upper Tribunal, direct that the case be so transferred. [*SI 2009 No 273, Rule 28*].

Costs

See **5.22** below for the taxpayer's option to request that a complex case be excluded from potential liability for costs.

The hearing

[5.17] Basic, standard and complex cases normally require a hearing before they are decided (and see **5.13** above for hearings in default paper cases).

This does not apply, however, if all of the parties consent to a decision without a hearing and the Tribunal considers that it is able to make a decision without a hearing. Hearings are also not required for the correction, setting aside, review or appeal of a Tribunal decision (see **5.18–5.20** below) or where the Tribunal strikes out a party's case (see **5.11** above).

Each party to the proceedings is normally entitled to attend the hearing and the Tribunal must give reasonable notice of its time and place. Where the hearing is to consider disposal of the proceedings, at least 14 days' notice must be given except in urgent or exceptional circumstances or with the consent of the parties.

Hearings are normally held in public. The Tribunal may, however, direct that a hearing should be private if it considers that restricting access is justified in the interests of public order or national security, to protect a person's right to respect for their private and family life, to maintain the confidentiality of sensitive information, to avoid serious harm to the public interest or because not to do so would prejudice the interest of justice.

[*SI 2009 No 273, Rules 29–32*].

Failure to attend hearing

If a party fails to attend a hearing, the Tribunal can nevertheless proceed with the hearing if it considers that it is in the interests of justice to do so. The Tribunal must be satisfied that the party was notified of the hearing or that reasonable steps were taken to notify the party. [*SI 2009 No 273, Rule 33*].

The following cases were decided under the rather different provisions applicable before 1 April 2009 to failure to attend a hearing of the General Commissioners, but may be relevant to the above provision. Determinations in the absence of the taxpayer or his agent were upheld where notice of the meeting was received by the appellant (*R v Tavistock Commrs (ex p. Adams) (No 1)* QB 1969, 46 TC 154; *R v Special Commr (ex p. Moschi)* CA, [1981] STC 465 and see *Fletcher & Fletcher v Harvey* CA 1990, 63 TC 539), but Commissioners were held to have acted unreasonably in refusing to re-open proceedings when the taxpayer's agent was temporarily absent when the appeal was called (*R & D McKerron Ltd v CIR* CS 1979, 52 TC 28). Where the taxpayer was absent through illness, a determination was quashed because the Commissioners, in refusing an adjournment, had failed to consider whether injustice would thereby arise to the taxpayer (*R v Sevenoaks Commrs (ex p. Thorne)* QB 1989, 62 TC 341 and see *Rose v Humbles* CA 1971, 48 TC 103). See also *R v O'Brien (ex p. Lissner)* QB, [1984] STI 710 where the determination was quashed when the appellant had been informed by the inspector that the hearing was to be adjourned.

Evidence and submissions

The Tribunal has wide powers to make directions as to issues on which it requires evidence or submissions, including the nature of such evidence or submissions, the way in which and time at which it must be provided and the need for expert evidence. It may also limit the number of witnesses whose evidence a party can put forward.

The Tribunal can accept evidence whether or not it would be admissible in a civil trial and can exclude evidence provided late or not in accordance with a direction.

[SI 2009 No 273, Rule 15(1)(2)].

The following cases relate to evidence given at hearings of the General Commissioners before 1 April 2009, but may be relevant to the above provision. A party to the proceedings could not insist on being examined on oath (*R v Special Commrs (in re Fletcher)* CA 1894, 3 TC 289). False evidence under oath would be perjury under criminal law (*R v Hood Barrs* CA, [1943] 1 All ER 665). A taxpayer was held to be bound by an affidavit he had made in other proceedings (*Wicker v Fraser* Ch D 1982, 55 TC 641). A remission to Commissioners to hear evidence directed at the credit of a witness was refused in *Potts v CIR* Ch D 1982, 56 TC 25. Rules of the Supreme Court under which evidence can be obtained from a witness abroad could not be used in proceedings before the Commissioners (*Leiserach v CIR* CA 1963, 42 TC 1). As to hearsay evidence under *Civil Evidence Act 1968*, see *Forth Investments Ltd v CIR* Ch D 1976, 50 TC 617 and *Khan v Edwards* Ch D 1977, 53 TC 597.

The Commissioners were under no obligation to adjourn an appeal for the production of further evidence (*Hamilton v CIR* CS 1930, 16 TC 28; *Noble v Wilkinson* Ch D 1958, 38 TC 135), and were held not to have erred in law in determining assessments in the absence abroad of the taxpayer (*Hawkins v Fuller* Ch D 1982, 56 TC 49).

Witnesses

The Tribunal, on the application of any party to the proceedings or its own initiative, can issue a summons (in Scotland, a citation) requiring any person either to attend the hearing of those proceedings to give evidence or to produce any relevant document in his possession or control. A witness required to attend a hearing must be given 14 days notice or a shorter period if the Tribunal so directs and, if the witness is not a party, the summons or citations must make provision for necessary expenses of attendance and state who is to pay them. If, before the summons or citation was issued, the witness did not have an opportunity to object, he may apply to the Tribunal for the summons to be varied or set aside. The application must be made as soon as reasonably practicable after the summons or citation is received.

A witness cannot be compelled to give evidence or produce documents which he could not be compelled to give or produce in an action in a court of law.

[*SI 2009 No 273, Rule 16*].

The Tribunal's decision

[5.18] In an appeal case, if the Tribunal decides:

(a)   that the appellant is overcharged or undercharged by a self-assessment;

(b)   that any amounts in a partnership statement (see **63.13 RETURNS**) are excessive or insufficient; or

(c)   that the appellant is overcharged or undercharged by an assessment other than a self-assessment,

the assessment or amounts are reduced or increased accordingly, but otherwise the assessment or statement stands good. The Tribunal is given the power to vary the extent to which a claim or election included in a tax return is disallowed following an enquiry. (Separate rules apply to claims and elections made outside returns, for which see **18.3 CLAIMS**.) In a case within (c) above, the Tribunal can normally only reduce or increase the amount assessed, and this determines the appeal; the Tribunal is not obliged to determine the revised tax payable. In a case within (b) above, HMRC must amend the partners' own tax returns to give effect to the reductions or increases made.

The Tribunal's decision is final and conclusive, subject to:

(i)   the correction of clerical mistakes etc. (see **5.19** below);

(ii)   the setting aside of a decision (see **5.19** below); and

(iii)   a further appeal against the decision (see **5.20** below).

[*TMA 1970, s 50(6)–(11); SI 2009 No 56, Sch 1 para 31*].

See **42.3 INTEREST AND SURCHARGES ON OVERDUE TAX** and **55.5 PENALTIES** for the Tribunal's options in an appeal against a surcharge or a late filing penalty, which turns on the question of whether the appellant had a 'reasonable excuse' for his non-compliance.

The Tribunal can give its decision orally at a hearing or in writing. In either case it will give each party a decision notice in writing within 28 days after making a decision which finally disposes of all the issues in the case or as soon as practicable. The notice will also inform the party of any further right of appeal.

Unless each party agrees otherwise the notice should also include a summary of the findings of fact and the reason for the decision. If it does not, any party to the case can apply for full written findings and reasons, and must do so before applying for permission to appeal (see **5.20** below). The application must be made in writing so that the Tribunal receives it within 28 days after the date it sent the decision notice.

[*SI 2009 No 273, Rule 35*].

Case law

The following cases relate to decisions of the General Commissioners before 1 April 2009, but may be relevant to the above provisions.

In reaching their decision, the Commissioners could not take into account matters appropriate for application for judicial review (*Aspin v Estill* CA 1987, 60 TC 549). They did not generally have the power to review on appeal the exercise of a discretion conferred on HMRC by statute (see *Slater v Richardson & Bottoms Ltd* Ch D 1979, 53 TC 155; *Kelsall v Investment Chartwork Ltd* Ch D 1993, 65 TC 750).

Onus of proof

The onus is on the appellant to displace an assessment. See *Brady v Group Lotus Car Companies plc* CA 1987, 60 TC 359 where the onus of proof remained with the taxpayer where the amount of normal time limit assessment indicated contention of fraud. The general principle emerges in appeals against estimated assessments in 'delay cases', which, before self-assessment, made up the bulk of appeals heard by the General Commissioners. For examples of cases in which the Commissioners have confirmed estimated assessments in the absence of evidence that they were excessive, see *T Haythornthwaite & Sons Ltd v Kelly* CA 1927, 11 TC 657; *Stoneleigh Products Ltd v Dodd* CA 1948, 30 TC 1; *Rosette Franks (King St) Ltd v Dick* Ch D 1955, 36 TC 100; *Pierson v Belcher* Ch D 1959, 38 TC 387. In a number of cases, the courts have supported the Commissioners' action in rejecting unsatisfactory accounts (e.g. *Cain v Schofield* Ch D 1953, 34 TC 362; *Moll v CIR* CS 1955, 36 TC 384; *Cutmore v Leach* Ch D 1981, 55 TC 602; *Coy v Kime* Ch D 1986, 59 TC 447) or calling for certified accounts (e.g. *Stephenson v Waller* KB 1927, 13 TC 318; *Hunt & Co v Joly* KB 1928, 14 TC 165; *Wall v Cooper* CA 1929, 14 TC 552). In *Anderson v CIR* CS 1933, 18 TC 320, the case was remitted where there was no evidence to support the figure arrived at by the Commissioners (which was between the accounts figure and the estimated figure assessed), but contrast *Bookey v Edwards* Ch D 1981, 55 TC 486. The Commissioners were entitled to look at each year separately, accepting the appellant's figures for some years but not all (*Donnelly v Platten* CA(NI) 1980, [1981] STC 504). Similarly, the onus is on the taxpayer to substantiate his claims to relief (see *Eke v Knight* CA 1977, 51 TC 121; *Talib v Waterson* Ch D, [1980] STC 563).

For the standard of proof required in evidence, see *Les Croupiers Casino Club v Pattinson* CA 1987, 60 TC 196.

Consent orders. The case can also be settled by the Tribunal making a consent order where the parties have reached agreement. Such an order is made at the request of the parties but only if the Tribunal considers it appropriate to do so. No hearing is necessary if such an order is made. [*SI 2009 No 273, Rule 34*].

Correction of mistakes in a decision

[5.19] The Tribunal can correct any clerical mistake or other accidental slip or omission in a decision at any time by notifying the parties of the amended decision. This rule applies also to directions and any other document produced by the Tribunal. [*SI 2009 No 273, Rule 37*].

Setting aside a decision

The Tribunal can set aside a decision disposing of a case and re-make the decision if it considers that to do is in the interests of justice and one of the following applies:

- a relevant document was not sent to, or was not received at an appropriate time by, a party or his representative;
- a relevant document was not sent to the Tribunal at a relevant time;
- there was some other procedural irregularity; or
- a party or representative was not present at a hearing.

A party to a case can apply for a decision to be set aside. The application must be in writing and must be received by the Tribunal within 28 days after the date on which the Tribunal sent the decision notice.

[*SI 2009 No 273, Rule 38*].

An application for a decision to be set aside was successful in *Wright v HMRC* FTT (TC 177), [2009] SFTD 748.

Appeal against the Tribunal's decision

[5.20] A further appeal to the Upper Tribunal can be made against the First-tier Tribunal's decision. The appeal can be made only on a point of law. No appeal can be made against a decision on whether or not to review a decision (see below), to set aside a decision (see **5.19** above) or to refer a matter to the Upper Tribunal.

A person wishing to appeal must make a written application to the First-tier Tribunal for permission to appeal. Such an application must be received by the Tribunal no later than 56 days after the date the Tribunal sent full reasons for the decision to that person. Where a decision has been amended or corrected following a review (see below) or an application (other than a late application) for a decision to be struck out has been unsuccessful (see **5.19** above), the 56 day limit runs from the date on which the Tribunal sent the notification of amended reasons or correction of the decision or of the failure of the striking out application.

The application must identify the alleged errors in the decision and state the result sought. Late applications must include a request for extension of time and the reason for lateness.

On receiving an application, the Tribunal will first consider whether to review the decision. It can do so only if satisfied that there was an error in law in the decision. Unless it decides to take no action following the review, the Tribunal will notify the parties of the outcome and must give them an opportunity to make representations before taking any action.

If the Tribunal decides not to review the decision or, following a review, decides to take no action, it will then consider whether to give permission to appeal to the Upper Tribunal. It will send a record of its decision to the parties as soon as practicable together with, where it decides not to give permission, a statements of its reasons for refusal and details of the right to apply directly to the Upper Tribunal for permission to appeal (see **5.25** below). The Tribunal's permission can be in respect of part only of the decision or on limited grounds.

[*TCEA 2007, s 11; SI 2009 No 273, Rules 39–41*].

Payment of tax pending further appeal

[5.21] Tax is payable or repayable in accordance with the decision of the Tribunal even if a party appeals to the Upper Tribunal. If the amount charged in the assessment concerned is subsequently altered by the Upper Tribunal, any amount undercharged is due and payable at the end of the thirty days beginning with the date on which HMRC issue the appellant a notice of the amount payable in accordance with the Upper Tribunal's decision. Any amount overpaid will be refunded along with such interest as may be allowed by the decision.

This provision applies equally to any further appeal from a decision of the Upper Tribunal to the Courts.

[*TMA 1970, s 56; SI 2009 No 56, Sch 1 para 35*].

Award of costs

[5.22] The Tribunal can make an order awarding costs (or, in Scotland, expenses):

(a)   under *TCEA 2007, s 29(4)* ('wasted costs');
(b)   where it considers that a party or representative has acted unreasonably in bringing, defending or conducting the case; and
(c)   in a complex case (see **5.16** above), where the taxpayer has not sent a written request that the case be excluded from potential liability for costs or expenses.

A request within (c) above must be sent within 28 days of the taxpayer receiving notice that the case has been allocated as a complex case.

'*Wasted costs*' are any costs incurred by a party because of an improper, unreasonable or negligent act or omission by any representative or employee of a representative, which the Tribunal considers it unreasonable for the party to pay.

Before making an order for costs, the Tribunal must give the person who will have to pay them the chance to make representations. If the payer is an individual, it must consider his financial means.

The Tribunal can make an order on its own initiative or on an application from one of the parties. Such an application must be sent both to the Tribunal and to the person from whom costs are sought, together with a schedule of the costs claimed. An application must be made no later than 28 days after the date on which the Tribunal sends a notice recording the decision which finally disposes of all the issues or notice of a withdrawal which ends the case.

The amount of costs will be decided either by agreement of the parties, by summary assessment by the Tribunal or, if not agreed, by assessment. Where the amount is to be decided by assessment, either the payer or the person to whom the costs are to be paid can apply to a county court, the High Court or the Costs Office of the Supreme Court for a detailed assessment of the costs on the standard basis or, where the Tribunal's order so specifies, the indemnity basis.

[*TCEA 2007, s 29(4); SI 2009 No 273, Rule 10*].

Upper Tribunal procedure

Case management

[5.23] The powers of the Upper Tribunal to regulate its own proceedings are broadly the same as the powers of the First-tier Tribunal. See *SI 2008 No 2698, Rules 5, 6, 9, 12* and **5.10** above.

Representation

The same rights to representation in a case before the Upper Tribunal apply as in a case before the First-tier Tribunal. See *SI 2008 No 2698, Rule 11* and **5.10** above.

Withdrawal from a case

A party can notify the Upper Tribunal of the withdrawal of its case, or part of it. This can be done in writing before a hearing or orally at a hearing. If the case is to be settled without a hearing, written notice must be given before the Tribunal disposes of the case. The withdrawal only takes effect, however, if the Tribunal consents (but this requirement does not apply to the withdrawal of an application for permission to appeal).

A party who has withdrawn its case can, however, apply (in writing) to the Tribunal to reinstate it. The application must be received by the Tribunal within one month after it received the withdrawal notice or the date of the hearing.

[SI 2008 No 2698, Rule 17].

Failure to comply with rules

[5.24] An irregularity resulting from any failure to comply with the Tribunal Procedure Rules, a practice direction or a direction by the Upper Tribunal does not in itself make the proceedings void.

Where a party fails to comply with the Rules etc. the Upper Tribunal can take such action as it considers just. This could be to require compliance or waive the requirement, to strike the case out (see below) or to restrict a party's participation in the case.

The Upper Tribunal has the same powers as the High Court to deal with the failure (which may include financial penalties).

[TCEA 2007, s 25; SI 2008 No 2698, Rule 7].

Striking out a case

The Upper Tribunal has similar powers to strike out a case as the First-tier Tribunal. See *SI 2008 No 2698, Rule 8* and **5.11** above. Note, however, that the Upper Tribunal cannot strike out an appeal from the decision of another Tribunal or judicial review proceedings on the grounds that there is no reasonable prospect of the appellant's case succeeding.

Appeal against decisions of the First-tier Tribunal

[5.25] A party to a case who disagrees with a decision of the First-tier Tribunal can apply for permission to appeal against it. Applications must first be made to the First-tier Tribunal (see **5.20** above), but if that Tribunal refuses permission a further application can be made to the Upper Tribunal.

Applications to the Upper Tribunal must be in writing and must be received no later than one month after the date on which the First-tier Tribunal sent the notice refusing permission to appeal. An application must include the grounds for appeal and state whether the appellant wants the application to be dealt with at a hearing. It must be accompanied by copies of any written record of the decision being challenged, any statement of reasons for that decision, and the notice of the First-tier Tribunal's refusal of permission to appeal. Late applications must include a request for extension of time and the reason for lateness.

If the application to the First-tier Tribunal for permission to appeal was refused because it was made out of time, the application to the Upper Tribunal must include the reason for the lateness of the first application. The Upper Tribunal can then admit the application only if it considers that it is in the interests of justice to do so.

If the Tribunal refuses permission to appeal it will notify the appellant of its decision and its reasons. If the refusal is made without a hearing the appellant can apply in writing for the decision to be reconsidered at a hearing. The application must be received by the Tribunal within 14 days after the date that written notice of its decision was sent. This rule applies also where the Tribunal gives permission on limited grounds or subject to conditions without a hearing.

If the Tribunal grants permission, the application for permission is then normally treated as a notice of appeal, and the case will proceed accordingly. If all the parties agree, the appeal can be determined without obtaining any further response.

[*SI 2008 No 2698, Rules 21, 22; SI 2009 No 274, Rule 14; SI 2009 No 1975, Rules 15, 16*].

Notice of appeal

[5.26] If the First-tier Tribunal gives permission to appeal to the Upper Tribunal (or the Upper Tribunal gives permission but directs that the application for permission should not be treated as a notice of appeal) an appellant can appeal to the Upper Tribunal by providing a notice of appeal. This must be received by the Tribunal within one month after the notice giving permission to appeal was sent.

The notice must include the grounds for appeal and state whether the appellant wants the application to be dealt with at a hearing. If the First-tier Tribunal gave permission to appeal, the notice must be accompanied by copies of any written record of the decision being challenged, any statement of reasons for that decision, and the notice of permission to appeal. Late applications must include a request for extension of time and the reason for lateness.

A copy of the notice and the documents provided will then be sent by the Upper Tribunal to the respondents who can provide a written response. The response must be received by the Tribunal not later than one month after the copy of the notice of appeal was sent. (Where an application for permission to appeal stands as the notice of appeal (see **5.25** above), the response must be received not later than one month after the Tribunal sent to the respondent notice that if had granted permission to appeal.)

The response must indicate whether the respondent opposes the appeal, and if so, the grounds for opposition (which can include grounds which were unsuccessful before the First-tier Tribunal) and whether the respondent wants the case to be dealt with at a hearing. Late responses must include a request for extension of time and the reason for lateness.

A copy of the response and any documents provided will then be sent by the Tribunal to the appellant and any other parties to the case who can, in turn, provide a written reply. The reply must be received by the Tribunal within one month of the date the Tribunal sent the copy of the respondent's response.

[*SI 2008 No 2698, Rules 23–25; SI 2009 No 1975, Rules 17, 18*].

Other cases before the Upper Tribunal

[5.27] Where a case has been transferred or referred to the Upper Tribunal from the First-tier Tribunal (see **5.16** above) or where a case is started by direct application to the Upper Tribunal, the Upper Tribunal will determine by direction the procedure for considering and disposing of the case. [*SI 2008 No 2698, Rule 26A; SI 2009 No 274, Rule 16; SI 2009 No 1975, Rule 19*].

The hearing

[5.28] The Upper Tribunal can make any decision with or without a hearing, but in deciding whether to hold a hearing, it must have regard to any view expressed by any party to the case.

Each party is normally entitled to attend the hearing and the Upper Tribunal must give reasonable notice of its time and place. At least 14 days' notice must normally be given except in urgent or exceptional circumstances or with the consent of the parties. In application for permission to bring judicial review cases, the notice period must normally be at least two days.

Hearings are normally held in public, but the Tribunal can direct that a hearing, or part of it, should be held in private.

[*SI 2008 No 2698, Rules 34–37; SI 2009 No 274, Rule 19; SI 2009 No 1975, Rule 29*].

Failure to attend hearing

If a party fails to attend a hearing, the Upper Tribunal can nevertheless proceed with the hearing if it considers that it is in the interests of justice to do so. The Tribunal must be satisfied that the party was notified of the hearing or that reasonable steps were taken to notify the party. [*SI 2008 No 2698, Rule 38*].

Evidence and witnesses

Similar rules apply in relation to evidence, submission and witnesses as apply to the First-tier Tribunal. See *SI 2008 No 2698, Rules 15, 16* and **5.17** above.

The Upper Tribunal's decision

[5.29] If the Upper Tribunal decides that the First-tier Tribunal's decision involved an error on a point of law it can set aside that decision and either remit the case back to the First-tier Tribunal or remake the decision itself.

If it remits the case to the First-tier Tribunal, the Upper Tribunal can direct that the case is reheard by different members.

If it decides to remake the decision itself, the Upper Tribunal is free to make any decision that the First-tier Tribunal could make if it were rehearing the case (see **5.18** above) and can make such findings of fact as it considers appropriate.

[*TCEA 2007, s 12*].

The Upper Tribunal can give its decision orally at a hearing or in writing. In either case it will give each party a decision notice in writing as soon as practicable. The notice will include written reasons for the decision unless the decision was made with the consent of the parties or the parties have consented to the Tribunal not giving written reasons. The notice will also inform the party of any further right of appeal. [*SI 2008 No 2698, Rule 40; SI 2009 No 274, Rule 21; SI 2009 No 1975, Rule 21*].

Consent orders

The case can also be settled by the Upper Tribunal making a consent order where the parties have reached agreement. Such an order is made at the request of the parties but only if the Tribunal considers it appropriate to do so. No hearing is necessary if such an order is made. [*SI 2008 No 2698, Rule 39; SI 2009 No 274, Rule 20*].

Correction of mistakes in a decision

Identical provisions to those applicable to decisions by the First-tier Tribunal apply to decisions of the Upper Tribunal. See *SI 2008 No 2698, Rule 42* and **5.19** above. Setting aside a decision. Virtually identical provisions to those applicable to decisions by the First-tier Tribunal apply to decisions of the Upper Tribunal. An application for a decision to be set aside must be received by the Upper Tribunal no later than one month after the date on which the Tribunal sent the decision notice. See *SI 2008 No 2698, Rule 43* and **5.19** above.

Appeal against the Tribunal's decision

[5.30] A further appeal to the Court of Appeal (in Scotland, the Court of Session) can be made against the Upper Tribunal's decision. The appeal can be made only on a point of law and the Tribunal will give permission to appeal only if the appeal would raise some important point of principle or practice or there is some other compelling reason for the Court to hear it.

A person wishing to appeal must make a written application to the Tribunal for permission to appeal. Such an application must be received by the Tribunal within one month after the date the Tribunal sent written reasons for the decision to that person. Where a decision has been amended or corrected following a review (see below) or an application (other than a late application) for a decision to be struck out has been unsuccessful (see **5.24** above), the one month limit runs from the date on which the Tribunal sent the notification of amended reasons or correction of the decision or of the failure of the striking out application.

The application must identify the alleged errors of law in the decision and state the result sought. Late applications must include a request for extension of time and the reason for lateness.

On receiving an application, the Upper Tribunal will first consider whether to review the decision. It can do so only if either it overlooked a legislative provision or binding authority which could have affected the decision or if a court has subsequently made a decision which is binding on the Upper Tribunal and could have affected the decision.

The Tribunal will notify the parties of the outcome of a review. If it decides to take any action following a review without first giving every party an opportunity to make representations, the notice must state that any party not given such an opportunity can apply for the action to be set aside and for the decision to be reviewed again.

If the Tribunal decides not to review the decision or, following a review, decides to take no action, it will then consider whether to give permission to appeal. It will send a record of its decision to the parties as soon as practicable together with, where it decides not to give permission, a statements of its reasons for refusal and details of the right to apply directly to the court for permission to appeal (see **5.32** below). The Tribunal's permission can be in respect of part only of the decision or on limited grounds.

[*TCEA 2007, s 13; SI 2008 No 2698, Rules 44–46; SI 2008 No 2834*].

See **5.21** above for the payment of tax pending an appeal from a decision of the Upper Tribunal.

Award of costs

[5.31] The Upper Tribunal can make an order awarding costs (or, in Scotland, expenses):

(a)   in proceedings on appeal from the Tax Chamber of the First-tier Tribunal
(b)   in judicial review cases (see **5.34** below);
(c)   in cases transferred from the Tax Chamber of the First-tier Tribunal
(d)   under *TCEA 2007, s 29(4)* (wasted costs — see **5.22** above); or
(e)   where the Tribunal considers that a party or representative has acted unreasonably in bringing, defending or conducting the case.

Before making an order for costs, the Tribunal must give the person who will have to pay them the chance to make representations. If the payer is an individual, it must consider his financial means.

The Tribunal can make an order on its own initiative or on an application from one of the parties. Such an application must be sent both to the Tribunal and to the person from whom costs are sought, together with a schedule of the costs claimed. An application must be made no later than one month after the date on which the Tribunal sends the notice recording the decision which finally disposes of all the issues in the case.

The amount of costs will be decided either by agreement of the parties, by summary assessment by the Tribunal or, if not agreed, by assessment. Where the amount is to be decided by assessment, either the payer or the person to whom the costs are to be paid can apply to a county court, the High Court or the Costs Office of the Supreme Court for a detailed assessment of the costs on the standard basis or, where the Tribunal's order so specifies, the indemnity basis.

[*SI 2008 No 2698, Rule 1; SI 2009 No 274, Rule 7*].

Appeal to the Court of Appeal

[5.32] As noted at **5.30** above a party who disagrees with a decision of the Upper Tribunal can ask the Tribunal for permission to appeal to the Court of Appeal (in Scotland, the Court of Session). The appeal can be made only on a point of law.

If the Tribunal refuses permission, the party can seek permission to appeal directly from the Court. The Court will give permission only if the appeal would raise some important point of principle or practice or there is some other compelling reason for the Court to hear it.

[*TCEA 2007, s 13; SI 2008 No 2834*].

There are no tax-specific rules governing the making of applications for permission to appeal or for notifying appeals where permission has been given by the Court or Upper Tribunal. The *Civil Procedure Rules 1998, SI 1998 No 3132* therefore apply.

The Court's decision. If the Court finds that the decision of the Upper Tribunal involved an error on a point of law it can set aside the decision. It must then either remake the decision itself or remit the case back to either the Upper Tribunal or the First-tier Tribunal, with directions for its reconsideration. Those directions can include a direction that the case is to be re-heard by different Tribunal members.

Where the case is remitted to the Upper Tribunal, it can itself decide to remit the case to the First-tier Tribunal.

If the Court decides to remake the decision itself, it can make any decision that the Upper Tribunal or first-tier Tribunal could have made, and can make such findings of fact as it considers appropriate.

[*TCEA 2007, s 14*].

Case law

The following cases relate to the pre-1 April 2009 appeal process (which involved initial appeal to the High Court rather than the Court of Appeal) but remain relevant to the new process.

Withdrawal etc.

Once set down for hearing, a case cannot be declared a nullity (*Way v Underdown* CA 1974, 49 TC 215) or struck out under *Order 18, Rule 19 of the Rules of the Supreme Court* (*Petch v Gurney* CA 1994, 66 TC 473), but the appellant may withdraw (*Hood Barrs v CIR (No 3)* CA 1960, 39 TC 209, but see *Bradshaw v Blunden (No 2)* Ch D 1960, 39 TC 73). Where the appellant was the inspector and the taxpayer did not wish to proceed, the Court refused to make an order on terms agreed between the parties (*Slaney v Kean* Ch D 1969, 45 TC 415).

Remission of cases to Tribunal

In *Consolidated Goldfields plc v CIR* Ch D 1990, 63 TC 333, the taxpayer company's request that the High Court remit a case to the Commissioners for further findings of fact was refused. Although the remedy was properly sought, it would only be granted if it could be shown that the desired findings were (a) material to some tenable argument, (b) reasonably open on the evidence adduced, and (c) not inconsistent with the findings already made. However, in *Fitzpatrick v CIR* CS 1990, [1991] STC 34, a case was remitted where the facts found proved or admitted, and the contentions of the parties, were not clearly set out, despite the taxpayer's request for various amendments and insertions to the case, and in *Whittles v Uniholdings Ltd (No 1)* Ch D, [1993] STC 671, remission was appropriate in view of the widely differing interpretations which the parties sought to place on the Commissioners' decision (and the case was remitted a second time (see [1993] STC 767) to resolve misunderstandings as to the nature of a concession made by the Crown at the original hearing and apparent inconsistencies in the Commissioners' findings of fact). If a case is remitted, the taxpayer had the right to attend any further hearing by the Commissioners (*Lack v Doggett* CA 1970, 46 TC 497) but the Commissioners could not, in the absence of special circumstances, admit further evidence (*Archer-Shee v Baker* CA 1928, 15 TC 1; *Watson v Samson Bros* Ch D 1959, 38 TC 346; *Bradshaw v Blunden (No 2)* Ch D 1960, 39 TC 73), but see *Brady v Group Lotus Car Companies plc* CA 1987, 60 TC 359 where the Court directed the Commissioners to admit further evidence where new facts had come to light suggesting the taxpayers had deliberately misled the Commissioners. Errors of fact in the case may be amended by agreement of the parties prior to hearing of the case (*Moore v Austin* Ch D 1985, 59 TC 110). See *Jeffries v Stevens* Ch D 1982, 56 TC 134 as regards delay between statement of case and motion for remission.

Appeal restricted to point of law

Many court decisions turn on whether the Commissioners' decision was one of fact supported by the evidence, and hence final. The courts will not disturb a finding of fact if there was reasonable evidence for it, notwithstanding that the evidence might support a different conclusion of fact. The leading case is *Edwards v Bairstow & Harrison* HL 1955, 36 TC 207, in which the issue was whether there had been an adventure in the nature of trade. The Commissioners' decision was reversed on the ground that the only reasonable conclusion from the evidence was that there had been such an adventure. For a recent discussion of the application of this principle, see *Milnes v J Beam Group Ltd* Ch D 1975, 50 TC 675.

A new question of law may be raised in the courts on giving due notice to the other parties (*Muir v CIR* CA 1966, 43 TC 367) but the courts will neither admit evidence not in the stated case (*Watson v Samson Bros* Ch D 1959, 38 TC 346; *Cannon Industries Ltd v Edwards* Ch D 1965, 42 TC 625; *Frowd v Whalley* Ch D 1965, 42 TC 599, and see *R v Great Yarmouth Commrs (ex p. Amis)* QB 1960, 39 TC 143) nor consider contentions of which evidence in support was not produced before the Commissioners (*Denekamp v Pearce* Ch D 1998, 71 TC 213).

Use of Parliamentary material

Following the decision in *Pepper v Hart* HL 1992, 65 TC 421, the courts are prepared to consider the parliamentary history of legislation, or the official reports of debates in Hansard, where all of the following conditions are met.

- Legislation is ambiguous or obscure, or leads to an absurdity.
- The material relied upon consists of one or more statements by a Minister or other promoter of the Bill together if necessary with such other parliamentary material as is necessary to understand such statements and their effect.
- The statements relied upon are clear.

Any party intending to refer to an extract from Hansard in support of any argument must, unless otherwise directed, serve copies of the extract and a brief summary of the argument intended to be based upon the extract upon all parties and the court not less than five clear working days before the first day of the hearing (Supreme Court Practice Note, 20 December 1994) (1995 STI 98).

Status of decision

A court decision is a binding precedent for itself or an inferior court except that the House of Lords, while treating its former decisions as normally binding, may depart from a previous decision should it appear right to do so. For this see *Fitzleet Estates Ltd v Cherry* HL 1977, 51 TC 708. Scottish decisions are not binding on the High Court but are normally followed. Decisions of the Privy Council and of the Irish Courts turning on comparable legislation are treated with respect. A court decision does not affect other assessments already final and conclusive (see **5.6** assessments) but may be followed, if relevant, in the determination of any open appeals against assessments and in assessments made subsequently irrespective of the years of assessment or taxpayers concerned (*Re Waring decd* Ch D, [1948] 1 All ER 257; *Gwyther v Boslymon Quarries Ltd* KB 1950, 29 ATC 1; *Bolands Ltd v CIR* SC(I) 1925, 4 ATC 526). Further, a court decision does not prevent the Crown from proceeding on a different basis for other years (*Hood Barrs v CIR (No 3)* CA 1960, 39 TC 209). A general change of practice consequent on a court decision may affect error or mistake relief (see **18.8** claims).

For joinder of CIR in non-tax disputes, see In re *Vandervell's Trusts* HL 1970, 46 TC 341.

Appeals open on 1 April 2009

[5.33] Appeals made before 1 April 2009 are, in general, dealt with on and after that date under the process outlined at **5.4** onwards above. The following special rules apply, however, to deal with the transition to the new regime.

HMRC review

A review by HMRC of its decision (see **5.5** above) can be requested or sought if neither the appellant nor HMRC have served notice on the Appeal Commissioners requesting a hearing before 1 April 2009.

Where a review is required or offered before 1 April 2010, HMRC have 90 days within which to give notice of their conclusions (rather than the normal 45 days).

[SI 2009 No 56, Sch 3 para 5].

Hearing requested before 1 April 2009

Where either HMRC or the appellant notified the Appeal Commissioners requesting a hearing before 1 April 2009, the proceedings continue on and after that date before the Tribunal. (If a hearing was actually under way, but was not concluded, on 31 March 2009, it continued on 1 April 2009 as a Tribunal hearing, with the same Commissioners acting as members of the Tribunal.)

The Tribunal can give directions to ensure that the case is dealt with fairly and justly, in particular by applying the procedural rules applicable before 1 April 2009 and disapplying those applying from that date. Directions in force immediately before 1 April 2009 continue in force on and after that date. Any time period (such as for the delivery of particulars) which began but did not expire before 1 April 2009 continues to apply after that date.

The Tribunal can award costs only if, and to the extent that, costs could have been awarded before 1 April 2009. Costs cannot therefore be awarded where the appeal was to the General Commissioners and, if the appeal was to the Special Commissioners, can be awarded only against a party who has, in their opinion, acted wholly unreasonably in connection with the hearing (see **5.37** below).

[SI 2009 No 56, Sch 3 paras 6, 7].

Cases to be remitted by courts

Any case heard by the Appeal Commissioners before 1 April 2009 which is to be remitted by a court on or after that date is remitted to the Tribunal. *[SI 2009 No 56, Sch 3 para 8]*.

Commissioners' decision made before 1 April 2009. Where a decision has been made by the Appeal Commissioners and immediately before 1 April 2009 there is a right of appeal to a court against that decision the same rights of appeal apply as apply in respect of a decision of the First-tier Tribunal (so that, initially, appeal will be to the Upper Tribunal).

Where, however, a party to a case decided by the General Commissioners before 1 April 2009 has, before that date, initiated an appeal to the High Court using the stated case procedure, the appeal will proceed to the High Court under that procedure (see **5.39** below). The General Commissioners concerned will be required to state and sign a case notwithstanding the general abolition of the Commissioners with effect from 1 April 2009.

Similarly the rules governing the correction of irregularities and the reviewing of a decision continue to apply to decisions of General Commissioners made before 1 April 2009. Again, the General Commissioners continue to function for that purpose notwithstanding their general abolition. See **5.38** below.

[SI 2008 No 2696, Art 3; SI 2009 No 56, Sch 3 para 11].

Judicial review

[5.34] A taxpayer who is dissatisfied with the exercise of administrative powers may in certain circumstances (e.g. where HMRC has exceeded or abused its powers or acted contrary to the rules of natural justice, or where the Tribunal has acted unfairly or improperly) seek a remedy in a mandatory or prohibiting order or a quashing order. This is done by way of application for judicial review to the High Court under *Supreme Court Act 1981, s 31* and *Part 54 of the Civil Procedure Rules*. With effect from 1 April 2009, the High Court can in certain cases transfer an application for judicial review or for leave to apply for judicial review to the Upper Tribunal (see *Supreme Court Act 1981, s 31A*).

The issue on an application for leave to apply for judicial review is whether there is an arguable case (*R v CIR (ex p Howmet Corporation and another)* QB, [1994] STC 413). The procedure is generally used where no other, adequate, remedy, such as a right of appeal, is available. See *R v Special Commrs (ex p Stipplechoice Ltd) (No 1)* CA 1985, 59 TC 396, *R v HMIT (ex p Kissane and Another)* QB, [1986] STC 152, *R v Sevenoaks Commrs (ex p Thorne)* QB 1989, 62 TC 341, *R v Hastings and Bexhill General Commrs and CIR (ex p Goodacre)* QB 1994, 67 TC 126 and *R v CIR (ex p Ulster Bank Ltd)* CA 1997, 69 TC 211.

There is a very long line of cases in which the courts have consistently refused applications where a matter should have been pursued through the ordinary channels as described above. See, for example, *R v Special Commrs (ex p Morey)* CA 1972, 49 TC 71; *R v Special Commrs (ex p Emery)* QB 1980, 53 TC 555; *R v Walton General Commrs (ex p Wilson)* CA, [1983] STC 464; *R v Special Commrs (ex p Esslemont)* CA, 1984 STI 312; *R v Brentford Commrs (ex p Chan)* QB 1985, 57 TC 651; *R v CIR (ex p Caglar)* QB 1995, 67 TC 335. See also, however, *R v HMIT and Others (ex p Lansing Bagnall Ltd)* CA 1986, 61 TC 112 for a successful application where the inspector issued a notice under a discretionary power on the footing that there was a mandatory obligation to do so, and *R v Ward, R v Special Commr (ex p Stipplechoice Ltd) (No 3)* QB 1988, 61 TC 391, where insufficient notice was given of revision of an accounting period under *ICTA 1988, s 12(8)* prior to appeal hearing.

In *R v CIR (ex p J Rothschild Holdings)* CA 1987, 61 TC 178, the Revenue were required to produce internal documents of a general character relating to their practice in applying a statutory provision, but in *R v CIR (ex p Taylor)* CA 1988, 62 TC 562 discovery of internal Revenue correspondence was refused as there was no material indication that it had any bearing on the question of whether the decision taken by the inspector could be challenged. In *R v CIR (ex p Unilever plc)* CA 1996, 68 TC 205, an application for judicial review for a Revenue decision to refuse a late loss relief claim was successful. The Revenue's refusal was 'so unreasonable as to be, in public law terms, irrational' in view of an administrative procedure established with the company over many years of raising assessments on estimates of net taxable profits, adjusted when the final accounts became available without regard to the loss claim time limit. A confirmation by the local inspector that capital allowances were available in relation to an enterprise zone property trust scheme was not binding where the promoters were aware that clearance applications were required to be made to a specialist department, and failed to disclose that the scheme involved 'artificial provisions' (*R v CIR (ex p Matrix-Securities Ltd)* HL 1994, 66 TC 587). As regards informal advice by the Revenue generally, they were not bound by anything less than a clear, unambiguous and unqualified representation (*R v CIR (ex p MFK Underwriting Agencies Ltd)* QB 1989, 62 TC 607), and in *R v CIR (ex p Bishopp and another)* QB, [1999] STC 531, an application for judicial review of informal advice given by the Revenue in relation to a proposed transaction was refused. See generally **34.6** HMRC — ADMINISTRATION. See also *R v CIR (ex p Camacq Corporation)* CA 1989, 62 TC 651, where a Revenue decision to revoke its authorisation to pay a dividend gross was upheld; *R v CIR (ex p S G Warburg & Co Ltd)* QB 1994, 68 TC 300, where a decision not to apply a published practice was upheld; *R (oao Bamber) v HMRC* QB 2005, [2006] STC 1035, where a Revenue decision to resile from a written agreement was upheld as being in the public interest; and *R (oao Huitson) v HMRC* QB, [2010] STC 715, where the court rejected the claimant's contention that retrospective tax legislation was in breach of *Human Rights Act 1998*. (In the Bamber case a subsequent claim for damages was rejected (*R (oao Bamber) v HMRC (No 2)* QB, [2008] STC 1864).)

The underlying facts in *Carvill v CIR (No 3)* Ch D, [2002] STC 1167 were that in two separate appeals relating to different tax years, income from an identical source had been held liable to tax for some years (the earlier years) but not others. An appeal against the Revenue's refusal to refund tax, and interest on tax, paid for the earlier years was rejected; the assessments for those years were valid assessments which the Special Commissioner in question had had jurisdiction to determine, and the taxpayer the right to challenge, and those assessments had not been set aside. An application for judicial review on the grounds that the Revenue's refusal to repay was unfair was dismissed (*Carvill (R oao) v CIR* QB 2003, 75 TC 477).

See **38.11** HMRC INVESTIGATORY POWERS as regards challenges to the validity of notices under *TMA 1970, s 20*.

The first step is to obtain leave to apply for judicial review from the High Court. Application for leave is made ex parte to a single judge who will usually determine the application without a hearing. The Court will not grant leave unless the applicant has a sufficient interest in the matter to which the application relates. See *CIR v National Federation of Self-employed and Small Businesses Ltd* HL 1981, 55 TC 133 for what is meant by 'sufficient interest' and for discussion of availability of judicial review generally, and cf. *R v A-G (ex p ICI plc)* CA 1986, 60 TC 1.

Time limit

Applications must be made **within three months** of the date when the grounds for application arose. The Court has discretion to extend this time limit where there is good reason, but is generally very reluctant to do so. See e.g. *R v HMIT (ex p Brumfield and Others)* QB 1988, 61 TC 589 and *R v CIR (ex p Allen)* QB 1997, 69 TC 442. Grant of leave to apply for review does not amount to a ruling that application was made in good time (*R v Tavistock Commrs (ex p Worth)* QB 1985, 59 TC 116).

Costs

[5.35] Costs may be awarded by the Courts in the usual way. In suitable cases, e.g. 'test cases', HMRC may undertake to pay the taxpayer's costs. See **5.22** and **5.31** above for the award of costs by the First-tier and Upper Tribunals. See **5.37** above as regards costs awarded by the Special Commissioners. Costs awarded by the Courts may include expenses connected with the drafting of the stated case (*Manchester Corporation v Sugden* CA 1903, 4 TC 595). Costs of a discontinued application for judicial review were refused where the Revenue was not informed of the application (*R v CIR ex p Opman International UK* QB 1985, 59 TC 352). Law costs of appeals not allowable for tax purposes (*Allen v Farquharson* KB 1932, 17 TC 59; *Rushden Heel and Smith's Potato cases* HL 1948, 30 TC 298 & 267, and see *Spofforth* KB 1945, 26 TC 310).

The appeal process before 1 April 2009

[5.36] As noted at **5.33** above, appeals made before 1 April 2009 but not concluded before that date generally transfer into the new system. The detailed procedures applying before 1 April 2009 are therefore not covered in this work. A brief summary of the rules is given at **5.37** below; for full details see the 2008/09 edition.

Certain provisions relating to decisions made by the General Commissioners before 1 April 2009 do, however, remain relevant in transitional cases as described at **5.33** above. These provisions are covered in detail at **5.37–5.39** below.

Summary of process

[5.37] Before 1 April 2009 there was no HMRC review procedure, so that appeals were settled either by agreement (see **5.8** above) or by determination by the Appeal Commissioners. Appeals were normally to the General Commissioners, subject to specific statutory exceptions and subject also to the appellant's limited right of election to bring an appeal before the Special Commissioners.

The procedures for appeals hearings were governed by regulations: see *SI 1994 No 1812* for cases before the General Commissioners and *SI 1994 No 1811* for cases before the Special Commissioners.

General Commissioners

General Commissioners were appointed by the Lord Chancellor and required no legal qualifications. The Commissioners were appointed to local divisions, each with its own Clerk, usually a local solicitor, who attended meetings to take minutes and give advice. Proceedings in a particular case would be heard by between two and five Commissioners. Any party to the proceedings could serve notice on the Clerk that he wished a date for a hearing to be fixed, although in practice it was usually HMRC which did so.

The Commissioners' powers to make a decision in an appeal were broadly the same as those of the First-tier Tribunal — see **5.18** above. Their decision was final and conclusive, subject to the correction of irregularities, any application for review or any further appeal. [*TMA 1970, ss 46(2), 50 as previously enacted; SI 1994 No 1812, Regs 17, 24*].

Further appeal on a point of law was initially to the High Court (in Scotland the Court of Session) through the case stated procedure: see **5.39** below. Further appeal could then be made to the Court of Appeal and thence (with leave) to the House of Lords.

There was no provision for the award of costs in General Commissioners' cases.

Special Commissioners

Special Commissioners were appointed by the Lord Chancellor and were required to satisfy certain requirements as to legal qualifications and experience. They heard cases only in a small number of locations, each case being heard by one, two or three Commissioners.

Appeal against a decision of the Special Commissioners on a point of law was to the High Court (in Scotland the Court of Session). Further appeal could be made to the Court of Appeal and thence (with leave) to the House of Lords.

The Special Commissioners could make an order awarding costs (in Scotland expenses) of, or incidental to, the hearing of any proceedings against any party who had, in their opinion, acted wholly unreasonably in connection with the hearing, but not without giving that party the opportunity of making representations against the award. The award could be of all or part of the costs of the other party or parties, such costs to be taxed in the county court (in Scotland the sheriff court) if not agreed. [*SI 1994 No 1811, Reg 21*]. For this purpose an act 'in connection with the hearing' included any action taken once the appeal has been consigned by one or both parties to the Special Commissioners (*Carter v Hunt* 1999 (Sp C 220), [2000] SSCD 17). Failure by the taxpayer to attend or be represented at the hearing without giving prior notification could be a contributory factor in an award of costs, as could a failure to comply with a Commissioners' direction (*Phillips v Burrows* 1998 (Sp C 229, 229A), [2000] SSCD 107, 112).

For cases in which costs were awarded, see *Scott and another (trading as Farthings Steak House) v McDonald* (Sp C 91), [1996] SSCD 381, *Robertson v CIR (No 2)* (Sp C 313), [2002] SSCD 242, *Jones v Garnett* (Sp C 432), [2005] SSCD 9, *Carvill v Frost* (Sp C 447), [2005] SSCD 208 and *Oriel Support Ltd v HMRC* (Sp C 615) [2007] SSCD 670 (on taxpayer application) and *Phillips v Burrows* (Sp C 229A), [2000] SSCD 112, *Morris and another v Roberts* (Sp C 407), [2004] SSCD 245 and *Businessman v HMRC* (Sp C 702), [2008] SSCD 1151 (on Inland Revenue/HMRC application).

For cases in which costs were refused, see *Salt v Young* (Sp C 205), [1999] SSCD 249 and *Nightswood BV v HMRC* (Sp C 651), [2008] SSCD 651 (on Inland Revenue/HMRC application) and *Carter v Hunt* (Sp C 220), [2000] SSCD 17, *Self-assessed v Inspector of Taxes (No 2)* (Sp C 224), [2000] SSCD

47, *Powell v Jackman* (Sp C 338), [2002] SSCD 488, *Lavery v Macleod (No 2)* (Sp C 375), [2003] SSCD 413, *Conlon v Hewitt* (Sp C 436), [2005] SSCD 46, *Collins and another v Laing* (Sp C 472), [2005] SSCD 453, *McEwan v O'Donoghue (No 2)* (Sp C 488), [2005] SSCD 681 (in which it was held that whilst in principle the Revenue had acted wholly unreasonably, the result of the appeal had been that each party had succeeded in roughly equal amounts) and *Kidney and others v HMRC* (Sp C 558), [2006] SSCD 660 (on taxpayer application).

Only in 'a very rare case' would the Court interfere with the Commissioners' decision as regards costs (see *Gamble v Rowe* Ch D 1998, 71 TC 190, where a refusal of costs was upheld). There is nothing to prevent costs being awarded on the indemnity basis (*Carvill v Frost (No 2)* (Sp C 468), [2005] SSCD 422).

General Commissioners' decisions — transitional provisions

[5.38] As indicated at **5.33** above, where a decision was made by the General Commissioners on or before 31 March 2009 certain provisions continue to apply after that date. The Commissioners must continue to operate their functions under the provisions, despite their general abolition with effect from 1 April 2009. The provisions are as follows.

Review of the Commissioners' final determination

The Commissioners may review and set aside or vary a final determination made before 1 April 2009 on the application of any party or of their own motion where they are satisfied that either:

- it was wrongly made as a result of administrative error, or
- a party entitled to be heard failed to appear or be represented for good and sufficient reason, or
- relevant information had been supplied to the Clerk or to the appropriate inspector or other HMRC officer prior to the hearing but was not received by the Commissioners until after the hearing.

A written application for such a review must be made to the Commissioners not later than 14 days after the date of the notice of the determination (or by such later time as the Commissioners may allow), stating the grounds in full. Where the Commissioners propose of their own motion to review a determination, they must serve notice on the parties not later than 14 days after the date of the notice of the determination.

The parties are entitled to be heard on any such review or proposed review. If practicable, the review is to be determined by the Commissioners who decided the case, and if they set aside the determination, they may substitute a different determination or order a rehearing before the same or different Commissioners. A decision to vary or substitute a final determination is to be notified in the same way as the original determination (see above).

[*SI 1994 No 1812, Reg 17; SI 2008 No 2696, Art 4; SI 2009 No 56, Sch 3 para 11*].

Irregularities

Although irregularities resulting from failure to comply with regulations or with any Commissioners' direction did not of themselves, render the proceedings void, any of the Commissioners concerned (or the Clerk if all the Commissioners have died or ceased to be Commissioners) can correct clerical errors in any document recording a direction or decision by certificate under his hand. [*SI 1994 No 1812, Reg 24; SI 2008 No 2696, Art 4; SI 2009 No 56, Sch 3 para 11*].

Appeal to the High Court by case stated procedure

[5.39] Within 30 days of the date of final determination before 1 April 2009 of an appeal any party dissatisfied with the determination as being erroneous in point of law may, before 1 April 2009, serve notice on the Clerk requiring the Commissioners to state and sign a case for the opinion of the High Court (in Scotland the Court of Session), setting forth the facts and final determination of the Commissioners. See *Grainger v Singer* KB 1927, 11 TC 704 as regards receipt of the case. The 30-day time limit for requesting a case does not apply to the payment of the fee (*Anson v Hill* CA 1968, 47 ATC 143). (Where no application for a stated case is made before 1 April 2009, the right of appeal against the Commissioners' decision is the same as that against a decision of the First-tier Tribunal — see **5.33** above.)

The Commissioners may serve notice on the person who required the stated case requiring him, within a specified period of not less than 28 days, to identify the question of law on which he requires the case to be stated. They may refuse to state a case until such notice is complied with, or if they are not satisfied that a question of law is involved, or if the requisite fee (see below) has not been paid. A requirement for a case to be stated becomes invalid if the determination to which it relates is set aside or varied. The case stated procedure does not apply to a final determination by the General Commissioners of an appeal in which a question has been referred to another Tribunal (the Lands Tribunal or the Special Commissioners) and all appeal rights have been exhausted. [*SI 1994 No 1812, Regs 20, 23; SI 1999 No 3293, Reg 6; SI 2008 No 2696, Art 4; SI 2009 No 56, Sch 3 para 11*].

A fee of £25 is payable to the Clerk by the person requiring the case before he is entitled to have it stated. [*TMA 1970, s 56(3) as previously enacted; SI 1994 No 1813; SI 2008 No 2696, Art 4; SI 2009 No 56, Sch 3 para 11*]. A single case may have effect as regards each of a number of appeals heard together (*Getty Oil Co v Steele and related appeals* Ch D 1990, 63 TC 376).

If the taxpayer dies, his personal representatives stand in his shoes (*Smith v Williams* KB 1921, 8 TC 321).

The case stated procedure is not open to a successful party to an appeal (*Sharpey-Schafer v Venn* Ch D 1955, 34 ATC 141), but where another party requires a case, the successful party may invite the Commissioners to include in the case an additional question relating to another ground on which the Commissioners had found against it (*Gordon v CIR* CS 1991, 64 TC 173).

In the case of a partnership, the procedure is available to any one of the partners, with or without the consent of the others (*Sutherland & Partners v Barnes and Another* CA 1994, 66 TC 663).

Consideration of draft case

Within 56 days of receipt of a notice requiring a stated case (or of the Commissioners being satisfied as to the question of law involved), the Clerk must send a draft of the case to all the parties. Written representations thereon may be made to the Clerk by any party within 56 days after the draft case is sent out, with copies to all the other parties, and within a further 28 days further representations may similarly be made in response. Any party to whom copies of representations are not sent may apply to the Clerk for a copy. The validity of a case after it has been stated and signed, and of any subsequent proceedings, is not affected by a failure to meet these time limits or by a failure to send copies of representations to all parties. [*SI 1994 No 1812, Reg 21; SI 2008 No 2696, Art 4; SI 2009 No 56, Sch 3 para 11*].

An application for the taxpayer's name to be withheld was refused (In re *H Ch D 1964, 42 TC 14*) as was an application for the deletion of a passage possibly damaging the taxpayer (*Treharne v Guinness Exports Ltd* Ch D 1967, 44 TC 161). An application for judicial review on the ground that the case did not cover all matters in dispute was refused in *R v Special Commrs (ex p. Napier)* CA 1988, 61 TC 206. In *Danquah v CIR* Ch D 1990, 63 TC 526, an application for the statement of a further case was refused where the case did not set out all the questions raised by the taxpayer in the originating motion by which he had sought an order directing the Commissioners to state a case. See also *Consolidated Goldfields plc v CIR* Ch D 1990, 63 TC 333 in which a request to remit a case to the Commissioners for further findings of fact was refused.

Preparation and submission of final case

As soon as may be after the final date for representations, the Commissioners, after taking into account any representations, must state and sign the case. In the event of the death of a Commissioner, or of his ceasing to be a Commissioner, the case is to be signed by the remaining Commissioner(s) or, if there are none, by the Clerk. The case is then sent by the Clerk to the person who required it to be stated, and the other parties notified accordingly.

In England, Wales and Scotland, the party requiring the case must transmit it to the High Court (in Scotland, the Court of Session) within 30 days of receiving it, and at or before the time he does so must notify each of the other parties that the case has been stated on his application and send them a copy of the case. The 30 day time limit (under the similar earlier provisions of *TMA 1970, s 56(4)*) is mandatory (*Valleybright Ltd (in liquidation) v Richardson* Ch D 1984, 58 TC 290; *Petch v Gurney* CA 1994, 66 TC 473), may run from the date the case is received by the taxpayer's authorised agent (*Brassington v Guthrie Ch D 1991, 64 TC 435*), and requires the case to be *received* by the High Court within the 30 days (*New World Medical Ltd v Cormack* Ch D, [2002] STC 1245). The notification (and copy) to the other parties is required only to give 'adequate notice' of the appeal and not to be 'too long delayed' (*Hughes v Viner* Ch D 1985, 58 TC 437). In Northern Ireland, slightly different rules apply (and see *CIR v McGuckian CA(NI)* 1994, 69 TC 1).

[*SI 1994 No 1812, Regs 22, 23; SI 2008 No 2696, Art 4; SI 2009 No 56, Sch 3 para 11*].

Key points

[5.40] Points to consider are as follows.

- Those wishing to lodge an appeal will be responsible for notifying the Tribunal under the new system, rather than HMRC. Those handling cases for clients should be aware of this aspect of the process.
- Notice of appeal is now initially made to the HMRC officer dealing with the case.
- Prior to the case being passed to the Tribunal the taxpayer can request HMRC to carry out a review, or HMRC may offer to carry out a review.
- HMRC's offer of a review is preceded by written notification of their view or decision on the matter. The appellant has only 30 days to accept the offer of a review or notify the Tribunal that he wishes to proceed to appeal. If he does neither within this time, HMRC's view becomes final and is deemed to form an agreement between the taxpayer and HMRC from which the appellant cannot withdraw. It is thus very important to react promptly to an offer of a review from HMRC.
- Early indications are that a significant proportion of reviews find wholly or mainly in favour of the taxpayer, so you may regard a review as a 'no-lose' option as the case can still proceed to Tribunal at the conclusion of the review.
- When an appeal has been allocated as a 'complex case' the appellant should ensure that a written notice is sent requesting that the case be excluded from potential costs or expenses, otherwise an award of costs may be made against him at the conclusion of the appeal.

6

Assessments

Cross-references. As regards particular assessments, see also **27 EMPLOYMENT INCOME** and **53 PAY AS YOU EARN** for assessments on employment income; **52 PARTNERSHIPS**; **68 SETTLEMENTS** for assessment on trust income.

Simon's Taxes. See A4.210, A4.3, A6.701–A6.704.

Introduction

[6.1] All assessments which are not self-assessments (see **65 SELF-ASSESSMENT**) must (unless otherwise provided) be made by an officer of HMRC, notice of such assessment to be served on the person assessed stating the date of issue and the time limit for making **APPEALS (5)**. The assessment may not then be altered except as expressly provided under the *Taxes Acts*. All income tax falling to be assessed other than by self-assessment may be included in a single assessment, notwithstanding that the liability may have arisen under more than one Part or Chapter of *ITEPA 2003* or *ITTOIA 2005*. [*TMA 1970, s 30A*].

Normal time limits

[6.2] The normal time limit for the making of an income tax assessment on or after 1 April 2010 is four years after the end of the tax year. Assessments made before 1 April 2010 had to be made within five years after 31 January following the tax year. [*TMA 1970, s 34(1); FA 2008, Sch 39 para 7; SI 2009 No 403*].

The latest time for assessing the personal representatives of a deceased person on or after 1 April 2010 is four years after the end of the tax year in which death occurred. Assessments made before 1 April 2010 had to be made within three years after 31 January following that tax year. [*TMA 1970, s 40(1); FA 2008, Sch 39 para 11(2); SI 2009 No 403*].

In relation to employment income, pension income or social security income chargeable to tax for 2004/05 or any subsequent year but received in a tax year later than that for which it is chargeable, an assessment made on or after 1 April 2010 can be made at any time within four years after the tax year in which the income is received. Assessments made before 1 April 2010 had to be made within six years after the end of that tax year. [*TMA 1970, s 35; FA 2008, Sch 39 para 8; SI 2009 No 403*].

In a case where the assessment relates to a tax year for which the taxpayer has not been given notice to make a return within one year after the end of the tax year (in effect, where the taxpayer is outside self-assessment), the above changes in the time limits for making assessments apply from 1 April 2012 rather than 1 April 2010. This only applies where tax has been *overpaid*, its purpose being to allow taxpayers extra time to take appropriate action. [*SI 2009 No 403, Art 10*].

For extended time limits in certain cases, see **6.3–6.5** below.

Extended time limits from 1 April 2010

[6.3] On and after 1 April 2010, the time limit for making an assessment on a person in a case involving a loss of income tax brought about 'carelessly' by that person (or by a person acting on his behalf) is no later than six years following the end of the tax year.

Also on and after 1 April 2010, the time limit for making an assessment on a person in a case involving a loss of income tax brought about deliberately by that person (or by a person acting on his behalf) is no later than 20 years following the end of the tax year.

The 20-year time limit also applies in the case of a loss of tax through failure to notify chargeability as in **55.2** penalties and in the case of a loss of tax attributable to arrangements in respect of which there has been a failure to comply with specified obligations to provide information to HMRC under **4.44–4.51** ANTI-AVOIDANCE (disclosure of tax avoidance schemes). In both cases, however, this does not apply where the tax year in question is 2008/09 or an earlier year unless the assessment is made for the purpose of making good a loss of tax attributable to the negligent conduct of the person assessed (or of a person acting on his behalf).

[*TMA 1970, s 36(1)(1A)(1B); FA 2008, Sch 39 para 9; SI 2009 No 403, Arts 2, 7*].

There is an overriding deadline for deceased persons — see **6.5** below.

For the above purposes, a loss of tax is brought about '*carelessly*' by a person if that person fails to take reasonable care to avoid bringing about that loss. Where information is provided to HMRC and the person who provided it (or the person on whose behalf it was provided) discovers later that it was inaccurate but then fails to take reasonable steps to inform HMRC, any loss of tax brought about by the inaccuracy is treated as having been brought about carelessly by that person.

References to a loss of tax brought about deliberately by a person include a loss of tax arising as a result of a deliberate inaccuracy in a document given to HMRC by or on behalf of that person.

[*TMA 1970, s 118(5)–(7); FA 2008, Sch 39 para 15*].

The extended time limits in new *TMA 1970, s 36(1)(1A)(1B)* above replace those previously provided for by *s 36* (see **6.4** below). Persons in partnership with a person responsible for a loss of tax as above may similarly be assessed in respect of additional partnership profits. If a person assessed so requires, the assessment may give effect to reliefs or allowances to which he would have been entitled had he made the necessary claims within the relevant time limits (excluding certain elections for the transfer of the married couple's allowance). The facility to claim late reliefs and allowances is similarly available in relation to an HMRC amendment to a personal or partnership tax return (see **63.9 RETURNS**).

[*TMA 1970, s 36(2)(3)(3A); FA 2008, Sch 39 para 9; SI 2009 No 403, Arts 2, 7*].

Any late assessment required to give effect to a late claim as above, or as a result of allowing such a claim, can be made within a year after the claim becomes final (i.e. becomes no longer capable of being varied, on appeal or otherwise); this applies to claims made as a consequence of either an assessment or an amendment to a return. [*TMA 1970, s 43C; FA 2008, Sch 39 para 14; SI 2009 No 403*].

Married couples and civil partners

Where total income is increased as a result of an extended time limit assessment as above, this does not affect the validity of any excess married couple's allowance or any blind person's allowance transferred between spouses or civil partners. In other words, the transferred allowance is not restored to the transferor. [*TMA 1970, s 37A; ITA 2007, Sch 1 para 252; FA 2008, Sch 39 para 10; SI 2009 No 403*].

Extended time limits before 1 April 2010

[6.4] In certain cases, as described below, extended limits apply to assessments for the purpose of making good a loss of tax. There is an overriding deadline for deceased persons — see **6.5** below. For the position on and after 1 April 2010, see **6.3** above.

Where the loss of tax arises due to the *fraudulent or negligent conduct* of a person (or of a person acting on his behalf), an assessment may be made at any time not later than 20 years after 31 January following the tax year to which it relates. Persons in partnership with a person responsible for fraudulent or negligent conduct may similarly be assessed in respect of additional partnership profits. If a person assessed so requires, the assessment may give effect to reliefs or allowances to which he would have been entitled had he made the necessary claims within the relevant time limits (excluding certain elections for the transfer of the married couple's allowance). [*TMA 1970, s 36; ITA 2007, Sch 1 para 251*]. The facility to claim late reliefs and allowances is similarly available in relation to an HMRC amendment to a personal or partnership tax return (see **63.9 RETURNS**). Also, any late assessment required to give effect to such a claim, or as a result of allowing such a claim, can be made within a year after the claim becomes final (i.e. becomes no longer capable of being varied, on appeal or otherwise); this applies to claims made as a consequence of either an assessment or an amendment to a return. [*TMA 1970, s 43C*].

For a case in which appeals against assessments raised out of the normal time limit were allowed on the grounds that, on the balance of probabilities, the Inland Revenue had not proved fraudulent or negligent conduct, see *York v Pickin* (Sp C 160), [1998] SSCD 138. For a case in which such appeals were allowed on the grounds that HMRC had failed to prove that there had been a loss of tax, see *Gaughan v HMRC* (Sp C 575), [2007] SSCD 148. For cases where 'fraudulent or negligent conduct' was found, see *Last Viceroy Restaurant v Jackson* Ch D, [2000] STC 1093; *Hurley v Taylor* CA 1998, 71 TC 268; *Hancock v CIR* (Sp C 213), [1999] SSCD 287; *Billows v Hammond* (Sp C 252), [2000] SSCD 430; and *Chartered Accountant v Inspector of Taxes* (Sp C 358), [2003] SSCD 166.

Married couples and civil partners

Where total income is increased as a result of fraudulent or negligent conduct assessments, this does not affect the validity of any excess married couple's allowance or any blind person's allowance transferred between spouses or civil partners). In other words, the transferred allowance is not restored to the transferor. [*TMA 1970, s 37A; ITA 2007, Sch 1 para 252*].

Simon's Taxes. See A4.321–A4.329.

Extended time limits — deceased persons

[6.5] On and after 1 April 2010, in a case involving a loss of tax brought about carelessly or deliberately by a person who has died (or another person acting on that person's behalf before that person's death), assessments to make good the tax lost can be made for any of the six tax years preceding the tax year in which death occurred. No such assessment can be made later than four years after the end of that tax year.

Before 1 April 2010, assessments to make good tax lost due to the deceased's fraudulent or negligent conduct could be made for any of the six tax years preceding the tax year in which death occurred, but any such assessment had to be made no later than the third anniversary of 31 January following that tax year.

[*TMA 1970, s 40(2); FA 2008, Sch 39 para 11(3); SI 2009 No 403*].

Simon's Taxes. See A4.327.

Further Assessments on 'Discovery'

[6.6] If an officer of HMRC or the Commissioners of HMRC 'discover', as regards any person (the taxpayer) and a chargeable period (i.e. for income tax and capital gains tax purposes, a year of assessment), that:

(a)   any income or chargeable gains which ought to have been assessed to tax (see **65.3 SELF-ASSESSMENT**) have not been assessed, or

(b)   an assessment is or has become insufficient, or

(c)   any relief given is or has become excessive,

then with the exceptions below, an assessment (a discovery assessment) may be made to make good to the Crown the apparent loss of tax. In limited circumstances, a discovery assessment may be made even though the deadline for opening an enquiry into the return (see **63.6 RETURNS**) has not passed (see Revenue Tax Bulletin August 2001 pp 875, 876).

No discovery assessment may be made, in respect of a chargeable period, where a return under *TMA 1970, s 8* or *s 8A* (see **63.2 RETURNS**) has been delivered:

(1)   if it would be attributable to an error or mistake in the return as to the basis on which the liability ought to have been computed and the return was, in fact, made on the basis, or in accordance with the practice, generally prevailing at the time when it was made; or

(2)   unless either

      (a)   (for assessments made on or after 1 April 2010) the loss of tax is brought about carelessly or deliberately by the taxpayer or a person acting on his behalf, or

      (b)   at the time when an officer of HMRC either ceased to be entitled to enquire (see **63.6 RETURNS**) into the return or informed the taxpayer of the completion of his enquiries, he could not have been reasonably expected, on the basis of the information so far made available to him (see below), to be aware of the loss of tax.

For assessments made before 1 April 2010, condition (a) above is that the loss of tax must be attributable to fraudulent or negligent conduct by the taxpayer or a person acting on his behalf (for an example of which see *Hancock v CIR (Sp C 213)*, [1999] SSCD 287).

For the purposes of (2)(b) above, information is regarded as having been made available to the officer if it has been included in:

(i)   the return (or accompanying accounts, statements or documents) for the chargeable period concerned or for either of the two immediately preceding it, or

(ii)   a partnership return (see **63.13 RETURNS**), where applicable, in respect of the chargeable period concerned or either of the two immediately preceding it, or

(iii)   any claim for the chargeable period concerned, or

(iv)   documents etc. produced for the purposes of any enquiries into such a return or claim,

or is information the existence and relevance of which could reasonably be expected to be inferred from the above-mentioned information or are notified in writing by the taxpayer to HMRC. See also below.

An objection to a discovery assessment on the grounds that neither (a) nor (b) in (2) above applies can be made only on an appeal against the assessment. (See **5.2 APPEALS** for right of appeal.)

[TMA 1970, s 29; FA 2008, s 113, Sch 36 para 71; FA 2008, Sch 39 para 3; SI 2009 No 403, No 404, Arts 2, 3].

See **65.8 SELF-ASSESSMENT** as regards due date of payment.

A change of opinion by HMRC on information previously made available to them is not grounds for a discovery assessment.

Particularly in large or complex cases, the standard accounts information details and other information included in the tax return (see **63.2 RETURNS**) may not provide a means of disclosure adequate to avoid falling within (2)(b) above. The submission of further information, including perhaps accounts, may be considered appropriate but will not necessarily provide protection against a discovery assessment beyond that arising from submission of the return alone. The reasonable expectation test (see (2)(b) above) must be satisfied. Where voluminous information beyond the accounts and computations is sent with the return, HMRC recommend that there should be a brief indication of the relevance of the material. HMRC will accept that for *TMA 1970, s 29* purposes documents submitted within a month of the return 'accompany' it (see (i) above) provided the return indicates that such documents have been or will be submitted. They will consider sympathetically a request that this condition be treated as satisfied where the time lag is longer than a month. (Revenue Press Release 31 May 1996 and Tax Bulletin June 1996 pp 313–315).

The categories in (i)–(iv) above constitute an exhaustive definition of 'information made available to an officer of HMRC' for the purpose of (2)(b) above; an officer is not precluded from making a discovery assessment simply because some other information (not normally part of the officer's immediate checks) might be available (in the instant case a form P11D) that might place doubt on the sufficiency of the self-assessment (*Langham v Veltema* CA 2004, 76 TC 259). Following this important CA decision, HMRC produced a guidance note in December 2004; this guidance was reclassified in January 2006 as HMRC SP 1/06. In particular, a taxpayer can protect himself from a discovery assessment by stating (truthfully) in his tax return:

- (in cases involving valuations) that a valuation has been used and that it was carried out by a named independent and suitably qualified valuer on an appropriate basis (but such protection is not available in the circumstances present in *Langham v Veltema*, i.e. where the same transaction is the subject of an agreed valuation in a tax return made by another party to the transaction);
- (in cases involving other judgmental issues, for example where expenditure on property is allocated between non-deductible capital expenditure, e.g. improvements to property, and deductible revenue expenditure, e.g. repairs) that a programme of work has been carried out and the expenditure allocated on a particular basis; and
- (where such is the case) that a view of the law has been taken which differs from a published view taken by HMRC.

In no case does the taxpayer need to supply sufficient information to *quantify* a possible insufficiency in the self-assessment; the object of the exercise is merely to draw HMRC's attention to the possible existence of such insufficiency.

In *R (oao Pattullo) v HMRC* CS, [2010] STC 107, an HMRC officer had newly discovered, as a result of expert examination of the taxpayer's return, that the taxpayer was probably a participant in a named tax avoidance scheme and he believed that this might lead there to be an insufficiency. It was held that this was a discovery (a new fact had come to light: the taxpayer's probable membership of the scheme). Although the taxpayer had disclosed certain related transactions in his return, these were held insufficient to alert the officer to a possible insufficiency.

In *Anderson and another (personal representatives of Anderson (deceased))* FTT (TC 206), 2009 STI 2938, the fact that HMRC had received the information they needed in the form of a chargeable event certificate did not prevent a discovery assessment being validly made. The certificate was provided to HMRC by an insurance company and not by the appellant or her representatives, and was therefore to be disregarded.

Simon's Taxes. See **A4.315, A6.702, A6.707.** See also generally HMRC Assessment Procedures Manual AP2144–2160.

See **18.9** CLAIMS for extended time limits for claims where a discovery assessment is made in a case where neither fraudulent nor negligent conduct is involved.

Amendment of partnership return on discovery

Provisions broadly similar to those described above apply as regards an understatement of profits or excessive claim for relief or allowance in a partnership statement (see **63.13** RETURNS), although HMRC's remedy in this case is to amend the partnership return, with consequent amendment of partners' own returns. [*TMA 1970, s 30B; FA 2008, Sch 39 para 4; SI 2009 No 403*]. See **5.2** APPEALS for right of appeal.

Double Assessment

[6.7] The taxing acts 'nowhere authorise the Crown to take income tax twice over in respect of the same source for the same period of time' (Lord Sumner in *English Sewing Cotton Co* HL 1923, 8 TC at 513). An *alternative* income tax assessment may, however, be raised in respect of transactions already the subject of a final CGT assessment (*Bye v Coren* CA 1986, 60 TC 116), and where more than one of a number of alternative assessments become final and conclusive, the Crown may institute collection proceedings in respect of any one (but not more than one) of them (*CIR v Wilkinson* CA 1992, 65 TC 28). For alternative assessments generally, see *Lord Advocate v McKenna* CS, [1989] STC 485.

Where there has been double assessment for the same cause and for the same chargeable period a claim may be made to HMRC (with a right of appeal against refusal) for the overcharge to be vacated. [*TMA 1970, s 32; SI 2009 No 56, Sch 1 para 22*]. See **18.7** CLAIMS for recovery of tax on or after 1 April 2010 and **18.8** CLAIMS for error or mistake relief before that date.

Finality of Assessments

[6.8] An assessment cannot be altered after the notice has been served except in accordance with the express provisions of the *Taxes Acts* (e.g. where the taxpayer appeals — see **5** APPEALS). [*TMA 1970, s 30A(4)*]. Where over-assessment results from a mistake in a return, see **18.7**, **18.8** CLAIMS. An assessment as determined on appeal or not appealed against is final and conclusive (but see **54.16** PAYMENT OF TAX for application of 'equitable liability').

Contract settlements

[6.9] In cases of fraudulent or negligent conduct, the taxpayer may be invited to offer a sum in full settlement of liability for tax, interest and penalties (a 'contract settlement') and such offers are often accepted by HMRC without assessment of all the tax. A binding agreement so made cannot be repudiated afterwards by the taxpayer or his executors.

See *CIR v Nuttall* CA 1989, 63 TC 148 for confirmation of power to enter into such agreements. Amounts due under such an agreement which are unpaid may be pursued by an action for a debt, but the Crown does not rank as a preferential creditor in respect of the sums due (*Nuttall* above; *CIR v Woollen* CA 1992, 65 TC 229).

See **55.22** PENALTIES for mitigation of penalties and certificates of full disclosure.

7

Bankruptcy

(See also HMRC factsheet EF5 (at www.hmrc.gov.uk/factsheets/ef5.pdf).)

Simon's Taxes. See **A1.608, B1.415, C4.240.**

[7.1] Income received by trustee during bankruptcy is not income of bankrupt for purposes of claiming personal allowances, etc. (*Fleming CS 1928, 14 TC 78*). Trustee is assessable on such income including profits of bankrupt's business continued by him notwithstanding requirement to hand over to creditors (*Armitage v Moore* QB 1900, 4 TC 199). And see *Hibbert v Fysh* CA 1962, 40 TC 305 (bankrupt assessable on remuneration retainable by him). The trustee continues generally to act following the death (undischarged) of the bankrupt as if he or she were still alive.

Bankruptcy

8

Banks

Simon's Taxes. See A4.403–A4.410, A4.415–A4.419, A4.426, B5.604, D7.701, D7.715.

Introduction

[8.1] The overriding rule is that interest payable in the UK to a UK bank, and interest paid by a UK bank, are both payable gross (see **24.12 DEDUCTION OF TAX AT SOURCE**), but this is subject to the significant exceptions in **8.2** below. For savings bank interest etc., see **30.24 EXEMPT INCOME**.

In general, the term 'bank' is defined by reference to the carrying on of a *bona fide* banking business, but for certain purposes it is specially defined as:

(a)   the Bank of England;

(b)   a person who has permission under *Financial Services and Markets Act 2000, Pt 4* to accept deposits (excluding building and friendly societies, credit unions and insurance companies);

(c)   an EEA firm within *Financial Services and Markets Act 2000, Sch 3 para 5(b)* which has permission under *para 15* of that *Schedule* (as a result of qualifying for authorisation under *para 12(1)*) to accept deposits;

(d)   the European Investment Bank; or

(e)   an international organisation of which the UK is a member and which is designated as a bank for the particular purpose by Treasury order (e.g. the European Investment Bank, see *SI 1996 No 1179*).

See **16.11 CHARITIES, 24.12 DEDUCTION OF TAX AT SOURCE, 63.14 RETURNS**.

[*ITA 2007, s 991; ICTA 1988, s 840A; SI 2001 No 3629, Art 46; SI 2002 No 1409*].

Returns. Banks must make returns of interest paid to depositors, see **63.14 RETURNS**.

Deduction of tax from interest

[8.2] Note that for 2007/08 onwards the rules relating to deduction by deposit-takers also apply to building societies (see **9.1 BUILDING SOCIETIES**).

With effect in relation to payments of interest made on or after 31 October 2008, the *Income Tax (Deposit-takers) (Interest Payments) Regulations 1990 (SI 1990 No 2232)* and the *Income Tax (Building Societies) (Dividends and Interest) Regulations 1990 (SI 1990 No 2231)*, to the extent that the latter had not already been rewritten in *ITA 2007*, are consolidated and rewritten as a single set of regulations, the *Income Tax (Deposit-takers and Building Societies) (Interest Payments) Regulations 2008 (SI 2008 No 2682)*.

Any 'relevant financial institution' paying or crediting interest on a 'relevant investment' must deduct therefrom a sum representing income tax thereon (at the basic rate for the tax year in which the payment is made), unless the conditions for gross payment contained in *SI 2008 No 2682* are met. (Before 2008/09, the deduction was at the savings rate of tax (20%) but as the basic rate itself fell to 20% for 2008/09, there was effectively no immediate change.) Income tax chargeable on such interest is computed on the full amount of the interest arising in the year (see **64.2 SAVINGS AND INVESTMENT INCOME**). The duty to deduct a sum representing income tax under *ITA 2007, s 874* (see **24.12 DEDUCTION OF TAX AT SOURCE**) does not apply to such payments.

Generally, **ALTERNATIVE FINANCE ARRANGEMENTS (3)** are treated as a deposit and these rules apply to returns under such arrangements as they do to interest. [*ITA 2007, s 564Q, Sch 1 para 602; FA 2005, ss 55, 56, Sch 2 paras 1, 6, 11; FA 2006, s 95(8);FA 2007, s 53(9); CTA 2009, Sch 1 para 664(4); TIOPA 2010, Sch 2 para 18*].

An 'investment' means a deposit, which is in turn defined as a sum of money paid on terms which mean it will be repaid, with or without interest, either on demand or at an agreed time or in agreed circumstances.

The relevant financial institution must treat all investments as relevant investments unless satisfied to the contrary, but if so satisfied may treat an investment as not being a relevant investment until he comes into possession of information reasonably indicative that the investment is, or may be, a relevant investment.

A 'relevant financial institution' means either a 'deposit-taker' or, for 2007/08 onwards, a building society.

For these purposes, a *deposit-taker*' means the Bank of England, persons authorised under the *Financial Services and Markets Act 2000* (including a European Economic Area firm but excluding building societies, friendly societies, credit unions and insurance companies), the Post Office (until its dissolution), any local authority or company in respect of which a local authority has passed an appropriate resolution, and any other deposit-taker prescribed by Treasury order. Any authorised person (i.e. under *Financial Services and Markets Act 2000*) whose business consists wholly or mainly of dealing as principal in 'financial instruments' (as defined) is included. As regards local authorities, see HMRC Brief 22/08, 9 April 2008.

A '*relevant investment*' (subject to the exclusions below) is an investment where either:

(a)   the person beneficially entitled to any interest is an individual (or the persons so entitled are all individuals), or is a Scottish partnership all the partners of which are individuals; or

(b)   the person entitled to the interest receives it as the personal representative of a deceased individual (but note particularly the ordinary residence requirement at (xii) below); or

(c)   the interest arises to the trustees of a discretionary or accumulation settlement (as defined in *ITA 2007, s 873*). This does not apply to deposits made before 6 April 1995 unless the relevant financial institution has, since that date but before the making of the payment, been notified by HMRC or the trustees that the interest is income of such a settlement (and HMRC have wide information powers in relation to such notices). The form of notification by the trustees is laid down by *SI 1995 No 1370*, under which payments may continue to be made gross for up to 30 days after receipt of notice (whether by the trustees or by HMRC) where deduction within that period has not become reasonably practicable. Notification may be cancelled by HMRC where appropriate.

Excluded are:

(i)   deposits in respect of which a CERTIFICATE OF DEPOSIT (**14**) has been issued for £50,000 or more (or foreign equivalent at the time the deposit is made) and which are repayable within five years (a 'qualifying certificate of deposit');

(ii)   non-transferable deposits of £50,000 or more (or foreign equivalent at the time the deposit is made) where neither partial withdrawals nor additions may be made, and which are repayable at the end of a specified period of not more than five years ('qualifying time deposits');

(iii)   a deposit in respect of which the relevant financial institution has issued a qualifying uncertificated eligible debt security unit (as defined);

(iv)   debentures (as defined in *Companies Act 2006, s 738*) issued by the relevant financial institution;

(v)   loans made *by* a relevant financial institution in the ordinary course of its business;

(vi)   debts on securities listed on a recognised stock exchange;

(vii)   deposits in a '*general client account deposit*', i.e. a client account, other than an account for specific clients, if the depositor is required by law to make payments representing interest to any of the clients whose money it contains;

(viii)   Lloyd's UNDERWRITERS (**74**) premiums trust funds;

(ix)   investments held at non-UK branches of UK resident relevant financial institutions;

(x)   investments with non-UK resident relevant financial institutions held other than in UK branches; and

(xi)   investments in respect of which the 'appropriate person' has declared in writing, by fax or by electronic means to the relevant financial institution that:

    (1)   where (a) above applies, the individual (or all of the individuals) concerned is (are), at the time of the declaration, not ordinarily resident in the UK; or

(2)   where (b) above applies, the deceased, at the time of his death, was not ordinarily resident in the UK; or

(3)   where (c) above applies, at the time of the declaration the trustees are not UK resident and do not have any reasonable grounds for believing that any of the beneficiaries (as defined for this purpose) is a UK ordinarily resident individual or a UK resident company.

The *'appropriate person'* is any person beneficially entitled to the interest, or entitled to receive it in his capacity as a personal representative or trustee, or to whom it is payable. The declaration must be in such form, and contain such information, as is required by HMRC, and must include an undertaking to notify the relevant financial institution should any individual concerned become ordinarily resident in the UK, or the trustees or any company concerned become resident in the UK, or any UK ordinarily resident individual or UK-resident company become a beneficiary of the trust to which the declaration relates. The declaration of non-ordinary residence must include the depositor's permanent address.

A person fraudulently or negligently giving incorrect information in a declaration is subject to a penalty of up to £3,000. [*TMA 1970 ss 98(2), 99B; ITA 2007, Sch 1 paras 260, 262*].

The Treasury and HMRC are given wide powers to alter the legislation by statutory instrument, in particular in relation to the declaration required at (xii) above.

In the case of investors who make the appropriate declaration for their investment to be excluded from being a relevant investment (see (xi) above) the normal deduction rules under *ITA 2007, s 874* are disapplied by *ITA 2007, s 876*. Before 2007/08, the deduction rules under *ICTA 1988, s 349(2)* were disapplied in relation to a deposit-taker other than a bank by *section 349(3)(h)* and in the case of banks by *section 349(3)(a)*.

The collection of income tax in respect of payments from which a relevant financial institution is required to make a deduction is provided for in *ITA 2007, Pt 15 Ch 15*. For years prior to 2007/08, the collection procedure of *ICTA 1988, Sch 16* applied to such payments whether or not the deposit-taker was UK-resident.

For repayment claims on behalf of persons incapable of managing their own affairs, see Revenue Tax Bulletin April 1996 p 301.

Certificate of non-liability to tax

Gross payment may be made where the person beneficially entitled to the interest is UK ordinarily resident (see **62.7 RESIDENCE, ORDINARY RESIDENCE AND DOMICILE**) and has supplied the appropriate certificate to the relevant financial institution to the effect that he is unlikely to be liable to income tax for the tax year of in which the payment is made or credited (taking into account for this purpose all interest arising in the tax year concerned which would, in the absence of such a certificate, be received under deduction of basic rate tax or, before 2008/09, savings rate tax). The certificate must be in prescribed form and must contain the name, permanent address, date of birth and (where applicable) National Insurance number of the person beneficially entitled to the interest, and the name (and if necessary branch) of the relevant financial institution and account number. It must also contain an undertaking to notify the relevant financial institution if the person beneficially entitled to the payment becomes liable to income tax for the year in which the payment is made or credited. The 'taxback' pages of the HMRC website (www.hmrc. gov.uk/taxback) outline the conditions for certification (which are described in detail below) and contain a link to the appropriate form R85 on which registration may be made. They also explain the procedure for reclaiming tax deducted, using form R40, where no registration is in place. Provision is made for use of electronic forms of communication.

A certificate of non-liability to tax may only be given by:

- a depositor aged 16 or over at the beginning of the tax year of assessment in which the payment is made or credited, or who attains age 16 during that year, who is beneficially entitled to the payment; or
- the parent or guardian of a person beneficially entitled to the payment who is under 16 at the beginning of that year; or
- a person authorised by power of attorney to administer the financial affairs of the person beneficially entitled to the payment; or
- the parent, guardian, spouse, civil partner, son or daughter of a mentally handicapped person, or any person appointed by a court to manage the affairs of a mentally handicapped person; or
- a person appointed by the Secretary of State to receive benefits on behalf of a person who is for the time being unable to act.

A certificate of non-liability to tax may not be given where the payment is treated as income of a parent of the person beneficially entitled to the payment, or where HMRC have issued a notice in relation to the account concerned requiring deduction of tax (see below).

The certificate of non-liability to tax must be supplied before the end of the tax year of in which the payment is made or credited, or, in the case of a certificate given by a person who will attain 16 years of age during the tax year, before the end of that year.

A person who gives a certificate of non-liability to tax fraudulently or negligently, or fails to comply with any undertaking contained in the certificate, is liable to a penalty of up to £3,000. [*TMA 1970, s 99A; ITA 2007, Sch 1 para 261*].

Tax deducted from payments in a year prior to receipt of a certificate of non-liability to tax relating to that year may be refunded, and a like amount recovered by the relevant financial institution from HMRC, provided that a statement or certificate of deduction of tax (see **24.5 DEDUCTION OF TAX AT SOURCE**) has not been furnished to the depositor prior to receipt of the certificate of non-liability.

The fact that payments are made gross does not mean that the interest is thereby exempted from the charge to tax.

In Revenue Press Release 13 August 1992, the Revenue position as regards incorrect certification for gross payment was explained. In asking those who had registered to reconsider their position (and, if appropriate, to ask for their registration with the bank or building society to be cancelled), the Revenue made clear that where, as a result of their audited sample, cases of incorrect registration were identified, gross payment would cease and tax (and possibly interest and penalties) would be imposed in respect of any interest already received. No interest and penalties would be applied in cases of simple misunderstanding of the position, and a penalty would be considered only where false or fraudulent declarations had knowingly been made on the registration form (or there had been a deliberate failure to cancel the registration).

A certificate of non-liability to tax ceases to be valid:

(A) where the relevant financial institution is notified (as above) that the person beneficially entitled to the payment is liable to income tax for the year in which the payment is made;

(B) where it was given by a parent or guardian, at the end of the tax year in which the person beneficially entitled to the payment attains 16 years of age;

(C) where it was given by a person who attained 16 years of age during the tax year in which a payment was made or credited, but who was not the holder of the account to which the certificate relates, and that person fails to become the holder before the first payment is made or credited after the end of that tax year;

(D) where the relevant financial institution is notified that the person by or on whose behalf the certificate was given has died; and

(E) where HMRC, having reason to believe that a person beneficially entitled to a payment of interest has become liable to income tax, give notice requiring the relevant financial institution to deduct tax from payments of interest made, more than 30 days after the issue of the notice (or from earlier payments, if practicable), to or for the benefit of that person on a specified account held by or on behalf of that person.

A notice under (E) above must be copied to the person to whom it refers, and a further certificate of non-liability to tax in respect of the account referred to in the notice may not be given by or on behalf of that person (unless the notice is subsequently cancelled, see below).

A notice under (E) above may be cancelled (and the relevant financial institution and person referred to in the notice so informed) if HMRC are satisfied that the person referred to in the notice was not at the date of the notice, and has not since become, liable to income tax, or is no longer so liable.

Declarations as to non-UK residence (see (xi) above) and certificates of non-liability to tax made or given to building societies which then incorporate are treated as having been made or given to the successor company. In relation to payments of interest made before 31 October 2008, this applied by concession (see HMRC ESC A69) but it now has statutory effect by virtue of *SI 2008 No 2682, Reg 19.*

Joint accounts

The position as regards certification by each of joint holders of an account is considered separately. Payments are apportioned equally to each joint holder, and tax deducted in respect of that part of a payment to which certification does not apply. The relevant financial institution may, however, deduct tax from the whole of payments in respect of joint accounts where certification does not apply to all the joint holders, after giving notice to HMRC of its intention to do so (which notice the relevant financial institution may subsequently cancel).

Information

HMRC may by notice require any relevant financial institution (within not less than 14 days) to furnish them with such information (including books, records etc.) as they require, in particular:

(I)   for verification of payments made without deduction of tax and of the validity of certification for gross payment; and
(II)   for verification of the amount of tax deducted from payments of interest.

Copies of the relevant financial institution's books, records etc. must be made available when required by HMRC. Declarations as to non-UK residence and certificates of non-liability to tax (or a record of such declarations or certificates) must be retained for at least two years after they cease to be valid.

Subject to *FA 1989, s 182(5)* (see **35.5** HMRC — CONFIDENTIALITY OF INFORMATION), information obtained under these provisions may not be used other than for the purposes of the provisions or for the ascertainment of the tax liability of the deposit-taker or of the person beneficially entitled to interest paid without deduction of tax to whom the information relates.

[*ITA 2007, ss 850–873, Sch 2 Part 15; FA 2008, Sch 1 paras 25, 65; SI 2008 No 954, Arts 1, 41; SI 2008 Nos 2682, 2688; SI 2009 No 2035, Sch para 51*].

9

Building Societies

Simon's Taxes. See A4.403–A4.410, A4.412, D7.810, D7.830–D7.832.

Interest and dividends paid to investors

[9.1] [*ITA 2007, ss 850–873, 889, 945–962, 975–987, Sch 1 para 88; FA 2008, Sch 1 paras 27, 65; CTA 2010, Sch 1 para 558; SI 2006 No 745, Reg 20; SI 2008 No 2682; SI 2009 No 2035, Sch para 51*].

For these purposes, a building society is one within the meaning of *Building Societies Act 1986*. [*ITA 2007, s 989; ICTA 1988, s 832(1)*].

See **64.2** SAVINGS AND INVESTMENT INCOME for the charge to tax on interest generally, and note that building society *dividends* are taxed as interest and not as dividends.

During the rewrite of the legislation in *ITA 2007* the opportunity was taken to bring building societies within the regime applying to deposit-takers in respect of the deduction of sums representing income tax. This has resulted in an alignment of the provisions in respect of banks and building societies (see Change 126 listed in Annex 1 to the Explanatory Notes to *ITA 2007*); accordingly the commentary at **8.2** BANKS applies also to building societies for 2007/08 onwards. For commentary on the position prior to 2007/08, see **9.2** below.

Returns

Building societies are required to make returns of dividends and interest paid to investors. [*TMA 1970, s 17; ITA 2007, Sch 1 para 247*]. See **63.14** RETURNS.

Marketable securities

Dividends or interest paid in respect of securities issued by a building society (other than 'qualifying certificates of deposit', a 'qualifying uncertificated eligible debt security unit', or a 'quoted Eurobond' — all as defined) which were listed, or capable of being listed, on a recognised stock exchange when the dividend etc. became payable are not within the deduction scheme referred to above, but are subject to deduction of tax under *ITA 2007, s 889*. 'Permanent interest bearing shares' (see Tolley's Corporation Tax under Building Societies) issued by a society are within these provisions.

199

Generally, these provisions apply to returns under **ALTERNATIVE FINANCE ARRANGEMENTS (3)** as they do to interest. [*ITA 2007, s 564Q, Sch 1 para 602; FA 2005, ss 55, 56, Sch 2 paras 1, 12; FA 2007, s 53(9); CTA 2009, Sch 1 para 664(4); TIOPA 2010, Sch 2 para 18*].

Payments under deduction prior to 2007/08

[9.2] Subject to the exceptions below, building societies are required under regulations (*SI 1990 No 2231 (now revoked)*) made under *ICTA 1988, s 477A* to deduct a sum representing income tax (at the savings rate for the tax year in which the payment is made) thereon from all payments or credits of dividends or interest in respect of shares in, deposits with or loans to the society, unless gross payment is authorised under the conditions described below. The deduction requirements of *ICTA 1988, s 349* (see **24.21 DEDUCTION OF TAX AT SOURCE**) do not apply to such payments.

These rules apply to returns under **ALTERNATIVE FINANCE ARRANGEMENTS (3)** (other than those in **3.4**) as they do to interest paid on a deposit or loan. [*FA 2005, ss 55, 56, Sch 2 paras 1, 5*].

For repayment claims on behalf of persons incapable of managing their own affairs, see Revenue Tax Bulletin April 1996 p 301.

Gross payment

Interest and dividends are payable without deduction of tax where, at the time of payment, they fall into one of the following categories.

(a)   A payment to an individual not ordinarily resident in the UK who is beneficially entitled to the payment, or jointly so entitled with other such individuals.

(b)   A payment to trustees of a trust in the income of which no person has an interest apart from individuals not ordinarily resident in the UK.

(c)   A payment to personal representatives in respect of an investment (or another investment representing an investment) forming part of the estate of a deceased person who was not ordinarily resident in the UK at the time of his death.

(d)   A payment to a charity exempt under *ICTA 1988, s 505(1)(c)*.

(e)   A payment of interest on a bank loan.

(f)   A payment under a **CERTIFICATE OF DEPOSIT (14)** under which the society is obliged within five years of issue to pay £50,000 or more (exclusive of interest); or on a non-transferable sterling deposit of £50,000 or more for a fixed period of less than five years (which must prohibit partial withdrawals or additions). Such certificates of deposit and other non-transferable deposits may be denominated in a foreign currency, the equivalent £50,000 limit being determined at the time of the deposit.

(g)   A payment on a deposit by a subsidiary of a building society with its parent society (where an election for gross payment is in force).

(h)   A payment in respect of a general client deposit account (see **8.2**(vii) **BANKS**).

(i)   A payment to a local authority.

(j)   A payment into a Lloyd's UNDERWRITERS (74) premiums trust fund.

(k)   All payments to companies (defined to include all bodies corporate and unincorporated associations other than partnerships and local authority associations), health service bodies and trustees of unit trust schemes (within *Financial Services and Markets Act 2000, s 237(1)*).

(l)   A payment in respect of a 'qualifying deposit right' (as defined below).

(m)   A payment in respect of an investment held at a non-UK branch.

(n)   A deemed interest payment under *ICTA 1988, s 730A(2)* (price differential on sale and repurchase of securities, see **4.8** ANTI-AVOIDANCE).

(o)   A payment to trustees of a discretionary or accumulation trust (within **68.11** SETTLEMENTS) where the trustees are non-UK resident and all beneficiaries (as widely defined) are either non-UK ordinarily resident individuals (or Scottish partnerships comprising such individuals) or non-UK resident companies.

(p)   A payment of interest in respect of cash received in connection with a sale and repurchase agreement to which *ICTA 1988, s 730A* (see **4.8** ANTI-AVOIDANCE) applies, and which is required as a result of a variation in the value of the securities concerned as security for performance by the parties to the agreement of their obligations thereunder.

(q)   A payment to a registered pension scheme.

Gross payment also applies where the person beneficially entitled to the interest is UK ordinarily resident (see **62.7** RESIDENCE, ORDINARY RESIDENCE AND DOMICILE) and has supplied the appropriate certificate to the society to the effect that he is unlikely to be liable to income tax for the year of assessment in which the payment is made or credited (taking into account for this purpose all interest arising in the year of assessment concerned which would, in the absence of such a certificate, be received under deduction of savings rate tax). The conditions for certification, and related Revenue information powers, are similar to those described at **8.2** BANKS.

Scottish partnerships consisting only of individuals not ordinarily resident in the UK are within the requirements at (a) and (b) above. A payment within (a)–(d) above may not be made gross unless the society has a written or electronic declaration in a prescribed form from the investor certifying that the relevant conditions are met. This requirement also applies to most companies and to unit trust scheme trustees.

Interest payments completely exempt from income tax (e.g. under ISAs, TESSAs or SAYE schemes or personal equity plans (see **30.21, 30.24** EXEMPT INCOME)) are also paid gross.

The fact that payments are made gross does not mean that the interest is thereby exempted from the charge to tax.

A *'qualifying deposit right'* is a right to receive an amount in pursuance of a deposit of money under an arrangement under which no certificate of deposit has been issued, although the person entitled to the right could call for the issue of such a certificate, which otherwise meets the same conditions as a qualifying certificate of deposit. [*ICTA 1988, s 349(3A)(3B)(4), s 477A(1A)*].

Simon's Taxes. See A4.412.

Transfer of building society business to company

[9.3] The acquisition by members of shares on such a transfer is granted certain reliefs from capital gains tax and from treatment as a distribution. [*FA 1988, s 145, Sch 12; TCGA 1992, ss 216, 217; FA 2006, Sch 12 para 20; CTA 2009, Sch 1 para 337*]. See Tolley's Corporation Tax under Building Societies.

Declarations as to non-UK residence and certificates of non-liability to tax made or given to building societies which then incorporate are treated as having been made or given to the successor company. In relation to payments of interest made before 31 October 2008, this applied by concession (see HMRC ESC A69) but it now has statutory effect by virtue of *SI 2008 No 2682, Reg 19.*

Simon's Taxes. See D7.830–D7.832.

10

Capital Allowances

Cross-references. See **11** CAPITAL ALLOWANCES ON PLANT AND MACHINERY.

Simon's Taxes. See Part B3.

Other sources. See Tolley's Capital Allowances.

Introduction

[10.1] The law relating to capital allowances was consolidated in *Capital Allowances Act 2001 (CAA 2001)* as part of the Tax Law Rewrite programme.

Capital allowances (balancing charges) are a deduction from (addition to) the profits etc. of trades and other qualifying activities in arriving at the taxable amount. The amount of depreciation charged in the accounts of a business is not so allowed. They are generally treated as trading expenses (receipts) of the period of account (see **10.2**(i) below) to which they relate. [*CAA 2001, ss 2, 6*].

Certain allowances are given only in relation to trades, some only in relation to particular kinds of trade, and some additionally given against particular sources of non-trading income — details are given in the relevant section of the chapter.

Capital allowances are available in respect of expenditure on plant and machinery, which is a sufficiently large and important subject to warrant its own chapter — see **11 CAPITAL ALLOWANCES ON PLANT AND MACHINERY**. They are also available in respect of certain other types of expenditure as detailed in **10.3–10.37** below.

Matters of general application

[10.2] The following matters are pertinent to more than one type of capital allowance.

(i)   **Meaning of 'chargeable period' and 'period of account'.** For capital allowances purposes, a *'chargeable period'* is a 'period of account'.
For persons carrying on a trade, profession or vocation, a *'period of account'* means a period for which accounts are drawn up, except that where such a period exceeds 18 months, it is deemed to be split into two or more periods of account, beginning on, or on an anniversary of, the date on which the actual period begins. Exceptionally, where there is an interval between two periods of account, it is deemed to form part of the first such period, and where two periods of account overlap, the common period is deemed to form part of the first such period only. For non-traders, a period of account is a tax year.
[*CAA 2001, s 6*].
See the examples at **11.32 CAPITAL ALLOWANCES ON PLANT AND MACHINERY**.

(ii)   **Claims.** Capital allowances are given only if a claim is made. Such a claim can only be made by inclusion in the annual tax return (subject to the very limited exceptions at *CAA 2001, s 3(4)* as amended). A claim for allowances under **10.5** below (business premises renovation) must be separately identified as such in the return. [*CAA 2001, s 3, Sch 2 para 103(2)*]. See **63.4 RETURNS** as regards amendments to income tax returns, and the time allowed for making them.

(iii)   **Capital expenditure.** References in the capital allowances legislation to the incurring of capital expenditure and the paying of capital sums exclude any sums allowed as deductions in computing the payer's profits or earnings and certain sums payable under deduction of tax. Corresponding rules apply as regards the receipt of such sums. [*CAA 2001, s 4, Sch 3 para 9; ITA 2007, Sch 1 para 397*].

(iv)   **Time expenditure incurred.** Capital expenditure (other than that constituted by an 'additional VAT liability' — see (viii) below) is generally treated, for capital allowances purposes, as incurred as soon as there is an unconditional obligation to pay it, even if all or part of it is not required to be paid until some later date. However, expenditure is treated as incurred on a later date in the following circumstances.

- Where any part of the expenditure is not required to be paid until a date more than four months after the date determined as above, it is treated as incurred on that later date.
- Where an obligation to pay becomes unconditional earlier than in accordance with normal commercial usage, with the sole or main benefit likely to be the bringing forward of the chargeable period in which the expenditure would otherwise be treated as incurred, it is instead treated as incurred on the date on or before which it is required to be paid.

Where, as a result of an event such as the issuing of a certificate, an obligation to pay becomes unconditional within one month after the end of a chargeable period, but at or before the end of that chargeable period the asset concerned has become the property of, or is otherwise attributed under the contract to, the person having the obligation, the expenditure is treated as incurred immediately before the end of that chargeable period.

The above provisions do not override any specific rule under which expenditure is treated as incurred later than the relevant time given above.

[*CAA 2001, s 5*].

Simon's Taxes. See B3.103, B3.104, B3.107.

(v)   **Exclusion of double allowances.** Where an allowance is made to a person under one of the following codes of allowances, he cannot obtain an allowance under another of those codes in respect of that expenditure or the provision of any asset to which that expenditure related:

- agricultural buildings allowances (**10.3** below);
- allowances for expenditure on business premises renovation (**10.5** below);
- allowances for expenditure on dredging (**10.6** below);
- allowances for dwelling-houses let on assured tenancies (**10.8** below);
- allowances for expenditure on flat conversion (**10.9** below);
- industrial buildings allowances (**10.10–10.22** below);
- allowances for mineral extraction (**10.24–10.34** below);
- research and development allowances (**10.37** below).

Similarly, no allowance under any of the above codes can be made in respect of any expenditure that has been allocated to a plant and machinery pool (see **11.23 CAPITAL ALLOWANCES ON PLANT AND MACHINERY**), and on which a plant or machinery allowance (or balancing charge) has consequently been given (or made), or any related asset (as above); and expenditure which has attracted an allowance under any of the above codes (and any related asset) cannot be allocated to a plant and machinery pool.

Additional rules apply under *CAA 2001, s 9* to prevent double allowances in relation to plant or machinery treated as fixtures (as at **11.33** *et seq.* **CAPITAL ALLOWANCES ON PLANT AND MACHINERY**).

[*CAA 2001, ss 7–10, Sch 3 para 10*].

Where an item of expenditure qualifies for more than one type of capital allowance, it is the taxpayer's choice as to which to claim, but he cannot alter his choice in later years. (HMRC Capital Allowances Manual CA16000, HMRC Brief 12/09, 31 March 2009).

Simon's Taxes. See B3.114.

(vi) **Expenditure met by another's contributions.** Subject to the exceptions below, a person is not regarded as incurring expenditure for capital allowances purposes (other than for dredging — see below) to the extent that it is met, or will be met, directly or indirectly by another person or by a *'public body'*, i.e. the Crown or any government or public or local authority (whether in the UK or elsewhere). For the scope of 'public authority', see *McKinney v Hagans Caravans (Manufacturing) Ltd* CA(NI) 1997, 69 TC 526. There is an exception where the expenditure is met by a Regional Development Grant or NI equivalent. In practice, applications for Regional Development Grants were no longer accepted after 31 March 1988, but NI equivalents did continue to be available until 31 March 2003. Expenditure met by insurance or other compensation money due in respect of a destroyed, demolished or defunct asset is not excluded from allowances.

As regards allowances for dredging (see **10.6** below), the above is replaced by a rule to the effect that a person is not regarded as incurring expenditure for the purposes of his trade or future trade to the extent that it is met, or will be met, directly or indirectly by a public body or by capital sums contributed by another person *for purposes other than those of the fore-mentioned trade.*

The main rule above (but not the rule for dredging) is disapplied, and allowances are thus available, if the contributor is not a public body and can obtain neither a capital allowance on his contribution by virtue of (vii) below nor a deduction against profits of a trade, profession or vocation.

[*CAA 2001, ss 532–536, Sch 2 para 19, Sch 3 paras 106–108*].

Repaid grants. Where a grant which has been deducted from expenditure qualifying for capital allowances (as above) is later repaid (in whole or part), the repayment will, by concession, be treated as expenditure qualifying for capital allowances. Where allowances were restricted in respect of a contribution from a person (other than a public body) who himself obtained either a capital allowance under (vii) below

or a trading deduction for his contribution (as above), this treatment is dependent upon the repayment falling to be taxed on the recipient through a balancing charge or as a trading receipt. (HMRC ESC B49 as revised).
Simon's Taxes. See **B3.111.**

(vii) **Contribution allowances.** Contributors towards another person's capital expenditure on an asset may receive allowances (*'contribution allowances'*) where the contribution is for the purposes of a trade, profession or vocation carried on (or to be carried on) by the contributor, and where the expenditure would otherwise have entitled the other person (assuming him not to be a public body) to agricultural buildings, industrial buildings, plant and machinery or mineral extraction allowances. Contribution allowances are not available where the contributor and the other person are CONNECTED PERSONS (21).

Contribution allowances are such as would have been made if the contribution had been expended on the provision for the contributor's trade etc. of a similar asset and as if the asset were at all material times used for the purposes of the contributor's trade etc. (so that balancing adjustments do not apply to such contributions). On a transfer of the trade etc., or part thereof, the allowances (or part) are subsequently made to the transferee.

In relation to agricultural buildings and industrial buildings allowances, the conditions are satisfied if the contribution is made for the purposes of a trade etc. carried on by a tenant of land in which the contributor has an interest. Entitlement to writing-down allowances passes to any person becoming entitled to the interest held by the contributor at the time of the contribution.
[*CAA 2001, ss 537–542, Sch 3 paras 109, 110; FA 2008, Sch 27 paras 8–11, 20, 23, 30*].

Capital contributions towards expenditure on dredging are treated as expenditure incurred by the contributor on that dredging. [*CAA 2001, s 543*].
Simon's Taxes. See **B3.112.**

(viii) **VAT capital goods scheme.** Under the VAT capital goods scheme, the input tax originally claimed on the acquisition of certain capital assets is subject to amendment within a specified period of adjustment in accordance with any increase or decrease in the extent to which the asset is used in making taxable, as opposed to exempt, supplies for VAT purposes. The items covered by the scheme are limited to land and buildings (or parts of buildings) worth at least £250,000 and computers (and items of computer equipment) worth at least £50,000. See Tolley's Value Added Tax under Capital Goods Scheme for a full description.

Special capital allowances provisions apply where a VAT adjustment is made under the capital goods scheme. These affect allowances for industrial buildings, business premises renovation and research and development, and the provisions specific to each are described in the appropriate sections of this chapter. General definitions and provisions are described below.

'*Additional VAT liability*' and '*additional VAT rebate*' mean, respectively,

- an amount which a person becomes liable to pay, or
- an amount which he becomes entitled to deduct

by way of adjustment under the VAT capital goods scheme in respect of input tax. Generally (but see below), such a liability or rebate is treated as incurred or made on the last day of the period

- which is one of the periods making up the applicable VAT period of adjustment under the VAT capital goods scheme, and
- in which occurred the increase or decrease in use giving rise to the liability or rebate.

However, for the purpose of determining the chargeable period (see (i) above) in which it accrues, an additional VAT liability or rebate is treated as accruing on whichever is the relevant day below.

- Where the liability or rebate is accounted for in a VAT return, the last day of the period covered by that return.
- If, before the making of a VAT return, HMRC assess the liability or rebate, the day on which the assessment is made.
- If the trade is permanently discontinued before the liability or rebate has been accounted for in a VAT return and before the making of an assessment, the last day of the chargeable period in which the cessation occurs.

Where an allowance or charge falls to be determined by reference to a proportion only of the expenditure incurred or a proportion only of what that allowance or charge would otherwise have been, a related additional VAT liability or rebate is similarly apportioned.

[*CAA 2001, ss 546–551; FA 2008, Sch 27 paras 12, 30*].

Simon's Taxes. See B3.103, B3.104, B3.110.

(ix) **Composite sales** may be apportioned by the Appeal Tribunal regardless of any separate prices attributed in the sale agreement. [*CAA 2001, ss 562–564; FA 2008, Sch 27 paras 13, 30; SI 2009 No 56, Sch 1 para 299*]. See *Fitton v Gilders & Heaton* Ch D 1955, 36 TC 233, and *Wood v Provan* CA 1968, 44 TC 701.

(x) **Recovery of assets under *Proceeds of Crime Act 2002, Pt 5*.** *Proceeds of Crime Act 2002, Pt 5 Ch 2* provides for the recovery, in civil proceedings before the High Court (or, in Scotland, the Court of Session), of property which is, or represents, property obtained through 'unlawful conduct' (as defined in the *Act*). If the Court is satisfied that any property is recoverable under the provisions, it will make a '*recovery order*', vesting the property in an appointed trustee for civil recovery. Alternatively, the Court may make an order under *section 276* of the *Act* staying (or, in Scotland, sisting) proceedings on terms agreed by the parties. The vesting of property in a trustee for civil recovery or any other person, either under a recovery order or in pursuance of a *section 276* order, is known as a *Pt 5* transfer. A '*compensating payment*' may in some cases be made to the person who held the property immediately before the transfer. If the order provides for the creation of any interest in favour of that person, he is treated as receiving (in addition to any other compensating payment) a compensating payment equal to the value of the interest. [*Proceeds of Crime Act 2002, ss 240(1), 266(1)(2), 276, 316(1), 448, Sch 10 para 2*].

Where the property in question is plant or machinery, the relevant interest in an industrial building or in a flat (within **10.9** below), or an asset representing qualifying expenditure on research and development (within **10.37** below), there are provisions to ensure that the *Pt 5* transfer has a tax-neutral effect, unless a compensating payment is made to the transferor in which case its amount and/or value must be brought into account as a disposal value or, as the case may be, as proceeds from a balancing event. [*Proceeds of Crime Act 2002, Sch 10 paras 12–29; FA 2008, Sch 27 paras 24, 30*].

(xi) **Avoidance affecting proceeds of balancing event.** There is an anti-avoidance rule to prevent a balancing allowance being created or increased by means of any tax avoidance scheme that depresses an asset's market value and thus the amount to be brought into account on a balancing event (e.g. a sale) or as a disposal value. The rule denies entitlement to a balancing allowance, though the unrelieved balance of expenditure immediately after the event must be computed as if the allowance had been made. The rule applies to allowances for industrial buildings, agricultural buildings, business premises renovation, flat conversion expenditure, dwelling-houses let on assured tenancies and mineral extraction. It applies in relation to any event that would otherwise occasion a balancing allowance, except where it occurs in pursuance of a contract entered into on or before that date and is not consequent upon the exercise after that date of any option or right. [*CAA 2001, s 570A; FA 2008, Sch 27 paras 17, 30*]. Simon's Taxes. See B3.110, B3.108C.

Agricultural buildings and works

[10.3] The current code of capital allowances for agricultural buildings and works (as described below) applies to expenditure incurred on or after 1 April 1986 (1 April 1987 where it was incurred under a contract entered into before 14 March 1984). [*CAA 2001, Sch 3 para 82*].

Withdrawal of the agricultural buildings allowances regime

Agricultural buildings allowances are being phased out. No allowances will be available for chargeable periods (as in **10.2**(i) above) beginning **on or after 6 April 2011**. In the meantime, the maximum writing-down allowance is equal to the following percentage of the allowance to which the person would otherwise have been entitled:

(i)   100% for 2007/08 and earlier years;
(ii)   75% for 2008/09;
(iii) 50% for 2009/10; and
(iv)   25% for 2010/11.

In the simple case where there has been no transfer of the relevant interest, this translates to writing-down allowances at 3% for 2008/09, 2% for 2009/10 and 1% for 2010/11 (compared to 4% for 2007/08 and earlier years).

If a chargeable period ending after 5 April 2008 (and beginning before 6 April 2011) does not coincide with a tax year, the writing-down allowance is determined as follows. Divide each chargeable period into the parts ending with 5 April and beginning with 6 April. Apply the following formula to each part and then add the results together. The result is the amount of the writing-down allowance available. The formula is:

$$\left(\frac{\text{RDCPY}}{\text{RDCP}}\right) \times \text{NWDA} \times \text{P}$$

Where

RDCPY = the number of 'relevant days' in the chargeable period which fall within the part of the chargeable period in question;

RDCP = the total number of 'relevant days' in the chargeable period;

NWDA = the normal writing-down allowance, i.e. the allowance to which the person would have been entitled had it not been for the phasing out of allowances; and

P = the percentage in either (i), (ii), (iii) or (iv) above depending on the tax year in which that part of the chargeable period falls (or 0% if it falls after 5 April 2011).

For the purposes of RDCPY and RDCP, a *'relevant day'* is any day on which the person in question has the 'relevant interest' (see below) in relation to the qualifying expenditure in respect of which the allowance is made.

However, the residue of expenditure carried forward is computed as if the normal writing-down allowance (NWDA in the above formula) had been made.

[FA 2008, ss 84, 85].

Qualifying buildings etc.

Writing-down, and previously (in certain cases) initial, allowances (see below) are given in respect of capital expenditure incurred for the purposes of 'husbandry' on the construction of buildings (such as farmhouses (but see (b) below), farm buildings or cottages), fences or other works. [CAA 2001, s 361(1)(2)]. 'Capital expenditure on construction' includes preliminary demolition costs (unless already taken into account for industrial buildings allowance purposes, see **10.16** below), expenditure on reconstruction, alteration or improvement and architect's fees, and 'other works' includes e.g. drainage and sewage works, water and electricity installations, walls, shelter belts of trees, silos, farm roads, land reclamation and hedge demolition. (HMRC Capital Allowances Manual CA 40100, 40200). Cottages occupied by retired farm workers and buildings constructed to provide welfare facilities for employees may qualify for allowances, as may farm shops to the extent that they sell produce of the farm. (HMRC Capital Allowances Manual CA40100). '*Husbandry*' includes any method of intensive rearing of livestock or fish on a commercial basis for the production of food for human consumption, and also 'short rotation coppice' (see **73.73**(k) TRADING INCOME). [*CAA 2001, s 362; CTA 2010, Sch 1 para 354*].

Market gardening

Market gardening, whether of plants or flowers or for the production of food, is treated in the same way as farming for allowance purposes, and a house which is the centre of such operations is treated as a farmhouse (see (b) below). (This commentary is not included in the current HMRC Capital Allowances Manual but was previously at CA4509 and is presumed still to be of application.)

Qualifying expenditure

Allowances are available where a person who has a 'freehold' or 'leasehold' interest in land in the UK occupied wholly or mainly for the purposes of husbandry incurs capital expenditure on qualifying buildings etc. (as set out above) for the purposes of husbandry on that land. The building etc. on which the expenditure is incurred does not have to be on the land in question, e.g. a farmworker's cottage in a nearby village might qualify (this commentary, although not included in the current HMRC Capital Allowances Manual having previously been at CA4504 and being presumed still to be of application). A '*freehold*' interest in land is the fee simple estate in the land or an agreement to acquire that interest (or Scottish equivalent), and a '*leasehold*' interest is the interest of a tenant in property subject to a lease (including an agreement for a lease if the lease term has begun and any tenancy, but excluding a mortgage). The expenditure is '*qualifying expenditure*' except that:

(a) expenditure on the acquisition of the land or rights over the land is excluded;

(b) a maximum of one-third of expenditure on the construction of a farmhouse may qualify (reduced as is just and reasonable where the accommodation and amenities are disproportionate to the nature and extent of the farm). For the meaning of 'farmhouse', see *Lindsay v CIR* CS 1953, 34 TC 289, *CIR v Whiteford & Sons* CS 1962, 40 TC 379, *Korner v CIR* HL 1969, 45 TC 287, and HMRC Capital Allowances Manual CA40100 (including the circumstances in which it may be accepted that a farm has two farmhouses); and

(c) only a just and reasonable proportion of expenditure on assets (other than the farmhouse) only partly used for the purposes of husbandry on the land in question may qualify.

[*CAA 2001, ss 361(1)(2), 363, 369, 393, Sch 3 para 81*].

As regards *buildings etc. bought unused*, similar provisions apply as in the case of industrial buildings (see **10.13** below), modified to take account of the restrictions and exclusions referred to above. [*CAA 2001, ss 370, 374*].

Where a person is entitled to different 'relevant interests' (see below) in different parts of the land, the expenditure is apportioned on a just and reasonable basis, and these provisions apply separately to the expenditure apportioned to each part.

Initial allowances

An initial allowance was available to a person incurring qualifying expenditure under a contract entered into in the twelve-month period 1 November 1992 to 31 October 1993 inclusive, or for the purpose of securing compliance with obligations incurred under a contract entered into during that period, but not for expenditure incurred under a contract entered into for the purpose of securing compliance with obligations under a contract entered into before 1 November 1992. The qualifying building must have come to be used for the purposes of husbandry before 1 January 1995, and, if this condition was not satisfied or if the building first came to be used for purposes other than husbandry, any initial allowance given will have been withdrawn. The initial allowance was **20%** of the expenditure incurred, and was given for the chargeable period related to the incurring of the expenditure. Either a smaller initial allowance could be claimed or the initial allowance not claimed at all. [*CAA 1990, s 124A(1)–(3), (5)–(7); FA 1993, Sch 12 para 3*].

Writing-down allowances

Writing-down allowances are made to the person who for the time being has the '*relevant interest*' in relation to the qualifying expenditure, i.e. (except as follows) the interest in the land in question to which the person incurring the expenditure was entitled when the expenditure was incurred. If there is more than one such interest and one was reversionary on all the others, that one is the relevant interest. The creation of a lease to which the relevant interest is subject is disregarded for these purposes. Where an interest in land has been conveyed or assigned by way of security subject to a right of redemption, it will still be treated as belonging to the person with the right of redemption. [*CAA 2001, ss 361(3), 364–366*]. When a leasehold relevant interest is surrendered or reverts, the interest into which it merges becomes the relevant interest, unless a new lease takes effect on the extinguishment. Otherwise, on a leasehold relevant interest coming to an end, if a new lease is granted to the former lessee, the lessee is treated as continuing to have the same relevant interest. (This applies equally where the new lease is of only part of the land subject to the old lease.) If the new lease is granted to a person other than the former lessee, the relevant interest is treated as acquired by the new lessee if he makes a payment to the former lessee for the assets representing the expenditure in question. In any other case, the interest of the landlord under the former lease is treated as becoming the relevant interest. [*CAA 2001, ss 367, 368*].

A person is entitled to an allowance for any chargeable period (see **10.2**(i) above) at any time during which he is entitled to the relevant interest. For 2007/08 and earlier years, allowances are given at the rate of **4% p.a.** of the qualifying expenditure (or such lesser amount as may be claimed) during a period of 25 years beginning on the first day of the chargeable period (of the person incurring the expenditure) during which the expenditure was incurred, so as to give aggregate allowances (including any initial allowance) up to the amount of that expenditure. See also above under Withdrawal of the agricultural buildings allowances regime. If the buildings etc. in fact come to be first used other than for the purposes of husbandry, no writing-down allowance can be made in respect of the related expenditure and any allowance previously given is withdrawn. A writing-down allowance could be given for the same chargeable period as an initial allowance under *CAA 1990, s 124A* (see above) in respect of the same expenditure, but only if the building etc. came to be used for the purposes of husbandry before the end of that chargeable period. [*CAA 2001, ss 372–374*]. If the conditions are met when the expenditure is incurred and the first use is for the purposes of husbandry, allowances continue throughout the writing-down period without regard to any change of use of the building in later years (HMRC Capital Allowances Manual CA41100).

Transfer of relevant interest

Where a person entitled to allowances in respect of capital expenditure as above ceases to own the relevant interest in the land (or part of the land) giving rise to that entitlement, and another person acquires that interest, the right to the writing-down allowances (or appropriate part) is transferred to the new owner of the interest (proportionate allowances being given where the transfer falls during a chargeable period (see **10.2**(i) above) of either the former or the new owner). See below as regards allowances where the transfer is a 'balancing event'. [*CAA 2001, s 375*]. If, by virtue of a transfer of the relevant interest, the total allowances which were or could have been claimed (disregarding any anti-avoidance etc. restrictions on balancing allowances) during the writing-down period would otherwise be less than the amount of the expenditure, then the difference is made up in the chargeable period in which the writing-down period ends. [*CAA 2001, s 379*].

Balancing events

A '*balancing event*' occurs when the relevant interest in land (or part) is acquired by another person (see above) or when the building etc. (or part) on construction of which the expenditure was incurred is demolished, destroyed, or otherwise ceases altogether to be used, *provided that* a written election to that effect is made. The election must be made no later than the first anniversary of 31 January following the tax year in which ends the chargeable period in which the balancing event occurs. The election must be made jointly in the case of acquisition of the relevant interest, but otherwise by the former owner only. An election may not be made by a person outside the charge to income tax or corporation tax, nor if the sole or main benefit of an acquisition was the obtaining of an allowance or greater allowance (but ignoring *CAA 2001, ss 568, 573*, see below). [*CAA 2001, ss 381, 382*].

Where a balancing event occurs in a chargeable (or basis) period for which an allowance would otherwise have been available, no such allowance is made, but a balancing adjustment arises for that period on or to the person entitled to the relevant interest immediately before the balancing event. If the residue of expenditure immediately before the balancing event (i.e. after deducting any allowances previously given and adding any balancing charges previously made) exceeds any sale, compensation etc. receipts, a balancing allowance equal to that excess is made (subject to the anti-avoidance rule at **10.2**(xi) above). If any sale, compensation etc. receipts exceed that residue, a balancing charge is made equal to the excess (but limited to the allowances previously given to the person on whom the charge arises). Allowances made to a husband before 6 April 1990 in respect of his wife's relevant interest are treated as having been made to the wife for these purposes on a balancing event on or after that date. [*CAA 2001, ss 377, 380, 383–388, Sch 3 para 80*].

Where a balancing event occurs on the transfer of the relevant interest, the writing-down allowances available to the new owner consist of the residue of expenditure (see above) immediately before the balancing event, plus any balancing charge or less any balancing allowance consequent on that event, spread over the period from the balancing event to the end of the original 25 year writing-down period. For this purpose, any balancing allowance which (on that or any previous balancing event) has been reduced or denied under *CAA 2001, s 389* (see below) is treated as having been made in full. [*CAA 2001, ss 376, 378*].

Balancing events occurring **on or after 21 March 2007** do not normally give rise to a balancing adjustment, i.e. either a balancing allowance or a balancing charge. It would appear that, in the absence of a balancing adjustment, writing-down allowances are due to the person entitled to the relevant interest immediately before the balancing event as if no election for a balancing event had been made. The writing-down allowances of the new owner (where the balancing event is the transfer of the relevant interest) are based on the residue of expenditure immediately before the balancing event. Balancing adjustments remain available where a balancing event occurs before 1 April 2011 in pursuance of a written contract made before 21 March 2007. Any conditions attaching to the contract must have been satisfied before that date. No terms must remain to be agreed, and the contract must not be varied in a significant way, on or after that date. [*FA 2007, s 36(4)–(7)*].

Making of allowances and charges

An initial, writing-down or balancing adjustment for a chargeable period is given or made in taxing a trade. If no trade is carried on in that chargeable period, then allowances and charges are treated as expenses and receipts of a UK property business (see **60.2 PROPERTY INCOME**) or, where the taxpayer is not, in fact, carrying on such a business, of a notional UK property business. [*CAA 2001, ss 391, 392; CTA 2009, Sch 1 para 504*]. See also **10.2**(i)(ii)(x) above, and see **60.15 PROPERTY INCOME** as regards property business losses.

Connected persons and other anti-avoidance provisions

There are connected person and anti-avoidance provisions in respect of certain balancing events, similar to those applicable to industrial buildings allowances (see **10.22**(i) below). [*CAA 2001, ss 389, 390, 567, 568, 570(1), 573; FA 2008, Sch 27 paras 14, 16, 18, 30*].

Simon's Taxes. See B3.5.

Example

[10.4]

Farmer Jones prepares accounts annually to 31 December and has incurred the following expenditure

		£
12.1.04	Extension to farmhouse	12,000
3.6.05	Construction of cattle court	15,000
26.4.06	Erection of barn	10,000
15.10.09	Replacement barn for that acquired on 26.4.06 which was destroyed by fire in September 2009	20,000
	The insurance proceeds totalled £5,200	

The agricultural buildings allowances are as follows.

Date of expenditure	Cost	Residue brought forward	Allowances WDA 4%	Residue carried forward
	£	£	£	£
2004/05 (period of account — year to 31.12.04)				
12.1.04	4,000		160	3,840
2005/06 (period of account — year to 31.12.05)				
12.1.04	4,000	3,840	160	3,680
3.6.05	15,000		600	14,400
	£19,000	£3,840	£760	£18,080
2006/07 (period of account — year to 31.12.06)				
12.1.04	4,000	3,680	160	3,520
3.6.05	15,000	14,400	600	13,800
26.4.06	10,000		400	9,600
	£29,000	£18,080	£1,160	£26,920
2007/08 (period of account — year to 31.12.07)				
12.1.04	4,000	3,520	160	3,360
3.6.05	15,000	13,800	600	13,200
26.4.06	10,000	9,600	400	9,200
	£29,000	£26,920	£1,160	£25,760

Date of expenditure	Cost	Residue brought forward	Allowances WDA 4%	Residue carried forward
	£	£	£	£
	2008/09 (period of account — year to 31.12.08)			
12.1.04	4,000	3,360	131	3,200
3.6.05	15,000	13,200	489	12,600
26.4.06	10,000	9,200	326	8,800
	£29,000	£25,760	£946	£24,600
	2009/10 (period of account — year to 31.12.09)			
12.1.04	4,000	3,200	90	3,040
3.6.05	15,000	12,600	336	12,000
26.4.06	10,000	8,800	224	8,400
15.10.09	20,000		450	19,200
	£49,000	£24,600	£1,100	£42,640
	2010/11 (period of account — year to 31.12.10)			
12.1.04	4,000	3,040	51	2,880
3.6.05	15,000	12,000	191	11,400
26.4.06	10,000	8,400	128	8,000
15.10.09	20,000	19,200	255	18,400
	£49,000	£42,640	£625	£40,680

The writing-down allowance for 2008/09 on the expenditure incurred on 12 January 2004 is computed as follows.

Period 1.1.08 to 5.4.08 (96 days)

$$\left(\frac{96}{366}\right) \times 160 \times 100\%$$

£42

Period 6.4.08 to 31.12.08 (270 days)

$$\left(\frac{270}{366}\right) \times 160 \times 75\%$$

£89

£131

However, the amount deducted in arriving at residue carried forward is the normal writing-down allowance of £160. The writing-down allowances for 2008/09 on the other items of expenditure are computed in the same way.

The writing-down allowance for 2009/10 on the expenditure incurred on 12 January 2004 is computed as follows.

Period 1.1.09 to 5.4.09 (95 days)

$$\left(\frac{95}{365}\right) \times 160 \times 75\%$$

£

31

Period 6.4.09 to 31.12.09 (270 days)

$$\left(\frac{270}{365}\right) \times 160 \times 50\%$$

59

£90

However, the amount deducted in arriving at residue carried forward is the normal writing-down allowance of £160. The writing-down allowances for 2009/10 on the other items of expenditure are computed in the same way. As regards the expenditure incurred on 15 October 2009, the normal writing-down allowance is £800 (£20,000 @ 4%).

The writing-down allowance for 2010/11 on the expenditure incurred on 12 January 2004 is computed as follows.

Period 1.1.10 to 5.4.10 (95 days)

$$\left(\frac{95}{365}\right) \times 160 \times 50\%$$

£

21

Period 6.4.10 to 31.12.10 (270 days)

$$\left(\frac{270}{365}\right) \times 160 \times 25\%$$

30

£51

However, the amount deducted in arriving at residue carried forward is the normal writing-down allowance of £160. The writing-down allowances for 2010/11 on the other items of expenditure are computed in the same way.

Business premises renovation

[10.5] For expenditure incurred on or after **11 April 2007** and subject to the conditions below, 100% capital allowances (known as business premises renovation allowances) are available for qualifying expenditure (see below) incurred by individuals and companies (whether as landlords or tenants) on the conversion or renovation of vacant business premises in designated development areas of the UK for the purpose of bringing those premises back into business use. The premises must have been unused for at least one year before the date the work begins. Certain trades are excluded. The scheme is expected to run for five years from date of commencement, but is capable of being extended. [*CAA 2001, ss 360A–360Z4; SI 2007 No 949*].

Business premises renovation allowances are available to the person (including a company) who incurred the qualifying expenditure and has the 'relevant interest' in the 'qualifying building'. [*CAA 2001, s 360A(2)*]. The '*relevant interest*' in relation to qualifying expenditure is determined in similar manner, with appropriate modifications, as for industrial buildings allowances (see **10.15** below), except that for the present purposes it cannot be transferred by the grant of a lease. In its simplest form, the relevant interest is the interest in the qualifying building to which the person incurring the expenditure was entitled when it was incurred. [*CAA 2001, ss 360E, 360F*]. As regards termination of leases, provisions similar to those of *CAA 2001, s 359* apply (see **10.15** below). [*CAA 2001, s 360Z3*]. '*Lease*' is defined (as are related expressions accordingly), and in particular includes an agreement for a lease whose term has begun and a tenancy. [*CAA 2001, s 360Z4*].

Qualifying expenditure

Qualifying expenditure means capital expenditure incurred before the 'expiry date' on, or in connection with:

- the conversion of a 'qualifying building' into 'qualifying business premises';
- the renovation of a 'qualifying building' if it is, or will be, 'qualifying business premises'; or
- repairs to a 'qualifying building' (or to a building of which the 'qualifying building' forms part), to the extent that they are incidental to either of the above (and for this purpose repairs are treated as capital expenditure if disallowable in computing the taxable profits of a property business (see **60.2 PROPERTY INCOME**) or of a trade, profession or vocation),

other than expenditure incurred on, or in connection with:

- the acquisition of, or of rights in or over, land;
- the extension of a qualifying building (except to the extent necessary to provide access to 'qualifying business premises');
- the development of adjoining or adjacent land; or
- the provision of plant and machinery, unless it is, or it becomes, a fixture as in **11.33** *et seq.* **CAPITAL ALLOWANCES ON PLANT AND MACHINERY.**

The '*expiry date*' is the fifth anniversary of the day appointed for these provisions to come into force, but may be a later date if the Treasury so decide and prescribe by regulations.

[*CAA 2001, s 360B(1)–(4)*].

A '*qualifying building*' is any building or structure (or part of a building or structure) which:

(a)   is situated in an area which, on the date the conversion or renovation work begins, is a 'disadvantaged area';

(b)   was unused for at least one year before the date the work begins;

(c)   was last in use for the purposes of a trade, profession or vocation or as an office or offices;

(d)   was not last in use as a dwelling or part of a dwelling; and

(e)   (in the case of part of a building or structure) had not last been occupied and used in common with another part of the building or structure which was last in use as a dwelling or which does not meet itself the one-year rule in (b) above.

A '*disadvantaged area*' is an area designated as such for these purposes by Treasury regulations or, in the absence of such regulations, an area for the time being designated as a disadvantaged area for stamp duty land tax purposes. Any such regulations may designate an area for a limited time only. If a building or structure is situated partly in a designated area and partly outside it, expenditure is to be apportioned on a just and reasonable basis in determining how much of it is qualifying expenditure. The areas designated from the outset are areas designated as development areas by the *Assisted Areas Order 2007 (SI 2007 No 107)* plus NI.

[*CAA 2001, s 360C(1)–(6); SI 2007 No 945, Reg 3*].

For any premises (i.e. a building or structure or part thereof) to be '*qualifying business premises*';

• they must be a qualifying building as above;

• they must be used, or available and suitable for letting for use, for '*qualifying purposes*', i.e. the purposes of a trade, profession or vocation or as an office or offices; and

• they must not be used, or available for use, as a dwelling or part of a dwelling.

Once premises are qualifying business premises, they do not cease to be so by reason only of *temporary* unsuitability for use, or for letting, for qualifying purposes.

[*CAA 2001, s 360D(1)–(3)*].

The above definitions of qualifying expenditure, qualifying building and qualifying business premises may be amended by Treasury regulations. [*CAA 2001, s 360B(5), s 360C(7), s 360D(4)*]. Consequently, *SI 2007 No 945, Reg 4* provides from the outset that premises are not qualifying business premises if they are converted or renovated by, or used by, a business engaged in any of the following trades: fisheries and aquaculture; shipbuilding; the coal industry; the steel industry; synthetic fibres; primary production of certain agricultural products; and the manufacture and marketing of products which imitate or substitute for milk products.

Initial allowances

The initial allowance is **100%** of the qualifying expenditure, may be claimed in whole or in part, and is made for the chargeable period (see **10.2**(i) above) in which the expenditure is incurred. The initial allowance is not available if the qualifying building is not qualifying business premises at the 'relevant time'; any initial allowance already made is withdrawn in such circumstances, and is also withdrawn if the person to whom the allowance was made has sold the relevant interest before the 'relevant time'. The *'relevant time'* is the time the premises are first used by the person with the relevant interest or, if not so used, are first suitable for letting for qualifying purposes. [*CAA 2001, ss 360G, 360H*].

Writing-down allowances

Writing-down allowances (WDAs) are available where the expenditure has not been wholly relieved by an initial allowance. The annual WDA is **25%** of the qualifying expenditure, on a straight line basis, proportionately reduced or increased if the chargeable period is less or more than a year, and may be claimed in whole or in part. The WDA cannot exceed the residue, i.e. the unrelieved balance, of the qualifying expenditure. The person who incurred the expenditure is entitled to a WDA for a chargeable period if *at the end of that period*:

- he is entitled to the relevant interest (see above) in the qualifying building;
- he has not granted, out of the relevant interest, a long lease (exceeding 50 years) of the qualifying building for a capital sum; and
- the qualifying building is qualifying business premises.

There is nothing to prevent a WDA being given in the same chargeable period as an initial allowance for the same expenditure.

[*CAA 2001, ss 360I–360K, 360Q, 360R*].

Effect of grants on entitlement to allowances

No initial allowance or WDA is available to the extent that the qualifying expenditure is taken into account for the purposes of a relevant grant or a relevant payment made towards that expenditure; any allowance already made is withdrawn to the appropriate extent. To the extent (if any) that a relevant grant or payment is repaid by the grantee, it is treated as having never been made. Any assessments, or adjustments of assessments, necessary to give effect to these rules are not out of time if made within three years after the chargeable period in which the grant or payment was made or, as the case may be, repaid. A grant or payment is *'relevant'* if it is a State aid notified to, and approved by, the European Commission or any other grant or subsidy nominated by Treasury order for these purposes. [*CAA 2001, s 360L*].

Balancing allowances and charges

If a 'balancing event' occurs, a balancing adjustment, i.e. a balancing allowance or balancing charge, is made to or on the person who incurred the qualifying expenditure and for the chargeable period in which the event occurs. If more than one balancing event occurs, a balancing adjustment is made only on the first of them. **No balancing adjustment** is made in respect of a balancing event occurring **more than seven years** after the time the premises were first used, or suitable for letting, for qualifying purposes. Any of the following is a *'balancing event'*:

(i)   the sale of the relevant interest (see above) in the qualifying building;

(ii)   the grant, out of the relevant interest, of a long lease (exceeding 50 years) of the qualifying building for a capital sum;

(iii)   (where the relevant interest is a lease) the coming to an end of the lease otherwise than on the person entitled to it acquiring the reversionary interest;

(iv)   the death of the person who incurred the qualifying expenditure;

(v)   the demolition or destruction of the qualifying building;

(vi)   the qualifying building's otherwise ceasing to be qualifying business premises.

The proceeds of a balancing event depend upon the nature of the event and are as follows.

(1)   On a sale of the relevant interest, the net sale proceeds receivable by the person who incurred the qualifying expenditure.

(2)   On the grant of a long lease, the capital sum involved or, if greater, the premium that would have been paid in an arm's length transaction.

(3)   In an event within (iii) above, where the persons entitled to, respectively, the lease and the superior interest are **CONNECTED PERSONS (21)**, the market value of the relevant interest in the qualifying building at the time of the event.

(4)   On death, the residue (see below) of qualifying expenditure.

(5)   On demolition or destruction, the net amount received for the remains by the person who incurred the qualifying expenditure, plus any insurance or capital compensation received by him.

(6)   On the qualifying building's otherwise ceasing to be qualifying business premises, the market value of the relevant interest in the qualifying building at the time of the event.

If the residue, i.e. the unrelieved balance, of qualifying expenditure immediately before the event exceeds the proceeds of the event (including nil proceeds), a balancing allowance arises, equal to the excess. (This is subject to the anti-avoidance rule at **10.2**(xi) above.) If the proceeds exceed the residue (including a nil residue), a balancing charge arises, normally equal to the excess but limited to the total initial allowances and WDAs previously given to the person concerned in respect of the expenditure.

[CAA 2001, ss 360M–360P].

Note that, by virtue of *CAA 2001, s 572*, a surrender for valuable consideration of a leasehold interest is treated as a sale (for equivalent proceeds), and thus falls within (1) above (if not caught by (3) above).

Any proceeds of sale of the relevant interest or other proceeds of a balancing event are, if attributable to both, apportioned on a just and reasonable basis between assets representing qualifying expenditure and other assets, and only the first part taken into account as above. *[CAA 2001, s 360Z2]*.

Demolition costs

Where a qualifying building is demolished, the net cost (after crediting any money received for remains) of demolition borne by the person who incurred the expenditure is added to the residue of qualifying expenditure immediately before the demolition, and is thus taken into account in computing the balancing adjustment; no amount included in gross demolition costs can then be included for any capital allowances purposes as expenditure on replacement property. [*CAA 2001, s 360S*].

Making of allowances and charges

If the person entitled to allowances or liable to charges under these provisions carries on a trade or occupies the qualifying building for the purposes of a trade, profession or vocation, the allowances/charges are treated as expenses/receipts of the trade, profession or vocation.

If the taxpayer's interest in the qualifying building is an asset of a property business (see **60.2 PROPERTY INCOME**) carried on by him at any time in the chargeable period (see **10.2**(i) above) in question, allowances/charges under these provisions are treated as expenses/receipts of that business. If the above is not the case but his interest in the building is nevertheless subject to a lease or a licence, he is deemed to be carrying on a property business anyway, and allowances/charges given effect accordingly. [*CAA 2001, ss 360Z, 360Z1*]. See **60.15 PROPERTY INCOME** as regards relief for property business losses.

Additional VAT liabilities and rebates

See **10.2**(viii) above as regards these generally. The initial allowance above is also available in respect of any additional VAT liability incurred at a time when the qualifying building is, or is about to be, qualifying business premises; the allowance is made for the chargeable period in which the liability accrues. For the purposes of WDAs, the residue of qualifying expenditure is treated as increased by the amount of an additional VAT liability at the time it accrues. The making of an additional VAT rebate is a balancing event, but it does not give rise to a balancing allowance and gives rise to a balancing charge only if it exceeds the residue (including a nil residue) of qualifying expenditure at the time the rebate accrues; otherwise the residue is treated as reduced by the amount of the rebate at the time it accrues. [*CAA 2001, ss 360T–360Y*].

Connected persons and other anti-avoidance provisions

The provisions at **10.22**(i) below for industrial buildings allowances apply equally to business premises renovation allowances, *except* that the election to treat a sale etc. as being at tax written-down value is *not* available in the instant case. [*CAA 2001, ss 567–570, 573, 575, 575A, 577(4); ITA 2007, Sch 1 para 411; FA 2008, Sch 27 paras 14–16, 18, 30; CTA 2010, Sch 1 para 362*].

Simon's Taxes. See **B3.11.**

Dredging

[10.6] Writing-down, balancing and, previously, initial allowances may be claimed for capital expenditure on **dredging** incurred for the purposes of a *qualifying trade* (provided that neither industrial buildings allowances (see **10.10** below) nor plant and machinery allowances (see **11 CAPITAL ALLOWANCES ON PLANT AND MACHINERY**) are available in respect of the same expenditure).

'*Dredging*' must be done in the interests of navigation, and either:

(i)   the qualifying trade must consist of the maintenance or improvement of navigation of a harbour, estuary or waterway; or

(ii)   the dredging must be for the benefit of vessels coming to, leaving or using docks or other premises used in the qualifying trade.

It includes removal, by any means, of any part of, or projections from, any sea or inland water bed (whether then above water or not), and the widening of any inland waterway.

A '*qualifying trade*' is one either within (i) above or within the industrial buildings allowance definitions at **10.12**(a)–(c) below. Expenditure only partly for a qualifying trade is apportioned as may be just and reasonable, and for this purpose, where part only of a trade qualifies, the qualifying and non-qualifying parts are treated as separate trades. [*CAA 2001, ss 484, 485; FA 2008, Sch 27 paras 34, 35*].

Initial allowances

Initial allowances were given for the tax year in whose basis period the expenditure was incurred at the following rates.

From 6 April 1956 —	10%
From 15 April 1958 —	15% (5% where certain investment allowances were payable between 8 April 1959 and 16 January 1966).

[*CAA 1968, s 67(1)(a)(8), Sch 1*].

Initial allowances were **abolished** for expenditure incurred **after 31 March 1986**, unless incurred before 1 April 1987 under a contract entered into before 14 March 1984 by the person incurring the expenditure. [*FA 1985, s 61*].

Writing-down allowances

Writing-down allowances are given to the person for the time being carrying on the trade during a writing-down period of 25 years (50 years for expenditure incurred before 6 November 1962) beginning with the first day of the chargeable period in which the expenditure was incurred, subject to an overall restriction on allowances (initial and writing-down) of the amount of the expenditure. No allowance is given for a chargeable period in which a balancing allowance arises (see below). The rates of allowance, fixed by the date expenditure was incurred, are as follows (although a lesser amount may be claimed).

Before 6 November 1962 — 2% p.a.
From 6 November 1962 — 4% p.a.

[*CAA 2001, ss 487, 489, Sch 3 para 103*].

Expenditure incurred for a trade before it is carried on attracts allowances as if it were incurred on the first day on which the trade was carried on. Similarly, expenditure incurred in connection with a dock etc. with a view to occupying it for the purposes of a qualifying trade other than one within (i) above attracts allowances as if it were incurred when the dock etc. is first so occupied. [*CAA 2001, s 486*].

Balancing allowances

A balancing allowance is given for the chargeable period of *permanent discontinuance* of the trade, equal to expenditure incurred less initial and writing-down allowances given, to the person last carrying on the trade. The allowance includes expenditure incurred before 6 April 1956, but in relation to such expenditure, all possible allowances (other than initial allowances) are deemed to have been given in respect of 1955/56 and earlier years as if the provisions introduced by *FA 1956* had always been in force.

Permanent discontinuance includes sale of the business (unless it is a sale between CONNECTED PERSONS (**21**), or without change of control, or one the sole or main benefit of which appears to be a capital allowance advantage), but not deemed discontinuance under **73.14 TRADING INCOME**.

[*CAA 2001, s 488, Sch 3 para 104*].

Contributions to expenditure

See **10.2**(vi)(vii) above.

Simon's Taxes. See B3.8.

Example

[10.7]

D is the proprietor of an estuary maintenance business preparing accounts to 30 June. Expenditure qualifying for dredging allowances is incurred as follows.

	£
Year ended 30.6.09	4,000
Year ended 30.6.10	5,000

On 2 January 2011, D sells the business to an unconnected third party. The allowances available are

Date of expenditure	Cost	Residue brought forward	Allowances WDA 4%	Residue carried forward
	£	£	£	£
2009/10 (year ended 30.6.09)				
2009	4,000		<u>160</u>	<u>£3,840</u>
2010/11				
Year ended 30.6.10				
2009	4,000	3,840	160	3,680
2010	5,000		<u>200</u>	<u>4,800</u>
			<u>£360</u>	<u>£8,480</u>
Six months ending 2.1.11				
Balancing allowance			<u>£8,480</u>	
Total allowances 2010/11 (360 + 8,480)			<u>£8,840</u>	

Dwelling-houses let on assured tenancies

[10.8] Legislation was introduced by *FA 1982* to give capital allowances on capital expenditure incurred by an *'approved body'* (i.e. a body specified by the Secretary of State under *Housing Act 1980, s 56(4)*), on the construction of buildings consisting of, or including, dwelling-houses let on assured and certain other tenancies, after 9 March 1982 and before 1 April 1992. [*CAA 2001, ss 490(1), 491, 492*]. The provisions were substantially modified following repeal of the relevant sections of the *Housing Act 1980* by the *Housing Act 1988*.

A dwelling-house is a *'qualifying dwelling-house'* when it is let on a tenancy being an assured tenancy within *Housing Act 1980, s 56* (or, not being an assured shorthold tenancy, within *Housing Act 1988*) and continues to qualify at any time when:

(i) it is subject to a regulated tenancy or a housing association tenancy (as defined in the *Rent Act 1977*); and

(ii) the landlord under the tenancy either is or has been an approved body.

[*CAA 2001, s 490(2)–(5)*].

A dwelling-house does not qualify:

(a) unless the landlord is a company (applicable to expenditure contracted and incurred after 4 May 1983, or where a person other than a company becomes entitled to the 'relevant interest' after that date) and either is entitled to the relevant interest in the dwelling-house or is the person who incurred the capital expenditure on the construction of the building containing it; or

(b)   if the landlord is a housing association approved under *CTA 2010, Pt 13 Ch 7* (previously *ICTA 1988, s 488*) (co-operative housing association) or is a self-build society under the *Housing Associations Act 1985*; or

(c)   if the landlord and tenant, or a company of which the tenant is a director, are CONNECTED PERSONS (**21**); or

(d)   if the landlord is a close company and the tenant is a participator, or associate of a participator, in that company; or

(e)   if the tenancy is part of a reciprocal arrangement between the landlords or owners of different dwelling-houses designed to counter the restrictions in (c) or (d) above.

[*CAA 2001, ss 504, 505; CTA 2010, Sch 1 para 358*].

Capital expenditure

Capital expenditure attributable to a dwelling-house is limited to £60,000 if it is in Greater London and £40,000 elsewhere, and is:

(A)   where the building consists of a single qualifying dwelling-house, the whole of the expenditure on its construction;

(B)   where the dwelling-house forms part of a building, (i) the proportion of capital expenditure attributable to that dwelling-house, and (ii) such proportion of the capital expenditure on any common parts of the building as is just and reasonable, but not exceeding one-tenth of the amount in (i).

[*CAA 2001, s 511*].

The acquisition of, or of rights in or over, any land is not included in expenditure incurred on the cost of construction of a building for these purposes. Any capital expenditure incurred on repairs is treated as if incurred on the construction for the first time of that part of the building. [*CAA 2001, s 493*].

Buildings bought unused

The provisions in *CAA 2001, ss 502, 503* are similar to those in *CAA 2001, ss 295, 296*, for which see **10.13, 10.14** below.

Expenditure met by another's contributions

See **10.2**(vi) above.

Initial and writing-down allowances

Initial allowances were, and writing-down allowances are, given in a similar manner, at similar rates and under similar conditions as for industrial buildings, for which see **10.14, 10.15** below. [*CAA 2001, ss 507–510, 519*].

References to 'temporary disuse' [*CAA 2001, s 506(2)*], 'residue of expenditure' [*CAA 2001, ss 512, 523–528*], and 'relevant interest' [*CAA 2001, ss 495–498, 500*] should be taken as they apply for industrial buildings allowances, but it should be noted that the creation of a subsidiary interest (e.g. leasehold out of freehold) does not transfer the relevant interest.

Balancing allowances and charges

Balancing allowances and charges are made in a similar manner and under similar conditions as for industrial buildings in *CAA 2001, s 314 et seq.* (see **10.16** below); this remains the case notwithstanding the abolition of balancing allowances and charges for industrial buildings allowances purposes and the pending abolition of industrial buildings allowances themselves. [*CAA 2001, s 513 et seq.*].

Where *cessation of qualifying use occurs* otherwise than by sale or transfer of the relevant interest, that interest is treated as having been sold at the time of cessation at the open market price. [*CAA 2001, s 506(1)*].

Making of allowances and charges

Allowances and charges are made in a similar way as they apply to lessors and licensors of industrial buildings, for which see **10.18** below. [*CAA 2001, s 529; CTA 2009, Sch 1 para 515*].

Holding over by lessee etc.

Where the relevant interest in relation to the capital expenditure incurred on the construction of a building is an interest under a lease, the following provisions apply. The lease will be treated as continuing where (i) with the consent of the lessor, a lessee remains in possession of any building after his lease ends and without a new lease being granted, (ii) where a lease ends and a new lease is granted to the same lessee under an option available in the first lease, and (iii) where a lease ends and another lease is granted to a different lessee who pays a sum to the first lessee (i.e. the transaction is treated as an assignment). However, where a lease ends and the lessor pays any sum to the lessee in respect of the building, the transaction is treated as if the lease had come to an end by reason of its surrender in consideration of the payment. [*CAA 2001, s 499*].

Connected persons and other anti-avoidance provisions

The provisions of *CAA 2001, ss 567–570* (and forerunners) apply to certain sales as they apply to sales of industrial buildings (see **10.22** below) but an election is only available if both the seller and the buyer are, at the time of the sale (or were at any earlier time), approved bodies. Any transfer of relevant interest which is not a sale will be treated as a sale other than at market price under these provisions but there is no balancing allowance or charge if the dwelling-house is treated as having been sold for a sum equal to the residue of expenditure before the sale. [*CAA 2001, ss 569(5), 570(4), 573*]. See also the anti-avoidance rule at **10.2**(xi) above.

Simon's Taxes. See B3.9.

Flat conversion

[10.9] Subject to the conditions below, 100% capital allowances (known as flat conversion allowances) are available for qualifying expenditure (see below) on converting former residential space above shops and other commercial premises in the UK into flats for letting or on renovating such flats. [*CAA 2001, ss 393A–393W*]. The allowances are available only in computing the profits of a UK property business (see **60.2 PROPERTY INCOME**) (though see **60.15 PROPERTY INCOME** as regards relief for property business losses).

Flat conversion allowances are available to the person (including a company) who incurred the qualifying expenditure and has the 'relevant interest' in the flat. [*CAA 2001, s 393A(2)*]. The *'relevant interest'* in relation to qualifying expenditure is determined in similar manner, with appropriate modifications, as for industrial buildings allowances (see **10.15** below), except that for the present purposes it cannot be transferred by the grant of a lease. In its simplest form, the relevant interest is the interest in the flat to which the person incurring the expenditure was entitled when it was incurred. [*CAA 2001, ss 393F, 393G*]. As regards termination of leases, provisions similar to those of *CAA 2001, s 359* apply (see **10.15** below). [*CAA 2001, s 393V*]. *'Lease'* is defined (as are related expressions accordingly), and in particular includes an agreement for a lease whose term has begun and a tenancy. [*CAA 2001, s 393W*].

For these purposes, a *'flat'* is a separate set of premises (covering one or more floors) forming part of a building and divided horizontally from another part. [*CAA 2001, s 393A(3)*]. See below for 'qualifying flat'.

Qualifying expenditure

Qualifying expenditure means capital expenditure incurred on, or in connection with:

- the conversion of part of a 'qualifying building' into a 'qualifying flat';
- the renovation of a flat in a 'qualifying building' if the flat is, or will be, a 'qualifying flat'; or
- repairs to a 'qualifying building', to the extent that they are incidental to either of the above (and for this purpose repairs are treated as capital expenditure if disallowable in computing the profits of a UK property business),

other than expenditure incurred on, or in connection with:

- the acquisition of, or of rights in or over, land;
- the extension of a qualifying building (except to the extent necessary to provide access to a 'qualifying flat');
- the development of adjoining or adjacent land; or
- furnishings or chattels.

The part of the building being converted, or the flat being renovated, must have been unused, or used only for storage, throughout the 12 months immediately preceding the commencement of the work.

[*CAA 2001, s 393B(1)–(4); ITTOIA 2005, Sch 1 para 559*].

Qualifying building

For a building to be a '*qualifying building*':

- all or most of its ground floor must be 'authorised for business use';
- its construction must have been completed before 1 January 1980 (disregarding any extension completed on or after that date but before 1 January 2001);
- it must have no more than four storeys above ground floor (disregarding an attic storey, unless used, or previously used, as a dwelling or part of a dwelling); and
- at time of construction, all such storeys must have been primarily for residential use.

[*CAA 2001, s 393C(1)(3)(4)*].

'*Authorised for business use*' is defined by reference to specified uses designated in the relevant ratings rules for England and Wales, Scotland and NI. [*CAA 2001, s 393C(2)*]. Included are retail shops, food and drink outlets, premises offering financial and professional services, other offices, medical and dental practices, and premises used for research and development and industrial processes which can be carried out in residential areas (Revenue Budget Notes REV BN 15, 7 March 2001).

Qualifying flat

For a flat to be a '*qualifying flat*':

(a) it must be in a qualifying building;

(b) it must be suitable for letting as a dwelling (disregarding any temporary unsuitability where previously suitable);

(c) it must be held for short-term letting, i.e. on leases of five years or less;

(d) it must be accessible by some means other than via the ground floor business area;

(e) it must have no more than four rooms (disregarding kitchens and bathrooms of whatever area, and closets, cloakrooms and hallways of no more than five square metres in each case);

(f) it must not be a 'high value flat';

(g) it must not be (or have been) created or renovated as part of a scheme involving the creation etc. of one or more 'high value flats'; and

(h) it must not be let to a person connected (within **21 CONNECTED PERSONS**) with the person who incurred the conversion or renovation expenditure.

[*CAA 2001, s 393D(1)–(4)*].

A flat is a '*high value flat*' if the 'notional rent' exceeds the relevant limit below.

No. of rooms (as in (e) above)	Greater London	Outside Greater London
1 or 2	£350 per week	£150 per week
3	£425 per week	£225 per week
4	£480 per week	£300 per week

The *'notional rent'* is the rent that could reasonably have been expected, at the time expenditure on the conversion etc. work is first incurred, if the work had been completed and the flat was then let furnished, on a shorthold tenancy (not applicable in NI), other than to a CONNECTED PERSON (21), and otherwise than for any additional payment, such as a premium.

[*CAA 2001, s 393E(1)–(5)(7)*].

General

The above definitions of qualifying expenditure, qualifying building and qualifying flat and the above notional rent limits may be amended by Treasury regulations. [*CAA 2001, s 393B(5), s 393C(5), s 393D(5), s 393E(6)*].

Initial allowances

The initial allowance is **100%** of the qualifying expenditure, may be claimed in whole or in part, and is made for the chargeable period (see **10.2**(i) above) in which the expenditure is incurred. The initial allowance is not available if the flat is not a qualifying flat at the time it is first suitable for letting as a dwelling or if the person who incurred the expenditure sells the relevant interest (see above) before that time; any initial allowance already made is withdrawn in such circumstances. [*CAA 2001, ss 393H, 393I*].

Writing-down allowances

Writing-down allowances (WDAs) are available where the expenditure has not been wholly relieved by an initial allowance. The annual WDA is **25%** of the qualifying expenditure, on a straight line basis, proportionately reduced or increased if the chargeable period is less or more than a year, and may be claimed in whole or in part. The WDA cannot exceed the residue, i.e. the unrelieved balance, of the qualifying expenditure. The person who incurred the expenditure is entitled to a WDA for a chargeable period if *at the end of that period*:

- he is entitled to the relevant interest (see above) in the flat;
- he has not granted, out of the relevant interest, a long lease (exceeding 50 years) of the flat for a capital sum; and
- the flat is a qualifying flat.

There is nothing to prevent a WDA being given in the same chargeable period as an initial allowance for the same expenditure.

[*CAA 2001, ss 393J–393L, 393Q, 393R; CTA 2009, Sch 1 para 506*].

Balancing allowances and charges

If a 'balancing event' occurs, a balancing adjustment, i.e. a balancing allowance or balancing charge, is made to or on the person who incurred the qualifying expenditure and for the chargeable period in which the event occurs. If more than one balancing event occurs, a balancing adjustment is made only on the first of them. **No balancing adjustment** is made in respect of a balancing event occurring **more than seven years** after the time the flat was first suitable for letting as a dwelling. Any of the following is a '*balancing event*':

(i)   the sale of the relevant interest (see above) in the flat;

(ii)   the grant, out of the relevant interest, of a long lease (exceeding 50 years) of the flat for a capital sum;

(iii)   (where the relevant interest is a lease) the coming to an end of the lease otherwise than on the person entitled to it acquiring the reversionary interest;

(iv)   the death of the person who incurred the qualifying expenditure;

(v)   the demolition or destruction of the flat;

(vi)   the flat's otherwise ceasing to be a qualifying flat.

The proceeds of a balancing event depend upon the nature of the event and are as follows.

(1)   On a sale of the relevant interest, the net sale proceeds receivable by the person who incurred the qualifying expenditure.

(2)   On the grant of a long lease, the capital sum involved or, if greater, the premium that would have been paid in an arm's length transaction.

(3)   In an event within (iii) above, where the persons entitled to, respectively, the lease and the superior interest are **CONNECTED PERSONS (21)**, the market value of the relevant interest in the flat at the time of the event.

(4)   On death, the residue (see below) of qualifying expenditure.

(5)   On demolition or destruction, the net amount received for the remains by the person who incurred the qualifying expenditure, plus any insurance or capital compensation received by him.

(6)   On the flat's otherwise ceasing to be a qualifying flat, the market value of the relevant interest in the flat at the time of the event.

If the residue, i.e. the unrelieved balance, of qualifying expenditure immediately before the event exceeds the proceeds of the event (including nil proceeds), a balancing allowance arises, equal to the excess. (This is subject to the anti-avoidance rule at **10.2**(xi) above.) If the proceeds exceed the residue (including a nil residue), a balancing charge arises, normally equal to the excess but limited to the total initial and writing-down allowances previously given to the person concerned in respect of the expenditure.

[*CAA 2001, ss 393M–393P*].

Note that, by virtue of *CAA 2001, s 572*, a surrender for valuable consideration of a leasehold interest is treated as a sale (for equivalent proceeds), and thus falls within (1) above (if not caught by (3) above).

Any proceeds of sale of the relevant interest or other proceeds of a balancing event are, if attributable to both, apportioned on a just and reasonable basis between assets representing qualifying expenditure and other assets, and only the first part taken into account as above. [*CAA 2001, s 393U*].

Demolition costs

Where a qualifying flat is demolished, the net cost (after crediting any money received for remains) of demolition borne by the person who incurred the expenditure is added to the residue of qualifying expenditure immediately before the demolition, and is thus taken into account in computing the balancing adjustment; no amount included in gross demolition costs can then attract capital allowances of any kind. [*CAA 2001, s 393S*].

Making of allowances and charges

If the taxpayer's interest in the flat is an asset of a UK property business (see **60.2** PROPERTY INCOME) carried on by him at any time in the chargeable period (see **10.2**(i) above) in question, allowances/charges under these provisions are treated as expenses/receipts of that business. If the above is not the case, he is deemed to be carrying on a UK property business anyway, and allowances/charges given effect accordingly. [*CAA 2001, s 393T; CTA 2009, Sch 1 para 507*]. See **60.15** PROPERTY INCOME as regards relief for property business losses.

Connected persons and other anti-avoidance provisions

The provisions at **10.22**(i) below for industrial buildings allowances apply equally to flat conversion allowances, *except* that the election to treat a sale etc. as being at tax written-down value is *not* available in the instant case. [*CAA 2001, ss 567–570, 573, 575, 575A, 577(4); ITA 2007, Sch 1 para 411; FA 2008, Sch 27 paras 14–16, 18, 30; CTA 2010, Sch 1 para 362*].

See generally the guidance at www.hmrc.gov.uk/specialist/flatsovershops.htm.

Simon's Taxes. See B3.10.

Industrial buildings

[10.10] Until the withdrawal of the regime (see **10.11** below), allowances are given in respect of certain capital expenditure (see **10.13** below) on industrial buildings (see **10.12** below), and are available to traders and to lessors and licensors of industrial buildings for use by traders.

The main elements of the industrial buildings allowances regime are dealt with in **10.12–10.22**.

Simon's Taxes. See B3.2.

Withdrawal of the industrial buildings allowances regime

[10.11] Industrial buildings allowances are being phased out. No allowances will be available for chargeable periods (as in **10.2**(i) above) beginning **on or after 6 April 2011**. In the meantime, the maximum writing-down allowance (see **10.15** below) is equal to the following percentage of the allowance to which the person would otherwise have been entitled:

(i)   100% for 2007/08 and earlier years;
(ii)   75% for 2008/09;
(iii)   50% for 2009/10; and
(iv)   25% for 2010/11.

In the simple case where the capital expenditure was incurred after 5 November 1962 and there has been no transfer of the relevant interest, this translates to writing-down allowances at 3% for 2008/09, 2% for 2009/10 and 1% for 2010/11 (compared to 4% for 2007/08 and earlier years).

If a chargeable period ending after 5 April 2008 (and beginning before 6 April 2011) does not coincide with a tax year, the writing-down allowance is determined as follows. Divide each chargeable period into the parts ending with 5 April and beginning with 6 April. Apply the following formula to each part and then add the results together. The result is the amount of the writing-down allowance available. The formula is:

$$\left(\frac{RDCPY}{RDCP}\right) \times NWDA \times P$$

Where

RDCPY   =   the number of days in the chargeable period which fall within the part of the chargeable period in question;

RDCP   =   the total number of days in the chargeable period;

NWDA   =   the normal writing-down allowance, i.e. the allowance to which the person would have been entitled had it not been for the phasing out of allowances; and

P   =   the percentage in either (i), (ii), (iii) or (iv) above depending on the tax year in which that part of the chargeable period falls (or 0% if it falls after 5 April 2011).

However, the residue of expenditure carried forward (see **10.15** below) is computed as if the normal writing-down allowance (NWDA in the above formula) had been made.

The abolition of industrial buildings allowances applies equally to enterprise zone expenditure (see **10.20** below) but the phasing out does not.

[*FA 2008, ss 84, 85*].

See Examples at **10.17** below.

Qualifying buildings

[**10.12**] An 'industrial building' is a building or structure, or part of a building or structure, in use either:

(a)   for the purposes of a trade, or part of a trade (see (A) below), consisting of:

        (i)   the manufacture or processing of goods or materials; or

(ii) the maintaining or repairing of goods or materials (but not goods etc. employed by the person carrying out the repair or maintenance in any trade or undertaking unless that trade etc. itself qualifies the building as an industrial building); or

(iii) the storage of (a) raw materials for manufacture, (b) goods to be processed, (c) goods manufactured or processed but not yet delivered to any purchaser, or (d) goods on arrival in the UK from a place outside the UK; or

(iv) the working of mines, oil wells etc. or foreign plantations; or

(v) agricultural operations on land not occupied by the trader; or

(vi) catching fish or shellfish; or

(b) for the purposes of:

(i) a transport, dock, inland navigation, water, sewerage, electricity, hydraulic power, bridge or tunnel undertaking; or

(ii) a toll road undertaking or a 'highway undertaking' (see below); or

(c) for the welfare of workers employed in a trade or undertaking within (a) or (b) above; or

(d) as a sports pavilion for the welfare of workers employed in any trade; or

(e) as a qualifying hotel (see **10.19** below).

As regards (a) above, following the decision in *Bestway (Holdings) Ltd v Luff* Ch D 1998, 70 TC 512, the Inland Revenue changed their view in two respects.

(A) Previously they had considered that, provided it was self-contained, anything done in the course of a trade was part of a trade for this purpose. Their revised view is that, whilst the activities in question do not need to be self-contained, they must be a significant, separate and identifiable part of the trade carried on. (HMRC Capital Allowances Manual CA32300).

(B) They previously considered the main test under (a)(iii) above to be whether the further conditions as to use of the goods or materials stored were satisfied. They have now adopted the Court's preliminary test that the determining factor in deciding whether a building is used for storage is the purpose for which the goods or materials are kept or held — it is used for storage only if the purpose of keeping them there is their storage as an end in itself and not some other purpose. (HMRC Capital Allowances Manual CA32224).

This change of view is most likely to be significant in wholesale trades where it has previously been accepted that there was a qualifying part trade of storage of goods or materials to be used in the manufacture of other goods or materials or subjected to a process. For allowances to continue to be available, the storage must be conducted as a purpose and end in itself, not just as a necessary and transitory incident of the conduct of the wholesale business. Where claims have previously been accepted under the earlier view, the revised view should be applied to claims for chargeable periods ending after 31 December 1999. (Revenue Tax Bulletin December 1999 pp 710, 711). See also the HL decision in *Maco Door and Window Hardware (UK) Ltd v HMRC* HL, [2008] STC 2594 in which allowances were denied on the grounds that a 'part of a trade' had to be not simply one of the activities carried out in the course of a trade but a viable section of a trade which would still be recognisable as a trade if separated from the whole.

A building the whole of which is in use partly for qualifying and partly for non-qualifying purposes may qualify for allowances in full provided that the qualifying use is at least 10% of the total use. (HMRC Capital Allowances Manual CA32315). See also *Saxone Lilley & Skinner (Holdings) Ltd* below.

Exclusions

Excluded from the definition of 'industrial building' are buildings or structures in use as, or as part of, dwelling-houses, retail shops, showrooms, offices or hotels (but see **10.19** below as regards expenditure on hotels), or for purposes ancillary thereto. See HMRC Capital Allowances Manual at CA32312 for what is an 'office' for these purposes, and at CA32313 for purposes 'ancillary' to those of a retail shop. In *Girobank plc v Clarke* CA 1998, 70 TC 387, a bank document and data processing centre was held not to be an office. In *Sarsfield v Dixons Group plc* CA 1998, 71 TC 121, a warehouse used by a group distribution company for receiving, storing and delivering goods purchased by the group for sale from its shops was held to be used for purposes ancillary to those of the group's retail shops. Where only part of a building or structure, representing 25% or less of the total cost, falls within these exclusions, the whole building or structure continues to qualify. Note that when alterations, extensions etc. or changes in use result in the 25% limit being exceeded, no amendment is made to allowances for chargeable (or basis) periods before that of the change, and allowances continue to be available in respect of that part of the building or structure not excluded. Similarly, where the 25% condition commences to be met, allowances are available for the whole of the building or structure only for the chargeable (or basis) period of the change and subsequent periods.

Buildings for employee use

Paragraph (c) above is regarded by HMRC as including canteens, day nurseries, garages, hard tennis courts, hostels and indoor sports halls. It does not, however, include buildings or structures excluded as above from being 'industrial buildings' (e.g. a grocery shop with extended hours for the convenience of workers, or holiday accommodation). Also as regards (c) above, the workers for whose welfare a building or structure is provided must be workers engaged directly in the productive, manufacturing or processing side of the business, rather than office staff or management, although the whole of a building or structure provided for staff generally may qualify provided use by production workers is not negligible. Similarly, use by outsiders as well as workers does not exclude the building or structure from relief. (HMRC Capital Allowances Manual CA32320).

Buildings or structures constructed for occupation by, or welfare of, employees in mines, oil wells etc. or foreign plantations, and likely to have little or no value on the ending of the working of the mine etc. or of the foreign concession, also qualify.

Buildings outside the UK

Buildings or structures outside the UK can only qualify if the trade for which they are in use is taxable in accordance with the rules that apply for calculating trading profits.

Buildings used by multi-licensees

A building or structure used by more than one licensee of the same person only qualifies if each of the licensees uses the building or structure, or his part of it, for the purposes of a trade as above under licences granted after 9 March 1982.

[*CAA 2001, ss 271(1)(2), 274–278, 280, 282, 283, Sch 3 paras 57, 59, 74*].

Highway undertakings and concessions

A '*highway undertaking*' (see (b)(ii) above) means so much of any undertaking relating to the design, building, financing and operation of roads as is carried on for the purposes of, or in connection with, the exploitation of 'highway concessions'. A '*highway concession*', in relation to a road, means any right, in respect of public use of the road, to receive sums from the State, or, in the case of a toll road, the right to charge tolls. [*CAA 2001, ss 274(1), 341(4)(5)*].

Case law

For cases in which industrial buildings allowances were **refused** see *Dale v Johnson Bros* KB(NI) 1951, 32 TC 487 (warehouse — contrast the non-tax case *Crusabridge Investments Ltd v Casings International Ltd* Ch D 1979, 54 TC 246); *CIR v National Coal Board* HL 1957, 37 TC 264 (colliery houses capable of alternative use); *Bourne v Norwich Crematorium* Ch D 1967, 44 TC 164 (furnace chamber etc.); *Abbott Laboratories Ltd v Carmody* Ch D 1968, 44 TC 569 (separate administrative block); *Buckingham v Securitas Properties Ltd* Ch D 1979, 53 TC 292 (building used for wage packeting); *Vibroplant Ltd v Holland* CA 1981, 54 TC 658 (depots of plant hire contractor, but now see (a)(ii) above); *Copol Clothing Co Ltd v Hindmarch* CA 1983, 57 TC 575 (inland storage of goods imported in containers); *Carr v Sayer* Ch D 1992, 65 TC 15 (quarantine kennels, claimed under (a)(iii)(d) above); *Girobank plc v Clarke* CA 1998, 70 TC 387 (bank document and data processing centre); *Bestway (Holdings) Ltd v Luff* Ch D 1998, 70 TC 512 (cash-and-carry wholesale warehouse); and *Sarsfield v Dixons Group plc* CA 1998, 71 TC 121 (warehouse used by retail group distribution company for receiving, storing and delivering goods); *Maco Door and Window Hardware (UK) Ltd v HMRC* HL, [2008] STC 2594 (storage not a part of the trade but simply an activity carried out in the course of the trade).

For cases where allowances were **granted**, see *CIR v Lambhill Ironworks Ltd* CS 1950, 31 TC 393 (drawing office); *Kilmarnock Equitable Co-operative Society Ltd v CIR* CS 1966, 42 TC 675 (coal packing not ancillary to retail shop); *Saxone Lilley & Skinner (Holdings) Ltd v CIR* HL 1967, 44 TC 122 (warehouse for shoes both bought and manufactured).

Temporary disuse

A building or structure which falls temporarily out of use after a period in which it qualified as an 'industrial building' is treated as continuing to so qualify during disuse. [*CAA 2001, s 285*]. All disuse other than that preceding demolition or dereliction is in practice regarded as temporary.

Simon's Taxes. See **B3.203–B3.213, B3.236**.

Qualifying expenditure

[**10.13**] Qualifying expenditure is the cost of construction of the building or structure including the cost of preparing, cutting, tunnelling or levelling land, but excluding expenditure on the land itself or on rights therein. [*CAA 2001, ss 272(1), 294*]. A just and reasonable apportionment is required to exclude unallowable expenditure (and see *Bostock v Totham* Ch D 1997, 69 TC 356 as regards the basis of such apportionment). [*CAA 2001, s 356*]. Anything with four walls and a roof is a building for these purposes, provided that it is of a reasonably substantial size. Anything smaller may be a structure. A structure is something which has been artificially erected or constructed, and which is distinct from the surrounding earth, e.g. roads, paved car parks or tennis courts, tunnels, culverts, bridges, walls and fences. (HMRC Capital Allowances Manual CA31110, 31120). The fees of professionals involved in the design and construction of a building or structure (e.g. architects, quantity surveyors and engineers) are also included. (HMRC Capital Allowances Manual CA31400). Expenditure on repairs which is, exceptionally, disallowable as capital expenditure in computing profits is treated as the cost of constructing that part of the building or structure [*CAA 2001, s 272(2)(3)*], and the cost of preparing etc. land as a site for the installation of plant or machinery is, if no relief would otherwise be available under industrial buildings or plant and machinery allowances, treated as attracting allowances as if the plant or machinery were a building or structure. [*CAA 2001, s 273*]. Where, for the purpose of erecting a new building or structure on the same site, costs are incurred in demolishing an existing building or structure, and the costs cannot be taken into account in calculating a balancing adjustment (see **10.16** below) on the demolished building or structure (e.g. because more than 25 (or 50) years has elapsed since it was first used), the demolition costs may be treated as expenditure on construction of the new building or structure. (HMRC Capital Allowances Manual CA31400).

Roads on an industrial trading estate most of the buildings on which are industrial buildings will themselves be treated as industrial buildings. [*CAA 2001, s 284*].

See **11.6** for certain expenditure on existing buildings or structures treated as being on plant or machinery.

The following are considered by HMRC to be excluded from being qualifying expenditure: expenditure on obtaining planning permission (although if a builder's costs are inclusive of such expenditure, no apportionment will be made); capitalised interest; public enquiry costs; land drainage and reclamation and landscaping; and legal expenses. (HMRC Capital Allowances Manual CA31400).

Abortive expenditure

Expenditure (including professional fees) incurred on the construction of a building or structure which never becomes an industrial building (e.g. because it is never completed) cannot be qualifying expenditure. (HMRC Capital Allowances Manual CA31410).

Buildings bought unused

If the 'relevant interest' (see **10.15** below) in a building or structure is sold before it is used, the purchaser (the last purchaser if more than one before the building or structure is used) is treated as having incurred on its construction, at the time the purchase price becomes payable, the lesser of the actual cost of construction and the net purchase price of the interest (excluding any part attributable to the land, see HMRC Capital Allowances Manual CA31305). Where the original expenditure was incurred by a builder as part of his trade of constructing such buildings or structures with a view to sale, the purchaser's deemed construction cost is the net purchase price paid by him or, if there have been previous sales unused, the lesser of the net purchase price paid by him and the net price paid to the builder on the first sale. (Note that this latter provision does not apply for agricultural buildings allowances purposes, for which the provisions are otherwise similar.) [*CAA 2001, ss 294–296, 299, 300*]. Except where the purchase price is specially defined by virtue of an election under *CAA 2001, s 290* (see **10.15** below), the net purchase price of the interest includes acquisition costs, i.e. legal fees, surveyors fees and stamp duty. (HMRC Capital Allowances Manual CA33520).

The initial allowance under *CAA 1990, s 2A* (see **10.14** below) could be claimed by the purchaser (or last purchaser) of an unused building or structure regardless of the date of sale providing some or all the actual construction expenditure fell within those provisions, i.e. it was incurred in, broadly, the year ending 31 October 1993. It could also be claimed where the actual construction expenditure was incurred by a builder (as above) *at any time* before 1 November 1993, the sale occurred between 1 November 1992 and 31 October 1993 inclusive and the vendor had been entitled to the relevant interest since before 1 November 1992. Such construction expenditure was deemed for these purposes to fall within *section 2A*. In both circumstances, it remained a condition that the building or structure came to be used before 1 January 1995 (see **10.14** below). Where only part of the actual construction expenditure was within *section 2A*, the purchaser's deemed construction cost was computed as above and then divided into a *section 2A* element qualifying for the initial allowance and a residual element qualifying only for writing-down allowances. The *section 2A* element was the proportion of the deemed expenditure that corresponded to the proportion of actual construction expenditure that was within *section 2A*. [*CAA 2001, Sch 3 para 77*].

Appropriation from trading stock

A building or structure appropriated by a builder from trading stock to capital account (with a corresponding market value credit to profit and loss) and let as an industrial building, is eligible for writing-down allowances based on the construction cost (rather than on the transfer value). Initial allowances were not available in these circumstances. (This commentary is not included in the current HMRC Capital Allowances Manual but was previously at CA1212 and is presumed still to be of application.)

Arrangements having an artificial effect on pricing

Where certain 'arrangements' have been entered into relating to, or with respect to, any interest in or right over a building or structure, special rules apply for determining any amount which is to be taken to be:

(a) for the purposes of the provisions relating to buildings bought unused or, after use, from original builder or, in certain cases, within two years after first use (see above and **10.20** below), the sum paid on the sale of the relevant interest; and

(b) for the purposes of allowances and charges generally (see above and **10.14–10.20** below), the amount of any proceeds from a subsequent balancing event where a person is deemed under any of the provisions referred to in (a) above to have incurred expenditure on the construction of the building or structure of an amount equal to the price paid on a sale of the relevant interest.

Where these provisions apply, the amount falling to be determined is reduced to the extent that the sale price or the amount of the sale etc. moneys is more than it would have been if the arrangements had not contained the provision in (iii) below.

The '*arrangements*' in question are those:

(i) entered into at or before the 'specified time';

(ii) having the effect at that time of enhancing the value of the relevant interest in the building or structure; and

(iii) containing any provision having an artificial effect on pricing,

and as regards (iii) above, arrangements are treated as containing such a provision to the extent that they go beyond what, at the time they were entered into, it was reasonable to regard as required by the prevailing market conditions in similar arm's length transactions. For examples of the sort of arrangements considered by HMRC to be most likely to be used, see HMRC Capital Allowances Manual CA39620.

The '*specified time*' is the time of the fixing of the sale price:

(A) in relation to the determination of an amount within (a) above, for the sale in question; and

(B) in relation to the determination of an amount within (b) above, for the sale by reference to which the amount of the deemed expenditure fell to be determined.

These provisions do not apply if the sale price referred to became payable before 29 November 1994 (6 April 1995 where the price was fixed under a contract entered into before 29 November 1994).

[*CAA 2001, ss 357, 564(3), Sch 3 para 78; FA 2008, Sch 27 paras 13, 30*].

Simon's Taxes. See B3.222–B3.224A.

Initial allowances

[10.14] In general, initial allowances were **abolished** for expenditure incurred after 31 March 1986, or after 31 March 1987 in the case of expenditure incurred after 13 March 1984 under a contract entered into before 14 March 1984 by the person incurring the expenditure. [*FA 1984, Sch 12 para 1*]. However, they continue at a rate of 100% for certain expenditure in enterprise zones (see **10.20** below), and were temporarily reinstated at a rate of 20% for general expenditure incurred in, broadly, the year ended 31 October 1993 (see below). They also continue to be available at the appropriate rate in respect of any additional VAT liability (see **10.2**(viii) above) in respect of such expenditure. [*CAA 2001, ss 305, 306, 346, Sch 3 paras 75–77*].

Initial allowances were temporarily reintroduced in respect of qualifying expenditure (see **10.13** above) incurred under a contract entered into in the twelve-month period **1 November 1992 to 31 October 1993 inclusive** or for the purpose of securing compliance with obligations incurred under a contract entered into during that period, but not for expenditure incurred under a contract entered into for the purpose of securing compliance with obligations under a contract entered into before 1 November 1992. The qualifying building or structure must have come to be used before 1 January 1995, and if this condition was not satisfied, any initial allowance given will have been withdrawn. The initial allowance was **20%** of the expenditure incurred. These provisions did not apply where initial allowances would otherwise have been available as above. They do apply to qualifying hotels (see **10.19** below), and also in respect of any 'additional VAT liability' (see **10.2**(viii) above) incurred in respect of expenditure falling within these provisions. [*CAA 2001, Sch 3 paras 75–77*].

The general conditions for the grant of initial allowances apply to the temporary allowances as above and (subject to the special provisions described in **10.20** below) to the 100% enterprise zone allowances generally in the same way as they applied to the pre-1984 allowances. The allowances are available to a person incurring qualifying expenditure (see **10.13** above) on a building etc. which is to be in use as an 'industrial building' (see **10.12** above) for a trade carried on by that person or by his lessee or, for licences granted after 9 March 1982, by his licensee. [*CAA 2001, s 305, Sch 3 para 64*]. See also **10.13** above as regards buildings or structures bought unused. An initial allowance is given for the chargeable period in which the expenditure is incurred. [*CAA 2001, s 306(3)*]. Expenditure for the purposes of a trade incurred by a person about to carry it on is treated as if incurred on the day the trade is actually commenced, but this applies only for the purpose of determining the chargeable period for which the allowance may be made (and not, for example, to determine the availability or otherwise of an initial allowance). [*CAA 2001, s 306(4)*]. See also **10.2**(iv) above generally as to the time at which expenditure is treated as being incurred.

Expenditure taken into account for the purposes of certain grants or payments specified by the Treasury for the purpose are excluded from initial allowances. [*CAA 2001, s 308, Sch 3 para 65*]. See also **10.2**(vi) above.

Initial allowances may be claimed in whole or part. [*CAA 2001, s 306(2)*]. They are withdrawn if, when the building or structure comes to be used, it is not an 'industrial building', or (in relation to the vendor) if it is sold before being used. [*CAA 2001, s 307*].

Earlier rates of initial allowance were as follows.

After 5 April 1944	— 10%	
After 5 April 1952	— Nil	
After 14 April 1953	— 10%	
After 6 April 1954	— Nil	
After 17 February 1956	— 10%	
After 14 April 1958	— 15%	
After 7 April 1959	— 5%	
After 16 January 1966	— 15%	
After 5 April 1970	— 30%	(40% if building or structure in development or intermediate area or N. Ireland)
After 21 March 1972	— 40%	
After 12 November 1974	— 50%	(20% on hotels and 100% in enterprise zones, from later dates, see **10.19** and **10.20** below)
After 10 March 1981	— 75%	(— as above —)
After 13 March 1984	— 50%	(— as above, omitting reference to workshops from 27 March 1985 —)
After 31 March 1985 to 31 March 1986	— 25%	(— as above —)

Simon's Taxes. See **B3.232, B3.254, B3.264.**

Writing-down allowances

[10.15] See also **10.11** above (withdrawal of the industrial buildings allowances regime).

These are available where a qualifying building or structure (see **10.12** above) is in use as such (or in temporary disuse following such use, see **10.12** above) at the end of a chargeable period. They are available to the person entitled to an interest which is the 'relevant interest' in the building or structure at the end of that period. A writing-down allowance can be given for the same chargeable period as an initial allowance (see **10.14** above) in respect of the same expenditure.

For expenditure incurred between 6 April 1946 and 5 November 1962 inclusive, the rate of allowance is 2% p.a. for 2007/08 and earlier years.

For expenditure incurred after 5 November 1962, the rate of allowance is **4% p.a.** for 2007/08 and earlier years (but see **10.20** as regards 25% annual allowances in certain cases) or such smaller amount as may be claimed.

The allowances are calculated on the qualifying expenditure (see **10.13** above) incurred, and continue until the 'residue of expenditure' is nil. The annual writing-down allowance is available in full where the expenditure is incurred during the chargeable period, but is proportionately reduced or increased where the chargeable period is less or more than twelve months. [*CAA 2001, ss 309, 310, 312, Sch 3 para 66*]. For lessors of industrial buildings, however, the chargeable period is the tax year itself, so that the full allowance is available regardless of the date of commencement of letting in the year. [*CAA 2001, s 6(2)*].

Additional VAT liabilities and rebates

Where an 'additional VAT liability' (see **10.2**(viii) above) is incurred in respect of any qualifying expenditure, the amount of the liability qualifies for writing-down allowances as if it were additional capital expenditure incurred on the construction in question; the 'residue of expenditure' is increased by that amount at the time the liability accrues. For chargeable periods ending after the time the liability accrues, writing-down allowances are given of the proportion of the residue of expenditure immediately after that time which the length of the chargeable period bears to the length of the period from the date of the incurring of the liability to the 25th anniversary of the first use of the building or structure for any purpose. Similar provisions apply where an 'additional VAT rebate' (see **10.2**(viii) above) is made, the residue being reduced by the amount thereof (but see **10.16** below where the rebate exceeds the residue). [*CAA 2001, ss 311, 347, 349–351*].

Effect of balancing events

If the 'relevant interest' in a building or structure is sold, and the sale is a balancing event (see **10.16** below), subsequent writing-down allowances are given to the purchaser and are calculated on the 'residue of expenditure' immediately after the sale, spread over the period from the date of sale to the 25th anniversary of the first use of the building or structure for any purpose (50th anniversary for expenditure incurred before 6 November 1962). [*CAA 2001, s 311, Sch 3 para 67*]. In a case of a sale on or after 21 March 2007 in relation to which no balancing adjustments are available (see **10.16** below), the residue of expenditure immediately after the sale is the same as the residue of expenditure immediately before the sale. [*FA 2007, s 36(2)(3)*].

Effect of sales before 18 December 1980

For a sale *before 18 December 1980* (or pursuant to a contract made before that date) at a time when the building or structure was not in use as an 'industrial building', so that no balancing adjustment arose (see **10.16** below), writing-down allowances to the purchaser (for subsequent chargeable (or basis) periods at the end of which the building or structure has reverted to use as an 'industrial building') continue at the rate after the most recent sale while in use as an 'industrial building' or, if there has been no such sale, the full 4% (or 2%) rate. [*CAA 1968, s 2; FA 1981, s 74*].

Residue of expenditure

'*Residue of expenditure*' is original capital expenditure

minus all industrial buildings and research and development allowances (see **10.37** below) granted, including balancing allowances, and

minus 'notional writing-down allowances' for periods, following first use of the building or structure for any purpose, at the end of which the building or structure was not in use as an 'industrial building', and

plus any balancing charges made, and

plus or *minus* any 'additional VAT liability' or 'additional VAT rebate' (see **10.2**(viii) above) incurred or made in respect of that expenditure.

Where the Crown is entitled to the relevant interest for a period immediately before a sale etc., allowances and charges which could have been made if the building or structure had been in use by a non-corporate trader entitled to that interest for that period are taken into account for this purpose. This treatment applies also to prior entitlement by any person not within the charge to income tax or corporation tax.

Where a balancing charge arises on the excess of allowances given over adjusted net cost following a sale after non-qualifying use (see **10.16** below), the residue after the sale is restricted to the net sale proceeds.

[*CAA 2001, ss 313, 332–339, 348, Sch 3 paras 72, 73*].

'*Notional allowances*' are calculated on the original qualifying expenditure or, if the building etc. has subsequently been sold in circumstances giving rise to a balancing adjustment (see **10.16** below), at the appropriate rate following that sale. [*CAA 2001, s 336(3)(4)*].

Relevant interest

'*Relevant interest*' is, in relation to any expenditure incurred on the construction of the building or structure, the interest (freehold or leasehold) in that building or structure to which the person who incurred the expenditure was entitled when he incurred it. If there is more than one such interest, and one was reversionary on all the others, the reversionary interest is the relevant interest. The creation of a subordinate interest (e.g. leasehold out of freehold) does not generally transfer the relevant interest (but see below). An interest arising on or as a result of completion of construction is treated as having been held when the expenditure was incurred. If a leasehold relevant interest is extinguished by surrender, or by the person entitled to it acquiring the interest reversionary on it, the interest into which it merges becomes the relevant interest. A highway concession (see **10.12** above) is not generally an interest in a road, but is treated as the relevant interest where the person who incurred expenditure on construction of the road was not then entitled to an interest in the road but was entitled to the highway concession in respect of it. [*CAA 2001, ss 286–289, 342*].

But where a lease of more than 50 years is granted out of a 'relevant interest' the lessor and the lessee may jointly elect for allowances to apply to the leasehold interest. The grant of the lease is then regarded as a sale to the lessee, the capital sum as the purchase price, and the lessee's interest as replacing all the lessor's relevant interest. The election is not available if lessor and lessee are

CONNECTED PERSONS (21) (unless the lessor controls the lessee and has statutory functions) or if the sole or main benefit which may be expected to accrue to the lessor is a balancing allowance (see **10.16** below). The election must be in writing to the inspector within two years after the date on which the lease takes effect. [*CAA 2001, ss 290, 291*].

Requisitioned land

Allowances may be available for buildings on land requisitioned by the Crown. See *CAA 2001, s 358*.

Termination of leases

(i) Where a lease ends and the lessee, with the lessor's consent, remains in possession without a new lease being granted, the lease is treated as continuing. (ii) A new lease granted on the termination of an old lease on exercise of an option available under the old lease is treated as a continuation of the old lease. (iii) If on termination of a lease the lessor pays any sum to the lessee in respect of a building comprised in the lease, the lease is treated as surrendered in consideration of the payment. (iv) If, on the termination of a lease, a lessee who is granted a new lease makes a payment to the lessee under the old lease, the two leases are treated as the same lease, the old lessee having assigned it to the new lessee for payment. [*CAA 2001, s 359*].

Buildings bought after use

Where a person carrying on a trade, consisting wholly or partly of the construction of buildings or structures with a view to their sale, incurs expenditure on such a construction and after the building or structure has been used, he sells the relevant interest in the course of the trade, the purchaser is entitled to allowances as if the original expenditure had been capital expenditure and all appropriate writing-down allowances and balancing allowances or charges (see **10.16** below) had been made to or on the vendor. Normally, the effect will be that the purchaser obtains allowances on the lesser of the net purchase price and the cost of construction. [*CAA 2001, s 297, Sch 3 para 60*].

Anti-avoidance

If there is a sale of the relevant interest in a building on or after 12 March 2008 and all the conditions set out below are met, the buyer's writing-down allowances for the chargeable period in which he buys the building are restricted by time-apportionment. The conditions are as follows.

- the sale is a balancing event (see **10.16** below);
- the buyer and seller have different chargeable periods;
- the buyer is a body of persons over whom the seller has control, or *vice versa*, or both the seller and the buyer are bodies of persons and another person has control over both of them, or the buyer and seller are CONNECTED PERSONS (21); and
- a main purpose of the sale is the obtaining of a tax advantage by the buyer under the industrial buildings allowances provisions.

The writing-down allowance to which the buyer would otherwise be entitled is:

$$\left(\frac{\text{DI}}{\text{CP}}\right) \times \text{NWDA}$$

Where

DI	=	the number of days in the chargeable period for which the buyer has the relevant interest;
CP	=	the total number of days in the chargeable period;
NWDA	=	the writing-down allowance to which the buyer would otherwise have been entitled.

These provisions do not apply if the sale is in pursuance of a written contract made before 12 March 2008 which is unconditional at that date, provided that no terms remain to be agreed at that date and that the contract is not significantly varied on or after that date.

[*CAA 2001, s 313A; FA 2008, s 87*].

Simon's Taxes. See **B3.221, B3.225–B3.227, B3.234–B3.234C.**

Balancing allowances and charges

[10.16] A balancing adjustment, i.e. either a balancing allowance or a balancing charge may arise to or on the person entitled to the 'relevant interest' (see **10.15** above) in a building or structure when it is sold, destroyed or permanently put out of use, or when the relevant interest is lost on termination of a lease or foreign concession, or when a highway concession (see **10.12** above) is brought to or comes to an end (see also below), *provided that* that event occurs within 25 years (50 years for expenditure incurred before 6 November 1962) of the building or structure's first being used. These events are known as balancing events. However, see below (and also **10.11** above) for the withdrawal of balancing adjustments in most cases where a balancing event occurs on or after 21 March 2007. On a sale etc. of a building or structure which has been an industrial building (or used for research and development — see **10.37** below) throughout the 'relevant period', the balancing adjustment is calculated as follows. If the 'residue of expenditure' (see **10.15** above) immediately before the sale etc. exceeds the proceeds of any sale, insurance, salvage or compensation, the difference is allowed as a balancing allowance (subject to the anti-avoidance rule at **10.2**(xi) above); if it is less, the difference is the subject of a balancing charge.

Where the building or structure has at any time in the 'relevant period' been neither an 'industrial building' nor in use for research and development, a balancing charge will be made to recover all allowances given where the proceeds of sale, insurance, salvage or compensation equal or exceed the 'starting expenditure'. Where those proceeds are nil or less than the 'starting expenditure', a balancing allowance will be given (or a balancing charge made) on the excess of the 'adjusted net cost' of the building or structure over the allowances given (or *vice versa*). For this purpose, the allowances given include all industrial buildings, research and development, and mills, factories or exceptional depreciation allowances, and any balancing charge raised may not exceed the total of such allowances, less any balancing charges previously made. Allowances made to a husband before 6 April 1990 in respect of his wife's relevant interest are treated as having been made to the wife for this purpose on a balancing event on or after that date.

'*Relevant period*' means the period beginning at the time when the building or structure was first used for any purpose and ending with the event giving rise to the balancing adjustment, unless there have been previous sales, when the relevant period begins on the day following the last sale.

'*Starting expenditure*' means the expenditure incurred on the construction of the building or structure (less any balancing charge made in respect of an 'additional VAT rebate' — see below) or, in the case of a second-hand building or structure, the residue of expenditure (see **10.15** above) at the beginning of the relevant period, together (in either case) with the net cost of demolition (see below) if appropriate.

'*Adjusted net cost*' means the amount by which starting expenditure exceeds the proceeds, reduced in the proportion that the period of qualifying use bears to the relevant period.

[*CAA 2001, ss 314(1)–(4), 315, 316, 318–324, 343, 350(5), Sch 3 paras 68–70*].

Successive sales etc. during non-use as industrial building

Where there are two or more sales etc. in a period during which a building or structure is not an 'industrial building', a balancing adjustment arises only on the first such sale etc. [*CAA 2001, s 314(5)*].

Additional VAT rebate

Where an 'additional VAT rebate' (see **10.2**(viii) above) is made in respect of qualifying expenditure, and this exceeds the residue of expenditure (see **10.15** above), a balancing charge, equal to the excess, will be made. [*CAA 2001, s 350*].

Highway concessions

In the case of a highway concession (see above), no balancing adjustment arises (and writing-down allowances continue) where, on the coming to an end of the concession, the period for which it was granted is extended, i.e. the person entitled to it is granted a renewal of the concession in respect of the whole or part of a road, or he or a CONNECTED PERSON (21) is granted a new concession in respect of the same road (or part of it or a road of which it is part). Where the extension relates to part only of a road, a 'just and reasonable' apportionment is made to determine the expenditure in respect of which a balancing adjustment arises. [*CAA 2001, s 344*].

Buildings for miners etc.

Special provisions apply to certain balancing allowances arising in the chargeable period in which a trade consisting of or including the working of a source of mineral deposits ceases, but which cannot be given effect because of an insufficiency of profits. Where the allowances are in respect of buildings occupied by, or for the welfare of, persons employed at or in connection with the working of the source, and they arise because of the source ceasing to be worked or the coming to an end of a foreign concession, the allowances may (subject to restrictions) be carried back to earlier chargeable periods. [*CAA 2001, s 355; ITA 2007, Sch 1 para 406; FA 2008, Sch 27 paras 27(4), 30*].

Balancing events occurring on or after 21 March 2007

Balancing events occurring on or after 21 March 2007 do not normally give rise to a balancing adjustment. This is the first phase of the withdrawal of industrial buildings allowances referred to at **10.11** above. Balancing adjustments remain available where a balancing event occurs before 1 April 2011 in pursuance of a written contract made before 21 March 2007. Any conditions attaching to the contract must have been satisfied before that date. No terms must remain to be agreed, and the contract must not be varied in a significant way, on or after that date. Balancing adjustments continue to apply where the qualifying expenditure in question is expenditure qualifying for enterprise zone allowances as in **10.20** below. [*FA 2007, s 36(1)(7)*].

Demolition

The net cost (after crediting sales of materials and scrap) of demolition borne by the person on whom a balancing adjustment arises is added to 'residue of expenditure' for balancing allowance and balancing charge calculations (and those costs are then not taken into account for capital allowance purposes except in the case of dwelling-houses let on assured tenancies, see **10.8** above). [*CAA 2001, s 340*]. Where this is not possible (e.g. because more than 25 (or 50) years has elapsed since the building or structure was first used), and if the holder of the relevant interest demolishes the building or structure for the purpose of erecting a new building or structure on the same site, the demolition costs may be treated as expenditure by the holder on construction of the new building or structure. (HMRC Capital Allowances Manual CA31400).

See also **10.22**(i) below as regards certain transactions between connected persons and other anti-avoidance provisions.

Simon's Taxes. See B3.237.

Examples

[10.17]

Writing-down allowances for periods spanning 6.4.08 to 5.4.2011

D prepares accounts to 30 June each year and incurred qualifying expenditure of £800,000 on an industrial building in May 2001. He claimed writing-down allowances of £32,000 p.a. for the years 2001/02 to 2007/08 inclusive. For 2008/09 (for which the basis period is the year to 30 June 2008), as a result of the phased withdrawal of industrial building allowances (see **10.11** above), his writing-down allowance is reduced to £30,120 (computed as follows).

Period 1.7.07 to 5.4.08 (280 days)

$$\left(\frac{280}{366}\right) \times 32,000 \times 100\%$$

£

24,481

Period 6.4.08 to 30.6.08 (86 days)

$$\left(\frac{86}{366}\right) \times 32,000 \times 75\%$$

5,639

£30,120

However, the amount deducted in arriving at residue carried forward is the normal writing-down allowance of £32,000. For 2009/10 (for which the basis period is the year to 30 June 2009), his writing-down allowance is £22,115 (computed as follows).

Period 1.7.08 to 5.4.09 (279 days)

$$\left(\frac{279}{365}\right) \times 32,000 \times 75\%$$

£

18,345

Period 6.4.09 to 30.6.09 (86 days)

$$\left(\frac{86}{365}\right) \times 32,000 \times 50\%$$

3,770

£22,115

For 2010/11 (for which the basis period is the year to 30 June 2010), his writing-down allowance will be £14,115 (computed as follows).

Period 1.7.09 to 5.4.10 (279 days)

$$\left(\frac{279}{365}\right) \times 32,000 \times 50\%$$

£

12,230

Period 6.4.10 to 30.6.10 (86 days)

$$\left(\frac{86}{365}\right) \times 32,000 \times 25\%$$

1,885

£14,115

For 2011/12 (for which the basis period is the year to 30 June 2011), his writing-down allowance will be £6,115 (computed as follows).

Period 1.7.10 to 5.4.11 (279 days)

$$\left(\frac{279}{365}\right) \times 32,000 \times 25\%$$

£

6,115

Period 6.4.11 to 30.6.11

<u>Nil</u>
<u>£6,115</u>

For 2012/13 onwards, D is not entitled to any industrial buildings allowances.

Writing-down allowances and balancing adjustments

(i) Prior to commencing business on 1 June 1996, P incurred the following expenditure.

	£
10.1.96 Plot of land	50,000
20.2.96 Clearing and levelling site	20,000
20.4.96 Construction of factory	<u>500,000</u>
	<u>£570,000</u>

The factory was brought into use for a qualifying purpose on commencement of trade, and remained in such use until 1 May 2006, when it was sold to Y for £550,000, being £480,000 for the factory and £70,000 for the land. P drew up accounts annually to 31 May. Y draws up accounts to 5 April, and uses the factory for a qualifying purpose.

The allowances available to P are as follows.

Period of account ended			Residue of expenditure £
31 May 1997	Qualifying expenditure		520,000
	Writing-down allowance	4% of £520,000	(20,800)
			499,200
31 May 1998	Writing-down allowance for 8 years	4% of £520,000 × 8	(166,400)
1999			
2000			
2001			
2002			
2003			
2004			
2005			
			332,800
31 May 2006	Sale proceeds		(480,000)

Period of account ended	Residue of expenditure £
Balancing charge	£147,200

The allowances available to Y are as follows.

Date of first use	1.6.96
Date of purchase by Y	1.5.06
Number of years remaining	15 years 1 month
Residue of expenditure	£480,000

Y is therefore entitled to writing-down allowances of £31,824 p.a. (i.e. the residue divided by 15.083 years). His first writing-down allowance will be given for the period of account ended 5 April 2007. For 2008/09 (for which the basis period is the year to 5 April 2009), as a result of the phased withdrawal of industrial building allowances (see **10.11** above), his writing-down allowance is reduced to £31,824 × 75% = £23,868. For 2009/10, his writing-down allowance is reduced to £31,824 × 50% = £15,912. For 2010/11, his writing-down allowance is reduced to £31,824 × 25% = £7,956.

Note

(a) No allowances are due on the cost of the land (see **10.13** above).

(ii) The facts are as in (i) above except that all dates are advanced by one year, so that P incurred the expenditure on the building in 1997 and sells it to Y on 1 May 2007 (and not under a pre-21 March 2007 contract).

P is entitled to a writing-down allowance of £166,400 spread equally over eight years, leaving a residue of expenditure of £332,800. There is no balancing charge for the year to 31 May 2007 (as the sale to Y took place after 20 March 2007) (see **10.16** above). Y inherits the residue of £332,800 and is entitled to a writing-down allowance of £22,065 (i.e. the residue divided by 15.083 years) for the year to 5 April 2008. For 2008/09 (for which the basis period is the year to 5 April 2009), his writing-down allowance is reduced to £22,065 × 75% = £16,549. For 2009/10, his writing-down allowance is reduced to £22,065 × 50% = £11,033. For 2010/11, his writing-down allowance is reduced to £22,065 × 25% = £5,517.

Non-qualifying purposes and balancing adjustments

A, B and C entered into partnership in 1976 and prepare accounts annually to 31 March. The partnership incurred £40,000 of capital expenditure in 1986 (and before 31 March 1986) on the construction of a building which was brought into use as an industrial building on 1 April 1987. After three years of use for a qualifying industrial purpose, it was used for three years, from 1 April 1990 to 31 March 1993, for non-qualifying purposes after which the original qualifying activity was resumed until the building was destroyed by fire.

The fire occurred on 1 October 2006 with an insurance recovery of (i) £50,000 (ii) £35,000. The partnership's industrial buildings allowance position for the period of account 1 April 2006 to 31 March 2007 will be as follows.

Year ended 31 March 2007: Balancing charge
(i) *Proceeds exceed cost*

Actual allowances given	note (a)	£34,000
Balancing charge		£34,000

		£
(ii) *Proceeds less than cost*		
Net cost (£40,000 – £35,000)		5,000
Reduction $\dfrac{3y}{19y6m}$	note (b)	(769)
Adjusted net cost		4,231
Allowances given	note (a)	34,000
Excess		£29,769
Balancing charge		£29,769

Notes

(a)   Allowances given in previous years are:

	£
Initial allowance £40,000 × 25%	10,000
Writing-down allowances £40,000 × 4% × 15	24,000
	£34,000

Writing-down allowances would not have been given for the three years 1991/92 to 1993/94 as the building was not an industrial building at the end of the basis period for each of those years (see **10.15** above).

(b)   In example (ii), the net cost is reduced by the proportion which the period of non-qualifying use bears to the total period from first use to date of balancing event (see **10.16** above).

(c)   No balancing charge would have arisen if the fire had occurred after 20 March 2007 (see **10.16** above).

Making of allowances and charges

[10.18] For traders, allowances and charges are given effect in calculating profits (see **10.1** above and see also below). This applies equally to professions and vocations. [*CAA 2001, s 352*]. Allowances must be claimed in the annual tax return (see **10.2**(ii) above). A highway undertaking (see **10.12** above) is treated as a trade. [*CAA 2001, s 341(1)*].

Allowances to, and charges on, traders are treated as trading expenses and receipts [*CAA 2001, s 352(1)*] and are calculated by reference to events in periods of account (see **10.2**(i) above).

Temporarily unused buildings

Where a period of temporary disuse follows on immediately from a time when a building was an industrial building, with the result that (by virtue of *CAA 2001, s 285* — see **10.12** above) the building is deemed to be an industrial building during the period of temporary disuse, then if on the last occasion upon which the building was in use as an industrial building,

- it was in use for the purposes of a trade which has ceased, or
- the relevant interest was subject to a lease which has since come to an end, or
- it was used under a licence which has since come to an end,

any allowance or charge falling to be made during any period for which the temporary disuse continues after the cessation of the trade or the coming to an end of the lease or licence is made, under *CAA 2001, s 353* (see below), as if the interest in the building were subject to a lease at that time.

Where a balancing charge falls to be made on any person following a period of temporary disuse of a building, and its most recent use was as an industrial building for the purposes of a trade carried on by that person which has since ceased, the same deductions can be made from the charge as can be made under from a post-cessation receipt (see **59.3 POST-CESSATION RECEIPTS AND EXPENDITURE**). This is without prejudice to the deduction of any amounts allowable against the balancing charge under other provisions.

[*CAA 2001, s 354*].

Lessors and licensors

Lessors (and licensors) of industrial buildings may claim allowances for a tax year. Allowances and balancing charges are treated as expenses and receipts of a UK property business (see **60.2 PROPERTY INCOME**) or, if the lease or licence is an asset of an overseas property business (see **60.2 PROPERTY INCOME**), of that business. Where it is not an asset of any property business, allowances and charges are treated as expenses and receipts of a notional UK property business. See **60.15 PROPERTY INCOME** as regards property business losses. [*CAA 2001, s 353*].

Simon's Taxes. See B3.236, B3.241.

Hotels

[10.19] Expenditure incurred after 11 April 1978 and before 1 April 1986, or before 1 April 1987 under a contract entered into before 14 March 1984 by the person incurring the expenditure, on construction or extension of a 'qualifying hotel' attracted an initial allowance of 20% and writing-down allowances of 4% p.a. The 20% initial allowance under *CAA 1990, s 2A* for expenditure incurred in, broadly, the year ending 31 October 1993 (see **10.14** above) applied equally to 'qualifying hotels'. For subsequent expenditure, 'qualifying hotels' attract writing-down allowances as industrial buildings in the normal way (see **10.15** above). Certain expenditure on safety measures and thermal insulation may be treated as expenditure on plant and machinery, see **11.8 CAPITAL ALLOWANCES ON PLANT AND MACHINERY.**

A *'qualifying hotel'* must have accommodation in building(s) of a permanent nature and be open for at least four months during April–October, and whilst open during those months: (i) must have at least ten letting bedrooms, i.e. private bedrooms for letting to the public generally and not normally in same occupation for more than a month; (ii) must offer sleeping accommodation consisting wholly or mainly of letting bedrooms; and (iii) its services must normally include providing breakfast and evening meals, making beds and cleaning rooms. The provision of breakfast and dinner must be offered as a normal event in the carrying on of the hotel business and must not be exceptional or available only on request. (HMRC SP 9/87). Buildings provided (and in use) for the welfare of employees are regarded as part of a qualifying hotel. Accommodation which, when the hotel is open during April–October, is normally used as a dwelling by an individual carrying on (including in partnership) the hotel (or by a member of his family or household) is excluded (unless the proportion of the total cost attributable to excluded accommodation is less than 25%, in which case the whole of the expenditure qualifies).

The meeting of the above conditions at any time during a chargeable period is determined by reference to their being met during a twelve month period as follows. If the hotel was in use for the trade throughout the twelve months ending with the last day of the chargeable period, it is that twelve month period. If the hotel was first used for the purposes of the trade after the beginning of such a period (or the ten-bedroom requirement commenced to be met after the beginning of such a period), it is the twelve months from commencement (or from the requirement being first met). The conditions are not met at any time in a chargeable period after the hotel has ceased altogether to be used. An hotel in temporary disuse (see **10.12** above) ceases to qualify two years after the end of the chargeable period in which it fell out of use. An hotel outside the UK may qualify provided that the profits etc. are taxable in accordance with the rules that apply for calculating trading profits.

Balancing adjustments arise on a balancing event falling within *CAA 2001, s 315* (see **10.16** above) (whether or not the hotel is at the time a 'qualifying hotel') or, if the hotel ceases to qualify and there is no such balancing event within two years of the end of the chargeable period in which it ceases to qualify, at the end of that two years, when the hotel is treated as having been sold at market value. The latter 'two-year' rule does not apply to qualifying hotels in enterprise zones (see **10.20** below).

[*CAA 2001, ss 271(1)(b), 279, 282, 283, 285, 317, Sch 3 para 58*].

Simon's Taxes. See **B3.251–B3.254**.

Enterprise zones

[10.20] An 'enterprise zone' is an area designated as such by the Secretary of State (or by Scottish Ministers, the National Assembly for Wales or, for NI, the Department of the Environment). [*CAA 2001, s 298(3); FA 2001, s 69, Sch 21 para 5*]. Areas designated are set out below but it should be noted that in every case the ten-year life of the zone expired before 1 April 2007.

Allerdale, see Workington (Allerdale)

Arbroath, see Tayside (Arbroath)

Ashfield, see East Midlands (No 7)

Barnsley, see Dearne Valley

Bassetlaw, see East Midlands (No 4)

Belfast (from 21 October 1981, *SR 1981 No 309*)

Clydebank (from 3 August 1981, *SI 1981 No 975*)

Corby (from 22 June 1981, *SI 1981 No 764*)

Dearne Valley (Nos 1 to 6) (from 3 November 1995, *SI 1995 No 2624*)

Delyn (from 21 July 1983, *SI 1983 No 896*)

Derbyshire (NE), see East Midlands (Nos 1 to 3)

Doncaster, see Dearne Valley

Dudley (Round Oak) (from 3 October 1984, *SI 1984 No 1403*)

Dudley (not Round Oak) (from 10 July 1981, *SI 1981 No 852*)

Dundee, see Tayside (Dundee)

Easington, see East Durham

East Durham (Nos 1 to 6) (from 29 November 1995, *SI 1995 No 2812*)

East Midlands (Nos 1 to 3) (from 3 November 1995, *SI 1995 No 2625*)

East Midlands (No 4) (from 16 November 1995, *SI 1995 No 2738*)

East Midlands (No 7) (from 21 November 1995, *SI 1995 No 2758*)

Flixborough, see Glanford (Flixborough)

Gateshead (from 25 August 1981, *SI 1981 No 1070*)

Glanford (Flixborough) (from 13 April 1984, *SI 1984 No 347*)

Glasgow (from 18 August 1981, *SI 1981 No 1069*)

Hartlepool (from 23 October 1981, *SI 1981 No 1378*)

Holmewood, see East Midlands (Nos 1 to 3)

Inverclyde (from 3 March 1989, *SI 1989 No 145*)

Invergordon (from 7 October 1983, *SI 1983 No 1359*)

Isle of Dogs (from 26 April 1982, *SI 1982 No 462*)

Kent (NW) (zones 1 to 5 only) (from 31 October 1983, *SI 1983 No 1452*)

Kent (NW) (zones 6 and 7 only) (from 10 October 1986, *SI 1986 No 1557*)

Lanarkshire (Hamilton) (from 1 February 1993, *SI 1993 No 23*)

Lanarkshire (Monklands) (from 1 February 1993, *SI 1993 No 25*)

Lanarkshire (Motherwell) (from 1 February 1993, *SI 1993 No 24*)

Lancashire (NE) (from 7 December 1983, *SI 1983 No 1639*)

Liverpool (Speke) (from 25 August 1981, *SI 1981 No 1072*)

London, see Isle of Dogs

Londonderry (from 13 September 1983, *SR 1983 No 226*)

Lower Swansea Valley (from 11 June 1981, *SI 1981 No 757*)

Lower Swansea Valley (No 2) (from 6 March 1985, *SI 1985 No 137*)

Middlesbrough (Britannia) (from 8 November 1983, *SI 1983 No 1473*)

Milford Haven Waterway (North Shore) (from 24 April 1984, *SI 1984 No 443*)

Milford Haven Waterway (South Shore) (from 24 April 1984, *SI 1984 No 444*)

Newcastle (from 25 August 1981, *SI 1981 No 1071*)

Rotherham (from 16 August 1983, *SI 1983 No 1007*), and see Dearne Valley

Salford Docks (from 12 August 1981, *SI 1981 No 1024*)

Scunthorpe (Normanby Ridge and Queensway) (from 23 September 1983, *SI 1983 No 1304*)

Speke, see Liverpool (Speke)

Sunderland (Castletown and Doxford Park) (from 27 April 1990, *SI 1990 No 794*)

Sunderland (Hylton Riverside and Southwick) (from 27 April 1990, *SI 1990 No 795*)

Swansea, see Lower Swansea Valley and Lower Swansea Valley (No 2)

Tayside (Arbroath) (from 9 January 1984, *SI 1983 No 1816*)

Tayside (Dundee) (from 9 January 1984, *SI 1983 No 1817*)

Telford (from 13 January 1984, *SI 1983 No 1852*)

Trafford Park (from 12 August 1981, *SI 1981 No 1025*)

Tyne Riverside (North Tyneside) (No 1) (from 19 February 1996, *SI 1996 No 106*)

Tyne Riverside (North Tyneside) (No 2) (from 26 August 1996, *SI 1996 No 1981*)

Tyne Riverside (North Tyneside and South Tyneside) (from 21 October 1996, *SI 1996 No 2435*)

Wakefield (Dale Lane and Kingsley) (from 23 September 1983, *SI 1983 No 1305*)

Wakefield (Langthwaite Grange) (from 31 July 1981, *SI 1981 No 950*)

Wellingborough (from 26 July 1983, *SI 1983 No 907*)

Workington (Allerdale) (from 4 October 1983, *SI 1983 No 1331*)

Advantageous provisions apply to expenditure on the construction of an industrial building, which for this purpose includes a 'qualifying hotel' or a 'commercial building or structure', which is incurred (or contract entered into) within ten years of the inclusion of the site in an enterprise zone. Expenditure incurred more than 20 years after a site was first included in an enterprise zone does not attract enterprise zone allowances, regardless of when the contract for the expenditure was entered into. [*CAA 2001, ss 271(1)(b), 298*].

These provisions will **cease to have effect from 6 April 2011** in line with the general abolition of industrial buildings allowances (see **10.11** above). There is no phased withdrawal, so allowances continue to be fully available, and normal balancing adjustments apply, for chargeable periods (as in **10.2**(i) above) beginning before 6 April 2011.

For a chargeable period straddling 6 April 2011, the writing-down allowance is determined in accordance with the following formula:

$$\left(\frac{\text{DCPY}}{\text{DCP}} \right) \times \text{NWDA}$$

Where

DCPY = the number of days in the chargeable period which fall before 6 April 2011;

DCP   =   the total number of days in the chargeable period; and

NWDA =   the normal writing-down allowance, i.e. the allowance to which the person would have been entitled had it not been for the phasing out of allowances.

[FA 2008, s 86].

Despite the abolition, a balancing charge can still arise in a chargeable period beginning on or after 6 April 2011 on the sale etc. of a building on which enterprise zone allowances have been claimed. This will be the case if an event occurs within seven years after the building is first used, and the event is such that, disregarding the abolition, it would have been a balancing event giving rise to a balancing charge. *[FA 2008, Sch 27 paras 31, 35]*. See **10.16** above as regards balancing events generally (and see also (iii) below).

Similarly, if an initial allowance falls to be withdrawn by virtue of *CAA 2001, s 307* (change of use or sale — see **10.14** above), it will be withdrawn notwithstanding the abolition, but only if the event giving rise to the withdrawal occurs within seven years after the end of the chargeable period for which the initial allowance was made. *[FA 2008, Sch 27 paras 32, 35]*.

'*Qualifying hotel*' has the same meaning as in **10.19** above. (Note that any hotel not qualifying under this heading will qualify as a commercial building.)

'*Commercial building or structure*' means a building or structure which is used for the purposes of a trade, profession or vocation or as an office for any purpose, but does not include any building in use as, or as part of, a dwelling house. *[CAA 2001, s 281]*.

Initial and writing-down allowances

An initial allowance of **100%** is given but the full amount need not be claimed. If any part of the initial allowance is not claimed, then writing-down allowances at **25%** p.a. of cost on the straight line basis will apply to the unclaimed balance. *[CAA 2001, s 306(1)(2), s 310(1)(a)]*. No writing-down allowances are available after 5 April 2011 — see above.

Special rules

For the general provisions relating to industrial buildings allowances, see **10.12** *et seq.* above. As regards enterprise zone allowances, the following special rules apply.

(i)   *Date expenditure incurred. CAA 2001, s 306(4)* (pre-trading expenditure treated as incurred on first day of trading, see **10.14** above) do not apply in determining whether expenditure attracts enterprise zone allowances (i.e. whether it is incurred at a time when the building or structure is in an enterprise zone).

      As regards buildings or structures bought unused, where the purchase price becomes payable after 15 December 1991, the normal rules under *CAA 2001, ss 294–296* apply (see **10.13** above), except that:

      (a)   where some or all of the actual construction expenditure is incurred (or incurred under a contract entered into) within ten years of the inclusion of the site in an enterprise zone, a corresponding proportion of the purchaser's deemed expenditure is treated as giving rise to entitlement to enterprise zone allowances, notwithstanding that it may be deemed to have been incurred outside that ten-year period;

(b)   where (a) does not apply, the purchaser's deemed expenditure is treated as not giving rise to entitlement to enterprise zone allowances, notwithstanding that it may be deemed to have been incurred during the ten-year period.

Where some of the actual construction expenditure fell within (a) above and some or all of the balance could qualify for a 20% initial allowance by virtue of the provisions in **10.13** above, the above provisions and those in **10.13** above interacted. The purchaser could thus obtain a 100% enterprise zone initial allowance on part of his deemed expenditure and the 20% initial allowance on another part or, where appropriate, on the balance.
[*CAA 2001, ss 300, 302, Sch 3 para 61*].

(ii)   *Buildings purchased within two years of first use.* Where some or all of the construction expenditure on a building or structure is incurred (or incurred under a contract entered into) within ten years of the inclusion of the site in an enterprise zone, and the 'relevant interest' (see **10.15** above) is sold during the two years (but see below) following the first use of the building or structure (whether or not there have been any sales while the building or structure was unused), then on that sale (or the first such sale) the normal balancing allowance or charge rules apply to the vendor (see **10.16** above), but the purchaser is deemed to have incurred expenditure on purchase of a building or structure bought unused (see **10.13** and (i) above). A proportion of the deemed expenditure corresponding to the proportion of the actual construction expenditure which was incurred within ten years of the inclusion of the site in the enterprise zone is treated as giving rise to entitlement to enterprise zone allowances, notwithstanding that it may be deemed to have been incurred outside the ten-year period. The balance of the deemed expenditure does not attract enterprise zone allowances. If the purchase is directly from a person who constructed the building or structure in the course of a trade of constructing such buildings or structures for sale, the part of the purchaser's deemed expenditure which does *not* attract enterprise zone allowances is calculated by reference to the actual expenditure of the vendor if that is less than the price actually paid by the purchaser. [*CAA 2001, ss 301, 303, 304, Sch 3 para 62*].

(iii)   *Balancing charge on realisation of capital value.* Where capital expenditure on construction of a building or structure in an enterprise zone has been incurred (or is deemed to have been incurred) under a contract entered into after 12 January 1994 (or which becomes unconditional after 25 February 1994), and 'capital value' is received in respect of the building or structure, a balancing charge (but not a balancing allowance) may arise. This applies generally where the payment is made (or an agreement to make it made) seven years or less after the date of the agreement relating to the expenditure (or the date on which that agreement became unconditional). Where, however, there are certain guaranteed exit arrangements, it applies throughout the normal balancing adjustment period (i.e. 25 years from first use, see **10.16** above). '*Capital value*' is realised when a sum is paid which is attributable to an interest in land to which the relevant interest in the building or structure in question is or will be subject, e.g. where a lease is granted out of the relevant interest, unless *CAA 2001, s 290* (see **10.15** above) applies to the grant of that interest. There are detailed provisions as to the form and amount of the capital value, and as to its attribution to the grant of the interest. See HMRC Capital Allowances Manual CA37730 *et seq.* [*CAA 2001, ss 327–331, Sch 3 para 71; CTA 2009, Sch 1 para 500*].

(iv) *Partially completed buildings.* For the HMRC interpretation of the allowances available where a partially completed building or structure is acquired in an enterprise zone, see Revenue Tax Bulletin June 1998 p 553.

(v) It should be noted that where a building or structure in an enterprise zone is sold and the purchaser is *not* treated as having incurred expenditure on its construction, the residue of expenditure (if any) is allowed over the balance of the period of 25 years from first use of the building etc., and not at the 25% writing-down rate (see HMRC Capital Allowances Manual CA37375).

(vi) The withdrawal of balancing allowances and balancing charges in relation to most balancing events occurring on or after 21 March 2007 (see **10.11** and **10.16** above) does not apply to expenditure qualifying for enterprise zone allowances.

Additional VAT liabilities

An 'additional VAT liability' (see **10.2**(viii) above) incurred in respect of qualifying expenditure, within ten years of the inclusion of the site in the enterprise zone, is itself qualifying expenditure for the chargeable period in which the liability accrues. [*CAA 2001, s 346*]. Where a 100% initial allowance was not claimed on the expenditure to which the additional VAT liability relates, a 100% allowance may nevertheless generally be claimed for the additional VAT liability. If less than the full 100% allowance is claimed for the additional VAT liability, writing-down allowances for the whole of the expenditure on the building or structure in question will be recomputed as under **10.15** above, resulting in a substantial reduction in the rate of annual allowance.

Plant and machinery

Expenditure on plant or machinery, or on thermal insulation treated as plant or machinery under **11.8 CAPITAL ALLOWANCES ON PLANT AND MACHINERY**, which is to be an integral part of an industrial or commercial building in an enterprise zone may be treated as part of the expenditure on construction of the building or structure, and so attract the 100% initial allowance. A claim for expenditure on plant or machinery to be so treated does not prevent a subsequent purchaser of the building or structure from claiming plant and machinery allowances on that expenditure and industrial buildings allowances on the fabric of the building. (This commentary is not included in the current HMRC Capital Allowances Manual, but was previously at CA1060 and is presumed still to be of application.)

General

For balancing adjustments after non-qualifying use, see **10.16** above. For transfers between connected persons etc., see **10.22**(i) below.

For the special treatment for tax purposes of investors in enterprise zone property schemes, see *SI 1988 No 267* and *SI 1992 No 571* (and see HMRC Savings and Investment Manual SAIM6160–6190).

Simon's Taxes. See **B3.261–B3.265.**

Examples

[10.21]

Example (i)

In 2007, J, a builder, incurred expenditure of £400,000 on the construction of a building in a designated enterprise zone. The whole of the expenditure was contracted for within ten years of the site's first being included in the zone. In January 2008, he sold the building unused to K for £600,000 (excluding land). In February 2008, K let the building to a trader who immediately brought it into use as a supermarket. K claims a reduced initial allowance of £50,000. In May 2010, he sells the building to L for £650,000 (excluding land).

K's allowances are as follows.

		£	Residue of expenditure £
2007/08	Qualifying expenditure		600,000
	Initial allowance (maximum 100%)	50,000	
	Writing-down allowance 25% of £600,000	150,000	
	Total IBA due	200,000	(200,000)
2008/09	Writing-down allowance	150,000	(150,000)
2009/10	Writing-down allowance	150,000	(150,000)
			100,000
2010/11	Writing-down allowance		
	Sale proceeds		(650,000)
			£550,000
	Balancing charge (restricted to allowances given)		£500,000

Notes

(a) K's qualifying expenditure would normally be the lesser of cost of construction and the net price paid by him for the building. However, on purchase from a builder, whose profit on sale is taxable as a trading profit, his qualifying expenditure is equal to the net price paid for the relevant interest (excluding the land). See **10.13**, **10.20**(i) above.

(b) K's allowances and balancing charges are treated as expenses and receipts of a UK property business. See **10.18** above. K could have claimed a 100% initial allowance in 2007/08 if he had so wished.

(c) Providing the building continues to be used for a qualifying purpose, L can claim writing-down allowances until 5 April 2011. His qualifying expenditure is restricted to £600,000, i.e. the residue of expenditure (£100,000) plus the balancing charge on K. See **10.15** above.

(d) In this example, the first sale after the building was first used took place just over three years after the date of first use. If the sale had taken place within two years after first use, the balancing charge on K would have been computed in the same manner, but L could have claimed an initial allowance and 25% writing-down allowances as if he had bought the building unused. His qualifying expenditure would again have been restricted to £600,000, being the lesser of the price paid by him for the relevant interest in the building and that paid on the original purchase by K from the builder. See **10.20**(ii) above.

Example (ii)

The facts are as in (i) above, except that, of the £400,000 construction expenditure actually incurred, only £360,000 was contracted for within ten years of the site's first being included in an enterprise zone, and the first sale occurred after the expiry of that ten-year period.

K's qualifying expenditure of £600,000 (arrived at as in (i) above) is divided into an enterprise zone element and a non-enterprise zone element.

The enterprise zone element is

$$£600,000 \times \frac{360,000}{400,000} = £540,000$$

The non-enterprise zone element is $£600,000 - £540,000 = £60,000$

The non-enterprise zone element does not qualify for enterprise zone allowances. See **10.20**(i) above. (It could have qualified for normal IBAs if the building had been an industrial building.)

K's allowances are as follows.

		£	Residue of expenditure £
2007/08	Qualifying expenditure (enterprise zone element)		540,000
	Initial allowance (maximum 100%)	50,000	
	Writing-down allowance (25% of £540,000)	<u>135,000</u>	
		<u>185,000</u>	(185,000)

		£	Residue of expenditure £
2008/09	Writing-down allowance	135,000	(135,000)
2009/10	Writing-down allowance	135,000	(135,000)
			85,000
2010/11	Writing-down allowance		
	Sale proceeds £650,000 × $\frac{540,000}{600,000}$		(585,000)
			£500,000
	Balancing charge (restricted to allowances given)		£455,000

L's qualifying expenditure is £540,000, i.e. the residue of £85,000 plus the balancing charge of £455,000 on K.

Note

The apportionment of sale proceeds in 2010/11 is considered to be 'just and reasonable'.

General Matters

[10.22] The following general matters apply.

(i)   *Connected persons and other anti-avoidance provisions.* Special provisions apply to sales of industrial buildings where:
(a)   the sale results in no change of control; or
(b)   the sole or main benefit apparently arising is the obtaining of an industrial buildings allowance.
Paragraph (a) also covers sales between CONNECTED PERSONS (**21**), and (b) includes cases where the anticipated benefit is a reduction in a charge or the *increase* of an allowance. Normally, where these provisions apply, market value is substituted for purchase price (if different), and this also applies to transfers other than by way of sale. However, provided that (b) above does not apply, for sales within (a) above and other transfers the parties may elect for the substitution of the residue of expenditure (see **10.15** above) if this is lower than market value, and for any subsequent balancing charge on the buyer to be calculated by reference to allowances etc. of both buyer and seller. Such an election is *not* available if the circumstances are such that an allowance or charge which otherwise would or might fall, in consequence of the sale, to be made to or on *any* of the parties to the sale cannot fall to be made. The

election must be made within two years after the sale. The election also covers qualifying hotels and commercial buildings etc. in enterprise zones. [*CAA 2001, ss 567–570, 573, 575, 575A, 577(4); ITA 2007, Sch 1 para 411; FA 2008, Sch 27 paras 14–16, 18, 30; CTA 2010, Sch 1 para 362*].

Balancing allowances (see **10.16** above) are restricted on sales after 13 June 1972 where the relevant interest (see **10.15** above) in an industrial building is sold subject to a subordinate interest (e.g. in a sale and lease-back) and either:

(1)   the seller, the purchaser of the interest, and the grantee of the subordinate interest (or any two of them) are CONNECTED PERSONS (**21**); or

(2)   the sole or main benefit appears to be the obtaining of an industrial buildings allowance.

In such cases the net sale proceeds are increased, in determining any balancing allowance, by:

(A)   where less than a commercial rent is payable under the subordinate interest, the difference between actual sale proceeds and market value had a commercial rent been payable; and

(B)   the amount of any premium receivable for the grant of the subordinate interest and not chargeable under **60.16** PROPERTY INCOME,

but not by more than is required to eliminate any balancing allowance. Special provisions apply if the terms of the subordinate interest are varied before the sale. The residue of expenditure (see **10.15** above) following the sale is, however, calculated as if the balancing allowance had been made without the application of these provisions.

[*CAA 2001, ss 325, 326; CTA 2009, Sch 1 para 499*].

(ii)   *Double allowances.* See **10.2**(v) above.

(iii)   *Partnerships* are entitled to industrial buildings allowances in respect of qualifying expenditure (see **10.13** above) on industrial buildings (see **10.12** above).

Following a change in the persons carrying on the trade etc., other than one resulting in the activity being treated as permanently discontinued, unexhausted allowances are carried forward, and subsequent balancing adjustments (see **10.16** above) made as if the new partnership etc. had carried on the trade etc. before the change. [*CAA 2001, ss 557, 558; CTA 2009, Sch 1 para 518*]. See also (iv) below as regards allowances on successions to trades.

(iv)   *Successions.* Following a change in the persons carrying on the trade etc., such that the activity is treated as permanently discontinued, any asset transferred, without being sold, to the new owner for continuing use in the trade is treated as sold at market value on the date of change, although no initial allowance is available to the new owner. [*CAA 2001, ss 557, 559; CTA 2009, Sch 1 para 519*].

'Know-how'

[**10.23**] Expenditure on acquiring 'know-how' (so far as not otherwise deductible for income tax purposes) gives rise to writing-down and balancing allowances (and balancing charges) where the person acquiring it either:

(i)   is then carrying on a trade for use in which it is acquired; or
(ii)   subsequently commences such a trade (in which case the expenditure is treated as incurred on commencement); or
(iii)   acquires it with a trade (or part) in which it was used, and either the parties to the acquisition make the appropriate joint election under *ITTOIA 2005, s 194* (see **73.91** TRADING INCOME), or corporation tax equivalent, or the trade was carried on wholly outside the UK before the acquisition.

The same expenditure may not be taken into account in relation to more than one trade.

Expenditure is, however, *excluded* where the buyer and seller are bodies of persons (which includes partnerships) under common control.

[*CAA 2001, ss 452(1), 454, 455*].

'*Know-how*' means any industrial information and techniques of assistance in (a) manufacturing or processing goods or materials, (b) working, or searching etc. for, mineral deposits, or (c) agricultural, forestry or fishing operations. [*CAA 2001, s 452(2)(3)*]. For expenditure on offshore divers' training courses treated as on know-how, see HMRC Capital Allowances Manual CA74000.

All qualifying expenditure of a trade is pooled, and:

(1)   if the 'available qualifying expenditure' exceeds the 'total disposal value', a writing-down allowance is available of **25%** of the excess, proportionately reduced or increased where the period is less or more than one year, or if the trade has been carried on for part only of a chargeable period (and subject to any lesser amount being claimed), *except that* if the chargeable period is that of permanent discontinuance of the trade, a balancing allowance of **100%** of the excess is available;
(2)   if the 'total disposal value' exceeds the 'available qualifying expenditure', a balancing charge arises of **100%** of the excess.

'*Available qualifying expenditure*' in a pool for a chargeable period consists of qualifying expenditure allocated to the pool for that period and any unrelieved qualifying expenditure brought forward in the pool from the previous chargeable period (usually referred to as the written-down value brought forward). In allocating qualifying expenditure to the pool, rules identical to those for patent rights at **10.35**(i) and (ii) below must be observed.

The '*total disposal value*' is the aggregate of any disposal values to be brought into account for the period, i.e. the net sale proceeds (being capital sums) from any disposal of know-how on which qualifying expenditure was incurred (but excluding any sale the consideration for which is treated as a payment for goodwill under *ITTOIA 2005, s 194(2)* (see **73.91** TRADING INCOME) or corporation tax equivalent).

The allowances and charges are given effect as deductions or receipts of the relevant trade.

[CAA 2001, ss 456–463].

For receipts arising from sales of know-how, see also **73.91 TRADING INCOME**.

Simon's Taxes. See **B3.615**, **B3.616**.

Mineral extraction

[10.24] Mineral extraction allowances are available in respect of qualifying expenditure (see **10.25** below) incurred by a person carrying on a 'mineral extraction trade'. A *'mineral extraction trade'* is a trade consisting of or including the working of a source of *'mineral deposits'*, i.e. such deposits of a wasting nature including any natural deposits or geothermal energy capable of being lifted or extracted from the earth. A *'source of mineral deposits'* includes a mine, an oil well and a source of geothermal energy. [CAA 2001, s 394]. A *share* in an asset may qualify for mineral extraction allowances. [CAA 2001, s 435].

Simon's Taxes. See **B3.4**.

Qualifying expenditure

[10.25] *'Qualifying expenditure'* means capital expenditure, incurred for the purposes of a mineral extraction trade, on:

(a)   *'mineral exploration and access'* (i.e. searching for or discovering and testing the mineral deposits of any source, or winning access to any such deposits);

(b)   acquisition of a *'mineral asset'* (i.e. any mineral deposits or land comprising mineral deposits, or any interest in or right over such deposits or land) (subject to the limitations in **10.26** below);

(c)   construction of works, in connection with the working of a source of mineral deposits, which are likely to become of little or no value when the source ceases to be worked;

(d)   construction of works which are likely to become valueless when a foreign concession under which a source of mineral deposits is worked comes to an end;

(e)   net expenditure incurred on the restoration of the site of a source of mineral deposits (or land used in connection with working such a source) within three years after the cessation of the trade, unless relieved elsewhere. In this case, the expenditure is treated as incurred on the last day of trading.

Included in (a) above is abortive expenditure (including appeal costs) on seeking planning permission for the undertaking of mineral exploration and access or the working of mineral deposits. Expenditure on the acquisition of, or of rights over, mineral deposits or the site of a source of mineral deposits falls into (b) rather than (a) above.

However, the following are *not* qualifying expenditure:

- expenditure on the provision of plant or machinery (except certain pre-trading expenditure — see below), and see **10.32** below;
- expenditure on acquisition of, or of rights in or over, the *site* of any works in (c) or (d) above;
- expenditure on works constructed wholly or mainly for processing the raw products, unless the process is designed to prepare the raw products for use as such;
- (subject to *CAA 2001, s 415* — see below) expenditure on buildings and structures for occupation by, or welfare of, workers;
- expenditure on a building constructed *entirely* for use as an office;
- expenditure on the office part of a building or structure constructed *partly* for use as an office, where such expenditure exceeds 10% of the capital expenditure on construction of the whole building.

[*CAA 2001, ss 395–399, 400(1), 403(1)(2), 414, 416*].

Qualifying expenditure also includes capital contributions, for the purposes of a mineral extraction trade carried on outside the UK, to the cost of accommodation buildings, and certain related utility buildings and welfare works, for employees engaged in working a source, provided that the buildings or works are likely to be of little or no value when the source ceases to be worked, that the expenditure does not result in the acquisition of an asset, and that relief is not due under any other tax provision. [*CAA 2001, s 415*].

Pre-trading expenditure

Pre-trading expenditure for the purposes of a mineral extraction trade is treated as incurred on the first day of trading. This applies equally to pre-trading expenditure on mineral exploration and access, but in determining whether such expenditure is qualifying expenditure within (a) above, the following limitations apply.

(i) In the case of pre-trading expenditure on plant or machinery which is used at a source but is sold, demolished, destroyed or abandoned before commencement of the mineral extraction trade, qualifying expenditure is limited to net expenditure after taking account of sale proceeds, insurance money or capital compensation.

(ii) In the case of pre-trading exploration expenditure other than on plant or machinery, qualifying expenditure is limited to net expenditure after taking into account any reasonably attributable capital sums received before the first day of trading.

In either case, if mineral exploration and access is not continuing at the source on the first day of trading, qualifying expenditure is further limited to net expenditure incurred in the six years ending on that day.

[*CAA 2001, s 400(2)–(5), 401, 402, 434*].

Simon's Taxes. See **B3.405–B3.410.**

Limitations on qualifying expenditure

[10.26] Qualifying expenditure within **10.25**(b) above (acquisition of mineral asset) is limited in the following circumstances.

If the mineral asset is an interest in land, an amount equal to the 'undeveloped market value' of the interest is excluded. *'Undeveloped market value'* is the market value of the interest at the time of acquisition ignoring the mineral deposits and assuming that development of the land (other than that already lawfully begun or for which planning permission has already been granted) is, and will remain, unlawful. Where the undeveloped market value includes the value of buildings or structures which, at any time after acquisition, permanently cease to be used, their value at acquisition (exclusive of land and after deducting any net capital allowances received in respect of them) is treated as qualifying expenditure incurred at the time of cessation of use. These provisions operate by reference to the actual time of acquisition, regardless of any different time given by the pre-trading expenditure provisions at **10.25** above. They do not apply where an election is made under *CAA 2001, s 569* or its forerunner (election to treat connected persons transactions as made at written-down value). [*CAA 2001, ss 403(3), 404, 405, Sch 3 para 84*].

Where a deduction has been allowed under *ITTOIA 2005, ss 60–67* (previously *ICTA 1988, s 87*) in respect of a premium under a lease (see **73.104 TRADING INCOME**), the qualifying expenditure allowable in respect of the acquisition of the interest in land to which the premium relates is correspondingly reduced. [*CAA 2001, s 406*].

Simon's Taxes. See B3.410.

Second-hand assets

[10.27] Where:

(a)   an asset is acquired from another person; and
(b)   either that person or any previous owner incurred expenditure on it in connection with a mineral extraction trade,

the buyer's qualifying expenditure is restricted to the seller's qualifying expenditure on the asset less net allowances given to him. If an oil licence (or an interest therein) is acquired, the buyer's qualifying expenditure is limited to the amount of the original licence fee paid (or such part of it as it is just and reasonable to attribute to the interest). However, these restrictions do not affect amounts treated under rules below as qualifying expenditure on mineral exploration and access.

Where:

(i)   the purchased asset above is a mineral asset; and
(ii)   part of its value is properly attributable to expenditure on mineral exploration and access incurred as in (b) above,

so much if any of the buyer's expenditure as it is just and reasonable to attribute to the part of the value in (ii) above (not exceeding the amount of original expenditure to which it is attributable) is treated as qualifying expenditure on mineral exploration and access, with the remainder treated as expenditure on acquisition of a mineral asset. Expenditure deducted by a previous owner in computing taxable profits is excluded for these purposes from the original expenditure.

Where:

- capital expenditure is incurred in acquiring assets for a mineral extraction trade from a person (the seller) who did *not* carry on a mineral extraction trade; and
- the assets represent expenditure on mineral exploration and access incurred by the seller,

the buyer's qualifying expenditure is limited to the amount of the seller's expenditure. Assets include any results obtained from any search, exploration or inquiry on which the expenditure was incurred. This restriction does not apply if the asset is an interest in an oil licence acquired by the buyer; in this case, so much if any of the buyer's expenditure as it is just and reasonable to attribute to the part of the value of the licence attributable to the seller's expenditure (but limited to the amount of that expenditure) is treated as qualifying expenditure on mineral exploration and access, with the cost of the oil licence being reduced by the buyer's expenditure so attributable (without limitation).

Where a mineral asset is transferred between companies under common control, and no election is made under *CAA 2001, s 569* or its forerunner (election to treat connected persons transactions as made at written-down value), the buyer's expenditure is limited to that of the seller. However, this does not affect amounts *treated* under rules above as qualifying expenditure on mineral exploration and access. Where the asset is an interest in land, the limitations at **10.26** above generally apply as if the buyer acquired the interest when the seller acquired it (or, in the case of a sequence of such transactions, when the first seller acquired it).

[*CAA 2001, ss 407–413, Sch 3 paras 85–87*].

Simon's Taxes. See **B3.411–.B3.414.**

Writing-down allowances and balancing adjustments

[10.28] For each item of qualifying expenditure (see **10.25** above), a **writing-down allowance (WDA)** is available for each chargeable period (see **10.2**(i) above) and is equal to a set percentage (as below) of the amount (if any) by which 'unrelieved qualifying expenditure' exceeds the total of any disposal values falling to be brought into account as in **10.29** below. The WDA is proportionately reduced or increased if the chargeable period is less or more than a year, or if the mineral extraction trade has been carried on for part only of the chargeable period.

In the circumstances listed at **10.30** below, a **balancing allowance** is available, instead of a WDA, equal to the excess (if any) of (1) 'unrelieved qualifying expenditure' over (2) total disposal values. (This is subject to the anti-avoidance rule at **10.2**(xi) above.) If, for any chargeable period, (2) exceeds (1), there arises a liability to a **balancing charge**, normally equal to that excess but limited to net allowances previously given. A claim for a WDA *or* a balancing allowance may require it to be reduced to a specified amount.

Rates of WDA are as follows:

Acquisition of a mineral asset (see **10.25**(b) above)	10% p.a.
Other qualifying expenditure	25% p.a.

'*Unrelieved qualifying expenditure*' means qualifying expenditure (other than first-year qualifying expenditure) incurred in the chargeable period and the tax written-down value brought forward (i.e. net of allowances and any disposal values) of qualifying expenditure (including first-year qualifying expenditure) incurred in a previous chargeable period.

[*CAA 2001, ss 417–419*].

The net demolition costs (i.e. the excess, if any, of demolition costs over money received for remains) of an asset representing qualifying expenditure is added to that expenditure in determining the amount of any balancing allowance or charge for the chargeable period of demolition, and is not then treated as expenditure incurred on any replacement asset. [*CAA 2001, s 433*].

There is no provision for pooling expenditure (in contrast to plant and machinery at **11.23 CAPITAL ALLOWANCES ON PLANT AND MACHINERY**). In practice, HMRC do not object to the grouping together of assets for computational convenience, provided individual sources are kept separate and assets attracting different rates of WDA are not grouped with each other. However, where a disposal value falls to be brought into account or a balancing allowance arises, it will sometimes be necessary to reconstruct separate computations for individual items of expenditure previously grouped. (HMRC Capital Allowances Manual CA50410).

Simon's Taxes. See B3.419–B3.422.

Disposal events and values

[10.29] A disposal value must be brought into account (by deduction from unrelieved qualifying expenditure — see **10.28** above), for the chargeable period in which the event occurs, on the occurrence of any of the following events.

(i)   An asset representing qualifying expenditure (see **10.25** above) is disposed of or permanently ceases to be used for the purposes of a mineral extraction trade (whether because of cessation of trade or otherwise).

(ii) A mineral asset begins to be used (by the trader or another person) in a way which constitutes development which is neither 'existing permitted development' nor development for the purposes of a mineral extraction trade. Development is '*existing permitted development*' if, at the time of acquisition, it had already lawfully begun or the appropriate planning permission had already been granted.

(iii)   In a case not within (i) or (ii) above, a capital sum is received which, in whole or in part, it is reasonable to attribute to qualifying expenditure.

The amount to be brought into account depends upon the nature of the event.

(a)   On an event within (i) or (ii) above, it is an amount determined in accordance with the list at **11.24**(a)–(g) CAPITAL ALLOWANCES ON PLANT AND MACHINERY (disregarding (f), the reference to abandonment at (d) and the text immediately following the list). However, if the asset is an interest in land, the amount so ascertained is then restricted by excluding the '*undeveloped market value*', determined as in **10.26** above but by reference to the time of disposal.

(b)   On an event within (iii) above, it is so much of the capital sum as is reasonably attributable to the qualifying expenditure.

[*CAA 2001, ss 420–425; TIOPA 2010, Sch 8 para 235*].

In relation to sales at other than market value, the connected person and other anti-avoidance provisions, and election potential, of *CAA 2001, ss 567–570* (and forerunners) apply with appropriate modifications for mineral extraction allowances as they do for industrial buildings allowances (see **10.22**(i) above).

Simon's Taxes. See B3.420.

Balancing allowances

[10.30] A person is entitled to a balancing allowance (instead of a writing-down allowance) for a chargeable period if:

- the chargeable period is that in which the first day of trading falls, and either the qualifying expenditure is pre-trading expenditure on plant or machinery within **10.25**(i) above or it is pre-trading exploration expenditure within **10.25**(ii) above where mineral exploration and access is not continuing at the source on the first day of trading; or

- the qualifying expenditure was on mineral exploration and access, and in that chargeable period he gives up the exploration, search or inquiry to which the expenditure related, without subsequently carrying on a mineral extraction trade consisting of or including the working of related mineral deposits; or

- in that chargeable period he permanently ceases to work particular mineral deposits, and the qualifying expenditure was on mineral exploration and access relating solely to those deposits or on the acquisition of a mineral asset consisting of those deposits or part of them; but where two or more mineral assets are comprised in, or derive from, a single asset, the above applies only when *all* the relevant mineral deposits cease to be worked; or

- the qualifying expenditure falls within *CAA 2001, s 415* (capital contributions to certain buildings or works for benefit of employees abroad — see **10.25** above), and in that chargeable period, the buildings or works permanently cease to be used for the purposes of or in connection with the mineral extraction trade; or

- the qualifying expenditure was on the provision of any assets, and in that chargeable period any of those assets is disposed of or otherwise permanently ceases to be used for purposes of the trade; or

- the qualifying expenditure is represented by assets, and in that chargeable period those assets are permanently lost or cease to exist (due to destruction, dismantling or otherwise) or begin to be used wholly or partly for purposes other than those of the mineral extraction trade; or
- the mineral extraction trade is permanently discontinued in that chargeable period.

[CAA 2001, ss 426–431].

Simon's Taxes. See **B3.421**.

Making of allowances and charges

[10.31] Mineral extraction allowances (or balancing charges) are given (or made) as trading expenses (or trading receipts) in calculating the profits of the mineral extraction trade. [CAA 2001, s 432].

Simon's Taxes. See **B3.423**.

Plant and machinery allowances

[10.32] Plant and machinery is normally excluded from relief under the current provisions, but certain pre-trading expenditure may qualify (see **10.25** above). The normal plant and machinery rules (see **11 CAPITAL ALLOWANCES ON PLANT AND MACHINERY**) apply to plant and machinery provided for mineral exploration and access in connection with a mineral extraction trade. [CAA 2001, ss 159, 160]. Where such expenditure is incurred prior to the date of commencement of a mineral extraction trade and the plant or machinery is still owned at that date, it is treated as if sold immediately before that date and re-acquired on that date. The capital expenditure on re-acquisition is deemed to be equal to the actual expenditure previously incurred. [CAA 2001, s 161, Sch 3 para 25].

Example

[10.33]

X has for some years operated a mining business with two mineral sources, G and S. Accounts are prepared to 30 September. On 31 December 2009 the mineral deposits and mineworks at G are sold at market value to Z for £80,000 and £175,000 respectively. A new source, P, is purchased on 30 April 2010 for £170,000 (including land with an undeveloped market value of £70,000) and the following expenditure incurred before the end of the period of account ended on 30 September 2010.

	£
Plant and machinery	40,000
Construction of administration office	25,000
Construction of mining works which are likely to have little value when mining ceases	50,000
Staff hostel	35,000

Winning access to the deposits	<u>150,000</u>
	<u>£300,000</u>

During the year to 30 September 2010, X also incurred expenditure of £20,000 in seeking planning permission to mine a further plot of land, Source Q. Permission was refused.

Residue of expenditure brought forward		£
(based on accounts to 30 September 2009)		
Mineral exploration and access	– Source G	170,000
	– Source S	200,000
Mineral assets	– Source G	95,250
	– Source S	72,000

The mineral extraction allowances due for the year ending 30 September 2010 are as follows.

Source G	£	£
Mineral exploration and access		
WDV b/f	170,000	
Proceeds	<u>175,000</u>	
Balancing charge	<u>£5,000</u>	(5,000)
Mineral assets		
WDV b/f	95,250	
Proceeds	<u>80,000</u>	
Balancing allowance	<u>£15,250</u>	15,250
Source S		
Mineral exploration and access		
WDV b/f	200,000	
WDA 25%	<u>(50,000)</u>	50,000
WDV c/f	<u>£150,000</u>	
Mineral assets		
WDV b/f	72,000	
WDA 10%	<u>(7,200)</u>	7,200
WDV c/f	<u>£64,800</u>	
Source P		
Mineral exploration and access		
Expenditure	150,000	
WDA 25%	<u>(37,500)</u>	37,500
WDV c/f	<u>£112,500</u>	
Mineral assets		
Expendi- note (c) ture	100,000	
WDA 10%	<u>(10,000)</u>	10,000

WDV c/f	£90,000	
Mining works		
Expenditure	50,000	
WDA 25%	(12,500)	12,500
WDV c/f	£37,500	
Source Q		
Mineral exploration and access		
Expendi- note (b)	20,000	
ture		
WDA 25%	(5,000)	5,000
WDV c/f	£15,000	
Total allowances (net of charges)		£132,450

Notes

(a)   Allowances are not due on either the office or staff hostel although the hostel may qualify for industrial buildings allowances (see **10.12** above). The plant and machinery qualify for plant and machinery allowances (see **11 CAPITAL ALLOWANCES ON PLANT AND MACHINERY**) rather than for mineral extraction allowances (see **10.32** above).

(b)   Abortive expenditure on seeking planning permission is qualifying expenditure as if it were expenditure on mineral exploration and access (see **10.25** above).

(c)   The undeveloped market value of land is excluded from qualifying expenditure (see **10.26** above).

Transition to current code of allowances

[10.34] The current code of allowances, as described at **10.24–10.31** above was introduced for expenditure incurred after 31 March 1986 (though a trader could elect to continue to apply the old code to certain expenditure incurred in the twelve months to 31 March 1987). Any unrelieved balance of expenditure at 1 April 1986 (or 1 April 1987 where applicable) under the old code was treated for the purposes of the current code as expenditure incurred on that day for the purposes for which the original expenditure was actually incurred. If expenditure had been fully relieved under the old code but the assets remained in use, the current code applies as if the expenditure had been incurred on 1 April 1986 and had been fully relieved under the current code (thus enabling balancing charges to accrue subsequently).

Expenditure on mineral exploration and access, or on acquisition of mineral assets, or on construction of certain works, which did not qualify for allowances under the old code because either the trade, or output from the source, had not commenced, or for some other reason, was treated as incurred on 1 April 1986 and relieved as appropriate under the new code.

Special rules apply where the old code expenditure on a mineral asset included the acquisition of an interest in land. The undeveloped market value of that interest was not excluded from the relievable expenditure where some relief had already been given under the old code, but nor is such value excluded under **10.29**(a) above from any disposal value to be brought into account.

In making balancing charges where old code expenditure has been brought under the new code, allowances given under the old code will be taken into account together with those given under the new code.

[*CAA 2001, Sch 3 para 88*].

Simon's Taxes. See **B3.401**.

Patent rights

[10.35] Allowances are available, and balancing charges made, in respect of 'qualifying expenditure' on the purchase of patent rights, i.e. the right to do or authorise the doing of anything which would, but for that right, be a patent infringement. The obtaining of a right to acquire future patent rights and the acquisition of a licence in respect of a patent are each treated for these purposes as a purchase of patent rights. '*Qualifying expenditure*' may be either:

- '*qualifying trade expenditure*', i.e. capital expenditure incurred by a person on purchase of patent rights for the purposes of a trade carried on by him and within the charge to UK tax; or
- '*qualifying non-trade expenditure*', i.e. capital expenditure incurred by a person on purchase of patent rights if the above does not apply but any income receivable by him in respect of the rights would be liable to tax.

Expenditure incurred by a person for the purposes of a trade he is about to carry on is treated as if incurred on the first day of trading, unless all the rights in question have been sold before then. The same expenditure cannot be qualifying trade expenditure in relation to more than one trade.

The grant of a licence in respect of a patent is treated as a sale of part of patent rights. The grant by a person entitled to patent rights of an exclusive licence, i.e. a licence to exercise the rights to the exclusion of the grantor and all others for the remainder of their term, is, however, treated as a sale of the whole of those rights.

[*CAA 2001, ss 464–469*].

Qualifying expenditure is pooled for the purpose of determining entitlement to writing-down allowances and balancing allowances and liability to balancing charges. A separate pool applies for each separate trade and for all qualifying non-trade expenditure.

For each pool of qualifying expenditure, a **writing-down allowance (WDA)** is available for each chargeable period (see **10.2**(i) above) other than the 'final chargeable period' and is equal to a maximum of **25%** of the amount (if any) by which 'available qualifying expenditure' exceeds the total of any disposal values falling to be brought into account. The WDA is proportionately reduced or increased if the chargeable period is less or more than a year, or if (where relevant) the trade has been carried on for part only of the chargeable period. A claim for a WDA may require it to be reduced to a specified amount. For the 'final chargeable period', a **balancing allowance** is available, equal to the excess (if any) of (1) 'available qualifying expenditure' over (2) total disposal values. If, for *any* chargeable period, (2) exceeds (1), there arises a liability to a **balancing charge**, equal to that excess.

The '*final chargeable period*', as regards a pool of qualifying trade expenditure, is the chargeable period in which the trade is permanently discontinued. As regards a pool of non-qualifying trade expenditure, it is the chargeable period in which the last of the patent rights in question either comes to an end (without any such rights being revived) or is wholly disposed of.

'*Available qualifying expenditure*' in a pool for a chargeable period consists of qualifying expenditure allocated to the pool for that period and any unrelieved qualifying expenditure brought forward in the pool from the previous chargeable period (usually referred to as the written-down value brought forward).

In allocating qualifying expenditure to a pool, the following must be observed.

(i)   Qualifying expenditure can be allocated to a pool for a chargeable period only to the extent that it has not been included in available qualifying expenditure for an earlier chargeable period. (There is now nothing to prohibit the allocation of *part only* of a particular amount of qualifying expenditure for a particular chargeable period.)

(ii)   Qualifying expenditure cannot be allocated to a pool for a chargeable period earlier than that in which it is incurred.

(iii)   Qualifying expenditure cannot be allocated to a pool for a chargeable period if in any earlier period the rights in question have come to an end (without any of them being revived) or have been wholly disposed of.

[*CAA 2001, ss 470–475*].

A *disposal value* falls to be brought into account for a chargeable period in which a person sells the whole or part of any patent rights on the purchase of which he has incurred qualifying expenditure. The disposal value is equal to the net sale proceeds (limited to *capital* sums), except that:

(1)   it cannot exceed the qualifying expenditure incurred on purchase of the rights in question; and

(2)   where the rights were acquired as a result of a transaction between **CONNECTED PERSONS (21)** (or a series of such transactions), (1) above shall have effect as if it referred to the greatest capital expenditure incurred on the purchase of those rights by any of those connected persons.

[*CAA 2001, ss 476, 477; TIOPA 2010, Sch 8 para 236*].

Connected persons and other anti-avoidance

Where a person incurs capital expenditure on the purchase of rights either from a connected person (see **21 CONNECTED PERSONS**), or so that it appears that the sole or main benefit from the sale and any other transactions would have been the obtaining of an allowance under these provisions, the amount of that expenditure taken into account as qualifying expenditure may not exceed an amount determined as follows:

(a)   where a disposal value (see above) falls to be brought into account, an amount equal to that value;

(b)   where no disposal value falls to be brought into account, but the seller receives a capital sum chargeable under *ITTOIA 2005, s 587* (see **40.6 INTELLECTUAL PROPERTY**), an amount equal to that sum;

(c)   in any other case, an amount equal to the smallest of
   • market value of the rights;
   • the amount of capital expenditure, if any, incurred by the seller on acquiring the rights;
   • the amount of capital expenditure, if any, incurred by any person connected with the seller on acquiring the rights.

[*CAA 2001, s 481, Sch 3 para 102*]. Previously, the restriction was by reference to the disposal value only. See also (2) above.

Making of allowances and charges

An allowance (or balancing charge) in respect of qualifying *trade* expenditure is given effect as a trading expense (or trading receipt). [*CAA 2001, s 478*].

An allowance in respect of qualifying *non-trade* expenditure is set against the person's 'income from patents' for the same tax year, with any excess being carried forward without time limit against such income for subsequent tax years. The allowance is given effect by deduction at Step 2 of the calculation of income tax liability (see **1.7 ALLOWANCES AND TAX RATES**). A balancing charge is assessed as taxable income. For these purposes, '*income from patents*' embraces royalties and similar sums, balancing charges under these provisions, and receipts from the sale of patent rights taxable under *ITTOIA 2005, s 587, 593* or *594* (see **40.6, 40.7 INTELLECTUAL PROPERTY**). [*CAA 2001, ss 479, 480, 483; ITA 2007, Sch 1 para 408*].

Trading partnerships and successions

Trading partnerships and successions are treated in the same way as for industrial buildings allowances (see **10.22**(iii)(iv)).

General

See **40 INTELLECTUAL PROPERTY** for treatment of patent royalties and capital sums received, and **73.99 TRADING INCOME** for trading income and expenses re patents.

Simon's Taxes. See B3.601–B3.609.

Example

[10.36]

P, who prepares accounts to 31 December, acquires two new patent rights for trading purposes.

	Date	Term	Cost
Patent 1	19.4.09	15 years	£4,500
Patent 2	5.10.10	5 years	£8,000

On 1.12.10 P sold part of his rights under patent 1 for £2,000.
The allowances for each patent are

	Pool	WDA
Y/e 31.12.09		
	£	£
Expenditure (patent 1)	4,500	
WDA 25%	(1,125)	£1,125
	3,375	
Y/e 31.12.10		
Expenditure (patent 2)	8,000	
Disposal proceeds (patent 1)	(2,000)	
	9,375	
WDA 25%	(2,344)	£2,344
WDV c/f	£7,031	

Research and development

[10.37] 'Qualifying expenditure' incurred by a trader on 'research and development' (R & D) attracts an allowance equal to **100%** of the expenditure. A claim for an allowance may require it to be reduced to a specified amount (but the part of the allowance thus forgone cannot be claimed for a later chargeable period).

'*Qualifying expenditure*' is capital expenditure incurred by a trader on R & D related to the trade and undertaken directly or on his behalf (i.e. by an agent or other person in a similar contractual relationship, see *Gaspet Ltd v Elliss CA 1987, 60 TC 91*). It includes such expenditure incurred before commencement of the trade (pre-commencement expenditure). Expenditure potentially leading to or facilitating an extension of the trade is related to that trade, as is expenditure of a medical nature specially related to the welfare of workers in the trade. A just and reasonable apportionment may be made of capital expenditure only partly qualifying.

Expenditure on the acquisition of, or of rights in or over, land cannot be qualifying expenditure, except insofar as, on a just and reasonable apportionment, such expenditure is referable to a building or structure already constructed on the land, or to plant or machinery which forms part of such a building or structure, and otherwise qualifies as R & D expenditure.

Expenditure on R & D includes all expenditure incurred for carrying out (or providing facilities for carrying out) R & D. Expenditure on the acquisition of rights in, or arising out of, R & D is, however, excluded. Also excluded is expenditure on provision of a *dwelling*, except where not more than 25% of the expenditure (disregarding any 'additional VAT liability' or 'rebate' — see **10.2**(viii) above) on a building consisting partly of a dwelling and otherwise used for R &D is attributable (on a just and reasonable apportionment) to the dwelling, in which case the dwelling can be ignored and the whole of the building treated as used for R & D.

An 'additional VAT liability' (see **10.2**(viii) above) incurred in respect of qualifying expenditure is itself qualifying expenditure, provided the same person still owns the asset in question and it has not been demolished or destroyed.

Meaning of research and development

'*Research and development*' means activities that fall to be treated as such in accordance with generally accepted accounting practice (see **73.18** above) and includes oil and gas exploration and appraisal (within *ITA 2007, s 1003*, previously *ICTA 1988, s 837B*). However, this is subject to Treasury regulations which narrow the definition by reference to guidelines issued by the Department of Trade and Industry (DTI). [*CAA 2001, s 437(2)(3); ITA 2007, Sch 1 para 407*]. The latest regulations have effect for 2004/05 onwards and refer to DTI guidelines issued on 5 March 2004 (for which see www.dti.gov. uk/support/rd-guidelines-2004.htm). [*SI 2004 No 712*].

For special provisions relating to oil licences, see *CAA 2001, ss 552–556, Sch 3 para 91* as amended.

Making of allowances

The allowance is given as a trading expense of the chargeable period (see **10.2**(i) above) in which the expenditure is incurred (or, in the case of pre-commencement expenditure, the chargeable period in which the trade commences). An allowance in respect of an additional VAT liability is similarly given, but by reference to the time the *liability* is incurred.

[*CAA 2001, ss 437(1), 438–441, 447, 450, Sch 3 paras 89, 90*].

Disposal events and balancing charges

If a disposal value (see below) falls to be brought into account for the same chargeable period as that for which the related allowance falls to be given, the allowance is given on the excess (if any) of the expenditure over the disposal value.

If a disposal value falls to be brought into account for the chargeable period after that for which the related allowance is given, liability to a balancing charge arises for that later chargeable period. Effect is given to the charge by treating it as a trading receipt. The charge is equal to disposal value (or, where a reduced allowance was claimed, the excess, if any, of disposal value over unrelieved expenditure), except that it cannot exceed the allowance given (less any earlier balancing charges arising from 'additional VAT rebates' — see below).

A disposal value falls to be brought into account for a chargeable period in which a disposal event occurs, or, if such an event occurs later, for the chargeable period in which the trade is permanently discontinued. If, exceptionally, a disposal event occurs *before* the chargeable period for which the related allowance falls to be given, it is brought into account for the later chargeable period.

Either of the following is a disposal event (unless it gives rise to a balancing charge under the rules for industrial buildings or plant and machinery allowances).

(a)   The trader ceases to own the asset representing the qualifying expenditure;

(b)   An asset representing the qualifying expenditure is demolished or destroyed before the trader ceases to own it.

On the sale of an asset, the seller is treated for these purposes as ceasing to own it at the earlier of the time of completion and the time when possession is given.

The amount of the disposal value depends on the nature of the disposal event, as follows.

• If the event is a sale of the asset at not less than market value, it is the net sale proceeds.

• If the event is the demolition or destruction of the asset, it is the net amount received for the remains, plus any insurance or capital compensation received (but see below as regards demolition costs).

• In any other event, it is the market value of the asset at the time of the event.

An 'additional VAT rebate' (see **10.2**(viii) above) made in respect of qualifying expenditure, before the asset in question ceases to belong to the trader or has been demolished or destroyed, must be brought into account as a disposal value (or as an addition to a disposal value otherwise arising) for the chargeable period in which the rebate accrues or, if later, the chargeable period in which the trade commences.

[*CAA 2001, ss 441(1), 442–444, 448, 449–451; FA 2008, Sch 27 paras 6, 7, 30*].

Demolition costs

On demolition of an asset (within (b) above), the disposal value is reduced (or extinguished) by any demolition costs incurred by the trader. If the demolition costs exceed the disposal value, then, provided the asset had not begun to be used for non-qualifying purposes, the excess is itself treated as qualifying R & D expenditure, incurred at time of demolition (or, if earlier and where relevant, immediately before cessation of the trade). The demolition costs cannot be treated for any capital allowances purposes as expenditure on any replacement asset.

[*CAA 2001, s 445*].

Connected persons and other anti-avoidance

Connected persons and other anti-avoidance provisions apply to substitute market value for sale consideration on certain 'sole or main benefit' transactions, sales without change of control and sales between connected persons. For most sales, the election referred to at **10.22**(i) above is available, with the result that an asset representing expenditure for which an R & D allowance has been made as above will be treated as transferred for nil consideration. [*CAA 2001, ss 567–570, 575, 575A; ITA 2007, Sch 1 para 411; FA 2008, Sch 27 paras 14–16, 30; CTA 2010, Sch 1 para 362*].

General

For R & D expenditure of a revenue nature, see **73.109 TRADING INCOME**.

Simon's Taxes. See **B3.108, B3.108B, B3.7.**

Example

[10.38]

C is in business manufacturing and selling cosmetics, and he prepares accounts annually to 30 June. For the purposes of this trade, he built a new laboratory adjacent to his existing premises, incurring the following expenditure.

		£
April 2008	Laboratory building	50,000
June 2008	Technical equipment	3,000
March 2009	Technical equipment	4,000
July 2009	Plant	2,500
August 2010	Extension to existing premises comprising 50% further laboratory area and 50% sales offices	30,000

In September 2009 a small fire destroyed an item of equipment originally costing £2,000 in June 2008; insurance recoveries totalled £3,000. In March 2010, the plant costing £2,500 in July 2009 was sold for £1,800.

The allowances due are as follows.

Y/e 30.6.08	£
Laboratory building	50,000
Technical equipment	3,000
	£53,000

Y/e 30.6.09	£
Technical equipment	4,000
	£4,000

Y/e 30.6.10

Net allowance on plant sold	(note (a))	£700
Balancing charge on equipment destroyed	(note (b))	(£2,000)
Y/e 30.6.11 Extension (qualifying R&D expenditure only)		£15,000

Notes

(a) As the plant is sold in the period of account in which the expenditure is incurred, the disposal value of £1,800 is set against the expenditure of £2,500, resulting in a net allowance of £700.

(b) The destruction of the equipment in the year to 30 June 2010 results in a balancing charge limited to the allowance given. The charge accrues in the period of account in which the event occurs.

Key points

[10.39] Points to consider are as follows.

- It is easy to overlook VAT adjustments relating to capital items which have a capital allowances impact. Where a client is partially exempt, or begins to use an affected asset for a non-taxable purpose, links will be needed from the VAT working papers through to the capital allowances working papers to ensure that the capital allowances impact is not overlooked. This applies both to Capital Goods Scheme adjustments, but also to the annual adjustment made by larger VAT registered traders — the computation of the initial cost needs to reflect the actual rate of VAT recovery after the annual adjustment has been made.

- Certain expenditure may qualify for allowances either under the industrial buildings/agricultural buildings regime or as plant and machinery. The choice of which allowances to claim is irreversible, and in view of the termination of the two types of building allowances in 2011, claims would be better made if possible under the plant and machinery regime. (See **11 CAPITAL ALLOWANCES ON PLANT AND MACHINERY**.)

- Note that business premises renovation allowance can be claimed by a purchaser of a building provided the relevant conditions have been met. There is nothing to prevent, for example, a taxpayer purchasing a run-down hotel on Anglesey to refurbish and bring back into use, claiming business premises renovation allowance on the expenditure, provided the property has been unused for at least 12 months before work starts.

- Business premises renovation allowance can also be claimed by investors in commercial property who intend to redevelop the premises for letting. In this case the allowance would normally produce a property business loss, which can be set against other income of the claimant to the extent that it relates to capital allowances (see **60.15 PROPERTY INCOME**). The careful use of partial claims can permit 50% taxpayers to restrict relief to the quantum of income within the 50% tax band. Investors should consider carefully the potential benefits of opting to tax the premises at the outset, as the VAT on the building works may not be recoverable if the option is not made until the completion of the redevelopment.

- Flat conversion allowances present a similar planning opportunity as in this case the flats created must be intended for letting. Targeting property losses against income bearing 40% or 50% tax presents a useful planning opportunity for those seeking to invest. Note that due to the restriction regarding 'luxury flats', significant ground work is needed at the planning permission stage to ensure that the rental figures are not exceeded; otherwise the entire redevelopment will fall outside the scheme.

- As flat conversion allowances depend on the flats being available for letting at the end of the chargeable period (the fiscal year) clients with developments in progress should be advised to liaise with their builders to ensure that the development is completed in time, to enable the allowances to be claimed at the earliest point. Note also that the expenditure may qualify as a reduced rate (5%) supply for VAT purposes.

- The notional rents in relation to luxury flats for the purposes of flat conversion allowance have not been uprated since the regime was introduced in 2001, and are therefore likely to be significantly more difficult to meet than previously. There is power for the Treasury to uprate these amounts by Order. Note also that the quoted rents apply to letting the flat furnished on a shorthold tenancy, irrespective of the intention as to actual letting. The test is applied only once — when the work is completed, so there is no need for existing developments to consider the rental limits further.

- Where an industrial building has been sold on or after 21 March 2007 and before 1 April 2011 there may still be a balancing adjustment where the sale was agreed prior to 21 March 2007, and the contract was unconditional, and is not varied. It is also possible to escape the transitional regime by deciding to vary the contract before completing the sale, which will eliminate any possible balancing adjustment.

- Buildings in Enterprise zones are not within the general abolition of balancing adjustments applying to industrial and agricultural buildings. There can still be a balancing charge in relation to a disposal event after March 2007.

11

Capital Allowances on Plant and Machinery

Cross-references. See **10 CAPITAL ALLOWANCES**. See also **73.84 TRADING INCOME** for gifts of plant or machinery to charities.

Simon's Taxes. See B3.303–B3.305, B3.311.

Other sources. See Tolley's Capital Allowances.

Introduction

[11.1] The law relating to capital allowances was consolidated in *Capital Allowances Act 2001 (CAA 2001)* as part of the Tax Law Rewrite programme.

Capital allowances (balancing charges) are a deduction from (addition to) the profits etc. of trades and other qualifying activities in arriving at the taxable amount. They are generally treated as trading expenses (receipts) of the period of account (see **11.2**(i) below) to which they relate. [*CAA 2001, ss 2, 6*].

For a full list of qualifying activities in relation to which plant and machinery allowances are available, see **11.4** below.

Matters applying to capital allowances generally

[11.2] The following matters are pertinent to capital allowances generally.

(i)   **Meaning of 'chargeable period' and 'period of account'.** For capital allowances purposes, a *'chargeable period'* is a 'period of account'.

For persons carrying on a trade, profession or vocation, a *'period of account'* means a period for which accounts are drawn up, except that where such a period exceeds 18 months, it is deemed to be split into two or more periods of account, beginning on, or on an anniversary of, the date on which the actual period begins. Exceptionally, where there is an interval between two periods of account, it is deemed to form part of the first such period, and where two periods of account overlap, the common period is deemed to form part of the first such period only. For non-traders, a period of account is a tax year.

[*CAA 2001, s 6*].

See the examples at **11.32** below.

(ii)   **Claims.** Capital allowances are given only if a claim is made. Such a claim can only be made by inclusion in the annual tax return (subject to the very limited exceptions at *CAA 2001, s 3(4)* as amended). [*CAA 2001, s 3, Sch 2 para 103(2)*]. See **63.4 RETURNS** as regards amendments to income tax returns, and the time allowed for making them.

(iii)   **Capital expenditure.** References in the capital allowances legislation to the incurring of capital expenditure and the paying of capital sums exclude any sums allowed as deductions in computing the payer's profits or earnings and certain sums payable under deduction of tax. Corresponding rules apply as regards the receipt of such sums. [*CAA 2001, s 4, Sch 3 para 9; ITA 2007, Sch 1 para 397*].

(iv)   **Time expenditure incurred.** Capital expenditure (other than that constituted by an 'additional VAT liability' — see (viii) below) is generally treated, for capital allowances purposes, as incurred as soon as there is an unconditional obligation to pay it, even if all or part of it is not required to be paid until some later date. However, expenditure is treated as incurred on a later date in the following circumstances.

•   Where any part of the expenditure is not required to be paid until a date more than four months after the date determined as above, it is treated as incurred on that later date.

•   Where an obligation to pay becomes unconditional earlier than in accordance with normal commercial usage, with the sole or main benefit likely to be the bringing forward of the chargeable period in which the expenditure would otherwise be treated as incurred, it is instead treated as incurred on the date on or before which it is required to be paid.

Where, as a result of an event such as the issuing of a certificate, an obligation to pay becomes unconditional within one month after the end of a chargeable period, but at or before the end of that chargeable period the asset concerned has become the property of, or is otherwise attributed under the contract to, the person having the obligation, the expenditure is treated as incurred immediately before the end of that chargeable period.

The above provisions do not override any specific rule under which expenditure is treated as incurred later than the relevant time given above.

[*CAA 2001, s 5*].

Simon's Taxes. See B3.103, B3.104, B3.107.

(v)   **Exclusion of double allowances.** No allowance under any of the codes listed below can be made in respect of any expenditure that has been allocated to a plant and machinery pool (see **11.23** below), and on which a plant or machinery allowance (or balancing charge) has consequently been given (or made), or any related asset (as above); and expenditure which has attracted an allowance under any of those codes (and any asset to which that expenditure related) cannot be allocated to a plant and machinery pool.

- Agricultural buildings allowances (**10.3** CAPITAL ALLOWANCES);
- Allowances for expenditure on business premises renovation (**10.5** CAPITAL ALLOWANCES);
- Allowances for expenditure on dredging (**10.6** CAPITAL ALLOWANCES);
- Allowances for dwelling-houses let on assured tenancies (**10.8** CAPITAL ALLOWANCES);
- Allowances for expenditure on flat conversion (**10.9** CAPITAL ALLOWANCES);
- Industrial buildings allowances (**10.10–10.22** CAPITAL ALLOWANCES);
- allowances for mineral extraction (**10.24–10.34** CAPITAL ALLOWANCES);
- Research and development allowances (**10.37** CAPITAL ALLOWANCES).

Additional rules apply under *CAA 2001, s 9* to prevent double allowances in relation to plant or machinery treated as fixtures (as at **11.33** *et seq.* below).

[*CAA 2001, ss 7–10, Sch 3 para 10*].

Where an item of expenditure qualifies for more than one type of capital allowance, it is the taxpayer's choice as to which to claim, but he cannot alter his choice in later years. (HMRC Capital Allowances Manual CA16000, HMRC Brief 12/09, 31 March 2009).

Simon's Taxes. See B3.114.

(vi)   **Expenditure met by another's contributions.** Subject to the exceptions below, a person is not regarded as incurring expenditure for capital allowances purposes to the extent that it is met, or will be met, directly or indirectly by another person or by a '*public body*', i.e. the Crown or any government or public or local authority (whether in the UK or elsewhere). For the scope of 'public authority', see *McKinney v Hagans Caravans (Manufacturing) Ltd* CA(NI) 1997, 69 TC 526. There is an exception where the expenditure is met by a Regional Development Grant or NI equivalent. In practice, applications for Regional Development Grants were no longer accepted after 31 March 1988, but NI equivalents did continue to be available until 31 March 2003. Expenditure met by insurance or other compensation money due in respect of a destroyed, demolished or defunct asset is not excluded from allowances.

The above rule is disapplied, and allowances are thus available, if the contributor is not a public body and can obtain neither a capital allowance on his contribution by virtue of (vii) below nor a deduction against profits of a trade, profession or vocation or any qualifying activity within **11.4**(iii)–(vi) below. [*CAA 2001, ss 532–536, Sch 2 para 19, Sch 3 paras 106–108*].

Repaid grants. Where a grant which has been deducted from expenditure qualifying for capital allowances (as above) is later repaid (in whole or part), the repayment will, by concession, be treated as expenditure qualifying for capital allowances. Where allowances were restricted in respect of a contribution from a person (other than a public body) who himself obtained either a capital allowance under (vii) below or a trading deduction for his contribution (as above), this treatment is dependent upon the repayment falling to be taxed on the recipient through a balancing charge or as a trading receipt. (HMRC ESC B49 as revised).

Simon's Taxes. See **B3.111**.

(vii) **Contribution allowances.** Contributors towards another person's capital expenditure on an asset may receive allowances (*'contribution allowances'*) where the contribution is for the purposes of a trade or 'relevant activity' carried on (or to be carried on) by the contributor, and where the expenditure would otherwise have entitled the other person (assuming him not to be a public body) to agricultural buildings, industrial buildings, plant and machinery or mineral extraction allowances. Contribution allowances are not available where the contributor and the other person are **CONNECTED PERSONS (21)**. A *'relevant activity'* is a profession or vocation or,an activity within **11.4**(iii)–(vi) below.

Contribution allowances are such as would have been made if the contribution had been expended on the provision for the contributor's trade etc. of a similar asset and as if the asset were at all material times used for the purposes of the contributor's trade etc. (so that balancing adjustments do not apply to such contributions). As regards plant and machinery, the contributor's deemed expenditure can only be allocated to a single asset pool (see **11.23** below). On a transfer of the trade etc., or part thereof, the allowances (or part) are subsequently made to the transferee. [*CAA 2001, ss 537–542, Sch 3 paras 109, 110; FA 2008, Sch 27 paras 8–11, 20, 23, 30*].

Capital contributions towards expenditure on dredging are treated as expenditure incurred by the contributor on that dredging. [*CAA 2001, s 543*].

Simon's Taxes. See **B3.112**.

(viii) **VAT capital goods scheme.** Under the VAT capital goods scheme, the input tax originally claimed on the acquisition of certain capital assets is subject to amendment within a specified period of adjustment in accordance with any increase or decrease in the extent to which the asset is used in making taxable, as opposed to exempt, supplies for VAT purposes. The items covered by the scheme are limited to land and buildings (or parts of buildings) worth at least £250,000 and computers (and items of computer equipment) worth at least £50,000. See Tolley's Value Added Tax under Capital Goods Scheme for a full description.

Special capital allowances provisions apply where a VAT adjustment is made under the capital goods scheme.

'*Additional VAT liability*' and '*additional VAT rebate*' mean, respectively:

- an amount which a person becomes liable to pay, or
- an amount which he becomes entitled to deduct,

by way of adjustment under the VAT capital goods scheme in respect of input tax. Generally (but see below), such a liability or rebate is treated as incurred or made on the last day of the period:

- which is one of the periods making up the applicable VAT period of adjustment under the VAT capital goods scheme, and
- in which occurred the increase or decrease in use giving rise to the liability or rebate.

However, for the purpose of determining the chargeable period (see (i) above) in which it accrues, an additional VAT liability or rebate is treated as accruing on whichever is the relevant day below.

- Where the liability or rebate is accounted for in a VAT return, the last day of the period covered by that return.
- If, before the making of a VAT return, HMRC assess the liability or rebate, the day on which the assessment is made.
- If the trade (or other qualifying activity — see **11.4** below) is permanently discontinued before the liability or rebate has been accounted for in a VAT return and before the making of an assessment, the last day of the chargeable period in which the cessation occurs.

Where an allowance or charge falls to be determined by reference to a proportion only of the expenditure incurred or a proportion only of what that allowance or charge would otherwise have been, a related additional VAT liability or rebate is similarly apportioned.

[*CAA 2001, ss 546–551; FA 2008, Sch 27 paras 12, 30*].

Simon's Taxes. See B3.103, B3.104, B3.110.

(ix) **Composite sales** may be apportioned by the Appeal Tribunal regardless of any separate prices attributed in the sale agreement. [*CAA 2001, ss 562–564; FA 2008, Sch 27 paras 13, 30; SI 2009 No 56, Sch 1 para 299*]. See *Fitton v Gilders & Heaton* Ch D 1955, 36 TC 233, and *Wood v Provan* CA 1968, 44 TC 701.

(x) **Finance leasing.** See **73.79** TRADING INCOME as regards restrictions on capital allowances where certain finance leasing arrangements are involved. These are disapplied from, broadly, 1 April 2006 in relation to long funding leases. See also **11.43** *et seq.*, **11.61**, **11.63** below.

(xi) **Recovery of assets under** *Proceeds of Crime Act 2002, Pt 5*. *Proceeds of Crime Act 2002, Pt 5 Ch 2* provides for the recovery, in civil proceedings before the High Court (or, in Scotland, the Court of

Session), of property which is, or represents, property obtained through 'unlawful conduct' (as defined in the *Act*). If the Court is satisfied that any property is recoverable under the provisions, it will make a '*recovery order*', vesting the property in an appointed trustee for civil recovery. Alternatively, the Court may make an order under *s 276* of the *Act* staying (or, in Scotland, sisting) proceedings on terms agreed by the parties. The vesting of property in a trustee for civil recovery or any other person, either under a recovery order or in pursuance of a *s 276* order, is known as a *Pt 5* transfer. A '*compensating payment*' may in some cases be made to the person who held the property immediately before the transfer. If the order provides for the creation of any interest in favour of that person, he is treated as receiving (in addition to any other compensating payment) a compensating payment equal to the value of the interest. [*Proceeds of Crime Act 2002, ss 240(1), 266(1)(2), 276, 316(1), 448, Sch 10 para 2*].

Where the property in question is plant or machinery, the relevant interest in an industrial building or in a flat (within **10.9** CAPITAL ALLOWANCES), or an asset representing qualifying expenditure on research and development (within **10.37** CAPITAL ALLOWANCES), there are provisions to ensure that the *Pt 5* transfer has a tax-neutral effect, unless a compensating payment is made to the transferor in which case its amount and/or value must be brought into account as a disposal value or, as the case may be, as proceeds from a balancing event. [*Proceeds of Crime Act 2002, Sch 10 paras 12–29; FA 2008, Sch 27 paras 24, 30*].

Qualifying expenditure

[**11.3**] Allowances are available in respect of 'qualifying expenditure' incurred by a person carrying on a trade or other 'qualifying activity' (see **11.4** below). Subject to **11.6–11.12** below and to other specific exclusions, expenditure is '*qualifying expenditure*' if it is 'capital expenditure' (see **11.2**(iii) above) incurred on the provision of plant or machinery wholly or partly for the purposes of the qualifying activity carried on by that person, and as a result of which that person owns the plant or machinery (for which see the paragraph on 'Ownership' in **11.15** below). [*CAA 2001, s 11*]. See **11.29** below as regards partial use for other purposes. Provided these tests are met (but subject to specific restrictions — see, for example, **11.63** below), it is irrelevant whether or not the object of the person incurring the expenditure was, or included, the obtaining of capital allowances (see the CA judgment in *Barclays Mercantile Business Finance Ltd v Mawson* HL 2004, 76 TC 446, a case involving complex 'finance leasing' arrangements).

Expenditure incurred for the purposes of, and prior to the commencement of, a qualifying activity is treated as incurred on the first day on which the activity is carried on. [*CAA 2001, s 12*].

Expenditure incurred on the provision of plant or machinery for long funding leasing is excluded from being qualifying expenditure in the hands of the lessor (see **11.46** below). See **11.33** *et seq.* below as regards fixtures which become part of land or buildings.

Whether plant or machinery is acquired new or second-hand is generally irrelevant (but see **11.63** below as regards certain sales between connected persons etc.). A *share* in plant or machinery can qualify for allowances [*CAA 2001, s 270*].

See also Eligible expenditure at **11.6–11.12** below.

Simon's Taxes. See B3.303–B3.305, B3.311.

Qualifying activities

[11.4] Any of the following is a '*qualifying activity*':

(i)   a trade, profession or vocation;

(ii)   an employment or office (excluding any duties the earnings for which are taxable on the remittance basis — see generally **27.4–27.10 EMPLOYMENT INCOME**);

(iii)   a UK property business or overseas property business (see **60.2 PROPERTY INCOME**);

(iv)   a furnished holiday lettings business (see **60.10 PROPERTY INCOME**);

(v)   any of the concerns listed in *ITTOIA 2005, s 12(4)* (mines, quarries and sundry other undertakings);

(vi)   managing the investments of a company with investment business;

(vii) special leasing, i.e. the hiring out of plant or machinery otherwise than in the course of another qualifying activity (see **11.50** below),

but (other than for the purposes of **11.51** and **11.63** below) to the extent only that the profits therefrom are within the charge to UK tax (or would be if there *were* any profits).

[*CAA 2001, ss 15–18, 19(1), 20*].

As regards (iii) and (vii) above, expenditure in providing plant or machinery for use in a dwelling-house (or flat — see HMRC Capital Allowances Manual CA20020, 20040) is not qualifying expenditure. Expenditure on plant and machinery partly for such use is apportioned as is just and reasonable. [*CAA 2001, s 35*]. See HMRC Brief 66/08, 29 December 2008 as regards university halls of residence and similar facilities (including other types of multiple occupancy accommodation, such as those provided to key workers).

As regards (ii) above, the plant or machinery must be *necessarily* provided for use in performing the duties of the employment etc. and mechanically propelled road vehicles and cycles are excluded. [*CAA 2001, s 36*]. Plant provided by a vicar so as to give visual sermons was held not to comply with this requirement (*White v Higginbottom* Ch D 1982, 57 TC 283). With minor exceptions, expenditure on plant or machinery used for providing business entertainment is excluded [*CAA 2001, s 269, Sch 2 para 51*], as is certain expenditure incurred by members of the House of Commons, the Scottish Parliament or the Wales or Northern Ireland Assemblies in or in connection with the provision or use of residential or overnight accommodation. [*CAA 2001, s 34*].

Simon's Taxes. See B3.303–B3.305, B3.311.

Making of allowances and charges

[11.5] Where the qualifying activity is within **11.**4(i) or (iii)–(v) above, plant and machinery allowances are treated as expenses of, and balancing charges are treated as receipts of, the trade, profession, vocation, UK property business, overseas property business, furnished holiday lettings business or *ITTOIA 2005, s 12(4)* concern. Where the qualifying activity is an employment or office (as in **11.**4(ii) above), allowances are given as deductions from taxable earnings and balancing charges are themselves treated as earnings. [*CAA 2001, ss 247–252, 262*].

Allowances and charges are computed for income tax purposes by reference to events in periods of account (see **11.**2(i) above). [*CAA 2001, ss 2(1), 6(1)*].

See **11.50** below as regards a qualifying activity of special leasing (as in **11.**4(vii) above).

See **11.**2(ii) above as regards the *claiming* of capital allowances.

Simon's Taxes. See B3.380–B3.386.

Eligible expenditure

[11.6] The capital expenditure eligible for allowances includes that on alteration of existing buildings incidental to the installation of plant or machinery for the purposes of a trade or other qualifying activity [*CAA 2001, s 25*] and on demolition of plant or machinery which it replaces [*CAA 2001, s 26(1)(2)*]. There is, however, a distinction between alterations incidental to the installation of plant or machinery and alterations consequential upon the installation of plant or machinery (*J D Wetherspoon plc v HMRC* (Sp C 657), [2008] SSCD 460). See also *J D Wetherspoon plc v HMRC (No 2)* FTT (TC 312), 2010 STI 1292 as regards a number of specific items claimed as alterations incidental in the context of public houses.

Costs of moving plant from one site to another and re-erecting it, so far as not deductible in computing profits, qualify for allowances (HMRC Capital Allowances Manual CA21190). Capital expenditure on animals and other living creatures kept for the purposes of farming or any other trade, or on shares in such animals etc., is excluded. [*CAA 2001, s 38*].

Simon's Taxes. See B3.305–B3.314.

Meaning of plant or machinery—leading cases

[11.7] 'Plant' and 'machinery' are not defined in the legislation. '*Machinery*' is accordingly given its ordinary meaning, but '*plant*' has been considered in many cases. It includes apparatus kept for permanent employment in the trade etc., but a line is drawn between that which performs a function in the business operations (which may be plant) and that which provides the place or setting in which these operations are performed (which is not). See *Cole Bros Ltd v Phillips* HL 1982, 55 TC 188 (electric wiring and fittings in department store held not to be plant) and *St. John's School v Ward* CA 1974, 49 TC 524 (prefabricated school buildings held not to be plant) and contrast *CIR v Barclay, Curle & Co Ltd* HL 1969, 45 TC 221 (dry docks, including cost of excavation, held to be plant) and *CIR v Scottish & Newcastle Breweries Ltd* HL 1982, 55 TC 252 (lighting and decor of licensed premises held to be plant). If an item used for carrying on a business does not form part of the premises and is not stock-in-trade, then it is plant (*Wimpy International Ltd v Warland* CA 1988, 61 TC 51).

Permanent employment in the trade

Permanent employment demands some degree of durability, see *Hinton v Maden & Ireland Ltd* HL 1959, 38 TC 391 (shoe manufacturer's knives and lasts, average life three years, held to be plant). In practice, a life of two years or more is sufficient, and this applies equally as regards animals functioning as apparatus with which a trade is carried on (see HMRC Capital Allowances Manual CA21100, 21220).

Film expenditure

Film production and acquisition expenditure incurred by a person carrying on a trade is treated for income tax purposes as revenue expenditure. In relation to certified films (broadly, British or European films), an election may be made to disapply this rule (and effectively to treat the expenditure as capital expenditure on plant) where the master version is expected to realise its value over a period of two years or more. See *Ensign Tankers (Leasing) Ltd v Stokes* HL 1992, 64 TC 617 for relief to investor in film production partnership. Otherwise, see **73.76 TRADING INCOME** as regards the above matters and film tax reliefs generally.

Held to rank as plant

Movable office partitions (*Jarrold v John Good & Sons Ltd* CA 1962, 40 TC 681); mezzanine platforms installed in a warehouse (but not ancillary lighting) (*Hunt v Henry Quick Ltd* Ch D 1992, 65 TC 108); swimming pools for use on caravan site (*Cooke v Beach Station Caravans Ltd* Ch D 1974, 49 TC 514); grain silos (*Schofield v R & H Hall Ltd* CA(NI) 1974, 49 TC 538); barrister's books (*Munby v Furlong* CA 1977, 50 TC 491); Building Society window screens (*Leeds Permanent Building Society v Proctor* Ch D 1982, 56 TC 293); light fittings (*Wimpy International Ltd v Warland* CA 1988, 61 TC 51; *J D Wetherspoon plc v HMRC (No 2)* FTT (TC 312), 2010 STI 1292); synthetic grass football pitch (*CIR v Anchor International Ltd* CS 2005, 77 TC 38); cubicle walls and doors in public house toilets (*J D Wetherspoon plc v HMRC* (Sp C 657), [2008] SSCD 460).

Held not to be plant

Stallions (*Earl of Derby v Aylmer* KB 1915, 6 TC 665); wallpaper pattern books (*Rose & Co Ltd v Campbell* Ch D 1967, 44 TC 500); canopy over petrol-filling station (*Dixon v Fitch's Garage Ltd* Ch D 1975, 50 TC 509); ship used as floating restaurant (*Benson v Yard Arm Club Ltd* CA 1979, 53 TC 67); false ceilings (*Hampton v Fortes Autogrill Ltd* Ch D 1979, 53 TC 691); a football stand (*Brown v Burnley Football Co Ltd* Ch D 1980, 53 TC 357); an inflatable tennis court cover (*Thomas v Reynolds* Ch D 1987, 59 TC 502); shop fronts, wall and floor coverings, suspended floors, ceilings and stairs etc. (*Wimpy International Ltd v Warland, Associated Restaurants Ltd v Warland* CA 1988, 61 TC 51); permanent quarantine kennels (allowances having been granted for movable kennels) (*Carr v Sayer* Ch D 1992, 65 TC 15); lighting ancillary to mezzanine platform installation qualifying as plant (*Hunt v Henry Quick Ltd* Ch D 1992, 65 TC 108); a planteria (a form of glasshouse — see also **11.8** below) (*Gray v Seymours Garden Centre (Horticulture)* CA 1995, 67 TC 401); access site and wash hall containing car wash equipment (*Attwood v Anduff Car Wash Ltd* CA 1997, 69 TC 575); housing for underground electricity sub-station (*Bradley v London Electricity plc* Ch D 1996, 70 TC 155); golf putting greens (*Family Golf Centres Ltd v Thorne* (Sp C 150), [1998] SSCD 106); an all-weather horse racing track (*Shove v Lingfield Park 1991 Ltd* CA 2004, 76 TC 363); decorative wood panelling in a public house (*J D Wetherspoon plc v HMRC* (Sp C 657), [2008] SSCD 460).

In *McVeigh v Arthur Sanderson & Sons Ltd* Ch D 1968, 45 TC 273, held that cost of blocks etc. of a wallpaper manufacturer (admitted to be plant) should include something for the designs but the designs, following *Daphne v Shaw* KB 1926, 11 TC 256, were not plant. (*Daphne v Shaw* has since been overruled by *Munby v Furlong* above.)

Borrowings

Interest etc. on money borrowed to finance purchases of plant and charged to capital, held not eligible for capital allowances (*Ben-Odeco Ltd v Powlson* HL 1978, 52 TC 459 and cf *Van Arkadie v Sterling Coated Materials Ltd* Ch D 1982, 56 TC 479). In *Tower MCashback LLP 1 v HMRC* CA, [2010] STC 809, by virtue of an arrangement involving 75% of the purchase price being funded by the making of non-recourse loans (on extreme terms) to the partners, the price ostensibly paid by an LLP for software was vastly in excess of its true market value. The CA concluded that the terms of the borrowing should be considered in relation to the fundamental question of whether the taxpayer suffered the economic burden of paying the full amount and that on this basis capital allowances were available on the full price.

Depreciation

Where it appears that any sums, not otherwise taxable, are to be payable, directly or indirectly, to the owner of plant or machinery in respect of, or to take account of, the *whole* of the depreciation of that plant or machinery, the expenditure incurred in providing that plant or machinery for the purposes of the qualifying activity is not qualifying expenditure. [*CAA 2001, s 37*]. As regards subsidies towards *partial* depreciation, see **11.69** below.

Buildings

[11.8] See **11.11** below for allowances for expenditure after 5 April 2008 on integral features (as defined) of buildings and structures.

See **11.12** below for provisions restricting allowances for certain expenditure on buildings and structures.

Certain expenditure on buildings, as below, is treated for capital allowance purposes as being on plant and machinery (unless tax relief could otherwise be obtained). On any disposal, the disposal value (see **11.24** below) in respect of expenditure within (i)–(iii) below is taken as nil [*CAA 2001, s 63(5)*].

(i) *Fire safety expenditure* incurred before 6 April 2008 in a trade or other qualifying activity in taking steps specified in a notice under *Fire Precautions Act 1971, s 5(4)* (or which might have been so specified but were in fact specified in a document from the fire authority on application for a fire certificate under that Act) and similarly for expenditure incurred in order to avoid restriction of use of premises by a prohibition notice under *s 10* of that Act. [*CAA 2001, ss 27, 29; FA 2008, s 72*]. Applies to NI by concession (HMRC ESC B16). Applies by Order to hotels and boarding houses (*SI 1972 No 238*) and to premises of factories, offices, shops and railways with minimum of 10 employees (*SI 1976 No 2009*). *Lessors of such premises* may claim allowances on contributions (see **11.2**(vii) above) towards tenants' qualifying expenditure or own similar direct expenditure (HMRC ESC B16).

This measure is repealed with effect for expenditure incurred after 5 April 2008. Either capital allowances or revenue deductions are available under general principles for most expenditure on fire prevention and safety, such as extinguishers, alarms and sprinkler systems (Treasury Explanatory Notes to the 2008 Finance Bill).

(ii) Expenditure on *thermal insulation of existing building* by a person occupying the building for the purposes of a trade carried on by him or letting the building in the course of a UK property business or overseas property business. This measure is subject to the overriding rule, where the building is let, that expenditure incurred in providing plant or machinery for use in a *dwelling-house* cannot be qualifying expenditure (see **11.3** above); in addition, expenditure is not qualifying expenditure if a deduction is available for it under **60.5**(c) PROPERTY INCOME (landlord's expenditure on energy-saving items) or would be so available if the expenditure did not potentially attract capital allowances. Expenditure incurred after 5 April 2008 within this category qualifies for writing-down allowances at the special 10% rate (see **11.25** below); expenditure incurred on or before that date qualified for the normal writing-down allowances at **11.23** below.

For expenditure incurred before 6 April 2008, the above applied only if the building in question was an *industrial building*.

[*CAA 2001, ss 27, 28; ICTA 1988, s 32(1B)(1C); FA 2008, s 71*].

(iii) *Sports ground expenditure* incurred by a person carrying on a trade or other qualifying activity to comply with a safety certificate issued or to be issued under the *Safety of Sports Grounds Act 1975* or certified by local authority as falling within requirements if such certificates had been (or could have been) applied for. Also, expenditure incurred by a trade in respect of a 'regulated stand' (as defined by the *Fire Safety and Safety of Places of Sport Act 1987*) to comply with a safety certificate (as defined by that *Act*) issued for the stand or to take steps specified by the local authority as being necessary under the terms, or proposed terms, of such a safety certificate issued, or to be issued, by it. [*CAA 2001, ss 27, 30–32*]. See also **11.2**(vi)(vii) above as regards certain contributions to expenditure.

(iv) *Hotels and restaurants*. HMRC regard as eligible for capital allowances expenditure on *apparatus* to provide electric light or power, hot water, central heating, ventilation or air conditioning, alarm and sprinkler systems. Also on cost of hot water pipes, baths, wash basins etc. (CCAB Statement, 9 August 1977.) See now *Cole Bros Ltd v Phillips* HL 1982, 55 TC 188 and *CIR v Scottish & Newcastle Breweries Ltd* HL 1982, 55 TC 252.

Professional fees

Fees such as survey fees, architects' fees, quantity surveyors' fees, structural engineers' fees, service engineers' fees or legal costs, only qualify as expenditure on the provision of plant or machinery if they relate directly to the acquisition, transport and installation of the plant or machinery. Where professional fees are paid in connection with a building project that includes the provision of plant or machinery, only the part, if any, which relates to services that can properly be regarded as on the provision of plant or machinery can be qualifying expenditure for plant or machinery allowances.

Preliminary expenses

The same applies to preliminary expenses, e.g. site management, insurance, general purpose labour, temporary accommodation and security, in connection with a building project. (HMRC Capital Allowances Manual CA20070). Where preliminary expenses are allocable or apportionable to expenditure on alterations to a building incidental to the installation of plant or machinery they can rank as eligible expenditure so long as the cost of the alterations is eligible expenditure (*J D Wetherspoon plc v HMRC* (Sp C 657), [2008] SSCD 460).

Cable television

The cost of provision and installation of ducting in connection with construction of cable television networks is regarded as expenditure on plant or machinery (Revenue Press Release 15 March 1984).

Glasshouses

Glasshouses are likely to be accepted as plant only where, during construction, sophisticated environmental control systems are permanently installed, incorporating e.g. a computer system controlling heating, temperature and humidity control, automatic ventilation systems and automatic thermal or shade screens (Revenue Tax Bulletins November 1992 p 46, June 1998 p 552). See, for example, *Gray v Seymours Garden Centre (Horticulture)* CA, 67 TC 401, where a 'planteria' was held to be premises. See also **11.12** below and, as regards whether glasshouses are 'long-life assets', **11.31** below.

Pig industry

HMRC have published guidance illustrating the range of assets on which the pig industry might claim plant and machinery capital allowances (HMRC Brief 03/10, February 2010).

Slurry storage systems

Slurry storage systems, used for the temporary storage of slurry, qualify as plant or machinery, but any building or structure which is part of a slurry storage facility does not qualify (HMRC Brief 66/08, 29 December 2008).

See generally HMRC Capital Allowances Manual CA21000 *et seq.*

Enterprise zones

Expenditure on plant or machinery which is to be an integral part of an industrial or commercial building in an enterprise zone may qualify for 100% industrial buildings allowance. See **10.20 CAPITAL ALLOWANCES**.

Expenditure on security assets

[11.9] Except where tax relief could otherwise be obtained, expenditure by an individual, or partnership of individuals, carrying on a trade or any other qualifying activity within **11.4**(i), (iii) or (iv) above, in connection with the provision for or use by the individual, or any of them, of a security asset (being an asset which improves personal security), is treated as if it were capital expenditure on plant or machinery. On any disposal the disposal value (see **11.24** below) is taken as nil. They apply only where certain conditions, very similar to those described in **73.110 TRADING INCOME**, are satisfied, both as regards the provision or use of the asset and the type of asset that may qualify. An appropriate proportion of the expenditure may qualify in cases where the asset is intended to be used *only partly* to improve personal physical security. [*CAA 2001, ss 27, 33, 63(5); FA 2009, Sch 11 paras 13, 26–28*]. See also **27.73 EMPLOYMENT INCOME**.

Computer software

[11.10] Where capital expenditure is incurred on the acquisition of computer software for the purposes of a trade or other qualifying activity, the software, if it would not otherwise be plant, is treated as such for capital allowances purposes. Similarly, where capital expenditure is incurred after that date in acquiring for such purposes a right to use or otherwise deal with computer software, both the right and the software are treated as plant provided for the purposes of the qualifying activity and (so long as entitlement to the right continues) as belonging to the person incurring the expenditure.

Where a right is granted to another person to use or deal with the whole or part of software or rights which are treated as plant, and the consideration for the grant consists of (or would if it were in money consist of) a capital sum, a disposal value (see **11.24** below) has to be brought into account (unless the software or rights have previously begun to be used wholly or partly for purposes other than those of the qualifying activity, or the activity for which they were used has been permanently discontinued). The amount of the disposal value to be brought into account is the net consideration in money received for the grant, plus any insurance moneys or other capital compensation received in respect of the software by reason of any event affecting that consideration. However, market value is substituted where the consideration for the grant was not, or not wholly, in money, or where:

- no consideration, or money consideration less than market value, was given for the grant;
- there is no charge under *ITEPA 2003* (i.e. on employment, pension or social security income); and
- the grantee cannot obtain plant and machinery or research and development allowances for his expenditure or is a dual resident investing company connected with the grantor.

Where a disposal value falls to be calculated in relation to software or rights, then for the purpose of determining whether it is to be limited by reference to the capital expenditure incurred (see **11.24** below), that disposal value is increased by any disposal value previously falling to be brought into account as above in respect of the same person and the same plant.

[*CAA 2001, ss 71–73, Sch 3 para 18*].

See also **73.98** TRADING INCOME.

Integral features of buildings and structures

[**11.11**] Where a person incurs expenditure **after 5 April 2008** on the provision of an 'integral feature' of a building or structure used by him for the purposes of a qualifying activity (see **11.4** above) that he carries on, that expenditure is treated for the purposes of plant and machinery allowances as qualifying expenditure on plant or machinery. Expenditure so treated qualifies for writing-down allowances at the special 10% rate (see **11.25** below). No deduction is then available for the expenditure in calculating income from the activity (whether or not such a deduction would be available under general principles).

For these purposes, an '*integral feature*' is any of the following:

- an electrical system (including a lighting system);
- a cold water system;
- a space or water heating system, a powered system of ventilation, air cooling or air purification, and any floor or ceiling comprised in such a system;
- a lift, escalator or moving walkway; or
- external solar shading.

The above list is not, however, to be taken as including any asset whose principal purpose is to insulate or enclose the interior of a building or to provide an interior floor, wall or ceiling which is intended to remain permanently in place. The Treasury may vary the above list by statutory instrument, but they can add an asset only if it would not otherwise qualify for plant and machinery allowances and can remove an asset only if it would thereby qualify for plant and machinery allowances at a rate other than the special rate.

Expenditure incurred on the *replacement* of an integral feature also qualifies as above. For this purpose, an integral feature is treated as replaced if the amount of the expenditure is more than half the cost of replacing the feature at the time the expenditure is incurred. If a person incurs expenditure which does not meet this test but, within twelve months, incurs further expenditure on the integral feature, the test is again applied but by reference to the aggregate expenditure. If the aggregate amount is more than half the cost of replacing the feature at the time the initial expenditure was incurred, both the initial expenditure and the further expenditure qualifies. It is not a requirement that the further expenditure be incurred in the same chargeable period as the initial expenditure; the tax return covering the earlier chargeable period can be amended if necessary.

[*CAA 2001, ss 33A, 33B; FA 2008, s 73(2)(6)*].

Restrictions on eligible expenditure

[11.12] With effect after 29 November 1993, legislation was introduced (see now *CAA 2001, ss 21–24*) to exclude certain expenditure from the definition of plant and machinery for capital allowances purposes. Assets which had been held to be plant under specific court decisions continued to qualify for plant and machinery allowances, and assets not covered by this legislation remain subject to prevailing case law on plant. (HMRC Press Release 17 December 1993).

General exceptions

Expenditure falling within any of *CAA 2001, ss 28–33, 71* and *ITTOIA 2005, s 143* or earlier equivalents (relating to thermal insulation, fire safety (before 6 April 2008), safety of sports grounds, security assets, computer software, and films and sound recordings — see **11.7**, **11.8** and **11.10** above) is not affected by the legislation described below. The same applies to expenditure within *CAA 2001, s 33A* (integral features of buildings and structures — see **11.11** above). [*CAA 2001, s 23(1)(2); FA 2008, ss 71(7)(8), 72(2)(4), 73(1)(6)*].

Expenditure on buildings which does not qualify for allowances

Expenditure on the construction or acquisition of a building does not qualify for plant and machinery allowances (subject to the general exceptions above and the specific exceptions listed at (1)–(33) below). For these purposes the expression 'building' includes:

- any assets incorporated in the building;
- any assets which, although not incorporated in the building (because they are movable or for some other reason), are nevertheless of a kind which are normally incorporated into buildings; and
- any of the following:
  - (i) walls, floors, ceilings, doors, gates, shutters, windows and stairs;
  - (ii) mains services, and systems, of water, electricity and gas;
  - (iii) waste disposal systems;
  - (iv) sewerage and drainage systems;
  - (v) shafts or other structures in which lifts, hoists, escalators and moving walkways are installed; and

(vi)   fire safety systems.

[*CAA 2001, s 21*].

Expenditure on structures which does not qualify for allowances

'*Structure*' means a fixed structure of any kind, other than a building. A structure is 'any substantial man-made asset' (see Revenue Press Release 17 December 1993).

Expenditure on the construction or acquisition of a structure or any other asset listed immediately below, or on any works involving the alteration of land, does not qualify for plant and machinery allowances (subject to the general exceptions above and the specific exceptions listed at (1)–(33) below).

- A tunnel, bridge, viaduct, aqueduct, embankment or cutting.
- A way, hard standing (such as a pavement), road, railway, tramway, a park for vehicles or containers, or an airstrip or runway.
- An inland navigation, including a canal or basin or a navigable river.
- A dam, reservoir or barrage (including any sluices, gates, generators and other equipment associated with it).
- A dock, harbour, wharf, pier, marina or jetty, or any other structure in or at which vessels may be kept or merchandise or passengers may be shipped or unshipped.
- A dike, sea wall, weir or drainage ditch.
- Any structure not included above, except:
  - (i)   a structure (other than a building) within the definition of an 'industrial building' (see **10.12 CAPITAL ALLOWANCES**);
  - (ii)   a structure in use for the purposes of a gas undertaking; or
  - (iii) a structure in use for the purposes of a trade consisting in the provision of telecommunications, television or radio services,

  and see *CIR v Anchor International Ltd CS 2005, 77 TC 38*, in which a synthetic football pitch was held not to be within this exclusion.

[*CAA 2001, s 22, Sch 3 para 13; FA 2008, Sch 27 paras 33, 35*].

Specific exceptions

The above exclusions do not affect the question as to whether expenditure on any of the items listed in (1)–(33) below qualifies for plant and machinery allowances. Note that items (1)–(16) below do not include any asset whose principal purpose is to insulate or enclose the interior of a building or to provide an interior wall, floor or ceiling which (in each case) is intended to remain permanently in place.

(1)   Any machinery (including devices for providing motive power) not within any other item in this list.

(2)   Gas and sewerage systems (and, for expenditure incurred before 6 April 2008, electrical systems (including lighting systems) and cold water systems) provided mainly to meet the particular requirements of the qualifying activity, or provided mainly to serve particular plant or machinery used for the purposes thereof.

(3)   For expenditure incurred before 6 April 2008, space or water heating systems; powered systems of ventilation, air cooling or air purification; and any ceiling or floor comprised in such systems.

(4)   Manufacturing or processing equipment; storage equipment, including cold rooms; display equipment; and counters, checkouts and similar equipment.

(5)   Cookers, washing machines, dishwashers, refrigerators and similar equipment; washbasins, sinks, baths, showers, sanitary ware and similar equipment; and furniture and furnishings.

(6)   Hoists (and, for expenditure incurred before 6 April 2008, lifts, escalators and moving walkways).

(7)   Sound insulation provided mainly to meet the particular requirements of the qualifying activity.

(8)   Computer, telecommunication and surveillance systems (including their wiring or other links).

(9)   Refrigeration or cooling equipment.

(10)   Fire alarm systems; sprinkler and other equipment for extinguishing or containing fires.

(11)   Burglar alarm systems.

(12)   Strong rooms in bank or building society premises; safes.

(13)   Partition walls, where movable and intended to be moved in the course of the qualifying activity.

(14)   Decorative assets provided for the enjoyment of the public in hotel, restaurant or similar trades.

(15)   Advertising hoardings; signs, displays and similar assets.

(16)   Swimming pools (including diving boards, slides and structures on which such boards or slides are mounted).

(17)   Any glasshouse constructed so that the required environment (namely, air, heat, light, irrigation and temperature) for the growing of plants is provided automatically by means of devices forming an integral part of its structure; see also below.

(18)   Cold stores.

(19)   Caravans provided mainly for holiday lettings. (Under *CAA 2001, s 23(5)*, 'caravan' includes, in relation to a holiday caravan site, anything treated as such for the purposes of the *Caravan Sites and Control of Development Act 1960* (or NI equivalent).

(20)   Buildings provided for testing aircraft engines run within the building.

(21)   Movable buildings intended to be moved in the course of the qualifying activity.

(22)   The alteration of land for the purpose only of installing plant or machinery.

(23)   The provision of dry docks.

(24)   The provision of any jetty or similar structure provided mainly to carry plant or machinery.

(25)   The provision of pipelines, or underground ducts or tunnels with a primary purpose of carrying utility conduits.

(26)   The provision of towers provided to support floodlights.

(27)   The provision of any reservoir incorporated into a water treatment works or any service reservoir of treated water for supply within any housing estate or other particular locality.

(28)   The provision of silos provided for temporary storage; or storage tanks.

(29)   The provision of slurry pits or silage clamps.

(30)   The provision of fish tanks or fish ponds.

(31) The provision of rails, sleepers and ballast for a railway or tramway.
(32) The provision of structures and other assets for providing the setting for any ride at an amusement park or exhibition.
(33) The provision of fixed zoo cages.

The omission, as regards expenditure incurred after 5 April 2008, of the assets in item (3) above and of certain assets in items (1) and (6) above is due to those assets now being included in *CAA 2001, s 33A* (integral features of buildings and structures — see **11.11** above) and thus automatically excluded from the scope of *CAA 2001, ss 21, 22* (see above).

As regards expenditure on *glasshouses* (item 17 above), see **11.8** above for the HMRC approach to allowances for such expenditure, and **11.31** below as regards whether glasshouses are 'long-life assets'.

[*CAA 2001, s 23(3)–(5); FA 2008, s 73(1)(4)*].

Interests in land

Expenditure on the provision of plant or machinery does not include expenditure incurred on the acquisition of an interest in land, but this restriction does not apply to any asset which is so installed or otherwise fixed in or to any description of land as to become, in law, part of that land. 'Land' does not include buildings or other structures but is otherwise as defined in *Interpretation Act 1978, Sch 1*. 'Interest in land' for these purposes has the same meaning as in *CAA 2001, s 175* (allowances for fixtures — see **11.33** *et seq.* below). [*CAA 2001, s 24*].

Simon's Taxes. See B3.306, B3.308.

Annual investment allowance

[11.13] A person is entitled to an annual investment allowance (AIA) of up to £100,000 (£50,000 before 6 April 2010) for a chargeable period (see **11.2**(i) above) in respect of any 'AIA qualifying expenditure' which he incurs in that period on plant or machinery which he owns at some time during that period. (See also below under *Modus operandi*.) Subject to the exclusions below, qualifying expenditure (see **11.3** above) is '*AIA qualifying expenditure*' if it is incurred **after 5 April 2008** by an individual or by a partnership consisting entirely of individuals (or after 31 March 2008 by a company, as regards which see Tolley's Corporation Tax under Capital Allowances — Plant and machinery: eligible expenditure and initial allowances). In determining whether expenditure is AIA qualifying expenditure, any effect of *CAA 2001, s 12* (pre-commencement expenditure — see **11.3** above) on the time at which it is to be treated as incurred is disregarded. Other entities, such as a trust or a partnership consisting of both companies and individuals, are not entitled to an AIA. As regards ownership of plant or machinery, see **11.15** below under *Ownership*.

The annual investment allowance is to be reduced to £25,000 from April 2012 (HMRC Budget Note BN04, 22 June 2010).

Exclusions

Expenditure is not AIA qualifying expenditure in any of the following circumstances.

(i)   The expenditure is incurred in the chargeable period in which the qualifying activity is permanently discontinued.

(ii)   The expenditure is incurred on the provision of a '*car*', defined for these purposes (by *CAA 2009, s 268A*, previously by *CAA 2001, s 81*) as a mechanically propelled road vehicle which is neither (1) of a construction primarily suited for the conveyance of goods or burden of any description nor (2) of a type not commonly used as a private vehicle and unsuitable for such use. A 'car' used to include a motor cycle. However, for new regime expenditure (as in **11.27** below — broadly expenditure incurred on or after 6 April 2009), motor cycles are excluded from the definition of 'car' and thus qualify for the AIA. It is confirmed on page 12 of an HMRC Technical Note published in December 2008 ('Modernising tax relief for business expenditure on cars') that the above definition means that black hackney cabs (e.g. London taxis) are not regarded as cars for this purpose. A double cab pick-up may also qualify as a car — see HMRC Employment Income Manual EIM23150, and see **11.71** below.

As regards (2), see employee benefits case of *Gurney v Richards* Ch D, [1989] STC 682 (fire brigade car equipped with flashing light held within excluded class), decided on similarly worded legislation (see **27.32 EMPLOYMENT INCOME**). See also *Bourne v Auto School of Motoring* Ch D 1964, 42 TC 217 (driving school cars) and *Roberts v Granada TV Rental Ltd* Ch D 1970, 46 TC 295 (mini-vans etc.).

(iii)   The provision of the plant or machinery is connected with a change in the nature or conduct of a trade or business carried on by a person other than the person incurring the expenditure on its provision, and the obtaining of an AIA was the main benefit, or one of the main benefits, which could reasonably be expected to arise from the making of the change.

(iv)   The provision of the plant of machinery is by way of gift (see **11.64** below).

(v)   The plant or machinery was previously used by the owner for purposes other than those of the qualifying activity (see **11.65** below), which includes the purposes of long funding leasing (see **11.46** below).

(vi)   The plant or machinery is acquired by means of a transaction with a connected person (within **21 CONNECTED PERSONS**), or a sale and leaseback transaction or a transaction the sole or main benefit of which would be the obtaining of a plant and machinery allowance (see *CAA 2001, s 217, 232; FA 2008, Sch 24 paras 8, 23*).

In addition, if an arrangement is entered into and a main purpose of it is to enable a person to claim an AIA to which he would not otherwise be entitled, the AIA is not made or, if already made, is withdrawn.

Modus operandi

The AIA is made for the chargeable period in which the AIA qualifying expenditure is incurred. Otherwise, see **11.2**(iv) above as regards the date on which expenditure is treated as having been incurred.

The amount of the AIA is equal to £100,000 or the amount of the AIA qualifying expenditure, whichever is the lower. A person may choose to claim less than the full AIA available. The £100,000 maximum is proportionately increased, or reduced, if the chargeable period is more than, or less than, twelve months.

Where a chargeable period straddles 6 April 2010, the monetary maximum is the sum of:

- the entitlement, based on the previous £50,000 maximum, for the portion of the chargeable period ending on 5 April 2010; and
- the entitlement, based on the current £100,000 maximum for the portion of the chargeable period beginning on 6 April 2010.

Thus, if exactly three-quarters of the chargeable period fell before 6 April 2010, the maximum for the full chargeable period would be £62,500 (three-quarters of £50,000 plus one-quarter of £100,000) or, if lower, the amount of the AIA qualifying expenditure. This is subject to an overriding rule that no more than £50,000 of expenditure incurred in the part of the chargeable period falling before 6 April 2010 can qualify for the AIA. So if the business in this example incurred £60,000 of AIA qualifying expenditure in the chargeable period but all of it was incurred in the first three-quarters of that period, the maximum for the chargeable period would effectively be £50,000 and not £62,500.

Where a chargeable period straddled 6 April 2008, the maximum was computed as if the period began on that date.

The taxpayer is free to decide how to allocate the AIA between different classes of AIA qualifying expenditure; he might, for example, choose to allocate it to expenditure qualifying for writing-down allowances at only 10% in priority to expenditure qualifying at 20%.

An AIA and an FYA cannot be claimed in respect of the same expenditure (see **11.14** below).

If expenditure is incurred partly for the purposes of a qualifying activity and partly for other purposes, any resultant AIA must be reduced as is just and reasonable.

Restriction where related qualifying activities are under common control

Where, in the same tax year, two or more qualifying activities are carried on by one or more persons (other than companies), are controlled by the same person and are 'related' to each other, they do not each attract the £100,000 maximum AIA. For this purpose, a person carries on a qualifying activity in a tax year if he carries it on at the end of the chargeable period for that activity ending in that tax year. If the activities in question are carried in by the same person, he is entitled to a single AIA. If the activities are carried on by more than one person, they are entitled to a single AIA between them. In each case, the amount of the AIA is determined by reference to the aggregate amount of AIA qualifying expenditure incurred in the chargeable periods for the qualifying activities ending in the tax year. The maximum in this case is £100,000 regardless of the length of the chargeable periods. The person or persons involved may allocate the AIA to the qualifying expenditure as he or they think fit; they could, for example, choose to allocate it to expenditure qualifying for 10% writing-down allowances in priority to expenditure qualifying for 20% writing-down allowances. The amount allocated to AIA qualifying expenditure cannot exceed the maximum amount that would have been available in respect of that expenditure if the restriction had not applied.

For the above purposes a qualifying activity is controlled by a person in a tax year if it is controlled by that person at the end of the chargeable period for that activity ending in that tax year. A qualifying activity carried on by an individual is treated as controlled by that individual. A qualifying activity carried on by a partnership is treated as controlled by the individual (if any) who controls the partnership (within the meaning of *CAA 2001, s 574(3)*). Where partners who between them control one partnership also between them control another partnership, the qualifying activities carried on by the partnerships are treated as controlled by the same person.

Where a qualifying activity has more than one chargeable period ending in the same tax year, each such period must be considered separately, i.e. as if it were the only chargeable period for that activity ending in the tax year, in determining if the restriction applies.

A qualifying activity (A1) is '*related*' to another qualifying activity (A2) in a tax year if they meet either of the two conditions below (or both of them). If A1 is thereby related to A2, A1 is also related to any qualifying activity to which A2 is related. The conditions are as follows.

(1)   The shared premises condition. This condition is met if, at the end of the 'relevant chargeable period' for one or both of the qualifying activities, they are carried on from the same premises.

(2)   The related activities condition. This condition is met if, at the end of the 'relevant chargeable period' for one or both of the qualifying activities, they are of the same NACE classification. This means the first level of the common statistical classification of economic activities in the EU established by Regulation (EC) No 1893/2006 of the European Parliament and the Council of 20 December 2006. Information on these classifications is to be included in the relevant HMRC guidance.

The '*relevant chargeable period*' for an activity is the chargeable period for that activity ending in the tax year in question.

If the restriction applies and the relevant chargeable period for one of the qualifying activities (A1) in question is longer than a year, an additional amount of AIA may be available for A1 if there is an amount of unused allowance for an earlier tax year which coincides at least in part with A1's long chargeable period (or for more than one such earlier tax year). Say that X controls two related businesses, A1 and A2. A1 is a new business commenced on 6 October 2010. In the tax year 2011/12, accounts for A1 are prepared for the 18 months to 5 April 2012 and accounts for A2 are prepared as usual for the year ended on that date. For 2011/12, A1 and A2 have AIA qualifying expenditure of £120,000 and £40,000 respectively but the restriction means that, in the absence of a special rule, X would be entitled to an AIA of only £100,000. For the year ended 5 April 2011, A2 had AIA qualifying expenditure of £36,000, so, in theory, there is unused AIA qualifying expenditure of £64,000 (£100,000 – £36,000); however, this is capped at £50,000 (£100,000 × $\frac{1}{2}$) as only six months of A1's long period of account falls within 2010/11. The unused amount of £50,000 is added to the 2011/12 amount of £100,000 to give a theoretical AIA of £150,000 for 2011/12; this must still be compared to the maximum available AIA for A2 in 2011/12, which in this case gives the same figure of £150,000 (£100,000 × 18/12). X can allocate this between A1 and A2 as he likes, except that the AIA for each business cannot exceed what would have been the available AIA if the related activity restriction had not applied, i.e. £150,000 for A1 (which will clearly not be exceeded) and £40,000 for A2.

The special rule above also applies if the relevant chargeable period for *two or more* of the qualifying activities in question is longer than a year, but with the modifications in *CAA 2001, s 51N* if those activities were related in an earlier tax year.

Additional VAT liabilities

In general, where expenditure was AIA qualifying expenditure, any 'additional VAT liability' (see **11.2**(viii) above), incurred in respect of that expenditure at a time when the plant or machinery in question is provided for the purposes of the qualifying activity, is also AIA qualifying expenditure — for the chargeable period in which the liability accrues. An additional VAT liability incurred at a time when the plant or machinery is used for overseas leasing other than protected leasing (see **11.56** below) is not AIA qualifying expenditure.

[*CAA 2001, ss 38A, 38B, 51A, 51H–51N, 205, 218A, 236, 237, 268A; FA 2008, Sch 24 paras 2, 3, 6, 9–11, 23; FA 2009, Sch 11 paras 2, 11, 26–28, Sch 32 paras 12, 17,18, 22; FA 2010, s 5*].

First-year allowances

[11.14] A person is entitled to a first-year allowance (FYA) for a chargeable period (see **11.2**(i) above) in respect of any 'first-year qualifying expenditure' which he incurs in that period on plant or machinery which he owns (see **11.15** below under *Ownership*) at some time during that period. He may claim the allowance in respect of the whole or a part of the first-year qualifying expenditure. In determining for these purposes the time at which expenditure is incurred, *CAA 2001, s 12* (pre-commencement expenditure — see **11.3** above) is disregarded. Otherwise, see **11.2**(iv) above as regards the date on which expenditure is treated as having been incurred.

For expenditure after 5 April 2008, FYAs remained available only for expenditure within (d)–(g) below and was replaced in general by the AIA in **11.13** above. General FYAs are **temporarily reintroduced** as in (*h*) below. An FYA and an AIA cannot be claimed in respect of the same expenditure; where both allowances are possible, the taxpayer can choose which, if any, to claim.

Subject to the exclusions below, qualifying expenditure (as in **11.3** above) is *'first-year qualifying expenditure'* if it is incurred:

(a)   **after 1 July 1997** by a **'small or medium-sized enterprise'** (see **11.16** below), in which case the maximum FYA is as follows:

    (i)   (except where (ii) below applies) **40%** (of the amount of the expenditure) for expenditure incurred **after 1 July 1998 and before 6 April 2008** (but long-life assets are excluded);

    (ii)   (in the case of a **'small enterprise'** only (see **11.16** below)) **50%** for expenditure incurred within the tax years **2004/05, 2006/07 and 2007/08** (but long-life assets remain excluded); and

    (iii)   **50%** for expenditure incurred **before 2 July 1998** (**12%** in the case of long-life assets — see **11.31** below); or

(b)   **after 31 March 2000 and before 1 April 2004** by a **'small enterprise'** (see **11.16** below) on **'information and communications technology'** (see **11.17** below), in which case the maximum FYA is **100%**; or

(c)   **after 11 May 1998 and before 12 May 2002** by a **'small or medium-sized enterprise'** (see **11.16** below) on the provision of plant and machinery for use primarily in **Northern Ireland**, in which case the maximum FYA is **100%**; or

(d)   **after 31 March 2001** by any person on **'energy-saving plant or machinery'** (see **11.18** below) which is unused and not second-hand, in which case the maximum FYA is **100%** (available for income tax periods of account ending after 5 April 2001); or

(e)   **after 16 April 2002 and before 1 April 2013** by any person on cars first registered after 16 April 2002 which are either **'electrically-propelled'** or have **'low CO_2 emissions'** (see **11.19** below), and which are unused and not second-hand, in which case the maximum FYA is **100%**; or

(f)   **after 16 April 2002 and before 1 April 2013** by any person on plant or machinery, unused and not second-hand, installed at a **'gas refuelling station'** (see **11.20** below) for use solely for or in connection with refuelling vehicles with natural gas, biogas (as regards expenditure incurred after 31 March 2008) or hydrogen fuel, in which case the maximum FYA is **100%**;

(g)   **after 31 March 2003** by any person on **'environmentally beneficial plant or machinery'** (see **11.21** below), unused and not second-hand, in which case the maximum FYA is **100%** (but long-life asset expenditure, see **11.31** below, does not qualify).

(h)   **after 5 April 2009 and before 6 April 2010** by any person on plant or machinery, provided the expenditure is not special rate expenditure as in **11.25** below (and provided the expenditure does not qualify under any of (d)–(g) above), in which case the maximum FYA is **40%**.

It is proposed to introduce a new 100% FYA for expenditure incurred after 5 April 2010 and before 6 April 2015 on zero-emission goods vehicles that are acquired unused and not second-hand. In order to comply with EU State aid rules, certain conditions will apply. The legislation will be included in a Finance Bill to be introduced in autumn 2010. (HMRC Budget Note BN05, 22 June 2010).

Exclusions

FYAs are not available under *any* of (a)–(h) above in the circumstances listed below (and note also the exclusion of long-life assets from (a)(i) and (a)(ii) above and from (g) above and the exclusion of special rate expenditure from (h) above).

(i) The expenditure is incurred in the chargeable period in which the qualifying activity is permanently discontinued.

(ii) The expenditure is incurred on the provision of a '*car*' (defined as in **11.13**(ii) above).

This exclusion does *not* apply as regards (e) above, in relation to which the above-mentioned definition of 'car' applies but with the specific inclusion of any mechanically-propelled road vehicle of a type commonly used as a hackney carriage. Motor cycles have always been excluded from the definition of car for the purposes of (e) above.

(iii) The expenditure is on a ship or railway asset of a kind excluded from being a long-life asset (see **11.31** below).

(iv) The plant or machinery would be a long-life asset but for the transitional provisions of *CAA 2001, Sch 3 para 20* (see **11.31** below).

(v) The expenditure is on plant or machinery for leasing (whether or not in the course of a trade). For this purpose, 'leasing' expressly includes the letting of a ship on charter or of any other asset on hire. This exclusion does *not* apply as regards expenditure incurred after 16 April 2002 and before 1 April 2006 within (d), (e) or (f) above or expenditure before 1 April 2006 within (g) above. The exclusion continues not to apply as regards expenditure incurred on or after 1 April 2006 within (d), (e) or (g) above, but, in the case of (d) and (g), only if the plant or machinery is leased under an 'excluded lease of background plant or machinery for a building' (see **11.45**(1)(B) below). To summarise, expenditure on or after 1 April 2006 on plant or machinery for leasing does not qualify for FYAs unless it is within (e) above or is on background plant or machinery and within (d) or (g) above.

As regards expenditure within (h) above, the leasing exclusion does apply but again not if the plant or machinery is leased under an excluded lease of background plant or machinery for a building.

Expenditure by a company on plant and machinery to be used by its subsidiary in return for an annual charge fell within the exclusion (*M F Freeman (Plant) Ltd v Jowett* (Sp C 376), [2003] SSCD 423).

In an article published initially on their website and subsequently in their Tax Bulletin, the Inland Revenue announced a change of view concerning the supply by a business of plant or machinery with an operator. Where the equipment is to be operated solely by the operator thus provided, they now accept that this is the provision of a service and not merely plant hire. FYAs are not excluded in such a case. Previously, this applied only where overall supervision and control rested with the operator and not, as is usual, with the hirer; the change of view cannot be used to reopen closed periods. They also now accept that the provision of building access services by the scaffolding industry (but not simply the supply of scaffolding poles etc. for use by others) is the provision of a service. (Revenue Internet Statement 2 June 2003; Revenue Tax Bulletin August 2003 p 1054).

(vi)   The provision of the plant or machinery is connected with a change in the nature or conduct of a trade or business carried on by a person other than the person incurring the expenditure on its provision, and the obtaining of an FYA was the main benefit, or one of the main benefits, which could reasonably be expected to arise from the making of the change.

(vii)   The provision of the plant of machinery is by way of gift (see **11.64** below).

(viii) The plant or machinery was previously used by the owner for purposes other than those of the qualifying activity (see **11.65** below), which includes the purposes of long funding leasing (see **11.46** below).

(ix)   The plant or machinery is acquired by means of a transaction with a connected person (within **21 CONNECTED PERSONS**), or a sale and leaseback transaction (or, where the sale etc. occurs before 9 October 2007, a sale and finance leaseback transaction), or a transaction the sole or main benefit of which would be the obtaining of a plant and machinery allowance (see *CAA 2001, ss 217, 223, 232; ITA 2007, Sch 1 para 403; FA 2008, Sch 20 para 6(8)(12)(19)* and note the definition of 'finance lease' at **11.63**(C) below).

Also excluded from (b) above (expenditure on information and communications technology) is expenditure incurred after 25 March 2003 on software (including software rights) if the person incurring the expenditure does so with a view to granting to another person a right to use or otherwise deal with any of the software in question. This is intended to exclude the *sub-licensing* of software rights; *leasing* activities were already excluded by virtue of (v) above.

Also excluded from (c) above (expenditure for NI purposes) is expenditure on long-life assets (see **11.31** below), on aircraft or hovercraft or on goods vehicles for use in a trade consisting primarily of the conveyance of goods, and unauthorised expenditure on plant or machinery for use primarily in agriculture, fishing or fish farming or in any transportation, storage, preparation, processing or packaging activities carried out in bringing any agricultural produce, fish or fish product to market. Expenditure is unauthorised for this purpose unless it is authorised by the Department of Agriculture and Rural Development in Northern Ireland, and provision is made for the necessary exchange of information between HMRC and that Department. Expenditure is also excluded where, when it is incurred, the person incurring it intends the plant or machinery to be used partly outside NI, and there are arrangements (of which the transaction under which the expenditure is incurred forms part) from which the main benefit, or one of the main benefits, which could reasonably be expected is the obtaining of an FYA (or greater FYA) in respect of so much of the expenditure as is attributable (on a just and reasonable basis) to the intended use outside NI. There are also provisions for the withdrawal of FYAs if, within two years of the expenditure being incurred (five years where the expenditure concerned exceeds £3.5 million), and at a time when the plant or machinery belongs to the person who incurred it (or a connected person), the primary use to which it is put is a use outside NI, or it is held for use otherwise than primarily in NI. Any person whose return is rendered incorrect by such a change of use must (subject to penalty) amend the return within three months of becoming aware that it has become incorrect.

[*CAA 2001, ss 39–45E, 45H–52A, 268A–268C, Sch 3 paras 14, 48–50; FA 2006, s 30, Sch 8 para 4, Sch 9 para 11; FA 2007, s 37; FA 2008, ss 75, 76, 77(2)(3)(5), 78, Sch 20 para 6(3)(19), Sch 24 para 4; FA 2009, s 24, Sch 11 paras 3, 11, 14, 26–28, Sch 32 paras 13, 17, 19, 22*].

Simon's Taxes. See B3.320–B3.326, B3.330.

Miscellaneous matters

[**11.15**] *Partial use for non-trade etc. purposes* results in FYAs being scaled down as is just and reasonable. [*CAA 2001, s 205*]. See **11.29** below as regards writing-down allowances in such cases.

See **11.69** below for the scaling down of FYAs where it appears that a *partial depreciation subsidy* will be payable.

See **11.67** below for the denial of FYAs on plant and machinery treated as changing hands by virtue of certain partnership changes and other *successions.*

Ownership

Before *CAA 2001* came into effect (see **11.1** above), the question of whether a person *owns* plant and machinery at some time in the chargeable period in which the expenditure is incurred was expressed in terms of whether it *belonged* to him at some time during the chargeable period related to the incurring of the expenditure. [*CAA 1990, s 22(1)*]. 'Belongs' has its ordinary meaning and normally entails a right of disposition over the thing possessed. See also *Bolton v International Drilling Co Ltd* Ch D 1982, 56 TC 449, *Ensign Tankers (Leasing) Ltd v Stokes* HL 1992, 64 TC 617, *Melluish v BMI (No 3) Ltd* HL 1995, 68 TC 1 and *BMBF (No 24) Ltd v CIR* Ch D, [2002] STC 1450. Following the decision in *Stokes v Costain Property Investments Ltd* CA 1984, 57 TC 688, specific provisions were introduced to determine entitlement to allowances for plant or machinery which are fixtures (see **11.33** *et seq.* below). See **11.61** below as regards plant and machinery acquired on hire-purchase, and **11.70** below as regards certain expenditure incurred by a lessee under the terms of a lease. For ownership of certain assets transferred under oil production sharing contracts to the government or representative of the production territory, see *CAA 2001, s 171*. The change in terminology in *CAA 2001* was not intended to be a change in the law.

Ships (postponement of FYAs)

Where a ship qualifies for an FYA (and note the exclusion at **11.14**(iii) above), the person entitled may, by written notice, *postpone* all or part of the allowance. The amount to be postponed must be specified in the notice. Where an FYA is claimed in respect of part only of the qualifying expenditure, the above applies in respect of the FYA claimed. The notice must be given no later than the first anniversary of 31 January following the tax year in which ends the chargeable period for which the allowance is due. Available qualifying expenditure for writing-down allowances (see **11.23** below) is computed as if the postponed FYA had, in fact, been made. Postponed FYAs may be claimed over one or more subsequent chargeable periods. [*CAA 2001, s 130(1)(3)–(6), s 131(1)(2)(4)(7); CTA 2010, Sch 1 para 337*]. See **11.28** below for postponement of writing-down allowances and deferment of balancing charges.

Additional VAT liabilities

See **11.22** below.

Size of enterprise

[11.16] *Small or medium-sized enterprise*' is defined for the purposes of **11.14**(a) and (c) above by reference to the definition of 'small or medium-sized company' in *Companies Act 2006, ss 382, 465* (previously *Companies Act 1985, s 247* or NI equivalent). Broadly, the requirement is that two of the following three conditions are fulfilled: that the turnover not exceed £22.8 million; that the assets not exceed £11.4 million; and that there be not more than 250 employees. If an enterprise which previously qualified fails to satisfy this requirement over two consecutive financial years, it will cease to qualify with effect from the second of those years, and an enterprise which did not previously qualify but which satisfies the requirement over two consecutive financial years will qualify with effect from the second of those years. In the case of a company which is a member of a group of companies, the requirements apply to the group as a whole. For expenditure incurred after 11 May 1998 (but not for the purposes of the allowances available for expenditure incurred before 2 July 1998, or for the purposes of those available for expenditure incurred thereafter where the contract was entered into before 12 May 1998), the group which has to be considered in this context includes any international group of which the company is a member.

'*Small enterprise*' is similarly defined for the purposes of **11.14**(a)(ii) and (b) above, but by reference to the *Companies Acts* definitions of 'small company', i.e. where two of the following three conditions are fulfilled: that the turnover does not exceed £5.6 million; that the assets are not more than £2.8 million; and that there be not more than 50 employees.

[*CAA 2001, s 44; FA 2008, s 75; SI 2008 No 954, arts 1, 28–30*].

Information and communications technology

[11.17] '*Information and communications technology*' is divided for the purposes of **11.14**(b) above into three classes: computers and associated equipment (but excluding computerised control or management systems or other systems that are part of a larger system whose principal function is not processing or storing information); other qualifying equipment (i.e. WAP and third generation mobile telephones and data network reception and transmission devices for use with television sets, and similar devices capable of receiving and transmitting information from and to data networks); and software (i.e. the right to use or otherwise deal with software for the purposes of equipment within the first two classes). The class of 'other qualifying equipment' may be further defined or added to by Treasury order. [*CAA 2001, s 45; FA 2008, s 76*].

Energy-saving plant or machinery

[11.18] '*Energy-saving plant or machinery*', for the purposes of **11.14**(d) above, is plant or machinery which, either at the time the expenditure is incurred or at the time the contract for its provision is entered into, is of a description specified by Treasury order *and* meets the energy-saving criteria specified by Treasury order for plant or machinery of that description. Expenditure incurred, or incurred under a contract entered into, after 31 March 2001 but before 16 July 2001 (the date of making of the first Treasury order) qualifies if it would have done so had that order already been made when the expenditure was incurred. A Treasury order may identify qualifying plant or machinery by reference to lists of technology or products issued by the relevant Secretary of State; the Treasury orders refer, in fact, to the Energy Technology Product List (ETPL) available at www.eca.gov.uk. An order may also provide that, in specified cases, no FYA is to be given under **11.14**(d) above unless a '*relevant certificate of energy efficiency*' is in force, i.e. a certificate issued by the Secretary of State, the Scottish Ministers, the Welsh Assembly or the relevant NI department, or by persons authorised by them, to the effect that a particular item, or an item constructed to a particular design, meets the relevant energy-saving criteria. The first order so specifies certain combined heat and power equipment. With effect after 4 August 2003, component based fixed systems falling within the technology class 'automatic monitoring and targeting equipment' (see below) were also specified. If a certificate is revoked, it is treated as having never been in issue, with the result that FYAs under **11.14**(d) above will not have been available. Subject to penalty under *TMA 1970, s 98* for non-compliance, a person who has consequently made an incorrect tax return must give notice to HMRC, specifying the amendment required to the return, within three months of his becoming aware of the problem. Technology classes initially included in the ETPL, subject to the appropriate criteria, certification or product approval, were boilers, combined heat and power, lighting, motors and drives, pipework insulation, refrigeration and (with effect up to and including 6 September 2006) thermal screens. The following classes have since been added:

- (with effect after 4 August 2002) heat pumps for space heating, radiant and warm air heaters, compressed air equipment and solar thermal systems;
- (with effect after 4 August 2003) automatic monitoring and targeting equipment;
- (with effect after 25 August 2004) air-to-air energy recovery equipment, compact heat exchangers and certain heating, ventilation and air conditioning equipment; and
- (with effect after 3 August 2009) uninterruptible power supplies.

If one or more components of an item of plant and machinery qualify under these provisions, but the whole item does not, normal apportionment rules are disapplied, and instead the first-year qualifying expenditure under **11.14**(d) above is limited to the amount (or aggregate amount) specified in the ETPL for that component (or those components); where relevant, each *instalment* of expenditure falls to be apportioned in the same way as the whole. See generally the detailed guidance notes at www.hmrc.gov.uk/capital_allowances/eca-guid ance.htm.

[*CAA 2001, ss 45A–45C; SI 2001 No 2541; SI 2006 No 2233; SI 2007 No 2165; SI 2008 No 1916; SI 2009 No 1863*].

Energy-efficient cars

[11.19] For the purposes of **11.14**(e) above, a car has 'low CO_2 emissions' if it is first registered on the basis of a qualifying emissions certificate (see *CAA 2001, s 268C*) and has CO_2 emissions (see *CAA 2001, s 268C*) of 110g/km or less. For expenditure incurred before 1 April 2008, the limit was 120g/km or less. A car is '*electrically-propelled*' if it is propelled solely by electrical power derived from an external source or from a storage battery not connected to any source of power when the car is in motion. See also HMRC Capital Allowances Manual CA23153. [*CAA 2001, s 45D; FA 2008, s 77(2)(3)(5); FA 2009, Sch 11 paras 14, 26–28*].

Gas refuelling stations

[11.20] For the purposes of **11.14**(f) above, a '*gas refuelling station*' is any premises (or part) where mechanically-propelled road vehicles are refuelled with natural gas, biogas (as regards expenditure after 31 March 2008) or hydrogen fuel. Plant or machinery installed for use solely for or in connection with such refuelling includes any storage tank for such fuels, any compressor, pump, control or meter used in the refuelling and any equipment for dispensing such fuels to vehicles' fuel tanks. [*CAA 2001, s 45E; FA 2008, s 78*].

Environmentally beneficial plant or machinery

[11.21] '*Environmentally beneficial plant or machinery*', for the purposes of **11.14**(g) above, is plant or machinery which, either at the time the expenditure is incurred or at the time the contract for its provision is entered into, is of a description specified by Treasury order *and* meets the environmental criteria specified by Treasury order for plant or machinery of that description. A Treasury order may identify qualifying plant or machinery by reference to technology lists or product lists issued by the relevant Secretary of State. The intention is to promote the use of technologies, or products, designed to remedy or prevent damage to the physical environment or natural resources (Revenue Press Release BN 26, 9 April 2003); the Treasury orders refer, in fact, to the Water Technology Product List (WTPL) available at www.eca-water.g ov.uk. Expenditure incurred, or incurred under a contract entered into, after 31 March 2003 but before 11 August 2003 (the date of making of the first

Treasury order) qualifies if it would have done so had that order already been made when the expenditure was incurred or the contract entered into. An order may provide that, in specified cases, no FYA is to be given under **11.14**(g) above unless a *'relevant certificate of environmental benefit'* is in force, i.e. a certificate issued by the Secretary of State, the Scottish Ministers, the Welsh Assembly or the relevant NI department, or by persons authorised by them, to the effect that a particular item, or an item constructed to a particular design, meets the relevant environmental criteria. If a certificate is revoked, it is treated as having never been in issue, with the result that FYAs under **11.14**(g) above will not have been available. Subject to penalty under *TMA 1970, s 98* for non-compliance, a person who has consequently made an incorrect tax return must give notice to HMRC, specifying the amendment required to the return, within three months of his becoming aware of the problem. Technology classes currently included in the WTPL, subject to the appropriate criteria or product approval, are listed below; the list was last updated with effect on and after 11 August 2008:

- flow controllers;
- leakage detection equipment;
- meters and monitoring equipment;
- efficient taps;
- efficient toilets;
- rainwater harvesting equipment;
- water reuse systems (see also below);
- cleaning in place equipment;
- efficient showers;
- efficient washing machines;
- small scale slurry and sludge dewatering equipment;
- vehicle wash waste reclaim units;
- water efficient industrial cleaning equipment; and
- water management equipment for mechanical seals.

Expenditure on the following items falling within the category of 'water reuse systems' will qualify only if a relevant certificate of environmental benefit (see above) is in force:

- efficient membrane filtration systems for the treatment of wastewater for recovery and reuse; and
- efficient wastewater recovery and reuse systems.

If one or more components of an item of plant and machinery qualify under these provisions, but the whole item does not, normal apportionment rules are disapplied, and instead the first-year qualifying expenditure under **11.14**(g) above is limited to the amount (or aggregate amount) specified in the WTPL for that component (or those components); where relevant, each *instalment* of expenditure falls to be apportioned in the same way as the whole. See generally the detailed guidance notes at www.hmrc.gov.uk/capital_allowances/eca-wate r.htm.

[*CAA 2001, s 45H–45J; SI 2003 No 2076; SI 2006 No 2235; SI 2007 No 2166; SI 2008 No 1917; SI 2009 No 1864*].

Additional VAT liabilities

[11.22] In general, where expenditure has qualified for an FYA, any 'additional VAT liability' (see **11.2**(viii) above), incurred in respect of that expenditure at a time when the plant or machinery in question is provided for the purposes of the qualifying activity, also qualifies — at the same rate and for the chargeable period in which the liability accrues. An additional VAT liability incurred at a time when the plant or machinery is used for overseas leasing other than protected leasing (see **11.56** below) does not qualify for an FYA, and nor does such a liability qualify if incurred at a time when an FYA given on the original expenditure has fallen to be withdrawn under the NI provisions in **11.14** above. However, there is nothing to prevent an FYA in respect of an additional VAT liability from being available in the chargeable period in which the qualifying activity is permanently discontinued, notwithstanding exclusion **11.14**(i) above, where the liability (but not the original expenditure) is incurred in that period. The fact that the FYAs in **11.14**(a)–(c) above are no longer available, and that the relevant legislation has been repealed, does not prevent any subsequent additional VAT liability from qualifying for an FYA as above. [*CAA 2001, ss 236, 237, Sch 3 paras 46–50; FA 2008, ss 75(6)(7), 76(4)(5)(7)(8)*].

Pooling, writing-down allowances and balancing adjustments

[11.23] Qualifying expenditure (as in **11.3** above) is *pooled* for the purpose of determining entitlement to writing-down allowances and balancing allowances and liability to balancing charges. In addition to the *main pool* for each qualifying activity, there may be a *single asset pool* and/or a *class pool*, and qualifying expenditure falling to be allocated to either of the latter (see **11.26–11.31**, **11.52**, **11.69** below) cannot be allocated to the main pool.

For each pool of qualifying expenditure, a **writing-down allowance (WDA)** is available for each chargeable period (see **11.2**(i) above) other than the 'final chargeable period' and is equal to a maximum of **20%** (after 5 April 2008) of the amount (if any) by which 'available qualifying expenditure' exceeds the total of any disposal values (see **11.24** below) falling to be brought into account. See **11.25** below (special rate expenditure), **11.31** below (long-life assets) and **11.52**, **11.53** below (overseas leasing) for exceptions to the 20% rate. The WDA is proportionately reduced or increased if the chargeable period is less or more than a year, or if the qualifying activity has been carried on for part only of the chargeable period. A claim for a WDA may require it to be reduced to a specified amount. For the 'final chargeable period', a **balancing allowance** is available, equal to the excess (if any) of (1) 'available qualifying expenditure' over (2) total disposal values. If, for *any* chargeable period, (2) exceeds (1), there arises a liability to a **balancing charge**, equal to that excess.

For chargeable periods beginning before 6 April 2008, the maximum WDA was 25% of the amount (if any) by which 'available qualifying expenditure' exceeded total disposal values. For chargeable periods straddling that date, the maximum WDA is a hybrid rate based on how much of the period fell before that date and how much of it falls on or after that date. The rate is found by applying the formula:

$$R = \left(25 \times \frac{BRD}{CP}\right) + \left(20 \times \frac{ARD}{CP}\right)$$

Where

R = the rate per cent (to be rounded up to two decimal places);

BRD = the number of days in the chargeable period before 6 April 2008;

ARD = the number of days in the chargeable period on and after 6 April 2008; and

CP = the total number of days in the chargeable period.

The WDA computed at the hybrid rate still falls to be proportionately reduced or increased if the chargeable period is less or more than a year etc.

HMRC provide an online 'ready reckoner' to assist in calculating the hybrid rate — see http://cahrcalculator.hmrc.gov.uk/CAHR01.aspx.

For any chargeable period beginning on or after 6 April 2008, the maximum rate of WDA in a main pool or a special rate pool is increased to 100% if the balance of the pool (i.e. 'available qualifying expenditure' less total disposal values) is £1,000 or less (proportionately reduced or increased if the chargeable period is less or more than a year, or if the qualifying activity has been carried on for part only of the chargeable period). This figure may be amended in future by Treasury order made by statutory instrument.

The writing-down allowance is to be reduced to 18% from 6 April 2012. A hybrid rate will apply for chargeable periods spanning that date. (HMRC Budget Note BN04, 22 June 2010).

The '*final chargeable period*', as regards the main pool, is the chargeable period in which the trade or other qualifying activity is permanently discontinued. As regards a single asset pool, it is normally the first chargeable period in which a disposal event (see **11.24** below) occurs. As regards class pools, see **11.25** (special rate expenditure), **11.31** (long-life assets) and **11.52** (overseas leasing) below.

'*Available qualifying expenditure*' in a pool for a chargeable period consists of qualifying expenditure allocated to the pool for that period and any unrelieved qualifying expenditure brought forward in the pool from the previous chargeable period (usually referred to as the written-down value brought forward). There are rules requiring an allocation to a pool in specific circumstances, for example where an item falls to be transferred from one type of pool to another, and prohibiting the allocation of certain excluded expenditure. These are listed in *CAA 2001, s 57(2)(3)*, as amended, and are covered elsewhere in this chapter where appropriate. See **11.63** below as regards restrictions under connected persons and other anti-avoidance provisions.

In allocating qualifying expenditure to the appropriate pool, the following rules must be observed (and see below for interaction with first-year allowances).

(a)   Qualifying expenditure can be allocated to a pool for a chargeable period only to the extent that it has not been included in available qualifying expenditure for an earlier chargeable period. (There is nothing to prohibit the allocation of *part only* of a particular amount of qualifying expenditure for a particular chargeable period.)

(b)   Qualifying expenditure cannot be allocated to a pool for a chargeable period earlier than that in which it is incurred.

(c)   Qualifying expenditure can be allocated to a pool for a chargeable period only if the person concerned *owns* the plant or machinery at some time in that period. (Before *CAA 2001* came into effect, see **11.1** above, this was expressed in terms of the item *belonging* to that person, but no change in the law is intended; see **11.15** above and **11.34** below for meaning of 'belongs'. See **11.70** below as regards certain expenditure by a lessee.)

Where an 'additional VAT liability' (see **11.2**(viii) above) is incurred in respect of qualifying expenditure, at a time when the plant or machinery in question is provided for the purposes of the qualifying activity, it is itself expenditure on that plant or machinery and may be taken into account in determining available qualifying expenditure for the chargeable period in which it accrues.

The net cost of demolition of plant and machinery demolished during a chargeable period, and not replaced, is allocated to the appropriate pool for that chargeable period.

Interaction with annual investment allowance

If an annual investment allowance (AIA) (see **11.13** above) is made in respect of an amount of AIA qualifying expenditure, the expenditure is nevertheless added to the appropriate pool (or pools). Such allocation is necessary to enable a disposal value to be properly brought into account when a disposal event occurs in relation to the item in question. Following the allocation, the available qualifying expenditure in the pool (or in each pool) is reduced by the amount of the AIA on the expenditure allocated. It follows that any excess of the AIA qualifying expenditure over the AIA made will qualify for WDAs beginning with the chargeable period in which the expenditure is incurred.

Interaction with first-year allowances

If a first-year allowance (FYA) (see **11.14** above) is made in respect of an amount of first-year qualifying expenditure, none of that amount can be allocated to a pool for the chargeable period in which the expenditure is incurred, and only the balance (after deducting the FYA) can be allocated to a pool for a subsequent chargeable period.

However, expenditure which qualifies for an FYA for a chargeable period is not excluded from being allocated to a pool for that period if either (1) the FYA is not claimed or (2) it is claimed in respect of part only of the expenditure (in which case the remaining part can be so allocated).

If an FYA is made in respect of an amount of qualifying expenditure, at least some of the balance (after deducting the FYA) must be allocated to a pool for a chargeable period no later than that in which a disposal event (see **11.24** below) occurs in relation to the item in question. It will usually be beneficial to choose to allocate the whole balance. A nil balance (following a 100% FYA) is deemed to be so allocated. Such allocation is necessary to enable a disposal value to be properly brought into account.

[*CAA 2001, s 26(3)–(5), ss 53–56, 56A, 57–59, 65, 235; FA 2008, s 80(2), (8)–(12), s 81, Sch 20 para 6(4)(19), Sch 24 para 5, Sch 26 paras 3–5, 14; FA 2009, Sch 11 paras 15, 17, 26–28, Sch 32 paras 14, 17, 20, 22*].

See the Examples at **11.32** below.

Simon's Taxes. See **B3.331–B3.333**.

Disposal events and values

[**11.24**] Where a person has incurred qualifying expenditure (see **11.3** above) on plant or machinery, a **disposal value** must be brought into account for a chargeable period (see **11.2**(i) above) in which any one of the following **disposal events** occurs (but normally only in relation to the first such event to occur in respect of that plant or machinery).

(i)   The person ceases to own the plant or machinery.

(ii)   He loses possession of it, and it is reasonable to assume the loss is permanent.

(iii) It has been in use for 'mineral exploration and access' (see **10.25**(a) **CAPITAL ALLOWANCES**) and the person abandons it at the site where it was so in use.

(iv)   It ceases to exist as such (by reason of its destruction, dismantling or otherwise).

(v)   It begins to be used wholly or partly for purposes other than those of the qualifying activity.

(vi)   It begins to be leased under a long funding lease (see **11.46** below).

(vii) The qualifying activity is permanently discontinued.

The amount to be brought into account depends upon the nature of the event.

(a)   On a sale (other than one within (b) below), it is the net sale proceeds plus any insurance or capital compensation received (by the person concerned) by reason of any event affecting the sale price obtainable.

(b)   On a sale at less than market value, it is market value, unless:

   (i)   the buyer (not being a dual resident investing company connected with the seller) can claim plant or machinery or research and development allowances for his expenditure; or

   (ii)   the sale gives rise to a charge to tax under *ITEPA 2003* (i.e. on employment, pension or social security income), in which case (a) above applies.

(c)   On demolition or destruction, it is the net amount received for the remains, plus any insurance or capital compensation received.

(d)   On permanent loss (otherwise than within (c) above), or on abandonment as in (iii) above, it is any insurance or capital compensation received.

(e)   On commencement of a long funding lease, it is as stated in **11.46** below.

(f)   On permanent discontinuance of the qualifying activity preceding an event in (a)–(e) above, it is whatever value would otherwise have applied on the occurrence of that event.

(g)   On a gift giving rise to a charge to tax on the recipient under *ITEPA 2003* (i.e. on employment, pension or social security income), it is nil. See also HMRC Capital Allowances Manual CA23250.

(h)   On any other event, it is market value at the time of the event.

However, the disposal value is in all cases limited to the qualifying expenditure incurred on the plant or machinery by the person in question. In addition, there is no requirement to bring a disposal value into account if none of the qualifying expenditure in question has been taken into account in determining the person's available qualifying expenditure (see **11.23** above) for any chargeable period up to and including that in which the disposal occurs. As regards both these rules, see also **11.63**(i) below as regards certain transactions between connected persons.

See **11.44** below for a further disposal event in the case of long funding leasing, and for the appropriate disposal value.

Additional VAT rebates

Where an 'additional VAT rebate' (see **11.2**(viii) above) is made in respect of an item of qualifying expenditure, a disposal value of an equivalent amount must be brought into account (on its own or as an addition to any other disposal value brought into account for that item) for the chargeable period in which the rebate accrues. Any disposal value brought into account for a subsequent chargeable period is limited to the original qualifying expenditure less all additional VAT rebates accrued in all chargeable periods up to (but not including) that chargeable period. If the disposal value is itself the result of an additional VAT rebate, it is limited to the original qualifying expenditure less *any* disposal values brought into account as a result of earlier events.

[CAA 2001, ss 60, 61, 62(1), s 63(1), s 64(1)(5), ss 238, 239; FA 2006, Sch 8 para 5; TIOPA 2010, Sch 8 para 234].

Anti-avoidance

In response to identified avoidance schemes, the disposal value is restricted on an event within (a), (b) or (h) above where:

- the plant or machinery is subject to a lease, and
- arrangements have been entered into that have the effect of reducing the disposal value in so far as it is attributable to rentals payable under the lease.

The disposal value is to be determined as if the arrangements had not been entered into. This applies to disposal events occurring on or after 9 December 2009. It does not apply where the arrangements take the form of a transfer of relevant receipts as in **4.34 ANTI-AVOIDANCE** such that an amount has been treated as taxable income.

[*CAA 2001, s 64A; FA 2010, Sch 5 para 3*].

See **11.63**(ii) below for other anti-avoidance rules.

Simon's Taxes. See **B3.331, B3.334, B3.335.**

Special rate expenditure

[11.25] Certain expenditure incurred **after 5 April 2008** qualifies for writing-down allowances (WDAs) at a reduced rate of **10%** of the amount (if any) by which available qualifying expenditure (see **11.23** above) exceeds the total of any disposal values (see **11.24** above) falling to be brought into account. This is known as '*special rate expenditure*' and comprises the following:

(i)   expenditure on thermal insulation within **11.8**(ii) above;
(ii) expenditure on integral features of buildings and structures (see **11.11** above);
(iii) long-life asset expenditure within **11.31** below;
(iv) (on or after 6 April 2009) expenditure on certain cars (see below); and
(v)   (on or after 1 April 2010) expenditure on the provision of cushion gas, i.e. gas that functions, or is intended to function, as plant in a particular gas storage facility.

In addition, long-life asset expenditure incurred on or before 5 April 2008 is also special rate expenditure if it is allocated to a pool in a chargeable period beginning after that date.

The special rate writing-down allowance is to be reduced to 8% from 6 April 2012. A hybrid rate will apply for chargeable periods spanning that date. (HMRC Budget Note BN04, 22 June 2010).

A car is within (iv) above if it is not one of the following:

• a car with 'low CO_2 emissions';
• an electrically-propelled car (as defined by *CAA 2001, s 268B*); or
• a car first registered before 1 March 2001.

A car has '*low CO2 emissions*' if, when first registered, it was registered on the basis of a qualifying emissions certificate (as defined by *CAA 2001, s 268C*) and its CO_2 emissions (see *CAA 2001, s 268C*) do not exceed 160g/km. '*Car*' is as defined by *CAA 2001, s 268A* (see **11.13**(ii) above) and excludes a motor cycle.

If only a part of the expenditure on any item is special rate expenditure, the part which is and the part which is not are treated as if they were separate items of plant or machinery; any necessary apportionments must be made on a just and reasonable basis.

If special rate expenditure is incurred wholly and exclusively for the purposes of the qualifying activity, and does not fall to be allocated to a single asset pool, it is allocated to a class pool known as the '*special rate pool*'. Even if allocated to a single asset pool, the 10% rate of WDAs still applies. As regards the special rate pool, see **11.23** above as regards the 100% rate of WDAs where the balance of the pool is no more than £1,000. The 10% WDA is proportionately reduced or increased if the chargeable period is less or more than a year, or if the qualifying activity has been carried on for part only of the chargeable period. A claim for a WDA can require it to be reduced to a specified amount. The final chargeable period (see **11.23** above) of a special rate pool is that in which the qualifying activity is permanently discontinued.

As regards (v) above, any disposal event within **11.24** above that occurs on or after 1 April 2010 and relates to expenditure on cushion gas is deemed to relate to post-31 March 2010 expenditure (if any) in priority to pre-1 April 2010 expenditure (if any). If, as a result of this rule, a single disposal event is taken as relating to both post-31 March 2010 and pre-1 April 2010 expenditure, it is treated as two separate disposal events. The purpose of the rule is to ensure that pre-1 April 2010 expenditure attracting WDAs at 20% is retained in preference to later expenditure which is in the special rate pool.

[*CAA 2001, ss 65(1), 104A, 104AA, 104B–104D, 104G; FA 2008, Sch 26 paras 2, 5, 14; FA 2009, Sch 11 paras 7, 8, 26–28; FA 2010, s 28(6)(7)(9)(10)*].

Long-life asset expenditure — transitional

At the end of the chargeable period straddling 6 April 2008 (the '*straddling period*'), the balance of the long-life asset pool (representing expenditure incurred before 6 April 2008) is transferred to the special rate pool. If a chargeable period ends on 5 April 2008, such that there is no straddling period, the balance of the long-life asset pool at the end of that day is transferred to a special rate pool. In either case, the balance transferred is generally treated in future as if it had always been special rate expenditure. Long-life asset expenditure in a single asset pool remains in that pool but is treated in future as special rate expenditure in a single asset pool. [*FA 2008, s 83*]. See also **11.31** below.

Connected persons transactions — transitional

If, after 5 April 2008, there is a sale between CONNECTED PERSONS (**21**) of an integral feature (see **11.11** above) on which expenditure was incurred on or before that date and the buyer's expenditure would otherwise be special rate expenditure, the buyer's expenditure is qualifying expenditure only if the original expenditure was qualifying expenditure or if the buyer's expenditure would have been qualifying expenditure if incurred at the time the original expenditure was incurred. If expenditure is thereby prevented from being qualifying expenditure, this rule is again applied if there is a further sale between connected persons, but reference to the original expenditure is always to the pre-6 April 2008 expenditure. [*FA 2008, Sch 26 para 15*]. This rule is designed to prevent allowances being claimed after 5 April 2008 on an integral feature if allowances would not have been available for that feature on or before that date (Treasury Explanatory Notes to the 2008 Finance Bill).

Other anti-avoidance

Where a disposal value less than the 'notional written-down value' would otherwise fall to be brought into account in respect of special rate expenditure which has attracted restricted allowances as above, an adjustment may be required. Where the event giving rise to the disposal value is part of a scheme or arrangement a main object of which is the obtaining of a tax advantage under the plant and machinery allowances provisions, the 'notional written-down value' is substituted for the disposal value. The *notional written-down value* is qualifying expenditure on the item in question less maximum allowances to date, computed on the assumptions that the item was the only item of plant or machinery, that the expenditure (if on a long-life asset) was not excluded from being long-life asset expenditure by the operation of a monetary limit and that all allowances have been made in full. [*CAA 2001, s 104E; FA 2008, Sch 26 paras 2, 14*].

Exclusions from the main pool

[**11.26**] The majority of items excluded from the main pool of qualifying expenditure are set out in **11.27–11.31** below. In addition to those, the following items are excluded:

- special rate expenditure (see **11.25** below);
- plant and machinery in respect of which a partial depreciation subsidy is received (see **11.69** below);
- plant and machinery used for overseas leasing (see **11.51** *et seq.* below).

Cars

[**11.27**] Qualifying expenditure (see **11.3** above) **before 6 April 2009** on a car costing **over £12,000** can only be allocated to a *single asset pool* (see **11.23** above). Writing-down allowances (WDAs) are limited to a maximum of £3,000 per chargeable period (proportionately reduced or increased for chargeable periods of less or more than a year). For this purpose, 'car' is broadly as defined at **11.13**(ii) above; it includes a motor cycle, but specifically excludes 'qualifying hire cars' and cars qualifying for first-year allowances under **11.14**(e) above.

Separate rules apply to reduce the maximum WDA in cases involving contributions towards capital expenditure (as in **11.2**(vi)(vii) above) and partial depreciation subsidies (as in **11.69** below). If the car begins to be used *partly* for purposes other than those of the qualifying activity, the single asset pool continues and no disposal value is brought into account. For a chargeable period in which such part use exists, the WDA and any balancing allowance or charge is reduced to such amount as is just and reasonable (though the full amount is deducted in arriving at any unrelieved qualifying expenditure carried forward).

A car is a *'qualifying hire car'* if it is provided wholly or mainly for hire to, or the carriage of, members of the public in the ordinary course of a trade and:

- it is not normally on hire etc. to the same person (or a person connected with him — see **21 CONNECTED PERSONS**) for 30 or more consecutive days or for 90 or more days in any 12-month period; or
- it is provided to a person who himself satisfied those conditions in using it wholly or mainly for a trade of hire etc. to members of the public (e.g. a taxi driver); or
- it is provided wholly or mainly for the use of a person receiving a disability living allowance (because of entitlement to the mobility component) or certain mobility supplements.

[*CAA 2001, ss 74–78, 81, 82, Sch 3 para 19; FA 2009, Sch 11 paras 4, 5, 24–29; SI 1984 No 2060*].

See **11.63**(iii) below for special rule determining the disposal value of a car within these provisions on a sale etc. to which the anti-avoidance provisions there mentioned apply.

Simon's Taxes. See B3.342.

New regime from 6 April 2009

The above rules (the so-called 'expensive car' rules) are **abolished** with immediate effect for expenditure incurred **on or after 6 April 2009** (*'new regime expenditure'*). They are abolished with effect for chargeable periods beginning on or after 6 April 2014 for expenditure incurred before 6 April 2009 (*'old regime expenditure'*). Any remaining written-down value carried forward to the first such chargeable period will then be immediately transferable to the main pool unless there is some other reason for it to be excluded from the main pool (of which non-business use is the most likely), in which case it remains in the single asset pool until disposed of. [*FA 2009, Sch 11 para 31*]. If expenditure is incurred under an agreement made after 8 December 2008 but the car is not required to be made available before 6 August 2009, the expenditure is treated for this purpose as new regime expenditure (but not so as to defer the chargeable period for which the first WDA is due). An agreement is treated as made as soon as there is an unconditional written contract for the provision of the car and no terms remain to be agreed. [*FA 2009, Sch 11 para 27*].

New regime expenditure on cars used exclusively for the purposes of the qualifying activity goes into the main pool unless the expenditure is special rate expenditure. Cars with an element of non-business use continue not to be pooled but attract only the 10% special rate of writing-down allowances if the expenditure is special rate expenditure. See **11.25** above for details of those cars the expenditure on which is special rate expenditure. A 'car' now excludes a motor cycle, which means that a motor cycle is treated like any other item of plant or machinery. There are no exceptions for qualifying hire cars.

It is conceivable that both old regime expenditure and new regime expenditure may be incurred on the same car or motor cycle. In this case, the item is treated for capital allowances purposes as if it were two separate but identical cars or motor cycles, with any disposal value being apportioned on a just and reasonable basis. [*FA 2009, Sch 11 para 30*].

See **73.42 TRADING INCOME** as regards expenditure on *hiring* a car.

As regards motor vehicles generally, see HMRC Brief 31/09, 14 May 2009, for the capital allowances implications of the Government's temporary vehicle scrappage scheme announced in the 2009 Budget.

Ships

[11.28] Qualifying expenditure (see **11.3** above) on the provision of a ship for the purposes of a trade or other qualifying activity can only be allocated to a *single asset pool* (see **11.23** above), known as a *single ship pool*. This does not apply if:

- an election is made to exclude such treatment (see below); or
- the qualifying activity is one of special leasing (see **11.50** below); or
- the ship is otherwise provided for leasing (which expressly includes letting on charter), *unless* it is not used for 'overseas leasing' (other than 'protected leasing') at any time in the 'designated period' *and* it appears that it will be used only for a 'qualifying purpose' in that period (see **11.51** *et seq.* below for meaning of expressions used here).

When a disposal event occurs in relation to a single ship pool, the available qualifying expenditure (see **11.23** above) in that pool for the chargeable period in question is transferred to the '*appropriate non-ship pool*' (i.e. the pool to which the expenditure would originally have been allocated in the absence of the single ship pool rules), and the single ship pool is brought to an end with no balancing allowance or charge. The disposal value is brought into account in the pool now containing the qualifying expenditure. In addition to the circumstances at **11.24** above, a disposal event occurs if a ship is provided for leasing or letting on charter and begins to be used otherwise than for a 'qualifying purpose' at some time in the first four years of the 'designated period' (see **11.51** *et seq.* below as regards expressions used).

If the ship ceases to be used by the person who incurred the qualifying expenditure, without his having brought it into use for the purposes of the qualifying activity, then, in addition to any adjustments required as above, any writing-down allowances (WDAs) previously made (or postponed — see below) are withdrawn, and the amount withdrawn is allocated to the 'appropriate non-ship pool' (see above) for the chargeable period in question.

A person who has incurred qualifying expenditure on a ship may elect, for any chargeable period, to disapply the single ship pool provisions in respect of:

- all or part of any qualifying expenditure that would otherwise be allocated to a single ship pool in that period; or
- all or part of the available qualifying expenditure (see **11.23** above) already in a single ship pool,

with the result that the amount in question is allocated to the 'appropriate non ship pool' (see above). The election must be made no later than the first anniversary of 31 January following the tax year in which ends the chargeable period in question.

Postponement of WDAs

A person entitled to a WDA for a chargeable period in respect of a single ship pool may, by written notice, postpone all or part of it to a later period. The amount to be postponed must be specified in the notice. Where a reduced WDA is claimed, all or part of the reduced amount may be postponed. The time limits for giving notice are the same as for the election referred to immediately above. Available qualifying expenditure (see **11.23** above) is computed as if the postponed WDA had, in fact, been made. Postponed WDAs may be claimed over one or more subsequent chargeable periods. See **11.15** above for postponement of first-year allowances.

[*CAA 2001, ss 127–129, s 130(2)(7), s 131(1)(3)–(7), ss 132, 133, 157(1); CTA 2010, Sch 1 para 337*].

Deferment of balancing charges on qualifying ships

Balancing charges on ships may be deferred and set against subsequent expenditure on ships for a maximum of six years from the date of disposal. A claim for deferment of the whole or part of a balancing charge may be made by the shipowner where a disposal event within **11.24**(i)–(iv) above occurs after 20 April 1994 in relation to a 'qualifying ship' (the old ship). A '*qualifying ship*' is, broadly, a ship of a sea-going kind of 100 gross registered tons or more, excluding offshore installations (as defined by *ITA 2007, s 1001*) and ships of a kind used or chartered primarily for sport or recreation (but passenger ships and cruise liners are not so excluded). The provisions also apply to ships of less than 100 tons in cases where the old ship is totally lost or is damaged beyond worthwhile repair. A ship brought into use in the trade on or after 20 July 1994 must within three months of first use (unless disposed of during those three months) be registered in the UK, the Channel Islands, Isle of Man, a colony (as to which see Revenue Tax Bulletins April 1995 p 208, June 1998 p 553), a European Union State or a European Economic Area State and must continue to be so until at least three years from first use or, if earlier, until disposed of to an unconnected person. It is a further condition that no amount in respect of the old ship has been allocated to an overseas leasing pool (see **11.52** below), a 'partial use' single asset pool (see **11.29** below), a 'partial depreciation subsidy' single asset pool (see **11.69** below) or a pool for a qualifying activity consisting of special leasing (see **11.50** below).

The balancing charge on the old ship is in effect calculated as if allowances had been granted, and the charge arises, in a single ship pool, with appropriate assumptions where that is not, in fact, the case (see *CAA 2001, s 139*).

Deferment is achieved by allocating the amount deferred to the 'appropriate non-ship pool' (see above) for the chargeable period in question, so that it is effectively set against the disposal value brought into account in that pool (see above) as a result of the disposal event concerned. The *maximum deferment* is the *lowest* of (i) the amount treated as brought into account in respect of the old ship under *CAA 2001, s 139* (see above), (ii) the amount to be expended on new shipping (see below), so far as not already set against an earlier balancing charge, in the six years starting with the date of disposal of the old ship, (iii) the amount which, in the absence of a deferment claim, would have been the total balancing charge for the chargeable period in question in the appropriate non-ship pool, and (iv) the amount needed to reduce the profit of the trade or other qualifying activity to nil (disregarding losses brought forward), no deferment being possible if no such profit has been made. If the amount actually expended within (ii) above turns out to be less than the amount deferred, the amount of the deficiency is reinstated as a balancing charge for the chargeable period to which the claim relates.

Where an amount is expended on new shipping within the six-year period allowed and is attributed by the shipowner, by notice to HMRC, to any part of an amount deferred, an amount equal to the amount so matched is brought into account as a disposal value, for the chargeable period in which the expenditure is incurred, in the single ship pool to which the expenditure is allocated, thus reducing the amount on which allowances may be claimed on the new ship. No amount of expenditure can be attributed to a deferment if there is earlier expenditure on new shipping within the said six-year period which has not been attributed to that or earlier deferments. An attribution may be varied by the trader by notice to the inspector within a specified time (see *CAA 2001, s 142*).

For the purposes of these provisions, an amount is expended on new shipping if it is qualifying expenditure, incurred by the claimant wholly and exclusively for the purposes of a qualifying activity, on a ship (the new ship) which will be a qualifying ship (see above) for at least three years from first use or, if earlier, until disposed of to an unconnected person. Expenditure is treated as incurred by the claimant if it is incurred by a successor following a partnership change (see **52.7 PARTNERSHIPS**) or company reconstruction (see Tolley's Corporation Tax) in consequence of which the qualifying activity was not treated as discontinued. Expenditure incurred on a ship which has belonged to either the shipowner or a connected person within the previous six years or which is incurred mainly for tax avoidance reasons does not qualify. The expenditure must be allocated to a single ship pool. If an election is made to disapply the single ship pool provisions, the expenditure is deemed never to have been expenditure on new shipping (but must nevertheless be treated as such in matching expenditure with deferments, so that the election prevents further matching of amounts already deferred). Expenditure does not qualify if the overseas leasing provisions at **11.51** below come to apply to the new ship.

For income tax purposes, the claim for deferment must be made within twelve months after 31 January following the tax year in which ends the chargeable period of deferment. Before the current year basis of assessment applied, the claim had to be made within two years after the end of that chargeable period. Where a claim for deferment is found to be erroneous as a result of subsequent circumstances, the shipowner must, within three months after the end of the chargeable period in which those circumstances first arise, notify HMRC accordingly (failure to do so incurring a penalty under *TMA 1970, s 98*); consequential assessments may be made within twelve months after notice is given, notwithstanding normal time limits.

[*CAA 2001, ss 134–158, Sch 3 para 24; ITA 2007, Sch 1 paras 400, 401; CTA 2010, Sch 1 paras 338–342; SI 1996 No 1323; SI 1997 No 133*].

Simon's Taxes. See **B3.350–B3.353.**

Plant and machinery partly used for non-trade etc. purposes

[11.29] Qualifying expenditure (see **11.3** above) incurred partly for the purposes of the trade or other qualifying activity and partly for other purposes can only be allocated to a *single asset pool* (see **11.23** above). (See **11.15** above as regards first-year allowances.) Where in other cases plant or machinery *begins to be used* partly for other purposes, such that a disposal value falls to be brought into account (see **11.24**(v) above) in a pool, an amount equal to the disposal value is allocated to a single asset pool for the chargeable period in question (but see **11.27** above as regards cars costing over £12,000). In respect of a single asset pool under these provisions, writing-down allowances and balancing allowances and charges are reduced to such amount as is just and reasonable (though the full amount is deducted in arriving at any unrelieved qualifying expenditure carried forward).

Where, after 20 March 2000, circumstances change such that the proportion of use for purposes other than those of the qualifying activity increases during a chargeable period, and the market value of the plant or machinery at the end of the period exceeds the available qualifying expenditure (see **11.23** above) in the pool for that period by more than £1 million, then if no disposal value would otherwise fall to be brought into account for the period, a disposal value must be brought into account (equal to market value — see **11.24**(g) above) and, in the next or a subsequent chargeable period, an equivalent amount may be allocated to a new single asset pool as if it were qualifying expenditure newly incurred.

[*CAA 2001, ss 206–208, Sch 3 para 42*].

See also *Kempster v McKenzie* Ch D 1952, 33 TC 193 and *G H Chambers (Northiam Farms) Ltd v Watmough* Ch D 1956, 36 TC 711 and HMRC Capital Allowances Manual CA 23530, 27100 as regards further adjustment for any element of personal choice.

Simon's Taxes. See B3.359.

Short-life assets

[11.30] A person who has incurred qualifying expenditure (see **11.3** above) on an item of plant or machinery may elect for it to be treated as a short-life asset, provided it is not an excluded item (see list below). There is no requirement as to the expected useful life of the item, but short-life asset treatment will be of no practical benefit where the item remains in use for five years or more. The election is irrevocable and must be made no later than the first anniversary of 31 January following the tax year in which ends the chargeable period in which the expenditure (or earliest expenditure) is incurred.

In general, inspectors will require sufficient information in support of an election to minimise the possibility of any difference of view at a later date (e.g. on a disposal) about what was and was not covered by the election, and to ensure that it does not incorporate any excluded items (see list below). Where separate identification of short-life assets acquired in a chargeable period is either impossible or impracticable, e.g. similar small or relatively inexpensive items held in very large numbers, perhaps in different locations, then the information required in support of the election may be provided by reference to batches of acquisitions. (HMRC SP 1/86).

Each of the following items of plant or machinery is excluded from being a short-life asset.

(i)   A car, defined as at **11.13**(ii) above with the exception of cars hired out to persons receiving certain disability allowances or mobility supplements. Note that for new regime expenditure (as in **11.27** above — broadly expenditure incurred on or after 6 April 2009), motor cycles are excluded from the definition of 'car' and are thus no longer excluded from being short-life assets.

(ii)   A ship.

(iii)   An item which is the subject of special leasing (see **11.50** below).

(iv)   An item acquired partly for the purposes of a trade or other qualifying activity and partly for other purposes.

(v)   An item which is the subject of a partial depreciation subsidy (see **11.69** below).

(vi)   An item received by way of gift or whose previous use by the person concerned did not attract capital allowances (see **11.64**, **11.65** below and, as regards long funding leasing, **11.46** below).

(vii)   An item the expenditure on which is long-life asset expenditure (see **11.31** below).

(viii)   An item the expenditure on which is special rate expenditure (see **11.25** above) unless it is a car hired out to persons receiving certain disability allowances or mobility supplements.

(ix)   An item provided for leasing, unless it will be used within the 'designated period' for a 'qualifying purpose' (see **11.51** *et seq.* below as regards these expressions), and with the exception in any case of cars hired out to persons receiving certain disability allowances or mobility supplements.

(x)   An item leased overseas such that it attracts only a 10% writing-down allowance (see **11.52** below).

(xi)   An item leased to two or more persons jointly such that *CAA 2001, s 116* applies (see **11.57** below).

Qualifying expenditure in respect of a short-life asset can only be allocated to a *single asset pool* (see **11.23** above), known as a *short-life asset pool*. If no disposal event within **11.24**(i)–(vi) above occurs in any of the chargeable periods ending on or before the fourth anniversary (referred to below as the *'four-year cut-off date'*) of the end of the chargeable period in which the expenditure is incurred (or the first such period in which any of it was incurred), the short-life asset pool is brought to an end on the four-year cut-off date but with no balancing allowance or charge and no denial of a writing-down allowance for the final period. The item ceases to be a short-life asset and the available qualifying expenditure in the pool is allocated to the main pool for the first chargeable period ending *after* the four-year cut-off date. (If the item is a car the expenditure on which was special rate expenditure (see **11.25** above), it is allocated to the special rate pool rather than the main pool.)

The following applies where short-life asset treatment has been claimed on the basis that the item has been provided for leasing, but will be used within the 'designated period' for a 'qualifying purpose' (so is not excluded by (ix) above). (See **11.51** *et seq.* below as regards expressions used here.) If, at any time in a chargeable period ending on or before the four-year cut-off date (as above), the item begins to be used otherwise than for such a purpose, and that time falls within the first four years of the 'designated period', the short-life asset pool is brought to an end at that time but with no balancing allowance or charge and no denial of a writing-down allowance for the final period. The item ceases to be a short-life asset and the available qualifying expenditure in the pool is allocated, for the chargeable period in which that time falls, to the main pool.

If at any time before the four-year cut-off date (as above), a short-life asset is disposed of to a connected person (within **21 CONNECTED PERSONS**), short-life asset treatment continues in the connected person's hands (though the original four-year cut-off date remains unchanged). If both parties so elect (within two years after the end of the chargeable period in which the disposal occurs), the disposal is treated as being at a price equal to the available qualifying expenditure (see **11.23** above) then in the short-life asset pool, and certain anti-avoidance provisions on transactions between connected persons are disapplied. If no election is made, the anti-avoidance provisions at **11.63** below apply in full, and the exception at **11.24**(b)(i) above is disapplied (so that market value can be substituted for a lesser sale price even where the buyer is entitled to capital allowances).

If a disposal event occurs in respect of a short-life asset pool such that the pool ends and a balancing *allowance* arises (see **11.23** above), and an 'additional VAT liability' (see **11.2**(viii) above) is subsequently incurred in respect of the item concerned, a further balancing allowance of that amount is given for the chargeable period in which the additional VAT liability accrues.

HMRC accept that it may not be practicable for individual pools to be maintained for every short-life asset, especially where they are held in very large numbers. Statement of Practice SP 1/86 sets out examples of acceptable bases of computation where the inspector is satisfied that the actual life in the business of a distinct class of assets with broadly similar average lives, before being sold or scrapped, is likely to be less than five years.

[CAA 2001, ss 83–89, 240, 268D; FA 2006, Sch 8 para 8; FA 2008, Sch 20 para 6(7)(19), Sch 26 paras 7, 14; FA 2009, Sch 11 paras 6, 19, 20, 22, 26–28, 32].

See *Example (A)* at **11.32** below.

Simon's Taxes. See B3.343.

Long-life assets

[11.31] There are special provisions relating to certain '*long-life asset expenditure*', i.e. qualifying expenditure (as in **11.3** above) incurred on the provision of a 'long-life asset' for the purposes of a qualifying activity (but see below for exclusions by reference to a monetary limit).

Subject to below, a '*long-life asset*' is plant or machinery which it is reasonable to expect will have a useful economic life of at least 25 years (or where such was a reasonable expectation when the plant or machinery was new, i.e. unused and not second-hand). For these purposes, the useful economic life of plant or machinery is the period from first use (by any person) until it ceases to be, or to be likely to be, used by anyone as a fixed asset of a business. Where part only of capital expenditure incurred before 6 April 2008 on an item of plant or machinery falls within these provisions, that part and the remainder are treated as expenditure on separate items, any necessary apportionments being made on a just and reasonable basis; for expenditure incurred after 5 April 2008, this rule is subsumed by an identical rule for special rate expenditure in **11.25** above. As an introduction to a detailed discussion of what constitutes a long-life asset (including twelve examples), HMRC have stated that they 'will generally accept the accounting treatment as determining whether an asset is long-life provided it is not clearly unreasonable' (Revenue Tax Bulletin August 1997 pp 445–450). For whether glasshouses (for which see generally **11.8** and **11.12**(17) above) are long-life assets, see Revenue Tax Bulletin June 1998 p 552. For aircraft, see Revenue Tax Bulletin June 1999 pp 671, 672, April 2000 pp 739, 740 and December 2003 pp 1074, 1075.

The following *cannot* be long-life assets.

(i)   Fixtures (see **11.33** below) in, or plant or machinery provided for use in, a building used wholly or mainly as a dwelling-house, showroom, hotel, office or retail shop or similar retail premises, or for purposes ancillary to such use.

(ii)   Cars, as defined at **11.13**(ii) above.

(iii)   (In relation to expenditure incurred before 1 January 2011) ships of a seagoing kind, other than offshore installations (as defined by *ITA 2007, s 1001*, previously *ICTA 1988, s 837C* — and for earlier definition see *CAA 2001, s 94 as originally enacted*), and not of a kind used or chartered primarily for sport or recreation (which expression does not encompass passenger ships or cruise liners).

(iv)   (In relation to expenditure incurred before 1 January 2011) 'railway assets' used only for a 'railway business' (as defined).

(v)   Motor cycles.

Long-life asset expenditure which is incurred wholly and exclusively for the purposes of a qualifying activity, and which does not require allocation under other rules to a single asset pool, can only be allocated to a *class pool* (see **11.23** above). If the expenditure was incurred on or before 5 April 2008, it was allocated to a class pool known as the *long-life asset pool*. The final chargeable period (see **11.23** above) of a long-life asset pool is that in which the qualifying activity is permanently discontinued. If the expenditure is incurred after 5 April 2008, it is allocated to the special rate pool in **11.25** above.

Writing-down allowances for a chargeable period in respect of long-life asset expenditure (whether in a class pool or a single asset pool) are restricted to:

•   6% for chargeable periods ending before 6 April 2008;
•   10% for chargeable periods beginning after 5 April 2008 (as in **11.25** above);

- a hybrid rate for chargeable periods straddling 6 April 2008, based on how much of the period fell before that date, how much of it falls on or after that date and whether the expenditure was incurred before or on or after that date (see further below),

proportionately reduced or increased if the chargeable period is less or more than a year, or if the qualifying activity has been carried on for part only of the chargeable period. A claim for a writing-down allowance may require it to be reduced to a specified amount. Where plant and machinery allowances have been claimed for long-life asset expenditure, any earlier or later expenditure on the same asset for which allowances are subsequently claimed, unless excluded by (i)–(iv) above, is treated as also being long-life asset expenditure if it would not otherwise be so. This over-rides the exclusion of expenditure within the monetary limit referred to below.

The hybrid rate for chargeable periods straddling 6 April 2008 is found by applying the formula:

$$R = \left(6 \times \frac{BRD}{CP}\right) + \left(10 \times \frac{ARD}{CP}\right)$$

Where

R	=	the rate per cent (to be rounded up to two decimal places);
BRD	=	the number of days in the chargeable period before 6 April 2008;
ARD	=	the number of days in the chargeable period on and after 6 April 2008; and
CP	=	the total number of days in the chargeable period.

HMRC provide an online 'ready reckoner' to assist in calculating the hybrid rate — see http://cahrcalculator.hmrc.gov.uk/CAHR01.aspx.

The hybrid rate applies only to expenditure incurred before 6 April 2008. Expenditure incurred after that date qualifies at 10% as in **11.25** above. At the end of the straddling period, the balance of the long-life asset pool (representing expenditure incurred before 6 April 2008) is transferred to the special rate pool. If a chargeable period ends on 5 April 2008, such that there is no straddling period, the balance of the long-life asset pool at the end of that day is transferred to a special rate pool. In either case, the balance transferred is generally treated in future as if it had always been special rate expenditure. Long-life asset expenditure in a single asset pool remains in that pool but is treated in future as special rate expenditure in a single asset pool.

Expenditure incurred on or before 5 April 2008 is treated in the same way as post-5 April 2008 expenditure if it is not allocated to a pool until a chargeable period beginning after that date.

Where a disposal value less than the 'notional written-down value' would otherwise fall to be brought into account in respect of pre-6 April 2008 long-life asset expenditure which has attracted restricted allowances as above, an adjustment may be required. Where the event giving rise to the disposal value is part of a scheme or arrangement a main object of which is the obtaining of a tax advantage under these provisions, the 'notional written-down value' is substituted for the disposal value. The *notional written-down value* is qualifying expenditure on the item in question less maximum allowances to date, computed on the assumptions that the expenditure was not excluded from being long-life asset expenditure by the operation of the monetary limit below and that all allowances have been made in full. For expenditure incurred after 5 April 2008, this rule is subsumed by an identical rule for special rate expenditure in **11.25** above.

Monetary limit

Expenditure is not long-life asset expenditure if it is expenditure to which the monetary limit (see below) applies and it is incurred in a chargeable period for which that limit is not exceeded. The limit applies to expenditure incurred by an individual who devotes substantially the whole of his time in that chargeable period to the carrying on of the qualifying activity for the purposes of which the expenditure was incurred. In the case of a partnership of individuals, at least half the partners must satisfy the requirement as to devotion of time, but a company falls outside that requirement. In any case, the monetary limit does not apply to the following types of expenditure:

- expenditure on a share in plant or machinery; or
- a contribution treated as plant or machinery expenditure under *CAA 2001, s 538* (see **11.2**(vii) above); or
- expenditure on plant or machinery for leasing (whether or not in the course of a trade).

The monetary limit is £100,000, proportionately reduced or increased for chargeable periods of less or more than a year and, as regards companies, divided by one plus the number of associated companies (as under *CTA 2010, ss 25–30*). For the purpose of applying the monetary limit, all expenditure under a contract is treated as incurred in the first chargeable period in which any expenditure under the contract is incurred.

Transitional rule for second-hand assets

A second-hand asset is excluded from the long-life asset provisions if:

- the previous owner properly claimed plant and machinery allowances for expenditure on its provision;
- his expenditure did not fall to be treated as long-life asset expenditure; and
- his expenditure would have fallen to be so treated if the long-life asset rules (apart from this transitional rule) had always been law.

A provisional claim to normal writing-down allowances may be made by a purchaser on this basis, before the vendor has made the appropriate return, provided that reasonable steps have been taken to establish that entitlement will arise, and that the appropriate revisions will be made, and assessments accepted, if entitlement does not in the event arise (Revenue Tax Bulletin August 1997 p 450).

[*CAA 2001, ss 56(5), 65(1), 90–104, 268A, Sch 3 para 20; FA 2008, s 80, Sch 26 paras 8–11, 14; FA 2009, Sch 11 paras 21, 26–28; CTA 2010, Sch 1 para 332*].

For an article explaining how HMRC interpret and operate these provisions, see Revenue Tax Bulletin August 1997 pp 445–450. For their application to modern equipment used in the printing industry, see Revenue Tax Bulletin February 2002 pp 916, 917.

See *Example (B)* at **11.32** below.

Simon's Taxes. See B3.344.

Examples

[11.32] The following examples illustrate a number of matters detailed above.

(A) Short-life assets

A runs a business classed as a 'small or medium-sized enterprise' (see **11.16** above). He prepares trading accounts to 30 September each year, and buys and sells machines, for use in the trade, as follows.

	Cost	Date of acquisition	Disposal proceeds	Date of disposal
Machine X	£40,000	30.4.05	£13,000	1.12.06
Machine Y	£25,000	1.9.05	£4,000	1.12.09

A elects under *CAA 2001, s 83* for both machines to be treated as short-life assets. His main pool of qualifying expenditure brought forward at the beginning of period of account 1.10.04–30.9.05 is £80,000.

A's capital allowances are as follows.

	Main Pool	Short-life asset pools		Total Allowances
		Machine X	Machine Y	
	£	£	£	£
Period of account 1.10.04–30.9.05				
WDV b/f	80,000			
Additions		40,000	25,000	
FYA 40%		(16,000)	(10,000)	26,000
WDA 25%	(20,000)	____	____	20,000
	60,000	24,000	15,000	£46,000
Period of account 1.10.05-30.9.06				
WDA 25%	(15,000)	(6,000)	(3,750)	£24,750
	45,000	18,000	11,250	

	Main Pool	Short-life asset pools		Total Allow- ances
		Machine X	Machine Y	
	£	£	£	£
Period of account 1.10.06-30.9.07				
Disposal		(13,000)		
Balancing allowance		£5,000		5,000
WDA 25%	(11,250)		(2,813)	14,063
				£19,063
	33,750		8,437	
Period of account 1.10.07–30.9.08				
WDA 22.57% — note (b)	(7,617)		(1,904)	£9,521
	26,133		6,533	
Period of account 1.10.08–30.9.09				
WDA 20%	(5,227)		(1,307)	£6,534
	20,906		5,226	
Period of account 1.10.09–30.9.10				
Transfer to pool	5,228		(5,228)	
	26,134		—	
Disposal	(4,000)			
	22,134			
WDA 20%	(4,427)			£4,427
WDV c/f	£17,707			
Period of account 1.10.10–30.9.11				
WDA 20%	(3,541)			£3,541
WDV c/f	£14,166			

Notes

(a) The fourth anniversary of the end of the chargeable period in which the expenditure is incurred is 30.9.09 (the four-year cut-off date). The balance of expenditure on Machine Y is thus transferred to the pool in the period of account 1.10.09–30.9.10, this being the first chargeable period ending after the four-year cut-off date.

(b) The hybrid rate of WDA for the year to 30 September 2008 is 22.57%, computed as follows (where 188 is the number of days from 1 October 2007 to 5 April 2008, 178 is the number of days from 6 April 2008 to 30 September 2008 and 366 is the total number of days in the period of account).

$$R = \left(25 \times \frac{188}{366}\right) + \left(20 \times \frac{178}{366}\right) \quad 22.57$$

(B) Long-life assets and special rate pool

B prepares trading accounts to 31 December. In the year to 31 December 2007, he has new factory premises built for use in his trade, which include a building mainly in use as offices (on which 20% of the cost of the premises is expended). Industrial buildings allowances are available on the construction expenditure. The main plant and machinery pool written-down value at 1 January 2007 is £800,000, and the disposal value to be brought into account in respect of plant and machinery in B's previous premises is £720,000. Machines installed in the new factory cost £920,000. No first-year allowances are available.

B also claims, for the year to 31 December 2007, plant and machinery allowances for expenditure of £520,000 incurred on fixtures integral to the new premises, which are agreed to have an expected life in excess of 25 years. Of this expenditure, it is agreed £120,000 should be apportioned to the offices.

On 1 May 2008 he incurs additional expenditure on upgrading the fixtures of £19,000, none of it relating to office fixtures.

On 1 March 2009 he moves to new premises, disposing of the old premises for a consideration including £425,000 relating to the integral fixtures (of which £95,000 relates to the office fixtures) and £510,000 relating to other plant and machinery.

Plant and machinery in the new premises costs £1,760,000, of which £200,000 is agreed to be long-life asset expenditure and £600,000 relates to integral features as defined in **11.11** above. All of the remaining expenditure was incurred before 6 April 2009 and therefore does not qualify for the temporary first-year allowance for expenditure incurred in the tax year 2009/10 (see **11.14** above). The full £1,760,000 is AIA qualifying expenditure.

The plant and machinery allowances computations for relevant periods are as follows.

	Main Pool £	Long-life asset pool £	Special rate pool £	Total allow-ances
Year ending 31.12.07				
WDV b/f	800,000	—		
Additions (see note (a))	1,040,000	400,000		
Disposals	(720,000)	—		
	1,120,000	400,000		
WDA 25%/6%	280,000	24,000		£304,000
WDV c/f	840,000	376,000		
Year ending 31.12.08				
Additions (see note (b))	—	19,000		

	Main Pool	Long-life asset pool	Special rate pool	Total allow-ances
	£	£	£	
	840,000	395,000		
WDA (see note (d))	179,004	35,353		£214,357
WDV c/f	660,996	359,647		
Transfer to special rate pool		(359,647)	359,647	
WDV c/f		—	359,647	
Year ending 31.12.09				
Additions	960,000		800,000	
	1,620,996		1,159,647	
AIA 100% (see note (c))			50,000	50,000
			1,109,647	
Disposals	(605,000)		(330,000)	
	1,015,996		779,647	
WDA (see note (d))	203,199		77,965	281,164
				£331,164
WDV c/f	£812,797		£701,682	

Notes

(a)   Expenditure on fixtures provided for use in offices is excluded from being long-life asset expenditure (regardless of whether the office building itself attracts industrial buildings allowances because it represents not more than 25% of the overall cost of premises otherwise qualifying). (Where incurred after 5 April 2008, such expenditure is nevertheless special rate expenditure if it relates to integral features as defined in **11.11** above.)

(b)   Additional expenditure on existing long-life assets is within the provisions even if within the annual monetary limit.

(c)   The annual investment allowance (AIA) is restricted to the first £50,000 of AIA qualifying expenditure (£100,000 on and after 6 April 2010). It has been allocated in this example to special rate expenditure as this maximises the writing-down allowances available in subsequent years.

(d)   The WDAs in the main pool and long-asset pool are at a hybrid rate for periods of account straddling 5 April 2008, calculated as follows.
Main pool (where 96 is the number of days from 1 January 2008 to 5 April 2008, 270 is the number of days from 6 April 2008 to 31 December 2008 and 366 is the total number of days in the period of account):

$$R = \left(25 \times \frac{96}{366}\right) + \left(20 \times \frac{270}{366}\right) \quad 21.31\%$$

Long-life asset pool

$$R = \left(6 \times \frac{96}{366}\right) + \left(10 \times \frac{270}{366}\right) \qquad 8.95\%$$

In subsequent years, the rate of WDA in the main pool is 20% unless the balance of the pool falls to £1,000 or less, in which case it will be 100%. The rate of WDA in the special rate pool is 10% from the outset (again unless the balance of the pool falls to £1,000 or less, in which case it will be 100%).

(e) The balance of the long-life asset pool at the end of the period of account straddling 5 April 2008 is transferred to the special rate pool, and the long-life asset pool ceases to exist.

(C) Pooling, annual investment allowance, writing-down allowances, cars, partial non-business use, acquisitions from connected persons and balancing adjustments

A is in business as a builder and demolition contractor. He makes up his accounts to 5 April. The accounts for the year to 5 April 2011 reveal the following additions and disposals.

	£
Additions	
Plant	
Dumper Truck	5,000
Excavator 1	32,000
Excavator 2	50,000
Bulldozer	20,000
	£107,000
Fittings	
Office furniture	£8,000
Motor Vehicles	
Land Rover	6,000
Van	5,000
Car 2	21,000
Car 3	2,000
	£34,000

Disposals	Cost	Proceeds
	£	£
Excavator 1	32,000	30,000
Digger loader	15,000	4,000
Car 1	14,200	4,200
Fittings	3,500	500

The dumper truck was bought second-hand from Q, brother of A, but had not been used in a trade or other qualifying activity. The truck had originally cost Q £6,000, but its market value at sale was only £2,000.

Excavator 1 was sold without having been brought into use.

The bulldozer and Car 3 were both purchased from P, father of A and had originally cost P £25,000 and £3,500 respectively. Both assets had been used for the purposes of a qualifying activity. In both cases, the price paid by A was less than the market value.

Car 1 sold and the new Car 2 are both used for private motoring by A. Private use has always been 30%. Car 2 has CO_2 emissions of over 160g/km. Car 3 is occasionally borrowed by A's daughter, and the private use proportion is 20%. Car 3 has CO_2 emissions of less than 160g/km.

The written-down values at 5 April 2010 of the main plant and machinery pool and Car 1 are £20,500 and £3,900 respectively.

The plant and machinery allowances for the 12-month period of account ending on 5 April 2011 are

	Expenditure qualifying for AIA	Main pool	Car 2 partial use pool	Car 3 partial use pool	Expensive car pool (Car 1)	Total allowances
	£	£	£	£	£	£
WDV b/f		20,500			3,900	
Additions						
Excavator 1 (note (a))	32,000	32,000				
Excavator 2	50,000	50,000				
Dumper truck (notes (b)(c))		2,000				
Bulldozer (notes (b)(d))		20,000				
Furniture	8,000	8,000				
Land Rover and van	11,000	11,000				
Cars			21,000	2,000		
	£101,000					
AIA (100% on £100,000)		(100,000)				100,000
Disposals						
Excavator		(30,000)				
Digger		(4,000)				
Fittings		(500)				

	Expendi-ture qualifying for AIA	Main pool	Car 2 partial use pool	Car 3 partial use pool	Expensive car pool (Car 1)	Total allow-ances
	£	£	£	£	£	£
Audi					(4,200)	
	9,000	21,000	2,000		(£300)	
WDA (20%)		(1,800)		(400)		2,200
WDA (10%)			(2,100)			2,100
Private use re-striction:						
Car 2 — £2,100 @ 30%						(630)
Car 3 — £400 @ 20%						(80)
WDV c/f		£7,200	£18,900	£1,600		
Total al-lowances						£103,590
Balancing charge (Car 1) £300 less 30% private use						£210

Notes

(a)   The annual investment allowance (AIA) (**11.13** above) and writing-down allowances (**11.23** above) are available even though an item of plant or machinery is disposed of without being brought into use, always provided that the expenditure is, respectively, AIA qualifying expenditure (see **11.13** above) and general qualifying expenditure (see **11.3** above). See **11.23** above as regards the requirement, where an AIA has been given, to allocate the expenditure to a pool.

(b)   No AIA is available in respect of an item of plant or machinery purchased from a connected person. See **11.13**(vi) above.

(c)   Qualifying expenditure (and AIA qualifying expenditure) on the dumper truck is restricted to the lowest of:
(i)   market value;
(ii)   capital expenditure incurred by the vendor (or, if lower, by a person connected with him);
(iii)   capital expenditure incurred by the purchaser.
See **11.63** below.

(d)   Qualifying expenditure on the bulldozer is the lesser of A's actual expenditure and the disposal value brought into account in the ven-dor's computations (see **11.63** below). (The vendor's disposal value would have been market value but for the fact that the purchaser is himself entitled to claim capital allowances on the acquisition (see **11.24**(b)(i) above).) A's qualifying expenditure is thus equal to his actual expenditure. The same applies to the purchase of Car 3.

(e) Cars 2 and 3 are allocated to separate single asset pools by virtue of their being used partly for non-business purposes (see **11.27** above), and the same applied to Car 1. Car 3 is allocated to a single asset pool by virtue only of its being used for non-business purposes (see **11.27** above). Car 2 qualifies for writing-down allowances (WDAs) at the special rate of 10% because of its CO_2 emissions level (see **11.25** above). See note (d) above as regards the amount of qualifying expenditure to be brought into account in respect of Car 3.

(D) Period of account not exceeding 18 months

James commences business on 1 October 2008 preparing accounts initially to 30 September. He changes his accounting date in 2010, preparing accounts for the 15 months to 31 December 2010. The following capital expenditure is incurred.

	Plant	Car
	£	£
1 October 2008 to 5 April 2009	64,400	4,000 (no private use)
6 April 2009 to 30 September 2009	Nil	
15 months to 31 December 2010	7,500	
Year ended 31 December 2011	4,000	

An item of plant was sold for £500 (original cost £1,000) on 25 September 2010. All of the expenditure on plant additions is AIA qualifying expenditure. The expenditure in the 15 months to 31 December 2010 was all incurred after 5 April 2010.

Profits *before* capital allowances but otherwise as adjusted for tax purposes are as follows:

	£
Year ended 30 September 2009	84,000
Period ended 31 December 2010	31,000
Year ended 31 December 2011	50,000

The capital allowances are:

	AIA qualifying expenditure	Main pool	Allowances
	£	£	£
Year ended 30.9.09			
Qualifying expenditure	64,400	4,000	
AIA 100% (maximum £50,000)	50,000		50,000
Transfer to main pool	(14,400)	14,400	
		18,400	
WDA 20%		(3,680))	3,680
WDV at 30.9.09		14,720	

	AIA qualify-ing expenditure	Main pool	Allow-ances
	£	£	£
Total allowances			£53,680
15 months ended 31.12.10			
Additions	7,500	7,500	
AIA 100%		(7,500)	7,500
Disposals		(500)	
		14,220	
WDA (note (b))		(3,556)	3,556
WDV at 31.12.10		10,664	
Total allowances			£11,056
Year ended 31.12.11			
Additions	4,000	4,000	
AIA 100%		(4,000)	4,000
		10,664	
WDA 20%		(2,133)	2,133
WDV at 31.12.11		£8,531	
Total allowances			£6,133

Taxable profits for the accounting periods concerned are:

	Before CAs	CAs	After CAs
	£	£	£
Year ended 30 September 2009	84,000	53,680	30,320
Period ended 31 December 2010	31,000	11,056	19,944
Year ended 31 December 2011	50,000	6,133	43,867

Taxable profits for the first four tax years of the business are:

	£	£
2008/09 (1.10.08–5.4.09) (£30,320 × $^6/_{12}$)		15,160
2009/10 (y/e 30.9.09)		30,320
2010/11 (1.10.09–31.12.10)	19,944	
Deduct Overlap relief £15,160 × $^3/_6$	7,580	12,364
2011/12 (y/e 31.12.11)		43,867

Notes

(a)   Capital allowances are calculated by reference to periods of account and are treated as trading expenses (see **11.1, 11.2**(i), **11.5** above).

(b)   Where a period of account exceeds 12 months, WDAs are proportionately increased (see **11.23** above). In this case, there are 458 days in the period, so the WDA is 20% x 458/365 = 25.01%.

(E) Period of account exceeding 18 months

Bianca commenced business on 1 October 2008 preparing accounts initially to 30 June. She changes her accounting date in 2010/11, preparing accounts for the 21 months to 31 March 2011. The following capital expenditure is incurred:

	Plant £	Car £
Period ended 30 June 2009	66,000	20,000 (no private use)
21 months to 31 March 2011	10,600	
Year ended 31 March 2012	2,150	

All of the expenditure incurred in the period to 30 June 2009 was incurred before 6 April 2009. Of the £10,600 of expenditure incurred in the 21-month accounting period to 31 March 2011, £3,600 was incurred in January 2010 and £7,000 in the nine months to 31 March 2011. Apart from the car, all expenditure is AIA qualifying expenditure.

An item of plant is sold for £880 (original cost £1,000) on 3 November 2010.

Profits *before* capital allowances but otherwise as adjusted for tax purposes are as follows:

	£
Period ended 30 June 2009	75,000
Period ended 31 March 2011	115,000
Year ended 31 March 2012	80,000

The capital allowances are:

	AIA qualifying expenditure £	Main pool £	Car £	Total allowances £
9 months ended 30.6.09				
Qualifying expenditure	66,000		20,000	
AIA 100% (maximum £50,000)	(50,000)			50,000
	16,000			
Transfer to main pool	(16,000)	16,000		
WDA 20% x⁹/₁₂		2,400		2,400
WDA £3,000 x⁹/₁₂			(2,250)	2,250
WDV at 30.6.09		13,600	17,750	

341

	AIA qualifying expenditure	Main pool	Car	Total allow-ances
	£	£	£	£
Total allowances				£54,650
12 months ended 30.6.10				
Additions	3,600			
AIA 100%	(3,600)			3,600
WDA 20%		(2,720)		2,720
WDA £3,000			(3,000)	3,000
WDV at 30.6.10		10,880	14,750	
Total allowances				£9,320
9 months ended 31.3.11				
Additions	7,000			
AIA 100%	(7,000)			7,000
Disposals		(880)		
		10,000		
WDA 20% × ⁹/₁₂		(1,500)	(2,213)	3,713
WDV at 31.3.11		8,500	12,537	
Total allowances				£10,713
Year ended 31.3.12				
Additions	2,150			
AIA 100%	(2,150)			2,150
WDA 20%		(1,700)	(2,507)	4,207
WDV at 31.3.12		£6,800	£10,030	
Total allowances				£6,357

Taxable profits for the periods of account concerned are:

	Before CAs	CAs	After CAs
	£	£	£
Period ended 30 June 2009	75,000	54,650	20,350
Period ended 31 March 2011	115,000	(9,320 + 10,713)	94,967
Year ended 31 March 2012	80,000	6,357	73,643

Taxable profits for the first four tax years of the business are:

	£	£
2008/09 (1.10.08 – 5.4.09) (£20,350 × 6/9)		13,567
2009/10 (1.10.08 – 30.9.09):		

1.10.08 – 30.6.09	20,350	
1.7.09 – 30.9.09 (£94,967 × ³/₂₁)	13,567	33,917
2010/11 (1.10.09 – 31.3.11) (£94,967 × ¹⁸/₂₁)	81,400	
Deduct Overlap relief	(13,567)	67,533
2011/12 (y/e 31.3.12)		73,643

Notes

(a) Where a period of account for capital allowances purposes would otherwise exceed 18 months, it is broken down into shorter periods, the first beginning on the first day of the actual period and each subsequent period beginning on an anniversary of the first day of the actual period. No period can therefore exceed 12 months. See **11.2**(i) above.

(b) The capital allowances computed for the notional periods of account referred to in (a) above are deductible in aggregate in arriving at the adjusted profit for the actual period of account.

(c) A period of account exceeding 18 months cannot normally result in an immediate change of basis period. However, the conditions at **73.7** **TRADING INCOME** do not have to be satisfied if the change of accounting date occurs in the second or third tax year of a new business, as in this example.

Fixtures

[11.33] There are special provisions to determine entitlement to allowances on fixtures, i.e. plant or machinery which, by law, becomes part of the building or land on which it is installed or otherwise fixed, including any boiler or water-filled radiator installed as part of a space or water heating system. A dispute may arise as to whether fixtures have, in law, become part of a building or land. Where two or more persons' tax liabilities are affected by the outcome of such a dispute, the question is determined for tax purposes by the Appeal Tribunal, and each of the parties concerned is entitled to be a party to the proceedings. [*CAA 2001, s 172(1)(2), s 173, s 204(1)–(3); SI 2009 No 56, Sch 1 para 298(2)(3)*].

In *J C Decaux (UK) Ltd v Francis* (Sp C 84), [1996] SSCD 281, automatic public conveniences and other street furniture such as bus shelters were held to be fixtures forming part of the land (and see **11.34** below).

These provisions determine ownership for capital allowances purposes of plant or machinery that is (or becomes) a fixture and determine entitlement to allowances in each of the various circumstances described at **11.34–11.39** below. See **11.47** below for the disapplication of these provisions in cases involving long funding leases of plant or machinery that is (or becomes) a fixture. The provisions do not affect the entitlement of a contributor towards capital expenditure (see **11.2**(vii) above). [*CAA 2001, s 172(1)(2)(5)*]. See, respectively, **11.40**, **11.41** and **11.42** below for provisions determining cessation of ownership (and consequent disposal values), acquisition of ownership in certain cases and restrictions of qualifying expenditure where allowances previously claimed.

Although the rules apply strictly on an asset-by-asset basis, HMRC accept that in practice they may be applied to groups of assets provided that this does not distort the tax computation (Revenue Tax Bulletin June 1998 p 552).

For the purposes of the fixtures provisions, an '*interest in land*' means:

(i)   the fee simple estate in the land;

(ii)   in Scotland, in the case of feudal property prior to abolition of feudal tenure, the estate or interest of the proprietor of the *dominium utile*, and in any other case, the interest of the owner;

(iii)   a lease (defined for these provisions in relation to land as any leasehold estate in (or, in Scotland, lease of) the land (whether a head-lease, sub-lease or under-lease) or any agreement to acquire such an estate (or lease));

(iv)   an easement or servitude;

(v)   a licence to occupy land,

and any agreement to acquire an interest as in (i)–(iv) above. Where an interest is conveyed or assigned by way of security subject to a right of redemption, the interest is treated as continuing to belong to the person having the redemption right. [*CAA 2001, ss 174(4), 175, Sch 3 para 29*]. As regards (v) above, for the HMRC view of when a licence to occupy land exists for these purposes, see Revenue Tax Bulletin June 2000 p 761.

See generally HMRC Capital Allowances Manual CA26000 *et seq.*

Finance leasing

See **73.79** TRADING INCOME as regards restrictions on capital allowances where certain finance leasing arrangements are involved. See also **11.43**, **11.61**, **11.63** below.

Expenditure incurred by holder of interest in land

[11.34] Where a person having an interest in land incurs capital expenditure on plant or machinery which becomes a fixture in relation to that land, for the purposes of a trade or other qualifying activity, then, subject to the election in **11.35** or **11.39** below, the fixture is treated as belonging to that person. If there are two or more such persons, with different interests, the only interest to be taken into account for this purpose is:

(i)   an easement or servitude, or any agreement to acquire same;

(ii)   if (i) does not apply to any of those interests, a licence to occupy the land;

(iii)   if neither (i) nor (ii) applies to any of those interests, that interest which is not directly or indirectly in reversion on any other of those interests in the land (in Scotland, that of whichever of those persons has, or last had, the right of use of the land).

[*CAA 2001, s 176; FA 2001, s 66, Sch 18 para 3*].

In *J C Decaux (UK) Ltd v Francis* (Sp C 84), [1996] SSCD 281, suppliers to local authorities of automatic public conveniences and other street furniture such as bus shelters, which were held to be fixtures forming part of the land, were held not to have an interest in the land.

Expenditure incurred by equipment lessor

[**11.35**] An 'equipment lease' exists where:

- a person incurs capital expenditure on an item of plant or machinery for leasing;
- an agreement is entered into for the lease, directly or indirectly from that person (the '*equipment lessor*'), of the item to another person (the '*equipment lessee*');
- the item becomes a fixture; and
- the item is not leased as part of the land in relation to which it is a fixture.

Such an agreement, or a lease entered into under such an agreement, is an '*equipment lease*'. Provided that:

(i) under the equipment lease, the plant or machinery is leased for the purposes of a trade or other qualifying activity carried on (or to be carried on in future) by the equipment lessee;

(ii) it is not for use in a dwelling-house;

(iii) the equipment lessor and equipment lessee are not **CONNECTED PERSONS** (**21**);

(iv) if the expenditure on the fixture had been incurred by the equipment lessee, he would have been entitled to allowances under **11.34** above,

the equipment lessor and equipment lessee may jointly elect for the fixture to be treated, from the time the expenditure is incurred by the equipment lessor (or, if later, from the commencement of the lessee's qualifying activity), as owned by the lessor and not the lessee.

Where the following conditions are met, (i) and (iv) above do not have to be satisfied (and the potentially later start date of the election is not relevant):

(1) the plant or machinery becomes a fixture by being fixed to land which is neither a building nor part of a building;

(2) the lessee has an interest in that land when he takes possession of the plant or machinery under the equipment lease;

(3) under the terms of the equipment lease the lessor is entitled, at the end of the lease period, to sever the plant or machinery from the land to which it is then fixed, whereupon it will be owned by the lessor;

(4) the nature of the plant or machinery and the way it is fixed to the land are such that its use does not, to any material extent, prevent its being used, after severance, for the same purposes on different premises; and

(5) the equipment lease is such as falls under generally accepted accounting practice (see **73.18 TRADING INCOME**) to be treated in the accounts of the equipment lessor as an operating lease.

In relation to agreements entered into before 19 March 1997, the election is not available where the lessee's trade was not being carried on at the time of the agreement, and the waiver of certain requirements (as above) where conditions (1)–(5) above are satisfied does not apply. For expenditure incurred by the equipment lessor before 24 July 1996, condition (ii) above does not apply, and (iv) above is replaced by a requirement that, if the expenditure had been incurred by the equipment lessee, the equipment would, under **(11.34)** above, have been treated as belonging to him (for which see *Melluish v BMI (No 3) Ltd* HL 1995, 68 TC 1).

The election must be made no later than the first anniversary of 31 January following the tax year in which ends the equipment lessor's chargeable period in which the expenditure is incurred.

Where expenditure is incurred before 1 January 2008 on plant or machinery consisting of a boiler, heat exchanger, radiator or heating control installed in a building as part of a space or water heating system, and the equipment lease is approved under the Affordable Warmth programme by the Secretary of State (or the responsible Scottish, Welsh or NI body), these provisions have effect without (i), (ii) and (iv) above having to be satisfied. If the approval is withdrawn, it is treated as never having had effect. The taxpayer must notify the inspector, within three months of his becoming aware that a return of his has become incorrect by reason of the withdrawal of approval, of the amendments to the return required in consequence of the withdrawal, subject to penalties for failure.

[*CAA 2001, s 174(1)–(3), ss 177–180, 203, Sch 3 paras 30–33*].

See **11.39** below as regards expenditure incurred by an energy services provider.

Expenditure included in consideration for acquisition of existing interest in land

[11.36] Where a person acquires a pre-existing interest in land to which a fixture is attached, for a consideration in part treated for capital allowance purposes as being expenditure on provision of the fixture, the fixture is treated as belonging to the person acquiring the interest. This applies equally where the fixture in question was previously let under an 'equipment lease' (see **11.35** above) and, in connection with the acquisition, the purchaser pays a capital sum to discharge the equipment lessee's obligations under that lease. It also applies where the fixture was provided under an energy services agreement (see **11.39** below) and, in connection with the acquisition, the purchaser pays a capital sum to discharge the client's obligations under that agreement.

[*CAA 2001, s 181(1)(4), s 182(1), 182A(1), Sch 3 paras 34, 35*].

Where the above provisions would otherwise apply, they are treated as not applying (and as never having applied) where the following conditions are met:

(i)   a person is treated as the owner of the fixture (other than under *CAA 2001, s 538* (contributions to expenditure — see **11.2**(vii) above)) immediately before the time of the above acquisition, in consequence of his having incurred expenditure on its provision; and

(ii)   that person is entitled to, and claims, an allowance in respect of that expenditure.

Where any person becomes aware that a return of his has become incorrect because of the operation of this provision, the necessary amendments to the return must be notified to HMRC within three months of his becoming so aware, subject to penalties for failure.

[*CAA 2001, s 181(2)(3), s 182(2)(3), s 182A(2)(3), s 203*].

Expenditure incurred by incoming lessee — election to transfer lessor's entitlement to allowances

[11.37] Where a person with an interest in land to which a fixture is attached grants a lease and he would (or if chargeable to tax would) be entitled, for the chargeable period in which the lease is granted, to capital allowances in respect of the fixture, and the consideration given by the lessee falls, in whole or in part, to be treated for plant and machinery allowances purposes as expenditure on the provision of the fixture, an election is available to the lessor and lessee. They may jointly elect (by notice to HMRC within two years after the date on which the lease takes effect) that, from the grant of the lease, the fixture is treated as belonging to the lessee and not to the lessor. No such election is available if lessor and lessee are **CONNECTED PERSONS** (**21.** These provisions apply to the entering into of an agreement for a lease as they apply to a grant of a lease. [*CAA 2001, ss 174(4), 183, Sch 3 para 36*].

Expenditure incurred by incoming lessee — lessor not entitled to allowances

[11.38] Where:

- a person with an interest in land to which a fixture is attached grants a lease;
- the provisions at **11.37** above do not apply, because the lessor is not entitled to capital allowances in respect of the fixture;
- before the lease is granted, the fixture has not been used for the purposes of a trade or other qualifying activity by the lessor or a person connected with him (see **21 CONNECTED PERSONS**); and
- the consideration given by the lessee includes a capital sum falling, in whole or in part, to be treated for plant and machinery allowances purposes as expenditure on the provision of the fixture,

the fixture is treated as belonging to the lessee from the time the lease is granted.

Rules similar to those of *CAA 2001, s 181(2)(3), s 182(2)(3), s 182A(2)(3), s 203* at **11.36** above apply (by reference to the time of grant).

[*CAA 2001, s 184, Sch 3 para 37*].

Expenditure incurred by energy services provider

[11.39] An *'energy services agreement'* is an agreement entered into by an 'energy services provider' and his client that provides, with a view to the saving or more efficient use of energy, for:

- the design of plant or machinery or of systems incorporating it;
- the obtaining and installation of the plant or machinery; and
- its operation and maintenance,

and under which any payment by the client in respect of the operation of the plant or machinery is wholly or partly linked to the energy savings or increased energy efficiency. An *'energy services provider'* is a person carrying on a qualifying activity consisting wholly or mainly in providing energy management services. [*CAA 2001, s 175A*].

Where:

- an energy services agreement is entered into;
- the energy services provider incurs capital expenditure under the agreement on an item of plant or machinery;
- the item becomes a fixture;
- at the time the item becomes a fixture, the client has an interest in the land in relation to which it is a fixture but the provider does not;
- the item is neither leased nor used in a dwelling-house;
- the operation of the item is carried out wholly or substantially by the provider or a person connected with him; and
- provider and client are not CONNECTED PERSONS (**21**),

the energy services provider and the client may jointly elect for the fixture to be treated, from the time the expenditure is incurred, as owned by the former and not the latter. This opens the way for the energy services provider to claim 100% first-year allowances where his expenditure is within **11.14**(d) above. The election must be made no later than the first anniversary of 31 January following the tax year in which ends the income tax period of account in which the expenditure is incurred. If the client would not have been entitled to allowances under **11.34** above if he had incurred the expenditure himself, the election is available only if the item belongs to the technology class 'Combined Heat and Power' in the Energy Technology Criteria List (see **11.18** above). The intention is that, in such specified cases, allowances to the provider are not to be denied only because the client is a non-taxpayer. [*CAA 2001, s 180A*]. See also HMRC Capital Allowances Manual CA23150.

Cessation of ownership

[11.40] The following points apply.

(A)   If a person is treated as owning a fixture under *CAA 2001, s 176* (see **11.34** above) *s 181, 182* or *182A* (see **11.36** above), *s 183* (see **11.37** above) or *s 184* (see **11.38** above), he is treated as ceasing to be the owner if and when he ceases to have the 'qualifying interest'. The '*qualifying interest*' is the interest in the land in question, except that where **11.37** or **11.38** apply it is the lease there referred to. There are rules (see *CAA 2001, s 189*) for identifying the qualifying interest in special cases.

(B) Where, under **11.37** above, the lessee begins to be treated as owning the fixture, the lessor is treated as ceasing to own it at that time.

(C) Where a fixture is permanently severed from the building or land, such that it is no longer owned by the person treated as owning it, he is treated as ceasing to own it at the time of severance.

(D) Where an equipment lessor is treated as owning a fixture (see **11.35** above) and either he assigns his rights under the equipment lease or the financial obligations of the equipment lessee (or his assignee etc.) are discharged, the equipment lessor is treated as ceasing to own the fixture at that time (or the earliest of those times).

(E) Where an energy services provider is treated as owning a fixture (see **11.35** above) and either he assigns his rights under the energy services agreement or the financial obligations of the client (or his assignee etc.) are discharged, the energy services provider is treated as ceasing to own the fixture at that time (or the earliest of those times).

[*CAA 2001, ss 188–192A*].

The *disposal value* to be brought into account in relation to a fixture depends upon the nature of the event.

(1) On cessation of ownership under (A) above due to a sale of the qualifying interest (other than where (2) below applies), and subject to the election below, it is that part of the sale price that falls (or would, if there were an entitlement, fall) to be treated for plant and machinery allowances purposes as expenditure by the purchaser on the provision of the fixture.

(2) On cessation of ownership under (A) above due to a sale of the qualifying interest at less than market value (unless the buyer (not being a dual resident investing company connected with the seller) can claim plant or machinery or research and development allowances for his expenditure, in which case (1) above applies), it is the amount that, if that interest were sold at market value (determined without regard to the disposal event itself) at that time, would be treated for plant and machinery allowances purposes as expenditure by the purchaser on provision of the fixture.

(3) On cessation of ownership under (A) above where neither (1) or (2) above applies but the qualifying interest continues (or would do so but for being merged with another interest), it is an amount determined as in (2) above.

(4) On cessation of ownership under (A) above due to the expiry of the qualifying interest, it is any capital sum received by reference to the fixture, or otherwise nil.

(5) On cessation of ownership under (B) above, and subject to the election below, it is that part of the capital sum given by the lessee for the lease as qualifies for plant and machinery allowances as the lessee's expenditure on the fixture.

(6)   On cessation of ownership under (C) above, it is market value at time of severance.

(7)   On cessation of ownership under (D) above, it is the consideration for the assignment or, as the case may be, the capital sum, if any, paid to discharge the equipment lessee's financial obligations.

(8)   On cessation of ownership under (E) above, it is the consideration for the assignment or, as the case may be, the capital sum, if any, paid to discharge the client's financial obligations.

(9)   On permanent discontinuance of the trade or other qualifying activity followed by the sale of the qualifying interest, it is an amount determined as in (1) above.

(10)   On permanent discontinuance of the qualifying activity followed by demolition or destruction of the fixture, it is the net amount received for the remains, plus any insurance or capital compensation received.

(11)   On permanent discontinuance of the qualifying activity followed by permanent loss (other than as in (10) above) of the fixture, it is any insurance or capital compensation received.

(12)   On the fixture's beginning to be used wholly or partly for purposes other than those of the qualifying activity, it is that part of the sale price that would fall to be treated for plant and machinery allowances purposes as expenditure by the purchaser on the provision of the fixture if the qualifying interest were sold at market value.

If, before 24 July 1996, a person is treated as ceasing to own a fixture by virtue of (A), (B) or (C) above, and another person incurs expenditure on the fixture, allowances are not available on so much (if any) of that expenditure as exceeds the former owner's disposal value.

[*CAA 2001, s 196, Sch 3 para 41*].

Fixtures are treated as disposed of at their 'notional written-down value' (if greater than would otherwise be the case) where the disposal event is part of a scheme or arrangement having tax avoidance (whether by increased allowances or reduced charges) as a main object. The '*notional written-down value*' is qualifying expenditure on the item in question less maximum allowances to date, computed on the assumption that all allowances have been made in full. [*CAA 2001, s 197*].

A special election is available where the disposal value of fixtures falls to be determined under (1) or (5) above. Subject as below and to *CAA 2001, ss 186, 187* (see **11.42** below) and *s 197* (above), the seller and purchaser (or, where (5) above applies, the lessor and lessee under **11.37** above) may jointly elect to fix the amount so determined at a figure not exceeding either the capital expenditure treated as incurred on the fixtures by the seller (or lessor) former owner or the actual sale price (or capital sum). The remainder (if any) of the sale price (or capital sum) is attributed to the other property included in the sale. The notice of election must be given within two years after the interest is acquired (or the lease granted), and is irrevocable. A copy must also accompany the return of the persons making the election. The notice must contain prescribed information and must quantify the amount fixed by the election, although if subsequent circumstances reduce the maximum below that fixed, the election is treated as being for that reduced maximum amount.

There are provisions for the determination of questions relating to such elections by the Appeal Tribunal. Where any person becomes aware that a return of his has become incorrect because of such an election (or because of subsequent circumstances affecting the election), the necessary amendments to the return must be notified to HMRC within three months of his becoming so aware, subject to penalties for failure. [*CAA 2001, ss 198–201, 203, 204(4)–(6); SI 2009 No 56, Sch 1 para 298(4)–(6)*]. In practice, HMRC normally accept an election covering a group of fixtures, or all the fixtures in a single property, but not one covering fixtures in different properties (e.g. where a portfolio of properties is sold) (Revenue Tax Bulletin June 1998 p 552).

Acquisition of ownership in certain cases

[11.41] If, on the termination of a lease, the outgoing lessee is treated under **11.40**(A) above as ceasing to own a fixture, the lessor is thereafter treated as the owner. This applies in relation to a licence as it does in relation to a lease. [*CAA 2001, s 193*].

The following apply where an election is made under **11.35** above (election to treat fixture as owned by equipment lessor), and either:

• the equipment lessor assigns his rights under the equipment lease; or
• the equipment lessee's financial obligations under the lease (or those of his assignee etc.) are discharged (on the payment of a capital sum).

If the former applies, then, from the time of the assignment, the fixture is treated as belonging to the assignee for capital allowance purposes, and the consideration for the assignment treated as consideration given by him on provision of the fixture. If the assignee makes any further assignment, he is treated under this provision as if he were the original lessor.

If the latter applies, the capital sum is treated as consideration for the fixture, and the fixture is treated from the time of the payment as belonging to the equipment lessee (or to any other person in whom his obligations under the lease have become vested).

[*CAA 2001, ss 194, 195*].

The same applies, with appropriate modifications, where the election in question was under **11.39** above (election to treat fixture as owned by energy services provider). [*CAA 2001, ss 195A, 195B*].

Restriction of qualifying expenditure where allowance previously claimed

[11.42] Where:

(i) a fixture is treated under these provisions as belonging to any person (the current owner) in consequence of his incurring capital expenditure on its provision; and
(ii) the plant or machinery is treated (other than under *CAA 2001, s 538* — contributions to expenditure, see **11.2**(vii) above) as having belonged at a 'relevant earlier time' to a person (who may be the same as the person

within (i) above) in consequence of his incurring expenditure other than that within (i) above; and that person, having claimed a plant and machinery allowance for that expenditure, must bring a disposal value into account,

so much (if any) of the expenditure referred to in (i) above as exceeds the 'maximum allowable amount' is left out of account in determining the current owner's qualifying expenditure or, as the case may be, is taken to be expenditure which should never have been so taken into account.

A *'relevant earlier time'* is any time before the earliest time when the plant or machinery is treated as belonging to the current owner in consequence of the expenditure referred to in (i) above. The relevant earlier time does not, however, include any time before an earlier sale of the plant or machinery other than as a fixture and other than between CONNECTED PERSONS (21).

The *'maximum allowable amount'* is the sum of the disposal value referred to in (ii) above and so much (if any) of the expenditure referred to in (i) above as is deemed under *CAA 2001, s 25* (installation costs, see **11.6** above) to be on provision of the plant or machinery. Where (ii) above is satisfied in relation to more than one disposal event, only the most recent event is taken into account for this purpose.

Where any person becomes aware that a return of his has become incorrect because of the operation of this provision, the necessary amendments to the return must be notified to HMRC within three months of his becoming so aware, subject to penalties for failure.

[*CAA 2001, ss 185, 203, Sch 3 para 38*].

Where:

(I)   a person has claimed industrial buildings allowances for expenditure partly on the provision of plant or machinery, and transfers the relevant interest in the building concerned; and

(II)   the transferee, or any other person to whom the plant or machinery is subsequently treated under these provisions as belonging, claims plant and machinery allowances for expenditure incurred thereon when it is a fixture in the building,

the claim in (II) above may not exceed the *'maximum allowable amount'*, i.e. an amount equal to the proportion of the residue of expenditure (see **10.15 CAPITAL ALLOWANCES**) attributable to the relevant interest immediately after the transfer referred to in (I) above (calculated on the assumption that the transfer was a sale) that the part of the consideration for the transfer attributable to the fixture bears to the total consideration.

As a consequence of the abolition of industrial buildings allowances, the above rule is modified where the transfer occurs in a chargeable period beginning after 5 April 2011. The residue of expenditure is taken to be what it would have been if the transfer had occurred immediately before abolition. If, however, the consideration for the transfer does not exceed that notional residue, the *'maximum allowable amount'* is restricted to the part of the consideration that is attributable to the fixture.

A similar restriction applies where research and development allowances have previously been claimed.

[*CAA 2001, ss 186, 187, Sch 3 paras 39, 40; FA 2008, Sch 27 paras 5, 30*].

Simon's Taxes. See B3.355–B3.358.

Long funding leasing

[**11.43**] The rules on leasing of plant and machinery are reformed by *FA 2006, s 81, Sch 8* as set out at **11.44–11.48** below with effect from, broadly, 1 April 2006 (and see **11.49** below for commencement and transitional provisions). For 'long funding leases', the new regime grants entitlement to capital allowances to the lessee rather than to the lessor as previously. There are corresponding changes to the tax treatment of lease rentals, to ensure that the lessor is no longer taxed on, and the lessee does not obtain a deduction for, the capital element of rentals (see **73.94** TRADING INCOME). The new regime applies only to leases which are essentially financing transactions, known as '*funding leases*', comprising mainly finance leases but also some operating leases. Leases of no more than five years' duration are excluded from the regime, as are pre-1 April 2006 leases (subject to transitional rules). There are transitional rules to enable leases finalised on or after 1 April 2006 to remain within the pre-existing regime in appropriate circumstances. The coverage below is divided into sections on lessees (**11.44**), relevant definitions (**11.45**), lessors (**11.46**), fixtures (**11.47**), miscellaneous (**11.48**) and commencement/transitional provisions (**11.49**).

For an HMRC Technical Note published on 1 August 2006 on the long funding leasing rules, see www.hmrc.gov.uk/leasing/tech-note.pdf. See also HMRC Business Leasing Manual BLM20000 *et seq.* (defining long funding leases), HMRC Business Leasing Manual BLM 40000 *et seq.* (taxation of income and expenditure under long funding leases) and HMRC Capital Allowances Manual CA23800 *et seq.* (capital allowances aspects of long funding leases).

Simon's Taxes. See B3.340Y–B3.340ZC.

Lessees

[**11.44**] Where a person carrying on a qualifying activity (see **11.4** above) incurs expenditure (whether or not capital expenditure) on the provision of plant or machinery for the purposes of that activity under a 'long funding lease' (see **11.45**(1) below), the plant or machinery is treated as owned by him at all times whilst he is the lessee. He is then treated as having incurred *capital expenditure* on the provision of the plant or machinery, of an amount determined as below depending on whether the lease is a 'long funding operating lease' (see **11.45**(3) below) or a 'long funding finance lease' (see **11.45**(4) below), at the 'commencement' (see *CAA 2001, s 70YI(1)*) of the term of the lease. The combined effect is to treat that capital expenditure as qualifying expenditure (as in **11.3** above) of the lessee for the purposes of plant and machinery capital allowances and, where appropriate, as first-year qualifying expenditure (as in **11.14** above) for the purposes of first-year allowances.

If the lease is a 'long funding operating lease' (see **11.45**(3) below), the capital expenditure is equal to the market value of the plant or machinery as at the commencement of the term of the lease or, if later, the date on which the plant or machinery is first brought into use for the purposes of the qualifying activity.

If the lease is a 'long funding finance lease' (see **11.45**(4) below), then, subject to the possible addition and restriction described below, the capital expenditure is equal to the present value, as at the commencement of the term of the lease or, if later, the date on which the plant or machinery is first brought into use for the purposes of the qualifying activity, of the 'minimum lease payments' (see **11.45**(5) below). Present value is computed as it would be if accounts were prepared in accordance with generally accepted accounting practice (GAAP) on the date on which that value is first recognised in the lessee's books or other financial records. If the lessee paid rentals under the lease before its term commenced, the capital expenditure also includes the amount of any such rentals for which tax relief is otherwise unavailable (and would still have been unavailable even if the plant or machinery had been used pre-commencement). If a main purpose of entering into the lease (or arrangements that include the lease) was to obtain capital allowances on an amount materially greater than the market value of the leased asset at the commencement of the term of the lease, the capital expenditure is restricted to that market value.

If the *lessor* under the long funding finance lease subsequently incurs additional expenditure such that the lease rentals increase, the *lessee* is treated as incurring further capital expenditure on the plant or machinery. The further expenditure is equal to the increase (if any) in the present value of the minimum lease payments and is treated as incurred on the date it is first recognised in the lessee's books or other financial records.

As regards long funding finance leases, the same principles apply whether the lease is accounted for as a lease or as a loan.

Consequences ensue where plant or machinery is the subject of a 'transfer and long funding leaseback' and the term of the long funding lease commences on or after 13 November 2008. A *'transfer and long funding leaseback'* occurs if:

- a person (S) transfers (see *CAA 2001, s 70Y(3)*) plant or machinery to another person (B); and
- at any time after the date of the transfer, the plant or machinery is available to be used by S, or by a person (other than B) who is connected (within **21 CONNECTED PERSONS**) with S (CS), under a long funding plant or machinery lease.

The consequences are that no annual investment allowance (see **11.13** above) or first-year allowance (see **11.14** above) is available in respect of the expenditure of S or CS under the lease. Also, in determining the qualifying expenditure of S or CS, there is disregarded any excess of his expenditure over the disposal value to be brought into account by S. Where no such disposal value falls to be brought into account, the qualifying expenditure of S or CS (if otherwise greater) is restricted to the lesser of the market value of the plant or machinery, the capital expenditure (if any) incurred on it by S before the transfer and any capital expenditure incurred on it before the transfer by any person connected with S.

Disposal events and values

Any of the following events occurring on or after 13 November 2008 is a disposal event, and a disposal value (see **11.24** above) must be brought into account by the lessee for the chargeable period in which that event occurs:

- the termination of the lease;
- the plant or machinery beginning to be used wholly or partly for purposes other than those of the qualifying activity; and
- the permanent discontinuance of the qualifying activity.

The disposal value is (QE − QA) + R where

QE is the person's qualifying expenditure on the provision of the plant or machinery;
QA is the 'qualifying amount' (see below); and
R is any 'relevant rebate' (see below).

If the lease is a 'long funding operating lease', the '*qualifying amount*' is the aggregate amount of the reductions made under *ITTOIA 2005, s 148I* (see **73.96 TRADING INCOME** under Lessees) (and its corporation tax equivalent) for periods of account in which the person concerned was the lessee.

If the lease is a 'long funding finance lease', the '*qualifying amount*' is the aggregate of the payments made to the lessor by the lessee (including any initial payment and any payment under a guarantee of any 'residual amount' (see **11.45**(5) below)). It excludes so much of any payment as, in accordance with GAAP, falls (or would fall) to be shown in the lessee's accounts as finance charges in respect of the lease. Any payment representing charges for services or representing 'taxes' (as in **11.45**(5) below) to be paid by the lessor is also excluded. If the long funding finance lease is not an arm's length transaction, the qualifying amount is reduced to so much of the aggregate payments (net of exclusions) as would reasonably be expected to have been made if the lease had been an arm's length transaction.

If the disposal event is the termination of the long funding operating or finance lease, '*relevant rebate*' means any amount payable to the lessee (or a person connected with him) that is calculated by reference to 'termination value' (as defined by *CAA 2001, s 70YH*), e.g. lease rental refunds. In any other case, '*relevant rebate*' means any such amount that would have been so payable if, when the relevant event occurred, the lease had terminated and the plant or machinery had been sold for its then market value. If the lease is not an arm's length transaction, the relevant rebate is reduced accordingly.

The termination of a long funding lease is a disposal event, and a disposal value (see **11.24** above) must be brought into account by the lessee for the chargeable period in which that event occurs, computed as follows. Before 13 November 2008, only the termination of the lease was a disposal event, and the disposal value is computed as follows.

If the lease is a 'long funding operating lease', the disposal value is equal to the sum of elements A and B below. Element A is the excess (if any) of the original amount of capital expenditure (computed as above) over the total *reductions* falling to be made under *ITTOIA 2005, s 148I* (see **73.96** TRADING INCOME under Lessees) (and its corporation tax equivalent) for periods of account in which the person concerned was the lessee. Element B is the total of any amounts payable to the lessee that are calculated by reference to 'termination value' (as defined by *CAA 2001, s 70YH*), e.g. lease rental refunds.

If the lease is a 'long funding finance lease', the disposal value is equal to the sum of Elements C and D below less any amount payable by the lessee to the lessor in consequence of the termination. Element C is the total of any amounts payable to the lessee that are calculated by reference to 'termination value' (as defined by *CAA 2001, s 70YH*), e.g. lease rental refunds. Element D applies only if the lease terminates short of its full term, and is the present value, immediately before the termination, of the excess of the original amount of the 'minimum lease payments' (see **11.45**(5) below), over what would have been the amount of the minimum lease payments had the lease been designed to expire when it did.

If the event in question would also give rise to a disposal event within **11.24** above in the case of the lessee, that disposal event is ignored.

[*CAA 2001, ss 70A–70D, 70DA, 70E; FA 2006, Sch 8 para 6; FA 2009, Sch 32 paras 7, 8, 15, 17; CTA 2010, Sch 1 para 329*].

Definitions

[11.45] The following definitions apply for these purposes.

(1)   A *'long funding lease'* is a 'funding lease' (as in (2) below) that is not a 'short lease' (see (A) below), is not an 'excluded lease of background plant or machinery for a building' (see (B) below) and is not excluded under the *de minimis* provision at (C) below for plant or machinery leased with land. Where, at the 'commencement' (see *CAA 2001, s 70YI(1)*) of the term of a plant or machinery lease (as widely defined by *CAA 2001, s 70K*), the plant or machinery is not being used for the purposes of a qualifying activity, but subsequently is so used, the lease is a long funding lease if it would otherwise have been a long funding lease at its 'inception' (see *CAA 2001, s 70YI(1)*); this covers, for example, the situation where either the lessor or the lessee is originally non-UK resident and subsequently becomes UK resident. However, the treatment of a lease as a long funding lease as regards the *lessee* is always subject to the following two conditions.
   •   The lessee must treat the lease as a long funding lease in his first tax return (and thus his first accounts) the profits declared by which are affected by the question of whether or not the lease is a long funding lease. Once a lease has or has not been so treated in a return, no subsequent error or mistake claim can be made before 1 April 2010, and nor can tax be recovered on a claim within **18.7** CLAIMS made on or after that date, due to the return having made on that basis.

A lessee cannot use the above to turn what would otherwise be a long funding lease into a non-long funding lease if

(i)   (in relation to leases entered into after 12 December 2007), at any time in the 'relevant period', he the lessee himself is a sub-lessor of any of the same plant or machinery under a long funding lease. The 'relevant period' is the period from inception of the first-mentioned lease to (i) the making of the said tax return or (ii) where relevant, the making of the final amendment to that tax return.; or

(ii)   (in relation to leases commenced on or after 13 November 2008) the lease is the leaseback in a 'transfer and long funding leaseback' (see above).

- A lease is not a long funding lease as regards the lessee if either the lessor or any superior lessor under a chain of leases (as defined) is entitled, at the commencement of the term of the lease, to any capital allowance (not necessarily a plant or machinery allowance) in respect of the leased plant or machinery. This also applies if such entitlement would have arisen but for *CAA 2001, s 70V* (see **11.48** below under Tax avoidance involving international leasing). It also applies if the entitlement arose at an earlier time but no requirement has yet arisen to bring into account a disposal value as described in **11.46** below. These conditions are applied on the assumption that the lessor in question is within the charge to UK tax, even if that is not, in fact, the case. However, where the inception of the lease is before 28 June 2006 and the lessor remains entitled to capital allowances by virtue only of the exception under (2)(iii) below the lease is still regarded as a long funding lease as regards the lessee.

[*CAA 2001, ss 70G, 70H, 70Q; FA 2006, Sch 8 para 7; FA 2008, Sch 20 para 8; FA 2009, s 100, Sch 32 paras 16, 17, Sch 52 para 9; CTA 2010, Sch 1 para 330*].

The above-mentioned exclusions from long funding lease treatment are defined in (A)–(C) below.

(A)   A '*short lease*' is defined as a lease whose term is five years or less or, if three conditions are met, a lease whose term is more than five years but no more than seven. (The 'term' of a lease is defined by *CAA 2001, s 70YF*.) The first two conditions are that (i) the lease falls to be treated under GAAP as a finance lease, (ii) the residual value of the plant or machinery implied in the terms of the lease must not be more than 5% of its market value at commencement of the lease term. The third condition compares the lease rentals due in each year of the lease term (ignoring any variations resulting from changes in published interest rates); the total rentals due in Year 1 must not be more than 10% less than those due in Year 2, and the total rentals due in any of Years 3 to 7 must not be more than 10% greater than those due in Year 2. There is an anti-avoidance rule at *section 70I(9)* (effective for leases entered into on or after 7 April 2006) aimed at preventing arrangements between **CONNECTED PERSONS** (**21**) being used to create artificially short leases.

The finance lease in a sale and finance leaseback caught by *CAA 2001, s 221* (see **11.63**(ii) below) is excluded from being a 'short lease' (if it otherwise would be) where the sale etc. part of the arrangement occurs after 8 October 2007. Where the sale etc. occurs after 11 March 2008, this treatment extends to *any* finance lease that is part of the leaseback arrangement. However, if certain conditions are satisfied, a joint (irrevocable) election may be made by the seller (or assignor) and the lessor (within two years of the sale etc.) to disapply the exclusion. The conditions are the same as those relating to the similar election in *CAA 2001, s 227* (see **11.63**(ii) below), in particular that the sale etc. takes place not more than four months after the plant or machinery is first brought into use; the effect of the election is also the same as that of the *CAA 2001, s 227* election.

The finance lease in a lease and finance leaseback caught by *CAA 2001, s 228A* (see **11.63**(iv) below) is excluded from being a 'short lease' (if it otherwise would be) where the original lease is granted after 11 March 2008. This treatment extends to any other finance lease that is part of the lease and finance leaseback arrangements except for the original lease.

[*CAA 2001, s 70I; FA 2006, Sch 8 para 7; FA 2008, Sch 20 paras 6(6)(19)(20), 7*].

(B)   An '*excluded lease of background plant or machinery for a building*' occurs where 'background plant or machinery' is affixed to (or otherwise installed in or on) land that consists of (or includes) a building and is leased with that land under a 'mixed lease' (as defined by *CAA 2001, s 70L* — broadly a lease of plant or machinery plus other assets — see also **11.48**below under Mixed leases). '*Background plant or machinery*' is plant or machinery of such description as might reasonably be expected to be installed in various buildings and whose sole or main purpose is to contribute to the functioning of the building or its site as an environment in which activities can be carried on. There is provision for the Treasury to supplement this definition by statutory instrument and to similarly designate particular types of plant or machinery as being, or as not being, background plant or machinery — see now *SI 2007 No 303*. There are anti-avoidance provisions to prevent this exclusion from applying if a main purpose of the mixed lease (or of transactions of which it is part) is to entitle the lessor to capital allowances on the background plant or machinery or if the rentals vary according to the value of allowances available to the lessor. [*CAA 2001, ss 70R–70T; FA 2006, Sch 8 para 7; SI 2007 No 303*].

(C)   The *de minimis* provision referred to above applies in a case in which relatively small amounts of plant and machinery are leased with land and the exclusion at (B) above would have applied but for the plant or machinery not being 'background plant or machinery'. The lease is excluded from long funding lease treatment if, at commencement of its term, the aggregate market value of all such plant or machinery does not exceed 10% of the aggregate market value of any 'background plant or machinery' leased with the land *and* does not exceed 5% of the market value of the land (including buildings and fixtures and assuming an absolute interest). [*CAA 2001, s 70U; FA 2006, Sch 8 para 7*].

See also HMRC Business Leasing Manual BLM20000 *et seq*.

(2)   A *'funding lease'* is a plant or machinery lease (as widely defined by *CAA 2001, s 70K*) which meets the 'finance lease test', the 'lease payments test' or the 'useful economic life test' (see bullet points below) (or meets more than one of these tests) and does not fall within either of the exceptions below. A plant or machinery lease whose inception is on or after 1 April 2010 is automatically a funding lease if the plant or machinery is cushion gas, i.e. gas that functions, or is intended to function, as plant in a particular gas storage facility.

- A lease meets the *'finance lease test'* as regards any person if it is one that, under GAAP, falls (or would fall) to be treated in that person's accounts as either a finance lease or a loan. A lease also meets the finance lease test as regards *the lessor* if is one that, under GAAP, falls (or would fall) to be so treated in the accounts of a person connected with him (within **21 CONNECTED PERSONS**). The Treasury has power to vary the finance lease test by statutory instrument.

- A lease meets the *'lease payments test'* if the present value of the 'minimum lease payments' (see (5) below) is not less than 80% of the 'fair value' of the leased plant or machinery. Present value is calculated using the interest rate implicit in the lease (applying normal commercial criteria including GAAP or, in default, the temporal discount rate contained in *FA 2005, s 70* or amending regulations). *'Fair value'* means market value less any grants receivable towards the purchase or use of the plant or machinery.

- A lease meets the *'useful economic life test'* if the term of the lease exceeds 65% of the remaining useful economic life (see *CAA 2001, s 70YI(1)*) of the leased plant or machinery. (The 'term' of a lease is defined by *CAA 2001, s 70YF*.)

Exceptions.

(i)   A contract within **11.61** below (hire-purchase contracts etc.) is not a funding lease.

(ii)   A lease is not a funding lease if, before the 'commencement' (see *CAA 2001, s 70YI(1)*) of its term, the lessor has leased the same plant or machinery under one or more other plant or machinery leases, none of which were funding leases, and the aggregate term of those other leases exceeds 65% of the remaining useful economic life of the plant or machinery at the commencement of the earliest lease; for this purpose only, any person who was a lessor under a pre-1 April 2006 lease is treated as the same person as the lessor under the first post-1 April 2006 lease.

(iii) A lease is not a funding lease as regards the lessor if, before 1 April 2006, the plant or machinery had, for a period or periods totalling at least ten years, been the subject of one or more leases and the lessor was also the lessor of the plant or machinery on the last day before 1 April 2006 on which it was leased.

[*CAA 2001, ss 70J, 70N–70P, 70YJ; FA 2006, Sch 8 para 7; FA 2010, s 28(2)–(5), (8)*].

(3) A '*long funding operating lease*' is any long funding lease that is not a long funding finance lease within (4) below. [*CAA 2001, s 70YI(1); FA 2006, Sch 8 para 7*].

(4) A '*long funding finance lease*' is a long funding lease that meets the *finance lease test* at (2) above (disregarding the connected persons rule). [*CAA 2001, s 70YI(1); FA 2006, Sch 8 para 7*].

(5) The '*minimum lease payments*' are the minimum payments under the lease over the term of the lease (including any initial payment). In the case of the lessee, they also include so much of any 'residual amount' as is guaranteed by him or a person connected with him. In the case of the lessor, they also include so much of any 'residual amount' as is guaranteed by the lessee or a person who is not connected with the lessor. Any payment representing charges for services or representing 'taxes' to be paid by the lessor must be excluded from 'minimum payments' for the purposes of this definition. ('*Taxes*' means UK or foreign taxes or duties, but not income tax, corporation tax or foreign equivalents.) '*Residual amount*' means so much of the 'fair value' (see the 'lease payments test' in (2) above) of the plant or machinery subject to the lease as cannot reasonably be expected to be recovered by the lessor from the payments under the lease. [*CAA 2001, s 70YE; FA 2006, Sch 8 para 7*]. This definition of 'minimum lease payments' is based on GAAP (Treasury Explanatory Notes to Finance Bill 2006).

(6) For the purposes of these provisions, the *market value* of any plant or machinery at any time is to be determined on the assumption of a disposal by an absolute owner free from all leases and other encumbrances. [*CAA 2001, s 70YI(2); FA 2006, Sch 8 para 7*].

Lessors

[11.46] Expenditure incurred on the provision of plant or machinery for leasing under a long funding lease is not qualifying expenditure for the purposes of plant and machinery capital allowances. [*CAA 2001, s 34A; FA 2006, Sch 8 para 3*].

Where expenditure on plant or machinery is already included in qualifying expenditure and the plant or machinery begins to be leased under a long funding lease, a disposal event then occurs and a disposal value must be brought into account as follows.

- If the lease is a 'long funding operating lease' (see **11.45**(3) above), the disposal value is the market value of the plant or machinery at commencement of the lease.
- If the lease is a 'long funding finance lease' (see **11.45**(4) above), the disposal value depends on the date of the 'inception' (see *CAA 2001, s 70YI(1)*) of the lease.

Where the inception of the lease is on or after 13 November 2008, the disposal value is the greater of the market value of the plant or machinery at commencement of the lease and the 'qualifying lease payments'. The *'qualifying lease payments'* means the minimum payments under the lease, including any initial payment but excluding so much of any payment as falls (or would fall) under GAAP to be treated as the gross return on investment, i.e. the interest element. Any payment representing charges for services or representing 'taxes' (as in **11.45**(5) above) to be paid by the lessor must also be excluded.

Where the inception of the lease was before 13 November 2008, the disposal value was the amount that would have fallen to be recognised as the lessor's net investment in the lease if accounts had been prepared in accordance with GAAP on the date (the *'relevant date'*) on which the lessor's net investment in the lease was first recognised in his books or other financial records. In relation to leases granted after 12 December 2007, any rentals made (or due) under the lease on or before the relevant date were treated for these purposes as made (and due) on the day after the relevant date. In relation to leases granted after 11 March 2008, the lessor's net investment in the lease was calculated for these purposes as if he had no liabilities of any kind at any time on the relevant date, but only if the effect of doing so was to increase the disposal value.

[*CAA 2001, s 61(1)(ee), (2), (6)–(9); FA 2006, Sch 8 para 5; FA 2008, Sch 20 para 4; FA 2009, Sch 32 paras 1,2, 5*]. (See **11.24** above as regards disposal events and disposal values generally.)

Where the owner of plant or machinery has been leasing it under a long funding lease and ceases to do so but continues to use it for the purposes of a qualifying activity (see **11.4** above), writing-down allowances are available to him as if he had, on the day after the cessation, incurred capital expenditure on the acquisition of that plant or machinery and as if he owned it as a result of that notional capital expenditure. The plant or machinery is thereafter treated as if it were not the same plant or machinery that existed previously. The amount of the notional capital expenditure is equal to the 'termination amount' in relation to the long funding lease under which the plant or machinery was last leased. [*CAA 2001, s 13A; FA 2006, Sch 8 para 2*]. However, neither a first-year allowance (see **11.14** above) nor an annual investment allowance (see **11.13** above) is available on the notional capital expenditure, and nor can it qualify for short-life asset treatment as in **11.30** above. The *termination amount'* is determined as follows.

- If that lease terminated as a result of a disposal event or if a disposal event is triggered by the termination, the termination amount is the disposal value that would have fallen to be brought into account by the lessor on the fictional assumptions that he had been entitled to capital allowances on the plant or machinery and had claimed his full entitlement. 'Disposal event' is itself to be construed in accordance with those assumptions. See generally **11.24** above as regards disposal events and disposal values.

- If the above does not apply and the lease is a 'long funding operating lease' (see **11.45**(3) above), the termination amount is the market value of the plant or machinery immediately after the termination.
- If the above does not apply and the lease is a 'long funding finance lease' (see **11.45**(4) above), the termination amount is the value at which, immediately after the termination, the plant or machinery is recognised in the lessor's books or other financial records.

[*CAA 2001, s 70YG; FA 2006, Sch 8 para 7*].

Note that where plant or machinery either begins or ceases to be leased under a long funding lease, there is also, by virtue of *TCGA 1992, s 25A*, as amended, a deemed disposal and reacquisition, at similar values as above, for CGT purposes. See Tolley's Capital Gains Tax.

Election available to lessors

The Treasury has made regulations enabling a lessor to elect for his plant and machinery leases to be treated as long funding leases if they would not otherwise be so treated; the election cannot be made on an individual lease by lease basis. For guidance, see the HMRC Technical Note referred to in **11.43** above and see also www.hmrc.gov.uk/leasing/long-funding-lease-election.pdf. The election (a 'long funding lease election') applies to all the lessor's 'eligible leases' (as defined by *SI 2007 No 304, Reg 3*) and 'qualifying incidental leases' that are finalised on or after the effective date, but does not affect the lessees' position. The election must be made during the period beginning with the end of the tax year to which it relates and ending on the first anniversary of 31 January following that tax year; it must be made in a tax return or an amended tax return. It can be revoked, by means of an amended return, within the permitted time for making it but is thereafter irrevocable. The election must specify the effective date, which cannot precede the period of account or (as the case may be) the tax year to which it relates and cannot in any case be earlier than 1 April 2006. Leases of less than 12 months' duration (except as below) and leases finalised before 1 April 2006 are excluded from being eligible leases for these purposes, as are certain other leases. A '*qualifying incidental lease*' is a plant or machinery lease that is wholly incidental to an eligible lease and which would itself have been an eligible lease if its term were 12 months or more. [*FA 2006, Sch 8 para 16; SI 2007 No 304*].

Fixtures

[11.47] The fixtures rules at **11.33** *et seq.* above do not apply, to determine either ownership or entitlement to allowances of either the lessee or the lessor, where plant or machinery that is (or becomes) a fixture is the subject of a long funding lease. If the lessee under the long funding lease himself leases out all or any of the plant or machinery under a lease that is not a long funding lease, the provisions at **11.33** *et seq.* are similarly disapplied as regards both the lessor and the lessee under that sub-lease. [*CAA 2001, ss 172(2A), 172A; FA 2006, Sch 8 para 9*]. Thus, the allowances (for expenditure on fixtures) available to any such lessors and lessees are to be determined under the rules applicable to long funding leases, rather than the rules applicable to fixtures.

Miscellaneous

[11.48] The following matters are relevant.

Mixed leases

There is provision for a situation where plant or machinery is leased with other types of asset (whether plant or machinery or not). In such case, different leases are deemed to exist so that the above rules (and those at **73.94–73.96 TRADING INCOME**) can be applied to each such notional lease (known as a '*derived lease*' — see, for example, **11.45**(1)(B) above). [*CAA 2001, ss 70L, 70M; FA 2006, Sch 8 para 7*].

Transfers, assignments etc.

Where a *lessor* of plant or machinery transfers it to a new lessor (other than by granting him a lease), it is treated for the purposes of these provisions (as regards lessors) as the termination of the existing lease and the creation of a new lease commencing at the date of transfer (which may or may not be the case in reality). Provided there is effectively no change to the term of the original lease or to the payments due under it, then, as regards the new lessor, the new lease retains the classification of the original lease (i.e. as a long funding lease or as a lease other than a long funding lease, as the case may be) and, as regards the lessee, the old and new leases are treated as a single continuing lease. [*CAA 2001, s 70W; FA 2006, Sch 8 para 7*].

The above also applies, with the appropriate modifications, where a *lessee* of plant or machinery transfers it to a new lessee. [*CAA 2001, s 70X; FA 2006, Sch 8 para 7*].

Extension of the term of a lease

Where the term of a *long funding operating lease* (see **11.45**(3) above) is extended as a result of one or more specified events (involving variations to the provisions of the lease, the granting or exercise of options etc.), a new lease is deemed to begin. [*CAA 2001, s 70YB; FA 2006, Sch 8 para 7*].

Where the term of a lease that is *not* a long funding lease is extended as a result of one or more specified events (as above), it is necessary to consider whether or not it thereby becomes a long funding lease. If, were it to be assumed that the lease has then terminated and a new lease commenced, the new lease would be a long funding lease, or at least that assumption is made, and the 'new' lease is a long funding lease as regards the lessor. If not, the term of the lease is taken to be the term as extended. [*CAA 2001, s 70YC; FA 2006, Sch 8 para 7*].

Tax avoidance involving international leasing

There are anti-avoidance rules aimed at arrangements made to lease plant and machinery into the UK, and then lease it back out again (other than under a long funding lease) in order to obtain the benefit of UK capital allowances. The rules deem the leasing by the UK resident to be long funding leasing, so that capital allowances are not available to him. They apply where the provision of the asset by the non-UK resident is itself long funding leasing as regards the UK resident or is under a contract within **11.61** below (hire-purchase contracts etc.), such that the UK resident would otherwise be entitled to capital allowances. They are not aimed at normal commercial arrangements (see also Treasury Explanatory Notes to Finance Bill 2006). [*CAA 2001, s 70V; FA 2006, Sch 8 para 7; ITA 2007, Sch 1 para 398; CTA 2010, Sch 1 para 331*].

Sale and leaseback/lease and leaseback arrangements

Where an existing long funding lessor transfers (e.g. by selling or leasing) the plant or machinery that is the subject of the existing lease to another person and leases the plant or machinery back from him, the leaseback is a long funding lease as regards both of them. Similar treatment is applied where the leaseback is via a series of leases. [*CAA 2001, s 70Y; FA 2006, Sch 8 para 7*].

Change in the accountancy classification of a long funding lease

There are rules to cater for changes in generally accepted accounting practice (GAAP) such that an operating lease falls to be reclassified as a finance lease for accounting purposes or *vice versa*. [*CAA 2001, s 70YA; FA 2006, Sch 8 para 7*].

Increase in proportion of residual amount guaranteed

The following applies as regards the lessor if, in the case of a lease other than a long funding lease and as a result of arrangements, there is an increase in the proportion of the residual amount that is guaranteed by the lessee (or by a person not connected with the lessor) (as to which see **11.45**(5) above) and the lease would have been a long funding lease if those arrangements had been made before its 'inception' (see *CAA 2001, s 70YI(1)*). The lease is treated as terminated, and a new lease treated as commenced, as at the time of the arrangement (or the latest arrangement if more than one). [*CAA 2001, s 70YD; FA 2006, Sch 8 para 7*].

Commencement/transitional provisions

[11.49] The long funding leasing rules above (and those at **73.94–73.96** TRADING INCOME) apply in respect of a lease where one of the conditions at (a) and (b) below is met. However, regardless of these conditions, a lease 'finalised' (see below) before 21 July 2005 cannot be a long funding lease (but this let-out is itself disapplied if the lessor does not come within the charge to UK tax until after 17 May 2006).

(a)   Condition 1 is that the lease is not an 'excepted lease' and that it is 'finalised' on or after 1 April 2006 or the 'commencement' (see *CAA 2001, s 70YI(1)*) of its term is on or after that date.

(b)   Condition 2 applies if the commencement of the term of the lease was before 1 April 2006 but the plant or machinery is not brought into use by the person concerned for the purposes of a qualifying activity (see **11.4** above) until on or after that date. (This covers, for example, the situation where the person concerned becomes UK resident on or after that date, such that his activity becomes a qualifying activity.) The person concerned may be the lessor or the lessee depending on from whose point of view one is applying the provisions.

There are regulations enabling a *lessor* to elect for a lease to be treated, as regards him only, as a long funding lease if it would not otherwise be such a lease, but the election cannot be made on an individual lease by lease basis. See **11.46** above.

For these purposes, a lease is '*finalised*' when there is a written contract for it between lessor and lessee, the contract is unconditional (or any conditions have already been met) and there are no terms still to be agreed.

For the purposes of (a) above, a lease is an '*excepted lease*' if it meets *all* the following conditions.

(i)   Condition 1 is that before 21 July 2005 there was written evidence of an agreement or common understanding (the '*pre-existing heads of agreement*') between (or effectively between) lessor and lessee as to the 'principal terms of the lease' (as defined).

(ii) Condition 2 is that the leased plant or machinery was 'under construction' (as defined) before 1 April 2006.

(iii) Condition 3 is that the lease is 'finalised' (see above) before 1 April 2007 (but see below).

(iv) Condition 4 is that the commencement of the term of the lease is before 1 April 2007 (but see below).

(v)   Condition 5 is that the lessee is the person(s) identified as such in the 'pre-existing heads of agreement' (within (i) above).

(vi) Condition 6 is that the principal terms of the lease are not materially different from those in the 'pre-existing heads of agreement' (within (i) above).

The date in (iii) and (iv) above is deferred to 1 April 2009 if construction of the asset proceeds continuously from 1 April 2006 (and at the normal pace for an asset of its type) and the lease commences as soon as is practicable after construction is substantially complete. There is provision to treat this condition as satisfied if it is failed only by reason of unforeseen events beyond the control of the parties (including the main constructor).

There are rules (see *FA 2006, Sch 8 paras 20, 25*) as to how these transitional provisions are to be applied in a case where the 'pre-existing heads of agreement' (see (i) above) relates to two or more assets.

If a person incurs expenditure before 19 July 2006 for leasing under a long funding lease which does not meet all the conditions in (i)–(vi) above, but in respect of which there was a 'pre-existing heads of agreement' before 21 July 2005 (as in (i) above), such expenditure (the '*old expenditure*') is treated as separate from any expenditure incurred on or after date (the '*new expenditure*'). *FA 2006, Sch 8 para 22* provides rules, for this purpose only, as to the time at which an amount of expenditure is treated as being incurred. The old and new expenditure are treated as if incurred on separate assets leased under separate leases; the notional lease relating to the old expenditure is then deemed to be an excepted lease. The lease rentals are apportioned between the two notional leases in a just and reasonable manner. These splitting provisions apply in determining the income tax or corporation tax liability of anyone who is at any time the lessor or the lessee under the actual lease.

Mixed leases

Where a lease is a mixed lease (see **11.48** above), it is first necessary to consider whether the mixed lease is itself an 'excepted lease' for the purposes of these transitional provisions. If it is not, one can then consider separately, in the case of each derived lease, whether that lease is an 'excepted lease'.

Transfers

There is provision to ensure that a lease that is outside the long funding leasing regime (by virtue of the commencement/transitional provisions) remains outside that regime if it is transferred from one lessor to another or from one lessee to another. For this to have effect, there must be no effective change to the term of the lease or to the payments due under it, and the lessor or lessee (as the case may be) must be within the charge to UK tax immediately before the transfer.

[*FA 2006, Sch 8 paras 15–27; ITA 2007, Sch 1 para 624*].

Special leasing

[11.50] '*Special leasing*' is the hiring out of plant or machinery otherwise than in the course of a trade or other qualifying activity. It is itself a qualifying activity for the purpose of claiming plant and machinery allowances. However, plant or machinery provided for use in a dwelling-house or flat is excluded from being qualifying expenditure. See **11.3** above.

Where a person hires out more than one item of plant and machinery, he has a *separate qualifying activity* in relation to each item. A qualifying activity of special leasing begins when the plant or machinery is first hired out. It is permanently discontinued if the lessor permanently ceases to hire it out. [*CAA 2001, s 19(2)–(4)*].

Manner of making allowances and charges for special leasing

For *income tax*, a plant and machinery allowance is given effect by deduction from the person's income for the tax year in question from qualifying activities of special leasing. If, however, the plant or machinery was not used for the whole (or for a part) of the tax year for the purposes of a qualifying activity carried on by the *lessee*, the allowance (or a proportionate part) can only be set against the lessor's income from that particular qualifying activity of special leasing. In all cases the deduction is given effect at Step 2 of the calculation of income tax liability (see **1.7 ALLOWANCES AND TAX RATES**). A claim for an allowance may be made outside a tax return. Any excess of allowances over the income for a tax year against which they may be set is carried forward without time limit against future such income. A balancing charge is taxed as income and is included in the income against which an allowance may be set as above.

[CAA 2001, s 3(4), ss 258, 259; ITTOIA 2005, Sch 1 para 548; ITA 2007, Sch 1 para 404].

Simon's Taxes. See B3.385.

Overseas leasing

[11.51] For the purposes of the provisions described at **11.52–11.59** below, plant or machinery is used for overseas leasing if it is leased to a person who:

(1) is not resident in the UK, and
(2) does not use the plant or machinery exclusively for earning profits chargeable to UK tax (which includes profits from exploration or exploitation activities carried on in the UK or its territorial sea).

However, in determining whether plant or machinery is used for overseas leasing, no account is to be taken of any lease finalised on or after **1 April 2006** (as to which see **11.49** above).

For the purpose of (2) above, profits chargeable to UK tax do not include profits in respect of which the trader etc. is entitled to tax relief under a double taxation agreement. This does not apply in the case of leases entered into before 16 March 1993 for which, in addition, the use of the plant or machinery does not have to be *exclusively* for the purposes stated.

[CAA 2001, s 105(2)–(4), Sch 3 para 21; FA 2006, Sch 9 para 13; TIOPA 2010, Sch 8 para 58].

From 24 May 2007, HMRC accept that in some circumstances the provisions described below may be contrary to European Community law. Therefore, in cases where the lessee is resident in a country within the European Economic Area (EEA), HMRC have adopted the following approach.

*   Where the EEA country in question gives the lessee a relief that is broadly equivalent to capital allowances, they will restrict the lessor's writing-down allowances to 10% as in **11.52** below but will not apply **11.53** below (prohibition of allowances).
*   Where the EEA country in question does not give the lessee a broadly equivalent relief, they will accept that neither **11.52** nor **11.53** below applies and that the lessor is entitled to the normal rate of writing-down allowances.

The EEA consists of all the EU countries plus Norway, Iceland and Liechtenstein.

(HMRC Brief 40/07, 24 May 2007).

For the purposes of the provisions described below, a 'lease' includes a sub-lease, with 'lessor' and 'lessee' being construed accordingly, and 'leasing' is regarded as including the letting of any asset on hire, or of a ship or aircraft on charter (see *Barclays Mercantile Industrial Finance Ltd v Melluish* Ch D 1990, 63 TC 95 at **11.55** below). *[CAA 2001, s 105(1)]*.

Where there is a chain of leases, HMRC consider that the provisions apply where any lessee in the chain falls within (1) and (2) above (Revenue Tax Bulletin April 1999 p 654). In determining whether or not overseas leasing is 'protected leasing' (see **11.52** and **11.56** below), HMRC take the view that every lease in the chain must be considered; if the leasing under any of the leases is not 'protected leasing', the overseas leasing restrictions apply to the whole chain (Revenue Internet Statement 3 February 2005).

The first-year allowances at **11.14**(a)–(h) above are not generally available in respect of expenditure on plant or machinery for leasing (see **11.14**(v) above for details and exceptions).

Simon's Taxes. See B3.340T–340X.

Separate pooling and restriction of writing-down allowances

[11.52] Separate pooling provisions apply to qualifying expenditure (see **11.3** above) if it is incurred on the provision of plant or machinery for leasing and if that plant or machinery is at any time in the 'designated period' (see **11.54** below) used for overseas leasing other than 'protected leasing' (see **11.56** below). They do not apply to long-life asset expenditure (see **11.31** above) or to expenditure which can only be allocated to a single asset pool (see **11.23** above). Qualifying expenditure meeting the above conditions can only be allocated to a *class pool* (see **11.23** above), known as the *overseas leasing pool*. The final chargeable period (see **11.23** above) of the overseas leasing pool is the chargeable period at the end of which circumstances are such that no further disposal values (see **11.24** above) could fall to be brought into account.

Writing-down allowances on qualifying expenditure meeting the above conditions are restricted to **10% p.a.** The restriction applies whether such expenditure falls to be allocated to the overseas leasing pool or to a single asset pool (including a pool for partial non-business use as in **11.29** above). The 10% rate does not, however, displace the 6% rate applicable to long-life asset expenditure (see **11.31** above). The 10% allowance is proportionately reduced or increased if the chargeable period is less or more than a year, or if the qualifying activity has been carried on for part only of the chargeable period. A claim for a writing-down allowance may require it to be reduced to a specified amount.

[*CAA 2001, ss 56(5), 65(4), 107, 109*].

When plant or machinery in the overseas leasing pool is disposed of to a CONNECTED PERSON (**21**) (otherwise than on a change in the members of a partnership or a company reconstruction in circumstances such that, in each case, the qualifying activity is treated as continuing) the disposal value to be brought into account (see generally **11.24** above) is its market value or, if lower, its original cost, and the person acquiring it may claim allowances on the same value. [*CAA 2001, s 108; ITTOIA 2005, Sch 1 para 537; CTA 2009, Sch 1 para 485; CTA 2010, Sch 1 para 334*].

Prohibition of allowances

[11.53] No writing-down or balancing allowances are available in respect of qualifying expenditure meeting the conditions in **11.52** above if the plant or machinery is used other than for a 'qualifying purpose' (see **11.55** below) *and*:

(i)   there is more than one year between consecutive payments due under the lease; or

(ii)   any payments other than periodical payments are due under the lease or under any collateral agreement; or

(iii) any payment expressed monthly under the lease or any collateral agreement is not the same as any other such payment, but disregarding variations due to changes in rates of tax, capital allowances, interest which is linked with rates applicable to inter-bank loans or changes in premiums for insurances of any kind by a person not connected with the lessor or lessee; or

(iv)   either the lease is for a period exceeding 13 years or there is any provision for its extension or renewal or for the grant of a new lease such that the leasing period could exceed 13 years; or

(v)   at any time, the lessor or CONNECTED PERSON (**21**) could be entitled to receive from the lessee or any other person a payment (not insurance money) of an amount determined before expiry of the lease and referable to the value of the plant or machinery at or after that expiry (whether or not the payment relates to a disposal of the plant or machinery).

[*CAA 2001, s 110*].

Where allowances (including any first-year allowance) have been made (and not fully withdrawn under the excess relief provisions in **11.58** below) but by reason of any event in the 'designated period' (see **11.54** below) the expenditure is brought within the above provisions, the net allowances are clawed back by means of a balancing charge. For this purpose only, the allowances made are determined as if the item of plant or machinery in question were the only item, i.e. as if it had not been pooled. A disposal value equal to the balance of the expenditure is also brought into account so as to effectively remove the item from the pool. Where the item was acquired from a CONNECTED PERSON (**21**), or as a part of a series of transactions with connected persons, allowances made to those persons are also taken into account in computing the balancing charge, with any actual consideration on a connected persons transaction being ignored and with the amount of such allowances being adjusted 'in a just and reasonable manner' where balancing allowances/charges have already been made in respect of the item in question. This does not apply in the case of transactions between connected persons which are treated as not involving a cessation of the quality activity, i.e. where there is a change in the members of a partnership but there is at least one continuing individual or corporate partner or where the activity is treated as continuing by virtue of *CTA 2010, Pt 22 Ch 1* (previously *ICTA 1988, s 343*) (company reconstructions without change of ownership). [*CAA 2001, ss 114, 115; CTA 2009, Sch 1 para 487; CTA 2010, Sch 1 para 336*].

Designated period

[11.54] For the purposes of these provisions, the '*designated period*' is the period of ten years after the item of plant or machinery in question is first brought into use by the person who incurred the expenditure. It is, however, brought to an end at any time within that ten-year period at which that person ceases to own the item, disregarding any disposal to a CONNECTED PERSON (21) or on a change in members of a partnership where there is at least one continuing individual or corporate partner. For leases entered into before 16 March 1993, the ten-year period was reduced to one of four years if the plant or machinery was used for a 'qualifying purpose' (see **11.55** below); for later leases, this continues to apply only for the purposes of the provisions for separate pooling of ships (see **11.28** above) and short-life assets (see **11.30** above). [CAA 2001, 106; CTA 2009, Sch 1 para 484].

Qualifying purpose

[11.55] Plant or machinery on which a person (the buyer) has incurred expenditure is used for a 'qualifying purpose' at any time if, at that time:

(i)   the lessee uses it for the purposes of a qualifying activity without leasing it; and had the lessee bought the plant or machinery himself at that time, his expenditure would have fallen to be wholly or partly included in his available qualifying expenditure (see **11.23** above) for a chargeable period; or

(ii)   the buyer uses it for 'short-term leasing' (see **11.56** below); or

(iii)   the lessee uses it for 'short-term leasing' and is either UK resident or so uses it in the course of a qualifying activity carried on in the UK; or

(iv)   the buyer uses it for the purposes of a qualifying activity without leasing it.

For the purposes of (ii) and (iv) above, where the plant or machinery is disposed of to a connected person, or on a change in the members of a partnership where there is at least one continuing individual or corporate partner, the new owner is treated as the 'buyer'.

[CAA 2001, ss 122, 125; CTA 2009, Sch 1 paras 488, 489].

As regards the reference to 'leasing' in (i) above, the word is to be construed in accordance with the narrow test applicable to leases of land, so that distribution agreements entered into by film lessee companies were not leases for these purposes but arrangements entered into in the ordinary course of their businesses (*Barclays Mercantile Industrial Finance Ltd v Melluish* Ch D 1990, 63 TC 95).

Ships, aircraft and transport containers

Without prejudice to (i)–(iv) above, a ship is also used for a 'qualifying purpose' at any time when it is let on charter in the course of a trade of operating ships if the lessor is resident, or carries on his trade, in the UK and is responsible as principal (or appoints another person to be responsible in his stead) for navigating and managing the ship and for defraying substantially all its expenses except those directly incidental to a particular voyage or charter period. The same applies with necessary modifications in relation to aircraft. However, neither ship nor aircraft chartering qualifies if the main object, or one of them, of the chartering (or of a series of transactions of which the chartering was one) was the obtaining by any person of an unrestricted writing-down allowance. A transport container is also used for a 'qualifying *purpose*' at any time when it is leased in the course of a trade carried on in the UK or by a UK resident if either the trade is one of operating ships or aircraft and the container is at other times used by the trader in connection with such operation, or the container is leased under a succession of leases to different persons who, or most of whom, are not connected with each other. [*CAA 2001, ss 123, 124, Sch 3 para 23*].

Protected leasing

[11.56] 'Protected leasing' means 'short-term leasing' (see below) or, in the case of a ship, aircraft or transport container, its use for a qualifying purpose (see **11.55** above). [*CAA 2001, s 105(5)*].

'*Short-term leasing*' means leasing an item of plant or machinery in such a manner:

(i)   that (A) the number of consecutive days for which it is leased to the same person will normally be less than 30 and (B) the total number of days to the same person in any period of 12 months will normally be less than 90; or

(ii)   that (A) the number of consecutive days for which it is leased to the same person will not normally exceed 365 and (B) the aggregate of the periods for which it is leased to lessees not falling within **11.55**(i) above in any period of 4 consecutive years within the 'designated period' (see **11.54** above) will not exceed 2 years.

For the above purposes, persons who are connected with each other (see **21 CONNECTED PERSONS**) are to be treated as the same person. Where plant or machinery is leased from a group of items of similar description and not separately identifiable, all the items in the group may be treated as used for short-term leasing if substantially the whole of the items in the group are so used.

[*CAA 2001, s 121*].

Joint lessees

[11.57] The following applies where an item of plant or machinery is leased (otherwise than by 'protected leasing' — see **11.56** above) to two or more persons jointly, and at least one of the joint lessees is a person within **11.51**(1) and (2) above (definition of overseas leasing). An unrestricted writing-down allowance is due if the lessees use the item for the purposes of a qualifying activity or activities (but not for leasing) but only to the extent that it appears that the profits therefrom throughout the 'designated period' (see **11.54** above), or the period of the lease if shorter, will be chargeable to UK income tax or corporation tax. The part of the expenditure so qualifying for unrestricted allowances is treated as if it were expenditure on a separate item of plant or machinery (outside the overseas leasing pool) with the remaining part treated as expenditure within the overseas leasing provisions, with such apportionments as are necessary.

Excess relief is recoverable under **11.58** below if at any time in the designated period while the item is so leased, no lessee uses it for the purposes of a qualifying activity the profits of which are chargeable to UK tax as above (referred to below as *'eligible use'*) or if, at the end of the designated period, it appears that the actual extent of eligible use was less than anticipated. In the latter case the amount of excess relief recoverable is in proportion to the reduction in eligible use and any disposal value subsequently brought into account is apportioned to the extent of the eligible use as determined at the end of the designated period.

Recovery of excess relief

[11.58] Where expenditure has qualified for a normal writing-down allowance (or for a first-year allowance) and the plant or machinery is used for overseas leasing (other than 'protected leasing' — see **11.56** above) at any time in the 'designated period' (see **11.54** above), any 'excess relief' is recovered. This is achieved by means of a balancing charge of an amount equal to the excess relief, to be made on the person who owns the item when it is first so used, for the chargeable period in which it is first so used. The item is removed from its existing pool by means of a disposal value equal to the item's written-down value for capital allowances purposes at the end of that period. The *'excess relief'* is the excess, if any, of the allowances made, up to and including the chargeable period in question, over the maximum allowances that could have been made if the expenditure had been within **11.52** or **11.53** above from the outset. The allowances made are determined for this purpose as if the item in question were the only item, i.e. as if it had not been pooled with any other item of plant or machinery. The sum of the excess relief and the disposal value is then allocated to the appropriate pool (usually the overseas leasing pool) for the following chargeable period.

Where the person on whom the balancing charge falls to be made acquired the item in question from a CONNECTED PERSON (**21**), or as part of a series of transactions with connected persons, the allowances taken into account in computing the excess relief include the allowances made to such person(s), any consideration passing between them for the item being ignored. The amount of excess relief is adjusted 'in a just and reasonable manner' where balancing allowances/charges have been made on any of the transactions. However, these modifications do not apply in the case of transactions between connected persons which are treated as not involving a cessation of the quality activity, i.e. where there is a change in the members of a partnership but there is at least one continuing individual or corporate partner or where the activity is treated as continuing by virtue of *CTA 2010, Pt 22 Ch 1* (previously *ICTA 1988, s 343*) (company reconstructions without change of ownership).

In the case of a ship, any allowance previously postponed (see **11.15**, **11.28** above) cannot be made for any chargeable period in or after that in which the ship is first used for overseas leasing (other than protected leasing) within the designated period. The total of any such allowances is instead allocated to the appropriate pool for the following chargeable period as if it were itself qualifying expenditure.

[*CAA 2001, ss 111–113; CTA 2009, Sch 1 para 486; CTA 2010, Sch 1 para 335*].

Information

[11.59] Information must be provided to HMRC, by the then owner, where expenditure on plant or machinery has qualified for a normal writing-down allowance (or for a first-year allowance) and the item is subsequently used for overseas leasing (other than 'protected leasing'— see **11.56** above) at any time in the 'designated period' (see **11.54** above). Information must also be provided to HMRC, by the lessor, where plant or machinery is leased to joint lessees as described in **11.57** above and, in addition, if circumstances occur such that excess relief is recoverable. In all cases, the time limit for providing the information is three months after the end of the chargeable period in which the item is first so used (or the said circumstances occur), extended to 30 days after the informant came to know that the item was being so used (if he could not reasonably have been expected to know earlier).

Where expenditure has not yet qualified for a normal writing-down allowance or a first-year allowance or for either and the item is used for overseas leasing which is protected leasing, a claim for a first-year allowance or writing-down allowance thereon must be accompanied by a certificate describing the protected leasing.

[*CAA 2001, ss 118–120, 126*].

Miscellaneous

[11.60] The matters discussed at **11.61–11.70** below also apply for the purposes of capital allowances on plant and machinery.

Hire-purchase and similar contracts

[11.61] The following applies where a person incurs capital expenditure, on the provision of plant or machinery for the purposes of a trade or other qualifying activity, under a contract providing that he will (or may) become the owner of it on performance of the contract. One example of such a contract is a hire-purchase agreement. That person is treated for the purposes of plant and machinery allowances as the sole owner of the plant or machinery for as long as he is entitled to the benefit of the contract. When the plant or machinery is brought into use for the purposes of the qualifying activity, the full outstanding capital cost (i.e. excluding the hire or interest element) attracts capital allowances immediately. Any such capital payments made before it is brought into use attract allowances as they fall due.

As regards any such contract finalised on or after 1 April 2006 (as to which see **11.49** above) that, in accordance with generally accepted accounting practice (GAAP), falls to be treated as a lease (or would so fall if the person prepared accounts), the person mentioned above is treated as owning the plant or machinery only if the contract falls (or would fall) under GAAP to be treated by that person as a *finance lease*. At any time at which, by virtue only of the preceding rule, the lessee is *not* treated as owning the plant or machinery, no-one else is treated as owning it either; so, in these circumstances, neither lessee nor lessor are entitled to capital allowances. According to the Treasury Explanatory Notes to Finance Bill 2006, the treatment of ordinary hire-purchase contracts, with a nominal option fee payable to acquire the plant or machinery at the end of the lease, remains unaltered as such contracts will fall to be accounted for as finance leases.

Also, as regards contracts finalised on or after 1 April 2006, these provisions are extended so as to apply where the plant or machinery is used for the purposes of any overseas activity that would be a qualifying activity within **11.4** above if the person carrying it on were UK resident.

Also, as regards contracts finalised on or after 1 April 2006, any two or more agreements (or undertakings) are treated for these purposes as a single contract if, when taken together, they have the effect that the person concerned will (or may) become the owner of the plant or machinery on performance of the 'contract'.

If the person mentioned above is treated as owning the plant or machinery but the contract is not completed, so that he does not, in fact, become the owner of the plant or machinery, he is treated as ceasing to own it when he ceases to be entitled to the benefit of the contract. The resulting disposal value (see **11.24** above) depends on whether the plant or machinery has been brought into use for the purposes of the qualifying activity. If it has, the disposal value is

(i)   the total of any capital sums received by way of consideration, compensation, damages or insurance in respect of the person's rights under the contract or the plant or machinery itself, plus

(ii)   the capital element of all instalments treated as paid (see above) but not, in fact, paid.

This is subject to the over-riding rule that the disposal value cannot exceed the qualifying expenditure brought into account (see **11.24** above).

If the plant or machinery has not been so brought into use, the disposal value is the total in (i) above (but see below as regards assignments).

[*CAA 2001, ss 67, 68, Sch 3 para 15; FA 2006, Sch 9 para 12*].

See **73.42** TRADING INCOME as regards hire-purchase agreements relating to cars whose retail price when new exceeded £12,000.

The above rules do not apply to expenditure incurred on 'fixtures' within *CAA 2001, ss 172–204* (see **11.33** *et seq*. above), and if plant or machinery which has been treated under the above rules as owned by a person becomes such a fixture, he is treated as ceasing to own it at that time (unless it is treated as belonging to him under *sections 172–204*). [*CAA 2001, s 69, Sch 3 para 16*].

The above rules similarly do not apply (except in relation to deemed ownership of the asset concerned) if the person mentioned above acquires the plant or machinery for leasing under a 'finance lease' (as defined in **11.63** below, and note the exclusion of long funding leases from that definition from, broadly, 1 April 2006). [*CAA 2001, s 229(3), Sch 3 para 44*]. See Revenue Tax Bulletin June 1998 pp 539–544 for a general article on how these and associated capital allowance restrictions are intended to operate. See also **11.63** below and **73.79** TRADING INCOME as regards finance lease allowance restrictions. See **11.43** above as regards long funding leasing.

If the person entitled to the benefit of a hire-purchase or similar contract assigns that benefit before the plant or machinery is brought into use, and the assignee's allowances fall to be restricted under the anti-avoidance provisions at **11.63**(ii) below, both the disposal value and the expenditure against which it is set are increased by the capital expenditure he would have incurred if he had wholly performed the contract. The same applies in finance lease cases. This is to protect the assignee against an undue repression of qualifying expenditure by reference to the assignor's disposal value (see **11.63**(ii) below). [*CAA 2001, s 229*].

Consequences ensue where:

- a person (S) transfers (see *CAA 2001, s 70Y(3)*) plant or machinery to another person (B);
- at any time after the date of the transfer, the plant or machinery is available to be used by S or by a person (other than B) who is connected (within **21** CONNECTED PERSONS) with S (CS);
- it is available to be so used under a contract entered into on or after 13 November 2008 which provides that S or CS will (or may) become the owner of the plant or machinery on the performance of the contract (e.g. a hire-purchase agreement); and
- S or CS incurs capital expenditure on the provision of the plant or machinery under that contract.

The consequences are that no annual investment allowance (see **11.13** above) or first-year allowance (see **11.14** above) is available in respect of the expenditure of S or CS under the contract. Also, in determining the qualifying expenditure of S or CS, there is disregarded any excess of his expenditure over the disposal value to be brought into account by S. Where no such disposal value falls to be brought into account, the qualifying expenditure of S or CS (if otherwise greater) is restricted to the lesser of the market value of the plant or machinery, the capital expenditure (if any) incurred on it by S before the transfer and any capital expenditure incurred on it before the transfer by any person connected with S. *CAA 2001, ss 214, 215* (see **11.63**(ii) below) do not then apply in relation to the contract.

[*CAA 2001, s 229A; FA 2009, Sch 32 paras 21, 22*].

For a further anti-avoidance rule, see **11.48** above under Tax avoidance involving international leasing.

Simon's Taxes. See B3.340A, B3.340G.

Abortive expenditure

[11.62] The rules at **11.61** above for hire-purchase and similar contracts can equally be applied to expenditure under other contracts which proves to be abortive. A disposal value falls to be brought into account as in **11.61** above when the contract fails to be completed. Thus, for example, plant and machinery allowances can be obtained in respect of a non-refundable deposit paid on an item of plant or machinery which is never actually supplied, notwithstanding the fact that the item is never owned by the person incurring the expenditure.

Connected persons, leasebacks and other anti-avoidance measures

[11.63] See **21 CONNECTED PERSONS** for the definition of that term for these purposes.

(i) For disposals of plant or machinery acquired as a result of transaction(s) between connected persons, the limit on the disposal value (see **11.24** above) is to the greatest amount of qualifying expenditure incurred on it by any of the participants in the transaction(s) (after deducting any 'additional VAT rebates' made — see **11.2**(viii) above).

The normal absence of any requirement to bring a disposal value into account if none of the qualifying expenditure in question has been taken into account in determining available qualifying expenditure (see **11.24** above) does not apply if the person concerned acquired the plant or machinery as a result of such transaction(s) as are mentioned above *and* any earlier participant was required to bring a disposal value into account. Instead, the current participant's qualifying expenditure is deemed to be allocated (if this is not actually the case), for the chargeable period in which the current disposal event occurs, to whichever pool is appropriate, thus requiring the bringing into account of a disposal value (which is then subject to the above-mentioned limit). [*CAA 2001, s 62(2)–(4), s 64(2)–(5), s 239(5)(6)*].

(ii) Where plant or machinery is purchased from a connected person, or in a 'sale and leaseback transaction', or in transaction(s) from which the sole or main benefit appears to be the obtaining of a plant and machinery allowance, no annual investment allowance or first-year allowances (where otherwise relevant) are available (see **11.13**(vi), **11.14**(ix) above), and, in determining the buyer's qualifying expenditure, there is disregarded any excess of his expenditure (including any 'additional VAT liability' incurred in respect thereof — see **11.2**(viii) above) over the disposal value to be brought into account by the seller. Where no such disposal value is to be brought into account (e.g. where the seller is non-UK resident), the buyer's qualifying expenditure (if otherwise greater) is restricted to the lesser of:

(a) market value at time of sale; and

(b) the capital expenditure, if any, incurred by the seller or any person connected with him,

with modifications to allow for 'additional VAT liabilities' and 'rebates' — see **11.2**(viii) above.

For these purposes, a sale is a '*sale and leaseback transaction*' if the plant or machinery:

(A) continues to be used for the purposes of a 'qualifying activity' carried on by the seller (or, for transactions on or after 22 April 2009, by a connected person other than the buyer); or

(B) is used at some time after the sale for the purposes of a 'qualifying activity' carried on by the seller (or by a connected person other than the buyer) without having been used in the meantime for the purposes of any other 'qualifying activity' except that of leasing the plant or machinery.

For the purposes of these provisions, a *'qualifying activity'* is any activity within **11.4**(i)–(vii) above regardless of whether or not profits therefrom are within the charge to UK tax.

The above provisions apply to contracts for future delivery, hire-purchase etc. contracts, and hire-purchase etc. contract assignments as they apply to direct sales. They do not apply to the supply of unused plant or machinery in the ordinary course of the seller's business.

[*CAA 2001, s 213(1)(2), ss 214–218, 230–233, 241, 242; ITA 2007, Sch 1 para 403; FA 2008, Sch 20 para 6(8)(9)(15)(16)(19), Sch 24 paras 8, 12, 23; FA 2009, Sch 32 paras 23, 25*].

The 'sole or main benefit' restriction referred to above does not generally apply to straightforward finance leasing transactions (*Barclays Mercantile Industrial Finance Ltd v Melluish Ch D 1990, 63 TC 95*). However, subject to the repeals referred to below for transactions after 8 October 2007, the above rules are extended to further restrict allowances in the case of 'sale and finance leasebacks'. A *'sale and finance leaseback'* is a transaction:

• in which the plant or machinery continues to be used for the purposes of an activity carried on by the seller or by a connected person other than the buyer (for transactions on or after 22 April 2009, previously for the purposes of a 'qualifying activity' (as defined above) carried on by the seller); or

• in which the plant or machinery is used at some time after the sale for the purposes of a qualifying activity carried on by the seller (or by a connected person other than the buyer) without having been used in the meantime for the purposes of any other qualifying activity except that of leasing the plant or machinery; or

• in which the plant or machinery is used at some time after the sale etc. for the purposes of a non-qualifying activity carried on by the seller (or by a connected person other than the buyer) without having been used in the meantime for the purposes of a qualifying activity except that of leasing the plant or machinery,

where the availability of the plant or machinery for the use in question is a direct or indirect consequence of its having been leased under a 'finance lease'.

Where an item of plant or machinery is the subject of a sale and finance leaseback, the buyer's qualifying expenditure (*and* in this case the seller's disposal value, if any) is further limited to the item's notional written-down value, computed on the assumption that all available allowances have been made in full. There are also restrictions on the qualifying expenditure of any future owner of the item. Where the finance lessor has substantially divested himself of any risk that the lessee will default, the lessor's expenditure does not qualify for plant and machinery allowances at all (and this applies regardless of any election as below). Modifications to these rules allow for any 'additional VAT liabilities' and 'rebates' — see **11.2**(viii) above.

A *'finance lease'* is any arrangements for plant or machinery to be leased or made available such that the arrangements (or arrangements in which they are comprised) would fall, in accordance with generally accepted accounting practice (see **73.18** TRADING INCOME), to be treated in the accounts of one or more of those companies as a finance lease or as a loan. With effect, broadly, from 1 April 2006 (but see **11.49** above), any arrangements which are a long funding lease (as in **11.45**) as regards the lessor were excluded from the definition of 'finance lease' for these purposes (and for the purposes of (iv) below). However, where the sale etc. part of the sale and finance leaseback occurs after 8 October 2007, such long funding leases are no longer excluded.

In the case of sale and leaseback transactions (and, prior to the repeals referred to below, sale and finance leaseback transactions) within the above provisions, a joint (irrevocable) election may be made by the seller (or assignor) and the lessor (within two years of the sale etc.) provided that:

- the seller (or assignor) incurred capital expenditure on acquiring the plant or machinery unused (and not second-hand) and not under a transaction itself within the above provisions;
- the sale etc. takes place not more than four months after the plant or machinery is first brought into use for any purpose; and
- the seller (or assignor) has not claimed capital allowances for the expenditure or included it in a pool of qualifying expenditure.

The effect of the election is that no allowances are made to the seller (or assignor) in respect of the expenditure, and that allowances which are accordingly available to the lessor are given by reference to the lesser of his expenditure and the amount in (b) above, i.e. disregarding the current market value at the time of the sale etc. (and, in the case of sale and finance leasebacks, the item's notional written-down value).

The rules restricting the seller's disposal value, the buyer's qualifying expenditure and the qualifying expenditure of any future owner, and those denying the buyer first-year allowances, are repealed for *sale and finance leasebacks* taking place after 8 October 2007, i.e. where the sale etc. part of the arrangement occurs after that date. Instead, sale and finance leasebacks are generally excluded from 'short lease' treatment and thus brought within the scope of the long funding leasing rules at **11.43** above (see **11.45**(1)(A) above). It remains the case, as above, that the finance lessor is denied plant and machinery allowances where he has divested himself of the risk that the lessee will default.

[*CAA 2001, ss 219, 221–228, 243–245, Sch 3 paras 45, 51; FA 2006, Sch 9 para 14; FA 2008, Sch 20 para 6(10)–(14)(17)(19); FA 2009, Sch 32 paras 24, 26*].

(iii) Where a disposal value is required to be brought into account in respect of a car costing over £12,000 (see **11.27** above) on a sale (or on the performance of a contract) within any of the provisions in (ii) above, the disposal value is equal to the lesser of market value at the time of the event and the capital expenditure incurred (or treated as incurred) on it by the person disposing of it. The new owner is treated as having incurred capital expenditure on the car of the same amount. [*CAA 2001, s 79; FA 2009, Sch 11 paras 4, 26–29*]. This rule ceases to be relevant following the repeal of the 'expensive car' rules at **11.27**, and is itself repealed. The repeal has effect immediately where the disposal value relates to new regime expenditure and has effect for chargeable periods beginning on or after 6 April 2014 where the disposal value relates to old regime expenditure. (See **11.27** for what is meant by new regime expenditure and old regime expenditure.)

A comparable rule applies where a disposal value is required to be brought into account in similar circumstances in respect of a car the expenditure on which is new regime expenditure and which is allocated to a single asset pool due to non-business use. If allowances fall to be restricted as in (ii) above, the disposal value is equal to the lesser of market value at the time of the disposal event and the capital expenditure incurred (or treated as incurred) on the car by the person disposing of it. The new owner is treated as having incurred capital expenditure on the car of the same amount. [*CAA 2001, s 208A; FA 2009, Sch 11 paras 10, 26–28*].

(iv) In a case where an item of plant or machinery is the subject of a sale and finance leaseback (as defined in (ii) above) and the seller's disposal value falls to be restricted as in (ii) above, further anti-avoidance provisions apply in relation to periods ending after 16 March 2004 (but subject to the transitional provisions below) so as to limit the amount of lease rentals deductible in computing the lessee's income or profits. These further provisions are repealed for sale and finance leasebacks taking place after 8 October 2007, i.e. where the sale etc. part of the arrangement occurs after that date (but, as regards the finance lessee, continue to apply to 'lease and finance leasebacks' — see below).

The amount deductible is limited to the aggregate of the finance charges shown in the accounts and the depreciation that would have been charged if the value of the item at the beginning of the leaseback had been taken for this purpose to be equal to the restricted disposal value. In the period of account in which the leaseback terminates:

- the above restriction on deductible lease rentals does not apply to any refund of lease rentals;
- the aforementioned aggregate is increased by a proportion of the net book value of the item immediately before the termination, such proportion to be computed in accordance with a formula in *CAA 2001, s 228B(4)*;
- the lessee's income/profits from the qualifying activity for the purposes of which the leased item was used immediately before the termination are increased by a proportion of the original consideration on the sale less the restricted disposal value, such proportion to be computed in accordance with a formula in *CAA 2001, s 228C(3)*.

The above rules do not apply to a lessee who became the lessee by means of an assignment of the lease.

For the above purposes and those below, a *'termination'* of a leaseback includes an assignment of the lessee's interest, the making of any other arrangements under which a person other than the lessee becomes liable to make payments under the leaseback and any variation as a result of which the leaseback ceases to be a finance lease.

In any case in which the above restriction on the lessee's deductible lease rentals potentially applies (or would do so if he had not obtained his interest by way of assignment), the following apply in computing the income/profits of the *lessor* for a period of account. Amounts receivable by the lessor under the leaseback are included as income without netting off any amounts due by the lessor to the lessee. However, amounts receivable are not included as income to the extent that they exceed the aggregate of the gross earnings under the leaseback as shown in the lessor's accounts (effectively the finance charge element of the lease rentals) and a proportion of the restricted disposal value, such proportion to be computed in accordance with a formula in *CAA 2001, s 228D(4)*. These rules do not apply if the lessee became the lessee by means of an assignment of the lease made before 17 March 2004.

Where the leaseback terminates and the lessor disposes of the plant or machinery in circumstances such that the resulting disposal value is limited under the general rule in **11.24** above (disposal value of plant or machinery to be limited to qualifying expenditure incurred on its acquisition) or by that rule as modified under (i) above, then, in computing the lessor's income/profits for the period of account in which termination occurs, any amount refunded to the lessee is deductible only to the extent that it does not exceed the limited disposal value.

Special provision is made for cases in which accounts are not drawn up in accordance with generally accepted accounting practice (GAAP). Additionally, the above rules are adapted, insofar as they relate to the lessee, in a case where the leaseback does not fall under GAAP to be treated in the lessee's accounts as a finance lease but does fall to be so treated in the accounts of a person connected with the lessee. If the leaseback falls to be so treated in the accounts of neither the lessee nor a person connected with him, those rules are disapplied. In that case, however, the lessee's income/profits for the period of account during which it begins are increased by the sale consideration less the restricted disposal value.

Where plant or machinery, whilst continuing to be the subject of a sale and finance leaseback, is leased to the original owner, or a person connected with him, under an operating lease (meaning, for this purpose, a lease that does not fall under GAAP to be treated in the lessee's accounts as a finance lease), the following apply. In computing the income/profits of the lessee (i.e. the lessee under the operating lease), the deduction for operating lease rentals is restricted to the 'relevant amount'. In computing the income/profits of the lessor (i.e. the lessor under the operating lease), amounts receivable by him under the operating lease are included as income without netting off any amounts due by the lessor to the lessee. However, amounts receivable are not included as income to the extent that they exceed the 'relevant amount'. In each case, the *'relevant amount'* is the maximum amount of finance lease rentals deductible in computing the finance lessee's income/profits (see above). In applying these rules, such apportionments are to be made as are just and reasonable where only some of the plant or machinery subject to the sale and finance leaseback is also subject to the operating lease. Note that these rules are retained for sale and finance leasebacks taking place after 8 October 2007.

Lease and finance leasebacks. Subject to below, the above rules also apply (subject to the transitional provisions below), to a 'lease and finance leaseback' but with appropriate modifications; in particular, depreciation is disregarded in computing the finance lessee's lease rentals and the above limitation on the finance lessor's income/profits applies by reference only to the gross earnings under the leaseback. A *'lease and finance leaseback'* occurs if a person leases plant or machinery to another in circumstances such that, had it been a sale, the transaction would have been a sale and finance leaseback as defined in (ii) above (except that the availability of the plant or machinery for the use in question must in this case be a *direct* consequence of its having been leased under a finance lease). For this purpose, a person is regarded as leasing an item of plant or machinery to another person only if he grants him rights over the item for consideration and is not required to bring all of that consideration into account under the plant and machinery capital allowances code; there is a let-out where the last condition is met only because a joint election under *CAA 2001, s 199* was made by lessor and lessee before 18 May 2004 in relation to a fixture (see **11.40** above).

The rules above for computing the income/profits of the *lessor* in a sale and finance leaseback ceased to apply to lease and finance leasebacks for periods of account ending on or after 6 December 2006 (but not so as to affect the taxation of rentals receivable before that date or of rentals receivable on or after that date to the extent that those rentals relate to any period before that date).

Any finance lease in a lease and finance leaseback occurring after 11 March 2008 (i.e. one in respect of which the original lease is granted after that date) is excluded from 'short lease' treatment and thus brought within the scope of the long funding leasing rules at **11.43** above (see **11.45**(1)(A) above).

Transitional provisions. In relation to any leasebacks whose term commenced before 17 March 2004, transitional rules seek to preserve the pre-existing treatment of lease rentals payable before that date or in respect of any period ending before that date and a time proportion of lease rentals payable for periods straddling that date. For the effect on the lease rental deductions due to the lessee, see *FA 2004, Sch 23 paras 2, 3*; for the equivalent rules affecting computation of the lessor's income/profits, see *FA 2004, Sch 23 paras 7, 8*.

The increase in the lessee's income/profits for the period of account in which the leaseback terminates is capped, in accordance with a formula in *FA 2004, Sch 23 para 5*, if a pre-17 March 2004 leaseback terminates early, i.e. other than by expiry of its term.

The increase in the lessee's income/profits for the period of account in which the leaseback terminates is abated if a pre-17 March 2004 leaseback terminates early, the lessee reacquires ownership of the plant or machinery and the lessee's capital expenditure on reacquisition is itself restricted under (ii) above. If the restriction equals or exceeds the increase in profits/income, the increase is cancelled; in other cases, the increase is reduced by the restriction. However, the increase is reinstated in modified form if a disposal event (see **11.24** above) occurs in relation to the whole or part of the plant or machinery within six years after the leaseback terminates. See *FA 2004, Sch 23 para 6*.

Where a pre-17 March 2004 lease and finance leaseback terminates and the finance lessee then disposes of the plant or machinery, there is provision for his chargeable gain to be reduced for capital gains tax purposes. See *FA 2004, Sch 23 para 10*.

See Tolley's Capital Allowances for more detail on these transitional provisions.

[*CAA 2001, ss 228A–228J; FA 2007, Sch 5 para 17; FA 2008, Sch 20 paras 12, 13*].

(v)   In relation to capital expenditure incurred on or after 9 December 2009, a lessor's qualifying expenditure for the purposes of plant and machinery allowances may fall to be restricted to the 'value of the asset to the lessor'. The restriction applies if, at the time the lessor incurs the capital expenditure on the asset (i.e. the plant or machinery):

- the asset is leased or arrangements exist under which it is to be leased; and

- arrangements have been entered into in relation to payments under the lease that reduce the value of the asset to the lessor.

The '*value of the asset to the lessor*' is the sum of (i) the present value of the lessor's anticipated taxable income from the lease of the asset and (ii) the present value of the residual value of the asset (reduced by the amount of any rental rebate).

In calculating the lessor's anticipated taxable income from the lease, one excludes any amount brought into account as a disposal value as in **11.24** above and any amounts that represent charges for services or 'taxes' to be paid by the lessor. ('*Taxes*' means UK or foreign taxes or duties, but not income tax, corporation tax or foreign equivalents.) Present value is calculated by using the 'interest rate implicit in the lease' (see *CAA 2001, s 228MB*). A rental rebate means any sum payable to the lessee that is calculated by reference to the value of the plant or machinery at or about the time when the lease terminates (see *CAA 2001, s 228MC*).

Where the lessor has previously incurred capital expenditure on the same asset, the qualifying expenditure falling to be restricted is his total qualifying expenditure on that asset. This covers the possibility that the lessor may incur the capital expenditure in instalments.

For the above purposes, a 'lease' includes any arrangements which provide for plant or machinery to be leased or otherwise made available by one person to another.

[*CAA 2001, ss 228MA–228MC; FA 2010, Sch 5 para 1*].

The above legislation is a response to identified avoidance schemes. There should be no need to consider whether it applies in the case of a normal commercial lease as the value of the asset to the lessor would not normally be less than the capital expenditure incurred by him (HMRC Technical Note 'Plant and machinery leasing: anti-avoidance' at www.hmrc.gov.uk/pbr2009/plant-machinery-aa-1280.pdf).

Simon's Taxes. See **B3.334, B3.340H–B3.340S, B3.342, B3.359, B3.365, B3.366, B3.377.**

See Revenue Tax Bulletin June 1998 pp 539–544 for a general article on how these and associated capital allowance restrictions are intended to operate. In particular the article considers sale and leaseback by novation or new contract, or on defeased terms, and assets with long build times. See also **11.61** above and **73.79** TRADING INCOME as regards finance lease allowance restrictions. See **11.43** above as regards long funding leasing.

See **11.67** below as regards succession to a trade or other qualifying activity carried on by a connected person.

Plant or machinery received by way of gift

[11.64] Where plant or machinery received by way of gift is brought into use for the purposes of a trade or other qualifying activity carried on by the donee, the donee is entitled to writing-down allowances as if he had purchased it from the donor at the time it is brought into use and at its market value at that time. The deemed expenditure cannot qualify for first-year allowances (see **11.14** above) or for the annual investment allowance (see **11.13** above). [*CAA 2001, ss 14, 213(3), Sch 3 paras 12, 43*]. **Simon's Taxes.** See **B3.303.**

Previous use outside the business

[11.65] Where a person brings into use, for the purposes of a trade or other qualifying activity carried on by him, plant or machinery which he previously owned for purposes not entitling him to plant and machinery allowances in respect of that activity, writing-down allowances are calculated as if the trader etc. had, at the time of bringing it into use, incurred expenditure on its acquisition equal to its market value at that time. If, however, actual cost is less than market value, the actual cost is used instead. The actual cost for this purpose is reduced to the extent that it would have been reduced under the anti-avoidance provisions of *CAA 2001, s 218* or (prior to its repeal) *CAA 2001, s 224* (see **11.63** above) had it been expenditure on plant or machinery for use in the qualifying activity.

The deemed expenditure cannot qualify for first-year allowances (see **11.14** above) or for the annual investment allowance (see **11.13** above).

[*CAA 2001, s 13, Sch 3 para 11; FA 2008, Sch 20 para 6(2)(19)*].

Simon's Taxes. See **B3.303.**

See also **11.46** above as regards an asset ceasing to be used for long funding leasing but being retained by the lessor for use in a qualifying activity.

Partnerships

[11.66] Partnerships are entitled to allowances in respect of an item of plant or machinery used for the trade or other qualifying activity carried on by the partnership, and owned by one or more partners without being partnership property. Any transfer of the item between partners, whilst it continues to be so used, does not require a disposal value to be brought into account. These provisions do not apply if such an item is *let* by one or more partners to the partnership or otherwise made available to it in consideration of a tax-deductible payment. [*CAA 2001, s 264*].

Following a change in the persons carrying on a trade or other qualifying activity, other than one resulting in the activity being treated as permanently discontinued, allowances are subsequently given and balancing charges subsequently made as if the new partnership etc. had carried on the activity before the change. For this purpose, a *'qualifying activity'* does not include an office or employment but otherwise includes any of the activities at **11.4**(i)–(vii) above regardless of whether or not the profits therefrom are within the charge to UK tax. [*CAA 2001, s 263; FA 2008, Sch 24 paras 13, 23; CTA 2009, Sch 1 para 495*]. See **11.67** below as regards partnerships treated as discontinued and successions to trades generally.

Simon's Taxes. See **B3.390**.

Successions

[11.67] Following a change in the persons carrying on a trade or other qualifying activity, such that the activity is treated as permanently discontinued, any plant or machinery transferred, without being sold, to the new owner for continuing use in the qualifying activity is treated as sold at market value on the date of change, although no annual investment allowance or first-year allowance (where otherwise applicable) is available to the new owner. For this purpose, a *'qualifying activity'* does not include an office or employment but otherwise includes any of the activities at **11.4**(i)–(vii) above regardless of whether or not the profits therefrom are within the charge to UK tax. These provisions apply equally to plant or machinery not in use but provided and available for use for the purposes of the qualifying activity. [*CAA 2001, s 265; FA 2008, Sch 24 paras 14, 23; CTA 2009, Sch 1 para 496*].

If a beneficiary succeeds to a 'qualifying activity' (as above) under a deceased proprietor's will or intestacy, he may elect for written-down value to be substituted (if less) for market value. [*CAA 2001, s 268, Sch 3 para 53*].

Where a person succeeds to a trade or other qualifying activity carried on by a person 'connected' with him, each is within the charge to UK tax on the profits, and the successor is not a dual resident investing company, they may jointly elect, within two years after the date of change, for plant or machinery to be treated as transferred at a price giving rise to neither a balancing allowance nor a balancing charge. This applies to plant or machinery which immediately before and after the succession is owned by the person concerned and either in use, or provided and available for use, for the purposes of the qualifying activity, and regardless of any actual sale by the predecessor to the successor. Allowances and charges are subsequently made as if everything done to or by the predecessor had been done to or by the successor. Where *CAA 2001* has effect, it is expressly provided that the deemed sale takes place when the succession takes place.

For this purpose, persons are '*connected*' if:

(a) they are CONNECTED PERSONS (**21**); or

(b) one of them is a partnership in which the other has the right to a share of assets or income, or both are partnerships in both of which some other person has the right to such a share; or

(c) one of them is a body corporate over which the other has control (within *CAA 2001, s 574*), or both are bodies corporate, or one a body corporate and one a partnership, over both of which some other person has control.

The above election precludes the application of *CAA 2001, s 104E* (disposal value in connection with special rate expenditure in avoidance cases — see **11.25** above), *CAA 2001, s 104* (disposal value of long-life assets in avoidance cases — see **11.31** above), *CAA 2001, s 265* (see above) and the similar provisions in *CAA 2001, s 108* (see **11.52** above), and their forerunners. An annual investment allowance would appear to be precluded by **11.13**(vi) above and first-year allowances by **11.14**(ix) above.

[*CAA 2001, ss 266, 267, Sch 3 para 52; ITA 2007, Sch 1 para 405; FA 2008, Sch 26 paras 12, 14*].

Simon's Taxes See **B3.390**.

Renewals basis

[11.68] A renewals basis is generally available as an alternative to capital allowances. A deduction is allowed in computing profits of the cost of a replacement item less the proceeds of sale (or scrap value) of the item replaced. Where, however, the replacement item is an improvement on that replaced, the deduction is restricted to the cost of replacing like with like. See *Caledonian Railway Co v Banks* CES 1880, 1 TC 487; *Eastmans Ltd v Shaw* HL 1928, 14 TC 218; *Hyam v CIR* CS 1929, 14 TC 479.

Cost of renewals of trade implements, utensils etc. are allowed as a deduction under *ICTA 1988, s 74(1)(d)*, but cf. *Hinton v Maden & Ireland Ltd* HL 1959, 38 TC 391 and also see *Peter Merchant Ltd v Stedeford* CA 1948, 30 TC 496 (provision for future renewals not allowable). Replacement of parts is allowed under general principles so far as identity of plant or machinery is retained. For further details of 'renewals basis' and change from renewals basis to normal capital allowances and *vice versa*, see HMRC ESC B1 and HMRC Business Income Manual BIM46935, 46950, 46955.

Simon's Taxes. See **B3.312**.

Valuation basis

A valuation basis is a variation of the renewals basis in which a class of assets, for example spare parts for plant and machinery, are dealt with in a similar way to trading stock, involving opening and closing valuations. For further detail, and for change from capital allowances to valuation basis, see HMRC Business Income Manual BIM46940, 46960.

Partial depreciation subsidies

[11.69] Partial depreciation subsidies, i.e. sums, not otherwise taxable on the recipient, are payable to him, directly or indirectly, by any other person in respect of, or to take account of, *part* of the depreciation of plant or machinery resulting from its use in the recipient's trade or other qualifying activity.

Where it appears that a partial depreciation subsidy will be payable, an annual investment allowance or first-year allowance (where available — see **11.13**, **11.14** above) can nevertheless be given, but must be scaled down as is just and reasonable (though the full amount is deducted in arriving at the balance of expenditure available for writing-down allowances).

Qualifying expenditure (see **11.3** above) which has been the subject of a partial depreciation subsidy can only be allocated to a *single asset pool* (see **11.23** above). Where qualifying expenditure has otherwise been allocated to a pool and a partial depreciation subsidy is received for the first time in respect of it, it must be transferred to a single asset pool. This is achieved by bringing in a disposal value (equal to market value — see **11.24**(g) above) in the original pool for the chargeable period in which the subsidy is paid and allocating an equivalent amount to the single asset pool. Writing-down allowances and balancing allowances and charges in respect of the single asset pool are reduced to such amounts as are just and reasonable (though the full amount is deducted in arriving at any unrelieved qualifying expenditure carried forward).

[*CAA 2001, ss 209–212; FA 2008, Sch 24 paras 7, 23*].

See **11.7** above as regards subsidies towards the whole of such depreciation. See **11.2**(vi)(vii) above as regards contributions by others towards *expenditure* qualifying for plant and machinery and other capital allowances.

Simon's Taxes See B3.360.

Lessee required to provide plant or machinery

[11.70] A lessee required to provide plant or machinery under the terms of the lease (including any tenancy), and using it for the purposes of a trade or other qualifying activity, is treated as if he owned it (for as long as it is used for those purposes), but is not required to bring in a disposal value (see **11.24** above) on termination of the lease. If:

- the plant or machinery continues to be so used until termination of the lease;
- the lessor holds the lease in the course of a qualifying activity; and
- on or after termination, a disposal event occurs at a time when the lessor owns the plant or machinery,

the *lessor* is required to bring in a disposal value, for the chargeable period in which the disposal event occurs, in the pool to which the expenditure would have been allocated if incurred by the lessor. These rules do not, however, apply where the plant or machinery becomes, by law, part of the building in which it is installed or attached (see **11.33** above) under a lease. [*CAA 2001, s 70, Sch 3 para 17*].

Key points

[11.71] Points to consider are as follows.

- The replacement of integral features in stages — possibly prompted by a major repair — may require what would otherwise be treated as revenue expenditure to be disallowed and capitalised as replacement features, qualifying instead for capital allowances. Due to the rolling 12 months nature of the test of replacement expenditure, adequate post-balance sheet events procedures should be implemented to identify expenditure which becomes capital by virtue of subsequent expenditure on the same features.
- The trigger for capital treatment of replacement expenditure on integral features is that it exceeds 50% of the cost of replacing the features at the date the first expenditure is incurred. Taxpayers should be made aware of the need to qualify the replacement cost at the time expenditure on repairing integral features is planned, and to retain evidence of that cost.
- The activity classifications used to determine whether two activities are 'related' for the purposes of the annual investment allowance are very wide. Advice on this area should not be given without reviewing the NACE list in detail. Each activity area is defined as the first level of classification (A, B, C etc.) only, rather than sub-levels such as A1, A2 etc. However, detailed study of the sub-classifications is needed to identify what business activities are classified under each heading. For example, accountancy services is in the same classification as photography.
- When deciding whether or not to elect for short-life asset treatment, it should be borne in mind that this is only beneficial if the asset is both disposed of within the period of 4 years, and for less than the current written-down value, which in relation to cost would be:

Period of Account after date of acquisition	% cost
1st	100
2nd	80
3rd	64
4th	51

- The election available under *CAA 2001, s 198* (see **11.40**) for fixtures in a building to be transferred at agreed value is more complex since 6 April 2008, and may not be beneficial for purchasers. On the first change of ownership of a building on or after 6 April 2008 the fixtures transferred will comprise main pool items and integral features, some of which will be recognised for capital allowances for the first time, and some of which would currently be in the main pool. Items which were previously excluded from any form of capital allowances will now attract allowances as integral features. However, these items cannot be included in an election, as the disposer was unable to claim capital allowances on them, and a valuation by conventional means will have to be arrived at. Subsequent changes of ownership will not present the same problem.

- Double cab pick-ups have a special status for capital allowances purposes. Although it is questionable whether they meet the definition of a 'car' for these purposes, it is accepted by HMRC that if the payload (defined as the gross vehicle weight less the unoccupied kerb weight) of the vehicle equals or exceeds 1 tonne (1,000 kg) then the vehicle is not a car, and will therefore qualify for annual investment allowance. However, the fitting of a hard top to the load bay is deemed to reduce the stated payload by 45kg (irrespective of its actual weight) which may take the payload below the limit.

- It is easy to overlook VAT adjustments relating to capital items which have a capital allowances impact. Where a client is partially exempt, or begins to use an affected asset for a non-taxable purpose, links will be needed from the VAT working papers through to the capital allowances working papers to ensure that the capital allowances impact is not overlooked. This applies both to Capital Goods Scheme adjustments, but also to the annual adjustment made by larger VAT registered traders — the computation of the initial cost needs to reflect the actual rate of VAT recovery after the annual adjustment has been made, and this will affect any assets purchased, not only those within the Capital Goods scheme.

12

Capital Gains Tax

For full details of CGT provisions, see Tolley's Capital Gains Tax. For date due, see **54.1 PAYMENT OF TAX**.

Capital gains tax (CGT)

[12.1] The legislation applying to individuals and companies was consolidated by the *Taxation of Chargeable Gains Act 1992* (*TCGA 1992*) and references to that Act are given throughout this book where appropriate. For full details see Tolley's Capital Gains Tax.

Exclusion of amounts otherwise taxed

[12.2] Gains for CGT purposes are calculated exclusive of receipts chargeable to income tax (except items giving rise to balancing charges or disposal values for capital allowances purposes). However, the capitalised value of a rent-charge, ground annual, feu duty or other series of income receipts can be taken into account for CGT purposes. [*TCGA 1992, s 37; CAA 2001, Sch 2 para 77; ITA 2007, Sch 1 para 299; SI 2004 No 2310, Sch para 48*].

Rates of CGT

[12.3] Rates of CGT are as follows.

Gains accruing on or after 23 June 2010

Subject to any available entrepreneurs' relief, the rate of CGT applicable to an individual is 18% or, where the individual is liable at the higher rate or dividend upper rate on any part of his taxable income, 28%. Where there is no higher rate or dividend upper rate income tax liability, but the amount chargeable to CGT exceeds the unused part of the basic rate band, the CGT rate on the excess is 28%. (For 2010/11, the amount chargeable to CGT does not for this purpose include gains accruing before 23 June 2010; in certain special cases, transitional rules apply to determine whether gains accrue before 23 June 2010 or on or after that date.)

See **1.3 ALLOWANCES AND TAX RATES** for the higher rate and the basic rate limit, and **1.5 ALLOWANCES AND TAX RATES** as regards the dividend upper rate. See **1.7 ALLOWANCES AND TAX RATES** (Step 3) as regards taxable income.

In determining for the above purposes the unused part of an individual's basic rate band and whether any income is liable at the higher rate or the dividend upper rate, account is taken of certain special provisions, such as top slicing relief on life assurance gains and life assurance deficiency relief. See *TCGA 1992, s 4A*.

The rate of CGT applicable to gains accruing to the trustees of a settlement or the personal representatives of a deceased person is 28%.

For 2010/11 onwards, if the gains accruing to a person in a tax year are chargeable to CGT at different rates, allowable capital losses may be deducted from those gains, and the CGT annual exempt amount may be used against those gains, in the way that is most beneficial to that person.

For entrepreneurs' relief, see the chapter of that name in Tolley's Capital Gains Tax.

2008/09 to 2010/11 (gains accruing before 23 June 2010 only)

Subject to any available entrepreneurs' relief for individuals, there was a single CGT rate of 18% for individuals, trustees and personal representatives.

2007/08 and earlier years

The rate of CGT applicable to an individual was equivalent to the savings rate of income tax or, where the individual was liable at the higher rate or dividend upper rate on any part of his taxable income, the higher rate. Where there was no higher rate or dividend upper rate income tax liability, but the amount chargeable to CGT exceeded the unused part of the basic rate band, the CGT rate on the excess was equivalent to the higher rate of income tax. For this purpose, the basic rate band was the whole of the amount up to the basic rate limit. The starting rate of income tax applied to CGT to the extent that taxable gains, if treated as though they were the top slice of taxable income, would have fallen within the starting rate band.

See **1.4 ALLOWANCES AND TAX RATES** for the savings rate, the higher rate, the basic rate limit and the starting rate, and **1.5 ALLOWANCES AND TAX RATES** as regards the dividend upper rate. See **1.7 ALLOWANCES AND TAX RATES** (Step 3) as regards taxable income.

In determining for the above purposes the unused part of an individual's basic rate band and whether any income was liable at the higher rate or the dividend upper rate, account was taken of certain special provisions, such as top slicing relief on life assurance gains and life assurance deficiency relief. See *TCGA 1992, s 6*.

The rate of CGT applicable to gains accruing to the trustees of a settlement or the personal representatives of a deceased person is equivalent to the trust rate of income tax (see **68.11 SETTLEMENTS**).

[*TCGA 1992, ss 4, 4A, 4B, 5, 6; ITA 2007, Sch 1 paras 295, 296; FA 2008, s 8; F(No 2)A 2010, Sch 1 paras 2, 3, 12, 13, 18–22*].

Simon's Taxes. See C1.107.

Set-off of income tax reliefs against capital gains

[**12.4**] See **45.7** LOSSES for set-off of trading losses against capital gains. See **59.5** POST-CESSATION RECEIPTS AND EXPENDITURE for relief for certain post-cessation expenditure, and **27.53** EMPLOYMENT INCOME for relief for certain post-employment expenditure.

13

Cash Basis for Barristers and Advocates

Introduction

[13.1] There is a statutory requirement for taxable business profits to be computed in accordance with generally accepted accounting practice (GAAP) (subject to any adjustment under specific legislation) (see **73.18** TRADING INCOME). This in turn requires profits to be computed on the earnings basis (see **73.18** TRADING INCOME). [*ITTOIA 2005, s 25; SI 2008 No 954, Arts 1, 24*].

Barristers and advocates

[13.2] Barristers and advocates in independent practice are exempt from the above requirement for periods of account ending not more than seven years after they first hold themselves out as available for fee-earning work. They may instead compute their profits either on the cash basis or by reference to fees earned whose amount has been agreed or in respect of which a fee note has been delivered. The basis adopted must be applied consistently. Under the cash basis, profits are measured by excess of cash receipts over cash outlay, ignoring debtors and creditors, accruals, unbilled or uncompleted work. Once an accounting basis complying with *ITTOIA 2005, s 25* (as in **13.1** above) is adopted for any period of account, the exemption ceases and that *section* applies for all subsequent periods of account.

Under the cash basis, profits are measured by excess of cash receipts over cash outlay, ignoring debtors and creditors, accruals, unbilled or uncompleted work.

[*ITTOIA 2005, s 160*].

If a change of accounting basis arises on a barrister or advocate ceasing to take advantage of the above exemption or on its ceasing to be available, any resulting adjustment income is automatically spread over ten years. See **73.20** TRADING INCOME for details.

14

Certificates of Deposit

Simon's Taxes. See E1.459–E1.461.

[14.1] A certificate of deposit is a document:

- relating to the deposit of money in any currency;
- recognising an obligation to pay a stated principal amount to bearer or to order, with or without interest; and
- by the delivery of which, with or without endorsement, the right to receive that stated amount, with or without interest, is transferable.

[*ITTOIA 2005, s 552(2); ITA 2007, s 1019*].

[14.2] Profits or gains on certificates of deposit acquired after 6 March 1973 are chargeable to income tax under *ITTOIA 2005, ss 551–554* (if not taxable as a trading receipt). These provisions do not apply to exempt pension funds. [*ITTOIA 2005, s 551; FA 2009, Sch 25 paras 9(2), 10*]. See **16.10 CHARITIES** for the exemption applicable to charitable trusts.

Relief for a loss on a certificate of deposit can be claimed against interest chargeable in respect of that certificate. [*ITA 2007, s 154; ICTA 1988, s 398; CTA 2010, Sch 1 para 36*].

[14.3] Where, in a transaction in which no certificate of deposit or security (as defined by *TCGA 1992, s 132*) is issued, but an amount becomes payable with interest (by a bank, similar institution or person regularly engaging in similar transactions), then if the right to receive the amount or interest is disposed of or exercised, any profit (or loss) will be treated as in **14.2** above. [*ITTOIA 2005, s 552(1)*]. Where a right to receive an amount (with or without interest) in pursuance of a deposit of money comes into existence without a certificate of deposit, but the person entitled to the right could call for the issue of such a certificate, a profit (or loss) on disposal of the right before the issue of such a certificate is similarly treated as in **14.2** above. A disposal of the right to receive the interest is taken outside these provisions on and after 22 April 2009, but see now the more general provisions on transfers of income streams at **4.34 ANTI-AVOIDANCE**. [*ITTOIA 2005, s 552(1)(2); FA 2009, Sch 25 paras 9(2), 10*].

[14.4] Neither **14.2** nor **14.3** above applies to a transfer of a right that is a *Pt 5* transfer under *Proceeds of Crime Act 2002* (as in **10.2(x) CAPITAL ALLOWANCES**) where no compensating payment is made to the transferor. [*Proceeds of Crime Act 2002, Sch 10 paras 6, 10*].

[14.5] Profits within **14.2** or **14.3** above arising to trustees of a settlement are chargeable at the trust rate. See **68.12 SETTLEMENTS**.

15

Certificates of Tax Deposit

Simon's Taxes. See A4.635, A4.636.

[**15.1**] Taxpayers may make deposits, evidenced by Certificates of Tax Deposit, with Collectors of Taxes for the subsequent payment of their own tax and Class 4 NIC liabilities generally (other than PAYE and tax deducted from payments to construction sub-contractors and corporation tax — see further below). If a deposit is tendered in respect of any liability, that liability will be treated as paid on the later of the certificate date and the normal due date for that liability (see **54 PAYMENT OF TAX**). The minimum initial deposit is £500 with minimum additions of £250.

Series 7 Certificates are *not* available for purchase for use against corporation tax liabilities.

Deposits made after 5 April 2003 in a partnership name are not accepted in settlement of an individual partner's tax liability.

Interest, which is payable gross but taxable, will accrue for a maximum of six years from the date of deposit to the date of payment of tax or, if earlier, the 'deemed due date' for payment of the liability against which the deposit (plus accrued interest) is set. The '*deemed due date*' is generally the normal due date for payment of the tax under the relevant legislation, and does not change if for any reason an assessment is made late or the liability is not payable until later (e.g. following settlement of an appeal). A deposit may be withdrawn for cash at any time but will then receive a reduced rate of interest. Where a certificate is used in settlement of a tax liability, interest at the higher rate up to the normal due date may be less than interest at the encashment rate up to the reckonable date. In such circumstances the taxpayer may instruct HMRC to calculate interest on the latter basis. (ICAEW Technical Release TAX 13/93, 30 June 1993). The rates of interest, published by the Treasury, and calculated by reference to the rate on comparable investment with the Government, vary with the size and period of the deposit, and the rate payable on a deposit is adjusted to the current rate on each anniversary of the deposit.

Deposits are not transferable except to personal representatives of a deceased person.

Rates of interest are given at **15.2, 15.3** and **15.4** below. Information on current rates may be obtained from www.hmrc.gov.uk/howtopay/ctd-interest-rates. pdf, from any HMRC Tax Collecting Office or from HMRC, Revenue Finance (CTD), Room B2 South Block, Barrington Road, Worthing, West Sussex, BN12 4XH (tel. 01903 509064 or 509066).

[**15.2**] The rates of interest on date of deposit or anniversary on Series 6 and Series 7 Certificates for deposits of under £100,000 are (from 5 August 2005 onwards) as follows:

	Used to pay tax	Withdrawals for cash
5 August 2005–3 August 2006	1%	0.5%
4 August 2006–9 November 2006	1.75%	0.75%
10 November 2006–10 May 2007	1.5%	0.75%
11 May 2007–5 July 2007	2%	1%
6 July 2007–6 December 2007	2.25%	1.1%
7 December 2007–7 February 2008	3%	1.5%
8 February 2008–8 October 2008	2%	1%
9 October 2008–6 November 2008	2.5%	1.25%
7 November 2008–4 December 2008	1.75%	0.75%
5 December 2008 onwards	nil	nil

[15.3] The rates of interest on date of deposit or anniversary on Series 6 or Series 7 Certificates for deposits of £100,000 or more used to meet a scheduled liability are (from 5 August 2005 onwards) as follows:

			Period of deposit in months		
	Under 1	1 but under 3	3 but under 6	6 but under 9	9 but under 12
5 August 2005–3 August 2006	1%	3.5%	3.25%	3%	3%
4 August 2006–9 November 2006	1.75%	4.25%	4.25%	4%	4%
10 November 2006–11 January 2007	1.5%	4%	4%	3.75%	3.75%
12 January 2007–10 May 2007	1.5%	4.25%	4%	4%	4%
11 May 2007–5 July 2007	2%	4.75%	4.5%	4.5%	4.5%
6 July 2007–6 December 2007	2.25%	5%	4.75%	4.75%	4.75%
7 December 2007–7 February 2008	3%	5.5%	5%	4.75%	4.5%
8 February 2008–10 April 2008	2%	4.5%	4.25%	4%	3.75%
11 April 2008–8 October 2008	2%	4.75%	4.5%	4.25%	4.25%
9 October 2008–6 November 2008	2.5%	5.25%	5%	5%	4.75%
7 November 2008–4 December 2008	1.75%	4.5%	4.25%	4.25%	4%
5 December 2008–8 January 2009	nil	2.5%	2.5%	2.5%	2.25%
9 January 2009–5 February 2009	nil	1.5%	1.25%	1.25%	1.25%
6 February 2009–5 March 2009	nil	1%	1%	1%	0.75%
6 March 2009 onwards	nil	0.75%	0.75%	0.75%	0.75%

[15.4] The rates of interest on date of deposit or anniversary on Series 6 or Series 7 Certificates for deposits of £100,000 or more withdrawn for cash are (from 5 August 2005 onwards) as follows:

	Period of deposit in months				
	Under 1	1 but under 3	3 but under 6	6 but under 9	9 but under 12
5 August 2005–3 August 2006	0.5%	1.75%	1.5%	1.5%	1.5%
4 August 2006–9 November 2006	0.75%	2%	2%	2%	2%
10 November 2006–11 January 2007	0.75%	2%	2%	1.75%	1.75%
12 January 2007–10 May 2007	0.75%	2%	2%	2%	2%
11 May 2007–5 July 2007	1%	2.25%	2.25%	2.25%	2.25%
6 July 2007–6 December 2007	1.1%	2.5%	2.25%	2.25%	2.25%
7 December 2007–7 February 2008	1.5%	2.75%	2.5%	2.25%	2.25%
8 February 2008–10 April 2008	1%	2.25%	2%	2%	1.5%
11 April 2008–8 October 2008	1%	2.25%	2.25%	2%	2%
9 October 2008–6 November 2008	1.25%	2.5%	2.5%	2.5%	2.25%
7 November 2008–4 December 2008	0.75%	2.25%	2%	2%	2%
5 December 2008–8 January 2009	nil	1.25%	1.25%	1.25%	1%
9 January 2009–5 February 2009	nil	0.75%	0.5%	0.5%	0.5%
6 February 2009–5 March 2009	nil	0.5%	0.5%	0.5%	0.25%
6 March 2009 onwards	nil	0.25%	0.25%	0.25%	0.25%

16

Charities

- For detailed guidance, see www.hmrc.gov.uk/charities/guidance-notes/intro.htm and www.hmrc.gov.uk/charities/index.htm.
- See also specialist HMRC guidance 'Giving to charity: businesses' at www.hmrc.gov.uk/businesses/giving/index.htm, 'Giving to charity: individuals' at www.hmrc.gov.uk/individuals/giving/index.htm, and 'Fund raising events: exemption for charities and other qualifying bodies' at www.hmrc.gov.uk/charities/fund-raising-events.htm.
- See also 'A guide to tax incentives for corporate giving', published jointly by the Treasury and Home Office (and available at www.hmrc.gov.uk/charities/guide_tax_incentives.pdf), which, despite its title, covers charitable giving by all businesses and not just by companies.

Cross-reference. 73.70 TRADING INCOME for employees seconded to charities.

Simon's Taxes. See C5.1.

Other sources. See Tolley's Charities Manual.

Introduction

[16.1] This chapter considers the income tax position of charitable trusts and also of persons within the charge to income tax who give to charity. In **16.2**, **16.3** below, the meaning of 'charity' is examined, and **16.4–16.6** then deal with the income tax position of a charitable trust, the exemptions available to it and the circumstances in which those exemptions are restricted or nullified. The remainder of the chapter covers donations to charity, with particular reference to the income tax position of the donor. Tax-efficient methods of giving to charity comprise Gift Aid (**16.15–16.19**), payroll giving by employees (**16.20**) and qualifying gifts of shares, securities or real property (**16.21**).

Charity, charitable purposes — general principles

[16.2] '*Charity*' means any body of persons or trust established for charitable purposes only. [*ITA 2007, s 989; ICTA 1988, s 506(1); ITTOIA 2005, s 878(1)*]. A new definition of charity has been introduced by *FA 2010* but with limited immediate effect (see **16.3** below for details). The meaning of charity is also governed by general law.

Before *Charities Act 2006* took effect not all charities were subject to the "public benefit" test (see below). This test now applies to all charities and control over this area is exercised by the Charity Commission in England and Wales. The Commission is statutorily charged with both setting guidance on the meaning of public benefit and ensuring that charities meet the test. To this end, charities may be subject to review and may be given a limited period to make changes sufficient to comply, or face removal from the register of charities with related tax consequences. [*Charities Act 2006, s 4*

Although not further defined for tax purposes, for the purposes of the law of England and Wales, a 'charitable purpose' is one which is for the public benefit and which is within one of the following categories:

(a)   the prevention or relief of poverty;
(b)   the advancement of education;
(c)   the advancement of religion;
(d)   the advancement of health or the saving of lives;
(e)   the advancement of citizenship or community development;
(f)   the advancement of the arts, culture, heritage or science;
(g)   the advancement of amateur sport;
(h)   the advancement of human rights, conflict resolution or reconciliation or the promotion of religious or racial harmony or equality and diversity;
(i)   the advancement of environmental protection or improvement;
(j)   the relief of those in need by reason of youth, age, ill-health, disability, financial hardship or other disadvantage;
(k)   the advancement of animal welfare;
(l)   the promotion of the efficiency of the armed forces of the Crown, or of the efficiency of the police, fire and rescue services or ambulance services;

(m)   any purposes not within (a) to (l) above but recognised as charitable purposes under existing charity law or under *Recreational Charities Act 1958, s 1*;

(n)   any purposes that may reasonably be regarded as analogous to, or within the spirit of, any purposes falling within (a) to (m) above; and

(o)   any purposes that may reasonably be regarded as analogous to, or within the spirit of, any purposes which have been recognised under charity law as falling within (n) above or this category.

[*Charities Act 2006, s 2; SI 2007 No 309; SI 2008 No 945*].

Before the above provision took effect, what was a charity rested largely on judicial interpretation. A leading case is *Special Commrs v Pemsel* HL 1891, 3 TC 53 in which Lord Macnaghten laid down that 'charity' should be given its technical meaning under English law and comprises 'four principal divisions; trusts for the relief of poverty, trusts for the advancement of education, trusts for the advancement of religion and trusts beneficial to the community and not falling under any of the preceding heads. The trusts last referred to are not the less charitable . . . because incidentally they affect the rich as well as the poor'. In the same case it was held that in relation to tax the English definition should be applied to Scottish cases (and cf. *Jackson's Trustees v Lord Advocate* CS 1926, 10 TC 460 and *CIR v Glasgow Police Athletic Assn* HL 1953, 34 TC 76). The concept of 'charity' may change with changes in social values (cf. *CIR v Trustees of Football Association Youth Trust* HL 1980, 54 TC 413).

Charities are regulated in England and Wales by the Charity Commission and in Scotland by the Office of the Scottish Charities Regulator. Under *Charities Act 1993, ss 10–10C*, HMRC may disclose information regarding charities to the Charity Commission.

The charity reliefs are not available to overseas charities (*Gull* KB 1937, 21 TC 374; *Dreyfus Foundation Inc v CIR* HL 1955, 36 TC 126).

Where land given for educational and certain other charitable purposes ceases to be used for such purposes and, under the *Reverter of Sites Act 1987*, is held by the trustees on a trust for sale for the benefit of the revertee, then unless the revertee is known to be a charity, there is a deemed disposal and reacquisition for capital gains purposes, which may give rise to a chargeable gain. Any income arising from the property will be liable to income tax, and a chargeable gain may also arise on a subsequent sale of the land. By concession, where the revertee is subsequently identified as a charity or disclaims all entitlement to the property (or where certain orders are made by the Charity Commission or the Secretary of State), provided that charitable status is re-established within six years of the date on which the land ceased to be held on the original charitable trust, any capital gains tax paid as above in the interim period will be discharged or repaid (with repayment supplement where appropriate) as will any income tax (provided that the income charged was used for charitable purposes). Partial relief will be given where the above conditions are only satisfied in respect of part of the property concerned. A request by the trustees for postponement of the tax payable will be accepted by HMRC where the revertee has not been identified and this concession may apply. (HMRC ESC D47). This concession will be withdrawn from 1 April 2010 (www.hmrc.gov.uk/budget2009/withdrawl-esc-6400.pdf).

The *Charitable Trusts (Validation) Act 1954* provides for validating as charitable a pre-1953 trust if its property was in fact applied for charitable purposes only, notwithstanding that the trust also authorised its application for non-charitable purposes (cf. *Vernon & Sons Ltd Employees Fund v CIR* Ch D 1956, 36 TC 484; *Buxton v Public Trustees* Ch D 1962, 41 TC 235).

A donation by one charity to another has been applied for charitable purposes even though merely added to the funds of the other charity (*Helen Slater Charitable Trust Ltd* CA 1981, 55 TC 230).

The application of income to the making of loans at interest to the subsidiaries from whom the income was derived was held to be for charitable purposes in *Nightingale Ltd v Price* (Sp C 66), [1996] SSCD 116.

As regards the time at which charitable purposes arise, see *Guild and Others (as Trustees of the William Muir (Bond 9) Ltd Employees' Share Scheme) v CIR* CS 1993, 66 TC 1 (trustees of share scheme required to repay loans out of proceeds of distribution and to apply balance to charitable purposes; held not to apply proceeds of distribution for charitable purposes).

For general restrictions on reliefs, see **16.11**, **16.12** below.

HMRC publish guidelines on the tax treatment of Appeal Funds set up following an accident, disaster or other misfortune; see www.hmrc.gov.uk/af g/afg.htm.

The Charity Commission publish advice for charity trustees in 'Charities and Fund-raising' (CC20), available at their website (www.charity-commission.go v.uk).

Simon's Taxes. See C5.105.

FA 2010 definition of charity

[16.3] *FA 2010, Sch 6 Pt 1* introduces a new statutory definition of a charity for tax purposes following the extension of UK charitable tax reliefs to bodies equivalent to charities and community amateur sports clubs in the EU and in Norway and Iceland. The new definition replaces the existing definition in *ITA 2007, s 989* (see **16.2** above) but, with one exception, does not apply in relation to any particular tax provision until the Treasury make a commencement order by statutory instrument. The exception is Gift Aid relief (see **16.15–16.19** below); in this case the new definition has effect in relation to gifts made on or after 6 April 2010. [*FA 2010, Sch 6 paras 33, 34*]

Under the new definition, a 'charity' is a body of persons or trust that:

- is established for charitable purposes only (see **16.2**(a)–(o) above), and
- meets the jurisdiction, registration and management conditions below.

New definitions of 'charitable trust' and 'charitable company' are also provided. A *'charitable company'* is a charity (within the new definition) that is a body of persons. A *'charitable trust'* is a charity (within the new definition) that is a trust. These replace the definitions at **16.4** below but only from a date to be appointed by the Treasury as above.

Jurisdiction condition

A body of persons or trust meets the jurisdiction condition if it falls to be subject to the control of:

- a UK court (the High Court, Court of Session or the High Court in NI) in the exercise of its jurisdiction with respect to charities; or
- any other court in the exercise of a corresponding jurisdiction under the law of another EU member State or a territory specified by statutory instrument.

Registration condition

In the case of a body of persons or trust that is a charity within the meaning of *Charities Act 1993*, the registration condition is met if the body or trust has complied with any requirement to be registered in the register of charities kept under s 3 of that Act. In any other case, the registration condition is met if the body of persons or trust has complied with any corresponding requirement under the law of a territory outside England and Wales.

Management condition

A body of persons or trust meets the management condition if its managers are fit and proper persons to be managers of the body or trust. For this purpose, the 'managers' are the persons having the general control and management of the administration of the body or trust.

In relation to any period for which the management condition is not met, it is nevertheless treated as met if the Commissioners for HMRC consider that:

- the failure to meet the condition has not prejudiced the charitable purposes of the body or trust; or
- it is just and reasonable in all the circumstances for the condition to be treated as met throughout the period in question.

For HMRC guidance on the 'fit and proper persons' test and how it will be applied in practice, see www.hmrc.gov.uk/charities/guidance-notes/chapter2/f p-persons-test.htm. HMRC assumes that all people appointed by charities are fit and proper persons unless they have information to suggest otherwise. Provided charities take appropriate steps on appointing personnel they may assume that they meet the test at all times unless, exceptionally, they are challenged by HMRC.

General

HMRC may publish the name and address of any body of persons or trust that appears to them to meet, or at any time to have met, the above definition of a charity.

[*FA 2010, Sch 6 paras 1–7*].

The extension of UK charitable tax reliefs to equivalent bodies in the EU and in Norway and Iceland follows a judgment in the European Court of Justice (ECJ) on 27 January 2009. For Questions and Answers on this topic, see www.hmrc.gov.uk/budget2010/char-tax-rel-qa.pdf. In particular, if an individual made a gift to a charitable organisation in an EU country, or Iceland or Norway, on or after 27 January 2009 and before 6 April 2010 (when the above legislation comes into force) he may be able to claim tax relief on the gift, depending on whether the recipient would have been a charity under English and Welsh law at the time of the gift.

Specific exemptions and reliefs from tax

[16.4] Apart from the exemptions at **16.5–16.10** below, charities are subject to tax on investment and rental income and gains and on profits from trades carried on in order to raise funds.

The exemptions, as they relate to income tax, were rewritten in *ITA 2007*, and are applied for 2007/08 onwards to 'charitable trusts'. The corresponding corporation tax exemptions apply to 'charitable companies'.

For this purpose, a *'charitable trust'* is a trust established for charitable purposes only. [*ITA 2007, s 519*]. A *'charitable company'* is a body of persons established for charitable purposes only. [*CTA 2010, s 467; ICTA 1988, s 506(1); ITA 2007, Sch 1 para 95(2)*]. The commentary at **16.5**, **16.6**, **16.7–16.12** below deals with the income tax position only. For convenience, the expression 'charitable trust' is used throughout. See Tolley's Corporation Tax for the provisions applying to charitable companies. Note that the above definitions of 'charitable trust' and 'charitable company' are to be replaced in due course by the corresponding new definitions at **16.3** above.

The exemptions are subject to the restrictions at **16.11**, **16.12** below.

Claims must be made for the exemptions (other than those at **16.10** below) to apply, generally within the time limit at **18.4 CLAIMS**, to HMRC Charities, St John's House, Merton Road, Bootle, Merseyside L69 9BB or, in Scotland, HMRC Charities, Meldrum House, 15 Drumsheugh Gardens, Edinburgh EH3 7UL. [*ITA 2007, s 538(1)(2); ICTA 1988, s 505(1)*].

HMRC have long since had powers to require the production of books, documents etc. relevant to any claim for exemption leading to the repayment of income tax or the payment of tax credits. [*F(No 2)A 1992, s 28; ITA 2007, Sch 1 para 350; FA 2008, s 113, Sch 36 para 86*]. From 1 April 2009, these are replaced by the more general powers at **38.3–38.10 HMRC INVESTIGATORY POWERS**. [*SI 2009 No 404*].

Simon's Taxes. See C5.117A–C5.124.

Property income

[16.5] The following income is exempt from income tax to the extent that it is applied to charitable purposes only.

- Income otherwise chargeable to income tax under *ITTOIA 2005, Pt 3* (property income) which arises from an estate, interest or right in or over any land vested in any person in trust for a charitable trust or for charitable purposes.

- Income otherwise chargeable to income tax under *ITTOIA 2005, Pt 2* (trading income) by virtue of *ITTOIA 2005, s 261* (provisions to be given priority over *Pt 3* — see **60.1 PROPERTY INCOME**) which arises from rents or other receipts from an estate, interest or right in or over any land vested in any person in trust for a charitable trust or for charitable purposes.

- Distributions out of tax-exempt profits of a UK Real Estate Investment Trust (as in **60.14 PROPERTY INCOME**).

[ITA 2007, s 531; ICTA 1988, s 505(1)(a)(aa); FA 2007, Sch 17 paras 17, 18; CTA 2010, Sch 1 para 531].

Where the letting of premises amounts to a trade otherwise than under *ITTOIA 2005, s 261* (because of the provision of other services), this exemption will not be available (see *Rotunda Hospital, Dublin v Coman HL 1920, 7 TC 517*). The trade may, however, qualify for the exemption at **16.8** below.

Savings and investment income

[16.6] Income of a charitable trust, or applicable for charitable purposes only under an Act, charter, court judgment, trust deed or will, is exempt so far as applied to charitable purposes only and consisting of:

(a) income within *ITTOIA 2005, Pt 4 Ch 2* (interest), *Ch 7* (purchased life annuity payments), *Ch 8* (profits from deeply discounted securities) or *Ch 10* (distributions from unauthorised unit trusts); or

(b) dividends or other distributions from UK resident companies; or

(c) distributions from non-UK resident companies; or

(d) non-trading royalties etc. from intellectual property within *ITTOIA 2005, s 579*; or

(e) non-trading income from telecommunications rights within *ITTOIA 2005, Pt 5 Ch 4*; or

(f) annual payments charged to tax under *ITTOIA 2005, Pt 5 Ch 7*.

Income within (a)–(c) above must be income which would otherwise fall within and be dealt with under *ITTOIA 2005, Pt 4* (see *ITTOIA 2005, s 366* for provisions given priority over *Pt 4*).

[ITA 2007, ss 532, 536; ICTA 1988, s 505(1)(c)(1AA)].

Where under a will, a business was bequeathed to trustees to carry it on and pay the net profits to a charity, the amounts so paid were held to be annual payments (*R v Special Commrs (ex p Shaftesbury Homes) CA 1922, 8 TC 367*). For annual payments generally, see **24.10 DEDUCTION OF TAX AT SOURCE.**

Public revenue dividends (as defined) on securities in the name of trustees are exempt so far as they are applicable and applied only towards repairs of any cathedral, college, church, chapel etc.

[ITA 2007, s 533; ICTA 1988, s 505(1)(d)].

Estate income

[16.7] For 2007/08 onwards, estate income (see **23.4** *et seq.* DECEASED ESTATES) of a trustee of a charitable trust is exempt so far as it is applied for the purposes of the charitable trust only. [*ITA 2007, s 537*]. This provision enables the trustee to recover any income tax suffered by the personal representatives on the income (see **23.3** DECEASED ESTATES).

Before 2007/08 there was no statutory provision to this effect, but HMRC policy was to allow repayment claims by trustees of charitable trusts in respect of estate income (see Change 97 listed in Annex 1 to the Explanatory Notes to *ITA 2007*).

Trading profits

[16.8] Profits of a trade carried on by, and applied solely for the purposes of, a charitable trust, are exempt if the profits are profits of a tax year in relation to which the trade is a 'charitable trade'.

The exemption is extended by *ITA 2007* to include adjustment income (see **73.20** TRADING INCOME) from such a trade arising in a tax year in which the trade is a charitable trade and POST-CESSATION RECEIPTS **(59)**from a trade which was a charitable trade in the tax year of cessation. As with trading profits, the adjustment income or post-cessation receipt must be applied to the purposes of the trust only. The extensions apply HMRC's previous practice (see Change 92 listed in Annex 1 to the Explanatory Notes to *ITA 2007*).

For this purpose, a trade is a '*charitable trade*' in relation to a tax year if throughout the basis period (see **73.3** TRADING INCOME) for the year:

(a)   the trade is exercised in the course of carrying out a primary purpose of the charitable trust; or

(b)   the work is mainly carried out by its beneficiaries.

A trade exercised partly as in (a) above and partly otherwise is treated as two separate trades for this purpose, receipts and expenditure being apportioned between them on a just and reasonable basis. Similarly, where the work is carried out partly, but not mainly, by beneficiaries (see (b) above), the part in connection with which work is carried out by beneficiaries and the other part are treated as separate trades.

[*ITA 2007, ss 524, 525; ICTA 1988, s 505(1)(e); ITTOIA 2005, Sch 1 para 198(2); FA 2006, s 56*].

For trades held to fall within the exemption, see *Glasgow Musical Festival Assn* CS 1926, 11 TC 154; *Royal Choral Society v CIR* CA 1943, 25 TC 263 and *Dean Leigh Temperance Canteen Trustees v CIR* Ch D 1958, 38 TC 315. For regular trading, see *British Legion, Peterhead Branch v CIR* CS 1953, 35 TC 509. (In practice, HMRC may in such cases allow a reasonable deduction for services etc. provided free.)

In practice, HMRC extend the exemptions above to related 'ancillary activities' such as the provision of a bar to theatre patrons and a coffee shop for patrons of a museum or similar concern. Guidance on the extent of and limitations to ancillary activities is at item 13 at www.hmrc.gov.uk/charities/guidance-notes/annex4/sectionb.htm#12.

There are also three specific exemptions as follows.

Exemption for small trades and miscellaneous income and gains

Profits of a trade not otherwise exempt from income tax which is carried on by, and applied solely for the purposes of, a charitable trust, are exempt for a tax year provided that the resources condition described below is met in relation to that year.

The exemption is extended by *ITA 2007* to include adjustment income (see **73.20** TRADING INCOME) and POST-CESSATION RECEIPTS (**59**) from a trade carried on by a charitable trust which are applied to the purposes of the trust only. Any adjustment income must arise in, and any post-cessation receipt must be received in, a tax year for which the resources condition below is met. These extensions apply HMRC's previous practice (see Change 92 listed in Annex 1 to the Explanatory Notes to *ITA 2007*).

The exemption also applies for a tax year to income or gains of a charitable trust which is chargeable to income tax under any of the provisions listed in *ITA 2007, s 1016* (see **49.8** MISCELLANEOUS INCOME) and is not otherwise exempted from income tax, provided that the income or gains are applied solely for the purposes of the trust and that the resources condition below is met in relation to that year.

The resources condition is that:

(i)   the sum of the trust's trading and miscellaneous incoming resources (broadly, the gross income potentially within this exemption and before deducting expenses) for the tax year does not exceed the 'requisite limit'; or

(ii)   the trustees had, at the beginning of the tax year, a reasonable expectation that its trading and miscellaneous incoming resources (as above) would not exceed that limit.

The '*requisite limit*' is 25% of the charitable trust's total incoming resources but must not be less than £5,000 or more than £50,000.

The extension of the exemption to miscellaneous income is intended to cover miscellaneous fund-raising activities not counted as trading. Certain specified tax charges listed in *ITA 2007, s 1016* are excluded from the exemption (see *ITA 2007, s 527(2)*).

[*ITA 2007, ss 526–528; FA 2000, s 46; CTA 2010, Sch 1 para 530; TIOPA 2010, Sch 8 para 81*].

HMRC will consider any evidence to satisfy the reasonable expectation test in (b) above. Such evidence may include minutes of meetings at which the expectations were discussed, cash-flow forecasts, business plans and previous years' accounts (see HMRC guidance on trading by charities in para 22 at www.hmrc.gov.uk/charities/guidance-notes/annex4/sectionb.htm#19).

Fund-raising events

The profits of a trade carried on by a charitable trust are exempt so far as they arise from a VAT-exempt event and are applied solely for the purposes of the trust. An event is VAT-exempt for this purpose if the supply of goods and services by the trust in connection with the event would be exempt from value added tax under Group 12 of *VATA 1994, Sch 9* (fund-raising events by charities and other qualifying bodies). *[ITA 2007, s 529]*. For 2006/07 and earlier years this exemption applied by way of extra-statutory concession (ESC C4).

There is guidance on this exemption and the corresponding VAT exemption at www.hmrc.gov.uk/charities/fund-raising-events.htm.

Lotteries

Lottery profits applied solely to the charitable trust's purposes are exempt, provided that:

- (on and after 1 September 2007) the lottery is an exempt lottery within the meaning of *Gambling Act 2005* by virtue of *Pt 1* or *Pt 4* of *Sch 11* of that *Act* or is promoted in accordance with a lottery operating licence within the meaning of *Pt 5* of that *Act* or is promoted and conducted in accordance with relevant NI legislation;
- (before 1 September 2007) the lottery is promoted and conducted in accordance with *Lotteries and Amusements Act 1976, s 3* or *s 5* (or NI equivalent).

[ITA 2007, s 530; ICTA 1988, s 505(1)(f); FA 2007, Sch 25 para 2; SI 2007 No 2532, Regs 2, 3].

Capital gains

[16.9] Charitable trusts are exempt from capital gains tax on gains applicable, and applied, for charitable purposes. *[TCGA 1992, s 256(1); ITA 2007, Sch 1 para 326(1)]*. But this exemption does not apply to gains arising where property which ceases to be subject to charitable trusts is then deemed to have been sold, and immediately re-acquired, at market value. Any CGT on such gains may be assessed within three years after the year of assessment in which the cessation occurs. *[TCGA 1992, s 256(2)]*. The exemption applies to liability under *TCGA 1992, s 87* in respect of capital payments received from offshore trusts. (Revenue Tax Bulletin August 1998 pp 573, 574).

Miscellaneous

[16.10] The following miscellaneous items are relevant.

Offshore income gains

Offshore income gains (see **51.3, 51.29 OFFSHORE FUNDS**) of a charitable trust are exempt if applicable and applied to charitable purposes. No claim is needed for the exemption to apply. *[ITA 2007, ss 535, 538(2); ICTA 1988, s 761(6); SI 2009 No 3001, Reg 129(4)]*.

Where property representing directly or indirectly an offshore income gain ceases to be subject to charitable trusts, the trustees are treated as if they had disposed of and immediately re-acquired the property at market value. Any offshore income gain accruing does not attract the above exemption. *[ICTA 1988, s 761(6)(6A)(6B)(6C); ITA 2007, Sch 1 para 179; SI 2009 No 3001, Reg 31(3)–(6)]*.

Transactions in deposits

Profits or gains arising to a charitable trust from the disposal, or (except so far as the right is a right to receive interest) the exercise, of 'exempt deposit rights' are exempt so far as applied solely for charitable purposes. For this purpose, *'exempt deposit rights'* are:

- a right to receive, with or without interest, a principal amount stated in, or determined in accordance with, the current terms of issue of an 'eligible debt security' (as defined), where in accordance with those terms the issue of 'uncertificated units' (as defined) of the security corresponds to the issue of a certificate of deposit (see **14 CERTIFICATES OF DEPOSIT**);
- a right to receive the principal amount stated in a certificate of deposit with or without interest; and
- an 'uncertificated right' (i.e. a right in respect of which no certificate of deposit has been issued, although the person entitled to it is entitled to call for the issue of such a certificate) to receive a principal amount, with or without interest, as a result of a deposit of money.

No claim is needed for the exemption to apply.

[ITA 2007, ss 534, 538(1); ICTA 1988, ss 56(3), 56A(3)].

Charitable unit trust schemes are excluded from the normal income tax treatment of unauthorised unit trusts, and are thus able to pass on their income to participating charitable trusts without deducting tax. *[SI 1988 No 267; SI 1994 No 1479].*

Restrictions on exemptions

[16.11] A restriction of the exemptions referred to in **16.4–16.10** above applies for any tax year in which a charitable trust incurs (or is treated as incurring) 'non-charitable expenditure' (see below).

Exemption is denied in respect of so much of any income or gains which are attributed to the 'non-exempt amount' for the year. For this purpose, the *'non-exempt amount'* for a tax year is equal to the non-charitable expenditure for the year or, if less, the *'attributable income and gains'* for the year (i.e. the total of the otherwise exempt income and gains for the year).

Attributable income and/or attributable gains are to be attributed to the non-exempt amount until the whole of that amount is used up. The charitable trust may itself specify by notice to HMRC which particular items of income and gains are to be so attributed; but if HMRC require a charitable trust to give such notice and the trust fails to comply within 30 days of the requirement being imposed, HMRC may then determine which amounts are to be treated as attributed.

[ITA 2007, ss 539–542, Sch 1 paras 326, 327; ICTA 1988, s 505(3)(4)(7); TCGA 1992, ss 256(3), (4)–(6), 256A, 256B; CTA 2010, Sch 1 para 254(4); SI 2007 No 3506, Reg 3(3); SI 2009 No 23, Regs 1, 3].

If the non-charitable expenditure exceeds the charity's 'available income and gains' for the tax year, the excess is carried back and treated as non-charitable expenditure of earlier tax years ending not more than six years before the end of the year in which the expenditure was actually incurred, taking later years in priority to earlier years. The amount of the excess to be attributed to an earlier year cannot be greater than the amount, if any, by which the available income and gains for that earlier year exceed the non-charitable expenditure for that year (including any excess expenditure attributed to the year as a result of a previous operation of these provisions).

For the above purpose, a charitable trust's *'available income and gains'* is the aggregate of its otherwise exempt income and gains, its chargeable income and gains and its other non-chargeable receipts such as donations and legacies.

[*ITA 2007, ss 562–564, Sch 2 para 107; ICTA 1988, s 505(5)(6)*].

A charitable trust's *'non-charitable expenditure'* for a tax year is:

(a) any loss made in the year (i.e. any loss made in the basis period for the year) in a trade other than a trade within one of the exemptions at **16.8** above;

(b) any payment made in the year in connection with a trade where post-cessation expenditure relief is available (see **59.5 POST-CESSATION RECEIPTS AND EXPENDITURE**) unless the trade was within one of the exemptions at **16.8** above at cessation;

(c) any loss made in the year in a trade, UK or overseas property business where the loss relates to land and any profits generated from the land for the year would not have been within the exemption at **16.5** above;

(d) any payment made in the year in connection with a trade or UK or overseas property business where post-cessation expenditure relief is available (see **59.5 POST-CESSATION RECEIPTS AND EXPENDITURE**) where the payment relates to land and any profits generated from the land immediately before cessation would not be within the exemption at **16.5** above;

(e) any loss made in the year in a 'miscellaneous transaction' entered into otherwise than in the course of carrying on a charitable purpose;

(f) any 'expenditure' incurred in the tax year not within (b) or (d) above which is not incurred solely for charitable purposes and is not required to be taken into account in calculating the profits or losses of any trade or property business or miscellaneous transaction;

(g) any amounts for the year treated as non-charitable expenditure under the substantial donor provisions at **16.12** below;

(h) the amount of any funds invested in the year in any investment which is not an 'approved charitable investment'; and

(i) any amount lent in the year by the trust, if the loan is neither an investment nor an 'approved charitable loan'.

Any amount falling within more than one of the above categories is treated as non-charitable expenditure only once.

For the purposes of (e) and (f) above, a *'miscellaneous transaction'* is a transaction any income or gains from which would have been chargeable to income tax under any of the provisions listed in *ITA 2007, s 1016* (see **49.8 MISCELLANEOUS INCOME**) but for the miscellaneous income and gains exemption at **16.8** above, where the trustees of the charitable trust would have been liable for the tax.

For the purposes of (f) above, '*expenditure*' includes capital expenditure but does not include the investment of any of the charitable trust's funds, the making of a loan by the trust or the repayment by the trust of the whole or part of a loan. Expenditure which is referable to commitments (contractual or otherwise) entered into before or during a particular tax year is treated as incurred in that year if, had accounts been drawn up in accordance with UK generally accepted accounting practice for the year, it would have had to be taken into account in preparing those accounts. A payment made (or to be made) to a body situated outside the UK is non-charitable expenditure within (f) above unless the charitable trust has taken all reasonable steps to ensure that the payment will be applied for charitable purposes. For payments representing expenditure incurred on or after 24 March 2010, any claim that such a payment is charitable expenditure must be supported by evidence sufficient to satisfy the Commissioners for HMRC that such reasonable steps were taken.

If, in any tax year, a charitable trust (wholly or partly) realises an investment made in that year which is not an approved charitable investment or is repaid a loan made in that year which is neither an investment nor an approved charitable loan, any further investment or lending in that year of the amount realised or repaid (to the extent that it does not exceed the amount originally invested or lent) cannot be treated for a second time as non-charitable expenditure.

Note that, prior to the enactment of *ITA 2007*, there was no detailed definition of 'non-charitable expenditure'. The *ITA 2007* definition given above does, however, reflect existing HMRC practice (see Change 98 listed in Annex 1 to the Explanatory Notes to the *ITA 2007*).

[*ITA 2007, ss 543–548, Sch 2 para 105; ICTA 1988, s 506; FA 2010, Sch 8 paras 2(1), 8(3)*].

The following are '*approved charitable investments*'.

(i)   An investment in securities (including shares, stocks and debentures (as defined)):

- issued or guaranteed by the government of an EU member state of the government or a governmental body of any territory or part of a territory;
- issued by an international entity listed in the Annex to Council Directive 2003/48/EC;
- issued by an entity meeting the four criteria set out at the end of that Annex;
- issued by a building society;
- issued by a credit institution operating on mutual principles which is authorised by an appropriate governmental body in the territory of issue;
- issued by an open-ended investment company (within *CTA 2010, ss 613, 615*);
- issued by a company and listed on a recognised stock exchange (within *ITA 2007, s 1005*); or
- issued by a company and not listed on a recognised stock exchange.

Further conditions (see *ITA 2007, s 560*) must be met in the case of certain of the above securities.

(ii)   An investment in a common investment fund established under *Charities Act 1960, s 22* (or NI equivalent) or *Charities Act 1993, s 24*.

(iii)   An investment in a common deposit fund established under *Charities Act 1960, s 22A* or *Charities Act 1993, s 25*.

(iv)   An investment in a fund which is similar to those in (ii) or (iii) above which is established for the exclusive benefit of charities by or under legislation relating to any particular charities or class of charities.

(v)   An interest in land other than an interest held as security for a debt.

(vi)   Any bills, certificates of tax deposit, savings certificates or tax reserve certificates issued in the UK by the Government.

(vii)   Northern Ireland Treasury bills.

(viii)   Units in a unit trust scheme within *Financial Services and Markets Act 2000, s 237(1)* or in a recognised scheme within *Financial Services and Markets Act 2000, s 237(3)*.

(ix)   A deposit with a bank (within *ITA 2007, s 991*) in respect of which interest is payable at a commercial rate, but excluding a deposit made as part of an arrangement under which the bank makes a loan to a third party.

(x)   A deposit with the National Savings Bank, a building society or a credit institution operating on mutual principles which is authorised by an appropriate governmental body in the territory in which the deposit is taken.

(xi)   CERTIFICATES OF DEPOSIT (**14**) within *ITTOIA 2005, s 552(2)*, including uncertificated eligible debt security units as defined in *ITA 2007, s 986(3)*.

(xii)   Any loan or other investment as to which HMRC are satisfied, on a claim, that it is made for the benefit of the charitable trust and not for the avoidance of tax (whether by the trust or any other person). Loans secured by mortgage etc. over land are within this heading.

[*ITA 2007, ss 558–560; ICTA 1988, Sch 20 Pt I; CTA 2010, Sch 1 para 536; SI 2001 No 3629, Art 50*].

As regards swap contracts, e.g. interest rate or currency swaps, see Revenue Tax Bulletin August 2003 p 1056.

The following are '*approved charitable loans*' if they are not made by way of investment.

- A loan made to another charity for charitable purposes only.
- A loan to a beneficiary of the charitable trust which is made in the course of carrying out the purposes of the trust.
- Money placed on a current account with a bank (within *ITA 2007, s 991*), but excluding a loan made as part of an arrangement under which the bank makes a loan to a third party.
- Any other loan as to which HMRC are satisfied, on a claim, that the loan is made for the benefit of the charitable trust and not for the avoidance of tax (whether by the trust or by some other person).

[*ITA 2007, s 561; ICTA 1988, Sch 20 Pt II*].

See the detailed guidance on all aspects of these provisions at www.hmrc.go
v.uk/charities/guidance-notes/annex2/annex_ii.htm. For HMRC guidance on
approved charitable investments and loans, see www.hmrc.gov.uk/charities/g
uidance-notes/annex3/annex_iii.htm.

Restrictions on exemptions — transactions with substantial donors

[16.12] Where a charitable trust participates in a 'substantial donor transaction' with a 'substantial donor' (see below), any payment made by the
charitable trust to the donor in the course of, or for the purposes of, the
transaction is treated for the purposes of **16.11** above as non-charitable
expenditure. If the terms of any such transaction are less beneficial to the
charitable trust than might be expected in the case of an arm's length
transaction, the trust is treated as incurring non-charitable expenditure of an
amount to be determined by HMRC (and at a time to be determined by
HMRC) as being the cost to the trust of the difference in terms. Either or both
of these rules may be applied to a single transaction, but any amount caught
by the first-mentioned rule is deductible from the amount determined under
the second rule.

Any payment of remuneration by a charitable trust to a 'substantial donor' is
treated as non-charitable expenditure unless it is remuneration, for services as
a trustee, that is approved by the Charity Commission, by any similar
regulatory body under legislation in effect in any part of the UK or by a court.
Where remuneration is paid otherwise than in money, the cash equivalent is
determined in accordance with the benefit-in-kind rules for employees (see
27.30 EMPLOYMENT INCOME).

In dealing with an appeal against an assessment, the Appeal Tribunal may
review any decision of HMRC in connection with these rules.

See the detailed guidance, including examples, at www.hmrc.gov.uk/charities/
guidance-notes/annex2/annex_ii.htm#11.

Meaning of 'substantial donor transaction'

The following types of transaction are *substantial donor transactions*.

(a) The sale or letting of property by a charitable trust to a substantial
donor or *vice versa*.

(b) The provision of services by a charitable trust to a substantial donor or
vice versa.

(c) An exchange of property between a charitable trust and a substantial
donor.

(d) The provision of financial assistance by a charitable trust to a substantial donor or *vice versa*. 'Financial assistance' includes, but is not
restricted to, the providing of a loan, guarantee or indemnity and the
entering into of **ALTERNATIVE FINANCE ARRANGEMENTS (3)**.

(e) Any investment by a charitable trust in the business of a substantial
donor.

The above list is subject to the following exceptions.

- As regards (a) and (b) above, the sale or letting or provision of services *by* a substantial donor *to* a charitable trust is outside these rules if HMRC determine that it occurs in the course of a business carried on by the donor, is on the equivalent of arm's length terms and is not part of tax avoidance arrangements.

- As regards (b) above, the provision of services *by* a charitable trust *to* a donor is outside the rules if HMRC determine that the services are provided in the course of carrying out a primary purpose of the charitable trust and are provided on terms no more beneficial to the donor than those on which services are provided to others.

- As regards (d) above, the provision of financial assistance *by* a donor *to* a charitable trust is outside the rules if HMRC determine that it is on the equivalent of arm's length terms and is not part of tax avoidance arrangements.

- As regards (e) above, an investment is outside the rules if it takes the form of the purchase of shares or securities listed on a recognised stock exchange.

- A gift of shares, securities or real property to a charitable trust at an undervalue and within **16.21** below (or equivalent corporation tax provisions) is not a transaction within these rules; this does not prevent its being taken into account in determining whether or not a donor is a 'substantial donor' (see below).

- A gift of an asset to a charitable trust, being a gift within *TCGA 1992, s 257*, is not a transaction within these rules; this does not prevent its being taken into account in determining whether or not a donor is a 'substantial donor' (see below).

- If, in relation to a gift aid donation, the charitable trust provides benefits to the donor that do not breach the allowable limits at **16.18** below (or equivalent limits relating to corporate gift aid), such benefits are disregarded for the purposes of these rules.

Meaning of 'substantial donor'

For these purposes, a person is a *'substantial donor'* to a charitable trust for a tax year if:

- the charitable trust receives from him 'relievable gifts' of £25,000 or more in any period of 12 months in which that tax year wholly or partly falls; or

- the charitable trust receives from him 'relievable gifts' of £150,000 or more (£100,000 or more before 23 April 2009) in any period of six years in which that tax year wholly or partly falls,

but if, by virtue of the above, a person is a substantial donor in respect of a tax year, he is also regarded as a substantial donor to the charitable trust in respect of the next five tax years. If a transaction is entered into in a tax year with a person who turns out to be a substantial donor in respect of that year, it is caught by these rules even if the person was not a substantial donor at the time of the transaction.

A company that is wholly owned by a charity (within the meaning of *CTA 2010, s 200*) is not treated as a substantial donor in relation to a charitable trust that owns it (or any part of it). A registered social landlord or housing association (both as defined) is not treated as a substantial donor in relation to a charitable trust with which it is connected (and for this purpose a body and a charitable trust are connected if one owns or controls the other or they are under common ownership or control).

'*Relievable gifts*' are effectively gifts and donations on which the donor is entitled to some form of income tax, corporation tax or capital gains tax relief; a full list of the types of gift covered is given (in terms of the legislation under which the tax relief is available) at *ITA 2007, s 550* (as amended) and is comprehensive. Non-monetary gifts are included in the rules by reference to their value. Both the sums and the periods of time referred to above may be varied in future by the Treasury by statutory instrument.

Connected persons rules

All references within these rules to a substantial donor or to any person include references to a person connected with the donor or with that person (within **21 CONNECTED PERSONS**). A charitable trust and any other charities with which it is 'connected' may be treated as a single charitable trust for the purposes of these rules; for this purpose, '*connected*' means connected in a matter relating to the structure, administration or control of a charity. This is intended to prevent the rules being circumvented by fragmenting a single charitable trust into two or more charities.

[*ITA 2007, ss 549–557, Sch 2 paras 105, 106; ICTA 1988, ss 506A–506C; CTA 2009, Sch 1 paras 703, 704; CTA 2010, Sch 1 paras 532–535; SI 2009 No 56, Sch 1 para 453; SI 2009 No 1029*].

Gifts to charitable trusts

[16.13] The receipt by a charitable trust of a '*qualifying donation*' under the Gift Aid scheme (see **16.17** below) is treated as the receipt, under deduction of basic rate income tax for the tax year in which the gift is made, of a gift equal to the 'grossed up amount of the gift' (i.e. the amount of the gift grossed up by reference to the basic rate for the tax year in which the gift is made).The income tax so treated as deducted is treated as income tax paid by the trustees, so that they can normally reclaim the tax from HMRC. So far as a gift is not applied to charitable purposes only, however, the grossed up amount of the gift is charged to income tax. The charge is on the amounts arising in the tax year and the trustees are liable for any tax so charged. [*ITA 2007, ss 520, 521; ICTA 1988, s 505(1)*].

In the case of a gift made via the self-assessment tax return (see above), the charity is treated as having made any necessary claim for exemption from tax, which means that it will receive back the basic rate tax without having to reclaim it. [*ITA 2007, s 538(3); CTA 2009, Sch 1 para 571*].

In the case of other gifts under the Gift Aid Scheme, a claim by the charity for exemption from tax can be made either within or outside a tax return. *ITA 2007, s 538A* puts this on a statutory footing and also gives HMRC power to make regulations limiting the number of claims that are made outside the return. [*TMA 1970, s 43(3ZA); ITA 2007, s 538A; FA 2010, Sch 8 paras 4, 5, 8(6)*].

The receipt by a charitable trust of a donation made on or after 24 March 2010 under the payroll giving scheme (see **16.20** below) is chargeable to tax to the extent that it is not applied to charitable purposes only. The charge is on the full amounts arising in the tax year and the trustees are liable for any tax so charged. [*ITA 2007, s 521A; FA 2010, Sch 8 paras 1(1), 8(1)*].

Gifts of money from companies (other than companies which are charities — see **16.14** below) are also charged to income tax except so far as applied to charitable purposes only. The charge is on the full amount of such gifts arising in the tax year and the trustees are liable for any tax so charged. [*ITA 2007, s 522; ICTA 1988, ss 339(4), 505(1); FA 2000, s 40(6); ITTOIA 2005, Sch 1 para 198*].

Transitional Gift Aid supplement

The reduction in the basic rate of income tax from 22% to 20% for 2008/09 onwards has the consequential effect of reducing the amount a charity can reclaim from HMRC in respect of a Gift Aid donation. For example, a cash gift of £78 in 2007/08 would be grossed up to £100, and the charity would reclaim £22. A cash gift of the same amount in 2008/09 would be grossed up to £97.50, and the charity would be able to reclaim only £19.50. However, for the three years 2008/09 to 2010/11 inclusive, a charity is able to reclaim the difference (i.e. £2.50 in the example given) by way of a tax-free supplement. In order to qualify for the supplement in relation to a Gift Aid donation, a charitable trust must make a successful claim for exemption from income tax in respect of that donation within two years after the end of the tax year in question. Any change in the basic rate for 2010/11 will affect the amount of supplement available. There are provisions enabling HMRC to recover, with interest, an amount of supplement wrongly paid or overpaid. [*ITA 2007, s 521(7); FA 2008, s 53, Sch 19*].

Simon's Taxes. See C5.117C.

Payments from other charities

[16.14] Any payments received by a charitable trust from other charities, other than in return for full consideration, which would otherwise not be chargeable to income tax (and which are not of a description which on a claim would be exempt from income tax under any of the relieving provisions at **16.5–16.8**, **16.10** above), are chargeable to income tax. The charge is on the full amount of the payments arising in the tax year and the trustees of the charitable trust are liable for the tax charged. The amount charged is subject, where relevant, to the provisions at **68.11** SETTLEMENTS regarding discretionary payments by trustees.

The above provision does not apply to payments arising from a source outside the UK or to payments so far as applied solely for charitable purposes.

[*ITA 2007, s 523; ICTA 1988, s 505(2); ITTOIA 2005, Sch 1 para 198(4)*].

Simon's Taxes. See C5.117C.

Gift aid donations by individuals

[16.15] Gifts of money made by individuals to charities which are 'qualifying donations' (see **16.17** below) attract tax relief under the Gift Aid scheme described below. For the Gift Aid scheme as it applies to company donors, see the corresponding chapter of Tolley's Corporation Tax.

For the purposes of these provisions, '*charity*' has the meaning in **16.3** above (**16.2** above in relation to gifts made before 6 April 2010) but also includes the Trustees of the National Heritage Memorial Fund, the Historic Buildings and Monuments Commission for England, the National Endowment for Science, Technology and the Arts, and registered community amateur sports clubs under *CTA 2010, ss 658–671* (and predecessor legislation) (but club membership fees are not gifts for the purposes of these provisions). [*ITA 2007, s 430; FA 1990, s 25(12)(a); CTA 2010, Sch 1 para 526; FA 2010, Sch 6 paras 23(6), 33, 34(1)*]. For the application of the relief to gifts to community amateur sports clubs, see Tolley's Corporation Tax under Voluntary Associations.

A detailed guide to Gift Aid is available at www.hmrc.gov.uk/charities/guidance-notes/chapter3/index.htm.

Simon's Taxes. See E1.810, E1.811.

The Gift Aid scheme

[16.16] Where a 'qualifying donation' to charity is made by an individual ('*the donor*') in a tax year, then, for that year, he is treated for the purposes of income tax (and capital gains tax) as if:

(a)   the gift had been made after deduction of income tax at the basic rate; and

(b)   the basic rate limit and (for 2010/11 onwards) the higher rate limit (see **1.3 ALLOWANCES AND TAX RATES**) were increased by an amount equal to the 'grossed up amount of the gift', i.e. the amount which, after deducting income tax at the basic rate for the tax year in which the gift is made, leaves the amount of the gift.

The donor obtains higher rate relief, where applicable, by virtue of (b) above. For this purpose, higher rate relief generally means relief for the excess of tax at the higher rate over tax at the basic rate for which relief is effectively given at source by virtue of (a) above (but see the second example at **16.19** below for the situation where there is dividend income, which also applied where there was non-dividend savings income before 2008/09). (The increase in the basic rate limit does not apply for the purposes of computing top slicing relief as in **44.8 LIFE ASSURANCE POLICIES**). For 2010/11 onwards, individuals liable at the additional (50%) rate will obtain relief at that rate in the same way.

To the extent, if any, necessary to ensure that the amount of income tax and capital gains tax to which the donor is charged for a tax year in which one or more gifts is made is an amount at least equal to the tax treated under (a) above as deducted from the gift or gifts, the donor is *not* entitled to the following reliefs for that year:

•   the personal allowance;

- the blind person's allowance;
- the married couple's allowance;
- children's tax credits; and
- the miscellaneous life assurance-related reliefs at **44.2 LIFE ASSURANCE POLICIES.**

The restriction does not adversely affect the donor's ability to transfer unused married couple's allowance to a spouse or civil partner as in **47.3 MARRIED PERSONS AND CIVIL PARTNERS.**

Where the tax treated as deducted exceeds the amount of income tax and capital gains tax to which the donor is charged for the year after taking into account the above restriction of reliefs, the donor is liable to an income tax charge for the year, the tax chargeable being equal to the excess.

The amount of income tax to which the donor is charged for a tax year for these purposes is calculated according to the steps at **1.7 ALLOWANCES AND TAX RATES,** but with the following modifications.

(i)   At Step 6 (tax reductions), the following tax reductions are ignored:
- relief for qualifying maintenance payments (see **47.9 MARRIED PERSONS AND CIVIL PARTNERS**); and
- any **DOUBLE TAX RELIEF (26)** (whether given under a double tax agreement or unilaterally).

(ii)   Step 7 is ignored.

(iii) The following amounts are deducted:
- any notional tax treated as having been paid under *ITTOIA 2005, s 399* or *s 400* (distributions without a tax credit — see **64.9, 64.10 SAVINGS AND INVESTMENT INCOME**), *ITTOIA 2005, s 414* (stock dividends — see **64.14 SAVINGS AND INVESTMENT INCOME**), *ITTOIA 2005, s 421* (release of loan to participator in close company — see **64.16 SAVINGS AND INVESTMENT INCOME**), *ITTOIA 2005 s 530* (life assurance gains — see **44.7 LIFE ASSURANCE POLICIES**), or *ITTOIA 2005, s 685A* (payments from settlor-interested settlements — see **68.26 SETTLEMENTS**);
- any tax treated as deducted from estate income under *ITTOIA 2005, s 656(3) or s 657(4)*, to the extent that it is treated as paid out of sums within *ITTOIA 2005, s 680(3)(b)* or *(4)* (see **23.6 DECEASED ESTATES**); and
- the amount of any tax credit attaching to a dividend or other distribution from a non-UK resident company (see **64.13 SAVINGS AND INVESTMENT INCOME**).

The amount of capital gains tax to which the donor is charged for a tax year for these purposes is similarly calculated without regard for any double tax relief due, whether under a double tax agreement or unilaterally.

See **1.14, 1.15 ALLOWANCES AND TAX RATES** for the deduction of the aggregate grossed up amount of a donor's qualifying donations for a tax year in calculating 'net income' for the purpose of applying the income limit for age-related personal allowance and married couple's allowance.

[ITA 2007, ss 414, 415, 423–425, Sch 1 para 536(4); FA 1990, s 25(1)(6)(a)(c), (8)–(9A)(12)(d); FA 2008, s 34, Sch 1 paras 20, 65, Sch 12 para 24; FA 2009, Sch 1 paras 6, 7, Sch 2 paras 6, 25; TIOPA 2010, Sch 8 paras 79, 80; SI 2009 No 2859, Art 4(3)].

See the examples at **16.19** below.

Carry-back of relief

The donor may elect for a qualifying donation to be treated for the purposes of the relief as having been made in the previous tax year, provided that the condition below is satisfied.

For amounts carried back from 2008/09 onwards, the condition is that the donor's 'charged amount' for that previous tax year must be at least equal to the 'increased total of gifts'. For this purpose, the donor's *'charged amount'* for a tax year is the sum of his 'modified net income' and the amount on which he is chargeable to capital gains tax for the year. The definition of *'modified net income'* at **1.9 ALLOWANCES AND TAX RATES** applies for this purpose as if the first modification listed there were omitted. The *'increased total of gifts'* is the aggregate of the sum of the grossed up amounts of all the gifts made in the current year which are to be, or have already been (by an earlier election) carried back to the previous year and the sum of the grossed up amounts of any qualifying donations actually made in the previous year (and not themselves carried back). All the grossed up amounts are calculated for this purpose as if the gifts were made in the previous year.

For amounts carried back from 2007/08 or an earlier year, the condition is that the grossed up amount of the gift would, if made in the previous year, be payable out of profits or gains brought into charge to income tax or capital gains tax for that year.

The election must be made in writing to HMRC by the date of delivery of the self-assessment return for the previous year, and not later than 31 January following the end of that year. The election affects only the tax position of the donor. As regards the recipient charity, the donation continues to be treated as made in the tax year in which it is in fact made. The 'date of delivery of the self-assessment return' means the date of delivery of the original return and not an amended return (*Cameron v HMRC* FTT (TC 415), [2010] SFTD 664).

The carry-back facility above is *not* available in respect of gifts made through the self-assessment return as below.

[ITA 2007, ss 426, 427, Sch 2 para 100; FA 2002, s 98; CTA 2010, Sch 1 para 525].

Giving through the self-assessment return

Where, as a result of his filing a personal self-assessment tax return, an individual is entitled to an income tax and/or capital gains tax repayment for one or more years, he may (within the tax return itself) authorise HMRC to make the repayment (or a specified part of it) by means of a gift to a single charity specified by him. (For these purposes, an individual is entitled to a repayment only if he is entitled to it after any set-off against liabilities, other than one made under *FA 2008, s 130*, and the amount of the repayment to be gifted is taken as including any repayment supplement due — see **41 INTEREST ON OVERPAID TAX**). The specified charity must be included on the list maintained for these purposes by HMRC. (Charities need to apply to HMRC to be included on the list.) The gift must meet the conditions at **16.17**(a)–(g) below. It is then treated as a qualifying donation made by the individual at the time the payment is received by the charity. [*ITA 2007, s 429; FA 2008, s 130(9); FA 2010, Sch 8 paras 3(4), 8(5)*]. In practice, taxpayers are required to enter on the return the unique reference code allocated to the charity of their choice; there is a search facility at www.hmrc.gov.uk/charities/charities-search. htm to assist in finding the code required.

See **16.13** above for the treatment of charitable trusts receiving qualifying donations. See the corresponding chapter of Tolley's Corporation Tax for the treatment of charitable companies.

Qualifying donations

[16.17] A *'qualifying donation'* is a gift to a charity by the donor which meets the following conditions:

(a)   it takes the form of a payment of a sum of money;

(b)   it is not subject to a condition as to repayment;

(c)   it is not deductible under the payroll deduction scheme — see **16.20** below;

(d)   it is not deductible in calculating the donor's income from any source;

(e)   it is not conditional on, or associated with, or part of an arrangement involving, the acquisition of property by the charity, otherwise than by way of gift, from the donor or a person connected with him;

(f)   neither the donor nor any person connected with him (see **21 CON-NECTED PERSONS**) receives any benefit, in consequence of making it, in excess of specified limits (see **16.18** below);

(g)   (in relation to gifts made before 6 April 2010) the gift is not a 'disqualified overseas gift'; and

(h)   the donor gives the charity a 'gift aid declaration' in relation to it.

For the purposes of (g) above, an *'overseas gift'* is a gift which would otherwise be a qualifying donation which is made at a time when the donor is neither UK-resident nor is in Crown employment (i.e. employment under the Crown which is of a public nature and the earnings from which are payable out of UK public revenue). For 2007/08 to 2009/10 inclusive, an overseas gift is a *'disqualified overseas gift'* if, as a result of the gift, the donor's overseas gift total (i.e. the total of the grossed up amounts of all overseas gifts made in the tax year in question) is more than his 'charged amount' (see **16.16** above). For 2006/07 and earlier years, an overseas gift is a disqualified overseas gift unless the grossed up amount of the gift would, if in fact made, be payable out of profits or gains brought into charge to income tax or capital gains tax.

Condition (g) is abolished in relation to gifts made on or after 6 April 2010. This aligns the position for non-UK resident donors with that for UK resident donors. Gift Aid can apply to the donation, and if the non-resident donor has not paid sufficient UK tax to cover the tax treated as deducted from the donation he is liable for the shortfall as in **16.16** above.

A *'gift aid declaration'* for the purposes of (h) above is a declaration which is given in the manner prescribed by regulations. It may be made in writing, by fax, over the internet or orally (e.g. by telephone). It must contain the donor's name and address, the name of the charity, a description of the gift(s) to which it relates, a statement that the gift(s) is (are) to be treated as qualifying donations for these purposes. In order for the declaration to have effect, it must have been explained to the donor that he must pay sufficient income tax or capital gains tax to cover the tax deemed to be deducted at source from the donation. No signature is required. It is unnecessary for the charity to send the donor a written record of an oral declaration, provided it maintains a satisfactory auditable (by HMRC) record of declarations given to it. A donor may still cancel the donation of his own volition. [*SI 2000 No 2074; SI 2005 No 2790*].

[*ITA 2007, ss 416, 417, 422, 428; FA 1990, s 25(1)–(3A)(11); FA 2010, Sch 8 paras 3(2)(3), 8(5)*].

As regards (f) above, the benefit does not have to be received from the charity to be taken into account (see *St Dunstan's v Major* (Sp C 127), [1997] SSCD 212, in which the saving of inheritance tax by personal representatives as a result of the variation of a will to provide for a donation which would otherwise qualify under these provisions constituted a benefit).

The release of a loan not for consideration and not under seal cannot amount to a gift of money (see *Battle Baptist Church v CIR and Woodham* (Sp C 23), [1995] SSCD 176).

Limits on donor benefits

[16.18] Where the donor or a person connected with him (see **21 CONNECTED PERSONS**) receives a benefit or benefits in consequence of making the gift, the gift will not be a qualifying donation if either:

(a) the aggregate value of the benefits received exceeds:
  (i) where the gift is £100 or less, 25% of the amount of the gift;
  (ii) where the gift is greater than £100 but not more than £1,000, £25;
  (iii) where the gift is greater than £1,000, 5% of the amount of the gift (in relation to gifts made in 2007/08 onwards, previously 2.5%); or
(b) the aggregate of the value of the benefits received in relation to the gift and the value of any benefits received in relation to any qualifying donations previously made to the charity by the donor in the same tax year exceeds £500 (in relation to gifts made in 2007/08 onwards, previously £250).

The operation of (a) above is modified where a benefit:

(1)   consists of the right to receive benefits at intervals over a period of less than twelve months;

(2)   relates to a period of less than twelve months;

(3)   is one of a series of benefits received at intervals in consequence of making a series of gifts at intervals of less than twelve months; or

(4)   is not one of a series of benefits but the gift is one of a series of gifts made at intervals of less than twelve months.

Where (1), (2) or (3) above apply, the value of the benefit and the amount of the gift are 'annualised' for the purposes of (a) above. Where (4) above applies, the amount of the gift (but not the value of the benefit) is likewise annualised. For these purposes a gift or benefit is '*annualised*' by multiplying the amount or value by 365 and dividing the result by the number of days in the period of less than twelve months or the average number of days in the intervals of less than twelve months as appropriate.

In determining whether a gift is a qualifying donation, the benefit of any 'right of admission' received in consequence of the gift is disregarded for the purpose of applying the above limits if all the following conditions are satisfied.

• The opportunity to make a gift and to receive an admission right as a consequence must be available to the public.

• The admission right must be a right granted by the charity to view property preserved, maintained, kept or created by a charity for its charitable purposes, including, in particular, buildings, grounds or other land, plants, animals, works of art (but not performances), artefacts and property of a scientific nature.

• Either:
   (i)   the admission right must be valid for a least a year and, during its period of validity, must include all times at which the public can gain admission; or
   (ii) a member of the public could purchase the same admission right, and the amount of the gift is greater by at least 10% than the purchase price.

For these purposes, a '*right of admission*' is a right granted to the donor, or to the donor and members of his family, to be admitted to premises or property for which a public admission fee applies and to be so admitted for no admission fee or for a reduced admission fee. An admission right is within (i) above even if it does not apply on certain days specified by the charity as an '*event day*' (i.e. a day on which an event is take place on the premises concerned), so long as no more than five such days are specified for the period of validity (if the period is one year) or for each calendar year of which the period of validity forms all or part (if the period is more than one year).

[ITA 2007, ss 417–421, Sch 2 para 99; FA 1990, s 25(2)(e), (4)–(5J)(11); FA 2007, s 60(1)(3)].

See www.hmrc.gov.uk/charities/guidance-notes/chapter3/chapter3-insert.htm for guidance on the post-5 April 2006 rules above.

Acknowledgement of a donor in the charity's literature does not amount to a benefit *provided that* it does not take the form of an advertisement for the donor's business (see para 3.27 of the HMRC guide referred to at **16.15** above).

Examples

[16.19]

Higher rate taxpayer (1). Ronan, a single man under 65, has total income of £45,300 for 2010/11 which consists entirely of employment income. During that year, he makes various single donations and covenanted payments to charity, all of them qualifying donations, amounting in total to £600.

		£
Total and net income		45,300
Less Personal Allowance		6,475
Taxable Income		£38,825
Tax Liability		
38,150	@ 20%	7,630.00
675	@ 40%	270.00
£38,825		
		£7,900.00

Note

The basic rate limit of £37,400 is increased by the grossed up amount of the qualifying donations (£600 × 100/80 = £750) and becomes £38,150. Ronan thereby saves tax of £150 (£750 × 20% (40% – 20%)). The charities will reclaim basic rate tax of £150 (£750 × 20%) and will thus receive £750 in all. The net cost to Ronan is £450 (£600 – £150), a saving of 40%.

Higher rate taxpayer (2). The tax relief can, in fact, exceed 40% where the effect of extending the basic rate limit is that an additional amount of dividend income falls within the basic rate band and is taxed at 10% instead of at 32.5%. Imagine the facts are as above but that £10,000 of Ronan's income is UK dividend income (chargeable at 10% if within the basic rate band) with the remaining £35,300 being employment income as before.

		£
Total and net income		45,300
Less Personal Allowance		6,475
Taxable Income		£38,825
Tax Liability		
28,825	@ 20%	5,765.00
9,325	@ 10%	932.50
38,150		
675	@ 32.5%	219.37
£38,825		
		£6,916.87

Note

Ronan now saves tax of £168.75 (£750 × 22.5% (32.5% – 10%)). The charities will still reclaim basic rate tax of £150 (£750 × 20%) and will receive £750 in all. The net cost to Ronan is £431.25 (£600 – £168.75), a saving of 42.5%.

Additional rate taxpayer. Rikki, a single man under 65, has total income of £175,000 for 2010/11, none of which is dividend income. During that year, he makes qualifying donations to charity of £2,400.

		£
Total and net income		175,000
Less Personal Allowance		Nil
Taxable Income		£175,000
Tax Liability		
40,400	@ 20%	8,080.00
112,600	@ 40%	45,080.00
22,000	@ 50%	11,000.00
£175,000		
		£64,120.00

Note

Both the basic rate limit of £37,400 and the higher rate limit of £150,000 are increased by the grossed up amount of the qualifying donations (£2,400 × 100/80 = £3,000) and become £40,400 and £153,000 respectively. Rikki thereby saves tax of £900 (£3.000 × 30% (50% – 20%)). The charities will reclaim basic rate tax of £600 (£3,000 × 20%) and will thus receive £3,000 in all. The net cost to Rikki is £1,500 (£2,400 – £900), a saving of 50%. (No personal allowance is available in this example as income is too high — see **1.14 ALLOWANCES AND TAX RATES.**)

Low income taxpayer. Rod, a single person of 66, has a pension of £6,840 and UK dividends of £2,700 (with tax credits of £300) for 2010/11. He makes a qualifying donation of £400 to charity.

		£
Pension income		6,840
Dividends plus tax credits		3,000
Total and net income		9,840
Less Personal Allowance	9,490	
Restricted by (note (a))	650	8,840
Taxable Income		£1,000
Tax Liability		
£1,000 @ 10% (dividend ordinary rate)		100.00
Deduct tax credits on dividends (note (b))		100.00
		Nil

Notes

(a) The personal allowance is restricted by such amount as is necessary to leave tax of £100.00 in charge, this being the amount of basic rate tax deemed to have been deducted at source from the qualifying donation (£400 × 20/80 = £100).

(b) Although dividend tax credits of £300 are available, the deduction is limited to 10% of the taxable income (as dividend tax credits are not repayable — see **64.8 SAVINGS AND INVESTMENT INCOME**).

Payroll giving schemes

[**16.20**] Under an 'approved payroll giving scheme', an individual may make charitable donations, without limit, by deduction from earnings (or pension income or taxable social security income) subject to **PAYE** (**53**). At the individual's request, the employer (or other payer) withholds sums from gross pay as 'donations'. The amount of the donations is allowed as a deduction from gross pay for PAYE purposes and in calculating the individual's taxable income. The deduction is made from the particular type of income (e.g. employment income) in respect of which the donations are made. The deduction is made for the tax year in which the donation is withheld or, as regards pension and social security income only, for the tax year in which the income out of which the deduction is made is chargeable to tax. A donation made under a payroll giving scheme is not a qualifying donation for Gift Aid purposes (see **16.17** above).

'*Donations*' are sums withheld by the payer under a scheme which at that time is an 'approved payroll giving scheme' and which constitute gifts by the individual to one or more charities specified by him and satisfy any conditions set out in the scheme. An '*approved payroll giving scheme*' is a scheme approved by (or of a kind approved by) HMRC under which the payer is required to pay to an 'approved agent' the sums withheld and the agent is required to pass them on to the specified charities. An '*approved agent*' is a body approved by HMRC for the purpose of paying donations to one or more charities; if the agent is itself a charity specified by the individual, it may retain any sum due to itself.

For these purposes, '*charity*' is as defined in **16.2** above, but also includes the bodies listed in *CTA 2010, s 468*.

Administrative regulations may be made by statutory instrument regarding such matters as:

(i) the grant or withdrawal of approval by HMRC of schemes and agents, and appeals against HMRC's decision;

(ii) the requirements of kinds of schemes and qualifications of agents;

(iii) production of other information to HMRC.

Such regulations are contained in *The Charitable Deductions (Approved Schemes) Regulations 1986 (SI 1986 No 2211)* as amended.

Penalties apply for failure to comply with (iii) above under *TMA 1970, s 98*.

[*ITEPA 2003, ss 713–715, Sch 6 paras 137, 243, Sch 8; ITA 2007, Sch 1 para 390; CTA 2010, Sch 1 para 394; SI 2009 No 56, Sch 1 para 339; SI 2009 No 3054, Arts 2, 3, Sch*].

For HMRC guidance on payroll giving, see www.hmrc.gov.uk/payrollgiving/index.htm.

Administrative costs

Voluntary contributions made by an employer to assist an approved agent with its costs in managing a payroll giving scheme on the employer's behalf are deductible in computing the profits of a trade, profession or vocation. [*ITTOIA 2005, s 72*].

Simon's Taxes. See B2.441, E4.1116.

Gifts of shares, securities and real property to charities

[16.21] Income tax relief is available on a non-arm's length disposal, by an individual to a 'charity', of the whole of the beneficial interest in a 'qualifying investment'. This is in addition to the pre-existing capital gains tax relief for assets generally, for which see the corresponding chapter of Tolley's Capital Gains Tax. '*Charity*' has the meaning in **16.2** above, but also includes the Trustees of the National Heritage Memorial Fund, the Historic Buildings and Monuments Commission for England and the National Endowment for Science, Technology and the Arts. A '*qualifying investment*' is any of the following:

(a)   shares or securities listed (or alternatively, before 19 July 2007, dealt in) on a recognised stock exchange (within *ITA 2007, s 1005*) or (on and after 19 July 2007) dealt in on any market in the UK that is designated for this purpose by HMRC Order;

(b)   units in an authorised unit trust (within *CTA 2010, ss 616, 619*);

(c)   shares in an open-ended investment company (within *CTA 2010, ss 613, 615*);

(d)   an interest in an **OFFSHORE FUND** (**51.24**); and

(e)   a 'qualifying interest in land'.

On a claim to that effect (within the time allowed at **18.4 CLAIMS**), the 'relievable amount' (see below) is deductible in computing the donor's net income for the tax year of disposal. See below as regards adjustments for incidental costs and consequential benefits. The deduction is disregarded for the purposes of computing top slicing relief in respect of gains on life assurance gains (see **44.8 LIFE ASSURANCE POLICIES**). Where the claim is made, no relief is available under **73.84 TRADING INCOME** or any other provision in respect of the same disposal.

The '*relievable amount*' is, subject to the adjustments below, the value of the 'net benefit to the charity' either at the time the disposal is made or immediately after that time (whichever gives the lower value), or the excess (if any) of that value over any consideration given for the disposal.

The *'net benefit to the charity'* is normally the market value of the investment. Where, however, the charity is, or becomes, subject to a 'disposal-related obligation' to *any* person (whether or not the donor or a connected person), it is the market value of the investment reduced by the aggregate *'disposal-related liabilities'* of the charity. An obligation is a *'disposal-related obligation'* if it is reasonable to suppose, taking into account all the circumstances, that the disposal would not have been made in its absence or if it relates to, or is framed by reference to, or is conditional upon the charity receiving, the investment in question or a disposal-related investment (as widely defined); 'obligation' is itself widely defined so as to include any scheme, arrangement or understanding (whether or not legally enforceable) and any series of obligations. A charity's *'disposal-related liabilities'* are its liabilities under the disposal-related obligation (or under each of them). Contingent obligations are taken into account if the contingency actually occurs.

The market value of the investment is determined as for capital gains tax purposes, but the market value of an interest in an offshore fund for which separate buying and selling prices are published is the buying price published on the date of the disposal or, if none were published on that date, the most recent published buying price.

In computing the relievable amount, any consideration for the disposal is brought into account without any discount for postponement of the right to receive any of it and without regard to any risk of part of it being irrecoverable or to the right to receive any part of it being contingent. Where any part of the consideration subsequently proves irrecoverable, the donor can make a claim for the relievable amount to be adjusted accordingly.

Adjustments are made to the relievable amount as follows. The amount is increased by any 'incidental costs of disposal' incurred by the person making it. Where consideration is received for the disposal, this increase is limited to the excess, if any, of the deemed consideration for capital gains tax purposes (disposal deemed to be at no gain/no loss) over the actual consideration.

The relievable amount is reduced by the value of any benefits received, in consequence of the disposal, by the person making it or a person connected with him (within **21 CONNECTED PERSONS**).

The *'incidental costs of disposal'* are:

- fees, commission or remuneration paid for the professional services of a surveyor, valuer, auctioneer, accountant, agent or legal adviser incurred by the person making the disposal wholly and exclusively for the purposes of the disposal;
- costs of transfer or conveyance wholly and exclusively incurred by that person for the purposes of the disposal;
- costs of advertising to find a buyer; and
- costs reasonably incurred in making any valuation or apportionment for the purposes of these provisions.

For disposal to a charity on or after 15 December 2009, an anti-avoidance rule applies if:

- the qualifying investment, or anything from which it derives or which it represents, was acquired by the individual making the disposal within the period of four years ending with the day on which the disposal is made;
- the acquisition was made as part of a scheme (as widely defined); and
- a main purpose of the individual in entering into the scheme was to obtain relief, or an increased amount of relief, under the above provisions.

Where the rule applies, the 'net benefit to the charity' is the 'acquisition value' of the qualifying investment if lower than its market value. The relievable amount is reduced accordingly. The *'acquisition value'* is the consideration given for the qualifying investment by the individual less any amount received in connection with the acquisition, by the individual or a person connected with him, as part of the scheme in question. In the case where the thing acquired was something from which the qualifying investment derives or which it represents, the acquisition value is first computed by reference to the thing acquired and is then reduced to such proportion of that value as it is just and reasonable to attribute to the qualifying investment.

A *'qualifying interest in land'* is a freehold interest (or a leasehold interest which is a term of years absolute) in UK land (but not an agreement to acquire freehold land or for a lease). The following two circumstances are additionally brought within the relief.

- Where there is a disposal of the beneficial interest in a qualifying interest in land, and there is also a disposal to the charity of any easement, servitude, right or privilege so far as benefiting that land, relief is also available for the latter disposal.
- Where a person with a freehold or leasehold interest in UK land grants to a charity a lease, for (except in Scotland) a term of years absolute, of the whole or part of that land, this is regarded as a disposal for which the relief is available.

In the application of the above in Scotland:

- references to a freehold interest in land are to the interest of the owner;
- references to a leasehold interest in land which is a term of years absolute are to a tenant's right over or interest in a property subject to a lease; and
- references to an agreement for a lease do not include missives of let that constitute an actual lease.

The following supplementary provisions apply to disposals of qualifying interests in land.

- Where two or more persons are entitled jointly or in common to a qualifying interest in land, the relief applies only if each person disposes of the whole of his beneficial interest in the land to the charity. Relief is then allowed to any of those persons who qualify (including companies qualifying under the equivalent corporation tax provisions), being apportioned between or amongst them as they may agree. See *ITA 2007, s 443* for the calculation of the relievable amount in these circumstances.

- The relief is dependent on the receipt by the person disposing of the interest of a certificate given by or on behalf of the charity specifying the description of the interest concerned and the date of the disposal, and stating that the charity has acquired the interest.
- If a 'disqualifying event' occurs at any time in the period from the date of the disposal to the fifth anniversary of 31 January following the tax year of the disposal, the person (or each of the persons) making the disposal is treated as never having been entitled to the relief in respect of the disposal (and HMRC has the necessary assessment etc. powers). A *'disqualifying event'* occurs if the person (or any one of the persons) who made the disposal, or any connected person (within **21 CONNECTED PERSONS**), either becomes entitled to an interest or right in relation to all or part of the land to which the disposal relates, or becomes party to an arrangement under which he enjoys some right in relation to all or part of that land, otherwise than for full consideration in money or money's worth. This does *not* apply if the person became entitled to such an interest or right as a result of a disposition of property on death, whether by will, by intestacy or otherwise.

[*ITA 2007, ss 431–438, 438A, 439–446, 989, 1005, Sch 1 para 536(4); ICTA 1988, ss 587B, 587C; FA 2007, Sch 26 para 12(10)(12); CTA 2010, Sch 1 paras 527–529, 562(2); FA 2010, Sch 7 paras 1–3, 9*].

The cost of the asset to the charity for capital gains tax purposes is reduced by the relievable amount as above, or, if it is less than that amount, is reduced to nil. [*TCGA 1992, s 257(2A)–(2C); ICTA 1988, s 587B(3); ITA 2007, Sch 1 para 328; CTA 2010, Sch 1 para 258(3)–(5)*].

On 15 December 2009, the Government gave notice of their intention to legislate against any future schemes that are designed to take advantage of the tax relief for disposal of qualifying investments to charities, with possible retrospective effect from 15 December 2009 (Written Ministerial Statement at www.hmrc.gov.uk/news/ministerial-statement.pdf.

Simon's Taxes. See E1.813.

Key points

[16.22] Points to consider are as follows.

- The definition of a charity extends to EEA bodies from 2010/11, so UK donors can benefit from tax relief on qualifying gifts.
- Gift Aid donations can benefit from very favourable rates of relief when made out of income triggering the restriction of personal allowances for elderly taxpayers, and (for 2010/11 onwards) taxpayers with relevant income in excess of £100,000.
- The carry back of Gift Aid donations can be used to benefit from this effect once the income for the previous year is determined; consider ensuring that clients who may be affected submit their information early so that the necessary computations can be prepared and advice delivered in time to act upon it.

- Charities should be advised to register with HMRC for gifts of tax refunds through the self-assessment return, and to publicise this fact and the relevant reference to supporters.
- Charities carrying on mixed trading activities where part will benefit from exemption as primary purpose or work carried out by beneficiaries, and part will not, should ensure that adequate records are maintained to enable the trades to be segregated for tax purposes.
- All charities should implement procedures to identify substantial donors and to monitor transactions with them.
- Charities making use of the limited exemption for small trading activity should be encouraged to review likely trading patterns for the coming year annually at trustee meetings to ensure that the limits are considered and action taken if they are to be exceeded. The likely solution is to move non-exempt trading activities into a separate trading vehicle, which will donate profits back to the charity.

17

Children

Cross-references. See **27.43** EMPLOYMENT INCOME for employer-provided childcare; **30.9** EXEMPT INCOME for Child Trust Funds; **70.4** SOCIAL SECURITY AND NATIONAL INSURANCE for child tax credit.

[17.1] All of a child's taxable income is chargeable on the child (subject to below) and he has full entitlement to personal allowances and reliefs. In most cases only the personal allowance (see **1.14** ALLOWANCES AND TAX RATES) will be available.

[17.2] Returns and claims may be made by a child in respect of income within his control but otherwise these are the responsibility of his parent, guardian, tutor or any trustee [*TMA 1970, ss 72, 118*] who is also liable for payment of any tax in default of payment by the child, with right of recovery. [*TMA 1970, s 73*]. Where assessment should primarily be made on the guardian, tutor or trustee, an assessment in the name of the child is not precluded (*R v Newmarket Commrs (ex p Huxley)* CA 1916, 7 TC 49).

[17.3] If a parent makes a settlement in favour of his child, then the income arising thereon is treated (subject to certain exceptions) as that of the parent and not of the child for tax purposes. The definition of 'settlement' for this purpose is wide enough to cover gifts e.g. of money, or shares. See **68.30** SETTLEMENTS. See also the other provisions in **68.26–68.34** SETTLEMENTS whereby income of a settlement can be treated as that of the settlor for tax purposes.

[17.4] Under general law throughout the UK, an **adopted child** is treated as if born as the child of the adopter(s). Thus, no specific provision to that effect is required or provided in tax law.

18

Claims

Cross-references. See ALLOWANCES AND TAX RATES at **1.11** onwards for claims to personal allowances and reliefs; **10.2**(ii) CAPITAL ALLOWANCES, **11.2**(ii) CAPITAL ALLOWANCES ON PLANT AND MACHINERY for capital allowances claims; **26** DOUBLE TAX RELIEF for claims under DTR agreements etc.; **43** INTEREST PAYABLE for relief for interest paid; **50.2** NON-RESIDENTS for reliefs claimable by non-residents; **68** SETTLEMENTS for claims by beneficiaries and contingent trust claims.

Introduction

[18.1] Claims and elections may be made to an officer of HMRC (or to the Commissioners of HMRC in certain specified cases) whenever the *Taxes Acts* provide for relief to be given or other thing to be done.

A formal procedure applies as regards the making of claims and elections. A claim for a relief, allowance or tax repayment (other than one to be given effect by a PAYE coding adjustment — see also **18.3** below) must be for an amount quantified at the time of the claim.

Where notice has been given by HMRC requiring the delivery of a return (see **63.2, 63.13** RETURNS), a claim etc. (other than one to be given effect by a PAYE coding adjustment) can only be made at any time by inclusion in such a return (or by virtue of an amendment to a return) *unless it could not be so included* either at that time or subsequently. See **16.13** CHARITIES for an exception to this as regards certain claims by charitable trusts.

In the case of a partnership business, a claim or election under any of numerous provisions specified in *TMA 1970, s 42(7)* must be made by a partner nominated by the partnership if it cannot be included in a partnership return (or amendment thereto). See **18.3** below for provisions applying where a claim etc. is made otherwise than by inclusion in a return.

Where a claimant discovers an error or mistake has been made in a claim (whether or not made in a return), he may make a supplementary claim within the time allowed for making the original claim.

[*TMA 1970, s 42; ITA 2007, Sch 1 para 253; CTA 2009, Sch 1 para 302; FA 2010, Sch 8 paras 4, 8(6)*].

Claims are personal matters and (except in the case of trustees for persons under disability etc.) can be made only by the person entitled to the relief (cf. *Fulford v Hyslop* Ch D 1929, 8 ATC 588). For claims to personal allowances etc. by persons receiving tax-free annuities, see **24.15 DEDUCTION OF TAX AT SOURCE**. See **63.2 RETURNS** for signing of claims by attorney.

Where an official form is provided for use in making a claim or election not included in a return, it is permissible to fill out a photocopy of the blank form, provided that, where double sided copying is not available, all the pages (including any notes) are present and attached in the correct order. Although such copying is in strictness a breach of HMSO copyright, this will only be pursued if forms are copied on a large scale for commercial gain. (HMRC SP 5/87). See also **63.2 RETURNS**.

See **18.5** below as regards the making of income tax claims by telephone or other method not in writing.

Simon's Taxes. See E1.260–E1.265.

Claims for relief involving two or more years

[18.2] The provisions described below are designed to facilitate the administration under self-assessment of claims, elections etc. which affect more than one tax year. They generally deem the claim to be that of the later year, with consequent effect on the dates from which interest on unpaid and overpaid tax will run.

Relief for losses and other payments

A claim, under whatever provision, for a loss incurred or payment made (for example, a personal pension contribution) in one year of assessment to be carried back to an earlier year need not be made in a return, is treated as a claim for the year of loss or payment (the later year), must be for an amount equal to what would otherwise have been the tax saving for the earlier year (after taking into account any associated claims, see below, to which effect has already been given) and is given effect *in relation to the later year* by repayment, set-off etc. or by treating the said amount for the purposes of **65.7 SELF-ASSESSMENT** as a tax payment made on account. See Revenue Tax Bulletin April 1996 p 299 for the practical effect.

HMRC have confirmed that under these provisions a carry-back claim (whether in the return for the year of loss or payment or not) will be given immediate effect provided that the tax return for the earlier year has been made and the tax calculated. Relief is given in terms of tax by set-off or repayment, and, provided that the claim (and, where appropriate, the payment) is made before 31 January in the year of loss or payment, may be by set-off against outstanding liabilities for the earlier year. Relief will be given by repayment where there are no outstanding liabilities. (Revenue Tax Bulletin December 1996 pp 361–365, June 1997 p 443; Revenue 'Working Together' Bulletin No 12, March 2003). See *Norton v Thompson* (Sp C 399), [2004] SSCD 163 for an illustration, and confirmation, of the principles involved.

See also **41.1 INTEREST ON OVERPAID TAX.**

Averaging of farming or market gardening profits

Where a farmer or market gardener makes a claim to average the profits of two consecutive years of assessment (see **73.74 TRADING INCOME**), the claim is treated as a claim for the later of those years. To the extent that the claim would otherwise have affected the profits of the earlier of those years, it must be for an amount equal to the tax that would consequently have become payable or repayable for that earlier year (after taking into account any associated claims, see below, to which effect has already been given) and is given effect *in relation to the later year* by increasing the tax payable or treating the said amount for the purposes of **65.7 SELF-ASSESSMENT** as a tax payment made on account, whichever is appropriate. Where the later year is included in a subsequent averaging claim, i.e. it is then averaged with the following year, the application of these provisions to the first claim is ignored in computing the effect of the subsequent claim.

See also **41.1 INTEREST ON OVERPAID TAX.**

Where, having made an averaging claim, a person then makes, amends or revokes any other claim for relief for either of the two years affected, which would be out of time but for the provisions of *ITTOIA 2005, s 224(4)*, the claim, amendment or revocation is treated as relating to the later of the two years. To the extent that it relates to income for the earlier year, the amount claimed (or, as appropriate, the increase or reduction therein) must be equal to the tax that would consequently have become payable or repayable for that earlier year (after taking into account any associated claims, see below, to which effect has already been given) and is given effect *in relation to the later year* by increasing the tax payable or treating the said amount for the purposes of **65.7 SELF-ASSESSMENT** as a tax payment made on account, whichever is appropriate.

For articles on these rules and on the completion of the relevant tax returns, see Revenue Tax Bulletin February 1997 pp 392–394 and August 1998 p 575.

Election for post-cessation receipts to be treated as if received on date of discontinuance

Where a person elects under *ITTOIA 2005, s 257* (formerly *ICTA 1988, s 108* — see **59.4 POST-CESSATION RECEIPTS AND EXPENDITURE**) for a post-cessation receipt to be treated as if received on the date of cessation of trade rather than in the year of receipt (the later year), the election is treated as a claim for the later year, must be for an amount equal to what would otherwise have been the additional tax payable for the year of assessment (the earlier year) in which the sum is treated as received (after taking into account any associated claims, see below, to which effect has already been given) and is given effect *in relation to the later year* by increasing the tax payable for that year.

Averaging of profits of creative artists

On a claim in specified circumstances, the profits of creative artists, i.e. authors, designers, composers etc. for two consecutive tax years may be averaged — see **73.52 TRADING INCOME**. Such an averaging claim is given effect in the same way as a claim to average the profits of a farmer or market gardener (see above). See also **41.1 INTEREST ON OVERPAID TAX**. The consequent making, amending or revoking of any other claim, where this would otherwise be out of time, is also given effect in the same way as for farmers etc. (see above).

General

For the purposes of all the above provisions, two claims, elections etc. (including, where appropriate, amendments and revocations) by the same person are *'associated'* in so far as the same year of assessment is the earlier year in relation to both.

[*TMA 1970, s 42(11A), Sch 1B*].

See Revenue Tax Bulletin August 2000 pp 774, 775 for an article concerning the admission of earlier year claims, including those affecting the liability of another taxpayer, consequential on carry-back claims as above.

Simon's Taxes. See E1.263.

Claims etc. not included in returns

[18.3] Subject to any specific provision requiring a claim or election to be made to the Commissioners of HMRC, a claim or election made otherwise than in a return (see **18.1** above) must be made to an officer of HMRC. The claim etc. must include a declaration by the claimant that all particulars are correctly stated to the best of his information or belief. No claim requiring a tax repayment can be made unless the claimant has documentary proof that the tax has been paid or deducted. The claim must be made in a form determined by HMRC and may require, *inter alia*, a statement of the amount of tax to be discharged or repaid and (except as below) supporting information and documentation. In the case of a claim by or on behalf of a person who is not resident (or who claims to be not resident or not ordinarily resident or not domiciled) in the UK, HMRC may require a statement or declaration in support of the claim to be made by affidavit.

A person who may wish to make a claim must keep all such records as may be requisite for the purpose and must preserve them until such time as HMRC may no longer enquire into the claim (see below) or any such enquiry is completed. There is a maximum penalty of £3,000 for non-compliance in relation to any claim *actually made*. Similar provisions and exceptions apply as in **63.5 RETURNS** as to the preservation of copies of documents instead of originals and the exception from penalty for non-compliance in relation to dividend vouchers, interest certificates etc.

Provisions similar to those in **63.4 RETURNS** (amendments of self-assessments) apply to enable a claimant (within twelve months of the claim) or officer of HMRC (within nine months of the claim) to amend a claim etc. HMRC have power of enquiry into a claim etc. (or amendment thereof) similar to that in **63.6, 63.7 RETURNS** (enquiries into returns). Notice of intention to enquire must be given by the first anniversary of 31 January following the year of assessment (or where the claim relates to a period other than a year of assessment the first anniversary of the end of that period) or, if later, the quarter day (meaning 31 January, 30 April etc.) next following the first anniversary of the date of claim etc. In the event of such an enquiry, HMRC had power to call for documents similar to that in **63.8 RETURNS**. These are replaced, where notice is given on or after 1 April 2009, with the powers at **38.3–38.10 HMRC INVESTIGATORY POWERS**. Where an enquiry is in progress, an officer of HMRC may give provisional effect to the claim etc. (or amendment thereof) to such extent as he thinks fit. Provisions similar to those in **63.9, 63.10 RETURNS** apply as regards completion of enquiries and amendments of claims upon completion. HMRC must give effect (by assessment, discharge or repayment) to an amendment arising out of an enquiry within 30 days after the date of issue of the closure notice. An appeal may be made against any conclusion stated, or amendment made, by a closure notice by giving written notice to the relevant officer within 30 days after the date of issue of the closure notice, extended to three months where certain specified issues concerning residence are involved. If an amendment is varied on appeal, HMRC must give effect to the variation within 30 days. Where a claim etc. does not give rise to a discharge or repayment of tax (for example, a claim to carry forward trading losses), there are provisions for disallowance of the claim on completion of enquiry, with appeal procedures similar to those above.

[*TMA 1970, s 42(11), Sch 1A; ITA 2007, Sch 1 para 264; FA 2008, ss 113, 115, Sch 36 para 77, Sch 37 para 3; FA 2009, s 100, Sch 52 paras 6, 7; SI 2009 No 56, Sch 1 paras 53–58; SI 2009 No 402; SI 2009 No 404, Arts 2, 5; SI 2009 No 2035, Sch para 9*].

See **18.5** below as regards the making of income tax claims by telephone or other method not in writing and also the use of photocopied blank claim forms.

HMRC accept that, following a claim, any interest, surcharge or penalty charged for the year to which the claim relates may be amended in line with the revised tax liability. Repayment supplement may be due on any overpayment of penalty or surcharge (see **41.1 INTEREST ON OVERPAID TAX**). (Revenue 'Working Together' Bulletin June 2003 p 12).

Claims given effect by PAYE coding adjustment

Claims for a tax year may be made during that year, and thus before a tax return is issued, and given effect by adjustment to a PAYE code (see **53.6 PAY AS YOU EARN**), for example a claim to married couple's allowance. Such in-year claims may subsequently be reflected in a tax return. Where no such return is issued, the claim will become final under the above provisions by the first anniversary of 31 January following the tax year, i.e. the final date for HMRC to give notice of intention to enquire. Except in cases of 'discovery' (see **6.6 ASSESSMENTS**), HMRC will in practice apply the same deadline to claims rolled forward from one year to the next and automatically included in code numbers and to those included on the basis of preliminary information given by the taxpayer before the start of the tax year. (Revenue Tax Bulletin October 1996 pp 350, 351).

Simon's Taxes. See E1.262.

Time limits for claims

[18.4] *Unless otherwise prescribed*, a claim with respect to income tax made before 1 April 2010 must be made no later than the fifth anniversary of 31 January following the tax year to which it relates. Where made on or after 1 April 2010, such claims must be made within four years after the end of the tax year to which they relate. [*TMA 1970, s 43(1); FA 2008, Sch 39 para 12; SI 2009 No 403*]. Thus, the time limit for 2003/04 was 31 January 2010, the time limit for 2004/05 was 31 March 2010 (the day before the new law came into force), the time limit for 2005/06 was 5 April 2010 and the time limit for 2006/07 is 5 April 2011.

In a case where the claim relates to a tax year for which the taxpayer has not been given notice to make a return within one year after the end of the tax year (in effect, where the taxpayer is outside self-assessment), the above change in the time limit for making claims applies from 1 April 2012 rather than 1 April 2010. This only applies where tax has been *overpaid*, its purpose being to allow taxpayers extra time to take appropriate action. [*SI 2009 No 403, Art 10*].

See **18.9** below for claims following late assessments, and see generally **71 TIME LIMITS — FIXED DATES** and **72 TIME LIMITS — MISCELLANEOUS**.

Simon's Taxes. See A4.204, E1.265.

Telephone claims and other services

[18.5] HMRC have powers to accept income tax claims by telephone (or by any other method not in writing), where a written claim would otherwise be required, for which purpose they must publish general directions as regards the circumstances in which, and conditions subject to which, such claims will be accepted. The time for making the claim and the contents may not be altered by the directions. No directions may be given in relation to claims by an individual as trustee, partner or personal representative, to capital allowances claims or to claims under *TMA 1970, Sch 1B* (see **18.2** above). Directions may similarly be given as regards the making of elections, the giving of notice, the amendment or withdrawal of claims, elections and notices and the amendment of returns. [*TMA 1970, ss 43E, 43F; FA 1998, s 118; TIOPA 2010, Sch 7 para 86*].

All tax offices offer certain telephone services, as set out in HMRC SP 2/03 and, for tax offices served by a Contact Centre, HMRC SP 1/10, 23 April 2010 (superseding SP 1/05) with which are published the appropriate directions.

These include acceptance of telephone claims for personal allowances, pension contributions, Gift Aid donations and certain employment expenses. They also enable taxpayers to notify items of income and changes in their personal details. Certain types of notification are accepted only if within specified monetary limits. Content Centres will additionally accept telephone amendments to self-assessment tax returns. These services are available to individuals and, subject to identity and authorisation checks, to agents acting for individuals.

Tax repayment claims

[18.6] A self-assessment tax return (see **63.2 RETURNS**) may give rise to a tax repayment. Otherwise, a tax repayment claim can be made on form R40. The form and related Guidance Notes are available on the HMRC website or from tax offices. There is no requirement to send vouchers, certificates or other supporting documents with the claim (though these *can* be sent if the taxpayer so wishes) but they must be retained under the record-keeping requirements at **63.5 RETURNS** as applied by **18.3** above. A tax repayment claim is also subject to the enquiry provisions at **18.3** above.

See **18.4** above for the time limit for making a claim. Where an overpayment of tax has arisen because of official error, and there is no doubt or dispute as to the facts, claims to repayment of tax are accepted outside the statutory time limit (HMRC ESC B41).

A tax repayment claim can be made *before* the end of the tax year to which it relates, though HMRC do not normally make in-year repayments of less than £50. If further income is expected between the making of the claim and the end of the tax year, i.e. the claim is an interim claim, a full-year estimate should be given for each such item of income as well as details of the actual income to date.

See **54.7 PAYMENT OF TAX** for the situation where the right to receive a tax repayment is transferred from one person to another.

Overpayment relief

[18.7] A claim under the following provisions can be made **on or after 1 April 2010**. These provisions replace the error or mistake relief provisions at **18.8** below, which are accordingly repealed.

Where a person has paid an amount of income tax (or capital gains tax) and believes that the tax is not due, he can make a claim to HMRC for repayment of the tax. Where a person has been assessed to pay an amount of tax, or there has been a determination or direction to that effect, he can likewise make a claim for the amount to be discharged if he believes that the tax is not due. For these purposes, tax paid by one person on behalf of another is treated as paid by the other person.

HMRC will not give effect to such a claim if:

(a)   the amount is excessive because of a mistake in an election, claim or notice or a mistake consisting of making or giving, or failing to make or give, an election, claim or notice; or

(b)   the amount is excessive because of a mistake in allocating (or not allocating) expenditure to a pool for capital allowances purposes; or

(c)   the amount is excessive because of a mistake in bringing into account (or not bringing into account) a disposal value for capital allowances purposes; or

(d)   the claimant can seek relief by taking other steps under tax legislation; or

(e)   the claimant could have sought relief by taking such other steps within a period which has expired by the time the claim is made, if he knew, or ought reasonably to have known, before the end of that period that such relief was available; or

(f)   the claim is made on grounds that have been put to a court or tribunal in the course of an appeal relating to the amount or on grounds that have been put to HMRC in the course of such an appeal settled by agreement (as in **5.8 APPEALS**); or

(g)   the claimant knew, or ought reasonably to have known, of the grounds for the claim before the latest of the date an appeal relating to the amount was determined by a court or tribunal, the date on which such an appeal was withdrawn by the claimant, and the end of the period in which the claimant could have appealed; or

(h)   the amount was due as a result of proceedings by HMRC against the claimant, or under an agreement between the claimant and HMRC settling such proceedings; or

(i)   the amount is excessive because of a mistake in calculating the claimant's liability where the liability was calculated in accordance with the practice generally prevailing at the time; or

(j)   the amount is excessive because of a mistake in a PAYE assessment or PAYE calculation where the assessment or calculation was made in accordance with the practice generally prevailing at the end of the period of 12 months following the tax year for which the assessment or calculation was made.

[*TMA 1970, s 33, Sch 1AB paras 1, 2; FA 2009, s 100, Sch 52 paras 1, 2*].

As regards (i) and (j) above, if a claim for overpayment relief relates to taxes paid in breach of EU law, HMRC will not seek to disallow it on the grounds that the tax liability was calculated in accordance with the prevailing practice (HMRC Brief 22/10, 3 June 2010).

Making a claim

For income tax (and capital gains tax) purposes, a claim must be made within four years after the end of the tax year concerned. Where the claim relates to tax overpaid, that year is the year in respect of which the payment was made or, where the amount paid is excessive due to a mistake in a tax return or returns, the year to which the return (or if more than one, the first return) relates. Where the claim relates to an assessment, determination or direction, the year concerned is the year to which that assessment etc. relates. The time limit is extended for claims made before 1 April 2012 relating to mistakes in returns if the return was not issued within one year after the end of the tax year to which it relates; in such a case, the claim must be made before the fifth anniversary of 31 January following the end of the tax year concerned.

A claim cannot be made in a tax return.

[*TMA 1970, Sch 1AB para 3; FA 2009, Sch 52 paras 2, 10*].

Where, under PAYE, the construction industry scheme or other tax legislation, one person (P) is accountable to HMRC for tax payable by another person or for any other amount that has been or is to be set off against another person's liability, a claim in respect of the amount can only be made by that other person. If, however, P has paid such an amount but was not in fact accountable to HMRC for it, P, and only P, can make a claim in respect of that amount. Effect will not be given to such a claim by P to the extent that the amount has been repaid to, or set against amounts payable by, the other person. [*TMA 1970, Sch 1AB para 4; FA 2009, Sch 52 para 2*].

Partnerships

A claim in respect of an amount paid or due by one or more partners in accordance with a self-assessment which is excessive because of a mistake in a partnership return must be made by a nominated partner (or his personal representative). The partner must have been a partner at some time in the period for which the return was made. [*TMA 1970, Sch 1AB para 5; FA 2009, Sch 52 para 2*].

Discovery assessment etc. following claim

Where the grounds for a claim also provide grounds for HMRC to make a discovery assessment or determination (see **6.6** ASSESSMENTS) for any period and such an assessment or determination could not otherwise be made as a result of one of the restrictions noted below, those restrictions are disregarded and an assessment or determination is not out of time if made before the final determination of the claim (i.e. before the time at which the claim can no longer be varied). The restrictions concerned are those at **6.6**(2) ASSESSMENTS and the expiry of a time limit for making a discovery assessment or determination (see **6.2, 6.3** ASSESSMENTS).

Similar provisions apply in relation to amendments of partnership returns following discovery. [*TMA 1970, Sch 1AB paras 6, 7; FA 2009, Sch 52 para 2*]

Contract settlements

The above provisions apply also to amounts paid under a contract settlement (see **6.9** ASSESSMENTS). If the person who paid the amounts due under the settlement (the '*payer*') was not the person from whom the tax was due (the '*taxpayer*'), then the provisions are modified accordingly. If an amount is repayable to the payer as a result of a claim, HMRC can set the amount repayable against any amount payable by the taxpayer under any discovery assessment or determination made as a result of the claim.

[*TMA 1970, Sch 1AB para 8; FA 2009, Sch 52 para 2*].

Error or mistake relief before 1 April 2010

[18.8] The following provisions (*TMA 1970, s 33* and *s 33A*) are replaced by those at **18.7** above and are accordingly **repealed** so that no claims can be made on or after **1 April 2010**.

Prior to 1 April 2010, if an income tax (or capital gains tax) assessment (or self-assessment) proves to be excessive due to an error or mistake in a return, the taxpayer may give written notice to that effect to HMRC (a claim for error or mistake relief) no later than the fifth anniversary of 31 January following the tax year to which the return relates. HMRC may give such relief as is reasonable and just. The relief is given because the return was wrong and hence these provisions do not apply where the assessment simply does not agree with the return. No relief is given if the return was made on the basis or in accordance with the practice generally prevailing at the time it was made. Where this last rule is in point, it is not possible to instead claim restitution under common law (*Monro v HMRC* CA, [2008] STC 1815).

The relief, which is given by repayment, is determined by HMRC, having regard to all relevant circumstances including, in particular, whether the granting of relief would result in income (or gains) being excluded from the charge to tax. They may take into account the taxpayer's liabilities, and assessments made on him, for years other than the year in question. The taxpayer may appeal to the Appeal Tribunal against the decision of HMRC, and the Tribunal's determination is final and conclusive except on a point of law arising in connection with the computation of the income etc. See *Rose Smith & Co Ltd v CIR* KB 1933, 17 TC 586; *Carrimore Six Wheelers Ltd* CA 1944, 26 TC 301 and CA 1947, 28 TC 422; *Arranmore Investment Co Ltd v CIR* CA(NI) 1973, 48 TC 623; *Eagerpath Ltd v Edwards* CA 2000, 73 TC 427; *Thompson v CIR* (Sp C 458), [2005] SSCD 320.

No relief is available in respect of an error or mistake in a claim which is included in a return (but see **18.1** above as regards supplementary claims) or an error or mistake consisting in the making of a claim for 2008/09 onwards for the REMITTANCE BASIS (**61**) to apply.

[*TMA 1970, s 33; FA 2008, Sch 7 paras 65, 81; SI 2009 No 56, Sch 1 para 23*].

Error or mistake relief cannot be used to rectify a failure to claim a particular tax relief within a stipulated time limit where that claim could have been made outside a return (*Howard v CIR* (Sp C 329), [2002] SSCD 408).

Error or mistake relief is extended to cover an error or mistake in a partnership return (see **63.13** RETURNS) by reason of which the partners allege that their self-assessments were excessive. The claim to relief must be made by one of the partners no later than a specified day. That day is the fourth anniversary of 31 January following the tax year for which the return is made. (If the return is for 2006/07 or an earlier year, that day is the fifth anniversary of the filing date specified in the notice requiring the return.) Where the claim results in an amendment to the partnership return, HMRC will, by notice, make any necessary amendments to the tax returns of all persons who were partners at any time in the period covered by the partnership return. [*TMA 1970, s 33A; FA 2007, s 91(6), s 92; SI 2009 No 56, Sch 1 para 24*].

Where a particular type of capital allowance (e.g. a plant and machinery allowance) has been claimed in respect of an item of expenditure, error or mistake relief cannot be used to substitute a different type of capital allowance (e.g. an industrial building allowance) (HMRC Brief 12/09, 31 March 2009).

A claim to error or mistake relief may still be made in relation to an amendment to a self-assessment notwithstanding an agreement with the inspector preceding that amendment (*Wall v CIR* (Sp C 303), [2002] SSCD 122).

HMRC accept that, following a successful error or mistake relief claim, any interest, surcharge or penalty charged for the year to which the claim relates may be amended in line with the revised tax liability. Repayment supplement may be due on any overpayment of penalty or surcharge (see **41.1 INTEREST ON OVERPAID TAX**). (Revenue 'Working Together' Bulletin June 2003 p 12).

For recovery of tax paid under *mistake of law*, see **54.14 PAYMENT OF TAX**. For relief for double assessment, see **6.7 ASSESSMENTS**. For alteration of past claims on farming and market gardening profits, see **73.74 TRADING INCOME**.

See generally HMRC Income Tax Claims Manual ITCM12005–12110.

Simon's Taxes. See A4.206–A4.208, E1.264.

Claims following further assessments

[18.9] A claim (including a supplementary claim) which could not have been allowed but for the making of an assessment to income tax or capital gains tax after the tax year to which it relates may be made before the end of the tax year following that in which the assessment was made. [*TMA 1970, s 43(2)*].

In the case of a discovery leading to an assessment under *TMA 1970, s 29* (see **6.6 ASSESSMENTS**) which is made:

- before 1 April 2010 other than for the purpose of making good a loss of tax attributable to fraudulent or negligent conduct (see **6.4 ASSESSMENTS**), or
- on or after 1 April 2010 other than for the purpose of making good a loss of tax brought about carelessly or deliberately (see **6.3 ASSESSMENTS**),

the following rules apply:

(a) any 'relevant' claim, election, application or notice which could have been made or given within the normal time limits may be made or given within one year after the end of the tax year in which the assessment is made; and

(b) any 'relevant' claim etc. previously made or given, except an irrevocable one, can, with the consent of the person(s) by whom it was made or given (or their personal representatives), be revoked or varied in the manner in which it was made or given.

Elections for the transfer of the basic married couple's allowance between spouses or civil partners are excluded from this treatment.

A claim under **18.7** above (recovery of tax overpaid) is '*relevant*' to an assessment for a tax year if it relates to that tax year. Any other claim etc. is '*relevant*' to an assessment for a tax year if:

(i) it relates to, or to an event occurring in, the tax year; and

(ii) it, or its revocation or variation, reduces, or could reduce:

- the increased tax liability resulting from the assessment; or
- any other liability of the person for that tax year or a later one ending not more than one year after the end of the tax year in which the assessment is made.

The normal APPEALS (**5**) provisions apply, with any necessary modifications.

If the making etc. of a claim etc. (as above) would alter another person's tax liability, the consent of that person (or his personal representatives) is needed. If such alteration is an increase, the other person cannot make etc. a claim etc. under the foregoing provisions.

If the reduction, whether resulting from one or more than one claim etc., would exceed the additional tax assessed, relief is not available for the excess. If the reduction, so limited, involves more than one period, or more than one person, the inspector will specify by notice in writing how it is to be apportioned; but within 30 days of the notice (or last notice if more than one person is involved) being given, the person, or persons jointly, can specify the apportionment by notice in writing to the inspector.

[*TMA 1970, ss 43A, 43B; ITA 2007, Sch 1 para 254; FA 2008, Sch 39 para 13; FA 2009, s 100, Sch 52 para 5; SI 2009 No 403*].

The provisions of *TMA 1970, ss 43(2), 43A, 43B* above have similar effect in relation to an HMRC amendment to a self-assessment personal or partnership tax return as they would have in relation to a further assessment (see **63.9** RETURNS). Also, any late assessment required to give effect to a claim etc. as above, or as a result of allowing such a claim etc., can be made within a year after the claim etc. becomes final (i.e. becomes no longer capable of being varied, on appeal or otherwise); this applies to claims etc. made as a consequence of either an assessment as above or an amendment to a return. [*TMA 1970, s 43C; FA 2008, Sch 39 para 14; SI 2009 No 403*].

See also **6.3, 6.4** ASSESSMENTS.

Key points

[18.10] Points to consider are as follows.

- Note the reduced time limit for claims from 1 April 2010 and the extended transitional rules for taxpayers not within self-assessment.
- Care is needed when applying to reduce self-assessment payments on account, to ensure that claims affecting the previous year are properly dealt with.
- Particular care is also needed in correctly dealing with the effect of averaging claims on payments on account.

- It is no longer necessary to submit evidence to support tax reclaims by those subject to deductions under the construction industry scheme, but sub-contractors should retain evidence of payments and deductions provided by contractors.
- Tax repayments may be donated directly to a nominated charity if the appropriate details are included on the relevant self-assessment return. (See **16.16 CHARITIES** under Giving through the self-assessment return.)

19

Community Investment Tax Relief

Simon's Taxes. See **A1.302, A1.303, E3.6.**

Introduction

[19.1] The Community Investment Tax Credit scheme provides tax relief to individuals and companies investing in Community Development Finance Institutions ('CDFIs') which have been accredited by the Government under the rules of the scheme. The intention is that CDFIs use investors' funds to finance small businesses and social enterprises in disadvantaged communities. The relief takes the form of a reduction in the investor's income tax or corporation tax liability. The quantum of the relief is a maximum of 25% of the 'invested amount' (as defined — see **19.4** below), spread over five years, but relief cannot exceed in any year the amount needed to reduce the investor's tax liability to nil. [*ITA 2007, ss 333–382, Sch 1 para 419; FA 2002, s 57, Sch 16*].

This chapter covers the relief due to investors who are individuals. For coverage of the relief due to corporate investors, see the corresponding chapter of Tolley's Corporation Tax.

No exemption is provided for chargeable gains on disposals of investments in CDFIs.

References in this chapter to the '*investment date*' are to the day on which the investment in the CDFI is made, and references to the '*five-year investment period*' are to the five years beginning with that day. [*ITA 2007, s 338; FA 2002, Sch 16 para 3*]. The investment term need not, however, be limited to five years.

Guidance on the relief is available in HMRC Community Investment Tax Relief Manual.

Eligibility for relief

[19.2] An individual who makes an investment in a body is eligible for community investment tax relief in respect of that investment if:

(a)   the body is accredited as a CDFI (see **19.24** below) at the time the investment is made;

(b)   the investment is a 'qualifying investment' (see **19.7** below); and

(c)   the general conditions at **19.11** below are satisfied.

[*ITA 2007, s 334; FA 2002, Sch 16 para 1*].

For these purposes, an individual makes an investment in a body when:

(i)   he makes a loan (whether secured or unsecured) to the body (otherwise than by providing overdraft facilities or acquiring securities); or

(ii)   an 'issue of securities or shares' (as defined) of or in the body, for which he has subscribed, is made to him.

Where a loan agreement authorises the body to draw down amounts of the loan over a period of time, the loan is treated for the purposes of (i) above as made when the first amount is drawn down.

[*ITA 2007, ss 336, 378; FA 2002, Sch 16 paras 2, 46*].

Form of relief

[19.3] Where an individual who is eligible for relief (see **19.2** above) makes a claim for relief for any 'relevant tax year', he is entitled to a reduction in his tax liability equal to 5% of the 'invested amount' (see **19.4** below) in respect of the investment in question.

The tax year in which the investment date falls and each of the four subsequent tax years (but no others) are *'relevant tax years'* for this purpose.

The order in which tax reductions are given against an individual's tax liability is set out at **1.8 ALLOWANCES AND TAX RATES,** which also makes clear that a tax reduction must be restricted to the extent (if any) that it would otherwise exceed the individual's remaining income tax liability after making all prior reductions.

Claims

The investor is entitled to make a claim for a 'relevant tax year' (see above) if he considers that the conditions for the relief are for the time being satisfied. He *must* also have received a tax relief certificate (see also **19.24** below) from the CDFI. No claim can be made before the end of the tax year to which it relates. Otherwise, by default, the general time limit for making claims applies (see **18.4 CLAIMS**). See **19.6** below for specific circumstances in which no claim for relief can be made.

No application can be made to postpone tax (see **54.5 PAYMENT OF TAX**), pending appeal, on the grounds that the appellant is entitled to community investment tax relief, unless a claim for the relief has been made.

[*ITA 2007, ss 335, 376; FA 2002, s 57, Sch 16 paras 19, 45, Sch 17 paras 2–4; ICTA 1988, s 289A(5)(ca), Sch 15B para 1(6)(da)*].

Meaning of the 'invested amount'

[19.4] For the purposes of **19.3**, in respect of a **loan**, the *'invested amount'* is as follows.

(a)   In the tax year in which the investment date falls, it is the 'average capital balance' (see below) for the first year of the five-year investment period (see **19.1** above).

(b)   In each subsequent tax year (subject to (c) below), it is the average capital balance for the one year beginning with the anniversary of the investment date falling in that tax year.

(c)   For the third, fourth and fifth tax years for which relief may be claimed, it is initially determined as in (b) above but is restricted to, if less, the average capital balance for the six-month period beginning eighteen months after the investment date. (This is a consequence of the eighteen-month rule for drawdown facilities referred to at **19.8** below. (Treasury Explanatory Notes to Finance Bill 2002).)

For the purposes of (a)–(c) above, the *'average capital balance'* of a loan for any period of time is the mean of the daily balances of capital outstanding during that period.

In respect of **securities or shares**, the *'invested amount'* for any tax year is the amount subscribed for them (not necessarily in that tax year).

[*ITA 2007, s 337; FA 2002, Sch 16 para 21*].

See **19.18, 19.19** below for restriction of the invested amount in certain circumstances where value is received.

Examples

[19.5]

(A) Loans

Faith makes a £50,000 loan to a CDFI on 1 September 2006 on terms that it be repaid in annual £10,000 instalments beginning on 1 September 2008. She agrees to increase the loan outstanding by £40,000 on 1 September 2010 (repayable on 1 September 2012). The 'invested amount', and the 5% maximum income tax reduction available, for the five tax years for which relief may be claimed, are as follows.

	Invested amount	Tax reduction
	£	£
2006/07	50,000	2,500
2007/08	50,000	2,500
2008/09	40,000	2,000
2009/10	30,000	1,500
2010/11	50,000*	2,500

* Initially determined at £60,000 (£20,000 + the £40,000 increase) but restricted to £50,000, being the average capital balance for the six-month period 1 March 2008 to 31 August 2008 inclusive (see **19.4**(c) above).

(B) Securities or shares

Bill subscribes £50,000 for shares in a CDFI on 1 September 2006 and holds them for at least five years. The 'invested amount', and the 5% maximum income tax reduction available for each of the tax years 2006/07 to 2010/11 inclusive, the five years for which relief may be claimed, are £50,000 and £2,500 respectively.

Circumstances in which no claim for relief can be made

[19.6] In the circumstances listed below, no claim for community investment tax relief can be made.

Loans — disposals and excessive repayments/receipts of value

No claim can be made for a tax year in respect of a loan if:

(a) the investor disposes of all or any part of the loan (disregarding any repayment of the loan) before the 'qualifying date' relating to that tax year; or

(b) at any time after the investment is made but before that 'qualifying date', the amount of the capital outstanding on the loan is reduced to nil; or

(c) before that 'qualifying date', cumulative loan repayments (or receipts of value treated as repayments — see **19.18** below) bring into play the withdrawal of relief provisions at **19.17** below.

The *'qualifying date'* relating to a tax year is the next anniversary of the investment date to occur after the end of that tax year.

[ITA 2007, s 354; FA 2002, Sch 16 para 22].

Thus, if, for example, a loan made on 1 October 2007 is repaid in full by the CDFI on 1 July 2011 (i.e. before 1 October 2011, the qualifying date for 2010/11), no claim for relief can be made for 2010/11, even though the loan remained outstanding throughout that tax year. No claim can be made for 2011/12 either.

Securities or shares — disposals and excessive receipts of value

No claim can be made for a tax year in respect of any securities or shares other than those held by the investor (as sole beneficial owner) continuously (see **19.25** below) throughout the period beginning when the investment is made and ending immediately before the 'qualifying date' (as in (a) above) relating to that tax year. In addition, no claim can be made for a tax year if, before the 'qualifying date' (as in (a) above) relating to that tax year, cumulative receipts of value bring into play the withdrawal of relief provisions at **19.19** below. *[ITA 2007, s 355; FA 2002, Sch 16 para 23; CTA 2010, Sch 1 para 512].*

Loss of accreditation by the CDFI

Where the CDFI ceases to be accredited as such during the first year of the five-year investment period, no claim for relief can be made. Where accreditation is lost at any later time within the five-year investment period, no claim can be made for the tax year in which falls the most recent anniversary of the investment date preceding (or coinciding with) the date the accreditation is lost, or for any subsequent tax year. (There is no withdrawal of relief for any earlier tax year.) *[ITA 2007, s 356; FA 2002, Sch 16 para 24; CTA 2010, Sch 1 para 513].*

Qualifying investments

[19.7] An investment is a *'qualifying investment'* in a CDFI (and thus meets condition (b) at **19.2** above) if:

- the investment consists of a loan, securities or shares satisfying the conditions at **19.8** or, as the case may be, **19.9** below;
- the investor receives from the CDFI a valid tax relief certificate (see also **19.24** below); and
- the conditions at **19.10** below (no pre-arranged protection against risks) are met.

[ITA 2007, s 344; FA 2002, Sch 16 para 8].

Conditions to be satisfied in relation to loans

[19.8] There are three such conditions. The first is that either the CDFI receives from the investor, on the investment date, the full amount of the loan or, in the case of a loan made under a drawdown facility, the loan agreement provides for the CDFI to receive the full amount of the loan within 18 months after the investment date. The second condition is that the loan must not carry any present or future right to be converted into, or exchanged for, a loan, securities, shares or other rights, any of which are redeemable within the five-year investment period. The third is that the loan must not be made on terms that allow any person to require:

(a)   repayment within years 1 and 2 (of the five-year investment period) of any of the loan capital advanced during those two years; or

(b)   repayment within year 3 of more than 25% of the balance of loan capital outstanding at the end of year 2; or

(c)   repayment before the end of year 4 of more than 50% of the balance of loan capital outstanding at the end of year 2; or

(d)   repayment before the end of year 5 of more than 75% of that balance.

Any of the above percentages may be altered by Treasury order, but only in relation to loans made on or after a date specified in the order. For the above purposes, there is disregarded any requirement to repay that may arise as a consequence of certain standard commercial default provisions in the loan agreement.

[*ITA 2007, s 345; FA 2002, Sch 16 para 9*].

Conditions to be satisfied in relation to securities or shares

[19.9] There are two such conditions. The first is that the securities or shares must be subscribed for wholly in cash and fully paid for as at the investment date. The second is that they must not carry:

•   any present or future right to be redeemed within the five-year investment period; or

•   any present or future right to be converted into, or exchanged for, a loan, securities, shares or other rights, any of which are redeemable within the five-year investment period.

[*ITA 2007, ss 346, 347; FA 2002, Sch 16 paras 10, 11; CTA 2010, Sch 1 para 510*].

No pre-arranged protection against risks

[19.10] Any arrangements (as very broadly defined) under which the investment in the CDFI is made (or arrangements preceding the investment but relating to it) must not include arrangements a main purpose of which is to provide (by means of any insurance, indemnity, guarantee or otherwise) complete or partial protection for the investor against the normal risks attaching to the investment. Arrangements are, however, allowed if they do no more than provide the kind of commercial protection, e.g. the use of property as security for a loan, that might be expected if the investment were made by a bank. [*ITA 2007, s 349; FA 2002, Sch 16 para 13*].

General conditions for eligibility

[19.11] The following conditions apply.

No control of CDFI by investor

The investor must not control the CDFI at any time in the five-year investment period. 'Control' is construed in accordance with *ITA 2007, s 995* where the CDFI is a body corporate, with similar rules applying in other cases, with any potential future rights and powers of the investor, and any rights and powers held or exercisable by another on his behalf, taken into account. References to 'the investor' include any person connected with him (within **21 CONNECTED PERSONS**).

Beneficial ownership

The investor must be the sole beneficial owner of the investment when it is made (which in the case of a loan means sole beneficial entitlement to repayment).

No acquisition of share in partnership

Where the CDFI is a partnership, the investment must not consist of or include any capital contributed by the investor on becoming a member of the partnership. This includes the provision of loan capital treated as partners' capital in the partnership accounts.

No tax avoidance purpose

The investment must not be made as part of a scheme or arrangement a main purpose of which is the avoidance of tax.

[*ITA 2007, ss 350–353, 1021; FA 2002, Sch 16 paras 14, 15, 17, 18, 51(3)*].

Withdrawal or reduction of relief

[19.12] Community investment tax relief may fall to be withdrawn or reduced on a disposal of the investment (see **19.15** below), on repayment of an investment consisting of a loan (see **19.17** below), or if value is received in respect of the investment (see **19.18–19.21** below).

Where relief given falls to be withdrawn or reduced, and also where it is found not to have been due in the first place, the withdrawal etc. is achieved by means of an income tax assessment for the tax year *for which the relief was obtained*. On and after 1 April 2010, it is specified that the assessment must be made no later than six years after the tax year for which the relief was obtained. This restriction is without prejudice to the extension of time limits in cases of loss of income tax brought about deliberately (see **6.3 ASSESSMENTS**). No such assessment can be made by reason of any event occurring after the investor's death. [*ITA 2007, ss 371, 372; FA 2002, Sch 16 para 27; FA 2008, Sch 39 para 60; SI 2009 No 403*].

Information

[19.13] Certain events giving rise to withdrawal or reduction of investment relief must be notified to HMRC by the investor. An individual investor must give such notice no later than 31 January following the tax year in which the event occurs. If the requirement arises from the receipt of value by a connected person, the above deadline is extended to, if later, the end of the period of 60 days beginning when the investor comes to know of the event. The penalty provisions of *TMA 1970, s 98* apply in the event of non-compliance. [*ITA 2007, s 373; FA 2002, s 57, Sch 16 para 42, Sch 17 para 1; CTA 2010, Sch 1 para 520*].

Attribution of relief

[19.14] Community investment tax relief is said to be 'attributable' to any investment in respect of a tax year if relief as in **19.3** above has been obtained in respect of that investment and has not been withdrawn (as opposed to reduced). Where for any tax year relief has been obtained by reason of a single investment (i.e. one loan, or securities or shares comprised in one issue), the relief attributable to it is the reduction made in the investor's tax liability. Where the relief has been obtained by reason of two or more investments, it is attributed to those investments in proportion to the invested amounts (see **19.4** above) for the year. Relief attributable to any one issue of securities or shares is attributed *pro rata* to each security or share in that issue, and any reduction of relief is similarly apportioned between the securities or shares in question. For these purposes, any bonus shares, issued in respect of the original shares and being shares in the same company, of the same class and carrying the same rights, are treated as if comprised in the original issue, and relief is apportioned to them accordingly. This applies only if the original shares have been continuously held (see **19.25** below) by the investor (as sole beneficial owner) since their issue, and, where it does apply, the bonus shares are themselves treated as having been continuously held since the time of the original issue. [*ITA 2007, ss 357, 358, 382(1)(2); FA 2002, Sch 16 paras 26, 51(2); FA 2007, Sch 26 para 12(8)*].

Disposals

[19.15] For the purposes below, an investment is regarded as being disposed of if it is so regarded for the purposes of tax on chargeable gains, and see also **19.23** below (certain company reconstructions treated as disposals). [*ITA 2007, s 379; FA 2002, Sch 16 para 48*].

Loans

Where the investment consists of a loan, and the investor disposes of the whole of it within the five-year investment period (see **19.1** above), otherwise than by way of a 'permitted disposal', or disposes of part of it during that period, any relief attributable to the investment (see **19.14** above), for any tax year, is withdrawn. See **19.12** above for consequences of withdrawal. Repayment of the loan does not count as a disposal. A disposal is a *'permitted disposal'* if it is:

- by way of a distribution in the course of dissolving or winding up the CDFI; or
- a disposal within *TCGA 1992, s 24(1)* (entire loss, destruction etc. of asset — see Tolley's Capital Gains Tax under Disposal); or

- a deemed disposal under *TCGA 1992, s 24(2)* (assets of negligible value — see Tolley's Capital Gains Tax under Losses); or
- made after the CDFI has ceased to be accredited as such.

[*ITA 2007, s 360; FA 2002, Sch 16 para 28*].

Securities or shares

Where the investment consists of securities or shares, and the investor disposes of the whole or any part of the investment within the five-year investment period, any relief attributable to the investment (see **19.14** above), in respect of any tax year, is withdrawn or reduced as set out below. This does not apply if the CDFI has ceased to be accredited before the disposal or if the disposal arises from the repayment, redemption or repurchase by the CDFI of any of the securities or shares. See **19.12** above for consequences of withdrawal etc.

In the case of a 'permitted disposal' (defined as for *Loans* above) or a disposal by way of a bargain made at arm's length, the relief attributable to the investment in respect of any tax year is withdrawn, or is reduced by 5% of the disposal consideration (if such reduction would not amount to full withdrawal). If the relief initially obtained for any tax year was less than 5% of the invested amount (see **19.4** above), i.e. because the investor's tax liability was insufficient to fully absorb the available relief, the reduction is correspondingly restricted. In the case of any other disposal, the relief for all tax years is withdrawn.

[*ITA 2007, s 361; FA 2002, Sch 16 para 29; CTA 2010, Sch 1 para 514*].

Identification rules on disposal of securities or shares

[19.16] The rules below apply, for the purpose of identifying shares disposed of, where the investor makes a part disposal of a holding of shares of the same class in the same company, and the holding includes shares to which community investment tax relief is attributable (see **19.14** above) and which have been held continuously (see **19.25** below) since the time of issue. The rules apply for the purposes of **19.15** above and this chapter generally and for the purposes of taxing chargeable gains; as regards the latter, the normal identification rules are disapplied. The rules below apply to securities as they apply to shares.

Where shares comprised in the holding have been acquired on different days, a disposal is identified with acquisitions on a first in/first out basis. In matching the shares disposed of with shares acquired on a particular day, shares to which relief is attributable, and which have been held continuously since issue, are treated as being disposed of *after* any other shares included in the holding and acquired on that day. If, on a reorganisation of share capital (e.g. a scrip issue), a new holding falls, by virtue of *TCGA 1992, s 127* (or any other chargeable gains enactment which applies that *section* — see Tolley's Capital Gains Tax under Shares and Securities, and see also **19.22** below), to be equated with the original shares, shares comprised in the new holding are deemed for these purposes to have been acquired when the original shares were acquired.

[ITA 2007, ss 377, 382(2), Sch 1 para 316; TCGA 1992, s 151BA; FA 2002, Sch 16 paras 47, 51(2); FA 2007, Sch 26 para 12(8)].

Excessive repayments of loan capital

[19.17] Where the investment consists of a loan, and the 'average capital balance' for the third, fourth or final year of the five-year investment period (see **19.1** above) is less than the 'permitted balance' for the year in question (other than by an amount of 'insignificant value'), any relief attributable to the investment (see **19.14** above), for any tax year, is withdrawn. See **19.12** above for consequences of withdrawal.

For these purposes, the *'average capital balance'* of the loan for any period of time is the mean of the daily balances of capital outstanding during that period, disregarding any 'non-standard repayments' made in that period or at any earlier time. The *'permitted balance'* of the loan is as follows:

- for the third year of the five-year investment period, 75% of the average capital balance for the six months beginning eighteen months after the investment date;
- for the fourth year, 50% of that balance; and
- for the final year, 25% of that balance.

For these purposes, an amount is of *'insignificant value'* if it does not exceed £1,000 or if it is insignificant in relation to the average capital balance for whichever year of the five-year investment period is under consideration.

'Non-standard repayments' are repayments made:

- at the choice or discretion of the CDFI and not under any obligation under the loan agreement; or
- as a consequence of certain standard commercial default provisions in the loan agreement.

[ITA 2007, s 362; FA 2002, Sch 16 para 30].

Value received by investor: loans

[19.18] Where the investment consists of a loan, and the investor 'receives value' (see **19.20** below), other than an amount of 'insignificant value', from the CDFI during the 'six-year period', the investor is treated as having received a repayment equal to the amount of value received. This may have consequences for **19.4** above (determination of invested amount) and **19.17** above (withdrawal of relief where excessive repayments made). Where the value is received in the first or second year of the 'six-year period', the repayment is treated as made at the beginning of that second year. Where the value is received in a later year, the repayment is treated as made at the beginning of the year in question. The repayment is not treated as a 'non-standard repayment' for the purposes of **19.17** above.

For these purposes, an amount is of *'insignificant value'* if it does not exceed £1,000 or if it is insignificant in relation to the 'average capital balance' for the year of the 'six-year period' in which the value is received (treating any value received in the first year as received at the beginning of the second). There are provisions to aggregate a receipt of value, whether insignificant or not, with amounts of insignificant value received previously, and treating that aggregate, if it is not itself an amount of insignificant value, as an amount of value received at the time of the latest actual receipt. The '*average capital balance*' of the loan for any year is the mean of the daily balances of capital outstanding during that year, disregarding the receipt of value in question.

[*ITA 2007, ss 363, 365; FA 2002, Sch 16 paras 31, 34; CTA 2010, Sch 1 paras 515, 517*].

The '*six-year period*' is the period of six years beginning one year before the investment date. [*ITA 2007, s 359(3); FA 2002, Sch 16 para 33*].

These provisions apply equally to receipts of value by and from persons connected (within **21 CONNECTED PERSONS**), at any time in the period of restriction, with the investor or, as the case may be, the CDFI. [*ITA 2007, s 370; FA 2002, Sch 16 para 39*]. See **19.20** below for the meaning of 'value received' and the determination of the *amount* of value received.

Value received by investor — securities or shares

[19.19] Where the investment consists of securities or shares, and the following circumstances are present, any relief attributable (see **19.14** above) to the 'continuing investment' (see (b) below), for any tax year, is withdrawn. See **19.12** above for consequences of withdrawal. The circumstances are that:

(a)   the investor 'receives value' (see **19.20** below), other than an amount of 'insignificant value', from the CDFI during the 'six-year period' (defined as in **19.18** above);

(b)   the investment or a part of it has been continuously held (and see **19.25** below) by the investor (as sole beneficial owner) since the investment was made (the '*continuing investment*'); and

(c)   the receipt wholly or partly exceeds the permitted level of receipts (see below) in respect of the continuing investment (other than by an amount of 'insignificant value').

The permitted level of receipts is exceeded where:

(i)   any value is received by the investor (disregarding any amounts of 'insignificant value') in the first three years of the 'six-year period'; or

(ii)   the aggregate value received by the investor (disregarding any amounts of 'insignificant value') exceeds,

- before the beginning of the fifth year of the 'six-year period', 25% of the amount subscribed for the securities or shares comprising the continuing investment;

- before the beginning of the final year of that period, 50% of that amount;

- before the end of that period, 75% of that amount.

Where a receipt of value in (a) above is not an amount of 'insignificant value' but is nevertheless insufficient to trigger any withdrawal of relief under the above rules, any tax relief subsequently due is computed as if the amount subscribed for the securities or shares comprising the continuing investment (and thus the invested amount at **19.4** above) were reduced by the amount of value received. This restriction applies for tax years ending on or after the anniversary of the investment date falling immediately before (or coinciding with) the receipt of value.

For the above purposes, an amount is of '*insignificant value*' if it does not exceed £1,000 or if it is insignificant in relation to the amount subscribed by the investor for the securities or shares comprising the continuing investment. There are provisions to aggregate a receipt of value, whether insignificant or not, with amounts of insignificant value received previously, and treating that aggregate, if it is not itself an amount of insignificant value, as an amount of value received at the time of the latest actual receipt.

[*ITA 2007, ss 364, 365, 369; FA 2002, Sch 16 paras 32, 34, 38; CTA 2010, Sch 1 paras 516, 517, 519*].

These provisions apply equally to receipts of value by and from persons connected (within **21 CONNECTED PERSONS**), at any time in the 'six-year period', with the investor or, as the case may be, the CDFI. [*ITA 2007, s 370; FA 2002, Sch 16 para 39*]. See **19.20** below for the meaning of 'value received' and the determination of the *amount* of value received.

Meaning of, and amount of, value received

[19.20] For the purposes of **19.18** and **19.19** above, the investor '*receives value*' from the CDFI at any time when the CDFI (and see **19.18, 19.19** above *re* connected persons):

(a)   repays, redeems or repurchases any securities or shares included in the investment;

(b)   releases or waives any liability of the investor to the CDFI (which it is deemed to have done if discharge of the liability is twelve months or more overdue) or discharges (or agrees to discharge) any liability of the investor to a third party;

(c)   makes a loan or advance to the investor which has not been repaid in full before the investment is made; for this purpose a loan includes any debt incurred, other than an ordinary trade debt (as defined), and any debt due to a third party which is assigned to the CDFI;

(d)   provides a benefit or facility for the investor, or for any associates (as defined) of the investor — except in circumstances such that, if a *payment* had been made of equal value, it would have been a 'qualifying payment';

(e)   disposes of an asset to the investor for no consideration or for consideration less than market value (as defined), or acquires an asset from the investor for consideration exceeding market value; or

(f)   makes a payment to the investor other than a 'qualifying payment'.

References above to a debt or liability do not include one which would be discharged by making a 'qualifying payment'. References to a payment or disposal include one made indirectly to, or to the order of, or for the benefit of, the person in question.

Each of the following is a '*qualifying payment*':

- a reasonable (in relation to their market value) payment for any goods, services or facilities provided by the investor in the course of trade or otherwise;
- the payment of interest at no more than a reasonable commercial rate on money lent;
- the payment of a dividend or other distribution which represents no more than a normal return on investment;
- a payment to acquire an asset at no more than its market value;
- a payment not exceeding a reasonable and commercial rent for property occupied;
- a payment discharging an 'ordinary trade debt' (as defined).

The amount of value received is:

- in a case within (a) above, the amount received;
- in a case within (b) above, the amount of the liability;
- in a case within (c) above, the amount of the loan etc. less any amount repaid before the making of the investment;
- in a case within (d) above, the cost to the CDFI (net of any consideration given for it by the investor or his associate) of providing the benefit etc.;
- in a case within (e) above, the difference between market value and the consideration received (if any); and
- in a case within (f) above, the amount of the payment.

[*ITA 2007, ss 366, 367, 381, 382(3); FA 2002, Sch 16 paras 35, 36, 50, 51(4)*].

Value received where more than one investment

[19.21] Where the investor makes more than one investment in the CDFI for which he is eligible for, and claims, relief, any value received (other than value within **19.20**(a) above) is apportioned between the investments by reference to the average capital balances of loans and the amounts subscribed for securities or shares. [*ITA 2007, s 368; FA 2002, Sch 16 para 37; CTA 2010, Sch 1 para 518*].

Company restructuring

Reorganisations of share capital

[19.22] The following apply where the CDFI is a company and the investment consists of shares or, in the case of **19.23** below, shares or securities.

Rights issues etc.

Where:

- a reorganisation (within *TCGA 1992, s 126*) involves an allotment of shares or debentures in respect of, and in proportion to, an existing holding of shares of the same class in the CDFI held by the investor in a single capacity;

- community investment tax relief is attributable (see **19.14** above) to the shares in the existing holding or to the allotted shares; and
- if the relief is attributable to the shares in the existing holding, those shares have been held continuously (and see **19.25** below) by the investor since they were issued,

the share reorganisation rules of *TCGA 1992, ss 127–130* are disapplied. The effect is that the allotted shares are treated as a separate holding acquired at the time of the reorganisation. This does not, however, apply in the case of bonus shares where these are issued in respect of shares comprised in the existing holding and are of the same class and carry the same rights as those shares. (For *TCGA 1992, ss 126–130*, see Tolley's Capital Gains Tax under Shares and Securities.)

Reorganisation involving issue of QCB

If, in a case otherwise within *TCGA 1992, s 116(10)* (see Tolley's Capital Gains Tax under Qualifying Corporate Bonds):

- the old asset consists of shares to which community investment tax relief is attributable (see **19.14** above) and which have been held continuously (see **19.25** below) by the investor since they were issued; and
- the new asset consists of a qualifying corporate bond,

the usual treatment is disapplied. The effect is that the investor is deemed to have disposed of the shares at the time of the reorganisation, and the resulting chargeable gain or allowable loss crystallises *at that time*.

[*TCGA 1992, s 151BB; FA 2002, Sch 16 paras 40, 51(2); ITA 2007, Sch 1 para 317*].

Company reconstructions

[19.23] *TCGA 1992, s 135* (exchange of securities for those in another company) and *s 136* (schemes of reconstruction involving issue of securities), which normally equate the new holding with the original shares, are disapplied in the following circumstances:

- an investor holds shares in or debentures of a company (company A);
- community investment tax relief is attributable (see **19.14** above) to those shares;
- those shares have been held continuously (see **19.25** below) by the investor since they were issued; and
- there is a reconstruction whereby another company issues shares or debentures in exchange for, or in respect of, company A shares or debentures.

The result is that the transaction is treated, both for the purposes of this chapter and for the purposes of taxing chargeable gains, as a disposal of the original securities or shares (and an acquisition of a new holding). (For *TCGA 1992, ss 135, 136*, see Tolley's Capital Gains Tax under Shares and Securities.)

[*TCGA 1992, s 151BC; FA 2002, Sch 16 paras 41, 48(2); ITA 2007, Sch 1 para 318*].

Accreditation and tax relief certificates

Accreditation

[19.24] A body may apply to the Department for Business, Enterprise and Regulatory Reform (previously the Department of Trade and Industry) for accreditation as a CDFI. The body's principal objective must be to provide (directly or indirectly) finance, or finance and access to business advice, for enterprises for disadvantaged communities. The latter term includes enterprises located in disadvantaged areas and enterprises owned or operated by, or designed to serve, members of disadvantaged groups. The body must also satisfy such other criteria as may be specified in Treasury regulations. Such regulations may distinguish between 'wholesale' CDFIs, i.e. those whose objective is to finance other, generally smaller, CDFIs, and 'retail' CDFIs, i.e. those whose objective is to invest directly in enterprises. The terms and conditions of accreditation are also to be set by regulations; these may include a right of appeal against a refusal to accredit, and provision for the withdrawal of an accreditation, and the possible imposition of penalties, in consequence of any breach of terms and conditions. See now *SI 2003 No 96*.

An accreditation normally has effect for three years. A new accreditation may, if the CDFI so claims, displace an existing accreditation.

[*ITA 2007, ss 340–343; FA 2002, Sch 16 paras 4–7; SI 2009 No 56, Sch 1 para 451*].

Tax relief certificates

Before an investment in a CDFI can qualify for tax relief, the CDFI must issue to the investor a tax relief certificate (see **19.3**, **19.7**(b) above) in a specified form. In relation to an accreditation period, a CDFI may issue tax relief certificates in respect of investments made in it within that period of an aggregate value of up to £20 million in the case of a wholesale CDFI (see above) or £10 million in the case of a retail CDFI. The Treasury may substitute other figures by order but not so as to reduce them for periods beginning before the order takes effect. Any tax relief certificate issued in contravention of these limits is invalid (and thus the investment in question does not satisfy **19.7**(b) above and does not attract tax relief). A CDFI is liable to a penalty of up to £3,000 for the issue of a tax relief certificate made fraudulently or negligently. [*ITA 2007, s 348; FA 2002, Sch 16 para 12; CTA 2010, Sch 1 para 511*].

Miscellaneous

Circumstances in which investment not held 'continuously'

[19.25] An investor is not treated for the purposes of this chapter as having held an investment (or a part of an investment) continuously throughout a period if:

* under any provision of *TCGA 1992*, the investment (or part) has been deemed to be disposed of and immediately reacquired by the investor at any time in that period; or

- there has been at any time in that period a transaction treated, by virtue of **19.23** above (company reconstructions etc.), as a disposal by the investor.

[*ITA 2007, s 380; FA 2002, Sch 16 para 49*].

Nominees and bare trustees

[19.26] For the purposes of this chapter, actions of a person's nominee or bare trustee in relation to loans, shares or securities are treated as actions of that person. [*ITA 2007, s 375; FA 2002, Sch 16 para 44*].

Disclosure of information

[19.27] There are provisions for the exchange of information between the Secretary of State and HMRC in so far as this is necessary to enable them both to discharge their functions appertaining to community investment tax relief. Information thus obtained cannot be further disclosed except for the purposes of legal proceedings arising out of those functions. [*ITA 2007, s 374; FA 2002, Sch 16 para 43*].

Alternative finance arrangements

[19.28] With effect on and after 10 July 2008, the provisions described in this chapter apply as if references to a loan included references to arrangements falling within **3.2** (alternative finance return — purchase and re-sale), **3.7** (profit share return — deposit) or **3.8** (profit share return — agency) ALTERNATIVE FINANCE ARRANGEMENTS and as if references to interest included references to alternative finance return or profit share return as appropriate. [*ITA 2007, ss 372A–372D; FA 2005, s 54A; CTA 2009, Sch 1 para 658; TIOPA 2010, Sch 2 paras 51-54; SI 2008 No 1821*]. ITA 2007, ss 372B–372D set out the mechanics of how the provisions have effect in relation to each of those types of arrangement.

20

Compensation for Loss of Employment (and Damages)

Cross-references. See **73.48** TRADING INCOME ('Compensation, Damages etc. — Receipts') and **73.48** ('Compensation, Damages etc. — Payments') for treatment in relation to trading profits and **73.65** for allowability of payments to employees; **27.70** EMPLOYMENT INCOME for Redundancy Payments, **27.72** for Restrictive Covenants, **27.78** for certain payments to MPs etc. and **27.94** for wages in lieu of notice.

Simon's Taxes. See E4.8.

Introduction

[20.1] The following paragraphs apply to lump sums paid on termination of an office or employment and, at **20.7** below, to the reduction of an award for damages by reference to the tax liability. The statutory exemption for the first £30,000 of a termination payment is covered at **20.4–20.6** below.

Payments and benefits on termination of office or employment — summary

[20.2] In determining the correct treatment for tax purposes of a sum receivable by a director or employee on termination of his office or employment, it is first necessary to see whether it is taxable as employment income under the rules for taxing general earnings (see **27.1** EMPLOYMENT INCOME). See **20.3** below for an outline of the principles to be applied. If it is within the general rules, it is taxable in full under PAYE (**53**) at the time of the payment.

If it is not within the general earnings rules, such a sum will generally be taxable as employment income by virtue of, and in accordance with, the special legislation in *ITEPA 2003, ss 401–416*. See **20.4**, **20.5** below for the application of this legislation, and **20.6** below for exemptions.

Compensation for termination of office or employment — general tax law

[20.3] The following principles apply in determining whether a sum received in compensation for termination of office or employment is taxable under the general earnings rules in **27 EMPLOYMENT INCOME**. See **20.4** *et seq.* below as regards such payments not within these rules.

A payment made to a director or employee by way of reward for services, past, present or future, is within the general earnings rules. It was considered by the Revenue that this could include any termination payment received under the terms of a contract of service, or where there was an expectation of receiving such a payment firm enough to allow the payment to be viewed as part of the reward for services. In *Mairs v Haughey* HL 1993, 66 TC 273, however, it was held that a non-statutory redundancy payment would not be within the general earnings charge, being compensation for the employee's not being able to receive emoluments from the employment rather than emoluments from the employment itself. (The case concerned a payment for the waiver of a contingent right to such a payment, which was to be accorded the same tax treatment.) Following the decision in *Mairs v Haughey*, the Revenue published Statement of Practice SP 1/94. This acknowledges that lump sum payments under a non-statutory redundancy scheme are liable to income tax only under what are now *ITEPA 2003, ss 401–416*), provided that they are genuinely made solely on account of redundancy as defined in *Employment Rights Act 1996, s 139*, whether the scheme is a standing scheme forming part of the conditions of service or an *ad hoc* scheme devised to meet a particular situation. SP 1/94 indicates, however, that the Revenue is concerned to distinguish payments which are in reality terminal bonuses or other reward for services, which are fully taxable under the general earnings rules, and that in view of the often complex arrangements for redundancy, and the need to consider each scheme on its own facts, employers may submit proposed schemes (together with any explanatory letter to be sent to employees) to the inspector for advance clearance. (HMRC SP 1/94).

The following decided cases reflect the different approaches the courts have adopted in relation to such compensation. Proper compensation for loss of office is usually exempt (see *Clayton v Lavender* Ch D 1965, 42 TC 607) except where payable under service agreement (see *Dale v De Soissons* CA 1950, 32 TC 118) or under rights conferred by company's articles (*Henry v Foster* CA 1932, 16 TC 605). But an agreed sum payable for waiving such rights was held not assessable (*Hunter v Dewhurst* HL 1932, 16 TC 605), as also a payment in lieu of agreed pension (*Wales v Tilley* HL 1943, 25 TC 136). Payment in settlement of claim re breach of service contract also exempt (*Du Cros v Ryall* KB 1935, 19 TC 444), but cf. *Carter v Wadman* CA 1946, 28 TC 41 and *Richardson v Delaney* Ch D 2001, 74 TC 167. Voluntary payments on retirement held to be personal testimonials and not assessable (*Cowan v Seymour* CA 1919, 7 TC 372; *Mulvey v Coffey* HC(I) 2 ITC 239). But voluntary payments of £30,000 each made to the former directors of a family company the day after their resignation and retirement and minuted as being 'in appreciation of [their] services to the company over many years' were held by a Special Commissioner to be for services rendered and chargeable to tax as general earnings (*Allum and another v Marsh* (Sp C 446), [2005] SSCD 191). An ex gratia payment of £150,000 to compensate a director for the benefits she was giving up as a result of her resignation for the good of the company were held not to be chargeable as general earnings (*Resolute Management Services Ltd v HMRC; Haderlein v HMRC* (Sp C 710), [2008] SSCD 1202). A transfer fee paid by his old club to a professional footballer held to be assessable under general earnings rules and not as a termination payment (*Shilton v Wilmshurst* HL 1991, 64 TC 78).

Sums paid on cessation of office in lieu of future income were held not to be assessable in *Duff v Barlow* KB 1941, 23 TC 633; *Carter v Wadman* CA 1946, 28 TC 41; *Henley v Murray* CA 1950, 31 TC 351; and *Clayton v Lavender* Ch D 1965, 42 TC 607. *Hofman v Wadman* KB 1946, 27 TC 192, in which the decision was against the taxpayer, was not followed in *Clayton v Lavender*. But the following items paid during continuance of office were held liable: agreed sum paid to director to remain in office (*Prendergast v Cameron* HL 1940, 23 TC 122); for surrender of rights to fees or commission (*Leeland v Boarland* KB 1945, 27 TC 71; *Wilson v Daniels* KB 1943, 25 TC 473; *Bolam v Muller* KB 1947, 28 TC 471 and *McGregor v Randall* Ch D 1984, 58 TC 110); and for accepting lower fees (*Wales v Tilley* HL 1943, 25 TC 136). See also *Williams v Simmonds* Ch D 1981, 55 TC 17. Statutory redundancy payments under *Employment Rights Act 1996* (or NI equivalent) are otherwise exempt from tax (see *ITEPA 2003, s 309*) but must be taken into account for the purposes of the special legislation in *ITEPA 2003, ss 401–416*. A proposed supplementary redundancy payment which, following a change in circumstances, was made to all employees whether or not made redundant, was held to be assessable under the general earnings rules where made to employees not made redundant (*Allan v CIR; Cullen v CIR* CS 1994, 66 TC 681). However, in *Mimtec Ltd v CIR* (Sp C 277), [2001] SSCD 101 a Special Commissioner held that certain payments made following redundancy negotiations 'in recognition of any entitlements under the consultation process including pay in lieu of notice etc.' were not taxable as earnings.

See **27.94** EMPLOYMENT INCOME for the Revenue view of payments in lieu of notice.

Sum paid as compensation for loss of benefit under an abandoned refuse salvage scheme held assessable (*Holland v Geoghegan* Ch D 1972, 48 TC 482).

See **4.28** ANTI-AVOIDANCE regarding capital sums received in lieu of earnings.

See generally HMRC Employment Income Manual EIM12800 *et seq.*

Termination payments and benefits — special legislation

[20.4] The general legal position in **20.3** above is modified by special legislation as explained in **20.5, 20.6** below. A payment taxable under any other provisions is not within this special legislation, but *a compensation payment which does not fall within the special legislation nevertheless remains subject to the general law.*

For the interaction of these provisions and *Gourley* principles (see **20.7** below) see *Stewart v Glentaggart Ltd* CS 1963, 42 ATC 318; *Bold v Brough* QB, [1963] 3 AER 849 and *Parsons v BNM Laboratories Ltd* CA, [1963] 2 AER 658.

Termination payments and benefits — the charge to tax

[20.5] Under the special legislation in *ITEPA 2003, ss 401–416*, payments and other benefits 'received' in connection with the termination of a person's office or employment (or with any change in the duties thereof or earnings therefrom), and not otherwise chargeable to income tax (see also **20.4** above), are chargeable to tax as employment income if *and to the extent that* they amount in aggregate to more than £30,000. The charge is as employment income for the tax year in which the payment or benefit is received. For these purposes, a cash benefit is treated as *'received'* when payment is made (including any payment on account) or when the recipient becomes entitled to require such payment. A non-cash benefit is treated as *'received'* when it is used or enjoyed. See **20.6** below for exceptions from this charge. The amount chargeable as above is treated as the highest part of the person's total income for the year (apart from life assurance gains subject to top-slicing relief).

A benefit includes anything which would be taxable earnings from the office or employment (or would be charged to tax as such) if received for performance of the duties thereof. However, a right to receive payments or benefits is not itself regarded as a benefit. A benefit also includes anything which would be taxable earnings, if received for the performance of duties, but for the availability of an 'earnings-only exemption'. However, the following earnings-only exemptions can be disregarded.

- Any benefit received in connection with a change in duties or earnings to the extent that, were it received for the performance of duties, it would fall within the exemption at **27.71** EMPLOYMENT INCOME (exempt removal benefits and expenses on relocation).
- Certain benefits received in connection with the termination of an office or employment which, were they received for the performance of duties, would fall within certain specified exemptions (see *ITEPA 2003, s 402(2)*).

An *'earnings-only exemption'* is defined in *ITEPA 2003, s 227*, but, unhelpfully, such exemptions are not listed; broadly, it is an exemption that removes a charge to tax as general earnings as opposed to a wider exemption that removes any charge to tax as employment income; this was explained in greater detail in the Explanatory Notes (on clause 227) to the Income Tax (Earnings and Pensions) Bill. See **27.51, 27.79** EMPLOYMENT INCOME for the termination-related exemptions of *ITEPA 2003, ss 310, 311* (counselling and retraining); these, for example, are not earnings-only exemptions and thus can be disregarded entirely for the purposes of these provisions.

The charge applies to payments and other benefits received directly or indirectly, in consideration or in consequence of, or otherwise in connection with, the termination (or change), by the employee himself, by a spouse (or civil partner), other relative or other dependant of his or by his personal representatives, or provided on his behalf or to his order. The charge is on the employee or, in the event of his death, on his personal representatives. Where an individual suffered constructive dismissal on grounds of discrimination, the amount awarded by a tribunal was within the charge to the extent that it related to loss of income but not to the extent that it covered injury to feelings (*Walker v Adams* (Sp C 344), [2003] SSCD 269). In another constructive dismissal case, HMRC allocated only £10,000 of a £250,000 award to 'injury to feelings', and this was upheld by the Sp C (*'A' v HMRC* (Sp C 734), [2009] SSCD 269). In *Crompton v HMRC* FTT (TC 12), [2009] SSCD 504, the Tribunal found that on the proper interpretation of 'in connection with' in the statute, there had to be some sort of link, joint or bond between two things. In this case there was no such link between a payment of compensation and the termination of the appellant's employment, and the compensation was not taxable. For the reporting requirements in relation to taxable termination payments, see **53.12 PAY AS YOU EARN.**

Where a payment or benefit could fall to be taxed under both these provisions and the benefits code (see **27.26 EMPLOYMENT INCOME**), the benefits code takes priority. (There will not usually be any overlap between the two charging provisions where payments or benefits are received in connection with *termination* of employment, as opposed to a change of duties etc.) (Revenue Tax Bulletin June 2003 pp 1036, 1037).

Non-cash benefits

The amount of a non-cash benefit is normally its cash equivalent as determined under the benefits code (see **27.30 EMPLOYMENT INCOME**) as applied, with the necessary modifications (including a modified version of the rules for valuing the benefit of living accommodation) by *ITEPA 2003, s 415.* If, however, a greater figure would thus result, the benefit is the amount of earnings it would give rise to if received by an employee for duties of the employment (money's worth), thus bringing into charge any appreciation in the value of an asset since its acquisition by the person providing it. Where the cash equivalent of a beneficial loan (see **27.40 EMPLOYMENT INCOME**) is charged under these provisions for any tax year, the taxpayer is treated as having paid interest for that year of an amount equal to that brought into charge (but not to the extent that the amount otherwise chargeable is covered by the £30,000 threshold); general principles then apply to determine whether such notional interest is allowable for tax purposes (see **43 INTEREST PAYABLE**).

Application of £30,000 threshold

The £30,000 threshold is utilised against payments and benefits received in earlier tax years before those of later years. In any one tax year, the threshold (or so much of it as remains unutilised in earlier years) is set firstly against any cash benefits as they are received and any balance is set against the aggregate of non-cash benefits for the year. The threshold applies to the aggregate of payments and benefits provided in respect of the same person in respect of the same employment or of different employments with the same employer or 'associated' employers (as defined in *ITEPA 2003, s 404*) or successors.

[*ITEPA 2003, ss 401–404, 404A, 415, 416; ITA 2007, Sch 1 para 437*].

A payment or benefit within *ITEPA 2003, ss 401–416* is 'taxable specific income', which means that the charge is not dependent on the employee's residence or domicile status. See **27.1** EMPLOYMENT INCOME and also *Nichols v Gibson* CA 1996, 68 TC 611.

A statutory redundancy payment under *Employment Rights Act 1996* (or NI equivalent) is specifically brought within these provisions. [*ITEPA 2003, s 309(3)*]. For the position as regards a payment under a non-statutory redundancy scheme, see **20.3** above.

For MPs see *ITEPA 2003, s 291*, and for European MPs, **27.78** EMPLOYMENT INCOME.

Compensation for unfair dismissal, in a case in which the employment tribunal also made a reinstatement order, was held to be within these provisions (and thus subject to the £30,000 threshold) notwithstanding that the effect of the reinstatement order was to treat the taxpayer as if he had never been dismissed (*Wilson v Clayton* CA 2004, 77 TC 1). In *Clinton v HMRC* FTT (TC 278), 2010 STI 487 a lump sum payment equivalent to three months' salary was held to be have been made either on an ex gratia basis or to settle the appellant's common law claim for constructive dismissal and was not a payment in lieu of notice; it was thus subject to the £30,000 threshold.

An award from a stock bonus plan, granted whilst in employment but subsequently included in a termination agreement and vesting two years after date of redundancy, was held to be within these provisions and not general earnings (*Porter v HMRC* (Sp C 501), [2005] SSCD 803).

Expenses incurred by taxpayer in obtaining an award for unfair dismissal or securing fresh employment held not deductible (*Warnett v Jones* Ch D 1979, 53 TC 283).

A gratuitous payment of £150,000 held to be within these provisions was nevertheless held not to be within the term 'salaries, wages and other similar remuneration' for the purposes of the UK/USA double tax agreement, with the result that the whole payment escaped UK tax (*Resolute Management Services Ltd v HMRC; Haderlein v HMRC* (Sp C 710), [2008] SSCD 1202).

See **27.52** EMPLOYMENT INCOME for exemption from these provisions for payment made or benefit provided to reimburse the employee for cost of indemnity insurance or certain liabilities relating to the employment.

As to whether *compensation to auditor* and others falls within these provisions, see **27.54** EMPLOYMENT INCOME.

Simon's Taxes. See E4.743, E4.811–E4.814, E4.824.

Exceptions from charge

[20.6] The following are **excepted from the charge** under **20.5** above on termination payments and benefits (or, in the case of (vi) below, may be subject to reduction).

(i) Payments and other benefits where termination arises from death, injury or disability of the employee or office holder. [*ITEPA 2003, s 406*]. 'Disability' covers not only a condition resulting from a sudden affliction but also continuing incapacity to perform the duties of an office or employment arising out of the culmination of a process of deterioration of physical or mental health caused by chronic illness. (HMRC SP 10/81). See e.g. *Horner v Hasted* Ch D, [1995] STC 766 (relief refused).

(ii) Benefits provided before 1 December 1993, or on or after that date under retirement benefit schemes entered into before that date and not varied on or after that date, for the provision of which the employee has been charged under *ICTA 1970, s 220* or *ICTA 1988, s 595* (subsequently re-enacted as *ITEPA 2003, s 386*). [*ICTA 1988, s 188(1)(c); FA 1994, s 108(7)(8)*].

(iii) Any payment or other benefit provided under a tax-exempt pension scheme (as defined) by way of compensation for loss of office or employment or for loss or diminution of earnings, in either case because of ill-health, or properly regarded as earned by past service. [*ITEPA 2003, s 407*].

(iv) Certain payments and other benefits (including redundancy payments/benefits and commutation of annual sums) provided to members of the armed forces. [*ITEPA 2003, s 411*].

(v) A benefit provided under a pension scheme administered by a Commonwealth government or a payment of compensation, for loss of career, interruption of service etc. in connection with constitutional change in a Commonwealth country, to a person employed in the public service of that country. [*ITEPA 2003, s 412*].

(vi) Payments and other benefits where the office or employment in question included foreign service (as defined). Depending on length of foreign service in relation to total service, payments etc. may be wholly excepted or the amount otherwise chargeable may be proportionately reduced. [*ITEPA 2003, ss 413, 414; FA 2008, Sch 7 paras 30, 81*].

(vii) A contribution to a registered pension scheme or an employer-financed retirement benefit scheme (see respectively **57.2, 57.26 PENSION PROVISION**) to provide benefits in accordance with the scheme as part of an arrangement relating to the termination of an office or employment. [*ITEPA 2003, s 408; FA 2004, Sch 35 para 63*].

(viii) Legal costs. Where an employee takes action to recover compensation for termination of office or employment, any legal costs recovered from the employer are strictly chargeable without any deduction for the costs incurred. By concession, tax will not be charged under **20.5** above on such recovered costs where either:

(a) the dispute is settled without recourse to the courts, and the costs are paid direct to the employee's solicitor under the settlement agreement, in full or partial discharge of the solicitor's bill of costs incurred by the employee only in connection with the termination of the office or employment; or

(b) the dispute goes to court, and the costs are paid in accordance with a court order (including where they are paid direct to the employee).

Other professional costs, such as accountancy fees, are not covered by this concession, but it does cover legal costs incurred by the employee's solicitor in consulting other professionals for the specific claim or in paying the expenses of expert professional witnesses. (HMRC ESC A81; Revenue Tax Bulletin October 1994 p 170).

- any payment received in connection with a change in duties or earnings to the extent that, were it received for the performance of duties, it would fall within the exemption at **27.71 EMPLOYMENT INCOME** (exempt removal benefits and expenses on relocation); and
- any contribution made, in connection with the termination of an office or employment, to the employee's approved personal pension scheme.
- [*ITEPA 2003, s 405*].

Simon's Taxes. See E4.815, E4.816, E4.827.

Damages — reduction for tax

[20.7] Tax liability is taken into account in fixing *damages* for injury, see *British Transport Commission v Gourley* HL 1955, 34 ATC 305. For application of *Gourley* principle see *West Suffolk CC v W Rought Ltd* HL 1956, 35 ATC 315 and contrast *Stoke-on-Trent City Council v Wood Mitchell & Co Ltd* CA 1978, [1979] STC 197 (compulsory purchase of land); *Lyndale Fashion Mfrs v Rich* CA 1972, [1973] STC 32 (tax on damages calculated as if top slice of income after expenses deducted); *In re Houghton Main Colliery* Ch D 1956, 23 ATC 320 (lump sum payable re pensions); *Stewart v Glentaggart* CS 1963, 42 ATC 318; *Parsons v BNM Labs* CA 1963, 42 ATC 200 (damages for wrongful dismissal); *McGhie & Sons v BTC* QB 1962, 41 ATC 144 (prohibition from mining under railway — cf. **73.48**(c) **TRADING INCOME**); and *John v James* Ch D, [1986] STC 352 (no deduction for tax paid by defendant on sums wrongfully retained or for tax plaintiff would have been liable for on these sums or on compound interest award). But cf. *Spencer v Macmillan's Trustees* CS 1958, 37 ATC 388 (breach of contract). A PAYE refund was deducted in *Hartley v Sandholme* QB, [1974] STC 434. In a case involving taxable damages paid to a large group of Lloyd's Names, it was held that the fact that certain of the Names would receive a tax benefit, due to the differential tax rates applicable to the damages and the corresponding loss reliefs, did not require a departure from the general principle that no account is to be taken of taxation where both damages and lost profits are taxable (*Deeny and others v Gooda Walker Ltd* HL 1996, 68 TC 458).

As regards whether interest on awarded damages should take account of the extent to which the damages are taxable, see *Deeny and others v Gooda Walker Ltd (in liquidation) and others (No 4)* QB, [1995] STC 696.

Simon's Taxes. See E4.831–836.

Key points

[20.8] Points to consider are as follows.

- To benefit from the £30,000 exemption the payment must first be excluded from charge under other areas, and in particular as employment income.

- Termination payments are frequently more tax efficient when made to a registered pension scheme on behalf of the taxpayer, but beware the tax implications of the annual allowance, lifetime allowance and for 2009/10 and 2010/11 the special annual allowance. (See **57 PENSION PROVISION**.)

- Employers providing non cash benefits to former employees should note the reporting requirements in respect of them. These arise only at the point of termination but should include details of benefits to be provided in future years. A copy must be provided to the employee to enable him to complete his tax return. Further reporting is not necessary unless the payment increases by more than £10,000.

- Payments in lieu of notice (PILONs) can sometimes fall within the termination payments legislation and therefore benefit from the exemption. (See **27.94**.)

- Note that non cash benefits provided on termination are taxable on all employees, not just those who would have been liable to tax on the benefit during their employment. This is because *ITEPA 2003, s 401* does not have the corresponding exemption for lower paid employees etc.

21

Connected Persons

[ITA 2007, ss 993, 994, Sch 1 para 411; CAA 2001, ss 575, 575A as amended; ICTA 1988, s 839 as amended]

Simon's Taxes. See A1.156.

[21.1] For many tax purposes, certain persons are treated as being so closely involved with each other that they must either be viewed as the same person or that transactions between them must be treated differently from transactions 'at arm's length'. These 'connected persons' are generally defined for tax purposes as below. It should, however, be noted that a modified definition may be applied in relation to any specific legislation, to which reference is made as appropriate in the text describing that legislation.

[21.2] An individual ('A') is connected with another individual ('B') if:

- A is B's spouse or civil partner;
- A is a relative of B;
- A is the spouse or civil partner of a relative of B;
- A is a relative of B's spouse or civil partner; or
- A is the spouse or civil partner of a relative of B's spouse or civil partner.

See definition of 'relative' in **21.8** below. A widow or widower is no longer a spouse (*Vestey's Exors and Vestey v CIR* HL 1949, 31 TC 1). Spouses divorced by decree nisi remain connected persons until the decree is made absolute (*Aspden v Hildesley* Ch D 1981, 55 TC 609).

[21.3] A trustee of a settlement, in his capacity as such, is connected with:

(a) any individual who is a settlor in relation to the settlement;
(b) any person connected with such an individual;
(c) any close company (see *CTA 2010, s 439* and Tolley's Corporation Tax under Close Companies) whose participators include the trustees of the settlement;
(d) any non-UK resident company which, if it were UK resident, would be a close company whose participators include the trustees of the settlement;
(e) any body corporate controlled (within *ITA 2007, s 995*) by a company within (c) or (d) above;
(f) (if the settlement is the principal settlement in relation to one or more sub-fund settlements — see **68.6** SETTLEMENTS), any trustee (in his capacity as such) of the sub-fund settlement(s); and
(g) (if the settlement is itself a sub-fund settlement), any trustee (in his capacity as such) of any other sub-fund settlements in relation to the same principal settlement.

See **21.8** below for relevant definitions.

[21.4] A partner in a partnership is connected with:

- any partner in the partnership;
- the spouse or civil partner of any individual who is a partner in the partnership; and
- a relative of any individual who is a partner in the partnership.

But none of the above applies in relation to acquisitions and disposals of partnership assets made pursuant to genuine commercial arrangements.

See **21.8** below for relevant definitions.

[21.5] A company is connected with another company if:

- the same person controls both; or
- a person has control of one company and persons connected with that person have control of the other company;
- a person ('A') has control of one company and A together with persons connected with A have control of the other company;
- the same group of persons controls both; or
- the companies are controlled by separate groups which could be regarded as the same group if (in one or more cases) a member of either group were replaced by a person with whom the member is connected.

See **21.8** below for relevant definitions.

[21.6] A company is connected with another person ('A') if:

- A has control of the company; or
- A together with persons connected with A have control of the company.

See **21.8** below for relevant definitions.

[21.7] **Persons acting together to secure or exercise control of a company** are treated in relation to that company as connected with each other and with any other person acting on the direction of any of them to secure or exercise such control. For the meaning of 'acting together to secure or exercise control', see *Steele v EVC International NV (formerly European Vinyls Corp (Holdings) BV)* CA 1996, 69 TC 88. Control may be 'exercised' passively. See *Floor v Davis* HL 1979, 52 TC 609.

[21.8] The following **definitions** apply for the above purposes.

'*Company*' includes any body corporate, unincorporated association or unit trust scheme (within *ITA 2007, s 1007*). It does not include a partnership.

'*Control*' is as defined by *CTA 2010, ss 450, 451* (previously *ICTA 1988, s 416*) (see Tolley's Corporation Tax under Close Companies) except in **21.3**(e) above.

'*Relative*' means brother, sister, ancestor or lineal descendant.

'*Settlement*' is given its wider definition so as to include any disposition, trust, covenant, agreement, arrangement or transfer of assets, wherever made. See **68.28** SETTLEMENTS.

'*Settlor*' is as defined in **68.3** SETTLEMENTS.

In relation to a settlement that would otherwise have no trustees, it is expressly provided that '*trustee*' means any person in whom the settled property or its management is for the time being vested.

22

Construction Industry Scheme (CIS)

Simon's Taxes. See E5.5.

Introduction

[22.1] A revised construction industry scheme was introduced in relation to payments made on or after 6 April 2007. [*FA 2004, s 77(1)(7); SI 2006 No 3240*]. The framework of the new scheme is provided for in *FA 2004*, but much of the detail is contained in regulations (see *FA 2004, ss 73, 75, 77(8)* for the principal regulation-making powers given to HMRC and the Treasury); see now *SI 2005 No 2045*.

Features of the new scheme include:

(a) the introduction of a verification service to enable contractors to check whether sub-contractors are registered for gross or net payment (see **22.11** below); and

(b) the introduction of periodic returns by contractors to replace the voucher system (see **22.11** below).

For HMRC guidance see Explanatory Booklet CIS340 Construction Industry Scheme — Guide for contractors and subcontractors. For links to other HMRC guidance on the new scheme, see www.hmrc.gov.uk/new-cis/index. htm.

Outline of the CIS

Where a contractor makes a contract payment to a sub-contractor under a construction contract, and that sub-contractor is either registered for payment under deduction (as opposed to being registered for gross payment), or is not registered at all, the contractor must make a deduction from the payment (see **22.6** below). The deduction is at 20% if the sub-contractor is registered for payment under deduction and 30% if he is unregistered. The terms 'contractor', 'contract payment', 'sub-contractor' and 'construction contract' are all defined by the legislation (see **22.2–22.6** below). The topic of registration is dealt with at **22.7–22.10** below.

It is up to the contractor to verify with HMRC the registration status of a sub-contractor (see **22.11** below). The contractor must then make periodic returns to HMRC concerning contract payments, as well as providing information about such payments to the sub-contractor (see **22.11** below).

Simon's Taxes. See E5.540–E5.567.

Payments from which tax must be deducted

[22.2] The scheme is concerned with payments (see **22.6** below) under a 'construction contract'. A contract of employment is specifically excluded from the definition of a construction contract, and it follows that the first question to be addressed before making any payment is whether the recipient is an employee. If so, the CIS is not in point (and the contractor will have to declare, in periodic returns to HMRC, that none of the contracts to which the return relates is a contract of employment — see **22.11** below). For the indicators of employment status, see **58.16 PERSONAL SERVICE COMPANIES ETC.** and **27.54 EMPLOYMENT INCOME.**

A *'construction contract'* must relate to 'construction operations' (see **22.3** below) and involve a 'sub-contractor' (see **22.4** below) and a 'contractor' (see **22.5** below).

[FA 2004, s 57].

Simon's Taxes. See E5.545.

Construction operations

[22.3] *'Construction operations'* include:

- construction, alteration, repair, extension, demolition or dismantling of buildings or structures, including offshore installations and temporary structures;
- construction, alteration, repair, extension or demolition of works forming part of the land, and this specifically includes walls, road-works, power-lines, electronic communications apparatus, aircraft runways, docks and harbours, railways, inland waterways, pipe-lines, reservoirs, water-mains, wells, sewers, industrial plant and installations for purposes of land drainage, coast protection or defence;
- installation of heating, lighting, air-conditioning, ventilation, power supply, drainage, sanitation, water supply or fire protection;
- internal cleaning if carried out during construction, alteration, repair, extension or restoration; and

- painting or decorating (internal and external).

Operations which are an integral part of, or are preparatory to, the operations in the above list are also included, for instance: site clearance, earth-moving, excavation, tunnelling and boring, laying of foundations, erection of scaffolding, site restoration, landscaping and the provision of roadways and other access works.

Specifically excluded from the definition of construction operations are:

- operations outside the UK;
- drilling for, or extraction of, oil or natural gas, and extraction of minerals;
- manufacture of building or engineering components or equipment, and delivery of these to site;
- manufacture of components for heating, ventilation etc. systems and delivery to site;
- the work of architects, surveyors and consultants;
- making, installing or repairing artistic works;
- signwriting, and erecting, installing or repairing signboards and advertisements;
- installation of seating, blinds and shutters; and
- installation of security systems and public address systems.

The Treasury may, by order, amend either of the above lists.

[*FA 2004, s 74*].

Carpet fitting is treated as outside the scope of the CIS (HMRC SP 12/81).

Simon's Taxes. See E5.541.

Sub-contractors

[22.4] A person is a '*sub-contactor*' if the contract imposes on him a duty to:

- carry out construction operations; or
- furnish his own labour or the labour of others in carrying out construction operations; or
- arrange for the labour of others to be furnished in carrying out construction operations.

Alternatively, a person may be a sub-contractor if, under the construction contract, he is answerable to the contractor for construction operations carried out by others (whether under a contract or other arrangements).

[*FA 2004, s 58*].

Simon's Taxes. See E5.543.

Contractors

[22.5] The term '*contractor*' in relation to a construction contract includes someone who is at the same time a party to that contract and a sub-contractor in another construction contract relating to any or all of the same construction operations. [*FA 2004, s 57(2)(b)*]. This would include, for instance, a gang-leader.

Other than that, the definition of a '*contractor*' may be divided into three categories.

(i)   Persons who are automatically classed as contractors. These are:

     (a)   any person carrying on a business which includes construction operations; and

     (b)   the Secretary of State if the contract is made by him under *Housing Associations Act 1985, s 89*.

(ii)   Persons carrying on a business which exceeds a set level of expenditure on construction operations. That level is:

- £1 million per year on average over the period of three years ending at the same time as the last period of account; or
- where the business was not being carried on at the beginning of that three-year period, £3 million over the whole of the truncated period.

Once defined as a contractor under this category, the person is deemed to continue to be a contractor until HMRC are satisfied that expenditure on construction operations has been less than £1 million for each of three successive years beginning in or after the period of account in which contractor status was acquired. For the purposes of all these limits, where a trade is transferred from one company to another and *CTA 2010, Pt 22 Ch 1* (no change of ownership) applies, the transferor's expenditure will be treated as the transferee's, with apportionment by HMRC (subject to appeal) when only part of the trade is transferred.

(iii)   Specified bodies or persons specified, provided their average annual expenditure on construction operations in any three-year period exceeds £1 million. Contractor status ceases to apply if, subsequently, there are three successive years in which expenditure on construction operations is less than £1 million. The bodies or persons specified are:

- any public office or department of the Crown (including any NI department and any part of the Scottish Administration);
- the Corporate Officer of the House of Lords, the Corporate Officer of the House of Commons, and the Scottish Parliamentary Corporate Body;
- any local authority;
- any development corporation or new town commission;
- the Commission for the New Towns;
- the Housing Corporation, a housing association, a housing trust, Scottish Homes, and the Northern Ireland Housing Executive;
- any NHS trust;
- any Health and Social Services trust.

HMRC may add to this list by means of regulations.

Under *FA 2004, s 73A* (see **25.1 DIPLOMATIC ETC. IMMUNITY**), the Treasury may designate any international organisation of which the UK is a member as being outside the above definition of a contractor.

[*FA 2004, s 59; ITA 2007, Sch 1 para 459; CTA 2010, Sch 1 para 426; SI 2009 No 56, Sch 1 para 420*].

Simon's Taxes. See D1.240, E5.542.

Deductions from contract payments

[22.6] Deductions on account of tax must be made from '*contract payments*'. These are defined as payments under a construction contract by the contractor to:

- a sub-contractor; or
- a nominee of the sub-contractor or the contractor; or
- a nominee of a person who is a sub-contractor under another construction contract relating to the construction operations.

Where the contractor makes a payment to a third party which discharges his obligation to pay a person within the above list, that payment is deemed to have been made directly to that person.

There are three exceptions to this definition of a contract payment:

- payments to agency workers treated, by virtue of *ITEPA 2003, Pt 2 Ch 7* as earnings from employment (see **27.95 EMPLOYMENT INCOME**);
- payments where the recipient is registered for gross payment (see **22.7** below) when the payment is made (although this is subject to certain qualifications in the case of nominees and partnerships — see below); and
- payments excepted by regulations; these comprise:
  - small payments, i.e. payments made by contractors within **22.5**(i)(b), (ii) or (iii) above and approved for this purpose, in a case where the total payments under the construction contract (excluding direct cost of materials) do not, or are not likely to, exceed £1,000;
  - payments made by a contractor within **22.5**(i)(a) above, and approved for this purpose, to a body or person for work carried out on land owned by that body or person or on agricultural property (as defined) of which that body or person is a tenant, in a case where the total payments under the construction contract (excluding direct cost of materials) do not, or are not likely to, exceed £1,000;
  - reverse premiums (within the meaning of *ITTOIA 2005, s 99* — see **73.105 TRADING INCOME** — as modified for this purpose);
  - payments by local authority maintained schools under devolved budgets;
  - payments made by contractors within **22.5**(ii) above in respect of construction operations relating to property used (as defined) in their own or in another group company's business;
  - payments made by public bodies within **22.5**(i)(b) or (iii) above under a private finance transaction (as defined); and
  - payments made by any body of persons or trust established for charitable purposes only.

The qualifications to the exception where the recipient is registered for gross payment are as follows.

- Where the recipient is a nominee, then the nominee, the person who nominated him and the person for whose labour (or the company for whose employees' labour) the payment is made must all be registered for gross payment when the payment is made.
- Where the recipient is registered for gross payment as a partner in a firm, the exception only applies to payments in respect of the firm's business (i.e. under contracts where the firm is a sub-contractor or, where the firm has been nominated to receive payments, the person who nominated the firm is a sub-contractor and is himself registered for gross payment).
- Where a person registered for gross payment other than as a partner in a firm becomes a partner in a firm, the exception does not apply to payments in respect of the firm's business (i.e. under contracts where the firm is a sub-contractor, or, where the firm has been nominated to receive payments, the person who nominated the firm is a sub-contractor).

[*FA 2004, s 60; SI 2005 No 2045, Regs 18–24; SI 2007 No 672, Regs 4–6*].

Upon making a contract payment, the contractor must make a deduction on account of tax. The deductible amount is calculated by first excluding the cost of materials and any VAT charged and then applying the 'relevant percentage', which is set by Treasury order. The *maximum* relevant percentage varies in accordance with the registration status of the person for whose labour (or, in the case of companies, for whose employees' labour) the payment is made, as follows.

- If registered for payment under deduction (see **22.7** below), the relevant percentage may not exceed the basic rate of tax for the tax year in which the payment is made;
- If unregistered, the relevant percentage may not exceed the higher rate of tax for that year.

The actual relevant percentages are **20%** if the sub-contractor is registered for payment under deduction and **30%** if he is not.

The contractor must pay the amount deducted to HMRC. For the purposes of computing the contractor's taxable profits, the full amount of the contract payment (i.e. the amount paid to the sub-contractor plus the amount paid to HMRC) is allowed as a deduction (assuming the payment itself is allowable under general principles).

Where the sub-contractor is not a company, the amounts deducted from contract payments are treated as income tax paid in respect of the profits of the trade. Any excess of those amounts over the income tax liability on those profits is treated as discharging any Class 4 National Insurance contributions payable in respect of those profits.

Where the sub-contractor is a company, the treatment of the amounts deducted is to be governed by regulations. The order of set-off is firstly against payments due to HMRC, for the tax year in which the deduction is made, under the contractor's obligations as an employer or contractor (e.g. PAYE, Class 1 National Insurance contributions, deductions under the CIS) and secondly against corporation tax. Any excess is repayable to the sub-contractor.

[*FA 2004, ss 61, 62; SI 2007 No 46*].

Simon's Taxes. See E5.545–E5.547.

Where the recipient is a managed service company (see **46 MANAGED SERVICE COMPANIES**) acting as an intermediary for the worker, the contractor must ensure that he correctly establishes the contractual relationships involved and the true nature of the services provided. The intermediary may not be a sub-contractor within **22.4** above, but a nominee of the worker, in which case it will not be sufficient that the intermediary is registered for gross payment. In order for payment to be made gross, the worker must be registered also — see the first qualification above. (HMRC Internet Statement, 3 December 2008 at www.hmrc.gov.uk/news/cis-msc.htm). See also www.hmrc.gov.uk/news/cis-ms c-faqs.htm (employment agencies or businesses placing workers in the construction sector).

Registration as a sub-contractor

[22.7] In order to be registered, an applicant must provide sufficient documents, records and information to establish, to the satisfaction of HMRC, his identity and address. If the required documents etc. have been provided, HMRC must register the applicant. If, in addition, the requirements for gross payment are met (see below) then the applicant must be registered for gross payment. There is provision for an appeal against HMRC's refusal to register for gross payment (see below). Otherwise, the applicant must be registered for payment under deduction. Once again, there is provision for an appeal against a refusal by HMRC to register.

There is a penalty of up to £3,000 for knowingly or recklessly making a statement, or supplying a document, which is false in a material particular (i.e. which contains a falsehood that is relevant to the decision regarding registration).

[*FA 2004, ss 63, 72*].

The requirements for registration for gross payment vary, depending upon whether the applicant is:

* an individual (see **22.8** below);
* a company (see **22.10** below); or
* an individual or company applying as a partner in a firm (see **22.9** below).

Details in respect of the documents, records and information to be provided to HMRC in support of an application for registration (for gross payment or for payment under deduction) are set out in regulations. [*SI 2005 No 2045, Reg 25*]. The Treasury is specifically empowered to alter, by means of an order, the conditions relating to registration for gross payment. [*FA 2004, Sch 11 para 13*].

Cancellation of registration

Failure to comply with the requirements of the CIS may result in the cancellation of a person's registration.

In the case of registration for gross payment, the conditions relating to cancellation may be divided into two by reference to the gravity of the offence. Lesser offences are if:

- at the time in question, HMRC would refuse a hypothetical application for gross payment registration;
- the person has made an incorrect return or provided incorrect information (whether as a contractor or a sub-contractor); or
- there is any failure to comply with the provisions of the CIS (whether as a contractor or a sub-contractor).

If it appears to HMRC that any of these apply, a determination may be made cancelling a person's registration with effect from 90 days after the date of notice of cancellation (see below). However, the effective date of cancellation may be delayed by an appeal (see below) to the latest of:

- the abandonment of the appeal;
- determination by the First-tier Tribunal; or
- determination by the Upper Tribunal or a court.

If gross payment registration is cancelled because of the above type of offence, the person must then be registered for payment under deduction.

More serious offences are:

- becoming registered for gross payment on the basis of false information;
- making a fraudulently incorrect return, or fraudulently providing incorrect information; or
- knowingly failing to comply with the provisions of the CIS.

HMRC must have reasonable grounds to suspect such an offence, and if so they may make a determination cancelling registration with immediate effect. HMRC then have discretion whether to register the person for payment under deduction.

On any cancellation, HMRC must, without delay, give a notice stating the reasons for the cancellation. The person whose registration is cancelled may not re-apply for gross payment registration for at least a year.

[FA 2004, ss 66, 67(5); SI 2005 No 2045, Reg 26; SI 2009 No 59, Sch 1 para 421(4)].

In the case of registration for payment under deduction, the conditions relating to cancellation (and appeal against such a decision) are governed by regulations. [FA 2004, s 68; SI 2005 No 2045, Reg 25; SI 2009 No 56, Sch 1 para 141].

Entering into a 'time to pay' arrangement (see **54.8, 54.9** PAYMENT OF TAX) before payment is due will not result in cancellation of the taxpayer's gross payment registration (www.hmrc.gov.uk/cis/business-payment-support.htm).

Appeals

An appeal may be made against the cancellation or refusal of a registration for gross payment by giving notice to HMRC within 30 days of the decision. The notice must state the reasons why the decision is believed to be unjustified. On appeal to the Appeal Tribunal, the Tribunal may review any relevant decision made in relation to registration. [*FA 2004, s 67; SI 2009 No 56, Sch 1 para 421*]. In the case of registration for payment under deduction, the conditions relating to refusal (and appeal against such a decision) are governed by regulations. [*SI 2005 No 2045, Reg 25*].

Simon's Taxes. See E5.547L, E5.550, E5.552–E5.554.

Registration for gross payment — individuals

[22.8] The conditions to be satisfied by individuals comprise three tests: a business test, a turnover test, and a compliance test.

The business test

The business carried on by the individual must be carried on in the UK. It must include either carrying out 'construction operations' (see **22.3** above), or furnishing labour for construction operations, or arranging for the furnishing of labour. Finally, it must, to a substantial extent, be carried on using an account with a bank; the phrase 'to a substantial extent' is not further defined in the legislation. The evidence required to prove the satisfaction of these conditions (prescribed by *SI 2005 No 2045, Reg 27*) includes the business address, invoices, contracts or purchase orders and payment details for the construction work, the business's books and accounts and details of the business bank account, including bank statements.

The turnover test

The applicant must satisfy HMRC that the likely receipt of 'relevant payments' in the year following the application is not less than £30,000. '*Relevant payments*' means payments under contracts relating to 'construction operations' (see **22.3** above), or contracts relating to the work of individuals in the carrying out of construction operations. Payments representing the cost of materials are excluded.

The evidence required to satisfy the turnover test (prescribed by *SI 2005 No 2045, Reg 29*) comprises:

- evidence of turnover during the twelve months prior to the application (the '*qualifying period*');
- evidence of relevant payments, which may include bank statements and paid cheques;
- evidence that total relevant payments received in the qualifying period equalled or exceeded £30,000;
- documentary evidence that construction operations were carried out during the qualifying period.

An individual who does not meet the turnover test can be treated as if he did if:

- the business does not consist mainly of construction operations;
- total turnover in the year prior to making the application exceeded £30,000; and
- in the year following making the application the individual is likely to receive relevant payments in relation to construction operations which are incidental to the main business.

This is designed to cover the situation where overall turnover exceeds the threshold but relevant payments derive from an ancillary part of the business and are less than the threshold.

The compliance test

In the twelve months prior to the application (the *'qualifying period'*) the individual must have complied with all his tax compliance obligations. Over the same period, the applicant must have supplied any requested information and accounts concerning any business of his (i.e. not just the business relating to the application). These requirements also apply to a company controlled by the applicant. Compliance must be within any required time limits or at the required time. That is to say, late compliance is no compliance at all for the purposes of this test.

The above compliance requirements are relaxed in two respects, as follows.

- There is a 'reasonable excuse' defence. This is accompanied by the usual requirement to have remedied any failure without unreasonable delay once the excuse ceased.
- There are disregards of specified compliance failures set out in regulations which are intended to make loss of gross payment status attach to quite serious combinations of defaults (see *SI 2005 No 2045, Reg 32, Table 3* or see www.hmrc.gov.uk/cis/gross-paid-review.htm). On and after 3 June 2008, late or non-payment of an amount due to HMRC is disregarded if the amount is less than £100 (*SI 2008 No 1282*).

The applicant may state that he was not subject to compliance obligations, e.g. because of absence abroad, or unemployment, or being in full-time education, but must provide evidence prescribed by *SI 2005 No 2045, Regs 33, 35, 36*. In the case of absence abroad, the applicant must also provide prescribed evidence of compliance with comparable obligations under the tax laws of the country in which he was living (see *SI 2005 No 2045, Reg 34*).

The applicant must have paid any national insurance contributions as they fell due. This is not subject to the 'reasonable excuse' defence.

Finally, there must be reason to expect that the applicant will continue to comply with compliance obligations and requests for documents etc., and continue to pay his National Insurance contributions, after the qualifying period.

[*FA 2004, s 64(2), Sch 11 paras 1–4, 13–16; CTA 2010, Sch 1 para 430; SI 2005 No 2045, Regs 27–29, 31–37*].

Unusually, in *Mutch v HMRC*, FTT (TC 232), 2010 STI 233 the Tribunal accepted insufficiency of funds as a reasonable excuse for compliance failures. Difficulty balancing childcare with full-time work during school holidays was accepted as a reasonable excuse in *Cormac Construction Ltd v HMRC* FTT (TC 315), 2010 STI 1296. A tribunal has no discretion to take the impact of a loss of gross payment status into account as it cannot consider proportionality, having regard to the decision in *Barnes v Hilton Main Construction* Ch D, [2005] STC 1532. The 'exceptional and extraordinary trading conditions' a company faced in a recession, coupled with the 'unhelpful banking environment' which prevailed during the period under review, were together accepted as a reasonable excuse for compliance failures, though the Tribunal emphasised that the decision should not be seen as providing a 'blanket excuse' for sub-contractors generally (*Prior Roofing Ltd v HMRC*, FTT (TC 246), 2010 STI 237.

Simon's Taxes. See E5.551.

Registration for gross payment — partners

[22.9] An individual applying for gross payment as a partner in a firm must first meet the compliance test for individuals (see **22.8** above). A company applying for gross payment as a partner in a firm must first meet all the tests applicable to companies (see **22.10** below). In addition, the firm itself must meet the following business, turnover and compliance tests.

The business test

The test for a firm's business is the same as that for a business carried on by an individual (see **22.8** above).

The turnover test

The partners must satisfy HMRC that the likely receipt of 'relevant payments' (see **22.8** above) in the year following the application is not less than a threshold figure. The threshold is the smaller of:

- £200,000; and
- the 'multiple turnover threshold'.

The '*multiple turnover threshold*' is obtained by adding together:

(i)   an amount found by multiplying the number of individuals in the partnership by the £30,000 turnover threshold for individuals (see **22.8** above); and

(ii)   in respect of each company (if any) in the partnership, the threshold that would obtain were the company to be applying in its own behalf (see **22.10** below).

In calculating the figure in (ii) above, there is disregarded any company whose only shareholders are other companies that are limited by shares and registered for gross payment.

The evidence required to satisfy the turnover test (prescribed by *SI 2005 No 2045, Reg 29*) is similar to the evidence prescribed for individuals as in **22.8** above but by reference to the above turnover threshold. Where the number of partners has fluctuated over the course of the qualifying period, the threshold is computed by reference to the greatest number of partners at any one time during that period. In a case where this evidence cannot be supplied because the business is new, the following evidence may be given instead, but only in relation to one application for registration for gross payment:

- evidence of relevant payments, which may include bank statements and paid cheques;
- evidence of turnover of partners during the qualifying period; and
- evidence of construction contracts entered into by the firm including payment schedules where the aggregate value of these contracts exceeds £200,000 and payments have been made of at least £30,000.

In similar circumstances as for individuals (see **22.8** above), a firm that does not meet the turnover test may be treated as if it did.

The compliance test

Each of the partners at the time of the application must, during the qualifying period (i.e. the twelve months prior to the application), have complied with all tax compliance obligations in relation to any income tax or corporation tax charge which was computed by reference to the firm's business. Over the same period, each partner must have supplied all requested information and accounts concerning the firm's business or his share of the profits of that business. Compliance must be within any required time limits or at the required time.

There are similar 'reasonable excuse' and regulatory relaxations as for individuals (see **22.8** above).

There must be reason to expect that, following the qualifying period, each of the persons who are from time to time partners in the firm will continue the record of compliance.

[*FA 2004, s 64(3), Sch 11 paras 5–8, 13–16; SI 2005 No 2045, Regs 27–37; SI 2009 No 1890, Regs 1, 6*].

Simon's Taxes. See E5.551.

Registration for gross payment — companies

[22.10] In order to register for gross payment, a company must pass the business, turnover and compliance tests described below.

In addition to those tests, HMRC may make a direction applying the conditions relating to individuals (see **22.8** above) to the directors of the company. If the company is a close company, this is extended to include the beneficial owners of shares. Rather than apply all the conditions to all of the directors or shareholders, the direction may specify which conditions are to apply, and to which directors or shareholders. In particular, HMRC may make such a direction where there has been a change in control of a company that either is, or is applying to be, registered for gross payment. HMRC are empowered to make regulations requiring the submission of information concerning changes in control of such companies. [*FA 2004, ss 64(5), 65; ITA 2007, Sch 1 para 460*].

The business test

The test for a company's business is the same as that for a business carried on by an individual (see **22.8** above).

The turnover test

A company may pass this test in either of two ways:

- satisfying HMRC that its only shareholders are companies limited by shares and registered for gross payment; or
- providing HMRC with evidence that 'relevant payments' (see **22.8** above) received in the year following the application are likely to equal or exceed a set threshold.

The set threshold is the smaller of:

(i) an amount found by multiplying the number of 'relevant persons' in relation to the company by the £30,000 turnover threshold for individuals (see **22.8** above); and

(ii) £200,000.

For a close company, a '*relevant person*' for the purposes of (i) above is a director or a beneficial owner of shares; for other companies, the definition is limited to a director. 'Director' is defined by reference to *ITEPA 2003, s 67*.

The evidence required to satisfy the turnover test (prescribed by *SI 2005 No 2045, Reg 29*) is similar to the evidence prescribed for individuals as in **22.8** above but by reference to the above set threshold. Where the number of relevant persons has fluctuated over the course of the qualifying period, the threshold is computed by reference to the greatest number of relevant persons at any one time during that period. In a case where this evidence cannot be supplied because the business is new, the following evidence may be given instead, but only in relation to one application for registration for gross payment:

- evidence of relevant payments, which may include bank statements and paid cheques;
- evidence of turnover of relevant persons during the qualifying period;
- evidence of construction contracts entered into by the company including payment schedules where the aggregate value of these contracts exceeds £200,000 and payments have been made of at least £30,000; and
- where the business was transferred from another person, firm or company, similar evidence in relation to the transferor as would otherwise be required from the applicant in relation to the business, together with evidence that the transferor would have passed the compliance test at the date of transfer.

In similar circumstances as for individuals (see **22.8** above), a company that does not meet the turnover test may be treated as if it did.

The compliance test

The provisions relating to companies mirror those relating to individuals (see **22.8** above). However, in addition to this a company must have complied with specified *Companies Acts* obligations during the qualifying period.

[FA 2004, s 64(4), Sch 11 paras 9–16; SI 2005 No 2045, Regs 27–37; SI 2009 No 1890, Regs 1, 6].

Simon's Taxes. See E5.551.

CIS procedures and administration

[22.11] Detailed procedures and administrative arrangements for the operation of the scheme are contained in *SI 2005 No 2045*. There are detailed provisions governing verification by contractors of sub-contractors' registration status, monthly returns by contractors, payments and recovery of tax deducted, electronic communications and methods of payment, and HMRC powers to inspect records.

Multiple contractors

A contractor may elect to be treated as different contractors in relation to different groups of sub-contractors. The election must be made (or revoked) by notice to an officer of HMRC before the beginning of the tax year for which it is to have effect. There are special provisions which apply where a contractor acquires the business of another contractor. [SI 2005 No 2045, Reg 3].

Verification of status of sub-contractors

Anyone making contract payments must verify with HMRC the registration status of the recipient, which can be done by telephone or online. HMRC will confirm whether the payment should be made gross or under deduction. Verification is not necessary if the recipient has been included in the contractor's returns (see below) in the current or previous two tax years. Where the contractor is a company, the return could be one made by another company in the same group and, where a multiple contractors election has been made (see above), the return could be one made in relation to a different group of sub-contractors. If the contractor acquired the contract under which the payment is to be made in a transfer of a business as a going concern and the transferor satisfied these conditions, the contractor does not need to verify if he has notified HMRC of the transfer. HMRC must notify a contractor if a person registered for gross payment becomes registered for payment under deduction, or vice versa, or if a registered person has ceased to be registered. Once a person has been verified or notified as being registered (whether for gross payment or payment under deduction) the contractor is entitled to assume that the person has not subsequently ceased to be so registered. [FA 2004, s 69; SI 2005 No 2045, Reg 6].

HMRC automatically notify affected contractors when a sub-contractor changes status.

Monthly returns by contractors

There are detailed provisions for monthly returns by contractors of payments made to sub-contractors. A contractor must make monthly returns to HMRC within 14 days after the end of every tax month and written information must also be provided to sub-contractors who are registered for payment under deduction or who are not registered. Where a return has been made, or should have been made, and no contract payments are made in the tax month following that return, the contractor must make a nil return for that month unless the contractor has notified HMRC that no further payments are to be made under construction contracts within the following six months. The returns are subject to the penalty provisions of *TMA 1970, s 98A* (see **55.21** **PENALTIES**). [*FA 2004, ss 70, 76, Sch 12 paras 7, 8; SI 2005 No 2045, Reg 4*]. This system of monthly returns replaces the pre-2007 requirement for end of year returns and also provides for the option of electronic submission to reduce the administrative burden of reporting.

Scheme representative

A contractor company may appoint another company in the same group ('a scheme representative') to act on its behalf in relation to the requirement to make a return or other such requirements under the regulations. [*SI 2005 No 2045, Reg 5*].

Collection and recovery of sums deducted

The arrangements for accounting for tax deductions, interest on unpaid and overpaid tax and (for 2010/11 onwards) penalties for late in-year payments broadly follow those for PAYE (see **53.11, 53.14 PAY AS YOU EARN** and HMRC Explanatory Booklet CIS340 referred to at **22.1** above). There are detailed provisions governing methods of payment, including electronic payment. [*FA 2004, s 71; CTA 2009, Sch 1 para 570; FA 2009, Sch 56; SI 2005 No 2045, Regs 7–17, 44–49, 58, 59; SI 2007 No 672, Reg 3; SI 2008 No 740, Regs 4–7; SI 2009 No 56, Sch 1 paras 139, 140, 142; SI 2010 No 466; SI 2010 No 717, Regs 1–3, 5*].

Simon's Taxes. See E5.542A–E5.542D, E5.546A–E5.547K, E5.555–E5.565.

Key points

[22.12] Points to consider are as follows.

- Businesses in the construction sector need to focus on effective engagement procedures so that the indicators of employment are adequately considered whenever labour is engaged, and that employees are identified and appropriately dealt with for tax purposes.

- HMRC's employment status indicator (ESI) tool provides an effective method by which the terms of any engagement can be tested, and evidence of the consideration printed and retained as evidence of the process. Use of the ESI tool is likely to satisfy any requirement for reasonable care under penalty legislation.

- It is essential that smaller contractors appreciate the need to make a return every month, even when no contract payments have been made. Each late return accrues a penalty which increases over time, and there is no cap which would limit penalties when nil returns have been overlooked. It is possible to make a an inactivity statement covering a period of six months, during which time no returns will be required, but contractors should be aware that should they make a payment under the scheme before the six months expires, the requirement to make returns recommences at that point.

- The adviser cannot over-emphasise the importance of adequate internal procedures to ensure that the compliance tests are met at all times by sub-contractors registered for gross payment. Loss of gross payment status can be catastrophic to some businesses, and the outcome of an appeal on grounds of reasonable excuse is far from guaranteed. Businesses will need adequate holiday and sickness arrangements to ensure that obligations remain covered in staff absence.

- The HMRC guide CIS340 provides excellent practical guidance on the scope of construction operations. Those unsure about the treatment of activities on the periphery of the sector, such as landscaping, should refer to this guide or seek help from the specialist HMRC helpline on 0845 366 7899.

23

Deceased Estates

Cross-references. See **42.7 INTEREST AND SURCHARGES ON OVERDUE TAX** and **43.11 INTEREST PAYABLE.**

Simon's Taxes. See A1.431–A1.436, C4.1.

Introduction

[23.1] The first part of this chapter (**23.2** and **23.3**) considers the liability to tax of the personal representatives of a deceased person (being either executors appointed under the will or administrators if there was no will). The next part of the chapter (**23.4–23.14**) examines entitlement of beneficiaries to income from deceased estates during administration: how it is computed (by reference to tax years) and how it is taxed in a beneficiary's hands. This will depend upon the type of interest a beneficiary has (an absolute interest, a limited interest or a discretionary interest) and whether the estate is a UK or foreign estate. See also the full contents list above.

Liability of personal representatives

[23.2] Personal representatives of a deceased person are liable for all tax due from the deceased to the date of his death. [*ICTA 1988, s 60(1); TMA 1970, s 74*]. Personal allowances may be claimed in full for the year of death.

Income may be assessed and charged on (and in the name of) any one or more of the persons who, in the tax year in which the income arises, are personal representatives of the deceased person or on any subsequent personal representatives. [*TMA 1970, s 30AA; FA 1989, s 151; ITA 2007, Sch 1 para 281; TIOPA 2010, Sch 7 para 58*].

See **73.9, 73.14** TRADING INCOME for cessation of a business on death and **73.29** TRADING INCOME for trading (or not) by the executors. See **6.2, 6.5** ASSESSMENTS for time limits for assessments. See Tolley's Capital Gains Tax for capital gains tax position on death.

Liability on estate income

[23.3] Personal representatives are also liable to income tax at the basic rate or (before 2008/09) the savings rate (as appropriate) on estate income which they receive subsequent to the death. Dividends falling due after death are treated as the income of the estate, and not of the deceased, for all tax purposes, including exemption claims, although they accrued before the death (*Reid's Trustees v CIR* CS 1929, 14 TC 512; *CIR v Henderson's Exors* CS 1931, 16 TC 282), and the same principle applies in respect of interest payments, including bank and building society interest, falling due after the date of death. The accrued annuity to the date of death of an annuitant is income of his estate and not his income (*Bryan v Cassin* KB 1942, 24 TC 468) and similarly as to the accrued income of which he was life-tenant (*Wood v Owen* KB 1940, 23 TC 541; *Stewart's Exors v CIR* Ch D 1952, 33 TC 184).

Strictly, the personal representatives should notify HMRC that they are liable to tax on estate income no later than six months after the tax year in which they become liable (in accordance with **55.2** PENALTIES) and should file self-assessment tax returns and pay any tax due on normal self-assessment payment dates (see **65.5–65.8** SELF-ASSESSMENT). However, HMRC operate informal procedures. They will accept a single computation and one-off payment of an estate's self-assessment liability (presumably including capital gains tax where relevant) if the estate is not 'complex' and the liability (over the whole of the administration period) is less than £10,000. For these purposes, an estate is '*complex*' if probate value exceeds £2.5 million *or* if administration continues into the third tax year from date of death *or* the personal representatives have disposed of a chargeable asset of the estate for more than £250,000. (Revenue Tax Bulletin August 2003 pp 1043, 1044). The Tax Bulletin article also provides information as to which tax office is likely to deal with an estate.

An annual payment made by personal representatives in satisfaction of a liability of the deceased was treated as if made by an individual for the purpose of applying provisions excluding such payments from being a charge on income (see **1.10** ALLOWANCES AND TAX RATES). The concept of 'charges on income' is abolished for 2007/08 onwards.

Income from deceased estates during administration (estate income)

[23.4] Beneficiaries of deceased estates in administration are chargeable to tax in respect of income treated as arising from their interest in the residue of the estate (referred to in *ITTOIA 2005* as *'estate income'*). For this purpose, where different parts of an estate are subject to different residuary dispositions, those parts are treated as if they were separate estates. [*ITTOIA 2005, s 649*]. Liability under these provisions depends on the type of interest that the beneficiary has (an 'absolute interest', a 'limited interest' or a 'discretionary interest') and whether the estate is a 'UK estate' or a 'foreign estate'. See **23.5** below for definitions.

Examples involving an absolute interest and a limited interest are given at **23.14** below.

Tax certificates

A personal representative has a duty to supply a beneficiary on request with a statement of income and tax borne for a tax year. [*ITTOIA 2005, s 682A; ICTA 1988, s 700(5)–(7); TIOPA 2010, Sch 7 para 47*].

Definitions

[23.5] The following definitions apply for the purposes of the provisions.

A person has an *'absolute interest'* in the whole or part of the residue of an estate if the capital of the residue (or part) is properly payable to him or would be so payable if the residue had been ascertained. A person has a *'limited interest'* in the whole or part of the residue of an estate during any period if he does not have an absolute interest and the income from the residue (or part) would be properly payable to him if it had been ascertained at the beginning of the period. A person has a *'discretionary interest'* in the whole or part of an estate if a discretion may be exercised in his favour so that any income of the residue during the whole or part of the administration period would be properly payable to him if the residue had been ascertained at the beginning of that period. For this purpose, an amount is only treated as properly payable to a person if it is properly payable to that person, or to another in his right, for his benefit (whether directly or through a trustee or other person). The personal representatives of a deceased person are treated as having an absolute or limited interest in the whole or part of the estate of another deceased person (A) if they have a right in their capacity as personal representatives and, were the right vested in them for their own benefit, they would have that interest in A's estate. [*ITTOIA 2005, s 650*].

An estate is a *'UK estate'* for a tax year if:

(i)   either of the following apply:
- all of the income of the estate (disregarding any life assurance gains and any sums treated as bearing income tax at the dividend ordinary rate) has either borne UK income tax by deduction or is income in respect of which the personal representatives are directly assessable to income tax for the year; and

- none of the income of the estate (disregarding any life assurance gains and any sums treated as bearing income tax at the dividend ordinary rate) is income for which the personal representatives are not liable to income tax for the year by virtue of being not resident or not ordinarily resident in the UK; or

(ii) the income of the estate for the year consists only of life assurance gains and/or sums treated as bearing income tax at the dividend ordinary rate.

If an estate is not a UK estate for a tax year it is a *'foreign estate'* for that year. [*ITTOIA 2005, s 651*].

The *'aggregate income'* of an estate for a tax year is the total of:

(a) income of the personal representatives in that capacity which is charged to income tax for the year, less any allowable deductions;

(b) income of the personal representatives in that capacity which would have been chargeable to income tax if it were income from a UK source of a person resident and ordinarily resident in the UK, less any deduction which would have been allowable;

(c) any stock dividends that would be chargeable on the personal representatives if such income were so chargeable (see **64.14** SAVINGS AND INVESTMENT INCOME);

(d) any amount that would be chargeable on the personal representatives on release of a loan to a participator in a close company if such amounts were so chargeable (see **64.16** SAVINGS AND INVESTMENT INCOME); and

(e) any gain from a life insurance contract that would have been treated as income of the personal representatives in that capacity if the condition for such gains to be so treated were met (see **44.3** LIFE ASSURANCE POLICIES).

Income from property devolving on the personal representatives otherwise than as assets for payment of the deceased's debts and income to which any person is or may become entitled under a specific disposition (as defined) is, however, excluded.

[*ITTOIA 2005, s 664*].

The *'residuary income'* of an estate for a tax year is the aggregate income of the estate for the year less deductions for:

- all interest paid in the year by the personal representatives in that capacity (other than interest on unpaid inheritance tax under *IHTA 1984, s 233*);

- all annual payments for the year which are properly payable out of residue;

- all expenses of management of the estate paid in the year (but only where, ignoring any specific direction in a will, properly chargeable to income); and

- any excess of allowable deductions for the previous year over the aggregate income of the estate for that year.

No deduction is allowed for any amount allowable in calculating the aggregate income of the estate.

[*ITTOIA 2005, s 666*].

For the reduction of residuary income of an estate in respect of income which accrued before the death of the deceased and which is taken into account in calculating for inheritance tax purposes the value of the estate on death, see **23.16** below.

A transfer of assets or the appropriation of assets by personal representatives to themselves is treated for the purposes of these provisions as the payment of an amount equal to the assets' value at the date of the transfer or appropriation. The set off or release of a debt is treated as the payment of amount equal to it. If at the end of the administration period there is an obligation to transfer assets to any person or the personal representatives are entitled to appropriate assets to themselves, an amount equal to the assets' value at that time is treated as payable then. If at that time there is an obligation to release or set off a debt owed by any person or the personal representatives are entitled to release or set off a debt in their own favour, a sum equal to the debt is treated as payable then. [*ITTOIA 2005, s 681*].

Grossing-up of estate income

[23.6] In the case of a UK estate, in arriving at the amount of estate income, the basic amounts treated as income of the beneficiary are 'grossed up' by the basic rate of tax or the dividend ordinary rate, depending on the type of income and the tax year in which it arose. (Certain income arising before 2008/09 fell to be grossed up at the 20% savings rate of tax.) The estate income is then treated as having borne income tax at that rate or rates. In determining the rate applicable it is assumed first that amounts are paid to beneficiaries out of the different parts of the aggregate income of the estate in such proportions as are just and reasonable for their different interests, and then that payments are made from those parts bearing tax at the basic rate before they are made from those parts bearing tax at the dividend ordinary rate. (Before 2008/09, payments were assumed to be made firstly from income bearing tax at the basic rate, then from income bearing tax at the savings rate and lastly from income bearing tax at the dividend ordinary rate.)

If some of the aggregate income of the estate is income treated as having suffered tax at source, e.g. life assurance gains and UK stock dividends, it is assumed that an amount is paid from other income in priority to that income. The above assumptions are then made in relation to each part of the payment.

Grossing up is applicable to payments out of a foreign estate only in respect of certain sums treated as having suffered tax at source, so that, for example, life insurance gains are grossed up at the basic rate (for 2008/09 onwards, previously at the savings rate) and UK stock dividends are grossed up at the dividend ordinary rate. No repayment of such notional tax can be made.

[*ITTOIA 2005, ss 656, 657, 663, 679, 680, Sch 2 para 137; ITA 2007, Sch 1 paras 564, 565; FA 2008, Sch 1 paras 35, 60, 61, 65*].

Income bearing tax at the dividend ordinary rate or, before 2008/09, the savings rate (see **1.5, 1.6 ALLOWANCES AND RATES**) is treated in the hands of the recipient as dividend income or savings income respectively; income in respect of a discretionary interest paid indirectly through a trustee and taxable under *ITTOIA 2005, s 662* on the ultimate recipient is treated as dividend income or, before 2008/09, savings income of the trustee. [*ITTOIA 2005, s 680A, Sch 1 para 288; ITA 2007, Sch 1 para 566; FA 2008, Sch 1 paras 62, 65*].

Absolute interests

[23.7] A beneficiary with an absolute interest is chargeable to income tax on income treated as arising in a tax year from the interest if he has an 'assumed income entitlement' for the year and a payment is made in respect of the interest in the year and before the end of the administration period. For the year in which the administration period ends (the *'final tax year'*), income is treated as arising if the beneficiary has an assumed income entitlement for the year (whether or not any payments are made).

Subject to the grossing-up provisions at **23.6** above, the amount so treated as income for a tax year is the lower of the total amount of all sums paid in the year in respect of the interest and the person's assumed income entitlement for the year. For the final tax year, the amount is the person's assumed income entitlement for the year. Where, however, the residuary income of the estate for the final tax year is nil as a result of the allowable deductions exceeding the aggregate income of the estate, the amount for the year is reduced by the excess (or, where the interest is in part of the residue only, a just and reasonable part of that excess).

A person's *'assumed income entitlement'* for a tax year is the excess of the total of the person's share of the residuary income of the estate (less, in the case of a UK estate, income tax on that amount at the appropriate rate) for the year and for each previous tax year for which he held the interest over the total of the amounts (before grossing-up) relating to the interest in respect of which he was liable to tax for all previous years (or would have been liable had he been within the charge to income tax).

If the total of all sums paid during or payable at the end of the administration period in respect of the interest (grossed-up, in the case of a UK estate, at the basic rate for the tax year of payment or the final tax year) are less than the total of the beneficiary's shares of the residuary income for all years, the deficiency is applied to reduce his share of the residuary income, firstly for the final tax year, then for the previous year and so on.

[*ITTOIA 2005, ss 652, 653, 659(1), 660, 665, 667, 668, 670, Sch 2 para 136(1)(2)*].

Limited interests

[23.8] Subject to the grossing up provisions at **23.6** above, sums paid (including assets transferred, debts released etc.) to a beneficiary with a limited interest *during administration* are treated as his income for the tax year of payment and are chargeable to tax accordingly. Any amount which remains payable in respect of the limited interest *on completion of administration* is treated as income of the beneficiary for the tax year in which the administration period ends. If the interest ceases earlier, any amount then remaining payable is treated as income for the tax year in which the interest ceased. [*ITTOIA 2005, ss 654, 659(1), 661*].

Discretionary interests

[23.9] The person in whose favour the discretion is exercised is charged to income tax on the total payments made in a tax year in exercise of the discretion, grossed up, where appropriate, as indicated at **23.6** above. [*ITTOIA 2005, ss 655, 659(2), 662*].

This applies whether the payments are out of income as it arises, or out of income arising to the personal representatives in earlier years and retained pending exercise of the discretion. See HMRC SP 4/93.

Foreign estates

[23.10] Where estate income arises from a foreign estate it is deemed to arise from a source outside the UK and is 'relevant foreign income' (see **32.2** FOREIGN INCOME). [*ITTOIA 2005, s 658*]. See **61** for the REMITTANCE BASIS, **32.4** FOREIGN INCOME for amounts deductible from income and **32.5** FOREIGN INCOME for relief for unremittable income.

Where income tax is charged for a tax year on estate income from a foreign estate and income tax has already been borne by part of the aggregate income of the estate for the year, the taxpayer may make a claim for the income tax charged to be reduced in accordance with the formulae in *ITTOIA 2005, ss 677, 678 as amended*. The relief is given by way of a tax reduction at Step 6 of the calculation of income tax liability at **1.7** ALLOWANCES AND RATES.

Successive interests

[23.11] Special rules apply to the calculation of estate income where there are two or more successive absolute or limited interests during the period of administration. [*ITTOIA 2005, ss 671–676, Sch 2 para 136(3)–(7); CTA 2009, Sch 1 para 634*].

Adjustments, assessments etc. after the administration period

[23.12] If, after the administration period ends, it is clear that a person's liability under **23.7–23.11** above for a tax year is greater or less than previously appeared, all necessary assessments, adjustments etc. can be made. Assessments may be made or adjusted and relief may be claimed within three years after 31 January following the tax year in which administration was completed. [*ITTOIA 2005, s 682; ITA 2007, Sch 1 para 567*].

Non-UK resident beneficiaries

[23.13] By concession, a beneficiary, who is not resident or not ordinarily resident in the UK, may claim to have his tax liability on income from an absolute or limited interest in a UK estate adjusted to what it would be if such income had arisen to him directly from the respective sources of residuary income. The relief or exemption must be claimed within five years and ten months of the end of the tax year in which the beneficiary is deemed to have received the income. It is dependent upon the personal representatives having made all required estate returns, paid all tax and any interest, surcharge and penalties, and keeping available for inspection any relevant tax certificates and copies of the estate accounts for all years of the administration period showing details of all sources of estate income and payments to beneficiaries. No tax will be repayable in respect of income treated as bearing income tax within *ITTOIA 2005, s 680.* (HMRC ESC A14; Revenue Press Release 1 April 1999).

However, where the beneficiary is resident in a country with which the UK has a double taxation agreement, and the 'Other Income' Article in that agreement gives sole taxing rights in respect of such income to that country, the above concession does not apply. The tax paid by the personal representatives will be repaid to the beneficiary, subject to the conditions in the Article being met. (HMRC SP 3/86).

Examples

Absolute interest

[23.14]

C died on 5 July 2008 leaving his estate of £400,000 divisible equally between his three children. The income arising and administration expenses paid in the administration period which ends on 25 January 2011 are as follows.

	Period to 5.4.09		Year to 5.4.10		Period to 25.1.11	
	£	£	£	£	£	£
UK dividends (net)		16,875		9,900		3,375
Administration expenses chargeable to income		(1,500)		(750)		(300)
		15,375		9,150		3,075
Other income (gross)	10,000		3,200		975	
Basic rate tax thereon payable by personal representatives	(2,000)		(640)		(195)	
		8,000		2,560		780
Net income distributed		£23,375		£11,710		£3,855
Each child's share		£7,792		£3,903		£1,285

Dates and amounts of payments to *each* child are as follows.

	Payment
	£
30.4.09	5,000
16.10.09	3,500
21.6.10	2,500
22.1.11	1,000
30.7.11	980

Each child's assumed income entitlement is as follows.

	2008/09	2009/10	2010/11
	£	£	£
Cumulative income entitlement (net)	7,792	11,695	12,980
Deduct net equivalents of amounts taxed in previous years	Nil	Nil	8,500
Assumed income entitlement	£7,725	£11,695	£4,480

For all years other than the final tax year (i.e. the year in which the administration period ends), compare the assumed income entitlement with the payments made.

	2008/09	2009/10
Assumed income entitlement	£7,725	£11,695
Payments made	Nil	£8,500
Lower amount is the taxable amount (subject to grossing up)	Nil	£8,500

For the final tax year (2010/11), the taxable amount (subject to grossing up) is the amount of the assumed income entitlement (£4,480).

The children's income from the estate for tax purposes is as follows.

	2008/08	2009/10	2010/11
Each child's share of income (net)	Nil	£8,500	£4,480
		£	£
Each child's share of basic rate income	Nil	3,520*	260
Basic rate tax	Nil	880	65
Gross basic rate income	Nil	£4,400	£325

* £(8,000 + 2,560) × ¹/₃ = £3,520

	2008/08	2009/10	2010/11
Each child's share of dividend income	Nil	4,980	4,220
Tax credit	Nil	553	469
Gross dividend income	Nil	£5,533	£4,689

Notes

(a)   Each beneficiary would receive tax certificates (Forms R185 (Estate Income)) showing the gross amount of his entitlement and the tax paid by the personal representatives. Where the estate has dividend income bearing tax at the dividend ordinary rate, the tax certificate shows such income separately from income which has borne tax at the basic rate.

(b)   In the hands of a beneficiary, estate income which has borne tax at the dividend ordinary rate is treated as dividend income. The beneficiary will have a further liability only to the extent that such income exceeds the basic rate limit. Dividend tax credits are not, however, repayable.

(c)   Payments to a beneficiary of an estate are deemed to be made out of his share of income bearing tax at the basic rate in priority to his share of income bearing tax at the dividend ordinary rate. This means that administration expenses chargeable to income are effectively relieved primarily against dividend income.

Limited interest

Mrs D died on 5 January 2007 leaving her whole estate with a life interest to her husband and then the capital to her children on his death. The administration of the estate is completed on 7 February 2009. Mr D receives payments on account of income of £1,200 on 30 September 2007, £2,500 on 31 December 2008, £1,050 on 7 February 2009 and £340 on 31 May 2009.

The actual income and deductible expenses of the estate were as follows.

	2006/07 (from 6.1.07)	2007/08	2008/09 (to 7.2.09)
	£	£	£
Interest received (net)	750	2,400	2,000
Other income (gross)	400	600	200
Basic rate tax thereon	(88)	(132)	(40)
Expenses	(150)	(450)	(400)
Net income available for distribution	£912	£2,418	£1,760

Mr D's income from the estate for tax purposes is calculated as follows.

	2006/07	2007/08 Basic rate income	Savings rate income	2008/09 Basic rate income
	£	£	£	£
Net income	Nil	780*	420*	3,890
Basic rate tax		220		972
Savings rate tax	—		105	
Gross income	Nil	£1,000	£525	£4,862

* The payments to the beneficiary in each year prior to 2008/09 must be allocated between (i) income bearing tax at the basic rate and (ii) income bearing tax at the savings rate, (i) taking priority over (ii). Total basic rate income for 2006/07 and 2007/08 is £780 (£400 + £600 − £88 − £132), so £780 of the £1,200 payment in 2007/08 is deemed to have been made out of basic rate income.

Note

(a)   The £340 paid in May 2009 remains payable on completion of administration and is thus treated as income of the beneficiary for the tax year in which the administration period ends, i.e. 2008/09.

Residence of personal representatives

[23.15] See **62.5 RESIDENCE, ORDINARY RESIDENCE AND DOMICILE** for special provisions where personal representatives are partly UK resident and partly non-UK resident.

Relief for inheritance tax attributable to income accrued at death

[23.16] Where, on a death, income accrued at the death is treated both as capital of the estate for inheritance tax purposes and as residuary income of the estate in the hands of a beneficiary having an absolute interest in the residue, in arriving at the 'excess liability' of the beneficiary the residuary income is reduced by the grossed-up amount of the inheritance tax attributable to the excess of the accrued income over any liabilities taken into account in both valuing the estate and arriving at the residuary income. '*Excess liability*' means the excess of income tax at the higher rate or dividend upper rate over income tax at the basic rate, savings rate (before 2008/09), starting rate for savings (for 2008/09 onwards) or dividend ordinary rate. For 2010/11 onwards, the definition is duly amended to take account of the introduction of the additional rate and the dividend additional rate (see **1.3 ALLOWANCES AND RATES**). [*ITTOIA 2005, s 669; ITA 2007, Sch 1 para 561; FA 2008, Sch 1 paras 59, 65; FA 2009, Sch 2 paras 22, 25*].

Miscellaneous

[23.17] Otherwise the tax position in respect of deceased estates is similar to that of settlements (or trusts as they are often called) and reference should be made to the following items under **68 SETTLEMENTS** which contain details of tax cases relating to both deceased estates and settlements.

68.8	Assessments on trust income
68.17	Personal position of trustee
68.18	Income of beneficiaries
68.22	Annuities etc. out of capital
68.23	Foreign trust income
68.24	Claims by trustees and beneficiaries

24

Deduction of Tax at Source

Cross-references. See **4.39** ANTI-AVOIDANCE re annual payments for non-taxable consideration; **8** BANKS and **9** BUILDING SOCIETIES for interest; **22** CONSTRUCTION INDUSTRY SCHEME; **26.10** DOUBLE TAX RELIEF for reduced rate of deduction on payments abroad; **26.9**(h) DOUBLE TAX RELIEF for alimony payable by non-resident; **27.72** EMPLOYMENT INCOME for payments for restrictive covenants; **43** INTEREST PAYABLE; **48** MINERAL ROYALTIES; **50.10** NON-RESIDENTS for non-resident entertainers and sportsmen; **53** PAY AS YOU EARN; **57.7** PENSION PROVISION for contributions to a registered pension scheme; **60.21** PROPERTY INCOME for non-resident landlords; **64.17** SAVINGS AND INVESTMENT INCOME as regards the income element of purchased life annuities; **68.11** SETTLEMENTS for distributions from discretionary and accumulation trusts.

Simon's Taxes. See A4.4.

Introduction

[24.1] In the process of rewriting income tax legislation into *ITA 2007*, the opportunity was taken to simplify the approach to 'charges on income' by moving away from the concept of alienation of income to a much more straightforward deduction in calculating net income coupled with deduction of tax at source from the payments involved (see **1.10 ALLOWANCES AND TAX RATES** and also Change 81 listed in Annex 1 to the Explanatory Notes to *ITA 2007*). This had a fundamental effect on the way the 'machinery sections' providing for deduction of tax (*ICTA 1988, ss 348, 349*) were rewritten. There is no longer any need for payments to be 'covered' by the payer's taxable income and the pre-2007/08 distinction between situations where the payer *may* pay under deduction and where the payer *must* pay under deduction becomes unnecessary; (the distinction is described in **24.20, 24.21** below in relation to years prior to 2007/08).

For 2007/08 onwards, the approach of the legislation is to set out which payments must be made under deduction whilst providing for certain exceptions [*ITA 2007, Pt 15*]. Deduction may be at the savings rate (no longer applicable after 2007/08) or the basic rate, but in either case the rate in force for the year in which the payment is made is applied (see **1.3, 1.4 ALLOWANCES AND TAX RATES**; for over-deductions and under-deductions, see **24.4** below). Collection of the tax involved is via the payer's self-assessment return or by direct assessment [*ITA 2007, ss 963, 964*, as amended]: it is identified separately from the payer's own liability to tax (see **24.17** below).

The duty to deduct income tax from a payment may be disapplied by regulations relating to double tax relief (see **26 DOUBLE TAX RELIEF**) or to the London Olympic Games (see **30.32 EXEMPT INCOME**). Where income is exempt from income tax it is disregarded for the purposes of deduction of tax at source. [*ITA 2007, s 849(1)(3)(5); TIOPA 2010, Sch 8 para 84*].

Deduction of tax at source for 2007/08 onwards

[24.2] A duty to deduct a sum representing income tax is imposed in relation to the following types of payment.

(a)   Certain payments of yearly interest (see **24.12** below).

(b)   Certain payments of UK public revenue dividends (see **24.12** below and **64.3 SAVINGS AND INVESTMENT INCOME**).

(c)   Certain annual payments (see **24.7–24.10** below).

(d)   Certain royalty payments (see **24.13** below).

(e)   Certain manufactured payments (see **4.10 ANTI-AVOIDANCE**).

(f)   Certain issues of funding bonds (see **64.6 SAVINGS AND INVESTMENT INCOME**).

(g)   Payments treated as made to unit holders in an unauthorised unit trust (this is a notional deduction — see **75.9 UNIT TRUSTS ETC**).

(h)   Certain payments to non-residents taxable under anti-avoidance provisions relating to transactions in land and sales of occupation income where HMRC direct that a deduction should be made (see **24.9** below).

The amount deducted is treated as income tax paid by the recipient, and as such taken into account in determining the tax payable by, or repayable to, the recipient (although this rule does not apply to income tax deducted under the rules relating to visiting performers (see **50.10 NON-RESIDENTS**) or non-resident landlords (see **60.21 PROPERTY INCOME**)). [*ITA 2007, s 848, Sch 1 paras 548, 549, 570; ITTOIA 2005, ss 602, 618, 686; FA 2010, Sch 13 paras 2(2), 3*].

A payment made under deduction of tax is income (equal to the grossed-up equivalent) of the tax year by reference to which the rate of tax deducted from the payment was determined, without regard to the period over which the income accrued (and see *CIR v Crawley* Ch D 1986, 59 TC 728). [*ITA 2007, s 31(2)*].

There are other regimes that involve the deduction of tax at source: see especially:

(i)   PAYE (see **53 PAY AS YOU EARN**);
(ii)   CIS (see **22 CONSTRUCTION INDUSTRY SCHEME**);
(iii)   visiting performers (see **50.10 NON-RESIDENTS**);
(iv)   non-resident landlords (see **60.21 PROPERTY INCOME**);
(v)   Real Estate Investment Trusts (see **60.14 PROPERTY INCOME**).

Note that from 6 April 2007, annuities from former retirement annuity contracts are brought within PAYE, and other deduction of tax at source rules thus cease to apply — see **53.17 PAY AS YOU EARN**. The same applies to annuities within *ITEPA 2003, s 610* (annuities under an occupational pension scheme that is not a registered pension scheme) — see **56.2**(e) **PENSION INCOME**.

Rate of tax deductible

[24.3] The rate of tax deductible is the basic rate. It used to be either the basic rate or the savings rate (no longer applicable after 2007/08), depending on the type of payment. This is dealt with in commentary on the particular types of payment from which sums must be deducted (see **24.2** above). The basic rate (or savings rate) to apply is that for the year in which payment is made. This is a change from the situation prior to 2007/08, which is described below (see Change 138 listed in Annex 1 to the Explanatory Notes to *ITA 2007*). As a consequence of the reduction in the basic rate to 20%, the savings rate (which was also 20%) is abolished for 2008/09 onwards.

Situation prior to 2007/08

For *ICTA 1988, s 348* purposes, the basic rate (or savings rate) when payment becomes due applies, see **24.20** below.

For *ICTA 1988, s 349* purposes, the basic rate (or savings rate) when payment is **made** applies, see **24.21**(i) and (ii) below.

In other words, the tax deductible is at the basic rate (or savings rate) in force for the year in which the payment is due if paid out of taxed profits or gains or, in any other case, the rate for the year in which the payment is made.

For 1995/96 and earlier years, tax was deductible at the basic rate. This continued for 1996/97 to 2006/07 except where the payment would constitute 'savings income' (including interest) (see **1.6 ALLOWANCES AND TAX RATES**) of the recipient (whatever his status), in which case tax was deductible at the savings rate. [*ICTA 1988, s 4*].

Alterations in tax rate

[24.4] Where deductions are made by reference to a tax rate greater or less than the rate subsequently fixed for the tax year:

(a) **under-deductions** in respect of any half-yearly or quarterly payments of interest, dividends or other annual payments, other than company dividends and other distributions, are charged under *ITTOIA 2005, Pt 4 Ch 2. [ICTA 1988, s 821(1); ITA 2007, s 849(2)]*;

(b) **under-deductions** in respect of any rent, interest, annuity or other annual payment, any copyright royalties, public lending right payments or design royalties paid to non-residents and patent royalties (and, where previously applicable, mining rents etc. under *ICTA 1988, s 119* and *s 120*) may be deducted from future payments or, if none, recovered from the payee. [*ICTA 1988, s 821(2)(3); ITA 2007, s 849(2), Sch 1 para 205*]. See *Nesta v Wyatt* KB 1940, 19 ATC 541;

(c) **over-deductions** of tax under the deduction at source rules can generally be recovered from HMRC provided that the tax has been accounted for and no adjustment made between the parties. See *Provisional Collection of Taxes Act 1968, s 2*; and

(d) **over-deductions** of tax by a 'body corporate' on interest (not being a distribution) on its securities may be adjusted in the next payment but any repayments must be made no later than a year from the passing of the Act imposing the tax, and enure to the benefit of the person entitled at date of adjustment or repayment. [*ICTA 1988, s 822; ITA 2007, s 849(2)*].

Statement of tax deducted

[24.5] For 2007/08 onwards, where a person makes a payment from which a sum representing income tax must be deducted (see items (a)–(h) in **24.2** above) or under the rules relating to deposit-takers (see **8.2 BANKS**) and if the recipient so requests, that person must provide a statement showing the gross amount of the payment, the amount deducted and the actual amount paid. [*ITA 2007, s 975*].

A similar rule applies where a payment representing interest has been made by the Financial Services Compensation Scheme ('FSCS') on or after 6 October 2008 and is made net of an amount equivalent to income tax (see **64.2 SAVINGS AND INVESTMENT INCOME**). [*ITA 2007, s 979A(5)(6); FA 2009, s 33(4)(5)*].

Prior to 2007/08, a certificate of tax deducted under various provisions of *ICTA 1988*, or under *SI 1990 No 2231 (now revoked)* (see **9.1 BUILDING SOCIETIES**) had to be given by the payer upon written request by the recipient. [*ICTA 1988, s 352*].

Omission to deduct tax

[24.6] The following should be noted.

(a) The provisions for the deduction of tax do not preclude assessment of the recipient if tax is not deducted (*Glamorgan County Quarter Sessions v Wilson* KB 1910, 5 TC 537; *Renfrew Town Council v CIR* CS 1934, 19 TC 13; *Grosvenor Place Estates Ltd v Roberts* CA 1960,

39 TC 433). These cases were decided when the legislation precluded assessment on the recipient if the payment was out of taxed income. This provision was abolished for 1973/74 onwards. However where in a case within *ICTA 1988, s 348* (**24.20** below), for years up to and including 2006/07, tax is not deducted, the Crown nevertheless effectively collected from the payer the tax he failed to deduct [*ICTA 1988, s 3, s 256(3)(c)(ii), s 276(1)(1A)*] and did not need to have recourse to the recipient. The position is similar for 2007/08 onwards under the rewritten legislation in *ITA 2007*: the provisions governing the collection of tax (see **24.17** below) operate on payments where there is a requirement to deduct a sum representing income tax. That requirement is not removed simply because the sum has not in fact been deducted.

(b)   Tax not deducted at the time of payment cannot generally be recovered afterwards. For this see *Shrewsbury v Shrewsbury* CA 1907, 23 TLR 224; *Re Hatch* Ch D 1919, 1 Ch 351; *Ord v Ord* KB 1923, 39 TLR 437; *Taylor v Taylor* CA 1937, 16 ATC 218; *Brine v Brine* KB 1943, 22 ATC 177; *Hemsworth v Hemsworth* KB 1946, 25 ATC 466; *Tenbry Investments Ltd v Peugeot Talbot Motor Co Ltd* Ch D, [1992] STC 791. But where trustees omitted to deduct tax from annuities through an honest error of fact, not an error of law, they were authorised to recoup the tax from future payments (*Re Musgrave, Machell v Parry* Ch D, [1916] 2 Ch 417). See also *Turvey v Dentons* (1923) Ltd QB 1952, 31 ATC 470. Only net amount of alimony available to satisfy contra account (*Butler v Butler* CA 1961, 40 ATC 19). See also *Fletcher v Young* CS 1936, 15 ATC 531; *Hollis v Wingfield* CA 1940, 19 ATC 98.

(c)   The Courts may rectify documents shown not to embody the intentions of the parties. For cases where rectification sought in relation to deduction of tax see *Burroughes v Abbott* Ch D 1921, 38 TLR 167; *Jervis v Howle & Talke Colliery Co Ltd* Ch D 1936, 15 ATC 529; *Fredensen v Rothschild* Ch D 1941, 20 ATC 1; *Van der Linde v Van der Linde* Ch D 1947, 26 ATC 348; *Whiteside v Whiteside* CA 1949, 28 ATC 479.

(d)   A penalty of £50 is incurred by refusal to allow the deduction of tax, and any 'agreement' not to deduct is void to that extent. [*TMA 1970, s 106*]. See **24.15** below for 'free of tax' payments.

Annual payments

[24.7] There is a duty to deduct a sum representing income tax from certain 'qualifying annual payments'. [*ITA 2007, ss 900, 901*]. See **24.8** below for the meaning of 'qualifying annual payments', **24.9** below for the duty to deduct and **24.10** below for the meaning of 'annual payment'. For the position regarding annual payments prior to 2007/08, see **24.20, 24.21** below.

Simon's Taxes. See A4.432 A4.434, B8.421–B8.426, E1.512, E1.1206.

Qualifying annual payments

[24.8] A '*qualifying annual payment*' is an annual payment (see **24.10** below) arising in the UK that is charged to income tax under:

(a) *ITTOIA 2005, Pt 4 Ch 7* (purchased life annuity payments);
(b) *ITTOIA 2005, Pt 4 Ch 10* (distributions from unauthorised unit trusts);
(c) *ITTOIA 2005, s 579* (royalties etc. from intellectual property);
(d) *ITTOIA 2005, Pt 5 Ch 4* (certain telecommunication rights: non-trading income);
(e) *ITTOIA 2005, Pt 5 Ch 7* (annual payments not otherwise charged);
(f) *ITEPA 2003, s 609* (annuities for the benefit of dependants); or
(g) *ITEPA 2003, s 611* (annuities in recognition of another's services).

Where the recipient is a company, the annual payment must be charged to income tax as in (a)–(e) above or under specified provisions of *CTA 2009* (previously under *Schedule D, Case III*).

However, the annual payment must *not* be a payment of interest, a qualifying donation for gift aid purposes (see **16.17 CHARITIES**), a payment where income tax is treated as paid by a beneficiary or settlor in relation to a discretionary trust (or would do so but for the trustees being non-UK resident) (see **68.11 SETTLEMENTS**), or an annual payment for non-taxable consideration (see **4.39 ANTI-AVOIDANCE**).

[*ITA 2007, s 899; CTA 2009, Sch 1 para 707; CTA 2010, Sch 1 para 554*].

Duty to deduct

[24.9] Where the payer is an individual, a sum representing income tax must be deducted from qualifying annual payments (see **24.8** above) that are made for genuine commercial reasons in connection with that individual's trade, profession or vocation. [*ITA 2007, s 900*]. The amount of the deduction is the basic rate of tax in force for the year of payment (this is different from the situation prior to 2007/08 described in **24.3** above; see Change 138 listed in Annex 1 to the Explanatory Notes to *ITA 2007*). The tax is collected through the individual's self-assessment return (see **24.17 COLLECTION OF TAX**).

Personal representatives fulfilling a liability incurred by the deceased need not make a deduction from a qualifying annual payment unless the payment would have been made for genuine commercial reasons in connection with the deceased's trade, profession or vocation. [*ITA 2007, s 901(2)*].

Where the payer of a qualifying annual payment is not an individual, the rate at which the deduction must be made was dependent before 2008/09 on whether the payer had some 'modified net income' (see **1.9 ALLOWANCES AND TAX RATES**) for the year of payment. Where the payer has some modified net income, the deduction was at the basic rate in force for the tax year of payment. This is collected through the person's self-assessment return (see **24.17 COLLECTION OF TAX**). Where the payer has no modified net income, the deduction was at the 'applicable rate', to be collected by HMRC assessment (unless the payer was a company, where a separate collection machinery applied). The '*applicable rate*' is the basic rate in force for the year of payment, unless the payment is an annuity under a purchased life annuity (see **64.17** SAVINGS AND INVESTMENT INCOME) and the income is savings income, in which case the applicable rate is the savings rate for the year of payment. For 2008/09 onwards, in consequence of the abolition of the savings rate, the deduction is at the basic rate regardless of whether the payer has any modified net income. [*ITA 2007, ss 901, 902; FA 2008, Sch 1 paras 29, 30, 65*].

For amounts taxable under *ITA 2007, Pt 13 Ch 3*, (tax avoidance: transactions in land) and *Ch 4* (tax avoidance: sales of occupation income) (see **4.28, 4.29** ANTI-AVOIDANCE), if the person entitled is resident abroad HMRC may direct that they be subject to deduction of tax at the basic rate in force for the year in which the payment is made. [*ITA 2007, s 944; ICTA 1988, s 777(9)*]. Such a direction may, however, only be made once there is entitlement to the consideration, i.e. on execution of a contract (*Pardoe v Entergy Power Development Corp* Ch D 2000, 72 TC 617).

For annual payments under certain life assurance policies (i.e. guaranteed income bonds) not treated as such for tax purposes, see **44.15** LIFE ASSURANCE POLICIES.

For an exemption from the duty to deduct in relation to superannuation funds for overseas employees, see **57.32** PENSION PROVISION.

See also **4.39** ANTI-AVOIDANCE where certain annual payments are made for non-taxable consideration.

Definition of 'annual payment'

[24.10] The broad rule is that annual payments are recurrent payments which, in the hands of the recipient, are 'pure income profit' and not e.g. elements in the computation of the profits of the recipient. Leading cases are *Earl Howe v CIR* CA 1919, 7 TC 289 (insurance premiums under covenant not annual payments) and *CIR v Epping Forest Conservators* HL 1953, 34 TC 293 (yearly contributions to meet the deficiencies of a charity held to be annual payments). Payments for the use of chattels not annual payments (*In re Hanbury, decd* CA 1939, 38 TC 588). See also *CIR v Whitworth Park Coal Co Ltd* HL 1959, 38 TC 531. Payments to a County Council under deed of covenant in consideration of the Council's paying special school fees of the covenantor's handicapped child held not annual payments (*Essex County Council v Ellam* CA 1989, 61 TC 615). The profits of a business bequeathed to a charity were held to be annual payments (*R v Special Commrs (ex p Shaftesbury Homes)* CA 1922, 8 TC 367). For covenanted subscriptions see *CIR v National Book League* CA 1957, 37 TC 455 and *Taw & Torridge Festival Society Ltd v CIR* Ch D 1959, 38 TC 603. Covenanted payments to a charity as part of arrangements under which it acquired the business of the payer not annual payments (*Campbell v CIR* HL 1968, 45 TC 427). Payments by a film company of a share of certain receipts as part of arrangements for cancellation of a contract were annual payments (*Asher v London Film Productions Ltd* CA 1943, 22 ATC 432) as were payments under a guarantee of the dividends of a company (*Aeolian Co Ltd v CIR* KB 1936, 20 TC 547;

Moss Empires Ltd v CIR HL 1937, 21 TC 264). But not payments by the principal subscribers to a newsfilm service to make good its operating deficit (*British Commonwealth International Newsfilm Agency Ltd v Mahany* HL 1962, 40 TC 550).

Instalments of the purchase price of a mine held not annual payments (*Foley v Fletcher* 1858, 7 WR 141) nor instalment repayments of a debt (*Dott v Brown* CA 1936, 15 ATC 147). Where the Secretary of State for India acquired a railway in consideration of annuities for 48 years, tax held to be deductible only from the interest element actuarially ascertained (*Scoble v Secretary of State for India* HL 1903, 4 TC 478, 618 and cf. the two *East India Railway* cases at 21 TLR 606 and 40 TLR 241). Similarly where shares were sold for payments over 125 years, the actuarially ascertained interest element in the payments was held to be income in the hands of the recipient for surtax (*Vestey v CIR* Ch D 1961, 40 TC 112). See also *Goole Corporation v Aire etc. Trustees* KB 1942, 21 ATC 156 (tax held deductible from interest element in yearly payments to local authority to meet street repairs). In *CIR v Church Commissioners* HL 1976, 50 TC 516 rent charges paid as the consideration for property were held wholly income and not (as contended for Crown) partly income and partly capital. The HL judgments are an important review of the possibility of dissecting periodical payments in return for valuable consideration between income and capital and *Vestey v CIR* above, although not overruled, was called 'the high water of dissection cases' (Lord Wilberforce) and some of the reasoning in it was not approved. See also *Chadwick v Pearl Life Insce* KB 1905, 21 TLR 456. For reimbursement of expenditure calculated by reference to an interest factor, see *Re Euro Hotel (Belgravia) Ltd* Ch D 1975, 51 TC 293 and *Chevron Petroleum (UK) Ltd v BP Petroleum Development Ltd* Ch D 1981, 57 TC 137.

Payments in satisfaction of the transfer of a business etc., and based on profits held not to be annual payments in *CIR v Ramsay* CA 1935, 20 TC 79 and *CIR v Ledgard* KB 1937, 21 TC 129 but contrast *CIR v Hogarth* CS 1940, 23 TC 491. Payments of a percentage of receipts over 40 years for the use of a secret process held to be annual payments (*Delage v Nugget Polish Co Ltd* KB 1905, 21 TLR 454) as were quarterly payments for the use of a firm's name etc. (*Mackintosh v CIR* KB 1928, 14 TC 15). See also *CIR v 36/49 Holdings Ltd* CA 1943, 25 TC 173. Where a business was bequeathed for life and the trustees were directed to carry a percentage of the profits to reserve, the amounts set aside were held to be annual payments (*Stocker v CIR* KB 1919, 7 TC 304).

In *Watkins v CIR* KB 1939, 22 TC 696, payments by a husband for the maintenance of his wife (of unsound mind) were held not to be annual payments. Payments to trustees as 'remuneration' are annual payments (*Baxendale v Murphy* KB 1924, 9 TC 76; *Hearn v Morgan* KB 1945, 26 TC 478) but not Schedule E remuneration (*Jaworski v Institution of Polish Engineers* CA 1950, 29 ATC 385).

Annuities

[24.11] The following matters are relevant.

(a) **General.** In order for an annuity to be subject to deduction of tax at source, it would have to fall within the definition of a qualifying annual payment (see **24.8** above). This will, in fact, generally be the case. Prior to 2007/08, in the absence of provisions to the contrary annuities were subject to deduction of tax under *ICTA 1988, ss 348, 349(1)* and this was so notwithstanding that the annuity may have been granted for valuable and sufficient consideration. Normally, an annuity cannot be dissected between the capital, if any, in consideration of the annuity and an 'interest element', but see **63.20** SAVINGS AND INVESTMENT INCOME as regards purchased life annuities. For a full discussion of this, see the HL opinions in *CIR v Church Commissioners* HL 1976, 50 TC 516. See also **24.7–24.10** above. For tax-free annuities see **24.15** below.
Statutory exceptions to this general rule are below.

(b) **Annuities for non-taxable consideration.** See **4.39** ANTI-AVOIDANCE.

(c) **Purchased life annuities.** See **64.17** SAVINGS AND INVESTMENT INCOME.

(d) **Annuities** charged under *ITEPA 2003* as **pension income** (see **56.2** PENSION INCOME), other than those arising from retirement annuity contracts and certain employment-related annuities from UK sources. From 6 April 2007, annuities from former retirement annuity contracts are brought within PAYE, and thus are within this exception — see **53.17** PAY AS YOU EARN. The same applies to annuities within *ITEPA 2003, s 610* (annuities under an occupational pension scheme that is not a registered pension scheme) — see **56.2**(e) PENSION INCOME.

(e) **'Capital and income'** policies are those where in the event of death within a selected period, a lump sum and an annuity for the rest of the period is paid. The annuity may (conditionally) be treated as instalments of capital, not subject to tax deduction. Some companies arrange for return of part of *capital* over a number of years, followed by an ordinary annuity subject to tax deduction. But if assigned or settled for benefit of a third party see **68.22** SETTLEMENTS.

(f) For **children's education policies** see *Perrin v Dickson* CA 1929, 14 TC 608 in which the yearly payments were held to be a return of the premiums with interest, only the interest being taxable. The decision was questioned in *Sothern-Smith v Clancy* CA 1940, 24 TC 1. Purchased life annuities are now regulated, see (c) above.

(g) For **guaranteed income bonds**, see **44.15** LIFE ASSURANCE POLICIES.

Simon's Taxes. See A4.432, A4.485.

Dividends and interest

[24.12] A sum representing income tax at the basic rate (for 2008/09 onwards, previously the savings rate) in force for the year of payment must be deducted from payments of **yearly interest** arising in the UK if made by a company (other than in a fiduciary or representative capacity), a local authority (other than in a fiduciary or representative capacity), or a partnership which includes a company; or if made to a person whose usual place of abode is outside the UK. Payments of yearly interest specifically include interest paid by a registered industrial and provident society in respect of any mortgage, loan, loan stock or deposit; or any interest, dividend or bonus in respect of a holding in its share capital. [*ITA 2007, s 874(1)(2)(5)(6); FA 2008, Sch 1 paras 26, 65*].

As regards local authorities, see HMRC Brief 22/08, 9 April 2008. As regards interest paid by a company that falls to be treated as a distribution, see HMRC Brief 47/08, 26 September 2008.

As to deduction at source on yearly interest payments prior to 2007/08, see **24.20, 24.21** below.

For the particular treatment of distributions by authorised investment funds, see **75.2 UNIT TRUSTS ETC.** [*ITA 2007, s 874(4)*].

For the collection of tax deducted at source, see **24.17** below.

The obligation to deduct tax on payments of yearly interest is subject to numerous exceptions, as listed below:

(a) payments of interest made by a building society (see **9.1 BUILDING SOCIETIES**);

(b) payments of interest by a deposit-taker where there is already a duty to deduct a sum representing income tax under the rules relating to deposit-takers, or would be but for a declaration of non-residence or a certificate that the recipient is unlikely to be liable to income tax (see **8.2 BANKS**);

(c) payments of interest in respect of public revenue dividends (see below and **64.3 SAVINGS AND INVESTMENT INCOME**);

(d) payments of interest by a bank if made in the ordinary course of its business (although see also the rules relating to deposit-takers in **8.2 BANKS**);

(e) payments of interest on advances from banks or building societies or from the European Investment Bank (providing, in the case of a bank, that the person beneficially entitled to the interest is within the charge to corporation tax);

(f) payments of interest on deposits with the National Savings Bank;

(g) payments of interest on a quoted Eurobond (see HMRC Brief 21/08, 7 April 2008);

(h) payments of interest on loans to buy a life annuity: such loans are already subject to deduction of tax, see **43.12 INTEREST PAYABLE**;

(i) payments of interest which are chargeable as relevant foreign income (as defined — see **32.2 FOREIGN INCOME**);

(j) payments of interest by a person authorised under *Financial Services and Markets Act 2000* whose business consists wholly or mainly of dealing as principal in financial instruments (as defined) and who pays the interest in the ordinary course of that business;

(k) payments of interest by a recognised clearing house or recognised investment exchange (both as defined) which are made in the ordinary course of carrying on the business of providing a central counterparty clearing service (as defined): this includes certain interest treated as paid under the rules relating to repo price differentials (see **4.8 ANTI-AVOIDANCE**);

(l)   payments of yearly interest by a registered industrial and provident society (as defined) in respect of any mortgage, loan, loan stock or deposit, or any interest, dividend or bonus in respect of a holding in its share capital, if made to a person whose usual place of abode is in the UK. The society must make returns of such payments to HMRC;

(m)   payments of interest under the *Late Payment of Commercial Debts (Interest) Act 1998* ('statutory interest').

[*ITA 2007, ss 875–888; FA 2007, s 47, Sch 14 para 24; SI 2007 No 2483, Reg 3; SI 2009 No 3227, Reg 7*].

These provisions apply to alternative finance return and profit share return (for which see **3.2–3.8** ALTERNATIVE FINANCE ARRANGEMENTS) as they do to interest. [*ITA 2007, s 564Q, Sch 1 para 602; FA 2005, ss 55, 56, Sch 2 para 12; CTA 2009, Sch 1 para 664(4); TIOPA 2010, Sch 2 para 18*]. For an exception from the duty to deduct tax from certain payments between companies, see **24.18** below.

Banks etc.

See **8** BANKS.

Building societies

See **9** BUILDING SOCIETIES.

UK public revenue dividends

A '*UK public revenue dividend*' is any income from securities which is paid out of the public revenue of the UK or Northern Ireland, excluding interest on local authority stock. Interest on gilt-edged securities (as defined) and securities which are the subject of a Treasury direction are payable gross (unless the holder of the security has made a deduction at source application). Otherwise, the person by or through whom the payment is made must deduct tax at the basic rate (for 2008/09 onwards, previously the savings rate) in force for the year of payment. HMRC have wide powers to make regulations governing the accounting arrangements and modifying the provisions governing the collection of tax deducted at source (see **24.17** below) in their application to UK public revenue dividends. [*ITA 2007, ss 890–892, 895; FA 2008, Sch 1 paras 28, 65; SI 2008 No 954, Arts 1, 40*].

See also **64.3** SAVINGS AND INVESTMENT INCOME.

Local authority and statutory corporation stock

Tax is deductible under *ITA 2007, s 874* (see above) except in the circumstances set out in **50.12** NON-RESIDENTS. [*ITA 2007, s 981*].

UK company dividends

See **1.5** ALLOWANCES AND TAX RATES.

Simon's Taxes. See A4.421–A4.425, B8.417.

Royalties

[24.13] Copyright royalties, public lending right payments and design royalties paid to non-UK residents are subject to deduction of tax at source provided they are within the charge to income tax or corporation tax. Deduction is at the basic rate in force for the year in which the payment is made and, where paid through a UK-resident agent, is applied net of commission (unless the entitlement or amount of commission is unknown). There is an exemption in relation to copies of works or articles which have been exported from the UK for distribution outside the UK. Where both apply, these rules take precedence over those relating to annual payments and patent royalties. [*ITA 2007, ss 906, 907, 908; ICTA 1988, ss 536, 537, 537B*]. This does not apply to professional authors (Hansard 10 November 1969, Vol 791, Col 31). Collection is by HMRC assessment (although there is a separate collection mechanism for companies) (see **24.17** below). The payer is assessable, even if he has not deducted the tax (*Rye & Eyre v CIR* HL 1935, 19 TC 164).

A payment is treated as made when it is made by the first person who makes it. The duty to make a deduction applies also to payment on account of royalties. If the rules requiring a deduction apply, any agreement to pay without deduction is void. [*ITA 2007, s 909*].

A payment to foreign author, for right to sell translation, has been held to be within the above provisions (*Longmans, Green* KB 1932, 17 TC 272). Solicitors remitting royalties to non-UK residents on behalf of the payers must deduct and account for tax (*Rye & Eyre v CIR* HL 1935, 19 TC 164).

HMRC may call for a return of payments. [*TMA 1970, s 16*]. See **63.17 RETURNS**.

Patent royalties

For 2007/08 onwards, a deduction must be made from a patent royalty if:

- it is *not* a qualifying annual payment (see **24.8** above) nor an annual payment for non-taxable consideration under *ITA 2007, s 904* (see **4.39 ANTI-AVOIDANCE**);
- it arises in the UK;
- it is chargeable to income tax or corporation tax.

Any deduction is to be made at the basic rate in force for the year in which the payment is made. Collection is via the self-assessment return or, if the payer is not an individual and has no modified net income (see **1.9 ALLOWANCES AND TAX RATES**), by HMRC assessment (although there is a separate collection mechanism for companies) (see **24.17** below).

[*ITA 2007, s 903*].

For years prior to 2007/08, patent royalties were payable under deduction of tax.

The sale by a non-UK resident of patent rights is subject to deduction at source provided the seller is chargeable to tax on profits of the sale under the provisions at **40.6 INTELLECTUAL PROPERTY**. The deduction is applied to the net proceeds, i.e. the proceeds less any incidental expenses of the sale which are deducted before payment. The rate is the basic rate in force for the year of payment. See **24.18** below for an exception for certain payments between companies. Collection is by HMRC assessment (although there is a separate collection mechanism for companies) (see **24.17** below). For the treatment of capital sums for the acquisition or from the sale of patents prior to 2007/08, see **24.21**(iii) below. [*ITA 2007, s 910; CTA 2009, Sch 1 para 709*].

Instalments of fixed amount for five-year use of patent were held to be capital (*Desoutter Bros Ltd* KB 1936, 15 ATC 49). A lump sum payment on signing a ten-year agreement held capital but ten fixed yearly payments royalties (*CIR v British Salmson Aero Engines Ltd* CA 1938, 22 TC 29). Awards by a Royal Commission for use of inventions and patents in 1914–1918 war held patent royalties (*Constantinesco v Rex* HL 1927, 11 TC 730; *Mills v Jones* HL 1929, 14 TC 769). See also *Jones v CIR* KB 1919, 7 TC 310; *Wild v Ionides* KB 1925, 9 TC 392; *International Combustion Ltd v CIR* KB 1932, 16 TC 532 and cf. *Rank Xerox Ltd v Lane* HL 1979, 53 TC 185.

Special provisions in relation to royalties

Companies may exercise a discretion to pay royalties under deduction at a treaty rate where there is a reasonable belief that the payee is entitled to relief under double taxation arrangements. If the payee was not so entitled, the company must account for the tax as if the above rule had never applied, and HMRC have powers to direct the company that it is not to apply to a particular payment or payments. [*ITA 2007, ss 911–913*]. For details, see Tolley's Corporation Tax under Income Tax in relation to a Company.

EU Interest and Royalties Directive

This Directive (*Directive 2003/49/EC* of 3 June 2003) has effect from 1 January 2004 and provides for the elimination of source taxation on interest and royalty payments between associated companies in different member states of the European Union. Companies may make gross payments if there is a reasonable belief that the exemption applies [*ITA 2007, ss 914–917*]. For details, see Tolley's Corporation Tax under Income Tax in relation to a Company.

Simon's Taxes. See **A4.435, A4.441, A4.442, A4.445, A4.454, A4.482, A4.483, B5.317, B5.319, B5.334, B5.336.**

Tax-free arrangements

[24.14] An agreement which provides for an annual payment without deduction of tax is void [*TMA 1970, s 106(2)*] but a provision to pay interest at a stated rate after deduction of tax is treated as requiring payment at the gross rate. [*ITA 2007, s 976(4)–(6); ICTA 1988, s 818(2); CTA 2009, Sch 1 para 717*]. An agreement to make payments 'free of tax' is not avoided by *TMA 1970, s 106(2)* (*CIR v Ferguson* HL 1969, 46 TC 1). See **24.15** below for tax-free annuities.

Tax-free annuities etc.

[24.15] The following matters are relevant.

(a) **General.** A direction under a will or settlement for an annuity to be paid 'free of tax' (or similar wording) is a direction to pay an annuity of such an amount which after deduction of the tax will produce the specified figure (cf. *CIR v Ferguson* HL 1969, 46 TC 1). This is a matter, however, in which it is important the wording used should express clearly and unambiguously what is intended. The large number of court cases referred to below have arisen mostly because of the imprecision of the relevant wording.

The wording was held *not* to confer freedom from tax in *Abadam v Abadam* 1864, 10 LT 53 ('payable without any deduction whatsoever'); *Shrewsbury v Shrewsbury* Ch D 1906, 22 TLR 598 ('clear of all deductions'); *In re Loveless* Ch D 1918, 34 TLR 356 ('clear'); *In re Well's Will Trusts* Ch D 1940, 19 ATC 158 ('clear of all deductions'); *In re Best's Marriage Settlement* Ch D 1941, 20 ATC 235 ('such a sum as shall after deductions'); *CIR v Watson* CS 1942, 25 TC 25 (annuity payable out of 'whole free residue' of income); *In re Hooper* Ch D 1944, 1 AER 227 ('free of all duty . . . and . . . free of all deductions whatsoever'); *In re Wright* Ch D 1952, 31 ATC 433 ('net'). The wording was held to confer freedom from tax in *In re Buckle* 1894, 1 Ch 286 ('free of legacy duty and every other deduction' under a codicil to a will in which originally 'clear of all deductions whatsoever, except income tax'); *In re Shrewsbury Estate Acts* CA 1923, 40 TLR 16 ('clear of all deductions whatsoever for taxes or otherwise'). *In re Hooper* above was not followed in *In re Cowlishaw* Ch D 1939, 18 ATC 377 where the wording was similar, but in a later case (*In re Best's Marriage Settlement* above) *Cowlishaw* was described as special to its context.

(b) **Excess liability.** All the decisions below relate to super-tax or surtax but it would seem that, suitably adapted, they are equally applicable to excess liability, i.e. the excess of income tax liability over what it would be if all taxable income were charged at the basic rate, savings rate (before 2008/09), starting rate for savings (for 2008/09 onwards) or dividend ordinary rate to the exclusion of the higher rate or dividend upper rate. Here it is relevant that an annuity is investment income.

An annuity of a sum such 'as after deduction of the income tax' would give the prescribed amount was held not to be free of super-tax (*In re Bates* Ch D 1924, 4 ATC 518). However an annuity 'free of income tax' was held to be free of surtax on the ground that surtax was an additional income tax and there was no indication in the will to restrict the wording to 'income tax as known for many years'. The previous decision was distinguished as there the wording referred to 'deduction' and surtax was not deductible at source (*In re Reckitt* CA 1932, 11 ATC 429; followed in *Prentice's Trustees* CS 1934, 13 ATC 612). A direction to pay an annuity free of super-tax was held to cover surtax (*In re Hulton* Ch D 1930, 9 ATC 570).

The surtax is normally taken as the part of the annuitant's total surtax proportionate to the ratio of the annuity grossed at the standard rate to the annuitant's total income (*In re Bowring* 1918, 34 TLR 575; followed in *In re Doxat* 1920, 125 LT 60 and other cases). In *Baird's Trustees* CS 1933, 12 ATC 407 the surtax was calculated on the basis that the annuity was the annuitant's only income, but this decision was distinguished in *Richmond's Trustees 1935* CS, 14 ATC 489 and *In re Bowring* was followed. See also *In re Horlick's Settlement* CA 1938, 17 ATC 549.

The surtax/excess liability borne on behalf of the annuitant by the trust fund is itself, grossed-up, income in his hands (*Meeking v CIR* KB 1920, 7 TC 603; *Lord Michelham's Trustees v CIR* CA 1930, 15 TC 737. See also *Shrewsbury & Talbot v CIR* KB 1936, 20 TC 538 and compare *CIR v Duncanson* KB 1949, 31 TC 257). The practice is to treat the liability so borne for year 1 as an addition for grossing-up purposes to the annuity for year 2.

(c) **Tax repayments of annuitants.** In a tax-free annuity the question arises whether the benefit conferred on the annuitant should be limited to the tax actually suffered by him after taking into account his allowances etc.

Where the annuity under a will was 'free of income tax' it was held that the annuitant must hand to the trustees a part of the tax repaid to her on account of her reliefs, in proportion to the ratio of the net annuity to her net income after tax (*In re Pettit, Le Fevre v Pettit* Ch D 1922, 38 TLR 787). But where the annuity was expressed to be of such an amount as after deduction of the tax at the current rate would give the prescribed sum it was held, distinguishing *In re Pettit*, that the annuitant was entitled to retain any tax repaid to him (*In re Jones* Ch D 1933, 12 ATC 595). For cases in which these two decisions were considered and applied as appropriate to the precise wording of the provision of the annuity, see *Richmond's Trustees* CS 1935, 14 ATC 489; *In re Maclennan* CA 1939, 18 ATC 121; *In re Eves* Ch D 1939, 18 ATC 401; *Rowan's Trustees* CS 1939, 18 ATC 378; *In re Jubb* Ch D 1941, 20 ATC 297; *In re Tatham* Ch D 1944, 23 ATC 283; *In re Williams* Ch D 1945, 24 ATC 199; *In re Bates's Will Trusts* Ch D 1945, 24 ATC 300; *In re Arno* CA 1946, 25 ATC 412. *Tatham* and *Arno* give useful reviews of the subject as does *CIR v Cook* HL 1945, 26 TC 489 (in which it was held that the Inland Revenue must repay the tax on the grossed-up amount of a tax-free annuity notwithstanding that the annuitant would not be liable to tax if the annuity was not grossed-up and that the whole of the repayment would be handed over to the trustees). The annuitant must, if required by the trustees, exercise his right to repayment (*In re Kingcombe* Ch D 1936, 15 ATC 37). If the annuitant is a married woman *In re Pettit* applies to tax repayable to the husband but, if necessary, she must apply for separate assessment (*In re Batley* CA 1952, 31 ATC 410). It applies to loss relief (*In re Lyons* CA 1951, 30 ATC 377). For the effect of an *In re Pettit* refund on the annuitant's total income for surtax see *CIR v Duncanson* KB 1949, 31 TC 257.

(d)   **Tax-free alimony etc. payments.** The *In re Pettit* rule (see (c) above) does not apply to tax-free Court Orders and in *CIR v Ferguson* HL 1969, 46 TC 1, Lord Diplock explicitly refrained from deciding whether it applied to a separation agreement. Whether a free of tax Court Order would confer freedom from surtax/ excess liability does not seem to have arisen. Subject to the foregoing (a), (b) and (c) above apply, where appropriate, to tax-free alimony payments etc.

For tax-free alimony payments by non-residents, see *Ferguson* above and *Stokes v Bennett* Ch D 1953, 34 TC 337.

(e)   For **overseas taxes** under tax-free annuities, see *Re Frazer* Ch D 1941, 20 ATC 73 and compare *Havelock v Grant* KB 1946, 27 TC 363.

Deduction of tax under foreign agreements or by non-residents

[24.16] UK tax legislation cannot alter rights not within the jurisdiction of UK courts. See *Keiner v Keiner* QB 1952, 34 TC 346 (tax not deductible from alimony under American agreement paid by UK resident ex-husband to non-resident ex-wife); *Bingham v CIR* Ch D 1955, 36 TC 254 (maintenance payments under foreign Court Order not deductible in arriving at total income as tax not deductible); *Westminster Bank v National Bank of Greece* HL 1970, 46 TC 472 (interest on foreign bonds paid in London by guarantor held within *Schedule D, Case IV* and tax not deductible). But where under a UK contract a non-UK resident paid interest to another non-UK resident and the payer died, held his executors (resident in UK) must deduct tax from interest they paid (*CIR v Broome's Exors* KB 1935, 19 TC 667). And where 'free of tax' alimony was payable under UK agreements etc., payments by the ex-husband no longer resident in the UK were held to have been paid subject to deduction of tax, the onus being on the Crown to collect the tax if the payments were within *ICTA 1988, s 349* (*Stokes v Bennett* Ch D 1953, 34 TC 337). See also *CIR v Ferguson* HL 1969, 46 TC 1.

Collection of tax

[24.17] There are three mechanisms to collect the income tax relating to payments made under deduction at source.

*   UK resident companies, deposit-takers and building societies are subject to a system of regular returns and payments during an accounting period. [*ITA 2007, Pt 15 Ch 15*]. For details, see Tolley's Corporation Tax under Income Tax in relation to a Company.
*   Tax on certain payments (listed at *ITA 2007, s 963(1)*) is collected by HMRC assessment. There is an accompanying requirement for the payer to deliver to HMRC an account of the payment 'without delay' and subject to a penalty under *TMA 1970, s 98*. [*ITA 2007, s 963*].
*   Tax in relation to certain annual payments and certain patent royalty payments is collected through the payer's self-assessment return. The tax is treated for the purposes of *TMA 1970* as if it were charged on the payer. It is taken into account in addition to (but separately from) the normal calculation of liability. [*ITA 2007, s 964; FA 2008, s 69*].

Exception for payments between companies etc.

[24.18] For payments made by one company to another, there is no requirement to deduct tax from interest, royalties, annuities or other annual payments where the recipient company is within the charge to corporation tax in respect of that income. There are detailed rules requiring the paying company to satisfy itself that the recipient company is eligible to receive the payment gross. Gross payment may also be made by companies to a wide range of tax-exempt bodies (and to their nominees), and the provisions are extended to apply to payments by local authorities subject to similar conditions. [*ITA 2007, Pt 15 Ch 11; ICTA 1988, ss 349A–349D; SI 2002 No 2931*]. For details, see Tolley's Corporation Tax under Income Tax in relation to a Company. See also Revenue Tax Bulletin August 2001 pp 867, 868 for an article outlining the original provisions.

Simon's Taxes. See A4.460.

Deduction of tax at source prior to 2007/08

[24.19] Income tax (at the basic rate or savings rate, whichever is applicable) *may* legally be deducted by the payer from certain annuities and other annual payments and certain royalties, which are paid out of taxed income, within the terms of *ICTA 1988, s 348* (see **24.20** below) and *must* be deducted from the payments listed in **24.21** below.

The **payer** thus obtains tax relief other than at the higher rate in respect of such payments. He may also be able to deduct the payments as charges on income in arriving at his excess liability, i.e. the excess of income tax liability over what it would be if all taxable income were charged at the basic rate (or, as appropriate, starting rate, savings rate or dividend ordinary rate) to the exclusion of the higher rate or dividend upper rate.

The **recipient** is treated as having paid income tax at the basic rate or savings rate (whichever is applicable) on the income. [*ITTOIA 2005, ss 602, 618, 686*]. If he is not liable, or not wholly liable, on such income at that rate, he can recover from HMRC any excess tax suffered so far as not adjusted in direct assessments on him. On the other hand, if his total income is high enough, further liability will arise on him at the higher rate of income tax. See **1.6 ALLOWANCES AND TAX RATES** as regards liability at the savings rate (as opposed to the basic rate) on savings income.

A payment made under deduction of tax is income (equal to the grossed-up equivalent) of the tax year by reference to the basic rate or savings rate of tax for which tax is deducted from the payment, without regard to the period of accrual (and see *CIR v Crawley* Ch D 1986, 59 TC 728). [*ITA 2007, s 31(2); ICTA 1988, s 835(6)*].

Circumstances where payer may deduct tax — years prior to 2007/08

[24.20] [*ICTA 1988, s 348*]

The permissible tax deduction, as **24.19** above, applies to:

(a)   any annuity or other annual payment, not being interest, charged with tax under *Schedule D, Case III* or, from 6 April 2003, under *ITEPA 2003, s 607* (annuities from retirement annuity contracts — and see below) or, if sourced in the UK, *ss 609–611* (see **56.2**(e) PENSION INCOME), or, from 6 April 2005, under *ITTOIA 2005, Pt 4 Ch 7* (purchased life annuity payments) and *Chapter 10* (distributions from unauthorised unit trusts), *s 579* (royalties etc. from intellectual property), *Part 5 Chapter 4* (certain telecommunication rights: non-trading income) and *Chapter 7* (annual payments not otherwise charged), provided none of these constitute relevant foreign income (but see **30.4** EXEMPT INCOME for certain annual payments excluded from the charge to tax, and also see **4.39** ANTI-AVOIDANCE re annual payments made for non-taxable consideration and **68.11** SETTLEMENTS re payments out of discretionary trusts),

(b)   any royalty or other sum paid in respect of the user of a patent,

provided that the payment is wholly out of profits or gains brought into charge to income tax. (Note that as the profits of UK companies are not charged to income tax, *ICTA 1988, s 348* does not apply to them and payments by them will be within *ICTA 1988, s 349* — see **24.21** below.) The following income is specifically treated as not having been brought within the charge to income tax for the purposes of both the permissible tax deduction (under *ICTA 1988, s 348*) and the compulsory deduction (under *ICTA 1988, s 349* — see **24.21** below):

(i)   distributions from UK resident companies etc. on which there is no tax credit (*ITTOIA 2005, ss 399(2), 400(2)*);

(ii)   stock dividend income (*ITTOIA 2005, s 413(2)(3)*);

(iii)   the release of a loan to a participator in a close company (*ITTOIA 2005, Pt 4 Ch 6*);

(iv)   gains from contracts for life insurance where income tax is treated as paid (*ITTOIA 2005, ss 465, 467, 530*);

(v)   income described in (ii)–(iv) above which is treated as arising to personal representatives (under *ITTOIA 2005, s 664(2)(c)–(e)*).

The payer is entitled to deduct tax and it will be detrimental to himself if he fails to do so. See **24.6** above regarding omission to deduct tax.

From 6 April 2007, annuities from former retirement annuity contracts were brought within PAYE, and deduction of tax at source thus ceased to apply — see **53.17** PAY AS YOU EARN. The same applies to annuities within *ITEPA 2003, s 610* (annuities under an occupational pension scheme that is not a registered pension scheme) — see **56.2**(e) PENSION INCOME.

The tax deductible is at the basic rate for the year in which the payment became due, irrespective of the date of actual payment. Where the payment would constitute 'savings income' (see **1.6** ALLOWANCES AND TAX RATES) of the recipient (whatever his status), deduction is at the savings rate instead (although the only type of payment within *section 348* to which this should apply is a purchased life annuity). [*ICTA 1988, s 4*]. (Cf. *Re Sebright* Ch D 1944, 23 TC 190.) It is accordingly income of the recipient of the year when due — an important point if the recipient wishes to claim repayment of the tax deducted (*CIR v Crawley* Ch D 1986, 59 TC 728).

Simon's Taxes. See A4.431, A4.463, A4.464, A4.481–A4.498.

Circumstances where payer must deduct tax — years prior to 2007/08

[24.21] [*ICTA 1988, ss 349, 350*]

Income tax *must* be deducted from the following.

(i)   Payments specified in **24.20**(a) and (b) above which are not payable, or not wholly payable, out of profits or gains brought into charge to income tax. [*ICTA 1988, s 349(1)*]. See **49.10** MISCELLANEOUS INCOME as regards certain payments to theatrical 'angels'.

The payer must deduct tax from such payments, and must inform HMRC, who will make an assessment to collect that tax. Appeals against that assessment were to the Special Commissioners. [*TMA 1970, s 31C(2)*]. Payments by UK companies are within *s 349(1)* but the tax is accounted for under *ICTA 1988, Sch 16*, see Tolley's Corporation Tax. See, however, **24.18** above as regards disapplication of the requirement to deduct tax from such payments.

The obligation to deduct is upon 'the person by or through whom' the payment is made and see *Rye & Eyre v CIR* HL 1935, 19 TC 164; *Aeolian Co Ltd v CIR* KB 1936, 20 TC 547 and *Howells v CIR* KB 1939, 22 TC 501. But liability under *section 350* does not arise until the annual payment is actually 'paid'.

Tax is deductible at the basic rate in force at the time of payment. Where the payment would constitute 'savings income' (see **1.6** ALLOWANCES AND TAX RATES) of the recipient (whatever his status), deduction is at the savings rate instead (but the same comment applies as in **24.20** above as regards application). [*ICTA 1988, s 4*].

Where a payment from which tax should have been deducted is made in full, there is no right to recover the under-deduction by deduction from later payments (*Tenbry Investments Ltd v Peugeot Talbot Motor Co Ltd* Ch D, [1992] STC 791).

If a payment is made by an individual in a later year than the year when due and it could have been made out of taxed income in that due year, an allowance will be made in any assessment to collect the tax for the tax which could have been deducted if the payment had been made when due. A similar allowance may be made in the case of a trust or other non-trading institution (not within the charge to corporation tax) in cases of hardship. (HMRC ESC A16).

The profits or gains to be taken into account are those assessed (or received less tax) for the year of assessment in which the payment was made. Hence, except where ESC A16 applies, accumulated income of previous years cannot be taken into account (*Luipaard's Vlei Estate v CIR* CA 1930, 15 TC 573) and, for a trader, the taxable profits for the year after deducting any losses forward and capital allowances are taken into account irrespective of the actual profits of the year (*A-G v Metropolitan Water Board* CA 1927, 13 TC 294; *Trinidad Petroleum Development Co Ltd v CIR* CA 1936, 21 TC 1). For the individual, *section 349(1)* will normally be applicable only if his annual payments etc. exceed his aggregate income of the year (cf. *CIR v Plummer* HL 1979, 54 TC 1). However, trustees may be liable under *s 350* where annual payments etc. are made out of capital of the trust fund irrespective of the trust income, see **68.22 SETTLEMENTS**.

Where payments are made under deduction of tax but the payer has no income chargeable to income tax the tax deducted will be collected by assessment under *ICTA 1988, s 350*. But if this position arises by reason of a loss sustained in a trade etc., the trader etc. may be able to treat amounts so assessed as if they were trading losses and carry them forward against profits of the same business for subsequent years. See **45.24 LOSSES** for the detailed provisions.

(ii)   Subject to the exclusion of certain payments by companies and local authorities (see **24.18** above), and interest chargeable as relevant foreign income, yearly interest of money which falls within *ITTOIA 2005, Pt 4 Ch 2* (excluding anything specially exempted from income tax and discounts treated as interest under *ITTOIA 2005, s 381*), but only if paid:

    (a)   by a company or local authority (otherwise than in a fiduciary or representative capacity); or

    (b)   by or for a partnership of which a company is a member; or

    (c)   to a person whose usual place of abode is outside the UK. [*ICTA 1988, s 349(2)(3)*].

As regards (c) above, tax need not be deducted from payments of interest to the UK branch of a non-UK resident company trading in the UK through that branch, where the branch profits are liable to corporation tax and not exempted under a double tax treaty. (Revenue Tax Bulletin August 1993 p 87). See **24.18** above for the general exclusion of certain payments by companies and local authorities.

Where interest received by a company is charged to tax as a trading receipt (see Tolley's Corporation Tax under Loan Relationships), this does not affect the requirement for deduction of tax by the payer (see Revenue Tax Bulletin August 1999 pp 685, 686). See **24.18** above for the general exclusion of certain payments by companies and local authorities.

Interest under the *Late Payment of Commercial Debts (Interest) Act 1998* (or under a contractual right but for which that Act would have applied) is *not* 'yearly interest'. (Revenue Tax Bulletin August 1999 pp 686, 687).

For advances made on or after 29 April 1996, interest payable on an advance from a bank (within *ICTA 1988, s 840A* — see **8.1 BANKS**) within the charge to corporation tax in respect of it, and interest paid by such a bank in the ordinary course of its business, is excluded. Previously, the exclusion applied to interest payable in the UK on an advance from a bank carrying on a *bona fide* banking business in the UK (see *Hafton Properties Ltd v McHugh* Ch D 1986, 59 TC 420) or paid by such a bank in the ordinary course of such a business (for which see HMRC SP 4/96). For whether interest is 'payable in the UK', see *Mistletoe Ltd v Flood* (Sp C 351), [2003] SSCD 66. There are transitional provisions preserving relief as regards interest payable or paid on or after 29 April 1996 on an advance made before that day. National Savings Bank interest is always paid without deduction of tax.

[ICTA 1988, s 349(3)(a)(b)(3AA)(3AB)]. See, however, **8.2 BANKS** as regards special deduction schemes. See **8.2 BANKS** also for exclusion from *section 349(2)* of certain interest payments by bodies other than banks where those payments are not within the special deduction scheme. *[ICTA 1988, s 349(3)(h)]*. See **24.18** above for the general exclusion of certain payments by companies and local authorities.

As regards payments by building societies, only interest and dividends on certain 'marketable securities' is within *s 349*. *[ICTA 1988, s 349(2)(3A)]*. See **BUILDING SOCIETIES (9)** generally and at **9.1** in particular. Interest paid to a society is payable gross. *[ICTA 1988, s 369(1)]*. See **24.18** above for the general exclusion of certain payments by companies and local authorities.

The requirement to deduct tax does not apply to a person authorised under the *Financial Services and Markets Act 2000* whose business consists wholly or mainly of dealing as principal in 'financial instruments' (as specially defined) and who pays the interest in the ordinary course of that business. *[ICTA 1988, s 349(3)(i)(5)(6)]*.

The requirement to deduct tax does not apply to:

- interest paid by a recognised clearing house or recognised investment exchange, in the course of providing a central counterparty clearing service (as defined), on margin or other collateral deposited with it by users of the service; or

- price differentials on repos where treated (under *ICTA 1988, s 730A* — see **4.8 ANTI-AVOIDANCE**) as interest paid by a recognised clearing house or recognised investment exchange in respect of contracts made by it as provider of a central counterparty clearing service.

[ICTA 1988, s 349(3)(j)(k)(6)].

'UK *public revenue dividends*' (i.e. any income from securities which is paid out of the UK or NI public revenue, but excluding interest on local authority stock (see (a) above)) are payable under deduction of tax, subject to any provision to the contrary in the *Taxes Acts* (and see in particular **64.3 SAVINGS AND INVESTMENT INCOME** for the general exemption of gilt-edged securities). HMRC have wide powers to make regulations governing the accounting arrangements and modifying *ICTA 1988, ss 349, 350* in their application to UK public revenue dividends. *[ICTA 1988, ss 349(3C)(4), 350A]*.

Interest paid on '*quoted Eurobonds*' (i.e. listed securities issued by a company and carrying a right to interest) is in all cases excluded from the above provisions for deduction of tax from interest. *[ICTA 1988, ss 124, 841A]*.

These provisions apply to alternative finance return and profit share return (for which see **3.2–3.6 ALTERNATIVE FINANCE ARRANGEMENTS**) as they do to interest. *[FA 2005, ss 55, 56, Sch 2 para 3]*.

Tax is deductible at the savings rate in force for the tax year in which payment is made. *[ICTA 1988, s 4]*.

(iii) The following, as under (i) above, except that they cannot qualify for the loss relief described.

    (a)   Net proceeds of sale of British patent rights by a non-resident where seller is chargeable to tax on profits of sale under the provisions at **40.6 INTELLECTUAL PROPERTY**. For this purpose, the net proceeds are the proceeds less any incidental expenses of the sale which are deducted before payment. [*ICTA 1988, ss 349ZA, 524*].

    (b)   Copyright royalties, public lending right payments and design royalties payable to a non-resident. [*ICTA 1988, ss 536, 537, 537B*]. See also **24.13** above.

Simon's Taxes. See **A4.424, A4.431, A4.463, A4.464, A4.481–A4.498.**

25

Diplomatic Immunity etc.

Simon's Taxes. See C1.221, D1.240, E1.575, E5.401, E5.401C, E6.464.

Diplomatic Agents etc.

[25.1] Diplomatic agents (i.e. heads of mission or members of diplomatic staff) of foreign states (recognised by HM Government, see *Caglar v Billingham* (Sp C 70), [1996] SSCD 150) are exempt from tax except on income or capital gains arising from *private* investments or immovable property in the UK under *Diplomatic Privileges Act 1964*. Similar exemption is given to *Agents-General* and their staffs and to certain official agents of Commonwealth countries [*ITA 2007, s 841*] (and see *SI 1997 No 1334* as regards certain Hong Kong officials). *Consuls* and *official agents* of foreign States in the UK (not British subjects or citizens of Eire and not trading) are exempt on income from their official employment [*ITEPA 2003, ss 300, 301*].

Subject to any Order in Council, consular officers and employees, provided they are foreign nationals and not British (or overseas British) citizens, are exempt from tax on employment income. Provided they are either permanent employees or were not ordinarily resident in the UK immediately prior to the employment, and are not otherwise engaged in any UK trade, profession, vocation or employment, they are also exempt from tax on relevant foreign income (see **32.2 FOREIGN INCOME**).

[*ITTOIA 2005, ss 771, 772; ITEPA 2003, ss 302, 646A, 681A, Sch 6 para 44*]. See also *Consular Relations Act 1968*.

In *Jimenez v CIR* (Sp C 419), [2004] SSCD 371, a person employed as a cook by the Namibian High Commission in London was denied income tax exemption on her earnings, otherwise available under *Diplomatic Privileges Act 1964* and *article 37(3)* of the *Vienna Convention on Diplomatic Relations* (which provides exemption for 'members of the service staff' of a diplomatic mission who are not 'permanently resident in the receiving State'), because she had not been notified to the UK authorities as a member of a diplomatic mission in the UK.

International organisations

[25.2] International organisations (e.g. the United Nations (*SI 1974 No 1261*)), their representatives, officers, members of committees, persons or missions etc. may be specified by Order in Council as exempt from certain taxes under *International Organisations Act 1968*. Also other bodies under the *European Communities Act 1972* (e.g. the North Atlantic Salmon Conservation Organisation (*SI 1985 No 1773*)) and certain financial bodies under the *Bretton Woods Agreements Act 1945* (e.g. the International Monetary Fund (*SI 1946 No 36*)).

Exemption from income tax is given to the remuneration of the Commissioners of the European Communities and their staffs under *Art. 13 of Chap. V of the Protocol on the Privileges and Immunities of the European Communities*. See *Hurd v Jones* CJEC, [1986] STC 127 as regards exemption of certain payments out of Community funds, although see now *SI 1990 No 237*. See also *Tither v CIR* CJEC, [1990] STC 416, where exclusion of EU official from MIRAS scheme upheld. Experts seconded to the European Commission under the detached national experts scheme are exempt from income tax on their daily subsistence allowances [*ITEPA 2003, s 304*], and certain education allowances under the Overseas Services Aid Scheme are similarly exempt (see HMRC ESC A44). The Treasury may also designate any of the international organisations of which the UK is a member for the purpose of exemption from various requirements for the deduction of tax from payments made in the UK (see e.g. *SI 1997 No 168*).

[*ITA 2007, s 979, Sch 1 para 461; ICTA 1988, s 582A*].

26

Double Tax Relief

Cross-references. See generally **50 NON-RESIDENTS**. See also HMRC's Digest of Double Taxation Treaties at www.hmrc.gov.uk/cnr/dtdigest.pdf and the various Double Taxation Guidance Notes at www.hmrc.gov.uk/cnr/dt_guide_not es.htm.

Simon's Taxes. See E6.4.

Introduction

[26.1] Where the same income is liable to be taxed in both the UK and another country, relief may be available:

(a)   under the specific terms of a double tax agreement between the UK and that other country — see **26.2** below [*TIOPA 2010, s 2; ICTA 1988, s 788*];

(b)   under special arrangements with Ireland — see **26.4** below; or

(c)   under the unilateral double tax relief provisions contained in UK tax legislation — see **26.6** below. [*TIOPA 2010, s 8; ICTA 1988, s 790*].

See **34.10 HMRC — ADMINISTRATION** as regards arrangements for exchange of information between the UK and other countries.

Double tax agreements

[26.2] A list is given below of the bilateral double tax agreements (also known as double tax treaties or double tax conventions) made by the UK. For texts of agreements, see **Simon's Taxes F1.6**. Representations on points interested parties would like to see addressed in negotiating particular treaties, or on other matters relating to the treaty negotiation programme or the treaty network, should be addressed to Jas Sahni, Customs & International (Tax Treaty Team), HM Revenue & Customs, 100 Parliament Street, London, SW1A 2BQ (email Jas.Sahni@hmrc.gsi.gov.uk).

Under these agreements certain classes of income derived from those countries by UK residents are given complete exemption from income taxes in the country from which they arise and reciprocal exemption from UK income tax is given to similar income derived from the UK by residents of those countries. Exemption may also be granted in respect of taxes on capital gains.

[*TIOPA 2010, ss 2–7; ICTA 1988, s 788*].

Other classes of income derived from those countries are not exempted, or only partially exempted, by the double tax agreements and in these cases relief from UK income tax is generally given in the agreement in the form of a credit, calculated by reference to the foreign tax suffered, which is set against and reduces the UK tax chargeable on the doubly taxed income. The relief is given as a tax reduction at Step 6 of the calculation of income tax liability (see **1.7, 1.8 ALLOWANCES AND TAX RATES**). [*TIOPA 2010, s 18; ICTA 1988, s 793; ITA 2007, Sch 1 para 192*]. See the Example at **26.12** below.

Relief by way of credit is not available against any UK tax for any tax year unless the person on whose income the UK tax is chargeable is resident in the UK for that year. [*TIOPA 2010, s 26(1); ICTA 1988, s 794(1)*].

See the **general anti-avoidance rule** at **26.5** below.

HMRC International Manual INTM153000 *et seq.* provides a brief description of the contents of each Article normally found in a double tax agreement to which the UK is party.

Double tax agreements normally contain a 'mutual agreement procedure' enabling a taxpayer who considers that the action of a tax authority has resulted, or will result, in taxation not in accordance with the agreement to present his case to the competent authority in his state of residence. The UK competent authority is the HMRC, and the address to which all relevant facts and contentions should be sent is International Division, Melbourne House, Aldwych, London WC2B 4LL. For the presentation of such cases, and for giving effect to solutions and agreements reached under such procedures, see *TIOPA 2010, ss 124, 125*. Details of the administrative arrangements for operating the procedure with the USA were set out in Revenue Press Release 13 November 2000.

Where relief by credit is available by double tax agreement, no deduction for foreign tax is generally allowed in taxing foreign income. [*TIOPA 2010, s 31(2); ICTA 1988, s 795(2)*]. However, if a taxpayer chooses not to take relief by credit (whether by double tax agreement or unilaterally — see **26.6** below), any tax paid on the foreign income in the place where it arises is *deductible* from the income for the purposes of charging it to UK tax — see **26.9**(a)(iii) below.

See **26.3** below for further points on double tax relief by agreement.

The following bilateral agreements (*SI* numbers in round brackets) supersede the provisions of *TIOPA 2010, ss 8–17* (unilateral relief) to the extent, and as from the operative dates, specified therein. Where more than one agreement is listed for a particular country or territory, readers should generally refer to the most recent, which may contain provision to the effect that the agreement wholly supersedes the preceding agreement(s) listed or does so to a specified extent.

Antigua and Barbuda (1947/2865; 1968/1096), **Argentina** (1997/1777), **Australia** (1968/305; 1980/707; 2003/3199), **Austria** (1970/1947; 1979/117; 1994/768), **Azerbaijan** (1995/762),

Bangladesh (1980/708), **Barbados** (1970/952; 1973/2096), **Belarus** (1995/2706 (not yet in force, and see note below under USSR)), **Belgium** (1987/2053), **Belize** (1947/2866; 1968/573; 1973/2097), **Bolivia** (1995/2707), **Bosnia-Herzegovina** (see note below), **Botswana** (1978/183; 2006/1925 (applies from 6 April 2007 (UK) and 1 July 2007 (Botswana))), **British Honduras** (see Belize), **Brunei** (1950/1977; 1968/306; 1973/2098), **Bulgaria** (1987/2054), **Burma** (see Myanmar),

Canada (1980/709; 1980/780; 1980/1528; 1985/1996; 1987/2071; 1996/1782; 2000/3330; 2003/2619) (2003 protocol applies from 6 April 2005 (UK) and 1 January 2005 (Canada)), **Chile** (2003/3200 (applies from 6 April 2005 (UK) and 1 January 2005 (Chile))), **China** (1981/1119; 1984/1826; 1996/3164) (and see note below), **Croatia** (see note below), **Cyprus** (1975/425; 1980/1529), **Czech Republic** (see note below),

Denmark (1980/1960; 1991/2877; 1996/3165),

Egypt (1980/1091), **Estonia** (1994/3207),

Falkland Islands (1997/2985), **Faroes** (2007/3469 (applies from 6 April 2009 (UK) and 1 January 2009 (Faroes))), **Fiji** (1976/1342), **Finland** (1970/153; 1980/710; 1985/1997; 1991/2878; 1996/3166), **France** (1968/1869; 1973/1328; 1987/466; 1987/2055; 2009/226 (applies from 6 April 2010 (UK) and 1 January 2010 (France))),

Gambia (1980/1963), **Georgia** (2004/3325 (applies from 6 April 2006 (UK) and 1 January 2006 (Georgia))), **Germany** (1967/25; 1971/874), **Ghana** (1993/1800), **Greece** (1954/142), **Grenada** (1949/361; 1968/1867), **Guernsey** (1952/1215; 1994/3209; 2009/3011 (Arrangement amending the 1952 Agreement applies from 6 April 2010 (UK) and 1 January 2010 (Guernsey) and Tax Information Exchange Agreement applies from 27 November 2009)), **Guyana** (1992/3207),

Hungary (1978/1056),

Iceland (1991/2879), **India** (1981/1120; 1993/1801), **Indonesia** (1994/769), **Ireland** (see **26.4** below), **Isle of Man** (1955/1205; 1991/2880; 1994/3208; 2009/228 (Arrangement amending the 1955 Agreement applies from 6 April 2009 (both in UK and Isle of Man) and Tax Information Exchange Agreement applies from 2 April 2009)), **Israel** (1963/616; 1971/391), **Italy** (1990/2590), **Ivory Coast** (1987/169),

Jamaica (1973/1329), **Japan** (1970/1948; 1980/1530; 2006/1924 (applies from 6 April 2007 (UK), but from 1 January 2007 as regards taxes withheld at source, and 1 January 2007 (Japan))), **Jersey** (1952/1216; 1994/3210; 2009/3012 (Arrangement amending the 1952 Agreement applies from 6 April 2010 (UK) and 1 January 2010 (Jersey) and Tax Information Exchange Agreement applies from 27 November 2009)), **Jordan** (2001/3924),

Kazakhstan (1994/3211; 1998/2567), **Kenya** (1977/1299), **Kiribati and Tuvalu** (1950/750; 1968/309; 1974/1271), **Korea (South)** (1996/3168), **Kuwait** (1999/2036),

Latvia (1996/3167), **Lesotho** (1997/2986), **Libya** (2010/243 (applies from 6 April 2010 (UK) and 1 January 2011(Libya))), **Lithuania** (2001/3925, 2002/2847), **Luxembourg** (1968/1100; 1980/567; 1984/364; 2010/237) (2010 protocol applies from 6 April 2011 (UK) and 1 January 2011 (Luxembourg)),

Macedonia (2007/2127 (applies from 6 April 2008 (UK) and 1 January 2008 (Macedonia) and see note below)), **Malawi** (1956/619; 1964/1401; 1968/1101; 1979/302), **Malaysia** (1973/1330; 1987/2056; 1997/2987), **Malta** (1995/763), **Mauritius** (1981/1121; 1987/467; 2003/2620), **Mexico** (1994/3212), **Moldova** (2008/1795 (applies from 6 April 2009 (UK) and 1 January 2009 (Moldova)), **Mongolia** (1996/2598), **Montserrat** (1947/2869; 1968/576), **Morocco** (1991/2881), **Myanmar** (1952/751),

Namibia (1962/2352; 1967/1490), **Netherlands** (1967/1063; 1980/1961; 1983/1902; 1990/2152; 2000/3330; 2009/227 (not yet in force)), **New Zealand** (1984/365; 2004/1274; 2008/1793) (2008 protocol applies on and after 28 August 2008 in both the UK and New Zealand), **Nigeria** (1987/2057), **Norway** (1985/1998; 2000/3247),

Oman (1998/2568),

Pakistan (1987/2058), **Papua New Guinea** (1991/2882), **Philippines** (1978/184), **Poland** (1978/282; 2006/3323 (applies from 6 April 2007 (UK) and 1 January 2007 (Poland))), **Portugal** (1969/599),

Qatar (2010/241 (not yet in force)),

Romania (1977/57), **Russia** (1994/3213),

St. Christopher (St. Kitts) and Nevis (1947/2872), **Saudi Arabia** (2008/1770 (applies from 6 April 2010 (UK) and 1 January 2010 (Saudi Arabia))), **Serbia and Montenegro** (see note below), **Sierra Leone** (1947/2873; 1968/1104), **Singapore** (1997/2988), **Slovak Republic** (see note below), **Slovenia** (2008/1796 (applies from 6 April 2009 (UK) and 1 January 2009 (Slovenia) and see note below)), **Solomon Islands** (1950/748; 1968/574; 1974/1270), **South Africa** (1969/864; 2002/3138), **South West Africa** (see Namibia), **Spain** (1976/1919; 1995/765), **Sri Lanka** (1980/713), **Sudan** (1977/1719), **Swaziland** (1969/380), **Sweden** (1961/619; 1984/366; 2000/3330), **Switzerland** (1978/1408; 1982/714; 1994/3215; 2007/3465 (applies from 6 April 2009 (UK), from 1 January 2009 (Switzerland) and from 22 December 2008 as regards exchange of information provisions),

Taiwan (2002/3137), Thailand (1981/1546), **Trinidad and Tobago** (1983/1903), **Tunisia** (1984/133), **Turkey** (1988/932),
Uganda (1993/1802), **Ukraine** (1993/1803), **USA** (1980/568; 2002/2848), **USSR** (see note below), **Uzbekistan** (1994/770),
Venezuela (1996/2599), **Vietnam** (1994/3216), **Virgin Islands** (2009/3013 (applies from 6 April 2011 (UK), from 1 January 2011 (Virgin Islands) and from 12 April 2010 as regards exchange of information provisions)),
Yugoslavia (see note below),
Zambia (1972/1721; 1981/1816), **Zimbabwe** (1982/1842).

Shipping & Air Transport only — Algeria (Air Transport only) (1984/362), Argentina (but see now above), Belarus (but see now above), Brazil (1968/572), Cameroon (Air Transport only) (1982/1841), China (Air Transport only) (1981/1119), Ethiopia (Air Transport only) (1977/1297), Hong Kong (Air Transport only) (1998/2566), Hong Kong (Shipping only) (2000/3248), Iran (Air Transport only) (1960/2419), Jordan (1979/300), Kuwait (Air Transport only) (1984/1825), Lebanon (1964/278), Russia (but see now above), Saudi Arabia (Air Transport only) (1994/767), Venezuela (but see now above), USSR (see note below), Ukraine (but see now above), Uzbekistan (but see now above), Zaire (1977/1298).

Exchange of Information only (see **34.10** HMRC — ADMINISTRATION)—Bermuda (2008/1789 (applies on and after 4 December 2008 in both the UK and Bermuda)). See also **63.15** RETURNS as regards agreements made in connection with the EU Savings Directive.

Notes

Copies of double tax agreements and other statutory instruments published from 1987 onwards are available on the Stationery Office website at www.opsi.gov.uk/stat.htm.

China

The Agreement published as *SI 1984 No 1826* does not apply to the Hong Kong or Macao Special Administrative Regions which came into existence on 1 July 1997. (Revenue Tax Bulletin October 1996 p 357).

Czechoslovakia

The Agreement published as *SI 1991 No 2876* between the UK and Czechoslovakia is treated as remaining in force between the UK and, respectively, the Czech Republic and the Slovak Republic. (HMRC SP 5/93).

USA

For HMRC's understanding of how certain provisions of the latest Agreement published as *SI 2002 No 2848* will be interpreted and applied, see Revenue Tax Bulletin Special Edition 6, April 2003.

USSR

The Agreement published as *SI 1986 No 224* (which also continued in force the Air Transport agreement published as *SI 1974 No 1269*) between the UK and the former Soviet Union was to be applied by the UK as if it were still in force between the UK and the former Soviet Republics until such time as new agreements took effect with particular countries. It later came to light that Armenia, Georgia, Kyrgyzstan, Lithuania and Moldova did not consider themselves bound by the UK/USSR convention and were not operating it in relation to UK residents. Accordingly, the UK ceased to apply it to residents of those countries from 6 April 2002 for income tax and capital gains tax. (The Agreement published as *SI 2001 No 3925* between the UK and Lithuania has effect from those dates, and note the new Agreements between the UK and, respectively, Georgia and Moldova.) The position for other former Republics (Belarus, Tajikistan and Turkmenistan) with which new conventions are not yet in force remains as before. (HMRC SP 4/01 (replacing SP 3/92) and Revenue Tax Bulletin June 2001 p 864).

Yugoslavia

The Agreement published as *SI 1981 No 1815* between the UK and Yugoslavia is regarded as remaining in force between the UK and, respectively, Bosnia-Herzegovina, Croatia, Macedonia, Serbia and Montenegro, and Slovenia. That Agreement ceased to be so regarded with respect to Macedonia when the new treaty between the UK and Macedonia (*SI 2007 No 2127*) came into force. (HMRC Statement of Practice SP 03/07, 29 November 2007 (replacing SP 3/04)). The Agreement published as *SI 1981 No 1815* ceases to be regarded as remaining in force between the UK and Slovenia when the new treaty between the UK and Slovenia (*SI 2008 No 1796*) comes into force.

See the general anti-avoidance rule at **26.5 below.**

Double tax treaty relief — further points

[26.3] As regards the concept of 'permanent establishment' on which taxation rights are based under most treaties, HMRC take the view that a website, or a server on which e-commerce is conducted through a website, is not of itself a permanent establishment (Revenue Press Release 11 April 2000).

Distributions

See *Memec plc v CIR* CA 1998, 71 TC 77 in which receipts under a silent partnership agreement were held not to attract relief. In this connection, see HMRC International Manual INTM180000 *et seq.* as regards the classification of foreign entities for UK tax purposes and for a list of such classifications.

In *Swift v HMRC* FTT (TC 399), [2010] SFTD 553, it was held by the Tribunal that the profits of a particular US Limited Liability Company (LLC) belonged to the individual members as they arose and that the UK member should be taxed accordingly. Since he was thereby taxed on the same income in both countries, he was entitled to double taxation relief for US tax paid on his share of the LLC's profits. HMRC arc appealing this decision and in the meantime intend to continue with their current general practice in relation to

US LLCs, which is to tax a UK resident member only if and when the LLC distributes profits to its members, with no double tax relief due against income tax. See www.hmrc.gov.uk/international/swift-v-hmrc.htm.

The general abolition of the repayment of dividend tax credits after 5 April 1999 did not affect the entitlement of a non-UK resident to payment in respect of a tax credit under double tax agreements (although it should be noted that in practice, with the rate of tax credit being only one-ninth of the net dividend, such repayments are probably very limited). [*F(No 2)A 1997, s 30(9)(10)*].

Employees working in the UK

Under many double tax agreements, employees working in the UK, who are resident in the overseas territory but not resident in the UK, and who are not physically present in the UK for more than 183 days in the tax year, are exempt from UK tax on earnings paid by or on behalf of a non-UK resident employer. For this purpose, fractions of days are counted. (CCAB Memorandum TR 508, 9 June 1983). This exemption does not usually apply to public entertainers (and see now **50.10** NON-RESIDENTS), nor, under certain agreements, does it extend to employees working on the UK continental shelf (Revenue Press Release 3 March 1989).

Before 6 April 2009, when counting up the 183 days, a part day counts as a part day and days of arrival and departure and all other days spent inside the UK should be included. On and after 6 April 2009, any part of a day counts as a full day. Any days during which the taxpayer is UK resident should not be included in the calculation. (HMRC Double Taxation Relief Manual DT1921).

For employees commencing a work assignment in the UK, claims will be refused where the cost of an employee's remuneration is borne by a UK resident company acting as the 'economic employer'. This would apply where, for example, the employee is seconded to the UK company, which obtains the benefit and bears the risks in relation to work undertaken by the employee, and to which the non-resident employer recharges the remuneration costs. It would also apply where the non-resident employer carries on a business of hiring out staff to other companies. (Revenue Tax Bulletin June 1995 p 220). In the absence of a formal contract of employment, HMRC would not consider a UK company to be the employer of a short-term business visitor who is in the UK for less than 60 days in a tax year (the '*60-day rule*'), provided that that period does not form part of a more substantial period (for example, a period spanning two tax years) when the taxpayer is in the UK (Revenue Tax Bulletins October 1996 p 358, December 2003 pp 1069–1071).

UK partnerships

A UK partnership cannot be classed as UK resident for the purposes of claiming reliefs under a double tax agreement (as the partnership is not itself an entity chargeable to UK tax). For the purpose of enabling UK resident partners to claim such reliefs, HMRC will, if requested, confirm that those partners are UK resident and entitled to benefit from those reliefs. The information required by HMRC before they will issue a certificate of residence in respect of those partners is listed in HMRC Tax Bulletin August 2006 pp 1308, 1309. HMRC will not confirm partners' UK residence if they are of the opinion that to do so would not be in accordance with the relevant double tax agreement.

Special relationships — interest

Double tax agreements making provision in relation to interest may also contain a rule (a '*special relationship rule*') dealing with cases where, owing to a special relationship, the amount of interest paid exceeds the amount which would have been paid in the absence of that relationship, and requiring the interest provision to be applied only to that lower amount. Any such special relationship rule has to be construed:

- as requiring account to be taken of all factors, including whether, in the absence of the relationship, the loan would have been made at all, or would have been in a different amount, or a different rate of interest and other terms would have been agreed; this does not apply, however, where the special relationship rule expressly requires regard to be had to the debt on which the interest is paid in determining the excess interest (and accordingly expressly limits the factors to be taken into account); and
- as requiring the taxpayer either to show that no special relationship exists or to show the amount of interest which would have been paid in the absence of that relationship.

[*TIOPA 2010, s 131; ICTA 1988, s 808A*].

Simon's Taxes. See **E1.570, F1.5**.

Special relationships — royalties

Double tax agreements may contain a special relationship rule in relation to royalties. Such a rule operates similarly to a special relationship rule in relation to interest (see above). The special relationship rule may expressly require regard to be had to the use, right or information for which the royalties are paid in determining the excess royalties (and accordingly expressly limits the factors to be taken into account). The special relationship rule is to be read as requiring the taxpayer to show either that no special relationship exists or the amount of royalties which would have been payable in the absence of the relationship.

If the asset in respect of which the royalties are paid, or any asset which it represents or from which it is derived, has previously been in the beneficial ownership of:

(a)   the person (P) who is liable to pay the royalties;
(b)   person who is, or has at any time been, an associate (as specially defined) of P;
(c)   a person who has at any time carried on a business which, at the time when the liability to pay the royalties arises, is being carried on wholly or in partly by P; or
(d)   a person who is, or has at any time been, an associate (as specially defined) of a person within (c) above.

the special relationship rule is to be read as requiring account to be taken of the following factors:

(i)   amounts paid under the transaction(s) which resulted in the asset falling into its present beneficial ownership;

(ii)   the amounts which would have been so paid in the absence of the special relationship; and

(iii)   the question as to whether the transaction(s) would have taken place at all in the absence of that relationship.

The special relationship rule is to be read as requiring the taxpayer to either show that (a)–(d) above are not applicable or show that the transaction(s) mentioned in (i)–(iii) above would have taken place in the absence of a special relationship and the amounts which would then have been paid under those transaction(s).

[*TIOPA 2010, ss 132, 133; ICTA 1988, s 808B*].

Simon's Taxes. See **E1.570, F1.522.**

Ireland

[26.4] [*SI 1976 Nos 2151, 2152; SI 1995 No 764; SI 1998 No 3151*].

A Convention and Protocol 1976 (as subsequently amended) replace previous provisions between UK and Ireland. Shipping and air transport profits, certain trading profits not arising through a permanent establishment, interest, royalties, pensions (other than Government pensions and salaries which are normally taxed by the paying Government only) are taxed in the country of residence. Salaries, wages and other similar remuneration (including directors) is taxed in the country where earned unless the employer is non-resident and the employee is present for not more than 183 days in the fiscal year and is not paid by a permanent establishment.

HMRC take the view that a website, or a server on which e-commerce is conducted through a website, is not of itself a permanent establishment (Revenue Press Release 11 April 2000).

Where income is taxable in both countries, relief is given in the country of residence for the tax payable in the country of origin.

The recipient of a dividend from a company resident in the other country is entitled to the related tax credit (except where the recipient is a company which controls, alone or with associates, 10% or more of the voting power of the paying company). Income tax up to 15% of aggregate of dividend and tax credit may be charged in country of source (but not on charity or superannuation scheme exempt in other country).

See also **61.25 REMITTANCE BASIS** and **27.10 EMPLOYMENT INCOME** for restrictions on the application of the remittance basis for 2007/08 and earlier tax years (no longer applicable for 2008/09 onwards).

Anti-avoidance — relief by credit under double tax agreement

[26.5] Wide-ranging anti-avoidance provisions were introduced with effect in relation to any credit for foreign tax which is connected either with a payment of foreign tax on or after the commencement date or with income received on or after that date from which foreign tax has been deducted (or treated as deducted) at source. The commencement date was 16 March 2005, except to the extent that the scheme or arrangement falls within (iv) below in which case the commencement date was 10 February 2005. In addition, the provisions apply in relation to any action (or failure to act) that occurs under any scheme or arrangement after 5 December 2006.

HMRC may issue a notice (a counteraction notice) to any person, requiring that he make adjustments to (or amend) his tax return for the year in question to nullify the effects of a scheme or arrangement, where they have reasonable grounds to believe that, in relation to any income or chargeable gain taken into account in determining the tax liability for that year:

- relief by way of credit against UK tax is available under a double tax agreement for the foreign tax suffered on that income or gain;
- there is a scheme or arrangement the main purpose of which is to provide for an amount of foreign tax to be taken into account;
- the scheme or arrangement is a 'prescribed scheme or arrangement'; and
- the aggregate amount of credit relief which can be or has been claimed for that tax year by that person, and by any persons connected with him (within **21 CONNECTED PERSONS**), is at least £100,000 (see HMRC International Manual INTM170120).

According to HMRC International Manual INTM170120, a counteraction notice will not be issued in the simple case of an individual holding foreign shareholdings within an investment portfolio where the dividends are taxed as investment income (with credit for foreign tax deducted), but this let-out will not apply if income is received by a person for the purpose of benefiting from the let-out, for example where income is deliberately diverted from one person to another for that purpose.

There is no formal clearance procedure but HMRC will be prepared to give advice concerning actual or proposed transactions and, where appropriate, will confirm that no counteraction notice will be issued in respect of the disclosed transactions (see HMRC International Manual INTM170110).

A scheme or arrangement is a *'prescribed scheme or arrangement'* if any one or more of the following applies to it.

(i)   The scheme enables foreign tax that is properly attributable to one source of income or gain to be paid in respect of a different source of income or gain.

(ii)   It enables any scheme participant to claim credit for a payment of foreign tax that increases the total amount of foreign tax paid by all the scheme participants by less than the amount which that person can claim (for example, because the payment made by the claimant is matched by a tax saving for another scheme participant). In relation to foreign tax payable on or after 6 April 2010, it is no longer a necessary part of the condition that the claimant himself has paid any foreign tax.

(iii) Under the scheme, there is an amount of notional foreign tax and either:

- when the claimant entered into the scheme, it could reasonably be expected that, under the scheme, no *real* foreign tax would be paid or payable by a participant; or

- when the claimant entered into the scheme, it could reasonably be expected that, under the scheme, some real foreign tax would be paid or payable by a participant but it increases the total amount of foreign tax paid by all the scheme participants by less than the amount which the claimant can claim in respect of the notional foreign tax.

This has effect in relation to foreign tax deemed to be paid or payable on or after 21 October 2009 and is aimed principally at foreign tax deemed to have been deducted from manufactured overseas dividends (see **4.10 ANTI-AVOIDANCE**). In relation to foreign tax deemed to be payable on or after 6 April 2010, it is no longer a necessary part of the condition that the claimant himself is deemed to have paid any foreign tax.

(iv) It involves a scheme participant making a claim or election etc. or omitting to make a claim or election etc. which in either case has the effect of increasing the credit for foreign tax available to any scheme participant. References here to claims and elections or suchlike are to claims etc. made under the law of any territory or under the terms of a double tax agreement. In relation to foreign tax payable on or after 6 April 2010, a step taken or not taken by a scheme participant can be a step taken or omitted before a scheme comes into existence, and the reason for taking or not taking a step does not matter provided the effect is to increase the credit for foreign tax available to a scheme participant.

(v) It has the effect of reducing a scheme participant's total UK tax liability on income and chargeable gains to less than it would have been in the absence of the transactions made under the scheme. This will be the case, for example, where the credit for foreign tax on the scheme income covers not only the UK tax on that income but at least some of the UK tax on other income, thereby reducing total liability.

(vi) Under the scheme, a tax deductible payment is made by a person, in return for which that person, or a person connected with him (within **21 CONNECTED PERSONS**), receives consideration which is taxable in a foreign territory (and thus on which credit relief can be obtained in respect of the foreign tax).

Where a tax return is made within 90 days after the issue of a counteraction notice, the notice may be disregarded when making the return, as long as the return is then amended in accordance with the notice before the end of that 90-day period.

Once a tax return has been made, HMRC can only issue a counteraction notice if a notice of enquiry has been issued in respect of the return (see **63.6 RETURNS**), but an enquiry may be opened for just that purpose. If a counteraction notice is then issued, the taxpayer must amend the return accordingly within the 90 days beginning with the date of issue of the notice.

Failure to make or amend a return in accordance with a counteraction notice results in the return becoming an incorrect return (so that penalties potentially apply — see, for example, **55.10 PENALTIES**). An enquiry cannot be closed until either the amendment is made or the 90-day period for making it expires. Disputes between HMRC and taxpayer are settled under the normal self-assessment enquiry procedures and with the normal rights of appeal (see HMRC International Manual INTM170080).

Where an enquiry into a return has been completed, a counteraction notice can only be issued where HMRC could not have been reasonably expected to realise that a notice was required on the basis of the information supplied before the enquiry was completed, or, had requests for information by HMRC in the course of the enquiry been complied with, it is reasonable to suppose that they would have issued a notice at that time. Once a counteraction notice is issued in such circumstances, a related 'discovery' assessment cannot be made until either the necessary amendment is made to the tax return or the 90-day period for making it expires. The conditions at **6.6**(2) **ASSESSMENTS** for making a discovery assessment are disapplied (being replaced by the above conditions for issuing the notice).

[*TIOPA 2010, ss 81–85, 85A, 86–95, Sch 8 para 5; TMA 1970, s 29(7A); ICTA 1988, ss 804ZA–804ZC, Sch 28AB; FA 2007, s 35; FA 2010, Sch 11 paras 1–6*].

See generally HMRC International Manual INTM170000–170140.

Unilateral relief by UK

[26.6] The following applies where no credit is available for foreign tax under the bilateral double tax agreements in **26.2** above. Where:

- tax is paid under the law of a territory outside the UK;
- the tax is calculated by reference to income arising in that territory; and
- the tax is charged on income and corresponds to UK income tax or is charged on income or gains and corresponds to UK corporation tax (see further below).

Credit for the foreign tax is allowed against any UK income tax calculated by reference to that income.

Profits from personal or professional services performed in a territory are to be treated as income arising in that territory. The same applies to remuneration for such services.

[*TIOPA 2010, s 9(1)(3)(4); ICTA 1988, ss 790(1)–(4)(12)*]

See the Example at **26.12** below.

Corresponding taxes

Tax may correspond to income tax, corporation tax or capital gains tax even if it is payable under the law of a province, state or other part of a country or it is levied by or on behalf of a municipality or other local body. [*TIOPA 2010, s 9(6); ICTA 1988, s 790(12)*]. In *Yates v GCA International Ltd and cross-appeal* Ch D 1991, 64 TC 37, a tax imposed on gross receipts less a fixed 10% deduction was held to correspond to UK income tax or corporation tax. Following that decision, HMRC amended their practice (HMRC SP 7/91). Foreign taxes will be examined to determine whether, in their own legislative context, they serve the same function as UK income tax and corporation tax in relation to business profits, and are thus eligible for unilateral relief. As regards those foreign taxes which HMRC considers admissible (or inadmissible) for relief, these are listed by country in HMRC Double Taxation Relief Manual at DT2100 *et seq*. See also HMRC Business Income Manual BIM45900. Inadmissible foreign taxes may nevertheless be an allowable expense in computing income taxable in the UK under normal trading income rules. (HMRC International Manual INTM161080).

Residence requirement

The general rule is that relief by way of credit is not available against any UK tax for any tax year unless the person on whose income the UK tax is chargeable is resident in the UK for that year. [*TIOPA 2010, s 26(1); ICTA 1988, s 794(1)*]. This is subject to the following exceptions as regards unilateral relief.

(a)   *Channel Islands and Isle of Man.* Credit is allowed for tax paid under the law of the Isle of Man or any of the Channel Islands, if the claimant is resident either in the UK or in the Isle of Man or any of the Channel Islands, as the case may be. [*TIOPA 2010, s 28; ICTA 1988, s 794(2)(a)*].

(b)   *Employment income.* Credit for overseas tax on income from an office or employment, the duties of which are wholly or mainly performed in the overseas territory is given, against income tax on employment income computed by reference to that income, if the claimant is resident either in the UK or in the overseas territory. [*TIOPA 2010, s 29; ICTA 1988, s 794(2)(b)*].

(c)   *UK branch or agency.* Credit is available for foreign tax paid on the income of the UK branch or agency of a non-UK resident person provided the overseas territory in question is not one in which the person is liable to tax by reason of domicile, residence or place of management. However, the relief may not exceed the relief that would have been available if the branch or agency were a UK resident person. [*TIOPA 2010, s 30; ICTA 1988, s 794(2)(bb)*].

Apportionment of income

Where appropriate an apportionment must be made to determine what part of income may be regarded as 'arising in' the overseas territory, and in making that apportionment it is the principles of UK tax law which are to be applied (see *Yates v GCA International Ltd and cross-appeal* Ch D 1991, 64 TC 37 and HMRC SP 7/91).

Circumstances where no unilateral relief permitted

Unilateral relief will not be allowed where credit could be claimed under a double tax agreement under **26.2** above, or in cases or circumstances in which a double tax agreement specifically prohibits relief. [*TIOPA 2010, s 11; ICTA 1988, s 793A(2)(3)*].

Channel Islands and Isle of Man

The restriction to tax on income arising *in the territory* does not apply in the case of the Channel Islands or Isle of Man. See also (a) above. [*TIOPA 2010, s 9(7); ICTA 1988, s 790(5)(a)*].

Community tax

For 2009/10 onwards, unilateral relief is available for Community tax deducted from the salaries, transitional allowances and pensions of members of the European Parliament (MEPs) under the Statute for Members of the European Parliament (2005/684/EC, Euratom). The enabling legislation treats such tax as if it were payable under the law of a territory outside the UK. [*FA 2009, s 56(1)(3)*].

Limits on relief

[26.7] Where income is chargeable to UK income tax, credit for foreign tax suffered on that income reduces the income tax chargeable in respect of the doubly taxed income. The reduction is made at Step 6 of the calculation of income tax liability — see **1.7, 1.8 ALLOWANCES AND TAX RATES**. This applies whether the credit is given under a double tax agreement or unilaterally. [*TIOPA 2010, ss 9(1)–(3), 18; ICTA 1988, ss 790(4), 793; ITA 2007, Sch 1 para 192*].

But the reduction is limited to the difference between the income tax to which the claimant would be liable (before double tax relief but after any other income tax reduction other than the reduction at **68.19 SETTLEMENTS** available to trusts with vulnerable beneficiaries):

(i)   if he were charged on his total income; and

(ii)   if he were charged on his total income *excluding* the income in respect of which the credit is to be allowed.

In all cases, the tax reduction is restricted to the extent (if any) that it would otherwise exceed the income tax liability after other reductions have been made — see **1.8 ALLOWANCES AND TAX RATES** and before making any additions at Step 7 at **1.7 ALLOWANCES AND TAX RATES**. For 2006/07 and earlier years, for this purpose, a person's income tax liability is reduced by any income tax he is entitled to charge against any other person. For 2007/08 onwards, for this purpose and for the purposes of the corresponding capital gains relief, a person's combined income tax and capital gains tax liability is reduced by any tax deemed to have been deducted by him from Gift Aid donations (see **16.16 CHARITIES**).

If credit for foreign tax is available in respect of income from more than one source, the comparison at (i) and (ii) above is made successively in relation to the income from each source, taking the sources in the order which will result in the greatest reduction in the person's income tax liability for the tax year. Each time a comparison is made after the first, all the income for which a comparison has previously been made is excluded from total income in (i) and (ii) above.

[*TIOPA 2010, ss 36, 41; ICTA 1988, s 796; ITA 2007, Sch 1 para 193; SI 2007 No 3506, Reg 3(5); SI 2009 No 2859, Art 4(6)*].

It is in addition provided that relief is limited to that which would be allowed if all reasonable steps had been taken, including all relevant claims, elections etc., under the law of the territory concerned or under a double tax agreement with that territory, to minimise the foreign tax payable. [*TIOPA 2010, s 33; ICTA 1988, s 795A*].

As regards what HMRC consider that taxpayers can and cannot reasonably be expected to do to minimise foreign tax payable, the former is likely to include appeals against excessive assessments, claims for reliefs generally known to be available, and selection of any option which produces a lower tax liability, and the latter is likely to include claims to reliefs whose availability is uncertain, and where disproportionate expenditure would be required to pursue a claim, substituting carry-forward claims for carry-back claims and *vice versa*, and attempting to exercise influence the taxpayer does not have. See the note on the HMRC website at www.hmrc.gov.uk/international/dtr26.htm. The taking of reasonable steps should not, however, be interpreted as meaning that the taxpayer should have entered into a completely different, albeit economically similar, transaction to the one actually entered into (*Hill Samuel Investments Ltd v HMRC* (Sp C 738), [2009] SSCD 315).

Trade income

The following additional restriction applies if the tax against which the credit is to be allowed is income tax on 'trade income'. For this purpose, *'trade income'* comprises profits of a trade, profession or vocation (see **73 TRADING INCOME**) or of a property business (see **60.2 PROPERTY INCOME**), post-cessation receipts from any of these (see **59 POST-CESSATION RECEIPTS AND EXPENDITURE** and **60.6 PROPERTY INCOME**) and overseas property income (see **60.3 PROPERTY INCOME**).

The comparison at (i) and (ii) above is to be undertaken on the basis of net income (after any allowable deductions) rather than, as before, gross income, i.e. the foreign tax credit is restricted by reference to profit rather than income. As well as deducting expenses etc. that are directly attributable to the income, one must also allocate and deduct a just and reasonable proportion of expenses etc. that are only partly attributable, e.g. overheads. In making the said comparison, royalties from different non-UK jurisdictions in respect of the same asset, and foreign tax credits in respect of such income, are to be aggregated.

In relation to foreign tax paid (or suffered at source) on or after 6 April 2008, it is made clear that the trade income to be taken into account as above is the trade income arising out of the transaction, arrangement or asset in connection with which the credit for foreign tax arises. The intention is that relief should not be given against UK tax due on income that is unrelated to the payment of the foreign tax.

[*TIOPA 2010, ss 37, 38; ICTA 1988, s 798; FA 2008, s 57*].

See HMRC International Manual INTM168010–168065.

Relief for disallowed credit

Where an amount of credit for foreign tax is disallowed because of the application of *TIOPA 2010, s 36* above, the taxpayer's income is treated as reduced by the amount of disallowed credit. This has effect in relation to a credit for foreign tax in connection with either with a payment of foreign tax or with income received in respect of which foreign tax has deducted at source, and has effect notwithstanding the general rule at **26.9**(a)(ii) below. The amount of the reduction is the lower of the disallowed credit and the amount of any loss, *after* deducting the foreign tax, that arises from the transaction that gives rise to the foreign tax payment; if there is no such loss, no reduction is available. [*TIOPA 2010, s 35; ICTA 1988, s 798C; ITA 2007, Sch 1 para 194*].

Claims for relief

[26.8] Claims made on or after 1 April 2010 for credit relief, whether under a double tax agreement or unilaterally, must be made on or before the later of:

- the fourth anniversary of the end of the tax year in which the income falls to be charged to tax; and
- 31 January following the tax year in which the foreign tax is paid.

Claims made before 1 April 2010 had to be made for income tax purposes on or before the later of

- the fifth anniversary of 31 January following the tax year in which the income falls to be charged to tax; and
- 31 January following the tax year in which the foreign tax is paid.

[*TIOPA 2010, s 19(2); ICTA 1988, s 806(1); FA 2008, Sch 39 para 24; SI 2009 No 403*].

In a case where the claim relates to a tax year for which the taxpayer has not been given notice to make a return within one year after the end of the tax year (in effect, where the taxpayer is outside self-assessment), the above change in the time limit for making claims applies from 1 April 2012 rather than 1 April 2010. This only applies where tax has been *overpaid*, its purpose being to allow taxpayers extra time to take appropriate action. [*SI 2009 No 403, Art 10*].

Written notice must be given to HMRC where any credit allowed for foreign tax has become excessive by reason of an adjustment of the amount of any foreign tax payable (except in the case of **UNDERWRITERS AT LLOYD'S (74)** where the consequences of such an adjustment are dealt with under regulations). The notice must be given within one year after the making of the adjustment. The maximum penalty for failure to comply is the amount by which the credit was rendered excessive by the adjustment. The time limit for assessments etc. to be revised following such an adjustment is extended to six years after the adjustment is finalised. See HMRC International Manual INTM162120.

[*TIOPA 2010, ss 79, 80; ICTA 1988, s 806(2)–(6); FA 2009, s 59(3)–(7), (13)*].

For appeals, see **62.8 RESIDENCE, ORDINARY RESIDENCE AND DOMICILE.** Pending final agreement, a provisional allowance can usually be obtained on application to HMRC.

Miscellaneous

[26.9] The following miscellaneous items are relevant.

(a)

(i) **Amounts chargeable in UK on the REMITTANCE BASIS (61).** Where double tax credit for foreign tax is allowable in respect of it, any income which is chargeable on the remittance basis is treated, for UK tax purposes, as increased by the foreign tax on that income (but ignoring any notional foreign tax under (d) below). [*TIOPA 2010, s 32(1)(2)(5)(6); ICTA 1988, s 795(1)(3)*].

(ii) **Amounts chargeable in UK on the arising basis.** Where income is chargeable to income tax on the basis of the full amount arising (i.e. not on the remittance basis as in (i) above), and double tax credit relief is allowable given by credit in respect of foreign tax suffered on it, no deduction may can be made for any foreign tax in computing the amount of the income for UK tax purposes. [*TIOPA 2010, s 31(1)(2); ICTA 1988, s 795(2)*].

(iii) **If the taxpayer does not take any credit** by way of either bilateral or unilateral relief, or if no UK double tax credit is otherwise allowable in respect of foreign income, any tax paid on that income in the place where it arises is generally deductible from the income for the purposes of charging it to UK tax, unless the charge to UK tax is on the remittance basis. Where foreign tax for which such a deduction has been given is subsequently adjusted, similar provisions to those which apply by virtue of *TIOPA 2010, s 80* in the case of foreign tax credits (see **26.8** above) apply as regards the requirement to notify HMRC of the adjustment and extended time limit for assessments etc. In relation to foreign tax paid on or after 6 April 2010, an amendment is made to ensure that the foreign tax can be deducted only once. [*TIOPA 2010, ss 112–115; ICTA 1988, ss 805, 811; ITA 2007, Sch 1 para 200; FA 2009, s 59(8)–(13); FA 2010, Sch 11 para 7*].

(b) **Exchange rate.** Foreign tax is normally converted into sterling at the rate of exchange obtaining on the date it became payable. (HMRC International Manual INTM162160). Where part of foreign tax repaid and sterling was devalued in the period between payment and repayment, held relief due on net tax in foreign currency at the old rate (*Greig v Ashton* Ch D 1956, 36 TC 581).

(c) **Lloyd's underwriters.** For special arrangements for double tax relief for Lloyd's underwriters, see *SI 1997 No 405*.

(d) **Notional foreign tax.** It may be provided in a double tax agreement that any tax which would have been payable in a foreign country but for a relief under the law of that territory given with a view to promoting industrial, commercial, scientific, educational or other development therein is nevertheless treated for purposes of credit against UK tax as if it had been paid. [*TIOPA 2010, ss 4, 20; ICTA 1988, s 788(5)*]. See, for example, HMRC Double Taxation Relief Manual at DT12758 in the case of Malaysia and at DT16911 in the case of Singapore.

(e) **Overlap profits** Credit for foreign tax paid in respect of 'overlap profits' (see **73.11** TRADING INCOME) arising in taxing a trade etc. is allowed against UK income tax chargeable for any year in respect of that income, notwithstanding that credit for that foreign tax has already been allowed in an earlier year. There are overriding provisions limiting the credit allowable for any year by reference to the total of credit due for all the relevant years as above, and for cases where the number of UK tax years exceeds the number of foreign periods of assessment. The relief requires a claim to be made on or before the fifth anniversary of 31 January following the tax year for which relief is claimed or, if there is more than one, following the later of those tax years.

Recovery of excess credit applies where, and to the extent that, relief is given for overlap profits either on cessation of the trade or on a change of accounting date resulting in a basis period of longer than twelve months. Recovery is achieved by reducing the credit otherwise available for the year of relief and, if there is still an excess, by charging an amount of income tax for that year.

[*TIOPA 2010, ss 22–24; ICTA 1988, s 804; ITA 2007, Sch 1 para 197*].

(f) **Partnerships.** It was held in the case of *Padmore v CIR* CA 1989, 62 TC 352 that, where profits of a non-UK resident partnership were exempt under the relevant double tax treaty, the profit share of a UK resident partner was thereby also exempt. This decision was, however, reversed by subsequent legislation with retrospective effect, see **52.20** PARTNER-SHIPS.

(g) **Prevention of double relief.** Credit will not be given for foreign tax for which relief is available in the territory in which it would otherwise be payable, either under a double tax agreement or under the law of that territory in consequence of any double tax agreement or in cases or circumstances in which such an agreement specifically prohibits relief. [*TIOPA 2010, s 25; ICTA 1988, s 793A(1)*].

(h) **Alimony.** Where alimony payments etc. under UK Court Order or agreement (technically a UK source) are made by an overseas resident, concessional relief by way of credit is allowed where (i) the payments are made out of the overseas income of the payer and subject to tax there, (ii) UK income tax if deducted from the payments is duly accounted for, and (iii) the payee is resident in the UK and effectively bears the overseas tax. (HMRC ESC A12).

(i) **Royalties and 'know-how' payments.** Notwithstanding that credit for overseas tax is ordinarily given only against income which arises (or is deemed to arise) in the overseas territory concerned, HMRC's treatment as regards this class of income is as follows.

Income payments made by an overseas resident to a UK trader for the use, in that overseas territory, of any *copyright, patent, design, secret process or formula, trade mark etc.*, may be treated, for credit purposes (whether under double tax agreements or by way of unilateral relief) as income arising outside the UK — *except* so far as they represent consideration for services (other than merely incidental) rendered in the UK by the recipient to the payer (HMRC ESC B8).

For the treatment of sales of 'know-how' etc., see **73.91** TRADING INCOME.

(j) **UK residents and foreign enterprises.** In relation to income arising on or after 12 March 2008, where a double tax agreement contains the following provision (however expressed), it is not to be taken as preventing income of a *UK resident* person being chargeable to income tax. For these purposes, a person is UK resident if he is UK resident for the purposes of the double tax agreement. The provision is that the profits of an enterprise which is resident outside the UK, or carries on a trade, profession or business the control or management of which is situated outside the UK, are not to be subject to UK tax except in so far as they are attributable to a permanent establishment of the enterprise in the UK. [*TIOPA 2010, s 130; ICTA 1988, s 815AZA; FA 2008, s 59; CTA 2009, Sch 1 para 264*].

(k) **Payments by reference to foreign tax.** Where a person (P) is entitled under a double tax agreement to a credit for foreign tax paid and, on or after 22 April 2009, a payment is made by a tax authority to P by reference to that foreign tax, the amount of the credit is reduced by the amount of the payment. The same applies if the payment is to a person connected with P (within **21** CONNECTED PERSONS). [*TIOPA 2010, s 130; ICTA 1988, s 804G; FA 2009, s 59(2)(13)*]. If relief for the foreign tax is given by way of deduction as opposed to credit (see (a)(iii) above), P's income is increased by the amount of the payment made. [*TIOPA 2010, s 112(3)(7); ICTA 1988, s 811(3A)(3B); FA 2009, s 59(9)(13)*].

Where any credit allowed for foreign tax has become excessive by reason of a reduction as above, *TIOPA 2010, s 80* (see **26.8** above) applies as regards the requirement to notify HMRC of the reduction and as regards the extended time limit for assessments and claims. A similar requirement and extension applies under *TIOPA 2010, ss 114, 115* where the amount of P's income falls to be increased as above.

Payments abroad by UK residents

[26.10] Under *SI 1970 No 488*, if a UK resident pays income to a resident of a country with which the UK has a double tax agreement income, and under that agreement the income is wholly or partially relieved, the payer may be required, by notice from the Commissioners for HMRC, to make such payments without deducting UK income tax, or under deduction of tax at, or not exceeding, a specified rate. Applications for such relief from deduction should be sent to IR International — Centre for Non-Residents, Fitz Roy House, PO Box 46, Nottingham NG2 1BD. Where a notice is given, the payer, if otherwise chargeable with, or liable to account for, tax on such payments (**24 DEDUCTION OF TAX AT SOURCE**) is exempted from that liability if the notice requires him to pay the income gross, and in other cases need account for tax only at the rate specified. Prior to 2007/08, the payer could, nevertheless, treat the gross amount of the payment as a loss for relief purposes (see **45.24 LOSSES**). Also prior to 2007/08, if the payment was made by a company it was treated for the purposes of treatment as a charge on income as if tax had been deducted from it and accounted for under *ICTA 1988, s 349, Sch 16*. Similarly, where the payer would have been entitled (under *ICTA 1988, s 348*) to retain the tax deducted (as having made the payment out of income subjected to income tax) he was given, against the income tax otherwise payable by him for that year, an allowance equal to the additional tax which, but for the notice, he would have been entitled to deduct from the payment.

For HMRC practice in relation to claims for payment of interest to non-residents without deduction of tax, and in particular where payments are made in full in advance of the issue (or refusal) of a gross payment notice, see Revenue Tax Bulletin August 1994 p 153.

For review of applications for relief from deduction where loans are re-denominated from one currency to another (e.g. to or from the euro), see Revenue Tax Bulletin February 1999 pp 631, 632.

Companies

[26.11] Companies enjoy the benefit of the foregoing double tax reliefs and they can in certain circumstances claim relief for 'underlying tax' in respect of overseas dividends receivable by them. 'Underlying tax' refers to the overseas taxes borne by the paying company on its profits). See the corresponding chapter of Tolley's Corporation Tax.

Example of relief by credit

[26.12]

A single man has, for 2010/11, UK earnings of £17,930 and foreign income from property of £2,000 on which foreign tax of £300 has been paid. He is entitled to the personal allowance of £6,475.

(a) *Tax on total income*	£	
Earnings	17,930	
Income from property	2,000	(foreign tax £300)
	19,930	
Personal allowance	6,475	
Taxable income	£13,455	
Tax on £13,455 @ 20%	£2,691.00	

(b) *Tax on total income less foreign income*	£
Earnings	17,930
Personal allowance	6,475
Taxable income	£11,455
Tax on £11,455 @ 20%	£2,291.00

The difference in tax between (a) and (b) is £400. The foreign tax is less than this and full credit of £300 is available against the UK tax payable. If the foreign tax was £600, the credit would be limited to £400 and the balance of £200 would be unrelieved.

EU Savings Directive — special withholding tax

[26.13] Under the EU Savings Directive (*Directive 2003/48/EC* (see **63.15** RETURNS), which came into force on 1 July 2005, three EU member States (Austria, Belgium and Luxembourg) will, for a transitional period, impose a 'special withholding tax' on the interest and other 'savings income' of individuals resident in the EU but outside the State in question. This is to be levied at 15% for the first three years, 20% for the next three and 35% thereafter, and is an alternative to the automatic exchange of information on cross-border payments which is envisaged by the Directive. Some of the non-EU countries applying similar measures as the Directive, and countries with which the UK has made equivalent arrangements, are also imposing a special withholding tax. These are Andorra, Liechtenstein, San Marino, Monaco and Switzerland, and the British Virgin Islands, Guernsey, the Isle of Man, Jersey, the Netherlands Antilles and the Turks and Caicos Islands.

The legislation described at **26.14, 26.15** below provides for relief to be given for the special withholding tax against UK income tax and capital gains tax liabilities or, to the extent that set-off is not possible, by repayment. It also provides, as an alternative, for application to be made to HMRC for a certificate which can be presented to a paying agent to enable savings income to be paid to the individual without deduction of the special withholding tax.

In these provisions, *'special withholding tax'* means a withholding tax (however described) levied under the law of a territory outside the UK implementing the relevant provision (*Article 11*) of the EU Savings Directive or, in the case of a non-EU member state, any corresponding provision of equivalent international arrangements (whatever the period for which the provision is to have effect). 'Savings income' means income within the scope of the EU Savings Directive or the equivalent international arrangements in question. [TIOPA 2010, s 136; FA 2004, s 107].

Pre-existing legislation giving double tax relief by way of credit, as described elsewhere in this chapter, does not apply for the purposes of special withholding tax, and such tax is not regarded as a foreign tax for the purposes of such provisions.

Relief by way of credit

[26.14] Where a UK resident is chargeable to income tax for a tax year on a payment of savings income (or would be so chargeable but for any exemption or relief available) and special withholding tax is levied, the special withholding tax is treated, on the making of a claim, as if it were tax deducted at source from the payment of income. To the extent that the special withholding tax so treated exceeds his income tax liability for the year, the excess is set against any capital gains tax liability of his for the year and any balance repaid to him. To the extent, however, that he is also resident in another territory in that tax year, or is treated as such under a double tax treaty, and obtains relief for the special withholding tax under the law of that territory, he is not entitled to the above relief.

A similar relief applies where a UK resident makes a disposal of assets which is within the scope of capital gains tax and the consideration for the disposal consists of or includes an amount of savings income subjected to special withholding tax. On the making of a claim, a credit is given against his capital gains tax liability (if any) for the tax year, with any excess given against his income tax liability and any balance repaid. For the purposes of certain specified self-assessment provisions (for example in determining the amount of a balancing payment as in **65.7 SELF-ASSESSMENT**) the credit is treated as if it were income tax deducted at source. For more details of the capital gains tax credit, see the equivalent coverage in Tolley's Capital Gains Tax.

Where, for any tax year, double tax relief by way of credit is available for any foreign tax suffered, the credit for foreign tax is given in priority to any credit due as above for special withholding tax. This is to ensure that the taxpayer gets maximum relief, since excess foreign tax is not repayable.

Special withholding tax is not deductible in computing amounts of chargeable income or chargeable gains.

Where an amount of savings income is chargeable to income tax on the **REMITTANCE BASIS (61)**, the amount received is treated as increased by any special withholding tax levied in respect of it and claimed under these provisions.

[TIOPA 2010, ss 135–143; FA 2004, ss 107–111].

Certificate to avoid levy of special withholding tax

[26.15] A person may make written application to HMRC for a certificate which he may then present to his paying agent. The paying agent will not then levy special withholding tax on savings income from the investment covered by the certificate. The application must include the person's name, address and national insurance number, the account number of the investment in question (or, if there is no such number, a statement identifying the investment), the name and address of the paying agent, the period for which the applicant would like the certificate to be valid (the maximum period of validity is three years) and any documents required by HMRC to verify the said information. HMRC must issue the certificate within two months after the applicant provides the said information and documents. These requirements may be modified as necessary where international arrangements differ from the EU Savings Directive as regards the issue of such certificates.

If HMRC are not satisfied that the applicant has provided them with the requisite information and documents, they must give the applicant written notice, stating their reasons, of their refusal to issue a certificate. The applicant may give written notice of appeal against the refusal within 30 days after the date of the refusal notice. On appeal to the Appeal Tribunal, the Tribunal may either confirm or quash the refusal notice.

[*TIOPA 2010, ss 144, 145; FA 2004, ss 113, 114; SI 2009 No 56, Sch 1 para 422*].

It would appear that certification is only possible in practice if the territory in which the savings income arises has adopted this option as a means of avoiding withholding tax (see www.hmrc.gov.uk/esd-guidance/app-for-cert.htm). An alternative option is for the individual to authorise the overseas paying agent to report details of the savings income payment to its own tax authority, who will in turn supply it to HMRC; the individual will have to follow whatever procedures are prescribed for this purpose by the territory where the paying agent is established (see www.hmrc.gov.uk/esd/paper-11-final.htm).

27

Employment Income

Cross-references. See **20 COMPENSATION FOR LOSS OF EMPLOYMENT (AND DAMAGES); 26 DOUBLE TAX RELIEF; 45.33 LOSSES; 46 MANAGED SERVICE COMPANIES; 62 RESIDENCE, ORDINARY RESIDENCE AND DOMICILE** for definitions of those terms; **53 PAY AS YOU EARN; 54 PAYMENT OF TAX; 56 PENSION INCOME; 57 PENSION PROVISION; 58 PERSONAL SERVICE COMPANIES ETC.; 69 SHARE-RELATED EMPLOYMENT INCOME AND EXEMPTIONS; 70 SOCIAL SECURITY AND NATIONAL INSURANCE** for taxation of benefits.

Simon's Taxes. See **Part E4.**

Introduction

[27.1] This chapter is concerned with the taxation of income from employment.

'Employment' is not exhaustively defined, but includes any employment under a contract of service or apprenticeship or in the service of the Crown. [*ITEPA 2003, s 4*]. Except as otherwise provided, the provisions apply equally to any 'office', which in particular includes any position which has an existence independent of the person holding it and may be filled by successive holders (and see HMRC Employment Status Manual ESM2502 *et seq.*). [*ITEPA 2003, s 5*].

The charge to tax on employment income is divided into a charge on 'general earnings' (see **27.20** below) and a charge on '*specific employment income*', i.e. amounts which count as employment income (in particular payments to and benefits from pension schemes, see **57 PENSION PROVISION** ; payments and benefits on termination of employments etc., see **20 COMPENSATION FOR LOSS OF EMPLOYMENT (AND DAMAGES)**; and share-related income, see **69 SHARE-RELATED EMPLOYMENT INCOME AND EXEMPTIONS**). The provisions described in **27.3–27.16** below relate only to the charge on general earnings. [*ITEPA 2003, ss 6, 7; FA 2007, s 25, Sch 3 para 2; FA 2008, Sch 7 paras 3, 80, 81*].

The amount of *general earnings* chargeable for a particular year from an employment is the net taxable earnings for the year from the employment. The taxable earnings are determined as described in **27.3–27.16** below.

Subject to the possible application of the remittance basis to share-related income (see **69.18 SHARE-RELATED EMPLOYMENT INCOME AND EXEMPTIONS**) the amount of *specific employment income* chargeable for a particular year from an employment is the net taxable specific income from the employment. The taxable specific income is the full amount which counts as employment income for that year under the relevant provision.

The deductions allowed in arriving at *net taxable earnings* or *net taxable specific income* from an employment are as described in **27.22–27.24** below, but such deductions may not reduce the taxable amount from any source below nil. If there is more than one kind of specific employment income from an employment in a year, a separate calculation is required for each. If, exceptionally, taxable earnings or net taxable earnings are negative, loss relief against general income may be available as in **45.33 LOSSES**.

[*ITEPA 2003, ss 9–12; ITA 2007, Sch 1 para 427; FA 2008, Sch 7 paras 4, 80, 81*].

For the tax treatment of particular occupations, see HMRC Employment Income Manual EIM50000 *et seq.*

Person liable for tax

[27.2] On *general earnings*, the person liable to tax thereon is the person to whose employment the earnings relate. If the tax is on such earnings received, or remitted to the UK, after the death of that person, the liability falls on the personal representatives, and is payable out of the estate. On *specific employment income*, the person liable to tax thereon is the person in relation to whom the income is to count as employment income under the provision in question. In relation to shares or share options acquired on or after 6 April 2008 (but not shares acquired on or after that date under an option acquired before that date), if the tax is on share-related income (see **69 SHARE-RELATED EMPLOY-**

MENT INCOME AND EXEMPTIONS) received, or remitted to the UK, after the death of that person, the liability falls on the personal representatives, and is payable out of the estate. [*ITEPA 2003, s 13; FA 2008, Sch 7 paras 5, 80, 81*]. See, however, HMRC Concession A37, referred to at **27.3**(v) below.

General earnings — basis of assessment

[27.3] The basis on which taxable general earnings for a tax year are determined **for 2008/09 onwards** depend on whether the employee is, in that year, (a) UK resident (see **62 RESIDENCE, ORDINARY RESIDENCE AND DOMICILE**), (b) a person to whom the remittance basis applies (see **61.2 REMITTANCE BASIS**) or (c) non-UK resident. See **27.4–27.8** below.

The basis on which taxable general earnings for a tax year are determined before 2008/09 depend on whether the employee is, in that year, (a) UK resident, ordinarily resident and domiciled in the UK or (b) either resident, ordinarily resident or domiciled outside the UK (for both of which see **62 RESIDENCE, ORDINARY RESIDENCE AND DOMICILE**). See **27.9** and **27.10** below.

Subject to any specific provision requiring earnings to be treated as 'for' a particular tax year, general earnings are earned 'for' a period if they are earned in, or in respect of, the period. If the period is or is within a tax year, they are earned for that year: if the period extends over two or more tax years, they are apportioned between those years on a just and reasonable basis. Earnings (other than benefits in kind, see **27.28** below) which would accordingly be treated as for a tax year in which the employee does not hold the employment are instead treated as for the first year in which the employment is held (if later) or the last such year (if earlier)(but not if any of the years concerned is earlier than 1989/90).

[*ITEPA 2003, ss 14, 16, 17, 20, 29, 30, Sch 7 para 8(4); FA 2008, Sch 7 paras 6, 7, 11, 81*].

The following **general matters** apply.

(i) **Leave periods etc.** If a person ordinarily performs the whole or part of the duties of an employment in the UK, general earnings for periods of absence from the employment are treated as for duties performed in the UK except insofar as, but for that absence, they would have been for duties performed outside the UK. [*ITEPA 2003, s 38*]. An airline pilot, the great majority of whose work was performed outside the UK, could not rely on this provision to treat his days of absence from work as days of absence from the UK in the same proportion as his working days (*Leonard v Blanchard* CA 1993, 65 TC 589).

(ii) **Incidental duties in the UK.** If an employment is substantially one where the duties for a year fall to be performed outside the UK, any duties incidental thereto performed in the UK are treated as if performed abroad. [*ITEPA 2003, s 39*]. As to whether duties 'incidental' to foreign duties see *Robson v Dixon* Ch D 1972, 48 TC 527 (airline pilot employed abroad but occasionally landing in UK where family home maintained, held UK duties more than incidental). HMRC will normally disregard a single take-off and landing on *de minimis* grounds. (HMRC SP A10). See also HMRC Pamphlet IR 20, paras 5.7, 5.8. Different rules apply in relation to the 100% foreign earnings deduction available to seafarers (see **27.17** below).

(iii) **Duties deemed to be performed in the UK.** As regards certain overseas *employments under the Crown*, see **27.5** and **27.10** below.

Duties of *seafarers and aircraft crew* are treated as performed in the UK if (i) the voyage does not extend to a port outside the UK or (ii) the person concerned is UK-resident and either (a) the voyage or flight begins or ends in the UK or (b) it is a part, beginning or ending in the UK, of a voyage or flight which does not begin or end in the UK. As regards seafarers' duties on board ship, this does *not* apply for the purpose of determining whether the duties of an 'associated employment' are performed wholly outside the UK (for which see **27.5** and **27.10** below); for this purpose, duties performed on a ship during a voyage beginning or ending outside the UK (other than any part of it beginning and ending there), or on a part beginning or ending outside the UK of any other voyage, are treated as performed outside the UK. The UK includes areas designated under *Continental Shelf Act 1964, s 1(7)* for this purpose. A 'ship' does not include an offshore installation (within *ITA 2007, s 1001*). [*ITEPA 2003, s 40*]. See **27.17** below for the meaning of 'seafarer'.

(iv) **United Kingdom** for these purposes includes the UK sector of the continental shelf (under *Continental Shelf Act 1964, s 1(7)* as regards duties performed there in connection with exploration or exploitation activities. [*ITEPA 2003, s 41*].

(v) **Directors' fees received by other companies.** Where a company has the right to appoint a director to the board of another company and the director is required to hand over to the first company any fees or other earnings received from the second company and does so, and the first company agrees to accept liability to corporation tax on the fees etc., the director is not charged to tax on thereon. Where the first company is not chargeable to corporation tax but to income tax (e.g. a non-resident company not trading through a branch or agency/permanent establishment in the UK) and agrees to accept liability, tax is deducted at the basic rate from the fees etc. This practice is extended to the case where the first company has no formal right to appoint the director to the board but the director is required to, and does, hand over his fees etc., provided the first company is (a) chargeable to corporation tax on its income and (b) not a company over which the director has control. '*Control*' for this purpose has the meaning given by *ITA 2007, s 995*, but in determining whether the director has control of the company the rights and powers of his spouse, his children and their spouses and his parents, will also be taken into account. (HMRC ESC A37). For directors' fees received by professional partnerships, see **27.54** below.

(vi) **Changes in practice.** Where income dealt with under PAY AS YOU EARN (53) was received more than twelve months before the beginning of the year *in* which the assessment on the income is made, that assessment, if made after the period of twelve months following the year *for* which it is made, is to accord with the practice generally prevailing at the end of that period. [*ITEPA 2003, s 709*]. This cannot, however, displace an unqualified statutory exemption relating to the income in question (*Walters v Tickner* CA 1993, 66 TC 174).

(vii)   **Divers.** See **73.24 TRADING INCOME** for treatment of earnings of certain divers etc. under Schedule D, Case I.

Simon's Taxes. See E4.101–E4.132, E4.403.

Employee resident in the UK — 2008/09 onwards

[27.4] Subject to **27.5** below, where general earnings are for a tax year in which the employee is resident in the UK, the full amount of such earnings 'received' in a tax year (see **27.16** below) is taxable earnings in that year, whether or not the employment is held when the earnings are received. [*ITEPA 2003, s 15; FA 2008, Sch 7 paras 8, 9, 81*].

See **27.5** below for the various circumstances in which the earnings of an employee to whom the remittance basis applies fall within the above paragraph.

Employee to whom the remittance basis applies — 2008/09 onwards

[27.5] For the question of whether the remittance basis applies to an individual for a tax year, see **61.2 REMITTANCE BASIS**) and note in particular that the remittance basis can only apply to an individual if he is (i) resident in the UK, but *either* (ii) not domiciled in the UK or (iii) not ordinarily resident in the UK, but that it does not automatically apply to such an individual.

Allowable deductions under the remittance basis

Expenses which would be allowable (see **27.22–27.24** below) against earnings taxed on the receipts basis are generally allowable against earnings taxed on the remittance basis. No deduction is, however, allowable for an amount paid in respect of the duties of an employment to which earnings taxed other than on the remittance basis relate. Capital allowances are not available for expenditure on plant or machinery (see **11.4**(ii) **CAPITAL ALLOWANCES ON PLANT AND MACHINERY**). [*ITEPA 2003, ss 353, 354*].

Employee ordinarily resident in UK

[27.6] To the extent that they are 'chargeable overseas earnings' for a tax year, the full amount of general earnings remitted to the UK in any tax year (not necessarily the year in which they arose) is taxable earnings in that year, whether or not the employment is held when the earnings are remitted. See **61 REMITTANCE BASIS** for the meaning of 'remitted to the UK' etc. To the extent that the earnings are not chargeable overseas earnings, they fall within **27.4** above.

General earnings are overseas earnings for a tax year if the employee is ordinarily resident in the UK, the remittance basis applies to him, the employment is with a 'foreign employer' and the duties of the employment are performed wholly outside the UK. Generally, *'chargeable overseas earnings'* are the full amount of overseas earnings reduced by any deductions which would be allowable if they were taxable earnings. *However*, where the duties of any 'associated' employment are not performed wholly outside the UK, the chargeable overseas earnings are then limited to a reasonable proportion of the aggregate earnings (after allowable deductions) from all the employments, having regard to the nature of and the time devoted to duties performed outside and in the UK and to all other relevant considerations. Employments are *'associated'* if they are with the same employer, or the employers are under common control or one controls the other, control being as in *CTA 2010, ss 450, 451* (for companies) and *ITA 2007, s 995* (for individuals and partnerships). The amount by which chargeable overseas earnings are thus restricted falls back into charge under **27.4** above.

'Foreign employer' means an individual, partnership or body of persons (including a company) resident outside, and not resident in, the UK.

The above applies equally to general earnings for 2007/08 and earlier years where those earnings are remitted to the UK in 2008/09 or a later year, but only if in the year the earnings arose the employee was UK resident and either not ordinarily resident or not domiciled in the UK. For these purposes only, the remittance basis is then treated as having applied to the employee for that earlier year. In relation to such pre-2008/09 general earnings, *'foreign employer'* means an individual, partnership or body of persons (including a company) resident outside, and not resident in, the UK *and not resident in the Republic of Ireland*. Pre-2008/09 general earnings that are not chargeable overseas earnings do not fall within **27.4** above as they will already have been taxed on the receipts basis (see **27.10, 27.16** below).

In their April 2005 Tax Bulletin, HMRC announced a change of emphasis in the way that they will approach enquiries into dual contract arrangements. A non-UK domiciled employee may, for example, be offered two employment contracts, one with a UK employer and the other with an associated 'foreign employer', the intended effect being to create or maximise 'chargeable overseas earnings'. The Tax Bulletin article explains HMRC's pre-existing approach to dual contract arrangements and their change of emphasis. In particular, they do not consider that the existence of separate and distinct employments is determined by the terms of dual contracts where the main distinction between each contract's duties is merely geographical, and are concerned that arrangements of this nature artificially divide a single job. They have apparently now received legal advice in support of this view, and such arrangements are thus increasingly vulnerable to challenge; dual contract arrangements seem unlikely to be accepted by HMRC as effective unless there are two distinguishable jobs. (Revenue Tax Bulletin April 2005 pp 1201–1204).

Employee not ordinarily resident in UK

[27.7] If they are 'foreign earnings' for a tax year, the full amount of general earnings remitted' to the UK in any tax year (not necessarily the year in which they arose) is taxable earnings in that year, whether or not the employment is held when the earnings are remitted. See **61 REMITTANCE BASIS** for the meaning of 'remitted to the UK' etc. If the earnings are not foreign earnings, they fall within **27.4** above.

General earnings are *'foreign earnings'* for a tax year if the employee is ordinarily resident in the UK, the remittance basis applies to him and the earnings are neither in respect of duties performed in the UK nor 'from overseas Crown employment subject to UK tax'.

General earnings are *'from overseas Crown employment subject to UK tax'* if they are from employment of a public nature under the Crown and payable out of UK or NI public revenue (which includes civil servants (*Graham v White* Ch D 1971, 48 TC 163 and *Caldicott v Varty* Ch D 1976, 51 TC 403) and HM Forces), unless excluded by an order made by the Commissioners of HMRC. See HMRC Employment Income Manual EIM40209 for the text of the Commissioners' Order as amended. See also **27.57** below and **30.6, 30.7** and **30.14** EXEMPT INCOME.

The above applies equally to general earnings for 2007/08 and earlier years where those earnings are remitted to the UK in 2008/09 or a later year, but only if in the year the earnings arose the employee was UK resident and either not ordinarily resident or not domiciled in the UK. Pre-2008/09 general earnings that are not foreign earnings do not fall within **27.4** above as they will already have been taxed on the receipts basis (see **27.10, 27.16** below).

[*ITEPA 2003, ss 20, 22–24, 26, 28, 721(1); FA 2008, Sch 7 paras 10–19, 39, 81, 82; CTA 2010, Sch 1 para 379*].

An HMRC Statement of Practice covers the apportionment of earnings where a person resident but not ordinarily resident in the UK performs duties of a single employment both inside and outside the UK. In such cases, the earnings will be taxable in full under *ITEPA 2003, s 15* in respect of the UK duties, but under *ITEPA 2003, s 26* on amounts remitted to the UK in respect of the non-UK duties. Apportionment of the earnings between UK and non-UK duties is a question of fact, but time apportionment based on working days inside and outside the UK will normally be applied, unless clearly inappropriate. Where part of the earnings are paid in the UK, the HMRC practice is to accept that, where a reasonable apportionment has been made between earnings chargeable under *section 15* and *section 26*, liability arises under *section 26* only on any excess of the aggregate of earnings paid and benefits received in the UK and earnings remitted to the UK over the amount chargeable under *section 15*. Where none of the earnings are paid in the UK, remittances are generally taken in the first instance as out of income liable under *section 15*. (HMRC SP 1/09). This Statement of Practice applies only from 6 April 2009 but replaces SP 5/84 (see **27.10** below) which made similar provision for 2007/08 and earlier years and continued to apply for 2008/09 onwards. It is to be given statutory effect by *Finance Act 2011* (HMRC Budget Note BN55, 22 April 2009; HMRC Internet Statement, 3 March 2010).

Employee non-resident in the UK — 2008/09 onwards

[27.8] If the earnings are either in respect of duties performed in the UK or 'from overseas Crown employment subject to UK tax' (see **27.5** above under Employee not ordinarily resident in UK), the full amount of the general earnings 'received' (see **27.16** below) in a tax year is taxable earnings in that year, whether or not the employment is held when the earnings are received.

[ITEPA 2003, s 27; FA 2008, Sch 7 paras 20, 81].

Employee resident, ordinarily resident and domiciled in the UK — 2007/08 and earlier years

[27.9] Where general earnings are for a tax year in which the employee is resident, ordinarily resident and domiciled in the UK, the full amount of such earnings 'received' in a tax year (see **27.16** below) is taxable earnings in that year, whether they are for that or another year and whether or not the employment is held when the earnings are received. *[ITEPA 2003, s 15].*

Employee resident, ordinarily resident or domiciled outside the UK — 2007/08 and earlier years

[27.10] Where the employee is resident, ordinarily resident or domiciled outside the UK for a tax year, determination of taxable general earnings depends upon which of the following applies. *[ITEPA 2003, s 20].*

Earnings for a year when the employee is resident and ordinarily resident, but not domiciled, in the UK

[27.11] The determination depends on whether the earnings are 'chargeable overseas earnings' for the year or not.

If they are not, the full amount of such earnings 'received' (see **27.16** below) in a tax year is taxable earnings in that year, whether they are for that or another year and whether or not the employment is held when the earnings are received.

If they are 'chargeable overseas earnings', the full amount of such earnings 'remitted to the UK' (see below) in a tax year is taxable earnings in that year, whether they are for that or another year and whether or not the employment is held when the earnings are remitted. See also below as regards relief for certain delayed remittances.

'Chargeable overseas earnings' are earnings from an employment with a 'foreign employer', the duties of which are performed wholly outside the UK. They are reduced by any deductions which would be allowed if they were taxable earnings. Where the duties of any 'associated' employment are not performed wholly outside the UK, then the chargeable overseas earnings are limited to a reasonable proportion of the aggregate earnings (after allowable deductions) from all the employments, having regard to the nature of and the time devoted to duties performed outside and in the UK and to all other relevant considerations. Any amount deducted by virtue of this limitation falls back into general earnings. Employments are *'associated'* if they are with the same employer, or the employers are under common control or one controls the other, control being as in *ICTA 1988, s 416* (for companies) and *ITA 2007, s 995* (for individuals and partnerships).

A *'foreign employer'* is one resident outside, and not resident within, the UK (and, in relation to a UK resident employee, not resident in the Republic of Ireland).

[ITEPA 2003, ss 21–24, 721(1); ITA 2007, Sch 1 para 428].

In their April 2005 Tax Bulletin, HMRC announced a change of emphasis in the way that they will approach enquiries into dual contract arrangements. A non-UK domiciled employee may, for example, be offered two employment contracts, one with a UK employer and the other with an associated 'foreign employer', the intended effect being to create or maximise 'chargeable overseas earnings'. The Tax Bulletin article explains HMRC's pre-existing approach to dual contract arrangements and their change of emphasis. In particular, they do not consider that the existence of separate and distinct employments is determined by the terms of dual contracts where the main distinction between each contract's duties is merely geographical, and are concerned that arrangements of this nature artificially divide a single job. They have apparently now received legal advice in support of this view, and such arrangements are thus increasingly vulnerable to challenge; dual contract arrangements seem unlikely to be accepted by the Revenue as effective unless there are two distinguishable jobs. (Revenue Tax Bulletin April 2005 pp 1201–1204).

Earnings for a year when the employee is resident, but not ordinarily resident, in the UK

[27.12] The determination depends on whether the earnings are UK-based or foreign earnings. The former applies if they are either in respect of duties performed in the UK or from overseas Crown employment subject to UK tax (for which see further below). The latter applies otherwise.

If they are UK-based earnings, the full amount of such earnings 'received' (see **27.16** above) in a tax year is taxable earnings in that year, whether they are for that or another year and whether or not the employment is held when the earnings are received.

If they are foreign earnings, the full amount of such earnings 'remitted to the UK' (see below) in a tax year is taxable earnings in that year, whether they are for that or another year and whether or not the employment is held when the earnings are remitted. See also below as regards relief for certain delayed remittances.

General earnings are '*from overseas Crown employment subject to UK tax*' if they are from employment of a public nature under the Crown and payable out of UK or NI public revenue (which includes civil servants (*Graham v White* Ch D 1971, 48 TC 163 and *Caldicott v Varty* Ch D 1976, 51 TC 403) and HM Forces), unless excluded by an order made by the Commissioners of HMRC. See HMRC Employment Income Manual EIM40209 for the text of the Commissioners' Order; this Order is amended so as to omit Gurkhas from the exclusion as from 13 June 2006 (www.hmrc.gov.uk/si/board-order.pdf). See also **27.57** below and **30.6**, **30.7** and **30.14 EXEMPT INCOME**.

An HMRC Statement of Practice covers the *apportionment of earnings* where a person resident but not ordinarily resident in the UK performs duties of a single employment both inside and outside the UK. In such cases, the earnings will be taxable in full under *ITEPA 2003, s 25* in respect of the UK duties, but under *ITEPA 2003, s 26* on amounts remitted to the UK in respect of the non-UK duties. Apportionment of the earnings between UK and non-UK duties is a question of fact, but time apportionment based on working days inside and outside the UK will normally be applied, unless clearly inappropriate. Where part of the earnings are paid in the UK, the HMRC practice is to accept that, where a reasonable apportionment has been made between earnings chargeable under *s 25* and *s 26*, liability arises under *s 26* only on any excess of the aggregate of earnings paid and benefits received in the UK and earnings remitted to the UK over the amount chargeable under *s 25*. Where none of the earnings are paid in the UK, remittances are generally taken in the first instance as out of income liable under *s 25*. (HMRC SP 5/84). See also Revenue Tax Bulletin February 2003 pp 996–998 for examples of how apportionment is applied in practice. (Note that SP 5/84 has no direct relevance for National Insurance contributions, for which see HMRC Tax Bulletin October 2005 pp 1235–1241.)

As regards *tax equalisation* payments to non-UK ordinarily resident employees, for 1997/98 and subsequent years these are treated as being chargeable wholly under Case II. (Revenue Tax Bulletin February 1997 pp 386, 387). They are treated as being wholly in respect of the UK duties to which they relate (i.e. they are not apportioned between UK and non-UK duties) (*Perro v Mansworth* (Sp C 286), [2001] SSCD 179). For an article on the treatment of tax equalisation payments following the decision in that case, see Revenue Tax Bulletin June 2002, pp 931–934. For self-assessment returns in cases involving tax equalisation, see Revenue Tax Bulletin October 1997 pp 467, 468 and June 1998 p 551. See **53.44 PAY AS YOU EARN** as regards modified PAYE procedures for tax equalised employees.

[*ITEPA 2003, ss 25, 26, 28*].

UK-based earnings for a year when the employee is not resident in the UK

[27.13] See **27.12** above for the meaning of 'UK-based earnings'. The full amount of such earnings 'received' (see **27.16** below) in a tax year is taxable earnings in that year, whether they are for that or another year and whether or not the employment is held when the earnings are received. [*ITEPA 2003, s 27*].

Meaning of 'remitted to the UK'

[27.14] Earnings are '*remitted to the UK*' at the time when they are paid, used or enjoyed in the UK, or transmitted or brought to the UK in any manner or form. There are special provisions treating as a remittance the use of earnings of employees not ordinarily resident in the UK to satisfy UK-linked debt. These are similar to the general 'constructive remittances' provisions at **61.27 REMITTANCE BASIS**. [*ITEPA 2003, ss 33, 34*]. Certain pre-1989/90 earnings remitted in 2003/04 or later are excluded. [*ITEPA 2003, Sch 7 para 8(3)*].

Relief for delayed remittances

Relief is available in respect of general earnings taxable on the remittance basis in a tax year (under *ITEPA 2003, s 22(2)* or *s 26(2)* — see above) which were received outside the UK before that year but which were not transferred to the UK until that year and could not be transferred to the UK before that year because of the laws of the country or territory in which they were received, the executive action of its government or the impossibility of obtaining non-local currency which could be transferred to the UK. A claim may be made for remittances to be taxable instead in an earlier tax year or years. This is normally the year(s) in which the earnings were received outside the UK. An irrevocable election may, however, be made as part of the claim for the earnings to be allocated to certain years (before that of receipt in the UK) for which there were *'blocked earnings'* from the employment, i.e. earnings which would have been taxable had they been remitted to the UK in that year but which could not be transferred to the UK in that year for the reasons referred to above. The amount which may be allocated to a particular tax year by election is restricted to the excess of the blocked earnings for that year over the amount of delayed remittances previously treated as taxable in that year. Claims for relief on delayed remittances must be made within five years after 31 January following the tax year of remittance to the UK. Where appropriate, these provisions apply to the personal representative of the taxpayer as they would have to the taxpayer. [*ITEPA 2003, ss 35–37*]. Special provision is made where any of the years concerned is before 2003/04, to ensure that the appropriate legislation applies. [*ITEPA 2003, Sch 7 paras 9–11*].

Allowable deductions

Expenses which would be allowable (see **27.22–27.24** below) against earnings taxed on the receipts basis are generally allowable against earnings taxed on the remittance basis. No deduction is, however, allowable for an amount paid in respect of the duties of an employment to which earnings taxed other than on the remittance basis relate. Capital allowances are not available for expenditure on plant and machinery (see **11.4**(ii) CAPITAL ALLOWANCES ON PLANT AND MACHINERY). [*ITEPA 2003, ss 353, 354, Sch 7 para 39; CAA 2001, s 20*].

Disputes on ordinary residence or domicile

[27.15] Disputes on ordinary residence or domicile in relation to employment income are referred to, and decided by, the Commissioners of HMRC, subject to appeal (by written notice within three months of HMRC's decision) to the Special Commissioners or, on and after 1 April 2009, the Appeal Tribunal. [*ITEPA 2003, ss 42, 43, Sch 7 para 12; SI 2009 No 56, Sch 1 para 335*]. This no longer applies for tax years after 2007/08.

This paragraph and 27.9–27.14 above relate only to 2007/08 and earlier years. See now **27.5, 27.8** above.

Receipts basis

[27.16] General earnings consisting of money (including money payments chargeable under the benefits code, see **27.26** below) are *'received'* at the earliest of the following times:

- the time when payment is actually made of, or on account of, the earnings;
- the time when a person becomes entitled to such payment; and

- where the person concerned is a 'director' of a company at any point in the tax year in which the time falls and the earnings are from employment with that company (whether or not as director), the earliest of:
  - the time when sums on account of earnings are credited in the company's accounts or records (regardless of any restriction on the right to draw those sums);
  - the time when a period of account ends and the amount of earnings for that period has already been determined; and
  - the time when the amount of earnings for a period of account is determined and that period has already ended.

A '*director*' is defined as being any of the following:

(a)   a member of a board of directors, or similar body, which manages the company;

(b)   a single director, or similar person, who manages the company;

(c)   a member of the company, in cases where the company is managed by its members;

(d)   any person in accordance with whose directions or instructions, given other than in a professional capacity, the directors, as defined in (a)–(c) above, are accustomed to act.

Non-money general earnings (e.g. benefits in kind) are generally treated as received in the tax year for which they are treated as earnings.

[*ITEPA 2003, ss 18, 19, 31, 32; FA 2008, Sch 7 paras 21, 81*].

Foreign earnings deduction for seafarers

[27.17]   Where the duties of a 'seafarer' resident and ordinarily resident in the UK are performed wholly or partly outside the UK, a deduction may be allowed from taxable earnings (other than chargeable overseas earnings) within any of **27.4–27.10** above. Employment as a '*seafarer*' for this purpose means an employment (other than certain employments under the Crown) consisting of the performance of duties on a ship (disregarding incidental duties elsewhere). For this purpose, a 'ship' does not include an offshore installation (within *ITA 2007, s 1001*). The distinction between a ship and an offshore installation was considered in *Torr v HMRC and related appeals* (Sp C 679), [2008] SSCD 679 and *Spowage v HMRC and related appeals* FTT (TC 142), [2009] SFTD 393. As a result of those appeals, HMRC have revised their interpretation of the distinction — see HMRC Employment Income Manual EIM33105, 33106.

For 2011/12 onwards, the requirement that the seafarer be resident and ordinarily resident in the UK is to be amended to allow EU and EEA residents to qualify for the relief. The amending legislation will be included in a Finance Bill to be introduced in autumn 2010. (HMRC Budget Note BN31, 22 June 2010).

Duties performed on a ship during a voyage beginning or ending outside the UK (other than any part of it beginning and ending there), or on a part beginning or ending outside the UK of any other voyage, are treated as performed outside the UK for these purposes. Overseas duties merely incidental to a UK employment are treated as performed in the UK, as are duties on a voyage not extending to a port outside the UK.

Where such duties are performed in the course of an 'eligible period' of 365 days or more (which can include days outside the tax year concerned), a deduction is made of 100% of the earnings for those duties attributable to that period (i.e. they are completely relieved from tax). Earnings for a tax year for this purpose are as reduced by capital allowances and all allowable deductions (including mileage allowance relief (see **27.87** below), post-5 April 2006 contributions to registered pension schemes and certain pre-6 April 2006 superannuation contributions). An *'eligible period'* consists either (a) entirely of consecutive days of absence from the UK or (b) of days of absence from the UK *plus* any earlier eligible period *plus* an intervening period in the UK not exceeding 183 days, provided that the total number of days in the UK in the intervening period and in the earlier eligible period is not more than one-half of the total number of days in the new eligible period. Successive intervening periods and periods of absence may continue to be eligible as long as these conditions are met in relation to each new period of absence.

A day of absence from the UK requires absence from the UK at the end of the day.

A period spent in the UK during a contract of employment but not followed by a period abroad may not be included in the eligible period (*Robins v Durkin* Ch D 1988, 60 TC 700).

The seafarer must have been resident and ordinarily resident in the UK for tax purposes throughout the eligible period (for which see *Carstairs v Sykes* Ch D 2000, 73 TC 225). It may therefore be more favourable for a taxpayer departing from or returning to the UK to be treated, in strict accordance with the statute, as UK resident throughout the tax year of departure or return, rather than only being so treated for the part of that year falling before the departure or after the return under HMRC Extra-statutory Concession A11 (see **62.6 RESIDENCE, ORDINARY RESIDENCE AND DOMICILE**). Liabilities on earnings from employment are normally calculated on the basis that the concession applies unless the application of the statutory basis is requested. (Revenue Tax Bulletin November 1992 p 40).

Leave periods

Earnings for duties attributable to an eligible period include earnings from that employment for a period of leave immediately following that period (and so qualify for the 100% deduction) to the extent that they are earnings for the tax year in which the eligible period ends.

Associated employments

Where the duties of the employment or any 'associated employment' (see **27.5** and **27.10** above) are not performed wholly outside the UK, the earnings relievable as above may not exceed a reasonable proportion of the total earnings from all such employments, having regard to the nature of, and time devoted to, duties performed outside and in the UK and to all other relevant considerations.

[*ITEPA 2003, ss 378–385; FA 2008, Sch 7 paras 29, 81*].

Overseas duties — travel etc. expenses

[27.18] For travelling expenses generally, see 27.80 *et seq.* below. For certain EU travel expenses of MPs etc., see 30.27 EXEMPT INCOME.

Where duties of an employment by an employee resident and ordinarily resident in the UK are performed abroad, the following deductions may be made from taxable earnings (if not 'chargeable overseas earnings', see 27.5 and 27.10 above). In each case, apportionment applies where expenses are only partly attributable to the purpose in question.

Where duties performed wholly outside the UK

(a)   Travelling expenses incurred by the employee from any place in the UK to take up the overseas employment and to return on its termination.

(b)   Board and lodging expenses outside the UK provided or reimbursed by the employer to enable the employee to perform the duties of the overseas employment.

Incidental duties performed in the UK are for these purposes treated as performed outside the UK.

[*ITEPA 2003, ss 341, 376*].

Where duties are performed partly outside the UK

Travel facilities, provided or reimbursed to the employee (so far as included in the taxable earnings), between any place in the UK and the place of performance outside the UK of any of the duties of an employment, either:

(i)   for the employee, provided that the duties concerned can only be performed outside the UK, and that either the outward and return journeys are wholly exclusively for the purpose of performing those duties or returning after performing them, or the absence from the UK is wholly and exclusively for the purpose of performing those duties and the journeys are from the place of employment of the duties to the UK and return; or

(ii)   where there is absence from the UK for a continuous period of 60 days or more, for his spouse (or civil partner) and any children of his under 18 (at beginning of outward journey) accompanying the employee at the beginning of the period of absence or visiting him during that period, including the return journey, but with a limit of two outward and return journeys per person in any tax year.

For these purposes, duties performed on a ship on a voyage extending to a port outside the UK are not treated under *ITEPA 2003, s 40(2)* (see 27.3(iii) above) as performed in the UK, and the requirements as to place of performance of duties are correspondingly modified.

[*ITEPA 2003, s 370–372; FA 2008, Sch 7 paras 27, 28, 81*].

More than one employment

Where two or more employments are held and at least one of them is performed wholly or partly outside the UK, and travelling expenses are incurred by the employee in travelling from one place where duties of one employment were performed to another place to perform duties of another, and either or both places are outside the UK, the expenses are deductible from the taxable earnings from the second employment.

[*ITEPA 2003, s 342*].

For travel on leave by HM Forces, see **27.57** below.

Simon's Taxes. See E4.782, E4.784.

Employees of non-UK domicile — travel costs etc.

[27.19] A deduction may be allowed from taxable earnings for duties performed in the UK for the cost of certain travel facilities provided or reimbursed to a non-UK domiciled employee (so far as included in taxable earnings) for journeys ending on the date of arrival in the UK to perform the duties of the employment, or within five years after that date. This applies to facilities provided:

(a)   for any journey between the employee's usual place of abode (i.e. the country outside the UK where he normally lives) and any place in the UK in order to perform, or after performing, any duties of the employment; and

(b)   where the employee is in the UK for the purpose of performing the duties of any such employment for a continuous period of 60 days or more, for any outward and return journey by his spouse (or civil partner) or child (under 18 at the beginning of the journey to the UK) between his usual place of abode and the place where any of those duties are performed in the UK, either to accompany him at the beginning of the period or to visit him during it (but limited to two outward and return journeys by any person in a tax year).

No deduction is, however, available unless, on a date on which he arrives in the UK to perform the duties, either:

(i)   he was not resident in the UK in either of the two tax years immediately preceding that in which that date falls; or

(ii)   he was not in the UK for any purpose at any time in the two years ending immediately before that date,

and if condition (i) is satisfied on more than one date in a tax year, relief is given by reference to the first such date only.

As regards the 60-day requirement under (b) above, HMRC accept that the 60-day requirement is satisfied where at least two-thirds of working days are spent in the UK over a period of 60 days or more, at both the start and end of which the employee is in the UK for the purpose of performing the duties of the employment. (Revenue Tax Bulletin December 2001 pp 900, 901 and HMRC Employment Income Manual EIM35050, 35055).

[*ITEPA 2003, ss 373–375, Sch 7 para 40*].

Foreign employer

Certain payments made by a non-UK domiciliary out of earnings from an employment with a 'foreign employer' (see **27.5** and **27.10** above) which do not reduce the employee's liability to UK income tax, but which are made 'in circumstances corresponding to those in which it would do so', may be allowed as a deduction from those earnings. [*ITEPA 2003, s 355*]. See HMRC Employment Income Manual EIM32661 *et seq.*

Simon's Taxes. See E4.783, E4.784.

General earnings

[27.20] The income taxable as '*general earnings*' from employment (see **27.1**, **27.3** above) consists of '*earnings*', i.e. any salary, wages or fee, any gratuity or other incidental benefit of any kind obtained by an employee consisting of money or money's worth, and anything else constituting an emolument of the employment, together with anything treated under any statutory provision as earnings (e.g. benefits, see **27.25** below). '*Money's worth*' means something of direct monetary value to the employee or capable of being converted into money or something of such value. [*ITEPA 2003, ss 7(3)(5), 62; FA 2007, s 25, Sch 3 para 2*].

Before 6 April 2003, tax was chargeable on the emoluments of offices and employments, including 'all salaries, fees, wages, perquisites and profits whatsoever'. The revised description of the charge as above did not entail any change in the scope of the charge on employment income. The pre-2003 case law accordingly continues to be of application, with references to 'emoluments' now being relevant to 'general earnings'.

The emoluments assessable are those arising from the office or employment, regardless of by whom they are provided (see e.g. *Shilton v Wilmshurst* HL 1991, 64 TC 78).

Where an employee was granted a share option, the emolument was the granting of the option (any subsequent increase in value not being an emolument) (*Abbott v Philbin* HL 1960, 39 TC 82). See, however, *Bootle v Bye; Wilson v Bye* (Sp C 61), [1996] SSCD 58, where payments under an agreement with a third party, and not the rights under the agreement, were held to be emoluments. Where a payment was made for two reasons which were not dissociable, if the payment came from the employment then it was taxable even if it could also fairly be said to come from something else or was also made for a second reason (*Kuehne + Nagel Drinks Logistics Ltd and others v HMRC* FTT (TC 314), [2010] SFTD 298.

For an early and important statement of the concept of 'money's worth', see *Tennant v Smith* HL 1892, 3 TC 158. Whether money's worth received by an employee comes to him as an emolument may be a difficult question of fact. For modern examples see *Hochstrasser v Mayes* HL 1959, 38 TC 673 (compensation for loss on sale of house on transfer, held not assessable); *Wilcock v Eve* Ch D 1995, 67 TC 223 (payment for loss of rights under share option scheme, held not assessable), and contrast *Hamblett v Godfrey* CA 1986, 59 TC 694 (payment for loss of trade union etc. rights, held assessable); *Laidler v Perry* HL 1965, 42 TC 351; *Brumby v Milner* HL 1976, 51 TC 583; *Tyrer v Smart* HL 1978, 52 TC 533.

The meeting by the employer of a *pecuniary liability* of the employee constitutes money's worth, see e.g. *Hartland v Diggines* HL 1926, 10 TC 247 (tax liability), *Nicoll v Austin* KB 1935, 19 TC 531 (rates etc. of employee's residence), and *Glynn v CIR* PC 1990, 63 TC 162 (payment direct to school of child's school fees); this applies to payment of the employee's council tax (Revenue Press Release 16 March 1993), and may apply to payment of employees' parking fines. In the latter case, the tax treatment depends on whether the vehicle is owned by employer or by employee and whether the fixed penalty notice is affixed to the car or handed to the driver (see HMRC Employment Income Manual EIM21686 for a full summary). Congestion charges paid by an employer in connection with an employee-owned vehicle are taxable (see HMRC Employment Income Manual EIM21680). For specific items and legislation modifying the general rule, see **27.25** onwards below.

Hence, subject to any special legislation, board, lodging, uniforms etc. provided by the employer and not convertible into money are not assessable, but cash allowances *in lieu* are generally assessable, e.g. a clothing allowance to a 'plain-clothes' policeman (*Fergusson v Noble* CS 1919, 7 TC 176); a meals allowance when working abnormal hours (*Sanderson v Durbridge* Ch D 1955, 36 TC 239); lodging allowances to army personnel (*Nagley v Spilsbury* Ch D 1957, 37 TC 178); an allowance to meet extra cost of living abroad (*Robinson v Corry* CA 1933, 18 TC 411). Allowances in lieu of uniform to uniformed staff are, however, not treated as emoluments (see HMRC Employment Income Manual EIM10400). See **27.69** below for meal vouchers. See also **30.27** **EXEMPT INCOME** as regards accommodation allowances for Members of Parliament and **27.59–27.68** below as regards living accommodation generally. Where deductions were made from salary for board etc., held gross amount assessable (*Cordy v Gordon* KB 1925, 9 TC 304; *Machon v McLoughlin* CA 1926, 11 TC 83). Where a higher salary may be taken in lieu of the provision of free board and lodging, the value of the provision is taxable. In this respect, HMRC ESC A60 provides a concession for agricultural workers, but it is considered to be no longer of any practical relevance and will be withdrawn from 1 April 2010 (www.hmrc.gov.uk/budget2009/withdrawl-esc-6400.pdf).

Where an employee used his car in the course of his duties, a lump sum and mileage allowances were held to be emoluments (*Perrons v Spackman* Ch D 1981, 55 TC 403). See **27.87** below as regards mileage allowances and travelling and subsistence allowances generally. 'Garage allowances' to salesmen with company cars were held to be assessable in *Beecham Group Ltd v Fair* Ch D 1983, 57 TC 733, but expenditure on the provision of car, cycle, motor cycle or van parking facilities for an employee at or near his place of work does not constitute an emolument, and where such a benefit is convertible into cash, e.g. under a salary sacrifice arrangement, no charge to tax on general earnings arises (see *ITEPA 2003, s 237*).

Financial loss allowances, or payments for loss of earnings, to members of public bodies, or to magistrates or those on jury service, are not taxable as employment income (although when received by the self-employed they are taxable as business receipts, see **73.48**(e) TRADING INCOME) (HMRC Employment Income Manual EIM01120). For the PAYE treatment of local councillors' attendance allowances, see **53.35** PAY AS YOU EARN.

For the exemption of cash allowances paid to miners in lieu of free coal, see **27.29**(xi) below.

Employer's gift of clothing assessable on *second-hand* value (*Wilkins v Rogerson* CA 1960, 39 TC 344), but gift voucher available for use only in specified shop assessable on face value (*Laidler v Perry* HL 1965, 42 TC 351) but see **27.90** below for legislation now applicable although the case remains an important authority on what constitutes an emolument. Also see *Heaton v Bell* HL 1969, 46 TC 211 (assessment on free use of car connected with reduction in wages, but see company car legislation at **27.32** *et seq.* below).

Interest on money loaned interest-free, subject to conditions and repayable on demand, by the employer to a trust for the benefit of an employee held to be assessable emoluments (*O'Leary v McKinlay* Ch D 1990, 63 TC 729).

Endowment premiums paid by employers are assessable (*Richardson v Lyon* KB 1943, 25 TC 497). But trustees' payments out of fund set up by employers for assisting education of employees' children held not assessable on parent (*Barclays Bank v Naylor* Ch D 1960, 39 TC 256) but see now educational scholarships under **27.47** below. In *Ball v Johnson* Ch D 1971, 47 TC 155, a discretionary payment to employee for passing an examination was held not assessable (but see HMRC Employment Income Manual EIM01100, and see also **27.28** below for treatment of such awards as benefits-in-kind). Commission applied in taking up shares held assessable (*Parker v Chapman* CA 1927, 13 TC 677). In *Clayton v Gothorp* Ch D 1971, 47 TC 168, a loan to a former employee for improving qualifications, which became non-repayable when the employee returned to employer's service after qualification, was held assessable for year in which it became non-repayable. Where wages paid in gold sovereigns, held their market value to be taken as the measure of the emoluments (*Jenkins v Horn* Ch D 1979, 52 TC 591).

There is no liability on payments to an employee (or the employee's spouse or civil partner) under an insurance policy covering health or employment risks taken out by the employer, provided the conditions relating to such policies in *ITTOIA 2005, s 735* are met, and the employee has made contributions in respect of the premiums (see **30.23** EXEMPT INCOME). [*ITEPA 2003, s 325A*].

Whether lump sum payments etc. on taking up an employment are emoluments of the employment or non-taxable inducements is a question of fact. Signing-on fees to an amateur footballer on joining a Rugby League club were held to be assessable in *Riley v Coglan* Ch D 1967, 44 TC 481, distinguishing *Jarrold v Boustead* CA 1964, 41 TC 701. In *Shilton v Wilmshurst* HL 1991, 64 TC 78, a transfer fee paid by his old club to a professional footballer was taxable as an emolument of his new employment. In *Sports Club plc and others v Inspector of Taxes* (Sp C 253), [2000] SSCD 443, payments by a sports club via third party companies under separate promotional contracts relating to employees' services were held not to be chargeable as employment income.

The value of shares allotted to an accountant on becoming managing director of a company was held not to be assessable in *Pritchard v Arundale* Ch D 1971, 47 TC 680, but an opposite conclusion was reached on the facts in *Glantre Engineering Ltd v Goodhand* Ch D 1982, 56 TC 165. A lump sum payment for giving up rights to trade union representation was assessable (*Hamblett v Godfrey* CA 1986, 59 TC 694).

In *McLoughlin v HMRC* (Sp C 542), [2006] SSCD 467, an agreement entitling a new employee to a percentage of the proceeds of the employer partnership in the event of its being dissolved or sold during his term of employment was held to have not given rise to an emolument at the time of the agreement; instead, an emolument arose when the contingency occurred and was equal to the amount realised by the employee from the entitlement.

For the effectiveness of 'salary sacrifice' arrangements, see www.hmrc.gov.uk/specialist/salary_sacrifice.pdf and see also www.hmrc.gov.uk/specialist/sal-sac-question-and-answers.htm.

The reimbursement by an employer of an employee's bank charges, where these arise solely because of the employer's failure to make a salary payment on time, does not give rise to a tax charge (Revenue Tax Bulletin June 2003 p 1039).

Goodwill transferred to a company on incorporation of a business, if deliberately overvalued as an inducement for the individual concerned to take up employment with the company or in return for future services to be provided by the individual to the company, may (to the extent of the overvalue) be taxed as general earnings or, exceptionally, as a benefit (Revenue Tax Bulletin April 2005 p 1200).

For HMRC's view of the taxation implications of guaranteed selling price (or similar) schemes for houses as part of employee relocation packages, see Revenue Tax Bulletin May 1994 p 122 and April 1995 p 211.

Simon's Taxes. See E4.4.

Homeworkers

[27.21] Payments made by an employer to a 'homeworker employee' in respect of reasonable additional 'household expenses' incurred by him after that date in carrying out the duties of his employment at home are exempt from income tax. For these purposes, a *'homeworker employee'* is one who, by arrangement with the employer, regularly performs all or some of those duties at home, and *'household expenses'* are expenses connected with the day-to-day running of his home. [*ITEPA 2003, s 316A*]. Up to £3 per week (£2 per week before 6 April 2008) can be paid without the need to justify the amount paid or to provide supporting evidence of the expenses incurred; for larger payments, the employer must be able to provide supporting evidence that the payment falls wholly within the exemption (Revenue Press Release REV BN 3, 9 April 2003). See also HMRC Employment Income Manual EIM01472–01478 and Revenue Tax Bulletin December 2003 pp 1068, 1069.

Unreimbursed homeworking expenses

In their October 2005 Tax Bulletin, HMRC set out guidance on the circumstances in which employees working at home can claim a deduction for a proportion of their household expenses. Any element of personal choice as to whether the employee works at home will fail the 'necessarily' test above and will thus preclude a deduction. HMRC will accept that a deduction is available where:

- the duties performed at home are substantive duties of the employment;
- those duties cannot be performed without the use of appropriate facilities;
- either no such facilities are available to the employee on the employer's premises or the nature of the job requires the employee to live too far away from the employer's premises for daily commuting to be a reasonable option; and
- at no time (either before or after the contract is drawn up) is the employee able to choose between working at the employer's premises or elsewhere.

If one or more of these conditions are not satisfied, HMRC will disallow any deduction, subject to the employee's normal right of appeal. The Tax Bulletin article gives examples of how the above conditions apply in a number of circumstances.

The expenses qualifying for relief under the guidance are limited to the additional unit costs of gas and electricity consumed while a room is being used for work, the metered cost of any water used in the performance of the duties and the unit costs of business telephone calls, including dial-up internet access. For simplicity, a deduction of £3 per week (£2 per week before 6 April 2008) (exclusive of business telephone calls) will be allowed by HMRC without the need for supporting evidence of the actual costs incurred; employees claiming more than that will need to be able to justify it. No proportion of the following expenses is allowed: council tax, rent, water rates, mortgage costs and household insurance.

(HMRC Tax Bulletin October 2005 pp 1231–1235; HMRC Employment Income Manual EIM32815).

In past decisions of the courts, use of room at home for business *Newlin v Woods* CA 1966, 42 TC 649 but cf. *Kirkwood v Evans* Ch D 2002, 74 TC 481) but not alternative room for son's homework (*Roskams v Bennett* Ch D 1950, 32 TC 129) or mortgage interest on loan to purchase property used as office (*Baird v Williams* Ch D 1999, 71 TC 390).

Rental of *second* telephone line at employee's home is allowed where used exclusively for business calls and there is a genuine business need for the line (but rental of first line or single line is not allowed) (HMRC Employment Income Manual EIM32940).

No deduction is permitted for broadband internet access where the employee is able to use the internet for non-business purposes (HMRC Employment Income Manual EIM32940).

Allowable deductions

[27.22] A deduction is generally allowed from earnings from employment charged on the receipts basis (see generally **27.4–27.15** above) for expenses the holder of an office or employment is obliged to incur and pay which are either qualifying travelling expenses (see **27.23** below) or other amounts incurred wholly, exclusively and necessarily (*ITEPA 2003, s 336*) in the performance of the duties of the employment. See **27.24** below. A deduction is similarly allowed for amounts paid on behalf of, or reimbursed to, the employee and included in the earnings from the employment. The deductions allowable against earnings may not exceed those earnings. There is a general prohibition on obtaining more than one deduction for any cost or expense. For deductions from earnings charged on the remittance basis, see **27.5** and **27.10** above.

- For travelling, subsistence and incidental overnight expenses etc. generally, see **27.80–27.89** below, and for other specific deductions, see below at **27.55** (flat rate expenses), **27.76** (subscriptions) and **27.79** (training etc.).
- For provision of security assets and services for employees, see **27.73** below.
- For capital allowances where plant or machinery is provided for the purposes of an employment, see **11.4 CAPITAL ALLOWANCES ON PLANT AND MACHINERY**.
- For expenditure by Members of Parliament on accommodation, see **27.68** below.
- For charitable donation payroll deduction scheme, see **16.20 CHARITIES**.
- For deduction of agents' fees by artistes, see **27.54** below.
- For expenditure on indemnity insurance and on certain liabilities such as legal costs in relation to the employment, see **27.52** below.
- For deductions from earnings charged on the remittance basis, see **27.5** and **27.10** above.

For HMRC's view on specific employments and expenses, see HMRC Employment Income Manual EIM31622 *et seq.*

Simon's Taxes. See E4.770–E4.799.

Qualifying travelling expenses

[27.23] '*Qualifying travelling expenses*' are amounts necessarily expended on travelling in the performance of the duties of the office or employment, or other travel expenses which:

(i)   are attributable to necessary attendance at any place of the holder of the office or employment in the performance of those duties; and

(ii)   are not expenses of either 'ordinary commuting' or 'private travel'.

Expenses of travel between two places at which duties are performed of different offices or employments under or with companies in the same group are treated as necessarily expended in the performance of the duties to be performed at the destination. Companies are members of the same group for this purpose if one is a 51% subsidiary (by reference to ordinary share capital) of the other or both are 51% subsidiaries of a third company.

Travelling expenses include the actual costs of travel and also the subsistence expenditure and other associated costs (e.g. overnight accommodation) that are incurred as part of the cost of making the journey (HMRC Employment Income Manual EIM31815, 31820).

'Ordinary commuting' means travel between home (or a place other than a 'workplace' in relation to the office or employment) and a place which is a 'permanent workplace' in relation to the office or employment. The fact that an employee may have a fully-equipped office at home does not prevent it from being her home (Lewis v HMRC (Sp C 690), [2008] SSCD 895) but see Kirkwood v Evans Ch D 2002, 74 TC 481 for a case in which weekly home to office travel by a homeworker was held to be ordinary commuting.) 'Private travel' means travel between home and a place that is not a 'workplace', or between two places neither of which is a 'workplace'. Travel which for practical purposes is substantially ordinary commuting or private travel is treated as such. As regards emergency call-outs, see **27.80** below.

A 'workplace' in relation to an employment is a place at which attendance is necessary in the performance of the duties of the office or employment. It is a 'permanent workplace' if it is not a 'temporary workplace' and attendance there in the performance of those duties is regular. Except as below, it is a 'temporary workplace' if the purpose of attendance there is to perform a task of limited duration or some other temporary purpose.

A workplace is *not* a 'temporary workplace' if attendance there is in the course of a 'period of continuous work' at that place lasting more than 24 months or comprising all (or almost all) of the period for which the office or employment is likely to be held, or if it is reasonable to assume that it will be in the course of such a period. See Phillips v Hamilton; Macken v Hamilton (Sp C 366), [2003] SSCD 286. A 'period of continuous work' at a place is a period over which the duties of the employment fall to be performed to a significant extent at that place (i.e. 40% or more of working time is spent there, see HMRC Booklet 490 para 3.13). Actual or contemplated modifications of the place at which the duties are performed which do not have any substantial effect on the journey or on the travelling expenses are disregarded.

A place regularly attended in the performance of the duties of the office or employment which forms the base from which those duties are performed, or which is the place at which the tasks to be carried out in the performance of those duties are allocated, is treated as a permanent workplace. Similarly where the duties are defined by reference to an area (whether or not requiring attendance outside the area), and attendance is required at different places in the area (none of them a permanent workplace) in the performance of the duties, then that area is treated as a permanent workplace if it would be so treated (as above) were it a place.

Where a vehicle other than a company vehicle is used for business travel, and either mileage allowance payments are received or mileage allowance relief is available in respect of that use (see **27.87** below), no deduction is available for qualifying travelling expenses incurred in connection with that use. However, this does *not* prevent relief for costs incurred other than 'in connection with' the use of the vehicle', e.g. subsistence and accommodation costs (HMRC Employment Income Manual EIM31815, 31820).

[ITEPA 2003, s 328(1), s 329(1)–(3), s 330, s 333(1)(2), s 334(1)(2), s 335(1)(2), ss 336–340, s 359].

For leading articles explaining the above rules, with numerous examples, see Revenue Tax Bulletin December 1997 pp 477–485, February 1998 pp 497–505 and April 1998 pp 524–527. See also Revenue Tax Bulletin December 2000 pp 805–809 for an article explaining HMRC's approach to benefits and expenses paid to employees sent on secondments not exceeding 24 months, in particular those sent by an overseas employer to work in the UK. HMRC Booklet 490 'Employee Travel: A Tax and NICs Guide for Employees' also provides comprehensive general guidance, and see generally HMRC Employment Income Manual EIM32005 *et seq.*

Restrictions on deductions

[27.24] The requirements that expenditure be incurred 'necessarily' and (other than in the case of qualifying travelling expenses within **27.23** above) 'in the performance of the duties' impose additional restrictions on the allowability of deductions from earnings compared with those generally deductible under the rules for computing trading income. 'Necessarily' has been held to require that every holder of the office or employment would have to incur the expenditure, regardless of personal circumstances (see *Ricketts v Colquhoun* HL 1925, 10 TC 118, *Lewis v HMRC* (Sp C 690), [2008] SSCD 895). As regards 'in the performance of the duties', it follows that expenses incurred prior to entering upon duties or merely in preparation for them or to better qualify the employee for performing them are not allowed (see, for example, *Ansell v Brown* Ch D 2001, 73 TC 338, *Emms v HMRC* (Sp C 668), [2008] SSCD 618 and, in relation to training costs, *Snowdon v Charnock* (Sp C 282), [2001] SSCD 152, *HMRC v Decadt* Ch D 2007, [2008] STC 1103 and *Perrin v HMRC* (Sp C 671), [2008] SSCD 672). See *Nolder v Walters* KB 1930, 15 TC 380, air pilot allowed hotel expenses because incurred *in course of duty*, but not car and telephone *merely in preparation for it*, and *Bhadra v Ellam* Ch D 1987, 60 TC 466 where a doctor's travelling and secretarial expenses in relation to locum posts obtained through medical agencies were not allowed, as his duties commenced only on arrival at the hospital concerned. But contrast *Pook v Owen* HL 1969, 45 TC 571 where a GP with a part-time hospital appointment was allowed his expenses of travelling to the hospital from his home (where his surgery was), not covered by his mileage allowance, because, on the facts, his home as well as the hospital was a place where he carried out the duties of his appointment. See also *Gilbert v Hemsley* Ch D 1981, 55 TC 419 and **27.80** below generally. Airline pilots who are obliged upon leaving their employment to repay costs of training cannot deduct the amount repaid (*Hinsley v HMRC; Milsom v HMRC* (Sp C 569), [2007] SSCD 63).

Employees' costs of provision, upkeep, replacement or repair of protective clothing or of uniforms (recognisable as such) are allowable where their duties require them to be worn (HMRC Employment Income Manual EIM32465 *et seq.*). See, in particular, the flat rate allowances for laundry costs at **27.55** below.

Expenses of a part-time appointment not allowable against employment income may not be deducted in computing the trading income of an associated business (*Mitchell & Edon v Ross* HL 1961, 40 TC 11).

Entertaining expenses are not allowed, but see **73.72** TRADING INCOME for exceptions. However where an employer is not allowed a deduction for expenditure on business entertainment paid by him, directly or indirectly, to a member of staff, and that sum is also taxable earnings of the employee, the employee is allowed an equivalent deduction from taxable earnings for expenses defrayed out of that sum. [*ITEPA 2003, ss 356–358; ITA 2007, Sch 1 para 436; CTA 2009, Sch 1 para 552; CTA 2010, Sch 1 para 385; SI 2004 No 2310, Sch para 68*].

Expenses not allowed include: employment agency fees (*Shortt v McIlgorm* KB 1945, 26 TC 262); meal expenses paid out of meal allowances (*Sanderson v Durbridge* Ch D 1955, 36 TC 239); living expenses paid out of living allowances when working away from home (*Elderkin v Hindmarsh* Ch D 1988, 60 TC 651); headmaster's course to improve background knowledge (*Humbles v Brooks* Ch D 1962, 40 TC 500); qualified psychiatrist's costs of continuing professional development (*Consultant Psychiatrist v HMRC* (Sp C 557), [2006] SSCD 653); articled clerk's examination fees (*Lupton v Potts* Ch D 1969, 45 TC 643); cost of ordinary clothing (*Hillyer v Leeke* Ch D 1976, 51 TC 90; *Woodcock v CIR* Ch D 1977, 51 TC 698; *Ward v Dunn* Ch D 1978, 52 TC 517; *Williams v HMRC* FTT (TC 397), 2010 STI 1638); rental of telephone installed at employer's behest, but not used *wholly* and *exclusively* in performance of duties (*Lucas v Cattell* Ch D 1972, 48 TC 353); telephone and other expenses of consultant anaesthetist (*Hamerton v Overy* Ch D 1954, 35 TC 73); journalists' expenditure on newspapers and periodicals (*Fitzpatrick and Others v CIR, Smith v Shuttleworth and Others* HL 1994, 66 TC 407); rugby player's expenditure on dietary supplements (*Ansell v Brown* Ch D 2001, 73 TC 338; *Emms v HMRC* (Sp C 668), [2008] SSCD 618); and payment by a director under a personal guarantee of the company's indebtedness (*Guarantor v HMRC* (Sp C 703), [2008] SSCD 1154).

Expenses not allowed also include: any excess cost of living in place where required by work *Bola v Barlow* KB 1949, 31 TC 136; *Collis v Hore (No 1)* KB 1949, 31 TC 173; *Robinson v Corry* CA 1933, 18 TC 411); cost of domestic assistance where wife employed (*Bowers v Harding* QB 1891, 3 TC 22); cost of looking after widower's children (*Halstead v Condon* Ch D 1970, 46 TC 289).

Benefits — general

[27.25] Generally, if an employee receives money or money's worth from his employment he is chargeable to tax on that amount (see **27.20** above). However, he or his family may receive benefits by reason of his employment where special legislation is required if taxation is to apply. That legislation (the 'benefits code') is contained in *ITEPA 2003, Pt 3 Chs 2–11*. For benefits derived by directors and certain employees from their employment, see **27.26** *et seq.* below. For other taxable benefits of general application, see **27.59–27.68, 27.90–27.93** below. A benefit provided by a third party (e.g. a car provided by a car dealer to a football player for promotional purposes) is potentially within the benefits charging provisions where it is provided by reason of the employment.

Where the provision charging a particular benefit does not specify the year of charge, the earnings are treated as received at the time the benefit is provided. [*ITEPA 2003, ss 19(4), 32(4)*].

See **56.1** PENSION INCOME as regards the provision of benefits to retired employees.

Many of the exceptions listed at **27.29** below from the special charge on benefits apply also to amounts in respect of which a charge might also arise under the general charge on employment income. As a general rule there is a relief from all income tax liability in respect of such amounts. Where an amount is assessable both as general earnings and under the benefits code, only the amount (if any) by which the charge under the benefits code exceeds that as general earnings is brought in under the benefits code. This does not apply to the provision of living accommodation (see **27.59** below) or in relation to certain employee shareholdings taxed under the benefits code (see **69.11** SHARE-RELATED EMPLOYMENT INCOME AND EXEMPTIONS). [*ITEPA 2003, s 64*]. See also HMRC Employment Income Manual EIM21640.

See **53.15** PAY AS YOU EARN as regards PAYE settlement agreements whereby the employer accounts for tax on minor benefits, which do not then count as employees' income.

Directors and employees — the benefits code

[27.26] The provisions of the benefits code described at **27.27–27.48** below apply to all directors (as widely defined, but subject to the exclusion below) and to employees who are not in 'lower-paid employment'. [*ITEPA 2003, ss 63, 66, 67, 216*]. See **27.59–27.68, 27.90–27.93** below as regards those parts of the benefits code which apply to *all* employees and directors.

A director is excluded if he has no material interest (i.e. broadly if his and/or his associates' interests in the company do not exceed 5%) in the company *and either* is a full-time working director (i.e. he devotes substantially the whole of his time to the service of the company in a managerial or technical capacity) *or* the company is either non-profit-making (i.e. it does not carry on a trade nor is its main function the holding of investments or other property) or charitable. [*ITEPA 2003, ss 67–69, 216(3); ITA 2007, Sch 1 para 430; CTA 2010, Sch 1 para 383*]. A director so excluded will nevertheless be subject to these provisions if he is not in 'lower-paid employment'.

Meaning of 'lower-paid employment'

An employee is in '*lower-paid employment*' for a tax year if the earnings rate for the employment for that year is less than £8,500. The earnings rate for an employment for a year is calculated as follows.

(a)   Determine the aggregate (after deducting any exempt income) of:

        (i)   the earnings (see **27.20** above) from the employment for that year;

        (ii)   the total of amounts treated as earnings for that year. This includes all amounts which would be so treated under the benefits code, disregarding the exclusion of lower-paid employees where it might otherwise apply;

        (iii)   any deemed employment payment for the year by an intermediary (see **58.6 PERSONAL SERVICE COMPANIES ETC.**); and

        (iv)   the total amount of any deemed employment payments for the year by managed service companies (see **46.3 MANAGED SERVICE COMPANIES**).

    As regards (ii) above: in the case of provision of living accommodation under **27.59** *et seq.* below, the additional charge at **27.64** where cost exceeds £75,000 does not apply for this purpose, the basic charge being applied regardless of the cost. Prior to 2007/08, where car or car fuel benefits were provided by means of a voucher or credit token, the legislation strictly required both the car or fuel benefit and the voucher or token benefit to be taken into account in determining whether or not earnings were at the £8,500 level (see *Allcock v King* (Sp C 396), [2004] SSCD 122); but HMRC ESC A104 ensured that the voucher or token benefit would not be so taken into account where a car or car fuel benefit would apply, thus removing the anomaly of double counting (Revenue Press Release 5 July 2004). For 2007/08 onwards, amendments are made to the legislation so as effectively to give statutory effect to the concession.

(b)   Where an alternative is offered to a company car such that, if it had been taxable as earnings rather than under the benefits code, the taxable amount would have exceeded the car and fuel benefits charge computed as in **27.33, 27.35** below, the excess is added to the amount determined under (a) above.

(c)   From the amount resulting from (a) and (b) above, subtract specified 'authorised deductions', which do *not* include general allowable deductions within **27.22** above or most general travelling expenses. The '*authorised deductions*' are those within **27.18** (other than those under *ITEPA 2003, s 341* or *s 342* (travelling expenses on commencement or termination of employment or between employments)) and **27.19** above, **27.52** (employee liabilities), **27.54** (artiste's percentage deduction) and **27.73** (personal security provision) below, **11.5 CAPITAL ALLOWANCES ON PLANT AND MACHINERY, 16.20 CHARITIES** (payroll deduction scheme) and **57.7 PENSION PROVISION** (contributions to a registered pension scheme).

(d)   The earnings rate is the figure resulting from (a)–(c) above, proportionately increased if the employment is held for less than the full number of days in the tax year concerned.

Earnings rates from different but 'related' employments during a year are aggregated and compared with £8,500 p.a. in determining whether all or none of them is lower-paid employment. Employments are '*related*' for this purpose where either they are with the same employer or one is with a body or partnership ('A') and the other either with an individual, partnership or body ('B') that controls A or with another partnership or body controlled by B.

[*ITEPA 2003, ss 216–220; FA 2007, ss 25, 62, Sch 3 para 5*].

Detailed application of the provisions is covered in **27.26–27.48** below, in which references to an 'employee' should (unless the context requires otherwise) be taken as referring to any director or employee to whom the provisions relate.

Simon's Taxes. See E4.601–E4.603.

Expenses

[27.27] All payments to an employee by reason of the employment in respect of expenses, including sums put at employee's disposal and paid away by him, are taxable. All payments by the employer are 'by reason of the employment' unless the employer is an individual and the payment is made in the normal course of his domestic, family or personal relationships. Deductions may be made as under **27.5** and **27.10** (remittances), **27.18** (under *ITEPA 2003, s 341* or *s 342* (travelling expenses on commencement or termination of employment or between employments)), **27.22**(general allowable deductions), **27.50** (clergymen etc.), **27.52** (employee liabilities) and **27.76** (professional fees and subscriptions). [*ITEPA 2003, ss 70–72*]. This includes use of employer's credit card. See **53.15** PAY AS YOU EARN as regards PAYE settlement agreements whereby employer accounts for tax on minor payments of expenses within the agreement, which do not then count as employees' income.

Benefits-in-kind generally

[27.28] All benefits or facilities of any kind (other than those within the special charging provisions at **27.32–27.48** below) provided for an employee (or for an employee's family or household) by reason of the employment are taxable on the cash equivalent of the benefit (see **27.30** below). Benefits are 'provided' by those at whose cost they are provided, and benefits provided by someone other than the employer may be included. All benefits provided by the employer are 'by reason of the employment' unless the employer is an individual and the provision is made in the normal course of his domestic, family or personal relationships. [*ITEPA 2003, ss 201, 202, 209*]. See also **27.59–27.68**, **27.90–27.93** below as regards provisions for the taxation of certain benefits which apply to *all* employees and directors.

In a case in which, by virtue of an earlier change in control agreement, the appellant had disposed of shares in his employer company *to* that company for more than their market value, the excess was held to be a benefit provided to the appellant by reason of his employment and thus chargeable to tax as a benefit (*Smith v HMRC* FTT (TC 163), [2009] SFTD 731).

The Treasury does, however, have powers to exempt minor benefits by order, such exemption being conditional on the benefit(s) in question being made available to the employer's employees generally on similar terms. From 6 April 2002, provision of a voucher evidencing entitlement to such an exempt minor benefit is also exempt from charge under *ITEPA 2003, s 87* (non-cash vouchers, see **27.91** below). The following minor benefits have been the subject of such regulatory exemption.

- Welfare counselling (excluding medical treatment and advice on finance (other than debt problems), tax, leisure or recreation and legal advice). HMRC has agreed with the UK Employee Assistance Professionals Association (EAPA) that legal information provided within the context of welfare counselling will not prevent the exemption from applying as long as it remains within agreed guidelines, for which see www.hmrc. gov.uk/specialist/welfare-counselling.htm.
- Cyclists' breakfasts.
- Provision of buses for journeys of ten miles or less from the workplace to shops etc. on a working day.
- Certain benefits provided to disabled employees (e.g. hearing aids or wheelchairs) to enable them to perform the duties of the employment.
- Pension information and advice given to an employee on the employer's behalf where the cash equivalent of the benefit (see **27.30** below) does not in total exceed £150 for the tax year; if there is an excess over £150, the full amount is taxable and not just the excess.
- (For 2007/08 and 2008/09) one health screening and one medical check-up per employee per year. Screenings must be available to all employees and check-ups must be available either to all employees or to all those identified by screening as needing a check-up. For this purpose, a '*health screening*' is an assessment to identify employees who might be at particular risk of ill health; a '*medical check-up*' is a physical examination by a health professional for the purpose of determining the employee's state of health and no more.

  A similar exemption was generally applied on a non-statutory basis before 6 April 2007 (see **27.29**(xviii) below) and concern has been raised that the statutory exemption does not always operate as intended in relation to some pre-existing health screening schemes. For 2007/08 and 2008/09, HMRC will not seek to collect tax in respect of health screening and/or medical check-ups where tax would not have been payable under the pre-2007/08 non-statutory basis. For 2009/10 onwards, legislation broadly restores the pre-6 April 2007 position by omitting the proviso that screenings and check-ups have to be available to all employees (see **27.29**(xviii) below). (HMRC Internet Statements 12 October 2007, 17 March 2008, 10 December 2008).

[*ITEPA 2003, ss 210, 266(4); SI 2000 No 2080; SI 2002 Nos 205, 1596; SI 2003 No 1434; SI 2004 No 3087; SI 2007 No 2090; SI 2009 No 695*].

In relation to the timing of a benefit, 'provided' refers to the receipt by the employee of the benefit, rather than to steps taken or costs incurred by the employer (*Templeton v Jacobs* Ch D 1996, 68 TC 735).

See **56.1 PENSION INCOME** as regards benefits provided to retired employees.

Following the decision in *Wicks v Firth* HL 1982, 56 TC 318, payments of cash are potentially within the benefits legislation, so that, for example, examination awards which would otherwise not be taxable following *Ball v Johnson* (see **27.20** above) fall within the benefits charge (ICAEW Technical Memorandum TR 786, 15 March 1990).

Legal expenses incurred by a company in defending a dangerous driving charge against a director were held to be a benefit (*Rendell v Went* HL 1964, 41 TC 641). Parking etc. fines met by employer would generally constitute a benefit (see **27.20** above). Legal costs incurred by a company in proceedings to which the managing director lent his name and from which he personally benefited were held to be a taxable benefit; the fact that the company also benefited was irrelevant, except that the benefit should be restricted to that proportion of total costs which is attributed to the employee on a fair basis (*XI Software Ltd v Laing* (Sp C 450), [2005] SSCD 249).

Allocations of moneys by trustees of an *employee benefit trust* to sub-funds for individual employees were not taxable as benefits-in-kind (*Macdonald v Dextra Accessories Ltd and Others* Ch D 2003, 77 TC 146).

See **27.73** below as regards provision of security assets and services for employees.

See **53.15** PAY AS YOU EARN as regards PAYE settlement agreements whereby employer accounts for tax on minor benefits within the agreement, which do not then count as employees' income.

Exceptions

[27.29] Exceptions from the charge on benefits-in-kind are listed below. See also the minor exemptions listed in **27.28** above.

(i)   **Provision of accommodation, supplies or services** used by the employee in performing the duties of the employment, provided that either:

    (a)   if the benefit is provided on premises occupied by the employer or other person providing it, any private use (i.e. use other than in performing those duties) by the employee (or by the employee's family or household) is not significant; or

    (b)   in any other case, the sole purpose of providing the benefit is to enable the employee to perform those duties, any private use (as in (a)) is 'not significant', and the benefit is not an 'excluded benefit'.

    Whether private use under (b) above meets the 'not significant' test will depend on all the circumstances of any given case, but provided that:

- the employer's policy is clearly stated to employees, setting out the circumstances in which occasional private use may be made; and
- any decision of the employer not to recover the costs of private use is a commercial decision, for example based on the impractical nature of doing so, rather than a desire to reward the employee,

HMRC will usually accept that the 'not significant' test is met. Employers are not expected to keep detailed records of private use. The 'not significant' condition should not be decided purely on the absolute time spent on different uses of the asset or service provided; instead, it should be considered in the context of the employee's duties and the necessity for the employee to have the asset or service in order to carry out those duties. (HMRC Employment Income Manual EIM21613).

Subject to Treasury regulations (which may provide that a benefit is an 'excluded benefit' only if prescribed conditions are met as to the terms on which, and persons to whom, it is provided), *'excluded benefit'* consists of the provision of a motor vehicle, boat or aircraft, or of a benefit which involves the extension, conversion or alteration of any living accommodation or the construction, extension, conversion or alteration of a building or other structure on land adjacent to and enjoyed with living accommodation. [*ITEPA 2003, s 316*].

The exemption can extend to the provision of a telephone line and/or broadband internet access in the employee's home (HMRC Employment Income Manual EIM21615–21617). See generally EIM21610–21614.

(ii) **Provision of living accommodation and connected expenses** in certain circumstances, see **27.62, 27.63, 27.66** below. [*ITEPA 2003, ss 313–315*].

(iii) **Provision made by the employer for any pension, annuity, lump sum, gratuity** or other like benefit to be given to the employee, his dependants or any other members of his family or household on his retirement or death. This exemption applies to (but is not restricted to) provision made under a registered pension scheme (as in **57.2 PENSION PROVISION**). It does not extend to any amount paid to insure against the risk that a retirement or death benefit under an employer-financed retirement benefits scheme (see **57.26 PENSION PROVISION**) cannot be paid due to the employer's insolvency. [*ITEPA 2003, s 307*].

(iv) **Provision by the employer of free or subsidised meals** in a canteen or on the employer's business premises where, in either case, the meals are provided on a reasonable scale and all of the employer's employees (or all of them at a particular location) may obtain such a meal or a voucher, ticket, pass etc. to enable them to obtain such a meal. Light refreshments are regarded as meals for these purposes. If the meals are provided in the restaurant or dining-room of a hotel or a catering etc. business at a time when meals are served to the public, the exemption applies only if the staff meals are taken in a part designated for staff use only.

For 2011/12 onwards, the exemption is not available where the employee's entitlement to free or subsidised meals arises in conjunction with salary sacrifice arrangements or 'flexible remuneration arrangements'. For example, the employee might agree to accept a reduced salary in return for being provided with food and drink (or the means of obtaining it) of a value that is commensurate with the amount of income given up. It matters not whether the arrangements are made before or after the employment commences. For this purpose, *'flexible*

remuneration arrangements' are arrangements under which employer and employee agree that the employee is to be provided with free or subsidised meals rather than receive some other description of employment income.
[ITEPA 2003, ss 266(3)(e), 317; FA 2010, s 60].
Where the provision of subsidised meals to employees is exempt as above, the provision of those meals to others who are working at the employer's premises but are not employees of that employer is also exempt. *[SI 2002 No 205, Reg 6].*

(v)   **Provision of travel, accommodation and subsistence** during public transport disruption caused by industrial action. *[ITEPA 2003, s 245].* See also **27.80** below.

(vi)   **Provision of means of transport between home and place of employment (or training) for disabled employees.** *[ITEPA 2003, ss 246, 247].* See also **27.32, 27.80** below.

(vii)   **Provision of transport for occasional late night journeys from work to home,** or following a failure of car-sharing arrangements, subject to certain conditions. *[ITEPA 2003, s 248].* See also **27.81** below.

(viii) **Provision of transport between mainland and offshore rig etc.,** and necessary overnight accommodation on the mainland, for offshore oil and gas workers. *[ITEPA 2003, s 305].*

(ix)   **Travelling expenses** (including reasonable hotel expenses) of:
        (a)   a director of two or more companies within a group of companies, between his main place where he acts as director and other places within the UK in the course of his duties as a director. Similarly where a person is a director of one company and an employee of another company in the same group;
        (b)   an unremunerated director of a company not managed with a view to dividends (e.g. a club);
        (c)   a director who holds the position as part of a professional practice, provided no claim is made to a deduction under the trading income rules;
        (d)   a spouse accompanying a director on his or her duties abroad because of his or her precarious health.
        (HMRC ESC A4). See also **27.80** below and, as regards (a), see **27.23** above for comparable statutory relief.

(x)   **Removal expenses.** For the statutory relief from charge as employment income of certain payments and benefits received in connection with job-related residential moves, see **27.71** below.
        For HMRC's view of the taxation implications of guaranteed selling price (or similar) schemes for houses as part of employee relocation packages, see Revenue Tax Bulletin May 1994 p 122 and, in relation in particular to the application of the concession at (xix) below, April 1995 p 211.

(xi)   **Miners' free coal and allowances in lieu thereof.**

(xii)   **Meal vouchers.** See **27.69** below.

(xiii) **Medical insurance** for treatment and medical services where the need for treatment arises **while abroad** in performance of duties. *[ITEPA 2003, s 325].*

(xiv) **Vehicle parking facilities.** No benefit arises from the provision for the employee of a car, a cycle, a motor cycle or a van parking space at or near his place of work, and where such a benefit is convertible into cash, e.g. under a salary sacrifice arrangement, no charge to tax on general earnings arises. [*ITEPA 2003, s 237(1)(3)*]. See also **27.20** above, **27.90** below.

(xv) **Entertainment by third parties.** No income tax liability arises from the provision of hospitality of any kind for the employee (or for his family or household), unless it is provided either:

- in recognition or anticipation of particular services by the employee in the course of the employment; or
- directly or indirectly by or on behalf of the employer or by any person connected with the employer (within **21 CONNECTED PERSONS**).

[*ITEPA 2003, s 265*].

'Hospitality' covers dinners, parties, hospitality tents at sporting events etc., and events such as theatrical performances or sporting events where a host invites someone to accompany him as a guest. It includes associated costs, such as transport or overnight accommodation. (HMRC Employment Income Manual EIM21836).

See also **27.90** below and, as regards concessionary relief in respect of gifts from third parties, **27.56** below.

(xvi) **Christmas parties etc.** No benefit arises from expenditure on an annual Christmas party or similar annual function open to the staff generally, or to staff at a particular location, of up to £150 per head per annum, including VAT and any transport or accommodation costs, or of non-cash vouchers for obtaining such provision (see **27.91** below). Where expenditure exceeds this amount the full amount will be taxable. The total cost is for this purpose divided by the total number of people attending the function to determine whether the limit is exceeded. The expenditure may be split between more than one annual event, and where the total expenditure for the year exceeds the £150 limit, a function or functions whose cost or the sum of whose costs is within the limit will not be taxed, the cost of the remaining functions being taxed in full. Casual hospitality is not regarded as constituting an annual function for these purposes. No P11D return (see **53.12 PAY AS YOU EARN**) is required in respect of expenditure not exceeding the limit. [*ITEPA 2003, s 264;*].

(xvii) **Certain training and counselling expenses,** see **27.51, 27.79** below.

(xviii) **Medical check-ups and health-screenings.** Before 2007/08, the provision of routine health checks or medical screening for employees did not confer a chargeable benefit, whether carried out by the employer's own medical staff or by an outside firm. (Revenue Tax Bulletin May 1993 p 74). This applied also to such provision for members of the employee's family or household (HMRC Employment Income Manual EIM21765).

For 2007/08 and 2008/09, a similar exemption operated under a combination of statutory instrument and non-statutory concession (see **27.28** above).

For 2009/10 onwards, the provision by an employer of one health-screening assessment and/or one medical check-up per employee per tax year does not confer a chargeable benefit. The provision of a voucher or credit-token (see generally **27.90** below) to obtain such screenings and/or check-ups is similarly exempt. Where the employee has more than one employer at the same time, the exemption applies only to one medical check-up and one health-screening per tax year provided by any of them. There is no requirement that these benefits be available to all employees of a particular employer. [*ITEPA 2003, ss 266(3), 267(2), 320B; FA 2009, s 55*].

(xix)   **Asset acquisition costs.** Normal purchaser's costs in relation to the sale or transfer of an asset by the employee to the employer (or to some other person by reason of the employment) are disregarded in calculating any benefit arising to the employee. [*ITEPA 2003, s 326*]. See Revenue Tax Bulletin April 1995 p 210 as regards the application of this exemption in relation to guaranteed selling price (or similar) schemes for houses as part of employee relocation packages (and see (x) above).

(xx)   **Incidental overnight expenses.** A benefit is exempt from tax where its provision is incidental to the employee's being away from home on business during a 'qualifying absence' in relation to which the authorised maximum (£5 per night spent in the UK and £10 per night spent abroad) is not exceeded, being a benefit the cost of which is not otherwise deductible from earnings. [*ITEPA 2003, ss 240, 241, Sch 7 paras 33, 34*]. See also **27.82** below.

(xxi)   **Mobile phones.** No benefit arises from the making available (without any transfer of property) of a single mobile phone to an employee (but *not* to any member of his family or household). The exemption covers line rental for, and calls from, a single mobile phone number. Where the benefit of the phone is convertible into cash, e.g. under a salary sacrifice arrangement, no charge to tax on general earnings arises.

Before 2006/07 the exemption could cover more than one phone and could also cover a phone provided to a member of an employee's family or household. Where a second or subsequent mobile phone was first provided to an employee before 6 April 2006 or a mobile phone was provided to a member of his family or household before that date, the pre-2006/07 exemption continues to have effect for 2006/07 onwards as regards that particular phone.

See also HMRC Employment Income Manual EIM21779.

The provision of a voucher or credit-token (see generally **27.90** below) to obtain use of a mobile phone is exempt if direct provision of the phone would have been exempt.

'*Mobile phone*' is defined so as to exclude a cordless extension to a land-line, but not so as to exclude a telephone provided in connection with a vehicle.

[*ITEPA 2003, ss 266(2), 267(2), 319*].

(xxii)   **Computer equipment.** For 1999/2000 to 2005/06 inclusive, the making available (without any transfer of property) of certain computer equipment to an employee (or to his family or household) gave rise to a benefits charge only to the extent that the aggregate cash equivalent of the benefit exceeded £500 for a tax year. For example, the provision of the use of £2,000 of equipment (at 20% cash equivalent) plus £100 of related expenses, or the provision of equipment rented at an annual rental of £500, would be within the exemption. The arrangements by the employer for providing employees with computer equipment could not be limited to directors, and could not make more favourable provision in relation to any director(s).

'Computer equipment' includes printers, scanners, modems, discs and other peripheral devices designed to be used with a computer, and the provision of a right to use software together with the provision of hardware is included (but not provision of access to, or use of, any public telecommunications system (within *Telecommunications Act 1984*)).

Computer equipment provided as above was also exempt from the general charge under *ITEPA 2003, s 62* on earnings (see **27.20** above), thus avoiding a charge where the employee is given the choice of the loan of computer equipment or additional salary.

The exemption was abolished for 2006/07 onwards. However, where computer equipment was first provided to an employee (or to a member of his family or household) before 6 April 2006, the exemption continues to have effect for 2006/07 onwards as regards that particular equipment. In most cases, there needs to have been a binding agreement in place before 6 April 2006 for loan of the equipment to the employee; but HMRC accept that, where employer and employee had agreed in writing before 6 April 2006 the terms on which the equipment would be made available (including equipment specifications, cost/value and details of the salary/tax impact upon the employee), the exemption will apply, even if, due to circumstances beyond his control, the employee was not able to take physical possession of the equipment before 6 April (HMRC Internet Statement 24 March 2006). For other points on the transition, see HMRC Employment Income Manual EIM21699. It was widely suggested that the abolition of the exemption would cause practical difficulties. However, where employers provide computer equipment to employees solely to enable them to carry out the duties of the employment at home, HMRC take the view that in many cases private use is likely to be 'not significant' (see (i) above), when compared with the primary business purpose of providing the equipment, in which case no taxable benefit should arise (HMRC Internet Statement 12 June 2006). For HMRC guidance (with examples) on how the term 'not significant' should be interpreted in this respect, see HMRC Employment Income Manual EIM21613.

[*ITEPA 2003, s 320; FA 2006, s 61*].

For the interaction between this exemption and *ITEPA 2003, s 206* (cost of benefit on subsequent transfer of asset), see HMRC Employment Income Manual EIM21652.

(xxiii) **Bus services.** Two exemptions apply in relation to bus services for employees.

    (a)   No benefit arises from the provision for employees of a '*works transport service*', i.e. a service provided by means of a 'bus' or a 'minibus' for conveying employees of one or more employers on 'qualifying journeys'. For this purpose a *'bus'* is a road passenger vehicle with a seating capacity of 12 or more, and a *'minibus'* is a vehicle constructed or adapted for the carriage of 9, 10 or 11 passengers (no account being taken in the case of a minibus of seats which do not meet the relevant 'construction and use requirements' under *Road Traffic Act 1988, Pt II* or NI equivalent). Seating capacity is determined as under *Vehicle Excise and Registration Act 1994, Sch 1 Pt III*. A *'qualifying journey'* for an employee is a journey (or part of a journey) between home and workplace (i.e. a place at which the employee's attendance is necessary in performance of the duties of the employment) or thereabouts (see Hansard Standing Committee B, 25 May 1999), or between workplaces, in connection with the performance of those duties. The service must be available generally to employees of the employer(s) concerned, and the main use must be for qualifying journeys by those employees. The service must also substantially be used only by those employees or their children aged under 18 (including step- and illegitimate children). Provision of a voucher for use of such a service is similarly exempt from charge under *ITEPA 2003, s 87* (non-cash vouchers — see **27.91** below), and it is made clear that the company car provisions (see **27.33** below) cannot apply to a works bus service.

(b) No income tax liability arises in respect of financial or other support for a public passenger transport service provided by means of a road vehicle and used by employees of one or more employers for 'qualifying journeys'. A *'qualifying journey'* is as under (a) above. The service must be available generally to employees of the employer(s) concerned. The terms on which it is available must not be more favourable than those available to other passengers, although this condition does not apply in the case of a 'local bus service' within *Transport Act 1985, s 2* and provision of a voucher for use of the service is similarly exempt from charge under *ITEPA 2003, s 87* (non-cash vouchers — see **27.91** below).

HMRC have become aware that this exemption is being used in salary sacrifice arrangements that are aimed at providing employees with bus passes and that the conditions for the exemption are not always satisfied. They will apply the law as intended where bus pass salary sacrifice arrangements are entered into after 18 December 2009. For their approach in transitional cases, see www.hmrc.gov.uk/specialist/cycles_bus_passes.pdf.

[*ITEPA 2003, ss 242, 243, 249, 266(2)*].

See **27.28** above as regards exemption of minor benefits of provision of transport to shops etc.

(xxiv) **Cycles and cyclists' safety equipment.** No benefit arises from the provision (without any transfer of property) for an employee of a cycle or cyclist's safety equipment, provided that:

(a) the facility is available generally to employees of the employer concerned; and

(b) the employee uses the cycle or equipment mainly for 'qualifying journeys' (as under (xxiii)(a) above). Employers are not, however, expected to monitor employees' other cycling journeys (see Hansard Standing Committee B, 25 May 1999).

Where such a benefit is convertible into cash, e.g. under a salary sacrifice arrangement, no charge to tax on general earnings arises.

Provision of a voucher for use of a cycle or safety equipment is similarly exempt from charge under *ITEPA 2003, s 87* (non-cash vouchers, see **27.91** below).

See also (xiv) above, **27.20** above and **27.91, 27.93** below as regards cycle parking facilities at work places.

[*ITEPA 2003, ss 244, 249, 266(2)*].

See also **27.28** above as regards exemption of minor benefit of cyclists' breakfasts.

HMRC are aware that some 'cycle to work' salary sacrifice arrangements based on the above exemption do not satisfy the condition that the offer of a cycle should be open to all employees. In such instances, the exemption does not apply, but HMRC have set out their approach where the only reason the exemption does not apply is that the offer excludes employees aged under 18 or earning at or around the National Minimum Wage. In those circumstances, HMRC will apply the letter of the law only where the 'cycle to work' salary sacrifice arrangements are entered into after 18 December 2009; for their approach in transitional cases, see www.hmrc.gov.uk/specialist/cycles_bus_passes.pdf.

(xxv) **Emergency vehicles.** No benefit arises where an emergency vehicle (as defined) is made available to a person employed in an emergency service (i.e. police or a fire, fire and rescue, ambulance or paramedic service) if the terms on which it is made available prohibit its private use otherwise than when the person is 'on call' or 'engaged in on-call commuting' and the person does not, in fact, make private use of the vehicle outside these terms. For this purpose, a person is '*on call*' when liable, as part of normal duties, to be called upon to use the vehicle to respond to emergencies. A person is '*engaged in on-call commuting*' when he is using the vehicle for ordinary commuting (see **27.23** above) (or for travel between two places that is for practical purposes substantially ordinary commuting) and is required to do so in order that the vehicle is available for use in responding to emergencies. [*ITEPA 2003, s 248A; FA 2004, s 81(1)(3)*].

(xxvi) **Eye tests and corrective glasses.** If health and safety legislation requires an employer to provide eye tests and eyesight tests for employees, particularly in relation to employees' use of Visual Display Units (VDUs), the provision of the tests themselves, and of any corrective glasses shown by the tests to be necessary, is exempt. The provision of a voucher or credit-token (see generally **27.90** below) to obtain such tests and/or glasses is similarly exempt. It is a condition that the benefit be made available to all employees for whom it is meant to be provided under the health and safety rules. [*ITEPA 2003, ss 266(3), 267(2), 320A*].

Cash equivalent of the benefit

[27.30] The cash equivalent of the benefit is the cost of the benefit (including a proper proportion of any expense relating partly to the benefit and partly otherwise) less any part made good by the employee to those providing the benefit. [*ITEPA 2003, ss 203, 204*]. VAT is included whether or not recoverable by the employer (HMRC SP A6). The cost of 'in-house' benefits (i.e. those consisting of services or facilities enjoyed by the employee which it is part of the employer's business to provide to members of the public) is the additional or marginal cost of their provision to the employee, rather than a proportionate part of total costs incurred in their provision both to employees and to the public. See *Pepper v Hart* HL 1992, 65 TC 421, in which only the marginal cost of providing school places for the children of masters at the school was assessable, regardless of whether or not the children occupied places which would otherwise have been provided to members of the public. (*Note.* This decision was based on consideration of statements by the Financial Secretary to the Treasury in Standing Committee debates on the enacting legislation. See **5.32 APPEALS** as regards the circumstances in which this is permissible.)

Following this decision, HMRC set out their view of how the marginal cost rule should apply in practice. In particular, nil or negligible cost arises in the case of:

- rail or bus travel by employees (provided fare-payers are not displaced);
- goods sold to employees for not less than the wholesale price; and
- provision of professional services not requiring additional staffing (excluding disbursements).

It is accepted that no additional benefit arises where teachers pay 15% or more of normal school fees.

The decision also affects the calculation of the benefit of the provision of assets for part business, part private use. Fixed costs need not now be taken into account where the private use is incidental to the business use. The cash equivalent is the proper proportion of the 'annual value' of the asset (see below) together with any *additional* running expenses.

(Revenue Press Release 21 January 1993).

See **27.91** below as regards valuation of incentive awards.

Where the benefit is the *use of an asset* other than a car or van (as to which see **27.33, 27.36** below), the cost of the benefit is the annual value (or if higher, the rent or hire charge paid by those providing the benefit) plus any expenses related to the asset's provision (excluding the cost of acquiring or producing it and excluding also any rent or hire charge payable for the asset by those providing the benefit). [*ITEPA 2003, s 205*].

Where the benefit is the *transfer of an asset after it has been used or depreciated* since the transferor acquired it, the cost of the benefit is the market value at the time of the transfer. However, if the asset (not a car or van) was first applied for the provision of any benefit for a person or for members of his family or household by reason of his employment after 5 April 1980 and a person (whether or not the present transferee) has been chargeable to tax on its use, the cost of the benefit (unless a higher benefit is obtained by taking market value at the time of transfer) is its market value when it was first so applied less the total cost of the benefit of the *use* of the asset (see above) in the years up to and including the year of transfer. [*ITEPA 2003, s 206, Sch 7 para 32(2)*]. The second alternative does not apply to computer equipment within **27.29**(xxii) above or to cycles within **27.29**(xxiv) above, with the result that the charge is always on market value at time of transfer. [*FA 2005, s 17*].

Annual value of the use of an asset is:

> *for land*, its 'annual rental value' under *ITEPA 2003, s 207*;
> *in any other case*, **20%** of market value at time asset was first provided as a benefit.

[*ITEPA 2003, ss 205(3), 207, 208*].

Apportionment

Where appropriate, e.g. where an asset is not available for the whole of a tax year or where it is available to more than one person, only a corresponding proportion of the cost etc. of the benefit (determined as above) is brought in. See *ITEPA 2003, s 204*, HMRC Employment Income Manual EIM21200 *et seq.* and *Kerr v Brown; Boyd v Brown* (Sp C 333, 333A), [2002] SSCD 434, [2003] SSCD 266.

Deductions

Deductions may be claimed from the cash equivalent calculated as above for allowable payments falling within **27.18, 27.19, 27.22–27.24** or **27.50** above or **27.52** (employee liabilities), **27.54** (artiste's percentage deduction), **27.73** (personal security provision) or **27.76** (professional fees and subscriptions) below. [*ITEPA 2003, s 365*].

Part business and part private use

A deduction may be available under *ITEPA 2003, s 365* (as above) from the full cash equivalent of a benefit within the general charge where there is mixed use of the benefit, or the cost of the benefit may be apportioned under *ITEPA 2003, s 204* (see above) if the expense relates partly to the benefit and partly to other matters. This does not apply to benefits for which there are special computational rules (see **27.32** *et seq.* below). See Revenue Tax Bulletin October 2000 pp 779–782 for an article on this subject and for the application of *Pepper v Hart* (see above) in cases of mixed use. The article also deals in particular with the provision of home telephones.

Simon's Taxes. See E4.611–E4.616, E4.7.

Example

[27.31]

During 2010/11 P Ltd transferred to R a television set which it had previously leased to him for a nominal rent of £2 per month. The company also leased a suit to R under the same arrangements. R's salary is £30,000 p.a.

Television

First leased to R in April 2009 (when its market value was £560); transferred to R on 6 March 2011 for £50, the market value at that time being £175.

R's benefits are	£	£
2009/10		
Cost of benefit 20% × £560		112
Deduct Rent paid by R		24
Cash equivalent of benefit		£88
2010/11		
Cost of benefit 20% × £560 × $^{11}/_{12}$		103
Deduct Rent paid by R (11 months)		22
Cash equivalent of benefit		81
Greater of		
(Market value at transfer	175	
Deduct Price paid by R	50	
	£125	
And		
(ii) Original market value	560	
Deduct Cost of benefits note (b)	215	
	345	
Deduct Price paid by R	50	
	£295	
		295
Total		£376

Suit

First leased to R on 6 November 2010 (when its market value was £340).

R's benefit for 2010/11 is	£
Cost of benefit 20% × £340 × $^{5}/_{12}$	28
Deduct Rent paid by R (5 months)	10
Cash equivalent of benefit	£18

Notes

(a)   On the transfer of the television set, the cost of the benefits to date (£112 + 103), not the cash equivalents, is deducted from the original market value.

(b)   It is assumed that the television set and suit have been bought by P Ltd and are not goods provided from within its own business. If the latter was the case, R would be assessed on the marginal cost to P Ltd in providing the benefit (in accordance with *Pepper v Hart* — see **27.30** above).

Motor vehicles provided for private use

[27.32] The provision by an employer, by reason of the employment, of a car or van partly or wholly for 'private use' by an employee (or by a member of his family or household), without the transfer of any property in it, is the subject of a special basis of charge. A car provided by the employer is provided 'by reason of the employment' unless the employer is an individual and the provision is made in the normal course of his domestic, family or personal relationships. '*Private use*' means any use other than for travel the expenses of which would, if incurred and paid by the employee, have been deductible from his earnings, and a car or van is deemed to be available for private use unless the terms on which it is made available prohibit such use *and* it is not so used. [*ITEPA 2003, ss 114, 116, 117, 118, 171(1)*].

See **27.33** below as regards cars and **27.36** below as regards vans.

See **27.80** below as regards business use where more than one place of work. See also *Gilbert v Hemsley* Ch D 1981, 55 TC 419. As regards special arrangements for employees in the motor industry, see HMRC Employment Income Manual EIM23800, 23885 for 2009/10 onwards and EIM23750–23775 for 2008/09 and earlier years. See **27.29**(xxv) above for an exemption for emergency vehicles.

The special basis of charge continues to apply where the car is in the *co-ownership* of the employer and employee (*Christensen v Vasili* Ch D 2004, 76 TC 116) and where the car is *leased* by the employer to the employee (*Whitby and another v HMRC* FTT (TC 255), 2010 STI 296).

A car provided by a third party (e.g. by a car dealer to a football player for promotional purposes) is within these provisions where it is provided by reason of the employment (HMRC Employment Income Manual EIM23260).

Where the special basis of charge applies, no other charge arises in respect of any expenses or reimbursements etc. in relation to the vehicle or in respect of vouchers for their provision (e.g. insurance, road tax, congestion charges). It appears that this does not apply to the payment of fines by the employer (although parking fines may escape liability in certain circumstances — see HMRC Employment Income Manual EIM21686). The provision of a driver is a separate benefit under **27.28** above (subject to an expense claim for business use). [*ITEPA 2003, ss 239, 269; FA 2008, s 48*]. See **27.29**(xxi) above for the general exemption of the provision of a mobile phone. The provision of a personalised registration number does not enter into the computation under the special basis of charge under **27.33** below, and is normally excluded from charge as above. (Revenue Tax Bulletin December 1994 p 177). The provision of a benefit which could equally be enjoyed by the employee when using a car of his own (e.g. a season ticket for a toll bridge) is not excluded from charge (HMRC Employment Income Manual EIM23035).

The mere fact that an employee is offered an alternative (for example, a cash alternative) to a company car or van does not make the benefit chargeable under the general earnings rules as opposed to the special company car or van provisions. [*ITEPA 2003, s 119*].

Compensation to an employee from whom a company car was withdrawn following a change of policy by the employer was held to be a taxable emolument in *Bird v Martland; Bird v Allen* Ch D 1982, 56 TC 89.

Where the special basis of charge applies to provision of a car, a separate charge also arises in respect of provision of any fuel for private use (see **27.35** below). In the case of provision of a van, no separate charge arose before 2007/08 on provision of fuel; for 2007/08 onwards, see **27.36** below.

As regards mileage allowances for the provision by employees of fuel for business travel in company cars, see **27.87** below.

Definition of car

A car is any mechanically propelled road vehicle *except* (i) a vehicle constructed primarily for carrying goods, (ii) a vehicle of a type unsuitable and not commonly used as a private vehicle, (iii) a motor cycle and (iv) an invalid carriage. [*ITEPA 2003, s 115*]. A car owned by the fire brigade and equipped with a flashing light and other emergency equipment was held to be within (ii) (*Gurney v Richards* Ch D 1989, 62 TC 287). A motor home was adjudged to be a car in *Morris v HMRC; County Pharmacy Ltd v HMRC* Ch D, [2006] STC 1593.

Definition of van

A van is a mechanically propelled road vehicle, other than a motor cycle, of a construction primarily suited for the conveyance of goods or burden and designed (or adapted) not to exceed a laden weight of 3,500 kgs. in normal use. [*ITEPA 2003, s 115*]. There was apparent confusion initially about the status of 'double cab pick-ups', and HMRC now follow the definitions used for VAT purposes. This means that a double cab pick-up that has a payload of 1 tonne (1,000 kg) or more is regarded as a van. Payload means gross vehicle weight (or design weight) less unoccupied kerb weight; for more details see HMRC Employment Income Manual EIM23150 and **27.96** below.

Disabled employees

There is a limited exemption for '*disabled employees*', i.e. those with a physical or mental impairment which has a substantial and long-term adverse effect on their ability to carry out normal day-to-day activities. Where a car is made available to such an employee, without any transfer of the property in it, no benefits charge arises on provision of the car, provided that:

(a)   the car has been adapted for the employee's special needs (or has an automatic transmission (see **27.33** below) because the employee can only drive such a car); and

(b)   the terms of its provision prohibit private use except for home-to-work travel or travel in connection with certain training course, and those terms are complied with.

The provision of, or payment or reimbursement of the cost of, fuel for the car does not give rise to an income tax liability where the conditions in (b) above are met. See also **27.80** below.

Parking facilities

The provision of car and van parking facilities for an employee at or near his place of work (including such provision in relation to a privately-owned vehicle) constitutes neither earnings nor a benefit. [*ITEPA 2003, ss 237, 247*].

Members of same family or household and shared cars

Where two members of the same family or household are each supplied with a car for their private use by the same employer, and neither is in lower-paid employment, each will be charged separately according to his/her own usage but will not be charged in respect of the car supplied to the other. Similarly, if one of them is not in such employment, but is supplied with the car in his/her own right either in equivalent circumstances to other employees in similar employment or in accordance with normal commercial practice for a job of that kind, the other will not be charged in respect of the car supplied to the lower-paid employee. This applies equally to any fuel scale charge. Where two or more persons are chargeable in respect of their shared use of the same car, the charge applicable to each of them will be reduced on a just and reasonable basis (and a similar reduction is made in any fuel scale charge). The reliefs for members of the same family or household apply to vans also. [*ITEPA 2003, s 169A*].

For pooled vehicles, see **27.38** below.

Simon's Taxes. See E4.625, E4.630.

Cars for private use

[27.33] The cash equivalent of the benefit (see **27.30** above) of a company car is a percentage of the 'price of the car' dependent on CO_2 emissions and certain related factors. The cash equivalent is reduced *pro rata* if the car was 'unavailable' for part of the tax year (see below). It is reduced finally by any payment made by the employee for private use (see below). The '*price of the car*' is its 'list price' or, if it has no list price, its 'notional price' (see below) plus in each case the price of any accessories that fall to be taken into account (see below).

Appropriate percentage

The percentage of the price of the car which determines the cash equivalent of the benefit (the '*appropriate percentage*') varies (except as further detailed below) from 15% to 35% depending on the 'applicable CO_2 emissions figure' for the car, expressed in grams per kilometre (g/km). The 15% rate applies if the emissions figure does not exceed the '*lower threshold*' for the year (140g/km for 2005/06, 2006/07 and 2007/08, 135g/km for 2008/09 and 2009/10, 130g/km for 2010/11, 125g/km for 2011/12, see below for 2012/13 onwards). For each 5g/km by which the emissions figure exceeds the lower threshold (rounding the emissions figure down to the nearest multiple of 5), the 15% rate is increased by one percentage point, up to the maximum rate of 35%.

For 2008/09 and 2009/10, the appropriate percentage is reduced to 10% in the case of a car (other than an electrically-propelled car) with an 'applicable CO_2 emissions figure' of no more than 120g/km. For 2010/11 and 2011/12, the appropriate percentage is reduced to 10% in the case of a car with an applicable CO_2 emissions figure of more than 75g/km but no more than 120g/km and to 5% in the case of a car with an applicable CO_2 emissions figure of no more than 75g/km. (For these purposes there is no rounding down of emissions figures.) See below as regards 2012/13 onwards.

The applicable CO_2 emissions figure

The 'applicable CO_2 emissions figure' is determined as follows.

(a)   If the car was first registered after 31 December 1997 but before 1 October 1999 and conformed to a vehicle type with an 'EC type-approval certificate' (as defined), or had a 'UK approval certificate' (as defined), specifying a CO_2 emissions figure in terms of g/km driven, it is that figure.

(b)   If the car is first registered after 30 September 1999 on the basis of an 'EC certificate of conformity' (as defined) or UK approval certificate specifying a CO_2 emissions figure in terms of g/km driven, it is that figure or, if more than one figure is quoted, the CO_2 emissions (combined) figure.

(c)   If a bi-fuel car is first registered after 31 December 1999 on the basis of an EC certificate of conformity or UK approval certificate specifying separate CO_2 emissions figures in terms of g/km driven for the different fuels, it is the lowest figure specified or, if more than one figure is specified in relation to each fuel, the lowest CO_2 emissions (combined) figure.

The official CO_2 emissions figures referred to in (a)–(c) above are recorded on the vehicle registration document from November 2000. For earlier registrations, an online CO_2 emissions enquiry service has been set up by the Society of Motor Manufacturers and Traders under an agreement with HMRC.

For 2012/13 onwards, the appropriate percentage will range from 5% to 35%. The 5% rate will apply if the CO_2 emissions figure does not exceed 75g/km but will cease to apply at all for 2015/16 onwards. A 10% rate will apply if the emissions figure is less than 100g/km (except where the 5% rate applies). The rate will be increased to 11% at an emissions level of 100g/km and then by one percentage point for each additional 5g/km, up to the maximum rate of 35%. The 15% rate will thus apply at 120g/km and the 35% rate at 220g/km, both down by 5g/km from 2011/12. (In computing rates at 11% or more, the car's emissions figure is rounded down to the nearest multiple of 5.)

Cars with no CO_2 emissions figure

If a car is first registered after 31 December 1997 but (a)–(c) above do not apply, then if the car has an internal combustion engine with reciprocating piston(s), the appropriate percentage is 15% if the cylinder capacity is 1,400 cc or less, 25% if it is 1,401–2,000 cc inclusive, 35% if it is more than 2,000 cc. For 2009/10 and earlier years, if a car which does not have such an engine is an '*electrically propelled vehicle*' (i.e. if it is propelled solely by electrical power derived from an external source or from a battery not connected to any source of power when the vehicle is in motion), the appropriate percentage is 15%.

Otherwise it is 35%. For 2010/11 onwards, if a car which does not have such an engine cannot in any circumstances emit CO_2 by being driven, the appropriate percentage is 0% (to be increased to 9% for 2015/16 onwards. Otherwise it is 35%.

Automatic cars for disabled drivers

Where an employee holding a disabled person's badge can only drive a car with automatic transmission, and an automatic car to which (a) or (b) above applies is made available to him (and not merely deemed to be made available to him or her because it is made available to a member of his family or household), then if the applicable CO_2 emissions figure for the car is higher than that for the 'equivalent manual car', the manual figure is substituted. The *equivalent manual car* is the closest non-automatic variant available of the same make and model of car first registered at or about the same time. A car has automatic transmission for these purposes if the gear ratio cannot be varied by the driver independently of the accelerator and brakes, or if the driver can independently vary the gear ratio but not by means of a manually-operated clutch pedal or lever. For 2009/10 onwards, if an employee holding a disabled person's badge can only drive a car with automatic transmission, and such a car is made available to him as above, the list price of the equivalent manual car, if lower, is substituted for that of the automatic car in calculating the benefit.

Diesel car supplement

Where a car propelled solely by diesel is first registered after 31 December 1997, the appropriate percentage, determined as above, is increased by 3%, subject to a maximum of 35%.

Discounts

The Treasury may make regulations providing for a reduction in any of the appropriate percentage figures as above in such circumstances, and subject to such conditions, as may be prescribed. Under *SI 2001 No 1123* (as amended), reductions are accordingly provided for as follows.

(1) Cars first registered after 31 December 1997 and before 1 January 2006, propelled solely by diesel and meeting the European standard for cleaner cars (*Council Directive 70/220/EEC, Annex 1, section 5.3.1.4, table row B*): the amount of the diesel supplement (as above). This discount is already abolished for cars registered on or after 1 January 2006 and is abolished entirely for 2011/12 onwards.

(2) Electrically-propelled cars (as above) first registered after 31 December 1997: 6%. This discount is abolished for 2010/11 onwards (in consequence of the reduction of the appropriate percentage to nil — see above).

(3) Cars first registered after 31 December 1997 and capable of being propelled by electricity and petrol: for 2006/07 onwards, 3%; for 2005/06 and earlier years, 2% + 1% for each 20g/km by which the CO_2 emissions figure is less than the lower threshold (as above). This discount is abolished for 2011/12 onwards.

(4) Cars first registered after 31 December 1997 and propelled solely by road fuel gas (e.g. LPG), and bi-fuel cars within (c) above: for 2006/07 onwards, 2%; for 2005/06 and earlier years, 1% + 1% for each 20g/km by which the CO_2 emissions figure is less than the lower threshold (as above). This discount is abolished for 2011/12 onwards.

(5) (For 2008/09 onwards) cars first registered after 31 December 1997 and capable of being propelled by bioethanol or by a mixture of 85% bioethanol and unleaded petrol (commonly known as 'E85'): 2%. This discount is abolished for 2011/12 onwards.

The discounts in (3) and (4) above for bi-fuel cars, cars capable of being propelled by electricity and petrol and cars propelled solely by road fuel gas do not apply to reduce the 10% appropriate percentage figure for 2008/09 onwards for cars with an 'applicable CO_2 emissions figure' of no more than 120g/km.

Cars registered before 1 January 1998

If the car has an internal combustion engine with reciprocating piston(s), the appropriate percentage is 15% if the cylinder capacity is 1,400 cc or less, 22% if it is 1,401–2,000 cc inclusive, 32% if it is more than 2,000 cc. In any other case the appropriate percentage is 32%.

Unavailability

A deduction is made from the cash equivalent of the benefit if the car was 'unavailable' on any day of the tax year. A car is *'unavailable'* on any day if it is a day falling before the first day on which it is made available to the employee (or a member of his family or household) or after the last day on which it is made so available, or on a day falling within a period of 30 or more consecutive days throughout which it is not so available. The deduction is given by the formula U/Y × C where U is the number of days for which the car was unavailable, Y is the total number of days in the tax year, and C is the cash equivalent of the benefit before taking account of any payment made by the employee for private use (see below).

If the car is unavailable for a period of less than 30 days and the employee is provided with a replacement car during that period, the replacement car is effectively ignored, provided that either it is not materially better than the normal car or it is not provided as part of an arrangement to supply a materially better car.

Payment by employee for private use

Where the employee is required, as a condition of the car being available for private use, to pay for that use and does so, the cash equivalent of the benefit for the tax year in question is reduced (or extinguished) by the amount so paid in respect of that year. This is the final part of the calculation. No reduction was allowed for a payment made to the employer to obtain a better car (*Brown v Ware* (Sp C 29) [1995] SSCD 155) or for a payment made for the insurance of the car for both private and business use (*CIR v Quigley* CS, [1995] STC 931).

Price of the car

The 'list price' of a car is the price published by the manufacturer, importer or distributor (as the case may be) as the inclusive price (including delivery charges and any car tax, value added tax, customs or excise duty or similar duty) appropriate for a car of that kind sold in the UK singly in an open market retail sale on the day before the date of its first registration. The price advertised by a car dealer cannot be used instead of that published by the manufacturer etc. (Revenue Tax Bulletin December 1994 p 177).

In the case of a car that is manufactured so as to be capable of running on road fuel gas and is not a bi-fuel car as within (c) above, the price of the car is reduced by so much of it as is reasonably attributable to the car's being manufactured to be so capable rather than only being capable of running on petrol.

The 'notional price' of a car is that which might reasonably be expected to have been its list price (as above) had such a price been published.

The price of the following 'accessories' must be added to the list price or notional price to find the price of the car:

(A) in the case of a car with a list price, any 'qualifying accessory' that is not a 'standard accessory', is available with the car when it is first made available to the employee and either has a price published by the manufacturer, importer or distributor of the car or is available with the car in the tax year for which the benefit is being computed; and

(B) in the case of *any* car, any 'qualifying accessory' that is available with the car in the tax year in question, was not so available when the car was first made available to the employee, was not made available with the car before 1 August 1993 and has a price of at least £100.

'Accessory' means any kind of equipment other than equipment necessarily provided for use in the performance of the duties of the employment, equipment by means of which a car is capable of running on road fuel gas, or 'equipment to enable a disabled person to use a car' (as defined by *ITEPA 2003, s 172*). A mobile phone is specifically excluded from being an accessory. A 'qualifying accessory' is an accessory that is made available for use with the car without any transfer of the property in the accessory, is made available by reason of the employment, and is attached to the car (whether permanently or not). A 'standard accessory' is a type of accessory assumed to be available with cars of the same kind as the car in question in arriving at the list price of the car.

The price of an accessory is its 'list price' or, if it has no list price, its 'notional price'. The 'list price' of an accessory within (A) above is the price published by the manufacturer, importer or distributor of the car or, if there is no such price, the price published by the manufacturer, importer or distributor of the accessory. The 'list price' of an accessory within (B) above is the price published by the manufacturer, importer or distributor of the accessory. The price published by the manufacturer, importer or distributor of the accessory means the inclusive price (including delivery charges, the price for permanently attaching it to the car where relevant, and any relevant taxes or duties) appropriate for an accessory of that kind sold in the UK singly in an open market retail sale at the time immediately before it is first made available for use with the car. The *'notional price'* of an accessory is that which might reasonably be expected to have been its list price (as above) had such a price been published.

Where an accessory within (B) above is available with the car in the tax year for which the benefit is being computed and that accessory replaced a qualifying accessory of the same kind in that year or in an earlier year, the new accessory is treated as a continuation of the old. If, however, the new accessory is superior to the one it replaced, and the old accessory was not a standard accessory, the cash equivalent of the benefit is to be computed ignoring the old accessory. A new accessory is superior to the old if its price exceeds the greater of the price of the old accessory and the price of an accessory equivalent to the old accessory at the time immediately before the new accessory is first made available for use with the car.

Capital contribution by employee

Where the employee makes a capital contribution to the cost of the car or of any qualifying accessories taken into account as above, the price of the car for the purposes of the charge on the employee for the tax year in which the contribution is made and subsequent years is reduced by the lesser of the amount of the contribution (or the sum of such contributions) and £5,000. An agreement for the employee to receive a proportionate return of his capital contribution on disposal of the car will not prejudice relief in respect of the contribution, and will not give rise to any employment income charge on the amount repaid. An agreement to refund the contribution in full will result in the contribution being disregarded. (Revenue Tax Bulletin December 1994 p 177).

Overall limit

There is an overall limit of £80,000 on the price of the car, whether list or notional, inclusive of accessories and after taking into account capital contributions by the employee. This limit is to be abolished for 2011/12 onwards.

Classic cars

There are special provisions substituting market value for the price determined as above where the market value is at least £15,000 and exceeds that price, and the car is 15 years or more old at the end of the tax year concerned. Capital contributions are taken into account on a similar basis to that described above, and the £80,000 overall limit similarly applies before 2011/12. Market value is judged as at the last day of the tax year or, if earlier, the last day in the tax year in which the car was available to the employee.

[*ITEPA 2003, ss 120–124, 124A–147, 170(1)–(4), 171, 172, Sch 7 paras 22, 23; FA 2006, s 59; FA 2008, s 47; FA 2009, s 54, Sch 28; FA 2010, ss 58(2)–(10), (18)(20), 59; SI 1994 Nos 777, 778; SI 2001 No 1123; SI 2005 No 2209; SI 2007 No 3068; SI 2010 No 695*].

See HMRC guidance at www.hmrc.gov.uk/cars/index.htm and see also **53.19 PAY AS YOU EARN.** HMRC also provide a company car and car fuel benefit calculator at www.hmrc.gov.uk/calcs/cars.htm.

Simon's Taxes. See E4.626A–E4.627A.

[27.34]

A, B and C are employees of D Ltd. Each earns at least £8,500 per annum and each is provided with a company car throughout 2010/11. The company also bears at least part of the cost of petrol for private motoring (see **27.35** below).

A is provided with a 1,800 cc car first registered in January 2008 with a list price (including VAT, car tax (but not road tax), delivery charges and standard accessories) of £19,000. The car was made available to A in April 2008. It has a diesel engine and an emissions figure of 185g/km. An immobiliser was fitted in September 2008 at a cost of £200. A is required to pay the company £250 per year as a condition of using the car for private motoring, and duly pays this amount.

B is provided with a 1,400 cc car first registered in March 1997 with a list price of £9,000. He was required to make a capital contribution of £1,000 on provision of the car in January 2009. B leaves the company in March 2011 and returns the car to D Ltd on 16 March. B was required to pay the company £50 per year as a condition of using the car for private motoring, and duly paid this amount.

C is provided with a luxury car first registered in February 2009 with a list price of £85,000 (which includes the list price of non-standard accessories). It has an emissions figure of 280g/km. C made a capital contribution of £3,000 in 2008/09.

Car and fuel benefits for 2010/11 are as follows.

		A £	B £	C £
List price		19,000	9,000	85,000
Later accessories (within **27.33**(B) above)		200	—	—
		19,200	9,000	85,000
Capital contributions		—	(1,000)	(3,000)
				£82,000
Overall limit				£80,000
Price of car		£19,200	£8,000	£80,000
Cash equivalent	£19,200 @ 29% (including 3% diesel supplement)	5,568		
	£8,000 @ 15%		1,200	
	£80,000 @ 35%			28,000
Deduction for unavailability (£1,200 × 20/365)			(66)	
			1,134	
Contribution for private use		(250)	(50)	—
Car benefit		5,318	1,084	28,000

	A £	B £	C £
Fuel benefit (£18,000 @ 29%)	5,220		
(£18,000 @ 15%)		2,700	
(£18,000 @ 35%)			6,300
Deduction for unavailability (£2,700 × 20/365)		(148)	
Total car and fuel benefits	£10,538	£3,636	£34,300

Car fuel for private use

[27.35] Tax is chargeable on the cash equivalent of the benefit of provision of free fuel for private motoring in a 'company car', i.e. a vehicle which attracts, or could attract, a charge within **27.33** above. The cash equivalent is obtained by applying the 'appropriate percentage' (see **27.33** above) used in determining the benefit of use of the car to an amount initially fixed at £14,400 (and variable by Treasury order). This amount remained unchanged for all years up to and including 2007/08. It was increased to £16,900 for 2008/09 and 2009/10. It is further increased to £18,000 for 2010/11 onwards. Within the normal range for the 'appropriate percentage' of 15% to 35%, the fuel charge thus ranges from £2,160 to £5,040 for 2007/08 and earlier years, from £2,535 to £5,915 for 2008/09 and 2009/10 and from £2,700 to £6,300 for 2010/11 onwards. 'Fuel' for these purposes does *not* include, for 2010/11 onwards, electrical energy or energy for a car which cannot in any circumstances emit CO_2 by being driven (previously electrical energy for an electrically propelled vehicle).

This charge does not apply to fuel provided for vans but a separate charge for van fuel applies for 2007/08 onwards, for which see **27.36** below.

If the employee is required to make good to his employer the cost of *all* company fuel used for private purposes, and in fact does so during the year in question (or without unreasonable delay thereafter — see HMRC Employment Income Manual EIM25660), the charge is reduced to nil. Travel between home and work is private for these purposes. In a case in which the cost was made good more than a year retrospectively, neither HMRC nor the Sp C accepted that the charge was so reduced (*Impact Foiling Ltd and others v HMRC* (Sp C 562), [2006] SSCD 764).

Where for any part of the tax year either:

- fuel is not provided for the car at all; or
- it is made available only for business travel; or
- the requirements for the 'making good' exemption referred to above are met,

and there is no subsequent time in the year when none of these three conditions is met, the cash equivalent of the fuel benefit is reduced in the proportion that the number of days on which at least one of these conditions is met bears to the number of days in the year. (For example, if for part of a year an employee makes good the cost of all fuel for private use but then ceases to do so later in the same tax year, without one of the other conditions being met, no reduction can be made to the cash equivalent of the benefit for that year.)

The cash equivalent of the fuel benefit is also proportionately reduced if the car is 'unavailable' (see **27.33** above) at any time in the tax year.

Where there is a charge under these provisions, there is no charge under other provisions in respect of the supply of fuel (e.g. on expense allowances or use of credit cards or vouchers which enable the employee to obtain private fuel). The *method* by which private fuel is obtained does not affect the employee's liability.

These provisions do not apply to fuel provided for private use in individuals' own cars, hire cars etc., where the general charging rules continue to apply (i.e. the employer will notify HMRC on form P11D of the actual cost of fuel provided by him). For fuel provided *by the employee* for business use in a car *other than* a company car, see **27.87** below.

[*ITEPA 2003, ss 149–152, 170(5)(6); FA 2010, s 58(11)(18); SI 2008 No 511; SI 2010 No 406, arts 1, 2*].

Providing that all the miles of private travel have been properly identified, HMRC will accept that there is no fuel charge where the employer uses the appropriate rate per mile from the table below (or any higher rate) to work out the cost of fuel used for private travel that the employee must make good. These advisory rates are not binding where the employer can demonstrate that employees cover the full cost of private fuel by repaying at a lower rate per mile. Even if it seems that the actual cost of the fuel could be more than the current advisory fuel rate, it is only in exceptional cases that HMRC will argue that a higher repayment rate should apply, for example where the employee drives a very large-engined company car that achieves fewer than 16 or 17 miles to the gallon; they will always accept the use of the advisory rates where the engine size is 3 litres or less.

Engine size	Petrol	Diesel	LPG*
1.7.05 to 30.6.06			
1400 cc or less	10p	9p	7p
1401 cc to 2000 cc	12p	9p	8p
Over 2000 cc	16p	13p	10p
1.7.06 to 31.1.07			
1400 cc or less	11p	10p	7p
1401 cc to 2000 cc	13p	10p	8p
Over 2000 cc	18p	14p	11p
1.2.07 to 31.7.07			
1400 cc or less	9p	9p	6p

1401 cc to 2000 cc	11p	9p	7p
Over 2000 cc	16p	12p	10p

1.8.07 to 31.12.07

1400 cc or less	10p	10p	6p
1401 cc to 2000 cc	13p	10p	8p
Over 2000 cc	18p	13p	10p

1.1.08 to 30.6.08

1400 cc or less	11p	11p	7p
1401 cc to 2000 cc	13p	11p	8p
Over 2000 cc	19p	14p	11p

1.7.08 to 31.12.08

1400 cc or less	12p	13p	7p
1401 cc to 2000 cc	15p	13p	9p
Over 2000 cc	21p	17p	13p

1.1.09–30.6.09

1400 cc or less	10p	11p	7p
1401 cc to 2000 cc	12p	11p	9p
Over 2000 cc	17p	14p	12p

1.7.09–30.11.09

1400 cc or less	10p	10p	7p
1401 cc to 2000 cc	12p	10p	8p
Over 2000 cc	18p	13p	12p

30.11.09–31.5.10

1400 cc or less	11p	11p	7p
1401 cc to 2000 cc	14p	11p	8p
Over 2000 cc	20p	14p	12p

After 31.5.10

1400 cc or less	12p	11p	8p
1401 cc to 2000 cc	15p	11p	10p
Over 2000 cc	21p	16p	14p

LPG = Liquid Petroleum Gas.

For 2008 onwards, the rates are reviewed twice a year. From 1 December 2009, any changes take effect on 1 December and 1 June, but HMRC will consider making interim changes if fuel prices fluctuate by 5% or more during the six-month period. For one month from the date of each change, employers may use either the previous or the new rates, as they choose. Employers may therefore require supplementary payments if they so wish, but are under no obligation to do so.

(www.hmrc.gov.uk/cars/fuel_company_cars.htm).

See **27.32** above for relief from the fuel scale charge in the cases of certain cars supplied to disabled employees or to members of the same family, and of shared cars, where there is relief from the charge on provision of the car.

Vans for private use

[27.36] The cash equivalent of the benefit of a 'van' (as defined in **27.32** above) depends on the degree to which private use is permitted or does, in fact, occur.

If the van is made available to the employee mainly for business travel and the terms on which it is made available prohibit its private use otherwise than for the purposes of 'ordinary commuting' (for which see **27.23** above), the cash equivalent of the benefit is nil. For this purpose, the term 'ordinary commuting' is extended to include travel between two places that is for practical purposes substantially ordinary commuting. It is a further condition that neither the employee nor any member of his family or household does, in fact, make private use of the van outside these terms. These requirements must be met throughout the tax year (or throughout that part of the tax year during which the van is available to the employee), but insignificant private use is disregarded. For some examples of what HMRC do and do not consider to be 'insignificant' in this context, see www.hmrc.gov.uk/employers/van-tax.htm or Revenue Tax Bulletin October 2004 p 1161.

If the restricted private use requirements above are not met, the cash equivalent of the benefit is:

- (for 2007/08 and subsequent years) **£3,000**;
- (for 2006/07) £500 if the van is less than four years old at the end of the tax year or £350 if is not.

The £3,000 rate is reduced to nil for 2010/11 to 2014/15 inclusive if the van cannot in any circumstances emit CO_2 by being driven.

The above figures are subject to reductions as outlined below for periods when the van is unavailable or if the van is shared or if the employee makes payments for private use. There is a separate fuel benefit charge (see below).

If the van is 'unavailable' on any one or more days during the tax year, the cash equivalent as above is reduced proportionately. For these purposes, a van is '*unavailable*' on any day in the tax year if that day falls before the first day on which it is available to the employee or after the last day on which it is so available or within a period of 30 days or more throughout which it is not so available.

If a van is shared, i.e. if it is made available to two or more employees concurrently by the same employer and is available concurrently for each of those employees' private use (or for private use by any member of their family or household), the cash equivalent as above to each such employee (reduced in each case for any periods of unavailability) is reduced on a just and reasonable basis. If any of the employees in question is a member of the family or household of another of them and the first-mentioned employee is outside the charge to tax on van benefits by virtue of his being in lower-paid employment (see **27.26** above), the availability of the van to him is disregarded in applying any reduction in the case of the second-mentioned employee.

If, as a condition for private use of a van, an employee is required to pay an amount of money (whether by deduction from earnings or otherwise) and does, in fact, make such payment, the cash equivalent (after applying any reductions as above) is reduced by the amount paid (or by so much of that amount as is required to reduce the cash equivalent to nil).

If the van normally available to the employee is not available to him for a period of less than 30 days and is replaced for all or part of that period by another van, the above provisions generally apply as if the replacement van were the normal van.

The rates on which the cash equivalent figures are based, including the nil rate for zero-emission vans, may be altered by the Treasury by statutory instrument.

For heavier commercial vehicles, see **27.39** below.

Fuel charge for vans

If fuel is provided for a van by reason of the employment and the cash equivalent of the benefit of the van itself falls to be computed on the basis that the restricted private use requirements above are not met, then for 2007/08 onwards, and subject to the exceptions below, there is a tax charge on fuel as well as on the van itself. For 2010/11 onwards, the fuel benefit charge does not apply if the cash equivalent of the benefit of the van itself is reduced to nil due to zero emissions. Fuel is treated as provided if *inter alia* a liability for such fuel is discharged, a non-cash voucher or credit-token is used to obtain fuel or to obtain money to buy fuel or if any sum is paid for expenses incurred in providing fuel. For 2009/10 and earlier years, the supply of electrical energy for an electrically-propelled vehicle does not count as provision of fuel for these purposes.

The cash equivalent of the benefit of fuel is £500 for 2009/10 and earlier years. It is increased to £550 for 2010/11 onwards. However, no charge applies for a tax year if either:

* the fuel is made available for business travel only; or
* the employee is required to make good the full cost of fuel provided for private use and does, in fact, do so.

Where for any part of the tax year either:

(a)   fuel is not provided for the van at all; or
(b)   it is made available only for business travel; or
(c)   the requirements for the 'making good' exemption referred to above are met,

and there is no subsequent time in the year when none of these three conditions is met, the cash equivalent of the fuel benefit is reduced in the proportion that the number of days on which at least one of these conditions is met bears to the number of days in the year. (For example, if for part of a year an employee makes good the cost of all fuel for private use but then ceases to do so later in the same tax year, without one of the other conditions being met, no reduction can be made to the cash equivalent of the benefit for that year.)

The cash equivalent of the fuel benefit is also proportionately reduced if the van is 'unavailable' (see above) at any time in the tax year. As above, a replacement van generally counts as the normal van.

If the cash equivalent of the benefit of the van itself falls to be reduced because the van is shared (see above), a corresponding reduction is made in the cash equivalent of the fuel benefit.

[*ITEPA 2003, ss 154–164, 170(1A)(2)(5); FA 2010, s 58(12)–(15), (18); SI 2010 No 406, arts 1, 3*].

Example

[27.37]

W is an employee of C Ltd, earning £37,000 per annum. From 1 October 2010 to 5 April 2011, W is provided by his employer with exclusive use of a one-year old company van (Van A) on terms such that the restricted private use requirements are not met and which provide for a deduction of £4 per month to be made from his net salary at the end of each month in consideration for private use. Van A was off the road and incapable of use for a three-week period in January 2011; no replacement was provided.

X, Y and Z are also employees of C Ltd, each earning £32,500 per annum. Throughout 2010/11, a single two-year old company van (Van B) is made available to the three of them. The terms are such that the restricted private use requirements are met in relation to X but not in relation to Y and Z. No payment for private use was required from any of them. Van B was damaged and incapable of use for 40 consecutive days in February/March 2011; no replacement was provided. The facts show that a just and reasonable allocation of the benefit for 2010/11 is 0% to X (whose private use was insignificant), 60% to Y and 40% to Z.

Both vans have a normal laden weight not exceeding 3,500 kilograms.

It is not the policy of C Ltd to provide fuel for private travel in its vans. All employees are required to make good the full cost of any fuel used for private purposes and have done so.

The taxable benefits to W, X, Y and Z for 2010/11 of company vans are calculated as follows.

		£
W		
Cash equivalent of benefit before adjustment		3,000
Exclude	Period of unavailability (see note below):	1,463
	$£3,000 \times \dfrac{178}{365}$ (6.4.10 – 30.9.10)	
		1,537
Deduct	Payment for private use (6 × £4 per month)	24
Cash equivalent of benefit		£1,513

X	
Cash equivalent of benefit	<u>Nil</u>

Y	
Cash equivalent of benefit before adjustment	3,000
Exclude Period of unavailability:	

$$£3,000 \times \frac{40}{365}$$ <u>329</u>

	2,671
Exclude Reduction for sharing (40%)	<u>1,068</u>
Cash equivalent of benefit	<u>£1,603</u>

Z	
Cash equivalent of benefit before adjustment	3,000
Exclude Period of unavailability (same as for Y)	<u>329</u>
	2,671
Exclude Reduction for sharing (60%)	<u>1,603</u>
Cash equivalent of benefit	<u>£1,068</u>

In W's case, the period of unavailability in January 2011 does not count towards the reduction as it is a period of less than 30 consecutive days.

Pooled vehicles

[27.38] Cars or vans provided as *pooled cars* or *pooled vans* will not be treated as being available for private use by any employee.

Conditions are:

(a) the vehicle must have been included for the year in a car or van pool for use of employees of one or more employers and actually used by more than one of those employees by reason of their employment and not ordinarily used by one of them to the exclusion of the others, and

(b) any private use of the vehicle in the year by an employee was merely incidental to his other use of it, and

(c) the vehicle was not normally kept overnight at or near any of the residences of the employees concerned (except on the employer's premises).

As regards (b) above, HMRC interpret the requirement that private use is 'merely incidental to' other use as a qualitative test requiring consideration, in the case of each employee using the vehicle during the year, of whether the private use is independent of the employee's business use (so that it is not 'merely incidental' to it) or follows from the business use (so that it is). Thus if a business journey requiring an early start cannot reasonably be undertaken starting from the normal place of work, the journey from work to home the previous day (although private) is merely incidental to the business use. Similarly minor private use (e.g. to visit a restaurant) while away from home on a business trip is merely incidental to the business use. On the other hand use for an annual holiday would not be merely incidental to business use, no matter how small in comparison to business travel in the year. As regards cars with drivers, carrying and working on confidential papers, whilst a factor in determining whether a journey is business or private (and if private whether merely incidental to business use), is not determinative of the issue. The need to deliver papers to a client, or to have them available for a meeting at the employee's home, may be additional relevant factors. Where a chauffeur is obliged to take the car home for the night, in order to collect or deliver passengers, this does not disqualify the car from treatment as a pooled vehicle. (HMRC SP 2/96).

[*ITEPA 2003, ss 167, 168*].

HMRC accept that condition (c) above is satisfied if the occasions on which the vehicle is taken home by employees do not amount to more than 60% of the year. However, where a vehicle is garaged at employees' homes on a large number of occasions (although less than 60% of the year), they consider it 'unlikely' that all home-to-work journeys would satisfy the 'merely incidental' test in (b) above. Such use by a chauffeur employed to drive a car does not prevent its being a pooled car. (HMRC Booklet 480).

Simon's Taxes. See E4.629, E4.630F.

Heavier commercial vehicles

[27.39] Where a 'heavier commercial vehicle' is made available to an employee in such circumstances that had it been a van it would have been chargeable under the provisions described at **27.36** above, no charge will arise in respect of its provision unless the vehicle is wholly or mainly used for private purposes. A benefit will, however, arise on the provision of any driver for the vehicle. A '*heavier commercial vehicle*' is defined in the same terms as a van under **27.36** above, but with a design laden weight limit exceeding 3,500 kgs in normal use. From 6 April 2003, this exemption is extended to apply to any income tax charge in these circumstances. [*ITEPA 2003, s 238*]. Simon's Taxes. See E4.630D.

Cheap loan arrangements

[27.40] Where a director or employee not in lower-paid employment (see **27.26** above) obtains an 'employment-related loan', and the loan is a 'taxable cheap loan' in relation to that year, the cash equivalent of the benefit of the loan is treated as earnings from the employment for that year, subject to the exceptions referred to below.

An '*employment-related loan*' is a loan (including any form of credit) made to an employee (or a 'relative' of an employee) by the employer, by a company or partnership under the employer's control, by a company or partnership controlling the employer (being a company or partnership), or by a company or partnership under common control with the employer (being a company or partnership). It also includes a loan by a person having a 'material interest' (broadly 5% — see *ITEPA 2003, s 68*) in a close company which was the employer or had control of or was controlled by the employer, or in a company or partnership controlling that close company. It does not include a loan made by an individual in the normal course of his domestic, family or personal relationships, or one made to a 'relative' of the employee from which the employee derives no benefit. Loans by a prospective employer are included, and 'making a loan' includes arranging, guaranteeing or in any way facilitating a loan or the continuation of an existing loan, and the assumption of the rights and liabilities of the person who originally made the loan. *'Relative'* means spouse or civil partner of the employee, or parent, ancestor, lineal descendant, brother or sister (or those persons' spouses or civil partners) of the employee or spouse/civil partner.

A *'taxable cheap loan'* is an employment-related loan for a tax year if it is outstanding at any time during that year when the employment is held and the interest (if any) paid on the loan for that year is less than would have been payable at the 'official rate'. The cash equivalent of the benefit of a loan (which applies to each loan separately) is the excess of the interest which would have been payable at the 'official rate' over the interest (if any) actually paid. A loan ceases to be outstanding on the death of the employee.

It is not necessary for the application of these provisions that there be any benefit from the loan in terms of something of an advantage to the employee (*Williams v Todd* Ch D 1988, 60 TC 727). A loan secured by a charge on a house purchased by a relocated employee, with an agreement that when the charge was called in the employing company would receive the same proportion of the sale price or valuation as the loan bore to the purchase price, was within these provisions (*Harvey v Williams* (Sp C 49), [1995] SSCD 329; (Sp C 168), [1998] SSCD 215). The payment of the expenses of an estate agency by a service company of which one of the partners in the agency was a director was within the provisions from the time the services were provided for so long as the payments were not reimbursed (with agreed mark-up) to the company (*Grant v Watton and cross-appeal* Ch D 1999, 71 TC 333).

The 'official rate' is set in advance for the whole year, although it may be decreased during the year should there be a sharp fall in typical mortgage rates (but will *not* be increased during the year). (Revenue Press Release 25 January 2000). The prescribed rates (from 6 January 2002) are as follows.

> 5% p.a. from 6 January 2002 to 5 April 2007
> 6.25% p.a. from 6 April 2007 to 28 February 2009
> 4.75% p.a. from 1 March 2009 to 5 April 2010
> 4.00% p.a. from 6 April 2010 onwards

See *SI 2007 No 684; SI 2009 No 199; SI 2010 No 415*; Revenue Press Releases 12 December 2002, 12 January 2004; Revenue Internet Statements 17 March 2005, 3 March 2008.

The average rate for 2008/09 is 6.1%.

Regulations may provide for a different official rate of interest in relation to a loan in the currency of a country or territory outside the UK, the benefit of which is obtained by reason of the employment of a person who normally lives in that country or territory and who has lived there at some time in the year in question or the preceding five years. In this context, 'lives' and 'has lived' are considered to connote a degree of continuance if not permanence, i.e. more than a return for a short holiday. (Revenue Tax Bulletin October 1994 p 162). The following different rates are applicable.

| *Japan* | 3.9% p.a. |
| *Switzerland* | 5.5% p.a. |

[*SI 1994 Nos 1307, 1567*]. For the circumstances in which loans taken out prior to an employee coming to work in the UK are within the beneficial loan provisions, see Revenue Tax Bulletin October 1994 p 161.

The amount taxable in respect of the loan for a tax year is treated as interest paid by the employee on the loan in that year of that amount (other than for the purpose of this or any other benefit charge). It is not treated as income of the lender, but it is treated as accruing during, and paid at the end of, the year (or, if different, the period during the year when the employee was in the employment and the loan was outstanding).

Where the lender is a close company (see Tolley's Corporation Tax under Close Companies) and the borrower a director, the lender may elect, by notice to HMRC on or before 6 July following the tax year, to treat as a single loan all loans with that borrower which are in the same currency, are not 'qualifying loans (see below), were obtained by reason of employment, and the rate of interest on which has been below the official rate throughout the year.

A claim may be made for late payments of interest to be related to the year to which they apply, and for assessments to be adjusted accordingly.

The above provisions do not apply where a loan made for a fixed and unvariable period and at a fixed and unvariable rate of interest (originally not less than the official rate) becomes a taxable cheap loan only by reason of an increase in the official rate, or on similar unvariable loans made before 6 April 1978 where the rate of interest is not less than could have been expected to apply between persons not connected with each other.

[*ITEPA 2003, ss 173–175, 177, 181, 184, 187, 190(2), 191(2)*].

Alternative finance arrangements

A 'loan' for these purposes includes arrangements entered into after 21 March 2006 which are alternative finance arrangements within **3.2** or **3.4** ALTERNATIVE FINANCE ARRANGEMENTS or which would be such arrangements if one of the parties thereto were a financial institution. In relation to such arrangements, all references in these provisions to interest are to be taken as references to alternative finance return. For an arrangement within **3.2**, the amount of the 'loan' treated as outstanding at any time is the excess of the purchase price of the asset therein referred to over such part of the aggregate payments to date as does not represent alternative finance return. For an arrangement within **3.4**, the amount treated as outstanding at any time is the excess of the amount of

X's original beneficial interest in the asset therein referred to over such part of the aggregate payments to date as does not represent alternative finance return. [*ITEPA 2003, s 173A; CTA 2009, Sch 1 para 683; TIOPA 2010, Sch 2 para 49*].

'Qualifying loans' — interest qualifying for relief

The above provisions do not apply to a loan in any tax year in which, if interest were paid on the loan (whether or not it is in fact so paid), the whole of the interest paid on it would either be eligible for relief under *ITA 2007, s 383* (see **43.5 INTEREST PAYABLE**) or would be an allowable deduction to the payer in computing the taxable profits of a trade, profession or vocation carried on wholly or partly in the UK or of a UK property business (see **73.89 TRADING INCOME, 60.4 PROPERTY INCOME**). [*ITEPA 2003, s 178; ITA 2007, Sch 1 para 431; CTA 2009, Sch 1 para 550*]. Where the interest would only partly so qualify for relief, the above provisions do apply but relief is given where appropriate for the amount chargeable as if it were an amount of interest paid. [*ITEPA 2003, s 184*].

Ordinary commercial loans

The above provisions do not apply to a loan on '*ordinary commercial terms*', i.e. a loan made in the ordinary course of business by a lender whose business includes either the lending of money or the supply of goods or services on credit, and in relation to which one of the following conditions is satisfied.

(a)   When the loan was made, loans for the same or similar purposes and on the same terms and conditions were available to all those who might be expected to avail themselves of the services provided by the lender in the course of business, and a substantial proportion (broadly 50% or more, see HMRC Employment Income Manual EIM26160) of such loans (including the loan in question) made at or about that time were made to members of the public (i.e. those with whom the lender deals at arm's length). All such loans so made to members of the public at or about that time must be held on the same terms as the loan in question, and any change in those terms since that time must have been imposed in the ordinary course of the lender's business. As regards loans made before 1 June 1994, terms and conditions are considered for this purpose disregarding any fees, commission or other incidental expenses incurred by the borrower to obtain the loan.

(b)   If the loan was varied before 6 April 2000, a substantial proportion (as in (a) above) of the loan in question, any existing loans varied at or about the same time so as to be held on the same post-variation terms and any new loans made by the same lender at or about the time of the variation must have been made to members of the public. All such loans so made to members of the public at or about the time of the variation must be held on the same terms as the loan in question, and any change in those terms since that time must have been imposed in the ordinary course of the lender's business. Terms and conditions are considered for these purposes disregarding any fees, commission or other incidental expenses incurred by the borrower to obtain the loan and any penalties, interest or similar amounts incurred by the borrower as a result of varying the loan.

(c) If the loan is varied on or after 6 April 2000, a substantial proportion (as in (a) above) of the loan in question, of any existing loans varied at or about the same time so as to be held on the same post-variation terms and of any new loans made by the same lender at or about the time of the variation must have been made to members of the public. At the time of the variation, members of the public who had loans from the lender for similar purposes must have had a right to vary their loans on the same terms and conditions as applied in relation to the variation of the loan in question, and the post-variation terms on which any existing loans so varied and the loan in question are held must be the same. Any change in those terms since that time must have been imposed in the ordinary course of the lender's business. Terms and conditions are considered for these purposes disregarding any fees, commission or other incidental expenses incurred by the borrower to obtain the loan and any penalties, interest or similar amounts incurred by the borrower as a result of varying the loan.

[*ITEPA 2003, s 176*].

De minimis exemption

No amount is treated as earnings (or as interest paid) in respect of a loan within the above provisions if the loan (or aggregate taxable loans) at no time in the year exceed £5,000. Additionally, if the aggregate taxable loans do exceed £5,000 but the aggregate loans that are not 'qualifying loans' (as above) do not exceed that figure, the above provisions do not apply to those non-qualifying loans.

[*ITEPA 2003, s 180; ITA 2007, Sch 1 para 432; CTA 2009, Sch 1 para 551*].

Bridging loans

By concession, reimbursement by an employer of the net interest on a bridging loan is not charged to tax, nor is the benefit of a bridging loan advanced by an employer in excess of the relief limit. See **27.71** below.

Expense advances

There is also no charge on advances for an employee's incidental overnight expenses (see **27.82** below) or other expenses necessarily incurred in performance of the duties of the employment, provided that:

- the maximum amount outstanding at any one time in the tax year does not exceed £1,000 (or such higher figure as may be set by Treasury order);
- the advances are spent within six months; and
- the employee accounts to his employer at regular intervals for the expenditure of the sum advanced.

Where there are good reasons for exceeding either the monetary limit or the time limit, the employer may apply for an increased limit. Where the conditions are met, no entry is required on form P11D for taxable loans but details of expense payments are still necessary.

[*ITEPA 2003, s 179*].

Calculation of interest at the official rate

The normal method for any tax year ('the relevant year') is as follows.

- Take the average of the maximum amounts of the loan outstanding on 5 April immediately preceding the relevant year and 5 April in the relevant year (or at the date the loan was made or discharged (or the employee died) if falling within that year).
- Multiply that figure by the number of whole months (a month begins on sixth day of each calendar month) during which the loan was outstanding in that year and divide by twelve.
- Multiply the result by the official rate of interest in force, or if the rate changed, the average rate (on a daily basis), for the period during which the loan was outstanding during the year.

[*ITEPA 2003, ss 182, 190(1)*].

A replacement loan is treated for averaging purposes as being the same loan as the original if it is a 'further employment-related loan' which replaces (i) the original loan or (ii) a non-employment related loan which itself replaced the original, the second replacement occurring in the same tax year, or within 40 days thereafter, as the first. A *'further employment-related loan'* is a loan the benefit of which is obtained by reason of the same employment or other employment with the same employer or a person connected with him (within **21 CONNECTED PERSONS**). [*ITEPA 2003, s 186*].

There is an alternative method which may be imposed by HMRC or for which the employee may elect. Notice of imposition or election must be given within twelve months after 31 January following the relevant tax year. This alternative method is to calculate the figures by reference to the daily amounts of the loan and official rates of interest. [*ITEPA 2003, s 183, Sch 7 para 26*].

See the example at **27.42** below.

General

Where two or more employees are chargeable under the above provisions in respect of the same loan, the cash equivalent is apportioned between them in a fair and reasonable manner, the portion allocated to each being treated as the cash equivalent as far as that employee is concerned. Any election for the alternative method of calculation in such a case must be made by all the employees concerned. [*ITEPA 2003, ss 183(4), 185*].

Interest on money loaned interest-free, subject to conditions and repayable on demand, by the employer to a trust for the benefit of an employee was held to be taxable earnings (*O'Leary v McKinlay* Ch D 1990, 63 TC 729).

Simon's Taxes. See E4.631–E4.638.

Loans written off

[27.41] Any amount released from, or written off, an 'employment-related loan' (see **27.40** above) will be charged as taxable earnings, unless otherwise taxable as income. Where, however, it would be taxable under *ITEPA 2003,* *s 403* (see **20.5 COMPENSATION FOR LOSS OF EMPLOYMENT (AND DAMAGES)**)) it will instead be taxable under this provision, and where the loan is one which is a capital sum within *ITTOIA 2005, s 633* (see **68.32 SETTLEMENTS**) the charge will be on the excess of the amount released over sums previously treated as the employee's income under *s 633*. These provisions continue to apply after termination of employment, and to a loan replacing the original loan, but they cease on death of the employee. If the loan is wholly or partly repaid after a charge has arisen under this provision, a claim may be made for the appropriate relief. They do not apply to arrangements to protect a person from a fall in value of shares. [*ITEPA 2003, ss 188–190, 191(3), Sch 7 paras 25, 27*].

Where the lender is a close company in which the employee is a participator and an amount is released or written off, a charge arises on the participator under *ITTOIA 2005, ss 415–421* (see **64.16 SAVINGS AND INVESTMENT INCOME**). The charge under *ITTOIA 2005, ss 415–421* takes priority over the charge described above, so that the same amount will not give rise to a charge under both provisions (HMRC Employment Income Manual EIM21746).

Example

[27.42]

D, who is an employee of A Ltd earning £25,000 per annum, obtained a loan of £10,000 from the company on 10 October 2007 for the purpose of buying a car. Interest at a nominal rate is charged on the outstanding balance while the principal is repayable by instalments of £1,000 on 31 December and 30 June commencing 31 December 2007. The interest paid by D amounted to £50 in 2007/08 and to £250 in 2008/09. The official rate of interest is 6.25% until 28 February 2009 and 4,75% thereafter; the average rate for 2008/09 is 6.1%. D is assessed for 2007/08 as follows.

Normal method (averaging)	£
Average balance for period $\dfrac{£10,000 + £9,000}{2}$	£9,500
£9,500 × $^5/_{12}$	£3,958
£3,958 × 6.25%	247
Deduct Interest paid in year	50
Cash equivalent of loan benefit	£197

Alternative method

Period	Balance of loan in period	Interest at official rate on balance	
	£		£
10.10.07 – 31.12.07	10,000	£10,000 × 6.25% × $^{83}/_{365}$	142

Period	Balance of loan in period	Interest at official rate on balance	
	£		£
1.1.08 – 5.4.08	9,000	$£9,000 \times 6.25\% \times {}^{95}/_{365}$	146
			288
De- Interest paid in *duct* year			50
Cash equivalent of loan benefit			£238
Amount chargeable to tax note (b)			£238

D is assessed for 2008/09 as follows.

Normal method (averaging) £

$$\text{Average balance for period } \frac{£9,000 + £7,000}{2}$$

	£8,000
$£8,000 \times 6.1\%$	488
De-duct	250
Cash equivalent of loan benefit	£238

Alternative method

Period	Balance of loan in period	Interest at official rate on balance	
	£		£
6.4.08 – 30.6.08	9,000	$£9,000 \times 6.25\% \times {}^{86}/_{365}$	132
1.7.08 – 31.12.08	8,000	$£8,000 \times 6.25\% \times {}^{184}/_{365}$	252
1.1.09 – 28.2.09	7,000	$£7,000 \times 6.25\% \times {}^{59}/_{365}$	71
1.3.09 – 5.4.09	7,000	$£7,000 \times 4.75\% \times {}^{36}/_{365}$	33
			488
De-duct Interest paid in year			250
Cash equivalent of loan benefit			£238
Amount chargeable to tax note (b)			£238

Notes

Notes

(a) The period 10 October 2007 to 5 April 2008 is, for the purpose of calculating the average balance, five complete months (months begin on the sixth day of each calendar month). However, in applying the interest rate change, the actual number of days during which the loan was outstanding is taken into account.

(b) HMRC will probably require the alternative method to be applied for 2007/08. For 2008/09, both methods happen to give the same result.

(c) This example illustrates the year 2008/09 as that was the latest year in which the official rate was changed in-year. The principles continue to apply for subsequent years.

Childcare provision

[27.43] The tax position differs according to whether the childcare is provided by the employer (see **27.44** below), otherwise contracted for by the employer (see **27.45** below) or provided by means of vouchers (see **27.46** below).

See also HMRC's general guidance at www.hmrc.gov.uk/childcare/index.htm.

Employer-provided childcare

[27.44] No liability to income tax arises in respect of the provision for an employee of 'care' for a 'child' where *all* of the following conditions are met:

* the child is the employee's child or stepchild and is maintained (wholly or partly) at his expense *or* is resident with the employee *or* is a person for whom the employee has parental responsibility (as defined);
* the premises on which the care is provided are not used wholly or mainly as a private dwelling, and any applicable registration requirement (under *Children Act 1989, Pt 10A* (before 18 July 2009) or *Childcare Act 2006, Pt 3* or Scottish or NI equivalents) is met;
* those premises are made available by the employer operating the childcare scheme (the scheme employer) or, where the care is provided under arrangements made by the scheme employer and other persons, those premises are made available by one or more of those persons with the scheme employer being wholly or partly responsible for financing and managing the care provision; and
* the childcare scheme is open to all the scheme employer's employees or to all those at a particular location and the employee in question is either an employee of the scheme employer or works at the same location as employees of the scheme employer to whom the scheme is open.

If the conditions are met in respect of part only of the childcare provision (for example if the arrangements change partway through the tax year), the exemption applies to that part.

For the above purposes:

* 'care' means any form of care or supervised activity not provided in the course of the child's compulsory education; and

- a person is regarded as a '*child*' until 1 September following his 15th birthday (or 16th birthday if he is disabled, as defined) and on until the end of the week in which that date falls.

Where the benefit of childcare is convertible into cash, e.g. under a salary sacrifice arrangement, no charge to tax on general earnings arises.

[*ITEPA 2003, ss 318, 318B; SI 2008 No 2170, Reg 2; SI 2009 No 1544, Reg 2*].

Other employer-contracted childcare

[27.45] In cases where the exemption at **27.44** above does not apply, no liability to income tax arises in respect of the provision for an employee of 'care' for a 'child' *except* to the extent that the cash equivalent of the benefit (see **27.30** above) exceeds £55 per week and the employee is not in lower-paid employment (see **27.26** above). (In practice, HMRC take £243 to be the monthly equivalent.) *All* of the following conditions must be met:

- the child must be the employee's child or stepchild and must be maintained (wholly or partly) at his expense *or* must be both resident with the employee and a person for whom the employee has parental responsibility (as defined);
- the care must be 'qualifying childcare' (see below); and
- the care scheme is open to all the employer's employees or to all those at a particular location.

If the conditions are met in respect of part only of the childcare provision, the exemption applies to that part. '*Care*' and '*child*' have the same meanings as for employer-provided childcare at **27.44** above.

The weekly exemption is applied to a tax year by multiplying it by the number of 'qualifying weeks' in the tax year to give an annual exempt amount. For employees not in lower-paid employment (see **27.26** above), income tax is chargeable on the excess, if any, of the cash equivalent of the benefit for the year over that exempt amount. For this purpose, a week begins on the first day of the tax year and on every 7th day after that, with the last day of the tax year (or 2 days if the tax year ends in a leap year) being treated as a week in itself. Any week in which care is provided in compliance with the above conditions counts as a '*qualifying week*'. An employee is entitled to only one exempt amount regardless of the number of children for whom care is provided, but two or more people can be entitled to an exempt amount in respect of the same child. If an employee would otherwise be entitled to an exemption both under these provisions and under the childcare vouchers provisions described at **27.46** below, he is entitled to only one such exemption for any one week. The Treasury has power to alter the amount of the weekly exemption by statutory instrument.

'*Qualifying childcare*' means 'registered or approved care'. This is defined by one of *subsections (2)–(6)* of *ITEPA 2003, s 318C* (as amended) depending on whether the care is being provided for a child in England, Wales, Scotland, NI or outside the UK. In England, for example, it currently includes care provided by a person registered under *Childcare Act 2006, Pt 3*, by or under the direction of the governors of a school on the school premises, and by a domiciliary care worker under the *Domiciliary Care Agencies Regulations 2002*. Care provided for a child in England on school premises is excluded if it is provided during school hours for a child who has reached compulsory school age or if it is provided in breach of a requirement to register under *Childcare Act 2006, Pt 3*. Care provided by the employee's domestic partner is excluded in all cases from being qualifying childcare, as is care provided by a relative (as defined) of the child wholly or mainly in the child's home or, if different, the home of a person having parental responsibility for the child and, on and after 18 July 2009, care provided by a foster parent in respect of a child whom that foster parent is fostering.

Where the benefit of childcare is convertible into cash, e.g. under a salary sacrifice arrangement, no charge to tax on general earnings arises.

[*ITEPA 2003, ss 318A–318D; SI 2005 No 770; SI 2006 No 882; SI 2007 No 849, SI 2007 No 2478; SI 2008 No 2170, Reg 3; SI 2009 No 1544, Reg 3, SI 2009 No 2888*].

It is proposed that for 2011/12 onwards, for people joining an employer's scheme on or after 6 April 2011, the £55 per week limit will be restricted in cases where an employee's earnings and taxable benefits are liable to tax at the higher or additional rate. The intention is to restrict tax savings to the basic rate. The employer will be required at the beginning of each tax year to estimate the level of employment earnings that the employee is likely to receive during that year, ignoring potential bonus and overtime payments, but including other known taxable benefits. This will fix the employee's limit for the entire tax year. See www.hmrc.gov.uk/employers/employersupportedchild care.pdf.

Childcare vouchers

[27.46] No liability to income tax arises in respect of the provision for an employee of 'qualifying childcare vouchers' *except* to the extent that the cash equivalent of the benefit (see **27.30** above) exceeds £55 per week 'plus the voucher administration costs'. (In practice, HMRC take £243 to be the monthly equivalent of the fixed weekly limit.) A '*qualifying childcare voucher*' is a non-cash 'childcare voucher' in relation to which *all* of the following conditions are met:

- the voucher is provided to enable the employee to obtain 'care' for a 'child' who is the employee's child or stepchild and is maintained (wholly or partly) at his expense *or* who is both resident with the employee and a person for whom the employee has parental responsibility (as defined);
- the voucher can be used only to obtain 'qualifying childcare'; and
- the voucher is provided under a scheme that is open to all the employer's employees or to all those at a particular location.

'Care', 'child' and 'qualifying childcare' have the same meanings as in **27.44**, **27.45** above. The 'voucher administration costs' are the difference between the face value of the vouchers provided and the cost of providing them; administration fees charged to the employer (or whoever provides the vouchers to the employee) are thus included within the exemption.

The exemption is applied to a tax year by multiplying the weekly limit by the number of 'qualifying weeks' in the tax year and then adding the voucher administration costs for the year to give an annual exempt amount. Income tax is chargeable on the excess, if any, of the cash equivalent of the benefit for the year over that exempt amount. For this purpose, a week begins on the first day of the tax year and on every 7th day after that, with the last day of the tax year (or 2 days if the tax year ends in a leap year) being treated as a week in itself. Any week in respect of which a qualifying childcare voucher is received counts as a 'qualifying week'. An employee is entitled to only one exempt amount regardless of the number of children for whom care is provided, but two or more people can be entitled to an exempt amount in respect of the same child. If an employee would otherwise be entitled to an exemption both under these provisions and those for employer-contracted childcare at **27.45** above, he is entitled to only one such exemption for any one week. The Treasury has power to alter the amount of the weekly exemption by statutory instrument.

See **27.90–27.93** below as regards tax liability on vouchers, including non-cash vouchers, generally. A 'childcare voucher' is a voucher, stamp or similar document intended to enable a person to obtain childcare (whether or not in exchange for the voucher).

[ITEPA 2003, ss 84(2A), 270A; SI 2006 No 882].

It is proposed that for 2011/12 onwards, for people joining an employer's scheme on or after 6 April 2011, the £55 per week limit will be restricted in cases where an employee's earnings and taxable benefits are liable to tax at the higher or additional rate. The intention is to restrict tax savings to the basic rate. The employer will be required at the beginning of each tax year to estimate the level of employment earnings that the employee is likely to receive during that year, ignoring potential bonus and overtime payments, but including other known taxable benefits. This will fix the employee's limit for the entire tax year. See www.hmrc.gov.uk/employers/employersupportedchild care.pdf.

Scholarships

[27.47] Where payments are made under scholarship awards, ITTOIA 2005, s 776 (see **30.41** EXEMPT INCOME) is not to be construed as conferring exemption from tax on any person other than the holder of the scholarship. If a scholarship (including an exhibition, bursary or other similar educational endowment) is provided to a member of the family or household of a director or employee (other than a lower-paid employee as in **27.26** above) by reason of the latter's employment the payments are chargeable on such director etc. under the benefits code. A scholarship is taken to have been provided by reason of a person's employment if provided, directly or indirectly, under arrangements entered into by, or by a person connected with, the employer, unless the employer is an individual and the arrangements are made in the normal course of his domestic, personal or family relationships.

However, the benefits code will not bring into charge a payment under a scholarship awarded out of a trust fund, or under a scheme, to a person receiving full-time instruction at an educational establishment, where 25% or less of the payments made out of the fund etc. in any tax year are scholarship payments provided, or treated as provided, by reason of a person's employment (regardless of whether or not the employment is director's or non-lower-paid or in the UK).

Payments which are *in fact* provided by reason of a person's employment are taxable even if the fund meets the 25% test.

[ITEPA 2003, ss 211–215, Sch 7 para 32(3)].

For administrative procedures in relation to educational trust scholarships, see HMRC Employment Income Manual EIM30006–30008.

See also **30.39** EXEMPT INCOME for payments to employees to attend sandwich courses and other full-time educational courses.

Simon's Taxes. See E4.618.

Sporting and recreational facilities

[27.48] The provision to an employee (or to a member of his family or household) of:

- any benefit consisting in, or in a right or opportunity to make use of, any sporting or other recreational facilities made available generally to, or for use by, the employees of the employer in question; or
- any non-cash voucher (see **27.91** below) capable of being exchanged only for such a benefit,

is exempted from any charge to income tax.

Excluded from the relief is any benefit consisting in:

(i)   an interest in, or the use of, any mechanically propelled vehicle (including ships, boats, aircraft and hovercraft);
(ii)   an interest in, or the use of, any holiday or other overnight accommodation or associated facilities;
(iii)   a facility provided on domestic premises (i.e. premises used wholly or mainly as a private dwelling, or belonging to or enjoyed with such premises);
(iv)   a facility available to, or for use by, the general public;
(v)   a facility not used wholly or mainly by persons whose right or opportunity to use it derives from employment; or
(vi)   a right or opportunity to make use of any facility within (i)–(v) above.

As regards (iv) above, where employers group together to provide facilities for members of all their staffs, this does not of itself mean that they are available to members of the general public. In practice, the opening of facilities to a restricted section of the public (e.g. those living in the immediate vicinity) as well as to employees will similarly not result in loss of the relief. (HMRC Employment Income Manual EIM22860, 22862).

As regards (v) above, a right or opportunity derives from employment only if it derives from the person's being (or having been) an employee of a particular employer (or a member of such a person's family or household) and the facility is available generally to employees of that employer.

The Treasury may by regulation prescribe exceptions from, and conditional inclusions in, this relief.

[*ITEPA 2003, ss 261–263*].

Where the provision of recreational facilities to employees is exempt as above, the provision of those facilities to others who are working at the employer's premises but are not employees of that employer is also exempt. [*SI 2002 No 205, Reg 6; SI 2004 No 3087*].

Simon's Taxes. See E4.716.

Dispensations (notices of nil liability)

[27.49] If an employer supplies HMRC with a statement of the cases and circumstances in which particular types of expense payments and benefits are made or provided by him for any employees (whether his own or those of anyone else) and HMRC are satisfied that such benefits etc. give rise to no tax liability, they may issue a notice of nil liability (but this can be revoked later). [*ITEPA 2003, s 65, Sch 7 para 15*]. Dispensations are not generally available for 'round sum' expense allowances, but are frequently given for e.g. travelling and subsistence expenses on an approved scale for business journeys in the UK. They are also unavailable in so far as they relate to expenses in connection with the use of a vehicle for business travel where mileage allowance payments are made or mileage allowance relief is available in respect of that use (see **27.87** below). [*ITEPA 2003, Sch 7 para 16*]. This does not, however, prevent the inclusion of congestion charges in a dispensation (see Revenue Internet Statement 6 February 2003). Scale rate payments merely reimbursing average expenditure are not regarded as round sum allowances (see HMRC Employment Income Manual EIM05200). The effect is to exclude such items from the PAYE scheme, returns etc. Dispensations are not given, however, where the effect would be to remove the employee from liability under the benefits legislation (see **27.26** above). A dispensation may be considered for a controlling director who decides his own expenses provided that there is independent documentation to vouch for the expenditure.

See www.hmrc.gov.uk/forms/p11dx.pdf for an application form and more information on dispensations. See also HMRC Employment Income Manual EIM30050 *et seq*.

Provided that the circumstances under which a dispensation was issued have not changed, it will also be accepted as evidence that the expenses covered are not earnings for national insurance contributions purposes (Revenue Tax Bulletin August 1995 p 245).

Simon's Taxes. See E4.651.

Clergymen etc.

[27.50] A clergyman or other minister of a religious denomination in full-time employment as such is not taxable on any sums paid for or reimbursed to him in respect of any statutory amount payable, or statutory deduction made, under any *Act* in connection with the residence made available to him by a charity or ecclesiastical corporation for carrying out his duties (except in so far as they relate to any part of the premises which he lets) and, provided he is in 'lower-paid employment' (see **27.26** above), no account is taken of the value of any expenses relating to his own living accommodation so provided. [*ITEPA 2003, s 290*].

No liability arises in respect of payment or reimbursement of a minister's heating, lighting, cleaning or gardening expenses, provided his employment is lower-paid employment. Where an allowance is paid to the minister to meet such costs it will not be taxed except to the extent that it exceeds the costs actually incurred. These rules used to apply by concession (HMRC ESC A61) but have statutory effect for 2010/11 onwards. [*ITEPA 2003, ss 290A, 290B; SI 2010 No 157, art 2(3)(4)*]. For the purpose of determining whether a minister is in lower-paid employment, these payments, reimbursements or allowances are included in the aggregate at **27.26**(a) above. [*ITEPA 2003, s 218(1); SI 2010 No 157, art 2(2)(4)*].

Expenses wholly, exclusively and necessarily incurred in performance of duties (e.g. postage, stationery, telephone, car etc.) may be deducted from earnings from any employment as a minister (although where a vehicle other than a company vehicle is used for business travel, and either mileage allowance payments are received or mileage allowance relief is available in respect of that use (see **27.87** below), no deduction is available for qualifying travelling expenses (see **27.23** above) incurred in connection with that use). If he pays rent in respect of a dwelling-house any part of which is used mainly or substantially for his duties, up to one-quarter thereof may be deducted from earnings, and in addition he may claim in total one-quarter of the aggregate of any expenses of maintenance, repair, insurance or management of the premises borne by him. [*ITEPA 2003, ss 351, 328(2), Sch 6 para 47*]. Relief may also be available for the cost of *locum tenens* for illness or holidays and lighting, heating, cleaning and rates of study (see HMRC Employment Income Manual EIM60046, 60048).

See generally HMRC Employment Income Manual EIM60001–60055.

The expenses of a minister in visiting his congregation were allowed (*Charlton v CIR* CS 1890, 27 SLR 647) but not expenses of a curate in moving from one curacy to another (*Friedson v Glyn-Thomas* KB 1922, 8 TC 302). In *Mitchell v Child* KB 1942, 24 TC 511, cost of opposing a Bill which would have dispossessed rector of parsonage was allowed.

Gifts to a clergyman including voluntary subscriptions and collections (*In re Strong* C/E/S 1878, 1 TC 207; *Slaney v Starkey* KB 1931, 16 TC 45), Easter offerings (*Cooper v Blakiston* HL 1908, 5 TC 347) and grants (*Herbert v*

McQuade CA 1902, 4 TC 489; *Poynting v Faulkner* CA 1905, 5 TC 145) are taxable but not where in recognition of past service (*Turner v Cuxson* QB 1888, 2 TC 422). The cost of maintenance of a priest living in communal presbytery held not taxable as not convertible into money (*Daly v CIR* CS 1934, 18 TC 641).

An unbeneficed clergyman was held to be within the charge on employment income (*Slaney v Starkey* above) as was a professed nun employed as a teacher (*Dolan v K* Supreme Court (IFS), 2 ITC 280) but not the headmaster of a school established by a congregation of secular priests (*Reade v Brearley* KB 1933, 17 TC 687).

For *self-employed* clergymen, see **73.45 TRADING INCOME**.

Simon's Taxes. See E4.731, E4.788.

Counselling services

[27.51] No income tax liability arises in respect of qualifying counselling services and certain necessary related travelling expenses provided for, or paid or reimbursed on behalf of, an employer in connection with the termination of his employment. This applies whether or not the services or expenses are provided or paid by the employer.

The counselling services which qualify are those consisting wholly of giving advice and guidance, imparting or improving skills, and/or providing or making available the use of office equipment or similar facilities to enable an employee to adjust to his job loss and/or find other employment. The employee must have been in the employment throughout the period of two years to the date the services are provided or, if earlier, the time he ceases to be employed. The opportunity to receive the services must be generally available to employees or a particular class of employees. Part-time employees are within the exemption.

[*ITEPA 2003, s 310*].

For relief to the employer, see **73.66 TRADING INCOME**.

Simon's Taxes.See E4.744, E4.828.

Employee liabilities and indemnity insurance

[27.52] There may be deducted from earnings from an employment which continues to be held:

(a)   any amount paid in or towards the discharge of a 'qualifying liability' of the employee;

(b)   costs or expenses incurred in connection with any claim that the employee is subject to a 'qualifying liability' or with any related proceedings; and

(c)   so much of any premium (or similar payment) paid under a 'qualifying contract' of insurance as relates to the indemnification of the employee against a 'qualifying liability' or to the payment of such costs and expenses as in (b) above.

Where any amount in (a)–(c) above is met by the employer or a third party, there may be made a deduction to offset a resultant taxable benefit (see **27.26** above). However, no deduction may be made for any such liability, costs or expenses if it would have been unlawful for the employer to insure against them (for example, costs arising from criminal convictions, and see Revenue Tax Bulletin October 1995 p 258).

A liability is a *'qualifying liability'* of the employee if it is imposed either:

- in respect of any acts or omissions of the employee in his capacity as such or in any other capacity in which he acts in the performance of his duties; or
- in connection with any proceedings relating to or arising from claims in respect of such acts or omissions.

A *'qualifying contract'* of insurance is one:

(a) which, as regards the risks insured against, relates exclusively to one or more of the following:
    (i) indemnification of any employee against any qualifying liability;
    (ii) indemnification of any person against any vicarious liability in respect of acts or omissions giving rise to a qualifying liability of another;
    (iii) payment of costs and expenses in connection with any claim that a person is subject to a liability to which the insurance relates or with related proceedings; and
    (iv) indemnification of any employer against any loss from the payment by him to an employee of his of any amount in respect of either a qualifying liability or costs and expenses as in (iii) above;
(b) which is not 'connected' with any other contract (see below);
(c) a significant part of the premium for which does not relate to rights to payments or benefits other than cover for the risks insured against and any right of renewal; and
(d) the period of insurance under which is not more than two years (disregarding renewals) and which the insured is not required to renew.

Two contracts are *'connected'* (see (b) above) if either was entered into by reference to the other or to enable the other to be, or to facilitate the other being, entered into on particular terms *and* the terms of either contract would have been significantly different if it had not been for the other. Connected contracts, each of which satisfy (a), (c) and (d), are qualifying contracts despite (b) above, where the only significant difference in terms consists in certain premium reductions.

Where applicable, for the purposes of these provisions, an insurance premium may be reasonably apportioned as between the different risks, persons or employments to which the contract relates.

For clarification of certain points on operation of the relief, see Revenue Tax Bulletin October 1995 pp 257, 258.

See **27.53** below as regards payments made after the employment has ceased.

Anti-avoidance

In response to a marketed avoidance scheme, legislation now denies a deduction under these provisions where the liability in respect of which the deduction would otherwise be due has been paid in connection with arrangements a main purpose of which is the avoidance of tax. The legislation applies to payments made on or after 12 January 2009, regardless of when the arrangements that resulted in the payments were entered into.

[*ITEPA 2003, ss 346–350; ITA 2007, Sch 1 para 435; FA 2009, s 67(2)(4)*].

Simon's Taxes. See E4.787.

Post-employment deductions

[27.53] Relief may be claimed for payments made by a former employee or office-holder which are made after the day the employment ceases and no later than six years after the end of the tax year in which it ceased and that are of a kind that would have been deductible under *ITEPA 2003, s 346* (see **27.52** above) if the employment had continued. Relief is given as a deduction in calculating net income for the year in which the payment is made (see Step 2 in the calculation of income tax liability at **1.7 ALLOWANCES AND TAX RATES**). Unused relief cannot be carried forward, but it can be set against capital gains of the same year — see below.

Payments made by the former employer, by a successor to the former employer's business or to his liabilities, or by a person connected with any of them (see **21 CONNECTED PERSONS**), is not deductible in calculating net income of the former employee *except* insofar as the payment falls to be treated either as general earnings received after the cessation of the employment by the former employee or as a taxable benefit received by the former employee under an employer-financed retirement benefits scheme (see **57.26 PENSION PROVISION**). Similarly where a payment made by the former employee is borne wholly or partly by the former employer or other persons mentioned above, so much of the payment as is such taxable earnings or taxable benefit of the former employee is deductible in calculating net income.

Relief against capital gains

Where a claim is made as above and the claimant's income for the year is insufficient to fully utilise the relief, he may claim to have the excess relief treated as an allowable loss for that year for capital gains tax purposes. The allowable loss may not exceed the amount of the claimant's gains for the year *before* deducting any losses brought forward, the capital gains tax annual exemption, any relief available under **45.7 LOSSES** (trading losses set against capital gains) or any relief available to a former trader etc. for post-cessation expenditure (see **59.5 POST-CESSATION ETC. RECEIPTS AND EXPENDITURE**); any excess over that amount is *not* available to carry forward against gains of a later year.

Anti-avoidance

Legislation now denies a deduction under these provisions where the payment in question is made in pursuance of arrangements a main purpose of which is the avoidance of tax. The legislation applies to payments made on or after 12 January 2009, regardless of when the arrangements under which they were made were entered into.

[*ITEPA 2003, ss 555, 556, 556A, 557–564, Sch 6 para 217; TCGA 1992, s 263ZA; ITA 2007, Sch 1 paras 333, 440; FA 2009, s 67(3)(4)*].

No tax is charged under *ITEPA 2003, s 403* (see **20.5 COMPENSATION FOR LOSS OF EMPLOYMENT (AND DAMAGES)**) in respect of any amount paid, or benefit provided, to reimburse the former employee for a payment, which, had he not been reimbursed, would have attracted relief under the above provisions; the same applies as regards amounts paid etc. to the former employee's executors or administrators. [*ITEPA 2003, ss 409, 410*].

Simon's Taxes. See E4.798.

Employment or self-employment?

[27.54] Whether a person holds an office or employment or carries on a trade, profession or vocation depends on the facts including the relevant contract(s). A distinction is drawn between a contract *of service* (employment) and a contract *for services* (profession or vocation). A vision mixer engaged under a series of short-term contracts was self-employed (*Hall v Lorimer* CA 1993, 66 TC 349), as was an artiste who entered into a series of engagements (*Davies v Braithwaite* KB 1933, 18 TC 198), but contrast *Fall v Hitchen* Ch D 1972, 49 TC 433 in which a ballet dancer engaged by a theatrical management under a standard form of contract, but able to work elsewhere when not required by the management, was held to be in employment. See now below as regards artistes. A barristers' clerk was not the holder of an office (*McMenamin v Diggles* Ch D 1991, 64 TC 286), but in *Horner v Hasted* Ch D, [1995] STC 766 an unqualified accountant contributing capital to, and sharing profits of, a firm of accountants was held not to be a partner. The provision of catering services under contract at a golf club was held to be a trade (*McManus v Griffiths* Ch D 1997, 70 TC 218). See *Andrews v King* Ch D 1991, 64 TC 332 as regards agricultural gangmasters. The relationship between a supplier of scaffolding services and the workers he recruited to provide the services was held on the facts to be an informal and undocumented verbal contract for services (*Lewis (t/a MAL Scaffolding) and others v HMRC, Armstrong and others, third parties* (Sp C 527), [2006] SSCD 253).

See also *Barnett v Brabyn* Ch D 1996, 69 TC 133 for a case in which the taxpayer unsuccessfully appealed against additional assessments on trading income on the grounds that he was employed, where the original assessments had been agreed on the basis of his contention that he was self-employed.

Problems may arise in relation to part-time activities. A part-time medical appointment of a doctor in private practice was held to be an employment (*Mitchell & Edon v Ross* HL 1961, 40 TC 11) as were the lecture fees of a full-time employed consultant (*Lindsay v CIR* CS 1964, 41 TC 661) and a non-practising barrister (*Sidey v Phillips* Ch D 1986, 59 TC 458), the evening class fees of a teacher (*Fuge v McClelland* Ch D 1956, 36 TC 571) and the remuneration as lecturer of a professional singer (*Walls v Sinnett* Ch D 1986, 60 TC 150), but *ad hoc* Crown appointments were held not to be employment (*Edwards v Clinch* HL 1981, 56 TC 367). Salaries of sub-postmasters carrying on a retail trade from the same premises as the sub-post office are in practice treated as part of their trading income. Where a company operates sub-post offices in its shops with its directors as nominee sub-postmasters, and the directors are required to, and do, hand over their salaries as sub-postmasters to the company, the salaries will similarly be brought into the company's trading income computation and not assessed on the directors as employment income. (HMRC Employment Status Manual ESM4400). As regards sub-postmasters generally, see *Dhendsa v Richardson* (Sp C 134), [1997] SSCD 265.

Certain appointments, such as auditorships and registrarships, are strictly offices, but if held by practising accountants or solicitors the annual remuneration therefrom is, in practice, usually included in computing the business profits of the profession. Fees from directorships of professional partnerships may be included in profits provided that the directorship is a normal incident of the profession and the practice concerned, and that the fees are only a small part of total profits and are pooled for division among the partners under the partnership agreement. A written undertaking must be given that the full fees received will be included in gross income of the basis period whether or not the directorship is still held in the tax year or the partner concerned is still a partner. (HMRC ESC A37). For directors' fees received by other companies see **27.3**(v) above. However, any compensation etc. payments on the termination of such appointments are dealt with under *ITEPA 2003, ss 401–416* — see **20.4 COMPENSATION FOR LOSS OF EMPLOYMENT (AND DAMAGES)** and *Brander & Cruickshank* HL 1970, 46 TC 574 and the cases referred to therein.

See generally HMRC Employment Status Manual ESM0500 *et seq.* and, for HMRC's approach to case law in this area, ESM7000 *et seq.* For questions likely to be raised in any interview in relation to the question of employment or self-employment, see ESM0525. See also HMRC online factsheets ES/FS1 and ES/FS2.

See also **58.3, 58.16 PERSONAL SERVICE COMPANIES ETC.** which are concerned with the question of whether an individual providing his services through an intermediary would be an employee if engaged directly by a client, but which are also of wider application.

An **apprenticeship** is an employment (see HMRC Employment Status Manual ESM1111).

A **dentist** employed by a Panamanian company, which contracted with a UK practice to supply his services in return for a proportion of the NHS fees and a management charge, was held to be employed, although the legality of the arrangements was in question (*Cooke v Blacklaws* Ch D 1984, 58 TC 255). See generally HMRC Employment Status Manual ESM4030.

Divers etc. employed in the UK area of the Continental Shelf are taxable under the trading income rules (see **73.24 TRADING INCOME**). See also HMRC Employment Status Manual ESM4050.

Artistes

HMRC accept that the earnings of most artistes (i.e. actors, singers, musicians, dancers and theatrical artists) should be assessed as trading income. Circumstances in which such earnings are employment income subject to **PAY AS YOU EARN (53)** would e.g. be where the artiste is engaged for a regular salary to perform in a series of different productions at the direction of the engager, and with a period of notice stipulated before termination of the contract. This might apply e.g. to permanent members of an opera, ballet or theatre company or an orchestra. (*Taxation* 8 September 1994, p 553). See HMRC Business Income Manual BIM50151 for a general discussion of this distinction. In such cases, a deduction of up to 17.5% of earnings may be claimed in respect of percentage fees (and VAT thereon) paid out of those earnings to a licensed employment agency within *Employment Agencies Act 1973* or to a *bona fide* non-profit-making co-operative society acting as agent for the artiste. [*ITEPA 2003, s 352*]. Two well-known television presenters/interviewers were held to be 'theatrical artists' for the purpose of the above deduction for agency fees, i.e. the term is not restricted to those who actually perform in the theatre (*Madeley and another v HMRC* (Sp C 547), [2006] SSCD 513); none of the agency fees in this case could be said to have been incurred in the performance of the duties of the employment and thus the fees did not alternatively qualify for a deduction under **27.22** above.

See generally HMRC Employment Status Manual ESM4121 *et seq.*

Film and television industry

Certain self-employed grades are specified in Appendix 1 of the Film and Television Industry Guidance Notes at http://www.hmrc.gov.uk/specialist/fi_guidance_notes2003.pdf. HMRC have reviewed the contractual and working arrangements applicable to these grades in detail and it is accepted that the terms of engagement do not normally constitute a contract of employment. See HMRC Employment Status Manual ESM4101 *et seq.* See also Revenue Tax Bulletin August 2000 pp 775, 776.

A vision mixer was held to be self-employed in *Hall v Lorimer* CA 1993, 66 TC 349.

Employment Status Indicator tool

HMRC have produced an interactive tool which can be used as a guide in working out the employment status of individuals or groups of workers. It must be borne in mind that this can do no more than provide a general indication of employment status and that it has no legal authority. See www.hmrc.gov.uk/calcs/esi.htm.

Simon's Taxes. See E4.205–E4.224.

Flat rate expenses for employees

[27.55] Deductions are allowed for tools, special clothing etc. necessarily provided by an employee without reimbursement, and which the employer does not make available. If tools or protective clothing are supplied, but not both, or if some of the tools are provided, the rate of allowance is reduced accordingly. These rates are mostly agreed with trade unions, but the agreed rates do not preclude further claims, if justified, under the general deduction provisions (see **27.22** above) and nor do they require union membership. [*ITEPA 2003, ss 330(2), 367*]. See also *Ward v Dunn* Ch D 1978, 52 TC 517.

Industry	Occupation	Deductions p.a. for 2004/05–2007/08 inclusive (2003/04 and earlier years in brackets)	Deductions p.a. for 2008/09 onwards
		£	£
Agriculture	All Workers	70 (70)	100
Aluminium	a. Continual Casting Operators, Process Operators, De-Dimplers, Driers, Drill Punchers, Dross Unloaders, Firemen, Furnace Operators and their helpers, Leaders, Mould-men, Pourers, Remelt Department Labourers, Roll Flatteners	130 (130)	140
	b. Cable Hands, Case Makers, Labourers, Mates, Truck Drivers and Measurers, Storekeepers	60 (60)	80
	c. Apprentices	45 (45)	60
	d. All Other Workers	100 (100)	120
Banks and Building Societies	Uniformed Doormen and Messengers	45	60
	Uniformed Bank Employees	(40)	—
Brass and Copper	Braziers, Coppersmiths, Finishers, Fitters, Moulders, Turners and All Other Workers	100	120
	All Workers	(100)	—
Building	a. Joiners and Carpenters	105 (105)	140
	b. Cement Works, Roofing Felt and Asphalt Labourers	55 (55)	80
	c. Labourers and Navvies	45 (40)	60
	d. All Other Workers	85 (85)	120
Building Materials	a. Stone Masons	85 (85)	120

Industry	Occupation	Deductions p.a. for 2004/05– 2007/08 inclusive (2003/04 and earlier years in brackets)	Deductions p.a. for 2008/09 onwards
		£	£
	b. Tilemakers and Labourers	45 (40)	60
	c. All Other Workers	55 (55)	80
Clothing	*a.* Lacemakers, Hosiery Bleachers, Dyers, Scourers and Knitters, Knitwear Bleachers and Dyers	45 (45)	60
	b. All Other Workers	45 (30)	60
Constructional Engineering	*a.* Blacksmiths and their Strikers, Burners, Caulkers, Chippers, Drillers, Erectors, Fitters, Holders Up, Markers Off, Platers, Riggers, Riveters, Rivet Heaters, Scaffolders, Sheeters, Template Workers, Turners and Welders	115 (115)	140
	b. Banksmen, Labourers, Shop-helpers, Slewers and Straighteners	60 (60)	80
	c. Apprentices and Storekeepers	45 (45)	60
	d. All Other Workers	75 (75)	100
Electrical and Electricity Supply	*a.* Those workers incurring laundry costs only	45 (25)	60
	b. All Other Workers	90 (90)	120
Engineering (ancillary trades)	*a.* Pattern Makers	120 (120)	140
	b. Labourers, Supervisory and Unskilled Workers	60 (60)	80
	c. Apprentices and Storekeepers	45 (45)	60
	d. Motor Mechanics in Garage Repair Shop	100 (100)	120
	e. All Other Workers	100 (100)	120
Fire Service	Uniformed Fire Fighters and Fire Officers	60 (60)	80
Food	All Workers	45 (40)	60
Forestry	All Workers	70 (70)	100
Glass	All Workers	60 (60)	80

Industry	Occupation	Deductions p.a. for 2004/05– 2007/08 inclusive (2003/04 and earlier years in brackets)	Deductions p.a. for 2008/09 onwards
		£	£
Health-care Staff in the NHS, Private Hospitals and Nursing Homes	a. Ambulance Staff on Active Service	110 (110)	140
	b. Nurses, Midwives, Chiropodists, Dental Nurses, Occupational, Speech, Physios and Other Therapists, Phlebotomists and Radiographers	70 (70)	100
	c. Plaster Room Orderlies, Hospital Porters, Ward Clerks, Sterile Supply Workers, Hospital Domestics, Hospital Catering Staff	60 (60)	100
	d. Laboratory Staff, Pharmacists and Pharmacy Assistants	45 (45)	60
	e. Uniformed Ancillary Staff — Maintenance Workers, Grounds Staff, Drivers, Parking Attendants and Security Guards, Receptionists and Other Uniformed Staff	45 (45)	60
Heating	a. Pipe Fitters and Plumbers	100 (100)	120
	b. Coverers, Laggers, Domestic Glaziers, Heating Engineers and all their Mates	90 (90)	120
	c. All Gas Workers and All Other Workers	70 (70)	100
Iron Mining	a. Fillers, Miners and Underground Workers	100 (100)	120
	b. All Other Workers	75 (75)	100
Iron and Steel	a. Day Labourers, General Labourers, Stockmen, Timekeepers, Warehouse Staff and Weighmen	60 (60)	80
	b. Apprentices	45 (45)	60
	c. All Other Workers	120 (120)	140
Leather	a. Curriers (Wet Workers), Fell-mongering Workers and Tanning Operatives (Wet)	55 (55)	80
	b. All Other Workers	45 (40)	60

Industry	Occupation	Deductions p.a. for 2004/05–2007/08 inclusive (2003/04 and earlier years in brackets)	Deductions p.a. for 2008/09 onwards
		£	£
Particular Engineering	*a*. Pattern Makers	120 (120)	140
	b. Chainmakers; Cleaners, Galvanisers, Tinners and Wire Drawers in the Wire Drawing industry; Toolmakers in the Lock Making Industry	100 (100)	120
	c. Apprentices and Storekeepers	45 (45)	60
	d. All Other Workers	60 (60)	80
Police Force	Uniformed Police Officers (ranks up to and including Chief Inspector)	Note 7 (55)	140
Precious Metals	All Workers	70 (70)	100
Printing	*a*. The following occupations in the Letterpress Section; Electrical Engineers (Rotary Presses), Electrotypers, Ink and Roller Makers, Machine Minders (Rotary), Maintenance Engineers (Rotary Presses) and Stereotypers	105 (105)	140
	b. Bench Hands (Periodical & Bookbinding Section), Compositors (Letterpress Section), Readers (Letterpress Section), Telecommunications &Electronic Section Wire Room Operators, Warehousemen (Paper Box Making Section)	45 (30)	60
	c. All Other Workers	70 (70)	100
Prisons	Uniformed Prison Officers	55 (55)	80
Public Service	i. Docks and Inland Waterways		
	a. Dockers, Dredger Drivers and Hopper Steerers	55 (55)	80
	b. All Other Workers	45 (40)	60
	ii. Public Transport		
	a. Garage Hands (including Cleaners)	55 (55)	80

Industry	Occupation	Deductions p.a. for 2004/05–2007/08 inclusive (2003/04 and earlier years in brackets)	Deductions p.a. for 2008/09 onwards
		£	£
	b. Conductors and Drivers	45 (40)	60
Quarrying	All Workers	70 (70)	100
Railways	All Workers except Craftsmen (Engineering, Vehicles etc. for which see the appropriate category)	70 (70)	100
Seamen	a. Carpenters — Passenger Liners	165 (165)	165
	b. Carpenters — Cargo Vessels, Tankers, Coasters and Ferries	130 (130)	140
Shipyards	a. Blacksmiths and their Strikers, Boilermakers, Burners, Carpenters, Caulkers, Drillers, Furnacemen (Platers), Holders Up, Fitters, Platers, Plumbers, Riveters, Sheet Iron Workers, Shipwrights, Tubers and Welders	115 (115)	140
	b. Labourers	60 (60)	80
	c. Apprentices and Storekeepers	45 (45)	60
	d. All Other Workers	75 (75)	100
Textiles and Textile Printing	a. Carders, Carding Engineers, Overlookers, and Technicians in Spinning Mills	85 (85)	120
	b. All Other Workers	60 (50)	80
Vehicles	a. Builders, Railway Vehicle Repairers and Railway Wagon Lifters	105 (105)	140
	b. Railway Vehicle Painters, Letterers and Builders' and Repairers' Assistants	60 (60)	80
	c. All Other Workers	45 (40)	60
Wood and Furniture	a. Carpenters, Cabinetmakers, Joiners, Wood Carvers and Woodcutting Machinists	115 (115)	140
	b. Artificial Limb Makers (other than in wood), Organ Builders and Packaging Case Makers	90 (90)	120

Industry	Occupation	Deductions p.a. for 2004/05–2007/08 inclusive (2003/04 and earlier years in brackets)	Deductions p.a. for 2008/09 onwards
		£	£
	c. Coopers not providing own tools, Labourers, Polishers and Upholsterers	45 (45)	60
	d. All Other Workers	75 (75)	100

Notes

(1) The expressions 'all workers' and 'all other workers' refer only to manual workers, or certain other workers who have to bear the cost of upkeep of tools or special clothing. They do not extend to other employees such as office staff.

(2) 'Cost of upkeep' means the cost of replacement, repair or cleaning, but not the initial cost of providing the tools or special clothing.

(3) 'Special clothing' means overalls or other protective clothing or uniform, but does not include ordinary clothing of the sort which is also worn off duty.

(4) In the entry relating to aluminium, 'firemen' means persons engaged to light and maintain furnaces.

(5) 'Constructional engineering' means engineering undertaken on a construction site, including buildings, shipyards, bridges, roads and other similar operations.

(6) 'Particular engineering' means engineering undertaken on a commercial basis in a factory or workshop for the purposes of producing components such as wire, springs, nails and locks.

(7) The rate for police officers is £110 for 2007/08 only and £55 for previous years.

(HMRC Employment Income Manual EIM32712).

As regards commercial **airline pilots** (including co-pilots, helicopter pilots, and other uniformed flight deck crew but not cabin crew) for 2006/07 onwards, see HMRC Employment Income Manual EIM50050.

Laundry costs

For employees *not* covered by one of the above deductions but who are required to wear protective clothing or uniforms, a flat rate deduction of £60 p.a. is allowed for 2008/09 onwards (£45 p.a. for earlier years) to cover the cost of laundering. If the expense is met partly by the employer the amount of the deduction should be restricted. Larger deductions will not be allowed without adequate evidence of the expenditure incurred. (HMRC Employment Income Manual EIM32712). For **nurses** (including midwives, auxiliaries, students, nursing assistants and healthcare assistants or workers) the agreed deduction is £100 p.a. for 2008/09 onwards (£70 p.a. for earlier years). (HMRC Employment Income Manual EIM67210, 67240).

Gifts, awards etc. received

[27.56] Gifts etc. are taxable when they arise out of the employment but not if they are given to the recipient in a personal capacity. The line between the two may be fine. Although payments may be voluntary and irregular, they are assessable. Also all commissions, Christmas presents, 'cost of living', cash and other bonuses. For 'tax-free' payments and awards, see **27.77** below. For payments to clergymen, see **27.50** above.

Bonus to a director described as a gift held assessable (*Radcliffe v Holt* KB 1927, 11 TC 621), and *ex gratia* payments to the retiring chairman of an action group for the successful outcome of litigation similarly held assessable (*McBride v Blackburn* (Sp C 356), [2003] SSCD 139). Proceeds of a *public benefit match* for a cricketer held to be a gift and not chargeable (*Reed v Seymour* HL 1927, 11 TC 625), but see *Moorhouse v Dooland* CA 1954, 36 TC 1 re collections. In *Davis v Harrison* KB 1927, 11 TC 707, *Corbett v Duff and other cases* KB 1941, 23 TC 763, payments to professional football players *in lieu of benefit* or on *transference to another club*, held assessable. World Cup bonus to professional footballer not assessable (*Moore v Griffiths* Ch D 1972, 48 TC 338). Present to *successful jockey* by owner of racehorse assessable (*Wing v O'Connell* Supreme Court (Ireland) 1926, 1 ITC 170) also *taxi driver's tips* (*Calvert v Wainwright* KB 1947, 27 TC 475) and gifts to Hunt servant (*Wright v Boyce* CA 1958, 38 TC 160). Betting winnings on own games by professional golfer not assessable (*Down v Compston* KB 1937, 21 TC 60).

Gift to employee by company to which his services were lent by employer held not assessable, *Morris* CS 1967, 44 TC 685. But amount to company secretary, agreed by directors for negotiating sale of works and paid by liquidator, held assessable (*Shipway v Skidmore* KB 1932, 16 TC 748) as were payments to a director for negotiating sale of a branch (*Mudd v Collins* KB 1925, 9 TC 297) and to a director for special services abroad (*Barson v Airey* CA 1925, 10 TC 609). Commission for work outside ordinary duties assessable (*Mudd v Collins* KB 1925, 9 TC 297). Sums paid as compensation for loss of benefit under an abandoned salvage scheme held assessable (*Holland v Geoghegan* Ch D 1972, 48 TC 482), also assets distributed to employees on termination of profit-sharing trust fund before termination of employment (*Brumby v Milner* HL 1976, 51 TC 583). See, however, *Bray v Best* HL 1989, 61 TC 705 as regards such a distribution after termination of employment.

See **27.74** below regarding gifts of shares.

Pensions (voluntary or otherwise) to retired employees are taxable (see **56.2 PENSION INCOME**) as are certain payments in consideration of, in consequence of, or in connection with the termination, or change, of employment (see **20 COMPENSATION FOR LOSS OF EMPLOYMENT (AND DAMAGES)**).

Suggestion scheme awards

Suggestion scheme awards are not liable to income tax provided that there is a formally constituted scheme open to all employees (or to a particular description of them) on equal terms, and that:

(a) the suggestion relates to the employer's activities;

(b) it could not reasonably have been expected to be made by the employee in the course of the duties of the employment in the light of the employee's experience; and

(c) it is not made at a meeting held for that purpose.

Awards under the scheme must either be 'encouragement' awards of £25 or less, for suggestions with intrinsic merit or showing special effort, or 'financial benefit' awards for suggestions relating to improvements in efficiency or effectiveness which the employer has decided to adopt with a reasonable expectation of financial benefit. The amount of a financial benefit award must not exceed 50% of the first year's expected net benefit, or 10% of the expected benefit over a period of up to five years, with an overall limit of £5,000. Any excess over £5,000 is not covered by the exemption. Where a suggestion is put forward by more than one employee, the award is limited *pro rata*, and any subsequent award(s) for the same suggestion must not exceed the residue of the maximum award. [*ITEPA 2003, ss 321, 322, Sch 7 para 38*].

Long service awards

Long service awards to employees, including directors, for service of 20 years or more, are not liable to income tax to the extent that the cost to the employer does not exceed £50 for each year of service and provided that no similar award has been made to the recipient within the previous ten years. Service may include that with predecessor employers. The award must consist of tangible articles, of shares in the employing company (or in another group company), or of other benefits provided that they are not payments (or cash vouchers or credit-tokens) or other shares or securities (or interests in or rights over them). [*ITEPA 2003, s 323; SI 2003 No 1361, Reg 3*]. Cash awards are assessable (*Weston v Hearn* KB 1943, 25 TC 425).

Gifts from third parties

Gifts received by an employee (or a member of the employee's family or household) from a person other than the employer (or person connected with the employer, see **21 CONNECTED PERSONS**), and not directly or indirectly procured by the employer or a connected person, are not liable to income tax, provided that:

(a) they are not made in recognition or anticipation of particular services by the employee in the course of the employment;

(b) they are of goods (i.e. not of cash, securities or the use of a service), or of non-cash vouchers or credit-tokens only capable of being used to obtain goods; and

(c) the total cost to the donor of all such gifts relating to an employee in a tax year is not more than £250 (inclusive of any VAT).

[*ITEPA 2003, ss 270, 324; SI 2003 No 1361, Regs 1, 4*].

Simon's Taxes. See E4.461-E4.471, E4.764–E4.766.

HM Forces

[27.57] Mess and ration allowances and certain bounties and gratuities are exempt. [*ITEPA 2003, s 297*]. No tax allowance may be claimed for lodging expenses paid out of assessable lodging allowance (*Evans v Richardson, Nagley v Spilsbury* Ch D 1957, 37 TC 178), nor for mess expenses (*Lomax v Newton* Ch D 1953, 34 TC 558).

The Operational Allowance introduced in October 2006 (for UK armed forces serving in designated combat zones) is exempt (see **30.6 EXEMPT INCOME**). Certain payments and other benefits (including redundancy payments/benefits and commutation of annual sums) are exempt from any charge under *ITEPA 2003, s 403* (see **20.6**(iv) **COMPENSATION FOR LOSS OF EMPLOYMENT (AND DAMAGES)**). See also **30.7** and **30.14 EXEMPT INCOME** and **56.3 PENSION INCOME**. Travel facilities (including allowances, vouchers and warrants) for going on, or returning from, leave are exempt from tax. [*ITEPA 2003, ss 266(3), 296*]. Territorial Army pay is chargeable but not annual bounty and training expenses. [*ITEPA 2003, s 298*].

Uniform allowances

Serving officers generally receive an annual tax-free allowance which, taking one year with another, covers the costs they are obliged to incur in maintaining their uniforms. The allowance is automatically included in their earnings, with a corresponding deduction being made in arriving at taxable earnings. [*ITEPA 2003, ss 328(3), 368*]. No further action is thus generally required.

Legal costs

[27.58] In *Eagles v Levy* KB 1934, 19 TC 23 it was held that (a) costs of action to recover remuneration were not an allowable deduction, and (b) a lump sum amount in settlement of action for balance remuneration was assessable in full.

Where company had special need of director's services and paid more than necessary in legal costs of defence on motoring charge, it was held that no apportionment was to be made between benefits to company and employee and that all the costs were assessable (*Rendell v Went* HL 1964, 41 TC 641).

Simon's Taxes. See E4.614, E4.778A.

Living accommodation

[27.59] Provision of living accommodation for an employee may be taxable earnings under general principles (see **27.20** above). In *Nicoll v Austin* KB 1935, 19 TC 531, a company maintained a large house owned and occupied by its managing director and controlling shareholder, paying the rates, fuel bills and other outgoings. The expenditure was held to be assessable on him as emoluments of his office.

There may, however, be liability under special legislation as described at **27.60–27.64** below. This takes priority over any charge under general principles, the latter applying only if, and to the extent that, the charge would exceed that under the special legislation. [*ITEPA 2003, s 109*].

'Living accommodation' for these purposes includes all kinds of residential accommodation – e.g. mansions, houses, flats, houseboats, holiday homes or apartments – but not overnight or hotel accommodation or board and lodging (HMRC Employment Income Manual EIM11321). Whether such accommodation is provided for an employee is a question of fact — see HMRC Employment Income Manual EIM11405, 11406.

For expenses related to living accommodation, see **27.66** below.

The basic charge

[27.60] For any employee, the 'cash equivalent' of any living accommodation provided to him, or to members of his family or household, by his employer for any period during or comprising a tax year is treated as earnings for that year unless:

- the accommodation is provided in the normal course of domestic, family and personal relationships; or
- it is provided by a local authority under its usual terms for non-employees; or
- any of the exemptions at **27.62, 27.63** below apply.

A deduction is allowed for any amounts which would have been allowed had the employee paid for the accommodation out of earnings.

A charge similarly arises where the accommodation is provided by someone other than the employer but 'by reason of' the employment, i.e. where the accommodation would not have been provided but for the employment. In practice HMRC normally assume that a benefit which is provided by someone other than the employer but which is plainly connected with the employment has been provided by reason of the employment. (HMRC Employment Income Manual EIM11408, 20503).

The '*cash equivalent*' of the provision of accommodation for a period is the 'rental value' of the accommodation for that period less any sum made good by the employee to the person at whose cost the accommodation is provided and attributable to that provision. The '*rental value*' is normally an amount equal to rent for the period at an annual rent equal to the annual value ascertained under *ITEPA 2003, s 110*, which for UK property is equivalent to the gross rateable value. In Scotland, where the 1985 rating revaluation produced annual values out of line with those in the rest of the UK, a figure lower than the gross rateable value is, by concession, used as annual value. The 1985 valuation figure is scaled back by the average increase in Scottish rateable values between 1978 and 1985 (170%), e.g. a 1985 value of £270 becomes £100 for this purpose. (HMRC ESC A56). For new properties which do not appear on the domestic rating lists, and for those where there has been a material change since the lists ceased to be maintained, estimates will be agreed of what the gross annual value would have been had domestic rates been continued. In the case of Scotland these will then be scaled back to 1978 values. (Revenue Press Release 19 April 1990).

For determination of the annual value of property situated outside the UK, see HMRC Employment Income Manual EIM11440, 11441. Disputes as to annual value may be referred to the Appeal Tribunal.

Alternatively, if the person at whose cost the accommodation is provided pays actual rent for the whole or part of the period at an annual rate greater than the annual value (as above), then that actual rent is the rental value for the period (or part). See **27.61** below for property acquired on a short lease at a premium.

[*ITEPA 2003, ss 97, 98, 102, 103, 105, 110, 111, 364; FA 2009, s 71(2), (4)–(6); SI 2009 No 56, Sch 1 para 336*].

See also the additional charge at **27.64** below.

Simon's Taxes. See E4.607, E4.607A.

Premium treated as rent

[27.61] In this paragraph the person at whose cost the accommodation is provided is known as P. Where the accommodation is leased by P under a lease entered into on or after 22 April 2009 of ten years or less and P pays a premium, the 'net premium' is treated for the purposes of **27.60** above as if it were a payment of rent (or additional rent). In determining the amount to be so treated for any tax year (or part of a tax year) the net premium is regarded as accruing evenly throughout the term of the lease. The *'net premium'* means the total amount paid or payable by P by way of premium, less any part of that amount that has been repaid or is (or will become) repayable. These rules come into play only if the premises are mainly used by P for providing employee living accommodation. They apply if the accommodation represents all or part of the premises leased. A pre-22 April 2009 lease is brought within the rules if it is extended on or after that date, but only by reference to the additional term of the lease and ignoring any premium payable in respect of the unextended term. A premium includes a premium under the lease or otherwise under the terms on which the lease is granted; in Scotland, a premium includes a grassum.

Special rules apply if a lease contains one or more 'break clauses' if the right to terminate the lease that any such clause confers is capable of being exercised in such a way that the term of the lease is then ten years or less. A *'break clause'* is a provision of a lease that gives a person a right to terminate the lease so that its term is shorter than it otherwise would be. In applying the above provisions, both the term of the lease and the net premium are to be determined on the assumption that any such break clause is exercised in such a way that the term of the lease is as short as possible. If, in fact, the break clause is not exercised, so that the lease continues, the parties to the lease are treated as if they had entered into a further lease. The above provisions are then applied to this notional lease, taking the net premium to be a time-apportioned amount of so much of the premium payable under the actual lease as has not already been treated as a payment of rent. Appropriate modifications apply if there is a further break clause in that part of the term of the actual lease that coincides with the notional lease.

[ITEPA 2003, ss 105A, 105B; FA 2009, s 71(3)–(6)].

This legislation was enacted in response to an apparently widely used scheme involving the use of lease premium arrangements by employers to provide living accommodation to employees with the intention of minimising the tax and national insurance charge on the benefit of the accommodation. The accommodation was often provided via an employee benefit trust or similar entity. HMRC always considered that such arrangements were ineffective and the aim of the legislation was to put this beyond doubt. For arrangements outside the scope of the legislation (generally where the lease was entered into before 22 April 2009), HMRC invited employers and employees to indicate their willingness to reach a financial settlement with HMRC. A response was required by 6 August 2010. See www.hmrc.gov.uk/news/lease-prem-sett.pdf for full details of the initiative.

Exemptions

[27.62] There is an exemption from the charge at **27.60** above where:

(a)   it is necessary for the proper performance of his duties for the employee to reside in the accommodation; or

(b)   the employment is such that it is customary for employees to be provided with accommodation for the better performance of their duties; or

(c)   there is a special threat to the employee's personal security, and he resides in the accommodation as part of special security arrangements in force; or

(d)   the accommodation is in Chevening House or certain related premises and the employee is a person nominated in accordance with the Chevening Estate trusts.

[ITEPA 2003, ss 99(1)(2), 100, 101].

See also **27.63** below (overseas holiday homes etc.).

See *Vertigan v Brady* Ch D 1988, 60 TC 624 as regards the scope of (a) and (b) above.

As regards (b) above, it is accepted that the following employees are within the exemption: police officers; MOD police; prison governors, officers and chaplains; clergymen and ministers of religion (unless engaged on purely administrative duties); members of HM forces; members of the Diplomatic Service; managers of newsagent shops with paper rounds; live-in managers of public houses; managers of off-licences with opening hours broadly equivalent to those of public houses; boarding school head teachers and certain other staff provided with accommodation on or near the school premises; stable staff of racehorse trainers who live on the premises and certain key workers who live close to the stables. Veterinary surgeons assisting in veterinary practices and managers of camping and caravan sites living on or adjacent to the site will be accepted as meeting the test that provision of accommodation is 'customary', but must individually satisfy the test that the provision is for the 'better performance' of their duties. (HMRC Employment Income Manual EIM11351, 11352).

Council tax and rates

Where (a), (b) or (c) above applies, there is also no liability if the water or sewerage charges or rates or council tax are paid or reimbursed by the employer. [*ITEPA 2003, s 314*].

Directors

Neither (a) nor (b) above applies to accommodation provided by a company, or associated company, to its director unless for each such directorship he has no material interest in the company (i.e. broadly if his and/or his associates' interests in the company do not exceed 5%) *and either* he is a full-time working director *or* the company is non-profit-making (i.e. it does not carry on a trade nor is its main function the holding of investments or other property) *or* the company is established for charitable purposes only. [*ITEPA 2003, ss 68, 99(3)–(5); CTA 2010, Sch 1 para 383*].

Overseas holiday homes etc.

[27.63] A further exemption from the charge at **27.60** above was introduced by *FA 2008, s 45* and treated as having always had effect. The exemption is intended mainly for UK resident individuals who set up or acquire an overseas company for the purpose of owning an overseas property, generally for use as a holiday home. It applies where a property outside the UK is owned by a company that is itself wholly owned (with or without other individuals) by the director or other officer on whom a taxable living accommodation benefit would otherwise arise. The company must be the '*holding company of the property*', i.e.

- it must own a '*relevant interest*' in the property, being an interest that confers (or would but for any inferior interest confer) a right to exclusive possession;
- its interest in the property must be its sole or main asset; and
- it must undertake no activities other than those incidental to its ownership of that interest.

A company can also be the '*holding company of the property*' if the property is owned by a wholly owned subsidiary of the company. The subsidiary must meet the three conditions above and the company itself must meet the second and third conditions by reference to its interest in the subsidiary.

The company must also have been the holding company of the property at all times since the 'relevant time'. The '*relevant time*' is normally the time the company first owned a relevant interest in the property. If, however, the director or officer acquired his interest in the company after that time, and otherwise than from a connected person (see **21 CONNECTED PERSONS**), the '*relevant time*' is the time the director or officer acquired that interest.

The exemption does *not* apply in any of the following circumstances:

- if the company's interest in the property was acquired from a 'connected company' at an undervalue (as defined) or derives from an interest that was so acquired;
- if, at any time after the relevant time (as above), expenditure in respect of the property has been incurred by a 'connected company' or any borrowing of the company from a 'connected company' has been outstanding (disregarding any borrowing at a commercial rate or which results in a charge under **27.40** above (cheap loan arrangements) on the director or officer concerned); or
- if the living accommodation is provided in pursuance of an arrangement (as widely defined) a main purpose of which is the avoidance of tax or National Insurance contributions.

For the purposes of the above, a *'connected company'* is a company connected with the director or officer concerned (or with a member of his family or with his employer) or a company connected with such a company. Reference to the company's acquiring an interest include an interest being granted to it.

[*ITEPA 2003, ss 100A, 100B; FA 2008, s 45*].

Advice and a contact address are available at www.hmrc.gov.uk/news/hol-hom e-abroad.htm for any individual who can show that he has paid income tax for any year before 2008/09 on the benefit of living accommodation which qualifies for the overseas property exemption and wishes to claim a refund.

Additional charge on properties costing over £75,000

[27.64] For all employees, if there is a liability to tax on living accommodation under the basic charge in **27.60** above (or there would be a liability if the employee's contributions towards the cost were disregarded) and the cost of providing the accommodation exceeds £75,000, the employee will, in addition to any basic charge, be taxable on the 'additional value' to him of the accommodation. Where, however, the basic charge is based on the full open market rent the property might fetch, HMRC will, by concession, not seek to impose an additional charge (HMRC ESC A91).

The *'additional value'* is the rent which would have been payable for the period if the annual rent was the 'appropriate percentage' of the amount by which the cost of providing the accommodation exceeds £75,000. The *'appropriate percentage'* is the 'official rate' in force, for the purposes of taxing cheap loan arrangements under *ITEPA 2003, s 181* (see **27.40** above), at the beginning of the tax year (e.g. 6.25% for 2007/08 and 2008/09, 4.75% for 2009/10, 4% for 2010/11). Any rent paid by the employee which exceeds the value of the accommodation as determined for the purposes of the basic charge is deducted from the additional value.

The cost of providing the accommodation is the aggregate of expenditure incurred by any 'relevant person' in acquiring the property together with any improvement expenditure incurred before the tax year in question *less* any payments by the employee to any relevant person as reimbursement of such expenditure or as consideration for the grant of a tenancy, or subtenancy, to him. Where the employee first occupies the property on a date after 30 March 1983 and an estate or interest in the property was held by a relevant person throughout the period of six years ending with the date of first occupation, then the cost of providing the accommodation, for the purposes of calculating the additional value (but not for determining whether the additional charge applies), is calculated as follows. Take the market value of the property at the date of first occupation and add any improvement expenditure incurred after that date and before the start of the tax year. Deduct from the total any payments made by the employee to any relevant person as reimbursement of any part of the cost of acquiring the estate or interest held when the employee first occupied the property (up to the market value on that date) or of the improvement expenditure, or as consideration for the grant of a tenancy, or subtenancy, to him. A *'relevant person'* is the person providing the accommodation, or, if different, the employee's employer, and any person, other than the employee, connected with such persons (within **21 CONNECTED PERSONS**). *'Market value'* is open market value assuming vacant possession and disregarding any options on the property held by the employee, a person connected with him or any relevant person as defined above.

Where an employee is provided with more than one property, the £75,000 limit is applied separately to each property (Revenue Press Release 22 November 1990). Where a property is provided as living accommodation to more than one employee or director in the same period, the total of the basic and additional charges cannot exceed the amount which would have been chargeable if the property had been provided to a single employee in that period.

[*ITEPA 2003, ss 104, 106–108, 112, Sch 7 para 21*].

Simon's Taxes. See **E4.608.**

Example

[27.65]

S, the founder and managing director of S Ltd, a successful transport company, has since April 2005 occupied a mansion house owned by S Ltd. The house was acquired by S Ltd in August 1999 for £150,000 and, since acquisition, but before 6 April 2009, £80,000 has been spent by S Ltd on alterations and improvements to the house. The gross annual value of the house for rating purposes before 1 April 1990 (when the community charge replaced general rates) was £1,663. S pays annual rental of £2,000 to the company for 2010/11 only. He pays all expenses relating to the property.

S will have taxable benefits in respect of his occupation of the house for 2009/10 and 2010/11 as follows.

	£	£
2009/10		
Gross annual value		1,663
Additional charge		
Acquisition cost of house	150,000	

Cost of improvements	<u>80,000</u>	
	230,000	
Deduct	<u>75,000</u>	
Additional value	£155,000	
Additional value at 4.75%		<u>7,362</u>
		<u>£9,025</u>
2010/11		
Gross annual value		Nil*
Additional charge		
Acquisition cost of house	150,000	
Cost of improvements	<u>80,000</u>	
	230,000	
Deduct	<u>75,000</u>	
Additional value	£155,000	
Additional value at 4%		<u>6,200</u>
		6,200
Rental payable by S	2,000	
De-duct Gross annual value	<u>1,663</u>	
		<u>337</u>*
		<u>£5,863</u>

* No taxable gross annual value arises in 2010/11 because the rental of £2,000 payable by S exceeds the gross annual value of £1,663. The excess is deductible from the amount of the benefit arising under the additional charge.

Expenses connected with living accommodation

[27.66] Certain expenses connected with the provision of living accommodation which are met on behalf of, or reimbursed to, the employee may give rise to liability either as benefits-in-kind for directors and certain employees or directly as earnings for all employees. The following reliefs apply.

(i)   *Alterations and repairs* to accommodation provided for directors and employees other than lower-paid employees (see **27.26** above) will not be treated as benefits if:
  • the alterations or additions are of a structural nature; or
  • the repairs would be the obligation of the lessor if the premises were leased and *Landlord and Tenant Act 1985, s 11* applied. [*ITEPA 2003, s 313*].

(ii)   Where one of the exemptions in **27.62**(a), (b) or (c) above applies, any amount to be treated as earnings in respect of expenditure on *heating, lighting, cleaning, repairs, maintenance, decoration, provision of furniture etc.* normal for domestic occupation is limited to 10% of the net earnings from the employment for the period concerned less any sum made good by the employee. Earnings include any from an associated company (i.e. where one company has control of the other or both are under control of the same person). Net earnings are after deducting capital allowances, allowable expenses, mileage allowance relief, and contributions to registered pension schemes and disregarding the benefit in question. [*ITEPA 2003, s 315*]. The earnings to be taken into account are those for the year under review, regardless of the year in which they are chargeable (HMRC Employment Income Manual EIM21723).

Simon's Taxes. See **E4.608A**.

Example

[27.67]

N is employed by the G Property Co Ltd, earning £12,700 p.a. He occupies, rent-free, the basement flat of a block of flats for which he is employed as caretaker/security officer. The annual value of the flat is determined at £250. In 2010/11, G Ltd incurred the following expenditure on the flat.

	£
Heat and light	700
Decoration	330
Repairs	210
Cleaning	160
	1,400
Conversion of large bedroom into two smaller bedrooms	3,000

In addition, the company pays N's council tax which amounts to £500.

As the company does not have a pension scheme, N pays a stakeholder pension premium of £160 net of tax (equivalent to £200 gross) into a registered scheme on 31 October 2010, but apart from his personal allowance, he has no other reliefs.

N's taxable income for 2010/11 is

	£
Salary	12,700
Annual value of flat	—
Heat and light, decoration, repairs, cleaning £1,400 restricted to	1,250
	13,950
Deduct	
Personal allowance	6,475
Taxable	£7,475

Notes

(a) N is not chargeable on the annual value of the flat as long as he can show that it is necessary for the proper performance of his duties for him to reside in the accommodation.

(b) The structural alterations costing £3,000 will not be regarded as a benefit.

(c) The earnings treated as having arisen in respect of the heat and light, decoration, repairs and cleaning costs will be restricted to the lesser of:
  (i)   the expenses incurred £1,400;
  (ii)   10% × £12,500 (net earnings) £1,250.
The contribution to a registered pension scheme is deductible in arriving at net earnings for this purpose. (The contribution is not shown above as a deduction from taxable income as basic rate relief has been given at source and higher rate relief is not applicable.)

Miscellaneous

[27.68] The following cases, decided under earlier legislation, may be relevant to a charge under the benefits code in respect of expenses related to living accommodation. *Butter v Bennett* CA 1962, 40 TC 402 ('representative occupier' held to be assessable on provisions for fuel and gardening); *Doyle v Davison* QB(NI) 1961, 40 TC 140 (repairs paid for by employer held to be benefits); *McKie v Warner* Ch D 1961, 40 TC 65 (flat provided at reduced rent held to be benefit); *Luke* HL 1963, 40 TC 630 (certain expenses held not to be benefits — house owned by employer); *Westcott v Bryan* CA 1969, 45 TC 476 (apportionment approved where company house provided to accommodate company guests).

As regards board and lodging allowances, see **27.20** above and for subsistence allowances, see **27.80** below. For deductibility of the cost of living accommodation etc., see **27.24** above.

Compulsory transfers

Guarantee payments making good loss on sale of employee's house when compulsorily transferred were held not assessable in *Hochstrasser v Mayes, Jennings v Kinder* HL 1959, 38 TC 673.

Members of Parliaments and Assemblies

Members of the House of Commons, the Scottish Parliament or the Wales or Northern Ireland Assemblies are not allowed a deduction for expenses incurred on residential or overnight accommodation to enable duties to be performed where the body of which they are a member sits or in the area which they represent. In relation to a member of the House of Commons, overnight stays in hotels that are excluded from the exemption in **30.27 EXEMPT INCOME** are also excluded from this disallowance. [*ITEPA 2003, s 360; F(No 2)A 2010, Sch 4 para 1(3)(6)*]. **Simon's Taxes.** See E4.790.

Meal vouchers

[27.69] The provision by the employer of meal vouchers is not taxable on the employee if the vouchers are:

- non-transferable;
- used for meals on working days only;
- limited to 15 pence per day; and
- if limited in issue, available to staff in lower-paid employment (see **27.26** above).

The value of any voucher or part voucher not satisfying these conditions is taxable (e.g. the excess over 15p where the voucher otherwise qualifies).

[ITEPA 2003, s 89, Sch 7 para 18]. See **27.29**(iv) above for canteen meals.

Redundancy payments

[27.70] Amounts received under *Employment Rights Act 1996*, or NI equivalent, may be taken into account for purposes of *ITEPA 2003, s 403* — see **20.5** COMPENSATION FOR LOSS OF EMPLOYMENT (AND DAMAGES), but are otherwise exempt earnings. *[ITEPA 2003, s 309]*. Other redundancy payments may be taxable earnings, see **20.5** *et seq.* COMPENSATION FOR LOSS OF EMPLOYMENT (AND DAMAGES). Simon's Taxes. See E4.743.

Relocation packages

[27.71] Certain payments and benefits received in connection with job-related residential moves are exempted from charge as taxable earnings. The statutory exemption applies to:

- any sums paid to the employee, or to another person on behalf of the employee, in respect of 'qualifying removal expenses'; and
- any 'qualifying removal benefit' provided for the employee or for members of his family or household (including sons- and daughters-in-law, servants, dependants and guests),

to the extent that they do not exceed a 'qualifying limit' (currently £8,000).

'*Qualifying removal expenses*' are 'eligible removal expenses' reasonably incurred by the employee, and '*qualifying removal benefits*' are 'eligible removal benefits' reasonably provided, on or before the 'limitation day' in connection with a change of the employee's sole or main residence. The change of residence does not require the disposal of the former residence, but the new residence must, on the facts of the particular case, become the main residence of the employee (see Revenue Press Release 14 April 1993).

The change of residence must result from the employee commencing employment with the employer, or from an alteration of his duties in the employment, or from an alteration of the place where those duties are normally to be performed. The change must be made wholly or mainly to bring the employee's residence within a reasonable daily travelling distance of the place he normally performs, or is to perform, those duties. What is a 'reasonable daily travelling distance' is not defined, but is a matter for common sense, taking account of local conditions. It may depend on either or both travelling time or distance (see Revenue Tax Bulletin November 1993 p 94).

The '*limitation day*' is the last day of the tax year following that in which the commencement or change of duties etc. took place, unless the Commissioners for HMRC grant an extension in a particular case to the end of a later tax year.

Eligible removal expenses

'*Eligible removal expenses*' fall into seven different categories.

(i) **Expenses of disposal,** i.e. legal expenses, loan redemption penalties, estate agents' or auctioneers' fees, advertising costs, disconnection charges, and rent and maintenance etc. costs during an unoccupied period, relating to the disposal of his interest (or of the interest of a member of his family or household) in the employee's former residence. Expenses of a sale which falls through are eligible provided that the residence is in fact still changed.

(ii) **Expenses of acquisition,** i.e. legal expenses, loan procurement fees, insurance costs, survey fees, Registry fees, stamp duty and connection charges, relating to the acquisition by the employee (and/or by a member of his family or household) of an interest in his new residence.

(iii) **Expenses of abortive acquisition,** i.e. expenses which would have been within (ii) above but for the interest not being acquired, for reasons beyond the control of the person seeking to acquire it or because that person reasonably declined to proceed with it.

(iv) **Expenses of transporting belongings,** i.e. expenses, including insurance, temporary storage and disconnection and reconnection of appliances, connected with transporting domestic belongings of the employee and of members of his family or household from the former to the new residence.

(v) **Travelling and subsistence expenses** (subsistence meaning food, drink and temporary accommodation). These are restricted to:

    (a) such costs of the employee and members of his family or household on temporary visits to the new area in connection with the change;

    (b) the employee's travel costs between his former residence and new place of work;

    (c) (other than in the case of a new employment) the employee's travel costs, before the change in the employment, between his new residence and old place of work or temporary living accommodation;

    (d) the employee's subsistence costs (not within (a));

    (e) the employee's travel costs between his old residence and any temporary living accommodation;

    (f) the travel costs of the employee and members of his family or household between the former and new residences;

    (g) certain costs incurred to secure continuity of education for a member of the employee's family or household who is under 19 at the beginning of the tax year in which the commencement or change of duties etc. takes place.

Expenses for which a deduction is allowable under *ITEPA 2003, ss 341, 342, 369–375* (certain foreign travel expenses, see **27.18, 27.19** above) are excluded, so that these are in effect allowed in addition to expenses up to the 'qualifying limit' referred to below (HMRC Employment Income Manual EIM03116).

(vi) **Bridging loan expenses**, i.e. interest payable by the employee (or by a member of his family or household) on a loan raised at least partly because there is a gap between the incurring of expenditure in acquiring the new residence and the receipt of the proceeds of disposal of the former residence. Interest on so much of the loan as either:

- exceeds the market value of his interest (or the interest of a member of his family or household) in the former residence (at the time the new residence is acquired); or
- is not used for the purpose of either redeeming a loan raised by the employee (or by a member of his family or household) on his former residence or acquiring his interest (or the interest of a member of his family or household) in the new residence,

is excluded.

(vii) **Duplicate expenses**, i.e. expenses incurred as a result of the change on the replacement of domestic goods used at the former residence but unsuitable for use at the new residence.

The Treasury may by regulation amend these categories so as to add any expenses from a day to be specified in the regulations, with effect for commencements or changes of duties etc. taking place on or after that day.

Eligible removal benefits

'*Eligible removal benefits*' fall into six different categories, consisting of the benefit of services corresponding, as applicable, to the expenses specified under (i)–(v) and (vii) above in relation to eligible removal expenses (but, under (v), excluding the provision of a company car or van also available for general private use (see **27.33, 27.36** above) in the same tax year in which it is provided for the move). They may include administration fees of a relocation management company charged to the employer. The Treasury has similar powers to those applicable in the case of eligible removal expenses.

Qualifying limit

The '*qualifying limit*' as regards any change of residence applies to the aggregate of qualifying removal expenses paid and the value of qualifying removal benefits received in respect of the change. The value attributed to such benefits is their cash equivalent under the general benefits legislation (**27.30** above) or, as appropriate, the amount of the living accommodation charge under **27.59** *et seq.* above (net of any attributable contribution by the employee and certain allowable deductions).

The amount of the '*qualifying limit*' is £8,000. This may be varied upwards by Treasury order from a day to be specified in the order, with effect for commencements or changes of duties etc. taking place on or after that day.

Bridging loan finance

Bridging loan finance obtained before the 'limitation day' (as above) by reason of the employment within the cheap loan provisions of *ITEPA 2003, s 173* (see **27.40** above) on a move meeting the above conditions may attract a measure of relief where the expenses and benefits for which relief is obtained in respect of the move are in total less than the £8,000 (or increased) limit. Relief is obtained by delaying the implementation of the cheap loan provisions for a number of days after the making of the loan such that the interest (at the official rate at the time the loan was made, see **27.40** above) on the maximum sum borrowed for those days would equate to the amount by which the £8,000 (or increased) limit exceeds the amount of expenses and benefits otherwise relieved. If the loan is discharged before those days have expired, no liability arises. Otherwise, the cheap loan provisions apply as if the loan had been made on the day after the last of the days for which the exemption applies. The tax payable by virtue of those provisions for a tax year ending before the limitation day may be decided on the basis that the maximum relief would be utilised against qualifying removal expenses and benefits, and subsequently adjusted if that is not in fact the case.

[*ITEPA 2003, ss 191(4), 271–289, Sch 7 paras 35, 36; FA 2008, Sch 7 paras 25, 81*].

General

PAYE should not be applied to payments made under a relocation package, even if the qualifying limit is exceeded. Flat rate allowances may be paid gross, provided that the inspector is satisfied that they do no more than reimburse employees' eligible expenses. Any taxable payments are to be included in the annual return of benefits (see **53.12 PAY AS YOU EARN**). See Revenue Press Release 14 April 1993.

For the application of these provisions to relocation company management fees, and in particular to guaranteed sale price schemes, see HMRC Employment Income Manual EIM03127–03137. See generally EIM03101 *et seq.* and guidance at www.hmrc.gov.uk/guidance/relocation.htm.

Simon's Taxes. See E4.723–E4.728.

Restrictive covenants

[27.72] Where the present, past or future holder of an office or employment, the earnings from which are taxable on the receipts basis (as opposed to the remittance basis — see generally **27.4–27.10** above), gives, in connection therewith, an undertaking (whether qualified or legally valid or not) restricting his conduct or activities, any sum paid to any person in respect of the giving or fulfilment (in whole or part) of the undertaking is, if it would not otherwise be so, treated as earnings from the office or employment for the tax year of payment. If such a payment is made after the death of the individual concerned, it is treated as having been paid immediately before his death. Where valuable consideration rather than money is given, a sum equal to the value of that consideration is treated as having been paid. [*ITEPA 2003, ss 225, 226; FA 2008, Sch 7 paras 24, 81*].

In *Kent Foods Ltd v HMRC* (Sp C 643), [2008] SSCD 307, the Sp C considered that the statutory phrase 'in connection with' used in the legislation was wide in scope and did not mean exclusively or solely in connection with.

Termination settlements

Financial settlements relating to the termination of an employment may require the employee to undertake that the agreement is in 'full and final settlement' of his claims relating to the employment, and/or not to commence, or to discontinue, legal proceedings in respect of those claims. They may also reaffirm undertakings about the employee's conduct or activity after termination which formed part of the employment terms. HMRC accept that such undertakings do not give rise to a charge under the above provisions, without prejudice to the treatment of other restrictive undertakings, whether or not contained in the settlement. (HMRC SP 3/96).

Where a compromise agreement made at termination of employment includes a repayment clause (typically a clause requiring full or partial repayment by the employee of the sum settled if he subsequently initiates litigation in respect of the employment or its termination), the attribution of any of the sum settled to the undertaking not to litigate would be outside SP 3/96 and thus within the above charging provisions. Other than in exceptional cases, e.g. where the sum settled is clearly excessive in the circumstances, HMRC will not seek to make such an attribution and a charge under the above provisions will not arise. It should be noted that if, exceptionally, a charge *does* arise, there can be no subsequent adjustment to the charge if a repayment is, in fact, made under the clause. (Revenue Tax Bulletin October 2003 p 1063).

Security of employees

[27.73] Where an asset or service which improves personal security is provided for an employee by reason of his employment, or is used by the employee, and the cost was (wholly or partly) borne by (or on behalf of) a person other than the employee, then a deduction is allowed to the extent that the provision gives rise to taxable earnings of the employee. The asset or service must be provided or used to meet a special threat to the employee's personal physical security arising wholly or mainly by virtue of the employment, and the sole object of the provider must be the meeting of that threat. In the case of an asset, relief is available only to the extent that the provider intends the asset to be used solely to improve personal physical security (ignoring any other incidental use), and in the case of a service, the benefit to the employee must consist wholly or mainly in such an improvement. Any improvement in the personal physical security of the employee's family resulting from the asset or service provided is disregarded for these purposes.

Excluded from relief is provision of a car, ship or aircraft, or of a dwelling (or grounds appurtenant thereto); but relief may be obtained in respect of equipment or a structure (such as a wall), and it is immaterial whether or not an asset becomes affixed to land and whether or not the employee acquires the property in the asset or (in the case of a fixture) an estate or interest in the land.

Similar relief applies where the employee incurs the expenditure out of his earnings and is reimbursed by some other person, and to office holders. [*ITEPA 2003, ss 369(1), 377*].

In *Lord Hanson v Mansworth* (Sp C 410), [2004] SSCD 288 (involving the meeting of a potential terrorist threat to the high profile executive chairman of a prominent public company), the above deduction was allowed on appeal.

See also **11.9** CAPITAL ALLOWANCES ON PLANT AND MACHINERY, **73.110** TRADING INCOME.

Simon's Taxes. See E4.793.

Shares etc.

[**27.74**] The value of a gift or transfer of shares to a director or employee, if regarded as a reward for services or part of his earnings, is taxable on him. Held, liability did not arise in *Bridges v Bearsley* CA 1957, 37 TC 289 (because gift of shares in default of legacy held to be testimonial not remuneration). Where shares were issued to employees at par value which was less than market value, the difference was held taxable (*Weight v Salmon* HL 1935, 19 TC 174; *Ede v Wilson* KB 1945, 26 TC 381; *Patrick v Burrows* Ch D 1954, 35 TC 138; *Bentley v Evans* Ch D 1959, 39 TC 132; *Tyrer v Smart* HL 1978, 52 TC 533).

A payment received from the parent company of a group after the employing company left the group, in consideration of loss of rights under the parent company's SAYE option scheme (see **69.47** SHARE-RELATED EMPLOYMENT INCOME AND EXEMPTIONS), was not taxable (*Wilcock v Eve* Ch D 1995, 67 TC 223).

For capital gains tax, such gifts are treated as an acquisition for nil consideration where there is no corresponding disposal of the shares, i.e. where the shares are issued by the company concerned. [*TCGA 1992, s 17*].

For the circumstances in which HMRC will accept that shares or share options were acquired by a director or employee in a different capacity and not by reason of the office or employment, see HMRC Share Schemes Manual SSM 4.4.

For priority allocations of shares for employees etc., see **69.74** SHARE-RELATED EMPLOYMENT INCOME AND EXEMPTIONS.

See generally **69** SHARE-RELATED EMPLOYMENT INCOME AND EXEMPTIONS.

Phantom share schemes

Some employers may set up incentive schemes involving 'phantom' or hypothetical shares; the employee is 'allocated' a number of shares in the employer company and potentially receives a future cash bonus linked to the value of those shares. No tax is chargeable at the time of the award (as no value passes), the bonus being chargeable as general earnings for, usually but not invariably, the tax year of receipt. (HMRC Employment Income Manual EIM01600). See also **69.3** SHARE-RELATED EMPLOYMENT INCOME AND EXEMPTIONS.

Sick pay and health insurance

[27.75] Continuing pay from an employer during sickness or other absence from work is taxable as earnings from employment. Any payments of statutory sick pay under *Social Security Contributions and Benefits Act 1992, s 151* are similarly taxable. *[ITEPA 2003, s 660]*.

Any sum paid to, or to the order or for the benefit of, an employee in respect of absence from work through sickness or disability (or to his spouse, a son or daughter or spouse, or a parent or dependant) is taxable earnings of the employee for the period of absence (unless otherwise taxable) where it is paid as a result of any arrangements entered into by the employer. There is no charge under the benefits code (see **27.26** above) on the right to receive such sums, and there is no liability to the extent that the contributions funding the arrangements are paid by the employee. *[ITEPA 2003, ss 202(1), 221;]*.

A lump sum received under a life, accident or sickness or insurance policy is not normally taxable.

See **30.23** EXEMPT INCOME for provisions exempting annual payments falling to be made under certain insurance policies.

See generally HMRC Employment Income Manual EIM01550, 06400 *et seq*.

See also **73.88** TRADING INCOME.

Subscriptions

Professional subscriptions etc.

[27.76] There may be deducted from taxable earnings:

(a) provided the registration, retention etc. is a condition of the performance of the duties, professional fees listed in the *Table* in *ITEPA 2003, s 343*. These include fees payable by health (or animal health) professionals, legal professionals, architects, teachers, patent and trade mark agents, driving instructors, aircraft maintenance engineers, air traffic controllers, aircraft flight crew, flight information service officers, HGV drivers and seafarers (including certain related technical and medical examination fees). The Commissioners for HMRC may add to the list by order. Additions in recent years have been fees paid by an airport employee (or prospective employee) for a criminal records check needed to qualify him for a security pass, fees paid by employees in the private security industry on application for a licence from the Security Industry Authority, fees payable for the entry or retention of a name in the register maintained by the General Teaching Council for Northern Ireland, and, from 6 April 2008, fees payable for the entry or retention of a name in the register maintained by the General Social Care Council, the Care Council for Wales, the Scottish Social Services Council, the Northern Ireland Social Care Council or the Animal Medicines Training Regulatory Authority;

(b) annual subscriptions, or parts thereof, to bodies approved by the Commissioners for HMRC whose activities are directed, otherwise than for profit, to advancing or spreading knowledge, maintaining or improving professional conduct and competence, or indemnifying or protecting professional persons against claims incurred in exercising their profession, and are relevant to the office or employment. The body must not be of a mainly local character.

[*ITEPA 2003, ss 343–345; SI 2009 No 56, Sch 1 para 337*].

As regards (b) above, for approval of bodies by HMRC, withdrawal of approval, apportionment of subscriptions and appeals generally, see *ITEPA 2003, ss 344(4)–(6), 345*. Applications for approval should be made in writing to HMRC, Personal Tax Division 5, Sapphire House, 550 Streetsbrook Road, Solihull, West Midlands B91 1QU. A list of bodies approved by HMRC for this purpose is available on the HMRC website at www.hmrc.gov.uk/list3/list3.htm.

Other subscriptions

Bank manager's club subscriptions reimbursed by bank not allowed (*Brown v Bullock* CA 1961, 40 TC 1) but subscriptions to clubs to obtain cheaper accommodation on visits to London were allowed (*Elwood v Utitz* CA (NI) 1965, 42 TC 482).

'Tax-free payments'

[27.77] If an employer pays an employee's tax, this constitutes the payment of a pecuniary liability of the employee as in **27.20** above. If, however, it is agreed between them that the employer will pay the employee such amount as leaves the employee with a stated sum after PAY AS YOU EARN (**53**) deductions, it follows that the employer must account for those deductions to HMRC under the PAYE system and that the employee's taxable earnings are equal to the gross amount before PAYE and not the net amount he actually receives. See *North British Rly v Scott* HL 1922, 8 TC 332; *Hartland v Diggines* HL 1926, 10 TC 247; *Jaworski v Institution of Polish Engineers* CA 1950, 29 ATC 385). See also HMRC Pamphlet P7 (Employer's Guide to PAYE).

Special forms and tax tables are available to assist employers who pay employees on a 'net of tax' basis to calculate how much tax is due (Revenue Press Release 2 March 1984).

Where an employer paying earnings of a director fails, in whole or in part, to deduct and account for PAYE tax at the proper time, and that tax is subsequently accounted for by someone other than the director, such tax paid, less so much as is made good by the director, will be treated as taxable earnings unless the director has no material interest in the company and either he is a full-time working director or the company is non-profit-making. Any amounts accounted for after cessation of employment are treated as having arisen in the tax year in which the employment ended but no amounts accounted for after the death of the director will be chargeable. [*ITEPA 2003, s 223*].

An agreement to reimburse tax as 'expenses' was held not to be enforceable as the contract was illegal (*Miller v Karlinski* CA 1945, 24 ATC 483, and see also *Napier v National Business Agency* CA 1951, 30 ATC 180).

Interim payments of tax under self-assessment made by an employer on an employee's behalf, as part of *tax equalisation* arrangements where full in-year gross up is used, should not figure in the employment pages of the employee's self-assessment tax return (see Revenue Tax Bulletin June 1998 p 551). See **53.44 PAY AS YOU EARN** as regards modified PAYE procedures for tax equalised employees.

Simon's Taxes. See E4.451, E4.483.

Taxed award schemes

Employers may, if they wish, enter into arrangements with HMRC to meet the liability of employees on the grossed-up value of non-cash incentive prizes and awards. The arrangements involve a legally binding contract for payment of the related tax together with simplified reporting arrangements. The arrangements may involve payment of tax at the basic rate or at the higher rate or both, although separate contracts are required in relation to basic rate and higher rate schemes. Where only basic rate liabilities are met, higher rate liabilities continue to be collected from employees in the usual way. Valuation of an award will depend on details of the scheme and whether or not the recipient is in lower-paid employment (see **27.26** above). Details of the arrangements may be obtained from HMRC, Incentive Award Unit, Manchester Blackfriars TDO, Trinity Bridge House, 2 Dearmans Place, Salford M3 5BH (tel. 0161–261 3269), which also deals with national insurance aspects. (Revenue Press Releases 2 November 1984, 18 January 1990; Revenue Tax Bulletin April 2000 p 747).

See generally HMRC Employment Income Manual EIM11235 *et seq.*

For the valuation of incentive awards generally, see **27.91** below and HMRC SP 6/85.

Termination payments

[27.78] See **20.3 COMPENSATION FOR LOSS OF EMPLOYMENT (AND DAMAGES)** for the assessment of such payments under general principles (see **27.20** above). See also **27.70** above for statutory redundancy payments and **27.94** below for wages in lieu of notice.

Certain payments to persons ceasing to be members of the House of Commons, the European Parliament, the Scottish Parliament, the Assembly for Wales, or the Northern Ireland Assembly or the Greater London Assembly, or to persons ceasing to hold a ministerial (or equivalent) office, including the office of Mayor of London, are exempted from the general charge on earnings. They are, however, liable in the normal way under *ITEPA 2003, s 403* (see **20 COMPENSATION FOR LOSS OF EMPLOYMENT (AND DAMAGES)**). [*ITEPA 2003, s 291; FA 2008, s 52; FA 2009, s 56(2)(3)*].

Training costs

[27.79] No income tax liability arises in respect of expenditure incurred by the employer in paying or reimbursing retraining course expenses of an employee (or past employee). The employee must begin the course during, or within one year of leaving, the employment, must have left that employment by two years after the end of the course, and must not be re-employed by the employer within two years of leaving. If, after the relief has been given, any of these conditions fail to be met, an assessment may be raised to withdraw the relief within six years of the end of the tax year in which the failure occurred. The employer must notify such failure to the inspector within 60 days of coming to know of it, and the inspector may require information from the employer in relation to any such failure where he has reason to believe that the employer has failed to give such notice. Penalties apply under *TMA 1970, s 98* for failure to give such notice or furnish such information.

The retraining course must:

- be designed to impart or improve skills or knowledge relevant to, and intended to be used in the course of, gainful employment (or self-employment) of any description; and
- be devoted entirely to the teaching and/or practical application of such skills or knowledge; and
- not last more than two years; and
- be available on similar terms to all, or to a particular class or classes of, past or present employees,

and the employee must be employed in the employment throughout the two years prior to starting the course (or prior to his earlier leaving that employment — see above). Part-time employees are within the exemption.

The qualifying expenses are:

- course attendance and examination fees; and
- costs of essential course books; and
- travelling expenses where, if attendance at the course was a duty of the employment and the employee was in that employment when the expenses were incurred and paid them himself, either they would have been deductible under *ITEPA 2003, Pt 5* (see **27.22** above) or mileage allowance relief would have been available if no mileage allowance had been paid (see **27.87** below).

[*ITEPA 2003, ss 311, 312, Sch 7 para 37*].

For relief to the employer, see **73.69** TRADING INCOME.

Work-related training

Subject to the exceptions below, where an employer pays or reimburses the cost of providing 'work-related training' to employees, no income tax liability arises in respect of such expenditure or of any benefit. Similar relief applies to any incidental costs incurred as a result of the employee's undertaking the training, any expenses in connection with an assessment of what the employee has gained from the training, and the costs of obtaining for the employee any consequent qualification, registration or award.

'*Work-related training*' means any training course or other activity designed to impart, instil, improve or reinforce any knowledge, skills or personal qualities likely to prove useful to the employee in performing the duties of the employment or a 'related employment', or which will qualify (or better qualify) the employee to perform such duties or to participate in any charitable or voluntary activities available to be performed in association with any such employment. Participation in a genuine Employee Development Scheme which seeks to improve the employee's attitude towards training by commencing with an enjoyable course, as an introduction to more concentrated job-related training, will qualify, as will participation in activities such as Outward Bound, Raleigh International or Prince's Trust where leadership skills are appropriate to the employee. (HMRC Employment Income Manual EIM01220). A 'related employment' is an employment, with the same employer or a person connected with him (within **21 CONNECTED PERSONS**), which the employee is to hold, has a serious opportunity of holding or can realistically expect to have a serious opportunity of holding in due course.

Exceptions

The above exemption does not apply to the extent that facilities or other benefits are provided or made available for any of the following purposes:

- to enable the employee to enjoy them for entertainment or recreational purposes, or in the course of any leisure activity, unconnected with the promotion of knowledge, skills or personal qualities (as above);
- to reward the employee for the performance of the duties of his employment or for the manner of their performance; or
- to provide the employee with an inducement, unconnected with the promotion of knowledge, skills or personal qualities (as above), to remain in or accept an employment with the employer or a connected person.

The cost of provision of any asset, or of the use of any asset, to the employee is excluded except where:

- the asset is not for use other than in the course of the training or in the performance of the duties of the employment;
- it consists of training materials, e.g. stationery, books, tapes, disks etc.; or
- it consists in something made by the employee during the training, or incorporated into something so made.

Travelling and subsistence expenses are not excluded provided that, if the training had been undertaken in the performance of the duties of the employment and the expenses incurred and paid by the employee, either they would have been allowable under the general deductions provisions or mileage allowance relief would have been available if no mileage allowance had been paid (see **27.87** below).

[*ITEPA 2003, ss 250–254*].

An MBA course costing £18,000 and reimbursed by way of a 'signing bonus' was held on the facts to be for the purpose of qualifying the taxpayer to undertake the employment as opposed to inducing her to accept the employment and was within the exemption; it did not matter that the training took place outside the currency of the employment (*Silva v Charnock* (Sp C 332), [2002] SSCD 426). However, HMRC do not see this case as supporting a general exemption for reimbursements of training costs incurred by individuals before the employment commences, though they will not pursue arrears of tax where such reimbursements have been made tax-free in accordance with specific advice given by tax offices (some of which may have given conflicting advice). HMRC do allow exemption for reimbursement of pre-commencement training costs where there is a strong and demonstrable link between the training and the employment, for example where an individual undergoes training for a job he has already accepted and which he is due to start in the near future. (Revenue Tax Bulletin April 2003 pp 1022, 1023).

See generally HMRC Employment Income Manual EIM01200 *et seq.*

Simon's Taxes. See **E4.711, E4.745.**

Training costs borne by employees

Training costs borne by employees may attract tax relief under *ITEPA 2003, s 336* (see **27.22** above) but only if they fully satisfy the stringent conditions for such relief. Relief was refused in *Snowdon v Charnock* (Sp C 282), [2001] SSCD 152, *Consultant Psychiatrist v HMRC* (Sp C 557), [2006] SSCD 653, *HMRC v Decadt* Ch D 2007, [2008] STC 1103 and *Perrin v HMRC* (Sp C 671), [2008] SSCD 672. Relief was allowed in *HMRC v Banerjee (No 1)* Ch D, [2009] STC 1915 in which the courses and training that the employee, an NHS trust specialist registrar, attended were compulsory and a pre-requisite of her maintaining her post and employment.

Travelling and subsistence

[27.80] See generally HMRC Booklet 490 'Employee Travel — A Tax and NICs Guide for Employers' and HMRC Employment Income Manual EIM31800 *et seq.*

The normal statutory relief for expenses in employment is extended to include certain additional travelling and associated expenses, broadly those of travelling to temporary workplaces (excluding ordinary commuting and private travel). See **27.23** above. The following commentary applies to all travelling and associated expenses which are not the subject of specific statutory relief (or exclusion).

See also:

- **27.81** below — Late night journeys home;
- **27.82** below — Incidental overnight expenses;
- **27.83** below — Benchmark scale rates for day subsistence;
- **27.84** below — Working Rule Agreements;
- **27.85** below — Lorry drivers;
- **27.86** below — Employment abroad;
- **27.87** below — Private vehicle used for employment;
- **27.88** below — Mileage allowances for business travel in company car;
- **27.89** below — Parking facilities.

The general relief for deductions from employment income is for expenses necessarily incurred in the performance of the duties of the office or employment (see **27.22** above). Subject to the special reliefs mentioned above and below relating to temporary workplaces, this excludes expenses of travelling to the place of employment from home or from a place at which a business or another employment is carried on. A leading case here is *Ricketts v Colquhoun* HL 1925, 10 TC 118 in which a barrister practising in London was refused his expenses of travelling to Portsmouth where he was employed as Recorder. See also *Cook v Knott* QB 1887, 2 TC 246; *Revell v Directors of Elworthy Bros & Co Ltd* QB 1890, 3 TC 12; *Nolder v Walters* KB 1930, 15 TC 380; *Burton v Rednall* Ch D 1954, 35 TC 435; *Bhadra v Ellam* Ch D 1987, [1988] STC 239 (see **27.24** above); *Parikh v Sleeman* CA 1990, 63 TC 75; *Smith v Fox* Ch D 1989, 63 TC 304; *Miners v Atkinson* Ch D 1995, 68 TC 629; *Warner v Prior* (Sp C 353), [2003] SSCD 109 and contrast *Pook v Owen*(see below and **27.24** above) and *Taylor v Provan* HL 1974, 49 TC 579 in both of which *Ricketts v Colquhoun* was distinguished. The deduction is refused notwithstanding that the taxpayer is unable to live nearer his place of employment (*Andrews v Astley* KB 1924, 8 TC 589; *Phillips v Keane* HC(IFS), 1 ITC 69). No allowance to an assistant required to attend classes (*Blackwell v Mills* KB 1945, 26 TC 468). For extra-statutory concession for directors and employees of two or more group companies, see **27.29**(ix) above (and note the comparable statutory relief at **27.23** above).

If an emergency call-out requires an employee to travel from home to the normal place of employment, reimbursed travel expenses will be taxable earnings unless the conditions underlying the decision in *Pook v Owen* HL 1969, 45 TC 571 (for which see also **27.24** above) are met, i.e. (i) advice on handling the emergency is given on receipt of the telephone call; (ii) responsibility for those aspects appropriate to the employee's duties is accepted at that time; and (iii) the employee has a continuing responsibility for the emergency whilst travelling to the normal place of employment. A claim for a deduction for expenses not reimbursed will be allowed on the same basis. Where an emergency call-out requires travel from home to a place other than the normal place of employment, reimbursed expenses are not chargeable emoluments, and a claim for expenses not reimbursed should be allowed. (HMRC Employment Income Manual EIM10040, 10050).

Reasonable reimbursement of expenses of home to work travel (or the provision of vouchers etc. for such travel, see **27.90** below) is not taxed where the expenses are incurred either (a) as a result of public transport disruption owing to industrial action, or (b) by disabled employees. [*ITEPA 2003, ss 245, 246*]. See also **27.29**(v)(vi) above.

A claim for a deduction corresponding to living allowances paid while working away from home was refused where an engineer without a permanent work base was required to undertake assignments necessitating his living away from home for long periods (*Elderkin v Hindmarsh* Ch D 1988, 60 TC 651).

In addition, reasonable reimbursement of expenditure on subsistence etc. is, by concession, not taxed where (a) an employee occupies overnight accommodation near his normal place of work as a result of public transport disruption owing to industrial action, or (b) it is necessary for an offshore oil or gas worker to take overnight accommodation near the point of his departure from the mainland for the offshore rig etc. [*ITEPA 2003, ss 245, 305*]. See also **27.29**(v)(vi) above.

See **27.29**(x) as regards certain removal expenses.

See **49.7** MISCELLANEOUS INCOME as regards **volunteer drivers**, e.g. hospital car service drivers.

Simon's Taxes. See E4.703–E4.707.

Late night journeys home

[27.81] The provision by an employer of private transport, e.g. taxis, hired cars etc., for the journey home of employees required to work late (or of vouchers etc. for such travel — see **27.90** below) will not result in a charge to income tax on the employee, provided that:

- the employee is required to work later than usual and until at least 9 pm,
- such occasions occur irregularly, and
- either public transport between the employee's place of work and his home has ceased for the day or it would not be reasonable to expect the employee to use it, for example if the journey would take significantly longer than usual due to the lateness of the hour.

This exemption is extended to cover the payment for or provision of transport home by the employer where regular home to work car-sharing arrangements with other employees fail on a particular occasion due to unforeseen or exceptional circumstances. The exemption applies to a maximum of 60 journeys in a tax year, and this applies to the aggregate of journeys under both legs of the exemption (i.e. late night journeys and car-share breakdowns).[*ITEPA 2003, s 248*].

See also HMRC Employment Income Manual 21831–21834 with particular reference to the three conditions above, the 60-journey rule and the standard of record-keeping required.

Incidental overnight expenses

[27.82] Payments made to or on behalf of an employee in respect of his overnight personal incidental expenses (e.g. laundry, newspapers, telephone calls home) while away from home on business are exempt from income tax provided that they do not exceed certain limits. Payments exceeding the limits are taxable in full. The exemption covers expenses incidental to the employee's being away from home during a 'qualifying absence' other than one in relation to which the overall exemption limit is exceeded, being expenses which would not otherwise be deductible. A '*qualifying absence*' is a continuous period throughout which the employee is obliged to stay away from home and which includes at least one overnight stay but does not include any such stay at a place the expenses of travelling to which would not be either deductible under normal rules or exempt under *ITEPA 2003, s 250* (work-related training costs, see **27.79** above) or exempt under *ITEPA 2003, s 255* (individual learning account training, see **27.79** above). The overall exemption limit, in relation to a qualifying absence, is £5 for each night spent in the UK and £10 for each night any part of which is spent outside the UK (such amounts being subject to increase by Treasury Order from a date specified therein). In determining whether the authorised maximum is exceeded, payments by non-cash voucher or credit token and the providing of benefits are taken into account as well as cash payments. [*ITEPA 2003, ss 240, 241, Sch 7 paras 33, 34*].

HMRC guidance notes for employers on the practical application of these provisions (see HMRC Booklet 480 and the Employer's Guide to PAYE (P7)) are available.

Benchmark scale rates for day subsistence

[27.83] With effect for 2009/10 onwards, HMRC have published benchmark scale rates which employers can use to make subsistence payments to employees. These do not cover overnight trips and are thus described as day subsistence rates. As long as the employee has incurred subsistence expenses whilst on a business journey, employers will be able to make subsistence payments up to the benchmark rates without agreeing them with HMRC, and these will be tax-free in the hands of the employee. Employers wishing to use the benchmark rates need to notify HMRC of their intention when applying for a dispensation (see **27.49** above). Benchmark scale rates must only be used where all the qualifying conditions are met. The qualifying conditions are that:

- the travel must be in the performance of the employee's duties or to a temporary place of work;
- the employee must be absent from his normal place of work or home for a continuous period in excess of five hours (for the five-hour rate) or ten hours (for the ten-hour rate); and
- the employee must have incurred a cost on a meal (food and drink) after starting his journey.

The five-hour rate is £5 and the ten-hour rate is £10. In addition, a 'breakfast' rate of £5.00 may be paid where an employee leaves home earlier than usual and before 6.00 am and incurs a cost on breakfast taken away from his home. A 'late evening meal' rate of £15.00 may be paid where the employee has to work later than usual, finishes work after 8.00 pm having worked his normal day and has to buy a meal which he would usually have at home. HMRC stress that these last two rates are for use in exceptional circumstances only and not intended for employees with regular early or late work patterns. An employer may pay less than the benchmark rate if he wishes. If he pays more than the benchmark rate without agreeing a tailored scale rate with HMRC, the excess will be chargeable to tax. A tax-free payment can only be made if an employee does actually incur an expense on meals after leaving home or his normal place of work (which excludes packed lunches). (HMRC Brief 24/09, 2 April 2009). For further details, see www.hmrc.gov.uk/briefs/income-tax/brief2409.htm.

Working Rule Agreements

[27.84] Where Working Rule Agreements are drawn up between employers and trade unions and include payments of allowances for daily travel and subsistence, HMRC have agreed that certain of these payments (or part) should not be taxed because of the high degree of mobility required in the industries concerned. Consistent treatment is accorded to site-based staff who work alongside operatives who are covered by a Working Rule Agreement and who have broadly the same working circumstances. Employers must obtain authority from their local tax district before making any such tax-free payments. (Revenue Press Release 13 February 1981).

Lodging allowances may generally be paid tax-free to an employee engaged under the terms of a Working Rule Agreement, provided that he is married, or has dependants living with him, and incurs extra expense while working away from home in addition to the cost of maintaining a permanent home. This treatment is extended to single men without dependants who maintain a permanent home. (ICAEW Memorandum TR 713, August 1988).

Lorry drivers

[27.85] Long distance lorry drivers normally receive a payment in respect of each rest period spent away from the home base. The payment includes a subsistence element and, sometimes, an additional round sum payment. Any additional round sum payment is taxable. As regards the subsistence element, HMRC accept the following payments per night as being no more than fair reimbursement of the costs of accommodation and subsistence in the UK: £30.75 per night from 1 January 2009; £29.85 for calendar year 2008; £28.62 for calendar year 2007; £27.55 for 2006. These figures are reduced by 25% where a sleeper cab is available. Greater amounts may, however, be paid without charge to tax if certain conditions are met. (See HMRC Employment Income Manual EIM66100–66190, which also cover lunch allowances).

Employment abroad

[27.86] Tax will not be charged on the reimbursement to an employee, whose duties are carried on wholly abroad and who retains an abode in the UK, of expenses, including reasonable hotel expenses necessarily incurred, in travelling (whether alone or with his wife and family) to the country where his duties are performed and returning to the UK. Similar relief applies for persons of non-UK domicile travelling between the UK and their abode in the home country. See **27.18**, **27.19** above. For allowances for travelling etc. expenses to members of the European Parliament, see *Lord Bruce of Donington v Aspden* CJEC, [1981] STC 761.

For overseas trips generally, see *Newlin v Woods* CA 1966, 42 TC 649 (cost of journey for health reasons disallowed); *Maclean v Trembath* Ch D 1956, 36 TC 653 (business trip accompanied by wife; expenses attributable to wife disallowed); *Thomson v White* Ch D 1966, 43 TC 256 (expenses of farmers and wives on organised trip partly for sightseeing and partly to see farms overseas disallowed); *Owen v Burden* CA 1971, 47 TC 476 (expenses of county surveyor voluntarily to attend overseas road conference disallowed). Expenses of spouse of director or higher-paid employee who accompanies director on business journey abroad because his or her health is too precarious for travel alone are not assessable on employee. (HMRC ESC A4). See **30.27** EXEMPT INCOME as regards certain overseas travel costs of MPs.

From March 2008 HMRC publish tables of country-by-country benchmark scale rates that employers can use to pay accommodation and subsistence expenses to employees whose duties require them to travel abroad. A link to the current rates is provided at HMRC Employment Income Manual EIM05250. Accommodation and subsistence payments made at or below the published rates are not liable for income tax, employers need not include them on forms P11D and employees do not have to produce receipts. If an employer pays less than the published rates the employees are not entitled to tax relief for the shortfall; they can obtain relief only for their actual, vouched expenses less any amounts borne by the employer. The scale rates can be paid in addition to the tax-free amounts for incidental overnight expenses referred to at **27.82** above. Employers are not obliged to use the published rates; they may reimburse actual vouched expenses or negotiate a scale rate amount which they believe more accurately reflects their employees' spending. (HMRC Employment Income Manual EIM05250).

Private vehicle used for employment

[27.87] There are statutorily exempt mileage allowances for employees (which includes office holders). These allowances are exempt from income tax when paid by the employer, and may also form the basis of a claim by the employee where no (or smaller) mileage allowances are payable.

The statutory exemption applies to:

- 'approved mileage allowance payments' for a 'qualifying vehicle', *provided that* the employee is not a passenger in the vehicle and the vehicle is not a 'company vehicle' (as broadly defined, see *ITEPA 2003, s 236(2)*); and
- 'approved passenger payments' made to an employee for a car or van, *provided that* 'mileage allowance payments' are made to the employee for the vehicle and, if it is made available to the employee by reason of the employment, the employee is chargeable in respect of it as a benefit-in-kind under **27.33** or **27.36** above.

Mileage allowance payments

'*Mileage allowance payments*' are payments (other than 'passenger payments') paid to an employee in respect of expenses in connection with the use by the employee of a 'qualifying vehicle' for 'business travel'. They are '*approved*' if and to the extent that, for a tax year, the total payments made to the employee for the kind of vehicle in question do not exceed the 'approved amount' for mileage allowance payments applicable to that kind of vehicle.

A '*qualifying vehicle*' is a car, van, motor cycle or cycle (each as defined in *ITEPA 2003, s 235*), and '*business travel*' is travel the expenses of which would be deductible under the general provisions (see **27.23** above) if incurred and paid by the employee. The '*approved amount*' for this purpose is obtained from the formula:

$$M \times R$$

where M is the number of business miles travelled by the employee (other than as a passenger) using the kind of vehicle in question, in the tax year; and

R is the rate applicable for that kind of vehicle. For a car or van, it is 40p per mile for the first 10,000 miles, 25p per mile thereafter. For motor cycles it is 24p per mile and for cycles it is 20p per mile. The 10,000 mile limit is applied by reference to business travel by car or van in all 'associated employments' (as defined — broadly where the employments are under the same employer or the employers are under common control). All these rates may be altered by the Treasury by regulation.

Passenger payments

'*Passenger payments*' are payments made to an employee because, while using a car or van for business travel, he carries one or more '*qualifying passengers*', i.e. fellow employee(s) for whom the travel is also business travel. They are '*approved*' if and to the extent that, for a tax year, the total passenger payments made to the employee do not exceed the 'approved amount' for passenger payments. The '*approved amount*' for this purpose is:

$$M \times R$$

where M is the number of business miles travelled by the employee by car or van carrying any qualifying passenger in the tax year and in respect of which passenger payments are made. If more than one qualifying passenger is carried, a separate addition is made to the amount in respect of each passenger; and

R is 5p per mile (alterable by the Treasury by regulation).

[*ITEPA 2003, ss 229, 230, 233–236; ITA 2007, Sch 1 para 433; CTA 2010, Sch 1 para 384*].

Mileage allowance relief

An employee (or office holder) who uses a qualifying vehicle for business travel is entitled to '*mileage allowance relief*' for a tax year if the approved amount for mileage allowance payments (as above) applicable to the kind of vehicle in question exceeds the total amount of mileage allowance payments (if any) made to the employee for the tax year for that kind of vehicle. As above, the relief is not available where the employee is a passenger in a vehicle or the vehicle is a company vehicle. The amount of the relief is the excess of the approved amount over any mileage allowance payments. Where available, the relief is allowed as a deduction from earnings taxable on the receipts basis (see generally **27.4–27.10** above). Any amount of relief which cannot be so given may be deducted from earnings taxable on the remittance basis (see **27.5** and **27.10** above), the deduction for any tax year being of amounts of relief available and otherwise unrelieved for that tax year and for any earlier tax year in which the employee was UK resident, and which would have been deductible from earnings for each such year if the receipts basis had applied. [*ITEPA 2003, ss 231, 232*].

Mileage allowances for business travel in company car

[27.88] Employers may negotiate dispensations for payments to employees for fuel provided by the employee for business travel in a company car. Advisory rates per mile are the same as those listed at **27.35** above, although it is open to the employer to make a case for paying higher rates in particular circumstances. The rates are currently reviewed twice a year. From 1 December 2009, any changes take effect on 1 December and 1 June, but HMRC will consider making interim changes if fuel prices fluctuate by 5% or more during the six-month period. For one month from the date of change, employers may use either the previous or new current rates, as they choose. Employers may therefore make supplementary payments if they so wish, but are under no obligation to do so

Parking facilities

[27.89] No income tax liability arises in respect of expenditure on the provision of car parking facilities for an employee at or near his place of work, whether the car etc. is company-owned or private. This exemption extends to parking facilities for cycles, motor cycles and vans. Where the benefit is convertible into cash, e.g. under a salary sacrifice arrangement, no charge to tax on general earnings arises. [*ITEPA 2003, s 237*].

Vouchers and credit tokens

[27.90] The items at **27.91–27.93** below, when provided for an employee (or a member of his family, i.e. his spouse, civil partner, parent, child or spouse/civil partner of his child or any dependant of the employee) by reason of the employment, are taxable earnings of the employment. [*ITEPA 2003, ss 74, 81, 83, 87, 91, 94*]. Their supply by the employer is regarded as 'by reason of the employment' unless the employer is an individual and the supply is made in the normal course of his domestic, family or personal relationships. [*ITEPA 2003, ss 73(2), 82(2), 90(2)*]. The provisions do not apply to vouchers etc. of a kind made available to the public generally and provided to the employee (or family) on no more favourable terms than to the public generally. [*ITEPA 2003, ss 78, 85, 93*]. Where they do apply (or would do so but for a dispensation, see below), no liability arises in respect of the money goods or services obtained for the voucher. [*ITEPA 2003, s 95*].

For a summary of the amounts chargeable and the tax year in which liability arises, see HMRC Employment Income Manual EIM16140.

For the exemption from income tax liability of the provision of vouchers or credit-tokens which can be used to obtain specified benefits the direct provision of which would be exempt, see *ITEPA 2003, ss 266, 267 as amended.* The Treasury are now empowered to specify further exempt benefits by means of statutory instrument. [*ITEPA 2003, s 96A; FA 2006, s 63*].

For the application of PAYE, see **53.3 PAY AS YOU EARN.**

Dispensations

The provisions do not apply if a person supplies an HMRC officer with a statement of the cases and circumstances in which vouchers or credit tokens are provided to any employee (whether his own or not) and the officer is satisfied that no additional tax is payable under these provisions and notifies that person accordingly. Such notification may be revoked retrospectively. [*ITEPA 2003, s 96, Sch 7 paras 19, 20*].

Non-cash vouchers

[27.91] 'Non-cash vouchers' are within the charge at **27.90** above. '*Non-cash vouchers*' means vouchers, stamps or similar documents or tokens capable of being exchanged, either singly or together, immediately or later, for money, goods or services or any combination of these but not cash vouchers — see also HMRC Employment Income Manual EIM16040). The tax charge is on the expense incurred by the person at whose cost the voucher, and the money, goods or services for which it is capable of being exchanged, are provided, and in or in connection with that provision, with 'just and reasonable' apportionment in the case of schemes relating to groups of employees, and less any amounts made good by the employee. The charge is reduced to the extent that general deductions would have been allowable if the costs had been incurred by the employee. The tax year in which the earnings are treated as received is the year in which the expense is incurred by the employer or, if different and later, the year in which the voucher is received by, or appropriated to, the employee, but for cheque vouchers it is the year in which the voucher is handed over in exchange for money, goods or services (time of posting is treated as time of handing over).

[*ITEPA 2003, ss 82, 83, 84(1)(2), 87, 88, 362*].

Expense incurred by the employer in providing vouchers or any other incentive awards includes expenses beyond the direct cost of buying the goods or services provided where the expenses contribute more or less directly to the advantage enjoyed by the employee, e.g. costs of selecting and testing goods or services, or of after-sales service, or of storage and distribution. More remote expenses, e.g. costs of planning or administering a scheme or of promotional literature etc., are excluded. See HMRC SP 6/85.

A voucher used by an employee to obtain the use of a *car parking space* (or a cycle, motor cycle or van parking space) at or near his place of work is excluded from these provisions. A voucher provided neither by the employer nor by a person connected with the employer (within **21 CONNECTED PERSONS**) and used to obtain *entertainment* for the employee (or a relation) is similarly excluded, subject to the same conditions as are specified in **27.29**(xv) above. [*ITEPA 2003, s 266(1)*]. See also **27.48** above for the exclusion of vouchers relating to certain sports and recreational facilities.

This provision does not affect the treatment of meal vouchers as in **27.69** above.

For a limited exemption in respect of *childcare vouchers*, see **27.46** above.

Transport vouchers

'Transport vouchers' are specifically included in the above provisions but *not included* is a voucher provided for an employee of a passenger transport undertaking under arrangements in operation on 25 March 1982 to enable that employee (including spouse or family, as in **27.90** above) to obtain passenger transport services from his employer or his employer's subsidiary or parent company or another passenger transport undertaking. *'Transport voucher'* means any ticket, pass or other document or token intended to enable a person to obtain passenger transport services (whether or not in exchange for it). [*ITEPA 2003, ss 84(3), 86, 87(4); SI 2009 No 1890, regs 1, 4(1)*]. See also **27.29**(xxiii)(xxiv) above.

Cheque vouchers

'Cheque vouchers' are also included in the above provisions. *'Cheque voucher'* means a cheque provided for an employee and intended for his use wholly or mainly for payment for particular goods or services or for goods or services of one or more particular classes. [*ITEPA 2003, s 84(4)*].

Incidental overnight expenses

There is excluded from these provisions a voucher used to obtain goods or services (or to obtain money to buy goods or services) incidental to the employee's being away from home on business during a 'qualifying absence' in relation to which the authorised maximum (£5 per night spent in the UK and £10 per night spent abroad) is not exceeded, where the cost of such goods or services is not otherwise deductible from earnings. [*ITEPA 2003, s 268, Sch 7 paras 33, 34*]. See also **27.82** above.

Simon's Taxes. See E4.605, E4.720.

Cash vouchers

[27.92] 'Cash vouchers' are within the charge at **27.90** above. *'Cash voucher'* means any voucher, stamp or similar document capable of being exchanged, either singly or together, immediately or later, for a sum of money not substantially less than the cost to the person at whose cost it is provided, but excluding any document for a sum which would not have been employment income if paid to the employee directly and excluding any savings certificate on which accumulated interest is exempt from tax. Where the sum of money is substantially less than the cost, any part of the difference representing benefits in connection with sickness, personal injury or death will be disregarded in deciding if the voucher is a cash voucher.

Where, as in some holiday pay schemes, a cash voucher is provided for an employee for redemption for cash which will be an emolument, tax is to be charged on the redemption amount when the voucher is received by, or appropriated to, the employee, with 'just and reasonable' apportionment in the case of schemes relating to groups of employees, *unless* the voucher is issued under a scheme which is approved by the Commissioners for HMRC as being practicable for PAYE to be applied at the time the vouchers are exchanged for cash.

[*ITEPA 2003, ss 73, 75–77, 79–81*].

Simon's Taxes. See E4.604.

Credit tokens

[27.93] 'Credit tokens' are within the charge at **27.90** above. Tax is charged when the employee (or a relative — see **27.90** above) uses a credit token to obtain money, goods or services, on the expense incurred by the person at whose cost the money, goods or services are provided, in or in connection with that provision, with 'just and reasonable' apportionment in the case of schemes relating to groups of employees. See **27.91** above as regards valuation of expenses incurred. The charge is reduced by any amounts made good by the employee and by deductions which would have been allowable if the costs had been incurred by the employee. [*ITEPA 2003, ss 90, 94, 363*].

'*Credit-token*' means a card, token or other thing given to a person by another person who undertakes that (a) on the production of it (whether or not some other action is also required) he will supply money, goods or services on credit or (b) on *similar* production to a third party, he will pay that third party for the money etc. supplied (whether or not taking any discount or commission). '*Production*' includes the use of an object provided to operate a machine. Not included is a non-cash voucher within **27.91** above or a cash voucher within **27.92** above. [*ITEPA 2003, s 92*].

A token used by an employee to obtain the use of a *car parking space* (or a cycle, motor cycle or van parking space) at or near his place of work is excluded from these provisions. A token provided neither by the employer nor by a person connected with the employer (within **21 CONNECTED PERSONS**) and used to obtain *entertainment* for the employee (or a relation) is similarly excluded, subject to the same conditions as are specified in **27.29**(xv) above. [*ITEPA 2003, s 267(2)*].

Incidental overnight expenses

There is excluded from these provisions a token used to obtain goods or services (or to obtain money to buy goods or services) incidental to the employee's being away from home on business during a 'qualifying absence' in relation to which the authorised maximum (£5 per night spent in the UK and £10 per night spent abroad) is not exceeded, where the cost of such goods or services is not otherwise deductible from earnings. [*ITEPA 2003, s 268, Sch 7 paras 33, 34*]. See also **27.82** above.

Simon's Taxes. See E4.606, E4.720.

Wages in lieu of notice

[27.94] The taxation treatment of payments in lieu of notice ('PILONs') is governed by the general principles applying to payments on cessation of employment, for which see **20.3** *et seq*. **COMPENSATION FOR LOSS OF EMPLOYMENT (AND DAMAGES)**. Where the payment is *not* within the general employment income charge, it will generally fall within *ITEPA 2003, s 403*, subject to the exemptions from charge under that *section* and, in particular, the exemption of the first £30,000.

HMRC have set out their approach to the application of the general employment income charge to PILONs, as follows.

(a) Where contractual arrangements provide for a PILON, the contract is terminated in accordance with its terms on a summary dismissal. The compensation is a contractual entitlement rather than liquidated damages and is chargeable as income from the employment under general principles.

(b) Where the employer and employee agree at the time of termination that the employment is to be terminated without proper notice but on the making of a PILON, and there was no existing understanding in this respect which could be construed as a contractual provision or amendment, the source of the payment lies only in the agreement to terminate the employment. The payment is therefore not income from the employment.

(c) In establishing whether contractual arrangements provide for a PILON, all relevant factors, e.g. rules in staff handbooks or wage agreements, or oral agreements, have to be considered. Even in the absence of any direct contractual arrangements, there may be an implied contractual term of service where an employer has established a practice of making PILONs instead of giving due notice (but see below for a change in HMRC's view on this aspect).

(d) Where neither (a) nor (b) above applies, failure to give due notice is a breach of contract, and a payment made for such a breach represents liquidated damages and is not an emolument from the employment.

(e) The existence of a reserved right or discretion of the employer to make a PILON where due notice is not given is not a determining factor where the right or discretion is not exercised. Where it is exercised, (a) above applies.

HMRC reject the view that a contractual PILON is properly analysed as a payment of damages for breach of contract (in particular by analysis of the true effect of (what is now) *Employment Rights Act 1996, s 86*). They also reject the view that a PILON is a redundancy payment.

Payments for a period where notice is given but not in fact worked ('garden leave') are income from the employment. (See *Redundant Employee v McNally* Ch D, 2005 ST1 652)

(Revenue Tax Bulletin August 1996 pp 325–327).

A further article in Revenue Tax Bulletin February 2003 pp 999–1001 updates the above in a number of respects.

(i) In the employment law case *Cerberus Software Ltd v Rowley* [2001] ICR 376, the Court of Appeal held that a contractual clause providing that an employer 'may' make a PILON meant that the employer was free to give neither notice nor a PILON, but instead to breach the contract and pay damages for that breach. Such damages would fall within *ITEPA 2003, s 403* (see **20.5 COMPENSATION FOR LOSS OF EMPLOYMENT AND DAMAGES**) rather than the normal employment income charging provisions. Whether such discretion has been thus exercised in any particular case is a question of fact, but HMRC sets out its views of indicative factors.

(ii) HMRC do not consider that *Cerberus* overrules the *EMI* case referred to below, since the general employment income charge is not expressed in contractual terms, so that many taxable payments are not dependent on any contractual obligation. What is required is that the source of the payment is the employer/employee relationship.

(iii) As regards (c) above, although HMRC now accept that it is unlikely that an implied contractual term in relation to PILONs can exist, they nevertheless consider that where, for example, a PILON is paid as an automatic response to a termination, the payment may be an 'integral part of the employer/employee relationship for the workplace', and as such be assessable under the normal employment income rules.

An article in *Taxation Magazine, 29 September 2005, p 714* confirms that, as suggested in (iii) above, HMRC are increasingly seeking to tax 'auto-PILONs' as general employment income. An *'auto-PILON'* is therein described as a payment made for unworked notice as an automatic response to the termination of a contract of employment in the same way as 'night follows day'. HMRC distinguish this from a payment made following a genuine critical assessment, on an individual by individual basis, to establish the true level of damages, which would fall within *ITEPA 2003, s 403*. Such a payment should reflect the likelihood of the employee's finding alternative employment within the notice period and should be made net of the tax and National Insurance contributions that would have been deductible from a payment made for notice actually worked (the *Gourley* principle).

A further article in *Taxation Magazine, 6 July 2006, p 379* considers HMRC's practice above in the light of the decision in *SCA Packaging Ltd v HMRC* Ch D, [2007] STC 1640 and concludes that, contrary to HMRC's view, the habitual or routine nature of the payment of PILONS does not in itself prevent such a payment being compensation for breach of contract and thus within *ITEPA 2003, s 403*.

In *EMI Group Electronics Ltd v Coldicott* CA 1999, 71 TC 455, it was held that payments following exercise by the employer of a reserved right as under (e) above were chargeable earnings. However, in *Mimtec Ltd v CIR* (Sp C 277), [2001] SSCD 101 a Special Commissioner held that certain payments made following redundancy negotiations 'in recognition of any entitlements under the consultation process including pay in lieu of notice etc.' were not taxable earnings.

Simon's Taxes. See E4.822.

Workers supplied by agencies

[27.95] Where an individual worker (including a partner in a firm and a member of an unincorporated body) has a contract or arrangement with another person (e.g. with an agency, which term includes an unincorporated body of which the worker is a member) under which he is obliged to render personal services to another person ('the client') which are subject to supervision, direction or control as to the manner in which the services are rendered, those services will be treated as duties performed under an employment with the agency. Any remuneration, whether from the agency or the client, is treated as earnings from that employment (if not already so chargeable), as is any remuneration paid by the agency during a period when the worker is not assigned to any particular client. 'Remuneration' includes every form of payment, gratuity, profit and benefit, but not anything which would not otherwise be employment income if receivable from an office or employment. [*ITEPA 2003, ss 44–46, 47(1)(3), Sch 7 para 13*]. For the existence of a contract, see *Brady v Hart* Ch D 1985, 58 TC 518.

See also *Bhadra v Ellam* Ch D 1987, 60 TC 466, where a doctor obtaining locum posts through medical agencies was held to be within the legislation.

The above provisions do not apply (a) to entertainers or fashion etc. models, or (b) if the services are wholly rendered in the worker's own home or at other premises which are neither under the control or management of the client nor at which the services are required by their nature to be rendered. [*ITEPA 2003, s 47(2)*].

The deemed employer must include the worker in his return of employees under *TMA 1970, s 15* — see **63.16 RETURNS**. Where a worker is engaged through a foreign agency which does not have a branch or permanent agency in the UK, the client is responsible for operating PAYE and national insurance arrangements (see HMRC Employment Status Manual ESM2012).

See **53.5 PAY AS YOU EARN** as regards application of PAYE generally.

As regards the scope of the legislation on agency workers, see generally HMRC Employment Status Manual ESM2003. These provisions are independent of, and are not affected by, the rules at **46 MANAGED SERVICE COMPANIES** and **58 PERSONAL SERVICE COMPANIES ETC.**

Simon's Taxes. See E4.225.

Key points

[27.96] Points to consider are as follows.

- Where an employee is internationally mobile, a body of case law is building up which will help establish whether the individual is UK resident, and to what extent the duties of the employment are performed in the UK. Those new to this area would be wise to study a selection of cases, particularly where employees in the airline industry are involved. See, for example, the more recent cases cited at **62.7 RESIDENCE, ORDINARY RESIDENCE AND DOMICILE**. A study should also be made of HMRC's most recent guidance on UK residence for tax purposes.

- The assumption is that any payment to an employee arises from the employment and is taxable as such, but see **27.20** for indications of payments which have been held not to arise from the employment. Where there is a personal relationship between the employer (an individual) and the employee, this general rule does not always apply.

- The treatment of employees based at home for some or all of their working hours differs according to whether the employer reimburses home running costs, or whether the employee makes a claim against employment income for the expenses. In short, the employee is in a much more favourable position if the employer elects to make a reimbursement, as the exemption for such payment is phrased more flexibly than the equivalent legislation supporting a claim. (See **27.21**).

- In deciding the treatment of travelling and subsistence expenses, it is essential that the advisor can correctly identify the one or more 'permanent workplaces' that relate to the employment, and can successfully distinguish these from 'temporary workplaces', as journeys to and from a temporary workplace will always be allowable. In this regard, it should be remembered that the '24 month rule' applies only when it has been established that the workplace is indeed a temporary workplace, and applies to set an upper limit on the temporary aspect. See **27.23**.

- Payment of parking fines for employees when incurred on company business can be liable to tax as employment income. Various factors are taken into account, but in particular whether the vehicle is owned by the employer and whether the penalty notice is fixed to the vehicle or handed to the employee can affect the tax status of the payment by the employer. HMRC's Employment Income Manual sets out the full details at EIM21686, and should be consulted, particularly where a high level of parking fines is incurred.

- Where a taxable company car is unavailable for a period of 30 days or more a deduction is made from the benefit-in-kind calculation. However, it is common to overlook a replacement vehicle which has been provided during the period of unavailability. Benefit-in-kind calculations should be made in respect of the replacement vehicle, even if provided by the garage performing the repair, as it is a benefit provided by a third party, but arranged or facilitated by the employer, and therefore taxable as if it were employer-provided.

- When an employee reimburses fuel used for private journeys to escape the benefit-in-kind charge on fuel the records of private mileage are most vulnerable to challenge. If found to be unreliable, a fuel benefit will apply, as this applies unless all private fuel is paid for by the employee. If employers choose to use this route to provide business fuel, rather than requiring employees to provide the fuel and claim for business journeys, it is essential to impress upon staff the need for rigorous records of private journeys — indeed a 100% record of mileage in the vehicle would seem an appropriate precaution to take.

- Double cab pick-ups are taxed as *vans* provided the payload exceeds 1 tonne (1,000kg). However, if a hard top is fitted to the vehicle, this will reduce the quoted payload, so employers purchasing these vehicles for employee use should ensure that they have taken this into account. HMRC's practice is to accord hard tops a generic weight of 45kg (see EIM23150). The rules also apply for VAT and capital allowances purposes.

- Claims that vehicles are 'pooled' vehicles are common, and frequently unsuccessful. Generally speaking a car is taxed as a benefit-in-kind where it is made available to an employee, whether or not it is used by them, and any claim that the car is a 'pool car' should be treated with care. See the detailed guidance in **27.38** to decide whether this is appropriate.

- Where a loan has been made or repaid during the year, the average method of calculating the benefit can be most favourable, as it measures the benefit in tax months only. For example a loan of £50,000 made on 8 January and repaid on 3 April is outstanding for only one complete tax month (6 February to 5 March), presenting a considerable saving. Note, however, that HMRC has a right to require the benefit to be calculated on a strict basis.

- Where the employer provides childcare vouchers or employer contracted childcare to employees, the tax exemption described at **27.45** requires that the care is qualifying care. It is essential that the employer ensures that the vouchers are used in respect of qualifying care, and that procedures are in place to check. Note in this context that the law regarding qualifying care has changed several times since the legislation was introduced — employers should follow the guidance on HMRC's website and document the checks they have made, alongside printed copies of the guidance they referred to.

- Although the results of the Employment Indicator Tool remain outside the bounds of a legally binding decision, HMRC's policy is to abide by the results if the tool has been used correctly. Employers using the tool should print the results and details of responses given to the questions and retain on file, as this will support their treatment of the particular worker, and also provide evidence of 'reasonable care' when considering penalties.

- An additional charge applies to taxable living accommodation which cost more than £75,000 (including improvements since purchase). However, the additional charge is based on the market value (plus subsequent improvements) of the property when first provided to that employee as a taxable benefit where it was owned by the employer for more than six years prior to that provision. This is easily overlooked, and most often arises where there is a change of occupant arising from the departure of the previous job holder.

- The most recent version of the exemption for medical screening allows up to one screening per annum to be exempt from tax; there is no requirement that screening is provided to all staff, and this can be a useful tax-free benefit where employers choose to provide medical check-ups for staff attaining a particular age, or performing certain functions.

28

Enterprise Investment Scheme

(See also HMRC guidance at www.hmrc.gov.uk/guidance/eis-index.htm and HMRC Venture Capital Schemes Manual.)

Introduction

[28.1] The Enterprise Investment Scheme (EIS) is a scheme whereby, subject to numerous conditions being met, individuals may obtain income tax relief and capital gains tax reliefs on an investment in newly-issued shares in an unquoted company. An investor is eligible for EIS income tax relief in respect of an amount invested by him on his own behalf for an issue of shares in a company if:

- the shares are issued to the investor;
- the general requirements at **28.26** below are met in respect of the shares;
- the investor is a 'qualifying investor' (see **28.34** below) in relation to the shares; and
- the company issuing the shares is a 'qualifying company' (see **28.38** below) in relation to the shares.

[*ITA 2007, s 157(1); ICTA 1988, ss 289(1), 291(1)*].

This chapter concentrates on the income tax relief but a brief summary of the CGT reliefs is included at **28.23, 28.24** below. For the form of the income tax relief see **28.4** *et seq.* below and for the restriction or withdrawal of relief in certain circumstances see **28.10** *et seq.* below.

Enquiries from companies as to whether they meet the conditions of the EIS should be directed to Small Company Enterprise Centre, HM Revenue and Customs, 1st Floor, Ferrers House, Castle Meadow Road, Nottingham, NG2 1BB (tel. 0115 974 1250; fax 0115 974 2954). However, where subscribers to the same issue of shares are expected to include company applicants claiming relief under the Corporate Venturing Scheme (see Tolley's Corporation Tax under Corporate Venturing Scheme), and the issuing company seeks formal advance clearance under that scheme, any request for informal EIS clearance should accompany the Corporate Venturing Scheme clearance application.

See generally HMRC guidance at www.hmrc.gov.uk/eis/index.htm and HMRC Venture Capital Schemes Manual VCM10000 *et seq.*

Simon's Taxes. See E3.1.

Approved funds

[28.2] EIS relief is also available where shares are subscribed for by a nominee for the individual claiming relief, including the managers of an investment fund approved by HMRC for this purpose (an *'approved fund'*). With regard to an approved fund closed for the acceptance of further investments, the provisions at **28.4, 28.6** below (dealing with the form and attribution of relief, see) apply as if the eligible shares were issued at the time at which the fund was closed, provided that the amount subscribed on behalf of the individual for eligible shares issued within twelve months after the closure of the fund is not less than 90% of the individual's investment in the fund. [*ITA 2007, ss 250(1), 251(1)(2); ICTA 1988, s 311(1)(2A)(2B); FA 2007, Sch 16 para 19*].

Enquiries about the circumstances in which an investment fund may be given approval can be made to HMRC CT&VAT (Technical), Room 3C35, 100 Parliament Street, London, SW1A 2BQ (telephone 020 7147 2626) (see HMRC Venture Capital Schemes Manual VCM21510).

Bare trustees and nominees

[28.3] EIS relief is available where shares which satisfy the requirement at **28.27**(i) below are held on a bare trust for two or more beneficiaries as if each beneficiary had subscribed as an individual for all of those shares, and as if the amount subscribed by each was the total subscribed divided by the number of beneficiaries. [*ITA 2007, s 250(2)(3); ICTA 1988, s 311(2)*].

EIS income tax relief

[28.4] Relief is (except as below) given for the tax year in which the shares were issued, by a reduction in what would otherwise be the individual's income tax liability (a *'tax reduction'*) equal to tax at the EIS rate (currently 20%) for the year on the amount (or aggregate amounts) subscribed for shares in respect of which he is eligible for and claims EIS relief (subject to the minimum and maximum limits at **28.5** below). For shares issued on or after 5 April 2007, investors may restrict a claim to EIS relief in respect of a single issue of shares so that relief is given only in respect of some of the shares.

The order in which tax reductions are given against an individual's tax liability is set out at **1.8 ALLOWANCES AND TAX RATES,** which also makes clear that a tax reduction must be restricted to the extent (if any) that it would otherwise exceed the individual's remaining income tax liability after making all prior reductions.

Where shares in respect of which the individual is eligible for relief are issued at any time in 2009/10 or a subsequent year, he may claim relief as if any number of shares up to the full number of shares issued to him had been issued in the preceding tax year.

Where shares in respect of which the individual is eligible for relief are issued before 6 October in 2008/09 or an earlier tax year, he may claim relief as if up to one half of the shares had been issued in the preceding tax year, subject to an overall limit of £50,000 (£25,000 for shares issued before 6 April 2006) on the amount of subscriptions which may be so treated.

These carry-backs are subject to the overriding rule that the total amount of investment on which relief can be obtained for any one year cannot exceed the annual maximum for that year at **28.5** below.

See **18.2** CLAIMS for general provisions regarding claims for payments made in one tax year to be carried back to an earlier year.

[ITA 2007, s 158; ICTA 1988, s 289A(1)–(5); FA 2008, s 31, Sch 1 paras 13, 65; FA 2009, Sch 8 paras 6, 13].

Simon's Taxes. See E3.143, E3.144.

Minimum and maximum amounts

[28.5] Except in the case of investments through 'approved funds' (see **28.2** above), relief is restricted to investments of £500 or more in any one company in any tax year.

There is in all cases an upper limit of £500,000 for 2008/09 onwards (£400,000 for 2006/07 and 2007/08) on the amount in respect of which an individual may obtain relief in a tax year (regardless of whether the shares were issued in that year or in the following year — see **28.4** above).

[ITA 2007, ss 157(2)(3), 158(2), 251(3); ICTA 1988, ss 290, 311(3); FA 2006, Sch 14 para 6; FA 2008, s 31, Sch 1 paras 13, 65; SI 2008 No 3165].

Simon's Taxes. See E3.136, E3.141.

Attribution of relief to shares

[28.6] Subject to any reduction or withdrawal of relief (see **28.10** et seq. below), where an individual's income tax liability is reduced for a tax year as in **28.4** above by reason of an issue or issues of shares made (or treated as made) in that year, the tax reduction is attributed to that issue or those issues (being apportioned in the latter case according to the amounts claimed for each issue (for shares issued before 6 April 2007, the amounts subscribed for each issue)). Issues of shares of the same class by a company to an individual on the same day are treated as a single issue for this purpose. A proportionate amount of the reduction attributed to an issue is attributed to each share in the issue in respect of which the claim was made (for shares issued before 6 April 2007, each share in the issue) and is adjusted correspondingly for any subsequent bonus issue of shares of the same class and carrying the same rights.

An issue to an individual part of which is treated as having been made in the preceding tax year (as in **28.4** above) is treated as two separate issues, one made on a day in the previous year.

Where relief attributable to an issue of shares falls to be withdrawn or reduced, the relief attributable to each of the shares in question is reduced to nil (if relief is withdrawn) or proportionately reduced (where relief is reduced).

[ITA 2007, ss 201, 255; ICTA 1988, s 289B].

Claims for relief

[28.7] A claim for relief must be made not earlier than the end of the four-month minimum period at **28.31** below, and not later than the fifth anniversary of 31 January following the tax year in which the shares are issued.

The claimant must have received a compliance certificate from the issuing company before making the claim. The certificate must state that the requirements for relief, except in so far as they fall to be satisfied by the investor, are for the time being satisfied in relation to the shares in question. A certificate may not be issued without the authority of an HMRC officer. Where a notice under *ITA 2007, s 241* (see **28.25** below), or a notice of certain chargeable events under the EIS capital gains deferral provisions mentioned at **28.24** below, has been given to HMRC, a compliance certificate must not be issued unless the authority is given or renewed after receipt of the notice. For appeal purposes, the inspector's refusal to authorise a certificate is treated as a decision disallowing a claim by the company.

Before issuing such a certificate, the company must supply to HMRC a compliance statement (Form EIS 1) that those requirements are fulfilled for the time being and have been fulfilled at all times since the shares were issued. The statement must contain such information as HMRC may reasonably require, and a declaration that it is correct to the best of the company's knowledge and belief. The statement must be provided to HMRC within two years after the end of the tax year in which the shares in question were issued (or, if the four-month minimum period at **28.31** below ends in the following year, within two years after the end of that four-month period). The statement cannot be provided to HMRC before the four-month minimum period expires.

References above to requirements being fulfilled for the time being are, in the case of requirements that cannot be fulfilled until a future date, references to nothing having occurred to prevent their being fulfilled.

If a certificate or statement is made fraudulently or negligently, or a certificate was issued despite being prohibited (as above), the company is liable to a fine of up to £3,000.

Special provisions (see *ITA 2007, s 251(4)–(7)*) apply in relation to the issue of certificates (Forms EIS 5) where shares are held through an approved fund (see **28.2** above).

No application for postponement of tax pending appeal can be made on the ground that relief is due under these provisions unless a claim has been duly submitted. No regard is to be had to EIS relief for the purposes of PAY AS YOU EARN (**53**) unless a claim for relief has been made.

For shares issued before 6 April 2007, for the purposes of INTEREST ON OVERDUE TAX (**41**), tax charged by an assessment is regarded as due and payable notwithstanding that relief is subsequently given on a claim under these provisions, but is regarded as paid on the date on which a claim is made resulting in relief being granted, unless it was either in fact paid earlier or not due and payable until later. Interest is not refunded in respect of any subsequent discharge or repayment of tax giving effect to relief under these provisions. This provision has not been reproduced in *ITA 2007* as it is considered unnecessary under self-assessment (see Change 53 listed in Annex 1 to the Explanatory Notes to *ITA 2007*).

[*ITA 2007, ss 202–207, 257(8), 989; ICTA 1988, ss 306, 311(4)–(6)*].

Relief for a year can only be claimed after the end of the year, and any in-year claims for relief by repayment through self-assessment will be rejected. This does not affect the right to claim a reduction in payments on account (see **65.5** SELF-ASSESSMENT), and relief may still be given through a PAYE coding. (Revenue Tax Bulletin April 2002 p 924).

In a case where a company inserted an incorrect issue date when completing Form EIS 1, HMRC withdrew a claimant's EIS relief on the grounds that there was no valid compliance certificate; the claimant's assertion on appeal that substance should prevail over form was rejected by the Sp C (*Ashley v HMRC* (Sp C 633), [2008] SSCD 219).

Simon's Taxes. See **E3.142, E3.143**.

Relief for loss on disposal

[28.8] See **45.25** LOSSES for income tax relief for certain losses on disposals of shares in unquoted trading companies, including shares to which EIS income tax relief is attributable.

Example

[28.9]

Mr Jones is a married man with a salary of £88,975 for 2009/10 and no other income. He is not entitled to married couple's allowance. For 2009/10, he is entitled to full income tax relief on an investment of £60,000 in a venture capital trust.

In 2009/10 he subscribes for ordinary shares in two unquoted companies issuing shares under the enterprise investment scheme (EIS).

A Ltd was formed by some people in Mr Jones' neighbourhood to publish a local newspaper. In August 2009, 200,000 ordinary £1 shares were issued at par and the company started trading in September 2009. Mr Jones subscribed for 16,000 of the shares. Mr Jones becomes a director of A Ltd in September 2009, receiving director's fees of £5,000 per annum (£2,500 in 2009/10), a level of remuneration which is considered reasonable for services rendered by him to the company in his capacity as a director.

B Ltd, which is controlled by an old friend of Mr Jones, has acquired the rights to manufacture in the UK a new type of industrial cleaning solvent and requires additional finance. Mr Jones subscribed for 8,000 ordinary £1 shares at a premium of £1.50 per share in October 2009. The issue increases the company's issued share capital to 25,000 ordinary £1 shares.

Mr Jones will obtain tax relief in 2009/10 as follows.

Amount eligible for relief

	£
A Ltd notes (a) and (b)	16,000
B Ltd note (c)	Nil
Total (being less than the maximum of £500,000)	£16,000

	£
Salary	88,975
Director's remuneration (A Ltd)	2,500
Total income	91,475
Deduct Personal allowance	6,475
Taxable income	£85,000

Tax payable:	£
37,400 @ 20%	7,480.00
47,600 @ 40%	19,040.00
	26,520.00
Deduct VCT relief £60,000 @ 30%	18,000.00
	8,520.00
Deduct EIS relief £16,000 @ 20%	3,200.00
Net tax liability 2008/09	£5,320.00

Notes

(a) Mr Jones is entitled to relief on the full amount of his investment in A Ltd regardless of the amount of relief claimed by other investors.

(b) The fact that Mr Jones becomes a paid director of A Ltd *after* an issue to him of eligible shares does not prevent his qualifying for relief in respect of those shares providing his remuneration as a director is reasonable and he is not otherwise connected with the company (see **28.35** below).

(c) Mr Jones is not entitled to relief against his income for his investment of £20,000 in B Ltd. As a result of the share issue he owns more than 30% of the issued ordinary share capital (8,000 out of 25,000 shares) and is therefore regarded as connected with the company and denied relief. See **28.35** below.

(d) The VCT investment relief must be deducted before the EIS investment relief.

In 2010/11, Mr Jones subscribes for shares in three more unquoted companies trading in the UK and issuing shares under the EIS.

C Ltd is a local company engaged in the manufacture of car components. It issues a further 540,000 ordinary £1 shares at £2 per share in June 2010 and Mr Jones subscribes for 14,800 shares costing £29,600, increasing his stake in the company to 2%. He had originally held 24,300 shares, acquired by purchase at arm's length in May 2008 for £32,400.

D Ltd has been trading as a restaurant for several years and requires an injection of capital to finance a new restaurant. Mr Jones and three other unconnected individuals each subscribe for 37,500 ordinary £1 shares at par in November

2010. The balance of 240,000 shares are held by Mr Jones' sister and niece. D Ltd has the equivalent of 40 full-time employees in November 2010 when the new shares are issued.

E Ltd is an electronics company, with 30 employees, controlled by two cousins of Mr Jones. The company has not issued any shares in the previous twelve months but is now seeking £2.6 million extra capital for expansion, and raises it via the EIS. Mr Jones subscribes for 467,000 ordinary £1 shares at par in December 2010.

Mr Jones's salary is increased to £93,000 for 2010/11. He makes a claim to treat 13,300 of his C Ltd shares (costing £26,600) to be regarded as issued in 2009/10, thus eliminating his income tax liability for that year.

Mr Jones will obtain tax relief as follows:

2009/10

C Ltd (note (a)) £26,600 @ 20% =	£5,320

2010/11
Amount eligible for relief

	£
C Ltd (£29,600 – £26,600 carried back)	3,000
D Ltd	37,500
E Ltd	467,000
Total	£507,500

But amount eligible for relief restricted to subscriptions of	£500,000

Relief given

	£
Salary	93,000
Director's remuneration	5,000
Total income	98,000
Deduct Personal allowance	6,475
Taxable income	£91,525

Tax payable:	
37,400 @ 20%	7,480.00
54,125 @ 40%	21,650.00
	29,130.00
Deduct EIS relief:	
£500,000 @ 20% = £100,000, but restricted to	29,130.00
Net tax liability 2010/11	Nil

Attribution of relief to shares (note (b))

$$\text{CLtd shares} \frac{3,000}{507,500} \times £29,130$$

	£
	172

$$\text{DLtd shares } \frac{37,500}{507,500} \times \text{£}29,130 \qquad\qquad 2,153$$

$$\text{ELtd shares } \frac{467,000}{507,500} \times \text{£}29,130 \qquad\qquad \underline{26,805}$$

$$\underline{\underline{\text{£}29,130}}$$

Notes

(a)   The investor may claim relief as if any number of the shares had been issued to him in the preceding tax year. The only restriction (not relevant in this example) is that relief in any one tax year may not be given on subscriptions of more than the annual maximum for that year. The relief will be given in addition to that previously claimed for 2009/10 (see above). See **28.4, 28.5** above.

(b)   Relief is restricted by (i) the £500,000 maximum (see **28.5** above) and (ii) an insufficiency in Mr Jones' tax liability. The relief attributable to each issue of shares (which will be relevant in the event of a disposal of the shares or withdrawal of relief—see **28.10** *et seq.* below) is found by apportioning the income tax reduction by reference to the amounts subscribed for each issue. (For this purpose, 13,300 of the C Ltd shares are regarded as having been separately issued in the previous year.) The relief so attributed to each issue is then apportioned equally between all the shares comprised in that issue. See **28.6** above.

Restriction or withdrawal of relief

[28.10] The following provisions apply to restrict or withdraw relief in certain circumstances. References to a reduction of relief include its reduction to nil, and references to the withdrawal of relief in respect of any shares are to the withdrawal of the relief attributable to those shares (see **28.6** above). Where no relief has yet been given, a reduction applies to reduce the amount which apart from the provision in question would be the relief, and a withdrawal means ceasing to be eligible for relief in respect of the shares in question. [*ITA 2007, s 257(4); ICTA 1988, s 312(4)*].

Where an event giving rise to complete withdrawal of relief occurs at the same time as a disposal at a loss, the disposal is regarded as occurring first, so that relief may be only partially withdrawn (as below). (HMRC Venture Capital Schemes Manual VCM26010).

Disposal of shares

[28.11] Where the investor disposes of shares (or an interest or right in or over shares) to which relief is attributable (see **28.6** above) or grants an option the exercise of which would bind him to sell the shares before the end of 'period A' (as in**28.35** below):

(a)   if the disposal is at arm's length, relief attributable to those shares (see **28.6** above) is withdrawn or, if that relief exceeds an amount equal to tax at the EIS rate of 20% on the disposal consideration, reduced by that amount;

(b)   otherwise, the relief is withdrawn.

Where the relief attributable to the shares was less than tax at the EIS rate on the amount subscribed for the issue, the amount referred to in (a) above is correspondingly reduced. Where the relief attributable to the shares has been reduced (otherwise than as a result of an issue of bonus shares (see **28.6** above)) before the relief was obtained, in calculating the amount referred to in (a) above, the gross relief attributable to the shares before that reduction is used.

A share exchange is treated as a disposal for these purposes unless it is within **28.22** below.

See **28.21** below for transfers of shares between spouses or civil partners.

Identification rules

For the above purposes, disposals are identified with shares of the same class issued earlier before shares issued later (i.e. first in/first out (FIFO)). Where shares within two or more of the categories listed below were acquired on the same day, any of those shares disposed of (applying the FIFO basis) are treated as disposed of in the order in which they are listed, as follows:

(i)   shares to which neither EIS income tax relief nor EIS capital gains deferral relief (see **28.24** below) is attributable;

(ii)   shares to which deferral relief, but not income tax relief, is attributable;

(iii)   shares to which income tax relief, but not deferral relief, is attributable;

(iv)   shares to which both of those reliefs are attributable.

Any shares within (iii) or (iv) above which are treated as issued on an earlier day by virtue of the carry-back provisions at **28.4** above are to be treated as disposed of before any other shares within the same category. Shares transferred between spouses or civil partners living together are treated as if they were acquired by the transferee spouse or partner on the day they were issued (see also **28.21** below). Shares comprised in a 'new holding' following a reorganisation to which *TCGA 1992, s 127* applies (see Tolley's Capital Gains Tax under Shares and Securities) are treated as having been acquired when the original shares were acquired.

Relief is also withdrawn where, during the relevant period, an option is granted to the investor, the exercise of which would bind the grantor to purchase shares. There are provisions for identifying the shares to which an option relates, where these form part of a larger holding.

[*ITA 2007, ss 209–212, 246, 254; ICTA 1988, ss 299, 312(3)(4B); FA 2008, Sch 1 paras 14, 15, 65*].

Simon's Taxes. See E3.146.

Value received by investor

[28.12] Where an investor subscribes for shares in a company, and during 'period C' that investor 'receives value' (other than 'insignificant value') from the company, any relief attributable to those shares (see **28.6** above) and not previously reduced in respect of the 'value received' is withdrawn or, if that relief exceeds an amount equal to tax at the EIS rate of 20% on the 'value received', reduced by that amount. See also **28.13** below for further computational provisions.

'*Period C*' is the period beginning one year before the issue of the shares and ending immediately before the third anniversary of the issue date or, if later and where relevant, the third anniversary of the date of commencement of the intended trade referred to in **28.49**(a) below. (In determining for these purposes the time at which a qualifying trade begins to be carried on by any 'qualifying 90% subsidiary' (see **28.48** below) of a company, any carrying on of the trade by it before it became such a subsidiary is disregarded.)

The provisions apply equally to value received from a person who is connected (within **21 CONNECTED PERSONS**) with the issuing company at any time in period A (as in**28.35** below), whether or not at the time value is received. As regards shares issued before 6 April 1998, they applied to 'value received' from a company which is a 51% subsidiary of the issuing company (i.e. a company more than 50% of whose ordinary share capital it owns) at any time in the period A (whether before or after the value is received).

An investor '*receives value*' from the issuing company if it:

(a) repays, redeems or repurchases any part of his holding of its share capital or securities, or makes any payment to him for giving up rights on its cancellation or extinguishment; or

(b) (in relation to shares issued after 16 March 2004) repays, in pursuance of any arrangements for or in connection with the acquisition of the shares in respect of which the relief is claimed, any debt owed to him other than one incurred by the company on or after the date of issue of those shares and otherwise than in consideration of the extinguishment of a debt incurred before that date; (but if the debt was incurred on or before 16 March 2004 but on or after the date the shares were subscribed for, (c) below applies instead of the foregoing); or

(c) (in relation to shares issued on or before 16 March 2004) repays, whether or not in pursuance of any such arrangements as are referred to in (b) above, any debt owed to him other than one incurred by the company on or after the date on which he subscribed for the shares in respect of which the relief is claimed and otherwise than in consideration of the extinguishment of a debt incurred before that date; or

(d) pays him for the cancellation of any debt owed to him other than an '*ordinary trade debt*' (i.e. one incurred for normal trade supply of goods or services on normal trade credit terms (not in any event exceeding six months)) or one in respect of a payment falling within **28.35**(A) or (F) below; or

(e)   releases or waives any liability of his to the company (which it is deemed to have done if discharge of the liability is twelve months or more overdue) or discharges or undertakes to discharge any liability of his to a third person; or

(f)   makes a loan or advance to him (defined as including any debt either to the company (other than an 'ordinary trade debt' (as above)) or to a third person but assigned to the company) which has not been repaid in full before the issue of the shares; or

(g)   provides a benefit or facility for him; or

(h)   transfers an asset to him for no consideration or for consideration less than market value, or acquires an asset from him for consideration exceeding market value; or

(i)   makes any other payment to him except one either falling within **28.35**(A)–(F) below or in discharge of an 'ordinary trade debt' (as above); or

(j)   is wound up or dissolved in circumstances such that the company does not thereby cease to be a 'qualifying company' (see **28.38** above), and he thereby receives any payment or asset in respect of ordinary shares held by him.

However, an individual does *not* receive value from a company by reason only of the payment to him (or to an 'associate' — see **28.35** below) of reasonable remuneration (including any benefit or facility) for services as a company director, and for this purpose, if the individual is also an employee of the company, references to him in his capacity as a director include him in his capacity as an employee.

The amount of value received by the individual is that paid to or received by him from the company; or the amount of his liability extinguished or discharged; or the difference between the market value of the asset and the consideration (if any) given for it; or the net cost to the company of providing the benefit. In the case of value received within (a), (b) or (c) above, the market value of the shares, securities or debt in question is substituted if greater than the amount receivable.

Additionally, the investor *'receives value'* from the company if any person connected with the company (within **28.35** below) purchases any shares or securities of the company from him, or pays him for giving up any right in relation to such shares or securities. The value received is the amount received or, if greater, the market value of the shares etc.

All payments or transfers, direct or indirect, to, or to the order of, or for the benefit of, the investor or associate are brought within these provisions.

Where relief is withdrawn or reduced by reason of a disposal (see **28.11** above), the investor is not treated as receiving value in respect of the disposal.

An individual who acquired shares by means of a transfer from a spouse or civil partner within **28.21** below is treated for these purposes as the investor.

[*ITA 2007, ss 159(4), 213, 214(1), 216, 217, 221, 256; ICTA 1988, ss 300, 301(3)–(6A), 312(1); FA 2008, Sch 1 paras 16, 65*].

Insignificant value

An amount of '*insignificant value*' is an amount of value which:

- does not exceed £1,000; or
- in any other case is insignificant in relation to the amount subscribed by the investor for the shares.

If, at any time in the period beginning one year before the date of issue of the shares and ending with the date of issue, there are in existence arrangements (as very broadly defined) providing for the investor (or an 'associate', within **28.35** below) to receive, or become entitled to receive, any value from the issuing company (or a 'connected person', within **21 CONNECTED PERSONS**) at any time in 'period C' (as above), no amount of value received by the individual is treated as an amount of insignificant value. References to an associate or person connected with the company include anyone who has such status at *any* time in period C.

There are provisions to aggregate a receipt of value, whether insignificant or not, with amounts of insignificant value received previously, and treating that aggregate, if it is not itself an amount of insignificant value, as an amount of value received at the time of the latest actual receipt.

[*ITA 2007, ss 214(2)(3), 215; ICTA 1988, ss 300(1)(1BC), 301A*].

Simon's Taxes. See **E3.147, E3.147A**.

Reduction in relief — further computational provisions

[28.13] Adjustments are made in the amount by which relief is to be reduced in the following circumstances. Where more than one circumstance is relevant, the adjustments are made in the order in which they are set out below.

(a) Where two or more issues of shares have been made by the same company to the same investor, in relation to each of which income tax relief is claimed, and value is received during the applicable period C for more than one such issue, the value received is apportioned between them by reference to the amounts of relief obtained for each of those issues (for shares issued before 6 April 2007, the amounts subscribed for each of those issues).

(b) Where any of the shares are treated as issued in the previous tax year by virtue of the carry-back provisions at **28.4** above, the value received is apportioned between the shares allocated to each year on the basis of the amount on which relief was obtained for each year. The normal provisions for reducing relief are then applied to each of the apportioned amounts as if there were separate issues of shares (taking (c) below into account where appropriate, but not (a) above) and the resulting amounts are added together. (Note that this provision was not explicit in the legislation prior to the enactment of *ITA 2007*, but is understood to be in line with existing practice (see Change 49 listed in Annex 1 to the Explanatory Notes to *ITA 2007*).)

(c) Where maximum relief is not obtained, the amount of value received is treated as reduced by multiplying that amount by the relief attributable to the shares divided by tax at the EIS rate of 20% on the amount on which the investor claims relief in respect of the shares (for shares issued before 6 April 2007, on the amount subscribed for the issue). For this purpose, where the relief attributable to the shares has been reduced (otherwise than as a result of an issue of bonus shares — see **28.6** above) before the relief was obtained, the gross relief attributable to the shares before that reduction is used in calculating the reduction in the value received.

[*ITA 2007, ss 218–220; ICTA 1988, ss 289B(5), 299(4), 300(1B)–(1BB), s 312(1); FA 2008, Sch 1 paras 17, 65*].

Replacement value

[28.14] The 'value received' provisions in **28.12** above (other than **28.12**(i)) are disapplied if the person from whom the value was received (the '*original supplier*') receives, by way of a 'qualifying receipt', and whether before or after the original receipt of value, at least equivalent replacement value from the original recipient. A receipt is a '*qualifying receipt*' if it arises by reason of:

(a)   any one, or any combination of, the following:
   (i)   a payment by the original recipient to the original supplier other than a payment within (1) to (6) below or a payment covered by (c) below;
   (ii)   the acquisition of an asset by the original recipient from the original supplier for consideration exceeding market value;
   (iii) the disposal of an asset by the original recipient to the original supplier for no consideration or for consideration less than market value; or
(b)   (where the original receipt of value falls within **28.12**(e) above) an event having the effect of reversing the original event; or
(c)   (where the original receipt of value arose from the purchase from the individual by a person connected with the company of shares or securities of the company, including for this purpose a payment for giving up any right in relation to them) the repurchase by the original recipient of the shares or securities in question, or reacquisition of the right in question, for consideration not less than the original value.

The amount of replacement value is:

*   in a case within (a) above, the amount of any such payment plus the difference between the market value of any such asset and the consideration received;
*   in a case within (b) above, the same as the amount of the original value; and
*   in a case within (c) above, the consideration received by the original supplier.

The receipt of replacement value is disregarded if:

*   it occurs before the start of period C relating to the shares in question; or
*   there was an unreasonable delay in its occurrence; or
*   it occurs more than 60 days after the relief falling to be withdrawn (or reduced) has been determined on appeal.

A receipt of replacement value is also disregarded if it has previously been set against a receipt of value to prevent any reduction or withdrawal of relief.

The following payments are excluded from (a)(i) above:

(1)   a reasonable (in relation to their market value) payment for any goods, services or facilities provided (in the course of trade or otherwise) by the original supplier;

(2)   a payment of interest at no more than a reasonable commercial rate on money lent to the original recipient;

(3)   a payment not exceeding a reasonable and commercial rent for property occupied by the original recipient;

(4)   a payment not exceeding market value for the acquisition of an asset;

(5)   a payment in discharge of an 'ordinary trade debt' (as in **28.12**(d) above);

(6)   a payment for any shares or securities in any company in circumstances not within (a)(ii) above.

Each reference in (1)–(3) above to the original supplier or recipient includes a reference to any person who at any time in period C is an 'associate' (as in **28.35** below) of his or, in the case of the supplier, is 'connected' with him (within **21 CONNECTED PERSONS**).

Where:

•   the receipt of replacement value is a qualifying receipt (as above); and
•   the event giving rise to the receipt is (or includes) a subscription for shares by the individual or by a person who is an 'associate' (as in **28.35** below) of his at any time in period C,

the subscriber is not eligible for EIS income tax relief or EIS capital gains deferral relief (see **28.24** below) in relation to those shares or any other shares in the same issue.

For the above purposes, any apportionment made of value received where there are two or more share issues (see **28.13** above) is disregarded in determining the amount of the original receipt of value; and payments to a person include any made indirectly or to his order or for his benefit.

[*ITA 2007, ss 222, 223; ICTA 1988, ss 300A, 301*].

Value received other than by investor

[28.15] Relief is also restricted or withdrawn where an individual has obtained relief attributable (see **28.6** above) to shares in a company, and at any time during 'period C', the company or any '51% subsidiary' of the company repays, redeems or repurchases any of its share capital belonging to a member other than:

(i)   the individual; or

(ii)   another individual whose relief is thereby withdrawn or reduced (as above) or who thereby suffers a qualifying chargeable event under the capital gains deferral provisions mentioned at **28.24** below; or

(iii)   a company whose investment relief under the Corporate Venturing Scheme (see Tolley's Corporation Tax) is thereby withdrawn or reduced,

or makes any payment to any such member for giving up rights on the cancellation or extinguishment of any of the share capital of the company or subsidiary. See below for the exception for insignificant repayments etc.

The absence of any withdrawal or reduction of the kind referred to in (ii) and (iii) above is disregarded if it is due only to the amount received being of insignificant value.

A '*51% subsidiary*' of a company is one of which the company owns more than 50% of the ordinary share capital at any time in period A (as in **28.35** below), whether or not at the time of the repayment etc.

'*Period C*' is the period beginning one year before the issue of eligible shares and ending immediately before the third anniversary of the issue date or, if later and where relevant, the third anniversary of the date of commencement of the intended trade referred to in **28.49**(a) below. (In determining for these purposes the time at which a qualifying trade begins to be carried on by any 'qualifying 90% subsidiary' (see **28.48** below) of a company, any carrying on of the trade by it before it became such a subsidiary is disregarded.)

This restriction of relief does not apply to the redemption, within twelve months of issue, of any share capital of nominal value equal to the authorised minimum issued to comply with *Companies Act 2006, s 761* (or earlier equivalent).

A repayment etc., is ignored for the above purpose to the extent that relief attributable to any shares has already been withdrawn or reduced on its account.

[*ITA 2007, ss 159(4), 224(1)(3)–(7), 230; ICTA 1988, ss 303(1)–(1C)(9)–(9B) 312(1); SI 2008 No 954, arts 1, 39*].

Computation

The relief is withdrawn or, if it exceeds an amount equal to tax at the EIS rate of 20% on the sum received by the member, reduced by that amount.

Adjustments are made in the amount by which relief is to be reduced in the following circumstances. Where more than one circumstance is relevant, the adjustments are made in the order in which they are set out below.

(1)   Where, in relation to the same repayment etc., relief attributable to two or more issues of shares falls to be reduced, the amount received by the member is apportioned between the issues by reference to the amounts of relief obtained for each of those issues (for shares issued before 6 April 2007, the amounts subscribed for each of those issues).

(2)   Where, in relation to the same repayment etc., relief attributable to shares held by two or more individuals falls to be reduced, the amount received by the member is apportioned between the individuals by reference to the amounts of relief obtained by each individual (for shares issued before 6 April 2007, the amounts subscribed by each individual).

(3)   Where any of the shares are treated as issued in the previous tax year by virtue of the carry-back provisions at **28.4** above, the amount received by the member is apportioned between the shares allocated to each year on the basis of the amount on which relief was obtained for each year. The normal provisions for reducing relief are then applied to each of the apportioned amounts as if there were separate issues of shares (taking (4) below into account where appropriate, but not (1) or (2) above) and the resulting amounts are added together. (Note that this provision was not explicit in the legislation prior to the enactment of *ITA 2007*, but is understood to be in line with existing practice (see Change 49 listed in Annex 1 to the Explanatory Notes to *ITA 2007*).)

(4)   Where maximum relief is not obtained, the amount received by the member is treated as reduced by multiplying that amount by the relief attributable to the shares divided by tax at the EIS rate of 20% on the amount on which the investor claims relief in respect of the shares (for shares issued before 6 April 2007, on the amount subscribed for the issue). For this purpose, where the relief attributable to the shares has been reduced (otherwise than as a result of an issue of bonus shares — see **28.6** above) before the relief was obtained, the gross relief attributable to the shares before that reduction is used in calculating the reduction in the amount received by the member.

[*ITA 2007, ss 224(2), 226–229; ICTA 1988, ss 303(1A)(1C)–(2); FA 2008, Sch 1 paras 18, 19, 65*].

Insignificant repayments etc.

A repayment etc. is disregarded if both the amount received by the member in question and the market value immediately before the event of the shares to which the event relates is insignificant in relation to the market value immediately after the event of the remaining issued share capital of the company or, as the case may be, 51% subsidiary. The assumption is made that the shares in question are cancelled at the time of the event. This let-out does not apply if, at any time in the period beginning one year before the date of issue of the shares and ending with the date of issue, there are in existence arrangements (as very broadly defined) providing for a payment within these provisions to be made, or entitlement to such a payment to come into being, at any time in period C. [*ITA 2007, s 225; ICTA 1988, s 303AA*].

Interaction with corporate venturing scheme provisions

Where, by virtue of provisions comparable to those above, a repayment, redemption etc. of share capital causes a withdrawal or reduction of investment relief given to one or more companies, in respect of the full amount repaid etc., under the Corporate Venturing Scheme ('CVS') (see Tolley's Corporation Tax), there is provision to ensure that no withdrawal or reduction is made under the above provisions. A withdrawal etc. of CVS investment relief is also disregarded for the purposes of *s 303* if the amount repaid etc. exceeds the amount in respect of which the relief was given by no more than £1,000. These exemptions are subject to the absence of any 'repayment arrangements' (as defined) throughout the one year ending with the date of issue of the shares to which the CVS investment relief is attributable. Where the above-mentioned excess (if any) is greater than the *de minimis* limit or the exemptions are prevented from applying, the amount of that excess is taken as the amount received by the member for the purposes of the above provisions.

Under the comparable CVS provisions mentioned above, a repayment etc. of an insignificant amount (judged by reference to the greater of the market value of the shares to which it relates and the amount received by the member in question, and to the market value of the remaining share capital) is disregarded. A repayment etc. disregarded under that provision was also disregarded for the purposes of the above provisions, but following the introduction of the insignificant repayments etc. provisions above, this rule becomes superfluous and is abolished.

[*ITA 2007, s 231; ICTA 1988, s 303A*].

Simon's Taxes. See E3.148.

Acquisition of a trade or trading assets

[28.16] Relief attributable (see **28.6** above) to any shares in a company held by an individual is withdrawn if, at any time in period A (as in **28.35** below), the company or any qualifying subsidiary (see **28.47** below), begins to carry on as its trade, business or profession (or part), a trade etc. (or part) previously carried on at any time in that period otherwise than by the company or a qualifying subsidiary, or acquires the whole or the greater part of the assets used for a trade etc. previously so carried on, and the individual is a person who, or one of a group of persons who together, either:

(a)   owned more than a half share in the trade etc. previously carried on at any time in period A, and also own or owned at any such time such a share in the trade etc. carried on by the company, or

(b)   control (within *CTA 2010, ss 450, 451*), or at any time in period A have controlled, the company, and also, at any such time, controlled another company which previously carried on the trade etc.

In determining, for the purposes of (a) above, the ownership of a trade and, if appropriate, the shares owned by multiple owners, *CTA 2010, s 941(6)* and *s 942* (previously *ICTA 1988, s 344(1)(a)(b), (2)(3)*) apply.

For the above purposes, interests etc. of 'associates' (see **28.35** below) are taken into account. There are special rules relating to shares held by certain directors of, or of a partner of, the issuing company or any subsidiary.

[*ITA 2007, ss 232, 257(3); ICTA 1988, s 302(1)(2)(4)–(5); CTA 2010, Sch 1 paras 502, 503*].

Simon's Taxes. See E3.151.

Acquisition of share capital

[28.17] Relief is also withdrawn if the company, at any time in period A (as in **28.35** below), comes to acquire all the issued share capital of another company, and where the individual is a person who, or one of a group of persons who together, control (within *CTA 2010, ss 450, 451*) or have, at any such time, controlled the company and who also, at any such time, controlled the other company. There are special rules relating to shares held by certain directors of, or of a partner of, the issuing company or any subsidiary.

[*ITA 2007, ss 233, 257(3); ICTA 1988, s 302(3)(4A)(4B); CTA 2010, Sch 1 para 503*].

Simon's Taxes. See E3.151.

Relief subsequently found not to have been due

[28.18] Relief is withdrawn if it is subsequently found not to have been due. Relief can be withdrawn on the ground that the issuing company is not a qualifying company (see **28.38** below) or that the purpose of the issue or use of money raised requirements at **28.29, 28.30** are not met only if:

* the issuing company has given notice under the provisions at **28.25** below (or the equivalent capital gains deferral provisions); or
* an HMRC officer has given notice to the issuing company of his opinion that the whole or part of the relief was not due because of the ground in question.

The issuing company may appeal against an HMRC notice as though it were refusal of a claim by the company. The determination of an appeal against an HMRC notice under the equivalent capital gains deferral provisions (see **28.24** below) is conclusive for the purposes of any income tax relief appeal.

[*ITA 2007, ss 234, 236; ICTA 1988, s 307(1)–(1B)*].

Procedure for withdrawing or reducing relief

[28.19] An assessment to income tax withdrawing or reducing EIS relief is made for the tax year for which the relief was given.

Such an assessment may not be made, and any notice by an HMRC officer under the provisions at **28.18** above may not be given, more than six years after the end of the tax year in which the time limit for the use of money raised requirement at **28.30** below expires or, if later, the event giving rise to withdrawal or reduction occurs. This restriction is without prejudice to the extension of time limits in cases of loss of income tax brought about deliberately (see **6.3** ASSESSMENTS) or fraudulent or negligent conduct (see **6.4** ASSESSMENTS). No assessment may be made by reason of any event occurring after the death of the person to whom the shares were issued.

Where a person has made an arm's length disposal or disposals of all the shares issued to him by a company in respect of which either relief is attributable or period A (as in **28.35** below) has not come to an end, no assessment may be made in respect of those shares by reason of any subsequent event unless he is at the time of that event 'connected with' the company (as in **28.35** below). As regards shares issued before 6 April 1998, this rule operated by reference to disposals of all the *ordinary* shares.

On and after 21 July 2009, the relevant date for the purposes of **42.2 INTEREST AND SURCHARGES ON OVERDUE TAX** is 31 January following the tax year for which the assessment is made.

Before 21 July 2009, the relevant date for those purposes was the date on which the event took place which gave rise to the withdrawal or reduction of relief, *except that*:

(a)   where relief is withdrawn due to a failure to meet the no linked loans requirement at **28.36** below, it is the date of the making of the loan;

(b)   where relief is withdrawn or reduced due to a disposal of the shares (see **28.11** above), it is the date of the disposal;

(c)   where relief is withdrawn as a result of the grant of an option the exercise of which would bind the grantor to purchase the shares (see **28.11** above), it is the date of grant of the option; and

(d)   where relief is withdrawn as a result of the receipt of value (see **28.12** above), it is the date of the receipt of value.

Slightly different rules applied in principle for shares issued before 6 April 2007, but the above is understood to reflect the position in practice (see Change 53 listed in Annex 1 to the Explanatory Notes to *ITA 2007*).

[*ITA 2007, ss 235, 237–239; ICTA 1988, s 307; FA 2007, Sch 16 para 5(4); FA 2008, Sch 39 para 59; FA 2009, s 105(1)–(3); SI 2009 No 403*].

Simon's Taxes. See E3.152, E3.153.

Example

[28.20]

In June 2011, Mr Jones, the investor in **28.9** above, sells 38,100 ordinary £1 shares in C Ltd (see **28.9** above), in an arm's length transaction, for £90,000. The position is as follows.

Income tax
2009/10   £

Relief attributable to 13,300 shares treated as issued in 2009/10:

13,300 shares at £2 per share = £26,600 @ 20%   5,320

$$\text{Consideration received}\left(\frac{13,300}{38,100}\times £90,000\right)=£31,417 \text{ @ } 20\%$$

                                                                                                                     6,283
Excess of tax at the EIS rate on consideration over relief   £963
Relief withdrawn by assessment   £5,320

2010/11   £

Relief attributable to 500 shares

Income tax

500/1,500 × £172   57

Consideration received

$$\left(\frac{500}{38,100} \times £90,000\right) = £1,181 \times 57/(1,000 @ 20\%) = £337 @ 20\%$$

                                                                                67

Excess of tax at the EIS rate on adjusted consideration over relief   £10

Relief withdrawn by assessment   £57

Capital gains tax

2011/12	£	£
Disposal proceeds (38,100 shares)		90,000
Cost: 24,300 shares acquired May 2008	32,400	
13,800 shares acquired June 2010	27,600	60,000
Chargeable gain		£30,000

Notes

(a)   For both income tax and capital gains tax purposes, a disposal is matched with acquisitions on a first in/first out basis (see **28.11** above and Tolley's Capital Gains Tax). Thus, the 38,100 shares sold in June 2011 are matched with 24,300 shares purchased in May 2008 and with 13,800 of the 14,800 EIS shares subscribed for in June 2010. For these purposes, 13,300 of the EIS shares are treated as having been issued in 2009/10 (by virtue of Mr Jones' carry-back claim — see **28.9** above). Therefore, those shares are treated as disposed of in priority to those on which relief was given in 2010/11.
Following the disposal, Mr Jones is left with 1,000 shares in C Ltd acquired in June 2010 for £2,000, to which the EIS relief attributable is £115 (172 – 57).

(b)   EIS relief is withdrawn if shares are disposed of before the end of the requisite three-year period. In this example, relief attributable to the shares sold is fully withdrawn as consideration received, reduced as illustrated, exceeds the relief attributable. See below for where the reverse applies. The consideration is reduced where the relief attributable (A) is less than tax at the EIS rate of 20% on the amount subscribed (B), and is so reduced by applying the fraction A/B. See **28.11** above.

(c)   Relief is withdrawn by means of an assessment for the year(s) in which relief was given (see **28.19** above).

(d)   The capital gain on the disposal is fully chargeable as the EIS shares are not held for the requisite three-year period (see Tolley's Capital Gains Tax).

In December 2011 Mr Jones disposes of his 37,500 ordinary £1 shares in D Ltd (see **28.9** above), in an arm's length transaction, for £30,000.

The position is as follows.

Income tax

2010/11	£
Relief attributable to shares sold	2,153
Consideration received:	

$$£30,000 \times \frac{2,153}{£37,500 \times 20\%} = £8,612 \text{ @ } 20\% \qquad \underline{1,722}$$

Excess of relief over tax at the EIS rate on adjusted consideration	<u>£431</u>
Relief withdrawn by assessment	<u>£1,722</u>

Capital gains tax

2011/12	£	£
Disposal proceeds (December 2011)		30,000
Cost (November 2010)	37,500	
Less Relief attributable to shares		
£2,153 – £1,722	431	<u>37,069</u>
Allowable loss		<u>£7,069</u>

Notes

(a)   The EIS relief withdrawn is limited to tax at the EIS rate of 20% on the consideration received, reduced as illustrated. If the disposal had been made otherwise than by way of a bargain made at arm's length, the full relief would have been withdrawn. See **28.11** above.

(b)   An allowable loss may arise for capital gains tax purposes on a disposal of EIS shares, whether or not the disposal occurs within the requisite three-year period. In computing such a loss, the allowable cost is reduced by EIS relief attributable to the shares (and not withdrawn). See Tolley's Capital Gains Tax.

(c)   A loss, as computed for capital gains tax purposes, may be relieved against income on a claim (see **45.25** LOSSES).

Married persons and civil partners

[28.21] The provisions for withdrawal of relief on the disposal of shares in respect of which relief has been given (see **28.11** above) do not apply to transfers between spouses or civil partners living together. On any subsequent disposal or other event, the spouse or partner to whom the shares were so transferred is treated as if:

- he or she were the person who subscribed for the shares;
- the amount he or she subscribed for the shares were the same amount as subscribed by the transferor spouse or partner;
- his or her liability to income tax had been reduced in respect of the shares by the same amount, and for the same tax year, as applied on the subscription by the transferor spouse or partner; and
- that amount of EIS income tax relief had continued to be attributable to the shares despite the transfer.

Where the amount of EIS relief attributable to the shares had been reduced before the relief was obtained by the transferor spouse or partner, the transferee is treated as if his or her relief had been correspondingly reduced before it was obtained (but this does not prevent the gross relief before reduction being used for the purposes of the calculations at **28.11**, **28.13**(c) and **28.15**(4) above).

Any assessment for reducing or withdrawing relief is made on the transferee spouse or partner. The identification rules for disposals at **28.11** above apply to determine the extent (if any) to which shares to which relief is attributable are comprised in the transfer.

[*ITA 2007, ss 209(4), 245, 246(1); ICTA 1988, s 304*].

EIS company becoming wholly-owned subsidiary of new holding company

[28.22] Where a company (Company A) has issued shares under the enterprise investment scheme (a certificate having been issued on Form EIS 3 — see **28.7** above) and subsequently, by means of an exchange of shares, all of its shares (the old shares) are acquired by a company (Company B) in which the only previously issued shares are subscriber shares, then, subject to the further conditions below being satisfied, the exchange is not regarded as involving a disposal of the old shares (and a consequent withdrawal of relief) and an acquisition of the Company B shares (the new shares). EIS relief attributable to the old shares is regarded as attributable instead to the new shares for which they are exchanged. For EIS purposes generally, the new shares stand in the shoes of the old shares, e.g. as if they had been subscribed for and issued at the time the old shares were subscribed for and issued and as if anything done by or in relation to Company A had been done by or in relation to Company B.

The further conditions are as follows.

(a) The consideration for the old shares must consist entirely of the issue of the new shares.

(b) The consideration for old shares of each description must consist entirely of new shares of the 'corresponding description'.

(c) New shares of each description must be issued to holders of old shares of the 'corresponding description' in respect of and in proportion to their holdings.

(d) Before the issue of the new shares, on the written application (for which see **4.5 ANTI-AVOIDANCE**) of either Company A or Company B, HMRC must have notified to that company their satisfaction that the exchange:

    (i)   is for genuine commercial reasons; and

    (ii)   does not form part of a scheme or arrangements designed to avoid liability to corporation tax or capital gains tax.

HMRC may, within 30 days of an application, request further particulars, which must then be supplied within 30 days of the request (or such longer period as they may allow in any particular case).

For the purposes of (b) and (c) above, old and new shares are of a '*corresponding description*' if, assuming they were shares in the same company, they would be of the same class and carry the same rights.

References above to 'shares' (other than those to 'shares issued under the enterprise investment scheme' or 'subscriber shares') include references to 'securities'.

An exchange within these provisions does not breach the control and independence requirement at **28.42** below.

[*ITA 2007, ss 247–249; ICTA 1988, s 304A; TCGA 1992, s 138(2); FA 2007, Sch 16 para 11(2)(8)*].

Simon's Taxes. See E3.121.

Capital gains tax

[28.23] In determining the gain or loss on a disposal of shares to which any income tax relief is attributable (see **28.6** above):

(a)   if a loss would otherwise arise, the consideration the individual is treated as having given for the shares is treated as reduced by the amount of the relief;

(b)   if the disposal is after the end of 'period A' and a gain would otherwise arise, the gain is not a chargeable gain (although this does not prevent a loss arising in these circumstances from being an allowable loss). Where the reduction in liability in respect of the issue of the shares was less than the amount corresponding to income tax at the EIS rate on the amount subscribed for the shares (other than because there is insufficient income tax liability to make full use of the relief), there is a corresponding reduction in the amount of the gain which is not chargeable.

'*Period A*' for this purpose is broadly the three years beginning with the date the shares are issued or, if later and where relevant, the date of commencement of the intended trade referred to in **28.49**(a) below. See **28.35** below.

Where a gain (or part of a gain) on a disposal is not a chargeable gain under (b) above, but the income tax relief on the shares disposed of is reduced on account of value received from the company by the claimant or by other persons (see **28.12–28.15**) before the disposal, then a corresponding proportion of the gain is brought back into charge.

The identification rules at **28.11** above apply for the above purposes.

See further *TCGA 1992, ss 150A, 150B*. For full coverage, see the corresponding chapter of Tolley's Capital Gains Tax.

Simon's Taxes. See **C3.10, E3.101.**

Capital gains deferral relief

[28.24] A chargeable gain can be deferred to the extent that it could be matched with an investment in EIS shares to which income tax relief was attributable (see **28.6** above).

It is not a requirement that the EIS shares qualify for income tax relief nor that the individual be unconnected with the company. However, the company itself must be a qualifying company (as in **28.38** below) and certain other EIS income tax relief conditions are adopted. The provisions are also extended to trustees. There is no limit on the amount of the gain that can be deferred, but the gross assets requirement at **28.43** below does limit the amount that may be invested in any one EIS company (or group).

Deferral relief applies where:

- a chargeable gain would otherwise accrue to an individual on the disposal by him of any asset;
- the individual makes a 'qualifying investment'; and
- the individual is UK resident or ordinarily resident both when the chargeable gain accrues to him and when he makes the qualifying investment, and is not, at the time he makes the investment, regarded as resident outside the UK for the purposes of any double taxation arrangements the effect of which would be that he would not be liable to tax on a gain arising on a disposal, immediately after their acquisition, of the shares comprising the qualifying investment, disregarding any exemption available under *TCGA 1992, s 150A* (see **28.23** above).

Subject to the further conditions referred to above, a '*qualifying investment*' is a subscription for shares within **28.27**(i) below (broadly, ordinary, non-preferential, shares) in a qualifying EIS company which are issued within the one year immediately preceding or the three years immediately following the time the chargeable gain in question accrues. These time limits may be extended by HMRC in individual cases. If the shares are issued *before* the gain accrues, they must still be held at the time it accrues. The deferred gain is brought back into charge on the occurrence of (and at the time of) any one of a number of specified chargeable events, in particular the disposal (at any time) of the shares in question.

For disposals on or after 23 June 2010, the gain on which (or part of the gain on which) attracts CGT entrepreneurs' relief and thus a CGT rate of 10%, the individual may claim the entrepreneurs' relief and pay tax at 10% or defer the gain (or that part of the gain) as above and pay a higher rate of tax (as in **12.3** CAPITAL GAINS TAX when it later comes into charge.

[*TCGA 1992, s 150C, Sch 5B; ITA 2007, Sch 1 para 345; FA 2007, Sch 16 paras 7, 8; FA 2009, Sch 8 paras 1–5, 11, 12; F(No 2)A 2010, Sch 1 paras 9, 14; SI 2008 No 954, arts 1, 18*].

The above is intended as a brief summary only. For full coverage, see the corresponding chapter of Tolley's Capital Gains Tax.

Simon's Taxes. See C3.10.

Notification requirements and information powers

[28.25] Certain events leading to withdrawal or reduction of income tax relief must be notified to HMRC, generally within 60 days, by either the individual who received the relief, the issuing company, or any person connected with the issuing company having knowledge of the matter. An HMRC officer may require such a notice and other relevant information where he has reason to believe it should have been made.

It should be noted that:

• the notification requirement extends to cases where income tax relief would have fallen to be withdrawn or reduced were it not for the 'replacement value' rules at **28.14** above; and in all cases a notice under these provisions should include details of any such replacement value received (or expected to be received) where this is within the knowledge of the person giving the notice; and

• HMRC's powers extend to cases where notice would have been required were it not for 'value received', or a repayment, redemption etc. of share capital, being of an insignificant amount (see **28.12, 28.15** above), and they may require notice and other information from persons giving or receiving such value or making or receiving such a repayment etc.

The penalty provisions of *TMA 1970, s 98* apply for failure to comply with the notification requirements.

HMRC also have broad powers to require information in other cases where relief may be withdrawn, restricted or not due. The obligations of secrecy do not prevent HMRC disclosing to a company that relief has been given or claimed on certain of its shares.

[*ITA 2007, ss 240–244, Sch 1 para 260; ICTA 1988, s 310*].

Simon's Taxes. See E3.155.

General requirements

[28.26] The general requirements mentioned at **28.1** above are described at **28.27–28.33** below.

The shares requirement

[28.27] The shares must:

(i) be ordinary shares which, throughout 'period B', carry no present or future preferential right to dividends or to assets on a winding-up and no present or future right to be redeemed; and

(ii)   unless they are 'bonus shares', be subscribed for wholly in cash and be fully paid up at the time of issue.

For the purposes of (ii) above, '*bonus shares*' are shares issued otherwise than for payment (whether in cash or otherwise). Shares are not fully paid up if there is any undertaking to pay cash to any person at a later date in respect of the acquisition.

For the purposes of (i) above, '*period B*' is the three years beginning with the date of issue. If the company satisfied the purpose of the issue requirement at **28.29** below by virtue of **28.49**(a) below and the trade had not yet commenced on the issue date, period B is the period from date of issue to immediately before the third anniversary of commencement. (In determining for this purpose the time at which a qualifying trade begins to be carried on by any 'qualifying 90% subsidiary' (see **28.48** below) of a company, any carrying on of the trade etc. by it before it became such a subsidiary is disregarded.)

[*ITA 2007, ss 159(3), 173, 256, 257(1); ICTA 1988, ss 289(1)(7)–(8A), 312(1)–(1A)*].

For the date on which shares are issued, see *National Westminster Bank plc v CIR; Barclays Bank plc v CIR* HL 1994, 67 TC 1.

The 'maximum amount raised' requirement

[28.28] In relation to shares issued on or after 19 July 2007, otherwise than to an approved fund (see **28.2** above) that closed before that date, the total amount of 'relevant investments' made in the issuing company in the twelve months ending with the date of issue must not exceed £2 million. Relevant investments in any company that was a subsidiary of the issuing company at any time in those twelve months also count towards this limit (regardless of whether or not it was a subsidiary when the investment was made). '*Relevant investments*' comprise:

(a)   investments (of any kind) made by a VENTURE CAPITAL TRUST (VCT) (**76**); and
(b)   money subscribed for shares issued by the investee company under the EIS or the Corporate Venturing Scheme (CVS) (see Tolley's Corporation Tax).

As regards (a) above, an investment is disregarded for these purposes if it was made before 6 April 2007 or if was an investment of money raised by the issue of shares or securities in the VCT before that date or money derived from the investment by the VCT of any such money.

As regards (b) above, shares are treated as having been issued under the EIS or CVS if at any time the investee company provides an EIS compliance statement (see **28.7** above) or CVS equivalent in respect of those shares; an investment is regarded as made when the shares are issued. Shares are disregarded for these purposes if they were issued before 19 July 2007 or issued on or after that date to an approved fund that closed before that date.

[*ITA 2007, s 173A; FA 2007, Sch 16 paras 5(3)(5)(6), 8*].

The 'purpose of the issue' requirement

[28.29] The shares, other than any bonus shares, must be issued to raise money (i.e. cash, see *Thompson v Hart* Ch D 2000, 72 TC 543) for the purpose of a 'qualifying business activity' (see **28.49** below). [*ITA 2007, s 174; ICTA 1988, s 289(1)(b)*].

This requirement may be satisfied where money is raised to acquire shares in a company carrying on a 'qualifying trade' (see **28.50** below). Money used to meet the expenses of issuing the shares should be regarded as employed in the same way as the remainder of the money raised. Where the company obtains a listing, for example on the Alternative Investment Market, at the same time as it issues the shares, the use of money to meet the expenses of flotation is normally acceptable. (HMRC Venture Capital Schemes Manual VCM12070).

The requirement was held to be satisfied where the money raised was loaned to overseas subsidiaries for the purpose of enabling them to supply information and analysis for the purposes of the issuing company's business (*4Cast Ltd v Mitchell* (Sp C 455), [2005] SSCD 287).

The requirement is *not* satisfied if the money raised by the issue is used partly to pay dividends to investors (*Forthright (Wales) Ltd v A L Davies* Ch D 2004, 76 TC 138). The requirement was not satisfied where a company issued convertible loan notes which it subsequently converted into shares; the issue of the shares was not then for the purpose of raising money (*Optos plc v HMRC* (Sp C 560), [2006] SSCD 687). It *was* satisfied where the money raised was loaned to another company, subsequently repaid and a qualifying trade then acquired; the loan was a means of 'parking' the money until it was needed and was no different to placing it on deposit with a bank (*G C Trading Ltd v HMRC* (Sp C 630), [2008] SSCD 178).

The 'use of money raised' requirement

[28.30] For shares issued on or after 22 April 2009, all of the 'money raised' must be employed wholly (disregarding insignificant amounts) for the purpose of the qualifying business activity for which it was raised by the end of the two years following the issue. If the only qualifying business activity falls within **28.49**(a) below, the deadline is extended until the end of the two years starting when the company (or, where applicable, a subsidiary) begins to carry on the qualifying trade.

For shares issued before 22 April 2009, the 'money raised' had to be employed wholly (disregarding insignificant amounts) for the purpose of the qualifying business activity for which it was raised by the end of the 24 months following the issue. If the only qualifying business activity fell within **28.49**(a) below, the deadline was extended until the end of the 24 months starting when the company (or, where applicable, a subsidiary) began to carry on the qualifying trade. Additionally, 80% of that money had to be so employed within 12 months after the issue/commencement of trade.

For these purposes, the '*money raised*' means the money raised by the issue of the shares in question (other than any of them which are bonus shares issued after 16 March 2004) and any other shares in the company of the same class (as defined) which are within **28.27**(i) above and which are issued on the same day. In determining the time at which a qualifying trade begins to be carried on by a 'qualifying 90% subsidiary' of a company, any carrying on of the trade etc. by it before it became such a subsidiary is disregarded.

[*ITA 2007, ss 175, 257(5); ICTA 1988, ss 289(1)(3)(3A); FA 2007, Sch 26 para 12(5); FA 2009, Sch 8 paras 7, 11*].

Money whose retention can reasonably be regarded as necessary or advisable for financing current business requirements is regarded as employed for trade purposes (see HMRC Venture Capital Schemes Manual VCM12080).

This requirement is *not* satisfied if the money raised by the issue is used partly to pay dividends to investors (*Forthright (Wales) Ltd v A L Davies* Ch D 2004, 76 TC 138).

The 'minimum period' requirement

[28.31] The trade or the research and development must have been carried on for a period of at least four months ending at or after the time of the share issue. The trade etc. must have carried on for those months by no person other than the qualifying company or a 'qualifying 90% subsidiary' (see **28.48** below) of that company.

A period shorter than four months is permitted if this is by reason only of the winding-up or dissolution of any company or anything done as a consequence of a company being in administration or receivership, provided the winding-up etc. is for genuine commercial reasons and not part of a tax avoidance scheme or arrangements.

[*ITA 2007, s 176; ICTA 1988, s 289A(6)–(8A)*].

The 'no pre-arranged exits' requirement

[28.32] The arrangements (as very broadly defined) under which the shares are issued to the investor (or arrangements preceding the issue but in relation or in connection to it) must not:

(a)   provide for the eventual disposal by the investor of the shares in question or other shares or securities of the company; or

(b)   provide for the eventual cessation of a trade of the company or of a person connected with it; or

(c)   provide for the eventual disposal of all, or a substantial amount (in terms of value) of, the assets of the company or of a person connected with it; or

(d)   provide (by means of any insurance, indemnity, guarantee or otherwise) complete or partial protection for investors against the normal risks attaching to EIS investment (but excluding arrangements which merely protect the company and/or its subsidiaries against normal business risks).

Arrangements with a view to the company becoming a wholly-owned subsidiary of a new holding company within the terms of *ITA 2007, s 247(1)* (see **28.22** above) are excluded from (a) above. Arrangements applicable only on an unanticipated winding-up of the company for genuine commercial reasons are excluded from (b) and (c) above.

[*ITA 2007, ss 177, 257(1); ICTA 1988, ss 299B, 312(1)*].

Simon's Taxes. See **E3.101–E3.104**.

The 'no tax avoidance' requirement

[28.33] The shares must be issued for genuine commercial reasons and not as part of a scheme or arrangement a main purpose of which is the avoidance of tax. [*ITA 2007, s 178; ICTA 1988, s 289(6)*].

Qualifying investor

[28.34] An individual is a '*qualifying investor*' in relation to shares if the requirements at **28.35–28.37** are met.

The 'no connection with the issuing company' requirement

[28.35] The investor must not (except as below) be at any time in the period specified below 'connected with' the issuing company (whether before or after its incorporation) (i.e. there must be no such connection at any time in that period, see *Wild v Cannavan* CA 1997, 70 TC 554). The specified period is the period beginning two years before the issue of the shares and ending immediately before the third anniversary of the issue date or, if later and where relevant, the third anniversary of the date of commencement of the intended trade referred to in **28.49**(a) below

In determining the time at which a qualifying trade begins to be carried on by any 'qualifying 90% subsidiary' (see **28.48** below) of a company, any carrying on of the trade by it before it became such a subsidiary is disregarded.

[*ITA 2007, ss 163, 256; ICTA 1988, ss 291(1), 312(1)(1ZA)*].

An investor is '*connected with*' the issuing company if he, or an 'associate' of his, is either:

(a)   an employee, partner, or director of, or an employee or director of a partner of, the issuing company or any 'subsidiary'; or

(b)   an individual who directly or indirectly possesses or is entitled to acquire (whether he is so entitled at a future date or will at a future date be so entitled):

    (i)   more than 30% of the voting power, the issued ordinary share capital, or the loan capital and issued share capital of the issuing company or any 'subsidiary' (loan capital including any debt incurred by the company for money borrowed, for capital assets acquired, for any right to income created in its favour, or for insufficient consideration, but excluding a debt incurred for overdrawing a bank account in the ordinary course of the bank's business), or

(ii) such rights as would entitle him to more than 30% of the assets of the issuing company or any 'subsidiary' available for distribution to the company's equity holders (as under *CTA 2010, Pt 5 Ch 6* — see Tolley's Corporation Tax under Groups of Companies); or

(c) an individual who has control (as defined by *ITA 2007, s 995*) of the issuing company or any 'subsidiary'; or

(d) an individual who subscribes for shares in the issuing company as part of an arrangement providing for another person to subscribe for shares in another company with which, were that other company an issuing company, the individual (or any other individual party to the arrangement) would be connected as above.

Rights or powers of associates are taken into account as regards (b) and (c) above (see *Cook v Billings* CA, [2001] STC 16 on the similar wording under the earlier BES provisions). An *'associate'* of any person is any 'relative' (i.e. spouse, civil partner, ancestor or linear descendant) of that person, the trustee(s) of any settlement in relation to which that person or any relative (living or dead) is or was a settlor and, where that person has an interest in any shares of obligations of a company which are subject to any trust or are part of a deceased estate, the trustee(s) of the settlement or the personal representatives of the deceased. For this purpose, 'settlor' is defined as in **68.3 SETTLEMENTS.**

As regards (b)(i) above, an individual is not connected with the company by virtue only of the fact that he or an associate is a shareholder if at that time the company has issued no shares other than subscriber shares and has neither commenced business nor made preparations for doing so.

A *'subsidiary'* for these purposes is a company more than 50% of whose ordinary share capital is at any time in 'period A' owned by the issuing company, regardless of whether or not that condition is fulfilled while the individual falls within (a)–(d) above in respect of it.

'Period A' for this purpose is the period beginning with the incorporation of the company or, if later, two years before the date of issue of the shares and ending immediately before the third anniversary of the issue date or, if later and where relevant, the third anniversary of the date of commencement of the intended trade referred to in **28.49**(a) below

(In determining for this purpose the time at which a qualifying trade begins to be carried on by any 'qualifying 90% subsidiary' (see **28.48** below) of a company, any carrying on of the trade by it before it became such a subsidiary is disregarded.)

[*ITA 2007, ss 159(2), 166, 167(1)(2), 170, 171, 253, 256; ICTA 1988, ss 291(2)(3)(5), 291B, 312(1)–(1ZA), 417(3)(4); CTA 2010, Sch 1 para 499; SI 2007 No 1820, Reg 2*].

As regards (a) above, directorships are taken into account only where the individual or an associate (or a partnership of which either of them is a member) receives or is entitled to receive, during the specified period above, a payment (whether directly or indirectly or to his order or for his benefit) from the issuing company or a 'related person' other than by way of:

(A)   payment or reimbursement of allowable expenditure against employment income;
(B)   interest at no more than a commercial rate on money lent;
(C)   dividends etc. representing no more than a normal return on investment;
(D)   payment for supply of goods at no more than market value;
(E)   rent at no more than a reasonable and commercial rent for property occupied; or
(F)   any reasonable and necessary remuneration for services rendered (other than secretarial or managerial services, or those rendered by the payer) which is taken into account in computing the recipient's trading profits.

A '*related person*' is any company of which the individual or an associate is a director and which is a subsidiary or partner of the issuing company, or a partner of the issuing company or a subsidiary, or any person connected (within *ITA 2007, s 993* — see **21 CONNECTED PERSONS**) with such a company; 'subsidiary' for this purpose requiring ownership of more than 50% of ordinary share capital at some time in the specified period.

For these purposes (and those below), in the case of a person who is both a director and an employee of a company, references to him in his capacity as a director include him in his capacity as an employee, but otherwise he is not treated as an employee.

An individual who is connected with the issuing company may nevertheless qualify for relief if he is so connected only by reason of his (or his associate's) being a director of (or of a partner of) the issuing company or any subsidiary receiving, or entitled to receive, remuneration (including any benefit or facility) as such, provided that:

(I)   the remuneration (leaving out any within (F) above) is reasonable remuneration for services rendered to the company as a director;
(II)   he subscribed for shares in the company meeting the general requirements at **28.26** *et seq.* above at a time when he had never been either:
   (i)   connected with the issuing company; or
   (ii)   involved (as sole trader, employee, partner or director) in carrying on its (or its subsidiary's) trade, business or profession (or any part thereof).

Where these conditions are satisfied in relation to an issue of shares, subsequent issues are treated as fulfilling (II) where they would not otherwise do so, provided that they are made within three years of the date of the last issue which did fulfil (II). Where relevant, the said three-year period is replaced by a longer period beginning with the date of the last such issue and ending with the date of commencement of the intended trade referred to in **28.49**(a) below. (In determining for these purposes the time at which a qualifying trade begins to be carried on by any 'qualifying 90% subsidiary' (see **28.48** below) of a company, any carrying on of the trade by it before it became such a subsidiary is disregarded.) For examples of this 'business angels' exception, see HMRC Venture Capital Schemes Manual VCM25080.

[*ITA 2007, ss 167(3), 168, 169, 256; ICTA 1988, ss 291(5), 291A, 312(1)–(1ZA)*].

Simon's Taxes. See E3.106–E3.113.

The 'no linked loans' requirement

[28.36] No loan may be made to the investor or to an associate (see **28.35** above) at any time in period A (see **28.35** above) if it would not have been made, or would not have been made on the same terms, if the investor had not subscribed, or had not been proposing to subscribe, for the shares. The giving of credit to, or the assignment of a debt due from, the investor or associate is counted as a loan for these purposes. [*ITA 2007, s 164; ICTA 1988, s 299A*].

The test under this requirement is whether the lender makes the loan on terms which are connected with the fact that the borrower (or an associate) is subscribing for the shares. The prime concern is why the lender made the loan rather than why the borrower applied for it. The requirement would be met, for example, in the case of a bank loan if the bank would have made a loan on the same terms to a similar borrower for a different purpose. But if, for example, a loan is made specifically on a security consisting of or including the shares (other than as part of a broad range of assets to which the lender has recourse), the requirement would not be met. Relevant features of the loan terms would be the qualifying conditions to be satisfied by the borrower, any incentives or benefits offered to the borrower, the time allowed for repayment, the amount of repayments and interest charged, the timing of interest payments, and the nature of the security. (HMRC SP 6/98).

Simon's Taxes. See E3.149.

The 'no tax avoidance' requirement

[28.37] The shares must be subscribed for by the investor for genuine commercial reasons and not as part of a scheme or arrangement a main purpose of which is the avoidance of tax. [*ITA 2007, s 165; ICTA 1988, s 289(6)*].

Qualifying company

[28.38] The issuing company is a '*qualifying company*' in relation to the shares if the requirements at **28.39**–**28.46** below are met. The company may be resident in the UK or elsewhere.

'*Period B*' for these purposes is the period beginning with the date of issue of the shares and ending either three years after that date or, where **28.49**(a) below applies and the company (or subsidiary) was not carrying on the qualifying trade on that date, three years after the date on which it begins to carry on the trade. In determining for these purposes the time at which a qualifying trade begins to be carried on by any 'qualifying 90% subsidiary' (see **28.48** below) of a company, any carrying on of the trade by it before it became such a subsidiary is disregarded. [*ITA 2007, s 159(3); ICTA 1988, s 312(1A)*].

Simon's Taxes. See E3.115–E3.123.

The trading requirement

[28.39] The company must, throughout 'period B' (as in **28.38** above), either:

(a)   exist wholly for the purpose of carrying on one or more 'qualifying trades' (see **28.50** below) (disregarding purposes having no significant effect on the extent of its activities); or

(b)   be a *'parent company'* (i.e. a company that has one or more 'qualifying subsidiaries' (see **28.47** below)) and the business of the *'group'* (i.e. the company and its qualifying subsidiaries) must not consist wholly or as to a substantial part (i.e. broadly 20% — see HMRC Venture Capital Schemes Manual VCM17040) in the carrying on of 'non-qualifying activities'.

Where the company intends that one or more other companies should become its qualifying subsidiaries with a view to their carrying on one or more qualifying trades, then, until any time after which the intention is abandoned, the company is treated as a parent company and those other companies are included in the group for the purposes of (b) above. (This provision is made explicit in *ITA 2007* but reflects previous practice (see Change 42 listed in Annex 1 to the Explanatory Notes to *ITA 2007*).)

For the purpose of (b) above, the business of the group means what would be the business of the group if the activities of the group companies taken together were regarded as one business. Activities are for this purpose disregarded to the extent that they consist in:

(i)   holding shares in or securities of any of the company's subsidiaries;
(ii)   making loans to another group company;
(iii)   holding and managing property used by a group company for the purposes of a qualifying trade or trades carried on by any group company; or
(iv)   holding and managing property used by a group company for the purposes of research and development from which it is intended either that a qualifying trade to be carried on by a group company will be derived or, for shares issued after 5 April 2007, a qualifying trade carried on or to be carried on by a group company will benefit.

References in (iv) above to a group company include references to any existing or future company which will be a group company at any future time.

Activities are similarly disregarded to the extent that they consist, in the case of a subsidiary whose main purpose is the carrying on of qualifying trade(s) and whose other purposes have no significant effect on the extent of its activities (other than in relation to incidental matters), in activities not in pursuance of its main purpose.

'Non-qualifying activities' are:

(I)   excluded activities within **28.50**; and
(II)   non-trading activities (not including research and development — see **28.49** below).

[*ITA 2007, ss 181, 257(1); ICTA 1988, s 293(2)(3A)–(3E)*].

For the ascertainment of the purposes for which a company exists, see HMRC Venture Capital Schemes Manual VCM15070.

Although a winding-up or dissolution in period B generally prevents a company meeting the above conditions, they are deemed met if the winding-up or dissolution is for genuine commercial reasons and not part of a scheme a main purpose of which is tax avoidance. A company does not cease to meet the above conditions by reason of anything done as a consequence of its being in administration or receivership (both as defined by *ITA 2007, s 252*), provided everything so done and the making of the relevant order are for genuine commercial (and not tax avoidance) reasons. These provisions are extended to refer also to the winding-up, dissolution, administration or receivership of any of the company's subsidiaries. [*ITA 2007, s 182; ICTA 1988, s 293(4A)–(6)(8A)*].

The 'issuing company to carry on the qualifying business activity' requirement

[28.40] At no time in period B (as in **28.38** above) must any of the following be carried on by a person other than the issuing company' or a 'qualifying 90% subsidiary' (see **28.48** below) of that company:

- the *'relevant qualifying trade'*, i.e. the 'qualifying trade' which is the subject of the 'qualifying business activity' referred to in **28.29** above;
- *'relevant preparation work'*, i.e. preparations to carry on a 'qualifying trade' where such preparations are the subject of that qualifying business activity (see **28.49**(a) below);
- research and development which is the subject of that qualifying business activity (see **28.49**(b) below); and
- any other preparations for the carrying on of the qualifying trade.

Where relevant preparation work is carried on by the issuing company or a qualifying 90% subsidiary, the carrying on of the relevant 'qualifying trade' by a company other than the issuing company or one of its subsidiaries is disregarded for these purposes if it occurs before the issuing company or a qualifying 90% subsidiary carries on that trade.

This requirement is not regarded as failing to be met if, by reason only of a company being wound up or dissolved or being in administration or receivership (both as defined by *ITA 2007, s 252*), the relevant qualifying trade ceases to be carried on in period B by the issuing company or any qualifying 90% subsidiary and is subsequently carried on by a person who is not connected (within **21 CONNECTED PERSONS**) with the company at any time in 'period C'. This let-out applies only if the winding-up, dissolution or entry into administration or receivership (and everything done as a consequence of the company being in administration or receivership) is for genuine commercial reasons and not part of a tax avoidance scheme or arrangements.

'Period C' is the period beginning one year before the issue of eligible shares and ending immediately before the third anniversary of the issue date or, if later and where relevant, the third anniversary of the date of commencement of the intended trade referred to in **28.49**(a) below. In determining for these

purposes the time at which a qualifying trade begins to be carried on by any qualifying 90% subsidiary (see **28.48** below) of a company, any carrying on of the trade by it before it became such a subsidiary is disregarded.

HMRC have revised their view of how the above requirement has effect in relation to partnerships. In contrast to their earlier view, they now consider that the requirement is not met where the relevant qualifying trade, preparation work or research and development is carried on by the company in partnership or by a limited liability partnership (LLP) of which the company is a member. This is because where any of these activities are carried on in partnership or by an LLP, there are persons other than the issuing company or a qualifying 90% subsidiary carrying on the activity. HMRC will apply this revised view in relation to shares issued after 9 December 2009. They will also apply it to shares issued on or before that date where they have not by that date authorised the issue of the compliance certificate in **28.7** above; the only exception is where, in full knowledge of the facts, they gave an advance assurance on or before 9 December 2009 that the share issue would qualify under the EIS. (HMRC Brief 77/09, 16 December 2009).

[ITA 2007, ss 159(4), 183; ICTA 1988, s 289(1A)–(1E)(9), s 312(1); SI 2007 No 1820, reg 2].

The 'unquoted status' requirement

[28.41] The issuing company must be 'unquoted' when the shares are issued and no arrangements must then exist for it to cease to be unquoted. If, at the time of issue, arrangements exist for the company to become a wholly-owned subsidiary of a new holding company by means of a share exchange within **28.22** above, no arrangements must exist for the new company to cease to be unquoted. A company is *'unquoted'* if none of its shares etc. are listed on a recognised stock exchange or on a foreign exchange designated for the purpose, or dealt in outside the UK by such means as may be designated for the purpose. Securities on the Alternative Investment Market ('AIM') are generally treated as unquoted for these purposes. (Revenue Press Release 20 February 1995; HMRC Internet Statement 29 March 2007 at www.hmrc.gov.uk/budg et2007/rec-stock-exch.htm). If the company is unquoted at the time of the share issue, it does not cease to be unquoted in relation to those shares solely because they are listed on an exchange which becomes a recognised stock exchange or is designated by an order made after the date of the issue (see HMRC Venture Capital Schemes Manual VCM15020).

[ITA 2007, ss 184, 989, 1005; ICTA 1988, ss 293(1A)(1B)(8A), 312(1)(1B)(1C); FA 2007, Sch 26 para 12(4)(12)].

The control and independence requirement

[28.42] The issuing company must not at any time in period B (as in **28.38** above) either:

(a)   (subject to **28.22** above) control another company other than a qualifying subsidiary (see **28.47** below), 'control' being construed in accordance with *CTA 2010, ss 450, 451* and being considered with or without **CONNECTED PERSONS (21)**; or

(b)   (subject to **28.22** above) be a 51% subsidiary of another company or otherwise under the control of another company, 'control' being construed in accordance with *ITA 2007, s 995* and again being considered with or without connected persons; or

(c)   be capable of falling within (a) or (b) by virtue of any arrangements (as very broadly defined).

[*ITA 2007, ss 185, 257(3); ICTA 1988, ss 293(8)–(8A), 312(1); CTA 2010, Sch 1 para 503; SI 2007 No 1820, reg 2*].

The gross assets requirement

[28.43] The value of the issuing company's gross assets must not exceed £7 million immediately before the issue of EIS shares and must not exceed £8 million immediately afterwards. In relation to shares issued before 6 April 2006, these limits were £15 million and £16 million respectively; the higher limits continue to apply in relation to: (i) shares issued after 5 April 2006 to a person who subscribed for them before 22 March 2006; and (ii) shares issued at any time to the managers of an approved investment fund as nominee for an individual (see **28.2** above) where the fund was approved before 22 March 2006 and accepted investments before 6 April 2006. If the issuing company is a parent company, the gross assets test applies by reference to the aggregate gross assets of the company and all its qualifying subsidiaries (disregarding certain assets held by any such company which correspond to liabilities of another). [*ITA 2007, s 186, Sch 2 para 58; ICTA 1988, s 293(6A)–(6C); FA 2006, Sch 14 para 1*].

The general approach of HMRC to the gross assets requirement is that the value of a company's gross assets is the sum of the value of all of the balance sheet assets. Where accounts are actually drawn up to a date immediately before or after the issue, the balance sheet values are taken provided that they reflect usual accounting standards and the company's normal accounting practice, consistently applied. Where accounts are not drawn up to such a date, such values will be taken from the most recent balance sheet, updated as precisely as practicable on the basis of all the relevant information available to the company. Values so arrived at may need to be reviewed in the light of information contained in the accounts for the period in which the issue was made, and, if they were not available at the time of the issue, those for the preceding period, when they become available. The company's assets immediately before the issue do not include any advance payment received in respect of the issue. Where shares are issued partly paid, the right to the balance is an asset, and, notwithstanding the above, will be taken into account in valuing the assets immediately after the issue regardless of whether it is shown in the balance sheet. (HMRC SP 2/00).

The 'number of employees' requirement

[28.44] In relation to shares issued on or after 19 July 2007, otherwise than to an approved fund (see **28.2** above) that closed before that date, the issuing company must have fewer than the equivalent of 50 full-time employees when the EIS shares are issued. If the company is a parent company (see **28.39**(b) above), this rule applies by reference to the aggregate number of full-time employees of itself and its qualifying subsidiaries (see **28.47** below). To ascertain the equivalent number of full-time employees of a company, take the actual number of full-time employees and add to it a just and reasonable fraction for each employee who is not full-time. For this purpose, an 'employee' includes a director but does not include anyone on maternity or paternity leave or a student on vocational training. [*ITA 2007, s 186A; FA 2007, Sch 16 para 2(3)–(5)*].

The subsidiaries requirements

[28.45] At any time in period B (as in **28.38** above) any subsidiary of the issuing company must be a 'qualifying subsidiary' (see **28.47** below). [*ITA 2007, s 187; ICTA 1988, ss 293(3A), 308(1)(5A)*].

The company must not at any time in period B have a 'property managing subsidiary' which is not a 'qualifying 90% subsidiary' (see **28.48** below) of the company. A *'property managing subsidiary'* is a subsidiary whose business consists wholly or mainly in the holding or managing of land or any 'property deriving its value from land'. For this purpose, *'property deriving its value from land'* includes any shareholding in a company, any partnership interest or interest in settled property, which derives its value directly or indirectly from land and any option, consent or embargo affecting the disposition of land. [*ITA 2007, s 188; ICTA 1988, s 293(6ZA)–(6ZC)(8A)*].

The financial health requirement (prospective)

[28.46] This is a prospective requirement which, when introduced, must be met at the beginning of period B (as in **28.38** above). The requirement is that the issuing company is not 'in difficulty'. A company is *'in difficulty'* if it is reasonable to assume that it would be regarded as an enterprise in difficulty for the purposes of the EC *Guidelines on State Aid for Rescuing and Restructuring Firms in Difficulty (2004/C 244/02)*. The legislation is to be included in a Finance Bill to be introduced in autumn 2010 and will have effect on and after a date to be appointed. (HMRC Budget Note BN11, 22 June 2010).

Qualifying subsidiaries

[28.47] In order to be a *'qualifying subsidiary'* a subsidiary must be a '51% subsidiary' (within *CTA 2010, Pt 24 Ch 3*) of the qualifying company and no person other than the qualifying company or another of its subsidiaries may have control (within *ITA 2007, s 995*) of the subsidiary. Furthermore, no arrangements (as very broadly defined) may exist by virtue of which either of these conditions would cease to be satisfied.

However, the above conditions are not regarded as ceasing to be satisfied by reason only of the subsidiary or any other company being wound up or dissolved or by reason only of anything done as a consequence of any such company being in administration or receivership (both as defined by *ITA 2007, s 252*), provided the winding-up, dissolution, entry into administration or receivership or anything done as a consequence of its being in administration or receivership is for genuine commercial reasons and is not part of a tax avoidance scheme or arrangements. Also, the above conditions are not regarded as ceasing to be satisfied by reason only of arrangements being in existence for the disposal of the interest in the subsidiary held by the qualifying company (or, as the case may be, by another of its subsidiaries) if the disposal is to be for genuine commercial reasons and is not to be part of a tax avoidance scheme or arrangements.

[*ITA 2007, ss 191, 989; ICTA 1988, ss 308, 312(1); CTA 2010, Sch 1 para 562(8); SI 2007 No 1820, reg 2*].

Simon's Taxes. See **E3.117A, E3.117B.**

Qualifying 90% subsidiaries

[28.48] A company (the subsidiary) is a '*qualifying 90% subsidiary*' of another company (the relevant company) if:

- the relevant company possesses at least 90% of both the issued share capital of, and the voting power in, the subsidiary;
- the relevant company would be beneficially entitled to at least 90% of the assets of the subsidiary available for distribution to equity holders on a winding-up or in any other circumstances;
- the relevant company is beneficially entitled to at least 90% of any profits of the subsidiary available for distribution to equity holders;
- no person other than the relevant company has control (within *ITA 2007, s 995*) of the subsidiary; and
- no arrangements (as very broadly defined) exist by virtue of which any of the above conditions would cease to be met.

For the above purposes, *CTA 2010, Pt 5 Ch 6* applies, with appropriate modifications, to determine the persons who are equity holders and the percentage of assets available to them.

The above conditions are not regarded as ceasing to be satisfied by reason only of the subsidiary or any other company being wound up or dissolved or by reason only of anything done as a consequence of any such company being in administration or receivership (both as defined by *ITA 2007, s 252*), provided the winding-up, dissolution, entry into administration or receivership or anything done as a consequence of its being in administration or receivership is for genuine commercial reasons and is not part of a tax avoidance scheme or arrangements. Also, the above conditions are not regarded as ceasing to be satisfied by reason only of arrangements being in existence for the disposal of the relevant company's interest in the subsidiary if the disposal is to be for genuine commercial reasons and is not to be part of a tax avoidance scheme or arrangements.

With effect on and after 6 April 2007, a company ('company A') which is a subsidiary of company B is a qualifying 90% subsidiary of company C if:

- company A is a qualifying 90% subsidiary of company B, and company B is a 'qualifying 100% subsidiary' of company C; or
- company A is a 'qualifying 100% subsidiary' of company B, and company B is a qualifying 90% subsidiary of company C.

For this purpose, no account is to be taken of any control company C may have of company A, and *'qualifying 100% subsidiary'* is defined similarly to 'qualifying 90% subsidiary' above but substituting '100%' for '90%'.

[ITA 2007, s 190; ICTA 1988, ss 289(9)–(13), 312(1); FA 2007, Sch 16 paras 16, 18; CTA 2010, Sch 1 para 500; SI 2007 No 1820, Reg 2].

Simon's Taxes. See E3.117B.

Qualifying business activity

[28.49] Either of the following is a *'qualifying business activity'* in relation to the issuing company.

(a) The issuing company or any 'qualifying 90% subsidiary' (see **28.48** above) (i) carrying on a 'qualifying trade' which, on the date of issue of the shares, the company or any such subsidiary is carrying on or (ii) preparing to carry on such a trade which, on the date of issue of the shares, is intended to be carried on 'wholly or mainly in the UK' (but see below) by the company or any such subsidiary and which is begun to be so carried on within two years after that date or (iii) actually carrying on the trade mentioned in (ii) above; provided that, at any time in period B (as in **28.38** above) when the qualifying trade is so carried on, it is carried on wholly or mainly in the UK.

(b) The issuing company or any 'qualifying 90% subsidiary' (see **28.48** above) carrying on 'research and development' which, on the date of issue of the shares, the company or any such subsidiary is carrying on or which company or any such subsidiary begins to carry on immediately afterwards, and from which it is intended on that date that a 'qualifying trade' which the company or any such subsidiary will carry on 'wholly or mainly in the UK' either will be derived or, for shares issued after 5 April 2007, will benefit; provided that, at any time in period B (as in **28.38** above) when the research and development or the qualifying trade derived or benefiting from it is carried on, it is carried on wholly or mainly in the UK.

In determining for the purposes of (a) and (b) above the time at which a qualifying trade or research and development begins to be carried on by a qualifying 90% subsidiary of the issuing company, any carrying on of the trade etc. by it before it became such a subsidiary is disregarded. References in (a) and (b) above to a qualifying 90% subsidiary include, in cases where the qualifying trade is not carried on at the time of issue of the shares, references to any exiting or future company which will be such a subsidiary at any future time.

'*Research and development*' in (b) above has the meaning given by *ITA 2007, s 1006* (see **73.109** TRADING INCOME.

[*ITA 2007, ss 179, 257(1); ICTA 1988, ss 289(2)(3A)(4)(5)(8), 312(1)(1A)(b)(1ZA); SI 2007 No 1820, Reg 2*].

As regards (a) above, 'preparing' to carry on a trade covers both the setting up of a new trade and the acquisition of an existing trade from its present owner. It does not cover preliminary activities such as market research aimed at discovering whether a trade would be likely to succeed or raising capital or research and development. (HMRC Venture Capital Schemes Manual VCM20030).

In considering whether a trade is carried on '*wholly or mainly in the UK*', the totality of the trade activities is taken into account. Regard will be had, for example, to where capital assets are held, where any purchasing, processing, manufacturing and selling is done, and where the company employees and other agents are engaged in its trading operations. For trades involving the provision of services, both the location of the activities giving rise to the services and the location where they are delivered will be relevant. No one factor is itself likely to be decisive in any particular case. A company may carry on some such activities outside the UK and yet satisfy the requirement, provided that the major part of them, that is over one-half of the aggregate of these activities, takes place within the UK. Thus relief is not excluded solely because a company's products or services are exported, or because its raw materials are imported, or because its raw materials or products are stored abroad. Similar principles apply in considering the trade(s) carried on by a company and its qualifying subsidiaries.

In the particular case of a ship chartering trade, the test is satisfied if all charters are entered into in the UK and the provision of crews and management of the ships while under charter take place mainly in the UK. If these conditions are not met, the test may still be satisfied depending on all the relevant facts and circumstances.

(HMRC SP 3/00).

The 'wholly or mainly in the UK' requirement is to be dropped and replaced by a requirement that the company must have a permanent establishment in the UK. The legislation is to be included in a Finance Bill to be introduced in autumn 2010 and will have effect in relation to shares issued on and after a date to be appointed. (HMRC Budget Note BN11, 22 June 2010).

For the manner in which the scheme operates where a company wishes to raise money by a single issue of shares either partly for preparing to carry on a trade and partly for the subsequent carrying on of that trade, or for more than one qualifying business activity (e.g. for a trade carried on by one subsidiary and for research and development carried on by another), see Revenue Tax Bulletin April 1996 pp 305, 306.

Simon's Taxes. See **E3.125–E3.134.**

Qualifying trade

[28.50] A trade is a *'qualifying trade'* if it is conducted on a commercial basis with a view to the realisation of profits and it does not, at any time in period B (as in **28.38** above), consist to a substantial extent in the carrying on of 'excluded activities'. For these purposes, 'trade' (except in relation to the trade mentioned in (m) below) does not include a venture in the nature of trade. *'Excluded activities'* are:

(a)   dealing in land, commodities or futures, or in shares, securities or other financial instruments; or

(b)   dealing in goods otherwise than in an ordinary trade of wholesale or retail distribution (see below); or

(c)   banking, insurance or any other financial activities; or

(d)   leasing or letting or receiving royalties or licence fees; or

(e)   providing legal or accountancy services; or

(f)   'property development';

(g)   farming or market gardening;

(h)   holding, managing or occupying woodlands, any other forestry activities or timber production;

(i)   (in relation to shares issued after 5 April 2008) shipbuilding (defined by reference to relevant EU State aid rules);

(j)   (in relation to shares issued after 5 April 2008) producing coal or steel (both defined by reference to relevant EU State aid rules and including the extraction of coal);

(k)   operating or managing hotels or comparable establishments (i.e. guest houses, hostels and other establishments whose main purpose is to offer overnight accommodation with or without catering) or property used as such;

(l)   operating or managing nursing homes or residential care homes (both as defined) or property used as such;

(m)   providing services or facilities for any trade, profession or vocation concerned in (a) to (l) and carried on by another person (other than a parent company), where one person has a 'controlling interest' in both trades.

HMRC regard as 'substantial' for the above purposes a part of a trade which consists of 20% or more of total activities, judged by any reasonable measure (normally turnover or capital employed) (HMRC Venture Capital Schemes Manual VCM17040). As regards (a) above, dealing in land includes cases where steps are taken, before selling the land, to make it more attractive to a purchaser; such steps might include the refurbishment of existing buildings (HMRC Venture Capital Schemes Manual VCM17050).

As regards (b) above, a trade of wholesale distribution is a trade consisting of the offer of goods for sale either to persons for resale (or processing and resale) (which resale must be to members of the general public for their use or consumption) by them. A trade of retail distribution is a trade in which goods are offered or exposed for sale and sold to members of the general public for their use or consumption. A trade is not an ordinary wholesale or retail trade if it consists to a substantial extent of dealing in goods collected or held as an investment (or of that and any other activity within (a)–(m) above), and a substantial proportion of such goods is held for a significantly longer period than would reasonably be expected for a vendor trying to dispose of them at market value. Whether such trades are 'ordinary' is to be judged having regard to the following features, those under (A) supporting the categorisation as 'ordinary', those under (B) being indicative to the contrary.

(A)

    (i)   The breaking of bulk.

    (ii)   The purchase and sale of goods in different markets.

    (iii)   The employment of staff and incurring of trade expenses other than the cost of goods or of remuneration of persons connected (within **21 CONNECTED PERSONS**) with a company carrying on such a trade.

(B)

    (i)   The purchase or sale of goods from or to persons connected (within **21 CONNECTED PERSONS**) with the trader.

    (ii)   The matching of purchases with sales.

    (iii)   The holding of goods for longer than would normally be expected.

    (iv)   The carrying on of the trade at a place not commonly used for wholesale or retail trading.

    (v)   The absence of physical possession of the goods by the trader.

As regards the application of (d) above, a trade is not excluded from being a qualifying trade solely because at some time in period B it consists to a substantial extent in the receiving of royalties or licence fees substantially attributable (in terms of value) to the exploitation of 'relevant intangible assets'. An intangible asset is an asset falling to be treated as such under generally accepted accounting practice (see **73.18 TRADING INCOME**), including all intellectual property and also industrial information and techniques (see HMRC Venture Capital Schemes Manual VCM17310). A *'relevant intangible asset'* is an intangible asset the whole or greater part of which (in terms of value) has been created by the issuing company or by a company which was a 'qualifying subsidiary' (within **28.47** above) of the issuing company throughout the period during which it created the whole or greater part of the asset. The definition also includes an intangible asset the whole or greater part of which was created by a company when it was not a qualifying subsidiary of the issuing company, provided it subsequently became a qualifying subsidiary under a particular type of company reconstruction. Where the asset is 'intellectual property', it is treated as created by a company only if the right to exploit it vests in that company (alone or with others). The term *'intellectual property'* incorporates patents, trade marks, copyrights, design rights, etc. and foreign equivalents.

The above definition of 'relevant intangible asset' applies on and after 6 April 2007 regardless of when the shares were issued (but see below). Before that date, a *'relevant intangible asset'* was an asset the whole or greater part of which (in terms of value) has been created by the company carrying on the trade or by a company which throughout the creation of the asset was the 'holding company' of that company or a qualifying subsidiary of that holding company. A *'holding company'* is for these purposes a company with one or more 51% subsidiaries which is not itself a 51% subsidiary. The stated purpose of the change of definition is to enable a trade involving the exploitation of relevant intangible assets to be transferred between companies in a group (Treasury Explanatory Notes to the 2007 Finance Bill). In a case where shares were issued before 6 April 2007 and, immediately before that date, the right to exploit an intangible asset which was then a relevant intangible asset was vested (solely or jointly with others) in the issuing company or in a subsidiary of it, the definition is effectively treated as unchanged if at any time on or after that date the new definition would alone cause the 'no excluded activities' requirement to be breached in relation to those shares.

Also as regards (d) above, a trade will not be excluded by reason only of its consisting of letting ships, other than offshore installations (previously oil rigs) or pleasure craft (as defined), on charter, provided that:

(i)   the company beneficially owns all the ships it so lets;
(ii)   every ship beneficially owned by the company is UK-registered;
(iii)   throughout period B, the company is solely responsible for arranging the marketing of the services of its ships; and
(iv)   in relation to every letting on charter, certain conditions as to length and terms of charter, and the arm's length character of the transaction, are fulfilled,

and if any of (i)–(iv) above is not fulfilled in relation to certain lettings, the trade is not thereby excluded if those lettings and any other excluded activities taken together do not amount to a substantial part of the trade.

In relation to (d) above, in the Revenue Tax Bulletin August 2001 pp 877, 878, the Inland Revenue set out their views on the scope of the exclusions. The *leasing and letting* exclusion covers all cases where (subject to reasonable conditions imposed by the trader) the customer is free to use the property for the purpose for which it is intended, e.g. television rental, video hire and the provision of self-storage warehousing facilities. In the case of car hire, a distinction has to be drawn between the provision of a *transportation service* and that of a *transportation facility*, only the latter falling within the exclusion. A taxi service would usually fall within the former category, a chauffeured car hire within the latter. *Royalties and licence fees* are received where property rights are exploited by the granting of permission to others to make use of the property. There will, however, be cases (e.g. the retailing of CDs) where, although the sales are made under licence, the receipts are nevertheless consideration for the supply of goods. In the case of *licence fees*, the grant of the right to use the property is often incidental to the supply of services (e.g. a cinema ticket), and the exclusion does not apply in such cases. The principle can be illustrated in relation to sports and leisure facilities provision. Simply making sports facilities available to the general public, with no service provision, would involve the receipt of licence fees. In the more commonly encountered activity of a health club providing a high level of services, including active supervision and advice from qualified staff, the licence to enter the premises and use the equipment would be merely incidental. Similarly where, although there is no direct provision of services, continuous work is required to keep the property in a fit state for use, the question to be considered is the extent to which the fees relate to the cost of such work.

In *Optos plc v HMRC* (Sp C 560), [2006] SSCD 687, the Sp C, in finding for the appellant company on this point, took the view that for these purposes the term 'leasing' should be construed to connote essentially a passive activity where consideration was charged for the use of an asset as opposed to the provision of services.

As regards (e) above, the provision of the services of accountancy personnel is the provision of accountancy services (*Castleton Management Services Ltd v Kirkwood* (Sp C 276), [2001] SSCD 95).

'*Property development*' in (f) above means the development of land by a company, which has (or has had at any time) an 'interest in the land' (as defined), with the sole or main object of realising a gain from the disposal of an interest in the developed land.

Exclusions (k) and (l) above apply only if the person carrying on the activity in question has an estate or interest (e.g. a lease) in the property concerned or occupies that property.

As regards (m) above, a person has a '*controlling interest*' in a trade etc. carried on by a company if he controls (within *CTA 2010, ss 450, 451*) the company; or if the company is a close company and he or an 'associate' is a director of the company and the owner of, or able to control, more than 30% of its ordinary share capital; or if at least half of its ordinary share capital is directly or indirectly owned by him. In any other case it is obtained by his being entitled to at least half of the assets used for, or income arising from, the trade etc. In either case, the rights and powers of a person's 'associates' are attributed to him. An '*associate*' of any person is any 'relative' (i.e. spouse, civil partner, ancestor or linear descendant) of that person, the trustee(s) of any settlement in relation to which that person or any relative (living or dead) is or was a settler and, where that person has an interest in any shares or obligations of a company which are subject to any trust or are part of a deceased estate, the trustee(s) of the settlement or the personal representatives of the deceased and, if that person is a company, any other company which has an interest in those shares or obligations. For this purpose, 'settlor' is defined as in **68.3 SETTLE-MENTS.**

[*ITA 2007, ss 189, 192–199, 253, 257(3), Sch 1 para 483; ICTA 1988, ss 297, 298; FA 2007, Sch 16 paras 11(1)(7), 13, 14; FA 2008, Sch 11 paras 4–6, 10, 11; CTA 2010, Sch 1 paras 501, 503; SI 2007 No 1820, Reg 2*].

The Treasury may, by statutory instrument, amend any of the above provisions. [*ITA 2007, s 200; ICTA 1988, s 298(4)*].

Simon's Taxes. See E3.126–E3.134.

Key points

[28.51] Points to consider are as follows.

* The qualifying conditions for EIS relief have changed during 2009/10 and 2010/11 to meet requirements for EU State Aid, these changes being implemented in stages during the two tax

years concerned. It is essential that those issuing or investing in shares during this period check the qualifying conditions at the time of issue of the shares to ensure that any new conditions have been complied with. The first raft of changes was in *FA 2009, Sch 8* and the remainder will be in the autumn 2010 Finance Bill.

- Withdrawal of relief for EIS is dealt with by HMRC assessment, so the notification requirements are important as they underpin this assessment, and trigger the related time limits. Those involved in EIS issues should ensure that they are conversant with the notification requirements and have procedures in place to ensure compliance with them.

- Where a claim is made to treat shares as issued in the preceding year it should be remembered that any resulting tax relief will be treated as available in the later year, and therefore there will be no reduction in amounts payable for the earlier year, nor in self-assessment payments on account calculated by reference to the liability of the earlier year. See **18.2** for more general details of carry-back claims.

- Where a company carries on the qualifying business activity in partnership or as a member of an LLP, HMRC do not accept that the requirement for the issuing company to carry on the qualifying business activity is met. This view applies to issues of shares on or after 9 December 2009. For this reason, the company will need to carry on the activity on its own behalf for EIS relief to apply to the issued shares. (See **28.40**).

29

European Community Legislation

Statements of the European Council and European Commission

[29.1] Statements of the European Council and European Commission are graded under the *EC Treaty* as follows.

- **Regulations** are binding in their entirety and have general effect in all member States. They are directly applicable in the legal systems of member States and do not have to be implemented by national legislation.
- **Directives** are binding as to result and their general effect is specific to named member States. The form and methods of compliance are left to individual member States, which are normally given a specific period in which to implement the necessary legislation.
- **Decisions** are binding in their entirety and are specific to a member State, commercial enterprise or private individual. They take effect on notification to the addressee.
- **Recommendations and opinions** are not binding and are directed to specific subjects on which the Council's or Commission's advice has been sought.

European Community law

[29.2] European Community law is effective in the UK by virtue of *European Communities Act 1972, s 2*, and the European Court of Justice has held that 'wherever the provisions of a Directive appear . . . to be unconditional and sufficiently precise, those provisions may . . . be relied upon as against any national provision which is incompatible with the Directive insofar as the provisions define rights which individuals are able to assert against the State' (*Becker v Finanzamt Munster-Innenstadt* [1982] 1 CMLR 499). Judgments in the European Court of Justice also have supremacy over domestic decisions, even if the proceedings commenced in another member State.

Direct tax measures

[29.3] In contrast to the extensive application of EU legislation in the VAT sphere, direct taxes are subject to only the following specific measures.

(a)   *Council Regulation 2137/85* (25 July 1985) concerning European Economic Interest Groupings.

(b)   *Directive 90/434/EEC* (23 July 1990) concerning mergers, divisions, transfers of assets and exchanges of shares concerning companies of different member States.

(c)   *Directive 90/435/EEC* (23 July 1990) concerning distributions of profits to parent companies.

(d)   *Directive 2003/48/EC* (3 June 2003) concerning the taxation of savings income.

(e)   *Directive 2003/49/EC* (3 June 2003) concerning interest and royalty payments.

As regards (a), see the related UK legislation at **52.26 PARTNERSHIPS**. As regards (b), the UK legislation is dealt with in Tolley's Corporation Tax under Capital Gains. As regards (c), a minor amendment is dealt with at **24.12 DEDUCTION OF TAX AT SOURCE**, and see also Tolley's Corporation Tax under Double Tax Relief. As regards (d), see **63.15 RETURNS** and **26.13 DOUBLE TAX RELIEF**, and as regards (e), see Tolley's Corporation Tax under Income Tax in relation to a Company. The Revenue Consultative Document on EC Direct Tax Measures published in December 1991 sets out the manner in which (b) and (c) are considered to be implemented by the UK legislative changes.

For a case on the application of *Directive 90/434/EEC*, see *Leur-Bloem v Inspecteur der Belastingdienst/Ondernemingen Amsterdam 2 (Case C-28/95)* ECJ, [1997] STC 1205.

In addition to the above, *Convention 90/436/EEC* is concerned with arbitration in double taxation disputes arising from transfer pricing adjustments. See **4.27 ANTI-AVOIDANCE** and **35.3**(o), **35.5 HMRC — CONFIDENTIALITY OF INFORMATION**.

European Company (Societas Europaea)

[29.4] *The European Company Statute Regulation (Council Regulation (EC) No 2157/2001)*, which was adopted on 8 October 2001, applies to all member States with effect from 8 October 2004. It creates the legal framework for a corporate entity, the European Company or 'Societas Europaea' (SE), to facilitate cross-border activities within the European Union including cross-border mergers. See the corresponding chapter of Tolley's Corporation Tax.

30

Exempt Income

UEFA Champions League Final 2011	**30.44**
Woodlands	**30.45**

Cross-references. See **18.6** CLAIMS for repayment of tax suffered; **64.17** SAVINGS AND INVESTMENT INCOME for exemption of capital portion of purchased life annuities; **31** EXEMPT ORGANISATIONS; **56.3, 56.4** PENSION INCOME; **60.12** PROPERTY INCOME for rent-a-room relief; **68.34** SETTLEMENTS — re heritage maintenance settlements.

Introduction

[30.1] The following income is exempt from income tax (to the extent and in the circumstances stated, where appropriate) and any tax suffered may be reclaimed. The paragraphs are arranged in alphabetical order.

Adopters, financial support to

[30.2] Financial support paid by local authorities and adoption agencies to adopters or potential adopters, to assist towards the extra costs faced when adopting, or seeking to adopt, a child, is exempted from income tax. The legislation lists the specific types of payment and reward within the exemption, by reference to *Adoption Act 1976* (and Scottish and NI equivalents) and *Adoption and Children Act 2002* (and to regulations under those Acts), and these extend to payment of legal and medical expenses in certain cases. The Treasury is given power to amend the list by order to take account of any future changes in the description of financial support payments. [*ITTOIA 2005, ss 744–747*]. Adoption allowances paid under the *Adoption Allowance Regulations 1991* (and Scottish equivalent) are included in this exemption.

Adult Placement carers

[30.3] Special tax arrangements apply to those who receive income for providing accommodation and care for up to three adults placed with them by local authorities (or Health and Social Services Trusts in NI) or by independent bodies under an adult placement scheme. These arrangements apply to schemes which are registered with the relevant care standards inspectorate and to unregistered schemes which comply with National Association of Adult Placement Services good practice standards. They do *not* apply to full-time carers with more than three adults in care at any one time during the year; they must compute their profits and losses based on actual income and expenditure in the same way as other businesses.

The nature of the arrangements depends on whether the carer is a respite carer, day carer or full-time carer.

Respite carers who provide no more than 182 days of care in the tax year are treated as having nil taxable profits/losses from adult placement care. For this purpose, a day of care is a day when respite care is provided to one person. If respite care is provided to two people on the same day, it counts as two days of care. If more than 182 days of respite care are provided in the tax year, see the arrangements below for full-time carers.

Day carers

If only day care is provided, the carer may choose to deduct fixed expenses of £15 per day per adult in arriving at his taxable income (though this cannot produce an allowable loss). He may alternatively use a sampling method to arrive at a fair estimate of his regular expenses for the year by keeping records for three months. Otherwise, he must compute his profits/losses based on actual income and expenditure.

Full-time carers (up to three adults in care at the carer's home)

These carers can choose one of the following three methods of calculating their profits.

- The Fixed Expenses method. The taxable profit is the total receipts from adult placement care less £400 per week for the first resident in care at any one time and £250 per week for each of the second and third residents in care at any one time. If the total of these fixed expenses exceeds receipts, taxable profits/losses are treated as nil.
- The Actual Income and Receipts method. Profits/losses are computed in accordance with actual income and expenditure.
- The Rent-a-Room method. The taxable profit is the excess of total receipts (before deducting expenses) from adult placement care over the rent-a-room threshold of £4,250 (see **60.12 PROPERTY INCOME**). If receipts do not exceed £4,250, taxable profits/losses are treated as nil.

The above is based on guidance provided by HMRC in August 2005 (see www.hmrc.gov.uk/individuals/adult-placement-carers.htm). For further background, see HMRC Business Income Manual BIM52780 *et seq.*

Qualifying shared lives carers from 6 April 2010

The above non-statutory guidance is to be superseded by legislation. This will be included in a Finance Bill to be introduced in autumn 2010, but will have backdated effect on and after 6 April 2010. There will be a single relief for qualifying shared lives carers, which will be known as *'qualifying care relief'* and will consist of a tax-free allowance. For 2010/11 only, 'qualifying shared lives carers' can choose between the above non-statutory arrangements for adult placement carers and the new qualifying care relief. The non-statutory arrangements will then be withdrawn for 2011/12 onwards.

Qualifying shared lives carers whose shared lives earnings do not exceed the tax-free allowance will not be taxed on their income from providing shared lives care. Qualifying shared lives carers whose shared lives earnings are more than the tax-free allowance have the option to choose a simplified method for calculating their profits. This will operate in a similar way to foster care relief at **30.15** below. The tax free allowance will be available per household and consist of:

- a £10,000 fixed amount per tax year;
- £200 per week (or part week) per placement aged under 11; and
- £250 per week (or part week) per placement aged 11 or over.

'*Qualifying shared lives carers*' are carers who:

- provide accommodation, care and support for up to three individuals who have been placed with them under a local authority shared lives placement scheme; and
- share their home and family life with the individuals placed with them under the shared lives scheme.

Qualifying shared lives carers may provide a maximum of three shared lives placements at any one time, but they may care for a number of different individuals during the tax year. Foster children are not counted as shared lives placements for this purpose. Siblings placed together in the same household will be counted as one shared lives placement for this purpose only.

Where there is more than one carer in the household, the household may provide care to a maximum of three shared lives placements, and the allowance will be shared equally between the carers. If a carer is entitled to both foster care relief and qualifying care relief, the household will only be entitled to claim one £10,000 fixed amount per tax year.

(HMRC Budget Note BN27, 22 June 2010).

See **30.43** below as regards special guardians and kinship carers.

Annual payments made by individuals

[30.4] An annual payment arising in the UK, made by an individual (or an individual's personal representatives) or by a Scottish partnership in which at least one partner is an individual, does not form part of the taxable income of the person to whom it is made or of any other person. This rule also applies to payments treated as income of the payer under *ITTOIA 2005, ss 624–628* or *ss 629–632* (see **68.26–68.30** SETTLEMENTS). Excluded from this rule are payments made for commercial reasons in connection with the payer's trade, profession or vocation and, subject to certain exceptions, payments for non-taxable consideration (see **4.39** ANTI-AVOIDANCE). Interest is also effectively excluded, as it is taxable as in **64.2** SAVINGS AND INVESTMENT INCOME.

As a result of the above, maintenance payments do not form part of the recipient's income for tax purposes; see also **47.9** MARRIED PERSONS AND CIVIL PARTNERS. A maintenance payment (as defined) arising outside the UK is similarly exempt if it would have been exempt had it arisen in the UK.

[*ITTOIA 2005, ss 727–730, Sch 2 para 146*].

Simon's Taxes. See B8.420, E1.514.

Armed forces — Council Tax Relief payments

[30.5] No liability to income tax arises in respect of payments of Council Tax Relief to members of the UK armed forces. The exemption covers all such payments made on or after 1 April 2008 when the Ministry of Defence's Armed Forces Council Tax Relief Scheme was due to begin. [*ITEPA 2003, s 297B; FA 2008, s 51*].

Armed forces — Operational Allowance

[30.6] No liability to income tax arises in respect of payments of the Operational Allowance to members of the UK armed forces. The Operational Allowance is paid to members of the armed forces serving in designated combat zones. [*ITEPA 2003, s 297A; FA 2007, s 64*].

Armed forces — training allowances etc

[30.7] Training allowances and bounties for reserve and auxiliary forces are generally exempt, as are armed forces' **food, drink and mess allowances**. [*ITEPA 2003, ss 297, 298*]. Civil Defence Corps bounties are not exempt because these are paid by local authorities and therefore not 'out of the public revenue' (*Lush v Coles* Ch D 1967, 44 TC 169).

Bravery awards

[30.8] Pensions and annuities are exempt if paid to holders of certain awards for bravery in respect of the award (see **56.3**(b) PENSION INCOME).

Child Trust Funds

[30.9] The Government announced on 24 May 2010 that it intends to reduce and then stop all Government contributions to Child Trust Funds. Contributions at birth will reduce, and contributions at age seven will cease, on 1 August 2010. The reduction will be from £500 to £100 for children in lower income families and from £250 to £50 for other children. Contributions at birth will cease altogether from early in 2011. Disability payments into CTF accounts will cease at the end of the tax year 2010/11. No CTF vouchers to open new accounts will be issued after 31 December 2010. Existing accounts will continue to be tax-free CTF accounts until the child's 18th birthday, with no withdrawals permitted in the meantime. Non-Government contributions of up to £1,200 per year will still be permitted. Note that the foregoing does not affect payments into CTF accounts paid by the Welsh Assembly for Welsh children. (Government Announcement on Child Trust Funds at www.hmrc.gov.uk/chancellors-statement/ctf-announce-qa.pdf).

Broadly, there is no tax on the income or gains of a Child Trust Fund (see below for more details). Similarly, there will be no tax charges when the fund matures on the child's 18th birthday.

The Child Trust Fund (CTF) was established in order to provide all children with a financial asset at the start of adult life, to encourage savings and investment, and to help people to engage with financial institutions. Given these aims, it is not surprising that the legislation detailing the characteristics of an account that may qualify as a CTF, and those who may provide such accounts, is carefully drawn to protect the assets until the child reaches 18.

An account with an approved provider may be opened in respect of a child born after 31 August 2002 where (broadly) there is an entitlement to Child Benefit (an 'eligible child'). CTFs became fully operational on 6 April 2005.

The process of opening an account begins with HMRC issuing a voucher to the person who is entitled to Child Benefit in respect of an eligible child. The voucher must be given to an account provider within twelve months of issue. After 5 April 2009, the account provider may choose to accept information taken from the voucher rather than the voucher itself. There is provision to appeal against an HMRC decision not to issue such a voucher. As stated above, no new vouchers will be issued after 31 December 2010, but vouchers issued on or before that date will continue to be valid up to their expiry date.

An account may be opened by a responsible person (broadly, a person with parental responsibility). If there is no responsible person, or if a voucher has been issued but not given to an account provider within twelve months, HMRC will open an account. At any time only a single responsible person, or only the child if over 16, is able to give instructions to the account provider as to the management of the account. This person is designated the 'registered contact'. There is provision for the Official Solicitor (in Scotland, the Accountant of Court) to manage the CTF accounts of looked after children for whom nobody (or nobody suitable) has parental responsibility.

In truth, the decisions to be made about the management of the account are limited. However, it is possible to swap to another account provider (at the cost only of incidental expenses) or to swap to an account of another description or type offered by the same account provider (once again, at the cost only of incidental expenses).

Accounts may be of two types: stakeholder accounts and non-stakeholder accounts. Stakeholder accounts are subject to stringent rules about the charges that may be deducted from them, and have a more restricted range of permissible investments and investment strategies (see below). Certain accounts, chiefly those opened by HMRC, have to be stakeholder accounts.

Contributions to the account

See above for the Government's intention to reduce and then cease making contributions to CTF accounts.

HMRC will make an initial payment into the account. The amount of this initial contribution is £250 (£500 for children in care), but there are small increases to this figure for eligible children born before 6 April 2005. The initial £250 contribution is supplemented by a further £250 if (broadly) income is below the child tax credit threshold, and either (i) child tax credit is claimed no later than the expiry date of the CTF voucher (see **70.4 SOCIAL SECURITY AND NATIONAL INSURANCE**) or (ii) certain other child-related State benefits were being paid when Child Benefit was first claimed. The amount of the supplementary payment was subject to small increases where Child Benefit was first paid prior to 6 April 2005.

A top-up payment will be made by HMRC to the account when the child reaches the age of seven. This will again be £250, once more doubled to £500 in the case of children in care and children in lower income families — judged as at the child's seventh birthday.

Top-up payments of £100 are also made by HMRC for each whole year following 1 April 2007 that a child is in care.

From 1 April 2010, HMRC make additional annual payments of £100 into the CTF accounts of all children in receipt of Disability Living Allowance. For severely disabled children (those who receive the High Care element of Disability Living Allowance), the payments are £200 per child.

There is provision for HMRC to recoup their contributions where the account is invalid and cannot be 'repaired' (see under Administration below) or where the basis for the supplementary contribution is removed because of a change in the tax credit/benefit position. Any decision not to pay a contribution, or to recoup contributions, is subject to a right of appeal.

In addition to these government payments, anyone, including the child, may pay into the account. However, there is a limit of £1,200 for such contributions in any one year. A 'year' for this purpose is the period from the opening of the account to the child's next birthday, and each succeeding period of twelve months. If the limit is not reached in any year, it is not possible to carry forward the unused part. Neither is there any provision for a carry-back of contributions.

Only monetary payments may be accepted, so there is no possibility of gifting shares or other assets into a CTF.

Withdrawals from the account

Withdrawals from the account are not permitted before the child reaches the age of 18. There are three exceptions to this. The first is that the account provider is allowed to make deductions in respect of management charges and incidental expenses. The second is where the child is terminally ill. The third is where the child dies before reaching 18.

The investments under a CTF are inalienable — any charge over them, or assignment of them is void. If the child is made bankrupt, creditors may not gain access to the account.

Qualifying investments

There are extensive strictures regarding permitted investments for a CTF account. In order to help account providers, the structure of the regulations governing CTF accounts has been modelled on the provisions relating to Individual Savings Accounts. Qualifying investments for CTFs are as follows.

(a) Shares issued by a company (other than an investment trust, but see (e) below) wherever incorporated, and officially listed on a recognised stock exchange. There are rules to allow the official listing condition to be treated as satisfied in the case of shares issued under a public offer and due to be listed. However, shares do not qualify if they have been acquired on favourable terms because of a connection with the allocation or allotment of other shares, securities or rights thereto.

(b) Securities issued by a company wherever incorporated, provided either the securities themselves, or the shares in the issuing company, or the shares in a parent company (of which the issuing company is a 75% subsidiary) are officially listed on a recognised stock exchange. In the case of securities in an investment trust, the investment trust must have no 'eligible rental income' (see Tolley's Corporation Tax under Investment Trusts).

(c) Gilt-edged securities.

(d) Securities issued by or on behalf of a government of any EEA State, and strips of such securities.

(e) Shares in an investment trust listed in the Official List of the Stock Exchange. Broadly, in order to qualify, an investment trust must have no 'eligible rental income' (see Tolley's Corporation Tax under Investment Trusts).

(f) Units in, or shares of, a securities scheme, warrant scheme or fund of funds scheme.

(g) Units in, or shares of, a money-market scheme.

(h) Units in, or shares of, a UCITS (Undertaking for Collective Investment in Transferable Securities).

(i) A depositary interest.

(j) Cash deposited in a share or deposit account with a building society or deposit account with a bank (as defined) or a relevant European institution. However, a deposit or share account is not a qualifying investment if it is 'connected' with any other investment. For this purpose, an account is 'connected' with another investment if either was opened or acquired with reference to the other, or with a view to enabling the other to be opened or acquired on particular terms, or with a view to facilitating the opening or acquisition of the other on particular terms *and* the terms on which the account was opened would have been significantly less favourable to the holder if the investment had not been acquired.

(k) Designated national savings products.

(l) Life insurance policies satisfying specified conditions (see below).

(m) ALTERNATIVE FINANCE ARRANGEMENTS(3) (e.g. Shari'a products).

(n) 'qualifying' units in, or shares of, a non-UCITS retail scheme (a category introduced by the New Collective Investment Schemes Sourcebook from March 2004 and covering all types of retail collective investment schemes authorised by the Financial Services Authority for sale in Great Britain other than UCITS schemes). Units or shares are 'qualifying' units or shares for this purpose if they do not restrict savers' ability to access their funds by more than two weeks.

In order to qualify, a life insurance policy must insure the life of the child only. Its terms and conditions must provide:

- that the policy may only be owned or held as a qualifying investment for a CTF account;
- that the policy will terminate if it comes to the notice of the account provider that there has been a breach of the CTF regulations relating to insurance policies, and the breach cannot be remedied as a repair to an invalid account (see below under Administration);
- for the express prohibition of payments resulting from termination or partial surrender to the child before age 18;
- that the policy etc. cannot be assigned other than by transfer of title between approved account providers or by its vesting in the child's personal representatives.

The contract of insurance must either fall within the *Financial Services and Markets Act 2000 (Regulated Activities) Order 2001, Sch 1 Pt 2* (contract of long-term insurance), *para 1* (life insurance) or *para 3* (life insurance where benefits linked to value of property), or be capable of falling within either of those paragraphs were the insurer to be a company with permission under *Financial Services and Markets Act 2000* to effect insurance contracts.

The policy must constitute life insurance and must not be a contract to pay a life annuity, a personal portfolio bond (see **44.17 LIFE ASSURANCE POLICIES**) or a contract constituting pension business (as defined). There must be no contractual obligation to pay any premium other than the first (so regular premium policies are excluded). The making of loans by, or by arrangement with, the insurer to, or at the direction of, the child or registered contact is prohibited.

Stakeholder accounts

There are further restrictions on investment, and investment strategy, for stakeholder accounts. Broadly, they must not invest directly in shares, investment trusts or certain types of insurance contract. Investment in securities, authorised unit trusts and open-ended investment companies is subject to specific conditions. Interest must accrue at a specified minimum rate (linked to base rate) in respect of cash held in deposit or share accounts (except where temporarily deposited while dealing in investments). As regards investment strategy, there is a requirement for the account to be exposed to equities. The account provider must have regard to the need for diversification, and must consider investment options in the light of the purpose of the account. For the last five years or so of the account, the account provider must consider the need to minimise fluctuations in the capital value of the account resulting from market conditions.

Tax treatment

No tax is chargeable in respect of interest, dividends, distributions or gains on account investments. (For capital gains tax purposes, assets in the fund are treated as sold and immediately re-acquired at market value just prior to the child's 18th birthday.) Capital losses on account investments are not allowable.

Any income from account investments is not to be regarded as income for any income tax purposes — this exemption specifically embraces the children's settlements provisions at **68.30 SETTLEMENTS**. The exemption on income extends to returns under **ALTERNATIVE FINANCE ARRANGEMENTS (3)** (e.g. Shari'a products). Annual building society bonuses are brought within the exemptions on both income and gains from 1 January 2007.

There are, in addition, disapplications of provisions taxing profits or gains under the **ACCRUED INCOME SCHEME (2)**, offshore income gains (see **51 OFFSHORE FUNDS**), and profits on deeply discounted securities (see **64.18 SAVINGS AND INVESTMENT INCOME**). Life assurance gains (see **44.3 LIFE ASSURANCE POLICIES**) are not taxable (and a deficiency on termination is not deductible from the child's total income) provided regulatory conditions are not breached (see below). Companies and local authorities may pay interest etc. gross.

It is up to the account provider to make tax claims, conduct appeals, and agree liabilities and reliefs on behalf of the child or registered contact. It is unlikely then that the child or registered contact will have to deal with any tax matters arising from the account. However, there is power for HMRC to make an assessment on the registered contact as an alternative to the account provider in order to withdraw relief or recover tax. This is subject to the right of appeal.

Where a life assurance policy becomes invalid because of a breach of the regulations (see above under Qualifying investments) a chargeable event then occurs. That event, and any prior chargeable event becomes taxable under the normal provisions relating to life assurance gains (see **44.3** *et seq.* **LIFE ASSURANCE POLICIES**). Basic rate tax (for 2008/09 onwards, previously savings rate tax) is payable by the account provider (with HMRC having the power to tax the registered contact). Any higher rate tax due is payable by the registered contact by assessment within five years after 31 January following the year in which the chargeable event or termination occurred.

Administration

Administration of the account largely rests with the account provider. Regulations cover: qualification as an account manager; HMRC approval and withdrawal thereof (and appeals against these decisions); appointment of UK tax representatives of non-UK account managers; account managers ceasing to act or qualify; transfer of accounts to other account providers; annual and fortnightly electronic returns of information; annual and interim tax repayment claims; record-keeping; and information to be provided to the named child (including annual statements).

The account provider and the registered contact are required to take any necessary steps to remedy any breach of the regulations surrounding the CTF account. Provided this is done the account remains valid during the period of the breach, although penalties may still be in point. There are, however, two breaches where no repair is possible:

- where the child has never been an eligible child; and
- where more than one account is held for the same child.

In the above circumstances, HMRC contributions, plus any consequent income and gains, will be recouped, the account provider, registered contact and named child being jointly and severally liable.

HMRC have wide powers to require information and to inspect records in relation to CTF accounts. This is subject to a penalty regime analogous to that for special returns in *TMA 1970, s 98* (see **55.21** PENALTIES).

There is a penalty of up to £300 for fraudulently opening, or making a withdrawal from, a CTF account.

[*Child Trust Funds Act 2004; SI 2004 Nos 1450, 2422, 2676, 3369, 3382; SI 2005 No 383; SI 2005 Nos 909, 3349; SI 2006 Nos 199, 2684, 3195; SI 2009 Nos 475, 694; SI 2009 No 56, Sch 1 paras 414–418, Sch 2 para 127; SI 2009 No 3054, Arts 2, 3, Sch; SI 2010 No 836*].

For practical guidance, see the Child Trust Fund website at www.childtrustfun d.gov.uk For HMRC's guidance for account providers, see www.hmrc.gov.u k/ctf/ctfguidancenotes.pdf. For key features, see www.hmrc.gov.uk/ctf/key-fea tures.htm.

Compensation for loss of employment etc. up to £30,000

[30.10] See **20.4** COMPENSATION FOR LOSS OF EMPLOYMENT for details of exemptions and reliefs for these and other terminal payments at the end of an employment.

Compensation for mis-sold pensions products (and interest thereon)

Personal pensions etc.

[30.11] Exemption from both income tax and capital gains tax is conferred on the receipt at any time of a capital sum (which may include a sum otherwise chargeable to income tax) by way of compensation for loss, or likely loss, caused by certain 'bad investment advice' concerning personal pensions etc. '*Bad investment advice*' is investment advice (as defined) in respect of which an action has been or may be brought against the adviser for negligence, breach of contract or fiduciary obligation or by reason of a contravention actionable under *Financial Services Act 1986, s 62* or *Financial Services and Markets Act 2000, s 150*. The exemption applies where a person (whether or not the person suffering loss), acting on such advice at least some of which was given after 28 April 1988 and before 1 July 1994 (at which date new regulatory safeguards came into force), either

(a)   joined a personal pension scheme or took out a retirement annuity contract whilst eligible, or reasonably likely to become eligible, to join an occupational pension scheme (i.e. an approved retirement benefits scheme, relevant statutory scheme or pre 6 April 1980 approved superannuation scheme); or

(b)   left, or ceased to pay into, an occupational pension scheme and instead joined a personal pension scheme or took out a retirement annuity contract; or

(c)   transferred to a personal pension scheme his accrued rights under an occupational pension scheme; or

(d)   left an occupational pension scheme and instead entered into arrangements for securing relevant benefits by means of an annuity contract with an insurance company.

Interest on the whole or part of a capital sum within the above exemption is itself exempt from income tax to the extent that it covers a period ending on or before the earliest date on which the amount of the capital sum is first determined, whether by agreement or by a court, tribunal, commissioner, arbitrator or appointee.

[*FA 1996, s 148*].

As regards interest on compensation for the mis-selling of other financial products, such as mortgage endowment policies, see **64.2** SAVINGS AND INVESTMENT INCOME.

Freestanding additional voluntary contribution schemes ('FSAVCSs')

By concession, where liability would otherwise arise, the following payments will not be chargeable to income tax (although this will not apply to annuities or other annual payments arising from the compensation), and their receipt will not be treated as the disposal of an asset for capital gains tax purposes.

(i)   The payment of a capital sum by way of compensation determined in accordance with the Financial Services Authority guidance for the performance of the review required by the Authority of specified categories of FSAVCSs sold between 28 April 1988 and 15 August 1999 inclusive, and made as a result of the review.

(ii)   The payment of interest on the whole or part of the sum within (i) for a period ending on or before the earliest date on which the capital sum was determined.

(HMRC ESC A99).

Damages and compensation for personal injury — periodical payments

[30.12] An income tax exemption is available where an agreement is made settling a claim or action for damages for personal injury (as widely defined) under which the damages are to consist wholly or partly of periodical payments, or where a court order incorporates such terms. (This applies equally in relation to interim court order payments and voluntary payments on account.) The payments are not regarded as income for income tax purposes, and are paid without deduction of tax under *ITA 2007, Pt 15 Ch 6*. This applies as regards the person ('A') entitled to the damages under the agreement or order, and also:

(a)   any person receiving the payments on behalf of A; and

(b)   any trustee receiving the payments on trust for A's benefit under a trust under which A is (during his lifetime) the sole beneficiary,

and sums paid on to (or for the benefit of) A by a person within (b) above are not regarded as A's income for income tax purposes.

Any or all of the periodical payments may (if the agreement etc., or a subsequent agreement, so provides) be under one or more annuities purchased or provided for (or for the benefit of) A by the person otherwise liable for the payments.

The above provisions apply equally to annuity payments under a compensation award under the Criminal Injuries Compensation Scheme. The Treasury may also apply them (with any necessary modifications) to any other scheme or arrangement making similar provision. The provisions are thus applied to recipients of payments from the Thalidomide Children's Trust established on 10 August 1973. On and after 1 April 2010, they are applied to a specified arrangement whereby payments funded by the Department of Health are made to persons infected with HIV through contaminated blood or blood products used by the NHS.

[*ITTOIA 2005, ss 731–734; SI 2004 No 1819; SI 2010 No 673*].

Simon's Taxes. See E1.515, E1.553–E1.555, E4.326.

Electricity microgeneration for home use

[30.13] For 2007/08 onwards, no income tax liability arises in respect of income arising to an individual from the sale of electricity generated by a microgeneration system (as defined) installed at or near domestic premises which he occupies, provided the intention is that the amount of electricity generated will not significantly exceed the amount consumed in those premises. [*ITTOIA 2005, s 782A; FA 2007, s 20*]. The exemption covers, for example, the sale of surplus power to an energy company. Before 2007/08 the tax treatment of such income was uncertain and the legislation is intended to put the position beyond doubt.

Also, for 2007/08 onwards and subject to the same criteria as above, no income tax liability arises in respect of the receipt by an individual of a renewables obligation certificate (as defined) in connection with the generation of electricity by a microgeneration system. [*ITTOIA 2005, s 782B; FA 2007, s 21*]. There is a corresponding exemption from CGT on a gain from the disposal of a renewables obligation certificate on or after 6 April 2007 (see *TCGA 1992, s 263AZA*).

Foreign service allowance

[30.14] Such allowance is exempt where paid to a person in the service of the Crown representing compensation for the extra cost of living abroad. [*ITEPA 2003, s 299*].

Foster care receipts

[30.15] These are exempt if they do not exceed a limit computed by reference to the individual recipient, and, if the recipient so elects, are subject to special computational rules if they do. See further below.

An individual's 'foster care receipts' are potentially within the above exemption if, for the tax year under consideration, he derives no taxable income, other than 'foster care receipts', from any trade, profession, vocation or non-trading foster care arrangement from which he derives 'foster care receipts'. In the remainder of this coverage, the word 'trade' is used to denote a trade, a profession or a vocation. Receipts are *'foster care receipts'* of an individual for a tax year if:

- they are receipts from the 'provision of foster care';
- they would otherwise be brought into account in computing the profits of a trade or taxed as miscellaneous income; and
- they accrue in the basis period for the trade (see **73.3 TRADING INCOME**) or, in the case of non-trading foster care arrangements, in the tax year itself.

For these purposes, the *'provision of foster care'* means the provision of accommodation and maintenance for a child by an individual, other than an 'excluded individual', with whom the child has been placed under specified statutory provisions governing foster care in the UK. Receipts from *private* foster care arrangements do not qualify for the exemption. Anyone who is a parent of the child, or has parental responsibility in relation to the child, is an *'excluded individual'* for this purpose, as is (where relevant) anyone in whose favour a residence order (or, in Scotland, a contact order) has been made and was in force immediately prior to the child's being placed in care.

The full exemption applies where the individual's total foster care receipts for the tax year or (as the case may be) the period of account, taking no account of any deduction for expenses etc., do not exceed the individual's limit. This limit is based on a fixed amount of £10,000 per 'residence' plus an amount per child per individual based on the number of weeks (or part weeks) during the income period (i.e. the basis period or, for non-trading arrangements, the tax year) in which the individual provides foster care for the child. The amount per child is £200 per week (or part week) for a child under 11 and £250 per week (or part week) for a child of 11 or over; a week in which the child reaches the age of 11 qualifies for the higher figure. A week, for these purposes, comprises the seven days beginning with a Monday. A week in which an income period ends is counted as belonging to that income period. Both the fixed and weekly amounts are subject to any amendment made by future Treasury order. If, *in the tax year*, the residence used to provide the foster care is also used for provision of foster care by one or more other individuals who also have foster care receipts for the year, the £10,000 fixed amount is divided equally between them. If an individual's income period is a period other than a year, the fixed amount or, where relevant, his share of it is adjusted proportionately. For these purposes, a *'residence'* is a building, or part of a building, occupied, or intended to be occupied, as a separate residence, with any temporary division of a single residence into two or more residences being disregarded; the term also extends to a caravan or houseboat.

Where the full exemption applies, the individual is treated, for the tax year in question, as making nil profit and nil loss from the trade or (as the case may be) from each non-trading foster care arrangement from which the foster care receipts arise. If, in the case of a trade, the individual would otherwise be entitled to relief for an overlap profit (see **73.11** TRADING INCOME), he is given the relief anyway.

If, for the tax year or (as the case may be) the period of account, the individual's total foster care receipts would be within the exemption were it not for the fact that they exceed his limit, he may make an election to be charged to income tax as if his profit were equal to the excess. The election for this alternative method of calculating profit must specify the tax year for which it is made, must be made no later than the first anniversary of 31 January following that tax year (or such later date as HMRC may, in a particular case, allow) and has effect for that tax year only. In the absence of an election, the normal rules for computing profits and losses apply. If no election is made before the deadline but his taxable foster care profits are adjusted after the deadline has passed, the individual is given additional time in which to make an election, the revised deadline being the first anniversary of 31 January following the tax year in which the adjustment is made (or, again, such later date as HMRC may, in a particular case, allow). Once made, an election can be withdrawn within the time limits specified for making it.

In computing the individual's limit in a case where the foster care receipts are those of a period of account (other than one ending on 5 April), the fixed amount is that prescribed for the tax year in which the period of account ends, e.g. £10,000 for a period ending in 2010/11. If, in future, the prescribed amounts per child alter, so that different rates apply for two tax years in which the period of account falls, the rates for the first of those tax years apply in respect of children cared for during that part of the period of account preceding 6 April and the new rates will apply in respect of children cared for during that part of the period of account falling after 5 April.

Example

Dave and Holly, a couple living together, provide foster care by way of trade. Each prepares accounts to 31 December. During their respective periods of account covering the year ending 31 December 2009, they provide care to a twelve-year old (child 1) for the full 52 weeks and to a nine-year old (child 2) for 15 weeks. *Each* of their individual limits is computed as follows.

		£
Fixed amount for 2009/10: £10,000 ÷ 2		5,000
Amounts per child:	child 1 (52 × £250)	13,000
	child 2 (15 × £200)	3,000
		£21,000

Some HMRC offices are believed to have taken the view that, in a case such as this, the amounts per child must be divided between the couple instead of being available separately to each individual. In this example, this would have the effect of reducing each individual's limit by £8,000. In the author's opinion, the legislation does not support such a view; if, however, a couple are trading in partnership (clearly not the case in this example) it becomes arguable that the partnership should take the place of an individual for the purpose of computing the limits.

For a chargeable period (see **11.2**(i) CAPITAL ALLOWANCES ON PLANT AND MACHINERY) corresponding to an income period for a tax year for which either the exemption applies or an election is made to apply the alternative method of calculating profit, the individual is not entitled to capital allowances on plant and machinery used to provide foster care. Where such allowances *were* available for the preceding chargeable period, a disposal event is deemed to have occurred immediately after the start of the current chargeable period and a disposal value must be brought into account equal to the unrelieved qualifying expenditure brought forward from the preceding chargeable period; consequently, no balancing allowance or charge arises (see generally **11.23** CAPITAL ALLOWANCES ON PLANT AND MACHINERY). For the first chargeable period for which neither the exemption nor the alternative method applies, but for which foster care receipts still arise, *CAA 2001, s 13* is brought into effect as if, on the first day of that chargeable period, the individual had brought into use for the purposes of his provision of foster care any such plant or machinery that he still owns and any plant or machinery acquired for those purposes during the time that allowances were not available. Such plant or machinery will normally fall to be brought in at its then market value — see **11.65** CAPITAL ALLOWANCES ON PLANT AND MACHINERY.

[*ITTOIA 2005, ss 803–828*].

Amending legislation is to be included in a Finance Bill to be introduced in autumn 2010 to ensure that the above capital allowances rules operate as intended, especially where the individual moves in and out of the foster care relief regime. The amendments will apply to chargeable periods ending on or after the date that the legislation receives Royal Assent. (HMRC Budget Note BN29, 22 June 2010).

See **30.3** above as regards the relationship between foster care relief and qualifying care relief for shared lives carers.

German and Austrian annuities and pensions for victims of Nazi persecution

[30.16] Such annuities and pensions payable under German or Austrian law are not treated as income for any income tax purpose. [*ITEPA 2003, s 642*].

Guaranteed income bonds

[30.17] See **44.15** LIFE ASSURANCE POLICIES as regards annuities and annual payments under certain life insurance policies which are excluded from treatment as such.

Housing grants

[30.18] Except where the expense recouped is deductible from profits, amounts received, under any relevant Act, towards expenses incurred, by the recipient or another, in providing, maintaining or improving residential accommodation are not assessable. [*ITTOIA 2005, ss 769, 879(4), 880(2)*].

Immediate needs annuities

[30.19] An annual payment made under an 'immediate needs annuity' is exempt from income tax to the extent that it is made to a care provider (as defined) or local authority in respect of the provision of care (as defined) for the person for whose benefit the annuity was made. For this purpose, an *'immediate needs annuity'* is a life annuity contract:

• the purpose of which, or one of the purposes of which, is to protect a person against the consequences of his being unable, at the time the contract is made, to live independently without assistance, due to permanent mental or physical impairment, injury, sickness or other infirmity; and
• under which benefits are payable in respect of the provision of care for that person.

The above definition, and the definition of care provider, may be amended by Treasury Order.

[*ITTOIA 2005, s 725*].

Incentives for electronic communications

[30.20] No liability to income tax arises in respect of anything received by way of incentive under any regulations made in accordance with primary legislation. See **34.9 HMRC — ADMINISTRATION**.

See **63.2 RETURNS** for initial incentives for making certain returns over the internet and see **53.12 PAY AS YOU EARN** as regards incentives for e-filing of PAYE returns where not mandatory.

Individual savings accounts

[30.21] Individuals aged 18 or over (16 or over in the case of cash accounts (as below)) who are resident and ordinarily resident in the UK are able to subscribe up to £10,200 in each tax year to an individual savings account (an ISA) set up in accordance with regulations. Of the annual subscription, no more than £5,100 may go into cash. Before 2005/06, the account could contain two components: cash (including National Savings) and stocks and shares. Before 2005/06, there was a third component, the life insurance component, but this was abolished. Shares acquired under approved SAYE option schemes or share incentive plans (see **69.47, 69.20 SHARE-RELATED EMPLOYMENT INCOME AND EXEMPTIONS**) may be transferred in at market value (with no capital gains tax liability) within the annual subscription limits, but public offer and demutualisation issues may not be transferred in. There is no minimum subscription, no lifetime limit and no loss of relief on withdrawals.

The overall limit was £7,200 before 2010/11 and £7,000 before 2008/09. The cash limit was £3,600 before 2010/11 and £3,000 before 2008/09. For investors aged 50 or over, the increased limits for 2010/11 onwards also had effect on and after 6 October 2009 for 2009/10. Thus, from 6 October 2009, those investors were able to deposit £10,200 into their 2009/10 ISA, up to £5,100 of which could be in cash. Investors who reached the age of 50 between 6 October 2009 and 5 April 2010 could nevertheless subscribe up to the new limits from 6 October 2009 without waiting for their 50th birthday.

From 6 April 2011 the subscription limits will be increased in line with the Retail Prices Index (RPI) on an annual basis (HMRC Budget Note BN21, 22 June 2010).

Personal equity plans (PEPs) were abolished for 2008/09 onwards and all existing PEPs automatically became stocks and shares ISAs on 6 April 2008..

There is exemption from income tax and capital gains tax on the investments..

The necessary regulation-making powers are provided in general by *ITTOIA 2005, ss 694–701 as amended.The Individual Savings Account Regulations 1998 (SI 1998 No 1870)* provide for the setting up by HMRC-approved accounts managers of plans (ISAs) under which individuals may make certain investments, for the conditions under which they may invest and under which the accounts are to operate, for relief from tax in respect of account investments, and for general administration.

General

An application to subscribe to an ISA may be made by an individual who is 18 or over (16 or over in the case of cash accounts) and who is resident and ordinarily resident in the UK (or who is non-UK resident but has general earnings 'from overseas Crown employment subject to UK tax' — see **27.5 EMPLOYMENT INCOME** — or who is a non-UK resident spouse (or civil partner) of an individual with such earnings). Joint accounts are not permitted. An investor who subsequently fails to meet the residence requirement may retain the account and the right to tax exemptions thereunder but can make no further subscriptions to the account until he again comes to meet that requirement. An application made on behalf of an individual suffering from mental disorder, by a parent, guardian, spouse, civil partner, son or daughter of his, is treated as if made by that individual. This replaced a rule specific to Scotland whereby a *curator bonis* appointed in respect of a qualifying individual incapable of managing his affairs could subscribe to an ISA in his capacity as such without affecting his right to subscribe in any other capacity.

2008/09 onwards

An ISA may be a stocks and shares account or a cash account.

A *stocks and shares account* is made up of a single stocks and shares component. An investor can subscribe to only one stocks and shares account for a tax year. The maximum subscription (per tax year) is £10,200 (previously £7,200 — see above). Stocks and shares accounts are not available to 16- and 17-year olds.

A *cash account* is made up of a single cash component. An investor can subscribe to only one cash account for a tax year. The maximum subscription (per tax year) is £5,100 (previously £3,600 — see above). But this is subject to an overall ISA subscription limit of £10,200 (previously £7,200 — see above). So an individual who subscribes, say, £8,000 to a stocks and shares account in 2010/11 can subscribe only £2,200 to a cash account in the same tax year and an individual who subscribes the maximum £5,100 to a cash account in 2010/11 can subscribe only £5,100 to a stocks and shares account. Cash accounts are available to any individual of 16 or over who satisfies the general conditions above; the overall subscription limit for 16- and 17-year olds is £5,100 (£3,600 before 2010/11).

For 2008/09 onwards, an investor is permitted to transfer some or all of the amount saved in ISAs in previous tax years to a stocks and shares account. Such transfers do not count towards the annual subscription limits. An investor is also permitted to transfer the amount saved in the current tax year in a cash account to a stocks and shares account. In this case the transfer must consist of the whole of the amount saved in that tax year in that cash account; for the purpose of applying the annual subscription limits, the cash transferred is treated as if it had been invested directly into a stocks and shares account in that tax year.

2007/08 and earlier years

Before 2008/09, an ISA was made up of *one or more* of the following: a stocks and shares component, a cash component (see below re qualifying investments for each of these components). It had to be designated from the outset as a maxi-account or mini-account, such designation continuing to have effect for any year in which the investor makes a subscription to the account.

A *maxi-account* had to comprise a stocks and shares component (*with or without* other components). The maximum subscription per tax year was £7,000 of which a maximum of £3,000 could be allocated to a cash component. Where the subscriber was aged 16 but under 18 at the end of the tax year, the overall limit was £3,000, which could only be invested in a cash component. In the year in which the subscriber attained the age of 18, that limit and restriction applied to subscriptions before his or her birthday. In any tax year in which an investor subscribed to a maxi-account he could not subscribe to any other ISA. A maxi-account in existence immediately before 6 April 2008 automatically became on that date a stocks and shares account to the extent that it comprised a stocks and shares component and a cash account to the extent (if any) that it comprised a cash component.

A *mini-account* had to consist of a single specified component. The maximum subscription (per tax year) was £4,000 if that component was stocks and shares and £3,000 if it was cash. In any tax year in which an investor subscribed to a mini-account, he could not subscribe to another mini-account consisting of the same component or to a maxi-account. A mini-account in existence immediately before 6 April 2008 automatically became on that date a stocks and shares account or a cash account, depending upon the component of which it consisted.

Subscriptions to an ISA

Subscriptions to an ISA must be made in cash (and must be allocated irrevocably to the agreed component) *except that* shares acquired by the investor under a SAYE option scheme (see **69.47 SHARE-RELATED EMPLOYMENT INCOME AND EXEMPTIONS**) or a share incentive plan (see **69.20 SHARE-RELATED EMPLOYMENT INCOME AND EXEMPTIONS**) may be transferred to a stocks and shares component. Such transfers count towards the annual subscription limits, by reference to the market value of the shares at the date of transfer. No chargeable gain or allowable loss arises on the transfer. A transfer of SAYE scheme shares must be made within 90 days after the exercise of the option, and a transfer of share incentive plan shares must be made within 90 days of the shares ceasing to be subject to the plan. From 13 December 2000, 'shares' in these cases includes a reference to those held in the form of depositary interests (see (k) below).

It is possible for the investor to sell investments and subscribe the proceeds to an ISA and for the ISA manager to then use those proceeds to acquire investments (often the same investments) within the ISA. This is sometimes known as 'Bed and ISAing'. Provided the funds generated by the disposal are available to meet the purchase on settlement day, the subscription date for the ISA can be the date of disposal, the settlement date for the purchase or any date in between that the investor chooses. (HMRC ISA Bulletin 15, August 2009).

Compensation paid into ISAs for loss of income or capital growth due to failures or delays on the part of ISA managers will not count towards the subscription limit. This does not apply to compensation paid in respect of a delay in opening an ISA, or in accepting a subscription to an ISA. See HMRC Guidance Notes for ISA Managers and PEP and ISA Bulletin 4, 13 December 2001.

Other matters

ISA investments cannot be purchased otherwise than out of cash held by the account manager under an account or component, and cannot be purchased from the investor or the investor's spouse or civil partner.

The title to ISA investments (other than cash deposits, national savings products and certain insurance policies) is vested in the account manager (or his nominee) either alone or jointly with the investor, though all ISA investments are in the beneficial ownership of the investor. The investor may elect to receive annual reports and accounts etc. in respect of ISA investments and/or to attend and vote at shareholders' etc. meetings.

The statements and declarations to be made when applying to subscribe to an ISA are specified. The maximum penalty for an incorrect statement or declaration is the amount (if any) of income tax and/or capital gains tax underpaid as a result. Assessments to withdraw tax relief or otherwise recover tax underpaid may be made on the account manager or investor. HMRC have power to require information from, and to inspect records of, account managers and investors.

The terms and conditions of an ISA cannot prevent the investor from withdrawing funds or from transferring his account (or a part of it) to another HMRC-approved account manager (subject to the conditions governing such transfers). The account manager is allowed a reasonable business period (usually not exceeding 30 days) to comply with the investor's instructions in this regard.

Tax exemptions

Except as stated below, no income tax or capital gains tax is chargeable on the account manager or the investor in respect of interest, dividends, distributions or gains on ISA investments. Capital losses are not allowable. The exemption on income extends to returns under ALTERNATIVE FINANCE ARRANGEMENTS (**3**) (e.g. Shari'a products). Annual building society bonuses are brought within the exemptions on both income and gains from 1 January 2007.

Interest on a cash deposit held within a stocks and shares component is, however, taxable at the basic rate of income tax (for 2008/09 onwards, previously at the savings rate), such tax to be accounted for by the account manager (by set-off against tax repayments or otherwise). There is no further liability; the interest does not form part of the investor's total income and the tax paid cannot be repaid to the investor.

Life assurance gains on policies held within an ISA are not subject to income tax (and a deficiency on termination is not deductible from the investor's total income). If it comes to the account manager's notice that such a policy is invalid, i.e. its terms and conditions do not provide (or no longer provide) that it be held only as a qualifying insurance component investment, a chargeable event then occurs, with any gain taxable. If the policy has already terminated, the chargeable event is deemed to have occurred at the end of the final insurance year (see **44.11** LIFE ASSURANCE POLICIES). Any previous chargeable event which actually occurred in relation to the policy is similarly taxed, by reference to the time it occurred. Basic rate income tax (or, before 2008/09, savings rate income tax) is payable by the account manager (with HMRC also having power to assess the investor). Any higher rate tax due is payable by the investor by assessment within five years after 31 January following the tax year in which the chargeable event occurred or was deemed to occur. Top slicing relief (see **44.8** LIFE ASSURANCE POLICIES) is available in the same way as for non-ISA-related chargeable events.

Exempt income and gains do not have to be reported in the investor's personal tax return.

Further capital gains matters

A transfer of ISA investments by an account manager to an investor is deemed to be made at market value, with no capital gain or allowable loss arising. An investor is treated as holding shares or securities in an ISA in a capacity other than that in which he holds any other shares etc. of the same class in the same company, so that share identification rules (see Tolley's Capital Gains Tax under Shares and Securities — Identification Rules) are applied separately to ISA investments (and separately as between different ISAs held by the same investor). The normal share reorganisation rules are disapplied in respect of ISA investments in the event of a reorganisation of share capital involving an allotment for payment, e.g. a rights issue. Shares transferred to an ISA in the limited circumstances described above are deemed for these purposes to have been ISA investments from, in the case of SAYE option scheme shares, their acquisition by the investor and, in the case of share incentive plan shares, their ceasing to be subject to the plan. Where the investor held shares eligible for transfer to an ISA and other shares of the same class but not so eligible, disposals are generally identified primarily with the latter, thus preserving to the greatest possible extent the eligibility of the remaining shares.

Qualifying investments

Qualifying investments for the various ISA components are as follows.

Stocks and shares account

Qualifying investments for a stocks and shares account or component are as follows.

(a) Shares issued by a company (other than an investment trust, but see (e) below) wherever incorporated, and officially listed on a recognised stock exchange (see below). There are rules to allow the official listing condition to be treated as satisfied in the case of shares issued under a public offer and due to be listed. Shares acquired after 6 October 2005 must satisfy the '5% test' outlined below.

(b) Securities (i.e. secured or unsecured loan stock and similar) issued by a company wherever incorporated, and with a minimum residual term of five years from the date when first held under the ISA. Either the securities must be officially listed on a recognised stock exchange (see below) or the shares in the issuing company or its 75% holding company must be so listed. In the case of securities of an investment trust, the trust must satisfy the two qualifying conditions at (f) below.

(c) Gilt-edged securities and gilt strips with at least five years to run to maturity from the date when first held under the ISA.

(d) Securities issued by or on behalf of a government of a European Economic Area State (comprising the EU plus Norway, Iceland and Liechtenstein and excluding for this purpose the UK), and strips of such securities, with at least five years to run to maturity from the date when first held under the ISA.

(e) Securities issued by multilateral institutions as defined by the Organisation for Economic Cooperation and Development (i.e. institutions contributions to which may be reported as official development assistance by governments and other official agencies).

(f)   Shares in a qualifying investment trust listed in the Official List of the Stock Exchange. Broadly, in order to qualify, not more than 50% in value of an investment trust's investments can be securities otherwise within any of (b)–(d) above but having less than five years to run to maturity from the date when first acquired by the trust.

(g)   Units in, or shares of, a 'UK UCITS' where the units or shares satisfy the '5% test' outlined below.
A '*UK UCITS*' is a authorised collective investment scheme which complies with the requirements to be a UCITS scheme (an Undertaking for Collective Investment in Transferable Securities) for the purposes of the Collective Investment Schemes Sourcebook made by the Financial Services Authority, or part of such a scheme equivalent to a sub-fund of an umbrella scheme.

(h)   Units in, or shares of, a 'recognised UCITS' where the units or shares satisfy the '5% test' outlined below.
A '*recognised UCITS*' is the broad equivalent of a UK UCITS in (g) above but constituted in another EEA Member State.

(i)   'Qualifying' units in, or shares of, a non-UCITS retail scheme (a scheme to which COLL 5.1, 5.4 and 5.6 of the Collective Investment Schemes Sourcebook apply and which comprises all types of retail collective investment schemes authorised by the Financial Services Authority for sale in Great Britain other than UCITS schemes) where the units or shares satisfy the '5% test' outlined below. Units or shares are '*qualifying*' units or shares for this purpose if they do not restrict savers' ability to access their funds by more than two weeks.

(j)   Shares acquired by the investor under a SAYE share option scheme or all-employee share ownership plan or appropriated to him under an approved profit sharing scheme which are transferred into the ISA as mentioned under '*General*' above.

(k)   A 'depositary interest' in or in relation to an investment which is itself a qualifying investment other than cash. A '*depositary interest*' means the rights of any person to investments held by another, effectively as his nominee. The underlying investment, if within (a), (g), (h) or (i) above, must satisfy the '5% test' outlined below.

(l)   Units in a relevant collective investment scheme specified as a stakeholder product by *SI 2004 No 2738, reg 5* (the *Financial Services and Markets Act 2000 (Stakeholder Products) Regulations 2004*) where the units satisfy the '5% test' outlined below.

(m)   Life insurance policies issued on or after 6 April 2005 which satisfy the conditions summarised below under Insurance component and which also satisfy the '5% test' outlined below.

(n)   Life insurance policies previously held in an insurance component and transferred to a stocks and shares component under the transitional provisions following abolition of the insurance component (see below under Insurance component).

(o)   Cash held on deposit pending investment in any of the above.

(p)   In the case of a stocks and shares account which immediately before 6 April 2008 was a PEP, qualifying investments held in the PEP immediately before 6 April 2001 and retained in the plan throughout the intervening period even though they no longer strictly qualified.

The term *'company'* does not for the above purposes include an OEIC, a UK UCITS, recognised UCITS or non-UCITS retail scheme or an industrial and provident society (or 51% subsidiary thereof).

As regards the 50% test in (f) above, securities transferred under stock lending arrangements are still considered to be held by the trust or scheme, and any collateral obtained under those arrangements is ignored (Revenue PEP and ISA Bulletin No 5, 29 April 2002).

For the purposes of (a), (g), (h), (i), (k), (l) and (m) above, an investment satisfies the *'5% test'* if, judged at the date on which the investment becomes held in the ISA (and having regard to the contractual terms and conditions then in existence), the investor will not be entitled to a 'secured minimum return' at any time falling within the following five years. For this purpose, an investor is entitled to a *'secured minimum return'* if:

- the contract under which the investments were acquired, or any other transaction entered into by the investor or any other person; or
- the nature of the underlying subject matter of the investments,

have the effect that the investor is not exposed, or not exposed to any significant extent, to the risk of loss from fluctuations in the value of the investments exceeding 5% of the capital consideration paid or payable for the acquisition of those investments. Thus, if the investor is certain or near certain of receiving back at least 95% of the investment within five years, for example if he is given a guarantee to that effect or if the product itself invests substantially in cash, the test is failed. Where a life insurance policy confers an option to have its terms changed or have a new policy issued in its place, any such potential change is taken into account in applying the 5% test.

Certain categories of investment held in an ISA on 6 April 2004 that would not have qualified after that date due to the '5% test' could continue to be held on and after that date notwithstanding that test. The same applies to depositary interests (see (k) above) where the underlying investment is within those categories. This treatment extends to similar investments held in a PEP on 6 April 2004.

Following a revision in HMRC's interpretation of the phrase 'listed on a recognised stock exchange', securities admitted to trading on a European Economic Area exchange where securities traded are not listed by the relevant competent authority may have ceased to be a qualifying investment from 28 November 2001. Amending regulations were passed to preserve the qualifying status of securities held on that date within an ISA (where such status would otherwise have been lost for the aforementioned reason and no other) for as long as the above circumstances continue (and see Revenue Press Release 28 November 2001). This extends to securities held in a PEP on 28 November 2001.

Cash account

Qualifying investments for a cash account or component are as follows.

(i)   Cash deposited in a deposit account with a building society, a credit union or a person within *ITA 2007, s 991(2)(b)* (see **8.1**(b) **BANKS**), or with certain European institutions entitled to accept deposits in the UK.

(ii)   Cash deposited in a building society share account.

(iii)   Designated national savings products.

(iv)   Investments that would fall within (h) above (stocks and shares account) but for their failing the '5% test'.

(v)   Depositary interests (see (k) above) in or in relation to an investment which is itself a qualifying investment for a cash component.

(vi)   Investments that would fall within (g) above (stocks and shares account) but for their failing the '5% test'.

(vii) A deposit account specified as a stakeholder product by *SI 2004 No 2738, Reg 4* (the *Financial Services and Markets Act 2000 (Stakeholder Products) Regulations 2004*).

(viii) Units in a relevant collective investment scheme specified as a stakeholder product by *SI 2004 No 2738, Reg 5* that would fall within (l) above (stocks and shares account) but for their failing the '5% test'.

(ix)   Life insurance policies issued after 5 April 2005 that would fall within (m) above (stocks and shares account) but for their failing the '5% test'.

(x)   Life insurance policies previously held in an insurance component and transferred to a cash component under the transitional provisions following abolition of the insurance component (see below under Insurance component).

(xi)   Investments that would fall within (a) above (stocks and shares account) but for their failing the '5% test'.

(xii) **ALTERNATIVE FINANCE ARRANGEMENTS** (**3**) (e.g. Shari'a products).

A deposit or share account within (i) or (ii) above is not a qualifying investment if is 'connected' with any other account held within those categories (whether or not by the investor). For this purpose, accounts are *'connected'* if either was opened with reference to the other or with a view to enabling the other to be opened, or facilitating the opening of the other, on particular terms *and* the terms on which the cash component account was opened would have been significantly less favourable to the investor if the other had not been opened. HMRC will accept that an account is not a connected account if it is a 'feeder' account opened to enable investors to fund future deposits into an ISA, provided that the interest on the feeder account is in line with the interest paid on the account manager's other savings accounts (see HMRC Guidance Notes for ISA Managers).

Insurance component

Qualifying investments for an insurance component before 2005/06 are policies of life insurance satisfying specified conditions and cash held on deposit pending investment in such policies. The insurance must be on the life of the ISA investor only and its terms and conditions must provide:

(A)   that the policy may only be owned or held as a qualifying investment for an ISA insurance component;

(B)   that, if found to be in breach of (A) above, it shall automatically terminate (and see also above under 'Tax exemptions');

(C)   for an express prohibition of any transfer to the investor of the policy or the rights conferred thereby or any share or interest therein (other than cash proceeds on termination or partial surrender); and

(D)   that the policy etc. cannot be assigned other than by transfer of title between approved ISA managers or by its vesting in the investor's personal representatives.

The policy must constitute life insurance and must not be a contract to pay a life annuity, a personal portfolio bond (see **44.17 LIFE ASSURANCE POLICIES**) or a contract constituting pension business (as defined). There must be no contractual obligation to pay any premium other than the first (so regular premium policies are excluded). 'Connected' policies are excluded in much the same way as connected accounts are excluded from a cash component (see above). The making of loans by, or by arrangement with, the insurer to, or at the direction of, the ISA investor is prohibited.

For 2005/06 onwards, the insurance component is abolished, but the same conditions as above apply to determine whether or not a policy is a qualifying investment for a stocks and shares account (see (l) above) or a cash account (see (ix) above). For these purposes, a *'policy'* includes rights under a linked long-term contract specified as a stakeholder product by *SI 2004 No 2738, Reg 6* (the *Financial Services and Markets Act 2000 (Stakeholder Products) Regulations 2004*).

Repairing of invalid accounts

Where, within a single tax year, an investor opens a valid ISA, closes it and opens a new ISA of the same designation and component, the new ISA used to be technically invalid (because transfers between ISAs can only be carried out by account managers). For 2003/04 to 2007/08 inclusive, where the account is a mini-account, the new ISA (i.e. the first such ISA to be opened after the said closure and in the same tax year) is treated as valid (and thus qualifying for tax relief) from the date it is opened.

Where the above circumstances occurred in 2001/02 or 2002/03 and HMRC give notice that the new account is invalid, the account becomes 'eligible for repair', i.e. it qualifies for tax relief *but only from the date of the notice*. Similar consequences ensue for 2001/02 and all subsequent years where an investor subscribes to an incompatible combination of maxi-accounts and mini-accounts in a single tax year. The account thus eligible for repair is the earliest invalid account opened in the year. Repairing of accounts is subject to normal subscription limits, and where necessary HMRC will apportion (i.e. between valid accounts and any one or more accounts eligible for repair) the total amount subscribed in the tax year.

For 2008/09 onwards, an account is eligible for repair if either the overall subscription limit is breached or it is the second stocks and shares account or cash account subscribed to by the same investor in the tax year. If the investor closes a cash account and opens another cash account, the new account (i.e. the first cash account to be opened after the said closure and in the same tax year) is treated as valid (and thus qualifying for tax relief) from the date it is opened.

HMRC will seek to void invalid subscriptions only where the investor has either subscribed to a disallowed combination of accounts for more than one year or has significantly exceeded the subscription limits. In all other cases, they will simply issue a letter, drawing the investor's attention to the ISA rules and advising him that they will take no action unless he subscribes to a disallowed combination of ISAs in a later tax year. If he then does so, they will take corrective action for both years. (HMRC PEP and ISA Bulletins No 31, 29 September 2006 and No 33, 10 November 2006).

Specific companies

Investors who withdrew funds from an ISA with Northern Rock plc between 13 September 2007 and 19 September 2007 inclusive were permitted to re-deposit (on or after 13 September) all or part of the amount withdrawn into an ISA with Northern Rock or any other provider in 2007/08 without losing their tax advantages as a result of the withdrawal. The amount reinvested did not count towards the subscription limits. If any amount was invested in the original account in 2007/08 (before 13 September), any excess of this amount over the amount reinvested did not count towards the subscription limits either. Investors wishing to re-deposit with another provider had to obtain a certificate from Northern Rock and present it to the new provider.

Similarly, investors who receive compensation under the Financial Services Compensation Scheme in respect of an Icesave cash ISA held on 8 October 2008 may reinvest into another ISA for 2008/09 without losing their tax advantages, provided they do so before 6 October 2009. The reinvestment, if made after 5 April 2009, does not count towards the subscription limit for 2009/10. Any amount invested in the original account in 2008/09 still counted towards the 2008/09 subscription limit. Investors receiving compensation will be given a certificate, which they must present to the new provider if they wish to reinvest. (HMRC ISA Bulletin 6, November 2008; HMRC ISA Bulletin 9, March 2009).

It was discovered that certain ISA investments sold by Keydata Investment Services Ltd, which went into liquidation on 8 June 2009, did not comply with the ISA rules. HMRC have stated that the vast majority of affected investors will not have to pay tax, as HMRC will pursue the company for the tax due prior to administration, and the Financial Services Compensation Scheme will pay the tax on behalf of the investors for the period since administration. (HMRC News Release, 13 November 2009). For more details, see HMRC guidance at www.hmrc.gov.uk/isa/keydata.pdf. Individuals who had Keydata ISAs holding SLS Capital S.A. Secure Income Bonds, issue 1, 2 or 3, may reinvest up to the amount subscribed for investment in the Bonds in another stocks and shares ISA by means of a single subscription before 6 April 2011. Such individuals will have received a certificate from the administrators of Keydata showing the maximum amount which can be so invested. The certificate must be handed to the new ISA provider. The amount so invested does not count towards the annual subscription limits.

Account managers

The regulations cover qualification as an account manager, HMRC approval and withdrawal thereof, appointment of UK tax representatives of non-UK account managers, account managers ceasing to act or to qualify, claims for tax relief and agreement of liabilities, annual returns of income and of information, annual and interim tax repayment claims, record-keeping, and information to be provided to investors.

[*SI 1998 No 1870; SI 1998 No 3174; SI 2006 No 3194; SI 2007 No 2119; SI 2008 Nos 704, 1934, 3025; SI 2009 No 56, Sch 2 paras 45–47; SI 2009 Nos 1550, 1994; SI 2010 No 835*].

Closure and death

Subject to the ISA terms and conditions, an investor may close an ISA at any time without affecting tax exemptions up to the date of closure. Where an investor dies, income and gains in respect of ISA investments which arise after the date of death but before the date of closure are not exempt.

See generally HMRC guidance at www.hmrc.gov.uk/leaflets/isa-factsheet.htm and the HMRC 'Guidance Notes for ISA Managers' at www.hmrc.gov.uk/is a/isa-guidance-notes-2008.pdf. PEP and ISA Bulletins are published on the HMRC website.

Simon's Taxes. See E3.3.

International organisations, income from

[30.22] Income from **international organisations** may be exempt under specific provisions, see **25 DIPLOMATIC IMMUNITY**.

Insurance policies, annual payments under

[30.23] Annual payments falling to be made under certain **insurance policies** are exempt from income tax. The exemption, described below, will most commonly apply to mortgage payment protection insurance, permanent health insurance, creditor insurance (to meet existing commitments, possibly including domestic utility bills, in event of accident, sickness, disability or unemployment) and certain kinds of long-term care insurance (but only where the policy is taken out before the need for care becomes apparent). (Revenue Press Release REV 6, 28 November 1995).

The exemption applies to policies insuring against a health or employment risk, provided that certain conditions are met and that no part of any premium is deductible in calculating the income of the insured. The exemption therefore does not apply if any premiums under the policy have to any extent qualified for tax relief, either as a deduction from total income or in computing income from any source (e.g. business profits). However, where an employer takes out a group policy to meet the cost of employees' sick pay and the policy would otherwise qualify under these provisions, the proportion of any payment attributable (on just and reasonable apportionment) to employees' contribu tions to premiums is not treated as employment or pension income despite the deduction available to the employer.

For an annual payment to qualify for the exemption:

(a)   it must be made under a policy (or part of a policy) providing insurance against a 'health or employment risk';

(b)   the provisions of the policy which insure against that risk must not be significantly affected by other benefits payable under the policy (see below);

(c)   the policy must make no provision for payments relating to that risk other than for specified periods (see below); and

(d)   the provisions of the policy relating to that risk must always have been such that the insurer runs a genuine risk of loss (i.e. proceeds payable must be capable of exceeding premiums received plus an investment return on those premiums).

A '*health or employment risk*' is either a risk of physical or mental illness, disability, infirmity or defect (including a risk of an existing condition deteriorating) or a risk of loss of employment (including loss of self-employment and loss of office). The persons at risk may include the insured, his spouse (or civil partner), any child under 21 of the insured or his spouse (or civil partner), and, for policies connected with the meeting of liabilities under an identified transaction, a person jointly liable with the insured or his spouse (or civil partner).

The specified periods for which payment may be made are: for as long as the illness etc. or unemployment continues (including in the case of illness etc. any related period of convalescence or rehabilitation) or for as long as the income of the insured etc. (apart from benefits under the policy) is less, in circumstances so insured against, than it otherwise would be. If any such period ends as a result of the death of the insured etc., it is extended to any period immediately following (so that benefits paid to the deceased's spouse or estate are brought within the exemption).

The requirement for the relevant provisions of the policy not to be affected by other benefits is an anti-avoidance measure. The provisions of a policy covering different kinds of benefits must ensure that the terms of the policy relating to the health or employment risk (possibly including the fixing of the amount of premiums), or the way in which they are given effect, would not have been significantly different if the policy insured only against the health or employment risk (where the only difference is that certain benefits are applied for reducing other benefits under the policy this is ignored). A broadly similar rule applies where there are multiple policies. In each case, regard must be had to all the persons for whose benefit insurance is provided against the qualifying risk.

There are provisions enabling benefits relating to illness etc. to qualify for the exemption if paid under an individual policy derived from and superseding an employer's group policy where an employee has left the employment as a consequence of the occurrence insured against.

[*ITTOIA 2005, ss 735–743*].

Where an insurance policy is taken out by a third party, no liability to income tax in respect of employment income arises on a payment, and no liability to income tax arises on a pension or annuity payment, provided the exemption criteria under *ITTOIA 2005, s 735* (see above) are met and two further conditions are satisfied:

- that payments are made: to a person who made payments or contributions in respect of premiums in respect of the insurance policy taken out by a third party wholly or partly for that person's benefit; or to that person's spouse (or civil partner); and
- that the payments are attributable (on a just and reasonable basis) to the contributions in respect of premiums.

[ITEPA 2003, ss 324A, 644A].

Benefits which are wholly exempt are paid without deduction of tax. Where they are partially exempt (e.g. in the case of a company policy to which the employee contributes) or the policy holder's income, including the maximum benefits payable, is below taxable income limits, the insurer may pay benefits gross on receipt of an appropriate declaration from the recipient (on form R91). (Revenue Tax Bulletin December 1996 p 377).

Interest received

[30.24] The receipt of interest is exempt from income tax where the interest is paid on:

(i)   damages for personal injuries or death including similar interest awarded by a foreign court if also exempt from tax in that country. [*ITTOIA 2005, s 751*];

(ii)   certain UK government stocks held by non-residents (see **64.3 SAVINGS AND INVESTMENT INCOME**) and certain borrowings in foreign currency by local authorities and certain statutory bodies (see **24.12 DEDUCTION OF TAX AT SOURCE**);

(iii)   **National Savings Bank** deposits other than investment deposits, **but** the exemption applies **only** to the first £70 per tax year per individual. [*ITTOIA 2005, s 691*]. In practice, the exemption only applies to National Savings Bank ordinary accounts and not to any other National Savings Bank products; no new ordinary accounts can be opened after 28 January 2004;

(iv)   **Government Savings Certificates;**

(v)   **Save As You Earn** savings arrangements (bonuses under such arrangements also being exempt), provided that they are linked to approved SAYE option schemes (see **69.51 SHARE-RELATED EMPLOYMENT INCOME AND EXEMPTIONS**). Share option linked savings arrangements may be offered by a wide range of providers, including certain European authorised institutions. Authorisation by HMRC (previously by the Treasury) is required for the operation of such schemes. [*ITTOIA 2005, ss 702–708; ITA 2007, Sch 1 para 571; FA 2009, s 50, Sch 26; SI 1995 No 1778; SI 2001 No 3629, Art 19*];

(vi)   overpaid inheritance tax. [*IHTA 1984, ss 233(3), 235(2)*];

(vii)   certain repayments, see **41 INTEREST ON OVERPAID TAX;**

(viii) refunds of amounts over-repaid by borrowers in respect of **student loans** made under specified statutory provisions. [*ITTOIA 2005, s 753*];

(ix)   tax reserve certificates issued by the Treasury. [*ITTOIA 2005, s 750*].

See also **30.29** below (payments to victims of Nazi persecution).

Long service awards

[30.25] Such awards to employees are exempt within the limits set out in **27.56 EMPLOYMENT INCOME.**

Meal vouchers

[30.26] Where provided to employees, such vouchers do not attract an income tax charge if the conditions shown in **27.69 EMPLOYMENT INCOME** are complied with; in particular, the exemption extends only to the first 15 pence per working day.

Members of Parliaments or Assemblies

[30.27] The following exemptions apply.

MPs' overnight accommodation expenses

No liability to income tax arises in respect of a payment made for 'accommodation expenses' to a member of the House of Commons under *Parliamentary Standards Act 2009, s 5(1)*. This applies equally to a payment related to, or in consequence of, a payment for accommodation expenses. '*Accommodation expenses*' are expenses necessarily incurred on overnight accommodation that is required for the performance of the member's parliamentary duties in or about the Palace of Westminster or the member's constituency. They do not include the cost of an overnight stay in a hotel that is required only because the House is sitting late, unless the House is sitting beyond 1 am. The exemption does not cover loans made to MPs for a deposit on a rented property.

The above has effect in relation to payments made on or after 7 May 2010, unless they are made in accordance with a Commons resolution passed before that date in which case the old rules apply. The old rules were not dissimilar but predated the introduction, by the Independent Parliamentary Standards Authority (IPSA), of a new scheme for paying MPs' expenses. The rules applied to an overnight expenses allowance paid to an MP in accordance with a Commons resolution; the above exclusions did not apply.

[*ITEPA 2003, s 292; F(No 2)A 2010, Sch 4 para 1(2)(4)(5)*].

See also **27.68 EMPLOYMENT INCOME.**

Overnight expenses of other elected representatives

Payments to members of the Scottish Parliament or the Wales or Northern Ireland Assemblies for necessary overnight expenses are also exempt from income tax. These are additional expenses necessarily incurred for the purpose of performing duties as a member in staying away from home overnight either where the body of which he is a member sits or in the area he represents. [*ITEPA 2003, s 293*].

MPs' UK travel and subsistence expenses

No liability to income tax arises in respect of a payment made for 'relevant UK travel expenses' or 'relevant subsistence expenses' to a member of the House of Commons under *Parliamentary Standards Act 2009, s 5(1)*. '*Relevant UK travel expenses*' are expenses necessarily incurred on journeys made by the member within the UK that are necessary for the performance of his parliamentary duties. If the member shares caring responsibilities with a spouse or partner, the cost of journeys made by the spouse or partner between the member's London Area residence and the member's constituency residence are also within the exemption. 'Caring responsibilities' and 'London Area residence' have the same meaning as they have in the MPs' expenses scheme for the time being in effect under *Parliamentary Standards Act 2009, s 5*. '*Relevant subsistence expenses*' are expenses necessarily incurred on an evening meal (excluding alcoholic drinks) eaten on the Parliamentary Estate in cases where the member is required to be at the Commons because the House is sitting beyond 7.30 pm.

The above has effect in relation to payments made on or after 7 May 2010, unless they are made in accordance with a Commons resolution passed before that date in which case the old rules apply. The old rules operated largely by concession and predated the introduction by IPSA (see above) of the current MPs' expenses scheme. Under the old rules, MPs were reimbursed the cost of certain travel by spouses and, by concession, no liability to income tax arose; the current rules are more restrictive. The costs of evening meals as above were in some circumstances previously paid under the allowance for overnight accommodation expenses and were within the exemption at *ITEPA 2003, s 292* above; under the IPSA scheme, payments for such meals are made separately from payments for accommodation expenses.

[*ITEPA 2003, s 293A; F(No 2)A 2010, Sch 4 para 2*].

European travel expenses of MPs and other representatives

No liability to income tax arises in respect of a sum that is paid in respect of 'European travel expenses' to a member of the House of Commons under *Parliamentary Standards Act 2009, s 5(1)*. '*European travel expenses*' means the cost of, and any additional expenses incurred in, travelling between the UK and 'a relevant European location'. A '*relevant European location*' is an EU institution or agency or the national parliament of another member State, of a candidate or applicant country or of any other country that is a member of the Council of Europe. Payments to members of the Scottish Parliament or the Wales or Northern Ireland Assemblies in respect of European travel expenses are similarly exempt.

The above has effect in relation to payments made on or after 7 May 2010, unless they are made in accordance with a Commons resolution passed before that date in which case the old rules apply. The old rules were similar but predated the introduction by IPSA (see above) of the current MPs' expenses scheme. The one substantive change is that the current exemption for travel to the national parliaments of Council of Europe member States previously applied to travel to the national parliaments of European Free Trade Association member States.

[*ITEPA 2003, s 294; F(No 2)A 2010, Sch 4 para 3*].

Transport and subsistence for Government ministers etc.

Ministers and certain other office-holders in the UK Government, the Scottish Parliament or the Wales or Northern Ireland Assemblies are exempt from income tax in respect of the provision of transport or subsistence to them or their families or households by or on behalf of the Crown, or the reimbursement of expenditure on such provision. 'Transport' for this purpose includes any car (with or without a driver) and any other benefit in connection with such a car (including fuel). 'Subsistence' includes food, drink and temporary accommodation. [*ITEPA 2003, s 295*].

Miners' free coal

[**30.28**] Miners' free coal, or cash in lieu thereof, is exempt (see **27.29**(xi) EMPLOYMENT INCOME and **56.3**(j) PENSION INCOME).

Nazi persecution, interest paid to victims of

[**30.29**] Interest paid to, or in respect of, a victim of Nazi persecution is exempt from income tax if it is paid under a 'qualifying compensation scheme', for a 'qualifying purpose' and in respect of a 'qualifying deposit' of the victim. A '*qualifying compensation scheme*' is a scheme constituted (whether under UK or foreign law) by written instrument and the purpose (or a purpose) of which is to make payments of interest of the kind contemplated by this exemption. Interest is paid for a 'qualifying purpose' if it either meets a liability to pay such interest on the deposit or is paid to compensate for the effects of inflation on the deposit. A '*qualifying deposit*' is a deposit made by, or on behalf of, the victim and on or before 5 June 1945. The exemption has retrospective effect for 1996/97 and subsequent years. In relation to the years 1996/97 to 2005/06 inclusive, all such adjustments are to be made as are necessary to give effect to the exemption (whether by repayment, discharge of tax or otherwise), provided the person entitled to the exemption makes a claim on or before 31 January 2012 for it to apply. [*ITTOIA 2005, s 756A; FA 2006, s 64(2)(7)(9)–(12); ITA 2007, Sch 1 para 575*].

Prior to *FA 2006*, a similar exemption applied by concession (ESC A100) but only in relation to payments made by UK banks and building societies, whereas the legislation applies also to payments by foreign banks and building societies, including payments made through the Claims Resolution Tribunal for Dormant Accounts in Switzerland. The concession applied to payments made after 7 May 2000 but is now made redundant by the retrospectivity of the legislation.

For further information, see www.hmrc.gov.uk/individuals/holocaust.htm.

Interest exempted by the legislation remains subject to the reporting requirements of *TMA 1970, ss 17, 18* at **63.14 RETURNS**.

Non-UK domiciliaries

[30.30] Where certain conditions are met, an exemption is introduced for **2008/09 onwards** for the foreign income and gains (see **61.5 REMITTANCE BASIS**) of low-income non-UK domiciled employees working in the UK. According to HMRC, such individuals will typically be migrant workers employed in seasonal work in the agricultural or service sectors in UK and in other countries in the same tax year and whose overseas income is subject to tax where it is earned (Treasury Explanatory Notes to the 2009 Finance Bill). The exemption removes in most cases the requirement for a self-assessment tax return to be filed.

The conditions (all of which must be met for the tax year in question) are that:

- the individual is UK resident but not domiciled in the UK (see **62.4 RESIDENCE, ORDINARY RESIDENCE AND DOMICILE**);
- the individual has not made a claim to be taxed on the remittance basis (see **61.2**(1) **REMITTANCE BASIS**);
- the individual has income from an employment the duties of which are performed wholly or partly in the UK;
- the individual's 'relevant foreign earnings' (if any) (see **61.5 REMITTANCE BASIS**) do not exceed £10,000 and are all subject to a foreign tax;
- the individual's income consisting of foreign interest (if any) does not exceed £100 and is all subject to a foreign tax;
- the individual has no other foreign income and gains other than 'relevant foreign earnings' or interest;
- the individual would not be liable to UK income tax at a rate other than the basic rate or the starting rate for savings if this exemption did not apply; and
- the individual does not file a tax return.

The exemption operates by calculating the individual's income tax liability (L1) without regard to the exemption and then reducing it by so much of that liability (L2) as relates to his foreign income and gains. In computing L2, the foreign income and gains must be reduced by personal reliefs to the extent that these were set against them in the calculation of L1. If any double tax relief is due in respect of the foreign income and gains, this must be deducted in arriving at L2.

[*ITA 2007, ss 828A–828D; FA 2009, s 52*].

Non-UK residents

[30.31] Non-UK residents are exempt from tax on income and capital gains from: certain government stocks (see **64.3 SAVINGS AND INVESTMENT INCOME**); securities of the Inter-American Development Bank [*ITTOIA 2005, s 773*]; securities of the OECD Support Fund [*OECD Support Fund Act 1975, s 4*] and certain other international organisations designated by statutory instrument [*ITTOIA 2005, s 774;*], including the Asian Development Bank (*SI 1984 No 1215*), the African Development Bank (*SI 1984 No 1634*), the European Bank for Reconstruction and Development (*SI 1991 No 1202*) and any of the European Communities or the European Investment Bank (*SI 1985 No 1172*); and from certain pensions, see **56.4 PENSION INCOME**. See also **26.2 DOUBLE TAX RELIEF**.

Olympic Games, London 2012 — competitors and staff

[30.32] The Treasury have power to make regulations conferring exemption from income tax to non-UK resident athletes in relation to income arising from their performance at these Games, and conferring similar exemptions to other non-UK resident persons in relation to income earned from specified classes of activity performed in relation to these Games. Such regulations may also disapply, as regards any related payments, various statutory requirements to deduct income tax at source. [*FA 2006, s 68; ITA 2007, Sch 1 para 614*]. See also **31.5 EXEMPT ORGANISATIONS**.

Overseas income

[30.33] Certain overseas income is exempt from UK tax under specific **DOUBLE TAX RELIEF (26)** agreements. If not so exempt, double tax relief may nevertheless be claimable. In some circumstances, overseas income is chargeable on the **REMITTANCE BASIS (61)**. See also **50 NON-RESIDENTS**.

Pensions

[30.34] Certain pensions are exempt — see **56.3, 56.4 PENSION INCOME**.

Premium savings bonds

[30.35] Prizes are free of both income tax and capital gains tax.

Redundancy payments

[30.36] Redundancy payments under *Employment Rights Act 1996* (or NI equivalent) are exempt. [*ITEPA 2003, s 309, Sch 6 para 63*]. See also **27.70 EMPLOYMENT INCOME**.

Repayment supplement

[30.37] Repayment supplement (i.e. interest on overpaid tax) in respect of income tax or capital gains tax repayments (see **41 INTEREST ON OVERPAID TAX**) is disregarded for income tax purposes. The same applies to VAT repayment supplement under *VATA 1994, s 79*, but interest payable on certain VAT repayments under *VATA 1994, s 80* is *not* exempt. [*ITTOIA 2005, ss 749, 777, Sch 1 para 331*].

Retirement, lump sums on

[30.38] Certain lump sums under **PENSION PROVISION (57)** are exempt. See **56.3**(a) **PENSION INCOME**.

Sandwich courses etc.

[30.39] Where an employee is released by employer to take a full-time educational course at a university, technical college or similar institution open to the public at large, payments made by employer to employee for periods of attendance are exempt from income tax subject to the following conditions: (i) that the course lasts at least one academic year, with an average of at least 20 weeks per year of full-time attendance, and (ii) that the total payments, including lodging, subsistence and travel allowances but excluding any tuition fees paid by the employer to the university etc., do not exceed

- (for academic year 2007/08, beginning on 1 September 2007, and subsequent years) £15,480;
- (for academic years 2005/06 and 2006/07, beginning on 1 September 2005 and 2006 respectively) £15,000.

Payments become taxable in full where the rate exceeds the annual limit. However, an increase in the rate of payment over the limit, partway through a course, does not prevent the exemption applying to any payments for the earlier part of the course.

(HMRC SP 4/86; HMRC Internet Statements 12 June 2006, 15 August 2007).

Savings certificates

[30.40] All income arising from savings certificates (as defined) (and including index-linked) and tax reserve certificates is exempt from tax except that arising from:

(i)   savings certificates purchased by or on behalf of a person in excess of the amount authorised under the regulations of the particular issue; or

(ii)   Ulster savings certificates, unless the holder is resident and ordinarily resident in NI when the certificates are repaid or he was so resident and ordinarily resident when he purchased them. Where repayment is made after the death of the holder, who was resident and ordinarily resident in NI when he purchased them, the exemption is allowed.

[*ITTOIA 2005, ss 692, 693*].

Scholarship income and bursaries

[30.41] Such income is exempt where arising from a scholarship held by a full-time student at an educational establishment. [*ITTOIA 2005, s 776*]. In *Clayton v Gothorp* Ch D 1971, 47 TC 168, discharge of loan made by employer for training course held not scholarship income but was emoluments. See **27.47** EMPLOYMENT INCOME for where scholarship awarded by employer of parent etc. Covenanted 'parental contributions' under *Education Act 1962* not an educational endowment (*Gibbs v Randall* Ch D 1980, 53 TC 513).

Social security benefits etc

[30.42] Exemption applies to certain social security benefits (see **70** SOCIAL SECURITY AND NATIONAL INSURANCE) and corresponding foreign benefits (HMRC ESC A24) and payments under Jobmatch programme (HMRC ESC A97). Disabled Person's Vehicle Maintenance Grants under *National Health Service Act 1977, Sch 2 para 2* or corresponding Scottish or NI Act. [*ITTOIA 2005, s 780*].

Special guardians and kinship carers

[30.43] On and after 6 April 2010, 'qualifying guardians' will be exempt from income tax on any 'qualifying payments' they receive. The legislation will be included in a Finance Bill to be introduced in autumn 2010, but will have backdated effect.

'*Qualifying guardians*' are individuals who care for one or more children placed with them under:

- a special guardianship order; or
- a residence order where the individual is not the child's parent or step-parent.

'*Qualifying payments*' are payments:

- by the child's parents or by, or on behalf of, the local authority;
- to a qualifying guardian,

which are made in relation to a special guardianship order or a residence order.

Before 6 April 2010, special guardians were able to compute their taxable care income using the non-statutory fixed expenses method for Adult Placement carers at **30.3** above; the fixed expenses were £400 per week for the first child placed with them and £250 per week for each of the second and third such children.

Kinship carers

Kinship carers who provide care to a child who has not been placed with them under a residence order will not be considered a qualifying guardian for the purposes of the income tax exemption from 6 April 2010. However, they will be entitled to claim the new income tax relief for shared lives carers at **30.3** above. Before 6 April 2010, they were able to compute their taxable income in the same way as special guardians.

(HMRC Budget Note BN26, 22 June 2010).

UEFA Champions League Final 2011

[30.44] The final of the UEFA Champions League is to be held in England in 2011. There are provisions conferring exemption from income tax to non-UK resident employees and contractors of competing overseas teams in relation to employment income or trading income arising from duties or services performed in the UK in connection with the final. The exemption does not apply to income from contracts entered into or amended after the final. Also, it does not apply if there are tax avoidance arrangements a main purpose of which is the obtaining of the exemption. Where the exemption applies, the deduction at source rules normally applicable to non-UK resident sportsmen (see **50.10** NON-RESIDENTS are accordingly disapplied. [*FA 2010, Sch 20*].

Woodlands

[30.45] Profits (and losses) from the commercial occupation of woodlands in the UK are ignored for income tax purposes. For this purpose, the occupation of woodlands is commercial if the woodlands are managed on a commercial basis and with a view to the realisation of profits. Land on which short rotation coppice (i.e. a perennial crop of tree species planted at high density, the stems of which are harvested above ground level at intervals of less than ten years) is cultivated is not woodlands. [*ITA 2007, s 996(4)(6), Sch 1 paras 369, 583; ITTOIA 2005, ss 11, 267, 768, 876(4)(6), Sch 1 para 481*].

In *Jaggers (trading as Shide Trees) v Ellis* Ch D 1997, 71 TC 164, land on which trees were planted and cultivated in a manner normally associated with Christmas tree production was held not to be woodland.

See **73.73**(p) TRADING INCOME for the tax treatment of certain Government grants.

For the purpose of computing the profits of a trade of dealing in land, there is disregarded any part of the cost of purchasing UK woodlands in the course of the trade that is attributable to trees or saleable underwood growing on the land. If the woodlands are subsequently sold in the course of the trade and any of the trees and underwood are still growing, the amount disregarded on purchase is excluded from the sale proceeds. These rules do not apply if the purchase was under a pre-1 May 1963 contract. [*ITTOIA 2005, s 156, Sch 2 para 42*].

31

Exempt Organisations

Introduction

[31.1] Exemption is given to the organisations etc. below to the extent indicated.

Non-resident central banks

[31.2] Non-UK resident central banks as specified by Order in Council are exempt from tax on certain classes of income. [*ITA 2007, s 840; ICTA 1988, s 516*]. The issue departments of the Reserve Bank of India and the State Bank of Pakistan are exempt from all taxes. [*ITA 2007, s 839; ICTA 1988, s 517; TCGA 1992, s 271(8)*].

Charities

[31.3] Charities are generally exempt but see full details at **16 CHARITIES**.

Local authorities etc.

[31.4] Local authorities and local authority associations, as defined by *ITA 2007, s 999* and *s 1000* respectively, are exempt from income tax. [*ITA 2007, s 838; ICTA 1988, s 519*].

Olympic Games, London 2012

[31.5] Olympic Games, London 2012. London Organising Committee of the Olympic Games Ltd (set up to organise, manage and promote the 2012 London Olympics) is exempt from corporation tax, and payments made to it are exempt from various statutory requirements to deduct income tax at source. The Treasury are given power to grant exemption from income tax and capital gains tax to the International Olympic Committee (IOC), to treat it as not having a permanent UK establishment for corporation tax purposes and to grant similar exemption as above in respect of payments (including interest payments) to the IOC. The Treasury may make regulations to extend or restrict these exemptions in specified circumstances. [*FA 2006, ss 65–67; ITA 2007, Sch 1 paras 612, 613*]. See also **30.32 EXEMPT INCOME.**

Registered pension schemes

[31.6] Registered pension schemes are exempt from income tax on income derived from investments (including futures contracts and option contracts) or deposits held for the purposes of the scheme. See **57.6 PENSION PROVISION.** See, however, **57.22–57.25 PENSION PROVISION** as regards the charge to tax where income is derived from certain property held by self-directed registered pension schemes.

Visiting forces etc.

[31.7] Visiting forces and associated civilians from designated countries. [*ITA 2007, s 833; ICTA 1988, s 323; FA 2009, Sch 1 paras 6, 7*]. See *SI 1961 No 580, SI 1964 No 924* and *SI 1998 Nos 1513, 1514.* See also **25 DIPLOMATIC ETC. IMMUNITY.**

32

Foreign Income

Cross-references. See **61 REMITTANCE BASIS; RESIDENCE, ORDINARY RESIDENCE AND DOMICILE** at **62.4** for domicile, **62.5** for residence, **62.6** for split-year treatment of persons becoming or ceasing to be resident in the UK, **62.7** for ordinarily resident; **25.1 DIPLOMATIC ETC. IMMUNITY — INDIVIDUALS AND ORGANISATIONS** for exemption from tax on foreign income of consular officers and employees in UK; **26.4 DOUBLE TAX RELIEF** regarding Ireland; **27.5, 27.10, 27.19 EMPLOYMENT INCOME** for foreign employment.

Introduction

[32.1] Each type of foreign (i.e. non-UK) income is charged to tax under the provisions charging the equivalent type of UK income (except for dividends from non-UK companies, which have their own charging provision). A number of special rules continue to apply to foreign income, however, and these are described in this chapter). *ITTOIA 2005* employs the expression 'relevant foreign income' to indicate the types of income to which many of those rules apply (see **32.2** below).

Relevant foreign income

[32.2] *'Relevant foreign income'* (see **32.1** above) means chargeable income which arises from a source outside the United Kingdom (see **32.3** below) and which falls within any of the following categories:

(a)   trade profits (see **73.1 TRADING INCOME**);
(b)   a partner's share of the profits of a trade arising outside the UK for a tax year if:
  •   the control and management of the trade is outside the UK; and
  •   the partner is a UK resident individual who is not domiciled in the UK (see **62.4 RESIDENCE, ORDINARY RESIDENCE AND DOMICILE**) or is not ordinarily resident in the UK (see **62.7 RESIDENCE, ORDINARY RESIDENCE AND DOMICILE**) and, in either case, the **REMITTANCE BASIS (61)** applies to him for the tax year;

(c)   adjustment income on change of basis in computing trade profits (see **73.20 TRADING INCOME**);

(d)   profits of a property business (which may be a UK property business or an overseas property business — see **60.2 PROPERTY INCOME**);

(e)   interest (see **64.2 SAVINGS AND INVESTMENT INCOME**);

(f)   dividends from non-UK resident companies (see **64.12 SAVINGS AND INVESTMENT INCOME**);

(g)   purchased life annuity payments (see **64.17 SAVINGS AND INVESTMENT INCOME**);

(h)   profits from the disposal of deeply discounted securities (see **64.18 SAVINGS AND INVESTMENT INCOME**) which are outside the UK;

(i)   sales of foreign dividend coupons (see **64.25 SAVINGS AND INVESTMENT INCOME**);

(j)   royalties and other income from intellectual property within *ITTOIA 2005, s 579* (see **40.1 INTELLECTUAL PROPERTY**);

(k)   films and sound recordings (non-trade businesses) (see **49.3 MISCELLANEOUS INCOME**);

(l)   non-trading income from telecommunication rights within **49.4 MISCELLANEOUS INCOME**;

(m)   estate income within *ITTOIA 2005, s 649* where the estate is not a UK estate (see **23.4 DECEASED ESTATES**);

(n)   annual payments not otherwise charged within *ITTOIA 2005, ss 683–686* (see **49.5 MISCELLANEOUS INCOME**);

(o)   income not otherwise charged within *ITTOIA 2005, ss 687–689* (see **49.7 MISCELLANEOUS INCOME**);

(p)   distributions by the Commonwealth Development Corporation;

(q)   foreign pension income within **56.2**(b) **PENSION INCOME**;

(r)   employment-related annuities within **56.2**(e) **PENSION INCOME**;

(s)   pre-1973 pensions paid under the *Overseas Pensions Act 1973* within **56.2**(h) **PENSION INCOME**;

(t)   annual payments within **56.2**(i) **PENSION INCOME**;

(u)   social security income from foreign benefits (see **70.2 SOCIAL SECURITY AND NATIONAL INSURANCE**);

(v)   (for 2008/09 onwards) accrued income profits (see **2.9 ACCRUED INCOME SCHEME**); and

(w)   (for 2008/09 onwards) foreign deemed income under the 'transfer of assets' abroad rules (see **4.14, 4.15 ANTI-AVOIDANCE**).

In a case where the **REMITTANCE BASIS** (**61**) applies, the reference above to chargeable income includes income that would be chargeable if the remittance basis did not apply.

See also **51.8, 51.29 OFFSHORE FUNDS** (offshore income gains treated as relevant foreign income in certain circumstances).

Income chargeable as a result of the withdrawal of relief for unremittable income under *ITTOIA 2005, s 844* (see **32.5** below) is not relevant foreign income.

Where a claim for relief is made, unremittable income is not taken into account for income tax purposes. Claims must be made within twelve months after 31 January following the tax year in which the income would otherwise be chargeable. A claim may not be made if a payment has been made in respect of the income under certain export credit guarantee arrangements (see *ITTOIA 2005, s 842(4)*).

Relief under the above provisions is withdrawn if the income ceases to be unremittable or if a payment under export credit guarantee arrangements is made. In such an event, the income is treated as arising at the time it so ceases to be unremittable or the payment is made, and it is valued for tax purposes as at that time (together with any foreign tax). If the source has ceased at that time then the income is treated as a post-cessation receipt (see **59.1 POST-CESSATION RECEIPTS AND EXPENDITURE**) if the source was a trade, profession or vocation or a property business, or in the case of income from another source, the income is taxed as if the source was continuing. Where appropriate, these provisions apply to the personal representative of the taxpayer as they would have to the taxpayer.

Relief under these provisions is not available in respect of profits which a person is treated as making under the accrued income scheme, but a similar relief is provided for in *ITA 2007, ss 668, 669* — see **2.10 ACCRUED INCOME SCHEME**.

Where no claim is made under the above provisions in respect of unremittable income, the amount chargeable to tax is determined by reference to the generally recognised market value in the UK of the currency in which the income is denominated or, if there is no such value, according to the official exchange rate of the territory where the income arises.

[*ITTOIA 2005, ss 841–845, Sch 2 para 153; ITA 2007, Sch 1 para 578; SI 2009 No 56, Sch 1 para 444*].

Interest does not run on the unpaid tax if HMRC are informed promptly, see details under **42.5 INTEREST AND SURCHARGES ON OVERDUE TAX**.

See **73.124 TRADING INCOME** for relief for certain unremittable income forming part of the profits of trades.

Simon's Taxes. See E1.607–E1.609.

33

Herd Basis

See generally HMRC Business Income Manual BIM55501–55640.

Simon's Taxes. See **B5.150–B5.154**.

Introduction

[33.1] Animals and other living creatures kept for the purposes of farming or similar trades (e.g. animal or fish breeding) are generally treated as trading stock (see **73.112 TRADING INCOME**) unless:

- they are part of a herd in relation to which an election is made under *ITTOIA 2005, ss 111–129* for the 'herd basis' (see **33.2** *et seq.* below) to apply; or
- the animals etc. are kept wholly or mainly for the work they do in connection with the trade or for public exhibition or racing or other competitive purposes.

[*ITTOIA 2005, ss 30, 111, 112(1)*].

Animals etc. are exempt from capital gains tax as wasting assets within *TCGA 1992, s 45*.

Herd basis — definitions

[33.2] For the purposes of the herd basis rules covered in the remainder of this chapter, an '*animal*' means any living creature, a '*herd*' includes a flock and any other collection of animals, and a '*production herd*' means a herd of animals of the same species, irrespective of breed, kept by a farmer or other trader wholly or mainly for the saleable produce obtainable from the living animal, which includes the young of the animal and any other product obtainable from it without slaughtering it. The herd basis provisions apply equally to animals kept singly and to shares in animals.

Immature animals kept in a production herd are generally not regarded as part of the herd for these purposes, but if:

- the nature of the land on which the herd is kept is such that replacement animals have to be bred and reared on that land (e.g. acclimatised hill sheep);
- the immature animals in question are bred and maintained in the herd for the purpose of replacing animals in the herd;
- it is necessary to maintain the immature animals for that purpose,

the immature animals are regarded as part of the herd insofar as they are required to prevent a fall in numbers.

An immature animal which is not regarded as part of the herd is regarded as added to the herd when it reaches maturity. Female animals are treated as becoming mature when they produce their first young or, in the case of laying birds, when they first lay.

[*ITTOIA 2005, ss 112, 113(5)*].

Herd basis elections

[33.3] An election for the herd basis to have effect must specify the class of production herd to which it relates and must be made on or before the first anniversary of 31 January following the tax year in which the 'first relevant period of account' ends. If, however, that tax year is the one in which the person commences the trade, and that person is not a partnership, the deadline is deferred to the second anniversary of that 31 January. The '*first relevant period of account*' is the first period of account in which the person making the election keeps a production herd of the class specified.

The election is irrevocable, and has effect in relation to all the production herds of the class to which it relates, including any which the trader has ceased to keep before making the election or starts to keep after making the election. The election cannot relate to more than one class of production herd, but separate elections can be made for different classes. Two or more production herds are of the same class if the animals kept in those herds are of the same species (irrespective of breed) and the saleable produce for which the herds are wholly or mainly kept is of the same kind. An election has effect for every period of account in which the trader carries on the trade and keeps a production herd of the relevant class.

Where there is a change in the persons carrying on a trade in partnership (see **52.7 PARTNERSHIPS**), whether or not the trade is treated as continuing, a further election is required if the herd basis is to continue to apply. In this case, the 'first relevant period of account' (see above) is that in which the 'new' firm keeps a production herd of the class to which the election relates.

[*ITTOIA 2005, ss 113(2), 124*].

See **33.7** below as regards a further opportunity to make an election in a case of compulsory slaughter.

Further assessments may be made for any year as necessary, and repayments may be made (on a claim), to give effect to a herd basis election. [*ITTOIA 2005, s 129*].

Five-year gap between keeping herds

If a trader has kept a production herd of a particular class, ceases to keep herds of that class for at least five years and then does so once more:

- any herd basis election previously made in relation to herds of that class ceases to have effect; but
- the trader may make a further election by reference to the first period of account in which he again keeps a production herd of that class.

[*ITTOIA 2005, s 125*].

Consequences of herd basis election

[33.4] Where a herd basis election is in force, the animals in the herd are in effect treated as capital assets instead of as trading stock. The initial cost of the herd is not deductible in computing trading profits, and its value is not brought into account. No deduction is allowed for additions to the herd (as opposed to replacement animals — see **33.5** below). If the additional animal was previously part of trading stock, a receipt must be brought into account equal to the cost of breeding it, or acquiring it, and rearing it to maturity. If it is not possible to ascertain actual costs of breeding and rearing, an alternative deemed cost method may be used (HMRC Business Income Manual BIM55410, 55530).

[*ITTOIA 2005, ss 114, 115*].

Replacement animals

[33.5] The replacement of an animal dying or ceasing to be a member of a herd gives rise to a trading receipt equal to the disposal proceeds (if any) of the animal replaced, and a trading deduction equal to the cost of the replacement animal (so far as not otherwise allowable) but limited to the cost of an animal of similar quality to that replaced (for which see Revenue Tax Bulletin October 2001 pp 890, 891). See **33.6** below for meaning of disposal proceeds. Where the animal replaced was slaughtered under a disease control order (as defined), and the replacement animal is of inferior quality, the trading receipt is restricted to the amount allowable as a deduction in respect of the new animal. [*ITTOIA 2005, ss 113(3), 116, 117*].

Whether a particular animal brought into the herd replaces an animal disposed of is a question of fact, requiring a direct connection between the disposal and the later addition rather than a simple restoration of numbers. As a practical matter, inspectors will accept that replacement treatment is appropriate where animals are brought into the herd within twelve months of the corresponding disposal. Where disposal and replacement are in different accounting periods, the overall profit or loss may either be brought in in the first period and any necessary adjustment made in the second, or the profit or loss arising in the first period may be held over to the second period. Where the interval is more than twelve months, there is unlikely to be sufficient evidence to support the necessary connection where the new animal is bought in. Where animals are home bred, however, a longer interval may be reasonable where e.g. there is insufficient young stock to replace unexpected disposals. (Revenue Tax Bulletin October 1994 p 169, February 1997 p 396).

Disposal of animals from the herd

[33.6] Where an animal is disposed of from the herd, any profit is brought into account as a trading receipt and any loss is deductible as an expense. This does not apply if the animal is replaced (for which see **33.5** above) or on a disposal of the whole or a substantial part of the herd within a 12-month period (for which see below). The profit or loss is computed by reference to disposal proceeds and the cost of breeding the animal, or acquiring it, and rearing it to maturity. Market value is substituted for acquisition cost if the animal was acquired other than for valuable consideration. [*ITTOIA 2005, s 118*]. For HMRC's interpretation of this provision, including a change of view on how the profit on such disposals is to be computed, see Revenue Tax Bulletin April 2003 pp 1024, 1025.

For the purposes of the herd basis rules, the disposal of an animal includes its death or destruction as well as its sale, and disposal proceeds include sale proceeds and, in the case of death or destruction, insurance or compensation money received and proceeds of carcass sales. [*ITTOIA 2005, s 113(3)(4)*].

On the disposal of the whole or a substantial part of the herd, either all at once or over a period of 12 months or less, any profit is not brought into account as a receipt and any loss is not deductible as an expense. (20% or more of the herd is regarded as a 'substantial' part of it (but this does not prevent a smaller percentage from being regarded as 'substantial' in any particular case). If, however, the disposal is of *the whole herd* and the trader acquires, or starts to acquire, a new production herd of the same class within 5 years of the disposal, the following rules apply.

(i)   The replacement rules at **33.5** above apply as if a number of animals, equal to the smaller of the number in the old herd and the number in the new, had been disposed of in the old herd and replaced in that herd. Disposal proceeds of any animal are brought into account when the 'replacement' animal is acquired.

(ii)   If the number of animals in the new herd is smaller than that in the old by an insubstantial margin (i.e. normally less than 20% — see above), the difference is subject to the normal disposal rules in *ITTOIA 2005, s 118* above.

(iii)   If the number of animals in the new herd is smaller than that in the old by a substantial margin (i.e. normally 20% or more — see above), the difference is treated as a disposal of a substantial part of the herd.

(iv)   If the number of animals in the new herd is greater than that in the old, the difference is treated as additions (within **33.4** above) to the herd.

If the disposal is of *a substantial part of the herd* and the trader acquires, or starts to acquire, a new production herd of the same class within 5 years of the disposal, the following rules apply.

(1) The replacement rules at **33.5** above apply insofar as the animals included in the part disposed of are replaced. Disposal proceeds of an animal included in the part sold are brought into account when the replacement animal is acquired.

(2) If some of the animals included in the part disposed of are not replaced, any profit on their disposal is not brought into account as a receipt and any loss is not deductible as an expense.

Where the disposal of all or a substantial part of a herd is for reasons wholly outside the trader's control and a 'replacement' animal is of inferior quality to the old, the replacement rules at **33.5** above (as applied by either (i) or (1) above) apply as they do when animals are slaughtered under a disease control order (whether or not that is indeed the case).

[*ITTOIA 2005, ss 113(6), 119–123*].

Elections following compulsory slaughter

[33.7] Where compensation is receivable in respect of the whole, or a substantial part (normally 20% or more), of a production herd slaughtered under a disease control order (as defined), the trader may, notwithstanding the time limits in **33.3** above, elect for the herd basis to apply. The time limit for making the election in these circumstances follows the rules in **33.3** above, except that the period of account in which the compensation falls (or would otherwise fall) to be brought into account in computing profits is treated as if it were the first period of account in which the trader kept a production herd of the class in question. The election has effect for that period of account and each subsequent period of account in which the trader carries on the trade and keeps a production herd of that class.

[*ITTOIA 2005, s 126*].

Compensation paid under the BSE Suspects Scheme and the BSE Selective Cull (where the animal was born after 14 October 1990) is for compulsory slaughter, and for these purposes includes Selective Cull 'top-up' payments. Payments under the Calf Processing Scheme, the Over Thirty Month Scheme and the BSE Selective Cull where the animal was born before 15 October 1990 are *not* for compulsory slaughter. See Revenue Tax Bulletin February 1997 pp 396, 397 for this and for the application of these provisions to BSE compensation generally. For compulsory slaughter in cases where the herd basis does not and could not apply, see **73.73**(b) TRADING INCOME.

Anti-avoidance

[33.8] There are provisions for the prevention of avoidance of tax in the case of a non-arm's length transfer of all or part of a production herd where either transferor and transferee are bodies of persons under common control or the sole or main benefit of the transfer relates to its effect on a herd basis election. [*ITTOIA 2005, s 127*].

Example

[33.9]

A farmer acquires a dairy herd and elects for the herd basis to apply. The movements in the herd and the tax treatment are as follows.

Year 1	No	Value £
Mature		
Bought @ £150	70	10,500
Bought in calf @ £180		
(Market value of calf £35)	5	900
Immature		
Bought @ £75	15	1,125
Herd Account		£
70 Friesians		10,500
5 Friesians in calf (5 × £(180 – 35))		725
75 Closing balance		£11,225
Trading Account		£
5 Calves (5 × £35)		175
15 Immature Friesians		1,125
Debit to profit and loss account		£1,300

Year 2	No	Value £
Mature		
Bought @ £185	15	2,775
Sold @ £200	10	2,000
Died	3	—
Immature		
Born	52	—
Matured @ 60% of market value of £200 note (a)	12	1,440

Herd Account		£	£
75	Opening balance		11,225
	Increase in herd		
15	Purchases	2,775	

Year 2			No	Value
				£
	12	Transferred from trading stock	1,440	
	—			
	27		4,215	
	(13)	Replacement cost £4,215 × $^{13}/_{27}$	2,029	
14		Non-replacement animals cost		2,186
89		Closing balance		£13,411

Trading Account	£
Sale of 10 mature cows replaced	(2,000)
Transfer to herd—14 animals	(1,440)
Cost of 13 mature cows purchased to replace those sold/deceased ($^{13}/_{15}$ × £2,775)	2,405
Net credit to profit and loss account note (b)	£1,035

Year 3	No	Value
		£
Mature		
Jerseys bought @ £250	70	17,500
Friesians slaughtered @ £175 (market value £185)	52	9,100
Immature		
Friesians born	20	—
Matured		
Friesians @ 60% of market value of £190 note (a)	15	1,710

Herd Account		£	£
89	Opening balance		13,411
	Increase in herd		
18	Jerseys		4,500
	52 Improvement Jerseys @	250	
	less Market value of Friesians	185	
	52 @	65	3,380
	Transfer from trading stock		
15	Friesians		1,710
122	Closing balance		£23,001

Trading Account	£
Compensation	(9,100)
Transfer to herd	(1,710)
Purchase of replacements note (c) (52 × £185)	9,620

Net credit to profit and loss account £(1,190)

Year 4

The farmer ceases dairy farming and sells his whole herd.

	No	Value £
Mature		
Jerseys sold @ £320	70	22,400
Friesians sold @ £200	52	10,400
Immature		
Friesians sold @ £100	65	6,500

Herd Account		£
Opening balance		23,001
52	Friesians	
70	Jerseys	
(122)	Sales	(32,800)
	Profit on sale note (d)	£(9,799)

Trading Account	£
Sale of 65 immature Friesians	(6,500)
Credit to profit and loss account	£(6,500)

Notes

(a) The use of 60% of market value was originally by agreement between the National Farmers' Union and the Inland Revenue (see now HMRC Business Economic Note 19: Farming — Stock Valuation for Income Tax purposes, at paragraph 7.2). Alternatively, the actual cost of breeding or purchase and rearing could be used.

(b) As the cost of rearing the 12 cows to maturity will already have been debited to the profit and loss account, no additional entry is required to reflect that cost. Due to the fact that the animals were in opening stock at valuation and will not be in closing stock, the trading account will in effect be debited with that valuation.

(c) The cost of the replacements is restricted to the cost of replacing like with like.

(d) Provided these animals are not replaced by a herd of the same class within five years the proceeds will be tax-free (see **33.6** above).

34

HMRC — Administration

Introduction

[34.1] From 18 April 2005, the collection and management of income tax is administered by the **Commissioners for Her Majesty's Revenue and Customs (HMRC)**. [*TMA 1970, s 1; Commissioners for Revenue and Customs Act 2005, Sch 4 para 12*]. Previously, this tax was administered by the Commissioners of Inland Revenue (normally referred to as 'the Board'). All the functions vested in the Board before that date (with the exception of prosecutions for tax offences — see below) are now vested in the Commissioners for HMRC. [*Commissioners for Revenue and Customs Act 2005, s 5; SI 2005 No 1126*].

Under the Commissioners for HMRC are officers of Revenue and Customs who are civil servants. In relation to income tax, officers of Revenue and Customs have broadly taken over the functions previously vested in officers of the Board of Inland Revenue, inspectors of taxes and collectors of taxes. [*Commissioners for Revenue and Customs Act 2005, ss 6, 7, Sch 1*]. As such they are responsible for processing returns, making assessments, dealing with claims, allowances and appeals, carrying out enquiries and collection and recovery of tax.

Criminal prosecutions of tax offences in England and Wales are conducted by an independent Revenue and Customs Prosecutions Office, whose director is appointed by the Attorney General. [*Commissioners for Revenue and Customs Act 2005, ss 34–42, Sch 3*]. See **38.14 HMRC INVESTIGATORY POWERS** for HMRC's practice in relation to prosecutions.

The HMRC website (www.hmrc.gov.uk/home.htm) provides access to detailed information on many aspects of income tax.

HMRC Charter

[34.2] A new Charter setting out what individuals, businesses and other groups dealing with HMRC can expect from the department, and what the department expects from them, was launched on 12 November 2009. Under the Charter, HMRC give a commitment to:

* respect their customers;
* help and support them to get things right;
* treat them as honest;
* treat them even-handedly;
* be professional and act with integrity;
* tackle people who deliberately break the rules and challenge those who bend the rules;
* protect their customers' information and respect their privacy;
* accept that someone else can represent their customers; and
* do all they can to keep the cost of dealing with HMRC as low as possible.

In return, HMRC expects their customers to be honest, respect HMRC staff, and take care to get things right. The Charter also provides links to further information on customers' rights and where they can get help and support. (HMRC News Release, 12 November 2009). The Charter is available at www.hmrc.gov.uk/charter/index.htm.

Appeal Tribunals

[34.3] See 5 APPEALS.

'Care and management' powers

[34.4] As noted at **34.1** above, the Commissioners for HMRC have responsibility for the 'collection and management' of taxes, including income tax. Before 18 April 2005, the Board of Inland Revenue had responsibility for the 'care and management' of direct taxes. The extent and limits of these care and management powers were considered before the courts on a number of occasions.

For the validity of amnesties by the Board, see *CIR v National Federation of Self-Employed and Small Businesses Ltd* HL 1981, 55 TC 133. HMRC EXTRA-STATUTORY CONCESSIONS (37) have been the subject of frequent judicial criticism (see Lord Edward Davies' opinion in *Vestey v CIR (No 1)* HL 1979, 54 TC 503 for a review of this) but their validity has never been directly challenged in the Courts. In *R v HMIT (ex p Fulford-Dobson)* QB 1987, 60 TC 168, a claim that the Revenue had acted unfairly in refusing a concession where tax avoidance was involved was rejected, but the taxpayer's right to seek judicial review of a Revenue decision to refuse the benefit of a concession was confirmed in *R v HMIT (ex p Brumfield and Others)* QB 1988, 61 TC 589. A decision by the Revenue to revoke its authorisation to pay a dividend gross was upheld in *R v CIR (ex p Camacq Corporation)* CA 1989, 62 TC 651. For a general discussion of the Board's care and management powers and an example of a ruling by the Court that the Board had exercised a discretionary power reasonably, see *R v CIR (ex p Preston)* HL 1985, 59 TC 1. Where a discretionary power is given to the Revenue, it is an error in law to proceed on the footing that the power is mandatory (*R v HMIT and Others (ex p Lansing Bagnall Ltd)* CA 1986, 61 TC 112). See also *R v CIR (ex p J Rothschild Holdings)* CA 1987, 61 TC 178, where the Revenue were required to produce internal documents of a general character relating to their practice in applying a statutory provision.

The Inland Revenue policy of selective prosecution for criminal offences in connection with tax evasion did not render a decision in a particular case unlawful or *ultra vires*, provided that the case was considered on its merits fairly and dispassionately to see whether the criteria for prosecution were satisfied, and that the decision to prosecute was then taken in good faith for the purpose of collecting taxes and not for some ulterior, extraneous or improper purpose (*R v CIR (ex p Mead and Cook)* QB 1992, 65 TC 1). See *R v CIR (ex p Allen)* QB 1997, 69 TC 442 for an unsuccessful application for judicial review of a Revenue decision to take criminal proceedings.

The making of a 'forward tax agreement', by which the Inland Revenue renounced their right and duty to investigate the true financial and other circumstances of the other party during the period of the agreement in return for payments of money, was not a proper exercise of the Inland Revenue's care and management powers, and was accordingly *ultra vires* and illegal (*Fayed and others v Advocate General for Scotland* CS 2004, 77 TC 273).

The social security authorities are authorised to disclose information held by them to the Commissioners for HMRC, or persons providing certain services to the Commissioners, for investigative purposes or in relation to national insurance contributions. [*FA 1997, s 110; Social Security Administration Act 1992, s 121F*].

HMRC clearances

[34.5] From 1 April 2008, HMRC have a commitment to provide all businesses with their view of the tax consequences of significant commercial issues wherever there is uncertainty. This applies regardless of when the legislation in question was enacted but businesses will be asked to demonstrate the commercial significance of the transaction where the clearance relates to direct tax legislation enacted earlier than the last four years. HMRC undertake to respond to such clearance applications within 28 days. See www.hmrc.gov.uk/news/extend-clearances.htm. See HMRC Code of Practice 10 (COP 10) for the extent to which advice on a proposed transaction is binding on HMRC.

Previously, HMRC would respond to queries on their interpretation of legislation passed in the last four Finance Acts, including its application to a proposed transaction. The query must arise from genuine uncertainty about the meaning of the law. They will not help with tax planning or give advice on transactions designed to save tax. See COP 10.

Certain types of transaction have specified clearance procedures. These are covered throughout this work where appropriate; see, for example, **4.5** ANTI-AVOIDANCE as regards transactions in securities etc.

HMRC rulings

[34.6] HMRC may provide a post-transaction ruling for a transaction after it has occurred but before the tax return is submitted. Rulings will only be given where the tax treatment of a transaction is in doubt, for example in relation to unusual transactions or transactions entered into in usual circumstances. See HMRC Code of Practice 10 (COP 10) for the types of transactions on which a ruling can be given, the extent to which HMRC will be bound by the ruling, the effect of the ruling on interest and penalties and the procedures in obtaining such a ruling.

HMRC error

[34.7] An HMRC factsheet 'Complaints' (available at www.hmrc.gov.uk/fac tsheets/complaints-factsheet.pdf) outlines the complaints procedures, and states that HMRC may consider refunding reasonable costs directly caused by HMRC's mistakes or unreasonable delays. Such costs could include postage, phone calls and professional fees. HMRC may pay additional compensation for worry or distress.

In *Neil Martin Ltd v HMRC* CA, [2007] STC 1802, an unsuccessful action for damages against HMRC, it was held that HMRC did not have a direct duty of care to process an application for a sub-contractors' tax certificate (under the old construction industry tax deduction scheme) with reasonable expedition, and that an officer of HMRC does not generally owe a common law duty of care for which his employers would be vicariously liable.

Adjudicator's Office

[34.8] A taxpayer who is not satisfied with HMRC's response to a complaint has the option of putting the case to an independent Adjudicator for HMRC. The Adjudicator's Office considers complaints about HMRC's handling of a taxpayer's affairs, e.g. mistakes, delays, misleading advice, staff behaviour or the exercise of HMRC discretion. Its services are free of charge. Matters subject to existing rights of appeal are excluded.

The address is The Adjudicator's Office, 8th Floor, Euston Tower, 286 Euston Road, London NW1 3US (tel. 0300 057 1111, website www.adjudicatorsoff ice.gov.uk/details.htm).

Complaints normally go to the Adjudicator only after they have been considered by, firstly, the Customer Relations or Complaints Manager and, secondly, the Director of the relevant HMRC office, and where the taxpayer is still not satisfied with the response received. The alternatives of pursuing the complaint to the HMRC's Head Office, to an MP, or (through an MP) to the Parliamentary Ombudsman continue to be available. The Adjudicator reviews all the facts, considers whether the complaint is justified, and, if so, settles the complaint by mediation or makes recommendations as to what should be done. HMRC normally accept the recommendations.

The Adjudicator publishes an annual report.

See also HMRC leaflet AO1 'The Adjudicator's Office' (available at www.hm rc.gov.uk/leaflets/ao1.pdf).

Leave to apply for judicial review of the rejection by the Adjudicator of a complaint concerning the use of information from unidentified informants was refused in *R v Revenue Adjudicator's Office (ex p Drummond)* QB 1996, 70 TC 235.

Use of electronic communications

[34.9] The Commissioners for HMRC have broad powers to make regulations by statutory instrument to facilitate electronic communication in the delivery of information, e.g. tax returns, and the making of tax payments. The regulations may allow or require the use of intermediaries such as internet service providers. They have effect notwithstanding any pre-existing legislation requiring delivery or payment in a manner which would otherwise preclude the use of electronic communications or intermediaries. [*FA 1999, ss 132, 133*]. The intention is to develop a range of electronic services which taxpayers can use as an alternative to paper. One of the first services to be offered was to allow taxpayers and their agents to file self-assessment tax returns online (see **63.2 RETURNS**). (Joint Revenue and Customs & Excise News Release CW 1, 9 March 1999).

See *The Income and Corporation Taxes (Electronic Communications) Regulations 2003 (SI 2003 No 282)* and directions thereunder by the Commissioners, which make provision for electronic communications in relation to delivery of returns and other information under various provisions of *TMA 1970* and payments or repayments in connection with the operation of those provisions.

Regulations (*SI 2003 No 3143*) provide for electronic delivery of dividend vouchers, interest vouchers and other tax deduction certificates by prior agreement between sender and recipient.

Incentives for electronic communications

Regulations may be made by statutory instrument by the Commissioners for HMRC in relation to matters under their care and management for the provision of incentives to use electronic communications. These may include discounts (or payments or repayments), or additional time for compliance or payment, or more convenient intervals for the delivery of information or the making of payments. The regulations may make provision as to the conditions of entitlement to incentives and for their withdrawal (which may be authorised to be made by direction), and may provide for penalties up to £1,000 for failure to comply with any specified provision. They may make different provision for different cases, and may make such incidental, supplemental, consequential or transitional provision as the Commissioners think fit. [*FA 2000, s 143(1), Sch 38*]. See, for example, *SI 2001 No 56; SI 2001 No 1081, Reg 22; SI 2003 No 2495; SI 2005 No 826; SI 2006 No 777, Regs 1, 6.*

See **53.12** PAY AS YOU EARN as regards incentives for e-filing of PAYE returns where not mandatory.

Anything received by way of incentive is not regarded as income for tax purposes. [*ITTOIA 2005, s 778*].

Mandatory e-filing

HMRC have been given wide powers to make regulations requiring the use of electronic communications for the delivery of information required or authorised to be delivered under tax legislation. [*FA 2002, ss 135, 136; FA 2007, s 93(1)–(3)*]. See **53.12** PAY AS YOU EARN as regards e-filing of PAYE returns.

International co-operation

[34.10] *FA 2006, ss 173–175* provide for international agreements on mutual assistance in tax enforcement, covering exchange of information foreseeably relevant to the administration, enforcement or recovery of any UK or foreign tax; the recovery of debts relating to any UK or foreign tax; and the service of documents relating to any UK or foreign tax. Where such agreements have effect, no obligation of secrecy, whether statutory or otherwise, prevents the disclosure of any information that is authorised to be disclosed under the agreement. However, such information cannot be disclosed by HMRC to a foreign tax authority unless HMRC are satisfied that the foreign tax authority is bound by, or has undertaken to observe, rules of confidentiality at least as strict as those applying in the UK. Most of HMRC's investigatory powers to obtain the production of accounts, books and other information relevant to income tax, corporation tax or capital gains tax liabilities can be used to obtain information in respect of foreign tax liabilities covered by such agreements (see **38.11** HMRC INVESTIGATORY POWERS).

See, for example, *SI 2007 No 2126*, which brings into effect arrangements relating to international tax enforcement contained in the joint Council of Europe/OECD Convention on mutual administrative assistance in tax matters which was signed on behalf of the UK on 24 May 2007. See also *SI 2007 No 3507*, which provides the necessary machinery for recovering foreign taxes on behalf of a non-EU country with which an appropriate international agreement on mutual assistance is in force.

Co-operation between tax authorities of EU member States

The Mutual Assistance Directive (*Directive 77/799/EEC*) provides for the exchange of information between tax authorities of EU member States to enable them to correctly assess liabilities to the taxes covered by the *Directive* (which include taxes on income and capital). By virtue of amending *Directive 2004/56/EC*, the Mutual Assistance Directive now extends to the notification of instruments and decisions by the tax authority of a member State, to persons residing in that State, at the request of the tax authority of the member State from which the instrument or decision emanates. This requirement is transposed into UK domestic law by *F(No 2)A 2005, s 68*.

Recovery of taxes etc. due in other EU member States

Provision is made for the recovery in the UK of amounts in respect of which a request for enforcement has been made in accordance with the Mutual Assistance Recovery Directive (*Directive 2008/55/EC* and earlier equivalent) by an authority in another EU member State. Disclosure of information by a UK tax authority (i.e. the Commissioners for HMRC or, in relation to certain agricultural levies, the relevant Minister) for these purposes (or for the purposes of a request for enforcement by the UK) is not generally precluded by any obligation of secrecy.

Broadly, the UK tax authority has the same powers it would have for a corresponding claim in the UK, in particular in relation to penalties and interest. Treasury regulations may make provision as to what UK claim corresponds to a foreign claim, and for other procedural and supplementary matters (see *SI 2004 No 674*). Regulations may also be made by the UK tax authority for the application, non-application or adaptation of the law applicable to corresponding UK claims, without prejudice to its application when not dealt with by such regulations.

No proceedings may be taken against a person under these provisions if he shows that proceedings relevant to the liability in question are pending (i.e. still open to appeal), or about to be instituted, before a competent body in the member State in question. This does not apply if the foreign proceedings are not prosecuted or instituted with reasonable expedition, or if regulations made by the UK tax authority apply a UK enactment that permits proceedings in the case of a corresponding UK claim. If a final decision on the foreign claim (i.e. one against which no further appeal lies or would be in time), or a part of it, has been given in favour of the taxpayer by a competent body in the member State in question, no proceeding may be taken under these provisions in relation to the claim (or part).

The Treasury may amend, replace or repeal any of the above provisions by regulations for the purpose of giving effect to future amendments to the Directive.

The Commission Directive which laid down detailed rules for implementing certain provisions of *Directive 2008/55/EC* was replaced by a new 'Implementing Regulation' (*Regulation (EC) No 1179/2008*) with effect on and after 1 January 2009. This Regulation is directly applicable and ensures that similar procedures are implemented across the EU. Many of the provisions of *SI 2004 No 674* were rendered superfluous and were repealed with effect on and after 6 April 2010.

[*FA 2002, s 134, Sch 39; SI 2005 No 1479; SI 2008 No 2871; SI 2010 No 792*].

HMRC functions carried out by the Serious Organised Crime Agency

[34.11] On 1 April 2008, the Assets Recovery Agency (ARA) merged with the Serious Organised Crime Agency (SOCA), which now undertakes civil recovery and tax investigations in England and Wales and Northern Ireland. Cases that were the responsibility of the ARA immediately before the merger were transferred to SOCA. The *Serious Crime Act 2007* extended the civil recovery and taxation powers of the ARA to SOCA.

Under the *Proceeds of Crime Act 2002, Pt 6*, the SOCA is empowered to carry out the functions vested in HMRC and its officers. SOCA must have reasonable grounds to suspect that:

(a)   income arising or a gain accruing to a person in respect of a chargeable period is chargeable to income tax or is a chargeable gain and arises or accrues as a result (whether wholly or partly, directly or indirectly) of the 'criminal conduct' of that person or another; or

(b)   a company is chargeable to corporation tax on its profits arising in a chargeable period and the profits arise as a result (whether wholly or partly, directly or indirectly) of the criminal conduct of the company or another person,

and must serve a notice on HMRC specifying the person or company, the period or periods concerned, and the functions which he intends to carry out. The periods involved may include periods beginning before the *Act* was passed.

For the purpose of the exercise by SOCA of any function so vested in them, it is immaterial that they cannot identify a source for any income. An assessment made by SOCA under *TMA 1970, s 29* (discovery assessment — see **6.6 ASSESSMENTS**) in respect of income charged to tax under *ITTOIA 2005, Pt 5 Ch 8* (income not otherwise charged — see **49.7 MISCELLANEOUS INCOME**) cannot be reduced or quashed only because it does not specify (to any extent) the source of the income.

SOCA may cease carrying out the functions specified in the notice at any time (by notifying HMRC), but *must* so cease where the conditions allowing the notice to be made are no longer satisfied. Any assessment made by them under *TMA 1970, s 29* is subsequently invalid to the extent that it does not specify a source for income.

For the above purposes, *'criminal conduct'* is conduct which constitutes an offence anywhere in the UK or which would do so if it occurred there, but does not include conduct constituting an offence relating to a matter under the care and management of HMRC.

It should be noted that the vesting of a function in SOCA under these provisions does not divest HMRC or its officers of the function (so that, for example, HMRC can continue to carry out routine work). Certain functions, as listed in *Proceeds of Crime Act 2002, s 323(3)*, cannot be carried out by SOCA. If SOCA serve notice in relation to a company and in respect of a chargeable period or periods, the general HMRC functions vested in SOCA do not include functions relating to any requirement which is imposed on the company in its capacity as an employer and relates to a tax year which does not fall wholly within the chargeable period(s).

[*Proceeds of Crime Act 2002, ss 317, 318(1)(2), 319, 320(1)–(3), 323(1)(3), 326(1)(2); SI 2003 No 120; FA 2007, s 84(4)–(6), Sch 22 para 15; Serious Crime Act 2007, s 74, Sch 8 paras 92–96; SI 2007 No 3166, Reg 3; SI 2008 No 755; SI 2009 No 56, Sch 1 para 333*].

An assessment made by SOCA in carrying out their HMRC functions does not constitute a criminal charge within the ambit of *Article 6* of the *European Convention on Human Rights* (*Khan v Director of the Assets Recovery Agency* (Sp C 523), [2006] SSCD 154).

See www.soca.gov.uk/financialIntel/assetsRecovery.html and the guidance at www.hmrc.gov.uk/specialist/ara-guidance_.pdf.

35

HMRC — Confidentiality of Information

Cross-reference. See **55.34** PENALTIES (publishing details of deliberate tax defaulters).

Introduction

[35.1] Subject to certain specified exceptions relating to the functions of HMRC (and those at **35.3** below), officials of HMRC may not disclose information held by HMRC. All Commissioners and officers of HMRC must make a declaration acknowledging their duty of confidentiality as soon as reasonably practicable following their appointment. [*Commissioners for Revenue and Customs Act 2005, ss 3, 18*]. Officers of the Inland Revenue were required to make similar declarations. [*TMA 1970, s 6, Sch 1; SI 2009 No 56, Sch 1 paras 6, 52*].

General

[35.2] Information acquired by HMRC in connection with one of their functions may be used by them in connection with any other of their functions. [*Commissioners for Revenue and Customs Act 2005, s 17(1)*].

As to production in Court proceedings of documents in HMRC's possession of , see *Brown's Trustees v Hay* CS 1897, 3 TC 598; *In re Joseph Hargreaves Ltd* CA 1900, 4 TC 173; *Shaw v Kay* CS 1904, 5 TC 74; *Soul v Irving* CA 1963, 41 TC 517; *H v H* HC 1980, 52 TC 454. For the overriding of confidentiality by the public interest in the administration of justice, see *Lonrho plc v Fayed and Others (No 4)* CA 1993, 66 TC 220.

Specifics

[35.3] HMRC are authorised to disclose information to the following.

(a) **Charity Commission for England and Wales.** There are wide powers under which information may be exchanged between the Charity Commission and HMRC and also between principal regulators of certain charities and HMRC. [*Charities Act 1993, ss 10–10C; CTA 2010, Sch 1 para 274; SI 2007 No 309*].

(b) **Business Statistics Office of the Department of Industry** or to the **Department of Employment.** HMRC are authorised to disclose, for the purposes of statistical surveys, the names and addresses of employers and employees and the number of persons employed by individual concerns. *[FA 1969, s 58].*

(c) **Tax authorities of other countries.** HMRC are authorised to disclose information where it is necessary to do so for the operation of double taxation agreements. *[TIOPA 2010, s 129; ICTA 1988, s 816; TCGA 1992, s 277(4); IHTA 1984, s 158(5); ITA 2007, Sch 1 para 202].* Disclosure may also be made to the tax authorities of other member States of the EU which observe similar confidentiality and use only for tax purposes *[FA 1990, s 125(5)(6); FA 2003, s 197(1)–(6); FA 2008, s 113, Sch 36 para 83; SI 2009 No 404];* (this legislation transposes into UK law the provisions of the EU Mutual Assistance Directive (*Council Directive 77/799/EEC* as amended) — see also **34.10** HMRC — ADMINISTRATION). See also the 'working arrangement' between USA and UK in Revenue Press Release 2 March 1978.

FA 2006, ss 173–175 provide for international agreements on mutual assistance in tax enforcement, covering the exchange of information foreseeably relevant to the administration, enforcement or recovery of any UK or foreign tax; the recovery of debts relating to any UK or foreign tax; and the service of documents relating to any UK or foreign tax. Where such agreements have effect, no obligation of secrecy, whether statutory or otherwise, prevents the disclosure of any information that is authorised to be disclosed under the agreement. However, such information cannot be disclosed by HMRC to a foreign tax authority unless HMRC are satisfied that the foreign tax authority is bound by, or has undertaken to observe, rules of confidentiality at least as strict as those applying in the UK. See also **34.10** HMRC — ADMINISTRATION.

(d) **Occupational Pensions Board.** HMRC are authorised to disclose information about pension schemes. *[Social Security Act 1973, s 89(2)].*

(e) **Social Security Departments.** Information held by HMRC relating to national insurance contributions, statutory sick pay or statutory maternity pay may, and must if an authorised social security officer so requires, be supplied to the social security authorities for use in relation to social security, child support or war pensions. Other information may similarly be supplied to those authorities in relation to the prevention, detection, investigation or prosecution of social security offences or in checking social security information. *[Social Security Administration Act 1992, ss 121E, 122; Social Security Administration (Fraud) Act 1997, s 1].* HMRC will also supply the names and addresses of absent parents and, where appropriate, their employers, in cases where they are liable under the *Social Security Acts* to maintain lone parent families receiving income support. (Revenue Press Release 9 May 1990). (See **34.4** HMRC — ADMINISTRATION for supply of information *by* social security authorities.) HMRC may, and must if an authorised social security officer so requires, supply to the social security authorities information held for the purposes of tax credit functions (see **70.4** SOCIAL SECURITY AND NATIONAL INSURANCE) and functions relating to child benefit or guardian's allowance for use by those authorities for the purposes of functions relating to social security benefits, child support, tax credits, war pensions or prescribed evaluation or statistical studies. [*Tax Credits Act 2002, Sch 5 para 4; SI 2002 No 3036*].

(f)   **Assistance to police investigation into suspected murder or treason.** [*Royal Commission on Standards of Conduct in Public Life 1976, para 93*].

(g)   **Non-UK resident entertainers and sportsmen.** In connection with the deduction of tax from certain payments to such persons, HMRC may disclose relevant matters to any person who appears to HMRC to have an interest. [*ITA 2007, s 970(2)(3); ICTA 1988, s 558(4)*].

(h)   **Land Registry.** Particulars of land and charges. [*Land Registration Act 1925, s 129*].

(i)   **Parliamentary Commissioner for Administration.** Information required for the purposes of his investigations. [*Parliamentary Commissioner Act 1967, s 8*].

(j)   **National Audit Office.** Information required for the purposes of the Office's examinations. [*National Audit Act 1983, s 8*].

(k)   **Data Protection.** Any information necessary for the discharge of the Registrar's or Tribunal's functions. [*Data Protection Act 1984, s 17*].

(l)   An **advisory commission** set up under the Convention (*90/463/EEC*) on the elimination of double taxation in connection with the adjustment of profits of associated enterprises (see **4.18I ANTI-AVOIDANCE**). [*TIOPA 2010, s 128; ICTA 1988, s 816(2A)*].

(m)   As regards information held for the purposes of tax credit functions (see **70.4 SOCIAL SECURITY AND NATIONAL INSURANCE**) and functions relating to child benefit or guardian's allowance, a **local authority** (or authorised delegate) for use in the administration of housing benefit or council tax benefit. Information must also be provided in the opposite direction if the Commissioners of HMRC so require but only for use for purposes relating to tax credits etc. [*Tax Credits Act 2002, Sch 5 paras 7, 8*].

Also as regards information held for the above-mentioned purposes, **Health Departments** for use for purposes of prescribed functions relating to health, relevant Government Departments for purposes of prescribed functions relating to **employment** or **training** (with provision also for certain information to pass in the opposite direction) and (as regards information held for child benefit and guardian's allowance functions only) any civil servant or other person for purposes of prescribed functions relating to provision of specified services concerning participation by young persons in **education and training**. [*Tax Credits Act 2002, Sch 5 paras 5, 6, 9, 10*].

(n)   The **Health and Safety Executive**, the **Government Actuary's Department**, the **Office for National Statistics** or the **Occupational Pensions Regulatory Authority** in relation to National Insurance contributions, statutory sick pay or statutory maternity pay. [*Social Security Administration Act 1992, s 122AA*].

(o) **Financial Services Authority.** The Commissioners of Inland Revenue were able to authorise the disclosure of information to the Financial Services Authority or the Secretary of State for the purposes of investigations under *Financial Services and Markets Act 2000, s 168.* [*Financial Services and Markets Act 2000, s 350*]. Note that HMRC may only disclose information in this way if it was obtained or is held in the exercise of a function previously vested in the Inland Revenue. [*Commissioners for Revenue and Customs Act 2005, Sch 2 para 18*].

(p) Under the *Anti-terrorism, Crime and Security Act 2001, ss 19, 20,* the Revenue and Customs & Excise (now collectively HMRC) are authorised to disclose certain information required for the purposes of that Act. A Code of Practice on this was published jointly by those departments.

(q) **Assets Recovery Agency.** HMRC may disclose information (including information obtained before that date) to the Director of the Assets Recovery Agency for the purpose of the exercise of his functions. [*Proceeds of Crime Act 2002, s 436; SI 2003 No 120*]. HMRC may also disclose information to the Lord Advocate and the Scottish Ministers in connection with the exercise of their functions in Scotland under *Proceeds of Crime Act 2002, Pt 3* and *Pt 5* respectively. [*Proceeds of Crime Act 2002, s 439*].

(r) **The Financial Reporting Review Panel.** HMRC may disclose certain information to this Panel for the purposes of facilitating their taking steps to discover whether there are grounds for an application to the courts for a declaration that the annual accounts of a company do not comply with *Companies Acts* requirements (or NI equivalents) or determining whether or not to make such an application (Memorandum of Understanding between HMRC and The Financial Reporting Review Panel, 24 June 2005). For detail and background, see HMRC Tax Bulletin October 2005 pp 1243–1245.

(s) After 14 February 2008, HMRC may disclose information to specified persons in relation to the **Criminal Assets Bureau** in Ireland for the purpose of the exercise of its functions in identifying and recovering proceeds of crime, or for a similar purpose to any public authority (in the UK or elsewhere) that may be specified by Treasury Order. [*Serious Crime Act 2007, s 85; SI 2008 Nos 219, 403*].

Prosecutions Office

[35.4] HMRC are permitted to disclose information to the Revenue and Customs Prosecutions Office for the purpose of enabling the Office to consider whether to institute criminal proceedings in respect of a matter considered in the course of an investigation by HMRC or to give advice in connection with a criminal investigation. In relation to Scotland, HMRC are similarly authorised to disclose information to the Lord Advocate or a procurator fiscal. In Northern Ireland disclosures to the Director of Public Prosecutions for Northern Ireland are likewise permitted. [*Commissioners for Revenue and Customs Act 2005, s 21*].

'Tax functions'

[35.5] It is a criminal offence for a person to disclose information held by him in the exercise of 'tax functions' about any matter relevant to tax in the case of an 'identifiable person' (as defined). *'Tax functions'* include functions relating to the First-tier Tribunal and Upper Tribunal, HMRC and its officers. This applies equally as regards HMRC's tax credit functions and social security functions. It does not apply if (or if he believes) he has lawful authority or the information has lawfully been made available to the public, or if the person to whom the matter relates has consented. [*FA 1989, s 182; ITA 2007, Sch 1 para 282; SI 2009 No 56, Sch 1 para 167*]. Similar provisions apply to members of an advisory commission set up under the Convention on transfer pricing arbitration (see **4.27 ANTI-AVOIDANCE**). [*FA 1989, s 182A*].

36

HMRC Explanatory Publications

HMRC explanatory leaflets

[36.1] HMRC publish explanatory leaflets on direct taxes. Those that relate to income tax are listed below, with the date of the latest edition in brackets, and are obtainable free of charge (with just a few exceptions) from any HMRC office, unless otherwise stated. Most of them (including some for which a charge is made for hard copy) are freely available on the HMRC website; some are available *only* on the website.

Since 2004, there has been a move towards withdrawing leaflets and replacing them with online guidance (which is cross-referred to in this work where appropriate). See list of withdrawn leaflets at www.hmrc.gov.uk/leaflets/obso lete.htm.

IR 8	Winding-Up Petitions (November 2002).
IR 10	Paying the Right Tax on Your Earnings or Pension (August 2004).
IR 111	Bank and Building Society Interest: Are You Paying Tax When You Don't Need To? (June 2009).
IR 115	Paying for Childcare — Getting Help from your Employer (December 2009).
IR 121	Approaching Retirement: A Guide to Tax and National Insurance Contributions (August 2009).
IR 160	Inland Revenue Enquiries under Self-Assessment (August 2009). Available online only.
IR 177	Share Incentive Plans and Your Entitlement to Benefits (October 2001).
480	Expenses and Benefits — A Tax Guide (April 2010).
490	Employee Travel — A Tax and NICs Guide (April 2010).
CWG2	Employer Further Guide to PAYE and NICs (April 2010).
AO1	The Adjudicator's Office (2009) (available at www.hmrc.go v.uk/leaflets/ao1.pdf).

CC/FS1   Compliance Checks — General Information (April 2010). See www.hmrc.gov.uk/compliance/cc-fs1.pdf.

CC/FS2   Compliance Checks — Requests for Information and Documents (April 2010). See www.hmrc.gov.uk/complianc e/cc-fs2.pdf.

CC/FS3   Compliance Checks — Visits – Pre-arranged (April 2009). See www.hmrc.gov.uk/compliance/cc-fs3.pdf.

CC/FS4   Compliance Checks — Visits – Unannounced (April 2009). See www.hmrc.gov.uk/compliance/cc-fs4.pdf.

CC/FS5   Compliance Checks — Visits – Unannounced – Tribunal Approved (April 2009). See www.hmrc.gov.uk/compliance/ cc-fs5.pdf.

CC/FS6   Compliance Checks — What Happens When We Find Something Wrong (April 2010). See www.hmrc.gov.uk/com pliance/cc-fs6.pdf.

CC/FS7   Compliance Checks — Penalties for Errors in Returns or Documents (April 2010). See www.hmrc.gov.uk/complianc e/cc-fs7.pdf.

CC/FS8T   Compliance Checks — Help and Advice (April 2009). See www.hmrc.gov.uk/compliance/cc-fs8-t.pdf.

CC/FS9   Compliance Checks — Human Rights Act (May 2010). See www.hmrc.gov.uk/compliance/cc-fs9.pdf.

CC/FS10   Compliance Checks — Suspending Penalties for Careless Errors in Returns or Documents (April 2010). See www.hm rc.gov.uk/compliance/cc-fs10.pdf.

CC/FS11   Compliance Checks — Penalties for Failure to Notify (April 2010). See www.hmrc.gov.uk/compliance/cc-fs11.pdf.

CC/FS13   Compliance Checks — Publishing Details of Deliberate Defaulters (April 2010). See www.hmrc.gov.uk/compliance/ cc-fs13.pdf.

C/FS   Complaints (December 2009). See www.hmrc.gov.uk/factsh eets/complaints-factsheet.pdf.

CIS340   Construction Industry Scheme — Guide for contractors and subcontractors (January 2007).

COP 8   Specialist Investigations (Fraud and Avoidance) (June 2009).

COP 9   Civil Investigation of Fraud (April 2009).

COP 10   Information and Advice (April 2008).

COP-AT   Anti-Terrorism, Crime and Security Act 2001: Code of Practice on the Disclosure of Information (February 2002).

EC/FS4   Compliance Checks — Penalties (December 2009). See www.hmrc.gov.uk/leaflets/ecfs4.pdf.

EF5   Bankruptcy — What You Must Do (April 2007) (available at www.hmrc.gov.uk/factsheets/ef5.pdf).

ES/FS1	Employed or Self-employed for Tax and National Insurance Contributions (June 2008). See www.hmrc.gov.uk/leaflets/es-fs1.pdf.
ES/FS2	Are Your Workers Employed or Self-employed for Tax and National Insurance Contributions (August 2008). See www.hmrc.gov.uk/leaflets/es-fs2.pdf.
E24	Tips, Gratuities, Service Charges and Troncs (October 2009) (available at www.hmrc.gov.uk/helpsheets/e24.pdf).
FEU 50	A Guide to Paying Foreign Entertainers (March 2000) (available at www.hmrc.gov.uk/feu/feu50_0300.pdf).
HMRC1	HMRC decisions — What to do if You Disagree (October 2009). See www.hmrc.gov.uk/factsheets/hmrc1.pdf.
HMRC6	Residence, Domicile and the Remittance Basis (February 2010). See www.hmrc.gov.uk/cnr/hmrc6.pdf.
Pride1	Taxes and Benefits — Information for our Lesbian, Gay, Bisexual and Transgender customers (June 2009).
WTC1	Child Tax Credit and Working Tax Credit — An Introduction (April 2010).
WTC2	Child Tax Credit and Working Tax Credit — A Guide (April 2010).
—	Giving your Business the Best Start with Tax (July 2009). See www.hmrc.gov.uk/startingup/working-yourself.pdf.
—	New Penalties for Errors in Tax Returns and Documents (April 2008). See www.hmrc.gov.uk/about/new-penalties/penalties-leaflet.pdf.
—	Take Care to Avoid a Penalty (July 2008), See www.hmrc.gov.uk/about/new-penalties/new-penalties.pdf.
—	Digest of Double Taxation Treaties (April 2010). See www.hmrc.gov.uk/cnr/dtdigest.pdf.
—	List of bodies approved by HMRC under *ITEPA 2003*, *ss 343, 344* (subscriptions to professional bodies). See www.hmrc.gov.uk/list3/list3.htm.

HMRC also publish Concessions and Statements of Practice, brief descriptions of which are included in Chapters 38 and 40 with appropriate cross-references to the main coverage.

HMRC guidance manuals

[36.2] The HMRC Guidance Manuals provide guidance to HMRC staff on the operation and application of tax law and the tax system and are available online at www.hmrc.gov.uk/manuals/index.htm. Among the more important of the Manuals, as far as income tax is concerned, are the Business Income Manual, the Employment Income Manual and the Capital Allowances Manual. References to HMRC Manuals are made throughout this work where appropriate.

Some material may be withheld from the online versions of the manuals under exemptions contained in the Government's 'Code of Practice on Access to Government Information'.

HMRC Tax Bulletin and HMRC Briefs

[36.3] Until December 2006, HMRC published a bi-monthly Tax Bulletin aimed at tax practitioners and giving the views of HMRC technical specialists on various issues. (Up to and including April 2005, the Tax Bulletin was published by the Inland Revenue.) Tax Bulletin was available in paper form by annual subscription but was also published free-of-charge online at www.hmrc.gov.uk/bulletins/index.htm.

The December 2006 Tax Bulletin was the last published. It is replaced in 2007 by HMRC Briefs, a free service covering both direct and indirect taxes which is published online only (see www.hmrc.gov.uk/briefs). These are issued as and when HMRC have news to impart.

HMRC Helpsheets

[36.4] HMRC produce a number of helpsheets designed to explain different aspects of the tax system and to assist in the completion of self-assessment tax returns. These can be downloaded from the self-assessment area of the HMRC website. Those currently available in connection with the personal and partnership tax returns are listed below (and see Tolley's Capital Gains Tax for helpsheets on that tax).

General

HS237	Community Investment Tax Relief.
HS305	Employee shares and securities — further guidance.
HS310	War widow's and dependant's pensions.
HS320	Gains on UK life insurance policies.
HS325	Other taxable income.
HS340	Interest and alternative finance payments eligible for relief on qualifying loans and alternative finance arrangements.
HS341	Enterprise Investment Scheme — income tax relief.
HS342	Charitable giving.
HS343	Accrued income scheme.
HS344	Exempt employers' contributions to an overseas pension scheme.
HS345	Pensions — tax charges on any excess over the Lifetime Allowance, Annual Allowance and Special Annual Allowance and on unauthorised payments.

HS346 Pension savings tax charges — guidance for members of overseas pension schemes that are not UK registered pension schemes.

Employment
HS201 Vouchers, credit cards and tokens.
HS202 Living accommodation.
HS203 Car benefits and car fuel benefits.
HS205 Seafarers' earnings deduction.
HS207 Non-taxable payments or benefits for employees.
HS208 Payslips and coding notices.
HS210 Assets provided for private use.
HS211 Employment — residence and domicile issues.
HS212 Tax equalisation.
HS213 Payments in kind — assets transferred.
HS52   Capital allowances and balancing charges.

Self-employment
HS220 More than one business.
HS222 How to calculate your taxable profits.
HS224 Farmers and market gardeners.
HS227 Losses.
HS229 Information from your accounts.
HS232 Farm stock valuation.
HS234 Averaging for creators of literary or artistic works.
HS236 Foster Carers and Adult Placement Carers.
HS238 Revenue recognition in service contracts — UITF 40.

Lloyd's underwriters
HS240 Lloyd's underwriters.

Land and property
HS223 Rent a Room for traders.
HS251 Agricultural land.

Foreign
HS260 Overlap.
HS262 Income and benefits from transfers of assets abroad and income from non-resident trusts.
HS263 Calculating foreign tax credit relief on income.
HS321 Gains on foreign life insurance policies.

Trusts
HS270   Trusts and settlements — income treated as the settlor's.

Non-residence
HS300   Non-residents and investment income.
HS302   Dual residents.
HS303   Non-resident entertainers and sports persons.
HS304   Non-residents — relief under Double Taxation Agreements.

Partnerships
HS231   Doctor's expenses.
HS380   Partnerships — foreign aspects.

Trusts
HS392   Trust Management Expenses (TMEs).

HMRC website

[36.5] The HMRC website at www.hmrc.gov.uk/home.htm gives access to news, leaflets, manuals, online guidance, Tax Briefs, Tax Bulletin, statutory instruments etc., has specialist areas devoted to such matters as self-assessment, employers, practitioners, non-residents etc., and includes online filing facilities where appropriate.

37

HMRC Extra-Statutory Concessions

Introduction

[**37.1**] The following is a summary of the concessions published online by HMRC at www.hmrc.gov.uk/specialist/esc.pdf at 10 August 2009 or subsequently announced, insofar as they relate to subjects dealt with in this book. It should be borne in mind that in a particular case there may be special circumstances which will require to be taken into account in considering the application of a concession. A concession will not be given in any case where an attempt is made to use it for tax avoidance (and see *R v HMIT (ex p Fulford-Dobson)* QB 1987, 60 TC 168). See also **34.4** HMRC — ADMINISTRATION.

On and after 21 July 2008, the Treasury have power to give statutory effect to any existing HMRC concession. 'Concession' is given a wide interpretation and is not restricted to the HMRC or Inland Revenue statements originally described as extra-statutory concessions and listed in this chapter. The Treasury's power is exercisable by statutory instrument (see now *SI 2009 No 730*). [*FA 2008, s 160*]. Where a concession listed in this chapter has been superseded by legislation, this is indicated in the listing.

A. APPLICABLE TO INDIVIDUALS

A4   **Directors' travelling expenses.** Certain expenses paid by employers are not assessable. See **27.29**(ix), **27.86** EMPLOYMENT INCOME.

A10   **Overseas pension schemes.** Income tax is not charged on certain lump sums on termination of employment overseas. See **56.3**(k) PENSION INCOME.

A11   **Residence in the UK: year of commencement or cessation of residence.** Liability to tax is computed by reference to the period of residence in that year. See **62.6** RESIDENCE, ORDINARY RESIDENCE AND DOMICILE.

A12   **Double taxation relief: alimony etc. under UK court order or agreement: payer resident abroad.** Relief by way of credit is allowed in certain circumstances. See **26.9**(h) DOUBLE TAX RELIEF.

A14 **Deceased person's estate: residuary income received during the administration period.** A legatee resident abroad may have his tax liability on estate income adjusted as if the income had arisen to him directly. See **23.13** DECEASED ESTATES.

A16 **Annual payments (other than interest) paid out of income not brought into charge to income tax.** If payment is made in a year later than when due, and it could have been made out of taxed income in that due year, an allowance will be made (when collecting under *ICTA 1988, s 350*) for the tax which the payer would have been entitled to deduct (under *ICTA 1988, s 348*) and retain if the payment had been made at the due date. See **24.21**(i) DEDUCTION OF TAX AT SOURCE.

A17 **Death of taxpayer before due date for payment of tax.** Interest on tax overdue may not begin to run until after probate or letters of administration are obtained. See **42.7** INTEREST AND SURCHARGES ON OVERDUE TAX.

A19 **Arrears of tax arising through official error.** Relief is given. See **54.11** PAYMENT OF TAX for current details.

A31 **Life assurance premium relief by deduction: pre-marriage policies: premium relief after divorce** continues where one party pays on life of the other. See **44.27**(h) LIFE ASSURANCE POLICIES.

A32 **Tax relief for life assurance premiums: position of certain pension schemes which are unapproved after 5 April 1980.** Relief is continued. See **44.33**(ii) LIFE ASSURANCE POLICIES.

A33 **Lump sum retirement benefits: changes after 5 April 1980.** Previous tax exemption is continued under certain conditions. Superseded by *SI 2009 No 730, Art 2* for 2009/10 onwards. See **57.28** PENSION PROVISION.

A37 **Tax treatment of directors' fees received by partnerships and other companies.** Under certain conditions, such fees may be included in computing the partnership profits — see **27.54** EMPLOYMENT INCOME, or in the corporation tax assessment of the other company — see **27.3**(v) EMPLOYMENT INCOME.

A41 **Qualifying life assurance policies: statutory conditions** may be relaxed in certain circumstances. See **44.35**(h) LIFE ASSURANCE POLICIES.

A43 Interest relief: investment in partnerships, close companies, employee-controlled companies and co-operatives continue to attract relief where the partnership is incorporated or the company's shares reorganised. Superseded by *ITA 2007, s 410*. See **43.7–43.10 INTEREST PAYABLE.**

A44 Education allowances under Overseas Service Aid Scheme, payable to officers in the public service of certain overseas territories, which the UK government has undertaken to exempt from income tax, are so exempted. See **25.1 DIPLOMATIC IMMUNITY.**

A45 Life assurance policies: variation of term assured policies. A term assurance policy for a term of ten years or less will not be disqualified under *ICTA 1988, Sch 15 paras 17(2)(b), 18* (see **44.35**(d) **LIFE ASSURANCE POLICIES**) because of a reduction in the rate of premium to less than half as a result of a similar reduction in the sum assured or an extension of the term (resulting in a total term still not exceeding ten years). To be withdrawn with effect from 9 December 2010.

A49 Widow's pension paid to widow of Singapore nationality, resident in the UK, whose husband was a UK national employed as a Public Officer by the Government of Singapore is included in the exemption provided by *ITEPA 2003, s 643*. See **56.3**(g) **PENSION INCOME.**

A56 Benefits in kind: tax treatment of accommodation provided by employers. The rules are modified in relation to Scotland. See **27.60 EMPLOYMENT INCOME.**

A60 Agricultural workers' board and lodging will, subject to conditions, not be charged to tax even where a higher wage in lieu could be taken. Withdrawn from 1 April 2010. See **27.20 EMPLOYMENT INCOME.**

A61 Clergymen's heating and lighting etc. expenses. Certain sums paid or reimbursed are not charged to tax. Superseded by legislation. See **27.50 EMPLOYMENT INCOME.**

A68 Payments out of a discretionary trust which are taxable as employment income. Trustees may reclaim tax on certain payments to beneficiaries. Superseded by legislation. See **68.15 SETTLEMENTS.**

A69 Composite rate tax: non-resident depositors. Certain declarations made to a society are treated as having been made to a successor company. Superseded by *SI 2008 No 2682, Reg 19*. See **8.2 BANKS, 9.3 BUILDING SOCIETIES.**

A78 **Residence in the UK: accompanying spouse.** A concessional treatment is available for the determination of the residence and ordinary residence status of spouses accompanying individuals in full-time employment abroad. See **62.6 RESIDENCE, ORDINARY RESIDENCE AND DOMICILE.**

A81 **Termination payments and legal costs.** Certain legal costs recovered from the employer will not be charged under *ITEPA 2003, ss 401–416*. See **20.6**(viii) **COMPENSATION FOR LOSS OF EMPLOYMENT (AND DAMAGES).**

A86 **Blind person's tax allowance.** The allowance will be granted for the year before registration where the evidence on which registration was based was available at the end of that year. Superseded by *ITA 2007, s 38*. See **1.16 ALLOWANCES AND TAX RATES.**

A91 **Living accommodation provided by reason of employment.** A charge will not be raised under the special provisions for accommodation costing £75,000 or more where the basic charge was based on the full market rent. See **27.64 EMPLOYMENT INCOME.**

A93 **Payments from offshore trusts to minor unmarried child of settlor: claim by settlor for credit of tax paid by trustees** against his liability to tax on income distributed to or for the benefit of the child will be allowed. See **68.15 SETTLEMENTS.**

A94 **Profits and losses of theatre backers (angels)** may in certain cases be treated as within *ITTOIA 2005, s 687*, and the requirement for deduction of tax from certain payments is waived. See **49.6 MISCELLANEOUS INCOME.**

A97 **Jobmatch programme.** Income tax is not charged on payments under the Jobmatch programme or in respect of training vouchers received under its terms. See **30.42 EXEMPT INCOME.**

A99 **Tax treatment of compensation for mis-sold freestanding additional voluntary contribution schemes.** Certain compensation payments are exempted from tax. See **30.11 EXEMPT INCOME.**

A100 **Tax exemption for compensation paid on bank accounts owned by Holocaust victims.** Compensation paid on unclaimed accounts opened by Holocaust victims and frozen during the Second World War is exempt from income tax and death duties. Superseded by *FA 2006, s 64* with retrospective effect for 1996/97 onwards. See now **30.29 EXEMPT INCOME.**

A103 **Approved employee share schemes: armed forces reservists.** Armed Forces Reservists called up to active service are enabled to maintain their participation in their civilian employers' approved share schemes during the period they are away on service. See **69.2** SHARE-RELATED EMPLOYMENT INCOME AND EXEMPTIONS.

A104 **Car and fuel benefits** provided to employees via vouchers or credit tokens are not double counted in determining whether or not the employment is 'lower paid'. Superseded by *FA 2007, s 62* for 2007/08 onwards. See **27.26** EMPLOYMENT INCOME.

B. **CONCESSIONS APPLICABLE TO INDIVIDUALS AND COMPANIES**

B1 **Machinery or plant: changes from 'renewals' to 'capital allowances' basis.** Capital allowances may be claimed provided all items of the same class are changed to new basis. See **11.68** CAPITAL ALLOWANCES ON PLANT AND MACHINERY.

B7 **Benevolent gifts by traders** are allowable in certain circumstances. To be withdrawn with effect from 9 December 2010. See **73.72** TRADING INCOME.

B8 **Double tax relief: income consisting of royalties and 'know-how' payments** arising to a UK resident from abroad. See **26.9**(i) DOUBLE TAX RELIEF.

B11 **Compensation for compulsory slaughter of farm animals** may be treated as profits spread over the following three years. See **73.73**(b) TRADING INCOME.

B16 **Fire safety: capital expenditure incurred on certain trade premises (a) in Northern Ireland, and (b) by lessors.** (a) Provisions relating to fire safety expenditure in the UK are extended to NI, and (b) relief is allowed where lessor incurs the expenditure himself, if similar expenditure by the tenant would have qualified for relief. No longer relevant as the said provisions are themselves repealed for expenditure after 5 April 2008. See **11.8**(i) CAPITAL ALLOWANCES ON PLANT AND MACHINERY.

B18 **Payments out of discretionary trusts.** Beneficiaries may claim certain reliefs as if they had received the income out of which the payment was made directly. See **68.15** SETTLEMENTS.

B40 **UK investment managers acting for non-resident clients.** The exemptions of *TMA 1970, ss 78(2), 82* are extended in certain cases. See **50.3, 50.7** NON-RESIDENTS.

B41   **Claims to repayment of tax.** Where an overpayment of tax has arisen because of official error, and there is no doubt or dispute as to the facts, claims to repayment of tax are accepted outside the statutory time limit. See **18.6 CLAIMS.**

B42   **'Free gifts' and insurance contracts.** Certain incentive gifts offered in connection with the issue of insurance policies are disregarded. See **44.29 LIFE ASSURANCE POLICIES.**

B46   **Automatic penalties for late employers' and contractors' end-of-year returns.** A short period of grace is allowed for submission of annual returns. This concession is to be withdrawn after 31 March 2011. See **55.21 PENALTIES.**

B47   **Furnished lettings of dwelling houses — wear and tear of furniture.** As an alternative to the renewals basis, an allowance of 10% of rent may be claimed. See **60.9 PROPERTY INCOME.**

B49   **Capital allowances — repaid grants.** Capital allowances will be given for repayments of grants which were deducted from expenditure qualifying for capital allowances. See **10.2**(vi) **CAPITAL ALLOWANCES, 11.2**(vi) **CAPITAL ALLOWANCES ON PLANT AND MACHINERY.**

C. CONCESSIONS APPLICABLE TO COMPANIES ETC.

C4   **Trading activities for charitable purposes.** Profits are not taxed under certain conditions. Superseded by *ITA 2007, s 529.* See **16.8 CHARITIES.**

C32   **Interest relief—companies with tax and NICs liabilities under the personal service rules where the payments for relevant contracts have been received after deduction of tax by virtue of the construction industry scheme provisions.** Corporation tax repayments due may be set against certain liabilities in respect of deemed employment payments for the purposes of interest on overdue tax and NICs on such payments. See **58.11 PERSONAL SERVICE COMPANIES ETC.**

C33   **Life assurance gains.** The information requirements are relaxed in relation to non-UK resident policy holders in specified circumstances. See **44.16 LIFE ASSURANCE POLICIES.**

D. CONCESSIONS RELATING TO CAPITAL GAINS

D47   **Temporary loss of charitable status due to reverter of school and other sites.** Liabilities which may arise in the period before charitable status is re-established will be discharged or repaid. Withdrawn from 1 April 2010. See **16.2 CHARITIES**.

38

HMRC Investigatory Powers

Cross-references. See **55** PENALTIES; **63** RETURNS.

See HMRC Compliance Handbook, in particular CH20000 *et seq.* (technical guidance: information and inspection powers) and CH200000 *et seq.* (operational guidance: how to do a compliance check).

See the series of factsheets CC/FS1 to CC/FS9 listed in **36.1** HMRC EXPLANATORY PUBLICATIONS.

Introduction

[38.1] HMRC have wide powers to enforce compliance with tax legislation. In most cases, the powers used are those for enquiries into self-assessment returns, for which see **38.2** below and **63.6–63.11** RETURNS. Those powers do, however, operate in tandem with further powers to obtain evidence both directly from the taxpayer and from third parties, which are described in this chapter.

FA 2008, Sch 36 introduces a common set of information and inspection powers for HMRC covering income tax, capital gains tax and other direct and indirect taxes and levies. The powers apply from 1 April 2009 (or, in some cases, from 1 April 2010). [*SI 2009 Nos 404, 3054*]. See **38.3–38.10** below.

The *FA 2008* powers replace the pre-existing powers at **38.11, 38.12** below to obtain documents and particulars and the pre-existing power to call for documents during self-assessment enquiries (see **38.2** below).

HMRC can require a tax accountant who has been convicted by, or before, any UK court of a tax offence or incurred a penalty under *TMA 1970, s 99* (see **55.19 PENALTIES**) to deliver 'documents' in his possession or power relevant to any tax liability of any of his clients. See **38.13** below.

With effect from 1 December 2007, HMRC are able to exercise certain powers under the *Police and Criminal Evidence Act 1984* when conducting direct tax criminal investigations. See **38.15** below. As a result of the availability of those powers, the pre-existing search and seizure powers at **38.17** below are no longer needed and are repealed. The pre-existing power to seek judicial authority to require the delivery of documents at **38.16** below is restricted to circumstances where the equivalent police power cannot be used.

There are special provisions relating to computer records (see **38.18** below).

Self-assessment enquiries

[38.2] The self-assessment enquiry procedures are explained at **63.6–63.11 RETURNS**; these operate in tandem with the provisions below. The enquiry procedures incorporate a separate power to call for documents but, from 1 April 2009, that power is repealed and replaced by the powers at **38.3–38.10** below. [*SI 2009 No 404, Arts 2, 3*]. See, in particular, **38.5** below for restrictions on HMRC's power to issue an information notice where a tax return has been made.

Information and inspection powers under FA 2008, Sch 36

[38.3] *FA 2008, Sch 36* introduces a common set of information and inspection powers for HMRC covering income tax, capital gains tax and other direct and indirect taxes and levies. The powers apply from 1 April 2009 (or in some cases from 1 April 2010), and are covered at **38.4–38.10** below to the extent that they apply for the purposes of income tax. The powers replace those at **38.11** below and the existing power to call for documents during self-assessment enquiries (see **63.8 RETURNS**). [*SI 2009 No 404, Arts 2, 3; SI 2009 No 3054, Art 2*].

Definitions

For the purposes of the provisions at **38.4–38.10** below, the following definitions apply.

'*Checking*' includes carrying out an investigation or enquiry of any kind. '*Document*' includes a part of a document (unless the context requires otherwise).

An '*authorised HMRC officer*' is an HMRC officer who is, or who is a member of a class of officers, authorised by the Commissioners for HMRC for the particular purpose.

The carrying on of a business includes the letting of property and the activities of a charity, a government department, a local authority (within *ITA 2007, s 999*), a local authority association (within *ITA 2007, s 1000*) or any other public authority. HMRC can make regulations specifying activities as businesses.

'*Tax*' means any or all of income tax, capital gains tax, corporation tax and VAT. It also includes taxes of EU member states in respect of which information can be disclosed and taxes of territories to which a tax enforcement agreement applies (see **35.3**(c) HMRC — CONFIDENTIALITY OF INFORMATION). With effect from 1 April 2010, '*tax*' will also include the other taxes listed at *FA 2008, Sch 36 para 63(1) as amended*.

A person's '*tax position*' is his position at any time and in relation to any period as regards any tax, including his position as to past, present and future liability to any tax, penalties and other amounts which have been paid or are, or may be, payable by or to him in connection with any tax, and any claims, elections, applications and notices that have or may be made or given in connection with the person's liability to pay any tax. A person's tax position also includes matters relating to the withholding by the person of another person's PAYE income (as defined in **53.2** PAY AS YOU EARN). References to a person's tax position also include the tax position of a company that has ceased to exist and an individual who has died.

In relation to income tax, references in this chapter to an '*involved third party*' are to any of the following:

(a)   an approved agent under the rules for payroll giving (see **16.20** CHARITIES);
(b)   an ISA account manager (see **30.21** EXEMPT INCOME);
(c)   an account provider in relation to a Child Trust Fund (see **30.9** EXEMPT INCOME); or
(d)   a person registered as a managing agent at Lloyd's in relation to a syndicate of underwriting members (see **74** UNDERWRITERS AT LLOYD'S).

In relation to an involved third party, references to '*relevant information and relevant documents*' are to information and documents relating to:

(i)   (in a case within (a) above) the donations;
(ii)   (in a case within (b) above) the account and investments that have been held in the account;
(iii)   (in a case within (c) above) the fund and investments that have been held under the fund; and
(iv)   (in a case within (d) above) the syndicate and its activities.

[*FA 2008, Sch 36 paras 58 60, 61A, 63, 64; FA 2009, s 96(1), Sch 47 para 22, Sch 48 para 14*].

Responsibility of company officers

Everything to be done by a company under the provisions at **38.4–38.10** below must be done by it through the '*proper officer*' (i.e. the secretary of a corporate body, except where a liquidator or administrator has been appointed when the latter is the proper officer, or the treasurer of a non-corporate body) or, except where a liquidator has been appointed, any authorised officer. The service of a notice on a company may be effected by serving it on the proper officer. [*TMA 1970, s 108; FA 2008, Sch 36 para 56; SI 2009 No 1890, Regs 1, 3(3)*].

Information and documents

[38.4] With effect from 1 April 2009, an HMRC officer may by notice in writing require a person to provide information or to produce a document if it is reasonably required by him:

(a)   for the purpose of checking that person's tax position;

(b)   for the purpose of checking the tax position of another person whose identity is known to the officer; or

(c)   for the purpose of checking the UK tax position of a person whose identity is not known to the officer or of a class of persons whose individual identities are not known to the officer.

Such a notice (an '*information notice*') may require either specified information or documents or information or documents described in the notice (so that a notice is not restricted to information or documents which HMRC can specifically identify). Where it is given with the approval of the Appeal Tribunal (see further below), the notice must say so.

The information or documents must be provided or produced within the time period and at the time, by the means and in the form (if any) reasonably specified in the notice. Documents must be produced for inspection either at a place agreed to by the recipient of the notice and an HMRC officer or at a place (other than one used solely as a dwelling) that an HMRC officer reasonably specifies. Subject to any conditions or exceptions set out in regulations made by HMRC, copies of documents can be produced unless the notice requires the production of the original document or an HMRC officer in writing subsequently requests the original document. Where an officer makes such a request, the document must be produced within the period and at the time and by the means reasonably requested by the officer.

An HMRC officer may take copies of, or make extracts from, a document (or copy) produced to him, and if it appears necessary to him, he may remove the document at a reasonable time and retain it for a reasonable period. The officer must, without charge, provide a receipt for a document which is removed where this is requested and must also provide, again without charge, a copy of the document if the person producing it reasonably requires it for any purpose. Where a document which has been removed is lost or damaged, HMRC are liable to compensate the owner for expenses reasonably incurred in replacing or repairing it.

The production or removal of a document under these provisions does not break any lien (i.e. any right) claimed on it.

Taxpayer notice

An information notice under (a) above can be given without the approval of the Tribunal, but where such approval is obtained the taxpayer has no right of appeal against the decision of the Tribunal to grant approval or against the notice or a requirement in it.

Where approval is sought from the Tribunal, the application for approval must be made by, or with the agreement of, an authorised HMRC officer. The taxpayer must normally have been told that the information or documents are required and have been given a reasonable opportunity to make representations to HMRC, and the Tribunal must be given a summary of any such representations. Where, however, the Tribunal is satisfied that informing the taxpayer would prejudice the assessment or collection of tax, it can approve the giving of the notice without the taxpayer having been informed.

Third party notice

A notice within (b) above cannot be given without either the agreement of the taxpayer (i.e. the person whose tax position is to be checked) or the approval of the Tribunal and must normally name the taxpayer. Where approval is obtained from the Tribunal, there is no right of appeal against the decision of the Tribunal to grant approval or against the notice or a requirement in it.

Where approval is sought from the Tribunal, the application for approval must be made by, or with the agreement of, an authorised HMRC officer. The taxpayer must normally have been given a summary of the reasons why an officer requires the information or documents. The person to whom the notice is to be given must normally have been told that the information or documents are required and have been given a reasonable opportunity to make representations to HMRC and the Tribunal must be given a summary of any such representations. These requirements can, however, be disapplied where the Tribunal is satisfied that informing the recipient of the notice or giving a summary of reasons to the taxpayer would prejudice the assessment or collection of tax.

The Appeal Tribunal can also disapply the requirement to name the taxpayer in the notice if it is satisfied that the officer has reasonable grounds for believing that naming him might seriously prejudice the assessment or collection of tax.

A copy of the notice must normally be given to the taxpayer. The Tribunal can, however, disapply this requirement if an application for approval is made by, or with the agreement of, an authorised HMRC officer and the Tribunal is satisfied that the officer has reasonable grounds for believing that giving a copy of the notice to the taxpayer might prejudice the assessment or collection of tax.

Where, on or after 1 April 2010, a third party notice is given to an 'involved third party' (see 38.3 above) for the purpose of checking a person's income tax position and refers only to relevant information or relevant documents (see 38.3 above), neither the agreement of the taxpayer nor the approval of the Tribunal is required and a copy of the notice need not be given to the taxpayer.

Similarly rules apply if a third party notice refers only to information or documents that relate to any pensions matter (as defined in *FA 2008, Sch 36 para 34B*, which also provides, however, that the HMRC officer must normally give a copy of the notice to certain persons — see also *SI 2010 No 650*).

Where a third party notice is given for the purpose of checking the tax position of more than one of the partners in a business carried on in partnership, in their capacity as such, the above provisions apply as if the taxpayer were at least one of the partners. The requirement for the notice to name the taxpayer is satisfied by stating in the notice that its purpose is checking the tax position of more than one of the partners and giving a name in which the partnership is registered for any purpose. Where a third party notice is given to one of the partners for the purpose of checking the tax position of any of the other partners, neither the agreement of any of the partners nor the approval of the Tribunal is required and a copy does not have to be given to any other partners.

Notice about persons whose identity is not known

The giving of a notice under (c) above requires the approval of the Tribunal. The Tribunal can approve the giving of the notice only if it is satisfied that:

- there are reasonable grounds for believing that the person or class of persons to whom the notice relates may have failed, or may fail, to comply with any provision of the Taxes Acts;
- any such failure is likely to have led, or to lead, to serious prejudice to the assessment or collection of tax; and
- the information or document is not readily available from another source.

There is no right of appeal against a decision of the Tribunal to grant approval.

The approval of the Tribunal is permitted but not required for a notice to be given to a partner in a business carried on in partnership for the purpose of checking the tax position of partners whose identities are not known to the officer giving the notice. With effect from 1 April 2010, approval is likewise permitted but not required for a notice to be given to an involved third party (see **38.3** above) for the purpose of checking the income tax position of persons whose identities are not known to the officer giving the notice, provided that the notice refers only to relevant information or relevant documents (see **38.3** above). Similarly, approval is permitted but not required if a notice refers only to information or documents that relate to any pensions matter (as defined in *FA 2008, Sch 36 para 34B*, which also provides that the HMRC officer must give a copy of the notice to certain persons — see also *SI 2010 No 650*).

[*FA 2008, Sch 36 paras 1–9, 15, 16, 34A–34C, 37; FA 2009, Sch 47 paras 2–4, 11, Sch 48 paras 2, 11; SI 2009 No 56, Sch 1 para 471(2)–(4); SI 2009 No 404; SI 2009 No 3054, Art 2; SI 2010 No 650*].

Approval was duly granted by the Tribunal in *Re an Application by HMRC for approval to serve notice on Financial Institution* FTT (TC 148), [2009] UKFTT 195 (TC); *Re an Application by HMRC for approval to serve notice on Financial Institution* FTT (TC 149), [2009] UKFTT 196 (TC); and *Re Applications by HMRC for approval to serve notices on Financial Institutions* FTT (TC 174), [2009] SFTD 780.

For further restrictions on the above powers, see **38.5** below. For appeals against information notices, see **38.6** below.

Restrictions on information notice powers

[38.5] An information notice does not require a person to:

(i)   produce a document if it is not in his possession or power;

(ii)   provide or produce information that relates to the conduct of a pending tax appeal or any part of a document containing such information;

(iii)   provide journalistic material (within *Police and Criminal Evidence Act 1984, s 13*) or information contained in such material;

(iv)   subject to the exceptions below, provide or produce 'personal records' (within *Police and Criminal Evidence Act 1984, s 12*); or

(v)   produce a document the whole of which originates more than six years before the giving of the notice, unless the notice is given by, or with the agreement of, an authorised officer.

With regard to (iv) above, an information notice may require a person to produce documents (or copies) that are personal records, omitting any personal information (i.e. information whose inclusion in the documents makes them personal records) and to provide any information in personal records that is not personal information.

[FA 2008, Sch 36 paras 18–20].

Notice where tax return made

Where a person has made a tax return under *TMA 1970, s 8, s 8A* or *s 12AA* (see **63.2, 63.13** RETURNS) in respect of a tax year, a taxpayer notice (see **38.4**(a) above) can be given for the purpose of checking his income tax or capital gains tax position for that year only if:

(a)   an enquiry notice under *TMA 1970, s 9A* or *s 12AC* (see **63.6, 63.13** RETURNS) has been given in respect of either the return or a claim or election for the year to which the return relates and the enquiry has not been completed;

(b)   an HMRC officer has reason to suspect, in relation to that person, that an amount that ought to have been assessed to tax may not have been assessed, that an assessment for the period may be or have become insufficient or relief from tax for the period may be or have become excessive;

(c)   the notice is given for the purpose of obtaining information or a document that is also required to check the taxpayer's VAT position (or, with effect from 1 April 2010, his position as regards any tax other than income tax, capital gains tax or corporation tax); or

(d)   the notice is given for the purpose of obtaining information or a document that is required to check the taxpayer's position as regards his obligation to make deductions or repayments under PAYE, the Construction Industry Scheme or any other provision.

Where a business is carried in partnership and a partnership return (see **63.13 RETURNS**) or a partnership claim or election (see **18.1 CLAIMS**) has been made by one of the partners, the above provisions apply as if the return, claim or election had been made by each of the partners.

Conditions (a)–(d) above do not have to be met if:

* the person is carrying on a trade to which the **HERD BASIS (33)** applies, and the taxpayer notice refers only to information or documents that relate to the animals kept for the purposes of the trade or their products; or

* it appears to an officer of HMRC that *ITA 2007, s 684* (see **4.2 ANTI-AVOIDANCE**) may apply to the person by reason of one or more transactions, and the taxpayer notice refers only to information or documents relating to the transaction (or to any of the transactions).

[*FA 2008, Sch 36 paras 21, 37(1)(2), 37A, 37B; FA 2009, Sch 47 paras 9, 11, 12, Sch 48 para 8; SI 2009 No 3054, Art 2*].

Deceased persons

An information notice for the purpose of checking the tax position of a deceased person cannot be given more than four years after death. [*FA 2008, Sch 36 para 22*].

Legal professional privilege

An information notice cannot require a person to provide information, or to produce any part of a document, in respect of which a claim to legal professional privilege (or, in Scotland, a claim to confidentiality of communications) could be maintained in legal proceedings.

HMRC can make regulations providing a means of resolving disputes over whether a document is privileged. See now *SI 2009 No 1916*, which sets out different procedures depending upon whether the information notice is given in the course of correspondence or in the course of an inspection of premises; both procedures involve recourse to the Appeal Tribunal. See HMRC Brief 54/09, 18 August 2009.

[*FA 2008, Sch 36 para 23; SI 2009 No 56, Sch 1 para 471(6)*].

Auditors

An information notice does not require an auditor (i.e. a person appointed as an auditor for the purpose of an enactment) to provide information held in connection with the performance of his functions under that enactment or to produce documents which are his property and which were created by him, or on his behalf, for or in connection with the performance of those functions.

This restriction does not apply to any information, or any document containing information, which explains any information or document which an auditor has, as tax accountant, assisted any client in preparing for, or delivering to, HMRC. Where the notice is given under **38.4**(c) above, the restriction also does not apply to information giving the identity or address of a person to whom the notice relates or of a person who has acted on behalf of such a person or to a document containing such information. Where the restriction is so disapplied, only that part (or parts) of a document which contains the relevant information has to be produced. The restriction is not disapplied if the information concerned, or a document containing the information, has already been provided or produced to an HMRC officer.

[FA 2008, Sch 36 paras 24, 26, 27].

Tax advisers

An information notice does not require a 'tax adviser' to provide information about, or to produce documents which are his property and which consist of, communications between him and a person in relation to whose tax affairs he has been appointed or between him and any other tax advisor of such a person, the purpose of which is the giving or obtaining of advice about any of those tax affairs. For this purpose, a *'tax adviser'* is a person appointed (directly or by another tax adviser) to give advice about the tax affairs of another person.

This restriction is disapplied in the same circumstances as the restriction applying to auditors is disapplied.

[FA 2008, Sch 36 paras 25–27].

Appeals against information notices

[38.6] A taxpayer can appeal against a taxpayer notice (see **38.4**(a) above) or any requirement in such a notice unless the notice was given with the approval of the Appeal Tribunal. No appeal can be made against a requirement to provide information or to produce a document which forms part of his 'statutory records'.

A person given a third party notice (see **38.4**(b) above) can appeal against the notice or any requirement in it on the ground that compliance would be unduly onerous. No appeal can be made, however, where the notice was given with the approval of the Tribunal or against a requirement to provide information or produce a document forming part of the taxpayer's statutory records.

Where a third party notice is given for the purpose of checking the tax position of more than one of the partners in a business carried on in partnership, no appeal can be made against a requirement to provide information or produce a document forming part of the statutory records of any of the partners. No appeal can be made against a requirement, in a notice given to a partner for the purpose of checking the tax position of other partners, to produce a document forming part of the statutory records of the partner receiving the notice.

A person given a notice about persons whose identity is not known (see **38.4**(c) above) can appeal against the notice or any requirement in it on the ground that compliance would be unduly onerous. No appeal can be made against a requirement, in a notice given to a parent undertaking for the purpose of checking the tax position of one or more subsidiary undertakings, to produce a document forming part of the statutory records of the parent undertaking or any of its subsidiary undertakings. Likewise, no appeal can be made against a requirement, in a notice given to a partner in a business carried on in partnership for the purpose of checking the tax position of other partners, to produce a document forming part of the statutory records of the partner receiving the notice.

For this purpose, '*statutory records*' are information and documents which a taxpayer is required to keep and preserve for tax purposes (see **18.3 CLAIMS, 63.5 RETURNS**), for VAT purposes and, with effect from 1 April 2010, for the purposes of the other taxes listed at *FA 2008, Sch 36 para 63(1) as amended*. To the extent that information or documents do not relate to the carrying on of a business and are not required to be kept or preserved for the purposes of VAT and other taxes, they form part of a taxpayer's statutory documents only to the extent that the tax to which they relate has ended. Information and documents cease to be statutory records when the period for which they are required to be preserved ends.

Notice of appeal under the above provisions must be given in writing to the HMRC officer who gave the information notice within the period of 30 days beginning with the date on which the information notice was given. A decision on an appeal by the Tribunal is final. Where the Tribunal confirms the notice or a requirement in it, the person to whom the notice was given must comply with the notice or requirement within the period specified by the Tribunal. If the Tribunal does not specify such a period, compliance must be within such period as an HMRC officer reasonably specifies in writing.

Subject to the above, the appeal provisions of *TMA 1970, Pt 5* (see **5 APPEALS**) apply to an appeal against an information notice as they apply to an appeal against an income tax assessment.

[*FA 2008, Sch 36 paras 29–33, 37, 62; FA 2009, Sch 47 para 11, Sch 48 para 15; SI 2009 No 56, Sch 1 para 471(2), (7)–(10); SI 2009 No 3054, Art 2*].

Concealing, destroying or disposing of documents

[38.7] A person to whom an information notice is addressed must not conceal, destroy or otherwise dispose of, or arrange for the concealment, destruction or disposal of, a document that is the subject of the notice. This does not apply if he does so after the document has been produced to HMRC in accordance with the notice, unless an HMRC officer has notified him in writing that the document must continue to be available for inspection (and has not withdrawn the notification). It also does not apply if a copy of the document was produced in compliance with the notice and the destruction, etc. takes place after the end of the period of six months beginning with the day on which the copy was produced unless within that period, an HMRC officer makes a request for the original document.

Similarly, where a person has been informed that a document is, or is likely, to be the subject of an information notice addressed to him, he must not conceal, destroy or otherwise dispose of, or arrange for the concealment, destruction or disposal of, the document. This does not apply if he acts more than six months after he was so informed (or was last so informed).

[FA 2008, Sch 36 paras 42, 43].

Failure to comply with the above provisions may be a criminal offence or result in penalties. See **38.10** below.

Inspection of business premises

[38.8] With effect from 1 April 2009, an HMRC officer may enter a person's 'business premises' and inspect the premises and any 'business assets' and 'business documents' that are on the premises if the inspection is reasonably required for the purpose of checking that person's tax position. The officer may not enter or inspect any part of the premises used solely as a dwelling.

With effect from 1 April 2010, an HMRC officer may enter business premises of an involved third party (see **38.3** above) and inspect the premises and any business assets and relevant documents that are on the premises if the inspection is reasonably required for the purpose of checking the tax position of any person or class of persons. It is not necessary that the officer know the identity of the person or persons. The officer may not enter or inspect any part of the premises used solely as a dwelling.

The officer may mark business assets and anything containing business assets to indicate that they have been inspected and may obtain and record information (electronically or otherwise) relating to the premises, assets and documents inspected. He may take copies of, or make extracts from, a document (or copy) which he inspects, and if it appears necessary to him, he may remove the document at a reasonable time and retain it for a reasonable period. He must, without charge, provide a receipt for a document which is removed where this is requested and must also provide, again without charge, a copy of the document, if the person producing it reasonably requires it for any purpose. Where a document which has been removed is lost or damaged, HMRC are liable to compensate the owner for expenses reasonably incurred in replacing or repairing it.

An inspection must normally be carried out at a time agreed to by the occupier of the premises. It can, however, be carried out at any reasonable time if:

(i)   the occupier has been given at least seven days' notice (in writing or otherwise) of the time of the inspection; or

(ii)   the inspection is carried out by, or with the agreement of, an authorised HMRC officer.

Where (ii) above applies, the officer carrying out the inspection must provide a notice in writing stating the possible consequences of obstructing the officer in the exercise of the power. If the occupier is present when the inspection begins, the notice must be given to him. If he is not present, the notice must be given to the person who appears to be the officer in charge of the premises, but if no such person is present, the notice must be left in a prominent place on the premises. The giving of such a notice does not require the approval of the Appeal Tribunal, but such approval can be applied for by, or with the agreement of, an authorised HMRC officer. A penalty for deliberate obstruction of an officer in the course of an inspection can only be charged where such approval has been obtained (see **38.10** below). A decision of the Tribunal to approve an inspection is final and there is no right of appeal.

An officer may not inspect a document if or to the extent that an information notice (see **38.4** above) given at the time of the inspection to the occupier of the premises could not require him to produce the document (see **38.5** above).

For the above purposes, *'business premises'* are premises (including any land, building or structure or means of transport), or a part of premises, that an HMRC officer has reason to believe are used in connection with the carrying on of a business by or on behalf of the taxpayer concerned. *'Business assets'* are assets, other than documents that are neither trading stock nor plant, that an HMRC officer has reason to believe are owned, leased or used in connection with the carrying on of any business. *'Business documents'* are documents, or copies of documents, relating to the carrying on of any business that form part of any person's statutory records.

[FA 2008, Sch 36 paras 10, 10A, 12–17, 28, 58; FA 2009, Sch 47 paras 5, 7, 8, Sch 48 paras 3, 4, 6, 10; SI 2009 No 56, Sch 1 para 471(2)(5); SI 2009 No 404; SI 2009 No 3054, Art 2].

Inspection of premises for valuation purposes

[38.9] With effect from 1 April 2010, an HMRC officer can enter and inspect any premises for the purpose of valuing them. The valuation must be reasonably required for the purpose of checking any person's position as regards income tax or corporation tax. The officer can be accompanied by a valuation expert.

The inspection must normally be carried out at a time agreed to by the occupier of the premises and he must be given notice in writing of the agreed time. If the occupier cannot be identified, agreement can be obtained from, and notice given to, a person who controls the premises. Where, however, the inspection has been approved by the Appeal Tribunal (see below), the only requirement is that the occupier or person controlling the premises be given at least seven days' notice in writing of the time of the inspection. Where such notice is given it must state that the inspection has been approved by the tribunal and indicate the possible consequences of obstructing the inspection (see below).

The giving of a notice does not require the approval of the Tribunal, but such approval can be applied for by, or with the agreement of, an authorised HMRC officer. A penalty for deliberate obstruction of an officer in the course of an inspection can only be charged where such approval has been obtained (see **38.10** below). A decision of the Tribunal to approve an inspection is final and there is no right of appeal. Both the person whose tax position is in question and the occupier of the premises (unless he cannot be identified) must be given a reasonable opportunity to make representations to the HMRC officer and a summary of any representations must be given to the Tribunal.

An officer carrying out an inspection under these powers must produce evidence of his authority to do so if asked by the occupier or any other person who appears to be in charge of the premises or property. He may obtain and record information (electronically or otherwise) relating to the premises and property inspected.

[*FA 2008, Sch 36 paras 12A, 12B, 13, 14, 17; FA 2009, Sch 47 para 8, Sch 48 paras 5–7; SI 2009 No 3054, Art 2*].

Offences and penalties under FA 2008, Sch 36

[38.10] For penalties for failure to comply with an information notice within **38.4** above or deliberately obstructing an HMRC officer in the course of an inspection of premises under the power at **38.8** or **38.9** above that has been approved by the Appeal Tribunal, see **55.17** PENALTIES.

It is an offence for a person required to produce a document by an information notice within **38.4** above which has been approved by the Appeal Tribunal to conceal, destroy or otherwise dispose of the document or to arrange for its concealment, destruction or disposal. This does not apply if he does so after the document has been produced to HMRC in accordance with the notice, unless an HMRC officer has notified him in writing that the document must continue to be available for inspection (and has not withdrawn the notification). It also does not apply if a copy of the document was produced in compliance with the notice and the destruction, etc. takes place after the end of the period of six months beginning with the day on which the copy was produced unless within that period, an HMRC officer makes a request for the original document.

It is also an offence for a person to conceal, destroy or otherwise dispose of, or to arrange for the concealment, destruction or disposal of, a document after an HMRC officer has informed him in writing that the document is, or is likely to be, the subject of an information notice approval for which is to be obtained from the Appeal Tribunal. This does not apply if the person so acts more than six months after he was so informed (or was last so informed).

On summary conviction of either of the above offences the offender is liable to a fine not exceeding the statutory maximum. On conviction on indictment the punishment is imprisonment for a maximum of two years and/or a fine.

[*FA 2008, Sch 36 paras 53–55; SI 2009 No 56, Sch 1 para 471(2)*].

Power to call for documents of taxpayer and others before 1 April 2009

[38.11] The provisions below are repealed with effect from 1 April 2009 and replaced by the provisions in *FA 2008, Sch 36* (see **38.3–38.10** above). These provisions continue, however, to have effect for the purposes of any notice given before 1 April 2009 under *TMA 1970, s 20* below. [*SI 2009 No 404, Arts 2, 4*].

For the purposes of these provisions, '*document*' means anything in which information of any description is recorded, but (except in relation to orders under *TMA 1970, s 20BA* — see **38.16** below) does not include personal records or journalistic material (within *Police and Criminal Evidence Act 1984, ss 12, 13*) (and those exclusions apply also to particulars contained in such records or material). The documents concerned are those in the possession or power of the person receiving the notice. Photographic etc. facsimiles may be supplied provided the originals are produced if called for, and documents relating to any pending tax appeal need not be delivered. In practice, the latter also applies to documents relating to a pending referral (see **63.11** RETURNS) during an enquiry (Hansard Standing Committee A 8 May 2001, Cols 172–174). There are special provisions relating to electronic records (see **38.18** below). Documents in a person's 'possession or power' are those actually in existence at the time the notice is given, and not any which would have to be brought into existence in order to satisfy the notice.

(a)   Where an HMRC officer is of the reasonable opinion that documents contain, or may contain, information relevant to any tax liability of a person he may (with the authority of the Commissioners for HMRC and the consent of a General or Special Commissioner (who is excluded from subsequent appeal proceedings)) by notice in writing require that person to deliver such documents to him (but only after that person has been given reasonable opportunity to produce them). Applications to a Commissioner for consent to issue a notice are held *ex parte* (see *Applicant v Inspector of Taxes* (Sp C 189), [1999] SSCD 128).

A notice may not require disclosure of material subject to legal professional privilege (*R v A Special Commr, ex p Morgan Grenfell & Co Ltd* HL 2002, 74 TC 511) but this does not extend to accountants' advice (*R (oao Prudential plc and another) v Special Commr of Income Tax and another* QB, [2009] All ER (D) 142 (Oct); *Re an Application by HMRC to serve Section 20 Notices* (Sp C 647), [2008] SSCD 358). For other challenges to the validity of notices, see *R v CIR (ex p T C Coombs & Co)* HL 1991, 64 TC 124; *R v CIR (ex p Taylor)* CA 1988, 62 TC 562; (No 2) CA 1990, 62 TC 578; also *Kempton v Special Commrs and CIR* Ch D 1992, 66 TC 249, where the validity of the notice was confirmed although the only evidence on which the Inspector of Taxes relied related to omissions from the returns of a fellow director of the taxpayer concerned, and *R v Macdonald and CIR (ex p Hutchinson & Co Ltd and others)* QB 1998, 71 TC 1, in which the notice was quashed in view of the failure of the Inland Revenue either to put before the Commissioner a letter setting out the taxpayer's substantive response to precursor notices (which had failed for technical reasons), or to address the issues raised by the taxpayer in their summary of reasons (see below) for applying for consent to the notice. In *R v CIR (ex p Banque Internationale à Luxembourg SA)* QB 2000, 72 TC 597, an application for judicial review based *inter alia* on the protections afforded by the European Convention on Human Rights was refused, although an opposite view (albeit *obiter*) was expressed in *R v A Special Commr, ex p Morgan Grenfell & Co Ltd* HL 2002, 74 TC 511.

(b) An HMRC officer may similarly by notice in writing require a person to furnish him with such particulars as he may reasonably require as being relevant to any tax liability of that person.

The notice is subject to the same authority and giving of consent requirements as at (a) above, and the requirements there relating to the giving of a written summary and the obligation imposed on the Special or General Commissioner giving consent apply similarly in relation to particulars as they do at (a) above to documents.

(c) An HMRC officer may similarly by notice in writing require any other person (including the Director of Savings) to deliver to him (or, if the person so elects, make available for inspection by a named officer) documents relevant to any tax liability of a 'taxpayer'. A copy of the notice must be given to the taxpayer concerned unless, in a case involving suspected fraud, a General or Special Commissioner so directs. Production of documents originating more than six years before the notice cannot be required (unless the Commissioner who gave consent to the notice specifically allows it on being satisfied that there is reasonable ground for believing loss of tax through fraud).

'*Taxpayer*' includes an individual who has died (but any notice must be given no more than six years after the death) and a company which has ceased to exist.

For general limitations on these powers, see *R v O'Kane and Clarke (ex p Northern Bank Ltd) and related application* QB 1996, 69 TC 187, and for a review of the procedural and other requirements, see *R v CIR (ex p Ulster Bank Ltd)* CA 1997, 69 TC 211, in which *ex p Northern Bank Ltd* was in part disapproved.

The notice is subject to the same authority and giving of consent requirements as at (a) above, and the requirements there relating to the giving of a written summary and the obligation imposed on the Special or General Commissioner giving consent apply similarly, except that the summary must be given to, and the obligation imposed relates to an appeal brought by, the taxpayer rather than the person to whom the notice is given, and no summary need be given if the taxpayer is not, as above, given a copy of the notice.

A notice cannot require the production by a statutory auditor of his audit papers, nor by a tax adviser of communications with a client (or with any other tax adviser of his client) relating to advice about the client's tax affairs. This exemption does not, however, apply to explanatory documents concerning any other documents prepared with the client for, or for delivery to, HMRC, unless HMRC already have access to the information contained therein in some other document. Similarly, where a notice does not identify the taxpayer to which it relates (see below), the exemption does not apply to any document giving the name or address of any taxpayer to whom the notice relates (or of a person acting on their behalf) unless HMRC already have access to the information contained therein. Where the exemption is so disapplied, either the document must be delivered or made available to HMRC or a copy of the relevant parts must be supplied (which parts must be available if required for inspection).

HMRC's application of these provisions in practice is set out in a Statement of Practice (HMRC SP 5/90). In particular, it is made clear that accountants' working papers will be called for only where voluntary access has not been obtained and it is considered absolutely necessary in order to determine whether a client's accounts or returns are complete and correct. Requests for access may on occasion extend to the whole or a particular part of the working papers, rather than just to information explaining specific entries, and HMRC will usually be prepared to visit the accountants' or clients' premises to examine the papers and to take copies or extracts. These restrictions on the use of its powers by HMRC do not apply in the circumstances described under **38.13** below. The restrictions also do not apply to 'link papers', i.e. those papers which show how the figures in a tax return are derived from the figures in the prime records (Revenue Tax Bulletin June 2003 pp 1031, 1032).

For guidance on the question of whether documents and records are the property of a statutory auditor or tax adviser, or of the client of such a person, see ICAEW Memorandum TR 781, 23 February 1990.

(d) Under *TMA 1970, s 20(8A)*, subject to conditions and with the specific consent of a Special Commissioner, a notice may be served as in (c) above which does not name the taxpayer(s) to whom it relates. The notice is subject to appeal (within 30 days) by the person on whom it is served on the ground that it would be onerous for him to comply with it.

For successful applications to serve notice under *TMA 1970, s 20(8A)*, see, for example, *Re an Application by HMRC to Serve section 20 Notice* (Sp C 517), [2006] SSCD 71 in which consent was granted to serve notice on a financial institution seeking information about UK credit card customers whose cards were associated with offshore bank accounts; *Re an Application by HMRC to Serve section 20 Notice (No 2)* (Sp C 536), [2006] SSCD 360 in which consent was granted to serve notice on the same financial institution, this time seeking information about customers with UK addresses and non-UK bank accounts; *Re an Application by HMRC to Serve section 20 Notice* (Sp C 533), [2006] SSCD 310 in which consent was granted to serve notice on an investment bank seeking information about UK-resident clients for whom it acted as prime broker and who conducted share transactions via a tax haven company; *Re an Application by HMRC to Serve section 20 Notice* (Sp C 537), [2006] SSCD 376 in which consent was granted to serve notice on a financial institution seeking information about UK-resident clients for whom it acted other than as prime broker and who conducted share transactions via a tax haven company; and, in similar vein, *Re An Application by HMRC to serve a Section 20 Notice on Financial Institution No 1* (Sp C 580), [2007] SSCD 202, *Re an Application by HMRC to serve a Section 20 Notice on Financial Institution No 2* (Sp C 581), [2007] SSCD 208, *Re an Application by HMRC to serve a Section 20 Notice on Financial Institution No 3* (Sp C 582), [2007] SSCD 216, *Re an Application by HMRC to serve a Section 20 Notice on Financial Institution No 4* (Sp C 583), [2007] SSCD 222, *Re an Application by HMRC to serve Section 20 Notice on*

Financial Institution No 5 FTT (TC 9), [2009] SSCD 488, *Re an Application by HMRC to serve Section 20 Notice on Financial Institution No 6 and 7* FTT (TC 10), [2009] SSCD 493 and *Re an Application by HMRC to serve Section 20 Notice on Financial Institution No 8* FTT (TC 11), [2009] SSCD 498. It was further decided in Sp C 533 above that the six-year restriction mentioned above does not apply to a notice served under *section 20(8A)*. For an unsuccessful application for judicial review of the issue of a *section 20(8A)* notice, see *R v CIR (ex p Ulster Bank Ltd)* QB 2000, 73 TC 209.

(e)   The **Commissioners for HMRC** may require, by notice in writing, a person to deliver or furnish, to a named officer of theirs, documents or information as specified in (a) and (b) above. Notices will not, however, be given under this power unless there are reasonable grounds for believing that that person may have failed, or may fail, to comply with any provision of the *Taxes Acts*, and that any such failure is likely to have led, or to lead, to serious prejudice to the proper assessment or collection of tax.

Supplementary

Where notice is given under (a), (b) or (c) above, the taxpayer concerned must be provided with a written summary of the officer's reasons for applying for consent to the giving of the notice (unless, in the case of (c), an Appeal Commissioner has directed that the taxpayer need not be sent a copy of the notice itself). Such a summary may exclude information which might identify an informant, or which the Appeal Commissioner is satisfied might prejudice the assessment or collection of tax, although a summary written so as not to compromise these requirements should nevertheless be provided. However, in a case within (c) above, the courts refused to quash such a notice where no written summary had been provided to the taxpayers whose liabilities were under investigation (*R v CIR (ex p Continental Shipping Ltd and Atsiganos SA)* QB 1996, 68 TC 665).

The notice must specify or describe the documents or particulars required, the time limit for production (generally not less than 30 days) and, except as above, the name of the taxpayer or client, as appropriate; and the person to whom they are delivered may take copies. There are severe penalties for the falsification, concealment, disposal or destruction of a document which is the subject of a notice or formal request (see (a) above), unless strict conditions and time limits are observed.

[*TMA 1970, s 20, s 20B(1)(1A)(1B)(2)(4)–(7)(9)–(14), s 20BB, s 20D; FA 2008, s 113, Sch 36 paras 67–70; SI 2009 No 56, Sch 1 para 11*].

For failure to comply with a notice, see **55.21** PENALTIES.

The person to whom notice is to be given is not entitled to attend or be legally represented at the meeting at which HMRC seek the consent of a Commissioner (*Applicant v Inspector of Taxes* (Sp C 189), [1999] SSCD 128).

Notices (other than those which relate to an unnamed taxpayer) may relate to tax liabilities in EU member states other than the UK [*FA 1990, s 125(1)(2)(6); FA 2008, Sch 36 para 83*] or in any other territory with which the UK has entered into arrangements providing for the obtaining of information. [*FA 2000, s 146(3)(4); FA 2006, s 174, Sch 26 Pt 8(2); FA 2008, Sch 36 para 91; SI 2009 No 404, Arts 2, 10*].

For an article setting out HMRC's view on the question of claims to legal or professional privilege in relation to requests for information under these provisions (other than where tax evasion or tax fraud is suspected), see Revenue Tax Bulletin April 2000 pp 743–746 (updated by Revenue Tax Bulletin December 2002 p 993 following the *Morgan Grenfell* case at (a) above).

Barristers, advocates or solicitors

[38.12] A notice under **38.11**(a), (b) or (c) above to a barrister, advocate or solicitor can be issued only by the Commissioners for HMRC (although that power may be delegated, see *R v CIR (ex p Davis Frankel & Mead)* QB 2000, 73 TC 185) and he cannot (without his client's consent) be required to deliver under **38.11**(*c*) above documents protected by professional privilege. [*TMA 1970, s 20B(3)(8); FA 2008, Sch 36 para 68(6)(9); SI 2009 No 404, Arts 2, 4*]. In this event the taxpayer concerned need not be provided with a written summary of HMRC's reasons for applying for consent to the giving of the notice (*R (oao Cooke) v HMRC* QB 2007, [2008] STC 1847). As regards the search and seizure powers in **38.17** below, there is an exclusion for documents protected by 'legal privilege' as more widely defined than 'professional privilege' but excluding items held with the intention of furthering a criminal purpose [*TMA 1970, s 20C(4); FA 1989, s 146(4); FA 2000, s 150(4)*], and see also **38.16** below as regards similar protection in relation to an order under *TMA 1970, s 20BA* in cases involving serious tax fraud. See *R v CIR (ex p Goldberg)* QB 1988, 61 TC 403 as regards nature of documents subject to privilege, but note that the decision in that case was doubted in *Dubai Bank Ltd v Galadari* CA, [1989] 3 WLR 1044, a non-tax case. In relation to search and seizure under **38.17** below, it was held in *R v CIR (ex p Tamosius & Partners)* QB, [1999] STC 1077 that the presence of independent counsel to determine the issue of privilege was 'to be encouraged', although it would not prevent action by the courts if counsel was wrong. The issue and execution of warrants to search a lawyer's offices was held not to be in breach of *Article 8* of the *European Convention on Human Rights* (*Tamosius v UK* ECHR, [2002] STC 1307).

For an article setting out HMRC's view on the question of claims to legal or professional privilege in relation to requests for information under these provisions (other than where tax evasion or tax fraud is suspected), see Revenue Tax Bulletin April 2000 pp 743–746 (updated by Revenue Tax Bulletin December 2002 p 993 following the *Morgan Grenfell* case at **38.11**(a) above).

Simon's Taxes. See A6.310, A6.313.

Power to call for papers of tax accountant

[38.13] An HMRC officer may (with the authority of the Commissioners for HMRC and the consent of a Circuit judge in England and Wales, a sheriff in Scotland or a county court judge in Northern Ireland) by notice in writing require a '*tax accountant*' (i.e. a person who assists another in the preparation of returns, etc. for tax purposes) who has been convicted by or before any UK court of a tax offence or incurred a penalty under *TMA 1970, s 99* (see **55.19** PENALTIES) to deliver 'documents' in his possession or power relevant to any tax liability of any of his clients. The tax accountant must be given an opportunity to deliver the documents in question before a notice is issued.

The notice must be issued within twelve months of the final determination of the conviction or penalty award and must specify or describe the documents required and the time limit for production (generally not less than 30 days).

A '*document*' is anything in which information of any description is recorded, but does not include personal records or journalistic material (within *Police and Criminal Evidence Act 1984, ss 12, 13*). Photographic, etc. facsimiles may be supplied provided the originals are produced if called for, and documents relating to any pending tax appeal need not be delivered.

The penalty for failure to comply with a notice is given by *TMA 1970, s 98* (see **55.21** PENALTIES). In addition there are severe penalties (in summary proceedings, a fine of the statutory maximum, and on indictment, imprisonment for two years and/or an unlimited fine) for the falsification, concealment, destruction or disposal of a document which is the subject of a notice, unless strict conditions and time limits are observed.

[*TMA 1970, ss 20A, 20B(1)(2)–(4)(8), 20BB, 20D; FA 2008, Sch 36 paras 68–70; SI 2009 No 404, Arts 2, 4; SI 2009 No 56, Sch 1 para 11*].

HMRC's practice in cases of serious tax fraud

[38.14] As from 1 September 2005, the former Inland Revenue's Hansard procedures and the former Customs & Excise Civil Evasion procedures are replaced with a common Civil Investigations of Fraud procedure for HMRC, to be used in suspected serious tax evasion cases. Where suspicions of evasion cut across direct and indirect taxes, one single meeting can be held to cover all regimes; however, the meeting will be structured so that each tax is covered separately using powers appropriate to that tax. Cases opened before 1 September 2005 will be worked to a conclusion under the old procedures. Under the Civil Investigations of Fraud procedure (in contrast to the Hansard procedure), interviews will not be conducted under caution or tape-recorded. As before, the taxpayer will be given an opportunity to make a full and complete disclosure of all irregularities in his tax affairs. In general, HMRC reserve complete discretion to pursue a criminal investigation with a view to prosecution where they consider it necessary and appropriate. However, where they decide to investigate using the Civil Investigations of Fraud procedure instead, they will not seek a prosecution for the tax fraud which is the subject of the investigation. But, where, in the course of a civil investigation, materially false statements are made or false documents are provided with intent to deceive, HMRC may then conduct a criminal investigation with a view to prosecuting those offences. Initially, the Civil Investigations of Fraud procedure will be used only by officers serving in HMRC Special Civil Investigations (SCI), but its use may spread to other specialist teams within HMRC. From 1 July 2006, its use is extended to newly-created specialist Civil Investigation of Fraud teams operating outside SCI (HMRC Internet Statement 29 June 2006).

For a useful article on the above procedure and how it differs from the earlier Hansard procedure, see *Taxation Magazine, 22 September 2005, p 686.*

See also HMRC Code of Practice COP 9.

Under its published Criminal Investigation Policy (see www.hmrc.gov.uk/pro secutions/crim-inv-policy.htm), HMRC reserve complete discretion to conduct a criminal investigation in any case, with a view to prosecution by the Revenue and Customs Prosecutions Office (RCPO) in England and Wales or the appropriate prosecuting authority in Scotland and Northern Ireland. Examples of the kind of circumstances in which HMRC will generally consider commencing a criminal, rather than civil, investigation are, *inter alia*, cases involving organised or systematic fraud including conspiracy; cases where an individual holds a position of trust or responsibility; cases where materially false statements are made or materially false documents are provided in the course of a civil investigation; cases where deliberate concealment, deception, conspiracy or corruption is suspected; cases involving the use of false or forged documents; cases involving money laundering; cases where there is a link to suspected wider criminality; and repeated offences.

See *R v CIR (ex p Mead and Cook)* QB 1992, 65 TC 1 as regards HMRC discretion to seek monetary settlements or institute criminal proceedings. See *R v CIR (ex p Allen)* QB 1997, 69 TC 442 for an unsuccessful application for judicial review of a Revenue decision to take criminal proceedings. HMRC have an unrestricted power to conduct a prosecution in the Crown Court, there being no requirement for the consent of the Attorney-General (*R (oao Hunt) v Criminal Cases Review Commission* DC, [2000] STC 1110). See also **34.4 HMRC — ADMINISTRATION.**

The Crown Prosecution Service ('CPS') is not precluded from instituting criminal proceedings in circumstances where the Revenue has accepted a monetary settlement. (*R v W and another* CA, [1998] STC 550). The Attorney-General made it clear, however, in a Parliamentary Written Answer, that proceedings brought by the CPS will ordinarily encompass charges relating to tax evasion only in circumstances where that is incidental to allegations of non-fiscal criminal conduct. A 'Convention between Prosecuting Authorities to provide arrangements for ensuring effective co-ordination of decision making and handling in related cases which are the responsibility of different authorities' was established on 11 February 1998 (for which see the Attorney-General's Press Release of that date). See Hansard Vol 310, No 155 at Cols 230, 231 and Revenue Tax Bulletin June 1998 pp 544, 545.

Statements made or documents produced by or on behalf of a taxpayer are admissible as evidence in proceedings against him notwithstanding that reliance on HMRC's practice above or on their policy for mitigating penalties (see **55.22 PENALTIES**) may have induced him to make or produce them. [*TMA 1970, s 105*].

Simon's Taxes. See A6.1007, A6.1008.

HMRC use of Police and Criminal Evidence Act 1984 powers

[38.15] Prior to the merger between the Inland Revenue and HM Customs and Excise in 2005, the latter department was able to exercise certain police powers under the *Police and Criminal Evidence Act 1984* when conducting criminal investigations. These powers continued to be available to HMRC following the merger, but only in respect of former Customs and Excise matters. *FA 2007* includes provisions enabling the Treasury by Order (made by statutory instrument) to make the powers (and similar powers in Scotland and NI) available to HMRC for the purposes of direct tax criminal investigations. Only HMRC officers authorised by the Commissioners for HMRC are able to exercise the powers. These powers are made available on and after 1 December 2007. They include powers to require production of information, to apply for search warrants, to make arrests and to search suspects and premises following arrest. They do not include power to take fingerprints or to charge and bail suspects, all of which can only be carried out by the police. Some of the powers in the *Police and Criminal Evidence Act 1984* are modified for the purposes of their use by HMRC. A list of the powers initially made available can be found in *SI 2007 No 3175, Sch 1* (or NI equivalent). See generally the document 'HMRC: criminal investigation powers and safeguards' published on 30 November 2007 (at www.hmrc.gov.uk/prosecutions/ci-powers-safeguards.pdf).

The search and seizure powers at **38.17** below are consequently no longer needed and are repealed with effect on and after 1 December 2007. The power to seek judicial authority to require the delivery of documents at **38.16** below is restricted to circumstances where the equivalent police power cannot be used because the material concerned cannot be obtained using those powers.

[*Police and Criminal Evidence Act 1984, s 114; FA 2007, ss 82–87, Schs 22, 23; SI 2007 Nos 3166, 3175; SI 2010 No 360*].

Order for delivery of documents in serious tax fraud cases

[38.16] Under *TMA 1970, s 20BA, Sch 1AA*, the Commissioners for HMRC may apply to the appropriate judicial authority (a circuit judge in England and Wales, a sheriff in Scotland or a county court judge in NI) for an order requiring any person who appears to have in his possession or power documents specified or described in the order to deliver them to an officer of

HMRC within ten working days after the day of service of the notice, or such longer or shorter period as may be specified in the order. The judicial authority must be satisfied, on information on oath given by an authorised officer of HMRC, that there is reasonable ground for suspecting that an offence involving serious tax fraud has been or is about to be committed, and that the documents may be required as evidence in proceedings in respect of the offence. In Scotland, a single sheriff may make orders in respect of persons anywhere in Scotland as long as one of the orders relates to a person residing or having a place of business at an address in the sheriff's own sheriffdom. Orders may not be made in relation to items subject to legal privilege (as defined) unless they are held with the intention of furthering a criminal purpose. Failure to comply with an order is treated as contempt of court, and there are severe penalties for falsification of documents.

On and after 8 November 2007, these provisions are restricted to circumstances where the equivalent power under the *Police and Criminal Evidence Act 1984* cannot be used because the material concerned cannot be obtained using those powers. [*Police and Criminal Evidence Act 1984, ss 14B, 114; FA 2007, ss 82(6), s 84(5)(6); SI 2007 No 3166, Reg 2*]. Similar rules apply for NI.

Schedule 1AA lays down detailed requirements in relation to applications under the main provisions, and these may be supplemented by regulations. In particular, a person is entitled to notice of intention to apply for such an order, and to appear and be heard at the application, unless the judicial authority is satisfied that this would seriously prejudice investigation of the offence. Until the application has been dismissed or abandoned, or an order made and complied with, any person given such notice must not conceal, destroy, alter or dispose of any document to which the order sought relates, or disclose information etc. likely to prejudice the investigation, except with the leave of the judicial authority or the written permission of HMRC. Professional legal advisers may, however, disclose such information etc. in giving legal advice to a client or in connection with legal proceedings, provided that it is not disclosed with a view to furthering a criminal purpose. Failure to comply with these requirements is treated as failure to comply with an order under these provisions. The procedural rules where documents are delivered in accordance with an order are as under *TMA 1970, s 20CC(3)–(9)* (see **38.17** below). For detailed procedural requirements, see *SI 2000 No 2875* (as amended by *SI 2005 No 1131* and by *SI 2007 No 881*).

Simon's Taxes. See A4.151, A6.313, A6.315, A6.1006.

Search and seizure

[38.17] Where there is reasonable suspicion of serious tax fraud, and there are reasonable grounds for believing that use of the procedure under *TMA 1970, s 20BA* (see **38.16** above) might seriously prejudice the investigation, the Commissioners for HMRC may apply to a circuit judge etc. (as in **38.13** above) for a warrant to enter premises within 14 days to search and to seize any things which may be relevant as evidence. There are detailed procedural rules governing searches and the removal of documents etc.

These provisions are **repealed** (and replaced by equivalent powers under the *Police and Criminal Evidence Act 1984*) with effect on and after 1 December 2007 (see **38.15** above).

[*TMA 1970, ss 20C, 20CC, 20D; FA 1989, ss 146, 147; FA 2000, s 150; Criminal Justice and Police Act 2001, Sch 2 para 13; FA 2007, s 84(4)–(6), Sch 22 paras 1, 4; FA 2008, s 113, Sch 36 para 70; SI 2007 No 3166, Reg 3; SI 2009 No 404, Arts 2, 4*].

The warrant need not specify the suspected fraud or the documents etc., searched for (*Rossminster Ltd* HL 1979, 52 TC 160). For the proper procedure in seeking and obtaining judicial review of a decision to grant such a warrant, and interim injunctions, see *R v CIR (ex p Kingston Smith (a firm))* QB 1996, 70 TC 264. For the validity of warrants, see *R v CIR (ex p Tamosius & Partners)* QB, [1999] STC 107. If an HMRC officer executing a warrant has reasonable cause to believe that the data on a computer's hard drive might be required as evidence, he can seize and remove that computer even though it may also contain irrelevant material (*H (R oao) v CIR* QB 2002, 75 TC 377).

Simon's Taxes. See A4.151, A6.312–A6.314, A6.1006.

Computer records etc.

[38.18] The following applies to any tax provisions requiring a person to produce a document or cause a document to be produced, furnished or delivered, or requiring a person to permit HMRC to inspect a document, to make copies of or extracts from, or remove, a document (i.e. including the provisions at **38.4**, **38.10**, **38.11**, **38.13**, **38.16** and **38.17** above).

For the purposes of such provisions, a reference to a document is a reference to anything in which information of any description is recorded, and a reference to a copy of a document is to anything onto which information recorded in the document has been copied, by whatever means and whether directly or indirectly.

Where a document has been, or may be, required to be produced, inspected etc. under any such provisions, a person authorised by the Commissioners for HMRC can obtain access to any computer and associated apparatus or material used in connection with the document at any reasonable time in order to inspect it and check its operation. Reasonable assistance can be required from the person by whom or on whose behalf the computer has been so used or any person in charge of the computer etc. or otherwise concerned with its operation.

A penalty of £300 (£500 before 21 July 2008) applies for obstruction of such access or refusal to provide assistance.

[*FA 1988, s 127; FA 2008, s 114*].

39

HMRC Statements of Practice

Introduction

[**39.1**] The following is a summary of those Statements of Practice published online by HMRC at www.hmrc.gov.uk/practitioners/sop.pdf at 23 April 2010, which are referred to in this work.

Statements are divided into those originally published before 18 July 1978 (which are given a reference letter (according to the subject matter) and consecutive number, e.g. A16) and subsequent Statements (which are numbered consecutively in each year, e.g. SP 1/09).

Certain Statements marked by HMRC as obsolete continue to be referred to in the text if they have been relevant at any time within the tax years referred to in that particular text.

A6	**Employment income — VAT.** Expenses and other benefits chargeable on an employee must include VAT, if any. See **53.12 PAY AS YOU EARN, 27.30 EMPLOYMENT INCOME.** For PAYE purposes, VAT is excluded from payments for services supplied by a person holding an office in the course of carrying on a trade, profession or vocation. See **53.48 PAY AS YOU EARN.**
A10	**Airline pilots.** HMRC practice re duties deemed to be performed in the UK. See **27.3**(ii) **EMPLOYMENT INCOME.**
A13	**Completion of return forms by attorneys.** In cases of illness, infirmity or old age of the taxpayer, HMRC will accept the signature of an attorney who has full knowledge of the taxpayer's affairs. See **63.2 RETURNS.**
A16	**Living expenses abroad: trades, professions and vocations.** A UK resident living abroad for the purposes of his trade etc. will have his personal living expenses allowed as a deduction. See **73.122 TRADING INCOME.**
A32	**Goods taken by traders for personal consumption.** HMRC's practice in applying *Sharkey v Wernher* is stated. See **73.114 TRADING INCOME.**

A33   **Relief for interest payments: loans applied in acquiring an interest in a partnership.** Salaried partners in a professional firm may claim relief in certain circumstances. Superseded by *ITA 2007, s 399*. See **43.10 INTEREST PAYABLE**.

B1   **Treatment of VAT.** Guidance on the general principles applied in dealing with VAT in tax computations. See **73.126 TRADING INCOME**.

B6   **Goods sold subject to reservation of title.** Such goods should normally be treated as purchases in the buyer's accounts and sales in the supplier's accounts provided that both parties agree. See **73.112 TRADING INCOME**.

C1   **Lotteries and football pools.** Where part of the cost of a ticket is to be donated to a club etc., that part is, in certain circumstances, not treated as a trading receipt. See **73.23 TRADING INCOME**.

SP 3/78   **Close companies: income tax relief for interest on loans applied in acquiring an interest in a close company.** Relief continues after company ceases to be close. See **43.7 INTEREST PAYABLE**.

SP 8/79   **Compensation for acquisition of property under compulsory powers.** Reimbursement of revenue costs are trading receipts. See **73.48**(d) **TRADING INCOME**.

SP 11/79   **Life assurance premium relief — children's policies.** Relief will be given in certain circumstances on premiums on policies taken out by children under twelve. See **44.27**(g) **LIFE ASSURANCE POLICIES**.

SP 3/80   **Cancellation of tax advantages from certain transactions in securities: procedure for clearance in advance.** The procedure is explained. See **4.5 ANTI-AVOIDANCE**.

SP 5/81   **Expenditure on farm drainage.** The net cost of restoring drainage is allowable as revenue expenditure. See **73.73**(c) **TRADING INCOME**.

SP 10/81   **Payments on account of disability resulting in cessation of employment.** The interpretation of 'disability' in *ITEPA 2003, s 406* is extended. See **20.6**(i) **COMPENSATION FOR LOSS OF EMPLOYMENT**.

SP 12/81   **Construction industry scheme (CIS): carpet fitting** is considered to be outside the scope of the scheme. See **22.3 CONSTRUCTION INDUSTRY SCHEME.**

SP 1/82   **Interaction of income tax and inheritance tax on assets put into settlement.** Income of a settlement will not be treated as income of the settlor solely because the trustees have power to pay, or do pay, inheritance tax on assets put into the settlement by the settlor. See **68.28**(e) **SETTLEMENTS.**

SP 5/84   **Employees resident but not ordinarily resident in the UK: general earnings chargeable under ITEPA 2003, ss 25, 26.** HMRC practice on apportionment of earnings between UK and non-UK duties of an employment is explained. Superseded by SP 1/09 with effect from 6 April 2009. See **27.12 EMPLOYMENT INCOME.**

SP 6/84   **Non-UK resident lessors: FA 1973, s 38 (now TMA 1970, ss 77B–77K.** The conditions under which profits of non-UK resident lessors of mobile drilling rigs etc. are exempt from tax are outlined. See **32.3 FOREIGN INCOME.**

SP 6/85   **Incentive awards.** The basis on which expenses are included is outlined. See **27.77, 27.91 EMPLOYMENT INCOME.**

SP 1/86   **Capital allowances: short-life assets.** Guidance is given on some practical aspects of the short-life asset provisions. See **11.30 CAPITAL ALLOWANCES ON PLANT AND MACHINERY.**

SP 2/86   **Offshore funds.** Various aspects of the pre-1 December 2009 legislation are clarified. See **51.24, 51.26 OFFSHORE FUNDS.**

SP 3/86   **Payments to a non-resident from UK discretionary trusts or UK estates during the administration period: double taxation relief.** A change of practice replaces extra-statutory concessions A14 and B18 in certain cases. See **23.13 DECEASED ESTATES, 68.15 SETTLEMENTS.**

SP 4/86   **Scholarship and apprenticeship schemes for employees.** Certain payments to employees attending full-time educational courses are exempt from income tax. See **30.39 EXEMPT INCOME.**

SP 9/86   **Partnership mergers and demergers.** The application of the succession rules is explained. See **52.9 PARTNERSHIPS**

SP 5/87   **Tax returns: the use of substitute forms.** The conditions for acceptance of facsimile and photocopied returns and other forms are set out. See **18.1 CLAIMS, 63.2 RETURNS.**

SP 9/87   **Capital allowances: hotels.** HMRC's interpretation of the provision of breakfast and evening meals by a qualifying hotel is set out. See **10.19 CAPITAL ALLOWANCES.**

SP 5/90   **Accountants' working papers.** HMRC's approach to the use of its information powers in relation to accountants' working papers is explained. See **38.11 HMRC INVESTIGATORY POWERS.**

SP 2/91   **Residence in the UK: visits extended because of exceptional circumstances.** Extra days spent in the UK may be ignored for certain purposes. See **62.5 RESIDENCE, ORDINARY RESIDENCE AND DOMICILE.**

SP 3/91   **Finance lease rental payments.** The practice in relation to deduction of rental payments is explained. See **73.78 TRADING INCOME.**

SP 7/91   **Double taxation: business profits: unilateral relief.** The practice as regards admission of foreign taxes for unilateral relief is revised. See **26.6 DOUBLE TAX RELIEF.**

SP 16/91   **Accountancy expenses arising out of accounts investigations.** HMRC's practice on the allowance of such expenses is explained. See **73.92 TRADING INCOME.**

SP 17/91   **Residence in the UK: when ordinary residence is regarded as commencing where the period to be spent here is less than three years.** See **62.7 RESIDENCE, ORDINARY RESIDENCE AND DOMICILE.**

SP 6/92   **Accident insurance policies: chargeable events and gains on policies of life insurance.** Certain accident insurance policies will no longer be considered policies of life insurance for these purposes. See **44.5 LIFE ASSURANCE POLICIES.**

SP 4/93   **Deceased persons' estates: discretionary interests in residue.** Payments out of income of the residue are treated as income of the recipient for the year of payment, whether out of income as it arises or out of income arising in earlier years. See **23.9 DECEASED ESTATES.**

SP 5/93   **UK/Czechoslovakia double taxation Convention.** The Convention is regarded as applying to the Czech and Slovak Republics. See **26.2 DOUBLE TAX RELIEF.**

SP 15/93   **Business tax computations rounded to nearest £1,000** will be accepted from certain large businesses. See **73.17 TRADING INCOME.**

SP 1/94   **Non-statutory redundancy payments.** HMRC's practice following the decision in *Mairs v Haughey* is explained. See **20.3 COMPENSATION FOR LOSS OF EMPLOYMENT.**

SP 4/94   **Enhanced stock dividends received by trustees of interest in possession trusts.** HMRC's view on the tax treatment of such dividends is explained. See **64.15 SAVINGS AND INVESTMENT INCOME.**

SP 6/95   **Legal entitlement and administrative practice** in relation to repayments of tax is revised. See **54.12 PAYMENT OF TAX.**

SP 8/95   **Venture capital trusts — default terms in loan agreements.** Certain event of default clauses will not disqualify a loan from being a security for the purposes of approval. See **76.12 VENTURE CAPITAL TRUSTS.**

SP 1/96   **Notification of chargeability to income tax.** Employees are relieved in certain circumstances of the obligation to notify chargeability in respect of benefits etc. See **55.2 PENALTIES.**

SP 2/96   **Pooled cars: incidental private use.** HMRC's interpretation of the requirement that private use of pooled vehicles be 'merely incidental' to business use is explained. See **27.38 EMPLOYMENT INCOME.**

SP 3/96   **ITEPA 2003, ss 225, 226 — termination payments made in settlement of employment claims.** The circumstances in which a charge will not arise are clarified. See **27.72 EMPLOYMENT INCOME.**

SP 4/96   **Income tax — interest paid in the ordinary course of a bank's business.** HMRC's interpretation of this requirement is explained. See **24.21 DEDUCTION OF TAX AT SOURCE.**

SP 5/96   **PAYE settlement agreements.** The detailed operation of the scheme is explained. See generally **53.15 PAY AS YOU EARN.**

SP 4/97   **Taxation of commission, cashbacks and discounts.** HMRC's views are outlined. See **73.46 TRADING INCOME.**

SP 6/98   **Enterprise investment scheme, venture capital trusts, capital gains tax reinvestment relief and business expansion scheme — loans to investors.** The no linked loan requirement is explained. See **28.36 ENTERPRISE INVESTMENT SCHEME, 76.3 VENTURE CAPITAL TRUSTS.**

SP 1/99   **Self-assessment enquiries — TMA 1970, ss 9A, 12AC.** Where an enquiry remains open for agreement of a capital gains tax valuation, HMRC will not take advantage of this fact to raise further enquiries which could otherwise not be made. See **63.7 RETURNS.**

SP 3/99   **Advance pricing agreements (APAs).** The detailed administration of the scheme of APAs relating to transfer pricing issues is explained. See **4.26 ANTI-AVOIDANCE.**

SP 2/00   **Venture capital trusts, the enterprise investment scheme, the corporate venturing scheme and enterprise management incentives — value of 'gross assets'.** HMRC's general approach to the valuation of gross assets is explained. See **28.43 ENTERPRISE INVESTMENT SCHEME, 69.38 SHARE-RELATED EMPLOYMENT INCOME AND EXEMPTIONS, 76.29 VENTURE CAPITAL TRUSTS.**

SP 3/00   **Enterprise investment scheme, venture capital trusts, corporate venturing scheme and enterprise management incentives — location of activity.** The requirement that trade(s) be carried on 'wholly or mainly in the UK' is clarified. See **28.49 ENTERPRISE INVESTMENT SCHEME, 69.39 SHARE-RELATED EMPLOYMENT INCOME AND EXEMPTIONS, 76.22 VENTURE CAPITAL TRUSTS.**

SP 1/01   **Treatment of investment managers and their overseas clients.** Guidance is given on the application of the rules introduced by *FA 1995*. Revised 20 July 2007. See **50.7 NON-RESIDENTS.**

SP 4/01   Double taxation relief — status of the UK's double taxation conventions with the former USSR and with newly independent states. The current position is clarified. See **26.2 DOUBLE TAX RELIEF**.

SP 2/02   **Exchange rate fluctuations.** HMRC set out their practice in relation to the tax treatment of exchange rate fluctuations in the tax computations of non-corporate traders. See **73.81 TRADING INCOME**.

SP 3/02   **Financial futures and options.** HMRC set out their views on the circumstances in which transactions in financial futures and options would be regarded as trading rather than taxed under the chargeable gains rules. See **73.25 TRADING INCOME**.

SP 2/03   **Business by telephone — non-Contact Centre taxpayers.** Details are given of the services available by telephone from tax offices not served by a Contact Centre. See **18.5 CLAIMS**.

SP 1/06   **Self-assessment: finality and discovery.** HMRC clarify how a taxpayer may protect himself from a later 'discovery' assessment by providing sufficient information in his self-assessment tax return. See **6.6 ASSESSMENTS**.

SP 3/07   **Double tax relief — Yugoslavia.** Details are given as to the application of the UK/Yugoslavia double tax agreement to the countries formerly known as Yugoslavia. See **26.2 DOUBLE TAX RELIEF**.

SP 1/09   **Employees UK resident but not ordinarily resident: remittance basis.** Covers apportionment of general earnings where duties of a single employment performed both inside and outside the UK and part of those earnings is remitted to the UK. Supersedes SP 5/84. See **27.7 EMPLOYMENT INCOME**.
Also sets out, by reference to the 'mixed funds' rules, how HMRC will treat transfers made from an offshore account holding only the income or gains relating to a single employment. See **61.16 REMITTANCE BASIS**.

SP 1/10   **Business by telephone — HMRC Taxes Contact Centres.** Details are given of expanded services available by telephone from Taxes Contact Centres dealing with the tax affairs of individuals. See **18.5 CLAIMS, 63.4 RETURNS**.

40

Intellectual Property

Cross-references. See **10.23** and **10.35** CAPITAL ALLOWANCES for allowances on capital expenditure in acquiring know-how and patent rights; **24.13** DEDUCTION OF TAX AT SOURCE for patent royalties and for other royalties paid to non-residents; **26.9**(i) DOUBLE TAX RELIEF for DTR treatment of royalties from abroad; **69.75** SHARE-RELATED EMPLOYMENT INCOME AND EXEMPTIONS as regards research institution spin-out companies; **73.51, 73.91** and **73.99** TRADING INCOME for trading receipts and expenses re intellectual property.

Simon's Taxes. See B5.3.

Introduction

[40.1] This chapter deals with the charge to tax on royalties and other income from 'intellectual property', income from disposals of know-how and income from sales of patent rights.

'Intellectual property' means:

- any patent, trade mark, registered design, copyright, design right or performer's or plant breeder's right;
- any rights under the law of any part of the UK which are similar to such rights;
- any rights under the law of any territory outside the UK which correspond or are similar to such rights; and
- any idea, information or technique not protected by a right within any of the above.

[*ITTOIA 2005, s 579(2)*].

Royalties and other income

[40.2] Subject to the priority provisions at **49.2** MISCELLANEOUS INCOME (which, for example, exclude income from a trade etc.), royalties and other income from 'intellectual property' (as in **40.1** above) are chargeable to income tax. The full amount of such income arising in the tax year is chargeable (but see below), the person liable for the tax being the person receiving or entitled to the income. Income from intellectual property which also falls within the charge at **49.4** MISCELLANEOUS INCOME (films and sound recordings) is excluded.

See **49.2** MISCELLANEOUS INCOME for the territorial scope of the charge. Where income within the charge arises from a source outside the UK it is 'relevant foreign income' (see **32.2** FOREIGN INCOME). See **32.4** FOREIGN INCOME for amounts deductible from income, **32.5** FOREIGN INCOME for relief for unremittable income and **61** for the REMITTANCE BASIS.

See also **40.4** below for the spreading of patent royalties etc. over several tax years.

[*ITTOIA 2005, ss 576, 579(1), 580, 581*].

Patent royalties are subject to DEDUCTION OF TAX AT SOURCE (**24.13**), as are other royalties paid to non-UK residents.

See **49.8** and **49.11** MISCELLANEOUS INCOME for apportionment rules and for relief for losses.

Expenses

[40.3] Expenses incurred wholly and exclusively for the purpose of generating income within **40.2** above are deductible in calculating the amount chargeable to tax, provided that, if they had been incurred for the purposes of a trade, they would have been deductible in calculating its profits. Where an expense is incurred for more than one purpose, if any identifiable part or proportion of the expense is incurred for the purpose of generating the income, a deduction is allowed for that part or proportion. Expenses for which any kind of relief is given under any other provision are not deductible.

No deductions can be made where the income consists of annual payments (see **24.10** DEDUCTION OF TAX AT SOURCE). In determining whether income consist of annual payments, the frequency with which payments are made is ignored. Deductions are also not permitted where the income is assessable on the REMITTANCE BASIS (**64**).

[*ITTOIA 2005, s 582*].

See also **40.4** below for relief for certain expenditure in relation to patents.

Patent income

[40.4] '*Patent income*' of an individual is any royalties or other sums paid in respect of the use of a patent charged to tax under **40.2** above, amounts on which tax is payable under **40.6** below, and any balancing charges under the capital allowances code for patent rights (see **10.35** CAPITAL ALLOWANCES).

Inventor's expenses etc.

Relief can be claimed for expenses:

- incurred by an individual on devising an invention for which a patent has been granted; and
- incurred by a person, otherwise than for the purposes of a trade, in connection with the grant, maintenance or extension of the term of a patent or in connection with a rejected or abandoned patent application, provided that, if the expenses had been incurred for the purposes of a trade, they would have been allowable in calculating the profits of that trade.

The relief is not available for any expenses for which relief is given under **40.3** above or any other provision. Expenses are also disregarded to the extent that they are met by a '*public body*' (i.e. the Crown or any government, local authority or other public authority in the UK or elsewhere) or by any other person. Where, however, the contributor is not a public body, expenses are not so disregarded if, on the assumption that he is within the charge to tax, the contributor can obtain neither a capital allowance for the contributions (see **10.2**(vii) CAPITAL ALLOWANCES) nor a deduction in calculating the profits of a trade, profession or vocation.

Where a claim is made, the expenses are deducted or set off against the person's 'patent income' for the tax year in which they are incurred with any unallowed balance being carried forward indefinitely against patent income without further claim. Any CAPITAL ALLOWANCES (**10.35**) must be deducted before relief is given for the expenses.

[*ITTOIA 2005, ss 600, 601, 603, 604, Sch 2 para 129; ITA 2007, Sch 1 para 547*].

Spreading of patent royalties

A relief can be claimed by a person who receives a payment of a royalty or other sum, under deduction of tax at source, for use of a patent that has extended over a period of two years or more. The relief is the excess (if any) of:

(a) the recipient's income tax liability on the payment for the tax year of receipt, over
(b) what would have been the recipient's income tax liability on the payment if the latter had been spread over a number of years.

For the purpose of (b), the payment is deemed to have been made in a number of equal instalments at yearly intervals, with the final instalment made on the date the actual payment was made. The number of instalments is equal to the number of complete years over which the use of the patent extended, subject to a maximum of six years. Once the amount of the relief is established, it is given by means of a tax reduction (see Step 6 at **1.7** ALLOWANCES AND TAX RATES). The order in which tax reductions are given against an individual's tax liability is set out at **1.8** ALLOWANCES AND TAX RATES. [*ITA 2007, s 461*].

Disposal of know-how

[40.5] Subject to the priority and territorial scope provisions at **49.2** MISCEL-LANEOUS INCOME, profits arising where consideration is received for the disposal of 'know-how' are chargeable to income tax. Tax is chargeable on the full amount of the profits arising in the tax year, the person liable for the tax being the person receiving the consideration. Also included within the charge are profits arising where consideration is received for giving, or wholly or partly fulfilling, an undertaking (whether or not legally enforceable) which is given in connection with a disposal of know-how and which restricts or is designed to restrict any person's activities in any way.

The profits chargeable to tax are the amount of the consideration less any expenditure incurred by the recipient wholly and exclusively in the acquisition or disposal of the know-how. Where know-how is acquired or disposed of together with other property, the acquisition costs or proceeds, as appropriate, must be apportioned on a just and reasonable basis. Expenditure can only be taken into account for tax purposes once (whether under this provision or otherwise).

Expenditure is disregarded in calculating the taxable profits to the extent that it is met by a public body (see **40.3** above) or by any other person. Where, however, the contributor is not a public body, the expenditure is not so disregarded if, on the assumption that he is within the charge to tax, the contributor can obtain neither a capital allowance for the contribution (see **10.2**(vii) CAPITAL ALLOWANCES) nor a deduction in calculating the profits of a trade, profession or vocation.

The charge does not apply if:

- the consideration is brought into account under **40.2** above;
- the consideration is brought into account as a disposal value under the capital allowances know-how code (see **10.23** CAPITAL ALLOWANCES);
- the consideration is treated as a trading receipt (see **73.91** TRADING INCOME);
- the consideration is received as part of the disposal of all or part of a trade and is treated as a capital receipt for goodwill under *ITTOIA 2005, s 194(2)* (see **73.91** TRADING INCOME); or
- the disposal is by way of a sale and the buyer is a body of persons (including a firm) over which the seller or buyer has control or the buyer and seller are both bodies of persons and another person has control over them both.

For the above purposes, '*know-how*' means any industrial information or techniques likely to assist in manufacturing or processing goods or materials, in working, or searching for etc., mineral deposits (as defined), or in carrying out any agricultural, forestry or fishing operations. References above to a sale or disposal of know-how include an exchange of know-how.

[*ITTOIA 2005, ss 583–586, 603–607, Sch 1 para 338(4)(5), Sch 2 para 129*].

See **49.8** and **49.11** MISCELLANEOUS INCOME for apportionment rules and for relief for losses.

Sales of patent rights

[40.6] Subject to the priority provisions at **49.2** MISCELLANEOUS INCOME, profits from sales of the whole or part of any 'patent rights' (including receipts for rights for which a patent has not yet been granted) are chargeable to tax.

The seller is charged to tax if a UK resident or, if not UK resident, where the patent is a UK patent. '*Patent rights*' for this purpose means the right to do or authorise the doing of anything which would, but for the right, be an infringement of a patent.

See also **24.13**, **24.21**(iii) DEDUCTION OF TAX AT SOURCE) for deduction of income tax by the purchaser in the case of a sale by a non-UK resident.

The profits chargeable are any capital sum (defined as for capital allowances purposes, see **10.2**(iii) CAPITAL ALLOWANCES) comprised in the proceeds less the 'capital cost' of the rights sold and any incidental costs incurred in connection with the sale.

For this purpose, the '*capital cost*' of patent rights means any capital sum included in any price paid by the seller to purchase the rights (or the rights out of which they were granted), less any capital sum received for a previous sale of part of the purchased rights. Expenditure is disregarded in calculating the capital cost to the extent that it is met by a public body (see **40.4** above) or by any other person. Where, however, the contributor is not a public body, the expenditure is not so disregarded if, on the assumption that he is within the charge to tax, the contributor can obtain neither a capital allowance for the contribution (see **10.2**(vii) CAPITAL ALLOWANCES) nor a deduction in calculating the profits of a trade, profession or vocation.

The deduction of the capital cost for this purpose does not affect the amount of income tax to be deducted by the purchaser in the case of a sale by a non-UK resident (see **24.13**, **24.21**(iii) DEDUCTION OF TAX AT SOURCE), and any adjustment required to give effect to such a deduction is made by repayment of tax.

References above to the sale of patent rights include the exchange of patent rights, and in the case of such an exchange, references above and in **40.7** below to the proceeds of sale and the price include the consideration for the exchange, and references to capital sums included in the proceeds include references to so much of the consideration for the exchange as would have been a capital sum if it had been a money payment. Where patent rights are acquired or disposed of together with other property, the acquisition costs or proceeds, as appropriate, must be apportioned on a just and reasonable basis.

Licences

The acquisition of a licence in respect of a patent is treated for the purposes of the above provisions as a purchase of patent rights, and the grant of a licence is treated as a sale of part of such rights. Where, however, the licence is a licence to exercise the rights to the exclusion of all other persons (including the grantor) for the whole of the period until the rights come to an end, the grant is treated as a sale of the whole of the rights. The use in certain circumstances of an invention, which is the subject of a patent, by the Crown or a foreign government is treated as use under a licence.

[*ITTOIA 2005, ss 587–589, 595(1)(2), 596–599, 603–608, Sch 2 para 129; ITA 2007, Sch 1 para 546*].

See **49.8** and **49.11** MISCELLANEOUS INCOME for apportionment rules and for relief for losses.

Spreading provisions

[40.7] In the case of a UK-resident seller, the profits from the sale of patent rights are chargeable spread equally over a period of six tax years, starting with the tax year in which the proceeds are received. If the proceeds are received in instalments, each instalment is likewise spread over six tax years. The seller may elect, by notice to an officer of HMRC, to disapply spreading, so that the profits (or instalments) are taxed in the year of receipt. If the seller is not UK-resident, an election is required for spreading to apply; in the absence of an election the profits (or instalments) are taxed in the year of receipt. The elections must be made within twelve months after 31 January following the tax year in which the profits or instalment were received.

Where the seller is a partnership and the sale is in the course of a trade carried on by the partnership, each amount chargeable under the above spreading provisions is chargeable on the partners for the time being carrying on the trade, unless there is a partnership change such that no partner who carried on the trade before the change continues to do so afterwards (i.e. there is a cessation of the partnership trade).

In the latter event, any amounts which would have been chargeable in later tax years are charged instead in the tax year of cessation. Any partner accordingly chargeable to an additional amount of tax in the year of cessation may elect for the amount to be reduced to what would have been chargeable had the amounts that would have been charged in subsequent years been charged in equal instalments in each of the tax years beginning with the year of receipt and ending with the year of cessation. The election must be made within twelve months after 31 January following the tax year of cessation.

Similar provisions apply where a seller dies during the period over which the charge is spread. The personal representatives of a deceased seller may make an election the effect of which is the same as that available to partners above. The same time limit applies.

The making of an election for spreading does not affect the amount of income tax to be deducted by the purchaser in the case of a sale by a non-UK resident (see 24.13, 24.21(iii) DEDUCTION OF TAX AT SOURCE), and any adjustment required as a result of such an election is made by repayment of tax on a year by year basis.

[ITTOIA 2005, ss 590–594, 595(1)(3), 596, 861, 862; ITA 2007, Sch 1 para 546; CTA 2009, Sch 1 paras 642, 643].

41

Interest on Overpaid Tax

Cross-reference. See also **53.11 PAY AS YOU EARN**.

Simon's Taxes. See A4.625, A4.630.

Interest on overpaid tax

[41.1] A repayment by HMRC of income tax (including payments on account — see **65.5 SELF-ASSESSMENT**) paid by or on behalf of an individual, a partnership, a trust, the scheme administrator of a registered pension scheme or the personal representatives of a deceased person carries interest at the rates listed below. The amount by which the repayment is so increased is known as a **repayment supplement**. The interest runs from the 'relevant time' until the date on which the order for the repayment is issued by HMRC. Repayment supplement is added in similar fashion to any repayment of a penalty imposed under any provision of *TMA 1970* (see **55 PENALTIES**) or of a surcharge imposed under *TMA 1970, s 59C* (see **42.3 INTEREST AND SURCHARGES ON OVERDUE TAX**). In 2009, following a period of zero rates, a minimum rate of interest of 0.5% was introduced; this will apply regardless of low base rates and first has effect from 29 September 2009. No liability to income tax arises in respect of repayment supplement. The *'relevant time'* is:

(a) as regards interim payments (see **65.5 SELF-ASSESSMENT**) and other payments of income tax not deducted at source, the date of the payment;

(b) as regards tax repaid as a result of a claim affecting two or more years (see **18.2 CLAIMS**), 31 January following the *later* year in relation to the claim, i.e. on a claim to carry back a loss or a payment, e.g. a pension contribution, the tax year in which the loss arises or the payment is made; on an averaging claim (for farmers or creative artists), the later of the two tax years to be averaged;

(c) as regards income tax deducted at source, 31 January following the tax year for which the tax is deducted;

(d) as regards a penalty or surcharge, the date on which the penalty or surcharge was paid; and

(e)   as regards tax repaid on a claim under *ITA 2007, s 496B* (relief for payments by discretionary trust taxable as employment income — see **68.15 SETTLEMENTS**), 31 January following the tax year to which the claim relates.

Income tax is deducted at source for a tax year if it is so deducted (or treated as deducted) from any income, or treated as paid on any income, in respect of that year (but excludes tax deducted under **PAY AS YOU EARN (53)** in respect of previous years). Repayments in respect of income tax for a tax year are attributed first to the final payment (see **65.7 SELF-ASSESSMENT**) of income tax for that year, secondly in two equal parts to the interim payments for that year, and finally to income tax deducted at source for that year. Where a payment was made in instalments, any repayment is attributed to later instalments before earlier ones.

It will be noted that the rates below are considerably lower than those by reference to which interest is charged on late paid tax (see **42.2 INTEREST AND SURCHARGES ON OVERDUE TAX**). The rates are adjusted automatically by reference to changes in the average of base lending rates of certain clearing banks, and are announced by HMRC News Release. For details of the relationship to base rates, see *SI 1989 No 1297, Reg 3AB* as inserted from 31 January 1997 by *SI 1996 No 3187* and as subsequently amended.

There is no requirement that the taxpayer be resident in the UK or EU.

Repayments relating to claims under *ITA 1952, s 228* (income accumulated under trusts, see **68.25 SETTLEMENTS**) are treated as repayments of tax paid for the tax year in which the contingency happened. The above provisions do not apply to repayments of post-war credits or amounts paid by order of a court having power to allow interest (for which see **54.6 PAYMENT OF TAX**).

Although interest on tax paid otherwise than at source runs from the date the tax was paid, even if this falls before the due date, HMRC will not pay repayment supplement on any amount deliberately overpaid (Revenue Press Release 12 November 1996). This is intended to deter taxpayers from using HMRC as a source of tax-free interest. Where a payment of tax is not set against any liability and repayment is not claimed, the payment remains on record until the next liability arises, but no repayment supplement will be given (Revenue Tax Bulletin June 1999 p 674). As regards the date on which payment is treated as made, see **54.2 PAYMENT OF TAX**. Repayment supplement is not paid in respect of out-of-date claims, since the amount repaid is regarded as an *ex gratia* payment made without acceptance of any legal liability. (HMRC Claims Manual RM5104).

Repayment supplement applies also to Class 4 national insurance contributions (see **70.5 SOCIAL SECURITY AND NATIONAL INSURANCE**) and to tax paid by employers under PAYE (see **53.11 PAY AS YOU EARN**).

[*ITTOIA 2005, s 749; ICTA 1988, s 824; FA 2008, s 34, Sch 12 para 15; SI 1989 No 1297; SI 1996 No 3187; SI 2008 Nos 778, 3234; SI 2009 No 2032; SI 2010 No 157, Art 4(1)*].

See **41.5** below as regards future changes.

Rates of interest

> **0.5% p.a. from 29 September 2009**
>   0% p.a. from 27 January 2009 to 28 September 2009
> 0.75% p.a. from 6 January 2009 to 26 January 2009
> 1.5% p.a. from 6 December 2008 to 5 January 2009
> 2.25% p.a. from 6 November 2008 to 5 December 2008
>   3% p.a. from 6 January 2008 to 5 November 2008
>   4% p.a. from 6 August 2007 to 5 January 2008
>   3% p.a. from 6 September 2006 to 5 August 2007
> 2.25% p.a. from 6 September 2005 to 5 September 2006

Earlier rates can be found at www.hmrc.gov.uk/rates/interest.htm and www.hmrc.gov.uk/rates/archive.htm.

Unauthorised demands for tax

[41.2] There is a general right to interest under *Supreme Court Act 1981, s 35A* in a case where a taxpayer submits to such an unauthorised demand, provided that the payment is not made voluntarily to close a transaction (*Woolwich Equitable Building Society v CIR HL 1992, 65 TC 265*). (*Note.* The substantive decision against the Inland Revenue which gave rise to the repayment was subsequently upheld in the HL. See *R v CIR (ex p Woolwich Equitable Building Society)* HL 1990, 63 TC 589.)

HMRC error

[41.3] HMRC publish a Code of Practice (No 1) setting out the circumstances in which they will consider paying a repayment supplement on money owed to the taxpayer for any period during which there has been undue delay on the part of HMRC. See **34.7 HMRC — ADMINISTRATION.**

Over-repayments

[41.4] Where a repayment supplement has been overpaid it may be recovered by an assessment — see **54.13 PAYMENT OF TAX.**

Interest harmonisation

[41.5] A new harmonised regime for interest is to be introduced to apply to all of the taxes and duties administered by HMRC. It is expected that the regime will be introduced for 2011/12 for income tax purposes. The new rules will replace those described in this chapter and those at **42 INTEREST AND SURCHARGES ON OVERDUE TAX**. They will provide for a single rate of simple interest on overpaid tax payable from the date of payment to the date of repayment. The legislation for the new regime is at *FA 2009, ss 101–104, Schs 53, 54*.

42

Interest and Surcharges on Overdue Tax

Cross-references. See also **53.11** PAY AS YOU EARN.

Simon's Taxes. See A4.535, A4.620, A4.621, A4.629, A6.601.

Introduction

[42.1] The provisions of *TMA 1970, s 86*, charging interest on income tax paid late, are described at **42.2** below. Income tax paid more than 28 days after the due date is subject also to a surcharge, with an additional surcharge where payment is more than six months late — see **42.3** below. See **42.4** below as regards special arrangements in relation to national disasters or emergencies. See **42.8** below as regards future changes.

Interest on overdue tax

[42.2] Interest is charged by HMRC on late payments of income tax, whether they be:

- interim payments or a balancing payment (see **65.5, 65.7** SELF-ASSESSMENT), or
- tax payable under an assessment made by HMRC or as a result of an HMRC amendment to a self-assessment following an enquiry (see **63.10** RETURNS), or
- tax becoming payable under *TMA 1970, s 55* (payment and postponement of tax pending appeal — see **54.5** PAYMENT OF TAX).

See below for rates of interest.

Interest accrues from the 'relevant date' (even if a non-business day) to the date of payment. For the two interim payments under **65.5** SELF-ASSESSMENT, the *'relevant dates'* are the due dates, i.e. 31 January in the tax year and the following 31 July. In any other case, the *'relevant date'* is 31 January following the tax year (with the one statutory exception that where the due date of a final payment is deferred until three months after notice is given to deliver a return – see **65.7 SELF-ASSESSMENT** – the relevant date is identically deferred). Where the due date for payment is *later* than the relevant date, either under the circumstances in **65.8 SELF-ASSESSMENT** or because a successful application is made to postpone tax (see **54.5 PAYMENT OF TAX**), this does *not* alter the relevant date for interest purposes.

There are provisions to remit interest charged on interim payments to the extent that an income tax repayment is found to be due for the year. There are also provisions covering the situation where a taxpayer makes a claim to dispense with or reduce his interim payments (see **65.5 SELF-ASSESSMENT**) and the total income tax liability for the year is found to be such that interim payments should have been made or should have been greater. Interest is chargeable as if each interim payment due had been equal to half the current year's liability or half the previous year's liability, whichever is less.

[*TMA 1970, s 86*].

In practice, where a self-assessment return is submitted by 30 September for calculation by HMRC of the tax due (see **65.4 SELF-ASSESSMENT**), the relevant date is deferred until 30 days after notification of the liability to the taxpayer if this occurs later than 31 December following the tax year (HMRC Self-Assessment Manual — Interest, penalties and surcharge section). This is of no significance where returns are filed over the internet (see **63.2 RETURNS**) as the tax due is automatically computed during the filing process. See also **42.7** below re executors.

As regards the date on which payment of tax is treated as made, see **54.2 PAYMENT OF TAX.**

Interest charges are calculated automatically and, however small, will appear on taxpayer statements of account under self-assessment. There is no *de minimis* limit for charging interest. It will be noted that the rates below are greater than those by reference to which interest is paid by HMRC (see **41.1 INTEREST ON OVERPAID TAX**). The rates are adjusted automatically by reference to changes in the average of base lending rates of certain clearing banks, and are announced by HMRC News Release. For the relationship to base rates, see *SI 1989 No 1297, Reg 3.*

Interest is also chargeable on late payment of surcharges (see **42.3** below) and penalties (see **55.20 PENALTIES**). [*TMA 1970, ss 59C(6), 103A; SI 1989 No 1297, Reg 3; SI 1998 Nos 310, 311; SI 2009 No 2032*].

Interest is payable gross and recoverable (as if it were tax) as a Crown debt; it is not deductible from profits or income [*ITTOIA 2005, ss 54, 869, Sch 1 para 378; TMA 1970, ss 69, 90; SI 2009 No 56, Sch 1 paras 438, 442*] and is refundable to the extent that tax concerned is subsequently discharged (and any repayment may be treated as a discharge for this purpose). [*TMA 1970, s 91; ITA 2007, Sch 1 para 259; FA 2008, Sch 1 paras 35, 39, 65*].

Interest is also charged on Class 4 national insurance contributions (see **70.5 SOCIAL SECURITY AND NATIONAL INSURANCE**) and on tax paid by employers under PAYE (see **53.11 PAY AS YOU EARN**).

See **42.4** below as regards special arrangements in relation to national disasters or emergencies generally, the 2007 foot and mouth outbreak and the June and July 2007 flooding in parts of the UK.

Rates of interest

3% p.a. from 29 September 2009

2.5% p.a. from 24 March 2009 to 28 September 2009

3.5% p.a. from 27 January 2009 to 23 March 2009

4.5% p.a. from 6 January 2009 to 26 January 2009

5.5% p.a. from 6 December 2008 to 5 January 2009

6.5% p.a. from 6 November 2008 to 5 December 2008

7.5% p.a. from 6 January 2008 to 5 November 2008

8.5% p.a. from 6 August 2007 to 5 January 2008

7.5% p.a. from 6 September 2006 to 5 August 2007

6.5% p.a. from 6 September 2005 to 5 September 2006

Earlier rates can be found at www.hmrc.gov.uk/rates/interest.htm and www.hmrc.gov.uk/rates/archive.htm.

Tax becoming due where notice of appeal given

See **54.5, 54.6** PAYMENT OF TAX as regards determination of the due and payable date where an assessment etc. is under appeal. The giving of notice of appeal, whether or not accompanied by a postponement application, does *not* affect the date from which interest accrues.

Tax becoming due after determination of an appeal by the Courts

See **54.6** PAYMENT OF TAX as regards the due and payable date where further tax is found to be chargeable on determination by the Courts of an appeal against an assessment etc. Those rules do *not* affect the date from which interest accrues.

Surcharges on overdue tax

[42.3] Where income tax has become payable, whether under a self-assessment in accordance with *TMA 1970, s 59B* (see **65.7, 65.8** SELF-ASSESSMENT) or an assessment raised by HMRC or as a result of an HMRC amendment to a self-assessment following an enquiry (see **63.10** RETURNS), and any of the tax remains unpaid more than 28 days after the due date (i.e. at any time after the end of the 28th day, see *Thompson v Minzly* Ch D 2001, 74 TC 340), the taxpayer is liable to a surcharge of 5% of the unpaid tax. An additional 5% surcharge is levied on any tax still unpaid more than six months after the due date. The due date is normally 31 January following the tax year, but see **65.7, 65.8** SELF-ASSESSMENT for exceptions (and note also the postponement rules at **54.5** PAYMENT OF TAX). As regards a pre 1996/97 assess ment first raised after 5 April 1998, the due date is 30 days after the issue of the notice of assessment, though this is deferred to the extent that any tax is postponed on appeal (see **54.5 PAYMENT OF TAX**).

Interest (at the rates in **42.2** above) will accrue on an unpaid surcharge with effect from the expiry of 30 days beginning with the date of the notice imposing the surcharge. An appeal may be made, within that same 30-day period, against the imposition of a surcharge as if it were an assessment to tax. The Appeal Tribunal may, on appeal, set aside the surcharge if it appears to them that, *throughout* the period from the due date until payment, the taxpayer had a reasonable excuse for not paying the tax. Inability to pay the tax, i.e. due to insufficient funds, is not to be regarded as a reasonable excuse. For HMRC's general approach to what constitutes a 'reasonable excuse' for late payment, see Revenue Tax Bulletin April 1998 pp 527–529.

Common examples which HMRC might regard as reasonable are where a cheque is lost in the post or by HMRC (although evidence may be required to show that every effort was made to pay by the due date); where a cheque is dishonoured solely through bank error (and payment made immediately after the taxpayer learned of the bank's action); serious illness of the taxpayer or a close relative or domestic partner which began shortly before the due date; or the death of a close relative or domestic partner at or around the due date. Examples of excuses *not* considered reasonable by HMRC are the fact that the return had not been submitted; pressure of work; failure by a tax agent; not knowing how much to pay; or the absence of a reminder that the tax is due. It is, however, stressed that these are HMRC's views, and that it is for the Appeal Tribunal to adjudicate where the taxpayer takes a different view. In *Rowland v HMRC* (Sp C 548), [2006] SSCD 536, the Sp C held that reasonable reliance on a third party (in this case the appellant's accountants) can be a reasonable excuse for these purposes. A taxpayer's political beliefs do not amount to a 'reasonable excuse' (*Gladders v Prior* (Sp C 361), [2003] SSCD 245).

Although, as stated above, the 'reasonable excuse' must strictly continue throughout the period of default in payment, in practice HMRC normally allow a further 14 days for payment to be made after the excuse has ceased.

See also *Steeden v Carver* (Sp C 212), [1999] SSCD 283, in which reliance on HMRC's advice as to the practical extension of a deadline, unequivocally given, was held to be 'as reasonable an excuse as could be found'.

There are provisions to prevent a double charge where tax has been taken into account in determining the tax-geared penalties of *TMA 1970, s 7* or *FA 2008, Sch 41* (see **55.3 PENALTIES**), *TMA 1970, s 93(5)* (tax-geared penalty for failure to make return — see **55.5 PENALTIES**), *TMA 1970, s 95* (incorrect return etc. — see **55.13 PENALTIES**) and *s 95A* (incorrect return etc. for partnerships — see **55.13 PENALTIES** and *FA 2007, Sch 24* (see **55.10, 55.14 PENALTIES**)). Any such tax will not be subject to a surcharge. The Commissioners for HMRC have discretion to mitigate, or to stay or compound proceedings for recovery of, a surcharge and may also, after judgment, entirely remit the surcharge.

[*TMA 1970, s 59C; SI 2009 No 56, Sch 1 para 39; SI 2009 No 571, Art 11; SI 2010 No 530, Sch para 2*].

'Time to Pay' agreements

No surcharge will be imposed where a taxpayer has entered into a 'Time to Pay' agreement (see **54.8** PAYMENT OF TAX), provided that the payment proposals lead to an acceptable agreement to defer the tax, and the taxpayer does not break the agreement. For this purpose, a taxpayer breaks an agreement if the tax is not paid by the agreed date or if a condition of the agreement is not complied with. If the taxpayer does break the agreement, HMRC can serve a notice reinstating the surcharge. [*FA 2009, s 108*]. This provision applies to agreements made on or after 24 November 2008, but similar provisions applied previously by concession (see HMRC Self-Assessment Manual — Payments section).

See **42.4** below as regards special arrangements in relation to national disasters or emergencies generally, the 2007 foot and mouth outbreak and the June and July 2007 flooding in parts of the UK.

National disasters or emergencies

[42.4] The Treasury are granted power by *FA 2008* to specify by order made by statutory instrument any disaster or emergency which they consider to be of national significance. This will then allow interest and surcharges on late paid tax to be waived where the late payment is attributable to that disaster or emergency. See, for example, *SI 2008 No 1936* below (flooding in June and July 2007). The regulation-making power envisages the making of agreements for deferred payment of tax between HMRC and individual taxpayers but the waiver will also apply in any case in which HMRC are satisfied that, although no agreement for deferred payment was made, such an agreement could have been made. In all cases no interest on the amount deferred is chargeable in respect of the 'relief period' and no liability to a surcharge (as in **42.3** above) on the deferred amount arises during that period.

The '*relief period*' is the period:

- beginning with a date specified in the Treasury order or, if the Commissioners of HMRC so direct, a later date from which the agreement for deferred payment has effect; and
- ending with the date on which the agreement for deferred payment ceases to have effect or, if earlier, the date on which the order is revoked.

The agreement for deferred payment ceases to have effect at the end of the period of deferment specified in the agreement or, if the Commissioners of HMRC agree to extend (or further extend) that period by reason of circumstances arising as a result of the disaster or emergency, with the end of that extended (or further extended) period.

[*FA 2008, s 135*].

Foot and mouth outbreaks — relief from interest on overdue tax

There are no special rules regarding the 2007 foot and mouth outbreak but, where appropriate, HMRC will consider using its powers to give up interest and surcharges on tax paid late due to the outbreak (HMRC News Release 8 August 2007).

Flooding in June and July 2007 — relief from interest on overdue tax

The Treasury has used the power given to them by *FA 2008, s 135* (see above) to enable HMRC to waive interest and surcharges on tax paid late where this was due to the flooding, caused by weather conditions, in parts of the UK in June and July 2007. The relief period begins on 1 June 2007. [*SI 2008 No 1936*]. Prior to enactment of these *regulations*, HMRC were able to exercise their discretionary power not to collect such interest and surcharges (HMRC News Release 25 July 2007). The News Release also announced a number of other measures that would be employed by HMRC to assist those affected by the flooding.

Exchange restrictions

[42.5] Where foreign income cannot be remitted to the UK due to government action in the country of origin, and tax thereon is held over by agreement with HMRC, interest ceases to run from the date when HMRC were first in possession of relevant facts — with *no interest charged* if that date falls within three months after the tax is due. Interest recommences from the date of any subsequent demand, but this *latter* interest remitted if payment made within three months of demand. [*TMA 1970, s 92*]. See **32.5 FOREIGN INCOME**.

HMRC error

[42.6] HMRC publish a Code of Practice (No 1) setting out the circumstances in which they will consider waiving a charge to interest on overdue tax where there has been undue delay on their part. See **34.7 HMRC — ADMINISTRATION**.

Executors

[42.7] Executors unable to pay tax before obtaining probate may have special treatment by concession so that interest on tax falling due after the date of death runs from 30 days after the date on which probate or letters of administration are obtained. (HMRC ESC A17). It is believed that the concession is similarly applied to surcharges (as in **42.3** above).

Interest harmonisation and penalty for late payment

[42.8] A new harmonised regime for interest is to be introduced to apply to all of the taxes and duties administered by HMRC. It is expected that the regime will be introduced for 2011/12 for income tax purposes. The new rules will replace those described in this chapter and those at **41 INTEREST ON OVERPAID TAX**. They will provide for a single rate of simple interest on overdue tax payable from the due date of payment to the date of payment. The legislation for the new regime is at *FA 2009, ss 101–104, Schs 53, 54*.

At the same time as the above provisions are introduced, a new penalty for failure to make payments on time is to be introduced. The penalty will apply not only to income tax and capital gains tax but to other taxes also. It will replace late payment surcharges (see **42.3** above). Broadly, there will be an initial 5% penalty where tax is unpaid 30 days after the due date. Further 5% penalties will be charged on the amount of tax still outstanding after a further five months and eleven months. Penalties will be suspended during a 'Time to Pay' agreement (see **54.8 PAYMENT OF TAX**) and no liability will arise where there is a reasonable excuse for the failure. See *FA 2009, s 107, Sch 56* for the detailed provisions.

As regards late in-year payments of PAYE, a new penalty applies for 2010/11 onwards — see **53.14 PAY AS YOU EARN**.

43

Interest Payable

Cross-references. See **3 ALTERNATIVE FINANCE ARRANGEMENTS; 4.36 ANTI-AVOIDANCE; 8 BANKS; 9 BUILDING SOCIETIES; 24 DEDUCTION OF TAX AT SOURCE; 64.6 SAVINGS AND INVESTMENT INCOME** for interest paid by issue of funding bonds; **42 INTEREST AND SURCHARGES ON OVERDUE TAX**.

Simon's Taxes. See E1.820–E1.832.

Introduction

[43.1] This chapter is concerned with the extent to which interest payable is deductible in computing taxable income for income tax purposes. The first part of the chapter (**43.2–43.4**) covers interest payable for the purposes of a business. The next part of the chapter (**43.5–43.12**) covers interest on particular categories of loan which, subject to conditions, is deductible by virtue of specific tax legislation. Provisions to prevent double tax relief are examined in **43.13**, and **43.14** details a general anti-avoidance rule.

Business interest payable

[43.2] For the purpose of computing the taxable profits of a trade, profession or vocation, interest payable is revenue expenditure, as opposed to capital, whatever the nature of the loan. [*ITTOIA 2005, s 29; ICTA 1988, s 74(1)(f)*].

Whether or not it is deductible in computing those profits depends on general principles, in particular the 'wholly and exclusively' rule at **73.36 TRADING INCOME**. Interest incurred wholly and exclusively for the purposes of a property business is similarly an allowable deduction from the profits of that business (see **60.4 PROPERTY INCOME**). For disallowance of interest where the proprietor's capital account was overdrawn, see *Silk v Fletcher* (Sp C 201), [1999] SSCD 220 and *(No 2)*(Sp C 262), [2000] SSCD 565 and see HMRC Business Income Manual BIM45705–45730.

No relief is given if the interest is within the anti-avoidance provisions of *ITA 2007, s 809ZG* — see **43.14** below.

The conditions in **43.5** *et seq.* below do not apply to interest deductible in computing business profits, but if interest so deductible is also allowable within those conditions, relief may instead be claimed under *ITA 2007, s 383* (or, before 2007/08, under *ICTA 1988, s 353*). See **43.13** below for the exclusion of double relief. Where interest wholly and exclusively for business purposes is dealt with under *ITA 2007, s 383* or its predecessor but not wholly relieved because of insufficiency of income, the unrelieved interest can be treated as a trading loss for certain purposes (see **45.23 LOSSES**).

See generally HMRC Business Income Manual BIM45650–45776.

Interest on loan for property bought by partner for partnership use

[43.3] The following applies where interest is paid by a partnership, and charged as an expense in its accounts, on a loan taken out by a partner to purchase land occupied rent-free by the partnership and used for business purposes. Relief as a trading expense for interest payable by the partnership on the individual's behalf should be available in the normal way. The individual's property income computation would include as a receipt the interest payments made by the partnership on his behalf, but these would be offset by a deduction for interest payable by the individual (which would be allowable regardless of the interest payments actually having been met by the partnership). The taxable property income would therefore generally be nil. (Revenue Tax Bulletin June 1997 pp 437, 438).

Interest on loan for property bought by controlling director for company use

[43.4] The following applies where interest is paid by a company, and charged as an expense in its accounts, on a loan taken out by a controlling director to purchase land occupied rent-free by the company and used for business purposes. Relief as a trading expense for interest payable by the company on the director's behalf should be available in the normal way as a deduction from the company's profits for tax purposes, and the payments would not normally constitute either emoluments or a benefit of the director. The director's property income computation would include as a receipt the interest payments made by the company on his behalf, but these would be offset by a deduction for interest payable by the director (which would be allowable regardless of the interest payments actually having been met by the company). The taxable property income would therefore generally be nil. (Revenue Tax Bulletin June 1997 pp 437, 438).

Other relief for interest paid

[43.5] Relief for interest on the categories of loan described in **43.6–43.12** below is given for income tax purposes for the tax year in which paid. [*ITA 2007, s 383(1)(2), Sch 1 para 62(2)–(5); ICTA 1988, s 353(1)*].

Relief is not, however, available for interest on overdrafts, credit cards or similar arrangements. Nor will relief be given to the extent that the interest exceeds a reasonable commercial rate. In response to a notified avoidance scheme, a further rule was introduced, in relation to interest paid after 8 October 2007, to effectively prevent relief for interest that relates to a tax year later than that in which it is paid. [*ITA 2007, s 384; ICTA 1988, s 353(3); FA 2008, Sch 22 para 21*].

In response to notified tax avoidance schemes, legislation is included in *FA 2009* to deny relief for interest if the loan is made as part of arrangements that are certain (ignoring insignificant risk) to enable the borrower to exit the arrangements with a profit by virtue of the interest being eligible for relief. Whilst the legislation is sufficiently wide-ranging to catch most likely variations to these schemes, it is not intended to catch genuine commercial investments in business where there is uncertainty as to the return that will be produced from the investment. The legislation applies to interest paid on or after 19 March 2009. [*ITA 2007, s 384A; FA 2009, Sch 30 para 1*].

Relief for interest is not granted unless the loan proceeds are so applied within a reasonable time, nor if the loan proceeds are used for some other purpose first (but these conditions do not apply to loans used to purchase plant or machinery as in **43.6** below). The giving of credit can be treated as a loan. [*ITA 2007, s 385(2)–(4); ICTA 1988, s 367(2)(4)*].

If a loan is a mixed loan, such that part of it qualifies under any of **43.6–43.12** below and part does not qualify at all, a corresponding proportion of the interest qualifies for relief. If the mixed loan is partly repaid, the repayment is applied rateably between the qualifying and non-qualifying parts, so the percentage of interest eligible for relief remains the same; this applied in practice before 2007/08 but now has statutory effect. [*ITA 2007, s 386; ICTA 1988, s 367(4)*].

Where the interest is business interest (see **43.2** above), see **43.13** below for the exclusion of double relief and **45.23** LOSSES for the treatment of unrelieved interest as a trading loss.

No relief is given if the interest is within the anti-avoidance provisions of *ITA 2007, s 809ZG* — see **43.14** below.

For interest paid to persons other than building societies or local authorities, the person to whom relief is due is entitled to require from the lender by written request a statement in writing showing the date and amount of the debt, the name and address of the debtor and the interest paid in the tax year. [*ITA 2007, s 412, Sch 1 para 70; ICTA 1988, s 366*]. See generally Revenue Tax Bulletin April 1995 p 210.

Method of giving relief

Interest on loans within **43.6–43.11** below is relieved by way of a deduction in arriving at net income for the tax year in question (see Step 2 at **1.7 ALLOWANCES AND TAX RATES**), and thus attracts relief at marginal rates. If the deduction exceeds net income, no relief is available for the excess except as in **43.11** below (loans to pay inheritance tax).

Relief for interest on a loan within **43.12** below (pre-9 March 1999 loans for purchasing a life annuity) is restricted to 23% of the eligible interest; the relief is normally given by deduction of tax at source but is otherwise given by way of an income tax reduction (see **1.8 ALLOWANCES AND TAX RATES**), and does not save tax at the higher rate (see **43.12** below for more details).

Where, for any tax year, an amount of interest is eligible for relief partly as a deduction in arriving at net income and partly as a tax reduction (for example, because the loan is a mixed loan), it is apportioned by reference to the proportions of the amount borrowed (not the amount still outstanding) applied for different purposes.

[*ITA 2007, s 383(3)(4), Sch 1 para 62(3)–(5); ICTA 1988, s 353(1A)–(1E)*].

Replacement loans

Where, under any of **43.7–43.11** below and subject to the conditions therein, interest is specifically eligible for relief if it is paid on a loan that is used to repay another (eligible) loan, the current loan and the loan it replaced are generally treated for these purposes as if they were one and the same loan. [*ITA 2007, s 408; ICTA 1988, s 363(4)*].

Hire purchase charges

Hire purchase charges (the excess of the hire purchase payments over the cash price) are not interest and therefore not within this relief. (Some hire purchase agreements may specify that the whole balance of the rental after the initial payment is payable within seven days but will leave the hirer the option of paying that balance over a defined period on interest terms. At the date the option is exercised a loan is created and the interest on that loan is true interest under *ITA 2007, s 383* or its predecessor and will qualify for relief if all other relevant conditions are satisfied.)

Loans for purchasing plant or machinery

[43.6] Relief is given under **43.5** above for interest paid by an individual on a loan for the purchase of plant or machinery:

(a)   for use for the purposes of a trade, profession or UK property business carried on by a partnership of which the payer is a member and which is entitled to a capital allowance, or liable to a balancing charge, on that item under *CAA 2001, s 264* (see **11.66** CAPITAL ALLOWANCES ON PLANT AND MACHINERY) for the period of account in which the interest is paid; or

(b)   for the purposes of an office or employment he holds, and in respect of which he is entitled to plant or machinery capital allowances, or liable to a balancing charge, under *CAA 2001, Pt 2* (or would be so entitled but for a contribution made by his employer).

Relief is given only for interest payable no later than three years after the end of the period of account (where (a) above is relevant), or the tax year (where (b) above is relevant), in which the loan was made. If the plant or machinery is only partly in use for the purposes stated in (a) or (b) above and partly for other purposes, a proportionate part of the interest, determined on a just and reasonable basis, is eligible for the relief.

For the above purposes, a partnership or an individual remains entitled to a capital allowance on an item for so long as no disposal value (see **11.24** CAPITAL ALLOWANCES ON PLANT AND MACHINERY) has been brought into account in respect of that item. As regards (a) above, there is some doubt over whether interest on a loan to buy plant or machinery for the purposes of a UK property business qualified for the relief for 2006/07 and earlier years; for 2007/08 onwards, it is made explicit that it does (see Change 68 in Annex 1 to the Explanatory Notes to *ITA 2007*).

[*ITA 2007, ss 388–391; ICTA 1988, s 359; CAA 2001, Sch 2 para 27*].

Simon's Taxes. See E1.826.

Loans for interests in close companies

[**43.7**] Subject to the conditions below, relief is given under **43.5** above for interest paid by an individual on a loan used

(i)   for acquiring ordinary shares in a close company (see Tolley's Corporation Tax); and/or

(ii)   for lending money to such a company; and/or

(iii)   to repay a loan used for any one or more of these purposes.

The company must not be a close investment-holding company (see Tolley's Corporation Tax under Close Companies), whether at the time the loan proceeds are applied or the time the interest is paid.

If the loan is within (i) above, relief is denied in relation to shares in respect of which a claim is made, in relation to shares acquired after 13 March 1989, to income tax relief under the EIS (see **28** ENTERPRISE INVESTMENT SCHEME) or, in relation to shares acquired after 5 April 1998, for deferral of a chargeable gain on reinvestment in an EIS investment, by the person acquiring them or their spouse or civil partner. If the loan is within (ii) above, the money must be used wholly and exclusively for the purposes of the business of the company or of an associated company (within *CTA 2010, s 449*); any such associated company must also be a close company and not a close investment-holding company.

For an interest payment to qualify for the relief, the individual must not have recovered any capital from the company in the period from the use of the loan to the payment of the interest, except as taken into account in treating the loan as repaid or partly repaid (see below under Capital recovery). In addition, *either* of the following two conditions must be met.

(a) **The material interest test.** The individual must have a 'material interest' in the company when the interest is paid. In addition, if the company exists wholly or mainly to hold investments or other property, no property of the company must be used by the individual as a residence, unless, in the period from the use of the loan to the payment of the interest, he has worked for the greater part of his time in the actual management or conduct of the company or an associated company (for which see (b) below). An individual has a *'material interest'* for this purpose if he (either alone or with 'associates') or an 'associate' of his (with or without other 'associates' of his) owns (or can control) more than 5% of the company's ordinary share capital or would be entitled to more than 5% of the assets available for distribution among the participators on a winding-up or in other circumstances. 'Control' is as defined in *CTA 2010, ss 450, 451* and 'participator' is as defined in *CTA 2010, s 454.*

(b) **The full-time working condition test.** The individual must have a holding of ordinary share capital of the company when the interest is paid and, in the period from the use of the loan to the payment of the interest, he must have worked for the greater part of his time in the actual management or conduct of the company or an associated company. The facts of each particular case must be considered, but individuals will normally be regarded as meeting the latter requirement if they are directors or have significant managerial or technical responsibilities. They must, however, be involved in the overall running and policy-making of the company as a whole — responsibility for just a particular area is not sufficient. (Revenue Tax Bulletin November 1993 p 102).

'Associate' is defined for the purposes of (a) above by *ITA 2007, s 395*. An individual's associates include his relatives (as defined), his business partners, the trustees of a settlement of which he or a relative is the settlor, the trustees of any settlement by virtue of which he has an interest in the company's shares or obligations and the personal representatives of a deceased person whose estate includes any of the company's shares or obligations in which the individual has an interest. But, in relation to loans made after 26 July 1989, an individual's associates do not generally include the trustees of an employee benefit trust (as defined), as a beneficiary of which the individual has an interest in shares or obligations of the company, unless the 5% ordinary share capital test would be satisfied without their inclusion (for which purpose certain payments received from the trust are treated as giving rise to beneficial ownership of ordinary share capital).

A slightly different definition of 'associate' applies to loans made before 14 November 1986 (see now *ITA 2007, Sch 2 para 93).*

[*ITA 2007, ss 392–395, Sch 2 paras 91–94; ICTA 1988, ss 360, 360A, Sch 9 para 39; FA 2006, Sch 13 para 11; CTA 2010, Sch 1 paras 521–523*].

The interest will continue to be allowed if the company ceases to be close after the application of the loan monies (HMRC SP 3/78). Conversely, it is understood that relief will be given where a loan is used to purchase shares in an 'open' company which by that acquisition becomes a close company (Tolley's Practical Tax Newsletter 1981 p 99).

Interest paid by the guarantor of a bank loan to a close company is not within the relief (*Hendy v Hadley* Ch D 1980, 53 TC 353).

Where shares were subscribed for in a 'shell' company to enable it to acquire a business, but the business had not been acquired at the time of the subscription, it could fairly be said that the company existed for the purpose of carrying on that business, so that interest on a loan for the purchase of the shares qualified for relief under these provisions (*Lord v Tustain* Ch D 1993, 65 TC 761).

Interest on a loan applied to the purchase of a close company's convertible loan stock can qualify for relief under these provisions. Relief will, however, cease from the date on which the loan stock is converted to ordinary share capital, since this constitutes a capital recovery (see below). (Revenue Tax Bulletin February 1992 p 13).

Capital recovery

If, at any time after the loan is used as above, the borrower recovers an amount of capital from the company, the loan is treated as repaid at that time to the extent of that amount. For 2007/08 onwards, this applies regardless of whether or not such repayment is actually made; previously it applied only if such repayment was not actually made (see Change 74 in Annex 1 to the Explanatory Notes to *ITA 2007*). Relief for subsequent interest payments is restricted accordingly. An individual recovers capital from the company if he sells, exchanges or assigns ordinary shares of the company, obtains a repayment of ordinary share capital, is repaid a loan or advance he has made to the company or assigns a debt due to him from the company. A sale or assignment is treated for this purpose as having been made at market value if it was not a bargain at arm's length. If a loan is used to repay another loan, so that it is within (iii) above, any capital recovery restrictions that were already affecting the original loan similarly affect the new loan. [*ITA 2007, ss 406–408; ICTA 1988, s 363(1)–(4)*].

Business successions and reorganisations

Relief on a loan qualifying as above does not cease where shares in the close company are exchanged for, or replaced by, shares in another close company, or by shares in a co-operative (see **43.8** below), or by shares in an employee-controlled company (see **43.9** below), provided that relief would have been available if the loan had been a new loan taken out to invest in the new entity. For 2006/07 and earlier years, this rule operated by concession (see HMRC ESC A43); it is given statutory authority for 2007/08 onwards. [*ITA 2007, s 410*].

Woodlands

Interest is ineligible for the above relief to the extent that the business carried on by the close company consists of the occupation of commercial woodlands, i.e. UK woodlands managed on a commercial basis with a view to realisation of profits. See **30.45 EXEMPT INCOME** for the general exemption of such woodlands. [*ITA 2007, s 411; FA 1988, Sch 6 para 3(3)–(5) (7)*].

Simon's Taxes. See E1.827.

Loans for investing in co-operatives

[43.8] Subject to the conditions below, relief is given under **43.5** above for interest paid by an individual on a loan used (i) for acquiring shares in a 'co-operative', and/or (ii) for lending money to a co-operative, and/or (iii) to repay a loan used for any one or more of these purposes. If the loan is within (ii) above, the money must be used wholly and exclusively for the purposes of the business of the co-operative or of a 'subsidiary' of the co-operative.

The conditions (all of which must be met) are that:

- the co-operative is still a co-operative when the interest is paid;
- in the period from the use of the loan to the payment of the interest, the individual must have worked for the greater part of his time as an employee of the co-operative or of a subsidiary of the co-operative; and
- in that period the individual must not have recovered any capital from the co-operative, except as taken into account in treating the loan as repaid or partly repaid under the capital recovery provisions referred to below.

'*Co-operative*' (and '*subsidiary*') means a common ownership enterprise or a co-operative enterprise as defined in the *Industrial Common Ownership Act 1976, s 2*.

[*ITA 2007, ss 401, 402, Sch 2 para 97; ICTA 1988, ss 361(1)(2), 363(5)*].

The capital recovery provisions at **43.7** above apply equally here (with the appropriate modifications), as does the rule for business successions and reorganisations.

Simon's Taxes. See E1.828.

Loans for investing in employee-controlled companies

[43.9] Subject to the conditions below, relief is given under **43.5** above for interest paid by an individual on a loan used (i) for acquiring ordinary shares in an 'employee-controlled company' and/or (ii) to repay a loan used for any one or more of these purposes. The individual must acquire the shares before, or not later than 12 months after, the company first becomes an employee-controlled company.

For this purpose, a company is an '*employee-controlled company*' if more than 50% of both the issued ordinary share capital and the voting power is beneficially owned by full-time employees (as defined in (c) below) of the company. But if any one individual's ownership exceeds 10% of either issued ordinary share capital or voting power, the excess is treated as owned otherwise than by a full-time employee.

The conditions (all of which must be met) are that:

(a)   throughout the period from the acquisition of the shares to the payment of the interest, the company must be resident only in the UK, unquoted, and either a trading company (i.e. its business consists wholly or mainly of the carrying on of trade(s)) or the holding company of a trading group (i.e. a group, being a company and one or more 75% subsidiaries, the business of whose members, taken together, consists wholly or mainly of carrying on trade(s));

(b)   the company must be an employee-controlled company throughout a period of at least nine months in the tax year in which the interest is paid, unless it is the year in which it first becomes an employee-controlled company;

(c)   throughout the period from the use of the loan to the payment of the interest, the individual is a full-time employee of the company (i.e. works for the greater part of his time as an employee or director of the company or of a 51% subsidiary); if such employment ceased before, but not more than 12 months before, the payment of the interest, the condition can instead be satisfied by reference to the period from the use of the loan to the date of ceasing full-time employment; and

(d)   in the period from the use of the loan to the payment of the interest, the individual must not have recovered any capital from the company, except as taken into account in treating the loan as repaid or partly repaid under the capital recovery provisions referred to below.

If the loan qualified before 6 April 1990, the reference in the definition of 'employee-controlled company' to full-time employees is a reference to such employees or their spouses. Ownership of husband and wife is then taken together in applying the 10% condition, unless they are *both* full-time employees. The condition at (c) above can be satisfied by the individual's spouse. Interest on a loan made on or after that date to repay a loan made before that date can be eligible (by virtue of (ii) above) only if interest on the original loan would have been eligible if the original loan had been used on or after that date.

[ITA 2007, ss 396, 397, 989, 1005, Sch 2 para 95; ICTA 1988, s 361(3)–(8); FA 2007, Sch 26 para 12(9)(12); SI 2007 No 3506, reg 3(2)].

The capital recovery provisions at **43.7** above apply equally here (with the appropriate modifications), as does the rule for business successions and reorganisations and the exclusion of businesses consisting of the occupation of commercial woodlands.

Simon's Taxes. See **E1.829.**

Loans for investing in partnerships

[43.10] Subject to the conditions and restrictions below, relief is given under **43.5** above for interest paid by an individual on a loan used (i) for purchasing a share in a partnership, and/or (ii) contributing money to the partnership (by way of capital or premium), and/or (iii) advancing money to a partnership, and/or (iv) to repay a loan used for any one or more of these purposes. If the loan is within (ii) or (iii) above, the money must be used wholly for the purposes of the trade or profession carried on by the partnership.

The conditions (both of which must be met) are that:

- throughout the period from the use of the loan to the payment of the interest, the individual has been a member of the partnership otherwise than as a limited partner in a limited partnership registered under *Limited Partnerships Act 1907* or as a member of an 'investment limited liability partnership' (see **52.22**, **52.25 PARTNERSHIPS**); and
- in that period the individual must not have recovered any capital from the partnership, except as taken into account in treating the loan as repaid or partly repaid under the capital recovery provisions referred to below.

In the case of a partnership carrying on a profession, certain individuals who are not members of the partnership, for example salaried partners, are treated for these purposes as if they were members. This apples to any individual who is employed by the partnership in a senior capacity, is allowed to act independently in dealing with clients and is allowed to act generally in such a way as to be indistinguishable from the partners in relations with those clients. For 2006/07 and earlier years, this rule applied by virtue of a Statement of Practice (see HMRC SP A33), but it is given statutory effect for 2007/08 onwards.

[*ITA 2007, ss 398, 399; ICTA 1988, s 362; Limited Liability Partnerships Act 2000, s 10(2)*].

For a case in which relief was denied where 'the true net result of the circular transaction [involving a series of payments between spouses] was that no money was contributed or advanced to the partnership which it did not already have', see *Lancaster v CIR* (Sp C 232), [2000] SSCD 138.

The capital recovery provisions at **43.7** above apply equally here (with the appropriate modifications and by reference to the individual's interest in the partnership); the return of capital by the partnership to the individual is one occasion of recovery. The exclusion at **43.7** above of businesses consisting of the occupation of commercial woodlands also applies equally here.

Business successions and reorganisations

Relief on a loan qualifying as above does not cease where the partnership is incorporated into a close company (see **43.7** above), a co-operative (see **43.8** above) or an employee-controlled company (see **43.9** above), provided that relief would have been available if the loan had been a new loan taken out to invest in the new entity. Also, relief does not cease where the partnership is dissolved and a new partnership (of which the individual is, or falls to be treated as, a member) succeeds to the whole or part of its undertaking; in this case the old and new partnerships are treated as the same partnership for the purposes of the relief. For 2006/07 and earlier years, these rules operated by concession (see HMRC ESC A43); they are given statutory authority for 2007/08 onwards. [*ITA 2007, ss 409, 410*].

Anti-avoidance measures on changeover to current year basis of assessment

Anti-avoidance provisions applied where a claim for interest relief under the above provisions was made by a partner for 1997/98 in respect of a loan made after 31 March 1994 and there was a transitional overlap profit (see **73.12 TRADING INCOME**) on the changeover to the current year basis. Subject to a *de minimis* limit of £7,500 for application of these provisions, that partner's transitional overlap profit (as reduced where applicable by the anti-avoidance provisions at **73.12**) was reduced by the amount of interest paid in respect of the transitional overlap period on any part of the loan proceeds which was contributed or advanced by him to the partnership otherwise than wholly or mainly for *bona fide* commercial reasons or wholly or mainly for a purpose other than the reduction of partnership borrowings for a period falling wholly or partly within the transitional overlap period. [*FA 1995, Sch 22 paras 5, 12; ITA 2007, Sch 1 para 370*].

Anti-avoidance measure involving film partnerships

In response to an identified avoidance scheme, legislation was included in *FA 2006* to restrict relief under *ICTA 1988, s 362* for the payment of interest accruing after 9 March 2006 in the circumstances set out below. The legislation is now in *ITA 2007* and restricts relief under *ITA 2007, s 398* in those circumstances. For any tax year for which these circumstances apply, relief for the interest on the loan is restricted to 40% of the amount that would otherwise be eligible for relief. The circumstances are that:

- a loan is used by an individual ('the borrower') to buy into (or advance money to) a *'film partnership'*, i.e. a partnership carrying on a trade in which the film tax reliefs at **73.76 TRADING INCOME** have been used in computing profits or losses;
- the borrower is, or has been, a member of another partnership (the *'investment partnership'*);
- the loan used to buy into (or to contribute or advance money to) the film partnership is secured (as widely defined) on an asset or activity of the investment partnership; and
- at any time in the tax year, the proportion of the taxable profits of the investment partnership to which the borrower is entitled is less than the proportion of the partnership's capital contributed by him at that time.

For this purpose, the investment partnership's capital comprises: (i) anything that is (or in accordance with generally accepted accounting practice, would be) accounted for as partners' capital or partners' equity; and (ii) amounts lent to the partnership by partners or persons connected with partners (within **21.2 CONNECTED PERSONS**). The proportion of the investment partnership's capital contributed by the borrower at any time includes, in particular:

- any amount paid by the borrower to acquire an interest in the investment partnership (insofar as he still has that interest at that time);
- any amount made available by the borrower (directly or indirectly) to another person who acquires an interest in the investment partnership (in so far as the other person still has that interest at that time);

- any amount lent by the borrower to the investment partnership and not repaid at that time;
- any amount made available by the borrower (directly or indirectly) to another person in so far as any amount lent by that person to the investment partnership has not been repaid at that time; and
- any amount made available in any other manner that may be prescribed by HMRC regulations made by statutory instrument (which may have retrospective effect).

All references above to the borrower include references to anyone connected with him (within **21.2 CONNECTED PERSONS**, i.e. spouses, civil partners and relatives).

[*ITA 2007, s 399(4), s 400, Sch 2 para 96; FA 2006, s 75*].

Simon's Taxes. See **E1.830**.

Loans to pay inheritance tax

[43.11] Relief is given under **43.5** above for interest on a loan to the personal representatives of a deceased person that is used (i) to pay inheritance tax that they are obliged to pay under *IHTA 1984, s 226(2)* (obligation of personal representatives to pay tax on delivery of their account in order to obtain a grant of representation or confirmation), or (ii) to pay interest on such inheritance tax, or (iii) to repay a loan used for any of these purposes. In order to attract relief, the loan interest paid must have been in respect of a period ending within one year from the making of the loan.

If the interest cannot be relieved in the tax year due to insufficiency of income, it is carried back to preceding tax years, latest year first, until it is fully relieved. If the interest cannot be relieved by carry-back, it may instead be carried forward to tax years following the year of payment, earliest year first, until it is fully relieved.

[*ITA 2007, ss 403–405; ICTA 1988, s 364*].

Simon's Taxes. See **E1.832**.

Pre-9 March 1999 loans for purchasing a life annuity

[43.12] Relief is given under **43.5** above for interest on a loan for the purchase of a life annuity by a borrower aged 65 or over under a scheme in which 90% or more of the proceeds of the loan are applied to the purchase by the borrower of an annuity ending with his death (or the last death of two or more annuitants aged 65 or over which include the borrower). The loan must be secured on land in the UK or Eire in which the borrower or one of the annuitants owns an estate or interest. Interest is not eligible unless payable by the borrower or one of the annuitants. The rate of tax relief on interest allowable under these provisions is fixed at 23% of the amount of the allowable interest.

The loan must have been made before 9 March 1999, or in pursuance of an offer made by the lender before that date (and either written or evidenced by a note or memorandum made by the lender before that date). However, replacement loans made on or after 27 July 1999 qualify for relief if the old loan did so, and this applies where only part of the new loan is applied in paying off the old loan, provided that at least 90% of the balance of the new loan not applied in paying off the old loan is applied to the purchase of an annuity ending with the life of the person to whom the loan is made (or of the survivor of two or more persons including that person).

As regards loans made from 27 March 1974 onwards: (a) the borrower or each of the annuitants must use the land as his only or main residence when the interest is paid or have so used it immediately before 9 March 1999; and (b) relief is granted on loans up to £30,000 only, with apportionment where payable by two or more annuitants. The condition at (a) is treated as satisfied where it ceased to be satisfied at a time falling within the twelve months ending with 8 March 1999 and it was then intended to take steps to dispose of the land within the following twelve months.

As stated at **43.5** above, relief is normally given by deduction of tax at source but is otherwise given by way of an income tax reduction as opposed to a deduction from total income. The reduction is 23% of the amount of interest eligible for relief. The order in which tax reductions are given against an individual's tax liability is set out at **1.8 ALLOWANCES AND TAX RATES,** which also makes clear that a tax reduction must be restricted to the extent (if any) that it would otherwise exceed the individual's remaining income tax liability after making all prior reductions.

Relief at source is given via the MIRAS (Mortgage Interest Relief At Source) system which generally applied to tax relief on mortgage interest prior to such relief being abolished with effect from 6 April 2000. Once relief is given under MIRAS, no further tax relief is available but nor is tax relief clawed back if the borrower has insufficient tax liability to cover it.

[ICTA 1988, s 353(1A)(1AA)(1AB)(1F)–(1H), s 357(1), s 365; ITA 2007, Sch 1 para 62(3)(6)].

Simon's Taxes. See E1.820.

Exclusion of double relief

[43.13] There are provisions to prevent double relief by different methods. The general rule is that any interest relieved under *ITA 2007, s 383* (see **43.5** above) is not deductible for any other purpose. If a payment of interest on a debt has been allowed under **43.2** above in computing the profits of a trade, profession, vocation or property business for a period of account, no relief can be given under *ITA 2007, s 383* for that payment and for any other interest on the same debt in any tax year for which that period is the basis period (see **73.3 TRADING INCOME** onwards). Conversely, if a payment of interest has been relieved under *section 383*, that payment cannot be deducted in computing profits for any tax year and any payment of interest on the same debt cannot be deducted in computing profits for any tax year for which the interest relieved under *section 383* could otherwise have been relieved as a trading etc. deduction. For these purposes, all business overdrafts are treated as one debt.

Interest is treated as having been relieved under *section 383* when it has been deducted in an assessment that can no longer be varied (whether on appeal or otherwise). For years prior to 2007/08, the above references to *ITA 2007, s 383* should be read as references to *ICTA 1988, s 353*. [*ITA 2007, s 387, Sch 1 para 498; ITTOIA 2005, s 52; ICTA 1988, s 368*].

Simon's Taxes. See **E1.823**.

Anti-avoidance

[43.14] Relief is not available under *any* part of this chapter to a person for a payment of interest if a 'tax relief scheme' has been effected, or 'tax relief arrangements' have been made, in relation to the transaction under which the interest is paid. It matters not whether the scheme is effected, or the arrangements are made, before or after the transaction. The restriction applies whether the relief would otherwise have been given as a deduction in calculating profits or as a deduction or set-off against income. A scheme is a *'tax relief scheme'* in relation to a transaction if it is such that the sole or main benefit that might be expected to accrue to the person from the transaction is the obtaining of a reduction in tax liability by means of interest relief. *'Tax relief arrangements'* are similarly defined.

[*ITA 2007, s 809ZG; ICTA 1988, s 787; TIOPA 2010, Sch 7 para 52*].

The above restriction has effect in relation to returns under ALTERNATIVE FINANCE ARRANGEMENTS (3) in the same way as it has effect in relation to interest. [*ITA 2007, s 564P; FA 2005, ss 55, 56, Sch 2 para 8; TIOPA 2010, Sch 2 para 17*].

See also *Cairns v MacDiarmid* CA 1982, 56 TC 556 and *Lancaster v CIR* (Sp C 232), [2000] SSCD 138.

Deduction of tax from interest payments

[43.15] In general, tax is not deductible at source from interest paid by individuals (except as in **43.12** above).

Key points

[43.16] Points to consider are as follows.

- Unless allowed as a deduction from profits (including those of a property business) interest on credit card debt and overdrafts never attracts tax relief.
- The widely phrased anti-avoidance rule at **43.14** in relation to interest is unusual. It prevents a tax deduction for interest against profits, or generally, where a scheme or arrangement entered into before or after the transaction to which the interest relates has as its sole or main purpose a reduction in tax liability as a result of the transaction, by way of tax relief on the interest.

- It is common for HMRC to challenge interest deductions where the proprietor's capital account has become overdrawn. It may be possible to counter argue when the overdrawn position is temporary as a result of a difficult trading period, but when the overdrawing relates to drawings consistently exceeding profits, it is unlikely that a deduction for interest can be obtained.
- Loans to facilitate a draw down of equity in a rental property will normally qualify for tax relief against the property business profits provided that the draw down does not exceed the equity in the property when the rental business commenced (or the property was introduced into the business). Drawing against subsequent revaluations does not similarly qualify.

44

Life Assurance Policies

(See also HMRC Insurance Policyholder Taxation Manual.)

Introduction

[**44.1**] Generally, tax relief for premiums paid on qualifying life assurance policies was abolished for insurances made on or after 14 March 1984. The relatively minor reliefs at **44.2** do, however, still apply. Due to its continuing application to premiums on pre-14 March 1984 insurances, the general life assurance premium relief continues to be covered at **44.24** *et seq.*, with the definition of a qualifying policy considered at **44.29** *et seq.*.

Income tax is charged on gains treated as arising from many life assurance policies, contracts for life annuities and capital redemption policies. A gain (a '*chargeable event gain*') arises when a chargeable event occurs in relation to the policy or contract. Chargeable events include *inter alia* death, maturity, total or partial surrender and total or partial assignment — see **44.5**. See **44.3–44.16** for the main coverage.

This chapter also covers personal portfolio bonds (**44.17**), offshore policies (**44.18–44.20**) and friendly society policies (**44.21–44.23**)

Miscellaneous life assurance-related reliefs

[44.2] The relatively minor reliefs listed below are not affected by the abolition of life assurance premium relief from 14 March 1984 (see **44.24** below). These reliefs are available to all UK resident individuals; they are also available to certain other claimants as set out at **50.2 NON-RESIDENTS**. Prior to 2007/08, the limit at **44.25**(a) below applied to the first two reliefs but not to the third. The limit at **44.25**(b) below operated as a combined limit to all three (as well as to relief within **44.24** below). For 2007/08 onwards, the limits at **44.25** below do not apply at all to these three reliefs; instead, each relief now has its own independent limit by reference to a figure of £100 as described below (see Change 84 in Annex 1 of the Explanatory Notes to *ITA 2007*).

These changes did not apply to individuals within **50.2**(i) and (ii) **NON-RESIDENTS**, who for 2007/08 continued to obtain their relief under the old rules in *ICTA 1988* as opposed to the rewritten rules in *ITA 2007*. For 2008/09 and 2009/10, only individuals within **50.2**(i) **NON-RESIDENTS** obtained their relief under the old rules; for 2010/11 onwards, such individuals are no longer entitled to relief.

For 2008/09 onwards, an individual who claims the remittance basis loses any entitlement he may have to these reliefs (see **61.7 REMITTANCE BASIS**).

Payments to trade unions

Relief is available (on a claim) for any part of a payment by an individual to a trade union (as defined) as is attributable to the provision of superannuation, life insurance or funeral benefits. The relief is given as a deduction in calculating net income (see Step 2 at **1.7 ALLOWANCES AND TAX RATES**). The deduction is restricted to one-half of the aggregate part of any such payments in the tax year as is so attributable, and the maximum amount deductible for any tax year is £100. [*ITA 2007, s 457, Sch 1 para 36(5); ICTA 1988, s 266(7); FA 2009, Sch 1 paras 3(6), 7*].

Payments to police organisations

Relief is available (on a claim) for any part of a payment by an individual to a police organisation (as defined) as is attributable to the provision of superannuation, life insurance or funeral benefits. The relief is available only if the sum of the parts so attributable in any tax year is at least £20. Otherwise, the relief works in the same way (and the deduction is subject to an identical maximum) as the relief under *ITA 2007, s 457* above. [*ITA 2007, s 458, Sch 1 para 36(5); ICTA 1988, s 266(7); FA 2009, Sch 1 paras 3(6), 7*].

Payments for benefit of family members

An individual is entitled (on a claim) to a tax reduction (see Step 6 at **1.7** ALLOWANCES AND TAX RATES) if he pays a sum (or has a sum deducted from his earnings) under an *Act* or under the terms and conditions of his employment and it is for the purpose of:

- securing a deferred annuity after his death for the individual's surviving spouse or civil partner; or
- making provision after his death for the individual's children.

The amount of the tax reduction is equal to tax at the basic rate on the total of all such sums paid (or deducted) in the tax year, except that the maximum reduction for any tax year is equal to tax at the basic rate on £100. The order in which tax reductions are given against an individual's tax liability is set out at **1.8** ALLOWANCES AND TAX RATES, which also makes clear that a tax reduction must be restricted to the extent (if any) that it would otherwise exceed the individual's remaining income tax liability after making all prior reductions.

[*ITA 2007, s 459, Sch 1 para 37; ICTA 1988, s 273; FA 2009, Sch 1 paras 2, 7*].

Life assurance gains

[44.3] Income tax is charged on gains treated as arising from those policies and contracts set out in **44.4** below. A gain from a policy or contract (a '*chargeable event gain*') arises when a chargeable event occurs in relation to the policy or contract — see **44.5** below. Tax is charged on the amount of the gains arising in the tax year. See **44.11** below as to the time at which a gain arises on a *partial* surrender or partial assignment.

An individual is liable for income tax on a chargeable event gain if he is UK resident in the tax year in which the gain arises and one of the following conditions is met:

- the individual beneficially owns the rights under the policy or contract in question;
- those rights are held on non-charitable trusts which the individual created; or
- those rights are held as security for a debt of the individual.

[*ITTOIA 2005, ss 461–465*].

Personal representatives of a deceased individual are liable to income tax on a chargeable event gain arising to them (see *ITTOIA 2005, s 466*). As regards liability of trustees, see **44.10** below.

For the determination of liability where two or more persons have an interest in a policy or contract, see *ITTOIA 2005, ss 469–472.*

See **44.6** below as regards computation of the gain and **44.7** below as regards the charge to tax. Top slicing relief (see **44.8** below) may be available to reduce the tax chargeable.

Simon's Taxes. See E1.440 *et seq.*

Policies and contracts within the charge

[44.4] The chargeable event gain rules apply to life assurance policies, contracts for life annuities and capital redemption policies. However, see **44.5** below for the exclusion of certain qualifying policies. The rules do not apply to a policy or contract made before 20 March 1968, unless it is a life insurance policy which has been varied after that date to extend the term or increase the benefits; this does not include a policy where the only variation is in the amount of the premium. Certain special types of policy are also excluded from the rules, namely certain mortgage protection policies, certain policies connected with pension schemes, certain group life policies (as defined) providing protection for loans made to individuals by credit unions and other group life policies meeting specified conditions. [*ITTOIA 2005, ss 473, 478–483, Sch 2 paras 86, 96, 116; ITA 2007, Sch 1 para 533; CTA 2010, Sch 1 para 468*].

Chargeable events

[44.5] Subject to the exclusions and disregards below, there is a chargeable event in relation to any kind of policy or contract within **44.4** above where:

- all rights under it are *surrendered* or *assigned* for money or money's worth;
- a sum is payable under a right to participate in profits, if there are no remaining rights;
- the calculation on a *partial* surrender or *partial* assignment shows a gain (see **44.11** below);
- a transaction-related calculation shows a gain (see **44.11** below); or
- a personal portfolio bond calculation shows a gain (see **44.17** below).

There is also a chargeable event:

- in the case of a life insurance policy, on a *death* giving rise to benefits;
- on the *maturity* of a life insurance or capital redemption policy;
- on a payment on death under a life annuity contract, provided the contract was made after 9 December 1974;
- on the payment of a capital sum under a life annuity contract as a complete alternative to annuity payments or to any further annuity payments.

[*ITTOIA 2005, s 484, Sch 2 para 99*].

Exclusion of certain qualifying policies

In the case of a *qualifying policy* (see **44.29** below), any of the events in (i)–(v) below is a chargeable event only:

(a)   if the policy has been converted into a paid-up policy within ten years of its issue or, if sooner, three-quarters of the term for which it has to run; or

(b)   if a company has an interest in the rights in the policy at the time of the event and the policy was issued after 13 March 1989.

If the policy has been varied to increase the premiums payable, (a) above applies by reference to the date of variation. As regards (b) above, a company has an interest in the rights if a company beneficially owns them, if they are held on trusts created by a company or if they are held as security for a company's debt. A policy is *treated* as issued after 13 March 1989 if it was varied after that date to extend the term or to increase the benefits.

The said events are:

(i)   death or maturity;

(ii)   the surrender or assignment of all rights;

(iii)   a final participation in profits;

(iv)   a partial surrender or assignment where the calculation shows a gain; and

(v)   where a transaction-related calculation in respect of a qualifying policy shows a gain; this applies only in relation to (a) above.

[ITTOIA 2005, s 485(1)–(6), Sch 2 para 107].

Replacement of qualifying policies

Where a qualifying policy is replaced by another qualifying policy as a result of a change in the life or lives insured, the two policies are treated as a single policy issued at the time of the old policy, provided that:

• the amount due on surrender of the old policy is retained by the insurer and applied in satisfaction of premiums due under the new policy;

• no other consideration is received by any person on the replacement of the old policy by the new policy;

• the replacement policy was issued after 24 March 1982.

[ITTOIA 2005, s 542, Sch 2 para 101].

Disregard of certain assignments

An assignment of rights under a policy or contract or a share in such rights is ignored if it is:

• by way of security for a debt;

• on the discharge of a debt secured by the rights or share; or

• between spouses or civil partners living together.

[ITTOIA 2005, s 487].

Pre-26 June 1982 assignments

Where the rights in a policy or contract were assigned before 26 June 1982 for money or money's worth, a subsequent event in respect of that policy or contract is a chargeable event only if, on a date after 23 August 1982.

- the rights have reverted to the original owner; or
- there is a further assignment for money or money's worth (other than between spouses or civil partners or as security for a debt or on the discharge of a debt so secured); or
- there is a payment under the policy or contract by way of premium; or
- loans are taken against security of the policy or contract (but see below).

The last of the above points does not apply if:

- the policy or contract was made before 27 March 1974; or
- the policy is a qualifying policy (see **44.29** below), and either a commercial rate of interest is payable on the loan or it is made to a full-time employee of the insurer to assist in the purchase or improvement of the employee's only or main residence.

[*ITTOIA 2005, Sch 2 para 102*].

Cessation of premium collection on old policies

Where an insurer decides to cease collecting premiums on certain types of policy held for a specified period, and any change to the benefits is limited to a deduction of no more than the premiums forgone, a chargeable event is only treated as occurring in relation to the policy if one would have been treated as occurring had the alteration not occurred. This is dependent upon the policy being at least 20 years old at the time of the change and there being no option under the policy (whether or not previously exercised) for reduction of the premiums to a nominal amount in connection with a right to make partial surrenders after the date of the reduction. [*ITTOIA 2005, ss 488, 489*].

Exclusion of certain accident insurance policies

See HMRC SP 6/92 as regards certain accident insurance policies providing cover against dying as a result of an accident, which are not regarded as life insurance policies for these purposes and therefore cannot give rise to chargeable events. The Statement of Practice applies mainly to group policies, under which a gain might otherwise arise on payment of a death benefit as a result of earlier payments under the policy.

Divorce settlements

The transfer under a Court Order (between spouses as part of a divorce settlement) of the rights conferred by a life policy etc. is not regarded as being for money or money's worth, and thus no chargeable event can arise (Revenue Tax Bulletin December 2003 pp 1071–1073).

Computation of chargeable event gain

[44.6] Subject to the disregards below, the amount of the chargeable event gain is given by the formula TB − (TD + PG) where:

TB is the 'total benefit value' of the policy or contract;
TD is the total allowable deductions; in broad terms, the premiums paid; and

PG is the total amount of gains treated as arising on previous chargeable events (if any) in relation to the policy (including any 'related policy') or contract.

A '*related policy*' is one which has been replaced by a new policy by way of an option conferred by the old policy.

The '*total benefit value*' of the policy or contract is the aggregate of:

(a) the value of the policy or contract;

(b) any capital sum paid under the policy or contract before the event;

(c) the value of any other capital benefit conferred by the policy before the event;

(d) any loan made before the event which was treated as a surrender of part of the rights;

(e) in the case of guaranteed income bonds (see **44.15** below), any amount paid before the event which was treated as a surrender of part of the rights; and

(f) in the case of an assignment, the amount or value of any share in the rights assigned before the event.

For the purposes of (b)–(f) above, any 'related policy' (as above) must be taken into account.

The value of a policy or contract

The value of a policy or contract (see (a) above) is determined as follows.

• In the case of a life insurance policy, the value on a death is the surrender value immediately before death.

• In the case of an assignment of all the rights under a policy, the value of the policy is the amount or value of the consideration received. But if the assignment is between CONNECTED PERSONS (**21**), the value is the market value of the policy or contract.

• In the case of a final surrender payment under a guaranteed income bond (see **44.15** below), the value is the amount of the surrender payment.

• In any other case, the value is the total of:

(i) any sum payable because of the event; and

(ii) in the case of a life insurance policy or capital redemption policy, the amount or value of any other benefits arising because of the event including the capital value of any periodic payments arising because of the event.

[*ITTOIA 2005, ss 491–494*].

Disregards in computing gain

A non-monetary benefit not exceeding £30 in value provided by an insurance company as an inducement to take out a policy or contract is ignored for the purposes of calculating any chargeable event gain.

In computing total benefit value, any sum paid or benefit conferred under a policy is ignored for the purposes of (b) and (c) above if it is attributable to a person's disability. For the purposes of (f) above, where a share in the rights under the policy or contract was assigned by way of gift in an 'insurance year' (see **44.11** below) beginning before 6 April 2001, the value of the share assigned is ignored.

Where a qualifying policy has been replaced, such that *ITTOIA 2005, s 542* applies (see **44.5** above) the premium paid by the insurer on the replacement is ignored in calculating both the total benefit value and the total allowable deductions.

[*ITTOIA 2005, ss 495, 497*].

Whilst not strictly a disregard, any receipt which is taken into account in calculating an amount chargeable to income tax under some other statutory tax provision or chargeable to corporation tax is deductible from the amount of the chargeable event gain. [*ITTOIA 2005, s 527*].

Deductions reduced by commission

For policies taken out on or after 21 March 2007, the amount of premiums deductible in computing most types of chargeable event gain (but not one arising from a death) is reduced by the amount of any commission attributable to those premiums that has effectively been returned to the policyholder or reinvested for his benefit; the intention is to restrict the deduction to the true cost of the policy to the policyholder. This only applies if the premiums paid exceed £100,000 in the tax year in which the chargeable event occurs or in any of the three preceding tax years. There is, however, a rule to prevent this condition being circumvented by the taking out of multiple policies. These rules also apply to a pre-21 March 2007 policy if its terms are varied or a right is exercised, so as to increase benefits, on or after that date. [*ITTOIA 2005, ss 541A, 541B; FA 2007, s 29(3)(4)*].

The charge to tax

[44.7] Income tax is charged on the amount of the chargeable event gains arising in the tax year. See **44.11** below as to the time at which a gain arises on a *partial* surrender or partial assignment.

A chargeable event gain is designated as savings income (see **1.6 ALLOWANCES AND TAX RATES**). The gain forms part of an individual's total income. If an individual falls to be treated as having paid tax at the basic rate (or, before 2008/09, the savings rate) on the amount charged (see below), the amount charged is treated as the highest part of his total income.

[*ITTOIA 2005, ss 465(5), 465A; ITA 2007, Sch 1 para 529; FA 2008, Sch 1 para 51*].

Notional tax credit

Subject to the exceptions below, individuals and trustees are treated as having paid income tax at the applicable rate on a chargeable event gain. The tax treated as paid is usually referred to as the '*notional tax credit*'. The applicable rate for 2008/09 onwards is the basic rate; previously it was the savings rate. The notional tax credit is not in any circumstances repayable. If the chargeable event gain is reduced by any deductions at Step 2 or 3 of the calculation of income tax liability at **1.7 ALLOWANCES AND TAX RATES**, the notional tax credit is computed by reference to the reduced amount.

[*ITTOIA 2005, s 530; ITA 2007, Sch 1 para 535; FA 2008, Sch 1 para 54*].

If the taxpayer is not liable to income tax on his total income at any rate above the basic rate, he will thus pay no tax on the chargeable event gain. If the gain falls to be charged at the higher rate (or additional rate), then, subject to possible top slicing relief at **44.8** below, he will be liable on the gain at the excess of the higher rate (or additional rate) over the basic rate.

Exceptions

A gain arising on the following types of policy or contract does not carry a notional tax credit:

(i)   a foreign policy of life insurance issued by a non-UK resident company (see **44.20** below and note the exceptions therein);

(ii) a foreign capital redemption policy (see **44.20** below);

(iii) a life insurance policy or contract for a life annuity issued by a friendly society in the course of exempt life or endowment business (see **44.22** below);

(iv) a contract for a life annuity which has at any time not formed part of any insurance company's or friendly society's basic life assurance and general annuity business the income and gains of which are subject to corporation tax, unless:

- the contract was made before 27 March 1974; or
- it was made in an accounting period of the insurer beginning before 1 January 1992; or
- it was an immediate needs annuity contract made before 1 January 2005.

For the sole purpose of calculating top slicing relief at **44.8** below, such gains are, however, treated as if they carried a notional tax credit.

[*ITTOIA 2005, s 531, Sch 2 paras 98, 109, 118*].

Top slicing relief

[44.8] Top slicing relief is a means by which the tax on a chargeable event gain may be reduced in the case of an individual. No claim is necessary for the relief to be given. It is only likely to be of benefit where the gain straddles the basic rate limit, such that it is partly chargeable at the higher rate, or straddles the higher rate limit, such that it is partly chargeable at the additional rate. The relief is given as a tax reduction (at Step 6 of the calculation of income tax liability at **1.7 ALLOWANCES AND TAX RATES**) or as a tax repayment.

Top slicing relief is computed as follows.

(a)   Find the '*annual equivalent*' of the chargeable event gain by dividing the amount of the gain by (normally but see below) the number of *complete* years for which the policy or contract has run before the chargeable event.

(b)   Compute the tax payable on the annual equivalent on the assumptions that the chargeable event gain is limited to that amount and that it forms the highest part of the individual's total income for the tax year. Deduct from it tax at the applicable rate (see **44.7** above) on the annual equivalent.

(c)   Multiply the amount given by (b) above by the number of years in (a) above.

(d)   Compute the individual's tax liability on the chargeable event gain as if no top slicing relief applied and on the assumption that the gain forms the highest part of the individual's total income for the tax year. This liability will be net of tax at the applicable rate (see **44.7** above) on the gain.

(e)   If the amount given by (d) above exceeds the amount given by (c) above, the difference is the amount of top slicing relief due. If there is no such excess, no top slicing relief is due.

In computing the tax liability in (b) and (d) above, ignore any lease premiums (as in **60.16 PROPERTY INCOME**) and any termination payments or benefits taxable as in **20.5 COMPENSATION FOR LOSS OF EMPLOYMENT**. See also **16.16** and **16.21 CHARITIES** (relief under Gift Aid and relief for gifts of property to charities to be ignored when computing top slicing relief).

If there is more than one chargeable event gain for the tax year, the above calculation is modified. The computation in (b) above is made by reference to the total of the annual equivalents in (a) above. Instead of applying (c) above, multiply the amount given by (b) by the total chargeable event gains and divide the result by the total of the annual equivalents. Then proceed with (d) and (e) as above.

Computing the annual equivalent

As stated in (a) above, the annual equivalent of the chargeable event gain is normally found by dividing the amount of the gain by the number of complete years for which the policy or contract has run before the chargeable event. If, however, there has been a previous chargeable event in respect of the policy or contract (except in relation to a foreign insurance policy or a foreign capital redemption policy), the amount of the gain is instead divided by the number of complete years since the previous event. (For this purpose, a partial surrender or partial assignment is deemed to take place at the end of the 'insurance year' (see **44.11** below) in question.) If this is not the case but the current policy is a life insurance policy which has replaced an earlier related one, the amount of the gain is divided by the number of complete years since the date the original policy was first replaced. See **44.20** below as regards foreign insurance policies and foreign capital redemption policies.

[*ITTOIA 2005, ss 535–537; ITA 2007, Sch 1 para 536; FA 2008, Sch 1 paras 55–57, 65*].

Example

[44.9]

A single policyholder realises, in 2010/11, a gain of £2,600 on a non-qualifying policy which she surrenders after 2½ years. Her other income for 2010/11 comprises employment income of £38,900 and dividends amounting to £3,895 (inclusive of tax credits).

The tax chargeable on the gain is calculated as follows.

	Normal basis	With top slicing re-lief
	£	£
Policy gain	2,600	1,300
Earnings	38,900	38,900
Dividends	3,895	3,895
	45,395	44,095
Personal allowance	6,475	6,475
	£38,920	£37,620

Tax applicable to policy gain
Higher rate

		£		£
£1,520 at 40%		608.00		—
£220 at 40%				88.00
		608.00		88.00

Deduct
Basic rate

		£		£
£1,520 at 20%		304.00		—
£220 at 20%				44.00
				£44.00

Appropriate multiple 2 × £44.00   £88.00

Tax chargeable lower of £304.00   &   £88.00

top slicing relief (£304.00 − £88.00) = £216.00

Tax payable is therefore as follows.

		£
32,425	@ 20% (basic rate)	6,485.00
3,895	@ 10% (dividend ordinary rate)	389.50
1,080	@ 20% (policy gain at basic rate)	216.00
37,400		
1,520	@ 40% (policy gain at higher rate)	608.00
£38,920		
		7,698.50
	Deduct: Top slicing relief (as above)	216.00
		7,482.50

De-duct:			
	Tax credits on dividends (£3,895 @ 10%)	389.50	
	Basic rate of tax on policy gain (£2,600 @ 20%)	520.00	909.50
	Tax liability (subject to PAYE deductions)		£6,573.00

Gains arising to trustees

[44.10] Trustees are liable for tax on chargeable event gains if, immediately before the chargeable event occurs, they are UK resident and any of the conditions below are met. Where the trustees are liable, the gain is treated for income tax purposes as their income. The conditions are that the rights under the policy or contract:

- are held by the trustees on charitable trusts;
- are held by the trustees on non-charitable trusts and one or more of the absent settlor conditions (see below) is met;
- are held by the trustees on non-charitable trusts, none of the absent settlor conditions (see below) is met and no individual or personal representatives are chargeable; or
- are held as security for a debt owed by the trustees.

The third condition does not apply if the policy was effected before 9 April 2003, it was not varied on or after that date so as to increase benefits or extend the term and none of the rights were assigned to non-charitable trusts on or after that date.

The absent settlor conditions are that the person who created the trusts:

- is non-UK resident;
- has died; or
- in the case of a company or foreign institution (as defined in *ITTOIA 2005, s 468* below), has been dissolved or wound up or has otherwise come to an end.

If a chargeable event gain arises to a non-charitable trust and none of the absent settlor conditions is met, a UK resident individual settlor may be liable to income tax on the gain as if it had arisen to him (see **44.3** above).

Rates at which tax charged

For charitable trusts, chargeable event gains are charged at the basic rate of tax for 2008/09 onwards; previously they were charged at the savings rate. Due to the availability of the notional tax credit at **44.7** above, no further tax is payable. (The charge does not apply, however, if the trusts were created before 17 March 1998, the policy was issued before that date (and not varied on or after that date so as to increase benefits or extend the term) and at least one settlor died before that date.)

For non-charitable trusts, gains are chargeable at the trust rate — see **68.12** SETTLEMENTS, but the notional tax credit remains available.

[*ITTOIA 2005, s 467, Sch 2 paras 112, 114; FA 2006, Sch 7 para 7, Sch 13 para 32(3)(4); ITA 2007, Sch 1 para 531; FA 2008, Sch 1 paras 53, 65*].

Recovery of tax paid from trustees

Where an individual is charged to tax on a chargeable event gain realised by a non-charitable trust (see **44.3** above), he is entitled to recover the amount of the tax charged (as reduced by top slicing relief) from the trustees. The amount recoverable cannot exceed the amount of any sums or benefits received by the trustees from the event giving rise to the gain. The individual may require an officer of HMRC to certify the amount recoverable; such a certificate is conclusive evidence of the amount. [*ITTOIA 2005, s 538*].

Bare trusts for minors

If a gain arises to a bare trust for a minor, HMRC's long-standing view was that the settlor was liable. Following legal advice, HMRC changed their opinion with effect for 2007/08 onwards and now regard the minor himself as the person chargeable. Where, however, either or both of the child's parents are the settlors of the bare trust (see **68.7 SETTLEMENTS**), the children's settlements rules at **68.30 SETTLEMENTS** continue to apply as before in these circumstances so that the parent is potentially the person chargeable. (HMRC Brief 51/08, 8 October 2008).

Non-resident trustees and foreign institutions

A chargeable event gain is taken into account under the 'transfer of asset abroad' rules at **4.14–4.17 ANTI-AVOIDANCE** (as modified for this purpose) if:

- it arises to trustees who are not resident in the UK but would be liable if they were so resident;
- immediately before the chargeable event: a share in the rights is owned by a foreign institution (i.e. a company or other institution resident or domiciled outside the UK) or the rights are held for the purposes of a foreign institution or a share in the rights is held as security for a debt of a foreign institution.

[*ITTOIA 2005, s 468; ITA 2007, Sch 1 para 532*].

Partial surrenders and partial assignments

[**44.11**] The following rules apply if a part of, or a share in, the rights under a policy or contract within the charging rules is surrendered or is assigned for money or money's worth. A calculation must be made as at the end of the 'insurance year' in which the surrender or assignment occurs, in order to determine whether a gain has arisen and, if so, the amount of the gain. Any such gain is generally treated as arising at the end of the insurance year and is thus chargeable to income for the tax year in which the insurance year ends (but see below under both Transaction-related calculations). No chargeable event occurs as a result of a gain arising under the above calculation if the insurance year is the final insurance year (which may actually consist of a period shorter or greater than one year — see below), but receipts from a partial surrender will fall to be taken into account under **44.6** above in computing a gain on the termination chargeable event that brings the final insurance year to an end.

See **44.5**(iv) above for the exclusion of certain qualifying policies from these rules. Partial surrenders or assignments are sometimes treated as occurring where they would not otherwise do so — see **44.14** below.

Insurance year

An *'insurance year'* is any period of twelve months beginning on the commencement date of the policy or contract or an anniversary of that date. The termination of a policy or contract (by death, maturity or total surrender etc.) brings the then current insurance year to an end. If two insurance years consequently end in a single tax year, they are aggregated and treated as one insurance year.

Computation

The chargeable event gain on a partial surrender or partial assignment is equal to the excess (if any) of the 'net total value of rights surrendered or assigned' over the 'net total allowable payments'. See also the Example at **44.12** below.

The *'net total value of rights surrendered or assigned'* is the total value of all surrenders and assignments of the policy since its commencement, less the total of such values which have been brought into account on earlier chargeable events. Surrenders or assignments are left out of this total if they occurred in an insurance year prior to the first such year falling wholly after 13 March 1975. Assignments are generally included only if made for money or money's worth, but assignments made otherwise than for money or money's worth are included if made in an insurance year beginning before 6 April 2001. The value of a partial surrender is normally the amount or value of the sum payable or other benefits arising because of the surrender. If, however, the surrender is a loan (see **44.14** below), the value is the amount of the loan. The value of a partial assignment is the surrender value of the part or share assigned as at the time of the assignment.

The *'net total allowable payments'* is the total of annual fractions of one-twentieth of the premiums paid since the policy commenced, less the total of such fractions which have been brought into account on earlier chargeable events. Annual fractions are left out of this total if they occurred in an insurance year prior to the first such year falling wholly after 13 March 1975. The total number of twentieths included in the total cannot exceed 20.

Transaction-related calculations

Special rules apply if the above computation produces a gain but, during the insurance year:

- there has been an assignment for money or money's worth of part of, or a share in, the rights conferred by the policy or contract; or
- there has been a surrender of part of, or a share in, the rights and a subsequent assignment, otherwise than for money or money's worth, of the whole or part of, or a share in, those rights.

In these cases, special calculations have to be made separately for each such event during the insurance year in accordance with *ITTOIA 2005, ss 510–512.* The main purpose of these calculations is to determine how much of the premiums can be set against the value of each transaction. The intention is that liability to tax should attach to the person who profits from the transaction, regardless of the change in ownership of the rights in the policy or contract. See **44.5**(v) above for the exclusion of certain qualifying policies from these rules.

The general rule above that the gain is treated as arising on the occurrence of a chargeable event at the end of the insurance year does not apply. If the special calculations show that a transaction resulted in a gain, the transaction is treated as a chargeable event. That chargeable event gain is deemed to arise at the date of the transaction, but is brought into charge for the tax year in which the insurance year ends. If the transaction occurs in the final insurance year, the chargeable event is treated as occurring before the chargeable event that ends that insurance year; there are also rules in *ITTOIA 2005, s 513* to limit the chargeable event gain.

[*ITTOIA 2005, ss 498, 499, 507–514, Sch 2 paras 88, 100, 105*].

Example

[44.12]

Yasmina took out a policy on 4 February 2003 for a single premium of £15,000. The contract permits periodical withdrawals.

(i)   Yasmina draws £750 p.a. on 4 February in each subsequent year. There is no taxable gain because at the end of each insurance year the total value of rights surrendered (VRS) does not exceed the total allowable payments (TAP).

	£	
At 3.2.07 withdrawals have been	2,250	(VRS)
Deduct 4 × ¹⁄₂₀ of the sums paid in	3,000	(TAP)
	No gain	

(ii)   On 20.7.07 Yasmina withdrew an additional £3,500.

	£	
At 3.2.08 withdrawals have been	6,500	(VRS)
Deduct 5 × ¹⁄₂₀ of the sums paid in	3,750	(TAP)
Chargeable 2007/08	£2,750	

(iii)   Yasmina made no annual withdrawal on 4.2.08 but on 4.2.09 made a withdrawal of £1,000.

In the year 2009/10 the position is:

	£	£	
At 3.2.10 withdrawals have been		7,500	
Deduct Withdrawals at last charge		6,500	
		1,000	(VRS)
Deduct 7 × ¹/₂₀ of the sums paid in	5,250		
less amount deducted at last charge	3,750		
		1,500	(TAP)
		No gain	

(iv) Yasmina surrendered the policy on 1.7.10 for £13,250, having made a further £1,000 withdrawal on 4.2.10.

In the year 2009/10, the position is:

		£	£
Proceeds on surrender			13,250
Previous withdrawals			8,500
			21,750
De-duct:	Premium paid	15,000	
	Gains previously charged	2,750	
			17,750
Chargeable 2010/11			£4,000

Notes

(a) The gain on final surrender of the policy is calculated under *ITTOIA 2005, s 491* (see **44.6** above).

(b) The gains in (ii) and (iv) above are subject to any available top slicing relief (see **44.8** above).

Deficiency relief

[44.13] Relief is given (on a claim) to higher rate taxpayers for a deficiency arising on termination of a policy or contract (by death, maturity, total surrender or assignment etc.). The relief is known as '*deficiency relief*'. Deficiency relief is limited to the excess of higher rate tax or dividend upper rate tax over basic rate tax (or, before 2008/09, savings rate tax) or dividend ordinary rate tax on the amount of the deficiency. The computation is illustrated by means of a series of Steps at *ITA 2007, s 539(5)*, and see also Change 3 in Annex 1 to the Explanatory Notes to *ITA 2007* and HMRC Tax Bulletin April 2006 pp 1286–1288. The relief is given by means of a tax reduction at Step 6 of the calculation of income tax liability at **1.7 ALLOWANCES AND TAX RATES**. (Different rules apply to deficiencies on life annuity contracts made in an accounting period of the insurance company etc. beginning before 1 January 1992 — see *ITTOIA 2005, Sch 2 para 109(4)*.)

With the introduction of the additional rate of tax and the dividend additional rate for 2010/11 onwards (see **1.3 ALLOWANCES AND TAX RATES**), it should be noted that deficiency relief remains limited to the excess mentioned above. There are no plans to extend the relief to the additional rates of tax (Budget Report 22 June 2010 p 51).

A deficiency is treated as arising from a policy or contract on a chargeable event if the termination chargeable event was preceded by one or more chargeable events on which gains accrued and no gain accrues on the termination chargeable event. If, in the calculation in **44.6** above for the termination event, the total allowable deductions equal or exceed the total benefit value, the amount of the deficiency is equal to the total previous gains. If the total benefit value exceeds the total allowable deductions, the amount of the deficiency is equal to the total previous gains less that excess.

For policies effected after 2 March 2004, the deficiency cannot exceed the aggregate amount of earlier gains on the policy that formed part of the same individual's total income for tax purposes for previous tax years; this applies equally where a policy was effected on or before 2 March 2004 but after that date is varied so as to increase the benefits (an exercise of rights conferred by the policy being treated for this purpose as a variation), assigned (in whole or in part) or becomes held as security for a debt.

[*ITTOIA 2005, ss 539–541, Sch 2 para 117; ITA 2007, Sch 1 paras 539; FA 2008, Sch 1 paras 58, 65*].

In *Mayes v HMRC* Ch D 2009, [2010] STC 1, relief for a deficiency supposedly arising from a complex marketed avoidance scheme was allowed (but this preceded current law).

Events treated as partial surrenders or assignments

[44.14] The following events are treated as partial surrenders for the purposes of **44.11** above:

(a) the falling due of a sum payable as a result of a right under a policy or contract to participate in profits where further rights remain under it;

(b) in the case of a contract for a life annuity which provides for a capital sum to be taken as an alternative in part to the annuity payments, taking the capital sum;

(c) the making of a loan as outlined below;

(d) the making of certain payments under guaranteed income bonds (see **44.15** below).

Loans

Subject to the exclusions below, (c) above applies to a loan made by the insurer under a policy or contract to an individual or trustees who would be liable to tax if a chargeable event gain were to arise on that policy or contract. A loan is treated as made by an insurer if it is made by arrangement with the insurer, and a loan is treated as made to a person if it is made at that person's direction. Policies or contracts made before 27 March 1974 are excluded. For policies or contracts made before 9 April 2003, loans to trustees are excluded.

These provisions do not apply to a loan made under a contract for a life annuity if all the interest on the loan is eligible for tax relief as in **43.12 INTEREST PAYABLE**. If part of the interest is eligible for tax relief, these provisions apply only to the part of the loan carrying interest which is not eligible.

These provisions do not apply if the policy is a qualifying policy (see **44.29** below) and:

- interest is payable on the loan at a commercial rate; and/or
- the loan was made before 6 April 2000 to a full-time employee of the body issuing the policy to assist the employee in purchasing or improving a dwelling to be used as his only or main residence.

Partial assignments on co-ownership transactions

Where, as a result of any transaction:

- the whole or part of (or a share in) the rights conferred by a policy or contract (the '*ownership interest*') becomes beneficially owned by one person or by two or more persons jointly or in common (the '*new ownership*');
- immediately before that transaction the ownership interest was in the beneficial ownership of one person or two or more persons jointly (the '*old ownership*'); and
- at least one person is common to both the old and the new ownership;

the transaction is treated as having been the assignment by each of the old owners of so much (if any) of his old share as exceeds his new share (if any). The old and new shares in cases of joint ownership are treated as having been equal shares. These provisions generally do not apply in relation to transactions that took place in an insurance year beginning before 6 April 2001.

[*ITTOIA 2005, ss 500–503, 505, 506, Sch 2 paras 87, 97, 115; FA 2008, Sch 14 paras 14, 18*].

Guaranteed income bonds

[44.15] A guaranteed income bond is a life assurance contract within *Financial Services and Markets Act 2000 (Regulated Activities) Order 2001 (SI 2001 No 544), Sch 1 Pt II para 1 or 3* which is neither an annuity contract nor a contract effected in the course of a company's pension business. Such a bond is designed to provide an income each year with a lump sum on maturity. A payment under a guaranteed income bond which would otherwise be treated as interest or an annual payment is not so treated but is instead treated as a partial surrender as in **44.11** above. However, this treatment does *not* apply to a payment if:

- it is a payment under provisions in the policy which, if taken alone, would constitute a different kind of policy, e.g. a permanent health policy; or
- it is interest on a late payment under the policy.

If a payment under the bond comprises the whole of the final benefit due under the policy (disregarding any interest on late payments) and would otherwise be treated as interest or an annual payment, it is not so treated but is instead treated as a surrender of all the rights under the contract.

[ITTOIA 2005, ss 490, 500(d), 504].

Information requirements

[44.16] To assist policyholders in completing their self-assessment tax returns, insurers must issue them with a certificate in relation to a chargeable event gain. In certain circumstances insurers must send a similar certificate to HMRC. In each case the certificate must normally show *inter alia* the amount of the gain, the number of years for computing top slicing relief and the notional tax credit (where available). [*ICTA 1988, ss 552, 552ZA; FA 2007, s 29(2); FA 2008, Sch 1 paras 43, 65, Sch 14 paras 4, 5*].

As regards non-UK resident policy holders, see HMRC ESC C33, Part 2. For the requirement for most overseas insurers (as widely defined) to nominate a UK tax representative responsible for providing such information, see *ICTA 1988, ss 552A, 552B* and regulations thereunder.

Personal portfolio bonds

[44.17] A 'personal portfolio bond' generally enables the holder to nominate a portfolio of investments on which the interest and capital gains are deferred until the bond matures. The legislation counters this deferral by imposing an annual income tax charge in addition to any other charge under the life assurance gains provisions.

A *'personal portfolio bond'* is a life assurance policy, life annuity contract or capital redemption policy which meets both the following conditions.

(a) Under the terms of the policy or contract, some or all of the benefits are determined by reference to:
  - fluctuations in, or in an index of, the value of property of any description; or
  - the value of, or the income from, property of any description.
  It does not matter whether or not the index or property is specified in the policy or contract.
(b) The terms of the policy or contract permit the policy holder to select the index or some or all of the property. This condition is extended to also include persons connected with the policy holder, persons acting on his behalf etc.

There are, however, exclusions where the only property or index which may be selected is of a description contained in *ITTOIA 2005, ss 517–521*.

The annual charge operates by applying, at the end of each 'insurance year' (as defined in **44.11** above) other than the final insurance year, the formula (PP + TPE − TSG) x 15%, where:

PP is the total amount of premiums paid up to the end of the insurance year in relation to that year;
TPE is the total amount of personal portfolio bond excesses (see below); and
TSG is the total amount of partial surrender gains (see below).

TPE is found by applying the same formula as above for each previous insurance year for which the policy has been in existence, starting with the first year, and aggregating the results. Any years when the policy was not a personal portfolio bond are nevertheless included in the calculation. If there is no previous insurance year, TPE is zero.

TSG is the aggregate of all previous chargeable event gains (if any) computed as in **44.11** above but ignoring any partial assignments.

If the policy is a personal portfolio bond at the end of an insurance year, the amount arrived at by applying the above formula is a chargeable event gain deemed to arise at the end of that insurance year. It will this be chargeable to income tax in the tax year in which that insurance year ends. No top slicing relief is available.

[*ITTOIA 2005, ss 515–526, 535(6); ITA 2007, Sch 1 para 534; CTA 2010, Sch 1 para 469*].

See HMRC Insurance Policyholder Taxation Manual IPTM7700 *et seq.*

Offshore policies

[44.18] A policy issued in respect of an insurance made after 17 November 1983 by a company resident outside the UK (a '*new non-resident policy*') will not be a qualifying policy under *ICTA 1988, Sch 15 Pt II* (see **44.29** below) until either:

(a)   the premiums are payable to, and are business receipts of, a UK branch/permanent establishment of the issuing company and the company is lawfully carrying on life assurance business in the UK; or

(b)   the policy holder is a UK resident and a portion of the issuing company's income from the investments of its life assurance fund is charged to corporation tax.

[*ICTA 1988, Sch 15 para 24*].

As regards chargeable events, special provisions apply to life assurance policies with non-UK residents. If, immediately before the happening of the event, they form part of the overseas life assurance business of an insurance company or friendly society, they are not treated as qualifying policies in relation to that event. The gains are fully chargeable to income tax as in **44.20** below, without the benefit of a notional tax credit.

[*ITTOIA 2005, ss 474(5), 476(3), 531(3)(b)*].

Similar treatment applies to foreign capital redemption policies with a non-UK policy holder (i.e. a capital redemption policy which forms part of the overseas life assurance business of an insurance company). [*ITTOIA 2005, ss 476(3), 531(3)(d)*].

Simon's Taxes. See B8.658, B8.666, E1.441, E1.443, E1.1340.

Substitution of policies

[44.19] Where one policy is substituted for another and the old policy was a new non-resident policy (as in 44.18 above) but the new policy is not, the rules in *ICTA 1988, Sch 15 paras 17–20* (see 44.35(d) below) are modified as follows.

(a)   If the old policy and any related policy (any preceding policy in a chain of substituted policies) would have been, or, where certification was required, would have been capable of being, a qualifying policy were it not for the new non-resident policy rules, then it is assumed to have been a qualifying policy for the purposes of *ICTA 1988, Sch 15 para 17(2)*.

(b)   If the new policy would otherwise be, or, where certification is still required, be capable of being, a qualifying policy, it will nevertheless not qualify unless the circumstances are those specified in *ICTA 1988, Sch 15 para 17(3)* (regarding residence, benefits, the issuing company etc.).

(c)   The company issuing the new policy must certify that the old policy for which it is substituted was issued by a company outside the UK with whom they have arrangements for issuing substitute policies to persons coming to the UK.

The modification in (c) above also applied where the old policy was a qualifying policy issued on or before 17 November 1983 which would have been a non-qualifying new non-resident policy if issued after that date while the new policy is issued after that date and is not a new non-resident policy.

If the new policy confers an option to have another policy substituted for it or to have any of its terms changed and thereby falls within *ICTA 1988, Sch 15 para 19(3)* it is to be treated for the purposes of that sub-paragraph as having been issued in respect of an insurance made on the same day as the old policy. [*ICTA 1988, Sch 15 paras 25, 26*].

Tax on chargeable events

[44.20] Gains from foreign policies of life insurance issued by a non-UK resident company are fully chargeable to income tax without the benefit of a notional tax credit. This denial of notional tax credit does not apply if the conditions in (a) or (b) in 44.18 above are fulfilled at all times between the date of issue and the date of the gain, or to gains on certain policies issued by non-UK resident companies within the charge to tax in a territory within the European Economic Area. Similarly, no notional tax credit is available on gains from foreign capital redemption policies, i.e. capital redemption policies issued by non-UK resident companies. [*ITTOIA 2005, ss 474(4), 476(3), 531, 532, Sch 2 paras 103, 104, 111, 113*].

There is special provision in respect of foreign policies of life insurance or capital redemption where the policy holder is non-UK resident (see 44.18 above with regard to notional tax credit in relation to these policies). Except as below, the gain which would be chargeable is reduced by multiplying it by the fraction of which the denominator is the number of days for which the policy (and any preceding related policy) has run before the chargeable event and the numerator is the number of those days when the policy holder was UK resident. No reduction is, however, made where, at any time during the life of the policy, it was held either:

(a) by a trustee resident outside the UK, or by two or more trustees any of whom was so resident, *unless* the policy was issued in respect of an insurance made on or before 19 March 1985 *and* it was on that date held by a trustee resident outside the UK or by two or more trustees any of whom was so resident, or

(b) by a '*foreign institution*' (i.e. a company or other institution of non-UK residence or domicile) *unless* the policy was issued in respect of an insurance made on or before 16 March 1998 *and* it was on that date held by a foreign institution.

The gain thus reduced is chargeable to tax in full (see above) but any top slicing relief due (see **44.8** above) is computed as if the notional tax credit were available.

[*ITTOIA 2005, ss 528, 529, 531(1), Sch 2 para 106, 110*].

The figure for the number of years in the top slicing relief calculation at **44.8** above is altered for these purposes to the number of complete years the policy has run before the chargeable event less any complete years in which the policy holder was not resident in the UK. [*ITTOIA 2005, s 536(7)(8)*]. The provisions of *ITTOIA 2005, s 536(2)* regarding the operation of top slicing relief when there is more than one chargeable event do not apply to foreign life assurance or capital redemption policies. [*ITTOIA 2005, s 536(6)*].

Where there is a substitution of policies within **44.19** above and the new policy is a qualifying policy there is no chargeable event on the surrender of rights under the old policy and the new policy is treated as having been issued in respect of an insurance made on the same day as the old policy. [*ITTOIA 2005, ss 485(7), 543*].

If at any time a previously qualifying new non-resident policy ceases to fulfil the conditions of either (a) or (b) in **44.18** above it is brought within the chargeable events legislation from that time onwards. [*ITTOIA 2005, s 474(4)*].

Friendly Society policies

Qualifying policies

[44.21] The proceeds from a qualifying policy with a friendly society are generally free of any income tax charge. Pre-14 March 1984 policies attract income tax relief on the premiums paid (as in **44.24** below).

Except as below, all policies issued by friendly societies before 19 March 1985 in the course of tax exempt life or endowment business are qualifying policies. [*ICTA 1988, Sch 15 para 6(1)*]. A policy issued *or varied* after 18 March 1985 in the course of such business is a qualifying policy only if it satisfies the conditions set out in *ICTA 1988, Sch 15 paras 3, 4.*

Certain policies issued under contracts made before 20 March 1991, and expressed at the outset not to be made in the course of tax-exempt life or endowment business, were subsequently determined to have been within the statutory definition of that business. A similar situation arose in relation to certain contracts for qualifying policies assumed, at the outset of the contract, not to be made in the course of tax-exempt life or endowment business (without being expressed either to be or not to be so). By concession, the policy holder is taxed in accordance with the original assumption he will have been given that no charge to tax would arise on the surrender or maturity of the policy. (Revenue Press Release 12 June 1991).

Non-qualifying policies

[44.22] A gain on a chargeable event in respect of a policy which is not a qualifying policy (see **44.21** above), or in respect of certain life annuity contracts, may give rise to a charge to income tax (see **44.4** above). If such a gain arises on a policy issued in the course of a society's tax exempt life or endowment business, it is fully chargeable to income tax, with no notional tax credit but with the availability of top slicing relief (see **44.8** above). [*ITTOIA 2005, s 531(1), (3)(a)*].

Individual limit

[44.23] The total amount of business which a person may have outstanding with registered or incorporated friendly societies is limited as set out below. If a person obtains a policy which causes his contracts to exceed these limits, the policy will not be a qualifying policy (as in **44.21** above), but earlier policies are not thereby disqualified. [*ICTA 1988 Sch 15 para 6(2)*].

Such business is limited to:

- an annuity or annuities totalling not more than £156 p.a. (£416 p.a. where all the contracts were made before 14 March 1984); and
- a gross sum assured under a contract or contracts under which the total premiums payable in any twelve-month period do not exceed any of the following limits:

for all contracts	£270
for contracts made after 24 July 1991 and before 1 May 1995	£200
for contracts made after 31 August 1990 and before 25 July 1991	£150
for contracts made before 1 September 1990	£100

unless all the contracts were made before 1 September 1987. For these purposes, a premium under an annuity contract made before 1 June 1984 by a 'new society' is brought into account as if the contract were for the assurance of a gross sum. For contracts made before 1 September 1987, a limit was imposed by reference to the gross sum(s) assured, the limit being £750 (£2,000 if all the contracts were made before 14 March 1984). Where the premium under a contract made after 31 August 1987 and before 1 May 1995 is increased by a variation after 24 July 1991 and before 1 August 1992 or after 30 April 1995 and before 1 April 1996, the contract is to be treated for these purposes as having been made at the time of the variation.

No account is, however, taken of:

- so much of any premium as relates to exceptional death risk;
- 10% of premiums payable more frequently than annually (which means, for example, that the current £270 limit is effectively £25 per month); and
- £10 of the premiums payable in a twelve-month period under any contract made before 1 September 1987 by a society which is not a 'new society'.

The restrictions on both gross sum and annuity contracts are applied without taking into account any bonus or addition declared upon an assurance or accruing thereon by reference to an increase in the value of any investments. An annuity contract made before 1 June 1984 by a 'new society' is for these purposes treated as providing both the annual sum assured and a gross sum equal to 75% of the premiums which would be payable if the annuity ran its full term or the person died at age 75.

In relation to contracts made after 18 July 2007, any friendly society policy transferred to an insurance company counts towards the above limits. This includes policies which have become insurance company policies because the friendly society converted to a company.

[ICTA 1988, s 464; FA 2007, Sch 12 paras 2, 6].

A 'new society' is a society which either was registered after 3 May 1966 or was registered in the three months before that date but did not carry on any life or endowment business during that period (or a successor incorporated society). [ICTA 1988, s 466(2)].

Life assurance premium relief (obsolescent)

[44.24] Relief for premiums paid on qualifying life assurance policies (see 44.29 below) is available only for insurances made before 14 March 1984 (subject to transitional provisions for certain industrial assurance policies — see 44.35(b) below). Relief ceases for a contract made before 14 March 1984 if the policy is terminated or varied (including the exercise of an option to change the terms of the policy) so as to increase the benefits secured or extend the term of the insurance (disregarding increased benefits in consideration of the cessation of house to house collection of premiums). [ICTA 1988, s 266(3)(c), Sch 14 para 8(3)–(8); ITA 2007, Sch 1 paras 36(2), 232(4)].

Tax relief where applicable is generally given to UK residents (except children under 12), whether they have taxable income or not, by deduction from admissible premiums (see **44.26** below) up to certain limits (see **44.25** below). The deduction is **12¹/₂%**. The deductions will normally be calculated by the life offices etc. (who will recover from HMRC) without a specific claim being required. HMRC may make regulations by statutory instrument to implement this scheme of 'premium relief by deduction'. [*ICTA 1988, s 266(4)(5), Sch 14 para 7; ITA 2007, Sch 1 para 36(3); FA 2009, Sch 1 paras 3(5), 7*]. Under the scheme relief will normally be allowed without the intervention of a tax office and PAYE taxpayers do not require a coding allowance for premiums.

See **57.7** PENSION PROVISION as regards contributions to registered pension schemes which are 'life assurance premium contributions' (as defined).

Simon's Taxes. See **E1.1300, E1.1310, E1.1313.**

Limits on amounts of admissible premiums

[44.25] Relief is not given on premiums to the extent that they exceed:

(a)   **£1,500 or one-sixth of total income**, whichever is the greater. [*ICTA 1988, s 274(1)*]. See also **44.27**(h) below for married persons and civil partners;

(b)   **£100** for policies not securing a capital sum at death. [*ICTA 1988, s 274(2)*].

The restrictions in (a) and (b) are not to take into account any additional 'war insurance premiums'. [*ICTA 1988, s 274(4)*]. Where the limits seem likely to be exceeded by the deductions, HMRC may require some premiums to be paid in full. Any over- or under-deductions in a year will be adjusted by assessment or claim to repayment. [*ICTA 1988, Sch 14 paras 4–6; ITA 2007, Sch 1 para 232(3); FA 2009, Sch 1 paras 5, 7*].

Admissible premiums

[44.26] Subject to the abolition of relief for policies made after 13 March 1984, the relief at **44.24** above is available in respect of life assurance premiums (and payments under contracts for deferred annuities (but see **44.27**(b) below and note limit at **44.25**(b) above)) paid by an individual in respect of policies (or deferred annuities) on either the individual's own life or that of his spouse or civil partner. The insurance or contract must be made by the individual or his spouse or civil partner. Policies effected after 19 March 1968 must be 'qualifying policies', see **44.29** below. [*ICTA 1988, s 266(1)–(3)*].

If, with a view to providing benefits for an employee under an employer-financed retirement benefits scheme (see **57.26** PENSION PROVISION), an employer pays a life assurance premium or makes a payment under a deferred annuity contract, then, with certain exceptions, life assurance premium relief is available to the employee to the extent, if any, that it would have been available if the employee had made the payment himself under a policy or contract of his own. [*ICTA 1988, ss 266A, 595(1)(b); ITEPA 2003, s 386(7)(b)*].

Notes

[44.27] The following should be taken into account.

(a)   Policies as under **44.26** above are only eligible for relief if they secure capital sum at *death* whether or not in conjunction with any other benefit e.g. disability benefit or option to receive an annuity.

(b)   No allowance during period of deferment on '*deferred policies*'. [*ICTA 1988, s 266(3)(a)(d)*].

But neither (a) nor (b) applies to policies (i) in connection with *bona fide* employees' pension schemes as defined or for the benefit of persons engaged in any particular trade, profession, vocation or business, or (ii) taken out by teachers in secondary schools (as so called in 1918) pending setting up of a pension scheme. [*ICTA 1988, s 266(11)*].

(c)   The payments must be made to either (i) insurance company legally established in UK, *or lawfully carrying on business in UK*, (ii) underwriters, (iii) registered or incorporated friendly society, (iv) (deferred annuities) National Debt Commissioners. From 1 December 2001, this was revised to require payments to be made to a person permitted under *Financial Services and Markets Act 2000, Pt 4* or *Sch 3 para 15* to effect or carry out long-term insurance contracts (as defined), or to a member of Lloyd's who effects or carries out such contracts in accordance with *Pt 19* of that Act. [*ICTA 1988, s 266(2)(a)(13); ITA 2007, Sch 1 para 36(7)*]. *Note.* Included under (i) is a policy issued and managed overseas but where the premium is paid to the UK branch of the insurance company (Revenue Press Release 4 February 1981).

(d)   Premiums allowed only so far as *paid* i.e. not covered by advances (*Hunter v A-G* HL 1904, 5 TC 13), nor repayment of advances (*R v Special Commissioners (ex parte Horner)* KB 1932, 17 TC 362). A premium paid otherwise than in the year in which it becomes due and payable is treated as paid in that year. [*ICTA 1988, s 266(4); ITA 2007, Sch 1 para 36(3)*].

Non-residents must pay their premiums in full but will be given relief as appropriate under the rules at **50.2 NON-RESIDENTS**. Premiums to foreign life assurance companies etc. will be payable in full without relief but see Note in (c) above. A member of the armed forces or the spouse or civil partner of such a member is treated as resident in the UK. [*ICTA 1988, s 266(1A)(8)(9), Sch 14 para 6; ITA 2007, Sch 1 paras 36(6), 232(3); FA 2009, Sch 1 paras 3(3)(7), 5, 7*].

(e)   No allowance for joint insurance on two directors' lives (*Wilson v Simpson* KB 1926, 10 TC 753).

(f)   *Accident and Sickness Policies*. Relief allowed only on proportion of premium relative to death benefit.

(g)   *Children's Policies*. Premiums allowable if paid by parent for (i) life endowment on his own life, maturing when school fees begin, or when child may go into business etc., or (ii) for securing series of payments on specified dates if parent dies earlier. But no relief to parent where policy is on life of *child* unless it is an industrial assurance policy or policy issued by a registered or incorporated friendly society on the life of a child or grandchild and the annual premiums do not exceed £64. [*ICTA 1988, Sch 14 paras 2, 3; ITA 2007, Sch 1 para 232(2)*].

Policy by child on own life. HMRC are of the opinion that no relief is in strictness due on premiums on a policy taken out by a child under age twelve, but are prepared to allow relief as follows. An industrial branch policy or friendly society policy as above will receive relief. Where an ordinary branch policy is taken out on the life of a child and is assigned to him or he possesses or acquires the whole interest in the policy, relief on premiums paid by him may be allowed (provided the other conditions are satisfied) where the policy was taken out (a) after the child had attained age twelve; (b) before 1 March 1979 and before the child attained age twelve; or (c) on or after 1 March 1979 before the child attained age twelve and he has attained that age. (HMRC SP 11/79).

(h) *Married persons and civil partners.* Premiums paid by one spouse on the life of the other (in addition to relief on premiums paid on his or her own life) will be eligible for relief to the paying spouse even after divorce, unless the divorce was before 6 April 1979. [*ICTA 1988, Sch 14 para 1(1)*]. This treatment is extended to premiums paid by a divorced person on policies taken out prior to the marriage (HMRC ESC A31). Civil partners are treated in the same way as spouses for these purposes.

The premium relief limits in **44.25** above apply separately and in full to each spouse.

(i) See **44.29** below regarding qualifying policies effected after 19 March 1968.

Clawback of life assurance premium relief

[**44.28**] The following matters are relevant.

(i) **Clawback of relief on early surrender etc. within four years**
There was a 'clawback' of the tax relief given on premiums payable on a qualifying policy (see **44.29** below) issued in respect of an insurance made after 26 March 1974 and before 14 March 1984 (when relief ceased to be available) where within four years:
(a) the policy was wholly or partly surrendered (including certain loans, see **44.14** above); or
(b) there was a sum payable on the policy (other than on death) by way of participation in profits; or
(c) the policy was wholly or partly made paid-up.
The body which issued the policy had to pay the clawback to the Inland Revenue out of the sum falling due at the following rate for 1988/89 and earlier years.

Time of surrender etc.	Clawback of total premiums payable to date	Clawback limit
In year 1 or 2	³/₆ths of 30% i.e. 15%	Surrender value less 85% of total premiums payable to date
In year 3	²/₆ths of 30% i.e. 10%	Surrender value less 90% of total premiums payable to date
In year 4	¹/₆th of 30% i.e. 5%	Surrender value less 95% of total premiums payable to date

For partial surrenders etc. the clawback limit could not exceed the value withdrawn or the surrender value if the policy was made paid-up and account was taken of any earlier clawbacks on the same policy. If the annual premium on a policy was increased by more than 25% over the first annual premium (or the annual premium at 26 March 1974 where a policy was issued before that date), the additional premiums and rights obtained were treated as relating to a new policy.

The above provisions did not apply to policies issued in connection with sponsored superannuation schemes or certain approved retirement benefit schemes or if the event under (a) or (c) arose because of the winding-up of the issuing body.

[ICTA 1988, s 268].

For replacement of one policy by another, see **44.35**(d) below.

(ii) **Clawback of relief on surrender etc. after four years**

If in the fifth or any later year from the making of an insurance either (a) or (b) (other than on death or maturity) in (i) above occurs and either event has occurred before, a clawback will be made of 12.5% (15% for 1988/89 and earlier years of assessment) on the lower of the premiums payable in that year and the sum payable by reason of the event.

If two or more events occur in the same year the total clawback is limited to the appropriate percentage (as above) of the premiums payable in that year. Account is taken of any clawback also due under s 268 (above) on a policy treated as new because of an increase in premiums, see (i) above.

The above provisions apply to qualifying policies made after 26 March 1974 but not to industrial assurance policies. [ICTA 1988, s 269].

(iii) **Reduction in relief where clawback occurs**

Where there has been a clawback under (i) or (ii) above, the tax relief on the relevant premiums is reduced by the same amount and the increased liability arising from the loss of the tax relief is set against the clawback suffered (earlier years first), with any excess clawback reclaimable by the taxpayer within six years after the end of the tax year in which the event happens.

The relevant premiums are, for (i) above, the total premiums payable under the policy up to the event giving rise to the clawback and, for (ii) above, the premiums payable in the year in which the event happens. [*ICTA 1988, s 270*].

(iv)　Provisions apply for the collection etc. of the clawback by HMRC from the life office and for the taxpayer to be given, within 30 days by the life office, a statement of the clawback amount and how calculated. [*ICTA 1988, s 272*].

Simon's Taxes. See E1.1350–E1.1352.

Qualifying policies

[44.29] A policy effected after 19 March 1968 qualifies for life assurance relief only if it provides no 'benefits' other than a capital sum (see **44.35**(a) below for definition) payable only on death (or on death or earlier disability) or survival for specified term and it also fulfils the conditions set out in **44.30–44.32** below, subject to the exemptions in **44.33** below. [*ICTA 1988, s 266(3)(b), Sch 15 Pt I*].

By concession, free gifts offered as incentives in connection with life insurance policies are disregarded in determining whether a policy is a qualifying policy, provided that the aggregate cost to the insurer of all gifts in connection with a policy (or a 'cluster' of policies) does not exceed £30. (HMRC ESC B42).

See **44.18** above for conditions relating to 'new non-resident policies' issued in respect of an insurance made after 17 November 1983 by a company not resident in the UK.

Note

From 1 April 1976, the certification of new qualifying policies (other than friendly society policies) was transferred from the issuing body to the Inland Revenue (with right of appeal if certificate refused). Certification of policies issued before 1 April 1976 but varied on or after that date remained the responsibility of the life office. [*ICTA 1988, Sch 15 Pt II*]. See *R (oao Monarch Assurance plc) v CIR* CA 2001, 74 TC 346 for the circumstances in which HMRC may exercise its discretionary power to refuse certification. Certification of policies was to be abolished altogether from a day to be appointed for the purpose by HMRC, except for certification in relation to a time before that day, and subject to the rights of appeal in relation to refusals. A certificate issued under the old rules continues to be conclusive evidence that a policy is a qualifying policy. No date for the abolition has ever been appointed. [*FA 1995, s 55(1)–(3)*].

Simon's Taxes. See E1.1311, E1.1326.

Policies payable only on death (or earlier disability) within a specified period (term assurance)

[44.30] The following apply.

(a)   If the period *does not exceed ten years*, any surrender value must not exceed the return of premiums paid. [*ICTA 1988, Sch 15 para 1(4)*].

(b)   If the specified term *exceeds ten years*, premiums must be payable at yearly, or shorter intervals, during at least ten years or three-quarters of the term, whichever is less, or until the assured's earlier death (or disability), and those payable in any one year, excluding any loading for exceptional mortality risk, must not exceed:

    (i)   twice the amount of the premiums payable in any other year; nor

    (ii)   one-eighth of the total premiums which would be payable if the policy ran for the full term (or, if appropriate, the sooner of ten years or three-quarters of the term). [*ICTA 1988, Sch 15 para 1(3)(8)*].

(c)   For policies issued on or after 1 April 1976, if the specified term ends after the age of 75 years and the policy provides for any payment on the whole or partial surrender of the policy, the capital sum payable on death must not be less than 75% of the total premiums payable if death occurred at 75 years of age. In the case of a policy payable on one of two lives, the age of the older is taken if the sum is payable on the death of the first, and the age of the younger is taken if payment arises on the death of the survivor. If limited to death after 16 (or some lower age) the benefit on earlier death must not exceed the return of premiums paid. [*ICTA 1988, Sch 15 para 1(5)*].

In calculating total premiums, there will be ignored any weighting due to premiums being payable at lesser than annual intervals (generally taken to be 10% if the reduction is not specified) and in calculating the capital sum, the smallest amount is used if more than one is payable. [*ICTA 1988, Sch 15 para 1(6)(9)*].

Short-term assurances

A policy will not be a qualifying policy under **44.29** above if the capital sum is payable only if death or disability occurs less than one year after making the insurance. [*ICTA 1988, Sch 15 para 10*].

Endowment policies

[44.31] Term must be for at least ten years, or until the assured's earlier death (or disability). The policy must not provide for any capital benefit to be paid (other than on whole or part surrender of the policy or bonus additions to it or on disability) during its continuance, but it must guarantee on death (or death after 16 or some lower specified age) a sum at least equal to 75% of the total premiums (less any weighting due to premiums being paid at lesser than annual intervals, generally taken to be 10% if the reduction is not specified) which would be payable if the policy ran full term. For a policy effected on or after 1 April 1976 by a person over 55 years of age, the 75% requirement is reduced by 2% for each year the age exceeds 55. If limited to death after 16 (or some lower age) the benefit on earlier death must not exceed the return of premiums paid.

Premiums must be payable annually, or at shorter intervals, for a period of not less than ten years or until death etc. Limitations (I) and (ii) under **44.30**(b) above apply, but with exclusion of wording in brackets at end of (ii). For a policy payable on one of two lives, the rules under **44.30**(c) above apply. [*ICTA 1988, Sch 15 para 2*].

Whole-life policies

[44.32] Premiums must be payable annually, or at shorter intervals, until the assured's death (or his earlier disability, if so provided) or for a specified period of at least ten years should he live longer than that period. Premium limitations (I) and (ii) under **44.30**(b) above apply except that the total premiums under (ii) are those for the first ten years or for the specified period, as above, if longer. The provisions under **44.30**(c) above also apply. [*ICTA 1988, Sch 15 para 1(2)*].

Exemptions

[44.33] The above restrictions do not apply to the following.

(i)   Policies solely for the payment on an individual's death (or disability) of a sum substantially equal to the then balance of a mortgage (repayable by annual, or shorter, instalments) on his residence or business premises. [*ICTA 1988, s 266(10)(a)*].

(ii)   Policies under a sponsored superannuation scheme (as defined by *ICTA 1988, s 624*), if at least half the cost of the scheme is borne by the employer. This provision was repealed on 6 April 1980, but is continued, for policies issued before that date, by extra-statutory concession (HMRC ESC A32).

(iii)   Policies issued in connection with a pre-6 April 2006 approved occupational pension scheme under *ICTA 1988, s 590 et seq*. [*ICTA 1988, s 266(10)(b)*].

Although the above policies are not qualifying policies, relief under **44.24** to **44.27** above is available on premiums paid (subject to the general restrictions) and they are not subject to the charge on life assurance gains (see **44.3** *et seq.* above).

(iv)   Certain policies issued by a friendly society in the course of its tax-exempt life business are qualifying policies. See **44.21** above.

Disqualification of certain life policies

[44.34] A policy (issued in the UK or elsewhere) evidencing a contract of long-term insurance (within *SI 2001 No 544, Sch 1 Pt II*) is not a 'qualifying policy' if it is 'connected with' another policy the terms of which provide benefits greater than would reasonably be expected if any policy 'connected with' it were disregarded.

A policy is 'connected with' another policy if:

(a)   they are at any time simultaneously in force; and

(b)   either of them is issued with reference to the other, or with a view to enabling or facilitating the other to be issued on particular terms. (See Revenue Press Release 16 June 1980 for guidelines.)

This applies to policies issued in respect of insurances made after 25 March 1980 and to an insurance made on or before that date which is connected with one made after it, but not in relation to premiums paid before that date on the earlier policy.

In relation to policies issued in respect of insurances made after 22 August 1983, the above restriction applies where either of the policies concerned provides such excessive benefits as are mentioned above. With respect to payments made after 22 August 1983, this extension of the restriction also applies to insurances made before that date if further premiums exceeding £5 p.a. are made after that date.

[*ICTA 1988, Sch 15 para 14; SI 2009 No 2035, Sch para 24*].

Notes

[44.35] The following should be taken into account.

(a)   '*Capital sum*' includes a series of capital sums, or a sum varying with the circumstances. Bonus additions, an option to take an annuity, a payment on whole or part surrender, or a waiver of premiums in the event of disability *do not constitute 'benefits'*. [*ICTA 1988, Sch 15 para 1(7)(9)*].

(b)   For *industrial assurance* policies and *family income* and *mortgage protection* policies, see *ICTA 1988, Sch 15 paras 7–9*. After 1 April 1976, industrial insurance policies are generally regarded as qualifying policies although not within the appropriate conditions. In addition, industrial assurance policies issued in respect of insurances made after 13 March 1984 continue to attract premium relief (see **44.24** above) as if issued on or before that date provided that:

    (i)   the proposal form was completed on or before that date;

    (ii)   the policy was prepared for issue before 1 April 1984; and

    (iii)   before 1 April 1984 the policy was permanently recorded in the issuer's books in accordance with its normal business practice. [*ICTA 1988, Sch 14 para 8(3); ITA 2007, Sch 1 para 232(4)*].

Industrial assurance ceases to be a distinct form of business for tax purposes for accounting periods beginning after 31 December 1995. However, the special treatment afforded to industrial assurance policies will continue to be given to policies issued by any company on or after 1 December 2001, provided that the company had previously issued qualifying policies in the course of industrial assurance business and was, on 28 November 1995, offering such policies of the same type as those offered on or after 1 December 2001. [*ICTA 1988, Sch 15 para 8A; SI 2001 No 3643*].

(c)   A variation after 19 March 1968 to a policy taken out before that date so as to increase benefits or extend term ranks as a new policy. [*ICTA 1988, Sch 14 para 8(1)(2)*]. See, however, **44.5** above as regards cessation of premium collection on certain old policies which is not regarded as a variation.

(d)   Where, after 24 March 1982, a qualifying policy is replaced by another qualifying policy as a result of a variation in the life or lives assured (e.g. on marriage or divorce), both policies are treated for the following purposes as a single qualifying policy made at the time of the earlier policy provided that (a) any sum becoming payable in connection with the earlier policy is retained by the insurer and applied towards any premium on the later policy and (b) no consideration (apart from the benefits under the new policy) is received by any person in connection with the ending of the earlier policy. Any sum applied as in (a) is treated neither as a premium for premium clawback purposes (see **44.28** above) nor for the purposes of life assurance gain computations (see **44.3** *et seq.* above) nor as a capital sum received for the latter purposes. The replacement policy is also treated as made at the same time as the original policy for relief purposes (see **44.24** above) provided that the benefits conferred by the replacement policy are substantially equivalent to those under the original policy. [*ICTA 1988, Sch 14 para 8(6), Sch 15 para 20*].

Where a premium increases or decreases in connection with an exceptional risk of disability or death, this is not considered for tax purposes as a variation in the terms of the policy and, consequently, there is no need to consider whether or not a qualifying policy retains its status as such. A similar disregard applies to any amendment made to the policy by the insertion, variation or removal of a provision under which, on the grounds of such exceptional risk, a sum may become chargeable as a debt against the capital sum guaranteed. These disregards were added by *FA 2003* and deemed always to have had effect, except to the extent that this retrospection would deny a policy qualifying status at any time before 9 April 2003. [*ICTA 1988, Sch 15 para 18(4)*].

The transfer under a Court Order (between spouses as part of a divorce settlement) of the rights conferred by a policy is regarded as being for no consideration, and thus the policy may continue to attract life assurance premium relief.

For the effect of other substitutions for, and variations to, policies generally, see *ICTA 1988, Sch 15 paras 17–20* and, until 8 December 2010, ESC A45.

(e)   A body issuing a policy which is certified by HMRC as being a qualifying policy (or which is in the appropriate standard form) must, within three months of receipt of a written request by the policyholder, supply a certificate to that effect. Such a certificate must similarly be supplied where a policy is varied in a significant respect, but continues to be a qualifying policy (although certain alterations to the method of calculating benefits secured and certain variations to pre-20 March

1968 policies are ignored for this purpose). [*ICTA 1988, Sch 15 para 22; FA 2006, s 87(3)–(6)*]. This requirement would cease to apply following the abolition of certification (see **44.29** above). [*FA 1995, s 55(4)*].

(f) Any option to vary a policy issued before 1 April 1976 is disregarded until it is exercised and the policy is then subject to the new qualifying conditions. A policy issued after 1 April 1976 with an option to vary the terms or to have another policy issued in substitution for it is only a qualifying policy if all the specified conditions would continue to be satisfied after the exercise of the option. [*ICTA 1988, Sch 15 para 19*].

(g) As a result of legal advice received, HMRC have not, since 24 February 1988, certified as a qualifying policy any new life assurance policy which may be converted or fundamentally restructured in such a way as to constitute, under contract law, a rescission of the original contract and the creation of a new one, e.g. the conversion of a whole life policy to an endowment policy or vice versa. Such conversions etc. may arise by means of an agreement between the policyholder and the insurer or by the exercising of an option contained in the terms of the policy. Previously, such alterations were regarded as variations of the existing contract which did not, therefore, prejudice the qualifying status of the policy. Policies certified and sold before 25 February 1988 will not lose their qualifying status even if subsequently converted or restructured. (Revenue Press Release 22 January 1988). Certification was to be abolished (see **44.29** above).

(h) HMRC may, by concession, disregard certain minor infringements of the conditions for recognition as a qualifying policy relating to:
   (i) policies back-dated by not more than three months, which may for certain purposes be treated as if the assurance was made on the earlier date;
   (ii) reductions in first year premiums which do not result in any value being credited to the policyholder;
   (iii) trivial non-recurring infringements of arithmetical tests; and
   (iv) policies which could have been certified as qualifying but which were not so certified when the assurance was made.
   (HMRC ESC A41).

(i) In determining whether any policy is a qualifying policy, there is to be disregarded so much of any premium as is charged on the grounds of exceptional risk of death or disability and any provision under which, on those grounds, a sum may become chargeable as a debt against the capital sum guaranteed on death or disability. References here to 'disability' were added by *FA 2003* and deemed always to have had effect, except to the extent that this retrospection would deny a policy qualifying status at any time before 9 April 2003. [*ICTA 1988, Sch 15 para 12*].

45

Losses

Cross-references. See **18.2** claims for claims involving more than one tax year; **49.11** MISCELLANEOUS INCOME; **52.10–52.17, 52.22, 52.24** PARTNERSHIPS; **60.15** PROPERTY INCOME for property losses; **73.13** TRADING INCOME as regards trades carried on wholly outside the UK.

Simon's Taxes. See E1.10, E3.7.

Other sources. See also HMRC Business Income Manual BIM75000–75760.

Introduction

[45.1] Unless otherwise stated or the context suggests otherwise, references in this chapter to trading losses are to losses sustained in the carrying on of a trade, profession or vocation.

Trading losses are generally computed according to the same rules as apply in computing profits. [*ITTOIA 2005, s 26*]. Relief may be obtained for trading losses:

* by **set-off** against general income of the same tax year or preceding year — see **45.2** below;
* by **set-off** against **capital gains** of the same tax year or preceding tax year if and to the extent that the loss remains unrelieved after applying (a) above — see **45.7** below.
* by **carry-back** of **losses in early years of a trade** — see **45.9** below;
* by **carry-forward** against subsequent profits of the same trade — see **45.20** below;
* by carry-back of a **terminal loss** — see **45.21** below;

The first three reliefs are sometimes referred to as 'sideways relief'. See **45.11–45.19** below for restrictions.

As a temporary measure, a loss sustained for 2008/09 or 2009/10 can be carried back three years but subject to restrictions — see **45.5** below.

It is not possible to anticipate a loss by claiming it before the end of the period of account in which the loss arises (and similarly where the results of more than one period are required to determine the loss for a tax year, claims may not precede the end of the last such period). See *Jones v O'Brien* Ch D 1988, 60 TC 706 and Revenue Tax Bulletin August 2001 pp 878, 879.

Where a loss can be relieved under more than one head and it is sufficiently large, the taxpayer can select the order in which the different heads are to be applied, but the whole of the income or profits available for relief under one head must be relieved before passing to the next (*Butt v Haxby* Ch D 1982, 56 TC 547).

Relief against income may be obtained for losses on shares in unlisted trading companies. See **45.25** below.

See **18.2** CLAIMS for further provisions regarding claims for a loss incurred in one tax year to be carried back to an earlier tax year.

Note regarding ITA 2007

For 2007/08 onwards, most of the loss reliefs described in this chapter are given under various provisions of *ITA 2007* instead of, as previously, *ICTA 1988*. Generally speaking, and in common with earlier Tax Law Rewrite Acts, *ITA 2007* made some (relatively minor) changes to pre-existing law. Subject to the election below and to a few stated exceptions, *ITA 2007* has effect, for income tax purposes, for 2007/08 and subsequent tax years. [*ITA 2007, s 967*]. Where a change in the law effected by *ITA 2007* alters the tax consequences for a period of account straddling 5 April 2007 of a transaction or event occurring before 6 April 2007, the person affected may elect for that change not to have effect as regards that period. Where the same transaction or event so affects more than one person, an election by one is of no effect unless all elect. For income tax purposes, the election must be made on or before the first anniversary of 31 January following the tax year in which the straddling period of account ends. [*ITA 2007, Sch 2 para 10*].

Set-off of trading losses against general income

[45.2] Where in any tax year a person sustains a loss in a trade, profession or vocation, carried on solely or in partnership, he may make a claim on or before the first anniversary of 31 January following that tax year for relief against general income of:

(i)   the tax year in which the loss is incurred; or
(ii)   the tax year preceding that in which the loss is incurred; or
(iii)   both those tax years.

See **45.3** below as regards *late* claims. See **45.5** below for an extended carry-back permitted for a 2008/09 or a 2009/10 loss only.

A person sustains a trading loss in a tax year if he sustains a loss in the basis period for that tax year (see **73.3–73.11** TRADING INCOME for basis period rules). A claim within (i) above is made under *ITA 2007, s 64(2)(a)* for 2007/08 onwards and under *ICTA 1988, s 380(1)(a)* for earlier years. A claim within (ii) above is made under *ITA 2007, s 64(2)(b)* where the year of loss is 2007/08 or any subsequent year and under *ICTA 1988, s 380(1)(b)* for earlier years. A claim within (iii) above is made under *ITA 2007, s 64(2)(c)* where the year of loss is 2007/08 or any subsequent year and under *ICTA 1988, s 380(1)(a)* and *(b)* for earlier years. If a claim is made within (i) above and the loss is not wholly exhausted, a subsequent claim can be made (within the time limit) within (ii) above, and *vice versa*.

A claim is given effect by deducting the loss in arriving at net income for the tax year in question (see Step 2 at **1.7** ALLOWANCES AND TAX RATES).

Where a claim is made for a loss to be set against income of both the same tax year and the preceding tax year, there is no statutory order of priority; the claimant must specify the tax year for which the deduction from income should be made first. For 2006/07 and earlier years, this was not explicit but it was always the practice that the claimant could choose the order of priority (Revenue booklet SAT 1(1995), para 4.15).

Where, against income of the same year, claims are made both under (i) above in respect of that year's loss and under (ii) above in respect of the following year's loss, (i) takes precedence.

[*ITA 2007, ss 61(2), 64, 65; ICTA 1988, ss 380, 382(3); FA 2008, s 66(4)(l)(8), Sch 21 paras 4, 6, 7; FA 2010, Sch 3 paras 3, 11*].

For restrictions on relief, see **45.11–45.19** below.

The income against which a loss is set is income *before* deduction of the personal allowance or, where applicable, blind person's allowance (see **1.7** ALLOWANCES AND TAX RATES), which will thus be wasted if the income of a particular tax year is fully covered by a loss claim. The effect on personal allowances, rates of tax etc. needs to be carefully considered. Partial claims against one year's income are not permitted; if a loss is set against income of a particular tax year, it must be fully set against that income until either the loss or the available income is exhausted.

See **18.2** CLAIMS for further provisions regarding claims for a loss incurred in one tax year to be carried back to an earlier tax year.

Simon's Taxes. See E1.1002.

Late claims

[45.3] Although there is no provision for the acceptance of late claims under the provisions at **45.2** above (or under those at **45.9** below), such relief may be granted as would have been due if a timeous claim had been made where the taxpayer or agent either:

(a)   was misled by some relevant and uncorrected HMRC error; or

(b)   made an informal claim within the time limit which he or she reasonably believed to be an acceptable claim, and the need to formalise the claim was not pointed out by HMRC within the time limit; or

(c)   was effectively prevented from making a timeous claim for reasons beyond his or her control,

and provided that the late claim is made within a reasonable period (not normally more than three months) after the expiry of the excuse. As regards (c) above, acceptable reasons do *not* normally include: delays in preparing the accounts (unless for reasons beyond the taxpayer's or agent's control); delays in HMRC's agreeing the accounts (although valid claims may be made before the accounts are either submitted or agreed, provided that the loss is clearly identified); misunderstandings and failures to communicate between taxpayer and agent; oversight or neglect by current or previous agents; ignorance of the statutory time limits; or deliberate delays because it was unclear at the expiry of the time limit whether the claim was advantageous. (Revenue Tax Bulletin December 1994 p 183). See further HMRC Business Income Manual BIM75225, 75230. See also BIM75220 as regards withdrawal of claims.

Examples

General

[45.4]

L, a single woman, commences to trade on 1 July 2006, preparing accounts to 30 June, and has the following results (as adjusted for tax purposes) for the first four years.

	Profit/(loss)
	£
Year ended 30 June 2007	18,000
Year ended 30 June 2008	6,000
Year ended 30 June 2009	(2,000)
Year ended 30 June 2010	(14,000)

L has other income of £12,000 for 2009/10 and £16,000 for 2010/11, having had no other income in the earlier years.

The taxable profits for the first four tax years of the business are as follows.

	£
2006/07 (1.7.06–5.4.07) (£18,000 × $^9/_{12}$)	13,500*
2007/08 (y/e 30.6.07)	18,000
2008/09 (y/e 30.6.08)	6,000
2009/10 (y/e 30.6.09)	Nil
2010/11 (y/e 30.6.10)	Nil

* Overlap relief accruing – £13,500.

L claims relief under *ITA 2007, s 64(2)(a)* (set-off against income of the same year) for the 2009/10 loss (£2,000). She also claims relief under *ITA 2007, s 64(2)(b)* (set-off against income of the preceding year) for the 2010/11 loss (£14,000), with a further claim being made under *ITA 2007, s 64(2)(a)* for the balance of that loss.

The tax position for 2009/10 and 2010/11 is as follows.

	£
2009/10	
Total income before loss relief	12,000
Deduct Claim under *ITA 2007, s 64(2)(a)* note (a)	2,000
	10,000
Deduct Claim under *ITA 2007, s 64(2)(b)*	10,000
Net income	Nil
2010/11	
Total income before loss relief	16,000
Deduct Claim under *ITA 2007, s 64(2)(a)* (balance)	4,000
Net income	12,000
Deduct Personal allowance	6,475
Taxable income	£5,525

Loss utilisation

	£
2009/10	
Loss available under *ITA 2007, s 64(2)(a)*	2,000
Deduct Utilised in 2009/10	2,000

Loss available under *ITA 2007, s 64(2)(b)*	14,000
Deduct Utilised in 2009/10	10,000
Loss available for relief in 2010/11 under *ITA 2007, s 64(2)(a)*	£4,000
2010/11	
Balance of loss available under *ITA 2007, s 64(2)(a)*	4,000
Deduct Utilised in 2010/11	4,000

Note

(a)   Where losses of two different years are set against the income of one tax year, then, regardless of the order of claims, relief for the current year's loss is given in priority to that for the following year's loss (see **45.2** above). This is beneficial to the taxpayer in this example as it leaves £4,000 of the 2010/11 loss to be relieved in that year.

Losses in early years

Q commenced trading on 1 February 2010 and prepared accounts to 31 December. He made a trading loss of £20,900 in the 11 months to 31 December 2010 and profits of £18,000 and £16,000 in the years to 31 December 2011 and 2012 respectively. He has substantial other income for 2009/10 and 2010/11 and makes a claim under *ITA 2007, s 64* for both years.

Taxable profits/(allowable losses) are as follows.

	£	£
2009/10 (1.2.10–5.4.10) (£20,900) × $^2/_{11}$		(3,800)
2010/11 (1.2.10–31.1.11)		
1.2.10–31.12.10	(20,900)	
Less already allocated to 2009/10	3,800	
	(17,100)	
1.1.11–31.1.11 £18,000 × $^1/_{12}$	1,500	
		(15,600)
2011/12 (y/e 31.12.11)		18,000
(Overlap relief accruing — £1,500)		
2012/13 (y/e 31.12.12)		16,000

Notes

(a)   Losses available for relief for 2009/10 and 2010/11 are £3,800 and £15,600 respectively. If both years' losses are carried forward under *ITA 2007, s 83* instead of being set against other income (under either *ITA 2007, s 64* or *s 72*), the aggregate loss of £19,400 will extinguish the 2011/12 profit and reduce the 2012/13 profit by £1,400. Note that although the actual loss was £20,900, there is no further amount available for carry-forward: the difference of £1,500 has been used in aggregation in 2010/11.

(b)   The net profit for the first three accounting periods is £13,100 (£18,000 + £16,000 – £20,900). The net taxable profit for the first four tax years is £14,600 (£18,000 + £16,000 – £3,800 – £15,600). The difference of

£1,500 represents the overlap relief accrued (see **73.11 TRADING INCOME**). Note that the overlap profit of £1,500 is by reference to an overlap period of *three* months, i.e. 1.2.10 to 5.4.10 (two months — overlap profit nil) and 1.1.11 to 31.1.11 (one month — overlap profit £1,500).

Extended carry-back for 2008/09 and 2009/10 losses

[45.5] A trade loss incurred sustained in the basis period for 2008/09 or 2009/10 (but no other year) can be carried back three years. This applies equally to a loss sustained in a profession or vocation. A person sustains a trading loss in a tax year if he sustains a loss in the basis period for that tax year (see **73.3–73.11 TRADING INCOME** for basis period rules). The amount that can be carried back more than one year is limited in total to £50,000, and any amount carried back under these provisions can only be set against taxable profits from the same trade. A separate £50,000 cap applies to each year's loss. The set-off must be made against later years' profits in priority to earlier years' profits. The deadline for claims is the same as for an *ITA 2007, s 64* claim at **45.2** above, i.e. 31 January 2011 for a 2008/09 loss and 31 January 2012 for a 2009/10 loss.

A claim for the extended carry-back relief is possible where a claim is made under *ITA 2007, s 64* to set a trade loss for 2008/09 against general income and relief for the loss cannot be fully given due to an insufficiency of income. Where the *section 64* claim is to set the loss against general income for 2008/09 only, a claim for the extended relief can be made against profits of the same trade for 2007/08, 2006/07 and 2005/06. A carry-back to 2007/08 will not be subject to the £50,000 cap. Where the *section 64* claim is to set the loss against general income for 2007/08 only or against general income for both 2008/09 and 2007/08, a claim for the extended relief can be made against profits of the same trade for 2006/07 and 2005/06. If no *section 64* claim is possible, due only to an insufficiency of general income, a claim for the extended relief can still be made against profits of the same trade for 2006/07 and 2005/06. Any unrelieved loss will still be available for carry-forward under **45.20** below. See the Example at **45.6** below.

Identical rules apply (with the appropriate modifications) where a claim is made under *ITA 2007, s 64* to set a trade loss for 2009/10 against general income.

[FA 2009, Sch 6 paras 1, 2].

See **18.2 CLAIMS** for further provisions regarding claims for a loss incurred in one tax year to be carried back to an earlier tax year.

Example

[45.6]

M has been trading for some years, preparing accounts to 30 April, and has the following income for recent years.

	Trade profit/(loss)	Other income
	£	£
Year ended 30 April 2006 (2006/07)	50,000	1,500
Year ended 30 April 2007 (2007/08)	40,000	5,000
Year ended 30 April 2008 (2008/09)	19,000	1,000
Year ended 30 April 2009 (2009/10)	(91,000)	1,000

In relation to the 2009/10 loss, M claims relief under both *ITA 2007, s 64(2)(a)* (set-off against income of the same year) and under *ITA 2007, s 64(2)(b)* (set-off against income of the preceding year). In addition, she makes a claim under *FA 2009, Sch 6* at **45.5** above.

The tax position for the four years in question is as follows.

2009/10	£
Total income before loss relief	1,000
Deduct Claim under *ITA 2007, s 64(2)(a)*	1,000
Net income	Nil

2008/09	
Total income before loss relief	20,000
Deduct Claim under *ITA 2007, s 64(2)(b)*	20,000
Net Income	Nil

2007/08	
Total income before loss relief	45,000
Deduct Claim under *FA 2009, Sch 6* against trade profit	40,000
Net income covered by personal allowance	£5,000

2006/07	
Total income before loss relief	51,500
Deduct Claim under *FA 2009, Sch 6* (restricted by £50,000 cap)	10,000
Net income subject to personal allowance	£41,500
Loss utilisation	

	£
2009/10	
Loss available	91,000
Deduct Utilised in 2009/10 — *ITA 2007, s 64(2)(a)*	1,000
	90,000
Deduct Utilised in 2008/09 — *ITA 2007, s 64(2)(b)*	20,000

	70,000
Deduct Utilised in 2007/08 — *FA 2009, Sch 6*	40,000
	30,000
Deduct Utilised in 2006/07 — *FA 2009, Sch 6*	10,000
Balance carried forward against future trade profits	£20,000

Set-off of trading losses against capital gains

[45.7] Where relief is available under *ITA 2007, s 64* as in **45.2** above for a tax year and either a claim is made under that section or the person's total income for the year is either nil or does not include any income from which the loss can be deducted, a claim may also be made under *TCGA 1992, s 261B* for the determination of the '*relevant amount*', which is so much of the trading loss as:

(a)   is not deducted in calculating the claimant's net income for the year of claim; and

(b)   has not already been relieved for any other year.

The claim is not deemed to be determined until the relevant amount for the year can no longer be varied, whether by the Tribunal on appeal or on the order of any court.

The relevant amount, as finally determined, is to be treated for the purposes of capital gains tax as an allowable loss accruing to the claimant in the tax year, except that it cannot exceed the 'maximum amount'. Any such excess remains an income tax loss.

The '*maximum amount*' for this purpose is the amount on which the claimant would be chargeable to capital gains tax for that year, disregarding the effect of this provision and of the capital gains tax annual exemption. In relation to claims in respect of trading losses sustained in years before 2008/09, taper relief is also disregarded (so that the maximum amount is equal to pre-tapered gains). (Taper relief is abolished for 2008/09 onwards.)

In computing the maximum amount, no account is taken of any event occurring after the determination of the relevant amount and in consequence of which the amount chargeable to capital gains tax is reduced by virtue of any capital gains tax legislation. Thus if, as a result of a subsequent reduction in the chargeable gains against which the maximum amount is set, the maximum amount exceeds those chargeable gains, the excess is carried forward as an allowable capital loss.

No amount treated as an allowable loss under this provision may be deducted from chargeable gains accruing in a tax year which begins after the claimant has ceased to carry on the trade in which the loss was sustained.

A claim must be made on or before the first anniversary of the normal self-assessment filing date for the tax year in which the loss was made. Before 2007/08, strictly the claim had to form part of the claim under what is now

ITA 2007, s 64. In practice, however, HMRC accepted separate claims where there was no income for the year against which the loss could be claimed (see Change 160 listed in Annex 1 to the Explanatory Notes to *ITA 2007*). They also accepted separate claims where (i) relief against general income had previously been claimed and a claim under these provisions could have been made, (ii) the separate claim was made within the time limits for the original claim, (iii) after the relief against general income there was a balance of unrelieved trading losses, and (iv) all other conditions for relief under these provisions were satisfied. (Revenue Tax Bulletin August 1993 p 87).

The above provisions apply also to employment losses relievable under *ITA 2007, s 128* (see **45.33** below).

For years prior to 2007/08, the claim was under *FA 1991, s 72.*

[*ITA 2007, ss 71, 130, Sch 1 para 329; TCGA 1992, ss 261B, 261C; FA 2008, Sch 2 paras 39, 56; SI 2009 No 56, Sch 1 paras 182, 183*].

Simon's Taxes. See **E1.1003.**

Example

[45.8]

M has carried on a trade for some years, preparing accounts to 30 June each year. For the year ended 30 June 2010 he makes a trading loss of £17,000. His assessable profit for 2009/10 is £5,000, and his other income for both 2009/10 and 2010/11 amounts to £2,000. He makes a capital gain of £14,200 and a capital loss of £1,000 for 2010/11 and has capital losses brought forward of £9,900. M makes claims for loss relief, against income of 2009/10 and income and gains of 2010/11, under *ITA 2007, s 64(2)(b), s 64(2)(a)* and *TCGA 1992, s 261B.*

Calculation of 'relevant amount'

	£
Trading loss—year ended 30.6.10	17,000
Relieved against other income for 2010/11 (*ITA 2007, s 64(2)(a)*)	(2,000)
Relieved against income for 2009/10 (*ITA 2007, s 64(2)(b)*)	(7,000)
Relevant amount	£8,000

Calculation of 'maximum amount'

		£
Gains for 2010/11		14,200
Deduct	Losses for 2010/11	(1,000)
	Unrelieved losses brought forward	(9,900)
Maximum amount		£3,300

Relief under *TCGA 1992, s 261B*

	£	£
Gains for the year		14,200
Losses for the year	1,000	

Relief under *TCGA 1992, s 261B*	3,300	
		4,300
Gain (covered by annual exemption)		£9,900
Capital losses brought forward and carried forward		£9,900

Loss memorandum

	£
Trading loss	17,000
Claimed under *ITA 2007, s 64(2)(a)*	(2,000)
Claimed under *ITA 2007, s 64(2)(b)*	(7,000)
Claimed under *TCGA 1992, s 261B*	(3,300)
Unutilised loss	£4,700

Note

In this example, £200 of the capital gains tax annual exemption of £10,100 is wasted, but the brought forward capital losses are preserved for carry-forward against gains of future years. If M had *not* made the claim under *TCGA 1992, s 261B*, his net gains for the year of £13,200 would have been reduced to the annual exempt amount by deducting £3,100 of the losses brought forward. Only £6,800 of capital losses would remain available for carry-forward against future gains and a further £3,300 of trading losses would have been available for carry-forward against future trading profits. So the effect of the claim is to preserve capital losses at the expense of trading losses.

Losses in early years of a trade

[45.9] If an individual sustains a loss in a trade, profession or vocation in any of the first four tax years in which the trade etc., is first carried on by him, he may claim relief for that loss against his other income of the *three* tax years preceding the year of loss. Income of earlier years is relieved in priority to that of later years. The trade (or if part of a larger undertaking, the whole undertaking) must have been carried on during the period of loss on a commercial basis with a reasonable expectation of profits during that period or within a reasonable time afterwards (an objective test — see *Walls v Livesey* (Sp C 4), [1995] SSCD 12 — and see generally *Walsh and Another v Taylor* (Sp C 386) 2003, [2004] SSCD 48). For 2007/08 onwards, it is made clear that the '*period of loss*' is the basis period, and not the tax year, in which the loss is sustained.

The relief is available to an individual trading etc. in partnership by reference to the first four tax years in which he is a partner. However, relief is not available to a married individual where the trade was being carried on by his or her spouse at a time earlier than the three tax years preceding the year of loss (which, for example, precludes relief to that extent where an individual takes his spouse into partnership); this applies to civil partners as it does to married couples. See **52.13–52.17 PARTNERSHIPS** for other restrictions on relief available to certain partners.

A claim is made under *ITA 2007, s 72* where the year of loss is 2007/08 or any subsequent year and under *ICTA 1988, s 381* where it is an earlier year. The claim is given effect by deducting the loss in arriving at net income for the earliest of the three years preceding the year of loss (see Step 2 at **1.7 ALLOWANCES AND TAX RATES**), then (assuming there is any unrelieved balance) the year after that and finally the latest of the three years. Any amount still unrelieved is potentially available for relief under any of the other trading loss reliefs described in this chapter.

Time limit for claims

Claims must be made on or before the first anniversary of 31 January following the tax year in which the loss is sustained. For late claims, see **45.3** above.

See **18.2 CLAIMS** for further provisions regarding claims for a loss incurred in one tax year to be carried back to an earlier tax year.

Capital allowances

Capital allowances are subject to the restrictions in **45.14, 45.15** below. See also the anti-avoidance legislation at **45.16–45.18** below.

General

The income against which a loss is set is income *before* deduction of the personal allowance or, where applicable, blind person's allowance (see **1.7 ALLOWANCES AND TAX RATES**), which will thus be wasted if the income of a particular tax year is fully covered by a loss claim. The effect on personal allowances, rates of tax etc. needs to be carefully considered. Partial claims are not permitted; if a loss is set against income of a particular tax year, it must be fully set against that income until either the loss or the available income is exhausted. Furthermore, it is not possible to claim to carry back a loss under these provisions against the income of one or two specified years as opposed to all of the three years in question.

[*ITA 2007, ss 61(2), 72–74; ICTA 1988, ss 381, 382(3)(4); FA 2008, s 66(4)(l)(8), Sch 21 paras 5–7; FA 2010, Sch 3 paras 4, 11*].

See also **73.102 TRADING INCOME** as regards **pre-trading expenditure**.

Simon's Taxes. See E1.1021.

Example

[45.10]

F, a single person, commenced to trade on 1 December 2007, preparing accounts to 30 November. The first four years of trading produce losses of £12,000, £9,000, £2,000 and £1,000 respectively, these figures being as adjusted for tax purposes and after taking account of capital allowances. For each of the four tax years 2004/05 to 2007/08, F had other income of £8,000.

The losses for tax purposes are as follows.

	£	£
2007/08 (1.12.07–5.4.08) (£12,000 × $^4/_{12}$)		4,000
2008/09 (y/e 30.11.08)	12,000	
Less already allocated to 2007/08	4,000	
		8,000
2009/10 (y/e 30.11.09)		9,000
2010/11 (y/e 30.11.10)		2,000
2011/12 (y/e 30.11.11) note (b)		1,000

Loss relief under *ITA 2007, s 72* is available as follows.

	2007/08	2008/09	2009/10	2010/11
	£	£	£	£
Losses available	4,000	8,000	9,000	2,000
Set against total income				
2004/05	4,000	—	—	—
2005/06	—	8,000	—	—
2006/07	—	—	8,000	—
2007/08	—	—	1,000	2,000
	£4,000	£8,000	£9,000	£2,000

Revised total income is thus £4,000 for 2004/05, nil for 2005/06 and 2006/07 and £5,000 for 2007/08.

Notes

(a) Losses are computed by reference to the same basis periods as profits. Where any part of a loss would otherwise fall to be included in the computations for two successive tax years (as is the case for 2007/08 and 2008/09 in this example), that part is excluded from the computation for the second of those years.

(b) The loss for the year ended 30 November 2011 in this example is not available for relief under *ITA 2007, s 72* as it does not fall into the first four *tax years* of the business (even though it is incurred in the first four years of trading). It is, of course, available for relief under *ITA 2007, s 64* (depending on other income for 2010/11 and 2011/12) or for carry-forward under *ITA 2007, s 83*.

Restrictions on above reliefs

[45.11] The restrictions set out in **45.12–45.15** below, in **45.17** below insofar as it relates to *ITA 2007, ss 74B–74D*, in **45.18** below and in **45.19** below insofar as it relates to *ITA 2007, s 80* apply equally to the extended carry-back relief under *FA 2009, Sch 6* at **45.5** above as they do to loss relief under *ITA 2007, s 64* at **45.2** above. [*FA 2009, Sch 6 para 1(11)(a)–(d); FA 2010, Sch 3 paras 10, 11*].

Simon's Taxes. See **B1.503, B5.175, B5.417, B5.508.**

Non-commercial trades

[45.12] Relief under *ITA 2007, s 64* (see **45.2** above) will not be given for a trade loss unless, throughout the basis period for the tax year in which the loss is sustained, the trade, profession or vocation was carried on:

- on a commercial basis; and
- with a view to the realisation of profits in that trade etc., or in any larger undertaking of which it forms part.

The test is a subjective one — see *Walls v Livesey* (Sp C 4), [1995] SSCD 12 on the similar test in *ICTA 1988, s 504(2)(a)*. In *Wannell v Rothwell* Ch D 1996, 68 TC 719 an individual's speculative dealing in stocks and shares and commodity futures was held to be trading but not on a commercial basis. See also *Brown v Richardson* (Sp C 129), [1997] SSCD 233, and the Revenue Tax Bulletin article (October 1997 pp 472, 473) commenting on that decision, and *Delian Enterprises v Ellis* (Sp C 186), [1999] SSCD 103.

A trade is treated as complying with the second of the above requirements at any time at which it was being carried on so as to afford a reasonable expectation of profit. If there was a change during the basis period in the way in which the trade etc., is carried on, it is treated as having been carried on throughout in the way in which it was being carried on at the end of the basis period.

For 2006/07 and earlier years, these provisions applied by reference to the tax year itself rather than the basis period for the tax year.

For the HMRC approach generally, see HMRC Business Income Manual BIM75705–75725.

(The above restrictions do not apply to losses incurred in the exercise of functions conferred by or under an Act (for which see *ITA 2007, s 1018* and Change 152 in Annex 1 to the Explanatory Notes to *ITA 2007*).)

[*ITA 2007, s 66; ICTA 1988, s 384(1)–(5)(9)(10)*].

Farming and market gardening

[45.13] Except as below, relief will not be given under *ITA 2007, s 64* (see **45.2** above) for any loss incurred in a trade of farming or market gardening if losses from that trade were also incurred in each of the five years preceding the tax year in which the loss is sustained. In ascertaining for the purposes of these provisions whether losses have been incurred in preceding tax years, capital allowances and balancing charges are disregarded and losses are computed by reference to actual tax years (apportioning where necessary) as opposed to basis periods.

Similarly, if such a trade is carried on by a company a loss incurred in any accounting period may not be set off against total profits if there would still be a loss if capital allowances were ignored and there was a loss (similarly computed) in each of the accounting periods wholly or partly comprised in the five years preceding that accounting period (see Tolley's Corporation Tax for details).

There is no disallowance under *ITA 2007, s 64* or its predecessor if the trade commenced during the preceding five tax years but if the trade was transferred during that time from one spouse to the other (or from one civil partner to the other) it is treated for this purpose as not having thereby ceased and a new trade commenced. The same applies if the trade was transferred between an individual and a company which he controls or which his spouse (or civil partner) controls or which they together control.

Relief is not disallowed by virtue of these provisions if:

* the trade is part of, and ancillary to, a larger trading undertaking; or
* the farming or market gardening activities in the year are carried on in a way which might reasonably be expected to produce profits in the future and the activities in the preceding five years could not reasonably have been expected at the beginning of the 'prior period of loss' to become profitable until after the year under review.

The expectations included in the second test are to be considered on the assumption that the activities are carried on by a competent person, and the activities must be regarded as a whole. The *'prior period of loss'* comprises the five preceding tax years plus, if losses were made in successive tax years before those five years, those successive tax years.

[*ITA 2007, ss 67–70, Sch 1 para 74; ICTA 1988, s 397; CTA 2010, Sch 1 para 495*].

By concession, HMRC extend the five-year time limits above to eleven years from commencement in the case of stud farming, i.e. the breeding of thoroughbred horses, provided that the business is potentially profitable (HMRC Business Income Manual BIM55725).

Leasing by individuals

[45.14] Where an individual (alone or in partnership) incurs expenditure on plant or machinery for leasing in the course of a trade, any plant or machinery capital allowances on that expenditure are not to be included in computing a loss for the purposes of *ITA 2007, s 64* (see **45.2** above) (previously *ICTA 1988, s 380*) or *ITA 2007, s 72* (see **45.9** above) unless:

* the individual carries on the trade for a continuous period of at least six months beginning or ending in the 'period of loss'; and

- he devotes substantially the whole of his time (see HMRC Business Income Manual BIM75730) to the trade throughout the 'period of loss' or, if the trade begins or ceases (or both) in that year, for a continuous period of at least six months beginning or ending in that year.

For 2007/08 onwards, the *'period of loss'* means the basis period for the tax year in which the loss is sustained; for earlier years it meant the tax year itself.

The same restriction applies if the asset is not leased but payments in the nature of royalties or licence fees are to arise from rights granted by the individual in connection with the asset.

Any relief erroneously given will be withdrawn by assessment. The foregoing provisions are without prejudice to (d) and (e) below.

[*ITA 2007, ss 75, 79*].

Capital allowances

[45.15] There are two separate restrictions involving capital allowances, as follows.

(a) **Leasing partnerships.** Where expenditure is incurred on plant or machinery for leasing in the course of a trade (or other qualifying activity — see **11.4 CAPITAL ALLOWANCES ON PLANT AND MACHINERY**) carried on, or to be carried on, by a partnership including a company and an individual (with or without other partners), any first-year allowance (see **11.14 CAPITAL ALLOWANCES ON PLANT AND MACHINERY**) on that expenditure is not to be included in computing a loss for the purposes of *ITA 2007, s 64* (see **45.2** above) or *ITA 2007, s 72* (see **45.9** above).

(b) **Arrangements.** Where an individual incurs expenditure on an asset, any plant and machinery annual investment allowance (see **11.13 CAPITAL ALLOWANCES ON PLANT AND MACHINERY**) or first-year allowance (see **11.14 CAPITAL ALLOWANCES ON PLANT AND MACHINERY**) on that expenditure is not to be included in computing a loss for the purposes of *ITA 2007, s 64* (see **45.2** above) (previously *ICTA 1988, s 380*) or *ITA 2007, s 72* (see **45.9** above) if, under an arrangement or scheme, such loss relief was expected as the sole or main benefit to the individual of incurring the expenditure and (i) he was in partnership then or later, or (ii) he transferred the trade etc. or the relevant asset to a **CONNECTED PERSON** (**21**), or (iii) he transferred the asset to any person at lower than its market value.

Any relief already given will be withdrawn under (a) or (b) above by assessment.

[*ITA 2007, ss 76–79; ICTA 1988, s 384A; FA 2008, Sch 24 paras 21–23*].

Losses derived from film tax reliefs

[45.16] There is a potential exit charge as described below where:

(i)   an individual has claimed relief under *ITA 2007, s 64* (see **45.2** above), *TCGA 2002, s 261B* (see **45.7** above) (previously *FA 1991, s 72*) or *ITA 2007, s 72* (see **45.9** above) in respect of a 'film-related loss' sustained by him in a trade (whether carried on solely or in partnership);

(ii)   there is a 'disposal' of a right of the individual to profits arising from the trade (a *'relevant disposal'*); and

(iii)   an 'exit event' occurs.

A loss is a *'film-related loss'* if the computation of profits or losses that it results from is made in accordance with any of *ITTOIA 2005, ss 130–144* (or their predecessors), which give relief, as revenue expenditure, for production and acquisition expenditure on films and sound recordings (see **73.76 TRADING INCOME**).

A *'disposal'* is very widely (but not exhaustively) defined (by *ITA 2007, s 799*) for the purposes of (ii) above to include, for example, the disposal, surrender or loss of a right to income, a default in the payment of income, certain changes in profit- or loss-sharing ratios and the individual's leaving a partnership (including a case where the partnership is dissolved). The disposal may be part of a larger disposal.

An *'exit event'* occurs when:

• the individual receives any consideration for the relevant disposal (whether or not as part of a larger sum) which is not otherwise chargeable to income tax; or

• the 'losses claimed' become greater than the individual's 'capital contribution' (whether because of a claim for losses or a decrease in that capital contribution); or

• there is an increase in the amount by which the losses claimed exceed the capital contribution.

A **chargeable event** occurs at the time the last of the conditions at (i)–(iii) above is satisfied (regardless of whether or not the individual is still carrying on the trade). The individual is treated as receiving at that time an amount of income equal to the total consideration received for relevant disposals and not otherwise chargeable to income tax plus the excess (if any) of 'losses claimed' over 'capital contribution' (such amounts being judged as at the time immediately after the chargeable event). That income does not form part of the trading profits but is separately chargeable to income tax for the tax year in which the chargeable event occurs. There is provision to avoid double counting where there are successive chargeable events. Consideration from which a deduction has been made in consideration of any person's agreeing to or facilitating a relevant disposal or exit event (e.g. an exit fee) is treated as received free of that deduction.

References above to *'losses claimed'* are to any film-related losses sustained in the trade in any tax year for which the individual has claimed relief under *ITA 2007, s 64, TCGA 2002, s 261B* or *ITA 2007, s 72* or any of their predecessors. But for members of partnerships, 'losses claimed' are treated as decreased for these purposes by the lesser of any amount clawed back under the recovery provisions at **52.13 PARTNERSHIPS** and the amount of *film-related* losses that could potentially have been clawed back under those provisions.

An individual's '*capital contribution*' is the amount he has contributed to the trade as capital, less so much of that amount as:

- he has, directly or indirectly, drawn out or received back; or
- he is entitled so to draw out or receive back; or
- he has had, directly or indirectly, reimbursed to him by any person; or
- he is entitled to require any person so to reimburse to him,

but not including any such amount drawn out or received back as is chargeable to income tax as profits of a trade. Anything brought into account on a chargeable event as consideration for a relevant disposal is not deducted in arriving at his capital contribution. For 2007/08 onwards, if the trade is carried on by the individual in partnership, his capital contribution is the amount he has contributed to the firm (as opposed to the trade) but is otherwise determined in like manner; a share of profits (as computed for accounting, rather than tax, purposes) is an amount contributed in so far as that share has been added to the firm's capital. In consequence, for 2007/08 onwards, the general rules apply with some modification in a case where a partnership carries on more than one trade.

The Commissioners for HMRC are empowered to make regulations (see now *SI 2005 No 2017*), with retrospective effect, excluding from an individual's capital contribution for these purposes any amounts of a description specified in the regulations. These will apply *only* where the individual carries on the trade *in partnership*. Under *SI 2005 No 2017*, such exclusions are made in the following circumstances.

(A)   Where an individual takes out a loan in connection with his financing of all or part of his contribution to the trade and either:

   (i)   there is, at any time, an agreement or arrangement under which another person will, or may, bear any of the financial cost of repaying the loan; or

   (ii)   any such financial cost is at any time borne by another person otherwise than under an agreement or arrangement caught by (i) above; or

   (iii)   the liability to repay the loan is at any time assumed (or released) by any other person; or

   (iv)   the financial cost to the individual of repaying the loan over a specified period is substantially less than it would have been on arm's length terms.

   The period specified in (iv) above is the earliest period of five years beginning on or after 2 December 2004 (or, if later, the date the loan was taken out) for which condition (iv) is satisfied. Where conditions (i), (ii) or (iii) are satisfied, the amount in question is excluded from the individual's capital contribution after the time in question. Where condition (iv) is satisfied, the exclusion applies after the end of the five-year period and is equal to the amount of the loan outstanding at the end of that period. References to loans include replacement loans.

(B)   Where, at any time, there is an agreement or arrangement under which any of the financial cost of making the capital contribution will be, or may be, reimbursed (directly or indirectly) to the individual by any other person, or where such cost is at any time reimbursed otherwise than under such an agreement or arrangement. The amount in question is excluded from the individual's capital contribution after the time in question.

Neither (A) nor (B) above applies in relation to any financial cost borne or reimbursed by another individual in the normal course of his domestic, family or personal relationships or to any loan repayments not made by the partner due to his financial inability to pay (arising from events outside his control and occurring after the taking out of the loan) or to any amount on which the partner is chargeable to income tax as profits of the trade.

The above provisions are further extended by *SI 2006 No 1639*. They apply where:

- the individual is a limited partner, a member of a limited liability partnership or a non-active partner in a partnership (see, respectively, **52.22, 52.24, 52.13 PARTNERSHIPS**);
- he disposes of his right to profits arising from the trade, such that his share of any profits is reduced or extinguished or his share of any losses is increased;
- another person becomes a partner; and
- the new partner contributes (or agrees to contribute) capital to the partnership.

The amount of the new partner's contribution must be apportioned between the partners in accordance with profit sharing arrangements in force immediately before the new partner becomes a partner. The amount thus apportioned to the individual in question is deducted from his capital contribution for the purposes of determining: (i) whether a chargeable event (as above) occurs; and (ii) the amount to be brought into account as income as a result of that event.

[*ITA 2007, ss 790, 796–803, Sch 2 paras 144–149; FA 2004, ss 119–123; FA 2007, Sch 4 paras 19, 21; SI 2005 No 2017; SI 2006 No 1639*].

See **52.17 PARTNERSHIPS** for other anti-avoidance provisions concerning losses derived from exploiting films.

Non-active traders

[45.17] Where a trade loss is sustained by an individual for 2007/08 (subject to the transitional provision below) or any subsequent year (otherwise than as a partner) and during that tax year he carries on the trade in a 'non-active capacity', the quantum of relief that he can claim for that loss under:

- *ITA 2007, s 64* against general income (and, consequently, *TCGA 1992, s 261B* against chargeable gains) (see **45.2, 45.7** above); or
- *ITA 2007, s 72* (losses in early years of trade) against general income (see **45.9** above),

is restricted to £25,000. If the individual sustains more than one such loss in a tax year, the £25,000 cap applies to the aggregate of all such losses. The cap applies to the balance of a trade loss after applying all other restrictions. If the individual is also a member of a partnership, the amount of the cap is reduced by any relief given under the above provisions for his share of any partnership loss which is sustained in the same tax year and to which the similar cap at **52.15 PARTNERSHIPS** applies in his case. The amount of the cap may be varied in future by the Treasury via statutory instrument. The cap does *not* apply:

- to so much of any loss as derives from 'qualifying film expenditure' (see below);
- to prevent relief for the loss against profits of the same trade; or
- to **UNDERWRITERS AT LLOYD'S (74)** in connection with their underwriting business.

For these purposes, an individual carries on a trade in a '*non-active capacity*' during a tax year if he carries it on at any time in that tax year and, in the 'relevant period' for that tax year, he does not devote a 'significant amount of time' to it. An individual devotes a '*significant amount of time*' to a trade in the 'relevant period' for a tax year if, in that period, he spends an average of at least 10 hours a week personally engaged in activities of the trade. Those activities must be carried on on a commercial basis and with a view to profit. Any relief erroneously given on the assumption that this requirement will be met will be withdrawn by means of an income tax assessment. The '*relevant period*' for a tax year is normally the basis period for that tax year. If, however, the basis period is less than six months because the tax year is the one in which the individual commenced or ceased the trade, the requirement must instead be met by reference to the six months beginning with the commencement date or ending with the cessation date, as the case may be.

Transitional provisions

If the basis year for 2007/08 ended before **12 March 2008**, the cap does not apply to a loss sustained in that basis period. For a tax year the basis period for which begins before, and includes, **12 March 2008** (a 'straddling basis period'), the loss subject to the cap is the loss that would otherwise be eligible for the above-mentioned reliefs (disregarding the cap but applying all other restrictions) reduced by any 'pre-announcement loss'.

A '*pre-announcement loss*' is computed as follows.

(1) Compute the profit or loss for the straddling basis period without regard to capital allowances or 'qualifying film expenditure'.

(2) If the computation in (1) above produces a loss, time-apportion that loss to that part of the straddling period that falls before 12 March 2008. If the computation in (1) above does not produce a loss, this step is irrelevant.

(3) Compute (on a just and reasonable basis) the amount of the loss for the straddling basis period (not the loss computed in (1) above) as is attributable to capital allowances on expenditure paid before 12 March 2008 and expenditure paid on or after that date pursuant to an unconditional obligation (as defined) in a contract made before that date.

(4) The pre-announcement loss is the time-apportioned figure (if any) from (2) above plus the amount (if any) in (3) above.

Qualifying film expenditure

Expenditure is *'qualifying film expenditure'* if it is:

- expenditure which is deducted, in computing the trade loss, under the statutory relief provisions for certified films, i.e. under any of *ITTOIA 2005, ss 137–142* (see **73.76** TRADING INCOME); or
- incidental expenditure (i.e. expenditure on management, administration or obtaining finance) that, whilst deductible other than under the statutory relief provisions for certified films, was incurred in connection with the production or the acquisition (as defined) of a film in relation to which expenditure was deducted under the said provisions.

It was made clear by the Treasury in relation to the identical definition for the purposes of **52.17** PARTNERSHIPS that qualifying film expenditure does not include expenditure on distribution of a film or 'print and advertising' or production of a film as trading stock (Treasury Explanatory Notes to the 2004 Finance Bill).

The extent to which a loss derives from qualifying film expenditure and the extent to which expenditure qualifies as incidental expenditure are to be determined on a just and reasonable basis.

[*ITA 2007, ss 74A, 74C, 74D; FA 2008, Sch 21 paras 2, 6*].

Tax-generated losses

In addition to the above restriction, if an individual carries on a trade (otherwise than as a partner) in a 'non-active capacity' (as defined above) and makes a trade loss arising (directly or indirectly) in consequence of, or otherwise in connection with, 'tax avoidance arrangements' made **on or after 12 March 2008** (subject to the transitional provision below), no relief is available for that loss under:

- *ITA 2007, s 64* against general income (and, consequently, *TCGA 1992, s 261B* against chargeable gains) (see **45.2, 45.7** above); or
- *ITA 2007, s 72* (losses in early years of trade) against general income (see **45.9** above).

This restriction is superseded by the broader legislation outlined in **45.18** below and does not apply to a loss to which **45.18** potentially applies.

'Tax avoidance arrangements' means arrangements (as widely defined) made by the individual a main purpose of which is to obtain a reduction in tax liability by means of one or more of the above-mentioned reliefs. This restriction does not apply to any loss that derives wholly from 'qualifying film expenditure' (see above).

Transitional provision

The above restriction does not apply if the arrangements in question are made pursuant to an unconditional obligation (as defined) in a contract made on or before 11 March 2008.

[*ITA 2007, ss 74B–74D; FA 2008, Sch 21 paras 2, 7; FA 2010, Sch 3 paras 6–8, 11*].

Tax-generated losses

[45.18] The following reliefs are denied in the case of a 'tax-generated loss':

- relief under *ITA 2007, s 64* against general income (and, consequently, *TCGA 1992, s 261B* against chargeable gains) (see **45.2**, **45.7** above); and

- relief under *ITA 2007, s 72* (losses in early years of trade) against general income (see **45.9** above),

A *'tax-generated loss'* is a loss sustained by a person in carrying on a trade, profession or vocation (whether alone or in partnership) which arises in consequence of, or in connection with, 'relevant tax avoidance arrangements'. *'Relevant tax avoidance arrangements'* are arrangements (as widely defined) to which the person is a party and a main purpose of which is the obtaining of a reduction in tax liability by means of one or more of the above-mentioned reliefs. This denial of relief does not apply in relation to a loss that derives wholly from 'qualifying film expenditure' (as in **45.17** above).

The denial of relief applies if the tax-generated loss arises in consequence of, or in connection with,

- arrangements entered into on or after 21 October 2009, or
- any transaction forming part of any such arrangements which is entered into on or after that date,

unless the arrangements or transaction were entered into pursuant to an unconditional obligation (as defined) in a contract made before that date.

[*ITA 2007, s 74ZA; FA 2010, Sch 3 paras 5, 11*].

For guidance, including examples, see www.hmrc.gov.uk/briefs/income-tax/si de-loss-relief.pdf.

To decide whether a main purpose of arrangements is to obtain a reduction in tax liability by way of one of the above-mentioned loss reliefs, it is necessary to look at all the circumstances in which the arrangements were entered into, including the participant's overall economic objective. If the loss arises in connection with a marketed tax avoidance scheme, it is almost certain that this will indeed be the case; but the legislation is by no means restricted to such instances.

Miscellaneous

[45.19] See **52.13–52.17** PARTNERSHIPS for restrictions on loss reliefs available to non-active members of partnerships. Special restrictions on the use of losses apply in relation to certain company partnership arrangements [*CTA 2010, ss 958–962*] — see **52.19** PARTNERSHIPS. See **52.22**, **52.24** PARTNERSHIPS for restrictions on loss reliefs available to, respectively, limited partners and members of limited liability partnerships. Loss relief cannot be claimed in respect of losses of certain partnerships dealing in commodity futures (see **4.40** ANTI-AVOIDANCE).

Relief under *ITA 2007, s 64* or *s 72* or their predecessors cannot be given against income from oil extraction activities or oil rights except to the extent (if any) that the loss arises from oil extraction activities or oil rights. [*ITA 2007, s 80; ITTOIA 2005, ss 225A, 225B; ICTA 1988, ss 492(2), 502(1); TIOPA 2010, Sch 1 para 2*].

Trading losses carried forward

[45.20] On a claim under *ITA 2007, s 83* (or, before 2007/08, *ICTA 1988, s 385*), any trading loss not used as above (or any unused balance) may be carried forward to subsequent years without time limit. A claim is given effect by deducting the loss in arriving at net income for subsequent tax years (see Step 2 at **1.7 ALLOWANCES AND TAX RATES**). However, it can only be deducted from profits of the same trade, profession or vocation carried on by the same individual. The deduction must be made from the first available profits (and then, if those profits are insufficient, from the next available, and so on until the loss is exhausted). The deduction is made in priority to any other deductions from available profits. The loss must be deducted from available profits even if those profits might otherwise have been covered by personal reliefs; partial deductions are not permitted. See the second example at **45.4** above as regards losses used in aggregation (for which see *CIR v Scott Adamson* CS 1932, 17 TC 379). See *Bispham v Eardiston Farming Co* Ch D 1962, 40 TC 322 as to effect of what is now *ITTOIA 2005, s 9(2)* (all farming by a person treated as one trade — see **73.73 TRADING INCOME**) on the carry-forward of farming losses. [*ITA 2007, ss 61(2), 83, 84; ICTA 1988, s 385(1)*].

Time limit for claims

By virtue of *TMA 1970, s 43(1)* (see **18.4 CLAIMS**), a claim to carry forward a loss must be made within four years after the end of the tax year in which the loss arose. The loss is relieved automatically against subsequent profits with no further claim being necessary.

For a case turning on the failure to establish the year(s) in which losses from an abortive business venture arose, see *Richardson v Jenkins* Ch D 1995, 67 TC 246.

Relief against trade-related interest and dividends

Where full relief for a carried-forward loss cannot be given for any particular year because of an insufficiency of trading profits, any interest or dividends for that year that 'relate to the trade' are treated for this purpose as profits of the trade. Interest or dividends for a tax year '*relate to the trade*' if they arise in the tax year and, were it not for the fact that they have been subjected to tax under other provisions, they would be brought into account in calculating the trading profits. [*ITA 2007, s 85; ICTA 1988, s 385(4)*]. See also **73.90 TRADING INCOME**.

Carry-forward on incorporation

If a trade or business carried on by an individual (or by individuals in partnership) is transferred to a company for consideration consisting wholly or mainly of the allotment (to the individual or his nominee) of shares in the company, any unrelieved pre-incorporation trading losses brought forward under the above provisions are deductible from income derived by the individual from the company, which may take the form of dividends on the shares or may be, for example, director's fees.

The brought-forward loss is deductible against such derived income for a particular tax year only if throughout that tax year the individual retains beneficial ownership of the allotted shares *and* the company continues to carry on the trade. In the tax year of incorporation, these conditions must be satisfied throughout the period from the transfer of the business to the following 5 April. In practice, relief should not be refused for any year throughout which shares representing at least 80% of the consideration received for the business are retained (HMRC Business Income Manual BIM75500).

[*ITA 2007, s 86; ICTA 1988, s 386*].

Change of residence

Where, on a sole trader becoming or ceasing to be UK resident, the trade is deemed to be permanently discontinued and a new one commenced, losses of the 'old' trade may be carried forward under the above provisions and set against profits of the 'new' trade. See **73.16 TRADING INCOME** (and see **52.20 PARTNERSHIPS** for a similar rule as regards an individual trading in partnership).

Miscellaneous

For the treatment in certain circumstances of interest and (before 2007/08) annual payments as losses carried forward, see respectively **45.23** and **45.24** below.

For the purpose of relieving a carried-forward loss from **oil-related activities**, profits from other activities may be treated as being from the same trade if that would have been the case apart from the rule at **73.1 TRADING INCOME** requiring oil-related activities to be treated as a separate trade. [*ITA 2007, s 87; ICTA 1988, s 492(4)*].

Simon's Taxes. See E1.1010–E1.1015.

Terminal loss relief

[45.21] If a person ceases to carry on a trade or profession in a tax year and makes 'terminal losses', he may make a claim under *ITA 2007, s 89* (or, before 2007/08, *ICTA 1988, s 388*) to set off the total amount of terminal losses against the profits of the trade etc. for the tax year in which the cessation occurs and the three preceding tax years. The claim is given effect by deducting this amount in arriving at net income for those tax years (see Step 2 at **1.7 ALLOWANCES AND TAX RATES**), with the deduction for each year being restricted to the profits available. The deduction must be made firstly for the latest tax year for which there are available profits and then, if those profits are insufficient, for the previous year, and so on until either the total amount of the terminal losses or the maximum three-year carry-back period is exhausted. Any amount still unrelieved is potentially available for relief under any of the other trading loss reliefs described in this chapter (subject to the conditions and time limits for claiming those reliefs). Subject to the maximum three-year carry-back period, terminal losses must be deducted from available profits even if those profits might otherwise have been covered by personal reliefs; partial deductions are not permitted.

Each of the following is a *'terminal loss'*:

(a)   the loss (if any) sustained in the final tax year (i.e. the period from 6 April to cessation); and

(b)   the loss (if any) sustained in that part of the penultimate tax year that falls within the twelve months immediately preceding cessation,

in so far as such losses have not otherwise been relieved. A terminal relief claim must cover both the loss (if any) at (a) and the loss (if any) at (b); it is not possible to include one and not the other. If there is a profit at (a) but a loss at (b), or *vice versa*, the profit is not netted off against the loss but is simply disregarded — see also the *Example* and note at **45.22** below. If periods of account do not coincide with tax years, time apportionment is used to arrive at the figures at (a) and (b) (unless, exceptionally, a more accurate method is available).

Time limit for claims

By virtue of *TMA 1970, s 43(1)* (see **18.4 CLAIMS**), a claim for relief must be made within four years after the end of the tax year in which cessation occurs.

See **18.2 CLAIMS** for further provisions regarding claims for a loss incurred in one tax year to be carried back to an earlier tax year.

Overlap relief (see **73.11 TRADING INCOME**) is a deduction in computing the profit or loss of the final tax year (not the final period of account) and thus falls to be included in full in a terminal loss claim (and may itself create a terminal loss).

Partnerships

Terminal loss relief is available to an outgoing member of a partnership in respect of losses sustained in his notional trade. All partners may claim terminal loss relief on cessation of the actual partnership trade. See **52 PARTNERSHIPS**.

Effect of pre-2007/08 charges on income

The profits against which a terminal loss may be set are treated as reduced by the gross amount of any payment made from which income tax was deducted at source but did not have to be accounted for to HMRC, i.e. because the payment was made out of taxed profits. In other words, the profits are treated as reduced by charges on income within *ICTA 1988, s 348* (see **24.20 DEDUCTION OF TAX AT SOURCE**), with no distinction between trade and non-trade charges. In such cases, the terminal loss itself is reduced by a like amount *unless* the payment in question (i) was made wholly and exclusively for the purposes of the trade etc., (ii) could have been assessed under *ICTA 1988, s 350* (see **24.20 DEDUCTION OF TAX AT SOURCE**) if not made out of taxed profits, *and* (iii) if so assessed, could have been treated as a loss under the provisions at **45.24** below.

For 2007/08 onwards, as a consequence of changes made by *ITA 2007* to the manner in which payments formerly treated as charges on income are relieved and to the mechanism for collecting tax deducted at source from such payments, the above provisions are no longer required and are repealed. For a full discussion of this, see Change 81 in Annex 1 to the Explanatory Notes to *ITA 2007*. The repeal does not affect the treatment of a post-5 April 2007 terminal loss carried back to any of the years 2004/05 to 2006/07.

Relief against trade-related interest and dividends

Where full relief for terminal losses cannot be given for any particular tax year because of an insufficiency of trading profits, any interest or dividends for that year that 'relate to the trade' are treated for this purpose as profits of the trade. Interest or dividends for a tax year *'relate to the trade'* if they arise in the tax year and, were it not for the fact that they have been subjected to tax under other provisions, they would be brought into account in calculating the trading profits. See also **73.90 TRADING INCOME**.

Miscellaneous

Where the trade in question is a mineral extraction trade (as defined for capital allowances purposes), special provisions (see *ITA 2007, s 93*) apply where a claim is made under both *ITA 2007, s 89* (or its predecessor) and *CAA 2001, s 355* (carry-back of balancing allowance — see **10.16 CAPITAL ALLOWANCES**).

For the inclusion in certain circumstances of interest and (before 2007/08) annual payments in a terminal loss, see respectively **45.23** and **45.24** below.

[*ITA 2007, ss 63, 89–93; ICTA 1988, ss 388, 389*].

Simon's Taxes. See **E1.1022**.

Example

[45.22]

B, a trader with a 30 September year end, ceases to trade on 30 June 2010. Tax-adjusted results for his last two periods of account (disregarding overlap relief) are as follows.

	Trading profit/ (loss)
Year ended 30 September 2009	£28,000
Nine months to 30 June 2010	(£9,000)

In addition, there is unused overlap relief (see **73.11 TRADING INCOME**) of £2,000. The terminal loss relief available is as follows.

	£	£
2010/11 (6.4.10 to 30.6.10)		
£9,000 × $^3/_9$		3,000
plus unused overlap relief		2,000
Terminal loss		5,000
2009/10 (1.7.09 to 5.4.10)		
1.10.09 to 5.4.10 £9,000 × $^6/_9$	6,000	
1.7.09 to 30.9.09 (£28,000) × $^3/_{12}$	(7,000)	
	(1,000)	
Terminal loss		Nil
Terminal loss relief		£5,000

Note

In determining the terminal loss arising in a part of the final twelve months (a terminal loss period) that falls into any one tax year, a profit made in that period must be netted off against a loss sustained in that period. In this example, no net loss is incurred in the terminal loss period falling within 2009/10. However, the two different tax years are considered entirely separately, so that the 'net profit' of £1,000 falling within 2009/10 does not have to be netted off against the 2010/11 loss and is instead disregarded. The losses which do not form part of the terminal loss claim may be relieved under *ITA 2007, s 64* (see **45.2** above), and in practice, where other income is sufficient, the whole of the losses would in many cases be claimed under *section 64*.

Treatment of interest as a trade loss

[45.23] Where relief is claimed under *ITA 2007, s 383* (or, before 2007/08, under *ICTA 1988, s 353*) (see **43.5 INTEREST PAYABLE**) in respect of interest paid wholly and exclusively for the purposes of a trade, profession or vocation carried on wholly or partly in the UK and full effect cannot be given to such relief due to an insufficiency of income, the amount unrelieved may be carried forward as a trading loss under *ITA 2007, s 83* or its predecessor (see **45.20** above) or treated as a trading loss for the purposes of computing a terminal loss under *ITA 2007, s 89* or its predecessor (see **45.21** above). The treatment is effectively restricted to interest within **43.6**(a) or **43.10 INTEREST PAYABLE** (loans to purchase plant or machinery for, or to invest in, a partnership). [*ITA 2007, ss 88, 94; ICTA 1988, s 390*].

Treatment of pre-2007/08 annual payments as a trade loss

[45.24] Amounts assessed under *ICTA 1988, s 350* in respect of annual payments, royalties etc., not paid out of taxed income (see **24.21 DEDUCTION OF TAX AT SOURCE**) may be treated as trading losses for the purposes of carry-forward under *ICTA 1988, ss 385, 386* (see **45.20** above) or of computing a terminal loss under *ICTA 1988, s 388* (see **45.21** above). Further, where such payments are made to residents of a country with which a DOUBLE TAX RELIEF (**26**) agreement is in force and are thereby exempt from UK tax, so that no assessment under *ICTA 1988, s 350* is made in respect of them, the amounts thereof can nevertheless be similarly carried forward (*SI 1970 No 488*). But these provisions do not apply to *section 350* assessments arising from:

- payments not made wholly and exclusively for the purposes of the trade etc.;
- payments charged to capital, or not ultimately borne by the person assessed;
- yearly interest paid under deduction of tax under *ICTA 1988, s 349(2)* (see **24.21**(ii) DEDUCTION OF TAX AT SOURCE);
- copyright royalties and design royalty and public lending right payments paid to non-residents (see **24.21**(iii) DEDUCTION OF TAX AT SOURCE);
- sales of patent rights by non-residents (see *ITTOIA 2005, s 595* and **40** INTELLECTUAL PROPERTY).

For 2007/08 onwards, as a consequence of changes made by *ITA 2007* to the manner in which annual payments, royalties, etc., are relieved and to the mechanism for collecting tax deducted at source from such payments, the above provisions are no longer required and are repealed. For a full discussion of this, see Change 81 in Annex 1 to the Explanatory Notes to *ITA 2007*. This does not prevent the continued carry-forward as a trading loss of amounts assessed under *ICTA 1988, s 350* for 2006/07 and earlier years.

[*ICTA 1988, ss 387, 389(1); ITA 2007, Sch 1 para 73*].

Losses on shares in unlisted trading companies

[45.25] See generally HMRC Venture Capital Schemes Manual VCM10000 *et seq.*, 45000 *et seq.*

An individual may claim relief from income tax, instead of from capital gains tax, for an allowable loss (as computed for capital gains tax purposes) on a disposal of 'qualifying shares'. For 2007/08 onwards, the claim is under *ITA 2007, s 132*.

Relief is available only if:

- the disposal is at arm's length; or
- it is by way of a distribution on a winding-up; or
- the value of the shares has become negligible and a claim to that effect made under *TCGA 1992, s 24(2)* (see Tolley's Capital Gains Tax under Losses); or
- a deemed disposal occurs under *TCGA 1992, s 24(1)* (which deems the entire loss, destruction, dissipation or extinction of an asset to be a disposal — see Tolley's Capital Gains Tax under Disposal).

Relief is not available where the shares are the subject of an exchange or arrangement within *TCGA 1992, ss 135* or *136* and, because of *TCGA 1992, s 137*, that exchange or arrangement involves a disposal of the shares.

'*Qualifying shares*' are ordinary shares or stock:

- in a 'qualifying trading company' for which the individual 'subscribed'; or
- to which EIS income tax relief is attributable (see **28 ENTERPRISE INVESTMENT SCHEME**).

For this purpose, an individual '*subscribes*' for shares if they are issued to him by the company in consideration of money or money's worth, or were transferred to him *inter vivos* by his spouse or civil partner who had similarly subscribed for them. The spouses or civil partners concerned must be living together at the time of the transfer, and the shares are treated as issued to the transferee at the time they were issued to the transferor. Where an individual has subscribed for shares, he is treated as having subscribed for any bonus shares subsequently issued to him in respect of those shares provided that the bonus shares are in the same company, of the same class and carry the same rights as the original shares. The bonus shares are treated as issued at the time the original shares were issued.

The definition of 'qualifying trading company' differs according to whether the shares are issued after 5 April 1998 (see **45.28** below) or were issued on or before that date (see **45.30** below).

Where, for shares subscribed for before 10 March 1981, the consideration was deemed equal to the market value under *CGTA 1979, s 19(3)*, the loss allowable on disposal cannot exceed what the loss would have been without applying that subsection. (For shares subscribed for after 9 March 1981, market value is not substituted where the consideration is less than market value.)

[*ITA 2007, ss 131, 135, 150, 151(1)(2)*].

Simon's Taxes. See E3.7.

Operation of (and claims for) relief

[45.26] A loss within **45.25** above may be claimed against income:

- of the tax year in which the loss is incurred; and/or
- of the tax year preceding that in which the loss is incurred.

If a claim is made in relation to both tax years, it must specify the year for which relief is to be given first. The loss is deducted in calculating net income for the specified tax year, and, if the claim relates to both tax years, any remaining part of the loss is then deducted in calculating net income for the other year.

Where, against income of the same year, claims are made both in respect of that year's loss and in respect of the following year's loss, the claim for the current year's loss takes precedence.

A claim for relief must be made in writing on or before the first anniversary of 31 January following the tax year *in which the loss is incurred.*

Relief under these provisions is given in priority to relief under *ITA 2007, s 64* (see **45.2** above) and *ITA 2007, s 72* (see **45.9** above) for the same tax year.

To the extent that relief in respect of a loss is obtained under these provisions, the loss is not an allowable loss for capital gains tax purposes. Any part of the loss for which income tax relief is not given does, however, remain an allowable loss for capital gains tax purposes.

[*ITA 2007, ss 132, 133, Sch 1 para 309; TCGA 1992, s 125A(1)*].

Limits on relief

Where an individual claims relief under these provisions in respect of a loss on the disposal of qualifying shares which form part of a 'section 104 holding' or a '1982 holding' (i.e. holdings of shares which are pooled for capital gains tax purposes) either at the time of disposal or at an earlier time, the relief is restricted to the sums that would have been allowable as deductions in computing the loss if the qualifying shares had not formed part of the holding.

Where the qualifying shares were acquired on the same day as other shares that are not capable of being qualifying shares (see below), such that, by virtue of *TCGA 1992, s 105(1)(a)*, all the shares are treated as acquired by a single transaction, the amount of relief is restricted to the sums that would have been allowable as deductions in computing the loss if the qualifying shares were treated as acquired by a single transaction and the other shares were not so treated.

Where the qualifying shares, taken as a single asset, and other shares or debentures in the same company which are not capable of being qualifying shares, also taken as a single asset, are treated for capital gains tax purposes as the same asset under *TCGA 1992, s 127*, the amount of relief is restricted to the sums that would have been allowable as deductions in computing the loss if the qualifying shares and the other shares were not to be treated as the same asset.

For the above purposes, shares to which EIS income tax relief is not attributable are not capable of being qualifying shares at any time if they were acquired otherwise than by subscription, if the condition at **45.28**(c) below was not met in relation to the issue of the shares or the condition at **45.28**(d) below would not be met if the shares were disposed of at that time. Additionally, for the purposes only of the 'same asset' restriction above, shares to which EIS income tax relief is not attributable are not capable of being qualifying shares at any time if they are shares of a different class from the qualifying shares concerned.

[*ITA 2007, s 147*].

HMRC Venture Capital Schemes Manual VCM47150 identifies four steps in the computation of loss relief under these provisions where a holding does not entirely consist of qualifying shares.

Step 1 is to compute the allowable loss for capital gains tax purposes under normal capital gains tax principles and identification rules (see Tolley's Capital Gains Tax under Shares and Securities — Identification Rules).

Step 2 is to identify the qualifying and non-qualifying shares included in the disposal (using the special identification rules described at **45.27** below).

If it is found that the disposal comprises both, Step 3 is to apportion the loss, on a just and reasonable basis, between qualifying and non-qualifying shares.

Step 4 is to compare the loss so attributed to the qualifying shares with the actual allowable expenditure incurred on those shares and to apply, if necessary, the restriction mentioned above.

Share identification rules

[45.27] The following provisions apply to identify whether a disposal of shares forming part of a mixed holding (i.e. a 'holding' of shares including shares that are not capable of being qualifying shares and other shares) is a disposal of qualifying shares and, if so, to which of any qualifying shares acquired at different times the disposal relates. Except as noted below, the normal capital gains tax identification rules apply and where shares are thereby identified with the whole or any part of a section 104 holding or a 1982 holding, they are further identified with acquisitions on a last in/first out (LIFO) basis.

The above rules do not apply where the holding includes *any* of the following:

*   shares in respect of which the long defunct Business Expansion Scheme relief was given and was not withdrawn;
*   shares to which Enterprise Investment Scheme (EIS) income tax relief is attributable (see **28 ENTERPRISE INVESTMENT SCHEME**);
*   shares to which EIS capital gains deferral relief is attributable (see **28.24 ENTERPRISE INVESTMENT SCHEME**).

Instead, disposals are identified in accordance with the identification rules generally applicable to BES and EIS shares (broadly, first in/first out (FIFO) — see, for example, **28.11 ENTERPRISE INVESTMENT SCHEME**). Special rules apply where an election under *TCGA 1992, s 105A* (election for alternative treatment: approved-scheme shares) is made.

Where the above rules cannot identify the shares disposed of, the identification is to be made on a just and reasonable basis.

A '*holding*' of shares for the above purposes is any number of shares of the same class held by one individual in the same capacity, growing or diminishing as shares of that class are acquired or disposed of. Shares comprised in a 'new holding' following a reorganisation to which *TCGA 1992, s 127* applies are treated as having been acquired when the original shares were acquired. Any shares held or disposed of by a nominee or bare trustees for an individual are treated as held or disposed of by that individual.

[*ITA 2007, ss 148, 149*].

Qualifying trading company — shares issued after 5 April 1998

[45.28] As regards shares issued after 5 April 1998, a '*qualifying trading company*', for the purposes of **45.25** above, is a company which:

(a) either
    (i) on the date of disposal meets the trading requirement, control and independence requirement, qualifying subsidiaries requirement and (for shares issued on or after 17 March 2004) the property managing subsidiaries requirement; or
    (ii) has ceased to meet any of those requirements within three years before the date of disposal and has not since that cessation been an 'excluded company', an investment company (as defined) or a trading company; *and*

(b) either
    (i) has met each of the requirements in (a)(i) above for a continuous period of at least six years prior to the disposal (or prior to the cessation in (a)(ii) above, as the case may be); or
    (ii) has met each of those requirements for a shorter continuous period ending with the disposal or cessation and has not previously been an excluded company, an investment company or a trading company; *and*

(c) met the gross assets requirement both immediately before and immediately after the issue of the shares and (for shares issued after 6 March 2001) met the unquoted status requirement at the 'relevant time'; *and*

(d) has carried on its business wholly or mainly in the UK throughout the period ending with the date of disposal of the shares and beginning with the incorporation of the company, or, if later, one year before the date on which the shares were issued.

See **45.29** below as regards the six requirements mentioned in (a)–(c) above.

For shares issued before 7 March 2001, it was also a condition that the company be an 'unquoted' company (as defined for the purposes of the unquoted status requirement) throughout that part of the period mentioned in (d) above that falls before 7 March 2001.

An '*excluded company*' is a company which has a trade consisting mainly of dealing in land, in commodities or futures or in shares, securities or other financial instruments or which is not carried on on a commercial basis with a reasonable expectation of profit, or a company which is the holding company of a group other than a 'trading group', or which is a building society (see **9 BUILDING SOCIETIES**) or a registered industrial and provident society (as defined).

A '*trading group*' is a group (i.e. a company and its 51% subsidiaries) the business of the members of which, taken together, consists wholly or mainly in the carrying on of a trade or trades (disregarding any trade carried on by a subsidiary which is an excluded company.

[ITA 2007, ss 134, 151(1)(7), Sch 2 paras 38, 50; CTA 2010, Sch 1 para 498(2); SI 2007 No 940].

The six requirements

[45.29] The six requirements referred to at **45.28**(a) to (c) above are as follows.

The trading requirement

The company must either:

(i)   exist wholly for the purpose of carrying on one or more 'qualifying trades' (see **28.50** ENTERPRISE INVESTMENT SCHEME) (disregarding purposes having no significant effect on the extent of its activities); or

(ii) be a *'parent company'* (i.e. a company that has one or more 'qualifying subsidiaries' (see **28.47** ENTERPRISE INVESTMENT SCHEME)) and the business of the *'group'* (i.e. the company and its qualifying subsidiaries) must not consist wholly or as to a substantial part in the carrying on of 'non-qualifying activities'.

Where the company intends that one or more other companies should become its qualifying subsidiaries with a view to their carrying on one or more qualifying trades, then, until any time after which the intention is abandoned, the company is treated as a parent company and those other companies are included in the group for the purposes of (ii) above. (This provision is made explicit in *ITA 2007* but reflects previous practice (see Change 42 listed in Annex 1 to the Explanatory Notes to *ITA 2007*).)

For the purpose of (ii) above, the business of the group means what would be the business of the group if the activities of the group companies taken together were regarded as one business. Activities are for this purpose disregarded to the extent that they consist in:

•   holding shares in or securities of any of the company's subsidiaries;
•   making loans to another group company;
•   holding and managing property used by a group company for the purposes of a qualifying trade or trades carried on by any group company; or
•   holding and managing property used by a group company for the purposes of research and development from which it is intended either that a qualifying trade to be carried on by a 'group company' will be derived or, for shares issued after 5 April 2007, a qualifying trade carried on or to be carried on by a group company will benefit. *'Group company'* includes, for this purpose, any existing or future company which will be a group company at any future time.

Activities are similarly disregarded to the extent that they consist, in the case of a subsidiary whose main purpose is the carrying on of qualifying trade(s) and whose other purposes have no significant effect on the extent of its activities (other than in relation to incidental matters), in activities not in pursuance of its main purpose.

'Non-qualifying activities' are:

•   excluded activities within **28.50** ENTERPRISE INVESTMENT SCHEME; and
•   non-trading activities (other than research and development (as defined)).

References in the definition of 'qualifying trade' and 'excluded activities' at **28.50** ENTERPRISE INVESTMENT SCHEME to 'period B' are to be taken for the above purposes to refer to the continuous period mentioned in **45.28**(b) above.

For the ascertainment of the purposes for which a company exists, see HMRC Venture Capital Schemes Manual VCM15070.

A company ceases to meet the trading requirement if before the time that is relevant for the purposes of **45.28**(a) above a resolution is passed or an order is made for the winding-up of the company or if the company is dissolved without winding-up. This does not, however, apply if the winding-up is for genuine commercial reasons and not part of a scheme a main purpose of which is tax avoidance and the company continues, during the winding-up, to be a trading company. (Note that the continuation of trading condition now applies in relation to shares issued after 5 April 2001 but did originally apply up to and including 20 March 2000, after which a drafting error inadvertently altered the law.) For shares issued after 20 March 2000, a company does not cease to meet the trading requirement by reason of anything done as a consequence of its being in administration or receivership (both as defined by *ITA 2007, s 252*), provided everything so done and the entry into administration or receivership are for genuine commercial (and not tax avoidance) reasons. For shares issued after 16 March 2004, these provisions are extended to refer also to the winding-up, dissolution, administration or receivership of any of the company's subsidiaries.

The control and independence requirement

Subject to, the share exchange provisions at **45.25** above, the issuing company must not:

(I)   control another company other than a qualifying subsidiary (see **28.47** ENTERPRISE INVESTMENT SCHEME) or, for shares issued before 21 March 2000, have a 51% subsidiary other than a qualifying subsidiary, 'control' being construed in accordance with *CTA 2010, ss 450, 451* and being considered with or without connected persons within *ITA 2007, s 993*;

(II)   be a 51% subsidiary of another company or otherwise under the control of another company, 'control' being construed in accordance with *ITA 2007, s 995* and again being considered with or without connected persons; or

(III)   be capable of falling within (I) or (II) by virtue of any arrangements (as very broadly defined).

The qualifying subsidiaries requirement

The company must not have any subsidiaries other than qualifying subsidiaries (see **28.47** ENTERPRISE INVESTMENT SCHEME).

The property managing subsidiaries requirement

For shares issued on or after 17 March 2004, any 'property managing subsidiary' (see **28.45** ENTERPRISE INVESTMENT SCHEME) that the company has must be a 'qualifying 90% subsidiary' (see **28.48** ENTERPRISE INVESTMENT SCHEME).

The gross assets requirement

The value of the company's gross assets must not exceed £7 million immediately before the issue of the shares in respect of which relief is claimed and must not exceed £8 million immediately afterwards. In relation to shares issued before 6 April 2006, these limits were £15 million and £16 million respectively; the higher limits continue to apply in relation to shares issued after 5 April 2006 to a person who subscribed for them before 22 March 2006. If the issuing company is a parent company, the gross assets test applies by reference to the aggregate gross assets of the company and all its qualifying subsidiaries (disregarding certain assets held by any such company which correspond to liabilities of another).

The general approach of HMRC to the gross assets requirement is that the value of a company's gross assets is the sum of the value of all of the balance sheet assets. Where accounts are actually drawn up to a date immediately before or after the issue, the balance sheet values are taken provided that they reflect usual accounting standards and the company's normal accounting practice, consistently applied. Where accounts are not drawn up to such a date, such values will be taken from the most recent balance sheet, updated as precisely as practicable on the basis of all the relevant information available to the company. Values so arrived at may need to be reviewed in the light of information contained in the accounts for the period in which the issue was made, and, if they were not available at the time of the issue, those for the preceding period, when they become available. The company's assets immediately before the issue do not include any advance payment received in respect of the issue. Where shares are issued partly paid, the right to the balance is an asset, and, notwithstanding the above, will be taken into account in valuing the assets immediately after the issue regardless of whether it is shown in the balance sheet. (HMRC SP 2/00).

The unquoted status requirement

For shares issued on or after 7 March 2001, the company must be 'unquoted' at the time (the 'relevant time') at which the shares are issued and no arrangements must then exist for it to cease to be unquoted. If, at the time of issue, arrangements exist for the company to become a wholly-owned subsidiary of a new holding company by means of a share exchange within the provisions at 45.31 below, no arrangements must exist for the new company to cease to be unquoted. A company is 'unquoted' if none of its shares etc., are listed on a recognised stock exchange or on a foreign exchange designated for the purpose, or dealt in outside the UK by such means as may be designated for the purpose. Securities on the Alternative Investment Market ('AIM') are treated as unquoted for these purposes (Revenue Press Release 20 February 1995). If the company is unquoted at the time of the share issue, it does not cease to be unquoted in relation to those shares solely because they are listed on an exchange which becomes a recognised stock exchange or is designated by an order made after the date of the issue (see HMRC Venture Capital Schemes Manual VCM15020).

[ITA 2007, ss 137 144, Sch 2 paras 40–47, 51–57; FA 2007, Sch 16 paras 11(5), 13, 14, Sch 26 para 12(2); CTA 2010, Sch 1 para 497].

Qualifying trading company — shares issued before 6 April 1998

[45.30] As regards shares issued before 6 April 1998, a *'qualifying trading company'*, for the purposes of **45.25** above, is a company none of whose shares have been listed on a recognised stock exchange at any time in the period ending with the date of disposal of the shares and beginning with the incorporation of the company, or, if later, one year before the date on which the shares were subscribed for, and which:

(a)   either (i) is a trading company (i.e. a company, other than an excluded company, whose business consists wholly or mainly of the carrying on of a trade or trades, or which is the holding company of a 'trading group') on the date of the disposal or (ii) has ceased to be a trading company within the previous three years and has not since that time been an investment company or an 'excluded company'; and

(b)   either (i) has been a trading company for a continuous period of six years ending on the date of disposal of the shares or the time it ceased to be a trading company; or (ii) if shorter, a continuous period ending on that date or that time and had not before the beginning of that period been an excluded company or an investment company; and

(c)   has been resident in the UK since incorporation until the date of disposal.

Securities on the Alternative Investment Market ('AIM') are generally treated as unquoted for these purposes (Revenue Press Release 20 February 1995; HMRC Internet Statement 29 March 2007 at www.hmrc.gov.uk/budget2007/rec-stock-exch.htm).

A *'trading group'* is a group (i.e. a company and its 51% subsidiaries) the business of the members of which, taken together, consists wholly or mainly in the carrying on of a trade or trades (disregarding any trade carried on by a subsidiary which is an excluded company or which is non-UK resident).

An *'excluded company'* is a company which has a trade consisting mainly of dealing in shares, securities, land, trades or commodity futures or which is not carried on on a commercial basis with a reasonable expectation of profit, or a company which is the holding company of a group other than a trading group, or which is a building society (see **9 BUILDING SOCIETIES**) or a registered industrial and provident society (as defined).

[*ITA 2007, s 134, Sch 2 para 38*].

Miscellaneous

[45.31] The following matters are relevant.

Anti-avoidance

Any claim to relief under **45.25** above will bring in the provisions of *TCGA 1992, s 30* (value-shifting to give a tax-free benefit) so that the relief may be adjusted for any benefit conferred whether tax-free or not. [*TCGA 1992, s 125A(2); ICTA 1988, s 576(2); ITA 2007, Sch 1 para 309*].

Company reorganisations etc.

The following applies only to shares to which EIS income tax relief is not attributable. Where shares are disposed of and represent a new holding identifiable under *TCGA 1992, s 127* with 'old shares' after a reorganisation or reduction of share capital, relief under **45.25** above is not available unless it could have been given if an allowable loss had arisen on the disposal of the old shares at arm's length at the reorganisation etc., had this legislation been in force. Where the reorganisation did not so qualify, but new consideration was given for the new shares, relief is limited to such of that new consideration as is an allowable deduction. '*New consideration*' is money or money's worth but excluding any surrender or alteration to the original shares or rights attached thereto, and the application of assets of the company or distribution declared but not made out of the assets.

For new shares issued on or after 6 April 2007, the above does not apply where the share exchange provisions below apply.

[*ITA 2007, s 136, Sch 2 para 39; CTA 2010, Sch 1 para 496*].

See HMRC Venture Capital Schemes Manual VCM48000 *et seq.*

Share exchanges

The following provisions apply in relation to shares to which EIS income tax relief is not attributable. Where, by means of an exchange of shares, all of the shares (the old shares) of a company (the old company) are acquired by a company (the new company) in which the only previously issued shares are subscriber shares, then, subject to the further conditions below being satisfied, the exchange is not regarded as involving a disposal of the old shares and an acquisition of the new company shares (the new shares). Where old shares held by an individual were subscribed for by him and EIS relief was not attributable to them, the new shares stand in the shoes of the old shares, e.g. as if they had been subscribed for and issued at the time the old shares were subscribed for and issued and as if any requirements under the above provisions met at any time before the exchange by the old company had been met at that time by the new company.

The further conditions are as follows.

(a) The shares must be issued after 5 April 1998.

(b) The consideration for the old shares must consist entirely of the issue of the new shares.

(c) The consideration for old shares of each description must consist entirely of new shares of the 'corresponding description'.

(d) New shares of each description must be issued to holders of old shares of the 'corresponding description' in respect of and in proportion to their holdings.

(e) For new shares issued on or after 6 April 2007, the exchange of shares is not treated for capital gains tax purposes as involving a disposal of the old shares or an acquisition of the new shares by virtue of *TCGA 1992, s 127.*

(f)   For new shares issued before 6 April 2007, before the issue of the new shares, on the written application (for which see **4.5 ANTI-AVOIDANCE**) of either the old or new company, HMRC must have notified to that company their satisfaction that the exchange:
(i)   is for genuine commercial reasons; and
(ii)   does not form part of a scheme or arrangements designed to avoid liability to corporation tax or capital gains tax.
HMRC may, within 30 days of an application, request further particulars, which must then be supplied within 30 days of the request (or such longer period as they may allow in any particular case).

For these purposes, old and new shares are of a '*corresponding description*' if, assuming they were shares in the same company, they would be of the same class and carry the same rights.

References above to 'shares' (other than those to 'shares to which EIS income tax relief is not attributable' or 'subscriber shares') include references to 'securities'.

An exchange within these provisions, or arrangements for such an exchange, do not breach the control and independence requirement at **45.29** above.

[*ITA 2007, ss 145, 146, Sch 2 paras 48, 49; FA 2007, Sch 16 para 11(6)*].

Example

[45.32]

X is a semi-retired business executive. Over the years he has acquired several shareholdings in unlisted companies and he has suffered the following losses.

(i)   500 shares in A Ltd (a qualifying trading company) which X subscribed for in 1995. Allowable loss for CGT purposes on liquidation in June 2009 — £12,000.
(ii)   500 shares in B Ltd which X subscribed for in 1996 at £10 per share. B Ltd traded as a builder until 2002 when it changed its trade to that of buying and selling land. X received an arm's length offer for the shares of £3 per share in May 2009 which he accepted.
(iii)   In 1994, X subscribed for 2,000 shares in C Ltd at £50 per share. In 1998 his aunt gave him a further 1,000 shares. The market value of the shares at that time was £60 per share.
        The company has been a qualifying trading company since 1990 but has fallen on hard times recently. A company offered X £20 per share in June 2010. X accepted the offer to the extent of 1,500 shares.

The treatment of these losses in relation to income tax would be as follows.

(i)   Loss claim — *ITA 2007, s 132*, 2009/10 or 2008/09 — £12,000.
(ii)   No loss claim under *ITA 2007, s 132* is possible as B Ltd is an 'excluded company' (see **45.28** above).
(iii)   *Step 1.* Compute the allowable loss for capital gains tax purposes.

Share pool

	Shares	Qualifying expenditure £
1994 subscription	2,000	100,000
1998 acquisition	1,000	60,000
	3,000	160,000
2010 disposal	(1,500)	(80,000)
Pool carried forward	1,500	£80,000

	£
Disposal consideration 1,500 × £20	30,000
Allowable cost $\dfrac{1,500}{3,000} \times £160,000$	80,000
Allowable capital loss	£50,000

Step 2. Applying a LIFO basis, identify the qualifying shares (500) and the non-qualifying shares (1,000) comprised in the disposal.

Step 3. Calculate the proportion of the loss attributable to the qualifying shares.

Loss referable to 500 qualifying shares $\dfrac{500}{1,500} \times £50,000 =$ £16,667

Step 4. Compare the loss in *Step 3* with the actual cost of the qualifying shares, *viz.*

Cost of 500 qualifying shares $\dfrac{500}{2,000} \times £100,000 =$ £25,000

No restriction is necessary as the cost of the qualifying shares exceeds the loss in *Step 3*.

Loss claim — *ITA 2007, s 132* for 2010/11 or 2009/10 — £16,667

(The loss not relieved against income (£50,000 − £16,667 = £33,333) remains an allowable loss for capital gains tax purposes.)

Utilisation of losses

X makes all possible claims under *ITA 2007, s 132* so as to obtain relief against the earliest possible income. He has total income of £7,000 for 2008/09, £11,500 for 2009/10 and £9,000 for 2010/11.

The losses available as above are as follows.

	2009/10 disposals	2010/11 disposals
	£	£
A Ltd shares	12,000	
C Ltd shares		16,667

Claims are made as follows.

	£
2008/09	
Total income	7,000
Claim under *ITA 2007, s 132(1)(b)*	(7,000)
Net income	Nil
2009/10	
Total income	11,500
Claim under *ITA 2007, s 132(1)(a)* note (b)	(5,000)
	6,500
Claim under *ITA 2007, s 132(1)(b)*	(6,500)
Net income	Nil
2010/11	
Total income	9,000
Claim under *ITA 2007, s 132(1)(a)*	(9,000)
Net income	Nil

Loss utilisation

	£
2009/10 loss	
Loss available	12,000
Relief claimed for 2008/09 (*ITA 2007, s 132(1)(b)*)	(7,000)
Relief claimed for 2009/10 (*ITA 2007, s 132(1)(a)*)	(5,000)
	£
2010/11 loss	
Loss available	16,667
Relief claimed for 2009/10 (*ITA 2007, s 132(1)(b)*)	(6,500)
Relief claimed for 2010/11 (*ITA 2007, s 132(1)(a)*)	(9,000)
Unused balance note (c)	£1,167

Notes

(a)   In this example, losses have been set against preceding year's income first, as X wished to obtain relief against earliest possible income, but this need not be the case.

(b)   Where two years' losses are set against one year's income, the current year's loss is relieved in priority to that of the following year.

(c)   The unused balance of the 2010/11 loss cannot be relieved under *ITA 2007, s 132* due to insufficiency of income and therefore reverts to being a capital loss available to reduce chargeable gains.

Employment losses

[45.33] Rules very similar to those at **45.2** above apply to enable a loss sustained in an employment or office (an '*employment loss*') in a tax year to be set against general income (i) of the tax year in which the loss is incurred, or (ii) of the tax year preceding that in which the loss is incurred, or (iii) of both those tax years. A claim must be made on or before the first anniversary of 31 January following the tax year in which the loss is made and is given effect by deducting the loss in arriving at net income for the tax year in question (see Step 2 at **1.7 ALLOWANCES AND TAX RATES**).

Examples of situations in which an employment loss might arise include managers etc. who are entitled to a share of profits but also have to bear a share of any losses and sales persons who are required to bear the cost of bad debts arising from orders they have obtained.

A claim within (i) above is made under *ITA 2007, s 128(2)(a)* for 2007/08 onwards and under *ICTA 1988, s 380(1)(a)* for earlier years. A claim within (ii) above is made under *ITA 2007, s 128(2)(b)* where the year of loss is 2007/08 or any subsequent year and under *ICTA 1988, s 380(1)(b)* for earlier years. A claim within (iii) above is made under *ITA 2007, s 128(2)(c)* where the year of loss is 2007/08 or any subsequent year and under *ICTA 1988, s 380(1)(a)* and *(b)* for earlier years. If a claim is made within (i) above and the loss is not wholly exhausted, a subsequent claim can be made (within the time limit) within (ii) above, and *vice versa*.

Where a claim is made for a loss to be set against income of both the same tax year and the preceding tax year, there is no statutory order of priority; the claimant must specify the tax year for which the deduction from income should be made first.

Where, against income of the same year, claims are made both under (i) in respect of that year's loss and under (ii) in respect of the following year's loss or under **45.2** above in respect of a trading loss made in that following year, (i) takes precedence.

The facility at **45.7** above to set off surplus trading losses against capital gains is also available in relation to an employment loss. The restrictions at **45.11–45.19** above on set-off of trading losses do not apply in relation to employment losses. Those at **45.15** did in theory apply in relation to employment losses before 2007/08 but are unlikely to have been of any practical effect.

Anti-avoidance

In response to known avoidance schemes, the legislation now denies relief for a loss if, and to the extent that, it is sustained as a result of anything done in pursuance of arrangements a main purpose of which is the avoidance of tax. This has effect in relation to losses incurred in 2009/10 and subsequent tax years, and also in relation to a loss incurred in 2008/09 if, or to the extent that, it is occasioned by an act or omission occurring on or after 12 January 2009. Where the taxpayer has paid less tax on 31 January 2009 than he should have done, due to a loss that now falls to be disallowed, the due date for surcharge purposes (see **42.3 INTEREST AND SURCHARGES ON OVERDUE TAX**) is deferred until 1 April 2009 (the date these measures were announced) so that no surcharge will be due if the extra tax was paid before 29 April 2009. (This applies equally to tax due on any other date prior to 1 April 2009.) Penalties are waived where a person made a claim under these provisions at any time between 12 January 2009 and 1 April 2009 inclusive and a return, statement or declaration made in connection with the claim contained an inaccuracy by reason only of the introduction of this anti-avoidance rule.

[*ITA 2007, ss 128–130; FA 2009, s 68*].

See **18.2 CLAIMS** for further provisions regarding claims for a loss incurred in one tax year to be carried back to an earlier tax year.

Key points

[45.34] Points to consider are as follows.

- While relief against total income under *ITA 2007, s 64* provides immediate relief for a trading loss, this can often provide limited actual tax savings due to the use of the losses against income which was not taxable in any event due to its being covered by personal allowances. This is often an inevitable consequence of claims under *s 64*, and may give very poor value for the loss.
- When exploring the best relief available for trading losses, advisers may wish to modify capital allowance claims in both the loss-making period and often the preceding period. This may allow the loss (and profit against which it is set) to be tailored to achieve a better rate of relief, allowing the expenditure to be carried forward in the capital allowances pool, providing allowances in the future.
- The temporary relief available for the tax years 2008/09 and 2009/10 in *FA 2009, Sch 6* can be particularly beneficial as relief is given only against trading profits, leaving other income in charge to tax, and potentially covered by personal allowances. Note that at least one claim must be made under *ITA 2007, s 64* (if there is available income) in order to access the relief.
- When trading losses are offset against other income — normally when claiming relief under *ITA 2007, s 64* or *s 72*, or against capital gains, the loss will not be given effect for the purposes of

Class 4 national insurance contributions. A separate loss record will have to be created and relief claimed against the next available trading profits. For more details see Tolley's National Insurance Contributions.

- Relief of trading losses against capital gains can represent quite poor value for money unless the gains realised are substantial. Losses must first be set against total income, leaving personal allowances unutilised, and there is also potential for a wasted CGT annual exempt amount. Further, relief will then be obtained at only 18%. When substantial gains have been realised, wasted annual exemption is less likely to be a problem, and relief may arise at 28% on gains realised after 22 June 2010.

- Advisers should also be aware that the treatment of trading losses for the purposes of working tax credit and child tax credit differs from the tax treatment. A further separate record of losses and their utilisation will be needed in the event that the individual makes tax credit claims.

46

Managed Service Companies

Cross-reference. See **58** PERSONAL SERVICE COMPANIES.

Introduction

[46.1] Managed service companies (MSCs) (which for this purpose include composite service companies) are intermediaries through which individual workers provide their services to clients. They differ from personal service companies in that the worker, though often a shareholder, is not in business on his own account, is not usually a director of the MSC and does not exercise control over the MSC. Instead, the MSC is controlled by a scheme provider who promotes the use of the MSC and makes its structure available to workers for a fee. The underlying nature of the contracts in which the worker is involved is said to be almost invariably one of employment.

It had always been HMRC's view that the personal service company legislation can be applied equally to MSCs where the conditions at **58.4** PERSONAL SERVICE COMPANIES were satisfied (see Revenue Tax Bulletins August 2002 pp 956, 957 and December 2004 pp 1165–1168). But apparently they found it difficult in practice to enforce the legislation against MSCs. Furthermore, even where a tax debt to HMRC has been established it was difficult to collect the debt as the MSC has no assets and can simply be wound up (with the workers transferring to a new MSC set up for that purpose).

As a result, the provisions described in this chapter take MSCs out of the ambit of the personal service company rules and apply a separate set of rules instead for 2007/08 onwards. Personal service companies remain within the rules described at **58** PERSONAL SERVICE COMPANIES.

For official guidance etc., see www.hmrc.gov.uk/employment-status/current. htm.

The operation of *ITEPA 2003, ss 44–47* (workers supplied by agencies — see **27.95** EMPLOYMENT INCOME) is not affected by the provisions in this chapter. Nothing in these provisions applies to a payment or transfer subject to deduction of tax under *ITA 2007, s 966(3)* or *(4)* (payments to non-resident entertainers and sportsmen — see **50.10 NON-RESIDENTS**). [*ITEPA 2003, s 61A(2); FA 2007, s 25, Sch 3 para 4*].

See also **22.6 CONSTRUCTION INDUSTRY SCHEME (CIS)** (payments to MSCs in the construction industry) and www.hmrc.gov.uk/news/cis-msc-faqs.htm (employment agencies or businesses placing workers in the construction sector).

Meaning of 'managed service company'

[46.2] For the purposes of these provisions, the meaning of '*company*' is extended to include a partnership (which would include a Limited Liability Partnership) as well as a body corporate. The term 'managed service company' must be read accordingly.

A company is a '*managed service company*' for these purposes if it meets all of the following criteria:

(a)   its business consists wholly or mainly of providing (directly or indirectly) the services of an individual to other persons;

(b)   payments are made (directly or indirectly) to the individual (or to 'associates' of his) of an amount equal to the amount the company is paid for those services or to the greater part of that amount;

(c)   the way in which the payments are made results in the individual (or associates) receiving a greater net amount (after tax and National Insurance) than would have been received if all the payments in respect of the individual's services had been taxable as employment income; and

(d)   a person who carries on a business of promoting or facilitating the use of companies to provide the services of individuals ('*an MSC provider*') is 'involved with the company'.

An MSC provider is '*involved with the company*' if he (or an 'associate' of his):

(i)   benefits financially on an ongoing basis from the provision of the individual's services; or

(ii)   influences or controls the provision of those services; or

(iii)   influences or controls the way in which the above-mentioned payments are made; or

(iv)   influences or controls the company's finances or any of its activities (other than by merely providing legal or accountancy services in a professional capacity); or

(v)   undertakes to indemnify the individual against a tax loss (see *ITEPA 2003, s 61C(5)(6)* for details) or promotes such an undertaking.

A person is not within (d) above merely by virtue of his providing legal or accountancy services in a professional capacity. Also, a person is not within (d) above if he merely carries on a business as an employment agency, i.e. placing individuals with persons who wish to obtain their services, unless he (or an 'associate' of his) does anything within (iii)–(v) above. The Treasury has power to exclude (by statutory instrument) further categories of person from being within (d) above.

HMRC are of the opinion that being an officer or partner in a service company does not preclude a person from being an MSC Provider involved with the company (HMRC Internet Statement, 3 December 2008 at www.hmrc.gov.u k/news/cis-msc.htm).

The question of whether a person is an *'associate'* of another person for the purposes of these provisions is determined by *ITEPA 2003, s 60I* (and note that this treats a man and woman cohabiting as a couple as if they were spouses and two people of the same sex cohabiting as a couple as if they were civil partners). For the purposes of (a)–(d) and of (i)–(v) above, an 'associate' of a person ('P') also includes any person who, in order to secure that the individual's services are provided by a company, acts in concert with P (or with P and others); this is particularly relevant in terms of an associate of the MSC provider.

[*ITEPA 2003, ss 61B, 61C, 61I; FA 2007, s 25, Sch 3 para 4*].

The 'deemed employment payment'

[46.3] If:

(a)   the services of an individual ('the worker') are provided (directly or indirectly) by a managed service company (MSC);

(b)   the worker, or an associate of his (within *ITEPA 2003, s 61I*), receives (from any person) a payment or benefit that can reasonably be taken to be in respect of those services; and

(c)   the payment or benefit is not earnings received by the worker directly from the MSC,

the MSC is treated as making to the worker, and the worker is treated as receiving, a payment which is to be treated as earnings from an employment ('the deemed employment payment'). The deemed employment payment is treated as made at the time the payment or benefit in (b) above is received.

The reference to a 'payment or benefit' in (b) above means anything that, if received by an employee for performing the duties of an employment, would be general earnings from the employment (for which see **27.20 EMPLOYMENT INCOME**). A payment or a cash benefit is treated as received when payment is made. A non-cash benefit is treated as received when it would have been treated as received (see *ITEPA 2003, s 19* or *s 32*) if the worker were an employee and the benefit were provided by reason of the employment.

[*ITEPA 2003, ss 61D, 61F(2)(5); FA 2007, s 25, Sch 3 para 4*].

Computation of deemed employment payment

[46.4] The deemed employment payment in **46.3** above is computed as follows.

(1)   Take the amount of the payment or benefit referred to at **46.3**(b) above.

The amount of a payment or a cash benefit is the amount received. The amount of a non-cash benefit is equivalent to the cash equivalent of the benefit; the latter is determined under the benefits code rules (see **27.29–27.48**, **27.59 EMPLOYMENT INCOME**), modified in the case of living accommodation. If a payment or benefit relates only partly to the provision of the worker's services and partly to other matters, it is to be apportioned on a just and reasonable basis.

(2)   Deduct any expenses met by the worker that would have been deductible under normal rules (see **27.22 EMPLOYMENT INCOME**) if the worker had been employed by the person to whom the worker's services are provided ('the client') and those expenses had been met from his earnings. See further below.

If the result is a negative amount, or is nil, there is no deemed employment payment. In any other case, the deemed employment payment is the amount which, together with employer's NICs thereon, is equal to the result of applying steps (1) and (2) above. In other words, allowance is made at this point for the fact that employer's NICs are chargeable on the deemed payment itself (see Tolley's National Insurance Contributions).

Note that step (2) effectively applies the rules on qualifying travelling expenses at **27.22**(a) **EMPLOYMENT INCOME** as if each engagement with a client were a separate employment at a permanent workplace (thus disallowing relief for travel between the worker's home and that workplace).

If the MSC is a partnership of which the worker is a member, expenses met by the worker on behalf of the partnership can be brought into account at step (2).

If a vehicle is provided by the MSC for the worker or, where the MSC is a partnership of which the worker is a member, a vehicle is provided by the worker for the purposes of the partnership business, mileage allowance relief (see **27.80 EMPLOYMENT INCOME**) can also be included in the expenses deductible at step (2) to the extent that it would have been deductible from earnings on the assumption that the worker was employed by the client and that the vehicle was not provided by the client.

[*ITEPA 2003, ss 61E, 61F(3)(4); FA 2007, s 25, Sch 3 para 4*].

Tax treatment of deemed employment payment

[46.5] The deemed employment payment is taxed (and **PAY AS YOU EARN (53)** must be applied) as it would be if the worker were employed by the MSC and the deemed payment were a payment by the MSC of earnings from that employment. However, no deductions can be made from the deemed payment in respect of expenses etc., or mileage allowance relief (such matters having been taken into account as appropriate in the computation of the deemed payment itself — see **46.4** above).

If the worker is UK resident and the services in question are provided in the UK, the MSC is treated as having a place of business in the UK (and is thus obliged to operate PAYE for example — see **53.37 PAY AS YOU EARN**) even if this is not, in fact, the case.

To the extent that, by reason of any combination of:

- the worker being resident, ordinarily resident or domiciled outside the UK;
- the client being resident or ordinarily resident outside the UK; and
- the services in question being provided outside the UK,

the worker would not be chargeable if employed directly by the client, he is not chargeable to tax in respect of the deemed employment payment. (See **27.5, 27.8, 27.10** EMPLOYMENT INCOME for the relevant charging provisions.)

If the MSC is a partnership of which the worker is a member, the deemed employment payment is treated as received by the worker in his personal capacity and not as income of the partnership.

[*ITEPA 2003, s 61G; FA 2007, s 25, Sch 3 para 4*].

The total amount of deemed employment payments for a tax year is taken into account in determining whether the worker is a higher- or lower-paid employee for the purpose of applying the benefits code (see **27.26** EMPLOYMENT INCOME). [*ITEPA 2003, s 218(1)(e); FA 2007, s 25, Sch 3 para 5*].

Recovery of tax from persons other than the MSC

[46.6] There is provision for regulations to be made by statutory instrument (see now *SI 2007 No 2069*) to enable a PAYE debt of an MSC to be recovered from other persons. This covers any amount that an officer of HMRC believes should have been deducted by an MSC from a payment of PAYE income (see **53.2** PAY AS YOU EARN) to an individual; it is not restricted to PAYE becoming due by virtue of the above provisions. The persons from whom such recovery may be made are as follows:

(a) a director or other office-holder, or an associate (within *ITEPA 2003, s 60I*), of the MSC;
(b) an MSC provider who is involved with the MSC (see **46.2** above);
(c) a person who (directly or indirectly) has encouraged, facilitated or otherwise been actively involved in the provision by the MSC of the individual's services; and
(d) a director or other office-holder, or an associate (within *ITEPA 2003, s 60I* but see also below), of a person who is not an individual but is within (b) or (c) above.

A person is not within (c) above merely by virtue of his providing legal or accountancy services in a professional capacity. For the purposes of (d) above, an 'associate' of a person ('P') also includes any person who, in order to secure that the individual's services are provided by a company, acts in concert with P (or with P and others).

The regulations apply on and after 6 August 2007 and set out the conditions under which a PAYE debt may be transferred to another person, the procedure and time limits for making such a transfer and an appeals procedure. Generally the transferee is required to settle the debt within 30 days of the transfer notice. A transfer notice cannot be served on a person within (c) above (or on the associate of such a person) in respect of a PAYE debt incurred before 6 January 2008.

[ITEPA 2003, s 688A; FA 2007, s 25, Sch 3 para 6; SI 2003 No 2682, regs 97A–97L; SI 2007 Nos 2069, 2296; SI 2009 No 56, Sch 2 paras 103–105].

Relief where dividends etc. paid by MSC

[46.7] A relief from double taxation is available where a **company** MSC is treated as making a deemed employment payment in any tax year and also pays a dividend (or otherwise makes a distribution) in that or a subsequent tax year. The provisions are similar to those for intermediaries at **58.13 PERSONAL SERVICE COMPANIES**.

[ITEPA 2003, s 61H; FA 2007, s 25, Sch 3 para 4].

Computation of MSC's business profits

[46.8] In computing for income tax purposes the profits of a trade, profession or vocation carried on by an MSC, a deduction may be made for any deemed employment payment (and related employer's NICs) treated as made in connection with the trade etc. The deduction is made for the period of account in which the deemed employment payment is treated as made. The deduction can reduce the profits to nil for tax purposes but it cannot create a loss.

[ITTOIA 2005, s 164A; FA 2007, s 25, Sch 3 para 9].

47

Married Persons and Civil Partners

Cross-references. See **1.14**, **1.15** ALLOWANCES AND TAX RATES; **28.21** ENTERPRISE INVESTMENT SCHEME; **52.18** PARTNERSHIPS; **62.5** RESIDENCE, ORDINARY RESIDENCE AND DOMICILE (residence); **68.28**(a), **68.29** SETTLEMENTS as regards settlements not involving use of trusts.

Simon's Taxes. See E5.1.

Note on civil partnerships

These became possible in the UK from 5 December 2005 as a result of *Civil Partnership Act 2004*. The effect of the Act is to enable same-sex couples to obtain legal recognition of their relationship by forming a civil partnership broadly parallel to marriage. Tax parity between married couples and civil partnerships was achieved by numerous amendments to pre-existing tax legislation made by *SI 2005 No 3229* and *SI 2005 No 3230*. In as far as these amendments relate to income tax, they are reflected throughout this work where appropriate. In some respects, the amendments went beyond their principal purpose by also removing certain perceived inequalities of treatment based on gender and, in the case of a parent, marital status. In certain limited circumstances, income tax law treats a cohabiting unmarried couple in the same way as a married couple, and the amendments reflect this by giving equal treatment, in those same limited circumstances, to all cohabiting same-sex couples whether or not they are civil partners. For an overview of the amendments, see HMRC Tax Bulletin December 2005 pp 1251–1258 (as amended — see HMRC Tax Bulletin February 2006 p 1276). All published Extra Statutory Concessions and Statements of Practice are now to be regarded as extended, wherever relevant, so as to apply to civil partners as they do to married couples.

Transfers of certain personal reliefs

[47.1] See **47.2–47.5** below for transfers of relief between spouses and civil partners, but note that married couple's allowance is available only where at least one individual was born before 6 April 1935. See **1.15 ALLOWANCES AND TAX RATES** for full details as to entitlement to, and the amount of, the married couple's allowance.

Note also that each individual is entitled to the *personal* allowance (see **1.14 ALLOWANCES AND TAX RATES**) in his or her own right and that this allowance can never be transferred between spouses or civil partners.

Simon's Taxes. See E1.924, E1.925, E1.931.

Transfer of basic married couple's allowance

[47.2] An individual can elect to be entitled to claim one-half of the *basic* married couple's allowance (see **1.15 ALLOWANCES AND TAX RATES**) otherwise due to his or her spouse or civil partner for any tax year. Alternatively, a couple may jointly elect for the full amount of the *basic* allowance to be transferred between them, although the spouse or civil partner initially entitled can subsequently elect to be able to transfer back one-half of the basic allowance. In either case, the transferee must be UK resident or entitled to personal reliefs by virtue of **50.2 NON-RESIDENTS** (but see **47.5** below) and must make a claim for the transferred amount.

An election under these provisions has to be made in prescribed form (i.e. form 18) before the first tax year for which it is to have effect (or within the first 30 days of that year if prior notification of intention to elect has been given to HMRC before the beginning of that year), and has effect until withdrawn or until a different election is made. If an election is to have effect for the tax year in which the marriage or civil partnership is entered into, it may be made during that year, but will only apply for that year to the fraction of the basic married couple's allowance available (see **1.15 ALLOWANCES AND TAX RATES**). An election may be withdrawn with effect from the year following that in which notice of withdrawal is given.

[*ITA 2007, ss 47–50, Sch 1 para 32; ICTA 1988, s 257BA*].

Transfer of excess married couple's allowance

[47.3] Where either spouse's or civil partner's entitlement to an income tax reduction in respect of married couple's allowance exceeds his or her 'comparable tax liability', that individual may give notice to HMRC to transfer the excess, i.e. the unused amount of the reduction to his spouse or civil partner (in addition to any reduction to which his spouse or civil partner is already entitled). The notice must be given in prescribed form, it has effect for that tax year only and cannot be withdrawn. It must be given within four years after the end of the tax year to which it relates (and see **18.4 CLAIMS**).

An individual's '*comparable tax liability*' is his income tax liability immediately after carrying out *Step* 6 (subtraction of tax reductions) in the calculation at **1.7 ALLOWANCES AND TAX RATES**, except that (for this purpose only):

- any reduction attributable to double tax relief under *TIOPA 2010, ss 2, 6* (double tax agreements) or *TIOPA 2010, s 18(1)(b), (2)* (unilateral relief) or predecessor legislation must be disregarded; and
- any necessary restriction to the individual's married couple's allowance to leave sufficient tax in charge to cover the tax deemed to be deducted at source from a gift aid donation (see **16.16 CHARITIES**) must be deducted; this leaves a greater amount of excess married couple's allowance available for transfer.

Although the legislation for 2007/08 onwards does not make it explicit, it would appear that the reduction attributable to the married couple's allowance itself must also be disregarded for the purpose of arriving at 'comparable tax liability' (see the Example at **47.6** below).

[*ITA 2007, ss 51–53, Sch 1 para 33; ICTA 1988, s 257BB; FA 2008, Sch 39 para 57; TIOPA 2010, Sch 8 para 78; SI 2009 No 403*].

Transfer of blind person's allowance

[47.4] Any excess of the blind person's allowance (see **1.16 ALLOWANCES AND TAX RATES**) over the 'remaining relievable income' of the individual entitled to it can be transferred from one spouse or civil partner to the other. For this purpose, an individual's *'remaining relievable income'* is his net income (i.e. his total income net of amounts, other than personal reliefs, deductible therefrom — see **1.7 ALLOWANCES AND TAX RATES**) less his personal allowance. It is a condition of the transfer that the couple be living together, whilst married to, or in a civil partnership with, each other for at least part of the tax year. The transferee must be UK resident or entitled to personal reliefs by virtue of **50.2 NON-RESIDENTS** (but see **47.5** below) and must make a claim for the transferred amount. The transferor must make an election to transfer the amount; the election must be made within four years after the end of the tax year to which it relates (and see **18.4 CLAIMS**). The election has effect for that tax year only, cannot be withdrawn and also has effect as a notice to transfer excess married couple's allowance as in **47.3** above.

[*ITA 2007, ss 39, 40, Sch 1 para 35; ICTA 1988, s 265(2)–(6); FA 2008, Sch 39 para 55; SI 2009 No 403*].

Non-UK residents

[47.5] If either (but not both) of the spouses or civil partners involved is non-UK resident *and* entitled to personal reliefs by virtue only of **50.2**(i) or (ii) **NON-RESIDENTS**, the transfers in **47.2–47.4** above are not possible for 2007/08 (subject to transitional provisions). If either (but not both) of the spouses or civil partners involved is non-UK resident *and* entitled to personal reliefs by virtue only of **50.2**(i) **NON-RESIDENTS**, the above transfers are not possible for 2008/09 and 2009/10 (subject to transitional provisions affecting 2008/09 only). This is no longer of any relevance for 2010/11 onwards. See **50.2** for details.

Example

[47.6]

Transfer of excess married couple's allowance

Mr Grey, who was born on 19 July 1933, has pension income of £7,660 and building society interest of £1,040 (net) for 2010/11 and his wife, who was born in December 1951, has a salary of £16,440 and building society interest of £2,000 (net). Mr and Mrs Grey receive interest of £2,240 (net) in 2010/11 from a bank deposit account in their joint names.

The couple have not made the joint election at **1.15 ALLOWANCES AND TAX RATES** to be treated in the same way as couples marrying on or after 5 December 2005 for the purposes of the married couple's allowance. Neither have they made the election at 47.2 above to transfer the basic married couple's allowance between them. However, Mr Grey gives notice under *ITA 2007, s 51(4)* to transfer the unused balance of his married couple's allowance for 2010/11 to his wife.

The couple's tax position for 2010/11 is as follows.

	Mr Grey	Mrs Grey
	£	£
Employment income	—	16,440
Pension income	7,660	—
Building society interest (gross)	1,300	2,500
Bank deposit interest (gross)	1,400	1,400
Total and net income	10,360	20,340
Deduct Personal allowance	9,640	6,475
Taxable income	£720	£13,865
Tax payable:		
720 @ 10% (starting rate for savings)	72.00	
13,865 @ 20% (basic rate)		2,773.00
	72.00	2,773.00
Deduct Married couple's allowance		
£6,965 @ 10% = £696.50, but restricted to	72.00	
Deduct Excess married couple's allowance (see Note)	—	624.50
Total tax liabilities	Nil	2,148.50
Deduct Tax at source:		
Building society interest	(260.00)	(500.00)
Bank deposit interest	(280.00)	(280.00)
Net tax (repayment)/liability (subject to PAYE deductions)	£(540.00)	£1,368.50

Note

Mr Grey's 'comparable tax liability' (see **47.3** above) is £72.00. Thus the excess married couple's allowance is £624.50 (£696.50 – £72.00).

Jointly-held property

[47.7] Special rules apply for the apportionment between spouses living together (see **47.8** below) of income arising from property held in their joint names. The rules extend to members of a civil partnership who are living together. Provided that at least one of them is beneficially entitled to that income, the spouses (or civil partners) are treated as beneficially entitled to it in equal shares, except in the following circumstances.

(i)   Where the income is partnership income falling within **52 PARTNER-SHIPS**. Prior to 5 April 2007, this exception applies where the income is earned income or, not being earned income, is income within **52 PARTNERSHIPS** (see Change 125 listed in Annex 1 to the Explanatory Notes to *ITA 2007*). The main effect of this change is to bring all income from patents (see **40.4 INTELLECTUAL PROPERTY**) and know-how (see **40.5 INTELLECTUAL PROPERTY**) within the 50:50 rule (but see the option of a joint declaration in (v) below).

(ii)   For 2007/08 onwards, where the income is from furnished holiday lettings (see **60.10 PROPERTY INCOME**). Prior to 2007/08 such income was covered by the exception in (i) above in relation to earned income.

(iii)   To the extent that the income is by any other provision of the *Income Tax Acts* treated as the income either of the spouse (or civil partner) who is not beneficially entitled to the income, or of a third party.

(iv)   Where the income consists of a distribution in respect of shares in, or securities of, a close company (broadly a company controlled by five or fewer participators — see Tolley's Corporation Tax) to which the spouses (or civil partners) are beneficially entitled (whether in equal or unequal shares) or to which one of them is beneficially entitled. (The intention behind this is to prevent the normal 50:50 rule being used to circumvent the application of the settlements legislation (see **68.28**(a) **SETTLEMENTS**) where income is diverted to a spouse (or civil partner) via the payment of dividends.)

(v)   Where the spouses (or civil partners) are not beneficially entitled to the income in equal shares, and they make a declaration of their beneficial interests in the income to which the declaration relates and the property from which that income arises, provided that the beneficial interests of the spouses (or civil partners) in the property correspond to their beneficial interests in the income.

A declaration under (v) above has effect in relation to income arising on and after the date of the declaration, and continues to have effect unless and until the beneficial interests of the spouses (or civil partners) in either the income or the property cease to accord with the declaration. Notice of a declaration must be given to HMRC, in a prescribed form (i.e. form 17) and manner, within 60 days of the date of the declaration.

[*ITA 2007, ss 836, 837; ICTA 1988, ss 282A, 282B; CTA 2010, Sch 1 para 553*].

Simon's Taxes. See E5.103A.

'Living together'

[47.8] Individuals who are married to, or are civil partners of, each other are treated for income tax purposes as '*living together*' unless they are:

• separated under a Court Order or deed of separation; or
• in fact separated in circumstances in which the separation is likely to be permanent.

[*ITA 2007, s 1011; ICTA 1988, s 282*].

A husband and wife may be separated even though living under the same roof if they have become two households (*Holmes v Mitchell* Ch D 1990, 63 TC 718).

Alimony, maintenance, separation allowances etc.

[47.9] Simon's Taxes. See E1.806, E5.104–E5.113.

By virtue of *ITTOIA 2005, s 727* (and its predecessor), see **30.4 EXEMPT INCOME**, payments of alimony and maintenance do not form part of the taxable income of the person to whom they are made or of any other person. Where any such payments are 'qualifying maintenance payments', the *payer* obtains a limited relief as below. Relief is restricted to cases where at least one party was **born before 6 April 1935**. The relief available is **10%** of the lesser of:

• the total amount of 'qualifying maintenance payments' made by the payer which fall due in the tax year; and
• the amount of the *basic* married couple's allowance for that year (see **1.15 ALLOWANCES AND TAX RATES**).

Relief is given by means of a tax reduction (see Step 6 at **1.7 ALLOWANCES AND TAX RATES**). The order in which tax reductions are given against an individual's tax liability is set out at **1.8 ALLOWANCES AND TAX RATES**, which also makes clear that a tax reduction must be restricted to the extent (if any) that it would otherwise exceed the individual's remaining income tax liability after making all prior reductions.

A '*qualifying maintenance payment*' is a periodical payment (other than an instalment of a lump sum) which:

(A) is made under a Court Order originating in the UK, another European Union (EU) member state or a European Economic Area (EEA) member state, or under a written agreement the law applicable to which is the law of a part of the EU or EEA, or under a maintenance assessment or maintenance calculation made under the *Child Support Act 1991* (or NI equivalent);
(B) is made *either*:
    (i) by one party to a marriage or civil partnership (or former marriage or civil partnership) to or for the benefit of, and for the maintenance of, the other party; *or*

(ii)   by one parent of a child to the other parent for the child's maintenance or by one person to another for the maintenance of a 'child of the family';

(C)   is due at a time when:

(i)   (in a case within (B)(i) above) the two parties are not a married couple, or civil partners, living together and the party to whom or for whose benefit the payment is made has not subsequently married or entered into a civil partnership; or

(ii)   (in a case within (B)(ii) above) the payer and the payee are not living together; and

(D)   does not otherwise attract tax relief for the person making the payment (i.e. apart from the relief under these provisions).

As regards (A) above, the extension of the provisions to the EEA is by virtue of an EEA Agreement that came into force on 1 January 1994 (Inland Revenue Press Release 9 February 1994 — see 1994 STI 166).

As regards (B) above, there is the additional requirement referred to above that at least one of the parties to the marriage (or former marriage) or civil partnership (or former civil partnership) or, in a case within (B)(ii) above, either the payer or the payee (or both), was born before 6 April 1935.

In (B) above, a child means a person under 21, and a *'child of the family'* is a child who is either the child of both parties or has been treated by them both as a child of their family (but not a child who has been boarded out with them by a public authority or voluntary organisation).

As regards (C) above, the fact that the subsequent marriage may itself have been dissolved does not alter the fact that the party to whom or for whose benefit the payment is made has remarried (*Norris v Edgson* Ch D 2000, 72 TC 553).

The above conditions were not satisfied by a payment made by the taxpayer to a former spouse for the maintenance of their child where the agreement required the payment to be made to the child (*Billingham v John* Ch D 1998, 70 TC 380), nor by payments made by one party to a marriage to pay off the joint mortgage on a house continuing to be occupied by the other (*Otter v Andrews* (Sp C 181), [1999] SSCD 67).

Paragraph (B) above is treated as satisfied in relation to periodical payments made to or retained by the Secretary of State (or equivalent NI Department) under a maintenance assessment or maintenance calculation under the *Child Support Act 1991* (or NI equivalent) by any person where another person is, for the purposes of that *Act*, a parent of the child(ren) to whom the assessment or calculation relates. Assessments or calculations under *section 7* of that *Act* (right of child in Scotland to apply for maintenance assessment or calculation) are excluded from this treatment.

Paragraph (B) above is also treated as satisfied in relation to periodical payments made to the Secretary of State (or equivalent NI Department) made by any person under a recovery of benefit order under *Social Security Administration Act 1992, s 106* or *Jobseekers Act 1995, s 23* (or NI equivalent of either) in respect of income support or income-based jobseeker's allowance claimed by another person.

[ITA 2007, ss 453–456, Sch 2 para 101, Sch 3 Pt 1; ICTA 1988, s 347B; FA 1988, ss 36, 38(3A), 40, Sch 3 para 13].

A maintenance payment (as defined for this purpose) arising outside the UK is exempt from tax on receipt if it would have been exempt as above had it arisen in the UK. *[ITTOIA 2005, s 730].*

General matters

Court Orders for alimony generally take into account the income and the tax liabilities of both parties.

In strict law, the retrospective variation of a Court Order is not effective for tax purposes (*Morley-Clarke v Jones* CA 1985, 59 TC 567). For Orders made or varied after 30 June 1988 which provide for retrospective payments, only payments made on or after the date of the Order count towards the limit on which tax relief is available in any year. Payments made under a legally binding written agreement before the Court Order may of course qualify in their own right. (Revenue Press Release 15 March 1988). Payments made under an agreement voluntarily entered into by a father in favour of his children, for their maintenance following separation, and later confirmed by a Court Order, were not made under that Order and were thus ineffective for tax purposes (*CIR v Craw* CS 1985, 59 TC 56).

Example

[47.10]

Mr Green, who was born on 7 October 1933, separated from his wife in June 2000 and, under a Court Order dated 15 July 2001, pays maintenance of £300 per month to his ex-wife and £100 per month to his daughter, payments being due on the first of each calendar month commencing 1 August 2001. Mr Green has pension income of £15,810 and net dividends of £4,500 for 2010/11. He re-marries on 6 October 2010.

	£	£
2010/11		
Mr Green		
Pension income		15,810
Dividends	4,500	
Add Tax credits (£4,500 × ¹/₉)	500	5,000
Total and net income		20,810
Deduct Personal allowance		9,640
Taxable income		£11,170
Tax payable:		
6,170 @ 20% (basic rate)		1,234.00
5,000 @ 10% (dividend ordinary rate)		500.00
		1,734.00
Deduct Maintenance relief — wife:		
£3,600 paid, but restricted to £2,670 @ 10%		267.00
		1,467.00

Deduct	Married couple's allowance	
	£6,965 × $^6/_{12}$ = £3,483 @ 10%	348.30
Tax liability		1,118.70
Deduct	Tax credits	500.00
Net liability (subject to PAYE deductions)		£618.70

Key points

[47.11] Points to consider are as follows.

*   Details of the availability and restriction of married couple's allowance for taxpayers born before 6 April 1935 are at **1.15 ALLOWANCES AND TAX RATES.**
*   The transfer of the basic married couple's allowance can only take effect if notice is given in the preceding tax year (unless the marriage takes place during the year).
*   The transfer of unused (excess) married couple's allowance can relate to the full age-related amount and notice can be given up to four years after the end of the tax year concerned.
*   Notice of transfer of the basic married couple's allowance remains in force until revoked.
*   When one partner or spouse moves into long-term care, the 'living together' condition required to claim married couple's allowance may no longer be satisfied.
*   Elections with regard to income arising on jointly held property are limited to situations where the beneficial ownership of the underlying property is unequal and entitlement to both income and the underlying property are the same.

48

Mineral Royalties

Simon's Taxes. See B5.663, B6.206, B6.501.

Relief for royalties receivable

[48.1] Where a person resident or ordinarily resident in the UK and within the charge to income tax is entitled to receive 'mineral royalties' under a 'mineral lease or agreement', only one-half of any such royalties receivable in any tax year is treated as income for tax purposes.

Expenses of management available for set-off against those royalties, whether under the general rules for computing **PROPERTY INCOME (60)** or under the special rules (in **60.24 PROPERTY INCOME**) for taxing a 'UK section 12(4) concern' (mines, quarries etc.), are similarly reduced by one-half.

For these purposes, *'mineral royalties'* means so much of any rent receivable under a 'mineral lease or agreement' as relates to the winning and working of 'minerals'. (See *ITTOIA 2005, s 342* for an extended meaning of mineral royalties in NI.) *'Minerals'* means all minerals or substances in or under land which are ordinarily worked for removal, by either underground or surface working, but does not include water, peat, top-soil or vegetation. Coal is *not* excluded (*HMRC v Bute* CS, [2009] STC 2138). A *'mineral lease or agreement'* means a lease, profit à prendre, licence or other agreement conferring a right to win and work minerals in the UK; a contract for the sale or conveyance of minerals in or under land in the UK; or a grant of a right (other than an ancillary right) under *Mines (Working Facilities and Support) Act 1966, s 1*.

Where Betterment Levy (which was abolished after July 1970) was not chargeable on the grant of the lease, or any subsequent renewal, extension or variation of it, the other half of the royalties receivable is treated as a chargeable gain for purposes of capital gains tax.

Where, on the last disposition (before 23 July 1970) affecting the lease, Betterment Levy was chargeable under Case B (as defined by *Land Commission Act 1967, Pt III*) the chargeable gain, as above, is limited to a fraction (base value of that disposition/ consideration received) of one-half of the royalties received. After 5 April 1988, this limitation applies only if it applied to a chargeable period ending on or before that date. But if such a lease is renewed, extended or varied after 22 July 1970, one-half of any subsequent royalty receipt is treated as a chargeable gain.

Where payments under a mineral lease etc. relate both to the winning and working of minerals and to other matters, the part to be treated as mineral royalties for these purposes will be calculated under regulations made by HMRC. See *SI 1971 No 1035*.

These chargeable gains are assessable in full, without any deduction on account of expenditure incurred.

Terminal Losses

If the mineral lease comes to an end while the person entitled to receive the royalties still has an interest in the land, and an allowable loss would then arise to him if he sold his interest for a price equal to its market value, he may claim to be treated for CGT purposes as if he had sold, and immediately reacquired, his interest at that price, the resultant loss being allowed, at his election, either (a) against CGT for the year in which the lease expires, or (b) against chargeable gains, in respect of mineral royalties under the lease, within the previous 15 years.

[ITTOIA 2005, ss 157, 319, 340–343; TCGA 1992, ss 201–203; CTA 2009, Sch 1 paras 377, 378].

49

Miscellaneous Income

Introduction

[49.1] *ITTOIA 2005, Pt 5* contains provisions relating to miscellaneous income, not chargeable under any other provisions (see **40.3** below), within the following categories:

(i)   income from **INTELLECTUAL PROPERTY** (**40**);
(ii)   films and sound recordings (see **49.3** below);
(iii)   telecommunications rights (see **49.4** below);
(iv)   amounts treated as income of settlors of **SETTLEMENTS** (**68.26**);
(v)   income of beneficiaries from **DECEASED ESTATES** (**23.4**);
(vi)   annual payments not otherwise charged to tax (see **49.5** below); and
(vii)   income not otherwise charged to tax (see **49.7** below).

[*ITTOIA 2005, s 574(1)*].

Before *ITTOIA 2005*, there was no direct equivalent of *Part 5*. Income now falling within (vii) above was within Schedule D, Case VI (see **49.9** below). [*ICTA 1988, s 18(3)*]. (If from a non-UK source such income fell within Schedule D, Case V.) But Case VI also applied specifically to various types of income (whether or not from a UK source) which are not now within *Part 5*, but are the subject of their own specific charge to income tax. Income within (ii) above and certain types of income within (i) and (iii) above were not subject to a specific charge and thus fell within Case VI (or Case V if from a non-UK source) on general principles. Income within (vi) and the remaining income within (i) and (iii) above fell within Case III (or Case V if from a non-UK source).

Apportionment rules for miscellaneous income, including those types of income formerly within Case VI but not within *Part 5*, are covered at **49.8** below and loss relief for such income is covered at **49.11** below.

Scope of ITTOIA 2005, Part 5

[49.2] The provisions charging to tax income within the categories listed below take priority over *ITTOIA 2005, Pt 5*. Any income otherwise within *Part 5* which also falls within one of the categories is not taxed under *Part 5*. Instead the provisions appropriate to the relevant category apply. The categories are:

- receipts of a trade, profession or vocation (see **73 TRADING INCOME**);
- receipts of a UK property business (see **60.2 PROPERTY INCOME**);
- interest and other income taxed as interest (see **64.2 SAVINGS AND INVESTMENT INCOME**);
- dividends and other distributions from a UK resident company; or
- **EMPLOYMENT INCOME (27), PENSION INCOME (56)** or social security income (see **70 SOCIAL SECURITY AND NATIONAL INSURANCE**).

[*ITTOIA 2005, s 575*].

Income within *ITTOIA 2005, Pt 5* arising to a UK resident is chargeable to tax whether or not from a source in the UK. Income arising to a non-UK resident is chargeable to tax only if from a source in the UK. If income does not have a source, it is treated as having a UK source if it has a comparable connection to the UK. [*ITTOIA 2005, s 577*]. The same applies to the provisions listed at **49.8** below (other than those of *ITTOIA 2005* itself). [*ITTOIA 2005, Sch 1 para 333*]. See also **40.6 INTELLECTUAL PROPERTY** for the charge on sale of patent rights, which has its own territoriality rules.

Films and sound recordings

[49.3] Subject to the provisions at **49.2** above, income from a business (a '*non-trade business*') involving the exploitation of films or sound recordings where the activities carried on do not amount to a trade is chargeable to income tax. The full amount of such income arising in the tax year is chargeable (but see below), the person liable for the tax being the person receiving or entitled to the income.

Expenses incurred wholly and exclusively for the purpose of generating the income are deductible in calculating the amount chargeable to tax, provided that, if they had been incurred for the purposes of a trade, they would have been deductible in calculating its profits. Where an expense is incurred for more than one purpose, if any identifiable part or proportion of the expense is incurred for the purpose of generating the income, a deduction is allowed for that part or proportion. Expenses for which any kind of relief is given under any other provision are not deductible. Relief is additionally available for expenditure incurred by a non-trade business on the production or acquisition of the original master version of a film or sound recording and preliminary expenditure in relation to a film under the rules at **73.76 TRADING INCOME**. In applying those rules to non-trade businesses, the basis period is taken to be the tax year and references to anything not constituting trading stock of a trade are treated as omitted.

The charge to tax under these provisions takes priority over the charge to tax on income from **INTELLECTUAL PROPERTY (40.2)**.

Where income within the charge arises from a source outside the UK it is 'relevant foreign income' (see **32.2** FOREIGN INCOME). See **32.4** FOREIGN INCOME for amounts deductible from income, **32.5** FOREIGN INCOME for relief for unremittable income and **61** for the REMITTANCE BASIS.

[*ITTOIA 2005, ss 609–613*].

See **49.8** below for apportionment rules and **49.11** below for relief for losses.

Telecommunications rights

[49.4] Subject to the provisions at **49.2** above, income from a 'relevant telecommunications right' that is not held or used for the purposes of a trade, profession or vocation is chargeable to income tax. The full amount of such income arising in the tax year is chargeable (but see below), the person liable for the tax being the person receiving or entitled to the income.

Unless the income consists of annual payments (see **24.10** DEDUCTION OF TAX AT SOURCE), expenses incurred wholly and exclusively for the purpose of generating the income are deductible in calculating the amount chargeable to tax, provided that, if they had been incurred for the purposes of a trade, they would have been deductible in calculating its profits. Where an expense is incurred for more than one purpose, if any identifiable part or proportion of the expense is incurred for the purpose of generating the income, a deduction is allowed for that part or proportion. The provisions at **73.119** TRADING INCOME as to the treatment of acquisition costs, disposal proceeds and amounts in respect of revaluation as revenue items apply as they apply for the purpose of calculating the profits of a trade etc.

No deductions can be made where the income consists of annual payments and, for this purpose, in determining whether income consists of annual payments, the frequency with which payments are made is ignored. Deductions are also not permitted where the income is chargeable on the REMITTANCE BASIS (**61**).

Where income within the charge arises from a source outside the UK it is 'relevant foreign income' (see **32.2** FOREIGN INCOME). See **32.4** FOREIGN INCOME for amounts deductible from income, **32.5** FOREIGN INCOME for relief for unremittable income and **61** for the REMITTANCE BASIS.

For the purpose of these provisions '*relevant telecommunications rights*' are the licences and rights covered at **73.119** TRADING INCOME.

Where the income consists of annual payments it may be subject to DEDUCTION OF TAX AT SOURCE (**24.7–24.10**). Any tax so deducted is treated as income tax paid by the recipient.

[*ITTOIA 2005, ss 614–618, Sch 2 paras 130, 131; ITA 2007, Sch 1 para 549; CTA 2010, Sch 1 para 471(4)*].

See **49.8** below for apportionment rules and **49.11** below for relief for losses.

Annual payments not otherwise charged

[49.5] There is a residual charge to income tax in respect of annual payments (see **24.10 DEDUCTION OF TAX AT SOURCE**) not charged to income tax under any other provision (other than any such payments not so charged only because of an exemption). In determining whether income consists of annual payments, the frequency with which payments are made is ignored.

Income tax is chargeable on the full amount of the annual payments arising in the tax year (unless the remittance basis applies — see below), the person liable for the tax being the person receiving or entitled to the income. Certain payments made by trustees in the exercise of a discretion are, however, subject to grossing up under the provisions at **68.15 SETTLEMENTS**.

Where annual payments within the charge arises from a source outside the UK they are 'relevant foreign income' (see **32.2 FOREIGN INCOME**). See **32.4 FOREIGN INCOME** for amounts deductible from income, **32.5 FOREIGN INCOME** for relief for unremittable income and **61** for the **REMITTANCE BASIS**.

[*ITTOIA 2005, ss 683–685; ITA 2007, Sch 1 para 568*].

See **68.26 SETTLEMENTS** for relief available to avoid double taxation where a discretionary annual payment is received from a trust and a settlor is chargeable on the underlying income from which it is made.

For an exemption for certain annual payments made by individuals, see **30.4 EXEMPT INCOME**.

See also **24 DEDUCTION OF TAX AT SOURCE**.

Theatrical angels

[49.6] UK-resident backers of theatrical productions ('angels'), although strictly chargeable under *ITTOIA 2005, s 683* in **49.5** above on any return over and above their original investment (with the capital gains tax rules applicable to any losses), may treat a profit or loss arising on any particular transaction as being within *ITTOIA 2005, s 687* at **49.7** below, so that the loss relief provisions at **49.11** below apply. Losses thus utilised against income cannot also qualify as capital losses. In cases where it would normally be required, HMRC will not insist on deduction of tax at source being applied to payments to angels whose usual place of abode is in the UK. (Non-UK resident angels may apply for authority for tax not to be deducted — see **26.10 DOUBLE TAX RELIEF**.) (HMRC ESC A94).

Income not otherwise charged

[49.7] There is a residual charge to income tax in respect of income not charged to income tax under any other provision (other than income not so charged only because of an exemption). Income tax is chargeable on the amount of the income arising in the tax year (but see below), the person liable for the tax being the person receiving or entitled to the income.

Income arising from a source outside the UK is 'relevant foreign income' (see **32.2 FOREIGN INCOME**). See **32.4 FOREIGN INCOME** for amounts deductible from income, **32.5 FOREIGN INCOME** for relief for unremittable income and **61** for the **REMITTANCE BASIS**.

[*ITTOIA 2005, ss 687–689; FA 2008, s 34, Sch 12 para 22*].

There is no express provision for deductions in calculating taxable income under the above provisions. Before *ITTOIA 2005* came into effect, HMRC accepted that the rules of Case I should be followed where applicable in calculating Case VI income (see *Curtis Brown Ltd v Jarvis* KB 1929, 14 TC 744 and HMRC Business Income Manual BIM80125), and this should continue to apply to income under the above provisions (see *ITTOIA 2005, Sch 2 para 159*).

See **49.10** below for case law on income within Case VI, which continues to be relevant in determining whether income falls within the above provisions. See **49.8** below for apportionment rules and **49.11** below for relief for losses.

See also **60.12 PROPERTY INCOME** for rent-a-room relief on amounts potentially within the above provisions, and **30.15 EXEMPT INCOME** in respect of foster care receipts.

Volunteer drivers

Volunteer drivers (e.g. hospital car service drivers) are taxable on the profit element in any mileage allowances. They may use the statutory tax-free mileage rates applicable to employees (see **27.87 EMPLOYMENT INCOME**) in determining any profit element, although they have the option of claiming their actual motoring expenses (see Revenue Press Release BN 2/01 7 March 2001). See also HMRC guidance at www.hmrc.gov.uk/cars/volunteer-drivers.htm.

Apportionment of miscellaneous income

[49.8] Where income is chargeable to income tax under any of the provisions listed below and any period for which accounts are drawn up (a '*period of account*') does not coincide with a tax year, the profits or losses for the tax year may, if necessary, be arrived at by apportioning the profits and losses of the relevant periods of account between tax years on a time basis, by reference to the number of days in the respective periods. The taxpayer may use a different method of determining the length of the relevant periods if it is reasonable to do so and that method is used consistently.

The provisions (listed in chronological order) are:

- (before 2010/11 — see now *CTA 2010, s 1086(2)*) *ICTA 1988, s 214(1)(ab)* (chargeable payments connected with exempt distributions — see Tolley's Corporation Tax);
- *ICTA 1988, s 571(1)* (schemes for rationalising industry: cancellation of certificates);
- (before 2007/08 — see now *ITA 2007, Pt 12 Ch 2*) *ICTA 1988, s 714* (transfer of securities within the **ACCRUED INCOME SCHEME** (**2.4**);

- (before 2007/08 — see now *ITA 2007, Pt 12 Ch 2*) *ICTA 1988, s 716(3)* (transfer of securities with unrealised interest where the settlement day follows the last interest period (see ACCRUED INCOME SCHEME **2.14**));
- (before 2007/08 — see now *ITA 2007, Pt 12 Ch 2*) *ICTA 1988, s 723* (proceeds of transfer of foreign securities within the ACCRUED INCOME SCHEME (**2.10**) ceasing to be unremittable);
- (for transfers before 22 April 2009) *ICTA 1988, s 730(4)* (transfers of income arising from securities — see **4.6** ANTI-AVOIDANCE);
- (before 2007/08 — see now *ITA 2007, s 720, s 727* or *s 731*) *ICTA 1988, s 740* or *s 743* (transfer of assets abroad — see **4.14, 4.15** ANTI-AVOIDANCE) but, in the case of *s 743*, not so far as relating to dividend income;
- (before 1 December 2009 — see now *SI 2009 No 3001, Reg 17*) *ICTA 1988, s 761(1)(b)(i)* (charge to tax on offshore income gains — see **51.29** OFFSHORE FUNDS);
- *ICTA 1988, s 774* (transactions between dealing company and associated company — see Tolley's Corporation Tax);
- (before 2007/08 — see now *ITA 2007, s 776*) *ICTA 1988, s 775* (sales of occupation income — see **4.28** ANTI-AVOIDANCE);
- (before 2007/08 — see now *ITA 2007, Pt 13 Ch 3*) *ICTA 1988, s 776* (transactions in land — see **4.29** ANTI-AVOIDANCE);
- (before 2010/11 — see now *ITA 2007, s 681BB(8)(9)*) *ICTA 1988, s 780(3A)(a)* (sale and lease-back: new lease of land after assignment or surrender — see **4.31** ANTI-AVOIDANCE);
- (before 2010/11 — see now *ITA 2007, s 681DD*) *ICTA 1988, s 781* (leased assets: capital sums — see **4.33** ANTI-AVOIDANCE);
- (before 2010/11 — see now *ITA 2007, s 809CZC(2)*) *ICTA 1988, s 786(5)* (loan or credit transactions — see **4.36**(ii) ANTI-AVOIDANCE);
- *FA 1989, s 68(2)* (chargeable event in relation to trustees of qualifying employee share ownership trusts);
- *FA 1989, s 71(4)* (qualifying employee share ownership trusts: borrowing);
- *CAA 2001, s 258(4)* (special leasing of plant or machinery: balancing charge — see **11.50** CAPITAL ALLOWANCES ON PLANT AND MACHINERY);
- *CAA 2001, s 479(4)* (allowances for patent rights of non-trader: balancing charge — see **10.35** CAPITAL ALLOWANCES);
- *ITEPA 2003, s 394(2)* (charge on administrators of non-approved retirement schemes for employees before 2006/07);
- *ITEPA 2003, s 476(5)* (unapproved share options: charge on occurrence of chargeable event as a result of operation of law— see **69.15** SHARE-RELATED EMPLOYMENT INCOME AND EXEMPTIONS);
- *ITTOIA 2005, s 242* (post-cessation receipts from trades, professions and vocations — see **59.1** POST-CESSATION RECEIPTS AND EXPENDITURE);
- *ITTOIA 2005, s 335* (rent receivable in connection with a UK concern within *ITTOIA 2005, s 12(4)* (mines, quarries etc.) — see **60.24** PROPERTY INCOME);
- *ITTOIA 2005, s 344* (rent receivable for UK electric-line wayleaves — see **60.23** PROPERTY INCOME);

- *ITTOIA 2005, s 349* (post-cessation receipts from UK property businesses — see **60.6 PROPERTY INCOME**);
- *ITTOIA 2005, Pt 4 Ch 2* as it relates to interest on funding bonds where the issue is treated as a payment of interest and the person by or through whom they are issued is required to retain bonds but it is impracticable for the person to do so (see **64.6 SAVINGS AND INVESTMENT INCOME**);
- *ITTOIA 2005, Pt 4 Ch 9* so far as relating to gains from a policy or contract specified in *ITTOIA 2005, s 531(3)* which do not fall within *ITTOIA 2005, s 532* (see **44.20 LIFE ASSURANCE POLICIES**) or *s 534*;
- *ITTOIA 2005, s 551* (disposal of deposit rights — see **14 CERTIFICATES OF DEPOSIT**);
- *ITTOIA 2005, s 555* (disposals of futures and options involving guaranteed returns — see **4.41 ANTI-AVOIDANCE**);
- *ITTOIA 2005, s 579* royalties and other income from **INTELLECTUAL PROPERTY** (**40.2**), but not so far as relating to annual payments;
- *ITTOIA 2005, s 583* (income from disposals of know-how — see **40.5 INTELLECTUAL PROPERTY**);
- *ITTOIA 2005, s 587* (income from sales of patent rights — see **40.6 INTELLECTUAL PROPERTY**);
- *ITTOIA 2005, s 609* (films and sound recordings: non-trade businesses — see **49.3** above);
- *ITTOIA 2005, s 614* (telecommunication rights: non-trading income), but not so far as relating to annual payments — see **49.4** above);
- *ITTOIA 2005, s 619* (amounts treated as income of settlor — see **68.26 SETTLEMENTS**) but not so far as relating to 'distribution income';
- *ITTOIA 2005, s 682(4)* (adjustments after the administration period — see **23.12 DECEASED ESTATES**);
- *ITTOIA 2005, s 687* (income not otherwise charged — see **49.7** above);
- *ITTOIA 2005, s 844(4)* (withdrawal of relief for unremittable foreign income after source ceases — see **32.5 FOREIGN INCOME**);
- (before 2007/08 — see now *ITA 2007, s 796*) *FA 2004, s 119(4)* (losses derived from film reliefs: chargeable event — see **45.16 LOSSES**);
- (before 2007/08 — see now *ITA 2007, s 804*) *FA 2004, s 127(2)* (claw-back of losses derived from exploiting licence: non-active partners — see **52.16 PARTNERSHIPS**);
- *ITA 2007, Pt 12 Ch 2* (accrued income profits — see **2 ACCRUED INCOME SCHEME**);
- *ITA 2007, s 681BB(8)(9)* (sale and lease-back: new lease of land after assignment or surrender — see **4.31 ANTI-AVOIDANCE**);
- *ITA 2007, s 681DD* (leased assets: capital sums — see **4.33 ANTI-AVOIDANCE**);
- *ITA 2007, s 720, s 727* or *s 731* (transfer of assets abroad — see **4.14, 4.15 ANTI-AVOIDANCE**) but, in the case of *s 720* or *s 727*, not so far as relating to dividend income;
- *ITA 2007, Pt 13 Ch 3* (transactions in land — see **4.29 ANTI-AVOIDANCE**);
- *ITA 2007, s 776* (sales of occupation income — see **4.28 ANTI-AVOIDANCE**);

- ITA 2007, s 796 (losses derived from film reliefs: chargeable event — see **45.16 LOSSES**);
- ITA 2007, s 804 (claw-back of losses derived from exploiting licence: non-active partners — see **52.16 PARTNERSHIPS**);
- ITA 2007, s 809CZC(2) (loan or credit transactions — see **4.36**(ii) **ANTI-AVOIDANCE**);
- CTA 2010, s 1086(2) (chargeable payments connected with exempt distributions — see Tolley's Corporation Tax); and
- (on and after 1 December 2009) SI 2009 No 3001, Reg 17 (charge to tax on offshore income gains — see **51.3 OFFSHORE FUNDS**).

[ITA 2007, s 1016, Sch 1 para 581; ICTA 1988, s 836B; ITTOIA 2005, s 871, Sch 1 para 340; FA 2009, Sch 25 paras 9(3), 10; CTA 2010, Sch 1 para 569; TIOPA 2010, Sch 8 paras 260, 274; SI 2006 No 959, Reg 2; SI 2009 No 3001, Reg 129(6)].

See **75.6 UNIT TRUSTS ETC.** for an addition to this list.

Schedule D, Case VI (pre-2005/06)

[49.9] Simon's Taxes. See B8.6.

Before *ITTOIA 2005*, tax was charged under Schedule D, Case VI in respect of any annual profits or gains not falling under any other case of Schedule D and not charged by virtue of any other Schedule. See also **49.1** above. Although otherwise of historical interest only, the scope of Case VI does continue to have some relevance in determining whether income now falls within the residual charge at **49.7** above.

Case VI was also specifically applied to various kinds of income including, for example, amounts chargeable under the **ACCRUED INCOME SCHEME (2)**; various charges under **ANTI-AVOIDANCE (4)**; withdrawal of relief under **28.19 ENTERPRISE INVESTMENT SCHEME**; sale of patent rights; **CERTIFICATES OF DEPOSIT (14)**; certain easements; certain under-deductions where tax rate changed — see **24 DEDUCTION OF TAX AT SOURCE**; interest paid by issue of bonds; gains on certain offshore life insurance policies — see **44.18–44.20 LIFE ASSURANCE POLICIES**; formerly unremittable overseas income where source has ceased — see **32.5 FOREIGN INCOME**; offshore income gains, see **51 OFFSHORE FUNDS**; recovery of tax over-repaid — see **54.13 PAYMENT OF TAX**; certain **POST-CESSATION ETC. RECEIPTS (59)**; lease premiums and assignments at under-value etc. — see **60.16** *et seq.* **PROPERTY INCOME**; certain settlement income — see **68.26 SETTLEMENTS**; charges on trustees of qualifying employee share ownership trusts; and recovery of various excess reliefs for double taxation, losses, capital allowances etc.

See **Simon's Taxes**. See B8.602.

See the case law at **49.10** below and also the list at **49.8** above which includes the types of income formerly within Case VI in respect of which a loss could arise or against which losses could be set.

Case law

[49.10] Following held to be income within Schedule D, Case VI: commission for guaranteeing overdrafts (*Ryall v Hoare* KB 1925, 8 TC 521 and *Sherwin v Barnes KB* 1931, 16 TC 278); underwriting commission (*Lyons v Cowcher* KB 1926, 10 TC 438); commission for negotiating a sale of shares (*Grey v Tiley* CA 1932, 16 TC 414); commission from an insurance company (*Hugh v Rogers* Ch D 1958, 38 TC 270 and see *Way v Underdown* CA 1974, 49 TC 648); shipping dues (the two *Forth Conservancy Board cases* HL 1928, 14 TC 709, HL 1931, 16 TC 103); share of prize monies for letting racehorses (*Norman v Evans* Ch D 1964, 42 TC 188).

Held to be capital were shares allotted to members of a mining finance development scheme (*Whyte v Clancy* KB 1936, 20 TC 679) and shares allotted for a guarantee of dividends (*National United Laundries v Bennet* KB 1933, 17 TC 420).

A payment to an architect for his services relating to a property deal was held income within Case VI in *Brocklesby v Merricks* KB 1934, 18 TC 576, but payments for services in deals are not income if made gratuitously in such circumstances that the recipient has no enforceable right to them. For cases in which such payments held *not* income see *Bradbury v Arnold* Ch D 1957, 37 TC 665; *Bloom v Kinder* Ch D 1958, 38 TC 77; *Dickinson v Abel* Ch D 1968, 45 TC 353. See also *Scott v Ricketts* CA 1967, 44 TC 303 in which a payment to an estate agent linked with a development scheme was held not to be income even though embodied in a contract.

Receipts of the use of copyright material were held income within Case VI in *Hobbs v Hussey* KB 1942, 24 TC 153 (sale of rights in life story to newspaper) and *Housden v Marshall* Ch D 1958, 38 TC 233 and *Alloway v Phillips* CA 1980, 53 TC 372 (receipt for material for newspaper articles by 'ghost writer') but held capital in *Earl Haig Trustees v CIR* CS 1939, 22 TC 725 (payment to trustees for permission to use diaries of deceased); *Beare v Carter* KB 1940, 23 TC 353 (payment for permission to re-print book); *Nethersole v Withers* HL 1948, 28 TC 501 (sale of film rights in work by deceased author).

For other copyright sales see **73.39** and **73.51** TRADING INCOME. For the line between Cases I and VI as regards surpluses on the sales of assets see **73.28** TRADING INCOME.

Losses

[49.11] Losses on transactions which, if profitable, would have been chargeable to income tax under any of the provisions listed at **49.8** above can be set off against income arising from any transaction chargeable under any of the provisions listed at **49.8** above for the same tax year or carried forward against the next available income chargeable under any of those provisions. For this purpose only, the list at **49.8** above is treated as if the following were omitted:

(a) (on and after 6 April 2007 and before 1 December 2009) *ICTA 1988, s 761(1)(b)(i)* (charge to tax on offshore income gains — see **51.29** OFFSHORE FUNDS); and

(b)   (on and after 1 December 2009) *SI 2009 No 3001, Reg 17* (charge to tax on offshore income gains — see **51.3 OFFSHORE FUNDS**); and

(c)   (for losses made in 2009/10 or any subsequent tax year, and see below) *ITTOIA 2005, Pt 4 Ch 9* (life assurance gains — see **44.3 LIFE ASSURANCE POLICIES**).

Loss relief cannot be claimed where any profits or gains from the transaction would have been relevant **FOREIGN INCOME** (**32.2**).

Subject to any express provision to the contrary, the same rules apply in calculating losses as apply in calculating the corresponding income.

Claims relating to the amount of losses must be made on or before the fifth anniversary of 31 January following the tax year in which they arose. If the claim is made on or after 1 April 2010 (and see **18.4 CLAIMS**), it must be made no later than four years after the end of that tax year. A further claim for relief for losses brought forward must be made on or before the fifth anniversary of 31 January following the tax year for which relief is claimed. Again, if the claim is made on or after 1 April 2010 (and see **18.4 CLAIMS**), it must be made no later than four years after the end of that tax year.

Relief is given effect by deducting the loss in arriving at net income for the tax year for which the relief is given (see Step 2 at **1.7 ALLOWANCES AND TAX RATES**). However, it can only be deducted from miscellaneous income, i.e. income chargeable under any of the provisions listed at **49.8** above. The deduction must be made from miscellaneous income (if any) of the year of loss (and then, if such income is insufficient, from miscellaneous income (if any) of the following tax year, and so on until the loss is exhausted). The deduction is made in priority to deductions of any other reliefs from the available income.

The exclusion at (c) above applies also to 2008/09 in relation to a loss arising under a life insurance policy, life annuity contract or capital redemption policy:

* made on or after 1 April 2009, or varied on or after that date so as to increase the benefits; or
* rights under which are assigned on or after 1 April 2009 to the person claiming the loss relief; or
* rights under which are become held on or after 1 April 2009 as security for a debt of the person claiming the loss relief.

Before *ITTOIA 2005*, the above loss relief applied to losses on transactions which, if profitable, would have been assessable under Schedule D, Case VI (other than losses on transactions falling under *ICTA 1988, ss 34–36*, see **60.16** *et seq.* **PROPERTY INCOME**), which losses could be set off against any profit or gains charged under Case VI. Any Case VI losses which were unrelieved when *ITTOIA 2005* came into effect in 2005/06 are carried forward as losses under the revised provisions above.

[*ITA 2007, ss 152, 153, 155, Sch 1 para 582; ITTOIA 2005, s 872, Sch 1 para 168; ICTA 1988, s 392; FA 2007, s 57(5)(9); FA 2008, Sch 39 para 58; FA 2009, s 69; SI 2009 No 403; SI 2009 No 3001, Reg 129(2)*].

50

Non-Residents

Cross-references. See **62 RESIDENCE, ORDINARY RESIDENCE AND DOMICILE** for the meaning of those terms. See also **4.14–4.17 ANTI-AVOIDANCE** regarding income payable to person abroad assessable on UK resident in certain circumstances; **4.18** for trading transactions with a non-resident under common control; **24 DEDUCTION OF TAX AT SOURCE** for certain payments to non-residents; **25 DIPLOMATIC IMMUNITY**, including international organisations etc.; **26 DOUBLE TAX RELIEF; 27.1–27.19 EMPLOYMENT INCOME** for earnings from work done abroad and expenses; **32 FOREIGN INCOME; 52 PARTNERSHIPS; 56 PENSION INCOME; 64.3 SAVINGS AND INVESTMENT INCOME** for exemption on certain stocks held by non-residents.

Introduction

[50.1] This chapter examines miscellaneous topics concerned with the income taxation of persons non-resident in the UK. **50.2** details the extent to which non-UK resident individuals are entitled to UK personal reliefs. The income tax chargeable on the total income of a non-resident cannot exceed a certain limit, and this is examined in **50.3**. The next part of the chapter (**50.4–50.9**) considers the position of non-residents trading in the UK via a branch or agency. There are special rules concerning payments made to, and the taxation of, performers, i.e. entertainers and sports persons, who are not resident in the UK but perform there from time to time; these are considered in **50.10**. See also the contents list above. See **62 RESIDENCE, ORDINARY RESIDENCE AND DOMICILE** as to a person's residence for tax purposes.

Personal reliefs for non-residents

[50.2] As mentioned under **62.3 RESIDENCE, ORDINARY RESIDENCE AND DOMICILE**, a non-UK resident individual is liable to UK tax without any deduction for personal reliefs (e.g. the personal allowance and married couple's allowance — see **1.14** *et seq.* **ALLOWANCES AND TAX RATES**) except under specific double tax treaties or in cases where the individual concerned is eligible for relief as below. (Foreigners resident here have the same rights to reliefs as British subjects, and where tax is chargeable on the grounds of *'residence'* in the UK, the taxpayer is entitled to the full personal reliefs. This does not apply to tax chargeable because a person is temporarily employed in the UK, but not technically 'resident'.)

The non-resident individuals eligible for personal reliefs are as follows.

(i)   (Before 2010/11), all Commonwealth citizens.

(ii)   All nationals of States within the European Economic Area (EEA), which comprises all EU States plus Norway, Iceland and Liechtenstein (see now *Interpretation Act 1978, Sch 1*, as amended).

(iii)   Persons who are or who have been employed in the service of the Crown.

(iv)   Persons employed in the service of a missionary society.

(v)   Persons employed in the service of any territory under British protection.

(vi)   Residents in the Isle of Man or Channel Islands.

(vii)   Persons abroad for health reasons (including the health of family members living with the person concerned) following residence in the UK.

(viii) Widows or widowers (or surviving civil partners) of Crown Servants.

For 2007/08, personal reliefs available to non-residents within any of (iii) to (viii) above are given by virtue of *ITA 2007, s 56*. Personal reliefs available to non-residents within (i) and (ii) above (and not also within any of (iii) to (viii) above) continue to be given by virtue of *ICTA 1988, s 278* as before and the reliefs themselves are given under *ICTA 1988* rather than *ITA 2007*. Also for 2007/08, the various transfers of married couple's allowance and blind person's allowance described at **47.2–47.4 MARRIED PERSONS AND CIVIL PARTNERS** are not possible if one of the two individuals involved qualifies for UK personal reliefs by virtue only of (i) or (ii) above and the other qualifies for reliefs by virtue of being UK resident or by virtue of any of (iii) to (viii) above. In other words, transfers cannot be made if one spouse or civil partner receives (or would receive) the allowance under *ICTA 1988* and the other receives it (or would receive it) under *ITA 2007*. *However*, if the individual initially entitled to the allowance was also entitled to that allowance immediately before 6 April 2007, this prohibition on transfers does not take effect until 2009/10; in other words, such transfers remain possible in 2007/08 and 2008/09. (See Change 7 in Annex 1 to the Explanatory Notes to *ITA 2007*.)

For 2008/09 and 2009/10, personal reliefs available to non-residents in (ii) above are brought within the ambit of *ITA 2007, s 56*, so that only personal reliefs available to non-residents within (i) above (and not also within any of (ii) to (viii) above) continue to be given by virtue of *ICTA 1988, s 278*. (The definition of an EEA national is also updated to ensure that it includes all current EU member states including Accession States and will automatically do so in future.) The various transfers of married couple's allowance and blind person's allowance described at **47.1–47.4 MARRIED PERSONS AND CIVIL PARTNERS** are not possible if one of the two individuals involved qualifies for UK personal reliefs by virtue only of (i) above and the other qualifies for reliefs by virtue of being UK resident or by virtue of any of (ii) to (viii) above. *However*, if the individual initially entitled to the allowance was also entitled to that allowance immediately before 6 April 2007, this prohibition on transfers does not take effect until 2009/10; in other words, such transfers remain possible in 2008/09.

For **2010/11 onwards,** personal reliefs are no longer available (other than by virtue of specific double tax treaties) to non-resident Commonwealth citizens, i.e. those in (i) above. Reliefs for non-residents within any of (ii) to (viii) above continue to be given under *ITA 2007, s 56*. Consequently, the relevant provisions of *ICTA 1988* are repealed.

The relatively minor reliefs at **44.2 LIFE ASSURANCE POLICIES** are treated in the same way as personal reliefs for the above purposes, except that in this case reliefs available to non-residents within any of (iii) to (viii) above (for 2007/08) and (ii) to (viii) above (for 2008/09 onwards) are given by virtue of *ITA 2007, s 460* (as opposed to *ITA 2007, s 56*).

[*ITA 2007, ss 56, 460, Sch 1 para 40, Sch 2 paras 14–17; ICTA 1988, ss 256–257, 257A, 257AB, 257C, 265, 278; FA 2008, ss 2, 3, 70, Sch 7 paras 78, 81; FA 2009, s 3, Sch 1 paras 2, 7; SI 2008 Nos 673, 3024*].

For the status of Hong Kong residents who were previously British Dependent Territories citizens following the transfer of sovereignty on 30 June 1997, see Revenue Tax Bulletin October 1996 pp 357, 358. It was expected that most would continue to be able to claim personal reliefs.

Claims should be made on Form R43 to HMRC Residency, Fitz Roy House, PO Box 46, Nottingham, England, NG2 1BD. A right of appeal, within three months of the notice of HMRC's decision, is given by *TMA 1970, Sch 1A para 9(2)* as amended by *ITA 2007, Sch 1 para 264*.

See www.hmrc.gov.uk/cnr/r43-2008-notes.pdf (in particular note 3) for more detail, including lists of those countries whose nationals and/or residents may be entitled to personal reliefs under double tax treaties.

Simon's Taxes. See E6.201, E6.202.

Limit on liability to income tax

[50.3] The income tax chargeable on the total income of a non-UK resident is not to exceed the aggregate of:

(i)   the tax which would otherwise be chargeable if 'disregarded income' and any personal allowances due (see **50.2** above) were both left out of account; and

(ii)   the tax deducted from so much of the 'disregarded income' as is subject to deduction of income tax at source (including tax credits and tax treated as deducted at source).

Income is *'disregarded income'* if it falls into one of the categories below and is not income in relation to which the non-resident has a UK representative for the purposes of the provisions at **50.5** to **50.9** below (i.e. income from or connected with a trade etc. carried on in the UK through a branch or agency, subject to the exclusions at **50.7** below). The categories are:

(a)   income chargeable under *ITTOIA 2005, Pt 4 Ch 2* (interest), *Pt 4 Ch 7* (purchased life annuity payments), *Pt 4 Ch 8* profits from deeply discounted securities), *Pt 4 Ch 10* (distributions from unauthorised unit trusts), *Pt 4 Ch 11* (transactions in deposits), *s 579* (royalties etc. from intellectual property) so far as it relates to annual payments, *Pt 5 Ch 4* (non-trading income from certain telecommunications rights) so far as it relates to annual payments, or *Pt 5 Ch 7* (annual payments not otherwise charged), but not (in any of these cases) income which is relevant foreign income (see **32.2 FOREIGN INCOME**);

(b)   income chargeable under *ITTOIA 2005, Pt 4 Ch 3* (dividends and other distributions from UK resident companies) and for 2007/08 onwards *Ch 5* (stock dividends from UK resident companies) (see Change 122 listed in Annex 1 to the Explanatory Notes to *ITA 2007*);

(c)   certain social security benefits (including state pensions);

(d)   retirement annuities under contracts that became registered pension schemes on 6 April 2006 (see **57.3 PENSION PROVISION**) and UK-sourced employment-related annuities within **56.2**(e) **PENSION INCOME**;

(e)   'disregarded transaction income', being income which arises as mentioned in **50.7**(2)(3) below (certain income from trading in the UK through a broker or investment manager) and not being Lloyd's underwriting profits; and

(f)   any income designated for these purposes by Treasury regulations.

As regards (e) above, the application of **50.7**(3)(vi) below is restricted to 2007/08 and earlier years.

These provisions do not apply to limit the income tax chargeable on a settlement if any actual or potential income beneficiary, whether his interest is absolute or discretionary, is an individual ordinarily resident in the UK or a UK resident company.

[*ITA 2007, ss 810–828; FA 1995, s 128; FA 2008, Sch 16 paras 5, 10, 11(3)–(6); FA 2009, Sch 1 paras 6, 7; TIOPA 2010, Sch 8 paras 282–284; SI 2006 No 1963, reg 3; SI 2009 No 23, regs 1, 5(3)*].

Simon's Taxes. See **E6.106–E6.109.**

Example

[50.4]

Hugh and Elizabeth are non-UK resident throughout 2010/11. They are each entitled to a UK personal allowance under the provisions in **50.2** above. Their tax liabilities on total UK income for 2010/11, disregarding the limit under **50.3** above, are as follows.

	Hugh	Elizabeth
	£	£
Net rental income (received gross)	2,500	6,300
Bank interest (received gross)	8,685	985
Dividends	3,600	—
Tax credits	400	—
Total UK income	15,185	7,285
Deduct Personal allowance	6,475	6,475
Taxable UK income	£8,710	£810

Tax on total UK income:

	£	£
£2,440/810 @ 10% (starting rate for savings)	244.00	81.00
£2,270 @ 20% (basic rate on interest)	454.00	
£4,000 @ 10% (dividend ordinary rate)	400.00	
	1,098.00	81.00
Deduct Tax credits	400.00	
	£698.00	£81.00

But tax is limited under **50.3** above as follows.

	£	£
Property income	2,500	6,300

(Bank interest and dividends are 'disregarded income' — see **50.3** above.)

	£	£
£2,500/£6,300 @ 20% (basic rate)	500.00	1,260.00
	£500.00	£1,260.00

Hugh's UK income tax liability is therefore restricted to £500.00 (plus £400.00 in tax credits, which cannot be reclaimed). The total of £900.00 is less than the figure of £1,098.00 in the normal computation and means that Hugh has to pay only £500.00 to HMRC as opposed to £698.00. Elizabeth's liability is not reduced under **50.3** above and is thus £81.00.

Non-residents trading via UK branch or agency

[50.5] The provisions described below apply where a non-UK resident carries on a trade, profession or vocation in the UK through a branch or agency. The legislation provides for the branch or agency to be treated as the UK representative of the non resident in relation to certain amounts chargeable to income tax. It sets out the tax obligations and liabilities of the UK representative. See also **65.11 SELF-ASSESSMENT**.

For whether activities of a non-resident person constitute trading *in the UK*, see HMRC International Manual INTM263000.

Where a non-resident carries on a trade partly in and partly outside the UK, the charge to UK tax is limited to the profits from the part of the trade carried on in the UK, whether or not through a branch or agency (see **73.1 TRADING INCOME**). HMRC have reaffirmed that the profits from a part of a trade carried on in the UK are to be measured on the arm's length principle set out in the OECD model tax convention and explained in OECD publications, irrespective of whether a double tax agreement applies (Revenue Tax Bulletin August 1995 pp 237–239).

Meaning of 'UK representative'

[50.6] For the purposes of **50.9** below and subject to **50.7** below (persons not treated as UK representatives), a branch or agency in the UK (which for this purpose means any factorship, agency, receivership, branch or management) through which a non-UK resident carries on (alone or in partnership) a trade, profession or vocation is his '*UK representative*' in relation to the following:

- such income from the trade etc. as arises, directly or indirectly, through or from the branch or agency, and
- any income from property or rights used by, or held by or for, the branch or agency.

Where the non-resident ceases to carry on the trade etc. through the branch or agency, it continues to be his UK representative for tax purposes in relation to amounts arising during the period of the agency. A UK representative is a legal entity distinct from the non-resident. Where the branch or agency is carried on in partnership, the partnership is the non-resident's UK representative.

If a partnership carries on a trade or profession in the UK through a branch or agency, the branch or agency is treated as the UK representative of any non resident partner in relation to that partner's share of the UK profits. If a trade etc. is carried on in the UK by a non-resident in partnership with at least one UK resident partner, the partnership itself is the UK representative in relation to that partner's share of the UK profits, notwithstanding that there may also be a branch or agency which is the non-resident partner's UK representative in respect of those profits. All the partners are therefore jointly liable for tax on the non- resident partner's share of the UK profits.

[*ITA 2007, ss 835C–835F, 835S; FA 1995, s 126; TMA 1970, s 118(1); CTA 2009, Sch 1 para 400; TIOPA 2010, Sch 6 paras 1–4, 17*].

Simon's Taxes. See B1.210.

Persons not treated as UK representatives

[50.7] The following are *not* treated as UK representatives for the purposes of these provisions.

(1) *Agents.* An agent is not treated as a non-UK resident's UK representative in relation to income arising from so much of the non-resident's business as relates to transactions carried out through the agent otherwise than in the course of carrying on a regular agency for the non-resident. This extends to income from property or rights which, as a result of any such transactions, are used by, or held by or for, the agent on the non-resident's behalf.

(2) *Brokers.* A broker is not treated as a non-UK resident's UK representative in relation to income arising from so much of the non-resident's business as relates to transactions carried out through the broker and meeting all the conditions below. This extends to income from property or rights which, as a result of any such transactions, are used by, or held by or for, the broker on the non-resident's behalf. The conditions are that:

    (i) the broker was carrying on the business of broker at the time of the transaction;

    (ii) the transaction was carried out in the ordinary course of that business;

    (iii) the broker's remuneration for the transaction was at a rate not less than is customary for that class of business; and

    (iv) the broker is not the non-resident's UK representative in relation to income chargeable to tax for the same tax year which is not within this let-out.

(3) *Investment managers.* An investment manager is not treated as a non-UK resident's UK representative in relation to income etc. arising from so much of the non-resident's business as relates to investment transactions (as defined) carried out through the investment manager and meeting all the conditions below. This extends to income from property or rights which, as a result of any such transactions, are used by, or held by or for, the investment manager on the non-resident's behalf. The conditions are that:

    (i) the investment manager was carrying on the business of providing investment management services at the time of the transaction;

    (ii) the transaction was carried out in the ordinary course of that business;

    (iii) the manager, when acting on the non-resident's behalf in that transaction, did so in an independent capacity (see below);

    (iv) the '20% rule' is met in relation to the transaction (see below); and

(v)   the remuneration for the investment management services in question was at a rate not less than is customary for that class of business.

In relation to investment transactions occurring before 21 July 2008, it was a further condition that the investment manager was not the non-resident's UK representative in relation to income chargeable to tax for the same tax year which is not within this let-out.

See also **50.8** below.

(4)   *Lloyd's agents.* Neither a Lloyd's members' agent nor a syndicate managing agent istreated as a non-UK resident Lloyd's underwriter's UK representative in relation to income arising from his underwriting business. See **74 UNDERWRITERS AT LLOYD'S** generally.

(5)   *Persons acting under alternative finance arrangements.* See **3.9 ALTERNATIVE FINANCE ARRANGEMENTS.**

General

Where a person acts as broker or investment manager as part only of a business, that part is deemed to be a separate business for the purposes of (2) and (3) above. A person carries out a transaction on behalf of another where he either undertakes it himself or instructs a third party to do so.

[ITA 2007, ss 835G–835M, 835R, 835S; FA 1995, s 127(1)–(3), (12)–(17), (19); ITA 2007, Sch 1 para 367; FA 2008, Sch 16 paras 1, 2, 11(1), (4)–(6); CTA 2009, Sch 1 para 401; TIOPA 2010, Sch 6 paras 5–11, 16, 17; SI 2003 No 2172; SI 2007 No 963].

Simon's Taxes. See **B1.211.**

Further rules on investment managers

[50.8] As regards **50.7**(3)(iii) above, a person is not regarded as acting in an independent capacity on behalf of the non-UK resident unless, having regard to its legal, financial and commercial characteristics, their relationship is on an arm's length basis as between independent businesses. HMRC SP 1/01 (revised 20 July 2007) clarifies the 'independent capacity' requirement. The test will be regarded as met where any of the following applies (although this list is not exhaustive). (A subsidiary may be considered independently of its parent for these purposes.)

*   The provision of services to the non-resident (and persons connected with the non-resident) is not a substantial part (i.e. it must be no more than 70%) of the investment management business (or that condition is satisfied within 18 months from the start of a new investment management business).
*   An intention to satisfy the above condition was not met for reasons outside the manager's control, despite reasonable steps being taken to fulfil that intention.
*   The non-resident person is a widely held collective fund or is being actively marketed so as to become one or is being wound up or dissolved. (This will apply mostly to non-transparent overseas funds, and will be regarded as satisfied if either no majority interest in the fund

was held by five or fewer persons (and persons connected with them), or no interest of more than 20% was held by a single person (and persons connected with that person).)

The '20% *rule*' (see **50.7**(3)(iv) above) is that there is a 'qualifying period' in relation to which the investment manager (and persons connected with him) must intend that any interest that they may have in the non-resident's 'relevant disregarded income' will not exceed 20% of that income. If that intention is not fulfilled, the 20% rule will nevertheless be met if the only reason why the intention is not fulfilled is because of matters outside the control of the investment manager (or connected persons) despite his having taken reasonable steps to mitigate the effect of those matters. The non-resident's '*relevant disregarded income*' is the total of his income for the tax years comprised in the qualifying period which derives from investment transactions carried out by the investment manager on his behalf and meeting the conditions for the let-out (disregarding the 20% rule itself). A '*qualifying period*', in relation to a transaction, may be any period consisting in or including the tax year for which the transaction income is chargeable to tax, being, in a case where it is not that tax year, a period of not more than five years comprising two or more tax years including that one.

If a transaction meets the conditions at **50.7**(3)(i) to (v) above except for the 20% rule, it is regarded as meeting the 20% rule to the extent of so much (if any) of the transaction income to which the investment manager (or a person connected with him) has no beneficial entitlement.

HMRC SP 1/01 clarifies the 20% rule and certain other aspects of the conditions for exclusion; in particular the definition of 'investment transactions', the customary rate test at **50.7**(3)(v) above and the interaction between the 'independent capacity test' and the '20% rule'. The SP was revised on 20 July 2007 with immediate effect except to the extent that the revision required a non-resident or his investment manager to make changes to then current circumstances or contractual arrangements, in which case the original SP 1/01 could continue to be applied until 31 December 2009.

Persons are connected for the above purposes if they are connected within *ITA 2007, s 993* (previously *ICTA 1988, s 839*) (see **21 CONNECTED PERSONS**).

Special rules apply (see *ITA 2007, s 835Q*) if amounts arise or accrue to the non-resident as a participant in a collective investment scheme. They apply for the purposes of determining whether the 20% rule is met in relation to a transaction carried out for the purposes of the scheme.

[*ITA 2007, ss 835N–835Q, 835S; FA 1995, s 127(4)–(11), (18); ITA 2007, Sch 1 para 367; TIOPA 2010, Sch 6 paras 12–15, 17*].

Obligations etc. imposed on UK representatives

[50.9] As regards the taxation of any amounts in relation to which a non-UK resident has a UK representative (see **50.6–50.8**, legislation making provision for (or in connection with) the assessment, collection and recovery of income tax (and interest on tax) has effect as if the obligations and liabilities of the non-resident were *also* obligations and liabilities of the UK representative. The discharge of an obligation or liability by either the non-resident or the UK representative is treated as discharging the corresponding obligation or liability of the other. The non-resident is bound by any acts or omissions of his UK representative. Where an obligation or liability depends on the serving of a notice or other document or the making of a request or demand, it is not treated as having been imposed on the UK representative unless the notice etc. was served on or copied to him or he was notified of the request or demand.

A person cannot, by virtue of the above, face criminal proceedings for an offence except where he committed the offence himself or consented to or connived in its commission.

Independent agents

An '*independent agent*', in relation to a non-UK resident (N), is any person who is N's UK representative in respect of any agency in which he is acting on behalf of N in an independent capacity (see **50.8** above). The provisions above apply equally to independent agents as to other UK representatives, with the following applying in addition.

As regards his obligations to furnish information (including anything contained in a return, self-assessment, account, statement or report provided to HMRC), the independent agent is not required to do anything beyond what is practicable by acting to the best of his knowledge and belief after having taken all reasonable steps to obtain the information. In such a case, the non-UK resident is not discharged from his own obligation to furnish the information. But the non-resident is also not bound by any mistakes in the information so furnished by the agent unless the mistakeresults from the non-resident's own act or omission or is one to which he consented or in which he connived.

An independent agent is entitled to be indemnified in respect of any liability discharged by him on the non-resident's behalf under these provisions and to retain, out of monies due by him to the non-resident, amounts sufficient to cover any such liability, whether or not he has already discharged it.

An independent agent is not liable to any civil penalty or surcharge in respect of any act or omission which is neither his own nor one to which he consented or in which he connived, providing he can show that he could not recover the penalty etc. out of monies due to the non-resident after being indemnified for his other liabilities.

[*ITA 2007, ss 835T–835Y; FA 1995, Sch 23; TIOPA 2010, Sch 6 paras 18–23*].

Simon's Taxes. See B1.210.

Non-resident performers

[50.10] Any person making a payment or transfer (including by way of loan) for, in respect of, or which in any way derives either directly or indirectly from, the performance of a 'relevant activity' performed in the UK by a performer, i.e. an entertainer (as broadly defined), sportsman or sportswoman who is not resident in the UK in the tax year in which that activity is performed, is required to deduct and account to HMRC for an amount representing income tax, at a rate which may not exceed the basic rate of income tax for the tax year (see further below). In the case of a transfer, the actual worth of what is transferred is treated as being a net amount corresponding to a gross amount from which income tax at the basic rate has been deducted. That gross amount is treated as the value of the transfer and the net value is the cost to the transferor less any contribution made by the performer.

A *'relevant activity'* is an activity performed in the UK by a performer in his character as such on or in connection with (including promotion of) a commercial occasion or event (including participation in live or recorded transmissions of any kind) for which he is entitled to receive a payment or transfer or which is designed to promote commercial sales or activity by any means. See *Set, Deuce and Ball v Robinson* (Sp C 373), [2003] SSCD 382 which analysed this definition in relation to non-resident tennis players performing at Wimbledon; on appeal to the HL, it was held that payments made by a foreign company with no UK tax presence are within these provisions (*Agassi v Robinson* HL 2006, [2006] STC 1056).

Payments or transfers from which tax need not be withheld under these provisions are as follows:

- a payment subject to deduction of tax under some provision of the *Taxes Acts* other than *ITA 2007, s 966* (or its predecessor) and the *Income Tax (Entertainers and Sportsmen) Regulations 1987 (SI 1987 No 530)*;
- an arm's length payment made to a person resident and ordinarily resident in the UK, who is not connected or associated with the payee, for services ancillary to the performance of a relevant activity;
- payments representing royalties from the sale of sound recordings;
- any total amount paid in a tax year by a payer, together with persons connected or associated with him, to a non-UK resident performer, together with persons connected or associated with him, which does not exceed £1,000.

The *Regulations* provide for arrangements to be made in writing between the payer, the performer, or other recipient of the payment, and the Commissioners of HMRC for a reduced tax payment representing, as nearly as may be, the actual liability of the performer, to apply. Such application must be made not later than 30 days before the payment (or transfer) falls to be made and the full basic rate deduction must be made from any payment or transfer made before approval is given by HMRC. There are provisions to prevent any payment suffering withholding tax more than once where it passes through an intermediary, and for reductions to apply where there is a double taxation agreement in force. Similarly, there are anti-avoidance provisions to prevent payments or transfers being routed through third parties such as controlled companies and similar entities.

The sum accounted for to HMRC is treated as paid on account of the income or corporation tax liability of a person other than the person so accounting for it, whether a liability under the *Regulations*, under the main charging provisions below or under any other provision of the *Taxes Acts*. The charge under *ITA 2007, s 966* applies in place of any charge on employment income (any amount charged on which is to be treated as an expense of the separate trade referred to below), under the settlements legislation (see **68.26** *et seq.* SETTLEMENTS) or under Schedule D (where the connected payment is a receipt falling to be included in the computation of profits of a company which provides the services of the performer). A recipient is entitled to claim in writing that a tax payment deducted is excessive and *TMA 1970, s 42* (see **18.1, 18.3** CLAIMS) applies to such claims.

Payment of tax is due, whether or not it has been withheld from the connected payment or transfer, before, or at the time when, a quarterly return (see below) is made, whether or not an assessment has been made.

Liability of the performer

Where a payment or other transfer connected with the relevant activity is made, then (regardless of whether or not there is a duty to deduct tax at source) the relevant activity is treated as performed in the course of a trade, profession or vocation carried on in the UK (insofar as it would not otherwise be so treated, for example because the performer already has a UK trade), unless it is performed in the course of an office or employment. Payments and transfers made to a prescribed (by the *Regulations*) person other than the performer himself (typically to a company controlled by the performer), and connected with the relevant activity, are treated, other than in prescribed circumstances, as if made to the performer himself in the course of that trade etc.

Income tax is charged on profits arising from payments and transfers within these provisions as if they were received in the course of a *separate* trade, profession or vocation (distinct from any other trade etc. carried on by the performer, e.g. his world-wide trade). However, for the purposes of loss relief under *ITA 2007, s 72* and *ITA 2007, s 83*, the separate trade and world-wide trade are treated as the same trade, although losses in early years will be relieved only by reference to the date of commencement of the world-wide trade. Terminal loss relief under *ITA 2007, s 89* will only be given in respect of the separate trade if the world-wide trade ceases in the same period.

All other provisions of the *Taxes Acts* as to the time within which an assessment may be made apply to such an assessment as do the provisions for out of time assessments. Tax charged by an assessment is payable within 14 days of the issue of the notice, or by the due date of payment of the tax (see above) if this is earlier. The collection and recovery procedures and the provisions relating to interest on overdue tax in *TMA 1970* apply to such assessments.

Returns (including returns of payments for which a nil deduction rate applied) must be made quarterly in respect of the periods to 30 June, 30 September, 31 December and 5 April within 14 days of the end of each period. HMRC may require, in writing, within a specified time, certain information regarding payments, payees and relevant activities. The penalty provisions of *TMA 1970, s 98* apply to failure to submit returns (see **55.21** PENALTIES).

[*ITA 2007, ss 965–970, Sch 1 para 495; ITTOIA 2005, ss 13, 14; SI 1987 No 530*].

The provisions are administered by the Foreign Entertainers Unit (FEU), a specialist unit within HMRC (see www.hmrc.gov.uk/feu/feu.htm).

See also HMRC booklet FEU50 and HMRC Help sheet IR303.

Specific sporting events

The Treasury have power to make regulations exempting non-UK resident athletes from income tax on income arising from their performance at the 2012 Olympic Games in London. [*FA 2006, s 68; ITA 2007, Sch 1 para 614*].

There are provisions conferring exemption from income tax to non-UK resident employees and contractors of competing overseas teams in relation to certain income arising in connection with the 2011 UEFA Champions League final in England. See **30.44 EXEMPT INCOME**.

Simon's Taxes. See E5.801–E5.809.

Non-resident dealers in securities etc. trading in the UK

[50.11] If in any tax year:

- a person who is not ordinarily resident in the UK carries on a trade in the UK consisting wholly or partly of dealing in securities or of banking or insurance, and
- in calculating the profits of the trade any amount is disregarded as a result of *ITTOIA 2005, s 714* (exemption of profits from FOTRA securities — see **64.3 SAVINGS AND INVESTMENT INCOME**) because of a condition subject to which any 3½% War Loan 1952 Or After was issued,

interest on money borrowed for the purposes of the trade is deductible in calculating the profits for that tax year only insofar as it exceeds the total cost of the 3½% War Loan.

[*ITTOIA 2005, s 154A; ICTA 1988, s 475; TIOPA 2010, Sch 7 para 43*].

Interest on foreign currency securities etc.

[50.12] Where foreign currency securities are issued by a local authority or a 'statutory corporation' *and the Treasury so direct*, the interest on the securities is exempt from income tax if their beneficial owner is a non-UK resident. The same applies to interest on a foreign currency loan made to a statutory corporation if the Treasury so direct and the person for the time being entitled to repayment or eventual repayment of the loan is a non-UK resident. In both cases, the exemption does not apply if the interest falls to be treated by tax law as another person's income.

A *'statutory corporation'* is a corporation (other than a company) incorporated by a statute or any other corporation on which functions connected with carrying on an undertaking are conferred by a statute or by an order made under or confirmed by a statute.

A security or loan is a foreign currency one if under its terms the currency to be used for repayment is not sterling. In the case of a security issued or loan made before 6 April 1982, the security or loan is a foreign currency one if under its terms the currency to be used for repayment is not that of a country specified in *Exchange Control Act 1947, Sch 1* at the time the security was issued or the loan was made. If there is an option as to the currency to be used for repayment, the security or loan is only to be treated as a foreign currency one if the option is exercisable only by the holder of the security or the person for the time being entitled to repayment or eventual repayment of the loan.

[*ITTOIA 2005, ss 755, 756, 879(3), 880(1); ITA 2007, Sch 1 para 574; SI 2009 No 1890, Regs 1, 3(6)*]

Where interest is exempt as above, the payer is not required to deduct tax at source — see **24.12 DEDUCTION OF TAX AT SOURCE**.

Payments of royalties to non-residents

[50.13] See **24.13 DEDUCTION OF TAX AT SOURCE** as regards the requirement to deduct tax at source from **copyright royalties, public lending right payments** and **design royalties** paid to non-UK residents.

Key points

[50.14] Points to consider are as follows.

- Non-UK resident taxpayers are generally entitled to personal allowances and reliefs through double taxation treaties, but there is also a general entitlement for all EEA Nationals.
- The limit on income tax liability applying to non-resident individuals should not be overlooked. Advisers computing income tax liabilities for non-residents manually will need to perform both computations to check whether the limit applies to their client. Those using tax software should ensure that they are familiar with the particular requirements of their software package in this regard.
- The tax system as it applies to non-resident performers — broadly entertainers and sportsmen – imposes obligations both on the performer and anyone who makes payments in respect of their services. Advisers dealing with this area will need to ensure that they arc fully conversant with the rules.

- The rules permitting the transfer of married couple's allowance between spouses and civil partners are constrained in the case of non-residents. **50.2** explains in detail when the transfer of allowances is not possible.

51

Offshore Funds

Cross-reference. See **64.4 SAVINGS AND INVESTMENT INCOME** (certain distributions of offshore funds treated as interest).

Simon's Taxes. See **B5.7, B8.622–B8.640.**

Introduction

[51.1] Since 1984, gains arising on disposals of certain investments in offshore funds have been chargeable to income tax rather than capital gains tax. Broadly, this applies to investments that accumulate income rather than distribute it. Without special rules the accumulated income would be reflected in the value on disposal and would be converted into a chargeable gain. The original statutory regime was enacted by *Finance Act 1984* and was later consolidated as *ICTA 1988, Pt XVII Ch V*. That regime was replaced by legislation in *Finance Acts 2008* and *2009* (now in *TIOPA 2010*) and in *SI 2009 No 3001 (The Offshore Funds (Tax) Regulations 2009)* with effect in relation to distributions and disposals made **on or after 1 December 2009** (subject to the transitional rules at **51.19, 51.20**). This new regime has the same purpose as the old but sets out to achieve it in a different manner. For official guidance on the new regime, see HMRC Offshore Funds Manual at www.hmrc.gov.uk/offshorefunds/offshore-funds-manual.pdf.

For the original (i.e. pre-1 December 2009) regime, see **51.21** below.

Definition of offshore fund

[51.2] A new definition of 'offshore fund' is introduced for the purposes of the new regime with effect in relation to distributions and disposals made on or after 1 December 2009 (subject to the transitional rules at **51.19, 51.20** below).

The old definition of 'offshore fund' (see **51.24** below) was based on the regulatory definition of a collective investment scheme as set out in *Financial Services and Markets Act 2000*. The new definition uses a characteristics based approach.

An *'offshore fund'* means:

(a)   a 'mutual fund' constituted by a non-UK resident body corporate (other than a limited liability partnership);

(b)   a 'mutual fund' under which property is held on trust for the participants where the trustees are non-UK resident; or

(c)   a 'mutual fund' constituted by other arrangements that create rights in the nature of co-ownership where the arrangements take effect by virtue of the law of a territory outside the UK, but not including a mutual fund constituted by two or more persons carrying on a trade or business in partnership.

'Mutual fund' means arrangements with respect to property of any description (including money) that meet all of the conditions set out below, subject to the exceptions in *TIOPA 2010, s 357* and any other exceptions that may be specified by the Treasury in regulations made by statutory instrument. The conditions are that:

•   the purpose or effect of the arrangements is to enable the participants to participate in the acquisition, holding, management or disposal of the property or to receive profits or income arising from the acquisition, holding, management or disposal of the property or to receive amounts paid out of such profits or income;

- the participants do not have day-to-day control of the management of the property; and
- under the terms of the arrangements, a reasonable investor participating in the arrangements would expect to be able to realise all or part of his investment on a basis calculated entirely (or almost entirely) by reference to net asset value or to an index of some description.

In the case of 'umbrella arrangements', each part of the arrangements is to be treated as separate arrangements. *'Umbrella arrangements'* means arrangements which provide for separate pooling of the contributions of the participants and the profits or income out of which payments are made to them. Where there is more than one class of interest in arrangements (the *'main arrangements'*), the arrangements relating to each class of interest are to be treated as separate arrangements.

[*TIOPA 2010, ss 354–363; FA 2008, ss 40A–40G, 41, 42, 42A; FA 2009, Sch 22 paras 2–5*].

Charge to tax on participants in non-reporting funds

[51.3] Any fund that is not a reporting fund (for which see **51.13** below) is a *'non-reporting fund'*. [*SI 2009 No 3001, Reg 4*].

Subject to the exceptions at **51.4** below, there is a charge to income tax if a person disposes of an interest (i.e. an investment) in a non-reporting fund and an offshore income gain (see **51.5** below) arises on the disposal. The offshore income gain is treated for tax purposes as miscellaneous income which arises at the time of the disposal to the person making the disposal, and the tax is charged on that person. [*SI 2009 No 3001, Regs 17, 18; SI 2010 No 294, Reg 27*].

The charge to income tax may also arise if the interest disposed of is an interest in a reporting fund which has been a non-reporting fund at some time since the interest was acquired — see **51.18** below for details.

A person is within the above charge if the offshore income gain arises in a tax year during any part of which he is resident in the UK or during which he is ordinarily resident in the UK. [*TCGA 1992, s 2(1); SI 2009 No 3001, Reg 22(1)(a)*]. See also **51.11** below.

Any offshore income gains arising to trustees of a settlement are charged at the trust rate of income tax (see **68.11** SETTLEMENTS).

A disposal may well give rise to both an offshore income gain chargeable as above and a chargeable gain for capital gains tax (CGT) purposes. See **51.7** below as regards relief from CGT. See **51.6** below as to what constitutes a disposal.

See **51.8** below as regards investors chargeable to tax on the remittance basis.

Special rules apply to authorised investment funds (either unit trusts or open-ended investment companies) which invest in non-reporting offshore funds. See **75.8** UNIT TRUSTS ETC.

Exceptions from charge

[51.4] No charge arises under **51.3** above if

- the interest in the non-reporting fund is held as trading stock; or
- the disposal of the interest is taken into account in computing the profits of a trade; or
- the interest consists of 'excluded indexed securities' (as defined by *ITTOIA 2005, s 433* — see **64.20 SAVINGS AND INVESTMENT INCOME**); or
- the interest is a right arising under a policy of insurance; or
- the interest is a loan (but not if it is a loan where the amount payable on redemption exceeds the issue price by an amount wholly or partly determined by reference to the income of the non-reporting fund); or
- the interest is in an offshore fund falling within **51.2**(b) or (c) above and the fund is a 'transparent fund' (see below for definition and qualifications); or
- the exemption in **16.10 CHARITIES** applies; or
- the transitional protection in **51.19** below applies.

A fund is a '*transparent fund*'

(a)   if, in the case of investors who are UK resident individuals, any sums which form part of the income of the fund are of such a nature that they fall within any of **32.2**(a), (c)–(o) **FOREIGN INCOME** (insofar as the sums are referable to those investors' interests); or

(b)   if (a) would apply were it not for the fact that the income is derived from assets within the UK.

If a fund is transparent, such as would be the case for certain unit trusts and contractual funds, then any income arising to the fund is treated as arising to an investor in proportion to his rights. This means that income is charged to tax as it arises, hence the exemption.

The exemption for disposals of interests in transparent funds does not apply if:

(i)   during a period beginning with the date the interest (or any part of it) was acquired and ending with the date of disposal, the offshore fund has at any time held interests in other non-reporting funds which amounted in total to more than 5% by value of the offshore fund's assets; or

(ii)   the fund is a non-reporting fund and it fails to make sufficient information available to its participants in to enable them to meet their UK tax obligations with respect to their shares of income.

If, on the disposal by an offshore fund of an interest in another non-reporting fund, no liability would arise by virtue of the exemption for disposals of interests in transparent funds, that interest is not taken into account for the purposes of (i) above.

[SI 2009 No 3001, Regs 11, 25(5)(6), 26, 28–31].

Computation of offshore income gain

[51.5] An offshore income gain is computed in the same way as a chargeable gain would be computed under CGT legislation. If such a computation would produce a loss, the offshore income gain is taken to be nil. If the disposal gives rise to a claim for CGT purposes under *TCGA 1992, s 162* (rollover relief on transfer of a business to a company) or *TCGA 1992, s 165 or 260* (gifts holdover relief), these claims have no effect in computing the offshore income gain. In other words, an offshore income gain cannot be deferred for income tax purposes by such a claim.

If a participant's rights in an offshore fund attract the transitional protection in **51.19** below, those rights cannot be pooled for CGT purposes with any rights in the same fund that he acquires on or after 1 December 2009 and which do not attract the transitional protection. Instead, any disposal is treated as being a disposal of the protected rights to the extent that those rights are not yet exhausted. As this affects the computation of the chargeable gain on any such disposal, it similarly affects the amount of the offshore income gain.

[*SI 2009 No 3001, Regs 38, 39, 41–43*].

What constitutes a disposal?

[51.6] Generally there is a disposal for these purposes whenever there would a disposal for CGT purposes. This is subject to the special rules outlined below.

Death is not an occasion of charge for CGT purposes. However, for the purposes of the offshore funds rules, the deceased is deemed to have disposed on the date of death of any interest of his in a non-reporting fund at its market value at its market value at that date. Thus, an offshore income gain, and an income tax charge, may arise.

In specified circumstances, by virtue of *TCGA 1992, s 135*, an *exchange of securities* in one company for securities in another is not treated as a disposal for CGT purposes. Whilst that rule can apply for the purposes of the offshore funds rules, it does not apply where an interest in a non-reporting fund is exchanged for an interest in an entity that is not a non-reporting fund. Instead, the participant is deemed to have made a disposal at market value at the time of the exchange.

Also in specified circumstances, by virtue of *TCGA 1992, s 136*, a *scheme of reconstruction* involving the issue of securities is not treated as a disposal for CGT purposes but as an exchange with similar consequences as above. Again, that rule can apply for the purposes of the offshore funds rules, but does not apply where an interest in a non-reporting fund is deemed to be exchanged for an interest in an entity that is not a non-reporting fund. Instead, the participant is deemed to have made a disposal at market value at the time of the deemed exchange.

[*SI 2009 No 3001, Regs 33–36*].

By virtue of *TCGA 1992, s 127*, a *reorganisation* of a company's share capital is not normally treated for CGT purposes as involving a disposal by the investor. Instead, the new holding of shares or securities stands in the shoes of the old and inherits its CGT acquisition cost. This rule can also apply for the purposes of the offshore funds rules but does not do so if:

- the offshore fund is constituted by a class of interest ('Class A') in 'main arrangements' (see **51.2** above);
- a participant exchanges an interest of Class A for an interest in another offshore fund constituted by a different class of interest (Class B) in those main arrangements;
- the interest of Class A is a non-reporting fund and the interest of Class B is an interest in an entity that is not a non-reporting fund.

Instead, the participant is deemed to have made a disposal at market value at the time of the exchange.

[*SI 2009 No 3001, Reg 37*].

Relief from capital gains tax

[51.7] A single disposal may well give rise to both an offshore income gain (chargeable to income tax as in **51.3** above) and a chargeable gain for CGT purposes. To avoid a double charge, a sum equal to the offshore income gain is deducted from the sum which would otherwise constitute the amount or value of the consideration for the disposal for CGT purposes. Special rules apply if the disposal is a *part* disposal for CGT purposes or is a disposal to which *TCGA 1992, s 162* applies (rollover relief on transfer of a business to a company); for these rules, see Tolley's Capital Gains Tax under Overseas Matters.

A special rule also applies if, on an exchange of securities, a scheme of reconstruction or a reorganisation, there is a disposal for the purposes of the offshore fund rules by virtue of **51.6** above. An amount equal to the offshore income gain on that disposal is treated as having been given by the person making the exchange as consideration for the new holding (so that *TCGA 1992, s 128* applies — see Tolley's Capital Gains Tax under Shares and Securities).

[*SI 2009 No 3001, Regs 44–47*].

Remittance basis

[51.8] If an offshore income gain arises to a non-UK domiciled individual who is chargeable (whether or not as a result of a claim) on the remittance basis) for the tax year in question, it is treated as 'relevant foreign income' (as in **32.2 FOREIGN INCOME**) with the consequences in **61.4 REMITTANCE BASIS**.

See **61 REMITTANCE BASIS** for the meaning of 'remitted to the UK' etc. For the purpose of applying the provisions in that chapter to a remittance of an offshore income gain:

- treat any consideration for the disposal of the interest in the fund as deriving from the offshore income gain; and

- if the consideration is less than the market value of the interest, treat the interest as deriving from the offshore income gain.

[*SI 2009 No 3001, Reg 19*].

Offshore income gains arising to non-UK resident settlements

[51.9] If an offshore income gain arises to a settlement the trustees of which are neither resident nor ordinarily resident in the UK in the tax year in question, the gain is not regarded as income for the purposes of applying the provisions at **68.26** SETTLEMENTS (amounts treated as income of settlor). If offshore income gains arise to the trustees of such a settlement, the attribution rules of *TCGA 1992, ss 87, 87A* are applied (with appropriate modifications) to attribute the gain to beneficiaries, who may then be chargeable to income tax depending on their residence/domicile status. See Tolley's Capital Gains Tax under Offshore Settlements for those attribution rules. See also the draft guidance at www.hmrc.gov.uk/offshorefunds/ofmanual-uk-investors.pdf at OFM09300–09325. [*SI 2009 No 3001, Reg 20*].

'Transfer of assets abroad' rules

[51.10] The 'transfer of assets abroad' rules at **4.14–4.17** ANTI-AVOIDANCE apply in relation to an offshore income gain arising to a person resident or domiciled outside the UK as if the offshore income gain were foreign income becoming payable to that person. This does not apply to an offshore income gain that arises to an offshore company and, as a result of the relevant rule in **51.11** below, is treated as arising to a person resident or ordinarily resident in the UK. It also does not apply that arises to an offshore income gain that arises to the trustees of a non-UK resident settlement and which is consequently treated under **51.9** above as arising to an individual resident or ordinarily resident in the UK. For more on the interaction between these rules and those at **51.9** above, see the draft guidance at www.hmrc.gov.uk/offshorefunds/ofma nual-uk-investors.pdf at OFM09350. [*SI 2009 No 3001, Reg 21*].

Adoption of certain CGT rules

[51.11] *Market value* for the purposes of the offshore funds rules is generally determined in accordance with CGT rules. However, in the case of an interest in an offshore fund for which there are separate published buying and selling prices, *TCGA 1992, s 272(5)* (market value in relation to rights in unit trust schemes) applies with the necessary modifications to determine market value. [*SI 2009 No 3001, Reg 10*].

UK branch or agency

A person carrying on a trade, profession or vocation in the UK through a branch or agency is chargeable to tax on offshore income gains arising on the disposal of a holding in an offshore fund if the interest was held for the purposes of the UK branch or agency. [*SI 2009 No 3001, Reg 22*].

Temporary non-UK residence

An individual who is temporarily non-UK resident (within the meaning of *TCGA 1992, s 10A* — see Tolley's Capital Gains Tax under Overseas Matters) is chargeable to income tax in the tax year of his return to the UK on offshore income gains arising during the period of temporary non-residence. [*SI 2009 No 3001, Reg 23*].

Attribution of gains to members of non-UK resident companies

TCGA 1992, s 13 applies to offshore income gains (with appropriate modifications) in the same way as it applies to chargeable gains. Broadly, *TCGA 1992, s 13* applies to gains arising to non-UK resident companies which would be close companies if they were UK resident, and apportions those gains between any participators in the company who are resident or ordinarily resident in the UK. See Tolley's Capital Gains Tax under Overseas Matters. [*SI 2009 No 3001, Reg 24*].

Treatment of certain amounts as distributions

[51.12] If a non-reporting fund which is a transparent fund (see **51.4** above) has an interest in a reporting fund, any such excess as is mentioned in **51.14**(b) below is treated as if it were additional income of the participants in the non-reporting fund in proportion to their rights. Such income is treated as arising on the same date as the excess is treated as made to the non-reporting fund (see **51.15** below) and is chargeable to income tax as 'relevant foreign income' (see **32.2 FOREIGN INCOME**). [*SI 2009 No 3001, Reg 16*].

Reporting funds

[51.13] As far as 'reporting funds' are concerned, the post-1 December 2009 offshore funds regime moves away from the previous requirement that an offshore fund distribute a minimum proportion of its income if its UK investors are to benefit from CGT treatment of gains on disposal as opposed to those gains being chargeable to income tax. Instead, the CGT treatment will apply if an offshore fund's income is reported to its UK investors in such a way that they are charged to income tax on their share of the reported income of the fund, regardless of whether that income is distributed to them or accumulated in the fund. See **51.15** below for the tax treatment of participants in reported funds. For non-reporting funds, the charge to income tax on disposals continues (see **51.3** above).

A '*reporting fund*' is an 'eligible offshore fund' that has applied for and been approved by HMRC as a reporting fund. (An '*eligible offshore fund*' is an offshore fund that is not a guaranteed return fund as defined by *SI 2009 No 3001, Reg 9*.) Funds that have applied and been approved are said to be in the reporting funds regime. An existing offshore fund may apply to HMRC for reporting fund status, as may a fund that has yet to be established. A fund cannot apply to be a reporting fund if it has previously been excluded from being a reporting fund as a result of an HMRC notice due to serious breaches of duties or if it has previously left the reporting fund regime voluntarily for any reason other than its ceasing to have any UK-resident participants. Regulations set out the required contents of an application (including undertakings that must be given) and make provision for the timing and withdrawal of applications, the manner in which HMRC must respond to applications and appeals against refusal of applications. [*SI 2009 No 3001, Regs 51–56; SI 2009 No 3139, Reg 3*].

A reporting fund must comply with various duties as to the preparation of accounts, the computation of its reportable income, the provision of reports to participants (see **51.14** below) and the provision of information to HMRC. [*SI 2009 No 3001, Regs 57–93, 106, 107*].

Regulations set out various potential breaches of duties and their consequences. In the event of certain breaches specified as serious, the consequence (subject to appeal) is exclusion from the reporting fund regime. [*SI 2009 No 3001, Regs 108–115*].

A fund may voluntarily leave the reporting fund regime by giving notice to HMRC. [*SI 2009 No 3001, Regs 116, 117*].

See **51.17** below as regards constant NAV funds, broadly reporting funds whose net asset value remains fairly constant as a result of the nature of their assets, and the frequency with which they distribute their income.

Reports to participants in reporting funds

[51.14] A reporting fund must make a report available to each of its participants for each 'reporting period', and must do so within the six months immediately following the end of the reporting period. The purpose is to provide participants with the information they need to enter on their self-assessment tax returns. A fund's '*reporting period*' is normally its period of account. If, however, a fund has a period of account exceeding 12 months, this is split into two reporting periods; the first reporting period is the first 12 months of the period of account and the second reporting period is the balance of the period of account.

The report must show:

(a)   the amount distributed to participants per unit of interest in the fund in respect of the reporting period;
(b)   the excess of the reportable income per unit for the reporting period over the amount in (a); this may be nil but cannot be a negative amount;
(c)   the dates on which distributions were made;
(d)   the fund distribution date; this is normally the date on which the report is issued, but if the fund issues the report after the six-month period referred to above, the fund distribution date is the last day of the reporting period; and
(e)   a statement of whether or not the fund remains a reporting fund at the date it makes the report available.

[*SI 2009 No 3001, Regs 90–93, 94(4)*].

Income tax treatment of participants in reporting funds

[51.15] Participants within the charge to income tax are taxed on actual distributions from the fund plus their share of any excess of reportable income over distributed income, i.e. the amount at **51.14**(b) above. The precise rules, as described below, depend on whether or not the reporting fund is a 'transparent fund' and also on whether or not it is a corporate fund. For the meaning of '*transparent fund*', see **51.4** above.

If the reporting fund is not a transparent fund, any such excess as is referred to above is treated as additional distributions made to the participants in the fund in proportion to their rights. Where the trustees of a charitable trust are participants in a reporting fund, they are not chargeable to tax on these additional distributions.

If the fund is a transparent fund, any excess of reportable income over the income of the fund (which may occur if the fund holds investments in other reporting funds) is treated as additional income of the participants in the fund in proportion to their rights. To the extent that the participant's rights in the fund are rights to which *SI 2009 No 3001, Reg 30* (rights in certain pre-existing holdings — see **51.19** below) applies, the excess is reduced proportionately.

In both cases, the excess is treated as made, on the fund distribution date (see **51.14**(d) above), to participants holding an interest in the fund at the end of the reporting period (see **51.14** above).

If the fund is a corporate fund, i.e. it falls within **51.2**(a) above, any actual distribution plus any amount treated as an additional distribution as above is taxed as dividends from a non-UK resident company (with entitlement to tax credits — see **64.12**, **64.13** SAVINGS AND INVESTMENT INCOME or, where the conditions at **64.4** SAVINGS AND INVESTMENT INCOME are met, as interest.

If the fund is a non-transparent fund and it falls within **51.2**(b) or (c) above, i.e. it is not a corporate fund, any actual distribution plus any amount treated as an additional distribution as above is taxed as miscellaneous income or, where the conditions at **64.4** SAVINGS AND INVESTMENT INCOME are met, as interest.

If the fund is a transparent fund, UK investors will be charged to tax on their proportionate share of income from underlying investments of the fund as it arises (less a deduction for trustees' expenses) as if they had made those investments directly. For example, where the fund holds interest-producing investments, investors will be chargeable to tax on income arising to the fund from those investments as if they had received interest. If any amount falls to be treated as additional income of the participants as above, it is chargeable to income tax as 'relevant foreign income' (see **32.2** FOREIGN INCOME).

[*SI 2009 No 3001, Regs 94–97, 101; SI 2009 No 3139, Reg 4*].

Special rules apply in calculating the income from interests held by 'financial traders' in diversely owned reporting funds. '*Financial traders*' include banks, insurance businesses (but not life assurance businesses) and businesses dealing in certain financial products such that profits arising from the holding of investments in reporting funds would form part of their trading profits. [*SI 2009 No 3001, Regs 102–105*]. See the draft guidance at www.hmrc.gov.uk/o ffshorefunds/ofmanual-uk-investors.pdf at OFM15900.

CGT treatment of disposals by participants in reporting funds

[51.16] A disposal by a participant of his interest in a reporting fund is a disposal of an asset for CGT purposes. Any amount charged to income tax under 51.15 above as an additional distribution made to the participant or as additional income of the participant is treated as part of the CGT acquisition cost of the asset. [SI 2009 No 3001, Reg 99].

If an offshore fund ceases to be a reporting fund and becomes a non-reporting fund, a participant may make an election to be treated for CGT purposes:

- as disposing of an interest in the reporting fund at the end of that fund's final period of account, and
- as acquiring an interest in the non-reporting fund at the beginning of that fund's first period of account.

The deemed disposal and acquisition are treated as made for a consideration equal to the net asset value of the participant's interest in the fund at the end of the period of account for which the final reported income is reported to him. The election must be made by being included in a tax return for the year which includes the final day of the reporting fund's final period of account, but cannot be made if a report has not been made available to the participant under 51.14 above for that period of account. The normal purpose of an election would be to crystallise the gain accrued to date as a chargeable gain within the charge to CGT; any subsequent gain on actual disposal would be an offshore income gain chargeable to income tax as in 51.3 above.

[SI 2009 No 3001, Reg 100].

See Tolley's Capital Gains Tax under Overseas Matters for more details of both rules above.

Constant NAV funds

[51.17] A 'constant NAV fund' is an offshore fund whose net asset value (expressed in the currency in which units are issued) does not fluctuate by more than an insignificant amount throughout the fund's existence, as a result of the nature of the fund's assets, and the frequency with which it distributes its income. The reporting fund rules at 51.13 above are modified for constant NAV funds. Neither the reporting requirements at 51.14 above nor the tax treatment at 51.15 and 51.16 above apply. If, however, the value of the fund's assets (expressed in the currency in which units are issued) increases by more than an insignificant amount and the fund has not notified HMRC that it has ceased to be a constant NAV fund, a participant who subsequently disposes of his interest in the fund and who makes a chargeable gain on the disposal is treated as making an offshore income gain (chargeable to income tax as in 51.3 above). [SI 2009 No 3001, Regs 118–124].

Conversion of a non-reporting fund into a reporting fund

[51.18] If an offshore fund ceases to be a non-reporting fund and becomes a reporting fund as in 51.13 above, a participant may make an election to be treated for tax purposes:

- as disposing of an interest in the non-reporting fund at the end of that fund's final period of account, and
- as acquiring an interest in the reporting fund at the beginning of that fund's first period of account.

The deemed disposal and acquisition are treated as made at market value as at the deemed date of disposal. The election must be made by being included in a tax return for the year which includes the deemed date of disposal. The election can be made only if the deemed disposal would trigger an offshore income gain (chargeable to income tax as in **51.3** above). The normal purpose of an election would be to crystallise the gain accrued to date as an offshore income gain, leaving any subsequent gain on actual disposal to be taxed within the CGT regime.

[SI 2009 No 3001, Reg 48].

If the above election is *not* made, any subsequent disposal of the interest in the fund will be within the income tax charge at **51.3** above, provided:

- a deemed disposal as above would have triggered an offshore income gain; and
- the interest was an interest in a non-reporting fund during some or all of the 'material period'.

The '*material period*' is the period beginning with the day on which consideration was given for the acquisition of the interest (or on 1st January 1984 if later) and ending with the day on which the fund became a reporting fund.

[SI 2009 No 3001, Reg 17(1)(3)(4)].

Transition to post-1 December 2009 regime

[51.19] If:

- a person acquired rights in an offshore fund before 1 December 2009,
- the fund is an offshore fund within the definition at **51.2** above (new regime), and
- on the date the rights were acquired, the fund was not an offshore fund within the definition at **51.24** below (old regime),

those rights do not come within the new regime. This rule applies equally if the person acquires the rights on or after 1 December 2009 but was obliged to acquire them by virtue of a legally enforceable written agreement made before 30 April 2009, provided any conditions attached to the agreement were satisfied before that date and that the agreement is not varied on or after that date.

[TIOPA 2010, Sch 9 paras 33, 34; FA 2009, Sch 22 para 6].

If a person disposes of rights in an offshore fund which he acquired before 1 December 2009 (or on or after that date in the circumstances mentioned above), no income tax charge under **51.3** above can arise on the disposal if, when he acquired them, the rights did not constitute a 'material interest in an offshore fund' (within **51.24** below). [SI 2009 No 3001, Reg 30].

Further transitional rules

[51.20] The following applies if a person holds an interest in an offshore fund on 1 December 2009 that fell within the old definition of offshore fund at **51.24** below and also falls within the new definition at **51.2** above. If the fund is a non-reporting fund and the person subsequently disposes of his interest, any gain on the disposal will be taxed under **51.3** above in respect of the entire period that the investor held the interest in the fund. [*SI 2009 No 3001, Sch 1 para 2*].

An offshore fund within the old definition (a pre-existing fund) may apply to HMRC to be treated as a distributing fund (i.e. a fund pursuing a full distribution policy — see **51.26** below) for its period of account spanning 1 December 2009 (the overlap period). If successful, it may apply to continue to be so treated for its following period of account (the succeeding period). Neither application is possible for a period of account ending after 31 May 2012. If the fund becomes a reporting fund immediately following the end of the overlap period or succeeding period, it is treated as if it had been a reporting fund continuously from the day that it actually became a distributing fund (provided it was, in fact, a distributing fund continuously throughout.

Where a pre-existing fund is part of umbrella arrangements or is part of arrangements comprising more than one class of interest (see in both cases **51.2** above), any separate arrangements under the umbrella arrangements, or any class of interest under the main arrangements, established on or after 1 December 2009, may apply to HMRC to be treated as a distributing fund in respect of a period of account if:

*   that period has the same accounting reference date as the overlap period or succeeding period of the pre-existing fund, and
*   the pre-existing fund is treated as a distributing fund in respect of the contemporaneous overlap period or succeeding period.

No such application is possible for a period of account ending after 31 May 2012.

[*SI 2009 No 3001, Sch 1 paras 3, 6; SI 2009 No 3139, Reg 5(3)*; see correction at www.hmrc.gov.uk/ct/si3139_offshorefunds.htm].

If a reporting fund (see **51.13** above) has an interest in a distributing fund, its income from that fund is treated as if it were income from a reporting fund. There is also special provision for the treatment of income of a distributing fund in relation to any interest it may have in a reporting fund. If an interest in a distributing fund is exchanged for an interest in a reporting fund, *TCGA 1992, s 127* is not prevented from applying by *SI 2009 No 3001, Reg 37* in **51.6** above. [*SI 2009 No 3001, Sch 1 paras 3A–3C; SI 2009 No 3139, Reg 5(4)*].

If a pre-existing fund does not become a reporting fund immediately following its last period of account as a distributing fund, a participant in the fund may make an election to be treated for CGT purposes:

*   as disposing of an interest in the distributing fund at the end of that fund's final period of account, and

- as acquiring an interest in the non-reporting fund immediately following that disposal.

The deemed disposal and acquisition are treated as made at the net asset value of the participant's interest in the fund at the end of the final period of account. The election must be made by being included in a tax return for the year which includes the deemed date of disposal. The normal purpose of an election would be to crystallise the gain accrued to date as a chargeable gain within the charge to CGT; any subsequent gain on actual disposal would be an offshore income gain chargeable to income tax as in **51.3** above.

[SI 2009 No 3001, Sch 1 para 4].

If a pre-existing fund was a non-qualifying fund (see **51.25** below) before 1 December 2009 and becomes a reporting fund from that date (because its period of account commences on that date and it successfully applies for reporting fund status), the provisions of *SI 2009 No 3001, Reg 48* (conversion of a non-reporting fund into a reporting fund — see **51.18** above) are modified so as to apply on the conversion of a non-qualifying fund into a reporting fund. *[SI 2009 No 3001, Sch 1 para 5]*.

A fund that was not an offshore fund within the definition in **51.24** below (old regime) but is an offshore fund within the definition at **51.2** above (new regime) can apply for reporting fund status in relation to its period of account current on 1 December 2009. The application must be received by HMRC no later than 31 May 2010. (Funds that *were* within the old definition may apply for reporting fund status only from the beginning of their first period of account commencing on or after 1 December 2009.) *[SI 2009 No 3001, Sch 1 para 7]*.

The pre-1 December 2009 regime

[51.21] As stated at **51.1** above, a new offshore funds regime has effect in relation to distributions and disposals made on or after 1 December 2009 (subject to the transitional rules in **51.19, 51.20** above). The old regime that preceded it is described in the following paragraphs.

Old regime — disposal of material interests in non-qualifying offshore funds

[51.22] The pre-1 December 2009 offshore fund rules apply to a disposal by any person of an asset:

(a)   if, at the time of the disposal, the asset constitutes a **'material interest'** in an **'offshore fund'** (see **51.24** below) which is or has at any 'material time' been a **'non-qualifying offshore fund'** (see **51.25** below); or

(b)   if:

  (i)   at the time of the disposal, the asset constitutes an interest in a UK resident company or in a unit trust scheme (within *ITA 2007, s 1007*) which has UK resident trustees; and

(ii)   at a 'material time' after 31 December 1984 the interest was a material interest in a 'non-qualifying offshore fund'. For this purpose the provisions of *TCGA 1992, s 127*, equating original shares with a new holding on reorganisation, apply.

[*ICTA 1988, s 757(1)*].

A '*material time*' is any time after 31 December 1983 or, if later, the earliest date on which any 'relevant consideration' was given for the acquisition of the asset. '*Relevant consideration*' is that given by or on behalf of the person making the disposal or a predecessor in title which would be taken into account in determining any gain or loss on disposal under *TCGA 1992*. [*ICTA 1988, s 757(7)*].

With some modifications, a disposal occurs for offshore fund purposes if there would be a disposal under *TCGA 1992*. Death is an occasion of charge as the deceased is deemed to have made a disposal at market value, immediately before his death, of any asset which was or had at any time been a 'material interest' in a 'non-qualifying offshore fund'. In addition, neither *TCGA 1992, s 135* nor *s 136* will apply, and there will therefore be a disposal at market value, if an exchange or arrangement is effected in such a way that an interest in a 'non-qualifying offshore fund', is exchanged for an interest in a distributing fund. The same principle applies to exchanges of different classes of interest where they form separate funds in their own right (see **51.24** below). [*ICTA 1988, s 757(2)–(6), s 762A*].

A *Pt 5* transfer under *Proceeds of Crime Act 2002* (as in **10.2**(x) CAPITAL ALLOWANCES) of an asset within (a) or (b) above is not treated as a disposal for offshore fund purposes where no compensating payment is made to the transferor. [*Proceeds of Crime Act 2002, Sch 10 paras 7, 10*].

Old regime — offshore funds operating equalisation arrangements

[51.23] There are specific provisions to enable funds operating 'equalisation arrangements' to satisfy the 'distribution test' (see **51.26** below) which the nature of such funds might otherwise preclude. As a corollary, provision is also made to ensure that the 'accrued income' paid to outgoing investors as part of their capital payments is treated as income for tax purposes when the fund qualifies as a distributor.

Definition

For these purposes, an offshore fund operates '*equalisation arrangements*' where the first distribution paid to a person acquiring a 'material interest' by way of 'initial purchase' includes a payment which is a return of capital (debited to the fund's 'equalisation account') determined by reference to the income which had accrued to the fund in the period before that person's acquisition. An acquisition is by way of '*initial purchase*' if it is by way of direct purchase from the fund's managers in their capacity as such.

Where a sub-fund or class of interest is treated as a fund in its own right (see **51.24** below), this definition applies with appropriate modifications.

'Accrued income' chargeable to income tax — application of offshore fund rules

A disposal is one to which the offshore fund provisions apply, subject to exception below, if it is a disposal by any person of a 'material interest' in an 'offshore fund' operating equalisation arrangements where:

(i)   the disposal proceeds are not a trading receipt; and
(ii) the fund *is not*, and *has not been*, at any material time (see above) a 'non-qualifying offshore fund' (see **51.25** below).

(I.e. the provisions apply also to *distributing* funds (see **51.26** below) with equalisation arrangements.)

Capital gains tax rules for disposals apply as they do for other offshore fund disposals (see **51.22** above) with some variations. Death is not treated as a disposal in this context. In addition, *TCGA 1992, s 127* (reorganisations etc.) (including that section as applied by certain other *TCGA 1992* provisions) does not apply and there is a disposal at market value in such circumstances.

Exception

The offshore fund legislation does *not* apply as indicated above to a disposal where the fund's income for the period preceding the disposal is of such a nature that the part relating to the interest in question is in any event chargeable as mentioned at **51.27**(b) below on the person disposing of the interest (or would be so chargeable if residence/domicile/situation of assets requirements were met).

[*ICTA 1988, s 757(2)(3), s 758; SI 2004 No 2572, Reg 3*].

Old regime — material interests in offshore funds

[51.24] An '*offshore fund*' is a collective investment scheme (defined by reference to *Financial Services and Markets Act 2000, Pt 17*) constituted by:

(a)   a company resident outside the UK; or
(b)   a unit trust scheme (within *ITA 2007, s 1007*) which has non-UK resident trustees; or
(c)   any other arrangements taking effect under overseas law which create rights in the nature of co-ownership under that law.

For account periods (see **51.25** below) ending on or after 22 July 2004, sub-funds of a main fund (the umbrella fund) and different classes of interest in a main fund constitute separate offshore funds. This allows the test for distributing status (see **51.26** below) to be applied to them independently. The offshore funds legislation is appropriately modified in its application to such sub-funds and classes of interest (see *SI 2004 No 2572*).

[*ICTA 1988, ss 756A–756C, s 759(1)(1A); FA 2007, s 57(2)*].

A '*material interest*' is one which, when acquired, could reasonably be expected to be realisable (by any means, either in money or in asset form) within seven years for an amount reasonably approximate to its proportionate share of the market value of the fund's assets. For these purposes, an interest in an offshore fund which at any time is worth substantially more than its proportionate share of the fund's underlying assets is not to be regarded as so realisable. [*ICTA 1988, s 759(2)–(4)*]. If shares in a quoted overseas company have habitually been traded at or near net asset value, and an investor in these shares had a reasonable expectation, on acquisition, of a future sale at or near such value, those shares are likely to represent a 'material interest'. (HMRC SP 2/86).

Exceptions

The following are not material interests.

(i) Interests in respect of loans etc. made in the ordinary course of banking business.

(ii) Rights under insurance policies.

(iii) Shares in a company resident outside the UK where:

    (a) the shares are held by a company and the holding is necessary or desirable for the maintenance and development of a trade carried on by the company, or by an associated company within *ICTA 1988, s 416*; and

    (b) the shares confer at least 10% of the voting rights and, on winding-up, a right to at least 10% of the assets after discharging all prior liabilities; and

    (c) the shares are held by not more than ten persons and all confer both voting rights and a right to assets on winding-up; and

    (d) at the time of acquisition of the shares the company could reasonably expect to realise its interest for market value within seven years only by virtue of (I) an arrangement requiring the company's fellow participators to purchase its shares and/or (II) provisions of either the overseas company's constitution or an agreement between the participators regarding that company's winding-up.

(iv) Interests in companies resident outside the UK at any time when the holder is entitled to have the company wound up and to receive in that event in the same capacity more than 50% of the assets after discharging all prior liabilities.

[*ICTA 1988, s 759(5)–(8)*].

HMRC have also indicated that normal commercial loans or other debt instruments entitling the lender to no more than a fixed return of principal on redemption, and which are not geared to the underlying asset value of the borrower's business, are not regarded as 'material interests'. (HMRC SP 2/86).

'*Market value*' for the purposes of the offshore funds legislation is determined according to capital gains tax rules with necessary modifications of *TCGA 1992, s 272(5)* (market value in relation to rights in unit trust schemes) where appropriate. [*ICTA 1988, s 759(9)*].

Old regime — non-qualifying offshore funds

[51.25] An offshore fund is '**non-qualifying**' except during an 'account period' in respect of which it is certified by HMRC as a distributing fund pursuing a 'full distribution policy' (see **51.26** below). For these purposes, the first '*account period*' begins when the fund begins to carry on its activities or, if later, on 1 January 1984. An '*account period*' ends on the fund's accounting date or, if earlier, twelve months from the beginning of the period or on the fund's ceasing to carry on its activities. In addition, if the fund is a non-UK resident company, an '*account period*' ends when it becomes UK resident, and if the fund is a unit trust with non-UK resident trustees, it ends when those trustees become UK resident. Where a sub-fund or class of interest is treated as a fund in its own right (see **51.24** above), references to '*account period*' are to the account period of the main fund. [*ICTA 1988, s 760(1)(2)(8)–(10A)*].

Condition for certification

Subject to the modifications in certain cases noted below, an offshore fund is not to be certified as a 'distributing fund' for any account period if, at any time in that period, more than 5% by value of the fund's assets consists of interests in other offshore funds (but see below). Where HMRC are satisfied that an apparent failure to comply occurred inadvertently and was remedied without unreasonable delay, that failure may be disregarded.

[*ICTA 1988, s 760(3)*].

Following a small change effective from 19 July 2007 in the definition of an offshore fund, it is made clear that the reference above to offshore funds does not include funds that are not collective investment schemes for the purposes of *Financial Services and Markets Act 2000, Pt 17*. [*ICTA 1988, s 756A(4); FA 2007, s 57(2)*].

Modifications of condition for certification

The above condition is modified in the following cases.

(a)   **Investments in second tier funds.** If offshore funds ('primary funds') would fail to meet the above conditions because of investments in other offshore funds (referred to below as 'second tier funds') which could themselves be certified as qualifying distributing funds, then the primary funds' interests in the second tier funds are left out of account, except for determining the total value of the primary funds' assets, in establishing whether the primary funds are prevented from being certified as distributing funds. (For account periods beginning before 1 January 2007 this rule did not apply to the primary fund if the second tier fund could be certified as a qualifying distributing fund only by virtue of applying this rule.) In addition, where the above applies, if at any time in a primary fund's account period that fund's assets include an interest in another offshore fund or in any company and the qualifying second tier fund's assets also include an interest in that other fund or company, then the primary fund's interest is aggregated with its proportionate share of the second tier fund's interest in determining whether the primary fund is within the stipulated limit. Its share of the second tier fund's interest is the proportion which the average value during its account period of its own holding of interests in the second tier fund bears to the average value during the period of all interests in the second tier fund. [*ICTA 1988, s 760(3), Sch 27 paras 6, 7, 9; FA 2007, s 57(4)(8)*].

(b)   **Wholly-owned subsidiaries.** Where an offshore fund has a wholly-owned subsidiary company, the receipts, expenditure, assets and liabilities of the fund and the subsidiary are aggregated so that the fund and the subsidiary are treated as one for the purposes of determining whether the fund is within the stipulated limit. In the same way, the interest of the fund in the subsidiary and any distributions or other payments between the fund and the subsidiary are left out of account. A wholly-owned subsidiary is one owned either directly and beneficially by the fund, or directly by the trustees of the fund for the benefit of the fund, or, in the case of a fund within **51.24**(c) above, in some other equivalent manner. Where the subsidiary has only one class of issued share capital, ownership of at least 95% of that capital by the offshore fund constitutes the subsidiary a wholly-owned subsidiary for this purpose, and only a corresponding proportion of the subsidiary's receipts, expenditure, assets and liabilities are then aggregated with those of the offshore fund. [*ICTA 1988, s 760(3), Sch 27 para 11; SI 2004 No 2572, Reg 4(1)(6)*].

Old regime — the distribution test

[51.26] An offshore fund pursues a '*full distribution policy*' with respect to an account period if:

(a)   a distribution is made for that account period or for some other period falling wholly or partly within that period; and

(b)   subject to modifications below, the distribution represents at least 85% of the fund's income and not less than 85% of its 'UK equivalent profits' for that period; and

(c)   the distribution is made during or within six months after the end of the account period (the six month limit may be extended at HMRC's discretion); and

(d)   the form of the distribution is such that if any part of it were received in the UK by an individual or company resident there and did not form part of the profits of a trade, profession or vocation, it would be chargeable to income tax under any of the provisions listed at *ITTOIA 2005, s 830(2)* (relevant foreign income — see **32.2 FOREIGN INCOME**) or, as the case may be, would be chargeable to corporation tax under the relevant corporation tax charging provision.

These conditions may equally be satisfied by any two or more distributions taken together.

[*ICTA 1988, Sch 27 para 1(1); CTA 2009, Sch 1 para 289(2)*].

The basic conditions in (a) to (d) above are modified in certain cases (see **51.27** below).

A fund is treated as pursuing a full distribution policy for any account period in which there is no income and no 'UK equivalent profits', or for which gross fund income does not exceed 1% of the average value of fund assets during the period, but it will not be so treated for any account period for which no accounts are prepared. [*ICTA 1988, Sch 27 para 1(2)(2A)(3)(3A); SI 2004 No 2572, Reg 4(1)(2)*].

Non-UK legal restrictions

Where in an account period an offshore fund is subject to non-UK legal restrictions on making distributions by reason of an excess of losses over profits as computed according to the law in question, a deduction is allowed from the fund's income of any amount which cannot be distributed but which would otherwise form part of the fund's income for that account period. [*ICTA 1988, Sch 27 para 1(6)(7); SI 2004 No 2572, Reg 4(1)(2)*].

Apportionment of income and distributions between account periods

Where a period for which accounts are made up or for which a distribution is made covers the whole or part of two or more account periods of the fund, the income or distribution is apportioned on a time basis according to the number of days in each period. A distribution made out of specified income but not for a specified period is attributed to the account period in which the income arose. Where no period or income is specified, a distribution is treated as made for the last account period ending before the distribution. If the distribution made, or treated as made, for an account period exceeds the income of that period the excess is reallocated to previous periods, to later periods before earlier ones, until exhausted, unless the distribution was apportioned on a time basis as mentioned above in which case the excess is first reapportioned on a just and reasonable basis to the other account period(s). [*ICTA 1988, Sch 27 para 1(4)(5)*].

'*UK equivalent profits*' of an offshore fund are the total profits, excluding chargeable gains, on which, after allowing for any deductions available, corporation tax would be chargeable, assuming that:

(i) the offshore fund is a UK resident company in the account period in question, but in no other; and

(ii) the account period is an accounting period of that company; and

(iii) any dividends or distributions from a UK resident company are included.

The special corporation tax rules for loan relationships and derivative contracts (see Tolley's Corporation Tax under Loan Relationships and under Derivative Contracts Legislation) used to be disregarded for this purpose, and it was assumed that income tax, rather than corporation tax, rules applied, as they did for unauthorised unit trusts. However, for account periods ending on or after 22 July 2004, the corporation tax rules relating to creditor loan relationships and profits/losses from derivative contracts apply as if the fund were an authorised unit trust. This change in treatment does not apply to funds in existence on or before 22 July 2004 unless they elect for it to apply. Such an election, once made, is irrevocable. Where, in a case where no election has been made, a new sub-fund or class of interest is established *after* 22 July 2004 and is regarded as a separate offshore fund by virtue of **51.24** above, the change in treatment does not apply to the sub-fund or class either, so that they always take the same treatment as the 'parent' fund.

Any UK government securities or securities of foreign states which are exempt from tax (see **64.3 SAVINGS AND INVESTMENT INCOME**) must be brought into account in determining the fund's total profits.

Whether a fund is trading will turn on the particular facts, but in general a fund would not normally be regarded as trading in respect of relatively infrequent transactions, or where the intention was merely to hedge specific investments which were not associated with trading activities (HMRC SP 2/86).

The deductions referred to above include a deduction equal to that allowed against a fund's income where non-UK legal restrictions prevent distribution (see above) and a deduction equal to any foreign capital tax allowed as a deduction in determining the fund's income for the account period in question.

Interest paid to a non-UK resident is deductible in the same way as if it were paid to a UK resident. UK income tax (whether suffered by deduction or by assessment) is available as a deduction (HMRC SP 2/86).

[*ICTA 1988, Sch 27 para 5; CTA 2009, Sch 1 paras 289(6)(7), 581; SI 2004 No 2572, Regs 4(1)(5), 6, 7*].

Old regime — modifications of distribution test

[51.27] The basic rules of the distribution test in **51.26**(a) to (d) above are modified in various circumstances.

(a)   **Funds operating equalisation arrangements.** Where an offshore fund operates such arrangements (see **51.23** above) throughout an account period (see **51.25** above), an amount equal to any 'accrued income' which is part of the consideration for certain disposals in that period is treated as a distribution for the purposes of the distribution test. This applies to a disposal:

(i)   which is a disposal of a material interest in the fund to either the fund or the fund managers in their capacity as such; and

(ii)   which is one to which the offshore fund rules apply (whether or not by virtue of their application to disposals from distributing funds with equalisation arrangements — see **51.23** above), or which is one to which the rules would apply if the provisions regarding the non-application of *TCGA 1992, ss 127, 135* applied generally and not only for the purpose of determining whether a disposal from a distributing fund with equalisation arrangements is brought within the rules (see **51.23** above); and

(iii)   which is not a disposal within the *exception* at **51.23** above (where the income of the fund is, or would be, chargeable to tax in any event).

The *'accrued income'* referred to above is that part of the consideration which would be credited to the fund's equalisation account if the interest were resold to another person by way of 'initial purchase' (see

51.23 above) on the same day. However, there are provisions to ensure that this accrued income figure is reduced where the interest disposed of was acquired by way of initial purchase (by any person) after the beginning of the account period by reference to which the accrued income is calculated. In addition, where an offshore commodity dealing fund (see also (c) below) operates equalisation and there is a disposal within (i) to (iii) above, one half of the accrued income representing commodity profits is left out of account in determining what part of the disposal consideration represents accrued income.

For the purposes of the distribution test, the distribution which the fund is treated as making on a disposal is treated as being paid to the person disposing of his interest, in the income form required by **51.26**(d) above, out of the income of the fund for the account period of disposal. Where a distribution is made to the managers (in their capacity as such) of a fund operating equalisation arrangements it is disregarded for the purposes of the distribution test except to the extent that it relates to that part of the period for which the distribution is made during which the managers (in that capacity) held that interest. [*ICTA 1988, Sch 27 paras 2, 4(4); SI 2004 No 2572, Reg 4(1)(3)*].

(b) **Funds with income taxable on investors.** Where sums forming part of the income of an offshore fund within **51.24**(b) or (c) above:

(i) are chargeable to income tax under any of the provisions listed at *ITTOIA 2005, s 830(2)* (relevant foreign income — see **32.2 FOREIGN INCOME**) in the hands of an individual (or would be so chargeable if the assets from which the income is derived were situated outside the UK where this is not, in fact, the case); or

(ii) are chargeable to corporation tax under the relevant corporation tax charging provision in the hands of a company (with the same proviso as in (i) above); or

(iii) would be so chargeable if the individual or company were UK resident or if the individual were domiciled in the UK and both resident and ordinarily resident there,

any such sums which are not actually part of a distribution complying with the part of the distribution test in **51.26**(c) and (d) above are treated as distributions which do so comply made out of the income of which they are part and paid to the holders of the interests in question. [*ICTA 1988, Sch 27 para 3; CTA 2009, Sch 1 para 289(3)(4)*].

(c) **Funds with commodity dealing income.** Where an offshore fund's income includes commodity dealing profits, half of those profits are left out of account in determining the fund's income and UK equivalent profits for the purposes of the distribution test in **51.26**(b) above. '*Commodities*' are defined as tangible assets dealt with on a commodity exchange, excluding currency, securities, debts or other financial assets. '*Dealing*' includes dealing by way of futures contracts and traded options. Where the fund's income includes both commodity dealing profits and other income, its expenditure is apportioned on a just and reasonable basis and the non-commodity dealing business is treated as carried on by a separate company when determining what expenditure, if any, is deductible as management expenses. See also (a) above for position where a commodity dealing fund operates equalisation arrangements. [*ICTA 1988, Sch 27 para 4; CTA 2009, Sch 1 para 289(5); SI 2004 No 2572, Reg 4(1)(4)*].

(d) **Wholly-owned commodity dealing subsidiaries.** In a situation within **51.25**(b) above, the fund and the subsidiary dealing company are similarly treated as a single entity for the purposes of the distribution test. [*ICTA 1988, Sch 27 para 11; SI 2004 No 2572, Reg 4(1)(6)*].

(e) **Investments in second tier funds.** In a situation within **51.25**(a) above, the UK equivalent profits of the primary fund for the period are increased by its 'share' of the 'excess income' (if any) of the second tier fund in determining whether not less than 85% of the primary fund's UK equivalent profits are distributed. The '*excess income*' of the second tier fund is the amount by which its UK equivalent profits exceeds its distributions. There are provisions for apportioning excess income between periods on a time basis when the account periods of the primary and second tier funds do not coincide. The primary fund's '*share*' of the excess income is the proportion which the average value during its account period of its own holding of interests in the second tier fund bears to the average value of all interests in that fund. [*ICTA 1988, Sch 27 paras 6, 8, 9*].

Old regime — certification procedure

Fund requesting certification

[51.28] Application for certification as a distributing fund for an account period must be made within six months of the end of that period and should be sent to the HMRC Offshore Funds Centre, 1st Floor, Concept House, 5 Young Street, Sheffield S1 4LB. The application must be accompanied by a copy of the fund's accounts covering or including the account period for which certification is sought and provision of the required information in relation to the account period in question will assist HMRC in its consideration of the application. For details of the information required see the HMRC Offshore Funds Guide Manual at OSFG01050.

Where HMRC are satisfied that the necessary conditions are met it must certify the fund as a distribution fund for the period in respect of which application was made. HMRC must give written notice if, after application, it determines that no certificate should be issued. It must also give notice where it appears that the accounts or other information provided do not make full and accurate disclosure of all relevant matters, in which case any notice of certification previously given is void. The fund may appeal to the Appeal Tribunal against HMRC decisions within ninety days. The Tribunal has jurisdiction to review any decision of HMRC relevant to a ground of the appeal. [*ICTA 1988, Sch 27 paras 15, 16; SI 2004 No 2572, Reg 4(1)(7); SI 2009 No 56, Sch 1 para 161(2)(3)*].

A list of offshore funds which have been granted UK distributor status is available on the HMRC website.

Investor requesting certification

No appeal may be brought against a tax assessment (see **51.29** below) on the grounds that a fund should have been certified as a distributing fund in respect of an account period. However, where a fund does not apply for certification, an investor, who is assessed to tax for which he would not be liable if the fund were certified, may by notice in writing require HMRC to take action with a view to determining whether the fund should be so certified.

If more than one request from an investor is received, HMRC is taken to have complied with each if it complies with one.

Broadly, the procedure is as follows.

(i)   HMRC invites the fund to apply for certification. The time limit for application (see above) is then extended, if necessary, to 90 days from the date of the HMRC's invitation.

(ii)   If the fund does not then apply for certification HMRC must determine the question as if such application had been made having regard to any accounts or information provided by the investor.

(iii)   If, after HMRC has determined that the fund should not be certified, other accounts or information are provided which were not previously available, HMRC must reconsider their determination.

(iv)   HMRC must notify the investor who requested them to take action of their decision.

(v)   HMRC has wide powers enabling it to disclose to interested parties information regarding HMRC or Special Commissioner decisions or details of any notice given to a fund regarding a lack of full and accurate disclosure of information (see above).

[*ICTA 1988, Sch 27 paras 17, 18, 20*].

Postponement of tax

There are provisions to enable an investor to apply for tax assessed to be postponed pending HMRC's determination of the question of certification. [*ICTA 1988, Sch 27 para 19; SI 2009 No 56, Sch 1 para 161(4)(5)*].

Old regime — charge to income tax on an offshore gain

[51.29] Where a disposal to which the offshore fund rules apply (including a disposal of a holding in a distributing fund operating equalisation arrangements — see **51.23** above) gives rise to an 'offshore income gain', then subject to below, that gain is treated for all purposes as income arising to the investor at the time of disposal and chargeable to income tax for the tax year in which the disposal is made. The charge is on the full amount of income so treated as arising in the tax year.

The following provisions have effect in relation to income tax on offshore income gains as they have in relation to capital gains tax on chargeable gains.

(a)   *TCGA 1992, s 2* (persons chargeable).

(b)   *TCGA 1992, s 10* (gains accruing to non-residents carrying on a trade in the UK through a branch or agency) except that assets need not be situated in the UK.

(c) (before 2008/09) *TCGA 1992, s 12* (foreign chargeable gains of non-UK domiciled individuals chargeable on remittance basis).

As regards (c) above, the remittance basis does continue to apply to offshore income gains of a non-UK domiciliary for 2008/09 onwards but under *ICTA 1988, s 762ZB*, and the rules are brought into line with **61 REMITTANCE BASIS**. The remittance basis can apply only where one of **61.2**(1)–(3) applies to the non-domiciled individual for the tax year in which the offshore income gain arises. If that is the case, the deemed income is treated as 'relevant foreign income' of the individual, with the consequences set out at **61.4 REMITTANCE BASIS**. See **61 REMITTANCE BASIS** for the meaning of 'remitted to the UK' etc. For the purpose of applying the provisions described in that chapter, treat any consideration obtained on the disposal as deriving from the deemed income and, unless the consideration is of an amount equal to the market value of the asset, treat the asset itself (i.e. the interest in the offshore fund) as deriving from the deemed income.

See **16.10 CHARITIES** for the exemption applicable to charitable trusts.

Where a disposal to which the offshore fund rules apply is one of settled property, any offshore income gain will escape the income tax charge provided that:

- (for disposals before 6 April 2007) the general administration of the trust is ordinarily carried on outside the UK and a majority of the trustees are not resident or not ordinarily resident in the UK;
- (for disposals on or after 6 April 2007) the trustees of the settlement are at the time of the disposal neither resident nor ordinarily resident in the UK for capital gains tax purposes.

[*ICTA 1988, ss 761, 762ZB; FA 2008, Sch 7 paras 92, 94, 98, 171*].

Old regime — computation of offshore income gain

[51.30] The computation of the gain depends upon whether the disposal is of an interest in a non-qualifying fund (see **51.31** below) or of an interest involving an equalisation element (see **51.32** below).

Old regime — disposals of interests in non-qualifying funds

[51.31] A '*material disposal*' (one to which the offshore fund rules apply otherwise than by virtue of the provisions regarding distributing funds operating equalisation arrangements — see **51.23** above and **51.32** below) gives rise to an '*offshore income gain*' equal to the 'unindexed gain' or, if less, the 'post-1983 gain'.

Subject to the modifications to the CGT rules mentioned in **51.22** above and to exceptions below, the '*unindexed gain*' is the gain calculated under CGT rules without indexation allowance and without regard to any income tax charge arising under the offshore fund rules. The exceptions are as follows.

(a)   Where there has been indexation on an earlier disposal on a no gain/no loss basis within *TCGA 1992, s 56(2)*, the unindexed gain on the material disposal is computed as if indexation had not been available on the earlier disposal and, subject to that, as if the earlier disposal had produced neither gain nor loss.

(b)   If the material disposal forms part of a transfer to which *TCGA 1992, s 162* applies (rollover relief on transfer of business), the unindexed gain is computed without any deduction falling to be made under that section in computing a chargeable gain.

(c)   Any claim for relief under *FA 1980, s 79* (relief for gifts) does not affect the computation of the unindexed gain on the disposal. (See now *TCGA 1992, s 67*.)

(d)   In the case of an insurance company carrying on life assurance business, where a profit from overseas life assurance business, attributable to a material disposal, is taken into account in the computation under *ICTA 1988, s 441*, the unindexed gain, if any, accruing on disposal is computed as if *TCGA 1992, s 37(1)* did not apply. For accounting periods beginning before 1 January 1992, this applies equally where a profit arising from general annuity business attributable to a material disposal is taken into account (or would be but for the provisions relating to offshore income gains of insurance companies (see **51.33** below)) in the computation under *ICTA 1988, s 436*.

(e)   Where the computation of the unindexed gain would otherwise produce a loss, the unindexed gain is treated as nil so that no loss can arise on a material disposal.

[*ICTA 1988, Sch 28 paras 1–3, 5*].

'Post-1983 gains'

A person making a material disposal who acquired, or is treated as having acquired, his interest in the offshore fund before 1 January 1984, is treated as having disposed of and immediately reacquired his interest at market value on that date. The offshore income gain from 1 January 1984 to the date of disposal is then calculated in the ordinary way. If the person making the material disposal acquired his interest by way of a deemed no gain/no loss disposal (other than those arising by virtue of the indexation provisions of *FA 1982, s 86(5), Sch 13*) any previous owner's acquisition of the interest is treated as his acquisition of it. [*ICTA 1988, Sch 28 para 4*].

Old regime — disposals involving an equalisation element

[51.32] A disposal is a '*disposal involving an equalisation element*' if it is a disposal to which the offshore fund rules apply by virtue of the provisions relating to distributing funds operating equalisation arrangements (see **51.23** above). Such a disposal gives rise to an '*offshore income gain*' of an amount equal, subject to below, to the 'equalisation element' relevant to the asset disposed of. [*ICTA 1988, Sch 28 para 6(1)(3); SI 2004 No 2572, Reg 5*].

The '*equalisation element*' is the amount which would be credited to the fund's equalisation account in respect of accrued income if, on the date of the disposal, the asset disposed of were acquired by another person by way of 'initial purchase' (see **51.23** above). However, where the person making the disposal acquired the asset in question after the beginning of the account period by reference to which the accrued income is calculated, or at or before the beginning of that period where that period began before and ended after 1 January 1984, there are provisions to ensure that the equalisation element is reduced to exclude any part which accrued prior to either 1 January 1984 or to the investor's period of ownership. Where any of the accrued income represents commodity dealing profits (within **51.27**(c) above) half of that income is left out of account in determining the equalisation element. [*ICTA 1988, Sch 28 para 6(2)(4)–(6); SI 2004 No 2572, Reg 5*].

'Part I gains'

Where the offshore income gain as computed above would exceed the 'Part I gain', the offshore income gain is reduced to the lower figure. If there is no 'Part I gain' there can be no offshore income gain. The '*Part I gain*' is, broadly, the amount which would be the offshore income gain on the disposal if the disposal were a 'material disposal' within **51.31** above (i.e. within *ICTA 1988, Sch 28 Pt I*) as modified by certain consequential amendments. [*ICTA 1988, Sch 28 paras 7, 8*].

Old regime — miscellaneous

[51.33] The following matters are relevant.

Offshore income gains accruing to persons resident or domiciled abroad

There are consequential provisions made in connection with gains accruing to certain non-resident investors in offshore funds which modify, for the purposes of the offshore fund legislation, provisions relating to:

(a)   chargeable gains accruing to certain non-resident companies under *TCGA 1992, s 13*;
(b)   gains of non-resident settlements under *TCGA 1992, ss 80–98*;
(c)   avoidance of tax by the transfer of assets abroad under *ITA 2007, Pt 13 Ch 2* (previously under *ICTA 1988, ss 739, 740*).

To the extent that an offshore income gain is treated by virtue of (a) or (b) above as having accrued to any person resident or ordinarily resident in the UK, that gain is not deemed to be the income of any individual under any provision of *ITTOIA 2005, Pt 5 Ch 5* (previously *ICTA 1988, Pt XV* (settlements)) or, before 2008/09, under *ITA 2007, Pt 13 Ch 2*.

[*ICTA 1988, s 761(8), ss 762, 762ZA; ITA 2007, Sch 1 para 180; FA 2008, Sch 7 paras 92–94, 98*].

See also **51.29** above for the application of the remittance basis where the investor is UK-resident but not domiciled in the UK.

Capital gains tax

There are provisions to prevent a double charge to tax when a disposal gives rise to both an offshore income gain and a chargeable gain for capital gains tax purposes.

Where an offshore income gain arises on a 'material disposal' within **51.31** above, that gain is deducted from the sum which would otherwise constitute the amount or value of the consideration in the calculation of the capital gain arising under *TCGA 1992* (on 'the 1992 Act disposal'), although the offshore gain is not to be taken into account in calculating the fraction under *TCGA 1992, s 42(2)* (part disposal).

Where the 1992 Act disposal forms part of a transfer within *TCGA 1992, s 162* (rollover relief on transfer of business wholly or partly for shares) then, in determining the amount of the deduction from the gain on the old assets, the offshore income gain is deducted from the value of the consideration received in exchange for the business.

Where an exchange of shares or securities constitutes a disposal of an interest in an offshore fund (see **51.22** and **51.23** above), the amount of any offshore income gain to which the disposal gives rise is treated as consideration for the new holding.

Where the offshore fund provisions apply to a disposal of an interest in a fund operating equalisation arrangements (see **51.23** above) and the disposal:

- is not to the fund or to its managers in their capacity as such; and
- gives rise to an offshore income gain in accordance with **51.32** above; and
- is followed subsequently by a distribution to either the person who made the disposal or to a person connected with him (within *ICTA 1988, s 839*) and that distribution is referable to the asset disposed of,

then the subsequent distribution (or distributions) is (are) reduced by the amount of the offshore income gain.

[*ICTA 1988, s 763; ITA 2007, Sch 1 para 181*].

Exemption from capital gains tax under *TCGA 1992, s 76(1)* is disapplied where the disposal is of an interest in a trust which has at any time been an offshore trust, or where the interest disposed of originated in a trust which has at any time been an offshore trust. [*TCGA 1992, s 76(1A)/(1B)/(3)*]. See Tolley's Capital Gains Tax under Offshore Settlements.

Offshore income gains of trustees

Any offshore income gains arising to trustees and chargeable to income tax are charged at the trust rate (see **68.12**(9) SETTLEMENTS) for the year in question.

Where trustees hold assets for a person who would be absolutely entitled as against the trustees but for being a minor, any offshore income gains liable to income tax which accrue on the disposal of those assets are deemed to be paid to that person for the purposes of the provisions regarding settlements on children at **68.30** SETTLEMENTS. [*ITTOIA 2005, s 632; ICTA 1988, s 660B(4)*].

Example

[51.34]

R, who is resident, ordinarily resident and domiciled in the UK, invests in non-qualifying offshore funds as follows.

			£
(i)	ABC fund		
	30.11.82	1,000 shares purchased at £10 per share	10,000
	1.1.84	Market value per share = £20	20,000
	1.11.09	On amalgamation with XYZ fund (an offshore fund which is not and has not been non-qualifying) the 1,000 original shares are exchanged for 2,000 new shares in XYZ which have a value of £15 per share	30,000
(ii)	**DEF fund**		£
	1.8.83	500 units purchased at £25 per unit	12,500
	1.1.84	Market value per unit = £20	10,000
	1.9.09	500 units sold for £40 per unit	20,000

R has offshore income gains and capital gains/losses in 2009/10 as follows.

Offshore income gains

Disposal on 1.9.09 of 500 DEF units

	Post-1983 gain	Unindexed gain
	£	£
Disposal proceeds	20,000	20,000
Market value at 1.1.84	10,000	
Cost		12,500
	£10,000	£7,500

As the unindexed gain is less than the post-1983 gain, the offshore income gain chargeable to income tax is £7,500.

Disposal on 1.11.09 of 1,000 ABC shares

Disposal consideration	30,000	30,000
Market value at 1.1.84	20,000	
Cost		10,000
	£10,000	£20,000

The offshore income gain chargeable to income tax is the £10,000 post-1983 gain as this is less than the unindexed gain.

Capital gains computation

Disposal on 1.9.09 of 500 DEF units

	£
Disposal proceeds	20,000
Offshore income gain	7,500
	12,500
Cost	12,500
Chargeable gain/allowable loss	Nil

Disposal on 1.11.09 of 1,000 ABC shares

There is no capital gains tax liability as the share exchange is not treated as a disposal for capital gains tax purposes. [*TCGA 1992, s 135*]. See Tolley's Capital Gains Tax.

Note

The £10,000 offshore income gain arising on the exchange of ABC shares for XYZ shares will be treated as part of the acquisition cost for capital gains tax purposes on a subsequent disposal of XYZ shares (see **51.33** above).

Key points

[51.35] Points to consider are as follows.

- The pre–1 December 2009 regime will not apply to holdings in offshore funds after 2009/10, but advisers with affected clients should ensure that they are fully conversant with the transitional protection detailed at **51.19**.
- Advisers unfamiliar with the special rules which create an income tax charge on disposals of an interest in an offshore fund should study the rules in **51.3** and **51.15** carefully when commencing to act for an affected client.

52

Partnerships

Cross-reference. See also **58 PERSONAL SERVICE COMPANIES ETC.**

Simon's Taxes. See Part B7.

Introduction

[52.1] An English partnership is not a legal entity in the same way as a company, but a collection of separate persons. In Scotland though, a firm is a legal person, see *Partnership Act 1890, s 4(2)*.

Under UK tax law, a partnership is *not* generally treated for tax purposes as an entity which is separate and distinct from its members. The taxable profits of a trade, profession or other business carried on in partnership are apportioned between the partners, each of whom is then taxed individually on his own share (see **52.4** below).

See the corresponding chapter of Tolley's Capital Gains Tax as regards the chargeable gains of partnerships and individual partners.

See **63.9**, **63.13** RETURNS for self-assessment provisions regarding partnership returns and general compliance.

Nature of partnership

[52.2] Whether a partnership exists and, if so, from what date is a question of fact (*Williamson* CS 1928, 14 TC 335; *Calder v Allanson* KB 1935, 19 TC 293). The existence of a formal partnership agreement is not conclusive of the existence of a partnership (*Hawker v Compton* KB 1922, 8 TC 306; *Dickenson v Gross* KB 1927, 11 TC 614). Equally, whether a partnership can ante-date the date of the agreement is a question of fact (*Ayrshire Pullman Services v CIR* CS 1929, 14 TC 754; *Waddington v O'Callaghan* KB 1931, 16 TC 187; *Taylor v Chalklin* KB 1945, 26 TC 463; *Alexander Bulloch & Co v CIR* CS 1976, 51 TC 563; *Saywell v Pope* Ch D 1979, 53 TC 40).

Joint transactions may amount to a partnership or joint trading for tax purposes — see *Morden Rigg & Eskrigge v Monks* CA 1923, 8 TC 450 (joint cotton transactions); *Gardner & Bowring Hardy v CIR* CS 1930, 15 TC 602 (temporary joint coal merchanting); *Lindsay Woodward & Hiscox v CIR* CS 1932, 18 TC 43 (joint transactions in whisky in violation of USA law); *George Hall & Son v Platt* Ch D 1954, 35 TC 440 (joint crop growing). See also *Fenston v Johnstone* KB 1940, 23 TC 29.

Where a partnership terminated with open forward contracts, subsequently completed, it was held to continue trading notwithstanding that some of the partners had formed a new partnership to carry on a similar business (*Hillerns & Fowler v Murray* CA 1932, 17 TC 77). A doctor who sold his practice, helping the purchaser for a short time on a profit-sharing basis, was held not to be a partner (*Pratt v Strick* KB 1932, 17 TC 459).

A partnership set up for tax avoidance purposes may nevertheless be a true partnership (*Newstead v Frost* HL 1980, 53 TC 525).

A Rotary Club is not a partnership (*Blackpool Marton Rotary Club v Martin* Ch D 1988, 62 TC 686).

The question of whether an operation conducted with an overseas entity is akin to an English partnership or to a silent partnership (which is not within the rules in this chapter) may arise for the purposes of DOUBLE TAX RELIEF (**26**). See *Memec plc v CIR* CA 1998, 71 TC 77 and *Training Consultant v HMRC* (Sp C 584), [2007] SSCD 231. But see also **26.3** DOUBLE TAX RELIEF under Distributions.

See **60.2** PROPERTY INCOME as regards joint ownership and exploitation of property.

See generally HMRC Business Income Manual BIM72001–72035.

See **52.22** below as regards limited partnerships and **52.23–52.25** below as regards limited liability partnerships (LLPs).

Simon's Taxes. See B7.102–B7.104.

Taxation of partnership income

[52.3] See **52.4** below as regards trading profits and losses and **52.5** below as regards non-trading income.

The assignment by a partner of part of his share in the partnership was ineffective for the purpose of displacing his liability to income tax on that part of his share of partnership profits (*Hadlee and Another v Commissioner of Inland Revenue (NZ)* PC, [1993] STC 294).

Company as partner

If a company is a partner, see **52.19** below.

Capital gains

Capital gains which arise from the disposal of partnership assets are charged on the partners individually. [*TCGA 1992, s 59; FA 2008, s 58(2)(4)–(6); CTA 2009, Sch 1 para 365*]. See Tolley's Capital Gains Tax.

Simon's Taxes. See B7.110–B7.121.

Trading/professional profits and losses

[52.4] For any period of account (see **73.1** TRADING INCOME) for which there is at least one partner who is a UK resident individual chargeable to income tax, the profits or losses of the partnership trade or profession are computed for income tax purposes in like manner as if the partnership were a UK resident individual. The taxable profits or allowable losses of the partnership for a period of account (as adjusted for income tax purposes) are apportioned in accordance with the partnership's profit-sharing arrangements during that period of account (but see also **52.11** below as regards losses). In computing profits for any period of account, no account is taken of any losses for any other period of account. The above rules, but not those below, apply equally where a partnership carries on a business other than a trade or profession.

Each individual's share of the profit or loss of a partnership trade or profession (as adjusted for income tax purposes) is taxed or relieved as if it derived from a trade or profession (the notional trade) carried on by him alone. The notional trade is treated as commencing at the time the individual becomes a partner (or, if later, when the partnership starts to carry on the actual trade or profession), or, if the actual trade or profession was previously carried on by the individual alone, at the time the actual trade commenced. Similar rules apply as regards cessations.

The notional trade is taxed in accordance with the normal basis period rules including the overlap relief rules (see **73.3–73.11** TRADING INCOME). A change of accounting date of the actual partnership trade that would result in a change of basis period if it were a sole trade changes the basis periods for each partner's notional trade. Where no such change of basis period would result (because the necessary conditions are not satisfied), the basis periods for partners' notional trades are determined by reference to the partnership's old accounting date. Notice of a change of accounting date must be given in a partnership tax return by nominated partner nominated by the partnership for that purpose, and any appeal against a refusal by HMRC to accept the change must similarly be made by a nominated partner. The rule whereby the necessary conditions do not have to be satisfied if the change occurs in the second or third tax year of the business applies only by reference to the second or third tax year of the actual partnership trade and not to the second or third tax year of a partner's notional trade. See **73.7** TRADING INCOME for the detailed rules on changes of accounting date and **63.13** RETURNS for partnership tax returns.

Where the partnership trade or profession commenced before 6 April 1994, transitional overlap relief (see **73.12** TRADING INCOME) applies to individual partners' notional trades as it does to sole trades, providing they were partners in 1997/98.

[ITTOIA 2005, ss 846–848, 849(1)(2), 850(1), 852(1)–(5), 853(1)–(3); CTA 2009, Sch 1 paras 638, 639].

Notes on computation of partnership profits

(i)   Legal costs and stamps re partnership deeds are not normally permissible deductions.

(ii)   Partners' salaries, domestic and personal expenses, interest credited on capital and any benefit of financial value given to a partner are not permissible deductions for tax purposes, being regarded as part of the taxable profits. See e.g. *PDC Copyprint (South) v George* (Sp C 141), [1997] SSCD 326 as regards partners' salaries (and see the example at **52.8** below). But this does not necessarily apply to payments to a partner for goods or services 'altogether disconnected with the partnership business as such' and where the firm's premises are owned by a partner, *bona fide* rent paid to him under legal agreement is a proper deduction for tax purposes (*Heastie v Veitch* CA 1933, 18 TC 305). Contributions towards partners' removal expenses, where partner moved in the interests of the firm, are not deductible (*MacKinlay v Arthur Young McClelland Moores & Co* HL 1989, 62 TC 704).

(iii)   (Before 2007/08) taxed charges, payable out of firm's income, are added back in computing the firm's taxable profits, and tax on them has to be accounted for. HMRC accept the view that a partner's personal taxed investment income is available to cover his share of partnership charges. Should there be an excess of partnership taxed charges over partnership income, an assessment under *ICTA 1988, s 350* would therefore be made only to the extent that each individual partner's share of the excess is not covered by his own private investment income. The concept of 'charges on income' is abolished for 2007/08 onwards — see **1.10** ALLOWANCES AND TAX RATES and Change 81 in Annex 1 to the Explanatory Notes to *ITA 2007*.

See *MacKinlay v Arthur Young McClelland Moores & Co* HL 1989, 62 TC 704 as to prohibition on deduction of certain payments made to partners in connection with partnership business.

Excessive payments to the service company of a professional firm were held not to be deductible (*Stephenson v Payne, Stone Fraser & Co* Ch D 1967, 44 TC 507).

See also **73** TRADING INCOME for adjustments to profits generally and **27.54** EMPLOYMENT INCOME for director's fees received by a professional partnership.

Non-trading income

[52.5] In the case of a trading or professional partnership to which non-trading income (or a relievable non-trading loss) accrues, each individual partner is taxed on his share, computed by reference to the profit sharing arrangements for the period of account of the trade or profession. In the case of untaxed income (i.e. income not taxed at source or carrying a tax credit) from one or more sources, the normal basis period rules for *trading* income (see **73.3–73.11** TRADING INCOME) apply as if each individual's share of the income (or loss) were profits (or losses) of a notional business carried on by him alone. The notional business is treated as commencing at the time the individual becomes a partner (or, if later, when the partnership commences a trade or profession) and ceasing when he ceases to be a partner, with each separate source of income treated as continuing until he ceases to be a partner. The same comments apply as in **52.4** above as regards changes of partnership accounting date. Where overlap relief (see **73.11**) in respect of untaxed income falls to be deducted in a tax year (because of a change of accounting date or a permanent cessation of the notional business) and the deduction exceeds the partner's share of untaxed income for that year, the excess is deductible in computing his taxable income for that year.

These special rules for non-trading untaxed income apply only where the associated trade or profession is carried on *in partnership*, so that, for example, if one partner is left to carry on the partnership business as a sole trader, his notional trade ceases at that time and his untaxed income is subsequently taxed on a fiscal year basis. Similarly, if an individual initially carries on the trade as a sole trader, the notional business does not commence until the partnership is set up.

[*ITTOIA 2005, ss 851, 854(1)–(4)(6), 855, 856*].

Example

[52.6]

X and Y began to trade in partnership on 1 July 2006, preparing first accounts to 30 September 2007 and sharing profits equally. Z joins the firm as an equal partner on 1 October 2008. Y leaves the firm on 31 March 2010. Accounts are prepared to that date to ascertain Y's entitlement, but the accounting date then reverts to 30 September and the partnership does not give notice to HMRC of a change of accounting date, so that there is no change of basis period. In addition to trading profits, the partnership had a source of lettings income which ceased in September 2009, and is in receipt of both taxed and untaxed interest, the latter from a source commencing in October 2007. Taxed interest is received on 31 March each year. Revised figures as adjusted for income tax purposes are as follows.

	Trading income	Property income	Savings income (untaxed interest)	Savings income (taxed interest) (gross)
	£	£	£	£
15 months to 30.9.07	30,000	4,500	—	750
Year to 30.9.08	24,000	5,000	1,000	1,500
Year to 30.9.09	39,000	3,000	600	300
6 months to 31.3.10	19,500	—	225	165
6 months to 30.9.10	14,000	—	140	—

The partners' shares of taxable income from the partnership for the years 2006/07 to 2010/11 inclusive are as follows. (See **52.7** below as regards changes in the membership of a partnership.)

	X £	Y £	Z £
Trading income			
2006/07			
1.7.06–5.4.07 (£30,000 × $^9/_{15}$)	9,000	9,000	
2007/08			
1.10.06–30.9.07 (£30,000 × $^{12}/_{15}$)	12,000*	12,000*	
* Overlap relief accrued:			
1.10.06–5.4.07 (£30,000 × $^6/_{15}$)	6,000	6,000	
2008/09			
Y/e 30.9.08	12,000	12,000	
1.10.08–5.4.09 (£39,000 × $^6/_{12}$ × $^1/_3$)			6,500
2009/10			
Y/e 30.9.09	13,000	13,000	13,000*

	X £	Y £	Z £
1.10.09–31.3.10		6,500	
		19,500	
Less overlap relief		(6,000)	
		13,500	
* Overlap relief accrued			
1.10.08–5.4.09 (as above)			6,500
2010/11			
Y/e 30.9.10			
1.10.09–31.3.10	6,500		6,500
1.4.10–30.9.10	7,000		7,000
	13,500		13,500
Property income			
2006/07			
1.7.06–5.4.07 (£4,500 × $^9/_{15}$)	1,350	1,350	
2007/08			
1.10.06–30.9.07 (£4,500 × $^{12}/_{15}$)	1,800*	1,800*	
* Overlap relief accrued			
1.10.06–5.4.07 (£4,500 × $^6/_{15}$)	900	900	
2008/09			
Y/e 30.9.08	2,500	2,500	
1.10.08–5.4.09 (£3,000 × $^6/_{12}$ × $^1/_3$)			500
2009/10			
Y/e 30.9.09	1,000	1,000	1,000*
1.10.09–31.3.10		—	
		1,000	
Less overlap relief		(900)	
		100	
* Overlap relief accrued			
1.10.08–5.4.09 (as above)			500
Savings income (untaxed)			
2008/09			
Y/e 30.9.08	500	500	
1.10.08–5.4.09 (£600 × $^6/_{12}$ × $^1/_3$)			100
2009/10			
Y/e 30.9.09	200	200	200*
1.10.09–31.3.10		75	
		275	
* Overlap relief accrued			
1.10.08–5.4.09 (as above)			100
2010/11			
Y/e 30.9.10			
1.10.09–31.3.10	75		75
1.4.10–30.9.10	70		70
	145		145

	X	Y	Z
	£	£	£
Savings income (taxed)			
2006/07 (received 31.3.07)	<u>375</u>	<u>375</u>	
2007/08 (received 31.3.08)	<u>750</u>	<u>750</u>	
2008/09 (received 31.3.09)	<u>100</u>	<u>100</u>	<u>100</u>
2009/10 (received 31.3.10)	<u>55</u>	<u>55</u>	<u>55</u>
2010/11	**	—	**

** Each to be based on one-half of interest received 31.3.11.

Note

Taxed savings income is taxed on a fiscal year basis as for an individual, but is apportioned between the partners according to their shares for the period of account in which the income arises.

Changes in members of a partnership

[52.7] A partnership trade or profession is *not* treated as having ceased and recommenced when a partner joins or leaves the firm providing there is at least one continuing partner (which also embraces the situation where a sole trader begins to carry on the trade or profession in partnership or a former partner begins to carry it on as a sole trader). Where, exceptionally, the trade or profession continues to be carried on but without any such continuing partner, it is notionally treated as having ceased at that point, with a new trade or profession treated as having commenced.

New partners are taxed on their profit share under the opening years provisions at **73.4 TRADING INCOME** and outgoing partners are taxed on their share under the closing year provisions at **73.9 TRADING INCOME** (see also **52.3–52.5** above).

Example

[52.8]

P, Q and R have carried on a profession in partnership for a number of years (since before 6 April 1994) sharing profits in the ratio 2:2:1. Accounts are made up to 30 June. P leaves the partnership on 30 June 2005 and Q and R share profits 3:2 for the year to 30 June 2006 and equally thereafter. On 30 June 2008, Q leaves the partnership and on 1 July 2008, S becomes a partner. Profits are then shared between R and S in the ratio 2:1 until 30 September 2010 when the practice comes to an end, neither partner continuing to carry it on as a sole practitioner thereafter. P, Q and R have transitional overlap relief of £18,400, £18,400 and £9,200 respectively by reference to an overlap period of nine months.

Results for the seven periods of account up to 30 September 2010 are as follows.

Period ended	Partners' salaries				Adjusted Profit
	P	Q	R	S	
	£	£	£	£	£
30.6.04	4,000	4,000	2,000	—	75,000
30.6.05	18,000	13,000	13,500	—	60,000
30.6.06	—	12,500	12,500	—	80,000
30.6.07	—	12,000	17,000	—	85,000
30.6.08	—	4,000	11,000	—	95,000
30.6.09	—	—	5,000	—	101,000
30.9.10	—	—	3,000	—	58,000

The adjusted profit figures above are after adding back partners' salaries (see **52.4**(ii) above).

The taxable profits for the years 2004/05 to 2010/11 are as follows.

Taxable profits of P, Q & R individually for 2004/05 and 2005/06

	P	Q	R
	£	£	£
2004/05			
Y/e 30.6.04			
Profits £75,000 − £(4,000 + 4,000 + 2,000)	26,000	26,000	13,000
Salaries	4,000	4,000	2,000
Taxable profits	£30,000	£30,000	£15,000
2005/06			
Y/e 30.6.05			
Profits £60,000 − £(18,000 + 13,000 + 13,500)	6,200	6,200	3,100
Salaries	18,000	13,000	13,500
	24,200	19,200	16,600

	P £	Q £	R £
Less transitional overlap relief	18,400	—	
Taxable profits	£5,800	£19,200	£16,600

Taxable profits of Q, R & S individually from 2006/07 to 2010/11

	Q £	R £	S £
2006/07			
Y/e 30.6.06			
Profits £80,000 – £(12,500 + 12,500)	33,000	22,000	
Salaries	12,500	12,500	
Taxable profits	£45,500	£34,500	
2007/08			
Y/e 30.6.07			
Profits £85,000 – £(12,000 + 17,000)	28,000	28,000	
Salaries	12,000	17,000	
Taxable profits	£40,000	£45,000	
2008/09			
Y/e 30.6.08			
Profits £95,000 – £(4,000 + 11,000)	40,000	40,000	
Salaries	4,000	11,000	
Taxable profits	44,000	51,000	
Less transitional overlap relief	18,400	—	
Taxable profits	£25,600	£51,000	
Y/e 30.6.09			
Profits £101,000 – £5,000 × $\frac{1}{3}$ = £32,000			
Taxable profit 1.7.08–5.4.09			
£32,000 × $\frac{9}{12}$			£24,000
2009/10			
Y/e 30.6.09			
Profits £101,000 – £5,000		64,000	32,000
Salary		5,000	—
Taxable profits		£69,000	£32,000*
*Overlap relief accrued			
1.7.08–5.4.09 as above			£24,000
2010/11			
15 months to 30.9.10			
Profits £58,000 – £3,000		33,000	22,000
Salary		3,000	—

	Q	R	S
	£	£	£
		36,000	22,000
Less overlap relief		9,200	24,000
Taxable profit/(allowable loss)		£26,800	(£2,000)

Note

See 52.6 above for a further example of partners joining and leaving a firm, which also illustrates the position where there is non-trading as well as trading income.

Partnership mergers and demergers

[52.9] Where two businesses carried on in partnership merge, it is a question of fact whether the new partnership has succeeded to the businesses of the old partnerships, or whether the old businesses have ceased and a new business resulted from the merger which is different in nature from either of the two old businesses. Disparity of size between the old partnerships will not of itself be a significant matter. Clearly the former is more likely to be the case where the two old businesses carried on the same sort of activities, and the latter where they were themselves different in nature. Where the former applies, both businesses are treated as continuing. Where the new partnership does not succeed to the old businesses, the trades are treated as having ceased and the closing year rule (see **73.9 TRADING INCOME**) will apply to the notional trades of the partners in both old partnerships; the opening year rules (see **73.4 TRADING INCOME**) will then apply to the notional trades of the partners in the new partnership.

Similar considerations apply where a partnership is divided up and two or more partnerships are formed, in determining whether any of the separate partnerships has succeeded to the business of the original partnership.

Similar principles apply where sole traders merge into partnership or a partnership business is demerged and carried on by sole traders.

(HMRC SP 9/86).

See *C Connelly & Co v Wilbey* Ch D 1992, 65 TC 208 for a case in which it was held that neither part of a demerged partnership succeeded to the former partnership trade (and in which legal costs relating to the dissolution were disallowed).

The amalgamation of two sole traders into partnership in *Humphries v Cook* KB 1934, 19 TC 121 was held to result in the commencement of a new business and the cessation of both the old businesses, but this is applied sparingly by HMRC, mainly where the new partnership business is of a different nature from those previously carried on.

Simon's Taxes. See B7.127.

Losses

[52.10] Subject to **52.11** below, partnership losses, as computed for tax purposes, are apportioned between the individual partners in the same way as are profits. The loss of each partner may be:

- set off against his other income (under *ITA 2007, s 64,* or, where applicable, *ITA 2007, s 72*); or
- carried forward against his share of subsequent profits of the partnership (under *ITA 2007, s 83*), including in certain circumstances where a partnership business is converted into a company (*ITA 2007, s 86*); or
- used in a terminal loss claim (under *ITA 2007, s 89*) where either the partnership trade or profession ceases or the individual leaves the partnership.

For full details of these loss claims, see **45 LOSSES**. It is for each partner to choose how to utilise his own losses and to make his own claim.

Similarly, losses made by a partner in other businesses may be set-off against his share of partnership profits under *ITA 2007, s 64*.

For restrictions on, and claw-back of, loss reliefs in the case of non-active partners, see **52.13–52.17** below. For restrictions in the case of limited partners and members of limited liability partnerships, see, respectively, **52.22** and **52.24** below.

Unusual allocations

[52.11] *Where the firm as a whole makes a profit* (as adjusted for tax purposes) but, after the allocation of prior shares (e.g. salaries and interest on capital) the result is that *an individual partner makes a loss*, the loss-making partner cannot claim tax relief for his loss. Instead, he is treated as making neither profit nor loss, and his 'loss' is reallocated to the profit-making partners in proportion to the profits already allocated to them, thus reducing those profits for tax purposes. Similarly, *where there is an overall partnership loss*, the aggregate losses allocated to loss-making partners cannot exceed the overall loss and no partner can be taxed on a share of profit. Instead, a profit-making partner is treated as making neither profit nor loss, and his 'profit' is reallocated to the loss-making partners in proportion to the losses already allocated to them, thus reducing those losses.

[*ITTOIA 2005, s 850(2)–(6), 850A, 850B; CTA 2009, Sch 1 para 640*].

Example

[52.12]

Janet, John and James are full equity partners, sharing profits and losses equally and preparing accounts to 31 May. The partnership agreement also makes provision for partners' salaries. For the year to 31 May 2010, Janet and John are entitled to salaries of £19,000 and £8,000 respectively. However, the firm has an unexpectedly bad year and makes a loss of £21,000. This is the tax adjusted figure after adding back the non-deductible partners' salaries of £27,000.

The initial allocation between the partners is as follows.

	Total	Janet	John	James
	£	£	£	£
Adjusted loss	(21,000)			
Salaries	27,000	19,000	8,000	
Loss after salaries	£48,000	(16,000)	(16,000)	(16,000)
Allocation	(£21,000)	£3,000	(£8,000)	(£16,000)

As the partnership has made a tax loss, no partner can make a taxable profit. A reallocation must be made to reduce Janet's allocated profit of £3,000 to nil. John's allocated loss is reduced by £1,000 (£3,000 x 8,000/(16,000 + 8,000)) and James's by £2,000 (£3,000 x 16,000/(16,000 + 8,000)). The final allocation is as follows.

	Total	Janet	John	James
Tax loss	(£21,000)	Nil	(£7,000)	(£14,000)

Non-active partners — restriction of loss reliefs

[52.13] Trade loss relief under:

(1) *ITA 2007, s 64* or its predecessor (and, consequently, *TCGA 1992, s 261B* (or, before 2007/08, *FA 1991, s 72*) against chargeable gains) (see **45.2**, **45.7** LOSSES); or

(2) *ITA 2007, s 72* or its predecessor (see **45.9** LOSSES),

is restricted in the case of an individual who is a '*non-active*' partner, i.e. who does not devote 'a significant amount of time' to the trade. The relief available, otherwise than against profits of the trade, is restricted to the amount of the partner's 'contribution to the firm' (see **52.14** below) as at the end of the basis period for the tax year in which the loss is sustained. The restriction applies to losses sustained in the tax year in which the partner first carries on the trade and in any of the next three tax years.

See **52.15** below for a cap on the amount of relief that can be given under any of the provisions at (1) and (2) above for a loss sustained by a non-active partner for 2007/08 (subject to transitional provisions) or any subsequent year. The operation of the cap is not limited to the first four years of trading.

Before 2007/08, the restriction operated by reference to the individual's 'contribution to the trade' (see **52.14** below) as opposed to his 'contribution to the firm' (see Change 16 in Annex 1 of the Explanatory Notes to *ITA 2007*). Also, the individual's contribution was measured at the end of the tax year in which the loss was sustained, rather than, as now, at the end of the basis period for that tax year.

The restrictions potentially apply to a loss sustained in any tax year:

- the basis period for which ends on or after 10 February 2004 (see **52.4** above as regards partners' basis periods and see below for transitional provisions);
- at any time during which the individual carried on the trade as a partner (other than a limited partner within **52.22** below) or as a member of a limited liability partnership (LLP) within **52.23** below and at no time during which he carried it on as a limited partner;
- which is the first, second, third or fourth tax year in which the individual carried on the trade; and
- in the 'relevant period' for which he did not devote 'a significant amount of time' to the trade.

Where relief under any of the provisions at (1) and (2) above has previously been given for losses sustained in tax years which meet the above conditions, such reliefs must be aggregated. The relief that can then be given, otherwise than against profits of the trade, for the current loss is limited to the excess (if any) of the amount of the partner's 'contribution to the firm' at the end of the basis period for the current tax year over the aggregate amount. This aggregate must also include any relief given for losses sustained in any tax year at any time during which the partner carried on the trade as a limited partner or member of an LLP and the basis period for which ends on or after 10 February 2004. It does not include any 'pre-announcement allowance' (see the transitional provisions below). But the aggregate is decreased by the amount of any claw-back under the recovery provisions described at **52.14** below.

These rules do not prevent or restrict a loss from being carried forward under *ITA 2007, s 83* (or its predecessor) (see **45.20 LOSSES**) against subsequent profits of the trade. They do not apply at all to **UNDERWRITERS AT LLOYD'S (74)** in connection with their underwriting business.

'Significant amount of time'

A partner devotes a '*significant amount of time*' to the trade in the 'relevant period' for a tax year if, for the whole of that period, he spends an average of at least 10 hours a week personally engaged in activities of the trade. Where the relevant period ends on or after 12 March 2008, it is further stipulated that those activities must be carried on on a commercial basis and with a view to profit. Any relief erroneously given on the assumption that this requirement will be met will be withdrawn by means of an income tax assessment. The '*relevant period*' for a tax year is normally the basis period for that tax year. However, if the basis period is less than six months because the tax year is the one in which the individual joined or left the partnership, the requirement must instead be met by reference to the six months beginning with his commencement date or ending with his cessation date. The legislation is silent as to what is meant by personal engagement in the activities of the trade. The Explanatory Notes to the 2004 Finance Bill suggest that this may include, for example, a management or service role such as personnel, accountancy or purchasing, but does not include time spent deciding whether or not to invest, and/or how much to invest, in the partnership or its trade.

Carry-forward

Where a partner's loss relief has been restricted as above, the total amount thereby unrelieved is carried forward to subsequent tax years in which he continues to carry on the trade in partnership. For any such subsequent tax year, that total amount, or so much of it as still remains unrelieved, is treated for the purposes of the provisions in (1) and (2) above as a loss sustained in that year (or as an increase to any loss actually sustained in that year). In ascertaining how much remains unrelieved, any relief given under general rules (e.g. carry-forward and set-off of losses under *ITA 2007, s 83* or its predecessor) is taken into account as is any relief given (or which could have been given had a claim been made) by virtue of this carry-forward rule. For the purpose only of determining whether an amount can be relieved in a subsequent year by virtue of this rule, that year is treated as a year to which these restrictions potentially apply even it is not actually so. Thus, this carry-forward rule does enable restricted relief to be obtained in a subsequent year but only to the extent that capital contributions have increased sufficiently. Any amount remaining unrelieved after applying this rule is again carried forward and the rule once more applied in the following year. An unrelieved amount can also be carried forward to a year in which the partner no longer carries on the trade but makes a contribution to the assets of the partnership on a winding-up; in this case certain conditions that otherwise apply to the loss reliefs in (1) and (2) above (in particular the condition that the trade be carried on commercially with a view to profit) are relaxed in relation to the carried-forward amount, and for 2007/08 onwards the partner's contribution to the firm is measured as at the end of the tax year itself.

Transitional provisions

Special rules apply to the tax year the basis period for which includes 10 February 2004 (the *'first restricted year'*). If there is more than one tax year whose basis period includes that date (for example, under the opening years' rules at **73.4 TRADING INCOME**), the first restricted year is the first such tax year and the rules apply to that year only. Losses for the first restricted year are split into two parts; the first part (the *'pre-announcement allowance'*) is the loss sustained in the part of the basis period ending with 9 February 2004 and the second part is the loss sustained in the remaining part of the basis period. The first part is allowable in full and the second part is allowable only to the extent that it does not exceed the partner's contribution to the trade at the end of the tax year. Each part of the basis period has to be treated as a separate period of account for the purpose of determining how much (if any) of a loss is sustained in that part; the loss cannot simply be time-apportioned. However, any capital allowances derived from expenditure incurred before 10 February 2004 are regarded as belonging to the first part of the basis period; a similar rule applies to any film production or acquisition expenditure incurred before that date but deductible over a three-year period (see **73.76 TRADING INCOME**). A loss for either part of the basis period is allocated between partners in accordance with their sharing arrangements for that part. This would normally prevent an individual who joined the partnership after 9 February 2004 from having any share of the loss for the part of the basis period ending on that date but if he joined before 26 March 2004 he can nevertheless be allocated such a share provided he was a partner at some time in the basis period for the first restricted year.

For tax years after the first restricted year, capital allowances on pre-10 February 2004 expenditure and any film production or acquisition expenditure incurred before that date are again excluded from the losses subjected to the restrictions; the extent to which a loss derives from such allowances or expenditure is determined on a just and reasonable basis.

[ITA 2007, ss 103, 103B, 110, 112, 113, 790–795, Sch 2 paras 30, 32, 33; ICTA 1988, ss 118ZE, 118ZF, 118ZH–118ZK, 118ZN, 118ZO; FA 2007, Sch 4 paras 8, 10, 11, 13, 21; FA 2008, s 61].

Partner's contribution to the firm/trade

[52.14] In relation to 2007/08 onwards, a partner's '*contribution to the firm*' for the purposes of **52.13** above is the sum of the amount he has contributed as capital (net of withdrawals) and any profits of the trade to which he is entitled but has not received in money or money's worth. To the extent that profits have been added to the firm's capital, they should be included as part of capital contributions but not as part of profit entitlement. In determining the profits to which the partner is entitled, any losses are disregarded, and references to profits are to accounting profits, calculated in accordance with generally accepted accounting practice, and not to taxable profits (if different). Profits of any other trade carried on by the partnership are taken into account also.

In relation to 2006/07 and earlier years, a partner's '*contribution to the trade*' at any time ('*the relevant time*') for the purposes of **52.13** above is the sum of the 'amount subscribed' by him, any profits of the trade to which he is entitled but has not received in money or money's worth and (where relevant) any amount he has contributed to the partnership assets on a winding-up. For this purpose, the '*amount subscribed*' by a partner is the amount of his capital contributions net of 'capital withdrawals'. '*Capital withdrawals*' are widely defined so as to include amounts of capital:

•   that the partner has previously, directly or indirectly, drawn out or received back; or

•   that he so draws out or receives back during the five years beginning with the relevant time; or

•   that he is or may be entitled so to draw out or receive back at any time when he carries on the trade as a member of the partnership; or

•   that he is or may be entitled to require another person to reimburse to him, but not so as to include any such amount drawn out or received back which is chargeable to income tax as profits of a trade.

Exclusions

The Commissioners for HMRC are empowered to make regulations (see *SI 2005 No 2017*) excluding from a partner's 'contribution to the firm' (or, before 2007/08, his 'contribution to the trade') for these purposes any amounts of a description specified in the regulations. The exclusion will apply in relation to the relief that may otherwise be given under the provisions in **52.13**(1) or (2) above for a 'post-1 December 2004 loss' (see below). Under *SI 2005 No 2017*, such exclusions are made in the following circumstances.

(a)   Where an individual takes out a loan in connection with his financing of all or part of his contribution to the firm/trade and either:

    (i)   there is, at any time, an agreement or arrangement under which another person will, or may, bear any of the financial cost of repaying the loan; or

    (ii)   any such financial cost is at any time borne by another person otherwise than under an agreement or arrangement caught by (i) above; or

    (iii)   the liability to repay the loan is at any time assumed (or released) by any other person; or

    (iv)   the financial cost to the individual of repaying the loan over a specified period is substantially less than it would have been on arm's length terms.

The period specified in (iv) above is the earliest period of five years beginning on or after 2 December 2004 (or, if later, the date the loan was taken out) for which condition (iv) is satisfied. Where conditions (i), (ii) or (iii) are satisfied, the amount in question is excluded from the individual's contribution to the firm/trade after the time in question. Where condition (iv) is satisfied, the exclusion applies after the end of the five-year period and is equal to the amount of the loan outstanding at the end of that period. References to loans include replacement loans.

(b)   Where, at any time, there is an agreement or arrangement under which any of the financial cost of making the contribution to the firm/trade will be, or may be, reimbursed (directly or indirectly) to the individual by any other person, or where such cost is at any time reimbursed otherwise than under such an agreement or arrangement. The amount in question is excluded from the individual's contribution to the firm/trade after the time in question.

Neither (a) nor (b) above applies in relation to any financial cost borne or reimbursed by another individual in the normal course of his domestic, family or personal relationships or to any loan repayments not made by the partner due to his financial inability to pay (arising from events outside his control and occurring after the taking out of the loan) or to any amount on which the partner is chargeable to income tax as profits of the trade.

For the purposes of the above exclusion from a partner's contribution to the firm/trade, a '*post-1 December 2004 loss*' is a loss sustained in a tax year whose basis period begins after 1 December 2004 or, as regards a tax year whose basis period straddles 2 December 2004, so much of any loss as is sustained in the part of the basis period beginning on that date (computed as if a separate period of account began on that date).

Recovery provisions

There are recovery provisions to claw back any relief given for a post-1 December 2004 loss against other income or gains where the partner's contribution to the firm/trade is *subsequently* reduced by any application of the HMRC regulations referred to above, such that the relief given becomes excessive. The recovery provisions apply equally in relation to losses sustained by a limited partner (see **52.22** below) or by a member of an LLP (see **52.24** below). The partner is treated as receiving, at the time of that subsequent reduction, income chargeable to tax, other than as part of the trading profits, for the tax year in which the reduction occurs. The amount of that chargeable income is the smallest of the following:

(i) the said reduction in the partner's contribution to the firm/trade;
(ii) the partner's post-1 December 2004 losses (decreased by any amount previously clawed back under these recovery provisions); and
(iii) the excess (decreased by any amount previously clawed back under these recovery provisions) of the total losses claimed by the partner under the provisions at **52.13**(1) and (2) above over the partner's contribution to the firm/trade.

The amounts at (ii) and (iii) are to be computed as at the time immediately following the event giving rise to the reduction. The reference in (iii) to total losses are to losses claimed for any tax year to which restrictions of loss reliefs apply (whether under these non-active partner provisions or under **52.22** or **52.24** below). In a case where the partnership carries on more than one trade, these recovery provisions are modified accordingly for 2007/08 onwards.

The purpose test

An amount contributed as capital on or after 2 March 2007 does not count towards a partner's 'contribution to the firm' (or, before 2007/08, his 'contribution to the trade') for these purposes if the main purpose, or one of the main purposes, of making the contribution is the obtaining of a reduction in tax liability by means of any of the provisions at **52.13**(1) and (2) above. However, this does not apply to restrict any loss that derives wholly from 'qualifying film expenditure' (as defined in **52.15** below). In determining whether this purpose test applies, a capital contribution is regarded as made only when the money is paid to the partnership or, in the case of a contribution consisting of a right or other asset, when the right or asset is transferred to the partnership. An amount contributed on or after 2 March 2007 is not subject to this purpose test if it is contributed pursuant to an obligation in a contract made before that date, provided the partner has no right to vary or cancel the obligation.

Transitional

Capital contributions include capital contributed before 10 February 2004 but this must be reduced by any 'pre-announcement allowance' (see the transitional provisions at **52.13** above) and by any relief claimed under the provisions in **52.13**(1) or (2) above for losses sustained in any tax year whose basis period ended before 10 February 2004 and which either (i) would otherwise be a tax year to which the restrictions potentially apply or (ii) is a tax year at any time during which the partner carried on the trade as a limited partner or member of an LLP. Capital withdrawals are treated as made out of capital contributed on or after 10 February 2004 in priority to capital contributed earlier.

[*ITA 2007, ss 111, 113A(1)(3)(4), 114, 790–795, Sch 2 paras 31, 33–35, 142, 143; ICTA 1988, s 118ZG; FA 2005, ss 74–76; FA 2007, Sch 4 paras 2, 3, 11, 14, 17, 21; SI 2005 No 2017*].

Losses cap

[52.15] Where a trade loss is sustained by an individual for **2007/08** (but see also below under 'Transitional provisions') or any subsequent year as a partner in a firm (which includes a member of an LLP — see **52.23** below) and at any time in that tax year he is a 'non-active' partner (as in **52.13** above) or a 'limited partner' (as in **52.22** below), the quantum of relief that he can claim for that loss under:

- *ITA 2007, s 64* or its predecessor (and, consequently, *TCGA 1992, s 261B* (or, before 2007/08, *FA 1991, s 72*) against chargeable gains) (see **45.2, 45.7** LOSSES); or
- *ITA 2007, s 72* or its predecessor (see **45.9** LOSSES),

is restricted to £25,000. If the individual sustains more than one such loss in a tax year, the £25,000 cap applies to the aggregate of all such losses. The cap applies to the balance of a trade loss after applying (as appropriate) the restrictions at **52.13** above and **52.17, 52.22** and **52.24** below. The amount of the cap may be varied in future by the Treasury via statutory instrument. The cap does *not* apply:

- to so much of any loss as derives from 'qualifying film expenditure' (see below);
- to prevent relief for the loss against profits of the same trade; or
- to UNDERWRITERS AT LLOYD'S (**74**) in connection with their underwriting business.

Transitional provisions

For a tax year the basis period for which begins before, and includes, 2 March 2007 (a 'straddling basis period'), the loss sustained for the above purposes is the loss that would otherwise be eligible for the above-mentioned reliefs (disregarding the cap but applying all other restrictions) reduced by any 'pre-announcement loss'. Thus, the part (if any) of the loss for the tax year as represents a pre-announcement loss is not subject to the cap.

A '*pre-announcement loss*' is computed as follows.

(1)   Compute the profit or loss for the straddling basis period without regard to capital allowances or 'qualifying film expenditure'.

(2)   If the computation in (1) above produces a loss, time-apportion that loss to that part of the straddling period that begins with the *'relevant date'* and falls before 2 March 2007. If the individual made a capital contribution to the firm on or before the first day of the straddling basis period, the *'relevant date'* is that first day. If that is not the case but the individual made a capital contribution to the partnership at a later date but before 2 March 2007, the *'relevant date'* is the date he made the contribution (or the first such date). If the computation in (1) above does not produce a loss or no capital contribution was made before 2 March 2007, this step is irrelevant. For this purpose, a capital contribution is counted only when the money is paid to the partnership or, in the case of a contribution consisting of a right or other asset, when the right or asset is transferred to the partnership.

(3)   Compute (on a just and reasonable basis) the amount of the loss for the straddling basis period (not the loss computed in (1) above) as is attributable to capital allowances on expenditure incurred before 2 March 2007 and expenditure incurred on or after that date pursuant to an unconditional obligation (as defined) in a contract made before that date.

(4)   The pre-announcement loss is the time-apportioned figure (if any) from (2) above plus the amount (if any) in (3) above.

[*ITA 2007, ss 103, 103C, Sch 1 para 580; ITTOIA 2005, s 863(2); FA 2007, Sch 4 paras 1, 3*].

Qualifying film expenditure

Expenditure is *'qualifying film expenditure'* if it is:

*   expenditure which is deducted, in computing the partnership loss, under the statutory relief provisions for certified films, i.e. under any of *ITTOIA 2005, ss 137–142* (see **73.76 TRADING INCOME**); or
*   incidental expenditure (i.e. expenditure on management, administration or obtaining finance) that, whilst deductible other than under the statutory relief provisions for certified films, was incurred in connection with the production or the acquisition (as defined) of a film in relation to which expenditure was deducted under the said provisions.

It was made clear by the Treasury in relation to the identical definition for the purposes of **52.17** below that qualifying film expenditure does not include expenditure on distribution of a film or 'print and advertising' or production of a film as trading stock (Treasury Explanatory Notes to the 2004 Finance Bill).

The extent to which a loss derives from qualifying film expenditure and the extent to which expenditure qualifies as incidental expenditure are to be determined on a just and reasonable basis.

[*ITA 2007, s 103D; FA 2007, Sch 4 paras 9, 21*].

Non-active partners — claw-back of losses derived from exploiting a licence

[52.16] There is a potential exit charge as described below where:

(a)   an individual carries on a trade in partnership or has done so previously;

(b)   he has claimed relief under *ITA 2007, s 64, TCGA 1992, s 261B* or *ITA 2007, s 72* or under any of their predecessors (see, respectively, **45.2, 45.7, 45.9** LOSSES), against his general income or chargeable gains, for a 'licence-related loss' sustained in the first, second, third or fourth tax year in which he carried on the trade;

(c)   the tax year in which the loss was sustained was one in which he did not devote a *'significant amount of time'* (as defined in **52.13** above) to the trade;

(d)   there is a 'disposal' of any licence acquired in carrying on the trade or any right to income under any agreement 'related' to, or which contains, such a licence; and

(e)   the individual receives any consideration for that disposal (whether or not as part of a larger sum) which is not otherwise chargeable to income tax.

In (b) above, a *'licence-related loss'* means a loss derived to any extent from expenditure incurred in the partnership trade in exploiting the licence referred to in (d) above.

For the purposes of (d) above, an agreement is *'related'* to a licence if they are entered into (in whatever order) under the same arrangement. An agreement which imposes an obligation to do something (as opposed to conferring a right to do it) may itself be a licence for the purposes of these provisions; and fulfilling such obligations may therefore count as exploiting the licence.

A *'disposal'* is very widely (but not exhaustively) defined (by *ITA 2007, s 808*) for the purposes of (d) above to include, for example, a revocation of the licence, the disposal, surrender or loss of rights or income, certain changes in profit- or loss-sharing ratios and the individual's leaving the partnership (including a case where the partnership is dissolved). The disposal may be part of a larger disposal.

Consideration is not within (e) above if its receipt is an exit event under **45.16** LOSSES in relation to film-related losses.

A **chargeable event** occurs at the time the claim in (b) above is made or at the time the consideration in (e) above is received, whichever is the later. For a tax year in which one or more chargeable events occur, so much of the 'total consideration' as does not exceed the 'chargeable amount' is treated as taxable income of the individual. The *'total consideration'* is the aggregate of all the otherwise non-chargeable consideration received in that tax year *and* in previous tax years in relation to the licence in question. The *'chargeable amount'* is found by taking so much of the total consideration as does not exceed the 'net licence-related loss' and reducing that amount by so much (if any) of the consideration as has been taxed in previous years under these provisions. The *'net licence-related loss'* is the amount, computed as at the end of the tax year concerned and in relation to the licence in question, by which the individual's 'claimed licence-related losses' exceed the total of his 'licence-related profits' for all tax years. An individual's *'claimed licence-related losses'* are so much of the losses claimed by the individual under the legislation mentioned in (b) above and potentially subject to claw-back under these provisions as derive from expenditure incurred in the partnership trade in exploiting the licence. An individual's *'licence-related profits'* are so much of his profits as derive from income arising from any agreement that is related to or contains the licence. The extent to which a loss or profit is derived from any particular expenditure or income is determined on a just and reasonable basis.

[*ITA 2007, ss 790, 804–809; Sch 2 paras 150–153; FA 2004, ss 126–130; FA 2007, Sch 4 paras 18, 21*].

Non-active partners: restriction of loss reliefs derived from exploiting films

[52.17] Relief under:

(1) *ITA 2007, s 64* or its predecessor (and, consequently, *TCGA 1992, s 261B* (or, before 2007/08, *FA 1991, s 72*) against chargeable gains) (see **45.2, 45.7** LOSSES); or

(2) *ITA 2007, s 72* or its predecessor (see **45.9** LOSSES),

is restricted in the circumstances outlined below. Such relief can be given only against income consisting of profits (if any) arising from the trade in question and not against other income or against chargeable gains. This measure is aimed at avoidance schemes which apparently use generally accepted accounting practice to generate large initial losses followed by a guaranteed income stream over several years, thus producing a tax deferral. The rules do not prevent a loss from being carried forward under *ITA 2007, s 83* or its predecessor (see **45.20** LOSSES) against subsequent profits of the trade.

The restriction potentially applies to a loss sustained by an individual, in a trade consisting of or including the exploitation of films, in any tax year:

- in which he carried on the trade in partnership;
- which is the first, second, third or fourth tax year in which he carried on the trade;
- in the 'relevant period' for which he did not devote '*a significant amount of time*' to the trade (see the definitions in **52.13** above); and
- at any time during which there existed a 'relevant agreement' guaranteeing him an amount of income.

For these purposes, a *'relevant agreement'* is an agreement made with a view to the individual's carrying on the trade or in the course of his carrying it on (including any agreement under which he is, or may be, required to contribute an amount to the trade). The definition is extended to include an agreement relating to such an agreement. An agreement guarantees an amount of income if it, or any part of it, is designed to secure the receipt by the individual of that amount (or at least that amount); it is irrelevant as to *when* the income would be received.

The restriction does not apply to the extent (if any) that the loss derives from 'qualifying film expenditure' (as in **52.15** above),

[ITA 2007, ss 115, 116; ICTA 1988, ss 118ZL, 118ZM; FA 2007, Sch 4 paras 10, 15, 16, 21].

See **45.16** LOSSES for other anti-avoidance provisions concerning losses derived by individuals (whether trading in partnership or not) from the exploitation of film tax reliefs. For restriction of relief for interest on a loan used to buy into a film partnership in certain circumstances, see **43.10** INTEREST PAYABLE.

Spouse as partner

[52.18] Where a spouse is taken into partnership, perhaps to maximise the benefit of personal reliefs and rate bands, HMRC cannot challenge the apportionment of profits as they could the payment of a salary to a spouse. There is no requirement for the spouse to contribute capital or to participate in management or even to take an active part in the business. Note, however, the possible application of the settlements legislation at *ITTOIA 2005, s 624* where one spouse takes the other into partnership with a share of profits but with no requirement, or insufficient requirement, to contribute capital and/or personal time and effort (see **68.31** SETTLEMENTS). See also HMRC Business Income Manual BIM72065, which, as well as discussing the above, also covers the less frequent event of minor children being taken into partnership. 'Spouse' must be taken to include a civil partner.

Corporate partners

[52.19] For any accounting period (see below) of a partnership carrying on a trade or business for which there is at least one partner who is a UK resident company, the profits or losses are computed for corporation tax purposes in like manner as if the partnership were a UK resident company. Similarly, for any accounting period for which there is at least one partner who is a non-UK resident company, the profits or losses are computed in like manner as if the partnership were a non-UK resident company. Thus, two separate computations of profits/losses are needed if the partnership includes both resident and non-resident companies (and a third computation is needed as in **52.4** above if it also includes one or more individuals). See HMRC Company Taxation Manual CTM36510, 36520. As regards non-resident companies, the computation will cover only those profits in respect of which the company is within the charge to UK corporation tax, generally those arising from a permanent establishment within the UK.

No account is taken of any losses for any other accounting period, e.g. losses brought forward. Any interest paid or other distribution made by the partnership is not regarded as a distribution, and is thus not precluded from being deductible in computing profits. The taxable profits or allowable losses of the partnership for the accounting period (as adjusted for corporation tax purposes) are apportioned in accordance with the partnership's profit-sharing arrangements during that accounting period (subject to the corporation tax equivalent of the rules at **52.11** above). If the partnership makes qualifying charitable donations, these are similarly apportioned by reference to the accounting period in which they are paid.

The above references to an accounting period of a partnership are to a period that would be an accounting period if the partnership were a company. If the accounting period of the partnership does not coincide with the company partner's own accounting period, the company's share of profit or loss must be apportioned between those of the company's accounting periods with which the partnership accounting period partially coincides.

Changes of partners are disregarded for corporation tax purposes so long as a company that carried on the trade or business in partnership before the change continues to carry it on in partnership after the change.

For further information, see the corresponding chapter of Tolley's Corporation Tax.

[*CTA 2009, ss 1256–1262, 1265; ICTA 1988, ss 111(1), 114, 115(4); CTA 2010, Sch 1 para 691*].

Where a payment of yearly interest arising in the UK is made by, or on behalf of, a partnership of which a company is a member and is chargeable to tax under *ITTOIA 2005* or *CTA 2009* (or previously under Schedule D, Case III), it must be paid under deduction of income tax at the basic rate in force for the tax year in which the payment is made. Before 2008/09, deduction was at the savings rate. [*ITA 2007, s 874(1)(2); ICTA 1988, s 349(2)(b); FA 2008, Sch 1 paras 26, 65*].

Anti-avoidance

There are restrictions that apply in certain circumstances (where there are arrangements for transferring relief for losses etc.) on the use (a) by a partner company's losses in a partnership against its other income and (b) of a partner company's losses outside the partnership against its partnership profits. [*CTA 2010, ss 958–962; ICTA 1988, s 116; CTA 2009, Sch 1 para 86*]. See Tolley's Corporation Tax under Losses. From 17 March 2004, there are provisions aimed at schemes which allocate profit shares disproportionate to the shares of capital contributed so as to enable a company to realise profits as capital rather than as taxable income. [*FA 2004, ss 131–133 as amended*]. See Tolley's Corporation Tax under Partnerships. See **4.40** ANTI-AVOIDANCE for withdrawal of losses from a company partnership dealing in commodity futures.

Simon's Taxes. See B7.204, D7.1.

Non-resident partners and partnerships controlled abroad

[52.20] There are a number of considerations as set out below.

Partner non-UK resident

The general charging rules in **52.3–52.5** above are applied to a non-UK resident member of a trading etc. partnership in such a way as to ensure that he is taxed only on his share of profits earned in the UK (whereas UK resident partners are taxed on their share of worldwide profits). (A similar rule applies to a non-UK resident company partner.)

Individual partner's change of residence

Where a partnership trade or profession is carried on wholly or partly outside the UK and an individual partner becomes or ceases to be UK resident, he is treated for income tax purposes as ceasing to be a partner at that time and becoming a partner again immediately afterwards. His share of a loss sustained before the change may nevertheless be carried forward under *ITA 2007, s 83* and set against his share of profits after the change.

Individual partner resident but not domiciled etc. in the UK

Where a partnership trade etc. is carried on wholly or partly outside the UK and controlled and managed outside the UK, and the REMITTANCE BASIS (**61**) applies for the tax year to an individual partner who is UK resident but either not domiciled in the UK or not ordinarily resident, his share of trading etc. profits arising outside the UK is treated as 'relevant foreign income' (see **32.2** FOREIGN INCOME), so that the remittance basis may apply to it.

[*ITTOIA 2005, ss 849(3)(4), 852(6)(7), 854(5), 857; ITA 2007, Sch 1 para 579; FA 2008, Sch 7 paras 70, 81; CTA 2009, Sch 1 para 639*].

Subject to the exception above, UK-resident partners are within the charge to tax on both UK and foreign profits, regardless of where the partnership is controlled.

Double tax arrangements

In the case of *Padmore v CIR* CA 1989, 62 TC 352, it was held that, where profits of a non-UK resident partnership were exempt under the relevant double tax treaty, the profit share of a UK resident partner was thereby also exempt. This decision was, however, reversed by legislation now in *ITTOIA 2005, s 858*, to the effect that arrangements under a double tax treaty relieving partnership income from UK tax are not to affect any UK tax liability in respect of a UK resident partner's share of such income. Such a partner is similarly entitled to the corresponding share of the tax credit in respect of a UK company qualifying distribution to a share of which he is entitled. Similar provisions apply to capital gains. Where a partnership includes a company, similar provisions apply for corporation tax purposes. The provisions apply where the partnership either resides outside the UK or carries on any trade etc. the control and management of which is outside the UK. For the purposes of all these provisions, the members of a partnership are deemed to include any person who is entitled to a share of the income or capital gains of the partnership. [*ITTOIA 2005, s 858, Sch 1 paras 95, 431; FA 2008, s 58(1)(3)–(6); TIOPA 2010, Sch 8 para 70*]. These changes were deemed always to have had effect. [*F(No 2)A 1987, s 62(2)*]. An appeal based on a claim that the said legislation was ineffective in bringing about the changes described above was dismissed in *Padmore v CIR (No 2)* Ch D 2001, 73 TC 470.

Simon's Taxes. See B7.203, B7.302, D7.105, E6.135.

Loans for purchasing interest etc. in a partnership

[52.21] See **43.10** INTEREST PAYABLE as regards relief for interest on a loan to an individual for purchasing a share of or making an advance to a partnership.

Limited partnerships

[52.22] The *Limited Partnership Act 1907* allows the formation of limited partnerships, in which the liability of one or more (but not all) of the partners for the firm's debts is limited to a specified amount.

Restriction on loss reliefs

In *Reed v Young* HL 1986, 59 TC 196, it was held that the share of the loss of a limited partner for the purposes of what is now *ITA 2007, s 64* (see **45.2** LOSSES) was not restricted to the amount of her contribution to the partnership capital. The decision was, however, reversed by legislation. Where a 'limited partner' in a partnership sustains a loss in a partnership trade, relief is restricted as below.

For these purposes, a *'limited partner'* is a partner who is an individual carrying on a trade:

- as a limited partner in a limited partnership registered under *Limited Partnerships Act 1907*; or
- as a general partner in a partnership, but who is not entitled to take part in the management of the trade, and who is entitled to have any liabilities (or those beyond a certain limit) for debts or obligations incurred for the purposes of the trade met or reimbursed by some other person; or
- who carries on the trade jointly with others but, under the law of a territory outside the UK, is not entitled to take part in the management of the trade, and is not liable beyond a certain limit for debts or obligations incurred for the purposes of the trade.

The restriction applies to any excess of the loss sustained by a limited partner in respect of a trade as above for a tax year over his contribution to the firm' at the end of the basis period for that tax year. That excess may not be relieved under:

(i) *ITA 2007, s 64* or its predecessor (and, consequently, *TCGA 1992, s 261B* (or, before 2007/08, *FA 1991, s 72*) against chargeable gains) (see **45.2**, **45.7** LOSSES); or

(ii) *ITA 2007, s 72* or its predecessor (see **45.9** LOSSES),

other than against profits arising from the same trade.

Before 2007/08, the restriction operated by reference to the individual's 'contribution to the trade' as opposed to his 'contribution to the firm' (see Change 16 in Annex 1 of the Explanatory Notes to *ITA 2007*). Also, the individual's contribution was measured at the end of the tax year in which the loss was sustained (or at the time he ceased to carry on the trade if he did so during that tax year) rather than, as now, at the end of the basis period for that tax year.

If relief has previously been given under any of the provisions at (i) and (ii) above to the individual for a loss in the partnership trade in any tax year at any time during which the individual carried on the trade as a limited partner (or to which the restrictions at **52.13** above potentially apply), relief for the loss for the tax year in question is restricted by the excess of the sum of the loss for that tax year and earlier amounts so relieved, over his 'contribution to the firm'. For this purpose, the amount previously relieved is decreased by the amount of any claw-back under the recovery provisions at **52.14** above.

Partner's contribution to the firm/trade

In relation to 2007/08 onwards, the individual's *'contribution to the firm'* at any time is the aggregate of:

(a)   capital contributed and not withdrawn (excluding any capital contributed that the partner is or may be entitled to withdraw at any time he carries on the trade as a limited partner, or which he is or may be entitled to require another person to reimburse to him); and

(b)   his total share of profits from the trade (or from all trades carried on by the firm) except in so far as that share has been added to the firm's capital or the individual has received it in money or money's worth.

The amount in (a) above should include the individual's share of any profits of the firm in so far as that share has been added to the firm's capital. References to capital being withdrawn include drawing it out or receiving it back, whether directly or indirectly in either case, but do not include anything withdrawn in circumstances such that it becomes chargeable to income tax as profits of a trade. In determining total share of profits in (b) above, any losses are disregarded. All references to profits are to accounting profits, calculated in accordance with generally accepted accounting practice, and not to taxable profits (if different).

In relation to 2006/07 and earlier years, the individual's *'contribution'* to the trade at any time is the aggregate of:

•   capital contributed and not directly or indirectly withdrawn (excluding any the partner is or may be entitled to withdraw at any time he carries on the trade as a limited partner, or which he is or may be entitled to require another person to reimburse to him); and

•   any profits of the trade to which he is entitled but which he has not received in money or money's worth.

The exclusions referred to in **52.14**(a) and (b) above of amounts from a partner's contribution (i.e. where the costs of providing those amounts is or could be borne by another person) apply equally to a limited partner's contribution to the firm or his contribution to the trade for the above purposes; they apply in relation to a 'post-1 December 2004 loss' as defined in **52.14**. See also the recovery provisions at **52.14**.

The purpose test at **52.14** above applies in relation to contributions by limited partners as it does to contributions by non-active partners, with the same exceptions and by reference to the same dates.

[*ITA 2007, ss 103–106, 113A(1)(3)(4), s 114, Sch 2 para 27; ICTA 1988, ss 117, 118ZN, 118ZO; FA 2007, Sch 4 paras 2, 3, 8, 10–12, 14, 21; SI 2005 No 2017*].

See **52.15** above for a cap on the amount of relief that can be given under any of the provisions at (i) and (ii) above for a loss sustained by a limited partner for 2007/08 (subject to transitional provisions) or any subsequent year.

See generally HMRC Business Income Manual BIM72101, 72105.

Simon's Taxes. See B7.305, B7.306.

Limited liability partnerships (LLPs)

[52.23] Where a trade, profession or other business is carried on by an LLP (within *Limited Liability Partnerships Act 2000, s 1*) with a view to profit, all the activities of the LLP (i.e. anything it does) are treated as carried on in partnership by its members and not by the LLP as such. Anything done by, to or in relation to the LLP for the purposes of, or in connection with, any such activities is treated as done by, to or in relation to the members as partners, and property of the LLP is treated as held by the members as partnership property. In the *Tax Acts*, references to a firm or partnership or to members of a firm or partnership include an LLP to which the above applies and members of such an LLP, and references to a company or to members of a company do not include an LLP or members of an LLP.

Where an LLP no longer carries on any trade, profession or other business with a view to profit, the above provisions continue to apply if the cessation is only temporary or during a winding up following a permanent cessation (provided, in the latter case, that the winding up is not for reasons connected in whole or part with tax avoidance and is not unreasonably prolonged). They cease to apply on the appointment of a liquidator or (if earlier) on the making of a winding-up order by the court, or on the occurrence of any corresponding event under the law of a country or territory outside the UK.

[*ITTOIA 2005, s 863; ICTA 1988, s 118ZA; Limited Liability Partnerships Act 2000, s 10(1); ITA 2007, Sch 1 para 580*].

Similar provisions apply for capital gains tax purposes (see *TCGA 1992, s 59A, TCGA 1992, s 156A* and *TCGA 1992, s 169A*). See Tolley's Capital Gains Tax under Partnerships and Hold-Over Reliefs.

For HMRC's views on how the members of a limited liability partnership carrying on a trade or profession are to be taxed, see Revenue Tax Bulletin December 2000 pp 801–805.

Simon's Taxes. See B7.140, B7.310, B7.311.

Restrictions on LLP loss reliefs

[52.24] Where an individual sustains a loss in any tax year in a trade which he carries on as a member of an LLP, relief is restricted. The restriction applies to any excess of the loss over the member's 'contribution to the LLP' at the end of the basis period for that tax year. That excess may not be relieved under:

(i)   *ITA 2007, s 64* or its predecessor (and, consequently, *TCGA 1992, s 261B* (or, before 2007/08, *FA 1991, s 72*) against chargeable gains) (see **45.2, 45.7** LOSSES); or

(ii)   *ITA 2007, s 72* or its predecessor (see **45.9 LOSSES**),

other than against profits arising from the same trade.

If relief has previously been given under any of the provisions at (i) and (ii) above to the individual for a loss in the LLP trade in any tax year at any time during which the individual carried on the trade as a member of an LLP (or to which the restrictions at **52.13** above potentially apply), relief for the loss for the tax year in question is restricted by the excess of the sum of the loss for that tax year and earlier amounts so relieved, over his 'contribution to the LLP'. For this purpose, the amount previously relieved is decreased by the amount of any claw-back under the recovery provisions at **52.14** above.

Before 2007/08, the restriction operated by reference to the individual's 'contribution to the trade' as opposed to his 'contribution to the LLP' (see Change 16 in Annex 1 of the Explanatory Notes to *ITA 2007*). Also, the individual's contribution was measured at the end of the tax year in which the loss was sustained (or at the time he ceased to carry on the trade if he did so during that tax year) rather than, as now, at the end of the basis period for that tax year.

Individual's contribution to the LLP/trade

In relation to 2007/08 onwards, the individual's '*contribution to the LLP*' at any time (the 'relevant time') is the aggregate of:

(a)   capital contributed (excluding any capital contributed that the partner is or may be entitled to withdraw at any time he is a member of the LLP, or which he is or may be entitled to require another person to reimburse to him) less so much of it (if any) as:
  •   he has previously withdrawn; or
  •   he withdraws during the five years beginning with the relevant time; and

(b)   his liability on a winding-up of the LLP in so far as that amount is not included in (a). The amount of the liability of a member on a winding up is the amount which he is liable to contribute to the assets of the LLP in the event of its being wound up, and which he remains liable so to contribute for at least the period of five years beginning with the relevant time (or until the LLP is wound up if that happens before the end of that period).

The amount in (a) above should include the individual's share of any profits of the LLP in so far as that share has been added to the LLP's capital. The reference to profits is to accounting profits, calculated in accordance with generally accepted accounting practice, and not to taxable profits (if different). References to capital being withdrawn include drawing it out or receiving it back, whether directly or indirectly in either case, but do not include anything withdrawn in circumstances such that it becomes chargeable to income tax as profits of a trade.

In relation to 2006/07 and earlier years, the individual's '*contribution to the trade*' at any time (the 'relevant time') is the greater of the 'amount subscribed' by him and the amount of his liability on a winding-up (as in (b) above). The '*amount subscribed*' by a member is the amount contributed to the LLP as capital, less so much of that amount (if any) as:

- he has previously, directly or indirectly, drawn out or received back; or
- he so draws out or receives back during the five years beginning with the relevant time; or
- he is or may be entitled so to draw out or receive back at any time when he is a member of the LLP; or
- he is or may be entitled to require another person to reimburse to him.

The exclusions referred to in **52.14**(a) and (b) above of amounts from a partner's contribution (i.e. where the costs of providing those amounts is or could be borne by another person) apply equally to a member's contribution to the LLP or his contribution to the trade for the above purposes; they apply in relation to a 'post-1 December 2004 loss' as defined in **52.14**. See also the recovery provisions at **52.14**.

Purpose test

An amount contributed as capital on or after 2 March 2007 does not count towards a individual's 'contribution to the LLP' (or, before 2007/08, his 'contribution to the trade') for these purposes if:

- in the basis period for the tax year in which he makes the contribution he is a 'non-active' partner (as defined in **52.13** above); and
- the main purpose, or one of the main purposes, of making the contribution is the obtaining of a reduction in tax liability by means of any of the provisions at (i) and (ii) above.

However, this does not apply to restrict any loss that derives wholly from 'qualifying film expenditure' (as defined in **52.15** above). For the purpose of applying this restriction, a capital contribution is made only when the money is paid to the partnership or, in the case of a contribution consisting of a right or other asset, when the right or asset is transferred to the partnership. An amount contributed on or after 2 March 2007 is not subject to the purpose test if it is contributed pursuant to an obligation in a contract made before that date, provided the individual has no right to vary or cancel the obligation.

Unrelieved losses

Previous years' losses which, as a result of the above restrictions, have not been relieved are referred to as the member's *'total unrelieved loss'*. In each subsequent tax year in which the member continues to carry on the trade and any of the total unrelieved loss remains outstanding, the balance of the total unrelieved loss is treated for the purposes of the loss reliefs at (i) and (ii) above, and also for the purposes of applying the above restrictions, as having been made in that subsequent tax year. The amount of the total unrelieved loss remaining outstanding in a tax year is the total amount less any part of it for which relief has been given in that or any earlier tax year *other than* by virtue of this provision and any part for which relief has been given for an earlier tax year *under* this provision (or would have been so given had a claim been made).

General

The restrictions at **52.13** above also apply to members of LLPs, and do so in priority to the above restrictions where both sets of restrictions would otherwise apply to the same loss.

[*ITA 2007, ss 107–109, s 113A(2)–(4), s 114, Sch 2 paras 28, 29; ICTA 1988, ss 118ZB–118ZD, 118ZN, 118ZO; Limited Liability Partnerships Act 2000, s 10; FA 2007, Sch 4 paras 2, 3, 10, 11, 14, 21; SI 2005 No 2017*].

See **52.15** above for a cap on the amount of relief that can be given under any of the provisions at (i) and (ii) above for a loss sustained by an individual who is a 'non-active' member of an LLP for 2007/08 (subject to transitional provisions) or any subsequent year.

Investment LLPs and property investment LLPs

[52.25] Certain tax exemptions for income and gains are disapplied where they are received by a member of a 'property investment LLP' as such, and interest relief under **43.10 INTEREST PAYABLE** (loan to individual to invest in a partnership) is denied where the partnership is an 'investment LLP'. An '*investment LLP*' is an LLP (see **52.23** above) whose business consists wholly or mainly in the making of investments and the principal part of whose income is derived therefrom, and a '*property investment LLP*' is similarly defined by reference to investments in land. The status of an LLP in this respect is determined for each period for which partnership accounts are drawn up.

In the case of a property investment LLP, the exemptions disapplied include those for pension funds under *ICTA 1988, ss 613(4), 614(3)–(5)* (see **57.32 PENSION PROVISION**). Corresponding exemption from the trust rate and dividend trust rate of income tax under *ITA 2007, s 479* (accumulated or discretionary income — see **68.11 SETTLEMENTS**) is also disapplied.

[*ITA 2007, ss 399(2)(b)(6), 1004, Sch 1 para 143; ICTA 1988, s 659E*].

See generally HMRC Business Income Manual BIM72110–72155.

Simon's Taxes. See B7.312.

European Economic Interest Groupings (EEIGs)

[52.26] A European Economic Interest Grouping (EEIG) within *EEC Directive No. 2137/85* (which applies to all EEIGs established within the European Economic Area), wherever it is registered, is regarded as acting as the agent of its members. Its activities are regarded as those of its members acting jointly, each member being regarded as having a share of EEIG property, rights and liabilities, and a person is regarded as acquiring or disposing of a share of the EEIG assets not only where there is an acquisition or disposal by the EEIG while he is a member but also where he becomes or ceases to be a member or there is a change in his share of EEIG property.

A member's share in EEIG property, rights or liabilities is that determined under the contract establishing the EEIG or, if there is no provision determining such shares, it will correspond to the profit share to which he is entitled under the provisions of the contract. If the contract makes no such provision, members are regarded as having equal shares.

Where the EEIG carries on a trade or profession, the members are regarded for income tax purposes as carrying on that trade or profession in partnership.

[*ITA 2007, s 842; ICTA 1988, s 510A*].

Contributions to an EEIG from its members are not assessable on the EEIG, and the members are not assessable on distributions from the EEIG (HMRC EEIGs Manual EEIG34).

For the purposes of securing that members of EEIGs are assessed to income tax, corporation tax or capital gains tax, an inspector may, in the case of an EEIG which is registered, or has an establishment registered, in Great Britain or Northern Ireland, by notice require the EEIG to make a return containing such information as the notice may require, accompanied by such accounts and statements as the notice may require, within a specified time. In any other case, he may issue a similar notice to any UK resident member(s) of the EEIG (or if none is so resident, to any member(s)). Notices may differ from one period to another and by reference to the person on whom they are served or the description of EEIG to which they refer. Where a notice is given to an EEIG registered in Great Britain or Northern Ireland (or having an establishment registered there), the EEIG must act through a manager, except that if there is no manager who is an individual, the EEIG must act through an individual designated as a representative of the manager under the *Directive*. The return must in all cases include a declaration that, to the best of the maker's knowledge, it is correct and complete, and where the contract establishing the EEIG requires two or more managers to act jointly for the EEIG to be validly bound, the declaration must be given by the appropriate number of managers. [*TMA 1970, s 12A*]. See **63.1** RETURNS as regards the form and content of returns.

A penalty not exceeding £300 (and £60 per day for continued failure) may be imposed in the case of failure to comply with a notice under the above provisions. No penalty may be imposed after the failure has been remedied, and if it is proved that there was no income or chargeable gain to be included in the return, the maximum penalty is £100. Fraudulent or negligent delivery of an incorrect return etc. or of an incorrect declaration may result in a penalty not exceeding £3,000 for each member of the EEIG at the time of delivery. The £300 and £60 penalties are multiplied by the number of members of the EEIG (but subject to the overall £100 maximum in the circumstances described above); the daily penalty may only be imposed by the Appeal Tribunal (on an application to them by HMRC) and has effect from the day following notification of imposition. [*TMA 1970, s 98B; SI 2009 No 56, Sch 1 para 44*].

The provisions of *TMA 1970, ss 36, 40* for extended time limits for assessments in cases of loss of income tax brought about deliberately (see **6.3** ASSESSMENTS) or fraudulent or negligent conduct (see **6.4**, ASSESSMENTS) are amended so that any act or omission on the part of the EEIG or a member thereof is deemed to be the act or omission of each member of the EEIG. [*TMA 1970, s 36(4), s 40(3)*].

Simon's Taxes. See D4.501–D4.503.

Key points

[52.27] Points to consider are as follows.

- Where a partner may be subject to a restriction of loss relief based on the non-active rule, detailed records of the time spent on the firm's business should be kept throughout the period of reduced activity. These records can then form the basis of a case to support claims for loss relief.

- Where partners are restricted in the loss relief they can claim based on the partners' contributions to the firm/trade, the tax files should include an ongoing record of partners' contributions and relief given. This records should be reviewed in the light of the exclusions listed at **52.14**.

- When there is a change in the members of the partnership of the profit sharing ratio, the firm will often prepare accounts to the date of change. There is no requirement that this change is notified to HMRC for tax purposes, so the accounting date for tax purposes can remain unchanged if the firm so wishes.

- When a new partner joins the firm, if they are not already within self-assessment, a Unique Taxpayer Reference (UTR) will be needed to file the partnership return online. Changes in partnerships (and the formation of new partnerships) are now dealt with by the Central Agent Authorisation Team (CAAT) at HMRC Longbenton.

- Although partnerships between spouses and civil partners can be run on informal lines, it is sensible to have a basic partnership agreement setting out the rights and obligations of each partner, and the agreed profit sharing ratio. The agreement may assist if the partnership is subject to challenge under the settlements legislation (see **68.31 SETTLEMENTS**).

53

Pay As You Earn

| Tips, organised arrangements for sharing | 53.47 |
| Value added tax | 53.48 |

Cross-references. See also **58.11** PERSONAL SERVICE COMPANIES ETC., **65.12** SELF-ASSESSMENT.

Simon's Taxes. See E4.11.

Introduction

[53.1] Pay As You Earn (PAYE) is a system of collection of tax from salaries, wages, pensions etc. See under **27** EMPLOYMENT INCOME for provisions regarding amount chargeable, allowable deductions etc. and see **70.1** SOCIAL SECURITY AND NATIONAL INSURANCE for taxable State benefits.

PAYE is subject to regulations (the 'PAYE regulations'), which were last consolidated in the *Income Tax (Pay As You Earn) Regulations 2003 (SI 2003 No 2682)*. The main regulation-making powers are in *ITEPA 2003, s 684* and enable provision to be made for, *inter alia*, requiring persons making a payment of, or on account of, PAYE income (see **53.2** below) to deduct, at the time of payment, an amount of income tax computed in accordance with HMRC tax tables (see **53.8** below). Specific regulation-making powers enable provision to be made for acceptance by HMRC of the use of electronic means of transmission by employers (see, for example, *SI 2003 No 2682, Pt 10*). [*ITEPA 2003, s 684(2), Sch 7 para 89*].

It does not matter for the purposes of PAYE if income is wholly or partly income for a tax year other than that in which payment is made. [*ITEPA 2003, s 684(6)*].

This chapter is intended as an outline of the PAYE system. Note that the coverage at **53.16** onwards is arranged in alphabetical order by subject matter. See www.hmrc.gov.uk/paye/index.htm for index to detailed HMRC guidance. See also HMRC PAYE Online Manual.

Employee's right to make a tax return

A person within PAYE for a tax year will not necessarily be required to file a self-assessment tax return but may, by written notice, require HMRC to send him such a return for completion and filing. Notice must be given no later than the third anniversary of 31 October following the tax year (but see below). For notices given before 1 April 2010, the deadline was the fifth anniversary of 31 October following the tax year. [*ITEPA 2003, s 711; FA 2008, Sch 39 para 49; SI 2009 No 403*].

In a case where the notice under *ITEPA 2003, s 711* above relates to a tax year for which the taxpayer has not been given notice to make a return within one year after the end of the tax year, the above change in the time limit for making claims applies from 1 April 2012 rather than 1 April 2010. This only applies where tax has been *overpaid*, its purpose being to allow taxpayers extra time to take appropriate action. [*SI 2009 No 403, Art 10*].

Scope of PAYE

[53.2] PAYE income (i.e. income potentially within the scope of PAYE) embraces taxable earnings from an employment (see **27 EMPLOYMENT INCOME**), 'taxable specific income' from an employment, most taxable pension income and taxable social security income. [*ITEPA 2003, s 683*]. '*Taxable specific income*' includes, in accordance with *ITEPA 2003, s 10(3)*, payments and benefits on termination of office or employment within the special legislation at **20.4–20.6 COMPENSATION FOR LOSS OF EMPLOYMENT (AND DAMAGES)**, and, subject to the specific inclusions and exclusions in **53.3**(a) and **53.3**(e)–(g) below, amounts falling to be taxed as employment income under **69 SHARE-RELATED EMPLOYMENT INCOME AND EXEMPTIONS**.

Not all PAYE income is subject to deduction of tax under PAYE but all *payments* of such income are subject to such deduction. See **53.3** below for items not normally regarded as payments but brought specifically within the scope of PAYE deductions.

See **56.5 PENSION INCOME** as regards the application of PAYE to State pension lump sums.

Payments only part of which are PAYE income have been held to be outside the scope entirely (*CIR v Herd* HL 1993, 66 TC 29). It was held in *Paul Dunstall Organisation Ltd v Hedges* (Sp C 179), [1999] SSCD 26 that 'payment', for PAYE purposes, need not be payment in money (but see Taxation Vol 142, No 3692 p 429, 4 February 1999 for an article doubting the correctness of this decision). In *Black and others v Inspector of Taxes* (Sp C 260), [2000] SSCD 540 it was held that, where units in unit trusts were provided in satisfaction of a pre-existing legal entitlement to a payment in money or money's worth, tax should have been deducted and the units provided out of the net sum. In *Spectrum Computer Supplies Ltd v HMRC; Kirkstall Timber Ltd v HMRC* (Sp C 559), [2006] SSCD 668, the assignment of trade debts to an employee was held to be a 'payment' to which PAYE should have been applied. In *Sempra Metals Ltd v HMRC* (Sp C 698), [2008] SSCD 1062, neither payments to an employee benefit trust nor payments to a trust the beneficiaries of which were members of employees' families were held to be subject to deduction under PAYE, no transfer of cash or its equivalent having been placed unreservedly at the disposal of the employees at that point.

For arrangements for relief where both foreign tax and tax under PAYE have to be deducted from the earnings of employees sent to work abroad, see Revenue Tax Bulletin February 2003 p 999.

For the application of the *Ramsay* principle (see **4.1 ANTI-AVOIDANCE**) to a PAYE avoidance scheme, see *DTE Financial Services Ltd v Wilson* CA 2001, 74 TC 14.

Extension of scope

[53.3] The following items, not otherwise regarded as *payments* of income, are specifically brought within the scope of PAYE deductions.

(a)   Readily convertible assets — see **53.4** below.

(b)   'Non-cash vouchers' (see **27.91 EMPLOYMENT INCOME**), where the voucher is capable of being exchanged for anything which, if provided at the time the voucher is provided, would be a readily convertible asset (see **53.4** below) or the voucher would itself be such an asset but for the exclusion of non-cash vouchers from **53.4**. For PAYE purposes, the payment is deemed to be made at the later of the time its cost of provision is incurred and the time of receipt by the employee. If, however, the voucher is a 'cheque voucher' (see **27.91 EMPLOYMENT INCOME**), the payment is deemed to be made when the voucher is exchanged for money, goods or services.

(c)   'Credit tokens' (see **27.93 EMPLOYMENT INCOME**), not used to meet expenses, on each occasion they are used to obtain money or anything which, if provided at that time, would be a readily convertible asset (see **53.4** below).

(d)   'Cash vouchers' (see **27.92 EMPLOYMENT INCOME**), not used to meet expenses, when received by the employee.

(e)   A gain on the exercise of a share option where the gain is chargeable as in **69.15 SHARE-RELATED EMPLOYMENT INCOME AND EXEMPTIONS** and the shares acquired are readily convertible assets (as in **53.4** below). For PAYE purposes, the payment is deemed to be made at the time the option is exercised and in respect of the employment by reason of which the chargeable person was granted the option. The amount subject to PAYE is the best estimate of the amount chargeable to tax. Account is taken of any deduction likely to be available for employer national insurance contributions borne by the employee.

(f)   A gain on the assignment or release of a share option where the gain is chargeable as in **69.15 SHARE-RELATED EMPLOYMENT INCOME AND EXEMPTIONS** and regardless of whether or not the shares subject to the option are readily convertible assets. PAYE applies, at the time of the chargeable event, where the consideration for the assignment or release takes the form of a payment or the provision of a readily convertible asset (as in **53.4** below), and the amount subject to PAYE is as in (e) above. The application of PAYE extends to a chargeable event within **69.15**(d) (receipt of benefit in connection with the option) where the benefit takes the form of a payment or the provision of a readily convertible asset.

(g)   Any amount taxable as employment income, in relation to 'employment-related shares', by virtue of a chargeable event under **69.5** or **69.8 SHARE-RELATED EMPLOYMENT INCOME AND EXEMPTIONS**, the charge on acquisition under **69.9 SHARE-RELATED EMPLOYMENT INCOME AND EXEMPTIONS**, the charge under **69.10 SHARE-RELATED EMPLOYMENT INCOME AND EXEMPTIONS**, the charge on discharge of a notional loan under **69.11 SHARE-RELATED EMPLOYMENT INCOME AND EXEMPTIONS**, the charge on acquisition in avoidance cases under **69.11 SHARE-RELATED EMPLOYMENT INCOME AND EXEMPTIONS**, or the charge under **69.12** or **69.13 SHARE-RELATED EMPLOYMENT INCOME AND EXEMPTIONS**.

PAYE applies as if the employee were provided with PAYE income in the form of the employment-related shares by the employer on the date of the event in question (or, in the case of **69.10**, on the valuation date in question). (See **69.4** for the meaning of '*employment-related shares*' and **69.3** SHARE-RELATED EMPLOYMENT INCOME AND EXEMPTIONS for the extended meaning of '*shares*' in this connection.) The amount subject to PAYE is the best estimate of the amount chargeable to tax. Where the employment-related shares are not themselves readily convertible assets (as in **53.4** below) but the event is one involving the receipt of consideration or a benefit (whether in the form of a payment or the provision of an asset), PAYE applies to the payment or, if it is a readily convertible asset, to the provision of the asset.

If, in a case within (e), (f) or (g) above, all or part of the amount chargeable is (or is likely to be) 'foreign securities income' (within **69.19** SHARE-RELATED EMPLOYMENT INCOME AND EXEMPTIONS), the amount of the payment treated as made for PAYE purposes is limited to the best estimate that can reasonably be made of the difference between the amount that is likely to count as employment income and the amount that is likely to be foreign securities income. This applies where the shares, or as the case may be, the share option is acquired on or after 6 April 2008 (but not where shares are acquired on or after that date under an option acquired before that date). See also www.hmr c.gov.uk/shareschemes/res-dom-rules.htm and HMRC Employment-Related Securities Manual ERSM161000.

[*ITEPA 2003, ss 693–696, 698, 700, 700A, 712; FA 2008, Sch 7 paras 36–38, 80, 81*].

See **53.7** below as regards accounting for tax in respect of items within (a)–(g) above. See Revenue Tax Bulletins May 1994 p 212, February 1997 p 385 and April 2000 pp 734, 735 for practical considerations in operating PAYE in these circumstances.

Readily convertible assets

[53.4] As stated at **53.3**(a) above, 'readily convertible assets' are brought within the scope of PAYE. The amount subject to PAYE is computed on the basis of the best estimate that can reasonably be made of the amount likely to be chargeable to tax.

A '*readily convertible asset*' is an asset (defined as below) capable of being sold on a recognised investment exchange or other specified market, an asset for which 'trading arrangements' exist or are likely to come into existence, an asset consisting of rights in respect of a money debt, property subject to a warehousing regime (as defined) (or rights in respect of such property), or anything likely (without any action by the employee) to give rise to, or become, a right enabling a person to obtain (by any means at all, including the use of the asset as security for a loan) an amount of money similar to or greater than the amount expended in providing the asset (see *ITEPA 2003, s 702*).

For this purpose, 'asset' is widely defined to include any property but specifically *excludes*:

- non-cash vouchers, credit tokens and cash vouchers (but see the separate provisions at **53.3**(b)–(d) above); and

- shares acquired under an approved SAYE option scheme or CSOP scheme. In each case, the reference to shares is to ordinary shares in (i) the employer company, or (ii) a company that controls it, or (iii) a member of a consortium (as defined) that owns a company within (i) or (ii), or (iv) a company that controls a consortium member within (iii), and 'share' includes stock. In relation to shares acquired under an approved CSOP scheme, the exclusion does not apply (and PAYE therefore does apply) if the shares are acquired by exercise of an option within three years after it was granted (other than in permissible circumstances — see **69.62 SHARE-RELATED EMPLOYMENT INCOME AND EXEMPTIONS**) or more than ten years after it was granted.

The exclusions for shares apply only at the instant of their acquisition and therefore do not exclude post-acquisition events from the scope of PAYE.

For this purpose, 'trading arrangements' are arrangements which enable the recipient of the asset (or a member of his family or household) to obtain (by any means at all, including the use of the asset as security for a loan) an amount of money similar to or greater than the amount expended in providing the asset (see *ITEPA 2003, s 702(2)–(5)*).

These provisions extend to anything *enhancing* the value of an asset in which the employee (or a member of his family or household) has an interest, where the asset, with its value enhanced, would be a readily convertible asset if provided at the time of enhancement.

An asset consisting in securities within **69.3 SHARE-RELATED EMPLOYMENT INCOME AND EXEMPTIONS** is treated as a readily convertible asset in all cases unless the securities are shares (or interests therein) that are 'corporation tax deductible'. Shares (and interests) are '*corporation tax deductible*' if they are acquired by reason of employment, or pursuant to an option granted by reason of employment, and the employer company is entitled to corporation tax relief under *CTA 2009, ss 1001–1038* (see **73.59 TRADING INCOME** and, for detailed coverage, Tolley's Corporation Tax under Trading Expenses and Deductions). See *ITEPA 2003, s 702(5A)–(5D)*.

See HMRC Employment Income Manual EIM11900 for further notes on the meaning of 'readily convertible assets'. See Revenue Tax Bulletin August 1998 pp 563–573 for a detailed HMRC view of the application of PAYE to such assets. For notes on the status of shares as readily convertible assets where there is either a long stop provision or a prohibition on employees selling shares, see Revenue Tax Bulletin April 2000 pp 735, 736.

[*ITEPA 2003, ss 696, 697, 701, 702, 712*].

Deduction of tax under PAYE

[53.5] All persons making payments of PAYE income are required to deduct the appropriate amount of tax from each payment (or repay over-deductions) by reference to PAYE Tax Tables, which are so constructed that, as near as may be, tax deducted from payments to date from previous 5 April corresponds with the correct time proportion to date of the net total tax liability (after allowances and reliefs) of the recipient on that income for the year. See *Andrews v King* Ch D 1991, 64 TC 332 as regards extended definition of 'employer' and *Booth v Mirror Group Newspapers plc* QB, [1992] STC 615 as regards application of the PAYE regulations where emoluments are paid by a third party. The 'total tax' may include adjustments for any previous year and it 'may be assumed' that payments to date bear the same proportion to the total emoluments as that part of the year bears to the whole. [*ITEPA 2003, s 685; FA 2009, Sch 58 para 9(3)*]. Employers are also required to deduct national insurance contributions at the same time as PAYE tax is deducted.

There are provisions to determine the time at which a payment of income is treated as being made for PAYE purposes. These equate to the rules in **27.16 EMPLOYMENT INCOME** for determining when money earnings are to be treated as being received. [*ITEPA 2003, s 686*].

Employers may elect to operate separate PAYE schemes for different groups of employees. [*SI 2003 No 2682, Regs 98, 99; SI 2010 No 668, Regs 1, 16*].

An employer cannot shift liability to account for PAYE to enterprises that are in substance no more than payroll agents (*R (oao Oriel Support Ltd) v HMRC* CA, [2009] STC 1397).

Payments by intermediaries

Where a payment of, or on account of, PAYE income is made by an 'intermediary' of the employer (i.e. a person acting on behalf, and at the expense, of the employer or a person 'connected' (within **21 CONNECTED PERSONS**) with the employer, or trustees holding property for persons including the employee), then unless the intermediary deducts and accounts for tax under PAYE (whether or not the PAYE regulations apply to him), the employer is to be treated for PAYE purposes as having made the payment (grossed up where the recipient is entitled to the amount after deduction of any income tax). [*ITEPA 2003, ss 687, 712, 718; ITA 2007, Sch 1 para 442*]. See **53.7** below as regards the method of accounting for tax in respect of such notional payments.

Non-UK employer

Where, during any period, an employee works for a person (the 'relevant person') other than his employer, and any payment of, or on account of, his PAYE income for work done in that period is made by the employer (or by an intermediary (see above) of the employer or of the relevant person) outside the scope of PAYE, the relevant person is treated for PAYE purposes as having made the payment (grossed up where the employee is entitled to the payment after deduction of any income tax). This applies also to any items brought within the scope of PAYE under **53.3**(a)–(g) above. [*ITEPA 2003, s 689*].

Agency workers

Where an individual's remuneration under a contract falls to be treated under the agency worker rules at **27.95 EMPLOYMENT INCOME** as earnings from an employment, *ITEPA 2003, ss 687, 689* (see above) and *ss 693–702* (see **53.3**,

53.4 above) have effect as if the agency, and not the client, were the employer. However, where payment is made on behalf of, and at the expense of, the client or a person connected with him (within **21 CONNECTED PERSONS**), the rules above on payments by intermediaries have effect as if the client, and not the agency, were the employer. [*ITEPA 2003, ss 688, 718; ITA 2007, Sch 1 para 442*].

Mobile UK workforce

Where a person (the 'relevant person') has entered, or is likely to enter, into an agreement that employees of another person (the 'contractor') will work for him, but not as his employees, for a period, and it is likely that PAYE will not be deducted or accounted for in accordance with the regulations on payments made by (or on behalf of) the contractor of, or on account of, PAYE income of those employees for that period, HMRC may by notice to the relevant person direct that he apply PAYE to any payments made by him in respect of work done in that period by such employees of the contractor. So much of the payment as is attributable to the work done by each such employee is treated for this purpose as a payment of PAYE income of that employee. The notice must specify the relevant person and the contractor to whom it relates, and may similarly be withdrawn by further notice, and notices must, where reasonably practicable, be copied to the contractor. [*ITEPA 2003, s 691*].

PAYE codes

[53.6] The tax deductions to be made are those appropriate to the employee's 'PAYE code' (calculated by HMRC, and notified to both employer and employee, to take account of personal allowances and reliefs due, certain higher rate liabilities and reliefs, underpayments from earlier years, and items within the benefits code (see **27.26 EMPLOYMENT INCOME**) from which deductions cannot be made). The PAYE code generally represents the total allowances due omitting the final digit. Notice of objection to a code or revised code may be made to HMRC, with the employee having a right of appeal. See **74.4 UNDERWRITERS AT LLOYD'S** for a case concerning a request to include an anticipated underwriting loss in a PAYE code.

HMRC often include amounts of non-PAYE income in PAYE codes as a matter of administrative convenience. However, they published confirmation on 19 September 2005 that if a taxpayer informs them that he does not want such income to be included in his code, it will be removed (see www.hmrc.gov.uk/workingtogether/news/non_paye_in_code.htm). This does not apply to items such as benefits-in-kind, which do constitute PAYE income.

See, respectively, **63.3 RETURNS** and **18.3 CLAIMS** as regards the coding out of self-assessment liabilities and as regards claims for reliefs etc. given effect by adjustments to codes.

Tax offices only notify an employer if there is a change in an employee's code. Until such notification an employer will continue to use the same code from year to year.

[SI 2003 No 2682, Pt 2].

Notional payments — accounting for tax

[53.7] A '*notional payment*' of PAYE income is a payment treated as made by virtue of any of **53.3**(a)–(g) above or, with the exception of grossed up payments, under the 'payment by intermediary' rules or 'non-UK employer' rules in **53.5** above. Where a notional payment of PAYE income is made, the income tax thereon is to be deducted from any *actual* payment(s) of PAYE income to the employee made simultaneously or made subsequently but in the same PAYE month or quarter. Where, due to an insufficiency of actual payments, all or part of the tax cannot be so deducted, the employer (or person treated as such) must account to HMRC, within 14 days after the end of the PAYE month or quarter, for any tax he is required, but unable, to deduct. The amount so deducted or accounted for is treated as an amount paid by the employee in respect of his own liability to income tax. For 2003/04 onwards, it is made clear that it is so treated *at the time the notional payment is made*.

As regards any amount the employer has accounted for (being unable to deduct it from any payments made to the employee), if the employee does not make good the amount to the employer within 90 days beginning with the date on which the employer is treated as making the notional payment, the employee is treated as receiving earnings of that amount on that date.

As a result of the legislation referred to in **69.2 SHARE-RELATED EMPLOYMENT INCOME AND EXEMPTIONS** under Share options (and possible future legislation), items may fall to be treated as PAYE income with retrospective effect. If the employer is treated by virtue of any *Act* as making a notional payment before the date of Royal Assent to that *Act*:

- the employer must deduct the tax from any actual payment(s) of PAYE income to the employee made simultaneously or made subsequently but before the end of the PAYE month or quarter following that in which Royal Assent date falls;
- the employer must account to HMRC, within 14 days after the end of the PAYE month or quarter following that in which Royal Assent date falls, for any tax he is required, but unable, to deduct; and
- the employee has 90 days beginning with Royal Assent date to make good the amount accounted for by the employer. Otherwise, the employee is treated as receiving earnings of that amount on that date.

In the case of notional payments treated as made by *FA 2006*, the above rules apply by reference to a date of 6 April 2007 instead of Royal Assent date to that Act.

[ITEPA 2003, ss 222, 710; FA 2006, s 94(2)(4)(5); SI 2007 No 1081].

The PAYE regulations were amended with effect on and after 6 April 2007 to allow for payments which are retrospectively re-characterised as PAYE income — see *SI 2007 No 1077*. These deal with the recording, reporting and payment to HMRC of PAYE, both where the payments were received in a tax year which has not yet ended (an open year) and in a closed year. They provide a new statutory return to enable employers to report payments made to employees in a closed tax year; remove the requirement for electronic reporting and payment in respect of PAYE due on payments made in closed tax years and treated retrospectively as PAYE income; and provide for employers to notify affected employees of their additional taxable income and tax paid on that income. Guidance is available at www.hmrc.gov.uk/employers/retrospective. htm.

For notes on the application of the above provisions to share-related benefits, see Revenue Tax Bulletin April 2000 pp 734, 735. For a case in which directors were held to have made good an amount of tax despite the amount in question having erroneously been held in their loan account beyond the 30-day time limit, see *Ferguson and others v CIR* (Sp C 266), [2001] SSCD 1.

Simon's Taxes. See E4.1120, E4.1145.

Tax Tables

[53.8] Tax Tables show, in relation to each 'code', the cumulative 'free pay' for each weekly (or monthly) period, which is subtracted from the total gross pay down to that period leaving 'taxable pay' on which is calculated the tax due from (or refundable to) the employee.

HMRC may authorise the use of simplified tax tables for personal employees, i.e. those employed in the home to provide personal or domestic services or those employed to personally assist a disabled employer. [*SI 2003 No 2682, Regs 34, 35*].

Deductions working sheets

[53.9] Deductions working sheets (Form P11) must be kept in each fiscal year by every employer in respect of each employee for recording the employee's pay, tax and related national insurance contributions. [*SI 2003 No 2682, Reg 66*].

Under-deductions

[53.10] As to recovery from employee of tax under-deducted see *SI 2003 No 2682, Reg 72*. Recovery from employee is subject to the condition that either:

(i)   the employer made an error in good faith having taken reasonable care; or

(ii)   with the employee's acquiescence, the employer wilfully failed to deduct the correct tax.

Where (i) above applies, the employer may request HMRC to make a direction to the effect that the employer is not liable. If HMRC agree, they will issue a direction notice, subject to right of appeal by the employee within 30 days. If not, they will issue a refusal notice, subject to similar right of appeal by the employer. Where (ii) above applies, HMRC will issue a direction notice, to the effect that the employer is not liable, to the employee, who again has 30 days in which to appeal. [*SI 2003 No 2682, Regs 72A–72D; SI 2008 No 782, Reg 6*]. See also Revenue Tax Bulletin April 2004 pp 1108–1110.

Likewise, HMRC may direct that the employer be relieved of tax determined under *SI 2003 No 2682, Reg 80* (see **53.11** below), with similar right of appeal available to the employee after 11 April 2004. [*SI 2003 No 2682, Regs 81, 81A; SI 2009 No 56, Sch 2 para 102*]. See also Revenue Tax Bulletin April 2004 pp 1108–1110.

The Sp C decision in *Demibourne Ltd v HMRC* (Sp C 486), [2005] SSCD 667 confirmed that, other than in the limited circumstances above, HMRC do not have discretion to choose whether to collect tax from the employer or the employee. This meant that HMRC were obliged to seek recovery of tax from the employer even if it is tax on income which has been self-assessed by the employee. This is of particular relevance where an individual has self-assessed on the grounds that he is self-employed but is subsequently classified as an employee. Regulations to address this took effect on 6 April 2008. They apply where an employee has received a payment on which the employer should have accounted for tax under PAYE, the employer has under-accounted for the tax, and it appears to HMRC that the tax has been self-assessed by the employee or has been accounted for as a self-assessment payment on account by the employee (see **65.5 SELF-ASSESSMENT**) or as tax deducted from payments to him under the CIS and treated as paid by him (see **22.6 CONSTRUCTION INDUSTRY SCHEME**). If any one of a number of trigger events occurs on or after 6 April 2008 (and none of the trigger events occurred before that date in relation to the payment), HMRC may direct that the liability be transferred from employer to employee. The employee has a right of appeal (on limited grounds only) but the employer does not. The trigger events are:

- issue of a notice of determination by HMRC under *SI 2003 No 2682, Reg 80* (see **53.11** below) that includes the tax in question;
- receipt by HMRC of a tax return, amended tax return or error or mistake claim from the employee in which the tax is treated as having been deducted under PAYE; and
- receipt by HMRC of a letter of offer from the employer to agree an amount in settlement of his liability that includes the tax in question.

[*SI 2003 No 2682, Regs 72E–72G; SI 2008 No 782, Reg 7; SI 2009 No 56, Sch 2 paras 96–100*].

See the official guidance at www.hmrc.gov.uk/employers/demibourne-case.pdf and FAQs at www.hmrc.gov.uk/employers/faq-transfer-paye.htm.

See also *Bernard & Shaw Ltd v Shaw* KB 1951, 30 ATC 187, and for wilful failure by employer to deduct correct tax, *R v CIR (ex p Chisholm)* QB 1981, 54 TC 722, *R v CIR (ex p Sims)* QB 1987, 60 TC 398 and *R v CIR (ex p Cook)* QB 1987, 60 TC 405. In *R v CIR (ex p McVeigh)* QB 1996, 68 TC 121, accounting entries purporting to deduct tax, where tax not paid over to HMRC, were held not to constitute deduction of tax for these purposes.

For tax accounted for by employer in respect of certain notional payments, see **53.7** above.

Payment to HMRC

[53.11] The net tax deducted by the employer must be paid to HMRC within 14 days after the end of each tax month (17 days for electronic payments), except in certain cases where payment may be made quarterly. Quarterly payment applies either where simplified tax tables are in use for personal employees (see **53.8** above) or where the employer has reasonable grounds for believing that the 'average monthly amount' otherwise payable to HMRC will be less than £1,500 and chooses to pay quarterly instead of monthly. The *'average monthly amount'* is the average, for tax months falling within the current tax year, of:

(a)   amounts deducted under PAYE and the CONSTRUCTION INDUSTRY SCHEME (**22**) (disregarding any adjustment thereto in respect of working tax credit),

(b)   national insurance contributions (again disregarding working tax credit adjustments and also disregarding any contributions for which liability has been transferred to the employee), and

(c)   student loan repayments,

less any payments of:

(i)   statutory maternity pay, statutory paternity pay, statutory sick pay or statutory adoption pay; and

(ii)   (in the case of company employers only) amounts suffered by deduction under the construction industry scheme.

Where quarterly payment applies, payment to HMRC must be made within 14 days (or 17 days) after the end of the tax quarter. A tax month ends on the 5th of each month; a tax quarter ends on 5 July, 5 October, 5 January and 5 April.

[*SI 2003 No 2682, Regs 2, 68–71; SI 2006 No 777, Reg 3*].

If no tax has been paid within that 14 days (or 17 days where applicable), or HMRC are not satisfied that any payment made satisfies the employer's liability, HMRC, if they are not aware of the amount the employer is liable to pay, can give notice requiring a return within 14 days showing the amount of that liability. [*SI 2003 No 2682, Reg 77*]. HMRC have powers to determine to the best of their judgement the amount of tax payable where it appears to them that tax may have been payable under these regulations but has not been paid. The determination applies as if it were an assessment to tax. [*SI 2003 No 2682, Reg 80; SI 2008 No 782, Reg 9; SI 2009 No 56, Sch 2 para 101; SI 2010 No 668, Regs 1(3), 3*]. See **53.10** above as regards recovery of tax from employee in certain cases.

Interest on overdue tax

Interest is charged at the prescribed rate (as in **42.2 INTEREST AND SURCHARGES ON OVERDUE TAX**) on tax unpaid by 19 April in the tax year following that for which it was payable (22 April for electronic payments) whether or not it is the subject of a determination. Interest on overpaid tax runs at the prescribed rate (see **41.1 INTEREST ON OVERPAID TAX**) from the 14th day after the end of the year in respect of which the tax was paid (or, if later, from the date of payment of the tax). [*ITEPA 2003, s 684(2); SI 2003 No 2682, Regs 82, 83, Sch 1 para 23; SI 2008 No 782, Reg 10*]. In either case, such interest is paid without deduction of tax and is not taken into account in computing income for tax purposes. [*ITEPA 2003, s 684(2)*]. Cheque payments are normally treated as made on the day of receipt by HMRC (and see **54.2 PAYMENT OF TAX**). [*SI 2003 No 2682, Reg 219*].

Interest may also arise in the case of late paid or overpaid Class 1 or 1A national insurance contributions (see Tolley's National Insurance Contributions).

An employer is not entitled to charge HMRC with costs of PAYE collection (*Meredith v Hazell* QB 1964, 42 TC 435). Where money is stolen, the employer is liable (*A-G v Antoine* KB 1949, 31 TC 213).

Penalty for late in-year payments of PAYE

FA 2009 introduces a new penalty for late in-year payments of PAYE. This applies to payments due in 2010/11 onwards. See **53.14** below.

Funding from HMRC

Normally, if an employer needs to make a tax refund to one or more employees, it reduces his monthly or quarterly payment to HMRC of amounts within (a) to (c) above. If the refunds exceed the payment due to HMRC, the excess can be used to reduce subsequent monthly or quarterly payments or the employer can apply to HMRC for funding to cover it. The rules that apply to funding, and the steps involved in claiming it, are explained at www.hmrc.go v.uk/employers/payefunding.htm.

Mandatory electronic payment for 'large employers'

For 2004/05 and subsequent years, employers who at the 'specified date' were 'large employers' (i.e. they were paying PAYE income to at least 250 recipients) are required, upon receipt of an e-payment notice issued by HMRC by 31 December in the tax year preceding the year of payment, to use an approved method of electronic payment of PAYE liabilities. An appeal may be made (within 30 days) against an e-payment notice on the grounds that the employer is not a 'large employer'. '*Specified dates*' are 19 October 2008 for 2009/10 and 18 October 2009 for 2010/11. A system of default surcharges, ranging from 0.17% to 0.83% of the annual net PAYE liability, applied for 2009/10 and earlier years for persistent failure to make payments in full by the due dates; a person is not in default if he has a reasonable excuse (excluding inability to pay). *FA 2009, s 108* (no surcharge to be imposed where taxpayer has entered into a 'Time to Pay' agreement — see **42.3 INTEREST AND SURCHARGES ON OVERDUE TAX**) applies to these surcharges where the agreement is made on or after 13 August 2009. Appeals may be made against default notices and surcharge notices.

Default surcharges are dropped for 2010/11 onwards in view of the introduction of the late payment penalties at **53.14** below. For 2011/12 onwards, the requirement for HMRC to issue e-payment notices is dropped, and all large employers will be required to make payments electronically. The specified date will be 31 October for each tax year.

[*FA 2003, ss 204, 205; FA 2007, s 94; SI 2003 No 2682, Regs 190, 191, 198A, 199–204; SI 2006 No 777, Regs 4, 5; SI 2009 No 56, Sch 2 para 110; SI 2009 No 2029, Regs 1, 4; SI 2010 No 466, Art 4; SI 2010 No 668, Regs 1, 5–7; Revenue Directions 16 July 2008, 13 August 2009*]. See also Revenue Tax Bulletin February 2004 p 1085 and HMRC guidance available at www.hmrc.gov.uk/employers/doitonline/index.htm.

PAYE returns

[53.12] After the end of each tax year the employer must, in respect of each employee for whom he was required to maintain a deductions working sheet, send the following to HMRC.

(a)   Not later than 19 May:
  (i)   an End of Year Return P14;
  (ii)   a declaration on form P35 (including a nil return where appropriate).
  [*SI 2003 No 2682, Reg 73*].
(b)   Not later than 6 July, annual returns of other earnings on form P9D and, for 'P11D employees' only, form P11D. '*P11D employees*' are employees who are not in 'lower-paid employment' (see **27.26 EMPLOYMENT INCOME**) and all directors (other than those excluded under **27.26**). Particulars (including, where applicable, amounts) of the following are required for *any* employee or director:
  • earnings received otherwise than in money, whether from the employer or a 'related third party';
  • payments made on the employee's behalf (and not repaid), whether by the employer or a 'related third party';
  • non-cash vouchers and credit tokens falling to be treated as earnings (see **27.91, 27.93 EMPLOYMENT INCOME**), whether provided by the employer or a 'related third party';
  • any tax on 'notional payments' of PAYE income which has not been made good by the employee (see **53.7** above);
  • living accommodation provided for the employee or his family (see **27.59** *et seq.* **EMPLOYMENT INCOME**), whether by the employer or a 'related third party';
  • any removal benefits or removal expenses in excess of the qualifying limit (see **27.71 EMPLOYMENT INCOME**);
  • whether any earnings relating to business entertainment will be disallowed in computing the employer's profits (see **73.72 TRADING INCOME, 27.24 EMPLOYMENT INCOME**).
  Particulars of the following are additionally required for a P11D employee:
  • expenses payments, whether made by the employer or a 'related third party';

- sums put at the employee's disposal, whether by the employer or a 'related third party', and paid away by the employee;
- details (including amounts) of taxable benefits provided (see **27.26** *et seq.* **EMPLOYMENT INCOME**), whether by the employer or a 'related third party'.

For the above purposes, a *'related third party'* is any person who makes payments or provides benefits to an employee by arrangement with the employer, which includes the employer's guaranteeing or in any way facilitating the payments etc.

For the use of substitute forms P11D, see Revenue Tax Bulletin August 1996 p 334.

[*SI 2003 No 2682, Regs 85–89*].

Supplementary returns (form P38A) must be submitted with form P35 for all employees for whom a deductions working sheet is not required. [*SI 2003 No 2682, Reg 74*].

See **55.21 PENALTIES** as regards a period of grace for submission of returns under (a) above.

A return by the employer is also required not later than 6 July following the end of the tax year in respect of any employee (or former employee) awarded termination payments and other benefits within *ITEPA 2003, ss 401–416* (see **20.5 COMPENSATION FOR LOSS OF EMPLOYMENT (AND DAMAGES)**) totalling more than £30,000 in the tax year. [*SI 2003 No 2682, Regs 91–93, 96*].

As regards information to be supplied by employers to employees, see **65.12 SELF-ASSESSMENT**.

Value added tax paid, if any (and whether or not recoverable), must be included in amounts of expenses and benefits. (HMRC SP A6). See also **53.48** below.

Returns are also required under **53.19** below (cars provided for private use).

See **63.16 RETURNS** for employers' returns generally.

Mandatory e-filing

The Commissioners for HMRC have extremely wide powers to make regulations requiring the use of electronic communications for the delivery of information required or authorised to be delivered under tax legislation. [*FA 2002, ss 135, 136*]. The Government adopted a three-stage move towards e-filing of PAYE returns (i.e. the information required at (a) above), as follows.

(A) Employers with 250 or more employees are required to file electronically from 2004/05.

(B) Employers with 50 or more employees are required to file electronically from 2005/06.

(C) Employers with less than 50 employees are required to file electronically from 2009/10, with an incentive for earlier adoption.

(Revenue/C&E Budget Press Release 2/02, 17 April 2002).

Under the regulations giving effect to (A)–(C) above, the mandatory e-filing requirement applies for 2004/05 to employers who at 26 October 2003 were 'large employers' (i.e. they were paying PAYE income to at least 250 recipients) and who received an e-filing notice issued by HMRC no later than 31 December 2003. Similar provisions apply for subsequent years but by reference to employers who at the specified date (to be announced by HMRC Direction, e.g. 29 October 2006 for 2007/08 and 28 October 2007 for 2008/09) were 'large or medium-sized employers' (i.e. they were paying PAYE income to at least 50 recipients) and who received an e-filing notice issued by HMRC no later than 31 December preceding the tax year in question. An appeal may be made (within 30 days) against an e-filing notice on the grounds that the employer does not fall into the specified category. Penalties for failure to comply range from £100 to £3,000 (£600 to £3,000 for 2008/09 and earlier years) depending upon the number of employees required to be included in the returns, the maximum penalty applying where there are 1,000 or more. Appeals may be made against penalty determinations on specified grounds including reasonable excuse throughout the default period.

The following employers are exempted from mandatory e-filing:

- practising members of religious societies or orders whose beliefs are incompatible with electronic communication;
- (for 2009/10 onwards) employers authorised to use the simplified PAYE scheme for personal employees (see **53.8** above);
- (for 2009/10 onwards) care and support employers, i.e. individuals employing a person to provide domestic or personal services at or from the employer's home where the recipient of the services, being the employer or a member of his family, is elderly, disabled or infirm; and
- any employer paying PAYE income to less than 50 recipients who ceases paying PAYE income in 2009/10 and files his PAYE return by the end of that tax year.

[*SI 2003 No 2682, Regs 190, 191, 205–210C; SI 2006 No 777, Reg 4; SI 2007 No 2969, Regs 1, 19, 20; SI 2009 No 2029, Regs 1, 5–15; SI 2010 No 668, Regs 1, 4, 8–12; Revenue Directions 21 October 2003, 22 September 2006, 23 July 2007*].

Although in-year PAYE returns can be filed online, HMRC do not insist on electronic filing where the returns cover the part of the tax year ending with the date of an insolvency event (e.g. liquidation, receivership, administration or bankruptcy); no online filing penalty will be charged in these circumstances provided a late filing penalty (see **55.21 PENALTIES**) does not fall to be charged (Revenue Tax Bulletin October 2004 p 1158).

Regulations were also made to give effect to the incentives referred to at (C) above. These are available to employers who at a specified date (announced by HMRC Direction) preceding the tax year in question were 'small employers' (i.e. they were paying PAYE income to less than 50 recipients) or who first started paying PAYE income after that date. The payments receivable were £250 for each of 2004/05 and 2005/06, £150 for 2006/07, £100 for 2007/08 and £75 for 2008/09. These were not chargeable to tax. Appeals were possible (within 30 days of the notice) against an officer's decision not to make an incentive payment or to recover a payment already made. There were provisions to deny an incentive payment where a small employer was established, employed employees or made payments of PAYE income, wholly or mainly for the purpose of obtaining an income tax, corporation tax or national insurance advantage, obtaining an incentive payment or avoiding any mandatory obligation to file any return electronically (see Revenue Tax Bulletin April 2005 p 1192). [*SI 2003 No 2495; SI 2006 No 777, Regs 1, 6; SI 2009 No 56, Sch 2 para 91; SI 2009 No 1890, Regs 1, 3(7)(8)*].

See *ZXCV 1 Ltd and others v HMRC* (Sp C 706), [2008] SSCD 1171 for an unsuccessful attempt to obtain incentive payments for 500 newly-incorporated companies the sole director of which was the appellant's wife.

Employers can either use incentive payments to reduce a subsequent PAYE liability or claim a repayment (Revenue Tax Bulletins February 2004 p 1085, April 2005 pp 1191, 1192).

See also Revenue Tax Bulletins February 2003 pp 995, 996, February 2004 pp 1084, 1085, April 2005 pp 1189–1192 and HMRC guidance available at www.hmrc.gov.uk/employers/doitonline/index.htm.

See **53.25** below as regards 'PAYE in-year online'.

Form P60

[**53.13**] Employers must give each employee annually a certificate (form P60) showing his total taxable earnings for the year and total tax deducted therefrom, his appropriate code, national insurance number, and the employer's name and address etc. [*SI 2003 No 2682, Reg 67*]. This certificate is produced automatically as the third sheet of the End of Year Return, or a substitute form P60 may be used or other document approved by HMRC. See **65.12** SELF-ASSESSMENT for the time limit for supplying form P60 and for other information to be supplied by employers to employees.

For 2010/11 onwards, employers may, if they wish, provide form P60 electronically. [*SI 2003 No 2682, Reg 211; SI 2010 No 668, Regs 1(3), 13*].

Penalties

[**53.14**] See also **55.10**, **55.21** PENALTIES and *TMA 1970, ss 98, 98A*. See www.hmrc.gov.uk/leaflets/ecfs4.pdf.

Penalty for late in-year payments

FA 2009 introduces a new penalty for late in-year payments of PAYE. This applies for 2010/11 onwards, i.e. for tax months or quarters beginning on or after 6 April 2010. The person (P) who is liable to make payments of PAYE tax to HMRC will be liable to a penalty of an amount determined by reference to the number of defaults he makes during a tax year. P makes a default if he fails to fully pay an amount of tax due under the PAYE regulations on or before the date on which it becomes due and payable (see **53.11** above). However, the first such failure during a tax year does not count as a default.

If P makes one, two or three defaults during a tax year, he is liable to penalty of 1% of the total amount of those defaults. If he makes four, five or six defaults during a tax year, the penalty is 2% of the total amount. For seven, eight or nine defaults, the penalty is 3%, and for ten or more defaults in one tax year it is 4% of the total amount of the defaults. The amount of a default is the amount which P fails to pay on or before the due date. If any tax remains unpaid six months after a penalty date (i.e. the day following the due date) in relation to that tax, P is liable to a penalty of 5% of the unpaid amount. If any of that tax is still unpaid after a further six months, P is liable to a further penalty of 5% of the unpaid amount. P is not liable to a penalty in relation to any failure or action in respect of which he has been convicted of a criminal offence.

[FA 2009, s 107, Sch 56 paras 1(4), 5–8; SI 2010 No 466].

The above penalty must be paid within 30 days beginning with the day on which the notice of assessment of the penalty is issued. There are provisions for HMRC to reduce the penalty in special circumstances, to suspend the penalty during the currency of a 'Time to Pay' agreement (see **54.8 PAYMENT OF TAX**) and to assess the penalty, and for P to appeal against the imposition or amount of the penalty. No penalty is due if P shows he had a reasonable excuse for late payment; an insufficiency of funds is not a reasonable excuse unless attributable to events outside P's control. [FA 2009, Sch 56 paras 9–16].

For the first year, it is HMRC's intention to charge the penalties only after the tax year has ended; the first penalty notices will be issued in April/May 2011.

See FAQs at www.hmrc.gov.uk/employers/paye-penalties-faqs.htm.

Senior accounting officers of large companies

FA 2009, s 93, Sch 46 provide that, for financial years beginning on or after 21 July 2009, senior accounting officers of large companies are required, subject to penalties, to take reasonable steps to ensure that the company and its subsidiaries (if any) establish and maintain 'appropriate tax accounting arrangements'. 'Appropriate tax accounting arrangements' means accounting arrangements that enable the company's tax liabilities to be calculated accurately in all material respects, and this includes its PAYE liabilities. A large company for this purpose is broadly one with turnover of more than £200 million or a balance sheet total of more than £2 billion in the financial year prior to the one in question. The turnover and balance sheet totals of any other companies in the same group are taken into account also. See Tolley's Corporation Tax under HMRC — Administration for details of these provisions. For HMRC guidance, see www.hmrc.gov.uk/largecompanies/duties-sen-acc-officer.pdf.

PAYE settlement agreements

[53.15] HMRC and an employer used to be able to make a non-statutory agreement, known as an 'annual voluntary settlement', whereby the employer settles by way of lump sum an amount approximating to the tax otherwise payable by his employees on items covered by the settlement, which will be minor, incidental benefits and expenses payments, e.g. reimbursement of telephone expenses, late night taxis home and benefits shared between a number of employees. The employer is then relieved of including such benefits and expenses in the returns at **53.12**(b) above and the employees do not have to declare them or include them in their total income.

A statutory framework for such arrangements, known as 'PAYE settlement agreements', is established by regulations provided for by *ITEPA 2003, ss 703–707*. See *SI 2003 No 2682, Regs 105–117* and HMRC Statement of Practice SP 5/96 for the detailed rules governing such agreements and the scope of payments and benefits covered. These are described in some detail in an article in the Revenue Tax Bulletin December 1996 pp 365–369. Separate legislation enables national insurance contributions to be comprised in such settlements.

See also the guidance at www.hmrc.gov.uk/guidance/paye-settlements.htm.

Simon's Taxes. See E4.11110.

Annual payments

[**53.16**] Tax on certain periodic redundancy and other similar payments by a former employer which are strictly chargeable to tax as annual payments, and payable under deduction of basic rate tax, may, where it is convenient and with the agreement of the parties and the inspector, be dealt with instead under PAYE (Revenue Tax Bulletin February 1995 p 196).

Annuities

[**53.17**] Annuities under approved retirement annuity contracts are not within PAYE before 2006/07. Where such a retirement annuity contract became a registered pension scheme on 6 April 2006 (see **57.3 PENSION PROVISION**), this situation continued for 2006/07 only. From 6 April 2007, such annuities are brought within PAYE. [*FA 2004, Sch 36 para 43*]. (Note that this is an exception to the general rule (*ITEPA 683(3)*) whereby pensions and annuities from registered pension schemes are within PAYE from 6 April 2006.) See HMRC Tax Bulletin October 2006 pp 1315, 1316 for an article on the migration of retirement annuities into the PAYE system for 2007/08 onwards. In this article, HMRC state that if, as a result of the migration process, it comes to light that tax has been underpaid before 2007/08 on a retirement annuity, they will not take action to recover the underpayment except where fraud has occurred.

For 2006/07 onwards, annuities under an occupational pension scheme that is not a registered pension scheme are also brought within PAYE (see **56.2**(e) **PENSION INCOME**).

See also **53.40** below (small pensions).

Annuities paid out of superannuation funds approved under *ICTA 1970, s 208* which have not sought approval under subsequent legislation and to which no contributions have been made since 5 April 1980 continue to be taxable pension income and subject to PAYE. This has no direct application on and after 6 April 2006, but if the fund became a registered pension scheme on that date (see **57.3 PENSION PROVISION**) pensions will be subject to PAYE in the normal way. [*ITEPA 2003, ss 590–592, 594, 683(3)*].

Benefits in kind

[53.18] Benefits in kind constitute PAYE income (see **53.2** above) but are not payments and are not, therefore, directly subject to PAYE deductions. They are usually dealt with by set-off against allowances in arriving at an employee's PAYE code (see **53.6** above and *R v Walton Commrs (ex p Wilson)* CA, [1983] STC 464). However, see **53.3**(a)–(g) above for items not normally regarded as payments but brought within the scope of PAYE deductions.

Cars provided for private use

[53.19] See **27.33 EMPLOYMENT INCOME** for computation of the charge. A return on form P46 (Car) is required no later than 28 days after a tax quarter (see **53.11** above) if, during that quarter, a company car on which a benefits charge will arise is newly provided to an employee or ceases to be provided to an employee (without being replaced), or an employee to whom a car is provided becomes a P11D employee (see **53.12**(b) above). The form asks for specified particulars required to compute the benefits charge. [*SI 2003 No 2682, Reg 90; SI 2009 No 588, Regs 1, 9*].

Charitable donations

[53.20] Such donations are an allowable deduction for PAYE purposes where made under an approved payroll giving scheme. See **16.20 CHARITIES**.

Collection of small tax debts via PAYE

[53.21] With effect on and after 21 July 2009, HMRC are given the power to collect small tax debts through the PAYE system, thus allowing their debtors to spread their payments. Their general aim is to secure immediate payment of debts in full or, where this is not possible, to set up a 'Time to Pay' agreement (see **54.8 PAYMENT OF TAX**). If neither of these options is feasible, they would consider collecting smaller debts through PAYE as one of a number of remedies available to them as a creditor. If the debtor does not want to pay in this way, HMRC will expect him to make other arrangements for payment. If no such arrangements were forthcoming, HMRC will be able to collect debts in this way at its own option. However, no more than £2,000 can be collected in any tax year without the taxpayer's consent. The right to object to collecting underpayments of income tax and capital gains tax under self-assessment where the due date has not already passed will not be disturbed, and neither will the taxpayer's right to appeal against his tax code. [*ITEPA 2003, s 684(2)(3A)(3B)(7AA)(7AB); FA 2009, Sch 58 paras 1–7*].

Contributory employment and support allowance

[53.22] Contributory employment and support allowance (see **70.1** SOCIAL SECURITY AND NATIONAL INSURANCE) was brought within PAYE with effect on and after 27 October 2008 when the allowance was introduced. The Department for Work and Pensions (or in NI, the Department for Social Development) maintain a record of the claimant's cumulative pay and tax in the tax year and of any payments of taxable allowance made to him. At the end of the claimant's period of claim (or at the end of the tax year, if earlier) the Department calculate his tax position, make any repayments of tax due to him and notify the details to him and to HMRC. [*SI 2003 No 2682, Regs 184A–184S; SI 2008 No 2601; SI 2009 No 2029, Regs 1, 3; SI 2010 No 668, Regs 1, 17*].

Director's remuneration

[53.23] Credit of remuneration voted to a director to an account with the company constitutes 'payment' for PAYE purposes. See generally ICAEW Technical Release TAX 11/93, 9 July 1993, as regards tax implications of payments to directors. [*ITEPA 2003, s 686(1)*]. See **53.5** above and **27.16** EMPLOYMENT INCOME.

Domestic workers and nannies

[53.24] See HMRC PAYE Manual PAYE20085 for the simplified PAYE deduction scheme for taxpayers employing domestic workers or nannies. See also **53.8** above and www.hmrc.gov.uk/simple_deduction/index.htm.

Employee arriving

[53.25] A new employee should produce a form P45 and the employer should start a Deductions Working Sheet from the particulars on that form and send Part 3 to the tax office. If a form P45 (or other code authorisation) is not produced, the employer should complete form P46, ask the employee to sign the appropriate certificate, and send to the tax office on making the first payment exceeding the lower earnings limit for Class 1 NIC purposes (for 2008/09 onwards, previously the PAYE threshold — see **53.28** below). A Deductions Working Sheet must be prepared and tax deducted in accordance with the emergency code or basic rate code as appropriate. [*SI 2003 No 2682, Regs 40–53; SI 2007 No 2969, Regs 1, 4–10; SI 2009 No 588, Regs 1, 3*].

In 2009/10 onwards (for employers with at least 50 employees) and in 2011/12 onwards (for all remaining employers), forms P45 and P46 must be submitted to HMRC online (known as 'PAYE in-year online' — see www.hmrc.gov.uk/e mployers/doitonline/index.htm for details). Penalties for failure to comply range from £100 to £3,000 depending upon the number of items in each quarter of the tax year to which the failure relates, the maximum penalty applying where the number is 1,000 or more. No penalty applies if the said number of items is fewer than six for 2009/10 and 2010/11 or fewer than three for 2011/12 and 2012/13. No penalties were chargeable at all in relation to the first three quarters of 2009/10. Appeals may be made against penalty determinations on specified grounds including reasonable excuse throughout the default period. The following employers are exempted from mandatory PAYE in-year online for 2011/12 onwards:

- practising members of religious societies or orders whose beliefs are incompatible with electronic communication;
- employers authorised to use the simplified PAYE scheme for personal employees (see **53.8** above); and
- care and support employers, i.e. individuals employing a person to provide domestic or personal services at or from the employer's home where the recipient of the services, being the employer or a member of his family, is elderly, disabled or infirm.

[*SI 2003 No 2682, Regs 205–207, 210, 210B, 210BA, 210C; SI 2007 No 2969, Regs 1, 19, 20; SI 2010 No 668, Regs 1(4), 8–12*].

Employee dying

[53.26] On death of employee, the employer must forthwith send all parts of completed form P45 to HMRC. [*SI 2003 No 2682, Regs 38, 39*].

Employee leaving

[53.27] Employee leaving must be given certificate (form P45) by former employer showing code, pay and tax deducted to date of leaving (split if more than one employment). [*SI 2003 No 2682, Reg 36*]. This produced to new employer [*SI 2003 No 2682, Reg 40*] ensures continuity and provides data for commencement of new deduction working sheet.

Payments to employees who have left and which are not included in P45 must have tax deducted at the basic rate. [*SI 2003 No 2682, Reg 37*].

Employee retiring

At retirement on pension of an employee, no P45 need be completed and tax must be deducted from the pension on a non-cumulative basis. The employer/pension payer must then complete a 'retirement statement' (to be redesignated as form P46(Pen) for 2009/10 onwards) containing specified details and send it to HMRC with a copy to the pensioner. [*SI 2003 No 2682, Regs 36(3), 55; SI 2007 No 2969, Regs 1, 12*].

In 2009/10 onwards (for employers with at least 50 employees) and in 2011/12 onwards (for all remaining employers), form P46(Pen) must be submitted to HMRC online (known as 'PAYE in-year online' — see www.hmrc.gov.uk/emp loyers/doitonline/index.htm for details and see **53.25** above as regards penalties and exemptions).

Exemption

[53.28] Where a new employee has no other employment and rate of payment is less than a weekly or monthly rate equal to $^1/_{52}$nd or $^1/_{12}$th respectively of the personal allowance (the 'PAYE threshold'), no tax is deductible. [*SI 2003 No 2682, Reg 9*].

Expense payments etc.

[53.29] Such payments must (except as regards pure reimbursement to subordinate employees of specific outlay incurred) be included with pay and taxed with it, unless given a dispensation by HMRC under *ITEPA 2003, s 65* (or corresponding earlier legislation — see *ITEPA 2003, Sch 7 para 15*).

Free of tax payments, awards etc.

[53.30] For remuneration payable free of tax, taxed incentive awards etc., see **27.75 EMPLOYMENT INCOME**.

HM Forces

[53.31] Prior to 6 April 2009, special rules applied to members of the reserve and auxiliary forces with the result that they would generally have tax deducted from pay at the basic rate. For 2009/10 onwards, those rules are abolished, and standard PAYE applies to members of those forces. [*SI 2003 No 2682, Regs 122–133; SI 2009 No 588, Regs 1, 10*].

Holiday pay funds

[53.32] Holiday pay paid by a holiday pay fund is taxed at the basic rate at the time of payment. [*SI 2003 No 2682, Regs 134, 136*].

Incapacity benefit

[53.33] Such benefit, where taxable (see **70.1 SOCIAL SECURITY AND NATIONAL INSURANCE**), is brought within PAYE by *SI 2003 No 2682, Regs 173–180*.

Jobseekers allowance

[53.34] Jobseekers allowance (so far as taxable, see **70.1 SOCIAL SECURITY AND NATIONAL INSURANCE**) is brought within PAYE by *SI 2003 No 2682, Regs 148–172*. The Department for Work and Pensions (or in NI, the Department for Social Development) maintain a record of the claimant's previous cumulative pay and tax in the tax year and of any taxable benefit paid to him. At the end of the claimant's period of benefit claim (or at the end of the tax year, if earlier) the Department calculate his tax position, make any repayments of tax due to him and notify the details to him and to his tax office. See also **53.45** below.

Local councillors' attendance allowances

[53.35] The councillor may opt for deduction of basic rate tax from such allowances (net of an appropriate amount in respect of allowable expenditure) rather than deduction by reference to the appropriate code. [*SI 2003 No 2682, Regs 118–121*].

Maternity, paternity and adoption pay

[53.36] Such pay is taxable social security income. [*ITEPA 2003, ss 658, 660*].

Overseas matters

[53.37] Where a non-UK resident employee, or an employee who is not ordinarily resident in the UK, works (or is likely to work) both inside and out of the UK in a tax year, and it appears to HMRC that some of the income paid to the employee is PAYE income and some may not be, HMRC may, on application by the employer or a person designated by the employer, by notice give a direction (a '*Section 690 direction*') that only a proportion of any payment made in the year is to be dealt with under PAYE. If no direction is made, the whole of any payment must be so dealt with. The direction may similarly be withdrawn (with at least 30 days' notice) by a further notice. These provisions apply only to payments made by the employer and to payments by a person acting on the employer's behalf and at the expense of the employer or a person connected with him (within **21 CONNECTED PERSONS**). They are without prejudice to any income assessment on the employee and to any rights to repayment, or obligations to repay, income tax over- or underpaid. The provisions enable direction to be given, where both these provisions and those of *ITEPA 2003, s 689* (see **53.5** above under Non-UK employer) apply, on application made by whoever is the 'relevant person' for the purposes of *section 689*. For 2008/09 onwards, in a case where the employee is UK resident but not ordinarily resident, HMRC may for the above purposes treat the employee as being within **61.2(1) REMITTANCE BASIS** even if no claim for remittance basis has been made, thus allowing the Section 690 directions procedure to remain available in such cases.

[*ITEPA 2003, ss 690, 718; ITA 2007, Sch 1 para 442; FA 2008, Sch 7 paras 35, 81*].

See **Simon's Taxes E4.1182.**

For a brief article on the correct application of the above provisions, and the relaxation of strict PAYE rules in respect of certain short-term business visitors, see Revenue Tax Bulletin February 2003 pp 998, 999 and HMRC PAYE Online Manual PAYE82000.

See *SI 2003 No 2682, Reg 57* as regards pensions.

A non-UK resident employer must operate PAYE in respect of any taxable earnings of his employees if he has a tax presence in the UK (*Clark v Oceanic Contractors Incorporated* HL 1982, 56 TC 183). See also *Bootle v Bye; Wilson v Bye* (Sp C 61), [1996] SSCD 58 and HMRC PAYE Online Manual PAYE81610. See also **53.5** above as regards payments by intermediaries.

PAYE threshold

[53.38] See **53.28** above.

Pension contributions (the 'net pay arrangement')

[53.39] Employees' allowable pension contributions deducted from salary (see *SI 2003 No 2682, Reg 3*) are also allowable for the purposes of computing PAYE deductions (though not for the purposes of computing national insurance contributions).

Pensions (small)

[53.40] According to a statement on the HMRC website on 3 June 2008 (see www.hmrc.gov.uk/pensionschemes/taxation-small-pensions-note.htm), some small private pensions paid by employer schemes and insurance companies had still not been properly brought within PAYE. In these cases it was anticipated that the pension would be brought within PAYE in 2009/10, and any underpayment of tax for 2008/09 would normally be collected in 2010/11 via the PAYE coding. Other than in exceptional circumstances (e.g. cases involving deliberate avoidance) pensioners will not normally be required to pay any tax which should have been paid on their pension before April 2008.

Records

[53.41] Wages sheets, deductions working sheets, certificates, documents relating to P11D and P9D information and other records required to be maintained under the PAYE regulations (and not required to be sent to HMRC) must be kept and preserved by the employer for at least three years after the end of the year to which they relate. [*SI 2003 No 2682, Reg 97; SI*

2009 No 588, Regs 1, 6]. See www.hmrc.gov.uk/leaflets/ecfs1.pdf (employers and contractors — reviewing your records) or www.hmrc.gov.uk/leaflets/ecfs2. pdf (large employers and contractors — reviewing your records).

Before 1 April 2009, *SI 2003 No 2682, Reg 97* itself gave HMRC the power to require an employer to produce PAYE records for inspection at such time as they required. On or after that date, such records have the status of 'statutory records' (see **38.6 HMRC INVESTIGATORY POWERS**), and HMRC will carry out compliance checks using their powers under *FA 2008, Sch 3.* See generally **38 HMRC INVESTIGATORY POWERS.**

Religious Centres

[53.42] If a Local Religious Centre does not expect to pay anyone £100 or more in a tax year, no action is required under PAYE. For anyone to whom the Centre does expect to pay £100 or more in a tax year, but who has no other job, records need to be kept for three years of name, address, national insurance number and the amount paid in the tax year. For any such person who has (or may have) another job, the Centre does not need to deduct tax, but should write to TIDO(LRC), Ty Glas, Llanishen, Cardiff CV4 5ZG giving details of name, address and national insurance number and of both the amount paid to the following 5 April and the amount expected to be paid in a full tax year. (Taxation, 16 February 1995, p 462).

Seamen

[53.43] Seamen are subject to standard PAYE procedures on wages from employment. Travelling expenses and subsistence allowances paid to seafarers making regular journeys to the same UK port are subject to PAYE. (Hansard 26 February 1981 Vol 999 Col 442).

Tax equalised employees

[53.44] There are modified PAYE procedures for tax equalised employees, i.e. employees who come from abroad to work in the UK and are guaranteed a specified level of earnings after tax. The procedures are set out in HMRC PAYE Online Manual PAYE82002. They were revised with effect from 6 April 2007, and employers who already operated such procedures had to apply before that date to operate the revised version. The revised procedures do not apply to employees who are resident, ordinarily resident and domiciled in the UK or to employees who are equalised on only part of their earnings (which includes non-cash earnings). For an article on the revised procedures, see HMRC Tax Bulletin February 2006 pp 1267–1270.

Tax refunds arising during unemployment

[53.45] Such refunds are made directly by HMRC, but refunds are withheld from the unemployed who claim jobseeker's allowance and from strikers until the end of the strike. [*ITEPA 2003, s 708; SI 2003 No 2682, Regs 64, 65*].

Termination payments

[53.46] For the reporting requirements in relation to taxable termination payments, see **53.12** above.

Tips, organised arrangements for sharing

[53.47] Gratuities and service charge shares under such arrangements (sometimes known as a 'tronc') are within PAYE and the 'tronc-master' (i.e. the person running the arrangements, being a person other than the employer) is regarded as responsible for the tax deductions. The employer, on becoming aware of their existence, must notify HMRC and give the name of the person running them, if known. [*ITEPA 2003, s 692; SI 2003 No 2682, Reg 100*]. For a case in which informal arrangements, under which directors of the employing company collected gratuities and divided them between themselves and the employees, were held not to constitute organised arrangements, see *Figael Ltd v Fox* CA 1991, 64 TC 441.

The above rules apply where the troncmaster acts independently of the employer. If the employer himself acts as troncmaster, or appoints an employee to make distributions in accordance with the employer's own formula or is otherwise involved in the distribution of monies from the tronc, payments made under the arrangements must be dealt with through the employer's own PAYE system. (Revenue Tax Bulletin February 2004 p 1081).

See generally HMRC helpsheet E24 'Tips, Gratuities, Service Charges and Troncs' (available at www.hmrc.gov.uk/helpsheets/e24.pdf), HMRC PAYE Manual PAYE20160 and 20161, Revenue Tax Bulletin February 2004 pp 1081–1084 and HMRC Tax Bulletin June 2005 pp 1207–1210.

Value added tax

[53.48] Earnings paid to a person holding an office in the course of carrying on a trade, profession or vocation and subject to VAT on services supplied by him should exclude the VAT element for PAYE purposes (HMRC SP A6). See also **53.12** above.

54

Payment of Tax

Cross-references. See **41 INTEREST ON OVERPAID TAX; 42 INTEREST AND SURCHARGES ON OVERDUE TAX** and **53 PAY AS YOU EARN.**

Simon's Taxes. See A4.6, E1.250–E1.258.

Introduction and due dates for payment

[54.1] A final payment is due for a tax year if a person's combined income tax and capital gains tax liabilities contained in his self-assessment (see **63.3 RETURNS**) exceed the aggregate of any payments on account (whether under *TMA 1970, s 59A* at **65.5 SELF-ASSESSMENT** or otherwise) and any income tax deducted at source. If the second total exceeds the first, a repayment will be made. Tax deducted at source has the same meaning as in **65.5**(b) **SELF-ASSESSMENT.**

Subject to the further provisions referred to below, the normal due date for payment (or repayment) is 31 January following the tax year. Where, however, the person gave notice of chargeability under *TMA 1970, s 7* (see **55.2 PENALTIES**) within six months after the end of the tax year, but was not given notice under *TMA 1970, s 8* or *s 8A* (see **63.2 RETURNS**) until after 31 October following the tax year, the due date is the last day of the three months beginning with the date of the said notice.

[*TMA 1970, s 59B(1)–(4)(7)(8); FA 2008, s 34, Sch 12 para 14*].

See **65.8 SELF-ASSESSMENT** for deferral of the due date for payment (or repayment) of an amount of tax as a result of an amendment or correction to a self-assessment or a consequential amendment arising from an amendment or correction to a partnership return or partnership statement (see **63.13 RETURNS**). It should, however, be noted that those rules do *not* defer the date from which interest accrues (for which see **42.2 INTEREST AND SURCHARGES ON OVERDUE TAX** (or **41.1 INTEREST ON OVERPAID TAX**), although they *do* determine the due date for surcharge purposes (see **42.3 INTEREST AND SURCHARGES ON OVERDUE TAX**).

Where an officer of HMRC enquires into a return (see **63.6 RETURNS**) and a repayment is otherwise due, the repayment is not required to be made until the enquiry is completed (see **63.9 RETURNS**), although the officer may make a provisional repayment at his discretion.

Subject to the appeal and postponement provisions in **5.2 APPEALS** and **54.5** below, the due date for payment of tax charged by assessment *otherwise* than by self-assessment (e.g. a discovery assessment under *TMA 1970, s 29*, see **6.6 ASSESSMENTS**) is 30 days after the date on which the notice of assessment is given (but see also **42.2 INTEREST AND SURCHARGES ON OVERDUE TAX**).
[*TMA 1970, s 59B(4A)(6)*].

Effective dates of payment

[54.2] HMRC take the date of payment in respect of each of the following payment methods to be as follows.

(1) *Cheques, cash, and postal orders* handed in at the HMRC office or received by post — the day of receipt by HMRC *unless* received by post following a day on which the office was closed for whatever reason, in which case it is the day on which the office was first closed.

(2) *Electronic funds transfer* — payment by BACS (transfer over two days) or CHAPS (same day transfer) — one day prior to receipt by HMRC (not applicable to payments by employers under **PAY AS YOU EARN (53)** and by contractors under the **CONSTRUCTION INDUSTRY SCHEME (22)**).

(3) *Bank giro or Girobank* — the date on which payment was made at the bank or post office.

(Revenue 'Working Together' Bulletin July 2000 p 3).

For the purposes of *TMA 1970* and *ICTA 1988, s 824* (see **41 INTEREST ON OVERPAID TAX**), where any payment to an officer of HMRC or the Commissioners for HMRC is received by cheque and the cheque is paid on its first presentation to the bank on which it is drawn, the payment is treated as made on the date of receipt of the cheque by the officer or the Commissioners. However, this is subject to any regulations that HMRC may make under *FA 2007, s 95* to the effect that, either generally or in particular circumstances, payment be treated as made only when the cheque clears. [*TMA 1970, s 70A; FA 2007, s 95(1)–(5)(7)*].

Mandatory electronic payment

[54.3] The Commissioners for HMRC have power to make regulations requiring a person to use electronic means in making specified payments under legislation relating to any tax or duty for which they are responsible.

Regulations under *FA 2007, s 95* (see **54.2** above) may, in particular, provide for a payment which is made by cheque in contravention of a requirement to pay electronically to be treated as made only when the cheque clears. [*FA 2003, ss 204, 205; FA 2007, ss 94, 95(6)*]. See, for example, **53.11** PAY AS YOU EARN as regards mandatory electronic payment for 'large employers'.

Credit card payment

[54.4] HMRC is now accepting certain types of payment by credit card. *FA 2008* included legislation enabling them to make *regulations* for passing on the associated transaction fees to the taxpayer. Current fees are 1.25% of credit card payments made by telephone (0.91% before 14 December 2009) and 1.25% of credit card payments made online. The legislation allows HMRC to make similar regulations for other methods of payment, but only where they expect to be charged a fee in connection with payments using that method. [*FA 2008, s 136; SI 2008 Nos 1948, 2991; SI 2009 No 3073*].

Payment and postponement of tax pending appeal

[54.5] The provisions described below apply in the case of appeals against:

(i)   a conclusion stated or amendment made by a closure notice on completion of enquiry (see **63.9** RETURNS);

(ii)   an HMRC amendment to a self-assessment during enquiry to prevent potential loss of tax (see **63.10** RETURNS); and

(iii) an assessment other than a self-assessment.

In the absence of any application for postponement of tax as below, tax is due and payable as if there had been no appeal.

If the taxpayer has grounds for believing that he is overcharged to tax by the amendment or assessment or as a result of the conclusion stated, as the case may be, he (or his agent) may, by notice in writing stating those grounds, apply to HMRC within 30 days after the 'relevant date' for postponement of a specified amount of tax pending determination of the appeal. In the event that the matter cannot be agreed, the taxpayer may refer the application to the Appeal Tribunal within 30 days after the date of the document notifying HMRC's decision. A postponement application to the Tribunal is heard in the same way as an appeal, and the Tribunal's decision is final and conclusive. The *'relevant date'* is the date of issue of the notice of amendment or assessment or, in the case of an appeal within (i) above, the date of issue of the closure notice.

If the taxpayer and HMRC come to an agreement as to the amount of tax (if any) to be postponed, it is not effective unless it is in writing. An agreement not in writing is nevertheless treated as such provided that its existence and terms are confirmed in writing by notice given by either party to the other. (In *Sparrow Ltd v Inspector* (Sp C 289), [2001] SSCD 206, an obvious error by the Inland Revenue, notifying a full rather than the nil postponement previously notified, was held not to constitute such an agreement.)

The amount of tax to be postponed pending determination of the appeal is the amount (if any) in which it appears that there are reasonable grounds for believing that the appellant is overcharged to tax. For a case in which no such 'reasonable grounds' were found, see *Sparrow Ltd* (above).

On the determination of (or agreement as to) the amount of tax to be postponed, the balance of tax *not postponed* (if any) becomes due and payable as if it had been charged by an amendment or assessment issued on the date of that determination or agreement (or on the date of notice of confirmation of the latter) and in respect of which there had been no appeal.

Application for postponement may be made outside the normal 30-day time limit if the appeal was itself made late or if there is a change in the circumstances of the case giving grounds for belief that the appellant is overcharged. In HMRC's view, this requires a change in the circumstances in which the original decision not to apply for postponement was made, not just a change of mind, e.g. further accounts work indicating a substantially excessive assessment, or further reliefs becoming due (see CCAB Statement TR 477, 22 June 1982). A late application does not defer the due date of any balance of tax not postponed.

If, after the determination of an amount of tax to be postponed and as a result of a change in the circumstances of the case, either party has grounds for believing that the amount postponed has become either excessive or insufficient, then unless the parties can agree the matter themselves, the said party may, at any time before the determination of the substantive appeal, apply to the Tribunal for a revised determination of the amount to be postponed. If, on a consequent revised determination, an amount of tax ceases to be postponed, that amount is treated as charged by an assessment issued on the date of the revised determination and in respect of which there had been no appeal. If, on the other hand, an amount of tax has been overpaid, it is repaid.

[TMA 1970, s 55; ITA 2007, Sch 1 para 257; SI 2009 No 56, Sch 1 para 34].

The giving of notice of appeal, whether or not accompanied by a postponement application, does *not* affect the date from which interest accrues, for which see **42.2 INTEREST AND SURCHARGES ON OVERDUE TAX.**

Payment of tax on determination of appeal

[54.6] Tax payable in accordance with the determination of an appeal within **54.5**(i)–(iii) above, being either postponed or additional tax, becomes due and payable as if it were charged by an amendment or assessment issued on the date on which HMRC issued to the taxpayer a notice of the total amount payable in accordance with the determination, and in respect of which no appeal was made. Any tax found to be overpaid becomes repayable. [*TMA 1970, s 55(9); SI 2009 No 56, Sch 1 para 34(12)*].

Collection and generally

[54.7] HMRC may distrain. [*TMA 1970, ss 61–64; FA 2008, ss 128, 129, Sch 43 paras 1, 12; SI 2009 No 3024*]. See also *Herbert Berry Associates Ltd v CIR* HL 1977, 52 TC 113. Where an amount of income tax due is less than

£2,000, the Collector may within one year after the due date take summary magistrates' court proceedings. HMRC may also recover tax by proceedings in the county court. [*TMA 1970, ss 65, 66*]. But for limitations in Scotland and NI, see *TMA 1970, s 65(4), s 66(3)(4), s 67*, and for time limits for proceedings see *Mann v Cleaver* KB 1930, 15 TC 367 and *Lord Advocate v Butt* CS 1992, 64 TC 471.

Unpaid tax (and arrears) may also be recovered (with full costs) as a Crown debt in the High Court. [*TMA 1970, s 68*]. The amount of an assessment which has become final cannot be re-opened in proceedings to collect the tax (*Pearlberg* CA 1953, 34 TC 57; *CIR v Soul* CA 1976, 51 TC 86), and it is not open to the taxpayer to raise the defence that HMRC acted *ultra vires* in raising the assessment (*CIR v Aken* CA 1990, 63 TC 395).

From a date to be appointed by statutory instrument, HMRC's previous power of distraint in *TMA 1970, s 61* is replaced in England and Wales by the procedure in *Tribunals, Courts and Enforcement Act 2007, Pt 3* (enforcement by taking control of goods). [*FA 2008, s 127*].

FA 2008 gives HMRC formal power (other than in Scotland) to set off an amount owed to a taxpayer against an amount due from that taxpayer. This power cannot be used to set off an amount becoming due by HMRC after the taxpayer's insolvency against an amount due by the taxpayer before insolvency. [*FA 2008, ss 130, 131*]. See also www.hmrc.gov.uk/finance-bill2008/s et-off-taxes.htm.

Where, after 24 June 2008, the right to receive a tax repayment is transferred from one person ('the original creditor') to another ('the new creditor'), the new creditor cannot receive any more from HMRC than if the original creditor had made the repayment claim. Any tax liability of the original creditor that would have been set against the repayment if the original creditor had made the claim will be set against any repayment made to the new creditor. [*FA 2008, s 133*].

For whether unpaid tax is a business liability for commercial etc. purposes, see *Conway v Wingate* CA 1952, 31 ATC 148; *Stevens v Britten* CA 1954, 33 ATC 399; *R v Vaccari* CCA 1958, 37 ATC 104; *In re Hollebone's Agreement* CA 1959, 38 ATC 142.

'Time to Pay' agreements

[54.8] By concession, under a 'time to pay' arrangement, a taxpayer enters into a negotiated agreement with HMRC, which takes full account of his circumstances (e.g. illness, unemployment, unforeseen short-term business difficulties), and thereby commits to settle his tax liabilities by regular instalments. Clear reasons for allowing settlement over an extended period that runs beyond the due date must be established during negotiations and any such arrangement is normally subject to adequate provision being made to settle future liabilities on time. INTEREST AND SURCHARGES ON OVERDUE TAX (42) is chargeable in the normal way on the full amount unpaid at the due date and not just on overdue instalments. However, a surcharge may be avoided where a 'Time to Pay' arrangement is in force (see **42.3 INTEREST AND SURCHARGES ON OVERDUE TAX**). (HMRC HINT/Self-Assessment Manual para 7.2.1, Personal Contact Manual para 4.8). See also **54.9**, **54.10** below.

Business Payment Support Service

[54.9] On 24 November 2008, HMRC launched a dedicated 'Business Payment Support Service' on 0845 302 1435 to assist businesses having difficulty paying their taxes in the then adverse economic conditions. HMRC staff will endeavour to agree a 'time to pay' arrangement (see **54.8** above) with the caller. Late payment surcharges will not apply to payments included in the arrangement (unless already incurred prior to the arrangement), but interest continues to be payable by reference to the original due date for payment. This Support Line is intended for new enquiries only, i.e. on or after the launch date. For details, see www.hmrc.gov.uk/pbr2008/business-payment.htm and (for agents and advisers) www.hmrc.gov.uk/pbr2008/bus-payment-addinfo.htm. If the taxpayer is a sub-contractor in the construction industry and is registered for gross payment (see **22.7 CONSTRUCTION INDUSTRY SCHEME (CIS)**, entering into a 'time to pay' arrangement before payment is due will not affect the sub-contractor's gross payment status (www.hmrc.gov.uk/cis/business-payment-support.htm).

On 22 April 2009, HMRC announced with immediate effect that, where relevant, the Business Payment Support Service will now take into account the fact that a business is likely to make a loss for its current year when deciding how much time HMRC can give a business to pay the tax due on its profits for the previous year. See www.hmrc.gov.uk/budget2009/bus-payment-support-582.pdf.

Managed payment plans

[54.10] Under a managed payment plan, a taxpayer agrees with HMRC to pay income tax or capital gains tax by instalments which are 'balanced' equally before and after the normal due date. If the taxpayer then pays all of the instalments in accordance with the plan, he is treated as having paid the total amount on the due date, so that no interest, late payment surcharge or penalty will arise. Managed payment plans can theoretically be entered into where the due date for the tax falls after 21 July 2009. However, the Government has decided to defer their implementation; no commencement date has been given (Budget Report 22 June 2010 p 46).

Where the taxpayer pays one or more of the instalments in accordance with the plan but then fails to pay one or more later instalments, the total of the instalments paid before the failure are treated as paid on the due date. Where the failure takes place before the due date, the taxpayer is, nevertheless, entitled to be paid any interest on the early payments made if he would have been so entitled but for the plan. Where, following a failure, the taxpayer makes payments after the due date, HMRC can notify him that any or all of those payments will not be liable to a late payment surcharge or penalty.

Instalments to be paid before the due date are '*balanced*' with instalments to be paid after it if the aggregate time value of each set of instalments is equal or approximately equal. HMRC can make regulations to determine when, for this purpose, two amounts are approximately equal. The time value of an instalment is calculated by multiplying it by the number of days between the payment date for the instalment and the due date for the tax.

[*TMA 1970, ss 59G, 59H; FA 2009, s 111; TIOPA 2010, Sch 7 para 80*].

Remission or repayment of tax in cases of official error

[54.11] **Arrears** of income tax or capital gains tax may be waived if they result from HMRC's failure to make proper and timely use of information supplied by:

(a)   a taxpayer about his or her own income, gains or personal circumstances;

(b)   an employer, where the information affects a taxpayer's coding; or

(c)   the Department for Work and Pensions about a taxpayer's retirement, disability or widow's State pension.

The waiver will normally apply only where the taxpayer could reasonably have believed that his or her tax affairs were in order, and either:

(i)   was notified of the arrears more than twelve months after the end of the tax year in which HMRC received the information indicating that more tax was due; or

(ii)   was notified of an over-repayment after the end of the tax year following the year in which the repayment was made.

Exceptionally, arrears notified less than twelve months after the end of the relevant tax year may be waived if HMRC either failed more than once to make proper use of the facts they had been given about one source of income, or allowed the arrears to build up over two whole tax years in succession by failing to make proper and timely use of information they had been given.

(HMRC ESC A19).

Where an **overpayment** of tax has arisen because of official error, and there is no doubt or dispute as to the facts, claims to repayment of tax are accepted outside the statutory time limits (HMRC ESC B41).

Overpayment of tax

[54.12] HMRC's administrative practice relating to repayments of tax is as below.

(i)   Where an assessment has been made and this shows a repayment due to the taxpayer, repayment is invariably made of the full amount.

(ii)   Under **SELF-ASSESSMENT** (**65**), any amount repayable will be repaid on request.

(iii)   Where the end-of-year check applied to PAYE taxpayers who have not had a tax return for the year in question shows an overpayment of £10 or less, the repayment is not made automatically.

(iv)   Where tax assessed has been paid to the Collector in excess of the amount due, and the discrepancy is not noted before the payment has been processed, the excess is not repaid routinely by the computer system unless it is £1 or more, or where clerical intervention is required unless it is £10 or more.

The above tolerances are to minimise work which is highly cost ineffective, they cannot operate to deny a repayment to a taxpayer who has claimed it. (HMRC SP 6/95). Provisional repayments will not be made during the tax year to which a claim or claims relate if the tax involved does not exceed £50 in total. (Revenue Press Release 29 March 1989).

See **54.11** above as regards claims in cases of official error. See also **18.6** CLAIMS as regards repayment procedures.

Allocation of overpayments against underpayments

Where there are underpayments of tax, overpayments will automatically be reallocated against any other tax or Class 4 NICs (or interest thereon) outstanding in respect of the amended assessment unless the amendment is processed before 1 June following the end of the tax year and either the amount to be reallocated to the second instalment is £1,000 or more or the tax is not yet due and the taxpayer requests that no reallocation should be made. (HMRC Assessed Taxes Manual AT 8.701 *et seq.*). For an article on HMRC practice re allocations of overpayments under SELF-ASSESSMENT (**65**), see Revenue Tax Bulletin June 1999 pp 673, 674.

Over-repayments of tax

[54.13] Tax over-repaid (by actual payment or set-off) and not assessable under *TMA 1970, s 29* (see **6.6** ASSESSMENTS) may be recovered by an income tax assessment as if it were unpaid tax. However, this rule is subject to the same exceptions (modified as appropriate) as apply to discovery assessments (see **6.6** ASSESSMENTS). Any excess repayment supplement may be included in the assessment or assessed separately as if it were unpaid tax. The normal time limit for such an assessment is extended, if necessary, to the later of the end of the chargeable period following that in which the repayment was made and, where relevant, the day on which an officer of HMRC's enquiries into a return delivered by the person concerned are statutorily completed (see **63.9** RETURNS), but this time limit is without prejudice to the extended time limits which apply in cases of loss of income tax brought about deliberately (see **6.3** ASSESSMENTS) or fraudulent or negligent conduct (see **6.4** ASSESSMENTS). [*TMA 1970, s 30(1B)(5)*].

The exercise by HMRC of their discretion to raise an assessment under *TMA 1970, s 30* can be challenged only by way of judicial review (see **5.34** APPEALS) and not by appeal (*Guthrie v Twickenham Film Studios Ltd* Ch D 2002, 74 TC 733).

Recovery of tax paid under mistake of law

[54.14] It was held in *R v CIR (ex p. Woolwich Equitable Building Society)* HL 1990, 63 TC 589 that at common law taxes extracted *ultra vires* are recoverable as of right and without need to invoke mistake of law by the taxpayer (and see **41.2 INTEREST ON OVERPAID TAX**).

It was further held, *inter alia*, in *Deutsche Morgan Grenfell Group plc v CIR and A-G* Ch D, [2003] STC 1017 that the common law remedy of restitution of payment made under a mistake of law applies to payments of tax as it does to other payments. By virtue of *Limitation Act 1980, s 32(1)(c)*, the six-year period of limitation in such a case does not begin to run until the plaintiff discovers the mistake (or could with reasonable diligence have discovered it). However, under legislation in *FA 2004* (reversing the effect of *Deutsche Morgan Grenfell*), *Limitation Act 1980, s 32(1)(c)* (and Scottish equivalent) does *not* apply in relation to a mistake of law relating to taxes administered by HMRC where the action for restitution is brought after 7 September 2003. The effect is that court actions for restitution based on mistake of law must generally be brought within six years (or five years under Scottish law) of the tax having been paid. If a pre-existing action is amended to include additional years, the amendment is not treated as backdated to the date of the original action. [*FA 2004, ss 320, 321*].

The Ch D decision in *Deutsche Morgan Grenfell* was eventually confirmed by the HL (*Deutsche Morgan Grenfell Group plc v CIR and another* HL 2006, [2007] STC 1). The Government subsequently announced that it would legislate to ensure that (for those cases not already caught by the *FA 2004* legislation above) the limitation period for the recovery of direct tax paid by mistake of law is six years from the date of payment (and not from the date of discovery of the mistake). The legislation would have retrospective effect, but not so as to disturb the entitlement of those who have secured what amounts to a final judgment in their favour prior to 6 December 2006. The legislation was duly enacted as *FA 2007, s 107*.

HMRC powers to obtain contact details for debtors

[54.15] With effect on and after 21 July 2009, an HMRC officer may by notice in writing require a third party to provide contact details (i.e. an address and any other information about how the person may be contacted) for a person in debt to HMRC. The third party must provide the details within such period, and at such time, by such means and in such form (if any), as is reasonably specified or described in the notice, subject to a £300 penalty for non-compliance. The third party may appeal against the notice, or any requirement in it, on the grounds that it would be unduly onerous to comply. In order for these provisions to apply,

- a sum must be payable by a person (the debtor) to HMRC under an enactment or a contract settlement (as in **6.9 ASSESSMENTS**);
- the officer must reasonably require contact details for the debtor for the purpose of collection and have reasonable grounds to believe that the third party has such details; and

- either the third party is a company, local authority or local authority association (within *ITA 2007, s 1000*) or the officer has reasonable grounds to believe that the third party obtained the details in the course of carrying on a business (which term includes a profession or a property business).

The above does not apply if the third party is a charity and obtained the details in the course of providing services free of charge or is not a charity but obtained the details in the course of providing free services on behalf of a charity.

[*FA 2009, s 97, Sch 49*].

Equitable liability

[54.16] Where, in the absence of a return, HMRC has determined a taxpayer's liability, the taxpayer has until three years after the statutory filing date (reduced from five years with effect on and after 1 April 2010), or, if later, one year after the determination, to displace the determination with his own self-assessment (see **63.12 RETURNS**). In the event of the taxpayer's failing to displace the determination within the permitted time, HMRC apply a concession whereby they collect only the amount of tax that would have been due had the taxpayer filed the return on time (Revenue Tax Bulletin August 1995 pp 245, 246). This concession is known as '*equitable liability*'. The taxpayer must demonstrate that the amount charged by the determination is excessive and show what the correct amount should have been. He must also bring his tax affairs up to date and pay all outstanding tax plus any interest and penalties. The concession can usually only apply once to any taxpayer, although it may then be used to cover more than one year's liability.

Legislation is to be introduced to permit HMRC to continue to apply this treatment, but on a statutory basis. The concession will continue to operate until the legislation comes into force. (HMRC Pre-Budget Report Note 34, 9 December 2009).

The concession is aimed at situations where tax remains unpaid. It is thought that it cannot be used to recover tax already paid but subsequently found to be excessive.

55

Penalties

Cross-references. See **18.3** CLAIMS, **63.5** RETURNS as regards failure to keep records and **63.23** RETURNS as regards reasonable excuse for failure to make returns.

Simon's Taxes. See **A4.502–A4.531, A6.602–A6.617, E1.257.**

See HMRC Compliance Handbook CH80000 *et seq.* (penalties for inaccuracies).

Introduction

[55.1] This chapter considers HMRC's powers to charge penalties in the event of various tax compliance failures.

HMRC will not charge penalties for missed deadlines where they are satisfied that the deadlines were missed due to the severe flooding in parts of the UK in July 2007 (HMRC News Release 25 July 2007). See also **42.4 INTEREST AND SURCHARGES ON OVERDUE TAX.**

Notification of chargeability

[55.2] A person chargeable to income tax or capital gains tax for a particular tax year who has not been required by a notice under *TMA 1970, s 8* (see **63.2 RETURNS**) to deliver a return for that year must, within six months after the end of that year, notify an officer of HMRC that he is so chargeable. From 1 April 2010, any penalty for non-compliance is charged under *FA 2008, Sch 41* (see **55.3** below).

A person is not required to give notice under these provisions if his total income for the year consists of income from the sources below and he has no chargeable gains. The said sources are those in respect of which:

(a)   all payments etc. are dealt with under PAYE; or
(b)   all income has been or will be taken into account either in determining the chargeable person's liability to tax or under PAYE; or
(c)   the income is chargeable under *ITTOIA 2005, Pt 4 Ch 3* (dividends etc. from UK resident companies) or is other income from which income tax has been, or is treated as having been, deducted, provided that the chargeable person is not liable for that year at a rate higher than the basic rate, dividend ordinary rate or starting rate for savings; or
(d)   all income for that year is income on which the chargeable person could not become liable to tax under a self-assessment under *TMA 1970, s 9* (see **63.3 RETURNS**) in respect of that year.

These provisions also apply with the appropriate modifications to 'relevant trustees' (as defined in **65.11 SELF-ASSESSMENT**) of settlements.

[*TMA 1970, s 7(1)–(7), (9); ITA 2007, Sch 1 para 244; FA 2008, s 123, Sch 1 paras 35, 38, 65, Sch 41 para 25*].

As regards items within (b) above, HMRC will normally accept that employees in receipt of copy form P11D (or equivalent particulars) from their employer (see **65.12 SELF-ASSESSMENT**) can assume that any items on it not already taken into account for PAYE will be so taken into account, so there is no need to notify chargeability in respect of such items. Notice of chargeability is, however, necessary to the extent that the P11D is incorrect or incomplete or if the employee knows that the actual form has not been submitted to HMRC. Employees are not relieved of any obligation to notify chargeability if they have not received a copy P11D or in respect of non-P11D items which ought to have been reported by the employer to HMRC on other returns. (HMRC SP 1/96).

Pension schemes

The trustees of approved occupational pension schemes with income or capital gains are within these provisions. See Pension Schemes Office Update No 49, 24 August 1998 and, for the detailed administrative arrangements, Revenue Tax Bulletin February 1999 pp 628, 629.

Simon's Taxes. See A4.516, A6.612–A6.617, E1.202.

Penalties for non-compliance

[55.3] Penalties for non-compliance with the requirement at **55.2** above were brought within a unified penalty code for failures relating to a range of taxes. The code is described below to the extent that it relates to income tax. It applies to obligations to notify that arise on or after 1 April 2010, i.e. in relation to chargeability for 2009/10 onwards. See www.hmrc.gov.uk/about/new-penalties/failure-to-notify.pdf.

A person is not liable to a penalty for a failure in respect of which he has been convicted of an offence.

Amount of penalty

The amount of the penalty depends on whether or not the failure is deliberate and is subject to reduction as detailed below.

With effect from a date to be appointed by the Treasury, the amount of this penalty will also depend on whether the inaccuracy involves a domestic matter or an offshore matter. It is anticipated that this will apply to tax periods commencing on or after 1 April 2011 (HMRC Budget Note BN68, 24 March 2010). The following summary assumes the inaccuracy involves a domestic matter; see **55.4** below as regards offshore matters.

For a deliberate and concealed failure (i.e. where the failure was deliberate and the taxpayer made arrangements to conceal the situation giving rise to the obligation), the penalty is 100% of the 'potential lost revenue' (see below).

For deliberate but not concealed failure (i.e. where the failure was deliberate but the taxpayer did not make arrangements to conceal the situation giving rise to the obligation), the penalty is 70% of the potential lost revenue.

For any other case, the penalty is 30% of the potential lost revenue.

The *'potential lost revenue'* is equal to the amount of tax payable for the year that, by reason of the failure, remains unpaid on 31 January following that year. The fact that potential lost revenue may be balanced by a potential overpayment by another person is ignored, except to the extent that that person's tax liability is required or permitted to be adjusted by reference to the taxpayer's.

No penalty is due in relation to a failure that is not deliberate if the taxpayer satisfies HMRC or, on appeal, the Appeal Tribunal, that there is a reasonable excuse for the failure. Insufficiency of funds is not a reasonable excuse for this purpose, unless attributable to events outside the taxpayer's control, and neither is the taxpayer's reliance on another person to do anything, unless he took reasonable care (see **55.10** below) to avoid the failure. For more on what is or is not a reasonable excuse, see www.hmrc.gov.uk/about/new-penalties/f aqs.htm#44. If the taxpayer had a reasonable excuse, he is treated as continuing to have a reasonable excuse after the excuse has ceased if the failure is remedied without unreasonable delay.

Reduction for disclosure

A reduction in a penalty will be given where the taxpayer discloses a failure to notify. The penalty will be reduced to a percentage which reflects the quality of the disclosure and the amount of the reduction will depend on whether the disclosure is 'prompted' or 'unprompted'.

In the case of an unprompted disclosure, a 100% penalty may not be reduced to a percentage below 30%, and a 70% penalty may not be reduced to a percentage below 20%. A 30% penalty may be reduced to any percentage, including 0%, unless HMRC do not become aware of the failure until twelve months or more after the time tax first becomes unpaid by reason of the failure, in which case the penalty may not be reduced below 10%.

In the case of a prompted disclosure, a 100% penalty may not be reduced to a percentage below 50%, a 70% penalty may not be reduced to a percentage below 35%, and a 30% penalty may not be reduced to a percentage below 10% (20% where HMRC do not become aware of the failure until twelve months after the time tax first becomes unpaid by reason of the failure).

A person is treated as making a disclosure for these purposes only if he tells HMRC about the failure, he gives them reasonable help in quantifying the tax unpaid and allows them access to records for the purpose of checking how much tax is unpaid. A disclosure is *'unprompted'* if made when the taxpayer has no reason to believe HMRC have discovered or are about to discover the failure. In all other cases, disclosures are *'prompted'*.

Reduction in special circumstances

HMRC can also reduce or stay a penalty or agree a compromise in relation to proceedings for a penalty if they think it right to do so because of special circumstances. Ability to pay and the fact that a potential loss of revenue from one taxpayer is balanced by a potential overpayment by another are not special circumstances for this purpose.

Reduction for other penalty or surcharge

The amount of a penalty in respect of a failure is reduced by the amount of any other penalty or late payment surcharge, the amount of which is determined by reference to the same tax liability. No reduction is made for a tax-related penalty within **55.17** below.

Agents

A person is liable to a penalty under the above provisions where the failure is by a person acting on his behalf. He is not, however, liable to a penalty in respect of anything done or omitted by his agent if he satisfies HMRC or, on appeal, the Appeal Tribunal, that he took reasonable care (see **55.10** below) to avoid the failure.

[FA 2008, s 123, Sch 41 paras 1, 5–7, 11–15, 20, 21, 23, 24; CTA 2010, Sch 1 para 583; SI 2009 No 56, Sch 1 para 473(4)(5); SI 2009 No 511].

See www.hmrc.gov.uk/about/new-penalties/failure-to-notify.pdf.

[FA 2008, s 123, Sch 41 paras 1, 5, 6, 6A, 6D, 7, 11–15, 20, 21, 23, 24; CTA 2010, Sch 1 para 583; FA 2010, s 35, Sch 10 paras 7–9; SI 2009 No 56, Sch 1 para 473(4)(5); SI 2009 No 511].

Pre-1 April 2010 position

As regards obligations to notify that arose before 1 April 2010, i.e. in relation to chargeability for 2008/09 and earlier years, the maximum penalty was the amount of tax in which the person was assessed for that year which was not paid on or before 31 January following that year. *[TMA 1970, s 7(8)]*.

Penalties for non-compliance — offshore matters

[55.4] With effect from a date to be appointed by the Treasury by statutory instrument, the amount of the penalty in **55.3** above continues to depend on whether or not the failure is deliberate but also depends on whether the failure involves a domestic matter or an offshore matter. It is anticipated that this will apply to tax periods commencing on or after 1 April 2011 (HMRC Budget Note BN68, 24 March 2010).

For these purposes, a failure involves an offshore matter if it results in a potential loss of revenue (see **55.3** above) that is charged on or by reference to:

- income arising from a source in a territory outside the UK; or
- assets situated or held in a territory outside the UK; or
- activities carried on wholly or mainly in a territory outside the UK; or
- anything having effect as if it were income, assets or activities of the kind above.

Otherwise the failure involves a domestic matter. Provision made by the Treasury under **55.12** below, as to where a source of income is located, where an asset is situated etc., has effect for the above purposes also.

Category 1

If the failure involves an offshore matter and the territory in question is a 'category 1 territory', the amounts of the penalties are the same as for domestic matters, i.e. the amounts in **55.3** above. A '*category 1 territory*' is a territory designated as such by order to be made by the Treasury.

Category 2

If the inaccuracy involves an offshore matter and the territory in question is a 'category 2 territory', the amounts of the penalties are as follows.

For a deliberate and concealed failure, the penalty is 150% of the 'potential lost revenue' (see **55.3** above).

For a deliberate but not concealed failure, the penalty is 105% of the potential lost revenue.

For any other case, the penalty is 45% of the potential lost revenue.

A *'category 2 territory'* is a territory that is neither a category 1 territory nor a category 3 territory.

Category 3

If the inaccuracy involves an offshore matter and the territory in question is a 'category 3 territory', the amounts of the penalties are as follows.

For a deliberate and concealed failure, the penalty is 200% of the 'potential lost revenue' (see **55.3** above).

For a deliberate but not concealed failure, the penalty is 140% of the potential lost revenue.

For any other case, the penalty is 60% of the potential lost revenue.

A *'category 3 territory'* is a territory designated as such by order to be made by the Treasury.

Failure in more than one category

If a single failure is in more than one category it is treated for these purposes as if it were separate failures, one in each relevant category according to the matters that it involves. The potential lost revenue for each separate failure is such share of the potential lost revenue in respect of the single failure as is just and reasonable.

Categorisation of territories

The classification by the Treasury of territories for the purposes of **55.12** below has effect for these purposes also. The above penalty provisions do not apply to obligations that are to be complied with before the date on which the relevant categorisation order comes into force.

Reduction for disclosure

See **55.3** above as regards reductions for disclosure generally.

In the case of an unprompted disclosure:

- a 200% penalty may not be reduced to a percentage below 60%;
- a 150% penalty may not be reduced to a percentage below 45%;
- a 140% penalty may not be reduced to a percentage below 40%;
- a 105% penalty may not be reduced to a percentage below 30%; but
- a 60% penalty may be reduced to any percentage, including 0%, unless HMRC do not become aware of the failure until twelve months or more after the time tax first becomes unpaid by reason of the failure, in which case the penalty may not be reduced below 20%; and
- a 45% penalty may be reduced to any percentage, including 0%, unless HMRC do not become aware of the failure until twelve months or more after the time tax first becomes unpaid by reason of the failure, in which case the penalty may not be reduced below 15%.

In the case of a prompted disclosure,

- a 200% penalty may not be reduced to a percentage below 100%;
- a 150% penalty may not be reduced to a percentage below 75%;
- a 140% penalty may not be reduced to a percentage below 70%;
- a 105% penalty may not be reduced to a percentage below 52.5%;
- a 60% penalty may not be reduced to a percentage below 20% (40% if HMRC do not become aware of the failure until twelve months or more after the time tax first becomes unpaid by reason of the failure); and
- a 45% penalty may not be reduced to a percentage below 15% (30% if HMRC do not become aware of the failure until twelve months or more after the time tax first becomes unpaid by reason of the failure).

Reduction in special circumstances

See **55.3** above.

Reduction for other penalty or surcharge

See **55.3** above.

[*FA 2008, s 123, Sch 41 paras 6, 6A, 12–14; FA 2010, s 35, Sch 10 paras 7–9; SI 2009 No 511*].

Failure to deliver tax return on time

[55.5] A person (the taxpayer) who is required by notice under *TMA 1970, s 8* or *s 8A* to deliver a return to HMRC but fails to do so on or before the deadline is liable to a penalty of £100. The deadline is as follows.

- As regards returns for **2007/08 and subsequent years:**
  - (i) if the return is a non-electronic return, **31 October** following the tax year to which it relates or, if later, within three months beginning with the date of the notice;
  - (ii) if the return is an electronic return, **31 January** following the tax year to which it relates or, if later, within three months beginning with the date of the notice.
- As regards returns for 2006/07 and earlier years, 31 January following the tax year to which the return relates or, if later, within three months beginning with the date of the above-mentioned notice.

See **63.2** RETURNS for further details as regards the filing of returns.

For continuing failure, a further penalty of up to £60 per day may be imposed by the Appeal Tribunal (but not at any time after the failure has been remedied) on application by an officer of HMRC, such daily penalty to start from the day after the taxpayer is notified of the Tribunal's direction (but not for any day for which such a daily penalty has already been imposed).

If the failure continues for more than six months beginning with the 'filing date' and no application for a daily penalty was made within those six months, the taxpayer is liable to a further £100 penalty. If failure continues after the anniversary of the filing date, and there would have been a liability under *TMA*

1970, s 59B (see **65.7 SELF-ASSESSMENT**), based on a proper return promptly delivered, the taxpayer is liable to a further penalty of an amount not exceeding that liability. See **65.11 SELF-ASSESSMENT** as regards trustees.

For the above purposes only, the *'filing date'* is 31 January following the tax year to which the return relates or, if later, the last day of the period of three months beginning with the day on which the notice to deliver the return is given. As regards returns for 2007/08 and subsequent years, this is the case regardless of whether or not the return is an electronic return.

If the taxpayer proves that his liability under *TMA 1970, s 59B*, based on a proper return promptly delivered, would not have exceeded a particular amount, his liability to penalties other than the daily and tax-geared penalties is reduced to that amount. Thus a payment on account, made under *TMA 1970, s 59A* or otherwise, which reduces the liability outstanding at 31 January to less than £100 will similarly reduce any automatic penalty otherwise chargeable (see HMRC Enquiry Manual EM4562, HMRC Income Tax Self-Assessment Manual: The Legal Framework SALF 208, paras 2.68, 2.69). Where a number of tax years are being finalised together following late returns, it is understood that HMRC will not regard earlier years' overpayments as set against later years' underpayments so as to reduce or extinguish fixed penalties for the later years (Tolley's Practical Tax Newsletter 2002 p 152).

On an appeal against either of the £100 penalties (reduced where appropriate), the Appeal Tribunal may either confirm the penalty or, if it appears to them that throughout the period of failure the taxpayer had a reasonable excuse for not delivering the return (see **55.6** below), set it aside.

[TMA 1970, s 93; FA 2007, s 91(7), s 92; SI 2009 No 56, Sch 1 para 41; SI 2009 No 2035, Sch para 7].

HMRC's original intention was to use the daily penalty sanction above where the tax at risk was substantial and they believed the fixed penalties to be an insufficient deterrent (Revenue booklet SAT 2 (1995), para 2.74 (now out of print)), but they have since stated that they will be increasing their use of such sanctions (Revenue Tax Bulletins February 2002 p 915, December 2003 p 1067).

See **55.9** below for the replacement of the above provisions expected to take effect for 2011/12 onwards.

Political objections do not justify failure to make returns (*Turton v Bird-forth Commrs* Ch D 1970, 49 ATC 346), nor do objections to the system of taxation (*Walsh v Croydon Commrs* Ch D 1987, 60 TC 442). The submission of a return marked 'to be advised' or some similar phrase does not satisfy the requirements and penalties may be incurred (*Cox v Poole General Commrs* Ch D 1987, 60 TC 445).

Simon's Taxes. See A4.505, A4.506.

Reasonable excuse

[55.6] For the HMRC's approach to 'reasonable excuse' for failure to deliver a return on time, see HMRC Self-Assessment Manual SAM10090 and, in the particular case of online filing problems, i.e. where the HMRC Online Service does not accept the return, www.hmrc.gov.uk/agents/reason-excuse0809.htm Common examples which HMRC might regard as reasonable are where they are satisfied that the taxpayer did not receive the return; where the return was posted in good time but held up by an unforeseen disruption to the postal service; where the taxpayer's records were lost through fire, flood or theft and could not be replaced in time to meet the deadline; where serious illness immediately before the filing date made timeous submission impossible; or the death of a close relative or domestic partner shortly before the deadline (provided that all necessary steps to meet the deadline had been taken). Examples of excuses *not* considered reasonable by HMRC are claims that the return is too difficult to complete; pressure of work on the taxpayer or agent; failure by an agent; unavailability of information needed to complete the return; or the absence of a reminder that the return was overdue. It is, however, stressed that these are HMRC's views, and that it is for the Appeal Tribunal to adjudicate where the taxpayer takes a different view. A taxpayer's political beliefs do not amount to a 'reasonable excuse' (*Gladders v Prior* (Sp C 361), [2003] SSCD 245)). Although, as stated above, the 'reasonable excuse' must strictly continue throughout the period of default, in practice HMRC normally allow a further 14 days for submission of the return after the excuse has ceased.

See also *Steeden v Carver* (Sp C 212), [1999] SSCD 283, in which reliance on HMRC's advice as to the practical extension of a deadline, unequivocally given, was held to be 'as reasonable an excuse as could be found'. Following the decision in this case, HMRC's practice is as follows. They regard a return due on 31 January as delivered on time if found in a tax office post box when first opened on 1 February (or if delivered before midnight on 31 January by hand, courier or electronically). They do not charge a late filing penalty for returns subsequently delivered to the post box no later than first opening on 2 February (or delivered any time on 1 February by other means); however, such returns are nevertheless late, and the enquiry window is automatically extended as in **63.6**(c) RETURNS. The same approach applies to later filing dates where the return is issued after 31 October (see **63.2** RETURNS).

As regards 2008/09 paper returns, for which the due date is 31 October 2009, HMRC's practice, bearing in mind the Royal Mail industrial action then ongoing, is as follows. They will not charge a late filing penalty for returns hand delivered on Monday 2 November; however, such returns are nevertheless late, and the enquiry window is automatically extended. They also will not charge a penalty for returns sent by mail if the return was posted before 31 October. Taxpayers unable to meet the deadline still had until 31 January 2010 to deliver the return online instead. See www.hmrc.gov.uk/news/royalm ail-action2.htm.

As regards paper returns for 2007/08 and subsequent years, agents may submit with the return a 'reasonable excuse' form (www.hmrc.gov.uk/carter/sa-reaso nableexcuse.pdf) if they tried to file online after 31 October but were unable to do so and are thus filing manually instead.

'Unsatisfactory' returns

[55.7] By concession, HMRC do not charge a fixed late-filing penalty where:

- they reject a return as being 'unsatisfactory';
- they consequently send it back (to whoever submitted it — taxpayer or agent) with an explanatory letter no earlier than the 13th day before the filing date (e.g. 18 January where the filing date is 31 January), and
- they then receive a satisfactory return within 14 days from the date of the said letter.

An 'unsatisfactory' return is not the same as an incomplete return (for example, a return omitting income) for which the correct redress would be an enquiry (see **63.6 RETURNS**) rather than rejection. A return is *'unsatisfactory'* if, for example, it is unsigned or incorrectly signed (see **63.2 RETURNS**), it is not on the standard HMRC form (or agreed alternative — see **63.2 RETURNS**) or supplementary pages are missing (see **65.2 SELF-ASSESSMENT**). The 14-day period of grace will not be given where the original return is itself late or where the taxpayer appears to be using deliberate delaying tactics. (Revenue Tax Bulletin June 2001 pp 848, 849, February 2002 p 916). See **63.2 RETURNS** for the circumstances in which a return is likely to be accepted even though it contains a provisional figure.

Partnership returns

[55.8] The same fixed penalties (including the daily penalty) as under *TMA 1970, s 93* (at **55.5** above) apply in the case of failure to submit a partnership return as required by a notice under *TMA 1970, s 12AA* (see **63.13 RETURNS**). However, there is no tax-geared penalty and no provision for reducing the £100 penalties by reference to the tax outstanding on 31 January. The definition of 'filing date' is appropriately modified where the partnership includes one or more companies. Each person who was a partner at any time during the period in respect of which the return was required is separately liable to each penalty. The penalties apply by reference to failure by the representative partner, i.e. the partner required by the notice under *TMA 1970, s 12AA* to deliver the return, or his successor (see **63.13 RETURNS**). Where penalties are imposed on two or more partners, an appeal cannot be made otherwise than by way of composite appeal by the representative partner (or successor). The same reasonable excuse provisions apply as under *TMA 1970, s 93* but by reference to the representative partner (or successor). [*TMA 1970, s 93A; FA 1994, ss 196, 199(2)(a), Sch 19 para 26; FA 1996, s 123(8)–(11); FA 2007, s 91(8)(9), s 92; SI 2009 No 56, Sch 1 para 42*].

Cross-tax penalty for failure to make returns

[55.9] A new single penalty regime for failure to make returns on or before the filing date is to replace the penalties at **55.5** above. It is expected that the new penalties will apply for 2011/12 onwards for income tax purposes.

Broadly, there will be an initial penalty of £100 and, if HMRC choose to apply it, a daily penalty of £10 for each day up to 90 days where the failure continues more than three months after the filing date. Where the failure continues more than six months after the filing date a further penalty of 5% of the tax liability which would have been shown in the return (or, if greater, £300) will be charged. If the failure continues for more than 12 months after the filing date, a further penalty will be charged, the amount being dependent on whether the taxpayer has withheld information which would enable HMRC to assess his tax liability. If the withholding of information was deliberate and concealed, the penalty is 100% of the liability which would have been shown in the return. If the withholding was deliberate but not concealed, the penalty is 70%. In other cases the penalty is 5%. In all cases, the penalty is £300 if greater than the amount given by applying the percentage rate. The 100% and 70% rates are reduced for disclosure, but not below a specified minimum.

Where the withholding of information concerns an offshore matter, the 100% and 70% rates are subject to increase — to a maximum of 200% and 140% respectively. All increased penalties are then subject to reduction for disclosure, but not below a specified minimum. The rules are similar to those described at **55.12** below for careless or deliberate errors in documents.

[*FA 2009, s 106, Sch 55; CTA 2010, Sch 1 para 723; FA 2010, s 35, Sch 10 paras 10–14*].

Careless or deliberate errors in documents

[55.10] The following provisions apply from a date appointed by the Treasury by statutory instrument and replace those at **55.13** below. The appointed date is 1 April 2008 in relation to any documents relating to a tax period (e.g. a tax year) beginning on or after 1 April 2008, but no person is to be charged a penalty under these provisions in respect of any tax year for which a return has to be made before 1 April 2009. Thus, for income tax purposes, the provisions effectively apply for 2008/09 onwards. The changes made from 1 April 2009 (noted below where relevant) have effect in relation to any documents relating to a tax period beginning on or after 1 April 2009, but no person is to be charged a resulting penalty in respect of any tax year for which a return has to be made before 1 April 2010. Thus, for income tax purposes, those changes effectively apply **for 2009/10 onwards**.

The provisions apply to a wide range of documents relating to direct and indirect taxes, duties and levies which may be given by a taxpayer to HMRC, including the following which are relevant for the purposes of income tax:

- a tax return under *TMA 1970, s 8* or *s 8A* (personal or trustees' return — see **63.2 RETURNS**);

- a return, statement or declaration in connection with a claim for an allowance, deduction or relief;
- accounts in connection with ascertaining liability to tax;
- a partnership return (see **63.13 RETURNS**);
- a statement or declaration in connection with a partnership return;
- accounts in connection with a partnership return;
- (from 1 April 2009) a quarterly return under *FA 2004, s 254* by the scheme administrator of a registered pension scheme (see **57.4 PENSION PROVISION**);
- a PAYE return (see **53.12 PAY AS YOU EARN**);
- a CIS return (see **22.11 CONSTRUCTION INDUSTRY SCHEME**); and
- any other document (other than one in respect of which a penalty is payable under *TMA 1970, s 98* — see **55.21** below) likely to be relied on by HMRC to determine, without further inquiry, a question about the taxpayer's liability to tax, his payments by way of or in connection with tax, other payments (such as penalties) by the taxpayer or repayments or any other kind of payment or credit to him.

A penalty is payable by a person ('P') who gives HMRC such a document if it contains a careless or deliberate inaccuracy on his part which amounts to, or leads to, an understatement of a tax liability or a false or inflated statement of a 'loss' or claim to 'repayment of tax'. If there is more than one inaccuracy in the document a penalty is payable for each inaccuracy.

From 1 April 2009, a penalty is also payable by a person ('T') if another person ('P') gives HMRC such a document, the document contains an inaccuracy amounting to, or leading to, an understatement of a tax liability or a false or inflated statement of a 'loss' or claim to 'repayment of tax' and the inaccuracy is due to T deliberately supplying false information to P, or deliberately withholding information from P, with the intention of the document containing the inaccuracy. This penalty applies regardless of whether or not P is liable to the main penalty above in respect of the same inaccuracy.

For these purposes, giving HMRC a document includes making a statement or declaration in a document and giving HMRC information in any form and by any method (including post, fax, email or telephone). A *'loss'* includes a charge, expense, deficit or any other amount which may be available for, or relied upon to claim, a deduction or relief. *'Repayment of tax'* includes allowing a credit against tax.

A person is not liable to either of the above penalties for an inaccuracy in respect of which he has been convicted of an offence.

Amount of penalties

See **55.11** below.

Suspension of penalty

HMRC can suspend all or part of a penalty for a careless inaccuracy. A notice in writing must be given to the taxpayer setting out what part of the penalty is to be suspended, the period of suspension (maximum two years) and the conditions of suspension with which the taxpayer must comply. The conditions can specify an action to be taken and a period within which it must be taken. A penalty can be suspended only if compliance with a condition of suspension will help the taxpayer to avoid further penalties under these provisions.

A suspended penalty will become payable:

- at the end of the suspension period, if the taxpayer does not satisfy HMRC that the conditions have been complied with; and
- if, during the suspension period, the taxpayer incurs another penalty under these provisions.

Otherwise, the penalty is cancelled at the end of the suspension period.

Agents

P is liable to a penalty under the above provisions where a document containing a *careless* inaccuracy is given to HMRC on his behalf. He is not, however, liable to a penalty in respect of anything done or omitted by his agent, if he satisfies HMRC that he took reasonable care (see below) to avoid the inaccuracy.

Partnerships

Where a partner is liable to a penalty arising from an inaccuracy in, or in connection with, a partnership return, and the inaccuracy affects the amount of tax payable by another partner, that other partner is also liable to a penalty. The potential lost revenue is calculated separately for each partner by reference to the proportions of any tax liability that would be borne by each of them. The suspension provisions above are, however, applied jointly to the partners' penalties.

Company officers

Where a company (as widely defined) is liable to a penalty under the above provisions for a deliberate inaccuracy and the inaccuracy was attributable to a company 'officer', the officer is liable to pay such portion of the penalty (which may be 100%) as HMRC specify by written notice. Various provisions of *FA 2007, Sch 24* (e.g. right of appeal) then apply as if the specified portion were itself a penalty incurred by the officer. In relation to a body corporate, a director, shadow director, manager or secretary of the company is an '*officer*'. In relation to an LLP, a member of the LLP is an '*officer*'. In any other case, a director, manager, secretary or any other person managing or purporting to manage any of the company's affairs is an '*officer*'.

Power to amend provisions

The Treasury may by order make any incidental, supplemental, consequential, transitional, transitory or saving provision in connection with the above provisions and those at **55.14** below.

[*FA 2007, s 97, Sch 24 paras 1, 1A, 3, 14, 18–23A, 24–28; FA 2008, s 122, Sch 40 paras 2, 3, 5, 15–20; FA 2009, Sch 57, para 7; CTA 2010, Sch 1 para 575; SI 2008 No 568; SI 2009 No 571*].

Reasonable care

Taking 'reasonable care' includes:

- keeping accurate records to make sure returns are correct;
- checking what the correct position is when something is not understood; and
- informing HMRC promptly about any error discovered in a submitted return or document.

(www.hmrc.gov.uk/about/new-penalties/index.htm). For further guidance on 'reasonable care', see HMRC Compliance Manual CH81120, CH81142 and CH431010.

Other

The Government announced in the 2009 Budget that anyone who incurs a penalty of £5,000 or more for deliberate understatement of tax will be required to provide more information on his tax affairs for up to five years to ensure he has proper systems to be able to make a correct tax return and to allow HMRC to monitor future compliance (Budget Press Notice PN03, 22 April 2009).

See HMRC Briefs 19/08, 1 April 2008 and 29/08, 12 June 2008, www.hmr c.gov.uk/about/new-penalties/penalties-leaflet.pdf, and see also www.hmrc.gov. uk/about/new-penalties/index.htm for FAQs and other guidance.

Amount of penalties

[55.11] The amount of the penalty payable by P in **55.10** above depends on whether the inaccuracy is careless or deliberate, and is subject to reduction as detailed below. For this purpose, an inaccuracy in a document which was neither careless nor deliberate is treated as careless if P or a person acting on his behalf discovered the inaccuracy after giving HMRC the document but did not take reasonable steps to inform them.

With effect from a date to be appointed by the Treasury, the amount of this penalty will also depend on whether the inaccuracy involves a domestic matter or an offshore matter. It is anticipated that this will apply to tax periods commencing on or after 1 April 2011 (HMRC Budget Note BN68, 24 March 2010). The remainder of this paragraph assumes the inaccuracy involves a domestic matter; see **55.12** below as regards offshore matters.

For careless action or omission (i.e. where P or a person acting on his behalf failed to take reasonable care — see below), the penalty is 30% of the 'potential lost revenue' (see below).

For deliberate but not concealed action or omission (i.e. where the inaccuracy was deliberate but P did not make arrangements to conceal it), the penalty is 70% of the potential lost revenue.

For deliberate and concealed action or omission (i.e. where the inaccuracy was deliberate and P made arrangements to conceal it, for example by submitting false evidence in support of an inaccurate figure), the penalty is 100% of the potential lost revenue.

The amount of the penalty payable by T in **55.10** above is 100% of the potential lost revenue. (This is the case regardless of whether the inaccuracy involves a domestic matter or an offshore matter.)

Reduction for disclosure

A reduction in a penalty will be given where a person discloses an inaccuracy in a document or, in relation to the penalty payable by T, a supply of false information or a withholding of information. The penalty will be reduced to a percentage which reflects the quality of the disclosure and the amount of the reduction will depend on whether the disclosure is 'prompted' or 'unprompted'.

In the case of an unprompted disclosure, a 100% penalty may not be reduced to a percentage below 30%, and a 70% penalty may not be reduced to a percentage below 20%. A 30% penalty may be reduced to any percentage, including 0%.

In the case of a prompted disclosure, a 100% penalty may not be reduced to a percentage below 50%, a 70% penalty may not be reduced to a percentage below 35% and a 30% penalty may not be reduced to a percentage below 15%.

A person is treated as making a disclosure for these purposes only if he tells HMRC about the inaccuracy etc., gives HMRC reasonable help in quantifying the inaccuracy etc. and allows them access to records for the purpose of ensuring that the inaccuracy etc. is fully corrected. A disclosure is '*unprompted*' if made when the taxpayer has no reason to believe HMRC have discovered, or are about to discover, the inaccuracy etc. In all other cases, disclosures are '*prompted*'.

Reduction in special circumstances

HMRC can also reduce, stay, or agree a compromise in relation to proceedings for, either of the penalties in **55.10** above if they think it right to do so because of special circumstances. Ability to pay and the fact that a potential loss of revenue from one taxpayer is balanced by a potential overpayment by another are not special circumstances for this purpose. It is expected that this power will be used only in rare cases (Treasury Explanatory Notes to the 2007 Finance Bill).

Reduction for other penalty or surcharge

The amount of a penalty payable by P in **55.10** above in respect of a document relating to a particular tax year is reduced by the amount of any other penalty, or surcharge for late payment of tax, the amount of which is determined by reference to P's tax liability for the year. No reduction is made for a tax-related penalty within **55.17** below.

Where penalties are imposed on P and T in **55.10** above in respect of the same inaccuracy, the aggregate penalty cannot exceed 100% of the potential lost revenue.

Potential lost revenue

The *'potential lost revenue'* is the additional tax (including NIC) due or payable as a result of correcting the inaccuracy in the document. This includes any amount payable to HMRC having been previously repaid in error and any amount which would have been repaid in error had the inaccuracy not been corrected. The fact that potential lost revenue may be balanced by a potential overpayment by another person is also ignored.

Where the amount of potential lost revenue (in relation to the penalty payable by P) depends on the order in which inaccuracies are corrected, careless inaccuracies are taken to be corrected before deliberate inaccuracies, and deliberate but not concealed inaccuracies are taken to be corrected before deliberate and concealed inaccuracies. Where there are inaccuracies in one or more documents relating to a particular tax year (in relation to the penalty payable by P) and those inaccuracies include both understatements and overstatements, the overstatements are taken into account in calculating the potential lost revenue and are set off against understatements in the order which reduces the level of penalties the least (i.e. against understatements not liable to a penalty first, then against careless understatements, and so on).

Special rules apply where an inaccuracy leads to there being a wrongly recorded loss which has not been wholly used to reduce a tax liability. The potential lost revenue in respect of that part of the loss which has not been so used is restricted to 10% of the unused part. Where, however, there is no reasonable prospect of a loss being used to support a claim to reduce a tax liability (of any person) because of the taxpayer's circumstances or the nature of the loss, the potential lost revenue is nil.

Where an inaccuracy results in an amount of tax being declared later that it would have been (otherwise than because of a wrongly recorded loss), the potential lost revenue is 5% of the delayed tax for each year of delay (applied pro rata for periods of less than a year).

[FA 2007, s 97, Sch 24 paras 4, 4A, 4B, 4D, 5–12, 24, 28; FA 2008, s 122, Sch 40 paras 6–11, 20; FA 2009, Sch 57, paras 3, 4; FA 2010, s 35, Sch 10 paras 2–4; SI 2008 No 568; SI 2009 No 571].

Amount of penalties — offshore matters

[55.12] With effect from a date to be appointed by the Treasury by statutory instrument, the amount of the penalty payable by P in **55.10** above continues to depend on whether the inaccuracy is careless or deliberate (see **55.11** above) but also depends on whether the inaccuracy involves a domestic matter or an offshore matter. It is anticipated that this will apply to tax periods commencing on or after 1 April 2011 (HMRC Budget Note BN68, 24 March 2010).

For these purposes, an inaccuracy involves an offshore matter if it results in a potential loss of revenue (see **55.11** above) that is charged on or by reference to:

- income arising from a source in a territory outside the UK; or
- assets situated or held in a territory outside the UK; or
- activities carried on wholly or mainly in a territory outside the UK; or

- anything having effect as if it were income, assets or activities of the kind above.

Otherwise the inaccuracy involves a domestic matter. The Treasury may make provision by statutory instrument for determining for the above purposes where a source of income is located, where an asset is situated or held and/or where activities are carried on. Different provision may be made for different cases and for income tax and capital gains tax.

Category 1

If the inaccuracy involves an offshore matter and the territory in question is a 'category 1 territory', the amounts of the penalties are the same as for domestic matters, i.e. the amounts in **55.11** above. A *'category 1 territory'* is a territory designated as such by order to be made by the Treasury.

Category 2

If the inaccuracy involves an offshore matter and the territory in question is a 'category 2 territory', the amounts of the penalties are as follows.

For careless action or omission (i.e. where P or a person acting on his behalf failed to take reasonable care — see **55.10** above), the penalty is 45% of the 'potential lost revenue' (see **55.11** above).

For deliberate but not concealed action or omission (i.e. where the inaccuracy was deliberate but P did not make arrangements to conceal it), the penalty is 105% of the potential lost revenue.

For deliberate and concealed action or omission (i.e. where the inaccuracy was deliberate and P made arrangements to conceal it, for example by submitting false evidence in support of an inaccurate figure), the penalty is 150% of the potential lost revenue.

A *'category 2 territory'* is a territory that is neither a category 1 territory nor a category 3 territory.

Category 3

If the inaccuracy involves an offshore matter and the territory in question is a 'category 3 territory', the amounts of the penalties are as follows.

For careless action or omission (i.e. where P or a person acting on his behalf failed to take reasonable care), the penalty is 60% of the potential lost revenue.

For deliberate but not concealed action or omission (i.e. where the inaccuracy was deliberate but P did not make arrangements to conceal it), the penalty is 140% of the potential lost revenue.

For deliberate and concealed action or omission (i.e. where the inaccuracy was deliberate and P made arrangements to conceal it, for example by submitting false evidence in support of an inaccurate figure), the penalty is 200% of the potential lost revenue.

A *'category 3 territory'* is a territory designated as such by order to be made by the Treasury.

Inaccuracy in more than one category

If a single inaccuracy is in more than one category it is treated for these purposes as if it were separate inaccuracies, one in each relevant category according to the matters that it involves. The potential lost revenue is to be calculated separately in respect of each separate inaccuracy.

Categorisation of territories

In considering how to classify a territory for these purposes, the Treasury must have regard to:

- the existence or otherwise of arrangements for the exchange of information between the UK and that territory;
- the quality of any such arrangements (in particular, whether they provide for information to be exchanged automatically or on request), and
- the benefit that the UK would be likely to obtain from receiving information from that territory, were such arrangements to exist.

Categorisation orders are to be made by statutory instrument. The above penalty provisions do not apply to inaccuracies in a document given to HMRC (or, where appropriate, to inaccuracies discovered by P — see **55.11** above) before the date on which the relevant categorisation order comes into force.

Reduction for disclosure

See **55.11** above as regards reductions for disclosure generally.

In the case of an unprompted disclosure:

- a 200% penalty may not be reduced to a percentage below 60%;
- a 150% penalty may not be reduced to a percentage below 45%;
- a 140% penalty may not be reduced to a percentage below 40%;
- a 105% penalty may not be reduced to a percentage below 30%; but
- a 60% or 45% penalty may be reduced to any percentage, including 0%.

In the case of a prompted disclosure:

- a 200% penalty may not be reduced to a percentage below 100%;
- a 150% penalty may not be reduced to a percentage below 75%;
- a 140% penalty may not be reduced to a percentage below 70%;
- a 105% penalty may not be reduced to a percentage below 52.5%;
- a 60% penalty may not be reduced to a percentage below 30%; and
- a 45% penalty may not be reduced to a percentage below 22.5%.

Reduction in special circumstances

See **55.11** above.

Reduction for other penalty or surcharge

Where penalties are imposed on P and T (in **55.10** above) in respect of the same inaccuracy, the aggregate penalty cannot exceed:

- 100% of the potential lost revenue for an inaccuracy in category 1, i.e. the same as in **55.11** above;

- 150% of the potential lost revenue for an inaccuracy in category 2; or
- 200% of the potential lost revenue for an inaccuracy in category 3.

See also **55.11** above.

[FA 2007, Sch 24 paras 4, 4A, 10, 12(4)(5), 21A, 21B, 23B; FA 2010, s 35, Sch 10 paras 1–6].

Negligence or fraud in connection with return or accounts

[55.13] The following provisions were repealed and replaced by the provisions at **55.10** above for, effectively, 2008/09 onwards. [FA 2007, s 97, Sch 24 para 29; SI 2008 No 568].

Subject to the above, where a person fraudulently or negligently:

- delivers an incorrect tax return under TMA 1970, s 8 or s 8A (personal or trustees' return — see **63.2 RETURNS**);
- makes any incorrect return, statement or declaration in connection with any claim for an allowance, deduction or relief; or
- submits to HMRC or to the Appeal Commissioners any incorrect accounts,

he is liable to a maximum penalty of an amount equal to the resulting tax underpayment. In arriving at the latter, one takes into account the tax year *in which* the return is delivered etc., the following tax year and any previous tax year.

[TMA 1970, s 95].

Liability to a penalty is supplementary to the liability to make good the tax underpayment itself.

For the above purposes, an innocent error is attributed to negligence unless it is rectified without unreasonable delay after its discovery by the taxpayer (or, following his death, by his personal representatives). Accounts submitted on a person's behalf are deemed to have been submitted by him unless he proves that they were submitted without his consent or connivance. [TMA 1970, s 97].

Use of a provisional or estimated figure in a return may result in its being incorrect, and subject to a penalty, if the figure was calculated without reasonable care or if the final figure could have been obtained before the return was filed (Revenue Tax Bulletin February 2002 p 916).

Partnerships

Where a partner (the representative partner) delivers an incorrect partnership return (see **63.13 RETURNS**), or, in connection with such a return, makes an incorrect statement or declaration or submits incorrect accounts, and either he does so fraudulently or negligently or his doing so is attributable to fraudulent or negligent conduct on the part of a 'relevant partner' (i.e. any person who was a partner at any time in the period covered by the return). Each relevant partner is liable to a penalty not exceeding the income tax (or corporation tax) underpaid by him as a result of the incorrectness. Where penalties are imposed on two or more partners, an appeal cannot be made otherwise than by way of composite appeal by the representative partner, or his successor (see **63.13** RETURNS). [*TMA 1970, s 95A*].

Simon's Taxes. See A4.510, A6.602.

Failure to notify HMRC of error in assessment

[55.14] With effect for 2008/09 onwards, a penalty is payable by a person if an assessment issued to him by HMRC understates his liability to income tax and he or a person acting on his behalf has failed to take reasonable steps to notify HMRC, within the 30 days beginning with the date of the assessment, of the under-assessment. The penalty is 30% of the potential lost revenue (defined as at **55.11** above, with the necessary modifications), subject to the same reductions that apply under the provisions at **55.11** for disclosure or special circumstances. HMRC must consider whether the taxpayer or a person acting on his behalf knew, or should have known, about the under-assessment and what steps would have been reasonable to take to notify HMRC.

For the above purposes, 'assessment' includes a determination.

A person is not liable to a penalty under this provision in respect of anything done or omitted by his agent, if he satisfies HMRC that he took reasonable care (see **55.10** above) to avoid failure to notify HMRC as above.

The amount of a penalty under this provision in respect of a document relating to a particular tax year is reduced by the amount of any other penalty the amount of which is determined by reference to the person's tax liability for the period.

A person is not liable to a penalty for a failure in respect of which he has been convicted of an offence.

[*FA 2007, s 97, Sch 24 paras 2, 4, 4C, 5–12, 18, 20, 21, 28; FA 2008, s 122, Sch 40 para 4; FA 2009, Sch 57 paras 2–4; FA 2010, s 35, Sch 10 paras 2–4; SI 2008 No 568; SI 2009 No 571*].

During the passage of the 2007 Finance Bill through Parliament, the Government gave an undertaking that this penalty would be applied only where HMRC make an assessment in the absence of a return (Hansard Standing Committee Debate, 12th Sitting, 5 June 2007 (afternoon), Column 472).

Failure to produce documents during enquiry

[55.15] These provisions are **repealed** from 1 April 2009 in consequence of the repeal of *TMA 1970, s 19A*. That provision is replaced by the powers at **38.3–38.10** HMRC INVESTIGATORY POWERS. See **55.17** below for penalties in relation to those powers. These provisions do, however, continue to have effect on and after 1 April 2009 for the purposes of any notice given before that date under *TMA 1970, s 19A*. [*SI 2009 No 404, arts 2, 3*].

Subject to the above, a penalty applies where a person fails to comply with a notice or requirement under *TMA 1970, s 19A* or *TMA 1970, Sch 1A para 6(2)(3A)(b)* (notice requiring production of documents etc. for purpose of an HMRC enquiry into a return — see **63.8 RETURNS**). He is liable to a fixed penalty of £50 and, for continuing failure after the fixed penalty is imposed, a daily penalty not exceeding the 'relevant amount'. No penalty may be imposed after the failure has been remedied. An officer of HMRC may determine the daily penalty under *TMA 1970, s 100* (see **55.25** below), in which case the '*relevant amount*' is £30, or may commence proceedings under *TMA 1970, s 100C* (see **55.27** below) for determination of the penalty by the Appeal Tribunal, in which case the '*relevant amount*' is £150. [*TMA 1970, s 97AA; FA 2008, s 113, Sch 36 para 72; SI 2009 No 56, Sch 1 para 43*].

See Revenue 'Working Together' Bulletin April 2000 p 8 as regards discharge of penalties raised after 14 December 1998 for non-compliance with notices subsequently determined to be invalid because they did not allow 30 days *from receipt* for compliance. For successful appeals against penalty notices containing basic errors, see *Austin v Price* (Sp C 426), [2004] SSCD 487 and *Jacques v HMRC* (Sp C 513), [2006] SSCD 40. The fixed penalty has been held not to be a criminal charge within the meaning of *Article 6* of the *European Convention on Human Rights* (*Harvard Sharkey v HMRC* Ch D 2006, 77 TC 484).

Simon's Taxes. See A4.509, A6.405.

Failure to keep and preserve records

[55.16] The maximum penalty for non-compliance with *TMA 1970, s 12B* (records to be kept and preserved for the purposes of self-assessment tax returns — see **63.5 RETURNS**) in relation to any tax year is £3,000. [*TMA 1970, s 12B(5)–(5B)*].

A separate maximum £3,000 penalty applies in relation to records relating to a claim made otherwise than in a self-assessment tax return (see **18.3 CLAIMS**). [*TMA 1970, Sch 1A para 2A(4)(5)*].

Simon's Taxes. See A4.508, E1.205.

Failure to comply with investigatory powers under FA 2008, Sch 36

[55.17] The penalties below apply to offences under the investigatory powers of *FA 2008, Sch 36* which apply from 1 April 2009.

Failure to comply — fixed and daily penalties

Where a person fails to comply with an information notice within *FA 2008, Sch 36 Pt 1* (see **38.4 HMRC INVESTIGATORY POWERS**) he is liable to a fixed penalty of £300 and, for each subsequent day of continuing failure, a further penalty not exceeding £60. For this purpose, failing to comply with a notice includes concealing, destroying or otherwise disposing of, or arranging for the concealment, destruction or disposal of, a document in breach of *FA 2008, Sch 36 paras 42, 43* (see **38.7 HMRC INVESTIGATORY POWERS**).

Where a person deliberately obstructs an HMRC officer in the course of an inspection of business premises under *FA 2008, Sch 36 Pt 2* (see **38.8, 38.9 HMRC INVESTIGATORY POWERS**) which has been approved by the Appeal Tribunal, he is liable to a fixed penalty of £300 and, for each subsequent day of continuing obstruction, a further penalty not exceeding £60.

No penalty is due where a person fails to do anything required to be done within a limited time period if he does it within such further time as an HMRC officer allows. A person is not liable to a penalty if he satisfies HMRC or (on appeal) the Tribunal that there is a reasonable excuse for the failure or obstruction. An insufficiency of funds is not a reasonable excuse for this purpose unless it is attributable to events outside the person's control. Where a person relies on another person to do anything, that is not a reasonable excuse unless the first person took reasonable care (see **55.10** above) to avoid the failure or obstruction. Where a person has a reasonable excuse which ceases, he is treated as continuing to have a reasonable excuse if the failure is remedied or the obstruction stops without unreasonable delay.

The Treasury can make regulations amending the amounts of the above penalties.

[*FA 2008, s 113, Sch 36 paras 39–41, 44, 45; FA 2009, Sch 47 paras 13, 14, 16; SI 2009 No 56, Sch 1 para 471(2)(12); SI 2009 No 404*].

Failure to comply — tax-related penalty

A tax-related penalty may be imposed by the Upper Tribunal where a person's failure or obstruction continues after a fixed penalty has been imposed under the above provisions. An HMRC officer must have reason to believe that the amount of tax that the person has paid, or is likely to pay is significantly less than it would otherwise have been as a result of the failure or obstruction, and the officer must make an application to the Upper Tribunal before the end of the twelve months beginning with the 'relevant date'. In deciding the amount of the penalty (if any), the Upper Tribunal must have regard to the amount of tax which has not been, or is likely not to be, paid by the person.

The *'relevant date'* is the date on which the person became liable to the penalty. Where, however, the penalty is for a failure relating to an information notice against which a person can appeal, the relevant date is the later of the end of the period in which notice of such appeal could have been given and, where an appeal is made, the date on which the appeal is determined or withdrawn.

A tax-related penalty is in addition to the fixed penalty and any daily penalties under the above provisions. No account is taken of a tax-related penalty for the purposes of **55.18** below and no reduction in a penalty charged under *FA 2007, Sch 24* (see **55.10, 55.14** above) or *FA 2008, Sch 41* (see **55.3** above) is to be made in respect of a penalty under these provisions.

[*FA 2008, Sch 36 para 50; SI 2009 No 404*].

Inaccurate information or documents

If, in complying with an information notice, a person provides inaccurate information or produces a document that contains an inaccuracy, he is liable to a penalty of up to £3,000 if either:

- the inaccuracy is careless (i.e. due to a failure to take reasonable care) or deliberate; or
- the person later discovers the inaccuracy and fails to take reasonable steps to inform HMRC.

If the information or document contains more than one inaccuracy, a penalty is payable for each inaccuracy.

The Treasury can make regulations amending the amounts of the above penalties.

[FA 2008, Sch 36 paras 40A, 41; FA 2009, Sch 47 paras 15, 16].

A person is not liable to a penalty under any of the above provisions in respect of anything for which he has been convicted of an offence. [FA 2008, Sch 36 para 52; SI 2009 No 404].

Two or more tax-related penalties in respect of the same tax

[55.18] Where two or more tax-related penalties are determined by reference to the same income tax, capital gains tax or corporation tax liability, the aggregate penalty is reduced to the greater or greatest of those separate penalties. The penalties at **55.10, 55.14** and **55.17** above are not taken into account for the purposes of this provision. [TMA 1970, s 97A; FA 2007, s 97, Sch 24 para 12(3); FA 2008, Sch 36 para 50(6); SI 2009 No 404]. See **55.22** below for mitigation of penalties.

Assisting in preparation of incorrect return etc.

[55.19] Assisting in or inducing the preparation or delivery of any information, return, accounts or other document known to be incorrect and to be, or to be likely to be, used for any tax purpose carries a maximum penalty of £3,000. [TMA 1970, s 99]. For the taxpayer's position where an agent has been negligent or fraudulent, see *Mankowitz v Special Commrs & CIR* Ch D 1971, 46 TC 707 and cf. *Clixby v Pountney* Ch D 1967, 44 TC 515 and *Pleasants v Atkinson* Ch D 1987, 60 TC 228.

Interest on penalties

[55.20] All of the above penalties (other than those under *FA 2008, Sch 41* at **55.3** above and those at **55.10, 55.14** and **55.17** above) carry interest, calculated from the due date (broadly, 30 days after issue of a notice of determination by an officer of HMRC — see **55.25** below, or immediately upon determination by the Appeal Tribunal — see **55.27, 55.28** below) to the date of payment. [TMA 1970, s 103A; SI 1998 No 311].

For income tax and capital gains tax, rates of interest on penalties are synonymous with those on overdue tax — see **42.2 INTEREST AND SURCHARGES ON OVERDUE TAX.**

Special returns

[55.21] Failure to render any information or particulars or any return, certificate, statement or other document which is required, whether by notice or otherwise, under the provisions listed in *TMA 1970, s 98* is the subject of a maximum penalty of £300, plus £60 for each day the failure continues after that penalty is imposed (but not for any day for which such a daily penalty has already been imposed). These penalties are increased by a factor of ten in the case of a failure under *ICTA 1988, s 765A* (movements of capital between residents of EC member states). The maximum penalty for an incorrect return etc. given fraudulently or negligently is £3,000. Penalties for failure to render information etc. required by notice cannot be imposed after the failure is rectified, and daily penalties can similarly not be imposed where the information etc. was required other than by notice. [*TMA 1970, s 98; ITA 2007, Sch 1 para 260; CTA 2009, Sch 1 para 307; SI 2009 No 2035, Sch para 8*].

Failure to allow access to computers renders a person liable to a maximum £300 penalty (£500 before 21 July 2008). [*FA 1988, s 127; FA 2008, s 114*].

See **52.26 PARTNERSHIPS** as regards penalties under *TMA 1970, s 98B* in relation to European Economic Interest Groupings.

PAYE returns etc.

Special penalties are imposed for failure to make annual returns required under PAYE (see **53.12**(a) **PAY AS YOU EARN**) or the construction industry scheme (see **22.11 CONSTRUCTION INDUSTRY SCHEME**) by the statutory filing date, i.e. by 19 May following the end of the tax year for which the return is required. These are a penalty of £100 for each month or part month (up to twelve) during which the failure continues and for each 50 persons (or part where the total is not a multiple of 50) in respect of whom particulars should have been included in the return, and, if the failure continues beyond twelve months, an additional penalty of the amount payable for the tax year to which the return relates which remained unpaid at 19 April following that year. If an incorrect return is fraudulently or negligently made, the penalty is the difference between the amount payable under the return and the amount which would have been payable had the return been correct. The latter rule is replaced by the provisions at **55.10** above for, effectively, 2008/09 and subsequent years. [*TMA 1970, s 98A; FA 2007, s 97, Sch 24 para 29; SI 2003 No 2682, Regs 73, 146; SI 2008 No 568*].

By concession, no penalty is charged if the return is received on or before the last business day within seven days following the filing date (HMRC ESC B46). This applies equally to returns filed online (Revenue Tax Bulletin April 2005 p 1190). This concession is to be withdrawn after 31 March 2011 (HMRC Brief 24/10, 2 June 2010).

The fact that *TMA 1970, s 98A* might produce a disproportionately harsh penalty for an employer with just one employee is of no consequence and is not in breach of *Human Rights Act 1998* (*Bysermaw Properties Ltd v HMRC* (Sp C 644), [2008] SSCD 322).

See **53.11, 53.12, 53.25** PAY AS YOU EARN as regards penalties for failure to make payments to HMRC electronically, and to file returns and other documents electronically, when required to do so.

See **53.14** PAY AS YOU EARN as regards penalties for late in-year payments of PAYE for 2010/11 onwards.

Simon's Taxes. See A4.517, A4.518, A6.409, E4.11122, E5.542B.

Mitigation of penalties

[55.22] The Commissioners of HMRC may mitigate penalties before or after judgment. [*TMA 1970, s 102*]. This rule does not apply to penalties under *FA 2007, Sch 24* (see **55.10, 55.14** above), *FA 2008, Sch 36* (see **55.17** above) and *FA 2008, Sch 41* (see **55.3** above), which include specific rules for the reduction of penalties in certain cases. [*TMA 1970, s 103ZA; FA 2009, Sch 57 para 13*]. A binding agreement by a taxpayer to pay an amount in composition cannot be repudiated afterwards by him or his executors (*A-G v Johnstone* KB 1926, 10 TC 758; *A-G v Midland Bank Trustee Co* KB 1934, 19 TC 136; *Richards* KB 1950, 33 TC 1).

Negotiated settlements

In the case of tax-based penalties (other than those under *FA 2008, Sch 41* at **55.3** above and those at **55.10, 55.14** and **55.17** above) where a maximum penalty of 100% is in strict law exigible, HMRC will start with the figure of 100% and then take the following factors into account in arriving at the penalty element which he will expect to be included in any offer in settlement of liabilities.

(a)   Disclosure. A reduction of up to 20% (or 30% where there has been full voluntary disclosure), depending on how much information was provided, how soon, and how that contributed to settling the enquiry.
(b)   Co-operation. A reduction of up to 40%.
(c)   Seriousness. A reduction of up to 40%, depending upon the nature of the offence, how long it continued and the amounts involved.

(HMRC Pamphlet IR 160). See, for example, *Caesar v Inspector of Taxes* (Sp C 142), [1998] SSCD 1.

For power of HMRC to enter into agreements in full settlement of liabilities in investigation cases, see **6.9** ASSESSMENTS.

See **55.3** and **55.11** above for the statutory reductions for disclosure in relation to penalties under *FA 2008, Sch 41* and *FA 2007, Sch 24* respectively.

See also **63.23** RETURNS as regards *TMA 1970, s 118(2)* (reasonable excuse for failure etc.).

For the validity of tax amnesties, see *R v CIR (ex p. National Federation of Self-Employed and Small Businesses Ltd)* HL 1981, 55 TC 133.

Certificates of full disclosure

Where it is established that tax has been lost due to a careless or deliberate inaccuracy (see **55.10** above — previously due to fraudulent or negligent conduct), HMRC may request that the taxpayer complete a 'certificate of full disclosure' stating that complete disclosure has been made of, inter alia, all banking, savings and loan accounts, deposit receipts, building society accounts, and accounts with other financial institutions; all investments including savings certificates and premium bonds and loans (whether interest-bearing or not); all other assets, including cash and life assurance policies, which the taxpayer now possesses, or has possessed, or in which he has or has had any interest or power to operate or control during the stated period; all gifts (in any form) by the taxpayer to his spouse, domestic partner, children or other persons during the stated period; all sources of income and all income derived therefrom; and all facts bearing on liability to income tax, capital gains tax and other duties for the stated period. Great care must be exercised before signing such a certificate, since subsequent discovery of an omission could lead to heavy penalties including, in serious cases, criminal prosecution.

Simon's Taxes. See A4.526, A6.420.

Specific disclosure opportunities

Offshore Disclosure Facility

[55.23] HMRC encouraged people to notify their intention on or before 22 June 2007 to make a disclosure of undeclared tax liabilities if they have held, directly or indirectly, one or more offshore accounts that is in any way connected to a loss of tax to the UK Exchequer. 'Offshore' means anywhere outside the UK and therefore includes the Channel islands and Isle of Man. Having notified the intention, the taxpayer had to make the disclosure and pay all related tax, interest and penalties no later than 26 November 2007. In return, HMRC undertook to limit the penalty to 10% of the previously undeclared tax and not to charge a penalty at all if the undeclared tax was less than £2,500. (HMRC News Release 17 April 2007).

A new offshore disclosure opportunity was announced in the 2009 Budget. Those who made a complete and accurate disclosure will have qualified for the reduced penalty of 10%. Intention to disclose had to be notified before 5 January 2010. The disclosure itself had to be made before 1 February 2010 on paper or before 13 March 2010 electronically. The 10% penalty rate applied only to those who were not written to by HMRC under the 2007 offshore disclosure facility. Those who were offered the 10% rate by HMRC under the 2007 facility but did not complete the disclosure procedure will have been subject to a minimum 20% penalty rate if they disclosed under this new opportunity. Now that this disclosure window has closed, those taxpayers who have not disclosed but are found to have evaded tax will face penalties of between 30% and 100% of the amount of tax involved, and also face an increased risk of criminal prosecution. (HMRC News Releases, 28 July 2009, 12 August 2009, 27 November 2009).

Liechtenstein Disclosure Facility

A separate disclosure facility was announced on 11 August 2009 involving investments held in Liechtenstein. This followed the signing of a Tax Information Exchange Agreement between the UK and Liechtenstein. The Liechtenstein Disclosure Facility runs from 1 September 2009 to 31 March 2015 inclusive. Penalties on unpaid tax will be capped at 10% of tax evaded. The recovery of unpaid tax (and thus the amount on which the penalty is based) will be restricted to a maximum of ten years up to and including 2008/09. Those who fail to make full disclosure by the end of the programme face having their accounts in Liechtenstein closed down in addition to increased penalties. (HMRC News Release, 11 August 2009). For further information see www.hmrc.gov.uk/international/liechtenstein.htm.

Medical professionals

In January 2010, HMRC announced the 'Tax Health Plan', a facility for medical professionals to disclose previously undeclared tax liabilities. Those who made a complete and accurate disclosure will qualify for a reduced penalty of 10% where the total of unpaid taxes or duties is £1,000 or more and no penalty at all where the total is less than that. Intention to disclose had to be notified before 1 April 2010. The disclosure itself had to be made in writing before 1 July 2010, and full payment including interest and penalties had also to be made by that date. For details, see www.hmrc.gov.uk/tax-health-plan/index.htm. (HMRC News Release, 10 January 2010).

Commissioners' precepts etc.

[55.24] Before 1 April 2009, summary penalties (to be treated as tax assessed and due and payable) could be determined by Appeal Commissioners against any party to proceedings before them who fails to comply with a precept, order for inspection etc. The maximum penalty was £300 in the case of the General Commissioners, £10,000 in the case of the Special Commissioners (and in the case of the General Commissioners, a daily penalty up to £60 could also be imposed for continuing failure). A penalty up to £10,000 could similarly be imposed for failure to comply with any other direction of the Special Commissioners (including in relation to a preliminary hearing) or, in relation to proceedings commenced after 27 January 2008, the General Commissioners. [*SI 1994 No 1811, Reg 24(1)(3); SI 1994 No 1812, Regs 10(1)(3)(4), 24A; SI 2007 No 3612, Regs 2, 6*]. Penalties could also be charged in relation to witness summonses: the maximum penalty was £1,000 in the case of the General Commissioners, £10,000 in the case of the Special Commissioners. [*SI 1994 No 1811, Reg 24(2)(3), SI 1994 No 1812, Reg 4(12)(13)*]. The Appeal Commissioners are replaced by the Tribunal with effect from 1 April 2009 (see **5 APPEALS**).

Appeal against such summary penalties lay to the High Court (or Court of Session). [*TMA 1970, s 53 (as inserted by SI 1994 No 1813)*]. For the procedure on such appeals, see *QT Discount Foodstores Ltd v Warley Com-*

mrs Ch D 1981, 57 TC 268 and, for a case in which penalties were quashed because the taxpayer's evidence that he was unable to supply the information in question was not properly tested, see *Boulton v Poole Commrs* Ch D 1988, 60 TC 718.

For appeals against penalties for non-compliance with precepts etc. see *Shah v Hampstead Commrs* Ch D 1974, 49 TC 651; *Chapman v Sheaf Commrs* Ch D 1975, 49 TC 689; *Toogood v Bristol Commrs* Ch D 1976, 51 TC 634 and [1977] STC 116; *Campbell v Rochdale Commrs* Ch D 1975, 50 TC 411; *B & S Displays Ltd v Special Commrs* Ch D 1978, 52 TC 318; *Galleri v Wirral Commrs* Ch D 1978, [1979] STC 216; *Beach v Willesden Commrs* Ch D 1981, 55 TC 663; *Stoll v High Wycombe Commrs and CIR* Ch D 1992, 64 TC 587; *Wilson v Leek Commrs and CIR* Ch D 1993, 66 TC 537.

Procedure

[55.25] *Except* in the case of:

(a)   penalties under *FA 2007, Sch 24* and *FA 2008, Schs 36, 41* (see further below); or

(b)   penalty proceedings instituted before the courts in cases of suspected fraud (see **55.28** below); or

(c)   penalties under:
- *TMA 1970, s 98(1)(i)* (£300 penalty for non-filing of returns etc. under the provisions listed in *TMA 1970, s 98* — see **55.21** above);
- *TMA 1970, s 98C(1)(a)* (penalty of up to £5,000 under **4.51** ANTI-AVOIDANCE); or

(d)   penalties in respect of which application to the Appeal Tribunal is specifically required, as mentioned where relevant in the preceding paragraphs of this chapter (for example, the daily penalty for late income tax and capital gains tax returns as in **55.5** above),

an authorised officer of HMRC may make a determination imposing a penalty under any tax provision and setting it at such amount as, in his opinion, is correct or appropriate.

The notice of determination must state the date of issue and the time within which an appeal can be made. It cannot be altered unless

- there is an appeal (see **55.26** below), or
- an authorised officer of HMRC discovers that the penalty is or has become insufficient (in which case he may make a further determination), or
- the penalty is an automatic or tax-related penalty under *TMA 1970, s 93* (late delivery of personal or trustees' tax returns — see **55.5** above) or arises under *TMA 1970, s 94(6)* or *FA 1998, Sch 18 para 18(2)* (tax-related penalty for late filing of company tax returns) or *FA 2004, s 260(1)(b)* (late filing of registered pension scheme returns), and an authorised officer of HMRC subsequently discovers that the amount of tax is or has become excessive (in which case it is to be revised accordingly).

A penalty under these provisions is due for payment 30 days after the issue of the notice of determination, and is treated as tax charged in an assessment which is due and payable.

Before 1 April 2008, a determination which could have been made on a person who has died can be made on his personal representatives, and is then payable out of his estate. *However*, HMRC have accepted that this is incompatible with *Human Rights Act 1998, Art 6* (HMRC Enquiry Manual EM1375 and see now HMRC Notice, 10 September 2007 reproduced at www.hmrc.gov.u k/workingtogether/news/sa100-a-news.htm).

[*TMA 1970, ss 100, 100A, 103ZA; FA 2007, Sch 24 para 29(b); FA 2008, Sch 36 para 74; FA 2009, Sch 57 para 13; SI 1994 No 1813; SI 2009 No 404*].

Penalties under *FA 2007, Sch 24* and *FA 2008, Sch 41*

Penalties under *FA 2007, Sch 24* (see **55.10** and **55.14** above) and *FA 2008, Sch 41* (see **55.3** above) are charged by HMRC assessment. The assessment is treated in the same way as an assessment to tax and can be enforced accordingly. It may also be combined with a tax assessment. The notice of assessment must state the tax year in respect of which the penalty is assessed. Subject to the time limits below, HMRC can make a supplementary assessment if an earlier assessment operated by reference to an underestimate of the 'potential lost revenue' (see **55.3** and **55.11** above).

Penalties must be paid before the end of the period of 30 days beginning with the day on which the notification of the penalty is issued.

An assessment of a penalty within **55.3** above must be made before the end of the twelve months beginning with the end of the 'appeal period' for the assessment of tax unpaid by reason of the failure or, where there is no such assessment, the date on which the amount of tax unpaid by reason of the failure is ascertained. The *'appeal period'* is the period during which an appeal could be brought or during which an appeal that has been brought has not been determined or withdrawn.

An assessment of either of the penalties within **55.10** above must be made before the end of the twelve months beginning with the end of the 'appeal period' for the decision correcting the inaccuracy or, where there is no tax assessment correcting it, the date on which the inaccuracy is corrected.

An assessment of a penalty within **55.14** above must be made before the end of the twelve months beginning with the end of the appeal period for the tax assessment which corrected the understatement or, where there is no tax assessment correcting it, the date on which the understatement is corrected.

[*FA 2007, s 97, Sch 24 paras 13, 28; FA 2008, ss 122, 123, Sch 40 para 12, Sch 41 para 16*].

Penalties under *FA 2008, Sch 36*

Fixed and daily penalties for failure to comply or obstruction and penalties for inaccuracies (see **55.17** above) are charged by HMRC assessment. The penalty can be enforced as if it were income tax charged in an assessment. An assessment to a fixed or daily penalty must be made within twelve months of the date on which the liability arose. Where, however, the penalty is for a failure relating to an information notice against which a person can appeal, the assessment must be made within twelve months of the later of the end of the period in which notice of such appeal could have been given and, where an appeal is made, the date on which the appeal is determined or withdrawn. An assessment to a penalty for an inaccuracy must be made within twelve months of HMRC's first becoming aware of the inaccuracy and within six years of the person becoming liable to the penalty. The penalty must be paid within the 30-day period beginning with the date on which HMRC issue notification of the penalty assessment or, if an appeal against the penalty is made, within the 30-day period beginning with the date on which the appeal is determined or withdrawn.

A liability to a tax-related penalty is notified by HMRC to the person liable and may be enforced as if it were income tax charged in an assessment. It must be paid within the 30-day period beginning with the date on which the notification is issued.

[*FA 2008, Sch 36 paras 46, 49, 50(4), 51; FA 2009, Sch 47 paras 17, 20; SI 2009 No 404*].

Simon's Taxes. See **A4.520, A6.610, A6.616.**

Appeals

[55.26] Subject to the following points, the general APPEALS (5) provisions apply to an appeal against a determination of a penalty as in **55.25** above.

TMA 1970, s 50(6)–(8) (see **5.18** APPEALS) do not apply. Instead (subject to below), on appeal the First-tier Tribunal can:

- in the case of a penalty which is required to be of a particular amount, set the determination aside, confirm it, or alter it to the correct amount; and

- in any other case, set the determination aside, confirm it if it seems appropriate, or reduce it (including to nil) or increase it as seems appropriate (but not beyond the permitted maximum).

Neither *TMA 1970, s 50(6)–(8)* nor the above apply on an appeal against a determination of an automatic late filing penalty for personal or partnership tax returns (see **55.5** above), where the 'reasonable excuse' let-out may have effect (see **55.6** above for the options open to the Tribunal in those cases).

In addition to the right to appeal to the Upper Tribunal on a point of law, the taxpayer can so appeal (with permission) against the amount of a penalty determined by the First-tier Tribunal.

[*TMA 1970, ss 100B, 103ZA; SI 1994 No 1813; SI 2009 No 56, Sch 1 para 45, SI 2009 No 571, art 12*].

Penalties under *FA 2007, Sch 24* and *FA 2008, Sch 41*

Assessments of penalties under *FA 2007, Sch 24* (see **55.10** and **55.14** above) and *FA 2008, Sch 41* (see **55.3** above) are subject to specific appeal provisions. An appeal can be made against an HMRC decision that a penalty is payable or against a decision as to the amount of a penalty. In relation to penalty within **55.10** above, an appeal can be brought against a decision not to suspend a penalty or against conditions of suspension. An appeal against a penalty is generally to be treated in the same way as an appeal against an income tax assessment, but not so as to require payment of the penalty before the appeal is determined.

The powers of the Appeal Tribunal are restricted in certain cases, to where it thinks that HMRC's decision was flawed when considered in the light of principles applicable in proceedings for judicial review. The decisions concerned are as follows:

- a decision as to the extent to which the provisions for reduction of a penalty in special circumstances apply;
- a decision not to suspend a penalty; and
- a decision as to the conditions of suspension.

Where the Tribunal orders HMRC to suspend a penalty, there is a further right of appeal against the provisions of HMRC's notice of suspension.

[*FA 2007, s 97, Sch 24 paras 15–17; FA 2008, ss 122, 123, Sch 40 paras 13, 14, Sch 41 paras 17–19; FA 2009, Sch 57 paras 6, 11; SI 2009 No 56, Sch 1 paras 466, 467, 472, 473(2)(3)*].

Penalties under *FA 2008, Sch 36*

Appeals can be made against an HMRC decision that a fixed or daily penalty (see **55.17** above) is payable or against a decision as to the amount of such a penalty. Notice of appeal must be given in writing within the 30-day period beginning with the date on which HMRC notification of the penalty assessment is issued, and must state the grounds of appeal. Subject to this, the general APPEALS (**5**) provisions apply as they apply to income tax assessments. [*FA 2008, Sch 36 paras 47, 48; FA 2009, Sch 47 paras 18, 19; SI 2009 No 56, Sch 1 para 471(13)(14), SI 2009 No 404*].

Simon's Taxes. See **A4.524, A6.610, A6.616.**

Proceedings before Tribunal

[55.27] For a penalty within **55.25**(c) above or the higher daily penalty within **55.15** above (failure to produce documents), an authorised officer of HMRC can commence proceedings before the First-tier Tribunal. The taxpayer will be a party to the proceedings. In addition to the right to appeal to the Upper Tribunal on a point of law, the taxpayer can so appeal (with permission) against the amount of a penalty determined by the First-tier Tribunal. The Upper Tribunal can set the determination aside, confirm it if it seems appropriate, or reduce it (including to nil) or increase it as seems appropriate (but not beyond the permitted maximum). The penalty is treated as tax charged in an assessment and due and payable. [*TMA 1970, s 100C; SI 2009 No 56, Sch 1 para 46*].

These rules do not apply to penalties under *FA 2007, Sch 24* (see **55.10, 55.14** above), *FA 2008, Sch 36* (see **55.17** above) and *FA 2008, Sch 41* (see **55.3** above). [*TMA 1970, s 103ZA; FA 2009, Sch 57 para 13*].

Simon's Taxes. See **A4.521, A5.605, A5.611.**

Proceedings before court

[55.28] If the Commissioners of HMRC consider that liability for a penalty arises from fraud by any person, proceedings can be brought in the High Court (or Court of Session). If the court does not find fraud proved, it can nevertheless impose a penalty to which it considers the person liable. [*TMA 1970, s 100D*].

This rule does not apply to penalties under *FA 2007, Sch 24* (see **55.10, 55.14** above), *FA 2008, Sch 36* (see **55.17** above) and *FA 2008, Sch 41* (see **55.3** above). [*TMA 1970, s 103ZA; FA 2009, Sch 57 para 13*].

Simon's Taxes. See **A4.522.**

General matters

[55.29] Non-receipt of notice of the hearing at which the Appeal Commissioners awarded penalties is not a ground of appeal to the courts *(Kenny v Wirral Commrs* Ch D 1974, 50 TC 405; *Campbell v Rochdale Commrs* Ch D 1975, 50 TC 411).

A mere denial of liability to penalties implies an intention by the taxpayer to set up a case in refutation, and details must be supplied *(CIR v Jackson* CA 1960, 39 TC 357).

For the validity of penalty proceedings while assessments remain open, see *A-G for Irish Free State v White* SC (RI) 1931, 38 TC 666 and *R v Havering Commrs (ex p. Knight)* CA 1973, 49 TC 161. For other procedural matters, see *Collins v Croydon Commrs* Ch D 1969, 45 TC 566; *Bales v Rochford Commrs* Ch D 1964, 42 TC 17; *Sparks v West Brixton Commrs* Ch D, [1977] STC 212; *Moschi v Kensington Commrs* Ch D 1979, 54 TC 403; and for other appeals against penalties for failure to make returns, see *Dunk v Havant Commrs* Ch D 1976, 51 TC 519; *Napier v Farnham Commrs* CA, [1978] TR 403; *Garnham v Haywards Heath Commrs* Ch D 1977, [1978] TR 303; *Cox v Poole Commrs and CIR (No 1)* Ch D 1987, 60 TC 445; *Montague v Hampstead Commrs & Others* Ch D 1989, 63 TC 145; *Cox v Poole Commrs (No 2)* Ch D 1989, 63 TC 277.

For variation etc. of penalties by the court, see *Dawes v Wallington Commrs* Ch D 1964, 42 TC 200; *Salmon v Havering Commrs* CA 1968, 45 TC 77; *Williams v Special Commrs* Ch D 1974, 49 TC 670; *Wells v Croydon Commrs* Ch D 1968, 47 ATC 356; *Taylor v Bethnal Green Commrs* Ch D 1976, [1977] STC 44; *Stableford v Liverpool Commrs* Ch D 1982, [1983] STC 162; *Sen v St. Anne, Westminster Commrs* Ch D, [1983] STC 415; *Jolley v Bolton Commrs* Ch D 1986, 65 TC 242; *Lear v Leek Commrs* Ch D 1986, 59 TC 247; *Walsh v Croydon Commrs* Ch D 1987, 60 TC 442; *Fox v Uxbridge Commrs & CIR* Ch D 2001, [2002] STC 455.

For the test used by the court in considering whether penalties are excessive, see *Brodt v Wells Commrs* Ch D 1987, 60 TC 436. Per Scott LJ, penalties awarded by different bodies of Commissioners 'should, in relation to similar cases, bear some resemblance to one another'.

In determining whether the taxpayer has been negligent, the civil standard of proof (of the balance of probabilities) should be applied and not the criminal standard of proof (of beyond reasonable doubt) (*HMRC v Khawaja Ch D*, [2008] STC 2880).

Statements made or documents produced by or on behalf of a taxpayer are admissible as evidence in proceedings against him notwithstanding that reliance on HMRC's practice in cases of full disclosure (see **38.14** HMRC INVESTIGATORY POWERS) or their policy on mitigating penalties (see **55.22** above) may have induced him to make or produce them. [*TMA 1970, s 105*].

Time limits

[55.30] The time within which a penalty (other than those within **55.10** and **55.14**, for which see **55.25** above) can be determined, or proceedings can be commenced, depends on the penalty, as follows.

(a)   If the penalty is ascertainable by reference to tax payable, the time is:
    (i)   six years after the date the penalty was incurred; or
    (ii)   (subject to below) a later time within three years after the final determination of the amount of tax.
(b)   If the penalty arises under *TMA 1970, s 99* (assisting in preparation of incorrect return etc. — see **55.19** above) the time is twenty years after the date it was incurred.
(c)   In any other case, the time is six years from the time when the penalty was, or began to be, incurred.

Where the person liable has died, and the determination falls to be made in relation to his personal representatives, the extension in (a)(ii) above does not apply if the tax is charged in an assessment made more than six years after 31 January following the chargeable period for which it is charged. This ceases to apply for, effectively, 2008/09 onwards.

[*TMA 1970, s 103; FA 2007, s 97, Sch 24 para 29(b); SI 2008 No 568; SI 2009 No 56, Sch 1 para 48*].

These rules do not apply to penalties under *FA 2007, Sch 24* (see **55.10**, **55.14** above), *FA 2008, Sch 36* (see **55.17** above) and *FA 2008, Sch 41* (see **55.3** above). [*TMA 1970, s 103ZA; FA 2009, Sch 57 para 13*].

Provisional agreement of the amount due subject to the HMRC officer being satisfied later with statements of assets etc. is not final determination of the amount of tax (*Carco Accessories Ltd v CIR CS 1985, 59 TC 45*).

Simon's Taxes. See **A4.523**.

Bankrupts

[55.31] Penalties awarded after a bankruptcy are provable debts, but in practice HMRC does not proceed for penalties during a bankruptcy where there are other creditors. The trustee may agree to compromise any penalties awarded but the compromise must also be agreed by the bankrupt (*Re Hurren Ch D 1982, 56 TC 494*).

Liability under criminal law

[55.32] 'False statements to the prejudice of the Crown and public revenue' are criminal offences (*R v Hudson* CCA 1956, 36 TC 561). False statements in income tax returns, or for obtaining any allowance, reduction or repayment may involve liability to imprisonment for up to two years, under *Perjury Act 1911, s 5*, for 'knowingly and wilfully' making materially false statements or returns for tax purposes. Also, in Scotland, summary proceedings may be taken under *TMA 1970, s 107*.

HMRC have an unrestricted power to conduct a prosecution in the Crown Court, there being no requirement for the consent of the Attorney-General (*R (oao Hunt) v Criminal Cases Review Commission DC*, [2000] STC 1110).

See **6.9** ASSESSMENTS as regards acceptance of money settlements instead of institution of criminal proceedings. See **38.14** HMRC INVESTIGATORY POWERS for HMRC's published criminal investigation/prosecution policy. See **34.4** HMRC — ADMINISTRATION as regards HMRC powers generally.

Penalties imposed for non-declaration of income and calculated as a percentage of the tax lost have been held to be criminal (rather than civil) penalties for the purposes of the *European Convention on Human Rights (King v United Kingdom (No 2)* ECHR, [2004] STC 911).

Falsification etc. of documents which are required to be produced as in **38.11** and **38.13** HMRC INVESTIGATORY POWERS is a criminal offence punishable, on summary conviction, by a fine of the statutory maximum or, on indictment, by a fine or imprisonment for up to two years or both. [*TMA 1970, s 20BB; FA 2008, s 113, Sch 36 para 69; SI 2009 No 404*]. Similar punishments apply for the concealment, destruction or disposal of documents required to be produced as in **38.4** HMRC INVESTIGATORY POWERS. See **38.10**.

Simon's Taxes. See A4.530, A6.11, A6.311.

Offence of fraudulent evasion of income tax

[55.33] A person who is knowingly concerned in the fraudulent evasion of income tax (by him or any other person) is liable, on summary conviction, to imprisonment for up to six months and/or a fine not exceeding the statutory maximum (£5,000), or on conviction on indictment, to imprisonment for up to seven years and/or an unlimited fine. [*TMA 1970, s 106A; TIOPA 2010, Sch 7 para 95*].

For an article giving HMRC's views on conduct amounting to this offence, see Revenue Tax Bulletin October 2000 pp 782, 783.

Simon's Taxes. See A6.1105.

Publishing details of deliberate tax defaulters

[55.34] With effect from 1 April 2010, the Commissioners for HMRC can publish information about a person (including his name and address) if as a result of an investigation one or more specified penalties have been incurred by him and the total 'potential lost revenue' in respect of which the penalty or penalties were calculated is more than £25,000.

The information can only be first published in the period of one year beginning with the last day on which any of the penalties becomes final. It cannot continue to be published for more than one year.

Before publishing the information, the Commissioners must inform the taxpayer that they are doing so and provide a reasonable opportunity to make representations about whether it should be published. No information will be published if the penalty is reduced, by reason of disclosure, to the full extent possible.

The specified penalties are those under **55.10** above (careless or deliberate errors in documents), **55.3** above (failure to notify chargeability) and certain VAT and duty penalties. See **55.3** and **55.11** for the meaning of '*potential lost revenue*' in each case.

HMRC will apply the above for tax periods starting on or after 1 April 2010 and for offences which are committed on or after that date (www.hmrc.gov. uk/news/details-defaulters.htm).

[*FA 2009, s 94; SI 2010 No 574*].

Key points

[55.35] Points to consider are as follows.

- The new penalty regime for inaccuracies in returns in *FA 2007* (see **55.10**) requires taxpayers to take reasonable care to avoid an inaccuracy, even when an agent is acting. Advisers should ensure that clients are aware of the requirement and what the implications are for them. This could be done through the letter of engagement.

- When voluntarily correcting errors on returns the adviser will need to consider the penalty implications. Merely submitting an amended return does not count as 'disclosure' for the penalty reduction provisions. If the inaccuracy is careless or deliberate, a separate disclosure, meeting the requirements of the law, should be made. This may take the form of a note in the white space on the amended return, or may form a separate communication with HMRC.

- When the new regime for late filing of tax returns commences (expected to be in respect of 2011/12) (see **55.9**) there will no longer be a cap on the £100 penalty for a late return where the tax outstanding on 31 January is less than this amount. Advisers will wish to consider how to prepare or warn their clients about this change.

- Penalties for failure to supply information and documents under *FA 2008, Sch 36* (see **55.17**) move immediately to a daily penalty rate once HMRC has levied the fixed penalty. It is likely, however, that the officer will not impose the full £60 per day available in the legislation, but will commence at a lower rate per day initially, escalating the penalty for further delays or failures.

- When a penalty for a careless inaccuracy is considered (see **55.10**), the adviser may wish to suggest the option of suspending the penalty if this is not offered. He may also be able to assist in identifying additional controls which could be implemented, thus reducing the risk of error in the future; such controls can then become the conditions of suspension and thus promote future compliance. The decision by the officer not to suspend a penalty can be subject to appeal or review, as can the conditions set.

56

Pension Income

Simon's Taxes. See E4.126, E4.127, E4.129, E4.314–E4.317, E4.319, E4.320, E4.323, E4.841, E7.103, E7.121, E7.237, E7.239, E7.267, E7.416, E7.508.

Introduction

[56.1] The pensions, annuities etc. listed in **56.2** below are chargeable to tax as pension income. *Except where otherwise stated* in **56.2**:

- the chargeable amount is the full amount accruing in the tax year (regardless of when paid); and
- the chargeable person is the person receiving or entitled to the income.

The chargeable amount is subject to any deductions due under the payroll giving scheme (see **16.20 CHARITIES**) and the 10% deduction mentioned in **56.2**(f) below.

[*ITEPA 2003, ss 565–568*].

Except where otherwise stated in **56.2** below, and subject also to the exemptions in **56.4** below, the charge applies regardless of the residence status of the recipient. See **56.3, 56.4** below for exempt pension income generally.

Most taxable pension income is within the scope of **PAY AS YOU EARN (53)** (see the list at *ITEPA 2003, s 683(3)*). Certain annuities were brought within PAYE from 6 April 2007 — see **56.2**(e) below and **53.17 PAY AS YOU EARN**.

See **56.5** below for the taxation of State pension lump sums (applicable for 2006/07 onwards).

A disability benefit paid to a redundant employee from the former employer company pension fund was held to be chargeable as a pension (*Johnson v Holleran* Ch D 1988, 61 TC 428; *Johnson v Farquhar* Ch D 1991, 64 TC 385).

Taxable income

[56.2] The chargeable pensions, annuities etc. referred to in **56.1** above are as listed below. These are subject to the exemptions in **56.3, 56.4** below.

(a) **UK pensions,** i.e. any pension paid by or on behalf of a person within the UK and not within any of (c)–(h) below. These include voluntary pensions and pensions capable of being discontinued. [*ITEPA 2003, ss 569–572*].

(b) **Foreign pensions,** i.e. any pension paid by or on behalf of a person outside the UK to a person resident in the UK and not within any of (c)–(h) below. These include voluntary pensions, and pensions capable of being discontinued, paid by former employers or their successors. The chargeable amount is **90%** of the amount of income arising in the tax year, other than where the remittance basis applies (for which see **61 REMITTANCE BASIS**). The income is relevant foreign income (see **32.2 FOREIGN INCOME**) for the purposes of the remittance basis and **32.4** (deductions and reliefs). [*ITEPA 2003, ss 573–576; FA 2008, Sch 7 paras 45, 81*]. See **32.5 FOREIGN INCOME** (and also, for 2007/08 and earlier years, **61.28 REMITTANCE BASIS**) for reliefs potentially available for unremittable income.

(c) **UK social security pensions,** i.e. the State pension and similar benefits included in the list at **70.1 SOCIAL SECURITY AND NATIONAL INSURANCE,** subject to the partial exemption at **56.3**(i) below for child dependency additions. [*ITEPA 2003, ss 577–579*].

It is possible to defer the State pension and take a lump sum as a reward for doing so. For more details and for special rules relating to the taxation of this lump sum, see **56.5** below.

(d) **Pensions** paid under a **registered pension scheme** (see **57.2 PENSION PROVISION**). For this purpose, a 'pension' includes an annuity under, or purchased with assets held for or representing acquired rights under, a registered pension scheme. It also includes an income withdrawal (within *FA 2004, Sch 28 para 7*) or dependant's income withdrawal (within *FA 2004, Sch 28 para 21*). No charge applies to the extent, if any, that the payment of the pension attracts an unauthorised payments charge (see **57.19**(d) **PENSION PROVISION**). [*ITEPA 2003, ss 579A–579D*].

(e) Other **employment-related annuities** (where not covered by (d) above but including annuities from a non-UK source if paid to a UK resident). These comprise annuities purchased by someone in recognition of another's services in an office or employment, annuities under an occupational pension scheme (within *FA 2004, s 150(5)*) that is not a registered pension scheme and annuities within *ICTA 1988, s 273* or *ITA 2007, s 459* (see **44.2 LIFE ASSURANCE POLICIES**). If the annuity arises from a UK source, the chargeable amount is the full amount of the annuity arising in the tax year. If the annuity arises from a non-UK source), the chargeable amount is determined on the same basis as for foreign pensions in (b) above. [*ITEPA 2003, ss 609–614; ITA 2007, Sch 1 para 441*].

For 2006/07 onwards, annuities under an occupational pension scheme that is not a registered scheme were brought within the PAYE system. [*ITEPA 2003, s 683(3)*].

(f) **Overseas government pensions** payable in the UK *to* a UK resident (or to his widow, widower, surviving civil partner, child, relative or dependant) in respect of overseas government service, and *by* (or on behalf of) the government of a British dominion or protectorate or a country mentioned in *British Nationality Act 1981, Sch 3* and otherwise than out of UK or NI public revenue. These include voluntary pensions and pensions capable of being discontinued. A **10%** deduction is allowed from the amount otherwise chargeable. [*ITEPA 2003, ss 615–618*]. In *Magraw v Lewis* KB 1933, 18 TC 222, the taxpayer was given no reduction for foreign exchange differences and no deduction for costs of unsuccessful litigation against the overseas government.

(g)   Periodical payments out of the **House of Commons Members& Fund.** The chargeable amount is the total amount of payments made in the tax year. [*ITEPA 2003, ss 619–622*].

(h)   **Pre-1973 pensions previously paid by Commonwealth governments** and for which, under *Overseas Pensions Act 1973*, the British Government took over responsibility for payment. (Any part of the pension representing statutory increases is excluded from this heading and instead falls within (a) above.) The chargeable amount is determined on the same basis as for foreign pensions in (b) above. [*ITEPA 2003, ss 629–632*]. See also **56.3**(g) below.

(i)   **Annual payments** made **voluntarily**, or **capable of being discontinued**, by former employers or their successors (including payments from a non-UK source to a UK resident). If the payment is from a UK source, the chargeable amount is computed as in **56.1** above. If from a non-UK source, the chargeable amount is determined on the same basis as for foreign pensions in (b) above. [*ITEPA 2003, ss 633–636*].

(j)   **Trivial commutation and winding-up lump sums** paid under a **registered pension scheme** (see **57.2** PENSION PROVISION). If a trivial commutation lump sum (within *FA 2004, Sch 29 para 7*) or a winding-up lump sum (within *FA 2004, Sch 29 para 10*) is paid to a member of a registered pension scheme, it is taxable as pension income for the year of payment. But if, immediately before the lump sum is paid, the member has uncrystallised rights (within *FA 2004, s 212*) under any one or more arrangements under the scheme, a deduction is allowable from the amount otherwise chargeable. If all the member's rights are uncrystallised rights, the deduction is **25%** of the lump sum; otherwise, the deduction is 25% of the value of the uncrystallised rights. [*ITEPA 2003, s 636B*]. (A trivial commutation lump sum can be paid only if the value of the member's pension rights does not exceed 1% of the standard lifetime allowance (for which see **57.15** PENSION PROVISION) and a winding-up lump sum cannot exceed 1% of that allowance.) See *FA 2004, Sch 36 para 35* for a transitional modification of the above rules, affecting only winding-up lump sums paid by certain pre-6 April 1980 superannuation funds to which no contributions had been made since that date but which became registered pension schemes on 6 April 2006 (see **57.3** PENSION PROVISION). See *SI 2006 No 572, Reg 37* for a further transitional modification concerning 'equivalent pension benefits commutation lump sums' as therein defined.

(k)   **Trivial commutation and winding-up lump sum death benefits** paid under a **registered pension scheme** (see **57.2** PENSION PROVISION). If a trivial commutation lump sum death benefit (within *FA 2004, Sch 29* *para 20*) or a winding-up lump sum death benefit (within *FA 2004, Sch 29 para 21*) is paid to a person under a registered pension scheme, it is taxable on that person as pension income for the year of payment. [*ITEPA 2003, s 636C*]. (Neither a trivial commutation lump sum death benefit nor a winding-up lump sum death benefit is permitted to exceed 1% of the standard lifetime allowance (for which see **57.15 PENSION PROVISION**).)

General exemptions

[56.3] General exemptions from the charge to tax on pension income are as listed below. See **56.4** below for exemptions specific to non-UK residents.

(a)   The following types of **lump sum** paid under a **registered pension scheme** (see **57.2 PENSION PROVISION**):

- a pension commencement lump sum (within *FA 2004, Sch 29 para 1* (see also *SI 2006 No 135*) — broadly a lump sum to which a person becomes entitled in connection with his becoming entitled to a pension);
- a serious ill-health lump sum (within *FA 2004, Sch 29 para 4*);
- a short service refund lump sum (within *FA 2004, Sch 29 para 5*);
- a refund of excess contributions lump sum (within *FA 2004, Sch 29 para 6*);
- a lifetime allowance excess lump sum (within *FA 2004, Sch 29 para 11*);
- a defined benefits lump sum death benefit (within *FA 2004, Sch 29 para 13*);
- a pension protection lump sum death benefit (within *FA 2004, Sch 29 para 14*);
- an uncrystallised funds lump sum death benefit (within *FA 2004, Sch 29 para 15*);
- an annuity protection lump sum death benefit (within *FA 2004, Sch 29 para 16*);
- an unsecured pension fund lump sum death benefit (within *FA 2004, Sch 29 para 17*);
- (in relation to deaths occurring before 6 April 2007) a transfer lump sum death benefit (within *FA 2004, Sch 29 para 19* — now repealed);
- a life cover lump sum (within *FA 2004, Sch 29 para 21A* as added by *SI 2006 No 572, Reg 8*).

Lump sums may, however, give rise to a **lifetime allowance charge** (see **57.15 PENSION PROVISION**). A pension commencement lump sum paid in excess of the permitted maximum (see *FA 2004, Sch 29 paras 2, 3* and, for transitional protection of lump sum rights accrued before 2006/07, *FA 2004, Sch 36 paras 25–34*) is liable to the unauthorised payments charge at **57.19**(d) **PENSION PROVISION**. There is a separate tax charge on short service refund lump sums (see **57.19**(a) **PENSION PROVISION**). There is also a separate tax charge on a pension protection lump sum death benefit, an annuity protection lump sum death benefit or an unsecured pension fund lump sum death benefit (see **57.19**(b) PENSION PROVISION). [*ITEPA 2003, s 636A; FA 2007, Sch 19 paras 28, 29(3); SI 2006 No 572, Reg 7*].

See **56.2**(j)(k) above as regards the charge to tax on trivial commutation lump sums and winding-up lump sums.

See **56.5** below as regards lump sums taken in connection with the *State* pension, which *are* taxable.

(b) Pensions and annuities paid to holders of an '**award for bravery**' in respect of the award. For this purpose, an '*award for bravery*' means the Victoria Cross, George Cross, Albert Medal, Edward Medal, Military Cross, Distinguished Flying Cross, Distinguished Conduct Medal, Conspicuous Gallantry Medal, Distinguished Service Medal, Military Medal or Distinguished Flying Medal. [*ITEPA 2003, s 638*].

(c) Pensions in respect of **death due to military or war service**, comprising pensions or allowances payable by the UK Government in respect of death due to service in the armed forces (including peacetime service before the 1939–1945 war), wartime service in the merchant navy or war injuries, and comparable pensions etc. paid under foreign law. Where such a pension is abated because of entitlement to another pension, the exemption extends to so much of the other pension as is equal to the abatement. [*ITEPA 2003, ss 639, 640*].

(d) **Lump sums provided under an armed forces early departure scheme** established by the *Armed Forces Early Departure Payments Scheme Order 2005 (SI 2005 No 437)*. [*ITEPA 2003, s 640A*].

(e) Certain **wounds, disablement, disability** and **injury** pensions granted to members of the armed forces (including nurses) or payable under War Risks Compensation Schemes for the Mercantile marine or under certain War Compensation Acts and Armed Forces Pensions Acts, and **retired pay** granted to a disabled officer on account of service-related medical unfitness. Where a pension or retired pay is certified by the Secretary of State as only partly attributable to disablement etc., only the part attributable attracts the exemption. The exemption extends to certain illness or injury benefits payable by way of lump sum or following termination of service in the armed or reserve forces. [*ITEPA 2003, s 641*]. Otherwise, the whole of the disability pension or retired pay is exempt provided that the immediate occasion of retirement was service-related disability, notwithstanding that a 'long service' element enters into the computation of the award. Further, where a member of the armed forces is invalided out in circumstances which qualify him for both a service-related disability pension and a service pension, the combined pension is regarded as within the above exemption. (HMRC Assessment Procedures Manual AP844).

(f) Pensions and annuities payable under provision of German or Austrian law for **victims of Nazi persecution**. [*ITEPA 2003, s 642*].

(g) Certain **pre-1973** pensions paid in respect of **government service** in **Malawi, Trinidad and Tobago** and **Zambia**. [*ITEPA 2003, s 643*]. See also HMRC ESC A49.

(h)   Where a person has ceased to hold an employment or office because of **disablement,** such amount (if any) of any pension as exceeds what would have been payable if the disablement had not been attributable to the performance of the duties of the employment or office or to war injuries. But this exemption does not apply to a pension within **56.2**(d) above. [*ITEPA 2003, s 644*].

(i)   So much of any **social security pension** (as in **56.2**(c) above or a foreign equivalent) as is attributable to an increase in respect of a child. [*ITEPA 2003, s 645*].

(j)   **Coal or smokeless fuel** provided to former colliery workers and their widows, widowers or surviving civil partners for personal use (and allowances paid in lieu of such provision). [*ITEPA 2003, s 646*].

(k)   (By concession) **lump sums** paid by **overseas pension schemes** received by an employee (or by his dependants or personal representatives) from

        (i)   a superannuation fund for overseas employees accepted as being within *ICTA 1988, s 615(6)* (see now **57.32 PENSION PROVISION**), or

        (ii)   an overseas retirement benefits scheme or provident fund where certain conditions as to the employee's foreign service are met.

        As regards (ii) above, exemption may be total or partial depending on the length of foreign service, and this is determined in the same way as the statutory exemption from charge under *ITEPA 2003, ss 413, 414* for foreign service payments (see **20.6**(vi) **COMPENSATION FOR LOSS OF EMPLOYMENT (AND DAMAGES)**). (HMRC ESC A10).

Where pensions are paid to or from overseas, relief from double taxation may be available under the specific terms of a double tax treaty with the country concerned or by means of unilateral relief granted in the UK. See **26 DOUBLE TAX RELIEF**.

Exemptions specific to non-UK residents

[56.4] The exemptions listed below apply only if HMRC are satisfied, on his making a claim to that effect, that the person to whom the pension is payable is not resident in the UK. For the purposes of these exemptions, 'pension' includes a gratuity or any sum payable on death and a return of contributions (including any interest or other addition included therein). [*ITEPA 2003, s 647*].

(a)   Pensions paid from the **Central African Pension Fund.** [*ITEPA 2003, s 648*].

(b)   Pensions paid out of a fund established in the UK by a **Commonwealth government** (as defined) for the sole purpose of providing pensions payable in respect of service under that government. [*ITEPA 2003, s 649*].

(c)   Pensions paid under the **Oversea Superannuation Scheme.** [*ITEPA 2003, s 650; Overseas Superannuation Act 1991, s 2*].

(d)   Pensions paid under *Overseas Pensions Act 1973, s 1*, whether or not out of a fund established under a scheme made under that *section* but excluding certain statutory increases. [*ITEPA 2003, s 651*].

(e)   Pensions paid under the authority of the *Overseas Service Act 1958* to the extent that the pension is certified by the Secretary of State as attributable to the employment of a person in the public services of an overseas territory. [*ITEPA 2003, s 652*].

(f)   Pensions paid out of the **Overseas Service Pensions Fund.** For this purpose only, 'pension' also includes any sum payable in respect of ill-health. [*ITEPA 2003, s 653*].

(g)   Pensions paid under the authority of the *Pensions (India, Pakistan and Burma) Act 1955*, excluding certain statutory increases. [*ITEPA 2003, s 654*].

See also **50.2** NON-RESIDENTS for availability of UK personal allowances to British and certain other residents abroad and **50.3** NON-RESIDENTS for limitation on income tax liability of non-UK residents.

Taxation of State pension lump sums

[56.5] Under legislation in *Pensions Act 2004*, it is possible to defer receipt of the State pension and, in consequence, eventually claim an increased pension or a one-off lump sum plus the normal pension. The lump sum is the total amount of weekly pension forgone plus compound interest. If a lump sum is chosen, it is normally receivable at the time that payment of the pension commences (subject to the right of election referred to below), and it is within the charge to income tax but subject to the special rules below. Pensions remain taxable in the normal way. For more on the subject of pension deferral and the increased pension or lump sum options generally, see the Department of Work and Pensions (DWP) guidance at www.direct.gov.uk/prod_consum_dg/groups/dg_digitalassets/@dg/@en/@over50/documents/digitalasset/dg_180189.pdf.

A State pension lump sum counts as income for tax purposes but does not count towards total income. This means, in particular, that it does not affect the availability or calculation of the age-related personal allowance or the married couple's allowance (for which see **1.14, 1.15** ALLOWANCES AND TAX RATES) and it has no effect on the rates at which income tax is payable on other income. The charge to tax is on the person entitled to the lump sum, regardless of whether or not he is resident, ordinarily resident or domiciled in the UK. Income tax is chargeable on the lump sum at a single rate as follows.

For 2010/11 onwards

*   If the taxpayer's taxable income is nil, no tax is due on the lump sum.
*   If his taxable income is greater than nil but does not exceed the basic rate limit, the whole of the lump sum is taxable at the basic rate (20%).
*   If his taxable income exceeds the basic rate limit but does not exceed the higher rate limit, the whole of the lump sum is taxable at the higher rate (40%).
*   If his taxable income exceeds the higher rate limit, the whole of the lump sum is taxable at the additional rate (50%).

For 2008/09 and 2009/10

*   If the taxpayer's taxable income is nil, no tax is due on the lump sum.

- If his taxable income is greater than nil but does not exceed the basic rate limit, the whole of the lump sum is taxable at the basic rate (20%).
- If his taxable income exceeds the basic rate limit, the whole of the lump sum is taxable at the higher rate (40%).

For 2006/07 and 2007/08

- If the taxpayer's taxable income is nil, no tax is due on the lump sum.
- If his taxable income is greater than nil but does not exceed the starting rate limit, the whole of the lump sum is taxable at the starting rate.
- If his taxable income exceeds the starting rate limit but does not exceed the basic rate limit, the whole of the lump sum is taxable at the basic rate.
- If his taxable income exceeds the basic rate limit, the whole of the lump sum is taxable at the higher rate.

All years

In all cases, the reference above to taxable income is to net income after carrying out Steps 2 and 3 in the calculation of income tax liability at **1.7 ALLOWANCES AND TAX RATES**. It excludes the lump sum itself, the tax on which is added at Step 7 of that calculation. For the current basic rate limit, see **1.3 ALLOWANCES AND TAX RATES**; for the basic and starting rates and limits before 2010/11, see **1.4 ALLOWANCES AND TAX RATES**.

The tax year in which the lump sum falls to be taxed is the tax year in which falls the first benefit payment day, i.e. the day on which the deferred pension actually becomes payable. This will normally also be the tax year in which the lump sum entitlement arises, but the actual date of payment of the lump sum plays no part in determining when it is taxed. If the taxpayer dies before the beginning of that tax year, the lump sum is instead taxable in the year of death; this appears to cover the situation where a person has claimed his pension, but with effect from a future date, and then dies before the period of deferral is due to end. (No lump sum entitlement arises where death occurs before the pension is claimed, though the entitlement may pass to a surviving spouse.) In a case where a surviving spouse inherits a person's lump sum entitlement on his or her death *and is already receiving State pension*, the first benefit payment day is deemed to be the date of death of the spouse whose deferral gave rise to the lump sum entitlement.

Under DWP *regulations*, a person is able to elect to delay his lump sum entitlement until the tax year following that in which payment of the State pension commences. A person might do this, for example, because he is still in employment for a part of the tax year in which the pension commences and is likely to be in a lower rate band in the following tax year when he no longer has any earnings. Where such an election is made, the tax year in which the lump sum falls to be taxed is the tax year following that in which falls the first benefit payment day. But if, having made the election, the taxpayer dies before the beginning of that following tax year, the lump sum is instead taxable in the year of death.

Provision is made by the PAYE regulations to enable the DWP to deduct tax at source when paying a lump sum. The recipient will be able to make a self-declaration as to the likely rate of tax that will apply. In the absence of a declaration, basic rate tax will be deducted. Any tax under- or over-deducted will become payable or repayable once the true applicable tax rate has been determined. It could possibly be the case that a person who has claimed a lump sum has to file a tax return for the year for which the lump sum is taxable, but the DWP has not actually paid the lump sum by the filing date; HMRC will not seek any further tax that may be due in respect of the lump sum until the actual payment has been made by the DWP (Treasury Explanatory Notes to the 2005 Finance Bill).

In addition to a 'State pension lump sum', the above provisions apply to a 'shared additional pension lump sum' (i.e. where a pension-sharing order has been made following divorce) and a 'graduated retirement benefit lump sum'. These expressions are defined by *F(No 2)A 2005, s 9* by reference to various social security and national insurance enactments. As regards the State pension, lump sums are not available for Category D (non-contributory) pensions. See the DWP guidance referred to above for more details.

[*F(No 2)A 2005, ss 7–9; ITA 2007, Sch 1 para 604; SI 2006 No 243; FA 2008, Sch 1 paras 64, 65; FA 2009, Sch 2 paras 24, 25; SI 2003 No 2682, Regs 133A–133H; SI 2008 No 782, Reg 13*].

Financial Assistance Scheme

[56.6] The Financial Assistance Scheme (FAS) is a Government scheme set up to assist individuals who have lost pension rights because they were members of underfunded pension schemes that started to wind up between 1 January 1997 and 5 April 2005 and the employer is insolvent or no longer exists, or a compromise agreement has been reached with the employer. The assistance takes the form of a top-up to the individual's pension. Payments from the FAS, like payments of pension income, are chargeable to income tax for the tax year to which they relate, and will normally be made within PAY AS YOU EARN (53).

On and after 4 June 2008, payments from the FAS were increased from 80% to 90% (subject to an upper limit) of the pension the individual was expecting to receive from the employer scheme at his normal retirement age. Also, payments are now made from the individual's normal retirement age (but not from before age 60) whereas previously they were made from age 65 regardless of normal retirement age. These changes will result in some backdated payments being made. HMRC have stated that any payments made relating to an earlier tax year will be treated as income of that earlier tax year and not as income of the year in which the backdated payment is made (HMRC Internet Statement 31 March 2008 — see www.hmrc.gov.uk/news/tax-treatm ent.htm).

57

Pension Provision

Simon's Taxes. See E7.5.

Introduction

[57.1] With effect for 2006/07 and subsequent years, the various pre-existing pension scheme regimes (broadly, retirement schemes for employees, personal pension schemes and retirement annuities) were replaced by *FA 2004, ss 149–284, Schs 28–36* with a single universal regime for tax-privileged pension provision.

Main features are as follows.

- The pre-existing requirement for pension schemes to obtain HMRC approval was replaced by a requirement to register the scheme with HMRC. Pre-6 April 2006 approved schemes are automatically treated as registered schemes unless, before 6 April 2006, they gave notice to opt out of deemed registration. See **57.2–57.5** below.
- A registered scheme is exempt from income tax on its investment income and from capital gains tax on disposals of investments. See **57.6** below.
- Contributions to registered schemes are not limited by reference to a fraction of earnings and there is no earnings cap. An individual may make unlimited contributions and tax relief is available on contributions of up to the full amount of his relevant earnings or, provided the scheme operates tax relief at source, on contributions of up to £3,600 even if relevant earnings are lower than that. There is no provision for the carry-back or carry-forward of contributions to tax years other than the year of payment. Subject to protection for certain pre-existing policies, *FA 2007* withdrew the availability of relief for contributions that are effectively life assurance premiums. See **57.7** below.
- For 2011/12 onwards, certain high income individuals were to have higher and additional rate tax relief on pension provision restricted — see **57.9** below. There are anti-forestalling provisions (the special annual allowance charge) to deter individuals from increasing their pension savings in excess of their normal regular pattern in the years prior to the restriction taking effect. However, following the change of Government in May 2010, it is by no means certain that the plan for 2011/12 will go ahead. The special annual allowance charge does remain in place though. See **57.10, 57.11** below.
- Employer contributions to registered schemes are generally deductible for tax purposes, with statutory provision for the spreading of abnormally large contributions over a period of up to four years, and do not count as taxable income of the employee. See **57.12–57.14** below.
- Where a member of a registered pension scheme becomes entitled to a scheme pension from a defined benefits scheme, the maximum permissible 'tax-free' lump sum payment by the scheme to the member is broadly the lower of 25% of the value of the pension rights and 25% of the member's lifetime allowance (see below). Where a member becomes entitled to a scheme pension from a money purchase scheme, the maximum is broadly the lower of one-third of the amount used to provide the pension and 25% of the lifetime allowance. There is an anti-avoidance rule to deter people from converting or transferring from money purchase to defined benefits arrangements for the sole or

main purpose of increasing the tax-free entitlement. Where, instead of becoming entitled to a scheme pension, the member becomes entitled to an income withdrawal or lifetime annuity, the maximum is broadly the lower of one-third of the amounts designated into an unsecured pension or of the amount paid to purchase the annuity and 25% of the lifetime allowance. [*FA 2004, Sch 29 paras 2, 3; FA 2006, s 161, Sch 23 paras 22, 23; FA 2007, Sch 20 paras 11(4), 24(3)*]. All registered schemes are able to offer lump sums. There is transitional protection of lump sum rights accrued before 6 April 2006 (see *FA 2004, Sch 36 paras 24–35*). The general tax exemption for lump sums received is covered at **56.3**(a) PENSION INCOME, *but* is subject to the lifetime allowance below. For the taxation of 'trivial commutation lump sums' and 'winding-up lump sums', which are outside this general exemption, see **56.2**(j)(k) PENSION INCOME.

• Each individual has a **lifetime allowance** (currently set at £1.8 million). When benefits crystallise, most commonly when a pension begins to be paid, the amount crystallised is measured against the individual's lifetime allowance and any excess taxed at 55% if taken as a lump sum and 25% in other cases. Any tax due may be deducted by the administrator from the individual's benefits. See **57.15**, **57.16** below.

• Each individual also has an **annual allowance** (currently set at £255,000). To the extent (if any) that the annual increase in an individual's rights under all registered schemes of which he is a member exceeds the annual allowance, the excess is chargeable to tax at 40% with the individual being liable for the tax. See **57.17**, **57.18** below.

• The minimum pension age rose from 50 to 55 on 6 April 2010. [*FA 2004, s 279(1)*]. Other than on ill-health grounds, a pension cannot be paid before the minimum age is reached. [*FA 2004, s 165(1)*]. There is an exception where, as at 5 April 2006, an individual had a right to take pension benefits from an occupational pension scheme before age 55 under a scheme rule in force on 10 December 2003. An individual who was a member of the scheme on 10 December 2003 must have had the right to take benefits before age 55 on 10 December 2003 as well as on 5 April 2006. There is also an exception for individuals who, as at 5 April 2006, had a right to take pension benefits from a personal pension scheme or retirement annuity contract before age 50 and were in certain prescribed occupations. *SI 2005 No 3451, Sch 2* prescribes for this purpose various occupations (mainly sports persons). However, except in the case of certain prescribed professions, e.g. police and armed forces, a reduced lifetime allowance will apply in the case of early retirement before age 50. [*FA 2004, Sch 36 paras 19, 22, 23, 23A; SI 2006 No 498; SI 2007 No 838*].

For HMRC's interpretation of the rules for payment of pension commencement lump sums and pension benefits around 6 April 2010 and about some of the practical aspects of the change in the minimum pension age, see Pension Schemes Newsletter 38, 16 December 2009, and see also www.hmrc.gov.uk/pensionschemes/min-pen-age.pdf.

The Government intend to introduce regulations to remove an unintended unauthorised payments charge where an individual aged 50 and over but under 55 transfers his pension in payment to another pension provider. The regulations will be backdated to cover transfers made on or after 6 April 2010. (www.hmrc.gov.uk/pensionschemes/people-aged -50-55.pdf).

- Benefits must normally be taken by the age of 75 at the latest. A member of a money purchase scheme may take a pension from the age of 75 by way of income withdrawal, known as an '*alternatively secured pension*', instead of taking a scheme pension or purchasing a lifetime annuity; the maximum alternatively secured pension is 90% of a comparable annuity.

  The current rules effectively require a member of a money purchase scheme to use his pension fund to buy an annuity by the age of 75. The Government intend to abolish this effective requirement with effect for 2011/12 onwards. Pending abolition, legislation has been introduced in *F(No 2)A 2010, Sch 3* to increase to 77 the age by which members of money purchase schemes have to buy an annuity or otherwise secure a pension income. The increase applies only to individuals who had not reached the age of 75 before 22 June 2010. For further details, see HMRC Budget Note BN22, 22 June 2010 and Treasury Explanatory Notes to the 2010 Finance Bill published on 1 July 2010.

- It is not necessary for an employee to leave his employment before accessing his occupational pension. Members of occupational schemes may, where permitted by the scheme rules, continue to work for the same employer whilst drawing retirement benefits from the employer's scheme.

- There are rules designed to prevent *self-directed* registered pension schemes from gaining tax advantages where there is investment by the scheme in residential property and certain tangible moveable property such as fine wines, classic cars, art and antiques. A self-directed scheme is one where a scheme member can direct which investments the scheme makes. See **57.22–57.25** below.

- Non-registered employer pension schemes (known as 'employer-financed retirement benefits schemes') are permitted to exist but without the tax advantages of registered schemes; they are treated like any other arrangement to provide employees with benefits. On the other hand, they are not subject to restrictions such as the lifetime allowance. See **57.26–57.30** below.

HMRC publish detailed guidance in the form of a Registered Pension Schemes Manual. They also publish regular online-newsletters on the subject. For links to both the guidance and the newsletters, see www.hmrc.gov.uk/pensionsche mes.

For information on how HMRC apply the 'last four Finance Acts' rule in COP 10 (see **34.5 HMRC — ADMINISTRATION**) to pensions tax legislation, see Pensions Tax Simplification Newsletter No. 34, July 2008.

Simon's Taxes. See E7.501.

Registered pension schemes

[57.2] A *'pension scheme'* for these purposes is a scheme or other arrangements comprised in one or more instruments or agreements, having effect (or capable of having effect) so as to provide benefits to (or in respect of) persons on retirement, on death, on having reached a particular age, on the onset of serious ill-health or incapacity or in similar circumstances to these. [*FA 2004, s 150(1)*]. *FA 2004, s 151* defines a 'member' in relation to a pension scheme, and *FA 2004, s 152* defines, *inter alia*, money purchase schemes and defined benefits (usually final salary) schemes, both already well-known concepts.

A scheme administrator may make application, containing specified information and declarations, to HMRC to register a pension scheme. HMRC must register the scheme unless it appears that it contains incorrect information or a false declaration. The scheme must be an occupational pension scheme (as defined by *FA 2004, s 150(5)* — i.e. an employer scheme) or a public service pension scheme (as defined by *FA 2004, s 150(3)* — broadly a scheme established by Government) or else must be a scheme established by a person with permission from the Financial Services Authority to establish in the UK a personal pension scheme or stakeholder pension scheme. A deferred annuity contract (made with an insurance company) which will eventually provide the benefits due from a registered scheme is treated as having become a registered scheme on the day it was made. The same applies to an annuity contract made with an insurance company, and paid for with monies repatriated to a pension scheme, by order of the Pensions Regulator or the courts.

HMRC must notify the scheme administrator of their decision whether or not to register the scheme; no time limit is stipulated. An appeal may be made, within 30 days of the notice, against a decision not to register.

HMRC may by notice withdraw a pension scheme's registration on any one or more of a number of grounds specified by *FA 2004, s 158*. An appeal may be made, within 30 days of the notice, against the decision to de-register the scheme. See **57.19**(g) below as regards the tax charge on de-registration.

[*FA 2004, ss 153–159; ITA 2007, Sch 1 para 466; FA 2007, Sch 20 paras 2, 3, 24(1); SI 2009 No 56, Sch 1 paras 423, 424*].

The registered pension schemes regime is administered by Pension Schemes Services, FitzRoy House, Castle Meadow Road, Nottingham, NG2 1BD.

A helpsheet for scheme administrators is available at www.hmrc.gov.uk/pens ionschemes/scheme-administrator-facts.pdf.

There are rules as to the payments a registered scheme is and is not permitted to make (authorised and unauthorised payments — see *FA 2004, ss 160–181, Schs 28–30 and SI 2005 No 3449, SI 2006 Nos 133, 137, 209, 499, 571, 574, 614, 1465, SI 2007 No 3532, SI 2009 No 1171* at **57.5** below) and dealing with unauthorised borrowing by registered schemes (see *FA 2004, ss 163, 182–185*); registered schemes may borrow up to 50% of the value of total scheme assets. The rules relating to payment of pensions are in *FA 2004, s 165, Sch 28 Pt 1* (see also *SI 2006 Nos 129, 138, 499, 568; SI 2007 Nos 493, 826* at **57.5** below), those relating to pension death benefits are in *FA 2004, s 167,*

Sch 28 Pt 2 (see also *SI 2006 Nos 129, 499, 568, SI 2007 No 493* at **57.5** below), those relating to payment of lump sums are in *FA 2004, s 166, Sch 29 Pt 1* (see also *SI 2006 No 135* at **57.5** below) and those relating to lump sum death benefits are in *FA 2004, s 168, Sch 29 Pt 2*. As regards maximum permissible lump sums, see the sixth bullet at **57.1** above. See **57.19**(d)(e) below for the tax charge in respect of unauthorised payments by a registered scheme.

HMRC have published guidance as to how payments made in genuine error are treated — see www.hmrc.gov.uk/pensionschemes/errors-guidance.pdf.

There is an anti-avoidance rule to deter recycling of a tax-free pension commencement lump sum (i.e. the lump sum generally available when an individual begins to be paid a pension). 'Recycling' occurs where the member takes a pension commencement lump sum from a registered scheme with the intention of using it to pay significantly greater contributions to the same scheme or to other registered schemes. There are *de minimis* limits within which the rule does not apply. Otherwise, the scheme is regarded as making an unauthorised payment of a specified amount. [*FA 2004, Sch 29 para 3A; FA 2006, s 159*].

Changes were made (broadly from 6 April 2007) to the rules on members' and dependants' alternatively secured pensions (ASPs) to *inter alia*:

- introduce a minimum withdrawal of income from an ASP fund of 55% of the annual amount of a comparable annuity that could be purchased with the sums and assets in the fund. Failure to comply will result in a scheme sanction charge (as in **57.19**(f) below) on the difference between the minimum income limit and the amount withdrawn;
- increase the maximum withdrawal of income that is permitted from an ASP fund from 70% to 90% of the annual amount of a comparable annuity that could be purchased with the sums and assets in the fund;
- stipulate that where, following the death of a member (or dependant), any remaining ASP funds are transferred to the pension funds of other members of the scheme, the scheme is treated as making an unauthorised payment (with consequences as in **57.19** below).

The first two of the above-mentioned changes have effect for alternatively secured pension years (see *FA 2004, Sch 28 para 12*) beginning on or after 6 April 2007. The third change has effect in relation to deaths occurring on or after that date.

[*FA 2004, ss 165(1), 167(1), 172BA, 181A; FA 2007, Sch 19 paras 2, 4, 13, 14, 29(1)(2)(5)*].

HMRC are empowered to make regulations (see *SI 2006 No 569*) to treat prescribed registered pension schemes as if they were a number of separate registered pension schemes, each with its own administrator; this is aimed at very large schemes, spread over a number of employers, particularly those in the public sector, whose administrative functions are generally devolved from the centre. [*FA 2004, s 274A; SI 2006 No 569; SI 2007 No 793*].

There are rules restricting the type of investment that can be made by a *self-directed* registered pension scheme — see **57.22–57.25** below.

Simon's Taxes. See E7.502, E7.508, E7.509.

Transitional

[57.3] Subject to the opt-out below, a pension scheme which, immediately before 6 April 2006, fell into one of the following categories became automatically a registered scheme:

- a retirement benefits scheme approved for purposes of *ICTA 1988, Pt 14 Ch 1*;
- a superannuation fund approved as at 5 April 1980 for purposes of *ICTA 1970, s 208* which has not since been approved for purposes of *ICTA 1988, Pt 14 Ch 1* and to which no contribution has since been made;
- a relevant statutory scheme or a scheme treated as such by HMRC as at 6 April 2006;
- a deferred annuity contract providing for the eventual payment of benefits under any of the above-listed schemes;
- a scheme or fund within *ICTA 1988, s 613(4)(b)–(d)* (Parliamentary pension schemes or funds);
- a retirement annuity contract approved under *ICTA 1988, s 620* or *s 621* (or a substituted contract within *ICTA 1988, s 622(3)*);
- a personal pension scheme approved under *ICTA 1988, Pt 14 Ch 4* (which includes a stakeholder scheme).

Where only part of a retirement benefits scheme was approved, only that part became automatically a registered scheme. A retirement benefits scheme or personal pension scheme approved after 5 April 2006 with retrospective effect for a period ending with that date becomes automatically a registered scheme with effect from 6 April 2006.

A scheme was able to opt out of becoming automatically a registered pension scheme by giving HMRC notice to that effect before 6 April 2006. Except in the case of a Parliamentary scheme or fund, this action gave rise to an income tax charge at 40% on the aggregate of the sums held for the purposes of the scheme immediately before 6 April 2006 and the market value of the scheme assets at that time.

HMRC regulations (*SI 2006 No 364*) make appropriate modifications to the rules of pre-existing pension schemes which become registered schemes. The modifications apply until the scheme itself rules that they should no longer apply or, if later, until 5 April 2011 (or such subsequent date as HMRC may prescribe). See also *SI 2006 No 365* and *SI 2009 No 3055*. In some cases, the scheme rules may have made use of the 'permitted maximum' (aka 'earnings cap') figure set by Treasury Orders under *ICTA 1988, s 590C*, for example by using it to limit the right to benefits under the scheme or the liability to make contributions. For this limited purpose only (and not so as to impose any limits on available tax reliefs), *SI 2006 No 364* preserves the concept of a 'permitted maximum'. It has subsequently been announced that, had *s 590C* continued in force, the 'permitted maximum' figures would have been £108,600 for 2006/07, £112,800 for 2007/08, £117,600 for 2008/09 and £123,600 for both 2009/10 and 2010/11 (Pensions Tax Simplification Newsletters No. 11, March 2006 and No. 25, 28 February 2007, HMRC Internet Statements 15 February 2008, 19 February 2009, 29 January 2010).

[FA 2004, Sch 36 paras 1–6].

Compliance

[57.4] A compliance regime for registered pension schemes is set out at *FA 2004, ss 250–274*. This covers such matters as completion and filing of returns, the providing of information to HMRC outside of returns and accounting for income tax (see below). See also *SI 2005 Nos 3456; SI 2006 Nos 136, 567* at **57.5** below.

Inevitably, there is also an extensive penalty regime covering all aspects of non-compliance (see *FA 2004, ss 257–266*).

The scheme administrator must account on a quarterly basis, and without the need for a notice or an assessment, for income tax for which he, as administrator, is liable, i.e. tax arising from the lifetime allowance charge at **57.15** below and the charges at **57.19**(a)(b)(c)(g) below. (The scheme sanction charge at **57.19**(f) below is outside these rules and can be made only by assessment.) Where such a charge arises in any quarter (ending on 31 March, 30 June, 30 September or 31 December), the scheme administrator must both make an accounting return and pay the tax within 45 days after the end of that quarter. *[FA 2004, s 254]*. In the event of non-compliance, HMRC may raise an assessment to collect the tax. *[FA 2004, s 255]*. For quarters ending on and after 30 September 2010, penalties similar to those in **53.14 PAY AS YOU EARN** apply to late payments. *[FA 2009, Sch 56; SI 2010 No 466]*. See also *SI 2005 No 3454* at **57.5** below.

See *SI 2006 No 570* (as amended) as to returns and other information which *must* be delivered *electronically* and the information which *may* be so delivered. See HMRC Pensions Tax Simplification Newsletters No 27, 10 April 2007 and No 30, 12 October 2007 for details).

Regulations

[57.5] Except where otherwise stated, the following applicable regulations have effect from the commencement of the regime on 6 April 2006. Note that this is not intended as a comprehensive list of all statutory instruments concerned with registered pension schemes; other statutory instruments are cited elsewhere in this chapter where appropriate.

The Registered Pension Schemes (Prescribed Interest Rates For Authorised Employer Loans) Regulations 2005 (SI 2005 No 3449) prescribe the minimum rate of interest to be charged on a loan by a registered scheme to a sponsoring employer or former sponsoring employer (see also *FA 2004, s 179*).

The Registered Pension Schemes (Discharge Of Liabilities Under Sections 267 And 268 Of The Finance Act 2004) Regulations 2005 (SI 2005 No 3452) make supplementary provision in connection with applications by scheme administrators and other persons for relief from certain charges.

The Registered Pension Schemes (Accounting And Assessment) Regulations 2005 (SI 2005 No 3454) make provision in relation to the making of assessments, and related matters (including interest on tax), in respect of certain charges to tax arising under the regime.

The Registered Pension Schemes And Employer-Financed Retirement Benefits Schemes (Information) (Prescribed Descriptions Of Persons) Regulations 2005 (SI 2005 No 3455) describe the persons to whom an officer of HMRC may give a notice requiring the production of documents and information about pension schemes.

The Registered Pension Schemes (Audited Accounts) (Specified Persons) Regulations 2005 (SI 2005 No 3456) (as amended) prescribe the persons who may audit the accounts of a registered pension scheme.

The Registered Pension Schemes (Relevant Annuities) Regulations 2006 (SI 2006 No 129) define the terms 'relevant annuity' and 'annual amount' as required by *FA 2004, Sch 28 para 14.* These terms are relevant in computing the 'basis amount' in Pension rules 5 & 7 (see *FA 2004, s 165)* and Pensions death benefit rule 6 (see *FA 2004, s 167).*

The Registered Pension Schemes (Co-ownership of Living Accommodation) Regulations 2006 (SI 2006 No 133) apply where living accommodation is owned partly by a registered pension scheme and partly by other persons, and determines how an unauthorised payment (see **57.2** above) is computed where the accommodation is used to provide a benefit for scheme members.

The Registered Pension Schemes (Meaning of Pension Commencement Lump Sum) Regulations 2006 (SI 2006 No 135) prescribe circumstances in which a lump sum may be treated as a pension commencement lump sum even though it fails to satisfy certain conditions of *FA 2004, Sch 29 para 1.* The circumstances are that there has been an overpayment of tax on the lifetime allowance charge which is refunded to the scheme by HMRC, and the scheme administrator passes on the overpayment to the member.

These regulations are amended by *SI 2007 No 3533* with effect on and after 7 January 2008 in consequence of amendments already made to primary legislation.

The Pension Benefits (Insurance Company Liable as Scheme Administrator) Regulations 2006 (SI 2006 No 136) provide that where an insurance company pays certain lump sum death benefits, it is treated as a scheme administrator, with the attendant compliance obligations. See also **57.19**(b) below.

The Registered Pension Schemes (Authorised Member Payments) Regulations 2006 (SI 2006 No 137) prescribe as authorised payments (see **57.2** above) certain demutualisation payments made by insurance companies to scheme members; *the Registered Pension Schemes (Authorised Payments) Regulations 2006 (SI 2006 No 209)* prescribe as authorised payments certain lump sums and state scheme premiums paid by a registered scheme under specified pre-existing legislation; *the Registered Pension Schemes (Authorised Member Payments) (No 2) Regulations 2006 (SI 2006 No 571)* transitionally prescribe as authorised payments certain lump sums paid within a specified time after 5 April 2006 but to which entitlement arose on or before that date (see also *SI 2006 No 572, Regs 38–41 as amended); the Registered Pension Schemes (Authorised Payments — Arrears of Pension) Regulations 2006 (SI 2006 No 614)* prescribe as an authorised payment a payment of arrears of pension to which the member is entitled when the pension begins to be paid and which is taxable pension income.

The Registered Pension Schemes (Reduction in Pension Rates) Regulations 2006 (SI 2006 No 138) supplement the pension payment rules in *FA 2004, Sch 28 para 2* by prescribing circumstances in which a pension may be stopped or reduced.

These regulations are amended by *SI 2009 No 1311* with retrospective effect to remove unintended tax consequences where there is a reduction to pensions paid to certain members during the winding-up of a scheme.

The Pensions (Transfer of Sums and Assets) Regulations 2006 (SI 2006 No 499) provide for the transfer of sums and assets between registered pension schemes and insurance companies where those sums and assets represent pensions already in payment. The sums and assets transferred must meet the rules set out in the regulations, which require that the recipient scheme (or insurance company) must provide the member with the same type of pension that was paid previously; otherwise, the transfer will be an unauthorised payment (see **57.2** above). The regulations also provide that the new pension will stand in the shoes of the old for certain purposes.

These regulations are amended by *SI 2008 No 1946* with effect on and after 10 October 2007 in consequence of amendments already made to primary legislation.

The Registered Pension Schemes (Provision of Information) Regulations 2006 (SI 2006 No 567) prescribe information which a scheme administrator is required to provide to HMRC in the form of an annual event report and other information which is required to be given to HMRC, to members (or their personal representatives) and to other schemes in connection with the administration of a registered pension scheme. They also set requirements for the keeping of records. These regulations include the information that scheme administrators and insurance companies must provide to scheme members as to the percentage of lifetime allowance thus far used up by benefit crystallization events (see **57.15** below). An obligation is imposed on an employer company to notify HMRC (on or before 31 January following the tax year) of any unauthorised payments received from a scheme. A person who ceases to be a scheme administrator must notify HMRC of that fact within 30 days.

These regulations are amended by *SI 2006 No 1961* with effect after 10 August 2006 to provide for reportable events, and in some cases impose information obligations on members, in relation to, *inter alia*, stand-alone lump sums, recycling of lump sums and investment-regulated schemes (as in **57.23** below).

The principal regulations are further amended by *SI 2008 No 720* with effect on and after 6 April 2008 and by *SI 2010 No 581* with effect on and after 6 April 2010. In particular the 2010 regulations introduce a requirement, where there is unauthorised borrowing in a scheme, for the scheme administrator to provide HMRC with information without having first been issued with a notice requiring that information.

The Registered Pension Schemes (Prescribed Manner of Determining Amount of Annuities) Regulations 2006 (SI 2006 No 568) provide for the amount by which certain annuities may vary where the amount of the annuity is linked with changes in one of the factors set out in the regulations, such as changes in the retail prices index or in the market value of assets.

The Taxation of Pension Schemes (Transitional Provisions) Order 2006 (SI 2006 No 572) supplements *FA 2004, Sch 36* by making further transitional provisions consequent upon the introduction of the new regime on 6 April 2006. These regulations are amended by *SI 2006 No 1962*. They are further amended by *SI 2006 No 2004* with effect after 24 July 2006 in relation to stand-alone lump sums, by *SI 2008 No 2990* with retrospective effect in relation to bridging pensions and pension commencement lump sums; by *SI 2009 No 1172* with effect on and after 1 June 2009 in relation to trivial commutation lump sums of up to £2,000; and by *SI 2009 No 1989* with retrospective effect in relation to pensions paid to children of deceased members of registered schemes where the child is aged 23 or over.

The Pension Schemes (Transfers, Reorganisations and Winding Up) (Transitional Provisions) Order 2006 (SI 2006 No 573) preserves the protection of certain pre-6 April 2006 rights in the event of particular types of transfer from one pension scheme to another.

This Order is amended by *SI 2010 No 529* with retrospective effect to extend the transitional protection to cover additional situations likely to occur when a pension scheme is reorganised or wound up.

The Registered Pension Schemes (Authorised Surplus Payments) Regulations 2006 (SI 2006 No 574) enable surplus funds in a registered occupational pension scheme to be paid to a sponsoring employer and to count as authorised payments subject to specified conditions. Such payments will, however, be subject to the tax charge at **57.19**(c) below.

The Registered Pension Schemes (Authorised Reductions) Regulations 2006 (SI 2006 No 1465) prevent a potential unauthorised payments charge where an armed forces pension is stopped upon admission of the pensioner to the Royal Chelsea Hospital.

The Tax and Civil Partnership Regulations 2007 (SI 2007 No 493), Reg 2 (with effect after 21 February 2007) adds references to 'entering into a civil partnership' to certain references to 'marrying' in *FA 2004, Sch 28*.

The Registered Pension Schemes (Bridging Pensions) Regulations 2007 (SI 2007 No 826) provide a formula for calculating the prescribed rate by which a scheme pension may be reduced in specified circumstances without incurring an unauthorised payments charge. The circumstances are that the member becomes entitled to a State pension and he has not exclusively been in contracted-out employment.

The Registered Pension Schemes (Authorised Member Payments) Regulations 2007 (SI 2007 No 3532) prescribe as authorised payments (see **57.2** above), with effect on and after 7 January 2008, certain payments made by a registered scheme to with-profits policy holders that do not reduce the total value of the sums and assets held for the purposes of the scheme.

The Registered Pension Schemes (Authorised Payments) Regulations 2009 (SI 2009 No 1171) prescribe as authorised payments (see **57.2** above), with effect on and after 1 December 2009, certain commutation payments that are not otherwise permitted by the rules in *FA 2004*. They also prescribe as authorised payments, with retrospective effect, pensions or lump sums paid or overpaid in error.

Tax exemptions

[57.6] A registered pension scheme is exempt from income tax on income derived from investments (including futures contracts and option contracts) or deposits held for the purposes of the scheme. (The exemption does not apply in relation to investments or deposits held as a member of a property investment LLP — see **52.25 PARTNERSHIPS.**) [*FA 2004, s 186; FA 2006, s 158, Sch 21 para 7*]. A gain accruing on a disposal of scheme investments is not a chargeable gain for capital gains tax purposes. [*TCGA 1992, s 271(1A)*]. See, however, **57.22–57.25** below as regards the separate charge to tax where income is derived from certain property held by self-directed schemes or where gains are realised from such property.

Simon's Taxes. See C1.216, E7.511.

Relief for contributions by individual members

[57.7] An individual aged under 75 is entitled to tax relief on the contributions he makes to a registered pension scheme during a tax year if he is a 'relevant UK individual' for that year. An individual is a '*relevant UK individual*' for a tax year if:

- he has 'relevant UK earnings' 'chargeable to income tax' for the year; or
- he is resident in the UK at some time during the year; or
- he was resident in the UK both at some time within the period of five years immediately preceding the tax year and at the time he became a member of the scheme; or
- he, or his spouse or civil partner, has general earnings for the tax year 'from overseas Crown employment subject to UK tax' (see **27.5, 27.10 EMPLOYMENT INCOME**).

But for 2011/12 onwards see also **57.9** below (restriction of tax relief on pension provision to the basic rate).

'*Relevant UK earnings*' means:

- employment income;
- income from a trade, profession or vocation (whether carried on individually or in partnership) chargeable under *ITTOIA 2005, Pt 2*;
- income immediately derived from a furnished holiday lettings business (whether carried on individually or in partnership) (see **60.10 PROPERTY INCOME**); or
- patent income (i.e. royalties or other sums paid in respect of the use of a patent charged to tax under *ITTOIA 2005, s 579* (see **40.2 INTELLECTUAL PROPERTY**), amounts on which tax is payable under *ITTOIA 2005, s 587 or s 593* (sale of patent rights — see **40.6, 40.7 INTELLECTUAL PROPERTY**) and any balancing charges under the capital allowances code for patent rights — see **10.35 CAPITAL ALLOWANCES**) but only where the individual, either alone or jointly, devised the invention for which the patent in question was granted. Certain minor restrictions are removed for 2007/08 onwards — see Change 125 in Annex 1 of the Explanatory Notes to *ITA 2007*.

The individual is entitled to relief on contributions up to the total amount of his relevant UK earnings 'chargeable to income tax' for the year. Provided, however, the scheme operates tax relief at source (see below), contributions of up to £3,600 (gross) attract relief even if total relevant UK earnings are less than that amount or there are no such earnings. (The £3,600 minimum may be increased from time to time by Treasury order.)

Relevant UK earnings are treated as *not* being *'chargeable to income tax'* if, by virtue of a double tax treaty, they are not taxable in the UK.

In the case of an employer scheme, the relief may be given under the so-called net pay arrangements, whereby the contributions are deducted by the employer from salary before applying PAY AS YOU EARN (53) and the individual's employment income to be included in his total income for tax purposes is net of such contributions.

Otherwise, a registered pension scheme must normally operate relief at source arrangements, whereby tax relief at the basic rate is deducted from the amount of the contribution payable and the scheme administrator recovers the tax deducted from HMRC. If the individual is a higher rate taxpayer, he then claims relief for the excess of the higher rate over the basic rate in his self-assessment tax return. Such relief is achieved by increasing his basic rate limit for the year by the gross amount of the contribution. The increased basic rate limit applies for the purposes of both income tax and capital gains tax. For the purposes only of age-related personal and married couple's allowances (see 1.14, 1.15 ALLOWANCES AND TAX RATES), the gross amount of the contribution is treated as a deduction in arriving at net income. The individual retains the basic rate relief given at source even if his tax liability is insufficient to cover it. Any excess of contributions over an individual's relevant UK earnings (but within the £3,600 minimum referred to above) can *only* be relieved if the scheme operates relief at source (and cannot be relieved under net pay arrangements).

For 2010/11 onwards, an individual liable at the additional rate (see 1.3 ALLOWANCES AND TAX RATES) is entitled to relief for his contributions at the excess of the additional rate over the basic rate. This is achieved by increasing the higher rate limit (as well as the basic rate limit) by the gross amount of the contributions. This is, however, subject to 57.9 below (restriction of tax relief to the basic rate).

The Registered Pension Schemes (Relief at Source) Regulations 2005 (SI 2005 No 3448 as amended) prescribe conditions which must be satisfied in order for relief to be given at source, provide for claims by the scheme for payment by HMRC of tax withheld at source and for recovery by HMRC of tax wrongly claimed, and grant relevant information and inspection powers to HMRC.

Contributions to pre-6 April 2006 retirement annuity contracts that have become registered pension schemes (see 57.3 above) are not required to be included in relief at source arrangements but can instead be relieved, on the making of a claim, by deduction in arriving at net income.

There are other limited circumstances in which relief can be given, on the making of a claim, by deduction in arriving at net income. These apply to contributions to public service pension schemes or marine pilots' benefits funds by individuals who are not employees in relation to the scheme or fund and third party contributions made on behalf of individuals who are within net pay arrangements.

In contrast to the pre-6 April 2006 position for personal and stakeholder pensions and retirement annuity contracts, there is no provision for the carry-back of contributions/premiums to tax years preceding the year of payment. Likewise, there is no provision for the carry-forward of contributions/premiums or of unused relief.

There is provision for shares acquired under an approved share incentive plan or SAYE option scheme (see, respectively, **69.20, 69.47** SHARE-RELATED EMPLOYMENT INCOME AND EXEMPTIONS) to be transferred to a registered scheme and treated as contributions made. The amount of the contribution is the market value of the shares at the date of transfer, and the transfer must be made within, broadly, 90 days after the shares are acquired by the individual.

Life assurance premium contributions

No relief is available under the above provisions for any contributions paid after the dates given below which are 'life assurance premium contributions'. Contributions are *'life assurance premium contributions'* if rights under a non-group life policy (as defined) are held (or later become held) for the purposes of the pension scheme and either the payment of the contributions constitutes the payment of premiums under the policy or the payer of the contributions intends them to be applied towards the payment of such premiums.

The above restriction applies in relation to contributions paid on or after 1 August 2007 if the scheme is an occupational pension scheme or on or after 6 April 2007 in any other case. However, it does not apply at all if the policy in question is a 'protected policy'. In the case of an occupational pension scheme, a *'protected policy'* is broadly either a pre-21 March 2007 policy or a pre-1 August 2007 policy in pursuance of a written proposal made and received by or on behalf of the insurance company before 29 March 2007 (provided the policy is consistent with the proposal in terms of sum assured and duration of the policy). In the case of a scheme *other than* an occupational scheme, a *'protected policy'* is broadly either a pre-6 December 2006 policy or a pre-1 August 2007 policy in pursuance of such a written proposal made and received before 14 December 2006. If, on the date of issue of the policy, the rights of the individual under the pension scheme included an actual or prospective entitlement to a pension, a date of 13 April 2007 applies instead of 14 December 2006. In all cases, a policy ceases to be a protected policy if and when the benefits under the policy are increased or its duration extended.

[FA 2004, ss 188–195, 195A, Sch 36 paras 39, 40; ITA 2007, s 58, Sch 1 paras 473–476; FA 2007, Sch 18, Sch 19 paras 7, 29(3); FA 2009, Sch 2 paras 11, 25; TIOPA 2010, Sch 8 para 63].

Refunds of excess contributions

A refund of excess contributions, i.e. any contributions paid in excess of the tax relief limit in any tax year, may be made by the registered pension scheme to the member within six years after the end of the tax year in question without adverse tax consequences. [*FA 2004, Sch 29 para 6; FA 2006, s 161, Sch 23 para 28*]. Such refunds are not compulsory in law, so it is possible, subject to the scheme rules, to make contributions which do not attract tax relief. However, the refunds facility, if offered by the scheme, does enable the making of contributions based on estimated relevant UK earnings; this is particularly relevant to the self-employed, who will not usually know their exact profits until after the end of the tax year.

Simon's Taxes. See E7.506.

Examples

[57.8]

(i) Henry, a single man aged 48, carries on a trade in the UK in which he makes an allowable loss of £1,000 for 2008/09 (for which he claims relief against 2007/08 income), a taxable profit of £16,000 for 2009/10 and a taxable profit of £44,000 for 2010/11. His only other income consists of building society interest of £4,800 (net) and UK dividends of £900; these figures remain constant for the three years in question. He makes net contributions to a registered pension scheme of £2,400 during the tax year 2008/09 and £4,000 during each of the tax years 2009/10 and 2010/11. Henry's tax liabilities are as follows.

2008/09

		£
Trading income		Nil
Taxed interest £4,800 × 100/80		6,000
UK dividends £900 × 100/90		1,000
Total and net income		7,000
Less Personal Allowance		6,035
Taxable Income		£965

Tax Liability		
965	@ 10% (dividend ordinary rate)	96.50
Deduct	tax credits on dividends	(96.50)
	tax paid at source on interest	(1,200.00)
		£(1,200.00)

Note

Henry is entitled to an income tax repayment of £1,200.00. (Dividend tax credits can be offset only to the extent that the dividends are chargeable to tax, and the excess cannot be repaid.) Henry has made gross pension contributions of £3,000 (£2,400 × 100/80). As his gross contributions do not exceed £3,600, He is entitled to tax relief even though he has no relevant UK earnings for the year. He is not required to repay the basic rate tax of £600 withheld at source from the contributions.

2009/10

		£
Trading income		16,000
Taxed interest (as before)		6,000
UK dividends (as before)		1,000
Total and net income		23,000
Less Personal Allowance		6,475
Taxable Income		£16,525
Tax Liability		
15,525	@ 20% (basic rate)	3,105.00
1,000	@ 10% (dividend ordinary rate)	100.00
£16,525		
		3,205.00
Deduct	tax paid at source on interest	(1,200.00)
	tax credits on dividends	(100.00)
		£1,905.00

Note

Henry has made gross pension contributions of £5,000 (£4,000 × 100/80). His relevant UK earnings are £16,000, which is more than sufficient to cover the gross contributions. He is entitled to full tax relief, which he has already obtained by deduction at source.

2010/11

		£
Trading income		44,000
Taxed interest (as before)		6,000
UK dividends (as before)		1,000
Total and net income		51,000
Less Personal Allowance		6,475
Taxable Income		£44,525
Tax Liability		
42,400	@ 20% (basic rate)	8,480.00
1,125	@ 40% (higher rate)	450.00
1,000	@ 32.5% (dividend upper rate)	325.00
£43,525		
		9,255.00
Deduct	tax paid at source on interest	(1,200.00)
	tax credits on dividends	(100.00)
		£7,955.00

Note

Henry has made gross pension contributions of £5,000 (£4,000 × 100/80). His relevant UK earnings are £44,000, which is more than sufficient to cover the gross contributions. He has obtained basic rate tax relief at 20% by deduction at source. He obtains higher rate relief by extension of the basic rate band; the normal basic rate limit of £37,400 is increased by £5,000 to £42,400. Without that increase, £125 of trading income and an additional £4,875 of taxed interest would have been taxable at 40% instead of 20% (a 20% saving). (Above the normal basic rate limit, the rate at which the pension contributions save tax will depend on the mix of taxable income, i.e. the extent to which it is dividend income or other income; see the Examples at **16.19 CHARITIES**.)

(ii) Celia is a self-employed professional with taxable profits of £200,000 for the year to 30 April 2010. She has bank deposit interest of £3,200 (net) for 2010/11. She makes net contributions to a registered pension scheme of £16,000 during the tax year ending on 5 April 2011, having previously made net contributions of £4,000 per annum in recent years. Her tax position is as follows.

2010/11

		£
Professional income		200,000
Taxed interest (£3,200 x 100/80)		4,000
Total and net income		204,000
Less Personal Allowance (note (b))		—
Taxable Income		£204,000

Tax Liability

57,400	@ 20% (basic rate)	11,480.00
112,600	@ 40% (higher rate)	45,040.00
34,000	@ 50% (additional rate)	17,000.00
£204,000		
		73,520.00
Deduct	tax paid at source on interest	(800.00)
		£72,720.00

Notes

(a)   Celia has made gross pension contributions of £20,000 (£16,000 × 100/80) and has obtained basic rate relief at source. She obtains additional rate relief by extension of the basic rate band; the normal basic rate limit of £37,400 is increased by £20,000 to £57,400. The higher rate limit of £150,000 is increased by the same amount, so that the higher rate band remains at £112,600. Without these adjustments, an additional £20,000 of income would have been taxable at 50% instead of 20% (a 30% saving).

(b)   No personal allowance is due as income is too far in excess of the £100,000 limit (see **1.14 ALLOWANCES AND TAX RATES**).

(c)   Although Celia is a high income individual as defined in **57.10** below and has significantly increased her level of pension contributions, she cannot be liable to the special annual allowance charge as her pension input amount (in this case her gross contributions) does not exceed £20,000.

High income excess relief charge

[57.9] Although the legislation described below is already on the statute book it is uncertain that it will go ahead following the change of Government in the UK in May 2010. The new Government will be considering, in consultation with interested parties, possible alternative means of raising the same tax revenue. One alternative would be to significantly reduce the annual allowance at **57.17** below to somewhere in the range of £30,000 to £45,000. (Budget Report 22 June 2010, pp 36, 46). Legislation has been introduced to give the Treasury the power to repeal by statutory instrument the provisions described below should they decide to do so. If exercised at all, the power must be exercised no later than 31 December 2010. [*F(No 2)A 2010, s 5*].

For 2011/12 onwards, for 'high income' individuals who are members of one or more registered pension schemes, relief on pension provision at the higher and additional rates will be restricted. This will be achieved by imposing a charge to income tax, to be known as the *'high income excess relief charge'*. The charge to tax is on the individual and applies whether or not the individual and the scheme administrator of the pension scheme(s) concerned are resident, ordinarily resident or domiciled in the UK. The amount of the tax is to be added at Step 7 of the calculation of income tax liability at **1.7 ALLOWANCES AND TAX RATES**. The amount on which the tax is charged (the total pension savings amount — see further below) is not treated for any other tax purposes as income, which means, for example, that losses, reliefs and allowances cannot be set against it and that it does not count as income for the purposes of any double tax treaty.

Finance Act 2009 included anti-forestalling provisions (the special annual allowance charge) to deter individuals from increasing their pension savings in excess of their normal regular pattern prior to the restriction taking effect — see **57.10** below.

High income individuals

A *'high income'* individual is one with both 'gross income' of £150,000 or more and 'relevant income' of £130,000 or more.

'Gross income' is computed as follows.

(1)   Start with the individual's total income for the year (see Step 1 of the calculation of income tax liability at **1.7 ALLOWANCES AND TAX RATES**).

(2)   Add back any relief given under the so-called net pay arrangements for employer schemes (see **57.7** above) and any relief given by virtue of *FA 2004, Sch 36 para 51* (migrant member relief — see **57.20** below).

(3)   Add back any deductions made against employment income under **16.20 CHARITIES** (donations via payroll giving schemes).

(4)   Deduct any reliefs deductible at Step 2 of the calculation of income tax liability at **1.7 ALLOWANCES AND TAX RATES** *other than* pension contributions and gifts of qualifying investments to charities (see **16.21 CHARITIES**).

(5)   Add the individual's total pension savings amount for the tax year (see below) net of any relievable pension contributions paid by the individual himself (or by someone else on his behalf) during the tax year. This net figure is broadly the value of pension benefits funded by the individual's employer.

'*Relevant income*' is computed as follows.

(i)   Start with the figure obtained by carrying out Steps 1 to 4 in the above calculation of gross income.

(ii)   Add any amount of employment income given up for the tax year under 'relevant salary sacrifice arrangements' or 'relevant flexible remuneration arrangements'.

'*Relevant salary sacrifice arrangements*' are arrangements made on or after 22 April 2009 under which the individual gives up the right to employment income in return for greater pension benefits. It matters not whether the arrangements were made before or after the employment began. '*Relevant flexible remuneration arrangements*' means broadly the same thing. An individual is provided with greater pension benefits if contributions (or additional contributions) are made (by the employer or any other person) to a pension scheme so as to secure an increase in the amount of benefits to which the individual, or any dependant of his, or any person connected with him (within **21 CONNECTED PERSONS**), is actually or prospectively entitled.

Rate of tax

The rate of tax to be applied to the total pension savings amount (see below) depends on the amount of the individual's taxable income for the tax year, i.e. the amount obtained by carrying out Steps 1 to 3 of the calculation of income tax liability at **1.7 ALLOWANCES AND TAX RATES** and on the amount of his gross income computed as above.

Where the individual's gross income is £180,000 or more, the rate is:

(a)   0% in relation to so much (if any) of the total pension savings amount as, when added to the individual's taxable income, does not exceed the basic rate limit;

(b)   20% in relation to so much (if any) of that amount as, when added to the individual's taxable income, exceeds the basic rate limit but does not exceed the higher rate limit; and

(c)   30% in relation to so much (if any) of that amount as, when added to the individual's taxable income, exceeds the higher rate limit.

For the basic rate limit and higher rate limit, see **1.3 ALLOWANCES AND TAX RATES**. Where these limits fall to be increased under **57.7** above or under **16.16 CHARITIES** (relief for Gift Aid donations), those increases also apply for the purposes of (a)–(c) above.

Where the individual's gross income is less than £180,000 or more, the percentages in subsection (b) and (c) above are each reduced by one percentage point for every £1,000 by which the gross limit is less than £180,000. Thus, the clawback of relief above the basic rate does not apply in full until gross income reaches £180,000. For example, where gross income is £160,000, the 20% charge in (b) will be eliminated and the charge in (c) will be reduced to 10% of so much (if any) of the total pension savings amount as, when added to the individual's taxable income, exceeds the higher rate limit.

Total pension savings amount

The total pension savings amount in the case of an individual for a tax year is arrived at by aggregating the pension savings amounts in respect of each arrangement relating to the individual under a registered pension scheme of which he is a member. The aggregate is reduced by any amount that is subject to the annual allowance charge at **57.17** below for the same tax year. Pension savings amounts are computed in accordance with *FA 2004, ss 213F–213N* depending on the type of arrangement (see (A)–(D) below). Where a pension savings amount would otherwise be a negative amount it is to be taken to be nil. The Treasury may by regulations make provision by statutory instrument to exclude, from the total pension savings amount, arrangements where the individual is a deferred member for the whole tax year and to modify the high income excess relief charge for individuals who are deferred members for part of the year. (A person is a deferred member of a pension scheme if he has accrued rights under the scheme and is neither an active member nor a pensioner member [*FA 2004, s 151(4)*].) If during the tax year the individual dies or becomes entitled under the arrangement to a serious ill-health lump sum (within *FA 2004, Sch 29 para 4*), the pension savings amount in respect of an arrangement is nil.

(A) **Money purchase arrangements other than cash balance arrangements.** The pension savings amount is broadly the total of any relievable pension contributions paid by or on behalf of the individual and contributions paid in respect of the individual by an employer of his during the tax year.

(B) **Cash balance arrangements.** The pension savings amount is broadly the amount by which the amount of the closing rights exceeds the amount of the opening rights. The amount of the closing rights is the amount which would be available for the provision of benefits to or in respect of the individual if he became entitled to the benefits at the end of the tax year. The amount of the opening rights is the corresponding figure at the end of the previous tax year. In measuring the excess, the amounts of the opening and closing rights are to be multiplied by age-related factors to be set out in Treasury regulations. There is provision for adjustment of the amount of the closing rights in certain eventualities (see *FA 2004, s 213I*) and for uprating the amount of the opening rights broadly in line with inflation (see *FA 2004, s 213M*).

(C) **Defined benefits arrangements.** The pension savings amount is broadly the aggregate of the 'pension increase' and the 'lump sum increase'. The *'pension increase'* is the amount by which the amount of the closing pension exceeds the amount of the opening pension. The amount of the closing pension is the annual rate of the pension to which the individual would be entitled if he became entitled to it at the end of the tax year. The amount of the opening pension is the corresponding figure at the end of the previous tax year. The '*lump sum increase*' is similarly defined but by reference to the amount of the lump sum to which the individual would be entitled at those times. In measuring the excess, the amounts of the opening and closing pensions and the opening and closing lump sums are to be multiplied by age-related factors to be set out in Treasury regulations. There is provision for adjustment of the amount of the closing pension and closing lump sum in certain eventualities (see *FA 2004, s 213K*) and for uprating the amount of the opening pension and opening lump sum broadly in line with inflation (see *FA 2004, s 213M*).

(D) **Hybrid arrangements.** A hybrid arrangement is one in which the ultimate form of benefits may be either an exclusively money purchase benefit (other than a cash balance benefit), an exclusively cash balance benefit or an exclusively defined benefit. To find the pension savings amount, determine the pension savings amount as above in relation to each possible eventuality and then choose the greatest of those amounts.

Anti-avoidance

Anti-avoidance rules come into play if a 'high income excess relief charge scheme' applies in the case of the individual for the tax year. The individual is treated for the above purposes as if his gross income, relevant income and total pension savings amount were what they would have been apart from the scheme. 'Scheme' includes any arrangement, agreement, understanding, transaction or series of transactions (whether or not legally enforceable).

A scheme is a '*high income excess relief charge scheme*' if all the following conditions are met:

- it is reasonable to assume that a main purpose of the scheme is to avoid the whole or any part of the liability of the individual to the high income excess relief charge for the tax year;
- the scheme produces a reduction in gross income or relevant income and/or a reduction in the total pension savings amount; and
- under the scheme, the said reduction (or any of the reductions) is redressed by:
  - an increase in the individual's gross income or relevant income, or the total pension savings amount, for a different tax year; or
  - the provision at any time of some other benefit to, or for the benefit, of the individual or any dependant of his or any person connected with him (within **21 CONNECTED PERSONS**).

General

The Treasury may by regulations make provision about the high income excess relief charge. This may include modifications or amendments of the above but may not include provision increasing any person's liability to tax.

[*FA 2004, ss 213A–213P; FA 2010, Sch 2 paras 2, 5*].

Non-UK pension schemes

The Commissioners for HMRC may by statutory instrument apply the above provisions, with appropriate modifications, to members of 'currently-relieved' non-UK pension schemes as if those schemes were registered pension schemes. [*FA 2004, Sch 34 para 7B; FA 2010, Sch 2 para 4*].

A scheme is '*currently-relieved*' if:

- relief from tax is given in respect of contributions paid under the scheme during the tax year by virtue of the migrant member relief provisions at **57.20** below or of double tax arrangements; or
- one or more members are given exemption under *ITEPA 2003, s 307* (see **27.29**(iii) **EMPLOYMENT INCOME**) in respect of provision for retirement or death benefits made under the scheme at any time during the tax year when it is an overseas scheme.

[*FA 2004, Sch 34 para 8(3)*].

Special annual allowance charge

[57.10] In order to discourage members of registered pension schemes from increasing their pension savings prior to the restriction of higher and additional rate tax relief for 2011/12 onwards (see **57.9** above), a new income tax charge was introduced with effect **on and after 22 April 2009**. This is known as the **special annual allowance charge**. Despite the uncertainty as to whether the planned restriction for 2011/12 onwards will go ahead, the special annual allowance charge remains in place.

The special annual allowance charge applies to a 'high-income' individual who is a member of one or more registered pension schemes, and arises where his 'total adjusted pension input amount' for a tax year exceeds the special annual allowance, which is set at £20,000 (but see below). The chargeable amount is the excess less any amount that is subject to the annual allowance charge at **57.17** below for the same tax year. The tax liability is 20% of the chargeable amount, and the person liable is the individual himself. The liability is added at Step 7 of the calculation of income tax liability at **1.7 ALLOWANCES AND TAX RATES**. The charge is not dependent upon the residence, ordinary residence or domicile status of the individual or the scheme administrator(s). The chargeable amount is not treated for any tax purposes as income, which means that, for example, losses, reliefs and allowances cannot be set against it and it does not count as income for the purposes of any double tax treaty. After 5 April 2010, instead of being at 20%, the rate is in each case to be determined by the rate of tax relief given on the chargeable excess referred to above; the intention is to restrict tax relief on that excess to the basic rate (HMRC Pre-Budget Report Note 19, 9 December 2009).

The special annual allowance is reduced by (i) any 'protected pension input amounts' and (ii) any pre-22 April 2009 pension input amount attributable to contributions under money purchase arrangements that are not cash balance arrangements, if these have been deducted in arriving at total adjusted pension input amount (see below).

High income individuals

A '*high-income*' individual is one whose 'relevant income' for the tax year is £150,000 or more. An individual's '*relevant income*' is computed as follows.

(1) Start with the individual's total income for the tax year (see Step 1 of the calculation of income tax liability at **1.7 ALLOWANCES AND TAX RATES**).

(2) Add back any relief given under the so-called net pay arrangements for employer schemes (see **57.7** above) and any relief given by virtue of *FA 2004, Sch 36 para 51* (migrant member relief — see **57.20** below).

(3) Deduct any reliefs deductible at Step 2 of the calculation of income tax liability at **1.7 ALLOWANCES AND TAX RATES** other than pension contributions.

(4) Deduct relievable pension contributions up to a maximum of £20,000.

(5) Add any amount by which what would otherwise be general earnings or specific employment income (see **27.1 EMPLOYMENT INCOME**) of the individual for the tax year has been reduced by a post-22 April 2009 salary sacrifice scheme (see below).

(6) Deduct the grossed up amount of any Gift Aid donations (see **16.16 CHARITIES**).

If the amount arrived at is less than £150,000, compute the individual's relevant income for the two preceding tax years using steps at (1) to (6) above. If the result for either year (or both years) is £150,000 or more, the individual's relevant income for the current year is assumed to be £150,000 so that he falls within the anti-forestalling provisions.

If there is a scheme a main purpose of which is to secure that the individual's relevant income for the tax year is less than £150,000, it is assumed to be £150,000.

For the purpose of (5) above, there is a salary sacrifice scheme if:

• the individual has given up the right to receive general earnings or specific employment income, and

• in return, his employer or any other person has agreed to pay contributions (or additional contributions) to a pension scheme in respect of the individual or otherwise to secure an increase in the amount of benefits to which any of the following is actually or prospectively entitled under a pension scheme: the individual, a dependant of the individual or a person connected with the individual (within **21 CONNECTED PERSONS**).

On and after 9 December 2009, the special annual allowance charge is extended to individuals with incomes of £130,000 or more (see **57.11** below).

Total pension input amount

The *total pension input amount* is computed in accordance with *FA 2009, Sch 35 paras 3–6*. The computation is similar, though not identical, to the calculation of the total pension input amount for the purposes of the annual allowance charge at **57.17** below, i.e. the increase in the individual's pension rights, but is made by reference to the tax year rather than pension input periods. Contributions by the individual, his employer or a third party are all taken into account. Special rules apply where there is an avoidance scheme whose purpose is to avoid or reduce liability to the lifetime allowance charge, the annual allowance charge or the special annual allowance charge by reducing the total pension input amount.

To find the '*total adjusted pension input amount*', certain protected amounts (known as 'protected pension input amounts') must be deducted from the total pension input amount, as must any 'contributions refund lump sum' and, for 2009/10 only, any pre-22 April 2009 pension input amount.

'*Protected pension input amounts*' are computed in accordance with *FA 2009, Sch 35 paras 7–14*, whichever is applicable to the type of pensions arrangements involved, and represent normal ongoing regular pension savings. Broadly, for individuals contributing to a money purchase arrangement, normal regular ongoing savings are the continuation of those contributions paid under agreements made prior to 22 April 2009 that are paid quarterly or more frequently and at a rate that does not increase. For individuals in defined benefit schemes, normal regular ongoing savings include any increases in pension benefits which arise under the existing rules of the scheme as at 22 April 2009. These include any increased benefits due as a result of normal pay rises and progression. Added years contributions and additional voluntary contributions are treated along similar lines to money purchase arrangements. There is an anti-avoidance rule that prevents any amount from being a protected pension input amount if the individual is party to a scheme a main purpose of which is to avoid or reduce liability to the lifetime allowance charge, the annual allowance charge or the special annual allowance charge. Note that protected pension input amounts reduce the special annual allowance (see above).

SI 2010 No 429 extends protection to:

•   contributions made following a change in pension provider on or after 22 April 2009; and
•   contributions to which an individual or an employer was contractually committed at 22 April 2009 but which had not actually commenced on that date.

See www.hmrc.gov.uk/pensionschemes/allowance-charge.htm for details of these extensions.

For the tax year 2009/10 only, the total adjusted pension input amount is net of any element of the total pension input amount that relates to the part of the tax year preceding 22 April 2009 (when these rules were first announced), computed in accordance with *FA 2009, Sch 35 para 16*. In relation to a defined benefits arrangement or cash balance arrangement, a pre-22 April 2009 pension input amount is such proportion of the total pension input amount as, on a just and reasonable apportionment, relates to the period beginning with 6 April 2009 and ending with 21 April 2009. In relation to a money purchase arrangement that is not a cash balance arrangement, a pre-22 April 2009 pension input amount is so much of the amount of the contributions as are paid in the period beginning with 6 April 2009 and ending with 22 April 2009, but does not include contributions paid on a quarterly or more frequent basis; note that in this case the pre-22 April 2009 pension input amount reduces the special annual allowance (see above).

Adjusted special annual allowance

A special rule may apply if any contributions (including employer contributions) under money purchase arrangements (other than cash balance arrangements) are paid less frequently than quarterly. Ascertain the amount of any such contributions paid in the three years 2006/07 to 2008/09. Restrict each year's amount, if it would otherwise be greater, to the amount of the annual allowance for that year. Take the aggregate of those amounts and then compute the mean of that aggregate (i.e. the aggregate divided by three). If the mean exceeds £20,000 but is less than £30,000, the special annual allowance is the amount of the mean and not £20,000. If the mean is £30,000 or more, the special annual allowance is £30,000. In both cases, the revised special annual allowance is potentially subject to the reductions referred to above.

Refunds of contributions

High-income individuals potentially liable to the special annual allowance charge may be able to claim a refund of contributions, a *'contributions refund lump sum'*, depending on the nature and rules of the pension arrangements. A contributions refund lump sum is deductible in computing the total adjusted pension input amount only if it is paid in the tax year following the tax year in question and does not exceed an amount computed in accordance with *FA 2009, Sch 35 para 15*. A contributions refund lump sum is treated as if it were a short service refund lump sum (see **57.19**(a) below) chargeable on the scheme administrator at 50% (40% for 2009/10 and earlier years).

General

The Treasury have power to amend the above provisions by statutory instrument. In keeping with the transient nature of the provisions, the Treasury may also bring them to an end by statutory instrument with effect for a future specified tax year onwards (presumably 2011/12).

[*FA 2009, Sch 35; FA 2010, s 48(5); SI 2009 No 2031, Regs 1, 11; SI 2010 No 429*].

For guidance, see HMRC Registered Pension Schemes Manual RPSM15100000 *et seq.* and RPSM15200000 *et seq.* For 'frequently asked questions', see www.hmrc.gov.uk/budget2009/anti-forestalling-qa.pdf.

Non-UK pension schemes

SI 2009 No 2031 applies the provisions, with appropriate modifications, to members of 'currently-relieved' non-UK pension schemes as if those schemes were registered pension schemes. See **57.9** above for the meaning of a 'currently-relieved' non-UK pension scheme.

Extension of special annual allowance charge to individuals with incomes of £130,000 or more

[57.11] The special annual allowance charge at **57.10** above is extended so as also to apply to individuals whose 'relevant income' for the tax year (see above) is £130,000 or more. This has effect in relation to contributions paid on or after 9 December 2009 under money purchase arrangements and increases on or after that date in the rights accrued under defined benefit arrangements. Where an individual's relevant income is £150,000 or more, the rules at **57.10** above continue to apply unchanged. Where an individual's relevant income is £130,000 or more but less than £150,000, those rules apply in the same way as they do for an individual with relevant income of £150,000 or more but with the following principal modifications.

- References in **57.10** above to £150,000 should be taken as references to £130,000.
- In computing relevant income, salary sacrifice schemes are taken into account only if entered into on or after 9 December 2009.
- For the tax year 2009/10, the total adjusted pension input amount is net of any element of the total pension input amount that relates to the part of the tax year preceding 9 December 2009.
- For the tax year 2009/10, the special annual allowance is reduced by any pre-9 December 2009 pension input amount attributable to contributions under money purchase arrangements that are not cash balance arrangements, if these have been deducted in arriving at total adjusted pension input amount.
- In computing protected pension input amounts, references in **57.10** above to agreements made prior to 22 April 2009 and to scheme rules as at 22 April 2009 should be taken as references to agreements made prior to 9 December 2009 and to scheme rules as at that date.
- Generally, references to 22 April 2009 should be taken as references to 9 December 2009, and the reference to 21 April 2009 should be taken as a reference to 8 December 2009.

[*FA 2009, Sch 35 paras 1, 2, 16A; FA 2010, s 48(2)–(4), (6)(7)*]

(See HMRC Technical Note 'Pensions: Special annual allowance charge' at www.hmrc.gov.uk/pbr2009/pen-annual-allow-2020.pdf; HMRC factsheet at www.hmrc.gov.uk/pbr2009/pension_factsheet.pdf).

Employer contributions

[57.12] Contributions made by an employer to a registered pension scheme in respect of an individual are deductible in computing profits for the period of account in which they are made (subject to the spreading provisions below). The contributions must meet the normal conditions for expenditure deductible in computing trading profits, in particular the 'wholly and exclusively' rule (see **73.36 TRADING INCOME** and see also **57.13** below), but it is specifically provided that they are not treated as capital expenditure even if they would fall to be so treated under general principles.

Certain payments an employer may make to discharge his statutory obligations in relation to an under-funded defined benefits scheme are treated as contributions to the scheme for the above purposes and, if made after cessation of the employer's business, are treated as if made immediately before cessation. Otherwise, no sums other than contributions are deductible in connection with the cost of providing benefits under the employer pension scheme; this overrides any contrary rule that might apply under generally accepted accounting practice.

The Commissioners of HMRC are empowered to make regulations (see *SI 2005 No 3458*) restricting the deductibility of contributions to a registered scheme in respect of an individual if the individual's benefits from the scheme are dependent on the non-payment of benefits from an employer pension scheme which is not a registered scheme or if the transfer value of the individual's rights under the registered scheme is reduced by virtue of benefits being payable out of the non-registered scheme.

[*FA 2004, ss 196, 196A, 199, 200; FA 2008, Sch 29 para 14(3)(4); CTA 2009, Sch 1 paras 573, 574, 576, 577*].

[*FA 2004, ss 197, 198, 199A; FA 2008, s 90, Sch 29 para 14(2); CTA 2009, Sch 1 para 575*].

No tax charge on employee

An employee is not liable to income tax in respect of a contribution by his employer to a registered pension scheme, i.e. it is not treated as a benefit-in-kind. [*ITEPA 2003, s 308; FA 2004, s 201(2)*].

Simon's Taxes. See E7.506.

Applying the 'wholly and exclusively' rule

[57.13] HMRC have published guidance on the application of the 'wholly and exclusively' rule to employer contributions to registered pension schemes. A pension contribution to a registered scheme is part of the cost of employing staff and will be allowable unless, exceptionally, there is an identifiable non-business purpose for the employer's decision to make the contribution or for the size of the contribution. Where the facts show that a definite part or proportion of an expense is not wholly and exclusively laid out or expended for business purposes, only that part or proportion is disallowable.

One situation where all or part of a contribution *may* not have been paid wholly and exclusively for business purposes is where it is paid in respect of a director who is also a controlling shareholder or in respect of an employee who is a close relative (e.g. a spouse) or friend of the business proprietor or of a controlling director. This will depend on the facts in each case. If the pension contribution paid for such directors or employees is the same as that paid for a third-party employee in similar circumstances, HMRC accept that there is no non-business purpose and will allow a deduction for the full amount of the contribution. Otherwise, HMRC will consider the taxpayer's object in making the payment, which includes his subjective intentions in making the payment.

If the contribution is part of a remuneration package paid wholly and exclusively for the purposes of the business, the contribution is an allowable expense. However, if the level of the remuneration package is excessive in relation to the value of the work undertaken by the employee, this might be seen as an indication that the whole amount of the remuneration package, not just the pension contribution, fails the 'wholly and exclusively' test.

A payment may be made exclusively for business purposes even though it also secures a benefit for someone other than the business. This will be the case if the securing of that benefit was not the object of the payment but merely a consequential and incidental effect of the payment. A contribution made as part of a salary sacrifice arrangement will also usually meet the 'wholly and exclusively' test.

The guidance also considers, *inter alia*, contributions made in connection with the purchase, sale or cessation of a business, industry-wide pension schemes and group schemes.

(HMRC Business Income Manual BIM 46001–46085).

Spreading of abnormally large contributions

[57.14] Where the contributions paid (or treated as paid) by an employer in a period of account exceed 210% of the contributions paid in the previous period of account, relief for the excess contributions may fall to be spread over more than one period of account as follows. Firstly, identify the amount of current period contributions that exceeds 110% of previous period contributions (the *'relevant excess contributions'*). If this amount is less than £500,000, spreading does not apply. Otherwise, relief for the relevant excess contributions is spread over the current and following periods of account as follows.

Amount of relevant excess contributions	Spread equally over
£500,000 to £999,999 inclusive	2 periods of account
£1,000,000 to £1,999,999 inclusive	3 periods of account
£2,000,000 or more	4 periods of account

If the current and previous periods of account are unequal in length, the amount of the previous period contributions is adjusted proportionately in order to determine the excess (if any). Any contributions paid in the current period to fund cost of living increases in current pensions are disregarded in determining any excess, as are any contributions to fund a future service liability for employees joining the scheme in the current period. If the employer ceases business, such that some of the excess contributions would otherwise remain unrelieved, the otherwise unrelieved amount is relieved in the period of account which ends with the date of cessation or, at the employer's option, is apportioned on a daily basis over the whole of the spreading period up to the date of cessation.

Legislation is included in *FA 2008* to ensure that the spreading rules cannot be circumvented by routing the contributions through a third party such as a new company. The measure has effect where the payment subject to spreading is made after 9 October 2007 (other than under a contract entered into before that date).

[*FA 2004, ss 197, 198, 199A; FA 2008, s 90, Sch 29 para 14(2); CTA 2009, Sch 1 para 575*].

Lifetime allowance

[57.15] Each individual has a '*lifetime allowance*' for the purposes of these provisions. The amount of the lifetime allowance is as follows.

2006/07	£1.5 million
2007/08	£1.6 million
2008/09	£1.65 million
2009/10	£1.75 million
2010/11 to 2015/16 inclusive	£1.8 million

Future increases will be pre-announced at five-yearly intervals (Revenue Budget Note BN 39, 17 March 2004).

Whenever a 'benefit crystallisation event' occurs in relation to an individual, the amount crystallised is measured against the individual's lifetime allowance (or so much of it, if any, as remains after previous benefit crystallisation events). Any excess is chargeable to tax (the '*lifetime allowance charge*').

On a second or subsequent benefit crystallisation event, the *proportion* of the lifetime allowance utilised in relation to previous events is taken into account in computing how much lifetime allowance remains. Thus, if an amount of £500,000 is crystallised in 2006/07, one-third of the lifetime allowance of £1.5 million is utilised against it (and no charge applies). If a further amount is crystallised in 2010/11, the lifetime allowance remaining to be utilised against it is £1.2 million, i.e. two-thirds of the 2010/11 figure.

The legislation (*FA 2004, s 216, Sch 32*) lists nine different '*benefit crystallisation events*' and gives the amount crystallised in each case. These events are intended to cover:

(i)   the commencement of the individual's entitlement to receive a pension (and the various different ways in which this can occur);

(ii) increases in an individual's pension (already being paid) by more than a defined annual rate and by more than a permitted margin (applied on a cumulative basis);

(iii) the attainment of age 75 by an individual in a defined benefits scheme without his having received a pension or lump sum;

(iv) the attainment of age 75 by an individual who has previously designated sums or assets held in a money purchase scheme as available for the payment of unsecured pension;

(v)   an individual's becoming entitled to receive a lump sum,

(vi)   the payment of certain lump sum death benefits; and

(vii)   the transfer of funds from registered schemes to certain overseas schemes.

The amount crystallised when an individual starts to receive a pension is generally the amount of pension that will be payable in the first 12 months, disregarding any actual increases during that period, multiplied by a factor of 20. If, however, the scheme is a money purchase scheme and the pension is an unsecured pension or lifetime annuity, the amount crystallised is the total sum (including market value of any assets) designated for the payment of the unsecured pension or used to purchase the annuity (and any related dependants' annuity — see *FA 2004, Sch 29 para 3(4A)*). In the case of an event within (iv) above, the amount crystallised is the growth (if any) in the individual's unsecured pension fund since the designation (though there is transitional exemption for certain drawdown funds already in payment on 6 April 2006). In the case of a lump sum payment, the amount crystallised is the amount of the lump sum received by the individual. Any abatement of a pension under a public service pension scheme is generally disregarded in determining the time that a benefit crystallisation event occurs and the amount crystallised.

To the extent that the amount chargeable to tax is paid as a lump sum to the individual (or as a lump sum death benefit in respect of the individual), the tax charge is at 55%. Otherwise it is at 25%. The tax is the joint and several liability of the individual and the scheme administrator (except in the case of a lump sum death benefit, where the tax is the liability of the person to whom the benefit is paid). The tax will normally be paid by the scheme administrator (see *FA 2004, s 254*). The charge is not dependent upon any person's being resident, ordinarily resident or domiciled in the UK. Although chargeable to income tax, the chargeable amount is not treated for any tax purposes as income, which means that, for example, losses, reliefs and allowances cannot be set against it and it does not count as income for the purposes of any double tax treaty.

For 2010/11 onwards, the rate of charge may be varied by Treasury Order made by statutory instrument, and different rates may apply in different circumstances.

The scheme administrator may meet the liability out of scheme funds or by deducting it from the individual's scheme benefits. If it is paid by the scheme administrator, the tax itself is added to the chargeable amount. If the tax paid is then netted off against a lump sum payment, the chargeable amount above is effectively the aggregate of the lump sum actually received by the individual and the tax paid by the scheme administrator. If the tax paid is set against the individual's scheme pension entitlement (other than where funds are designated to pay an unsecured pension or to purchase an annuity), the reduction is ignored in computing the amount crystallised in events (i) to (iii) above; but if, applying normal actuarial practice, the reduction in pension fully reflects the amount of tax paid, the tax is not then regarded as having been paid by the scheme administrator. The intention is that the amount tested against the lifetime allowance should be the gross amount of benefits crystallised and not the net amount after deducting tax funded by the scheme.

Enhancement

An individual's lifetime allowance is enhanced (in accordance with *FA 2004, ss 221–223*) if, at any time during his membership of a registered pension scheme (treated for this purpose as commencing no earlier than 6 April 2006), either (i) he is not a 'relevant UK individual' (see **57.7** above) or (ii) he is such an individual only because he was UK resident at some time in the previous five tax years *and* he is not employed by a person resident in the UK. This is to reflect the fact that his pension provision will not have entirely benefited from UK tax reliefs. An individual's lifetime allowance is also enhanced (in accordance with *FA 2004, ss 224–226*) if pension rights of his are transferred from a recognised overseas pension scheme into a UK registered scheme, again reflecting the fact that rights will have built up without the benefit of UK tax relief. An individual who intends to benefit from either of these enhancements must give notice of that intention to HMRC in accordance with regulations made by the Commissioners of HMRC (see *SI 2006 No 131* which, *inter alia*, prescribes rules to determine the closing date for such notifications — see *Regs 7, 8*).

Where, exceptionally, an individual acquires a new or increased lifetime allowance enhancement factor between two benefit crystallisation events, there is provision for this to be taken into account in computing the proportion of the total lifetime allowance already utilised.

[*FA 2004, ss 214–226, Sch 32; FA 2006, s 161, Sch 23 paras 30, 31; FA 2007, Sch 20 paras 10, 24(3); FA 2008, Sch 29 para 1(3), paras 4–12, para 15; FA 2009, Sch 2 paras 14, 25; F(No 2)A 2010, Sch 3 para 6; SI 2006 Nos 131, 3261; SI 2007 No 494; SI 2009 No 56, Sch 1 paras 147–152; SI 2010 No 651; SI 2010 No 922, Reg 2*].

Simon's Taxes. See E7.504.

Transitional

[57.16] In relation to the lifetime allowance, there are two kinds of protection available in relation to pension rights built up before 6 April 2006 — primary protection and enhanced protection.

Primary protection

Primary protection applies where an individual's 'relevant pre-commencement pension rights' exceed £1.5 million (the amount of the lifetime allowance for 2006/07). The individual's lifetime allowance for each tax year is enhanced by the proportion which the excess bears to £1.5 million; for example, an individual with relevant pre-commencement pension rights of £2 million will have his lifetime allowance increased by one-third. An individual's '*relevant pre-commencement pension rights*' is the aggregate of (i) the value of his uncrystallised pension rights under all schemes of the kind listed at **57.3** above, rights being 'uncrystallised' if at 5 April 2006 the individual has not become entitled to the present payment of benefits, and (ii) the value of his crystallised rights (if any) at 5 April 2006, calculated at 25 times the annual rate of pensions payable at that date. In the case of occupational schemes, the value of uncrystallised pension rights is limited by a ceiling of 20 times the maximum permitted pension (as defined). An individual who intends to benefit from this enhancement must give notice of that intention to HMRC in accordance with regulations to be made by the Commissioners of HMRC (see *SI 2006 No 131* which, *inter alia*, prescribes 5 April 2009 as the closing date for such notifications and also enables an individual to notify HMRC that he no longer wishes to benefit — see *Reg 3*).

Primary protection is extended in certain circumstances where the entitlement to death benefits in relation to an individual (his 'pre-commencement rights to death benefits', as defined and assuming his hypothetical death on 5 April 2006) is greater than the amount of his relevant pre-commencement pension rights. In relation to benefit crystallisation events consisting of the payment of lump sum death benefits, the amount of the enhancement is computed as above but by reference to the greater amount. For this to apply, lump sum death benefits must actually become payable in respect of the individual, and notice of intention to benefit from this enhancement must be given to HMRC (in accordance with HMRC regulations) by the recipient of those benefits (see *SI 2006 No 131*, as amended by *SI 2006 No 3261*, which, *inter alia*, prescribes rules to determine the closing date for such notifications — see *Reg 3A*).

Enhanced protection

Enhanced protection exempts an individual from the lifetime allowance charge if he has ceased active membership of a pre-existing pension scheme that becomes a registered scheme on 6 April 2006 and continues for so long as he does not resume active membership or join any registered scheme. An individual is taken to have resumed active membership if, in the case of a money purchase scheme, a contribution to the scheme is made by (or on behalf of) him or his employer or, in the case of a defined benefits scheme, crystallised benefits exceed the 'appropriate limit' set out in *FA 2004, Sch 36 para 15* (see also *SI 2006 No 130*) or if pensionable earnings exceed a permitted maximum set out at *FA 2004, Sch 36 paras 16, 17* (see also *SI 2006 No 130*). Contributions consisting of the payment of life assurance premiums on a pre-6 April 2006 policy (or in some cases a replacement policy) are disregarded in certain circumstances, as are certain employer contributions made solely to provide certain lump sum death benefits. Enhanced protection also ceases to be available if certain transfers are made into or out of the scheme. An individual who intends to benefit from enhanced protection must give notice of that intention to HMRC in accordance with regulations to be made by the Commissioners of HMRC (see *SI 2006 No 131* which, *inter alia*, prescribes 5 April 2009 as the closing date for such notifications — see *Regs 4, 5*). A consequence of claiming enhanced protection is that the individual cannot be paid a lifetime allowance excess lump sum (within *FA 2004, s 166, Sch 29 para 11*).

Enhanced protection is extended where certain lump sum death benefits become payable in respect of an individual. The enhancement operates by computing the 'appropriate limit' as set out in *FA 2004, Sch 36 para 15A*, i.e. by reference to the value of the individual's 'pre-commencement rights to death benefits' (as defined and assuming his hypothetical death on 5 April 2006) and comparing it to the original 'appropriate limit' referred to above. In relation to benefit crystallisation events consisting of the payment of such lump sum death benefits, the greater of the two limits is used. Notice of intention to benefit from this enhancement must be given to HMRC (in accordance with HMRC regulations) by the recipient of the lump sum death benefit (see *SI 2006 No 131*, as amended by *SI 2006 No 3261*, which, *inter alia*, prescribes rules to determine the closing date for such notifications — see *Reg 4A*).

[*FA 2004, Sch 36 paras 7–20; FA 2006, s 161, Sch 23 paras 36–41, 45; ITA 2007, Sch 1 para 485; FA 2007, Sch 19 paras 10, 29(3), Sch 20 paras 15, 17–19, 24(3); CTA 2010, Sch 1 para 432(2); SI 2006 Nos 131, 211, 3261; SI 2009 No 56, Sch 1 paras 147–152; SI 2010 No 651*].

Annual allowance

[57.17] In addition to the lifetime allowance at **57.15** above, each individual has an '*annual allowance*' for the purposes of these provisions. The amount of the annual allowance is as follows.

2006/07	£215,000
2007/08	£225,000
2008/09	£235,000
2009/10	£245,000
2010/11 to 2015/16 inclusive (but see below)	£255,000

Future increases will be pre-announced at five-yearly intervals (Revenue Budget Note BN 39, 17 March 2004; Explanatory Notes to 2004 Finance Bill). But see **57.9** above for the possibility of the annual allowance being very significantly reduced for 2011/12 onwards.

The annual increase in an individual's rights under all registered pension schemes of which he is a member is measured against his annual allowance, and any excess over the annual allowance is chargeable to tax (the '*annual allowance charge*') at the rate of **40%**. The individual himself is liable to the tax. The charge is not dependent upon the residence, ordinary residence or domicile status of the individual or the scheme administrator. Although chargeable to income tax, the chargeable amount is not treated for any tax purposes as income, which means that, for example, losses, reliefs and allowances cannot be set against it and it does not count as income for the purposes of any double tax treaty.

For 2010/11 onwards, the rate of charge may be varied by Treasury Order made by statutory instrument, and different rates may apply in different circumstances.

The annual increase in an individual's pension rights is computed in terms of his total '*pension input amount*' for the tax year. This is found by aggregating the pension input amounts for all registered schemes of which he is a member. There is no pension input amount in respect of a pension arrangement if, before the end of the tax year, all the benefits under that arrangement have crystallised or the individual dies. The calculation of the pension input amount depends on the type of scheme and on the 'pension input period' that ends in the tax year. For money purchase schemes (other than cash balance arrangements — as defined by *FA 2004, s 152(3)*), the pension input amount is broadly the amount of contributions paid by or on behalf of the individual (including contributions by his employer) in that pension input period. For defined benefits schemes and cash balance arrangements, it is the excess (if any) of the value of his pension rights at the end of that pension input period over the value of his pension rights at the beginning of that pension input period. For this purpose, the value of an individual's pension rights at a particular time is:

- (in the case of a defined benefits scheme) the aggregate of any lump sum to which the individual would have been entitled (otherwise than by commutation of pension) if he had become entitled to payment of it at that time and 10 times the annual pension that would have been payable if the individual had become entitled to payment of it at that time;
- (in the case of a cash balance arrangements) the amount that would have been available for provision of benefits if the individual had become entitled to the benefits at that time.

In determining any amount to which an individual would have been entitled if he became entitled to it at a particular time, certain assumptions are made as set out in *FA 2004, s 277*.

In ascertaining the pension input amount, the value of the pension rights at the beginning of the pension input period is increased by the greatest of 5%, the increase in the retail prices index during that period and such percentage as may be determined by regulations made by the Commissioners of HMRC (see *SI 2006 No 130*), *but* in the case of a defined benefits scheme this uprating applies only if no pension rights accrue to the individual during the pension input period (whether by means of contributions or by accruing years of pensionable service). There is also provision for the adjustment in certain circumstances of the value of the pension rights at the end of the pension input period.

The first '*pension input period*' begins on the day the pension rights begin to accrue or, in the case of a money purchase scheme (other than cash balance arrangements) the day on which the first contribution to the scheme is made. The period ends a year after commencement or, if earlier, on a day nominated for the purpose. This enables the period to end on a convenient date, e.g. the end of the tax year or the date to which the scheme prepares its accounts; the nomination is made by the scheme administrator but, in the case of a money purchase scheme (other than cash balance arrangements), may also be made by the individual. Each subsequent pension input period begins immediately after the end of the previous one and ends a year later or, if earlier, on a nominated date falling in the tax year following that in which the previous pension input period ended. The final pension input period in relation to a scheme comes to an end on the first day on which the individual has no benefits remaining to be provided.

[*FA 2004, ss 227–238; FA 2009, Sch 2 paras 15, 25; SI 2007 No 494; SI 2010 No 922, Reg 3*].

Simon's Taxes. See E7.503.

Transitional

[57.18] Where an individual has notified HMRC of his intention to benefit from *enhanced protection* from the *lifetime allowance charge* (see **57.16** above), the individual is exempt from the annual allowance charge for any tax year throughout the whole of which the enhanced protection continues to apply. If at some point during a tax year the enhanced protection terminates (because the individual resumes active membership of a scheme or joins a new scheme), the annual allowance charge applies in full for that tax year. [*FA 2004, Sch 36 para 49; FA 2009, Sch 35 para 22*]. There is also provision for the pension input amount for the pension input period ending in 2006/07 to be reduced by any employer contribution made between 6 April 2006 and 7 July 2006 inclusive to consolidate unfunded unapproved pension promises made before 6 April 2006 into a registered scheme. [*FA 2004, Sch 36 para 48*].

Other tax charges

[57.19] In addition to the lifetime allowance charge at **57.15** above, the annual allowance charge at **57.17** above, the high income excess relief charge at **57.9** above and the special annual allowance charge at **57.10** above, other income tax charges may arise in relation to registered schemes as listed below. These are in addition to the normal taxation under *ITEPA 2003* of individuals' pension income, which is covered in **56 PENSION INCOME**. See **57.22–57.25** below as regards charges arising from investment restrictions applicable to self-directed registered schemes.

(a) **Short service refund lump sum charge.** This is a charge on the scheme administrator at **20%** or, to the extent that the lump sum exceeds £20,000 (£10,800 for 2009/10 and earlier years), **50%** (40% for 2009/10 and earlier years). A '*short service lump sum*' is defined by *FA 2004, Sch 29 para 5* and is broadly a refund in specified circumstances of a member's contributions to an occupational pension scheme. The charge is not dependent upon the residence, ordinary residence or domicile status of the scheme administrator or the person to whom the lump sum is paid. Although chargeable to income tax, a short service refund lump sum is not treated for any tax purposes as income. The tax may be deducted at source by the scheme administrator from the lump sum payment if the scheme rules so permit. [*FA 2004, s 205; SI 2010 No 536, Art 3*].

(b) **Special lump sum death benefits charge.** This is a charge on the scheme administrator at **35%** where a pension protection lump sum death benefit, an annuity protection lump sum death benefit or an unsecured pension fund lump sum death benefit is paid. These terms are defined by *FA 2004, Sch 29 paras 14, 16, 17*. The same comments apply as in (a) above as regards residence status etc., non-treatment as income and deduction at source. [*FA 2004, s 206*]. HMRC are empowered to make regulations to the effect that an insurance company paying certain types of lump sum death benefit be treated as a scheme administrator for this purpose — see now *SI 2006 No 136*. [*FA 2004, s 273A*].

(c) **Authorised surplus payments charge.** This is a charge on the scheme administrator at **35%** where an authorised surplus payment (i.e. a return of surplus funds — see *SI 2006 No 574* at **57.2** above) is made to the employer by an occupational scheme. The charge is not dependent upon the residence, ordinary residence or domicile status of the scheme administrator or the employer. Although chargeable to income tax, an authorised surplus payment is not treated for any tax purposes as income. If the employer is a charity or is otherwise exempt from tax, the charge does not apply. [*FA 2004, s 207*].

(d) **Unauthorised payments charge.** Where an unauthorised payment is made, a charge at **40%** arises on the amount thereof (and see also (*e*) below). The person liable is the scheme member (or former member) to whom (or in respect of whom) the payment is made (or, if made after the member's or former member's death, the recipient) or, where applicable, the employer to whom (or in respect of whom) it is made. If more than one person is liable, liability is joint and several. The charge is not dependent upon the residence, ordinary residence or domicile status of the scheme administrator or any person who is liable. Although chargeable to income tax, an unauthorised payment is not treated for any tax purposes as income.

The rate of charge may be varied by Treasury Order made by statutory instrument, and, for 2010/11 onwards, different rates may apply in different circumstances.

[*FA 2004, s 208; FA 2006, s 161, Sch 23 para 14; FA 2009, Sch 2 paras 12, 25*].

See *FA 2004, ss 160–181* as regards authorised and unauthorised payments by registered schemes. These include circumstances in which an unauthorised payment is treated as having being made, even though the scheme makes no actual payment. Examples, subject to detailed rules and conditions, are the assignment or surrender of benefits by the member, the reallocation within the scheme of members' benefits or employer contributions, the providing of non-cash benefits to a member and the shifting of value between scheme assets and members' assets. See *FA 2004, ss 172, 172A, 172B, 172BA, 172B, 172C, 172D, 173, 174, SI 2006 No 133* and **57.22** below. Certain of the pension rules and pension death benefit rules in *FA 2004, Sch 28* also treat an unauthorised payment as having being made; see, for example, *Sch 28 paras 2A, 16(2B), 16C(1)*. See also the anti-avoidance rule at **57.2** above on recycling of lump sums. In applying the rules on unauthorised payments, 'member' generally includes a former member. For relief from the unauthorised payments charge, and the surcharge at (e) below, in cases where monies are repatriated to the scheme by order of the Pensions Regulator or the courts, see *FA 2004, s 266A* as amended.

Amendments are made to the unauthorised payment rules by *FA 2008* to seek to ensure that tax-relieved pension savings diverted into inheritance using scheme pensions and lifetime annuities are subject to unauthorised payment charges and, where appropriate, inheritance tax. These have effect for assignments and surrenders of rights (and agreements to assign or surrender) made after 9 October 2007 and for increases in pension rights attributable to the death of a member after 5 April 2008. [*FA 2008, Sch 28 paras 1–4, 15*]. See also Tolley's Inheritance Tax under Pension Schemes.

(e) **Unauthorised payments surcharge.** This is payable at **15%**, in addition to the unauthorised payments charge at (d) above, in respect of:

- unauthorised payments to or for a member (or former member) where, broadly, such payments made over a 12-month period use up at least 25% of the value of that person's pension fund; and

- unauthorised payments to or for a scheme employer (or former scheme employer) where, broadly, such payments made over a 12-month period use up at least 25% of the aggregate value of sums and assets held for the purposes of the pension scheme.

  The rate of charge may be varied by Treasury Order made by statutory instrument, and, for 2010/11 onwards, different rates may apply in different circumstances.

  [*FA 2004, ss 209–213; FA 2006, s 161, Sch 23 paras 15–19; FA 2009, Sch 2 paras 13, 25*].

(f) **Scheme sanction charge.** This is a charge on the scheme administrator at **40%** in respect of unauthorised payments made by the scheme (with certain specified exemptions) and payments which the scheme is treated as having made by virtue of *FA 2004, s 181A* (minimum level of alternatively secured pension) or *FA 2004, s 183* or *s 185* (unauthorised borrowing). The charge is not dependent upon the residence, ordinary residence or domicile status of any person liable. If payments subjected to this charge are also charged under (d) above, credit is given for the tax *paid* (as opposed to the tax charged) under (d); however, the available credit is limited to 25% of the chargeable payment.

  For 2010/11 onwards, both the rate of charge and the rate of credit may be varied by Treasury Order made by statutory instrument, and different rates may apply in different circumstances.

  [*FA 2004, ss 239–241; FA 2006, s 158, Sch 21 paras 8, 9; FA 2007, Sch 19 paras 15, 29(2); FA 2009, Sch 2 paras 16, 25; SI 2006 No 365*].

  See **57.22** below for the application of this charge to income and gains arising from certain investments held by self-directed schemes. For relief from the scheme sanction charge in cases where monies are repatriated to the scheme by order of the Pensions Regulator or the courts, see *FA 2004, s 266B*.

(g) **De-registration charge.** This is a charge on the scheme administrator at **40%** of the aggregate value of sums and assets held for the purposes of the pension scheme immediately before the withdrawal by HMRC of the scheme's registration (see **57.2** above). It is not dependent upon the residence, ordinary residence or domicile status of any person liable.

  For 2010/11 onwards, the rate of charge may be varied by Treasury Order made by statutory instrument, and different rates may apply in different circumstances.

  [*FA 2004, s 242; FA 2009, Sch 2 paras 17, 25*].

For capital gains tax purposes, the scheme assets are then deemed to have been acquired immediately before withdrawal of registration for the amount on which they are charged to tax under *FA 2004, s 242*. [*TCGA 1992, s 239A*].

Simon's Taxes. See E7.508, E7.514.

Overseas pension schemes — migrant member relief

[57.20] Where an individual comes to work in the UK and is already a member of an overseas pension scheme, UK tax relief may be available for his contributions to the scheme and on his employer contributions. This is known as *'migrant member relief'*. It replaces the pre-existing 'corresponding relief' in *ITEPA 2003, s 355* (see **27.19 EMPLOYMENT INCOME**), although where an individual obtains relief under that *section* for contributions made in 2005/06, HMRC may in certain circumstances continue to allow relief for contributions made in subsequent years to the same scheme (see *FA 2004, Sch 36 para 51* and *SI 2006 No 572, Regs 15–17*).

Migrant member relief is available for contributions made by an individual:

- who is a 'relevant migrant member' of a 'qualifying overseas pension scheme';
- who has relevant UK earnings chargeable to income tax for the tax year in which the contributions are made (see **57.7** above); and
- who has notified the scheme manager of his intention to claim the relief.

Relief is given as in **57.7** above, but is so given by deduction from total income on the making of a claim rather than by deduction at source and extension of the basic rate band. Relief for employer contributions applies as in **57.12** above.

An individual is a *'relevant migrant member'* of an overseas pension scheme if he:

- was non-UK resident when he joined the scheme;
- was a member of the scheme at the beginning of the period of UK residence in which the contributions in question are made;
- was, either immediately before or at any time in the 10 years before the start of that period of UK residence, entitled to tax relief on his contributions in the country in which he was then resident; and
- has been notified by the scheme manager that information on benefit crystallisation events (see **57.15** above) will be given to HMRC.

HMRC have power to modify the above definition by statutory instrument (see now *SI 2006 No 1957*) so that, in prescribed circumstances, the first three bullet points apply equally by reference to any earlier overseas pension scheme of which the individual was a member.

A *'qualifying overseas pension scheme'* is an overseas pension scheme which has provided certain notifications, evidence and undertakings to HMRC, including an undertaking to comply with information requirements regarding benefit crystallisation events, and which has not been excluded by HMRC from being a qualifying overseas pension scheme by reason of previous significant failures to comply with such information requirements. A scheme manager has the right of appeal against a decision of HMRC to exclude the scheme from qualifying.

[*ITEPA 2003, s 308A; FA 2004, ss 150(7), 170, 243, Sch 33; FA 2006, s 161, Sch 23 para 32; SI 2006 Nos 206, 212; SI 2007 No 1600; SI 2009 No 56, Sch 1 paras 425, 435*].

SI 2006 No 208 prescribes the information which a qualifying overseas pension scheme must undertake to provide to HMRC, and the time limits within which the information must be provided.

Simon's Taxes. See E4.740, E7.506, E7.507, E7.514.

Overseas pension schemes — tax charges

Lifetime allowance charge

[57.21] The lifetime allowance charge at **57.15** above applies, with appropriate modifications, in relation to a member of a non-UK pension scheme if:

- UK tax relief has been given, on contributions to the scheme made by the member or on his behalf, either under the migrant member relief provisions at **57.20** above or under a double tax treaty; or
- the member has been given exemption under *ITEPA 2003, s 307* (see **27.29**(iii) **EMPLOYMENT INCOME**) in respect of provision for retirement or death benefits made under the scheme at a time after 5 April 2006 when it was an overseas scheme.

[*FA 2004, s 244, Sch 34 paras 13–20; TIOPA 2010, Sch 8 para 64*].

Annual allowance charge

The annual allowance charge at **57.17** above applies, with appropriate modifications, in relation to a member of a non-UK pension scheme for any tax year in respect of which:

- UK tax relief is obtained, on contributions to the scheme made by the member or on his behalf, either under the migrant member relief provisions at **57.20** above or under a double tax treaty; or
- the member is given exemption under *ITEPA 2003, s 307* (see **27.29**(iii) **EMPLOYMENT INCOME**) in respect of provision for retirement or death benefits made under the scheme while it is an overseas scheme.

[*FA 2004, s 244, Sch 34 paras 8–12, 20; FA 2008, Sch 29 para 19*].

Other tax charges

The charges at **57.19**(a)(b)(d) and (e) above apply, in certain circumstances and with appropriate modifications, in relation to payments made to or in respect of a member of a non-UK pension scheme at a time when he is UK resident, if:

(a)   UK tax relief has been given, on contributions to the scheme made by the member or on his behalf, either under the migrant member relief provisions at **57.20** above or under a double tax treaty; or

(b)   the member has been given exemption under *ITEPA 2003, s 307* (see **27.29**(iii) **EMPLOYMENT INCOME**) in respect of provision for retirement or death benefits made under the scheme at a time after 5 April 2006 when it was an overseas scheme; or

(c)   the member's pension rights have been transferred from a registered pension scheme to the non-UK scheme at a time when it was a 'qualifying recognised overseas pension scheme' (see *FA 2004, s 150(7)(8), s 169; SI 2006 No 206* and HMRC Registered Pension Schemes Manual RPSM14101050).

The charges at **57.19**(a)(b)(d) and (e) above similarly apply in relation to payments made to or in respect of a member of a non-UK scheme at a time when he is non-UK resident, provided he has been UK resident at some time earlier in the tax year in which the payment is made or at some time in the five preceding tax years.

The above provisions do not have effect where the unauthorised payments charge at **57.19**(d) above applies by virtue of **57.22** below (self-directed schemes). However, HMRC have power to make regulations imposing that charge, insofar as it so applies, on a member who is within the scope of (c) above; see now *SI 2006 No 1960*. HMRC may also make regulations imposing the unauthorised payments charge on a member within the scope of any of (a)–(c) above in circumstances similar to those in which a scheme administrator would be liable to the scheme sanction charge at **57.19**(f) above by virtue of *FA 2004, s 181A* (minimum level of alternatively secured pension).

[*FA 2004, s 244, Sch 34 paras 1–7, 7ZA, 7A, 20; FA 2006, s 158, Sch 21 para 14; FA 2007, Sch 19 paras 18, 29(3); FA 2008, Sch 29 para 16; SI 2006 No 207; SI 2007 No 493, Reg 3; SI 2009 No 2047*].

SI 2006 No 208 prescribes the information which a 'qualifying recognised overseas pension scheme' must undertake to provide to HMRC, and the time limits within which the information must be provided.

Simon's Taxes. See E7.514.

Self-directed registered pension schemes — investment restrictions

[57.22] There are provisions designed to prevent *self-directed* registered pension schemes from gaining tax advantages where there is investment by the scheme in residential property and certain tangible moveable property such as fine wines, classic cars, art and antiques (all collectively described below as 'taxable property' — see also **57.24** below). A self-directed scheme is broadly one where a scheme member can direct which investments the scheme makes, and is described below as an 'investment-regulated pension scheme' (see **57.23** below for the full definition). For transitional provisions, see **57.25** below.

See HMRC Registered Pension Schemes Manual at RPSM07109000 *et seq.*

Charges to tax

An 'investment-regulated pension scheme' (see **57.23** below) is treated as making an unauthorised payment to a member (thus subject to the tax charge at **57.19**(d) above, potentially the surcharge at **57.19**(e) above and the scheme sanction charge at **57.19**(f) above) if:

(a) the scheme acquires 'taxable property' which is held by it for the purposes of an arrangement relating to the member; or

(b) 'taxable property' that the scheme holds for such purposes is improved; or

(c) property that the scheme holds for such purposes is converted into, or adapted to become, 'residential property' (see **57.24** below).

References to acquiring or holding property are to acquiring or holding an interest in the property.

[FA 2004, s 174A; FA 2006, s 158, Sch 21 para 5].

There are extensive provisions for determining the timing and the amount of the unauthorised payment. In the simplest case within (a) above, the unauthorised payment is treated as made at the time of the acquisition and the taxable amount is the acquisition cost of the taxable property (including incidental costs of acquisition). However, this is subject to rules applying where the property is held only indirectly by the investment-regulated pension scheme and where property is acquired for less than market value.

In a case within (b) above, the unauthorised payment is treated as made whenever a payment is made in connection with the improvement works, and the taxable amount is equal to the amount of that payment.

In a case within (c) above, the unauthorised payment is treated as made when the conversion or adaptation works are substantially completed or, if earlier, when the property ceases to be held by the pension scheme after it has become residential property. However, if the property becomes residential property more than three years after the first payment in respect of the said works, the unauthorised payment is treated as made at the expiry of that three-year period. The taxable amount is broadly acquisition cost plus development costs if the works commenced within twelve months of the acquisition of the pension scheme's interest in the property or market value (as defined) plus development costs if the works commenced at a later date.

In all cases, there is provision for apportioning only a part of the taxable amount to the pension scheme where its interest in the property is less than 100%; the amount of the unauthorised payment is then the amount so apportioned. Where the taxable property is held by the pension scheme for the purposes of more than one arrangement, the amount of the unauthorised payment is apportioned between those arrangements on a just and reasonable basis; otherwise, the whole of the payment is treated as made to the member to which the arrangement relates.

[FA 2004, s 174A, Sch 29A paras 31–45; FA 2006, s 158, Sch 21 para 13].

The above rules are to be supplemented by Treasury regulations made by statutory instrument (see now *SI 2006 No 1958, Regs 3–9*).

In addition to the above, for any tax year in which an 'investment-regulated pension scheme' (see **57.23** below) holds 'taxable property', the scheme sanction charge at **57.19**(f) above is imposed on the net income from the property or, if there is no such income or if actual net income is lower, on a notional amount of income. The notional income is computed in accordance with *FA 2004, ss 185A–185C*. In the most straightforward case where the scheme holds an interest in taxable property directly for the whole of the tax year, the notional income is equal to 10% of a deemed market value of the property. Where the scheme holds its interest in the property indirectly, there are rules as to what proportion of the otherwise chargeable amount should be charged on the scheme. Where the scheme holds its interest in the property indirectly and a person receives profits on which he has paid tax, there is provision for a similar proportion of the tax paid to be allowed as a credit against the tax liability resulting from the scheme sanction charge.

Gains on disposals of taxable property (net of any losses on such disposals) are also subject to the scheme sanction charge — in accordance with *FA 2004, ss 185F–185H*. A disposal is also deemed to arise for this purpose if the scheme ceases to hold all or part of an interest in a vehicle through which the scheme holds its interest in the property indirectly. There is provision for a proportion of any tax paid by another person in connection with a disposal to be allowed as a credit against the tax liability resulting from the scheme sanction charge.

[*FA 2004, ss 185A–185I; TCGA 1992, s 271(1B); FA 2006, s 158, Sch 21 paras 1, 6*].

The Treasury has power to make regulations (see now *SI 2006 No 1958, Reg 10*) imposing the scheme sanction charge where 'taxable property' situated outside the UK is held by a non-UK resident 'investment-regulated pension scheme'. The regulations may, in particular, transfer liability to such a charge from the scheme administrator to the member(s) for the purposes of whose arrangement(s) the interest in the property is held. [*FA 2004, s 273ZA; FA 2006, s 158, Sch 21 para 10*].

Definition of 'investment-regulated pension scheme'

[57.23] For the purposes of **57.22** above, a registered pension scheme that is *not* an occupational scheme is an '*investment-regulated pension scheme*' if one or more of its members (or persons 'related' to them) is (or has been) able (directly or indirectly) to direct, influence or advise on the manner of investment of any of the sums and assets held for the purposes of an arrangement under the pension scheme relating to the member.

A registered pension scheme that *is* an occupational scheme is an '*investment-regulated pension scheme*' if the scheme has 50 or fewer members and one or more of them (or persons 'related' to them) is (or has been) able (directly or indirectly) to direct, influence or advise on the manner of investment of any of the sums and assets held for the purposes of the scheme.

If an occupational scheme does not meet the above condition, it is nevertheless an '*investment-regulated pension scheme*' if one or more of its members (or persons 'related' to them) is (or has been) able (directly or indirectly) to direct, influence or advise on the manner of investment of any sums and assets that are held for the purposes of an arrangement under the pension scheme relating to the member (unless this is merely by reason of a just and reasonable apportionment of the sums and assets held for the purposes of the pension scheme). The Treasury has power to amend this rule by statutory instrument and to modify the investment-regulated pension scheme provisions insofar as they apply to such an arrangement.

For the above purposes, a person is 'related' to a member of a pension scheme if he and the member are CONNECTED PERSONS (21) or if he acts on behalf of the member or a person connected with the member.

Where an investment-regulated pension scheme holds sums or assets otherwise than for the purposes of the administration or management of the scheme, then, to the extent that they do not otherwise fall to be treated as held for the purposes of arrangements relating to members, they are apportioned between all such arrangements according to the respective rights of the members and treated as held for the purposes of those arrangements.

[FA 2004, Sch 29A paras 1–5; FA 2006, s 158, Sch 21 para 13; ITA 2007, Sch 1 para 484; FA 2008, Sch 29 para 3].

Taxable property

[57.24] For the purposes of 57.22 above, property is 'taxable property' if it is residential property or tangible moveable property. 'Residential property' is defined for these purposes to include buildings used (or suitable for use) as dwellings and their gardens or grounds. It includes property located outside the UK. It does not include, for example, certain care homes, children's homes, hospices and students' halls of residence. The Treasury may include or exclude other types of building by means of statutory instrument. Residential property is not 'taxable property' if it is:

(a)   occupied by an employee as a condition of his employment; or
(b)   used in connection with business premises held as an investment of the pension scheme,

provided that the occupant is neither a member of the pension scheme nor connected (within 21 CONNECTED PERSONS) with a member or, in the case of (a), with the employer.

'Tangible moveable property' has its general meaning and will include, for example, fine wines, classic and vintage cars, art, antiques, jewellery, boats, stamp collections and rare books. The Treasury may exclude particular items by statutory instrument; SI 2006 No 1959 excludes gold bullion (as defined) and any items with a market value not exceeding £6,000 held by a vehicle solely for the purposes of its administration or management, being property in which the pension scheme does not hold an interest directly and which no member of the scheme (or connected person) occupies or uses (or has a right to do so).

[FA 2004, Sch 29A paras 6–11; FA 2006, s 158, Sch 21 para 13; SI 2006 No 1959].

There are extensive provisions determining what is meant by an investment-regulated pension scheme acquiring or holding an interest in property, defining both direct and indirect holdings and, in both cases, providing exceptions. There are also rules whereby a scheme is deemed to have acquired property in particular circumstances. An indirect holding in property is broadly a holding by the pension scheme in a vehicle (such as a company, collective investment scheme or trust) that holds the property (whether directly or indirectly). [*FA 2004, Sch 29A paras 12–30; FA 2006, s 158, Sch 21 para 13; FA 2007, Sch 20 paras 14, 24(8); CTA 2010, Sch 1 para 431*]. Generally, self-directed pension schemes are permitted to invest in genuinely diverse commercial vehicles that hold what would be otherwise be 'taxable property', but subject to rules preventing the use of such vehicles as a means to facilitate investment in prohibited assets where there remains scope for personal use of those assets (HMRC Technical Note, 5 December 2005).

Transitional

[57.25] Subject to below, the charges at **57.22** above do not apply if the pension scheme acquired the property in question before 6 April 2006 and it is property that the scheme was not prohibited from holding under the rules in force before that date (see, for example, *SI 1991 No 1614* and *SI 2001 No 117*), such that approval to the scheme could have been withdrawn. The same applies if the property is held directly by another person and the scheme was not prohibited from holding its interest in that other person. The exemption also applies where the acquisition occurs on or after 5 April 2006 under a pre-6 April 2006 contract.

References to acquiring or holding property are to acquiring or holding an interest in the property.

The above exemption ceases to apply in any of the following scenarios.

- There is a change in the occupation or use of the property that, had it occurred before 6 April 2006, would have prohibited the pension scheme from holding the property; in this case, the exemption ceases to apply on the date of change (or, if later, on the date the scheme acquires the property).
- The property was residential property as at 6 April 2006 and improvement works are begun on it on or after that date; the exemption ceases to apply on the date the works are substantially completed (or, if later, on the date the scheme acquires the property). There are provisions as to what is meant by 'improvement works' for this purpose and as to when such works are to be treated as having begun (see *FA 2004, Sch 36 para 37B(9)–(12)*).
- There is a change in the pension scheme's interest in any person who holds the property directly or any person who has contracted to acquire it, such that, had the change occurred before 6 April 2006, the scheme would have been prohibited from holding the interest in that person; the exemption ceases to apply on the date of change (or, if later, on the date the scheme acquires the property).

The pension scheme is treated for the purposes of **57.22** above as acquiring the property on the date the exemption ceases to apply. There are provisions to determine the taxable amount for the purposes of any unauthorised payments charge arising from that deemed acquisition (see *FA 2004, Sch 36 para 37B(7)*).

If the above exemption does not apply and this is due to the pension scheme being prohibited from holding the property (or from holding its interest in the person who holds the property directly) under the pre-6 April 2006 rules, the scheme is treated for the purposes of **57.22** above as acquiring the property on 6 April 2006. There are provisions to determine the taxable amount for the purposes of any unauthorised payments charge arising from that deemed acquisition (see *FA 2004, Sch 36 para 37C(4)*).

Where the exemption would otherwise apply, special rules apply if: (i) the pension scheme was, immediately before 6 April 2006, either a small self-administered scheme (SSAS) or a self-invested personal pension scheme (SIPP); (ii) the property was residential property on 6 April 2006; and (iii) improvement works are begun on it on or after 5 December 2005. If the scheme was a SASS, the special rules apply if it held the property directly on 6 April 2006 and acquired it before 5 August 1991 or if it held the property indirectly on 6 April 2006 (or, if later, the date of acquisition). If the scheme was a SIPP, the special rules apply if it held the property indirectly on 6 April 2006 (or, if later, the date of acquisition). The special rules are that:

- if the improvement works are completed on or after 6 April 2006, they are treated as having begun on or after that date, such that the exemption ceases to apply (see above); and
- if the improvement works are completed before 6 April 2006, the exemption does not apply and the scheme is treated as acquiring the property on 6 April 2006 (as above).

The exemption does not apply to an occupational pension scheme approved under *ICTA 1988, s 590* after 5 December 2005. Unless it is still to acquire the property on that date, the scheme is treated as acquiring the property on 6 April 2006 (as above).

[*FA 2004, Sch 36 paras 37A–37E; FA 2006, s 158, Sch 21 para 15*].

There is a separate exemption from the charges at **57.22** above in the following circumstances:

- the pension scheme acquires the property on or after 6 April 2006 but only because a person in whom the scheme holds an interest comes to hold the property directly;
- the pension scheme acquired its interest in that person before 6 April 2006 and was not prohibited from holding that interest under the rules then in force;
- at no time between 6 April 2006 and the acquisition of the property has the pension scheme's interest in that person been such as would have been prohibited under the pre-6 April 2006 rules;
- (in the case of tangible moveable property) the property is acquired by the person for use in its trade, profession or vocation or for the purposes of its administration or management; and

- (in the case of residential property) the property is acquired by the person for the purposes of its property rental business, and, after its acquisition, the property is not occupied or used by a member of the pension scheme or a person connected with such a member (within **21 CONNECTED PERSONS**). It is a further condition that the property rental business was in operation (by the same person) immediately before 6 April 2006 and involved the direct holding of at least five assets consisting of interests in residential property.

Again, there are provisions whereby the exemption ceases in specified circumstances and for determining the taxable amount for the purposes of any unauthorised payments charge arising from the resulting deemed acquisition of the property by the pension scheme.

[*FA 2004, Sch 36 paras 37F–37I; FA 2006, s 158, Sch 21 para 15*].

Employer-financed retirement benefits schemes

[57.26] The term 'employer-financed retirement benefits scheme' is used after 5 April 2006 to describe, broadly, any UK occupational pension scheme that is not a registered pension scheme. Payments and other benefits from an employer-financed retirement benefits scheme are taxable on the employee on receipt. Employer contributions to the scheme are deductible against profits at the time when payments are made to, or benefits provided for, employees out of those contributions. Employees are not charged tax in respect of contributions made to the scheme by their employer on their behalf. Employer-financed retirement benefits schemes are not subject to the tax charges at **57.15–57.19** above (lifetime allowance charge etc.) For HMRC guidance on employer-financed retirement benefits schemes, see HMRC Employment Income Manual EIM15000–15429.

Definitions

[57.27] The statutory definition of '*employer-financed retirement benefits scheme*' is a 'scheme' for the provision of benefits consisting of, or including, 'relevant benefits' to, or in respect of, employees and former employees of an employer. Registered pension schemes (as in **57.2** above) are specifically excluded from the definition, as are superannuation funds within *ICTA 1988, s 615(3)* (superannuation funds for overseas employees — see **57.32** below). '*Scheme*' is very widely defined to include any deed, agreement, series of agreements or other arrangements. [*ITEPA 2003, s 393A; FA 2004, s 249(3)*].

For the above purposes, '*relevant benefits*' means any lump sum, gratuity or other benefit (including a non-cash benefit) provided (or to be provided) on (or in anticipation of) retirement or on death or in connection with any change in nature of service or, following retirement or death, in connection with past service. Benefits under a 'pension sharing order or provision' (as defined) are also included. But *excluded* from relevant benefits are any benefits charged to tax as **PENSION INCOME 56**, any benefits charged to tax under *FA 2004, Sch 34* (overseas pension schemes — see **57.21** above), benefits in respect of the death by accident, or the disablement or ill-health, of an employee during service, benefits under certain life policies and benefits excluded by statutory instrument (see below). Note also the £100 exemption referred to in **57.28** below.

HMRC may add to the list of excluded benefits by statutory instrument and may do so with retrospective effect. See *SI 2006 No 132*, under which benefits from the Armed Forces Compensation Scheme are excluded benefits from the outset, i.e. 6 April 2006, and *SI 2006 No 210* under which non-accidental death lump sum benefits are excluded benefits if provided for under the rules of a scheme on 6 April 2006. The list has been expanded, with backdated effect from 6 April 2006, to include a number of exclusions similar to those applicable to employee benefits (with necessary modifications to reflect the fact that the recipient is retired). The additional exclusions relate to continued provision of accommodation and related expenses (including removal expenses), welfare counselling, recreational benefits, annual parties and similar functions, continued provision of equipment for disabled former employees and yearly health screenings and medical check-ups. Also excluded are the provision of a service for the writing of wills where the cash equivalent of the benefit (see **27.30 EMPLOYMENT INCOME**) does not exceed £150, and non-cash benefits provided in connection with the termination before 6 April 1998 of the employee's employment. [*SI 2007 No 3537; SI 2009 No 2886*]. For official guidance, see www.hmrc.gov.uk/pensionschemes/excluded-benefits.pdf.

Relevant benefits provided during a tax year must be reported to HMRC by the 'responsible person' no later than 7 July following that year. Guidance on the reporting of non-cash benefits is included in HMRC Pensions Tax Simplification Newsletter No 28, 2 July 2007.

[*ITEPA 2003, s 393B; FA 2004, s 249(3); FA 2007, Sch 20 para 21; SI 2005 No 3453*].

The 'responsible person' in relation to an employer-financed retirement benefits scheme is determined as follows.

(a)   If there are one or more trustees of the scheme who are UK resident, the responsible person is that trustee or each of those trustees.

(b)   If no-one qualifies under (a) above but there are one or more persons who control the management of the scheme, the responsible person is that person or each of those persons.

(c)   If no-one qualifies under (a) or (b) above, the responsible person (if still alive or in existence) is the employer who established the scheme (or any such employers where more than one) or anyone who has succeeded that employer (or those employers) in relation to the provision of benefits under the scheme.

(d)   If no-one qualifies under (a), (b) or (c) above, the responsible person is anyone who employs employees to whom benefits are provided under the scheme.

(e)   If no-one qualifies under (a), (b), (c) or (d) above but there are one or more trustees of the scheme who are non-UK resident, the responsible person is that trustee or each of those trustees.

[*ITEPA 2003, s 399A; FA 2004, s 249(11)*].

Charge to tax on benefits

[57.28] *Pensions* from employer-financed retirement benefits schemes are charged to tax as in **56.2**(a) or **56.2**(e) PENSION INCOME.

If a *non-pension* benefit within the above rules is received by an individual, the amount of the benefit is charged to tax as employment income of the individual for the tax year of receipt. There is an exemption where all such benefits received by the individual in the tax year do not exceed £100. If a benefit within these rules is received by a person other than an individual, the 'responsible person' (see **57.27** above) in relation to the scheme is charged income tax at 50% for the tax year of receipt (40% for 2009/10 and earlier years). Where the benefit is a *lump sum*, any contributions made by the employee towards its provision are deductible in arriving at the amount chargeable on the employee or, where applicable, the 'responsible person'. See also the transitional provisions at **57.30** below.

[*ITEPA 2003, ss 394, 395; FA 2004, s 249(4)–(8); SI 2010 No 536, Art 2*].

Non-pension benefits from certain closed or frozen schemes that enjoyed approval under *ICTA 1970, s 222* immediately before 6 April 1980 are excluded from the charge above. This has statutory effect for 2009/10 onwards but previously applied by concession (HMRC ESC A33). [*ITEPA 2003, s 395A; SI 2009 No 730, Art 2*].

Valuation of benefits

The amount of a cash benefit is the amount received. The amount of a non-cash benefit for these purposes is the greater of the 'cash equivalent of the benefit' and the amount chargeable under the normal employment income rules if the benefit were taxable as earnings. The '*cash equivalent of the benefit*' is determined under the benefits code rules (see **27.26–27.48, 27.59–27.68** EMPLOYMENT INCOME), modified as appropriate in the case of living accommodation and cheap loan arrangements (with relief being potentially available in the latter case for the notional interest as it is under those rules — see **27.40** EMPLOYMENT INCOME). [*ITEPA 2003, ss 398, 399; FA 2004, s 249(9)(10)*].

Relief for employer contributions and other expenses

[57.29] Relief for employer contributions to an employer-financed retirement benefits scheme is given under the employee benefit contribution rules in *ITTOIA 2005, ss 38–44* (see **73.57** TRADING INCOME for details). Broadly, the employer is entitled to make a deduction for contributions in computing trading etc. profits for a period of account to the extent that, during that period or within nine months after the end of it, payments are made to or benefits provided to employees out of those contributions. Contributions made in one period of account may thus remain non-deductible until a later period of account.

The following applies to expenses incurred by an employer in providing benefits under an employer-financed retirement benefits scheme and shown in the employer's accounts in accordance with generally accepted accounting practice. If the recipient is chargeable to income tax on receipt of the benefits, then, provided they are deductible under general principles, the expenses are deductible in computing trading etc. profits for the period of account in which they are paid. Otherwise the expenses are not deductible at all. [*FA 2004, s 246; CTA 2009, Sch 1 para 578*].

An employer's contributions and other expenses in providing 'relevant benefits' (see **57.27** above) to an employee are not, however, deductible where the provision of those benefits is linked to a reduction in the benefits payable to the same employee under a registered pension scheme. But if relief for contributions to the registered pension scheme has been restricted in accordance with *SI 2005 No 3458* (see **57.12** above), contributions and other expenses in providing the relevant benefits are not prevented from being deductible to an extent that is just and reasonable. [*FA 2004, s 246A; CTA 2009, Sch 1 para 579*].

Transitional

[57.30] Under the pre-6 April 2006 regime for non-approved occupational pension schemes, payments by an employer towards the provision of benefits for employees were generally taxed on the employee as employment income for the year in which the payments were made. This treatment does not continue after 5 April 2006 for employer-financed retirement benefits schemes, and the relevant legislation (*ITEPA 2003, ss 386–392*) is repealed by *FA 2004, s 247*. Included in this legislation was a provision (*ITEPA 2003, s 392*) enabling the tax charge to be refunded, or otherwise relieved, where the employee (or his personal representative) proves to the satisfaction of HMRC that no benefit has yet been provided and that an event has occurred by reason of which no benefit will subsequently be provided (in both cases other than as a result of a pension sharing order or provision — as defined). The tax would be refunded or otherwise relieved on an application made within six years after the occurrence of the said event. In appropriate circumstances and on a just and reasonable basis, *partial* repayment could be made. Notwithstanding its repeal, *ITEPA 2003, s 392* continues to have effect after 5 April 2006 so as to give relief in a case where the tax charge was for 2005/06 or an earlier year but the said event occurs after 5 April 2006. [*FA 2004, Sch 36 para 52*].

Transitional relief is provided as in (a) and (b) below where a lump sum benefit is provided by an employer-financed retirement benefits scheme after 5 April 2006, such that the charge in *ITEPA 2003, ss 394, 395* at **57.28** above applies, and the employee was taxed for 2005/06 and/or earlier years under *ITEPA 2003, ss 386–392* (see above) or their predecessors.

(a) Where all of the scheme's income and gains are charged to tax or the scheme was in existence before 1 December 1993 and has not since been varied, no charge arises under **57.28** above if the employer has paid no sums to the scheme after 5 April 2006. If the employer has paid sums to the scheme since that date, the amount charged is restricted to any excess of: (i) the lump sum over; (ii) the employee's share of the market value of the scheme assets at 5 April 2006 as adjusted for inflation since that date. Post-5 April 2006 employee contributions are deductible from that excess.

(b)   In any case not within (a) above, the amount charged is restricted to any excess of the lump sum over the amount taxed on the employee for 2005/06 and earlier years. Post-5 April 2006 employee contributions are deductible from that excess.

[*FA 1994, Sch 36 paras 53–55; FA 2006, s 161, Sch 23 para 46*].

Inducement payments

[57.31] Where an employer offers employees an inducement to agree to a reduction in their benefits from the employer scheme or to transfer from one kind of employer scheme to another, the tax treatment depends on the form of the inducement. Such inducements are most likely to be offered to members of a defined benefit (final salary) scheme and may involve a transfer from that scheme to a defined contribution (money purchase) scheme.

If, or to the extent that, the inducement payment takes the form of an enhancement to a transfer value of the pension fund, such that it is included in the funds transferred between schemes, it is treated like any other employer contribution to a scheme.

If, or to the extent that, the inducement payment takes the form of a direct payment to the scheme member, HMRC's view is that such inducement payments paid to encourage scheme members to give up future pension rights or to move from one pension scheme to another are subject to income tax (and NIC). The income tax liability arises under *ITEPA 2003, s 394* at **57.28** above (and this is the case regardless of the fact that the scheme in question and/or the scheme to which the fund is to be transferred is a registered pension scheme).

(HMRC Internet Statement 24 January 2007).

For further details of why a charge arises under *ITEPA 2003, s 394*, see www.hmrc.gov.uk/pensionschemes/inducements.pdf.

Other pension funds

[57.32] The Trustees of the **House of Commons Members' Fund** are exempt from income tax on all income derived from that Fund and its investments. [*ICTA 1988, s 613(4)*].

Income from investments or deposits of any fund within **56.4**(a)–(d) PENSION INCOME (certain **overseas funds**) is exempt from tax. Any tax deducted from such income is repayable by HMRC to the recipient. [*ICTA 1988, s 614(3)*].

Exemption (as for a person not domiciled, resident or ordinarily resident in the UK) applies to income from investments or other property of a fund: (i) established under irrevocable trusts in connection with a trade carried on wholly or partly overseas; (ii) solely to provide **superannuation benefits to overseas employees** (incidental duties in UK being ignored); and (iii) recognised by both employer and employees. Annuities to non-UK residents are payable gross, and trustees are not liable under *ICTA 1988, s 349(1)*. *[ICTA 1988, s 614(5), s 615(3)(6); ITA 2007, Sch 1 para 140]*.

Judicial pension schemes are subject to their own legislation and are outside the registered pension schemes regime — see *SI 2006 No 497*.

National Employment Savings Trust

[57.33] The National Employment Savings Trust (NEST) is a national workplace pension scheme to be launched in 2011 and designed to meet the needs of low-to-moderate earners and their employers. The intention is that it will be a low cost, easy to use, online pension scheme that is open to any employer and will be run by a not-for-profit trustee corporation called NEST Corporation. Legislation to be included in a Finance Bill to be introduced in autumn 2010 will allow NEST to be treated as an occupational pension scheme. An application can then be made to HMRC for NEST to be a registered pension scheme so that members and contributing employers will be able to benefit from the available tax reliefs. The legislation will have effect on and after the date of Royal Assent. (HMRC Budget Note BN23, 22 June 2010).

Pension Protection Fund

[57.34] The Pension Protection Fund (PPF) was set up by *Pensions Act 2004*. Its purpose is to assume responsibility for final salary occupational pension schemes (and other pension schemes with defined benefit elements) whose sponsoring employers have become insolvent, leaving insufficient assets in the scheme. The PPF will pay compensation to pension scheme members in lieu of the benefits that would have been payable under the scheme. The PPF came into existence in April 2005, but compensation could not be paid from it earlier than April 2006. The Board of the PPF also takes over responsibility for the fund previously held by the Pension Compensation Board (PCB), hold that fund as the Fraud Compensation Fund, and pay compensation to pension schemes in cases of fraud.

The PPF is a body corporate and is funded by statutory levies on eligible schemes, for which tax relief would not necessarily be given. As it is not itself a pension scheme, the PPF would not be able to pay tax-free lump sums. In order to remove these and other anomalies, the PPF is given broadly equivalent tax treatment to that of a registered pension scheme (as in **57.2** above) for 2006/07 onwards. *FA 2005, s 102* gives the Treasury a wide-ranging power to make appropriate regulations giving effect to these matters. See *SI 2006 No 575*, which provides that tax legislation applies in relation to the PPF in the same way as it applies in relation to a registered pension scheme and goes on to make detailed modifications of that legislation with the object of ensuring that the tax treatment of the PPF is equivalent to the tax treatment of a registered scheme.

Payment of the PPF levy by an employer is part of the everyday cost of employing staff and will usually be an allowable deduction in computing the employer's trading profits for tax purposes (HMRC Business Income Manual BIM 46090). A transfer of the property, rights and liabilities of a registered pension scheme to the PPF is an authorised payment (see **57.2** or **57.19**(d) above) by the scheme (*SI 2006 No 134*).

Financial assistance scheme

[57.35] The financial assistance scheme (FAS) was established under *Pensions Act 2004, s 286* and has since been expanded. The scheme provides assistance to members of certain defined benefit occupational pension schemes that are no longer able to meet all their pension obligations. It only applies in relation to pension schemes wound up between 1 January 1997 and 5 April 2005, since when the PPF at **57.34** above performed a similar function. In its expanded form, the FAS will take over the assets of failed pension schemes. It will then make assistance payments to members of those pension schemes in lieu of their retirement benefits.

As the FAS is not a registered pension scheme, individuals who receive assistance payments from it would not necessarily benefit from the same tax treatment as if the payments were made by such a scheme. Tax charges could apply to some assistance payments received by individuals, such as certain lump sum payments, which would not arise if the payment had been made by the pension scheme. Under *FA 2009, s 73, regulations* have been made by statutory instrument (see *SI 2010 No 1187*) to ensure that individuals who receive assistance payments from the FAS will be subject to the same tax treatment as if they had received pension benefits from a registered pension scheme. The *regulations* have effect for all payments made by the FAS, whenever made.

Intervention by FSCS

[57.36] The Financial Services Compensation Scheme (FSCS) is an independent body established by *Financial Services and Markets Act 2000*. Among other things, the FSCS protects policyholders of authorised insurance companies that are unable, or likely to be unable, to meet claims made against them. Such insurance companies may be providers of registered pension schemes.

Individuals who have tax-relieved pension savings with an insurance company that gets into financial difficulties and becomes subject to an intervention by the FSCS could find that adverse tax consequences arise from that intervention. For example, as the FSCS is not a registered pension scheme, those individuals would not benefit from the tax exemptions available to members of such a scheme. Under *FA 2009, s 74, regulations* may be made by statutory instrument to suitably adapt the tax treatment in a case where the FSCS intervenes. The *regulations* may have retrospective effect but not so as to increase anyone's tax liability.

58

Personal Service Companies etc.

Cross-reference. See **46 MANAGED SERVICE COMPANIES**.

Simon's Taxes. See E4.9, E4.10.

Introduction

[58.1] There are provisions designed 'to remove opportunities for the avoidance of tax and Class 1 National Insurance contributions (NICs) by the use of intermediaries, such as [personal] service companies or partnerships, in circumstances where an individual worker would otherwise be an employee of the client or the income would be income from an office held by the worker'. (Annex to Revenue Press Release 23 September 1999). These are based on rules first published as Revenue Budget Press Release IR35 on 9 March 1999 (though significant changes were made subsequently) and are commonly referred to as the 'IR35' rules.

The rules do not prevent an individual providing his services through an intermediary. Instead, where the individual would otherwise have been categorised under pre-existing case law and practice as an employee in relation to a particular engagement, his income from that engagement is deemed to have been paid to him (if not *actually* paid to him) by the intermediary as earnings from an employment and is subject to **PAY AS YOU EARN (53)** and NICs. This applies even if the income is, in fact, paid to the individual in some other way, for example in the form of dividends from a personal service company (but see **58.13** below) or as a share of partnership profits, or is retained within the intermediary. Some allowance is made for deductible expenses (see **58.7, 58.8** below). Although proposed as an attack on avoidance, the provisions apply to any situation within their ambit (see **58.2, 58.4** below) and are not dependent on the taxpayer's motive.

The tax provisions are contained in *ITEPA 2003, ss 48–61* and are described in this chapter. For the NIC position, see *The Social Security Contributions (Intermediaries) Regulations 2000 (SI 2000 No 727)* (or, as regards Northern Ireland, *SI 2000 No 728*), and see Tolley's National Insurance Contributions.

See generally the guidance at www.hmrc.gov.uk/ir35/index.htm, HMRC Employment Status Manual ESM3000 *et seq.* and Revenue Tax Bulletins June 2000 pp 751–757 and February 2001 pp 819–826.

The operation of *ITEPA 2003, ss 44–47* (workers supplied by agencies — see **27.95 EMPLOYMENT INCOME**) is not affected by these provisions. Those *sections* apply only where the worker engaged through the agency is an individual. If a service company, for example, is engaged by a client via an independent agency, the provisions in this chapter may well apply but will not directly affect the agency. Nothing in these provisions applies to a payment or transfer subject to deduction of tax under *ITA 2007, s 966(3)* or *(4)* (payments to non-resident entertainers and sportsmen — see **50.10 NON-RESIDENTS**). [*ITEPA 2003, s 48(2); ITA 2007, Sch 1 para 429; FA 2007, s 25, Sch 3 para 3*].

Separate legislation applies for 2007/08 onwards to 'managed service companies' (see **46A MANAGED SERVICE COMPANIES**).

Simon's Taxes. See E4.1001.

Services provided through an intermediary

[58.2] The provisions apply in relation to an engagement where the following conditions are all present:

(a)   an individual (the worker) personally performs, or is under an obligation personally to perform, services for another person (the client);

(b)   the services are provided not under a contract directly between worker and client but under arrangements involving a third party (the 'intermediary') to which these provisions apply (see **58.4** below); and

(c)   if the services had been provided under a direct contract as mentioned in (b) above, the worker would have fallen to be categorised for income tax purposes as an employee of the client (see **58.3, 58.16** below).

The term *'intermediary'* in (b) above can refer to a company or to an individual. It is expressly provided that the term also refers to a partnership or unincorporated body of which the worker is a member.

[*ITEPA 2003, ss 49, 61(1); CTA 2009, Sch 1 para 549*].

Whether or not employment?

[58.3] In applying the test at **58.2**(c) above, i.e. whether or not the worker would have been an employee if engaged directly, the circumstances to be taken into account include the terms on which the services are provided, having regard to the terms of contracts forming part of the arrangements (as in **58.2**(b) above) under which the services are provided. [*ITEPA 2003, s 49(4)*]. Otherwise, no statutory rules are provided, the test instead being based on pre-existing case law and practice as to the distinction between employment and self-employment — see **27.54 EMPLOYMENT INCOME**, Tolley's National Insurance Contributions under Categorisation, and HMRC online factsheets ES/FS1 and ES/FS2. See also Revenue Tax Bulletin February 2000 pp 715–723 for a comprehensive article and practical illustrations devoted to the provisions in this chapter. The main text of this article is summarised at the end of this chapter — at **58.16** below. It is the reality of the working relationship that counts, irrespective of whether the parties have chosen to attach a different label to it (*Massey v Crown Life Insurance Co CA 1977*, [1978] 2 All ER 576).

Taxpayers may seek an opinion from HMRC as to whether or not a contract falls within the provisions in this chapter. The request, together with copies of contracts and any other relevant information, should be sent to IR35 Unit, HM Revenue & Customs, North East Metropolitan Area, Fountain Court, 119 Grange Road, Middlesbrough, TS1 2XA (fax 0845 302 3535). No opinion will be given on a *draft* agreement. (Revenue Tax Bulletin February 2001 p 820). See also HMRC Employment Status Manual ESM3280 *et seq*.

A number of cases have come before the Appeal Tribunal (previously the Special Commissioners) and the Courts on the question of whether an individual would have been an employee if engaged directly by the client rather than via a service company. These have tended to be brought under the equivalent National Insurance legislation referred to in **58.1** above, and each turns entirely on its own facts. For summaries of these cases, see Tolley's Tax Cases under National Insurance Contributions.

HMRC also identified a standard contract said to be common to service company workers engaged, through agencies, in the information technology industry. Such a contract requires the worker:

(a)   to work where the client requests, for an agreed number of hours per week, and at an agreed hourly rate;

(b)   to keep a timesheet for checking by the client;

(c)   to be subject to the client's control; and

(d)   not to sub-contract the work to anyone else.

Where a worker is engaged for a month or more on a contract of this type, and cannot demonstrate a recent history of work including engagements which have the characteristics of self-employment, HMRC will treat the engagement as being within the provisions in this chapter. (Note that whilst this may be a convenient rule of thumb, the taxpayer is not precluded from arguing for a different treatment.) Where the contract is for less than a month, HMRC will consider each case on its merits. (Revenue Press Release 7 February 2000 and Revenue Tax Bulletin February 2000 p 717).

The income tax legislation on personal service companies does not bite if the worker's only relationship with the client is as non-executive director of the client, as the wording in **58.2**(c) above refers to an 'employee' rather than an office-holder. (There is no such exemption for National Insurance purposes.) If, however, a non-executive director performs other services for the client through an intermediary, such that under a direct contract he would have been an employee as well as an office-holder, those services do fall within the legislation. (Revenue Internet Statement 29 April 2003).

Simon's Taxes. See E4.1003, E4.1007, E4.1008.

Intermediaries to which these provisions apply

[58.4] The provisions apply only if the intermediary meets the relevant conditions below.

Companies

Where the intermediary is a company, the provisions apply in relation to an engagement if either:

(a) the worker has a 'material interest' (see below) in the intermediary; or
(b) the payment or benefit in **58.6**(ii) below is received or receivable by the worker directly from the intermediary and can reasonably be taken to represent remuneration for services provided by the worker to the client.

The provisions do not, however, apply if either of the above is satisfied but the intermediary is an associated company (within *CTA 2010, s 449*) of the client by reason of both the client and itself being under the control of the worker (or of the worker and other persons).

For these purposes, the worker has a *'material interest'* in a company if he, and/or certain 'associates' of his (within *ITEPA 2003, s 60* and with the extended meaning of 'husband and wife' at **58.5**(c) below):

(i)   beneficially owns or is able to control (directly or indirectly) more than 5% of the ordinary share capital; or
(ii)   possesses, or is entitled to acquire, rights to more than 5% of any distributions that the company may make; or
(iii) (where the company is a close company) possesses, or is entitled to acquire, rights to more than 5% of the assets available for distribution among the participators (within *CTA 2010, s 454*) in a winding-up or in any other circumstances.

[*ITEPA 2003, ss 51, 61(1); CTA 2010, Sch 1 paras 380, 382*].

Providing (a) or (b) above is satisfied, the provisions apply equally to a 'composite service company' employing several workers as to a service company employing only one or two workers. (Revenue Tax Bulletin August 2002 pp 956, 957). For more on composite service companies and also on managed service companies (i.e. one-worker service companies set up and run by a promoter for an administration fee), see Revenue Tax Bulletin December 2004 pp 1165–1168; and see now **46 MANAGED SERVICE COMPANIES**.

In both places in which it is mentioned above, *'control'* is as defined by *ITA 2007, s 995* (previously *ICTA 1988, s 840*). [*ITEPA 2003, s 719; ITA 2007, Sch 1 para 443*].

Partrnerships

Where the intermediary is a partnership, the provisions apply in relation to payments or benefits received or receivable by the worker as a member of the partnership if:

(A)   the worker, *alone or with one or more 'relatives'*, is entitled to at least 60% of partnership profits; or

(B)   most of the partnership profits derive from provision of services under engagements within **58.2** above to a single client (or to a single client and his 'associates' — within *ITEPA 2003, s 60*); or

(C)   the partnership profit sharing arrangements are such that the income of any of the partners is based on the income which that partner generates from engagements within **58.2** above.

'Relative' is broadly defined to include a spouse or civil partner (or cohabitant treated as such — as in **58.5**(c) below), parent or child or remoter relation in the direct line, or brother or sister). Most family partnerships are thus potentially within these rules.

In addition, the provisions apply in relation to payments or benefits received or receivable by the worker directly from the partnership, but in a capacity other than as a member of the partnership, if they can reasonably be taken to represent remuneration for services provided by the worker to the client.

[*ITEPA 2003, ss 52, 61(4)*].

Individuals

Where (exceptionally) the intermediary is an individual, the provisions apply in relation to a payment or benefit if it is received or receivable by the worker directly from the intermediary and can reasonably be taken to represent remuneration for services provided by the worker to the client. [*ITEPA 2003, s 53*].

Overseas intermediaries

There is no requirement that the intermediary be resident or incorporated in the UK. An offshore service company, for example, can fall within these provisions (and see **58.10** below as regards place of business). See also HMRC guidance — as in **58.1** above.

Supplementary

[58.5] For the purposes of the above (and of these provisions generally):

(a)   whether a person is an *'associate'* of an individual is construed in accordance with *CTA 2010, s 448* (with the extended meaning of 'spouse or civil partner' at (c) below), except that special rules apply to determine whether an individual is an associate of an employee benefit trust of which he is a beneficiary;

(b)   a payment or benefit receivable from a partnership or unincorporated association includes any such payment or benefit to which a person may be entitled in his capacity as a member of the partnership or association;

(c)   a payment or benefit provided to a member of an individual's family or household (within *ITEPA 2003, s 721(4)(5) as amended* but treating a man and woman cohabiting as a couple as if they were spouses and treating two people of the same sex cohabiting as a couple as if they were civil partners) is treated as provided to the individual; and

(d)   anything done by an 'associate' (as defined) of an intermediary is treated as done by the intermediary.

[*ITEPA 2003, ss 60(1)(a) (2)–(6), 61(2)–(5), 721(4)(5); CTA 2010, Sch 1 para 381*].

The 'deemed employment payment'

[58.6] If, as regards any engagement within **58.2** above, in any tax year:

(i)   the intermediary is within these provisions by virtue of **58.4** above; and

(ii)   the worker (or an 'associate' of his) receives, is entitled to receive, or has rights entitling him to receive, from the intermediary (directly or indirectly) a payment or benefit that is not employment income,

the intermediary is deemed to have made to the worker, normally on 5 April in that tax year (though see **58.14** below for exceptions), a payment (a '*deemed employment payment*') the amount of which is computed as in **58.7** below and which is treated as earnings from an employment. Where such payments would be treated as having been made in respect of multiple engagements, a single such payment is deemed to have been made. See **58.11** below as regards the application of PAYE. [*ITEPA 2003, s 50*].

See **58.5** above for the meaning of 'associate' in relation to an individual and other supplementary provisions.

Computation of deemed employment payment

[58.7] The deemed payment in **58.6** above is computed as follows (and see the supplementary points at **58.8** below).

(1)   Take the total of all 'payments' and 'benefits' (see **58.8** below) received by the intermediary in the tax year in respect of engagements falling within **58.6** above by reference to the worker (the '*relevant engagements*') and reduce it by 5% (see **58.8** below).
        Where a payment received by the intermediary has been subjected to deduction of tax at source under the CONSTRUCTION INDUSTRY SCHEME (**22**), it is the gross amount before tax that must be brought into account in arriving at this total.

(2)   Add in any 'payments' and 'benefits' (see **58.8** below) received direct by the worker (and see **58.5**(c) above) in that tax year in respect of the relevant engagements, *from anyone other than the intermediary*, that are not chargeable as employment income but would have been if the worker had been employed by the client.

(3)   Deduct:
- (a)   any expenses met by the intermediary (see below) in that tax year which, if incurred by the worker as an employee of the client, would have been deductible under normal rules — see **27.22 EMPLOYMENT INCOME;**
- (b)   any capital allowances which on that basis could have been deducted by the worker from employment income under *CAA 2001, s 262* (plant and machinery allowances — see **11.5 CAPITAL ALLOWANCES ON PLANT AND MACHINERY**); and
- (c)   any contributions made to a registered pension scheme by the intermediary in that tax year for the benefit of the worker which, if made by an employer for the benefit of an employee, would not be regarded as the employee's income for tax purposes — see **57.12 PENSION PROVISION.**

(4)   Deduct:
- (a)   any 'payments' and 'benefits' (see **58.8** below) received in that tax year by the worker from the intermediary and chargeable as employment income in his hands (but excluding anything already deducted under (3)(a) above); and
- (b)   any employer's Class 1 and Class 1A NICs (on salary and benefits) payable by the intermediary for that tax year in respect of the worker.

If the result is a negative amount, or is nil, there is no deemed employment payment. In any other case, the deemed employment payment is the amount which, together with employer's NICs thereon, is equal to the result of applying steps (1)–(4) above. In other words, allowance is made at this point for the fact that employer's NICs are chargeable on the deemed payment itself (see Tolley's National Insurance Contributions).

[*ITEPA 2003, ss 54(1)(2), 61(1)*].

For the purposes of (3)(a) above, an intermediary 'meets' an expense on the date it pays the bill. (HMRC guidance — as in **58.1** above). Expenses met by an intermediary include expenses met by the worker and reimbursed by the intermediary and also, in the case of a partnership intermediary of which the worker is a member, expenses met by the worker for and on behalf of the intermediary. In a situation where the intermediary provides a vehicle for the worker, expenses deductible under (3)(a) above include any 'mileage allowance relief' (see **27.87 EMPLOYMENT INCOME**) that would have been due to the worker if he had been an employee of the client and had provided the vehicle himself. This also applies, in the case of a partnership intermediary of which the worker is a member, in a situation where the worker provides the vehicle for the purposes of the partnership business. Any 'approved mileage allowance payments' or 'approved passenger payments' made by the intermediary to the worker and exempt from the charge to tax on **EMPLOYMENT INCOME (27.87)** are deductible under (4)(a) above (if not deductible under (3)(a) above), notwithstanding the said exemption. The duties performed under the relevant engagements are treated, for the purpose of determining the deductibility under (3)(a) above of any travelling expenses (see **27.18, 27.23 EMPLOYMENT INCOME**), as duties of a continuous employment with the intermediary. [*ITEPA 2003, s 54(3)–(7)*].

For notes on the deductibility of travel and subsistence expenses reimbursed to workers in a composite service company or managed service company, see Revenue Tax Bulletin December 2004 pp 1166–1168; and see **46 MANAGED SERVICE COMPANIES**.

See the Example at **58.9** below.

Simon's Taxes. See **E4.1011–E4.1017.**

Supplementary

[58.8] For the purposes of computing the deemed employment payment as in **58.7** above, any amounts received by the intermediary that refer to more than one worker, or partly to a worker and partly to other matters, are to be apportioned on a just and reasonable basis. [*ITEPA 2003, s 54(8)*].

For the purposes of **58.7**(1), (2) and (4) above, a '*payment*' or '*benefit*' means anything that, if received by an employee for performing the duties of an employment, would be earnings from the employment. The amount of a payment or cash benefit is taken to be the amount received. The amount of a non-cash benefit is computed in the same way as if it were earnings of an employment, which means that it will normally, in practice, be computed under the employee benefit rules at **27.26–27.48 EMPLOYMENT INCOME**. A payment or cash benefit is treated as received when payment is actually made (or a payment is made on account). A non-cash benefit calculated by reference to a period within the tax year is treated as received at the end of that period; otherwise the time of receipt is determined under normal rules (see **27.25 EMPLOYMENT INCOME**). [*ITEPA 2003, s 55*].

Where the intermediary is VAT-registered, the amount to be brought into account at **58.7**(1) above is the VAT-exclusive amount, and this applies even where the optional flat-rate scheme is used (though in that case the VAT-exclusive amount is the amount inclusive of output VAT at the normal rate less the flat-rate VAT payable) (Revenue Tax Bulletin April 2003 p 1024).

The 5% deduction

The 5% deduction at **58.7**(1) above is a standard allowance intended to cover the intermediary's running costs. It is given regardless of the actual occurrence or amount of such running costs, and does not have to be justified or supported by records. The limited deductions at **58.7**(3) above, based on actual expenditure, are given in addition to the 5% deduction. The 5% deduction applies purely for the purpose of computing the deemed employment payment under these provisions, and is not deductible in computing the business profits of the intermediary (actual running costs being deductible or not, as the case may be, under normal rules — see **73 TRADING INCOME** and see also **58.12** below as regards partnerships). See **58.12** below as regards deductibility of the deemed employment payment itself.

Example

[58.9]

Harry is a systems analyst trading through his own personal service company, ABC Ltd, in which he owns 99% of the ordinary shares. During 2010/11, he is engaged at different times by two independent companies, DEF Ltd and GHJ Ltd (the client companies), in each case under a contract between the client company and ABC Ltd. It is accepted that each engagement is in the nature of employment and is within the provisions covered in this chapter. ABC Ltd is paid £40,000 by DEF Ltd and £20,000 by GHJ Ltd for the services provided by Harry.

For 2010/11, Harry draws a salary of £28,000 from ABC Ltd which is taxed under PAYE and on which employer's NICs of, say, £3,000 are due. He is also provided with a company car on which the taxable benefit is £4,000 and on which Class 1A NICs of, say, £510 are due. ABC Ltd makes pension contributions of £3,100 into a registered pension scheme on Harry's behalf and reimburses motor expenses of £1,500 which, if Harry had been employed directly by the client companies, would have been qualifying travelling expenses within **27.23 EMPLOYMENT INCOME**. It pays a salary of £5,720 to Harry's wife who acts as company secretary and administrator.

The deemed employment payment for 2010/11 is computed, using steps numbered in accordance with **58.7** above, as follows.

		£	£	£
Step (1)	Total amount from relevant engagements			60,000
	Deduct 5%			3,000
				57,000
Step (2)	Not applicable			
Step (3)	*Deduct* (a) Expenses	1,500		
	(b) Not applicable	—		
	(c) Pension contributions	3,100	4,600	
Step (4)	*Deduct* Salary	28,000		
	Benefits	4,000		
	Employer's Class 1 NICs	3,000		
	Employer's Class 1A NICs	510	35,510	£40,110
Total				£16,890

Deemed employment payment $£16,890 \times \dfrac{100}{112.8}$ 14,973

Employer's NICs due on deemed payment £14,973 @ 12.8%   £1,917

Total as above   £16,890

Note

The salary paid by ABC Ltd to Harry's wife is not deductible in arriving at the deemed employment payment, except to the extent that it, and other expenses of the company, are covered by the 5% deduction at **58.7**(1) above. (The salary may of course be deductible under the normal TRADING INCOME (**73**) rules in computing ABC Ltd's taxable business profits.)

Tax treatment of deemed employment payment

[58.10] The deemed employment payment is generally treated in the same way as an actual payment of employment income, as if the worker were employed by the intermediary and as if the relevant engagements (see **58.7**(1) above) were undertaken by him in the course of performing the duties of that employment. The PAYE provisions are applied as in **58.11** below. Where:

- the worker is UK resident, and
- the services in question are provided in the UK,

the intermediary is treated as having a place of business in the UK (and is thus obliged to operate PAYE for example — see **53.37** PAY AS YOU EARN) even if this is not, in fact, the case.

To the extent that, by reason of any combination of:

- the worker being resident, ordinarily resident or domiciled outside the UK;
- the client being resident or ordinarily resident outside the UK; and
- the services in question being provided outside the UK,

the worker would not be chargeable if employed directly by the client, he is not chargeable to tax in respect of the deemed employment payment. (See **27.5**, **27.8**, **27.10** EMPLOYMENT INCOME for the relevant charging provisions.)

In particular, the deemed employment payment counts:

- to determine whether the worker is a higher- or lower-paid employee for the purpose of applying the benefits code (see **27.26** EMPLOYMENT INCOME);
- as taxable earnings for the purpose of deducting qualifying travelling expenses and other necessary expenses incurred by the worker (see **27.22–27.24** EMPLOYMENT INCOME) or mileage allowance relief (see **27.87** EMPLOYMENT INCOME); and
- as relevant UK earnings for registered pension scheme contributions purposes (see **57.7** PENSION PROVISION).

[*ITEPA 2003, ss 56, 218(1)(d)*].

Where the work is carried out outside the UK, and the worker is UK resident and ordinarily resident, a service company may suffer foreign tax. Where the company's tax liability is insufficient to give full effect to DOUBLE TAX RELIEF (**26**), HMRC suggest that the balance of foreign tax may be allowed against UK tax (but not NICs) on the deemed employment payment, but only where it is possible to directly link the work in the overseas country and the deemed payment. (HMRC guidance — as in **58.1** above).

For an article, including case studies, on the international issues surrounding the personal service company legislation, concentrating mainly on the National Insurance aspects, see Revenue Tax Bulletin April 2003 pp 1016–1020.

PAYE

[58.11] By virtue of **58.10** above, the intermediary must account for tax under PAY AS YOU EARN (**53**) as if the deemed employment payment to the worker were an actual payment of employment income. Where, as is normally the case, the employment payment is deemed to be made on 5 April in the tax year (see **58.6** above), then, strictly, the total tax, employee's NICs and employer's NICs due in respect of the deemed payment must be paid over to HMRC on or before 19 April following the tax year (as in **53.11** PAY AS YOU EARN), which may leave insufficient time for the amount of the deemed payment to be computed. In practice, HMRC will accept a lower, provisional amount on account. They must be notified on Employer's Annual Return Form P35 (due by the following 19 May — see **53.12** PAY AS YOU EARN) that the amount paid is provisional (if this remains the case). The balance due must be paid (and a supplementary P35 submitted) by the following 31 January. Provided that deadline is met, HMRC will not seek to recover the underpaid tax in the meantime and will not seek PENALTIES (**55.21**). Subject to the concession described below, **interest on overdue tax** will, however, accrue from 19 April following the tax year as normal (see **53.11** PAY AS YOU EARN). (HMRC guidance — as in **58.1** above).

Simon's Taxes. See E4.1020.

Where the intermediary fails to account for PAYE on a deemed employment payment, then, in addition to their powers to recover such tax and impose interest and penalties, HMRC also have the option of using pre-existing rules (see **53.10** PAY AS YOU EARN) to collect the tax and NICs direct from the worker. (Annex to Revenue Press Release 23 September 1999).

See **58.15** below as regards joint and several liability of multiple intermediaries.

Interaction with construction industry scheme — concession

Where a deemed employment payment is based on amounts received by a company under deduction of tax under the CONSTRUCTION INDUSTRY SCHEME (**22**), the amounts deducted are treated as corporation tax paid in respect of company profits, and are therefore not available for offset against any liability in respect of the deemed employment payment. By concession, where, as a result of such deductions, a company is entitled to a corporation tax repayment for an accounting period which overlaps a tax year for which a deemed employment payment is treated as made, the company may claim to set off the corporation tax repayment against any outstanding tax and NICs due in respect of the deemed employment payment, using 19 April in the following tax year as the effective date of payment for the set-off. Provided that the claim is made by the following 31 January (and is accepted), no interest will be charged on the amount of any late-paid tax and NICs in respect of the deemed employment payment which is matched by the corporation tax repayment. (HMRC ESC C32). See also Revenue Tax Bulletin June 2001 p 861 and HMRC Employment Status Manual ESM3262, 3269 *et seq.*

Computation of intermediary's business profits

[58.12] Subject to the special rules below for partnerships, a deemed employment payment (and related employer's NICs) is an allowable expense in computing the business profits (or losses) of the intermediary for the period of account in which the payment is treated as made (but for no other period of account). [*ITTOIA 2005, s 163; CTA 2009, s 139*].

Partnerships — special rules

The above applies equally where the intermediary is a partnership except that:

(a)   the deduction for the deemed employment payment can reduce the partnership profits to nil for tax purposes but it cannot create a trading loss; and

(b)   the expenses of the partnership in connection with the relevant engagements (see **58.7**(1) above) for the period of account are deductible only to the extent that they do not exceed the sum of:

    (i)   the 5% deduction at **58.7**(1) above; and

    (ii)   the deduction at **58.7**(3)(a) above.

[*ITTOIA 2005, s 164; CTA 2009, s 140*].

Simon's Taxes. See B5.645, E4.1021.

Relief where dividends etc. paid by intermediary

[58.13] A relief from double taxation is available where a **company** intermediary is treated as making a deemed employment payment in any tax year and also pays a dividend (or otherwise makes a distribution) in that or a subsequent tax year. A claim for relief must be made in writing by the intermediary within five years after 31 January following the tax year in which the dividend is paid. Relief is given by reducing the dividend (not the deemed employment payment) but only if HMRC are satisfied that this is necessary to avoid a double charge to tax. The reduction is made, as far as practicable, by setting the amount of the deemed payment against:

- dividends etc. of the same tax year in priority to those of other years;
- dividends etc. received by the worker before those received by another person; and
- dividends etc. of earlier years before those of later years.

Where a dividend is reduced, the associated tax credit is correspondingly reduced. See **1.5 ALLOWANCES AND TAX RATES** for taxation of dividends and other distributions generally.

[*ITEPA 2003, s 58*].

Simon's Taxes. See E4.1025.

Earlier date of deemed employment payment in certain cases

[58.14] As stated in **58.6** above, the deemed employment payment is normally treated as made on 5 April in the relevant tax year. If, however, a 'relevant event' occurs in relation to the intermediary in that tax year and before that date, the deemed employment payment is treated as made immediately before that event, or, if there is more than one, immediately before the first of them. The fact that the deemed payment is treated as made before the end of the tax year does not affect the way in which it is computed and the receipts and other matters that are taken into account.

In relation to a **company** intermediary, any of the following is a 'relevant event':

- where the worker is a member of the company (which normally means a shareholder), his ceasing to be a member;
- where the worker holds an office with the company (for example, as a director), his ceasing to hold that office;
- where the worker is an employee of the company, his ceasing to be an employee;
- the company ceasing to trade.

In relation to a **partnership** intermediary, any of the following is a 'relevant event':

- the dissolution of the partnership or cessation of the partnership trade;
- a partner ceasing to act as such;
- where the worker is an employee of the partnership, his ceasing to be an employee.

Where the intermediary is an **individual** and the worker is employed by him, a 'relevant event' occurs if the worker ceases to be so employed.

[*ITEPA 2003, s 57*].

Multiple intermediaries

[58.15] Where, in the case of an engagement within **58.2** above, the arrangements (as in **58.2**(b) above) involve one or more intermediaries within **58.4** above, then, except as below, these provisions apply separately in relation to each such intermediary.

Where a payment or other benefit has been made or provided, directly or indirectly, by one such intermediary to another in respect of the engagement, the amount taken into account at **58.7**(1) or (2) above (computation of deemed employment payment) in relation to any intermediary is to be reduced as necessary so as to avoid double-counting.

All such intermediaries are jointly and severally liable to account for **PAYE (53)** on a deemed employment payment treated as made by any of them in respect of the engagement in question, or in respect of multiple engagements which include the engagement in question, except that an intermediary is excepted from such liability if has not received any payment or benefit in respect of the engagement(s).

[*ITEPA 2003, s 59*].

Simon's Taxes. See **E4.1026.**

Deciding employment status — summary of Revenue Tax Bulletin article

[58.16] The following is a summary of the main text of the article in Revenue Tax Bulletin February 2000 pp 716–723 referred to at **58.3** above. The views expressed are those of the Inland Revenue, who emphasise that their role is 'to provide advice and guidance about the employment status resulting from a given set of circumstances, not to impose any particular status. The terms and conditions of any engagement are entirely a matter for the parties involved.' Those views are reproduced here for the sole purpose of providing some general guidance on what is itself a specialist topic, and readers are advised to seek an independent view also. See also **58.3** above as regards HMRC's identification of a 'standard contract' and their advice thereon (which is included in the said article but not covered again below). See also **27.54** EMPLOYMENT INCOME, particularly as regards relevant case law, and HMRC Employment Status Manual.

Although not covered by the article, it is accepted that, in order for a contract for service to exist, there must be an irreducible minimum of mutual obligation. That irreducible minimum is that the engager must be obliged to pay remuneration and that the worker must be obliged to provide his own work or skill (HMRC Employment Status Manual ESM0514).

The summary of the article follows immediately below.

Whether a worker would have fallen to be treated as an employee of the client if engaged directly by the client rather than though an intermediary depends on a range of factors. However, it is not a mechanical exercise of running through a checklist with a view to adding up, and comparing, the number of factors pointing towards employment and self-employment respectively. The overall effect must be evaluated, which is not necessarily the same as the sum of the individual factors; the factors may not be of equal weight or importance in a given situation and may also vary in importance from one situation to another. See also *Hall v Lorimer* CA 1993, 66 TC 349. The intention of the parties may be conclusive if, but only if, the evidence is otherwise evenly balanced.

It is first necessary to establish the terms and conditions of the engagement, which is usually achieved mainly by considering the contract (whether written, oral or implied — or a mixture of those) between the client and the intermediary. Next, it is necessary to consider any relevant surrounding facts, for example whether the worker has other clients and a business organisation. In this context, other contracts under which the worker's services are supplied by the intermediary may be taken into account, as may any business organisation of the intermediary which is relevant to that supply.

Relevant factors in determining whether a contract is a 'contract of service' (i.e. employment) or a 'contract for services' (self-employment) are listed below.

- Does the client have the right to exercise **control** over the worker? This may be a right to control what work is done, where or when it is done and/or how it is done. A working relationship involving no control at all is unlikely to be employment. Where the client has the right to determine *how* the work is done or *what* work is carried out, this is, in either case, a strong pointer towards employment.

- Personal service is an essential element of a contract of employment. If the worker has the freedom to choose whether to do the job himself or hire a **substitute** to do it for him or a helper to provide substantial help, this points towards self-employment.

- The provision by the worker of significant **equipment** and/or materials which are fundamental to the engagement is a strong pointer towards self-employment. If the client provides the office space (where relevant) and equipment, this points towards employment. Note that in some trades it is not uncommon for *employees* to provide their own small tools.

- The taking on by the worker of **financial risk**, for example his buying significant assets and materials and/or quoting a fixed price for the job with the consequent risk of bearing the extra costs if it overruns, is a strong pointer towards self-employment.

- **Basis of payment.** Employees tend to be paid a fixed wage or salary, weekly or monthly, and possibly bonuses or overtime. A self-employed contractor tends to be paid a fixed sum for a particular job. (Piece work or payment by commission can be a feature of both employment and self-employment.)

- A person who may **profit from sound management**, i.e. his reward for the job varies according to his ability to organise the work effectively and reduce overheads, may well be self-employed. Though not mentioned in the Tax Bulletin text, an obligation to correct unsatisfactory work in the worker's own time and at his own expense suggests self-employment.

- A person who becomes '**part and parcel' of the client's organisation** may well be an employee.

- A **right of dismissal** is a common feature of employment. A contract for services, on the other hand, usually ends only when it is completed or is breached.

- The right to sick pay, holiday pay, pensions, expenses and/or other **employee benefits** points towards employment, though their absence does not necessarily indicate self-employment — especially where the engagement is short-term.

- **Length of engagement.** A long period working for one engager is typical of employment, but is not conclusive. Where a single engagement is covered by a series of short contracts, it is the length of the engagement that is relevant, and not the length of each contract.

- It may be appropriate to take into account factors which are personal to the worker and have little to do with the terms of the particular engagement. For example, if a skilled worker works for a number of clients and has a business-like approach to securing his engagements (perhaps involving expenditure on office accommodation, office equipment etc.), this points towards self-employment. Such **personal factors** carry less weight in the case of an unskilled worker, where factors like a high degree of control exercised by the client are more likely to be conclusive of employment.

Key points

[58.17] Points to consider are as follows.

- Compliance with this legislation is addressed by question 6 on form P35. Advisers may need to refer to the guidance supporting the form to ascertain how the question should be answered, as it is not clearly phrased. Note that answering part 1 'Yes' and part 2 'No' does not necessarily mean that there is a failure to comply with IR35.

- Advisers should not overlook the fact that although rare, partnerships can be affected by this legislation.

- When advising clients on whether they are subject to the deemed payment rules it is important to consider a wider picture than that presented by the contract alone. The behaviour of the parties day-to-day is often considered when a case goes to appeal.

- In practice, although there is relief from double taxation on dividends distributed to those subject to a deemed employment payment, it is often simpler and more transparent to pay out the income subject to IR35 as salary during the tax year.

- Personal service companies with income only from relevant engagements may suffer corporation tax losses as a result of having actual running costs in excess of the 5% allowed under IR35. There is little prospect of relief for those losses unless the company can secure other forms of income (including interest).

59

Post-Cessation Receipts and Expenditure

Simon's Taxes. See B2.8.

Post-cessation receipts of trades etc.

Introduction

[59.1] Income tax is charged under *ITTOIA 2005, ss 241–257* on 'post-cessation receipts' (see **59.2** below) arising from a trade, profession or vocation to the extent that they have not been brought into account in computing trading profits for any period and that they are not otherwise chargeable to tax. The charge is not subject to the rules covering TRADING INCOME (**73**), but is made on the full amount of post-cessation receipts received in the tax year (subject to any allowable deductions at **59.3** below and any carry-back election at **59.4** below). The person liable is the person receiving, or entitled to, the post-cessation receipts.

In the rest of this chapter, the word 'trade' is used to denote a trade, a profession or a vocation.

A post-cessation receipt is not chargeable as above if:

• it represents income arising outside the UK and accruing to a non-UK resident; or
• it arises from a trade carried on wholly outside the UK; or
• (in the case of a member of a partnership) it represents partnership trading income arising outside the UK and the partner's share of such income falls to be taxed on the remittance basis (see **52.20** PARTNERSHIPS); or
• the person who would be liable to tax on the receipt was born before 6 April 1917 *and* the cessation occurred before 6 April 2000.

If an individual has permanently ceased to carry on a trade and his income from the trade was 'relevant UK earnings' (see **57.7** PENSION PROVISION), his post-cessation receipts are similarly relevant UK earnings.

[ITTOIA 2005, ss 241–245, 256, Sch 2 paras 60, 61; ITA 2007, Sch 1 para 506].

Simon's Taxes. See B2.803.

Meaning of 'post-cessation receipt'

[59.2] For these purposes, a *'post-cessation receipt'* is a sum which is received after a person ceases to carry on a trade (including his leaving a partnership and thus ceasing his notional trade — see **52.4 PARTNERSHIPS**) but which arises from the carrying on of the trade before cessation. Certain sums as below are specifically treated as being, or as not being (as the case may be), post-cessation receipts. Certain enactments listed at *ITTOIA 2005, s 247* also specifically treat certain amounts as being, or as not being, post-cessation receipts; these are referred to elsewhere in this work where relevant. *[ITTOIA 2005, ss 246, 247; CTA 2009, Sch 1 para 612; FA 2009, Sch 11 paras 40, 65–67].*

Receipts within the legislation will include, *inter alia*, royalties and similar amounts which under decisions such as *Carson v Cheyney's Exor HL* 1958, 38 TC 240, prior to the original legislation being enacted, had been held not to be taxable.

See **59.5** below for circumstances in which amounts relieved as post-cessation expenditure may be clawed back as post-cessation receipts.

Debts

To the extent that a deduction has been made, in computing the profits of the trade, for a bad or doubtful debt (see **73.40 TRADING INCOME**), any amount received after cessation in settlement of that debt is a post-cessation receipt. If an amount owed *by* the trader is released, in whole or in part, after cessation, the amount released is a post-cessation receipt; this applies only if a trading deduction was allowed for the expense giving rise to the debt and does not apply if the release of the debt is part of a statutory insolvency arrangement (as defined in **73.40**). *[ITTOIA 2005, ss 248, 249, 259; CTA 2009, Sch 1 para 613; SI 2008 No 954, Arts 1, 37].*

Transfers of rights

If the right to receive a post-cessation receipt is transferred for value to another person (other than one who succeeds to the trade), the transferor is treated as receiving at that point a post-cessation receipt equal to the consideration for the transfer or, if the transfer is not at arm's length, the value of the rights transferred. The post-cessation receipts themselves are not then charged when received by the transferee.

If, however, the right to receive any sums arising from the transferors trade are transferred to someone who does succeed to the trade, then, to the extent (if any) that they were not brought into account in computing the transferor's profits for any pre-cessation period, those sums are treated as trading receipts of the transferee as and when received. They are not post-cessation receipts. This rule was applied in *Rafferty v HMRC* (Sp C 475), [2005] SSCD 484.

[*ITTOIA 2005, ss 98, 251*].

Stock and work in progress

A sum realised by the transfer of trading stock or work in progress is not a post-cessation receipt provided that a valuation of the stock or work in progress at cessation has been properly brought into account under *ITTOIA 2005, s 173 et seq.* (see **73.113 TRADING INCOME**). In the case of work in progress, this is subject to any election for valuation at cost on cessation (again see **73.113**). [*ITTOIA 2005, s 252*].

Lump sums paid to personal representatives for copyright etc.

A lump sum paid to the personal representatives of the deceased author of a literary, dramatic, musical or artistic work for the assignment by them, in whole or in part, of the copyright or public lending right in the work is not a post-cessation receipt. A similar rule applies in relation to personal representatives of the designer of a design in which a design right subsists. [*ITTOIA 2005, s 253*].

Allowable deductions

[59.3] A deduction from post-cessation receipts is allowed for any loss, expense or debit that would have been deductible if the trade had not ceased, has not been relieved in any other way and which does not arise directly or indirectly from the cessation itself. In the case of a loss, relief is given against the first available post-cessation receipts, i.e. receipts for an earlier year in priority to those for a later year, but not so as give relief for a loss against receipts charged for a tax year before that in which the loss is made. [*ITTOIA 2005, ss 254, 255(1)–(3); ITA 2007, Sch 1 para 505*].

Election to carry back

[59.4] If a post-cessation receipt is received in a tax year beginning no later than six years after the date of cessation, an election may be made (by the former trader or his personal representatives) to treat the receipt as having been received on the date of cessation. See **18.2 CLAIMS** for the way in which effect is given to this election. The election must be made no later than the first anniversary of 31 January following the tax year of actual receipt. [*ITTOIA 2005, s 257*].

Post-cessation expenditure

[59.5] Relief against income (and capital gains, see below) is available (on a claim under *ITA 2007, s 96*) for certain payments made by a person in connection with a trade, profession or vocation which he has permanently ceased to carry on (including his leaving a partnership and thus ceasing his notional trade — see **52.4 PARTNERSHIPS**). The relief applies where such payments are made within seven years after cessation. Relief is given for the year in which the payment is made and unused relief cannot be carried forward (but may qualify as a deduction from post-cessation receipts within **59.1** above). Relief is available (under *ITA 2007, s 125*) in relation to a UK property business (see **60.2 PROPERTY INCOME**).The relief is given by deducting the payment in arriving at net income for the tax year in which it is made (see Step 2 at **1.7 ALLOWANCES AND TAX RATES**).

Payments qualifying for relief

Payments qualifying for this relief are those made wholly and exclusively:

(a)   in remedying defective work done, goods supplied or services provided or by way of damages (awarded or agreed) in respect of defective work etc.;

(b)   in meeting legal and professional fees in connection with a claim that work done etc. was defective;

(c)   in insuring against such a claim or against the incurring of such legal etc. fees; or

(d)   for the purpose of collecting a debt taken into account in computing profits of the former trade etc.

In addition, where, within seven years after cessation, an unpaid debt taken into account in computing profits of the former trade etc. proves to be bad or is wholly or partly released as part of a statutory insolvency arrangement (see **73.40 TRADING INCOME**), then, to the extent that the former trader is entitled to the benefit of that debt, he is treated in the same way as if he had made a payment qualifying for relief under these provisions and equal to the amount lost or released. In the case of a debt proving to be bad, the claimant must specify the tax year for which relief is to be given, which may be the tax year in which the debt proves to be bad or any subsequent tax year throughout which it remains bad and which begins within the seven years after cessation. In the case of a debt released, relief is given for the year in which the release occurs. Before 2007/08, the reference above to a statutory insolvency arrangement was to a 'relevant arrangement or compromise' as defined by *ICTA 1988, s 74(2)*. To the extent that relief has been given under these provisions, any subsequent recovery of the debt is taxed as a post-cessation receipt (see **59.1** above) with no deduction available against it under **59.3** above.

Where relief becomes available in respect of a payment within any of (a) to (d) above, the following are taxed as post-cessation receipts with no deduction available against them under **59.3** above: (i) in the case of (a) or (b), any insurance proceeds, or similar, to allow the payment to be made or to reimburse it, (ii) in the case of (c), any refund of the insurance premium, or similar receipt, and (iii) in the case of (d), any sum received to meet the costs of collecting the debt. Where the receipt occurs in an earlier tax year than the related payment, it is treated as instead having been received in the year of payment.

Set-off of unpaid expenses against relief

Where a deduction was made in computing profits or losses of the former trade etc. in respect of an expense not actually paid, relief otherwise due and claimed under these provisions is reduced by the amount of any such expenses remaining unpaid at the end of the year to which the claim relates (to the extent that those expenses have not so reduced relief for an earlier year). If an unpaid expense has reduced relief but is subsequently paid, wholly or partly, the amount paid (or, if less, the amount of the reduction) is treated as a payment qualifying for relief under these provisions for the year of payment.

Exclusion of double relief

Relief is not available in respect of an amount for which income tax relief is otherwise available. In determining whether an amount could otherwise be relieved under **59.3** above (allowable deductions from post-cessation receipts), amounts not available for relief under these provisions are assumed to be relieved under **59.3** above in priority to amounts that are so available.

Time limit

The relief must be claimed on or before the first anniversary of 31 January following the tax year for which relief is due.

Relief against capital gains

Where a claim is made as above and the claimant's total income for the year is insufficient to fully utilise the relief (or is nil), he may claim to have the excess relief treated as an allowable loss for that year for capital gains tax purposes. The allowable loss may not exceed the amount of the claimant's gains for the year *before* deducting any losses brought forward, the capital gains tax annual exemption and any relief due and claimed under **45.7 LOSSES** for trading losses or under these provisions.

[*ITA 2007, ss 96–101, 125, 126, Sch 1 paras 12, 329, 503, 504, Sch 2 para 26; ICTA 1988, ss 109A, 110; TCGA 1992, ss 261D, 261E; ITTOIA 2005, s 248(3)(4), 250, 255(4), Sch 1 paras 89, 90*].

See generally Revenue Tax Bulletin October 1995 pp 256, 257.

Simon's Taxes. See B2.807, B2.809–B2.811.

Example

[59.6]

Simcock ceased trading in October 2009. In 2010/11 the following events occur in connection with his former trade.

(i)   He pays a former customer £9,250 by way of damages for defective work carried out by him in the course of the trade.

(ii)   He incurs legal fees of £800 in connection with (i) above.

(iii) He incurs debt collection fees of £200 in connection with trade debts outstanding at cessation and which were taken into account as receipts in computing profits.

(iv) He writes off a trade debt of £500, giving HMRC notice of his having done so.

(v)   He incurs legal fees of £175 in relation to a debt of £1,000 owing by him to a supplier which, although disputed, was taken into account as an expense in computing his trading profits.

(vi)   He eventually agrees to pay £500 in full settlement of his liability in respect of the debt in (v) above, paying £250 in March 2011 and the remaining £250 in May 2011.

In 2011/12 he receives £3,000 from his insurers in full settlement of their liability with regard to the expense incurred in (i) above.

For 2010/11, his total income before taking account of the above events is £9,000, and he also has capital gains of £11,300 (with £1,000 capital losses brought forward from 2009/10).

He makes a claim under *ITA 2007, s 96* for 2010/11 and a simultaneous claim under *TCGA 1992, s 261D* to have any excess relief set against capital gains.

Simcock's tax position is as follows.

2010/11

	£	£
Income		
Total income before claim under *ITA 2007, s 96*		9,000
Deduct post-cessation expenditure —		
(i)	9,250	
(ii)	800	
(iii)	200	
(iv)	500	
(v)	—	
(vi) *less* expenses unpaid at 5.4.11 (£1,000 – £250)	(750)	
	10,000	
Restricted to total income	(9,000)	(9,000)
Excess relief	£1,000	
Capital gains		
Gains before losses brought forward and annual exemption		11,300
Deduct excess post-cessation expenditure (as above)		1,000
Net gains for the year		10,300
Losses brought forward	1,000	
Used 2010/11	200	200
Losses carried forward	£800	
Net gains (covered by annual exemption)		£10,100

2011/12

He will have taxable post-cessation receipts of £3,000 arising from the insurance recovery. He will be able to offset expenses of £175 under (v) above which, whilst not within 59.5 above, should qualify as a deduction under 59.3 above. He will also have post-cessation expenditure of £250 in respect of the further payment under (vi) above, the 2010/11 post-cessation expenditure having been restricted by more than that amount.

60

Property Income

Simon's Taxes. See **B6**, **B9**.

Other sources. See HMRC Property Income Manual.

Introduction

[60.1] Income tax is charged on rents etc. (see **60.2** below) less deductible expenses (see **60.4**, **60.5** below). Certain lease premiums etc. are also taxable (see **60.16** below).

See **10.9** CAPITAL ALLOWANCES for flat conversion allowances and **10.10** *et seq.* CAPITAL ALLOWANCES for allowances available in respect of leased industrial buildings.

Where this work refers simply to a '*property business*', then unless the context clearly suggests otherwise, it means either a UK property business or an overseas property business (see in both cases **60.2** below). Any reference to something being charged to tax as property income or within the charge to tax on property income is a reference to its having to be brought into account in computing the profits of a property business.

In this chapter, '*lease*' includes an agreement for a lease (insofar as the context permits) and any tenancy. '*Premises*' includes land. [*ITTOIA 2005, s 364*]. '*Land*' includes an estate or interest in land.

ITTOIA 2005, ss 4(1), 261, 262 set out certain priority rules where a receipt or other credit item could be dealt with either as trading income or as property income or either as property income within **60.23, 60.24** below or as other property income. See **73.90** TRADING INCOME as regards the inclusion in trading profits of receipts from, and expenses of, the letting of **surplus business accommodation**. See **73.41** TRADING INCOME as regards the inclusion in trading profits of receipts and expenses in respect of **tied premises** which would otherwise be brought into account in calculating profits of a property business.

UK and overseas property businesses

[60.2] Income tax is chargeable on the profits of a property business, whether it be a 'UK property business' or an 'overseas property business'. Profits of a UK property business are chargeable whether or not the business is carried on by a UK resident. Profits of an overseas property business are chargeable only if the business is carried on by a UK resident. The charge is on the full amount of profits arising in the tax year; there are no basis periods as there are for trading income. Normally, one would expect profits to be computed by reference to a 5 April accounting date, but see **60.4** below as regards apportionment of profits to a tax year where accounts are prepared to some other date. For more on overseas property income, including the remittance basis, see **60.3** below.

See **60.4** below as regards the computation of the profits of a property business. The person liable to tax is the person in receipt of, or entitled to, the profits.

For these purposes, a person's '*UK property business*' consists of every business which he carries on for 'generating income from land' (see below) in the UK and any other transaction which he enters into for that purpose. An '*overseas property business*' is similarly defined, but by reference to land outside the UK. Note that a person cannot have more than one UK property business or more than one overseas property business; a property business carried on by a partnership is separate from any property businesses carried on by its individual members.

See **60.4** below as regards the computation of the profits of a property business.

Where this work refers simply to a '*property business*', it means either a UK or an overseas property business (unless the context clearly suggests otherwise). Any reference to something being charged to tax as property income or within the charge to tax on property income is a reference to its having to be brought into account in computing the profits of a property business.

'*Generating income from land*' means exploiting an estate, interest or right in or over land as a source of rent or other receipts. Expenditure by a tenant on maintenance and repairs which the lease does not require him to carry out counts as rent in the landlord's hands. The reference above to 'any other transaction' brings into charge, for example, one-off or casual lettings. 'Other receipts' include:

- payments in respect of a licence to occupy or otherwise use land or in respect of the exercise of any other right over land; and
- rent charges and any other annual payments reserved in respect of, or charged on or issuing out of, land.

For the above purposes, the following activities are *not* treated as carried on for generating income from land:

- farming or market gardening in the UK, which is instead treated as a trade — see **73.73 TRADING INCOME**;
- any other *occupation* of land, but commercial occupation of land is treated as a trade (with the exemption for woodlands) — see **73.1 TRADING INCOME**; and
- activities for the purposes of a concern within *ITTOIA 2005, s 12* (mines, quarries etc.) — see **73.1 TRADING INCOME** — but see also **60.24** below.

[*ITTOIA 2005, ss 263–271, 859(2)(3); FA 2008, Sch 7 para 48*].

Caravans, caravan sites and houseboats

Income from the letting of immobile caravans or permanently moored houseboats is specifically brought within the charge to income tax on property income. [*ITTOIA 2005, s 266(4)*]. See *ITTOIA 2005, s 875* for the meaning of 'caravan' and *ITTOIA 2005, s 878(1)* for the meaning of 'houseboat'.

Income from letting caravan pitches, i.e. site rents, is chargeable to income tax as property income to the extent that it arises from exploitation of land. However, if a person carries on material activities connected with the operation of a caravan site and those activities themselves constitute a trade or a part of a trade, the income and expenses of letting the caravans and/or pitches can be included in computing the profits of that trade instead of being treated as those of a property business. [*ITTOIA 2005, s 20*].

Miscellaneous

Receipts from sales of turf have been held to be within the charge to tax on property income although they may alternatively be taxed as trading income (*Lowe v J W Ashmore Ltd* Ch D 1970, 46 TC 597); but receipts from sale of colliery dross bings held to be capital (*Roberts v Lord Belhaven's Exors* CS 1925, 9 TC 501). Sums received for licence to tip soil on land held to be capital (*McClure v Petre* Ch D 1988, 61 TC 226). Note that these cases were decided under the pre-1995/96 property income regime, which differed in a number of material respects from the current rules.

Partnerships

Ancillary property income of a trading or professional partnership is taxable on an accounts year basis (see **52.5 PARTNERSHIPS**). Joint ownership of property does not, of itself, create a partnership. Where the letting is not ancillary to a trade or profession, there will only be a partnership if, exceptionally, the exploitation of property constitutes the carrying on of a business (using that term without regard to the concept of a property business) jointly with a view to profit. See Revenue Tax Bulletin December 1995 pp 271, 272 and HMRC Property Income Manual PIM1030.

Mutual businesses

The normal exemption for mutual trading (see **73.33 TRADING INCOME** does not extend to property businesses, the transactions and relationships involved in mutual business being instead treated as if they were between persons between whom no relationship of mutuality existed. The taxable person is the person who would be taxable if the business were not mutual business. (This does not affect the treatment of Co-operative Housing Associations — see Tolley's Corporation Tax). [*ITTOIA 2005, s 321*].

Rules on commencements/cessations in particular cases

If a property business is being carried on by trustees of a trust or by personal representatives of a deceased person, a mere change of trustee etc. does not give rise to a cessation and re-commencement of the property business. [*ITTOIA 2005, s 361*].

Non-resident companies are within the charge to income tax (not corporation tax) in certain circumstances (see Tolley's Corporation Tax under Residence). Where a company starts or ceases to be within the charge to income tax in respect of a UK property business, it is treated as starting or permanently ceasing to carry on the business at that time. [*ITTOIA 2005, s 362*].

See generally HMRC Property Income Manual.

Simon's Taxes. See B6.201, B6.202, B6.211, B9.101, B9.102, B9.105.

Overseas property income

[60.3] See **60.2** above as regards an overseas property business generally. As regards the application of the property income legislation to an overseas property business and to overseas land, domestic concepts of law are to be interpreted to produce the result most closely corresponding with that produced in relation to a UK property business or land in the UK. [*ITTOIA 2005, s 363*].

The **REMITTANCE BASIS** (**61**) can apply to overseas property income where appropriate. Before 2008/09, the charge was under *ITTOIA 2005, ss 357–360 (previously ICTA 1988, ss 18(1)–(3), 65(4)(5), 68(1))*. For 2008/09 onwards, those *sections* are repealed by *FA 2008, Sch 7 para 49* but the remittance basis continues to apply, due to profits of an overseas property business being classed as relevant foreign income (see **32.2 FOREIGN INCOME**). The one change is that, for 2008/09 onwards, the remittance basis can apply if the land in question is in the Republic of Ireland, which was not the case previously.

Under general principles, relief is available for travelling expenses incurred wholly and exclusively for the purposes of an overseas property business. Interest on a loan to purchase an overseas property is deductible as an expense to the extent that it is incurred wholly and exclusively for the purposes of the overseas property business, with the interest being apportioned accordingly where the owner occupies the property, or it is otherwise unavailable for letting, for part of the year or if only part of the property is used exclusively for letting. (Revenue booklet SAT 1(1995), paras 9.151–9.153). For the application of capital allowances to an overseas property business, see **10.18**, **11.4 CAPITAL ALLOWANCES ON PLANT AND MACHINERY**. Although all overseas let properties are regarded as a single business (see **60.2** above), the income from each must be calculated separately for the purposes of computing **DOUBLE TAX RELIEF** (**26**) (SAT 1(1995), para 9.160).

For years before 1998/99, deficiencies of income from overseas lettings could by concession be carried forward for set-off against future income from the same property. For 1998/99 onwards, the loss regime at **60.15** below operates instead, but any unrelieved losses at 5 April 1998 (including any incurred after 5 April 1995 on properties where letting ceased before 1998/99) could by concession be carried forward against future profits of the overseas property business. (HMRC ESC B25; Revenue Booklet SAT 1(1995), paras 9.157–9.159).

Simon's Taxes. See B6.214, B8.506.

Computing the profits of a property business

[60.4] The profits (or losses) of a property business are computed in the same way as those of a trade (see **81 TRADING INCOME**). The specific trading income provisions of *ITTOIA 2005* which apply to property businesses are, however, limited to those listed at *ITTOIA 2005, s 272(2)* and reproduced below. These do include the fundamental rules that profits or losses be computed in accordance with generally accepted accounting practice (GAAP), that capital receipts and expenditure be excluded and that, subject to any specific rule to the contrary, expenditure is not deductible unless incurred wholly and exclusively for the purposes of the business. As stated at **60.2** above, the basis period rules for trades do not apply to property businesses. Although property income is computed similarly to trading income, it retains its nature as investment income as opposed to earnings and does not count as relevant earnings for pension contribution purposes (subject to the rules at **60.10** below for furnished holiday lettings).

The list of included trading income provisions is as follows.

ITTOIA 2005	Brief description	See main coverage at
s 25	true and fair view/use of GAAP	**73.18** TRADING INCOME
s 26	losses computed on same basis as profits	**45.1** LOSSES
s 27	meaning of 'receipts' and 'expenses'	**73.18** TRADING INCOME
s 29	interest payable	**43.2** INTEREST PAYABLE
s 33	capital expenditure non-deductible	**73.35** TRADING INCOME
s 34	'wholly and exclusively' rule for expenditure	**73.36** TRADING INCOME
s 35	bad and doubtful debts	**73.40** TRADING INCOME
ss 36, 37	timing of deductions for re-muneration	**73.56** TRADING INCOME
ss 38–44	timing of deductions for em-ployee benefit contributions	**73.57** TRADING INCOME
ss 45–47	expenditure on business en-tertainment and gifts	**73.72** TRADING INCOME
ss 48–50B	car hire	**73.42** TRADING INCOME
s 51 (re-pealed for 2007/08 onwards)	patent royalties paid	**73.99** TRADING INCOME
s 52	interest payable — exclusion of double relief	**43.13** INTEREST PAYABLE
s 53	employee and employer Na-tional Insurance contribu-tions	**73.68** TRADING INCOME

ITTOIA 2005	Brief description	See main coverage at
s 54	interest, surcharges and penalties in relation to tax — non-deductible	**73.89, 73.126** TRADING INCOME
s 55	illegal payments non-deductible	**73.87** TRADING INCOME
s 55A	expenditure on integral features of buildings and structures	**73.106** (a) TRADING INCOME
s 57	pre-trading expenditure	**73.102** TRADING INCOME
ss 58, 59	incidental costs of obtaining finance	**73.93** TRADING INCOME
s 68	replacement of tools	**73.108** TRADING INCOME
s 69	payments for restrictive undertakings	**73.71** TRADING INCOME
ss 70, 71	employees seconded to charities or educational bodies	**73.70** TRADING INCOME
s 72	payroll deduction schemes: contributions to agents' administrative costs	**16.20** CHARITIES
s 73	counselling etc. services to employees	**73.66** TRADING INCOME
ss 74, 75	retraining employees	**73.69** TRADING INCOME
ss 76–80	redundancy payments etc.	**73.65** TRADING INCOME
s 81	expenditure on personal security	**73.110** TRADING INCOME
ss 82–86	subscriptions and contributions	**73.116** TRADING INCOME

ITTOIA 2005	Brief description	See main coverage at
ss 87, 88	research and development and scientific research	**73.109** TRADING INCOME
ss 89, 90	expenditure on trademarks, designs and patents	**73.98, 73.99** TRADING INCOME
s 91	payments to Export Credits Guarantee Department	**73.98** TRADING INCOME
s 94A	costs of setting up SAYE option scheme or CSOP scheme	**73.59** TRADING INCOME
s 96	capital receipts excluded from profits	**73.101** TRADING INCOME
s 97	debts incurred and later released	**73.102** TRADING INCOME
s 104	distribution of assets of mutual concerns	**73.98** TRADING INCOME
s 105	industrial development grants	**73.117** TRADING INCOME
s 106	insurance recoveries	**73.88** TRADING INCOME
s 109	receipt by donor etc. of benefit attributable to certain gifts	**73.84** TRADING INCOME
ss 148A–148J	long funding leases of plant and machinery	**73.95, 73.96** TRADING INCOME
s 155	levies and repayments under *Financial Services and Markets Act 2000*	**73.111** TRADING INCOME
ss 188–191	unremittable amounts	**73.124** TRADING INCOME

[ITTOIA 2005, s 272; FA 2006, Sch 8 para 14; ITA 2007, Sch 1 para 507; FA 2008, s 73(5)(6); FA 2009, Sch 11 paras 41, 65–67; TIOPA 2010, Sch 7 para 29].

For a general article on what constitutes an allowable *repair* in a property business, see Revenue Tax Bulletin June 2002, pp 935, 936.

See generally HMRC Property Income Manual.

In practice, a cash basis may be used instead of a full earnings basis (as required by GAAP) where gross annual receipts do not exceed £15,000, provided that it is used consistently and gives a reasonable overall result not substantially different from that produced on an earnings basis (see HMRC Property Income Manual PIM1101).

Profits or losses on contracts taken out to hedge interest payments deductible in computing profits or losses of the property business will normally be taxed or relieved as receipts or deductions of that business. Such profits or losses would generally be computed on an accruals basis in accordance with normal accountancy practice.

Similarly deposits paid to landlords by tenants or licensees will ordinarily be receipts of the business, to be recognised in accordance with generally accepted accountancy practice, normally by being deferred and matched with the related costs. Excess deposits which are refunded should be excluded from the business receipts. (Revenue Tax Bulletin October 1996 p 349).

As regards allowable legal and professional costs, see HMRC Property Income Manual PIM2205 and Revenue Tax Bulletin December 1996 p 375.

Apportionment of profits to tax year

Where, exceptionally, a period of account of a property business does not coincide with a tax year, profits must be apportioned to tax years. This must normally be done by reference to the number of days in the periods concerned, but the taxpayer may choose any other method, e.g. months and part-months, if it is reasonable to do so and so long as the chosen method is applied consistently. [*ITTOIA 2005, s 275, Sch 2 para 62*].

Miscellaneous deductions

[60.5] Special deductions may be available as follows.

(a)   *Capital allowances on plant and machinery.* A property business is a qualifying activity for the purposes of such allowances under *CAA 2001, Pt 2* (see **11.4 CAPITAL ALLOWANCES ON PLANT AND MACHINERY**). Allowances are thus given as expenses, and charges treated as receipts, of the business. Plant or machinery provided for use in a dwelling-house is excluded (with a just and reasonable apportionment of expenditure where such use is partial). [*CAA 2001, ss 15, 16, 35*].

(b)   *Sea walls.* For allowances for expenditure on making sea walls, see *ITTOIA 2005, ss 315–318; CTA 2009, Sch 1 para 628* and *Hesketh v Bray* CA 1888, 2 TC 380.

(c)   *Landlord's expenditure on energy-saving items.* Where the land in question consists of or includes a dwelling-house, a deduction is available, in computing the profits of a property business for income tax purposes, for expenditure incurred within any of the tax years **2004/05 to 2014/15** inclusive which:

- is capital expenditure incurred in the acquisition, and installation in the dwelling-house or alternatively, in relation to expenditure incurred on or after 6 April 2007 and insofar as the expenditure is for the benefit of the dwelling-house, in a building containing the dwelling-house, of a 'qualifying energy-saving item'; and
- is incurred wholly and exclusively for the purposes of the property business, is not otherwise deductible in computing the profits of that business and does not qualify for any capital allowance.

'*Qualifying energy-saving item*' is defined so as to comprise cavity wall insulation; loft insulation; (from 7 April 2005) solid wall insulation; (from 6 April 2006) hot water system insulation and draught proofing; and (from 6 April 2007) floor insulation.

The deduction is limited to a maximum of £1,500 per dwelling-house, irrespective of the number of persons incurring expenditure or entitled to make a deduction in respect of that dwelling-house. Before 6 April 2007, the deduction was limited to a maximum of £1,500 per *building*, irrespective of the number of dwelling-houses contained in the building and the number of persons eligible to make a deduction in respect of it. For 2004/05 only, it was necessary to make a claim for the deduction to be given.

The deduction is not available if, at the time the item is installed, the dwelling-house is under construction or is comprised in land in which the taxpayer does not have an interest or is in the course of acquiring an interest or a further interest. The property business must not consist in the commercial letting of furnished holiday accommodation (within **60.10** below) or, if it does so consist to any extent, the dwelling-house must not itself constitute any of that accommodation for the tax year in question. The taxpayer must not also be taking rent-a-room relief (within **60.12** below) in respect of any qualifying residence which consists of or includes the dwelling-house.

Where the qualifying conditions are satisfied in relation to part only of any expenditure, a deduction is allowed on the basis of a just and reasonable apportionment of the expenditure. Relief under *ITTOIA 2005, s 57* (previously *ICTA 1988, s 401*) for *pre-trading expenditure* (see **73.102 TRADING INCOME** as applied by **60.4** above) is allowed only for expenditure incurred within the *six months* before the claimant commences the property business.

The Treasury are given wide powers to vary these provisions by regulation; this includes the power to vary the definition of a 'qualifying energy-saving item' and to impose conditions by reference to which a specified item will qualify. Regulations apply (i) to determine entitlement to the deduction where different people have different interests in the land in question, (ii) to apportion to a particular dwelling-house expenditure which benefits more than one dwelling-house or a combination of dwelling-houses and other properties in a building, and (iii) to apportion relief between joint tenants or tenants in common; in all cases, a just and reasonable apportionment applies. Any contribution received from another person towards the expenditure must be ex-

cluded in arriving at the deductible amount. The regulations set out an appeals procedure where their application raises any question as to the amount of deduction to which a person is entitled. Note that the current regulations are in *SI 2007 No 3278*, all earlier versions of the regulations having been revoked.
[*ITTOIA 2005, ss 312–314, Sch 2 para 73; SI 2007 No 3278*].

Simon's Taxes. See B3.304, B6.207, B6.208, B9.301–B9.305.

Post-cessation receipts and expenditure

[60.6] Income tax is charged on any 'post-cessation receipts' of a UK property business by adopting the rules applicable to trades at **59.1–59.4 POST-CESSATION RECEIPTS AND EXPENDITURE** in suitably modified form. A '*post-cessation receipt*' is a sum which is received after a person permanently ceases to carry on a UK property business and which arises from the carrying on of the business before cessation. The charge for any tax year is on the full amount of post-cessation receipts for that year. In contrast to the rules for trades, post-cessation receipts of a UK property business do not count as relevant earnings for the purposes of making pension contributions. The charge does not apply in relation to an overseas property business. [*ITTOIA 2005, ss 310, 349–356; ITA 2007, Sch 1 para 512; CTA 2009, Sch 1 para 629; FA 2009, Sch 11 paras 43, 65–67*].

Relief for post-cessation expenditure is available (under *ITA 2007, s 125* or, before 2007/08, *ICTA 1988, s 109A*) in relation to a UK property business in the same way as in relation to a trade, profession or vocation (see **59.5 POST-CESSATION RECEIPTS AND EXPENDITURE**).

Adjustments on change of basis

[60.7] An adjustment similar to that described at **73.20 TRADING INCOME** is required where:

- there is, from one period of account of a UK property business to the next, a 'change of basis' in computing taxable profits;
- the old basis accorded with the law or practice applicable in relation to the period of account before the change; and
- the new basis accords with the law and practice applicable in relation to the period of account following the change.

A '*change of basis*' for this purpose is either (i) a change of accounting principle or practice that, in accordance with generally accepted accounting practice (see **73.18 TRADING INCOME**), gives rise to a prior period adjustment, or (ii) a change in the statutory tax adjustments applied (including a change resulting from a change of view as to application of the statute but excluding a change made to comply with an amendment to the statute which was not applicable to the earlier period of account).

The rules are based on those described at **73.20 TRADING INCOME**, as suitably modified.

Tax is charged on the full amount of any adjustment income arising in a tax year. The adjustment income is charged separately from the profits of the UK property business. However, for loss relief purposes adjustment income is treated as profits of the UK property business for the tax year in which tax is charged on it.

These rules are of no application to an overseas property business.

[*ITTOIA 2005, ss 329–334, 860, Sch 2 para 76; ITA 2007, Sch 1 para 511; CTA 2009, Sch 1 para 641*].

Three-line accounts

[60.8] Landlords whose total annual gross income from UK property is below the VAT registration threshold (£70,000 for 2010/11, £68,000 for 2009/10), or the appropriate proportion of that amount where they have been receiving income from property for less than a full tax year, need only show rental income, total expenses and net profit or loss in their self-assessment tax returns.. There is, of course, still a need to keep accurate records to ensure the correctness of the three-line accounts. (www.hmrc.gov.uk/factsheet/three-line-account.pdf). See generally **63.2, 63.5** RETURNS.

Furnished lettings

[60.9] Furnished lettings are taxable as, or as part of, a property business (and the computational rules at **60.4** above thus apply). See **60.10, 60.12** below for, respectively, special rules for furnished holiday lettings and rent-a-room relief.

A furnished letting is a lease or other arrangement under which a sum is payable for the use of premises (which expression includes a caravan or houseboat, as in **60.2** above) and the person entitled to the use of the premises is also entitled to the use of furniture. Any consideration receivable for the use of furniture is chargeable as property income in the same way as rent (and expenditure incurred in providing furniture is treated accordingly). This does not apply to any amount taken into account in computing profits of a trade involving the making available of furniture for use in premises. [*ITTOIA 2005, s 308*].

Dependent on the nature of the lettings, including their frequency and the extent to which the landlord provides services, e.g. cleaning, laundry and meals, the letting may amount to a trade of providing serviced accommodation and be chargeable to tax as trading income rather than property income. Alternatively, the provision of services may amount to a trade separate to the letting (cf. *Salisbury House Estate Ltd v Fry* HL1930, 15 TC 266). In *Gittos v Barclay* Ch D 1982, 55 TC 633, the letting of two villas in a holiday village was held not to amount to trading. A similar decision was reached in *Griffiths v Jackson; Griffiths v Pearman* Ch D 1982, 56 TC 583 in relation to the extensive letting of furnished rooms to students. Note that these cases were decided under the pre-1995/96 property income regime, which differed in a number of material respects from the current rules.

Capital allowances are not due on plant or machinery let for use in a dwelling house (see **11.4 CAPITAL ALLOWANCES ON PLANT AND MACHINERY**) (but see **60.10** below as regards furnished holiday lettings). Furniture and furnishing may be dealt with on the renewals basis but an alternative HMRC concession is to allow as depreciation 10% of the rents received as reduced by any council tax and water rates or material payments for services borne by landlord but normally a tenant's burden. Where the 10% deduction is allowed, no further deduction is given for the cost of renewing furniture or furnishings, nor for fixtures such as cookers, dishwashers or washing machines which, in unfurnished accommodation, the tenant would normally provide for himself. However, the cost of renewing fixtures which are an integral part of the building (e.g. baths, toilets, washbasins) may be claimed in addition, provided that they are revenue repairs to the fabric. (HMRC ESC B47; Revenue Press Release IR28, 29 November 1994). See *Abidoye v Hennessey* Ch D 1978, [1979] STC 212.

Furnished holiday lettings

[60.10] In so far as a property business consists in the 'commercial letting' of 'furnished holiday accommodation' in the UK (a 'furnished holiday lettings business') for a tax year, it is treated for the following purposes as a trade.

(i)   Relief for losses under any of **45.2, 45.5, 45.7, 45.9, 45.20,** or **45.21 LOSSES**).

(ii)   Disapplication of the 50:50 joint property rule for spouses and civil partners (see **47.7 MARRIED PERSONS AND CIVIL PARTNERS**).

(iii)   Relief for contributions to a registered pension scheme (see **57 PENSION PROVISION**).

(iv)   Before 2007/08 but now no longer relevant, classification as earned income.

In addition, a furnished holiday lettings business is a qualifying activity for the purposes of capital allowances on plant and machinery (see **11.4 CAPITAL ALLOWANCES ON PLANT AND MACHINERY**). In contrast to furnished lettings generally, plant or machinery provided for use in a dwelling-house is not precluded, but the 10% wear and tear allowance in **60.9** above cannot be claimed as an alternative.

The letting of furnished holiday accommodation outside the UK has hitherto been treated as an overseas property business, and the special treatment above has not been available. This may not be compliant with European law. HMRC will accept claims to apply the special treatment to the commercial letting of qualifying furnished holiday accommodation in the European Economic Area (EEA) for all open years up to and including 2009/10. Late claims for 2006/07 were accepted until 31 July 2009. Certain transitional rules apply where, as a result of this change, the special treatment applies to a letting for the first time; for example, the letting will not generally be regarded as a new business for tax purposes. (HMRC Technical Note, 22 April 2009 at www.hmrc.gov.uk/budg et2009/furnished-hol-lets-1015.pdf).

All commercial lettings of furnished holiday accommodation by a particular person (including a partnership) are treated as a single trade or, for capital allowances purposes, as a single qualifying activity, separate from any genuine trade or other qualifying activity carried on by that person.

If a UK property business consists only partly of the commercial letting of furnished holiday accommodation, the profits and losses of the separate parts of the business must be separately calculated. If there is a letting of accommodation only part of which is holiday accommodation, such apportionments are to be made as are just and reasonable.

Relief as at (i) above under *ITA 2007, s 72* (or its predecessor) (see **45.9 LOSSES**) is not available for a tax year if any of the accommodation concerned was first let by the same person as furnished accommodation more than three years before the beginning of that tax year. *ITA 2007, s 75* (and its predecessor) (restriction on relief for capital allowances etc., in a part-time letting trade — see **45.14 LOSSES**) does not apply to furnished holiday accommodation losses.

HMRC consider that the requirement under **45.9 LOSSES** that there be a reasonable expectation of profits in the period concerned or within a reasonable time afterwards normally requires a reasonable and realistic expectation of profits emerging within five years from the date of commencement of furnished holiday letting activities (Revenue Tax Bulletin October 1997 p 473).

'*Commercial letting*' is letting (whether or not under a lease) on a commercial basis and with a view to the realisation of profits, and accommodation is let '*furnished*' if the tenant is entitled to use of the furniture. For a case in which the 'commercial letting' test was satisfied despite a significant excess of interest over letting income, see *Walls v Livesey* (Sp C 4), [1995] SSCD 12, but see also *Brown v Richardson* (Sp C 129), [1997] SSCD 233 in which the opposite conclusion was reached. See Revenue Tax Bulletin October 1997 pp 472, 473 for HMRC's view of the requirements in this respect.

For any tax year, '*holiday accommodation*' is accommodation which:

(a)   is available for commercial letting to the public generally as holiday accommodation for at least 140 days in the twelve-month period referred to below; and

(b)   is so let for at least 70 such days.

Any period of more than 31 consecutive days during which the accommodation is in the same occupation (otherwise than because of abnormal circumstances), does not count towards the 70 days in (b) above. Any such period is known as a '*period of longer-term occupation*', and if, during the twelve-month period referred to below, more than 155 days fall during periods of longer-term occupation, the accommodation is *not* '*holiday accommodation*'. The words 'in the same occupation' refer to tenants and do not prevent relief being due where the owner himself occupies the property outside the holiday season (HMRC Property Income Manual PIM4110).

The twelve-month period referred to above is the tax year in question, unless:

(1)   the accommodation was not let by the person concerned as furnished accommodation in the preceding tax year, in which case the twelve-month period runs from the date such letting commenced in the tax year in question; or

(2)   the accommodation was let by the person concerned as furnished accommodation in the preceding tax year but is not so let in the succeeding tax year, in which case the twelve-month period is the twelve months ending with the date such letting ceased in the tax year in question.

In satisfying the 70-day test in (b) above, averaging may be applied to the number of let days of any or all of the accommodation let by the same person which either is 'holiday accommodation' or would be 'holiday accommodation' if it satisfied the 70-day test on its own. An election for averaging must be made no later than the first anniversary of 31 January following the tax year to which it is to apply. It must specify the accommodation to be included in the averaging calculation; 'holiday accommodation' cannot be included in more than one averaging election for a tax year. See below for an example of how averaging works.

[ITTOIA 2005, ss 322–328, Sch 1 paras 197, 526, 528, Sch 2 paras 74, 75; CAA 2001, ss 15, 17; ITA 2007, s 127, Sch 1 paras 508–510; FA 2009, Sch 6 para 2(5)].

Furnished holiday accommodation may include caravans (Revenue Press Release 17 May 1984).

See Tolley's Capital Gains Tax as regards relief from capital gains tax in respect of furnished holiday lettings.

Simon's Taxes. See **B6.4, B9.110.**

Example

[60.11]

Mr B owns and lets out furnished holiday cottages. None is ever let to the same person for more than 31 consecutive days. Three cottages have been owned for many years but Rose Cottage was acquired on 1 June 2010 (and first let on that day) while Ivy Cottage was sold on 30 June 2010 (and last let on that day).

In 2010/11, days available for letting and days let are as follows.

	Days available	Days let
Honeysuckle Cottage	180	160
Primrose Cottage	130	100
Bluebell Cottage	150	60
Rose Cottage	150	60
Ivy Cottage	30	5

Additional information

Rose Cottage was let for 30 days between 6 April and 31 May 2011.

Ivy Cottage was let for 50 days in the period 1 July 2009 to 5 April 2010 but was available for letting for 110 days in that period.

Qualification as 'furnished holiday accommodation'

Honeysuckle Cottage qualifies as it meets both the 140-day availability test and the 70-day letting test.

Primrose Cottage does *not* qualify although it is let for more than 70 days as it fails to satisfy the 140-day test. Averaging (see below) is only possible where it is the 70-day test which is not satisfied.

Bluebell Cottage does not qualify by itself as it fails the 70-day test. However it may be included in an averaging election.

Rose Cottage qualifies as furnished holiday accommodation. It was acquired on 1 June 2010 so qualification in 2010/11 is determined by reference to the period of twelve months beginning on the day it was first let, in which it was let for a total of 90 days.

Ivy Cottage was sold on 30 June 2010 so qualification is determined by reference to the period from 1 July 2009 to 30 June 2010 (the last day of letting). It does not qualify by itself as it was let for only 55 days in this period but it may be included in an averaging election.

Averaging election for 2010/11

	Days let
Honeysuckle Cottage	160
Bluebell Cottage	60
Rose Cottage	90
Ivy Cottage	55

$$\frac{160 + 60 + 90 + 55}{4} = 91.25 \text{ days} \quad \text{note (a)}$$

Note

(a)   All four cottages included in the averaging election now qualify as furnished holiday accommodation as each is deemed to have been let for 91.25 days in the year 2010/11. If the average had been less than 70, the two cottages which qualify in any case could have been included in an averaging election together with one of the non-qualifying cottages (leaving the other as non-qualifying). If averaging three cottages still did not improve the position, an average of just two could be tried.

Rent-a-room relief

[60.12] The taking in of domestic lodgers may be treated as the carrying on of a trade, where services other than accommodation are provided, or as furnished lettings.

An individual qualifies for a special relief (rent-a-room relief) for a tax year if he has 'rent-a-room receipts' for that year and does not derive any taxable income other than rent-a-room receipts from any trade, letting or agreement from which the rent-a-room receipts are derived. Receipts are *'rent-a-room receipts'* if:

- they arise from the use of furnished accommodation in a 'residence' (see below) in the UK or from goods or services (e.g. meals, cleaning, laundry) supplied in connection with such use;
- they accrue to the individual during the 'income period' (see below);
- the residence in question is the individual's only or main residence for all or part of the income period; and
- the receipts would otherwise be brought into account in computing trading income or property income or, from 2005/06 onwards, be chargeable to income tax as miscellaneous income.

For these purposes, a *'residence'* is a building, or part of a building, occupied or intended to be occupied as a separate residence; a caravan or houseboat can also be a residence. If a building (or part) designed for permanent use as a single residence is *temporarily* divided into two or more separate residences, it is still treated as a single residence.

If the receipts would otherwise be brought into account in computing the profits of a trade, the *'income period'* is the basis period for that trade for the tax year in question; see **73.3** *et seq.* TRADING INCOME for basis periods generally. Otherwise, the *'income period'* is the tax year itself, but disregarding any part of the tax year before the letting in question commenced or after it ceased.

Full rent-a-room relief

If an individual meets the 'exclusive receipts condition' and his total rent-a-room receipts for the tax year, *before* deducting any expenses or capital allowances but *after* adding any 'relevant balancing charges', are £4,250 or less (or such sum as may be specified for the future by Treasury order), the receipts are exempt from tax. This means that neither the receipts themselves nor any related expenses, relevant allowances or relevant balancing charges are included in computing any trading profits, letting income or miscellaneous taxable income. A *'relevant balancing charge'* or *'relevant allowance'* is a balancing charge or an allowance falling to be made under the plant and machinery capital allowances code in respect of any plant or machinery provided for the purposes of a trade or letting from which the rent-a-room receipts are derived. If an individual does not meet the 'exclusive receipts condition', the above applies with the substitution of £2,125 for the figure of £4,250, i.e. the limit is halved.

An individual meets the *'exclusive receipts condition'* for a tax year if, for each residence of his from which he derives rent-a-room receipts, no receipts accrue to any other person during the 'relevant period', for the use of residential accommodation (furnished or not) in that residence or for goods or services supplied in connection with such use, at a time when the residence is the individual's only or main residence. The *'relevant period'* is normally the income period (see above) for the tax year, except that if the income period is less than 12 months, the relevant period is extended to the 12 months beginning or ending at the same time as the income period begins or ends.

An election can be made to disapply the relief, for example if the individual would otherwise make an allowable loss. The election is made under *ITTOIA 2005, s 799*. It must specify the tax year to which it applies and has effect for that year only. It must be made, and can be withdrawn, no later than the first anniversary of 31 January following the tax year to which it applies (or such later date as HMRC may, in a particular case, allow — see HMRC Property Income Manual PIM4050).

Alternative method of calculation

If an individual's total rent-a-room receipts for the tax year, *before* deducting any expenses or capital allowances but *after* adding any relevant balancing charges (as above), exceed the limit for full rent-a-room relief (whether the limit be £4,250 or £2,125), he may make an election to use an alternative method of calculating profits. Under this method, an individual's taxable rent-a-room receipts are restricted to the said excess. No deduction is given for any expenditure or capital allowances. If the individual's rent-a-room receipts are derived from different sources, e.g. a trade and a letting, there is provision for apportioning the limit between the sources for the purpose of applying this method.

The election is made under *ITTOIA 2005, s 800*. It must specify the tax year for which it is made, but has effect for that year and all subsequent years until withdrawn. It must be made no later than the first anniversary of 31 January following the year for which it first has effect (or such later date as HMRC may, in a particular case, allow — see HMRC Property Income Manual PIM4050). A similar time limit applies to a notice of withdrawal, by reference to the tax year for which the withdrawal is to first have effect. A notice of withdrawal is without prejudice to the right to make a fresh election for a subsequent year. Where an election would otherwise apply to a tax year for which the individual's total rent-a-room receipts do *not* exceed the limit, the individual is treating as having withdrawn the election with effect from that year (again without prejudicing the right to make a fresh election for a subsequent year).

Before 2005/06, the election for the alternative calculation was not available if total rent-a-room receipts exceeded the limit only because of the addition of balancing charges; this anomaly is corrected by *ITTOIA 2005*.

Assessments

If an assessment is necessary to give effect to either of the above elections being made or withdrawn, the pre-2005/06 legislation specified that the assessment, if otherwise time-barred, could be made at any time no later than the first anniversary of 31 January following the tax year *in which* the election was made or withdrawn. *ITTOIA 2005* incorporates this rule but with the words 'for which' instead for 'in which'; this is thought to be a drafting error.

[*ITTOIA 2005, ss 784–802*].

Rent-a-room relief will not normally be available to taxpayers who are living abroad (or in job-related accommodation) and letting their home while they are away; this applies even in the years of departure and return since the property will not normally have been their residence at any time during the income periods for those years. If, however, the letting commences *before* departure and/or ceases *after* return, relief may then be due for the year of departure and/or return (HMRC Property Income Manual PIM4010, 4015).

HMRC consider that rent-a-room relief is inapplicable to the letting of a residence (or part) as an office or for other trade or business purposes (other than the business of providing furnished living accommodation) (Revenue Tax Bulletin August 1994 p 154).

Simon's Taxes. See **B6.6, B9.111.**

Example

[60.13]

Emily and Charlotte are single persons sharing a house as their main residence. They have for some years taken in lodgers to supplement their income. As Emily contributed the greater part of the purchase price of the house, she and Charlotte have an agreement to share the rental income in the ratio 2:1, although expenses are shared equally.

For the year ended 5 April 2005, gross rents amounted to £5,700 and allowable expenses were £1,100. In the year ended 5 April 2006, the pair face a heavy repair bill after uninsured damage to one of the rooms. Gross rents for that year amount to £3,600 and expenses to £4,400. For the years ended 5 April 2007 and 2008, gross rents are £6,600 and expenses £2,200, and for the year ended 5 April 2009 they are £6,000 and £2,500 respectively. For the year ended 5 April 2010, they are £8,100 and £4,500 respectively. For the year ended 5 April 2011, they are £9,000 and £3,000 respectively.

For 2004/05, the position is as follows.

Normal Schedule A computation

	Emily	Charlotte
	£	£
Gross rents (y/e 5.4.05)	3,800	1,900
Allowable expenses	550	550
Net rents	£3,250	£1,350

Charlotte's share of *gross* rents is less than £2,125, i.e. half of the £4,250 limit. It is assumed that she would not make the election for full rent-a-room relief not to apply. Her share of net rents is thus treated as nil.

Emily's share of gross rents exceeds £2,125, so full rent-a-room relief cannot apply. She can, however, elect to apply the alternative method of calculation. Under that method, she is taxed on the excess of *gross* rents over £2,125. It is assumed that she will make the election as she will then be taxed on £1,675 rather than £3,250.

For 2005/06, the position is as follows.

Normal computation of property income

	Emily	Charlotte
	£	£
Gross rents (y/e 5.4.06)	2,400	1,200
Allowable expenses	2,200	2,200
Net rents	£200	£(1,000)

Charlotte's share of gross rents continues to be less than £2,125. Under full rent-a-room relief, her share of net rents will be treated as nil. However, she will obtain no relief, by carry-forward or otherwise, for her loss. In order to preserve her loss, she could elect for full rent-a-room relief not to apply, the election having effect for 2005/06 only.

Emily's share of gross rents exceeds £2,125. Therefore, her previous election for the alternative method will not be automatically treated as withdrawn. She will be taxed under the alternative method on £275 (£2,400 – £2,125). However, this is greater than the amount taxable on the normal property income computation (£200), so it is assumed she would withdraw the election with effect for 2005/06 and subsequent years. The notice of withdrawal does not prejudice the making of a fresh election for 2006/07 or any subsequent year.

For 2006/07, the position is as follows.

Normal computation of property income

	Emily	Charlotte
	£	£
Gross rents (y/e 5.4.07)	4,400	2,200
Allowable expenses	1,100	1,100
Net rents	£3,300	£1,100

Charlotte's share of gross rents now exceeds £2,125, so full rent-a-room relief will not apply. She could elect for the alternative method to apply, and her chargeable income will then be reduced to £75 (£2,200 – £2,125). This is further reduced to nil by the bringing forward of her £1,000 loss for 2005/06. If Charlotte did not make the election, her chargeable income would be £100 with the whole of her 2005/06 loss having been utilised.

Emily can make a fresh election to apply the alternative method, with effect from 2006/07, and she will then be taxed on £2,275 (£4,400 – £2,125).

For 2007/08, the position is as follows.

The normal computation of property income is as for 2006/07. Assuming Emily and Charlotte both elected to apply the alternative method for 2006/07, the elections will continue to apply for 2007/08, so that their respective chargeable property incomes are £2,275 and £75. Charlotte's chargeable property income is reduced to nil by the brought forward balance of £925 of the 2005/06 loss (of which the balance of £850 is carried forward to 2008/09).

For 2008/09, the position is as follows.

Normal computation of property income

	Emily	Charlotte
	£	£
Gross rents (y/e 5.4.09)	4,000	2,000
Allowable expenses	1,250	1,250
Net rents	£2,750	£750

Charlotte's share of gross rents is now below £2,125, so that the election to apply the alternative method is treated as having been withdrawn, and full rent-a-room relief applies instead (assuming no election to disapply it). The balance of £850 of her 2005/06 loss is carried forward to 2009/10. Emily's election to apply the alternative method will continue to have effect (unless withdrawn), so that her chargeable property income will be £1,875 (£4,000 – £2,125).

For 2009/10, the position is as follows.

Normal computation of property income

	Emily	Charlotte
	£	£
Gross rents (y/e 5.4.10)	5,400	2,700
Allowable expenses	2,250	2,250
Net rents	£3,150	£450

For both Emily and Charlotte, their share of gross rents now exceeds £2,125, so that full rent-a-room relief will not apply, and since their share of the expenses also exceeds £2,125, the election to apply the alternative method will be unfavourable. It is therefore assumed that Emily withdraws her election (by 31 January 2012). They are accordingly both charged to tax on the basis of the normal property income computation, with Charlotte's £850 loss brought forward being set against her share, the balance of £400 being carried forward to 2010/11.

For 2010/11, the position is as follows.

Normal computation of property income

	Emily	Charlotte
	£	£
Gross rents (y/e 5.4.11)	6,000	3,000
Allowable expenses	1,500	1,500
Net rents	£4,500	£1,500

Both could now elect to apply the alternative method of calculation (the election to be made by 31 January 2013). Emily's chargeable property income will be reduced to £3,875 (£6,000 – £2,125) and Charlotte's to £875 (£3,000 – £2,125). Charlotte's is further reduced to £475 by the balance of her 2005/06 loss brought forward.

Property Income Distributions (PIDs) from Real Estate Investment Trusts (REITs)

[60.14] A distribution received from a Real Estate Investment Trust (REIT) (see below) by a shareholder within the charge to income tax is treated in the shareholder's hands as profits of a UK property business to the extent that it is paid out of the tax-exempt profits (including tax-exempt chargeable gains) of the REIT. Basic rate tax is deducted at source by the REIT; the shareholder remains liable for any excess liability, i.e. excess of the higher rate of tax over the basic rate. The distribution does not carry a tax credit. Manufactured dividends (see **4.10** ANTI-AVOIDANCE) that are representative of such dividends are treated similarly; however, where the payer is non-UK resident regulations may provide for the recipient to account for and pay the tax in respect of the manufactured dividend.

Distributions made by an REIT out of profits other than tax-exempt profits are taxed, and carry tax credits, in the same way as any other distribution made by a UK resident company, for which see **64.7** *et seq.* SAVINGS AND INVESTMENT INCOME. A distribution made by a company that has ceased to be an REIT is subject to the special treatment to the extent that it is paid out of tax-exempt profits made while the company was an REIT.

Distributions within the special treatment (known as Property Income Dividends or PIDs) are treated in the shareholder's hands as profits of a single business, regardless of the fact that they may come from different REITs or be received by the shareholder in different capacities. The single business is separate from any property business carried on by the shareholder. These rules apply to an individual partner's share of any PIDs received by a partnership as if it were received by him as a direct shareholder.

If the shareholder is non-UK resident, a PID is again treated as profits of a UK property business, but this does not preclude its being dealt with under the relevant dividend article of a double tax agreement (Treasury Explanatory Notes to Finance Bill 2006 and see www.hmrc.gov.uk/cnr/dt-guide-note-9.h tm). PIDs are outside the non-resident landlords regime at **60.21** below.

The special treatment does not apply to distributions falling to be taken into account in computing the recipient's trading profits (see **73.111** TRADING INCOME under Dealers in securities) or on shares held in a Lloyd's underwriter's premium trust fund or ancillary trust fund (see **74.3** UNDERWRITERS AT LLOYD'S).

The requirements concerning deduction of basic rate tax at source are set out in regulations (see *SI 2006 No 2867 as amended*). These *inter alia* specify classes of shareholder to whom PIDs can be made without deduction of tax (e.g. local authorities, health service bodies, public offices and Crown departments, charities, ISAs, Child Trust Funds, registered pension schemes). They also require REITs to provide shareholders with tax deduction certificates (e.g. to assist with preparation of self-assessment tax returns) and provide the framework for returns and payment to HMRC of the tax deducted by the REIT.

There are rules to determine the extent to which a distribution of an REIT is made out of its tax-exempt profits. It is one of the conditions of tax-exempt status that at least 90% of the profits of an REIT's property rental business is paid out as dividends within a specified time; distributions are thus attributed firstly to those profits (i.e. to tax-exempt profits) until the 90% condition is met. Once that condition is met with regard to an accounting period, the REIT may identify as much as it chooses of the balance (if any) of the distributions as being paid out of income (not gains) from activities of a kind in respect of which corporation tax is chargeable (i.e. out of profits other than tax-exempt profits). This apparently includes distributable profits of the tax-exempt business to the extent that such profits differ from the profits as computed for tax purposes, but any part of the distribution so attributed is nevertheless regarded as a distribution out of profits other than tax-exempt profits (Treasury Explanatory Notes to Finance Bill 2006). Any remaining balance of the distribution is next attributed to profits of the property rental business (i.e. to tax-exempt profits) to the extent that these have not yet been matched with distributions; these may include profits of an earlier accounting period. Next, the distribution is matched with any tax-exempt gains on disposals of assets used in the property rental business. Any part of the distribution still not attributed is regarded as a normal distribution out of profits other than tax-exempt profits. For worked examples on these attribution rules, see the Treasury Explanatory Notes to Finance Bill 2006.

[*CTA 2010, ss 548–550, Sch 1 paras 537, 555, 560, 561; ITA 2007, ss 576, 918, 973, 974, Sch 1 para 619; FA 2006, ss 121–123; FA 2007, s 52, Sch 17 para 10*].

See HMRC Savings and Investment Manual SAIM5300–5340.

There is a tax charge on an REIT if it makes a distribution to a shareholder with a 10% interest or more in the company or its dividends. A distribution that is withheld in order to prevent or reduce such a charge is nevertheless treated as having been made for the purposes of the regulations dealing with deduction of basic rate tax at source. [*CTA 2010, ss 530(6), 551–554; ITA 2007, s 974(3); FA 2006, ss 107(9)(b), 114, 122(4); FA 2007, s 52, Sch 17 para 3*].

General note on REITs

A listed UK resident company may opt into REIT status with effect for any accounting period beginning on or after 1 January 2007. It then continues to have REIT status for subsequent accounting periods until it opts out or its status is withdrawn by HMRC or it ceases to meet fundamental conditions. The company must carry on a property rental business (as defined), and both the company and the business must satisfy a number of conditions. The property rental business may include overseas properties, but certain properties are excluded; it must account for at least 75% of the company's business. At least 90% of the profits of the property rental business must be distributed as dividends. For so long as a company has REIT status, the profits and gains of its property rental business are exempt from corporation tax. The regime extends, with the appropriate modifications, to groups of companies. The intention of the REIT regime is to provide a collective investment vehicle for property investment where the returns received by investors mirror the treatment of direct holding in property; the legislation effectively shifts the burden of taxation of property rental from a company to its investors. A company within the regime may elect to apply it to a joint venture carried on by a group of companies in which it has an interest. For detailed coverage of REITs themselves, the corporation tax exemption, the conditions that the companies and their businesses must satisfy and the consequences flowing from breaches of those conditions, see Tolley's Corporation Tax under Investment Trusts.

Property AIFs

On and after 6 April 2008, new *regulations* enable open-ended investment companies to become Property AIFs (Property Authorised Investment Funds). This is a separate regime for collective investment in real property and in REITs and foreign equivalents. The regime is similar to the REIT regime itself. For more details and, in particular, the treatment of distributions to individual investors, see **75.4 UNIT TRUSTS ETC.**

Losses

Carry-forward

[60.15] Where a person carrying on a UK property business or an overseas property business (see **60.2** above) (alone or in partnership) makes a loss in that business for a tax year, the loss is automatically carried forward to subsequent tax years without time limit. The carried-forward loss is relieved by deduction in arriving at net income for subsequent tax years (see Step 2 at **1.7 ALLOWANCES AND TAX RATES**). However, it can only be deducted from profits of the same property business. The deduction must be made from the first available profits (and then, if those profits are insufficient, from the next available, and so on until the loss is exhausted). The deduction is made in priority to deducting any other reliefs from available profits. A loss is not carried forward to the extent that it is set against general income under the provisions described below. [*ITA 2007, ss 118, 119; ICTA 1988, ss 379A(1)(7), 379B*].

Limited set-off against general income

Where a person carrying on a UK property business or an overseas property business (see **60.2** above) (alone or in partnership) makes a loss in that business for a tax year (the year of loss) and as regards that year:

(a)   there is a net amount of capital allowances, (i.e. capital allowances exceed any balancing charges); and/or

(b)   the property business has been carried on in relation to land that consists of or includes an 'agricultural estate', and 'allowable agricultural expenses' (see below) deducted in computing the loss are attributable to that estate,

a claim may be made under *ITA 2007, s 120* (or, before 2007/08, under *ICTA 1988, s 379A(3)*) to set the available loss relief against his general income for the year of loss or the following tax year.

The available loss relief is the lower of the loss itself and either:

•   the net capital allowances (where (a) above applies); or
•   the allowable agricultural expenses (where (b) applies); or
•   the sum of those two items (where both (a) and (b) apply).

A claim is given effect by deducting the loss in arriving at net income for the tax year in question (see Step 2 at **1.7 ALLOWANCES AND TAX RATES**).

Relief cannot normally be claimed for both the year of loss and the following year in respect of the same loss, but where the whole of the available loss relief cannot be given in one year (i.e. due to an insufficiency of income), the balance may be separately claimed for the other year. Where, against income of the same year, claims are made both (i) in respect of the previous year's loss and (ii) in respect of the current year's loss, (i) takes precedence over (ii).

A claim must be made no later than the first anniversary of 31 January following *the year to which the claim relates* (i.e. the year for which relief is to be given). If the loss was previously being carried forward, the claim must be accompanied by any necessary amendments to the claimant's tax return for any year for which relief has been given on that basis and is now superseded by the claim.

An *'agricultural estate'* (see (b) above) means any land (including any houses or other buildings) which is managed as one estate and which consists of or includes land occupied wholly or mainly for husbandry. *'Allowable agricultural expenses'* (see (b) above) are any deductible expenses attributable to the agricultural estate in respect of maintenance, repairs, insurance or estate management (but excluding loan interest). For these purposes, expenses are taken into account only if they are attributable to the parts of the estate used for husbandry, with those attributable to parts used *partly* for other purposes being proportionately reduced.

Tax-generated losses attributable to annual investment allowance

An anti-avoidance rule applies if a loss arises directly or indirectly in consequence of, or otherwise in connection with, 'relevant tax avoidance arrangements' entered into on or after 24 March 2010 and (a) above applies. The rule applies equally if any transaction forming part of such arrangements is entered into on or after that date. No property loss relief against general income may be given to the person making the loss for so much of the available loss relief as is attributable to an annual investment allowance (AIA) (see **11.13 CAPITAL ALLOWANCES ON PLANT AND MACHINERY**). For this purpose, the available loss relief is treated as attributable to capital allowances before anything else and to an AIA before any other capital allowance.

'Relevant tax avoidance arrangements' are arrangements (as widely defined) to which the person making the loss is a party and a main purpose of which is to be in a position to make use of an AIA in reducing a tax liability by means of property loss relief against general income.

The above restriction does not apply where the arrangements are, or the transaction is, entered into pursuant to an unconditional obligation (as defined) in a contract made before 24 March 2010.

[*ITA 2007, ss 120–124, 127A; ICTA 1988, ss 379A(2)–(10), 379B; FA 2010, s 25*].

Simon's Taxes. See B6.203, B9.410.

Lease premiums etc.

[60.16] If a premium is payable under a *'short-term lease'* (i.e. a lease whose effective duration, see below, is 50 years or less), or under the terms on which such a lease is granted, the person to whom it is due (whether or not the landlord) is treated as entering into a transaction for the purpose of generating income from land. An amount must be brought into account as a receipt in computing the profits of the property business which consists of or includes that transaction (see **60.2** above) for the tax year in which the lease is granted. The amount to be brought into account is:

$$P \times \frac{50 - Y}{50}$$

where:

P = the amount of the premium; and

Y = the number of *complete* periods of twelve months (*other than the first*) comprised in the effective duration of the lease.

> *Example*
>
> Tom grants a 14-year lease of premises for a premium of £50,000 in June 2010. The amount to be included as a receipt in computing the profits of his property business for 2010/11 is as follows:
>
> $$£50,000 \times \frac{50 - 13}{50} = £37,000$$

Note that these provisions refer to leases granted and not to leases assigned. See *Banning v Wright* HL 1972, 48 TC 421. *ITTOIA 2005, ss 303, 304, Sch 2 paras 70, 71* (as amended) contain rules for ascertaining the effective duration of a lease, which is not necessarily the same as its contractual duration; in particular, any rights the tenant has to extend the lease, or any entitlement of his to a further lease of the same premises, may possibly be taken into account.

If the terms on which a lease is granted oblige the tenant to carry out work on the premises (other than work such as normal repairs or maintenance which, if incurred by the landlord, would be deductible expenditure in computing the profits of his property business), the lease is treated as requiring the payment of a premium (or additional premium) to the landlord of the amount by which the value of the landlord's interest increases as a result of the obligation.

If the terms on which a lease is granted require the tenant to pay a sum in lieu of rent for a period, and that period is less than 50 years, the person to whom the sum is due (whether or not the landlord) is treated as if he were entitled to a premium equal to that sum. *ITTOIA 2005* makes it explicit that this applies irrespective of the duration of the lease itself, and in particular whether or not it is a short-term lease, though HMRC have always taken that view in any case (see Change 68 listed in Annex 1 to the Income Tax (Trading and Other Income) Bill). The charge to tax is made for the tax year in which the sum becomes payable. The value of Y in the above formula is the number of complete periods of twelve months (other than the first) comprised in the period in relation to which the sum is payable (but excluding any part of that period falling after the expiry of the effective duration of the lease).

'Premium' is widely interpreted for the above purposes by *ITTOIA 2005, ss 306, 307* and, in particular, includes payments to a person connected with the landlord (as in **21 CONNECTED PERSONS**).

See generally HMRC Property Income Manual PIM1200–1214.

Payment by instalments

Where any premium etc. is payable by instalments, the tax thereon may itself be paid by such instalments as HMRC may allow in the particular case; the tax instalment period cannot exceed eight years or, if less, the period during which the premium instalments are payable. See HMRC Property Income Manual PIM1220.

[*ITTOIA 2005, ss 276(6), 277–279, 299, 303–307, Sch 2 paras 63, 64, 70, 71; CTA 2009, Sch 1 paras 614, 625–627, 646(2)(3); SI 2009 No 2035, Sch paras 44, 45*].

Determinations affecting liability of more than one person

Special rules apply where a determination is needed of an amount to be brought into account as a receipt under the lease premium rules and the determination could affect another person's tax liability. HMRC will issue a provisional determination to both the taxpayer and the other party, to which either (or both) may object (within 30 days). Where an objection is made, the said amount must be determined in the same way as an appeal. HMRC may require any person to give them any information that they feel is required in deciding whether to issue to any person a provisional determination. [*ITTIOA 2005, ss 302A–302C; ICTA 1988, s 42; TIOPA 2010, Sch 7 para 22; SI 2009 No 56, Sch 1 para 133*].

Capital gains tax

See Tolley's Capital Gains Tax for the treatment of chargeable gains arising from disposal by way of a lease. Note particularly that the part of the premium chargeable to income tax is omitted from the computation of the chargeable gain.

Surrender under the terms of a lease

If, under the terms on which a short-term lease is granted, a sum becomes payable by the tenant as consideration for the surrender of the lease, consequences ensue as above as if that sum were a premium. See HMRC Property Income Manual PIM1214. [*ITTOIA 2005, s 280, Sch 2 para 65*].

Variation or waiver of terms of lease

If:

- a sum becomes payable by a tenant (otherwise than by way of rent) as consideration for the variation or waiver of the terms of a lease, and
- the sum is due to the landlord or to a person connected with the landlord, and
- the period for which the variation or waiver has effect is 50 years or less,

consequences ensue as above as if that sum were a premium. This applies irrespective of the duration of the lease itself, and in particular whether or not it is a short-term lease. The charge to tax is made for the tax year in which the contract for the variation or waiver is entered into. The value of Y in the above formula is the number of complete periods of twelve months (other than the first) comprised in the period for which the variation or waiver has effect (but excluding any part of that period falling after the expiry of the effective duration of the lease). See HMRC Property Income Manual PIM1216. [*ITTOIA 2005, s 281; CTA 2009, Sch 1 para 616*].

Trustees

Chargeable lease premiums etc. arising to trustees of a settlement (including those deemed to arise under **60.17** below) are treated as being income chargeable at the trust rate. See **68.12 SETTLEMENTS**.

Factoring of income receipts etc.

The lease premium rules at *ITTOIA 2005, ss 277–281* above are disapplied where the grant of the lease constitutes the disposal of an asset for the purposes of applying the income factoring provisions at **4.35 ANTI-AVOIDANCE**. [*ITTOIA 2005, s 281A; TIOPA 2010, Sch 8 para 270*].

Simon's Taxes. See B6.301–B6.313, B9.201–B9.213.

Anti-avoidance — leases granted at undervalue etc.

[60.17] If a short-term lease (as in **60.16** above) was granted at an undervalue and is assigned at a profit, similar consequences ensue as in **60.16** above as regards the assignor as if he had received a premium (except that the opportunity to pay the tax by instalments is not available). The charge to tax is made for the tax year in which the consideration for the assignment becomes payable. The value of P in the formula in **60.16** above is the lesser of the profit on the assignment and the amount of the undervalue (adjusted to take account of any profits on earlier assignments of the same lease). This does not apply in relation to a lease granted before 6 April 1963 or pursuant to a contract entered into before that date. [*ITTOIA 2005, ss 282, 283, Sch 2 para 66*].

If land is sold subject to terms requiring it to be reconveyed on a future date to the seller or a person connected with him (within **21 CONNECTED PERSONS**) for a price lower than the sale price, similar consequences ensue as in **60.16** above as regards the assignor as if he had received a premium. This applies only if the period beginning with the sale and ending with the earliest date on which, under the said terms, the land could fall to be reconveyed is 50 years or less. The charge to tax is made for the tax year in which the sale occurs. The value of P in the formula in **60.16** above is the excess of the sale price over the price at which the land is to be reconveyed. The value of Y is the number of complete periods of twelve months (other than the first) comprised in the period of 50 years or less referred to above.

Similar provisions apply (with appropriate modifications) if, instead of being reconveyed, the land is to be leased back to the seller or to a person connected with him. (They do not, however, apply if the lease is granted and begins to run within one month after the sale.) In this case, the sale price is compared to the total of (i) any premium payable for the lease and (ii) the value on the date of sale of the right to lease back the land.

If the date for the reconveyance (or leaseback) is not fixed under the terms of the sale and the reconveyance price (or the total of (i) and (ii) above) varies dependent upon that date, the price (or total) is taken to be the lowest possible under the terms of the sale. There is provision for any overpaid tax to be repaid if the actual date of reconveyance (or of the grant of the lease) turns out to be different to the date by reference to which the tax charge was calculated. A claim for repayment must be made no later than six years after the reconveyance (or the grant of the lease). Where it is made on or after 1 April 2010 (and see **18.4** CLAIMS), such a claim must be made no later than *four* years after the reconveyance (or the grant of the lease).

[*ITTOIA 2005, ss 284–286, 301, 302; FA 2008, Sch 39 paras 51, 52; SI 2009 No 403*].

See HMRC Property Income Manual PIM1222, 1224, 1226. For the so-called 'treasury arrangement' to avoid a charge under these provisions where there is a genuine commercial reason for the owner of mineral-bearing land to sell with a right to repurchase, see HMRC Property Income Manual PIM1228. See **4.31** ANTI-AVOIDANCE for other provisions concerning the sale and leaseback of land.

Sub-leases etc.

[60.18] Relief is due if any of the charges at **60.16** above apply, or the charge on assignment (but not the other charges) at **60.17** above applies, and the grant of the lease in question is out of a 'taxed lease' or, as the case may be, the assignment in question is of a 'taxed lease'. A *'taxed lease'* is one in respect of which there has already been such a charge (or there would have been a charge but for the availability of this relief). Thus, in broad terms, the relief applies where the taxable person is himself a tenant and his own landlord has received a premium or other taxable sum in respect of the same property.

The amount given by the formula in **60.16** above is reduced by an amount found by the formula:

$$\frac{PC \times LRP}{TRP}$$

where

PC   =   the amount given by the formula in **60.16** above in respect of
the previous charge,

LRP =   the 'receipt period' of the receipt under calculation, and

TRP =   the 'receipt period' of the receipt by reference to which the previous charge was made.

The '*receipt period*' is:

• in the case of a premium (or similar sum) or a sum payable for the
surrender of a lease, the effective duration of the lease (see **60.16** above);

• in the case of a sum payable in lieu of rent, the period for which it is
payable;

• in the case of a sum payable for variation or waiver, the period for
which the variation or waiver has effect; and

• in the case of an assignment, the effective duration of the lease
remaining at the date of the assignment.

If the current charge is under **60.16** above and the sub-lease relates to only part
of the premises subject to the head-lease, the relief is reduced proportionately
on a just and reasonable basis.

Example

Tom grants a 14-year lease of premises to Jerry for a premium of £50,000 in June
2010. The amount to be included as a receipt in computing the profits of
Tom's property business for 2010/11 is £37,000 as computed in the *Example* in
60.16 above.

After 4 years, i.e. in June 2014, Jerry grants a 10-year sub-lease for which he
receives a premium of £60,000. The amount to be included as a receipt in
computing the profits of Jerry's property business for 2014/15 is as follows.

		£
Normal calculation	$£60,000 \times \dfrac{50-9}{50}$	49,200
Less relief as above	$\dfrac{£37,000 \times 10}{14}$	26,429
		£22,771

The relief is restricted to the 'unrelieved balance' of the value of PC in the
above formula. The '*unrelieved balance*' is found by deducting the following
from the value of PC:

- any relief previously given under these provisions;
- any deductions allowed under **60.19** below; and
- any deductions allowed under *ITTOIA 2005, ss 60–67* (deductions allowed where the land is used for the purposes of a trade etc. — see **73.104** TRADING INCOME),

so far as attributable to the charge to which PC relates.

If there is more than one previous charge in relation to which there is an unrelieved balance, an amount of relief is computed separately for each previous charge and then aggregated, but the total relief cannot exceed the total of the unrelieved balances.

For these purposes, in a case where the previous charge resulted from the tenant's obligation to carry out work on the premises (see **60.16** above), the value of PC in the above formula is recomputed as if that obligation had not included the carrying out of any work that results in expenditure qualifying for capital allowances.

If the relief would otherwise exceed the amount from which it is deductible, it is restricted to that amount.

[*ITTOIA 2005, ss 287–290, Sch 2 paras 67–69; CTA 2009, Sch 1 paras 617–619*].

Before 2005/06, the above provisions applied equally for the purposes of income tax and corporation tax. For 2005/06 onwards, the income tax rules are in *ITTOIA 2005* but the equivalent corporation tax rules are elsewhere. *ITTOIA 2005, ss 296–298* seek to ensure that the two sets of rules interact, for example where the landlord is a company and the tenant is an individual. The tenant remains entitled to the above relief even though the previous charge, i.e. the charge on the landlord etc., is a charge to corporation tax rather than income tax.

See generally HMRC Property Income Manual PIM2300–2340.

Other deductions available to tenant

[60.19] A tenant is allowed a deduction, in computing the profits of a property business carried on by him, by reference to a premium etc. charged on the landlord. The deduction is available to a tenant under a 'taxed lease'. A *'taxed lease'* is a lease by reference to which any of the charges at **60.16** have arisen, or the charge on assignment (but not the other charges) at **60.17** above has arisen (or would have done so but for the availability of the relief at **60.18** above). The deduction is available for any 'qualifying day' on which the whole or part of the premises subject to the taxed lease is either occupied by the tenant for the purposes of carrying on his property business or sub-let. It is given by treating an amount calculated as below as a revenue expense of the tenant's property business, but *not* so as to override any statutory rule, e.g. the 'wholly and exclusively' rule, governing deductible expenditure generally (see **60.4** above). A *'qualifying day'* is a day that falls within the 'receipt period' (as defined in **60.18** above) of the receipt charged under **60.16** or **60.17** above).

The amount of the expense for *each* qualifying day is the amount given by the formula in **60.16** above in respect of the charge under **60.16** or **60.17** above divided by the number of days in its receipt period.

> *Example (i)*
>
> Tom grants a 14-year lease of premises to Jerry for a premium of £50,000 on 1 June 2010. The amount to be included as a receipt in computing the profits of Tom's property business for 2010/11 is £37,000 as computed in the *Example* in **60.16** above. Jerry immediately sub-lets the premises but does not receive any premium.
>
> The number of days in the 14-year receipt period is 5,113. The deduction due to Jerry in calculating the profits of his property business for any one qualifying day is £37,000 divided by 5,113 = £7.24. For a full tax year, Jerry is entitled to a deduction of £7.24 × 365 = £2,643. For the tax year 2010/11, the available deduction is £7.24 × 309 (1.6.10 to 5.4.11) = £2,237.

If, however, the tenant is also entitled to relief under **60.18** above, he is treated as incurring a revenue expense for a qualifying day only to the extent (if any) that the daily amount computed as above exceeds the daily amount of the relief under **60.18**.

> *Example (ii)*
>
> The sub-letting in *Example (i)* above ceases in 2012/13. On 6 April 2013, Jerry again grants a sub-lease of the premises but this time for a period of 11 years at a premium of £70,000. The amount to be included as a receipt in computing the profits of Jerry's property business for 2013/14 is as follows.
>
> | | | £ |
> |---|---|---|
> | Normal calculation as in **60.16** | $£70,000 \times \dfrac{50-10}{50}$ | 56,000 |
> | *Less* relief as in **60.18** | $\dfrac{£37,000 \times 11}{14}$ | |
> | | | 29,071 |
> | | | £26,929 |
>
> The number of days in the 11-year receipt period of the sub-lease is 4,017. The daily amount of the relief given is therefore £29,071 divided by 4,017 = £7.24. This equals the daily expense computed in *Example (i)*; as there is no excess, Jerry is not entitled to any deduction for a revenue expense under these provisions for any of the 4,017 qualifying days covered by the sub-lease.
>
> Supposing Jerry had been able to obtain a premium of only £30,000 for the 11-year sub-lease. The amount to be included as a receipt in computing the profits of Jerry's property business for 2013/14 would then be as follows.

		£
Normal calculation as in **60.16**	$£30,000 \times \dfrac{50-10}{50}$	24,000
Less $\dfrac{£37,000 \times 11}{14}$	= £29,071 but restricted to	24,000
		Nil

The daily amount of the relief given is now £24,000 divided by 4,017 = £5.97. This is less than the daily expense of £7.24 computed in *Example (i)*, the deficit being £1.27. Jerry would be entitled to a deduction of £1.27 as a revenue expense for each of the 4,017 qualifying days covered by the sub-lease.

If a sub-lease relates to only part of the premises covered by the main lease, the above rules are applied separately to the different parts of the premises, the premium under the main lease being apportioned between those parts on a just and reasonable basis.

If the premises subject to the taxed lease are used for the purposes of a trade, profession or vocation instead of for those of a property business, very similar rules apply under *ITTOIA 2005, ss 60–67*, with the deduction being given as an expense in computing the profits of the trade etc. See **73.104** TRADING INCOME.

The total of the deductions allowed under these provisions, any deductions allowed under *ITTOIA 2005, ss 60–67* referred to above and any relief given under **60.18** above cannot exceed the amount charged under **60.16** or, where appropriate, **60.17** above.

[*ITTOIA 2005, ss 291–295, Sch 2 paras 67–69; CTA 2009, Sch 1 paras 620–622*].

Before 2005/06, the above provisions applied equally for the purposes of income tax and corporation tax. For 2005/06 onwards, the income tax rules are in *ITTOIA 2005* but the equivalent corporation tax rules remained in *ICTA 1988*. For company accounting periods ended before 1 April 2009, *ITTOIA 2005, ss 296–298* (as amended) sought to ensure that the two sets of rules interact, for example where the landlord is a company and the tenant is an individual. The tenant remained entitled to the above deduction even though the lease premium was charged to corporation tax rather than income tax. For later accounting periods, the above provisions are directly linked to equivalent rules in *CTA 2009* so as to achieve similar outcomes.

See generally HMRC Property Income Manual PIM2300–2340.

Simon's Taxes. See **B6.310, B9.221–B9.223**.

Reverse premiums

[60.20] There are provisions to ensure that reverse premiums are taxable as revenue receipts. They apply in relation to any 'reverse premium' (as defined but broadly a payment made or benefit provided by a landlord to a prospective tenant as an inducement to enter into a lease). Other than in cases where the transaction is entered into for purposes of the recipient's trade, profession or vocation. (or prospective trade etc.), a reverse premium is to be treated as a receipt of a UK property business, or (as the case may be) an overseas property business, carried on by the recipient. Subject to a specific anti-avoidance rule where the transaction involves connected persons, it is understood that accountancy principles require the receipt to be brought into account by spreading over the period of the lease or, if shorter, the period to the first rent review. See **73.105 TRADING INCOME** for the full provisions. [*ITTOIA 2005, s 311, Sch 2 para 72*].

Simon's Taxes. See B6.205.

Non-resident landlords — collection from agents or tenants

[60.21] Where a landlord is non-resident (i.e. his usual place of abode is outside the UK), tax is to be deducted at source by the agent for the property or, where there is no agent, the tenant, with a final settling up with the non-resident landlord. [*ITA 2007, ss 971, 972; ICTA 1988, s 42A; CTA 2009, Sch 1 para 714; CTA 2010, Sch 1 para 559*]. The regulations giving effect to these requirements provide broadly as follows.

(i) Letting agents who receive or have control over UK property income of a non-resident must operate the scheme.

(ii) Where there is no letting agent acting, tenants of a non-resident must operate the scheme.

(iii) Tenants who pay less than £100 per week do not have to operate the scheme unless asked to do so by HMRC.

(iv) Letting agents and tenants who have to operate the scheme must pay tax at the basic rate each quarter on the non-resident's UK property income less certain allowable expenses and deductions, and must give the non-resident an annual certificate showing details of tax deducted.

(v) Non-residents whose property income is subject to deduction of tax may set the tax deducted against their UK tax liability through their self-assessment.

(vi) Non-residents may apply to HMRC for approval to receive their UK property income without deduction of tax provided that:
(a) their UK tax affairs are up to date;
(b) they have never had any obligations in relation to UK tax; or
(c) they do not expect to be liable to UK income tax,
and that they undertake to comply with all their UK tax obligations in the future. An appeal may be made against refusal or withdrawal of approval.

The regulations also make provision for interest on unpaid tax and for payments on account under self-assessment, and set out details of the annual information requirements on those operating the scheme, and of other information to be supplied on request. Penalties apply under *TMA 1970, s 98* for non-compliance with these return and information provisions.

[*ITA 2007, s 972, Sch 2 para 169; ICTA 1988, s 42A(4)–(7); SI 2009 No 56, Sch 2 paras 28–32*].

HMRC publish detailed guidance notes for those required to operate the scheme (see www.hmrc.gov.uk/cnr/nrl_guide_notes.pdf). See also HMRC guidance at www.hmrc.gov.uk/cnr/nr_landlords.htm, Information Bulletin No. 1 (March 2010) at www.hmrc.gov.uk/cnr/nrl-bulletin1.pdf and Revenue Tax Bulletin December 1995 pp 261–263.

Simon's Taxes. See B6.217, B9.503.

Items apportioned on sale of land

[60.22] If, on a sale of land, receipts and outgoings due to be received or paid by the buyer are apportioned to the seller, then, in computing the profits of the seller's property business, the part apportioned to him is treated as being of the same nature, i.e. revenue or capital, as the receipt or outgoing itself. [*ITTOIA 2005, s 320*]. So, for example, if rent is receivable in arrears and the sale price includes an adjustment for rent receivable up to date of sale, the amount of that adjustment is income in the hands of the seller and not capital.

Electric-line wayleaves

[60.23] Rent receivable for a UK electric-line wayleave is chargeable to income tax as property income. If a person carries on a UK property business in relation to some or all of the land to which the wayleave relates and the business has other receipts for the tax year in question, the rent receivable for the wayleave is brought into account in the property business. Otherwise, it is taxed as a separate item; the charge is on the full amount of profits arising in the tax year, and the person liable to tax is the person in receipt of, or entitled to, the rent.

Rent is receivable for a UK electric-line wayleave if it is receivable in respect of an easement, servitude or right, in or over land in the UK, enjoyed in connection with an electric, telegraph or telephone wire or cable, including supporting poles or pylons and related apparatus. All references above to 'rent' include any other receipt in the nature of rent and, in particular, the 'other receipts' referred to in **60.2** above.

If, however, a person carries on a trade, profession or vocation on some or all of the land to which the wayleave relates and, apart from rent receivable, or expenses incurred, in respect of the wayleave, no other receipts or expenses in respect of any of the land are included in computing the profits of any property business of the trader, rent receivable, or expenses incurred, in respect of the wayleave may be brought into account, at the trader's option, in computing the profits of the trade etc. instead of being charged as above. This treatment extends to certain wayleaves other than those described above and to wayleaves relating to land outside the UK which would otherwise be included in an overseas property business.

[*ITTOIA 2005, ss 22, 344–348; CTA 2009, Sch 1 para 588*].

Mines, quarries etc.

[60.24] As stated at **73.1 TRADING INCOME**, profits of mines, quarries, gravel pits, sand pits, brickfields, ironworks, gas works, canals, railways, rights of fishing, rights of markets, fairs and tolls and like concerns are computed and charged to income tax as if the concern were a trade carried on in the UK. The full list of the types of concern to which this applies is at *ITTOIA 2005, s 12(4)*, and such concerns are referred to elsewhere in *ITTOIA 2005* as 'UK section 12(4) concerns'.

Where *rent* is receivable 'in connection with' (see *ITTOIA 2005, s 336*) a 'UK section 12(4) concern' it is chargeable to income tax as property income. The charge is on the full amount of profits arising in the tax year, and the person liable to tax is the person in receipt of, or entitled to, the rent. Where the letting is of a right to work minerals, a deduction is allowed for any sum paid wholly and exclusively as an expense of management or supervision of the minerals.

All references above to 'rent' include any other receipt in the nature of rent and, in particular, the 'other receipts' referred to in **60.2** above.

[*ITTOIA 2005, ss 335–339*].

See also **48 MINERAL ROYALTIES**.

Information re leases

[60.25] Information, including consideration for their grant or assignment etc., may be required by HMRC, subject to penalty for non-compliance, from present or former lessees or occupiers, or from agents managing property or receiving rents etc. [*TMA 1970, ss 19, 98*].

Key points

[60.26] Points to consider are as follows.

•   Rent-a-room relief is available where small scale bed and breakfast activities are carried on in the proprietor's home. Advisers should consider whether a claim may be beneficial.

•   The reprieve for the furnished holiday lettings regime in June 2010 means that investment in this sector may increase — particularly in view of the availability of CGT entrepreneurs' relief on qualifying disposals. Note that the qualifying conditions for FHL treatment may be amended with effect from April 2011.

- HMRC has provided guidance on the capital/revenue divide, which is particularly helpful for landlords refurbishing properties in the residential sector. The key relaxation is the use of the term 'changing technology' (See HMRC Business Income Manual at BIM46904) where the nearest current replacement for an item may well not be regarded as an improvement. A useful example is the replacement of single glazed windows with double glazed.
- Capital allowances can be claimed on plant and machinery in communal areas in multiple occupancy dwellings such as student accommodation. HMRC's guidance on the interpretation of the term 'dwelling house', issued in December 2008 is in HMRC Brief 66/08.
- Where an investor has refurbished a property and has benefitted from capital allowances under either the flat conversion scheme or the business premises renovation allowance there may be losses attributable to capital allowances for several periods. Careful tailoring of the capital allowances claims to maximise tax relief when offsetting losses against general income will be necessary.
- Property income arising on a jointly-owned property is not necessarily partnership income. For simplicity the relevant shares of income and expenses should be reported on the property pages of each owner's personal self-assessment return.
- The share of income to which each of the joint owners is entitled is reported on their tax return. This is not necessarily an equal split between the owners — each will report the sums to which he or she is entitled and pay tax on this amount; this does not necessarily reflect their underlying ownership of the property concerned. This does not apply to married couples or civil partners who are taxed on an equal share unless they indicate that the property (and therefore the income) is owned in unequal shares (see **47.7 MARRIED PERSONS AND CIVIL PARTNERS**).

61

Remittance Basis

Cross-references. See **62 RESIDENCE, ORDINARY RESIDENCE AND DOMICILE** for the meaning of these terms; **27.5, 27.10 EMPLOYMENT INCOME** for the charge to tax on the remittance basis on chargeable overseas earnings and foreign earnings; **30.30 EXEMPT INCOME** for an exemption for low-income non-UK domiciled employees; **32.2 FOREIGN INCOME** for the meaning of 'relevant foreign income'; **69.18, 69.19 SHARE-RELATED EMPLOYMENT INCOME AND EXEMPTIONS** for the charge to tax on the remittance basis on foreign securities income.

See www.hmrc.gov.uk/cnr/cgt-qa-jan09.pdf for questions and answers on the remittance basis as it applies for 2008/09 onwards. For more detailed guidance, see www.hmrc.gov.uk/cnr/rdrm-remittances.pdf.

Introduction

[61.1] UK residents are normally liable to UK tax on the whole of their worldwide income and chargeable gains arising in a tax year (the arising basis). The remittance basis is available to UK resident individuals who are not domiciled in the UK or are not ordinarily resident in the UK. It provides for foreign source income (and, in the case of non-domiciled individuals only, foreign source chargeable gains) to be charged to tax by reference to the extent to which they are remitted to, or received in, the UK.

The remittance basis applies to 'relevant foreign income' as defined at **32.2 FOREIGN INCOME**, relevant foreign earnings (see **61.3** below) and, for non-domiciled individuals only, foreign chargeable gains. For aspects of the remittance basis that are specific to chargeable gains, see the corresponding chapter of Tolley's Capital Gains Tax.

Fundamental changes were made to the remittance basis by *FA 2008, s 25, Sch 7*. Except where otherwise stated, this chapter covers the remittance basis for 2008/09 onwards, i.e. after the changes made by *FA 2008*.

Application of the remittance basis

[61.2] The remittance basis can only apply to an individual for a particular tax year if, in that tax year, the individual is (i) resident in the UK, but *either* (ii) not domiciled in the UK or (iii) not ordinarily resident in the UK.

The remittance basis does apply to an individual for a particular tax year if he makes a claim as in (1) below or if either (2) or (3) below apply to him.

(1)   An individual who meets the residence/domicile conditions at (i)–(iii) above for a tax year can make a claim to be chargeable on the remittance basis for that year. The claim must contain a statement to the effect that conditions (ii) or (iii) above (or both) are met. No time limit is specified for making the claim, so the default deadline at **18.4 CLAIMS** applies. An individual who claims the remittance basis loses entitlement to personal reliefs (see **61.7** below). An additional £30,000 tax charge applies to a 'long-term UK resident' who makes a claim for the remittance basis to apply for a particular tax year (see **61.8** below).
No error or mistake relief is available if the error consists in the making of a claim as above (see **18.8 CLAIMS** — no longer applicable on or after 1 April 2010).

(2)   No claim is required if an individual meets the residence/domicile conditions at (i)–(iii) above but the total of his 'unremitted foreign income and gains' for the tax year amounts to less than £2,000. An individual's *'unremitted foreign income and gains'* is the total of his 'foreign income and gains' (see **61.3** below) for the tax year less the total amount of those income and gains that are remitted to the UK in that year. Where the condition is satisfied, it is assumed that the remittance basis applies unless the individual is not domiciled in the UK and satisfies the conditions for the exemption at **30.30 EXEMPT INCOME**. If, however, the individual does not wish the remittance basis to apply for any year, he may give notice of that fact in a self-assessment tax return for the year.

If the condition is satisfied and the individual's remittances for a tax year amount to less than £500 and are in cash, he will not be required to complete a self-assessment tax return just for the sake of paying UK tax on the amount remitted. However where such an individual is required to complete a self-assessment tax return for any other reason, or if HMRC gives him notice to make a return, he will need to include those small remittances on the return and pay the tax due. (HMRC Brief 17/09, 25 March 2009).

Even if split-year treatment applies under ESC A11 upon an individual's becoming or ceasing to be UK resident (see **62.6 RESIDENCE, ORDINARY RESIDENCE AND DOMICILE**), the level of unremitted foreign income and gains for the whole tax year is taken into account in considering whether or not the 'less than £2,000' threshold is exceeded.

(3)   Additionally, no claim is required if an individual meets the residence/domicile conditions at (i)–(iii) above but also meets all the following conditions:

    (a)   he has no 'UK income or gains' for the tax year other than taxed investment income of no more than £100 gross;

    (b)   no 'relevant income' or 'gains' are remitted to the UK in the tax year; and

    (c)   he is either under 18 or has been UK resident in no more than six of the nine immediately preceding tax years.

If, however, the individual does not wish the remittance basis to apply for any year, he may give notice of that fact in a self-assessment tax return for the year.

For the purposes of (3)(a) above, an individual's '*UK income and gains*' means the total of his income and gains other than his 'foreign income and gains' (see **61.3** below). For the purposes of (3)(b) above, an individual's '*relevant income*' and '*gains*' comprise his 'foreign income and gains' for the tax year in question, his foreign income and gains for every other tax year for which (1), (2) or (3) applies to him and his foreign income and gains for any tax year before 2008/09 in which he was UK resident and either not ordinarily resident or not domiciled in the UK. For this purpose, an individual's foreign income and gains for a year prior to 2008/09 include 'relevant foreign income' (as in **32.2 FOREIGN INCOME**) only if the remittance basis applied to him for that year (whether as the result of a claim in the case of 2005/06 to 2007/08 inclusive or by default for years prior to 2005/06 — see **61.25** below). The point of (3) above is to ensure that an individual does not have to complete a tax return only for the purpose of claiming the remittance basis if he would have no tax to pay on that basis.

[*ITA 2007, ss 809A, 809B, 809D, 809E; FA 2008, Sch 7 paras 1, 81, 85; FA 2009, Sch 27 paras 3, 4, 15*].

Effect of the remittance basis applying

[61.3] Where any one of **61.2**(1)–(3) above applies to an individual for a tax year, the following income and gains of his for that year are chargeable to tax on the remittance basis (even if they are remitted in a tax year for which none of **61.2**(1)–(3) above apply):

(a) 'relevant foreign income' as in **32.2 FOREIGN INCOME** (see **61.4** below);

(b) 'relevant foreign earnings' (see **61.5** below);

(c) 'foreign securities income' as in **69.19 SHARE-RELATED EMPLOYMENT INCOME AND EXEMPTIONS**; and

(d) foreign chargeable gains, but only if the individual is not domiciled in the UK in that tax year; and

[ITA 2007, s 809F; FA 2008, Sch 7 paras 1, 81].

The items in (a)–(d) above together comprise an individual's *'foreign income and gains'* for a tax year. *[ITA 2007, s 809Z7(2); FA 2008, Sch 7 paras 1, 81]*.

Charge on relevant foreign income

[61.4] The charge on relevant foreign income for any tax year is on the full amount remitted to the UK (see **61.10** below) in that year. This applies to relevant foreign income for a year for which any one of **61.2**(1)–(3) above applies to the individual; it applies regardless of whether or not the source still exists when the income is remitted and regardless of whether or not any one of **61.2**(1)–(3) above applies to the individual for the year in which it is remitted. It does not apply if the individual is non-resident in the UK for the year in which the income is remitted, but see below under Temporary non-UK residence.

The only circumstance in which any deductions are allowed is where the income is from a trade, profession or vocation carried on outside the UK, in which case the same deductions are allowed as for trades etc. carried on in the UK.

In contrast to the position before 2008/09 (see **61.25** below), relevant foreign income arising in the Republic of Ireland is treated in the same way as relevant foreign income from any other non-UK source; the remittance basis thus applies to such income.

The above charge applies equally to relevant foreign income for 2007/08 and earlier years where it is remitted to the UK in 2008/09 or a later year, but only if the remittance basis applied to the individual for the year in which the income arose (whether as the result of a claim in the case of 2005/06 to 2007/08 inclusive or by default for years prior to 2005/06 — see **61.25** below). Income that arose in the Republic of Ireland is excluded.

Temporary non-UK residence

The following applies where an individual has left the UK for a period of temporary residence outside the UK, and:

• four out of the seven tax years immediately preceding the 'year of departure' were years for which the individual satisfied 'the residence requirements'; and

• there are fewer than five tax years (the *'intervening years'*) falling between (and not including) the 'year of departure' and the 'year of return'.

For the purposes of these provisions, the '*year of departure*' means the last tax year before the year of return for which the taxpayer satisfied the 'residence requirements'. The '*year of return*' is any tax year for which the individual satisfies the 'residence requirements' and which immediately follows one or more tax years for which he did not satisfy those requirements.

An individual satisfies the '*residence requirements*' for a tax year if during any part of the year he is resident in the UK and not 'treaty non-resident' or if for the year he is ordinarily resident in the UK and not treaty non-resident.

An individual is '*treaty non-resident*' at any time if he falls at that time to be regarded for the purposes of double tax arrangements (see **26.2 DOUBLE TAX RELIEF**) as resident in a territory outside the UK.

Where the above conditions are satisfied, relevant foreign income remitted during the intervening years (but not in a year preceding 2008/09) may fall to be treated for income tax purposes as if it were remitted in the year of return. This is the case if the income in question arose in the year of departure or in any earlier year, where the year in which it arose was a year for which any one of **61.2**(1)–(3) above applied to the individual.

[*ITTOIA 2005, ss 832, 832A, 832B; FA 2008, Sch 7 paras 53, 81, 83*].

Relevant foreign earnings

[61.5] An individual's '*relevant foreign earnings*' for a tax year depend on whether or not he is ordinarily resident in the UK. If he is ordinarily resident, his relevant foreign earnings are his 'chargeable overseas earnings'. If the individual is not ordinarily resident, his relevant foreign earnings are his 'foreign earnings'. For both these expressions and for the charge to tax on chargeable overseas earnings and foreign earnings, see **27.5 EMPLOYMENT INCOME**. [*ITA 2007, s 809Z7(3); FA 2008, Sch 7 paras 1, 81*].

Costs of claiming the remittance basis

[61.6] Where, for any tax year, an individual makes a claim as in **61.2**(1) above for the remittance basis to apply (but not where either **61.2**(2) or (3) above apply to an individual), he loses entitlement to personal reliefs (see **61.7** below) and, if he is a 'long-term UK resident', he is also liable to an additional tax charge of £30,000 (see **61.8** below).

Loss of personal reliefs etc.

[61.7] An individual who claims the remittance basis for any tax year is not entitled to any personal reliefs for that tax year and is not entitled to the annual exemption for capital gains tax. Personal reliefs comprise the personal allowance, married couple's allowance, blind person's allowance and the miscellaneous reliefs at **44.2 LIFE ASSURANCE POLICIES**.

[*ITA 2007, s 809G; FA 2008, Sch 7 paras 1, 81*].

It is possible under the terms of some double tax agreements for non-UK residents to claim the remittance basis and still obtain personal reliefs. This can occur where the individual is resident in both the UK and another territory and, under the provisions of the agreement with that territory, is treated as 'treaty resident' in the other territory. See www.hmrc.gov.uk/cnr/cgt-qa-jan09.pdf.

Charge of £30,000

[61.8] An individual who claims the remittance basis for any tax year incurs an additional tax charge of £30,000 for that year if the following circumstances apply to him:

- he is 18 years of age or over in that tax year; and
- he has been UK resident in at least seven of the nine tax years immediately preceding that tax year. (These preceding years may include years prior to 2008/09.)

The £30,000 charge is made on income and gains not remitted to the UK and is thus in addition to the tax charge on remitted income and gains. The individual can nominate the income and/or gains on which this charge is to be levied, and the remittance basis does not then apply to the nominated amount. For example, the taxpayer could nominate £75,000 of interest on an overseas bank deposit on which tax is then chargeable at 40%, giving a liability of £30,000. The point of nominating is that the nominated income and/or gains are not then charged to tax again if they are remitted in a later year. The nomination is made in the individual's claim within **61.2**(1) above, and the nominated amount must be part (or all) of his 'foreign income and gains' for the year (see **61.3** above). If the nominated amount is insufficient to increase the taxpayer's total income tax and CGT liability by £30,000 (after taking into account all reliefs and deductions due), he is treated for this purpose only as if he had nominated sufficient additional *income* to bring the tax increase up to £30,000; this remains the case even if in reality he has insufficient income to nominate. Income *treated as* nominated does not count as nominated income for the purpose of **61.9** below.

As the £30,000 is a charge to tax (whether it be income tax or CGT), the normal self-assessment payment dates apply. It is also available to cover Gift Aid payments. The Treasury are of the view that it should be recognised as tax for the purposes of double tax agreements. If, however, insufficient income and gains are nominated, the income *treated as* nominated, and the tax on that income, does not qualify for double tax relief as it is not tax on specific income. (Treasury Explanatory Notes to the 2008 Finance Bill).

[ITA 2007, ss 809C, 809H; FA 2008, Sch 7 paras 1, 81; FA 2009, Sch 27 paras 2, 5, 15].

Direct payments to HMRC from untaxed foreign income or gains in settlement of the £30,000 charge are not treated for tax purposes as remittances to the UK (see **61.18** below).

All years of actual residence in the UK count towards the years of residence test, even if for some or all of those years the taxpayer was treated as 'treaty resident' in another territory under a double tax agreement. See www.hmrc.g

ov.uk/cnr/cgt-qa-jan09.pdf. If, for any tax year, split-year treatment applies under ESC A11 upon an individual's becoming or ceasing to be UK resident (see **62.6 RESIDENCE, ORDINARY RESIDENCE AND DOMICILE**), that year still counts in full towards the years of residence test.

Nominated income and gains subsequently remitted

[61.9] For the purpose of applying the exemption from charge of nominated income and gains if later remitted, nominated income and gains are treated as not remitted (even if, in fact, they have been) until all other previously unremitted foreign income and gains have been remitted. In considering the extent to which other previously unremitted foreign income and gains have been remitted, one takes into account income and gains arising in the tax year under review and all other years for 2008/09 onwards for which the remittance basis has applied to the individual (on a claim or otherwise).

'Nominated income and gains' means income and gains actually nominated and does not include income merely treated as nominated (see **61.8** above).

Where nominated income and gains are, in fact, remitted but are to be treated as above as having not been remitted, the following steps determine the income and gains that are to be treated as having been remitted instead.

(i)   Find the amount of nominated income and gains remitted in the tax year (taking account of nominated income and gains for the tax year in question and all earlier tax years). Add this to the amount of other foreign income and gains remitted in the tax year that has arisen in any year for 2008/09 onwards for which the remittance basis has applied to the individual.

(ii)   Next, find the amount (if any) of the individual's foreign income and gains for the year (other than nominated income and gains) that fall within each of the following categories:
   * 'relevant foreign earnings' (see **61.3** above), other than those subject to a foreign tax;
   * 'foreign specific employment income' (see **69.19 SHARE-RELATED EMPLOYMENT INCOME AND EXEMPTIONS**), other than income subject to a foreign tax;
   * 'relevant foreign income' (see **32.2 FOREIGN INCOME**), other than income subject to a foreign tax;
   * foreign chargeable gains, other than gains subject to a foreign tax;
   * 'relevant foreign earnings' subject to a foreign tax;
   * 'foreign specific employment income' subject to a foreign tax;
   * 'relevant foreign income' subject to a foreign tax; and
   * foreign chargeable gains subject to a foreign tax.
   If the tax year is one to which the remittance basis does not apply, ignore this step and step (iii) below.

(iii)   Compare the total in step (i) to each of the amounts in step (ii) in the order in which those amounts are listed. If the first such amount does not exceed the total in step (i), regard the total in step (i) as containing the income and gains in that category. Reduce the total in step (i) by the amount of that income and gains and compare what remains with the next of the amounts in step (ii) and so on.

If the first such amount does exceed the total in step (i), regard the total in step (i) as containing the appropriate proportion of each kind of income and gains in that category; similarly if the amount in any subsequent category exceeds what remains of the amount in step (i).

(iv)   If, after going through all the categories, the total in step (i) is still not fully matched, repeat the process by reference to income and gains of the 'appropriate tax year' that had not yet been remitted (or treated under these provisions as remitted) by the beginning of the tax year mentioned in (i). The *'appropriate tax year'* is the latest of the preceding years (ignoring years before 2008/09) for which the remittance basis applied.

If the tax year in (i) is one to which the remittance basis does not apply, carry out this step instead of steps (ii) and (iii).

(v)   If the total in step (i) is still not fully matched, repeat steps (ii) and (iii) by reference to the next latest of the preceding years for which the remittance basis applied, and so on.

[*ITA 2007, ss 809I, 809J; FA 2008, Sch 7 paras 1, 81*].

Meaning of 'remitted to the UK'

[61.10] Subject to **61.17** below, an individual's income is, or his chargeable gains are, *'remitted to the UK'* in any of circumstances (a)–(c) below.

(a)   Property (which may include money) is brought to, or received or used in, the UK by, or for the benefit of, a 'relevant person' (see **61.11** below) or a service is provided in the UK to, or for the benefit of, a relevant person, and:
  (i)   the property, service or consideration for the service (as the case may be) is (wholly or in part) the income or gains; or
  (ii)   the property, service or consideration derives from the income or gains and, in the case of property or consideration, is property of, or consideration given by, a relevant person; or
  (iii) the income or gains are used outside the UK (directly or indirectly) in respect of a 'relevant debt' (see **61.12** below); or
  (iv)   anything deriving from the income or gains is used as mentioned in (iii) above.
       The references in (ii) and (iv) above to something 'deriving from the income or gains' are references to its so deriving wholly or in part and directly or indirectly.

(b)   'Qualifying property' of a 'gift recipient' (see in both cases **61.13** below):
  (i)   is brought to, or received or used in, the UK, and is enjoyed by a relevant person; or
  (ii)   is consideration for a service that is enjoyed in the UK by a relevant person; or
  (iii) is used outside the UK (directly or indirectly) in respect of a relevant debt.

(c)   Property of a person other than a relevant person (apart from qualifying property of a gift recipient as in (b) above):

   (i)   is brought to, or received or used in, the UK, and is enjoyed by a relevant person; or

   (ii)   is consideration for a service that is enjoyed in the UK by a relevant person; or

   (iii)   is used outside the UK (directly or indirectly) in respect of a relevant debt,

in circumstances where there is a 'connected operation' (see **61.14** below).

In (a)(iii), (b)(iii) and (c)(iii) above, 'used . . . in respect of a relevant debt' includes repayment or partial repayment of a relevant debt, payment of interest on a relevant debt and use as collateral for a relevant debt.

In a case where (b)(i) or (ii) or (c)(i) or (ii) above applies to the importation or use of property, the income or gains are taken to be remitted at the time the property or service is first enjoyed by a relevant person by virtue of that importation or use.

Enjoyment of property or a service by a relevant person is to be disregarded for the above purposes if it is minimal (i.e. the property or service is enjoyed virtually to the entire exclusion of all relevant persons); if the relevant person gives full consideration in money or money's worth for the enjoyment; or if the property or service is enjoyed by relevant persons in the same way (and on the same terms) that it may be enjoyed by the public (or a section of the public).

[ITA 2007, ss 809L(1)–(6)(9)(10), 809N(9), 809O(6); FA 2008, Sch 7 paras 1, 81; FA 2009, Sch 27 paras 6, 15].

In determining whether a remittance has been made in the case of a foreign chargeable gain on a disposal at undervalue (and if so, how much), the amount of the gain is taken to be the gain that would have arisen if the disposal had been at least equal to market value. [ITA 2007, s 809T; FA 2008, Sch 7 paras 1, 81; FA 2009, Sch 27 paras 9, 15].

If income (or a gain) would otherwise be treated as remitted to the UK before the income arises (or the gain accrues), by virtue of anything done in relation to anything regarded as deriving from the income (or gain), the remittance is instead treated as made at the time the income arises (or the gain accrues). [ITA 2007, s 809U; FA 2008, Sch 7 paras 1, 81].

Transitional

In either of the following cases, an individual's relevant foreign income (as in **32.2 FOREIGN INCOME**) is treated as not remitted to the UK on or after 6 April 2008 if it otherwise would be treated as so remitted:

*   if, before 6 April 2008, property (including money) consisting of or deriving from the relevant foreign income was brought to, or received or used in, the UK by, or for the benefit of, a relevant person; and

*   if, before 12 March 2008, property (other than money) consisting of or deriving from the relevant foreign income was acquired by a relevant person.

[FA 2008, Sch 7 para 86(1)–(3)(5)].

Relevant persons

[61.11] The following are *'relevant persons'* for the purposes of **61.10** above and these provisions generally:

(a)   the individual;

(b)   the spouse or civil partner of the individual;

(c)   a child or grandchild (under 18) of any person within (a) and (b) above;

(d)   a close company in which any other person within this definition is a participator;

(e)   (on and after 22 April 2009) a 51% subsidiary of a close company within (d) above;

(f)   a company in which any other person within this definition is a participator and which would be a close company if it were UK resident;

(g)   (on and after 6 April 2010) a 51% subsidiary of a company within (f) above;

(h)   the trustees of a settlement of which any other person within this definition is a beneficiary;

(i)   a body connected with a settlement within (h) above.

For the above purposes, a cohabiting couple are treated as husband and wife or, as the case may be, civil partners; a close company has the meaning given in *CTA 2010, Pt 10 Ch 2* (broadly a company with five or fewer participators); in relation to a settlement that would otherwise have no trustees, a 'trustee' means any person in whom the settled property or its management is for the time being vested; a body is 'connected with' a settlement if the body falls within any of **21.3**(c)–(f) CONNECTED PERSONS as regards the settlement.

The question of whether a person whose property is dealt with as in **61.10**(c) above is a relevant person is to be determined at the time the property is so dealt with.

[ITA 2007, ss 809M, 809O(2); FA 2008, Sch 7 paras 1, 81; FA 2009, Sch 27 paras 7, 15; CTA 2010, Sch 1 para 552; FA 2010, s 33].

Transitional

In relation to an individual's income or chargeable gains for any year before 2008/09, only the individual himself is a relevant person for the purposes of the provisions in **61.10** above (other than the transitional provision). *[FA 2008, Sch 7 paras 86(4)(4A), 87, 88; FA 2009, Sch 27 paras 14, 15].*

Relevant debts

[61.12] For the purposes of **61.10** above, a *'relevant debt'* is a debt that relates (wholly or in part, and directly or indirectly) to property within **61.10**(a); a service within **61.10**(a); property dealt with as in **61.10**(b)(i) or (c)(i); or a service falling within **61.10**(b)(ii) or (c)(ii).

[ITA 2007, s 809L(7)(8); FA 2008, Sch 7 paras 1, 81; FA 2009, Sch 27 paras 6, 15].

Gift recipient and qualifying property

[61.13] For the purposes of **61.10**(b) above, a '*gift recipient*' is a person (other than a relevant person as in **61.11** above) to whom the individual makes a gift of money or property that is (or derives from) income or chargeable gains of the individual. The question of whether a person is a relevant person is determined by reference to the time of the gift; but if a person subsequently becomes a relevant person, he then ceases to be a gift recipient. A disposition of property at less than full consideration is a gift to the extent of the deficit. Property is considered to have been gifted even in a case where the disponor retains an interest in it or a right to benefit from it.

'*Qualifying property*' in **61.10**(b) above, in relation to a gift recipient, means the property gifted or anything that derives from it (as widely defined). It also means any other property if it is dealt with as in **61.10**(b)(i), (ii) or (iii) above by virtue of an operation effected with reference to, or to enable or facilitate, the gift of the property to the gift recipient.

[*ITA 2007, s 809N(1)–(8)(10); FA 2008, Sch 7 paras 1, 81*].

Transitional

In relation to an individual's income or chargeable gains for any year before 2008/09, the initial reference above to a relevant person is to the individual, and the subsequent references are to be disregarded. [*FA 2008, Sch 7 para 87*].

Connected operations

[61.14] A '*connected operation*' in relation to property dealt with as mentioned in any of **61.10**(c)(i)–(iii) above is an operation which is effected with reference to, or to enable or facilitate, a 'qualifying disposition'. A '*qualifying disposition*' is a disposition made by a relevant person (as in **61.11** above) to or for the benefit of the person whose property is dealt with as in **61.10**(c) above, which is a disposition of money or other property that is, or derives from, income or chargeable gains of the individual. There is no qualifying disposition if the disposition represents, or is part of, the giving of full consideration for the fact that the property is so dealt with.

[*ITA 2007, s 809O(1)(3)–(5)(7); FA 2008, Sch 7 paras 1, 81*].

Transitional

In relation to an individual's income or chargeable gains for any year before 2008/09, only the individual is a relevant person for the above purposes. [*FA 2008, Sch 7 para 88*].

Determining the amount remitted to the UK

[61.15] *ITA 2007, s 809P* provides rules to determine the amount remitted by reference to **61.10** above. In the most straightforward case, where the property, service or consideration for a service is the income or chargeable gains, or derives from them, the amount remitted is equal to the amount of the income or gains or (as the case may be) the amount of income or gains from which the property, service or consideration derives. If the income or gains, or anything deriving from them, are used outside the UK in respect of a relevant debt, the amount remitted is equal to the amount of income or gains used, or the amount from which what is used derives. In cases within **61.10**(b) and (c), the amount remitted is in each case equal to an amount of income or gains determined by reference to the definitions in **61.13** and **61.14** above.

In all cases involving a relevant debt, if the debt relates only partly to the property or service in question (see **61.12** above), the amount remitted is limited (if it would otherwise be greater) to the amount the debt would be if it related wholly to the property or service.

On and after 22 April 2009, where the property remitted is part of a set, the amount remitted is an appropriate proportion of the value of the whole set.

In all cases, where the amount remitted, together with amounts previously remitted, would otherwise exceed the amount of the income or gains, the amount remitted is limited to an amount equal to the amount of income or gains.

[*ITA 2007, s 809P; FA 2008, Sch 7 paras 1, 81; FA 2009, Sch 27 paras 8, 15*].

Mixed funds

[61.16] Where money or other property is brought to, or received or used in, the UK by, or for the benefit of, a relevant person or a service is provided in the UK to, or for the benefit of, a relevant person (i.e. the first leg of **61.10**(a) above), the property or the consideration for the service may be, or may derive from, a transfer from a 'mixed fund' (or part of it may), or a transfer from a mixed fund (or something deriving from such a transfer) may be used in respect of a relevant debt (as in **61.10**(a)(iii) above). in such cases, there are rules to determine if the second leg of **61.10**(a) above (i.e. any of **61.10**(a) (i)–(iv)) applies and, if so, to determine the amount remitted.

A '*mixed fund*' is broadly a source that consists partly of amounts of taxable income or gains and partly of amounts that have already been taxed or are not taxable. Its statutory definition is money or other property containing (or deriving from) income or capital of more than one of the following nine categories, or income or capital for more than one tax year:

(a)   employment income (other than income within (b) or (c) below or income subject to a foreign tax);

(b)   'relevant foreign earnings' (see **61.3** above), other than those subject to a foreign tax;

(c)   'foreign specific employment income' (see **69.19 SHARE-RELATED EM- PLOYMENT INCOME AND EXEMPTIONS**), other than income subject to a foreign tax;

(d)   'relevant foreign income' (see **32.2 FOREIGN INCOME**), other than income subject to a foreign tax;

(e)   foreign chargeable gains, other than gains subject to a foreign tax;
(f)   employment income subject to a foreign tax;
(g)   'relevant foreign income' subject to a foreign tax;
(h)   foreign chargeable gains subject to a foreign tax; and
(i)   any income or capital not within any of (a)–(h) above.

For each of categories (a)–(j), find the amount of income and capital for the 'relevant tax year' in the mixed fund immediately before the transfer in question. The *'relevant tax year'* is the tax year in which the transfer takes place. For the purpose of determining the composition of the mixed fund, treat property which derives wholly or in part (and directly or indirectly) from an individual's income or capital for a tax year as consisting of or containing that income or capital. If a debt relating (wholly or in part, and directly or indirectly) to property is at any time satisfied (wholly or in part) by an individual's income or capital for a tax year (or anything deriving from such income or capital), treat the property from that time as consisting of or containing the income or capital if, and to the extent that, it is just and reasonable to do so. If an 'offshore transfer' is made from a mixed fund, it is to be regarded as containing the same proportion of each kind of income or capital as was contained in the fund before the transfer. A transfer is an *'offshore transfer'* if these rules (i.e. the rules in *ITA 2007, s 809Q*) do not apply to it; a transfer is *treated as* an offshore transfer if, and to the extent that, these rules do not apply to it at the end of the tax year in which it is made and will not do so on the best estimate that can reasonably be made at that time. If these rules apply to part only of a transfer, apply the rules in relation to that part before applying the 'offshore transfer' rule to the remaining part.

If the amount in category (a) does not exceed the amount of the transfer in question, regard the transfer as containing the income and gains in that category for the relevant tax year. Reduce the amount of the transfer by the amount in (a) and compare what remains with the amount in category (b). Continue by reference to each category, in the order in which they are listed, until the amount of the transfer is reduced to nil.

If, after going through all the categories, the amount of the transfer is still not fully matched, repeat the process by reference to income and capital of the preceding tax year, and so on until the amount of the transfer is fully matched.

If the amount in category (a) does exceed the amount of the transfer, regard the transfer as containing the appropriate proportion of each kind of income and gains in that category for the relevant tax year; similarly if the amount in subsequent category exceeds what remains of the amount of the transfer.

For the purposes of these rules, nothing is to be regarded as deriving from income or capital within (j) above if it is itself (or if it derives from) income or gains within any of (a)–(h) above.

[*ITA 2007, ss 809Q, 809R; FA 2008, Sch 7 paras 1, 81*].

Transitional

The above rules do not apply for the purposes of determining whether income or chargeable gains for any tax year before 2008/09 are remitted to the UK in 2008/09 or any subsequent year (or of determining the amount of any such income or chargeable gains so remitted). [*FA 2008, Sch 7 para 89*].

Anti-avoidance

If, by reason of an arrangement (as widely defined) a main purpose of which is to secure an income tax advantage or a CGT advantage (both as defined), a mixed fund would otherwise be regarded as containing income or capital within any of (f) to (j) above, the mixed fund should be treated as containing so much of such income or capital as is just and reasonable. [*ITA 2007, s 809S; FA 2008, Sch 7 paras 1, 81; FA 2010, Sch 12 paras 11, 15*].

Transfers made from an offshore account holding only the income or gains relating to a single employment. In practice, from 6 April 2009, and subject to the conditions below, HMRC will accept that, notwithstanding the statutory rules above, individuals who are UK resident but not ordinarily resident may, if they wish, calculate their tax liability by reference to the total amount transferred out of a mixed fund during a tax year, rather than by reference to individual transfers. The statutory rules are then applied to the total amount transferred out of the fund to the UK in the tax year as if it were a single transfer. The conditions are that the duties of a single employment (or office) are performed both inside and outside the UK, that the mixed fund is an account held solely by the employee (but see below) and that the account contains only the income from that employment, which may include income within any of (a), (b), (c) and (f) above, plus other permitted items. Those other permitted items comprise interest arising on the account, gains arising from foreign exchange transactions in respect of the funds in the account and proceeds from, or gains arising on, employee share scheme transactions. (HMRC SP 1/09). Where an account is held in joint names with a spouse or civil partner who has no income or gains of his or her own, except a share in any interest that arises on the account, HMRC has agreed that SP 1/09 can apply (HMRC Internet Statement, 3 March 2010).

Property treated as not remitted to the UK

[61.17] To the extent described at **61.18–61.20** below, money and other property brought into the UK are treated for tax purposes as not remitted to the UK. See also **61.24** below (offshore mortgages).

Payment of the £30,000 charge

[61.18] Direct payments to HMRC from untaxed foreign income or gains in settlement of the £30,000 charge in **61.8** above are not treated for tax purposes as remittances to the UK. This exemption applies only if the £30,000 is paid in respect of the tax due for a tax year for which the remittance basis has been claimed and for which the charge applies. The exemption covers any number of direct payments up to the £30,000 total. If any of the money is repaid by HMRC, for example because the taxpayer withdraws his claim, the exemption is to that extent deemed never to have applied. [*ITA 2007, s 809V; FA 2008, Sch 7 paras 1, 81*].

To qualify for this exemption, the money must be sent direct from an overseas bank account to HMRC by way of a cheque drawn on the overseas bank account or a form of electronic transfer, and not via a UK bank account (Treasury Explanatory Notes to the 2008 Finance Bill).

Consideration for certain services

[61.19] An exemption applies if:

- income or gains would otherwise be regarded as remitted to the UK because of **61.10**(a) above;
- the first leg of **61.10**(a) is met because a service is provided in the UK;
- the second leg of **61.10**(a) is met because **61.10**(a)(i) or (ii) applies to the consideration for that service; and
- both Conditions A and B below are met.

Where this exemption applies, income or gains are treated as not remitted to the UK.

Condition A is that the service provided relates wholly or mainly to property situated outside the UK.

Condition B is that the whole of the consideration for the service is given by way of payments to bank accounts held outside the UK by, or on behalf of, the person providing the service.

This exemption does not apply if the service relates (to any extent) to the provision in the UK of:

- a benefit treated as deriving from the income by virtue of *ITA 2007, s 735* (application of 'transfer of assets abroad' rules to non-UK domiciled individuals to whom the remittance basis applies — see **4.15 ANTI-AVOIDANCE**);or
- a relevant benefit within *TCGA 1992, s 87B* that is treated by virtue of that *section* as deriving from the gains. (That *section* is concerned with the attribution of gains of non-UK resident settlements to non-UK domiciled individuals to whom the remittance basis applies — see Tolley's Capital Gains Tax under Offshore Settlements.)

[*ITA 2007, s 809W; FA 2008, Sch 7 paras 1, 81*].

Condition A would cover, for example, fees paid to a UK bank for managing an individual's overseas investments. It would also cover legal or brokerage fees in respect of offshore assets, such as legal fees on the sale of a foreign house. The term 'wholly or mainly' in Condition A is not statutorily defined, but will be taken to mean more than half (Treasury Explanatory Notes to the 2008 Finance Bill).

Exempt property

[61.20] 'Exempt property' which is brought to, or received or used in, the UK, such that the first leg of **61.10**(a) above applies, is treated as not remitted to the UK.

The following are '*exempt property*' for this purpose:

(a)   property which meets the 'public access rule' (i.e. works of art etc. — see **61.21** below);

(b)   clothing, footwear, jewellery and watches which meet the 'personal use rule' (see **61.22** below); and

(c)   property of any kind if:
    (i)   the 'notional remitted amount' (see **61.23** below) is less than £1,000; or
    (ii)   the property meets the 'repair rule' (see **61.22** below); or
    (iii)   the property meets the 'temporary importation rule' (see **61.22** below).

For these purposes, 'property' does not include money (or specified items equivalent to money). If property ceases to be exempt property at any time after it is brought to, or received or used in, the UK, it is treated as remitted to the UK at that time. Property ceases to be exempt property if it (or part of it) is sold (or otherwise converted into money or specified items equivalent to money) whilst in the UK. Property which is exempt by virtue of one or more of the 'public access rule', the 'personal use rule', the 'temporary importation rule' and the 'repair rule' also ceases to be exempt property if it ceases to meet the rule(s) relied upon whilst in the UK, provided it does not meet any of the remaining rules.

[*ITA 2007, ss 809X, 809Y, 809Z6; FA 2008, Sch 7 paras 1, 81; FA 2009, Sch 27 paras 10, 15*].

Public access rule

[61.21] The *'public access rule'* in **61.20**(a) above allows certain property to be imported into the UK, without giving rise to a tax charge on the remittance basis, if all the conditions set out below are met. The property must be a work of art, a collectors' item or an antique, within the meaning of *Council Directive 2006/112/EC* (and, in particular, *Annex IX* to that *Directive*).

The property must be available for public access (as defined) at an approved museum, gallery or similar establishment or in storage at, or in transit to or from, the establishment (or other commercial premises in the UK used by the establishment for storage) pending or following public access.

Whilst in the UK, the property must meet the above condition for no more than two years (or such longer period as HMRC may in a particular case allow).

The property must attract a 'relevant VAT relief' (for which see *ITA 2007, s 809Z1*).

[*ITA 2007, ss 809Z, 809Z1; FA 2008, Sch 7 paras 1, 81*].

Personal use, repair and temporary importation rules

[61.22] The *'personal use rule'* in **61.20**(b) above is that the clothing, footwear, jewellery or watches are property of a relevant person (see **61.11** above) and are for the personal use of the individual with the income or gains, the spouse or civil partner (or co-habiting partner) of the individual, or a child or grandchild (under 18) of any of the aforementioned. [*ITA 2007, s 809Z2; FA 2008, Sch 7 paras 1, 81*].

The *'repair rule'* in **61.20**(c)(ii) above is that the property must be under repair or restoration at premises in the UK, in storage at the restorers pending or following repair or restoration or in transit between there and a place outside the UK. This rule interacts with the public access rule at **61.21** above in that if these conditions are met for only part of the time the property is in UK the repair rule is nevertheless treated as met provided the property meets the public access rule for the remainder of that time. [*ITA 2007, s 809Z3; FA 2008, Sch 7 paras 1, 81*].

The '*temporary importation rule*' in **61.20**(c)(iii) above is that the property is in the UK for no more than 275 'countable days' (approximately 9 months). The 275-day limit applies cumulatively to all periods of importation. A '*countable day*' is a day on which (or on part of which) the property is in the UK by virtue of its being brought to, or received or used in, the UK such that **61.10**(a) above applies. A day is not a countable day if on any part of that day the property meets the personal use rule or the repair rule or if the notional remitted amount (see **61.23** below) in relation to the property is less than £1,000. A day is also not a countable day if on any part of that day the property meets the public access rule provided other conditions are met. Broadly, the property must meet the public access rule during the whole of the period it is in the UK in which that day falls, or must meet the public access rule and the repair rule (and no other rule) during the whole of that period, or it must be imported under the temporary importation rule prior to a period of public access and then exported after the period of public access. [*ITA 2007, s 809Z4; FA 2008, Sch 7 paras 1, 81*].

Notional remitted amount

[61.23] The '*notional remitted amount*' in **61.20**(c)(i) above is the amount that would be regarded as remitted to the UK if the exemption did not apply. [*ITA 2007, s 809Z5; FA 2008, Sch 7 paras 1, 81; FA 2009, Sch 27 paras 11, 15*].

Offshore mortgages

[61.24] In the circumstances set out below, relevant foreign income of an individual used outside the UK before 6 April 2028 to pay the interest on a debt is treated as not remitted to the UK.

The circumstances are that:

- before 12 March 2008, money was lent to the individual outside the UK for the sole purpose of his acquiring an interest in residential property in the UK; and
- before 6 April 2008, the money was received in the UK and used by the individual to acquire such an interest, and repayment of the debt (or of payments made under a guarantee of that repayment) is secured on the interest in property acquired.

If at any time on or after 12 March 2008, any term on which the loan was made (or any term of the guarantee) is varied or waived, or repayment of the debt (or of payments made under the guarantee) ceases to be secured on the interest in the property, or repayment of any other debt is secured on the same interest(or is guaranteed by the same guarantee), or the interest ceases to be owned by the individual, the exemption does not apply to any relevant foreign income used to pay the interest after that time.

For these purposes, a 'guarantee' includes an indemnity.

Remortgaging

A similar exemption applies to interest on a subsequent loan if:

- before 12 March 2008, money was lent to the individual outside the UK (the subsequent loan) for the sole purpose of his repaying the above-mentioned loan; and
- before 6 April 2008, the money was used by the individual to repay the above-mentioned loan, and repayment of the subsequent loan (or of payments made under a guarantee of that repayment) is secured on the same interest in property as above.

This can apply to a third loan taken out to repay the second loan, and so on, provided all the conditions are met in relation to the loan in question.

[*FA 2008, Sch 7 para 90*].

Remittance basis before 2008/09

[61.25] For years before 2008/09, the remittance basis could be claimed by certain UK residents (see (i) and (ii) below) in respect of 'relevant foreign income' (as in **32.2 FOREIGN INCOME**).

A claim was required for the remittance basis to apply to a person's income for a tax year. For 2005/06 to 2007/08 inclusive, the claim had to be to an officer of HMRC and had to indicate that the person met either of the following conditions:

(i)   he was not domiciled in the UK (see **62.4 RESIDENCE, ORDINARY RESIDENCE AND DOMICILE**); or
(ii)   he was not ordinarily resident in the UK (see **62.7 RESIDENCE, ORDINARY RESIDENCE AND DOMICILE**).

No time limit was specified for making the claim, so by default the deadline is as stipulated in **18.4 CLAIMS**.

The effect of a claim for a tax year was that income tax was charged on the full amount of the sums received in the UK in the tax year in respect of relevant foreign income. It did not matter whether the income arose in the year for which the claim was made or in an earlier year in which the person was UK resident. No charge arose if income for the tax year to which the claim related was remitted in a subsequent year for which no claim was made (but see **61.4** above where the income is remitted in 2008/09 or a subsequent year).

The charge was normally on the actual remittances in respect of the income in the tax year without any deduction (subject to the addition of any foreign tax for which credit is allowable — see **26.9**(a)(i) **DOUBLE TAX RELIEF**). However, where the income was from a trade, profession or vocation carried on outside the UK, the same deductions were allowed as for trades etc. carried on in the UK. See also **61.28** below for relief for delayed remittances.

The remittance basis did not apply for any year before 2008/09 to relevant foreign income arising in the Republic of Ireland. See also **26.4 DOUBLE TAX RELIEF**.

[*ITTOIA 2005, ss 831, 832, Sch 2 para 150; ITEPA 2003, ss 575, 613, 631, 635, 679* (as originally enacted)].

Simon's Taxes. See E1.603.

Case law

[61.26] The following decisions pre-dated the fundamental legislative changes made to the remittance basis for 2008/09 onwards.

A remittance of capital is not taxable as such (unless within the provisions of capital gains tax, see Tolley's Capital Gains Tax) but a taxable remittance may include the proceeds of investments made abroad out of overseas income (*Scottish Provident Institution v Farmer CS 1912, 6 TC 34*). Where the proceeds were of investments made before the taxpayer came to reside in the UK, there was no liability (*Kneen v Martin CA 1934, 19 TC 33*). Similarly, a remittance from a foreign bank into which overseas income had been paid may be assessable, dependent on the circumstances. For this see *Walsh v Randall KB 1940, 23 TC 55* (sterling draft on foreign bank in favour of London hospital received by taxpayer before handing to hospital, held to be remittance) and *Thomson v Moyse HL 1960, 39 TC 291* (dollar cheques on US bank sold to Bank of England held to be remitted) and compare *Carter v Sharon KB 1936, 20 TC 229* (drafts on foreign bank posted abroad to taxpayer's daughter for maintenance, held not to be remittance as, under relevant foreign law, gift to daughter completed on posting of draft). See also *Fellowes-Gordon v CIR CS 1935, 19 TC 683*. In *Harmel v Wright Ch D 1973, 49 TC 149* an amount received via two South African companies, ending as a loan from one of them, was held to be a remittance of South African emoluments within Schedule E, Case III. Where, contrary to the customer's instructions, a bank erroneously remitted untaxed overseas income to him, it was held there was no liability (*Duke of Roxburghe's Exors v CIR CS 1936, 20 TC 711*). In *Grimm v Newman & another CA, [2002] STC 1388* (a negligence case in which the Revenue were not a party), an absolute inter-spousal gift, perfected abroad, of overseas assets subsequently used to purchase a matrimonial home in the UK was held not to be a remittance.

Constructive remittances

[61.27] Income arising abroad to a person ordinarily resident but not domiciled in the UK and which he applied abroad towards the satisfaction (wholly or in part) of:

(a)   a debt (or interest thereon) for money lent to him in the UK; or
(b)   a debt for money lent to him abroad and received in or brought to the UK; or
(c)   a debt incurred to satisfy such debts,

was treated as received by him in the UK at the time when it was so used.

For this purpose, if any of the money lent was used to satisfy a debt, the debt for the money so used was treated as incurred for satisfying that other debt, and a debt incurred to satisfy, wholly or in part, a debt within (c) above was itself treated as falling within (c) above.

In the case of a debt for money lent abroad (within (b) or (c) above), it was immaterial whether the money lent was received in, or brought to, the UK before or after the income was used to satisfy the debt, except that, if the money lent was received in or brought to the UK at a time *after* the income was so used, the income was treated as received in the UK at that later time.

Income hypothecated in any form to the lender so that the amount of a loan debt, or the time of its repayment, depended directly or indirectly on the amount of money or property so available to the lender, was treated as having been applied towards satisfaction of the loan. '*Lender*' includes any person for the time being entitled to repayment.

[*ITTOIA 2005, ss 833, 834; ITEPA 2003, ss 575, 613, 631, 635, 679* (as originally enacted)].

Similar provisions applied to employment income under *ITEPA 2003, ss 33, 34*.

All the above provisions are repealed for 2008/09 onwards, but see now **61.10** above. [*FA 2008, Sch 7 paras 54, 81*].

Simon's Taxes. See E1.604.

Relief for delayed remittances

[61.28] Relief was available in respect of income taxable on the remittance basis in a tax year which arose before that year if it could not have been transferred to the UK before that year because of the laws, or the executive action of the government, of the territory in which it arose or because of the impossibility of obtaining currency there that could be transferred to the UK. A claim could be made for some or all of the remittances to be taxable instead in the tax year in which the income arose.

The claim to relief had to be made within five years after 31 January following the tax year of remittance. Where appropriate, the above provisions apply to the personal representative of the taxpayer as they would have to the taxpayer.

[*ITTOIA 2005, ss 835, 837, Sch 2 para 151; ITEPA 2003, ss 575, 613, 631, 635, 679* (as originally enacted); *ICTA 1988, s 585*].

There were further provisions which treated income from pensions or annuities within **56.2** (b)(e)(i) PENSION INCOME, or an increase in such a pension or annuity, which were granted retrospectively, as arising, for the purpose of the above provisions, in the tax year in respect of which the pension, annuity or increase was paid, if that is earlier than the year in which it was paid. [*ITTOIA 2005, s 836; ICTA 1988, s 585(2)*].

All the above provisions are repealed for 2008/09 onwards. [*FA 2008, Sch 7 paras 54, 81*].

Simon's Taxes. See E1.605.

Key points

[61.29] Points to consider are as follows.

- For the purposes of the residence test, split year treatment applying under ESC A11 to either a year of arrival or departure still counts as a full year in the UK in determining whether the individual has been UK resident for at least seven of the nine preceding tax years. Taxpayers are also treated as UK resident when actually resident but treated as 'treaty resident' elsewhere.

- Where the remittance basis charge applies and the taxpayer has insufficient unremitted income to nominate and arrive at a tax charge of £30,000, he is treated as nominating additional income to make up the £30,000 charge. However, as this additional income does not in reality exist, that portion of the £30,000 remittance basis charge will not be available for double tax relief, nor will an equivalent amount of unremitted income be treated as already taxed when subsequently remitted. The taxpayer thus gets the worst of all worlds in that tax is due but no credit will ever be given in respect of this. Advisers should be aware of this situation during each tax year, and control remittances (increasing unremitted income correspondingly) or elect to pay tax on an arising basis as appropriate.

- Payment of the remittance basis charge direct from an overseas account to HMRC is not treated as a remittance for these purposes, but remitting a sum to a UK bank for onwards payment would be taxed as a remittance of overseas income, thus incurring an additional tax charge.

- Advisers new to this area must appreciate the special meaning of remitted to the UK for these purposes. Remittances as defined go far beyond the simple transfer of money, and include the enjoyment of property and services in the UK which has been paid for from foreign income or gains, including the repayments of debts and the provision of gifts to 'relevant persons'. **61.10** provides a full definition, but see also **61.17** onwards for exceptions and exemptions.

- It will also be clear that it is necessary to keep very detailed records of foreign income arising and remittances made, in addition to the nominated income for each year, in order to track remittances and deemed remittances and arrive at an appropriate tax charge, taking into account the remittance basis charges paid. Where there are mixed funds this becomes even more exacting.

- The remittance basis charge will normally be due twice when acting for a couple (whether married or civil partners) with joint financial arrangements. In this case it is important for the adviser to ascertain whether he is to act for both, or whether one has appointed another adviser. Where this is the case, liaison between the parties will need careful handling, and record keeping becomes even more challenging.

62

Residence, Ordinary Residence and Domicile

Cross-reference. See **50 NON-RESIDENTS** for situations in which the residence, ordinary residence or domicile of an individual may be of relevance for income tax purposes.

Simon's Taxes. See E6.1, E6.301–E6.323.

Introduction

[62.1] UK tax liability may depend on a person's **domicile** (the country or state which is his 'natural home' — see **62.4** below), on whether or not he is **resident** in the UK for tax purposes in a particular tax year (which is primarily a matter of physical presence — see **62.5** below) or, occasionally, on whether or not he is **ordinarily resident** in the UK (see **62.7** below). EU law does not prevent a member State from imposing more onerous fiscal charges on nationals resident in another member State than those imposed on its own resident nationals (*Werner v Finanzamt Aachen-Innenstadt (Case C–112/91)* CJEC, [1996] STC 961).

See generally HMRC Leaflet HMRC6 (Residence, Domicile and the Remittance Basis) (available at www.hmrc.gov.uk/cnr/hmrc6.pdf), to which reference is made throughout this chapter. This replaced Leaflet IR20 with effect from 6 April 2009, though the latter remains available at www.hmrc.gov.uk/pdfs/ir20.pdf in relation to 2008/09 and earlier years.

Residents

[62.2] A person who is resident in the UK is liable to UK tax on all his income and gains, whether from UK or overseas sources, subject to limited categories of **EXEMPT INCOME (30)**.

In certain circumstances, the charge to UK tax is limited to remittances to the UK out of the income or gains. See **61 REMITTANCE BASIS**.

Deductions are made from the amounts assessable as follows.

Seafarers

Employments wholly abroad where the employee is abroad for a qualifying period (as defined) of 365 days or more — a deduction of 100% is made (i.e. complete exemption) from taxable earnings if all relevant conditions are satisfied. See **27.17 EMPLOYMENT INCOME**.

Overseas pensions

A deduction of 10% may be made, as set out in **56.2 PENSION INCOME**.

Non-residents

[62.3] Non-UK residents are liable to UK tax on UK income, including income from property etc. in the UK, income from trades, professions etc. exercised in the UK and on employment income for duties performed in the UK.

See also **30.31 EXEMPT INCOME** and **64.3 SAVINGS AND INVESTMENT INCOME** for the special exemption to non-UK residents in respect of certain government stocks and **24.12 DEDUCTION OF TAX AT SOURCE** for a similar relief in respect of the interest or dividends on certain foreign stocks and securities payable in the UK.

The appropriate double tax agreement should be examined for exemptions and for restrictions on the rates of tax to be borne. Otherwise non-UK residents are chargeable at the full rate and not entitled to personal or other reliefs. Thus a person carrying on a business in the UK but claiming to be non-resident may thereby have his tax allowances reduced or even refused. But see **50.2 NON-RESIDENTS** for reliefs available to certain non-UK residents.

Non-UK residents have no UK income tax liability on overseas income.

Domicile

[62.4] It may be necessary to determine domicile in relation, *inter alia*, to the application of the **REMITTANCE BASIS (61)** to foreign income and chargeable gains. See also **30.30 EXEMPT INCOME** for an exemption for 2008/09 onwards for low-income non-UK domiciled employees working in the UK.

A person may have only one place of domicile at any given time denoting the country or state considered his permanent home. He acquires a **domicile of origin** at birth (normally that of his father). It may be changed to a **domicile of choice** (to be proved by subsequent conduct). If a domicile of choice is established but later abandoned (by actual action, not by intention or declaration only — see *Faye v CIR* below) reversion to domicile of origin is automatic.

Domicile is a highly technical matter and does not necessarily correspond with either residence or nationality (see *Earl of Iveagh v Revenue Commissioners Supreme Court* (IFS) [1930] IR 431, *Fielden v CIR* Ch D 1965, 42 TC 501, and *CIR v Cohen* KB 1937, 21 TC 301). This last case shows how difficult it is to displace a domicile of origin by a domicile of choice, but contrast *In re Lawton* Ch D 1958 37 ATC 216. A new domicile of choice may be acquired whilst continuing to be resident in the domicile of origin, but only if the residence in the domicile of choice is the 'chief residence' (*Plummer v CIR* Ch D 1987, 60 TC 452). See also *In re Wallach* HC 1949, 28 ATC 486, *Faye v CIR* Ch D 1961, 40 TC 103, *Buswell v CIR* CA 1974, 49 TC 334, *Steiner v CIR* CA 1973, 49 TC 13, *CIR v Bullock* CA 1976, 51 TC 522, *In re Furse decd., Furse v CIR* Ch D, [1980] STC 597, *Re Clore decd. (No 2)* Ch D, [1984] STC 609, *Anderson v CIR* (Sp C 147), [1998] SSCD 43, *Mrs F and S2 (personal representatives of F (dec'd)) v CIR* (Sp C 219), [2000] SSCD 1, *Civil Engineer v CIR* (Sp C 299), [2002] SSCD 72, *Moore's Executors v CIR* (Sp C 335), [2002] SSCD 463, *Surveyor v CIR* (Sp C 339), [2002] SSCD 501 and *Gaines-Cooper v HMRC* Ch D 2007, [2008] STC 1665.

In determining domicile for income tax purposes, no action taken at any time in relation to registration as an 'overseas elector', or in voting as such, is taken into account in determining domicile, unless the person whose liability is being determined (whether or not the person whose domicile is in question) wishes it to be taken into account (in which case the domicile determination applies only for the purpose of ascertaining the liability in question). An '*overseas elector*' is broadly a non-UK resident British citizen to whom the parliamentary franchise is extended under *Representation of the People Act 1985, s 1* or *s 3*. [*ITA 2007, s 835B; FA 1996, s 200; TIOPA 2010, Sch 7 paras 74, 77*].

See Leaflet HMRC6, chapter 4 and, for more technical guidance, www.hmrc.gov.uk/cnr/domicile-tier2.pdf.

See **62.5** below for administrative procedures for determination of domicile in certain cases.

Married women

Up to 31 December 1973, a woman automatically acquired the domicile of her husband on marriage. From 1 January 1974 onwards, the domicile of a married woman is to be ascertained 'by reference to the same factors as in the case of any other individual capable of having an independent domicile' except that a woman already married on that date will retain her husband's domicile until it is changed by acquisition or revival of another domicile. [*Domicile and Matrimonial Proceedings Act 1973, ss 1, 17(5)*]. But an American woman who married a husband with UK domicile before 1974 will be treated, for determining her domicile, as if the marriage had taken place in 1974. See Article 4(4) of the US/UK Double Tax Agreement. A **widow** retains her late husband's domicile unless she later acquires a domicile of choice (and see *CIR v Duchess of Portland* Ch D 1981, 54 TC 648).

Minors

The domicile of a minor normally follows that of the person on whom he is legally dependent. Under *Domicile and Matrimonial Proceedings Act 1973, s 3* (which does not extend to Scotland), a person first becomes capable of having an independent domicile when he attains 16 or marries under that age. Under *section 4* of that *Act*, where a child's father and mother are alive but living apart, his domicile is that of his mother if he has his home with her and has no home with his father.

Simon's Taxes. See E6.301–E6.323.

Residence

[62.5] There is relatively little statutory guidance on the determination of the 'residence' of an individual, despite its importance in determining the individual's tax liabilities (see **62.1–62.3** above). It has been held by the courts that residence is a question of fact for the Appeal Tribunal (previously the Appeal Commissioners) to decide on the particular circumstances of each case, and there are a number of important decisions indicative of the courts' views (see below). See also **62.8** below regarding appeals. A person can be resident for a particular tax year in more than one country for tax purposes (or may even be resident in none).

For practical purposes, HMRC's interpretation as set out in Leaflet HMRC6 and other sources referred to below is, subject to appeal, likely to determine the issue in any particular case.

There are three circumstances in which the residence status of an individual is subject to statutory provisions.

(a)   An individual in the UK for some temporary purpose only, and not with the intention of establishing his residence here, is UK resident for any tax year in which he spends 183 days or more (in aggregate) in the UK, and is not resident for any tax year in which spends less than 183 days in the UK. Prior to 5 April 2007, the statute referred to a period of six months rather than 183 days, the latter being introduced in *ITA 2007* (see Change 124 listed in Annex 1 to the Explanatory Notes to *ITA 2007*). The change brought the statutory language into line with HMRC practice. In determining whether the individual is in the UK for some temporary purpose only and not with the intention of establishing his residence here one of the considerations is that an individual is regarded as resident if visits to the UK average 91 days or more per tax year, calculated over a maximum of four years (see Leaflet HMRC6, para 7.6 for method of averaging). Any days which are spent in the UK due to exceptional circumstances beyond the individual's control, for example illness, can be excluded from the calculation (HMRC SP 2/91). The question is determined without regard to any available accommodation in the UK.
Strictly, periods of time in terms of hours are relevant in determining a period of presence in the UK (see *Wilkie v CIR* Ch D 1951, 32 TC 495). But, for 2008/09 onwards, an individual is treated as spending a day in the UK if (and only if) he is in the UK at the end of that day. If, however, an individual arrives in the UK on one day and departs on the next, he is not treated as spending a day in the UK (despite his presence at the end of the day of arrival) if between arrival and departure he does not

engage in activities that are to a substantial extent unrelated to his passage through the UK, i.e. he is merely a passenger in transit. Note that this precludes not only his engaging in activities relating to business or employment but also in many activities of a non-business nature such as spending time with family; the Treasury Explanatory Notes to the 2008 Finance Bill give a number of examples of how this passenger-in-transit test will be applied. Before 6 April 2008, in practice, days of arrival in and departure from the UK were not normally counted as days spent in the UK.

[*ITA 2007, ss 831, 832; ICTA 1988, s 336; FA 2008, s 24(1)–(4)(8); SI 2006 No 1963, Reg 4*].

(b) An individual who is both resident and ordinarily resident (see **62.7** below) in the UK, and who leaves the UK for the purpose only of occasional residence abroad, continues to be UK resident. [*ITA 2007, s 829; ICTA 1988, s 334*]. 'Occasional residence' is not defined, but generally refers to short stays on holiday or business trips (and see *Reed v Clark* Ch D 1985, 58 TC 528).

(c) The residence of an individual working full time in a trade, profession or vocation no part of which is carried on in the UK, or in an office or employment all of the duties of which are performed outside the UK (other than any whose performance is merely incidental to the duties abroad), is determined without regard to any place of abode maintained for his use in the UK. [*ITA 2007, s 830; ICTA 1988, s 335*]. As to whether duties are incidental, see *Robson v Dixon* Ch D 1972, 48 TC 527 (airline pilot employed abroad but occasionally landing in UK where family home maintained, held UK duties more than incidental). See also Leaflet HMRC6, para 10.6. 'Full-time' employment, in an ordinary case involving a standard pattern of hours, requires an individual working hours clearly comparable with those in a typical UK working week. See Leaflet HMRC6, sidenote to para 8.5 for this and for HMRC's interpretation of the requirement in less straightforward cases.

Case law

Resident in Eire making monthly visits to UK as director of British company (having no UK residence, but a permanent one in Eire) held to be resident and ordinarily resident in UK (*Lysaght v CIR* HL 1928, 13 TC 511) (but cf. *CIR v Combe* CS 1932, 17 TC 405). Officer succeeding to Eire estate, intending to return there permanently but prevented by military duties in UK, held on facts to be resident in both countries (*Lord Inchiquin v CIR* CA 1948, 31 TC 125). In *CIR v Brown* KB 1926, 11 TC 292 and *CIR v Zorab* KB 1926, 11 TC 289, however, held that retired Indian civil servants making periodical visits to the UK, but having no business interests here, were not UK resident.

An American holding a lease of a shooting box in Scotland and spending two months there every year (*Cooper v Cadwalader* CES 1904, 5 TC 101), and a merchant usually resident and doing business in Italy but owning house in UK where he resided less than six months (*Lloyd v Sulley* CES 1884, 2 TC 37) were both held to be UK resident.

A Belgian who had at his disposal, for the visits he paid here, a house owned not by him but by a company which he controlled, so that it was in fact available whenever he chose to come, was held to be UK resident (*Loewenstein v De Salis* KB 1926, 10 TC 424). In *Withers v Wynyard* KB 1938, 21 TC 724, however, an actress (after 18 months abroad) performing in UK, and for 3½ months in 1933/34 occupying a leasehold flat (unable to be disposed of and sublet when possible), was held to be non-resident for that year.

Where neither the individual nor spouse physically present in UK during tax year, although children here, the individual was non-resident (*Turnbull v Foster* CES 1904, 6 TC 206). See also *Reed v Clark* Ch D 1985, 58 TC 528, where individual held non-resident for tax year of absence from UK during which continuing trade carried on. If, however, either an individual or spouse, while they are still living together, has established a UK family home, any visit during a tax year, however short, to that home, may render the individual UK resident for that tax year (although cf. *Withers v Wynyard* above).

HMRC practice

Leaflet HMRC6 (to which paragraph numbers in the following text refer) considers the application of the above tests first generally, then in relation to those leaving the UK, then in relation to those coming to the UK.

General

The only occasion when the number of days that an individual is physically present in the UK will determine his UK residence status is when he is physically present in the UK for 183 days or more during a tax year (para 2.2).

Full personal allowances are available for the year UK residence begins or ends (subject, for 2008/09 onwards, to any claim for the REMITTANCE BASIS (**61**)) (para 6.7).

For detailed HMRC procedures in relation to matters concerned with residence, see HMRC Residence Guide Manual.

Leaving the UK

Short trips abroad, e.g. on holiday or business trips, do not alter the residence status of a person who usually lives in the UK (see (b) above) (para 8.1).

An individual (and accompanying spouse) leaving to work abroad 'full-time' (see (c) above) under a contract of employment is treated as non-UK resident provided that both the absence from the UK and the employment cover a complete tax year, and that any interim visits to the UK do not amount to either 183 days or more in any tax year or an average of 91 days or more per tax year (averaged over a maximum of four years (see para 8.3 for method of averaging), and ignoring days spent in the UK for exceptional circumstances beyond the person's control, for example own or family illness). Similar conditions apply to an individual leaving to work abroad full-time in a trade, profession or vocation. These conditions are applied separately in relation to the employee and the accompanying spouse, but must be satisfied by the employee for the concession to be available to the accompanying spouse. See also **62.7** below as regards ordinary residence of the accompanying spouse. (paras 8.4–8.9). See *R (oao Davies and another) v HMRC; R (oao Gaines-Cooper) v HMRC* CA, [2010] STC 860 for discussion of the operation of this rule.

An individual leaving the UK permanently is nevertheless treated as continuing to be UK resident if visits to the UK average 91 days or more per tax year (subject to exceptional circumstances, as above). Some evidence will normally be required in support of a claim to have become non-resident (and not ordinarily resident — see **62.7** below), e.g. steps taken to acquire a permanent home abroad, and, if UK property is retained, a reason consistent with the stated aim of permanent residence abroad. If such evidence is satisfactory, UK residence (and ordinary residence) will be treated as ceasing on the day after departure from the UK. (para 8.2). In *R (oao Davies and another) v HMRC; R (oao Gaines-Cooper) v HMRC* CA, [2010] STC 860, the taxpayer failed to establish non-UK residence under this rule as he had not established 'a distinct break' from his social and family ties in the UK.

See *Barrett v HMRC* (Sp C 639), [2008] SSCD 268 in which the Sp C gave a list of reasons as to why the appellant had not, as he claimed, ceased to be UK resident.

Coming to the UK

UK residence (and ordinary residence, see **62.7** below) will commence on the date of arrival in the UK where an individual whose home has been abroad comes to the UK to live here permanently or intending to stay for three years or more (disregarding holidays or short business trips abroad) (para 7.2). Otherwise, short-term visitors will be treated as resident for a tax year in which they are in the UK for 183 days or more in the year (see (a) above), or from the fifth tax year where in the preceding four tax years regular visits have been made to the UK averaging 91 days or more per tax year (subject to exceptional circumstances, as above). If such visits are clearly intended on arrival in the UK, residence will commence with the first of those four years, and if the decision to make such visits is taken before the start of the fifth year, residence will commence with the year in which the decision was taken. (para 7.5). Longer-term visitors are treated as resident throughout any period for which they come to the UK for a purpose (such as employment) that will mean remaining (apart from holidays or short business trips) for at least two years. This will also apply if accommodation is owned or is acquired or taken on a lease of three years or more in the year of arrival. Otherwise, such visitors will be treated as ordinarily resident from the beginning of the tax year in which such accommodation is acquired or leased. (paras 7.4, 7.7.1–7.7.4).

As regards visits for education, see **62.7** below.

91-day tests

Before 6 April 2008, in counting the days spent in the UK for the purposes of the 91-day tests referred to above (and in **62.7** below), HMRC normally disregarded days of arrival in and departure from the UK. It was suggested by some commentators that the Sp C decision in *Gaines-Cooper v HMRC* (Sp C 568), [2007] SSCD 23 superseded HMRC practice and changed the basis on which the 91-day test was applied. HMRC stated that this was incorrect and that the practice continued as before (HMRC Brief 01/07, 4 January 2007). However, for 2008/09 onwards, the same criteria is applied for the 91-day tests as for the 183-day test in (a) above, i.e. an individual is treated as spending a day in the UK if he is in the UK at the end of that day, but with the same exclusion as in (a) above for passengers in transit (Treasury Explanatory Notes to the 2008 Finance Bill).

Mobile workers

For how HMRC consider the residence and ordinary residence rules apply to individuals who usually live in the UK but make frequent and regular trips abroad in the course of their employment or business (e.g. lorry or coach drivers driving to and from the Continent and those working on cross-Channel transport), see the article in Revenue Tax Bulletin April 2001 pp 836–838. For this purpose individuals 'usually live' in the UK if their home and settled domestic life continue to be there, and trips abroad are 'frequent and regular' where they are made every two or three weeks or more often. Only in exceptional cases are HMRC likely to accept that such workers are other than resident and ordinarily resident in the UK.

Administrative procedures

Individuals who come to the UK to take up employment used to be asked to complete Form P86 to enable their residence status to be considered. This form also used to include a section on domicile so that, in straightforward cases (where, e.g., a person never domiciled in the UK came here only to work and with the intention of leaving the UK when the employment ceases), the two matters could be dealt with together. On leaving the UK, a shortened Form P85 (Form P85(S)) enables any repayment to be claimed in straightforward cases. Otherwise, Form P85 continues to be used. The domicile section of Form P86 was withdrawn with effect from 25 March 2009 (HMRC Brief 17/09, 25 March 2009). The requirement to complete Form P86 itself is withdrawn from 1 June 2010.

As regards individuals who are not regarded as ordinarily resident in the UK on arrival, enquiries as to any change in circumstances now begin only after a complete tax year has elapsed since arrival, although individuals are expected to report any actual changes in their circumstances without delay, whether or not that period has elapsed. (Revenue Press Release 8 September 1994).

Under self-assessment, individuals who regard themselves as not resident, not ordinarily resident or not domiciled in the UK are required to self-certify their status in the self-assessment tax return and to complete the 'non-residence etc.' supplementary pages to the return. HMRC queries on residence status and domicile aspects may be made by way of, or as part of, an enquiry into the self-assessment return or into an initial claim made outside the return (see **63.6 RETURNS, 18.3 CLAIMS**). See Revenue Tax Bulletin June 1997 pp 425–427.

Residence of personal representatives

Where at least one of the personal representatives of a deceased person is non-UK resident and at least one is UK resident, then provided that the deceased was resident, ordinarily resident or domiciled in the UK at the time of his death, the non-UK resident personal representative(s) is (are) treated as UK resident for income tax purposes. Otherwise, the UK resident personal representative(s) is (are) treated as not resident in the UK. [*ITA 2007, s 834; FA 1989, s 111*].

As regards the residence of **trustees**, see **68.5** SETTLEMENTS.

Simon's Taxes. See C4.104, E6.101–E6.113, E6.120–E6.124.

Split-year treatment

[62.6] Strictly, residence status applies only by reference to whole tax years. By concession, however, an individual coming to the UK to take up permanent residence or to stay for at least two years, or leaving the UK to live abroad permanently (or for at least three years), is treated as UK resident only from the date of arrival or up to and including the date of departure, tax liabilities which are affected by residence status being calculated on the basis of the period of residence. In either case, HMRC must be satisfied that the person was not ordinarily resident in the UK (see **62.7** below) prior to arrival or on departure. Similarly, subject to the further conditions as described in **62.5** above in relation to leaving the UK, an individual (and accompanying spouse) going abroad under a contract of employment will be so treated only up to and including the date of departure and from the date of return to the UK. The provisions limiting the income chargeable on non-residents (see **50.3** NON-RESIDENTS) do not apply to the non-resident part of a split year. (Leaflet HMRC6, para 2.4; HMRC ESCs A11 and A78).

There has been uncertainty in the past over whether HMRC regards ESC A11 as applying to income within *ITEPA 2003, Pt 7* (security-related employment income — see **69** SHARE-RELATED EMPLOYMENT INCOME AND EXEMPTIONS). In an online statement on 17 July 2008 (www.hmrc.gov.uk/esc/esc-a11.htm), HMRC announced that, whilst they had previously been of the view that the ESC does not apply to such income in the year of arrival in the UK, they will treat it as applying for open years and until further notice. Earlier years which are settled will not be reopened, whether ESC A11 has been applied to such income or not. With regard to the year of departure from the UK, ESC A11 has always been regarded as not applicable where the charge to tax is within **69.11** SHARE-RELATED EMPLOYMENT INCOME AND EXEMPTIONS (shares acquired for less than market value). As regards other chargeable income under *ITEPA 2003, Pt 7*, HMRC will treat the concession as applying in the year of departure for open years and until further notice. Earlier years which are settled will not be reopened, whether ESC A11 has been applied to such income or not. As regards both the year of arrival and the year of departure, HMRC reserve the right to depart from their stated position in cases of tax avoidance. (In certain cases, a charge to tax can arise where securities are acquired by exercise of an option granted overseas and this remains the case, as explained in the HMRC statement.)

Earnings from overseas employment

If an individual leaves the UK and becomes non-UK resident from the day following departure, he is not charged UK tax on earnings from an employment carried on wholly abroad which arise after his departure. Similarly, if an individual comes to the UK and becomes UK-resident from the date of arrival, he is not charged UK tax on earnings from an employment carried on wholly abroad which arise before his arrival. If an individual is paid for a period of leave spent in the UK following work overseas, HMRC treat this as arising during the leave period to which it relates, even if the individual's entitlement to it was built up over a period of employment carried on wholly abroad. (Leaflet HMRC6, para 10.7).

Overseas investment income

Before 6 April 2009, if an individual left the UK and became non-UK resident from the day following departure, HMRC applied the following rules in practice.

(a)   Where overseas investment income was chargeable *other than* on the
        REMITTANCE BASIS (**61**), the charge for the year in which permanent
        residence ceases was on the lesser of:
        (i)   income arising between 6 April in that year and the date of
                departure; and
        (ii)   the proportion of the income otherwise chargeable for the year
                which corresponded to the period of UK residence in that year
                (Leaflet IR 20, para 6.15).
(b)   Where overseas investment income was chargeable on the remittance
        basis, (a) above applied with the substitution of 'remitted' for 'arising'
        (Leaflet IR 20, para 6.16).

If an individual came to the UK and became UK resident from the date of arrival, HMRC applied the following rules in practice.

(A)   Where overseas investment income was chargeable other than on the
        remittance basis, no tax charge is made in respect of a source of
        overseas investment income ceasing before the date of arrival in the UK
        (Leaflet IR 20, para 6.19). Before 2007/08, this applied equally where
        untaxed overseas investment income was chargeable on the remittance
        basis, but for 2008/09 tax was chargeable on income remitted from any
        such source in existence on or after 5 April 2007 (Leaflet IR 20,
        para 6.20).
(B)   Where untaxed overseas investment income was chargeable *other than*
        on the remittance basis:
        (i)   if the source ceased in the period between arrival and the end of
                the tax year of arrival, tax would only be charged on the income
                arising in that period;
        (ii)   if the source ceased in the tax year following that of arrival, the
                tax charge for the year of arrival would be on a proportion of the
                income for the year of arrival. The proportion was that which
                corresponded to the period of UK residence in the year of arrival.
                For the following year, the tax charge would be on the income
                arising during that year to the date the source ceased;
        (iii)   if income from a continuing source first arose in the tax year of
                arrival but before arrival, the tax charge for the year of arrival
                was restricted to the same proportion as in (ii) above of the
                income for that year (Leaflet IR 20, para 6.19).

(C)   Where untaxed overseas investment income was chargeable on the remittance basis:

    (i)   if the source ceased in the period between arrival and the end of the tax year of arrival, tax would only be charged on the lesser of remittances in the tax year and income arising between arrival and cessation;

    (ii)   if the source ceased in the tax year following that of arrival, the charge for the year of arrival was on the lesser of (I) remittances in that year and (II) a proportion (as in (B)(ii) above) of the income arising in that year. The sum of the chargeable amounts for the year of arrival and the following year was then restricted to the sum of the amount arrived at under (II) and the income arising in the year following that of arrival up to the date the source ceased (Leaflet IR 20, para 6.20).

For 2009/10 onwards the above practices do not appear in Leaflet HMRC6 and are presumed to have been withdrawn. Applying ESC A11 above, liability for the year of departure is on untaxed overseas investment income arising (or, where applicable, remitted) up to the date of departure (Leaflet HMRC6, paras 10.14.2–10.14.4), with comparable rules for the year of arrival (Leaflet HMRC6, para 10.14.1).

Trading income etc.

For the effect of a change of residence on a trade, profession or vocation carried on by an individual wholly or partly outside the UK, see **73.16 TRADING INCOME.**

Ordinary residence

[62.7] The term 'ordinary residence' is not defined in the *Taxes Acts*. See below for the case law on its interpretation. Broadly, it denotes greater permanence than the term 'residence' (see **62.5** above), and is equivalent to habitual residence; if an individual is resident year after year, he is ordinarily resident. An individual may be resident in the UK under the 183-day rule (see **62.5**(a) above) without becoming ordinarily resident. Equally, he may be ordinarily resident without being resident in a particular year, e.g. because he usually lives in the UK but is absent on an extended holiday throughout a tax year. (Leaflet HMRC6, para 1.5.15).

An individual will be treated as ordinarily resident in the UK if he visits the UK regularly and his visits average 91 days or more per tax year (ignoring days spent in the UK for exceptional circumstances beyond his control, for example his own or family illness). Ordinary residence will commence from 6 April in the tax year of first arrival if the intention to make such visits to the UK for at least four tax years is clear on that first visit, or from 6 April in the fifth tax year after four years of such visits (unless the decision to make regular visits was made in an earlier tax year, in which case it applies from 6 April in that earlier year). (Leaflet HMRC6 paras 3.2, 7.5, 7.6).

See **62.5** above for administrative procedures in certain cases.

Longer-term visitors — commencement of ordinary residence

If it is clear on arrival in the UK that the intention is to stay for at least three years (disregarding holidays and short business trips abroad), ordinary residence commences on arrival. An individual coming to the UK, but not intending to stay more than three years (and not buying or leasing for three years or more accommodation for use in the UK), is treated as ordinarily resident from the beginning of the tax year in which falls the third anniversary of arrival. (This is according to Leaflet HMRC6, but SP 17/91 says 'from the beginning of the tax year after the third anniversary of arrival'.) If, before the beginning of that tax year, either there is a change in the individuals' intention (i.e. to an intention to stay in the UK for three years or more in all) or accommodation for use in the UK is bought (or leased for three years or more), ordinary residence is treated as commencing at the beginning of the tax year in which either of those events happens. If an individual is treated as ordinarily resident solely because he has accommodation in the UK and he disposes of the accommodation and leaves the UK within three years of arrival, he will be treated as not ordinarily resident for the duration of his stay. (HMRC SP 17/91 and Leaflet HMRC6, paras 7.7–7.7.4).

Education

A student who comes to the UK for a period of study or education and will be in the UK for less than four years will be treated as not ordinarily resident providing (i) he does not own or buy (or lease for three years or more) accommodation in the UK, and (ii) he will not, following his departure from the UK, be returning regularly for visits averaging 91 days or more per tax year. (Leaflet HMRC6, para 7.3).

91-day tests

See **62.5** above.

Mobile workers

See **62.5** above.

Relevant case law

In *Reid v CIR* SC 1926, 10 TC 673, British subject was held '*ordinarily resident*' in the UK although no fixed residence either in the UK or abroad and regularly absent abroad 8¹/₂ months every year. But she had here an address, family ties, banking account and furniture stored.

Levene v CIR HL 1928, 13 TC 486 was decided similarly. (British subject abroad for health reasons since 1918, no fixed residence in the UK since (or abroad till 1925), but having ties with the UK and in the 'usual ordering of his life', making habitual visits to the UK 20 weeks yearly for definite purposes.) The judgments in this case interpreted the meaning of 'ordinarily resident' by the following phrases: 'habitually resident', 'residence in a place with some degree of continuity', and 'according to the way a man's life is usually ordered'. In *Peel v CIR* CS 1927, 13 TC 443, although appellant had his business and house in Egypt, he was held ordinarily resident in the UK because he also had a house there, and spent an average of 139 days of each year in the UK.

In *Kinloch v CIR* KB 1929, 14 TC 736, a widow living mostly abroad with a son at school in the UK, who had won an appeal in previous years but continued regular annual visits, was held to be resident and ordinarily resident.

In *Elmhirst v CIR* KB 1937, 21 TC 381 appellant held on facts to have been ordinarily resident although denying any intention at the time to become so. And see *Miesegaes v CIR* CA 1957, 37 TC 493 (minor at school in the UK for five years, spending the occasional vacation with his father in Switzerland, held ordinarily resident). See also cases under **62.5** above.

In *R v Barnet London Borough Council (ex p Nilish Shah)* HL 1982, [1983] 1 AER 226 (a non-tax case), the words 'ordinarily resident' were held to mean 'that the person must be habitually and normally resident here, apart from temporary or occasional absence of long or short duration'.

In *Shepherd v HMRC*, Ch D, [2006] STC 1821, an airline pilot born and domiciled in the UK, and previously habitually resident in the UK, had during 1999/2000 spent 80 days in the UK, 77 days in Cyprus, 180 days flying in the course of his employment, and 28 days holidaying elsewhere. Whilst in the UK, he had stayed in the house which he shared with his wife. The Sp C held that the appellant's absences from the UK were temporary absences. The appellant was held to be resident and ordinarily resident in the UK for 1999/2000.

In *HMRC v Grace* Ch D 2008, [2009] STC 213, a South Africa-born airline pilot (G) moved to the UK in 1986 and began to work for a British airline, purchasing a house near Gatwick Airport. In 1997 he bought a house in Cape Town. He continued to work for a British airline and to own the house near Gatwick, where he stayed for about two or three days before and after long-haul flights to and from the UK. The Inland Revenue issued a determination that he had continued to be resident and ordinarily resident in the UK from 1997/98 to 2002/03 inclusive. On appeal, the Sp C found that G was neither resident nor ordinarily resident in the UK during that period and visited the UK 'for temporary and occasional purposes only'. The decision was reversed by the Ch D on appeal by HMRC: the recurring presence of the taxpayer in the UK in order to fulfil duties under a permanent (or at least indefinite) contract of employment could not be described as casual or transitory and thus was not for a temporary purpose. On the facts the only possible conclusion was that the taxpayer was resident in the UK. The case has, however, been remitted to the First Tier Tribunal (Tax Chamber) for reconsideration (CA, [2009] STC 2707).

Simon's Taxes. See E6.101–E6.109, E6.114–E6.124.

Claims and appeals

[62.8] Claims for the special reliefs referred to at **62.3** above are made to the Commissioners for HMRC.

If, on an appeal in connection with any claim, the issues arising include any question of residence, ordinary residence or domicile, the normal time limit of 30 days in which to appeal is extended to three months. [*TMA 1970, Sch 1A para 9(2)(b)*]. Other disputes regarding residence are settled by way of appeal against the relevant assessment in the normal way.

63

Returns

Cross-reference. See **55.2–55.13** PENALTIES as regards duty to notify chargeability to tax and penalties for late or incorrect returns. See also generally **65** SELF-ASSESSMENT.

Simon's Taxes. See A4.1, A6.4, E1.202A–E1.223.

Introduction

[63.1] HMRC have considerable powers to obtain information and these are generally exercised initially by the requirement to complete and submit various returns, with PENALTIES (**55**) for non-compliance, omissions or incorrect statements. Explanatory notes are usually issued with the returns. See **63.23** below as regards reasonable excuse for failure to comply with any such requirement.

Annual returns of income and chargeable gains

[63.2] For the purposes of establishing a person's income, chargeable gains and net income tax liability, an officer of HMRC may by notice require that person to deliver a return. See **55.5 PENALTIES** as regards failure to deliver the return on time. The return must contain such information and be accompanied by such accounts, statements, documents and other records as may reasonably be required. The return must include a declaration that, to the best of the knowledge of the person making it, it is complete and correct. The information, accounts and statements required by the notice may differ in relation to different periods, or different sources of income, or different descriptions of person.

As regards returns for 2007/08 and subsequent years, the deadline for delivering the completed return is determined as follows.

• If the return is an electronic return, it must be delivered to HMRC on or before **31 January** following the tax year to which it relates or, if later, within three months beginning with the date of the notice.
• If the return is a non-electronic return, it must be delivered to HMRC on or before **31 October** following the tax year to which it relates or, if later, within three months beginning with the date of the notice.

The question of whether a return is electronic or not depends on the method of delivery. HMRC have power to prescribe what constitutes an electronic return. Broadly, it will be a return that is capable of passing through HMRC's electronic (online) gateway; all other returns will be non-electronic returns. It is recognised that there are small categories of people for whom the facility to file online is not yet available; for those categories, HMRC can for the time being use pre-existing powers to extend the deadline to 31 January for paper returns. (Treasury Explanatory Notes to the 2007 Finance Bill).

[*TMA 1970, ss 8, 12; FA 2007, ss 88, 92; FA 2008, s 34, Sch 12 para 8; CTA 2009, Sch 1 para 296; SI 2009 No 2035, Sch para 2*].

Similar provisions apply in relation to returns by trustees, by reference to any 'relevant trustee' (see **65.11 SELF-ASSESSMENT**). [*TMA 1970, ss 8A, 12; FA 2007, ss 89, 92; FA 2008, s 34, Sch 12 para 9; CTA 2009, Sch 1 para 296; SI 2009 No 2035, Sch para 2*].

See **63.13** below as regards partnership returns.

HMRC will, on request, issue a return before the end of the tax year:

(a) in which the taxpayer dies (or administration of the estate is completed), to the personal representatives of the deceased; or
(b) in which a trust is wound up, to the trustees.

(Revenue Press Release 4 April 1996).

Under current criteria, fewer taxpayers (including higher rate taxpayers) whose affairs can be adequately dealt with using the PAYE system are asked to complete a return, though they may choose to do so if they wish. There is also a Short Tax Return (STR) for those with relatively straightforward tax affairs which can be issued by HMRC as an alternative to the standard self-assessment return. See Guidelines for Individuals completing Tax Returns at w ww.hmrc.gov.uk/sa/guidelines.htm and at www.hmrc.gov.uk/sa/guidelines-sa-returns.htm, guidance on the Short Tax Return at www.hmrc.gov.uk/sa/shortt axreturn.htm and Revenue Tax Bulletin April 2005 pp 1187–1189.

Persons in receipt of taxable income belonging to others

Returns may also be required from any person who, in whatever capacity, receives money or value etc. belonging to another person who is chargeable to income tax in respect thereof, or could be so chargeable if resident in UK and not an incapacitated person (although information may not be sought in relation to tax years ending more than three years before the date of the notice). [*TMA 1970, s 13*]. This applies whether a person is in receipt of chargeable profits or gains of another or of gross receipts representing an element in the determination of such profits or gains (*Fawcett v Special Commrs and Lancaster Farmers' Auction Mart Co Ltd* CA 1997, 69 TC 279).

Provisional figures

A return containing a provisional figure will be accepted provided that the figure is reasonable, taking account of all available information, and is clearly identified as such. An explanation should be given as to why the final figure is not available, all reasonable steps having been taken to obtain it, and when it is expected to be available (at which time it should be notified without unreasonable delay). The absence of such explanation and expected date will influence HMRC in selecting returns for enquiry (see **63.6** below). Pressures of work and complexity of tax affairs are not regarded as acceptable explanations. If the final figure is not provided by the expected date HMRC will take appropriate action to obtain it, which may mean opening an enquiry. See HMRC Tax Return Guide, Revenue Tax Bulletins October 1998 pp 593–596, December 1999 p 705, June 2001 p 848 and February 2002 p 916, and Revenue 'Working Together' Bulletin July 2000 p 5. Note that a provisional figure is different in concept to an estimate that is not intended to be superseded by a more accurate figure. See also **55.7 PENALTIES**.

Where the replacement of a provisional figure by a final figure leads to a *decrease* in the self-assessment, and the time limit for making amendments (see **63.10** below) has passed, the amendment may be made by way of claim for recovery of tax on or after 1 April 2010 (see **18.7 CLAIMS**) or by way of error or mistake relief claim before that date (see **18.8 CLAIMS**) where the conditions for such relief are otherwise met. Where such replacement leads to an *increase* in the self-assessment, a discovery assessment (see **6.6 ASSESSMENTS**) may be made to collect the additional tax due. (Revenue Tax Bulletin December 2000 p 817).

Rounding

As regards the use of pence in returns, see Revenue Tax Bulletin October 1997 pp 470, 471. Broadly, income (or aggregate income) figures may be rounded down and tax credits and deductions (or aggregate figures) rounded up.

Accounts

Business accounts are not generally required with the return. Instead, the taxpayer must complete the self-employment supplementary pages to the return, of which there are now full and short versions (to be used according to various criteria such as turnover and complexity). See also **73.17 TRADING INCOME**. See **6.6 ASSESSMENTS** re the option of submitting accounts (in addition to completing the supplementary pages) to possibly reduce the risk of a discovery assessment. Accounts should otherwise be retained in case of enquiry (see **63.6** below). (Revenue Press Release 31 May 1996, Tax Bulletins June 1996 pp 313–315, June 1997 p 436 and HMRC Income Tax Self-Assessment: The Legal Framework Manual SALF203, paras 2.18, 2.19).

Tax equalisation

For details of special instructions on practical measures to make the completion of the Employment Pages of returns more straightforward for foreign nationals working in the UK who have made tax equalisation arrangements with their employer, see Revenue Tax Bulletin October 1997 pp 467?469 and June 1998 p 551. (See also Help Sheet HS212 issued with the Employment Pages of the return, which reflects these instructions.) Interim tax payments (see **65.5 SELF-ASSESSMENT**) made by an employer on any employee's behalf, as part of tax equalisation arrangements where full in-year gross up is used, should not figure in the employment pages of the employee's self-assessment tax return (see Revenue Tax Bulletin June 1998 p 551). See **53.44 PAY AS YOU EARN** as regards modified PAYE procedures for tax equalised employees.

Signature of returns etc.

HMRC will accept returns signed by an attorney acting under a general or enduring power where the taxpayer is physically unable to sign (and not merely unavailable to do so). The attorney must have full knowledge of the taxpayer's affairs, and provide the original power or a certified copy when such a return is first made. In cases of mental incapacity, the signature of an attorney appointed under an enduring power registered with the Court of Protection (or of a receiver or committee appointed by that Court) will be accepted. Similar requirements apply to the signature of claims on behalf of physically or mentally incapacitated taxpayers, and to other documents. (HMRC SP A13 as revised and Revenue Tax Bulletin February 1993 p 51). Although this practice pre-dates self-assessment, the Inland Revenue published further information in their Tax Bulletin, which confirms that the only exceptions to the personal signature requirement are where, due to his age, physical infirmity or mental incapacity, the taxpayer is unable to cope adequately with the management of his affairs or where his general health might suffer if he were troubled for a personal signature. In all other cases, HMRC expect the return to be signed personally and will reject the return as unsatisfactory, and send it back to whoever submitted it (taxpayer or agent), if it is not (see also **55.7 PENALTIES**). In the case of a return submitted online, the taxpayer's personal authentication (password and User ID) takes the place of his signature. (Revenue Tax Bulletin June 2001 pp 847, 848).

Substitute return forms

The Inland Revenue issued a Statement of Practice (HMRC SP 5/87, 15 June 1987) concerning the acceptability of facsimile and photocopied tax returns. Whenever such a substitute form is used, it is important to ensure that it bears the correct taxpayer's reference.

Facsimiles must satisfactorily present to the taxpayer the information which HMRC have determined shall be before him when he signs the declaration that the return is correct and complete to the best of his knowledge. They should be readily recognisable as a return when received by HMRC, and the entries of taxpayers' details should be distinguishable from the background text. Approval must be obtained from HMRC, Corporate Communications Office, Room 9/3A, 9th Floor, NW Wing, Bush House, London WC2B 4PP before a facsimile return is used, and the facsimile must bear an agreed unique imprint for identification purposes.

Photocopies must bear the actual, not photocopied, signature of the relevant person. They are acceptable provided that they are identical (except as regards use of colour) to the official form. Where double-sided copies are not available, it is sufficient that all pages are present and attached in the correct order. Although the copying of official forms is in strictness a breach of HMSO copyright, action will be taken only where forms are copied on a large scale for commercial gain.

Online filing

Agents are authorised to file individual clients' personal tax returns online, subject to conditions as to authorisation of the agent by the client, authentication of the information by the client and use of HMRC-approved software. (Revenue Directions under *SI 2000 No 945, Reg 3*, 21 August 2001). For online filing and payment generally, see Revenue Tax Bulletin June 2000 pp 757, 758, and see www.hmrc.gov.uk/online/index.htm.

Simon's Taxes. See **A4.105–A4.115, A4.165–A4.171, E1.210–E1.212, E1.220, E1.221.**

Self-assessments

[63.3] Every return under *TMA 1970, s 8* or *s 8A* (see **63.2** above) must include, subject to the exception below, an assessment (a self-assessment) of the amounts in which, based on the information in the return and taking into account any reliefs and allowances claimed therein, the person making the return is chargeable to income tax and capital gains tax for the tax year and of his net income tax liability for the year, taking into account tax deducted at source and tax credits on dividends.

The tax to be self-assessed does not include any chargeable on the scheme administrator of a registered pension scheme (see **57.2 PENSION PROVISION**) or the responsible person in relation to an employer-financed retirement benefits scheme (see **57.27 PENSION PROVISION**).

A person need not comply with this requirement if he makes and delivers his return on or before 31 October following the tax year to which the return relates or, if later, within two months beginning with the date of the notice to deliver the return. This deadline is of no significance where returns are filed online (see **63.2** above) as the tax due is automatically computed during the filing process. In the event of a person making no self-assessment, an officer of HMRC *must* make the assessment on his behalf, based on the information in the return, and send the person a copy. Such assessments are treated as self-assessments by the person making the return and as included in the return.

A self-assessment must not show as repayable any notional tax treated as deducted from certain income deemed to have been received after deduction of tax, for example stock dividends.

[*TMA 1970, s 9(1)–(3A); FA 2007, ss 91(1), 92; FA 2008, s 34, Sch 12 para 10*].

HMRC need not give notice to deliver a return under **63.1** above, and thus a self-assessment will not be required, in cases where tax deducted under PAY AS YOU EARN (**53**) equates to the total tax liability for the year. See, however, **53.1** PAY AS YOU EARN for the taxpayer's right to request that a return be issued to him.

Taxpayers with employment income who wish to have a liability of less than £2,000 coded out through PAY AS YOU EARN (**53**) must file their return by an earlier date than the 31 January deadline at **63.2** RETURNS. That date is 31 October (following the tax year) if the return is filed manually and 30 December if it is filed online (see **63.2** RETURNS). A 2009/10 underpayment, for example, will be coded out for 2011/12. (HMRC Income Tax Self-Assessment: The Legal Framework Manual SALF204, para 2.33; Revenue Tax Bulletin June 1996 p 315; Revenue 'Working Together' Bulletin February 2001 p 2; Revenue Press Release 23 September 2002). Coding out of an underpayment for a tax year has the consequential effect of reducing any payments on account (see **65.5** below) due for the following tax year.

Simon's Taxes. See **E1.204, E1.230**.

Amendments of returns other than where enquiries made

[63.4] At any time within twelve months after the 'filing date', a person may by notice to an officer of HMRC amend his return. It should, however, be noted that amendment of a return does not preclude penalty action by HMRC where there is evidence that the taxpayer has acted fraudulently or negligently (see Revenue Tax Bulletin October 1998 p 597). For this purpose, and regardless of whether or not the return is filed electronically, the '*filing date*' is regarded as 31 January following the tax year to which the return relates, except that, if later, it is the last day of the period of three months beginning with the date of the notice requiring the return.

At any time within nine months after the delivery of a person's return, an officer of HMRC may by notice to that person amend his return to correct obvious errors and omissions (whether of principle, arithmetical or otherwise). From 1 April 2010, an officer may also correct anything else in the return that he has reason to believe is incorrect in the light of information available to him. Where a correction is required in consequence of an amendment by the taxpayer as above, the nine-month period begins immediately after the date of the taxpayer's amendment. The taxpayer has the right to reject an officer's correction, by notice within 30 days beginning with the date of the notice of correction. In practice HMRC will reverse a correction regardless of this 30-day limit, unless they are no longer empowered to do so, i.e. if all deadlines for corrections and amendments (by HMRC or taxpayer) have passed and the HMRC enquiry window (see **63.6** below) has closed. (Revenue Tax Bulletin June 2001 pp 850, 851).

[*TMA 1970, s 9(4)(6), s 9ZA, s 9ZB; FA 2007, s 91(2), s 92; FA 2008, s 119(1)(13); SI 2009 No 405*].

HMRC have published online a useful table illustrating enquiry and amendment windows in a number of scenarios (see www.hmrc.gov.uk/sa/enq-amen d-windows.htm).

Individuals whose tax office is served by a Contact Centre may notify certain amendments by telephone (HMRC SP 1/10, 23 April 2010 (superseding SP 1/05). See also **18.5** CLAIMS. It is HMRC policy to itself make increasing use of the telephone to resolve minor queries arising in connection with completed returns (Revenue Tax Bulletin February 2004 p 1080).

Otherwise, amendments may be made in the form of a letter, an amended return form, an extra supplementary page or an amended supplementary page. HMRC will normally accept an amendment to a return or self-assessment whether notified by the taxpayer or by an agent authorised to act on the taxpayer's behalf, but it must be supplied in writing. (HMRC Working Together' Bulletin September 2007 p 4).

See **63.10** below for amendments to returns where HMRC make enquiries into the return.

Simon's Taxes. See E1.213, E1.214.

Record-keeping

[63.5] Any person who may be required to make and deliver a return under **63.1** above (personal and trustee's returns) or **63.13** below (partnership returns) for a tax year or other period is statutorily required to keep all necessary records and to preserve them until the end of the 'relevant day'. The *'relevant day'* is normally:

(a) in the case of a person carrying on a trade (including, for these purposes, any letting of property), profession or business alone or in partnership, the fifth anniversary of 31 January following the tax year or, for partnership returns, the sixth anniversary of the end of the period covered by the return; and

(b) otherwise, the first anniversary of 31 January following the tax year,

or, in either case, from 1 April 2009, such earlier day as the Commissioners for HMRC may specify in writing.

Where, as is normal, notice to deliver the return is given before the day in whichever is the applicable of (a) or (b) above, the *'relevant day'* is the *later* of that day and whichever of the following applies:

(i)   where HMRC enquiries are made into the return, the day on which the enquiries are statutorily completed (see **63.9** below);

(ii)   where no such enquiries are made, the day on which HMRC no longer have power to enquire (see **63.6** below).

Where notice to deliver the return is given *after* the day in whichever is the applicable of (a) and (b) above, (i) and (ii) above still apply to determine the relevant day but only in relation to such records as the taxpayer has in his possession at the time the notice is given.

In the case of a person within (a) above, the records in question include records concerning business receipts and expenditure and, in the case of a trade involving dealing in goods, all sales and purchases of goods. All supporting documents (including accounts, books, deeds, contracts, vouchers and receipts) relating to such items must also be preserved.

Generally, copies of documents may be preserved instead of the originals. (See Revenue Tax Bulletin February 1996 p 283 as regards the use of optical imaging to preserve records.) Exceptions to this are vouchers, certificates etc. which show tax credits or deductions at source of UK or foreign tax, e.g. dividend vouchers, interest vouchers (including those issued by banks and building societies) and evidence of tax deducted from payments to sub-contractors under the CONSTRUCTION INDUSTRY SCHEME (**22**), which must be preserved in their original form.

The maximum penalty for non-compliance in relation to any tax year is £3,000. This penalty does not apply where the failure relates to records which might have been requisite only for the purposes of claims, elections or notices which are *not* included in the return (but see **18.3** CLAIMS for the requirement as regards records relating to such claims etc. and the penalty for non-compliance), or to vouchers, certificates etc. showing UK tax credits or deductions at source (e.g. dividend vouchers and interest certificates) where an HMRC officer is satisfied that other documentary evidence supplied to him proves any facts he reasonably requires to be proved and which the voucher etc. would have proved.

[TMA 1970, s 12B; ITA 2007, Sch 1 para 246; FA 2008, s 115, Sch 37 para 2; TIOPA 2010, Sch 8 para 3; SI 2009 No 402; SI 2009 No 2035, Sch para 4].

See HMRC Compliance Handbook at CH10000 *et seq.* (technical guidance: record-keeping).

Enquiries into returns

Notice of enquiry

[63.6] An officer of HMRC may enquire into a personal or trustees' return, and anything (including any claim or election) contained (or required to be contained) in it. He must give notice that he intends to do so (notice of enquiry) within whichever of the following periods is appropriate:

(a)   in the case of a return for 2007/08 or any subsequent year delivered on or before the filing date (i.e. the date on or before which the return must be delivered — see **63.2** above), the twelve months after the day on which the return was delivered;

(b)   in the case of a return for 2006/07 or any earlier year delivered on or before the filing date, the twelve months after the filing date;

(c)   in the case of a return delivered after the filing date, the period ending with the 'quarter day' next following the first anniversary of the delivery date;

(d)   in the case of a return amended by the taxpayer under **63.4** above, the period ending with the 'quarter day' next following the first anniversary of the date of amendment.

For these purposes, the *'quarter days'* are 31 January, 30 April etc. A return cannot be enquired into more than once, except in consequence of an amendment (or further amendment). If notice under (d) above is given at a time when the deadline in (a), (b) or (c) above, as the case may be, has expired or after a previous enquiry into the return has been completed, the enquiry is limited to matters affected by the amendment.

[*TMA 1970, s 9A; FA 2007, ss 91(3), 96(1)(5); TIOPA 2010, Sch 8 para 2*].

HMRC have published online a useful table illustrating enquiry and amendment windows in a number of scenarios (see www.hmrc.gov.uk/sa/enq-amend-windows.htm).

As regards (b) above, it was held by a Special Commissioner that service of a notice is treated as effected at the time at which the letter would be delivered in the ordinary course of post, i.e. on the second working day after posting for first class mail or on the fourth working day after posting for second class mail (*Wing Hung Lai v Bale* (Sp C 203), [1999] SSCD 238). See also *Holly v Inspector of Taxes* (Sp C 225), [2000] SSCD 50. HMRC now accept that it is the time of receipt of the notice, rather than that of its issue, by reference to which the time limit applies (Revenue 'Working Together' Bulletin April 2000 p 8).

In the case of a return by the personal representatives of a deceased taxpayer (for the year of death or of completion of administration of the estate), HMRC will give early written confirmation if they do not intend to enquire into the return (although, in exceptional circumstances, an enquiry at a later date would not thereby be precluded if the return was discovered to be incomplete or incorrect). Such early confirmation will also be given to trustees in relation to the return for the year in which the trust is wound up. (Revenue Press Release 4 April 1996). See also **63.1** above as regards early issue of returns in such cases.

See **63.13** below as regards similar provisions as regards enquiries into partnership returns.

Simon's Taxes. See A6.302A, A6.401–A6.406.

Conduct of enquiry

[63.7] A Code of Practice (COP 11, or, in certain simple cases, a short, single-page version) is issued at the start of every such enquiry. This sets out the rules under which enquiries are made into income tax returns and explains how taxpayers can expect HMRC to conduct enquiries. It describes what HMRC do when they receive a return and how they select cases for enquiry, how they open and carry out enquiries, and what happens if they find something wrong.

Where an enquiry remains open after the time by which notice to enquire into the return had to be given solely because of an unagreed capital gains tax valuation, HMRC will not raise further enquiries into matters unrelated to that capital gains tax computation unless, had the enquiry already been completed, a discovery under *TMA 1970, s 29* (see **6.6 ASSESSMENTS**) could have been made. (HMRC SP 1/99).

HMRC also publish an Enquiry Manual as part of their series of internal guidance manuals (see **34 HMRC — ADMINISTRATION**) and, as an extended introduction to the material on operational aspects of the enquiry regime covered in the manual, a special edition of their Tax Bulletin (Special Edition 2, August 1997). The following points are selected from the Bulletin.

(i)   Early submission of a tax return will not increase the likelihood of selection for enquiry.

(ii)   HMRC do not have to give reasons for opening an enquiry — and they *will not do so.*

(iii) Enquiries may be full enquiries or 'aspect enquiries'. An aspect enquiry will fall short of an in-depth examination of the return (though it may develop into one), but will instead concentrate on one or more aspects of it.

(iv)   Greater emphasis than before will be placed on examination of underlying records. HMRC will make an informal request for information before, if necessary, using their powers under *TMA 1970, s 19A* (see **63.8** below) or under **38.3–38.10 HMRC INVESTIGATORY POWERS**.

(v)   Where penalties are being sought, HMRC will aim to conclude the enquiry by means of a contract settlement (see **6.9 ASSESSMENTS**) rather than by the issue of a closure notice under *TMA 1970, s 28A* (see **63.9** below).

In March 2002, the Inland Revenue published a framework within which enquiries will be worked and to which professional advisers are encouraged to adhere. Particular topics covered are the opening enquiry letter, requests for and conduct of interviews and meetings, and requests for non-business bank and building society accounts (plus credit/charge/store card details). (Revenue 'Working Together' Bulletin March 2002 pp 1–6).

Where income is received from co-owned property where the letting activity does not amount to a partnership (see **60.2 PROPERTY INCOME**), and the name and address of the managing co-owner is provided in co-owners' returns, HMRC will confine initial enquiries relating to that income to the managing co-owner's return. (Revenue Tax Bulletin October 1996 p 350).

For the allowability of additional accountancy expenses incurred in connection with self-assessment enquiries, see **73.92 TRADING INCOME** and Revenue Tax Bulletin October 1998 p 596.

Power to call for documents

[63.8] These provisions are repealed from 1 April 2009, and replaced with the powers at **38.3–38.10** HMRC INVESTIGATORY POWERS. These provisions do, however, continue to have effect on and after that date for the purposes of any notice given before that date under *TMA 1970, s 19A* below. [*SI 2009 No 404, Arts 2, 3*].

At the same time as giving notice of enquiry under **63.6** above to any person, or subsequently, an officer of HMRC may by notice in writing require that person, within a specified period of at least 30 days (from the date of receipt of the notice — see *Self-assessed v Inspector of Taxes* (Sp C 207), [1999] SSCD 253 and Revenue 'Working Together' Bulletin April 2000 p 8), to produce to the officer such documents (including computer records) as are in the person's possession or power, and such accounts or particulars as the officer may reasonably require to check the validity of the return (or, where applicable, the amendment to the return). Copies of documents may be produced but the officer has power to call for originals, and may himself take copies of, or make extracts from, any document produced. A person is not obliged under these provisions to produce documents etc. relating to the conduct of any pending appeal by him or any pending referral (see **63.11** below) to which he is a party. There is provision for a person to appeal, within 30 days beginning with the date of the notice, against any requirement imposed by a notice as above. However, the Sp C can set aside the notice only if it is found to relate to documents etc. that are not reasonably required, and were unable to do so in a case where a notice was issued to a taxpayer whom HMRC were aware had recently been diagnosed with cancer (*A v HMRC* (Sp C 650), [2008] SSCD 380). In restricted cases, an officer may, alternatively or in addition, require documents, accounts etc. to enable him to exercise the 'Crown Option' (see **63.6** above). [*TMA 1970, s 19A; FA 2008, s 113, Sch 36 para 66*].

For cases on the scope of such notices, see *Mother v Inspector of Taxes* (Sp C 211), [1999] SSCD 279, *Accountant v Inspector of Taxes* (Sp C 258), [2000] SSCD 522, *Parto v Bratherton* (Sp C 414), [2004] SSCD 339, *Clarke v HMRC* (Sp C 735), [2009] SSCD 278. See **55.15** PENALTIES as regards penalties for non-compliance.

The provisions of *TMA 1970, s 19A* 'override the contractual duty of confidence owed by a solicitor to his clients', and 'the rule of legal professional privilege is excluded because it is not expressly preserved by *s 19A*' (*Guyer v Walton* (Sp C 274), [2001] SSCD 75). See also Revenue Tax Bulletin April 2000 pp 743–746. However, in *R v A Special Commr ex p Morgan Grenfell & Co Ltd* HL 2002, 74 TC 511, the HL quashed a notice under *TMA 1970, s 20(1)* (see **38.11**(a) HMRC INVESTIGATORY POWERS) on the grounds that the inspector was not entitled to require delivery of documents subject to legal professional privilege (of the person under enquiry), a fundamental human right not expressly overridden by that *subsection*; HMRC accept that the same reasoning applies as regards their power under *section 19A* (see Revenue Tax Bulletin December 2002 p 993). In cases not involving legal professional privilege, a notice under *s 19A* does not contravene a taxpayer's right under *Human Rights Act 1998, Sch 1, Article 8* to respect for his private and family life (*Afsar v HMRC* (Sp C 554), [2006] SSCD 625).

Completion of enquiry

[63.9] An enquiry is completed when an officer of HMRC gives the taxpayer notice (closure notice) that he has completed his enquiries and states his conclusions. The closure notice takes effect when it is issued and must either make the necessary amendments to the return to give effect to the stated conclusions or state that no amendment of the return is required. Before the enquiry is complete, the taxpayer may apply to the Appeal Tribunal for a direction requiring HMRC to give closure notice within a specified period, such application to be heard and determined in similar manner to an appeal. The Tribunal must give the direction unless satisfied that there are reasonable grounds for not giving closure notice within a specified period. [*TMA 1970, s 28A; SI 2009 No 56, Sch 1 para 17*].

In an application for closure as above, the Sp C considered that an investigation into the applicant's personal expenditure aimed at establishing the correct amount of tax due did not breach his rights under *Human Rights Act 1998, Sch 1, Art 8* (right to private life) (*Gould and another (t/a Garry's Private Hire) v HMRC* (Sp C 604), [2007] SSCD 502).

Similar provisions apply in the case of an enquiry into a partnership return. Where a partnership return is amended under these provisions, HMRC will, by notice, make any necessary consequential amendments to the partners' returns (including those of company partners). [*TMA 1970, s 28B; SI 2009 No 56, Sch 1 para 18*].

See **5.2 APPEALS** for right of appeal against any conclusion stated or amendment made by a closure notice.

Where a personal or partnership return is amended, the taxpayer is given the same rights to make, revise and withdraw claims, elections, applications and notices as he would have had if a 'discovery' assessment had been raised under *TMA 1970, s 29* (see **6.6 ASSESSMENTS**). This is achieved by giving effect to *TMA 1970, ss 43A, 43B* (see **18.9 CLAIMS**), to *TMA 1970, s 36(3)* (which enables the same reliefs and allowances to be given as if the necessary claims etc. had been made within the relevant time limits — see **6.3, 6.4 ASSESSMENTS**), and to *TMA 1970, s 43(2)* (extended time limit for claims — see **18.9 CLAIMS**). These sections are given similar effect in relation to an amendment as they would have in relation to an assessment. Any late assessment required to give effect to such a claim etc., or as a result of allowing such a claim etc., can be made within a year after the claim etc. becomes final (i.e. becomes no longer capable of being varied, on appeal or otherwise). [*TMA 1970, s 43C; FA 2008, Sch 39 para 14; SI 2009 No 403*].

Amendment of returns where enquiries made

[63.10] If a return is amended by the taxpayer under 63.4 above while an enquiry into it is in progress (i.e. during the inclusive period between notice of enquiry and closure notice), the amendment does not restrict the scope of the enquiry but may itself be taken into account in the enquiry. The amendment does not take effect to alter the tax payable until the enquiry is completed and closure notice is issued (see 63.9 above). It may then be taken into account separately or, if the officer so states in the closure notice, in arriving at the amendments contained in the notice. It does not take effect if the officer concludes in the closure notice that the amendment is incorrect. [*TMA 1970, s 9B*]. See 63.13 below as regards similar provisions for partnership returns. [*TMA 1970, s 9(5), s 12AB(3)*].

If in his opinion there is otherwise likely to be a loss of tax to the Crown, an officer may amend a self-assessment contained in the return while an enquiry is still in progress. If the enquiry is itself limited to an amendment to the return (see 63.6 above), the officer's power in this respect is limited accordingly. [*TMA 1970, s 9C, s 28A(2)*]. No similar power exists in the case of partnership returns.

Referral of questions during enquiry

[63.11] There is provision to enable specific contentious points to be litigated while an enquiry is still open, instead of waiting until it is completed. Enquiries into personal, trustees' and partnership returns are all included.

At any time whilst the enquiry is in progress (i.e. during the inclusive period between notice of enquiry as in 63.6 above and closure notice as in 63.9 above), any one or more questions arising out of it may be referred, jointly by the taxpayer and an officer of HMRC, to the Appeal Tribunal for their determination. More than one notice of referral may be given in relation to the enquiry. Either party may withdraw a notice of referral. Until the questions referred have been finally determined (or the referral withdrawn), no closure notice may be given or applied for in relation to the enquiry.

The determination of the question(s) by the Tribunal is binding on both parties in the same way, and to the same extent, as a decision on a preliminary issue in an appeal. HMRC must take account of it in concluding their enquiry. Following completion of the enquiry, the question concerned may not be reopened on appeal except to the extent (if any) that it could have been reopened had it been determined on appeal following the enquiry rather than on referral during the enquiry.

[*TMA 1970, ss 28ZA–28ZE; SI 2009 No 56, Sch 1 paras 12–16, Sch 2 para 187*].

Determination of tax where no return delivered

[63.12] Where a notice has been given under *TMA 1970, ss 8, 8A* (notice requiring an individual or trustee to deliver a return — see 63.2 above) and the return is not delivered by the 'filing date', an officer of HMRC may make a determination of the amounts of taxable income, capital gains and income tax payable which, to the best of his information and belief, he estimates for the tax year. The officer must serve notice of the determination on the person concerned. Tax is payable as if the determination were a self-assessment, with no right of appeal. No determination may be made after the expiry of three years beginning with the filing date (reduced from five years with effect on and after 1 April 2010).

For these purposes, and regardless of whether or not the return is filed electronically, the *'filing date'* is regarded as 31 January following the tax year to which the return relates, except that, if later, it is the last day of the period of three months beginning with the date of the notice requiring the return.

A determination is automatically superseded by any self-assessment made (whether by the taxpayer or HMRC), based on information contained in a return. Such self-assessment must be made within the three years beginning with the filing date (reduced from five years with effect on and after 1 April 2010) or, if later, within twelve months beginning with the date of the determination. Any tax payable or repayable as a result of the supersession is deemed to have fallen due for payment or repayment on the normal due date, usually 31 January following the tax year (see **65.7 SELF-ASSESSMENT**).

Any recovery proceedings commenced before the making of such a self-assessment may be continued in respect of so much of the tax charged by the self-assessment as is due and payable and has not been paid.

[*TMA 1970, ss 28C, 59B(5A); FA 2007, s 91(5), s 92; FA 2008, Sch 39 para 2; SI 2009 No 403*].

Simon's Taxes. See A6.304, E1.203.

Partnerships

[63.13] Any partner may be required by notice to complete and deliver a return of the partnership profits (a 'partnership return') together with accounts, statements, documents and other records (and see further below). The return must include information as to taxable partnership income, reliefs and allowances claimed, tax at source and tax credits plus the names, residences and tax references of all persons (including companies) who were partners during the period specified in the notice and such other information as may reasonably be required by the notice, which may include information relating to disposals of partnership property. The general requirements are similar to those for personal returns under *TMA 1970, s 8* (see **63.2** above).

The notice will specify the period (the relevant period) to be covered by the return and the date by which the return should be delivered (the filing date). For a partnership including at least one individual, the relevant period will be a tax year. For a partnership including one or more companies, it will usually be the partnership accounting period ending in the tax year. HMRC accept that if there is no such accounting period or if the partnership does not carry on a trade or profession, the relevant period is the tax year. For detailed guidance on partnership return filing dates, see www.hmrc.gov.uk/sa/partship -filing-v0-01.pdf.

As regards returns for 2007/08 and subsequent years, for a partnership including at least one individual, the filing date is determined as follows.

- If the return is an electronic return, it will be no earlier than **31 January** following the tax year to which the return relates.
- If the return is a non-electronic return, it will be no earlier than **31 October** following the tax year to which the return relates.

As regards returns for a relevant period beginning on or after 6 April 2007, for a partnership including at least one company, the filing date is determined as follows.

- If the return is an electronic return, it will be no earlier than the first anniversary of the end of the relevant period.
- If the return is a non-electronic return, it will be no earlier than the end of the period of nine months beginning at the end of the relevant period.

In all cases, the filing date will be deferred until, at the earliest, the last day of the three-month period beginning with the date of the notice, if this is a later date than that given above. See **63.2** above for what is meant by electronic and non-electronic returns.

Where the partner responsible for dealing with the return ceases to be available, a successor may be nominated for this purpose by a majority of the persons (or their personal representatives) who were partners at any time in the period covered by the return. A nomination (or revocation of a nomination) does not have effect until notified to HMRC. Failing a nomination, a successor will be determined according to rules on the return form or will be nominated by HMRC.

[*TMA 1970, s 12AA; FA 2007, ss 90, 92; FA 2008, s 34, Sch 12 para 11; SI 2009 No 2035, Sch para 3*].

See **55.5** PENALTIES as regards penalties for non-compliance.

It is not possible for individual partners to make, in their personal tax returns, supplementary claims for expenses incurred on the partnership's behalf or capital allowances on personal assets used in the partnership. If not included in the accounts, adjustments for such expenditure etc. must be included in the tax computation forming part of the partnership return. (Revenue booklet SAT 1(1995), para 5.17 and see Revenue Tax Bulletin August 1997 p 453).

Provisions similar to those in **63.4** above apply as regards amendments and corrections to partnership returns. Where a return is so amended or corrected (and, in the case of an HMRC correction, it is not rejected by the taxpayer), the partners' returns will be amended by HMRC accordingly, by notice to each partner concerned. [*TMA 1970, ss 12ABA, 12ABB; FA 2007, s 91(4), s 92; FA 2008, s 119(2)(13); SI 2009 No 405*].

Enquiries into returns

Provisions similar to those in **63.6** above apply as regards enquiries into partnership returns. The notice of enquiry may be given to a successor (see above) of the person who made the return. The giving of such notice is deemed to include the giving of notice under *TMA 1970, s 9A* (or, where applicable, the equivalent corporation tax provision) to each partner affected. Similarly the rules in **63.9–63.11** above apply in relation to partnership returns, except that there is no provision equivalent to *TMA 1970, s 9C* for amendment of returns by HMRC while an enquiry remains in progress. There is also appropriate provision to consequentially amend partners' own returns, including those of company partners. [*TMA 1970, ss 12AC, 12AD, 28ZA–28ZE, 28B; FA 2007, s 96(2)(5); SI 2009 No 56, Sch 1 paras 12–16, 18*].

Partnership statements

Every partnership return as above must include a statement (a partnership statement) showing, in respect of the period covered by the return and each period of account ending within that period:

(a)   the partnership income or loss from each source, after taking into account any relief or allowance due to the partnership and for which a claim is made under any of the provisions in *TMA 1970, s 42(7)* (see **18.1 CLAIMS**);

(b)   the amount of consideration for each disposal of partnership property;

(c)   the amounts of any tax deducted at source from or tax credits on partnership income; and

(d)   (before 2007/08) the amount of each charge on partnership income,

and each partner's share of that income, loss, consideration, tax, credit or (before 2007/08) charge.

In the case of an individual carrying on a trade etc. in partnership, the return under *TMA 1970, s 8* (see **63.2** above) must include each amount which, according to any '*relevant partnership statement*' (i.e. one falling to be made, as respects the partnership, for a period which includes all or any part of the tax year or its basis period), is the individual's share of any income, loss, tax, credit or charge for the period covered by the statement.

[*TMA 1970, ss 8(1B)(1C), 12AB; ITA 2007, Sch 1 para 245; FA 2008, s 34, Sch 12 para 12*].

Simon's Taxes. See **A6.406, B7.130, E1.220–E1.223**.

Bankers etc. and paying agents — returns of interest

[63.14] On receipt of notice, any person paying or crediting interest on money received or retained, in the UK, in the ordinary course of his business, and any bank (within *ITA 2007, s 991* — see **8.1 BANKS**) or building society, must make a return, for any specified tax year (ending not more than three years previously), showing the names and addresses of the recipients and the gross amount of interest paid or credited to each and the amount (if any) of tax deducted therefrom. In the case of a building society, 'interest' includes dividends and similar distributions. The payer may exclude from that return interest paid to a person who has so requested and has given written notice that the person beneficially entitled to the interest is a non-UK resident company. Notices may be issued re parts or branches of a business. HMRC have powers by statutory instrument to make regulations requiring further prescribed information with the return, or providing that prescribed information is *not* required, or requiring information or returns to be in prescribed form, or providing for inspection of books, documents, records etc. [*TMA 1970, s 17; SI 2001 No 405*].

Returns may similarly be required from any other person paying interest (including building society dividends) or receiving it on behalf of others [*TMA 1970, s 18; SI 2001 No 405*] and from persons collecting interest on securities on behalf of others. [*TMA 1970, s 24; ITA 2007, Sch 1 para 249; TIOPA 2010, Sch 8 para 4*].

SI 2001 No 405 excludes certain payments from the application of *TMA 1970, s 17* and *s 18*. For guidance on the making of information returns under *TMA 1970, s 17* and *s 18*, see www.hmrc.gov.uk/esd-guidance/s17-s18-si-reportin g.htm#3.

References in *TMA 1970, s 17* and *s 18* above include references to alternative finance return or (for which see **3.2–3.8** ALTERNATIVE FINANCE ARRANGEMENTS). [*TMA 1970, ss 17(8), 18(5); FA 2005, ss 55, 56, Sch 2 para 2; CTA 2009, Sch 1 paras 298, 299, 664(2)*].

EU Savings Directive

[**63.15**] Under *TMA 1970, ss 18B–18E* (previously *FA 2003, s 199*), the Treasury may make regulations by statutory instrument (see *SI 2003 No 3297*) to implement into UK law the EU Directive on the Taxation of Savings (*Directive 2003/48/EC*, 3 June 2003), designed to counter cross-border tax evasion by individuals on their savings income. The Directive is commonly referred to as either the Savings Directive or the Savings Tax Directive, and came into force on 1 July 2005.

Under the Directive, prescribed UK paying agents, e.g. businesses and public bodies that pay savings income to, or collect savings income for, individuals resident elsewhere in the EU will have to report details of the income and the payee to HMRC, who will then pass on the information to the corresponding tax authority in the payee's country of residence. Similar information regarding UK-resident payees will flow in the opposite direction. (Austria, Belgium and Luxembourg will impose, for a transitional period, a withholding tax as an alternative to exchanging information.) The regulations prescribe the types of paying agent and payee within the scheme, the information required, the time limits for compliance and the penalties for non-compliance, and they provide for inspection of paying agents' records. For these purposes, '*savings income*' means interest (including premium bond winnings but not interest unrelated to a money debt or penalty charges for late payments), interest accrued or capitalised at the sale, refund or redemption of a money debt, and certain income distributed by or realised upon the sale, refund or redemption of shares or units in a collective investment fund. Treasury regulations may also implement any similar arrangements made with non-EU countries (see further below).

For detailed savings income reporting guidance prepared by HMRC plus notes for UK investors and other related items, see www.hmrc.gov.uk/esd-guidance/index.htm. See also Treasury Explanatory Notes to Finance Bill 2003, European Commission Press Release 4 June 2003, Revenue Press Releases 30 June 2003, 22 September 2003 and Revenue Internet Statement 19 December 2003.

The Savings Directive applies to all 26 EU member states (including, for payments of income on and after their accession on 1 January 2007, Bulgaria and Romania). The EU has concluded similar savings taxation agreements with Andorra, Liechtenstein, San Marino, Monaco and Switzerland. These territories will apply a withholding tax and will exchange information at the request of tax authorities of EU member states in all criminal or civil cases of tax fraud etc. on a reciprocal basis.

Similar agreements have been concluded by individual EU member states with ten dependent and associated territories of the UK and the Netherlands (Anguilla, Aruba (*SI 2005 No 1458*), the British Virgin Islands (*SI 2005 No 1457*), the Cayman Islands, Guernsey (*SI 2005 No 1262*), the Isle of Man (*SI 2005 No 1263*), Jersey (*SI 2005 No 1261*), Montserrat (*SI 2005 No 1459*), the Netherlands Antilles (*SI 2005 No 1460*) and the Turks & Caicos Islands). The British Virgin Islands, Guernsey, the Isle of Man, Jersey, the Netherlands Antilles and the Turks and Caicos Islands will apply a withholding tax during the same transitional period as applies to Austria, Belgium and Luxembourg. The agreements with Anguilla, Aruba, the Cayman Islands and Montserrat provide for exchange of information. The agreements with Anguilla, Cayman Islands and Turks and Caicos Islands do not, for the time being, have a reciprocal effect as the residents of those territories are not taxable on their savings income.

As the UK and Gibraltar are not separate member states, the Directive does not apply between them (HMRC Internet Statement 5 July 2005), but a bilateral agreement was signed on 19 December 2005 between the UK and Gibraltar (and came into force on 1 April 2006) under which those territories will exchange information with each other and by virtue of which Gibraltar will operate a withholding tax during the above-mentioned transitional period (see *SI 2006 No 1453*).

Where, under the Savings Directive or equivalent arrangements made with non-EU member states, a withholding tax is levied as an alternative to exchanging information, relief is available for such withholding tax against UK income tax and capital gains tax liabilities or, to the extent that set-off is not possible, by repayment. See **26.14 DOUBLE TAX RELIEF**. As an alternative, application may be made to HMRC for a certificate which can be presented to a paying agent to enable savings income to be paid to the applicant without deduction of such withholding tax. See **26.15 DOUBLE TAX RELIEF**.

Simon's Taxes. See A6.1205, E6.455.

Employers

[63.16] Employers (including deemed employers of agency workers) must, on application by HMRC (made no later than the fifth anniversary of 31 January following the tax year(s) specified), furnish particulars, for employees (i.e. any person whose earnings are within the charge to tax on employment income) and periods specified, of:

- payments made by the employer to employees, including expenses, payments made on employees' behalf and not repaid and payments made for services rendered in connection with a trade or business (whether or not rendered in the course of the employment), and taxable benefits provided by the employer to employees;
- payments (as above) made, and benefits provided, by third parties by arrangement with the employer (including name and business address of third party);
- payments (as above) made, and benefits provided, to the employer's knowledge, by third parties other than by arrangement with the employer (including name and business address of third party).

Third parties may similarly be required by notice to furnish particulars of payments made and benefits provided to employees of other persons. A similar time limit applies.

As regards benefits, particulars required may include the amounts chargeable to tax.

[*TMA 1970, ss 15, 16A*].

See also **53.12 PAY AS YOU EARN** as regards employers' returns.

Person in UK treated as employer

Where a person (A) performs duties for a continuous period of 30 days or more in the UK for a non-UK resident employer but for the benefit of a person (B) resident or carrying on a trade etc. in the UK, then B must include A in any returns of employees, and A may be required to include any such earnings in a tax return. [*TMA 1970, s 8(4A)(4B), ss 8ZA, 15A; FA 1974, s 24; TIOPA 2010, Sch 7 paras 12–14*].

Fees, commissions, copyrights etc.

[63.17] Any person carrying on any trade etc., and any body of persons carrying on any non-trading activity (including Crown departments, public or local authorities and any other public bodies), may, by notice, be required to give particulars of all payments made (including commissions or expenses), or valuable consideration given, for services rendered by persons not employed by him, including, in the case of a trade etc., services in connection with the formation, acquisition, development or disposal thereof. Applies also to periodical or lump-sum payments in respect of any copyright or public lending right or design right. But returns are limited to payments from which tax is not deductible, and those (a) exceeding £15 in total to any one person, or (b) made during the three tax years ending prior to the notice. [*TMA 1970, s 16*].

Grants, subsidies, licences etc.

[63.18] Any person paying grants or subsidies directly or indirectly out of public funds (whether UK or European Union), or issuing licences or approvals or maintaining entries in a register which subsist after that date, may be required to furnish particulars to the inspector where they may be relevant to the determination of any tax liability. [*TMA 1970, s 18A*].

Hotels and boarding houses

[63.19] Returns of all lodgers and inmates resident in any dwelling house must be made by the proprietor, if required by notice from the inspector. [*TMA 1970, s 14*].

Issuing houses, stockbrokers, auctioneers etc.

[63.20] For the purposes of obtaining particulars of chargeable gains, an inspector may require a return of parties to transactions and description and consideration of assets dealt with from (i) an issuing house or any other person concerned in effecting public issues or placing of shares etc. or (ii) a member of a stock exchange (other than a market maker) or any other person acting as an agent or broker in share transactions or (iii) any person or body managing a clearing house for any terminal market in commodities or (iv) an auctioneer and any person carrying on a trade of dealing in any description of tangible movable property or acting as agent in such where the value in the hands of the recipient exceeds £6,000. Returns are limited to transactions effected within three years prior to the issue of the notice requiring the return. [*TMA 1970, s 25; FA 2009, Sch 22 paras 11, 13*].

HMRC may make regulations by statutory instrument, effective from a day to be appointed therein, making appropriate provision in regard to recognised investment exchanges other than the Stock Exchange. [*FA 1986, s 63, Sch 18 para 8*].

See also *TMA 1970, s 21* as regards other transactions by market makers. Simon's Taxes. See **A4.128**.

Pay as you earn

[63.21] See **53.12** PAY AS YOU EARN and **65.12** SELF-ASSESSMENT.

Trustees

[63.22] A return may be required from a trustee under *TMA 1970, ss 8A, 13* — see **63.2** above.

Reasonable excuse

[63.23] It is generally provided that a person is deemed not to have failed to do anything required to be done where there was a reasonable excuse for the failure and, if the excuse ceased, provided that the failure was remedied without unreasonable delay after the excuse had ceased. Similarly, a person is deemed not to have failed to do anything required to be done within a limited time if he did it within such further time as HMRC, or the Appeal Tribunal or officer concerned, may have allowed. [*TMA 1970, s 118(2); SI 2009 No 56, Sch 1 para 51(4)*]. In *Creedplan Ltd v Winter* (Sp C 54), [1995] SSCD 352, the Special Commissioner, in confirming a penalty under *TMA 1970, s 94(1)(a)*, considered that 'there is no reasonable excuse . . . for sending in a return which was less than was required' (but cf. *Akarimsons Ltd v Chapman* (Sp C 116), [1997] SSCD 140 in which a penalty under *TMA 1970, s 94(1)(b)* was quashed). See, however, *Steeden v Carver* (Sp C 212), [1999] SSCD 283, in which reliance on the Inland Revenue's advice as to the practical extension of a deadline, unequivocally given, was held to be 'as reasonable an excuse as could be found'.

Reliance on a third party is capable of being a reasonable excuse for direct tax purposes, though in determining whether a person had a reasonable excuse for failing to perform a particular task it is proper to have regard to the nature of that task (*Research & Development Partnership Ltd v HMRC* FTT (TC 271), 2010 STI 382). See also *Huntley Solutions Ltd v HMRC* FTT (TC 272), 2010 STI 571.

Under self-assessment, there are separate 'reasonable excuse' let-outs as regards penalties for late returns (see **55.6 PENALTIES**) and surcharges for late payment of tax (see **42.3 INTEREST AND SURCHARGES ON OVERDUE TAX**).

Key points

[63.24] Points to consider are as follows.

- As the enquiry window in relation to returns is now determined by the date on which the return was received by HMRC, the receipt of an enquiry notice should be checked against the date on which the return was filed. For returns filed online, this is available from the SA Online system. For returns filed on paper, advisers will need to retain a record of the date the return was filed to check the validity of enquiry notices.
- Partnership returns must include the UTR for every partner during the tax year. It is therefore important to ensure that any new partners obtain a UTR in sufficient time, as after 31 October partnership returns must be filed online to avoid incurring a penalty, and this is not possible without valid UTR's for each partner.
- Where a return cannot be filed online for technical reasons the adviser should file a 'reasonable excuse' form with the return to avoid penalty notices being raised unnecessarily. Details of those

cases which cannot be filed online are shown as SA excluded cases on HMRC's website each year. For individual returns the current exclusions are listed at www.hmrc.gov.uk/carter/sa-exclusions.htm.

- All employer annual returns must now be filed online, although there are very restrictive and limited exceptions available on religious grounds and for some domestic employers. Details of the exemptions can be found at www.hmrc.gov.uk/paye/payroll/year-end/paper-filing.htm

- HMRC can from 1 April 2010 amend any aspect of a self-assessment return which he has reason to believe is incorrect in the light of information available to him. The taxpayer (or his agent) can reject this amendment within 30 days of being notified. Advisers should be aware that HMRC amendments are likely to be much wider in scope than previously.

64

Savings and Investment Income

Cross-references. See **1.5 ALLOWANCES AND TAX RATES** for rates of tax on dividend income; **1.6 ALLOWANCES AND TAX RATES** for rates of tax on 'savings income'; **24 DEDUCTION OF TAX AT SOURCE**; **28 ENTERPRISE INVESTMENT SCHEME**; **30 EXEMPT INCOME**; **44.3** *et seq.* **LIFE ASSURANCE POLICIES** for gains on such policies; **69 SHARE-RELATED EMPLOYMENT INCOME AND EXEMPTIONS**; **73.51 TRADING INCOME** re copyrights and royalties; **75 UNIT TRUSTS ETC.**; **76 VENTURE CAPITAL TRUSTS**.

Simon's Taxes. See B8.4, D5.4, E1.4.

Other sources. See HMRC Savings and Investment Manual.

Introduction

[64.1] A list of the types of income included within the charge to tax on savings and investment income can be found at *ITTOIA 2005, s 365*. The term 'savings and investment income' includes income arising to UK residents, whether or not the source is in the UK, and to non-UK residents to the extent that the income arises from a UK source (see *ITTOIA 2005, s 368*).

If an item of income is both a trade receipt and potentially within the charge to tax as savings and investment income (including dividend income), priority is given to the charge on trade profits. See **73.90 TRADING INCOME** for circumstances in which investment income may be a trade receipt. Similarly, where an item of income is employment, pension or social security income and also potentially savings and investment income, then priority is given to the charge to tax under *ITEPA 2003*, though this priority rule does not apply either to dividends from UK companies or to the charge at **64.16** below. [*ITTOIA 2005, s 366*].

Interest

[64.2] Income tax is charged on the full amount of interest arising in the tax year, whether from a source within or outside the UK, (unless the **REMITTANCE BASIS (61)** applies). The person liable for any tax charged is the person receiving or entitled to the interest.

[*ITTOIA 2005, ss 369(1), 370, 371*].

Interest is receivable net of tax if tax is deductible at source under the provisions in **24 DEDUCTION OF TAX AT SOURCE** or under paying and collecting agent arrangements or if received from a building society (see **9.1 BUILDING SOCIETIES**) or from a bank (see **8.2 BANKS**) without a gross payment certificate being in force. Otherwise, interest is receivable gross. See **1.6 ALLOWANCES AND TAX RATES** as regards the rates of tax applicable to 'savings income'.

Any interest element included in a compensation package for the mis-selling of certain financial products, such as mortgage endowment policies, is normally taxable as savings income under general principles. If the package includes a payment for personal injury, interest on such payment is tax-exempt, as is interest on compensation for mis-sold pensions (see **30.11 EXEMPT INCOME**). (Revenue Tax Bulletin August 2004 pp 1131, 1132).

The definition of interest is extended to include:

- building society dividends and other distributions;
- open-ended investment company interest distributions (see **75.3 UNIT TRUSTS ETC.**);
- authorised unit trust interest distributions (see **75.2 UNIT TRUSTS ETC.**);
- industrial and provident society payments;
- (on and after 22 April 2009) certain distributions of offshore funds (see **64.4** below);
- (on and after 1 September 2009) any dividend paid by an investment trust company which the company has opted to treat as an interest distribution (see **64.5** below);

- funding bonds (see **64.6** below);
- (on and after 6 October 2008) payments from the Financial Services Compensation Scheme (see below); and
- discounts.

[*ITTOIA 2005, s 369(2); FA 2009, ss 33(2)(5), 39(2)(5)*].

For details of certain types of interest which are exempt from tax, see **30.24, 30.29 EXEMPT INCOME**.

Building society dividends and other distributions are charged to tax as interest and not as dividends. [*ITTOIA 2005, s 372; ITA 2007, Sch 1 para 514*].

Payments from the Financial Services Compensation Scheme ('FSCS') that are made on or after 6 October 2008 and which represent interest are treated as interest. A payment represents interest if it is calculated in the same way as interest which would have been paid to the recipient but for the circumstances giving rise to the making of payments under the FSCS, e.g. the failure of a bank or other financial institution. If the financial institution in default would have deducted tax from interest, the FSCS deducts an equivalent amount from the payment representing the interest; the payment is then treated in the hands of the recipient as an amount received net of basic rate tax. [*ITTOIA 2005, s 380A; ITA 2007, s 979A(1)–(4), (7); FA 2009, s 33(3)–(5)*].

Discounts are treated as interest for the purposes of the charge to tax. [*ITTOIA 2005, s 381*]. See **64.18–64.24** below for the separate charge to tax in relation to deeply discounted securities.

Premium bond prizes are free of income tax (and capital gains tax). For other National Savings products, see www.nsandi.com/index.jsp.

Designated client account interest passed on to the client by a solicitor is within the definition of 'savings income' (see **1.6 ALLOWANCES AND TAX RATES**) and payments made to clients in respect of money held in undesignated client accounts are similarly treated (Revenue Tax Bulletin February 1998 pp 512, 513).

Any dividend, bonus or other sum payable to a shareholder in either:

- a registered industrial and provident society; or
- a UK agricultural or fishing co-operative,

is treated as interest for income tax purposes if it is payable by reference to the amount of the shareholder's holding in its share capital. [*ITTOIA 2005, s 379*].

See **3.2, 3.7 ALTERNATIVE FINANCE ARRANGEMENTS** for the treatment of alternative finance return and profit share return, both as therein defined, as if it were interest.

Government stocks

[64.3] As regards deduction arrangements for UK public revenue dividends (other than gilt-edged securities), see **24.12 DEDUCTION OF TAX AT SOURCE**.

Interest on gilt-edged securities is paid without deduction of tax. The option of deduction is, however, available (see **24.12 DEDUCTION OF TAX AT SOURCE**). [*ITA 2007, s 893; ICTA 1988, s 50(A1)*].

Tax exemption for non-residents

The Treasury has powers to issue securities ('FOTRA securities') on terms that the profits or gains arising from the securities are exempt from tax provided that they are beneficially owned by persons not ordinarily resident in the UK (see **RESIDENCE, ORDINARY RESIDENCE AND DOMICILE (62)**). 'FOTRA' means 'Free of Tax to Residents Abroad'. From 6 April 1998, *all* gilt-edged securities are issued with that status, and *FA 1998, s 161* provided for gilt-edged securities issued before that date without that status to be treated as if they were FOTRA securities (except 3.5% War Loan, which is in effect treated in the same way as FOTRA securities under its terms of issue). For further information, see www.hmrc.gov.uk/cnr/fotra_sec.htm.

Provided that any conditions imposed are complied with, nothing in the *Tax Acts* overrides such exemption, although this does not confer any exemption from charge where income is treated under anti-avoidance provisions as income of a UK resident etc. (see **68.29, 68.30 SETTLEMENTS, 4.14–4.17 ANTI-AVOIDANCE**).

If interest forms part of the profits of a UK trade, exemption does not generally apply (depending on the Treasury conditions of issue) (see *Owen v Sassoon* Ch D 1950, 32 TC 101).

Interest from a FOTRA security held in trust is exempt (and therefore the beneficial ownership test is satisfied) where none of the beneficiaries of the trust is ordinarily resident in the UK at the time when the interest arises.

[*ITTOIA 2005, ss 713–716; ITA 2007, Sch 1 paras 384, 572*].

See **50.11 NON-RESIDENTS** for the special position of *non-resident banks, insurance companies and dealers in securities* carrying on business in the UK.

For the exemption of non-residents from income tax on interest on local authority securities expressed in a foreign currency, see **24.12 DEDUCTION OF TAX AT SOURCE**.

Offshore fund distributions

[64.4] On and after 22 April 2009, certain dividends of 'offshore funds' that would previously have been treated as dividend income are instead treated as interest for income tax purposes. This applies to dividends arising on or after that date and to manufactured overseas dividends (see **4.10 ANTI-AVOIDANCE**) representing distributions arising on or after that date, but only where the offshore fund fails to meet the 'qualifying investments test' at any time in the 'relevant period'. For this purpose, a dividend includes any distribution that would otherwise be treated as a dividend for income tax purposes. Where the qualifying investments test is met throughout the relevant period, distributions continue to be taxed as dividends and not as interest.

For the meaning of *'offshore funds'*, see **51.2 OFFSHORE FUNDS** (or, before 1 December 2009, **51.24 OFFSHORE FUNDS**).

An offshore fund fails to meet the *'qualifying investments test'* if the market value of the fund's 'qualifying investments' exceeds 60% of the market value of all of the assets of the fund (excluding cash awaiting investment). The term 'qualifying investments' refers broadly to interest-bearing investments and to investments that are economically similar in substance to interest-bearing investments; for the full list, see *CTA 2009, s 494(1)*.

The '*relevant period*' is the last period of account of the offshore fund that ends before the dividend is paid, provided that the profits available for distribution at the end of that period (and not since used, by distribution or otherwise) equal at least the amount of the dividend (aggregated with any simultaneous distribution made by the offshore fund). In any other case, the relevant period is the period of account of the offshore fund in which the dividend is paid. In both cases, if the period of account in question is less than 12 months, the relevant period is taken to be the 12 months ending on the last day of the period of account in question.

[*ITTOIA 2005, s 378A; FA 2009, s 39(3)(5); TIOPA 2010, Sch 8 para 168; SI 2009 No 3001, Reg 128(2)*].

Designated distributions from investment trust companies

[64.5] *FA 2009, s 45* gave the Treasury power to make regulations (see now *SI 2009 No 2034*) enabling investment trust companies (within *CTA 2010, s 1158*, previously *ICTA 1988, s 842(1)*)) to designate specified dividends as payments of interest. The *regulations* have effect in relation to dividends paid **on or after 1 September 2009.** They set out the conditions under which an investment trust company may opt to designate a dividend (or part thereof) as an interest distribution. A recipient of such an interest distribution who is within the charge to income tax is treated for income tax purposes as if the interest distribution were a payment of yearly interest on the date it is made. Basic rate tax is deductible at source under *ITA 2007, s 874* unless:

- the recipient is either a company or the trustees of a unit trust scheme; or
- either the 'residence condition' or the 'reputable intermediary condition' is met with respect to the recipient on the date of the distribution.

The '*residence condition*' and '*reputable intermediary condition*' are similar to those described in relation to interest distributions by authorised unit trusts at **75 UNIT TRUSTS ETC.**

An investment trust must supply the recipient of any distribution with a certificate showing *inter alia* the date and amount of the distribution, the extent to which it is an interest distribution and the extent to which it is a dividend, and the amount of any tax deducted.

[*FA 2009, s 45; CTA 2010, Sch 1 para 710; SI 2009 No 2034*].

Funding bonds

[64.6] Issues of 'funding bonds' to a creditor in respect of a liability to pay interest on a debt are charged to tax as interest. The issue is treated for income tax purposes as if it were a payment of interest equal to the market value of the bond at the date of issue. Charities are exempt from tax on all funding bond interest. *'Funding bonds'* includes bonds, stocks, shares, securities or certificates of indebtedness, whether issued by a government, a public institution, a public authority or a body corporate. Where the issue of funding bonds has been so treated, the redemption of the bonds is not treated as a payment of interest.

The person by or through whom the bonds are issued must retain bonds equal in value to income tax on the deemed interest at the basic rate (for 2008/09 onwards, previously the savings rate) in force for the year of issue of the bonds. The retained bonds can then be tendered to HMRC. Where this is impractical, information as to the recipients and the amount received must be supplied to HMRC.

In relation to funding bonds issued on or after 12 March 2008, HMRC may use the bonds tendered to it by the issuer to satisfy a tax repayment claim by the creditor.

[*ITTOIA 2005, ss 380, 754; ITA 2007, ss 939, 940, 940A; FA 2008, s 134, Sch 1 paras 32, 65; CTA 2009, Sch 1 paras 636, 712*].

The reference above to interest on a debt includes a return under **ALTERNATIVE FINANCE ARRANGEMENTS (3)**. [*ITA 2007, ss 564M(2), 564Q(4), Sch 1 para 602; FA 2005, ss 55, 56, Sch 2 paras 10, 13; CTA 2009, Sch 1 para 664(4); TIOPA 2010, Sch 2 paras 14, 18*].

Dividends and other distributions from UK-resident companies

[64.7] Dividends and other distributions of UK-resident companies are treated as income for income tax purposes (even if the distribution would otherwise be treated as capital) and charged to income tax.

The amount charged to tax in the year is the value of the dividend paid (or distribution made) in the year, plus any tax credit to which the recipient is entitled (see **64.8** below). The person liable for the charge is the one to whom the distribution is made (or treated as made) or the person receiving or entitled to the distribution.

Special rules apply to stock dividends (see **64.14** below).

Any income falling within both *ITEPA 2003* and *ITTOIA 2005* provisions is to be dealt with under the *ITTOIA 2005* provisions.

[*ITTOIA 2005, s 383–385, Sch 1 para 615; ITEPA 2003, s 716A*].

See **1.5 ALLOWANCES AND TAX RATES** for the rates of tax applicable to dividend income.

An excess of the value of goodwill transferred to a company on incorporation of a business over its true value may be treated as a distribution. If, however, it is clear that there was no intention to transfer the goodwill at excess value, and that reasonable efforts were made to carry out the transaction at market value by using a professional valuation, the distribution may be 'unwound'. (Revenue Tax Bulletin April 2005 pp 1200, 1201).

Tax credits on dividends etc.

[64.8] A UK resident or 'eligible non-UK resident' receiving a dividend or other qualifying distribution made by a UK resident company is normally entitled to a tax credit equal to one-ninth of the amount or value of the distribution. Where a person is entitled to a tax credit, the income chargeable to tax is the aggregate of the dividend plus the tax credit. The credit may be deducted from income tax charged on total income for the year in which the distribution is made, but is not repayable. Where an individual's total income is reduced (e.g. by personal reliefs), such that the qualifying distributions are not, or not wholly, brought within the charge to tax, the value of the tax credit attaching to the distribution is reduced (see the example at **1.18**(v)(c) ALLOWANCES AND TAX RATES). See *CTA 2010, s 1136* for the meaning of 'qualifying distribution'.

For the above purposes, an *'eligible non-UK resident'* is one who at any time in the tax year in which the dividend is received, is a non-resident within **50.2**(i)–(viii) NON-RESIDENTS.

[*ITTOIA 2005, ss 397, 398; ITA 2007, Sch 1 para 515; FA 2008, s 34, Sch 12 para 3*].

Tax credits set off or repaid which ought not to have been set off or repaid may be assessed, the tax due on such an assessment being payable (subject to the normal appeal procedures) within 14 days after the issue of the notice of assessment. [*ITTOIA 2005, s 401A; ICTA 1988, s 252; CTA 2010, Sch 1 para 456*].

HMRC may by notice require any person in whose name any shares or loan capital are registered to provide details as to the ownership of those investments. [*ITTOIA 2005, s 401B(1); FA 1989, Sch 12 para 3*].

See **1.5** ALLOWANCES AND TAX RATES for the rates of tax applicable to dividend income.

Dividends etc. received by persons not entitled to tax credits

[64.9] Where a person receives a dividend or other qualifying distribution, but is not entitled to a tax credit, e.g. because he is non-UK resident and does not fall within the definition of 'eligible non-resident' (see **64.8** above), he is treated as having paid income tax at the dividend ordinary rate (see **1.5** ALLOWANCES AND TAX RATES) on the 'amount or value of the distribution'. The tax treated as paid is not repayable. See *CTA 2010, s 1136* for the meaning of 'qualifying distribution'.

The *'amount or value of the distribution'* for these purposes is the distribution grossed up at the dividend ordinary rate. See **68.11** SETTLEMENTS for the similar position as regards discretionary or accumulation trusts.

[*ITTOIA 2005, s 399; ITA 2007, Sch 1 para 516; FA 2008, s 34, Sch 12 para 6*].

Non-qualifying distributions

[64.10] A non-qualifying distribution does not carry a tax credit. (For the definition of qualifying distribution, see *CTA 2010, s 1136*.) The recipient of a non-qualifying distribution is treated as having paid income tax at the dividend ordinary rate on the actual amount of the distribution (i.e. there is no grossing up), such tax being non-repayable. In the case of trustees of discretionary or accumulation trusts, the trustees are taxed on the distribution at the dividend trust rate, but their tax liability is reduced by an amount of income tax equivalent to the dividend ordinary rate.

[ITTOIA 2005, s 400; ITA 2007, Sch 1 para 517].

Where a person has paid tax at the excess of the dividend upper rate over the dividend ordinary rate on a non-qualifying distribution consisting of the issue of share capital or security, the amount so paid reduces his excess liability on a subsequent qualifying distribution consisting of the repayment of that share capital or of the principal of that security. The reduction is made at Step 6 of the calculation of income tax liability (see **1.7, 1.8 ALLOWANCES AND TAX RATES**). *[ITTOIA 2005, s 401; ITA 2007, Sch 1 para 518; CTA 2010, Sch 1 para 455].*

Distributions from Real Estate Investment Trusts (REITs)

[64.11] A distribution received from a Real Estate Investment Trust (REIT) by a shareholder within the charge to income tax is treated in the shareholder's hands as profits of a UK property business to the extent that it is paid out of the tax-exempt profits of the REIT. Basic rate tax is deducted at source by the REIT. The distribution does not carry a tax credit. Distributions made by an REIT out of profits other than tax-exempt profits are taxed, and carry tax credits, in the same way as any other distribution made by a UK resident company. See **60.14 PROPERTY INCOME** for more details.

Dividends from non-UK resident companies

[64.12] Income tax is also charged on dividends from companies not resident in the UK. The charge is on the amount of dividends arising in the tax year (though **DOUBLE TAX RELIEF (26)** may be available for any foreign tax suffered). Dividends of a capital nature are excluded from the charge. *[ITTOIA 2005, ss 402–404; FA 2008, s 34, Sch 12 para 18].*

Tax credits on dividends etc.

[64.13] For 2008/09, a UK resident or 'eligible non-UK resident' receiving a dividend or other qualifying distribution made by a non-UK resident company in which he is a 'minority shareholder' at the time of receipt is entitled to a tax credit equal to one-ninth of the amount or value of the 'grossed up distribution'. (This does not apply if the company is an offshore fund, as defined at **51.24 OFFSHORE FUNDS**.) Previously, no tax credit was available at all, and this continues to be the case for those who do not meet the minority shareholder condition.

Where a person is entitled to a tax credit, the income chargeable to tax is the aggregate of the dividend plus the tax credit. The credit may be deducted from income tax charged on total income for the year in which the distribution is made, but is not repayable. Where an individual's total income is reduced (e.g. by personal reliefs), such that the qualifying distributions are not, or not wholly, brought within the charge to tax, the value of the tax credit attaching to the distribution is reduced (as in the example at **1.18**(v)(c) **ALLOWANCES AND TAX RATES** in relation to UK dividends). See *CTA 2010, s 1136* for the meaning of 'qualifying distribution'.

For the above purposes, an *'eligible non-UK resident'* is one who at any time in the tax year in which the dividend is received, is a non-resident within any of **50.2**(ii)–(viii) **NON-RESIDENTS**. The *'grossed up distribution'* is the distribution plus any foreign tax attributable to it.

For the above purposes, a *'minority shareholder'* is a person whose shareholding in the company is less than 10% of its issued share capital (see below as regards 2009/10 onwards). Shares are considered to be part of the shareholding of a person ('P') for this purpose if:

- P is beneficially entitled to the shares or to a distribution arising from them (or both); or
- the shares are comprised in a settlement of which P is a settlor, and the circumstances are such that income arising from shares in the settlement fall to be treated as P's income for tax purposes; or
- the shares are held by a person connected with P (within **21 CONNECTED PERSONS**) and were transferred to him by P (or P arranged for the person to acquire them) for the purpose of avoiding tax; or
- P has transferred the shares to someone under a repo (sale and repurchase) or stock lending arrangement.

A person in receipt of a manufactured overseas dividend (see **4.10 ANTI-AVOIDANCE**) is treated as having received a distribution made by a non-UK resident company (and thus as potentially entitled to a tax credit) if, and only if, the manufactured overseas dividend is representative of such a distribution. In this case, the tax credit is equal to one-ninth of the gross amount of the overseas dividend of which the manufactured overseas dividend is representative, disregarding any overseas tax credit.

For 2009/10 onwards, tax credits continue to be available in the circumstances described above, except that:

- distributions from offshore funds made on or after 22 April 2009 are no longer excluded); and
- in relation to any distribution made or after 22 April 2009, where the company has more than one class of share in issue, a minority shareholder is a person whose shareholding in the company is less than 10% of its issued share capital of the same class as the share in respect of which the distribution is made. (Shares are not of the same class if the amounts paid up on them, other than by way of share premium, are different.)

Tax credits are also available in the circumstances below where the dividend or other qualifying distribution is made by the non-UK resident company on or after **22 April 2009** (or where a manufactured overseas dividend is paid representing such a distribution). Broadly, individuals with shareholdings of 10% or more are now entitled to a tax credit if either of the two following conditions are met.

The first condition (the 'residence condition') is that the company making the distribution is a resident of (and only of) a 'qualifying territory' at the time the distribution is received. If the distribution is one of a series of distributions made as part of a scheme (as very widely defined), it is further provided that the scheme must not be a 'tax advantage scheme' and that each company that makes a distribution in the series must meet the residence condition. A company is a resident of a territory for this purpose if, under the laws of that territory, it is liable to tax there by virtue of its domicile, residence or place of management, but not if it is so liable only in respect of its income from sources in that territory or capital situated there. A 'tax advantage scheme' is one designed solely to enable the obtaining of tax credits or any other tax relief on distributions.

The second condition is that the company making the distribution is an offshore fund (as defined at **51.24 OFFSHORE FUNDS**).

For the purpose of the residence condition, a *'qualifying territory'* is defined as the UK and any territory which has a double tax agreement with the UK that contains a 'non-discrimination provision'. A *'non-discrimination provision'* is a provision whereby nationals (as defined) of one party to the agreement are not subject to taxation, or any requirement connected with taxation, that is more burdensome than that to which the nationals of the other party are subject in similar circumstances. A list of qualifying territories is provided in HMRC Brief 76/09, 18 December 2009.

The Treasury has power to make regulations by statutory instrument designating as qualifying territories specific countries that do not meet the above definition and/or removing specific countries from the scope of the definition. Any such regulations could have retrospective effect from the beginning of the tax year in which they are made. In this connection, *SI 2009 No 3333* provides, with retrospective effect from 22 April 2009, that a territory is not a qualifying territory in relation to the company making the distribution if that company is an 'excluded company'. An *'excluded company'* is one which is excluded from one or more of the benefits of any double taxation agreement for the time being in force in relation to that territory.

[*ITTOIA 2005, ss 397A, 397AA, 397B, 397BA–397C, 398; FA 2008, s 34, Sch 12 paras 4, 5; FA 2009, Sch 19 paras 2–7, 14; TIOPA 2010, Sch 8 paras 66, 67; SI 2009 No 3333*].

For the years 2003/04 to 2007/08 inclusive, although there was no statutory entitlement to tax credits on dividends from non-UK resident companies, HMRC have stated that they will accept claims for tax credits on dividends from companies in Finland, Greece and Ireland. (In these cases a form of corporation tax is paid in the other country and there is no withholding tax on outbound dividends.) This does not apply, however, to dividends from Irish investment funds which are not chargeable to Irish tax on their relevant income or gains; these include Irish International Financial Services Centre funds. The tax credit will be equal to one-ninth of the grossed up distribution as normal. Any claim by a self-assessment taxpayer for 2003/04 or 2004/05 must be made by 31 May 2010. PAYE taxpayers who are not asked to file a tax return have until 31 January 2011 to claim for those years. For later years, normal time limits apply (see **71.2**, **71.3** TIME LIMITS—FIXED DATES). (HMRC Brief 73/09, 1 December 2009).

Stock dividends

Income tax

[**64.14**] Shares issued by a UK company in lieu of a cash dividend are chargeable to income tax on the individual beneficial shareholder on an amount equal to the cash equivalent grossed up by reference to the dividend ordinary rate (see **1.5** ALLOWANCES AND TAX RATES). The shareholder is then deemed to have paid the notional tax but it is not repayable. If his income is reduced by any deductions falling to be made (at Step 2 or 3 in the calculation of income tax liability at **1.7** ALLOWANCES AND TAX RATES) out of the stock dividend income, the amount on which he is treated as having paid the notional tax is similarly reduced.

Similarly chargeable are bonus shares issued in respect of shares held under terms which carry the right to the bonus.

The cash equivalent is normally the amount of the cash dividend alternative. If, however, the difference between the cash dividend alternative and the market value of the shares received is at least 15% of the market value of the shares received, the cash equivalent is taken to be that market value instead. If there is no cash dividend alternative, as in the case of bonus shares, the cash equivalent is the market value of the shares received. For listed shares, market value is determined as at the first day of dealing; for other shares, it is determined as at the earliest day on which the company was required to issue the shares.

The shareholder is treated as receiving the shares on the earliest date on which the company was required to issue the shares. Where more than one person is entitled to the shares issued, apportionment is made according to their respective interests.

If the shareholder is a settlement and a cash dividend would have been 'accumulated or discretionary income', the trustees are chargeable under these provisions (see also **68.11** SETTLEMENTS). 'Accumulated or discretionary income' is as defined in **68.11** except that it does not include income arising under a trust established for charitable purposes only.

[*ITTOIA 2005, ss 409, 410, 410A, 411–414, 414A, Sch 2 para 78A; ITA 2007, Sch 1 paras 519, 520; CTA 2009, Sch 1 para 630; CTA 2010, Sch 1 paras 458–461, 471(3)*].

Stock dividends issued to personal representatives during the administration period are grossed as above and deemed part of the aggregate income of the estate (see **23** DECEASED ESTATES).

Capital gains tax

The issue of shares treated as income as in above does not constitute a reorganisation of share capital within *TCGA 1992, ss 126–128*. The person acquiring the shares is treated for capital gains tax purposes as having acquired them for whichever of the cash dividend alternative or the market value was used in determining the amount treated as income. [*TCGA 1992, s 142*].

Enhanced stock dividends received by trustees of interest in possession trusts

[64.15] Where the trustees of an interest in possession trust have concluded that either:

(a)   an enhanced stock dividend belongs to the income beneficiary; or
(b)   it forms part of the trust's capital; or
(c)   while adding the enhanced stock dividend to capital, the trustees should compensate the income beneficiary for the loss of the cash dividend he would otherwise have received,

and the view they have taken of the trust law position is supportable on the facts, HMRC will not seek to challenge what the trustees have done. The income tax consequences of each of the views at (a)–(c) above are as follows.

(i)   As in (a) above the beneficiary is beneficially entitled to the shares comprised in the dividend, the provisions described at **64.14** above apply.
(ii)   As in (b) above the stock dividend is regarded as capital, there is no income tax liability.
(iii)   The payment in (c) above to the beneficiary is an annual payment from which basic rate tax must be deducted.

For full details of this treatment and of the capital gains tax consequences, and for differences under Scottish law, see HMRC SP 4/94.

Release of loan to participator in close company

[64.16] Where a close company that is chargeable to tax under *CTA 2010, s 455* (previously *ICTA 1988, s 419*, in respect of a loan or advance to a participator (or to an associate of a participator) (see Tolley's Corporation Tax under Close Companies), releases or writes off the debt, the amount released or written off is grossed up by reference to the dividend ordinary rate (see **1.5 ALLOWANCES AND TAX RATES**) and included in the taxable income of the borrower. That person is deemed to have paid the notional tax but it is not repayable. If his income is reduced by any deductions falling to be made (at Step 2 or 3 in the calculation of income tax liability at **1.7 ALLOWANCES AND TAX RATES**) out of the income so included, the amount on which he is treated as having paid the notional tax is similarly reduced.

[*ITTOIA 2005, ss 415–421, 421A; FA 2006, Sch 13 paras 13, 31(1)(3); ITA 2007, Sch 1 paras 521, 522; CTA 2009, Sch 1 para 631; CTA 2010, Sch 1 paras 462–465*].

Where an amount released or written off is charged as above, that amount is not charged as taxable earnings under *ITEPA 2003, ss 188–190* — see **27.41** EMPLOYMENT INCOME.

Purchased life annuities

[64.17] The income element of a 'purchased life annuity' payment is regarded as income for income tax purposes from which tax is deducted under *ITA 2007, s 901* (see **24.7–24.10** DEDUCTION OF TAX AT SOURCE). Tax is charged on the full amount of the payment arising in the year, subject to the special rules for foreign income (see **32** FOREIGN INCOME) and a credit for the tax deducted at source. The capital element is not treated as income and is thus exempt from the charge to income tax (see **24.11** DEDUCTION OF TAX AT SOURCE).

A *'purchased life annuity'* is one which is purchased for money or money's worth from a person whose business it is to grant annuities and which is payable for a term ascertainable only by reference to the end of a human life (notwithstanding that the annuity may in some circumstances end before or after the life).

[*ITTOIA 2005, ss 422–426; ITA 2007, Sch 1 para 523*].

The charge to tax on the income element of a purchased life annuity is at the rate of tax applicable to savings income (see **1.6 ALLOWANCES AND TAX RATES**). Tax is deductible at source at the basic rate for 2008/09 onwards and previously at the savings rate.

A proportion of a purchased life annuity payment is regarded as capital, and therefore exempt from income tax, and is thus not within the above charge. Prior to 2008/09, this exemption required the making of a claim by the annuitant. The exemption does not apply to annuities purchased wholly or partly with sums satisfying the conditions for relief under *ICTA 1988, s 266* (life assurance premiums), annuities purchased following a direction in a will or annuities purchased to provide for an annuity payable as a result of a will or settlement out of income of property disposed of by the will or settlement. It also does not apply to annuities forming part of the income of a trade or to annuities chargeable as pension income under *ITEPA 2003* (due to the priority rules at **64.1** above).

If the amount of the annuity payments depends solely on the duration of a human life or lives, the same proportion of each payment is the exempt amount of that payment. The proportion is that which the purchase price bears to the actuarial value of the annuity payment, determined by reference to mortality tables or, failing that, by the Government Actuary. For prescribed mortality tables see *SI 1956 No 1230* as amended by *SI 1991 No 2808*, and *Rose v Trigg* Ch D 1963, 41 TC 365. If the amount of the annuity payments depends on an additional contingency, each payment is regarded as exempt to the extent it does not exceed a fixed sum given by a formula in *ITTOIA 2005, s 721*. If a particular payment falls short of the fixed sum, the shortfall is added to the fixed sum for the next payment, and so on. If the term of the annuity does not depend solely on the duration of a human life or lives, the exempt proportion or the fixed sum is adjusted as is just and reasonable, having regard to the contingencies affecting the annuity. Consideration given partly for an annuity and partly for something else is apportioned on a just and reasonable basis in determining the purchase price of the annuity for these purposes.

Any question of whether an annuity is a purchased life annuity for these purposes, and any question as to how much of an annuity payment is exempt are (before 2008/09) determined by HMRC, with a right of appeal (to the Special Commissioners before 1 April 2009). If the payer of an annuity has been notified of such a determination, it is conclusive for fixing the amount of tax he must deduct at source from each payment. In the absence of any such notice, he must deduct tax from the full amount. Any tax over- or under-deducted from payments made before the notification is repaid to or charged on the payee, subject to time limits.

[*ITTOIA 2005, ss 717–724, Sch 2 paras 143–145; ITA 2007, Sch 1 para 573; SI 2008 No 562, Reg 28*].

Changes for 2008/09 onwards

The earlier regulations, which dated back to 1956, are replaced by modernised regulations for 2008/09 onwards. In this connection the following changes are made to the primary legislation with effect for those years.

* The above requirement for the annuitant to claim the exemption for the capital element of the annuity is dropped.
* The above requirement for certain questions to be determined by HMRC is also abolished.

The new regulations apply to any annuity under which the first payment to the annuitant is made on or after 6 April 2008. Under these regulations, the annuity provider will send the annuitant a form on which he must enter or confirm certain basic information and make a declaration as to whether the annuity is a purchased life annuity which is eligible for the partial tax exemption. The annuitant must then return the form to the annuity provider. Until the annuitant returns the completed form, the annuity must be treated as one for which no part of the payments are eligible for the tax exemption. Upon receipt of the form, the annuity provider must calculate and enter the exempt capital element of the annuity, if any, in accordance with prescribed mortality tables. He must then return the form to the annuitant within 30 days of receipt or, if later, within 30 days of the date of the first payment under the annuity, and send a photocopy to HMRC within three months of the date of that first payment. If the annuitant fails to provide a completed form, the annuity provider must supply HMRC with the known details of the annuity within that three-month period.

If the annuity is purchased from a non-UK insurer, the latter must usually nominate a UK-resident tax representative in accordance with set procedures. The representative will normally undertake the above compliance instead of the annuity provider.

[*FA 2007, s 46(5)–(7)(9); SI 2008 Nos 561, 562, 1481; SI 2009 No 56, Sch 1 para 183*].

Simon's Taxes. See B8.433, E1.428–E1.430C.

Deeply discounted securities

Charge to tax

[64.18] A profit on the disposal of a 'deeply discounted security' (as defined at **64.20** below) is treated as taxable income. Tax is charged on the full amount of such profits arising in the tax year. The person liable is the person making the disposal. The profit on disposal is the excess (if any) of the disposal proceeds over the acquisition cost and is taken to arise when the disposal occurs. See below for certain disposals treated as made at market value. No deduction is available for incidental costs of acquisition or disposal, except to the extent that any such costs were incurred before 27 March 2003 (and see also the special rules at **64.19** below for listed securities held since before 27 March 2003). No relief is available for a loss on disposal, again subject to the special rules at **64.19** below for listed securities held since before 27 March 2003.

If the securities are located outside the UK, the REMITTANCE BASIS (**61**) applies where appropriate.

See **64.21** below for special rules on strips of government securities and **64.22** below for special rules on corporate strips.

A disposal of a deeply discounted security occurs:

- when it is redeemed; or
- when it is transferred by sale, exchange, gift or otherwise; or
- when it is converted under its terms into shares in a company or other securities (including other deeply discounted securities).

A transfer or acquisition under an agreement is treated as taking place when the agreement is made if entitlement to the security passes at that time. A conditional agreement is treated as made when the condition is met.

Where a conversion into euros of deeply discounted securities from the currency of a State which has adopted the euro (a '*euroconversion*' — see *SI 1998 No 3177, Reg 3*) is effected solely by means of an exchange or conversion of those securities, the conversion is not treated as constituting either a transfer or a conversion. Provision is made for an adjustment to the acquisition cost in respect of any cash payment received as a result of the conversion.

Where the holder of a deeply discounted security dies, he is treated as having transferred the security immediately before his death to his personal representatives and thus as having made a disposal.

Market value disposals and acquisitions

The following transfers are treated for the above purposes as made at market value (determined as for capital gains tax purposes) at the time of the disposal:

(a)   a transfer made otherwise than by way of bargain at arm's length;

(b)   a transfer between CONNECTED PERSONS (21);

(c)   a transfer for consideration not wholly in money or money's worth;

(d)   a transfer treated as made on death (see above); and

(e)   a transfer by personal representatives to a legatee (as defined by *ITTOIA 2005, s 440(6)(7)*).

In each case, the transferee is also treated as having acquired the security at market value.

Where a deeply discounted security is converted under its terms into shares in a company or other securities, such that a disposal is treated as occurring (see above), the proceeds of the disposal are the market value of the shares or other securities at the time of the conversion. Where the conversion is into securities which are themselves deeply discounted securities, the acquisition cost of those securities for the purposes of these provisions is their market value.

Where a security is issued to a person in accordance with the terms of a 'qualifying earn-out right', the amount paid for the acquisition is taken to be the sum of the market value, immediately before the issue, of the right to be issued with the security in accordance with those terms and any amount payable for the issue in accordance with those terms. A *'qualifying earn-out right'* is so much of any right conferred on a person as:

(i)   constitutes the whole or any part of the consideration for the transfer by him of shares in or debentures of a company or for the transfer of the whole or part of a business or interest in a business carried on alone or in partnership;

(ii)   consists in either a right to be issued with securities of another company or a right which is capable of being discharged in accordance with its terms by the issue of such securities; and

(iii)   is such that the value of the consideration referred to in (i) above is unascertainable at the time when the right is conferred.

[*ITTOIA 2005, ss 427–429, 437–442, 460(1)(3), Sch 2 para 79; FA 2007, Sch 26 para 11(3)*].

Simon's Taxes. See **D9.5**.

Listed securities held since before 27 March 2003

[64.19] Where a deeply discounted security has been held continuously since before 27 March 2003 by the person making the disposal *and* the security was listed on a recognised stock exchange (within *ICTA 1988, s 841(1)*) at some time before that date, relief is available for losses and for incidental costs of acquisition and disposal as follows.

A loss on disposal, i.e. the excess (if any) of acquisition cost over disposal proceeds (together with any incidental costs of disposal and/or acquisition), is allowed as a deduction in computing net income for the year of disposal (at Step 2 of the calculation of income tax liability at **1.7 ALLOWANCES AND TAX RATES**). A claim for the relief must be made no later than the first anniversary of 31 January following the tax year in which the disposal occurs. See **64.23** below as regards trustees.

Where the loss is sustained by a charity or a pension scheme, such that a profit on the disposal would have been relieved from tax under any of the provisions listed at *ITTOIA 2005, Sch 2 paras 82, 83* (i.e. general tax reliefs for charities and pension funds), the loss can only be set off against profits from other disposals of deeply discounted securities in the tax year in which the loss is sustained.

A profit on disposal is reduced by any incidental costs of acquisition and/or disposal, regardless of when those costs are incurred (i.e. whether or not they were incurred before 27 March 2003).

See **64.21** below for special rules on strips of government securities.

Restriction of a loss: connected persons transactions

Notwithstanding the above, no loss relief is available to a person on the transfer of a deeply discounted security to a person connected with him (within **21 CONNECTED PERSONS**), where:

* the transferor acquired the security on issue;
* the amount paid by transferor in respect of the acquisition exceeded the market value of the security at the time of issue; and
* either:
  (a) the transferor was, at the time of issue, connected (as above) with the issuer; or
  (b) the following conditions are met:
    (i) the security was issued by a close company (as in *CTA 2010, Pt 10 Ch 2*, but without the exclusion of non-UK resident companies); and
    (ii) the transferor controlled (within *CTA 2010, ss 450, 451*) that company at the time of issue together with other persons to whom securities of the same kind were also issued.

[*ITTOIA 2005, ss 453–456, Sch 2 paras 82, 83; ITA 2007, Sch 1 paras 525, 589; CTA 2010, Sch 1 para 466*].

Meaning of 'deeply discounted security'

[64.20] Subject to the exceptions below, a security is a *'deeply discounted security'* if, at the time it is issued, the amount payable on maturity or any other possible occasion of redemption exceeds (or may exceed) the issue price by more than:

$R \times 0.5\% \times Y$

Where:

R = the amount payable on maturity or any other possible occasion of redemption; and

Y = the number of years in the 'redemption period' up to a maximum of 30.

The *'redemption period'* is the period between the date of issue and the date of the occasion of redemption in question. So if a security is issued at £80 and is redeemable in 35 years' time at £100, the calculation is £100 × 0.5% × 30 =

£15. As this is less than the £20 difference between issue price and maturity value, the security is a deeply discounted security. If, however, the issue price is £135 and the security is redeemable in 20 years' time at £150, the calculation is £150 × 0.5% × 20 = £15, and the security is not, therefore, a deeply discounted security.

If the redemption period is not a complete number of years but is less than 30 years, the value of Y in the above calculation is increased by a twelfth for each month or part month in excess of a whole number of years. Any interest payable on an occasion of redemption is disregarded in establishing the value of R. Where a security is issued in accordance with the terms of a qualifying earn-out right, its issue price is taken to be the amount paid to acquire it, determined as in **64.18** above.

Notwithstanding the above, none of the following can be deeply discounted securities:

(a)   shares in a company;
(b)   gilt-edged securities (other than strips — see below);
(c)   'excluded indexed securities' (but see below);
(d)   **LIFE ASSURANCE POLICIES (44)**; and
(e)   capital redemption policies.

Strips of government securities are always treated as being deeply discounted securities (see **64.21** below).

A possible occasion of redemption (other than maturity) is ignored for the purposes of the above calculation if either of the following two conditions is met. The first is that:

•   the security may be redeemed on the occasion at the option of a person other than its holder;
•   it is issued to a person not connected with the issuer; and
•   the obtaining of a tax advantage (within *CTA 2010, s 1139*) by any person is not one of the main benefits that might have been expected to accrue from the provision for redemption on that occasion.

The second condition is that redemption on that occasion can be achieved only on the exercise of an option that is exercisable only on an event adversely affecting the holder (see *ITTOIA 2005, s 431(8)*) or the default of any person, but the condition is met only if exercise of the option on that occasion appears unlikely at the time of issue.

If a security was not a deeply discounted security only because the first of these conditions is met, but at some time after its issue it is acquired by, or its holder becomes, a person connected with the issuer, the security is treated as a deeply discounted security from that time onwards. Notwithstanding (c) above, an 'excluded indexed security' (see below) can be a deeply discounted security in these circumstances.

If a person (P) not connected with the issuer acquires a security issued to or held by a person connected with the issuer and treated as a deeply discounted security for that reason alone, the security ceases to be a deeply discounted security from the time of P's acquisition of it.

For the above purposes, the rules in **21 CONNECTED PERSONS** apply to determine whether persons are connected, but without taking any account of the security under review or any security issued under the same prospectus.

Meaning of 'excluded indexed security'

For the above purposes, a security is an *'excluded indexed security'* if, broadly, its redemption value is found by indexing its issue price by reference to the value of chargeable assets of a particular description or by an index of the value of such assets (but not the retail prices index or similar price indices). See *ITTOIA 2005, s 433* for the full definition. If the terms of issue provide that the redemption value will exceed the issue price by at least a specified percentage regardless of movements in the index, the security cannot be an excluded indexed security if the specified minimum increase is over 10%.

Securities issued in separate tranches

The following special rules apply where securities are issued under the same prospectus but on separate occasions. If securities in any one of the separate issues are not deeply discounted securities, securities in the subsequent issues are not deeply discounted securities either, *unless* they fall to be treated as such only because of their being issued to, or coming to be held by, a person connected with the issuer (see the rules above).

If none of the securities in the first issue is a deeply discounted security, but at least some of the securities in one or more later issues are deeply discounted securities (or would be were it not for the foregoing rule), the rule below applies for any disposal or acquisition after the time when the following condition is first met. The condition is that the aggregate nominal value of the deeply discounted securities exceeds the aggregate nominal value of all other securities so far issued under the prospectus. The rule is that all securities issued under the prospectus at any time (including subsequent issues) are treated as being deeply discounted securities and as having been acquired as such. For the purpose only of applying this rule in the case of a person not connected with the issuer, securities falling to be treated as deeply discounted securities only because of their being issued to, or coming to be held by, a person connected with the issuer (see above) are treated as if they were not deeply discounted securities.

[ITTOIA 2005, ss 430–436, 460(1)(2); ITA 2007, Sch 1 para 528; CTA 2010, Sch 1 para 467].

In determining whether a security is a 'deeply discounted security' it is necessary, on a purposive construction of the statutory definition, that there should be a real possibility of a deep gain occurring. In the instant case, terms of issue which were essential for the securities to qualify as deeply discounted securities had to some extent no practical reality and had therefore to be disregarded. (*Astall and another v HMRC* CA, [2010] STC 137).

Strips of government securities

[64.21] Every strip is treated as a deeply discounted security, even it would not otherwise be so. This and the following rules were originally limited to strips of UK Government (i.e. gilt-edged) securities. In relation to securities acquired on or after 27 March 2003, strips of overseas government securities are also within the rules. However, for these purposes, strips do not include 'corporate strips', for which see **64.22** below. A strip, in relation to any stock or bond (the underlying security), is a security that meets the conditions in *ITTOIA 2005, s 444*.

For the purposes of applying the deeply discounted security provisions:

- on the exchange of a security for strips of that security, the acquisition cost of each strip is determined by apportioning the market value of the security *pro rata* to the market value of each strip;
- when a person consolidates strips into a single security by exchanging them for that security, each strip is treated as being redeemed at market value;
- any person holding a strip on 5 April in any tax year, and not disposing of it on that day, is treated as having transferred it at market value on that day and to have immediately re-acquired it at the same value (without incurring any incidental costs in connection with the notional transactions); and
- the Treasury has wide powers to modify by regulations the deeply discounted security provisions as they apply to strips.

Losses

A loss on disposal, i.e. the excess (if any) of acquisition cost over disposal proceeds (*disregarding* any incidental costs of disposal and/or acquisition), is allowed as a deduction in computing net income for the year of disposal (at Step 2 of the calculation of income tax liability at **1.7 ALLOWANCES AND TAX RATES**). A claim for the relief must be made no later than the first anniversary of 31 January following the tax year in which the disposal occurs. But see the anti-avoidance rules below and see **64.23** below as regards trustees. For disposals before 27 March 2003, incidental costs could be taken into account in determining the amount of a loss; they may still be taken into account where the disposal falls within **64.19** above.

Special rules for determining market value

The market value of a strip or of any security exchanged for strips of that security is determined in accordance with *ITTOIA 2005, ss 450, 451* which require use of prices quoted in the London Stock Exchange Daily Official List or, for overseas government strips or securities not quoted in that list, an equivalent foreign stock exchange list. For valuations falling to be made on or after a date to be appointed by the Treasury, these rules are to be replaced by regulations made by statutory instrument.

Anti-avoidance

The following anti-avoidance provisions apply.

(i)   With effect in relation to any strip held on 15 January 2004 or subsequently acquired (disregarding any notional re-acquisition as above): where, as a result of a scheme or arrangement aimed at securing a tax advantage, a person acquires (or acquired) a strip at more than market value or transfers or redeems a strip at less than market value (disregarding any costs incurred in connection with any acquisition, transfer etc.), market value is substituted for the purpose of determining both profits and losses. Market value for these purposes is determined in accordance with *ITTOIA 2005, ss 450, 451* (referred to above).

(ii)   Where, as a result of a scheme or arrangement aimed at securing a tax advantage or producing an allowable loss for capital gains tax purposes, the circumstances are (or might have been) as in (i) above and a payment resulting in a capital loss falls to be made other than in respect of the acquisition or disposal of a strip, that loss is not allowable for capital gains tax purposes.

(iii) With effect in relation to any strip acquired on or after 15 January 2004 (disregarding any notional re-acquisition as above): a loss on the disposal of a strip is restricted for tax purposes *by* the amount (if any) by which proceeds are less than 'original acquisition cost'. A profit is restricted *to* the amount (if any) by which disposal proceeds exceed 'original acquisition cost'. These rules cannot reduce a loss or a profit to a negative amount, i.e. a profit cannot be converted into a loss or *vice versa*. '*Original acquisition cost*' is determined without taking account of any earlier notional transfers and re-acquisitions by the person concerned but otherwise takes account of any rule requiring market value to be substituted for actual cost.

[*ITTOIA 2005, ss 443–452, 460(2)(3), Sch 1 para 437, Sch 2 paras 80, 81; TCGA 1992, s 151C; ITA 2007, Sch 1 paras 319, 524, 528; FA 2007, Sch 26 paras 5, 11*].

In *Berry v HMRC* FTT (TC 321), 2010 STI 1449, a gilt strip planning scheme failed to produce an allowable loss. No amount was paid by the claimant for the gilt strips nor was there any transfer of the strips; the claimant did not take a position in the gilt strips market at a real and significant risk to himself. The scheme was to be regarded for tax purposes as a single transaction.

Corporate strips

[64.22] Every 'corporate strip' is treated as a deeply discounted security, even it would not otherwise be so, in the hands of any person who acquires such a strip on or after 2 December 2004 and otherwise than in pursuance of an agreement entered into before that date. This is an anti-avoidance measure designed to thwart schemes that involve taking normal interest-bearing securities issued by companies and stripping the rights to some or all of the coupons away from the right to the repayment of the principal. The resultant rights have a value which is less than the amount which will eventually be paid by the issuer in respect of them, and thus produce the effect of discount. But, in the absence of this measure, the rights may not have been deeply discounted securities because the underlying security from which they derive was not issued at a discount.

For the purposes of these provisions, a person converts an 'interest-bearing corporate security' into corporate strips of the security if, as a result of any scheme or arrangements, he acquires, in place of the security, two or more separate assets each of which satisfies Condition A below and all of which (taken together) satisfy Condition B below. The rules equally apply where a corporate strip is itself stripped into separate assets.

Condition A is that the asset represents the right to, or secures, one or more 'stripped payments'. A *'stripped payment'* is a payment of (or corresponding to) the whole or a part of one or more payments (whether of interest or principal) remaining to be made under the security. Condition B is that the assets represent the right to, or secure, every payment so remaining to be made. Once a security has gone ex-dividend in respect of the next interest payment, that payment is no longer treated as one 'remaining to be made'.

A *'corporate strip'* is then defined as any asset which is, or has at any time been, one of the separate assets referred to above. However, an asset cannot be a corporate strip if it represents the right to, or secures, payments of (or corresponding to) a part of every payment remaining to be made under an 'interest-bearing corporate security' or a corporate strip. This is to ensure that a corporate strip is not created merely by the re-denomination of the principal into smaller amounts. Also, an asset cannot be a corporate strip in the case of any person if he acquired it, or entered into an agreement to acquire it, before 2 December 2004.

An *'interest-bearing corporate security'* is any interest-bearing security, including loan stock, other than one issued by a government (for which see **64.21** above) or a share in a company.

Where a person sells or transfers the right to one or more payments remaining to be made under a security, that is treated as a conversion into corporate strips followed by a sale of one or more of the assets created by that conversion.

The acquisition cost for income tax purposes of a corporate strip acquired by conversion is found by taking the cost of the original security (excluding any incidental costs of acquisition) and apportioning it between all the assets resulting from the conversion by reference to the proportion that the market value of each asset bears to the market value of all of them. If the converted security was itself a deeply discounted security, the conversion is treated as a transfer of that security, but for an amount equal to its acquisition cost. Where corporate strips are consolidated into a single security, they are treated as being thereby disposed of at their then market value.

There are anti-avoidance rules similar to those at **64.21**(i) above (disregarding the reference there to losses). For the purposes of those rules, market value is determined without regard to any increase or diminution in the value of a corporate strip as a result of the scheme or arrangement in question. Where, as a result of a scheme or arrangement aimed at securing a tax advantage or producing an allowable loss for capital gains tax purposes, the circumstances are (or might have been) as in **64.21**(i) above (as applied to corporate strips) and a payment resulting in a capital loss falls to be made other than in respect of the acquisition or disposal of a corporate strip, that loss is not allowable for capital gains tax purposes.

[ITTOIA 2005, ss 452A–452G; TCGA 1992, s 151D; ITA 2007, Sch 1 para 320].

Trustees

[64.23] Profits chargeable under these provisions on the disposal of a deeply discounted security by trustees are treated for the purposes of *ITTOIA 2005, ss 619–648* (income treated as that of the settlor — see **68.26–68.32** SETTLEMENTS) as income arising under the settlement from the security, and for the purposes of **68.11** SETTLEMENTS as income arising to the trustees. To the extent that tax on such profits is chargeable on the trustees, it is chargeable at the trust rate (see **68.11** SETTLEMENTS). These rules do not apply to trustees of unauthorised unit trusts (see **75.9** UNIT TRUSTS ETC.) to the extent that the profits are shown in the scheme's accounts as income available for payment to unit holders or for investment.

In the case of trustees, relief for losses under **64.19** above can be set off only against profits from other disposals of deeply discounted securities in the tax year in which the loss is sustained.

See **64.21** above for special rules on strips of government securities. The above rule restricting the set-off of losses does *not* apply to a loss sustained by trustees on the disposal of a strip.

Non-resident trustees

Tax is not charged, and losses are not relieved, under the deeply discounted securities rules if the disposal is made by a settlement of which the trustees are non-UK resident.

[*ITTOIA 2005, s 454(5), 457, 458; FA 2006, Sch 13 para 32(1)(2)(4); ITA 2007, Sch 1 para 526*].

Miscellaneous

Accrued income scheme

[64.24] Deeply discounted securities within these provisions are outside the accrued income scheme, except where the person making the disposal has held the security continuously since before 27 March 2003 and the security was listed at some time before that date (see **2.2** ACCRUED INCOME SCHEME).

Transfer of assets abroad

For the purposes of *ITA 2007, Pt 13 Ch 2* (transfer of assets abroad — see **4.14–4.17** ANTI-AVOIDANCE), a profit chargeable under these provisions realised by a person resident or domiciled outside the UK is taken to be income of that person. [*ITTOIA 2005, s 459; ITA 2007, Sch 1 para 527*].

Recovery of assets under Proceeds of Crime Act 2002, Pt 5

Where the transfer of a deeply discounted security is a *Pt 5* transfer under *Proceeds of Crime Act 2002* (as in **10.2**(x) CAPITAL ALLOWANCES) and no compensating payment is made to the transferor, it is not treated as a transfer for the purposes of these provisions. [*Proceeds of Crime Act 2002, Sch 10 paras 5, 10*].

Sales of foreign dividend coupons

[64.25] The provisions described below are repealed with effect on and after 22 April 2009 as a consequence of the introduction of general provisions regarding transfers of income streams at **4.34 ANTI-AVOIDANCE**.

A charge to tax arises under *ITTOIA 2005, Pt 4 Ch 13* on income which is treated as arising from foreign holdings of shares or securities (i.e. shares or securities outside the UK that are issued by or on behalf of a public authority in a country outside the UK or a non-UK resident body of persons).

Income is treated as arising from such holdings in two cases:

(a)   where a bank's office in the UK either pays over or carries to an account the proceeds of a sale or other realisation of dividend coupons (as defined) in respect of the holdings;

(b)   where dividend coupons in respect of the holdings are sold to a person dealing in coupons in the UK and the seller is neither a bank (as defined) nor a dealer in coupons.

Tax is charged on the full amount of the proceeds in (*a*) and on the full amount of the proceeds arising in the tax year in (b) (unless the **REMITTANCE BASIS (61)** applies). The person liable for the tax is the person receiving or entitled to the proceeds.

[*ITTOIA 2005, ss 570–573; ITA 2007, Sch 1 para 545*].

Trustees

Income treated as above as arising to trustees of a settlement is chargeable at the trust rate. See **68.12 SETTLEMENTS**.

Key points

[64.26] Points to consider are as follows.

*   Where savings and investment income other than dividends from UK companies potentially falls within the charge to tax as trading income or as employment income, then generally speaking either *ITTOIA 2005* or *ITEPA 2003* take precedence.
*   Where an investor receives part compensation for the loss of a bank deposit under the financial services compensation scheme, some of the payment will represent interest — even where the scheme does not cover the investor's entire capital sum. The amount which represents interest is taxable as savings income in spite of the loss of capital.
*   Interest arising on all current issues of gilts is tax exempt to non-UK residents under the FOTRA scheme. See **64.3**.
*   The treatment of income arising on offshore funds and indeed the classification of such funds changed significantly during 2009. See **51 OFFSHORE FUNDS**. Holders will need to ascertain the classification of the fund to check whether distributions are treated as interest or dividends.

- Note that distributions by UK REITS are treated as property income, and do not carry a tax credit, although basic rate tax is deducted at source.
- Where a stock dividend is taxed as income, the taxpayer should retain a record of the cash dividend alternative as this will normally count as the cost of the shares issued for capital gains tax purposes.
- Where a loan to a participator in a close company is written off, the principal is taxed as a distribution carrying a dividend tax credit. The amount cannot be taxed as employment income, although Class 1 national insurance contributions will apply to the amount written off (but not the tax credit).
- Advisers should not overlook the application of the accrued income scheme, which is dealt with in **2 ACCRUED INCOME SCHEME.**

65

Self-Assessment

Cross-reference. See also **66 SELF-ASSESSMENT — KEY DATES**.

Simon's Taxes. See E1.2.

See also HMRC Manual, 'Income Tax Self-Assessment: The Legal Framework'.

Introduction

[65.1] Self-assessment became part of the UK tax system in 1996/97. The term 'self-assessment' refers to a system whereby the annual tax return filed by individuals, partnerships and trustees should itself include an assessment of the taxpayer's liability to income tax and capital gains tax. Payment of tax is due automatically, based on this self-assessment, without the need for HMRC to issue its own tax assessments.

See **66 SELF-ASSESSMENT — KEY DATES** for a calendar of key dates and events.

Summary of the self-assessment system

[65.2] The tax return for individuals consists of a basic return to which will be attached any supplementary pages relevant to the individual concerned, forming a single 'customised' tax return. The supplementary pages cover employment, share schemes, self-employment, partnership income, land and property, foreign income, trust income, capital gains and non-UK residence etc. Each individual will also receive a tax return guide containing explanatory notes relevant to his circumstances. It is the individual's responsibility to obtain any supplementary pages he needs but has not received, which he may do by downloading from the HMRC website or telephoning an HMRC Orderline, by which means he may also obtain the relevant explanatory notes and/or 'helpsheets' on specific topics. Each return sent out will be accompanied by a tax calculation guide designed to assist the individual in calculating his tax liability if he chooses to do so. See generally **63.2 RETURNS**. Partnership returns follow a similar pattern (see **63.13 RETURNS**).

Returns must be filed on or before a specified date following the tax year (see **63.2 RETURNS**). As regards returns for 2007/08 onwards, different dates are specified for online filing and paper returns. Taxpayers who do not file online must file their return earlier than those who do (see **63.3 RETURNS**). Taxpayers with employment income must also file their return by an earlier specified date if they wish to have a liability of less than £2,000 coded out through **PAY AS YOU EARN (53)** (see **63.3 RETURNS**). Penalties will be imposed for late submission of returns, subject to appeal on the grounds of reasonable excuse (see **55.5 PENALTIES**). There are provisions for making amendments to returns (see **63.4 RETURNS**). HMRC are given a window in which to give notice of their intention to enquire into the return (see **63.6 RETURNS**). A formal procedure is laid down for such enquiries (see **63.6–63.11 RETURNS**). If HMRC do not give such notice, the return becomes final and conclusive, subject to any overpayment claim by the taxpayer (see **18.7 CLAIMS**) or 'discovery' assessment by HMRC (see **6.6 ASSESSMENTS**). In the event of non-submission of a return, HMRC are able to make a determination of the tax liability; there is no right of appeal but the determination can be superseded upon submission of the return (see **63.12 RETURNS**). Capital losses must be quantified if they are to be allowable losses (see Tolley's Capital Gains Tax).

A special return has to be filed by partnerships. This must include a statement of the allocation of partnership income between the partners. See **63.13 RETURNS**.

A Short Tax Return (STR) for those with relatively straightforward tax affairs was issued nationwide for the first time in April 2005 as an alternative to the standard self-assessment return. Also, under criteria applicable to returns for 2004/05 and subsequent years, fewer taxpayers (including higher rate taxpayers) whose affairs can be adequately dealt with using the PAYE system will be asked to complete a tax return of any kind, though they may choose to do so if they wish. See Guidelines for Individuals completing Tax Returns at w ww.hmrc.gov.uk/sa/guidelines.htm and www.hmrc.gov.uk/sa/guidelines-sa-ret urns.htm, guidance on the Short Tax Return at www.hmrc.gov.uk/sa/shorttax return.htm and Revenue Tax Bulletins February 2004 pp 1079, 1080 and April 2005 pp 1187–1189. From April 2004, it is HMRC policy to make increased use of the telephone to resolve minor queries arising in connection with completed returns.

Payment of tax

Income tax (on all sources of taxable income) for a tax year is payable by means of two interim payments of equal amounts, based normally on the liability for the previous year and due on 31 January in the tax year and the following 31 July, and a final balancing payment due on the following

31 January (on which date any capital gains tax liability is also due for payment). Taxpayers have the right to reduce their interim payments if they believe their liability will be less than that for the previous year or to dispense with interim payments if they believe they will have no liability. Interim payments are not in any case required where substantially all of a taxpayer's liability is covered by deduction of tax at source, including PAYE, or where the amounts otherwise due are below *de minimis* limits prescribed by regulations. See **65.5–65.8** below.

Interest on overdue payments runs from the due date to the date of payment (see **42.2** INTEREST AND SURCHARGES ON OVERDUE TAX). There is also a 5% surcharge on any tax unpaid by 28 February following the tax year and a further 5% surcharge on any tax unpaid by the following 31 July, such surcharges being subject to appeal on the grounds of reasonable excuse (see **42.3** INTEREST AND SURCHARGES ON OVERDUE TAX). Interest on tax overpaid runs from the due date (or date of payment if later) to the date of repayment (see **41.1** INTEREST ON OVERPAID TAX); the rate of interest is lower than that on overdue tax.

Miscellaneous

There is a statutory requirement for taxpayers to keep records for the purpose of making returns and to preserve such records for specified periods (see **63.5** RETURNS). A formal procedure applies to the making of claims and elections and the giving of notices (see **18.1** CLAIMS).

Interpretation of references to assessments etc.

[65.3] References in the legislation to an individual (or trustee) being assessed to tax, or being charged to tax by an assessment, are to be construed as including a reference to his being so assessed, or being so charged, by a self-assessment under *TMA 1970, s 9* (see **65.4** below) or by a determination under *TMA 1970, s 28C* (see **63.12** RETURNS) which has not been superseded by a self-assessment. [*FA 1994, s 197*].

Self-assessments

[65.4] Every return under *TMA 1970, s 8* or *s 8A* (see **63.2** RETURNS) must include, subject to the exception below, an assessment (a self-assessment) of the amounts in which, based on the information in the return and taking into account any reliefs and allowances claimed therein, the person making the return is chargeable to income tax and capital gains tax for the tax year and of his net income tax liability for the year, taking into account tax deducted at source and tax credits on dividends. In the event of non-compliance, an officer of HMRC *may* make the assessment on his behalf, based on the information in the return, and send the person a copy.

The tax to be self-assessed does not include any chargeable on the scheme administrator of a registered pension scheme (see **57.2** PENSION PROVISION) or the responsible person in relation to an employer-financed retirement benefits scheme (see **57.27** PENSION PROVISION).

A person need not comply with this requirement if he makes and delivers his return on or before 31 October following the tax year to which the return relates or, if later, within two months beginning with the date of the notice to deliver the return. This deadline is of no significance where returns are filed online (see **63.2** above) as the tax due is automatically computed during the filing process. In the event of a person making no self-assessment under this option, an officer of HMRC *must* make the assessment on his behalf, based on the information in the return, and send the person a copy. Such assessments are treated as self-assessments by the person making the return and as included in the return.

A self-assessment must not show as repayable any notional tax treated as deducted from certain income deemed to have been received after deduction of tax, for example stock dividends.

[*TMA 1970, s 9(1)–(3A); FA 2007, ss 91(1), 92; FA 2008, s 34, Sch 12 para 10*].

Taxpayers with employment income who wish to have a liability of less than £2,000 coded out through PAY AS YOU EARN (**53**) must file their return by an earlier date than the 31 January deadline at **63.2 RETURNS**. That date is 31 October (following the tax year) if the return is filed manually and 30 December if it is filed online (see **63.2 RETURNS**). A 2009/10 underpayment, for example, will be coded out for 2011/12. (HMRC Income Tax Self-Assessment: The Legal Framework Manual SALF204, para 2.33; Revenue Tax Bulletin June 1996 p 315; Revenue 'Working Together' Bulletin February 2001 p 2; Revenue Press Release 23 September 2002). Coding out of an underpayment for a tax year has the consequential effect of reducing any payments on account (see **65.5** below) due for the following tax year.

Simon's Taxes. See E1.202A, E1.204.

Interim payments of tax on account

[65.5] Where, as regards the year immediately preceding the tax year in question:

(a) a person is assessed to income tax under *TMA 1970, s 9* (self-assessment — see **63.3 RETURNS**);

(b) the assessed amount exceeds any income tax deducted at source (including tax deducted under PAYE, taking in any deduction in respect of that year but to be made in a subsequent year but subtracting any amount paid in that year but in respect of a previous year, tax treated as deducted from, or as paid on, any income, and tax credits on dividends); and

(c) the said excess (the 'relevant amount') and the proportion which the relevant amount bears to the assessed amount are not less than, respectively, £1,000 and 20%,

the person must make two interim payments on account of his income tax liability for the tax year in question, each payment being equal to 50% of the relevant amount (see (c) above) and the payments being due on or before, respectively, 31 January in the tax year and the following 31 July. If the preceding year's self-assessment is made late or is amended, the relevant amount is determined as if the liability as finally agreed had been shown in a timeous self-assessment, with further payments on account then being required where appropriate. If a discovery assessment (see **6.6** ASSESSMENTS) is made for the preceding year, each payment on account due is deemed always to have been 50% of the relevant amount plus 50% of the tax charged by the discovery assessment as finally determined.

The £1,000 *de minimis* was doubled from £500 for 2009/10 onwards, first affecting payments on account due on 31 January 2010 and 31 July 2010.

At any time before 31 January following the tax year, the taxpayer may make a claim stating his belief that he will have no liability for the year or that his liability will be fully covered by tax deducted at source and his grounds for that belief, in which case each of the interim payments is not, and is deemed never to have been, required to be made. Within the same time limit, the taxpayer may make a claim stating his belief that his liability for the year after allowing for tax deducted at source will be a stated amount which is less than the relevant amount, and stating his grounds for that belief, in which case each of the interim payments required will be, and deemed always to have been, equal to 50% of the stated amount. Either claim should be made on form SA 303. The maximum penalty for an incorrect statement made fraudulently or negligently in connection with either claim is the amount or additional amount he would have paid on account if he had made a correct statement. Interim payments of tax are subject to the same recovery provisions as any other payments of tax.

An officer of HMRC may direct, at any time before 31 January following a tax year, that a person is not required to make payments on account for that year, such adjustments being made as necessary to give effect to the direction. For the circumstances in which such a direction will be made, see Revenue Tax Bulletin August 2001 p 875.

[*TMA 1970, s 59A; FA 2008, s 34, Sch 12 para 13; SI 1996 No 1654; SI 1997 No 2491; SI 2008 No 838*].

For an article on HMRC practice on repayment, and allocations and reallocations of overpayments, see Revenue Tax Bulletin June 1999 pp 673, 674. For the interaction of loss relief claims and payments on account, see Revenue Tax Bulletin August 2001 pp 878, 879.

Interim payments made by an employer on an employee's behalf, as part of *tax equalisation* arrangements where full in-year gross up is used, should not figure in the employment pages of the employee's self-assessment tax return (see Revenue Tax Bulletin June 1998 p 551).

These provisions, and those described at **65.7** and **65.8** below (and, as regards surcharges, **42.3** INTEREST AND SURCHARGES ON OVERDUE TAX), apply equally (with the necessary modifications) to Class 4 national insurance contributions. [*Social Security Contributions and Benefits Act 1992, s 16(1)(b)*].

Simon's Taxes. See E1.251.

Example

[65.6]

Calculation of interim payments for 2010/11

For 2009/10, Kylie's self-assessment shows the following.

	£
Total income tax liability	8,664
Capital gains tax liability	2,122
Class 4 NIC liability	198
PAYE tax deducted (all relating to 2009/10)	3,740
Tax credits on dividends received	200
Tax deducted from interest received	300

The payments on account for 2010/11 (unless, on a claim, Kylie chooses to pay different amounts) are based on relevant amounts as follows.

	£
Income tax (£8,664 – £3,740 – £200 – £300 =)	4,424
Class 4 NIC	198

Half of the relevant amounts is due on each of 31 January 2011 and 31 July 2011. No payment on account is required in respect of capital gains tax liability.

Final payment (repayment) of tax

[65.7] A final payment (known as a '*balancing payment*') is due for a tax year if a person's combined income tax and capital gains tax liabilities contained in his self-assessment (see **63.3 RETURNS**) exceed the aggregate of any payments on account (whether under *TMA 1970, s 59A*, see **65.5** above, or otherwise) and any income tax deducted at source. If the second total exceeds the first, a repayment will be made. Tax deducted at source has the same meaning as in **65.5**(b) above.

Subject to **65.8** below, the due date for payment (or repayment) is 31 January following the tax year. The one exception is where the person gave notice of chargeability under *TMA 1970, s 7* (see **55.2 PENALTIES**) within six months after the end of the tax year, but was not given notice under *TMA 1970, s 8* or *s 8A* (see **63.2 RETURNS**) until after 31 October following the tax year; in such case, the due date is the last day of the three months beginning with the date of the said notice.

[*TMA 1970, s 59B(1)–(4)(7)(8); FA 2008, s 34, Sch 12 para 14*].

See **65.5** above as regards notifications to agents.

Simon's Taxes. See E1.252.

Due date — further provisions

[65.8] Where an amount of tax is payable (repayable) as a result of an amendment or correction to an individual's or trustees' self-assessment under any of (a)–(e) below, then, subject to the appeal and postponement provisions in **5.2** APPEALS and **54.5** PAYMENT OF TAX, the due date for payment (repayment) is as stated below (if this is later than the date given under the general rules in **65.7** above). Note that these rules do *not* defer the date from which interest accrues, which is as in **42.2** INTEREST AND SURCHARGES ON OVERDUE TAX or **41.1** INTEREST ON OVERPAID TAX, although they do determine the due date for surcharge purposes — see **42.3** INTEREST AND SURCHARGES ON OVERDUE TAX.

(a)   Taxpayer amendment to return as in **63.4** RETURNS: 30 days after the date of the taxpayer's notice of amendment.

(b)   HMRC correction to return as in **63.4** RETURNS: 30 days after the date of the officer's notice of correction.

(c)   Taxpayer amendment to return whilst enquiry in progress as in **63.10** RETURNS, where accepted by HMRC: 30 days after the date of the closure notice (see **63.9** RETURNS).

(d)   HMRC amendment to return where amendment made by closure notice following enquiry (see **63.9** RETURNS): 30 days after the date of the closure notice.

(e)   HMRC amendment of self-assessment to prevent potential loss of tax to the Crown (see **63.10** RETURNS): 30 days after the date of the notice of amendment.

As regards amendments and corrections to partnership returns, (e) above is not relevant, and the equivalent date in each of (a)–(d) above as regards each partner is 30 days after the date of the officer's notice of consequential amendment to the partner's own tax return. The same applies in the case of a consequential amendment by virtue of any of the following: an amendment of a partnership return on discovery (see **6.6** ASSESSMENTS), a partnership error or mistake relief claim made before 1 April 2010 (see **18.8** CLAIMS), or a reduction or increase in the partnership tax liability made by the Appeal Tribunal (see **5.2**, **5.18** APPEALS).

[*TMA 1970, s 59B(5), Sch 3ZA; FA 2009, s 100, Sch 52 para 8*].

Where an officer of HMRC enquires into the return (see **63.6** RETURNS) and a repayment is otherwise due, the repayment is not required to be made until the enquiry is completed (see **63.9** RETURNS) although the officer may make a provisional repayment at his discretion.

Subject to the appeal and postponement provisions in **5.2** APPEALS and **54.5** PAYMENT OF TAX, the due date for payment of tax charged by any assessment other than a self-assessment, e.g. a discovery assessment under *TMA 1970, s 29* (see **6.6** ASSESSMENTS), is 30 days after the date of the assessment (but, for interest consequences, see **42.2** INTEREST AND SURCHARGES ON OVERDUE TAX).

[*TMA 1970, s 59B(4A)(6)*].

Appeals

[65.9] For appeals generally, see **5.1** *et seq.* **APPEALS**. For postponement of tax pending appeal and payment of tax on determination of the appeal, see respectively **54.5** and **54.6 PAYMENT OF TAX**.

Claims etc.

[65.10] For full details as to the making of, and the ramifications of, claims and elections under self-assessment, see **18.1–18.4 CLAIMS**.

Liability of relevant trustees

[65.11] In relation to income and chargeable gains, the *'relevant trustees'* of a settlement are the persons who are the trustees when the income arises or in the tax year in which the chargeable gain or life assurance policy gain accrues or arises and, in both cases, any persons who subsequently become trustees. Where the relevant trustees are liable to a penalty under the self-assessment regime, to interest on a penalty, to a surcharge and/or interest thereon, to make interim and final payments of income tax and payments on an assessment to recover tax over-repaid, or to interest on overdue tax, the penalty etc. may be recovered (but only once) from any one or more of them. As regards penalties and surcharges (and interest on either), the liability of any relevant trustee is, however, restricted to those incurred after the day that he became a relevant trustee (a daily penalty being regarded as incurred on a daily basis). The 'reasonable excuse' provisions in **42.3 INTEREST AND SURCHARGES ON OVERDUE TAX** and **55.6 PENALTIES** have effect by reference to each of the relevant trustees. [*TMA 1970, ss 7(9), 107A; FA 2008, s 113, Sch 36 para 75; SI 2009 No 404, Arts 2, 3; SI 2009 No 571, Art 13; SI 2010 No 530, Sch para 3*].

Trustees of 'bare' (or 'simple') trusts treated as such for tax purposes (see **68.7 SETTLEMENTS**) are not required to complete self-assessment returns or make payments on account, the beneficiaries under such trusts being liable to give details of the income and gains in their own tax returns. The trustees may, if they and the beneficiaries so wish, make returns of income (but *not* of capital gains or capital losses), accounting for tax at the basic rate or (before 2008/09) the savings rate or the dividend ordinary rate, as appropriate to the class of income, provided that they so notify the trust district and follow this course consistently from year to year. This does not, however, affect the liability of the beneficiaries to make the appropriate self-assessment returns of income and gains. (Revenue Tax Bulletin February 1997 p 395, December 1997 pp 486, 487).

Information to be provided to employees

[65.12] Various measures are included in the *Income Tax (Pay As You Earn) Regulations 2003 (SI 2003 No 2682)* to ensure that sufficient information is given to employees, and in good time, to enable them to complete their self-assessment tax returns. The measures are as follows.

(a)   A time limit applies for providing an employee with form P60 (certificate of pay and tax deducted — see **53.13 PAY AS YOU EARN**). It must be provided no later than 31 May following the tax year to which it relates. [*SI 2003 No 2682, Reg 67*].

(b)   There is a requirement for the employer to provide each employee for whom form P11D or P9D (see **53.12 PAY AS YOU EARN**) is relevant with particulars of the information stated therein. This must be provided no later than 6 July following the tax year. An employer is not obliged to provide the above particulars to an employee who left during the tax year in question unless requested to do so within three years after the end of that tax year; the information must then be provided within 30 days of receipt of the request if later than the normal 6 July deadline. [*SI 2003 No 2682, Regs 85(1), 94, Sch 1 para 16*].

(c)   Where a third party makes payments or provides benefits which if done by arrangement with the employer would have fallen to be included on forms P11D and P9D (see **53.12 PAY AS YOU EARN**), he must provide particulars, including cash equivalents, to the employee by 6 July following the tax year. (The third party is not obliged to provide such particulars to HMRC unless required to do so by notice under *TMA 1970, s 15* (see **63.16 RETURNS**).) [*SI 2003 No 2682, Reg 95*].

Penalties under *TMA 1970, s 98* for failure to provide information to HMRC (see **55.21 PENALTIES**) apply equally to failure to comply with the above requirements for providing particulars to employees.

Taxation of non-UK residents

[65.13] Individuals who regard themselves as not resident, not ordinarily resident or not domiciled in the UK are required to self-certify their status in the self-assessment tax return. See **62.5 RESIDENCE, ORDINARY RESIDENCE AND DOMICILE** under Administrative procedures.

66

Self-Assessment — Key Dates

Cross-references. See also 65 SELF-ASSESSMENT.

[66.1] The Table below sets out key dates and events in the operation of the self-assessment regime.

Date	Event
31 January 2010	2008/09 tax return to be filed on or before this date if filed online (see **63.2 RETURNS**).
31 January 2010	Balancing payment of income tax and payment of capital gains tax due for 2008/09 (see **65.7 SELF-ASSESSMENT**).
31 January 2010	First interim payment on account due for 2009/10 (see **65.5 SELF-ASSESSMENT**).
February 2010	HMRC begin to issue fixed penalty notices, and in some cases take daily penalty action, for non-filing of 2008/09 tax returns (see **55.5 PENALTIES**).
28 February 2010	Initial surcharge due of 5% of any 2008/09 income tax and capital gains tax due on 31 January 2010 and remaining unpaid after this date (see **42.3 INTEREST AND SURCHARGES ON OVERDUE TAX**).
April 2010	HMRC issue majority of 2009/10 self-assessment tax returns (see **63.2 RETURNS**).
31 May 2010	Deadline for employers to provide employees with Form P60 for 2009/10 (see **65.12 SELF-ASSESSMENT**).
6 July 2010	Deadline for employers to provide both HMRC and employees with P11D/P9D information etc. for 2009/10 (see **53.12 PAY AS YOU EARN** and **65.12 SELF-ASSESSMENT**).
31 July 2010	Second interim payment on account due for 2009/10 (see **65.5 SELF-ASSESSMENT**).

Date	Event
31 July 2010	Further surcharge due of 5% of any 2008/09 income tax and capital gains tax due on 31 January 2010 and remaining unpaid on this date (see **42.3 INTEREST AND SURCHARGES ON OVERDUE TAX**).
1 August 2010	Further £100 penalty due where 2008/09 tax return not filed before this date (see **55.5 PENALTIES**).
1 August 2010	If 2009/10 tax return issued after this date, normal 31 October deadline for manual filing is deferred until three months from date of issue (see **63.2 RETURNS**).
5 October 2010	Chargeability to tax for 2009/10 to be notified to HMRC on or before this date if no tax return received (see **55.2 PENALTIES**).
31 October 2010	2009/10 tax return to be filed on or before this date if not filed online (see **63.2 RETURNS**).
1 November 2010	If 2009/10 tax return issued on or after this date, normal 31 January deadline for online filing is deferred until three months from date of issue (see **63.2 RETURNS**) as is due date of balancing payment and payment of capital gains tax provided notice of chargeability given timeously (see above, and **65.7 SELF-ASSESSMENT**).
30 December 2010	2009/10 tax return to be filed on or before this date if taxpayer filing online wishes 2009/10 tax underpayment of less than £2,000 to be collected by adjustment to 2011/12 PAYE code (see **65.4 SELF-ASSESSMENT**).
31 January 2011	2009/10 tax return to be filed on or before this date if filed online (see **63.2 RETURNS**).
31 January 2011	Balancing payment of income tax and payment of capital gains tax due for 2009/10 (see **65.7 SELF-ASSESSMENT**).
31 January 2011	First interim payment on account due for 2010/11 (see **65.5 SELF-ASSESSMENT**).
February 2011	HMRC begin to issue fixed penalty notices, and in some cases take daily penalty action, for non-filing of 2009/10 tax returns (see **55.5 PENALTIES**).

Date	Event
Date	*Event*
28 February 2011	Initial surcharge due of 5% of any 2009/10 income tax and capital gains tax due on 31 January 2011 and remaining unpaid after this date (see **42.3 INTEREST AND SURCHARGES ON OVERDUE TAX**).
April 2011	HMRC issue majority of 2010/11 self-assessment tax returns (see **63.2 RETURNS**).
31 May 2011	Deadline for employers to provide employees with Form P60 for 2010/11 (see **65.12 SELF-ASSESSMENT**).
6 July 2011	Deadline for employers to provide both HMRC and employees with P11D/P9D information etc. for 2010/11 (see **53.12 PAY AS YOU EARN** and **65.12 SELF-ASSESSMENT**).
31 July 2011	Second interim payment on account due for 2010/11 (see **65.5 SELF-ASSESSMENT**).
31 July 2011	Further surcharge due of 5% of any 2009/10 income tax and capital gains tax due on 31 January 2011 and remaining unpaid on this date (see **42.3 INTEREST AND SURCHARGES ON OVERDUE TAX**).
1 August 2011	Further £100 penalty due where 2009/10 tax return not filed before this date (see **55.5 PENALTIES**).
1 August 2011	If 2010/11 tax return issued after this date, normal 31 October deadline for manual filing is deferred until three months from date of issue (see **63.2 RETURNS**).
5 October 2011	Chargeability to tax for 2010/11 to be notified to HMRC on or before this date if no tax return received (see **55.2 PENALTIES**).
31 October 2011	2010/11 tax return to be filed on or before this date if not filed online (see **63.2 RETURNS**).

67

Self-Employed Persons

Introduction

[67.1] The individual in business, whether full-time or part-time, on his own or in partnership with others, is subject to particular tax legislation and practices. Such legislation etc. is covered in this work under various subject headings, and the following paragraphs indicate where the detailed provisions are to be found.

See the HMRC Guide 'Giving your business the best start with tax', available at www.hmrc.gov.uk/startingup/working-yourself.pdf.

See **27.54 EMPLOYMENT INCOME** as regards the distinction between employment and self-employment.

See **58 PERSONAL SERVICE COMPANIES ETC.** as regards individuals providing their services through an intermediary in circumstances such that they would fall to be categorised as employees if engaged directly.

Charge to income tax etc.

[67.2] Profits are chargeable to tax under the rules in **73 TRADING INCOME.** Special provisions relate to the opening and closing years of a business. Particular items of expenditure or receipt may, or may not, be included in the computation of taxable profits. Where a business is discontinued, see also **59 POST-CESSATION RECEIPTS AND EXPENDITURE.** Partnership matters are dealt with under **52 PARTNERSHIPS.** Farmers may elect for the **HERD BASIS (33)** to apply to their animals. Special provisions apply to **UNDERWRITERS AT LLOYD'S (74).**

Some transactions may result in a tax charge because they contravene legislation on **ANTI-AVOIDANCE (4).**

For general procedure, see **SELF-ASSESSMENT (65).** See also **6 ASSESSMENTS** and **5 APPEALS.**

Property

See **60 PROPERTY INCOME.**

Assets

The acquisition or ownership of business assets may give rise to capital allowances as the tax substitute for the disallowable depreciation charge (if any) in the accounts (see **10 CAPITAL ALLOWANCES** and **11 CAPITAL ALLOWANCES ON PLANT AND MACHINERY**). The disposal of assets may result in balancing adjustments for capital allowances purposes, and also to a charge to capital gains tax (see Tolley's Capital Gains Tax) unless certain exemptions and reliefs apply.

Overseas

Income from trades etc. carried on wholly abroad by a UK resident is within the charge to tax (see **73.1 TRADING INCOME**). See **50.5 NON-RESIDENTS** for non-residents trading in the UK.

Losses

If trading losses are incurred, relief may be obtained by various alternatives, see under **45 LOSSES.**

Employees

[67.3] If staff are employed, then the regulations under the **PAY AS YOU EARN** (**53**) system must be complied with.

Payment of tax

[67.4] For times of payment, see under **SELF-ASSESSMENT** (**65**). See also **54 PAYMENT OF TAX** and **42 INTEREST AND SURCHARGES ON OVERDUE TAX**. Special provisions relate to the construction industry, see **CONSTRUCTION INDUSTRY SCHEME** (**22**).

See **15 CERTIFICATES OF TAX DEPOSIT** for a method of payment.

Provision for retirement

[67.5] Special legislation allows tax relief for payments made to secure a pension in retirement. See **57 PENSION PROVISION.**

National insurance contributions

[67.6] Class 4 contributions are charged on business profits, see **70 SOCIAL SECURITY AND NATIONAL INSURANCE.**

Value added tax

[67.7] The detailed provisions of VAT are outside the scope of this book but registration is generally required when the 'taxable turnover' of the business will exceed £70,000 (£68,000 before 1 April 2010) in a year. See Tolley's Value Added Tax.

68

Settlements

Cross-references. See **4.14–4.17** ANTI-AVOIDANCE for transfer of assets abroad; **23** DECEASED ESTATES for the income of estates of deceased persons in course of administration; **24** DEDUCTION OF TAX AT SOURCE generally and at

24.7–24.10 for annuities etc. and **24.15** for tax-free annuities under wills etc.; **55.2 PENALTIES, 63.2 RETURNS, 65.11 SELF-ASSESSMENT** for administrative provisions relating to trustees under self-assessment.

Simon's Taxes. See C4.

Introduction

[68.1] Trustees of settlements are taxed in their representative capacities (see **68.8** below). They are charged to income tax at the basic rate or the dividend ordinary rate (see **1.5 ALLOWANCES AND TAX RATES**) or (before 2008/09) the savings rate (see **1.6 ALLOWANCES AND TAX RATES**), as appropriate to the class of income, except in the case of discretionary and accumulation trusts (see **68.11** below). The latter are generally charged at the 'trust rate' or, in respect of dividend income, the 'dividend trust rate', with a 'basic rate' band of £1,000. Certain narrow categories of income are charged at the trust rate or dividend trust rate regardless of the type of trust involved (see **68.12**(1)–(11) below).

The trustees of a settlement are together treated for income tax purposes as if they were a single person (distinct from the persons who are the actual trustees from time to time). Where part of the property comprised in a single settlement is vested in one trustee or body of trustees and part in another, those two trustees or bodies of trustees are together treated as constituting a single body of trustees. In a case where the trustees of a settlement carry on a trade, profession or vocation, the introduction of this rule or the definition of settled property at **68.2** below cannot in itself invoke the cessation and/or commencement rules for trades etc. [*ITA 2007, s 474; ICTA 1988, s 685E(1)(8)(9)*].

For residence of trustees, see **68.5** below.

Beneficiaries receive income from settlements which is treated as net of the tax accounted for by the trustees. The grossed-up amount of the income is treated as part of the total income of the beneficiary for tax purposes. If the total income of a beneficiary is high enough, he will suffer income tax at the excess of the higher rate or the dividend upper rate over the tax accounted for by the trustees on the grossed-up income from the trust. He may alternatively be entitled to a repayment of some or all of the tax suffered by the trustees where it exceeds his own liability (although this does not extend to non-repayable tax or non-payable tax credits of the trustees). See also **68.15** below for tax repayments to non-residents.

The following should also be noted.

(a)   **Trusts with vulnerable beneficiaries.** Special income tax and capital gains tax treatment is given if the trustees and the vulnerable beneficiary concerned opt for it to apply. The income tax liability is computed as if the beneficiary had received the income directly, i.e. applying his own tax rates and allowances. See **68.19** below.

(b)   **Scottish trusts.** Provided that the trustees are UK resident, the rights of a beneficiary of a Scottish trust are treated for income tax purposes as including an equitable right in possession to any trust income to which such a right does not arise under the law of Scotland but would have arisen if the trust had effect under the law of England and Wales. [*ITA 2007, s 464; FA 1993, s 118*].

(c)   **Demergers.** For the income and capital gains tax treatment of shares received by trustees as a result of exempt demergers (for which see Tolley's Corporation Tax under Groups of Companies), see HMRC Capital Gains Tax Manual CG33900 *et seq.*

(d)   **Trustees are also liable to capital gains tax.** See the corresponding chapter of Tolley's Capital Gains Tax for full coverage.

Definition of settled property

[68.2] A statutory definition of 'settled property' is provided for income tax purposes as follows. It applies unless 'the context otherwise requires' and, in particular, does not alter the wide definition of 'settlement' given in **68.28** below for the purposes therein stated.

'*Settled property*' means any property held in trust other than:

(a)   property held by a person as nominee for another; and
(b)   property held by a person as trustee for another person who is absolutely entitled as against the trustee or who would be so entitled were he not an infant or otherwise lacking legal capacity; (any such trustee is generally referred to as a bare trustee).

Any reference in income tax legislation to 'property comprised in a settlement' has the same meaning as above.

For the purposes of (b) above, and for general income tax purposes, a person is absolutely entitled to property as against the trustee if he has the exclusive right to direct how the property is to be dealt with (subject only to the trustees' right to resort to the property for payment of duties, taxes, costs or other outgoings). Any reference in income tax legislation to a person being so entitled is to be taken as including a reference to two or more persons being so entitled.

[*ITA 2007, s 466; ICTA 1988, s 685A*].

Definition of 'settlor'

[68.3] A statutory definition of 'settlor' is provided for income tax purposes as set out below. The definition applies 'except where the context otherwise requires', and it should be noted that a separate definition continues to have effect as in **68.28** below for the purposes therein stated.

'*Settlor*' in relation to a settlement means the person, or any of the persons, who has made, or is treated for income tax purposes as having made, the settlement. A person is treated as having made a settlement if:

- he has made or entered into the settlement, directly or indirectly; or
- the settlement arose on his death, whether by will, intestacy or otherwise, and the settled property (see **68.2** above), or property from which the settled property is derived (see below), is (or includes) property which he could have disposed of by will (if certain assumptions were made and powers ignored) or which represented his severable share in property as a joint tenant.

In particular, a person is treated as having made a settlement if he has provided property (directly or indirectly), or has undertaken to provide property (directly or indirectly), for the purposes of the settlement.

Where one person (A) makes or enters into a settlement in accordance with reciprocal arrangements with another person (B), B is treated as having made the settlement and A is not treated for that reason alone as having made it. 'Arrangements' is widely defined to include any scheme, agreement or understanding, whether or not legally enforceable.

A person ceases to be a settlor in relation to a settlement if:

- no property of which he is the settlor remains in the settlement;
- he has not undertaken to provide property (directly or indirectly), for the purposes of the settlement in the future; and
- he has not made reciprocal arrangements with another person for that other person to enter into the settlement in the future.

A person is a settlor of any property which is settled property by reason of his having made the settlement (or by reason of an event which causes him to be treated as having made the settlement) or which derives (see below) from such property.

For the above purposes, property is derived from other property if it derives (directly or indirectly and wholly or partly) from the other property or any part of it. In particular, property is derived from other property if it derives (as before) from *income* from the other property or any part of it.

[*ITA 2007, ss 465(7)(8), 467–469; ICTA 1988, s 685B*].

Identification of settlor

[68.4] Rules apply for identifying the settlor of property that has been transferred between settlements otherwise than for full consideration and other than by way of arm's length bargain. The rules apply 'except where the context otherwise requires'. For these purposes, a transfer of property involves a disposal by the trustees of a settlement (Settlement 1) and an acquisition by the trustees of another settlement (Settlement 2) of either the property disposed of by Settlement 1 or property created by the disposal (an example of the latter being the grant by Settlement 1 of a leasehold interest out of a freehold interest in land). The '*transferred property*' (see below) is the property thus acquired by Settlement 2. The question of whether there is a disposal or an acquisition is determined as for CGT purposes.

Broadly, the settlor of the property disposed of by Settlement 1 is treated, from the time of the disposal, as having made Settlement 2. If there is more than one such settlor, all the settlors are treated as having made Settlement 2, and each of the settlors is treated in relation to Settlement 2 as the settlor of a proportionate part of the transferred property. The transferred property is treated, from the time of the disposal, as provided for the purposes of Settlement 2 (to the extent that the property disposed of was provided for the purposes of Settlement 1). The person who provided the property for the purposes of Settlement 1 (or property from which it was derived — see **68.3** above) is treated as having provided the transferred property. If there is more than one such person, each of them is treated as having provided a proportionate part of the transferred property.

These rules are disapplied in relation to a transfer of property:

(a) that occurs by reason only of the assignment, by a beneficiary of Settlement 1 to the trustees of Settlement 2, of an interest in Settlement 1;

(b) that occurs by reason only of the exercise of a general power of appointment; or

(c) in particular circumstances (as mentioned below) which involve the variation of a will or an intestacy.

[*ITA 2007, ss 470, 471; ICTA 1988, s 685C*].

The following rules apply to identify the settlor in a case where a disposition of property (whether by will or intestacy) following a person's death is varied within two years after the death in a case where the instrument of variation requires that *TCGA 1992, s 62(6)* should apply. (*Section 62(6)* treats the variation as having effectively been made by the deceased and as not itself constituting a CGT disposal — see Tolley's Capital Gains Tax under Death.)

Where property becomes 'settled property' (see **68.2** above) by reason only of the variation, the person treated as having made the settlement and as having provided the property for the purposes of the settlement is the person who immediately before the variation was entitled to the property, or to property from which it derives (see **68.3** above), absolutely as legatee (which is given a broad meaning for this purpose). This rule is extended to include a person who would, but for the variation, have become so entitled and a person who would have fallen into either of these two categories but for his being an infant or otherwise lacking legal capacity.

Where property would have become comprised in a settlement that arose on or pre-dated the deceased person's death, but in consequence of the variation becomes comprised in another settlement, the deceased is treated as having made the other settlement.

Where, immediately before the variation, property is comprised in a settlement and is property of which the deceased is a settlor and, immediately after the variation, it becomes comprised in another settlement, the deceased is treated as having made the other settlement. These are the circumstances referred to at (c) above.

References in the two rules immediately above to the property becoming comprised in another settlement include references to property derived from that property (see above) becoming so comprised. In both rules, the time at which the deceased is treated as having made the other settlement is immediately before his death (other than where the other settlement actually arose on his death).

[*ITA 2007, ss 472, 473; ICTA 1988, s 685D*].

Residence of trustees

[68.5] The rules set out below have effect on and after 6 April 2007 for the purpose of determining the residence status of the trustees of a settlement (whenever created).

As stated at **68.2** above, the trustees of a settlement are together treated for income tax purposes as if they were a single person (distinct from the persons who are the actual trustees from time to time). That notional single person is treated for income tax purposes as UK resident and ordinarily resident at any time when *either* of the following two conditions are satisfied. If neither condition is satisfied, the notional person is treated as neither resident nor ordinarily resident in the UK.

Condition A is that all the trustees are UK resident.

Condition B is that at least one trustee is UK resident (with at least one trustee being non-UK resident) *and* that a settlor in relation to the settlement meets Condition C (see below).

For the purposes of Conditions A and B, a trustee who is non-UK resident is nevertheless treated as UK resident at any time when he is acting as trustee in the course of a business that he carries on in the UK through a branch, agency or permanent establishment there (see HMRC guidance on this at www.hmrc.gov.uk/cnr/trustee-res-guidance.pdf).

If the settlement arose on the settlor's death and, immediately prior to death, the settlor was resident, ordinarily resident or domiciled in the UK, the settlor meets Condition C from the time of his death until such time as he ceases to be a settlor in relation to the settlement. If the settlement arose otherwise than on the settlor's death and the settlor made it (or is treated for income tax purposes as making it) at a time when he was resident, ordinarily resident or domiciled in the UK, the settlor meets Condition C from that time until such time as he ceases to be a settlor in relation to the settlement.

Where there has been a transfer within *ITA 2007, ss 470, 471* between settlements (see **68.4** above), then Condition C is met by the person treated as having made Settlement 2 if it was met by him, immediately before the transfer, as a settlor in relation to Settlement 1.

[*ITA 2007, ss 475, 476; ICTA 1988, s 685E(2)–(7)*].

Prior to 6 April 2007, the rules are not dissimilar to those above. Where at least one of the trustees of a settlement is non-UK resident and at least one is UK resident, then provided that the settlor (including any person providing or undertaking to provide funds directly or indirectly for the settlement) satisfies the condition below (or, if there is more than one settlor, that at least one of them satisfies that condition), the non-UK resident trustee(s) is (are) treated as UK resident for income tax purposes. Otherwise, the UK resident trustee(s) is (are) treated as not resident in the UK and as resident elsewhere for income tax purposes. The said condition is that the settlor is resident, ordinarily resident or domiciled in the UK at a 'relevant time'. A 'relevant time' is the time of the settlor's death in relation to a testamentary disposition or an intestacy, otherwise it is the time, or each of the times, when he has provided funds for the settlement. [FA 1989, s 110; FA 2006, Sch 13 para 28(2)(c)(6)].

Sub-fund settlements

[68.6] Under *TCGA 1992, Sch 4ZA*, subject to conditions, the trustees of a settlement may make an irrevocable election ('a sub-fund election') to treat a fund or other specified portion of the settled property ('the sub-fund') as a separate settlement ('the sub-fund settlement') for CGT purposes. The election must specify the date on which it is to be treated as having taken effect, which can be earlier, but not later, than the date it is made. For the full rules, conditions, procedures and consequences, see the corresponding chapter of Tolley's Capital Gains Tax. See also HMRC Tax Bulletin August 2006 pp 1305, 1306.

Where a sub-fund election has been made, the following consequences ensue for income tax purposes.

- The sub-fund settlement is treated as a settlement, and as having been created on the 'effective date' (see below).
- Each trustee of the trusts on which the property comprised in the sub-fund settlement is held is treated as a trustee of the sub-fund settlement.
- Each trustee of the sub-fund settlement is treated from the 'effective date' as having ceased to be a trustee of the principal settlement unless he is also a trustee of trusts on which property comprised in the principal settlement is held.
- No trustee of the principal settlement is treated as a trustee of the sub-fund settlement unless he is also a trustee of trusts on which property comprised in the sub-fund settlement is held.
- The trustees of the sub-fund settlement are treated as having become absolutely entitled, from the 'effective date', to the property comprised in that settlement as against the trustees of the principal settlement.

References above to the '*effective date*' are to the date the sub-fund election is treated as having taken effect (see above). However, *TCGA 1992, Sch 4ZA para 2* contains rules as to exactly when on that date the election takes effect (see Tolley's Capital Gains Tax), and these apply equally for the above income tax purposes.

[ITA 2007, s 477; ICTA 1988, s 685G].

Bare trusts

[68.7] Trustees of 'bare' (or 'simple') trusts treated as such for tax purposes are not required to deduct tax from payments to beneficiaries or to complete self-assessment returns or make payments on account. The beneficiaries under such trusts are liable to give details of the income and gains in their own tax returns. The trustees may, if they and the beneficiaries so wish, make returns of income (but *not* of capital gains or capital losses), accounting for tax at the basic rate or the dividend ordinary rate or (before 2008/09) the savings rate, as appropriate to the class of income, provided that they so notify the trust district and follow this course consistently from year to year. This does not, however, affect the liability of the beneficiaries to make the appropriate self-assessment returns of income and gains. (Revenue Tax Bulletin February 1997 p 395, December 1997 pp 486, 487). See **68.2**(b) above as regards what is meant by bare trusts.

Where a chargeable event gain arises on a life policy held in a bare trust for a minor, HMRC's long-standing view was that the settlor was chargeable on the gain. Following legal advice, HMRC have changed their view with effect for 2007/08 onwards and now regard the minor himself as the person chargeable. Where, however, either or both of the child's parents are the settlors of the bare trust, the children's settlements rules at **68.30** below continue to apply as before in these circumstances so that the parent is potentially the person chargeable. (HMRC Brief 51/08, 8 October 2008).

Assessments on trust income

[68.8] Income may be assessed and charged on (and in the name of) any one or more of the persons who are trustees in the tax year in which the income arises or on any one or more subsequent trustees. [*TMA 1970, s 30AA; FA 1989, s 151; FA 2006, Sch 13 para 29; ITA 2007, Sch 1 para 281; TIOPA 2010, Sch 7 para 58*]. References here to assessment include self-assessment.

Untaxed income

The untaxed income of a trust may be assessed on the trustee as the person receiving it (see, for example, *ITTOIA 2005, s 271* and *Reid's Trustees v CIR* CS 1929, 14 TC 512) but if, under his authority, it is paid direct to the beneficiary and he returns it under *TMA 1970, s 13*, he will not be assessable. [*TMA 1970, s 76*]. See also *Williams v Singer* HL 1920, 7 TC 387 (trustees not assessable where overseas income paid direct to non-resident beneficiary) and compare *Kelly v Rogers* CA 1935, 19 TC 692 (UK trustee of foreign trust held assessable in respect of overseas income as there was no ascertainable non-resident beneficiary entitled to the income) and *Dawson v CIR* HL 1989, 62 TC 301 (sole UK resident trustee of foreign trust with three trustees held not assessable in respect of income not remitted). See, however, **62.5 RESIDENCE, ORDINARY RESIDENCE AND DOMICILE** as regards special residence provisions. Held in *Pakenham* HL 1928, 13 TC 573 that settlement trustees not assessable in respect of beneficiary's super-tax liability.

Expenses of administering the trust

Expenses of administering the trust are not deductible in the assessments on the trustee (*Aikin v Macdonald Trustees* CES 1894, 3 TC 306; *Inverclyde's Trustees v Millar* CS 1924, 9 TC 14) even though deductible in arriving at the beneficiaries' income as in **68.9** below. However, see **68.14** below for the effect of trust expenses on the rates of tax applicable to income otherwise chargeable at special rates.

Returns

Trustees are within the self-assessment regime (see **63.2 RETURNS, 65.4, 65.11 SELF-ASSESSMENT**). Trustees cannot make separate returns for different funds into which the settlement may be split (unless a sub-fund election has been made as in **68.6** above) (HMRC Tax Bulletin August 2006 p 1305).

Effect of trustees' expenses on beneficiaries' income

[68.9] Trustees' expenses (sometimes called 'management expenses') can be used to reduce the taxable income of the beneficiary as set out below. These rules apply only if, before being distributed, some or all of the income arising to the trustees in the tax year is the income of another person (i.e. the beneficiary). They thus apply to an interest in possession trust but not to a discretionary trust (for which see **68.14** below). The beneficiary is regarded as not entitled to the income used to pay the expenses; therefore, such income does not enter into any calculation of his income tax liability.

Expenses can be used in this way only if they are chargeable to income by the trustees either under a term of the settlement (subject to any overriding law) or, if the settlement deed contains no such term, under general trust law (subject to any overriding term of the settlement). The expenses to be considered are those incurred by the trustees in the current tax year or brought forward from an earlier tax year. For 2007/08 onwards, the foregoing rules had no statutory authority but were applied in practice — see Change 91 in Annex 1 to the Explanatory Notes to *ITA 2007*.

HMRC take the view that, except in 'rare circumstances where it can be demonstrated [that] the payments are solely for managing income, payments of trustees' remuneration are linked to the management of the trust as a whole and are therefore regarded as attributable to capital'. In other words, trustees' remuneration is not regarded as chargeable to income under general law. (HMRC Tax Bulletin August 2005 p 1228).

HMRC have prepared detailed guidance on trustees' expenses (see www.hmrc.gov.uk/trusts/tmes-paper.pdf). This guidance has been largely agreed with trust representatives but there are some areas of disagreement, particularly in relation to HMRC's view on trustees' fees (see above).

In *HMRC v Trustees of the Peter Clay Discretionary Trust* CA 2008, [2009] STC 469, it was held in the Ch D that trustees' remuneration fell to be regarded as incurred for the benefit of the whole estate and, therefore, to be treated as a capital expense; there had to be a heavy evidential burden upon those who asserted a contrary conclusion, and that burden was not satisfied in the instant case. However, whilst reasserting that it was generally only those expenses which had been incurred exclusively for the benefit of the income beneficiaries that might be charged against income, the CA nevertheless held that, on the particular facts of this case, a proportion of trustees' fees could be so charged. The CA also held that investment management fees had to be charged to capital; significantly the fees were incurred *after* the trustees had resolved to accumulate the trust income.

The order of set-off of expenses is determined by *ITA 2007, s 503*; firstly against dividend income (see **1.5 ALLOWANCES AND TAX RATES**), then against savings income (see **1.6 ALLOWANCES AND TAX RATES**) and finally against basic rate income. Expenses set against dividend income is set against UK dividend income in priority to dividends from non-UK resident companies. The beneficiary's taxable income is computed by subtracting from the gross amount of each of those three types of income the amount of income tax payable on it by the trustees and the expenses set against it. The resulting net amount of each of type of income is then grossed up at the rate of tax applicable to that type of income to give the beneficiary's taxable income of that type from the trust.

See the examples at **68.10** below.

Where a beneficiary is not liable to income tax on part of his share of the trust income, by virtue wholly or partly of his being non-UK resident or being deemed under a double tax agreement to be resident in a territory outside the UK, the trustees' expenses otherwise available to reduce his income are reduced in the same proportion as that which such non-taxable income bears to his full share of income (using in each case the income net of UK and foreign tax). Where the beneficiary's income tax liability is limited under the provisions at **50.3 NON-RESIDENTS**, excluded income (see **50.3**), other than that which has suffered deduction of UK income tax at source, must be included in non-taxable income for the purposes of this apportionment.

[*ITA 2007, ss 499–503; ICTA 1988, ss 689A, 689B; FA 2006, Sch 13 paras 19, 20*].

Example

[68.10]

A is sole life-tenant of a settlement which has income and expenses in the year 2010/11 as follows.

	£	£
Property income		500
Taxed investment income (tax deducted at source £300)		1,500
Dividends	900	
Add Tax credits	100	
		1,000

£3,000

Expenses chargeable to income £400

The tax assessable on the trustees will be £100 (£500 at 20%). The expenses are not deductible in arriving at the tax payable by the trustees. The starting rate for savings applies only to individual taxpayers and not to trustees, although the dividend ordinary rate does apply to trustees.

A is sole life-tenant of the above settlement and as such is absolutely entitled to receive the whole settlement income.

A's income for 2010/11 will include the following.

		£	£	£
Trust dividend income (gross)		1,000		
Trust interest income			1,500	
Other trust income				500
Deduct: dividend ordinary rate tax (10%)		(100)		
Basic rate tax (20%)			(300)	(100)
		900	1,200	400
Deduct Expenses (note (b))		400		
Net income entitlement		£500	£1,200	£400
Grossed-up amounts:	£500 × $^{100}/_{90}$	£556		
	£1,200 × $^{100}/_{80}$		£1,500	
	£400 × $^{100}/_{80}$			£500

Notes

(a)   This income falls to be included in A's return even if it is not actually paid to him, as he is absolutely entitled to it. He will receive a tax certificate (form R185 (Trust Income)) from the trust agents, showing three figures for gross income (£556, £1,500 and £500), tax deducted (£56, £300 and £100) and net income (£500, £1,200 and £400).

(b)   The trust expenses are deducted from dividend income in priority to other income (see **68.9** above).

(c)   That part of A's trust income which is represented by dividend income (£500 net) is treated in A's hands as if it were such income received directly by A. It is thus chargeable at the dividend ordinary rate, the liability being satisfied by the 10% tax credit, except to the extent, if any, that it exceeds his basic rate limit.

Similarly, that part of A's trust income which is represented by savings income (£1,200 net) is treated in A's hands as if it were such income received directly by A. It will thus qualify wholly or partly for the 10% starting rate for savings (see **1.6 ALLOWANCES AND TAX RATES**) to the extent (if any) that A's other taxable income is less than the starting rate limit of £2,440.

Special trust rates of tax

[68.11] 'Accumulated or discretionary income' arising to the trustees of a settlement (other than under a trust established for charitable purposes only) is taxed at either the 'trust rate' or the 'dividend trust rate' (rather than at the basic rate, higher rate or the dividend ordinary and higher rates or, before 2008/09, the savings rate). The *'trust rate'* is **50%** for 2010/11 onwards (previously 40%). The *'dividend trust rate'* is **42.5%** for 2010/11 onwards (previously 32.5%).

The dividend trust rate applies if the income is 'dividend income' (as defined in **1.5 ALLOWANCES AND TAX RATES**). See Revenue Tax Bulletin February 1999 pp 629, 630 for an illustrative interpretation of the application of the dividend trust rate. See *Howell & Morton (Robin Settlement Trustees) v Trippier* CA 2004, 76 TC 415 in which it was held that the dividend trust rate applies to stock dividends (see **64.14 SAVINGS AND INVESTMENT INCOME**) received by discretionary trusts even if treated under the terms of the settlement as a capital receipt in the hands of the trustees.

Income is *'accumulated or discretionary income'* for the above purpose in so far as it must be accumulated or it is payable at the discretion of the trustees or any other person. However, income is excluded from being 'accumulated or discretionary income' in so far as:

(a)   before being distributed, the income is the income of any person other than the trustees; or

(b)   the income arises from property held for the purposes of an overseas employee superannuation fund within *ICTA 1988, s 615(3)* (see **57.32 PENSION PROVISION**) or certain pre-2006/07 retirement benefit or personal pension schemes; or

(c)   (for 2007/08 onwards) the income is from 'service charges' which are paid in respect of UK dwellings and which are held on trust; (for this purpose, *'service charges'* has the meaning given by *Landlord and Tenant Act 1985, s 18* but as if that *section* also applied in relation to dwellings in Scotland and NI); or

(d)   (for 2006/07 only, and thereafter effectively subsumed in (c) above) the income is from service charges (within *Landlord and Tenant Act 1985, s 18(1)*) held on trust by a relevant housing body (as defined and including local authorities, registered social landlords, charitable housing associations and charitable housing trusts).

The exclusion at (b) above does not apply to property held as a member of a property investment LLP (see **52.25 PARTNERSHIPS**). In a case in which the facts pre-dated (c) above, income arising from service charges held on trust was held to be liable at the trust rate (*Retirement Care Group Ltd (as trustees) v HMRC* (Sp C 607), [2007] SSCD 539).

The trust rate and dividend trust rate thus apply mainly to discretionary trusts and accumulation trusts, but see **68.12** below for items treated as income within these provisions when arising to the trustees of any settlement.

See **68.13** below for the 'basic rate' band available to trustees liable at the trust rate and/or dividend trust rate. See **68.14** below for the treatment of trust expenses.

See **68.19** *et seq.* below as regards special treatment of trusts with vulnerable beneficiaries.

[ITA 2007, ss 9, 479, 480; ICTA 1988, s 686(1)(1AA)(1A)(2)(5A)(5B) (6ZA)(6ZB)(6A); FA 2006, s 90, Sch 13 paras 2, 15; FA 2007, s 65; FA 2009, s 6(4)(6)].

Any sum received by trustees of a settlement from personal representatives on or before completion of the administration of an estate that would be accumulated or discretionary income or income within **68.12** below if the personal representatives were trustees is regarded as income of the trustees and treated as having borne tax at the applicable rate (for which see **23.6 DECEASED ESTATES**). *[ITA 2007, s 483; ICTA 1988, s 686(6); FA 2006, Sch 13 para 15].*

Where the income of non-resident trustees includes a qualifying distribution which is grossed up at the dividend ordinary rate (see **1.5 ALLOWANCES AND RATES**), a credit is allowed for the dividend ordinary rate tax (which cannot, however, be repaid). *[ITTOIA 2005, s 399(4)–(6); ITA 2007, Sch 1 para 516(2)].* See CTA 2010, s 1136 for meaning of 'qualifying distribution'.

Where the income of the trustees includes a distribution other than a qualifying distribution, liability is restricted to the difference between the dividend trust rate and the dividend ordinary rate on so much of the distribution as otherwise falls to be charged at the dividend trust rate. *[ITTOIA 2005, s 400(4)(5); ITA 2007, Sch 1 para 517(2)].*

Other items chargeable at the special trust rates

[68.12] The items listed at (1)–(11) below are chargeable at the special rates in **68.11** above where they arise to the trustees of any settlement (and not just a discretionary trust or an accumulation trust). However, the following exclusions apply for 2007/08 onwards:

(a)   income arising to a trust established for charitable purposes only;

(b)   'accumulated or discretionary income' (within **68.11** above);

(c)   income that would be 'accumulated or discretionary income' were it not for the exclusions at **68.11**(a), (c) or (d) above; and

(d)   income from property held for the purposes of an overseas employee superannuation fund within *ICTA 1988, s 615(3)* (see **57.32 PENSION PROVISION FOR 2006/07 ONWARDS**).

Similar exclusions applied for 2006/07 and earlier years but for the purposes only of Item (1) below. See Change 85 in Annex 1 to the Explanatory Notes to ITA 2007.

Item (1) below is chargeable at the dividend trust rate and items (2)–(11) at the trust rate.

(1)   Payments receivable from a company for the purchase, redemption or repayment of its own shares or for the purchase of rights to acquire its own shares. The amount chargeable is restricted to the qualifying distribution element of the payment and excludes that part of the payment that represents the original subscription price received for the shares by the issuing company.

(2)   Chargeable event gains on life policies other than where the settlement is a charitable trust (see **44.10 LIFE ASSURANCE POLICIES**).

(3)   Profits on disposals of deeply discounted securities unless the trustees are non-UK resident (see **64.23 SAVINGS AND INVESTMENT INCOME**).

(4)   Lease premiums etc. (see **60.16, 60.17 PROPERTY INCOME**).

(5)   Profits on disposals of futures and options within the 'guaranteed returns' provisions in **4.41 ANTI-AVOIDANCE**, but with certain exceptions as therein noted.

(6)   Profits on disposals of **CERTIFICATES OF DEPOSIT (14)**.

(7)   Proceeds of sale of foreign dividend coupons (see **64.25 SAVINGS AND INVESTMENT INCOME**).

(8)   Chargeable events occurring in relation to a qualifying employee share ownership trust (QUEST).

(9)   Offshore income gains (see **51.3 OFFSHORE FUNDS** or, before 1 December 2009, **51.33 OFFSHORE FUNDS**).

(10)   Gains on disposals of land that are brought within the charge to income tax as in **4.29 ANTI-AVOIDANCE**.

(11)   Accrued income profits chargeable under **2.4** or **2.14 ACCRUED INCOME SCHEME**.

[*ITA 2007, ss 481, 482; ICTA 1988, s 686A; FA 2006, Sch 13 para 3; FA 2007, s 55; SI 2009 No 3001, Reg 129(3)*].

'Basic rate' band

[68.13] A 'basic rate' band is available for any trust whose income for the tax year consists of or includes income otherwise chargeable at the special rates at **68.11** above, i.e. the trust rate or the dividend trust rate. The 'basic rate' band is £1,000. So much of that income as does not exceed that amount is chargeable not at the said rates but at the basic rate or the dividend ordinary rate (see **1.3, 1.5, 1.6 ALLOWANCES AND TAX RATES**) or, before 2008/09, at the savings rate depending on the type of income. For the purpose of determining which income falls within the 'basic rate' band (where the total income otherwise chargeable at the special rates exceeds that band), income normally chargeable on trustees at the basic rate is deemed to form the lowest part of that total income, income normally chargeable on trustees at the savings rate (before 2008/09) is deemed to form the next slice of that total income, and income normally chargeable on trustees at the dividend ordinary rate is deemed to form the highest part of that total income. For the purposes of applying the 'basic rate' band, chargeable event gains on life policies count as savings income. To the extent that UK dividends and other savings income fall within the band, there will be no further tax liability on them, due to their carrying a tax credit or having suffered deduction of basic rate tax (or, before 2008/09, savings rate tax) at source. There may, however, be further tax to pay if the trustees make discretionary payments to beneficiaries out of such income (see below and the *Examples* at **68.16** below). For an article on the 'basic rate' band, see HMRC Tax Bulletin August 2005 pp 1215–1218.

The £1,000 'basic rate' band is divided equally between all settlements made by any one settlor and in existence for any part of the tax year in question, subject to a minimum band of £200 for each such settlement. In the case of a settlement with more than one settlor, the band is determined by reference to the settlor with the greatest number of settlements.

[ITA 2007, ss 463(2), 491, 492; ICTA 1988, ss 686D, 686E; FA 2006, s 90, Sch 13 para 4].

Treatment of trustees' expenses

[68.14] The trustees may offset their expenses (sometimes referred to as management expenses) against trust income for the purpose of determining income chargeable at the special rates, i.e. the trust rate or the dividend trust rate, although income so relieved remains subject to basic rate, savings rate (before 2008/09) or dividend ordinary rate tax, as the case may be. They must, however, be expenses properly chargeable to income (or which would be so chargeable but for any express terms of the settlement) (see *Carver v Duncan*; *Bosanquet v Allen* HL 1985, 59 TC 125). HMRC take the view that, except in 'rare circumstances where it can be demonstrated [that] the payments are solely for managing income, payments of trustees' remuneration are linked to the management of the trust as a whole and are therefore regarded as attributable to capital'. In other words, trustees' remuneration is not regarded as properly chargeable to income. (HMRC Tax Bulletin August 2005 p 1228). Generally, the expenses allowable are those incurred in exercising the trustees' powers and duties in so far as they relate to managing the trust assets to produce or maintain an income flow.

HMRC have published detailed guidance on trustees' expenses (see www.hm rc.gov.uk/trusts/tmes-paper.pdf). This guidance has been largely agreed with trust representatives but there are some areas of disagreement, particularly in relation to HMRC's view on trustees' fees (see above).

In *HMRC v Trustees of the Peter Clay Discretionary Trust* CA 2008, [2009] STC 469, it was held in the Ch D that trustees' remuneration fell to be regarded as incurred for the benefit of the whole estate and, therefore, to be treated as a capital expense; there had to be a heavy evidential burden upon those who asserted a contrary conclusion, and that burden was not satisfied in the instant case. However, whilst reasserting that it was generally only those expenses which had been incurred exclusively for the benefit of the income beneficiaries that might be charged against income, the CA nevertheless held that, on the particular facts of this case, a proportion of trustees' fees could be so charged. The CA also held that investment management fees had to be charged to capital; significantly the fees were incurred after the trustees had resolved to accumulate the trust income.

Before 2007/08, expenses were generally taken into account when 'defrayed' (i.e. paid), though the Ch D in *Peter Clay Discretionary Trust* (above) disagreed with HMRC that this was mandatory. For 2007/08 onwards, expenses are to be taken into account when incurred. A rule is also introduced for 2007/08 onwards whereby expenses remaining unrelieved in a tax year, due to an insufficiency of income chargeable at the special rates, can be carried forward and treated as if incurred in a subsequent tax year.

As income properly covered by expenses is no longer income chargeable at the special rates, it is left out of account in applying the 'basic rate' band at **68.13** above.

The order of set-off of expenses is determined by *ITA 2007, s 486*. First, reduce the expenses by any unallowable proportion computed as described below; then set them firstly against dividend income (see **1.5 ALLOWANCES AND TAX RATES**), then against savings income (see **1.6 ALLOWANCES AND TAX RATES**) and finally against basic rate income. The expenses set against each type of income must be grossed up by reference to the normal rate of tax applicable to that type of income, e.g. the amount set against dividend income should be such amount as, when grossed up by reference to the dividend ordinary rate, equals the dividend income (inclusive of tax credits) or, if less, the total allowable expenses grossed up by reference to that rate. Expenses set against dividend income is set against UK dividend income in priority to dividends from non-UK resident companies (but are in either case grossed up by reference to the dividend ordinary rate). See the *Examples* at **68.16** below.

Where the trust has income not chargeable to income tax, by virtue wholly or partly of the trustees being non-UK resident or being deemed under a double tax agreement to be resident in a territory outside the UK, the trustees' expenses otherwise available for offset are reduced in the same proportion as that which such non-taxable income bears to the total trust income for the year. Where the trustees' income tax liability is limited under the provisions at **50.3 NON-RESIDENTS**, excluded income (see **50.3**), other than that which has suffered deduction of UK income tax at source, must be included in non-taxable income for the purposes of this apportionment.

[*ITA 2007, ss 484–487, Sch 2 para 102; ICTA 1988, ss 686(2AA)(2A)(2B) 689B; FA 2006, Sch 13 paras 15, 20; FA 2008, Sch 1 paras 21, 65*].

Discretionary payments by trustees

[68.15] A discretionary payment is treated as a net amount corresponding to a gross amount from which the trustees have deducted income tax *at the trust rate*. That gross amount is chargeable to income tax on the beneficiary as an annual payment, and the beneficiary is treated as having paid the income tax deducted. This treatment applies only if the discretionary payment is income of the beneficiary for tax purposes by virtue of its having been paid to him or if the payment is made to the settlor's minor children (neither married nor in a civil partnership) such that the payment is treated under *ITTOIA 2005, s 629* as the settlor's income (see **68.30** below) (in which case it is the settlor who is treated as having paid the income tax). The treatment normally applies only if the trustees are UK resident for the tax year in which the payment is made. By concession and subject to conditions, tax paid by trustees of a *non-UK resident* trust may similarly be set against any liability of the settlor under *ITTOIA 2005, s 629* (HMRC ESC A93).

For whether a payment is received as income, see *Stevenson v Wishart and Others (Levy's Trustees)* CA 1987, 59 TC 740. A payment received as employment income is excluded from these provisions but see ESC A68 below. A payment in money's worth is potentially within the provisions as is a payment to a company (see Tolley's Corporation Tax for the treatment of discretionary payments in the company's hands).

Note that, in contrast to the position for interest in possession trusts in **68.9** above, no distinction is made between dividend income, savings income and other income in the hands of the beneficiary. Also, the beneficiary's position is unaffected by the availability of the 'basic rate' band to the trustees. The full amount of the payment to him is treated having suffered tax at a single rate, i.e. the trust rate.

Trustees' tax pool

The total tax treated as deducted by the trustees from discretionary payments in the tax year is chargeable on the trustees but only if, and to the extent that, it exceeds the amount of the 'trustees' tax pool'. The trustees are liable for any tax chargeable. The *'trustees' tax pool'* is computed by taking the balance brought forward (if any) from the previous tax year (net of the tax treated as deducted from payments in that year) and adding the following items (except that none of these items can be added to the pool for a year for which the trustees are non-UK resident):

- tax suffered by them at the trust rate or, in the case of dividend income (for which see **1.5 ALLOWANCES AND TAX RATES**), at the excess of the dividend trust rate over the dividend ordinary rate;
- tax suffered by them at the basic rate or (before 2008/09) at the savings rate (due to the income in question falling within the 'basic rate' band — see **68.13** above); and
- tax suffered by them under the special tax treatment at **68.19** below for trusts with vulnerable beneficiaries; and
- tax suffered by them, in relation to chargeable event gains on life policies, at the excess of the trust rate over the basic rate (or, for 2004/05 to 2007/08 inclusive, at the excess of the trust rate over the savings rate); but see below as regards 2006/07 only.

Also included in the trustees' tax pool where relevant (and on the making of a claim by the trustees) is tax treated as suffered on income available for distribution at the end of the 1972/73 tax year; for this purpose, the tax suffered is taken as two-thirds of the net amount of that available income. Note that tax credits on UK dividends do not form part of the pool. See Revenue Tax Bulletins February 1999 p 630, June 2004 pp 1120, 1121, and see the *Examples* at **68.16** below. Due to a legislative error, and for the year 2006/07 only, the notional 20% tax credit on a chargeable event gain on a life policy could enter the pool; the position has been corrected for 2007/08 onwards.

Certificate of tax deducted

A person in receipt of a discretionary payment on which he is treated as having paid tax at source has power to require from the trustees a certificate of tax deducted. For 2007/08 onwards this power is extended to a settlor whom *ITTOIA 2005, s 629* treats as having received the income and paid the tax.

[*ITA 2007, ss 493–498, Sch 2 para 104; ICTA 1988, ss 352, 687; FA 2006, Sch 13 para 17; FA 2007, s 56; FA 2008, Sch 1 paras 22, 65*].

Double tax relief

Where 'taxed overseas income' arises to a settlement and the trustees make a discretionary payment out of such income, the trustees may certify

- that the payment is one made out of income consisting of, or including, taxed overseas income of an amount, and from a source, stated in the certificate; and
- that the said amount of taxed overseas income arose to the trustees not earlier than tax years before the end of the tax year in which the discretionary payment is made.

The effect of certification is that the beneficiary to whom the payment is made may claim that the payment, up to the certified amount, is to be treated for the purposes of **DOUBLE TAX RELIEF** (26) as income received by him from the certified source and in the tax year in which the discretionary payment is made. '*Taxed overseas income*' means income in respect of which the trustees are entitled to relief by way of credit for tax under the law of a territory outside the UK. That entitlement is effectively transferred from the trustees to the beneficiary.

[*TIOPA 2010, s 111; ICTA 1988, s 809; ITA 2007, Sch 1 para 199*].

Employee benefit settlements

Employee benefit settlements are able to reclaim from HMRC tax at the trust rate on discretionary payments to employee beneficiaries which are taxable earnings in the hands of the employees without credit being available for the tax deducted at source from the payments. The repayment is limited to the amount of the trustees' tax pool, which is then treated as reduced or extinguished by the amount of the repayment. This used to apply by concession (HMRC ESC A68) but has statutory effect for 2010/11 onwards (i.e. for payments made by trustees on or after 6 April 2010). [*ITA 2007, ss 496A, 496B, 497(1); SI 2010 No 157, art 3*].

Payments to beneficiaries — reliefs given by concession

A non-resident beneficiary of a UK resident discretionary trust who receives income treated as net of tax may claim relief in respect of the tax exemption on 'FOTRA' securities (see **64.3 SAVINGS AND INVESTMENT INCOME**) or under the terms of a double taxation agreement, where such relief would have been available had the beneficiary received the income directly instead of through the trustees. Repayment may similarly be claimed where the beneficiary would not have been chargeable to UK tax in those circumstances. Relief is granted provided that the payment is out of income which arose to the trustees not earlier than six years before the end of the tax year in which the payment was made to the beneficiary. The trustees must have submitted trust returns supported by tax certificates and relevant information. They must also have paid all tax, interest, surcharge and penalties and must keep available for inspection any relevant tax certificates, and the beneficiary must claim the relief or exemption within five years and ten months after the end of the tax year in which the payment was received from the trustees.

A similar concession applies where a beneficiary receives a discretionary payment from trustees which is not within the main provisions above (e.g. a payment from a non-resident trust). A non-resident beneficiary who, had he received the income out of which the payment was made, would have been liable to UK tax thereon may claim personal reliefs under **50.2 NON-RESIDENTS** and may be treated as if he received the payment from a UK resident trust, but credit may be claimed only for UK tax actually paid by the trustees on the income out of which the payment was made. Exemption may also be claimed in respect of income arising from 'FOTRA' securities (as above). A UK resident beneficiary of a non-UK resident trust may similarly claim credit for tax actually paid by the trustees on the income out of which the payment was made as if the payment were from a UK resident trust. In all cases, the trustees must have submitted trust returns supported by tax certificates and relevant information. They must also have paid all tax due and any interest, surcharge and penalties, and must keep available for inspection any relevant tax certificates, and the beneficiary must claim the relief or exemption within five years and ten months after the end of the tax year in which the payment was received from the trustees. No credit is given for tax treated as paid on income received by the trustees which would not be available for set-off under the main provisions above if they applied, and that tax is not repayable and is not taken into account in calculating the beneficiary's gross income.

(HMRC ESC B18).

However, where the beneficiary is resident in a country with which the UK has a double taxation agreement, and the 'Other Income' Article in that agreement gives sole taxing rights in respect of such income to that country, the above concession does not apply, and the tax paid by the trustees will be repaid in full to the beneficiary, subject to the conditions in the Article being met (HMRC SP 3/86).

Simon's Taxes. See C4.212, C4.507, C4.509.

Examples

(i) 'Basic rate' band

[68.16]

For 2010/11, a small discretionary trust has property income of £500, building society interest of £240 (net of £60 tax deducted at source) and UK dividends of £450 (carrying a tax credit of £50). It has no other income or expenses. The settlor has made no other settlements.

The tax liability of the trust for 2010/11 is as follows.

	£
'Basic rate' band (£1,000)	
Property income — £500 @ 20%	100.00
Gross interest — £300 @ 20%	60.00
Dividends and tax credits — (£180 × $^{100}/_{90}$) = £200 @ 10%	20.00
	180.00
Income exceeding 'basic rate' band	
Dividends and tax credits — (£270 × $^{100}/_{90}$) = £300 @ 42.5%	127.50
	307.50
Less: Tax deducted at source	(60.00)
Tax credits	(50.00)
Net tax liability	£197.50

Notes

(a)   The property income and building society interest form the lowest slice of the total income; thus, it all falls within the 'basic rate' band and is charged at basic rate. £800 of the £1,000 'basic rate' band is now used up; thus, £200 of the dividend income falls within the 'basic rate' band and is charged at the dividend ordinary rate. The remainder of the dividend income is charged at the dividend trust rate.

(b)   Note that if the trustees were to distribute the whole of the net income of £992.50 (£500 + £240 + £450 – £197.50) to beneficiaries, they will have further tax to pay (assuming no balance, or insufficient balance, brought forward from earlier years in the trustees' tax pool). The total tax payable will be £992.50 (£992.50 × 50/50), from which can be deducted tax paid of £257.50 (£100.00 + £60.00 + (£127.50 – £30.00)), leaving a further £735.00 to pay (if no balance is brought forward in the pool). See also note (c) to *Example (ii)* below.

(c)   See *Example (ii)* below for the position of a beneficiary to whom income is distributed by the trustees.

(ii) General

The XYZ trust, an accumulation and maintenance settlement set up by W for his grandchildren in 1992 now comprises quoted investments and an industrial property. The property is let to an engineering company. Charges for rates, electricity etc. are paid by the trust and recharged yearly in arrears to the tenant. As a result of the delay in recovering the service costs, the settlement incurs overdraft interest. There are no other settlements in existence in relation to which W is a settlor.

The relevant figures for the year ended 5 April 2011 are as follows.

	£
Property rents	40,500
UK dividends (including tax credits of £500)	5,000
Taxed interest (before tax deducted at source £700)	3,500
	£49,000
Trust administration expenses — proportion chargeable to income	1,350
Overdraft interest	1,050
	£2,400

The tax liability of the trust for 2010/11 is as follows

	£	£
Property income — £1,000 @ 20%, £39,500 @ 50%		19,750
Gross interest — £3,500 @ 30% (50 – 20)		1,050
Net dividends	4,500	
Deduct Expenses	(2,400)	
	£2,100	
£2,100 grossed at $^{100}/_{90}$ = £2,333 @ 32.5% (42.5 – 10)		758
Tax payable by assessment		21,558
Add: Tax deducted at source		700
Tax credits		500
Total tax borne		£22,758

Notes

(a) Expenses (including in this example the overdraft interest) are set firstly against the dividend income and then against non-dividend savings income and then non-savings income (see **68.14** above). The effect is that the expenses, grossed-up at 10%, save tax at 32.5% (the difference between the 10% rate applicable to dividend income and the dividend trust rate of 42.5%).

(b) The net revenue available for distribution to the beneficiaries, at the trustees' discretion, will be £23,842 (£49,000 – £22,758 – £2,400), but see note (c) below.

(c) Of the tax borne, only £22,258 goes into the trustees' tax pool. Tax credits on dividends cannot enter the pool. Unless there is sufficient balance brought forward from earlier years, the effect is that if the whole of the distributable income is in fact distributed, there will be insufficient tax in the pool to frank the distribution (£23,842 × 50/50 = £23,842), and the trustees will have a further liability which they may not have the funds to settle.

(d) The property income and savings income form the lowest slice of the total income. Thus, the first £1,000 of such income falls within the 'basic rate' band; as it is normally basic rate income, that £1,000 is chargeable at the basic rate of 20%.

M, the 17-year-old grandson of W, is one of the beneficiaries to whom the trustees of the XYZ trust can pay the settlement income. The trustees make a payment of £4,200 to M on 31 January 2011. He has no other income in the year 2010/11.

M's income from the trust is:

	£
Net income	4.200
Tax at $^{50}/_{50}$	4,200
Gross income	£8,400

He can claim a tax repayment for 2010/11 as follows

	£
Total income	8,400
Deduct Personal allowance	6,475
	£1,925

Tax thereon at 20% (within basic rate band)	385.00
Tax accounted for by trustees	4,200.00
Repayment due	£3,815.00

Note

Unlike the position with interest in possession trusts (see **68.10** above), no distinction is made between dividend income, non-dividend savings income and other income in the beneficiary's hands, the full amount of the payment to him having suffered tax at a single rate of 50% in the hands of the trustees. The beneficiary is not entitled to the starting rate for savings (see **1.6 ALLOWANCES AND TAX RATES**) as a payment from a discretionary trust is not savings income in his hands.

Personal position of trustee

[68.17] Annual remuneration paid to a trustee under a will or settlement is an annual payment from which tax is deductible at source (*Baxendale v Murphy* KB 1924, 9 TC 76; *Hearn v Morgan* KB 1945, 26 TC 478 and cf. *Clapham's Trustees v Belton* Ch D 1956, 37 TC 26). Where a trustee is empowered to, and does, charge for his professional services, his fees are part of his receipts for the purposes of computing his professional profits (*Jones v Wright* KB 1927, 13 TC 221) even where he is also a beneficiary (*Watson & Everitt v Blunden* CA 1933, 18 TC 402).

Income of beneficiaries

[68.18] In the case of life-tenants and those with similar interests in trust income, the beneficiary's income for tax purposes is the grossed-up amount of the net income after deducting any trust outgoings payable out of the income

(*Lord Hamilton of Dalzell* CS 1926, 10 TC 406; *Murray v CIR* CS 1926, 11 TC 133; *MacFarlane v CIR* CS 1929, 14 TC 532) — see **68.9** above re trust expenses generally. In other cases, the tax treatment of payments under a trust depends on the circumstances. Payments to a parent for the maintenance of children were held to be income of the children assessable on the parent in *Drummond v Collins* HL 1915, 6 TC 525 (remittances to mother as guardian of minors, all resident in UK, of income of American trust) and *Johnstone v Chamberlain* KB 1933, 17 TC 706. Payments for the rates etc. and the super-tax of a beneficiary and payments for the maintenance of beneficiaries were held to be income in their hands in *Lord Tollemache v CIR* KB 1926, 11 TC 277; *Shanks v CIR* CA 1928, 14 TC 249; *Waley Cohen v CIR* KB 1945, 26 TC 471. In a number of cases, the outgoings of a residence provided for the beneficiary, grossed-up, have been held to be income of the beneficiary (*Donaldson's Exors v CIR* CS 1927, 13 TC 461; *Sutton v CIR* CA 1929, 14 TC 662; *Lady Miller v CIR* HL 1930, 15 TC 25). Income applied in reducing charges on the trust fund was held not to be income of the life-tenant (*Wemyss* CS 1924, 8 TC 551). Shares allotted to trustees in consideration of arrears of dividends were held to be income and not capital of the trust fund (*In re MacIver's Settlement* Ch D 1935, 14 ATC 571).

Interest on money loaned interest-free, subject to conditions and repayable on demand, by the employer to a trust for the benefit of an employee held to be earnings within the charge to tax on employment income (*O'Leary v McKinlay* Ch D 1990, 63 TC 729).

The tax treatment of income accumulated (e.g. during the minority of a beneficiary) has arisen in a number of cases. The test is whether the beneficiary's interest under the trust is vested or contingent. If vested, the accumulated income is his income as it arises. (N.B. If the accumulated income is the beneficiary's, **68.11** above does not apply. If the interest was contingent, see **68.25** below). Decision involves the general law of trusts, outside the scope of this book. For tax cases in which the accumulated income has been treated as income of the beneficiary, see *Gascoigne v CIR* KB 1926, 13 TC 573; *Stern v CIR* HL 1930, 15 TC 148, and *Brotherton v CIR* CA 1978, 52 TC 137; for cases where the income was held not to be the beneficiary's, see *Stanley v CIR* CA 1944, 26 TC 12 (where the position under the *Trustee Act 1925, s 31* was considered); *Cornwell v Barry* Ch D 1955, 36 TC 268, and *Kidston* CS 1936, 20 TC 603. For the release of accumulated income on the termination of a trust, see *Hamilton-Russell's Exors v CIR* CA 1943, 25 TC 200, and on termination of legally permissible period of accumulation, see *Duncan v CIR* CS 1931, 17 TC 1.

See also **23 DECEASED ESTATES**.

Simon's Taxes. See C4.501–C4.509.

Trusts with vulnerable beneficiaries

[68.19] Special income tax and capital gains tax (CGT) treatment is given if the trustees and the vulnerable beneficiary concerned opt for it to apply. The income tax treatment is described below. For the CGT treatment, see the corresponding chapter of Tolley's Capital Gains Tax. For income tax purposes, the special treatment is most likely to be beneficial where the income would otherwise be chargeable at the trust rate or the dividend trust rate. For HMRC guidance on the special treatment (including CGT treatment), see www.hmr c.gov.uk/trusts/vb-guidance.htm.

The special treatment applies to income arising to trustees from property held on 'qualifying trusts' (see **68.20** below) for a 'vulnerable person' and to chargeable gains accruing to trustees from the disposal of such property. '*Vulnerable person*' means a disabled person (see **68.20** below) or a person under 18 at least one of whose parents has died. The trustees can claim the special treatment for any tax year in which they hold such property and for all or part of which a 'vulnerable person election' is in force (see **68.21** below). But the special treatment does not apply if the property from which the income arises is property in which the settlor is regarded for the purposes of **68.29** below as having an interest.

The special treatment operates for income tax purposes by comparing:

(i)   what would otherwise be the trustees' liability on the income in question (the '*qualifying trusts income*') (computed as below); and

(ii)   what would be the beneficiary's liability on the qualifying trusts income if it were income arising to him directly (computed as below).

The excess (if any) of (i) over (ii) is then treated as a reduction in the trustees' income tax liability for the tax year. The reduction is given at Step 6 in the calculation of income tax liability and is given effect after any other tax reductions have been made (see **1.7, 1.8 ALLOWANCES AND TAX RATES**).

In computing the amount in (i), any allowable trustees' expenses of the trust (within **68.14** above) are apportioned between the qualifying trusts income and other income (if any).

The amount in (ii) is the excess of:

(a)   the beneficiary's total income tax liability *and capital gains tax* liability for the year if the qualifying trusts income were his own income over

(b)   what would otherwise be his total income tax liability and capital gains tax liability for the year.

But in computing *both* (a) and (b), the following are ignored:

• any income distributed by the trustees to the beneficiary in the tax year (regardless of when that income arose); and

• any reliefs to which he is entitled which are given by way of a reduction of income tax liability (e.g. married couple's allowance).

Where the beneficiary is neither UK resident for any part of the tax year nor ordinarily resident for the tax year, the income tax elements of both (a) and (b) are computed as if he were resident and domiciled in the UK throughout the year; see Tolley's Capital Gains Tax as regards the CGT element.

Where the vulnerable person election in **68.21** below is in force for part only of a tax year, the above applies only as respects qualifying trusts income arising in that part of the year, and any necessary apportionment of allowable trustees' expenses as above is made by reference to the income and expenses of that part of the year only.

The rule at **68.30** below, which treats income paid to an unmarried minor child of the settlor as the settlor's income, is disapplied for any tax year in respect of which the child in question is a vulnerable person, the income is qualifying trusts income and the trustees have successfully claimed the special income tax treatment above.

[*FA 2005, ss 23–29, 39, 41(2); FA 2006, Sch 13 paras 35(2)–(4), (7), 36; ITA 2007, Sch 1 paras 594, 595*].

These provisions, including those in **68.20**, **68.21** below, are appropriately modified in their application to Scotland by *FA 2005, s 42 as amended* so that they conform with Scottish trust law generally.

Qualifying trusts

[68.20] Where property is held on trusts for the benefit of a 'disabled person', those trusts are *'qualifying trusts'* for the purposes of **68.19** above if they secure that the conditions below are met during the lifetime of the disabled person or until the termination of the trusts (if that precedes his death). The conditions are:

- that if any of the property is applied for the benefit of a beneficiary it is applied for the benefit of the disabled person; and
- either that the disabled person is entitled to all the income (if any) arising from any of the property or that no such income may be applied for the benefit of any other person.

But the above is not to be regarded as failed by reason only of:

(i) a power of advancement conferred on the trustees by *Trustee Act 1925, s 32* (or its NI equivalent); or

(ii) a similar power of advancement conferred on the trustees by the law of a jurisdiction other than England and Wales or NI; or

(iii) a power of advancement conferred on the trustees by instrument and subject to similar restrictions as those in *Trustee Act 1925, s 32*.

If the property is held on trusts of the kind described in *Trustee Act 1925, s 33* (protective trusts), the reference above to 'the lifetime of the disabled person' is to be interpreted as the period during which the property is held on trust for him.

For the purposes of these provisions, a *'disabled person'* is:

(a) a person who by reason of mental disorder is incapable of administering his property or managing his affairs; or

(b) a person in receipt of attendance allowance or of a disability living allowance by virtue of entitlement to the care component at the highest or middle rate.

A person is treated as being within (b) above if he satisfies HMRC that he would be entitled to the said benefits if he satisfied the residence requirements appropriate to those benefits. A person does not cease to be within (b) above (or treated as such) by reason only that he ceases to be entitled to the benefit (or would cease to be so entitled) due to his undergoing treatment in hospital for renal failure or being provided with certain accommodation.

Where property is held on trusts for the benefit of a minor at least one of whose parents have died, those trusts are *'qualifying trusts'* for the purposes of **68.19** above if they are:

- statutory trusts under *Administration of Estates Act 1925, ss 46, 47(1)* (rules relating to intestacy);
- trusts established under the will of a deceased parent which secure that the conditions set out below are met; or
- trusts established under the Criminal Injuries Compensation Scheme (as defined) which secure that the conditions set out below are met.

The said conditions are:

- that the minor will become entitled to the property, any income arising from it and any accumulated income on reaching the age of 18;
- that, in the meantime and for so long as the minor is living, if any of the property is applied for the benefit of a beneficiary it is applied for the benefit of the minor; and
- that, in the meantime and for so long as the minor is living, either the minor is entitled to all the income (if any) arising from any of the property or no such income may be applied for the benefit of any other person.

But trusts are not to be regarded as failing to secure the meeting of these conditions by reason only of a power of advancement as in (i)–(iii) above.

Parts of assets

For the purposes of these provisions, property held on trusts includes a part of an asset if that part (and any income arising from it) can be identified for the purpose of determining whether the trusts are qualifying trusts.

[FA 2005, ss 34–36, 38; FA 2006, Sch 12 para 48(2)(3)(5)].

Vulnerable person election

[68.21] The *'vulnerable person election'* referred to at **68.19** above is an irrevocable election that may be made jointly in relation to qualifying trusts by the trustees and the vulnerable person. It must be made in such form as HMRC may require (form VPE 1), must specify the date on which it is to come into force (the 'start date') and must be made by notice to HMRC no later than the first anniversary of 31 January following the tax year in which the start date falls (or within such further time as the Commissioners of HMRC may allow in a particular case). It must contain certain specified information relating to the trusts, the trustees, the vulnerable person, the entitlement of the vulnerable person, and any other person connected with the trusts. It must also contain certain declarations including a declaration of its accuracy and the vulnerable person's authority for the trustees to claim the special tax treatment for any tax year for which they feel it is appropriate.

An election ceases to be in force when the vulnerable person ceases to be a vulnerable person, when the trusts cease to be qualifying trusts or when the trusts are terminated. If the trustees become aware that any such event has occurred, they must notify HMRC accordingly within 90 days of their becoming so aware.

Where the property held on qualifying trusts becomes treated as comprised in a sub-fund settlement (see **68.6** above), there is provision to treat a pre-existing vulnerable person election as made by the trustees of the sub-fund settlement (and the vulnerable person) from the date the sub-fund election is treated as having taken effect.

[*FA 2005, s 37; FA 2006, Sch 12 para 48(4)(5), Sch 13 para 35(2)(7)*].

HMRC powers

Where a vulnerable person election has been made, HMRC are given powers to require information from the trustees and/or the vulnerable person. In appropriate circumstances, HMRC may give notice to the effect that the election is deemed never to have come into force or that it has ceased to be in force from a specified date. An aggrieved person has a right of appeal; the notice of appeal must be given to HMRC within 30 days. [*FA 2005, s 40; SI 2009 No 56, Sch 1 para 445*].

Penalties under *TMA 1970, s 98* (see **55.21** PENALTIES) apply for failure to comply with any of the information requirements referred to above. For penalty purposes, any information, statements or declarations given or made jointly by the trustees and the vulnerable person are treated as given or made by the trustees. [*FA 2005, s 43; FA 2006, Sch 13 para 35(6)(7)*].

Annuities and other annual payments

[68.22] Annuities and other annual payments under settlements or wills are subject to the normal rules for DEDUCTION OF TAX AT SOURCE (**24**). Annual remuneration to a trustee is an annual payment for this purpose (see **68.17** above). Where the annuity etc. is paid out of the capital of the trust fund, the tax deducted is assessed on the trustees. (Where tax is not deducted, the beneficiary may be assessed instead.) Payments out of capital may be directed or authorised by the settlor or testator, as where he directs a stipulated annual amount to be paid out of capital (*Jackson's Trustees v CIR* KB 1942, 25 TC 13; *Milne's Exors v CIR* Ch D 1956, 37 TC 10) or authorises the beneficiary's income to be augmented to a stipulated amount out of capital (*Brodie's Trustees v CIR* KB 1933, 17 TC 432; *Morant Settlement Trustees v CIR* CA 1948, 30 TC 147), or direct payments out of capital for the maintenance etc. of the recipient (*Lindus & Hortin v CIR* KB 1933, 17 TC 442; *Esdaile v CIR* CS 1936, 20 TC 700) even though discretionary (*Cunard's Trustees v CIR* CA 1945, 27 TC 122). For position if annuity exceeds income of fund on which charged, see *Lady Castlemaine* KB 1943, 25 TC 408. Annuities directed to be paid out of capital but paid out of accumulated income forming part of the capital were held to have been paid out of income (*Postlethwaite v CIR* Ch D 1963, 41 TC 244).

For 'free of tax' annuities, see **24.15 DEDUCTION OF TAX AT SOURCE.**

Foreign trust income

[68.23] There are no special provisions for the income tax treatment of foreign trust income. For the liability of trustees within the jurisdiction as regards foreign trust income, see the case of *Williams v Singer, Dawson v CIR* and *Kelly v Rogers* at **68.8** above.

The income of a life-tenant of a foreign trust fund depends first on the nature of his interest under the relevant foreign law. See for this the cases of *Archer-Shee v Baker* HL 1927, 11 TC 749 and *Garland v Archer-Shee* HL 1930, 15 TC 693, dealing with the same life-tenancy. In the first, with no evidence as to the foreign law, the life-tenant was held to be assessable on the basis that the investments forming part of the fund were separate foreign possessions or securities. In the second case, relating to later years, it was held that having regard to evidence given as to the foreign law, she was assessable on the basis that the income was from a single foreign possession. (N.B. The decisions have lost some of their practical importance because of subsequent changes in the basis rules of Schedule D, Cases IV and V, but the principles established remain important.) See also *Nelson v Adamson* KB 1941, 24 TC 36 and *Inchyra v Jennings* Ch D 1965, 42 TC 388. Stock dividends received by trustees of an American trust fund were part of the trust income under the relevant American law but held not to be income of a UK life-tenant, as not of an income nature under UK principles (*Lawson v Rolfe* Ch D 1969, 46 TC 199).

Discretionary remittances from foreign trustees are assessable and become income when the discretion is exercised (*Drummond v Collins* HL 1915, 6 TC 525) but cf. *Lawson v Rolfe.*

See **32.5 FOREIGN INCOME** for unremittable foreign income and **32.1 FOREIGN INCOME** for overseas income generally.

Claims by trustees and beneficiaries

[68.24] Only such claims as relate to the trust can be made by the trustee — except as regards incapacitated persons for whom he is assessable, e.g. under *TMA 1970, s 72.* [*TMA 1970, s 42(6)*]. Beneficiaries other than these must claim in their own name. See **68.2**(b) and **68.15** above. Beneficiaries claiming a refund on their share of trust income must each make a separate claim showing their total income from all sources and tax paid on it.

In claim by non-resident life-tenants of residue subject to annuity, held that (where no 'appropriation') latter not to be treated as paid out of UK taxed income but rateably out of all investments. (*Crawshay* CA 1935, 19 TC 715).

Claims for personal allowances etc. on income up to 1968/69 — from specified 'contingent interests' on obtaining a specified age or marrying

[68.25] Under *ITA 1952, s 228*, where an individual has an interest under a will or settlement that is contingent on his or her attaining a specified age or marrying, and income is directed to be accumulated meantime, claims by that individual for personal allowances etc. may be made within six years after the end of the tax year in which the contingency happens, in respect of all income so compulsorily accumulated prior to 6 April 1969. [*ICTA 1970, Sch 14 para 1*]. Such claims cannot be made in respect of income which is deemed to be the income of the settlor as below. See **41 INTEREST ON OVERPAID TAX**.

Where income is legally vested in beneficiaries, relief as above is refused; it is important, therefore, to ascertain whether income legally vested or contingent (*Roberts v Hanks* KB 1926, 10 TC 351; *Jones v Down* KB 1936, 20 TC 279), and when the 'contingency' happens (*Stonely v Ambrose* KB 1925, 9 TC 389, and *Lynch v Davies* Ch D 1962, 40 TC 511).

The section applies only when the contingency is the claimant's attainment of a specified age or marriage (*Bone* CS 1927, 13 TC 20 and *White v Whitcher* KB 1927, 13 TC 202). Claimant's right must depend solely on happening of one of these contingencies *and on nothing else*, and no claim can be made if right to receive income is wholly at trustee's discretion (*Dain v Miller* KB 1934, 18 TC 478, and see *Maude-Roxby* CS 1950, 31 TC 388). See also *Cusden v Eden* KB 1939, 22 TC 435 as to accumulations.

Tax on income accumulated but directed to be capitalised on happening of contingency may nevertheless be claimed under this section (*Dale v Mitcalfe* CA 1927, 13 TC 41).

The amount recovered belongs to the beneficiary (*Fulford v Hyslop* Ch D 1929, 8 ATC 588). In *Chamberlain v Haig Thomas* KB 1933, 17 TC 595 where accumulations directed (from 1913 onwards) for infant children subject to power of appointment (which not in fact exercised until 1922), section held to apply to income of intervening period.

Liability of settlor

[68.26] Where:

(a) the settlor retains an interest in a settlement;

(b) payments are made out of, or, in certain cases, income is accumulated in, a settlement to or for a minor child of the settlor who is neither married nor in a civil partnership;

(c) capital sums are paid to the settlor by the trustees of a settlement; or

(d) capital sums are paid to the settlor by a body connected with a settlement,

income of the settlement, or (in the case of (c) or (d) above) the sum of the capital sums received, is treated as income of the settlor, and income tax is charged accordingly. See **68.29–68.32** below for the calculation of the amounts chargeable.

In calculating the amount chargeable on the settlor, the same deductions and reliefs are allowed as if the income had actually been received by the settlor. Where the charge is under (a) or (b) above, the income treated as the settlor's is charged in his hands at the rates that would have applied if the income had arisen to him directly.

Income treated under (a) or (b) above as income of the settlor is deemed to be the top slice of his income, but before taking into account income chargeable under *ITEPA 2003, s 403* (payments on loss of office, see **20.5 COMPENSATION FOR LOSS OF EMPLOYMENT (AND DAMAGES)**) or *ITTOIA 2005, s 465* (life assurance gains, see **44.3 LIFE ASSURANCE POLICIES**) and subject to the rules at **1.5, 1.6 ALLOWANCES AND TAX RATES**.

[*ITTOIA 2005, ss 619, 619A, 621–623, Sch 1 paras 272, 338(2); ICTA 1988, ss 660C, 677(7)(8), 833(3); FA 2006, Sch 13 paras 5, 31(2)(3); ITA 2007, Sch 1 paras 550, 551*].

The settlor is entitled to recover tax paid under (a) or (b) above from any trustee or any person to whom the income is payable under the settlement, and to that end can obtain from HMRC a certificate specifying the amount of income charged on him and the tax paid. If the settlor receives a tax repayment by virtue of setting an allowance or relief against income chargeable on him under these provisions, he must pay it over to the trustee or any person(s) to whom the income is payable under the settlement, with the Appeal Tribunal having the final decision on any question as to the amount payable or how it should be apportioned. Nothing in these provisions precludes tax being charged on the trustees as persons by whom any income is received. [*ITTOIA 2005, s 646; ICTA 1988, ss 660D, 682A(1); SI 2009 No 56, Sch 1 para 441*].

ITTOIA 2005, s 646 is to be amended so as to require a settlor to pay over to the trustees *all* repayments of tax received by the settlor in relation to the trust income. The amending legislation will be included in a Finance Bill to be introduced in autumn 2010, but will have backdated effect for all repayments that arise on or after 6 April 2010. (HMRC Budget Note BN25, 22 June 2010).

Settlors have an obligation to notify their tax office of any liability under the provisions even if they do not normally receive a tax return. (Revenue Press Release 4 January 1995).

HMRC information powers

HMRC can, by notice, require from any party to a settlement such particulars as they think necessary (subject to penalty under *TMA 1970, s 98* for non-compliance). [*ITTOIA 2005, s 647; ICTA 1988, ss 660F, 682A(1)*]. See *Cutner v CIR QB 1974, 49 TC 429* and *Wilover Nominees v CIR CA 1974, 49 TC 559* in connection with similar information powers under pre-Finance Act 1995 provisions.

Relief for recipients of annual payments

Where a person receives a discretionary annual payment of income from a trust and a settlor is chargeable as above (whether in the same tax year or a previous year) on the trust income out of which the payment is made, the recipient is treated as having paid higher rate tax on the income. The income is then treated as the highest part of the recipient's total income apart from chargeable event gains on life policies etc. (see **44.3 LIFE ASSURANCE POLICIES**). The notional higher rate tax credit is not repayable and cannot be used to reduce the tax chargeable on other income. For 2006/07, the payment is treated for the purposes of *ICTA 1988, s 348, 349* (see **24.20, 24.21 DEDUCTION OF TAX AT SOURCE**) as payable wholly out of profits or gains not brought into charge to income tax, but this ceases to be relevant for 2007/08 onwards. If only a proportion of the total trust income is chargeable on the settlor, only a similar proportion of the annual payment carries the higher rate credit. If the recipient is himself a settlor in relation to the settlement, the foregoing does not apply but the payment is not treated as taxable income in his hands. The normal tax treatment of discretionary payments by trustees (see **68.15** above) is disapplied insofar as the payment falls within these provisions.

For 2010/11 onwards, in consequence of the increase in the trust rate (see **68.11** above), the recipient will be treated as having paid *additional* rate tax (see **1.3 ALLOWANCES AND TAX RATES**) on the income.

[*ITTOIA 2005, s 685A; ITA 2007, Sch 1 para 569; FA 2008, s 67; FA 2009, Sch 2 paras 21, 25*].

Simon's Taxes. See C4.320, C4.329, C4.353.

Exclusion for income given to charity

[68.27] The charge to tax on the settlor under **68.26**(a) or (b) above does not apply to 'qualifying income' which arises to a 'UK settlement' and which either:

(a)   is given by the trustees to a 'charity' in the tax year in which it arises; or

(b)   is income to which a 'charity' is entitled under the terms of the settlement.

For these purposes, a '*UK settlement*' is a settlement the trustees of which are resident and ordinarily resident in the UK (see **68.5** above). '*Charity*' has the meaning in **16.2 CHARITIES** but also includes the Trustees of the National Heritage Memorial Fund, the Historic Buildings and Monuments Commission for England and the National Endowment for Science, Technology and the Arts. '*Qualifying income*' is widely defined to cover the income of accumulation, discretionary and interest in possession trusts.

Where the qualifying income arises from different sources (e.g. interest, dividends etc.) and *part* of that income for any tax year is excluded as above, the remainder is rateably apportioned for tax purposes between the different sources. However, this rule is overridden by any requirement in the terms of the settlement that the whole or part of a *particular* source of income be given to charity. For the purposes of **68.9** and **68.14** above, trustees' expenses are rateably apportioned between income excluded as above, with the effect that relief is to that extent available for such expenses, and any remainder.

[*ITTOIA 2005, ss 628, 630, 646A, Sch 1 para 512; FA 2006, Sch 13 para 33(1)–(3), (5); ITA 2007, Sch 1 paras 391, 555, 560*].

Definitions etc.

[68.28] The following apply for the purposes of **68.26** above and **68.29–68.32** below.

(a)   '*Settlement*' includes any disposition, trust, covenant, agreement, arrangement or transfer of assets, wherever made. [*ITTOIA 2005, s 620(1)(4); ICTA 1988, s 660G(1), 682A(1); FA 1995, Sch 17 paras 1, 11* The latter includes a gift of shares (*Hood Barrs v CIR* CA 1946, 27 TC 385) or of National Savings Bank deposit (*Thomas v Marshall* HL 1953, 34 TC 178). For shares in new company issued at par, see *Butler v Wildin* Ch D 1988, [1989] STC 22. See also *Yates v Starkey* CA 1951, 32 TC 38 re Court Orders and *Harvey v Sivyer* Ch D 1985, 58 TC 569 re provision for children whether under compulsion or not.

The creation of a new class of preference shares in a company, and their allotment to the wives of the directors, who had previously also been the sole shareholders, was held to be a settlement by the directors (*Young v Pearce; Young v Scrutton* Ch D 1996, 70 TC 331).

Parent's release of expectant life interest is a settlement (*Buchanan* CA 1957, 37 TC 365) and see *D'Abreu v CIR* Ch D 1978, 52 TC 352.

A distinction can be made between arrangements which amount to a settlement and bona fide commercial transactions without any element of bounty which do not (*Copeman v Coleman* KB 1939, 22 TC 594; *Bulmer v CIR* Ch D 1966, 44 TC 1) and this notwithstanding that tax avoidance was a motive for the transactions (*CIR v Plummer* HL 1979, 54 TC 1). See also *CIR v Levy* Ch D 1982, 56 TC 67. For whether 'arrangements' are a settlement, see also *Prince-Smith* KB 1943, 25 TC 84; *Pay* Ch D 1955, 36 TC 109; *Crossland v Hawkins* CA 1961, 39 TC 493; *Leiner* Ch D 1964, 41 TC 589; *Wachtel* Ch D 1970, 46 TC 543; *Mills v CIR* HL 1974, 49 TC 367; *Chinn v Collins* HL 1980, 54 TC 311; *Butler v Wildin* Ch D 1988, 61 TC 666; *Bird v HMRC* (Sp C 720) at **68.30** below.

For 'property comprised in a settlement', see *Vestey v CIR* HL 1949, 31 TC 1. Where the settlement is of shares in a company controlled by the settlor, the assets of the company are not comprised in the settlement (*Chamberlain v CIR* HL 1943, 25 TC 317; *Langrange Trust v CIR* HL 1947, 28 TC 55).

Where the trust is imperfect, income not disposed of reverts to the settlor (*Hannay's Exors v CIR* CS 1956, 37 TC 217).

A foreign settlement of UK income by a non-resident was held to be within the ambit of the pre-Finance Act 1995 settlements legislation (*Kenmare* HL 1957, 37 TC 383).

A settlement does not include any arrangement consisting of a loan of money by an individual to a charity (as defined in **68.27** above) either for no consideration or for a consideration consisting only of interest. [*ITTOIA 2005, s 620(1)(5); ITA 2007, Sch 1 para 552*].

See also **68.31** below (settlements not involving trusts).

(b)   '*Settlor*', in relation to a settlement, means any person by whom the settlement was made. A person is deemed to have made a settlement if he has made or entered into it directly or indirectly and/or has provided or undertaken to provide funds directly or indirectly for the purpose of the settlement or has made reciprocal arrangements for another person to make or enter into the settlement. [*ITTOIA 2005, s 620(1)–(3)*]. See *Crossland v Hawkins* CA 1961, 39 TC 493, *Leiner* Ch D 1964, 41 TC 589 and *Mills* HL 1974, 49 TC 367.

(c) If there is *more than one settlor*. Each is to be treated as the sole settlor, but only in respect of income or property he has himself provided, directly or indirectly. [*ITTOIA 2005, ss 644, 645*].

(d) '*Income arising under a settlement*' includes any income chargeable to income tax, by deduction or otherwise, or which would have been so chargeable if received in the UK by a person domiciled, resident and ordinarily resident in the UK. However, it does not include income for a tax year on which the settlor, if he were himself entitled to it, would not have been chargeable by reason of his being non-UK resident in the tax year.

If, for a tax year, the settlor is chargeable on the REMITTANCE BASIS (61), '*income arising under a settlement*' includes, in relation to any 'relevant foreign income' (see 32.2 FOREIGN INCOME) arising under the settlement in that tax year, only such of it as is remitted to the UK (whether in that tax year or any subsequent tax year) in circumstances such that, if the settlor had remitted it, the settlor would have been chargeable to income tax. The remitted income is then treated as arising under the settlement in the tax year in which it is remitted. (For the purpose only of applying the transitional rule at 61.11 REMITTANCE BASIS, the income is treated as arising in the tax year in which it did, in fact, arise to the settlement.)

Before 22 April 2009, the rule was that income arising under a settlement did not include income for a tax year on which the settlor, if he were himself entitled to it, would not have been chargeable by reason of his being non-UK domiciled, resident or ordinarily resident. Such income was treated as arising under the settlement in a tax year in which it was subsequently remitted to the UK if, had the settlor been entitled to the income when remitted, he would have been chargeable to income tax by reason of his being UK resident. The rule required clarification following the fundamental changes made to the remittance basis the previous year (see 61 REMITTANCE BASIS).

[*ITTOIA 2005, s 648; ICTA 1988, ss 660G(3)(4), 682A(1); FA 2008, Sch 7 para 86(4A); FA 2009, Sch 27 paras 13–15*].

(e) *Payment of inheritance tax by trustees on assets put into settlement by settlor.* Where the trustees have power to pay, or do in fact pay, inheritance tax on assets which the settlor puts into the settlement, HMRC will not argue that such a power renders that income the settlor's income for income tax purposes. This is because both the settlor and the trustees are liable for such inheritance tax (HMRC SP 1/82).

Settlor retaining an interest

[68.29] As indicated at **68.26** above, income arising under a settlement during the life of the settlor is treated for all income tax purposes as the income of the settlor (and not of any other person), *unless* the income arises from property in which the settlor has no interest (see below). See **68.27** above for the exclusion for income given to charity and **68.28** above for definitions.

These provisions do not apply in respect of an outright gift between spouses or civil partners of property from which income arises (but a gift which does not carry a right to the whole of that income is not excluded, nor is a gift of a right to income).

A gift is not an outright gift if it is conditional or if the property or any 'related property' could in any circumstances become payable to the giver or be applied for his benefit. See also **68.31** below as regards the application of the above exception in cases involving income shifting.

The following income is excluded from these provisions:

(i)   income arising under a marriage settlement (or civil partnership settlement) made between spouses (or civil partners) after separation, divorce or annulment, being income payable to or for the benefit of the spouse (or civil partner) being provided for;

(ii)   annual payments by an individual for *bona fide* commercial reasons in connection with his trade, profession or vocation;

(iii)   qualifying donations within **16.17** CHARITIES (Gift Aid); and

(iv)   benefits under a registered pension scheme or foreign government pension scheme or any such pension arrangements as may be specified in regulations under *Welfare Reform and Pensions Act 1999* (or NI equivalent).

A settlor has an *interest in property* if that property or any 'related property' could in any circumstances become payable to the settlor or the settlor's spouse or civil partner or be applied for the benefit of either. For this purpose, a spouse does not include a possible future spouse, a separated spouse or a widow/widower of the settlor; and similar exclusions apply in the case of a civil partner. A settlor does *not* have an interest in property if it could become so payable or be so applied only in the event of:

(A)   the bankruptcy of a current or potential beneficiary;

(B)   an assignment of, or charge on, the property or 'related property' being made or given by a current or potential beneficiary;

(C)   in the case of a marriage settlement or civil partnership settlement, the death of both parties to the marriage or civil partnership and of all or any of the children of one or both parties;

(D)   the death of a child of the settlor who has become beneficially entitled to the property etc. at an age not exceeding 25,

or if (and so long as) there is a beneficiary alive under the age of 25 during whose life the property etc. cannot become so payable etc. except in the event of the beneficiary becoming bankrupt or assigning or charging his interest.

'*Related property*', in relation to any property, means income from that property or any other property directly or indirectly representing proceeds of, or of income from, that property or income therefrom.

Where the settlement is a trust, expenses of the trustees do not reduce the income attributed to the settlor under these provisions.

[*ITTOIA 2005, ss 624–627, Sch 2 para 132; ITA 2007, Sch 1 paras 553, 554*].

See also **49.8** and **49.11** MISCELLANEOUS INCOME for apportionment rules and relief for miscellaneous losses.

Simon's Taxes. See **C4.325–C4.329**.

Children's settlements

[68.30] As indicated at **68.26** above, income arising under a settlement which during the life of the settlor is paid (whether in money or money's worth) to or for the benefit of an unmarried minor child (i.e. a child under 18, including a stepchild or illegitimate child) of the settlor in any tax year is treated for all income tax purposes as income of the settlor (and not of any other person) for that year. A child is not regarded for this purpose as 'unmarried' if he is in a civil partnership. See **68.27** above for the exclusion for income given to charity and **68.28** above for definitions.

However, the above rule does *not* apply for any tax year if the aggregate amount that would otherwise be treated as the settlor's income for that year in relation to any particular child does not exceed £100. Nor does it apply if the income falls to be treated under **68.29** above as that of the settlor. The rule is also disapplied in the circumstances described in **68.19** above (trusts with vulnerable beneficiaries).

As regards income arising under a settlement made on or after 9 March 1999, and income arising directly or indirectly from funds added on or after that date to a pre-existing settlement (any necessary apportionment being made on a just and reasonable basis), the provisions are extended to apply the same treatment as above to undistributed income which would otherwise be treated as income of an 'unmarried' minor child of the settlor in any tax year. This is intended to catch income accumulated in a bare trust. The above-mentioned £100 limit applies, per parent per child, by reference to the aggregate of income paid out or accumulated.

Retained or accumulated income

Where the trustees retain or accumulate income, any payment made on or after 9 March 1999 under the settlement to or for the child is taken into account as above only to the extent that there is available retained or accumulated income, i.e. aggregate income arising since the settlement was made exceeds the aggregate amount of such income which has been:

(a)   treated as income of the settlor;
(b)   paid (as income or capital) to or for the benefit of, or otherwise treated as the income of, a beneficiary other than an 'unmarried' minor child of the settlor; or

(c)   treated as the income of an unmarried minor child of the settlor, and 'subject to income tax', in any of the years 1995/96, 1996/97 or 1997/98; or

(d)   used to pay expenses of the trustees which were properly chargeable to income (or would have been so chargeable but for express terms of the settlement).

For the purposes of (c) above, the income so treated is '*subject to income tax*' to the extent that it does not exceed the child's taxable income (i.e. total income, inclusive of the settlement income, after allowances and deductions). For payments made before 9 March 1999, similar rules applied as above, the main difference being that any income treated as the income of an unmarried minor child, whether charged to tax or not, was deductible in arriving at available retained or accumulated income.

Where trustees hold assets for a person who would be absolutely entitled as against the trustees but for being a minor, any offshore income gains (see **51.3 OFFSHORE FUNDS** or, before 1 December 2009, **51.31 OFFSHORE FUNDS**) liable to income tax which accrue on the disposal of those assets are deemed to be paid to that person for the purposes of these provisions.

[*ITTOIA 2005, ss 629, 631, 632, Sch 2 para 133; FA 2006, Sch 13 paras 33(4)(5), 34; ITA 2007, Sch 1 para 556; SI 2009 No 3001, Reg 128(3)*].

Any provision by a parent for his child may create a settlement, whether made under compulsion or merely under parental obligation (*Harvey v Sivyer* Ch D 1985, 58 TC 569), although in practice HMRC do not treat payments made under a Court Order as being under a settlement for this purpose. '*Stepchild*' includes a child of the wife by a previous marriage (*CIR v Russell* CS 1955, 36 TC 83). In *Bird v HMRC* (Sp C 720), the issue to children of shares in the family company was held to be a settlement within these provisions with the result that dividends were taxable as the parents' income, though the Sp C also found that there had been no negligent conduct on the part of the parents in failing to declare this dividend income in their tax returns.

Simon's Taxes. See C4.330, C4.331.

Settlements not involving trusts — income shifting

[68.31] In its 2008 Pre-Budget Report, the then Government stated that 'given the current economic challenges' they would *not* be bringing forward new legislation on the matters detailed below, but that the issue would be kept under review.

The history

In April 2003, the Inland Revenue (now HMRC) published guidance, including some examples, as to how they intend to apply the settlements legislation at **68.26** above in situations not involving trusts and especially in relation to businesses carried on by companies and partnerships, but see now the HL decision in the *Arctic Systems* case below. Subject to that HL judgment, situations in which the settlements legislation might be applied include: the issue or gifting of shares (to spouses or other relatives, for example) carrying no right (or a restricted right) to a share of the assets on a winding-up, and the payment of dividends on those shares; the issue or gifting to another person, typically a spouse, of shares in a company with minimal capital value that derives its income from the work of one person; the gifting, or transfer at undervalue, of a share of profits in a partnership; the waiving of dividends by one or more shareholders so that other shareholders can receive larger dividends; the payment of larger dividends than would otherwise be possible on one or more classes of shares but not on others; and the gifting to children of shares by a parent, or by someone other than a parent where the company's profits, and decisions on the level of dividends, are made by a parent. The guidance also includes examples of situations in which the settlements legislation would not be applied, mainly involving transactions in which there is no element of bounty and outright gifts between spouses which are not wholly or substantially a right to income (see **68.29** above). (Revenue Tax Bulletin April 2003 pp 1011–1016). References above to spouses must be taken to include civil partners.

A detailed joint response by seven professional bodies, including CIOT and ICAEW, was published on 11 September 2003 (and reproduced at *2003 STI 1605*). This reflected the bodies' concerns both as to HMRC's interpretation of the settlements legislation as summarised above, and as to the retrospective nature of that interpretation, and made clear that they do not accept a number of key technical issues that underpin the above guidance.

HMRC responded with a further article. It contained no relaxation of their views. The examples included in the original article were revisited purely for the purpose of setting out the entries required on self-assessment tax returns where the settlements legislation applies. A number of new examples were also included. (Revenue Tax Bulletin February 2004 pp 1085–1094).

The Arctic Systems case

HMRC initially won a case before the courts involving the issue of one of the two shares in an information technology personal service company to a spouse (in this case the wife), the payment of only a small salary to the husband and the subsequent payment of dividends, but subsequently *lost* the case on appeal to the HL. The HL decision meant that dividends paid on the wife's share-holding do *not* fall to be taxed as the income of the husband (*Jones v Garnett* HL 2007, [2007] STC 1536 known colloquially as the *Arctic Systems* case). The HL held that the arrangement did constitute a settlement but that it fell within the exception at **68.29** above (outright gifts between spouses which are not wholly or substantially a right to income). In their judgment, the arrangement had the necessary element of bounty to be a settlement; it was not an arrangement that the taxpayer would have entered into with someone with whom he was dealing at arm's length. It was the husband's consent to the issue of the ordinary share to the wife that gave the arrangement the element of bounty but the share was not wholly or even substantially a right to income. It was an ordinary share conferring a right to vote, to participate in the distribution of assets on a winding-up, to block a special resolution etc.; those were all rights over and above the right to income.

Most recent guidance

Following the HL decision in *Jones v Garnett*, HMRC published guidance on 30 July 2007 (see www.hmrc.gov.uk/practitioners/sba.htm) as to how they would approach open cases. They would consider each case on the basis of its own facts but, unless there are additional factors which might lead them to take a different view, they expect that most cases involving inter-spouse settlements where the settled property comprises ordinary shares in a company or a non-limited interest in a partnership will fall within the exemption at **68.29** above.

HMRC have now made available their detailed guidance on the settlements legislation following *Jones v Garnett*. See HMRC Trusts, Settlements and Estates Manual TSEM4000 *et seq.*

The future?

Almost immediately following the HL decision in *Jones v Garnett*, the Government announced its intention to legislate to reverse the effect of that decision (see www.hmrc.gov.uk/practitioners/sba.htm). This was reiterated in the 2007 Pre-Budget Report. The Government believe it is unfair for one person to arrange their affairs so that their income is diverted to a second person, subject to a lower tax rate, to obtain a tax advantage (income shifting). They originally stated that they would consult on legislation to address the issue and to take effect for 2008/09 onwards (but see below). The legislation would apply only where 'the income is in the form of distributions from a company (dividends) or partnership profits. Income from employment, interest on savings and any other source will not be affected.' 'Relevant factors to consider when establishing whether or not income shifting has taken place could include the work done by the individuals in the business, the investments made and the risks to which they are subject through the business.' (Pre-Budget Report Press Notice 02, 9 October 2007). A consultation document including illustrative legislation was published on 6 December 2007. *However*, in the 2008 Budget the Government expressed the need for further consultation and said they would defer introducing legislation until *FA 2009* (Budget Press Notice 03, 12 March 2008). Subsequently, as stated above, the then Government announced that they would not now be bringing forward such legislation, but that the issue would be kept under review (Pre-Budget Report Press Notice 03, 24 November 2008).

Capital sums, loans and repayments of loans to settlor from settlement or connected body corporate

[68.32] As indicated at **68.26** above, where in any tax year the trustees of a settlement pay any 'capital sum' to the settlor or spouse or civil partner (or to the settlor (or spouse or civil partner) jointly with another person), such an amount (grossed up at the trust rate) is treated as income of the settlor to the extent that it falls within the amount of 'income available' in the settlement up to the end of that tax year or, to the extent that it does not fall within that amount, to the end of the next and subsequent years of assessment up to a maximum of ten years after the year of payment.

There is a corresponding reduction in the amount so treated as a settlor's income for any amount included in his income under *ITTOIA 2005, s 415* (see **64.16 SAVINGS AND INVESTMENT INCOME**) in respect of a loan. See also **68.34** below.

The amount charged on the settlor is taxed as part of his total income but he receives credit for the grossing up. The notional tax credit can only be set against the tax charged on the amount treated as the settlor's income. The credit is restricted to, broadly, the tax actually paid by the trustees on the equivalent amount of income; though, for this purpose and for the purpose of the grossing up itself, there is disregarded the fact that dividend income is in reality charged at the dividend trust rate as opposed to the trust rate.

[*ITTOIA 2005, ss 633, 634(7), 639, 640; ICTA 1988, s 677(1)(3)(6)(7)(7A)–(7C)(9); ITA 2007, Sch 1 para 559; FA 2009, Sch 2 paras 20, 25*].

Income available' in the settlement' up to the end of any tax year is the aggregate amount of income arising under the settlement (see **68.28** above), for that and any previous year, which has not been distributed, less:

(a) any amount of that income which has already been 'matched' against a capital sum for assessment on the settlor (see above);
(b) any income taken into account under these provisions in relation to capital sums previously paid to the settlor;
(c) sums treated as income of the settlor under *ITTOIA 2005, s 624* or *s 629* or their predecessors (see **68.29, 68.30** above);
(d) sums treated as income of the settlor under *ICTA 1988, ss 671–674A* or *s 683*;
(e) sums not allowed as an income deduction to the settlor under *ICTA 1988, s 676*;
(f) sums from an accumulation settlement for children treated as income of the settlor under *ICTA 1988, s 664(2)(b)*;
(g) sums included in the income arising under the settlement as amounts which have been or could have been apportioned to a beneficiary under *ICTA 1988, s 681(1)(b)*; and
(h) the tax at the trust rate on the accumulated undistributed income less the amounts in (c) to (g) above.

The amount of income arising under a settlement for a tax year which is treated as income which has not been distributed for this purpose is calculated according to rules in *ITTOIA 2005, ss 636, 637*.

[*ITTOIA 2005, ss 635–637, Sch 2 para 134(1)–(3); ITA 2007, Sch 1 paras 557, 558*].

'Capital sum' includes a loan or loan repayment and any other sum (other than income) paid otherwise than for full consideration (but excluding sums which could not have become payable to the settlor except in one of the events mentioned in **68.29**(A)–(D) above (or on the death under the age of 25 of the person referred to in the paragraph following **68.29**(A)–(D) above) or under earlier legislation. As regards loans and repayment of loans, see *Potts' Exors*

v CIR HL 1950, 32 TC 211; *De Vigier* HL 1964, 42 TC 24; *Bates v CIR* HL 1966, 44 TC 225; *McCrone v CIR* CS 1967, 44 TC 142; *Wachtel* Ch D 1970, 46 TC 543 and *Piratin v CIR* Ch D 1981, 54 TC 730.

There is also treated as a capital sum paid to the settlor any sum paid to a third party at the settlor's direction or by assignment of his right to receive it and any other sum otherwise paid or applied for the settlor's benefit.

[*ITTOIA 2005, s 634, Sch 2 para 134(4)(5)*].

Loan to settlor

Where the capital sum represents a loan to the settlor, there will be no tax charge on him for any tax year after the year in which the loan is repaid. If previous loans have been made and wholly repaid, any new loan will only be charged on its excess, if any, over so much of the earlier loans as have been treated as his income. [*ITTOIA 2005, s 638(1)–(3)*].

Repayment to settlor of loan

Where the capital sum is repayment of a loan by a settlor, a charge arises on him but will not apply for any year after the year in which he makes a further loan at least equal in amount to the loan repaid. [*ITTOIA 2005, s 638(4)(5)*].

Payment of IHT by trustees, see **68.28** above.

Connected companies

A capital sum (as above) paid to a settlor by a body corporate connected with the settlement (see **21.8 CONNECTED PERSONS**) is treated as paid to him by the trustees of the settlement irrespective of whether or not the funds originated from that settlement if there has been an 'associated payment' (made directly or indirectly) to the body (or to another body corporate associated with that body under *CTA 2010, s 449* at that time) from the settlement. Such payments to the settlor in a tax year will be 'matched' with associated payments from the trustees to the body corporate up to the end of that year (less any amounts already 'matched') in order to determine the amount deemed paid to the settlor by the trustees in the year, any 'unmatched' balance being 'matched' with associated payments in subsequent years.

'*Associated payment*' is any capital sum paid, or any other sum paid or asset transferred for less than full consideration, to the body corporate by the trustees within five years before or after the capital sum paid to the settlor by the body corporate.

Loans

The above provisions do not apply to any payment to the settlor by way of loan or repayment of a loan if (i) the whole of the loan is repaid within twelve months and (ii) the total period during which loans are outstanding in any period of five years does not exceed twelve months.

[*ITTOIA 2005, ss 641–643, Sch 2 para 135; CTA 2010, Sch 1 para 470*].

Simon's Taxes. See **C4.335–C4.340.**

Example

[68.33]

The trustees of a settlement with undistributed income of £1,375 at 5 April 2004 made a loan of £15,000 to B, the settlor, on 30 September 2004.

B repays the loan on 31 December 2006. Undistributed income of £3,500 arose in 2004/05, £6,500 in 2005/06 and £5,500 in 2006/07. The trustees duly settle all their liabilities to tax on trust income.

The following income amounts will be treated as part of B's total income.

		£
2004/05	£4,875 × $^{100}/_{60}$	8,125
2005/06	£6,500 × $^{100}/_{60}$	10,833
2006/07	£3,625 × $^{100}/_{60}$ note (a)	6,041

The notional tax credit available to B is

		£	£
2004/05	£1,375 × 100/66 at 34%	708.33	
	£3,500 × 100/60 at 40%	2,333.33	3,041.66
2005/06	£10,833 at 40%		4,333.20
2006/07	£6,041 at 40%		2,416.40

Notes

(a) The amount treated as income in 2006/07 is limited to the amount of the loan less amounts previously treated as income (£15,000 – (£4,875 + £6,500)).

(b) B's notional tax credit for 2004/05 would otherwise be £8,125 @ 40% = £3,250, but is restricted by the fact that £1,375 of the net income attributed to him for that year arose before 6 April 2004 and thus at a time when the trust rate was 34% rather than 40%.

Heritage maintenance settlements — tax exemptions for settlors etc.

[68.34] Where the Treasury has directed under *IHTA 1984, Sch 4 para 1* (a '*heritage direction*') that funds put into a settlement (a '*heritage maintenance settlement*') for the maintenance of, or for making provision of public access to, 'qualifying property' are exempt for inheritance tax purposes, the trustees may elect, in relation to any tax year, that:

(a) any income arising from the settlement property in respect of which the heritage direction has effect ('*heritage maintenance property*') which would otherwise be treated as income of the settlor (see **68.26–68.33** above) shall not be so treated; and

(b)   any sum applied out of heritage maintenance property for the mainte-
        nance of, or for making provision of public access to, qualifying
        property shall not be treated as income of any person by virtue of his
        interest in, or occupation of, the property in question or by virtue of
        ITTOIA 2005, s 633 — see **68.32** above).

The election must be made no later than the first anniversary of 31 January
following the tax year to which it relates. There is provision for splitting the
tax year if there is a change of circumstances, e.g. if a heritage direction takes
effect, or ceases to have effect, during the year; an election can then be made
for part of the year only.

If no election is made for a tax year and income arises from the heritage
maintenance property which is treated as income of the settlor, the exemption
at (b) above nevertheless applies to any excess of the sum applied as in (b) over
that income.

'*Qualifying property*' is defined at *IHTA 1984, Sch 4 para 3(2)* and includes:

- land of outstanding scenic, historic or scientific interest;
- buildings of outstanding historical or architectural interest and land
  essential to protect the character and amenities of such buildings; and
- objects historically associated with such buildings.

If a settlement comprises both heritage maintenance property and other
property, the heritage maintenance property and the other property are treated
as comprised in separate settlements for a number of purposes now listed at
ITA 2007, s 507(3).

Prevention of double taxation — reimbursement of settlor

Where income arising from heritage maintenance property (i) is treated as
income of the settlor by virtue of **68.26–68.33** above; (ii) the income is paid to
the settlor to reimburse him for expenditure incurred by him on the maintenance of, or for making provision of public access to, qualifying property; *and*
(iii) the expenditure is deductible in computing the profits of a trade or UK
property business (see **60.2 PROPERTY INCOME**) carried on by the settlor, the
reimbursed amount does not count as a taxable receipt of the trade or business
and is not regarded as income of the settlor otherwise than by virtue of
68.26–68.33 above.

Application of property for non-heritage purposes; charge to tax

An income tax charge potentially arises on the trustees of a heritage maintenance settlement in any of the circumstances below. The rate of tax applicable
is equal to the excess (if any) of the higher rate of income tax over the trust
rate, i.e. the rate was 6% before 2004/05 but is nil for 2004/05 to 2009/10
inclusive (so that no such charge arises). For 2010/11 onwards, the rate of tax
applicable is equal to the excess of the additional rate of income tax over the
trust rate, i.e. the rate continues to be nil.

The circumstances are as follows:

- where any property comprised in the settlement (whether capital or income) is applied otherwise than for the maintenance of, or for making provision of public access to, qualifying property or, in the case of income not so applied and not accumulated, for the benefit of a '*heritage body*' (i.e. a body or charity of a kind mentioned in *IHTA 1984, Sch 4 para 3(1)(a)(ii)*);
- where any of that property, on ceasing to be comprised in the settlement, devolves otherwise than on a heritage body;
- where the heritage direction ceases to have effect in respect of the settlement; and
- where any of that property, on ceasing at any time to be comprised in the settlement, devolves on a heritage body and at or before that time an interest under the settlement is or has been acquired for money or money's worth by that or another such body (but any acquisition from another such body will be disregarded).

The charge is on all income which has arisen from the property comprised in the settlement since the last charge under this provision or, otherwise, since the creation of the settlement, and has not been applied for the maintenance of, or for making provision of public access to, qualifying property or for the benefit of a heritage body. The charge will not apply to income which is treated as income of the settlor under **68.26–68.33** above, and sums applied otherwise than for the above-mentioned purpose are treated as paid first out of income treated as the settlor's. There is no charge where the whole of the settlement property is transferred to another settlement by means of a '*tax-free transfer*', i.e. a transfer in respect of which *IHTA 1984, Sch 4 para 9* provides an exception from charge or a transfer where both immediately before and after the transfer the property is heritage maintenance property. Instead, the transferee settlement stands in the shoes of the transferor settlement.

[*ITA 2007, ss 507–517; ICTA 1988, ss 690–694; FA 2009, Sch 2 paras 7, 25*].

Simon's Taxes. See **C4.355–C4.357**.

Key points

[68.35] Points to consider are as follows.

- For 2010/11 onwards, the new trust rate and dividend trust rate mean that beneficiaries of affected trusts are more likely to be in a position of needing to reclaim tax as their own liability is unlikely to be at the same rate. Advisers may wish to consider scheduling tax return work to enable early repayments to be claimed (before, in fact, the corresponding liability is due for payment by the trustees the following January).
- The £100 restriction on income of minor children does not apply where the invested funds derive from someone other than the parents. Funds given to the children by, for example, their grandparents are not therefore subject to the restriction, and the child's personal allowance will be available to use against the income arising.

- Where a business is jointly owned by spouses or civil partners so that tax is sheltered by sharing the income arising between the partners, advisers should ensure that they are fully conversant with the decision of the House of Lords in *Jones v Garnett* (see **68.31**) and the implications for their client. Advisers should also be alert to any change in interpretation or practice published by HMRC, particularly from 2010/11 onwards when the tax savings can be considerable.

69

Share-Related Employment Income and Exemptions

For HMRC's own guidance on this subject, see www.hmrc.gov.uk/shareschem es and HMRC Employment-Related Securities Manual.

Simon's Taxes. See E4.5.

Introduction

[69.1] For general tax liability in respect of shares given to directors or other employees as part of their employment income, see **27.74 EMPLOYMENT INCOME**. For tax deductions (against trading profits etc.) available to employer companies in connection with employee share schemes, see **73.59–73.62 TRADING INCOME**.

The expression 'shares' is used in this chapter in its broadest sense. For the application of the chapter to stocks and securities, as well as shares, see **69.3** below.

Legislation applies where there are arrangements to allow a person to acquire shares by reason of their (or in some cases another person's) employment, as follows.

(a)   Restricted shares under *ITEPA 2003, ss 422–432* — see **69.4** below.
(b)   Convertible shares under *ITEPA 2003, ss 435–444* — see **69.7** below.
(c)   Shares with artificially depressed market value, under *ITEPA 2003, ss 446A–446J* — see **69.9** below.
(d)   Shares with artificially enhanced market value, under *ITEPA 2003, ss 446K–446P* — see **69.10** below.

(e) Shares disposed of for more than market value, under *ITEPA 2003, ss 446X–446Z* — see **69.12** below.

(f) Post-acquisition benefits under *ITEPA 2003, ss 447–450* — see **69.13** below.

(g) Unapproved share options under *ITEPA 2003, ss 471–484* — see **69.14** below.

(h) Share incentive plans under *ITEPA 2003, ss 488–515, Sch 2* — see **69.20** below.

(i) Enterprise management incentives under *ITEPA 2003, ss 527–541, Sch 5* — see **69.35** below.

(j) SAYE option schemes under *ITEPA 2003, ss 516–520, Sch 3* see **69.47** below.

(k) Company share option plan (CSOP) schemes under *ITEPA 2003, ss 521–526, Sch 4* — see **69.61** below.

(l) Priority share allocations under *ITEPA 2003, ss 542–548* — see **69.74** below.

See also the notional loan provisions of *ITEPA 2003, ss 446Q–446W* at **69.11** below for shares acquired partly-paid, and see **69.75** below as regards research institution spin-out companies. For reporting obligations, see **69.17** below.

Legislation was introduced by *FA 2008* to bring employees who are resident but not ordinarily resident, and who receive employment-related shares, within those charging provisions of this chapter which previously had effect only for employees both resident and ordinarily resident, i.e. the provisions referred to at (a), (b), (f) and (j) above. The legislation applies to shares or, as the case may be, share options acquired on or after 6 April 2008. The effect of this can be seen under the sub-headings Exclusions in **69.4** below and Exceptions from charge in **69.15** below, where it will be noted that different criteria apply in relation to the earnings exclusion depending on when the shares or the share option were acquired. For the effect of the REMITTANCE BASIS **(61)**, where applicable, see **69.18** below; this also applies to the charging provisions at (e) above and in **69.11** below, again where the shares in question are acquired on or after 6 April 2008. For official guidance on the changes, see www.hmrc.gov.uk/shareschemes/res-dom-rules.htm and HMRC Employment-Related Securities Manual ERSM160000 *et seq.*

General matters

[69.2] The following miscellaneous items are dealt with in alphabetical order.

Armed Forces Reservists

By concession, backdated to 7 January 2003 (the date of the first call-up order for service in Iraq), a reservist called up for service under *Reserve Forces Act 1996* will have his consequent employment with the Ministry of Defence (MOD) treated as fulfilling the employment conditions for the approved schemes at **69.20**, **69.47** and **69.61** below and for enterprise management incentives at **69.35** below. In addition, employers and scheme providers may take such action as is necessary to maintain the reservist's participation in the scheme for the period they are away serving with the MOD; provided the action does no more than that, it will not compromise the approval of the scheme. (See HMRC ESC A103). Guidance notes for employers, setting out possible courses of action within the concession, are attached to the published concession.

Banks taken into public ownership

HMRC Brief 32/08, 9 July 2008 sets out the consequences of the transfer on 22 February 2008 of Northern Rock plc into public ownership in relation to the income tax and capital gains tax position of employees who held shares and share options under employee share schemes. HMRC Brief 16/09, 2 April 2009 sets out the consequences of the transfer on 29 September 2008 of Bradford & Bingley plc into public ownership in relation to those same matters.

Earn-outs

Where the consideration passing on the sale of a business includes an earn-out, typically a right to receive securities in the purchasing company after a certain period of time has elapsed and dependent on the performance of the newly taken-over business, any element of remuneration for services as an employee or prospective employee included in the earn-out may give rise to a tax charge under the provisions at **69.5** below (restricted shares), **69.8** below (convertible shares) or **69.14** below (unapproved share options), whichever is relevant, always bearing in mind the extended meaning of 'shares' at **69.3** below. Guidance has been issued as to how the rules will be applied and how to identify if an earn-out is 'remuneration' or further sale consideration or an element of both. See HMRC Employment-Related Securities Manual ERSM110900—110940.

Electronic information reporting

With effect from 6 April 2007, *SI 2007 No 792* provides statutory authority to companies who wish to submit information electronically about employee share scheme events. The regulations (supplemented by HMRC Directions dated 4 April 2007) specify (by means of statutory references to *ITEPA 2003*) the type of information that may be submitted via an HMRC-approved method of electronic communications. See also FAQs at www.hmrc.gov.uk/s hareschemes/online-filing-faqs.htm.

HMRC Share Focus Newsletter

HMRC publish very sporadically a newsletter, Share Focus, designed to provide practitioners with information on new interpretations on technical employee share schemes issues, together with guidance on practical issues, and to publicise the work of the HMRC Employee Shares and Securities Unit (ESSU) — see www.hmrc.gov.uk/shareschemes.

Memoranda of Understanding

Two Memoranda of Understanding between the Inland Revenue (as it then was) and the British Venture Capital Association, covering certain matters arising from substantial changes made by *FA 2003* to the provisions at

69.3–69.17 below, were published on 25 July 2003 and are reproduced in the HMRC Employment-Related Securities Manual at ERSM 30520 and 30530. As regards ratchet arrangements (commonly seen in management buy-outs), both within and without the relevant Memorandum, a change of opinion was published by HMRC on 21 August 2006 — see now ERSM90500.

Residence: split-year treatment

For the application of HMRC ESC A11 (split-year treatment for individual coming to the UK to take up permanent residence or to stay for at least two years, or leaving the UK to live abroad permanently) to share-related employment income, see **62.6 RESIDENCE, ORDINARY RESIDENCE AND DOMICILE.**

Retrospective legislation: statement of intent

On 2 December 2004, the then Government gave notice, in a statement made by the Paymaster General, of their intention 'to deal with any arrangements that emerge in future designed to frustrate our intention that employers and employees should pay the proper amount of tax and NICs on the rewards of employment'. Where the Government become aware of such arrangements, they will move to legislate against them and, 'where necessary', such legislation will take effect from the date of this statement of intent. The first such legislation appears in *FA 2006* — see **69.3** below for details.

Transfer pricing

For links to HMRC guidance on the implications of transfer pricing (see **4.18 ANTI-AVOIDANCE**) on employee share schemes operated by groups of companies, see www.hmrc.gov.uk/international/transfer-pricing.htm under Employee share schemes.

Extended meaning of 'shares'

[69.3] For the purposes of **69.4–69.15** below, the meaning of 'shares' is extended to embrace a broader range of financial products, including, for example, government and local authority stocks. All of the following are now 'shares' for these purposes:

- shares (including stock) in any body corporate, wherever incorporated, or in any unincorporated body constituted under the law of a foreign country;
- debentures, debenture stock, loan stock, bonds, certificates of deposit and other instruments creating or acknowledging indebtedness (other than contracts of insurance);
- warrants and other instruments entitling the holders to subscribe for securities;
- certificates and other instruments conferring rights in respect of securities held by persons other than the persons on whom the rights are conferred and which may be transferred without the consent of those persons;

- units in a collective investment scheme (as defined by *ITEPA 2003, s 420(2)*);
- futures (as defined by *ITEPA 2003, s 420(3)*);
- rights under contracts for differences (or under similar contracts — as defined by *ITEPA 2003, s 420(4)*) (other than contracts of insurance);
- rights under contracts of insurance, whenever acquired, other than: (i) contracts for annuities which are, or will be, pension income; (ii) contracts of long-term insurance, other than annuity contracts, which do not have, and cannot acquire, a surrender value; and (iii) contracts of general insurance which would not fall to be accounted for under generally accepted accounting practice as financial assets or liabilities;
- options acquired on or after 2 December 2004 (but see below);
- (on and after 17 August 2007) arrangements falling within **3.5 ALTERNATIVE FINANCE ARRANGEMENTS** (alternative finance investment bond arrangements).

However, none of the following are 'shares' for these purposes:

- cheques, bills of exchange, bankers' drafts and letters of credit (other than bills of exchange accepted by a banker);
- money and statements showing balances on a current, deposit or savings account;
- leases and other dispositions of property and heritable securities;
- 'share options' — see below.

The above lists can be amended by Treasury order.

Share options

In the list of exclusions above, *'share options'* are rights to acquire shares (with 'shares' having its extended meaning for this purpose). *However*, the term does not include a right to acquire shares that is itself acquired pursuant to a right or opportunity made available under arrangements having as one of their main purposes the avoidance of tax or national insurance contributions; such options are therefore omitted from the list of exclusions and do count as 'shares'. The effect of this is that such an option is a convertible share within **69.7** below (as it can be converted into 'shares' of a different description). In particular, it means that a tax charge may arise on acquisition of the option, and, for that purpose, the market value of the option may be determined on the basis that there is an immediate and unfettered right to convert (see **69.7** below). This contrasts with the normal treatment of share options at **69.14** below where there is usually no tax charge on the grant of the option. A share option that remains within the above list of exclusions (i.e. it is not acquired as part of avoidance arrangements) continues to be within **69.14** below rather than **69.7** below. These rules were introduced by *FA 2006* in response to identified avoidance schemes and were the first example of the Government's stated intention at **69.2** above to legislate with retrospective effect from 2 December 2004.

General

It is important to note that the above extended meaning of 'shares' does *not* apply for the purposes of the approved schemes at **69.20** *et seq.* below. For the purposes of **69.35** *et seq.* below, 'shares' includes stock but not securities, and see also the specific rules at **69.30**, **69.41**, **69.55** and **69.68** below.

An '*interest in shares*', for the purposes of **69.4–69.15** below, means an interest which is less than full beneficial ownership. It includes an interest in their sale proceeds but not a right to acquire them.

[*ITEPA 2003, ss 420, 516(4), 521(4), 548(1), Sch 5 para 58; FA 2006, s 92; CTA 2009, Sch 1 para 553; TIOPA 2010, Sch 8 para 204; SI 2007 No 2130*].

See FAQs at www.hmrc.gov.uk/shareschemes/faq_emprelatedsecurity-ch1.htm for further detail.

Phantom share schemes

In the context of the addition of options to the list of items treated as 'shares'. HMRC have stated that participation in a typical phantom share scheme (see **27.74 EMPLOYMENT INCOME**) does not mean that the employee is regarded for tax purposes as having acquired an option (HMRC Internet Statement 6 April 2006).

Restricted shares

[69.4] These provisions apply to 'employment-related shares' if, at the time of acquisition, they are 'restricted shares' (or a 'restricted interest in shares'). For the extended meaning of 'shares', in relation to these provisions, see **69.3** above. See below for exclusions from the charge and **69.6** below for the possibility of electing to disapply or moderate these provisions. See **69.17** below as regards reporting obligations. See also the anti-avoidance provisions at **69.9**, **69.10** below.

'*Employment-related shares*' are shares (or an interest in shares) acquired by a person by virtue of a right or opportunity made available by reason of the employment (present, past or prospective) of that or any other person. For this purpose, shares are deemed to be acquired when the beneficial entitlement to them is acquired and not, if different, at the time of conveyance or transfer. Any right or opportunity made available by a person's employer, or by a person connected (within **21 CONNECTED PERSONS**) with a person's employer, is treated as made available by reason of the employment of that person, other than in the case of an individual conferring a right or opportunity in the normal course of his domestic, family or personal relationships. There are rules dealing with company reorganisations (such as conversions, scrip issues and rights issues); these treat replacement shares or additional shares acquired on such a reorganisation as acquired by virtue of the same right or opportunity as the original interest and treat any consequent reduction in the market value of the original shares as consideration given for the replacement shares or additional shares.

For the circumstances in which HMRC will accept that shares or share options were acquired by an employee by virtue of a family or personal relationship and not by reason of the employment, see HMRC Employment-Related Securities Manual ERSM20220.

A right etc. is made available to the taxpayer even though he may himself have stipulated its being granted (*CIR v Herd* CS 1992, 66 TC 29).

An increase in a person's interest in shares is treated for the purposes of these provisions as a separate interest acquired by virtue of the same right or opportunity as the original interest. A decrease in a person's interest is treated as a disposal, otherwise than to an 'associated person', of a separate interest proportionate to the reduction.

For the purposes of these provisions, consideration given for the acquisition of employment-related shares includes consideration given by the employee or by the person who acquired the shares (if not the employee) and any consideration given for a *right* to acquire the shares. Any consideration given partly for one thing and partly for another is apportioned as is just and reasonable. Rules similar to those at **69.15** below (under Option exchanged for another) apply to determine the amount of consideration where a right to acquire the shares is assigned or released for consideration consisting of or including another right to acquire the shares.

Definition of restricted shares

Employment-related shares are '*restricted shares*' (or a '*restricted interest in shares*') if there is a contract, agreement, arrangement or condition that imposes any of the three types of restriction listed below *and* the market value of the shares or interest (determined as for capital gains purposes) is less than it otherwise would have been. The types of restriction covered are as follows:

(a)   any provision for the transfer, reversion or forfeiture of the shares etc. if certain circumstances arise or do not arise, such that the holder will cease to be beneficially entitled to them and will not be entitled to receive an amount at least equal to their unfettered market value;

(b)   any restriction (not within (a) above) on the freedom of the holder to dispose of the shares etc. (or to retain the proceeds if they are sold) or on his right to retain the shares or proceeds or on any right conferred by the shares themselves;

(c)   any provision (not within (a) or (b) above) whereby the disposal or retention of the shares etc., or the exercise of a right conferred by them, may result in a disadvantage to the holder or (if different) the employee or a connected person (within **21 CONNECTED PERSONS**) of either.

However, neither of the following is sufficient in itself to confer 'restricted shares' status on employment-related shares:

•   (in the case of unpaid or partly paid shares) a provision for forfeiture in the event of non-payment of calls (provided the meeting of calls is not itself restricted);

•   a requirement that the shares be offered for sale or transfer in the event of the employee's losing his employment by reason of misconduct;

These disregards are disapplied if the arrangements under which the right or opportunity to acquire the shares was made available have as one of their main purposes the avoidance of tax or national insurance contributions.

Exclusions

These provisions do not apply:

- (in relation to acquisitions on or after 6 April 2008 other than under an option acquired before that date) if, at the time of acquisition, the earnings from the employment in question were not (or would not have been if there were any) general earnings within **27.4 EMPLOYMENT INCOME** (earnings for year when employee resident in UK), chargeable overseas earnings (within **27.5 EMPLOYMENT INCOME**) or foreign earnings (within **27.5 EMPLOYMENT INCOME**); or
- (in relation to other acquisitions) if, at the time of acquisition, the earnings from the employment in question were not (or would not have been if there were any) general earnings within **27.9 EMPLOYMENT INCOME** (earnings for year when employee resident, ordinarily resident and domiciled in UK) or within *ITEPA 2003, s 21* (earnings, other than chargeable overseas earnings, for year when employee resident and ordinarily resident but not domiciled in UK — see **27.10 EMPLOYMENT INCOME**); or
- (in the case of a former employment) if they would not have applied had the acquisition taken place in the last tax year in which the employment was held; or
- (in the case of a prospective employment) if they would not apply if the acquisition had taken place in the first tax year in which the employment is held; or
- in relation to shares acquired under the terms of a public offer (including an 'employee offer' as in **69.74** below); but this exclusion does not apply if one of the main purposes of the arrangements under which the shares are acquired, or for which the shares are held, is the avoidance of tax or national insurance contributions.

These provisions cease to apply to shares (or an interest in shares):

- following a disposal to a person other than an 'associated person'; or
- immediately before the death of the employee (so that no charge arises on death); or
- on the seventh anniversary of the first date on which the employee is employed neither by the employer who made available the right or opportunity to acquire the shares nor by the company that issued the shares (where applicable) nor by a connected person (within **21 CONNECTED PERSONS**) of either that employer or that issuing company.

Associated persons

For the purposes of these provisions, any of the following are *'associated persons'* in relation to employment-related shares:

- the person who acquired them;
- (if different) the employee; and

- any 'relevant linked person'.

A *'relevant linked person'* is any person who is either connected (within **21 CONNECTED PERSONS**) with, or is a member of the same household as, either the person who acquired the shares or the employee. The statutory definition also embrace past connections etc. so as to ensure the link cannot be broken. However, a *company* cannot be a relevant linked person if it is the employer or (if different) the person by whom the right or opportunity to acquire the shares was made available or the person from whom the shares were acquired or by whom they were issued.

Tax exemption in certain cases on acquisition

No liability to income tax arises on the *acquisition* of employment-related shares under the normal rules at **27.74 EMPLOYMENT INCOME** if the shares are restricted under (a) above and will cease to be so within five years after the acquisition (whether or not they may remain restricted under either (b) or (c) above). However, the employer and employee may jointly and irrevocably elect to disapply this exemption. The point of an election would be to reduce the charge to tax on a future chargeable event (see **69.5** below). (See **69.6** below for the separate possibility of electing to disapply or moderate *all* these provisions.) The election is implemented by way of an agreement (between employer and employee), in a form approved by HMRC, that must be made no later than 14 days after the acquisition; there is no requirement for it to be submitted to HMRC or for HMRC's approval to be sought. Prescribed forms of election are available on the HMRC website. Whether or not the election is made, and where relevant, income tax charges may arise on acquisition under **69.14** below (unapproved share options), **69.7** below (conversion) or **69.11** below (acquisition for less than market value).

[*ITEPA 2003, ss 419, 421, 421A–421D, 421E(1)(3)–(5), 421F–421I, 422–425, 432, 718; ITA 2007, Sch 1 para 442; FA 2008, Sch 7 paras 31, 80; CTA 2010, Sch 1 para 386*].

In relation to shares acquired on or after 6 April 2008, see **69.18** below for the effect of the **REMITTANCE BASIS (61)** where relevant.

See also www.hmrc.gov.uk/shareschemes/faq_emprelatedsecurity-ch2.htm.

The charge to tax

[69.5] If a chargeable event occurs in relation to restricted shares, there is a charge to tax on the employee for the tax year in which it occurs; the amount chargeable, computed as below, counts as employment income for tax purposes. This is subject to the exception from charge detailed below. Any of the following is a chargeable event:

(i)   the employment-related shares ceasing to be restricted shares (or a restricted interest in shares) without their having been disposed of to a person who is not an 'associated person' (see **69.4** above);

(ii)   the variation or removal of any restriction without the employment-related shares having been disposed of to a person who is not an associated person and without their ceasing to be restricted shares (or a restricted interest in shares);

(iii) the disposal for consideration of the employment-related shares (or any interest in them) by an 'associated person' otherwise than to another associated person at a time when they are still restricted shares (or a restricted interest in shares).

Computation of chargeable amount

The chargeable amount is found by applying a formula, UMV × (IUP – PCP – OP) – CE (see *ITEPA 2003, s 426*), where:

UMV = Unrestricted Market Value, i.e. what would be the market value of the employment-related shares immediately after the chargeable event but for any restrictions;

IUP   = Initial Uncharged Proportion. This is that part, expressed as a proportion (e.g. 0.25), of the Initial Unrestricted Market Value (IUMV) in respect of which an income tax charge is still required. It is found by taking the difference between IUMV and any deductible amounts and dividing it by IUMV. IUMV is what would have been the market value of the shares at the time of acquisition but for any restrictions. Deductible amounts include any consideration given for the shares and amounts previously charged to income tax;

PCP   = Previously Charged Proportion. This is the aggregate obtained by applying the formula, IUP – PCP – OP, on each previous chargeable event since acquisition. If there has not been a previous chargeable event, PCP is nil;

OP   = Outstanding Proportion. This is the proportion of the share value that is still reduced by restrictions and is found by taking the difference between UMV and the actual market value of the shares immediately after the chargeable event and dividing it by UMV; and

CE   = Consideration and Expenses. This consists of any consideration given by the shareholder for, and any expenses incurred by him in connection with, the lifting or variation of restrictions, plus (where relevant) any expenses incurred by him in connection with the disposal of the shares.

If the employment-related shares are convertible shares (see **69.7** below), or an interest in convertible shares, their market value is to be determined for the purposes of the above formula as if they were not.

If the chargeable event is a disposal for less than actual market value, the chargeable amount as determined above is reduced in the proportion that the consideration given on the disposal bears to the market value of the shares. However, this reduction is unavailable if something that affects the shares has been done at or before the time of the chargeable event as part of arrangements which have as one of their main purposes the avoidance of tax or national insurance contributions.

The employer and employee may jointly and irrevocably elect to omit OP from the above formula. The effect is to preclude any further application of these provisions. The election is implemented by way of an agreement (between employer and employee), in a form approved by HMRC, that must be made no later than 14 days after the chargeable event; there is no requirement for it to be submitted to HMRC or for HMRC's approval to be sought. Prescribed forms of election are available on the HMRC website.

HMRC can provide a calculator (based on an Excel 97 spreadsheet) to apply the above formula — see www.hmrc.gov.uk/shareschemes/faq_emprelatedsec urity-ch2.htm#c.

PAYE

For the requirement to operate PAYE on chargeable amounts, see **53.3**(g) PAY AS YOU EARN.

Relief for employer national insurance contributions

Where, under a voluntary agreement or a joint election under *Social Security Contributions and Benefits Act 1992, Sch 1 para 3A or para 3B* (or NI equivalent), whenever made, a liability to secondary Class 1 national insurance contributions (i.e. employer contributions) on an amount chargeable to tax under these provisions is borne by the employee, the amount so borne is deductible from the chargeable amount computed as above. In the case of a voluntary agreement, or an election to which HMRC approval is withdrawn, no such amount is deductible to the extent that it is borne by the employee later than 4 June following the tax year in which the chargeable event occurs.

Exception from charge

No charge to tax arises on the occurrence of a chargeable event if the restriction in question applies to all the company's shares of the same class, all the company's shares of that class are affected by an event similar to the chargeable event (disregarding the references in (i)–(iii) above to associated persons) and *either* of the conditions below is satisfied. (The extended meaning of shares in **69.3** above does not apply for this purpose.) This exception from charge does not apply if anything that affects the shares is done at or before the time of the chargeable event as part of arrangements which have as one of their main purposes the avoidance of tax or national insurance contributions.

The first of the conditions mentioned above is that, immediately before the event, the company is 'employee-controlled' (within *ITEPA 2003, s 421H*) by virtue of holdings of shares of the class in question. The second condition is that, immediately before the event, the majority of the company's shares of the class in question are not 'employment-related shares' (see **69.4** above).

[*ITEPA 2003, ss 426–430; FA 2008, s 49(4)(11)*].

Capital gains tax

For capital gains tax purposes, the consideration for the acquisition is taken as the aggregate of the actual amount or value given for the restricted shares (or restricted interest in shares), any amount charged to income tax as earnings in relation to the acquisition and any amount charged on the occurrence of a chargeable event. (No account is taken of any relief given for employer national insurance contributions — see above.) This does not affect the calculation of the consideration received by the person from whom the acquisition is made. If any amount that would otherwise be charged to income tax is unremitted 'foreign securities income' (within **69.19** below) it does not form part of the consideration given, but the taxpayer may make a claim to adjust that consideration if any amount is subsequently remitted. [*TCGA 1992, ss 119A, 119B, 149AA; FA 2008, s 49(1)(9), Sch 7 paras 63, 64, 80; SI 2004 No 1945*]. See Tolley's Capital Gains Tax for full details.

Election to disapply or moderate the provisions

[69.6] The employer and employee may jointly and irrevocably elect to disapply the provisions at **69.4, 69.5** above in full and to disregard the restrictions attaching to the shares when computing their acquisition value for the purposes of any charge to tax on employment income (including the charge on conversion at **69.8**(a) below and the provisions at **69.11** and **69.14** below). The election is implemented by way of an agreement (between employer and employee), in a form approved by HMRC, that must be made no later than 14 days after the acquisition; there is no requirement for it to be submitted to HMRC or for HMRC's approval to be sought. Prescribed forms of election are available on the HMRC website.

Alternatively, an election may be made, in similar manner, to disregard one or more specified restrictions in applying the provisions at **69.4, 69.5** above and in computing acquisition value for the above-mentioned purposes.

The employer and the employee are deemed to have made the election to disapply the provisions in full if the shares in question are acquired under an approved share incentive plan (as in **69.20** below), SAYE option scheme (as in **69.47** below) or CSOP scheme (as in **69.61** below) or by the exercise of an enterprise management incentive qualifying option (as in **69.35** below) in circumstances such that (in each case) no income tax liability arises on acquisition.

The employer and the employee are deemed to have made the election to disapply the provisions in full if the arrangements under which the right or opportunity to acquire the shares was made available have as one of their main purposes the avoidance of tax or national insurance contributions.

If shares were acquired between 6 April 2008 and 31 July 2008 inclusive and the restricted shares provisions apply to them by virtue only of amendments made by *FA 2008, Sch 7* (remittance basis), employer and employee were given until 14 August 2008 to make either of the above elections.

[*ITEPA 2003, ss 431, 431A, 431B; FA 2008, Sch 7 para 91*].

Convertible shares

[69.7] These provisions apply to 'employment-related shares' if, at the time of acquisition, they are 'convertible shares' (or an interest in 'convertible shares'). For the extended meaning of 'shares', in relation to these provisions, see **69.3** above. See below for exclusions from the charge. See **69.17** below as regards reporting obligations. See also the provisions at **69.9** below.

'*Employment-related shares*' are defined as in **69.4** above. There are rules dealing with company reorganisations (such as conversions, scrip issues and rights issues); these treat replacement shares or additional shares acquired on such a reorganisation as acquired by virtue of the same right or opportunity as the original interest and treat any consequent reduction in the market value of the original shares as consideration given for the replacement shares or additional shares.

An increase in a person's interest in shares is treated for the purposes of these provisions as a separate interest acquired by virtue of the same right or opportunity as the original interest. A decrease in a person's interest is treated as a disposal, otherwise than to an 'associated person' (as defined in **69.4** above), of a separate interest proportionate to the reduction.

For the purposes of these provisions, consideration given for the acquisition of employment-related shares includes consideration given by the employee or by the person who acquired the shares (if not the employee) and any consideration given for a *right* to acquire the shares. Rules similar to those at **69.15** below (under Option exchanged for another) apply to determine the amount of consideration where a right to acquire the shares is assigned or released for consideration consisting of or including another right to acquire the shares.

Definition of convertible shares

Employment-related shares are '*convertible shares*' if:

- they confer on the holder an entitlement (whether immediate or deferred and whether conditional or unconditional) to convert them into shares of a different description; or
- a contract, agreement, arrangement or condition authorises or requires the grant of such an entitlement to the holder if certain circumstances arise, or do not arise (for example, where the shares can only be converted following a stipulated period after acquisition) or makes provision for the conversion of the shares (otherwise than by the holder) into shares of a different description.

Exclusions

The same exclusions from charge apply as in **69.4** above.

Tax relief on acquisition

For the purposes of any liability to tax in respect of the acquisition of shares (under the general charging rules at **27.74 EMPLOYMENT INCOME**, under **69.14** below (unapproved share options) or under **69.11** below (acquisition for less than market value)), the market value of the employment-related shares is to be determined as if they were not convertible shares or an interest in convertible shares. Thus, if the market value per share is £1,100 with a conversion right and would be £1,000 without the conversion right, only £1,000 is taxed; previously, any tax charge on acquisition would have been calculated by reference to the full market value (£1,100). However, this rule is disapplied if the arrangements under which the right or opportunity to acquire the shares was made available have as one of their main purposes the avoidance of tax or national insurance contributions. Instead, market value is determined on the basis that there is an immediate and unfettered right to convert (even if this is not, in fact, the case). But if this would produce a lower market value than that produced by the main rule above (i.e. ignoring the right to convert), the main rule applies instead.

[*ITEPA 2003, ss 419, 421, 421A–421D, 421E(1)(3)–(5), 421F–421I, 435–437, 444; FA 2008, Sch 7 paras 31, 80*].

In relation to shares acquired on or after 6 April 2008, see **69.18** below for the effect of the **REMITTANCE BASIS** (**64**) where relevant.

The charge to tax

[69.8] If a chargeable event occurs in relation to convertible shares, there is a charge to tax on the employee for the tax year in which it occurs; the amount chargeable, computed as below, counts as employment income for tax purposes. This is subject to the exception from charge referred to below. Any of the following is a chargeable event:

(a)   the conversion of the employment-related shares (or the shares in which they are an interest) into shares of a different description, where an 'associated person' (see **69.4** above) is beneficially entitled to the shares into which the employment-related shares are converted;

(b)   the disposal for consideration of the employment-related shares (or any interest in them) by an associated person otherwise than to another associated person at a time when they are still convertible shares (or an interest in convertible shares);

(c)   the release, for consideration, of the conversion right;

(d)   the receipt by an associated person of a benefit in money or money's worth in connection with the conversion right; this could be, for example, compensation for loss of the conversion right but excludes any benefit received on account of disability (as defined) or anything within (a)–(c) above.

Computation of chargeable amount

The chargeable amount is found by computing the gain (if any) realised on the occurrence of the chargeable event (see below) and deducting from it any consideration given for the conversion right and any expenses incurred by the shareholder in connection with the conversion, disposal, release or receipt (whichever is applicable). For this purpose, consideration given for the conversion right is the excess (if any) of the consideration given for the acquisition of the shares (or interest in shares) over their market value, at the time of acquisition, determined as if they were not convertible shares (or an interest in convertible shares).

The gain realised on the chargeable event depends on the nature of the event, as follows:

(i)   on an event within (a) above, it is the amount given by the formula, CMVCS – (CMVERS + CC), see below;

(ii)   on an event within (b) above, it is the amount given by the formula, DC – CMVERS, see below;

(iii)   on an event within (c) above, it is the amount of the consideration received by an associated person in respect of the release; and

(iv)   on an event within (d) above, it is the amount or market value of the benefit.

For the purposes of (i) and (ii) above:

CMVCS	=	the market value, at the time of the event, of the shares acquired on conversion (determined, if those shares are themselves convertible shares, as if they were not); in the case of an interest in shares, a proportionate amount of the market value is taken instead;
CMVERS	=	the market value, at the time of the event, of the convertible shares (or the interest in them), again disregarding the effect on value of the conversion right;
CC	=	the amount of any consideration given for the conversion; and
DC	=	the amount of any consideration given on the disposal in (b) above.

If, in computing the tax charge on acquisition, the market value of the shares was determined on the basis that there was an immediate and unfettered right to convert (see **69.7** above under Tax relief on acquisition), the chargeable amount (on the occurrence of the chargeable event) is reduced by the amount by which that value exceeded what would otherwise have been the market value (i.e. ignoring the right to convert).

For the purposes of these provisions generally, market value is determined as for capital gains tax purposes and *ITEPA 2003, ss 421(2), 421A* apply in determining the amount of any consideration given.

PAYE

For the requirement to operate PAYE on chargeable amounts, see **53.3**(g) PAY AS YOU EARN.

Relief for employer national insurance contributions

Where, under a voluntary agreement or a joint election under *Social Security Contributions and Benefits Act 1992, Sch 1 para 3A* or *para 3B* (or NI equivalent), whenever made, a liability to secondary Class 1 national insurance contributions (i.e. employer contributions) on an amount chargeable to tax under these provisions is borne by the employee, the amount so borne is deductible from the chargeable amount computed as above. In the case of a voluntary agreement, or an election to which HMRC approval is withdrawn, no such amount is deductible to the extent that it is borne by the employee later than 4 June following the tax year in which the chargeable event occurs.

Exception from charge

The exception from charge detailed at **69.5** above, in relation to chargeable events under the restricted shares provisions, applies equally, subject to the necessary modifications, in relation to chargeable events under these provisions.

[*ITEPA 2003, ss 438–443*].

Capital gains tax

For capital gains tax purposes, the consideration for the acquisition is taken as the aggregate of the actual amount or value given for the convertible shares (or interest in convertible shares), any amount charged to income tax as earnings in relation to the acquisition and any amount charged on the occurrence of a chargeable event within (a) above. (No account is taken of any relief given for employer national insurance contributions — see above.) This does not affect the calculation of the consideration received by the person from whom the acquisition is made. If any amount that would otherwise be charged to income tax is unremitted 'foreign securities income' (within **69.19** below) it does not form part of the consideration given, but the taxpayer may make a claim to adjust that consideration if any amount is subsequently remitted. [*TCGA 1992, ss 119A, 119B, 149AA; FA 2008, s 49(1)(9), Sch 7 paras 63, 64, 80*]. See Tolley's Capital Gains Tax for full details.

Shares with artificially depressed market value

[69.9] The following provisions are 'designed to ensure that if the value of employment-related securities is depressed by means of non-commercial transaction(s), then that reduction in value is taxed on the employee' (Treasury Explanatory Notes to Finance Bill 2003). They apply in certain cases where the market value of 'employment-related shares' (or, where relevant, other shares or interests in shares) is reduced by things done otherwise than for genuine commercial purposes; this specifically includes anything done as part of a scheme or arrangement a main purpose of which is to avoid tax or *national insurance contributions* and any transaction (other than a payment for corporation tax group relief) between members of a 51% group of companies otherwise than on arm's length terms. See **69.3** above for the extended meaning of 'shares', in relation to these provisions.

For these purposes, '*employment-related shares*' and 'consideration given for the acquisition of employment-related shares' are defined as in **69.4** above.

Exclusions

The same exclusions from charge apply as in **69.4** above, except that the exclusion for shares acquired under the terms of a public offer does not apply, and the exclusion relating to the nature of the earnings of the employment is more widely drawn (whatever the date of acquisition) in that these provisions are disapplied only if, at the time of acquisition, the earnings from the employment in question were not (or would not have been if there were any) general earnings to which any of the charging provisions in **27.4–27.10** EMPLOYMENT INCOME apply.

Subject to the rules below requiring the importing of certain fictions into the determination of **market values**, such values are to be determined as for capital gains tax purposes.

Charge on acquisition

If anything done otherwise than for genuine commercial purposes within the seven years ending with the acquisition reduces the market value of employment-related shares at acquisition by at least 10%, there is a charge to tax on the employee for the tax year in which the acquisition occurs; the amount chargeable (see below) counts as employment income for tax purposes. This does not apply in the case of *restricted shares* if the tax exemption on acquisition at **69.4** above applies. The charge does not displace other income tax charges that may arise on acquisition.

The chargeable amount is the amount by which market value has been reduced. If the consideration given for the shares is greater than actual market value, the chargeable amount is reduced by the excess. Where the shares are convertible shares as in **69.7** above (or an interest in convertible shares), the chargeable amount is determined as if they were not. Where the shares are restricted shares as in **69.4** above (or a restricted interest in shares), the chargeable amount is the excess of what would have been their market value, disregarding both the avoidance device and the effect of restrictions, over their actual market value taking account of restrictions; in such circumstances though, there is no charge under **69.5** above on any chargeable event.

Other tax charges

Restricted shares

The consequences described below ensue where the market value of restricted shares (or a restricted interest in shares) as in **69.4** above is 'artificially low' at any of the following times:

(a)   immediately after a chargeable event within **69.5**;
(b)   immediately before the shares are disposed of (in circumstances not giving rise to a chargeable event within (a) above) or are cancelled without being disposed of; or
(c)   on 5 April in any year.

For this purpose, market value is *'artificially low'* where it has been reduced by at least 10% as a result of anything done otherwise than for genuine commercial purposes within the 'relevant period'. The *'relevant period'* is normally the seven years ending with the event in question or, in the case of (c) above, with that 5 April. If, however, the tax exemption on acquisition at **69.4** applied in relation to the shares, the start of the relevant period is extended back to a point seven years before the acquisition.

The consequences are as follows.

- In a case within (b) above, a chargeable event within **69.5**(i) (lifting of restrictions) is deemed to occur on the date of disposal or cancellation. The reference to OP (Outstanding Proportion) in the formula in **69.5** (for charging tax on chargeable events) is deemed to be omitted (so that all remaining untaxed proportions are brought into charge).
- In a case within (c) above, a chargeable event within **69.5**(i) is deemed to occur on that 5 April.
- In *all* cases, the value of UMV (Unrestricted Market Value) in the formula in **69.5** (for charging tax on chargeable events) is suitably modified so as to disregard the things done otherwise than for commercial purposes and also, where (b) above applies, the fact that the shares are about to be disposed of or cancelled.
- In a case within (a) above, where the chargeable event concerned is a disposal for less than actual market value, the normal reduction in the chargeable amount determined by the formula in **69.5** is disapplied.

Convertible shares

As detailed in **69.8** above, any consideration given for the right to convert shares enters into the computation of the chargeable amount on a chargeable event. If anything done otherwise than for genuine commercial purposes within the seven years ending with the acquisition reduces the market value of the shares (or interest in shares) at acquisition by at least 10%, the market value of the shares at acquisition (determined as if they were not convertible shares or an interest in convertible shares) is taken as what would be their market value (as so determined) if it were not for the reduction. This has the effect of reducing the amount deductible in the said computation.

If, on a chargeable event within **69.8**(a) above (conversion of the shares), the market value, at the time of conversion, of the shares *into which* the shares are converted is reduced by 10% or more as a result of anything done otherwise than for genuine commercial purposes within the seven years ending with the event, the value of CMVCS in the formula at **69.8**(i) above is adjusted to what it would have been without the reduction.

Adjustments to consideration etc.

Where the consideration or benefit referred to in specific provisions contained in **69.4**, **69.7** above and **69.12**, **69.13** below (as listed at *ITEPA 2003, s 446I(1)*) consists wholly or partly of shares (or an interest in shares) whose market value at that time is reduced by 10% or more as a result of anything done otherwise than for genuine commercial purposes within the seven years ending with the receipt of the consideration or benefit, that market value is taken for the purpose of that provision to be what it would have been if it were not for the reduction. This rule also applies for the purpose of determining 'consideration given for the shares' under 'Charge on acquisition' above.

Exceptions from charge disapplied

The exception from charge in **69.5** above (restricted shares) and the similar exceptions in **69.8** above (convertible shares), **69.11** below (shares acquired for less than market value) and **69.13** below (post-acquisition benefits) do not apply if a charge or an adjustment to market value or consideration would otherwise arise under the above provisions.

[ITEPA 2003, ss 419, 421, 421A–421D, 421E(2)–(5), 421F–421I, 446A–446J; CTA 2010, Sch 1 paras 386, 387].

PAYE

For the requirement to operate PAYE on chargeable amounts, see **53.3**(g) PAY AS YOU EARN.

Shares with artificially enhanced market value

[69.10] The following provisions are 'designed to ensure that if the value of employment-related securities is enhanced by means of non-commercial transaction(s) during any tax year, then that appreciation in value is taxed on the employee at the earlier of the disposal of the employment-related securities or 5 April.' (Treasury Explanatory Notes to Finance Bill 2003). They apply in certain cases where the market value of 'employment-related shares' is increased by things done otherwise than for genuine commercial purposes (a '*non-commercial increase*'); this specifically includes anything done as part of a scheme or arrangement a main purpose of which is to avoid tax *or national insurance contributions* and any transaction (other than a payment for corporation tax group relief) between members of a 51% group of companies otherwise than on arm's length terms. See **69.3** above for the extended meaning of 'shares', in relation to these provisions. See **69.17** below as regards reporting obligations.

For these purposes, '*employment-related shares*' are defined as in **69.4** above.

Exclusions

The same exclusions from charge apply as in **69.4** above, except that the exclusion for shares acquired under the terms of a public offer does not apply. The exclusion relating to the nature of the earnings of the employment is more widely drawn in that these provisions are disapplied only if, at the time of acquisition, the earnings from the employment in question were not (or would not have been if there were any) general earnings to which any of the charging provisions in **27.4–27.10** EMPLOYMENT INCOME apply.

Subject to the rules below requiring the importing of certain fictions into the determination of **market values**, such values are to be determined as for capital gains tax purposes.

Charge on non-commercial increases

Where, on the 'valuation date' for a 'relevant period', the market value of employment-related shares is at least 10% greater than it would be if any 'non-commercial increases' (see above) during the relevant period were disregarded, the whole of the excess is taxed as employment income of the employee for tax purposes for the tax year in which the valuation date falls. In determining both actual and notional market values for this purpose, one must ignore any restrictions (of the kind at **69.4**(a)–(c) above) having effect in relation to the shares on the valuation date and any non-commercial reductions (i.e. the opposite to non-commercial increases) during the relevant period. For these purposes:

- the '*valuation date*' is the last day of the 'relevant period'; and
- the '*relevant period*' means any tax year, except that the first such period runs from date of acquisition to the following 5 April and the last runs from 6 April to the date in the tax year on which the provisions cease to apply (see **69.4** above under Exclusions). If these provisions cease to apply to an interest in the shares, the relevant period ends at that time in relation to that interest, but these provisions apply separately to that interest and to what remains.

Special provision applies where on the valuation date the employment-related shares are restricted shares (as in **69.4** above) (or a restricted interest in shares) and no election has been made to wholly disapply the restricted shares provisions in full or to ignore outstanding restrictions (i.e. to omit OP from the formula) in relation to a chargeable event preceding the valuation date. See **69.5, 69.6** above for these elections. The chargeable amount determined above (i.e. the excess) is reduced by the proportion of the non-commercial increase that remains to be taxed when the restriction is eventually lifted. This is achieved by multiplying the otherwise chargeable amount by $(1 - OP)$, where OP is determined in accordance with **69.5** above on the assumption that a chargeable event (resulting in no tax charge) occurs on the valuation date. This rule is suitably modified where an election has been made to disregard one or more specified restrictions in applying the restricted shares provisions.

Where the employment-related shares have been restricted shares (or a restricted interest in shares) at any time during the relevant period and there have been one or more chargeable events during that period, the otherwise chargeable amount under these provisions is reduced by the excess of chargeable amounts under **69.5** above over what they would have been if one were to disregard non-commercial increases during the relevant period (and before the chargeable event). In relation to shares acquired on or after 6 April 2008 (other than under an option acquired before that date), no such reduction is made for amounts representing 'foreign securities income' (within **69.19** below).

Exceptions from charge disapplied

The exception from charge in **69.5** above (restricted shares) and the similar exceptions in **69.8** above (convertible shares), **69.11** below (shares acquired for less than market value) and **69.13** below (post-acquisition benefits) do not apply if the market value of the shares in question at the time of acquisition has been increased by at least 10% by non-commercial increases in the seven years preceding acquisition. If the above charge on non-commercial increases applies in relation to any shares, the exception from charge in **69.5** above does not subsequently apply in relation to those shares.

[ITEPA 2003, ss 419, 421, 421B–421D, 421E(2)–(5), 421F–421H, 446K–446P; FA 2008, Sch 7 paras 32, 80; CTA 2010, Sch 1 paras 386, 388].

PAYE

For the requirement to operate PAYE on chargeable amounts, see **53.3**(g) **PAY AS YOU EARN.**

Shares acquired for less than market value

[69.11] The following provisions deal with the acquisition of 'employment-related shares' for less than their market value and do so by creating the fiction of a notional interest-free loan on the amount of the under-value. The provisions apply to all employees including those in 'lower-paid employment' (see **27.26 EMPLOYMENT INCOME**). They are aimed principally at shares that are acquired partly-paid, such that the employee pays an amount for the shares (which may well be equal to their market value) but does so wholly or partly by instalments.

For these purposes, *'employment-related shares'* are defined as in **69.4** above.

For the extended meaning of 'shares', see **69.3** above.

See **69.17** below as regards reporting obligations.

Exclusions

The same exclusions from charge apply as in **69.4** above. The exclusion relating to the nature of the earnings of the employment is more widely drawn (whatever the date of acquisition) in that these provisions are disapplied only if, at the time of acquisition, the earnings from the employment in question were not (or would not have been if there were any) general earnings to which any of the charging provisions in **27.4–27.10 EMPLOYMENT INCOME** apply.

When the provisions apply

The provisions apply, subject to the exception referred to below, where, at the time of acquisition of employment-related shares, either no payment is (or has been) made for them or a payment is (or has been) made of an amount which is less than market value (determined as for capital gains tax purposes and as if, where it is not the case, the shares were fully paid up). For this purpose, any obligation to make further payment(s) after the time of acquisition is disregarded.

If the tax exemption at **69.4** above applies on an acquisition of restricted shares, the current provisions apply as if the acquisition took place at the first occurrence of a chargeable event within **69.5** above.

The application of these provisions does not displace the application of other tax charges arising in respect of the acquisition of employment-related shares under specified provisions at *ITEPA 2003, s 446V.*

Exception from charge

An exception similar to that applying on chargeable events in **69.5** above is imported into the current provisions; the provisions are disapplied if *all* the company's shares of the same class are acquired at an under-value and *either* of the conditions detailed at **69.5** above is satisfied. (The extended meaning of shares in **69.3** above does not apply for this purpose.) This exception from charge does not apply if anything that affects the shares is done at or before the time of the acquisition as part of arrangements which have as one of their main purposes the avoidance of tax or national insurance contributions.

Interest-free notional loan

Where these provisions do apply, an interest-free notional loan is deemed to have been made to the employee by the employer at the time the employment-related shares are acquired. For so long as the employment continues, the loan counts as an 'employment-related loan' for the purposes of applying *ITEPA 2003, s 175* (benefit of cheap loan arrangements) and related provisions (see **27.40 EMPLOYMENT INCOME**). The initial amount of the loan is the market-value of the shares (or the interest in them) at the time of acquisition (determined as above) less any payment made at or before that time by the employee or (if different) the person who acquired the shares, any amount on which tax is charged as earnings by reason of the acquisition and any amounts on which tax is charged under specified other provisions relating to unapproved share options, restricted shares and convertible shares (see *ITEPA 2003, s 446T(3)*). The loan may be reduced subsequently by payments or further payments for the shares.

The notional loan is treated as discharged upon:

(a) the disposal, otherwise than to an 'associated person' (as defined at **69.4** above), of the shares (or the interest in shares); or

(b) (in the case of shares not fully paid up at time of acquisition) the release, transfer or adjustment, so as no longer to bind any associated person, of the outstanding or contingent liability to pay for the shares; or

(c) the doing of anything that affects the shares and is part of arrangements which have as one of their main purposes the avoidance of tax or national insurance contributions; or

(d) the making by associated persons of sufficient payments to clear the loan; or

(e) the death of the employee.

If the discharge of the loan is within (a), (b) or (c) above, the amount outstanding immediately before the discharge is taxed as employment income of the employee for the tax year of discharge, and this applies regardless of whether or not the employment has terminated.

The notional loan rules above do not apply if the arrangements under which the right or opportunity to acquire the shares was made available had as one of its main purposes the avoidance of tax or national insurance contributions. Instead, an amount equal to what would have been the initial amount of the notional loan is taxed as employment income of the employee for the tax year in which he acquires the shares.

[*ITEPA 2003, ss 192–197, 419, 421, 421B–421D, 421E(2)–(5), 421F–421H, 446Q–446W, Sch 7 paras 28, 29; FA 2008, s 49(5)(12); CTA 2010, Sch 1 para 386*].

See also FAQs at www.hmrc.gov.uk/shareschemes/faq_emprelatedsecurity-ch3 c.htm.

PAYE

For the requirement to operate PAYE on the chargeable amount on discharge of the loan, see **53.3**(g) PAY AS YOU EARN.

In relation to shares acquired on or after 6 April 2008, see **69.18** below for the effect of the REMITTANCE BASIS (**61**) where relevant.

For *capital gains tax* purposes, any amount taxed as employment income on discharge of the notional loan normally counts as part of the acquisition cost of the shares. [*TCGA 1992, ss 119A, 119B, 120; FA 2008, Sch 7 paras 63, 64, 80*]. See Tolley's Capital Gains Tax under Employee Share Schemes for full details.

Shares disposed of for more than market value

[69.12] The following provisions impose an income tax charge on the employee when an 'associated person' (as defined at **69.4** above) disposes of 'employment-related shares' for more than their market value. They apply to all employees including those in 'lower-paid employment' (see **27.26** EMPLOYMENT INCOME).

For these purposes, '*employment-related shares*' are defined as in **69.4** above.

For the extended meaning of 'shares', see **69.3** above.

See **69.17** below as regards reporting obligations.

Exclusions

The same exclusions from charge under the current provisions apply as in **69.4** above, except that the exclusion for shares acquired under the terms of a public offer does not apply. The exclusion relating to the nature of the earnings of the employment is more widely drawn in that these provisions are disapplied only if, at the time of acquisition, the earnings from the employment in question were not (or would not have been if there were any) general earnings to which any of the charging provisions in **27.4–27.10** EMPLOYMENT INCOME apply.

When a charge to tax arises

The charge to income tax arises where employment-related shares are disposed of by an associated person, such that no associated person is any longer beneficially entitled to them, for consideration which exceeds their market value (determined as for capital gains tax purposes) at the time of disposal. *ITEPA 2003, ss 421(2), 421A* apply in determining the amount of any consideration given.

The chargeable amount is the excess of the consideration given for the shares (or the interest in shares) over the market value of the shares (or interest). Any expenses incurred in connection with the disposal are also deductible in arriving at the chargeable amount. The chargeable amount is taxed as employment income of the employee for the tax year of disposal.

A *Pt 5* transfer of shares under *Proceeds of Crime Act 2002* (as in **10.2**(x) CAPITAL ALLOWANCES) does not give rise to an income tax charge under these provisions.

[*ITEPA 2003, ss 198–200, 419, 421, 421A–421D, 421E(2)–(5), 421F–421H, 446X–446Z, Sch 7 paras 30, 31, 61A; CTA 2010, Sch 1 para 386*].

The first appeal to reach the courts in relation to the above was decided in favour of HMRC (*Grays Timber Products Ltd v HMRC* SC, [2010] UKSC 4).

PAYE

For the requirement to operate PAYE on chargeable amounts, see **53.3**(g) PAY AS YOU EARN.

In relation to shares acquired on or after 6 April 2008, see **69.18** below for the effect of the REMITTANCE BASIS (**61**) where relevant.

Post-acquisition benefits from shares

[69.13] For these purposes, '*employment-related shares*' are defined as in **69.4** above. See **69.17** below as regards reporting obligations.

Exclusions

The same exclusions from charge apply as in **69.4** above, except that the exclusion for shares acquired under the terms of a public offer does not apply.

The charge

These provisions apply if an 'associated person' (as defined at **69.4** above) receives a benefit in connection with 'employment-related shares'. The amount or market value (determined as for capital gains tax purposes) of the benefit is taxed as employment income of the employee for the tax year in which the benefit is received.

Exceptions

These provisions do not apply if the benefit is otherwise chargeable to income tax. However, this let-out is unavailable if something that affects the shares is done as part of arrangements which have as one of their main purposes the avoidance of tax or national insurance contributions. In addition, an exception similar to that applying on chargeable events in **69.5** above is imported into the current provisions; the provisions are disapplied if a similar benefit is received by the owners of *all* the company's shares of the same class and *either* of the conditions detailed at **69.5** above is satisfied. (The extended meaning of shares in **69.3** above does not apply for this purpose, though the term does include stock.) This exception from charge does not apply if anything that affects the shares is done as part of arrangements which have as one of their main purposes the avoidance of tax or national insurance contributions.

[*ITEPA 2003, ss 421, 421B–421D, 421E(1)(3)–(5), 421F–421H, 447–450, Sch 7 para 54; FA 2008, Sch 7 paras 31, 80; CTA 2010, Sch 1 para 386*].

PAYE

For the requirement to operate PAYE on chargeable amounts, see **53.3**(g) PAY AS YOU EARN.

In relation to shares acquired on or after 6 April 2008, see **69.18** below for the effect of the REMITTANCE BASIS (**61**) where relevant.

See generally HMRC Employment-Related Securities Manual ERSM 90000 *et seq.*

Unapproved share options

[69.14] This section is essentially concerned with *unapproved* share options. For EMI options, approved SAYE option schemes and approved CSOP schemes, see respectively **69.35, 69.47** and **69.61** below. However, as noted in those sections where relevant, the breach of certain conditions under EMI options and approved schemes can lead to a charge under the provisions at **69.15** below.

In relation to options acquired on or after 6 April 2008, see **69.18** below for the effect of the REMITTANCE BASIS (**61**) where relevant.

For reporting obligations, see **69.17** below.

Meaning of 'share option'

A '*share option*' is a right to acquire '*shares*'. '*Shares*' has the extended meaning in **69.3** above.

A share option is outside the above definition (and thus outside the rules below) if it is a right to acquire '*shares*' that is itself acquired pursuant to a right or opportunity made available under arrangements having as one of their main purposes the avoidance of tax or national insurance contributions — see **69.3** above under Share options. [*ITEPA 2003, s 420(8)*].

Application of these provisions

These provisions apply to a share option (an '*employment-related share option*') acquired by a person where the right or opportunity to acquire it is available by reason of the employment (past, present or prospective) of that person or any other person. Any right or opportunity made available by a person's employer, or by a person connected (within **21** CONNECTED PERSONS) with a person's employer, is treated as made available by reason of the employment of that person, other than in the case of an individual conferring a right or opportunity in the normal course of his domestic, family or personal relationships. A right to acquire a share option becoming available by reason of an existing holding of 'employment-related shares' (as defined at **69.4** above) is treated for these purposes as available by reason of the employment by reason of which the right or opportunity to acquire those shares was available.

For the circumstances in which HMRC will accept that shares or share options were acquired by an employee by virtue of a family or personal relationship and not by reason of the employment, see HMRC Employment-Related Securities Manual ERSM20220.

A gain realised following cessation of the employment on the exercise, assignment, release etc. of an employment-related share option falls within *these* provisions and not those at **20 COMPENSATION FOR LOSS OF EMPLOYMENT (AND DAMAGES)** (*Bluck v Salton* (Sp C 378), [2003] SSCD 439).

Grant of option

If an employment-related share option is potentially within the charge to tax in **69.15** below on exercise, assignment, release etc., no income tax liability arises in respect of the receipt of the option.

Where the option is outside the charge to tax in **69.15** below on exercise, assignment, release etc. (because the earnings from the employment in question were within the relevant exceptions from charge), a charge to tax can arise on receipt of the option (regardless of when it is capable of being exercised) but not on its exercise etc. See also *Abbott v Philbin* HL 1960, 39 TC 82 and HMRC Employment-Related Securities Manual ERSM110100.

[*ITEPA 2003, ss 419, 421–421B, 421D, 471, 475, 484, 718; ITA 2007, Sch 1 para 442*].

Chargeable events

[69.15] Subject to the exceptions detailed below, the occurrence of a chargeable event in relation to an employment-related share option (as in **69.14** above) results in the chargeable amount (computed as below) being taxed as employment income of the employee for the tax year in which the event occurs. For these purposes, any of the following is a chargeable event:

(a)   the acquisition of shares on the **exercise** of the option by an 'associated person' (see below);

(b)   the **assignment** (for consideration) of the option by an associated person otherwise than to another associated person;

(c)   the **release** (for consideration) of the option by an associated person;

(d)   the receipt by an associated person of a benefit in connection with the option.

The reference in (a) above to the '*exercise*' of an option embraces any acquisition of shares in pursuance of a right to acquire them, which includes, for example, a right under a so-called long-term incentive plan to receive shares after a specified period of time without the need to exercise the right.

For the purposes of (a) above, shares are deemed to be acquired when the beneficial interest is acquired and not, if different, at the time of conveyance or transfer. Specifically included in (d) above is consideration received for omitting, or undertaking to omit, to exercise the option, or granting, or undertaking to grant, to another person a right to acquire the option shares (or an interest in them). Specifically excluded from (d) above is any benefit received on account of disability (as defined) and anything already covered by (a)–(c) above.

For the purposes of these provisions, any of the following are 'associated persons' in relation to an employment-related share option:

- the person who acquired it;
- (if different) the employee; and
- any 'relevant linked person'.

A 'relevant linked person' is any person who is either connected (within **21 CONNECTED PERSONS**) with, or is a member of the same household as, either the person who acquired the option or the employee. The statutory definition also embraces past connections etc. so as to ensure the link cannot be broken. However, a *company* cannot be a relevant linked person if it is the employer or (if different) the person by whom the right or opportunity to acquire the option was made available or the person from whom the option was acquired.

The **chargeable amount** depends on the type of chargeable event. On an event within (a) above (exercise of option), it is the excess (if any) of:

- the market value, at time of acquisition, of the shares acquired, over
- the consideration given (if any) for the shares acquired.

If the chargeable event is within (b) or (c) above, the chargeable amount is the amount of consideration given for the assignment or release of the option. On an event within (d) above, it is the amount or market value of the benefit. However, if that consideration or that benefit consists wholly or partly of shares (or an interest in shares) the market value of which has been reduced by 10% or more as a result of things done otherwise than for genuine commercial purposes (see **69.9** above) within the preceding seven years, such reduction is added back.

For the purposes of these provisions generally, market value is determined as for capital gains tax purposes and *ITEPA 2003, ss 421(2), 421A* apply in determining the amount of any consideration given for anything.

Whatever the type of event, any consideration given for the option itself (on its original acquisition) is also deductible, as are any expenses incurred in connection with the exercise, assignment or release or the receipt of benefit. Where, in consequence of the acquisition of the option itself or the acquisition of shares under the option or any transaction of which either forms part, there is a reduction in the market value of any employment-related shares held by an associated person, the amount of that reduction is deductible as if it were consideration given for the option. Any amount charged on *grant* of the option is also deductible. Where there is more than one chargeable event in relation to the same option, the same deductions cannot be made more than once.

The charge on exercise etc. is independent of any charge on grant of the option (see also above), and depends solely on the above conditions being satisfied (*Ball v Phillips* Ch D 1990, 63 TC 529).

A special rule applies if an employee is divested of a share option by operation of law; in such case, there is an income tax charge on a chargeable event and it is on the person who exercises the option or receives the consideration or benefit (whichever is applicable).

Exceptions from charge

No charge arises on any event within (a)–(d) above:

- if it occurs on or after the death of the employee; or
- (in relation to options acquired on or after 6 April 2008) if, at the time the option is acquired, the earnings from the employment were not (or would not have been if there were any) general earnings within **27.4 EMPLOYMENT INCOME** (earnings for year when employee resident in UK), chargeable overseas earnings (within **27.5 EMPLOYMENT INCOME**) or foreign earnings (within **27.5 EMPLOYMENT INCOME**); or
- (in relation to options acquired before 6 April 2008) if, at the time the option is acquired, the earnings from the employment in question were not (or would not have been if there were any) general earnings within **27.9 EMPLOYMENT INCOME** (earnings for year when employee resident, ordinarily resident and domiciled in UK) or within *ITEPA 2003, s 21* (earnings, other than chargeable overseas earnings, for year when employee resident and ordinarily resident but not domiciled in UK — see **27.10 EMPLOYMENT INCOME**); or
- (in the case of an option acquired after the employment has ceased) if no charge would have arisen had the acquisition taken place in the last tax year in which the employment was held; or
- (in the case of an option acquired before the employment has begun) if no charge would have arisen had the acquisition taken place in the first tax year in which the employment is held.

Where one option has been exchanged for another (see below) the acquisition referred to is that of the 'old' option.

Option exchanged for another

The following rules apply where an employee-related share option is assigned or released for consideration consisting of or including another share option. For the purpose of computing the chargeable amount (if any) on the assignment or release, the new option is not treated as consideration given for the old. For the purposes of computing the charge on any future chargeable event, the consideration (if any) given for the new option consists of any actual consideration given (apart from the old option) plus the excess (if any) of any consideration given for the old option over any consideration received (apart from the new option) for its assignment or release. There are provisions (see *ITEPA 2003, s 483(5)(6)*) which in specified circumstances treat for these purposes two or more transactions as a single transaction by which an option is assigned for consideration consisting of or including another share option.

Relief for employer national insurance contributions

Where, under a voluntary agreement or a joint election under *Social Security Contributions and Benefits Act 1992, Sch 1 para 3A* or *para 3B* (or NI equivalent), whenever made, a liability to secondary Class 1 national insurance contributions (i.e. employer contributions) on a share option gain chargeable to tax under these provisions is borne by the employee who realised the gain, the amount so borne is deductible in arriving at the amount on which the employee is chargeable to tax. In the case of a voluntary agreement, or an election to which HMRC approval is withdrawn, no such amount is deductible to the extent that it is borne by the employee later than 4 June following the tax year in which the chargeable event occurs. (Any deduction for national insurance contributions is disregarded in determining the allowable cost of the shares for capital gains tax purposes — see also below.)

[ITEPA 2003, ss 472–474, 476–483, Sch 7 paras 63, 64, 65; ITA 2007, Sch 1 para 438; FA 2008, s 49(6)(11), Sch 7 paras 33, 80; CTA 2010, Sch 1 para 390].

PAYE

For the requirement to operate PAYE on chargeable events, see **53.3**(e)(f) PAY AS YOU EARN.

Capital gains tax

For capital gains tax purposes, when shares acquired on exercise of an employment-related share option are disposed of, any sum charged to income tax as employment income is normally treated as part of the cost of acquiring the shares. The Inland Revenue's defeat in *Mansworth v Jelley* CA 2002, 75 TC 1 in December 2002 meant that persons exercising unapproved share options (or options granted under approved schemes but exercised in breach of the statutory provisions) could deduct the market value of the shares at time of exercise plus any amount charged to income tax on the exercise (see Revenue Internet Statements 8 January 2003, 17 March 2003). In May 2009, however, HMRC published a revised view to the effect that, for options exercised before 10 April 2003, the acquisition cost for capital gains tax purposes is not augmented by any amount charged to income tax, and that the full measure of that cost is therefore the market value of the shares at time of exercise. HMRC have indicated that they will apply this view in cases where there was an enquiry or appeal open on 13 May 2009. (HMRC Briefs 30/09, 12 May 2009 and 60/09, 11 September 2009).

With effect for options exercised on or after 10 April 2003, *FA 2003* reversed the effect of the decision in *Mansworth v Jelley* above, so that the cost of acquisition for capital gains tax purposes once again comprises the actual consideration given for the shares, any consideration given for the option itself, and, as stated above, any amount charged to income tax on the exercise. In computing the latter amount, for this purpose only, relief given for national insurance contributions (see above) is added back, as is any deduction made in respect of any tax charged on *grant* of the option (mainly relevant to long-term options under pre-*FA 2003* rules). If any amount that would otherwise be charged to income tax is unremitted 'foreign securities income' (within **69.19** below) it does not form part of the cost of acquisition of the shares, but the taxpayer may make a claim to adjust that cost if any amount is subsequently remitted.

[TCGA 1992, ss 119A, 119B, 120, 144ZA; FA 2008, Sch 7 paras 63, 64, 80].

For full coverage of this subject, see Tolley's Capital Gains Tax under Employee Share Schemes.

Internationally mobile employees

For an article on the imposition of income tax charges under the above provisions in the case of internationally mobile employees, including examples and the impact of double tax agreements, see Revenue Tax Bulletins August 2002 pp 951–954 and April 2005 pp 1193–1199 (the latter superseding Revenue Tax Bulletin October 2001 pp 883–887). For associated national insurance contributions liabilities, see Revenue Tax Bulletin December 2001 pp 895–899. See also HMRC Employment-Related Securities Manual ERSM160100.

Example

[69.16]

An employee is granted an option exercisable within five years to buy 1,000 shares at £5 each. The option costs 50p per share. He exercises the option in 2010/11 when the shares are worth £7.50. The option is not granted under an approved scheme.

The amount taxable as employment income in 2010/11 is as follows:

	£	£
Open market value of shares 1,000 × £7.50		7,500
Price paid 1,000 × £5 — shares	5,000	
1,000 × 50p — option	500	
		5,500
Amount taxable as employment income		£2,000

Notes

(a) The result would be the same if, instead of exercising the option, the employee transferred his option to a third party for £2,500.

(b) The capital gains tax cost of the shares is £7,500 (£5,000 + £500 + £2,000) — see **69.15** above.

Reporting obligations

[69.17] For the purposes generally of **69.4–69.15** above, there are extensive requirements for employers and others to provide HMRC with information concerning any of the events listed below. The reportable events are as follows:

• an acquisition (or event treated as such) of shares, an interest in shares or a share option pursuant to a right or opportunity available by reason of employment;

- chargeable events within either **69.5** above (restricted shares) or **69.8** above (convertible shares);
- the doing of anything that gives rise to an income tax charge under **69.10** above (shares with artificially enhanced market value);
- an event discharging a notional loan as in **69.11** above (shares acquired for less than market value);
- a disposal within **69.12** above (shares disposed of for more than market value);
- the receipt of a benefit within **69.13** above (post-acquisition benefits from shares);
- the assignment or release of a share option acquired pursuant to a right or opportunity available by reason of employment;
- the receipt of a benefit in money or money's worth received in connection with a share option (see **69.15**(d) above).

See **69.3** above for the extended meaning of 'shares' in these respects. The persons obliged to report such events are the employer, the 'host employer' if any, the person from whom the shares, interest or option was acquired and, unless the shares are excluded from these requirements, the person by whom they were issued. A *'host employer'* is a person for whom the employee works at the time of the event and who would be treated as making payments of PAYE income if such payments were actually made by a non-UK employer (see **53.5 PAY AS YOU EARN** under 'Non-UK employer'). Shares excluded from these requirements are, broadly, government and local authority stocks/bonds and quoted shares issued by a person who, at the time of the event, is not connected (within **21 CONNECTED PERSONS**) with the employer.

Every person obliged to report the event in question must give HMRC written particulars of the event (in specified form) before 7 July following the end of the tax year in which the event took place, but once one such person complies there is no need for others to comply in relation to the same event. In addition, HMRC may give notice to any person, requiring him to provide written particulars of reportable events which take place during a period specified in the notice (and in relation to which that person is a person obliged to report such events) or to state that there are no such events. Such notice must specify a deadline for compliance, which must be at least 30 days after the notice is given. Again, once such particulars are provided in relation to a particular event, others are released from their original obligation to report the event. In both cases, penalties are exigible under *TMA 1970, s 98* for non-compliance.

[*ITEPA 2003, ss 421J–421L, 718; ITA 2007, Sch 1 para 442; FA 2007, Sch 26 para 10(2)*].

Particulars should be sent to HMRC, Employee Shares and Securities Unit, Nottingham Team, 1st Floor, Ferrers House, Castle Meadow Road, Nottingham, NG2 1BB. The standard form for reporting the events listed above is Form 42. Detailed guidance is available on the reporting requirements generally and on the completion of Form 42 (see www.hmrc.gov.uk/sharesch emes/form42-guidance-2007.pdf)..

Effect of remittance basis

[69.18] Legislation was introduced by *FA 2008* to bring employees who are resident but not ordinarily resident, and who receive employment-related shares, within those charging provisions of this chapter which previously had effect only for employees both resident and ordinarily resident, i.e. the provisions at **69.4** (restricted shares), **69.7** (convertible shares), **69.13** (post-acquisition benefits) and **69.14** (unapproved share options) above. The legislation applies to shares or, as the case may be, share options **acquired on or after 6 April 2008** (but not to shares acquired on or after that date under an option acquired before that date). The effect of this can be seen under the sub-headings Exclusions in **69.4** and Exceptions from charge in **69.15**, where it will be noted that different criteria apply in relation to the earnings exclusion depending on when the shares or the share option were acquired. Consequently, the rules referred to below were introduced simultaneously to cover the situation where the **REMITTANCE BASIS (61)** applies to an individual within the charge to tax under those provisions. These rules also have effect where the remittance basis applies to an individual within the charge to tax under **69.11** or **69.12** above (shares acquired for less than, or disposed of for more than, market value), again where the shares in question are acquired on or after 6 April 2008.

For official guidance on the changes, see www.hmrc.gov.uk/shareschemes/res-d om-rules.htm and HMRC Employment-Related Securities Manual ERSM160000 *et seq.*

The extended meaning of 'shares' at **69.3** above applies throughout, and 'share option' should be construed accordingly.

The rules apply where any amount (the '*securities income*') counts as employment income of an individual for a tax year under any of the charging provisions referred to above (with one exception) and any part of 'the relevant period' is within a tax year for which the remittance basis applies to the individual by virtue of any one of **61.2(1)–(3) REMITTANCE BASIS**. (The exception is the specific anti-avoidance charge in **69.11** above under which an amount equal to what would have been the initial amount of the notional loan is instead taxed as employment income of the employee for the tax year in which he acquires the shares.) If an amount counts as employment income under any of those charging provisions but by virtue of **69.9** or **69.10** above (shares with artificially depressed or artificially enhanced market value) it is disregarded for these purposes.

The definition of the '*the relevant period*' depends on the charging provision in question, as follows.

- If an amount counts as employment income by virtue of **69.4** above (restricted shares) or **69.7** above (convertible shares), the relevant period is period from the acquisition of the shares to the date of the chargeable event.
- If an amount counts as employment income by virtue of the discharge of the notional loan in **69.11** above (shares acquired for less than market value), the relevant period is normally the tax year in which the notional loan is treated as made or, if the chargeable event occurs in that

year, a part of the tax year ending with the day of that event. If, however, the shares are acquired by means of a share option, the relevant period begins with the day the option is acquired and ends with the day on which the option is first capable of being exercised.

- If an amount counts as employment income by virtue of **69.12** above (shares disposed of for more than market value) or **69.13** above (post-acquisition benefits), the relevant period is the tax year in which the chargeable event occurs.
- If an amount counts as employment income by virtue of **69.15** above (unapproved share options), the relevant period begins with the day the option is acquired and ends with the day of the chargeable event or, if earlier, the day on which the option is first capable of being exercised.

[*ITEPA 2003, s 41A(1)(2)(3)(10), s 41B; FA 2008, Sch 7 paras 22, 80*].

There are two rules to ascertain the employee's taxable specific income from the employment for a tax year in respect of securities income (as defined above). (See **27.1 EMPLOYMENT INCOME** for the charge to tax on taxable specific income.) See **69.19** below.

[69.19] The first of the rules referred to in **69.18** above is that the excess of securities income (as in **69.18** above) over so much of that income as is 'foreign securities income' is taxable specific income for the tax year for which the securities income counts as employment income of the individual. This has nothing to do with what, if anything, is remitted to the UK.

The second rule is that the full amount of any of the foreign securities income that is remitted to the UK in any tax year is taxable specific income from the employment for that year. This applies whether or not the employment is held when the amount is remitted. See **61 REMITTANCE BASIS** for the meaning of 'remitted to the UK' etc. For the purpose of applying the provisions described in that chapter, generally treat the shares or the option as deriving from the foreign securities income; but where the chargeable event is the disposal of the shares, or the assignment or release of the share option, in question for consideration equal to or exceeding market value, treat the consideration (and not the shares or the option) as deriving from the foreign securities income.

The extent to which the securities income is '*foreign securities income*' is determined as set out below. For these purposes, treat the securities income as accruing evenly over 'the relevant period' (as defined in **69.18** above).

If any part of the relevant period is within a tax year for which all of the following apply, then, subject to what is said below regarding associated employments, the securities income treated as accruing in that part of the relevant period is foreign securities income:

- the remittance basis applies to the individual by virtue of any one of **61.2**(1)–(3) **REMITTANCE BASIS**;
- the individual is ordinarily resident in the UK;
- the employment is with a 'foreign employer'; and
- the duties of the employment are performed wholly outside the UK.

'*Foreign employer*' means an individual, partnership or body of persons (including a company) resident outside, and not resident in, the UK.

If the individual also holds 'associated employments' the duties of which are not performed wholly outside the UK, the foreign securities income is then limited to such amount as is just and reasonable, having regard to the employment income from all the employments, the proportion of that employment income that is 'chargeable overseas earnings' (see **27.5 EMPLOY-MENT INCOME**), the nature of and the time devoted to duties performed outside and in the UK, and all other relevant circumstances. Employments are 'associated' if they are with the same employer, or the employers are under common control or one controls the other, control being as in *CTA 2010, ss 450, 451* (for companies) and *ITA 2007, s 995* (for individuals and partnerships).

If any part of the relevant period is within a tax year for which all of the following apply:

- the remittance basis applies to the individual by virtue of any one of **61.2**(1)–(3) **REMITTANCE BASIS**;
- the individual is not ordinarily resident in the UK;
- some or all of the duties of the employment are performed outside the UK,

the securities income treated as accruing in that part of the relevant period is foreign securities income to the following extent. If the duties of the employment are performed wholly outside the UK, all of the securities income treated as accruing in that part of the relevant period is foreign securities income. If only some of the duties of the employment are performed outside the UK, then (having regard to the extent to which the duties are performed outside the UK) a just and reasonable proportion of the securities income treated as accruing in that part of the relevant period is foreign securities income.

For the purposes only of determining the extent to which securities income is foreign securities income, an individual who is non-resident in the UK in a tax year is treated as if the remittance basis applied to him for that year.

If, after taking into account all of the above (apart from the associated employments rule), the proportion of the securities income that would otherwise be regarded as foreign securities income is not, having regard to all the circumstances, just and reasonable, the foreign securities income is amended to such amount as is just and reasonable. See HMRC Employment-Related Securities Manual ERSM161900 for guidance.

[*ITEPA 2003, s 41A(4)–(10), ss 41C–41E, 721(1); FA 2008, Sch 7 paras 22, 39, 80, 81*].

For the purposes of **61 REMITTANCE BASIS**, an individual's '*foreign specific employment income*' for a tax year is such of his specific employment income (see **27.1 EMPLOYMENT INCOME**) for the year as is foreign securities income. [*ITA 2007, s 809Z7(4); FA 2008, Sch 7 paras 1, 81*].

Share Incentive Plans

[69.20] A share incentive plan ('SIP') is a plan established by a company and approved by HMRC (see **69.33** below), providing for shares to be appropriated without payment to employees ('*free shares*' — see **69.22** below) and/or for shares to be acquired on employees' behalf from sums deducted from their salary (*'partnership shares'* — see **69.23** below). A plan providing for partnership shares may also provide for shares to be appropriated without payment to employees (*'matching shares'* — see **69.24** below) in proportion to the partnership shares acquired by them. See **69.26, 69.27** below for tax consequences in each case. See **69.25** below as to reinvestment of dividends on plan shares. Where a plan provides for more than one of the above kinds of shares, it may leave it to the company to decide when each such provision is to have effect. A plan established by a company which controls (within *ITA 2007, s 995*) other companies (a *'parent company'*) may extend to one or more of those other companies, whereupon it is known as a *'group plan'*. Companies that for the time being are party to a group plan are known as *'constituent companies'*. [*ITEPA 2003, ss 488, 719, Sch 2 paras 1–4; ITA 2007, Sch 1 para 443*].

See **73.59, 73.60** TRADING INCOME as regards deductions which the employer company may make for corporation tax purposes.

Guidance for employers and advisers is provided by HMRC at www.hmrc.gov.uk/shareschemes/share_incentive/sip-guide-employers-advisors.pdf. Guidance for employees is at www.hmrc.gov.uk/shareschemes/sip-info-employees.rtf.

General requirements

[69.21] The purpose of the plan must be to provide benefits to employees by way of shares which give them a continuing stake in a company. A plan must contain no features which are neither essential nor reasonably incidental to that purpose. It *must* provide that every employee who is eligible (as in **69.28** below) in relation to an award of shares under the plan, and who is a 'UK resident taxpayer', may participate in the award and be invited to do so, and it should not contain any features (other than those required or authorised under these provisions) to discourage participation. It *may* provide for an eligible employee to be invited to participate in an award even though he is not a 'UK resident taxpayer'. An individual who *must* be invited, or who under terms as above *may* be invited, to participate in an award is a *'qualifying employee'* in relation to that award.

For the above purposes, an employee is a *'UK resident taxpayer'* if his earnings, from the employment by reference to which he meets the employment requirement at **69.28** below, are (or would be if there were any):

- (before 2008/09) general earnings within **27.9** EMPLOYMENT INCOME or *ITEPA 2003, s 21* (earnings, other than chargeable overseas earnings, for year when employee UK resident and ordinarily resident); or
- (for 2008/09 onwards) general earnings within **27.5** EMPLOYMENT INCOME (earnings for year when employee UK resident), and those general earnings are (or would be if there were any) earnings for a tax year in which the employee is ordinarily resident in the UK.

All employees invited to participate in an award must be invited to participate on the same terms, and those who do participate must actually do so on the same terms. Free shares may be awarded by reference to remuneration, length of service or hours worked, or (within confines) more than one of these factors, but not by reference to other factors. Free shares may, however, be allocated, in accordance with **69.29** below, by reference to performance. Subject to the above, no feature of the plan must have the likely effect of conferring benefits wholly or mainly on directors or on employees receiving higher levels of remuneration. In the case of a group, the identity of the company, or of the constituent companies in a group plan, must not be such as to have similar likely effect. No conditions may be imposed on an employee's participation in an award, except as required or permitted under these provisions. The arrangements (as broadly defined) for the plan must not provide for loans to employees of the company (or of constituent companies in a group plan), and neither those arrangements nor the operation of the plan must in any way be associated with any such loans.

[*ITEPA 2003, Sch 2 paras 6–12; FA 2008, Sch 7 paras 41, 81*].

Awards of shares

Shares are '*awarded*' under a plan on each occasion when, in accordance with the plan, free or matching shares are appropriated to employees or partnership shares are acquired on behalf of employees. Shares are awarded to a particular employee (a '*participant*') when free or matching shares are appropriated to him, or partnership shares are acquired on his behalf, as part of the global award. [*ITEPA 2003, Sch 2 para 5*].

Shares leaving the plan

Shares '*cease to be subject to the plan*' when:

(a)   they are 'withdrawn from the plan'; or

(b)   the participant ceases to be in '*relevant employment*' (which term comprises employment by the company and employment by any 'associated' company), in which case his shares cease to be subject to the plan on the date of leaving (but see below for exception); or

(c)   the plan trustees dispose of the shares in order to meet PAYE obligations (see **69.26** below).

For the purpose of determining any charge to income tax, shares cease to be subject to the plan in the order in which they were awarded to the participant. Shares awarded on the same day cease to be subject to the plan in the order which results in the lowest income tax charge. (Dividend shares are treated as awarded when the trustees acquire them on behalf of, or appropriate them to, the participant.)

Shares are '*withdrawn from the plan*' (see (a) above) when, on the direction of the participant (or, after his death, of his personal representatives), the plan trustees either transfer them (whether to the participant etc. or to another person) or dispose of them and similarly account for the proceeds, or when the participant etc. assigns, charges or otherwise disposes of his beneficial interest in them.

For the purposes of (b) above and of these provisions generally (except where otherwise stated), two companies are '*associated*' if one controls the other or they are under common control, 'control' being interpreted in accordance with *CTA 2010, ss 450, 151*.

Where an individual ceases to be in relevant employment during the 'acquisition period' relating to an award of partnership shares, he is treated for the purposes of (b) above as ceasing to be in such employment immediately after the shares are awarded. The *'acquisition period'* begins with the deduction from salary and ends with the 'acquisition date' or, where relevant, begins with the end of the 'accumulation period' and ends immediately before the 'acquisition date' (see **69.23** below for meaning of terms used here).

[*ITEPA 2003, s 508, Sch 2 paras 94–97; CTA 2010, Sch 1 para 396(7)*].

Jointly owned companies

To enable a jointly owned company to take part in a group plan (though it cannot thereby take part in more than one), such a company, and any company under its control (within *ITA 2007, s 995*), is treated as being under the control of each of its two joint owners (though not for the purposes of **69.30**(ii) below). A company controlled *by* a jointly owned company may not take part in more than one group plan or in a different plan to that (if any) in which the jointly owned company (or any other company controlled by it) takes part. [*ITEPA 2003, s 719, Sch 2 para 91, Sch 7 para 70; ITA 2007, Sch 1 para 443*].

In the case of a company registered outside the UK, **shares** include fractions of shares for the purposes of these provisions, where such fractions are recognised under local law. [*ITEPA 2003, Sch 2 para 99(2)*].

Free shares

[69.22] The 'initial market value' of free shares awarded (see **69.21** above) to a participant in any tax year under a plan providing for free shares (see **69.20** above) must not exceed £3,000. The *'initial market value'* of shares is their market value (determined as for capital gains tax purposes) on the date of the award. Where the market value of shares on any date falls to be determined, HMRC and the plan trustees may agree that it be determined by reference to a different date or a number of specified dates. In arriving at the market value of restricted shares as in **69.4** above, the restrictions (or risk of forfeiture) are disregarded. [*ITEPA 2003, Sch 2 paras 34, 35, 92*]. For HMRC practice on the determination of market value, see Revenue Share Focus Newsletter May 2007 pp 3–5.

As regards each award of free shares, the plan must require the company to specify a period (the holding period) during which a participant is bound by contract, for so long as he remains in relevant employment (see **69.21** above), to permit his shares to remain in the hands of the trustees and not to assign, charge or otherwise dispose of his beneficial interest. The holding period must not be less than three years, nor more than five, beginning with the date the shares are awarded to the participant, and must be the same for all shares in the same award. See **69.26** below for income tax consequences of free shares leaving the plan. The plan *may* enable different holding periods to be specified from time to time, though not so as to increase the holding period for free shares already awarded. Notwithstanding the foregoing, the participant may direct the trustees to accept or agree to:

(a)   an offer resulting in a new holding being equated with his original free shares for capital gains tax purposes (see Tolley's Capital Gains Tax under Shares and Securities); or

(b)   an offer of cash and/or a qualifying corporate bond (see Tolley's Capital Gains Tax), with or without other assets, which is part of a general offer designed to give the person making it control of the company; or

(c)   a transaction pursuant to a compromise, arrangement or scheme affecting all the shares or all the shares of the particular class concerned or all those held by a class of shareholders (identified otherwise than by reference to employment or participation in the plan).

[ITEPA 2003, Sch 2 paras 36, 37; CTA 2010, Sch 1 para 396(4)].

The holding period requirement is subject to the provisions for termination of plans (see **69.34** below) and those requiring the trustees to be enabled to meet certain PAYE obligations (see **69.26** below).

Partnership shares

[69.23] A plan providing for partnership shares (see **69.20** above) must provide for qualifying employees (see **69.21** below) to enter into agreements (*'partnership share agreements'*) with the company whereby the employee authorises the employer company to make deductions from his salary for the purchase of partnership shares to be awarded to him under the plan. It must specify the amount or percentage to be deducted from salary and the intervals at which deductions are to be made, although the company and employee may agree to vary both of these. It must also contain a notice giving prescribed information in prescribed form (see *SI 2000 No 2090*) as to the possible effect of deductions on an employee's entitlement to social security benefits, statutory sick pay and statutory maternity pay.

The amount deducted from salary must not exceed **£1,500** in any tax year. Furthermore, it must not exceed 10% of the employee's salary for the tax year. The plan may authorise the setting of maximum limits which are lower than the aforementioned; different limits may be set for different awards. A lower limit may be expressed in terms of a monetary amount, a percentage or a stipulation that earnings of a specified kind (e.g. overtime payments, bonuses etc.) be excluded from employees' salaries for these purposes. Any amount deducted from salary in excess of the applicable limits must be returned to the employee. The plan may also set a minimum amount that can be deducted on any occasion (previously in any month, regardless of actual pay intervals); the specified minimum must not exceed £10.

Subject to the above, for these purposes an employee's salary means his earnings (from the employment in question) otherwise subject to PAYE, excluding any taxable benefits and expenses within **27.26–27.48 EMPLOYMENT INCOME**. HMRC take this to mean salary after deduction of allowable pension contributions and charitable donations made under payroll giving schemes (Revenue Share Focus Newsletter December 2003 p 8). The term is extended to include emoluments which are outside the scope of the charge to tax on employment income, excluding benefits etc., which would have been chargeable had the individual been within the scope of that charge. See **69.26** below as regards tax relief for amounts deducted.

[ITEPA 2003, Sch 2 paras 43–48; SI 2000 No 2090; SI 2007 No 109].

Amounts deducted from salary are to be paid over to the trustees and held by them (in a bank, building society etc.) on the employee's behalf until applied in acquiring partnership shares on his behalf (which includes their appropriating to him shares already held by them). If such monies are held in an interest-bearing account, the plan must require the trustees to account to the employee for the interest.

If the plan does not provide for an accumulation period (see below), it must provide for deductions from salary to be applied as above on the *'acquisition date'*, which for *this* purpose is a date which is set by the trustees and is within 30 days after the date of the last salary deduction in relation to the partnership share award in question. Subject to any restriction imposed in accordance with the plan (see below), the number of shares awarded (see **69.21** above) to each employee is to be determined by reference to market value at the acquisition date.

A plan may provide for accumulation periods not exceeding 12 months. If it does so, the partnership share agreement must specify when each such period begins (which in the case of the first period must be no later than the date of the first salary deduction) and ends. The accumulation period for each award of shares must be same for all individuals entering into the partnership share agreements. Subject to this, the agreement may specify that an accumulation period shall end on the occurrence of a specified event, and may additionally provide that salary deductions be in such cases returned to participants. The plan may provide for continuity in the event of certain share exchanges. The plan must provide for deductions from salary to be applied by the trustees in acquiring, on the employee's behalf, partnership shares on the *'acquisition date'*, which for *this* purpose is a date which is set by the trustees and is within 30 days after the end of the accumulation period applicable to the partnership share award in question. Subject to any restriction imposed in accordance with the plan (see below), the number of shares awarded to each employee is to be determined by reference to the lower of market value at the beginning of the accumulation period and market value at the acquisition date. If an employee ceases to be in relevant employment (see **69.21** above) during an accumulation period, salary deductions made must be paid over to him.

Any surplus monies held after acquiring shares as above may, with the employee's agreement, be carried forward to the next deduction or, where applicable, carried forward to the next accumulation period; otherwise they must be paid over to the employee.

The plan *may* authorise the company to restrict the number of shares to be included in a particular partnership share award to a specified maximum, subject to its giving employees advance notification. Where necessary, in such case, the number of shares in each individual award is to be scaled down.

[ITEPA 2003, Sch 2 paras 43(3), 49–53; ITA 2007, Sch 1 para 447(2)].

An employee may, by written notice to the company, stop salary deductions under a partnership share agreement. He may similarly re-start deductions (though the plan *may* impose a limit of one re-start per accumulation period, where applicable) but is not permitted to make up deductions missed. The company must give effect to a notice to stop or re-start within 30 days of receiving it, unless the employee specifies a later date in the notice. An employee may also, again by written notice to the company, withdraw from a partnership share agreement, such notice to take effect within 30 days unless a later date is specified therein. Any monies deducted and still held on his behalf must then be paid over to him. On withdrawal of HMRC approval to a plan (see **69.33** below) or on the issue of a plan termination notice (see **69.34** below), any monies deducted and still held on an employee's behalf must be paid over to him as soon as practicable. [*ITEPA 2003, Sch 2 paras 54–56*].

Access to partnership shares

An employee may at any time withdraw from the plan any or all of the partnership shares awarded to him. See **69.26** below for income tax consequences of withdrawal. [*ITEPA 2003, Sch 2 para 57*].

Matching shares

[69.24] In a plan providing for matching shares (see **69.20** above), the partnership share agreement (see **69.23** above) must specify the ratio of matching shares to partnership shares for the time being offered by the company and the circumstances and manner in which the ratio may be changed. The ratio must apply by reference to the *number* of shares and must not be greater than **two matching shares to each partnership share**. If the ratio changes before partnership shares are awarded under the agreement, employees must be notified accordingly. Matching shares must be of the same class and carry the same rights as the partnership shares to which they relate. They must be awarded (see **69.21** above) on the day the related partnership shares are awarded and must be awarded to all participants on exactly the same basis. See **69.30** below as to permitted provision for forfeiture. The provisions of *ITEPA 2003, Sch 2 paras 36, 37* (holding period and related matters — see **69.22** above) apply to matching shares as they apply to free shares. [*ITEPA 2003, Sch 2 paras 58–61*].

Dividend shares

[69.25] The plan *may* provide that, where the company so directs and subject to the limit below, all cash dividends on plan shares are to be reinvested in further shares ('*dividend shares*') on participants' behalf. Participants may be allowed to choose whether or not to reinvest. The company may revoke a direction. Where cash dividends are not required to be reinvested, they must be paid over to the participants.

The maximum dividend reinvestment per participant per tax year is £1,500. This is a global limit embracing all approved SIPs established by the company and its associated companies (within *ITEPA 2003, Sch 2 para 94*). Any cash dividends in excess of the limit must be paid over to the participant.

Dividend shares must be of the same class and carry the same rights as the shares on which the dividend is paid and must not be subject to any provision for forfeiture. The trustees must acquire dividend shares on participants' behalf (which includes their appropriating to participants shares already held by them) on the '*acquisition date*', which for this purpose is a date which is set by the trustees and is within 30 days after they receive the dividend. The number of shares acquired on behalf of each participant is to be determined by reference to market value at the acquisition date. There are provisions for carrying forward for future reinvestment, as a separately identifiable amount, any remaining balance, and for such amounts to be paid over to the participant in certain circumstances.

The holding period, during which dividend shares must not leave the plan (other than on cessation of employment), must be three years. In other respects, the provisions of *ITEPA 2003, Sch 2 paras 36, 37* (holding period and related matters — see **69.22** above) apply to dividend shares as they apply to free shares.

[*ITEPA 2003, Sch 2 paras 62–69; ITTOIA 2005, s 397A(7); FA 2008, s 34, Sch 12 para 4*].

Income tax consequences for participants

[69.26] An award of shares (see **69.21** above) to an employee, or an acquisition of dividend shares (see **69.25** above) on his behalf, under an approved SIP does not attract an income tax charge.

Neither the employer's nor the plan trustees' incidental expenses in running the plan can give rise to any income tax charge. This exemption is extended to cover any such incidental expenses of the company which established the plan (if different from the employer).

Neither the above exemption nor the income tax consequences below apply to an individual if, at the time of the award in question, his earnings (from the employment by reference to which he meets the employment requirement at **69.28** below) are not (or would not be if there were any) within the charge to UK tax on employment income.

The income tax exemptions do not apply if the shares are awarded or acquired under arrangements one of the main purposes of which is the avoidance of tax or national insurance contributions.

[*ITEPA 2003, ss 489–491, 494, 495, 499, 500; CTA 2010, Sch 1 para 391*].

Capital receipts

Where a 'capital receipt' is received by a participant in respect of, or by reference to, free, matching or partnership shares awarded to him fewer than five years previously or dividend shares acquired on his behalf fewer than three years previously, the amount or value of that receipt is chargeable to tax as employment income of the participant for the tax year of receipt (see below as regards PAYE). For these purposes, a '*capital receipt*' means any money or money's worth except to the extent that:

(A) it constitutes taxable income of the recipient (or would do so but for the exemptions conferred by these provisions);

(B) it consists of the disposal proceeds of the shares;

(C) it consists of the proceeds of a part disposal by the trustees (at the direction of the participant) of rights under a rights issue where those proceeds are used to take up other such rights;

(D) it consists of 'new shares' following a company reconstruction (see **69.31** below); or

(E) it is received by the participant's personal representatives after his death.

[*ITEPA 2003, ss 501, 502, Sch 2 para 99*].

Free or matching shares leaving plan

If free shares (see **69.22** above) or matching shares (see **69.24** above) cease to be subject to the plan (see **69.21** above) within less than five years of their being awarded to him, an amount is chargeable to tax as employment income of the participant (subject to the exceptions at (a)–(c) below) for the tax year in which the shares cease to be subject to the plan. If the shares leave the plan in less than three years, the chargeable amount is their market value (determined as in **69.22** above) when they leave the plan. If they leave the plan after three years or more but less than five years, the chargeable amount is the lower of their market value when they leave the plan and their market value at the date they were awarded. If the latter, the tax is reduced by any tax paid on 'capital receipts' (see above) in respect of the shares.

Any tax due as above is reduced by any tax paid by virtue of **69.10** above (shares with artificially enhanced market value) in relation to the shares.

If, within the holding period (see **69.22, 69.24** above) specified for the award of free or matching shares, the participant, in breach of his obligations under the plan, assigns, charges or otherwise disposes of his beneficial interest, then, instead of the above, the market value of the shares at the time they cease to be subject to the plan is chargeable to tax as employment income of the participant for the tax year in which that time falls.

There is no charge on free or matching shares leaving the plan after five years or more, nor is there any charge on the forfeiture of such shares.

[*ITEPA 2003, ss 497(1), 505, 507*].

There is no income tax charge on shares ceasing to be subject to the plan within five years by reason of the participant's ceasing to be in relevant employment (see **69.21** above) due to

(a) injury, disability, redundancy (as defined), his employer company losing its 'associated company' status (see **69.21** above), or a transfer within the *Transfer of Undertakings (Protection of Employment) Regulations 1981 (SI 1981 No 1794)*; or

(b) his retirement on or after reaching a retirement age specified in the plan, which must be not less than 50 and the same for men and women; or

(c) his death.

[*ITEPA 2003, s 498, Sch 2 paras 98, 99*].

Partnership shares generally

Deductions from an employee's salary in accordance with a partnership share agreement (see **69.23** above) are allowable deductions for income tax purposes. [*ITEPA 2003, s 492*].

Any amount deducted from an individual's salary but subsequently returned to him under any of the relevant provisions in **69.23** above is chargeable to tax as employment income of the individual for the tax year in which the amount is paid over to him. Any money or money's worth received by an individual in respect of the cancellation of a partnership share agreement entered into by him is chargeable to tax as employment income of the individual for the tax year of receipt. [*ITEPA 2003, ss 503, 504*].

Partnership shares leaving plan

If partnership shares (see **69.23** above) cease to be subject to the plan (see **69.21** above) within less than five years of the 'acquisition date', an amount is chargeable to tax as employment income of the participant (subject to the same exceptions as for free and matching shares — see (a)–(c) above) for the tax year in which the shares cease to be subject to the plan. (The *'acquisition date'* depends on whether or not there is an accumulation period, and is separately defined in **69.23** above for each such possibility.) If the shares leave the plan in less than three years, the chargeable amount is their market value (determined as in **69.22** above) when they leave the plan. If they leave the plan after three years or more but less than five years, the chargeable amount is the lower of their market value when they leave the plan and the amount of salary deductions used to acquire them. If the latter, the tax is reduced by any tax paid on 'capital receipts' (see above) in respect of the shares. Any tax due is reduced by any tax paid by virtue of **69.10** above (shares with artificially enhanced market value) in relation to the shares. There is no charge on partnership shares leaving the plan after five years or more. [*ITEPA 2003, ss 497(2), 506*].

Dividend shares generally

The amount applied by the trustees in acquiring dividend shares (see **69.25** above) on behalf of a participant is not treated as his income for any tax purposes. He is not entitled to a dividend tax credit in respect of amounts so applied (see *ITTOIA 2005, s 397*). Any balance carried forward as in **69.25** above is treated in the same way, but any amount eventually paid over to the participant is chargeable to income tax as if it were a dividend received by him (with accompanying tax credit) in the tax year in which it is paid over (see **1.5** ALLOWANCES AND TAX RATES and **64.7** *et seq.* SAVINGS AND INVESTMENT INCOME for taxation of dividends generally). (If the dividend was from a non-UK resident company, it potentially attracts a tax credit (see **64.13** SAVINGS AND INVESTMENT INCOME) if it is paid over in 2008/09 or a subsequent year, even if it arose before 2008/09. [*ITTOIA 2005, ss 393, 396, 405, 406, 770, Sch 1 paras 600, 601; ITEPA 2003, ss 493, 496, Sch 2 para 80(4), Sch 6 paras 10, 34; FA 2008, s 34, Sch 12 para 19; CTA 2010, Sch 1 para 396(5)*].

Dividend shares leaving the plan

If dividend shares (see **69.25** above) cease to be subject to the plan (see **69.21** above) within less than three years after their acquisition on the participant's behalf, the participant is chargeable to income tax on a notional dividend (subject to the same exceptions as for free and matching shares — see (a)–(c) above). The notional dividend is equal to the amount of cash dividend applied to acquire the shares, and is chargeable to income tax as if it were a dividend received by the participant (with accompanying tax credit) in the tax year in which the shares cease to be subject to the plan (see **1.5 ALLOWANCES AND TAX RATES** and **64.7** *et seq.* **SAVINGS AND INVESTMENT INCOME** for taxation of dividends generally). (If the cash dividend was from a non-UK resident company, the question of whether the notional dividend potentially attracts a tax credit (see **64.13 SAVINGS AND INVESTMENT INCOME**) is determined by reference to the date the shares cease to be subject to the plan.) The tax due (after deduction of tax credits) is reduced by any tax paid on 'capital receipts' (see above) in respect of the shares. There is no charge on dividend shares leaving the plan after three years or more. [*ITTOIA 2005, ss 394–396, 397A(7), 407, 408. Sch 1 para 602; ITEPA 2003, s 497(3), Sch 2 para 80(4)(5), Sch 6 paras 10, 34; FA 2008, s 34, Sch 12 paras 20, 21; CTA 2010, Sch 1 para 396(5)*].

PAYE

Where a tax charge arises as above on any shares leaving the plan and those shares are 'readily convertible assets', PAYE must be applied by the 'employer company'. A *'readily convertible asset'* is as defined in *ITEPA 2003, s 702* (see **53.4 PAY AS YOU EARN**) except that, in determining for these purposes whether or not shares fall within that definition, there is disregarded:

- any market for the shares which is created by virtue of the trustees acquiring shares for the plan and which exists solely for the purposes of the plan; and
- *ITEPA 2003, s 702(5A)–(5D)*, which in certain circumstances treat shares and securities as readily convertible assets even if they would otherwise not be (see **53.4 PAY AS YOU EARN**).

The *'employer company'* is the company which employs the participant in 'relevant employment' (see **69.21** above) at the time the shares cease to be subject to the plan, or , if the participant is not employed in relevant employment at that time, the company which last so employed him. The plan may require the participant to pay to the employer company a sum sufficient to meet the PAYE liability. Otherwise, the trustees must make such payment to the employer company (see **69.32** below as regards the raising of the necessary funds). The company must account for PAYE and return any unused balance to the participant. If there is no employer company, or if HMRC consider that it is impracticable for the employer company to make a PAYE deduction and they so direct, the obligation to make the deduction falls on the trustees instead. *ITEPA 2003, s 689* (non-UK employers — see **53.5 PAY AS YOU EARN**) is then disapplied.

[*ITEPA 2003, ss 509–512*].

Where the trustees receive a sum of money by way of a capital receipt chargeable to tax on receipt by the participant (see above), the trustees must pay to the 'employer company' (defined as above but by reference to the time of receipt by the trustees) the amount on which such tax is chargeable. The employer company must make a PAYE deduction and account to the participant for the net amount. The obligation to deduct PAYE and account for the net amount may be transferred to the trustees in similar circumstances to those described above. [*ITEPA 2003, ss 513, 514*].

Plan trustees

For the tax position of the trustees in respect of dividends on unappropriated shares, see **69.32** below.

Capital gains tax

[69.27] A participant is treated for capital gains tax purposes as absolutely entitled as against the plan trustees to any shares awarded to him under an approved SIP. Shares ceasing to be subject to the plan (see **69.21** above) at any time are deemed to have been disposed of and immediately reacquired by the participant at their then market value, but no chargeable gain or allowable loss arises on the deemed disposal. If any of a participant's shares are forfeited (see **69.30** below as regards provision for forfeiture), they are deemed to have been disposed of by the participant and acquired by the plan trustees at their market value at the date of forfeiture, but again no chargeable gain or allowable loss arises. [*TCGA 1992, Sch 7D paras 1, 3, 5, 7*]. A form of rollover relief is available for shares transferred (other than by a company) to the trustees of an approved SIP. [*TCGA 1992, s 236A, Sch 7C; ITA 2007, Sch 1 para 348*].

For details, see Tolley's Capital Gains Tax under Employee Share Schemes.

Eligibility of employees

[69.28] An approved SIP must provide that only an individual who is eligible may participate in an award of shares (see **69.21** above), such eligibility to be judged, in the case of free shares, at the time the award is made and, in the case of partnership shares (and related matching shares), at the time of the salary deduction relating to the award or, if there is an accumulation period (see **69.23** above), the first such salary deduction. An individual is eligible only if the requirements (as detailed below) as to employment, no material interest and participation in other schemes are met. An individual who is not a 'UK resident taxpayer' (as defined in **69.21** above) must satisfy any further eligibility requirements set out in the plan. [*ITEPA 2003, Sch 2 para 14*].

Employment

The individual must be an employee of the company which established the plan or, in the case of a group plan, of a constituent company (see **69.20** above). The plan *may* provide for a qualifying period, in which case the individual is required to have been at all times during that period an employee of the company or of a company that is a constituent company at the end of that period. This condition can also be satisfied by reference to employment with an associated company (as in **69.21** above and judged as at the time of that employment) and, in the case of a group plan, with a company that was a constituent company at the time of that employment or with a then associated company of such a company. The qualifying period, if any, must be:

(i)   (in the case of free shares) a period of not more than 18 months ending with the date of the award; and

(ii)   (in the case of partnership shares and related matching shares) a period of not more than 18 months ending with the salary deduction related to the award, or, where relevant, a period of not more than six months ending with the start of the accumulation period (see **69.23** above) related to the award.

In relation to an award, the same qualifying period must apply in relation to all employees of the company or, where applicable, of the constituent companies. The plan may authorise the company to specify different qualifying periods in respect of different awards.

[*ITEPA 2003, Sch 2 paras 15–17*].

No material interest

An individual is not eligible to participate in an award if he has, or has had within the preceding 12 months, a 'material interest' in:

(a)   a close company whose shares may be awarded under the plan; or

(b)   a company which has control (within *ITA 2007, s 995*) of such a company or is a member of a consortium which owns such a company. (For this purpose, a company is a member of a consortium owning another company if it is one of a number of companies which between them beneficially own at least 75% of, and each of which beneficially owns at least 5% of, the other company's ordinary share capital.)

For these purposes, an individual has a '*material interest*' in a company if he, and/or certain associates of his (within *ITEPA 2003, Sch 2 paras 22–24 as amended*):

(1)   beneficially owns or controls (directly or indirectly) more than 25% of ordinary share capital; or

(2)   (where the company is a close company, or would be but for being a non-UK resident company or a quoted company) possesses or is entitled to acquire rights to more than 25% of the assets available for distribution among the participators (within *CTA 2010, s 454*) in a winding-up or in any other circumstances.

Rights to acquire shares must be taken into account (in accordance with *ITEPA 2003, Sch 2 para 21*). Shares or rights held by trustees of an approved SIP and *not* appropriated to, or acquired on behalf of, any individual are disregarded.

[*ITEPA 2003, s 719, Sch 2 paras 19–24, 99(3), Sch 7 para 87; ITA 2007, Sch 1 para 443; CTA 2010, Sch 1 para 396(2)*].

Participation in other schemes

An individual is not eligible to participate in an award of free, matching or partnership shares under an approved SIP at the same time as participating in an award under another approved SIP established by the same company or by a 'connected company' (simultaneous participation). It also used to be the case that an individual was also not eligible to participate in an award if he had in the same tax year participated in an award under another approved SIP established by the same company or by a 'connected company' (successive participation). From 10 July 2003, successive participation *is* permitted but the limits on the number of free shares an individual can obtain, the amount of salary he can invest in partnership shares and the amount that can be reinvested on his behalf in dividend shares apply as if all such plans were a single plan. For these purposes, an individual is treated as having participated in an award of free shares under a SIP if he would have done so but for his failure to obtain a performance allowance (see **69.29** below).

For these purposes, a *'connected company'* is:

(I)   a company which controls (within *ITA 2007, s 995*) the first company, or which is controlled by the first company, or which is controlled by a company which also controls the first company; or

(II)   a company which is a member of a consortium (as in (b) above) owning the first company or which is owned in part by the first company as a member of a consortium.

[*ITEPA 2003, s 719, Sch 2 paras 18, 18A; ITA 2007, Sch 1 para 443*].

Performance allowances

[69.29] If the plan provides for performance allowances, i.e. for the award of free shares, or the number or value of free shares awarded, to be conditional on performance targets being met, the company must use one of the two methods described below.

Under *Method 1*, in relation to a particular award of shares (see **69.21** above):

(a)   at least 20% of the shares must be awarded other than by reference to performance; and

(b)   the highest performance-related award (in terms of the number of shares) made to any individual must not exceed four times the highest non-performance-related award so made.

If different classes of share are awarded, the above applies separately in relation to each class. The overall requirement (at **69.21** above) to award free shares on similar terms to all participating employees is disapplied as regards the performance-related shares.

Under *Method 2*, in relation to a particular award of shares, some or all of the shares must be awarded by reference to performance, and the overall requirement to award free shares on similar terms to all participating employees is applied separately as regards each performance unit. The performance targets set must be consistent, which means they must be capable of being reasonably viewed as being comparable in terms of the likelihood of their being met by the performance units to which they apply.

Whichever method is used, performance allowances in relation to an award must be available to each qualifying employee. Performance targets must be set for performance units comprising one or more employees, and performance measures must be based on business results or other objective criteria and be fair and objective measures of the performance of the applicable units. An employee cannot belong to more than one performance unit for the purposes of a particular award of free shares. The plan must require:

(i)   performance targets and measures to be notified to prospective participants; and

(ii)   (in general terms and subject to reasonable considerations as to commercial confidentiality) performance measures to be notified to all qualifying employees (see **69.21** above) of the company (or of all constituent companies under a group plan),

such notifications to be given as soon as reasonably practicable.

[*ITEPA 2003, Sch 2 paras 34(4), 38–42*].

Requirements as to type of share used

[69.30] The requirements below must all be met with respect to any shares ('*eligible shares*') that may be awarded under an approved SIP.

Eligible shares must form part of the ordinary share capital of:

(a)   the company which established the plan;

(b)   a company which has control (within *ITA 2007, s 995*) of the company in (a) above;

(c)   a company which is a member of a consortium (as in **69.28**(b) above) owning either the company in (a) above or a company within (b) above; or

(d)   a company which has control of a company within (c) above.

Eligible shares must be:

(i)   shares of a class listed on a recognised stock exchange;

(ii)   shares in a company not under the control (within *ITA 2007, s 995*) of another company; or

(iii)   shares in a company under the control of a company (other than a close company) whose shares are listed on a recognised stock exchange. Reference here to a close company includes a company which would be a close company if it were UK resident.

Eligible shares must be fully paid up and, except in relation to shares in certain co-operatives (as defined), not redeemable (or capable of becoming redeemable). Shares are not fully paid up for this purpose if there is any undertaking to pay cash to the company at a future date.

Eligible shares must not be subject to any restrictions (as to their disposal or the exercise of rights conferred etc. — see *ITEPA 2003, Sch 2 para 30(2)–(4)* for full definition and disregards) other than:

(A)   those involved in there being a holding period (i.e. for free, matching and dividend shares — see respectively **69.22, 69.24, 69.25** above);

(B)   those affecting all ordinary shares in the company; or

(C)   permitted restrictions as to voting rights, provision for forfeiture or pre-emption conditions (see below in each case).

Eligible shares must not be shares in a '*service company*', i.e. a company whose business is substantially the provision of the services of its employees either to persons, including partnerships, who control the company or to associated companies (as specially defined for this purpose). The prohibition extends to shares in certain companies which have control of service companies. '*Control*' for these purposes is determined in accordance with *CTA 2010, ss 450, 451*.

[*ITEPA 2003, s 719, Sch 2 paras 2(2), 25–30; ITA 2007, Sch 1 para 443; CTA 2010, Sch 1 para 396(3)*].

Voting rights

Eligible shares may be shares carrying no voting rights or limited voting rights.

Provision for forfeiture

Provision for forfeiture (i.e. provision to the effect that a participant shall cease to be beneficially entitled to the plan shares on the occurrence of certain events). As regards free or matching shares (see **69.22, 69.24** above), provision may be made for forfeiture if the participant:

(1)   ceases to be in relevant employment (see **69.21** above); or

(2)   withdraws the shares from the plan (see **69.21** above),

within the '*forfeiture period*', i.e. a period not exceeding three years as specified in the plan and beginning with the date on which the shares were awarded (see **69.21** above) to the participant. However, shares cannot be made subject to provision for forfeiture in the event of shares ceasing to be subject to the plan for any of the reasons at **69.26**(a)–(c) above. As regards matching shares only, provision may be made for forfeiture if the participant withdraws from the plan, within the said forfeiture period, the partnership shares in respect of which the matching shares were awarded to him. Forfeiture cannot be linked to performance, and the same provision for forfeiture, if any, must apply to all free or matching shares included in the same award.

Pre-emption conditions

Eligible shares may be made subject to provision requiring shares awarded to an employee and held by him (or by a permitted transferee under the company's articles) to be offered for sale on his ceasing to be in relevant employment (see **69.21** above). Such provision can be made only if, under the company's articles, the same provision applies to all employees, the shares must be offered for sale at a specified price, and anyone disposing of shares of the class in question (whether or not as an employee) is required to offer them for sale on no better terms.

[*ITEPA 2003, Sch 2 paras 31–33, 99(1)*].

Company reconstructions

[69.31] For the purposes of the SIP provisions (and subject to the rules below for rights issues):

(a)   a company reconstruction (see below) is treated as not involving a disposal of shares comprised in the original holding;

(b)   new shares (see below) are deemed to have been awarded to (or acquired on behalf of) a participant on the date the corresponding original shares were awarded or so acquired;

(c)   the requirements at **69.30** above are treated as fulfilled with respect to new shares if they were fulfilled (or treated as fulfilled) with respect to the original shares;

(d)   references throughout the provisions to a participant's plan shares are to be construed as including any new shares; and

(e)   the tax provisions at **69.26, 69.27** above apply to new shares as they would have applied to the original shares.

If, as part of a company reconstruction, the trustees become entitled to a capital receipt, their entitlement is deemed to arise before the new holding comes into being.

For the above purposes, a '*company reconstruction*' is a transaction in relation to any of a participant's plan shares:

(i)   which results in a new holding being equated with the original holding for capital gains tax purposes (see Tolley's Capital Gains Tax under Shares and Securities); or

(ii)   which would do so but for the new holding consisting of or including a qualifying corporate bond (see Tolley's Capital Gains Tax under Qualifying Corporate Bonds),

and '*new shares*' means shares, securities and rights comprised in the new holding. Certain share issues treated as distributions chargeable to income tax are treated for the purposes of these provisions as *not* forming part of the new holding.

[*ITEPA 2003, Sch 2 paras 86, 87; CTA 2010, Sch 1 para 396(6)*].

Rights issues

Subject to the exceptions below, where the trustees take up rights under a rights issue in respect of a participant's plan shares, the resulting new shares or securities or rights are treated as synonymous with the original shares. This does not apply where:

(A)   the funds used to acquire the new shares etc. are provided other than by the part disposal of rights in order to take up other rights under the issue; or

(B)   the rights are not conferred in respect of all ordinary shares in the company.

Where the rule is disapplied, the new shares etc. are not plan shares and do not fall to be equated with the original shares for capital gains tax purposes.

[*ITEPA 2003, Sch 2 paras 88, 99(1)*].

The plan trustees

[69.32] A SIP must provide for the establishment of a trust, constituted under UK law and consisting of UK-resident trustees, the principal duties of the trustees being to acquire shares and appropriate them as free or matching shares to employees, and to acquire partnership and dividend shares on behalf of employees, in accordance with the plan. The trustees' other duties must include:

(a) giving an employee notice of shares awarded to him and of dividend shares acquired on his behalf, such notice to include specified information;

(b) maintaining such records as may be necessary for the purposes of their own, and the employer's, plan-related PAYE obligations (see **69.26** above);

(c) (where relevant) giving a participant notice of any foreign tax deducted at source from plan share dividends from a non-UK resident company;

(d) informing a participant of the facts relevant to determining any income tax liability which he incurs under these provisions; and

(e) maintaining records of individuals who have participated in other approved SIPs established by the same company or a connected company (see **69.28** above).

The trust instrument must require the trustees to act only at the direction of a participant as regards disposing of his plan shares and dealing with rights issues, but, except in the case of partnership shares, must also prohibit them from disposing of shares (to the participant or otherwise), except in certain specified circumstances, within the holding period for those shares (see **69.22, 69.24, 69.25** above), unless the participant has ceased to be in relevant employment (see **69.21** above). The plan may provide for participants' directions to be given in general terms. Subject to the above, the trustees may partly dispose of rights under a rights issue in order to raise funds to take up other rights under the issue. With certain exceptions, the trust instrument must require the trustees to account to participants for any money or money's worth received by them in respect of or by reference to plan shares.

The plan must provide for the trustees to raise funds to meet PAYE obligations on shares leaving the plan (see **69.26** above), either by disposing of a participant's plan shares (including a disposal to themselves as trustees) or by obtaining the necessary amount from the participant.

If authorised by the trust instrument, the trustees may borrow to acquire shares and for other specified purposes.

The trust instrument:

(i) must provide that shares acquired by the trustees by way of qualifying transfer of relevant shares from a qualifying employee share ownership trust are not awarded under the plan as partnership shares but are otherwise awarded in priority to other available shares; and

(ii) must not contain any terms which are neither essential nor reasonably incidental to complying with the statutory requirements.

The trust instrument *may* contain provision for at least half of the non-professional trustees to be selected from the employees of participating companies.

[*ITEPA 2003, Sch 2 paras 70–80, 99(1)*].

Tax exemption for dividends on unappropriated shares

Tax is not chargeable at the dividend trust rate (see **68.11** SETTLEMENTS) in respect of dividends or other distributions on shares held by the trustees on their own account, provided that the shares satisfy the requirements at **69.30** above as to the type of share that may be used in the plan and are awarded (see **69.21** above) (or acquired as dividend shares) within a statutory period. The period within which shares must be awarded depends on whether or not any of the shares in the company in question are 'readily convertible assets' (see **69.26** above under PAYE) at the time of the acquisition of shares by the trustees. If they are, the period is the two years from acquisition. Otherwise, it is five years from acquisition, but if within those five years any of the shares in the company become readily convertible assets the period ends no later than two years after the date on which they did so. For these purposes:

(A)   shares of a particular class are deemed to be awarded by the trustees on a first in/first out basis; and

(B)   shares subject to provision for forfeiture (see **69.30** above) are deemed to be acquired by the trustees if and when forfeiture occurs.

The period within which shares must be awarded is extended to ten years from acquisition if the shares are part of a significant block of shares acquired by the trustees in relation to which the employer company has been given an up-front corporation tax deduction (see **73.60** TRADING INCOME).

[*ITA 2007, ss 488–490; ICTA 1988, ss 686B, 686C; CTA 2009, Sch 1 para 70*].

For *capital gains tax* matters relevant to the trustees, see Tolley's Capital Gains Tax under Employee Share Schemes.

HMRC approval

[69.33] On written application by the company, HMRC will approve a SIP if they are satisfied that it meets the statutory requirements. Applications must contain such particulars and be supported by such evidence as HMRC may require. The company may appeal within 30 days against refusal of HMRC approval. On a successful appeal to the Appeal Tribunal, the Tribunal may direct HMRC to approve the plan from a specified date no earlier than the original date of application. [*ITEPA 2003, Sch 2 paras 81, 82; SI 2009 No 56, Sch 1 para 341*].

Withdrawal of approval

If any disqualifying event occurs, HMRC may by notice withdraw their approval of the plan with effect from, at the earliest, the time of the disqualifying event. The withdrawal does not affect the treatment of shares awarded to participants (see **69.21** above) before the effective time of withdrawal. Any of the following is a disqualifying event:

(a)   a contravention, in relation to the operation of the plan, of any of the statutory requirements, the plan itself or the plan trust;

(b)   an alteration made in a 'key feature' of the plan or in the terms of the plan trust without HMRC approval (see further below);

(c)   the setting under *Method 2* of performance targets that are not consistent (see **69.29** above);

(d)   an alteration in the share capital of the company whose shares are the subject of the plan, or in the rights attaching to any of its shares, that materially affects the value of plan shares;

(e)   plan shares of a particular class receiving different treatment from the other shares of that class, particularly in respect of dividends (other than in limited circumstances as specified), repayment, restrictions, or any offer of substituted or additional shares, securities or rights of any kind in respect of the shares (see further below);

(f)   the trustees, the company, or, in the case of a group plan, any company which is or has been a constituent company failing to furnish any information called for under HMRC's information powers below.

HMRC are not to withhold approval to an alteration within (b) above unless it appears to them that the plan, as altered, would not receive approval on an initial application. As regards (e) above, there is no disqualifying event where the difference in treatment arises from a 'key feature' or from any participants' shares being subject to provision for forfeiture (see **69.30** above). For the above purposes, a *'key feature'* of a plan is a provision of the plan that is necessary in order to meet the statutory requirements.

The company may appeal, within 30 days, against a withdrawal of approval, an associated withdrawal of corporation tax relief (see **73.60** TRADING INCOME), or a refusal to approve an alteration as in (b) above.

[*ITEPA 2003, Sch 2 paras 83–85, Sch 7 para 68(4)9; CTA 2009, Sch 1 para 557; FA 2010, s 42(2)(3)(7); SI 2009 No 56, Sch 1 para 342*].

Applications for approval should be sent to HMRC, Employee Shares and Securities Unit, Nottingham Team, 1st Floor, Ferrers House, Castle Meadow Road, Nottingham, NG2 1BB.

HMRC information powers

HMRC have wide-ranging powers to require any person to furnish them with such information as they reasonably require and as that person possesses or can reasonably obtain. The information must be supplied within a period specified in the notice, which must not be less than three months. Penalties under *TMA 1970, s 98* are exigible for non-compliance. [*ITEPA 2003, Sch 2 para 93, Sch 6 para 137*].

Termination of plan

[69.34] A SIP may provide for the company to terminate the plan in such circumstances as the plan may specify. This is accomplished by the issue of a plan termination notice, a copy of which must be given without delay to HMRC, the plan trustees and each individual who has plan shares or has entered into a current partnership share agreement. Any money held on an individual's behalf by the plan trustees must be paid over to him as soon as practicable after the plan termination notice is issued. Plan shares must be removed from the plan as soon as practicable after the end of three months following the distribution of the plan termination notice or, if later, after the first date on which they may be removed without giving rise to an income tax charge (see **69.26** above). Shares may be removed earlier with the consent of the participant (or, after his death, his personal representatives). The trustees can remove shares from the plan either by transferring them to, or at the direction of, the participant (or his personal representatives) or by disposing of them and similarly accounting for the proceeds.

[*ITEPA 2003, Sch 2 paras 89, 90*].

Enterprise Management Incentives

[69.35] 'Small higher risk' trading companies are able to grant options over shares worth (at time of grant) up to £120,000 (£100,000 before 6 April 2008) to eligible employees without income tax consequences (except to the extent that the option is to acquire shares at less than their market value at time of grant). The total value of shares in respect of which unexercised options exist must not exceed £3 million. Any gain on sale of the shares by the employee is chargeable to capital gains tax (see **69.37** below).

The company may be quoted or unquoted but must be an independent company trading or preparing to trade wholly or mainly in the UK (but see below), whose gross assets do not exceed £30 million and (for options granted on or after 21 July 2008) which has less than 250 full-time employees. A company carrying on certain specified activities does not qualify, such exclusions being similar to those at **28.50**(a)–(m) ENTERPRISE INVESTMENT SCHEME. Broadly, an employee is eligible if he is employed by the company for at least 25 hours per week or, if less, at least 75% of his total working time, and he controls no more than 30% of the company's ordinary share capital. Companies are not required to obtain HMRC approval to schemes but must give notification to HMRC within 92 days after an option is granted.

[*ITEPA 2003, ss 527–541, Sch 5; FA 2008, s 33*].

It is proposed to relax the requirement that the company be trading etc. wholly or mainly in the UK. Instead, a company will be required only to have a permanent establishment in the UK. The legislation will be included in a Finance Bill to be introduced in autumn 2010. The change will have effect for options granted on or after the date that the legislation receives Royal Assent. (HMRC Budget Note BN10, 22 June 2010).

HMRC will on request give written advance assurance that a company will be a qualifying company for these purposes, though not about any other aspect of the scheme. Applications should be made in writing to Small Company Enterprise Centre, HM Revenue and Customs, 1st Floor, Ferrers House, Castle Meadow Road, Nottingham, NG2 1BB and must be accompanied by all relevant information, including latest accounts, memorandum and articles, and details of trading activities, covering in each case the company and each of its subsidiaries. (Revenue Press Release BN6, 7 March 2001).

See generally the guidance at www.hmrc.gov.uk/shareschemes/emi-new-guida nce.htm.

Qualifying options

[69.36] A qualifying option is an option (i.e. a right to acquire shares) in relation to which the general requirements below and the further requirements at **69.38–69.41** below are met at the time it is granted, and of which notice is given to HMRC as in **69.43** below. [*ITEPA 2003, s 527, Sch 5 para 1*].

The option must be granted for commercial reasons in order to recruit or retain an employee in a company, and not as part of a tax avoidance scheme or arrangement. It must be granted to the employee by reason of his employment with the '*relevant company*' (i.e. the company whose shares are the subject of the option) or, if the relevant company is a parent company, his employment with that company or another member of the group. See **69.38** below as to qualifying companies and **69.40** below as to eligible employees. See **69.41** below for requirements as to the terms of the option, including the type of share that may be acquired.

The total value (see below) of shares in the relevant company in respect of which unexercised qualifying options exist must not exceed £3 million. If the limit is already exceeded at the time an option is granted, that option is not a qualifying option. If the grant of an option causes the limit to be exceeded, that option is not a qualifying option so far as it relates to the excess. For this purpose, where more than one option is granted simultaneously, the excess is divided *pro rata* between them according to the value of shares which each represents.

Maximum entitlement

An employee cannot at any time hold unexercised qualifying options in respect of shares with a total value (see below) of more than £120,000 (£100,000 before 6 April 2008). If the limit is already exceeded at the time an option is granted, that option is not a qualifying option. If the grant of an option causes the limit to be exceeded, that option is not a qualifying option so far as it relates to the excess. Where an employee has been granted qualifying options in respect of shares with a total value of £120,000, then, whether or not those options remain unexercised (and disregarding any release of options), no further *qualifying* option may be granted to him within three years after the date of grant of the last qualifying option. If, at the time an option is granted under these provisions, the employee holds unexercised options under an approved CSOP scheme (as in **69.49** below), those options count towards the limit as if they were qualifying options.

The £120,000 limit is a global limit covering options granted by reason of employment with one company or with any number of companies in the same group. The legislation is framed to prevent the above provisions being circumvented if options are granted to an individual by reference to his employment with different companies within a group.

For the above purposes, the value of shares is the market value (determined as for capital gains tax purposes), *at the time the option is granted*, of shares of the same class, and an option is treated as granted in respect of the maximum number of shares that may be acquired under it. Where the market value of shares on any date falls to be determined for any purpose of these provisions, HMRC and the employer company may agree that it be determined by reference to a different date or a number of specified dates. If market value is not agreed between HMRC and the employer company, HMRC have power to determine it. The employer company may appeal within 30 days against a notice of determination (see also **69.46** below as regards compliance with time limits). Alternatively, the company may, by notice to HMRC before a notice of determination is given, refer the question of market value to the Appeal Tribunal, who must then determine it in like manner as on appeal. In arriving at the market value of restricted shares as in **69.4** above, the restrictions (or risk of forfeiture) are disregarded.

[*ITEPA 2003, Sch 5 paras 1(3)(d), 2–7, 54–57; SI 2008 No 706; SI 2009 No 56, Sch 1 paras 355, 356*].

For HMRC practice on the determination of market value, see Revenue Share Focus Newsletter May 2007 p 3.

See **69.43** below re possibility and consequences of HMRC enquiry into an option.

Tax consequences of qualifying option

[69.37] No income tax is chargeable on the *receipt* of a qualifying option. The *exercise* of a qualifying option attracts the following special treatment (but only if it occurs within ten years after the time of the grant). Subject to any disqualifying event (see below), no income tax charge arises under **69.15** above on the exercise of a qualifying option to acquire shares at not less than their market value at the time of the grant. On the exercise of a qualifying option to acquire shares at nil cost or otherwise at less than their market value at the time of the grant, an amount is chargeable under **69.15** above, but is limited (if it would otherwise be greater) to the excess of the 'chargeable market value' over the aggregate of any consideration given for the option itself and (if any) the amount for which the shares are acquired. If there is no such excess, no charge arises. The '*chargeable market value*' is the lower of:

(a)   the market value of the shares at the time of grant; and
(b)   the market value of the shares at the time the option is exercised.

[*ITEPA 2003, ss 419, 475, 528–531, 532(6)*].

For guidance on the interaction between the above rules and the restricted shares rules at **69.4** above (where the shares acquired on exercise are restricted shares), see www.hmrc.gov.uk/shareschemes/faq_emprelatedsecurity-ch2.htm w.

In their application in relation to a 'UK resident employee', the notional loan provisions at **69.11** above in respect of shares acquired at less than market value do not apply in relation to shares acquired by the exercise of a qualifying option (whether or not at a discount). For this purpose, an employee is a '*UK resident employee*' if, judged at the time of either the grant or the exercise of the option, the earnings from the employment are (or would be if there were any) general earnings within **27.4 EMPLOYMENT INCOME** (earnings for year when employee resident in UK) or, before 2008/09, within **27.9 EMPLOYMENT INCOME** (earnings for year when employee resident, ordinarily resident and domiciled in UK) or *ITEPA 2003, s 21* (earnings, other than chargeable overseas earnings, for year when employee resident and ordinarily resident but not domiciled in UK — see **27.10 EMPLOYMENT INCOME**). [*ITEPA 2003, s 540; FA 2008, Sch 7 paras 34, 81*].

Other than on *exercise* of the qualifying option, there is no exemption from the charge at **69.15** above (e.g. on release of the option). In addition, the provisions at **69.4–69.10, 69.12** and **69.13** above all apply to shares acquired under a qualifying option as they would to other employment-related shares. However, amounts deductible in computing the chargeable amount under **69.5** above (restricted shares), i.e. in ascertaining the value of IUP in the given formula, include the amount (or additional amount) that would have been chargeable under **69.15** above on exercise if the shares had not been acquired under a qualifying option. [*ITEPA 2003, s 541*].

Disqualifying events

Where a 'disqualifying event' occurs in relation to a qualifying option before it is exercised, and the option is not exercised within 40 days after the date of that event, an amount is chargeable under **69.15** above on the eventual exercise of the option. The amount chargeable is:

- (where there would otherwise be no charge) the 'post-event gain' (if any) less any consideration given for the option itself; or
- the amount otherwise chargeable under *ITEPA 2003, s 531* (above) plus the 'post-event gain',

but not so as to substitute a greater chargeable amount than would be the case if these provisions (including *ITEPA 2003, ss 530, 531*) were disregarded. The 'post-event gain' is the amount (if any) by which the market value of the shares on exercise exceeds their market value immediately before the disqualifying event.

Any of the following is a '*disqualifying event*' in relation to a qualifying option.

(i) The 'relevant company' (see **69.36** above) becomes a 51% subsidiary of another company or otherwise comes under the control of another company (with or without the aid of **CONNECTED PERSONS (21)**). In a case where a replacement option has been granted (see **69.42** below), such an event is not a disqualifying event in relation to the original option if it occurred during the period beginning at the same time as the period within which the replacement had to be granted and ending with the release of rights under the old option.

(ii) The relevant company ceases to meet the trading activities requirement (see **69.38** below).

(iii) The relevant company was a qualifying company by virtue only of its *preparing to carry on* a qualifying trade (see **69.38, 69.39** below), and either the preparations cease or two years elapse from the date of grant without the relevant company or any company in its group commencing that trade.

(iv)   The employee ceases to be an eligible employee in relation to the relevant company by reason of his ceasing to satisfy the requirements at **69.40**(a) or (b) below (and see also below as to actual working time).

(v)   A variation is made of the terms of the option, the effect of which is to increase the market value of the option shares or that the statutory requirements would no longer be met in relation to the option.

(vi)   An alteration of a specified kind (see *ITEPA 2003, s 537(2)*) is made to the share capital of the relevant company where the effect is either:

- to increase the market value of the option shares, where the alteration is not made by the relevant company for commercial reasons or the said increase is one of its main purposes; or

- that the statutory requirements would no longer be met in relation to the option.

(vii)   Any of the shares to which the option relates are converted to shares of a different class. There is an exception, and subject to conditions, where all the shares of one class only are converted into shares of one other class only.

(viii)   The employee is granted a CSOP option (i.e. an option under an approved CSOP scheme — see **69.61** below) by reason of his employment with the same company or by a company in the same group as that company, *and* immediately afterwards holds unexercised 'employee options' in respect of shares with a total value of over £120,000 (£100,000 before 6 April 2008). For this purpose, *'employee options'* include the qualifying option in question and any other qualifying option or CSOP option granted by reason of employment with the same company or group.

In addition, a disqualifying event is treated as occurring in relation to a qualifying option *at the end of any tax year* if, during that year (disregarding any part of it before the option was granted), the average amount per week of the employee's 'reckonable time in relevant employment' was less than 25 hours or, if less, 75% of his 'working time' (as defined in **69.40**(b) below). An employee's *'reckonable time in relevant employment'* is the time he spent, as an employee in 'relevant employment' (as defined in **69.40**(b) below), on the business of the relevant company or, if it is a parent company, of its group (inclusive of any permissible periods of absence as in **69.40**(b) below).

[*ITEPA 2003, ss 419, 532–539, 718, Sch 5 paras 2, 54, Sch 7 para 78(2); ITA 2007, Sch 1 para 442; CTA 2010, Sch 1 para 392; SI 2008 No 706*].

The comments in **69.36** above regarding the market value of shares apply equally for the above purposes.

Internationally mobile employees

For an article on the imposition of income tax charges under the above provisions in the case of internationally mobile employees, including examples and the impact of double tax agreements, see Revenue Tax Bulletins August 2002 pp 951–954 and April 2005 pp 1193–1199 (the latter superseding Revenue Tax Bulletin October 2001 pp 883–887). For associated national insurance contributions liabilities, see Revenue Tax Bulletin December 2001 pp 895–899. See also HMRC Employment-Related Securities Manual ERSM160100.

Capital gains tax consequences

The cost of acquisition of shares acquired under a qualifying option is computed according to the rules at **69.15** above. In contrast to the rule for other types of option though, the period of ownership of the shares for taper relief (now abolished) normally runs from the date a qualifying option is granted and not the date it is exercised, though special rules apply if a disqualifying event (as above) occurs. For the detailed provisions, see Tolley's Capital Gains Tax under Employee Share Schemes.

Qualifying companies

[69.38] The company whose shares are the subject of the option must be a qualifying company. [*ITEPA 2003, Sch 5 para 1(3)(b)*]. To be a qualifying company, it must, at the time the option is granted, meet the requirements detailed below as to independence, qualifying subsidiaries, property managing subsidiaries, gross assets, number of employees (for options granted on or after 21 July 2008) and trading activities. [*ITEPA 2003, Sch 5 paras 1(4), 8; FA 2008, s 33(2)(6)*]. The company may be quoted or unquoted, and there is no requirement that it be UK resident (though see **69.39**(i) below as regards qualifying trades).

Independence

The company must not be a 51% subsidiary of another company or otherwise under the control (within *ITA 2007, s 995*) of another company, or of another company and persons connected with it (within **21 CONNECTED PERSONS**). No arrangements must exist whereby the company could become such a subsidiary or fall under such control. 'Arrangements' is very broadly defined, but for this purpose any arrangements with a view to a 'qualifying exchange of shares' (see **69.42** below) are disregarded. [*ITEPA 2003, ss 718, 719, Sch 5 paras 9, 58; ITA 2007, Sch 1 paras 442, 443*].

Qualifying subsidiaries

If the company has subsidiaries, each 'subsidiary' must be a 'qualifying subsidiary'. A *'subsidiary'* is a company which the company controls (within *CTA 2010, ss 450, 451*), with or without the aid of **CONNECTED PERSONS (21)**. A subsidiary is a *'qualifying subsidiary'* of a company (the holding company) if the following conditions are met.

The subsidiary must be a **51%** subsidiary (see *CTA 2010, Pt 24 Ch 3*) of the holding company and no person other than the holding company or another of its subsidiaries may have control (within *ITA 2007, s 995*) of the subsidiary. Furthermore, no arrangements (as very broadly defined) may exist by virtue of which either of these conditions would cease to be satisfied.

The above conditions are not regarded as ceasing to be met by reason only of the subsidiary or any other company being in the process of being wound up or by reason only of anything done as a consequence of its being in administration or receivership (both as defined by *ITA 2007, s 252*), provided the winding-up, entry into administration or receivership or anything done as a consequence of its being in administration or receivership is for commercial reasons and is not part of a tax avoidance scheme or arrangements.

The above conditions are not regarded as ceasing to be satisfied by reason only of arrangements being in existence for the disposal of the interest in the subsidiary held by the holding company (or, as the case may be, by another of its subsidiaries) if the disposal is to be for commercial reasons and is not to be part of a tax avoidance scheme or arrangements.

[*ITEPA 2003, ss 718, 719, Sch 5 paras 10, 11, 58; ITA 2007, s 989, Sch 1 paras 442, 443, 450(2); CTA 2010, Sch 1 paras 399(2), 562(8)*].

Property managing subsidiaries

The company must not have a 'property managing subsidiary' which is not a 'qualifying 90% subsidiary' of the company. A *'property managing subsidiary'* is a qualifying subsidiary (see above) whose business consists wholly or mainly in the holding or managing of land or any 'property deriving its value from land' (as defined by *ITA 2007, s 188(3)* — see **4.29 ANTI-AVOIDANCE**).

A company (the subsidiary) is a *'qualifying 90% subsidiary'* of another company (the holding company) if:

- the holding company possesses at least **90%** of both the issued share capital of, and the voting power in, the subsidiary;
- the holding company would be beneficially entitled to at least **90%** of the assets of the subsidiary available for distribution to shareholders on a winding-up or in any other circumstances;
- the holding company is beneficially entitled to at least **90%** of any profits of the subsidiary available for distribution to shareholders;
- no person other than the holding company has control (within *ITA 2007, s 995*) of the subsidiary; and
- no arrangements (as very broadly defined) exist by virtue of which any of the above conditions would cease to be met.

The above conditions are not regarded as ceasing to be met by reason only of the subsidiary or any other company being in the process of being wound up or by reason only of anything done as a consequence of its being in administration or receivership (both as defined by *ITA 2007, s 252*), provided the winding-up, entry into administration or receivership or anything done as a consequence of its being in administration or receivership is for commercial reasons and is not part of a tax avoidance scheme or arrangements. Nor are they regarded as ceasing to be met by reason only of arrangements being in existence for the disposal of the holding company's interest in the subsidiary if the disposal is to be for commercial reasons and is not to be part of a tax avoidance scheme or arrangements.

[*ITEPA 2003, s 719, Sch 5 paras 11A, 11B, 58; ITA 2007, Sch 1 para 443; CTA 2010, Sch 1 para 399(3)*].

Gross assets

The value of the company's gross assets must not exceed £30 million. If the company is the parent company of a group, that limit applies by reference to the aggregate value of the gross assets of the group (disregarding certain assets held by any member of the group which correspond to liabilities of another member). The limit may be amended in the future by Treasury Order. [*ITEPA 2003, Sch 5 paras 12, 54; SI 2001 No 3799*].

See HMRC SP 2/00 (at **28.43 ENTERPRISE INVESTMENT SCHEME**) for HM-RC's approach to the gross assets requirement.

Number of employees

In relation to options granted on or after 21 July 2008, the company must have less than 250 full-time employees. If the company has qualifying subsidiaries, the company and its subsidiaries must have less than 250 full-time employees in aggregate. In applying this test, any employee who is not full-time is given such numerical value as is just and reasonable, so that, for example, two employees each working half the normal hours would count as one full-time employee. Directors are employees for these purposes; but employees on maternity or paternity leave are excluded, as are students on vocational training. [*ITEPA 2003, Sch 5 para 12A; FA 2008, s 33(3)(6)*].

Trading activities

If the company is a single company (i.e. not the parent company of a group), it must exist wholly for the purpose of carrying on one or more qualifying trades (see **69.39** below) and must actually be carrying on such a trade or preparing to do so. Purposes having no significant effect (other than in relation to incidental matters) on the extent of the company's activities are disregarded. For the ascertainment of the purposes for which a company exists, see HMRC Venture Capital Schemes Manual VCM15070.

If the company is a parent company, the business of the group (treating the activities of the group companies, taken together, as a single business) must not consist wholly or as to a substantial part (i.e. broadly 20% — see HMRC Venture Capital Schemes Manual VCM17040) in the carrying on of 'non-qualifying activities', and at least one group company must satisfy the above trading activities requirement for a single company. '*Non-qualifying activities*' means 'excluded activities' (as in **69.39** below) and non-trading activities.

Purposes for which a company exists are disregarded to the extent that they consist of:

(i)   (as regards a single company) the holding and managing of property used by the company for one or more qualifying trades carried on by it; or

(ii) (as regards a group company) any activities within (a)–(c) below.

For the purposes of determining the business of a group, activities of a group company are disregarded to the extent that they consist of:

(a)   holding shares in or securities of, or making loans to, another group company;

(b)   holding and managing property used by a group company for the purposes of one or more qualifying trades carried on by a group company; or

(c)   incidental activities of a company which meets the above trading activities requirement for a single company.

Amendments to the trading activities requirement (including the provisions at **69.39** below) may be made in the future by Treasury Order.

[ITEPA 2003, Sch 5 paras 13, 14, 58].

Informal clearance

Enquiries from companies as to whether they meet the conditions of the enterprise management incentives scheme should be directed to Small Company Enterprise Centre, HM Revenue and Customs, 1st Floor, Ferrers House, Castle Meadow Road, Nottingham, NG2 1BB (tel. 0115 974 1250; fax 0115 974 2954).

Qualifying trades

[69.39] A trade is a qualifying trade (see the trading activities requirement at **69.38** above) if:

(i)   it is carried on wholly or mainly in the UK (but see the proposed amendment in **69.35** above);

(ii)   it is conducted on a commercial basis and with a view to profit;

(iii)   it does not consist wholly or as to a 'substantial' part in the carrying on of 'excluded activities' (see below).

See HMRC SP 3/00 (at **28.49 ENTERPRISE INVESTMENT SCHEME**) for HMRC's approach to the requirement at (i) above. '*Substantial*' in (iii) above is not defined, but in its application to similar legislation is taken by HMRC to mean 20% or more of total activities (see **28.50 ENTERPRISE INVESTMENT SCHEME**).

Activities of 'research and development' from which it is intended that a 'connected qualifying trade' will be derived or will benefit are treated as a notional qualifying trade, but preparing to carry on such activities is not treated as preparing to carry on a qualifying trade. A '*connected qualifying trade*' is a qualifying trade carried on either by the company carrying out the research and development or, where applicable, by another member of the group. '*Research and development*' is as defined by *ITA 2007, s 1006* (see **73.109 TRADING INCOME**).

'*Excluded activities*' are as follows:

(a)   dealing in land, commodities or futures, or in shares, securities or other financial instruments;

(b)   dealing in goods otherwise than in an ordinary trade of wholesale or retail distribution (see further below);

(c)   banking, insurance, money-lending, debt-factoring, hire purchase financing or other financial activities;

(d)   leasing (including letting ships on charter or other assets on hire) or receiving royalties or licence fees (see further below);

(e)   providing legal or accountancy services;

(f)   property development (see further below);

(g)   farming or market gardening;

(h)   holding, managing or occupying woodlands, any other forestry activities or timber production;

(i)   (in relation to options granted on or after 21 July 2008) shipbuilding (defined by reference to relevant EU State aid rules);

(j)   (in relation to options granted on or after 21 July 2008) producing coal or steel (both defined by reference to relevant EU State aid rules and including the extraction of coal);

(k)   operating or managing hotels or comparable establishments (including guest houses, hostels and other establishments whose main purpose is to offer overnight accommodation with or without catering) or property used as such (see further below);

(l)   operating or managing nursing homes or residential care homes (both as defined) or property used as such (see further below);

(m)   providing services or facilities for any business consisting to a substantial extent of activities within (a)–(k) above and carried on by another person, where a person (other than a parent of the service provider company) has a controlling interest (see below) in both that business and the business of the service provider company.

The exclusions at (j) and (k) above apply only if the person carrying on the activity has an estate or interest (e.g. a lease) in the property concerned or occupies that property.

As regards the application of (d) above, a trade is not excluded from being a qualifying trade solely because it consists to a substantial extent in the receiving of royalties or licence fees substantially (in terms of value) attributable to the exploitation of 'relevant intangible assets'. An intangible asset is an asset falling to be treated as such under generally accepted accounting practice (see **73.18 TRADING INCOME**). A *'relevant intangible asset'* is an intangible asset the whole or greater part of which (in terms of value) has been created by the 'relevant company' (see **69.36** above) or by a company which was a 'qualifying subsidiary' (within **69.38** above) of the relevant company throughout the period during which it created the whole or greater part of the asset. The definition also includes an intangible asset the whole or greater part of which was created by a company when it was not a qualifying subsidiary of the relevant company, provided it subsequently became a qualifying subsidiary under a particular type of company reconstruction. Where the asset is 'intellectual property', it is treated as created by a company only if the right to exploit it vests in that company (alone or with others). The term *'intellectual property'* incorporates patents, trade marks, copyrights, design rights etc. and foreign equivalents.

The above definition of 'relevant intangible asset' applies in relation to options granted on or after 6 April 2007. If an option granted before that date remained unexercised immediately before 6 April 2007 and no disqualifying event (see **69.37** above) had occurred in relation to it, the above definition applies in relation to that option at all times on after that date in determining whether an activity is an excluded activity. In relation to other options granted before 6 April 2007, a 'relevant intangible asset' was an intangible asset the whole or greater part of which (in terms of value) had been created by the company carrying on the trade or by a company which throughout the creation of the asset was the parent company of that company or a qualifying subsidiary of that parent company. The stated purpose of the change of definition is to enable an intangible asset to be transferred to a subsidiary that was not in the group at the time the asset was created (Treasury Explanatory Notes to the 2007 Finance Bill). In a case where, immediately before 6 April

2007, the right to exploit an intangible asset which was then a relevant intangible asset was vested (solely or jointly with others) in the relevant company or in a subsidiary of it, the definition is effectively treated as unchanged if at any time on or after that date the new definition would alone cause the 'no excluded activities' requirement to be breached in relation to an option.

As regards (b), (d), (e), (f) and (m) above, the additional comments in **28.50** ENTERPRISE INVESTMENT SCHEME, on the similar list of exclusions there, apply equally to the above provisions.

[*ITEPA 2003, Sch 5 paras 15–23, 58; ITA 2007, Sch 1 para 450(3); FA 2007, s 61; FA 2008, s 33(4)–(6); CTA 2010, Sch 1 para 399(4)*].

Eligible employees

[69.40] The individual to whom the option is granted must be an eligible employee in relation to the 'relevant company' (see **69.36** above). An individual is an eligible employee in relation to the relevant company if he satisfies the following three requirements at the time the option is granted.

(a)   *Employment.* He must be an employee of that company or, if it is a parent company, of that company or a qualifying subsidiary (see **69.38** above).

(b)   *Commitment of working time.* The average amount per week of his 'committed time' must be at least 25 hours or, if less, 75% of his 'working time'. (See **69.39** above for disqualifying event where *actual* working time falls below this average.) His *'committed time'* is the time he is required, as an employee in 'relevant employment', to spend on the business of the relevant company or, if it is a parent company, of its group (inclusive of certain permissible periods of absence, for example through ill-health, maternity leave, reasonable holiday entitlement, gardening leave etc.) His *'working time'* is time spent on 'remunerative work' as an employee or self-employed person (including the same permissible periods of absence). *'Remunerative work'* means work undertaken to produce income taxable as employment income or trading income (or which would be so taxable if the employee were UK resident and ordinarily resident and the remittance basis did not apply). An employee is in *'relevant employment'* if he is employed by the relevant company or, if it is a parent company, by any company in its group.

(c)   *Material interest test.* He must not have a 'material interest' in the company or, where applicable, in any of its subsidiaries. For these purposes, an individual has a *'material interest'* in a company if he, and/or certain 'associates' of his (within *ITEPA 2003, Sch 5 paras 31–33*):

　　(i)   beneficially owns or controls (directly or indirectly) more than 30% of ordinary share capital (as defined by *ITA 2007, s 989*); or

(ii)   (where the company is a close company, or would be but for its being non-UK resident or having a stock exchange quotation) possesses or is entitled to acquire rights to more than 30% of the assets available for distribution among the participators (within *CTA 2010, s 454*) in a winding-up or in any other circumstances.

Rights to acquire shares must be taken into account (in accordance with *ITEPA 2003, Sch 5 para 30*, though see below as regards qualifying options). Shares or rights held by trustees of an approved share incentive plan (see **69.20** above) and *not* appropriated to, or acquired on behalf of, any individual are disregarded.

In applying the material interest test, no account is taken of shares that the individual may acquire under a qualifying option, although account *is* taken of shares already so acquired.

[*ITEPA 2003, Sch 5 para 1(3)(c), (4), paras 24–33, 59, Sch 7 para 87; ITA 2007, Sch 1 para 450(4); FA 2008, Sch 7 paras 43, 81; CTA 2010, Sch 1 para 399(5)*].

Requirements as to terms of option etc

[69.41] An option is not a qualifying option unless all the requirements set out below are met at the time of grant. [*ITEPA 2003, Sch 5 para 34*].

The *shares that can be acquired* under the option must be fully paid up shares forming part of the 'ordinary share capital' (within *ITA 2007, s 989* of the 'relevant company' (see **69.36** above), and must be neither redeemable nor capable of becoming redeemable. Shares are not fully paid up for this purpose if there is any undertaking to pay cash to the company at a future date. [*ITEPA 2003, Sch 5 paras 35, 59; ITA 2007, Sch 1 para 450(4)*].

The option must be *capable of being exercised within ten years* beginning with the date of grant. If the exercise of the option is dependent on conditions being fulfilled, it is treated as so capable if the conditions may be fulfilled within those ten years. [*ITEPA 2003, Sch 5 para 36*].

The option must take the form of a *written agreement* between the person granting the option and the employee, which states:

(a)   the date on which the option is granted;
(b)   that it is granted under *ITEPA 2003, Sch 5*;
(c)   the number, or maximum number, of shares that may be acquired;
(d)   the price (if any) for which the shares may be acquired, or the method by which that price is to be determined;
(e)   when and how the option may be exercised;
(f)   any conditions, e.g. performance conditions, affecting the employee's entitlement; and
(g)   details of any restrictions attaching to the shares.

[*ITEPA 2003, Sch 5 para 37*].

Non-assignability of rights

The terms on which the option is granted must prohibit the grantee from transferring any of his rights under it. The terms *may* permit the option to be exercised within up to one year after the grantee's death. [*ITEPA 2003, Sch 5 para 38*].

Replacement options

[69.42] A company (the acquiring company) which obtains control (within *ITA 2007, s 995*) of a company whose shares are subject to an as yet unexercised qualifying option (as a result of a general offer to acquire the whole of its issued share capital or all the shares of the same class as those to which the option relates) may grant to the holder of a qualifying option (by agreement with him, and in consideration of his releasing his rights under the option) equivalent rights (a *'replacement option'*) relating to shares in the acquiring company. The replacement option must be granted within six months after the acquiring company obtains control and any condition subject to which the offer is made is satisfied. The replacement is a qualifying option only if the requirements listed below are met.

The same applies where the acquiring company obtains such control in pursuance of a compromise or arrangement with creditors and members which is sanctioned by the court under *Companies Act 2006, s 899* (or earlier equivalent) (in which case the replacement option must be granted within six months after the acquiring company obtains control) or becomes bound or entitled to acquire shares (of the same class as those to which the option relates) under *Companies Act 2006, ss 979–982* (or earlier equivalents) (in which case the replacement option must be granted within the period during which the acquiring company remains so bound or entitled).

The above also applies where the acquiring company obtains all the shares of the company (the old company) whose shares are subject to such an option as a result of a 'qualifying exchange of shares' (in which case the replacement option must be granted within six months after the acquiring company obtains control). A *'qualifying exchange of shares'* means arrangements whereby the old company becomes a wholly-owned subsidiary of a new holding company (the new company) by means of an exchange of shares. All the following conditions must be met (and for these purposes, references to 'shares', other than to 'subscriber shares', include references to securities).

(1) The consideration for the shares in the old company (the old shares) must consist wholly of the issue of shares (new shares) in the new company.

(2) The new shares must be issued only at times when the new company has no issued shares other than subscriber shares (and any new shares already issued in consideration of old shares).

(3) The consideration for new shares of each description must consist wholly of old shares of the corresponding description (i.e. shares of equivalent class and carrying equivalent rights).

(4)   New shares of each description must be issued to holders of old shares of the corresponding description in respect of, and in proportion to, their holdings.

(5)   The exchange of shares must not fall to be treated as a disposal and acquisition for capital gains tax purposes.

Requirements for replacement option to be a qualifying option

The replacement option is itself a qualifying option if it is granted to the holder of the old option by reason of his employment with the acquiring company or with a member of a group of which it is the parent company, and:

(a)   at the time of the release of rights under the old option:

    (i)   the replacement option is granted for the reasons given in **69.36** above;

    (ii)   the limit on the total value of unexercised qualifying options (previously the limit of 15 on the number of employees holding qualifying options) (see **69.36** above) is met in relation to the replacement option;

    (iii)   the requirements in **69.38** above as to independence and trading activities are met in relation to the acquiring company;

    (iv)   the individual to whom the replacement option is granted is an eligible employee (see **69.40** above) in relation to the acquiring company; and

    (v)   the requirements at **69.41** above (terms of option etc.) are met in relation to the replacement option;

(b)   the total market value, immediately before the release, of shares which were subject to the old option is equal to the total market value, immediately after the grant of the replacement option, of the shares in respect of which it is granted; and

(c)   the total amount payable by the employee for shares under the option remains the same.

General

For the purposes of the enterprise management incentives provisions, a replacement option which is a qualifying option is treated as if granted on the date the original option was granted. (This does not apply for the purposes of the 'notice of grant' provisions at **69.43** below — Revenue Share Focus Newsletter December 2003 pp 8, 9.) Such a replacement option may be replaced by a further replacement option if one of the above circumstances and the above qualifying requirements are again satisfied. For the purpose of applying the monetary tests at **69.36** above, the value of the shares in the acquiring company that are subject to a replacement option is taken to be equal to the value of the shares that were subject to the old option immediately before the release of rights under the old option (or the appropriate proportion of that value in a case where the replacement option has been partially exercised).

[ITEPA 2003, s 719, Sch 5 paras 39–43; ITA 2007, Sch 1 para 443; SI 2007 No 2194, Sch 4 para 101; SI 2008 No 954, arts 1, 34].

Notice of grant of option

[69.43] Notice of an option must be given (in prescribed form — form EMI 1) to HMRC by the employer company within 92 days after the option is granted, failing which the option is not a qualifying option (see **69.36** above). The notice must incorporate such information as HMRC may require (the standard form can be downloaded from the HMRC website), and must contain:

(i)   a declaration by a director or the company secretary (of the employer company) that, in his opinion, the statutory requirements are met in relation to the option and that the information provided is to the best of his knowledge correct and complete; and

(ii)   a declaration by the employee that he meets the requirement at **69.40**(b) above as to commitment of working time.

The notice should be sent to the HMRC's Small Company Enterprise Centre at the address given at **69.35** above.

HMRC may correct obvious errors or omissions in the notice. They must give notice of such correction to the employer company within nine months after the notice of grant is given, and the company may give notice to HMRC rejecting the correction within three months from the date of issue of the notice of correction.

HMRC enquiry

Where notice of grant of an option is given as above, HMRC may:

(a)   enquire into the option, by giving the employer company notice of enquiry; and/or

(b)   enquire into the employee's commitment of working time, in which case notice of enquiry must be given to the employee, with a copy to the employer company.

In either case, notice of enquiry must normally be given no later than twelve months after the end of the period within which notice of the grant of the option must be given (see above), but it may be given at any time if HMRC *discover* that any of the information provided was false or misleading in a material respect. In the absence of such discovery, no more than one enquiry can be made under either of (a) or (b) above.

While an enquiry under (a) above remains open, the employer company may apply to the Appeal Tribunal for a direction that it be closed within a specified period, such application to be heard and determined in the same way as an appeal. The Tribunal must give such a direction unless satisfied that HMRC have reasonable grounds for keeping the enquiry open. On completion of the enquiry, HMRC must issue a 'closure notice' informing the company that the enquiry is complete and stating their decision as to whether the statutory requirements are met in relation to the option. If that decision is negative, HMRC must also notify the employee. The employer company may appeal, within 30 days after a closure notice is given, against an HMRC decision that the statutory requirements have not been met or that notice of grant was not properly given. These provisions also apply, with appropriate modifications, to an enquiry under (b) above.

In the absence of an enquiry, the option can be taken to be a qualifying option. In the event of an enquiry, HMRC's decision, as stated in the closure notice, is conclusive, subject any appeal and, where the option has been found to be a qualifying option, to any further enquiry as a result of an HMRC discovery (see above).

[*ITEPA 2003, Sch 5 paras 1(4), 44–50; SI 2009 No 56, Sch 1 paras 353, 354*].

See also **69.46** below as regards compliance with time limits.

Returns

[69.44] A company whose shares are the subject of a qualifying option at any time in a tax year is required to make a return, containing such information as HMRC may require, before 7 July following the end of that tax year. Penalties are exigible under *TMA 1970, s 98* for non-compliance. [*ITEPA 2003, Sch 5 para 52, Sch 6 para 137*]. See also **69.46** below as regards compliance with time limits.

HMRC information powers

[69.45] HMRC have wide-ranging powers to require any person to furnish them with such information as they reasonably require and as that person possesses or can reasonably obtain. The information must be supplied within a period specified in the notice, which must not be less than three months. Penalties are exigible under *TMA 1970, s 98* for non-compliance. [*ITEPA 2003, Sch 5 para 51, Sch 6 para 137*]. See also **69.46** below as regards compliance with time limits.

The reporting obligations at **69.17** above also apply in relation to options under these provisions, but not in relation to particulars given in a notice under **69.43** above. [*ITEPA 2003, s 421J(11)*].

Compliance with time limits

[69.46] For the purposes of **69.43–69.45** above and for determining market value as in **69.36** above, a person is not taken to have failed to do anything within a time limit if he had a reasonable excuse and, if the excuse ceased, did it without unreasonable delay thereafter. In such circumstances, any further time limit expressed by reference to the original time limit operates by reference to the actual time of performance of the original task. [*ITEPA 2003, Sch 5 para 53*].

SAYE option schemes

[69.47] Approved SAYE option schemes (also known as savings-related share option schemes) are covered in *ITEPA 2003, ss 516–520, Sch 3*. A company may establish a scheme, subject to HMRC approval, for its directors and employees to obtain options to acquire shares in itself or another company without any charge to income tax on the receipt of the options and on any increase in value of the shares between the date of the option being granted and the date on which it is exercised. The shares must be paid for from the proceeds of an approved savings arrangement (see **69.51** below). Up to a limit (see **69.56**(a) below), the share option price may be set at a discount to the value of the shares at the time the option is granted, and such discount is also exempt from income tax.

See **73.59, 73.61** TRADING INCOME as regards deductions available to the employer company for corporation tax purposes.

See generally HMRC Employee Share Schemes User Manual at ESSUM30000 *et seq.*

Simon's Taxes. See E4.570–E4.580.

General

[69.48] To qualify for the favourable income tax treatment described at **69.49** below, the share option must be granted to an individual under an approved SAYE option scheme (see **69.53** below as regards the requirements for approval and **69.59** below for the approval procedure) and by reason of his office or employment as a director or employee of a company (not necessarily the company whose shares are the subject of the option). [*ITEPA 2003, ss 516, 517*]. The taxation of *unapproved* share options is covered at **69.14** above.

Income tax treatment

[69.49] No income tax liability arises in respect of the receipt of the option. [*ITEPA 2003, ss 475, 518*]. No income tax liability arises in respect of the exercise of the option if it is exercised in accordance with the scheme at a time when the scheme is approved (or treated as still approved — see **69.59** below). The exemption on exercise does not, however, apply if the option is exercised before the third anniversary of the date of grant by virtue of the inclusion in the scheme of a non-compulsory provision within **69.56**(h) or **69.57**(b) below. The exemption on exercise does not apply if the option was granted, or is exercised, under arrangements one of the main purposes of which is the avoidance of tax or national insurance contributions. Where the exemption does not apply, **69.15** above (exercise of unapproved share options) applies instead. [*ITEPA 2003, ss 519, 520*].

Other than on *exercise* of the qualifying option, there is no exemption from the charge at **69.15** above (e.g. on release of the option).

For an article on the imposition of income tax charges under the above provisions in the case of internationally mobile employees, including examples and the impact of double tax agreements, see Revenue Tax Bulletins August 2002 pp 951–954 and April 2005 pp 1193–1199 (the latter superseding Revenue Tax Bulletin October 2001 pp 883–887). For associated national insurance contributions liabilities, see Revenue Tax Bulletin December 2001 pp 895–899. See also HMRC Employment-Related Securities Manual ERSM160100.

Capital gains tax treatment

[69.50] There is no special capital gains tax treatment on the disposal of shares acquired under an approved SAYE option scheme and exempt from income tax on exercise of the option, except that *TCGA 1992, s 17(1)* (under which acquisitions are treated as made at their market value rather than their actual cost) is disapplied in relation to such acquisitions. [*TCGA 1992, Sch 7D paras 9, 10*]. The date of acquisition of the shares is the date the option is exercised. For details, see Tolley's Capital Gains Tax under Employee Share Schemes.

Approved savings arrangements

[69.51] As a condition of approval, a SAYE option scheme must provide for shares acquired on the exercise of options granted under the scheme to be paid for from the proceeds (including any interest or bonus added) of a 'certified SAYE savings arrangement' (within the meaning of *ITTOIA 2005, s 702* — see also **30.24**(vi) **EXEMPT INCOME**) which has been approved by HMRC for these purposes. The SAYE scheme must link the amount of a person's contributions under the approved savings arrangement to the total amount needed to acquire at the option price the number of shares in respect of which options are granted to him. The maximum total amount of contributions a person may make at any time to savings arrangements linked to approved SAYE schemes cannot exceed £250 per month. A SAYE scheme may impose a minimum contribution, but this must not exceed £10 per month. These amounts can be altered by Treasury Order. Subject to any such minimum that may be imposed, monthly contributions of as low as £5 are permitted. The savings arrangement may provide for a bonus to be added in respect of a person's contributions; this is to be determined at the time the options are granted and is to be taken into account in linking the contributions made to the number of shares that may be acquired. [*ITEPA 2003, Sch 3 paras 23–26*].

Interest and bonuses from the savings arrangement are exempt from income tax. [*ITTOIA 2005, s 702*]. Three- or five-year savings contracts are available, and five-year contracts may offer the option of repayment on the seventh anniversary. The Treasury may alter permitted levels of interest and bonuses, but not so as to affect pre-existing savings contracts.

Group schemes

[69.52] A SAYE option scheme established by a company that controls (within *ITA 2007, s 995*) one or more other companies may extend to all or any of those other companies. A scheme which so extends is a '*group scheme*' and each company to which it extends (including the parent) are '*constituent companies*'. [*ITEPA 2003, s 719, Sch 3 para 3; ITA 2007, Sch 1 para 443*].

Jointly owned companies

To enable a jointly owned company to take part in a group scheme (though it cannot thereby take part in more than one), such a company, and any company under its control (within *ITA 2007, s 995*), is treated as being under the control of each of its two joint owners. A company controlled by a jointly owned company may not take part in more than one group scheme or in a different scheme to that (if any) in which the jointly owned company (or any other company controlled by it) takes part. [*ITEPA 2003, s 719, Sch 3 para 46; ITA 2007, Sch 1 para 443*].

Requirements for approval

[69.53] In order to qualify for HMRC approval, a SAYE option scheme must meet the requirements at **69.54–69.58** below as well as the savings arrangement requirement at **69.51** above. It must not contain features that are neither essential nor reasonably incidental to the purpose of providing director and employee benefits in the form of share options. [*ITEPA 2003, Sch 3 paras 1, 4, 5*].

Eligibility of employees

[69.54] Eligible employees must include every person who:

(a)   is an employee or a full-time director of the company which established the scheme or, in the case of a group scheme, a constituent company; and

(b)   has been such an employee or director at all times during a qualifying period, not exceeding five years; and

(c)   whose earnings from the office or employment in question are (or would be if there were any):

- (before 2008/09) general earnings within **27.9 EMPLOYMENT INCOME** or *ITEPA 2003, s 21* (earnings, other than chargeable overseas earnings, for year when employee UK resident and ordinarily resident); or

- (for 2008/09 onwards) general earnings within **27.5 EMPLOY-MENT INCOME** (earnings for year when employee UK resident), and those general earnings are (or would be if there were any) earnings for a tax year in which the employee is ordinarily resident in the UK; and

(d)   is not excluded by the 'no material interest' test below.

The scheme *must* ensure that, other than as required or authorised under the statutory provisions, no-one is eligible to participate in the scheme at a particular time unless he is at that time a director or employee of the company or, as regards a group scheme, a constituent company. It *may*, however, include part-time directors and any employees and directors whose earnings are not within (c) above and/or who do not meet the condition in (b) above.

The scheme must not contain any feature, other than as required or authorised under the statutory provisions, which is likely to discourage any description of persons within (a)–(d) above from participating. Every person within (a)–(d) above must be eligible to participate on similar terms, and those who participate must actually do so on similar terms. However, the rights of participants to obtain and exercise share options may vary according to such factors as remuneration levels and length of service. If the company which established the scheme is a member of a group (comprising for this purpose a company and any companies it controls) the scheme must not have the likely effect of conferring benefits wholly or mainly on directors or on the more highly-paid employees.

[*ITEPA 2003, Sch 3 para 2(2), paras 4–10; FA 2008, Sch 7 paras 42, 81*].

No material interest

The scheme must ensure that an individual is not eligible to participate in the scheme if he has, or has had within the preceding 12 months, a 'material interest' in a 'close company':

- whose shares may be acquired under the scheme; or
- which has control (within *ITA 2007, s 995*) of a company whose shares may be acquired under the scheme; or
- is a member of a consortium which owns a company whose shares may be acquired under the scheme. (For this purpose, a company is a member of a consortium owning another company if it is one of a number of companies which between them beneficially own at least 75% of, and each of which beneficially owns at least 5% of, the other company's ordinary share capital.)

For these purposes, an individual has a '*material interest*' in a company if he, and/or certain associates of his (within *ITEPA 2003, Sch 3 paras 14–16*):

- beneficially owns or controls (directly or indirectly) more than 25% of ordinary share capital; or
- possesses or is entitled to acquire rights to more than 25% of the assets available for distribution among the participators (within *CTA 2010, s 454*) in a winding-up or in any other circumstances.

Rights (including SAYE options) to acquire shares must be taken into account (in accordance with *ITEPA 2003, Sch 3 para 13*). Shares or rights held by trustees of an approved SIP (see **69.20** above) and not appropriated to, or acquired on behalf of, any individual are disregarded.

For these purposes, '*close company*' has the meaning given by *CTA 2010, Pt 10 Ch 2* but also includes a company which would be a close company but for its being a non-UK resident company or a quoted company.

[*ITEPA 2003, s 719, Sch 3 paras 11–16, 48(2), Sch 7 para 87; ITA 2007, Sch 1 para 443; CTA 2010, Sch 1 para 397(2)(3)*].

Scheme shares

[69.55] Scheme shares (i.e. the shares which may be acquired under the scheme) must be fully paid up and not redeemable and must:

(a) form part of the ordinary share capital of:
    (i) the company which established the scheme; or
    (ii) a company which has control (within *ITA 2007, s 995*) of that company; or
    (iii) a member of a consortium (as in **69.54** above) which owns the company within (i) above or a company within (ii) above; or

(iv)   a company which has control of a member of a consortium within (iii) above; and

(b)   be either shares of a class listed on a recognised stock exchange, or shares in a company not under the control of another company, or shares in a company under the control of a listed company (other than a company which is, or would be if UK resident, a close company).

Scheme shares must not be subject to any restrictions (as to their disposal or the exercise of rights conferred etc. — see *ITEPA 2003, Sch 3 para 21(4)–(6)* for full definition and disregards) other than those attaching to all shares of the same class. Scheme shares can, however, be subject to a restriction imposed by the company's articles of association (or foreign company equivalent) which requires (i) shares held by directors or employees to be disposed of, or offered for sale, on cessation of the office or employment and (ii) shares acquired by persons who are not directors or employees, but in pursuance of rights or interests obtained by directors or employees, to be disposed of, or offered for sale, when they are acquired. The required disposal must be a sale for money on specified terms, and the articles must also provide that anyone disposing of shares of the same class (however acquired) may be required to sell them on those same specified terms.

Except where the scheme shares are in a company whose ordinary share capital consists of shares of one class only, the majority of the issued shares of the same class as the scheme shares must be either 'open market shares' or 'employee-control shares'. *'Open market shares'* are shares held by persons other than (i) persons who acquired them by virtue of their being directors or employees, or (ii) trustees for such persons, or (iii) (in the case of unlisted shares in a company under the control of a listed company — see (b) above) companies which control the company concerned or of which that company is an 'associated company' (within the meaning of *ITEPA 2003, Sch 3 para 47*). *'Employee-control shares'* are shares held by persons who are or have been directors or employees, and who are together able to control the company by virtue of their holdings.

[ITEPA 2003, s 719, Sch 3 paras 2(2), 17–22, 48(2); ITA 2007, Sch 1 para 443].

Share options

[69.56] A SAYE option scheme *must* meet all the following requirements.

(a)   The price at which shares may be acquired under the scheme must be fixed and stated at the time the option is granted and must not be less than 80% of the market value of shares of the same class at that time (or, if the company and HMRC agree in writing, at a stated earlier time). The scheme *may* provide for (i) the stated price, or (ii) the number or description of shares that may be acquired, to be varied as necessary, subject to prior HMRC approval, to take account of any variation in the share capital of which the scheme shares form part.

(b)   Options granted under the scheme must be non-transferable.

(c)   Except as otherwise permitted under any of (d)–(h) below and **69.57** below, options granted under the scheme must not be capable of being exercised before the 'bonus date' or more than six months after it. The '*bonus date*' is the date on which the proceeds of the approved savings arrangement are due to be released to the participant; that date is taken to be, in a case where those proceeds will include the maximum bonus under the scheme, the earliest date on which that bonus is payable and, in any other case, the earliest date on which a bonus is payable.

(d)   The scheme must provide that, if a participant dies before exercising his options and before the bonus date (defined as in (c) above), the options may be exercised after death, provided they are so exercised within twelve months after the date of death. It must also provide that, if death occurs before exercise and on, or within six months *after*, the bonus date, the options may be exercised within twelve months after the bonus date.

(e)   The scheme must provide that, if a participant continues in the office or employment (by reference to which he is eligible for the scheme) after reaching the 'specified age' (see below), he may exercise his options within six months after reaching that age. (This is subject to the overriding six-month rule at (c) above.)

(f)   The scheme must provide that, if a participant 'ceases to hold scheme-related employment' (see below) because of injury, disability or redundancy or because of retirement upon reaching the 'specified age' (see below) (or, if different, an age at which his employment contract requires him to retire), he has six months (after so ceasing) in which to exercise his options. (This is subject to the overriding six-month rule at (c) above.)

(g)   The scheme must provide that, if a participant 'ceases to hold scheme-related employment' (see below) for any reason other than those in (f) above, options granted more than three years previously either may not be exercised at all or may only be exercised within six months after so ceasing, whichever of those alternatives is specified in the scheme. (This is subject to the overriding six-month rule at (c) above.)

(h)   The scheme must provide that, if a participant 'ceases to hold scheme-related employment' (see below) for any reason other than those in (f) above, options granted within the immediately preceding three years may not be exercised at all. The scheme *may*, however, permit such exercise where the scheme-related employment ceases only because it is in a company of which the company that established the scheme ceases to have control (within *ITA 2007, s 995*) or because it relates to a business (or part) which is transferred to a person other than an 'associated company' (within the meaning of *ITEPA 2003, Sch 3 para 47*). If the scheme does permit such exercise, it must provide either that the options may be exercised within six months after the participant 'ceases to hold scheme-related employment' or that they may be exercised within six months after the participant subsequently leaves the employment for the reasons given in (f) above. (This is subject to the overriding six-month rule at (c) above.) Note that the income tax exemptions on exercise are forgone in these circumstances (see **69.49** above).

The scheme must specify the age that is to be the *'specified age'* for the purposes of (e) and (f) above. This must be between 60 and 75 (inclusive) and the same for men and women.

For the purposes of (f)–(h) above, a participant normally *'ceases to hold scheme-related employment'* on the date when he ceases (other than by reason of his death) to hold the office or employment by reference to which he is eligible for the scheme. If, however, he continues after that date to hold office or employment with the company that established the scheme or with any 'associated company' (within the meaning of *ITEPA 2003, Sch 3 para 35(4)*), he *'ceases to hold scheme-related employment'* not on that earlier date but on the date he ceases to hold office or employment with any company of such description.

[*ITEPA 2003, s 719, Sch 3 paras 2(2), 27–35, Sch 6 para 168; ITA 2007, Sch 1 para 443; CTA 2010, Sch 1 para 397(4)*].

Discretionary provisions

[69.57] A SAYE option scheme may make provision as follows.

(a) It may provide that options may be exercised within six months after the bonus date (defined as in **69.56**(c) above) if at that date the participant holds an office or employment in a company which is not a constituent company in a group scheme but which is an 'associated company' (within the meaning of *ITEPA 2003, Sch 3 para 47*) of the company that established the scheme.

(b) It may provide that options may be exercised in any of the following circumstances (in relation to the company whose shares may be obtained under the scheme) within six months after the 'relevant date'.

    (i) A person obtains control of the company as a result of making a general offer to acquire the whole of its issued share capital or of all the shares of the same class as the scheme shares. In this case, the *'relevant date'* is the date when the person obtains unconditional control. For this purpose, a person obtains control of a company if he and others acting in concert obtain control of it (within *ITA 2007, s 995*).

    (ii) A court sanctions, under *Companies Act 2006, s 899* (or earlier equivalent), a compromise or arrangement proposed in connection with a scheme for the reconstruction or amalgamation of the company. In this case, the *'relevant date'* is the date of the sanction.

    (iii) The company passes a resolution for voluntary winding up. In this case, the *'relevant date'* is the date the resolution is passed.

Options may also be exercised at any time when any person is bound or entitled to acquire shares in the company under *Companies Act 2006, ss 979–982* (or earlier equivalents) (power to acquire shares of dissenting shareholders).

All of the above are subject to the overriding six-month rule at **69.56**(c) above. Note that the income tax exemptions on exercise are forgone in any of the above circumstances if the option is thus exercised within three years after it was granted (see **69.49** above).

[*ITEPA 2003, s 719, Sch 3 paras 27, 36, 37; ITA 2007, Sch 1 para 443; SI 2007 No 1093, Sch 3 para 3; SI 2008 No 954, arts 1, 32(1)(2)*].

Exchange of share options

[69.58] A SAYE option scheme *may* provide that, if any other company (the 'acquiring company') obtains control of the company whose shares are scheme shares, or is bound or entitled to acquire shares in the company, in any of the circumstances described in **69.57**(b) above (disregarding (b)(iii) above), a participant may agree with the acquiring company to release his options to acquire scheme shares in consideration of being granted options to acquire shares in the acquiring company (or in some other company falling within **69.55**(a)(ii)–(iv) above). The new share options must be equivalent to the options under the pre-existing scheme as regards their being subject to the provisions of the scheme, the manner in which they are exercisable, the total market value of shares to which they are subject and the total amount payable by the participant on exercise. The new options are then treated as having been granted at the time the original options were granted. The agreement must be made within six months of the acquiring company's obtaining unconditional control or of the court's sanctioning the compromise or arrangement or within the period during which the acquiring company remains bound or entitled to acquire shares, whichever of these is applicable.

[*ITEPA 2003, Sch 3 paras 38, 39; SI 2008 No 954, Arts 1, 32(3)*].

HMRC approval

[69.59] On written application by the company, containing such particulars and supported by such evidence as HMRC require, HMRC will approve a SAYE option scheme if satisfied that it meets the statutory requirements outlined above. They must give notice of their decision to the company, who may appeal within 30 days against a refusal to give approval. On a successful appeal to the Appeal Tribunal, the Tribunal may direct HMRC to approve the scheme from a specified date no earlier than the original date of application.

Withdrawal of approval etc.

If any of the statutory requirements ceases to be met or the company fails to provide information requested by HMRC under their powers at **69.60** below or a 'key feature' of the scheme is altered without HMRC approval, HMRC may by notice withdraw their approval of the scheme with effect from, at the earliest, the time of the failure in question. The withdrawal does not affect the favourable tax treatment of options granted before withdrawal and exercised afterwards; in its application to such options, the scheme is treated for these purposes as if it were still approved at the time of exercise. HMRC are not to withhold approval to an alteration unless it appears to them that the scheme, as altered, would not receive approval on an initial application. For these purposes, a '*key feature*' is a provision of the scheme that is necessary in order to meet the statutory requirements. The company may appeal within 30 days against a withdrawal of approval or a decision to refuse approval of an alteration.

[*ITEPA 2003, Sch 3 paras 2(2), 40–44, Sch 7 para 71(4); SI 2009 No 56, Sch 1 paras 345, 346*].

See *CIR v Burton Group plc* Ch D 1990, 63 TC 191 where an appeal against an Inland Revenue refusal to approve an alteration imposing performance conditions was upheld. In *CIR v Reed International plc and cross-appeal* CA 1995, 67 TC 552, a similar decision was reached where the alteration removed a contingency on which options would be exercisable and would be required to be exercised within a specified period; this did not amount to the acquisition of a new and different right to acquire scheme shares. See also *CIR v Eurocopy plc* Ch D 1991, 64 TC 370.

Applications for approval should be sent to HMRC, Employee Shares and Securities Unit, Nottingham Team, 1st Floor, Ferrers House, Castle Meadow Road, Nottingham, NG2 1BB.

HMRC information powers

[69.60] HMRC have wide-ranging powers to require any person to furnish them with such information as they reasonably require, in relation to a SAYE option scheme, and as that person possesses or can reasonably obtain. The information must be supplied within a period specified in the notice, which must not be less than three months (30 days for 2002/03 and earlier years). Penalties are exigible under *TMA 1970, s 98* for non-compliance. [*ITEPA 2003, Sch 3 para 45, Sch 6 para 137*].

Company Share Option Plan (CSOP) schemes

[69.61] Company share option plan (CSOP) schemes are approved share option schemes and are covered in *ITEPA 2003, ss 521–526, Sch 4*. Unlike SAYE schemes above, CSOP schemes are discretionary schemes, in that there is no requirement to include all employees.

To qualify for the favourable income tax treatment on exercise described at **69.62** below, the share option must be granted to an individual under an approved CSOP scheme (see **69.65** below as regards the requirements for approval and **69.72** below for the approval procedure) and by reason of his office or employment as a director or employee of a company (not necessarily the company whose shares are the subject of the option). [*ITEPA 2003, ss 521, 522*]. The taxation of *unapproved* share options is covered at **69.14** above.

See **73.59, 73.61** TRADING INCOME as regards deductions available to the employer company for corporation tax purposes.

See generally HMRC Employee Share Schemes User Manual at ESSUM40000 *et seq*.

Simon's Taxes. See E4.581–E4.590.

Income tax treatment

[69.62] If, exceptionally, the aggregate of:

- the amount payable by the grantee, on exercise, in order to acquire the maximum number of shares that may be acquired under the option; and
- the amount or value of consideration given (if any) for the grant of the option,

is less than the market value, at the time the option is granted, of a similar quantity of issued shares of the class in question (in other words, if the option is granted at a discount), the difference is taxed as employment income of the grantee for the tax year in which the option is granted. Any amount thus taxed is deductible in computing any amount that subsequently falls to be taxed under **69.15** above (charge on exercise, assignment or release etc. of unapproved share option), e.g. because the scheme has ceased to be approved, or in determining the amount of any notional loan as in **69.11** above.

Except as above, no income tax liability arises in respect of the receipt of a CSOP option.

[*ITEPA 2003, ss 475, 523, 526*].

No income tax liability arises in respect of the *exercise* of an option if it is exercised in accordance with a CSOP scheme at a time when the scheme is approved, provided that the option is exercised no earlier than the third anniversary of the date it was granted and no later than the tenth anniversary of that date. There is an exception for options exercised within three years of grant but no later than six months after the individual ceases to be a full-time director or qualifying employee of the scheme organiser (or of a constituent company in a group scheme — see **69.64** below) because of injury, disability or redundancy or because he retires on or after reaching an age specified in the scheme (where the scheme rules allow such early exercise — see **69.70** below). (Any retirement age so specified must be the same for both sexes and must be at least 55.)

The exemption on exercise does not apply if the option was granted, or is exercised, under arrangements one of the main purposes of which is the avoidance of tax or national insurance contributions.

Where the exemption does not apply, **69.15** above (exercise of unapproved share options) applies instead.

[*ITEPA 2003, ss 524, 525, Sch 4 para 35A*].

Other than on *exercise* of the qualifying option, there is no exemption from the charge at **69.15** above (e.g. on release of the option).

For an article on the imposition of income tax charges under the above provisions in the case of internationally mobile employees, including examples and the impact of double tax agreements, see Revenue Tax Bulletins August 2002 pp 951–954 and April 2005 pp 1193–1199 (the latter superseding Revenue Tax Bulletin October 2001 pp 883–887). For associated national insurance contributions liabilities, see Revenue Tax Bulletin December 2001 pp 895–899. See also HMRC Employment-Related Securities Manual ERSM160100.

Capital gains tax treatment

[69.63] There is no special capital gains tax treatment on the disposal of shares acquired under an approved CSOP scheme and exempt from income tax on exercise of the option, except that:

- *TCGA 1992, s 17(1)* (under which acquisitions are treated as made at their market value rather than their actual cost) is disapplied in relation to such acquisitions; and
- where, exceptionally, an income tax charge arose on receipt of the option (see **69.62** above), the amount thus taxed forms part of the cost of acquisition of the shares for capital gains tax purposes; this applies equally if the scheme has ceased to be approved at time of exercise or if the exercise is made otherwise than in accordance with the scheme and/or if the income tax charge arose under earlier legislation preceding **69.62** above.

[*TCGA 1992, Sch 7D paras 11–13*].

The date of acquisition of the shares is the date the option is exercised. For further detail, see Tolley's Capital Gains Tax under Employee Share Schemes.

Group schemes

[69.64] A CSOP scheme established by a company that controls (within *ITA 2007, s 995*) one or more other companies may extend to all or any of those other companies. A scheme which so extends is a '*group scheme*' and each company to which it extends (including the parent) are '*constituent companies*'. [*ITEPA 2003, s 719, Sch 4 para 3*].

Jointly owned companies

To enable a jointly owned company to take part in a group scheme (though it cannot thereby take part in more than one), such a company, and any company under its control (within *ITA 2007, s 995*), is treated as being under the control of each of its two joint owners. A company controlled by a jointly owned company may not take part in more than one group scheme or in a different scheme to that (if any) in which the jointly owned company (or any other company controlled by it) takes part. [*ITEPA 2003, s 719, Sch 4 para 34; ITA 2007, Sch 1 para 443*].

Requirements for approval

[69.65] In order to qualify for HMRC approval, a CSOP scheme must meet the requirements at **69.66–69.71** below. It must not contain features that are neither essential nor reasonably incidental to the purpose of providing director and employee benefits in the form of share options. [*ITEPA 2003, Sch 4 paras 1, 4, 5*].

Limit on value of shares subject to options

[69.66] The scheme must provide that an individual cannot be granted options under it which would cause the value referred to below to exceed (or to further exceed) £30,000. The value in question is the aggregate market value (determined at time of grant or, where applicable, at the earlier time mentioned in **69.69** below) of the shares which the individual may acquire by exercising outstanding share options under the scheme or under any other approved CSOP scheme established by the same company or by an 'associated company' (within the meaning of *ITEPA 2003, Sch 4 para 35*). [*ITEPA 2003, Sch 4 paras 2(2), 6, 36(1)*].

Where an option is granted that causes the £30,000 limit to be exceeded, the whole of that option (and not just the excess) becomes an unapproved share option (Revenue Share Focus Newsletter December 2003 p 3).

Eligibility of employees

[69.67] The scheme *must* ensure that no-one is eligible to be granted share options under it at a particular time unless he is at that time a 'full-time' director or an employee (full-time or part-time) of the company or, as regards a group scheme, a constituent company. [*ITEPA 2003, Sch 4 paras 2(2), 7, 8*]. A director is treated as a 'full-time' director for these purposes if he works more than 25 hours per week for the company or, as regards a group plan, for constituent companies. See also **69.70** below.

No material interest

The scheme must ensure that an individual is not eligible to participate in the scheme if he has, or has had within the preceding 12 months, a 'material interest' in a 'close company':

- whose shares may be acquired under the scheme; or
- which has control (within *ITA 2007, s 995*) of a company whose shares may be acquired under the scheme; or
- is a member of a consortium which owns a company whose shares may be acquired under the scheme. (For this purpose, a company is a member of a consortium owning another company if it is one of a number of companies which between them beneficially own at least 75% of, and each of which beneficially owns at least 5% of, the other company's ordinary share capital.)

For these purposes, an individual has a *'material interest'* in a company if he, and/or certain associates of his (within *ITEPA 2003, Sch 4 paras 12–14*, as amended):

- beneficially owns or controls (directly or indirectly) more than 25% of ordinary share capital; or
- possesses or is entitled to acquire rights to more than 25% of the assets available for distribution among the participators (within *CTA 2010, s 454*) in a winding-up or in any other circumstances.

Rights (including CSOP options) to acquire shares must be taken into account (in accordance with *ITEPA 2003, Sch 4 para 11*). Shares or rights held by trustees of an approved SIP (see **69.20** above) and not appropriated to, or acquired on behalf of, any individual are disregarded.

For these purposes, *'close company'* has the meaning given by *CTA 2010, Pt 10 Ch 2* but also includes a company which would be a close company but for its being a non-UK resident company or a quoted company.

[ITEPA 2003, s 719, Sch 4 paras 9–14, 36(2), Sch 7 para 87; ITA 2007, Sch 1 para 443; CTA 2010, Sch 1 para 398(2)(3)].

Scheme shares

[69.68] CSOP scheme shares (i.e. the shares which may be acquired under the scheme) must satisfy broadly the same conditions as apply for SAYE option schemes, for which see **69.55** above. There is an exception in relation to options granted on or after 24 September 2010 in that CSOP scheme shares must not be shares in a company which is under the control of a listed company.

As regards the above exception (referred to below as the post-23 September requirement), the six-month period beginning with 24 March 2010 and ending with 23 September 2010 is a transitional period. The following transitional rules apply.

(a)   If during the transitional period:
- a share option is granted to an individual under an approved CSOP scheme, and
- the shares which can be acquired on the exercise of the option are shares in a company which is under the control of a listed company,

then, *unless* the shares themselves are of a class listed on a recognised stock exchange, the share option is treated as *not* having been granted under an approved CSOP scheme.

(b)   The company may alter the scheme during the transitional period in order to meet the post-23 September requirement. This will be regarded as an alteration made in a key feature of the scheme, which HMRC may approve as in **69.72** below.

(c)   If at the end of the transitional period the scheme does not meet the post-23 September requirement, HMRC will withdraw their approval to the scheme. For this purpose, the requirement is regarded as ceasing to be met immediately after the end of the transitional period, with the result that the withdrawal of approval will have effect from that time at the earliest (see **69.72** below). Whatever the effective date of withdrawal, it will affect options granted on or after 24 September 2010 only.

Where, on after 24 March 2010, old options are exchanged for new in the event of a company takeover etc. (see **69.71** below), the new options are *not* treated for the purposes of applying the post-23 September requirement or the transitional rules as having been granted at the time the original options were granted.

[ITEPA 2003, Sch 4 paras 15–20; FA 2010, s 39].

Share options

[69.69] A CSOP scheme *must* meet the following requirement. The price at which shares may be acquired must be stated at the time the option is granted and must not be less than the market value of shares of the same class at that time (or, if the company and HMRC agree in writing, at a stated earlier time).

The scheme *may* provide for (i) the stated price, or (ii) the number or description of shares that may be acquired, to be varied as necessary, subject to prior HMRC approval, to take account of any variation in the share capital of which the scheme shares form part.

The scheme must also ensure that share options granted are non-transferable. *[ITEPA 2003, Sch 4 paras 21–23].*

Discretionary provisions

[69.70] A CSOP scheme may make provision for share options to be exercised after a grantee has ceased to meet the requirement in **69.67** above to be a full-time director or an employee.

A CSOP scheme may also provide that a participant's options can be exercised within the twelve months following his death.

[ITEPA 2003, Sch 4 paras 24, 25].

Exchange of share options

[69.71] A CSOP scheme *may* make provision comparable to that for SAYE option schemes in **69.58** above to allow old options to be exchanged for new in the event of a company takeover etc. and for the new options to be treated as having been granted at the time the original options were granted. *[ITEPA 2003, Sch 4 paras 26, 27; SI 2008 No 954, arts 1, 33].*

HMRC approval

[69.72] On written application by the company, containing such particulars and supported by such evidence as HMRC require, HMRC will approve a CSOP scheme if satisfied that it meets the statutory requirements outlined above. They must give notice of their decision to the company, who may appeal within 30 days against a refusal to give approval. On a successful appeal to the Appeal Tribunal, the Tribunal may direct HMRC to approve the scheme from a specified date no earlier than the original date of application.

Withdrawal of approval etc.

If any of the statutory requirements ceases to be met or the company fails to provide information requested by HMRC under their powers at **69.73** below or a 'key feature' of the scheme is altered without HMRC approval, HMRC may by notice withdraw their approval of the scheme with effect from, at the earliest, the time of the failure in question. HMRC are not to withhold approval to an alteration unless it appears to them that the scheme, as altered, would not receive approval on an initial application. For these purposes, a '*key feature*' is a provision of the scheme that is necessary in order to meet the statutory requirements. The company may appeal within 30 days against a withdrawal of approval or a decision to refuse approval of an alteration.

[ITEPA 2003, Sch 4 paras 2(2), 28–32, Sch 7 para 73(4); SI 2009 No 56, Sch 1 paras 349, 350].

HMRC's refusal to accept an alteration to the rules of an approved scheme, allowing for the imposition or variation, after the date of grant of options, of 'key task' conditions on whose fulfilment the number of shares to which an employee was entitled under the scheme depended, was reversed on appeal in *CIR v Burton Group plc* Ch D 1990, 63 TC 191. A similar conclusion was reached in *CIR v Reed International plc and cross-appeal* CA 1995, 67 TC 552, where the alteration removed a contingency on which options would be exercisable and would be required to be exercised within a specified period; this did not amount to the acquisition of a new and different right to acquire scheme shares. In *CIR v Eurocopy plc* Ch D 1991, 64 TC 370, however, HMRC's refusal to accept (in relation to existing options) an alteration to a scheme, bringing forward the earliest date on which options could be exercised, was upheld; a different right would be acquired as a result of the alteration, so that the option price set at the time of the original grant would be less than the market value of the shares at the time the new right was acquired.

The existence of a 'phantom' scheme alongside an approved scheme, designed merely to provide the employee with the cash needed to exercise options under the approved scheme, does not affect either the approval of the option scheme or the tax relief on exercise of the option. If, however, the phantom scheme effectively gave a participant a choice between exercising an option and receiving a cash payment, the arrangements would not meet the conditions for approval. (Revenue Tax Bulletin May 1992 p 19). For further points on phantom schemes, see **27.74 EMPLOYMENT INCOME.**

Applications for approval should be sent to HMRC, Employee Shares and Securities Unit, Nottingham Team, 1st Floor, Ferrers House, Castle Meadow Road, Nottingham, NG2 1BB.

HMRC information powers

[69.73] HMRC have wide-ranging powers to require any person to furnish them with such information as they reasonably require, in relation to a CSOP scheme, and as that person possesses or can reasonably obtain. The information must be supplied within a period specified in the notice, which must not be less than three months. Penalties are exigible under *TMA 1970, s 98* for non-compliance. [*ITEPA 2003, Sch 4 para 33, Sch 6 para 137*].

Priority share allocations

[69.74] Where a director or employee (or future or past director or employee and whether or not of the company in question) is entitled, as such, to priority allocation of shares in a genuine public offer at fixed price or by tender, no liability to income tax in respect of earnings arises by virtue of any benefit derived therefrom, provided that:

(a)   the shares reserved for such priority allocation do not exceed:
- 10% of the total shares subject to the offer; or

- (if the offer is part of arrangements under which shares of the same class are offered to the public under more than one offer), either 40% of the total shares subject to the offer or 10% of all the shares of that class subject to any such offers;

(b)   all persons entitled to priority allocation are so entitled on similar terms (which may, however, vary according to level of remuneration, length of service or similar factors); and

(c)   the persons entitled to priority allocation are not restricted to directors or to those whose remuneration exceeds a particular level.

Paragraph (b) above is still satisfied where allocations to directors and employees of the company are greater than those to other persons, provided that:

- the aggregate value of priority allocations made under the offer and under other public offers made at the same time in respect of the shares of other companies to those persons; and
- the aggregate value of the shares allocated to comparable directors and employees of the company,

are, as nearly as reasonably practicable, the same.

The above exemption does not apply to the benefit of any discount given to the director or employee on the fixed price or lowest price successfully tendered. Any 'registrant discount' is disregarded for this purpose. Broadly, the 'registrant discount' is any discount which, subject to any conditions imposed, may be available in respect of all or some part of the shares allocated to any person, whether a member of the public or an employee or director applying for shares as such. For the disregard to apply, at least 40% of the shares allocated to members of the public (other than employees or directors entitled, as such, to priority allocation) must be allocated to individuals entitled either to the discount or to some alternative benefit of similar value for which they may elect.

The above exemption is extended to cases where:

- there is a genuine offer to the public of a combination of shares in two or more companies at a fixed price or by tender (the 'public offer'); and
- there is at the same time an offer (the 'employee offer') of shares, or a combination of shares, in one or more but not all of those companies to directors or employees (with or without others) of any company; and
- any of those directors or employees is entitled, by reason of his office or employment, to an allocation of shares under the employee offer in priority to any allocation to members of the public under the public offer.

The conditions at (a)–(c) above apply in relation to this extended exemption, and, for each company included in the employee offer, the limits in (a) above must be satisfied by reference to both offers. Where the extended exemption applies, the denial of exemption on any director- or employee-discount on the offer price (see above) is imposed by reference to an 'appropriate notional price' for shares in each company concerned, i.e. the fixed price at which the shares might reasonably have been expected to be offered in a separate offer to the public, proportionately varied where the sum of the notional prices for all the companies concerned would otherwise differ from the actual fixed price, or lowest successfully tendered price, for the combination of shares subject to the public offer.

The term '*director*' is widely defined for the purposes of these provisions (see *ITEPA 2003, s 548(1)(2)*) and includes, for example, any person in accordance with whose instructions (disregarding advice given in a professional capacity) the directors are accustomed to act.

[*ITEPA 2003, ss 542–548*].

For capital gains tax purposes, *TCGA 1992, s 17(1)* (under which acquisitions are treated as made at their market value rather than their actual cost) is disapplied in relation to acquisitions within the above exemption. [*TCGA 1992, s 149C*].

Simon's Taxes. See E4.506.

Research institution spin-out companies

[69.75] It is common for universities, public sector research establishments, entities such as NHS Trusts and some charities to own intellectual property (IP) created by their own employees. These institutions may have IP Sharing Policies (sometimes also called employee incentive or compensation schemes) to reward the employees (the researchers) who created the IP in the event of its being subsequently exploited. The reward may be in cash form, representing a share of royalties received by the university etc. from licensing or selling the IP, in which case normal income tax rules apply. But alternatively, it could be in the form of a transfer of value to researchers via their ownership of shares in a spin-out company set up to further develop the IP to the point where it can be exploited commercially. The value of the shares in the spin-out company held by the researcher will be affected by an agreement for the transfer of the IP into the spin-out or by the transfer of the IP pursuant to such an agreement. Consequently, a charge to tax can arise under the general earnings rules on the acquisition of the shares (see **27.74 EMPLOYMENT INCOME**) or under the rules for unapproved share schemes in this chapter, and the tax liability can arise before funds are available to meet it. The legislation summarised below seeks to address these and related issues.

The legislation applies where:

- an agreement (an IP agreement) is made for one or more transfers of IP from one or more research institutions (RIs) to a company (a 'spin-out company');
- a person (the researcher) acquires shares in the spin-out company either before the IP agreement is made or within 183 days after it is made;
- the right or opportunity to acquire the shares was available by reason of employment by the RI (or any of them) or by the spin-out company; and
- the person is involved in research in relation to any of the IP that is the subject of the IP agreement.

The legislation does not, however, apply where one of the main purposes of the arrangements under which the above right or opportunity is made available is the avoidance of tax or national insurance contributions.

References in this coverage to shares include an interest in shares. For these purposes, 'shares' includes stock but does not have the extended meaning in **69.3** above. '*Intellectual property*' is defined by *ITEPA 2003, s 456*, and the '*transfer*' of IP includes any of the following: a sale, the grant of a licence or other right in respect of it or the assignment of a licence etc. in respect of it. '*Research institution*' includes a university or a similar publicly funded institution and any institution that carries out research activities other than for profit and that is neither controlled nor wholly or mainly funded by a person who carries on activities for profit. A person is '*involved in research in relation to IP*' if he has been actively engaged (as an employee or otherwise) for the RI (or any of them) in connection with research which is relevant to anything to which the IP relates. If an RI has control (within *CTA 2010, ss 450, 451*) of a company, a transfer of IP from the company is treated for the purposes of these provisions as a transfer from the RI (and similarly where two or more RIs together have control of a company).

Tax relief on acquisition

For the following purposes, the market value of the shares at time of acquisition by the researcher is to be calculated disregarding the effect on that value of the IP agreement and any transfer of IP under it:

(a) the determining of any amount that is to constitute earnings from the employment;

(b) the determining of the amount of any gain realised on the occurrence of a chargeable event within **69.8**(a) above (conversion of convertible shares);

(c) the operation of the provisions at **69.11** above (shares acquired for less than market value); and

(d) the determining of any amount counting as employment income by virtue of **69.15** above (unapproved share options).

Post-acquisition benefits

If the shares are acquired before IP agreement is made, or before any transfer of any IP under it, and any benefit deriving from the agreement or any such transfer is received by the employee in connection with the shares, the taxable amount of the benefit for the purposes of **69.13** above (post-acquisition benefits) is treated as nil. (The receipt of the benefit continues to be a reportable event under **69.17** above.) But this is disapplied if something affecting the shares is done as part of an avoidance scheme at or before the time the IP agreement is made or the IP is transferred.

Restricted shares

If the shares are restricted shares (within **69.4** above), the employer and employee are treated as making the election referred to in **69.6** to fully disapply the restricted shares provisions. This means that on acquisition of the shares, relief can be given as above by reference to their unrestricted market value and that no later charges will arise under the restricted shares rules. As regards shares acquired before 2 December 2004, the notional election is treated as made on that date.

However, employer and employee may agree to disregard the foregoing. This course of action may be chosen if the unrestricted market value at acquisition reflects things other than the transfer of IP, so that bringing it into charge would result in a larger taxable amount. The agreement to disregard must be in a form approved by HMRC and must be made within 14 days after the acquisition.

For examples of both the notional election and the agreement to disregard, see the Treasury Explanatory Notes to the 2005 Finance (No 2) Bill.

If the agreement to disregard is made, then in determining the taxable amount on the occurrence of a chargeable event, the value of IUMV in **69.5** above is to be calculated disregarding the effect on that value of the IP agreement and any transfer of IP under it.

Shares with artificially enhanced market value

For the purposes of **69.10** above, neither the IP agreement nor any transfer of IP under it are things done otherwise than for genuine commercial purposes.

[*ITEPA 2003, ss 451–460; CTA 2010, Sch 1 para 389*].

The above provisions cease to apply to shares in the same circumstances as those at **69.4** cease to apply to shares (disposal to a person other than an associated person etc.). [*FA 2005, s 20(3)*].

Capital gains tax

Consequential amendments are made to the CGT legislation with the aim of ensuring that the correct amount is charged to CGT on disposal of the shares after taking account of the changes to income tax liability brought about by the above provisions. See Tolley's Capital Gains Tax under Employee Share Schemes for details.

Guidance

See generally HMRC's guidance at www.hmrc.gov.uk/shareschemes/ch4-guidance.pdf.

70

Social Security and National Insurance

Cross-references. See Tolley's Social Security and State Benefits and Tolley's National Insurance Contributions.

Taxable social security benefits

[70.1] The provisions for the taxation of social security benefits are in *ITEPA 2003, Pt 10.*

Benefits taxable (as earned income) are as follows:

Bereavement allowance	Jobseeker's allowance (up to 'taxable maximum')
Carer's allowance (previously invalid care allowance)	Old persons' pension
	Retirement pension
Contributory employment and support allowance	Retirement pension taken as lump sum (see **56.5 PENSION INCOME**)
Incapacity benefit (see below)	Statutory adoption pay
Income support when paid to strikers (see below)	Statutory maternity pay
Industrial death benefit (if paid as pension)	Statutory paternity pay
Invalidity allowance when paid with retirement pension	Statutory sick pay
	Widowed parent's allowance

[*ITEPA 2003, ss 577–579, 660–662, 670–675; Welfare Reform Act 2007, Sch 3 para 24; SI 2008 No 787*].

See **30 EXEMPT INCOME** for certain exemptions on war widow's pension and **30.42** for other exemptions. See inside back cover for **rates** of main taxable benefits.

For the application of PAYE to payments of contributory employment and support allowance (applicable on and after 27 October 2008), see *SI 2003 No 2682, Regs 184A–184S* inserted by *SI 2008 No 2601.*

Incapacity benefit

Incapacity benefit is taxable (and may be within PAYE) *except for* short-term benefit payable otherwise than at the higher rate, i.e. benefit payable for the first 28 weeks of incapacity (and except for any child addition). There is also an exclusion for certain payments where invalidity benefit was previously payable in respect of the same period of incapacity. [*ITEPA 2003, ss 663, 664*]. For the application of PAYE to taxable payments of incapacity benefit, see *SI 2003 No 2682, Regs 173–180*.

Income support

Income support is taxable only if the claimant is one of a couple (whether or not married and including a same-sex couple) and *Social Security Contributions and Benefits Act 1992, s 126* (or NI equivalent) (trade disputes) applies to the claimant but not to the other person (i.e. broadly if the claimant is on strike). There is a maximum amount in any period which is taxable, and this maximum applies to the sum of income support and jobseeker's allowance where both are in payment. There is provision for notification of, and objection to, determination of the taxable amount by the benefit officer. [*TMA 1970, ss 54A–54C; ITEPA 2003, ss 665–669; TIOPA 2010, Sch 7 para 32*]. See HMRC Pamphlet IR 41 (Income Tax and Job Seekers).

See also **53.45 PAY AS YOU EARN** regarding the withholding of tax refunds from the unemployed and strikers.

Statutory sick pay etc.

Statutory sick pay, statutory maternity pay, statutory paternity pay and statutory adoption pay paid by employers is taxable.

Simon's Taxes. See E4.129, E4.328, E4.329.

Non-taxable social security benefits

[70.2] Benefits not taxable are as follows:

Income-related benefits	*Short-term benefits*
Child tax credit (see **70.4** below)	Incapacity benefit (not at the higher rate, see **70.1** above)
Council tax benefit	Maternity allowance
Educational maintenance allowance	
Hospital patients' travelling expenses	*War disablement benefits*
Housing benefit	
Income-related employment and support allowance	Disablement pension, including

Income-related benefits

Income support (if not taxable as in **70.1** above)

Social fund payments

State pension credit

Student grants

Working tax credit (see **70.4** below)

Short-term benefits

Age allowance

Allowance for lowered standard of occupation

Clothing allowance

Comforts allowance

Constant attendance allowance

Dependant allowance

Education allowance

Exceptionally severe disablement allowance

Invalidity allowance

Medical treatment allowance

Mobility supplement

Severe disablement occupational allowance

Unemployability allowance

Industrial injury benefits

Industrial death benefit child allowance

Disablement benefit, including

Constant attendance allowance

Exceptionally severe disablement allowance

Reduced earnings allowance

Retirement allowance

Unemployability supplement

Other benefits

Attendance allowance

Back to work bonus (paid by way of jobseeker's allowance or income support)

Bereavement payment

Child benefit

Child dependency additions *paid with* widowed mother's allowance, retirement pension, invalid care allowance or unemployment benefit

Child's special allowance

Christmas bonus for pensioners

Cold weather payments

Disability living allowance

Employment rehabilitation allowance

Employment training allowance

Fares to school

Guardian's allowance

Health in pregnancy grant (for 2009/10 onwards)

Home renovation grants

Invalidity allowance when paid with invalidity pension

Other benefits
Invalidity pension
In-work credit (for 2008/09 onwards)
In-work emergency discretion fund payment (for 2008/09 onwards)
In-work emergency fund payment (for 2008/09 onwards)
Jobfinder's grant
Jobmatch payments and training vouchers
Jobseeker's allowance (in excess of 'taxable maximum')
Job search allowances
Return to work credit (for 2008/09 onwards)
Severe disablement allowance
Vaccine damage payment
War orphan's pension
War widow's pension
Winter fuel payments

See also **56.3 PENSION INCOME** for general exemptions from the charge to tax on such income.

[*ITEPA 2003, ss 641, 645, 656, 677, Sch 7 para 88, Sch 8; Welfare Reform Act 2007, Sch 3 para 24; FA 2008, s 46(1)(3); Health and Social Care Act 2008, s 138; SI 2008 Nos 787, 3137*]. See also **70.1** above.

New Deal 50 plus programme

In-work training grants are disregarded for income tax purposes. [*ITTOIA 2005, s 781*].

Employment Zones programme

Payments to a person as a participant in an Employment Zones programme are disregarded for income tax purposes. [*ITTOIA 2005, s 782*].

Foreign benefits

Foreign social security benefits substantially similar to UK taxable benefits are brought into charge by *ITEPA 2003, ss 678–680*, the taxable amount being the full amount arising in the tax year. The income is relevant foreign income (see **32.2 FOREIGN INCOME**) for the purposes of **32.4 FOREIGN INCOME** (deductions and reliefs) and **61 REMITTANCE BASIS**. See also **32.5 FOREIGN INCOME** for relief for unremittable income. There is an exemption if the corresponding UK benefit is exempt. [*ITEPA 2003, s 681*].

Benefits under Government pilot schemes

[70.3] The question as to whether or not, or to what extent, any benefit under a Government pilot scheme is to be within the charge to income tax is to be determined by Treasury Order. The Treasury may also by order provide for any such benefit to be wholly or partly left out of account in determining whether expenditure otherwise qualifying for capital allowances has been met by the Crown etc. (see **10.2**(vi) CAPITAL ALLOWANCES). For these purposes, a Government pilot scheme means, broadly, any arrangements made for a trial period by the Government which provide for new social security benefits or benefits under work incentive schemes. [*FA 1996, s 151*]. So far, payments under the following schemes have been exempted.

Name of scheme	Treasury Order
Earnings Top-up	*SI 1996 No 2396*
Employment Retention and Advancement	*SI 2003 No 2339*
Return to Work Credit	*SI 2003 No 2339*
Working Neighbourhoods Pilot	*SI 2004 No 575*
In-Work Credit	*SI 2004 No 575*
Up-Front Childcare Fund (exempt from 1 July 2008)	*SI 2008 No 1464*
Better off in Work Credit (exempt from 27 October 2008)	*SI 2008 No 2603*

Child tax credit and working tax credit

[**70.4**] Both Child tax credit ('CTC') and working tax credit ('WTC') are administered by HMRC through their Tax Credit Office, are awarded in respect of a tax year and are computed initially on the claimant's income of the preceding tax year (see further below). They are non-taxable and are neither related to nor deducted from the claimant's income tax liability. Thus, they are not 'tax credits' in the conventional sense, but social security benefits. The main provisions are in *Tax Credits Act 2002*, but most of the detail is provided by regulations made by statutory instrument.

Same-sex couples, who are living together as partners (whether or not they have formed a civil partnership), are treated the same way for tax credits purposes as opposite-sex couples.

Child tax credit

Child tax credit is payable to UK resident single parents and couples, married or otherwise, who are responsible for a child aged under 16 (tax credits will continue to be paid until 1 September following their 16th birthday) or a young person (generally a person aged over 16 and under 19 in full-time, non-advanced, education or on approved training (other than where provided by virtue of employment) or who, from 16 August 2007 onwards, is enrolled or has been accepted to undertake such training) and whose income is within a set limit (see further below). It includes: a family element for all who qualify for CTC (£545 for 2009/10 and 2010/11), increased where the family has a child under the age of one year (to £1,090 for 2009/10 and 2010/11), and a child element for each child or young person (£2,235 for 2009/10, £2,300 for 2010/11), increased if the child or young person is disabled (to £4,905 for 2009/10, £5,015 for 2010/11) and further increased where the child or young person is severely disabled (to £5,980 for 2009/10, £6,110 for 2010/11).

Working tax credit

Working tax credit is payable to UK residents who are at least 16 years old and who work (or in the case of a couple, one of whom works) at least 16 hours a week and whose income is within a set limit (see further below). Additionally, the claimant (or one of the claimants in the case of a couple) must either:

- have dependent children, or a mental or physical disability which puts them at a disadvantage in getting a job and have been previously in receipt of some form of disability benefit, or be over 50 and qualify for the 50+ element of WTC (see below); or
- be at least 25 years old and work for at least 30 hours a week.

It may consist of:

- a basic element which is paid to all who qualify for WTC (£1,890 for 2009/10, £1,920 for 2010/11);
- a second adult element in the case of a couple cohabiting (whether married or unmarried) or a lone parent element where the claimant has a dependent child (£1,860 for 2009/10, £1,890 for 2010/11);
- a 30 hour element where the claimant works (or, in the case of a couple, one of whom works) at least 30 hours a week or where the couple have a dependent child or young person and one of the couple works at least 16 hours a week and in aggregate they work at least 30 hours a week (£775 for 2009/10. £790 for 2010/11);
- a disability element where the claimant satisfies (or, in the case of a couple, one of whom satisfy) one of a wide range of disability conditions (£2,530 for 2009/10, £2,570 for 2010/11);
- a severe disability element where the claimant receives (or, in the case of a couple, one of whom receives) either higher rate attendance allowance or the higher rate care component of the disability living allowance (or would do so if not in hospital) (£1,075 for 2009/10, £1,095 for 2010/11);
- a 50+ element (paid for up to 12 months) for a claimant who is (or, in the case of a couple, one of whom is) 50 or over and has been out of work for at least six months and claiming certain benefits and who starts work within the three months preceding the claim (for 2009/10 £1,300 where the claimant works at least 16 hours a week and £1,935 where the claimant works at least 30 hours a week, for 2010/11 £1,320 and £1.965 respectively); and
- a childcare element equal to 80% of eligible childcare costs up to a maximum of £175 a week for one child or £300 a week for two or more children.

Income thresholds

The tax credits are subject to tapering if relevant gross annual income, or in the case of a couple aggregate joint income, exceeds specified thresholds. For claimants entitled to only WTC or to both CTC and WTC, the maximum credits, apart from the family element of CTC, are withdrawn at the rate of 39p for each £1 of the excess of relevant income (see below) over £6,420. For claimants entitled only to CTC the maximum credits, apart from the family element, are withdrawn at the rate of 39p for each £1 of the excess of relevant income over (£16,040 for 2009/10, £16,190 for 2010/11). For all claimants, the family element of CTC is withdrawn at the rate of £1 for every £15 (6.67%) of the excess of relevant income over £50,000. The taper is applied first to the non-childcare elements of WTC, then to the childcare element of WTC then to CTC. Where the tax credits are awarded at different rates within the same tax year, the figures are calculated for each relevant period (in which the rates remain the same) on a daily basis and the amounts for each period then aggregated.

Relevant income

The income taken into account is the annual gross income of the claimant or, in the case of a couple (of opposite sex) cohabiting (whether married or unmarried), the aggregate gross annual income of the couple. Claims are based on income for the preceding tax year. These awards are provisional only and will be altered retrospectively to the extent that income in the year in which tax credits are received (the current year) increases or decreases by more than £25,000 from that in the year on which the award is based. Any resulting underpayment will be paid to the claimant and any overpayment collected from him (see further below).

Gross annual income includes the aggregate amount (if it exceeds £300) of pension income, investment income, property income, foreign income and notional income (as defined in *SI 2002 No 2006, Regs 5, 10–17*). It also includes taxable income from employment (including most taxable benefits-in-kind), trading income, social security benefits (with some specific exclusions), student grants (other than for dependent children, travel, books or equipment) and other taxable income not covered above by the regulations. Certain types of income are specifically excluded such as maintenance payments and student loans, and certain deductions are allowed such as trading losses, charitable donations and pension contributions.

Claims

Claims for CTC and WTC can be made on form TC600 or via the internet (www.hmrc.gov.uk). Couples must make a joint claim. Claims must be made after the commencement of the tax year but must be made within three months after commencement if maximum entitlement is to be awarded, as claims can only be backdated for a maximum of three months (providing the claimant is entitled to the tax credit in that earlier period). Claims have to be renewed annually, normally by 31 July.

Payment by HMRC

CTC and WTC are paid by HMRC, at weekly or four-weekly intervals, to the main carer, normally through a bank account. In the case of a joint claim, the couple may jointly nominate the main carer, otherwise HMRC will decide who is the main carer (normally the mother or the person who receives child benefit).

Notifiable changes in circumstances

Certain in-year changes of circumstances must be notified to HMRC, normally within one month of the change, if tax credit entitlement will fall to be reduced as a result. Notifiable changes include, *inter alia*, marriage, start of cohabitation, separation, leaving the UK, and decreases in average weekly childcare charges where the childcare element of WTC is claimed.

Underpayments and overpayments

After the year-end, once entitlement to tax credits for the tax year has been determined, any underpayment will be paid by HMRC in a lump sum to the designated claimant. Overpayments are recovered by deduction from tax credit entitlement in the following year, or through the PAYE system, or by assessment as if they were unpaid tax. HMRC must serve notice on the claimants of the overpayment to be recovered specifying how it is to be recovered. Liability for the overpayment in the case of a couple is joint and several.

Interest and penalties

If a person fraudulently or negligently makes an incorrect statement or declaration in connection with a claim for CTC or WTC or incorrectly notifies a change of circumstances or provides incorrect information or evidence, a penalty may be imposed up to a maximum of £3,000. A penalty up to £3,000 may also be imposed on the other claimant in a joint claim (but not exceeding £3,000 in aggregate for both claimants) unless the other claimant was not, and could not reasonably have been expected to have been, aware of the fraud or neglect. Interest may also be charged on overpayments arising through fraud or neglect of the claimant(s). If a person fails to provide any information or evidence which is required in connection with the claim or fails to notify in-year changes of circumstances (where these must be notified), a penalty may be imposed of up to £300. If the failure persists, an additional penalty of up to £60 a day can be imposed for each day the failure continues after the initial penalty has been imposed.

See also HMRC leaflets WTC1 and WCT2 (listed at **36 HMRC EXPLANATORY PUBLICATIONS**).

National insurance contributions

[70.5] National Insurance contributions for **2010/11** (and for 2009/10 in brackets where different) are as set out below. With the one exception noted below under Class 1 (Contracted out), the 2010/11 figures are, in fact, the same as those for 2009/10. See Tolley's National Insurance Contributions for more details.

Class 1 (earnings-related)

Not contracted out

The employee contribution is **11%** of earnings between **£110** p.w. and **£844** p.w. and **1%** of all earnings above **£844** p.w.

The employer contribution is **12.8%** of all earnings in excess of the first £110 p.w.

Contracted out

The 'not contracted out' rates for employees are reduced on the band of earnings from £110 p.w. to £770 p.w. by **1.6%**. For employers, they are reduced on the band of earnings from £110 p.w. to £770 p.w. by **3.7%** for employees in salary-related schemes or **1.4%** for employees in money-purchase schemes. In addition, there is an employee rebate of **1.6%** and an employer rebate of **3.7%** or **1.4%**, as appropriate, on earnings from £97 p.w. (£95 p.w.) up to £110 p.w.

Married women

The reduced employee rate for certain married women and widows with a certificate of election is **4.85%** of earnings between £110 p.w. and £844 p.w. and **1%** of all earnings above £844 p.w.

Class 1A (cars and car fuel and other benefits)

Employer contributions at **12.8%** are required on the benefit of cars and fuel made available to employees for private use and on most other employment-related benefits.

Class 1B (PAYE settlement agreements)

Employer contributions at **12.8%** are required on the value of all items included in a PAYE settlement agreement and the tax paid under the agreement (see **53.15 PAY AS YOU EARN**).

Class 2 (self-employed, flat rate)

The flat weekly rate of contribution is **£2.40**. The annual limit of net earnings for exception from Class 2 liability is £5,075. Special rates apply for share fishermen and for volunteer development workers.

Class 3 (voluntary contributions)

The flat weekly rate of contribution is **£12.05**.

Class 4 (self-employed, profit-related)

The 2009/10 and 2010/11 contribution rate is **8%** on the band of profits between £5,715 and £43,875 and **1%** on all profits above £43,875. See below for earlier years' figures.

Class 4 contributions are levied, generally, on the profits of any trade, profession or vocation (not carried on wholly outside the UK) which are chargeable to income tax under *ITTOIA 2005, Pt 2*. Class 4 contributions are dealt with separately in the self-assessment tax return (or notice of assessment where applicable) and are payable at the same time as the income tax on the profits (see **65.5–65.8 SELF-ASSESSMENT**). Profits for this purpose are after capital allowances, loss reliefs and certain interest and annual payments for trade purposes. [*Social Security Contributions and Benefits Act 1992, Sch 2 paras 2, 3(1)(5); ITA 2007, Sch 1 para 293(3); FA 2009, Sch 6 para 2(6); SI 2010 No 588*]. Trading losses set against other income may, *for Class 4 purposes*, be carried forward and set against the first available profits. [*SSCBA 1992, Sch 2 para 3(4); ITA 2007, Sch 1 para 293(3)*].

Contributions to registered pension schemes do not reduce profits for Class 4 purposes as they are not deductible from any particular type of income (see **57.7 PENSION PROVISION**).

There are various exceptions from Class 4 liability, including persons over State pensionable age, divers etc. within the charge to tax on trading income (see **73.24 TRADING INCOME**) and, on application, those under 16 at the beginning of the tax year. [*SI 1979 No 591, Regs 58–60*]. Non-UK residents and sleeping partners are not within the scope of Class 4.

Interest is chargeable on overdue Class 4 contributions under *TMA 1970, s 86* as it is for income tax purposes (see **42 INTEREST AND SURCHARGES ON OVERDUE TAX**), and repayment supplement (see **41 INTEREST ON OVERPAID TAX**) is similarly available. [*SSCBA 1992, Sch 2 para 6; SI 1993 No 1025*].

The Class 4 rates and bands for earlier years are as follows.

	Rate	Band
2008/09	8% + 1%	£5,435 – £40,040
2007/08	8% + 1%	£5,225 – £34,840
2006/07	8% + 1%	£5,035 – £33,540

National Insurance contributions made by employees or by the self-employed are not allowable for tax purposes. An employer is allowed his contributions for employees as an expense or deduction. [*ITEPA 2003, s 360A; ITTOIA 2005, ss 53, 272, 868; SI 2004 No 2310, Sch para 31*]. See **73.68 TRADING INCOME**.

71

Time Limits — Fixed Dates

Introduction

[71.1] This chapter lists fixed date time limits falling in the year to 30 September 2011. See also **72 TIME LIMITS — VARIABLE DATES**, and see **53.12 PAY AS YOU EARN, 65.12 SELF-ASSESSMENT, 66 SELF-ASSESSMENT — KEY DATES.**

Recent changes to time limits generally

[71.2] From 1 April 2010 (subject to **71.3** below), a number of the current income tax time limits were altered. The amendments were made by *FA 2008, s 118, Sch 39* and brought into force by *SI 2009 No 403* (which also makes transitional provisions — see **71.3** below).

Broadly, where the time limit was previously the fifth anniversary of 31 January following the end of the tax year (roughly five years and ten months after the tax year), this became the fourth anniversary of 5 April in the tax year (i.e. four years after the tax year). Thus, the time limit for 2003/04 was 31 January 2010, the time limit for 2004/05 was 31 March 2010 (the day before the new law came into force), the time limit for 2005/06 was 5 April 2010 and the time limit for 2006/07 is 5 April 2011. Shorter time limits generally remained unchanged.

Transitional

[71.3] Under the transitional provisions, the coming into force of the new time limits is in some cases deferred two years until 1 April 2012. This only applies where tax has been overpaid, its purpose being to allow taxpayers extra time to take appropriate action. Subject to that proviso, the trigger for the deferral is the making of an assessment on the taxpayer, the making of a claim by (or on behalf of) the taxpayer or the exercise by the taxpayer of his right to make a tax return, where, in each case, the taxpayer has not been given notice, within twelve months after the end of that year, to make a tax return for the tax year in question. [*SI 2009 No 403, Art 10*].

Time limits of one year or less

[71.4] The following are miscellaneous short time limits.

(a)   **5 October 2010** for action in respect of 2009/10.
Notification of chargeability. Any person who is chargeable to tax for a tax year must give notice to HMRC that he is so chargeable, unless his income comes solely from certain sources (e.g. income dealt with under PAYE or dividend income chargeable at the dividend ordinary rate) and he has no chargeable gains. [*TMA 1970, s 7*]. See **55.2 PENALTIES**.

(b)   **31 October 2010** for action in respect of 2009/10.
Returns under self-assessment for 2009/10 when required by notice given before 2 August 2010 and filed manually. See **63.2 RETURNS**.

(c)   **31 January 2011** for action in respect of 2009/10 or 2010/11 (whichever is stated below).

    (i)   *Returns under self-assessment* for 2009/10 when required by notice given before 2 November 2010 and filed online. See **63.2 RETURNS**.

    (ii)   *Gift Aid donations to charity by individuals.* Election for qualifying donation(s) made in 2010/11 to be relieved as if made in 2009/10; election must be made no later than the date the 2009/10 self-assessment tax return is filed. See **16.16 CHARITIES**.

    (iii) *Change of accounting date.* Notice of change to be given (in a return) where it affects basis period for 2009/10. See **73.7 TRADING INCOME**.

    (iv)   *Charge on benefits from pre-owned assets.* Election to disapply the charging provisions for 2009/10 and subsequent years where 2009/10 is the first tax year for which a charge under those provisions would otherwise arise by reference to enjoyment of the property in question (or any substituted property). See **4.43 ANTI-AVOIDANCE**.

(d)   **5 April 2011** — advance time limits for action in respect of 2011/12.

    (i)   *Transfer of married couple's allowance (where available) and blind person's allowance.* Election by non-claimant spouse to receive one-half of the married couple's allowance, or by spouses jointly for non-claimant spouse to receive the whole of the allowance, or by claimant spouse to receive one-half where a joint election has been made for non-claimant spouse to receive the whole of the allowance, must be made before the start of the first tax year to which the election is to apply (subject to a 30-day extension where notice of intention to elect was given to HMRC before the start of that year). Withdrawals of such elections similarly do not have effect until the tax year after that in which notice of withdrawal was given. Similar rules apply to transfers between spouses of blind person's allowance and to transfers between civil partners of married couple's allowance and/or blind person's allowance. See **47.2 MARRIED PERSONS AND CIVIL PARTNERS**.

    (ii)   *Election by couple married before 5 December 2005 to opt into the married couple's allowance rules for couples marrying on or after that date.* The election must be made before the start of the first tax year for which it is to have effect but then continues to have effect for all succeeding tax years and is irrevocable. See **1.15 ALLOWANCES AND TAX RATES.**

(e) **5 April 2011** for action in respect of 2009/10.

Claims following late assessments. A claim (including a supplementary claim) which could not have been allowed but for the making of an assessment to income tax or capital gains tax after the tax year to which it relates may be made before the end of the tax year following that in which the assessment was made. This applies in relation to an HMRC amendment to a self-assessment personal or partnership tax return as it does in relation to an assessment. See **18.9 CLAIMS, 63.9 RETURNS.**

(f) **6 July 2011** for action in respect of 2010/11.

(i) *Election for treatment as a single loan of beneficial loans to director* by close company lender. [*ITEPA 2003, s 187*]. See **27.40 EMPLOYMENT INCOME.**

(ii) *Employment-related shares (outside approved employee share schemes).* Information on 'reportable events' to be supplied to HMRC by employer or other specified parties. See **69.17 SHARE-RELATED EMPLOYMENT INCOME AND EXEMPTIONS.**

Time limits of one to two years

[71.5] 31 January 2011 for action in respect of 2008/09.

(i) *Capital allowances.* The following time limits apply.

(A) *Ships.* Notice requiring the postponement of first-year allowances, see **11.15 CAPITAL ALLOWANCES ON PLANT AND MACHINERY.** Also notice requiring postponement of writing-down allowances, and disapplying the 'single ship pool' provisions, see **11.28 CAPITAL ALLOWANCES ON PLANT AND MACHINERY.** Also claim for deferment of balancing charge, see **11.28 CAPITAL ALLOWANCES ON PLANT AND MACHINERY.**

(B) *Short-life assets.* Election for certain expenditure to be treated as on short-life assets. See **11.30 CAPITAL ALLOWANCES ON PLANT AND MACHINERY.**

(C) *Equipment leasing.* Election for fixtures to be treated as belonging to the lessor and not the lessee. See **11.35 CAPITAL ALLOWANCES ON PLANT AND MACHINERY.**

(D) *Long funding leasing.* Election by lessor for all his plant and machinery leases finalised on or after a date of his choosing to be treated in his hands as long funding leases if they would not otherwise be so treated. See **11.46 CAPITAL ALLOWANCES ON PLANT AND MACHINERY.**

(ii) *Beneficial loan arrangements.* Election (or requirement by HMRC officer) for alternative method of calculating benefit. See **27.40 EMPLOYMENT INCOME.**

(iii) *Foster care receipts.* Election for the alternative method of calculating profits to apply for 2008/09. See **30.15 EXEMPT INCOME.**

(iv) *Unremittable overseas income.* Claim for relief from assessment. See **32.5 FOREIGN INCOME.**

(v)   *Herd basis.* Election where 2008/09 was either the first tax year (after that in which trading commenced) during whose basis period a herd was kept, or the first tax year in the basis period for which compensation was received for compulsory slaughter. See **33.3, 33.7 HERD BASIS**.

(vi)   *Sale of patent rights.* Election to disapply or apply spreading provisions (depending on whether UK resident or non-UK resident). See **40.7 INTELLECTUAL PROPERTY**.

(vii) *Sale of patent rights by a partnership followed by cessation of trade.* Election by partner to reduce amount chargeable in tax year of cessation. Time limit operates by reference to tax year of cessation. See **40.7 INTELLECTUAL PROPERTY**.

(viii) *Claim for loss in trade etc.* to be set off against general income (see **45.2 LOSSES**) or capital gains (see **45.7 LOSSES**) or to be carried back (see **45.5, 45.9 LOSSES**).

(ix)   *Claim for losses on shares* in unlisted companies. See **45.25 LOSSES**.

(x)   *Post-cessation receipts.* Election for such receipts to be treated as received on date of cessation. See **59.4 POST-CESSATION RECEIPTS AND EXPENDITURE**.

(xi)   *Post-cessation expenditure.* Claim for relief against total income. See **59.5 POST-CESSATION RECEIPTS AND EXPENDITURE**.

(xii) *Furnished holiday lettings.* Election for averaging treatment. See **60.10 PROPERTY INCOME**.

(xiii) *Rent-a-room relief.* Election (or withdrawal of election) for relief not to apply, or for profits to be treated as equal to excess of gross rents over relief limit. See **60.12 PROPERTY INCOME**.

(xiv) *Property losses.* Claim for relief, against general income, for certain capital allowances and agricultural expenses. See **60.15 PROPERTY INCOME**.

(xv)   *Amendment of self-assessment tax return.* Amendments by taxpayer to return must be made within 12 months after the filing date (itself normally 31 January following the tax year). See **63.4 RETURNS**.

(xvi) *Deeply discounted securities.* Claim for relief for loss on disposal where security has been held continuously since before 27 March 2003 by the person making the disposal *and* the security was listed on a recognised stock exchange at some time before that date. See **64.19 SAVINGS AND INVESTMENT INCOME**. Claim for relief for loss on disposal of a strip of a government security. See **64.21 SAVINGS AND INVESTMENT INCOME**.

(xvii) *Vulnerable person election.* Election must be made jointly in relation to qualifying trusts by the trustees and the vulnerable person by the first anniversary of 31 January following the tax year for which it is first to apply. See **68.21 SETTLEMENTS**.

(xviii) *Heritage maintenance settlements.* Election for tax exemption on income. See **68.34**.

(xix) *Opening years of a business.* Election for accounts prepared to 31 March or on any of the first four days in April *not* to be treated as if prepared to 5 April. See **73.4 TRADING INCOME**.

(xx)   *Accounts prepared to a variable date.* Election to treat such accounts as if prepared to a fixed date so that change of accounting date rules are not triggered by slight variations. See **73.7 TRADING INCOME**.

(xxi) *Change from realisation basis of computing profits to a mark to market basis.* Election for adjustment income to be spread equally over six periods of account beginning with the first period to which the new basis applies. See **73.20 TRADING INCOME.**

(xxii) *Change of basis in computing barrister's or advocate's profits.* Election for increased adjustment charge to be made for 2008/09 under the spreading provisions. See **73.20 TRADING INCOME.**

(xxiii) *Farming.* Claim to average profits of 2007/08 and 2008/09, see **73.74 TRADING INCOME.**

(xxiv) *Creative artists.* Claim to average profits of 2007/08 and 2008/09, see **73.52 TRADING INCOME.**

(xxv) *Films and sound recordings.* For certified films, an election may be made to disapply special rules treating production and acquisition expenditure as revenue expenditure. The time limit operates by reference to the tax year in which ends the period of account in which the original master version is completed. See **73.76 TRADING INCOME.**

(xxvi) *Appropriations to and from trading stock.* Election for market value to be adjusted in certain cases where a chargeable gain or allowable loss would otherwise arise. See **73.114 TRADING INCOME.**

(xxvii) *Valuation of trading stock on cessation.* Election for transfers between connected persons to be reduced below arm's length value in certain cases. See **73.113 TRADING INCOME.**

(xxviii) *Work in progress on cessation.* Election for work in progress to be taken at cost on cessation in 2008/09. See **73.113 TRADING INCOME.**

(xxix) *Spreading of UITF Abstract 40 adjustment.* Election for increased adjustment charge to be made for 2008/09 under the spreading provisions. See **73.115 TRADING INCOME.**

Time limits of three to four years

[71.6] 31 January 2011 for action in respect of 2006/07.

- Claim for adjustment of assessments where administration was completed in 2006/07. See **23.12 DECEASED ESTATES.**

Time limits of four years or more

[71.7] Claims by 31 October 2010 in respect of 2006/07.

- PAYE taxpayer to request that a return be issued to him. See **53.1 PAY AS YOU EARN.**

Claims by 31 October 2010 in respect of 2004/05.

- PAYE taxpayer to whom **71.3** above applies to request that a return be issued to him. See **53.1 PAY AS YOU EARN.**

Claims by 31 January 2011 in respect of 2004/05.

- Claim for income tax relief in respect of **ENTERPRISE INVESTMENT SCHEME** shares issued in 2004/05. See **28.7 ENTERPRISE INVESTMENT SCHEME.**

- Claims within (a)–(k) below where **71.3** above applies to the claimant.

Claims by 5 April 2011 in respect of 2006/07. Except where other time limits are prescribed, claims must be made within four years after the end of the tax year to which they relate (see **18.4 CLAIMS**).

(a) *Error or mistake claims.* See **18.8 CLAIMS**.

(b) *Claim against double assessment* where the same person has been assessed 'for the same cause' in the same year. [*TMA 1970, s 32*].

(c) **DOUBLE TAX RELIEF (26)**.

(d) **INTEREST PAYABLE (43)**.

(e) *Claim for loss in trade etc.* for 2006/07 to be carried forward against future profits of the same trade (see **45.20 LOSSES**).

(f) *Claim for terminal loss relief* in relation to a trade etc. that ceased in 2006/07 (see **45.21 LOSSES**).

(g) **MINERAL ROYALTIES (48)**.

(h) *Delayed remittances of overseas income or gains.* See **61.28 REMITTANCE BASIS**.

(i) *Post-employment deductions* (for employee liabilities and indemnity insurance) to be relieved against total income of former employee. See **27.53 EMPLOYMENT INCOME**.

(j) **VENTURE CAPITAL TRUSTS** at **76.3**. Claim for income tax relief in respect of investments.

(k) Any other matter not specified in this chapter for which relief from income tax is claimed.

72

Time Limits — Variable Dates

Introduction

[72.1] Certain time limits that operate by reference to variable dates are set out in this chapter. In some (but not all) cases, the periods can be extended at the discretion of HMRC. See also **65.5–65.8 SELF-ASSESSMENT** as regards payment of tax; **66 SELF-ASSESSMENT — KEY DATES; 71 TIME LIMITS — FIXED DATES.**

Time limits of one year or less

[72.2] The following are miscellaneous short time limits.

(a) **14 days**
Various elections to disapply or moderate the restricted shares provisions at **69.4 SHARE-RELATED EMPLOYMENT INCOME AND EXEMPTIONS.** Such elections are implemented by way of agreement between employer and employee to be made no later than 14 days after acquisition or after a chargeable event (whichever is applicable); there is no requirement for elections to be submitted to HMRC.

(b) **30 days**
    (i)   Rejection of HMRC corrections to self-assessment tax return or partnership return. See **63.4, 63.13 RETURNS.**

    (ii)   Appeals against assessments, amendments to self-assessment return or partnership return or claim made outside return, and HMRC conclusions on completion of enquiry. Lodging of notice of appeal. See **5 APPEALS, 18.3 CLAIMS.**

    (iii)   Generally, appeals against refusal or withdrawal of HMRC approval to an employee share scheme. See e.g. **69.33 SHARE-RELATED EMPLOYMENT INCOME AND EXEMPTIONS.**

    (iv)   There are many instances in which HMRC information powers and clearance procedures require a response within 30 days, see, for example, **4.4, 4.5 ANTI-AVOIDANCE.**

(c) **40 days**
Qualifying option under Enterprise Management Incentives scheme to be exercised within 40 days after a disqualifying event, if adverse tax consequences would otherwise ensue. See **69.37 SHARE-RELATED EMPLOYMENT INCOME AND EXEMPTIONS.**

(d)   **60 days**

    (i)   There are a number of circumstances in which information is required to be provided within 60 days, see, for example, **28.25 ENTERPRISE INVESTMENT SCHEME.**

    (ii)   Notice of declaration by husband and wife (or civil partners) of their beneficial interests in jointly-held property, and income arising from it, where these are not equal. See **47.7 MARRIED PERSONS AND CIVIL PARTNERS.**

(e)   **Three months**

    (i)   Returns of income, partnership returns etc., following notice requiring delivery (if this gives a date later than the normal filing date for the year for which return required). See **63.2, 63.13 RETURNS.**

    (ii)   Appeals relating to questions of (i) personal reliefs for non-residents, (ii) residence, ordinary residence or domicile, (iii) pension funds for service abroad. [*TMA 1970, Sch 1A para 9*].

    (iii)   Application for judicial review must be made within three months of the date when the grounds for application arose. See **5.34 APPEALS.**

    (iv)   There are instances in which HMRC information powers require a response within three months. See e.g. **69.33, 69.45, 69.60, 69.73 SHARE-RELATED EMPLOYMENT INCOME AND EXEMPTIONS.**

(f)   **92 days**

Notice of grant of option under Enterprise Management Incentives scheme to be given to HMRC within 92 days after option granted. See **69.43 SHARE-RELATED EMPLOYMENT INCOME AND EXEMPTIONS.**

(g)   **Twelve months**

Double tax relief. Notice must be given to HMRC within one year of a foreign tax credit becoming excessive. See **26.8 DOUBLE TAX RELIEF.**

Two-year time limits

[72.3] The following have a deadline of two years after a specific event.

(a)   *Industrial buildings.* Election for allowances to apply to holder of long lease out of relevant interest within two years of lease taking effect. See **10.15 CAPITAL ALLOWANCES.**

(b)   *Sales without change of control.* Election for transfer of assets at tax written-down value. See **10.22**(i) **CAPITAL ALLOWANCES.**

(c)   *Short-life assets.* Election for certain transfers between connected persons to be treated as at tax written-down value. See **11.30 CAPITAL ALLOWANCES ON PLANT AND MACHINERY.**

(d)   *Equipment leasing.* Election for certain fixtures on which expenditure incurred by incoming lessee to be treated as belonging to lessee within two years of date of lease taking effect. See **11.37 CAPITAL ALLOWANCES ON PLANT AND MACHINERY.**

(e)   *Long funding leasing.* Joint election by seller (or assignor) and lessor within two years of sale etc. to prevent a finance lease that is part of sale and finance leaseback arrangements from losing 'short lease' status. See **11.45**(1)(A) CAPITAL ALLOWANCES ON PLANT AND MACHINERY.

(f)   *Successions.* Election for transfers between 'connected persons' to be at tax written-down value. See **11.67** CAPITAL ALLOWANCES ON PLANT AND MACHINERY.

(g)   *Know-how disposal.* Joint election by vendor and purchaser within two years of disposal for the consideration not to be treated as a payment for goodwill. See **73.91** TRADING INCOME.

73

Trading Income

Cross-references. See subjects dealt with separately under **4** ANTI-AVOIDANCE; **10** CAPITAL ALLOWANCES; **11** CAPITAL ALLOWANCES ON PLANT AND MACHINERY; **13** CASH BASIS FOR BARRISTERS AND ADVOCATES; **26** DOUBLE TAX RELIEF; **33** HERD BASIS; **43** INTEREST PAYABLE; **45** LOSSES; **50** NON-RESIDENTS; **52** PARTNERSHIPS; **54** PAYMENT OF TAX; **58** PERSONAL SERVICE COMPANIES ETC.; **59** POST-CESSATION RECEIPTS AND EXPENDITURE and **65** SELF-ASSESSMENT.

Introduction

[73.1] For 'Basis Periods', see **73.3–73.12** below; for 'Whether a Trade Carried On', see **73.22–73.32** below; and for 'Chargeable Income and Allowable Deductions', see **73.34–73.127** below. See also the full contents list above.

The law relating to the taxation of 'trading income' was consolidated in *Income Tax (Trading and Other Income) Act 2005 (ITTOIA 2005)* as part of the Tax Law Rewrite programme. *ITTOIA 2005* has effect for 2005/06 onwards. [*ITTOIA 2005, s 883(1)*]. See HMRC Tax Bulletin June 2005 pp 1210, 1211 for a note on the purposes, nature and structure of *ITTOIA 2005*.

'Trading income' comprises profits from a trade, profession or vocation. Income tax is charged for any tax year on the full amount of the profits of the basis period for that tax year. For basis periods, see **73.3–73.10** below. The person liable for the tax is the person receiving or entitled to the profits. The charge extends to profits arising to a non-UK resident from a trade etc. carried on wholly in the UK or, where a trade etc. is carried on partly in the UK and partly elsewhere, from that part of the trade etc. carried on in the UK. See also **50.5** NON-RESIDENTS. Before 2005/06, the charge was made under *Schedule D, Case I* (for trades), *Schedule D, Case II* (for professions and vocations) or

Schedule D, Case V (for trades, professions and vocations carried on wholly abroad by a UK resident — see **73.13 below), but these labels were removed by *ITTOIA 2005*. [*ITTOIA 2005, ss 5, 6, 7(1)(2), 8*].

Trade 'includes every venture in the nature of trade' [*ITA 2007, s 989*]. For what is a trade, see generally **73.22–73.32 below and in particular, in relation to isolated or speculative transactions, 73.28 below. For a discussion on the** *scope* **of a trade, see HMRC Business Income Manual BIM21000–21040.**

There is no statutory definition of 'profession or vocation'. There are certain provisions applicable only to trades and others applicable only to professions or vocations but the distinction between the two is of limited practical importance. There is no reported case in which it was necessary to decide between the two for income tax purposes, but in a Hong Kong case it was held that stockbrokers were carrying on a trade, not a profession or business (*Kowloon Stock Exchange Ltd v Commr of Inland Revenue* PC, [1984] STC 602). **There are a number of cases turning on whether a business was an exempt profession as specially defined for the purposes of (now defunct) excess profits duty and similar taxes. For these see Tolley's Tax Cases. For professions or vocations (e.g. actor) which necessarily involve carrying out numerous engagements see 73.39 below and 27.54 EMPLOYMENT INCOME.**

In the rest of this chapter, 'trade' includes 'profession or vocation' unless otherwise stated or the context indicates otherwise.

For whether income is liable to tax as trading income or as employment income, see **27.54 EMPLOYMENT INCOME. See also 73.24 below for special treatment of certain divers and diving supervisors.**

Income from land

Rents and other income derived from the exploitation of proprietary interests in land are charged to income tax as **PROPERTY INCOME (60)** and not as income derived from a trade. [*ITTOIA 2005, s 4(1)*]. The leading case is *Salisbury House Estate Ltd v Fry* HL 1930, 15 TC 266, and see also *Sywell Aerodrome Ltd v Croft* CA 1941, 24 TC 126; *Webb v Conelee Properties Ltd* Ch D 1982, 56 TC 149. For relaxations to this rule, see **73.41** below (tied premises), **73.90** below (surplus business accommodation), **60.2 PROPERTY INCOME** (caravan sites) and **60.23 PROPERTY INCOME** (electric-line wayleaves). The commercial *occupation* of UK land with a view to realisation of profits is treated as the carrying on of a trade (though this does not apply to woodlands, for which see also **30.45 EXEMPT INCOME** or if the land in question is being prepared for forestry purposes). [*ITTOIA 2005, ss 10, 11*]. See **73.73** below as regards farming and market gardening.

It is possible for a person to have a separate trade of providing services in conjunction with a letting activity but the services provided must go well beyond those normally provided by a landlord. Even then, the provision of those services does not make the letting activity a trade.

Profits of mines, quarries, gravel pits, sand pits, brickfields, ironworks, gas works, canals, railways, rights of fishing, rights of markets, fairs and tolls and like concerns are computed and charged to income tax *as if* the concern were a trade carried on in the UK, with corresponding treatment for losses. This applies only where the concern is not, in fact, a trade on first principles and is not treated as such under the commercial occupation rule above. It does not impose a charge to tax on a non-UK resident in respect of a non-UK concern. [*ITTOIA 2005, s 12; ITA 2007, Sch 1 para 494*]. As regards rent received in connection with such concerns, see **60.24 PROPERTY INCOME**.

Oil-related activities

The carrying on of oil-related activities (i.e. oil extraction activities within *ITTOIA 2005, s 225A* and any activities consisting of the acquisition, enjoyment or exploitation of oil rights) as part of a trade is treated for income tax purposes as a separate trade in itself. [*ITTOIA 2005, s 16*].

Periods of account

A '*period of account*' in relation to a trade, profession, vocation or other business means a period for which accounts are drawn up. [*ITA 2007, s 989*].

Companies

[73.2] Companies (and other bodies corporate, unincorporated associations and authorised unit trusts — but not partnerships, local authorities or local authority associations) are chargeable to corporation tax on their trading income. Many of the provisions below from **73.22** onwards (relating to chargeable income, allowable deductions and other trading income matters) apply in similar fashion to companies, but from the mid-1990s the move has been towards a separate computational regime for corporation tax, with special rules on, for example, interest (the 'loan relationships' rules), intangible assets and research and development. Due to this diversification, and the fact that the income tax rules are in *ITTOIA 2005* and the corporation tax rules are in *CTA 2009*, it cannot now be assumed that the coverage in this chapter of any particular type of trading receipt or deduction etc. applies equally for corporation tax purposes. Instead, see Tolley's Corporation Tax. The basis period rules at **73.3** *et seq.* below do not apply to companies, which are instead charged to tax by reference to accounting periods (as defined). See **73.14** below for 'notional' commencements or cessations by companies.

Basis periods

[73.3] The basis period for a tax year is the period by reference to which the profits of a business are taxed for that year. The basis period rules are set out in detail in **73.4–73.11** below. In summary the basis periods are generally as follows (subject to any change of accounting date — see **73.7** below).

Opening years of the business (see **73.4** below)

Year 1   Actual

Year 2   12 months ending with the accounting date in the year or, if the period from commencement to the accounting date in the year is less than 12 months, the first 12 months or, if there is no accounting date in the second year, actual

See **73.11** below for relief (overlap relief) where the above rules have the effect of the same profits being taxed in each of two successive tax years.

Intermediate years (see **73.6** below)

The assessment is based on the profits shown by the annual accounts ended within the current tax year.

Closing year (see **73.9** below)

Period from the end of the basis period in the penultimate year to the date of cessation in the year (which may exceed 12 months).

Accounting date

For the purposes of computing basis periods, an 'accounting date' is the date in the tax year to which accounts are drawn up or, if there are two or more such dates, the latest of them. [*ITTOIA 2005, s 197*].

Apportionment of profits to basis periods

Power is given to apportion profits or losses, on a time basis in proportion to the number of days in the respective periods, if required for the purposes of arriving at the profits or losses of a basis period that does not coincide with a period of account. But any reasonable time-based method of apportionment may be used, at the taxpayer's discretion, instead of days, provided it is used consistently for the particular trade; the worked examples in this chapter use months for instance. [*ITTOIA 2005, s 203*]. This applies only where such time apportionment is necessary (see *Marshall Hus & Partners Ltd v Bolton* Ch D 1980, 55 TC 539) and only to the *extent* that it is necessary (see *Lyons v Kelly* (Sp C 334), [2002] SSCD 455).

Simon's Taxes. See B4.101–B4.106.

Opening years

[73.4] On the commencement of a business by an individual (which includes his commencing to carry on an existing business in partnership), the following rules apply. As to what constitutes a commencement etc. see **73.14** below.

First tax year

The assessment will be on the profits (as adjusted for tax purposes) from the commencement date to the following 5 April. [*ITTOIA 2005, s 199*].

Second tax year

If there is an accounting date in the year, the assessment is based on the twelve months to that date. If the period from commencement to the accounting date in the second year is less than twelve months, the assessment is based on the profits for the first twelve months of the business. If there is no accounting date in the second year, the second year's assessment will be on the actual profits for the year, i.e. 6 April to 5 April. [*ITTOIA 2005, s 200*].

See **73.11** below for relief (overlap relief) where the above rules have the effect of the same profits being taxed in each of two successive tax years.

Accounts prepared to 31 March etc. treated as prepared to 5 April

Where the first accounting date (or the first intended accounting date) of the business falls on 31 March or on any of the first four days in April, and that first accounting date falls in the tax year of commencement or either of the next two tax years, the accounts are treated as if prepared to 5 April. (If the business commences after 31 March, profits and losses are treated as nil for that tax year and the actual profits or losses for the short period to 5 April are treated as arising in the basis period for the following tax year.) This treatment avoids creating very short overlaps of basis periods and therefore small amounts of overlap profit. The taxpayer may elect for it *not* to have effect in relation to any tax year. The election must be made on or before the first anniversary of 31 January following the tax year to which it relates. [*ITTOIA 2005, ss 208–210*].

Simon's Taxes. See **B4.102, B4.103, B4.108.**

Example

[73.5]

Owen commences trade on 1 September 2009 and prepares accounts to 30 April, starting with an eight-month period of account to 30 April 2010. His profits (as adjusted for tax purposes) for the first three periods of account are as follows.

	£
Eight months to 30 April 2010	24,000
Year to 30 April 2011	39,000
Year to 30 April 2012	40,000

His taxable profits for the first four tax years are as follows.

	Basis period		£	£
2009/10	1.9.09 – 5.4.10	£24,000 × ⁷/₈		21,000
2010/11	1.9.09 – 31.8.10:			
	1.9.09 – 30.4.10		24,000	
	1.5.10 – 31.8.10	£39,000 × ⁴/₁₂	13,000	
				37,000
2011/12	Y/e 30.4.11			39,000
2012/13	Y/e 30.4.12			40,000

Basis period	£	£
Overlap relief accrued:		
1.9.09 – 5.4.10 — 7 months		21,000
1.5.10 – 31.8.10 — 4 months		13,000
Total overlap relief accrued (see **73.11** below)		£34,000

Intermediate years

[73.6] (Intermediate years are tax years for which the special rules for Opening Years, as in **73.4** above, or for the Closing Year, see **73.9** below, do not apply).

The general rule is that the basis period for a tax year is the period of twelve months ending with the accounting date falling in that tax year. This is subject to any change of accounting date, for which see **73.7** below. If, in a case where neither the opening years rules nor the change of accounting date rules apply (e.g. the next but one tax year after the year of commencement), there is no accounting date in the tax year, the basis period for that tax year is the twelve months immediately following the end of the basis period for the previous tax year. [*ITTOIA 2005, ss 198, 201*].

Change of accounting date

[73.7] Where a change from one accounting date (the old date) to another (the new date) is made in a tax year, the conditions below must be satisfied if the change of accounting date is to result in a change of basis period. (This does not apply if the year is the second or third tax year of the business.) A change of accounting date is made in a tax year if accounts are not made up to the old date in that year or are made up to the new date in that year. The conditions, *all of which must be satisfied*, are as follows.

(1)   The period of account ending with the new date does not exceed 18 months.

(2)   Notice of the change is given to HMRC in a personal (or, where appropriate, a partnership or trust) tax return on or before the day on which that return is required to be delivered (see **63.2, 63.13** RETURNS).

(3)   Either:

(i)   no change of accounting date resulting in a change of basis period has been made in any of the previous five tax years;

or

(ii)   the change is made for commercial reasons (which does not include the obtaining of a tax advantage). If this condition is relied upon, the notice in (2) above must set out the reasons for the change and HMRC then have 60 days, beginning with receipt of the notice, in which to give notice to the trader, if they wish, that they are *not* satisfied that the change is made for commercial reasons. (An appeal may be made against such an

HMRC notice, within 30 days beginning with the date of issue, and the Appeal Tribunal may either confirm the notice or set it aside.)

Where all the conditions are satisfied, or the change of accounting date is made in the second or third tax year of the business, the basis period for the tax year is as follows.

(a) If the year is the second tax year of the business, the basis period is the twelve months ending with the new date in the year (unless the period from commencement of the business to the new date in the second year is less than twelve months, in which case the basis period is the first twelve months of the business).

(b) If the 'relevant period' is a period of less than twelve months, the basis period is the twelve months ending with the new date in the year.

(c) If the 'relevant period' is a period of more than twelve months, the basis period consists of the relevant period.

The '*relevant period*' is the period beginning immediately after the end of the basis period for the preceding year and ending with the new date in the year.

It will be seen that a basis period can be of more than twelve months' duration but cannot be less than twelve months. If not all of the above conditions are satisfied (and the year is not the second or third tax year of the business), the basis period for the year is the twelve months beginning immediately after the end of the basis period for the preceding year. However, the change of accounting date is then treated as made in the following tax year and can thus result in a change of basis period for that following year if all the above conditions are satisfied as regards that year. A change of accounting date can continue to be 'carried forward' in this way until such time, if any, as a change of basis period results or the old accounting date is reverted to.

[*ITTOIA 2005, ss 214–219; SI 2009 No 56, Sch 1 para 440*].

See **73.11** below for relief (overlap relief) where the rules in (a) or (b) above have the effect of the same profits being taxed in each of two successive tax years, and for the use of overlap relief brought forward in computing profits in a situation within (c) above.

For partnership trades, notice in (2) above and an appeal within (3)(ii) above must be given or brought by such one of the partners as is nominated by them for the purpose (any resulting change of basis period affecting the notional trades of individual partners — see **52.4 PARTNERSHIPS**). [*ITTOIA 2005, s 853(3)*].

Accounts prepared to a variable date

Sometimes accounts are prepared to a particular day in the year (e.g. the last Friday in September) rather than a particular date. Provided that day can fall on one of only seven consecutive dates (or eight where 29 February is involved), there are provisions enabling the fourth of those seven or eight dates (the '*middle date*') to be treated, for these purposes only, as the normal accounting date, so that the change of accounting date rules above are not triggered by these minor changes from one year to the next. These provisions apply in relation to any particular tax year only if the taxpayer makes an election to that effect. The election must be made on or before the first anniversary of 31 January following the tax year to which it relates, and must specify both the actual accounting date for that tax year and the middle date. A change from an accounting date determined under these rules to an actual accounting date is, however, treated as a change of accounting date, even if those two dates happen to be the same. On cessation or a change of accounting date, basis periods are determined as if the basis period for the previous tax year had ended on the actual accounting date in that year and not on the middle date. [*ITTOIA 2005, ss 211–213, 214(2)*].

Simon's Taxes. See **B4.109, B4.110.**

Examples

[73.8]

(i) Change to a date earlier in the tax year

Miranda commenced trade on 1 September 2007, preparing accounts to 31 August. In 2010, she changed her accounting date to 31 May, preparing accounts for the nine months to 31 May 2010. The conditions in **73.7**(1)–(3) above are satisfied in relation to the change. Her profits (as adjusted for tax purposes) are as follows.

	£
Year ended 31 August 2008	18,000
Year ended 31 August 2009	21,500
Nine months to 31 May 2010	17,000
Year ended 31 May 2011	23,000

Taxable profits for the first five tax years are as follows.

	Basis period		£	£
2007/08	1.9.07 – 5.4.08	£18,000 × $^7/_{12}$		10,500
2008/09	Y/e 31.8.08			18,000
2009/10	Y/e 31.8.09			21,500
2010/11	1.6.09 – 31.5.10:			
	1.6.09 – 31.8.09	£21,500 × $^3/_{12}$	5,375	
	1.9.09 – 31.5.10		17,000	
				22,375
2011/12	Y/e 31.5.11			23,000

Overlap relief accrued (see **73.11** below)

	£
1.9.07 – 5.4.08 — 7 months	10,500
1.6.09 – 31.8.09 — 3 months	5,375
Total overlap relief accrued	£15,875

Note

(a)   In this example, the 'relevant period' is that from 1 September 2009 (the day following the end of the basis period for 2009/10) to 31 May 2010 (the new accounting date in the year 2010/11 — the year of change). As the relevant period is less than 12 months, the basis period for 2010/11 is the 12 months ending on the new accounting date.

(ii) Change to a date later in the tax year

Dennis starts a business on 1 July 2007, preparing accounts to 30 June. In 2010, he changes his accounting date to 31 December, preparing accounts for the six months to 31 December 2010. The conditions in **73.7**(1)–(3) above are satisfied in relation to the change. His profits (as adjusted for tax purposes) are as follows.

	£
Year ended 30 June 2008	18,000
Year ended 30 June 2009	21,500
Year ended 30 June 2010	23,000
Six months to 31 December 2010	12,000
Year ended 31 December 2011	27,000

Taxable profits for the first five years are as follows.

	Basis period		£	£
2007/08	1.7.07 – 5.4.08	£18,000 × $^9/_{12}$		13,500
2008/09	Y/e 30.6.08			18,000
2009/10	Y/e 30.6.09			21,500
2010/11	1.7.09 – 31.12.10:			
	1.7.09 – 30.6.10		23,000	
	1.7.10 – 31.12.10		12,000	
			35,000	
	Deduct Overlap relief		9,000	
				26,000
2011/12	Y/e 31.12.11			27,000

Overlap relief accrued:

1.7.07 – 5.4.08 — 9 months	£13,500
Less utilised in 2010/11	£9,000
Carried forward	£4,500

Utilisation of overlap relief in 2010/11

$$\text{Apply the formula: } A \times \frac{B - C}{D}$$

(see **73.11** below)

Where

A = aggregate overlap relief accrued (£13,500);
B = length of basis period for 2010/11 (18 months);
C = 12 months; and
D = the length of the overlap period(s) by reference to which the aggregate over-lap profits accrued (9 months).

Thus, the deduction to be given in computing profits for 2010/11 is:

$$£13,500 \times \frac{18-12}{9} = £9,000$$

Notes

(a) In this example, the 'relevant period' is that from 1 July 20089 (the day following the end of the basis period for 2009/10) to 31 December 2010 (the new accounting date in the year 2010/11 — the year of change). As the relevant period is more than 12 months, the basis period for 2010/11 is equal to the relevant period. Note that a basis period of 18 months results in this case, even though accounts were prepared for a period of only 6 months to the new date.

(b) The overlap relief accrued (by reference to an overlap period of 9 months) is given on cessation or, as in this example, on a change of accounting date resulting in a basis period exceeding 12 months (the relief given depending on the extent of the excess). The balance of overlap relief (£4,500) is carried forward for future relief on the happening of such an event. See **73.11** below. If Dennis had changed his accounting date to, say, 31 March or 5 April (instead of 31 December), the use of the formula in **73.11** below would have resulted in overlap relief of £13,500 being given in full in 2010/11.

Closing year

[73.9] On cessation of a business carried on by an individual (which includes his leaving a continuing partnership and his transferring the ownership of a business, e.g. on sale, incorporation or death), the following rule applies. As to what constitutes a cessation, see **73.14** below.

The basis period for the **final tax year**, i.e. that in which cessation occurs, is the period beginning immediately after the end of the basis period for the penultimate year and ending with the date of cessation. (If a business starts and ceases in the same tax year, the basis period is the actual period of trading.) [*ITTOIA 2005, s 202*].

The basis period may thus exceed twelve months, but see **73.11** below as regards the use of overlap relief brought forward in computing profits for the final year.

See **45.21** LOSSES for terminal losses and **45.20** LOSSES for the carry-forward of certain losses where a private business is converted into a company.

Simon's Taxes. See **B4.105**.

Example

[73.10]

Robin commenced to trade on 1 May 2006, preparing accounts to 30 April. He permanently ceases to trade on 30 June 2010, preparing accounts for the two months to that date. His profits (as adjusted for tax purposes) are as follows.

	£
Year ended 30 April 2007	24,000
Year ended 30 April 2008	48,000
Year ended 30 April 2009	96,000
Year ended 30 April 2010	36,000
Two months ended 30 June 2010	5,000
	£209,000

Taxable profits for the five tax years of trading are as follows.

	Basis period		£	£
2006/07	1.5.06 – 5.4.07	£24,000 × $^{11}/_{12}$		22,000
2007/08	Y/e 30.4.07			24,000
2008/09	Y/e 30.4.08			48,000
2009/10	Y/e 30.4.09			96,000
2010/11	1.5.09 – 30.6.10:			
	1.5.09 – 30.4.10		36,000	
	1.5.10 – 30.6.10		5,000	
			41,000	
	Deduct Overlap relief		22,000	
				19,000
				£209,000

Overlap relief accrued (see **73.11** below):

	£
1.5.06 – 5.4.07 — 11 months	22,000
Utilised in 2010/11	(22,000)

Overlap relief

[73.11] An 'overlap profit' is an amount of profits which, by virtue of the basis period rules above, is included in the computations for two successive tax years. It may arise as a result of the opening year rules in **73.4** above or on a change of basis period within **73.7**(a) or (b) above (i.e. resulting from a change of accounting date). An 'overlap period' in relation to an overlap profit is the number of days in the period for which the overlap profit arose. For example (working in terms of months for simplicity), if a business commences on

1 May 2009 and prepares its first accounts for the year to 30 April 2010 showing tax-adjusted profits of £24,000, the 2009/10 assessment is based on the period 1 May 2009 to 5 April 2010 (£24,000 × $^{11}/_{12}$ = £22,000) and the 2010/11 assessment is based on the year ended 30 April 2010 (£24,000). The overlap profit is £22,000 by reference to an overlap period of 11 months.

Relief for an overlap profit is given, by way of a deduction in computing profits, on a change of accounting date resulting in a basis period of more than twelve months (see **73.7**(c) above) and/or in the final tax year of the business (see **73.9** above).

Change of accounting date

On the first such change of accounting date, if any, the deduction is:

$$A \times \frac{B - C}{D}$$

Where

A	=	the aggregate of any overlap profits;
B	=	the number of days in the basis period (i.e. more than 365 or 366);
C	=	the number of days in the tax year (365 or 366); and
D	=	the aggregate of the overlap periods by reference to which the overlap profits in A are calculated.

For example (working in terms of months for simplicity), if the overlap profit brought forward is £22,000 by reference to an overlap period of 11 months, and the basis period for a tax year is 15 months, the overlap relief deductible in computing profits for that year is £22,000 × $^{3}/_{11}$ = £6,000, leaving an overlap profit of £16,000, by reference to an overlap period of eight months, to be carried forward. On subsequent applications of this formula, A and D are reduced by, respectively, the overlap profit previously relieved and the number of days referable to the previous relief.

At the taxpayer's discretion, a change of accounting date to 31 March or to any of the first four days in April can be treated for overlap relief purposes as if it were a change to 5 April, thus enabling all outstanding overlap relief to be deducted.

In the above formula, any reasonable measure may be used at the taxpayer's discretion instead of days, provided that measure is used consistently for the particular trade, so that, over the lifetime of the business, the taxable profit charged equals the taxable profit made (see also **73.3** above under Apportionment of profits to basis periods). (The worked examples in this chapter use months for instance.)

If days are used in the formula and the change is to 5 April (or is treated as such, as above), the occurrence of 29 February can be ignored in making the calculation if the overlap relief would not otherwise be relieved in full.

Cessation

On cessation, the deduction in computing profits for the final tax year is equal to the total overlap profits previously unrelieved.

Effect of overlap relief on losses

Relief for an overlap profit is not restricted to the amount of profits available, and may convert a taxable trading profit into an allowable trading loss, or increase an allowable trading loss, which may be relieved in the same way as any other trading loss (see **45 LOSSES**). Where it creates or augments a terminal loss claim (see **45.21 LOSSES**), the full amount of the overlap profit is included, without any apportionment.

[*ITTOIA 2005, ss 204, 205, 220*].

See **73.12** below for overlap profits arising under transitional rules for businesses commenced before 6 April 1994.

Overlap losses

Where an amount of loss would otherwise fall to be included in the computations for two successive tax years, that amount (the '*overlap loss*') is not to be so included for the second of those years. [*ITTOIA 2005, s 206*].

Simon's Taxes. See B4.105, B4.107.

Transitional rules for businesses commenced before 6 April 1994

[73.12] A business commenced before 6 April 1994 is treated as having a transitional overlap profit for 1997/98. This is equal to the amount of profits taxable for 1997/98, but before deduction/addition of capital allowances/balancing charges (except in the case of a partnership with a corporate partner), which arises after the end of the basis period for 1996/97 and before 6 April 1997. For example, if accounts are regularly made up to 30 June and those for the year to 30 June 1997 showed tax-adjusted profits of £20,000 before capital allowances, the 1997/98 assessment would have been £20,000 *less* capital allowances and there will be a transitional overlap profit of £15,000 by reference to a transitional overlap period of nine months, 1 July 1996 to 5 April 1997 (working in terms of months rather than days, for simplicity). The transitional overlap profit is carried forward indefinitely in the same way as other overlap profits until fully relieved (see **73.11** above). [*FA 1994, Sch 20 para 2(4)–(4B)*].

Trades carried on abroad

[73.13] Trading profits arising to a UK resident are chargeable to income tax wherever the trade is carried on. [*ITTOIA 2005, s 6(1)(3)*]. This encompasses trades, professions and vocations carried on either wholly or partly abroad.

A non-UK resident is chargeable to income tax to the extent that he carries on a trade etc. in the UK (see **73.1** above and **50.5 NON-RESIDENTS**).

Where a business is 'carried on' for these purposes depends on from where it is managed and controlled, irrespective of where the day-to-day business activities are conducted. See for this *Trustees of Ferguson, decd v Donovan Supreme Court* (IFS) 1927, 1 ITC 214 (trustees delegated control of Australian business to Australian company and did not interfere in any way; held not within Case I) and contrast *Ogilvie v Kitton* CES 1908, 5 TC 338 (Canadian business managed by Canadians but 'head and brains' in UK where owners resided; Case I applied) and *Spiers v Mackinnon* KB 1929, 14 TC 386.

See **73.16** below for provisions applying where an individual carrying on a business wholly or partly outside the UK becomes or ceases to be UK resident.

For special considerations concerning partnership trades carried on wholly or partly outside the UK, see **52.20 PARTNERSHIPS**.

Trades carried on wholly abroad — remittance basis

For trades carried on wholly outside the UK (see *ITTOIA 2005, s 7(5)*), the remittance basis may apply to individuals who are either not domiciled or not ordinarily resident in the UK. See **61 REMITTANCE BASIS**. Before 2008/09 this did not apply in the case of trades carried on in Ireland.

Trades carried on wholly abroad — loss reliefs

Where the trade is carried on wholly outside the UK, loss reliefs under **45.2**, **45.9**, **45.20** and **45.21 LOSSES** are available only against the profits of trades carried on wholly abroad, chargeable overseas earnings (see **27.5**, **27.10 EMPLOYMENT INCOME**), overseas government pensions (as in **56.2**(f) **PENSION INCOME**) and certain other foreign pensions (see **56.2**(b)(e)(h)(i) **PENSION INCOME**), but excluding any 'relevant foreign income' (see **32.2 FOREIGN INCOME**) charged on the **REMITTANCE BASIS** (**61**). Relief under **45.7 LOSSES** (set-off against chargeable gains) is not available at all. [*ITA 2007, s 95; ICTA 1988, ss 68(4), 391*].

Trades carried on wholly abroad — travelling etc. expenses

If, either alone or in partnership, an individual carries on a trade wholly outside the UK (a 'foreign trade'), a deduction is available for certain expenditure on travel, board and lodging which is incurred in connection with that trade and which would not otherwise be allowable due to its failing to meet the 'wholly and exclusively' rule at **73.36** below. The deduction is given in computing profits of the foreign trade, but is not available where such profits are charged on the remittance basis. It is given only where the trader's absence from the UK is wholly and exclusively for the purpose of carrying on either the foreign trade or that trade and one or more other trades (be they foreign trades or not).

The deductible expenses are as follows.

(a)　Expenses incurred by the trader in travelling between a UK location and the location of the foreign trade.

(b)　Expenses incurred by the trader on board and lodging at the location of the foreign trade.

(c)   Expenses incurred by the trader in travelling between the location of the foreign trade and the non-UK location of any other trade carried on by him wholly or partly outside the UK.

(d)   If the trader's continuous absence from the UK lasts 60 days or more, expenses of a journey made by his spouse (or, from 5 December 2005, civil partner) or by any child of his between a UK location and the location of any of the trades in question where that journey is made in order to accompany the trader at the beginning of his period of absence or to visit him during that period or is a return journey in connection with a journey of either of those kinds. The deduction is limited to the expenses of two such outward journeys and two return journeys per person per tax year. 'Child' includes a stepchild or an illegitimate child but does not include a person aged 18 or over at the start of the outward journey.

Where more than one foreign trade is carried on at the overseas location, expenses within (a) and (b) above are allocated between the trades on a just and reasonable basis. Where the trader's absence is for the purpose of carrying on more than one foreign trade, expenses within (d) above are likewise allocated on a just and reasonable basis. Expenses within (c) above are allocated to the trade carried on at the journey's destination if that is a foreign trade; otherwise they are allocated to the foreign trade carried on at the place of departure. If more than one foreign trade is carried on at the place of destination or at the place of departure, as the case may be, the expenses are again allocated between the foreign trades on a just and reasonable basis.

[ITTOIA 2005, ss 92–94].

Simon's Taxes. See B1.207, B1.302, B2.440, E1.1025.

Whether or not there has been a commencement or cessation

[73.14] The rules at 73.4 and 73.9 above for the opening and closing years apply (i) on the commencement of a new business or the permanent cessation of a business by an individual (including a transfer of the ownership of a business, e.g. when it is sold or incorporated or it passes on death) and (ii) on an individual becoming or ceasing to be a member of a partnership (*but not so as to affect the continuing partners*) — see 52.4 PARTNERSHIPS.

See 52.9 PARTNERSHIPS as regards partnership mergers and demergers.

If a trade is being carried on by trustees of a trust or by personal representatives of a deceased person, a mere change of trustee etc. does not give rise to a cessation and re-commencement of the trade. [ITTOIA 2005, s 258].

Non-resident companies are within the charge to income tax (not corporation tax) in certain circumstances (see Tolley's Corporation Tax under Residence). Where a company starts or ceases to be within the charge to income tax in respect of a trade, it is treated as notionally starting or permanently ceasing to carry on the trade at that time. [ITTOIA 2005, s 18].For a short article on the distinction between succession to a trade, extension of an existing trade and commencement of a new trade, see Revenue Tax Bulletin February 1996 pp 285, 286. For an in-depth discussion, see HMRC Business Income Manual BIM70500–70690.

Simon's Taxes. See B1.6.

Case law

[73.15] Whether or not a person has commenced/ceased trading and, if so, the date, are questions of fact. Preliminary activities in setting up a business do not amount to trading (*Birmingham & District Cattle By-Products Co Ltd v CIR* KB 1919, 12 TC 92). Negotiations to enter into the initial contracts are part of setting up the trade and do not mean trading has commenced (*Mansell v HMRC* (Sp C 551), [2006] SSCD 605). For pre-trading expenditure, see **73.102** below. For whether the sale of a business can be effective for tax purposes before the vending agreement, see *Todd v Jones Bros Ltd* KB 1930, 15 TC 396 and contrast *Angel v Hollingworth & Co* Ch D 1958, 37 TC 714. 'Permanent discontinuance' does not mean a discontinuance which is everlasting (see *Ingram v Callaghan* CA 1968, 45 TC 151) but a trade may continue notwithstanding a lengthy break in active trading (*Kirk & Randall Ltd v Dunn* KB 1924, 8 TC 663 but contrast *Goff v Osborne & Co (Sheffield) Ltd* Ch D 1953, 34 TC 441). An intensification by a freelance television producer of his freelance activities could not effect a discontinuance and commencement of a new business (*Edmunds v Coleman* Ch D 1997, 70 TC 322).

In a case where the global business of a company was run on the basis of divisions operating autonomously with their own operational management and reporting lines, supply chain, products, manufacturing, premises, sales organisation, notepaper, invoicing and accounting, the closure of two out of six UK divisions, all concerned with electronics products, did not amount to cessation for purposes of terminal loss relief; the company was held to be carrying on a single trade (*Electronics Ltd v HM Inspector of Taxes* (Sp C 476), [2005] SSCD 512).

A company which used to deal in computers and computer software and subsequently went on to provide IT consultancy services instead was held for loss relief purposes to have carried on two different trades at different times; it was inappropriate to regard both activities as part of a single trade carrying the general description of IT-related activities (*Kawthar Consulting Ltd v HMRC* (Sp C 477), [2005] SSCD 524).

The trade was held to have been continuous when the owner of a drifter continued to manage it after its war-time requisition (*Sutherland v CIR* CS 1918, 12 TC 63); when a merchant sold stock on hand after announcing retirement (*J & R O'Kane v CIR* HL 1922, 12 TC 303); when a flour miller and baker gave up a mill (*Bolands Ltd v Davis* KB(IFS) 1925, 4 ATC 532); when a barrister took silk (*Seldon v Croom-Johnson* KB 1932, 16 TC 740); when a partnership was dissolved but completed open forward contracts (*Hillerns & Fowler v Murray* CA 1932, 17 TC 77); when a building partnership transferred construction activities to a company but retained building land and continued to sell land with houses built thereon by the company (*Watts v Hart* Ch D 1984, 58 TC 209). A new trade was held to have commenced when the vendor of a business retained the benefit of outstanding hire-purchase agreements (*Parker v Batty* KB 1941, 23 TC 739) and when the vendor of a business got commission on open contracts completed by the purchaser (*Southern v Cohen's Exors* KB 1940, 23 TC 566).

It is similarly a question of fact whether a trader expanding by taking over an existing business and operating it as a branch has succeeded to the trade. See e.g. *Bell v National Provincial Bank of England Ltd* CA 1903, 5 TC 1 (bank succeeded to trade of single-branch bank taken over); *Laycock v Freeman Hardy & Willis Ltd* CA 1938, 22 TC 288 (shoe retailer did not succeed to trade of manufacturing subsidiaries taken over); *Briton Ferry Steel Co Ltd v Barry* CA 1939, 23 TC 414 (steel manufacturer succeeded to trade of tinplate manufacturing subsidiaries taken over); and *Maidment v Kibby* Ch D 1993, 66 TC 137 (fish and chip shop proprietor did not succeed to trade of existing business taken over). See also *H & G Kinemas Ltd* KB 1933, 18 TC 116 (cinema company disposed of existing cinemas and opened new one, held to commence new trade).

Change of residence

[73.16] A special rule applies where a sole trader carrying on his trade wholly or partly outside the UK either becomes or ceases to be resident in the UK. The trade is deemed to have been permanently discontinued at the time of the change of residence and, in so far as the individual continues to carry on the actual trade, a new trade is deemed to have been set up immediately afterwards. This applies equally for the purposes of loss reliefs except that a loss incurred in the 'old' trade may be carried forward under *ITA 2007, s 83* (see **45.20** LOSSES) and set against profits of the 'new' trade. [*ITTOIA 2005, s 17; ITA 2007, Sch 1 para 496*].

Similar rules apply to individuals trading in partnership (see **52.20** PARTNERSHIPS).

Accounts and accounts information

[73.17] Under self-assessment, it is not a requirement that accounts should accompany tax returns. Instead (except in cases where the annual turnover is less than the VAT registration threshold (see below), accounts information has to be provided on the self-employment supplementary pages to the return. There are full and short versions of these supplementary pages; the version to be used depends on various criteria such as turnover and complexity (see HMRC's Notes on Self-Employment — SA103F for the criteria).

Three-line accounts

Where turnover is less than the VAT registration threshold (£70,000 for 2010/11, £68,000 for 2009/10), or the appropriate proportion of that amount where the period of account is less than a year, only turnover, total expenses and profit or loss need be shown in the return. There are, however, strict requirements as to maintenance and preservation of records. (www.hmrc.gov.uk/factsheet/three line-account.pdf). See **63.5** RETURNS.

See **73.92** below for deductibility of accountancy fees.

Rounding of tax computations

To reduce the compliance burden on large businesses whose statutory accounts are produced in round thousands, HMRC are generally prepared to accept profit returns for tax purposes in figures rounded to the nearest £1,000 from single businesses with an annual turnover of at least £5 million (including investment and estate income) in the accounts in question or in the preceding year, where rounding at least to that extent has been used in preparing the accounts. Such returns must be accompanied by a certificate by the person preparing the computations stating the basis of rounding, and confirming that it is unbiased, has been applied consistently and produces a fair result for tax purposes (and stating the program or software used where relevant), or, if there have been no changes from the previous year in these respects, confirming the unchanged basis. The rounding may not extend to the tax payable or other relevant figures of tax. Rounding is not acceptable where it would impede the application of the legislation, or where recourse to the underlying records would normally be necessary to do the computation. Thus it is not acceptable e.g. in computations of chargeable gains (except in relation to the incidental costs of acquisition and disposal), in accrued income scheme computations (see **2 ACCRUED INCOME SCHEME**), in computations of tax credit relief or in certain capital allowance computations. HMRC officers may exceptionally insist that rounding is not used in other circumstances. (HMRC SP 15/93).

Examination of accounts information by HMRC

For HMRC's enquiry powers under self-assessment, see **63.6** *et seq.* **RETURNS**. An enquiry into a tax return may well include an examination of the accounts information included in the return and/or the underlying accounts themselves. See generally HMRC Pamphlet COP 11. See also **55.10, 55.13, 55.22 PENAL-TIES.**

Business Economic Notes

Business Economic Notes (BENs) relating to various trades, which were once used by HMRC as background information in examining accounts information, are available on the HMRC website at www.hmrc.gov.uk/bens/index.htm. However, see also below under Tactical and Information Packages (TIPs). The full list of published BENs is as follows.

1. Travel agents.
2. Road haulage.
3. The lodging industry.
4. Hairdressers.
5. Waste materials reclamation and disposals.
6. Funeral directors.
7. Dentists.

14. The pet industry.
15. Veterinary surgeons.
16. Catering — general.
17. — restaurants.
18. — fast-foods, cafes and snack-bars.
19. Farming — stock valuation for income tax purposes.
20. Insurance brokers and agents.

8. Florists.

9. Licensed victuallers.

10. The jewellery trade.

11. Electrical retailers.

12. Antiques and fine art dealers.

13. Fish and chip shops.

21. Residential rest and nursing homes.

22. Dispensing chemists.

23. Driving instructors.

24. Independent fishmongers.

25. Taxicabs and private hire vehicles.

26. Confectioners, tobacconists and newsagents.

Tactical and Information Packages

No new BENs have been published since November 1997 and it is understood that they have been replaced internally within HMRC by Tactical and Information Packages (TIPs). These were not originally made available to the public at all but were to be placed on the HMRC website over a period of time with sensitive material withheld. The first published TIPs appeared on the website in September 2006. TIPs are described by HMRC as trade/profession-based notes for internal use by HMRC officers; they combine sector/trade information, together with risk reviews and tactical information, with the primary purpose of supporting compliance activity throughout HMRC; they are designed to promote commercial awareness within HMRC and to provide information on trading practices, markets, competition etc. but are not intended to provide a definitive picture of any particular trade. However, HMRC have since **withdrawn** all published TIPs from their website following 'a review of our publication policy'.

Understated profits

The measure of understated profits is calculated from the available data, but if this is unsatisfactory, on the increase of capital from year to year, with adjustments for cost of living etc. See for this, cases mentioned at **6.4** ASSESSMENTS and *Deacon v Roper* Ch D 1952, 33 TC 66; *Horowitz v Farrand* Ch D 1952, 33 TC 221; *Moschi v Kelly* CA 1952, 33 TC 442; *Kilburn v Bedford* Ch D 1955, 36 TC 262; *Roberts v McGregor* Ch D 1959, 38 TC 610; *Chuwen v Sabine* Ch D 1959, 39 TC 1; *Erddig Motors Ltd v McGregor* Ch D 1961, 40 TC 95; *Hellier v O'Hare* Ch D 1964, 42 TC 155; *Hurley v Young* Ch D 1966, 45 ATC 316; *Hope v Damerel* Ch D 1969, 48 ATC 461; *Driver v CIR* CS 1977, 52 TC 153; *Kovak v Morris* CA 1985, 58 TC 493 and cf. *Rose v Humbles* CA 1971, 48 TC 103. For a case in which similar principles were applied in determining directors' true remuneration, see *Billows v Robinson* Ch D 1989, 64 TC 17.

HMRC officers will not automatically insist on annual capital statements (see above) where understated profits can be measured satisfactorily in other ways, such as by use of expected rates of gross trading profits (Revenue Press Release 1 August 1977).

Adherence to GAAP

[73.18] The profits of a trade, profession or vocation must be computed in accordance with '*generally accepted accounting practice*' (GAAP) (see also **73.19** below), which is defined (by *ITA 2007, s 997*) by reference to the practice adopted in UK company accounts that are drawn up to give a true and fair view. Despite this reference to 'company accounts', it must be emphasised that the requirement applies for income tax as well as corporation tax purposes. The requirement is, however, subject to any adjustment required or authorised by law; see, for example, the prohibition at **73.35** below on deducting capital expenditure. GAAP also incorporates international accounting standards in cases where accounts are prepared in accordance with such standards; in all other cases, the expression is restricted to UK GAAP.

The above requirement imposes a general requirement to apply an earnings basis (see below) for tax purposes, whilst at the same time importing the accountancy concept of 'materiality', allowing a practical view to be taken of the time at which immaterial amounts are recognised. It requires neither the auditing of accounts, nor additional disclosure, nor the preparation of a balance sheet. Neither does it require accounts to be drawn up on any particular basis (provided the necessary adjustments are made in the tax computation). For HMRC's view of what is meant by 'true and fair view', see Revenue Tax Bulletin December 1998 pp 606–615. See HMRC Business Income Manual BIM31045–31047 as regards the concept of materiality. See also **73.19** below.

The special computational rules for **UNDERWRITERS AT LLOYD'S (74)** are not affected by the above requirement.

There is an exemption for barristers and advocates in the early years of practice (see **13.2 CASH BASIS FOR BARRISTERS AND ADVOCATES** and **73.20** below).

[*ITTOIA 2005, s 25; ITA 2007, s 997; SI 2008 No 954, Arts 1, 24, 36*].

The earnings basis

Prior to the introduction of the above requirement, case law had previously established that the legal basis for computation of profits was the earnings basis with provision for debtors, creditors, accruals and stock and work in progress (cf. *CIR v Gardner Mountain & D'Ambrumenil Ltd* HL 1947, 29 TC 69). Hence profits and losses which have not accrued cannot be anticipated (cf. *Willingale v International Commercial Bank Ltd* HL 1977, 52 TC 242) nor can future expenses. Conversely an expense actually incurred may be allowable in full even though the benefit from it will not accrue until later years (*Vallambrosa Rubber Co Ltd v Farmer* CES 1910, 5 TC 529; *Duple Motor Bodies Ltd v Ostime* HL 1961, 39 TC 537).

See **73.49** below as regards future and contingent liabilities generally.

Meaning of 'receipts' and 'expenses'

Wherever they appear in income tax legislation in the context of computing trading profits, the words 'receipts' and 'expenses' refer generally to items brought into account as credits or debits in computing those profits, and contain no implication that an amount has been actually received or paid. [*ITTOIA 2005, s 27*].

Application of accountancy principles

[**73.19**] See **73.18** above as regards the requirement that generally accepted accounting practice (GAAP) be adhered to in the computation of taxable profits. Even prior to the introduction of this requirement, it had long since been the case that, since the starting figure in computing profits was that brought out by the accounts of the business, accountancy principles were of the greatest importance. They could not, however, override established income tax principles (*Heather v P-E Consulting Group Ltd* CA 1972, 48 TC 293; *Willingale v International Commercial Bank Ltd* HL 1977, 52 TC 242; but see *Threlfall v Jones* CA 1993, 66 TC 77; *Johnston v Britannia Airways Ltd* Ch D 1994, 67 TC 99). See also *RTZ Oil & Gas Ltd v Elliss* Ch D 1987, 61 TC 132. A 'provision for a future operating loss', whose inclusion could not be said to have 'violated existing accounting principles', was disallowed in *Meat Traders Ltd v Cushing* (Sp C 131), [1997] SSCD 245). See *Robertson v CIR* (Sp C 137), [1997] SSCD 282 as regards timing of inclusion of insurance agents' advance commission. See also *Herbert Smith v Honour* Ch D 1999, 72 TC 130 for the timing of deductions in respect of future rents under leases of premises ceasing to be used for business purposes, and Revenue Press Release 20 July 1999 for Inland Revenue practice following that decision.

Per Sir Thomas Bingham MR in *Threlfall v Jones*: ' . . . I find it hard to understand how any judge-made rule could override the application of a generally accepted rule of commercial accountancy which (a) applied to the situation in question, (b) was not one of two or more rules applicable to the situation in question and (c) was not shown to be inconsistent with the true facts or otherwise inapt to determine the true profits or losses of the business'. FRS 18 now requires companies to choose accounting policies that are most appropriate to their particular circumstances (see Revenue Tax Bulletin April 2002 p 924).

For HMRC's view on the relationship between accounting profits and taxable profits, see HMRC Business Income Manual BIM31000–31120 and Revenue Tax Bulletin December 1997 pp 485, 486, February 1999 pp 623–625, April 1999 pp 636–641, December 1999 pp 707–709, June 2001 pp 859, 86. For generally accepted accounting practice and accounting standards, see BIM31020–31070. For the timing of deductions where an expense is taken to the balance sheet rather than charged immediately against profits, i.e. *deferred revenue expenditure*, see HMRC Business Income Manual BIM42215, 42220. For *provisions*, see HMRC Business Income Manual BIM46500 *et seq.* and Revenue Press Release 20 July 1999, Revenue Tax Bulletin December 1999 pp 707–709.

Adjustments on a change of basis

[73.20] The adjustment described below is required where:

- there is, from one period of account of a trade, profession or vocation to the next, a 'change of basis' in computing taxable profits;
- the old basis accorded with the law or practice applicable in relation to the period of account before the change; and
- the new basis accords with the law and practice applicable in relation to the period of account following the change.

A *'change of basis'* for this purpose is either (i) a change of accounting principle or practice that, in accordance with generally accepted accounting practice (see **73.18** above), gives rise to a prior period adjustment, or (ii) a change in the statutory tax adjustments applied (including a change resulting from a change of view as to application of the statute but excluding a change made to comply with an amendment to the statute which was not applicable to the earlier period of account).

A *'change of basis'* also includes a change from using UK GAAP (see **73.18** above) to using international accounting standards.

Tax treatment of adjustment

Subject to the exceptions at (i)–(iv) below, an adjustment of a positive amount ('adjustment income') is treated for income tax purposes as income arising on the last day of the first period of account for which the new basis is adopted. Tax is charged on the full amount of any adjustment income arising in a tax year. The adjustment income is charged separately from the trading profits. However, for loss relief purposes it is treated as profits of the trade etc. for the tax year in which tax is charged on it. In the case of an individual for whom the income from the trade etc. is 'relevant UK earnings' (see **57.7 PENSION PROVISION**) the adjustment income is similarly relevant UK earnings. An adjustment of a negative amount (an 'adjustment expense') is treated as an expense of the trade arising on the last day of the first period of account for which the new basis is adopted.

Calculation of adjustment

Subject to the exceptions at (i)–(iv) below, the calculation of the required adjustment can be summarised as follows.

(a) Taxable receipts and allowable expenses of the trade etc. for periods of account before the change are determined and compared on both the old and new bases to give a net understatement (or overstatement) of profits or losses on the old basis (when compared with the new). See *ITTOIA 2005, s 231, Step 1 (Items 1 & 2) and Step 2 (Items 1 & 2)*.

(b) That figure is then adjusted for any difference between the closing stock or work in progress for the last period of account before the change and the opening stock or work in progress for the first period of account after the change, also taking account of any change in the basis of calculating those amounts. See *ITTOIA 2005, s 231, Step 1 (Item 3) and Step 2 (Item 3)*.

(c)   Finally an adjustment is made for depreciation to the extent that it was not the subject of an adjustment for tax purposes in the last period of account before the change but would be the subject of such an adjustment on the new basis. See *ITTOIA 2005, s 231, Step 1 (Item 4)*.

The resultant figure, be it positive or negative, is accorded the tax treatment described above. Amounts deducted in making the calculation cannot again be deducted in computing the profits of any period of account.

Exceptions

Exceptions to the above are as follows.

(i)   *Expenses spread over more than one period of account after the change* on the new basis which were brought into account before the change on the old basis are excluded from the calculation at (a) above, but may not be deducted for any period of account after the change.

(ii)   *Adjustment not required until asset realised or written off.* Where the change of basis results from a tax adjustment affecting the calculation of amounts within (b) or (c) above, the adjustment required by (b) or (c) is brought into account only when the asset concerned is realised or written off.

(iii) *Change from realisation basis to mark to market*, i.e. from recognition of a profit or loss on an asset only when it is realised to bringing assets into account in each period of account at fair value. Any adjustment required by (a) above for an understatement of profit (or overstatement of loss) in relation to an asset that is trading stock within *ITTOIA 2005, s 174* is not given effect until the period of account in which the value of the asset is realised. An election may, however, be made for the adjustment income to be spread equally over six periods of account beginning with the first period to which the new basis applies. The election must be made on or before the first anniversary of 31 January following the tax year in which the change of basis occurs. If the person permanently ceases to carry on the trade before the whole of the adjustment income has been brought into charge, the uncharged balance is charged as if it arose immediately before cessation.

(iv)   *Barristers and advocates*. See below.

Partnerships

In the case of trades, professions or vocations carried on in partnership, the adjustment (as above) is calculated as if the partnership were an individual resident in the UK. Each partner's share of any adjustment income is determined according to the profit-sharing arrangements for the twelve months immediately before the first day of the first period of account for which the new basis was adopted, and an election for spreading of an adjustment under (iii) above must be made jointly by all persons who were partners in that twelve-month period.

Death

In the case of the death of an individual otherwise chargeable to tax on adjustment income, his personal representatives assume the outstanding liabilities and may make any election under these provisions that the deceased might have made.

Barristers and advocates

If a change of basis arises on a barrister or advocate ceasing to take advantage of the exemption at *ITTOIA 2005, s 160* (see **13.2 CASH BASIS FOR BARRISTERS AND ADVOCATES**) or on its ceasing to be available, any resulting adjustment income is automatically spread over ten years, as follows. In each of the nine tax years beginning with that in which the full adjustment income would otherwise be charged to tax, the amount charged is instead 10% of the full amount or, if less, 10% of taxable profits *before* capital allowances or balancing charges. In the tenth tax year, the outstanding balance is brought into charge. If, within the ten years, the individual permanently ceases to carry on the profession, the annual charge continues to be made as before but without the '10% of taxable profits' alternative. An individual may elect for an additional amount of his own choosing to be added to the amount otherwise chargeable for a particular tax year. The election must be made on or before the first anniversary of 31 January following the tax year concerned, and must specify the additional amount. The maximum charge for each remaining year is then reduced proportionately. An election may be made more than once during the ten-year period.

[*ITTOIA 2005, ss 226–240, 860, Sch 2 paras 56–58; ITA 2007, Sch 1 para 502; CTA 2009, Sch 1 para 641*].

See HMRC Business Income Manual BIM34000–34135.

See **73.115** below for special rules on the spreading of adjustment income arising from the adoption of UITF Abstract 40, which affects the manner in which service providers must account for work in progress. The spreading rules above for barristers and advocates take precedence over those rules.

Whether a trade carried on

[73.21] See also **73.33** below (mutual trading) and see generally **73.1** above.

Simon's Taxes. See B1.4.

Avoidance schemes

[73.22] A line is drawn between transactions of a trading nature which remain trading even though entered into to secure tax advantages and transactions so remote from ordinary trading as to be explicable only as fiscal devices and hence not trading.

In *Ransom v Higgs and Kilmorie (Aldridge) Ltd v Dickinson etc.* HL 1974, 50 TC 1 the taxpayers entered into complex arrangements to siphon development profits into the hands of trustees. They succeeded, the Crown failing to establish that, looked at as a whole, the arrangements constituted trading. In *Johnson v Jewitt* CA 1961, 40 TC 231 an elaborate and artificial device to manufacture trading losses was held not to amount to trading, but see *Ensign Tankers (Leasing) Ltd v Stokes* HL 1992, 64 TC 617, where the company's investment in two film production partnerships was entered into with a view to obtaining first-year capital allowances. See also *Black Nominees Ltd v Nicol* Ch D 1975, 50 TC 229 and *Newstead v Frost* HL 1980, 53 TC 525. See generally ANTI-AVOIDANCE (**4**).

Betting

[73.23] Betting by professional bookmakers is assessable (*Partridge v Mallandaine* QB 1886, 2 TC 179) even if carried on in an unlawful way (*Southern v A B* KB 1933, 18 TC 59) but not private betting however habitual (*Graham v Green* KB 1925, 9 TC 309). Also exempt from CGT. [*TCGA 1992, s 51(1)*]. Receipts from newspaper articles based on betting system held assessable in *Graham v Arnott* KB 1941, 24 TC 157.

Lotteries and football pools promotion constitutes trading, but where a pool or small lottery is run by a supporters club or other society on terms that a specified part of the cost of the ticket is to be donated to a club or body within the purposes in *Lotteries and Amusements Act 1976, s 5(1)*, the donation element is not treated as a trading receipt (HMRC SP C1). For further detail, see HMRC Business Income Manual BIM61600–61615. See **16.8** CHARITIES as regards charitable lotteries.

Divers and diving supervisors

[73.24] The performance of his duties by a person employed in the UK (including a designated area under *Continental Shelf Act 1964, s 1(7)*, see **32.3** FOREIGN INCOME) as a diver in operations to exploit the sea-bed, or as a supervisor in relation to such operations, is treated for income tax purposes as the carrying on of a trade and not as an employment. [*ITTOIA 2005, s 15*]. Simon's Taxes. See **B1.516, E5.7**.

Futures, options and swap contracts

[73.25] Any gain arising in the course of dealing, other than in the course of trade, in commodity or financial futures or in traded or financial options on a recognised exchange, and not chargeable under *ITTOIA 2005, ss 555–569* (see **4.41** ANTI-AVOIDANCE), is dealt with under the chargeable gains rules and is not chargeable to tax as trading income. [*ITTOIA 2005, s 779; CTA 2009, Sch 1 para 369; SI 2006 No 959, Reg 3(2)*]. See Tolley's Capital Gains Tax under Disposal.

Where dealing is in the course of a trade, any profit or loss is chargeable as trading income or deductible as a trading loss. In general, relatively infrequent transactions, and transactions to hedge specific investments, would not be regarded as trading, nor would purely speculative transactions. For HMRC's view on what constitutes trading in this context, see HMRC SP 3/02.

Special rules are applied (by regulation) to the market formed by the merger of the London International Financial Futures Exchange (LIFFE) and the London Traded Options Market (LTOM), which operates outside the Stock Exchange. These relate to bond-washing and to stamp duty and stamp duty reserve tax. See *SI 1992 Nos 568, 570*.

Pension schemes etc.

For the purposes of approved retirement benefit schemes, futures and options contracts are treated as investments (and thus as attracting tax exemption for income and capital gains). Any income derived from transactions relating to such a contract is regarded as arising from the contract, and a contract is not excluded from these provisions by the fact that any party is, or may be, entitled to receive and/or liable to make only a payment of a sum in full settlement of all obligations, as opposed to a transfer of assets other than money. This continues to apply after 5 April 2006 for the purposes of funds within *ICTA 1988, s 613(4)* and *s 614(3)* at **57.32 PENSION PROVISION**. [*ICTA 1988, s 659A; TCGA 1992, s 271(10)(11)*].

Swaps

The word 'swap' is not defined for tax purposes but is taken to mean any financial arrangement that would be regarded by the financial markets as a swap. Profits or losses on a swap are chargeable as trading income if on trading account and are otherwise chargeable as miscellaneous income (if not of a capital nature). When considering whether or not a swap transaction constitutes trading, HMRC apply the general principles set out in SP 3/02 referred to above, and for an overview see also Revenue Tax Bulletin August 2003 pp 1054, 1055.

Pension schemes etc.

ICTA 1988, s 659A referred to above has no bearing on the tax status of swaps. Where a swap transaction by an approved scheme falls close to the trading/investment borderline, HMRC judge the case on its merits. Where an approved scheme uses interest rate swaps, currency swaps, equity swaps, credit derivatives or similar instruments to hedge risks inherent in, or as part of a strategy to enhance the return from, its existing investment portfolio or (in line with its normal policies of investing directly in such investments) to create a synthetic exposure to investments of a particular type or in a particular market, HMRC normally regard such swaps as investments (and thus as attracting tax exemptions for income and capital gains). (Revenue Tax Bulletin August 2003 pp 1055, 1056).

Horse racing etc.

[73.26] 'Private' horse racing and training is not normally trading (cf. *Sharkey v Wernher* HL 1955, 36 TC 275). But racing and selling the progeny of a brood mare held to constitute trading in *Dawson v Counsell* CA 1938, 22 TC 149 and in *Norman v Evans* Ch D 1964, 42 TC 188 share of prize monies for letting racehorses held within Schedule D, Case VI (now miscellaneous income). Profits from stallion fees are assessable and assessments under both

Schedule D, Case I (trading income) and Case VI have been upheld (*Malcolm v Lockhart* HL 1919, 7 TC 99; *McLaughlin v Bailey* CA (I) 1920, 7 TC 508; *Jersey's Exors v Bassom* KB 1926, 10 TC 357; *Wernher v CIR* KB 1942, 29 TC 20; *Benson v Counsell* KB 1942, 24 TC 178) but wear and tear allowances (the forerunner of modern capital allowances on plant etc.) for stallions refused in *Derby v Aylmer* KB 1915, 6 TC 665. Profits from greyhound breeding held trading in *Hawes v Gardiner* Ch D 1957, 37 TC 671.

Illegal trading

[73.27] Crime, e.g. burglary, is not trading but the profits of a commercial business are assessable notwithstanding the business may be carried on in an unlawful way, e.g. 'bootlegging' (*Canadian Minister of Finance v Smith* PC 1926, 5 ATC 621 and cf. *Lindsay Woodward & Hiscox v CIR* CS 1932, 18 TC 43), operating 'fruit machines' illegal at the time (*Mann v Nash* KB 1932, 16 TC 523), street bookmaking illegal at the time (*Southern v A B* KB 1933, 18 TC 59) and prostitution (*CIR v Aken* CA 1990, 63 TC 395). But penalties for trading contrary to war-time regulations held not deductible (*CIR v E C Warnes & Co* KB 1919, 12 TC 227; *CIR v Alexander von Glehn & Co* CA 1920, 12 TC 232). See also **73.23** above. **Simon's Taxes.** See **B1.420**.

See **73.87** below as regards prohibition on deduction of expenditure involving crime.

Isolated or speculative transactions

[73.28] For futures, property transactions and share dealing see **73.25**, **73.31** and **73.32** respectively.

Whether the surplus on the acquisition and sale of assets, otherwise than in the course of an established commercial enterprise, is derived from an 'adventure or concern in the nature of trade' (see **73.1** above) depends on the facts. Para 116 of the Final Report of the Royal Commission on the Taxation of Profits and Income (1955 HMSO Cmd. 9474) lists six 'badges of trade': (i) the subject matter of the sale; (ii) length of period of ownership; (iii) frequency or number of similar transactions; (iv) supplementary work on assets sold; (v) reason for sale; (vi) motive. Other relevant factors may be the degree of organisation, whether the taxpayer is or has been associated with a recognised business dealing in similar assets, how the assets were acquired and, if purchased, how the purchase was financed. For a recent review of the factors to be considered, see *Marson v Morton* Ch D 1986, 59 TC 381.

HMRC provide brief guidance on the status (i.e. trading or otherwise) of items sold online, through classified advertisements and at car boot sales (see www.hmrc.gov.uk/guidance/selling/index.htm).

Although in disputed cases the Inland Revenue could make alternative Schedule D, Case I and Schedule D, Case VI assessments, it would seem from *Pearn v Miller* KB 1927, 11 TC 610 and *Leeming v Jones* HL 1930, 15 TC 333 (see **73.31** below) that as regards isolated transactions the income tax liability, if any, was under Case I. As regards commodity futures, see **73.25** above.

Case I assessments were upheld on a purchase and resale of war surplus linen (*Martin v Lowry* HL 1926, 11 TC 297 — a leading case); a purchase, conversion and resale of a ship (*CIR v Livingston* CS 1926, 11 TC 538); transactions in brandy (*Cape Brandy Syndicate v CIR* CA 1921, 12 TC 358), whisky (*Lindsay Woodward* at **73.27** above), whisky in bond (*P J McCall decd v CIR* KB(IFS) 1923, 4 ATC 522; *CIR v Fraser* CS 1942, 24 TC 498); 'turning over' cotton mills (*Pickford v Quirke* CA 1927, 13 TC 251); purchase and resale of cotton spinning plant (*Edwards v Bairstow & Harrison* HL 1955, 36 TC 207); and purchase and resale of toilet rolls (*Rutledge v CIR* CS 1929, 14 TC 490). But in *Jenkinson v Freedland* CA 1961, 39 TC 636 the Commissioners' finding that a profit on the purchase, repair and sale (to associated companies) of stills was not assessable, was upheld, and in *Kirkham v Williams* CA 1991, 64 TC 253, the Commissioners' decision that the sale of a dwelling house built on land partly acquired for storage etc. was an adventure in the nature of trade was reversed in the CA.

Case I and Case VI do not apply for income tax purposes for 2005/06 onwards; the alternatives are now a charge to tax on trading income or a charge to tax on miscellaneous income.

Simon's Taxes. See **B1.401, B1.405, B1.447.**

Liquidators etc. and personal representatives

[73.29] Whether a liquidator or receiver is continuing the company's trade or merely realising its assets as best he can, is a question of fact and similarly for the personal representatives of a deceased trader. For liquidators or receivers see *Armitage v Moore* QB 1900, 4 TC 199; *CIR v 'Old Bushmills' Distillery* KB(NI) 1927, 12 TC 1148; *CIR v Thompson* KB 1936, 20 TC 422; *Wilson Box v Brice* CA 1936, 20 TC 736; *Baker v Cook* KB 1937, 21 TC 337.

Personal representatives were held to be trading while winding up the deceased's business in *Weisberg's Executrices v CIR* KB 1933, 17 TC 696; *Wood v Black's Exor* HC 1952, 33 TC 172; *Pattullo's Trustees v CIR* CS 1955, 36 TC 87 but not in *Cohan's Exors v CIR* CA 1924, 12 TC 602 (completion of ship under construction at death) and *CIR v Donaldson's Trustees* CS 1963, 41 TC 161 (sale of pedigree herd). For property sales after death of partner in property dealing firm, see *Marshall's Exors v Joly* KB 1936, 20 TC 256 and contrast *Newbarns Syndicate v Hay* CA 1939, 22 TC 461.

Miscellaneous

[73.30] Assessments under *Schedule D, Case I* (trading income) were upheld on a committee operating golf links owned by a Town Council (*Carnoustie Golf Course Committee v CIR* CS 1929, 14 TC 498); trustees under a private Act managing a recreation ground (*CIR v Stonehaven Recreation Ground Trustees* CS 1929, 15 TC 419); temporary joint coal merchanting (*Gardner and Bowring Hardy & Co v CIR* CS 1930, 15 TC 602); promotion of mining companies to exploit mines (*Murphy v Australian Machinery etc. Co Ltd* CA 1948, 30 TC 244 and cf. *Rhodesia Metals v Commr of Taxes* PC 1940, 19 ATC 472); purchase and resale of amusement equipment (*Crole v Lloyd* HC 1950, 31 TC 338).

A company which made loans to another company to finance a trading venture was held not to be trading itself (*Stone & Temple Ltd v Waters; Astrawall (UK) Ltd v Waters* Ch D 1995, 67 TC 145).

The activities of the British Olympic Association (which included the raising of funds through commercial sponsorship and the exploitation of its logo, but many of which were non-commercial) were held as a whole to be uncommercial and not to constitute a trade (*British Olympic Association v Winter* (Sp C 28), [1995] SSCD 85).

For whether or not an *athlete* is within the charge to tax on trading income, see HMRC Business Income Manual BIM50605; for the treatment of Lottery Sports Fund Athlete Personal Awards, see BIM50651–50690.

For whether *ostrich farming* (i.e. the ownership of ostriches which are looked after on the owner's behalf by others) amounts to trading, and for the consequences of such trading, see Revenue Tax Bulletin June 1996 pp 318, 319.

See also *Smith Barry v Cordy* CA 1946, 28 TC 250 in which a taxpayer was held liable on his surplus from the sale or maturing of endowment policies he had purchased, *J Bolson & Son Ltd v Farrelly* CA 1953, 34 TC 161 (deals in vessels by company operating boat services held a separate adventure) and *Torbell Investments Ltd v Williams* Ch D 1986, 59 TC 357 (dormant company revived for purpose of acquiring certain loans held to have acquired them as trading stock). But a company formed to administer a holidays with pay scheme for the building etc. industry was held not trading (*Building & Civil Engineering etc. Ltd v Clark* Ch D 1960, 39 TC 12). Assessments on profits from promoting a series of driving schools were upheld in *Leach v Pogson* Ch D 1962, 40 TC 585; in concluding that the profit from *first* sale was assessable, Commissioners were entitled to take into account the subsequent transactions.

For circumstances in which the profits of a trade may not accrue to the proprietor, see *Alongi v CIR* CS 1991, 64 TC 304.

Property transactions

[73.31] This paragraph relates to transactions in land and buildings otherwise than in the course of an established business of property development, building etc. For HMRC's view, see HMRC Business Income Manual BIM60000–60165. For other sales of property see **73.103** below.

A line is drawn between realisations of property held as an investment or as a residence and transactions amounting to an adventure or concern in the nature of trade. The principles at **73.28** above apply suitably adapted.

In *Leeming v Jones* HL 1930, 15 TC 333 an assessment on the acquisitions and disposal of options over rubber estates was confirmed by Commissioners. The Crown had defended the assessment under both Schedule D, Case I (trading income) and Schedule D, Case VI (miscellaneous income). In a Supplementary Case the Commissioners found there had been no concern in the nature of the trade. The Court held there was no liability. Per Lawrence LJ 'in the case of an isolated transaction . . . there is really no middle course open. It is either an adventure in the nature of trade, or else it is simply a case of sale and resale of property.' See also *Pearn v Miller* KB 1927, 11 TC 610 and *Williams v Davies* below.

Property transactions by companies were held to be trading in *Californian Copper Syndicate v Harris* CES 1904, 5 TC 159 (purchase of copper bearing land shortly afterwards resold); *Thew v South West Africa Co* CA 1924, 9 TC 141 (numerous sales of land acquired by concession for exploitation); *Cayzer, Irvine & Co v CIR* CS 1942, 24 TC 491 (exploitation of landed estate acquired by shipping company); *Emro Investments v Aller* and *Lance Webb Estates v Aller* Ch D 1954, 35 TC 305 (profits carried to capital reserve on numerous purchases and sales); *Orchard Parks v Pogson* Ch D 1964, 42 TC 442 (land compulsorily purchased after development plan dropped); *Parkstone Estates v Blair* Ch D 1966, 43 TC 246 (industrial estate developed—land disposed of by sub-leases for premiums); *Eames v Stepnell Properties Ltd* CA 1966, 43 TC 678 (sale of land acquired from associated company while resale being negotiated). See also *Bath & West Counties Property Trust Ltd v Thomas* Ch D 1977, 52 TC 20. Realisations were held to be capital in *Hudson's Bay v Stevens* CA 1909, 5 TC 424 (numerous sales of land acquired under Royal Charter — contrast *South West Africa Co* above); *Tebrau (Johore) Rubber Syndicate v Farmer* CES 1910, 5 TC 658 (purchase and resale of rubber estates — contrast *Californian Copper* above).

In *Rand v Alberni Land Co Ltd* KB 1920, 7 TC 629 sales of land held in trust were held not trading but contrast *Alabama Coal Iron Land v Mylam* KB 1926, 11 TC 232; *Balgownie Land Trust v CIR* CS 1929, 14 TC 684; *St Aubyn Estates v Strick* KB 1932, 17 TC 412; *Tempest Estates v Walmsley* Ch D 1975, 51 TC 305. Sales of property after a period of letting held realisations of investments or not trading in *CIR v Hyndland Investment Co Ltd* CS 1929, 14 TC 694; *Glasgow Heritable Trust v CIR* CS 1954, 35 TC 196; *Lucy & Sunderland Ltd v Hunt* Ch D 1961, 40 TC 132 but held trading in *Rellim Ltd v Vise* CA 1951, 32 TC 254 (notwithstanding that company previously admitted as investment company); *CIR v Toll Property Co* CS 1952, 34 TC 13; *Forest Side Properties (Chingford) v Pearce* CA 1961, 39 TC 665. But sales by liquidator of property owned by companies following abandonment of plan for their public flotation held not trading in *Simmons v CIR* HL 1980, 53 TC 461 (reversing Commissioners' decision). In *Rosemoor Investments v Inspector of Taxes* (Sp C 320), [2002] SSCD 325, it was not open to the Commissioners to recharacterise as trading a complex transaction routed via an investment company subsidiary and structured to produce capital.

Property transactions by individuals and partnerships were held to be trading in *Reynold's Exors v Bennett* KB 1943, 25 TC 401; *Broadbridge v Beattie* KB 1944, 26 TC 63; *Gray & Gillitt v Tiley* KB 1944, 26 TC 80; *Laver v Wilkinson* KB 1944, 26 TC 105; *Foulds v Clayton* Ch D 1953, 34 TC 382 and *Kirkby v Hughes* Ch D 1992, 65 TC 352; in all of which the taxpayers were or had been associated with building or estate development, and contrast *Williams v Davies* KB 1945, 26 TC 371 in which the taxpayers were closely associated with land development but a profit on transactions in undeveloped land in the names of their wives held not assessable. The acquisition and resale of land for which planning permission had been or was obtained held trading in *Cooke v Haddock* Ch D 1960, 39 TC 64; *Turner v Last* Ch D 1965, 42 TC 517 and *Pilkington v Randall* CA 1966, 42 TC 662 (and cf. *Iswera v Ceylon Commr* PC 1965, 44 ATC 157), but contrast *Taylor v Good* CA 1974, 49 TC 277 in which a house bought as a residence was found unsuitable and resold to a developer after obtaining planning permission and held not an adventure. In *Burrell v Davis* Ch D 1948, 38 TC 307; *Johnston v Heath* Ch D 1970, 46 TC 463; *Reeves v Evans, Boyce & Northcott* Ch D 1971, 48 TC 495 and *Clark v Follett* Ch D 1973, 48 TC 677 the short period of ownership or other evidence showed an intention to purchase for resale at a profit and not for investment, but contrast *CIR v Reinhold* CS 1953, 34 TC 389, *Marson v Morton* Ch D 1986, 59 TC 381 and *Taylor v Good* above. For other cases in which profits held assessable see *Hudson v Wrightson* KB 1934, 26 TC 55 and *MacMahon v CIR* CS 1951, 32 TC 311.

For sales after a period of letting see *Mitchell Bros v Tomlinson* CA 1957, 37 TC 224 and *Cooksey & Bibby v Rednall* KB 1949, 30 TC 514.

For sale of houses built by taxpayer and used as residences see *Page v Pogson* Ch D 1954, 35 TC 545 and *Kirkham v Williams* CA 1991, 64 TC 253.

For sales after death of partner in property dealing transactions, see cases at **73.29** above. See also re partnership sales *CIR v Dean Property Co* CS 1939, 22 TC 706 and *Dodd and Tanfield v Haddock* Ch D 1964, 42 TC 229.

Simon's Taxes. See B5.2.

Share dealing

[73.32] Share dealing with the public is strictly controlled by the *Financial Services and Markets Act 2000*. This paragraph is concerned with share transactions entered into (generally through the Stock Exchange) by persons not authorised to deal under that Act and the question arises whether they amount to an adventure or concern in the nature of trade. The principles of **73.28** above apply suitably adapted. The prudent management of an investment portfolio may necessitate changes in the holdings but this is not normally trading. Stock Exchange speculation, particularly by individuals, may be quasi-gambling and not trading — see Pennycuick J in *Lewis Emanuel & Son Ltd v White* Ch D 1965, 42 TC 369 in which, reversing the Commissioners' finding, he held that the Stock Exchange losses of a fruit etc. merchanting company were from a separate trade of share dealing but observed that gambling by the company would at that time have been *ultra vires*. In *Cooper v C & J Clark Ltd* Ch D 1982, 54 TC 670, the losses of a manufacturing company on its sale of gilts, in which it had invested temporarily surplus cash, were allowed as a set-off against its general trading profits. An individual speculating in stocks and shares and commodity futures was held to be trading in *Wannell v Rothwell* Ch D 1996, 68 TC 719 (although loss relief was refused on the grounds that the trading was 'uncommercial', see **45.12 LOSSES**), but the opposite conclusion was reached in *Salt v Chamberlain* Ch D 1979, 53 TC 143.

For share dealing by investment companies see *Scottish Investment Trust Co v Forbes* CES 1893, 3 TC 231 and *Halefield Securities Ltd v Thorpe* Ch D 1967, 44 TC 154. For trading in secured loans, see *Torbell Investments Ltd v Williams* Ch D 1986, 59 TC 357.

For share sales connected with an existing business see **73.111** below.

Mutual trading

[73.33] A person cannot derive a taxable profit from trading with himself except in certain cases of self-supply by a trader of trading stock, see *Sharkey v Wernher* HL 1955, 36 TC 275 and **73.114** below. This extends to a group of persons engaged in mutual activities of a trading nature if there is an identifiable 'fund' for the common purpose with complete identity between contributors to, and participators in, the fund (the *mutuality principle*). A body not liable as regards transactions with members may nevertheless be within the charge to tax on trading transactions with non-members and is liable in the ordinary way on investment income.

Whether the mutuality principle applies depends on the facts. For mutual insurance, see *Styles v New York Life Insce Co* HL 1889, 2 TC 460 (an early leading case on the mutuality principle but there are now special provisions for life insurance companies); *Jones v South-West Lancs Coal Owners' Assn* HL 1927, 11 TC 790; *Cornish Mutual Assce Co Ltd* HL 1926, 12 TC 841; *Municipal Mutual Insce Ltd v Hills* HL 1932, 16 TC 430; *Faulconbridge v National Employers' Mutual General Insce Assn Ltd* Ch D 1952, 33 TC 103.

For other cases see *Liverpool Corn Trade Assn Ltd v Monks* KB 1926, 10 TC 442 (trade association providing corn exchange etc. held to be trading and not 'mutual' — but see **73.116** below for special arrangement available for trade associations); *English & Scottish CWS Ltd v Assam Agricultural IT Commr* PC 1948, 27 ATC 332 (wholesale co-operative with two members held to be trading and not mutual — there was no 'common fund'). Similarly a members' club is not trading and is not liable on its surplus from the provision of its facilities for members (*Eccentric Club Ltd* CA 1923, 12 TC 657) but liable on the surplus attributable to non-members (*Carlisle and Silloth Golf Club v Smith* CA 1913, 6 TC 48; *NALGO v Watkins* KB 1934, 18 TC 499; *Doctor's Cave Bathing Beach (Fletcher) v Jamaica IT Commr* PC 1971, 50 ATC 368).

For a detailed discussion of mutual trading, see HMRC Business Income Manual BIM24000–24995.

For distribution of assets by a mutual concern to a trader, see **73.98** below.

Simon's Taxes. See B1.436 *et seq.*.

Chargeable income and allowable deductions

[73.34] Apart from **73.35** below (capital expenditure and receipts) and **73.36** below (the 'wholly and exclusively' rule), which are arguably the most fundamental rules on the calculation of taxable business profits, the remainder of this chapter is arranged in alphabetical order — with a general example at the end. See the contents list at the head of the chapter.

See **73.18** above for the requirement to adhere to generally accepted accounting practice (GAAP), **73.19** above re the application of accountancy principles generally and **73.20** above re adjustments required on a change of basis. See also **10 CAPITAL ALLOWANCES** and **11 CAPITAL ALLOWANCES ON PLANT AND MACHINERY.**

ITTOIA 2005, s 31 introduced a rule intended to resolve any conflict between statutory rules prohibiting a deduction in computing trading profits and statutory rules permitting such a deduction. It does so by giving priority, with specified exceptions, to the rule permitting the deduction. In practice, such conflict will rarely occur.

See HMRC Business Income Manual BIM50000 et seq. for HMRC guidance on measuring the profits of a wide range of particular trades.

Capital expenditure and receipts

[73.35] In computing trading profits, no deduction is allowed for items of a capital nature. [*ITTOIA 2005, s 33*]. By the same token, capital receipts are not brought into account. [*ITTOIA 2005, s 96*].

As to the distinction between capital and revenue expenditure and between capital and income receipts, 'no part of our law of taxation presents such almost insoluble conundrums as the decision whether a receipt or outgoing is capital or income for tax purposes' (Lord Upjohn in *Strick v Regent Oil Co Ltd* HL 1965, 43 TC 1 q.v. for a comprehensive review of the law). A widely used test is the 'enduring benefit' one given by Viscount Cave in *Atherton v British Insulated & Helsby Cables Ltd* HL 1925, 10 TC 155. For recent reviews of the cases, see *Lawson v Johnson Matthey plc* HL 1992, 65 TC 39 and *Halifax plc v Davidson* (Sp C 239), [2000] SSCD 251. In the latter case, costs incurred by a building society on conversion to a public limited company were disallowed as capital expenditure to the extent that they related to payment of statutory cash bonuses to non-voting members of the society, but otherwise allowed.

It is by virtue of the rule in *ITTOIA 2005, s 33* above that depreciation of fixed assets is not allowable in computing profits (see **10.1 CAPITAL ALLOWANCES**) (*In re Robert Addie & Sons* CES 1875, 1 TC 1). Where the depreciation charge in the accounts is reduced by capitalising part of it and including that part in the balance sheet value of stock (i.e. as an overhead cost), only the net depreciation (i.e. the amount after reduction) falls to be added back to trading profits in order to arrive at taxable profits (*HMRC v William Grant & Sons Distillers Ltd; Small v Mars UK Ltd* HL, [2007] STC 680). See HMRC Business Income Manual BIM33190.

A gain or loss on the sale of a capital asset not included in trading profits is dealt with according to the provisions relating to capital gains tax. A sale of a fixed asset on which capital allowances have been claimed may result in a balancing charge or allowance, see **10 CAPITAL ALLOWANCES** and **11 CAPITAL ALLOWANCES ON PLANT AND MACHINERY.**

The revenue or capital nature of a payment is fixed at the time of its receipt (*Tapemaze Ltd v Melluish* Ch D 2000, 73 TC 167, following *Morley v Tattersall* CA 1938, 40 TC 671).

A sum paid for, in effect, the acquisition of a business was held to be capital in *Triage Services Ltd v HMRC* (Sp C 519) [2006] SSCD 85. Where a lump sum payment is made to extinguish an obligation to make payments of capital expenditure (in this case an obligation to pay an annuity assumed as part of the consideration for the acquisition of a business), it is a capital payment (*Parnalls Solicitors Ltd v HMRC* FTT (TC 261), [2010] SFTD 284).

A property acquired by a company for the purpose of remunerating a director was adjudged to have been acquired, and to have been held, on capital account (*Lion Co v HMRC* FTT (TC 295), [2010] SFTD 454).

For a brief note on HMRC's approach to challenging schemes or arrangements designed to turn income into capital (or capital expenditure into a revenue deduction), see Revenue Tax Bulletin June 1997 p 438.

For the HMRC's own guidance on capital *v* income, see HMRC Business Income Manual BIM35000–35910.

The 'wholly and exclusively' rule

[73.36] For an expense to be deductible, it must, *inter alia*, have been incurred 'wholly and exclusively for the purposes of the trade'. It is specifically provided that if an expense is incurred for a *dual purpose*, this rule does not prohibit a deduction for any *identifiable* part or *identifiable* proportion of the expense which is incurred wholly and exclusively for the purposes of the trade; but this simply reflects a long-established principle (see below). [*ITTOIA 2005, s 34*].

For a review of the leading cases on the 'wholly and exclusively' rule, see *Harrods (Buenos Aires) Ltd v Taylor-Gooby* CA 1964, 41 TC 450 and for a frequently quoted analysis of the words see *Bentleys, Stokes & Lowless v Beeson* CA 1952, 33 TC 491. Following that case the dual purpose rule now in *ITTOIA 2005, s 34* has figured prominently in Court decisions. If an expense is for a material private or non-business purpose, the whole is strictly disallowable as it is thereby not wholly and exclusively for business purposes. For examples of its application see **73.100** and **73.122** below. 'Dual expenditure is expenditure that is incurred for more than one reason. If one of the reasons is not for business purposes, the expenditure fails the statutory test and there is no provision that allows a "business" proportion' (HMRC Business Income Manual BIM37007). *However*, where an *identifiable* part or proportion of an expense has been laid out wholly and exclusively for the purposes of the trade,

HMRC do not disallow that part or proportion on the grounds that the expense is not *as a whole* laid out wholly and exclusively for the purposes of the trade (BIM37007). For rent etc. of premises used both for business and as residence, see **73.104** below.

See *Mallalieu v Drummond* (**73.100** below) for an important HL discussion of the 'wholly and exclusively' rule, in which it was held that ascertaining the purposes of the relevant expenditure involved looking into the taxpayer's mind at the time of the expenditure, later events being irrelevant except as a reflection of that state of mind. However, the taxpayer's conscious motive at the time was not conclusive; an object, not a conscious motive (in this case the human requirement for clothing), could be taken into account.

A purely incidental consequence of a business expense does not, however, preclude its being wholly and exclusively for business purposes (HMRC Business Income Manual BIM37007, 37400). See, for example, *Robinson v Scott Bader Ltd*, **73.55** below and *McKnight v Sheppard* HL 1999, 71 TC 419, **73.92**, **73.100** below. *Mallalieu v Drummond* was applied in *Watkis v Ashford, Sparkes and Harward* Ch D 1985, 58 TC 468, where expenditure on meals supplied at regular partners' lunchtime meetings was disallowed, overruling the Commissioner's finding that the expenditure was exclusively for business purposes. Expenditure on accommodation, food and drink at the firm's annual weekend conference was, however, allowed as a deduction. For deduction of payments by partnerships to individual partners generally, see *MacKinlay v Arthur Young McClelland Moores & Co* HL 1989, 62 TC 704. Salaries paid to partners are not deductible as trading expenses (*PDC Copyprint (South) v George* (Sp C 141), [1997] SSCD 326).

See also **73.100** below as regards personal and domestic expenses.

It should be borne in mind that the trade for whose purposes the expenditure is incurred must be that in which the expense arose. For a successful appeal against a decision in favour of the Inland Revenue on this point, see *Vodafone Cellular Ltd v Shaw* CA 1997, 69 TC 376.

For HMRC's own guidance on the 'wholly and exclusively' rule, see HMRC Business Income Manual BIM37000–38600.

Advertising

[73.37] Expenditure generally is allowable (but not capital outlay such as fixed signs (but see *Leeds Permanent Building Society v Proctor* Ch D 1982, 56 TC 293), nor initial costs etc. of new business). Contribution to campaign for Sunday opening held allowable (*Rhymney Breweries* Ch D 1965, 42 TC 509). As to political campaign see *Tate & Lyle* HL 1954, 35 TC 367, contrasted with *Boarland v Kramat Pulai* Ch D 1953, 35 TC 1. See HMRC Business Income Manual BIM42550–42555.

In *McQueen v HMRC* (Sp C 601), [2007] SSCD 457 the Sp C found on the evidence that expenditure on motor rallying and capital allowances on rally cars were deductible trading expenses and that any private benefit to the taxpayer was a merely incidental effect of the expenditure rather than its purpose; in this case the taxpayer, a keen rally driver, owned a minibus business and used motor rallying as a means of advertising that business.

Application of profits

[73.38] A requirement that a trading surplus is to be applied in a particular way does not remove the trade from the charge to tax on trading income (*Mersey Docks and Harbour Board v Lucas* HL 1883, 2 TC 25) and applications of the profits under the requirement are not allowable deductions (*City of Dublin Steam Packet Co v O'Brien* KB(I) 1912, 6 TC 101; *Hutchinson & Co v Turner* HC 1950, 31 TC 495; *Young v Racecourse Betting Control Board* HL 1959, 38 TC 426 and cf. *Pondicherry Rly Co* PC 1931, 10 ATC 365; *Tata Hydro-Electric Agencies* PC 1937, 16 ATC 54; *India Radio & Cable Communication Co* PC 1937, 16 ATC 333).

For circumstances in which the profits of a trade may not accrue to the proprietor, see *Alongi v CIR* CS 1991, 64 TC 304.

Artistes

[73.39] For creative artists, see **73.51** below.

An actress based in the UK but with engagements abroad was held to be carrying on a single profession. Hence receipts from her overseas engagements fell to be included in her *Schedule D, Case II* (professional income) assessment (*Davies v Braithwaite* KB 1933, 18 TC 198 and compare *Withers v Wynyard* KB 1938, 21 TC 724).

An artiste engaged by a theatre under a standard contract was held to be within the charge to tax on employment income (*Fall v Hitchen* Ch D 1972, 49 TC 433), but see now **27.54 EMPLOYMENT INCOME** as regards application of trading income rules to artistes generally.

A sum received by a company, formed to exploit the services of an actor, on cancellation of an agreement giving another his exclusive services was held a trading receipt (*John Mills Productions Ltd v Mathias* Ch D 1967, 44 TC 441). Payment to actor for entering into restrictive covenant held not assessable (*Higgs v Olivier* CA 1952, 33 TC 136).

For deductibility of expenses of actors and other entertainers, including clothing, costume, grooming and cosmetic surgery, see HMRC Business Income Manual BIM50160.

See **4.28 ANTI-AVOIDANCE** for the treatment as income of certain capital sums received in lieu of earnings and **50.10 NON-RESIDENTS** as regards certain non-resident entertainers and sportsmen.

Bad and doubtful debts

[73.40] See generally HMRC Business Income Manual BIM42700–42750.

Bad debts, and doubtful debts to the extent they are estimated to be bad, are deductible. Where the debtor is bankrupt or insolvent, the debt is deductible except to the extent that any amount may reasonably be expected to be received on it.

A debt is also deductible to the extent that it is released wholly and exclusively for the purposes of the trade as part of a statutory insolvency arrangement, i.e. either:

(i)   a voluntary arrangement under, or by virtue of, *Insolvency Act 1986* (or Scottish or NI equivalents); or

(ii)   a compromise or arrangement under *Companies Act 2006, Pt 26* (or earlier equivalent); or

(iii)   for periods of account beginning on or after 1 January 2005, any foreign law equivalents of (i) or (ii).

Where a trade is treated as notionally discontinued (see **52.7 PARTNERSHIPS** and **73.14** above), the relief applies to debts taken over by the successor. [*ITTOIA 2005, ss 35, 259; SI 2008 No 954, Arts 1, 37*].

If a debt owed *by* a trader is released (otherwise than as part of a statutory insolvency arrangement — see above), and the expense giving rise to the debt has been allowed as a deduction for tax purposes, the amount released counts for tax purposes as a trading receipt arising on the date of release. [*ITTOIA 2005, ss 97, 259*]. As regards trade debts *not* released but nevertheless written back, HMRC take the view that the requirement that GAAP be adhered to in computing taxable profits (see **73.18** above) requires such write-backs to be taxed, subject only to the exception provided by *ITTOIA 2005, s 97* for releases under statutory insolvency arrangements (Revenue Tax Bulletin December 2001 pp 901, 902 and see now HMRC Business Income Manual BIM40265). See generally Business Income Manual BIM40201 *et seq*.

For debt recoveries and releases after the cessation of a trade, see **59 POST-CESSATION RECEIPTS AND EXPENDITURE**. Bad debt allowances are not applicable where, exceptionally, the business is assessed on a cash basis (see **13 CASH BASIS FOR BARRISTERS AND ADVOCATES**). For VAT on bad debts, see **73.126** below.

The provision for a bad or doubtful debt for a period of account may reflect events after the balance sheet date insofar as they furnish additional evidence of conditions that existed at the balance sheet date. See Revenue Tax Bulletin August 1994 p 154, which also outlines the evidence which inspectors may require in support of the allowance of a provision. It is not possible to employ hindsight to revisit a past computation of taxable profit so as to provide for a debt in a period of account in which there was no evidence that it would eventually prove to be bad (*Thompson v CIR* (Sp C 458), [2005] SSCD 320).

Where an asset accepted in satisfaction of a trading debt is of market value (as at the date of acceptance) less than the outstanding debt, the deficit may be allowed as a deduction, provided the trader agrees that, on a disposal of the asset, any excess of disposal proceeds over that value (up to the amount by which the debt exceeds that value) will be brought in as a trading receipt (such receipt being excluded from any chargeable gain computation on the disposal) (HMRC Business Income Manual BIM42735).

An allowance agreed under conditions of full disclosure cannot be withdrawn because of a subsequent change in the circumstances (*Anderton & Halstead Ltd v Birrell* KB 1931, 16 TC 200) but an allowance for year 1 may be revised, upwards or downwards, in the year 2 computation by reference to the circumstances for year 2 and similarly for later years. The amount of the allowance depends on the likelihood of recovery. This is a question of fact but the fact that the debtor is still in business is not itself a reason for refusing an allowance (*Dinshaw v Bombay IT Commr* PC 1934, 13 ATC 284). See also *Lock v Jones* KB 1941, 23 TC 749.

General bad debt provisions, i.e. not relating to specific debts, are not deductible. However where there are a large number of comparatively small debts, making the 'valuation' of individual debts impracticable, HMRC may agree to an allowance in accordance with a formula based on the bad debt experience of the business. Typical businesses are mail-order firms and firms with a large proportion of hire-purchase sales. Where hire-purchase is involved the formula may also cover the spread of the profit on hire-purchase sales. But no provision for the estimated cost of collecting future debt instalments is permissible (*Monthly Salaries Loan Co Ltd v Furlong* Ch D 1962, 40 TC 313).

For small credit traders who collect their debts by weekly instalments (sometimes called travelling drapers or Scotch drapers) a special arrangement is available. For details see Form 189 obtainable from inspectors.

Where a builder sold houses leaving part of the sale proceeds with building societies as collateral security for mortgages by the purchasers, held the amounts should be brought in at valuation when houses sold and if practicable and otherwise when released by Building Society (*John Cronk & Sons Ltd v Harrison* HL 1936, 20 TC 612 and cf. *Chibbett v Harold Brookfield & Son Ltd* CA 1952, 33 TC 467). A similar decision was reached in *Absalom v Talbot* HL 1944, 26 TC 166 where amounts were left on loan to the purchasers. See also *Lock v Jones* above. The HL judgments in *Absalom v Talbot* are an important review of the treatment of trading debts.

The normal debt considered for allowance under *ITTOIA 2005, s 35* is a debt for goods or services supplied or a debt in a business, such as banking or money-lending, which consists of advancing money (see e.g. *AB Bank v Inspector of Taxes* (Sp C 237), [2000] SSCD 229). Losses on advances by a brewery company to its customers were allowed as on the evidence it habitually acted as banker for them in the course of its brewing business (*Reid's Brewery v Male* QB 1891, 3 TC 279). But losses on advances to clients by solicitors were refused as there was no evidence that they were money-lenders (*CIR v Hagart & Burn-Murdoch* HL 1929, 14 TC 433; *Rutherford v CIR* CS 1939, 23 TC 8. See also *Bury & Walkers v Phillips* HC 1951, 32 TC 198 and contrast *Jennings v Barfield* Ch D 1962, 40 TC 365). An allowance was refused for an irrecoverable balance due from the managing director of a company as outside the company's trade (*Curtis v J & G Oldfield Ltd* KB 1925, 9 TC 319). See also *Roebank Printing Co Ltd v CIR* CS 1928, 13 TC 864.

Advances to finance or recoup the losses of subsidiary or associated companies are capital. Allowances were refused in *English Crown Spelter v Baker* KB 1908, 5 TC 327 and *Charles Marsden & Sons v CIR* KB 1919, 12 TC 217 for losses on advances to facilitate the supply of materials for the trade of the lender as were losses on an advance to a company under the same control (*Baker v Mabie Todd & Co Ltd* KB 1927, 13 TC 235), amounts written off in respect of the losses of a subsidiary (*Odhams Press Ltd v Cook* HL 1940, 23 TC 233) and payments to meet the operating losses of a subsidiary (*Marshall Richards Machine Co Ltd v Jewitt* Ch D 1956, 36 TC 511). See also *CIR v Huntley & Palmers Ltd* KB 1928, 12 TC 1209; *Henderson v Meade-King Robinson & Co Ltd* KB 1938, 22 TC 97; and *Stone & Temple Ltd v Waters; Astrawall (UK) Ltd v Waters* Ch D 1995, 67 TC 145.

Losses relating to trade debts with a subsidiary were, however, held allowable in *Sycamore plc and Maple Ltd v Fir* (Sp C 104), [1997] SSCD 1.

Payments by the purchaser to discharge the unpaid liabilities of the vendor to preserve goodwill etc. allowed in *Cooke v Quick Shoe Repair Service* KB 1949, 30 TC 460.

See **73.124** below for relief for certain unremittable overseas debts of trades carried on at least partly in the UK.

For losses under guarantees see **73.85** below.

Simon's Taxes. See B2.206, B2.410.

Breweries, distilleries, licensed premises

[73.41] See **73.120** below for rules on 'tied premises'. Those rules are of general application, although of most common application in the licensed trade.

Repairs, rates, insurance premiums paid on behalf of tied tenants allowable (*Usher's Wiltshire Brewery v Bruce* HL 1914, 6 TC 399) but not extra expenditure incurred to keep licensed houses open while undergoing rehabilitation (*Mann Crossman & Paulin Ltd v Compton* KB 1947, 28 TC 410) or compensation to a tenant displaced on a licence transfer (*Morse v Stedeford* KB 1934, 18 TC 457). For compensation paid on the termination of tenancies of tied houses, see *Watneys (London) Ltd v Pike* Ch D 1982, 57 TC 372. Losses on advances to 'customers and connections' held allowable (*Reid's Brewery v Male* QB 1891, 3 TC 279).

The expenses of an unsuccessful application for licences were held not allowable (*Southwell v Savill Bros* KB 1901, 4 TC 430 — it was conceded that expenses of successful applications are capital) nor expenses of applying for licence transfers (*Morse v Stedeford* above; *Pendleton v Mitchells & Butlers* Ch D 1968, 45 TC 341). Contributions by a brewer to a trade association to promote Sunday opening in Wales allowed in *Cooper v Rhymney Breweries* Ch D 1965, 42 TC 509. Compensation Fund levies deductible (*Smith v Lion Brewery* HL 1910, 5 TC 568) but not monopoly value payments (*Kneeshaw v Albertolli* KB 1940, 23 TC 462; *Henriksen v Grafton Hotels Ltd* CA 1942, 24 TC 453).

Damages paid to hotel guest injured by falling chimney held not allowable — see *Strong & Co v Woodifield* at **73.47** below. For accrued whisky storage rents see *Dailuaine-Talisker Distilleries v CIR* CS 1930, 15 TC 613; *CIR v Oban Distillery Co* CS 1932, 18 TC 33 and *CIR v Arthur Bell & Sons* CS 1932, 22 TC 315.

Where a brewery company ceased brewing but continued to sell beer brewed for it by another company it was held to have discontinued its old trade and commenced a new one (*Gordon & Blair Ltd v CIR* CS 1962, 40 TC 358).

Simon's Taxes. See B5.611–B5.614.

Car and motor cycle hire

[73.42] The new regime described below applies where a car is hired under an agreement under which the hire period begins **on or after 6 April 2009**. For this purpose, a hire period is treated as beginning on the first day on which the car is required to be made available for use under the agreement. Unlike the old regime, this regime does not apply at all to the hire of a motor cycle.

If an agreement for the hire of a car or motor cycle was entered into on or before 8 December 2008 and the hire period begins on or after 6 April 2009 but before 6 April 2010, the trader may irrevocably elect for the old regime described below to have effect instead of the new. The election must be made no later than the first anniversary of 31 January following the tax year in which ends the first period of account in which the trader incurred any expenditure on the provision of the car or motor cycle under the agreement. For this purpose, an agreement is treated as entered into as soon as there is an unconditional written contract for the use of the car or motor cycle by the trader and no terms remain to be agreed.

In all other cases, the old regime described below applies.

[*FA 2009, Sch 11 paras 65–67*].

New regime

The deduction allowed for the expenditure incurred in hiring a 'car' for the purposes of a trade falls to be restricted if it is not one of the following:

- a car with 'low CO_2 emissions';
- an electrically-propelled car (as defined by *CAA 2001, s 268B*);
- a 'qualifying hire car'; or
- a car first registered before 1 March 2001.

The deduction which would otherwise be due is reduced by 15%. See below for exceptions in cases of short-term hire or long-term sub-hire. No restriction applies if the car falls into one of the above categories.

Where the restriction has applied, any subsequent rental rebate (or debt release other than as part of a statutory insolvency arrangement — see **73.40** above) is also reduced for tax purposes by 15%. This treatment extends to amounts brought in as post-cessation receipts (see **59.1** POST-CESSATION RECEIPTS AND EXPENDITURE) after the trade has ceased.

For this purpose, a *'car'* is a mechanically propelled road vehicle which is neither:

(1)   of a construction primarily suited for the conveyance of goods or burden of any description; nor

(2)   of a type not commonly used as a private vehicle and unsuitable for such use; nor

(3)   a motor cycle.

As regards (2), see the case law referred to at **11.13**(ii) CAPITAL ALLOWANCES ON PLANT AND MACHINERY.

A car has *'low* CO_2 *emissions'* if its CO_2 emissions (see *CAA 2001, s 268C*) do not exceed 160g/km or if, when first registered, it was registered on the basis of a qualifying emissions certificate (as defined by *CAA 2001, s 268C*).

A car is a *'qualifying hire car'* if:

*   it is hired under a hire-purchase agreement (as defined by *ITA 2007, s 998A*) under which there is no option to purchase or an option to purchase that is exercisable on payment of a sum of not more than 1% of the retail price when new; or

*   it is leased under a long funding lease (for which see **11.45**(1) CAPITAL ALLOWANCES ON PLANT AND MACHINERY).

Expenditure is *excepted* from these provisions if either Condition A or Condition B is satisfied. Condition A is that the hire period is no more than 45 consecutive days. Condition B is that the expenditure relates to a period (the *'sub-hire period'*) throughout which the taxpayer makes the car available to another person and the sub-hire period is more than 45 consecutive days.

For the purpose of applying Condition B, the expenditure on hiring the car is apportioned on a time basis between the hire period and the sub-hire period. For the purpose of applying either condition, where arrangements for the hiring of a car include arrangements for the provision of a replacement car in the event that the first car is not available, the first car and any replacement car are to be treated as if they were the same car.

For the purposes of both conditions, two or more hire periods of the same car are aggregated in determining the number of consecutive days if those periods are no more than 14 days apart.

Neither condition is met if the car is hired under tax avoidance arrangements. Condition B is not met if the sub-lessee is an employee of the taxpayer or of a person connected with the taxpayer (within **21** CONNECTED PERSONS) or if, during any part of the period in question, the sub-lessee himself makes any car available to an employee of the taxpayer (under arrangements with the taxpayer) or of a person connected with the taxpayer.

Where there is a chain of leases involving CONNECTED PERSONS (**21**), the 15% restriction applies only to expenditure incurred by a *'commercial lessee'* or, where there is more than one, by the first *'commercial lessee'* in the chain. A *'commercial lessee'* is someone who incurs the expenditure under commercial arrangements, i.e. arrangements the terms of which are such as would reasonably have been expected if the parties thereto had been dealing at arm's length. If one or more persons in the chain is a company, the similar restriction that applies for corporation tax purposes is taken into account also, so that only one restriction applies overall.

[*ITTOIA 2005, ss 48, 49, 50A, 50B; FA 2009, Sch 11 paras 36–39; TIOPA 2010, Sch 8 para 254*].

Old regime

Where a 'car or motor cycle' of which the retail price when new (i.e. unused and not second-hand) exceeds £12,000 is hired for the purposes of a trade, the hire charge is reduced for tax purposes by multiplying it by the fraction:

$(12,000 + RP) \div 2RP$

where RP is the retail price when new. If the price paid for the car by the lessor when new is known, it can be used as the retail price when new, but otherwise the manufacturer's list price, net of any discount generally available but inclusive of extras and VAT, should be used (Revenue Tax Bulletin April 2000 p 746).

For this purpose, a '*car or motor cycle*' is a mechanically propelled road vehicle which is neither (1) of a construction primarily suited for the conveyance of goods or burden of any description nor (2) of a type not commonly used as a private vehicle and unsuitable for such use. As regards (2), see the case law referred to at **11.13**(ii) CAPITAL ALLOWANCES ON PLANT AND MACHINERY.

The restriction does *not* apply to 'qualifying hire cars' as defined in **11.27** CAPITAL ALLOWANCES ON PLANT AND MACHINERY. As regards hire-purchase agreements (as defined) under which there is an option to purchase, exercisable on payment of a sum of not more than 1% of the retail price when new, the finance charge element, which strictly falls within the definition of a hire charge, is also excluded from the restriction. This exclusion is extended to hire-purchase agreements under which there is no option to purchase.

Also *excluded* from the restriction is expenditure incurred after 16 April 2002 on hiring cars (but *not* motor cycles) first registered after that date which are 'electrically-propelled' or have 'low carbon dioxide emissions' (for which see **11.19** CAPITAL ALLOWANCES ON PLANT AND MACHINERY) for a period of hire beginning before 1 April 2013 under a contract entered into before that date. The reduction (referred to at **11.19**) from 120g/km to 110g/km in the maximum carbon dioxide emissions limit does not apply where the period of hire began before 1 April 2008 (even if it continues on and after that date) under a contract entered into before that date.

'Hire charges' for these purposes were held to include payments under a finance lease providing a revolving facility for the purchase of vehicles for use in a contract hire operation (*Lloyds UDT Finance Ltd and Another v Britax International GmBH and Another* CA 2002, 74 TC 662).

Where the above restriction has applied, any subsequent rental rebate (or debt release other than as part of a statutory insolvency arrangement — see **73.40** above) is reduced for tax purposes in the same proportion as the hire charge restriction. This treatment extends to amounts brought in as post-cessation receipts (see **59.1** POST-CESSATION RECEIPTS AND EXPENDITURE) after the trade has ceased.

[ITTOIA 2005, ss 48–50 as originally enacted; FA 2008, s 77(4)(6); CTA 2009, Sch 1 paras 589, 590].

See HMRC Business Income Manual BIM47715–47720.

See **11.27 CAPITAL ALLOWANCES ON PLANT AND MACHINERY** for the restriction of writing-down allowances in respect of *capital* expenditure on the acquisition of a car costing over £12,000.

Cemeteries and crematoria

[73.43] In computing profits of a trade consisting of, or including, the carrying on of a cemetery or the carrying on of a crematorium (and, in connection therewith, the maintenance of memorial garden plots), a deduction as a trading expense for any period of account is allowed for:

* the capital cost of purchasing and preparing land (including cost of levelling, draining or otherwise making suitable) sold for interments or memorial garden plots *in that period*; and
* a *proportion* (based on the ratio of number of grave-spaces/garden plots sold in the period to that number plus those still available — see *Example* below) of 'residual capital expenditure'.

'*Residual capital expenditure*' is the total 'ancillary capital expenditure' incurred before the end of the period of account in question after subtracting:

(i)   amounts previously deducted under these provisions;
(ii) any sale, insurance or compensation receipts for assets representing ancillary capital expenditure and sold or destroyed; and
(iii) certain expenditure before the basis period for 1954/55.

'*Ancillary capital expenditure*' is capital expenditure incurred on any building or structure (other than a dwelling-house), or on the purchase or preparation of other land not suitable or adaptable for interments or garden plots, which is in the cemetery or memorial garden and is likely to have little or no value when the cemetery or garden is full; it also includes capital expenditure on the purchase or preparation of land taken up by said buildings and structures.

For these purposes, sales of land in a cemetery include sales of interment rights, and sales of land in a memorial garden include appropriations of part of the garden in return for dedication fees etc. Expenditure met by subsidies cannot be deducted as above (the detailed rules being similar to those at **10.2**(vi) **CAPITAL ALLOWANCES**).

Any change in the persons carrying on the trade is ignored; allowances continue as they would to the original trader, disregarding any purchase price paid in connection with the change itself.

[ITTOIA 2005, ss 169–172; CTA 2009, Sch 1 paras 603, 604].

For the treatment of lump sums for grave maintenance etc., see HMRC Business Income Manual BIM52505, 52510. For the treatment of expenditure and receipts in connection with the provision of niches and memorials, see BIM52520, 52525.

As regards crematoria, see also *Bourne v Norwich Crematorium* Ch D 1967, 44 TC 164.

Simon's Taxes. See B5.620.

Example

[73.44]

GE, who operates a funeral service, owns a cemetery for which accounts to 31 December are prepared. The accounts to 31.12.10 reveal the following:

(i)	Cost of land representing 110 grave spaces sold in period	£3,400
(ii)	Number of grave spaces remaining	275
(iii)	Residual capital expenditure on buildings and other land unsuitable for interments	£18,250

The allowances available are		£
(a)	Item (i)	3,400
(b)	$\dfrac{110}{110+275} \times £18,250$	5,214
		£8,614

Note

£8,614 will be allowed as a deduction in computing GE's trading profits for the period of account ending on 31 December 2010.

Clergymen

[73.45] The following apply for the purpose of computing the profits of the profession or vocation of a minister of religious denomination. See **27.50 EMPLOYMENT INCOME** as regards clergymen in employment.

If the minister pays rent for a dwelling-house any part of which is used mainly and substantially for the purposes of his duty, a deduction is allowed for such part of the rent as on a just and reasonable apportionment is attributable to that part, subject to a maximum deduction of one-quarter of the rent.

If a charity or ecclesiastical corporation owns an interest in the premises in which the minister resides and from which he performs his duty, one-quarter of any expenses he incurs on the maintenance, repair, insurance or management of the premises is deductible even if it would not be so under general principles, e.g. the 'wholly and exclusively' rule at **73.36** above. The deduction may exceed one-quarter to the extent that it is allowable under general principles.

[*ITTOIA 2005, s 159, Sch 2 para 43*].

Commission, cashbacks and discounts

[73.46] HMRC Statement of Practice SP 4/97 sets out HMRC's views on the tax treatment of commissions, cashbacks and discounts. The types of payment with which the Statement is concerned are as follows.

- **Commissions.** Sums paid by the providers of goods, investments or services to agents or intermediaries as reward for the introduction of business, or in some cases paid directly by the provider to the customer. Sums paid to an agent or intermediary may be passed on to the customer or to some other person.
- **Cashbacks.** Lump sums received by a customer as an inducement for entering into a transaction for the purchase of goods, investments or services and received as a direct consequence of having entered into that transaction. The payer may be either the provider or another party with an interest in ensuring that the transaction takes place.
- **Discounts,** i.e. where the purchaser's obligation to pay for goods, investments or services is less than the full purchase price, other than as a result of commissions or cashbacks.

The Statement also deals with commissions or cashbacks which are netted off, or invested or otherwise applied for the benefit of the purchaser, or where extra value is added to the goods, investments or services supplied (e.g. the allocation of bonus units in an investment) (although in the case of the addition of value to investments this may represent a return on the investment, which is outside the scope of the Statement).

The Statement provides detailed guidance on the circumstances in which liability may arise, either as trading income or as miscellaneous income, on receipts of commission etc. It also considers deductibility of commission etc. passed on to customers. It also considers possible liabilities to tax on employment income or to capital gains tax, and the effect of commissions etc. on life insurance policies.

Generally, ordinary retail arm's length customers will not be liable to income tax or capital gains tax. The Statement outlines the circumstances in which receipts are treated as tax-free, or payments qualify for tax relief, and contains an element of concession for those who, in the ordinary course of their business, earn commission relating to their own transactions. It contains a warning that the principles outlined may not be followed where tax avoidance schemes are involved, or where the arrangements for the commission etc. include an increase in the purchase price of the goods etc. involved. The tax treatment of the payer and the recipient are in all cases considered independently of one another.

For an article explaining the legal basis of this approach, see Revenue Tax Bulletin February 1998 pp 505–509.

Compensation, damages etc. — payments

[73.47] For compensation and redundancy payments to directors or employees see **73.65** below. An important case is *Anglo-Persian Oil Co Ltd v Dale* CA 1931, 16 TC 253 in which a substantial payment by a company for the cancellation of its principal agency, with ten years to run, was held to be allowable. It was not for a capital asset nor to get rid of an onerous contract (cf. *Mallett v Staveley Coal* CA 1928, 13 TC 772) but to enable it to rationalise its working arrangements. The decision was applied in *Croydon Hotel & Leisure Co Ltd v Bowen* (Sp C 101), [1996] SSCD 466, in which a payment for the termination of a hotel management agreement was held to be allowable. See also *Vodafone Cellular Ltd v Shaw* CA 1997, 69 TC 376 (payment for release from onerous agreement), in which the principle under-lying the decision in *Van den Berghs Ltd v Clark* (see **73.48**(b) below) was applied, but cf. *Tucker v Granada Motorway Services Ltd* HL 1979, 53 TC 92, where a payment to modify the method of calculating the rent was held to be capital, and *Whitehead v Tubbs (Elastics) Ltd* CA 1983, 57 TC 472, where a payment to alter the terms of a capital loan by removing borrowing restrictions on the borrower was held to be capital.

A payment by a shipping company for cancelling an order it had placed for a ship was held capital (*'Countess Warwick' SS Co Ltd v Ogg* KB 1924, 8 TC 652 and contrast *Devon Mutual Steamship Insce v Ogg* KB 1927, 13 TC 184). A payment to an associated company in return for its temporarily ceasing production held allowable (*Commr of Taxes v Nchanga Consolidated Copper Mines* PC 1964, 43 ATC 20) as were statutory levies on a brewery for a Compensation Fund where a licence is not renewed (*Smith v Lion Brewery Co Ltd* HL 1910, 5 TC 568) and a payment to secure the closure of a rival concern (*Walker v The Joint Credit Card Co Ltd* Ch D 1982, 55 TC 617). Payments by a steel company to secure the closure of railway steel works were held capital (*United Steels v Cullington (No 1)* CA 1939, 23 TC 71) as were payments to safeguard against subsidence on a factory site (*Bradbury v United Glass Bottle Mfrs* CA 1959, 38 TC 369; compare *Glenboig Union Fireclay* at **73.48**(c) below) and a payment for cancelling electricity agreement on closure of a quarry (*CIR v Wm Sharp & Son* CS 1959, 38 TC 341). For compensation paid on the termination of tied houses of breweries, see *Watneys (London) Ltd v Pike* Ch D 1982, 57 TC 372.

Where damages awarded by a Court against a solicitor were later compounded, the compounded amount (accepted as allowable) was held to be an expense of the year in which the Court award was made (*Simpson v Jones* Ch D 1968, 44 TC 599). See also *CIR v Hugh T Barrie Ltd* CA(NI) 1928, 12 TC 1223.

Damages paid by a brewery to a hotel guest injured by a falling chimney were held to have been incurred by it *qua* property owner and not *qua* trader and not deductible (*Strong & Co of Romsey Ltd v Woodifield* HL 1906, 5 TC 215). Penalties for breach of war-time regulations and defence costs not allowed (*CIR v Warnes & Co* KB 1919, 12 TC 227; *CIR v Alexander von Glehn & Co Ltd* CA 1920, 12 TC 232), nor fines imposed by professional regulatory body (*McKnight v Sheppard* Ch D 1996, 71 TC 419), nor damages for breach of American 'anti-trust' law (*Cattermole v Borax & Chemicals Ltd* KB 1949, 31 TC 202). See also *G Scammell & Nephew v Rowles* CA 1939, 22 TC 479; *Fairrie v Hall* KB 1947, 28 TC 200; *Golder v Great Boulder Proprietary* HC 1952, 33 TC 75; *Knight v Parry* Ch D 1972, 48 TC 580; *Hammond Engineering v CIR* Ch D 1975, 50 TC 313.

Compensation, damages etc. — receipts

[73.48] The following matters are relevant.

(a) **Capital sums** (i.e. sums not taken into account in computing income) received as compensation for damage, injury, destruction or depreciation of assets are subject to capital gains tax [*TCGA 1992, s 22(1)*] (or corporation tax in the case of a company), but this does not apply to compensation or damages to an individual for wrong or injury to his person or in his profession or vocation. [*TCGA 1992, s 51(2)*]. See Tolley's Capital Gains Tax.

(b) **Cancellation or variation of trading contracts and arrangements.** An important case is *Van den Berghs Ltd v Clark* HL 1935, 19 TC 390 in which a receipt on the termination of a profit-sharing arrangement was held to be capital. The arrangement related to the whole structure of the recipient's trade, forming the fixed framework within which its circulating capital operated. Compensation etc. receipts were also held to be capital in *Sabine v Lookers Ltd* CA 1958, 38 TC 120 (varying car distributor's agreement); *British-Borneo Petroleum v Cropper* Ch D 1968, 45 TC 201 (cancelling a royalty agreement); *Barr Crombie & Co Ltd v CIR* CS 1945, 26 TC 406 (terminating agreement as ship-managers); but the opposite conclusion was reached in *Consultant v Inspector of Taxes* (Sp C 180), [1999] SSCD 63 (termination of profit participation agreement). A payment by the liquidator of a shipping company to its managers as authorised by the shareholders held not assessable (*Chibbett v Robinson & Sons* KB 1924, 9 TC 48).

Compensation etc. receipts on the cancellation of contracts receipts from which, if completed, would have been trading receipts are normally themselves trading receipts, to be credited in the computations for the period in which cancelled. See *Short Bros Ltd v CIR* and *Sunderland Shipbuilding Co Ltd v CIR* CA 1927, 12 TC 955 (cancellation of order for ships); *CIR v Northfleet Coal Co* KB 1927, 12 TC 1102; *Jesse Robinson & Sons v CIR* KB 1929, 12 TC 1241 (cancellation of contracts for sale of goods etc.); *Greyhound Racing Assn v Cooper* KB 1936, 20 TC 373 (cancellation of agreement to hire greyhound track); *Shove v Dura Mfg Co Ltd* KB 1941, 23 TC 779 (cancellation of commission agreement). Similarly compensation to a merchanting company on cancellation of a contract to supply goods to it was held a trading receipt (*Bush, Beach & Gent Ltd v Road* KB 1939, 22 TC 519). See also *United Steel v Cullington (No 1)* CA 1939, 23 TC 71; *Shadbolt v Salmon Estates* KB 1943, 25 TC 52; *Sommerfelds Ltd v Freeman* Ch D 1966, 44 TC 43; *Creed v H & M Levinson Ltd* Ch D 1981, 54 TC 477.

Compensation received on the termination of agencies is a trading receipt unless the agency, by reason of its relative size etc., is part of the 'fixed framework' (see *Van den Berghs* above) of the agent's business. See *Kelsall Parsons* CS 1938, 21 TC 608; *CIR v Fleming & Co* CS 1951, 33 TC 57; *CIR v David MacDonald & Co* CS 1955, 36 TC 388; *Wiseburgh v Domville* CA 1956, 36 TC 527; *Fleming v Bellow*

Machine Co Ch D 1965, 42 TC 308; *Elson v James G Johnston Ltd* Ch D 1965, 42 TC 545 (in all of which the compensation etc. was held to be a trading receipt). See also *Anglo-French Exploration Co Ltd v Clayson* CA 1956, 36 TC 545.

For payments received on termination of building society agencies, see HMRC Capital Gains Tax Manual CG13050 *et seq*.

The treatment of compensation on the termination of posts held in the course of a business (particularly a profession), the yearly remuneration having been included in the business receipts (see **27.54 EMPLOYMENT INCOME**), has arisen in a number of cases. In *Blackburn v Close Bros Ltd* Ch D 1960, 39 TC 164, compensation on the cancellation of an agreement by a merchant banker to provide secretarial services was held to be a trading receipt but in *Ellis v Lucas* Ch D 1966, 43 TC 276 compensation on the termination of an auditorship was held to be within the ambit of the special legislation on termination payments (see **20.4 COMPENSATION FOR LOSS OF EMPLOYMENT (AND DAMAGES)**) and hence could not be included in the profits for Schedule D, Case II (professional income) purposes (except a small part of the payment held to be compensation for the loss of general accountancy work). Similar decisions were reached in *Walker v Carnaby Harrower, Barham & Pykett* Ch D 1969, 46 TC 561 (loss of auditorship by firm of accountants) and *CIR v Brander & Cruickshank* HL 1970, 46 TC 574 (loss of company secretaryships by firm of Scottish advocates) and in *Carnaby Harrower* the payment was also held not to be a professional receipt because of its *ex gratia* nature. For *ex gratia* payments, see also (e) below. For compensation on cancellation of contracts of actors, authors etc. see **73.39** above, **73.51** below.

(c)   **Compensation etc. relating to capital assets.** Compensation to a company making fireclay goods for refraining from working a fireclay bed under a railway line was held to be capital (*Glenboig Union Fireclay Co Ltd v CIR* HL 1922, 12 TC 427 and cf. *Thomas McGhie & Sons v BTC* QB 1962, 41 ATC 144 and *Bradbury v United Glass Bottle* CA 1959, 38 TC 369), but compensation to a colliery from the Government for requisition of part of its mining area was held to be a trading receipt (*Waterloo Main Colliery v CIR (No 1)* KB 1947, 29 TC 235). Compensation to a shipping company for delay in the overhaul of a ship was held to be a trading receipt (*Burmah Steam Ship Co v CIR* CS 1930, 16 TC 67) as was compensation to a jetty owner for loss of its use after damage by a ship (*London & Thames Haven v Attwooll* CA 1966, 43 TC 491) and compensation for the detention of a ship (*Ensign Shipping Co v CIR* CA 1928, 12 TC 1169 but contrast *CIR v Francis West* CS 1950, 31 TC 402). Compensation for what turned out to be only a temporary loss of the use of land was held to be a trading receipt (*Able (UK) Ltd v HMRC* CA 2007, [2008] STC 136).

For insurance recoveries see **73.88** below.

(d)   **Compensation on compulsory acquisition etc.** Where compensation is paid for the acquisition of business property by an authority possessing powers of compulsory acquisition, any amounts included as compensation for temporary loss of profits or losses on trading stock or to reimburse revenue expenditure, such as removal expenses and interest, are treated as trading receipts. (See HMRC SP 8/79. This Statement of Practice was originally issued as consequence of *Stoke-on-Trent City Council v Wood Mitchell & Co Ltd* CA 1978, [1979] STC 197.)

(e)   **Other compensation etc. receipts.** Voluntary payments to an insurance broker on the loss of an important client company (made by its parent company) were held, approving *Chibbett v Robinson* and *Carnaby Harrower* (see (b) above), not to be assessable (*Simpson v John Reynolds & Co* CA 1975, 49 TC 693) and similarly for voluntary payments from a brewer to a firm of caterers for the surrender of the leases of tied premises (*Murray v Goodhews* CA 1977, 52 TC 86) but *ex gratia* payments to an estate agent who had not been given an agency he expected were held, on the facts, to be additional remuneration for work already done and assessable. (*McGowan v Brown & Cousins (Stuart Edwards)* Ch D 1977, 52 TC 8). A payment to a diamond broker under informal and non-binding arbitration as damages for the loss of a prospective client was held assessable (*Rolfe v Nagel* CA 1981, 55 TC 585). Compensation for 'loss of profits' following the destruction of the premises of a business not recommenced was held to be of a revenue nature in *Lang v Rice* CA (NI) 1983, 57 TC 80. For compensation receipts relating to the terms on which business premises are tenanted, see **73.104** below.

For the treatment of compensation received by businesses as customers of e.g. utility companies for interruptions and other service deficiencies, see Revenue Tax Bulletin December 1997 pp 490, 491.

Financial loss allowances paid to e.g. jurors, members of certain local authorities and magistrates to compensate them for loss of profit in their trade or profession are chargeable as trading receipts. (Revenue Tax Bulletin May 1992 p 20). Such payments are not taxable as employment income (see **27.20 EMPLOYMENT INCOME**).

Damages awarded to a theatrical company for breach of a licence it had, were held to be assessable (*Vaughan v Parnell & Zeitlin* KB 1940, 23 TC 505) as was compensation received by a development company under legislation for restricting development (*Johnson v W S Try Ltd* CA 1946, 27 TC 167). A retrospective award for a war-time requisition of trading stock was held to be a trading receipt of the year of requisition (*CIR v Newcastle Breweries Ltd* HL 1927, 12 TC 927).

Contingent and future liabilities

[73.49] For forward contracts see **73.50** below.

Where a company is required under overseas legislation to make leaving payments to its employees, a provision in its accounts for its prospective liability is permissible if capable of sufficiently accurate calculation (*Owen v Southern Railway of Peru* HL 1956, 36 TC 602). The allowance each year is the actual payments as adjusted for any variation between the opening and closing provisions but the deductible provision for the year in which the legislation was enacted may include an amount in respect of previous services of the employees (*CIR v Titaghur Jute Factory Ltd* CS 1978, 53 TC 675).

No deduction is normally permissible for future repairs or renewals (*Clayton v Newcastle-under-Lyme Corpn* QB 1888, 2 TC 416; *Naval Colliery Co Ltd v CIR* HL 1928, 12 TC 1017; *Peter Merchant Ltd v Stedeford* CA 1948, 30 TC 496). However, this rule is now subject to Financial Reporting Standard FRS 12 (see **73.107** below). No deduction is permissible for the future cost of collecting debts (*Monthly Salaries Loan Co v Furlong* Ch D 1962, 40 TC 313) or for future payments of damages in respect of accidents to employees unless liability has been admitted or established (*James Spencer & Co v CIR* CS 1950, 32 TC 111). See also *Albion Rovers Football Club v CIR* HL 1952, 33 TC 331 (wages deductible when paid). A provision for regular major overhaul work accrued due on aircraft engines was allowed in *Johnston v Britannia Airways Ltd* Ch D 1994, 67 TC 99 (but see now Revenue Tax Bulletin February 1999 p 624 and further below as regards changes in accounting practice superseding this decision).

For provisions by insurance companies for unexpired risks etc., see *Sun Insurance Office v Clark* HL 1912, 6 TC 59. For the liability of cemetery companies in receipt of lump sums for the future maintenance of graves, see *Paisley Cemetery Co v Reith* CES 1898, 4 TC 1 and *London Cemetery Co v Barnes* KB 1917, 7 TC 92.

A provision by a company engaged in the exploitation of a North Sea oil field, for anticipated future expenditure on the completion of the exploitation, in dismantling installations used and (as required under its licence) in 'cleaning up' the sea bed, was disallowed as capital when incurred in *RTZ Oil & Gas Ltd v Elliss* Ch D 1987, 61 TC 132.

See generally HMRC Business Income Manual BIM42201, 46500–46565. See also Revenue Press Release 20 July 1999, and FRS 12 and articles in the Revenue Tax Bulletin April 1999 pp 636–639 and December 1999 pp 707–709 commenting on its implications for the treatment of provisions in tax computations.

Simon's Taxes. See B2.504.

Contracts

[73.50] For compensation etc. on the cancellation or variation of contracts see **73.47** and **73.48** above. For work in progress under contracts see **73.112** below.

Where a taxpayer took over a coal merchanting business on the death of his father, an amount paid for the benefit of contracts between his father and suppliers was held capital (*John Smith & Son v Moore* HL 1921, 12 TC 266 and see *City of London Contract Corpn v Styles* CA 1887, 2 TC 239). The completion of outstanding contracts following a partnership dissolution (*Hillerns & Fowler v Murray* CA 1932, 17 TC 77) and on a company going into liquidation (*Baker v Cook* KB 1937, 21 TC 337) held to be trading.

Where under a long-term contract goods were invoiced as delivered, the sale proceeds are receipts of the year of delivery (*J P Hall & Co Ltd v CIR* CA 1921, 12 TC 382). If contract prices are varied retrospectively the resultant further sums are assessable or deductible for the years applicable to the sums at the original prices (*Frodingham Ironstone Mines Ltd v Stewart* KB 1932, 16 TC 728; *New Conveyor Co Ltd v Dodd* KB 1945, 27 TC 11). Compare *English Dairies Ltd v Phillips* KB 1927, 11 TC 597; *Isaac Holden & Sons Ltd v CIR* KB 1924, 12 TC 768 and contrast *Rownson Drew & Clydesdale Ltd v CIR* KB 1931, 16 TC 595.

Losses because of a fall in prices fixed under forward contracts etc. cannot be anticipated (*Edward Collins & Sons Ltd v CIR* CS 1924, 12 TC 773; *Whimster & Co v CIR* CS 1925, 12 TC 813) and cf. *Wright Sutcliffe Ltd v CIR* KB 1929, 8 ATC 168; *J H Young & Co v CIR* CS 1924, 12 TC 817; *CIR v Hugh T Barrie Ltd* CA(NI) 1928, 12 TC 1223.

Creative artists

[73.51] A taxpayer who, after writing plays in his spare time which were not sold, wrote a successful play was held to be carrying on the vocation of dramatist (*Billam v Griffith* KB 1941, 23 TC 757). Receipts from the occasional writing of articles are normally chargeable as miscellaneous income but *Schedule D, Case II* (i.e. professional income) assessments on a regular newspaper contributor were upheld in *Graham v Arnott* KB 1941, 24 TC 157. Receipts from the sale of an author's notebooks and memorabilia were held to be taxable as part of the fruits of his profession (*Wain v Cameron* Ch D 1995, 67 TC 324).

A sum received by an author on cancellation of his contract as script writer was held a revenue receipt (*Household v Grimshaw* Ch D 1953, 34 TC 366). Film writer's loss under guarantee of indebtedness of film company held allowable (*Lunt v Wellesley* KB 1945, 27 TC 78).

Whether a literary prize or award is a receipt of the author's profession depends on the precise facts, see HMRC Business Income Manual BIM50710, 50715.

See **73.52** below for averaging of profits. See **73.39** above for the taxation of *artistes*. See **4.28** ANTI-AVOIDANCE for the treatment as income of certain capital sums received in lieu of earnings.

Copyright and royalties

Amounts held to be assessable include advance payments of gramophone royalties to a singer (*Taylor v Dawson* KB 1938, 22 TC 189); commutations of future royalties paid to an authoress (*Glasson v Rougier* KB 1944, 26 TC 86); receipts from sale of film rights in books (*Howson v Monsell* HC 1950, 31 TC 529); sales of copyright in novels written when the author was non-resident (with no deduction for his expenses then incurred — *Mackenzie v Arnold* CA 1952, 33 TC 363). But contrast *Mitchell v Rosay* CA 1954, 35 TC 496. *Sharkey v Wernher* (see **73.114** below) does not apply to a gift of copyright (*Mason v Innes* CA 1967, 44 TC 326). Royalties etc. arising after an author etc. dies or otherwise ceases to carry on his profession or vocation may be chargeable as POST-CESSATION RECEIPTS AND EXPENDITURE (**59**).

Copyright and design royalties or public lending right payments paid by publisher etc. are deductible in computing their profits but royalties to non-residents must be paid net of tax (see **24.13 DEDUCTION OF TAX AT SOURCE**).

Simon's Taxes. See B5.326–B5.328.

Creative artists — averaging of profits

[73.52] The averaging provisions below apply in respect of profits of a 'qualifying trade, profession or vocation', i.e. one whose profits derive wholly or mainly from 'creative works'. *'Creative works'* means literary, dramatic, musical or artistic works, or designs, created by the individual personally or, in the case of a partnership, by one or more of the partners personally. The potential for averaging is extended to profits of a qualifying trade, profession or vocation carried on wholly outside the UK by a UK resident. Averaging does not apply to profits chargeable to corporation tax.

Where, in relation to two consecutive tax years, the profits for one year are less than 75% of the profits for the other (or the profits for one year, but not both, are nil, e.g. where a loss is incurred), an averaging claim can be made, with the following results. If the profits for either year do not exceed 70% of the profits for the other (or are nil), the profits for each year are adjusted to average of both years. If either year's profits exceed 70% of the other's, but are less than 75%, the profits are adjusted by adding to the lower and subtracting from the higher the amount obtained by first multiplying the difference by three and then deducting 75% of the higher figure. (Thus, if the profits are £29,200 and £40,000, the averaged profits would be £31,600 and £37,600.)

'Profits' for this purpose are those before any deduction for losses. An averaging claim does not prevent a claim for loss relief. (Thus, if there were a loss of £10,000 for one tax year and a profit of £30,000 for the other, the averaged profits for each year are £15,000, but the loss of £10,000 remains eligible for loss relief in the normal way.)

If an averaging claim is made for a pair of tax years, Years X and Y, a claim is also permitted for Years Y and Z, the profits for Year Y being taken as those adjusted on the first claim, and so on for subsequent years. However, no averaging claim is subsequently permissible involving any year prior to Year X. No averaging claim can be made for the tax year in which the taxpayer starts, or permanently ceases, to carry on the trade. This includes the tax years in which an individual joins and leaves a partnership. Neither can a claim be made involving any tax year in which the business begins, or ceases, to be a 'qualifying trade, profession or vocation' (see above).

An averaging claim must be made on or before the first anniversary of 31 January following the later of the two tax years to which it relates. An averaging claim can be made only by an individual. In the case of a partnership, an individual partner may make his own claim, based on his own profit shares, irrespective of whether or not other partners make claims.

If, after a claim, the profits of either or both years are adjusted for some other reason, the claim lapses but a new one may then be made, in respect of the adjusted profits, on or before the first anniversary of 31 January following the tax year in which the adjustment is made.

See **18.2** CLAIMS for the method of giving effect to an averaging claim.

A claim for relief under any other provision of the *Income Tax Acts* for a tax year included in an averaging claim can be made, amended or revoked at any time on or before the latest possible date on which the averaging claim itself could have been made. See **18.2** CLAIMS for the method of giving effect to such a claim, amendment or revocation that would otherwise be out of time.

[*ITTOIA 2005, ss 221–225*].

Simon's Taxes. See **B5.326–B5.328**.

Example

[73.53]

Richard is an established author by profession and has the following profits/losses as adjusted for income tax purposes (including a deduction for capital allowances) for the five years mentioned.

Year ended	Tax-adjusted profit/loss £
31.12.06	35,000
31.12.07	30,000
31.12.08	6,000
31.12.09	25,000
31.12.10	(2,000)

Averaged profits for all years would be

		No averaging claims £	Averaging claims for all possible years £
2006/07	note (i)	35,000	35,000
2007/08	note (ii)	30,000	18,000
2008/09	note (iii)	6,000	20,250
2009/10	note (iv)	25,000	11,375
2010/11	note (iv)	Nil	11,375
		£96,000	£96,000

Notes

(i) 2006/07   35,000
     2007/08   30,000
                             £65,000

As £30,000 is not less than 75% of £35,000, no averaging claim is possible.

(ii) 2007/08   30,000
     2008/09   6,000
                             £36,000   ÷ 2 = £18,000

As £6,000 does not exceed 70% of £30,000, straight averaging applies. Still no claims can be made to average 2007/08 (as adjusted) with 2006/07, even though this would now be possible purely on the figures.

(iii) 2008/09   18,000
      2009/10   25,000
                            £43,000

As £18,000 exceeds 70% of £25,000 (but is less than 75%), the adjustment proceeds as follows.

Difference £7,000 × 3		21,000
Deduct 75% × £12,000		18,750
Adjustment	2,250	(2,250)
Existing 2008/09	18,000	
Existing 2009/10		25,000
Averaged profits 2008/09/2009/10	£20,250	£22,750

(iv) 2009/10   22,750
     2010/11   Nil
                             22,750   ÷ 2 = £11,375

The loss of £2,000 for 2010/11 does not enter into the averaging claim, but is available to reduce either the 2009/10 or the 2010/11 averaged profits of £11,375 on a claim under *ITA 2007, s 64* (see **45.2 LOSSES**).

The 2010/11 averaged profits of £11,375 may themselves be averaged with 2011/12 profits if the 75% rule is satisfied. Any loss claim against income of 2010/11 is disregarded for this purpose.

Embezzlement etc.

[73.54] Losses from embezzlement are allowed as deductions, but misappropriations by a partner or director are not deductible. See *Bamford v ATA Advertising* Ch D 1972, 48 TC 359 and cf. *Curtis v J & G Oldfield Ltd* KB

1925, 9 TC 319. Where defalcations were made good by the auditor who admitted negligence, refund held to be a trading receipt for the year in which made (*Gray v Penrhyn* KB 1937, 21 TC 252).

See **73.87** below as regards prohibition on deduction of expenditure involving crime.

Employees (and directors)

[73.55] *Bona fide* remuneration is deductible including bonuses, commissions, tax deducted under PAYE and the cost of board, lodging, uniforms and benefits provided. The deduction is for the remuneration etc. payable; future payments cannot be anticipated (*Albion Rovers Football Club v CIR* HL 1952, 33 TC 331). The remuneration etc. must be shown to be wholly and exclusively for the purposes of the trade. In *Stott & Ingham v Trehearne* KB 1924, 9 TC 69 an increase in the rate of commission payable to the trader's sons was disallowed as not on a commercial footing. See also *Johnson Bros & Co v CIR* KB 1919, 12 TC 147, *Copeman v Wm Flood & Sons Ltd* KB 1940, 24 TC 53 and *Earlspring Properties Ltd v Guest* CA 1995, 67 TC 259. Payments by a farming couple to their young children for help on the farm were disallowed in *Dollar v Lyon* Ch D 1981, 54 TC 459. For excessive payments to 'service company' see *Payne, Stone Fraser* at **52.4 PARTNERSHIPS**. For wife's wages see *Thompson v Bruce* KB 1927, 11 TC 607; *Moschi v Kelly* CA 1952, 33 TC 442. The salary etc. of an employee for service in an overseas subsidiary was allowed in computing the profits of the parent in *Robinson v Scott Bader & Co Ltd* CA 1981, 54 TC 757. The secondment was wholly and exclusively for the purposes of the parent's business, notwithstanding the benefit to the subsidiary's business.

Any excess of the market value over the par value of shares issued to employees at par is not deductible (*Lowry v Consolidated African Selection Trust Ltd* HL 1940, 23 TC 259). For payments to trustees to acquire shares for the benefit of employees, see *Heather v P-E Consulting Group* CA 1972, 48 TC 293, *Jeffs v Ringtons Ltd* Ch D 1985, 58 TC 680 and *E Bott Ltd v Price* Ch D 1985, 59 TC 437, and contrast *Rutter v Charles Sharpe & Co Ltd* Ch D 1979, 53 TC 163 and *Mawsley Machinery Ltd v Robinson* (Sp C 170), [1998] SSCD 236. See also **73.59** below.

For **payroll giving schemes**, see **16.20 CHARITIES**.

Simon's Taxes. See B2.421.

Timing of deductions

[73.56] In calculating trading profits for a period of account, no deduction is allowed for an amount charged in the accounts in respect of employees' remuneration unless it is paid no later than nine months after the end of the period of account. Remuneration paid at a later time (and otherwise deductible) is deductible for the period of account *in which* it is paid. For these purposes, 'remuneration' includes any amount which is, or falls to be treated as, earnings for income tax purposes, and includes remuneration of office holders as well as other employees. Remuneration is treated as paid when it falls to be treated for tax purposes as received by the employee (see **27.16 EMPLOYMENT INCOME**). These provisions apply whether the amount charged is in respect of particular employments or employments generally and apply equally to remuneration for which provision is made in the accounts with a view to its becoming employees' remuneration. Computations prepared before the end of the said nine-month period must be prepared on the basis that any still unpaid remuneration will not be paid before the expiry of that nine-month period and thus will not be deductible for the period of account in question. If, in fact, such remuneration *is* paid by the end of the nine-month period, then the matter may be dealt with by way of amendment to the self-assessment tax return (see **63.4 RETURNS**).

These provisions apply to non-trade businesses as they do to trades, professions and vocations.

[*ITTOIA 2005, ss 36, 37, 865, Sch 2 para 12*].

Payments to an employee benefit trust were held to fall within these restrictions in *Macdonald v Dextra Accessories Ltd and Others* HL 2005, 77 TC 146 and in *Sempra Metals Ltd v HMRC* (Sp C 698), [2008] SSCD 1062. But see now **73.57** below.

Employee benefit contributions

[73.57] There are statutory rules for the timing of deductions for 'employee benefit contributions'. They apply instead of the more general rules at **73.56** above. For these purposes, an *'employee benefit contribution'* was originally defined as a payment of money, or the transfer of an asset, by the employer to a scheme manager (e.g. the trustees of an employee benefit trust) who is entitled or required, under the terms of an employee benefit scheme, to hold or use the money or asset to provide benefits to employees (including former employees). With effect after 20 March 2007, this definition is extended so as also to include any other act (for example, a declaration of trust), or any omission, which results in property being held, or becoming capable of being used, under such a scheme or which increases the total net value of property already so held or capable. A deduction is allowed only to the extent that, during the period in question or within nine months after the end of it, 'qualifying benefits' are provided, or 'qualifying expenses' are paid, out of the contributions. (If the employer's contribution is itself a qualifying benefit, it is sufficient that the contribution be made during the period or within those ensuing nine months.) Any amount thus disallowed remains available for deduction in any subsequent period during which it is used to provide qualifying benefits. For these purposes, qualifying benefits are treated as provided, and expenses are treated as paid, as far as possible out of employee benefit contributions, with no account being taken of any other receipts or expenses of the scheme manager.

A *'qualifying benefit'* is a payment of money or transfer of assets (other than by way of loan) that gives rise to *both* a charge to tax on employment income and a charge to NICs (or would do so but for available exemptions for duties performed outside the UK) or is made in connection with termination of employment or is made under an employer-financed retirement benefits scheme (see **57.26** PENSION PROVISION). Money benefits are treated for these purposes as provided at the time the money is treated as received (applying the rules at **27.16** EMPLOYMENT INCOME, except where paid under an employer-financed retirement benefits scheme). 'Qualifying expenses' are those expenses (if any) of the scheme manager in operating the scheme that would have been deductible in computing profits if incurred by the employer. Where a qualifying benefit takes the form of the transfer of an asset, the amount provided is the aggregate of the amount that would otherwise be deductible by the employer (in a case where the scheme manager acquired the asset from the employer) and the amount expended on the asset by the scheme manager. If, however, the amount charged to tax under *ITEPA 2003* (or which would be so charged if the duties of employment were performed in the UK) is lower than that aggregate, any amount deductible under these provisions at any time is limited to that lower amount; this rule is aimed at a situation where the asset falls in value after its acquisition by the scheme manager but before its transfer to the employee (Treasury Explanatory Notes to the 2003 Finance Bill).

These restrictions do not apply to disallow deductions for consideration given for goods or services provided in the course of a trade or profession or for contributions to a registered pension scheme (see **57.2** PENSION PROVISION), qualifying overseas pension scheme (if the employee is a relevant migrant member — see **57.20** PENSION PROVISION) or accident benefit scheme (as defined).

Computations prepared before the end of the said nine-month period must be prepared by reference to the facts at the time of computation. If any contributions are used for qualifying purposes after that time, but within the nine months, the computation may be adjusted accordingly (subject to the normal time limits for amending self-assessment tax returns).

[*ITTOIA 2005, ss 38–44, 866, Sch 2 paras 13–15; FA 2007, s 34(7)–(13)*].

Payments to a trust the beneficiaries of which were members of employees' families were held to fall within these restrictions in *Sempra Metals Ltd v HMRC* (Sp C 698), [2008] SSCD 1062.

Employees' council tax

[73.58] An employer who pays the council tax for an employee will normally be able to claim a deduction for it. If such payments are also made on behalf of members of the employee's family, they too are deductible if they are part of the employee's remuneration package (which would normally mean they were paid under the contract of employment). (Revenue Press Release 16 March 1993).

Employee share schemes

[73.59] By their very nature, the rules below and at **73.60–73.62**) apply for the purposes of corporation tax only but they are included in this work because of their relevance to **69** SHARE-RELATED EMPLOYMENT INCOME AND EXEMPTIONS.

There is a statutory corporation tax deduction regime for the cost of providing shares for employee share schemes where the employees are taxable in respect of shares acquired or would be taxable:

- if the scheme were not an approved share option scheme; or
- in the case of an enterprise management incentive scheme option (see **69.35 SHARE-RELATED EMPLOYMENT INCOME AND EXEMPTIONS**) if the option were non-qualifying; or
- if the employee were UK-resident and ordinarily resident and the duties of the employment were performed in the UK.

The deduction is normally based on the market value of the shares, at the time they are awarded or the share option is exercised (whichever is applicable), less any contribution given (by the recipient or anyone else) in respect of the shares. The relief relates only to the cost of providing shares; it does not affect, and is not restricted by, other reliefs for costs of setting up or administering schemes, costs of borrowing and incidental expenses of acquiring shares, e.g. fees, commissions, stamp duty. The shares themselves must be fully-paid, non-redeemable, ordinary shares in a listed company, a subsidiary of a listed company or an unlisted company not under the control of another company. The relief is generally given for the accounting period in which the employee acquires the shares. There are, however, special rules for restricted shares (within **69.4 SHARE-RELATED EMPLOYMENT INCOME AND EXEMPTIONS**) and convertible shares (within **69.7 SHARE-RELATED EMPLOYMENT INCOME AND EXEMPTIONS**) that also give relief, in subsequent accounting periods in which chargeable events occur, in amounts broadly equal to the amounts chargeable on employees as a result of such events. If the shares are acquired on or after 20 July 2005 (other than in pursuance of an option) and are not restricted shares, no relief is available if *ITEPA 2003, s 446UA* applies in relation to the shares. (That section applies if the shares are acquired at less than market value and the arrangements under which the right or opportunity to acquire them was made available had as one of its main purposes the avoidance of tax or national insurance contributions.)

For full details of the above provisions, see Tolley's Corporation Tax under Trading Expenses and Deductions. For an article on the interaction of the provisions with the transfer pricing rules (see **4.18** *et seq.* **ANTI-AVOIDANCE**), see Revenue Tax Bulletin February 2003 pp 1002–1007.

[*CTA 2009, ss 1001–1038; CTA 2010, Sch 1 para 665*].

Other reliefs available in connection with employee share schemes are described at **73.60–73.62** below.

Share incentive plans

[73.60] Subject to the exceptions below, the items at (a)–(d) below are allowable deductions in computing company trading profits in connection with an approved share incentive plan within *ITEPA 2003, Sch 2* (see **69.20–69.34 SHARE-RELATED EMPLOYMENT INCOME AND EXEMPTIONS**). If the company is carrying on a property business (as in **60 PROPERTY INCOME**), the items are similarly treated as allowable deductions in computing the profits. If the company is one with investment business (other than a property business) they are treated as management expenses.

(a)   The market value (at time of acquisition by the plan trustees, and see below) of free and matching shares awarded to employees under the plan (the deduction being given *to the employer company* for the period of account in which the shares are awarded).

(b)   Any excess of the market value (at time of acquisition by the plan trustees, and determined as for capital gains tax purposes) of partnership shares over the amounts paid by participating employees to acquire them (the deduction being given *to the employer company* for the period of account in which the shares are acquired on participants' behalf).

(c)   Expenditure incurred by a company in establishing a plan (the deduction being given for the period of account in which the expenditure is incurred, unless HMRC approve the plan more than nine months after the end of that period, in which case the deduction is given for the period of account in which approval is given).

(d)   Contributions by a company to the expenses of plan trustees in operating a plan, *excluding* expenses in acquiring shares (other than incidental costs such as fees, commission, stamp duty etc.) but *including* interest on money borrowed to acquire shares.

Once a deduction is made under (a) or (b) above, no other deduction (other than any within (c) or (d) above) may be made by the employer company or any associated company (as defined) in respect of the provision of the shares, and no deduction within (a) or (b) above may then be made by any other company in that respect. Once a deduction is made under (c) above, no other deduction may be made in respect of the costs of setting up the plan.

For the purposes of (a) above, market value is determined as for capital gains tax purposes, and, for the purposes of that determination (and also for those of (iii) below), shares acquired by the trustees on different days are deemed to be awarded under the plan on a first in/first out basis. In the case of a group plan (i.e. a plan established by a parent company and extending to one or more companies under its control), the total market value of the shares awarded is apportioned between the relevant employer companies by reference to the number of shares awarded to the employees of each company.

No deduction is allowed under (a) or (b) above:

(i)   in respect of shares awarded to an individual whose earnings from the eligible employment are not, at the time of the award, taxable earnings (whether or not subject to the remittance basis in the case of overseas earnings);

(ii)   in respect of shares that are liable to depreciate substantially in value for reasons that do not apply generally to shares in the company;

(iii) if a deduction has been made (on whatever basis), by the company, or an associated company (as defined) in respect of providing the same shares for the plan trust or for another trust (whatever its nature or purpose); or

(iv)   in respect of the subsequent award of shares previously forfeited by participants (such shares being treated as acquired by the trustees at time of forfeit for no consideration).

No deduction is allowed under (c) above if any employee acquires rights under the plan, or the trustees acquire any shares, before the plan receives HMRC approval. Subject to (d) above, no deduction is allowed for expenses in providing dividend shares.

On withdrawal of HMRC approval to a plan, HMRC may, by notice, direct that any deductions made under (a) or (b) above be withdrawn also, in which case the company is deemed to have received an amount equal to the aggregate deductions for the period of account in which HMRC notify withdrawal of approval. See **69.24** SHARE-RELATED EMPLOYMENT INCOME AND EXEMPTIONS for right of appeal.

The notional receipt is treated as a receipt of the company's trade or property business if applicable. If the business has ceased, it is treated as a post-cessation receipt; for accounting periods ending before 1 April 2009, this was not explicit — see Change 76 listed in Annex 1 to the Explanatory Notes to *CTA 2009*. In any other case, it is treated as a receipt within the charge to corporation tax on income; for accounting periods ending before 1 April 2009, the charge was under Schedule D, Case VI.

A payment made by the employer company to the trustees sufficient to enable them to acquire (other than from a company) a significant block of shares (at least 10% of the employer company's ordinary share capital) attracts a deduction (in computing trading profits etc.) which, in contrast to the above, is not deferred until the shares are awarded to employees. For payments on or after 24 March 2010, the deduction is not available if the payment is made in pursuance of tax avoidance arrangements, i.e. arrangements entered into by the paying company a main purpose of which is to obtain a deduction or an increased deduction. The deduction falls to be given for the period of account in which falls the first anniversary of the date of acquisition, provided the 10% requirement is then met. The deduction will, however, be clawed back unless at least 30% of those shares are awarded within five years of acquisition by the trustees and all of the shares are awarded within ten years. On clawback, the company is deemed to have received an amount equal to the deduction at the time that HMRC direct that the deduction be withdrawn, the notional receipt being treated as above. If all the shares are subsequently awarded, the deduction is reinstated at that later time. An appropriate proportion of the original deduction is also subject to clawback if the plan terminates before all the shares have been awarded or if shares are awarded to an individual within (i) above. In the event of HMRC withdrawing their approval to the plan, the same provisions apply as above as regards potential withdrawal of deductions.

[CTA 2009, ss 983–998, Sch 2 paras 105, 106; ICTA 1988, s 85B, Sch 4AA; CTA 2010, Sch 1 para 396(7); FA 2010, s 42(5)(6)(8)].

Approved share option schemes

[73.61] Expenditure on establishing an approved SAYE option scheme or CSOP scheme (see **69.47, 69.61** SHARE-RELATED EMPLOYMENT INCOME AND EXEMPTIONS) is deductible in computing the company's trading profits provided that no employee or director obtains rights under the scheme before it is approved. If the company is carrying on a property business (as in **60**

PROPERTY INCOME), the expenditure is similarly deductible in computing the profits. If the company is one with investment business (other than a property business) the expenditure is treated as management expenses.

If the scheme is approved more than nine months after the end of the period of account in which the expenditure is incurred, the deduction is made for the period of account in which the approval is given. (In the case of a company with investment business (other than a property business) the expenditure is treated as referable to the accounting period in which the approval is given.)

[*CTA 2009, s 999; ITTOIA 2005, s 94A; ICTA 1988, s 84A; TIOPA 2010, Sch 7 para 28*].

Employee share ownership trusts

[**73.62**] Expenditure incurred in setting up a qualifying employee share ownership trust (QUEST) (within *FA 1989, Sch 5*) is deductible in computing the company's trading profits. If the company is carrying on a property business (as in **60 PROPERTY INCOME**), the expenditure is similarly deductible in computing the profits. If the company is one with investment business (other than a property business) the expenditure is treated as management expenses.

If the deed establishing the trust is executed more than nine months after the end of the period of account in which the expenditure is incurred, the deduction is made for the period of account in which the deed is executed. (In the case of a company with investment business (other than a property business) the expenditure is treated as referable to the accounting period in which the deed is executed.)

[*CTA 2009, s 1000; ICTA 1988, s 85A*].

Non-qualifying employee share ownership trusts. For the treatment of contributions to employee share ownership trusts not within the above provisions which are not capital expenditure on general principles but which are required under UITF 13 to be treated as giving rise to an asset in the employer's accounts, see Revenue Tax Bulletin February 1997 pp 399, 400. Broadly, relief for the contributions is deferred until the rights in the shares are transferred to employees, although this would not prevent a deduction for a properly calculated provision reflecting employees' accruing entitlement to such benefits.

Employment income

[**73.63**] Employment income received by a trader should in law be excluded from his trading income but in practice the strict position is modified in certain circumstances. See HMRC Employment Income Manual EIM 03002. See *Walker v Carnaby Harrower* Ch D 1969, 46 TC 561 and *CIR v Brander & Cruickshank* HL 1970, 46 TC 574 for the inclusion in professional profits of remuneration as auditor etc. For the tax treatment of directors' fees received by partnerships and other companies and the distinction between employment income and trading income, see **27.3**(v) and **27.54 EMPLOYMENT INCOME**. See **27.70 EMPLOYMENT INCOME** as regards certain payments to redundant steel workers.

Retirement and benevolent provisions for employees

[73.64] See 57.12 PENSION PROVISION for the deductibility of payments by the employer under registered pension schemes. *Bona fide* voluntary pensions and retirement gratuities, including pensions to widows, are deductible (*Smith v Incorporated Council of Law Reporting* KB 1914, 6 TC 477). The cost of an annuity to replace a pension is deductible but not the cost of a policy to secure payment *to the employer* of an annuity equal to pensions payable by him (*Hancock v General Reversionary & Investment Co Ltd* KB 1918, 7 TC 358; *Morgan Crucible Co Ltd v CIR* KB 1932, 17 TC 311). For provisions for directors of 'family companies' see *Samuel Dracup & Sons Ltd v Dakin* Ch D 1957, 37 TC 377.

Payments directly or indirectly for the benefit of employees are generally allowed as deductions, including donations to hospitals and charities, unless capital or abnormal (*Rowntree & Co v Curtis* CA 1924, 8 TC 678; *Bourne & Hollingsworth v Ogden* KB 1929, 14 TC 349). See also *Hutchinson & Co v Turner* HC 1950, 31 TC 495 and **73.84** below. Subscriptions to BUPA and similar group schemes for employees are deductible (see **27.75** EMPLOYMENT INCOME for position regarding the employees).

See also **73.57** above (employee benefit contributions).

Redundancy payments

[73.65] Redundancy payments, or other employer's payments, under *Employment Rights Act 1996* (or NI equivalent) are allowable. Rebates recoverable are trading receipts. [*ITTOIA 2005, ss 76–78, 80; ITEPA 2003, s 309; CTA 2009, Sch 1 para 599*].

Non-statutory redundancy and similar payments are normally deductible unless made on the cessation of trading (but now see following paragraphs) (*CIR v Anglo-Brewing Co Ltd* KB 1925, 12 TC 803; *Godden v Wilson's Stores* CA 1962, 40 TC 161; *Geo Peters & Co v Smith* Ch D 1963, 41 TC 264) or as part of the bargain for the sale of shares of the company carrying on the business (*Bassett Enterprise Ltd v Petty* KB 1938, 21 TC 730; *James Snook & Co Ltd v Blasdale* CA 1952, 33 TC 244). See also *Overy v Ashford Dunn & Co* KB 1933, 17 TC 497 and contrast *CIR v Patrick Thomson Ltd* CS 1956, 37 TC 145. A payment to secure the resignation of a life-director who had fallen out with his co-directors was allowed in *Mitchell v B W Noble Ltd* CA 1927, 11 TC 372. See also *O'Keeffe v Southport Printers Ltd* Ch D 1984, 58 TC 88. For provisions for future leaving payments see **73.49** above.

Payments made, to employees taken on for trade purposes, under a pre-existing contractual or statutory obligation which was a consequence of their being so taken on are not disallowed by virtue of the 'wholly and exclusively' rule at **73.36** above merely because it is the cessation of the trade that crystallises the liability to pay (Revenue Tax Bulletin February 1999 pp 630, 631).

Payments in addition to the statutory payment made on cessation of trading are allowable deductions if they would have been allowable had there been no cessation. Allowance is up to three times the statutory payment. On a change in the persons carrying on the trade, the trade is treated as ceasing only if no person who carried on the trade before the change does so after the change. [*ITTOIA 2005, ss 79, 79A; CTA 2009, Sch 1 paras 597, 598*]. Relief is similarly given under these provisions for such payments made on cessation of *part* of a trade.

A gratuitous payment made on partial cessation of a company's trade to a managing director who nevertheless continued thereafter to be a director was held non-deductible in *Relkobrook Ltd v Mapstone* (Sp C 452), [2005] SSCD 272.

Relief under *ITTOIA 2005, ss 76–80* above is given for the period of account in which the payment is made (or, if paid after cessation, for the period of account in which falls the last day on which the trade is carried on). Where, instead, relief is due under general principles, a provision for future payments may be allowed as a deduction for a period of account provided that:

• it appears in the commercial accounts in accordance with generally accepted accounting principles;
• it was accurately calculated (normally requiring the identification of the individual employees affected) using the degree of hindsight permitted by SSAP 17;
• a definite decision to proceed with the redundancies was taken during the period; and
• payment was made within nine months of the end of the period.

(Revenue Tax Bulletin February 1995 p 195).

See generally HMRC Business Income Manual BIM46600–46615.

Counselling services etc.

[**73.66**] Expenditure on counselling and other outplacement services which falls within the earnings exemption of *ITEPA 2003, s 310* (see **27.51 EMPLOYMENT INCOME**) is deductible in computing the profits of the employer's trade. [*ITTOIA 2005, s 73*].

Key employee insurance

[**73.67**] Premiums on policies in favour of the employer insuring against death or critical illness of key employees are generally allowable, and the proceeds of any such policies trading receipts. However, in *Beauty Consultants Ltd v Inspector of Taxes* (Sp C 321), [2002] SSCD 352, premiums on a policy insuring a company against the death of either of its controlling shareholder-directors were disallowed; the 'dual purpose rule' at **73.36** above applied, in that the premiums benefited the shareholders personally by improving the value of their shares. In *Greycon Ltd v Klaentschi* (Sp C 372), [2003] SSCD 370, it was held that the company's sole purpose in taking out key man policies was to meet a requirement of an agreement under which funding and other benefits were obtained from another company, that the policies had a capital purpose and that, consequently, the proceeds of those policies were not trading receipts. See generally HMRC Business Income Manual BIM45525, 45530.

National insurance contributions (NICs)

[73.68] Secondary (i.e. employers') Class 1 NICs are deductible in computing profits. Relief is similarly available for Class 1A NICs (payable by an employer where benefits-in-kind are provided to employees) and for Class 1B NICs (payable in respect of PAYE settlement agreements — see **53.15 PAY AS YOU EARN**). (But no deduction is allowed for any NICs paid for the benefit of the trader himself, e.g. Class 2 or Class 4 contributions.) [*ITTOIA 2005, ss 53, 272, 868*].

Training costs

[73.69] Costs incurred by an employer in respect of employee training are generally allowable as a trading expense. For HMRC's view of the circumstances in which such relief may be prohibited by the 'wholly and exclusively' rule at **73.36** above, see Revenue Tax Bulletin February 1997 pp 400, 401 (which also indicates that it is extremely unlikely that such expenditure would be disallowed as a deduction on the grounds that it was of a capital nature).

Retraining course expenses paid or reimbursed by an employer and satisfying the conditions of the earnings exemption in *ITEPA 2003, s 311* (see **27.79 EMPLOYMENT INCOME**) are deductible in computing the profits of the employer's trade. Similar provisions relating to recovery of tax, information and penalties as apply in relation to the earnings exemption apply in relation to this deduction. [*ITTOIA 2005, ss 74, 75, Sch 2 paras 22, 23; SI 2009 No 2035, Sch para 42*]. See **73.116** below as regards contributions to training and enterprise councils.

Employees seconded to charities or educational bodies

[73.70] If an employer seconds an employee temporarily to a charity (as defined at **16.2 CHARITIES**), any expenditure of the employer which is attributable to the employment is deductible in computing the employer's profits. This relief is extended to secondments to educational establishments (as defined and including education authorities, educational institutions maintained by such authorities, and certain other educational bodies). [*ITTOIA 2005, ss 70, 71; CTA 2009, Sch 1 para 596*].

Payments for restrictive undertakings

[73.71] Payments to employees for restrictive undertakings, falling to be treated as earnings of the employee under *ITEPA 2003, s 225* (see **27.72 EMPLOYMENT INCOME**), are deductible in computing profits. [*ITTOIA 2005, s 69*].

Entertainment and gifts

[73.72] Subject to the exceptions below, no deduction is allowed in computing profits for expenses incurred in providing entertainment or gifts. This includes sums paid to or on behalf of an employee (including a director), or put at his disposal, *exclusively* for meeting expenses incurred, or to be incurred, by the employee in providing the entertainment or gift. See **27.24 EMPLOYMENT INCOME** for the employee position. It also includes expenses incidental to providing entertainment or gifts.

Entertainment expenditure is not within the above prohibition if:

• the entertainment is of a kind which it is the trader's trade to provide and it is provided in the ordinary course of that trade either for payment or free of charge for advertising purposes; or

• the entertainment is provided for the trader's employees (except where such entertainment is incidental to the entertainment of non-employees).

Gifts are not within the above prohibition if:

• they are of an item which it is the trader's trade to provide and are made for advertising purposes; or

• they incorporate a conspicuous advertisement for the trader *and* do not consist of food, drink, tobacco or a token or voucher exchangeable for goods *and* the cost to the trader of all such gifts to the same person in the same basis period does not exceed £50; or

• they are provided for the trader's employees (except where such gifts are incidental to the providing of gifts for non-employees); or

• they are made to a charity (i.e. a body of persons or trust established for charitable purposes only) or to either of the similar organisations specified in *ITTOIA 2005, s 47(5)*.

[*ITTOIA 2005, ss 45–47, 867; ITA 2007, s 989*].

By concession, other gifts are allowed as deductions provided that they are:

(i) wholly and exclusively for the purposes of the business;

(ii) made for the benefit of a body or association established for educational, cultural, religious, recreational or benevolent purposes which is local to the donor's business activities and not restricted to persons connected with the donor; and

(iii) reasonably small in relation to the scale of the donor's business (HMRC ESC B7).

Given the *Charities Act 2006* definition of 'charitable purposes' at **16.2 CHARITIES**, HMRC consider that any deduction that could have been claimed under this concession is now available by statute; in view of this, the concession is to be withdrawn with effect from 9 December 2010. In *Bourne & Hollingsworth v Ogden* KB 1929, 14 TC 349 an abnormally large donation was disallowed. See also **73.84** below. For donations of part of cost of ticket in football pools and lotteries, see **73.23** above.

The cost of hiring a room for a function to which potential customers were invited was held to be deductible (although the catering costs of the function were disallowed as being expenditure on business entertainment); as far as the room-hire was concerned, it was held to be for the purposes of attracting business; the entertainment was incidental to that purpose (*Netlogic Consulting Ltd v HMRC* (Sp C 477), [2005] SSCD 524).

Deductions were allowed for items provided in the ordinary course of a trade of providing entertainment in *Fleming v Associated Newspapers Ltd* HL 1972, 48 TC 382. See also the VAT cases of *C & E Commissioners v Shaklee International and Another* CA, [1981] STC 776 and *Celtic Football and Athletic Co Ltd v C & E Commissioners* CS, [1983] STC 470.

There is also a restriction on capital allowances where plant or machinery is used to provide entertainment, with similar exceptions as above where relevant (see **11.4 CAPITAL ALLOWANCES ON PLANT AND MACHINERY**).

For an article on the scope and application of these rules, see Revenue Tax Bulletin August 1999 pp 679–682 as supplemented by Revenue Tax Bulletin February 2000 p 729. For further comprehensive guidance on business entertainment, see HMRC Business Income Manual BIM45000–45090.

Simon's Taxes. See B2.432, B2.320, B2.441, B2.442.

Farming and market gardening

[73.73] Farming or market gardening in the UK is treated for income tax purposes as trading. All the UK farming carried on by a particular person (other than as part of a different trade) is treated as a single trade. Farming carried on by a partnership is, however, separate from any farming carried on by individual partners. [*ITTOIA 2005, ss 9, 859(1); ITA 2007, s 996*]. See *Bispham v Eardiston Farming Co* Ch D 1962, 40 TC 322 and *Sargent v Eayrs* Ch D 1972, 48 TC 573. The matters listed below are of particular application to farming or (where relevant) market gardening.

(a)   **Averaging of profits.** See **73.74** below.

(b)   **Compensation for compulsory slaughter.** Where compensation is received for compulsory slaughter of animals to which the **HERD BASIS** (**33**) does not and could not apply, any excess of the amount received over the book value or cost of those animals may, by concession, be excluded from the year of receipt and treated, by equal instalments, as profits of the next three years. (HMRC ESC B11). (In practice, the profit on an animal born in the year of slaughter is deemed to be 25% of the compensation received.) For a worked example of this spreading relief, see HMRC Business Income Manual BIM55185.

Compensation paid under the BSE Suspects Scheme and the BSE Selective Cull (where the animal was born after 14 October 1990) is for compulsory slaughter, and for these purposes includes Selective Cull 'top-up' payments. Payments under the Calf Processing Scheme, the Over Thirty Month Scheme and the BSE Selective Cull where the animal was born before 15 October 1990 are *not* for compulsory slaughter. (Revenue Tax Bulletin February 1997 pp 396, 397).

(c)   **Drainage.** Where land is made re-available for cultivation by the restoration of drainage or by re-draining, the net expenditure incurred (after crediting any grants receivable) will be allowed as revenue expenditure in farm accounts provided it excludes (i) any substantial element of improvement (e.g. the substitution of tile drainage for mole drainage) and (ii) the capital element in cases in which the present owner is known to have acquired the land at a depressed price because of its swampy condition (HMRC SP 5/81).

(d) **Farmhouses.** The apportionment of the running costs of a farmhouse between business and private use should be based on the facts of the case for the year of account in question (Revenue Tax Bulletin February 1993 p 54).

(e) **Gangmasters.** A special unit within HMRC, the Agricultural Compliance Unit (based within Special Compliance Office in Sheffield) monitors compliance by agricultural gangmasters in relation to PAYE and National Insurance in respect of their workers and their own returns. (Revenue Press Release 2 September 1988). For whether a worker also responsible for selection of other workers acts as gangmaster, see *Andrews v King* Ch D 1991, 64 TC 332.

(f) **Grants and subsidies.** See generally **73.117** below. As regards the time at which a receipt should be brought in for tax purposes, a distinction should be drawn between grants to meet particular costs and those subsidising the sale proceeds of a specific crop. The former should reduce the costs in question (and if those costs are included in the closing stock valuation, the net cost should be used), whereas the latter should be recognised as income of the year in which the crop is sold. (Revenue Tax Bulletin February 1993 p 53). A grant subsidising trading income generally is a trading receipt of the period when the entitlement to the grant was established, provided that it can be quantified with reasonable accuracy. As regards instalments of grant, the tax treatment should follow accounting practice, which provides that information available before accounts are completed and signed should be taken into account as regards those to which entitlement arose in the period of account. (Revenue Tax Bulletin February 1994 p 108).

As regards animal grants and subsidies, these are generally recognised either at the end of the retention period or on receipt. Either of these bases will be accepted for tax purposes provided that it is consistently applied, as will any other basis which reflects generally accepted accounting practice provided that it does not conflict with tax law. A change of basis should be made only where the need for change outweighs the requirement for accounts to be prepared on a consistent basis. (Revenue Tax Bulletin December 1994 p 182).

The following relate to specific types of farm support payment.

(i) *Advances under British Sugar Industry (Assistance) Act 1931*, linked with sugar production and prices, were held to be assessable as trading receipts (*Smart v Lincolnshire Sugar Co Ltd* HL 1937, 20 TC 643).

(ii) *Arable area payments.* Payments under the 1992 scheme for land set aside may be treated as sales subsidies, and hence recognised when the crops are sold. Valuations based on 75% of market value (see (l) below) should include the same proportion of the related arable area payments. (Revenue Tax Bulletin February 1994 p 109). See (v) below for specific comment on oilseed support payments. Note that the Arable Area Payments Scheme is superseded by the Single Payment Scheme at (g) below.

    (iii)   *Dairy herd conversion scheme.* Grants for changing from dairy-ing to meat production were held to be assessable as trading receipts (*White v G & M Davis* Ch D 1979, 52 TC 597; *CIR v Biggar* CS 1982, 56 TC 254).

    (iv)   *Flood rehabilitation grants* in excess of rehabilitation costs (admitted to be capital) were held to be capital receipts (*Watson v Samson Bros* Ch D 1959, 38 TC 346).

    (v)   *Oilseed support scheme.* Payments of aid under the 1992 scheme are a subsidy towards the selling price, and as such should be recognised as income at the time of sale. If the final amount is not known when the accounts are prepared, but it is reasonably certain that a further payment will be received, the tax compu-tations should be kept open to admit the final figure. If a reasonable estimate is included in the accounts and the differ-ence when the final amount is known has only a small effect on the overall tax liability, the inspector may agree to recognise the difference in arriving at profits of the following year. (Revenue Tax Bulletin February 1993 p 53).

    (vi)   *Ploughing subsidies* were held to be assessable as trading receipts (*Higgs v Wrightson* KB 1944, 26 TC 73).

(g)   **EU Common Agricultural Policy Single Payment Scheme.** Under this Scheme, direct payments to farmers are no longer linked to production; a farmer can cease to produce agricultural products and still receive support, but must comply with certain standards covering, for example, the environment, health and animal welfare. Each single payment covers a calendar year. In June 2005, HMRC published a comprehen-sive special edition of their Tax Bulletin dedicated to the Single Payment Scheme (available at www.hmrc.gov.uk/bulletins/tb-se-june05.pdf). This explains the Scheme itself, covers income tax, corporation tax, capital gains tax, inheritance tax and value added tax issues arising from it and also includes guidance on accounting issues including the recognition of Single Payments in accounts (which in turn will deter-mine when they are taxed). The income tax treatment is that, broadly, all Single Payments are chargeable to tax, whether as trading receipts or, depending on the circumstances, as miscellaneous income. If it can be shown that expenditure has been incurred wholly and exclusively to secure a Single Payment, such expenditure would be deductible, but HMRC consider that this is rarely likely to be the case. Generally, Single Payments should not be taken into account in stock valuations.

(h)   **Milk.** *SLOM compensation.* HMRC's view is that such compensation is on revenue account, and should be recognised for income tax purposes in one sum in the accounting period in which legal entitlement to it arises and the amount can be quantified with reasonable certainty using information available at the time of preparation of the accounts. Additions for interest to the date of payment should be dealt with under the normal Schedule D, Case III (now savings income) rules. (Revenue Tax Bulletin May 1994 p 127).

Superlevy. HMRC's view is that superlevy is an allowable trading deduction, but that the purchase of additional quota to avoid superlevy does not give rise to a deduction for either the superlevy thus avoided or the sum which would have been paid to lease rather than purchase the additional quota (Revenue Tax Bulletin August 1994 p 151). A deduction for the cost of milk quota purchased to avoid superlevy was refused, on grounds of its being capital expenditure, in *Terry and Terry (t/a C & J Terry & Sons) v HMRC* (Sp C 482), [2005] SSCD 629.

Residuary Milk Marketing Board receipts. B Reserve Fund distributions and sums repaid to producers under the Rolling Fund arrangements on the flotation of Dairy Crest (in the latter case whether taken in cash or in shares) are income receipts of the trade. Any element of a B Reserve Fund payment described as interest may also be treated as a trade receipt. Post-cessation treatment (see **59.1 POST-CESSATION RECEIPTS AND EXPENDITURE**) will apply where appropriate. (Revenue Tax Bulletin August 1997 p 461).

Dairy Farmers of Britain (DFB). This organisation went into receivership on 3 June 2009. For the implications for farmers who sold produce to DFB, see HMRC Brief 05/10, 11 February 2010.

(i) **Pig industry — plant and machinery capital allowances.** Following the Government's decision to phase out agricultural buildings allowances by April 2011, HMRC have published guidance illustrating the range of assets on which the pig industry might claim plant and machinery capital allowances (HMRC Brief 03/10, February 2010).

(j) **Share farming.** HMRC consider that both parties to a share farming agreement based on the Country Landowners Association model may be considered to be carrying on a farming trade for tax purposes. In the case of the landowner, he must take an active part in the share farming venture, at least to the extent of concerning himself with details of farming policy and exercising his right to enter onto his land for some material purpose, even if only for the purposes of inspection and policy-making. (Country Landowners Association Press Release 19 December 1991).

(k) **Short rotation coppice.** The cultivation of 'short rotation coppice' (i.e. a perennial crop of tree species planted at high density, the stems of which are harvested above ground level at intervals of less than ten years) is treated for tax purposes as farming and not as forestry, so that UK land under such cultivation is farm or agricultural land and not woodlands. [*ITA 2007, s 996(4)(6); ITTOIA 2005, s 876(3)(4)(6)*]. For HMRC's view of the taxation implications of short rotation coppice, see Revenue Tax Bulletin October 1995 p 252.

(l) **Stock valuations.** See generally Business Economic Notes No 19 'Farming — stock valuations for income tax purposes' (for which see **73.17** above) and, for a commentary thereon relating particularly to changes in the basis of valuation, Revenue Tax Bulletin May 1993 p 63. See also **33 HERD BASIS** and, for trading stock generally, **73.112** below. In general, livestock is treated as trading stock unless the herd basis applies, and home-bred animals may be valued, if there is no adequate record of cost, at 75% for sheep and pigs (60% for cattle) of open market value. Deadstock may be taken at 75% of market value.

Where an animal grant or subsidy for which application has been made has not been taken into account for a particular period but has been applied for, and that application materially affects the value of the animal, the grant or subsidy should be taken into account as a supplement to the market value when deemed cost is computed. Grants or subsidies applied for but not recognised as income in the period concerned should also be taken into account in arriving at net realisable value for stock valuation purposes. (Revenue Tax Bulletin December 1994 p 182).

(m) **Subscriptions** to the **National Farmers Union** are allowable in full.

(n) **Sugar beet outgoers scheme.** Receipts and payments derived from the disposal of contract tonneage entitlement under contracts between farmers and British Sugar are to be dealt with on revenue and not capital account, i.e. as taxable receipts and allowable deductions in computing profits. Payments for entitlement which are amortised in the accounts over the period for which the entitlement may reasonably be expected to be of value to the business are similarly allowed for tax purposes. (Revenue Tax Bulletin October 2001 pp 891, 892).

(o) **Trading profits.** Proceeds from the sale of trees (mostly willows planted by the taxpayer) were held to be farming receipts (*Elmes v Trembath* KB 1934, 19 TC 72), but no part of the cost of an orchard with nearly ripe fruit purchased by a fruit grower was an allowable deduction in computing his profits, which included receipts from the sale of the fruit (*CIR v Pilcher* CA 1949, 31 TC 314). Proceeds from sales of turf were held to be trading receipts from farming (*Lowe v J W Ashmore Ltd* Ch D 1970, 46 TC 597).

(p) **Woodlands grants.** The Forestry Commission's Woodland Grant Scheme (WGS) provides grants for the establishment and maintenance of woodlands. These grants are not taxable. Where the woodland concerned is being established on agricultural land, WGS participants can also apply to join the Farm Woodland Premium Scheme (FWPS). This is administered by the Department for Environment, Food and Rural Affairs (Defra)and provides annual payments of up to £300 per hectare for up to 15 years to the farmer to compensate for lost farming income as a result of converting the land to woodland. Because the annual payments are made in lieu of farming income, they must be included in trading profits and are chargeable to income tax. It matters not that the woodlands are likely to be commercial woodlands and thus outside the charge to income tax. (Sources: Defra and HMRC Business Income Manual BIM55165). For the general tax exemption for woodlands, see **30.45 EXEMPT INCOME.**

For these and other aspects of farming taxation, see HMRC Business Income Manual BIM55000–55730, 73000–73190 and 75600–75650.

Simon's Taxes. See B1.502–B1.505, B5.1.

Farming and market gardening — averaging of profits

[73.74] Where for two consecutive tax years the profits of an individual or partnership from a trade of farming or market gardening in the UK for one year are less than 75% of the profits for the other (or the profits for one year, but not both, are nil, e.g. where a loss is incurred), a claim for relief may be made as described below.

The potential for averaging is extended to the intensive rearing of livestock or fish on a commercial basis for the production of food for human consumption.

If the profits for either year do not exceed 70% of the profits of the other (or are nil), the profits for each year are adjusted to average of both years. If either year's profits exceed 70% of the other's, but are less than 75%, the profits are adjusted by adding to the lower and subtracting from the higher the amount obtained by first multiplying the difference by three and then deducting three-quarters of the higher figure. (Thus, if the profits are £21,900 and £30,000, the adjusted profits after relief would be £23,700 and £28,200.)

'*Profits*' for this purpose are those before any deduction for losses. The adjustments made under averaging relief are effective for all income tax purposes but do not prevent a claim for loss relief. Thus, if there was a loss of £5,000 in the basis period for one year and a profit of £15,000 in that for the other, the profits chargeable for each year become £7,500 but the loss of £5,000 remains eligible for loss relief in the normal way.

A claim must be made on or before the first anniversary of 31 January following the *second* year. If an averaging claim is made for a pair of tax years, Years X and Y, a claim is also permitted for Years Y and Z, the profits for Year Y being taken as those adjusted on the first claim, and so on for subsequent years. However, no averaging claim is subsequently permissible involving any year prior to Year X. In the case of a partnership, an individual partner may make his own claim, based on his share of profits, regardless of whether or not other partners make claims. See **18.2** CLAIMS for further provisions regarding claims.

No claim is available for the tax year in which the taxpayer starts, or permanently ceases, to carry on the trade. This includes the tax years in which an individual joins and leaves a partnership.

If, after a claim, the profits of either or both years are adjusted for some other reason, the claim lapses but a new one may then be made, in respect of the adjusted profits, on or before the first anniversary of 31 January following the tax year in which the adjustment is made.

A claim or election for other relief for either of the two years affected by an averaging claim can be made, amended or revoked at any time on or before the latest possible date on which the averaging claim itself could have been made. See also **18.2** CLAIMS for the way in which claims for other relief are given effect.

[*ITTOIA 2005, ss 221–225*].

For articles on the making, calculating and implementing of averaging claims under self-assessment and on the completion of the relevant tax returns, see Revenue Tax Bulletin February 1997 pp 392–394 and August 1998 p 575.

Example

[73.75]

A, who has been farming for many years, earns the following profits as adjusted for income tax purposes.

Year ended	Tax-adjusted profit/(loss) £
30.9.03	8,500
30.9.04	12,000
30.9.05	15,000
30.9.06	10,000
30.9.07	4,000
30.9.08	(1,000)
30.9.09	(10,000)
30.9.10	1,600

Averaged profits for all years would be

		No averaging claims £	Averaging claims for all years £
2003/04	note (i)	8,500	10,000
2004/05	notes (i)(ii)	12,000	12,750
2005/06	note (ii)(iii)	15,000	12,750
2006/07	notes (iii)(iv)	10,000	7,000
2007/08	notes (iv)(v)	4,000	3,500
2008/09	notes (v)(vi)	Nil	1,750
2009/10	notes (vii)(viii)	Nil	1,750
2010/11	note (ix)	1,600	1,600
		£51,100	£51,100

Notes

(i) 2003/04   8,500
     2004/05   12,000
                    £20,500

As £8,500 exceeds $7/10$ of £12,000 but is less than $3/4$, the adjustment is computed as follows.

Difference £3,500 × 3   10,500

Deduct ³/₄ × £12,000		9,000	
Adjustment		1,500	(1,500)
Existing 2003/04		8,500	
Existing 2004/05			12,000
Revised averaged profits 2003/04 & 2004/05		£10,000	£10,500

(ii) 2004/05   10,500
      2005/06   15,000
                 £25,500   ÷ 2 = £12,750

As £10,500 does not exceed ⁷/₁₀ of £15,000, the straight average applies.

(iii) 2005/06   12,750
      2006/07   10,000
                 £22,750

As £10,000 is not less than ³/₄ of £12,750, no averaging is permitted.

(iv) 2006/07   10,000
      2007/08   4,000
                 £14,000   ÷ 2 = £7,000

As £4,000 does not exceed ⁷/₁₀ of £10,000, the straight average applies.

(v)   2007/08   7,000
      2008/09   Nil
                  £7,000   ÷ 2 = £3,500

(vi) The loss for the year to 30 September 2008 is not taken into account for averaging, but would be available to reduce the averaged profits for 2008/09 on a claim under *ITA 2007, s 64* (see **45.2 LOSSES**).

(vii) 2008/09   3,500
      2009/10   Nil
                  £3,500   ÷ 2 = £1,750

(viii) The loss for the year to 30 September 2009 is not taken into account for averaging, but would be available to set off against the balance of the averaged profits for 2008/09 and against the averaged profits for 2009/10 on a claim under *ITA 2007, s 64* (see **45.2 LOSSES**), with the balance being carried forward.

(ix) 2009/10   1,750
      2010/11   1,600
                  £3,350

As £1,600 is not less than ³/₄ of £1,750, no averaging is permitted.

See generally HMRC Business Income Manual BIM73000–73190.

Films and sound recordings

[73.76] A new film reliefs regime was introduced in *FA 2006* to replace the rules below insofar as they relate to films. The relief is available only to corporate filmmakers and applies to culturally British films as defined by a test devised by the Department for Culture, Media and Sport (for which see www.culture.gov.uk/what_we_do/Creative_industries/film/culturaltest_british film.htm). The new relief applies to films beginning principal photography on or after 1 January 2007 and to certain films started before that date but which are not completed before that date. As the new regime has no application for income tax, it is covered not here but in Tolley's Corporation Tax under Trading Expenses and Deductions.

ITTOIA 2005, s 134 and *s 135* below (and relevant definitions) do, however, continue to apply for income tax purposes in relation to sound recordings only.

The rules now largely replaced are described below insofar as they apply for income tax purposes. For detailed coverage, with examples, of how these provisions are applied in practice, see HMRC Business Income Manual BIM56000–56725

Treatment of expenditure as revenue

If there were no legislation to the contrary, expenditure on the production or acquisition of a film or sound recording would generally be capital expenditure (and may qualify for plant and machinery capital allowances under general principles — see **11 CAPITAL ALLOWANCES ON PLANT AND MACHINERY**). Instead, 'production expenditure' or 'acquisition expenditure' (see (a) and (b) below) incurred by a person carrying on a trade is treated for income tax purposes as revenue expenditure. See below, however, as regards an available election for this rule *not* to apply to expenditure on certain 'certified master versions' (see (f) below) of films. Where expenditure is treated as revenue, any receipts from the disposal of any interest or right in or over the 'original master version' and any insurance, compensation etc. derived from it are treated as revenue receipts.

The above does **not** apply to production or acquisition expenditure on a film that commenced principal photography on or after **1 January 2007**. It also does **not** apply to acquisition expenditure incurred on or after **1 October 2007** on a film that commenced principal photography before 1 January 2007. In relation to films that commenced principal photography before 1 January 2007 but were uncompleted on that date, the above does not apply to films certified as British films and intended for theatrical release and does not apply to acquisition expenditure incurred on or after **31 March 2008**. The above continues to apply to production and acquisition expenditure on sound recordings.

[*ITTOIA 2005, s 134, Sch 2 paras 31, 32; FA 2006, s 47(1), Sch 26 Pt 3(4); SI 2006 No 3265; SI 2007 No 1050, reg 7*].

Definitions

Definitions for the purposes of the provisions both above and below.

(a)   'Production expenditure' is expenditure incurred on the production of the 'original master version' of a film or sound recording. It does not include interest or incidental costs of obtaining finance (the normal rules for deducting such expenditure applying instead).

(b)   'Acquisition expenditure' is expenditure incurred on the acquisition of the 'original master version' of a film or sound recording. Again, it does not include interest or incidental costs of obtaining finance (see (a) above).

(c)   The 'original master version' means, in relation to a film, the original master negative, tape or disc or, in relation to a sound recording, the original master audio tape or disc. The expression includes any rights in the original master version of the film or sound recording that are held or acquired with it. The original master version of a film also includes the original master version of its soundtrack (if any).

(d)   A film is 'completed' when it is first in a form in which it can reasonably be regarded as ready for copies to be made and distributed for public exhibition.

(e)   'Preliminary expenditure' (see below) means, in relation to a film, non-refundable expenditure incurred with a view to deciding whether to make the film and payable before the first day of principal photography. It is generally known in the industry as development expenditure or pre-production expenditure.

(f)   'Certified master version' (see below) means, in relation to a film, an original master negative, tape or disc which is certified by the Secretary of State (in practice, the Department for Culture, Media and Sport (DCMS)) as a qualifying film, tape or disc. Certification is under *Films Act 1985, Sch 1* or *Sch 1A*, each of which applies certain criteria as to the British, EU or Commonwealth nature of the film; for more details, see the DCMS website at www.culture.gov.uk/what_we_do/Creative_i ndustries/film/british_film_certificates.htm.

Each part of a series of films is treated as a separate film unless the DCMS give a direction to the contrary.

[*ITTOIA 2005, ss 130–132, Sch 2 para 31; FA 2006, Sch 26 Pt 3(4); SI 2007 No 1050, reg 12*].

Allocation of expenditure to periods of account

In a trade consisting of or including the exploitation of the original master versions (see (c) above) of films and sound recordings, production or acquisition expenditure (see (a) and (b) above) otherwise deductible is allocated to periods of account on a just and reasonable basis. In so allocating expenditure to any period of account, regard must be had to the expenditure unallocated at the beginning of the period, the expenditure incurred in the period, the proportion which the estimated value of the original master version realised in the period (whether by way of income or otherwise) bears to the sum of the value so realised and the estimated remaining value at the end of the period, and the need to bring the whole expenditure into account over the time during which the value of the original master version is expected to be realised (known as the 'income matching' method of allocation). The amount thus allocated to the period can then be increased up to an amount equal to the value of the original master version realised in the period (whether by way of income or otherwise) (known as the 'cost recovery' method). Before 2005/06, such further amount could only be allocated if a claim is made for that purpose within twelve months after 31 January following the tax year in which the period of account ends.

These provisions do not apply if the original master version in question constitutes trading stock under *ITTOIA 2005, s 174* (see **73.113** below).

Expenditure cannot be allocated to a period of account under the above rules if it is allocated to any period under any other of these film and sound recording provisions. If any expenditure in respect of an original master version is allocated to a period of account under those other provisions, no other production or acquisition expenditure in respect of that original master version can be allocated to that period under the above rules.

See below as regards an available election for these rules *not* to apply to expenditure on certain certified films.

These rules do **not** apply to production or acquisition expenditure on a film that commenced principal photography on or after **1 January 2007**. They also do **not** apply to acquisition expenditure incurred on or after **1 October 2007** on a film that commenced principal photography before 1 January 2007. In relation to films that commenced principal photography before 1 January 2007 but were uncompleted on that date, the above rules do not apply to films certified as British films and intended for theatrical release and do not apply to acquisition expenditure incurred on or after **31 March 2008**. The above rules continue to apply to production and acquisition expenditure on sound recordings.

[*ITTOIA 2005, s 135, Sch 2 para 32; FA 2006, s 47(1), Sch 26 Pt 3(4); SI 2006 No 3265; SI 2007 No 1050, Reg 7*].

If, exceptionally, no accounts are drawn up, any reference above and in the special rules below to a period of account is to be taken as a reference to the basis period for the tax year. [*ITTOIA 2005, s 133*].

Certified films

Each of the special rules below applies where:

- the trade consists of or includes the exploitation of films;
- the films do not constitute trading stock under *ITTOIA 2005, s 174* (see **73.113** below);
- the expenditure in question is of a revenue nature (whether or not by virtue of *ITTOIA 2005, s 134* above);
- the original master version (see (c) above) of the film in question is a '*certified master version*' (see (f) above);
- the theatrical release condition below is met; and

- no election has been made as below to disapply these rules in relation to the expenditure.

[*ITTOIA 2005, s 136; FA 2006, Sch 26 Pt 3(4)*].

For an appeal relying inter alia on the first two of these conditions, see *HMRC v Micro Fusion 2004-I LLP* CA, [2010] STC 1541.

Theatrical release condition

Unless an application for certification (as below) was received before 17 April 2002, the special rules below are restricted, for films completed after 16 April 2002, or completed before 1 January 2002 but not certified before 17 April 2002, to films genuinely intended for theatrical release, i.e. for exhibition to the paying public at the commercial cinema. The relevant intention for this purpose is the intention, at the time the film is completed (see (d) above), of the person then entitled to determine how the film is to be exploited. A film is not regarded as genuinely intended for theatrical release unless it is intended that a significant proportion of the film's earnings should be obtained by such exhibition.

[*ITTOIA 2005, s 144, Sch 2 para 35; FA 2006, Sch 26 Pt 3(4)*].

Preliminary expenditure

A deduction is allowed for any preliminary expenditure (see (e) above) allocated to a period of account and not otherwise disallowable. Up to 100% of the preliminary expenditure may be allocated to a period of account, except that the aggregate amount allocated to periods of account cannot exceed 20% of budgeted total expenditure on the film, calculated as at the first day of principal photography. It must be reasonably likely that if the film had been completed, where this is not actually the case, the original master version of it would have been a certified master version.

Expenditure cannot be allocated to a period of account under the above rules if it is allocated to any period under any other of these film and sound recording provisions. If any preliminary expenditure in connection with the film is allocated to a period of account under the general allocation rules above, no other preliminary expenditure in connection with the film can be allocated to that period under the above rules.

These rules do **not** apply to expenditure incurred after **19 July 2006**. [*ITTOIA 2005, s 137, Sch 2 para 33; FA 2006, s 47(2), Sch 26 Pt 3(4)*].

Production or acquisition expenditure

As an alternative to the general allocation rules above, up to **one-third** of the total deductible production or acquisition expenditure (see (a) and (b) above) in respect of a certified master version of a film can be allocated to any period of account (no earlier than that in which the film is completed — see (d) above). Before making the one-third calculation, the expenditure must be reduced by any preliminary expenditure already allocated as above and any expenditure allocated under the accelerated deductions below for limited budget films. For a period of account of less than 12 months, the one-third fraction is reduced proportionately. The expenditure allocated to any period cannot exceed the total production or acquisition expenditure not already allocated to that period or any other period. If any production or acquisition expenditure in respect of the original master version is allocated to a period of account under the general allocation rules above, no other production or acquisition expenditure in respect of the original master version can be allocated to that period under the above rules.

The following changes were made by *Finance Act 2005*.

(i)   For expenditure incurred on or after 2 December 2004 (excluding any 'pre-announcement expenditure' — see (ii) below), other than in relation to a film in production on that date, these allocation rules apply only if, in relation to production expenditure, the original master version (see (c) above) was owned by the person carrying on the trade at the time the film was completed (see (d) above) or, in relation to acquisition expenditure, the original master version (see (c) above) has not previously been acquired by the person carrying on the trade.

(ii)   Also with effect from 2 December 2004 and in relation to both production and acquisition expenditure (but not in relation to a film in production on that date), these allocation rules apply only if there has not been a previous deduction in relation to the film, taking into account deductions made to other persons and deductions made under the rules for limited-budget films below as well as those made under the instant rules. The intention is that relief should be given only once on any film, either for production or acquisition expenditure, but not both, and that the relief is given for the deduction first made. In the case of simultaneous deductions, HMRC are given power to decide which one is to be treated as made first. But double deductions are not prevented if both deductions relate *entirely* to 'pre-announcement expenditure'. *'Pre-announcement expenditure'* is expenditure incurred before 2 December 2004. However, expenditure incurred on or after that date in pursuance of an unconditional obligation is treated as if incurred before that date and is thus included in pre-announcement expenditure; the question of whether an obligation was unconditional is decided on the facts immediately before 2 December 2004, and certain possible conditions are disregarded for this purpose (see *FA 2005, Sch 3 para 32(2)*).

(iii)   For films *in production* on 2 December 2004, there are transitional rules to prevent a deduction for acquisition expenditure if the acquisition is not the first acquisition of the original master version of the film by the acquirer or if there has been a previous deduction for another acquisition of the film.

(iv)   In relation to expenditure on films whose first day of principal photography is on or after 2 December 2004 (but not where any of the expenditure being allocated is 'pre-announcement expenditure' — see (ii) above), these allocation rules cannot be used if the film is within the rules for limited-budget films below.

(v)   In relation to expenditure on films whose first day of principal photography is on or after 2 December 2004 (but not 'pre-announcement expenditure' — see (ii) above), any expenditure which remains unpaid when the film is completed (see (d) above), and which is not at that time the subject of an unconditional obligation to pay within four months after completion, is excluded from production expenditure for the purposes of these allocation rules. (A similar prohibition already applied for limited-budget films under the rules below). The rules as to *when* expenditure is incurred for these purposes follow those for capital allowances (see **10.2**(iv) CAPITAL ALLOWANCES).

(vi)   In relation to expenditure on films whose first day of principal photography is on or after 2 December 2004 (but not where any of the expenditure being allocated is 'pre-announcement expenditure' — see (ii) above), the total amount of acquisition expenditure to be allocated under these rules is restricted to the 'total production expenditure in respect of the original master version'. (A similar prohibition already applied for limited-budget films under the rules below.) Where the acquisition expenditure includes pre-announcement expenditure in excess of the total production expenditure, the restriction is to the total pre-announcement expenditure instead of the total production expenditure. Subject to the exclusion in (v) above, *'total production expenditure in respect of the original master version'* includes all the production expenditure (see (a) above) in respect of the original master version (see (c) above), whenever incurred and whether or not incurred by the trader in question.

These rules do **not** apply to production or acquisition expenditure on a film that commenced principal photography on or after **1 January 2007**. They also do **not** apply to acquisition expenditure incurred on or after **1 October 2007** on a film that commenced principal photography before 1 January 2007. In relation to films that commenced principal photography before 1 January 2007 but were uncompleted on that date, these rules do not apply to films certified as British films and intended for theatrical release and do not apply to acquisition expenditure incurred on or after **31 March 2008**.

[*ITTOIA 2005, ss 138, 138A, 140A, 141, 142, Sch 2 para 34; FA 2006, s 47(3), Sch 26 Pt 3(4); SI 2006 No 3265; SI 2007 No 1050, Reg 7*].

Accelerated deductions for limited-budget certified films

These are available for expenditure incurred on a film completed before 1 January 2007 with a 'total production expenditure in respect of the original master version' of **£15 million** or less. The rules as to *when* expenditure is incurred for these purposes follow those for capital allowances (see **10.2**(iv) CAPITAL ALLOWANCES).

'*Total production expenditure in respect of the original master version*' includes all the production expenditure (see (a) above) in respect of the original master version (see (c) above), whenever incurred and whether or not incurred by the trader in question. But any expenditure which remains unpaid when the film is completed (see (d) above), and which is not at that time the subject of an unconditional obligation to pay within four months after completion, is ignored. Where any of the expenditure relates to transactions between CONNECTED PERSONS (**21**), the equivalent arm's length amount is substituted if greater; for films whose first day of principal photography is on or after 2 December 2004, this rule has effect only for the purpose of applying the £15 million rule and for no other purpose.

Where these conditions are satisfied, up to **100%** of the total deductible production expenditure or acquisition expenditure (see (b) above) in respect of a certified master version of a film can be allocated to any period of account (no earlier than that in which the film is completed — see (d) above). In the case of production expenditure, any unpaid expenditure falling to be ignored as above cannot be so allocated.

In the case of acquisition expenditure, the total amount that can be allocated under these provisions is restricted to the total production expenditure in respect of the original master version. Where the first day of principal photography was on or after 2 December 2004, any of the expenditure being allocated is 'pre-announcement expenditure' (see (ii) above) and the total production expenditure would have been greater if it were not for the disapplication for these purposes of the connected persons rule above, the restriction is to the lower of the pre-announcement expenditure and what would otherwise have been the total production expenditure.

If any production or acquisition expenditure in respect of the original master version is allocated to a period of account under the general allocation rules above, no other production or acquisition expenditure in respect of the original master version can be allocated to that period under the above rules.

Similar changes are made by *Finance Act 2005* as are outlined at (i) and (ii) above.

These rules do **not** apply to production or acquisition expenditure on a film that commenced principal photography on or after **1 January 2007**. They also do **not** apply to acquisition expenditure incurred on or after **1 October 2007** on a film that commenced principal photography before 1 January 2007. As stated above, they do not apply in any case in relation to any film completed (see (d) above) on or after **1 January 2007**. In relation to films that commenced principal photography before 1 January 2007 but were uncompleted on that date, these rules do not apply to films certified as British films and intended for theatrical release and do not apply to acquisition expenditure incurred on or after **31 March 2008**.

[*ITTOIA 2005, ss 139–142, Sch 2 paras 36–38; FA 2006, s 47(3), Sch 26 Pt 3(4); SI 2006 No 3265; SI 2007 No 1050, Reg 7*].

Election to disapply the above rules in the case of certified films

A person carrying on a trade consisting of, or including, the exploitation of original master versions of films could elect for the above provisions of *ITTOIA 2005, ss 134–142 not* to apply in relation to expenditure incurred on the production or acquisition of an original master version (see (c) above) of a film, where:

- the original master version is a certified master version (see (f) above);
- its value is expected to be realisable over a period of not less than two years; and

- the theatrical release condition, described above under Certified films, is met.

The election, which is irrevocable, must relate to the whole of the expenditure incurred, or to be incurred, on the production or acquisition of the original master version in question. It must be made no later than the first anniversary of 31 January following the tax year in which ends the period of account in which the original master version is completed. For this purpose, the master version of a film is completed when the film is first in a form in which it can reasonably be regarded as ready for copies to be made and distributed for public exhibition or, in relation to acquisition expenditure, at the time of acquisition if later. The principal effect of the election is to treat production or acquisition expenditure as capital expenditure, except to the extent (if any) that it would qualify as revenue expenditure under general principles. No election is available in relation to expenditure on the production or acquisition of the original master version of a film if any of that expenditure has been allocated under *ITTOIA 2005, ss 137–142* above or equivalent earlier legislation (i.e. under the special rules for certified films).

[*ITTOIA 2005, s 143; FA 2006, s 47(3), Sch 26 Pt 3(4)*].

Anti-avoidance

For deferred income agreements, see **73.77** below. For claw-back in certain circumstances of reliefs for trading losses derived from the above film reliefs, see **45.16 LOSSES**. For restrictions on relief for partnership losses derived from expenditure, *other* than under the special rules for certified films, in a trade involving the exploitation of films, see **52.17 PARTNERSHIPS**. For restriction of relief for interest on a loan used to buy into a film partnership in certain circumstances, see **43.10 INTEREST PAYABLE**. For modification of the long funding leasing rules where the subject of the lease is a film, see **73.95** below.

Leasing

See **73.79** below as regards restrictions on relief under the above provisions where finance leasing arrangements are involved.

Simon's Taxes. See B5.501–B5.507.

Film reliefs — deferred income agreements

[73.77] The following provisions are designed to counter tax avoidance by persons who have benefited from film tax reliefs as in **73.76** above and defer income from the film for more than 15 years; they have effect where any deferred income agreements are entered into on or after 2 December 2004. There are two sets of provisions, depending on whether the deferred income agreement was already in existence when the relief was given or was entered into after that time.

For these purposes, a person is not to be regarded as entering into an agreement on or after 2 December 2004 if he did so in pursuance of an obligation of his which immediately before that date was an unconditional obligation; and an obligation is not to be regarded as conditional if it depended on a condition the fulfilment of which was outside that person's control.

The first set of provisions applies where:

- a deduction is made by a person (P) under any of *ITTOIA 2005, ss 138–140* in **73.76** above (production and acquisition expenditure on certified films, whether or not limited-budget films) for expenditure relating to a film; and
- there are in existence at that time one or more 'deferred income agreements' in respect of the film, being agreements to which P is or has been a party and which he entered into on or after 2 December 2004.

An amount of excess relief, computed as below, is brought into account as a receipt in computing P's trading profits for the period of account for which the deduction was made. If, however, immediately after the end of the '15-year period', P is still carrying on the trade, he is treated as incurring at that time production or acquisition expenditure of an amount equal to the excess relief, but this notional expenditure can be allocated to periods of account only under the normal allocation rules of *ITTOIA 2005, s 135* above and not under the special rules for certified films. The excess relief for these purposes is:

$$D \times \left(1 - \frac{T1}{T2}\right)$$

Where

D = the deduction made;

$T1$ = the number of days in the '15-year period'; and

$T2$ = the number of days from the 'operative date' to the 'final deferral date' inclusive.

The '*15-year period*' is the 15 years beginning with the 'operative date'. The '*operative date*' is the date of acquisition where the expenditure deducted is acquisition expenditure; in any other case, it is the date the film is completed (see **73.76**(d) above). The '*final deferral date*' is the 'last date of deferral' in relation to the deferred income agreement or, where there is more than one such agreement, the latest of those dates. The '*last date of deferral*' is the last date on which an amount of guaranteed income will or may arise under the 'deferred income agreement. A '*deferred income agreement*' is an agreement which:

- (whether or not it supplements or varies another agreement) guarantees an amount of income arising from exploitation of the film and has the effect that the 'last date of deferral' (as above) falls after the end of the 15-year period referred to above; or
- supplements or varies an earlier agreement which guarantees an amount of income arising from exploitation of the film and has the effect that the 'last date of deferral' (as above) falls after the end of the 15-year period and after the last date of deferral (if any) in relation to the earlier agreement.

The fact that any earlier agreement may have existed before 2 December 2004 does not prevent the deferred income agreement in question from falling within these provisions if it is entered into on or after that date, and 'agreement' includes a series of agreements. An agreement guarantees income for these purposes if it sets out to achieve the receipt of at least that amount.

The second set of provisions is similar, but applies where the deduction had already been made before the deferred income agreement is entered into. This time, the excess relief is brought into account as a receipt in computing P's trading profits for the period of account in which he enters into the agreement and is reduced by any amounts already recovered under these provisions, including any amounts recovered by virtue of P's entering into any previous deferred income agreements in respect of the film concerned after the deduction or claim was made.

[*ITTOIA 2005, ss 142A–142E*].

For a successful attempt by HMRC to apply this legislation in a particular case, see *HMRC v Micro Fusion 2004-1 LLP* CA, [2010] STC 1541.

Finance leasing

[73.78] The rules on leasing of *plant or machinery* were reformed by *FA 2006, s 81, Sch 8* with effect from, broadly, 1 April 2006 (see **11.43–11.49** CAPITAL ALLOWANCES ON PLANT AND MACHINERY for the detailed commencement and transitional provisions). For 'long funding leases' (within **11.45**(1)), the current regime grants entitlement to capital allowances to the lessee rather than to the lessor as previously. See also **73.94** below. It follows that the Statement of Practice described below can have no application to a long funding lease of plant or machinery. The *ITA 2007, Pt 11A* anti-avoidance provisions at **73.79, 73.80** below are specifically disapplied in relation to such leases.

Statement of Practice

HMRC's practice described below applies to rentals payable by a lessee under a finance lease, i.e. a lease which transfers substantially all the risks and rewards of ownership of an asset to the lessee while maintaining the lessor's legal ownership of the asset. The treatment of such rentals depends upon whether or not SSAP 21 has been applied. This practice has no implications for the tax treatment of rentals receivable by the lessor, nor for the availability of capital allowances to the lessor. (HMRC SP 3/91 and Revenue Press Release 11 April 1991).

Finance lease rentals are revenue payments for the use of the asset, and, both under normal accounting principles and for tax purposes, should be allocated to the periods of account for which the asset is leased in accordance with the accruals concept. Where there is an option for the lessee to continue to lease the asset after expiry of the primary period under the lease, regard should be had, in allocating rentals to periods of account, to the economic life of the asset and its likely period of use by the lessee, as well as to the primary period.

Under SSAP 21, the lessee is required to treat a finance lease as the acquisition of an asset subject to a loan, to be depreciated over its useful life, with rentals apportioned between a finance charge and a capital repayment element. This treatment does not, however, affect the tax treatment, which remains as described above.

Where SSAP 21 has not been applied, the lessee's accounting treatment of rental payments is normally accepted for tax purposes, provided that it is consistent with the principles described above. If not, computational adjustments are made to secure the proper spreading of the rental payments.

Where SSAP 21 has been applied, the finance charge element of the rental payments for a period of account is normally accepted as a revenue deduction for that period. In determining the appropriate proportion of the capital repayment element to be deducted for tax purposes, a properly computed commercial depreciation charge to profit and loss account will normally be accepted. Where, however, the depreciation charge is not so computed, the appropriate proportion for tax purposes will be determined in accordance with the principles described above.

For comment on the principles set out in SP 3/91, and on their application to particular arrangements, see Revenue Tax Bulletin February 1995 pp 189–193. This considers in particular: sums paid before the asset comes into use; depreciation of leased assets (and the interaction with SSAP 21); long-life assets; termination adjustments; fixtures leases; and the interaction of SP 3/91 with statutory restrictions on relief for rental payments.

See generally HMRC Business Income Manual BIM61000–61075 (leasing: general), BIM61100–61195 (finance leasing) and HMRC Business Leasing Manual BLM00001 *et seq.* (introduction to leasing).

General

See **11.23, 10A.62, 10A.64** CAPITAL ALLOWANCES ON PLANT AND MACHINERY for other finance lease capital allowance restrictions. It was held in *Caledonian Paper plc v CIR* (Sp C 159), [1998] SSCD 129 that annual or semi-annual payments of commitment fees, guarantee fees and agency fees relating to guarantees required in relation to finance leasing arrangements were deductible in computing profits, but that a one-off management fee was not.

Finance leases — return in capital form

[73.79] FA 1997, Sch 12 Pt I applied from 26 November 1996 in relation to asset leasing arrangements which fall to be treated under generally accepted accounting practice (GAAP) (see **73.18** above) as finance leases or loans, and whose effect is that some or all of the investment return is or may be in the form of a sum that is not rent and would not, apart from these provisions, be wholly taxed as lease rental. Those provisions are now in *ITA 2007, Pt 11A Ch 2 (ss 614B–614BY)* and are referred to below as the Chapter 2 provisions. The principal purposes of the Chapter 2 provisions are to charge any person entitled to the lessor's interest to income tax by reference to the income return for accounting purposes (taking into account the substance of the matter as a whole, e.g. as regards connected persons or groups of companies); and to recover reliefs for capital and other expenditure as appropriate by reference to sums received which fall within the provisions.

The Chapter 2 provisions apply where an asset lease (as widely defined) is or has at any time been granted in the case of which the conditions at (a)–(e) below are or have been met at some time (the *relevant time*) in a period of account of the current lessor. Where the conditions have been met at a relevant time, they are treated as continuing to be met unless and until the asset ceases to be leased under the lease or the lessor's interest is assigned to a person not connected with any of the following: (i) the assignor, (ii) any other person who was the lessor at some time before the assignment, and (iii) any person who at some time after the assignment becomes the lessor under arrangements made by a person who was the lessor (or was connected with the lessor) at some time before the assignment. A lease to which the Chapter 2 provisions cease to apply can come within those provisions again if the conditions for their application are again met.

For the purposes of these provisions generally, and those at **73.80** below, **20 CONNECTED PERSONS** applies initially to determine if persons are connected. But persons who are thus connected at any time in the 'relevant period' are then treated as being connected throughout that period. The *relevant period* runs from the earliest time at which any of the leasing arrangements were made to the time when the current lessor finally ceases to have an interest in the asset or any arrangements relating to it.

The Chapter 2 provisions do *not* apply if (or to the extent that), as regards the current lessor, the lease falls to be regarded as a long funding lease (within **11.45 CAPITAL ALLOWANCES ON PLANT AND MACHINERY**) of plant or machinery.

The conditions referred to above are as follows.

(a)   At the 'relevant time' (see above), and in accordance with GAAP, the leasing arrangements fall to be treated as a finance lease or loan, and either:

    (i)   the lessor (or a connected person) is the finance lessor in relation to the finance lease or loan; or

    (ii)   the lessor is a member of a group of companies for the purposes of whose consolidated accounts the finance lease or loan is treated as subsisting.

(b)   under the leasing arrangements, there is or may be payable to the lessor (or to a connected person), a sum (a *major lump sum*) that is not rent but falls to be treated, in accordance with GAAP, partly as a repayment of some or all of the investment in respect of the finance lease or loan and partly as a return on that investment.

(c)   Not all of the part of the major lump sum which is treated as a return on the investment (as in (b) above) would, apart from these provisions, be brought into account for income tax purposes, as 'normal rent' (see below) from the lease for periods of account of the lessor, in tax years ending with the 'relevant tax year'. The *relevant tax year* is the tax year (or latest tax year) consisting of or including all or part of the period of account in which the major lump sum is or may be payable under the arrangements.

(d)   The period of account of the lessor in which the relevant time falls (or an earlier period during which he was the lessor) is one for which the 'accountancy rental earnings' in respect of the lease exceed the normal rent. The normal rent is determined by treating rent as accruing and falling due evenly over the period to which it relates (unless a payment falls due more than twelve months after any of the rent to which it relates is so treated as accruing).

(e)   At the relevant time, either:

(i)   arrangements exist under which the lessee (or a person connected with the lessee) may directly or indirectly acquire the leased asset (or an asset representing it — see *ITA 2007, s 614DD*) from the lessor (or a person connected with the lessor), and in connection with that acquisition the lessor (or connected person) may directly or indirectly receive a 'qualifying lump sum' from the lessee (or connected person); or

(ii)   in the absence of such arrangements, it is in any event more likely that the acquisition and receipt described in (i) above will take place than that, before any such acquisition, the leased asset (or the asset representing it) will have been acquired in an open market sale by a person who is neither the lessor nor the lessee nor a person connected with either of them.

In (i) above, a '*qualifying lump sum*' is a sum which is not rent but at least part of which would be treated under GAAP as a return on investment in respect of a finance lease or loan.

For the purposes of the Chapter 2 provisions (and also the provisions at **73.80** below):

*   a '*normal rent*' for a period of account of a lessor is the amount which (apart from these provisions) the lessor would bring in for income tax purposes in the period as rent arising from the lease;
*   '*rental earnings*' for any period is the amount that falls for accounting purposes to be treated, in accordance with GAAP, as the gross return for that period on investment in respect of a finance lease or loan in respect of the leasing arrangements; and
*   the '*accountancy rental earnings*' in respect of a lease for a period of account of the lessor is the greatest of the following amounts of rental earnings for that period in respect of the lease:

(i)   the rental earnings of the lessor;

(ii)   the rental earnings of any person connected with the lessor;

(iii)   the rental earnings for the purposes of consolidated group accounts of a group of which the lessor is a member.

Where (ii) or (iii) applies and the lessor's period of account does not coincide with that of the connected person or the consolidated group accounts, amounts in the periods of account of the latter are apportioned as necessary by reference to the number of days in the common periods.

Current lessor to be taxed by reference to accountancy rental earnings. If for any period of account of the current lessor (L):

- the Chapter 2 provisions apply to the lease, and
- the accountancy rental earnings exceed the normal rent,

L is treated for income tax purposes as if in that period of account L had been entitled to, and there had arisen to L, rent from the lease of an amount equal to those accountancy rental earnings (instead of the normal rent). That rent is deemed to have accrued at an even rate throughout the period of account (or so much of the it as corresponds to the period for which the asset is leased).

Reduction of taxable rent by cumulative rental excesses

If a period of account of the current lessor is one in which the normal rent in respect of the lease exceeds the accountancy rental earnings, and there is a 'cumulative accountancy rental excess', the rent otherwise taxable for the period (the '*taxable rent*') is reduced by setting that excess against it. It cannot be reduced to less than the accountancy rental earnings.

There is an '*accountancy rental excess*' for a period if the period is one in which the current lessor is taxed by reference to accountancy rental earnings as above; it is the excess of the accountancy rental earnings over the normal rent. If, however, the taxable rent for that period is reduced by a 'cumulative normal rental excess' (see below), the accountancy rental excess for the period is limited to the excess (if any) of the accountancy rental earnings, reduced by the same amount as the taxable rent, over the normal rent. A '*cumulative accountancy rental excess*' is so much of the aggregate of accountancy rental excesses of previous periods of account as has not already been used, whether under these rules, the bad debt rules below or the rules below on disposals.

If a period of account of the current lessor is one in which the current lessor is taxed by reference to accountancy rental earnings, and there is a 'cumulative normal rental excess', the taxable rent is reduced by setting that excess against it. It cannot be reduced to less than the normal rent.

The '*normal rental excess*' for a period of account is the excess (if any) of normal rent over accountancy rental earnings. If, however, the taxable rent for that period is reduced by a cumulative accountancy rental excess (as above), the normal rental excess for the period is limited to the excess (if any) of the normal rent, reduced by the same amount as the taxable rent, over accountancy rental earnings. A '*cumulative normal rental excess*' is so much of the aggregate of normal rental excesses of previous periods of account as has not already been used, whether under these rules or the bad debt rules below.

Bad debts

Where accountancy rental earnings for a period of account are substituted for normal rent for income tax purposes (as above), and a 'bad debt deduction' in excess of the accountancy rental earnings falls to be made for the period, any cumulative accountancy rental excess for the period is reduced (but not below nil) by that excess. If the accountancy rental earnings do not exceed the normal rent, any bad debt deduction acts to reduce the amount of the normal rent against which a cumulative accountancy rental excess may be set, and the cumulative accountancy rental excess is reduced (but not below nil) by any excess of the bad debt deduction over the normal rent. There is provision for such reductions in the cumulative accountancy rental excess to be reversed in the event of subsequent bad debt recoveries or reinstatements. A '*bad debt deduction*', in relation to a period of account of the lessor, means the total of any sums falling within *ITTOIA 2005, s 35* (see **73.40** above), in respect of rents from the lease of the asset, which are deductible as expenses for that period.

There are similar provisions relating to the effect of bad debt deductions on cumulative normal rental excesses.

Effect of disposals

If the current lessor (or a connected person) disposes of its interest under the lease or the leased asset or an asset representing the leased asset (see *ITA 2007, s 614DD*), the Chapter 2 provisions have effect as if immediately before the disposal (or simultaneous such disposals) a period of account of the current lessor ended and another began.

In determining the amount of any chargeable gain on the disposal, the disposal consideration is reduced by setting against it any cumulative accountancy rental excess (as above) for the period of account in which the disposal occurs. *TCGA 1992, s 37* does not exclude any money or money's worth from the disposal consideration so far as it is represented by any cumulative accountancy rental excess set off under this rule (whether on the current disposal or previously). On a part disposal, the cumulative accountancy rental excess is apportioned in the same manner as the associated acquisition costs. Where there are simultaneous disposals, the cumulative accountancy rental excess is apportioned between them on a just and reasonable basis.

On an assignment of the current lessor's interest under the lease treated under *TCGA 1992* as a no gain/no loss disposal (see *TCGA 1992, s 288(3A)*), a period of account of the assignor is treated as ending, and a period of account of the assignee as beginning, with the assignment. Any unused cumulative accountancy rental excess or cumulative normal rental excess at the time of the assignment is transferred to the assignee.

Capital allowances etc.

Where an occasion occurs on which a major lump sum (as in (b) above) falls to be paid, there are provisions (see *ITA 2007, ss 614BR–614BW*) for the withdrawal of earlier reliefs for expenditure incurred by the current lessor in respect of the leased asset. This applies to capital allowances and to reliefs for capital expenditure under **73.43** above (cemeteries and crematoria) and **73.127** below (waste disposal). Deductions allowed under any of *ITTOIA 2005, ss 135, 138, 138A, 139, 140* (films and sound recordings — see **73.76** above) are similarly withdrawn. The earlier reliefs are withdrawn either by the bringing in of a disposal value or by the imposition of a balancing charge or, in the case of expenditure allowed in respect of cemeteries etc., waste disposal or films etc., by the bringing in of a countervailing receipt. These provisions apply equally to capital allowances for contributors to capital expenditure under *CAA 2001, ss 537–542*.

Pre-existing schemes for which (a)–(e) above are first met after 26 November 1996

Where a lease of an asset forms part of a 'pre-existing scheme' (as below) for which conditions (a)–(e) above are first met after 26 November 1996, the Chapter 2 provisions apply as if a period of account of the current lessor ended and another began both immediately before and immediately after those conditions came to be met, i.e. as if there was a brief separate period of account during which they came to be met. Any cumulative accountancy rental excess which would have arisen for that period, had the conditions been met in relation to the lease at all times on or after 26 November 1996, is treated as so arising, and the current lessor is treated as if, at the end of the immediately preceding period, there had accrued an additional amount of rent equal to that excess. (That rent is, however, left out of account in determining normal rent for comparison with accountancy rental earnings, as above.) Similarly a cumulative normal rental excess which would have arisen on those assumptions is treated as having arisen in the period in which the conditions came to be met.

A lease of an asset forms part of a *'pre-existing scheme'* if a contract in writing for the lease was made before 26 November 1996 and either:

(i)   no terms of the contract remained to be agreed on or after that date, and any conditions were met before that date; or

(ii)   the requirements in (i) were met before the end of the period ending with the later of 31 January 1997 and the expiry of six months after the making of the contract, or within such further time as HMRC may have allowed in any particular case, and in its final form the contract does not differ materially from how it stood when originally made.

Post-25 November 1996 schemes to which Chapter 3 provisions applied first

If the Chapter 2 provisions come to apply to a lease to which the Chapter 3 provisions at **73.80** below applied immediately beforehand, the cumulative accountancy rental excess and the cumulative normal rental excess are determined as if the Chapter 2 provisions had applied throughout the period for which the Chapter 3 conditions in fact applied.

[*ITA 2007, ss 614A, 614AA–614AC, 614B–614BY, 614D–614DG; TCGA 1992, s 37A; FA 1997 Sch 12 paras 1–7, 9–14, 20–30; FA 2006, Sch 9 para 7(1)(2)(4); CTA 2009, Sch 1 para 448; TIOPA 2010, Sch 3 paras 2, 3, 5, 7; SI 2008 No 954, Art 22*].

For HMRC's views on various points of interpretation regarding the Chapter 2 provisions, see HMRC Business Leasing Manual BLM70005 *et seq.*

Simon's Taxes. See **B3.340E, B5.416.**

Finance leases not within the above provisions

[73.80] *ITA 2007, Pt 11A Ch 3 (ss 614C–614CD)* (the Chapter 3 provisions) apply to arrangements, not within the Chapter 2 provisions at **73.79** above, which involve the lease of an asset and would fall to be treated under generally accepted accounting practice (GAAP) as finance leases or loans. The Chapter 3 provisions were previously in *FA 1997, Sch 12 Pt II* and applied from 26 November 1996. The main purpose of the Chapter 3 provisions is to charge any person entitled to the lessor's interest to income tax on amounts falling to be treated under GAAP as the income return on investment in respect of the finance lease or loan (taking into account the substance of the matter as a whole, e.g. as regards connected persons or groups of companies). The Chapter 3 provisions accordingly apply where:

• a lease of an asset is granted on or after 26 November 1996;
• the lease forms part of a post-25 November 1996 scheme (i.e. a scheme that is not a pre-existing scheme as defined in **73.79** above);
• condition (a) at **73.79** above (or its corporation tax equivalent) is met at some time on or after 26 November 1996 in a period of account of the current lessor; and
• the Chapter 2 provisions described at **73.79** above do not apply because not all of conditions (b)–(e) at **73.79** above (or their corporation tax equivalents) have been met at that time.

Where condition (a) at **73.79** above was met at some time on or after 26 November 1996, it is treated as continuing to be met until either the asset ceases to be leased under the lease or the lessor's interest is assigned to a person not connected with any of the following: (i) the assignor, (ii) any other person who was the lessor at some time before the assignment, and (iii) any person who at some time after the assignment becomes the lessor under arrangements made by a person who was the lessor (or was connected with the lessor) at some time before the assignment. A lease to which the Chapter 3 provisions cease to apply can come within those provisions again if the conditions for their application are again met.

If for any period of account of the current lessor (L):

• the Chapter 3 provisions apply to the lease, and
• the 'accountancy rental earnings' (**73.79** above) exceed the 'normal rent' (**73.79** above),

L is treated for income tax purposes as if in that period of account L had been entitled to, and there had arisen to L, rent from the lease of an amount equal to those accountancy rental earnings (instead of the normal rent). That rent is deemed to have accrued at an even rate throughout the period of account (or so much of the it as corresponds to the period for which the asset is leased).

The provisions at **73.79** above relating to reduction of taxable rent by cumulative rental excesses, bad debt relief and the effect of disposals apply equally for the purposes of the Chapter 3 provisions.

The Chapter 3 provisions do *not* apply if (or to the extent that), as regards the current lessor, the lease falls to be regarded as a long funding lease (within **11.45 CAPITAL ALLOWANCES ON PLANT AND MACHINERY**) of plant or machinery.

[ITA 2007, ss 614C–614CD, 614D–614DG; FA 1997, Sch 12 paras 15–17, 20–30; FA 2006, Sch 9 para 7(1)(3)(4); TIOPA 2010, Sch 3 paras 4, 5].

For HMRC's views on various points of interpretation regarding the Chapter 3 provisions, see HMRC Business Leasing Manual BLM74600 *et seq*.

Simon's Taxes. See B3.340E, B5.416.

Foreign exchange gains and losses

[73.81] In general, for income tax purposes, foreign exchange differences are taken into account in computing trading profits if they relate to the circulating capital of the business but not otherwise. In *Overseas Containers (Finance) Ltd v Stoker* CA 1989, 61 TC 473, exchange losses arising on loans transferred to a finance subsidiary set up to convert the losses to trading account were held not to arise from trading transactions.

In *Davies v The Shell Co of China Ltd* CA 1951, 32 TC 133, a petrol marketing company operating in China required agents to deposit Chinese dollars with it, repayable on the ending of the agency. Exchange profits it made on repaying the deposits were held to be capital. In *Firestone Tyre & Rubber Co Ltd v Evans* Ch D 1976, 51 TC 615, a company repaid in 1965 a dollar balance due to its US parent, the greater part of which represented advances in 1922–1931 to finance the company when it started. The Commissioners' finding that 90% of the resultant large exchange loss was capital and not allowable, was upheld. A profit by an agent on advances to the principal to finance purchases by the agent on behalf of the principal, was held to be a trading receipt (*Landes Bros v Simpson* KB 1934, 19 TC 62) as was a profit by a tobacco company on dollars accumulated to finance its future purchases (*Imperial Tobacco Co v Kelly* CA 1943, 25 TC 292). See also *McKinlay v H T Jenkins & Son* KB 1926, 10 TC 372; *Ward v Anglo-American Oil* KB 1934, 19 TC 94; *Beauchamp v F W Woolworth plc* HL 1989, 61 TC 542; and contrast *Radio Pictures Ltd v CIR* CA 1938, 22 TC 106. Where a bank operated in foreign currencies and aimed at, and generally succeeded in, matching its monetary assets and liabilities in each currency, it was held that there could be no profit or loss from matched transactions where there were no relevant currency conversions (*Pattison v Marine Midland Ltd* HL 1983, 57 TC 219). In *Whittles v Uniholdings Ltd (No 3)* CA 1996, 68 TC 528 it was held that a dollar loan and a simultaneous forward contract with the same bank for dollars sufficient to repay the loan had to be treated, for tax purposes, as separate transactions, each giving rise to its own tax consequences.

Following the *Marine Midland Ltd* case (above) the Inland Revenue issued a Statement of Practice setting out their views on the general treatment of exchange differences for tax purposes. The principles outlined in this Statement, as subsequently revised, are broadly summarised below. These extend to trades, professions and property businesses.

In accordance with the rule that generally accepted accounting practice (GAAP) be adhered to in computing taxable profits (see **73.18** above), tax computations should follow the accounting treatment where the latter is based on GAAP (and, in particular, on SSAP 20). Where, for example, under SSAP 20, gains and losses on monetary assets and liabilities are taken to reserve rather than profit and loss account, then, even if they are not capital items, they should not be recognised for tax purposes. Previously, the nature of the assets and liabilities had to be considered to determine whether or not a tax adjustment was required.

Where currency assets are matched by currency liabilities in a particular currency, so that a translation adjustment on one would be cancelled out by a translation adjustment on the other, no adjustment is required for tax purposes.

Where currency assets are not matched, or are incompletely matched, with currency liabilities in a particular currency, the adjustment required to the net exchange difference debited or credited in the profit and loss account is determined along the following lines:

(i)   the aggregate exchange differences, positive and negative, on capital assets and liabilities in the profit and loss account figure are ascertained;

(ii)   if there are no differences as at (i), no adjustment is required;

(iii) if the net exchange difference as at (i) is a loss, and the net exchange difference in the profit and loss account is also a loss, the smaller of the two losses is the amount disallowed for tax purposes as relating to capital transactions;

(iv)   if the net exchange difference as at (i) is a profit, and the net exchange difference in the profit and loss account is also a profit, the smaller of the two profits is allowed as a deduction for tax purposes;

(v)   if the net exchange difference as at (i) is a loss, and the net exchange difference in the profit and loss account is a profit, or *vice versa*, no adjustment is required for tax purposes.

In considering whether a trader is matched in a particular foreign currency, *forward exchange contracts* and *currency futures* entered into for hedging purposes may be taken into account, provided the hedging is reflected in the accounts on a consistent basis from year to year and in accordance with accepted accounting practice. *Currency swap agreements* are treated as converting the liability in the original currency into a liability in the swap currency for the duration of the swap. Hedging through *currency options* does not result in any matching.

Where the profits on disposal of assets held by a financial concern other than as trading stock fall to be treated as trading receipts and the concern does not account for those assets on a mark to market basis, such profits are taxable only on disposal (the 'realisation basis'). It may, however, be the practice to revalue the assets in the accounts to reflect exchange rate fluctuations. Where the resulting exchange differences are taken to profit and loss account or set against exchange differences on liabilities, the accounts treatment *must* be followed for tax purposes.

Where an *overseas trade*, or an *overseas branch* of a trade, is carried on primarily in a non-sterling economic environment, accounts are usually drawn up in the local currency and translated into sterling using the 'closing rate/net investment' method (SSAP 20 paras 25, 46). Under the revised Statement of Practice, tax computations *must* now be based on those translated accounts. (Under the original Statement of Practice, other specified methods of preparing computations were allowed if applied consistently.) The principles outlined in the Statement of Practice should be applied in considering any adjustment necessary in respect of exchange differences in the foreign currency accounts.

(HMRC SP 2/02).

For further discussion, see HMRC Business Income Manual BIM39500–39528.

If not taken into account in computing trading profits, a profit/loss on the sale of currency is within the ambit of CGT unless exempted by *TCGA 1992, s 269* as currency required for an individual's (or his dependant's) personal expenditure abroad (including provision or maintenance of a residence abroad).

Simon's Taxes. See **B2.433, B2.704–B2.707.**

Franchising

[73.82] Under a business system franchising agreement (i.e. an agreement under which the franchisor grants to the franchisee the right to distribute products or perform services using that system), there is generally an initial fee (payable in one sum or in instalments) and continuing, usually annual, fees.

The capital or revenue treatment of the initial fee depends on what it is for. To the extent that it is paid wholly or mainly for substantial rights of an enduring nature, to initiate or substantially extend a business, it is a capital payment (as are any related professional fees). (See **73.35** above for general principles.) It is immaterial that the expenditure may prove abortive, and the treatment of the payment in the hands of the franchisor is irrelevant. However, where goods or services of a revenue nature are supplied at the outset (e.g. trading stock or staff training), HMRC will accept that an appropriate part of the initial fee is a revenue payment, provided that the sum claimed fairly represents such items, and that it is clear that the items are not separately charged for in the continuing fees. The costs of the franchisee's own initial training are not normally allowable.

The continuing fee payable by the franchisee is generally a revenue expense.

(Revenue Tax Bulletin June 1995 p 224).

See generally HMRC Business Income Manual BIM57600–57620.

Gifts and other non-contractual receipts and payments

[73.83] See also **73.72** above (entertainment and gifts).

The fact that a receipt is gratuitous is not in itself a reason for its not being a trading receipt. See *Severne v Dadswell* Ch D 1954, 35 TC 649 (payments under war-time arrangements held trading receipts although *ex gratia*); *CIR v Falkirk Ice Rink* CS 1975, 51 TC 42 (donation to ice rink from associated curling club held taxable); *Wing v O'Connell Supreme Court* (IFS) 1926, [1927] IR 84 (gift to professional jockey on winning race taxable).

In relation to *ex gratia* payments on the termination of long-standing business arrangements, a distinction is drawn between parting gifts as personal testimonials (not taxable as business receipts) and payments which, on the facts, can be seen as additional rewards for services already rendered or compensation for a loss of future profits (taxable). For cases see **73.48**(e) above and compare the position for employees, see **27.56 EMPLOYMENT INCOME**.

Cremation fees (often known as 'ash cash') assigned in advance, and paid directly, to a medical charity may escape liability to tax on miscellaneous income where the doctor entitled to them is not chargeable to tax on trading income, but liability to tax on trading income is not affected by such assignment. See HMRC Business Income Manual BIM54015.

Simon's Taxes. See B2.320.

Gifts to charities and educational establishments

[73.84] A relief is available for certain gifts by traders for the purposes of a charity (within **16.2 CHARITIES**), any of the similar bodies listed in *ITTOIA 2005, s 108(4)*, a 'designated educational establishment' or a registered community amateur sports club (see Tolley's Corporation Tax under Voluntary Associations).

Where the gift is of an article manufactured by the trader, or of a type sold by him, in his trade, the trader is not required to bring in any amount as a trading receipt in respect of the disposal of the article.

Where the gift is of an item of plant or machinery used in the course of the donor's trade, its disposal value for capital allowances purposes (see **11.24 CAPITAL ALLOWANCES ON PLANT AND MACHINERY**) is nil.

The value of any benefit received by the donor or by a person connected with him (see **21 CONNECTED PERSONS**), which is in any way attributable to the making of a gift for which relief has been given as above, must be brought into account as a trading receipt arising on the date of receipt of the benefit or, if the trade has ceased, as a post-cessation receipt within **59.1 POST-CESSATION RECEIPTS AND EXPENDITURE**.

'*Designated educational establishment*' means any educational establishment designated (or of a category designated) in regulations, broadly all UK universities, public or private schools and further and higher educational institutions (see *SI 1992 No 42*).

[*ITTOIA 2005, ss 107–110; CAA 2001, s 63(2)–(4); ITA 2007, Sch 1 para 500; CTA 2010, Sch 1 paras 328, 446*].

Where the above relief does not apply, donations of trading stock to charities are dealt with on normal trading income principles; see Revenue Tax Bulletin June 1996 p 319 for HMRC's view of the application of those principles.

An ordinary annual subscription by a trader to a charity, made for the benefit of his employees, may be allowed as a trade expense where the availability of the charity to the employees can reasonably be regarded as a direct and valuable advantage to the employer's business and the amount is not unreasonably high (see *Bourne & Hollingsworth v Ogden* KB 1929, 14 TC 349). This would include reasonable annual subscriptions made by a trader to, for example, a general hospital in the locality of his place of business, or to a trade charity maintained primarily for the benefit of employees in the type of trade in question. It can also include subscriptions made to charities of benefit to a specific category of the employees.

A deduction for a contribution made to a charity in response to a special appeal may be allowed if an annual subscription would be allowed as above, provided that the employer has been or has become an annual subscriber, the proceeds of the appeal are to be used to meet revenue as opposed to capital expenditure, and the amount is reasonable.

(HMRC Business Income Manual BIM47410).

Simon's Taxes. See B2.442.

Guarantees

[73.85] Losses under guarantees of the indebtedness of another are analogous to bad debt losses (see **73.40** above) and similar principles apply. Losses allowed as a deduction to a solicitor under the guarantee of a client's overdraft (*Jennings v Barfield* Ch D 1962, 40 TC 365) and to a film-writer under guarantee of loans to a film company with which he was associated (*Lunt v Wellesley* KB 1945, 27 TC 78) but refused to a company under a guarantee of loans to an associated company with which it had close trading connections (*Milnes v J Beam Group Ltd* Ch D 1975, 50 TC 675) and a guarantee of loans to a subsidiary (*Redkite Ltd v Inspector of Taxes* [1996] SSCD 501). See also *Bolton v Halpern & Woolf* CA 1980, 53 TC 445 and *Garforth v Tankard Carpets Ltd* Ch D 1980, 53 TC 342.

A loss by an asphalt contractor under a guarantee to an exhibition (for which he hoped but, in the event, failed to work) allowed (*Morley v Lawford & Co* CA 1928, 14 TC 229). For commission paid to guarantors see *Ascot Gas Water Heaters Ltd* at **73.89** below.

Payments under guarantees made to a trader for the setting up or the purposes of his trade and irrecoverable are in certain circumstances allowable as a loss for capital gains tax. See Tolley's Capital Gains Tax.

Hire-purchase

[73.86] Where assets are purchased under hire-purchase agreements, the charges (the excess of the hire-purchase price over the cash price, sometimes referred to as interest) are, appropriately spread, allowable deductions (*Darngavil Coal Co Ltd v Francis* CS 1913, 7 TC 1). See **73.40** above for the bad debt etc. provisions of hire-purchase traders. For relief on capital element, see **11.61** CAPITAL ALLOWANCES ON PLANT AND MACHINERY.

For whether goods sold under hire-purchase are trading stock, see *Lions Ltd v Gosford Furnishing Co Ltd & CIR* CS 1961, 40 TC 256 and cf. *Drages Ltd v CIR* KB 1927, 46 TC 389.

See generally HMRC Business Income Manual BIM40550–40555 (hire-purchase receipts) and BIM45350–45365 (hire-purchase payments).

Illegal payments etc.

[73.87] In computing profits, no deduction may be made in respect of expenditure incurred:

• in making a payment the making of which constitutes a criminal offence; or

• in making a payment outside the UK where the making of a corresponding payment in any part of the UK would constitute a criminal offence there.

A deduction is similarly denied for any payment induced by a demand constituting blackmail or extortion.

[*ITTOIA 2005, ss 55, 870*].

For a discussion of the circumstances in which the above may apply, see HMRC Business Income Manual BIM43100–43185.

Simon's Taxes. See B2.420.

Insurance

[73.88] Premiums for business purposes are normally allowable including insurance of assets, insurance against accidents to employees, insurance against loss of profits and premiums under mutual insurance schemes (cf. *Thomas v Richard Evans & Co* HL 1927, 11 TC 790; for trade associations, see **73.116** below).

Any corresponding recoveries are trading receipts (or set off against trading expenses) or capital, according to the nature of the policy. Where a deduction was allowed for a loss or expense and the trader recovers a capital sum under an insurance policy or contract of indemnity in respect of that loss or expense, the sum must be brought into account, up to the amount of the deduction, as a trading receipt. [*ITTOIA 2005, s 106*]. Otherwise, if capital, the recovery may be taken into account, where appropriate, for the purposes of capital allowances or capital gains tax.

The whole of a recovery in respect of the destruction of trading stock was held to be a trading receipt of the year of destruction, notwithstanding that it exceeded the market value of the stock lost or not all the stock was replaced (*Green v J Gliksten & Son Ltd* HL 1929, 14 TC 364; *Rownson Drew & Clydesdale Ltd v CIR* KB 1931, 16 TC 595). The total recovery under a loss of profits was held a trading receipt although in excess of the loss suffered (*R v British Columbia Fir & Cedar* PC 1932, 15 ATC 624). See also *Mallandain Investments Ltd v Shadbolt* KB 1940, 23 TC 367. For recoveries under accidents to employees see *Gray & Co v Murphy* KB 1940, 23 TC 225; *Keir*

& Cawder Ltd v CIR CS 1958, 38 TC 23. Where a shipping company insured against late delivery of ships being built for it, both premiums and recoveries held capital (*Crabb v Blue Star Line Ltd* Ch D 1961, 39 TC 482).

Premiums on policies in favour of the employer insuring against death or critical illness of key employees are generally allowable, and the proceeds of any such policies trading receipts. However, in *Beauty Consultants Ltd v Inspector of Taxes* (Sp C 321), [2002] SSCD 352, premiums on a policy insuring a company against the death of either of its controlling shareholder-directors were not allowed as deductions; the 'dual purpose rule' at **73.36** above applied, in that the premiums benefited the shareholders personally by improving the value of their shares. In *Greycon Ltd v Klaentschi* (Sp C 372), [2003] SSCD 370, it was held that the company's sole purpose in taking out key man policies was to meet a requirement of an agreement under which funding and other benefits were obtained from another company, that the policies had a capital purpose and that, consequently, the proceeds were not trading receipts.

Accountancy fee protection insurance

See **73.92** below.

Health insurance

See **30.23** EXEMPT INCOME.

Locum and fixed practice expenses insurance

HMRC take the view that premiums for such policies are deductible, and benefits taxable, under the trading income rules, whether the professional person is obliged to insure (e.g. under NHS regulations) or does so as a matter of commercial prudence. This view relates to premiums paid by professional people such as doctors and dentists to meet locum and/or fixed overhead costs. It does not apply to any part of a premium relating to other, non-business, risks such as the cost of medical treatment for accident or sickness. (Revenue Press Release 30 April 1996).

Professional indemnity insurance

Professional indemnity insurance premiums are normally allowable on general principles, and HMRC will not seek to disallow a premium paid prior to cessation of trading on the grounds that the cover extends to claims lodged after cessation. (Premiums paid after cessation will generally be relievable as post-cessation expenditure, see **59.5** POST-CESSATION RECEIPTS AND EXPENDITURE.) (Revenue Tax Bulletin October 1995 p 257).

Commissions

HMRC Statement of Practice SP 4/97 (see **73.46** above) deals widely with commissions, cashbacks and discounts.

See also *Robertson v CIR* (Sp C 137), [1997] SSCD 282 as regards timing of inclusion of insurance agents' advance commission.

Interest and other payments for loans

[73.89] Interest paid for business purposes, if not claimed as a relief under *ITA 2007, s 383*, is deductible, subject to certain restrictions, as described at **43.2 INTEREST PAYABLE**. For hire-purchase charges, see **73.86** above.

Premium on repayment of mortgage (*Arizona Copper Co v Smiles* CES 1891, 3 TC 149) and on repayment of loan to finance estate development (*Bridgwater v King* KB 1943, 25 TC 385) held not allowable, as were exchange losses attendant on foreign borrowings by a company to finance its purchase of a controlling interest in another company (*Ward v Anglo-American Oil Co Ltd* KB 1934, 19 TC 94). A share of profits paid as partial consideration for a loan was held to be distribution of profits and not allowed in *Walker & Co v CIR* KB 1920, 12 TC 297.

INTEREST AND SURCHARGES ON OVERDUE TAX **(42)** are not allowable deductions in computing profits. This applies equally to interest (and certain penalties and surcharges) in respect of unpaid or under-declared value added tax, insurance premium tax, landfill tax, climate change levy, aggregates levy, stamp duty land tax, excise duties and customs, excise or import duties. It also applies to penalties under *FA 2007, Sch 24* and *FA 2008, Sch 41*. For a list of the specific charges to which this prohibition applies, see *ITTOIA 2005, s 54*. [*ITTOIA 2005, ss 54, 869; TMA 1970, s 90; ICTA 1988, s 827(1)–(1F); SI 2009 No 56, Sch 1 paras 438, 442; SI 2009 No 571, Arts 38, 39; SI 2010 No 530, Sch paras 8, 9*].

For the treatment of the incidental costs of obtaining loan finance, see **73.93** below.

Investment income (including letting income)

[73.90] Investment income may be treated as a trading receipt where it is the fruit derived from a fund employed and risked in the business (see *Liverpool and London and Globe Insurance Co v Bennett* HL 1913, 6 TC 327). This treatment is not confined to financial trades, but the making and holding of investments at interest must be an integral part of the trade. See *Nuclear Electric plc v Bradley* HL 1996, 68 TC 670, in which (in refusing the company's claim) the crucial test was considered to be whether the investments were employed in the business (of producing electricity) in the tax year in question. The Court of Appeal, whose judgment was approved, considered decisive the facts that the liabilities against which the investments were provided were liabilities to third parties, not to customers, and that, in view of the long-term nature of the liabilities, the business could be carried on for a long period without maintaining any fund of investments at all. See also *Bank Line Ltd v CIR* (above).

See **45 LOSSES** for treatment of certain investment income as trading profits for loss relief purposes.

Payments received in lieu of dividends in contango operations held trading receipts (*Multipar Syndicate Ltd v Devitt* KB 1945, 26 TC 359); also co-operative society 'dividends' on trading purchases (*Pope v Beaumont* KB

1941, 24 TC 78). For interest received by underwriters on securities deposited with Lloyd's see *Owen v Sassoon* HC 1950, 32 TC 101 and for discount receivable on bills see *Willingale v International Commercial Bank Ltd* HL 1978, 52 TC 242.

In certain cases pre-dating *ITTOIA 2005* (which abolished all the remaining labels under which income was charged to tax, e.g. Schedule D), income received under deduction of tax was unable to be included in a *Schedule D, Case I* or *II* assessment (cf. *F S Securities Ltd v CIR* HL 1964, 41 TC 666; *Bucks v Bowers* Ch D 1969, 46 TC 267; *Bank Line Ltd v CIR* CS 1974, 49 TC 307), and nor, subject to the Crown option between Cases (see **6.1** ASSESSMENTS), could income received gross from sources within Schedule D, Cases III, IV or V (cf. *Northend v White & Leonard & Corbin Greener* Ch D 1975, 50 TC 121) and also from sources *explicitly* within Schedule D, Case VI.

Letting income

Rents receivable and other letting income are within the charge to tax on property income as opposed to trading income (see **73.1** above).

Letting of surplus business accommodation

If, however, a trader lets surplus business accommodation and the conditions below are satisfied, he may choose to include the receipts and expenses of the letting in computing his trading profits instead of treating them as receipts and expenses of a property business. The conditions are that the let accommodation must be 'temporarily surplus to requirements', it must not be part of trading stock, it must be part of a building of which another part is used to carry on the trade, and the letting receipts must be relatively small. For these purposes, 'letting' includes a licence to occupy. Once the receipts and expenses of a letting are included in trading profits, all subsequent receipts and expenses of the letting must similarly be so included. For accommodation to be '*temporarily surplus to requirements*', it must have been used for trading within the last three years or acquired within that period; the trader must intend to use it for trading in future; and the letting itself must be for a term of no more than three years. The position is judged as at the beginning of a period of account. [*ITTOIA 2005, s 21*].

See **60.2 PROPERTY INCOME** for a further relaxation of the main rule above, this time in relation to caravan site operators.

Know-how

[73.91] '*Know-how*' is any industrial information and techniques likely to assist in (a) manufacturing or processing goods or materials, (b) working, or searching for etc., mineral deposits, or (c) agricultural, forestry or fishing operations. For capital allowances on purchases of know-how, see **10.23 CAPITAL ALLOWANCES.**

Where know-how used in the vendor's trade is disposed of, with the trade thereafter continuing, the consideration received is treated as a trading receipt, except to the extent that it is brought into account as a disposal value for capital allowances purposes (see **10.23 CAPITAL ALLOWANCES**). This does not apply to a sale between bodies of persons (which includes partnerships) under the same control.

If the know-how is disposed of as part of the disposal of all or part of the trade, both vendor and purchaser are treated for income tax purposes as if the consideration for the know-how were a capital payment for goodwill (in which case capital gains tax may apply). They may, however, jointly elect to disapply this treatment (within two years of the disposal, and provided they are not bodies under common control), and it is disapplied in any event in relation to the purchaser if, prior to his acquiring it, the trade was carried on wholly outside the UK. In either case, the purchaser may then claim capital allowances on his expenditure (see **10.23**(iii) **CAPITAL ALLOWANCES**).

Any consideration received for a restrictive covenant in connection with a disposal of know-how is treated as consideration received for the disposal of the know-how. An exchange of know-how is treated as a sale of know-how.

[*ITTOIA 2005, ss 192–195; CTA 2009, Sch 1 para 611*].

For disposals of know-how by non-traders, see **40.5 INTELLECTUAL PROPERTY**.

In *Delage v Nugget Polish Co Ltd* KB 1905, 21 TLR 454, payments for the use of a secret process, payable for 40 years and based on receipts, were held to be annual payments subject to deduction of tax at source. See also *Paterson Engineering v Duff* KB 1943, 25 TC 43.

For patents, see **73.99** below.

Simon's Taxes. See B5.343–B5.346.

Legal and professional expenses

[73.92] The expenses of a company incorporated by charter in obtaining a variation of its charter etc. were allowed (*CIR v Carron Co* HL 1968, 45 TC 18). See also *McGarry v Limerick Gas* HC(IFS) [1932] IR 125 and contrast *A & G Moore & Co v Hare* CS 1914, 6 TC 572. In general, the costs of maintaining existing trading rights and assets are revenue expenses (*Southern v Borax Consolidated* KB 1940, 23 TC 597; *Bihar etc. IT Commr v Maharaja of Dharbanga* PC 1941, 20 ATC 337 and compare *Morgan v Tate & Lyle Ltd* HL 1954, 35 TC 367). But the incidental costs of acquiring new assets etc. are part of their capital cost. The expenses of obtaining or renewing a lease of business premises are strictly capital but, in practice, the expenses of renewing leases under 50 years are generally deductible (although a proportionate disallowance may apply where a lease premium is involved — see HMRC Business Income Manual BIM46420). The cost of an unsuccessful application to vary a carrier's licence was disallowed (*Pyrah v Annis & Co* CA 1956, 37 TC 163) as was the cost of an unsuccessful application for planning permission (*ECC Quarries Ltd v Watkis* Ch D 1975, 51 TC 153 but see **10.12**(b) **CAPITAL ALLOWANCES**). For excise licences, see **73.41** above.

Legal expenses in defending charges brought by a professional regulatory body were allowed as deductions on the grounds that they were incurred to prevent suspension or expulsion and thus to protect the taxpayer's business (applying *Tate & Lyle Ltd* (above)), although the fines imposed were disallowed (see **73.47** above) (*McKnight v Sheppard* HL 1999, 71 TC 419).

Costs incurred by a partner in connection with the dissolution of the partnership were disallowed in *C Connelly & Co v Wilbey Ch D 1992, 65 TC 208.*

The cost of tax appeals, even if successful, is not deductible (*Allen v Farquharson Bros & Co* KB 1932, 17 TC 59; *Smith's Potato Estates v Bolland* HL 1948, 30 TC 267; *Rushden Heel Co v Keene* HL 1948, 30 TC 298). Where an accountant etc. agrees the tax liabilities based on the accounts he prepares, normal annual fees are allowed as a deduction but not fees for a special review of settled years (*Worsley Brewery Co v CIR* CA 1932, 17 TC 349).

Additional accountancy expenses incurred as a result of an investigation by HMRC of a particular year's accounts (see **73.17** above) will normally be allowed as a deduction if the investigation does not result in an adjustment to the profits of any earlier year or in the imposition of interest or interest and penalties in relation to the current year. Where the investigation reveals discrepancies and additional liabilities for earlier years, or results in a settlement for the current year including interest (with or without penalties), the expenses will be disallowed. Where, however, the investigation results in no addition to profits, or an adjustment to profits for the year of review only without a charge to interest or to interest and penalties, the additional accountancy expenses will normally be allowed. (HMRC SP 16/91).

It is HMRC's view that premiums for a fee protection insurance policy, which entitles the policy holder to claim for the cost of accountancy fees incurred in negotiating additional tax liabilities resulting from negligent or fraudulent conduct, are not allowable. Even if the policy covers other risks as well, the premiums cannot be apportioned between allowable and non-allowable elements. (Revenue Tax Bulletin June 2003 p 1036).

Simon's Taxes. See B2.449.

Loan finance incidental costs

[73.93] In computing profits, a deduction is allowed for 'incidental costs of obtaining finance' by means of a loan (or the issue of loan stock) the interest on which would be deductible in computing profits (see **73.89** above and **43.2 INTEREST PAYABLE**) and which does not carry a right, exercisable within three years, of conversion into, or to the acquisition of, shares or other (non-qualifying) securities. The said restriction does not apply if the right is not wholly exercised within the three-year period; in such a case, incidental costs incurred within the three-year period are treated as incurred immediately after that period. Where part only of the loan or loan stock is so converted, only the corresponding proportion of the incidental costs is disallowed.

'*Incidental costs of obtaining finance*' are expenses incurred on fees, commissions, advertising, printing and other incidental matters which are incurred wholly and exclusively for the purpose of (i) obtaining the loan finance or (ii) providing security for it or (iii) repaying it. Expenses within (i) and (ii) are deductible under these provisions even if the loan finance is not in fact obtained. But incidental costs of obtaining finance do not include stamp duty, sums paid because of foreign exchange losses (or sums paid for protection against them) or the cost of repaying the loan or loan stock so far as attributable to its being repayable at a premium or its having been obtained at a discount.

[*ITTOIA 2005, ss 58, 59*].

See also **3.2, 3.7 ALTERNATIVE FINANCE ARRANGEMENTS**.

Costs incidental to the taking out of a life insurance policy as a condition of obtaining the loan finance are deductible, but not premiums payable on such a policy (Revenue Tax Bulletin February 1992 p 13). Costs of a flotation the proceeds of which were used to repay loan finance were held not allowable as the motive of the company in arranging for the flotation was not wholly and exclusively to repay the debt (*Focus Dynamics plc v Turner* (Sp C 182), [1999] SSCD 71).

It was held in *Cadbury Schweppes plc v Williams* (Sp C 302), [2002] SSCD 115 that the period for which the relief is available is that in which the finance is obtained, rather than that in which the facility is used, notwithstanding the accountancy treatment. See, however, Revenue Tax Bulletin April 1996 p 306 for HMRC's view that the timing of the deduction must be in accordance with normal principles (i.e. it follows the accounting treatment, provided that the accounts are correctly drawn up in accordance with applicable UK accounting standards).

In *Kato Kagaku Co Ltd v HMRC* (Sp C 598) [2007] SSCD 412, it was held that part of an indemnity payment was deductible as an incidental cost of obtaining finance. The appellant had repaid a bank loan before the scheduled repayment date, and became liable to pay the bank approximately £21 million under an indemnity agreement. The Sp C disallowed all but about £3 million of this on the grounds that, on the facts of the case, the disallowed amount was a payment made in consequence of foreign exchange losses.

Simon's Taxes. See B2.437.

Long funding leases of plant or machinery

[73.94] The rules on leasing of plant and machinery were reformed by *FA 2006, s 81, Sch 8* with effect from, broadly, 1 April 2006. For 'long funding leases', the new regime grants entitlement to capital allowances to the lessee rather than to the lessor as previously (see **11.43–11.49 CAPITAL ALLOWANCES ON PLANT AND MACHINERY**). There were corresponding changes to the tax treatment of lease rentals, to ensure that the lessor is no longer taxed on, and the lessee does not obtain a deduction for, the capital element of rentals (see below). The current regime applies only to leases which are essentially financing transactions, known as '*funding leases*', comprising mainly finance leases but also some operating leases. Leases of no more than five years' duration are excluded from the regime, as are pre-1 April 2006 leases. There are transitional rules to enable leases finalised on or after 1 April 2006 to remain within the pre-existing regime in appropriate circumstances. See **11.49** CAPITAL ALLOWANCES ON PLANT AND MACHINERY. The coverage below considers firstly the lessor's position (**73.95**) and then the lessee's (**73.96**).

For an HMRC Technical Note published on 1 August 2006 on the long funding leasing rules, see www.hmrc.gov.uk/leasing/tech-note.pdf. See also HMRC Business Leasing Manual BLM 40000 *et seq.*

As regards finance leases that fall outside the definition of a long funding lease or preceded the introduction of those rules, see **73.78–73.80** above.

Long funding leases — lessors

[73.95] The treatment depends on whether the lease is a long funding operating lease or a long funding finance lease.

For any period of account for the whole or any part of which the trader is the lessor of plant or machinery under a 'long funding operating lease' (see **11.45**(3) CAPITAL ALLOWANCES ON PLANT AND MACHINERY), he is entitled to a deduction as follows in computing his profits (so as to compensate him for non-entitlement to capital allowances). Firstly, determine the 'starting value' in accordance with *ITTOIA 2005, ss 148DA, 148DB*. This varies depending on whether or not there has been any previous use of the plant or machinery by the lessor and on the nature of any such previous use. In the most straight-forward case where the sole use has been leasing under the long funding operating lease, the starting value is equal to cost. Secondly, deduct from the starting value the amount that is expected (at the commencement of the term of the lease — see *CAA 2001, s 70YI(1)*) to be the 'residual value' of the plant or machinery (i.e. its estimated market value assuming a disposal at the end of the term of the lease, less the estimated costs of that disposal). This gives the expected gross reduction in value over the term of the lease. Next, time-apportion that figure between all periods of account that coincide wholly or partly with the term of the lease. The resulting figure for each period of account is the amount deductible for that period.

Where the lessor (as above) incurs additional capital expenditure on the plant or machinery that is not reflected in its market value at the commencement of the term of the lease, an additional deduction is due as follows. Determine the amount which, at the time the additional expenditure is incurred, is expected to be the residual value of the plant or machinery. Deduct the amount previously expected to be the residual value. If this produces a positive amount, determine how much of that amount is attributable to the additional expenditure. Next, deduct the attributable amount from the amount of the additional expenditure. This gives the expected reduction in value of the additional expenditure over the remainder of the term of the lease. Time-apportion that figure between all periods of account that coincide wholly or partly with the term of the lease and which end after the additional expenditure is incurred. The resulting figure for each such period of account is the additional amount deductible for that period.

In the period of account in which a long funding operating lease *terminates*, any profit arising to the lessor from the termination must be brought into account as trading income and any loss so arising must be brought into account as a revenue expense. The profit or loss is computed as follows.

(1)   Determine the 'termination amount' (for which see **11.46 CAPITAL ALLOWANCES ON PLANT AND MACHINERY**) and subtract from it any sums paid to the lessee that are calculated by reference to the 'termination value' (as defined by *CAA 2001, s 70YH*), e.g. lease rental refunds.

(2)   Determine the 'starting value' as above and subtract from it all deductions (other than additional deductions) allowable as above to that same lessor up to the date of termination.

(3)   If any additional capital expenditure has been incurred as above, determine the total amount thereof and subtract from it all additional deductions allowable as above to that same lessor up to the date of termination.

(4)   If the total in (1) above exceeds the aggregate of the totals in (2) and (3), a profit arises equal to the excess.

(5)   If the total in (1) above falls short of the aggregate of the totals in (2) and (3), a loss arises equal to the deficit.

In computing the lessor's profits for the period of account in which termination occurs, no trading deduction is allowed for any sums paid to the lessee that are calculated by reference to the 'termination value' (as these are brought into account in (1) above).

[*ITTOIA 2005, ss 148D, 148DA, 148DB, 148E, 148EA, 148EB, 148F, 148J(2)(4); CTA 2010, Sch 1 paras 447–451*].

Long funding finance leases

For any period of account in which the trader is the lessor of plant or machinery under a 'long funding finance lease' (see **11.45**(4) **CAPITAL ALLOWANCES ON PLANT AND MACHINERY**), the amount to be brought into account as his taxable income from the lease is the amount of the 'rental earnings' in respect of the lease. The *'rental earnings'* for any period is the amount that, in accordance with generally accepted accounting practice (GAAP), falls to be treated as the gross return on investment for that period in respect of the lease. If, in accordance with GAAP, the lease falls to be treated as a loan in the accounts in question, so much of the lease rentals as fall to be treated as interest are treated for these purposes as rental earnings. There is also provision for exceptional profits or losses (including capital items) arising from the lease to be brought into account for tax purposes, as trading income or as revenue expenditure, if they fall to be brought into account under GAAP in the period of account in question but otherwise than as part of the profits calculation.

Where the lease *terminates* and any sum calculated by reference to 'termination value' (as defined by *CAA 2001, s 70YH*) is paid to the lessee, e.g. lease rental refunds, no deduction is allowed for that sum in computing the lessor's trading profits, except to the extent (if any) that it is brought into account in determining rental earnings.

[*ITTOIA 2005, ss 148A–148C, 148J(4)*].

Legislation introduced by *FA 2008* disapplies *ITTOIA 2005, ss 148A–148F* above where:

(a) expenditure incurred on the leased plant or machinery is (apart from anything in *ITTOIA 2005, ss 148A–148F*) allowable as a deduction in computing the lessor's trading profits because the plant or machinery is held, or comes to be held, as trading stock; or

(b) the long funding lease is part of an arrangement, including one or more other transactions, entered into by the lessor a main purpose of which is to secure that, over the term of the lease, there is a substantial difference between the amounts brought into account under GAAP and the amounts brought into account in computing taxable profits, such difference being at least partly attributable to the application of any of *ITTOIA 2005, ss 148A–148F*.

Sub-paragraph (a) above applies where the expenditure is incurred after 8 October 2007 or the lessor becomes entitled to a deduction as a result of plant or machinery forming part of the trading stock on or after that date. Sub-paragraph (b) above applies where the arrangement is entered into on or after that date.

Legislation was also included in *FA 2008* to counter an avoidance scheme involving a mismatch in the treatment of lease rentals under a head lease and a sub-lease of the same plant or machinery. Under a typical scheme, the head lease from A to B will not be a long funding lease from B's (the lessee's) point of view but the sub-lease from B to C will be a long funding lease from B's (the lessor's) point of view. The result is that B would be entitled to tax relief on the full amount of the lease rentals under the head lease (i.e. including the capital element) but would not be chargeable to tax on the capital element of the sub-lease rentals. The legislation seeks to ensure that B is taxed on the full amount of the sub-lease rentals by disapplying *ITTOIA 2005, ss 148A–148F* above in these circumstances in relation to the sub-lease. It applies where the sub-lease is entered into after 12 December 2007. There are additional provisions to ensure that a sub-lease already in existence at the beginning of 13 December 2007 is taxed broadly as if it were not a long-funding lease as regards rentals relating to any time on or after that date.

[*ITTOIA 2005, ss 148FA–148FC; FA 2008, Sch 20 paras 10, 11*].

Film lessors

Legislation was included in *Finance Act 2009* to disapply *ITTOIA 2005, ss 148A–148F* above where the subject of the long funding lease is a film. This has effect where the 'inception' (see *CAA 2001, s 70YI(1)*) of the lease is after 12 November 2008. In addition, there are changes to the treatment of a long funding finance lease of a film where its inception was on or before 12 November 2008 and rentals are due after that date and relate to time falling after that date. The lessor will be taxed on both the finance charge element of the rentals and so much of the capital element of the rentals as relates to the time falling after 12 November 2008; the other rules in *ITTOIA 2005, ss 148A–148C* above are suitably modified. [*ITTOIA 2005, s 148FD; FA 2009, Sch 33 paras 2–9*].

Long funding leases — lessees

[73.96] The treatment depends on whether the lease is a long funding operating lease or a long funding finance lease.

Long funding operating leases

In computing the profits of a trader for any period of account in which he is the lessee of plant or machinery under a 'long funding operating lease' (see **11.45**(3) CAPITAL ALLOWANCES ON PLANT AND MACHINERY), the otherwise allowable deductions in respect of amounts payable under the lease must be reduced as follows. Firstly, determine the 'relevant value' in accordance with *ITTOIA 2005, s 148I(4)(5)*. In the straightforward case where the sole use of the plant or machinery has been in a qualifying activity (within **11.4** CAPITAL ALLOWANCES ON PLANT AND MACHINERY) carried on by the lessee, the relevant value is equal to the market value of the plant or machinery at the commencement (see *CAA 2001, s 70YI(1)*) of the term of the lease. Secondly, deduct from the relevant value the amount that is expected (at the commencement of the term of the lease) to be the market value of the plant or machinery at the end of the term of the lease. This gives the expected gross reduction over the term of the lease. Next, time-apportion that figure between all periods of account that coincide wholly or partly with the term of the lease. The resulting figure for each period of account is the amount of the reduction for that period.

[*ITTOIA 2005, ss 148I, 148J*].

Long funding finance leases

In computing the profits of a trader for any period of account in which he is the lessee of plant or machinery under a 'long funding finance lease' (see **11.45**(4) CAPITAL ALLOWANCES ON PLANT AND MACHINERY), the amount deducted in respect of amounts payable under the lease must not exceed the amount that, in accordance with GAAP, falls to be shown in the lessee's accounts as finance charges in respect of the lease. If, in accordance with GAAP, the lease falls to be accounted for as a loan, it is for this purpose treated as if it fell to be accounted for as a finance lease.

Where the lease *terminates* and a sum calculated by reference to 'termination value' (as defined by *CAA 2001, s 70YH*) is paid to the lessee, e.g. lease rental refunds, that sum is not brought into account in computing the lessee's trading profits for any period. (It is, however, brought into account in calculating the disposal value of the plant or machinery for capital allowances purposes — see **11.44** CAPITAL ALLOWANCES ON PLANT AND MACHINERY).

[*ITTOIA 2005, ss 148G, 148H, 148J(4)*].

Mines, quarries etc.

[73.97] See **10.24** *et seq.* CAPITAL ALLOWANCES for mining etc. expenditure so allowable. The relevant legislation originated in 1945 and may therefore affect any pre-1945 decisions below.

The cost of sinking (*Coltness Iron Co v Black* HL 1881, 1 TC 287), deepening (*Bonner v Basset Mines* KB 1912, 6 TC 146) or 'de-watering' (*United Collieries v CIR* CS 1929, 12 TC 1248) a pit is capital.

A lump sum paid at the end of a mining lease for surface damage was held capital (*Robert Addie & Sons v CIR* CS 1924, 8 TC 671) but not periodic payments during the currency of the lease based on acreage worked (*O'Grady v Bullcroft Main Collieries* KB 1932, 17 TC 93). *Bullcroft* was decided before the enactment of what is now *ICTA 1988, s 119* and rents and tonnage payments for the right to withdraw surface support are easements within *s 119* (*CIR v New Sharlston Collieries* CA 1936, 21 TC 116). For the deduction of tax under *s 119* see **24.13 DEDUCTION OF TAX AT SOURCE** and also for periodic payments for rights to minerals, sand and gravel etc. For shortworkings, see *Broughton & Plas Power v Kirkpatrick* QB 1884, 2 TC 69; *CIR v Cranford Ironstone* KB 1942, 29 TC 113. Provision for the future costs of abandoning an oil field and of restoring hired equipment used therein to its original state held capital (*RTZ Oil and Gas Ltd v Elliss* Ch D 1987, 61 TC 132).

For HMRC's view of the treatment of payments by mining concerns to landowners for restoration for surface damage, see HMRC Business Income Manual BIM62025. In particular, a payment of compensation for ascertained past damage is allowable, as is a provision for such expenditure where made in accordance with generally accepted accounting practice and accurately quantified.

Purchase of unworked deposits by sand and gravel merchant held capital (*Stow Bardolph Gravel Co Ltd v Poole* CA 1954, 35 TC 459) as was purchase of land with nitrate deposits by chemical manufacturer (*Alianza Co v Bell* HL 1905, 5 TC 172) and payment by oil company for unwon oil in wells it took over (*Hughes v British Burmah Petroleum* KB 1932, 17 TC 286). See also *Golden Horse Shoe v Thurgood* CA 1933, 18 TC 280 (purchase of tailings for gold extraction, allowable) and *CIR v Broomhouse Brick* CS 1952, 34 TC 1 (purchase of blaes for brick manufacture, allowable).

See generally HMRC Business Income Manual BIM62000–62085.

Production wells etc.

The costs of drilling the second and subsequent production wells in an area are not generally allowable. [*ITTOIA 2005, s 161*]. Although not specifically stated in the statute, this prohibition applies particularly to intangible drilling costs. For a discussion of this, see HMRC Oil Taxation Manual OT26237. Such costs may attract mineral extraction capital allowances (see **10.24** *et seq.* **CAPITAL ALLOWANCES**).

Miscellaneous expenses and receipts

[73.98] The items below are arranged in alphabetical order. See also *Thompson v Magnesium Elektron* CA 1943, 26 TC 1 (payments based on purchases, held trading receipts); *British Commonwealth International Newsfilm v Mahany* HL 1962, 40 TC 550 (payments to meet operating expenses, trading receipts); *CIR v Pattison* CS 1959, 38 TC 617 (weekly instalments for business, capital).

Card winnings

Card winnings of club proprietor were held to be trading receipts (*Burdge v Pyne* Ch D 1968, 45 TC 320). For lotteries and football pools, see **73.23** above.

Carers

Any profits arising from payments by local authorities for taking the elderly or infirm into the home as family are chargeable as trading income (although the availability of 'rent-a-room' exemption (see **60.12 PROPERTY INCOME**) will often obviate the need for further enquiry). See HMRC Business Income Manual BIM52780–52800 for HMRC's approach to determination of the chargeable profit (if any) in such cases. See **30.3 EXEMPT INCOME** as regards adult placement carers and **30.15 EXEMPT INCOME** as regards foster carers.

Computer software

HMRC's views on the treatment of expenditure on computer software are summarised as follows.

Software acquired under licence

Regular payments akin to a rental are allowable revenue expenditure, the timing of deductions being governed by correct accountancy practice (see **73.18** above). A lump sum payment is capital if the licence is of a sufficiently enduring nature to be considered a capital asset in the context of the licencee's trade (see **73.35** above), e.g. where it may be expected to function as a tool of the trade for several years. Equally the benefit may be transitory (and the expenditure revenue) even though the licence is for an indefinite period. Inspectors will in any event accept that expenditure is on revenue account where the software has a useful economic life of less than two years. Timing of the deduction in these circumstances will again depend on correct accountancy practice.

Where the licence is a capital asset, capital allowances are available (see **11.10 CAPITAL ALLOWANCES ON PLANT AND MACHINERY**).

Expenditure on a package containing both hardware and a licence to use software must be apportioned before the above principles are applied.

Software owned outright

The treatment of expenditure on such software (including any in-house costs) follows the same principles as are described above in relation to licensed software.

(Revenue Tax Bulletin November 1993 p 99).

See HMRC Business Income Manual BIM35800–35865 for a detailed analysis of HMRC's views generally.

DVD/video rental

Relief for the cost of acquiring video tapes for hire may be obtained by way of either:

(i)   capital allowances (provided the useful economic life is at least two years);
(ii)   valuation basis (where the useful economic life is two years or less); or
(iii)   renewals basis.

The tax treatment of DVDs and similar items follows the same lines. See HMRC Business Income Manual BIM67200–67220.

Export Credits Guarantee Department

A deduction is allowed for amounts payable by a trader to that Department under an agreement entered into by virtue of arrangements made under *Export and Investment Guarantees Act 1991, s 2* or with a view to entering into such an agreement. [*ITTOIA 2005, s 91*].

Mutual concerns, distribution of assets from

If a deduction has been allowed (in computing trading profits) for a payment to a corporate mutual concern for the purposes of its mutual business and the trader receives a distribution in money or money's worth upon the winding-up or dissolution of the mutual concern, the amount or value received is a trading receipt. This applies only if the assets being distributed represent profits of the mutual concern. It does not apply to distributions of chargeable gains. If the trade has ceased by the time of the distribution, the amount or value received is a post-cessation receipt (within **59.1 POST-CESSATION RECEIPTS AND EXPENDITURE**). [*ITTOIA 2005, s 104*]. For mutual trading generally, see **73.33** above.

Overpayments

Overpayments received, due to errors by customers or their banks which the taxpayer neither caused nor facilitated, held not to be trading receipts (*Anise Ltd and others v Hammond* (Sp C 364), [2003] SSCD 258).

Purchases/sales of assets

See *T Beynon & Co v Ogg* KB 1918, 7 TC 125 (profits of colliery agent from deals in wagons held trading receipts); *Gloucester Railway Carriage v CIR* HL 1925, 12 TC 720 (sale by wagon manufacturer of wagons previously let, held trading receipts); *Bonner v Frood KB 1934, 18 TC 488* (sale of rounds by credit trader, held trading receipts).

Reimbursements of capital expenditure

Reimbursements of capital expenditure spread over 30 years held capital as regards both payer and recipient (*Boyce v Whitwick Colliery* CA 1934, 18 TC 655). For allowances from railway in respect of traffic on sidings paid for by trader see *Westcombe v Hadnock Quarries* KB 1931, 16 TC 137; *Legge v Flettons Ltd* KB 1939, 22 TC 455.

Rental rebates

With effect in relation to rebates payable on or after 9 December 2009, there is a restriction on the amount of the trading deduction allowable to a lessor of plant or machinery where he makes a rental rebate to the lessee. A rental rebate means any sum payable to the lessee that is calculated by reference to the value of the plant or machinery at or about the time when the lease terminates. The deduction is limited to the aggregate of all the amounts receivable in connection with the lease that have been brought into account in computing the lessor's taxable income. In calculating this aggregate, however, one excludes any amount brought into account as a disposal value as in **11.24 CAPITAL ALLOWANCES ON PLANT AND MACHINERY** and any amounts that represent charges for services or 'taxes' to be paid by the lessor. ('*Taxes*' means UK or foreign taxes or duties, but not income tax, corporation tax or foreign equivalents.) In the case of a finance lease, one also excludes the finance charge element of the rentals (as defined). The limit does not apply where the lease is a long funding finance lease as in **73.95** above.

Where the whole or part of a rental rebate is disallowed as above as a deduction in computing trading profits, an amount may be treated as an allowable loss for capital gains tax purposes accruing to the lessor on the termination of the lease. The amount which may be so treated is the lower of the amount disallowed and the amount by which the rental rebate exceeds the lessor's capital expenditure. The loss is deductible only from chargeable gains accruing to the lessor on the disposal of the plant or machinery.

[*ITTOIA 2005, s 55B; FA 2010, Sch 5 para 2*

The legislation is aimed at identified tax avoidance schemes. In circumstances not involving tax avoidance, the rebate would not normally exceed the taxable income from the lease and the restriction would not be relevant.

Solicitor's fees as trustee

Solicitor's fees as trustee were held to be professional receipts (*Jones v Wright* KB 1927, 13 TC 221) even if the solicitor is also a beneficiary (*Watson & Everitt v Blunden* CA 1933, 18 TC 402).

Sub-postmasters

Introductory fees paid by sub-postmasters were held not to be allowable (*Dhendsa v Richardson* (Sp C 134), [1997] SSCD 265).

Timber purchases and sales

For purchases and sales of standing timber by timber merchants see *Murray v CIR* CS 1951, 32 TC 238; *McLellan, Rawson & Co v Newall* Ch D 1955, 36 TC 117; *Hood Barrs v CIR (No 2)* HL 1957, 37 TC 188; *Hopwood v C N Spencer Ltd* Ch D 1964, 42 TC 169; *Russell v Hird and Mercer* Ch D 1983, 57 TC 127. For sales of trees by farmer see *Elmes v Trembath* KB 1934, 19 TC 72.

Trade marks or designs

Expenses are deductible if incurred in obtaining, for the purposes of a trade (not a profession or vocation), the registration of a trade mark or design, the renewal of registration of a trade mark or the extension of the period for which the right in a registered design subsists. [*ITTOIA 2005, s 90*].

Websites

The cost of setting up a website is likely to be capital expenditure; the regular update costs are likely to be revenue expenses (see HMRC Business Income Manual BIM35870).

Patents

[73.99] Expenses (agent's charges, patent office fees etc.) are deductible if incurred in obtaining, for the purposes of a trade (not a profession or vocation), the grant of a patent or the extension of its term or in connection with a rejected or abandoned application for a patent made for the purposes of the trade. [*ITTOIA 2005, s 89*].

For capital expenditure on the purchase of patent rights see **10.35** CAPITAL ALLOWANCES.

Sums received on the sale of patent rights may, dependent on the facts, be trading receipts (*Rees Roturbo Development v Ducker* HL 1928, 13 TC 366; *Brandwood v Banker* KB 1928, 14 TC 44; *CIR v Rustproof Metal Window* CA 1947, 29 TC 243 and cf. *Harry Ferguson (Motors) v CIR* CA(NI) 1951, 33 TC 15). Other sums are taxable under *ITTOIA 2005, ss 587–599*, see **40.6, 40.7** INTELLECTUAL PROPERTY.

Where a company held a patent for renovating car tyres, lump sums received by it under arrangements for giving the payer a *de facto* franchise in his area, were held to be capital receipts (*Margerison v Tyresoles Ltd* KB 1942, 25 TC 59).

Prior to 2007/08, royalties and other sums paid for the use of patents were not deductible in computing trading profits. This restriction is now removed as part of the abolition of the concept of 'charges on income'; see **1.10** ALLOWANCES AND TAX RATES and Change 81 in Annex 1 to the Explanatory Notes to *ITA 2007*. [*ITTOIA 2005, s 51; ITA 2007, Sch 1 para 497*].

For spreading of patent royalties received, see **40.4** INTELLECTUAL PROPERTY and for DTR treatment of royalties from abroad, see **26.9**(i) DOUBLE TAX RELIEF.

For copyright, know-how and trade marks, see **73.51**, **73.91** and **73.98** respectively.

Personal and domestic expenses

[73.100] Expenditure incurred for domestic and private purposes is by its very nature incurred otherwise than wholly and exclusively for business purposes and is thus disallowable by virtue of *ITTOIA 2005, s 34* at **73.36** above.

The 'dual purpose rule' at **73.36** above is relevant here. Hence the cost of treatment at a nursing home was disallowed even though motivated by need for room from which to conduct business (*Murgatroyd v Evans-Jackson* Ch D

1966, 43 TC 581) as was the cost of a minor finger operation to enable a professional guitarist to continue playing as, on the evidence, he also played the guitar as a hobby (*Prince v Mapp* Ch D 1969, 46 TC 169) and expenditure on child care by a graphic designer working from home (*Carney v Nathan* (Sp C 347), [2003] SSCD 28). Medical expenses where illness said to be due to working conditions were not allowed in *Norman v Golder* CA 1944, 26 TC 293. Expenditure on ordinary clothing is not normally allowable, the leading case here being *Mallalieu v Drummond* HL 1983, 57 TC 330, in which, reversing the decisions in the lower Courts, it was held that the cost of sober clothing worn by a lady barrister to comply with Bar Council guidelines was for the dual purpose of her profession and her requirements as a human being, and not allowable. See also **73.36** above and the 'clothing' cases at **27.24 EMPLOYMENT INCOME**. In *Watkis v Ashford, Sparkes and Harward* Ch D 1985, 58 TC 468, expenditure on meals at regular partners' lunchtime meetings was disallowed, whilst expenditure on accommodation, food and drink at the firm's annual weekend conference was allowed.

In *McKnight v Sheppard* HL 1999, 71 TC 419, legal expenses in defending charges brought by a professional regulatory body were allowed despite the fact that the taxpayer's 'personal reputation was inevitably involved'. In *MacKinlay v Arthur Young McClelland Moores & Co* HL 1989, 62 TC 704, contributions towards the removal expenses of a partner moved in the interests of the firm were not allowed. For rent etc. of premises used both as residence and for business see **73.104** below and for travelling and subsistence expenses see **73.122** below. See also *Mason v Tyson* Ch D 1980, 53 TC 333 (expenses of occasional use of flat) and *McLaren v Mumford* Ch D 1996, 69 TC 173 (expenses of residential accommodation required to be occupied with licensed premises).

The personal costs (e.g. accommodation, food and drink) of a UK resident individual of living abroad on business are not disallowed under *ITTOIA 2005, s 34* (HMRC Business Income Manual BIM47710 and HMRC SP A16).

For the 'dual purpose rule' in relation to expenditure with an intrinsic duality of purpose, e.g. food, warmth, health and shelter, see also HMRC Business Income Manual BIM37900–37970.

Simon's Taxes. See B2.318, B2.458.

Pooling of profits

[73.101] Where traders pool profits or act together in consortia but so as not to form **PARTNERSHIPS** (**52**) or trade jointly (cf. *Gardner and Bowring Hardy v CIR* CS 1930, 15 TC 602; *Geo Hall & Son v Platt* Ch D 1954, 35 TC 440) each trader's share of the pooled profits will normally be treated as a receipt of his main trade and any payment under the arrangement by one trader to another will be deductible in computing his profits (*Moore v Stewarts & Lloyds Ltd* CS 1905, 6 TC 501 and cf. *United Steel v Cullington (No 1)* CA 1939, 23 TC 71). In *Utol Ltd v CIR* KB 1943, 25 TC 517 payments by one company to another under a profit sharing arrangement were held to be dividends payable less tax under the law then in force. For compensation received on the termination of a profit sharing arrangement see *Van den Berghs* at **73.48**(b) above.

Pre-trading expenditure

[73.102] The general principle is that trading expenditure is deductible when incurred and hence is not allowable if incurred before trading commenced (cf. *Birmingham & District Cattle By-Products Ltd v CIR* KB 1919, 12 TC 92). The rule is modified for certain pre-trading capital expenditure, including scientific research expenditure and abortive exploration expenditure by mining concerns (see **10 CAPITAL ALLOWANCES**).

However, there is a statutory relief for expenditure incurred by a person within the seven years before he commences to carry on a trade which, had it been incurred on the first day of trading, would have been deductible in computing the profits. The expenditure is treated as if it was incurred on the on the first day of trading and is thus deductible. Expenditure otherwise deductible, e.g. pre-trading purchases of stock or advance payments of rent, is not within this special relief. [*ITTOIA 2005, s 57*].

Property sales and other property receipts

[73.103] As to whether a trade of property dealing carried on, see **73.31** above; for rents receivable, see **73.90** above. For builders and property developers generally, see HMRC Business Income Manual BIM51500–51665.

Sales of property by builders in special circumstances have been considered in a number of cases. Profits held trading receipts in *Spiers & Son v Ogden* KB 1932, 17 TC 117 (building activities extended); *Sharpless v Rees* KB 1940, 23 TC 361 (sale of land acquired for hobby abandoned for health reasons); *Shadford v H Fairweather & Co* Ch D 1966, 43 TC 291 (sale of site after development plan dropped); *Snell v Rosser, Thomas & Co* Ch D 1967, 44 TC 343 (sale of land surplus to requirements); *Bowie v Reg Dunn (Builders)* Ch D 1974, 49 TC 469 (sale of land acquired with business); *Smart v Lowndes* Ch D 1978, 52 TC 436 (sale of land in wife's name). Sales of property built but let meanwhile held trading in *J & C Oliver v Farnsworth* Ch D 1956, 37 TC 51; *James Hobson & Sons v Newall* Ch D 1957, 37 TC 609; *W M Robb Ltd v Page* Ch D 1971, 47 TC 465 and this notwithstanding active building given up (*Speck v Morton* Ch D 1972, 48 TC 476; *Granville Building Co v Oxby* Ch D 1954, 35 TC 245). But in *Harvey v Caulcott* HC 1952, 33 TC 159 the sales were held realisations of investments and in *West v Phillips* Ch D 1958, 38 TC 203 some houses were treated as investments and others as trading stock. See also *Andrew v Taylor* CA 1965, 42 TC 557. Sales of houses retained after business *transferred* held sales of investments in *Bradshaw v Blunden (No 1)* Ch D 1956, 36 TC 397; *Seaward v Varty* CA 1962, 40 TC 523. See also *Hesketh Estates v Craddock* KB 1942, 25 TC 1 (profit on sale of brine baths held trading receipt of mixed business including land development).

For house sales subject to ground rents etc., see *CIR v John Emery & Sons* HL 1936, 20 TC 213; *B G Utting & Co Ltd v Hughes* HL 1940, 23 TC 174; *McMillan v CIR* CS 1942, 24 TC 417; *Heather v Redfern & Sons* KB 1944, 26 TC 119. For ground rents (England) and feu duties (Scotland) there should be credited the lower of their market value and cost, the cost being taken as the proportion of the cost of the land and building in the ratio of the market value to the sum of the market value and the sale price. For ground annuals (Scotland) which are perpetual the realisable value is brought in. The right to receive the rent then becomes part of the fixed capital of the trade, whose subsequent sale is not taken into account for income tax purposes. Any premiums on the grant of leases are part of the sale proceeds.

Turf sales by a farmer were held to be farming receipts in *Lowe v J W Ashmore Ltd* Ch D 1970, 46 TC 597. For timber sales see **73.98** above and for woodlands managed on a commercial basis see **30.45 EXEMPT INCOME**.

A lump sum received by a property investment company in return for the assignment for a five-year term of a stream of rental income was held to be a capital receipt for part disposal of the company's interest (*CIR v John Lewis Properties plc* CA, [2003] STC 117), but see now Tolley's Corporation Tax under Property Income as regards special rent factoring provisions.

Any excess of allowable deductions over rent received by a builder from property held as trading stock may be allowed as a trading expense (HMRC Business Income Manual BIM51555).

See also **4.29 ANTI-AVOIDANCE** for provisions affecting land or land development.

Simon's Taxes. See B5.106, B5.226–B5.232, B9.107.

Rents, premiums etc. for business premises

[73.104] Rents paid for business premises are deductible in computing profits. For repairs see **73.106** below. As regards rents receivable, see **73.90** above.

For allowance for use of home for business, see *Thomas v Ingram* Ch D 1979, 52 TC 428. See also *Mason v Tyson* Ch D 1980, 53 TC 333 (expenses of flat used occasionally to enable professional man to work late not allowed as a deduction).

Where premises became redundant or were closed down, continuing rents (less sub-letting receipts) were allowed as a deduction (*CIR v Falkirk Iron* CS 1933, 17 TC 625; *Hyett v Lennard* KB 1940, 23 TC 346) but not payments to secure the cancellation of leases no longer required (*Mallett v Staveley Coal & Iron* CA 1928, 13 TC 772 (the leading case here); *Cowcher v Richard Mills & Co* KB 1927, 13 TC 216; *Union Cold Storage v Ellerker* KB 1939, 22 TC 547; *Dain v Auto Speedways* Ch D 1959, 38 TC 525; *Bullrun Inc v Inspector of Taxes* (Sp C 248), [2000] SSCD 384). See also *West African Drug Co v Lilley* KB 1947, 28 TC 140. Where the rent of a motorway service station was calculated by reference to takings, a lump sum payment for the exclusion of tobacco duty from takings was held capital (*Tucker v Granada Motorway Services* HL 1979, 53 TC 92), but, distinguishing *Granada Motorways*, an amount received by a company in respect of its agent's negligent failure to serve its landlord with counter-notice of a notice of an increase in its rent, was held to be a trading receipt in *Donald Fisher (Ealing) Ltd v Spencer* CA 1989,

63 TC 168. Rent for a building not required for occupation for business purposes but to control access to the lessee's works was held deductible (less sub-let rents) in *Allied Newspapers v Hindsley* CA 1937, 21 TC 422.

For allowance of a provision in respect of future rents under leases of premises ceasing to be used for business purposes, see *Herbert Smith v Honour* Ch D 1999, 72 TC 130. Following that decision, HMRC changed their opinion and accepted that there is no tax rule denying provisions for anticipated loses or expenses (see Revenue Press Release 20 July 1999).

Additional rent liability incurred to obtain the freehold reversion to premises already rented held capital (*Littlewoods Mail Order v McGregor* CA 1969, 45 TC 519 following *CIR v Land Securities* HL 1969, 45 TC 495), as were periodical payments to reimburse capital expenditure incurred by landlord (*Ainley v Edens* KB 1935, 19 TC 303) and payments based on production for grant of sisal estates (*Ralli Estates v East Africa IT Commr* PC 1961, 40 ATC 9). But payments for the use of a totalisator calculated by reference to its cost were allowed (*Racecourse Betting Control Board v Wild* KB 1938, 22 TC 182) as were rents subject to abatement dependent on profits (*Union Cold Storage v Adamson* HL 1931, 16 TC 293). For Scottish duplicands see *Dow v Merchiston Castle School* CS 1921, 8 TC 149. Rent paid by partnership to partner owning business premises allowed (*Heastie v Veitch & Co* CA 1933, 18 TC 305). For excessive payments to professional 'service company' see *Payne, Stone Fraser* at **52.4 PARTNERSHIPS**.

Rates and council tax

Business rates are deductible in the same way as rent. Council tax may similarly be deducted where it is attributable to premises (or part) used for trade purposes. (Revenue Press Release 16 March 1993).

Premiums

Certain lease premiums etc. in relation to leases not exceeding 50 years are chargeable on the landlord to an extent which varies with the length of the lease (see **60.16 PROPERTY INCOME**). For any part of the 'receipt period' (as defined in *ITTOIA 2005, s 288(6)* — generally the duration of the lease) during which the lessee occupies the premises for the purposes of a trade or (with certain limitations) deals with his interest therein as property employed for the purposes of a trade, he is treated as incurring expenditure of a revenue nature. This is deductible in computing his trading profits, subject to any rule that might prohibit such deduction in a particular case (e.g. the 'wholly and exclusively' rule). For each day of the receipt period on which the above conditions are satisfied, the amount of revenue expenditure treated as incurred is the 'taxed receipt' (as defined in *ITTOIA 2005, s 287(4)* — broadly the amount which falls to be included in computing the landlord's property income) divided by the total number of days in the receipt period. If only part of the leased land is used for trading purposes, the amount is proportionately reduced. The amount is also proportionately reduced to the extent, if any, to which the lessee is entitled to an allowance under *CAA 2001, s 403* (mineral asset expenditure — see **10.25**(b) **CAPITAL ALLOWANCES**).

If the lessee himself grants a sublease out of the leased property at a taxable premium, he is treated as incurring revenue expenditure only to the extent, if any, that the daily amount computed above exceeds the daily reduction in his own taxable premium. For more detail of how this rule operates, see **60.19 PROPERTY INCOME.** If the sublease relates to only part of the premises covered by the main lease, the above rules are applied separately to the different parts of the premises, the premium under the main lease being apportioned between those parts on a just and reasonable basis.

The above rules apply whether the premium is chargeable to income tax or corporation tax in the hands of the landlord. They also apply in relation to leases of property *outside* the UK where the landlord's property business is an overseas property business.

[*ITTOIA 2005, ss 60–67; CTA 2009, Sch 1 paras 591–595*].

Otherwise, lease premiums are not deductible in computing trading profits (cf. *MacTaggart v Strump* CS 1925, 10 TC 17).

In the case of a person dealing in land, there is provision to prevent a lease premium or similar sum being taxed as both (i) a trading receipt and (ii) a receipt of a property business (as in **60.16** *et seq.* **PROPERTY INCOME**). This is achieved by reducing the amount at (i) by the amount at (ii). [*ITTOIA 2005, s 158; CTA 2009, Sch 1 para 602*].

See **73.105** below as regards *reverse* premiums.

General

See **4.30** ANTI-AVOIDANCE regarding restrictions where there is a lease-back at a non-commercial rent and **4.31** ANTI-AVOIDANCE for taxation of capital sums received on certain lease-backs.

Simon's Taxes. See **B2.208, B2.411, B2.447, B2.448, B2.465.**

Reverse premiums

[73.105] In *New Zealand Commissioner of Inland Revenue v Wattie and another* PC 1998, 72 TC 639, it was held that a lump sum paid by a landlord to a prospective tenant as an inducement to enter into a lease at an above-market rental (generally known as a reverse premium) was a receipt of a capital nature. Legislation was introduced in the UK to counter this decision. For the purposes of the legislation, a '*reverse premium*' is a payment or other benefit received by way of inducement in connection with a transaction (the '*property transaction*') entered into by the recipient or a person 'connected' with him (see below), where:

(a)   the property transaction is one under which the recipient or connected person becomes entitled to an estate or interest in, or a right in or over, land; and

(b)   the payment (or other benefit) is made (or provided) by:

(i)   the person (the '*grantor*') by whom that estate, interest or right is granted, or was granted at an earlier time; or

(ii)   a person 'connected' with the grantor; or

(iii) a nominee of (or a person acting on the directions of) the grantor or a person connected with the grantor.

As regards (b)(i) above, the use of the word 'grantor' means that the provisions do not apply when a freehold is conveyed. The most common occasion on which the provisions will apply will be a payment by a landlord as an inducement to a tenant to take a new lease, but they may apply where an existing tenant pays a new tenant an inducement to take over the remaining term of a lease if (and only if) (b)(ii) or (iii) applies to the existing tenant (Revenue Tax Bulletin December 1999 pp 711–713).

For the purposes of these provisions, persons are 'connected' with each other if they are connected within **21 CONNECTED PERSONS** at any time during the period when the 'property arrangements' are entered into. The 'property arrangements' comprise the property transaction and any arrangements entered into in connection with it (whether earlier, simultaneously or later).

A reverse premium is treated for income tax purposes as a receipt of a revenue nature. Where the property transaction is entered into by the recipient of the reverse premium for the purposes of a trade carried on (or to be carried on) by him, the reverse premium must be taken into account in computing the trading profits. In any other case, the reverse premium is to be treated as a receipt of a UK property business, or (as the case may be) an overseas property business (see **60 PROPERTY INCOME**), carried on by the recipient.

It is understood that accountancy principles require the receipt to be brought into account by spreading over the period of the lease or, if shorter, to the first rent review. This treatment must normally be followed for tax purposes (see **73.18** above) but, as an anti-avoidance measure, is overridden where:

(A)   two or more parties to the property arrangements (see above) are connected persons (see above); and

(B)   the terms of the those arrangements differ significantly from those which, at that time and under prevailing market conditions, would be regarded as reasonable and normal between persons dealing at arm's length in the open market.

In such case, the full amount or value of the reverse premium must be brought into account in the period of account in which the property transaction (see above) is entered into or, where applicable, the first period of account of the trade which the recipient subsequently begins to carry on.

None of these provisions apply where the recipient is an individual and the property in question is, or will be, occupied by him as his only or main residence. Nor do they apply to the extent that the payment or benefit is consideration for the first leg of a sale and leaseback arrangement within **4.30** or **4.31 ANTI-AVOIDANCE** or is taken into account under *CAA 2001, s 532* (contributions to expenditure) to reduce the recipient's expenditure qualifying for capital allowances (see **10.2**(vi) **CAPITAL ALLOWANCES**).

[*ITTOIA 2005, ss 99–103; CTA 2010, Sch 1 para 445; TIOPA 2010, Sch 8 para 255*].

It will be seen that a reverse premium within the above provisions is not confined to a lump sum payment and that 'other benefit' may include, for example, a contribution to the tenant's costs or an assumption of the recipient's liabilities under an existing lease. 'Other benefit' must, however, represent money or something capable of being turned into money. It does not include a sum foregone or deferred by the provider, rather than actually expended, such as a rent free period. See the article in the Revenue Tax Bulletin December 1999 pp 711–713, in particular in relation to the meeting of the tenant's costs.

Payment of reverse premium

The payment of a reverse premium by a company to achieve the assignment of a lease which had become disadvantageous (due to the company's failure to meet its obligations under a repairing covenant) was held to be on capital account (*Southern Counties Agricultural Trading Society Ltd v Blackler* (Sp C 198), [1999] SSCD 200). HMRC take the view that where a reverse premium is paid by a developer trading in property, it is deductible in computing his trading profits (Revenue Press Release 9 March 1999).

For HMRC's approach to these rules, see HMRC Business Income Manual BIM41050–41145.

Simon's Taxes. See B9.235, B6.205.

Repairs and renewals

[73.106] Any allowable expenditure is deductible in the period when incurred and not when the repairs etc. accrued (*Naval Colliery Co Ltd v CIR* HL 1928, 12 TC 1017). Provisions for future repairs and renewals were held not allowable in *Clayton v Newcastle-under-Lyme Corpn* QB 1888, 2 TC 416 and *Peter Merchant Ltd v Stedeford* CA 1948, 30 TC 496, but see now **73.18** above, and HMRC Business Income Manual BIM46515, 46901, for the wider current acceptance of the application of normal accountancy principles in this context. Hence a provision for regular major overhaul work accrued due on aircraft engines was allowed as a deduction in *Johnston v Britannia Airways Ltd* Ch D 1994, 67 TC 99 (but see now Revenue Tax Bulletin February 1999 p 624 as regards changes in accounting practice superseding this decision). See also **73.107** below.

No deduction is available for expenditure incurred after 5 April 2008 on providing or replacing an integral feature of a building or structure if the expenditure is qualifying expenditure for plant and machinery capital allowances purposes. [*ITTOIA 2005, s 55A; FA 2008, s 73(4)(6)*]. See **11.11** CAPITAL ALLOWANCES ON PLANT AND MACHINERY.

See generally HMRC Business Income Manual BIM46900–46970.

Simon's Taxes. See B2.409, B2.411, B2.466.

Business premises

[73.107] The general rule is that expenditure on additions, alterations, expansions or improvements is capital but the cost of repairs, i.e. restoring a building to its original condition, is allowable. However, the use of modern materials in repairing an old building does not make the expenditure capital (*Conn v Robins Bros Ltd* Ch D 1966, 43 TC 266), and HMRC now consider that this applies to the replacement of single-glazed windows by double-glazed equivalents (see Revenue Tax Bulletin June 2002 p 936). If the expenditure is capital, the estimated cost of 'notional repairs' obviated by the work is not allowable (see *Wm P Lawrie* and *Thomas Wilson (Keighley)* below).

Where on taking a lease of dilapidated property the dilapidations were made good under a covenant in the lease, the cost was held disallowable as attributable to the previous use of the premises (*Jackson v Laskers Home Furnishers* Ch D 1956, 37 TC 69) but when cinemas were acquired in a state of disrepair (but still fit for public showings) because of war-time restrictions on building work, the cost of the repairs was allowed (*Odeon Associated Theatres Ltd v Jones* CA 1971, 48 TC 257). See also **73.108** below. In practice, expenditure on repairing and redecorating newly acquired premises is allowed unless abnormal (and likely to be reflected in the purchase price or rent payable). See generally HMRC Business Income Manual BIM46906.

A renewal of a building, i.e. a complete re-construction, is capital (*Fitzgerald v CIR Supreme Court* (IFS) 1925, 5 ATC 414; *Wm P Lawrie v CIR* CS 1952, 34 TC 20). The cost of rebuilding a factory chimney was held capital in *O'Grady v Bullcroft Main Collieries* KB 1932, 17 TC 93 but allowed in *Samuel Jones & Co v CIR* CS 1951, 32 TC 513 where the chimney was an integral part of the building. For roof replacements see *Wm P Lawrie* (above) and *Thos Wilson (Keighley) v Emmerson* Ch D 1960, 39 TC 360. The replacement of the ring in a cattle auction mart and of a stand in a football ground were held not to be repairs in *Wynne-Jones v Bedale Auction Ltd* Ch D 1976, 51 TC 426 and *Brown v Burnley Football Co Ltd* Ch D 1980, 53 TC 357 respectively in which the problem is reviewed.

Cost of barrier against coastal erosion held to be capital (*Avon Beach & Cafe v Stewart* HC 1950, 31 TC 487); also replacing a canal embankment (*Phillips v Whieldon Sanitary Potteries* HC 1952, 33 TC 213) and building new access road (*Pitt v Castle Hill Warehousing* Ch D 1974, 49 TC 638).

For a modern case (involving the insertion of plastic pipes within dilapidated metal ones over substantial lengths of a gas pipe network, held to be capital), see *Auckland Gas Co Ltd v CIR* PC, [2000] STC 527. *Auckland Gas* was considered but distinguished in *Transco plc v Dyall* (Sp C 310), [2002] SSCD 199, in which the insertion of plastic pipes in cast iron ones was on a selective basis and had not changed the character of the pipeline system as a whole.

Dilapidations of a repair nature on the termination of a lease are generally deductible.

For repairs to tied premises see **73.41** above.

Disability Discrimination Act 1995 requires service providers to make 'reasonable adjustments' to their premises to tackle any physical features that prevent disabled people from using their services. Whilst this does not give rise to any substantive changes to pre-existing tax treatment, HMRC published online some related guidance covering such matters as ramps, toilets and washing facilities, signs, hand rails, lighting, doors, lifts, steps and stairs, alterations to walls and floors, car parks and paths. See www.hmrc.gov.uk/sp ecialist/disability-act-guidance.htm.

Provisions for future expenditure

HMRC once considered that no deduction was available for such provisions (see HMRC Business Income Manual BIM46901). An Inland Revenue contention to this effect was rejected by the Special Commissioners in *Jenners Princes Street Edinburgh Ltd v CIR* (Sp C 166), [1998] SSCD 196. HMRC now accept that provisions properly made under Financial Reporting Standard 12 are tax deductible except where there is an express rule to the contrary (e.g. provisions for capital expenditure). (Revenue Press Release 20 July 1999). FRS 12 imposes a requirement that for a provision to be allowable:

- it must be a present obligation (either legal or constructive) as a result of a past event;
- it must be probable that a transfer of economic benefits will be required to settle the obligation; and
- it must be possible to make a reliable estimate of the amount of that obligation.

See Revenue Tax Bulletin April 1999 pp 636–639, December 1999 pp 707–709. It should be noted that HMRC's opinion is that *Jenners* would have been decided differently if FRS 12 had been in operation at the time (see HMRC Business Income Manual BIM46550).

Plant and other business assets

[73.108] The general rules at **73.107** above apply also to plant but with the modification that expenditure on the renewal of plant may be allowed as a deduction as an alternative to capital allowances. For this see **11.68 CAPITAL ALLOWANCES ON PLANT AND MACHINERY**. Replacements and alterations of trade tools (meaning any implement, utensil or article) are allowable deductions notwithstanding the fact that the expenditure would otherwise be capital. [*ITTOIA 2005, s 68*]. The cost of initial and additional tools is capital and not deductible but may well attract plant and machinery capital allowances.

For repairs soon after the acquisition of an asset see *Law Shipping v CIR* CS 1923, 12 TC 621 and *CIR v Granite City SS Co* CS 1927, 13 TC 1 in which the cost of repairs to ships attributable to their use before acquisition, was held capital. But see *Odeon Associated Theatres* at **73.107** above in which *Law Shipping* was distinguished. See also *Bidwell v Gardiner* Ch D 1960, 39 TC 31 in which the replacement of the furnishings of a newly acquired hotel was held capital.

Expenditure on renewal of railway tracks was allowed in *Rhodesia Railways v Bechuanaland Collector* PC 1933, 12 ATC 223, distinguishing *Highland Railway v Balderston* CES 1889, 2 TC 485 in which held capital. Abnormal expenditure on dredging a channel to a shipyard was held capital in *Ounsworth v Vickers Ltd* KB 1915, 6 TC 671 but the cost to a Harbour Board of removing a wreck (*Whelan v Dover Harbour Board* CA 1934, 18 TC 555) and of renewing moorings (*In re King's Lynn Harbour* CES 1875, 1 TC 23) was allowed. For shop fittings see *Eastmans Ltd v Shaw* HL 1928, 14 TC 218; *Hyam v CIR* CS 1929, 14 TC 479. See also *Lothian Chemical v Rogers* CS 1926, 11 TC 508.

Assets held under an operating lease

A deduction may be allowed for a provision to cover future repairs of assets held under an operating lease which contains a repairing obligation (for example, tenants' repairing leases of property). The obligation, required under FRS 12 (see **73.107** above), subsists from the signing of the lease. (HMRC Business Income Manual BIM46535). It is unlikely the Inland Revenue would have accepted such a deduction prior to the decision in *Jenners* at **73.107** above.

Research and development and scientific research

[73.109] Revenue expenditure incurred by a trader on 'research and development' related to his trade, whether undertaken directly or on his behalf, is allowable as a deduction in computing profits. Expenditure incurred in the acquisition of rights in, or arising out of, the research and development is excluded, but the allowable expenditure otherwise includes all expenditure incurred in, or providing facilities for, carrying it out. Research and development 'related' to a trade includes any which may lead to or facilitate an extension of the trade, or which is of a medical nature and has a special relation to the welfare of workers employed in the trade. These provisions apply equally to expenditure on oil and gas exploration and appraisal (within *ITA 2007, s 1003*).

A deduction is similarly allowed for any sum paid to an approved scientific research association having as its object 'scientific research' related (with the extended meaning given above) to the class of trade concerned, and for any sum paid to an approved university, college research institute etc. to be used for such research. '*Scientific research*' means any activities in the fields of natural or applied science for the extension of knowledge. Any question as to what constitutes scientific research is to be referred by HMRC to the Secretary of State, whose decision is final. In relation to sums paid to a scientific research association in an accounting period of the association beginning on or after 1 January 2008 (see *SI 2007 No 3424*), these provisions, insofar as they apply to sums paid to such associations, are amended in line with amendments made to the tax legislation granting exemption to scientific research associations (see Tolley's Corporation Tax under Exempt Organisations). The scientific research association to which the sum is paid no longer has to be approved, but it does have to be potentially within the exemption for such associations at *CTA 2010, s 469*; and it must have as its object the undertaking of 'research and development' which may lead to or facilitate an extension of the class of trade to which the payer's trade belongs.

The above reliefs are *not* available to professions or vocations.

[ITTOIA 2005, ss 87, 88; ITA 2007, Sch 1 para 499; CTA 2009, Sch 1 para 600].

'*Research and development*' means activities that fall to be treated as such in accordance with generally accepted accounting practice (see **73.18** above). However, this is subject to Treasury regulations which narrow the definition by reference to guidelines issued by the Department of Trade and Industry (DTI). *[ITA 2007, s 1006; ICTA 1988, s 837A].* The latest regulations refer to DTI guidelines issued on 5 March 2004 (for which see www.dti.gov.uk/support/r d-guidelines-2004.htm). *[SI 2004 No 712].*].

For *capital expenditure* on research and development, see **10.37** CAPITAL ALLOWANCES.

Security (personal)

[73.110] If an individual carries on a trade (either alone or as a member of a partnership of individuals) and there is a special threat to his personal physical security arising wholly or mainly because of the trade, expenditure incurred in connection with his use, or the provision for him, of a service or asset to meet that threat is not subject to the 'wholly and exclusively' rule at **73.36** above (and may therefore be deductible in computing profits), subject to the following conditions.

- In the case of a service, the benefit to the trader must consist wholly or mainly of an improvement to his personal physical security.
- In the case of an asset, the person incurring the expenditure must intend the asset to be used to improve personal physical security. If he intends it to be solely used for that purpose, any incidental use of the asset may be disregarded. If he intends it to be only partly used for that purpose, the potential deduction is restricted to the appropriate proportion of the expenditure.

The fact that a member of the trader's family or household also benefits from improved personal physical security does not preclude the potential deduction.

An 'asset' for these purposes includes equipment and a structure (e.g. a wall), but does not include a car, ship or aircraft. It is immaterial whether or not the asset becomes fixed to land and whether or not the trader acquires the property in the asset or (in the case of a fixture) an estate or interest in the land. But the provision or use of a dwelling or grounds appurtenant to a dwelling are excluded from the relief.

[ITTOIA 2005, s 81].

See also **11.9** CAPITAL ALLOWANCES ON PLANT AND MACHINERY, **27.73** EMPLOYMENT INCOME.

Simon's Taxes. See B2.471.

Shares and securities

[73.111] For whether a trade of 'share dealing' carried on see **73.32** above.

Profits and losses on realisations of investments by a bank in the course of its business enter into its *Schedule D, Case I* profits (*Punjab Co-operative Bank v Lahore IT Commr* PC 1940, 19 ATC 533 and see *Frasers (Glasgow) Bank v CIR* HL 1963, 40 TC 698) and similarly for insurance companies (*Northern Assce Co v Russell* CES 1889, 2 TC 551; *General Reinsurance Co v Tomlinson* Ch D 1970, 48 TC 81 and contrast *CIR v Scottish Automobile* CS 1931, 16 TC 381). Profits/losses held capital in *Stott v Hoddinott* KB 1916, 7 TC 85 (investments acquired by architect to secure contracts); *Jacobs Young & Co v Harris* KB 1926, 11 TC 221 (shares held by merchanting company in subsidiary wound up); *Alliance & Dublin Consumers' Gas Co v Davis* HC(IFS) 1926, 5 ATC 717 (investments of gas company earmarked for reserve fund). A profit by a property dealing company on the sale of shares acquired in connection with a property transaction was held a trading receipt (*Associated London Properties v Henriksen* CA 1944, 26 TC 46) but contrast *Fundfarms Developments v Parsons* Ch D 1969, 45 TC 707 and see now **4 ANTI-AVOIDANCE**.

Shares allotted for mining concessions granted by company dealing in concessions held trading receipts at market value (*Gold Coast Selection Trust v Humphrey* HL 1948, 30 TC 209). See also *Murphy v Australian Machinery & Investment Co* CA 1948, 30 TC 244 and *Scottish & Canadian Investment Co v Easson* CS 1922, 8 TC 265.

For options, see *Varty v British South Africa Co* HL 1965, 42 TC 406 (no profits or loss until shares sold). See also *Walker v Cater Securities* Ch D 1974, 49 TC 625.

Conversion etc. of shares and securities held as circulating capital

Where a new holding of shares or securities (as defined) is issued in exchange for an original holding a profit on sale of which would fall to be treated as part of trading profits, the transaction is treated as not involving any disposal of the original holding, the new holding being treated as the same asset as the original holding. This applies only to transactions which result in the new holding being equated with the original holding under *TCGA 1992, ss 132–136* (capital gains rollover in cases of conversion etc.) or *TCGA 1992, s 134* (compensation stock). The above rule does not apply to shares or securities for which unrealised profits or losses (computed on a mark to market basis by reference to fair value) are brought into account in the period of account in which the transaction takes place. Where consideration is receivable in addition to the new holding, the above rule applies only to a proportion of the original holding, computed by reference to the market value of the new holding and the other consideration received. [*ITTOIA 2005, s 150; FA 2009, Sch 22 paras 11(3), 12*].

Gilt-edged securities — stripping and consolidation

Where the profit on the sale of a gilt-edged security (as defined) or strips (as defined) of a gilt-edged security would fall to be brought into account in computing the profits of a trade, there are special provisions dealing with the exchange of such a security for strips of the security and *vice versa*. On an exchange for strips, the security is treated as having been redeemed at its market value, and the strips as having been acquired at that market value apportioned *pro rata* to their market value at the time of the exchange. Similarly on a consolidation, each strip is treated as having been redeemed at its market value, and the security as having been acquired at the aggregate market value of the strips. The Treasury may make regulations for determining market value for these purposes.

The above rules on conversion etc. of securities held as circulating capital do not apply where these provisions apply. These provisions have the opposite effect as they effectively require a profit on the exchange to be brought into account for tax purposes.

[*ITTOIA 2005, ss 151–154*].

Stock lending fees

Such fees relating to investments eligible for relief under *FA 2004, s 186* (pension scheme funds — see **57.6, 57.32 PENSION PROVISION**) are themselves eligible for relief under that *section*. [*ICTA 1988, s 129B*].

Dealers in securities

Any distribution by a UK resident company (or payment representative of such a distribution) *received by* a dealer in securities is taken into account (exclusive of any tax credit) in computing the dealer's trading profits. This takes precedence over the normal charge on dividends at **64.7 SAVINGS AND INVESTMENT INCOME.** The exclusion of the tax credit does not apply in the case of **UNDERWRITERS AT LLOYD'S (74)**. Any payment *made by* a dealer which is representative of a UK company distribution is similarly brought into the computation of trading profits.

[*ITTOIA 2005, ss 366(1), 398(2)*].

In cases where, in accordance with generally accepted accounting practice (see **73.18** above), profits and losses on the sale of securities are calculated by reference to the fair value of the securities and taken to reserves rather than profit or loss account, they are nevertheless brought into account in computing trading profits. [*ITTOIA 2005, s 149; FA 2009, Sch 22 paras 11(3), 12*].

FISMA levies

A deduction is available for certain levies payable under *Financial Services and Markets Act 2000* ('FISMA') where, exceptionally, such levies would not otherwise be deductible. A deduction is also available for payments made as a result of an award of costs under costs rules (as defined). Certain repayments under FISMA must be brought into account as a trading receipt. [*ITTOIA 2005, s 155; Financial Services and Markets Act 2000, s 411; CTA 2009, Sch 1 para 601*].

Extra return on new issues of securities

Where:

(a) securities of a particular kind are issued (being the original issue of securities of that kind);

(b)   new securities of the same kind are issued subsequently;

(c)   a sum (the 'extra return') is payable by the issuer in respect of the new securities, to reflect the fact that interest is accruing on the old securities and calculated accordingly; and

(d)   the issue price of the new securities includes an element (separately identified or not) representing payment for the extra return,

the extra return is treated for income tax purposes as a payment of interest (so far as it would not otherwise be treated as such), but the issuer is not entitled to tax relief, either as a deduction in computing profits or otherwise as a deduction or set-off, for the payment. [*ITA 2007, ss 845, 846; ICTA 1988, s 587A*].

General

See also **4.2–4.5** ANTI-AVOIDANCE (transactions in securities to obtain tax advantage).

Stock and work in progress

[73.112] See generally HMRC Business Income Manual BIM33000–33630. Following the adoption of the rule that GAAP be adhered to in computing taxable profits (see **73.18** above), HMRC Statement of Practice SP 3/90 (to which references are made below) was generally superseded and was accordingly withdrawn. However, the principles drawn from that Statement continue to be relevant for subsequent accounting periods (except as referred to below).

Basis of valuation

The general rule has long been that stock is to be valued at the lower of cost and market value. Leading cases are *Minister of National Revenue v Anaconda American Brass Co* PC 1955, 34 ATC 330 and *BSC Footwear v Ridgway* HL 1971, 47 TC 495. Market value held to be replacement price for a merchant (*Brigg Neumann & Co v CIR* KB 1928, 12 TC 1191) and retail price for a retailer in *BSC Footwear* above (Inland Revenue prepared to take price net of any selling commission). Stock may be valued partly at cost and partly at market value where lower (*CIR v Cock Russell & Co* KB 1949, 29 TC 387). The base stock method is not permissible (*Patrick v Broadstone Mills* CA 1953, 35 TC 44) nor is 'LIFO' (*Anaconda American Brass* above). See also *Ryan v Asia Mill* HL 1951, 32 TC 275. The cost should include as a minimum the cost of materials and direct labour but the accounts treatment of overheads is normally accepted (*Duple Motor Bodies v Ostime* HL 1961, 39 TC 537).

However, HMRC now take the view that any valuation of stock included in financial statements prepared in accordance with generally accepted accounting practice (see **73.18** above) should be accepted provided that:

- it reflects the correct application of the principles of normal accountancy;
- the method pays sufficient regard to the facts; and
- the basis does not violate the taxing statutes as interpreted by the courts.

(HMRC Business Income Manual BIM33115).

A mark to market basis of valuation, used mainly by financial institutions and commodity dealers and under which stock is valued at market value, may also be acceptable (HMRC Business Income Manual BIM33160).

The principal accounting standard governing stock is SSAP 9.

For the use of formulae in computing stock provisions and write-downs, see Revenue Tax Bulletin December 1994 p 184. Broadly, HMRC will accept formulae which reflect a realistic appraisal of future income from the particular category of stock and which result in the stock being included at a reasonable estimate of net realisable value. Where computations are accepted without enquiry, it is on the assumption that profits are arrived at in accordance with such principles.

For the treatment of depreciation taken into account in arriving at stock valuations, see Revenue Tax Bulletin June 2002 pp 936, 937.

For motor dealer stock valuations, see Revenue Tax Bulletin August 1994 p 156.

As regards valuation of professional work in progress, it is understood that, subject to the introduction of UITF Abstract 40 (see below), the following principles were, in broad terms, accepted by HMRC:

- nothing should be included for partners' time;
- direct employment costs of fee-earners and direct overheads applicable, such as secretarial salaries, stationery, telephone costs etc. should be included;
- general production overheads for general office areas, conference rooms etc. should be excluded, whilst those for individual office areas directly applicable should be discounted by, say, 30% for non-productive time; and
- contingent fees should be included.

(Taxation Magazine, 30 April 1998, p 126).

For a discussion on the application of GAAP to the valuation of the work in progress of a contractor in the construction industry, see *Smith v HMRC* FTT (TC 403), 2010 STI 1672.

UITF Abstract 40

UITF (Urgent Issues Task Force) Abstract 40, an accounting statement published on 10 March 2005 (see www.frc.org.uk/images/uploaded/documents/UITF%2040.pdf), changed the way that all service providers (not just those providing professional services) must account for uncompleted (and unbilled) work at the year end. The accounting treatment required by the Abstract is to be adopted in financial statements relating to accounting periods ending on or after 22 June 2005 (though earlier adoption was encouraged). Under the Abstract, firms must recognise turnover in respect of ongoing work by reference to the proportion of the work completed, rather than only when the contract is completed. This may require, for example, the bringing into account of a sole proprietor's (or partner's) own time (at its charge-out value) as well as that of his staff. ICAEW guidance on the application of Abstract 40 can be downloaded at www.icaew.co.uk/index.cfm?route=142496. See also HMRC Business Income Manual BIM74201–74275. Owing to the requirement that taxable trading or professional profits be computed in accordance with generally accepted accounting practice (see **73.18** above), the change of accounting basis will have impacted on taxable profits and was likely to result in a one-off uplift. Legislation is included in *FA 2006* to enable the uplift to be spread over more than one year for tax purposes — see **73.115** below. However, spreading relief is not available for businesses that voluntarily adopted the new accounting treatment in periods ended *before* 22 June 2005.

Changes in basis of valuation

Where the stock was found to be grossly undervalued it was held that an assessment to rectify the closing undervaluation must be reduced by the opening undervaluation to bring out the true profits (*Bombay IT Commr v Ahmedabad New Cotton Mills Co* PC 1929, 9 ATC 574). But where a company altered its method of dealing with accrued profits on long-term contracts and the closing work in progress in the year 1 accounts on the old basis was substantially below the opening figure in the year 2 accounts on the new basis, held, distinguishing *Ahmedabad*, the difference must be included in the year 2 profits (*Pearce v Woodall-Duckham Ltd* CA 1978, 51 TC 271). See also HMRC SP 3/90.

Where there is a change in the basis of valuation, the following practice is applied for tax purposes. If the bases of valuation both before and after the change are valid bases, the opening figure for the period of change must be the same as the closing figure for the preceding period. If the change is from an invalid basis to a valid one, the opening figure for the period of change must be arrived at on the same basis as the closing figure for that period, and liabilities for earlier years will be reviewed where it is possible to do so. (HMRC SP 3/90 and see now HMRC Business Income Manual BIM33199). See, however, *Woodall-Duckham Ltd* (above) as regards long-term contracts.

Valuation of stock and work in progress on cessation of trade

See **81.93A** below.

Long-term contracts

HMRC accept that accurate provisions for foreseen losses on long-term contracts (e.g. in the construction industry) made in accordance with correct accounting practice are tax deductible. (Revenue Press Release 20 July 1999 and see HMRC Business Income Manual BIM33025).

In *Symons v Weeks and Others* Ch D 1982, 56 TC 630, it was held that progress payments under the long-term contracts of a firm of architects did not fall to be brought into account for tax before the relevant contract was completed, notwithstanding that they exceeded the figure brought in for work in progress, calculated on the correct principles of commercial accounting.

See above for changes of basis.

What constitutes stock

The provisions in *ITTOIA 2005, ss 172A–172F* have their own definition of stock (see **73.114** below). For other purposes, case law applies as follows. Greyhounds kept by greyhound racing company not trading stock (*Abbot v Albion Greyhounds (Salford)* KB 1945, 26 TC 390). Payments by cigarette manufacturer for cropping trees (not owned by it) for leaves used in manufacture, held to be for materials (*Mohanlal Hargovind of Jubbulpore v IT Commr* PC 1949, 28 ATC 287). For payments for unworked minerals, sand and gravel etc., (including tailings etc.) by mines, quarries etc. see **73.97** above. For payments for oil by oil companies, see *Hughes v British Burmah Petroleum* KB 1932, 17 TC 286; *New Zealand Commr v Europa Oil (NZ)* PC 1970, 49 ATC 282; *Europa Oil (NZ) v New Zealand Commr* PC, [1976] STC 37. For timber see **73.98** above and *Coates v Holker Estates Co Ch D 1961, 40 TC 75*.

Trading stock acquired or disposed of other than in the course of trade

See 81.93B below.

Goods sold subject to reservation of title etc.

Where the supplier of goods reserves the title in them until payment is made (as a protection should the buyer become insolvent) and meanwhile the goods are treated by both parties for accountancy purposes as having been sold/purchased, HMRC will follow the accounts treatment (HMRC SP B6). See Note A of Financial Reporting Standard No 5 and HMRC Business Income Manual BIM33375.

Goods on consignment stock are normally treated as stock in the hands of the supplier until disposed of by the consignee (e.g. sale or return) (HMRC SP B6).

For **forward contracts**, see **73.50** above.

Insurance recoveries

See **73.88** above.

Recovery of assets under Proceeds of Crime Act

Where the transfer of trading stock is a *Pt 5* transfer under *Proceeds of Crime Act 2002* (as in **10.2**(x) CAPITAL ALLOWANCES) and the stock is to be treated, as a result of the transfer, as if sold in the course of the trade, it is treated, for the purpose of computing taxable profits and notwithstanding *ITTOIA 2005, s 173* at **73.113** below (if applicable), as sold at cost price. [*Proceeds of Crime Act 2002, Sch 10 para 11; CTA 2009, Sch 1 para 547(3)*].

Valuation of stock and work in progress on cessation of trade

[73.113] If a person permanently ceases to carry on a trade, any 'trading stock' at cessation must be valued as set out in (a) and (b) below in computing taxable profits. This does not apply on the death of a sole trader (see also below for HMRC practice where the trade continues); neither does it apply on a change in the persons carrying on the trade which does not fall to be treated as a cessation (see **52.7 PARTNERSHIPS**). '*Trading stock*' is widely defined for these purposes by *ITTOIA 2005, s 174* and includes any work in progress of a trade (though not of a profession or vocation, for which see below).

(a) If the trading stock at cessation is sold to a person carrying on (or intending to carry on) a trade, profession or vocation in the UK who can deduct the cost as an expense for income tax or corporation tax purposes, the stock is valued at the amount realised on the sale. If, however, the two parties to the sale are connected persons (defined more broadly than in **21 CONNECTED PERSONS** — see *ITTOIA 2005, s 179*), arm's length value is to be taken instead. (Neither rule applies to a transfer of farm animals where the anti-avoidance rules at **33.8 HERD BASIS** apply.) If the stock is sold with other assets, the amount realised is arrived at on a just and reasonable apportionment. For the purposes of these rules, a 'sale' includes a transfer for valuable consideration, with related expressions then being defined accordingly. Where arm's length value exceeds both (i) actual sale price and (ii) acquisition value (broadly, the amount that would have been deductible in respect of the stock had it been sold in the course of trade immediately before cessation), connected persons may jointly elect to substitute the greater of (i) and (ii) for the arm's length value. The election must be made no later than the first anniversary of 31 January following the tax year in which the cessation occurred.

The cost of the trading stock to the buyer is taken to be the value determined under the above rules (or the corresponding corporation tax rules) in relation to the seller.

Any question as to the application of these rules is to be determined in the same way as an appeal.

These rules are not applicable to woodlands managed on a commercial basis (*Coates v Holker Estates* above). For their application to 'hire-purchase debts' see *Lions Ltd v Gosford Furnishing Co Ltd & CIR* CS 1961, 40 TC 256. A contention by the Inland Revenue that the rules did not apply to a transfer of closing stock simultaneous to a cessation was rejected in *Moore v Mackenzie* Ch D 1971, 48 TC 196.

(b) In all cases not within (a) above, trading stock is to be valued at the price it would have realised if sold in the open market at the time of the cessation.

The above provisions are disapplied in relation to any trading stock if a transfer pricing adjustment (see **4.18** *et seq.* **ANTI-AVOIDANCE**) falls to be made in connection with any provision made or imposed in relation to that stock and having effect in connection with the cessation.

Similar rules as above apply in relation to '*work in progress*' (as defined by *ITTOIA 2005, s 183*) on cessation of a profession or vocation, except that there is no special rule for a transfer of work in progress to a connected person. Additionally, an election is available to the effect that, in computing profits to the date of cessation, closing work in progress is valued at cost and any realised excess over cost is then treated as a post-cessation receipt (see **59.1 POST-CESSATION RECEIPTS AND EXPENDITURE**); the election must be made no later than the first anniversary of 31 January following the tax year in which the cessation occurred. Again, the rules do not apply either on the death of a sole practitioner etc. or on a change in the persons carrying on a profession which does not fall to be treated as a cessation.

[*ITTOIA 2005, ss 173–186; ITA 2007, Sch 1 para 501; CTA 2009, Sch 1 paras 605–610; TIOPA 2010, Sch 8 para 121; SI 2009 No 56, Sch 1 para 439*].

If, following the death of a sole trader, the executors continue trading, or if the business passes direct to a beneficiary, the opening stock can be brought in at market value even if valued at cost on death (HMRC Business Income Manual BIM33520).

See ICAEW Technical Release TAX 7/95, 15 February 1995, for a guidance note on the taxation implications of various treatments of transfers of work in progress and debtors on incorporation of a professional partnership.

Trading stock acquired or disposed of other than in the course of trade

[73.114] The tax treatment of changes in trading stock on or after 12 March 2008 are placed on a statutory footing. (See below for the case law that previously established the correct tax treatment.) These provisions cover:

(i)   trading stock appropriated by the trader for another purpose (e.g. for his own consumption), in which case market value is brought into account as a receipt on the date of appropriation and any actual consideration received is left out of account;

(ii)   items owned by the trader otherwise than as trading stock being appropriated to trading stock, in which case the cost for tax purposes (treated as incurred at the time it became trading stock) is the market value of the item on the date it became trading stock, with any actual value given for it being left out of account;

(iii)   trading stock disposed of otherwise than in the course of a trade where (i) above does not apply, in which case market value is brought into account as a receipt on the date of disposal and any actual consideration is left out of account;

(iv)   trading stock acquired other than in the course of a trade where (ii) above does not apply, in which case the cost for tax purposes (treated as incurred at time of acquisition) is the market value of the item at time of acquisition, with any actual value given for it being left out of account.

Where they have effect, the transfer pricing rules at **4.18** *et seq*. **ANTI-AVOIDANCE** take precedence over (iii) and (iv) above.

For these purposes only, trading stock is defined as stock held for sale in the course of a trade, or partially completed or immature items which are intended for sale when complete or mature. It does not include materials used for manufacture etc., services carried out in the course of a trade or materials used in the performance of these services.

[*ITTOIA 2005, ss 172A–172F; FA 2008, s 37, Sch 15 para 2; TIOPA 2010, Sch 8 para 121*].

Case law

Where trading stock is disposed of otherwise than by way of trade, the realisable value is to be credited for tax purposes. This was established by *Sharkey v Wernher* HL 1955, 36 TC 275 approving *Watson Bros v Hornby* KB 1942, 24 TC 506. It applies, *inter alia*, to goods taken out of stock by a retailer for his own use (see below). It was applied in *Petrotim Securities Ltd v Ayres* CA 1963, 41 TC 389 to a disposal of shares at gross under-value as part of a tax avoidance scheme, but in *Ridge Securities Ltd v CIR* Ch D 1963, 44 TC 373, dealing with the other end of the same scheme, it was held that the same principle applied to acquisitions of trading stock otherwise than by way of trade, market price being substituted for the actual purchase price. But the principle is not applicable to sales or purchases by way of trade notwithstanding not at arm's length. Hence when a share dealing company acquired shares at substantial overvalue from an associated company, the claim by the Inland Revenue for market value failed (*Craddock v Zevo Finance Co* HL 1946, 27 TC 267), and when a property dealing company acquired property from its controlling shareholder at substantial undervalue, its claim to substitute market value failed (*Jacgilden (Weston Hall) v Castle* Ch D 1969, 45 TC 685). See also *Skinner v Berry Head Lands* Ch D 1970, 46 TC 377 and *Kilmorie (Aldridge) v Dickinson* HL 1974, 50 TC 1.

The leading case of *Sharkey v Wernher* above established the principle that stock taken for own use or disposed of otherwise than by sale in the normal course of trade should be treated as if it were a sale at market value. HMRC officers have been authorised to take a reasonably broad view in applying this principle. The case is not considered to apply to:

(a)   services rendered to the trader personally or to his household the cost of which should be disallowed under the 'wholly and exclusively' rule at **73.36** above;

(b)   the value of meals provided for proprietors of hotels, boarding houses, restaurants etc. and members of their families, the cost of which should be disallowed as in (a) above;

(c)   expenditure incurred by a trader on the construction of an asset which is to be used as a fixed asset in the trade.

(HMRC SP A32).

General

For HMRC's view of the application of normal trading income principles to donations of trading stock to charities, see Revenue Tax Bulletin June 1996 p 319.

Where a chargeable gain or allowable loss would otherwise arise for capital gains tax purposes under *TCGA 1992, s 161(1)* on the appropriation to trading stock of an asset held in another capacity, the trader may elect for the market value of the asset to be reduced for income tax purposes by the amount of the chargeable gain (or increased by the amount of the allowable loss), the trading profits being computed accordingly and the appropriation being disregarded for capital gains tax purposes. The election must be made within twelve months after 31 January following the tax year in which ends the period of account in which the asset is appropriated. [*TCGA 1992, s 161(3)(3A)*].

Spreading of UITF Abstract 40 adjustment

[73.115] Described below are the spreading rules referred to in **73.112** above (insofar as they apply for income tax purposes) in relation to the one-off adjustment arising from the adoption, for a period of account ending on or after 22 June 2005, of UITF Abstract 40, which alters the manner in which service providers must account for uncompleted work. See also HMRC Business Income Manual BIM74201–74275 and the ICAEW Guidance (TAXGUIDE 8/06) at www.icaew.co.uk/index.cfm?route=142496. For the period of account for which Abstract 40 is first adopted, generally accepted accounting practice (GAAP) requires the opening position in a set of accounts to be computed on the same basis as the closing position. As a result, the opening figure for uncompleted work will differ from, and usually exceed, the closing figure for uncompleted work (i.e. the work in progress) in the previous period of account. In accordance with the rules in **73.20** above (adjustments on change of basis), the difference (assuming it to be a positive amount, i.e. an excess) is treated for income tax purposes as income arising on the last day of the period of account for which Abstract 40 is adopted. It is this amount (the 'adjustment income') that is subject to the spreading rules below.

In computing the adjustment income subject to the spreading relief, it is to be assumed (where it is not the case) that no other change of accounting approach takes place in the period of account concerned. The relief is also available if accounts are drawn up in accordance with international accounting standards rather than UK GAAP. The relief may apply to a trade, a profession, a vocation or a property business (as in **60.2 PROPERTY INCOME** and whether UK or overseas). The relief is automatic and does not require a claim or election for it to apply. It does not, however, apply if the separate and more generous spreading relief available to barristers and advocates in **73.20** above would apply instead.

In each of the first three tax years beginning with that in which the full adjustment income would otherwise be chargeable to tax, the amount charged is instead one-third of the full amount or, if less, one-sixth of the taxable profits (see below) for that year. In each of the fourth and fifth tax years (assuming there remains any adjustment income as yet untaxed), the chargeable amount is computed as before, except that it cannot exceed the portion as yet untaxed. In the sixth tax year, any outstanding balance is brought into charge. If, within the six years, the individual permanently ceases to carry on the trade etc., the annual charge continues to be made as before but without the 'one-sixth of taxable profits' alternative. For the above purpose only, 'taxable profits' are before including capital allowances or balancing charges and before deducting any adjustment expenses as in **73.20** above. As adjustment income generally is treated as being separate from trading profits (see **73.20** above), it follows that such income must also be excluded from 'taxable profits'.

A person may elect for an additional amount of his own choosing to be added to the amount otherwise chargeable for a particular tax year. The election must be made on or before the first anniversary of 31 January following the tax year concerned, and must specify the additional amount. The maximum charge for each remaining year (i.e. the one-third of adjustment income) is then reduced proportionately. An election may be made more than once during the six-year period.

Thus if the change of practice occurs in the year ended 30 April 2006 and gives rise to adjustment income of £30,000, a maximum of £10,000 is taxable in 2006/07, 2007/08 and 2008/09. However, if profits (measured as above) amount to £36,000 in each of those years, only £6,000 is taxable in each year. If profits are then £54,000 and £12,000 in 2009/10 and 2010/11 respectively, the amount chargeable is £9,000 in 2009/10 and £2,000 in 2010/11. So far £29,000 has been taxed, so the remaining £1,000 is taxed in 2011/12 (year 6) regardless of profit levels. Supposing the trader has some relievable losses available from a separate business in 2008/09 and elects to bring an extra £6,000 of the adjustment income into charge for that year. The *maximum* chargeable amount for each of the two subsequent years (assuming no election for those years) is now £8,000 (i.e. one-third of (£30,000 – £6,000)); in fact, the *actual* chargeable amounts are now £6,000 for 2006/07 and 2007/08, £12,000 for 2008/09 and £6,000 for 2009/10 (i.e. the untaxed balance, being less than either the revised £8,000 one-third of adjustment income or the £9,000 one-sixth of profits).

Following the death of the person liable to tax on the adjustment income, liability passes to his personal representatives as a debt due from his estate.

If the trade etc. is carried on in partnership, a partner's share of the amount charged to tax for the first tax year is computed in accordance with the profit-sharing arrangements in force for the 12 months immediately preceding the period of account for which the change of accounting practice is adopted. For any subsequent tax year, the partner's share is computed in accordance with the profit-sharing arrangements in force for the 12 months following the 12 months used to determine his share for the previous tax year. An election to accelerate the charge for any tax year must be made by all persons who have been partners during the 12 months relevant to that year and who are chargeable to income tax. If the trade etc. ceases, each partner's share of any amount charged to tax after the cessation is determined:

(a)   (if cessation occurs on the first day of the period of account for which the change of basis is adopted) in accordance with the profit-sharing arrangements in force for the 12 months immediately preceding that date;

(b)   (if cessation occurs after the day mentioned in (a) above but on or before its first anniversary) in accordance with the profit-sharing arrangements in force for the period from the day in (a) above to the date of cessation; and

(c)   (in any other case) in accordance with the profit-sharing arrangements in force for the period from the immediately preceding anniversary of the day in (a) above to the date of cessation;

and any elections to accelerate a post-cessation charge are to be made on an individual basis. This applies equally if the partnership is a limited liability partnership (regardless of the normal rules for LLPs at **52.23 PARTNERSHIPS**).

[*FA 2006, Sch 15 Pt 1; FA 2007, s 91(10), s 92*].

Subscriptions and contributions

[73.116] The following are relevant.

Local enterprise organisations

Ordinary annual subscriptions to local associations, including Chambers of Commerce, are normally allowed as deductions in computing profits. Subscriptions to larger associations are deductible, and receipts therefrom chargeable, if the association has entered into an arrangement with HMRC under which it is assessed on any surplus of receipts over allowable expenditure (the association should be asked). Most associations enter into the arrangement but if not the deduction is restricted to the proportion applied by the association for purposes such that it would have been deductible if so applied by the subscriber (*Lochgelly Iron & Coal Co Ltd v Crawford* CS 1913, 6 TC 267). For other cases see Tolley's Tax Cases. Subscriptions to the Economic League are not deductible (*Joseph L Thompson & Sons Ltd v Chamberlain* Ch D 1962, 40 TC 657).

The payment of an ordinary annual subscription to a local trade association by a non-member is normally deductible as expenditure incurred for the purposes of the subscriber's trade with members of the association (HMRC Business Income Manual BIM47430).

Contributions to mutual insurance associations are deductible even though used to create a reserve fund (*Thomas v Richard Evans & Co Ltd HL 1927, 11 TC 790*).

Local enterprise organisations

Expenditure incurred in making any contribution (whether in cash or kind) to a 'local enterprise organisation' is specifically allowed as deduction in computing profits if it would not otherwise be deductible. If, however, in connection with the making of the contribution, the trader or a person connected with him (see **21 CONNECTED PERSONS**) receives (or is entitled to receive) a 'disqualifying benefit' of any kind, whether or not from the organisation itself, the value of the benefit is subtracted from the deduction otherwise available. Any such benefit received after such a deduction has been given is recovered by treating its value as a trading receipt for the period of account in which it is received. If received after the trade has permanently ceased, it is treated as a post-cessation receipt (within **59.1 POST-CESSATION RECEIPTS AND EXPENDITURE**). A '*disqualifying benefit*' is a benefit the expenses of obtaining which would not be deductible if incurred directly by the trader in an arm's length transaction.

For these purposes, a '*local enterprise organisation*' means any of the following.

- A local enterprise agency, i.e. a body for the time being approved as such by the relevant national authority (e.g. for England and NI, by the Secretary of State). Various conditions are prescribed for approval. In particular, the body's sole aim must be the promotion or encouragement of industrial and commercial activity or enterprise in a particular area of the UK, with particular reference to small businesses. If that is only one of its main aims, it must maintain a separate fund for the sole purpose of pursuing that aim and the above relief applies only to contributions to that fund. Also, the body must be precluded from transferring its income or profits to its members or its managers, other than as a reasonable return for goods, labour or services provided, money lent or premises occupied. Approval may be conditional and may be withdrawn retrospectively.
- A training and enterprise council, i.e. a body which has an agreement with the Secretary of State to act as such.
- A Scottish local enterprise company, i.e. a company which has an agreement with Scottish Enterprise or Highlands and Islands Enterprise to act as such.
- A business link organisation, i.e. a person authorised by the Secretary of State to use a trade mark designated for these purposes.

[*ITTOIA 2005, ss 82–85*].

Urban regeneration companies

Identical provisions to those described above in relation to local enterprise organisations apply to a contribution made to an urban regeneration company designated as such by Treasury order. A body may be so designated only if its sole or main function is to co-ordinate the regeneration of a specific urban area in the UK in association with public and local authorities. Designation orders may be backdated by up to three months. [*ITTOIA 2005, ss 82, 86; SI 2004 No 439*].

Subsidies, grants etc.

[**73.117**] See **10.2**(vi) CAPITAL ALLOWANCES for effect of grants and subsidies on capital allowances.

See **63.18** RETURNS as regards returns of certain grant and subsidy payments.

The following items are dealt with in alphabetical order.

Business Start-up scheme

Payments under the Business Start-up scheme, to assist unemployed people in setting up their own businesses, are made under *Employment and Training Act 1973, s 2(2)(d)* (or Scottish or NI equivalent). Such payments are generally taxed as trading income. If such a payment, other than a lump sum payment, is received in a period which falls within two basis periods, it is taken into account in computing trading profits in the first only of those basis periods. [*ITTOIA 2005, ss 207, 853(4)*]. The payments are made by training and enterprise councils (in Scotland, local enterprise companies). Where the business is run through a company, the payments are made to the individual as agent of the company and are treated as income of the company. (HMRC Business Income Manual BIM40400, 40405).

Farming support payments

See **73.73** above.

Fishing grants

For the tax treatment of decommissioning grants, laying-up grants, exploratory voyage grants and joint venture grants under *SI 1983 No 1883*, see HMRC Business Income Manual BIM57001.

Football pools promoters etc.

If the person carrying on the trade is liable to pool betting duty, e.g. he is a football pools promoter and he makes a 'qualifying payment' in consequence of his receiving a reduction in duty, he is allowed a deduction for that payment in computing his profits for income tax purposes. A *'qualifying payment'* is a payment to meet (directly or indirectly) capital expenditure incurred by any person in improving spectator safety or comfort at a soccer ground or a payment to trustees established mainly for the support of athletic sports or games but with power to support the arts. [*ITTOIA 2005, s 162*].

Industrial development grants

Grants to a trader under *Industrial Development Act 1982, s 7 or s 8* (or corresponding NI legislation)are trading receipts, unless the grant is designated as made towards the cost of specified capital expenditure or as compensation for loss of capital assets or, exceptionally, is made towards the meeting of a corporation tax liability. This is of no application to professions or vocations. [*ITTOIA 2005, s 105*].

An earlier interest relief grant under *Industry Act 1972* was held to be assessable in *Burman v Thorn Domestic Appliances (Electrical) Ltd* Ch D 1981, 55 TC 493, as was a similar grant undifferentiated between revenue and capital in *Ryan v Crabtree Denims Ltd* Ch D 1987, 60 TC 183, applying *Gayjon Processes Ltd* (below) and distinguishing *Seaham Harbour* (below).

Research grants

A research grant by trading company to a medical practitioner was held to be taxable (*Duff v Williamson* Ch D 1973, 49 TC 1). For research grants and fellowships generally, see HMRC Business Income Manual BIM65151.

Temporary employment subsidy

Temporary employment subsidy was paid under *Employment and Training Act 1973, s 5* (as amended by *Employment Protection Act 1975, Sch 14 para 2*) as a flat-rate weekly payment or (in the textile, clothing and footwear industries) by way of reimbursement of payments made to workers on short time.

Such payments were held to be taxable as trading receipts in *Poulter v Gayjon Processes Ltd* Ch D 1985, 58 TC 350, distinguishing the grants made by the Unemployment Grants Committee in *Seaham Harbour* (below).

Unemployment grants

Subsidy to dock company (from Unemployment Grants Committee) for extension work to keep men in employment held, although grant made in terms of interest, not a 'trade receipt' for tax purposes (*Seaham Harbour v Crook* HL 1931, 16 TC 333).

Taxation

[73.118] Income tax liabilities are not deductible in computing profits (cf. *Allen v Farquharson Bros & Co* KB 1932, 17 TC 59). Overseas taxes may be subject to DOUBLE TAX RELIEF (**26**) but any such tax not relieved by credit on overseas income included in the profits may generally be deducted [*TIOPA 2010, s 112*] but not on UK income, e.g. profits of UK branches (*CIR v Dowdall O'Mahoney & Co Ltd* HL 1952, 33 TC 259).

In *Harrods (Buenos Aires) v Taylor-Gooby* CA 1964, 41 TC 450 an annual capital tax imposed by the Argentine on foreign companies trading there was not a tax on the profits and was allowable.

As regards relief for national insurance contributions by employers in respect of employees, see **73.68** above.

For taxation appeals, see **73.92** above. For VAT, see **73.126** below.

Simon's Taxes. See B2.472.

Telecommunications rights

[73.119] Special rules apply in relation to licences granted under *Wireless Telegraphy Act 1949, s 1* as a result of bidding for such licences under *Wireless Telegraphy Act 1998, s 3* regulations, and to rights derived directly or indirectly therefrom. This would include, for example, the licences granted in response to the Government auction of third generation mobile phone licences in April 2000. The rules also apply to an indefeasible right to use a telecommunications cable system, and to rights derived from such a licence or indefeasible right.

Acquisition costs and disposal proceeds in respect of such rights which, in accordance with generally accepted accounting practice (see **73.18** above), are taken into account in determining accounting profit or loss are treated as being of a revenue nature in computing profits chargeable to income tax. This applies equally to costs of extension of attached rights or of cancellation or restriction of rights attached to derivative rights, and to receipts from cancellation or restriction of attached rights or from granting derivative rights or extensions of rights attached to derivative rights.

If, in accordance with generally accepted accounting practice, an amount in respect of the revaluation of such rights is recognised in the accounts (whether or not in determining accounting profit or loss), that amount is also treated for income tax purposes as being of a revenue nature. In computing profits for those purposes, it is brought into account for the period of account in which it is so recognised.

[*ITTOIA 2005, ss 145–148; CTA 2010, Sch 1 para 471(2)*].

For articles giving the HMRC's view on the interpretation of the above legislation, see Revenue Tax Bulletins December 2000 pp 815–817, February 2004 p 1094.

Tied premises

[73.120] Receipts and expenses in respect of 'tied premises' which would otherwise be brought into account in calculating profits of a property business (see **60.2 PROPERTY INCOME**) are instead brought into account as trading receipts or expenses. Any necessary apportionment (e.g. where rents etc. relate only in part to the tied premises or where only part of the premises qualifies) is on a just and reasonable basis. '*Tied premises*' are premises through which goods supplied by a trader are sold or used by another person, where the trader has an estate or interest in the premises which he treats as property employed for trade purposes. [*ITTOIA 2005, s 19*].

These rules are of general application, although of most common application in the licensed trade. As regards the licensed trade generally, see **73.41** above.

'Exclusivity payments' by petrol company to retailers undertaking to sell only its goods were allowed in computing its profits in *Bolam v Regent Oil Co Ltd* Ch D 1956, 37 TC 56 (payments for repairs carried out by retailer), *BP Australia Ltd* PC 1965, 44 ATC 312 (lump sums paid for sales promotion) and *Mobil Oil Australia Ltd* PC 1965, 44 ATC 323, but held capital in *Strick v Regent Oil* HL 1965, 43 TC 1 where the payment took the form of a premium to the retailer for a lease of his premises (immediately sub-let to him).

In the hands of the retailer, exclusivity payments were held capital when for capital expenditure incurred by him (*CIR v Coia* CS 1959, 38 TC 334; *McLaren v Needham* Ch D 1960, 39 TC 37; *Walter W Saunders Ltd v Dixon* Ch D 1962, 40 TC 329; *McClymont and Another v Jarman* (Sp C 387) 2003, [2004] SSCD 54) but revenue when for repairs etc. (*McLaren v Needham* above) or sales promotion (*Evans v Wheatley* Ch D 1958, 38 TC 216) or where petrol sales were a relatively small part (some 30%) of the company's turnover (*Tanfield Ltd v Carr* (Sp C 200), [1999] SSCD 213]).

For a summary of HMRC's view of such arrangements, see Revenue Tax Bulletin August 1993 p 88.

Training costs

[73.121] Costs incurred by an employer in respect of employee training are generally allowable as a trade expense. See **73.69** above for this and as regards certain other allowable employee training costs, and **73.116** above as regards contributions to training and enterprise councils.

In general, the expenses of a training course undertaken by a self-employed person are allowed as a trade deduction under general principles only where the training is undertaken for the purposes of the trade and relates to the updating of existing expertise rather than the acquisition of new skills. See HMRC Business Income Manual BIM47651. This principle was confirmed in *Dass v Special Commissioner and others* Ch D 2006, [2007] STC 187.

Travelling and subsistence expenses

[73.122] The cost of travelling in the course of the business activities is allowable but not that of travelling between home and the place at or from which the business is conducted. For this see *Newsom v Robertson CA 1952, 33 TC 452* in which the expenses of a barrister between his home and his chambers were refused and contrast *Horton v Young* CA 1971, 47 TC 60 in which a 'self-employed' bricklayer was allowed his expenses between his home and the sites at which he worked as, on the evidence, his business was conducted from his home. In *Jackman v Powell* Ch D, 76 TC 87, a milkman was not allowed the costs of travelling between his home and the dairy-owned depot from which he collected his supplies and to which his milk round was adjacent. Any expenses of an employment ancillary to a profession that are not allowable against employment income may not be deducted in computing the profits of the profession (*Mitchell & Edon v Ross* HL 1961, 40 TC 11).

The 'dual purpose rule' (see **73.36** above) entails the disallowance of *all* travelling expenses with a material private purpose, i.e. the part attributable to business purposes is not allowable. Thus the expenses of a solicitor in travelling abroad partly for a holiday and partly to attend professional conferences were disallowed in *Bowden v Russell & Russell* Ch D 1965, 42 TC 301 (but the expenses of an accountant to attend a professional conference abroad were allowed in *Edwards v Warmsley, Henshall & Co* Ch D 1967, 44 TC 431). Similarly the expenses of a dentist in travelling between his home and surgery were disallowed even though he collected dentures from a laboratory on the way (*Sargent v Barnes* Ch D 1978, 52 TC 335). The expenses of a farmer in visiting Australia with a view to farming there were held inadmissible (*Sargent v Eayrs* Ch D 1972, 48 TC 573). Car expenses are normally apportioned if the car is used partly for private purposes. Parking and other motoring fines are normally disallowed in their entirety either under the 'dual purpose rule' (see **73.36** above) or under the general principles applicable to allowable trading deductions (see *CIR v Alexander von Glehn & Co Ltd* CA 1920, 12 TC 232, in which penalties for breach of wartime regulations were disallowed), although reimbursement of employees is normally allowable (but see **27.20 EMPLOYMENT INCOME** as regards the employee's liability).

The 'dual purpose rule' also requires the disallowance of costs of food, drink and accommodation. The extra cost of lunching away from home was disallowed in *Caillebotte v Quinn* Ch D 1975, 50 TC 222. However, by law for 2009/10 onwards and in practice for earlier tax years (see HMRC Business Income Manual BIM47705), a deduction is allowed for any reasonable expenses incurred on food or drink for consumption by the trader at a place to which he travels in the course of carrying on the trade, or while travelling to a place in the course of carrying on the trade, but only if conditions A and B below are met.

- Condition A is that a deduction is available for the associated travelling costs (or, in a case where such costs are not incurred by the trader, a deduction would be available if they were so incurred).
- Condition B is that either:
    (i)   at the time the expenses on food and drink are incurred, the trade is by its nature itinerant (for example a commercial traveller); or
    (ii) the trader does not visit the place more than occasionally in the course of the trade and the travel is undertaken otherwise than as part of a normal pattern of travel in the course of the trade.

[*ITTOIA 2005, s 57A; SI 2009 No 730, Art 3*].

The above legislation deals only with food and drink and not with overnight accommodation. However, in practice, where a business trip necessitates one or more nights away from home (and away from the business base), the hotel accommodation is deductible (HMRC Business Income Manual BIM47705).

Where a UK resident individual trader spends time outside the UK on business, his personal living expenses are not disallowed if the absence abroad is for the purpose of the trade. Living expenses include for these purposes the cost of accommodation, food and drink attributable to the individual. If he is accompanied by his family or other dependants, the costs attributable to them are non-deductible. (HMRC SP A16).

Motoring expenses

As an alternative to claiming their actual business motoring costs in their accounts, taxpayers with a turnover not exceeding the VAT registration threshold (currently £70,000), judged at the time they first used the vehicle, are permitted to use the statutory tax-free mileage rates applicable to employees (see **27.87 EMPLOYMENT INCOME**) to arrive at the accounts figure. No other motoring expenses or related capital allowances may then be claimed (other than interest on a loan to purchase the vehicle). The basis of claim may only be changed when a vehicle is replaced. (HMRC Business Income Manual BIM47701; Revenue Press Release BN 2/01 7 March 2001).

See **73.13** above for extended relief for travelling expenses in overseas trade.

For car hire, see **73.42** above. For travelling and subsistence generally, see HMRC Business Income Manual BIM47700–47710. For the 'dual purpose rule' in relation to travel and subsistence costs, see BIM37600–37635, 37660.

Simon's Taxes. See B2.318, B2.476.

Unclaimed balances

[73.123] Unclaimed balances for which a firm was liable to account were held not assessable despite their being distributed to partners (*Morley v Tattersall* CA 1938, 22 TC 51). Such balances held by a pawnbroker are, however, assessable when claimants' rights expire (*Jay's, the Jewellers v CIR* KB 1947, 29 TC 274). Deposits on garments not collected were held to be trade receipts assessable when received (*Elson v Prices Tailors* Ch D 1962, 40 TC 671); the same applied to refundable deposits in respect of returnable containers in which goods were supplied to customers (*Gower Chemicals Ltd v HMRC* (Sp C 713), [2008] SSCD 1242). The fact that trading receipts were subsequently, and correctly, treated for accountancy purposes as an element in a sale of fixed assets did not alter their nature for tax purposes (*Tapemaze Ltd v Melluish* Ch D 2000, 73 TC 167). See **73.40** above for releases of debts owing.

Unremittable amounts

[73.124] Where a trade is carried on at least partly in the UK, so that liability to UK income tax arises on the profits, amounts received or receivable overseas (e.g. from export sales) which cannot be brought to the UK because of foreign exchange restrictions would nevertheless fall to be included in computing profits, with no relief being available under *ITTOIA 2005, ss 841–845* (unremittable overseas income — see **32.5 FOREIGN INCOME**), i.e. because the overall profits of the trade do not arise outside the UK, or under *ITTOIA 2005, s 35* (bad and doubtful debts — see **73.40** above), i.e. because a debt is not bad merely because it is unremittable. The provisions described below are designed to give relief in such circumstances.

The relief applies where an amount received by, or owed to, a trader is brought into account as a receipt in computing his profits, it is paid or owed in a territory outside the UK, and some or all of it is 'unremittable'. For these purposes, an amount is *'unremittable'* if:

- it is received but cannot be transferred to the UK because, and only because, of 'foreign exchange restrictions'; or
- it is owed but temporarily cannot be paid in the overseas territory, due only to such restrictions; or
- it is owed and can be paid in the overseas territory but the amount paid there would not be transferable to the UK, due only to such restrictions.

'Foreign exchange restrictions' are restrictions imposed by the law of the overseas territory, by any executive action of its government or by the impossibility of obtaining there currency which is transferable to the UK.

Relief is given for the amount in question by deducting it from profits but not so as to create a trading loss. Any excess of unremittable amounts over profits for any period of account is carried forward to the next period of account, aggregated with any unremittable amounts for that period and used to reduce or extinguish profits for that period, and so on *ad infinitum*. If no profit has been made for a period of account, any unremittable amounts are similarly carried forward.

However, no such deduction is allowed to the extent that:

- the amount in question is used to finance expenditure or investment outside the UK or is otherwise applied outside the UK; or

- a deduction is allowed for it under *ITTOIA 2005, s 35* (see **73.40** above) because it represents a bad or doubtful debt; or
- it is an amount owed and an insurance recovery is received in respect of it,

and no deduction is allowed if relief under *ITTOIA 2005, s 842* (see **32.5 FOREIGN INCOME**) could be claimed instead.

Relief given for an unremittable amount or any part of it is withdrawn if, subsequently, the amount (or part) ceases to be unremittable or is exchanged for (or discharged by) a remittable amount, or is used to finance overseas expenditure etc., or is deducted as a bad or doubtful debt or, in the case of an amount owed, is the subject of an insurance recovery. The amount (or part) is treated as a trading receipt for the period of account in which the said event occurs.

[*ITTOIA 2005, ss 187–191*].

Use of home for business purposes

[73.125] If part of a trader's home is for any period used solely for business purposes, he may be able to deduct part of the household expenses in computing his trading profit for tax purposes. The deductible expenditure will represent the costs incurred on that part of the home for that period. As it is unlikely that such costs will be separately billed, this means apportioning household bills. The factors to be taken into account when apportioning an expense include the following.

- Area: what proportion in terms of area of the home is used for business purposes?
- Usage: how much is consumed? This is appropriate where there is a metered or measurable supply such as electricity, gas or water.
- Time: how long is that part used for business purposes as compared to its total use?

At Business Income Manual BIM47820, HMRC provide a (non-exhaustive) list of, and commentary on, the types of expenditure that may be allowable, split between fixed costs and running costs. The types of expenditure considered are rent, mortgage interest, council tax, heat, light and power, telephone, internet connection charges, water rates, repairs and maintenance, cleaning and insurance.

If there is only minor use of the home, for example writing up the business records at home, HMRC officers will usually accept a reasonable estimate. The examples in HMRC's own manual suggest that £2 per week might be accepted as a reasonable estimate, but this is not to say that a higher figure would not be accepted.

(HMRC Business Income Manual BIM47800 *et seq.*).

Value added tax

[73.126] For treatment in computing business profits see HMRC SP B1.

In general, if the trader is not a 'taxable person' for VAT his expenditure *inclusive* of any VAT on it, is treated in the ordinary way.

If he is a taxable person, the receipts and expenses (including capital items) to be taken into account will generally be exclusive of VAT but if he suffers VAT on any expenditure which does not rank as 'input tax' (e.g. entertaining expenses and certain expenditure relating to motor cars) that expenditure inclusive of VAT will be taken into account for income tax etc. purposes (although any such inclusive sum in respect of entertaining expenses may also be disallowed for income tax purposes). Any allowance for bad debts (see **73.40** above) is inclusive of any VAT not recovered but accounted for to Customs and Excise. (*VATA 1994, s 36* and regulations made thereunder now provide for VAT on bad debts to be refunded in certain cases.)

VAT interest, penalties and surcharge are not allowed as a deduction for income tax purposes (see **73.89** above). Repayment supplement is disregarded for income tax purposes (see **30.37** EXEMPT INCOME).

Where the trader uses the optional *flat-rate scheme* for smaller businesses, receipts and expenses to be taken into account will generally be *inclusive* of normal output and input VAT, but the flat-rate VAT itself can either be deducted from turnover or treated as a separate expense and in either case is an allowable deduction for income tax purposes. Any irrecoverable VAT on capital items will form part of their cost for the purposes of capital allowances. (Revenue Tax Bulletin April 2003 pp 1023, 1024).

VAT refunds

See Revenue Tax Bulletin October 1995 pp 255, 256 for the timing of the recognition, for the purposes of computing trading profits, of certain VAT refunds (specifically, of refunds to opticians following acceptance by Customs and Excise that they had incorrectly required VAT to be charged on certain outputs).

See HMRC Business Income Manual BIM31500–31625, and see generally Tolley's Value Added Tax.

Waste disposal

[73.127] Expenditure on purchase and reclamation of tipping sites by a company carrying on a waste disposal business was held to be capital in *Rolfe v Wimpey Waste Management Ltd* CA 1989, 62 TC 399, as were instalment payments for the right to deposit waste material in *CIR v Adam* CS 1928, 14 TC 34. See also *McClure v Petre* Ch D 1988, 61 TC 226, where the receipt of sum for licence to tip soil was also held to be capital.

Site preparation and restoration expenditure

A deduction is allowed as below in computing profits where a person incurs, in the course of a trade, 'site preparation expenditure' in relation to a 'waste disposal site', and, at the time when he first deposits waste materials on the site in question, he holds a current 'waste disposal licence'. Expenditure incurred for trade purposes by a person about to carry on the trade is for this purpose treated as incurred on the first day of trading. The deduction is not available where the person incurring the expenditure recharges it to another person who holds the licence when first depositing waste (see Revenue Tax Bulletin April 1998 p 533). No claim is required but any supporting documentation should still be retained in case of an HMRC enquiry into a return.

A *'waste disposal site'* is a site used (or to be used) for the disposal of waste materials by their deposit on the site, and in relation to such a site, *'site preparation expenditure'* is expenditure on preparing the site for the deposit of waste materials. This includes expenditure incurred before the waste disposal licence is granted, and in particular expenses associated with obtaining the licence itself (Revenue Tax Bulletin November 1992 p 45). For preparation expenditure generally, see also Revenue Tax Bulletin April 1998 p 533, February 2001 p 828. A *'waste disposal licence'* is a disposal licence under *Control of Pollution Act 1974, Pt 1* (or NI equivalent), a waste management licence under *Environmental Protection Act 1990, Pt 2* (or NI equivalent), a permit under regulations under *Pollution Prevention and Control Act 1999, s 2* (or NI equivalent), an authorisation for the disposal of radioactive waste, or a nuclear site licence.

The deductible amount of site preparation expenditure for a period of account is the amount allocated to that period, which itself is given by the formula:

$$RE \times \frac{WD}{SV + WD}$$

Where

RE   =   residual expenditure (see below);

WD   =   volume of waste materials deposited on the site during the period; and

SV   =   volume of the site not used up for the deposit of waste materials at the end of the period.

The residual expenditure for a period of account is the site preparation expenditure incurred by the trader at any time before and up to the end of that period, less any expenditure which either has been allowed as a trading deduction for a prior period or is capital expenditure qualifying for capital allowances. If the trade commenced before 6 April 1989, a proportion of the expenditure incurred before that date (OE) is excluded, such proportion being calculated by reference to the volume of materials deposited before that date (OWD) and the unused volume of the site immediately before that date (OSV). The reduction is the amount given by the formula:

$$OE \times \frac{OWD}{OSV + OWD}$$

Any site preparation expenditure incurred by a predecessor of the current trader is brought into account above as if it had been incurred by the trader. For this purpose, a predecessor of the trader is a person who, on or after that date, has ceased to carry on the trade carried on by the trader or has ceased to carry on a trade so far as relating to the site in question and who, in either case, has transferred the whole of the site to the trader (though not necessarily the same estate or interest in the site).

Site restoration payments

A person making a 'site restoration payment', in the course of carrying on a trade, may deduct the payment in computing profits for the period of account in which the payment is made. A payment cannot, however, be deducted to the extent that it represents either expenditure allowed as a trading deduction for prior periods or capital expenditure qualifying for capital allowances. A provision made in the accounts for future site restoration payments is not deductible (*Dispit Ltd v HMRC* (Sp C 579), [2007] SSCD 194).

A '*site restoration payment*' is a payment made:

- in connection with the restoration of a site (or part thereof); and
- in order to comply with (i) any condition of a waste disposal licence (as defined above), or (ii) any condition imposed on the grant of planning permission to use the site for the carrying out of 'waste disposal activities', or (iii) a 'relevant planning obligation'.

'*Waste disposal activities*' means the collection, treatment, conversion and final depositing of waste materials, or any one or more of those activities.

A 'relevant planning obligation' is defined by *ITTOIA 2005, s 168(6)* by reference to *Town and Country Planning Act 1990* and Scottish and NI equivalents.

[*ITTOIA 2005, ss 165–168, Sch 2 paras 44–46; SI 2000 No 1973*].

See generally HMRC Business Income Manual BIM67405–67520. For restoration expenditure generally (including provisions for such expenditure), see also Revenue Tax Bulletin April 1998 p 534.

Leasing

See **73.79** above as regards restrictions on relief under the above provisions where finance leasing arrangements are involved.

Simon's Taxes. See **B2.478**.

Landfill tax

HMRC's views on the deductibility of landfill tax in computing trading income are as follows.

Site operators

Treatment of landfill tax charged on to customers will follow the generally accepted accounting practice. As regards self-generated waste, landfill tax (net of any credit following a contribution to an environmental trust) will be allowed as a deduction so long as the other costs incurred in disposing of the waste are deductible.

Customers of site operators

The landfill tax element of the global charge does not need to be separately invoiced, and deductibility of the landfill tax element will follow that of the non-landfill tax element of the charge.

Environmental trust contributions

Site operators may obtain relief from landfill tax by making such contributions, the deductibility of which is to be determined in the circumstances of each particular case under the normal test of whether the expenditure is incurred wholly and exclusively for trade purposes. In the case of an unconnected trust engaged in projects of possible use to the operator, the payment would *prima facie* be deductible. If the operator has some degree of control over the trust, or the income of the trust is ultimately received by a person connected with the operator, it might be less clear that the payment was for the purposes of the operator's own trade. Similarly if the trust's objects were insufficiently related to the operator's trade, it might be considered that contributions were for a general philanthropic, and hence non-trade, purpose.

(Revenue Tax Bulletin June 1996 pp 317, 318).

General example

[73.128]

A UK trader commences trading on 1 October 2009. His profit and loss account for the year to 30 September 2010 is:

			£	£
Sales				110,000
Deduct	Purchases		75,000	
	Less	Trading stock at 30.9.10	15,000	
				60,000
Gross profit				50,000
Deduct				
Salaries (all paid by 30.6.11)			15,600	
Rent and rates			2,400	
Telephone			500	
Heat and light			650	
Depreciation			1,000	
Motor expenses			2,700	
Entertainment			600	
Bank interest			900	
Hire-purchase interest			250	
Repairs and renewals			1,000	
Accountant's fee			500	
Bad debts			200	
Sundries			700	
				27,000

	£	£
Net profit		23,000
Gain on sale of fixed asset		300
Rent received		500
Bank interest received (net)		150
Profit		£23,950

Further Information

- Rent and rates. £200 of the rates bill relates to the period from 1.6.09 to 30.9.09.
- Telephone. Telephone bills for the trader's private telephone amount to £150. It is estimated that 40% of these calls are for business purposes.
- Motor expenses. All the motor expenses are in respect of the proprietor's car. 40% of the annual mileage relates to private use and home to business use.

		£
Entertainment	Staff	100
	UK customers	450
	Overseas customers	50
		£600

- Hire-purchase interest. This is in respect of the owner's car.
- Repairs and renewals. There is an improvement element of 20% included.
- Bad debts. This is a specific write-off.
- Sundries. Included is £250 being the cost of obtaining a bank loan to finance business expenditure, £200 for agent's fees in obtaining a patent for trading purposes and a £50 inducement to a local official.
- Other. The proprietor obtained goods for his own use from the business costing £400 (resale value £500) without payment.
- Capital allowances for the year to 30 September 2010 amount to £1,520.

Computation of taxable trading income — Year to 30.9.10

		£	£
Profit per the accounts			23,950
Add			
Repairs — improvement element			200
Hire-purchase interest (40% private)			100
Entertainment	note (e)		500
Motor expenses (40% private)			1,080
Depreciation			1,000
Telephone (60% × £150)			90
Goods for own use	note (f)		500
Illegal payment	note (g)		50

Deduct

Bank interest received (savings and investment income)	150
Rent received (property income)	500
Gain on sale of fixed asset	300
	950
	26,520
Less Capital allowances	1,520
Chargeable trading income	£25,000

Notes

(a) Costs of obtaining loan finance are specifically allowable (see **73.93** above).

(b) Capital allowances are deductible as a trading expense (see **10.1 CAPITAL ALLOWANCES, 11.1 CAPITAL ALLOWANCES ON PLANT AND MACHINERY**).

(c) The adjusted profit of £25,000 would be subject to the commencement provisions for assessment purposes (see **73.4** above).

(d) Pre-trading expenses are treated as incurred on the day on which trade is commenced if they are incurred within seven years of the commencement and would have been allowable if incurred after commencement. See **73.102** above.

(e) All entertainment expenses, other than staff entertaining, are non-deductible (see **73.72** above).

(f) Trading stock appropriated for personal use must be accounted for at market value (see **73.114** above).

(g) Expenditure incurred in making a payment which itself constitutes the commission of a criminal offence is specifically disallowed as a deduction. This includes payments which are contrary to the Prevention of Corruption Acts. See **73.87** above.

74

Underwriters at Lloyd's

Simon's Taxes. See E5.6.

Introduction

[74.1] Special tax provisions for Lloyd's underwriters are contained in *FA 1993, ss 171–184, Schs 19, 20.*

As regards underwriters who are Scottish limited partnerships or limited liability partnerships, see *SI 1997 No 2681* as amended by *SI 2006 No 111.*

Basis of assessment

[74.2] The profits or losses in a tax year are those declared in the underwriting year ending in the tax year, i.e. profits of underwriting year 2007 are generally declared in 2010 and assessed for 2010/11. [*FA 1993, s 172(1)*].

On cessation (on death or otherwise), the final tax year is that which corresponds to the underwriting year in which the underwriter's Lloyd's deposit is paid over to him or his personal representatives or assigns. Any underwriting profits or losses which do not fall to be taken as profits or losses of an earlier tax year are taken to be profits or losses of the final tax year. [*FA 1993, s 179*]. Where a member dies:

- he is treated for these purposes as having died on 5 April in the underwriting year in which he actually died; and
- the business is treated as continuing until the member's deposit is paid over to his personal representatives, whose carrying on of the business is not treated as a change in the persons so engaged.

[*FA 1993, s 179A*].

An underwriting year '*corresponds*' to the tax year in which it ends and *vice versa*, i.e. the 2010 underwriting year ends on 31 December 2010 and thus corresponds to the tax year 2010/11. [*FA 1993, s 184(2)*].

If underwriting commenced before 2 January 1971 and a cessation occurs, a claim may be made for assessments:

- for the final tax year for which underwriting profits or losses fall to be included (being profits or losses declared in the underwriting year following the closing year) to be based on the actual profits from 6 April to 31 December in that underwriting year, and
- for the preceding year to be reduced by the lesser of the whole of the profits of that year and the underwriting profits for the underwriting year 1972.

[*SI 1995 No 351, Reg 13*].

For double tax relief arrangements, see *SI 1997 No 405.*

Underwriting profits

[74.3] The aggregate of a member's underwriting profits is chargeable to tax as the profits of a trade carried on in the UK. Underwriting profits include income from premium trust fund assets and income from 'ancillary trust fund' assets. An '*ancillary trust fund*' does not include a premium trust fund or special reserve fund but otherwise means any trust fund required or authorised by Lloyd's rules or required by an underwriter's member's agent. [*FA 1993, s 171(1)(2)(4), s 184(2)(b)*].

Distributions in respect of any asset of a premium trust fund do not carry any entitlement to a tax credit (and see the provisions against arrangements to pass on the value of tax credits at **4.42 ANTI-AVOIDANCE**). [*FA 1993, s 171(2B); FA 2008, s 34, Sch 12 para 16*].

Annual appreciation in value of and profits on disposal of premium trust fund assets are included in underwriting profits for income tax purposes and annual depreciation in value and losses on disposal are deducted in arriving at such profits. For the purposes of computing appreciation and depreciation in value of premium trust fund assets, there is an exemption similar to that in **2.5**(d) **ACCRUED INCOME SCHEME** (FOTRA securities). [*FA 1993, ss 174, 184(2)*]. Gains and losses on ancillary trust fund assets are subject to the capital gains tax regime. [*FA 1993, s 176(2)*].

Underwriting profits are treated as derived from the carrying on of a business and thus count as relevant UK earnings for pension purposes (see **57.7 PENSION PROVISION**). [*FA 1993, s 180; ITA 2007, Sch 1 para 358*].

Stop-loss premiums

Stop-loss insurance premiums are allowable as an expense in computing underwriting profits, and insurance money received in respect of a loss is a trading receipt of the tax year corresponding to the underwriting year in which the loss was declared. This treatment is extended to payments into and receipts out of the High Level Stop Loss Fund, i.e. the fund of that name established under Lloyd's rules. A repayment of insurance money received etc. is likewise allowed as an expense, as is any amount payable under a quota share contract, i.e. a contract made in accordance with Lloyd's rules and practice between the underwriter and another person which provides for that other person to take over any rights and liabilities of the underwriter under any of his syndicates. As regards quota share contracts, the deduction may be limited by reference to certain prior 'transferred losses', and if such losses exceed the amount payable under the contract, a trading receipt will arise. Amounts paid in respect of conditional contracts which do not come into effect are, however, allowed in full, and certain cash calls in respect of undeclared transferred losses are treated as payments under the contract. The treatment of insurance receipts etc. is modified where the inspector is not notified of the receipt in time to raise the necessary assessment for the year corresponding to that in which the loss arose; in such a case, the trading receipt is treated as arising in the tax year corresponding to the underwriting year in which the payment of insurance money etc. was made to the underwriter. [FA 1993, ss 178, 184(1)].

Reinsurance premiums

A restriction is placed on relief for such premiums payable in respect of liabilities outstanding at the end of an underwriting year for the purpose of closing the accounts for the underwriting year, where the member by whom the premium is payable is also a member of the syndicate as a member of which the reinsurer is entitled to receive it. Relief is restricted to an amount which must not exceed an assessment, arrived at with a view to producing neither profit nor loss to the member to whom it is payable, of the value of the liabilities in respect of which it is payable, and a corresponding reduction is made in his profits or gains as a member of the reinsurer syndicate. [FA 1993, s 177].

See Revenue Tax Bulletin October 1998 p 599 as regards the proportion of such premiums generally allowable for tax purposes.

General insurance reserves

There are provisions for bringing in as a trading receipt or expense an amount representing interest on any allowance in respect of technical provisions to the extent that it subsequently becomes apparent that it was excessive or insufficient. [FA 2000, s 107; SI 2001 No 1757]. For guidance notes, including rates of interest, see www.hmrc.gov.uk/specialist/gir.htm.

Miscellaneous deductions

It is understood that subscriptions to the **Association of Lloyd's members** are allowable, as is the cost of League Tables and Syndicate Results. Two-thirds of the cost of prospective names seminars, and one-half of the cost of most other conferences and meetings, is also allowable, with proportionate allowance of travelling expenses other than to or from London (the place of business).

Bank guarantee fees paid initially to secure membership as a Lloyd's underwriter are not deductible, but annual payments for the maintenance of such facilities are deductible.

Personal accountancy fees are allowed on the usual 'wholly and exclusively' basis applicable to traders generally, by reference to the amount paid in the year of account.

Compensation payments from managing or members' agents are likely to be treated as trading receipts of the underwriting year in which the entitlement to compensation arises, and thus as not being chargeable to capital gains tax. Any legal fees incurred, together with any payments out of the compensation to stop-loss insurers, are deductible for tax purposes. (Revenue Tax Bulletin May 1992 p 17). For confirmation that such compensation payments are taxable, see *Deeny and others v Gooda Walker Ltd* HL 1996, 68 TC 458.

Members' agent pooling arrangements (MAPAs)

For the tax treatment of individuals' shares of the various syndicate membership rights held through each MAPA, see Tolley's Capital Gains Tax under Underwriters at Lloyd's. [*FA 1999, ss 82–84*].

Simon's Taxes. See E5.611–E5.619A.

Losses

[74.4] An underwriting loss can be **carried forward** for relief against underwriting profits in subsequent tax years (under the normal provisions for carry-forward of losses under *ITA 2007, s 83*).

An underwriting loss for a tax year can also be **offset against other income** of the underwriter under the normal provisions of *ITA 2007, s 64*.

An underwriting loss in the early years of the business may be carried back and offset against other income under *ITA 2007, s 72*.

See **45 LOSSES**.

An *anticipated* underwriting loss may not be taken into account in a PAYE coding until title to it has been established, i.e. until it has actually been sustained (*Blackburn v Keeling* CA, 75 TC 608).

Simon's Taxes. See E5.621–E5.628.

Carry-forward of losses against income from successor company or partnership

[74.5] Where, under a conversion arrangement made under the rules or practice of Lloyd's (conversion to limited liability underwriting), a member transfers the whole of his outstanding syndicate capacity to a company (the successor company) for a consideration consisting entirely of shares in the company, any income which he derives from the company (e.g. earnings or dividends) is treated for the purposes of carry-forward of losses under *ITA 2007, s 83* as if it were profits of the member's former underwriting business, thus enabling any unrelieved losses brought forward to be set against it. The successor company must be one which the member controls (within the meaning of *CTA 2010, ss 450, 451*) and of which he owns more than 50% of the ordinary share capital and, for the relief to apply in respect of income of a particular tax year, these conditions must continue to be satisfied from the time of transfer until the end of that tax year.

The transfer of syndicate capacity must take effect from the beginning of the underwriting year immediately following the member's final underwriting year, and the successor company must commence underwriting in that following year. The member must also have given notice of resignation to Lloyd's and must not undertake any new insurance business at Lloyd's after the end of his final underwriting year. If the member withdraws his resignation after claiming relief under these provisions, the relief fails; the member must give HMRC written notice of the withdrawal within six months after it occurs, subject to penalty under *TMA 1970, s 95* (see **55.13 PENALTIES**) in the event of his fraudulently or negligently failing to do so.

A similar relief applies if a member transfers the whole of his outstanding syndicate capacity to a Scottish limited partnership, provided he is the only person who disposes of syndicate capacity under a conversion arrangement to that partnership. The income to which the relief applies is the profits of the successor partnership's underwriting business to which the member is beneficially entitled and, for the relief to apply in respect of income of a particular tax year, the member must be beneficially entitled to more than 50% of such profits throughout the period from the time of transfer to the end of that tax year. The relief is extended to cover a transfer to a UK limited liability partnership.

[*FA 1993, s 179B, Sch 20A paras 1, 2, 5–11; ITA 2007, Sch 1 para 361; CTA 2010, Sch 1 para 279; SI 2006 No 112*].

Syndicate managing agents — tax obligations

[74.6] The administrative machinery under which syndicate managing agents must operate with regard to their tax obligations is set out in regulations (*SI 2005 No 3338*). These provide for the determination of the syndicate profit/loss and its apportionment between the members, the filing of returns and HMRC's powers to determine syndicate profits in certain cases. For the purpose of determining the liability to tax of each member of the syndicate, a determination of a syndicate's profit or loss for an underwriting year and its apportionment between members is conclusive against that member. For the purpose of the extended time limits at **6.3–6.5 ASSESSMENTS**, anything done or omitted to be done by a syndicate's managing agent is deemed to have been done or omitted to be done by each member of the syndicate.

The regulations also provide for the managing agent to claim from HMRC the repayment of tax suffered by way of deduction on the syndicate's investment income, to apportion the amount repaid between the members of the syndicate and (except in so far as it is required to meet a share of a loss of the syndicate) pay the amount so apportioned to each member, within 90 days of the repayment, to the members' agent of that member. Such repayment does not attract repayment supplement as in **41.1 INTEREST ON OVERPAID TAX.**

[*SI 2005 No 3338*].

Special reserve fund

[74.7] An underwriter may set up a Special Reserve Fund into which he may make payments (eligible for tax relief — see **74.9** below) for the purpose of meeting future losses.

A special reserve fund may be set up in relation to each underwriter under arrangements complying with the requirements of *FA 1993, Sch 20 Pt I* and approved by HMRC (who may consent to any variation of the arrangements). The fund must be vested in trustees who have control over it, and there must be appointed a fund manager, authorised under Lloyd's rules and who may be the trustees or one or more of them, to invest the capital and vary the investments. Payments into and out of the fund (which, unless a contrary intention appears in the legislation, must be in money) must be allowed only where required or permitted (expressly or by necessary implication) by the provisions of *Sch 20*. Otherwise, the income arising from the fund must be added to capital and retained in the fund. The underwriter is absolutely entitled as against the trustees to the fund assets, but subject to the rules of cessation (see **74.11** below) and without affecting the operation of capital gains tax on a disposal of an asset by the underwriter to the trustees. The fund manager must value the fund in a manner prescribed by regulations (see *SI 1995 No 353*) as at the end of each underwriting year, and must report the value (and such other matters as may be prescribed by regulations) to the underwriter. [*FA 1993, s 175(1)(2), Sch 20 paras 1(1), 2, 6(1), 8*].

Payments into and out of the special reserve fund are, respectively, deductions and additions in arriving at the underwriter's profit. [*FA 1993, Sch 19 para 10(2)(a)(3)(a), Sch 20 para 10*].

Where a member dies and his personal representatives carry on his underwriting business after his death, the special reserve fund provisions are modified to apply to the personal representatives. [*SI 1995 No 353, Regs 7, 7A*].

Simon's Taxes. See E5.641, E5.642.

Tax exemption

[74.8] Profits arising from special reserve fund assets are exempt from both income tax and capital gains tax, and losses are not allowable. The fund manager may, at any time after the end of an underwriting year, claim repayment of income tax deducted from such profits for that year. [*FA 1993, Sch 20 para 9*].

Payments into the fund out of syndicate profits

[74.9] For the purposes of the provisions described below, an underwriter's '*syndicate profit*' for an underwriting year is the excess of his aggregate profits over his aggregate losses, profits or losses being those shown in syndicate accounts as arising to him and disregarding payments into or out of the special reserve fund. Profits of a run-off underwriting year are attributable to the last underwriting year but one preceding the run-off year. An underwriter's *'syndicate loss'* is to be construed accordingly. *[FA 1993, Sch 20 para 1; SI 1995 No 353]*.

If an underwriter has made a syndicate profit for an underwriting year, he may pay into his special reserve fund, before the end of a period prescribed by regulations (see *SI 1995 No 353*), the lesser of:

(i)   50% of that profit; and

(ii)   the excess, if any, of an amount equal to 50% of the underwriter's 'overall premium limit' for the closing year (i.e. the year next but one following the underwriting year) over the value of the fund at the end of that year.

An underwriter's *'overall premium limit'* for an underwriting year means the maximum amount which, under Lloyd's rules, he may accept by way of premiums in that year. If the underwriter did not accept premiums in the closing year, the reference in (ii) above to the closing year is to be taken as a reference to the latest underwriting year in which he did so. The above provisions are not to apply, in the case of any underwriter, to any tax year after a tax year in which HMRC cancel their approval of the arrangements referred to in **74.7** above, having first given notice to Lloyd's of their intention to do so.

The payment into the fund in respect of an underwriting year is deductible as an expense in arriving at underwriting profits. It is made for the tax year next but two after the tax year to which the underwriting year corresponds (i.e. a payment made in underwriting year 2007 is deducted in 2010/11).

[FA 1993, s 175(3), Sch 20 paras 1(1), 3, 10(1)].

Payments out of the special reserve fund

[74.10] Payments *must* be made out of the fund in the following circumstances.

(i)   To cover 'cash calls'. A *'cash call'* means a request for funds made to the underwriter by an agent of a syndicate of which he is a member, being made in pursuance of a contract made in accordance with Lloyd's rules and practices. If a cash call is made in respect of an underwriting year, there must be paid out of the underwriter's special reserve fund into a premium trust fund of his an amount equal to the amount of the call (or, if less, the amount of the special reserve fund). There are provisions for a payment to be made back into the special reserve fund if a stop-loss payment (i.e. a payment of insurance money under a stop-loss insurance or a payment out of the High Level Stop Loss Fund — see **74.3** above) is made to the underwriter, and for a further payment out of the fund if a stop-loss payment is wholly or partly repaid. *[FA 1993, Sch 20 para 4; SI 1995 No 353]*.

(ii)   To cover syndicate losses. If an underwriter sustains a syndicate loss for an underwriting year, there must be paid out of his special reserve fund into a premium trust fund of his an amount equal to the 'net amount of the loss' (or, if less, the amount of the special reserve fund). The '*net amount of the loss*' is the amount of the syndicate loss as reduced by any payment made out of the special reserve fund for the year to cover a cash call (see (i) above). As in (i) above, there are provisions for payments into and out of the special reserve fund in the event of stop-loss payments and repayments of stop-loss payments. If a stop-loss payment is made in respect of the loss before any payment out of the special reserve fund in respect of the loss, no payment is required into the fund but the said payment out of the fund is determined as if the net amount of the loss were reduced by the amount of the stop-loss payment. [*FA 1993, Sch 20 para 5*].

(iii) To eliminate excess amounts. If on the valuation (see **74.7** above) of the special reserve fund at the end of the underwriting year, it is found that the value of the fund exceeds 50% of the higher of the underwriter's overall premium limit (see **74.9** above) for that year and the corresponding figure for the previous year (or 50% of his overall premium limit for the last year in which he accepted premiums), the excess must be paid to the underwriter (or to his personal representatives or assigns). [*FA 1993, Sch 20 para 6(2)*].

(iv) On cessation. On a person ceasing to be an underwriter (on death or otherwise), the amount of his special reserve fund (net of any amount required to be paid out to cover cash calls or syndicate losses) must be paid over to the underwriter (or to his personal representatives or assigns), the payment to be in money or in assets forming part of the fund, as the recipient may direct. [*FA 1993, Sch 20 para 7*].

Any payments required to be made out of or into the fund under (i)–(iii) above must be made before the end of a period to be prescribed in each case by regulations (see *SI 1995 No 353*). [*FA 1993, Sch 20 paras 4(8), 5(10), 6(3)*].

In computing underwriting profits for a tax year, payments into the special reserve fund under (i) and (ii) above in respect of the 'relevant' underwriting year are deductible as expenses, and the following are treated as trading receipts:

- payments out of the fund in respect of the 'relevant' underwriting year to cover cash calls and losses;
- payments out of the fund as a result of the repayment of stop-loss payments (see (i) and (ii) above) in the 'relevant' underwriting year; and
- any payment out of the fund under (iii) above in respect of the 'relevant' underwriting year's closing year (i.e. the underwriting year next but one following the 'relevant' underwriting year).

The '*relevant*' underwriting year for this purpose is the underwriting year next but two before the corresponding underwriting year, i.e. for 2010/11, for which the corresponding underwriting year is 2010, the relevant underwriting year is 2007.

[*FA 1993, Sch 20 para 10(2)–(4)*].

Cessation

[74.11] The aggregate of any payments made out of the special reserve fund under **74.10**(iv) above is treated, in computing underwriting profits for the 'relevant tax year', as made immediately after the end of the 'relevant underwriting year' and as being a trading receipt. Where cessation occurs by reason of death, such payments are treated for the purposes of INTEREST AND SURCHARGES ON OVERDUE TAX (**42**) as if made immediately after the beginning of the member's final tax year. The amount of the said trading receipt is the value of the fund at the end of the 'penultimate underwriting year' as reduced by subsequent payments out (other than under **74.10**(iii) or (iv) above) and as increased by:

- subsequent payments in;
- subsequent repayments of tax in respect of fund income;
- the amount of any subsequent profits, net of any losses, arising to the trustees from assets (any net deficit being deducted), leaving aside any gain or loss on an asset transferred to the member etc. and treated as an acquisition by him for capital gains tax purposes (see below); and
- any payments made before the end of the penultimate underwriting year by the trustees to the member etc., whether under **74.10**(iv) above or otherwise than out of the special reserve fund, including the market value of any asset transferred by way of such payment.

On the transfer of an asset by the trustees to the member, his personal representatives or assigns, whether under **74.10**(iv) above or otherwise, there are rules to determine for capital gains tax purposes both the date and cost of acquisition by the member etc., for which see the corresponding chapter of Tolley's Capital Gains Tax.

The '*relevant tax year*' is the final tax year except that, where a member dies before the occurrence of certain events, it is the tax year at the end of which he is treated as having died (see **74.2** above). The events in question are where the member's deposit is paid over to any person (or a substituted arrangement ceases) or the last open year of account of any syndicate of which he was a member is closed or is regarded as having closed. The '*relevant underwriting year*' is the underwriting year corresponding to the tax year immediately preceding the final tax year except that, where the member dies before the occurrence of certain events (as above), it is the underwriting year immediately preceding that corresponding to the relevant tax year (as above). The '*penultimate underwriting year*' is the underwriting year corresponding to the tax year immediately preceding the final tax year.

[*FA 1993, Sch 20 para 11*].

75

Unit Trusts etc.

Simon's Taxes. See **D8.1**.

Introduction

[75.1] This chapter (at **75.2–75.8** below) covers authorised investment funds (see below), principally from the point of view of an investor within the charge to income tax. From a similar viewpoint the chapter also covers unauthorised unit trusts (**75.9** below) and court common investment funds (**75.10** below). For the corporation tax provisions applicable to authorised investment funds and the treatment of distributions in the hands of corporate participants in authorised investment funds, see Tolley's Corporation Tax under Investment Funds. See **51 OFFSHORE FUNDS** for unit trusts which are offshore funds. For official guidance on unit trusts and other collective investment schemes, see www.hmrc.gov.uk/collective/index.htm.

An authorised investment fund may be either an authorised unit trust (see **75.2** below), an open-ended investment company (see **75.3** below) or a qualified investor scheme (see **75.5** below where a condition is met as to diversity of ownership — otherwise see **75.2** or **75.3** below, whichever is appropriate); different rules applied before 1 January 2009 — see **75.6** below. With effect on and after 1 September 2009, UK authorised investment funds that meet certain conditions may elect to be treated as a tax elected fund (see **75.7** below). With effect on and after 6 July 2010, a special regime is available for authorised investment funds which invest in non-reporting offshore funds (see **75.8** below).

Authorised unit trusts (AUTs)

[75.2] An '*authorised unit trust*' (AUT) is a 'unit trust scheme' which is the subject of an order under *Financial Services and Markets Act 2000, s 243* for the whole or part of an accounting period. A '*unit trust scheme*' is defined by

Financial Services and Markets Act 2000, s 237 as a collective investment scheme under which the property is held on trust for the participants. A unit holder is a person entitled to a share of the investments subject to the trusts of the scheme. The *Tax Acts* have effect as if the trustees were a company resident in the UK, and the rights of unit holders were shares in the company (but without prejudice to the making of 'interest distributions' (see below)). [*CTA 2010, s 617(1); ICTA 1988, s 468(1); ITA 2007, s 1007; SI 2006 No 964, Reg 88; SI 2009 No 23, Regs 1, 5(5)*]. For capital gains tax (CGT) purposes, any unit trust scheme is treated as if the scheme were a company and the rights of the unit holders were shares in the company, and, in the case of an AUT, as if the company were UK resident and ordinarily resident. [*TCGA 1992, s 99(1)*]. See the corresponding chapter of Tolley's Capital Gains Tax.

A special rate of corporation tax applies to the trustees of an AUT, equivalent to the basic rate of income tax (for 2008/09 onwards, previously the savings rate) for the tax year beginning in the financial year concerned. [*CTA 2010, s 618; ICTA 1988, s 468(1A); ITA 2007, Sch 1 para 85(1); FA 2008, Sch 1 paras 41, 65*].

'*Umbrella schemes*' (i.e. schemes which provide separate pools of contributions between which participants may switch) which are AUTs are treated as if each of the separate pools were an AUT. [*CTA 2010, s 619; ICTA 1988, s 468(7)–(9); FA 1994, s 113*].

Distributions

The rules on distributions are largely contained in the *Authorised Investment Funds (Tax) Regulations 2006 (SI 2006 No 964)*. See also *ITTOIA 2005, ss 376–378, 389–391 as amended*.

The total amount available for distribution to unit holders is to be allocated either for distribution as dividends or for distribution as yearly interest (which may not include any amount deriving from property income). This and the other distribution rules below do not apply to an AUT that is a registered pension scheme (see **57.2 PENSION PROVISION**).

A '*distribution period*' of an AUT is the period by reference to which the amount available for distribution is ascertained. The '*distribution date*' for a distribution period is the date specified for that purpose under the terms of the trust or instrument of incorporation or, if there is no such date specified, the last day of the distribution period.

Where the total amount available is allocated for distribution as dividends, it is treated for tax purposes as if it were dividends on shares paid on the distribution date to the unit holders in proportion to their holdings. Where the total amount available is allocated for distribution as yearly interest, it is treated for tax purposes as if it were yearly interest paid on the distribution date to the unit holders in proportion to their holdings. See **1.5, 1.6 ALLOWANCES AND TAX RATES** as regards taxation of dividends and other savings income (including interest) generally.

The retention and reinvestment by an AUT of an otherwise distributable amount in respect of a unit holder's accumulation units counts as a distribution.

There is a *de minimis* provision whereby an authorised investment trust may choose to waive a distribution if, in accordance with rules made by the Financial Services Authority, the trust has an agreed *de minimis* limit and the total amount available to be allocated for distribution is below that limit. The amount available must then be carried forward to the next distribution period as income available for distribution for that period. It is a condition that none of the units of the fund in issue on the distribution date are in bearer form. Where these conditions are satisfied, the amount carried forward is treated as not having been distributed.

No amount may be allocated for distribution as yearly interest unless the AUT satisfies the qualifying investments test throughout the distribution period, which it does if, at all times in that period, the market value of 'qualifying investments' exceeds 60% of the market value of all the investments of the trust (disregarding cash awaiting investment). '*Qualifying investments*' are any of the following:

(a) money placed at interest;

(b) building society shares;

(c) securities (other than company shares);

(d) units in another AUT or in an open-ended investment company, provided that, throughout the distribution period in question, more than 60% of the market value of the other unit trust's or the open-ended investment company's investments is represented by investments falling within (a)–(c) above and (f)–(i) below;

(e) units in an offshore fund, provided that, throughout the distribution period in question, more than 60% of the market value of the offshore fund's investments is represented by investments falling within (a)–(c) above and (f)–(i) below;

(f) derivative contracts whose underlying subject matter consists wholly of any one or more of (a)–(d) above and currency;

(g) contracts for differences (within *CTA 2009, s 582*) whose underlying subject matter consists wholly of any one or more of interest rates, creditworthiness or currency;

(h) derivative contracts (not within (f) or (g) above) where there is a hedging relationship between the derivative contract and an asset within (a)–(d) above; and

(i) alternative finance arrangements (see **3 ALTERNATIVE FINANCE ARRANGEMENTS**).

Tax deductible at source from interest distributions

Tax is deductible at source under *ITA 2007, s 874* from interest distributions unless either:

• the unit holder to whom the payment is made is either a company or the trustees of a unit trust scheme; or

• either the 'residence condition' or the 'reputable intermediary condition' is met with respect to the unit holder on the distribution date.

For 2008/09 onwards, the deduction is at the basic rate; previously it was at the savings rate.

The '*residence condition*' requires that any one of the following be met:

- the unit holder has made a valid declaration that he is not ordinarily resident in the UK; or
- the units are held by the personal representative of a deceased person in his capacity as such and the deceased had made a declaration, valid at the time of his death, that he is not ordinarily resident in the UK; or
- the units are held by the personal representative of a deceased person in his capacity as such and the personal representative makes a valid declaration that the deceased, immediately before his death, was not ordinarily resident in the UK; or
- the distribution is made to a trust under which the whole of the income is the income of a person other than the trustees and that person has made a valid declaration that he is not ordinarily resident in the UK or, if the person is a company, that the company is not resident in the UK; or
- the distribution is made to a trust to which the above does not apply and the trustees have made a valid declaration that they are not resident in the UK and that each beneficiary is not ordinarily resident in the UK or, in the case of a corporate beneficiary, not resident in the UK.

Declarations as above must be made to the trustees of the AUT in prescribed form and must contain specified details and undertakings.

The *'reputable intermediary condition'* requires broadly that the interest distribution is paid on behalf of the unit holder to a company which is subject to certain money laundering controls, and that the trustees of the AUT have reasonable grounds for believing the unit holder to be not ordinarily resident in the UK. If it subsequently transpires that the unit holder was in fact ordinarily resident, the tax which should have been deducted is payable to HMRC by the trustees of the AUT. See *TMA 1970, s 98(4E)* (as amended) for penalty provisions.

Compliance and HMRC powers

The trustees of an AUT are required to notify HMRC about distributions made without deduction of tax, within a specified time and subject to penalties for non-compliance. HMRC have power to require information about such distributions and to inspect records (including residence declarations and certificates of non-liability) (see now *SI 2006 No 964, regs 71–75 as amended*).

[*ITTOIA 2005, ss 376–378, 389–391; FA 2005, ss 55, 56, Sch 2 paras 1, 4; F(No 2)A 2005, ss 17–19; ITA 2007, Sch 1 para 605; CTA 2009, Sch 1 para 669; CTA 2010, Sch 1 paras 454, 479; SI 2006 No 964, Regs 8, 15–33, 70–75; SI 2006 No 982; SI 2007 No 794; SI 2008 No 705; SI 2009 No 2036, Regs 5, 11, 25–29; SI 2010 No 294, Regs 7–13, 24*].

For guidance on the tax treatment of income from AUTs, see www.hmrc.gov.uk/collective/treatment-investors.htm.

Simon's Taxes. See **D8.115–D8.120, E1.408, E1.413.**

Open-ended investment companies (OEICs)

[75.3] The rules on distributions are largely contained in the *Authorised Investment Funds (Tax) Regulations 2006 (SI 2006 No 964)*. Those rules are the same as those described at **75.2** above, subject only to a few minor necessary modifications. See also *ITTOIA 2005, ss 373–375, 386–388*, which mirror the equivalent provisions for authorised unit trusts.

For guidance on the tax treatment of income from OEICs, see www.hmrc.go v.uk/collective/treatment-investors.htm.

Property AIFs

[75.4] On and after 6 April 2008, *SI 2006 No 964, Pt 4A* enables OEICs (see **75.3** above) to become Property AIFs (Property Authorised Investment Funds). This is a separate regime for collective investment in real property and in Real Estate Investment Trusts (REITs) (see **60.14 PROPERTY INCOME**) and foreign equivalents. The regime is similar to the REIT regime itself. An OEIC carrying on a property investment business (as defined) and meeting the other required conditions can elect for the Property AIF regime to have effect. Its property-related income is then exempt from tax in the OEIC's hands. A distribution received from a Property AIF by an individual investor is treated in his hands as profits of a UK property business to the extent that it is paid out of the tax-exempt profits of the AIF. Basic rate tax is deducted at source by the Property AIF; the shareholder remains liable for any excess liability, i.e. excess of the higher rate of tax over the basic rate. The distribution does not carry a tax credit. A distribution of taxable income (not including dividends) is treated as interest in the hands of the investor and is also subject to deduction of basic rate tax at source. A distribution out of UK dividend income is treated as a dividend in the hands of the investor and carries a (non-repayable) tax credit. [*SI 2006 No 964, Pt 4A; SI 2008 No 705, SI 2008 No 3159, Regs 18–27; SI 2009 No 56, Sch 1 para 156–158, SI 2009 No 2036, Regs 15–23; SI 2010 No 294, Regs 16–19*].

Qualified Investor Schemes

[75.5] A Qualified Investor Scheme (QIS) is a type of (non-retail) authorised investment fund (either an open-ended investment company or a unit trust) authorised by the Financial Services Authority and aimed at sophisticated and institutional investors. The instrument constituting the scheme must contain a statement that the scheme is a QIS. The taxation of investors in a QIS is determined in accordance with the *Authorised Investment Funds (Tax) Regulations 2006 (SI 2006 No 964)*.

A QIS is treated for tax purposes in the same way as any other open-ended investment company or authorised unit trust provided that it meets a 'genuine diversity of ownership condition'. This rule applies to QISs established on or after 1 January 2009 and to existing QISs with effect on and after that date. A QIS authorised before 1 January 2009 is, however, automatically deemed to satisfy the condition for its accounting period straddling that date.

Where the genuine diversity of ownership condition is not satisfied for an accounting period of the scheme, the QIS is treated for tax purposes as if it were a close investment holding company within *ICTA 1988, s 13A* (see Tolley's Corporation Tax).

[SI 2006 No 964, reg 14B; SI 2008 No 3159, Regs 1, 11, 30; SI 2010 No 294, Reg 6].

Previously, a QIS fell to be treated in the same way as any other open-ended investment company or authorised unit trust, but investors were subject to the substantial holdings regime at **75.6** below.

A QIS meets the '*genuine diversity of ownership condition*' for an accounting period if:

(a) the scheme documents contain a statement that units in the scheme will be widely available and must specify the intended categories of investor and that the scheme manager must market and make available the units in accordance with (c) below;

(b) neither the specification of intended investor categories nor any other terms or conditions of investing in the scheme have the effect of either restricting investors to a limited number of specified persons or specified groups of connected persons (within *ITA 2007, s 993* or *ICTA 1988, s 839*) or of deterring any reasonable investor within the intended categories from investing in the scheme;

(c) units in the scheme are marketed and made available sufficiently widely to reach the intended categories of investor and in a way appropriate to attract those categories; and

(d) any person within one of the specified categories of intended investor can, on request to the scheme manager, obtain information about the scheme and acquire units in it.

Conditions (c) and (d) above are treated as met even where the scheme has no current capacity to receive additional investments, unless the capacity to receive investments is fixed and a pre-determined number of specified persons (or groups of connected persons) make investments which collectively exhaust all, or substantially all, of that capacity.

Before 1 September 2009, a QIS also met the genuine diversity of ownership condition if an investor in the scheme was a unit trust and the conditions at (a)–(d) above were met after taking into account investors in the unit trust. Both the QIS and the unit trust had to have the same manager (or proposed manager). This now applies only if the scheme is a property AIF (see **75.4** above).

[SI 2006 No 964, regs 9A, 14C; SI 2008 No 3159, Reg 11; SI 2009 No 2036, Regs 6, 9].

There are procedures under which a QIS may obtain clearance from HMRC that it satisfies the genuine diversity of ownership condition. See *SI 2006 No 964, Regs 9B, 14D*.

For CGT aspects of holding and disposing of units in a QIS, see the corresponding chapter of Tolley's Capital Gains Tax.

Substantial holdings regime before 1 January 2009

[75.6] Prior to the introduction of the genuine diversity of ownership condition in **75.5** above, a special tax regime applied as set out below to investors with a 'substantial holding' in a QIS. Certain classes of investor were excluded from this regime, e.g. charities, registered pension schemes and any person for whom a profit on the sale of units would have fallen to be treated as part of his trading profits.

An investor (referred to below as a participant) has a 'substantial holding' in a QIS if he owns units representing rights to 10% or more of the net asset value of the fund. Units held by CONNECTED PERSONS (**21**) or associates (within *ICTA 1988, s 417* — now *CTA 2010, s 448*) are taken into account for this purpose. Once a substantial holding has been established, it continues to be regarded as a substantial holding until *all* the units are disposed of, regardless of whether or not the 10% condition continues to be satisfied.

The charge to income tax is made by reference to the difference in market value of a substantial holding between two 'measuring dates'. For this purpose, the market value of the holding is established as at the beginning of the current measuring date and compared to the corresponding figure as at the end of the previous measuring date. (Where both buying and selling prices of units are published regularly by the scheme manager, market value means the buying price, i.e. the lower price.) The differences in value calculated by reference to each 'chargeable measuring date' in a tax year are aggregated. If the aggregate is a positive figure, the participant (if within the charge to income tax) is charged to income tax on that aggregate under *ITTOIA 2005, Pt 5 Ch 8* (income not otherwise charged). If the aggregate is a negative figure, the participant (if within the charge to income tax) is treated as having sustained a loss of that amount in a transaction; the *regulation* under which this applies (*SI 2006 No 964, Reg 57*) is then deemed to be included in the list at **49.8** MISCELLANEOUS INCOME so that the loss relief provisions at **49.11** apply.

Each of the following is a *'measuring date'*:

- the first measuring date (see below), but this is not a *'chargeable measuring date'*;
- any date on which a participant already with a substantial holding acquires additional units;
- each 'reporting date' — a *'reporting date'* is the final day of each half-yearly and annual accounting period of the scheme;
- any date on which there is a disposal (construed as for CGT purposes) of all or part of the substantial holding; and
- the date of the participant's death.

The first measuring date is the date as at which the participant is first required to value his holding. The general rule is that a participant is required to value his holding as at the first date on which he has a substantial holding, but this is subject to the following modifications.

- The first modification applies if the participant had a substantial holding on 6 April 2006, the first day of the new regime. If, on the first measuring date after 30 June 2006, the participant still has a substantial holding (but not otherwise), he is first required to value his holding as at 6 April 2006.

- The second modification applies when a new QIS is launched. If, on the first anniversary of the date of issue of the first prospectus, the participant has a substantial holding, the general rule above applies. If not, he is not required to value his holding either as at that first anniversary or as at any earlier date.

- The second modification applies if a participant comes to have a substantial holding other than as a result of acquiring additional units. If, on both the next reporting date (see above) and the one following, he does not have a substantial holding on the next reporting date (see above) or the one following, he is not required to value his holding at any time and is not treated as having a substantial holding either at the second of those reporting dates or at any earlier time. If, on the second of those reporting dates, he does have a substantial holding, the general rule applies.

For the purpose of bringing the substantial holdings regime to an end with effect on and after 1 January 2009, 31 December 2008 is treated as a final measuring date.

[SI 2006 No 964, Regs 8, 53–57, 59–64; SI 2008 No 3159, Regs 17, 31].

Capital Gains Tax

Broadly, an accrued gain (or loss) is computed when the substantial holding is established. The gain is subsequently brought into charge (or the loss becomes allowable), wholly or partly as the case may be, as and when the holding is disposed of or partly disposed of. Once the substantial holding is established, subsequent increases and reductions in its value are within the income tax regime above and thus fall outside the CGT regime.

Tax elected funds

[75.7] A new regime is introduced with effect on and after 1 September 2009 whereby a UK authorised investment fund (AIF) that meets certain conditions may elect to be treated as a tax elected fund (TEF). The effect is to move the point of taxation from the AIF to the investor, so that investors are taxed as though they had invested in the underlying assets directly. TEFs are required to make two types of distribution of the income they receive — a dividend distribution and a non-dividend (interest) distribution. For all income that is distributed as interest, the TEF obtains a corresponding tax deduction.

Of the total amount shown in the distribution accounts of a TEF as available for distribution to participants, dividends, property investment income and property business income must be attributed to dividend distributions, and all other income must be attributed to interest distributions. If an amount distributed by the TEF includes sums attributed to dividend distributions, the same tax consequences ensue as if those sums were dividends on shares paid on the distribution date by the fund to the participants in proportion to their rights. If an amount distributed by the TEF includes sums attributed to interest distributions, the same tax consequences ensue as if those sums were payments of yearly interest made on the distribution date by the fund to the participants in proportion to their rights. As regards the deduction of basic rate tax at source from interest distributions, the same rules and exceptions apply as in **75.2** above.

An TEF may elect out of the regime or have its TEF status terminated by HMRC.

[*SI 2006 No 964, Pt 4B; SI 2009 No 2036, Reg 24*].

Funds investing in non-reporting offshore funds (FINROFs)

[75.8] A special regime is available for authorised investment funds (AIFs) which invest in 'non-reporting offshore funds' (as in **51.3 OFFSHORE FUNDS**). Such AIFs are known as 'FINROFs'. The regime moves the point of taxation from the AIF to the investor in the AIF. The regime came into effect on 6 March 2010 but applies from 6 July 2010 to AIFs which met the 'investment condition' below on 6 March; such an AIF is treated as first meeting the investment condition on 6 July 2010, provided it did in fact meet it on that date.

The regime applies to:

(a)   an AIF which meets the 'investment condition' below;
(b)   an AIF which has elected into the regime;
(c)   a participant in an AIF in (a) or (b) above; and
(d)   a participant in an AIF which has left the FINROF regime, where the participant has not made the 'deemed disposal election' outlined below.

The '*investment condition*' in (a) above is that the total amount invested by the AIF in non-reporting offshore funds or other FINROFs is more than 20% of the gross asset value of the fund. For this purpose, gross asset value does not include cash awaiting investment. The election in (b) above must be made in writing by the fund manager and must specify the date from which the fund is to enter the FINROF regime. That date cannot be more than three months before the date of the election.

An AIF enters the regime from the date that the investment condition is first met or, if earlier, the date specified in an election. The AIF must notify its participants within three months that the fund has entered the FINROF regime and inform them that any gains made on the disposal of units in the fund shall be treated as income gains (see below) rather than as capital gains. If an AIF inadvertently and temporarily meets the investment condition, there is provision for it to be treated as if it had never met that condition.

A participant in an AIF that enters the FINROF regime may elect to be treated for CGT purposes as having disposed of and immediately reacquired his fund units at market value on the date the AIF enters the regime. If the participant is chargeable to income tax, the election can be made only by being included in his tax return for the year which includes that date.

Where an AIF ceases to meet the investment condition, the fund manager may, subject to certain conditions, elect for the fund to cease to be a FINROF. The AIF must notify its participants within three months that the fund has left the FINROF regime. The regime nevertheless continues to apply to the participants. However, a participant may elect to be treated as having disposed of and immediately reacquired his fund units at market value on the date the AIF leaves the regime (the '*deemed disposal election*' referred to at (d) above), in which case the regime ceases to apply to him. If the participant is chargeable to income tax, the election can be made only by being included in his tax return for the year which includes that date. The election can be made only if the deemed disposal produces a gain (which will then be charged to tax as income as below).

The charge to tax

Where a participant in an AIF is within (c) or (d) above, a gain on a disposal of his units is charged to tax as income and is referred to as an '*income gain*'. The income gain is treated for tax purposes as miscellaneous income which arises at the time of the disposal to the person making the disposal. The tax is charged on that person. An income gain is computed in the same way as a chargeable gain would be computed under CGT legislation. If such a computation would produce a loss, the income gain is taken to be nil. In a computation of a gain arising on the disposal for CGT purposes, a sum equal to the income gain is deductible from the consideration for the disposal. The detailed rules are not dissimilar to the rules for offshore income gains at **51.3–51.7, 52.1J** OFFSHORE FUNDS.

[*SI 2006 No 964, Pt 6A; SI 2010 No 294, Regs 21, 25*].

Unauthorised unit trusts

[75.9] The following provisions apply to a unit trust scheme not within **75.2** above (an 'unauthorised unit trust'), the trustees of which are UK resident. Such a trust is outside the rules in **75.2** above. Income arising to the trustees is treated as income of the trustees (as opposed to income of the unit holders). The unit holders are treated as receiving annual payments, under deduction of basic rate tax, equal to their respective entitlements to the grossed-up income available for distribution or investment. The date the payment is treated as having been made is the latest (or only) date for distribution under the terms of the trust or (if there is no such date or it is more than twelve months after the end of the distribution period) the last day of the distribution period. For the definition of 'distribution period', see *ITTOIA 2005, s 548(5)–(7)*.

The income of the trustees is chargeable at the basic rate of income tax to the extent that it would otherwise be chargeable at the savings rate (before 2008/09) or at the dividend ordinary rate. The charge on certain income (at

68.12 SETTLEMENTS) at the special trust rates does not apply. The income of the unit holders is also chargeable at the basic rate (to the extent, in the case of an individual, that it falls within the basic rate band).

No tax credit is attached to any qualifying distributions received by the trustees. Similarly, no notional tax credit is attached to non-qualifying distributions.

The liability of the trustees to account for tax deducted from annual payments treated as made by them is dealt with in their self-assessment returns. The liability is reduced where there is a cumulative uncredited surplus of modified net income on which they are chargeable to tax over such annual payments.

The trustees (and not the unit holders) are treated as the persons to or on whom any capital allowance or balancing charge is to be made.

Legislation has been enacted to thwart identified avoidance schemes involving unauthorised unit trusts in receipt of foreign income in respect of which the trustees claim double tax relief. It is in response to schemes that seek to take advantage of the tax rules applicable to unauthorised unit trusts by using them to convert foreign income subject to withholding tax into receipts of UK income with an associated UK tax credit. The aim of the schemes is to generate repayment of the tax credit or to avoid restrictions on the use of credits for foreign tax. The legislation has effect in relation to payments treated as made by the trustees to the unit holders on or after 21 October 2009. It means that in appropriate circumstances part of the payment is treated in the unit holders' hands as foreign income from which overseas tax has been deducted rather than UK income from which basic rate tax has been deducted. The foreign income is regarded as having arisen in a territory which has no double tax treaty with the UK. The overseas tax is accordingly treated as if it were tax payable under the law of such a territory.

For any tax year in which the trustees of an unauthorised unit trust are deemed to have made a payment of income to a unit holder, they must, as soon as reasonably practicable after the end of that year, give the unit holder an annual statement. The statement must include the following information in relation to each such deemed payment: the date on which it was treated as made; its gross amount; the foreign element (if any); the tax deduction deemed to have been made at source; and the foreign element (if any) of that deduction. This applies in relation to payments deemed to have been made on or after 21 October 2009 and is enforceable by the unit holder. The references to the foreign element of the income and of the tax deduction are to the amounts to be treated under the anti-avoidance legislation outlined above as foreign income and as overseas tax.

[ITA 2007, ss 504, 504A, 505, 506, 941–943, 943A–943D, 989, 1007, Sch 1 paras 87, 541, 542, Sch 2 paras 167, 168; CTA 2010, ss 621, 622; ITTOIA 2005, ss 547–550; ICTA 1988, s 469; FA 2008, ss 34, 66(4)(l)(8), Sch 1 paras 23, 65, Sch 12 para 25; CTA 2009, Sch 1 para 713; FA 2010, Sch 13; SI 2009 No 23, Regs 1, 5(2)(5); SI 2010 No 157, Art 3(6)(9)].

Pension fund pooling

Regulations make special provision to ensure that certain international pooled pension funds (registered as 'pension fund pooling vehicles') are transparent for UK tax purposes, by disapplying the tax rules for unauthorised unit trusts (as above). Participants in such schemes must be approved by HMRC, and are treated for income tax, capital allowances and CGT purposes as though they themselves owned directly a share of each of the trust assets. There is also relief from stamp duty (or stamp duty reserve tax) on transfers of assets (other than land or buildings) by participants into the scheme. Participation in pension fund pooling vehicles is restricted to registered pension schemes (or, before 2006/07, exempt approved pension schemes), UK-based superannuation funds used primarily by companies employing British expatriates working overseas, and recognised overseas pension schemes within *FA 2004, s 150(8)* (or, before 2006/07, pension funds established outside the UK broadly equivalent to UK exempt approved pension schemes). [*SI 1996 Nos 1583, 1584, 1585* as amended]. See generally HMRC Savings and Investment Manual SAIM6200–6230. The position in the country in which any overseas participator is based will of course be crucial to the operation of such schemes.

Simon's Taxes. See **C1.209, D8.130–D8.133, E1.457, E1.458.**

Court common investment funds

[75.10] Court common investment funds (CCIFs) are a form of unit trust set up by the Lord Chancellor under *Administration of Justice Act 1982, s 42(1)*. They are available only for individuals whose money is under control of certain Courts, e.g. road accident victims and the mentally incapacitated. CCIFs are treated for tax purposes as authorised unit trusts within **75.2** above. The investment manager is treated as the trustee, and the persons with qualifying interests are treated as the unit holders. For the above purposes, the persons with qualifying interests are, in relation to shares in the fund held by the Accountant General (or other person authorised by the Lord Chancellor), the persons whose interests entitle them, as against him, to share in the fund's investments. They also include any persons authorised by the Lord Chancellor to hold shares in the fund on their own behalf. [*CTA 2010, s 620; ICTA 1988, s 469A*].

76

Venture Capital Trusts

Simon's Taxes. See **C3.11, D8.2, E3.2.**

Introduction

[76.1] The venture capital trust scheme described at **76.2** *et seq.* below was introduced to encourage individuals to invest in unquoted trading companies through such trusts. It sets out to achieve this by a combination of income tax and capital gains tax reliefs.

The Treasury has wide powers to make regulations governing all aspects of the reliefs applicable to venture capital trust investments, and for the requirements as regards returns, records and provision of information by the trust. [*ITA 2007, ss 272, 284; FA 2007, Sch 16 para 21*]. See *SI 1995 No 1979; SI 1999 No 819; SI 2008 No 1893.*

See generally HMRC Venture Capital Schemes Manual VCM10000–17320, 60000 *et seq.* and the guidance at www.hmrc.gov.uk/guidance/vct.htm.

Income tax reliefs

[76.2] Relief from income tax is granted in respect of both investments in VCTs and dividends from VCTs.

Investment relief

[76.3] Subject to the conditions described below, an individual may claim relief ('investment relief') for a tax year for the amount (or aggregate amounts) subscribed by him on his own behalf for 'eligible shares' issued to him in the tax year by a VCT (or VCTs) for raising money. There is a limit of £200,000 on the amount in respect of which relief can be claimed for any one tax year.

'*Eligible shares*' means ordinary shares in a VCT which, throughout the five years following issue, carry no present or future preferential right to dividends or to assets on a winding up and no present or future right (before 6 April 1998, present or future preferential right) to redemption.

Relief is given by a reduction (a '*tax reduction*') in what would otherwise be the individual's income tax liability for the tax year by:

(i)   (for shares issued in 2006/07 and subsequent years) 30% of the amount eligible for relief;

(ii)   (for shares issued in 2004/05 and 2005/06 only) tax at the higher rate (40%) on the amount eligible for relief (regardless of whether or not the individual is a higher rate taxpayer);

(iii)   (for shares issued in any tax year before 2004/05) 20% of the amount eligible for relief.

Investors may restrict a claim to relief in respect of a tax year to only some of the shares issued to them. The order in which tax reductions are given against an individual's tax liability is set out at **1.8 ALLOWANCES AND TAX RATES**, which also makes clear that a tax reduction must be restricted to the extent (if any) that it would otherwise exceed the individual's remaining income tax liability after making all prior reductions.

An individual is **not** entitled to relief where:

(a)   he was under 18 years of age at the time of issue of the shares;

(b)   circumstances have arisen which, had the relief already been given, would have resulted in the withdrawal or reduction of the relief (see **76.5** below);

(c)   the shares were issued or subscribed for other than for genuine commercial purposes or as part of a scheme or arrangement a main purpose of which was the avoidance of tax; or

(d)   a loan is made to the individual (or to an 'associate') by any person at any time in the period beginning with the incorporation of the VCT (or, if later, two years before the date of issue of the shares) and ending five years after the date of issue of the shares, and the loan would not have been made, or would not have been made on the same terms, if he had not subscribed, or had not been proposing to subscribe, for the shares. The granting of credit to, or the assignment of a debt due from, the individual or associate is counted as a loan for these purposes.

For the purposes of (d) above, an *'associate'* of any person is any 'relative' (i.e. spouse, civil partner, ancestor or linear descendant) of that person, the trustee(s) of any settlement in relation to which that person or any relative (living or dead) is or was a settler and, where that person has an interest in any shares of obligations of a company which are subject to any trust or are part of a deceased estate, the trustee(s) of the settlement or the personal representatives of the deceased. For this purpose, 'settlor' is defined as in *ITA 2007, ss 467–473*.

An individual is *not* eligible for relief by reference to any shares *treated as* issued to him by virtue of *FA 2003, s 195(8)*, which provides for a disposal to a person by a company of its own shares (so-called 'treasury shares') to be treated as a new issue of shares and for the recipient to be treated as having subscribed for them. In such a case, the VCT must, at the time the shares are issued, give the individual a notice stating that he is not eligible for relief, and must copy that notice to HMRC within three months after the issue.

[*ITA 2007, ss 261–265, 271(4), 273, 332, Sch 2 paras 59–61, 63; ICTA 1988, Sch 15B paras 1, 2, 6; FA 2006, Sch 14 paras 4(1)(3), 7(2)(4)(5); SI 2003 No 3077*].

As regards (d) above, for this restriction to apply, the test is whether the lender makes the loan on terms which are connected with the fact that the borrower (or an associate) is subscribing for eligible shares. The prime concern is why the lender made the loan rather than why the borrower applied for it. Relief would not be disallowed, for example, in the case of a bank loan if the bank would have made a loan on the same terms to a similar borrower for a different purpose. But if, for example, a loan is made specifically on a security consisting of or including the eligible shares (other than as part of a broad range of assets to which the lender has recourse), relief would be denied. Relevant features of the loan terms would be the qualifying conditions to be satisfied by the borrower, any incentives or benefits offered to the borrower, the time allowed for repayment, the amount of repayments and interest charged, the timing of interest payments, and the nature of the security. (HMRC SP 6/98).

An individual subscribing for eligible shares may obtain from the VCT a certificate giving details of the subscription and certifying that certain conditions for relief are satisfied. [*SI 1995 No 1979, Reg 9; SI 2008 No 1893, Reg 10*].

Relief for a year can only be claimed after the end of the year, and any in-year claims for relief by repayment through self-assessment will be rejected. This does not affect the right to claim a reduction in payments on account (see **65.5 SELF-ASSESSMENT**), and relief may still be given through a PAYE coding. (Revenue Tax Bulletin April 2002 p 924).

Simon's Taxes. See E3.211.

Example

[76.4]

On 1 May 2010, Miss K, who has annual earnings of £80,000, subscribes for 100,000 eligible £1 shares issued at par to raise money by VCT plc, an approved venture capital trust. On 1 September 2010 she purchases a further 225,000 £1 shares in VCT plc for £175,000 on the open market. The trust makes no distribution in 2010/11. Miss K's other income for 2010/11 consists of dividends of £16,200. PAYE tax deducted is £21,930.00.

Miss K's tax computation for 2010/11 is as follows.

	£	£
Employment income		80,000
Dividends	16,200	
Add Tax credit	1,800	18,000
Total and net income		98,000
Deduct Personal allowance		6,475
Taxable income		£91,525
Tax payable:		
37,400 @ 20%		7,480.00
36,125 @ 40%		14,450.00
18,000 @ 32.5% (dividend upper rate)		5,850.00
		27,780.00
Deduct Relief for investment in VCT plc:		
30% of £100,000 subscribed = £30,000		
but restricted to		27,780.00
Net tax payable		—

PAYE tax of £21,930.00 is repayable. Dividend tax credits are not repayable.

Withdrawal of investment relief

[76.5] Where an individual disposes of eligible shares, in respect of which relief has been claimed as under **76.3** above, within five years of their issue (three years for shares issued after 5 April 2000 and before 6 April 2006) and other than to a spouse or civil partner when they are living together (see below), then:

(a)   if the disposal is otherwise than at arm's length, relief given by reference to those shares is withdrawn;

(b)   if the disposal is at arm's length, the relief given by reference to those shares is reduced by the appropriate percentage of the consideration received for the disposal and is withdrawn entirely if thereby reduced to nil. The appropriate percentage is 30% in relation to shares issued in 2006/07 or a subsequent year, 40% in relation to shares issued in 2004/05 or 2005/06 and 20% in relation to shares issued in 2003/04 or an earlier year, i.e. it mirrors the rate at which investment relief was available.

For the above purposes, disposals of eligible shares in a VCT are identified with those acquired earlier rather than later. As between eligible shares acquired on the same day, shares by reference to which relief has been given are treated as disposed of after any other eligible shares.

Relief is *not* reduced or withdrawn where the disposal is by one spouse or civil partner to the other at a time when they are living together. However, on any subsequent disposal the spouse or civil partner to whom the shares were transferred is treated as if he or she were the person who subscribed for the shares, as if the shares had been issued to him or her at the time they were issued to the transferor spouse or civil partner, and as if his or her liability to income tax had been reduced by reference to those shares by the same amount, and for the same tax year, as applied on the subscription by the transferor spouse or civil partner. Any assessment for reducing or withdrawing relief is made on the transferee spouse or civil partner.

[*ITA 2007, ss 266, 267, Sch 2 para 62; ICTA 1988, Sch 15B para 3; FA 2006, Sch 14 paras 4(2), 7(3)*].

Withdrawal of approval

Where approval of a company as a VCT is withdrawn (but not treated as never having been given) (see **76.14** above), relief given by reference to eligible shares in the VCT is withdrawn as if on a non-arm's length disposal immediately before the withdrawal of approval. [*ITA 2007, s 268; ICTA 1988, Sch 15B para 3(9)*].

Relief subsequently found not to have been due

Relief which is subsequently found not to have been due is withdrawn. [*ITA 2007, s 269; ICTA 1988, Sch 15B para 4(1)*].

Assessments withdrawing or reducing relief

Such assessments are made for the tax year for which the relief was given. No such assessment is, however, to be made by reason of an event occurring after the death of the person to whom the shares were issued. [*ITA 2007, s 270; ICTA 1988, Sch 15B para 4*].

Information

Particulars of all events leading to the reduction or withdrawal of relief must be notified to HMRC by the person to whom the relief was given within 60 days of his coming to know of the event. The requirements of secrecy do not prevent HMRC disclosing to a VCT that relief has been given or claimed by reference to a particular number or proportion of its shares. [*ITA 2007, s 271(1)–(3)(5); ICTA 1988, Sch 15B para 5; SI 2009 No 2035, Sch para 47*].

Simon's Taxes. See E3.212.

Example

[76.6]

On 1 May 2012, Miss K in the *Example* at **76.4** above, who has since 2010/11 neither acquired nor disposed of any further shares in VCT plc, gives 62,500 shares to her son. On 1 January 2013, she disposes of the remaining 262,500 shares for £212,500. The relief given as in **76.4** above is withdrawn as follows.

Disposal on 1 May 2012

The shares disposed of are identified, on a first in/first out basis, with 62,500 of those subscribed for, and, since the disposal was not at arm's length, the relief given on those shares is withdrawn.

£

$$\text{Relief withdrawn} \quad \frac{62,500}{100,000} \times 27,780 =$$

17,362

Disposal on 1 January 2013

The balance of £10,418 of the relief originally given was in respect of 37,500 of the shares disposed of. The disposal consideration for those 37,500 shares is

$$212,500 \times \frac{37,500}{262,500} = £30,357$$

The relief withdrawn is the lesser of the relief originally given (£10,418) and 30% of the consideration received, i.e.

30% of £30,357 = £9,107

Relief withdrawn is therefore	9,107
The 2010/11 assessment to withdraw relief is therefore	£26,469

Dividend relief

[76.7] A 'VCT dividend' to which a 'qualifying investor' is beneficially entitled is not treated as income for income tax purposes, provided that certain conditions are fulfilled as regards the obtaining of an 'enduring declaration' from the investor, and that the VCT claims the related tax credit, which it is required to pass on to the investor.

A *'qualifying investor'* is an individual aged 18 or over who is beneficially entitled to the distribution either as the holder of the shares or through a nominee (including the trustees of a bare trust).

A *'VCT dividend'* is a dividend paid in respect of ordinary shares in a company which is a VCT which were acquired at a time when it was a VCT by the recipient of the dividend, and which were not shares acquired in excess of the 'permitted maximum' for the year. The shares must also have been acquired for genuine commercial reasons and not as part of a tax avoidance scheme or arrangements. A 'VCT dividend' does not include any dividend paid in respect of profits or gains of any accounting period ending when the company was not a VCT.

Shares are acquired in excess of the *'permitted maximum'* for a year where the aggregate value of ordinary shares acquired in VCTs by the individual or his nominee(s) in that year exceeds £200,000, disregarding shares acquired other than for genuine commercial reasons or as part of a scheme or arrangement a main purpose of which is the avoidance of tax. Shares acquired later in the year are identified as representing the excess before those acquired earlier, and in relation to same-day acquisition of different shares, a proportionate part of each description of share is treated as representing any excess arising on that day. Shares acquired at a time when a company was not a VCT are for these purposes treated as disposed of before other shares in the VCT. Otherwise, disposals are identified with earlier acquisitions before later ones, except that as between shares acquired on the same day, shares acquired in excess of the permitted maximum are treated as disposed of before any other shares. There are provisions for effectively disregarding acquisitions arising out of share exchanges where, for capital gains purposes, the new shares are treated as the same assets as the old.

[*ITTOIA 2005, ss 709–712*].

Simon's Taxes. See E3.213.

Example

[76.8]

In 2011/12, Miss K in the *Example* at **76.4** above, whose circumstances are otherwise unchanged, receives a dividend from VCT plc of 9p per share.

The shares in VCT plc were acquired in 2010/11 for £275,000, so that dividends in respect of shares representing the £75,000 excess over the permitted maximum of £200,000 are not exempt. The 100,000 shares first acquired for £100,000 are first identified, so that the shares representing the excess are three-sevenths (75,000/175,000) of the 225,000 shares subsequently acquired for £175,000, i.e. 96,429 of those shares.

Miss K's tax computation for 2011/12 (assuming, for illustrative purposes only, that there are no changes in rates and allowances since 2010/11) is as follows.

	£	£
Employment income		80,000
Dividends (other than VCT plc)	16,200	
Add Tax credit	1,800	18,000
VCT plc distribution in respect of 96,429 shares	8,679	
Add Tax credit (¹/₉)	964	9,643
Total and net income		107,643
Deduct Personal allowance	6,475	
Restricted by excess of income over £100,000: (£7,643 x /)	3,821	2,654
Taxable income		£104,989
Tax payable:		
37,400 @ 20%		7,480.00
39,946 @ 40%		15,978.40
27,643 @ 32.5% (dividend upper rate)		8,983.97
Tax payable		32,442.37
Deduct Tax credits		2,764.30
Net tax liability (subject to PAYE)		£29,678.07

Capital gains tax reliefs

[76.9] The capital gains of a VCT are not chargeable gains. [*TCGA 1992, s 100(1); FA 1995, s 72(2)*].

In addition, individual investors in VCTs are entitled to exemption on the disposal of VCT shares (see **76.10** below).

Withdrawal of approval

Where approval of a company as a VCT is withdrawn (but not treated as never having been given) (see **76.14** above), shares which (apart from the withdrawal) would be eligible for the relief on disposal (see **76.10** below) are treated as disposed of at their market value at the time of the withdrawal. For the purposes of the relief on disposal, the disposal is treated as taking place while the company is still a VCT, but the re-acquisition is treated as taking place immediately after it ceases to be so. [*TCGA 1992, s 151B(6)(7); ITA 2007, Sch 1 para 315(3)*].

Exemption on disposal

[76.10] A gain or loss accruing to an individual on a 'qualifying disposal' of ordinary shares in a company which was a VCT throughout his period of ownership is not a chargeable gain or an allowable loss. A disposal is a *'qualifying disposal'* if:

(a)   the individual is 18 years of age or more at the time of the disposal;
(b)   the shares were not acquired in excess of the 'permitted maximum' for any tax year; and
(c)   the shares were acquired for genuine commercial purposes and not as part of a scheme or arrangement a main purpose of which was the avoidance of tax.

The identification of those shares which were acquired in excess of the *'permitted maximum'* is as under **76.7** above (in relation to dividend relief — broadly those in excess of an annual limit of £200,000), and the identification of disposals with acquisitions for this purpose is similarly as under **76.7** above.

[*TCGA 1992, ss 151A, 151B; ITA 2007, Sch 1 paras 314, 315*].

See **76.9** above as regards relief on withdrawal of approval of the VCT.

Simon's Taxes. See **C3.1103**.

Example

[76.11]

On the disposals in the *Example* at **76.6** above, a chargeable gain or allowable loss arises only on the disposal of the shares acquired in excess of the permitted maximum for 2010/11. As in the *Example* at **76.8** above, these are 96,429 of the shares acquired for £175,000 on 1 September 2010. The disposal identified with those shares is a corresponding proportion of the 262,500 shares disposed of for a consideration of £212,500 on 1 January 2013.

Miss K's capital gains tax computation for 2012/13 is therefore as follows.

	£
Disposal consideration for 96,429 shares —	
$212,500 \times \dfrac{96,429}{262,500} =$	78,061
Deduct Cost —	
$175,000 \times \dfrac{96,429}{225,000} =$	75,000
Chargeable gain	£3,061

Conditions for approval of a VCT

[76.12] A 'venture capital trust' ('VCT') is a company approved for this purpose by HMRC, close companies being excluded. The time from which an approval takes effect is specified in the approval, and may not be earlier than the time the application for approval was made. [ITA 2007, ss 259, 283; ICTA 1988, s 842AA(1)].

Approval may not be given unless HMRC are satisfied that the following conditions are met in relation to the most recent complete accounting period of the company and will be met in relation to the accounting period current at the time of the application for approval.

Where any of the conditions are not met, approval may nevertheless be given where HMRC are satisfied as to the meeting of those conditions (and in some cases other conditions imposed by regulations) in future accounting periods. [ITA 2007, s 275; ICTA 1988, s 842AA(4)].

See 76.14 below as regards withdrawal of approval, 76.15 below for special rules where two or more VCTs merge and 76.16 below for special rules where a VCT is wound up.

The listing condition

The company's ordinary shares (or each class thereof) must be included in the official UK list (within Financial Services & Markets Act 2000, Pt 6) throughout those periods. This is to be amended to a requirement that the shares must be admitted to trading on an EU regulated market. The legislation is to be included in a Finance Bill to be introduced in autumn 2010 and will have effect on and after a date to be appointed. (HMRC Budget Note BN11, 22 June 2010).

The nature of income condition

The company's income (as defined) must be derived wholly or mainly from shares or 'securities'.

'*Securities*' for these purposes are deemed to include liabilities in respect of certain loans not repayable within five years, and any stocks or securities relating to which are not re-purchasable or redeemable within five years of issue. Provided that the loan is made on normal commercial terms, HMRC will not regard a standard event of default clause in the loan agreement as disqualifying a loan from being a security for this purpose. If, however, the clause entitled the lender (or a third party) to exercise any action which would cause the borrower to default, the clause would not be regarded as 'standard'. (HMRC SP 8/95).

The income retention condition

An amount greater than 15% of its income (as defined) from shares and securities must not be retained by the company.

This condition does not apply for an accounting period if the amount the company would be required to distribute is less than £10,000 (proportionately reduced for periods of less than twelve months), or if the company is required by law to retain income in excess of the 15% limit. The latter exclusion only applies, however, if the aggregate of the excess of retentions over those required by law and any distribution is less than £10,000 (proportionately reduced for periods of less then twelve months).

The 15% holding limit condition

No 'holding' in any company other than a VCT (or a company which could be a VCT but for the listing condition above) may represent more than 15% of the value of the company's investments at any time in those periods.

For this purpose, and that of the 70% qualifying holdings condition below, the meaning of 'the company's investments' is extended after 5 April 2007 to include (if it would not otherwise include) money in the company's possession and any sum owed to the company over which the company has 'account-holder's rights', i.e. the right to require payment either to the company or at its direction. Anything to which the company is not beneficially entitled is excluded (though, for this purpose, a company *is* beneficially entitled to sums subscribed for shares issued by it and anything representing such sums).

If this condition was met when a holding in a company was acquired, it is treated as continuing to be met until any more shares or securities of the company are acquired (otherwise than for no consideration).

'*Holding*' means the shares or securities of whatever class or classes held in any one company. Where, in connection with a 'scheme of reconstruction' (within *TCGA 1992, s 136*), a company issues shares or securities to persons holding shares or securities in another in respect of, and in proportion to (or as nearly as may be in proportion to) such holdings, without the recipients' becoming liable for any consideration, the old and the new holdings are treated as the same. Holdings in companies which are members of a group (i.e. a company and its 51% subsidiaries), whether or not including the company whose holdings they are ('company A'), are treated as holdings in a single company if they are not excluded from the 15% holding limit condition. If company A is a member of a group, money owed to it by another group member is treated as a security and, as such, as part of its holding in that other group member.

See **76.13** below for the value of the company's investments.

The 70% qualifying holdings condition

Throughout the accounting periods at least 70% by value of the company's investments must be represented by shares or securities in 'qualifying holdings' (see **76.17** below).

Where this limit is breached inadvertently, and the position is corrected without delay after discovery, approval will in practice not be withdrawn on this account. Full details of any such inadvertent breach should be disclosed to HMRC as soon as it is discovered. (Revenue Press Release 14 September 1995).

On a second and subsequent issue of shares by an approved VCT, this condition and the eligible shares condition below do not have to be met, in relation to the money raised by the further issue, in the accounting period of the further issue or any later accounting period ending no more than three years after the making of the further issue. *SI 2004 No 2199, Reg 14* limits the operation of this rule by stipulating that the money raised by the further issue must be for the purposes of acquiring additional investments which do fulfil the conditions. Where any of that money (or assets derived therefrom) is used for another purpose, then from a time immediately before that use the whole of the money raised by the issue is deemed to be included in the company's investments in applying the percentage tests in the two conditions. If any of the money is used by the VCT to buy back its own shares, this stipulation is treated, in particular, as not fulfilled if HMRC regard the purchase as not insignificant in relation to the issued ordinary share capital of the VCT or if it is made as a result of a general offer to members. If the money is raised by a successor VCT (in a merger) and used to buy shares in the merging companies, the stipulation is treated, in particular, as not fulfilled if the money so used exceeds the least of three specified limits.

Where, on or after 6 April 2007, a VCT disposes of a holding that was comprised in its qualifying holdings throughout the six months ending immediately before the disposal, both the fact of the disposal and any monetary consideration for it are disregarded for a period of six months beginning with the disposal in determining whether or not the 70% qualifying holdings condition is met. This does not apply if the holding was acquired with money raised by a second or subsequent issue of shares such that the 70% qualifying holdings condition does not for the time being have to be met in relation to that money (see above). It also does not apply if the consideration for the disposal consists entirely of new qualifying holdings. If the consideration for the disposal consists partly of new qualifying holdings, the above treatment applies only to an appropriate proportion of the holding disposed of. The treatment does not apply at all to disposals between companies that are merging.

See the 15% holding limit condition above for the meaning of 'the company's investments' and see **76.13** below for the value of investments.

The eligible shares condition

At least 30% of the company's qualifying holdings (by value) must be represented throughout the accounting periods by holdings of *'eligible shares'*, i.e. ordinary shares carrying no present or future preferential right to dividends or to assets on a winding up and no present or future right to redemption.

See the 70% qualifying holdings condition above where a VCT makes a second or subsequent issue of shares and see **76.13** below for the value of investments.

The eligible shares condition is to be amended by increasing the 30% requirement to 70%. In addition, some changes are to be made to the definition of 'eligible shares' so as to include shares which may carry certain preferential rights to dividends. The legislation is to be included in a Finance Bill to be introduced in autumn 2010. The amendments will have effect on and after a date to be appointed but will not apply in relation to monies raised by the VCT before that date. (HMRC Budget Note BN11, 22 June 2010).

[*ITA 2007, ss 274, 276, 277, 280, 280A, 285, 989, 1005, Sch 2 paras 64, 66, 67; ICTA 1988, ss 842(1A)(1AB)(2)–(3), 842AA(2)(5A)(5B)(11); FA 2006, Sch 14 para 8; FA 2007, Sch 16 para 20, Sch 26 paras 1, 12(6)(12); CTA 2009, Sch 1 para 701; SI 2009 No 2860, art 5*].

Simon's Taxes. See D8.215–D8.212.

Value of investments

[76.13] The value of any investment for the purposes of the 15% holding limit condition, the 70% qualifying holdings condition and the eligible shares condition in **76.12** above, is the value when the investment was acquired, except that where it is added to by a further holding of an investment of the same description (otherwise than for no consideration), or a payment is made in discharge of any obligation attached to it which increases its value, it is the value immediately after the most recent such addition or payment.

For this purpose, where, in connection with a 'scheme of reconstruction' (within *TCGA 1992, s 136*; previously a 'scheme of reconstruction or amalgamation'), a company issues shares or securities to persons holding shares or securities in another in respect of, and in proportion to (or as nearly as may be in proportion to) such holdings, without the recipients' becoming liable for any consideration, the old and the new holdings are treated as the same.

Where:

• shares or securities in a company are exchanged for corresponding shares and securities in a new holding company; or

- a VCT exercises conversion rights in respect of certain convertible shares and securities,

then, subject to detailed conditions (see *ITA 2007, ss 326–329*), the value of the new shares is taken to be the same as the value of the old shares when they were last valued for these purposes.

Where, under a company reorganisation or other arrangement:

- a VCT exchanges a qualifying holding for other shares or securities (with or without other consideration); and
- the exchange is for genuine commercial reasons and not part of a tax avoidance scheme or arrangements,

regulations provide a formula which values the new shares or securities by reference to the proportion of the value of the old shares or securities that the market value of the new shares or securities bears to the total consideration receivable. If no other consideration is receivable, the value of the new is identical to that of the old. The provisions extend to new shares or securities received in pursuance of an earn-out right (see Tolley's Capital Gains Tax under Shares and Securities) conferred in exchange for a qualifying holding, in which case an election is available (under *SI 2002 No 2661, Reg 10*) to modify the formula by effectively disregarding the earn-out right itself.

[*ITA 2007, ss 278, 279, Sch 2 para 65; ICTA 1988, ss 842(3), 842AA(5)–(5AE)(11); SI 2002 No 2661*].

Withdrawal of approval

[76.14] Approval may be withdrawn where there are reasonable grounds for believing that either:

- the conditions for approval were not satisfied at the time the approval was given; or
- a condition that HMRC were satisfied would be met has not been or will not be met; or
- in either the most recent complete accounting period or the current accounting period, one of the conditions in **76.12** above has failed or will fail to be met (unless the failure was allowed for); or
- where, in relation to a second or further issue by an approved VCT, the 70% qualifying holdings condition and the eligible shares condition above do not have to be met in the period of issue or certain following accounting periods (see **76.12** above), one of the conditions in **76.12** above will fail to be met in the first period for which those two conditions must be met; or
- any other conditions prescribed by regulations have not been met in relation to, or to part of, an accounting period for which the 70% qualifying holdings condition and the eligible shares condition in **76.12** above do not have to be met.

The withdrawal is effective from the time the company is notified of it, except that:

- where approval is given on HMRC's being satisfied as to the meeting of the relevant conditions in future accounting periods, and is withdrawn before all the conditions in **76.12** above have been satisfied in relation to either a complete twelve-month accounting period or successive complete accounting periods constituting a continuous period of twelve months or more, the approval is deemed never to have been given; and
- for the purposes of relief for capital gains accruing to a VCT under *TCGA 1992, s 100* (see **76.9** above), withdrawal may be effective from an earlier date, but not before the start of the accounting period in which the failure occurred (or is expected to occur).

An assessment consequent on the withdrawal of approval may, where otherwise out of time, be made within three years from the time notice of the withdrawal was given.

For the detailed requirements as regards granting, refusal and withdrawal of approval, and appeals procedures, see *SI 1995 No 1979, Pt II.*

The Treasury have power to make regulations setting out circumstances in which HMRC will not withdraw approval from VCTs that breach the conditions for approval. See now *SI 1995 No 1979, Regs 8–8J* as inserted by *SI 2008 No 1893, Reg 9* with effect on and after 1 September 2008 which enable HMRC to determine that they will not withdraw their approval in a particular case provided that:

- the circumstances in which the VCT breached the conditions are outside its control;
- the VCT took all reasonable measures to continue to meet the conditions; and
- the breach is rectified by the VCT as soon as is reasonably possible or, in a case in which no measures could be taken by the VCT to rectify it, is nevertheless rectified in the course of events.

[*ITA 2007, ss 281, 282, 284; ICTA 1988, s 842AA(6)–(10); FA 2007, Sch 16 para 21*].

Mergers

[76.15] For mergers (as defined) of two or more VCTs, Treasury regulations (*SI 2004 No 2199, Regs 9–13*) enable the merging VCTs to retain VCT status and provide for investors in the merged VCTs who continue as investors in the successor company (as defined) to retain their tax reliefs. Broadly, the shares issued to effect the merger stand in the place of the shares for which they are exchanged or in respect of which they are issued. But these rules apply only where HMRC have notified their approval to the merger in advance of its taking place. The regulations lay down the detailed conditions for approval and the procedure for obtaining approval (including right of appeal against non-approval); approval will not be granted to mergers carried out other than for genuine commercial reasons or as part of tax avoidance arrangements. [*ITA 2007, ss 321–325; SI 2004 No 2199; SI 2008 No 954, Arts 1, 54; SI 2009 No 56, Sch 2 para 129*].

Winding-up

[76.16] Treasury regulations (*SI 2004 No 2199, Regs 3–7*) enable a VCT to retain its status as a VCT for a maximum of three years from the commencement of the winding-up. To qualify for this extension, the VCT must normally have been approved for at least three years prior to commencement of winding-up (five years in the case of VCTs first issuing shares between 6 April 2004 and 5 April 2006 inclusive). The intention is to provide a period of grace during which investors' reliefs can continue; the grace period does not, however, prevent a withdrawal of income tax investment relief (see **76.5** above) where the minimum holding period is not otherwise met (Treasury Explanatory Notes to Finance Bill 2002).

Regulations (*SI 2004 No 2199, Reg 8*) also permit a VCT commencing winding-up to transfer investments to another VCT and for such investments to be treated as meeting the requirements of a qualifying holding (see **76.17** below) in the hands of the recipient VCT to the same extent as they did in the hands of the first VCT. The transfer must be by way of arm's length bargain or for consideration not below market value, and it must occur within the period of grace referred to above and after all other reasonable endeavours to sell the investments at or near to market value have failed. No more than 7.5% of the value of investments at the commencement of winding-up can be transferred in this way.

In all cases, the winding-up must be for genuine commercial reasons and not part of tax avoidance arrangements.

[*ITA 2007, ss 314–320, 324, 325; SI 2004 No 2199; SI 2008 No 954, Arts 1, 54; SI 2009 No 56, Sch 2 para 129*].

Qualifying holdings of a VCT

[76.17] A VCT's holding of shares or securities in a company is comprised in its '*qualifying holdings*' at any time if the shares or securities were first issued to the VCT, and have been held by it ever since, and the requirements at **76.18–76.32** below are satisfied at that time. See also the supplementary provisions at **76.33** below.

Where any of the 'maximum qualifying investment' requirement (**76.18**), 'use of money raised' requirement (**76.25**) or 'relevant company to carry on the relevant qualifying activity' requirement (**76.26**) would be met as to only part of the money raised by the issue, and the holding is not otherwise capable of being treated as separate holdings, it is treated as two separate holdings, one from which that part of the money was raised, the other from which the rest was raised, with the value being apportioned accordingly to each holding. In the case of the use of money raised requirement, this does not require an insignificant amount applied for non-trade purposes to be treated as a separate holding.

[*ITA 2007, ss 286, 293(7); ICTA 1988, Sch 28B paras 1, 6(3); FA 2007, Sch 16 paras 3(2), 6(2)*].

The Treasury have power to modify by statutory instrument the trading requirement (**76.21**), the 'carrying on of a qualifying activity' requirement (**76.23**) and the qualifying subsidiaries requirement (**76.31**) as they consider expedient, and to alter the cash limits referred to in the 'maximum qualifying investment' requirement (**76.18**) and the gross assets requirement (**76.29**). [*ITA 2007, s 311; ICTA 1988, Sch 28B para 12*].

Informal clearance

Enquiries from potential investee companies as to whether they meet the conditions for investment by a venture capital trust should be directed to Small Company Enterprise Centre, HM Revenue and Customs, 1st Floor, Ferrers House, Castle Meadow Road, Nottingham, NG2 1BB (tel. 0115 974 1250; fax 0115 974 2954).

The 'maximum qualifying investment' requirement

[76.18] The holding in question must not, when it was issued, have represented an investment in excess of the 'maximum qualifying investment' for the period from six months before the issue in question (or, if earlier, the beginning of the tax yea of the issue) to the time of the issue. For this purpose, the maximum qualifying investment for a period is exceeded so far as the aggregate amount of money raised in that period by the issue to the VCT during that period of shares or securities of the company exceeds £1 million. Where this limit is exceeded, the shares or securities which represent the excess are treated as not being part of the holding concerned (so that £1 million can be included as a qualifying holding) and the money raised by those shares or securities is ignored for the purpose of any subsequent application of this requirement. Disposals are treated as far as possible as eliminating any such excess. The £1 million limit is proportionately reduced where, at the time of the issue, the qualifying trade is carried on, or to be carried on, in partnership or as a joint venture, and one or more of the other parties is a company. [*ITA 2007, s 287, Sch 2 para 68; ICTA 1988, Sch 28B para 7*].

The 'no guaranteed loan' requirement

[76.19] The holding in question must not include any securities (as defined in **76.12** above) relating to a guaranteed loan. A security relates to a guaranteed loan if there are arrangements entitling the VCT to receive anything (directly or indirectly) from a 'third party' in the event of a failure by any person to comply with the terms of the security or the loan to which it relates. It is immaterial whether or not the arrangements apply in all such cases. '*Third party*' means any person other than the investee company itself and, if it is a parent company that meets the trading requirement at **76.21** below, its subsidiaries. This condition applies for accounting periods (of the VCT) ending after 1 July 1997, but does not apply in the case of shares or securities acquired by the VCT by means of investing money raised by the issue by it before 2 July 1997 of shares or securities (or money derived from the investment of any such money raised). [*ITA 2007, s 288, Sch 2 para 69; ICTA 1988, Sch 28B para 10A*].

The 'proportion of eligible shares' requirement

[76.20] At least 10% (by value) of the VCT's *total* holding of shares in and securities of the company must consist of 'eligible shares' (as defined for the purposes of the eligible shares condition at **76.12** above — broadly, ordinary, non-preferential, shares). For this purpose, the value of shares etc. at any time is taken to be their value immediately after the most recent of the events listed below, except that it cannot thereby be taken to be less than the amount of consideration given by the VCT for the shares etc. The said events are as follows.

- The acquisition of the shares etc. by the VCT.
- The acquisition by the VCT (other than for no consideration) of any other shares etc. in the same company which are of the same description as those already held.
- The making of any payment in discharge (or part discharge) of any obligation attached to the shares etc. in a case where such discharge increases the value of the shares etc.

[*ITA 2007, s 289, Sch 2 para 70; ICTA 1988, Sch 28B para 10B*].

The trading requirement

[76.21] The company must either:

(a)   exist wholly for the purpose of carrying on one or more 'qualifying trades' (see **76.22** below), disregarding any purpose having no significant effect on the extent of its activities, or

(b)   be a *'parent company'* (i.e. a company that has one or more 'qualifying subsidiaries' — see the subsidiaries requirements at **76.31** below) and the business of the *'group'* (i.e. the company and its qualifying subsidiaries) must not consist wholly or as to a substantial part (i.e. broadly 20% — see HMRC Venture Capital Schemes Manual VCM17040) in the carrying on of 'non-qualifying activities'.

Where the company intends that one or more other companies should become its qualifying subsidiaries with a view to their carrying on one or more qualifying trades, then, until any time after which the intention is abandoned, the company is treated as a parent company and those other companies are included in the group for the purposes of (b) above. (This provision is made explicit in *ITA 2007* but reflects previous practice (see Change 61 listed in Annex 1 to the Explanatory Notes to *ITA 2007*).)

For the purpose of (b) above, the business of the group means what would be the business of the group if the activities of the group companies taken together were regarded as one business. Activities are for this purpose disregarded to the extent that they consist in:

(i)   holding shares in or securities of any of the company's subsidiaries;

(ii)   making loans to another group company;

(iii)   holding and managing property used by a group company for the purposes of a qualifying trade or trades carried on by any group company; or

(iv)   holding and managing property used by a group company for the purposes of research and development from which it is intended either that a qualifying trade to be carried on by a group company will be derived or, for shares issued after 5 April 2007, a qualifying trade carried on or to be carried on by a group company will benefit.

References in (iv) above to a group company include references to any existing or future company which will be a group company at any future time.

Activities are similarly disregarded to the extent that they consist, in the case of a subsidiary whose main purpose is the carrying on of qualifying trade(s) and whose other purposes have no significant effect on the extent of its activities (other than in relation to incidental matters), in activities not in pursuance of its main purpose.

'*Non-qualifying activities*' are:

* activities within **28.50**(a)–(m) ENTERPRISE INVESTMENT SCHEME (other than those within **28.50**(d) which do not result in a trade being excluded from being a qualifying trade); and
* non-trading activities.

[*ITA 2007, ss 290, 332, Sch 2 para 71; ICTA 1988, Sch 28B paras 3, 10*].

A company does not cease to meet this requirement by reason only of anything done as a consequence of its being in administration or receivership (both as defined — see *ITA 2007, s 331*), provided everything so done and the making of the relevant order are for genuine commercial (and not tax avoidance) reasons. [*ITA 2007, s 292, Sch 2 para 73; ICTA 1988, Sch 28B para 11A*].

Qualifying trades

[76.22] A trade is a '*qualifying trade*' if it is conducted on a commercial basis with a view to the realisation of profits and it does not, at any time in the period since the issue of the shares to the VCT consist to a substantial extent in the carrying on of 'excluded activities'. For these purposes, 'trade' (except in relation to the trade mentioned in (m) below) does not include a venture in the nature of trade. '*Excluded activities*' are:

(a)   dealing in land, commodities or futures, or in shares, securities or other financial instruments; or

(b)   dealing in goods otherwise than in an ordinary trade of wholesale or retail distribution (see below); or

(c)   banking, insurance or any other financial activities; or

(d)   leasing or letting or receiving royalties or licence fees; or

(e)   providing legal or accountancy services; or

(f)   'property development';

(g)   farming or market gardening;

(h)   holding, managing or occupying woodlands, any other forestry activities or timber production;

(i)   shipbuilding (defined by reference to relevant EU State aid rules);

(j)   producing coal or steel (both defined by reference to relevant EU State aid rules and including the extraction of coal);

(k)   operating or managing hotels or comparable establishments (i.e. guest houses, hostels and other establishments whose main purpose is to offer overnight accommodation with or without catering) or property used as such;

(l)   operating or managing nursing homes or residential care homes (both as defined) or property used as such;

(m)   providing services or facilities for any trade, profession or vocation concerned in (a) to (l) and carried on by another person (other than a parent company), where one person has a 'controlling interest' in both trades.

HMRC regard as 'substantial' for the above purposes a part of a trade which consists of 20% or more of total activities, judged by any reasonable measure (normally turnover or capital employed) (HMRC Venture Capital Schemes Manual VCM17040). As regards (a) above, dealing in land includes cases where steps are taken, before selling the land, to make it more attractive to a purchaser; such steps might include the refurbishment of existing buildings (HMRC Venture Capital Schemes Manual VCM17050).

As regards (b) and (d)–(f) above, see the comments in **28.50 ENTERPRISE INVESTMENT SCHEME** on the corresponding exclusions there.

Exclusions (i) and (j) above (and the reference to those in exclusion (m)) do not apply in relation to shares and securities issued before 6 April 2008 or to shares and securities acquired by the VCT after that date by means of the investment of:

- money raised by the issue before 6 April 2008 of shares in or securities of the VCT; or
- money derived from the investment by the VCT of money so raised.

As regards (k), (l) and (m) above, see the comments in **28.50 ENTERPRISE INVESTMENT SCHEME** on the corresponding exclusions there.

[ITA 2007, ss 300(1)(4), 303–310, 313(5)–(7), Sch 2 paras 81–85; ICTA 1988, Sch 28B paras 4, 5, 10, 13; FA 2007, Sch 16 paras 12–14; FA 2008, Sch 11 paras 7–9, 10, 12, 13; CTA 2010, Sch 1 para 505].

Research and development

'Research and development' from which it is intended that a qualifying trade carried on 'wholly or mainly in the UK' (see below) either will be derived or, for shares issued to the VCT after 5 April 2007, will benefit is treated as the carrying on of a qualifying trade. Preparing to carry on such research and development does not, however, count as preparing to carry on a trade. 'Research and development' has the meaning given by ITA 2007, s 1006 — see **73.109 TRADING INCOME**. [ITA 2007, s 300(2)(3), Sch 2 para 78; ICTA 1988, Sch 28B para 4(1)].

Meaning of 'wholly or mainly in the UK'

In considering whether a trade is carried on 'wholly or mainly in the UK', the totality of the trade activities is taken into account. Regard will be had, for example, to where capital assets are held, where any purchasing, processing, manufacturing and selling is done, and where the company employees and other agents are engaged in its trading operations. For trades involving the provision of services, both the location of the activities giving rise to the services and the location where they are delivered will be relevant. No one factor is itself likely to be decisive in any particular case. A company may carry on some such activities outside the UK and yet satisfy the requirement, provided that the major part of them, that is over one-half of the aggregate of these activities, takes place within the UK. Thus relief is not excluded solely because a company's products or services are exported, or because its raw materials are imported, or because its raw materials or products are stored abroad. Similar principles apply in considering the trade(s) carried on by a company and its qualifying subsidiaries.

In the particular case of a ship chartering trade, the test is satisfied if all charters are entered into in the UK and the provision of crews and management of the ships while under charter take place mainly in the UK. If these conditions are not met, the test may still be satisfied depending on all the relevant facts and circumstances. (HMRC SP 3/00).

The 'wholly or mainly in the UK' requirement is to be dropped in relation to shares or securities issued on or after an appointed day and replaced by a requirement that the company must have a permanent establishment in the UK. The legislation is to be included in a Finance Bill to be introduced in autumn 2010. (HMRC Budget Note BN11, 22 June 2010).

The 'carrying on of a qualifying activity' requirement

[76.23] In relation to shares or securities issued to the VCT after 16 March 2004, a 'qualifying company' (whether or not the same such company at all times) must, when the shares were issued to the VCT and at all times since, have been carrying on one of the following two *'qualifying activities'*:

(a) carrying on a 'qualifying trade' (see **76.22** above) 'wholly or mainly in the UK' (see **76.22** above); or

(b) preparing to carry on a qualifying trade which, at the time the shares were issued, was intended to be carried on wholly or mainly in the UK.

The second of these conditions is, however, relevant only for a period of two years after the issue of the shares, by which time the intended trade must have been commenced by a 'qualifying company', and ceases to be relevant at any time within those two years after the intention is abandoned.

The 'wholly or mainly in the UK' requirement is to be dropped in relation to shares or securities issued on or after an appointed day and replaced by a requirement that the company must have a permanent establishment in the UK. The legislation is to be included in a Finance Bill to be introduced in autumn 2010. (HMRC Budget Note BN11, 22 June 2010).

For these purposes, *'qualifying company'* means the issuing company itself or any 'qualifying 90% subsidiary' of that company. (In determining the time at which a qualifying trade begins to be carried on by a 'qualifying 90% subsidiary', any carrying on of the trade by it before it became such a subsidiary is disregarded.) For the purposes of (b) above only, a qualifying 90% subsidiary includes any existing or future company which will be a qualifying 90% subsidiary at any future time.

A company (the subsidiary) is a *'qualifying 90% subsidiary'* of the issuing company at any time when:

- the issuing company possesses at least 90% of both the issued share capital of, and the voting power in, the subsidiary;
- the issuing company would be beneficially entitled to at least 90% of the assets of the subsidiary available for distribution to equity holders on a winding-up or in any other circumstances;
- the issuing company is beneficially entitled to at least 90% of any profits of the subsidiary available for distribution to equity holders;
- no person other than the issuing company has control (within *ITA 2007, s 995*) of the subsidiary; and
- no arrangements exist by virtue of which any of the above conditions would cease to be met.

For the above purposes, *CTA 2010, Pt 5 Ch 6* applies, with appropriate modifications, to determine the persons who are equity holders and the percentage of assets available to them. A subsidiary does not cease to be a qualifying 90% subsidiary by reason only of it or any other company having commenced winding up or by reason only of anything done as a consequence of any such company being in administration or receivership, provided the winding-up, entry into administration or receivership (both as defined) or anything done as a consequence of its being in administration or receivership is for genuine commercial reasons and is not part of a tax avoidance scheme or arrangements. Also, the listed conditions are not regarded as ceasing to be satisfied by reason only of arrangements being in existence for the disposal of the issuing company's interest in the subsidiary if the disposal is to be for genuine commercial reasons and is not to be part of a tax avoidance scheme or arrangements.

With effect on and after 6 April 2007, a company ('company A') which is a subsidiary of company B (a company that is not the issuing company) is a qualifying 90% subsidiary of the issuing company if:

- company A would be a qualifying 90% subsidiary of company B (if company B were the issuing company), and company B is a 'qualifying 100% subsidiary' of the issuing company; or
- company A is a 'qualifying 100% subsidiary' of company B, and company B is a qualifying 90% subsidiary of the issuing company.

For this purpose, no account is to be taken of any control the issuing company may have of company A, and *'qualifying 100% subsidiary'* is defined similarly to 'qualifying 90% subsidiary' above but substituting '100%' for '90%'.

In relation to shares or securities issued to the VCT on or before 16 March 2004, the issuing company or a 'relevant qualifying subsidiary' must, when the shares were issued to the VCT and at all times since, have been either:

- carrying on a qualifying trade wholly or mainly in the UK; or
- preparing to carry on a qualifying trade which, at the time the shares were issued, it intended to carry on wholly or mainly in the UK,

but the second of these conditions is relevant only for a period of two years after the issue of the shares, by which time the trade must have commenced as intended, and ceases to be relevant at any time within those two years after the intention is abandoned. For this purpose, a *'relevant qualifying subsidiary'* is, broadly, a company which is 90% owned by the issuing company (or by a subsidiary of the issuing company) and which otherwise satisfies the conditions of *ICTA 1988, Sch 28B para 10* (as amended prior to *FA 2004*).

[*ITA 2007, ss 291, 301, Sch 2 paras 72, 79; ICTA 1988, Sch 28B paras 3, 5A; FA 2007, Sch 16 paras 17, 18; CTA 2010, Sch 1 para 504*].

A company does not cease to meet this requirement by reason only of anything done as a consequence of its being in administration or receivership (both as defined), provided everything so done and the making of the relevant order are for genuine commercial (and not tax avoidance) reasons. [*ITA 2007, s 292, Sch 2 para 73; ICTA 1988, Sch 28B para 11A*].

The 'maximum amount raised annually through risk capital schemes' requirement

[76.24] In relation to shares or securities issued to the VCT on or after 6 April 2007, the total amount of 'relevant investments' made in the issuing company in the twelve months ending with the date of issue to the VCT must not exceed £2 million. Relevant investments in any company that was a subsidiary of the issuing company at any time in those twelve months also count towards this limit (regardless of whether or not it was a subsidiary when the investment was made). This requirement does not apply in relation to shares or securities issued by an investee company on or after 6 April 2007 if they are acquired with money raised by the issue of shares in the VCT before that date or money derived from the investment by the VCT of any such money.

'Relevant investments' comprise:

(a)   investments (of any kind) made by a VCT; and
(b)   money subscribed for shares issued by the investee company under the ENTERPRISE INVESTMENT SCHEME (EIS) (28) or the Corporate Venturing Scheme (CVS) (see Tolley's Corporation Tax).

As regards (a) above, an investment is disregarded for these purposes if it was made before 6 April 2007 or if it was an investment of money raised by the issue of shares or securities in a VCT before that date or money derived from the investment by a VCT of any such money.

As regards (b) above, shares are treated as having been issued under the EIS or CVS if at any time the investee company provides an EIS compliance statement (see **28.7** ENTERPRISE INVESTMENT SCHEME) or CVS equivalent in respect of those shares; an investment is regarded as made when the shares are issued. Shares are disregarded for these purposes if they were issued before 19 July 2007 or issued on or after that date to an approved fund (see **28.2** ENTERPRISE INVESTMENT SCHEME) that closed before that date. If the provision of a compliance statement causes this requirement not to be met, the requirement is treated as having been met from the time the shares in question were issued to the VCT to the time the compliance statement was provided.

[*ITA 2007, s 292A; FA 2007, Sch 16 para 6(3)–(6), para 8*].

The 'use of the money raised' requirement

[76.25] The money raised by the issue of shares to the VCT must be employed *wholly* (disregarding insignificant amounts) for the purposes of the 'relevant qualifying activity'.

For shares or securities issued on or after 22 April 2009, this condition does not have to be met in the first two years after the issue (or in the two years after the commencement of the qualifying trade where this was later than the date of issue).

For shares or securities issued before 22 April 2009, this condition was treated as satisfied at any time within 12 months after the issue (or after the date of commencement of the qualifying trade where this was later than the date of issue) if at least 80% of that money had been, or was intended to be, so employed. At any time within the following 12 months, the condition was treated as satisfied if at least 80% of that money *had been* so employed.

For these purposes, a qualifying activity is a '*relevant qualifying activity*' if it was a qualifying activity at the time the shares were issued or if it is a qualifying trade and preparing to carry it on was a qualifying activity at that time.

[*ITA 2007, s 293, Sch 2 para 74; ICTA 1988, Sch 28B para 6; FA 2009, Sch 8 paras 9, 14*].

Money whose retention can reasonably be regarded as necessary or advisable for financing current business requirements is regarded as employed for trade purposes (HMRC Venture Capital Schemes Manual VCM12080, 62150–62153).

In relation to buy-outs (and in particular management buy-outs), HMRC will usually accept that where a company is formed to acquire a trade, and the funds raised from the VCT are applied to that purchase, the requirement that the funds be employed for the purposes of the trade is satisfied. Where the company is formed to acquire another company and its trade, or a holding company and its trading subsidiaries, this represents an investment rather than employment for the purposes of the trade. However, HMRC will usually accept that the requirement is satisfied if the trade of the company, or all the activities of the holding company and its subsidiaries, are hived up to the acquiring company as soon as possible after the acquisition. In the case of a holding company and its subsidiaries, to the extent that the trades are not hived up, the holding cannot be a qualifying holding. (Revenue Tax Bulletin August 1995 pp 243, 244).

The 'relevant company to carry on the relevant qualifying activity' requirement

[76.26] In relation to shares or securities issued to the VCT after 16 March 2004, at all times after the issue of the holding the relevant qualifying activity by reference to which the use of money raised requirement is satisfied must not be carried on by any person other than the issuing company or a 'qualifying 90% subsidiary' (see **76.23** above) of that company.

This requirement is not treated as not met merely because the trade in question is carried on by a person other than the issuing company or a qualifying subsidiary at any time after the issue of the shares and before the issuing company or a qualifying 90% subsidiary carries on the trade. The carrying on of the trade by a partnership of which the issuing company or a qualifying 90% subsidiary is a member, or by a joint venture to which any such company is a party, is permitted.

The requirement is also not regarded as failing to be met if, by reason only of a company being wound up or dissolved or being in administration or receivership (both as defined), the qualifying trade ceases to be carried on by the issuing company' or a qualifying 90% subsidiary and is subsequently carried on by a person who has not been connected (within **21 CONNECTED PERSONS** — but with the modifications to the meaning of 'control' that apply for the purposes of the control and independence requirement at **76.28** below) with the issuing company at any time in the period beginning one year before the shares were issued. This let-out applies only if the winding-up, dissolution or entry into administration or receivership (and everything done as a consequence of the company being in administration or receivership) is for genuine commercial reasons and not part of a tax avoidance scheme or arrangements.

In relation to shares or securities issued to the VCT on or before 16 March 2004, where the company is a 'parent company' within **76.21**(b) above, the '*trader company*' (i.e. the company carrying on (or preparing to carry on) the required qualifying trade) must either:

- satisfy the requirements in **76.21**(a) above; or
- be a company in relation to which those requirements would be satisfied if activities within **76.21**(i) to (iv) above, or consisting of a subsidiary making loans to its parent, were disregarded; or
- be a 'relevant qualifying subsidiary' which either:
  - (1) exists wholly for the purpose of carrying on activities within **76.21**(iii) or (iv) above (disregarding purposes capable of having no significant effect (other than in relation to incidental matters) on the extent of its activities); or
  - (2) has no corporation tax profits and no part of its business consists in the making of investments.

A '*relevant qualifying subsidiary*' is, broadly, a company which is 90% owned by the investee company (or by a subsidiary of that company) and which otherwise satisfies the conditions of *ICTA 1988, Sch 28B para 10* (as amended prior to *FA 2004*).

[*ITA 2007, s 294, Sch 2 para 75; ICTA 1988, Sch 28B para 6(AB)–(AG); SI 2007 No 1820, reg 4*].

The unquoted status requirement

[76.27] The issuing company must be an *'unquoted company'* (whether or not UK resident), i.e. none of its shares, stocks, debentures or other securities must be:

- listed on a recognised stock exchange, or a designated exchange outside the UK; or
- dealt in outside the UK by such means as may be designated for the purpose by order.

Securities on the Alternative Investment Market ('AIM') are generally treated as unquoted for these purposes (Revenue Press Release 20 February 1995; HMRC Internet Statement 29 March 2007 at www.hmrc.gov.uk/budget2007/rec-stock-exch.htm).

If the company ceases to be an unquoted company at a time when its shares are comprised in the qualifying holdings of the VCT, this requirement is treated as continuing to be met, in relation to shares or securities acquired before that time, for the following five years.

[ITA 2007, ss 295, 989, 1005; ICTA 1988, Sch 28B para 2; FA 2007, Sch 26 para 12(7)(12)].

The control and independence requirement

[76.28] The company must not 'control' (with or without 'connected persons') any company other than a 'qualifying subsidiary' (see the subsidiaries requirements at **76.31** below), nor must another company (or another company and a person connected with it) control it. Neither must arrangements be in existence by virtue of which such control could arise. For these purposes, *'control'* is as under *CTA 2010, ss 450, 451*, except that possession of, or entitlement to acquire, fixed-rate preference shares (as defined) of the company which do not, for the time being, carry voting rights is disregarded, as is possession of, or entitlement to acquire, rights as a loan creditor of the company. *'Connected persons'* are as under *ITA 2007, s 993* (see **21 CONNECTED PERSONS**) except that the definition of 'control' therein is similarly modified. *[ITA 2007, ss 296, 313(4)–(7); ICTA 1988, Sch 28B paras 9, 13; CTA 2010, Sch 1 para 506]*.

For the application of the control and independence requirement to co-investors in a company, and in particular the question of whether co-investors are connected by virtue of their acting together to secure or exercise control of the company, see Revenue Tax Bulletin October 1997 pp 471, 472.

The gross assets requirement

[76.29] The value of the company's gross assets or, where the company is a parent company, the value of the 'group assets', must not have exceeded £7 million immediately before the issue or £8 million immediately thereafter. In relation to shares and securities issued by investee companies before 6 April 2006, these limits were £15 million and £16 million respectively. For the purpose of determining whether shares or securities acquired by the VCT are to be regarded as comprised in its qualifying holdings, the higher limits continue to apply in relation to shares or securities issued by investee companies on or after 6 April 2006 but acquired with money raised by the issue of shares in the VCT before that date or money derived from the investment by the VCT of any such money.

'*Group assets*' are the gross assets of each of the members of the group, disregarding assets consisting in rights against, or shares in or securities of, another member of the group.

[*ITA 2007, s 297, Sch 2 para 76; ICTA 1988, Sch 28B para 8; FA 2006, Sch 14 para 2*].

The general approach of HMRC is that the value of a company's gross assets is the sum of the value of all the balance sheet assets. Where accounts are actually drawn up to a date immediately before or after the issue, the balance sheet values are taken provided that they reflect usual accounting standards and the company's normal accounting practice, consistently applied. Where accounts are not drawn up to such a date, such values will be taken from the most recent balance sheet, updated as precisely as practicable on the basis of all the relevant information available to the company. Values so arrived at may need to be reviewed in the light of information contained in the accounts for the period in which the issue was made, and, if they were not available at the time of the issue, those for the preceding period, when they become available. The company's assets immediately before the issue do not include any advance payment received in respect of the issue. Where shares are issued partly paid, the right to the balance is an asset, and, notwithstanding the above, will be taken into account in valuing the assets immediately after the issue regardless of whether it is stated in the balance sheet. (HMRC SP 2/00).

The 'number of employees' requirement

[76.30] In relation to shares or securities issued to the VCT on or after 6 April 2007 (and see also below), the company must have fewer than the equivalent of 50 full-time employees when the shares or securities are issued. If the company is a parent company (see **76.21**(b) above), this rule applies by reference to the aggregate number of full-time employees of itself and its qualifying subsidiaries (see **76.31** below). To ascertain the equivalent number of full-time employees of a company, take the actual number of full-time employees and add to it a just and reasonable fraction for each employee who is not full-time. For this purpose, an 'employee' includes a director but does not include anyone on maternity or paternity leave or a student on vocational training. This requirement does not apply in relation to shares or securities issued by an investee company on or after 6 April 2007 if they are acquired with money raised by the issue of shares in the VCT before that date or money derived from the investment by the VCT of any such money. [*ITA 2007, s 297A; FA 2007, Sch 16 para 3(3)(5)–(7)*].

The subsidiaries requirements

Qualifying subsidiaries

[76.31] Any subsidiary that the issuing company has must be a 'qualifying subsidiary'.

A subsidiary is a '*qualifying subsidiary*' of the issuing company if the following conditions are satisfied in relation to that subsidiary and every other subsidiary of the issuing company.

In relation to shares or securities issued to the VCT after 16 March 2004, the subsidiary must be a **51%** subsidiary (see *CTA 2010, Pt 24 Ch 3*) of the issuing company and no person other than the issuing company or another of its subsidiaries may have control (within *ITA 2007, s 995*) of the subsidiary. Furthermore, no arrangements may exist by virtue of which either of these conditions would cease to be satisfied.

The conditions are not regarded as ceasing to be satisfied by reason only of the subsidiary or any other company being in the process of being wound up or by reason only of anything done as a consequence of its being in administration or receivership, provided the winding-up, entry into administration or receivership or anything done as a consequence of its being in administration or receivership is for genuine commercial reasons and is not part of a tax avoidance scheme or arrangements.

In relation to shares or securities issued to the VCT on or before 16 March 2004, the issuing company, or another of its subsidiaries, must possess at least 75% of the issued share capital of, and the voting power in, the subsidiary, and be beneficially entitled to at least 75% of the assets available for distribution to equity holders on a winding-up etc. and of the profits available for distribution to equity holders. No other person may have control (within *ITA 2007, s 995*) of the subsidiary. Furthermore, no arrangements may exist by virtue of which any of these conditions could cease to be satisfied. A subsidiary does not fail these conditions by reason only of the fact that it is being wound up, provided that the winding-up is for *bona fide* commercial reasons and not part of a tax avoidance scheme or arrangements.

The conditions above are not regarded as ceasing to be satisfied by reason only of arrangements being in existence for the disposal of the interest in the subsidiary held by the issuing company (or, as the case may be, by another of its subsidiaries) if the disposal is to be for genuine commercial reasons and is not to be part of a tax avoidance scheme or arrangements.

[*ITA 2007, ss 298, 302, 989, Sch 2 para 80; ICTA 1988, Sch 28B paras 3(6), 10; CTA 2010, Sch 1 para 562(8)*].

Property managing subsidiaries

The company must not have a 'property managing subsidiary' which is not a 'qualifying 90% subsidiary' (see **76.23** above) of the company. A '*property managing subsidiary*' is a subsidiary whose business consists wholly or mainly in the holding or managing of 'land' or any 'property deriving its value from land' (as defined). [*ITA 2007, s 299, Sch 2 para 77; ICTA 1988, Sch 28B para 10ZA*].

The financial health requirement (prospective)

[76.32] This is a prospective requirement that will have to be met at the time of issue of the holding in question. The requirement is that the company is not 'in difficulty'; a company is *'in difficulty'* if it is reasonable to assume that it would be regarded as an enterprise in difficulty for the purposes of the *EC Guidelines on State Aid for Rescuing and Restructuring Firms in Difficulty (2004/C 244/02)*. The legislation is to be included in a Finance Bill to be introduced in autumn 2010 and will have effect on and after a date to be appointed. (HMRC Budget Note BN11, 22 June 2010).

Supplementary provisions

Winding-up of the issuing company

[76.33] Where the company is being wound up, none of the requirements listed at **76.18–76.32** above are regarded on that account as not being satisfied provided that those conditions would be met apart from the winding-up, and that the winding-up is for genuine commercial reasons and is not part of a scheme or arrangement a main purpose of which is the avoidance of tax. [*ITA 2007, s 312, Sch 2 para 86; ICTA 1988, Sch 28B para 11*].

Restructuring

Where shares or securities in a company are exchanged for corresponding shares and securities in a new holding company, then subject to detailed conditions, including HMRC approval, to the extent that any of the requirements listed below was satisfied in relation to the old shares, it will generally be taken to be satisfied in relation to the new shares. The consideration for the old shares must consist wholly of the issue of shares in the new company. Certain deemed securities (see **76.12** above) which are not thus acquired by the new company may be disregarded where these provisions would otherwise be prevented from applying.

The requirements to which the above provision applies are:

- the maximum qualifying investment requirement;
- the proportion of eligible shares requirement;
- the trading requirement;
- the carrying on of a qualifying activity requirement;
- the use of money raised requirement;
- the relevant company to carry on the relevant qualifying activity requirement;
- the control and independence requirement;
- the gross assets requirement;
- the number of employees requirement; and
- the size requirement.

[*ITA 2007, ss 326–328, Sch 2 para 87; ICTA 1988, Sch 28B para 10C; FA 2007, Sch 16 para 3(4)*].

Conversion of shares

Where a VCT exercises conversion rights in respect of certain convertible shares and securities, then subject to detailed conditions, for the purposes of the requirements listed below, the conversion is treated as an exchange of new shares for old shares to which the restructuring provisions above apply. The requirements are:

- the maximum qualifying investment requirement;
- the proportion of eligible shares requirement;
- the carrying on of a qualifying activity requirement;
- the use of money raised requirement;
- the relevant company to carry on the relevant qualifying activity requirement; and
- the gross assets requirement.

[ITA 2007, s 329, Sch 2 para 87; ICTA 1988, Sch 28B para 10D].

Reorganisations etc.

Where, under a company reorganisation or other arrangement:

- a VCT exchanges a qualifying holding for other shares or securities (with or without other consideration); and
- the exchange is for genuine commercial reasons and not part of a tax avoidance scheme or arrangements,

the new shares or securities may be treated as being qualifying holdings for a specified period even if some or all of the requirements at **76.18–76.32** above are not otherwise satisfied. Regulations specify the circumstances in which, and conditions subject to which, they apply and which requirements are to be treated as met. Where the new shares or securities are those of a different company than before and they do not meet any one or more of the above requirements (disregarding the maximum qualifying investment requirement and the use of the money raised requirement), those requirements are treated as met for, broadly, three years in the case of shares or five years in the case of securities, reduced in either case to, broadly, two years where the company is not, or ceases to be, an unquoted company as in the unquoted status requirement above. A formula is provided for valuing the new shares or securities for the purposes of the proportion of eligible shares requirement above. The provisions extend to new shares or securities received in pursuance of an earn-out right (see Tolley's Capital Gains Tax under Shares and Securities) conferred in exchange for a qualifying holding, in which case an election is available (under *Reg 10*) to modify the said valuation formula by effectively disregarding the earn-out right itself. *[ITA 2007, s 330, Sch 2 para 88; ICTA 1988, Sch 28B para 11B; SI 2002 No 2661; SI 2009 No 2035, Sch para 48]*.

77

Finance Act 2010 — Summary of Income Tax Provisions

[77.1] (Royal Assent: 8 April 2010)

s 1   **Income tax: charge, rates, thresholds and allowances for 2010/11.** The annual charge to income tax is renewed, the basic rate is set at 20% and the higher rate is set at 40% (both unchanged from 2009/10). The additional rate is 50%. See **1.3** ALLOWANCES AND TAX RATES.

The basic rate limit, starting rate limit for savings, personal allowance, married couple's allowance, blind person's allowance and income limit for age-related allowances are all set at the same level as for 2009/10. See **1.6, 1.14, 1.15, 1.16** ALLOWANCES AND TAX RATES.

s 5   **Capital allowances.** The annual investment allowance is increased from £50,000 to £100,000 for expenditure incurred on or after 6 April 2010. See **11.13** CAPITAL ALLOWANCES ON PLANT AND MACHINERY.

s 23, Sch 2   **Tax relief on pension provision.** These provisions impose for 2011/12 onwards the previously announced restriction of pension tax relief to the basic rate for high income individuals and sets out the mechanics of how this is achieved (the high income excess relief charge). High income individuals are broadly those whose income, plus any employer-funded pension provision, is £150,000 or more, subject to a floor so as to exclude those whose income without adding employer-funded pension provision is less than £130,000. But see also *F(No 2)A 2010, s 5*. See **57.9** PENSION PROVISION.

s 24, Sch 3   **Relief for trading losses.** Relief is denied against general income and capital gains where, broadly, the loss arises from tax avoidance arrangements entered into on or after 21 October 2009. See **45.18** LOSSES.

s 25   **Relief for property losses.** Relief is denied against general income for so much of available loss relief as is attributable to an annual investment capital allowance on plant and machinery and, broadly, the loss arises from tax avoidance arrangements entered into on or after 24 March 2010. See **60.15** PROPERTY INCOME.

s 27, Sch 5   **Leasing of plant and machinery — anti-avoidance.** This legislation is aimed at two identified avoidance schemes involving the leasing of plant or machinery. See **11.24**, **11.63**(v) CAPITAL ALLOWANCES ON PLANT AND MACHINERY and **73.98** TRADING INCOME (under Rental rebates).

s 28   **Cushion gas.** Capital expenditure incurred on or after 1 April 2010 on cushion gas is special rate expenditure qualifying for writing-down allowances at 10%. A plant or machinery lease commencing on or after 1 April 2010 is automatically a funding lease if the plant or machinery is cushion gas. See **11.25**, **11.45** CAPITAL ALLOWANCES ON PLANT AND MACHINERY.

s 30, Sch 6   **Charity.** A new statutory definition of a charity is introduced for tax purposes though with limited immediate effect. As regards Gift Aid relief, the new definition does have effect in relation to gifts made on or after 6 April 2010. See **16.3** CHARITIES.

s 31, Sch 7   **Gifts of shares, securities and real property to charity.** Legislation is introduced to block tax avoidance schemes that exploit the rules for tax relief on gifts of qualifying investments to charities. The legislation applies to gifts made on or after 15 December 2009 and operates by restricting the tax relief to the donor. See **16.21** CHARITIES.

s 32, Sch 8   **Charities — miscellaneous.** The receipt by a charitable trust of a payroll giving donation made on or after 24 March 2010 under the payroll giving scheme is chargeable to tax to the extent that it is not applied to charitable purposes only. See **16.13** CHARITIES.

     A pre-existing condition that disqualifies a payment, made by a charity to a body outside the UK, from qualifying as charitable expenditure is tightened with effect for payments representing expenditure incurred on or after 24 March 2010. **16.11** CHARITIES.

     The law is amended for donations made on or after 6 April 2010 by non-UK resident donors under Gift Aid where the donor has not paid sufficient UK tax to cover the tax treated as deducted from the donation. See **16.17** CHARITIES.

In relation to donations under Gift Aid, a claim by the charity for exemption from tax can be made either within or outside a tax return. The legislation puts this onto a statutory footing and also gives HMRC power to make regulations limiting the number of claims that are made outside the return. See **16.13** **CHARITIES**.

s 33 **Remittance basis.** A minor amendment is made, with effect on and after 6 April 2010, to the definition of a 'relevant person' for the purposes of the rules determining whether sums are remitted to the UK. See **61.11 REMITTANCE BASIS**.

s 35, Sch 10 **Penalties — offshore matters.** With effect from a date to be appointed by the Treasury by statutory instrument, the existing penalties for careless or deliberate errors in documents and failure to notify chargeability to tax are materially increased where the non-compliance involves an offshore matter, e.g. non-disclosure of offshore income. The size of the increase depends on the tax transparency of the offshore jurisdiction concerned; there is no increase if the jurisdiction automatically exchanges information with the UK. It is anticipated that the increases will apply to tax periods commencing on or after 1 April 2011. See **55.4, 55.12 PENALTIES**.

s 36, Sch 11 **Double tax relief.** The targeted anti-avoidance rules at **26.5** **DOUBLE TAX RELIEF** (relief by credit under double tax agreement) are amended. The majority of amendments apply in relation to foreign tax payable on or after 6 April 2010. One amendment has effect in relation to foreign tax deemed to be paid or payable on or after 21 October 2009 and is aimed principally at foreign tax deemed to have been deducted from manufactured overseas dividends.

Where double tax relief is obtained by deducting the foreign tax from the foreign income, an amendment is made to ensure that the foreign tax can be deducted only once. This applies in relation to foreign tax paid on or after 6 April 2010. See **26.9**(b)(iii) **DOUBLE TAX RELIEF**.

s 38, Sch 12 **Transactions in securities.** The anti-avoidance legislation to counter tax advantages arising from transactions in securities is substantially amended. The scope is widened to include all close companies (except where there has been a fundamental change in ownership) but is targeted more effectively at arrangements involving tax avoidance. The substantive amendments have effect in relation to income tax advantages obtained on or after 24 March 2010. See **4.2–4.4 ANTI-AVOIDANCE**.

s 39 **Company Share Option Plans (CSOPs).** On or after 24 September 2010, share options can no longer be granted under CSOPs in relation to shares in an unlisted company which is under the control of a listed company. Special rules apply throughout a six-month transitional period beginning with 24 March 2010 and ending with 23 September 2010. See **69.68 SHARE-RELATED EMPLOYMENT INCOME AND EXEMPTIONS.**

s 40, Sch 13 **Unauthorised unit trusts.** Legislation is enacted to thwart identified avoidance schemes involving unauthorised unit trusts in receipt of foreign income in respect of which the trustees claim double tax relief. It has effect in relation to payments treated as made by the trustees to the unit holders on or after 21 October 2009, and means that in appropriate circumstances part of the payment is treated in the unit holders' hands as foreign income from which overseas tax has been deducted rather than UK income from which basic rate tax has been deducted. See **75.9 UNIT TRUSTS ETC.**

s 42 **Share incentive plans (SIPs).** For payments made on or after 24 March 2010 by an employer company to the trustees of a SIP, the company does not obtain a trading deduction if the payment is made in pursuance of tax avoidance arrangements. See **73.59 TRADING INCOME.**

Section 42 also closes certain potential loopholes in the provisions allowing HMRC to withdraw its approval of a SIP.

s 48 **Pension provision — special annual allowance charge.** *Section 48* enacts the 2009 Pre-Budget Report announcement extending the special annual allowance charge to individuals with incomes of £130,000 or more with effect on and after 9 December 2009. This is in anticipation of the legislation at *section 23* above. See **57.11 PENSION PROVISION.**

s 56, Sch 17 **Disclosure of tax avoidance schemes.** With effect from a date to be appointed by the Treasury by statutory instrument, a number of amendments are made to the disclosure requirements. In particular, the amendments add to the obligations and duties of a promoter and substantially increase the potential penalties for non-compliance. See **4.44–4.51 ANTI-AVOIDANCE.**

s 58   **Car and van benefits — zero and low emission vehicles.** Company cars and vans which cannot produce CO_2 emissions under any circumstances when driven qualify for an appropriate percentage of 0% in the case of a car and for a cash equivalent of nil in the case of a van. A car with emissions of 75g/km or less qualifies for an appropriate percentage of 5%. These reduced rates apply for the years 2010/11 to 2014/15 inclusive. See **27.33, 27.36 EMPLOYMENT INCOME.**

s 59   **Car benefits — cars with a CO_2 emissions figure.** Company car appropriate percentages will be extended down to a new 10% band for 2012/13 onwards. The 10% rate will apply if the emissions figure is less than 100g/km (except where the 5% rate in *section 58* above applies). The rate will be increased to 11% at an emissions level of 100g/km and then by one percentage point for each additional 5g/km, up to the maximum rate of 35%. See **27.33 EMPLOYMENT INCOME.**

s 60   **Provision by an employer of free or subsidised meals.** For 2011/12 onwards, the exemption is not available where an employee's entitlement to such meals arises in conjunction with salary sacrifice arrangements or flexible remuneration arrangements. See **27.29**(iv) **EMPLOYMENT INCOME.**

s 63, Sch 20   **2011 UEFA Champions League final in England.** This measure confers exemption from income tax to non-UK resident employees and contractors of competing overseas teams in relation to employment income or trading income arising from duties or services performed in the UK in connection with this final. See **30.44 EXEMPT INCOME.**

78

Finance (No 2) Act 2010 — Summary of Income Tax Provisions

[78.1] (Royal Assent: 27 July 2010)

s 5	**Tax relief on pension provision.** *FA 2010, s 23, Sch 2* imposed for 2011/12 onwards the previously announced restriction of pension tax relief to the basic rate for high income individuals (the high income excess relief charge). This *section* gives the Treasury the power to repeal that legislation by statutory instrument. This power cannot be exercised after 31 December 2010. See **57.9** PENSION PROVISION.
s 6, Sch 3	**Pension provision — treatment of persons reaching age 75.** The Government intend to end the existing rules that create an effective obligation to purchase an annuity by age 75. Pending the requisite legislation (expected to apply for 2011/12 onwards) this *section* provides that certain tax rules which would otherwise have had effect when a member of a money purchase registered pension scheme reaches age 75 do not apply until the member reaches age 77. This applies to individuals who reach the age of 75 on or after 22 June 2010. See **57.1** PENSION PROVISION.
s 7, Sch 4	**MPs' expenses.** Following the introduction, by the Independent Parliamentary Standards Authority, of a new scheme for paying MPs' expenses, consequential changes are made with effect on and after 7 May 2010 to the income tax treatment of such expenses. See **30.27** EXEMPT INCOME.

Finance (No 2) Act 2010 — Summary of Income Tax Provisions

78.1] Royal Assent, 27 July 2010.

79 Table of Statutes

80 Table of Statutory Instruments

Note. The Statutory Instruments (SIs) listed at **10.20 CAPITAL ALLOWANCES,** those listed at the head of **41 INTEREST ON OVERPAID TAX** and those referred to at **26.2 DOUBLE TAX RELIEF** are not listed below.

The list below is in chronological order.

89 Table of Leading Cases

This Table lists those of the 2,000 or so cases referred to in this book which are considered to be of most general application and interest. For fuller details of these cases, and of all other tax cases relevant to current or recent legislation, see Tolley's Tax Cases.

A

C

F

I

J

K

L

M

Ch D 1965, 42 TC 301; [1965] 1 WLR 711; [1965] 2 All ER 258.

U

V

W

Y

90 Index

This index is referenced to the chapter and paragraph number. The entries printed in bold capitals are main subject headings in the text.

A

Accommodation,
employee, provided to, 27.59–27.68
expenses (MPs etc.), 27.68, 30.27
surplus business, 73.90
Accountancy expenses, 73.92
fee protection insurance, 73.92
underwriters, 74.3
Accountancy principles, 73.18, 73.19
Accountants,
HMRC power to call for tax
papers, 38.13
Accounting basis, 73.18
change of, 60.7, 73.20
— UITF Abstract 40
adjustment, 73.115
Accounting date,
change of, 73.7
Accounting periods,
change of, 73.7
Accounts, 73.17
penalty for negligence, 55.13
self-assessment, 63.2
Accrued income and accumulations,
accrued income scheme, **2**
deeply discounted securities, 64.18–64.25
death, at, 23.16
dividends after death, 23.3
securities, on, **2**, 4.6, 4.9
unit trusts, 75.2
ACCRUED INCOME SCHEME, 2
accrued income profits/losses, 2.4
anti-avoidance provisions, interaction
with, 2.25
bearer securities, 2.14
capital gains tax interaction, 2.23
charities, 2.17
conversions, 2.13
death, 2.11
deemed payments, 2.3

ACCRUED INCOME SCHEME, – *cont.*
determination of accrued income profit/
loss, 2.4
double taxation relief, 2.24
euroconversions, 2.2, 2.3, 2.15, 2.19
excluded transferors/transferees, 2.5
foreign currency, 2.8
foreign securities, delayed
remittances, 2.10
gilt strips, 2.20
interest in default, 2.16
new issues, 2.22
nominees, 2.7
pension funds. 2.18
profit/loss, 2.4
remittance basis 2.9
retirement schemes, 2.18
securities, sale and repurchase of, 2.19
stock lending, 2.21
trading stock, appropriations, 2.12
transfer of unrealised interest, 2.14
trustees, 2.7, 68.12(11)
unrealised interest, transfer of, 2.14
variable rate bonds, 2.15
Accumulated or discretionary income, 68.11
Accumulation trusts, 68.11
vulnerable beneficiaries, 68.19–68.21
Actors, 27.54
Additional rate, 1.3
Addresses, HMRC etc.,
Adjudicator's Office, 34.8
Anti-Avoidance Group (Intelligence)
Unit, 4.44
Centre for Non-Residents, 26.10
Clearance and Counteraction Team, 4.5
Corporate Communications Office, 63.2
CT & VAT (International), 4.26
CT & VAT (Technical), 28.2
Customs and International (Tax Treaty
Team), 26.2

N